Presented

TO

_____

BY

_____

ON

_____

I remember the days
   of long ago,
I meditate on all your works
   and consider what your
   hands have done.

PSALM 143:5

NIV

THE SPIRITUAL FORMATION BIBLE

Growing in Intimacy

With God

Through Scripture

New International
Version

Zondervan Publishing House
Grand Rapids, Michigan, 49530, U.S.A.

CONTENTS

ALPHABETICAL LIST
OF BIBLE BOOKS

The books of the New Testament are in *italic*.

HOW TO USE
THE SPIRITUAL FORMATION BIBLE

The editors and writers of the *Spiritual Formation Bible* (many associated with *The Upper Room* and *Weavings* magazines) believe that the written Word is a living word, that its readers should come to Scripture with the expectancy that God will speak to them. With that in mind The Upper Room and Zondervan Publishing House have teamed up to bring you *The Spiritual Formation Bible*. Spiritual formation, that process whereby we grow in our relationship with God and become conformed to Jesus Christ, takes place as we interact with God's words in Scripture. "The Bible is alive, it speaks to me," sixteenth-century reformer Martin Luther once said. "It has feet, it runs after me; it has hands, it lays hold of me." We meet God personally in the Bible.

This Bible provides simple and practical ways to help you listen for a word from God for your own life. Page after page and feature after feature, its attractive, easy-to-use format will help you linger over each precious passage of Scripture. Even if your life tends to be harried and hurried, using this Bible will encourage you to dig deeply and read reflectively. It can help you to be "transformed by the renewing of your mind" (Romans 12:2).

The *Spiritual Formation Bible* is designed to help you:

- reflect on the treasured stories and passages of Scripture until they come alive for you
- ask while reading the Bible, "What is God saying to me in this passage?"
- read Scripture prayerfully, expectantly and in ways that deeply touch you
- incorporate the riches of classical spiritual wisdom into your prayer times

The *Spiritual Formation Bible* offers you these benefits through the following features:

Getting Started Articles on pages x–xv will provide a wealth of wisdom on spiritual formation.

Book Introductions at the beginning of each book point to the primary themes of each book of the Bible. These will help you grasp the Bible's great and recurring spiritual truths and provide the context for each book.

Entry Points appear on each page of the Bible text. Each short article is based on a particular passage on or near the page of Scripture on which it appears, and each one will lead you to explore themes of special importance for spiritual growth. Each "Entry Point" follows one of the methods of approaching Scripture listed in "Meeting God in Scripture" (pages 1094-97). Many of the "Entry Points" contain quotations from spiritual classics to stir your thoughts and emotions. These insightful, reflective notes will help you enter the passage and make it come alive for you in a personal way. They allow you to *listen* to the Bible as never before. They are also linked to articles on "Ways of Meeting God." The entry points were designed to allow you the freedom to interact with Scripture at your own pace. You can use these "Entry Points" consecutively by reading through the Bible from Genesis to Revelation, or you can enter the text at any point. You may also want to try an in-depth reading of a particular book or books. Whatever method you choose, the "Entry Points" will assist you in interacting with God's word.

Ways of Meeting God tie many of the "Entry Points," and their corresponding passages to spiritual disciplines or practices that provide a framework and structure for spiritual growth. Each article provides the reader with background that helps make sense of the "big picture." These general articles provide a wonderful resource for individual reflection or small group or church school discussion. Each of the "Ways of Meeting God" articles can be identified by a distinctive woodcut that also identifies that practice in the Entry Points. Refer to the Table of Contents to locate these articles.

Glimpses from the Classics are brief excerpts from some of the wisest and most profound writings on the spiritual life. You will find these scattered throughout the text in beautiful, full-page calligraphy, providing a feast for the eyes as well as the spirit.

Indexes help you find topics of special relevance to spiritual formation and provide information about the quotations included in this Bible.

New International Version Far more important than any of the tools we've provided is the text itself, the Word of God. The Bible you are holding in your hands is a supernaturally powerful book. The life-giving truth it offers is startlingly simple, yet deeply layered. Our prayer for you is that, as you use *The Spiritual Formation Bible,* the Word of God will enter and enrich you with its message of God's love and grace.

About the Upper Room

"THE UPPER ROOM was prayed into existence," a church leader declared. At the worst of the Great Depression in 1935, a group of Texas church people asked for help with family and home worship. In response to that call, an interdenominational daily devotional magazine was created. From that small beginning, the magazine has grown to a publication in sixty-three editions and forty-three languages in more than eighty countries. Domestic circulation alone exceeds two and a quarter million copies per issue. *El Aposento Alto* is the Spanish language edition.

The organization publishes four additional magazines: *Alive Now* and *Weavings: A Journal of the Christian Spiritual Life* for adults; *Pockets* magazine for children and *Devo'Zine* for teens. Upper Room Books publishes a variety of resources in spiritual formation. In addition to publishing, The Upper Room's ministries have grown to include several spiritual formation programs, among them, The Walk to Emmaus, the Academy for Spiritual Formation, the Adventure in Healing and Wholeness, the Pathways Center for Spiritual Leadership and the Living Prayer Center. To find out more, log on to The Upper Room website: www.upperroom.org.

CONTRIBUTORS

THE EDITORS wish to especially thank **Keith Beasley-Topliffe, Jan Johnson, Robert Morris** and **Mary Lou Redding** for the advice and editorial assistance they provided far beyond the call of duty. Many thanks also to the writers who contributed to this project:

ENTRY POINT NOTES

The Reverend Mary Lou Santillan Baert
United Methodist minister and writer, Dallas, TX.
Proverbs

The Reverend Keith Beasley-Topliffe
United Methodist clergyperson and editor of the
Upper Room Spiritual Classics series.
1&2 Chronicles, Acts

The Reverend Eugene Blair
Director of Congregational Development, Northern Illinois Conference of the United Methodist church; curriculum writer for United Methodist Publishing House and the African Methodist Episcopal Church.
1&2 Kings

The Reverend Anne Broyles
A United Methodist minister and writer of novels, children's books and religious materials, who lives in Malibu, CA.
Haggai, Zechariah, Lamentations, Nehemiah

Professor Doris Donnelly, Ph.D.
Professor of Theology at John Carroll University, Cleveland, OH.
and
Ms. Carol Edkins, M.A.
President of Qualified Pension/Profit Sharing Consultants, Inc. Cleveland, OH.
1&2 Thessalonians, Philemon

Mr. Robert Durback
A former monk of Mepkin Abbey, Order of Cistercians of the Strict Observance and editor of *Seeds of Hope: A Henri Nouwen Reader* (Doubleday, 1997).
Exodus

Reverend Paul L. Escamilla
Pastor of Munger Place United Methodist Church in Dallas, TX and author of *Seasons of Communion* (1984).
James, Habakkuk

The Reverend Bernard John Franklin
A minister of the Presbyterian Church of Aotearoa, New Zealand, Reverend Franklin ministers in spiritual direction, leadership, teaching and preaching in Palmerston North, New Zealand.
John, Jeremiah

Eli Fisher, Ph.D.
Associate Editor of *Alive Now* magazine, Nashville, TN.
Leviticus

The Reverend Kent Ira Groff
Director, Oasis Ministries for Spiritual Development, Inc., Camp Hill, PA, and writer and Presbyterian minister.
Luke

Dr. E. Glenn Hinson
Professor of Spirituality and John Loftis Professor of Church History, Baptist Theological Seminary, Richmond, VA.
and
Ms. Stephanie Ford
A graduate of Baptist Theological Seminary in Richmond, VA as well as graduate studies in spirituality at The Catholic University of America, Washington, DC.
Psalms

Dr. Carol Caruth Johnson
Professor of Pastoral Care, Oral Roberts University, Tulsa, OK and a licensed marriage and family therapist.
Hosea, Joshua

Ms. Jan Johnson
Journalist, retreat leader, trained spiritual director and author of *Enjoying the Presence of God* and *Listening to God*, Ms. Johnson lives in Simi, CA.
Mark, Judges

Ms. Jan Knight
Editor of *Pockets* magazine, Nashville, TN.
Micah, Amos

The Reverend Robert Corin Morris
Founding Director of Interweave, an interfaith adult center in Summit, NJ, and an Episcopal priest.
Isaiah

The Reverend M. Robert Mulholland, Jr.
Vice President and Chief Academic Officer, Asbury Theological Seminary, Wilmore, KY. Among his books are *Shaped by the Word* (Upper Room Books) and *Invitation to a Journey* (IVP).
Revelation

Susan Muto, Ph.D.
Executive Director of the Epiphany Association, Pittsburgh, PA and the author or co-author of over thirty books.
1&2 Corinthians

The Reverend Bruce R. Ough
Senior Pastor, St. Paul's United Methodist Church, Cedar Rapids, IA , and writer.
Joel

Ms. Virginia Stem Owens
Esther

Dr. Elizabeth L. Patterson, M.A., Ph.D.
Associate Dean, School of Theology, Fuller Theological Seminary, Pasadena, CA
Romans

The Reverend Larry Peacock
A United Methodist pastor, retreat leader, author and spiritual director currently serving Malibu United Methodist Church, CA
Ezekiel, Obadiah, Nahum, Zephaniah, Malachi

Ms. Sheila Mary Pritchard, MTh, Dip. R.E.
Teacher, spiritual director, retreat leader; developed the Spiritual Formation department of the Bible College of New Zealand.
1&2 Peter, Jude

Ms. Mary Lou Redding
Managing Editor, *The Upper Room* magazine, Nashville, TN
Numbers, Daniel, Job, Ezra

Dr. Tom Schwanda
An ordained minister in the Reformed Church of America who serves as the associate for spiritual formation and family ministry in the RCA, Grand Rapids, MI
Galatians, Ephesians, Philippians, Colossians, Hebrews, 1,2,3 John

Mr. Gary Thomas
Director of the Center for Evangelical Spirituality, Bellingham, WA and author of *Seeking the Face of God, Sacred Pathways* and *The Glorious Pursuit.*
Matthew, 1&2 Timothy, Titus, Deuteronomy

The Reverend Douglas Vest
Episcopal priest, author, spiritual director and retreat leader, Altadena, CA
Jonah, Ecclesiastes, 1&2 Samuel

Ms. Norvene Vest
Author of *Gathered in the Word* and frequent writer on Benedictine spirituality. Ms. Vest is an Episcopal laywoman who lives with her husband, Douglas, in Altadena, CA
Genesis, Ruth

Wendy Wright
Professor of Theology, Creighton University, Omaha, NE and author of *Sacred Dwelling: A Spirituality of Family Life*
Song of Songs

WAYS OF MEETING GOD

The Reverend Keith Beasley-Topliffe
United Methodist clergyperson and editor of the *Upper Room Spiritual Classics* series
"Meeting God in Worship" (co-author)

Stephen D. Bryant
Publisher, The Upper Room, Nashville, TN
"Meeting God in Prayer"

Janice T. Grana
Former Editor and Publisher, The Upper Room, now Executive Editor, Upper Room Books, Nashville, TN
"Meeting God in Service"

J.Steven Harper, Ph.D.
Former Dean of the Chapel, The Upper Room, now Vice President and Dean, Asbury Theological Seminary, Orlando Campus
"Meeting God in Scripture"

Reuben P. Job
Former Publisher, The Upper Room, and a retired bishop in the United Methodist Church
"Meeting God in Worship" (co-author)

Timothy Jones
Author, editor and retreat leader, author of *Awake My Soul* and *The Art of Prayer*
"Meeting God in Everyday Life"

Mary Lou Redding
Managing Editor, The Upper Room magazine, Nashville, TN, author *of Breaking and Mending* (1998)
"Meeting God in Community"

Marjorie Thompson
Presbyterian Minister and Director of the Pathways Center for Spiritual Leadership, Nashville, TN; author of *Soul Feast* and *Family: The Forming Center*
"Meeting God in the Created Order"

GETTING STARTED IN SPIRITUAL FORMATION

J. Steven Harper, Ph.D.
Former Dean of the Chapel, The Upper Room, now Vice President and Dean, Asbury Theological Seminary, Orlando Campus.
"Moving Forward in Spiritual Formation"

John Mogabgab
Editor *Weavings* magazine, Nashville, TN and the husband of Marjorie Thompson.
"What is Spiritual Formation?"

The Reverend M. Robert Mulholland, Jr.
Adapted from Chapters Two and Five of *Shaped by the Word: The Power of Scripture in Spiritual Formation* (Upper Room Books,1985) by Jan Johnson
"Reading the Scriptures Devotionally"

Marjorie Thompson
Director, The Pathways Center for Spiritual Leadership, Nashville, TN and the wife of John Mogabgab.
"Praying the Scriptures"

GETTING STARTED
in SPIRITUAL FORMATION

What is Spiritual Formation?

Human beings are creatures of the future. Unlike other inhabitants of creation whose lives are fixed within the boundaries of genetics and instinct, human existence is open-ended, laced with mystery, like moist clay in a potter's hand. We are works in progress, shaped by the constant rhythms of nature and the unexpected turns of history. Sometimes elated and sometimes burdened by our unfinished condition, we live our days conscious that "what we will be has not yet been made known" (1 John 3:2). A sense of our true identity is always just beyond our grasp, always awaiting us, it seems, just around the next bend in the road.

As nature and history interact with a human existence that is incomplete, pliable and rich with significant potential, personal formation occurs. Human beings are formed by the sculpting of will, intellect and emotion into a distinct way of being in the world. Such formation of personal character will assume a wide range of expression depending on our location geographically, socially, economically and culturally. Family values, social conventions, cultural assumptions, the great turning points of an epoch, the painful secrets of a heart—these and many other factors combine to form or deform the direction, depth and boundaries of our lives. Formation is therefore a fundamental characteristic of human life. It is happening whether or not we are aware of it, and its effect may as often inhibit as promote the development of healthy, fulfilled humanity.

For people of Biblical faith, nature and history of themselves are not the final sources of personal formation. Rather, they are means through which the God who formed all things molds human beings into the contours of their truest destiny, the unfettered praise of God (see Isaiah 43:21). To be shaped by God's gracious design is a particular expression of personal formation—spiritual formation. Irenaeus, third-century bishop of Lyons, echoed this ancient Biblical theme when he observed that "the glory of God is the human being fully alive." The God known in Scripture is a God who continuously forms something out of nothing—earth and heaven, creatures great and small, a people who call upon God's name, the "inmost being" (Psalm 139:13) of every human life. Yet the majestic sweep of God's formational activity never eclipses the intimacy God desires and seeks with us. Having carefully and lovingly formed each of us in the womb, God knows us by name and will not forget us (see Isaiah 43:1; 44:21,24). In the Biblical perspective, to be a person

Personal spiritual practices also prime us to be responsive to the Holy Spirit's approach. The meditative reading of Scripture encouraged in this Bible enables us to become at home in God's Word. As this occurs, we develop a growing familiarity with the Holy Spirit who fashioned and continues to dwell in holy writ. According to twelfth-century Cistercian abbot Peter of Celle, such reading is nothing less than "the soul's food, light, lamp, refuge, consolation, and the spice of every spiritual savor." Prayer, that royal road to deepening intimacy with God, will inevitably acquaint us with the guiding grace of the Spirit. It is in the Spirit that we pray and through the Spirit that the inarticulate yearnings of our heart receive coherent expression before God (see Romans 8:27). Various "spiritual fitness" exercises, including abstaining from self-destructive activities and attitudes, allocating personal resources in a godly manner and following simple rules of life, help to remind us that God is the center of each day. Such exercises produce stamina for continued acceptance of the Holy Spirit's invitation to "come and follow."

Following the leading of the Holy Spirit builds in us a growing capacity for extraordinary witness to God's kingdom, such as extending forgiveness where there has been genuine injury. It also reinforces in us the knowledge that our new humanity in Jesus Christ is the work of the Spirit and not our own achievement. In our human weakness, we need the strength and sustenance of the Holy Spirit to maintain the Godward direction of our life. Such assistance is clearly promised by Jesus: "When he, the Spirit of truth, comes, he will guide you into all truth" (John 16:13). This truth is what the author of Ephesians calls "the fullness of Christ" (Ephesians 4:13). The measure of this truth is nothing other than love. Love is the first gift of the Spirit and the final test of our freedom in Jesus Christ (see 1 Corinthians 13; Galatians 5:22; Colossians 1:8). All other marks of our new humanity—joy, peace, patience, kindness, generosity, faithfulness, self-control—are manifestations of this love, a love that binds us to Jesus Christ in the unity of the Holy Spirit for the sake of the world God loves so much. "Since we live by the Spirit, let us keep in step with the Spirit" (Galatians 5:25).

> In a life increasingly given to the guidance of the Holy Spirit, our new humanity in Jesus Christ gradually becomes more visible and effective in the world.

In the World. In a life increasingly given to the guidance of the Holy Spirit, our new humanity in Jesus Christ gradually becomes more visible and effective in the world. Far from removing us from the messiness of the world, spiritual formation plunges us into the middle of the world's rage and suffering. It was to this place of pain and bewilderment that Jesus Christ was sent as the visible image of the invisible God (see John 14:9; Colossians 1:15). It was to this place of bitterness and infirmity that Jesus Christ was sent, not to condemn, but to save (see John 3:17). Those who are being formed in his image take the same path. Love, the full measure of Christian maturity, impels us with kindly urgency in this direction. Love desires to be seen, known and received, for by these actions it grows wider and deeper. Through us love is extended to the furthest recesses of human sorrow and need. Thus, God's love for the world—in us because we are in Jesus Christ—becomes a sign of hope and a source of transformation in the world.

"No one is richer, no one more powerful, no one more free," observed Thomas à Kempis, "than the person who can give his whole life to God and freely serve others with deep humility and love." To embody in thought, word and deed the love of God made known in our Lord Jesus Christ is the signal mark of faithful discipleship, the inexhaustible strength of vital congregations and the ultimate goal of spiritual formation.

GETTING STARTED
in SPIRITUAL FORMATION

Praying the Scriptures

A longtime member of a well-established Protestant church recounted a turning point in her spiritual life: She discovered that the Bible could be prayed as well as read. She had read, studied and reflected on the Bible for many years, yet the notion of "praying the Scriptures" seemed quite foreign when a friend first suggested it. Nonetheless, as soon as she began to practice praying the Scriptures, it made complete sense. For the first time in her adult life, the Bible truly came alive. She experienced the Word of God as "living and active" (Hebrews 4:12), a means through which God searched, invited, challenged and comforted her. It seemed so natural that she felt as if she had spiritually "come home."

> To pray the Scriptures means to allow the words of the sacred text to form our prayer —either directly or indirectly.

To pray the Scriptures means to allow the words of the sacred text to form our prayer—either directly or indirectly. Prayer entails heart-to-heart communication with God that moves in both directions. God speaks, we listen and respond; we speak, God listens and responds.

To pray the Scriptures requires first of all that we approach the Word in a spirit of prayer. We acknowledge that we are seeking the living, active presence

of God in and through God's Word. We bring ourselves consciously into the divine presence and affirm the reality of this presence even if we cannot feel it. Whatever we read and reflect on in the Word is part of our ongoing dialogue with God.

From this basic stance, we may take any number of approaches to praying the Scriptures. One of the most central and ancient practices of Christian prayer is called *lectio divina,* or spiritual reading. In *lectio divina,* we begin by reading and savoring a short passage of Scripture. Our inner posture is one of a listening heart filled with an unhurried expectation that God has a message to convey especially suited to our condition and circumstance. We read and ruminate with the ears of our heart open, alert to connections the Spirit may reveal between the passage and our life situation. We ask, "What are you saying to me today, Lord? What am I to hear in this story, parable, prophecy?" Listening in this way requires an attitude of patient receptivity in which we let go of our own agendas and open ourselves to God's shaping purpose.

Lectio Divina. Once we have heard a word that we know is meant for our ears, we are naturally drawn to prayer. From listening we move to speaking—perhaps in anguish, confession or sorrow; perhaps in joy, praise, thanksgiving or adoration; perhaps in anger, confusion or hurt; perhaps in quiet confidence, trust or surrender. Finally, after pouring out our heart to God, we come to rest simply and deeply in that wonderful, loving presence of God. Reading, reflecting, responding and resting—this is the basic rhythm of a venerable and often-used approach to Scripture called *lectio divina.*

Perhaps an example will help to bring this rhythm alive in your imagination. Recently I read in 2 Kings about the origins of the people called Samaritans. Samaria once belonged to the ancient kingdom of Israel. When the king of Assyria invaded, taking Israelites captive to his own land, he forcibly repopulated Samaria with people from surrounding regions who decided to worship "the god of the land." The passage reads, "They worshiped the LORD, but they also served their own gods in accordance with the customs of the nations from which they had been brought" (2 Kings 17:33). I hadn't read this book in a long time, and I found myself fascinated by the history. It would make for interesting Bible study, I thought, or a good sermon. Then suddenly I heard in my mind's ear a shocking indictment: "You are a Samaritan." Recalling that I was reading for the purpose of prayer, I asked, "Are you really saying that I'm like this, God?" The answer was there in my own heart: Yes, you worship God but also the gods of this land—success, prosperity, "the American Dream." This was clearly a very uncomfortable word that God had addressed personally to me. It prompted me to reflect on all the ways I do, in fact, give my heart and allegiance to the idols of my culture. Recognition of that reality propelled me into prayers of confession and repentance, then prayer for the strength of will to desire God above all else. Finally, I had to confess my guilt to God and rest in the assurance of God's mercy. The whole cycle took perhaps ten or fifteen minutes.

The Ignatian Method. *Lectio divina* is but one way to pray the Scriptures. We can also pray the Bible by using our God-given imagination by means of an ancient method referred to as Ignatian. This approach invites us to enter the narrative, picturing the situation and identifying with characters that populate the drama. This may eventually lead us to dialogue beyond what is given in the text, a dialogue that becomes part of our prayer. Some passages of Scripture are better suited to this process than others. The Gospels are especially rich in stories that easily engage our imagination as a way to enter into prayer.

Read, for example, a story such as the tax collector and the Pharisee (see Luke 18:9–14). Picture the two men in the temple, the Pharisee standing proudly upfront, grateful not to be like the man behind him. Imagine what it is like to be in the shoes of someone who represents such high standards of righteousness according to Israelite law, who sees his life as a model of religious conduct for others. Have you ever felt like this? If so, in what kinds of situations or with what sorts of people? Then step into the shoes of the tax collector, the hated "tool of Rome." Imagine how many times you have skimmed a hefty sum for yourself from the taxes you have collected from fellow Jews for the Roman occupiers. What emotions are your experiencing—the misery of being an outcast in your own community, the self-loathing that comes from betraying your people and your integrity, the despair at your weakness of character, your desperate hope for mercy from God? With which of these two characters do you most identify? What do you have to say to God about your own experience in relation to these two characters? Do you see how the story and your personal engagement with it lead you into prayer?

This approach to praying the Scriptures is rich and fruitful for people who can readily exercise their God-given imagination. Perhaps you can imagine yourself as Peter, looking at the awesome catch of fish, feeling the power of the One standing before you whose eyes you dare not even look into (see Luke 5:1–11). Does this speak to your experience before God? Or perhaps you identify strongly with Martha as your sister sits idly listening to Jesus while you, in an anxious dither, rush to complete meal preparations. Do you hear Jesus' words to you as rebuke or invitation? What are you really longing for in your own heart (see Luke 10:38–42)? Maybe you are in the boat with the disciples facing a sudden and terrifying storm. You sense the limits of your vision and power is limited by your fear. How do Jesus' words affect your spirit as you imagine being part of this story? Are you facing a storm in your life just now? Does identification with the story make your prayer more concrete? Is God speaking a word to you through this passage (see Mark 4:35–41)? Or picture yourself as the woman who suffered from an issue of blood for twelve years, as you shyly thread your way through the crowd to touch the edge of Jesus' clothing. Or as Jairus, desperate for Jesus to come quickly before your daughter dies, watching Jesus turn around to find out who touched him, taking precious time to deal with the needs of someone else before he comes with you to your home (see Mark 5:21–43). Where do you connect with these powerful stories? What insight into yourself, into God, into your relationships comes through praying the Gospels in this way? It can be especially helpful to write down the basic outline of your imaginative encounter with the text, your insights and any dialogue with story characters or with God that naturally occur as part of your prayer.

> The Gospels are especially rich in stories that easily engage our imagination as a way to enter into prayer.

The Prayers and Songs of Scripture. There are other ways to pray Scripture as well. The Bible gives us categories for prayer, expands our language for prayer and tutors us in speaking to God as we hear God speak to us through the Word. The Bible contains prayers and canticles (songs) that give us words to pray and praise. Many, such as the Lord's Prayer, the Magnificat and the Canticle of Simeon, have become part of the common prayer of church liturgy. Yet any of these may also give voice to the joys, yearnings and struggles of our personal lives. We truly pray the Lord's Prayer when we take each phrase and make it our own, finding its truth reflected in our beliefs, needs, fears and aspirations. Mary's Magnificat can become our own song of exultation, hope and trust. There are times when we recognize with her that "the Mighty One has done great things for me" (Luke 1:49). We may know from experience what it means to be lifted up from lowliness, or we may see the emptiness of those who seem powerful and self-satisfied. Thus, we know that the truths spoken in Mary's words are universal precisely because they are so personal.

Sometimes we can personalize a passage of Scripture by placing our own name in it. Some passages from the books of the Prophets lend themselves to becoming personal prayers as we make ourselves the recipients of God's Word. Take, for example, God's invitation to the abundant life in Isaiah. Insert your name in the blanks to get a feel for how to pray Scripture this way:

> Come, _____ who is thirsty,
>> come to the waters;
> and _____ who has no money,
>> come, buy and eat!
> _____, why spend money on what is not bread,
>> and your labor on what does not satisfy?
> Listen, listen to me, _____, and eat what is good . . .
>> hear me, that your soul may live.
> I will make an everlasting covenant with you, _____ (Isaiah 55:1–3).

Here you allow yourself to receive personally the promises (or the judgments) of God and to respond from the heart. Try this out with Isaiah 43:1–7; Jeremiah 1:4–8 or 18:1–6.

Praying the Book of Psalms. The words of Scripture can also become words through which we address God directly. Nowhere is this more apparent than in the book of Psalms. The book of Psalms has been called "the prayer book of the Bible" in both the Jewish and Christian traditions. It is a collection of sung prayers that has been used in corporate liturgy from the time of ancient Israel up to the present. Because the psalms range so widely in emotional expression, from the heights of adoration and praise to the depths of vengeful curses against the enemy, they have special pertinence to our prayer life. They teach us to hide nothing from God but to bring all that is real into the only relationship that can bless the best and heal the worst in us. Surely this is why German theologian Dietrich Bonhoeffer summoned the earthy wit of Martin Luther when he declared, "Whoever has begun to pray the Psalter seriously and regularly will soon give a vacation to other little devotional

spiritual formation—the process of being conformed to the image of Jesus Christ. Reading formationally helps us open our "rational filter," which can sift out so much of God's voice. We begin to hear at the heart and soul level. Jesus frequently reminded those who had "ears to hear" (Mark 4:9,23; Luke 8:8; 14:35).

Formational reading often helps us develop those ears to hear. Let me share with you a personal experience of formational reading. I was following a prescribed plan for Bible reading and had come to the exodus event. I'd read about the struggle between God and Pharaoh many times before but only informationally. As I read the daily assigned portion, I sat before it and said, "Lord, what are you seeking to say to me through this?" All sorts of thoughts went through my mind—who said what, Pharaoh's resistance, God's hardening Pharaoh's heart. I got nothing from it after wrestling with it for a week or more. Finally, each day's portion moved one by one through the ten plagues. I was met each time with silence—or my own noisy understanding of the passage.

As I moved toward the end of the passage about the plagues and asked that same question, an answer came: "You are Pharaoh!" "What?" I replied. "Me, Pharaoh? Moses, perhaps, even one of the Hebrews, but Pharaoh? Perhaps a servant or slave, but Pharaoh?" Things began to open up in the text and inside me. I realized God had given me certain gifts, abilities and personality traits. All these were God's "children," but I had enslaved them to my own purposes, desires, intentions and plans. Truly I was the Pharaoh of my life! I came to the last plague—the death of the firstborn. I saw that for me to cease to be Pharaoh in my life, there had to be a death of my "firstborn" desires to use God's gifts for my own purposes. If those gifts were to be liberated for God's use in my life, I would have to cease to be Pharaoh.

> **F**ormational Scripture reading invites us to open ourselves to allow God to set the agenda for our lives through the text.

Characteristics of Formational Scripture Reading.

Depth. Informational reading seeks to cover as much material as possible as quickly as possible, while formational reading involves smaller portions of Scripture. The point is not to just get through the text, but to become personally involved in it. Formational reading is concerned with depth, so we may find ourselves "holding on" to just one sentence or paragraph or page for quite a while. We allow the passage to open out to us its deeper dynamics and multiple layers of meaning. We let the text intrude into our life and address us.

Openness. In formational reading, we let the text master us. We come to the text with an openness to hear, to receive and to respond. This may feel risky because it lays us open to unforeseen conclusions.

Humility. Formational reading requires a humble and willing approach, which requires a new inner posture in which we are willing to relinquish our insights and purposes. We stand ourselves before Scripture and await its address.

Mystery. Informational reading can be characterized by a problem-solving mentality. When we do respond, we often read our needs and desires into the Scripture, asking, Does this passage solve my problems, answer my questions, meet my needs? Formational reading invites us to become open to the whole mystery of God. We allow God to address us however he may wish. Eventually, we may discover that problem-solving dynamics emerge from the encounter, but we relinquish the right to solve our problems with Scripture.

Suggestions for Formational Scripture Reading.

Make listening for God's voice a top priority. Focus your attention on what God is saying to you as you read. Listen for God to speak to you in and through, around and within, over and behind the words. Keep asking yourself, "What is God seeking to say to me in all of this?" Allow the text to become an instrument of God's control in your life. Respond to what you read with your heart and spirit.

Let your response take place down in the deeper levels of your being. Ask yourself questions such as: How do I feel about what is being said? How am I reacting? How am I responding down deep within myself? What is going on inside of me? Then begin to ask yourself "why" questions: Why do I feel this way? Why am I responding in this manner? Why do I have these feelings within?

Let this exercise be an opportunity to get in touch with the deeper layers of your being. What do your reactions tell you about your habits, your attitudes, your perspectives, your responses and your reactions to life? Are you beginning to see something about yourself? Thomas à Kempis said, "A humble knowledge of ourselves is a surer way to God than is the search for depth of learning." That humble knowledge of yourself can come when you read Scripture if you balance your cognitive response pattern with this affective response from deep within your being.

Prepare to read by quieting yourself. You can't run in, sit down, pick up the text and read Scripture formationally. You have to "center down," to use the old Quaker phrase—become still, relinquish your agenda and acknowledge the presence of God. You may have to relax first in order to do this. When you do this, you may find that no word addresses you out of that text on that day, but the constant discipline of preparing yourself and entering into formational reading will itself be spiritually forming to your soul.

Allow the two kinds of reading—informational and formational—to work together. You may begin reading a Scripture passage with informational dynamics, but then you must be sensitive to the need to move to the formational dynamics of reading. Allow yourself to become open and receptive to the intrusion of the living Word of God into your garbled, distorted self. You may get tripped up on an informational point and need to move back to an informational mode. There is a necessary interplay between these two approaches, but you'll ultimately need to arrive at a disciplined development of the formational mode of approaching the text. As we become skilled at shifting to that inner posture of becoming listeners, we develop "ears to hear." We become receptive and accessible to being addressed by the living Word of God.

GETTING STARTED
in SPIRITUAL FORMATION

Moving Forward in Spiritual Formation

In his article "What is Spiritual Formation," John Mogabgab defines spiritual formation as "a lifelong process through which our new humanity, hidden with Jesus
Christ in God, becomes ever more visible and effective through the leading of the
Holy Spirit." As noted evangelist E. Stanley Jones said, "We are Christians under
construction." Thinking of our spiritual life as a
process, as a journey, helps us to continually make
progress toward the goal of being conformed to the
image of Jesus Christ.

First, we journey forward in faith. The Christian life
is lived in relationship with Jesus Christ. We express
our faith in Jesus through the character and conduct
that emerge from that relationship. Our "belief system" is the total expression of who we are and what
we do. The ongoing process of spiritual formation begins and continues with faith. Having given ourselves
to God through an initial commitment, we subsequently respond to God, so that our faith grows deeper and stronger. The Holy Spirit is the dynamic
energy that conforms us to the likeness of Jesus
Christ in both personal and social holiness.

> Thinking of our spiritual life as a process, as a journey, helps us to continually make progress toward the goal of being conformed to the image of Jesus Christ.

We never "graduate" from the spiritual life. Instead, we awaken each day to discovery. Frank
Laubach began each day by praying, "God, what are
you doing in the world today that I can help you
with?" We move forward in spiritual formation believing that God does indeed invite us into holy partnership.

Second, we move forward with a sense of "fit." When David volunteered to fight
Goliath, King Saul clothed him with the royal armor (see 1 Samuel 17:38). Because
the armor didn't fit, David gave it back to Saul, preferring his own clothing and his
own weaponry—five stones and a slingshot. David's strategy may have been contrary to all standards of military preparedness, but it worked! Likewise, our ap-

proach to God in spiritual formation must "fit" each of us individually. The Christian life is a way of the heart, and we must follow our hearts in the way we move forward in spiritual formation. Spiritual formation is not random or subjective however. On the contrary, the choices we make will conform to the larger patterns of faith development in our lives.

As you use this Bible, you will undoubtedly find that certain approaches will be more valuable and meaningful than others. They may seem more comfortable. Go forward in the directions that have benefited you most. Don't worry about what you are *not* selecting; concentrate on the tradition or path that produces righteousness, peace and joy in your life (see Romans 14:17).

Along the way, you may find yourself circling back to a previous method or expanding into new areas. Just as with clothing so also with the soul, there will come those times when you "outgrow" the methods you are using and feel the need to develop in new and different ways. Remember that outgrowing something does not mean leaving it behind. It merely means increasing the size. You will inevitably arrive at such turning points in your spiritual life. When the time is ripe for change, you will know it. For now, work with the principles and practices that best fuel your desire for deeper life in God.

A sense of "fit" also means tailoring your spiritual practices to the realities of your life. What are you experiencing now? Develop a devotional life that takes your circumstances into consideration. In fact, you will not continue to move forward if you deny your needs and your emotions. When they change, you can alter your particular practices to fit a new circumstance or emotion. God knows what you are going through. Don't be afraid to follow wherever God might be leading you on your spiritual formation journey.

Third, we move forward in the presence of friends. Spiritual formation does not occur in isolation. One sign of our genuine progress is the desire to be in "communion with the saints"—in community with others. Community is the context in which much authentic spiritual formation takes place.

Through community we express our faith in Jesus Christ—a faith that includes the conviction that Jesus has many brothers and sisters whom we are called to love and with whom we are called to live. Our faith community consists of our particular affiliation with a congregation and the related smaller groups that exist within it, as well as our spiritual friends, mentors and teachers. Living in community educates, guides, protects, restores, inspires, forgives, heals and sustains us and sends us out into the world.

Community is also the laboratory in which we learn what it means to be compassionate, not only to fellow Christians, but to people located throughout the world; our community extends to our wider ecumenical and mission associations with Christians around the globe.

The saints are not only those with whom we live in ongoing fellowship—they are those of renown from the past. Being in community with others means developing a devotional life that includes reading and reflecting on the classics of Christian spirituality. Quotations from godly men and women have been scattered throughout this Bible, not only for inspiration, but also as a reminder that the spiritual life is always one of connecting to others. When we read the classics we connect with those who have gone before us. Far from being outdated or irrelevant, the classic writers are part of the great "cloud of witnesses" (see Hebrews 12:1) who both inform us and encourage us in our journey.

We are blessed to have many of the spiritual classics in print today. The Paulist Press series *Classics of Western Spirituality* is one of the most extensive offerings in this regard. The Upper Room has produced *Great Devotional Classics,* a boxed set of booklets with excerpts from the writings of many men and women of Christian history, and has more recently launched a series entitled *Upper Room Spiritual Classics.*

You can also find individual classics in print. Works like Augustine's *Confessions* or Julian of Norwich's *Revelations of Divine Love* are but two of hundreds of such works available for your enrichment. Anthologies are another wonderful way to connect with the classics. John Baillie's *A Diary of Readings* is one of the best known, containing one-page excerpts for every day of the year. Woodeene Koenig-Bricker's volume *365 Saints* summarizes the thoughts and contributions of well-known and little-known Christians.

Form provides the concrete structure on which spiritual formation is built.

Finally, we move forward by adopting a form. Faith and form are inseparable. Form provides the concrete structure on which spiritual formation is built. We are offered a variety of forms and styles, plans and programs to shape and sustain our discipleship. As we become rooted in the spiritual life, we will likely gravitate toward particular resources and practices that suit us and satisfy our needs. Our choices are determined by factors such as gender, race, personality, faith tradition, age and stage in life. There is nothing wrong with settling into a particular form of spiritual formation. It is as normal as our choices in areas such as literature, art and music. We never have to apologize for finding and developing those patterns to which we are drawn.

God is gracious to provide many avenues for spiritual development. This Bible is designed to provide a means to enter into the Scriptures in a very personal way. Or you may find a daily-office format like *The Book of Common Prayer* or *A Guide to Prayer for All God's People* very helpful. You may enjoy feeding for an extensive period of time on the writings of a single author like Oswald Chamber's *My Utmost for His Highest* or Lloyd Ogilvie's *Silent Strength.*

Though it's perfectly acceptable to choose a form that suits us, we also need to be open to broadening our experience by trying new forms, traditions, writers and so on. There is indeed a great variety in the ways God speaks to us. A look back through church history reveals that the saints were not only deeply spiritual people, they were also people with broad interests that expanded and informed their spiritual formation. Catherine of Siena was involved in the political affairs of her day. John Wesley was fascinated with medicine. Peter Marshall was a great game player.

There is a world of blessing and benefit available to us when we embrace all the experiences God offers us. If our spiritual formation is grounded in the Bible, we stand on a sure foundation that enables us to reach upward and outward to every dimension of development that God—who created the earth in all its fullness—has provided.

When you use this Bible you will not only encounter Holy Scripture directly, you will also encounter the elements that will enable you to move forward in spiritual formation: faith, fit, friends and form. These are the roadmaps that will guide your journey—a journey that none of us can plan or control.

The earliest Christian creed contained only three words: "Jesus is Lord!" It was the simplest way believers knew to declare their utter confidence in the risen Christ to lead and guide them into an abundant and everlasting life. Wherever you are right now, there is good news: God loves you more than you can imagine. Move forward with assurance. The best is yet to be!

PREFACE
TO THE NIV

THE NEW INTERNATIONAL VERSION is a completely new translation of the Holy Bible made by over a hundred scholars working directly from the best available Hebrew, Aramaic and Greek texts. It had its beginning in 1965 when, after several years of exploratory study by committees from the Christian Reformed Church and the National Association of Evangelicals, a group of scholars met at Palos Heights, Illinois, and concurred in the need for a new translation of the Bible in contemporary English. This group, though not made up of official church representatives, was transdenominational. Its conclusion was endorsed by a large number of leaders from many denominations who met in Chicago in 1966.

Responsibility for the new version was delegated by the Palos Heights group to a self-governing body of fifteen, the Committee on Bible Translation, composed for the most part of biblical scholars from colleges, universities and seminaries. In 1967 the New York Bible Society (now the International Bible Society) generously undertook the financial sponsorship of the project—a sponsorship that made it possible to enlist the help of many distinguished scholars. The fact that participants from the United States, Great Britain, Canada, Australia and New Zealand worked together gave the project its international scope. That they were from many denominations—including Anglican, Assemblies of God, Baptist, Brethren, Christian Reformed, Church of Christ, Evangelical Free, Lutheran, Mennonite, Methodist, Nazarene, Presbyterian, Wesleyan and other churches—helped to safeguard the translation from sectarian bias.

How it was made helps to give the New International Version its distinctiveness. The translation of each book was assigned to a team of scholars. Next, one of the Intermediate Editorial Committees revised the initial translation, with constant reference to the Hebrew, Aramaic or Greek. Their work then went to one of the General Editorial Committees, which checked it in detail and made another thorough revision. This revision in turn was carefully reviewed by the Committee on Bible Translation, which made further changes and then released the final version for publication. In this way the entire Bible underwent three revisions, during each of which the translation was examined for its faithfulness to the original languages and for its English style.

All this involved many thousands of hours of research and discussion regarding the meaning of the texts and the precise way of putting them into English. It may well be that no other translation has been made by a more thorough process of review and revision from committee to committee than this one.

From the beginning of the project, the Committee on Bible Translation held to certain goals for the New International Version: that it would be an accurate translation and one that would have clarity and literary quality and so prove suitable for public and private reading, teaching, preaching, memorizing and liturgical use. The Committee also sought to preserve some measure of continuity with the long tradition of translating the Scriptures into English.

In working toward these goals, the translators were united in their commitment to the authority and infallibility of the Bible as God's Word in written form. They believe that it contains the divine answer to the deepest needs of humanity, that it sheds unique light on our path in a dark world, and that it sets forth the way to our eternal well-being.

The first concern of the translators has been the accuracy of the translation and its fidelity to the thought of the biblical writers. They have weighed the significance of the lexical and grammatical details of the Hebrew, Aramaic and Greek texts. At the same time, they have striven for more than a word-for-word translation. Because thought patterns and syntax differ from language to language, faithful communication of the meaning of the writers of the Bible demands frequent modifications in sentence structure and constant regard for the contextual meanings of words.

A sensitive feeling for style does not always accompany scholarship. Accordingly the Committee on Bible Translation submitted the developing version to a number of stylistic consultants. Two of them read every book of both Old and New Testaments twice—once before and once after the last major revision—and made invaluable suggestions. Samples of the translation were tested for clarity and ease of reading by various kinds of people—young and old, highly educated and less well educated, ministers and laymen.

Concern for clear and natural English—that the New International Version should be idiomatic but not idiosyncratic, contemporary but not dated—motivated the translators and consultants. At the same time, they tried to reflect the differing styles of the biblical writers. In view of the international use of English, the translators sought to avoid obvious Americanisms on the one hand and obvious Anglicisms on the other. A British edition reflects the comparatively few differences of significant idiom and of spelling.

As for the traditional pronouns "thou," "thee" and "thine" in reference to the Deity, the translators judged that to use these archaisms (along with the old verb forms such as "doest," "wouldest" and "hadst") would violate accuracy in translation. Neither Hebrew, Aramaic nor Greek uses special pronouns for the persons of the Godhead. A present-day translation is not enhanced by forms that in the time of the King James Version were used in everyday speech, whether referring to God or man.

For the Old Testament the standard Hebrew text, the Masoretic Text as published in the latest editions of *Biblia Hebraica,* was used throughout. The Dead Sea Scrolls contain material bearing on an earlier stage of the Hebrew text. They were consulted, as were the Samaritan Pentateuch and the ancient scribal traditions relating to textual changes. Sometimes a variant Hebrew reading in the margin of the Masoretic Text was followed instead of the text itself. Such instances, being variants within the Masoretic tradition, are not specified by footnotes. In rare cases, words in the consonantal text were divided differently from the way they appear in the Masoretic Text. Footnotes indicate this. The translators also consulted the more important early versions—the Septuagint; Aquila, Symmachus and Theodotion; the Vulgate; the Syriac Peshitta; the Targums; and for the Psalms the *Juxta Hebraica* of Jerome. Readings from these versions were occasionally followed where the Masoretic Text seemed doubtful and where accepted principles of textual criticism showed that one or more of these textual witnesses appeared to provide the correct reading. Such instances are footnoted. Sometimes vowel letters and vowel signs did not, in the judgment of the translators, represent the correct vowels for the original consonantal text. Accordingly some words were read with a different set of vowels. These instances are usually not indicated by footnotes.

The Greek text used in translating the New Testament was an eclectic one. No other piece of ancient literature has such an abundance of manuscript witnesses as does the New Testament. Where existing manuscripts differ, the translators made their choice of readings according to accepted principles of New Testament textual criticism. Footnotes call attention to places where there was uncertainty about what the original text was. The best current printed texts of the Greek New Testament were used.

There is a sense in which the work of translation is never wholly finished. This applies to all great literature and uniquely so to the Bible. In 1973 the New Testament in the New International Version was published. Since then, suggestions for corrections and revisions have been received from various sources. The Committee on Bible Translation carefully considered the suggestions and adopted a number of them. These were incorporated in the first printing of the entire Bible in 1978. Additional revisions were made by the Committee on Bible Translation in 1983 and appear in printings after that date.

As in other ancient documents, the precise meaning of the biblical texts is sometimes uncertain. This is more often the case with the Hebrew and Aramaic texts than with the Greek text. Although archaeological and linguistic discoveries in this century aid in understanding difficult passages, some uncertainties remain. The more significant of these have been called to the reader's attention in the footnotes.

In regard to the divine name *YHWH,* commonly referred to as the *Tetragrammaton,* the translators adopted the device used in most English versions of rendering that name as "LORD" in capital letters to distinguish it from *Adonai,* another Hebrew word rendered "Lord," for which small letters are used. Wherever the two names stand together in the Old Testament as a compound name of God, they are rendered "Sovereign LORD."

Because for most readers today the phrases "the LORD of hosts" and "God of hosts" have little meaning, this version renders them "the LORD Almighty" and "God Almighty." These renderings convey the sense of the Hebrew, namely, "he who is sovereign over all the 'hosts' (powers) in heaven and on earth, especially over the 'hosts' (armies) of Israel." For readers unacquainted with Hebrew this does not make clear the distinction between *Sabaoth* ("hosts" or "Almighty") and *Shaddai* (which can also be translated "Almighty"), but the latter occurs infrequently and is always footnoted. When *Adonai* and *YHWH Sabaoth* occur together, they are rendered "the Lord, the LORD Almighty."

As for other proper nouns, the familiar spellings of the King James Version are generally retained. Names traditionally spelled with "ch," except where it is final, are usually spelled in this translation with "k" or "c," since the biblical languages do not have the sound that "ch" frequently indicates in English—for example, in *chant*. For well-known names such as Zechariah, however, the traditional spelling has been retained. Variation in the spelling of names in the original languages has usually not been indicated. Where a person or place has two or more different names in the Hebrew, Aramaic or Greek texts, the more familiar one has generally been used, with footnotes where needed.

To achieve clarity the translators sometimes supplied words not in the original texts but required by the context. If there was uncertainty about such material, it is enclosed in brackets. Also for the sake of clarity or style, nouns, including some proper nouns, are sometimes substituted for pronouns, and vice versa. And though the Hebrew writers often shifted back and forth between first, second and third personal pronouns without change of antecedent, this translation often makes them uniform, in accordance with English style and without the use of footnotes.

Poetical passages are printed as poetry, that is, with indentation of lines and with separate stanzas. These are generally designed to reflect the structure of Hebrew poetry. This poetry is normally characterized by parallelism in balanced lines. Most of the poetry in the Bible is in the Old Testament, and scholars differ regarding the scansion of Hebrew lines. The translators determined the stanza divisions for the most part by analysis of the subject matter. The stanzas therefore serve as poetic paragraphs.

As an aid to the reader, italicized sectional headings are inserted in most of the books. They are not to be regarded as part of the NIV text, are not for oral reading, and are not intended to dictate the interpretation of the sections they head.

The footnotes in this version are of several kinds, most of which need no explanation. Those giving alternative translations begin with "Or" and generally introduce the alternative with the last word preceding it in the text, except when it is a single-word alternative; in poetry quoted in a footnote a slant mark indicates a line division. Footnotes introduced by "Or" do not have uniform significance. In some cases two possible translations were considered to have about equal validity. In other cases, though the translators were convinced that the translation in the text was correct, they judged that another interpretation was possible and of sufficient importance to be represented in a footnote.

In the New Testament, footnotes that refer to uncertainty regarding the original text are introduced by "Some manuscripts" or similar expressions. In the Old Testament, evidence for the reading chosen is given first and evidence for the alternative is added after a semicolon (for example: Septuagint; Hebrew *father*). In such notes the term "Hebrew" refers to the Masoretic Text.

It should be noted that minerals, flora and fauna, architectural details, articles of clothing and jewelry, musical instruments and other articles cannot always be identified with precision. Also measures of capacity in the biblical period are particularly uncertain (see the table of weights and measures following the text).

Like all translations of the Bible, made as they are by imperfect man, this one undoubtedly falls short of its goals. Yet we are grateful to God for the extent to which he has enabled us to realize these goals and for the strength he has given us and our colleagues to complete our task. We offer this version of the Bible to him in whose name and for whose glory it has been made. We pray that it will lead many into a better understanding of the Holy Scriptures and a fuller knowledge of Jesus Christ the incarnate Word, of whom the Scriptures so faithfully testify.

The Committee on Bible Translation

June 1978
(Revised August 1983)

Names of the translators and editors may be secured
from the International Bible Society,
translation sponsors of the New International Version,
1820 Jet Stream Drive, Colorado Springs, Colorado
80921-3696 U.S.A.

Old Testament

GENESIS
Created for Relationship

KEY VERSES:

"I am God Almighty; walk before me and be blameless . . . I will establish my covenant as an everlasting covenant between me and you and your descendants after you for the generations to come, to be your God."—Genesis 17:1,7

The book of Genesis contains the "old, old stories" of our faith, the record of God's interaction with his people, an account that has been faithfully handed down to us for our encouragement. Perhaps the elements are so familiar that we overlook the stunning importance of the event itself. God chooses to create to be in covenant with us! We are not separate from, but intimately related to, the unimaginable God. Our relationship with God endures day by day, through challenges, opportunities, losses and joys. Our covenant with God endures though we fall short. Our intimacy with God satisfies our high aspirations for union with every breath and beyond death.

The record of Genesis is fascinating reading, for it is real, even harsh and cruel, yet often piercingly joyful. In its pages we find people not unlike ourselves, whose lives are always under God's watchful eye. Like us, these people are creatures formed by God's hand and inspirited with the very breath of God. Astonishingly, they are transformed even in the midst of their struggles; they deepen in their capacity to respond to God's care.

As you read Genesis slowly and prayerfully, seek to enter into the events described. Step into the "shoes" of the people you meet and ask how their situations might apply to your own life. Each reading is a new opportunity for God to speak to you through the Holy Spirit and for you to marvel at the ways God loved and formed Abraham and Sarah, Isaac and Rebekah, Jacob, Leah and Rachel.

> "(I said) Ah, good Lord, how could all things be well, because of the great harm which has come through sin to your creatures? . . . And to this our blessed Lord answered . . . that I should contemplate the glorious atonement, for this atoning is more pleasing to the blessed divinity and more honourable for man's salvation, without comparison, than ever Adam's sin was harmful. So then this is our blessed Lord's intention, and in this teaching we should pay heed to this: For since I have set right the greatest of harms, then it is my will that you should know through this that I shall set right everything which is less."
>
> —JULIAN OF NORWICH,
> *Showings*

God's Word Works

GENESIS 1:9

Over and over we read, "God said . . . And it was so." Verse 9 is one of many such refrains in this first chapter of Genesis. God spoke, and creation leaped into being in joyful response to the overwhelming power of God's Word. Great comfort can be found in knowing that God's Word is *always* fruitful. God doesn't just *try*. God *does*. Is there a place in your prayer today where this fact might bring you assurance? The next time you wonder how anything good can possibly emerge from your current situation, remember that God's response to prayer is immediate, even though the effects may not at first be visible. When God speaks, things happen—both within us and around us!

See *Meeting God in Prayer*

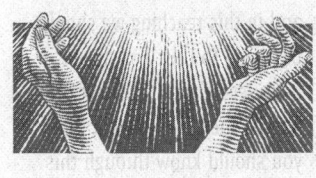

The Beginning

1 In the beginning God created the heavens and the earth. ²Now the earth was*ᵃ* formless and empty, darkness was over the surface of the deep, and the Spirit of God was hovering over the waters.

³And God said, "Let there be light," and there was light. ⁴God saw that the light was good, and he separated the light from the darkness. ⁵God called the light "day," and the darkness he called "night." And there was evening, and there was morning—the first day.

⁶And God said, "Let there be an expanse between the waters to separate water from water." ⁷So God made the expanse and separated the water under the expanse from the water above it. And it was so. ⁸God called the expanse "sky." And there was evening, and there was morning—the second day.

⁹And God said, "Let the water under the sky be gathered to one place, and let dry ground appear." And it was so. ¹⁰God called the dry ground "land," and the gathered waters he called "seas." And God saw that it was good.

¹¹Then God said, "Let the land produce vegetation: seed-bearing plants and trees on the land that bear fruit with seed in it, according to their various kinds." And it was so. ¹²The land produced vegetation: plants bearing seed according to their kinds and trees bearing fruit with seed in it according to their kinds. And God saw that it was good. ¹³And there was evening, and there was morning—the third day.

¹⁴And God said, "Let there be lights in the expanse of the sky to separate the day from the night, and let them serve as signs to mark seasons and days and years, ¹⁵and let them be lights in the expanse of the sky to give light on the earth." And it was so. ¹⁶God made two great lights—the greater light to govern the day and the lesser light to govern the night. He also made the stars. ¹⁷God set them in the expanse of the sky to give light on the earth, ¹⁸to govern the day and the night, and to separate light from darkness. And God saw that it was good. ¹⁹And there was evening, and there was morning—the fourth day.

²⁰And God said, "Let the water teem with living creatures, and let birds fly above the earth across the expanse of the sky." ²¹So God created the great creatures of the sea and every living and moving thing with which the water teems, according to their kinds, and every winged bird according to its kind. And God saw that it was good. ²²God blessed them and said, "Be fruitful and increase in number and fill the water in the seas, and let the birds increase on the earth." ²³And there was evening, and there was morning—the fifth day.

²⁴And God said, "Let the land produce living creatures according to their kinds: livestock, creatures that move along the ground, and wild animals, each according to its kind." And it was so. ²⁵God made the wild animals according to their kinds, the livestock according to their kinds, and all the creatures that move along the

ᵃ 2 Or possibly became

ground according to their kinds. And God saw that it was good. [26]Then God said, "Let us make man in our image, in our likeness, and let them rule over the fish of the sea and the birds of the air, over the livestock, over all the earth,[a] and over all the creatures that move along the ground."

[27]So God created man in his own image,
in the image of God he created him;
male and female he created them.

[28]God blessed them and said to them, "Be fruitful and increase in number; fill the earth and subdue it. Rule over the fish of the sea and the birds of the air and over every living creature that moves on the ground."
[29]Then God said, "I give you every seed-bearing plant on the face of the whole earth and every tree that has fruit with seed in it. They will be yours for food. [30]And to all the beasts of the earth and all the birds of the air and all the creatures that move on the ground—everything that has the breath of life in it—I give every green plant for food." And it was so. [31]God saw all that he had made, and it was very good. And there was evening, and there was morning—the sixth day.

2 Thus the heavens and the earth were completed in all their vast array.

[2]By the seventh day God had finished the work he had been doing; so on the seventh day he rested[b] from all his work. [3]And God blessed the seventh day and made it holy, because on it he rested from all the work of creating that he had done.

Adam and Eve

[4]This is the account of the heavens and the earth when they were created.

When the LORD God made the earth and the heavens— [5]and no shrub of the field had yet appeared on the earth[c] and no plant of the field had yet sprung up, for the LORD God had not sent rain on the earth[c] and there was no man to work the ground, [6]but streams[d] came up from the earth and watered the whole surface of the ground— [7]the LORD God formed the man[e] from the dust of the ground and breathed into his nostrils the breath of life, and the man became a living being.

[8]Now the LORD God had planted a garden in the east, in Eden; and there he put the man he had formed. [9]And the LORD God made all kinds of trees grow out of the ground—trees that were pleasing to the eye and good for food. In the middle of the garden were the tree of life and the tree of the knowledge of good and evil.

[10]A river watering the garden flowed from Eden; from there it was separated into four headwaters. [11]The name of the first is the Pishon; it winds through the entire land of

God Forms Us

GENESIS 2:7

Here we find a wonderful image of the way God forms us both physically and spiritually. Take a piece of clay or some malleable substance in your hands. Start by just feeling the weight and temperature of the clay you are holding, attentive to its basic nature—its pliability. Begin to knead the clay, gently but firmly working with it until it is soft. Think of a shape and begin to mold the clay to your purpose, noticing both its resistance and its receptivity. Based on this exercise, what do you think spiritual formation means? How is God molding or forming you continually, even today? How do you resist or receive God's attentions?

See Meeting God in the Created Order

---

[a] 26 Hebrew; Syriac *all the wild animals*   [b] 2 Or *ceased*; also in verse 3
[c] 5 Or *land*; also in verse 6   [d] 6 Or *mist*   [e] 7 The Hebrew for *man (adam)* sounds like and may be related to the Hebrew for *ground (adamah)*; it is also the name *Adam* (see Gen. 2:20).

It Is Not Good to Be Alone

GENESIS 2:18

Over and over God has found creation "good," but here is something "not good": that the man should be alone. From the very beginning, God has seen that we require not only divine companionship, but also the comfort and assistance that comes from being in community. We long for another who is so like us that we can cry out: "This is bone of my bone!" Who has God given you for companionship? Where do you find those who help you to be all that God has made you? Whatever your situation, God intends for you to have a friend of the heart; look for them among the many "givens" of your life.

See *Meeting God in Community*

Havilah, where there is gold. ¹²(The gold of that land is good; aromatic resin*ᵃ* and onyx are also there.) ¹³The name of the second river is the Gihon; it winds through the entire land of Cush.*ᵇ* ¹⁴The name of the third river is the Tigris; it runs along the east side of Asshur. And the fourth river is the Euphrates.

¹⁵The LORD God took the man and put him in the Garden of Eden to work it and take care of it. ¹⁶And the LORD God commanded the man, "You are free to eat from any tree in the garden; ¹⁷but you must not eat from the tree of the knowledge of good and evil, for when you eat of it you will surely die."

¹⁸The LORD God said, "It is not good for the man to be alone. I will make a helper suitable for him."

¹⁹Now the LORD God had formed out of the ground all the beasts of the field and all the birds of the air. He brought them to the man to see what he would name them; and whatever the man called each living creature, that was its name. ²⁰So the man gave names to all the livestock, the birds of the air and all the beasts of the field.

But for Adam*ᶜ* no suitable helper was found. ²¹So the LORD God caused the man to fall into a deep sleep; and while he was sleeping, he took one of the man's ribs*ᵈ* and closed up the place with flesh. ²²Then the LORD God made a woman from the rib*ᵉ* he had taken out of the man, and he brought her to the man.

²³The man said,

"This is now bone of my bones
    and flesh of my flesh;
she shall be called 'woman,'*ᶠ*
    for she was taken out of man."

²⁴For this reason a man will leave his father and mother and be united to his wife, and they will become one flesh.

²⁵The man and his wife were both naked, and they felt no shame.

The Fall of Man

3 Now the serpent was more crafty than any of the wild animals the LORD God had made. He said to the woman, "Did God really say, 'You must not eat from any tree in the garden'?"

²The woman said to the serpent, "We may eat fruit from the trees in the garden, ³but God did say, 'You must not eat fruit from the tree that is in the middle of the garden, and you must not touch it, or you will die.' "

⁴"You will not surely die," the serpent said to the woman. ⁵"For God knows that when you eat of it your eyes will be opened, and you will be like God, knowing good and evil."

⁶When the woman saw that the fruit of the tree was good for food and pleasing to the eye, and also desirable for gaining wisdom, she took some and ate it. She also gave some to her husband, who was with her, and he ate it. ⁷Then the eyes of both of them were opened, and they realized they were naked; so they sewed fig leaves together and made coverings for themselves.

ᵃ 12 Or *good; pearls*   *ᵇ 13* Possibly southeast Mesopotamia   *ᶜ 20* Or *the man*   *ᵈ 21* Or *took part of the man's side*   *ᵉ 22* Or *part*   *ᶠ 23* The Hebrew for *woman* sounds like the Hebrew for *man.*

⁸Then the man and his wife heard the sound of the LORD God as he was walking in the garden in the cool of the day, and they hid from the LORD God among the trees of the garden. ⁹But the LORD God called to the man, "Where are you?"

¹⁰He answered, "I heard you in the garden, and I was afraid because I was naked; so I hid."

¹¹And he said, "Who told you that you were naked? Have you eaten from the tree that I commanded you not to eat from?"

¹²The man said, "The woman you put here with me—she gave me some fruit from the tree, and I ate it."

¹³Then the LORD God said to the woman, "What is this you have done?"

The woman said, "The serpent deceived me, and I ate."

¹⁴So the LORD God said to the serpent, "Because you have done this,

> "Cursed are you above all the livestock
> and all the wild animals!
> You will crawl on your belly
> and you will eat dust
> all the days of your life.
> ¹⁵And I will put enmity
> between you and the woman,
> and between your offspring*a* and hers;
> he will crush*b* your head,
> and you will strike his heel."

¹⁶To the woman he said,

> "I will greatly increase your pains in childbearing;
> with pain you will give birth to children.
> Your desire will be for your husband,
> and he will rule over you."

¹⁷To Adam he said, "Because you listened to your wife and ate from the tree about which I commanded you, 'You must not eat of it,'

> "Cursed is the ground because of you;
> through painful toil you will eat of it
> all the days of your life.
> ¹⁸It will produce thorns and thistles for you,
> and you will eat the plants of the field.
> ¹⁹By the sweat of your brow
> you will eat your food
> until you return to the ground,
> since from it you were taken;
> for dust you are
> and to dust you will return."

²⁰Adam*c* named his wife Eve,*d* because she would become the mother of all the living.

²¹The LORD God made garments of skin for Adam and his wife and clothed them. ²²And the LORD God said, "The man has now become like one of us, knowing good and evil. He must not be allowed to reach out his hand and take also from the tree of life and eat, and live forever." ²³So the LORD God banished him from the Garden of Eden to work the ground from which he had been taken. ²⁴After he drove the man out, he placed on the east side*e* of the Garden of Eden

---

What Have You Done?

GENESIS 3:13

Amid all the gifts of God, we seem always to want what we don't have. We know better, yet we continue to act in acquisitive or destructive ways. At such moments, God appears before us, asking: "What have you done?" God asks the question, not because he doesn't know the answer, but because he is giving us the opportunity to admit our fault and be forgiven. Admitting sin is also admitting that God's power can strengthen the good in us. Today, ask if there is something God wants you to reassess and repent of. What goodness are you avoiding?

See Meeting God in Prayer

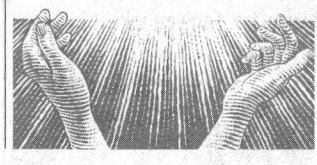

---

a 15 Or *seed*   *b 15* Or *strike*   *c 20* Or *The man*   *d 20* Eve probably means *living.*   *e 24* Or *placed in front*

More Than I Can Bear

GENESIS 4:13

Sin brings its own inevitable consequences. Imagine that you are Cain. You have murdered your own brother. You may have felt driven to it, but you also know you deserve punishment. Yet the punishment is crushing, like a too-heavy burden placed upon your shoulders, so that you cannot even stand up. Place yourself in this scene, feeling the weight that burdens you, tasting the bitterness of shame and grief, experiencing the hopeless future.

What is your reaction to God's unexpected grace—the touch of his anointing finger—protecting you from the worst harm? God kneels to share your yoke and lighten your load, sinner that you are. Can you take it in?

See *Meeting God in Scripture*

cherubim and a flaming sword flashing back and forth to guard the way to the tree of life.

Cain and Abel

4 Adam[a] lay with his wife Eve, and she became pregnant and gave birth to Cain.[b] She said, "With the help of the LORD I have brought forth[c] a man." ²Later she gave birth to his brother Abel.

Now Abel kept flocks, and Cain worked the soil. ³In the course of time Cain brought some of the fruits of the soil as an offering to the LORD. ⁴But Abel brought fat portions from some of the firstborn of his flock. The LORD looked with favor on Abel and his offering, ⁵but on Cain and his offering he did not look with favor. So Cain was very angry, and his face was downcast.

⁶Then the LORD said to Cain, "Why are you angry? Why is your face downcast? ⁷If you do what is right, will you not be accepted? But if you do not do what is right, sin is crouching at your door; it desires to have you, but you must master it."

⁸Now Cain said to his brother Abel, "Let's go out to the field."[d] And while they were in the field, Cain attacked his brother Abel and killed him.

⁹Then the LORD said to Cain, "Where is your brother Abel?"

"I don't know," he replied. "Am I my brother's keeper?"

¹⁰The LORD said, "What have you done? Listen! Your brother's blood cries out to me from the ground. ¹¹Now you are under a curse and driven from the ground, which opened its mouth to receive your brother's blood from your hand. ¹²When you work the ground, it will no longer yield its crops for you. You will be a restless wanderer on the earth."

¹³Cain said to the LORD, "My punishment is more than I can bear. ¹⁴Today you are driving me from the land, and I will be hidden from your presence; I will be a restless wanderer on the earth, and whoever finds me will kill me."

¹⁵But the LORD said to him, "Not so[e]; if anyone kills Cain, he will suffer vengeance seven times over." Then the LORD put a mark on Cain so that no one who found him would kill him. ¹⁶So Cain went out from the LORD's presence and lived in the land of Nod,[f] east of Eden.

¹⁷Cain lay with his wife, and she became pregnant and gave birth to Enoch. Cain was then building a city, and he named it after his son Enoch. ¹⁸To Enoch was born Irad, and Irad was the father of Mehujael, and Mehujael was the father of Methushael, and Methushael was the father of Lamech.

¹⁹Lamech married two women, one named Adah and the other Zillah. ²⁰Adah gave birth to Jabal; he was the father of those who live in tents and raise livestock. ²¹His brother's name was Jubal; he was the father of all who play the harp and flute. ²²Zillah also had a son, Tubal-Cain, who forged all kinds of tools out of[g] bronze and iron. Tubal-Cain's sister was Naamah.

---

[a] 1 Or *The man*   [b] 1 *Cain* sounds like the Hebrew for *brought forth* or *acquired*.   [c] 1 Or *have acquired*   [d] 8 Samaritan Pentateuch, Septuagint, Vulgate and Syriac; Masoretic Text does not have "*Let's go out to the field.*"   [e] 15 Septuagint, Vulgate and Syriac; Hebrew *Very well*   [f] 16 *Nod* means *wandering* (see verses 12 and 14).   [g] 22 Or *who instructed all who work in*

[23]Lamech said to his wives,

> "Adah and Zillah, listen to me;
>   wives of Lamech, hear my words.
> I have killed[a] a man for wounding me,
>   a young man for injuring me.
> [24]If Cain is avenged seven times,
>   then Lamech seventy-seven times."

[25]Adam lay with his wife again, and she gave birth to a son and named him Seth,[b] saying, "God has granted me another child in place of Abel, since Cain killed him." [26]Seth also had a son, and he named him Enosh.

At that time men began to call on[c] the name of the LORD.

From Adam to Noah

5 This is the written account of Adam's line.

When God created man, he made him in the likeness of God. [2]He created them male and female and blessed them. And when they were created, he called them "man.[d]"

[3]When Adam had lived 130 years, he had a son in his own likeness, in his own image; and he named him Seth. [4]After Seth was born, Adam lived 800 years and had other sons and daughters. [5]Altogether, Adam lived 930 years, and then he died.

[6]When Seth had lived 105 years, he became the father[e] of Enosh. [7]And after he became the father of Enosh, Seth lived 807 years and had other sons and daughters. [8]Altogether, Seth lived 912 years, and then he died.

[9]When Enosh had lived 90 years, he became the father of Kenan. [10]And after he became the father of Kenan, Enosh lived 815 years and had other sons and daughters. [11]Altogether, Enosh lived 905 years, and then he died.

[12]When Kenan had lived 70 years, he became the father of Mahalalel. [13]And after he became the father of Mahalalel, Kenan lived 840 years and had other sons and daughters. [14]Altogether, Kenan lived 910 years, and then he died.

[15]When Mahalalel had lived 65 years, he became the father of Jared. [16]And after he became the father of Jared, Mahalalel lived 830 years and had other sons and daughters. [17]Altogether, Mahalalel lived 895 years, and then he died.

[18]When Jared had lived 162 years, he became the father of Enoch. [19]And after he became the father of Enoch, Jared lived 800 years and had other sons and daughters. [20]Altogether, Jared lived 962 years, and then he died.

[21]When Enoch had lived 65 years, he became the father of Methuselah. [22]And after he became the father of Methuselah, Enoch walked with God 300 years and had other sons and daughters. [23]Altogether, Enoch lived 365 years. [24]Enoch walked with God; then he was no more, because God took him away.

[25]When Methuselah had lived 187 years, he became the father of Lamech. [26]And after he became the father of Lamech, Methuselah lived 782 years and had other sons and daughters. [27]Altogether, Methuselah lived 969 years, and then he died.

In God's Likeness

GENESIS 5:1

"Dignity is acting as if we believe the facts of our creation are true: that we are indeed created in God's image, that we are created out of love, that we are good because God created us, and that we have the goodness of God within us. Dignity is risking that, as the popular saying goes, 'God don't make junk' . . . Dignity always says we are meant for greater things than those we ever could aspire to. Choosing dignity, then, is not selecting another self-image. It is choosing an open-endedness in which we know all our images will be insufficient. It is an act of faith."

—GERALD MAY,
Addiction and Grace

---

[a] 23 Or *I will kill*   [b] 25 *Seth* probably means *granted*.   [c] 26 Or *to proclaim*
[d] 2 Hebrew *adam*   [e] 6 *Father* may mean *ancestor*; also in verses 7–26.

God's Grief

GENESIS 6:6

Can we imagine God feeling grief? Seeing how far humans have fallen away from his intention for them, God's heart, we are told, is filled with pain. God grieves for the human soul that is dead because of sin. Early Christians thought that the primary remedy for the soul was to weep tears of compunction, sharing God's grief at its misery and folly. Gregory of Nyssa's words at the death of his friend, St. Ephrem, suggest the inevitability of a "flood" of sorrow: "When I start to remember his floods of tears I myself begin to weep, for it is almost impossible to pass dry-eyed through the ocean of his tears." Might this great flood have been caused not only by God's wrath but also by God's sorrow?

²⁸When Lamech had lived 182 years, he had a son. ²⁹He named him Noah*a* and said, "He will comfort us in the labor and painful toil of our hands caused by the ground the LORD has cursed." ³⁰After Noah was born, Lamech lived 595 years and had other sons and daughters. ³¹Altogether, Lamech lived 777 years, and then he died.

³²After Noah was 500 years old, he became the father of Shem, Ham and Japheth.

The Flood

6 When men began to increase in number on the earth and daughters were born to them, ²the sons of God saw that the daughters of men were beautiful, and they married any of them they chose. ³Then the LORD said, "My Spirit will not contend with*b* man forever, for he is mortal*c*; his days will be a hundred and twenty years."

⁴The Nephilim were on the earth in those days—and also afterward—when the sons of God went to the daughters of men and had children by them. They were the heroes of old, men of renown.

⁵The LORD saw how great man's wickedness on the earth had become, and that every inclination of the thoughts of his heart was only evil all the time. ⁶The LORD was grieved that he had made man on the earth, and his heart was filled with pain. ⁷So the LORD said, "I will wipe mankind, whom I have created, from the face of the earth—men and animals, and creatures that move along the ground, and birds of the air—for I am grieved that I have made them." ⁸But Noah found favor in the eyes of the LORD.

⁹This is the account of Noah.

Noah was a righteous man, blameless among the people of his time, and he walked with God. ¹⁰Noah had three sons: Shem, Ham and Japheth.

¹¹Now the earth was corrupt in God's sight and was full of violence. ¹²God saw how corrupt the earth had become, for all the people on earth had corrupted their ways. ¹³So God said to Noah, "I am going to put an end to all people, for the earth is filled with violence because of them. I am surely going to destroy both them and the earth. ¹⁴So make yourself an ark of cypress*d* wood; make rooms in it and coat it with pitch inside and out. ¹⁵This is how you are to build it: The ark is to be 450 feet long, 75 feet wide and 45 feet high.*e* ¹⁶Make a roof for it and finish*f* the ark to within 18 inches*g* of the top. Put a door in the side of the ark and make lower, middle and upper decks. ¹⁷I am going to bring floodwaters on the earth to destroy all life under the heavens, every creature that has the breath of life in it. Everything on earth will perish. ¹⁸But I will establish my covenant with you, and you will enter the ark—you and your sons and your wife and your sons' wives with you. ¹⁹You are to bring into the ark two of all living creatures, male and female, to keep them alive with you. ²⁰Two of every kind of bird, of every kind of animal and of every kind of creature that moves along the ground will come to you to be kept

---

a 29 Noah sounds like the Hebrew for *comfort.*   *b 3* Or *My spirit will not remain in*   *c 3* Or *corrupt*   *d 14* The meaning of the Hebrew for this word is uncertain.   *e 15* Hebrew *300 cubits long, 50 cubits wide and 30 cubits high* (about 140 meters long, 23 meters wide and 13.5 meters high)   *f 16* Or *Make an opening for light by finishing*   *g 16* Hebrew *a cubit* (about 0.5 meter)

alive. ²¹You are to take every kind of food that is to be eaten and store it away as food for you and for them."

²²Noah did everything just as God commanded him.

7 The LORD then said to Noah, "Go into the ark, you and your whole family, because I have found you righteous in this generation. ²Take with you seven*a* of every kind of clean animal, a male and its mate, and two of every kind of unclean animal, a male and its mate, ³and also seven of every kind of bird, male and female, to keep their various kinds alive throughout the earth. ⁴Seven days from now I will send rain on the earth for forty days and forty nights, and I will wipe from the face of the earth every living creature I have made."

⁵And Noah did all that the LORD commanded him.

⁶Noah was six hundred years old when the floodwaters came on the earth. ⁷And Noah and his sons and his wife and his sons' wives entered the ark to escape the waters of the flood. ⁸Pairs of clean and unclean animals, of birds and of all creatures that move along the ground, ⁹male and female, came to Noah and entered the ark, as God had commanded Noah. ¹⁰And after the seven days the floodwaters came on the earth.

¹¹In the six hundredth year of Noah's life, on the seventeenth day of the second month—on that day all the springs of the great deep burst forth, and the floodgates of the heavens were opened. ¹²And rain fell on the earth forty days and forty nights.

¹³On that very day Noah and his sons, Shem, Ham and Japheth, together with his wife and the wives of his three sons, entered the ark. ¹⁴They had with them every wild animal according to its kind, all livestock according to their kinds, every creature that moves along the ground according to its kind and every bird according to its kind, everything with wings. ¹⁵Pairs of all creatures that have the breath of life in them came to Noah and entered the ark. ¹⁶The animals going in were male and female of every living thing, as God had commanded Noah. Then the LORD shut him in.

¹⁷For forty days the flood kept coming on the earth, and as the waters increased they lifted the ark high above the earth. ¹⁸The waters rose and increased greatly on the earth, and the ark floated on the surface of the water. ¹⁹They rose greatly on the earth, and all the high mountains under the entire heavens were covered. ²⁰The waters rose and covered the mountains to a depth of more than twenty feet.*b,c* ²¹Every living thing that moved on the earth perished—birds, livestock, wild animals, all the creatures that swarm over the earth, and all mankind. ²²Everything on dry land that had the breath of life in its nostrils died. ²³Every living thing on the face of the earth was wiped out; men and animals and the creatures that move along the ground and the birds of the air were wiped from the earth. Only Noah was left, and those with him in the ark.

²⁴The waters flooded the earth for a hundred and fifty days.

8 But God remembered Noah and all the wild animals and the livestock that were with him in the ark, and he sent a wind over the earth, and the waters receded. ²Now

The Gift of Water

GENESIS 7:11

Water is a critical element in many stories throughout Scripture: in the beginning of creation, in the exodus of the children of Israel from Egypt, and especially in Jesus' baptism. Meditate on the place of water in your life, its power for creation and destruction. Can you recall insights you've experienced during a renewing spring rain shower or while fishing a rushing stream? Do you remember your own baptism, or one you have attended recently? What truths has God shown you through the gift of water?

See *Meeting God in the Created Order*

---

a 2 Or *seven pairs*; also in verse 3   *b* 20 Hebrew *fifteen cubits* (about 6.9 meters)   *c* 20 Or *rose more than twenty feet, and the mountains were covered*

A Sign of Hope

GENESIS 8:11

Place yourself on the crowded deck of Noah's ark, confined for many days in a small space filled with every kind of creature. You have experienced the violent destruction of your whole environment and for days have seen nothing but water. Imagine the eagerness with which you anticipate the return of the dove, the mixture of hope and dread with which you wonder what the future will be. When you see the dove returning, you notice something in its mouth, but what? A freshly plucked olive leaf! Amidst all this loss, new life is emerging! Somewhere a tree grows, and fragile shoots bloom, and a safe place for you is being created. Praise God!

See Meeting God in Scripture

the springs of the deep and the floodgates of the heavens had been closed, and the rain had stopped falling from the sky. ³The water receded steadily from the earth. At the end of the hundred and fifty days the water had gone down, ⁴and on the seventeenth day of the seventh month the ark came to rest on the mountains of Ararat. ⁵The waters continued to recede until the tenth month, and on the first day of the tenth month the tops of the mountains became visible.

⁶After forty days Noah opened the window he had made in the ark ⁷and sent out a raven, and it kept flying back and forth until the water had dried up from the earth. ⁸Then he sent out a dove to see if the water had receded from the surface of the ground. ⁹But the dove could find no place to set its feet because there was water over all the surface of the earth; so it returned to Noah in the ark. He reached out his hand and took the dove and brought it back to himself in the ark. ¹⁰He waited seven more days and again sent out the dove from the ark. ¹¹When the dove returned to him in the evening, there in its beak was a freshly plucked olive leaf! Then Noah knew that the water had receded from the earth. ¹²He waited seven more days and sent the dove out again, but this time it did not return to him.

¹³By the first day of the first month of Noah's six hundred and first year, the water had dried up from the earth. Noah then removed the covering from the ark and saw that the surface of the ground was dry. ¹⁴By the twenty-seventh day of the second month the earth was completely dry.

¹⁵Then God said to Noah, ¹⁶"Come out of the ark, you and your wife and your sons and their wives. ¹⁷Bring out every kind of living creature that is with you—the birds, the animals, and all the creatures that move along the ground—so they can multiply on the earth and be fruitful and increase in number upon it."

¹⁸So Noah came out, together with his sons and his wife and his sons' wives. ¹⁹All the animals and all the creatures that move along the ground and all the birds—everything that moves on the earth—came out of the ark, one kind after another.

²⁰Then Noah built an altar to the LORD and, taking some of all the clean animals and clean birds, he sacrificed burnt offerings on it. ²¹The LORD smelled the pleasing aroma and said in his heart: "Never again will I curse the ground because of man, even though*ᵃ* every inclination of his heart is evil from childhood. And never again will I destroy all living creatures, as I have done.

> ²²"As long as the earth endures,
>   seedtime and harvest,
>   cold and heat,
>   summer and winter,
>   day and night
>   will never cease."

God's Covenant With Noah

9 Then God blessed Noah and his sons, saying to them, "Be fruitful and increase in number and fill the earth. ²The fear and dread of you will fall upon all the beasts of the earth and all the birds of the air, upon every creature

ᵃ 21 Or man, for

Canaan reached from Sidon toward Gerar as far as Gaza, and then toward Sodom, Gomorrah, Admah and Zeboiim, as far as Lasha.

²⁰These are the sons of Ham by their clans and languages, in their territories and nations.

The Semites

²¹Sons were also born to Shem, whose older brother was[a] Japheth; Shem was the ancestor of all the sons of Eber.

²²The sons of Shem:

Elam, Asshur, Arphaxad, Lud and Aram.

²³The sons of Aram:

Uz, Hul, Gether and Meshech.[b]

²⁴Arphaxad was the father of[c] Shelah,
and Shelah the father of Eber.

²⁵Two sons were born to Eber:

One was named Peleg,[d] because in his time the earth was divided; his brother was named Joktan.

²⁶Joktan was the father of

Almodad, Sheleph, Hazarmaveth, Jerah, ²⁷Hadoram, Uzal, Diklah, ²⁸Obal, Abimael, Sheba, ²⁹Ophir, Havilah and Jobab. All these were sons of Joktan.

³⁰The region where they lived stretched from Mesha toward Sephar, in the eastern hill country.

³¹These are the sons of Shem by their clans and languages, in their territories and nations.

³²These are the clans of Noah's sons, according to their lines of descent, within their nations. From these the nations spread out over the earth after the flood.

The Tower of Babel

11 Now the whole world had one language and a common speech. ²As men moved eastward,[e] they found a plain in Shinar[f] and settled there.

³They said to each other, "Come, let's make bricks and bake them thoroughly." They used brick instead of stone, and tar for mortar. ⁴Then they said, "Come, let us build ourselves a city, with a tower that reaches to the heavens, so that we may make a name for ourselves and not be scattered over the face of the whole earth."

⁵But the LORD came down to see the city and the tower that the men were building. ⁶The LORD said, "If as one people speaking the same language they have begun to do this, then nothing they plan to do will be impossible for them. ⁷Come, let us go down and confuse their language so they will not understand each other."

⁸So the LORD scattered them from there over all the earth, and they stopped building the city. ⁹That is why it was called Babel[g]—because there the LORD confused the language of the whole world. From there the LORD scattered them over the face of the whole earth.

---

[a] 21 Or *Shem, the older brother of*   [b] 23 See Septuagint and 1 Chron. 1:17; Hebrew *Mash*   [c] 24 Hebrew; Septuagint *father of Cainan, and Cainan was the father of*   [d] 25 *Peleg* means *division.*   [e] 2 Or *from the east;* or *in the east*   [f] 2 That is, Babylonia   [g] 9 That is, Babylon; *Babel* sounds like the Hebrew for *confused.*

A Name for Ourselves

GENESIS 11:4

What is wrong with trying to build a tower to heaven? Don't humans naturally aspire to heavenly things? In this account the problem is with the reason the people are building the tower; it is not to be nearer God, or to glorify God, but to exalt themselves. In our own lives, we often embark on projects designed to help us feel like little gods, in control, independently successful. All such projects, large or small, deny our creatureliness and minimize our dependence upon God. Often it is easier to see others "playing god" than to notice it in ourselves. What is your own most recent "tower" project? What clues show that it is *your* project and not God's?

See *Meeting God in Scripture*

13

What Do We Tell?

GENESIS 11:10–11

In this genealogy, each person is defined by name, age at death, and age at birth of the oldest son. If you were to give an account of your life and your family, what would be the important things you would want to tell? Today we rarely name our children when we identify ourselves, much less our own age at their births. When first meeting someone, we are most likely to describe ourselves in terms of our primary occupation. Yet our titles and job descriptions do not paint an adequate picture of who we are. How would you best identify yourself in terms of values important to you? What are the essential things you would want others to know about your life?

See Meeting God in Community

From Shem to Abram

¹⁰This is the account of Shem.

Two years after the flood, when Shem was 100 years old, he became the father*ᵃ* of Arphaxad. ¹¹And after he became the father of Arphaxad, Shem lived 500 years and had other sons and daughters.

¹²When Arphaxad had lived 35 years, he became the father of Shelah. ¹³And after he became the father of Shelah, Arphaxad lived 403 years and had other sons and daughters.*ᵇ*

¹⁴When Shelah had lived 30 years, he became the father of Eber. ¹⁵And after he became the father of Eber, Shelah lived 403 years and had other sons and daughters.

¹⁶When Eber had lived 34 years, he became the father of Peleg. ¹⁷And after he became the father of Peleg, Eber lived 430 years and had other sons and daughters.

¹⁸When Peleg had lived 30 years, he became the father of Reu. ¹⁹And after he became the father of Reu, Peleg lived 209 years and had other sons and daughters.

²⁰When Reu had lived 32 years, he became the father of Serug. ²¹And after he became the father of Serug, Reu lived 207 years and had other sons and daughters.

²²When Serug had lived 30 years, he became the father of Nahor. ²³And after he became the father of Nahor, Serug lived 200 years and had other sons and daughters.

²⁴When Nahor had lived 29 years, he became the father of Terah. ²⁵And after he became the father of Terah, Nahor lived 119 years and had other sons and daughters.

²⁶After Terah had lived 70 years, he became the father of Abram, Nahor and Haran.

²⁷This is the account of Terah.

Terah became the father of Abram, Nahor and Haran. And Haran became the father of Lot. ²⁸While his father Terah was still alive, Haran died in Ur of the Chaldeans, in the land of his birth. ²⁹Abram and Nahor both married. The name of Abram's wife was Sarai, and the name of Nahor's wife was Milcah; she was the daughter of Haran, the father of both Milcah and Iscah. ³⁰Now Sarai was barren; she had no children.

³¹Terah took his son Abram, his grandson Lot son of Haran, and his daughter-in-law Sarai, the wife of his son Abram, and together they set out from Ur of the Chaldeans to go to Canaan. But when they came to Haran, they settled there.

³²Terah lived 205 years, and he died in Haran.

The Call of Abram

12 The LORD had said to Abram, "Leave your country, your people and your father's household and go to the land I will show you.

²"I will make you into a great nation
    and I will bless you;

ᵃ 10 Father *may mean* ancestor; *also in verses 11–25.* *ᵇ 12,13* Hebrew; Septuagint (see also Luke 3:35, 36 and note at Gen. 10:24) *35 years, he became the father of Cainan.* ¹³*And after he became the father of Cainan, Arphaxad lived 430 years and had other sons and daughters, and then he died. When Cainan had lived 130 years, he became the father of Shelah. And after he became the father of Shelah, Cainan lived 330 years and had other sons and daughters*

I will make your name great,
> and you will be a blessing.
> [3] I will bless those who bless you,
> and whoever curses you I will curse;
> and all peoples on earth
> will be blessed through you."

[4] So Abram left, as the LORD had told him; and Lot went with him. Abram was seventy-five years old when he set out from Haran. [5] He took his wife Sarai, his nephew Lot, all the possessions they had accumulated and the people they had acquired in Haran, and they set out for the land of Canaan, and they arrived there.

[6] Abram traveled through the land as far as the site of the great tree of Moreh at Shechem. At that time the Canaanites were in the land. [7] The LORD appeared to Abram and said, "To your offspring[a] I will give this land." So he built an altar there to the LORD, who had appeared to him.

[8] From there he went on toward the hills east of Bethel and pitched his tent, with Bethel on the west and Ai on the east. There he built an altar to the LORD and called on the name of the LORD. [9] Then Abram set out and continued toward the Negev.

Abram in Egypt

[10] Now there was a famine in the land, and Abram went down to Egypt to live there for a while because the famine was severe. [11] As he was about to enter Egypt, he said to his wife Sarai, "I know what a beautiful woman you are. [12] When the Egyptians see you, they will say, 'This is his wife.' Then they will kill me but will let you live. [13] Say you are my sister, so that I will be treated well for your sake and my life will be spared because of you."

[14] When Abram came to Egypt, the Egyptians saw that she was a very beautiful woman. [15] And when Pharaoh's officials saw her, they praised her to Pharaoh, and she was taken into his palace. [16] He treated Abram well for her sake, and Abram acquired sheep and cattle, male and female donkeys, menservants and maidservants, and camels.

[17] But the LORD inflicted serious diseases on Pharaoh and his household because of Abram's wife Sarai. [18] So Pharaoh summoned Abram. "What have you done to me?" he said. "Why didn't you tell me she was your wife? [19] Why did you say, 'She is my sister,' so that I took her to be my wife? Now then, here is your wife. Take her and go!" [20] Then Pharaoh gave orders about Abram to his men, and they sent him on his way, with his wife and everything he had.

Abram and Lot Separate

13 So Abram went up from Egypt to the Negev, with his wife and everything he had, and Lot went with him. [2] Abram had become very wealthy in livestock and in silver and gold.

[3] From the Negev he went from place to place until he came to Bethel, to the place between Bethel and Ai where his tent had been earlier [4] and where he had first built an altar. There Abram called on the name of the LORD.

[5] Now Lot, who was moving about with Abram, also had flocks and herds and tents. [6] But the land could not support

---

The Call

GENESIS 12:1–4

God's covenant with his people begins with this simple yet earthshaking command, stated simply: "Leave what you know and go into the unknown." The command is united with a promise of blessing, yet it is no less fearful for that. God calls to each of us: "Leave what you know and go into the unknown. I will be with you and I will bless you, but you must act in faith in response to my word." Usually we are given many opportunities, and we need them, because we often deflect a call, ask for more information, distract ourselves, even run away. When you hear God's call, how do you usually respond? What is your preferred strategy when faced with this breathtaking word?

See Meeting God in Prayer

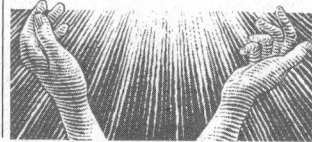

God's Designs

GENESIS 13:5–7

"The Old Testament is the history of a process whereby God prepares the human race for Christ . . . slowly and gradually, but inexorably . . . God speaks and we answer—very inadequately; so he speaks again and again, undeterred by our fumbling replies until he finally speaks the ultimate Word in Jesus. This is the Word we are still striving to answer—not perhaps very successfully, but that does not matter, for God's designs cannot be thwarted in the end, and he can use our very failures as instruments which will achieve his purpose."

—CYPRIAN SMITH, O.S.B.,
The Path of Life

them while they stayed together, for their possessions were so great that they were not able to stay together. ⁷And quarreling arose between Abram's herdsmen and the herdsmen of Lot. The Canaanites and Perizzites were also living in the land at that time.

⁸So Abram said to Lot, "Let's not have any quarreling between you and me, or between your herdsmen and mine, for we are brothers. ⁹Is not the whole land before you? Let's part company. If you go to the left, I'll go to the right; if you go to the right, I'll go to the left."

¹⁰Lot looked up and saw that the whole plain of the Jordan was well watered, like the garden of the LORD, like the land of Egypt, toward Zoar. (This was before the LORD destroyed Sodom and Gomorrah.) ¹¹So Lot chose for himself the whole plain of the Jordan and set out toward the east. The two men parted company: ¹²Abram lived in the land of Canaan, while Lot lived among the cities of the plain and pitched his tents near Sodom. ¹³Now the men of Sodom were wicked and were sinning greatly against the LORD.

¹⁴The LORD said to Abram after Lot had parted from him, "Lift up your eyes from where you are and look north and south, east and west. ¹⁵All the land that you see I will give to you and your offspring*ᵃ* forever. ¹⁶I will make your offspring like the dust of the earth, so that if anyone could count the dust, then your offspring could be counted. ¹⁷Go, walk through the length and breadth of the land, for I am giving it to you."

¹⁸So Abram moved his tents and went to live near the great trees of Mamre at Hebron, where he built an altar to the LORD.

Abram Rescues Lot

14 At this time Amraphel king of Shinar,*ᵇ* Arioch king of Ellasar, Kedorlaomer king of Elam and Tidal king of Goiim ²went to war against Bera king of Sodom, Birsha king of Gomorrah, Shinab king of Admah, Shemeber king of Zeboiim, and the king of Bela (that is, Zoar). ³All these latter kings joined forces in the Valley of Siddim (the Salt Sea*ᶜ*). ⁴For twelve years they had been subject to Kedorlaomer, but in the thirteenth year they rebelled.

⁵In the fourteenth year, Kedorlaomer and the kings allied with him went out and defeated the Rephaites in Ashteroth Karnaim, the Zuzites in Ham, the Emites in Shaveh Kiriathaim ⁶and the Horites in the hill country of Seir, as far as El Paran near the desert. ⁷Then they turned back and went to En Mishpat (that is, Kadesh), and they conquered the whole territory of the Amalekites, as well as the Amorites who were living in Hazazon Tamar.

⁸Then the king of Sodom, the king of Gomorrah, the king of Admah, the king of Zeboiim and the king of Bela (that is, Zoar) marched out and drew up their battle lines in the Valley of Siddim ⁹against Kedorlaomer king of Elam, Tidal king of Goiim, Amraphel king of Shinar and Arioch king of Ellasar—four kings against five. ¹⁰Now the Valley of Siddim was full of tar pits, and when the kings of Sodom and Gomorrah fled, some of the men fell into them and the rest fled to the hills. ¹¹The four kings seized all the goods of Sodom and Gomorrah and all their food; then they went

ᵃ 15 Or *seed*; also in verse 16   ᵇ 1 That is, Babylonia; also in verse 9
ᶜ 3 That is, the Dead Sea

away. ¹²They also carried off Abram's nephew Lot and his possessions, since he was living in Sodom.

¹³One who had escaped came and reported this to Abram the Hebrew. Now Abram was living near the great trees of Mamre the Amorite, a brother*ᵃ* of Eshcol and Aner, all of whom were allied with Abram. ¹⁴When Abram heard that his relative had been taken captive, he called out the 318 trained men born in his household and went in pursuit as far as Dan. ¹⁵During the night Abram divided his men to attack them and he routed them, pursuing them as far as Hobah, north of Damascus. ¹⁶He recovered all the goods and brought back his relative Lot and his possessions, together with the women and the other people.

¹⁷After Abram returned from defeating Kedorlaomer and the kings allied with him, the king of Sodom came out to meet him in the Valley of Shaveh (that is, the King's Valley).

¹⁸Then Melchizedek king of Salem*ᵇ* brought out bread and wine. He was priest of God Most High, ¹⁹and he blessed Abram, saying,

"Blessed be Abram by God Most High,
Creator*ᶜ* of heaven and earth.
²⁰And blessed be*ᵈ* God Most High,
who delivered your enemies into your hand."

Then Abram gave him a tenth of everything.

²¹The king of Sodom said to Abram, "Give me the people and keep the goods for yourself."

²²But Abram said to the king of Sodom, "I have raised my hand to the LORD, God Most High, Creator of heaven and earth, and have taken an oath ²³that I will accept nothing belonging to you, not even a thread or the thong of a sandal, so that you will never be able to say, 'I made Abram rich.' ²⁴I will accept nothing but what my men have eaten and the share that belongs to the men who went with me—to Aner, Eshcol and Mamre. Let them have their share."

God's Covenant With Abram

15 After this, the word of the LORD came to Abram in a vision:

"Do not be afraid, Abram.
I am your shield,*ᵉ*
your very great reward.*ᶠ*"

²But Abram said, "O Sovereign LORD, what can you give me since I remain childless and the one who will inherit*ᵍ* my estate is Eliezer of Damascus?" ³And Abram said, "You have given me no children; so a servant in my household will be my heir."

⁴Then the word of the LORD came to him: "This man will not be your heir, but a son coming from your own body will be your heir." ⁵He took him outside and said, "Look up at the heavens and count the stars—if indeed you can count them." Then he said to him, "So shall your offspring be."

⁶Abram believed the LORD, and he credited it to him as righteousness.

⁷He also said to him, "I am the LORD, who brought you

A Sacred Encounter

GENESIS 14:18–20

Who is this priest of God Most High who appears from nowhere with a blessing for Abram? This mystical encounter fascinated the authors of Scripture, with Psalm 110 describing "a priest forever, in the order of Melchizedek" and the book of Hebrews speculating in chapter 7 that the ancient priest prefigured the Son of God. Was there a time in your life when, unexpectedly, you felt that you were in the presence of God Most High? Who else was there, and what happened beforehand? Recall everything about that incident, what you saw and felt, all the sounds and smells you experienced, and above all, what your heart told you. Return to that moment regularly for refreshment and joy!

See Meeting God in Worship

Covenant

GENESIS 15:17

Perhaps when you were a child you made a pact with a close friend, pricking your fingers to mingle your blood or exchanging rings as a sign of solemn covenant. As we become adults, sometimes we neglect the importance of enacting a ritual to mark the importance of an event. What symbolic actions help you confirm your commitment to something? The next time a rite of passage occurs in your family, think of a special way to make a simple ritual for it: Collect armfuls of flowers and shower them on a graduate. Or at a wedding form a circle around the newly married couple and sing to them. Be imaginative and serious but not solemn.

See Meeting God in Community

out of Ur of the Chaldeans to give you this land to take possession of it."

⁸But Abram said, "O Sovereign LORD, how can I know that I will gain possession of it?"

⁹So the LORD said to him, "Bring me a heifer, a goat and a ram, each three years old, along with a dove and a young pigeon."

¹⁰Abram brought all these to him, cut them in two and arranged the halves opposite each other; the birds, however, he did not cut in half. ¹¹Then birds of prey came down on the carcasses, but Abram drove them away.

¹²As the sun was setting, Abram fell into a deep sleep, and a thick and dreadful darkness came over him. ¹³Then the LORD said to him, "Know for certain that your descendants will be strangers in a country not their own, and they will be enslaved and mistreated four hundred years. ¹⁴But I will punish the nation they serve as slaves, and afterward they will come out with great possessions. ¹⁵You, however, will go to your fathers in peace and be buried at a good old age. ¹⁶In the fourth generation your descendants will come back here, for the sin of the Amorites has not yet reached its full measure."

¹⁷When the sun had set and darkness had fallen, a smoking firepot with a blazing torch appeared and passed between the pieces. ¹⁸On that day the LORD made a covenant with Abram and said, "To your descendants I give this land, from the river*ᵃ* of Egypt to the great river, the Euphrates— ¹⁹the land of the Kenites, Kenizzites, Kadmonites, ²⁰Hittites, Perizzites, Rephaites, ²¹Amorites, Canaanites, Girgashites and Jebusites."

Hagar and Ishmael

16 Now Sarai, Abram's wife, had borne him no children. But she had an Egyptian maidservant named Hagar; ²so she said to Abram, "The LORD has kept me from having children. Go, sleep with my maidservant; perhaps I can build a family through her."

Abram agreed to what Sarai said. ³So after Abram had been living in Canaan ten years, Sarai his wife took her Egyptian maidservant Hagar and gave her to her husband to be his wife. ⁴He slept with Hagar, and she conceived.

When she knew she was pregnant, she began to despise her mistress. ⁵Then Sarai said to Abram, "You are responsible for the wrong I am suffering. I put my servant in your arms, and now that she knows she is pregnant, she despises me. May the LORD judge between you and me."

⁶"Your servant is in your hands," Abram said. "Do with her whatever you think best." Then Sarai mistreated Hagar; so she fled from her.

⁷The angel of the LORD found Hagar near a spring in the desert; it was the spring that is beside the road to Shur. ⁸And he said, "Hagar, servant of Sarai, where have you come from, and where are you going?"

"I'm running away from my mistress Sarai," she answered.

⁹Then the angel of the LORD told her, "Go back to your mistress and submit to her." ¹⁰The angel added, "I will so increase your descendants that they will be too numerous to count."

ᵃ 18 Or Wadi

thought, "After I am worn out and my master[a] is old, will I now have this pleasure?"

[13]Then the LORD said to Abraham, "Why did Sarah laugh and say, 'Will I really have a child, now that I am old?' [14]Is anything too hard for the LORD? I will return to you at the appointed time next year and Sarah will have a son."

[15]Sarah was afraid, so she lied and said, "I did not laugh."

But he said, "Yes, you did laugh."

Abraham Pleads for Sodom

[16]When the men got up to leave, they looked down toward Sodom, and Abraham walked along with them to see them on their way. [17]Then the LORD said, "Shall I hide from Abraham what I am about to do? [18]Abraham will surely become a great and powerful nation, and all nations on earth will be blessed through him. [19]For I have chosen him, so that he will direct his children and his household after him to keep the way of the LORD by doing what is right and just, so that the LORD will bring about for Abraham what he has promised him."

[20]Then the LORD said, "The outcry against Sodom and Gomorrah is so great and their sin so grievous [21]that I will go down and see if what they have done is as bad as the outcry that has reached me. If not, I will know."

[22]The men turned away and went toward Sodom, but Abraham remained standing before the LORD.[b] [23]Then Abraham approached him and said: "Will you sweep away the righteous with the wicked? [24]What if there are fifty righteous people in the city? Will you really sweep it away and not spare[c] the place for the sake of the fifty righteous people in it? [25]Far be it from you to do such a thing—to kill the righteous with the wicked, treating the righteous and the wicked alike. Far be it from you! Will not the Judge[d] of all the earth do right?"

[26]The LORD said, "If I find fifty righteous people in the city of Sodom, I will spare the whole place for their sake."

[27]Then Abraham spoke up again: "Now that I have been so bold as to speak to the Lord, though I am nothing but dust and ashes, [28]what if the number of the righteous is five less than fifty? Will you destroy the whole city because of five people?"

"If I find forty-five there," he said, "I will not destroy it."

[29]Once again he spoke to him, "What if only forty are found there?"

He said, "For the sake of forty, I will not do it."

[30]Then he said, "May the Lord not be angry, but let me speak. What if only thirty can be found there?"

He answered, "I will not do it if I find thirty there."

[31]Abraham said, "Now that I have been so bold as to speak to the Lord, what if only twenty can be found there?"

He said, "For the sake of twenty, I will not destroy it."

[32]Then he said, "May the Lord not be angry, but let me speak just once more. What if only ten can be found there?"

He answered, "For the sake of ten, I will not destroy it."

[33]When the LORD had finished speaking with Abraham, he left, and Abraham returned home.

How Many Is Enough?

GENESIS 18:23–24

Abraham ventures to plead with God on behalf of his nephew Lot for the people of Sodom. While we appreciate his loyalty, we are inclined to become impatient as he haggles over numbers. Write the names of ten friends on blank index cards, and lay out all ten cards face up on a flat surface. If it were important, would you walk five miles for these ten people? Now remove five cards at random; for the five remaining friends, would you still walk five miles? Remove one more card; for four friends, would you walk? Remove one; for three friends? Remove one more. At last only two are left: Are they alone worth your trouble?

See Meeting God in Scripture

---

[a]12 Or *husband*   [b]22 Masoretic Text; an ancient Hebrew scribal tradition but *the LORD remained standing before Abraham*   [c]24 Or *forgive*; also in verse 26   [d]25 Or *Ruler*

Wrath and Love

"God's wrath is not incompatible with his love; they are aspects of the same character. His wrath is the clear shining of his light which of its nature burns up injustice and oppression. The opposite of wrath is not love but neutrality: Wrath and love are essentially one. The wrath of God is the Bible's expression for his essential hostility to all evil. The Bible does not see the love and wrath of God as two conflicting impulses, wrath restraining love from time to time; on the contrary, wrath is tempered with mercy . . . To reject, and live apart from, the love of God is to enter the world of wrath, or ruin, or disaster."

—KENNETH LEECH,
True Prayer

See Meeting God in Community

Sodom and Gomorrah Destroyed

19 The two angels arrived at Sodom in the evening, and Lot was sitting in the gateway of the city. When he saw them, he got up to meet them and bowed down with his face to the ground. ²"My lords," he said, "please turn aside to your servant's house. You can wash your feet and spend the night and then go on your way early in the morning."

"No," they answered, "we will spend the night in the square."

³But he insisted so strongly that they did go with him and entered his house. He prepared a meal for them, baking bread without yeast, and they ate. ⁴Before they had gone to bed, all the men from every part of the city of Sodom—both young and old—surrounded the house. ⁵They called to Lot, "Where are the men who came to you tonight? Bring them out to us so that we can have sex with them."

⁶Lot went outside to meet them and shut the door behind him ⁷and said, "No, my friends. Don't do this wicked thing. ⁸Look, I have two daughters who have never slept with a man. Let me bring them out to you, and you can do what you like with them. But don't do anything to these men, for they have come under the protection of my roof."

⁹"Get out of our way," they replied. And they said, "This fellow came here as an alien, and now he wants to play the judge! We'll treat you worse than them." They kept bringing pressure on Lot and moved forward to break down the door.

¹⁰But the men inside reached out and pulled Lot back into the house and shut the door. ¹¹Then they struck the men who were at the door of the house, young and old, with blindness so that they could not find the door.

¹²The two men said to Lot, "Do you have anyone else here—sons-in-law, sons or daughters, or anyone else in the city who belongs to you? Get them out of here, ¹³because we are going to destroy this place. The outcry to the LORD against its people is so great that he has sent us to destroy it."

¹⁴So Lot went out and spoke to his sons-in-law, who were pledged to marry*a* his daughters. He said, "Hurry and get out of this place, because the LORD is about to destroy the city!" But his sons-in-law thought he was joking.

¹⁵With the coming of dawn, the angels urged Lot, saying, "Hurry! Take your wife and your two daughters who are here, or you will be swept away when the city is punished."

¹⁶When he hesitated, the men grasped his hand and the hands of his wife and of his two daughters and led them safely out of the city, for the LORD was merciful to them. ¹⁷As soon as they had brought them out, one of them said, "Flee for your lives! Don't look back, and don't stop anywhere in the plain! Flee to the mountains or you will be swept away!"

¹⁸But Lot said to them, "No, my lords,*b* please! ¹⁹Your*c* servant has found favor in your*c* eyes, and you*c* have shown great kindness to me in sparing my life. But I can't flee to the mountains; this disaster will overtake me, and I'll die.

a 14 Or *were married to*   *b 18* Or *No, Lord;* or *No, my lord*   *c 19* The Hebrew is singular.

²⁰Look, here is a town near enough to run to, and it is small. Let me flee to it—it is very small, isn't it? Then my life will be spared."

²¹He said to him, "Very well, I will grant this request too; I will not overthrow the town you speak of. ²²But flee there quickly, because I cannot do anything until you reach it." (That is why the town was called Zoar.ᵃ)

²³By the time Lot reached Zoar, the sun had risen over the land. ²⁴Then the LORD rained down burning sulfur on Sodom and Gomorrah—from the LORD out of the heavens. ²⁵Thus he overthrew those cities and the entire plain, including all those living in the cities—and also the vegetation in the land. ²⁶But Lot's wife looked back, and she became a pillar of salt.

²⁷Early the next morning Abraham got up and returned to the place where he had stood before the LORD. ²⁸He looked down toward Sodom and Gomorrah, toward all the land of the plain, and he saw dense smoke rising from the land, like smoke from a furnace.

²⁹So when God destroyed the cities of the plain, he remembered Abraham, and he brought Lot out of the catastrophe that overthrew the cities where Lot had lived.

Lot and His Daughters

³⁰Lot and his two daughters left Zoar and settled in the mountains, for he was afraid to stay in Zoar. He and his two daughters lived in a cave. ³¹One day the older daughter said to the younger, "Our father is old, and there is no man around here to lie with us, as is the custom all over the earth. ³²Let's get our father to drink wine and then lie with him and preserve our family line through our father."

³³That night they got their father to drink wine, and the older daughter went in and lay with him. He was not aware of it when she lay down or when she got up.

³⁴The next day the older daughter said to the younger, "Last night I lay with my father. Let's get him to drink wine again tonight, and you go in and lie with him so we can preserve our family line through our father." ³⁵So they got their father to drink wine that night also, and the younger daughter went and lay with him. Again he was not aware of it when she lay down or when she got up.

³⁶So both of Lot's daughters became pregnant by their father. ³⁷The older daughter had a son, and she named him Moabᵇ; he is the father of the Moabites of today. ³⁸The younger daughter also had a son, and she named him Ben-Ammiᶜ; he is the father of the Ammonites of today.

Abraham and Abimelech

20 Now Abraham moved on from there into the region of the Negev and lived between Kadesh and Shur. For a while he stayed in Gerar, ²and there Abraham said of his wife Sarah, "She is my sister." Then Abimelech king of Gerar sent for Sarah and took her.

³But God came to Abimelech in a dream one night and said to him, "You are as good as dead because of the woman you have taken; she is a married woman."

⁴Now Abimelech had not gone near her, so he said, "Lord, will you destroy an innocent nation? ⁵Did he not say

---

Preserve Our Family

GENESIS 19:32

This account troubles us: It seems to suggest that evil begets more evil. Try to imagine the catastrophe that has overtaken these young women who have been betrayed by their father, lost their mother and seen their home leveled. Consider their obligation to be fruitful and to preserve their line. They make the only choice they know in order to choose life in the midst of death. We, too, often find ourselves struggling in deeply troubling situations; how do we choose life? For one month, write in a journal about the little deaths and green shoots of new life you experience each day. Praying for God's help, note how you try to choose life daily.

See *Meeting God in Everyday Life*

ᵃ 22 *Zoar* means *small*.   ᵇ 37 *Moab* sounds like the Hebrew for *from father*.
ᶜ 38 *Ben-Ammi* means *son of my people*.

The Promise Fulfilled

GENESIS 21:2

So much turmoil intervenes in these few verses after God promised an heir to Abraham and Sarah (Genesis 17:19) that we almost forget the promise. Often this happens: Our life with God is filled with ups and downs, with passions and problems, and we cannot see the big picture. By the time God answers a prayer, we have forgotten we asked! What seemed impossible has happened, and we take it for granted rather than receive it as a gift. Is there some answered prayer in your life for which you have neglected to give thanks? Start writing down your prayers today, and in six months look back over your petitions to see how many God has answered.

See Meeting God in Prayer

to me, 'She is my sister,' and didn't she also say, 'He is my brother'? I have done this with a clear conscience and clean hands."

⁶Then God said to him in the dream, "Yes, I know you did this with a clear conscience, and so I have kept you from sinning against me. That is why I did not let you touch her. ⁷Now return the man's wife, for he is a prophet, and he will pray for you and you will live. But if you do not return her, you may be sure that you and all yours will die."

⁸Early the next morning Abimelech summoned all his officials, and when he told them all that had happened, they were very much afraid. ⁹Then Abimelech called Abraham in and said, "What have you done to us? How have I wronged you that you have brought such great guilt upon me and my kingdom? You have done things to me that should not be done." ¹⁰And Abimelech asked Abraham, "What was your reason for doing this?"

¹¹Abraham replied, "I said to myself, 'There is surely no fear of God in this place, and they will kill me because of my wife.' ¹²Besides, she really is my sister, the daughter of my father though not of my mother; and she became my wife. ¹³And when God had me wander from my father's household, I said to her, 'This is how you can show your love to me: Everywhere we go, say of me, "He is my brother." ' "

¹⁴Then Abimelech brought sheep and cattle and male and female slaves and gave them to Abraham, and he returned Sarah his wife to him. ¹⁵And Abimelech said, "My land is before you; live wherever you like."

¹⁶To Sarah he said, "I am giving your brother a thousand shekels*ᵃ* of silver. This is to cover the offense against you before all who are with you; you are completely vindicated."

¹⁷Then Abraham prayed to God, and God healed Abimelech, his wife and his slave girls so they could have children again, ¹⁸for the LORD had closed up every womb in Abimelech's household because of Abraham's wife Sarah.

The Birth of Isaac

21 Now the LORD was gracious to Sarah as he had said, and the LORD did for Sarah what he had promised. ²Sarah became pregnant and bore a son to Abraham in his old age, at the very time God had promised him. ³Abraham gave the name Isaac*ᵇ* to the son Sarah bore him. ⁴When his son Isaac was eight days old, Abraham circumcised him, as God commanded him. ⁵Abraham was a hundred years old when his son Isaac was born to him.

⁶Sarah said, "God has brought me laughter, and everyone who hears about this will laugh with me." ⁷And she added, "Who would have said to Abraham that Sarah would nurse children? Yet I have borne him a son in his old age."

Hagar and Ishmael Sent Away

⁸The child grew and was weaned, and on the day Isaac was weaned Abraham held a great feast. ⁹But Sarah saw that the son whom Hagar the Egyptian had borne to Abraham was mocking, ¹⁰and she said to Abraham, "Get rid of

---

ᵃ 16 That is, about 25 pounds (about 11.5 kilograms)   *ᵇ 3 Isaac* means *he laughs.*

that slave woman and her son, for that slave woman's son will never share in the inheritance with my son Isaac."

¹¹The matter distressed Abraham greatly because it concerned his son. ¹²But God said to him, "Do not be so distressed about the boy and your maidservant. Listen to whatever Sarah tells you, because it is through Isaac that your offspring*ᵃ* will be reckoned. ¹³I will make the son of the maidservant into a nation also, because he is your offspring."

¹⁴Early the next morning Abraham took some food and a skin of water and gave them to Hagar. He set them on her shoulders and then sent her off with the boy. She went on her way and wandered in the desert of Beersheba.

¹⁵When the water in the skin was gone, she put the boy under one of the bushes. ¹⁶Then she went off and sat down nearby, about a bowshot away, for she thought, "I cannot watch the boy die." And as she sat there nearby, she*ᵇ* began to sob.

¹⁷God heard the boy crying, and the angel of God called to Hagar from heaven and said to her, "What is the matter, Hagar? Do not be afraid; God has heard the boy crying as he lies there. ¹⁸Lift the boy up and take him by the hand, for I will make him into a great nation."

¹⁹Then God opened her eyes and she saw a well of water. So she went and filled the skin with water and gave the boy a drink.

²⁰God was with the boy as he grew up. He lived in the desert and became an archer. ²¹While he was living in the Desert of Paran, his mother got a wife for him from Egypt.

The Treaty at Beersheba

²²At that time Abimelech and Phicol the commander of his forces said to Abraham, "God is with you in everything you do. ²³Now swear to me here before God that you will not deal falsely with me or my children or my descendants. Show to me and the country where you are living as an alien the same kindness I have shown to you."

²⁴Abraham said, "I swear it."

²⁵Then Abraham complained to Abimelech about a well of water that Abimelech's servants had seized. ²⁶But Abimelech said, "I don't know who has done this. You did not tell me, and I heard about it only today."

²⁷So Abraham brought sheep and cattle and gave them to Abimelech, and the two men made a treaty. ²⁸Abraham set apart seven ewe lambs from the flock, ²⁹and Abimelech asked Abraham, "What is the meaning of these seven ewe lambs you have set apart by themselves?"

³⁰He replied, "Accept these seven lambs from my hand as a witness that I dug this well."

³¹So that place was called Beersheba,*ᶜ* because the two men swore an oath there.

³²After the treaty had been made at Beersheba, Abimelech and Phicol the commander of his forces returned to the land of the Philistines. ³³Abraham planted a tamarisk tree in Beersheba, and there he called upon the name of the Lᴏʀᴅ, the Eternal God. ³⁴And Abraham stayed in the land of the Philistines for a long time.

And She Sobbed

GENESIS 21:16

This situation seems unfair to Hagar. In everything, she has done as she was told, and now she is about to lose not only her life, but also her beloved child. Questioning just this kind of justice, Teresa of Avila is reputed to have charged God: "If this is how you treat your friends, no wonder you have so few of them!" What *does* God promise when we dedicate our lives to him? Are we promised that there will be no hardship, no difficulties? Instead, we are promised that we will never be alone. Is that enough for us? In your own difficulties, what is your "well of water"? What restores your hope? What opens your eyes to the utter fullness of God's companionship?

See Meeting God in Scripture

ᵃ 12 Or *seed*   *ᵇ 16* Hebrew; Septuagint *the child*   *ᶜ 31 Beersheba* can mean *well of seven* or *well of the oath.*

The Test

What kind of God would present such a test as this? We recoil from this difficult passage, which has caused wise ones to wonder for centuries. Perhaps the real question is "What kind of creatures benefit from such a test?" for no one here is exempt from its rigors. Hagar's hope is tested in the desert, as are Sarah's faith in "the impossible" and Lot's capacity for hospitality. Apparently there comes a time in our relationship with God when we need to be tested, even though he already knows our capabilities. Might God's purpose in the tests be to reveal something to us about ourselves? Think of a time when you felt God was absent, yet you sensed that he was testing you. What did you learn?

See Meeting God in Everyday Life

Abraham Tested

22 Some time later God tested Abraham. He said to him, "Abraham!"

"Here I am," he replied.

²Then God said, "Take your son, your only son, Isaac, whom you love, and go to the region of Moriah. Sacrifice him there as a burnt offering on one of the mountains I will tell you about."

³Early the next morning Abraham got up and saddled his donkey. He took with him two of his servants and his son Isaac. When he had cut enough wood for the burnt offering, he set out for the place God had told him about. ⁴On the third day Abraham looked up and saw the place in the distance. ⁵He said to his servants, "Stay here with the donkey while I and the boy go over there. We will worship and then we will come back to you."

⁶Abraham took the wood for the burnt offering and placed it on his son Isaac, and he himself carried the fire and the knife. As the two of them went on together, ⁷Isaac spoke up and said to his father Abraham, "Father?"

"Yes, my son?" Abraham replied.

"The fire and wood are here," Isaac said, "but where is the lamb for the burnt offering?"

⁸Abraham answered, "God himself will provide the lamb for the burnt offering, my son." And the two of them went on together.

⁹When they reached the place God had told him about, Abraham built an altar there and arranged the wood on it. He bound his son Isaac and laid him on the altar, on top of the wood. ¹⁰Then he reached out his hand and took the knife to slay his son. ¹¹But the angel of the Lord called out to him from heaven, "Abraham! Abraham!"

"Here I am," he replied.

¹²"Do not lay a hand on the boy," he said. "Do not do anything to him. Now I know that you fear God, because you have not withheld from me your son, your only son."

¹³Abraham looked up and there in a thicket he saw a ram*ᵃ* caught by its horns. He went over and took the ram and sacrificed it as a burnt offering instead of his son. ¹⁴So Abraham called that place The Lord Will Provide. And to this day it is said, "On the mountain of the Lord it will be provided."

¹⁵The angel of the Lord called to Abraham from heaven a second time ¹⁶and said, "I swear by myself, declares the Lord, that because you have done this and have not withheld your son, your only son, ¹⁷I will surely bless you and make your descendants as numerous as the stars in the sky and as the sand on the seashore. Your descendants will take possession of the cities of their enemies, ¹⁸and through your offspring*ᵇ* all nations on earth will be blessed, because you have obeyed me."

¹⁹Then Abraham returned to his servants, and they set off together for Beersheba. And Abraham stayed in Beersheba.

Nahor's Sons

²⁰Some time later Abraham was told, "Milcah is also a

ᵃ 13 Many manuscripts of the Masoretic Text, Samaritan Pentateuch, Septuagint and Syriac; most manuscripts of the Masoretic Text *a ram behind him* *ᵇ 18* Or *seed*

mother; she has borne sons to your brother Nahor: ²¹Uz the firstborn, Buz his brother, Kemuel (the father of Aram), ²²Kesed, Hazo, Pildash, Jidlaph and Bethuel." ²³Bethuel became the father of Rebekah. Milcah bore these eight sons to Abraham's brother Nahor. ²⁴His concubine, whose name was Reumah, also had sons: Tebah, Gaham, Tahash and Maacah.

The Death of Sarah

23 Sarah lived to be a hundred and twenty-seven years old. ²She died at Kiriath Arba (that is, Hebron) in the land of Canaan, and Abraham went to mourn for Sarah and to weep over her.

³Then Abraham rose from beside his dead wife and spoke to the Hittites.ª He said, ⁴"I am an alien and a stranger among you. Sell me some property for a burial site here so I can bury my dead."

⁵The Hittites replied to Abraham, ⁶"Sir, listen to us. You are a mighty prince among us. Bury your dead in the choicest of our tombs. None of us will refuse you his tomb for burying your dead."

⁷Then Abraham rose and bowed down before the people of the land, the Hittites. ⁸He said to them, "If you are willing to let me bury my dead, then listen to me and intercede with Ephron son of Zohar on my behalf ⁹so he will sell me the cave of Machpelah, which belongs to him and is at the end of his field. Ask him to sell it to me for the full price as a burial site among you."

¹⁰Ephron the Hittite was sitting among his people and he replied to Abraham in the hearing of all the Hittites who had come to the gate of his city. ¹¹"No, my lord," he said. "Listen to me; I giveᵇ you the field, and I giveᵇ you the cave that is in it. I giveᵇ it to you in the presence of my people. Bury your dead."

¹²Again Abraham bowed down before the people of the land ¹³and he said to Ephron in their hearing, "Listen to me, if you will. I will pay the price of the field. Accept it from me so I can bury my dead there."

¹⁴Ephron answered Abraham, ¹⁵"Listen to me, my lord; the land is worth four hundred shekelsᶜ of silver, but what is that between me and you? Bury your dead."

¹⁶Abraham agreed to Ephron's terms and weighed out for him the price he had named in the hearing of the Hittites: four hundred shekels of silver, according to the weight current among the merchants.

¹⁷So Ephron's field in Machpelah near Mamre—both the field and the cave in it, and all the trees within the borders of the field—was deeded ¹⁸to Abraham as his property in the presence of all the Hittites who had come to the gate of the city. ¹⁹Afterward Abraham buried his wife Sarah in the cave in the field of Machpelah near Mamre (which is at Hebron) in the land of Canaan. ²⁰So the field and the cave in it were deeded to Abraham by the Hittites as a burial site.

Isaac and Rebekah

24 Abraham was now old and well advanced in years, and the Lord had blessed him in every way. ²He said to the chiefᵈ servant in his household, the one in

---

Holiness

GENESIS 23:2–4

"As humans, we are holy insofar as we have come into contact with divine holiness . . . The divine initiative cannot be over stressed, but at the same time there is need of our most generous effort and concentration. The hard part is doing our utmost and then having to count it as nothing. Far from seeing ourselves growing in insight and closeness to God, the opposite happens. We are beset by weaknesses of all kinds and fail to make a good show in our own estimation. All we do seems paltry and shabby, even our sufferings are not worthy of the name. We have nothing to fall back on . . . except the one thing which is everything—faith in God's goodness and fidelity."

—RUTH BURROWS,
To Believe in Jesus

ª 3 Or *the sons of Heth*; also in verses 5, 7, 10, 16, 18 and 20   ᵇ 11 Or *sell*
ᶜ 15 That is, about 10 pounds (about 4.5 kilograms)   ᵈ 2 Or *oldest*

The Lord Will Send His Angel Ahead

GENESIS 24:17–21

Enter this scene fully in your imagination. Let your senses create the sight of the well, the smell of the water, the shuffling noises of the tired camels. First imagine yourself as Abraham's servant, entrusted with an important task, praying earnestly for God's help. Now imagine yourself as Rebekah, going about your hard daily work, interrupted by a stranger, asked to do yet more. Finally, imagine that you are the well itself, silent repository of many ancient secrets. Listen carefully for what God speaks to you as you enter each of these roles. When you have explored each in turn, sit quietly for a time, receptive to what God might be saying to you today through this incident in Scripture.

See *Meeting God in Scripture*

charge of all that he had, "Put your hand under my thigh. ³I want you to swear by the LORD, the God of heaven and the God of earth, that you will not get a wife for my son from the daughters of the Canaanites, among whom I am living, ⁴but will go to my country and my own relatives and get a wife for my son Isaac."

⁵The servant asked him, "What if the woman is unwilling to come back with me to this land? Shall I then take your son back to the country you came from?"

⁶"Make sure that you do not take my son back there," Abraham said. ⁷"The LORD, the God of heaven, who brought me out of my father's household and my native land and who spoke to me and promised me on oath, saying, 'To your offspring*a* I will give this land'—he will send his angel before you so that you can get a wife for my son from there. ⁸If the woman is unwilling to come back with you, then you will be released from this oath of mine. Only do not take my son back there." ⁹So the servant put his hand under the thigh of his master Abraham and swore an oath to him concerning this matter.

¹⁰Then the servant took ten of his master's camels and left, taking with him all kinds of good things from his master. He set out for Aram Naharaim*b* and made his way to the town of Nahor. ¹¹He had the camels kneel down near the well outside the town; it was toward evening, the time the women go out to draw water.

¹²Then he prayed, "O LORD, God of my master Abraham, give me success today, and show kindness to my master Abraham. ¹³See, I am standing beside this spring, and the daughters of the townspeople are coming out to draw water. ¹⁴May it be that when I say to a girl, 'Please let down your jar that I may have a drink,' and she says, 'Drink, and I'll water your camels too'—let her be the one you have chosen for your servant Isaac. By this I will know that you have shown kindness to my master."

¹⁵Before he had finished praying, Rebekah came out with her jar on her shoulder. She was the daughter of Bethuel son of Milcah, who was the wife of Abraham's brother Nahor. ¹⁶The girl was very beautiful, a virgin; no man had ever lain with her. She went down to the spring, filled her jar and came up again.

¹⁷The servant hurried to meet her and said, "Please give me a little water from your jar."

¹⁸"Drink, my lord," she said, and quickly lowered the jar to her hands and gave him a drink.

¹⁹After she had given him a drink, she said, "I'll draw water for your camels too, until they have finished drinking." ²⁰So she quickly emptied her jar into the trough, ran back to the well to draw more water, and drew enough for all his camels. ²¹Without saying a word, the man watched her closely to learn whether or not the LORD had made his journey successful.

²²When the camels had finished drinking, the man took out a gold nose ring weighing a beka*c* and two gold bracelets weighing ten shekels.*d* ²³Then he asked, "Whose daughter are you? Please tell me, is there room in your father's house for us to spend the night?"

a 7 Or *seed*   *b* 10 That is, Northwest Mesopotamia   *c* 22 That is, about 1/5 ounce (about 5.5 grams)   *d* 22 That is, about 4 ounces (about 110 grams)

²⁴She answered him, "I am the daughter of Bethuel, the son that Milcah bore to Nahor." ²⁵And she added, "We have plenty of straw and fodder, as well as room for you to spend the night."

²⁶Then the man bowed down and worshiped the LORD, ²⁷saying, "Praise be to the LORD, the God of my master Abraham, who has not abandoned his kindness and faithfulness to my master. As for me, the LORD has led me on the journey to the house of my master's relatives."

²⁸The girl ran and told her mother's household about these things. ²⁹Now Rebekah had a brother named Laban, and he hurried out to the man at the spring. ³⁰As soon as he had seen the nose ring, and the bracelets on his sister's arms, and had heard Rebekah tell what the man said to her, he went out to the man and found him standing by the camels near the spring. ³¹"Come, you who are blessed by the LORD," he said. "Why are you standing out here? I have prepared the house and a place for the camels."

³²So the man went to the house, and the camels were unloaded. Straw and fodder were brought for the camels, and water for him and his men to wash their feet. ³³Then food was set before him, but he said, "I will not eat until I have told you what I have to say."

"Then tell us," ⌞Laban⌟ said.

³⁴So he said, "I am Abraham's servant. ³⁵The LORD has blessed my master abundantly, and he has become wealthy. He has given him sheep and cattle, silver and gold, menservants and maidservants, and camels and donkeys. ³⁶My master's wife Sarah has borne him a son in her*ᵃ* old age, and he has given him everything he owns. ³⁷And my master made me swear an oath, and said, 'You must not get a wife for my son from the daughters of the Canaanites, in whose land I live, ³⁸but go to my father's family and to my own clan, and get a wife for my son.'

³⁹"Then I asked my master, 'What if the woman will not come back with me?'

⁴⁰"He replied, 'The LORD, before whom I have walked, will send his angel with you and make your journey a success, so that you can get a wife for my son from my own clan and from my father's family. ⁴¹Then, when you go to my clan, you will be released from my oath even if they refuse to give her to you—you will be released from my oath.'

⁴²"When I came to the spring today, I said, 'O LORD, God of my master Abraham, if you will, please grant success to the journey on which I have come. ⁴³See, I am standing beside this spring; if a maiden comes out to draw water and I say to her, "Please let me drink a little water from your jar," ⁴⁴and if she says to me, "Drink, and I'll draw water for your camels too," let her be the one the LORD has chosen for my master's son.'

⁴⁵"Before I finished praying in my heart, Rebekah came out, with her jar on her shoulder. She went down to the spring and drew water, and I said to her, 'Please give me a drink.'

⁴⁶"She quickly lowered her jar from her shoulder and said, 'Drink, and I'll water your camels too.' So I drank, and she watered the camels also.

⁴⁷"I asked her, 'Whose daughter are you?'

Come, You Who Are Blessed

GENESIS 24:31

In the culture of the desert, hospitality is a serious obligation. The stranger depends for life itself on various tribes' willingness to provide shelter, drink and food as he travels through the desert. The tribes are also aware that generosity is not merely an obligation. The stranger may bring blessing; angels are often entertained "unawares." What is your response to strangers at your door, especially if they seem "different" from you? Consider making a deliberate decision to give a certain percentage of your time or money for a period of time to the care of someone in need. Do this unconditionally, but be alert to the possibility that Jesus Christ may be revealed in those you encounter (see Matthew 25:34–46).

See Meeting God in Community

ᵃ 36 Or his

This Is From the Lord

GENESIS 24:50–51

How do we know when an opportunity is from the Lord? How do we discern God's desire among several good choices? We know that Abraham's servant has been praying, and we can reasonably assume that Laban, Bethuel and Rebekah root their lives in a regular rhythm of prayer; this is the foundation of all discernment. Today, take the phrase "This is from the LORD" and repeat it over and over until it begins to pulse with the rhythm of your heartbeat. Ponder the phrase; be open not only to ordinary insights, but to images or hymn verses that accompany your reflection. Finally, be receptive to an invitation to be or do something today in response to your meditation in the Spirit.

See *Meeting God in Prayer*

"She said, 'The daughter of Bethuel son of Nahor, whom Milcah bore to him.'

"Then I put the ring in her nose and the bracelets on her arms, ⁴⁸and I bowed down and worshiped the LORD. I praised the LORD, the God of my master Abraham, who had led me on the right road to get the granddaughter of my master's brother for his son. ⁴⁹Now if you will show kindness and faithfulness to my master, tell me; and if not, tell me, so I may know which way to turn."

⁵⁰Laban and Bethuel answered, "This is from the LORD; we can say nothing to you one way or the other. ⁵¹Here is Rebekah; take her and go, and let her become the wife of your master's son, as the LORD has directed."

⁵²When Abraham's servant heard what they said, he bowed down to the ground before the LORD. ⁵³Then the servant brought out gold and silver jewelry and articles of clothing and gave them to Rebekah; he also gave costly gifts to her brother and to her mother. ⁵⁴Then he and the men who were with him ate and drank and spent the night there.

When they got up the next morning, he said, "Send me on my way to my master."

⁵⁵But her brother and her mother replied, "Let the girl remain with us ten days or so; then you*ᵃ* may go."

⁵⁶But he said to them, "Do not detain me, now that the LORD has granted success to my journey. Send me on my way so I may go to my master."

⁵⁷Then they said, "Let's call the girl and ask her about it." ⁵⁸So they called Rebekah and asked her, "Will you go with this man?"

"I will go," she said.

⁵⁹So they sent their sister Rebekah on her way, along with her nurse and Abraham's servant and his men. ⁶⁰And they blessed Rebekah and said to her,

> "Our sister, may you increase
> to thousands upon thousands;
> may your offspring possess
> the gates of their enemies."

⁶¹Then Rebekah and her maids got ready and mounted their camels and went back with the man. So the servant took Rebekah and left.

⁶²Now Isaac had come from Beer Lahai Roi, for he was living in the Negev. ⁶³He went out to the field one evening to meditate,*ᵇ* and as he looked up, he saw camels approaching. ⁶⁴Rebekah also looked up and saw Isaac. She got down from her camel ⁶⁵and asked the servant, "Who is that man in the field coming to meet us?"

"He is my master," the servant answered. So she took her veil and covered herself.

⁶⁶Then the servant told Isaac all he had done. ⁶⁷Isaac brought her into the tent of his mother Sarah, and he married Rebekah. So she became his wife, and he loved her; and Isaac was comforted after his mother's death.

The Death of Abraham

25 Abraham took*ᶜ* another wife, whose name was Keturah. ²She bore him Zimran, Jokshan, Medan, Mid-

ᵃ 55 Or *she*   *ᵇ 63* The meaning of the Hebrew for this word is uncertain.
ᶜ 1 Or *had taken*

ian, Ishbak and Shuah. ³Jokshan was the father of Sheba and Dedan; the descendants of Dedan were the Asshurites, the Letushites and the Leummites. ⁴The sons of Midian were Ephah, Epher, Hanoch, Abida and Eldaah. All these were descendants of Keturah.

⁵Abraham left everything he owned to Isaac. ⁶But while he was still living, he gave gifts to the sons of his concubines and sent them away from his son Isaac to the land of the east.

⁷Altogether, Abraham lived a hundred and seventy-five years. ⁸Then Abraham breathed his last and died at a good old age, an old man and full of years; and he was gathered to his people. ⁹His sons Isaac and Ishmael buried him in the cave of Machpelah near Mamre, in the field of Ephron son of Zohar the Hittite, ¹⁰the field Abraham had bought from the Hittites.ᵃ There Abraham was buried with his wife Sarah. ¹¹After Abraham's death, God blessed his son Isaac, who then lived near Beer Lahai Roi.

Ishmael's Sons

¹²This is the account of Abraham's son Ishmael, whom Sarah's maidservant, Hagar the Egyptian, bore to Abraham.

¹³These are the names of the sons of Ishmael, listed in the order of their birth: Nebaioth the firstborn of Ishmael, Kedar, Adbeel, Mibsam, ¹⁴Mishma, Dumah, Massa, ¹⁵Hadad, Tema, Jetur, Naphish and Kedemah. ¹⁶These were the sons of Ishmael, and these are the names of the twelve tribal rulers according to their settlements and camps. ¹⁷Altogether, Ishmael lived a hundred and thirty-seven years. He breathed his last and died, and he was gathered to his people. ¹⁸His descendants settled in the area from Havilah to Shur, near the border of Egypt, as you go toward Asshur. And they lived in hostility towardᵇ all their brothers.

Jacob and Esau

¹⁹This is the account of Abraham's son Isaac.

Abraham became the father of Isaac, ²⁰and Isaac was forty years old when he married Rebekah daughter of Bethuel the Aramean from Paddan Aramᶜ and sister of Laban the Aramean.

²¹Isaac prayed to the LORD on behalf of his wife, because she was barren. The LORD answered his prayer, and his wife Rebekah became pregnant. ²²The babies jostled each other within her, and she said, "Why is this happening to me?" So she went to inquire of the LORD.

²³The LORD said to her,

"Two nations are in your womb,
    and two peoples from within you will be
        separated;
    one people will be stronger than the other,
        and the older will serve the younger."

²⁴When the time came for her to give birth, there were twin boys in her womb. ²⁵The first to come out was red, and his whole body was like a hairy garment; so they named him Esau.ᵈ ²⁶After this, his brother came out, with

---

Living in Conflict

GENESIS 25:22

Again conflict rears its head: The sons of Isaac and Ishmael live in hostility toward one another, and even the babies in Rebekah's womb jostle each other. In light of the record of Genesis, we might consider that the peace of God that we seek must surely encompass the inevitable conflicts of life. Perhaps our spiritual formation involves not eliminating conflict and suffering, but allowing ourselves to learn how they strengthen us in faith and love. Reflect on some current conflict in your life from which you have prayed for release. Ask God for insight into how you can *live with* the conflict, letting it teach you what he wishes you to learn.

See *Meeting God in Scripture*

ᵃ 10 Or *the sons of Heth*   ᵇ 18 Or *lived to the east of*   ᶜ 20 That is, Northwest Mesopotamia   ᵈ 25 *Esau* may mean *hairy*; he was also called Edom, which means *red*.

The Soul's Birthright

GENESIS 25:31–34

"If self-sacrifice is, as we are told, 'glorious madness,' then certainly undeviating self-assertion is inglorious madness. Either path leads alike to annihilation. We have come upon one of those deep paradoxes of life. To become a person, one must both affirm and deny oneself. Each involves the other. They are not totally different things, but diverse aspects of the same thing. They belong together as indissolubly as the two sides of the board do."

—RUFUS JONES,
Daily Readings from Quaker Spirituality

his hand grasping Esau's heel; so he was named Jacob.[a] Isaac was sixty years old when Rebekah gave birth to them.

²⁷The boys grew up, and Esau became a skillful hunter, a man of the open country, while Jacob was a quiet man, staying among the tents. ²⁸Isaac, who had a taste for wild game, loved Esau, but Rebekah loved Jacob.

²⁹Once when Jacob was cooking some stew, Esau came in from the open country, famished. ³⁰He said to Jacob, "Quick, let me have some of that red stew! I'm famished!" (That is why he was also called Edom.[b])

³¹Jacob replied, "First sell me your birthright."

³²"Look, I am about to die," Esau said. "What good is the birthright to me?"

³³But Jacob said, "Swear to me first." So he swore an oath to him, selling his birthright to Jacob.

³⁴Then Jacob gave Esau some bread and some lentil stew. He ate and drank, and then got up and left.

So Esau despised his birthright.

Isaac and Abimelech

26 Now there was a famine in the land—besides the earlier famine of Abraham's time—and Isaac went to Abimelech king of the Philistines in Gerar. ²The LORD appeared to Isaac and said, "Do not go down to Egypt; live in the land where I tell you to live. ³Stay in this land for a while, and I will be with you and will bless you. For to you and your descendants I will give all these lands and will confirm the oath I swore to your father Abraham. ⁴I will make your descendants as numerous as the stars in the sky and will give them all these lands, and through your offspring[c] all nations on earth will be blessed, ⁵because Abraham obeyed me and kept my requirements, my commands, my decrees and my laws." ⁶So Isaac stayed in Gerar.

⁷When the men of that place asked him about his wife, he said, "She is my sister," because he was afraid to say, "She is my wife." He thought, "The men of this place might kill me on account of Rebekah, because she is beautiful."

⁸When Isaac had been there a long time, Abimelech king of the Philistines looked down from a window and saw Isaac caressing his wife Rebekah. ⁹So Abimelech summoned Isaac and said, "She is really your wife! Why did you say, 'She is my sister'?"

Isaac answered him, "Because I thought I might lose my life on account of her."

¹⁰Then Abimelech said, "What is this you have done to us? One of the men might well have slept with your wife, and you would have brought guilt upon us."

¹¹So Abimelech gave orders to all the people: "Anyone who molests this man or his wife shall surely be put to death."

¹²Isaac planted crops in that land and the same year reaped a hundredfold, because the LORD blessed him. ¹³The man became rich, and his wealth continued to grow until he became very wealthy. ¹⁴He had so many flocks and herds and servants that the Philistines envied him. ¹⁵So all the wells that his father's servants had dug in the time of

---

[a] 26 *Jacob* means *he grasps the heel* (figuratively, *he deceives*).   [b] 30 *Edom* means *red*.   [c] 4 Or *seed*

his father Abraham, the Philistines stopped up, filling them with earth.

16Then Abimelech said to Isaac, "Move away from us; you have become too powerful for us."

17So Isaac moved away from there and encamped in the Valley of Gerar and settled there. 18Isaac reopened the wells that had been dug in the time of his father Abraham, which the Philistines had stopped up after Abraham died, and he gave them the same names his father had given them.

19Isaac's servants dug in the valley and discovered a well of fresh water there. 20But the herdsmen of Gerar quarreled with Isaac's herdsmen and said, "The water is ours!" So he named the well Esek,*a* because they disputed with him. 21Then they dug another well, but they quarreled over that one also; so he named it Sitnah.*b* 22He moved on from there and dug another well, and no one quarreled over it. He named it Rehoboth,*c* saying, "Now the LORD has given us room and we will flourish in the land."

23From there he went up to Beersheba. 24That night the LORD appeared to him and said, "I am the God of your father Abraham. Do not be afraid, for I am with you; I will bless you and will increase the number of your descendants for the sake of my servant Abraham."

25Isaac built an altar there and called on the name of the LORD. There he pitched his tent, and there his servants dug a well.

26Meanwhile, Abimelech had come to him from Gerar, with Ahuzzath his personal adviser and Phicol the commander of his forces. 27Isaac asked them, "Why have you come to me, since you were hostile to me and sent me away?"

28They answered, "We saw clearly that the LORD was with you; so we said, 'There ought to be a sworn agreement between us'—between us and you. Let us make a treaty with you 29that you will do us no harm, just as we did not molest you but always treated you well and sent you away in peace. And now you are blessed by the LORD."

30Isaac then made a feast for them, and they ate and drank. 31Early the next morning the men swore an oath to each other. Then Isaac sent them on their way, and they left him in peace.

32That day Isaac's servants came and told him about the well they had dug. They said, "We've found water!" 33He called it Shibah,*d* and to this day the name of the town has been Beersheba.*e*

34When Esau was forty years old, he married Judith daughter of Beeri the Hittite, and also Basemath daughter of Elon the Hittite. 35They were a source of grief to Isaac and Rebekah.

Jacob Gets Isaac's Blessing

27 When Isaac was old and his eyes were so weak that he could no longer see, he called for Esau his older son and said to him, "My son."

"Here I am," he answered.

2Isaac said, "I am now an old man and don't know the day of my death. 3Now then, get your weapons—your

---

We've Found Water!

GENESIS 26:32

Find a lovely bowl and fill it with water. Place the bowl near the main entrance to your home and gather your family around. Thank God for the gift of water and pray together over the bowl. Then, each time any one of you passes through the door, dip your fingers into the bowl and remember that God is with you, blessing your going in and your coming out. Refill the bowl from time to time with fresh water, and keep it there as long as it continues to remind you of God's presence.

See *Meeting God in the Created Order*

---

a 20 Esek means *dispute.* *b 21 Sitnah* means *opposition.* *c 22 Rehoboth* means *room.* *d 33 Shibah* can mean *oath* or *seven.* *e 33 Beersheba* can mean *well of the oath* or *well of seven.*

Just Do What I Say

GENESIS 27:13

Many strong wills are clashing in this account, bringing to a head the conflict that has simmered in this family from the beginning. So many people are determined to control the outcome that God's will seems to have been eclipsed. Notice how a stubborn desire to manage things prevails, creating a rigidity that inevitably pits individuals against each other. As you consider these Biblical events, choose one person in this story with whom you most identify. How is that person's situation and motivation like your own? And how unlike yours? How do you resist God's will in your life? In contrast, what can you do to allow God's will to flow through and permeate your life?

See Meeting God in Scripture

quiver and bow—and go out to the open country to hunt some wild game for me. ⁴Prepare me the kind of tasty food I like and bring it to me to eat, so that I may give you my blessing before I die."

⁵Now Rebekah was listening as Isaac spoke to his son Esau. When Esau left for the open country to hunt game and bring it back, ⁶Rebekah said to her son Jacob, "Look, I overheard your father say to your brother Esau, ⁷'Bring me some game and prepare me some tasty food to eat, so that I may give you my blessing in the presence of the LORD before I die.' ⁸Now, my son, listen carefully and do what I tell you: ⁹Go out to the flock and bring me two choice young goats, so I can prepare some tasty food for your father, just the way he likes it. ¹⁰Then take it to your father to eat, so that he may give you his blessing before he dies."

¹¹Jacob said to Rebekah his mother, "But my brother Esau is a hairy man, and I'm a man with smooth skin. ¹²What if my father touches me? I would appear to be tricking him and would bring down a curse on myself rather than a blessing."

¹³His mother said to him, "My son, let the curse fall on me. Just do what I say; go and get them for me."

¹⁴So he went and got them and brought them to his mother, and she prepared some tasty food, just the way his father liked it. ¹⁵Then Rebekah took the best clothes of Esau her older son, which she had in the house, and put them on her younger son Jacob. ¹⁶She also covered his hands and the smooth part of his neck with the goatskins. ¹⁷Then she handed to her son Jacob the tasty food and the bread she had made.

¹⁸He went to his father and said, "My father."

"Yes, my son," he answered. "Who is it?"

¹⁹Jacob said to his father, "I am Esau your firstborn. I have done as you told me. Please sit up and eat some of my game so that you may give me your blessing."

²⁰Isaac asked his son, "How did you find it so quickly, my son?"

"The LORD your God gave me success," he replied.

²¹Then Isaac said to Jacob, "Come near so I can touch you, my son, to know whether you really are my son Esau or not."

²²Jacob went close to his father Isaac, who touched him and said, "The voice is the voice of Jacob, but the hands are the hands of Esau." ²³He did not recognize him, for his hands were hairy like those of his brother Esau; so he blessed him. ²⁴"Are you really my son Esau?" he asked.

"I am," he replied.

²⁵Then he said, "My son, bring me some of your game to eat, so that I may give you my blessing."

Jacob brought it to him and he ate; and he brought some wine and he drank. ²⁶Then his father Isaac said to him, "Come here, my son, and kiss me."

²⁷So he went to him and kissed him. When Isaac caught the smell of his clothes, he blessed him and said,

> "Ah, the smell of my son
>   is like the smell of a field
>   that the LORD has blessed.
> ²⁸ May God give you of heaven's dew
>   and of earth's richness—
>   an abundance of grain and new wine.

²⁹ May nations serve you
    and peoples bow down to you.
Be lord over your brothers,
    and may the sons of your mother bow down to
        you.
May those who curse you be cursed
    and those who bless you be blessed."

³⁰ After Isaac finished blessing him and Jacob had scarcely left his father's presence, his brother Esau came in from hunting. ³¹ He too prepared some tasty food and brought it to his father. Then he said to him, "My father, sit up and eat some of my game, so that you may give me your blessing."

³² His father Isaac asked him, "Who are you?"

"I am your son," he answered, "your firstborn, Esau."

³³ Isaac trembled violently and said, "Who was it, then, that hunted game and brought it to me? I ate it just before you came and I blessed him—and indeed he will be blessed!"

³⁴ When Esau heard his father's words, he burst out with a loud and bitter cry and said to his father, "Bless me—me too, my father!"

³⁵ But he said, "Your brother came deceitfully and took your blessing."

³⁶ Esau said, "Isn't he rightly named Jacob*ᵃ*? He has deceived me these two times: He took my birthright, and now he's taken my blessing!" Then he asked, "Haven't you reserved any blessing for me?"

³⁷ Isaac answered Esau, "I have made him lord over you and have made all his relatives his servants, and I have sustained him with grain and new wine. So what can I possibly do for you, my son?"

³⁸ Esau said to his father, "Do you have only one blessing, my father? Bless me too, my father!" Then Esau wept aloud.

³⁹ His father Isaac answered him,

"Your dwelling will be
    away from the earth's richness,
    away from the dew of heaven above.
⁴⁰ You will live by the sword
    and you will serve your brother.
But when you grow restless,
    you will throw his yoke
    from off your neck."

Jacob Flees to Laban

⁴¹ Esau held a grudge against Jacob because of the blessing his father had given him. He said to himself, "The days of mourning for my father are near; then I will kill my brother Jacob."

⁴² When Rebekah was told what her older son Esau had said, she sent for her younger son Jacob and said to him, "Your brother Esau is consoling himself with the thought of killing you. ⁴³ Now then, my son, do what I say: Flee at once to my brother Laban in Haran. ⁴⁴ Stay with him for a while until your brother's fury subsides. ⁴⁵ When your brother is no longer angry with you and forgets what you did to him, I'll send word for you to come back from there. Why should I lose both of you in one day?"

He Deceived Me

GENESIS 27:36

Esau's way of handling the conflict seems all too familiar. Each of us has been taken advantage of by someone close to us. At such a time we have a choice: Will we grow bitter and cynical, holding a grudge and waiting for revenge? What other options exist? We can humbly accept the situation, praying for compassion for ourselves and the other, though acting thus requires the grace of God's help. Compare the two choices, recalling first an event about which you grew bitter and vengeful; try to remember how that felt, and notice its effect on your body. Now set that memory aside and bring to mind another event that you accepted fully. Observe the differences and compare the costs.

See Meeting God in Community

ᵃ 36 *Jacob* means *he grasps the heel* (figuratively, *he deceives*).

35

Awe and Gladness

"When you had been thinking you were the hunter, it is scary suddenly to discover that all the time you have actually been the hunted one: when you imagined that you had taken the initiative in pursuit of the Holy One and then realize that in truth it was the Holy One who initiated the pursuit. 'This is a terrifying place,' declared Jacob when he woke at Bethel; 'this is the house of God.' Yet Jacob had been attracted to that very spot; he had been drawn to it, fascinated by the dream of holy angels. The Holy One is both attractive and terrifying."

—DONALD NICHOLL,
Holiness

See Meeting God in Worship

⁴⁶Then Rebekah said to Isaac, "I'm disgusted with living because of these Hittite women. If Jacob takes a wife from among the women of this land, from Hittite women like these, my life will not be worth living."

28 So Isaac called for Jacob and blessed*ᵃ* him and commanded him: "Do not marry a Canaanite woman. ²Go at once to Paddan Aram,*ᵇ* to the house of your mother's father Bethuel. Take a wife for yourself there, from among the daughters of Laban, your mother's brother. ³May God Almighty*ᶜ* bless you and make you fruitful and increase your numbers until you become a community of peoples. ⁴May he give you and your descendants the blessing given to Abraham, so that you may take possession of the land where you now live as an alien, the land God gave to Abraham." ⁵Then Isaac sent Jacob on his way, and he went to Paddan Aram, to Laban son of Bethuel the Aramean, the brother of Rebekah, who was the mother of Jacob and Esau.

⁶Now Esau learned that Isaac had blessed Jacob and had sent him to Paddan Aram to take a wife from there, and that when he blessed him he commanded him, "Do not marry a Canaanite woman," ⁷and that Jacob had obeyed his father and mother and had gone to Paddan Aram. ⁸Esau then realized how displeasing the Canaanite women were to his father Isaac; ⁹so he went to Ishmael and married Mahalath, the sister of Nebaioth and daughter of Ishmael son of Abraham, in addition to the wives he already had.

Jacob's Dream at Bethel

¹⁰Jacob left Beersheba and set out for Haran. ¹¹When he reached a certain place, he stopped for the night because the sun had set. Taking one of the stones there, he put it under his head and lay down to sleep. ¹²He had a dream in which he saw a stairway*ᵈ* resting on the earth, with its top reaching to heaven, and the angels of God were ascending and descending on it. ¹³There above it*ᵉ* stood the LORD, and he said: "I am the LORD, the God of your father Abraham and the God of Isaac. I will give you and your descendants the land on which you are lying. ¹⁴Your descendants will be like the dust of the earth, and you will spread out to the west and to the east, to the north and to the south. All peoples on earth will be blessed through you and your offspring. ¹⁵I am with you and will watch over you wherever you go, and I will bring you back to this land. I will not leave you until I have done what I have promised you."

¹⁶When Jacob awoke from his sleep, he thought, "Surely the LORD is in this place, and I was not aware of it." ¹⁷He was afraid and said, "How awesome is this place! This is none other than the house of God; this is the gate of heaven."

¹⁸Early the next morning Jacob took the stone he had placed under his head and set it up as a pillar and poured oil on top of it. ¹⁹He called that place Bethel,*ᶠ* though the city used to be called Luz.

²⁰Then Jacob made a vow, saying, "If God will be with me and will watch over me on this journey I am taking and will

ᵃ 1 Or greeted   ᵇ 2 That is, Northwest Mesopotamia; also in verses 5, 6 and 7   ᶜ 3 Hebrew El-Shaddai   ᵈ 12 Or ladder   ᵉ 13 Or There beside him   ᶠ 19 Bethel means house of God.

give me food to eat and clothes to wear ²¹so that I return safely to my father's house, then the LORD*ᵃ* will be my God ²²and*ᵇ* this stone that I have set up as a pillar will be God's house, and of all that you give me I will give you a tenth."

Jacob Arrives in Paddan Aram

29 Then Jacob continued on his journey and came to the land of the eastern peoples. ²There he saw a well in the field, with three flocks of sheep lying near it because the flocks were watered from that well. The stone over the mouth of the well was large. ³When all the flocks were gathered there, the shepherds would roll the stone away from the well's mouth and water the sheep. Then they would return the stone to its place over the mouth of the well.

⁴Jacob asked the shepherds, "My brothers, where are you from?"

"We're from Haran," they replied.

⁵He said to them, "Do you know Laban, Nahor's grandson?"

"Yes, we know him," they answered.

⁶Then Jacob asked them, "Is he well?"

"Yes, he is," they said, "and here comes his daughter Rachel with the sheep."

⁷"Look," he said, "the sun is still high; it is not time for the flocks to be gathered. Water the sheep and take them back to pasture."

⁸"We can't," they replied, "until all the flocks are gathered and the stone has been rolled away from the mouth of the well. Then we will water the sheep."

⁹While he was still talking with them, Rachel came with her father's sheep, for she was a shepherdess. ¹⁰When Jacob saw Rachel daughter of Laban, his mother's brother, and Laban's sheep, he went over and rolled the stone away from the mouth of the well and watered his uncle's sheep. ¹¹Then Jacob kissed Rachel and began to weep aloud. ¹²He had told Rachel that he was a relative of her father and a son of Rebekah. So she ran and told her father.

¹³As soon as Laban heard the news about Jacob, his sister's son, he hurried to meet him. He embraced him and kissed him and brought him to his home, and there Jacob told him all these things. ¹⁴Then Laban said to him, "You are my own flesh and blood."

Jacob Marries Leah and Rachel

After Jacob had stayed with him for a whole month, ¹⁵Laban said to him, "Just because you are a relative of mine, should you work for me for nothing? Tell me what your wages should be."

¹⁶Now Laban had two daughters; the name of the older was Leah, and the name of the younger was Rachel. ¹⁷Leah had weak*ᶜ* eyes, but Rachel was lovely in form, and beautiful. ¹⁸Jacob was in love with Rachel and said, "I'll work for you seven years in return for your younger daughter Rachel."

¹⁹Laban said, "It's better that I give her to you than to some other man. Stay here with me." ²⁰So Jacob served

---

You Are My Own Flesh and Blood

GENESIS 29:14

What a wonderful feeling to be welcomed as kin! The language Laban uses here is reminiscent of Adam's joyful word to Eve: "This now is bone of my bones!" (Genesis 2:23). We feel truly at home when we are with others who have similar features, coloring, speech patterns, gestures or attitudes; no sense of strangeness separates us. Ironically, flesh and blood can separate as well as unite; no person is quite like any other, and often a sense of intimacy can also remind us of a foundational isolation. What helps you feel "at home"— physically, mentally and spiritually? Notice how both similarity and difference play a part in making us feel we have found our place.

See Meeting God in Community

ᵃ 20,21 Or *Since God . . . father's house, the LORD*   *ᵇ 21,22* Or *house, and the LORD will be my God, ²²then*   *ᶜ 17* Or *delicate*

37

She Was Not Loved

GENESIS 29:31

Leah's tragedy reminds us how important love is. The whole sad situation created from Jacob's multiple marriages could have been averted if each person—from Laban to Jacob to Leah to Rachel—would have acted more lovingly. Even though God ultimately works through this troubled family to accomplish his will, its members' lack of love causes much suffering and produces jealousy and conflict both in this generation of God's people and in subsequent generations.

In our frail humanity, we are limited in our ability and capacity to love. But God has given us the grace to love (see 1 John 4:7–12), and God has told us what love in action looks like (see 1 Corinthians 13). Practice living today as a conduit through which God's love flows continuously. Start at home. How does this change your usual behavior?

See Meeting God in Everyday Life

seven years to get Rachel, but they seemed like only a few days to him because of his love for her. ²¹Then Jacob said to Laban, "Give me my wife. My time is completed, and I want to lie with her."

²²So Laban brought together all the people of the place and gave a feast. ²³But when evening came, he took his daughter Leah and gave her to Jacob, and Jacob lay with her. ²⁴And Laban gave his servant girl Zilpah to his daughter as her maidservant.

²⁵When morning came, there was Leah! So Jacob said to Laban, "What is this you have done to me? I served you for Rachel, didn't I? Why have you deceived me?"

²⁶Laban replied, "It is not our custom here to give the younger daughter in marriage before the older one. ²⁷Finish this daughter's bridal week; then we will give you the younger one also, in return for another seven years of work."

²⁸And Jacob did so. He finished the week with Leah, and then Laban gave him his daughter Rachel to be his wife. ²⁹Laban gave his servant girl Bilhah to his daughter Rachel as her maidservant. ³⁰Jacob lay with Rachel also, and he loved Rachel more than Leah. And he worked for Laban another seven years.

Jacob's Children

³¹When the LORD saw that Leah was not loved, he opened her womb, but Rachel was barren. ³²Leah became pregnant and gave birth to a son. She named him Reuben,ᵃ for she said, "It is because the LORD has seen my misery. Surely my husband will love me now."

³³She conceived again, and when she gave birth to a son she said, "Because the LORD heard that I am not loved, he gave me this one too." So she named him Simeon.ᵇ

³⁴Again she conceived, and when she gave birth to a son she said, "Now at last my husband will become attached to me, because I have borne him three sons." So he was named Levi.ᶜ

³⁵She conceived again, and when she gave birth to a son she said, "This time I will praise the LORD." So she named him Judah.ᵈ Then she stopped having children.

30 When Rachel saw that she was not bearing Jacob any children, she became jealous of her sister. So she said to Jacob, "Give me children, or I'll die!"

²Jacob became angry with her and said, "Am I in the place of God, who has kept you from having children?"

³Then she said, "Here is Bilhah, my maidservant. Sleep with her so that she can bear children for me and that through her I too can build a family."

⁴So she gave him her servant Bilhah as a wife. Jacob slept with her, ⁵and she became pregnant and bore him a son. ⁶Then Rachel said, "God has vindicated me; he has listened to my plea and given me a son." Because of this she named him Dan.ᵉ

⁷Rachel's servant Bilhah conceived again and bore Jacob a second son. ⁸Then Rachel said, "I have had a great strug-

---

ᵃ 32 *Reuben* sounds like the Hebrew for *he has seen my misery*; the name means *see, a son.*   ᵇ 33 *Simeon* probably means *one who hears.*   ᶜ 34 *Levi* sounds like and may be derived from the Hebrew for *attached.*   ᵈ 35 *Judah* sounds like and may be derived from the Hebrew for *praise.*   ᵉ 6 *Dan* here means *he has vindicated.*

gle with my sister, and I have won." So she named him Naphtali.[a]

[9]When Leah saw that she had stopped having children, she took her maidservant Zilpah and gave her to Jacob as a wife. [10]Leah's servant Zilpah bore Jacob a son. [11]Then Leah said, "What good fortune!"[b] So she named him Gad.[c]

[12]Leah's servant Zilpah bore Jacob a second son. [13]Then Leah said, "How happy I am! The women will call me happy." So she named him Asher.[d]

[14]During wheat harvest, Reuben went out into the fields and found some mandrake plants, which he brought to his mother Leah. Rachel said to Leah, "Please give me some of your son's mandrakes."

[15]But she said to her, "Wasn't it enough that you took away my husband? Will you take my son's mandrakes too?"

"Very well," Rachel said, "he can sleep with you tonight in return for your son's mandrakes."

[16]So when Jacob came in from the fields that evening, Leah went out to meet him. "You must sleep with me," she said. "I have hired you with my son's mandrakes." So he slept with her that night.

[17]God listened to Leah, and she became pregnant and bore Jacob a fifth son. [18]Then Leah said, "God has rewarded me for giving my maidservant to my husband." So she named him Issachar.[e]

[19]Leah conceived again and bore Jacob a sixth son. [20]Then Leah said, "God has presented me with a precious gift. This time my husband will treat me with honor, because I have borne him six sons." So she named him Zebulun.[f]

[21]Some time later she gave birth to a daughter and named her Dinah.

[22]Then God remembered Rachel; he listened to her and opened her womb. [23]She became pregnant and gave birth to a son and said, "God has taken away my disgrace." [24]She named him Joseph,[g] and said, "May the LORD add to me another son."

Jacob's Flocks Increase

[25]After Rachel gave birth to Joseph, Jacob said to Laban, "Send me on my way so I can go back to my own homeland. [26]Give me my wives and children, for whom I have served you, and I will be on my way. You know how much work I've done for you."

[27]But Laban said to him, "If I have found favor in your eyes, please stay. I have learned by divination that[h] the LORD has blessed me because of you." [28]He added, "Name your wages, and I will pay them."

[29]Jacob said to him, "You know how I have worked for you and how your livestock has fared under my care. [30]The little you had before I came has increased greatly, and the LORD has blessed you wherever I have been. But now, when may I do something for my own household?"

[31]"What shall I give you?" he asked.

My First Responsibility

GENESIS 30:20

Recall that these early generations took quite seriously God's command to be fruitful and multiply. The first responsibility of a couple was to continue their family line, and those who did not have children were pitied and even shamed. Is there anything in your life that you value above everything else? Does its presence or absence make all the difference to you? Look at how you actually live: What do you prize so greatly that you are tempted to hoard it? What do you hold so tightly that you pity those who don't possess it? Is that something you *choose* to value, or has it been a less-than-conscious decision? Does it draw you nearer to God or drive you farther from him?

See *Meeting God in Everyday Life*

---

[a]8 *Naphtali* means *my struggle.*   [b]11 Or *"A troop is coming!"*
[c]11 *Gad* can mean *good fortune* or *a troop.*   [d]13 *Asher* means *happy.*
[e]18 *Issachar* sounds like the Hebrew for *reward.*   [f]20 *Zebulun* probably means *honor.*   [g]24 *Joseph* means *may he add.*   [h]27 Or possibly *have become rich and*

Relocated

GENESIS 30:25–43

"Our life of faith consists in moving with God in terms of (a) being securely *oriented*, (b) being painfully *disoriented*, and (c) being surprisingly *reoriented* . . . [Contrast that with] being well-settled, knowing that life makes sense and God is well placed in heaven, presiding but not bothering . . . [This latter mood] exists in the Bible, but it is a minor theme in the Psalms and is not very provocative. People are driven to poignant prayer and song precisely by *experiences of dislocation and relocation*. It is experiences of being overwhelmed, nearly destroyed, and surprisingly given life which empower us to pray and to sing."

—WALTER BRUEGGEMANN,
Praying the Psalms

See *Meeting God in Scripture*

"Don't give me anything," Jacob replied. "But if you will do this one thing for me, I will go on tending your flocks and watching over them: ³²Let me go through all your flocks today and remove from them every speckled or spotted sheep, every dark-colored lamb and every spotted or speckled goat. They will be my wages. ³³And my honesty will testify for me in the future, whenever you check on the wages you have paid me. Any goat in my possession that is not speckled or spotted, or any lamb that is not dark-colored, will be considered stolen."

³⁴"Agreed," said Laban. "Let it be as you have said." ³⁵That same day he removed all the male goats that were streaked or spotted, and all the speckled or spotted female goats (all that had white on them) and all the dark-colored lambs, and he placed them in the care of his sons. ³⁶Then he put a three-day journey between himself and Jacob, while Jacob continued to tend the rest of Laban's flocks.

³⁷Jacob, however, took fresh-cut branches from poplar, almond and plane trees and made white stripes on them by peeling the bark and exposing the white inner wood of the branches. ³⁸Then he placed the peeled branches in all the watering troughs, so that they would be directly in front of the flocks when they came to drink. When the flocks were in heat and came to drink, ³⁹they mated in front of the branches. And they bore young that were streaked or speckled or spotted. ⁴⁰Jacob set apart the young of the flock by themselves, but made the rest face the streaked and dark-colored animals that belonged to Laban. Thus he made separate flocks for himself and did not put them with Laban's animals. ⁴¹Whenever the stronger females were in heat, Jacob would place the branches in the troughs in front of the animals so they would mate near the branches, ⁴²but if the animals were weak, he would not place them there. So the weak animals went to Laban and the strong ones to Jacob. ⁴³In this way the man grew exceedingly prosperous and came to own large flocks, and maidservants and menservants, and camels and donkeys.

Jacob Flees From Laban

31 Jacob heard that Laban's sons were saying, "Jacob has taken everything our father owned and has gained all this wealth from what belonged to our father." ²And Jacob noticed that Laban's attitude toward him was not what it had been.

³Then the LORD said to Jacob, "Go back to the land of your fathers and to your relatives, and I will be with you."

⁴So Jacob sent word to Rachel and Leah to come out to the fields where his flocks were. ⁵He said to them, "I see that your father's attitude toward me is not what it was before, but the God of my father has been with me. ⁶You know that I've worked for your father with all my strength, ⁷yet your father has cheated me by changing my wages ten times. However, God has not allowed him to harm me. ⁸If he said, 'The speckled ones will be your wages,' then all the flocks gave birth to speckled young; and if he said, 'The streaked ones will be your wages,' then all the flocks bore streaked young. ⁹So God has taken away your father's livestock and has given them to me.

¹⁰"In breeding season I once had a dream in which I looked up and saw that the male goats mating with the

flock were streaked, speckled or spotted. [11]The angel of God said to me in the dream, 'Jacob.' I answered, 'Here I am.' [12]And he said, 'Look up and see that all the male goats mating with the flock are streaked, speckled or spotted, for I have seen all that Laban has been doing to you. [13]I am the God of Bethel, where you anointed a pillar and where you made a vow to me. Now leave this land at once and go back to your native land.' "

[14]Then Rachel and Leah replied, "Do we still have any share in the inheritance of our father's estate? [15]Does he not regard us as foreigners? Not only has he sold us, but he has used up what was paid for us. [16]Surely all the wealth that God took away from our father belongs to us and our children. So do whatever God has told you."

[17]Then Jacob put his children and his wives on camels, [18]and he drove all his livestock ahead of him, along with all the goods he had accumulated in Paddan Aram,[a] to go to his father Isaac in the land of Canaan.

[19]When Laban had gone to shear his sheep, Rachel stole her father's household gods. [20]Moreover, Jacob deceived Laban the Aramean by not telling him he was running away. [21]So he fled with all he had, and crossing the River,[b] he headed for the hill country of Gilead.

Laban Pursues Jacob

[22]On the third day Laban was told that Jacob had fled. [23]Taking his relatives with him, he pursued Jacob for seven days and caught up with him in the hill country of Gilead. [24]Then God came to Laban the Aramean in a dream at night and said to him, "Be careful not to say anything to Jacob, either good or bad."

[25]Jacob had pitched his tent in the hill country of Gilead when Laban overtook him, and Laban and his relatives camped there too. [26]Then Laban said to Jacob, "What have you done? You've deceived me, and you've carried off my daughters like captives in war. [27]Why did you run off secretly and deceive me? Why didn't you tell me, so I could send you away with joy and singing to the music of tambourines and harps? [28]You didn't even let me kiss my grandchildren and my daughters good-by. You have done a foolish thing. [29]I have the power to harm you; but last night the God of your father said to me, 'Be careful not to say anything to Jacob, either good or bad.' [30]Now you have gone off because you longed to return to your father's house. But why did you steal my gods?"

[31]Jacob answered Laban, "I was afraid, because I thought you would take your daughters away from me by force. [32]But if you find anyone who has your gods, he shall not live. In the presence of our relatives, see for yourself whether there is anything of yours here with me; and if so, take it." Now Jacob did not know that Rachel had stolen the gods.

[33]So Laban went into Jacob's tent and into Leah's tent and into the tent of the two maidservants, but he found nothing. After he came out of Leah's tent, he entered Rachel's tent. [34]Now Rachel had taken the household gods and put them inside her camel's saddle and was sitting on them. Laban searched through everything in the tent but found nothing.

You Made a Vow to Me

GENESIS 31:13

In many ways Jacob is a rascal, weak and morally immature. Yet his heart has been deeply touched by God, and he struggles to stay centered in that relationship.

Again and again God calls us back to our true selves by reminding us that we belong to him. Thankfully, each of us has been given occasional moments of *knowing* that God is with us, and we are meant to return to those moments again and again in memory, continuing to be nourished by them, and allowing them to strengthen our commitment to God. Remember one or two of your own personal "holy encounters." How can you establish a rhythm of deep reflection on their truth?

---

[a] 18 That is, Northwest Mesopotamia   [b] 21 That is, the Euphrates

God Is a Witness

GENESIS 31:50

The stone heap serves as a symbol for Laban and Jacob of their promises to one another. The symbol points to God as a true witness. God is a steady and objective witness to all we are and do, always setting our behavior beside his own loving vision of our intended wholeness. The good news is that we can always turn back to God in fidelity; the "bad" news is that God always notices when we are unfaithful. Can you think of some symbol that will remind you of this loving watchfulness of God in your life? Draw or build that symbol for yourself, and set it up on your desk or in another prominent place.

See Meeting God in Everyday Life

³⁵Rachel said to her father, "Don't be angry, my lord, that I cannot stand up in your presence; I'm having my period." So he searched but could not find the household gods.

³⁶Jacob was angry and took Laban to task. "What is my crime?" he asked Laban. "What sin have I committed that you hunt me down? ³⁷Now that you have searched through all my goods, what have you found that belongs to your household? Put it here in front of your relatives and mine, and let them judge between the two of us.

³⁸"I have been with you for twenty years now. Your sheep and goats have not miscarried, nor have I eaten rams from your flocks. ³⁹I did not bring you animals torn by wild beasts; I bore the loss myself. And you demanded payment from me for whatever was stolen by day or night. ⁴⁰This was my situation: The heat consumed me in the daytime and the cold at night, and sleep fled from my eyes. ⁴¹It was like this for the twenty years I was in your household. I worked for you fourteen years for your two daughters and six years for your flocks, and you changed my wages ten times. ⁴²If the God of my father, the God of Abraham and the Fear of Isaac, had not been with me, you would surely have sent me away empty-handed. But God has seen my hardship and the toil of my hands, and last night he rebuked you."

⁴³Laban answered Jacob, "The women are my daughters, the children are my children, and the flocks are my flocks. All you see is mine. Yet what can I do today about these daughters of mine, or about the children they have borne? ⁴⁴Come now, let's make a covenant, you and I, and let it serve as a witness between us."

⁴⁵So Jacob took a stone and set it up as a pillar. ⁴⁶He said to his relatives, "Gather some stones." So they took stones and piled them in a heap, and they ate there by the heap. ⁴⁷Laban called it Jegar Sahadutha,ᵃ and Jacob called it Galeed.ᵇ

⁴⁸Laban said, "This heap is a witness between you and me today." That is why it was called Galeed. ⁴⁹It was also called Mizpah,ᶜ because he said, "May the LORD keep watch between you and me when we are away from each other. ⁵⁰If you mistreat my daughters or if you take any wives besides my daughters, even though no one is with us, remember that God is a witness between you and me."

⁵¹Laban also said to Jacob, "Here is this heap, and here is this pillar I have set up between you and me. ⁵²This heap is a witness, and this pillar is a witness, that I will not go past this heap to your side to harm you and that you will not go past this heap and pillar to my side to harm me. ⁵³May the God of Abraham and the God of Nahor, the God of their father, judge between us."

So Jacob took an oath in the name of the Fear of his father Isaac. ⁵⁴He offered a sacrifice there in the hill country and invited his relatives to a meal. After they had eaten, they spent the night there.

⁵⁵Early the next morning Laban kissed his grandchildren and his daughters and blessed them. Then he left and returned home.

ᵃ47 The Aramaic *Jegar Sahadutha* means *witness heap*.   ᵇ47 The Hebrew *Galeed* means *witness heap*.   ᶜ49 *Mizpah* means *watchtower*.

Jacob Prepares to Meet Esau

32 Jacob also went on his way, and the angels of God met him. ²When Jacob saw them, he said, "This is the camp of God!" So he named that place Mahanaim.ᵃ

³Jacob sent messengers ahead of him to his brother Esau in the land of Seir, the country of Edom. ⁴He instructed them: "This is what you are to say to my master Esau: 'Your servant Jacob says, I have been staying with Laban and have remained there till now. ⁵I have cattle and donkeys, sheep and goats, menservants and maidservants. Now I am sending this message to my lord, that I may find favor in your eyes.' "

⁶When the messengers returned to Jacob, they said, "We went to your brother Esau, and now he is coming to meet you, and four hundred men are with him."

⁷In great fear and distress Jacob divided the people who were with him into two groups,ᵇ and the flocks and herds and camels as well. ⁸He thought, "If Esau comes and attacks one group,ᶜ the groupᶜ that is left may escape."

⁹Then Jacob prayed, "O God of my father Abraham, God of my father Isaac, O LORD, who said to me, 'Go back to your country and your relatives, and I will make you prosper,' ¹⁰I am unworthy of all the kindness and faithfulness you have shown your servant. I had only my staff when I crossed this Jordan, but now I have become two groups. ¹¹Save me, I pray, from the hand of my brother Esau, for I am afraid he will come and attack me, and also the mothers with their children. ¹²But you have said, 'I will surely make you prosper and will make your descendants like the sand of the sea, which cannot be counted.' "

¹³He spent the night there, and from what he had with him he selected a gift for his brother Esau: ¹⁴two hundred female goats and twenty male goats, two hundred ewes and twenty rams, ¹⁵thirty female camels with their young, forty cows and ten bulls, and twenty female donkeys and ten male donkeys. ¹⁶He put them in the care of his servants, each herd by itself, and said to his servants, "Go ahead of me, and keep some space between the herds."

¹⁷He instructed the one in the lead: "When my brother Esau meets you and asks, 'To whom do you belong, and where are you going, and who owns all these animals in front of you?' ¹⁸then you are to say, 'They belong to your servant Jacob. They are a gift sent to my lord Esau, and he is coming behind us.' "

¹⁹He also instructed the second, the third and all the others who followed the herds: "You are to say the same thing to Esau when you meet him. ²⁰And be sure to say, 'Your servant Jacob is coming behind us.' " For he thought, "I will pacify him with these gifts I am sending on ahead; later, when I see him, perhaps he will receive me." ²¹So Jacob's gifts went on ahead of him, but he himself spent the night in the camp.

Jacob Wrestles With God

²²That night Jacob got up and took his two wives, his two maidservants and his eleven sons and crossed the ford of the Jabbok. ²³After he had sent them across the stream, he

Bless Me

GENESIS 32:22–27

"The divine antagonist seemed anxious to depart as the day was about to dawn; and Jacob held him more convulsively fast, as if aware that the daylight was likely to rob him of his anticipated blessing . . . God is approached more nearly in that which is *indefinite* than in that which is definite and distinct. [God] is felt in *awe* and *wonder* and *worship* rather than in clear *conception*. There is a sense in which *darkness* has more of God than light has. Moments of tender, vague mystery often bring distinctly the feeling of [God's] presence . . . If Jacob had got a word, that word might have satisfied him . . . Instead, [God] impressed on Jacob's soul a religious awe."

—F.W. ROBERTSON,
"Jacob's Wrestling" in *Ten Sermons*

ᵃ2 *Mahanaim* means *two camps.*   ᵇ7 Or *camps*; also in verse 10   ᶜ8 Or *camp*

And They Wept

GENESIS 33:4

Turn back to chapter 27 and read how Jacob and Esau parted. Compare that occasion to this greeting. Jacob's anxiety about the meeting and Esau's need for the company of four hundred men suggest that both vividly remembered their parting. What changed? The tenderness of their reunion can only be called a miracle, a miracle resulting in part from Jacob's intense and touching struggle with God the previous night. Seeing God does change us, even when we struggle through the encounter. Is there something in your life that you need to have transformed? Pray intensely about it, and risk a face to face encounter with the Most High.

See Meeting God in Prayer

sent over all his possessions. ²⁴So Jacob was left alone, and a man wrestled with him till daybreak. ²⁵When the man saw that he could not overpower him, he touched the socket of Jacob's hip so that his hip was wrenched as he wrestled with the man. ²⁶Then the man said, "Let me go, for it is daybreak."

But Jacob replied, "I will not let you go unless you bless me."

²⁷The man asked him, "What is your name?"

"Jacob," he answered.

²⁸Then the man said, "Your name will no longer be Jacob, but Israel,ᵃ because you have struggled with God and with men and have overcome."

²⁹Jacob said, "Please tell me your name."

But he replied, "Why do you ask my name?" Then he blessed him there.

³⁰So Jacob called the place Peniel,ᵇ saying, "It is because I saw God face to face, and yet my life was spared."

³¹The sun rose above him as he passed Peniel,ᶜ and he was limping because of his hip. ³²Therefore to this day the Israelites do not eat the tendon attached to the socket of the hip, because the socket of Jacob's hip was touched near the tendon.

Jacob Meets Esau

33 Jacob looked up and there was Esau, coming with his four hundred men; so he divided the children among Leah, Rachel and the two maidservants. ²He put the maidservants and their children in front, Leah and her children next, and Rachel and Joseph in the rear. ³He himself went on ahead and bowed down to the ground seven times as he approached his brother.

⁴But Esau ran to meet Jacob and embraced him; he threw his arms around his neck and kissed him. And they wept. ⁵Then Esau looked up and saw the women and children. "Who are these with you?" he asked.

Jacob answered, "They are the children God has graciously given your servant."

⁶Then the maidservants and their children approached and bowed down. ⁷Next, Leah and her children came and bowed down. Last of all came Joseph and Rachel, and they too bowed down.

⁸Esau asked, "What do you mean by all these droves I met?"

"To find favor in your eyes, my lord," he said.

⁹But Esau said, "I already have plenty, my brother. Keep what you have for yourself."

¹⁰"No, please!" said Jacob. "If I have found favor in your eyes, accept this gift from me. For to see your face is like seeing the face of God, now that you have received me favorably. ¹¹Please accept the present that was brought to you, for God has been gracious to me and I have all I need." And because Jacob insisted, Esau accepted it.

¹²Then Esau said, "Let us be on our way; I'll accompany you."

¹³But Jacob said to him, "My lord knows that the children are tender and that I must care for the ewes and cows that are nursing their young. If they are driven hard just one

ᵃ *28 Israel* means *he struggles with God.*   ᵇ *30 Peniel* means *face of God.*
ᶜ *31 Hebrew Penuel,* a variant of *Peniel*

day, all the animals will die. ¹⁴So let my lord go on ahead of his servant, while I move along slowly at the pace of the droves before me and that of the children, until I come to my lord in Seir."

¹⁵Esau said, "Then let me leave some of my men with you."

"But why do that?" Jacob asked. "Just let me find favor in the eyes of my lord."

¹⁶So that day Esau started on his way back to Seir. ¹⁷Jacob, however, went to Succoth, where he built a place for himself and made shelters for his livestock. That is why the place is called Succoth.ᵃ

¹⁸After Jacob came from Paddan Aram,ᵇ he arrived safely at theᶜ city of Shechem in Canaan and camped within sight of the city. ¹⁹For a hundred pieces of silver,ᵈ he bought from the sons of Hamor, the father of Shechem, the plot of ground where he pitched his tent. ²⁰There he set up an altar and called it El Elohe Israel.ᵉ

Dinah and the Shechemites

34 Now Dinah, the daughter Leah had borne to Jacob, went out to visit the women of the land. ²When Shechem son of Hamor the Hivite, the ruler of that area, saw her, he took her and violated her. ³His heart was drawn to Dinah daughter of Jacob, and he loved the girl and spoke tenderly to her. ⁴And Shechem said to his father Hamor, "Get me this girl as my wife."

⁵When Jacob heard that his daughter Dinah had been defiled, his sons were in the fields with his livestock; so he kept quiet about it until they came home.

⁶Then Shechem's father Hamor went out to talk with Jacob. ⁷Now Jacob's sons had come in from the fields as soon as they heard what had happened. They were filled with grief and fury, because Shechem had done a disgraceful thing inᶠ Israel by lying with Jacob's daughter—a thing that should not be done.

⁸But Hamor said to them, "My son Shechem has his heart set on your daughter. Please give her to him as his wife. ⁹Intermarry with us; give us your daughters and take our daughters for yourselves. ¹⁰You can settle among us; the land is open to you. Live in it, tradeᵍ in it, and acquire property in it."

¹¹Then Shechem said to Dinah's father and brothers, "Let me find favor in your eyes, and I will give you whatever you ask. ¹²Make the price for the bride and the gift I am to bring as great as you like, and I'll pay whatever you ask me. Only give me the girl as my wife."

¹³Because their sister Dinah had been defiled, Jacob's sons replied deceitfully as they spoke to Shechem and his father Hamor. ¹⁴They said to them, "We can't do such a thing; we can't give our sister to a man who is not circumcised. That would be a disgrace to us. ¹⁵We will give our consent to you on one condition only: that you become like us by circumcising all your males. ¹⁶Then we will give you our daughters and take your daughters for ourselves. We'll

The Sins of the Fathers

GENESIS 34:13

Deceit breeds deceit. This family has a history of dishonesty, and even with the reconciliation recently effected between Jacob and Esau, the deeply ingrained tendency to lie and cheat does not disappear. The pride and anger that Jacob's sons display accomplishes nothing except to increase their neighbors' hostility. Today we talk about "family systems"; our modern language struggles with the same troublesome multigenerational patterns that we read about so often in the Biblical account. But the slightest honest effort on our part to break free of "disease" is always supported by God's healing power. Share with someone else one way in which you have been freed from a troublesome family habit through the power of God.

See *Meeting God in Community*

ᵃ17 Succoth means *shelters*.   ᵇ18 That is, Northwest Mesopotamia
ᶜ18 Or *arrived at Shalem, a*   ᵈ19 Hebrew *hundred kesitahs*; a kesitah was a unit of money of unknown weight and value.   ᵉ20 *El Elohe Israel* can mean *God, the God of Israel* or *mighty is the God of Israel*.   ᶠ7 Or *against*
ᵍ10 Or *move about freely*; also in verse 21

I Will Build an Altar

GENESIS 35:3

"Consecration means dedication to God. It occurs when we claim our deepest desire for God, beneath, above, and beyond all other things. We may not understand the full meaning of consecration: the ups and downs, the joys and agonies of the journey that must follow. And certainly we will be unable to grasp the overarching cosmic meaning of our small assent, the joy it gives to God, the deepening love it will bring to humanity, the universal covenant it has enriched. But our yes comes from some bare recollection of all these things. In a tiny space our hearts can say yes."

—GERALD MAY,
Addiction and Grace

See Meeting God in Worship

settle among you and become one people with you. [17]But if you will not agree to be circumcised, we'll take our sister[a] and go."

[18]Their proposal seemed good to Hamor and his son Shechem. [19]The young man, who was the most honored of all his father's household, lost no time in doing what they said, because he was delighted with Jacob's daughter. [20]So Hamor and his son Shechem went to the gate of their city to speak to their fellow townsmen. [21]"These men are friendly toward us," they said. "Let them live in our land and trade in it; the land has plenty of room for them. We can marry their daughters and they can marry ours. [22]But the men will consent to live with us as one people only on the condition that our males be circumcised, as they themselves are. [23]Won't their livestock, their property and all their other animals become ours? So let us give our consent to them, and they will settle among us."

[24]All the men who went out of the city gate agreed with Hamor and his son Shechem, and every male in the city was circumcised.

[25]Three days later, while all of them were still in pain, two of Jacob's sons, Simeon and Levi, Dinah's brothers, took their swords and attacked the unsuspecting city, killing every male. [26]They put Hamor and his son Shechem to the sword and took Dinah from Shechem's house and left. [27]The sons of Jacob came upon the dead bodies and looted the city where[b] their sister had been defiled. [28]They seized their flocks and herds and donkeys and everything else of theirs in the city and out in the fields. [29]They carried off all their wealth and all their women and children, taking as plunder everything in the houses.

[30]Then Jacob said to Simeon and Levi, "You have brought trouble on me by making me a stench to the Canaanites and Perizzites, the people living in this land. We are few in number, and if they join forces against me and attack me, I and my household will be destroyed."

[31]But they replied, "Should he have treated our sister like a prostitute?"

Jacob Returns to Bethel

35 Then God said to Jacob, "Go up to Bethel and settle there, and build an altar there to God, who appeared to you when you were fleeing from your brother Esau."

[2]So Jacob said to his household and to all who were with him, "Get rid of the foreign gods you have with you, and purify yourselves and change your clothes. [3]Then come, let us go up to Bethel, where I will build an altar to God, who answered me in the day of my distress and who has been with me wherever I have gone." [4]So they gave Jacob all the foreign gods they had and the rings in their ears, and Jacob buried them under the oak at Shechem. [5]Then they set out, and the terror of God fell upon the towns all around them so that no one pursued them.

[6]Jacob and all the people with him came to Luz (that is, Bethel) in the land of Canaan. [7]There he built an altar, and he called the place El Bethel,[c] because it was there that God revealed himself to him when he was fleeing from his brother.

[a] 17 Hebrew *daughter*   [b] 27 Or *because*   [c] 7 *El Bethel* means *God of Bethel*.

[8]Now Deborah, Rebekah's nurse, died and was buried under the oak below Bethel. So it was named Allon Bacuth.[a]

[9]After Jacob returned from Paddan Aram,[b] God appeared to him again and blessed him. [10]God said to him, "Your name is Jacob,[c] but you will no longer be called Jacob; your name will be Israel.[d]" So he named him Israel.

[11]And God said to him, "I am God Almighty[e]; be fruitful and increase in number. A nation and a community of nations will come from you, and kings will come from your body. [12]The land I gave to Abraham and Isaac I also give to you, and I will give this land to your descendants after you." [13]Then God went up from him at the place where he had talked with him. [14]Jacob set up a stone pillar at the place where God had talked with him, and he poured out a drink offering on it; he also poured oil on it. [15]Jacob called the place where God had talked with him Bethel.[f]

The Deaths of Rachel and Isaac

[16]Then they moved on from Bethel. While they were still some distance from Ephrath, Rachel began to give birth and had great difficulty. [17]And as she was having great difficulty in childbirth, the midwife said to her, "Don't be afraid, for you have another son." [18]As she breathed her last—for she was dying—she named her son Ben-Oni.[g] But his father named him Benjamin.[h]

[19]So Rachel died and was buried on the way to Ephrath (that is, Bethlehem). [20]Over her tomb Jacob set up a pillar, and to this day that pillar marks Rachel's tomb.

[21]Israel moved on again and pitched his tent beyond Migdal Eder. [22]While Israel was living in that region, Reuben went in and slept with his father's concubine Bilhah, and Israel heard of it.

Jacob had twelve sons:

[23]The sons of Leah:
Reuben the firstborn of Jacob,
Simeon, Levi, Judah, Issachar and Zebulun.
[24]The sons of Rachel:
Joseph and Benjamin.
[25]The sons of Rachel's maidservant Bilhah:
Dan and Naphtali.
[26]The sons of Leah's maidservant Zilpah:
Gad and Asher.
These were the sons of Jacob, who were born to him in Paddan Aram.

[27]Jacob came home to his father Isaac in Mamre, near Kiriath Arba (that is, Hebron), where Abraham and Isaac had stayed. [28]Isaac lived a hundred and eighty years. [29]Then he breathed his last and died and was gathered to his people, old and full of years. And his sons Esau and Jacob buried him.

Israel Moved On

GENESIS 35:21

From this point on in the Biblical account, Jacob is sometimes called Jacob and sometimes Israel. Israel is the name the angel gives him, with a blessing, after Jacob spends the night wrestling with God (see 32:28). The name directly refers to the struggle, but it eventually belongs to the nation, the beloved of God. Jacob grows into his new name, and, though his behavior is inconsistent for a time, there is no longer any doubt that he has God's blessing. Think about the name God might have for you, the one that describes your deepest wholeness as his beloved. Do a little research, as if you were going to name a new baby. Let your dreams suggest possibilities; be open to the name that is yours alone.

---

[a]8 Allon Bacuth means oak of weeping.   [b]9 That is, Northwest Mesopotamia; also in verse 26   [c]10 Jacob means he grasps the heel (figuratively, he deceives).   [d]10 Israel means he struggles with God.   [e]11 Hebrew El-Shaddai   [f]15 Bethel means house of God.   [g]18 Ben-Oni means son of my trouble.   [h]18 Benjamin means son of my right hand.

The People of God

GENESIS 36:9

The need that prompted these Biblical listings of generations of God's people also stands behind our contemporary interest in genealogies: Knowing our name is not enough; our identity is connected to and interrelated with a whole people. We ask: Who were my grandparents, and who were theirs? What kind of people were they and what was important to them? The question of *who* I am expands to include the question of *whose* I am. Reading these Biblical accounts, we discover one crucial element of our holy history: We are members of the people of God!

Find several people in your church with whom you share similar interests. Ask them to join you in planning, writing and presenting a short play that dramatizes your understanding of what it means to be the people of God.

See Meeting God in Community

Esau's Descendants

36

This is the account of Esau (that is, Edom).

[2] Esau took his wives from the women of Canaan: Adah daughter of Elon the Hittite, and Oholibamah daughter of Anah and granddaughter of Zibeon the Hivite— [3] also Basemath daughter of Ishmael and sister of Nebaioth.

[4] Adah bore Eliphaz to Esau, Basemath bore Reuel, [5] and Oholibamah bore Jeush, Jalam and Korah. These were the sons of Esau, who were born to him in Canaan.

[6] Esau took his wives and sons and daughters and all the members of his household, as well as his livestock and all his other animals and all the goods he had acquired in Canaan, and moved to a land some distance from his brother Jacob. [7] Their possessions were too great for them to remain together; the land where they were staying could not support them both because of their livestock. [8] So Esau (that is, Edom) settled in the hill country of Seir.

[9] This is the account of Esau the father of the Edomites in the hill country of Seir.

[10] These are the names of Esau's sons:
Eliphaz, the son of Esau's wife Adah, and Reuel, the son of Esau's wife Basemath.
[11] The sons of Eliphaz:
Teman, Omar, Zepho, Gatam and Kenaz.
[12] Esau's son Eliphaz also had a concubine named Timna, who bore him Amalek. These were grandsons of Esau's wife Adah.
[13] The sons of Reuel:
Nahath, Zerah, Shammah and Mizzah. These were grandsons of Esau's wife Basemath.
[14] The sons of Esau's wife Oholibamah daughter of Anah and granddaughter of Zibeon, whom she bore to Esau:
Jeush, Jalam and Korah.

[15] These were the chiefs among Esau's descendants:
The sons of Eliphaz the firstborn of Esau:
Chiefs Teman, Omar, Zepho, Kenaz, [16] Korah,[a] Gatam and Amalek. These were the chiefs descended from Eliphaz in Edom; they were grandsons of Adah.
[17] The sons of Esau's son Reuel:
Chiefs Nahath, Zerah, Shammah and Mizzah. These were the chiefs descended from Reuel in Edom; they were grandsons of Esau's wife Basemath.
[18] The sons of Esau's wife Oholibamah:
Chiefs Jeush, Jalam and Korah. These were the chiefs descended from Esau's wife Oholibamah daughter of Anah.
[19] These were the sons of Esau (that is, Edom), and these were their chiefs.

[20] These were the sons of Seir the Horite, who were living in the region:

---

a 16 Masoretic Text; Samaritan Pentateuch (see also Gen. 36:11 and 1 Chron. 1:36) does not have *Korah*.

Lotan, Shobal, Zibeon, Anah, 21Dishon, Ezer and Dishan. These sons of Seir in Edom were Horite chiefs.

22 The sons of Lotan:

Hori and Homam.[a] Timna was Lotan's sister.

23 The sons of Shobal:

Alvan, Manahath, Ebal, Shepho and Onam.

24 The sons of Zibeon:

Aiah and Anah. This is the Anah who discovered the hot springs[b] in the desert while he was grazing the donkeys of his father Zibeon.

25 The children of Anah:

Dishon and Oholibamah daughter of Anah.

26 The sons of Dishon[c]:

Hemdan, Eshban, Ithran and Keran.

27 The sons of Ezer:

Bilhan, Zaavan and Akan.

28 The sons of Dishan:

Uz and Aran.

29 These were the Horite chiefs:

Lotan, Shobal, Zibeon, Anah, 30Dishon, Ezer and Dishan. These were the Horite chiefs, according to their divisions, in the land of Seir.

The Rulers of Edom

31 These were the kings who reigned in Edom before any Israelite king reigned[d]:

32 Bela son of Beor became king of Edom. His city was named Dinhabah.

33 When Bela died, Jobab son of Zerah from Bozrah succeeded him as king.

34 When Jobab died, Husham from the land of the Temanites succeeded him as king.

35 When Husham died, Hadad son of Bedad, who defeated Midian in the country of Moab, succeeded him as king. His city was named Avith.

36 When Hadad died, Samlah from Masrekah succeeded him as king.

37 When Samlah died, Shaul from Rehoboth on the river[e] succeeded him as king.

38 When Shaul died, Baal-Hanan son of Acbor succeeded him as king.

39 When Baal-Hanan son of Acbor died, Hadad[f] succeeded him as king. His city was named Pau, and his wife's name was Mehetabel daughter of Matred, the daughter of Me-Zahab.

40 These were the chiefs descended from Esau, by name, according to their clans and regions:

Timna, Alvah, Jetheth, 41Oholibamah, Elah, Pinon, 42Kenaz, Teman, Mibzar, 43Magdiel and Iram. These were the chiefs of Edom, according to their settlements in the land they occupied.

This was Esau the father of the Edomites.

---

a 22 Hebrew *Hemam,* a variant of *Homam* (see 1 Chron. 1:39)
b 24 Vulgate; Syriac *discovered water;* the meaning of the Hebrew for this word is uncertain.   *c 26* Hebrew *Dishan,* a variant of *Dishon*   *d 31* Or *before an Israelite king reigned over them*   *e 37* Possibly the Euphrates
f 39 Many manuscripts of the Masoretic Text, Samaritan Pentateuch and Syriac (see also 1 Chron. 1:50); most manuscripts of the Masoretic Text *Hadar*

Life and Death

GENESIS 36:33

"When we compare the present life of man with that time of which we have no knowledge, it seems to me like the swift flight of a lone sparrow through the banqueting-hall in winter . . . This sparrow flies swiftly in through one door of the hall, and out through another. While he is inside, he is safe from the winter storms; but after a few moments of comfort, he vanishes from sight into the darkness whence he came.

Similarly, man appears on earth for a little while, but we know nothing of what went before this life, and what follows. Therefore if [Christianity] can reveal more certain knowledge, it seems only right that we should follow it."

—BEDE,
A History of the English Church and People

See Meeting God in the Created Order

He Kept the Matter in Mind

GENESIS 37:11

Jacob listened intently to his son's dream, and "kept the matter in mind." His words here remind us of Mary, who, on finding Jesus in the temple, treasures the events in her heart (see Luke 2:51). "Treasuring" is noticing that God is mysteriously at work and then reflecting on that work. Is there something in your life that disturbs you even as you sense that God is somehow involved? Be attentive to an event, a thought, idea or dream you may have set aside for safe-keeping. Regularly examine and tend it, so that God can eventually illuminate it. Every so often, bring it out from the back of your mind and gently reflect on it, asking God for guidance. Then send it back and remember it again at intervals until illumination comes.

See Meeting God in Prayer

Joseph's Dreams

37 Jacob lived in the land where his father had stayed, the land of Canaan.

²This is the account of Jacob.

Joseph, a young man of seventeen, was tending the flocks with his brothers, the sons of Bilhah and the sons of Zilpah, his father's wives, and he brought their father a bad report about them.

³Now Israel loved Joseph more than any of his other sons, because he had been born to him in his old age; and he made a richly ornamented[a] robe for him. ⁴When his brothers saw that their father loved him more than any of them, they hated him and could not speak a kind word to him.

⁵Joseph had a dream, and when he told it to his brothers, they hated him all the more. ⁶He said to them, "Listen to this dream I had: ⁷We were binding sheaves of grain out in the field when suddenly my sheaf rose and stood upright, while your sheaves gathered around mine and bowed down to it."

⁸His brothers said to him, "Do you intend to reign over us? Will you actually rule us?" And they hated him all the more because of his dream and what he had said.

⁹Then he had another dream, and he told it to his brothers. "Listen," he said, "I had another dream, and this time the sun and moon and eleven stars were bowing down to me."

¹⁰When he told his father as well as his brothers, his father rebuked him and said, "What is this dream you had? Will your mother and I and your brothers actually come and bow down to the ground before you?" ¹¹His brothers were jealous of him, but his father kept the matter in mind.

Joseph Sold by His Brothers

¹²Now his brothers had gone to graze their father's flocks near Shechem, ¹³and Israel said to Joseph, "As you know, your brothers are grazing the flocks near Shechem. Come, I am going to send you to them."

"Very well," he replied.

¹⁴So he said to him, "Go and see if all is well with your brothers and with the flocks, and bring word back to me." Then he sent him off from the Valley of Hebron.

When Joseph arrived at Shechem, ¹⁵a man found him wandering around in the fields and asked him, "What are you looking for?"

¹⁶He replied, "I'm looking for my brothers. Can you tell me where they are grazing their flocks?"

¹⁷"They have moved on from here," the man answered. "I heard them say, 'Let's go to Dothan.' "

So Joseph went after his brothers and found them near Dothan. ¹⁸But they saw him in the distance, and before he reached them, they plotted to kill him.

¹⁹"Here comes that dreamer!" they said to each other. ²⁰"Come now, let's kill him and throw him into one of these cisterns and say that a ferocious animal devoured him. Then we'll see what comes of his dreams."

---

[a] 3 The meaning of the Hebrew for *richly ornamented* is uncertain; also in verses 23 and 32.

[21] When Reuben heard this, he tried to rescue him from their hands. "Let's not take his life," he said. [22] "Don't shed any blood. Throw him into this cistern here in the desert, but don't lay a hand on him." Reuben said this to rescue him from them and take him back to his father.

[23] So when Joseph came to his brothers, they stripped him of his robe—the richly ornamented robe he was wearing—[24] and they took him and threw him into the cistern. Now the cistern was empty; there was no water in it.

[25] As they sat down to eat their meal, they looked up and saw a caravan of Ishmaelites coming from Gilead. Their camels were loaded with spices, balm and myrrh, and they were on their way to take them down to Egypt.

[26] Judah said to his brothers, "What will we gain if we kill our brother and cover up his blood? [27] Come, let's sell him to the Ishmaelites and not lay our hands on him; after all, he is our brother, our own flesh and blood." His brothers agreed.

[28] So when the Midianite merchants came by, his brothers pulled Joseph up out of the cistern and sold him for twenty shekels[a] of silver to the Ishmaelites, who took him to Egypt.

[29] When Reuben returned to the cistern and saw that Joseph was not there, he tore his clothes. [30] He went back to his brothers and said, "The boy isn't there! Where can I turn now?"

[31] Then they got Joseph's robe, slaughtered a goat and dipped the robe in the blood. [32] They took the ornamented robe back to their father and said, "We found this. Examine it to see whether it is your son's robe."

[33] He recognized it and said, "It is my son's robe! Some ferocious animal has devoured him. Joseph has surely been torn to pieces."

[34] Then Jacob tore his clothes, put on sackcloth and mourned for his son many days. [35] All his sons and daughters came to comfort him, but he refused to be comforted. "No," he said, "in mourning will I go down to the grave[b] to my son." So his father wept for him.

[36] Meanwhile, the Midianites[c] sold Joseph in Egypt to Potiphar, one of Pharaoh's officials, the captain of the guard.

Judah and Tamar

38 At that time, Judah left his brothers and went down to stay with a man of Adullam named Hirah. [2] There Judah met the daughter of a Canaanite man named Shua. He married her and lay with her; [3] she became pregnant and gave birth to a son, who was named Er. [4] She conceived again and gave birth to a son and named him Onan. [5] She gave birth to still another son and named him Shelah. It was at Kezib that she gave birth to him.

[6] Judah got a wife for Er, his firstborn, and her name was Tamar. [7] But Er, Judah's firstborn, was wicked in the LORD's sight; so the LORD put him to death. [8] Then Judah said to Onan, "Lie with your brother's wife and fulfill your duty to her as a brother-in-law to produce offspring for your brother." [9] But Onan knew that the offspring would not be his; so whenever he lay with his brother's wife, he spilled his semen on the ground to keep from

---

The Ornamented Robe

GENESIS 37:32–33

The robe is a beautiful symbol of love. Think of someone in whom you delight. Then find or buy some bits of beautiful fabric and sew the pieces together in a simple design that suits your fancy. Obtain several lovely buttons or beads and sew them on at random. Don't worry whether your creation looks fashionable or even useful; just pour all your creative, loving energy into making a gift for that person you love. When your creation feels complete to you, give it to that person with a prayer that God will always be with them. Then watch with awe as God cares for your loved one!

See Meeting God in Community

---

[a] 28 That is, about 8 ounces (about 0.2 kilogram)   [b] 35 Hebrew *Sheol*
[c] 36 Samaritan Pentateuch, Septuagint, Vulgate and Syriac (see also verse 28); Masoretic Text *Medanites*

51

More Righteous Than I

GENESIS 38:26

Why this troubling interruption? Genesis shows the lineage of God's people, and Perez, son of Tamar and Judah, is an ancestor of David and ultimately of Jesus. Here Judah admits that Tamar is righteous, for in fearing to lose another of his sons to her, he deprived her of her contribution to the community. This feisty woman fought for her right to bear children. Through them, the Davidic line gains Tamar's shrewdness and courage, as well as Judah's willingness to accept responsibility. Is there something God wants for you that is rightfully yours, but which you have relinquished because of how it might look to others? Write down a few possibilities, and consider whether you are being called to reclaim something for God.

See Meeting God in Everyday Life

producing offspring for his brother. ¹⁰What he did was wicked in the LORD's sight; so he put him to death also.

¹¹Judah then said to his daughter-in-law Tamar, "Live as a widow in your father's house until my son Shelah grows up." For he thought, "He may die too, just like his brothers." So Tamar went to live in her father's house.

¹²After a long time Judah's wife, the daughter of Shua, died. When Judah had recovered from his grief, he went up to Timnah, to the men who were shearing his sheep, and his friend Hirah the Adullamite went with him.

¹³When Tamar was told, "Your father-in-law is on his way to Timnah to shear his sheep," ¹⁴she took off her widow's clothes, covered herself with a veil to disguise herself, and then sat down at the entrance to Enaim, which is on the road to Timnah. For she saw that, though Shelah had now grown up, she had not been given to him as his wife.

¹⁵When Judah saw her, he thought she was a prostitute, for she had covered her face. ¹⁶Not realizing that she was his daughter-in-law, he went over to her by the roadside and said, "Come now, let me sleep with you."

"And what will you give me to sleep with you?" she asked.

¹⁷"I'll send you a young goat from my flock," he said.

"Will you give me something as a pledge until you send it?" she asked.

¹⁸He said, "What pledge should I give you?"

"Your seal and its cord, and the staff in your hand," she answered. So he gave them to her and slept with her, and she became pregnant by him. ¹⁹After she left, she took off her veil and put on her widow's clothes again.

²⁰Meanwhile Judah sent the young goat by his friend the Adullamite in order to get his pledge back from the woman, but he did not find her. ²¹He asked the men who lived there, "Where is the shrine prostitute who was beside the road at Enaim?"

"There hasn't been any shrine prostitute here," they said.

²²So he went back to Judah and said, "I didn't find her. Besides, the men who lived there said, 'There hasn't been any shrine prostitute here.' "

²³Then Judah said, "Let her keep what she has, or we will become a laughingstock. After all, I did send her this young goat, but you didn't find her."

²⁴About three months later Judah was told, "Your daughter-in-law Tamar is guilty of prostitution, and as a result she is now pregnant."

Judah said, "Bring her out and have her burned to death!"

²⁵As she was being brought out, she sent a message to her father-in-law. "I am pregnant by the man who owns these," she said. And she added, "See if you recognize whose seal and cord and staff these are."

²⁶Judah recognized them and said, "She is more righteous than I, since I wouldn't give her to my son Shelah." And he did not sleep with her again.

²⁷When the time came for her to give birth, there were twin boys in her womb. ²⁸As she was giving birth, one of them put out his hand; so the midwife took a scarlet thread and tied it on his wrist and said, "This one came out first." ²⁹But when he drew back his hand, his brother came out, and she said, "So this is how you have broken out!" And he

was named Perez.[a] ³⁰Then his brother, who had the scarlet thread on his wrist, came out and he was given the name Zerah.[b]

Joseph and Potiphar's Wife

39 Now Joseph had been taken down to Egypt. Potiphar, an Egyptian who was one of Pharaoh's officials, the captain of the guard, bought him from the Ishmaelites who had taken him there.

²The LORD was with Joseph and he prospered, and he lived in the house of his Egyptian master. ³When his master saw that the LORD was with him and that the LORD gave him success in everything he did, ⁴Joseph found favor in his eyes and became his attendant. Potiphar put him in charge of his household, and he entrusted to his care everything he owned. ⁵From the time he put him in charge of his household and of all that he owned, the LORD blessed the household of the Egyptian because of Joseph. The blessing of the LORD was on everything Potiphar had, both in the house and in the field. ⁶So he left in Joseph's care everything he had; with Joseph in charge, he did not concern himself with anything except the food he ate.

Now Joseph was well-built and handsome, ⁷and after a while his master's wife took notice of Joseph and said, "Come to bed with me!"

⁸But he refused. "With me in charge," he told her, "my master does not concern himself with anything in the house; everything he owns he has entrusted to my care. ⁹No one is greater in this house than I am. My master has withheld nothing from me except you, because you are his wife. How then could I do such a wicked thing and sin against God?" ¹⁰And though she spoke to Joseph day after day, he refused to go to bed with her or even be with her.

¹¹One day he went into the house to attend to his duties, and none of the household servants was inside. ¹²She caught him by his cloak and said, "Come to bed with me!" But he left his cloak in her hand and ran out of the house.

¹³When she saw that he had left his cloak in her hand and had run out of the house, ¹⁴she called her household servants. "Look," she said to them, "this Hebrew has been brought to us to make sport of us! He came in here to sleep with me, but I screamed. ¹⁵When he heard me scream for help, he left his cloak beside me and ran out of the house."

¹⁶She kept his cloak beside her until his master came home. ¹⁷Then she told him this story: "That Hebrew slave you brought us came to me to make sport of me. ¹⁸But as soon as I screamed for help, he left his cloak beside me and ran out of the house."

¹⁹When his master heard the story his wife told him, saying, "This is how your slave treated me," he burned with anger. ²⁰Joseph's master took him and put him in prison, the place where the king's prisoners were confined.

But while Joseph was there in the prison, ²¹the LORD was with him; he showed him kindness and granted him favor in the eyes of the prison warden. ²²So the warden put Joseph in charge of all those held in the prison, and he was made responsible for all that was done there. ²³The warden paid no attention to anything under Joseph's care, because

---

The Lord Was With Him

GENESIS 39:2,20–21

"It was just when, because I saw no escape, nothing to wish and no reason to expect any good thing, I abandoned all effort—it was then that the mere necessity I fell back upon proved to be 'the good and perfect and acceptable will of God' on which my soul could rest with a rest and peace that are better to me than any pleasure . . . It is as if my painted roof had been smashed and, instead of the darkness I had dreaded, I had found the stars shining."

—CAROLINE STEPHEN,
Daily Readings from Quaker Spirituality

All Belongs to God

GENESIS 40:8

This story of Joseph's life is sometimes called "wisdom" writing, part of the Biblical tradition of seeking how best to live. Observing this series of disasters in that light, we look carefully at Joseph's responses. Above all, Joseph believed that God was with him and that everything is in God's hands. Trusting, he looked for God's presence in all the details of his life, even in his dreams. Are there areas of your life that you have not yet entrusted to God? With what do you think it improbable that God would be concerned: driving the car, making business deals, disciplining children, sitting in noisy airports? Notice one or two areas in which you have kept God at a distance, and deliberately watch for his presence there.

See Meeting God in Everyday Life

the LORD was with Joseph and gave him success in whatever he did.

The Cupbearer and the Baker

40 Some time later, the cupbearer and the baker of the king of Egypt offended their master, the king of Egypt. [2]Pharaoh was angry with his two officials, the chief cupbearer and the chief baker, [3]and put them in custody in the house of the captain of the guard, in the same prison where Joseph was confined. [4]The captain of the guard assigned them to Joseph, and he attended them.

After they had been in custody for some time, [5]each of the two men—the cupbearer and the baker of the king of Egypt, who were being held in prison—had a dream the same night, and each dream had a meaning of its own.

[6]When Joseph came to them the next morning, he saw that they were dejected. [7]So he asked Pharaoh's officials who were in custody with him in his master's house, "Why are your faces so sad today?"

[8]"We both had dreams," they answered, "but there is no one to interpret them."

Then Joseph said to them, "Do not interpretations belong to God? Tell me your dreams."

[9]So the chief cupbearer told Joseph his dream. He said to him, "In my dream I saw a vine in front of me, [10]and on the vine were three branches. As soon as it budded, it blossomed, and its clusters ripened into grapes. [11]Pharaoh's cup was in my hand, and I took the grapes, squeezed them into Pharaoh's cup and put the cup in his hand."

[12]"This is what it means," Joseph said to him. "The three branches are three days. [13]Within three days Pharaoh will lift up your head and restore you to your position, and you will put Pharaoh's cup in his hand, just as you used to do when you were his cupbearer. [14]But when all goes well with you, remember me and show me kindness; mention me to Pharaoh and get me out of this prison. [15]For I was forcibly carried off from the land of the Hebrews, and even here I have done nothing to deserve being put in a dungeon."

[16]When the chief baker saw that Joseph had given a favorable interpretation, he said to Joseph, "I too had a dream: On my head were three baskets of bread.[a] [17]In the top basket were all kinds of baked goods for Pharaoh, but the birds were eating them out of the basket on my head."

[18]"This is what it means," Joseph said. "The three baskets are three days. [19]Within three days Pharaoh will lift off your head and hang you on a tree.[b] And the birds will eat away your flesh."

[20]Now the third day was Pharaoh's birthday, and he gave a feast for all his officials. He lifted up the heads of the chief cupbearer and the chief baker in the presence of his officials: [21]He restored the chief cupbearer to his position, so that he once again put the cup into Pharaoh's hand, [22]but he hanged[c] the chief baker, just as Joseph had said to them in his interpretation.

[23]The chief cupbearer, however, did not remember Joseph; he forgot him.

a 16 Or three wicker baskets   b 19 Or and impale you on a pole   c 22 Or impaled

Pharaoh's Dreams

41 When two full years had passed, Pharaoh had a dream: He was standing by the Nile, ²when out of the river there came up seven cows, sleek and fat, and they grazed among the reeds. ³After them, seven other cows, ugly and gaunt, came up out of the Nile and stood beside those on the riverbank. ⁴And the cows that were ugly and gaunt ate up the seven sleek, fat cows. Then Pharaoh woke up.

⁵He fell asleep again and had a second dream: Seven heads of grain, healthy and good, were growing on a single stalk. ⁶After them, seven other heads of grain sprouted—thin and scorched by the east wind. ⁷The thin heads of grain swallowed up the seven healthy, full heads. Then Pharaoh woke up; it had been a dream.

⁸In the morning his mind was troubled, so he sent for all the magicians and wise men of Egypt. Pharaoh told them his dreams, but no one could interpret them for him.

⁹Then the chief cupbearer said to Pharaoh, "Today I am reminded of my shortcomings. ¹⁰Pharaoh was once angry with his servants, and he imprisoned me and the chief baker in the house of the captain of the guard. ¹¹Each of us had a dream the same night, and each dream had a meaning of its own. ¹²Now a young Hebrew was there with us, a servant of the captain of the guard. We told him our dreams, and he interpreted them for us, giving each man the interpretation of his dream. ¹³And things turned out exactly as he interpreted them to us: I was restored to my position, and the other man was hanged.ᵃ"

¹⁴So Pharaoh sent for Joseph, and he was quickly brought from the dungeon. When he had shaved and changed his clothes, he came before Pharaoh.

¹⁵Pharaoh said to Joseph, "I had a dream, and no one can interpret it. But I have heard it said of you that when you hear a dream you can interpret it."

¹⁶"I cannot do it," Joseph replied to Pharaoh, "but God will give Pharaoh the answer he desires."

¹⁷Then Pharaoh said to Joseph, "In my dream I was standing on the bank of the Nile, ¹⁸when out of the river there came up seven cows, fat and sleek, and they grazed among the reeds. ¹⁹After them, seven other cows came up—scrawny and very ugly and lean. I had never seen such ugly cows in all the land of Egypt. ²⁰The lean, ugly cows ate up the seven fat cows that came up first. ²¹But even after they ate them, no one could tell that they had done so; they looked just as ugly as before. Then I woke up.

²²"In my dreams I also saw seven heads of grain, full and good, growing on a single stalk. ²³After them, seven other heads sprouted—withered and thin and scorched by the east wind. ²⁴The thin heads of grain swallowed up the seven good heads. I told this to the magicians, but none could explain it to me."

²⁵Then Joseph said to Pharaoh, "The dreams of Pharaoh are one and the same. God has revealed to Pharaoh what he is about to do. ²⁶The seven good cows are seven years, and the seven good heads of grain are seven years; it is one and the same dream. ²⁷The seven lean, ugly cows that came up afterward are seven years, and so are the seven

ᵃ 13 Or *impaled*

One in Whom Is the Spirit of God

GENESIS 41:38

"When you feel by the grace of God that he is calling you to this work, and you intend to respond, lift your heart to God with humble love. And really [attend] God himself who created you, and bought you, and graciously called you to this state of life . . . It all depends on your desire. A naked intention directed to God, and himself alone, is wholly sufficient. If you want this intention summed up in a word, to retain it more easily, take a short word, preferably of one syllable . . .

And fix this word fast to your heart, so that it is always there come what may. It will be your shield and spear in peace and war alike."

ANONYMOUS,
The Cloud of Unknowing

See Meeting God in Prayer

worthless heads of grain scorched by the east wind: They are seven years of famine.

²⁸"It is just as I said to Pharaoh: God has shown Pharaoh what he is about to do. ²⁹Seven years of great abundance are coming throughout the land of Egypt, ³⁰but seven years of famine will follow them. Then all the abundance in Egypt will be forgotten, and the famine will ravage the land. ³¹The abundance in the land will not be remembered, because the famine that follows it will be so severe. ³²The reason the dream was given to Pharaoh in two forms is that the matter has been firmly decided by God, and God will soon do it soon.

³³"And now let Pharaoh look for a discerning and wise man and put him in charge of the land of Egypt. ³⁴Let Pharaoh appoint commissioners over the land to take a fifth of the harvest of Egypt during the seven years of abundance. ³⁵They should collect all the food of these good years that are coming and store up the grain under the authority of Pharaoh, to be kept in the cities for food. ³⁶This food should be held in reserve for the country, to be used during the seven years of famine that will come upon Egypt, so that the country may not be ruined by the famine."

³⁷The plan seemed good to Pharaoh and to all his officials. ³⁸So Pharaoh asked them, "Can we find anyone like this man, one in whom is the spirit of God*ª*?"

³⁹Then Pharaoh said to Joseph, "Since God has made all this known to you, there is no one so discerning and wise as you. ⁴⁰You shall be in charge of my palace, and all my people are to submit to your orders. Only with respect to the throne will I be greater than you."

Joseph in Charge of Egypt

⁴¹So Pharaoh said to Joseph, "I hereby put you in charge of the whole land of Egypt." ⁴²Then Pharaoh took his signet ring from his finger and put it on Joseph's finger. He dressed him in robes of fine linen and put a gold chain around his neck. ⁴³He had him ride in a chariot as his second-in-command,*ᵇ* and men shouted before him, "Make way*ᶜ*!" Thus he put him in charge of the whole land of Egypt.

⁴⁴Then Pharaoh said to Joseph, "I am Pharaoh, but without your word no one will lift hand or foot in all Egypt." ⁴⁵Pharaoh gave Joseph the name Zaphenath-Paneah and gave him Asenath daughter of Potiphera, priest of On,*ᵈ* to be his wife. And Joseph went throughout the land of Egypt.

⁴⁶Joseph was thirty years old when he entered the service of Pharaoh king of Egypt. And Joseph went out from Pharaoh's presence and traveled throughout Egypt. ⁴⁷During the seven years of abundance the land produced plentifully. ⁴⁸Joseph collected all the food produced in those seven years of abundance in Egypt and stored it in the cities. In each city he put the food grown in the fields surrounding it. ⁴⁹Joseph stored up huge quantities of grain, like the sand of the sea; it was so much that he stopped keeping records because it was beyond measure.

⁵⁰Before the years of famine came, two sons were born to Joseph by Asenath daughter of Potiphera, priest of On.

ª 38 Or of the gods   ᵇ 43 Or in the chariot of his second-in-command; or in his second chariot   ᶜ 43 Or Bow down   ᵈ 45 That is, Heliopolis; also in verse 50

[51]Joseph named his firstborn Manasseh[a] and said, "It is because God has made me forget all my trouble and all my father's household." [52]The second son he named Ephraim[b] and said, "It is because God has made me fruitful in the land of my suffering."

[53]The seven years of abundance in Egypt came to an end, [54]and the seven years of famine began, just as Joseph had said. There was famine in all the other lands, but in the whole land of Egypt there was food. [55]When all Egypt began to feel the famine, the people cried to Pharaoh for food. Then Pharaoh told all the Egyptians, "Go to Joseph and do what he tells you."

[56]When the famine had spread over the whole country, Joseph opened the storehouses and sold grain to the Egyptians, for the famine was severe throughout Egypt. [57]And all the countries came to Egypt to buy grain from Joseph, because the famine was severe in all the world.

Joseph's Brothers Go to Egypt

42 When Jacob learned that there was grain in Egypt, he said to his sons, "Why do you just keep looking at each other?" [2]He continued, "I have heard that there is grain in Egypt. Go down there and buy some for us, so that we may live and not die."

[3]Then ten of Joseph's brothers went down to buy grain from Egypt. [4]But Jacob did not send Benjamin, Joseph's brother, with the others, because he was afraid that harm might come to him. [5]So Israel's sons were among those who went to buy grain, for the famine was in the land of Canaan also.

[6]Now Joseph was the governor of the land, the one who sold grain to all its people. So when Joseph's brothers arrived, they bowed down to him with their faces to the ground. [7]As soon as Joseph saw his brothers, he recognized them, but he pretended to be a stranger and spoke harshly to them. "Where do you come from?" he asked.

"From the land of Canaan," they replied, "to buy food."

[8]Although Joseph recognized his brothers, they did not recognize him. [9]Then he remembered his dreams about them and said to them, "You are spies! You have come to see where our land is unprotected."

[10]"No, my lord," they answered. "Your servants have come to buy food. [11]We are all the sons of one man. Your servants are honest men, not spies."

[12]"No!" he said to them. "You have come to see where our land is unprotected."

[13]But they replied, "Your servants were twelve brothers, the sons of one man, who lives in the land of Canaan. The youngest is now with our father, and one is no more."

[14]Joseph said to them, "It is just as I told you: You are spies! [15]And this is how you will be tested: As surely as Pharaoh lives, you will not leave this place unless your youngest brother comes here. [16]Send one of your number to get your brother; the rest of you will be kept in prison, so that your words may be tested to see if you are telling the truth. If you are not, then as surely as Pharaoh lives, you are spies!" [17]And he put them all in custody for three days.

[18]On the third day, Joseph said to them, "Do this and you

It Came to Pass

GENESIS 42:1–5

This is the record of *God's action* in human history. Sometimes we become so intrigued with the story and the characters' responses that we forget that God is the main actor. Nonetheless, even as God's will is unfolding as it should, we must account for our actions before him. Make a time line for your own life, dividing it into units of ten years. Give each decade a "name" and note your major life tasks and concerns during each period. Then evaluate how you prayed and the quality of your relationship with God during each decade. Finally, look over your time line and notice any patterns in the way God deals with you and the way you typically respond. Pray about what you find.

See Meeting God in Everyday Life

---

[a] 51 *Manasseh* sounds like and may be derived from the Hebrew for *forget*.
[b] 52 *Ephraim* sounds like the Hebrew for *twice fruitful*.

Punished or Invited to Return?

GENESIS 42:21

"For your prayer, your journey into God, may you be given a small storm, a little hurricane named after you, persistent enough to get your attention, violent enough to awaken you to new depths, strong enough to shake you to the roots, majestic enough to remind you of your origin: made of earth yet steeped in eternity, frail human dust yet soaked with infinity . . . In the midst of these holy winds, in the midst of this divine wrestling, your storm journey, like all hurricanes, leads you into the eye, into the Eye of God."

—MACRINA WIEDERKEHR,
A Tree Full of Angels

will live, for I fear God: ¹⁹If you are honest men, let one of your brothers stay here in prison, while the rest of you go and take grain back for your starving households. ²⁰But you must bring your youngest brother to me, so that your words may be verified and that you may not die." This they proceeded to do.

²¹They said to one another, "Surely we are being punished because of our brother. We saw how distressed he was when he pleaded with us for his life, but we would not listen; that's why this distress has come upon us."

²²Reuben replied, "Didn't I tell you not to sin against the boy? But you wouldn't listen! Now we must give an accounting for his blood." ²³They did not realize that Joseph could understand them, since he was using an interpreter.

²⁴He turned away from them and began to weep, but then turned back and spoke to them again. He had Simeon taken from them and bound before their eyes.

²⁵Joseph gave orders to fill their bags with grain, to put each man's silver back in his sack, and to give them provisions for their journey. After this was done for them, ²⁶they loaded their grain on their donkeys and left.

²⁷At the place where they stopped for the night one of them opened his sack to get feed for his donkey, and he saw his silver in the mouth of his sack. ²⁸"My silver has been returned," he said to his brothers. "Here it is in my sack."

Their hearts sank and they turned to each other trembling and said, "What is this that God has done to us?"

²⁹When they came to their father Jacob in the land of Canaan, they told him all that had happened to them. They said, ³⁰"The man who is lord over the land spoke harshly to us and treated us as though we were spying on the land. ³¹But we said to him, 'We are honest men; we are not spies. ³²We were twelve brothers, sons of one father. One is no more, and the youngest is now with our father in Canaan.'

³³"Then the man who is lord over the land said to us, 'This is how I will know whether you are honest men: Leave one of your brothers here with me, and take food for your starving households and go. ³⁴But bring your youngest brother to me so I will know that you are not spies but honest men. Then I will give your brother back to you, and you can trade[a] in the land.' "

³⁵As they were emptying their sacks, there in each man's sack was his pouch of silver! When they and their father saw the money pouches, they were frightened. ³⁶Their father Jacob said to them, "You have deprived me of my children. Joseph is no more and Simeon is no more, and now you want to take Benjamin. Everything is against me!"

³⁷Then Reuben said to his father, "You may put both of my sons to death if I do not bring him back to you. Entrust him to my care, and I will bring him back."

³⁸But Jacob said, "My son will not go down there with you; his brother is dead and he is the only one left. If harm comes to him on the journey you are taking, you will bring my gray head down to the grave[b] in sorrow."

The Second Journey to Egypt

43 Now the famine was still severe in the land. ²So when they had eaten all the grain they had brought

a 34 Or move about freely   *b 38 Hebrew Sheol*

from Egypt, their father said to them, "Go back and buy us a little more food."

³But Judah said to him, "The man warned us solemnly, 'You will not see my face again unless your brother is with you.' ⁴If you will send our brother along with us, we will go down and buy food for you. ⁵But if you will not send him, we will not go down, because the man said to us, 'You will not see my face again unless your brother is with you.' "

⁶Israel asked, "Why did you bring this trouble on me by telling the man you had another brother?"

⁷They replied, "The man questioned us closely about ourselves and our family. 'Is your father still living?' he asked us. 'Do you have another brother?' We simply answered his questions. How were we to know he would say, 'Bring your brother down here'?"

⁸Then Judah said to Israel his father, "Send the boy along with me and we will go at once, so that we and you and our children may live and not die. ⁹I myself will guarantee his safety; you can hold me personally responsible for him. If I do not bring him back to you and set him here before you, I will bear the blame before you all my life. ¹⁰As it is, if we had not delayed, we could have gone and returned twice."

¹¹Then their father Israel said to them, "If it must be, then do this: Put some of the best products of the land in your bags and take them down to the man as a gift—a little balm and a little honey, some spices and myrrh, some pistachio nuts and almonds. ¹²Take double the amount of silver with you, for you must return the silver that was put back into the mouths of your sacks. Perhaps it was a mistake. ¹³Take your brother also and go back to the man at once. ¹⁴And may God Almighty*ᵃ* grant you mercy before the man so that he will let your other brother and Benjamin come back with you. As for me, if I am bereaved, I am bereaved."

¹⁵So the men took the gifts and double the amount of silver, and Benjamin also. They hurried down to Egypt and presented themselves to Joseph. ¹⁶When Joseph saw Benjamin with them, he said to the steward of his house, "Take these men to my house, slaughter an animal and prepare dinner; they are to eat with me at noon."

¹⁷The man did as Joseph told him and took the men to Joseph's house. ¹⁸Now the men were frightened when they were taken to his house. They thought, "We were brought here because of the silver that was put back into our sacks the first time. He wants to attack us and overpower us and seize us as slaves and take our donkeys."

¹⁹So they went up to Joseph's steward and spoke to him at the entrance to the house. ²⁰"Please, sir," they said, "we came down here the first time to buy food. ²¹But at the place where we stopped for the night we opened our sacks and each of us found his silver—the exact weight—in the mouth of his sack. So we have brought it back with us. ²²We have also brought additional silver with us to buy food. We don't know who put our silver in our sacks."

²³"It's all right," he said. "Don't be afraid. Your God, the God of your father, has given you treasure in your sacks; I received your silver." Then he brought Simeon out to them.

²⁴The steward took the men into Joseph's house, gave them water to wash their feet and provided fodder for their

The Best of the Land

GENESIS 43:11

Balm and honey, spices and myrrh, pistachio nuts and almonds! If money were scarce for you, and you wanted to give a precious gift to someone, a gift that would convey the best of your life, what would you give? Put your five senses to work in your daily environment and notice the pleasant treasure of sight, of smell, of sound, taste and touch. Enjoy fully the gifts God has given you to nourish and stimulate your senses, and think of how you might best share them with another. Start today by sharing them with those you live with, by showing them what you see and giving thanks together.

See Meeting God in the Created Order

Can Trouble Be Treasure?

GENESIS 43:23

"We who try to evade suffering at any cost may be rejecting the Truth knocking at our door, asking that we sup with him and he with us, including most significantly the drinking of his cup. The Good News is that suffering is not itself alien and terrible, or hostile to the nature of God, but that suffering is that peculiar environment in which the love and power of God can shine most clearly, for it was God who suffered for us, who suffers with us, and shares our travail."

—THOMAS BROWN,
Daily Readings from Quaker Spirituality

donkeys. ²⁵They prepared their gifts for Joseph's arrival at noon, because they had heard that they were to eat there.

²⁶When Joseph came home, they presented to him the gifts they had brought into the house, and they bowed down before him to the ground. ²⁷He asked them how they were, and then he said, "How is your aged father you told me about? Is he still living?"

²⁸They replied, "Your servant our father is still alive and well." And they bowed low to pay him honor.

²⁹As he looked about and saw his brother Benjamin, his own mother's son, he asked, "Is this your youngest brother, the one you told me about?" And he said, "God be gracious to you, my son." ³⁰Deeply moved at the sight of his brother, Joseph hurried out and looked for a place to weep. He went into his private room and wept there.

³¹After he had washed his face, he came out and, controlling himself, said, "Serve the food."

³²They served him by himself, the brothers by themselves, and the Egyptians who ate with him by themselves, because Egyptians could not eat with Hebrews, for that is detestable to Egyptians. ³³The men had been seated before him in the order of their ages, from the firstborn to the youngest; and they looked at each other in astonishment. ³⁴When portions were served to them from Joseph's table, Benjamin's portion was five times as much as anyone else's. So they feasted and drank freely with him.

A Silver Cup in a Sack

44 Now Joseph gave these instructions to the steward of his house: "Fill the men's sacks with as much food as they can carry, and put each man's silver in the mouth of his sack. ²Then put my cup, the silver one, in the mouth of the youngest one's sack, along with the silver for his grain." And he did as Joseph said.

³As morning dawned, the men were sent on their way with their donkeys. ⁴They had not gone far from the city when Joseph said to his steward, "Go after those men at once, and when you catch up with them, say to them, 'Why have you repaid good with evil? ⁵Isn't this the cup my master drinks from and also uses for divination? This is a wicked thing you have done.'"

⁶When he caught up with them, he repeated these words to them. ⁷But they said to him, "Why does my lord say such things? Far be it from your servants to do anything like that! ⁸We even brought back to you from the land of Canaan the silver we found inside the mouths of our sacks. So why would we steal silver or gold from your master's house? ⁹If any of your servants is found to have it, he will die; and the rest of us will become my lord's slaves."

¹⁰"Very well, then," he said, "let it be as you say. Whoever is found to have it will become my slave; the rest of you will be free from blame."

¹¹Each of them quickly lowered his sack to the ground and opened it. ¹²Then the steward proceeded to search, beginning with the oldest and ending with the youngest. And the cup was found in Benjamin's sack. ¹³At this, they tore their clothes. Then they all loaded their donkeys and returned to the city.

¹⁴Joseph was still in the house when Judah and his brothers came in, and they threw themselves to the ground be-

fore him. ¹⁵Joseph said to them, "What is this you have done? Don't you know that a man like me can find things out by divination?"

¹⁶"What can we say to my lord?" Judah replied. "What can we say? How can we prove our innocence? God has uncovered your servants' guilt. We are now my lord's slaves—we ourselves and the one who was found to have the cup."

¹⁷But Joseph said, "Far be it from me to do such a thing! Only the man who was found to have the cup will become my slave. The rest of you, go back to your father in peace."

¹⁸Then Judah went up to him and said: "Please, my lord, let your servant speak a word to my lord. Do not be angry with your servant, though you are equal to Pharaoh himself. ¹⁹My lord asked his servants, 'Do you have a father or a brother?' ²⁰And we answered, 'We have an aged father, and there is a young son born to him in his old age. His brother is dead, and he is the only one of his mother's sons left, and his father loves him.'

²¹"Then you said to your servants, 'Bring him down to me so I can see him for myself.' ²²And we said to my lord, 'The boy cannot leave his father; if he leaves him, his father will die.' ²³But you told your servants, 'Unless your youngest brother comes down with you, you will not see my face again.' ²⁴When we went back to your servant my father, we told him what my lord had said.

²⁵"Then our father said, 'Go back and buy a little more food.' ²⁶But we said, 'We cannot go down. Only if our youngest brother is with us will we go. We cannot see the man's face unless our youngest brother is with us.'

²⁷"Your servant my father said to us, 'You know that my wife bore me two sons. ²⁸One of them went away from me, and I said, "He has surely been torn to pieces." And I have not seen him since. ²⁹If you take this one from me too and harm comes to him, you will bring my gray head down to the grave[a] in misery.'

³⁰"So now, if the boy is not with us when I go back to your servant my father and if my father, whose life is closely bound up with the boy's life, ³¹sees that the boy isn't there, he will die. Your servants will bring the gray head of our father down to the grave in sorrow. ³²Your servant guaranteed the boy's safety to my father. I said, 'If I do not bring him back to you, I will bear the blame before you, my father, all my life!'

³³"Now then, please let your servant remain here as my lord's slave in place of the boy, and let the boy return with his brothers. ³⁴How can I go back to my father if the boy is not with me? No! Do not let me see the misery that would come upon my father."

Joseph Makes Himself Known

45 Then Joseph could no longer control himself before all his attendants, and he cried out, "Have everyone leave my presence!" So there was no one with Joseph when he made himself known to his brothers. ²And he wept so loudly that the Egyptians heard him, and Pharaoh's household heard about it.

³Joseph said to his brothers, "I am Joseph! Is my father

Playing Cat and Mouse

GENESIS 44:15

Place yourself in this scene, in the role of each character in turn. Imagine that you are Joseph. How do you feel about your brothers' cruelty, your isolation from home, your wish to hurt as you have been hurt? Imagine that you are Reuben, Simeon or Levi, proud and quick to react with physical violence, but out of your element in Pharaoh's courts. Be Judah now, a good but weak man, seldom defending the truth. Or perhaps be Israel, waiting at home, expecting to lose your second beloved son, just as Joseph was taken so long ago. Experience all these emotions in yourself, and offer them one by one to God, asking that your heart be purified, freeing you to cooperate with his divine purpose in your life.

See Meeting God in Scripture

The Eyes of Faith

GENESIS 45:8

At last Joseph releases his desire for revenge and sees the events of his life with the eyes of faith. His brothers meant him evil, but God has brought goodness from the harm they intended. With this certainty, Joseph can be forgiving and generous. Seeing how much God has done for him, he weeps in gratitude. Is there a bitterness in your heart that has been eating away at your trust in God? Do not suppress it or act out because of it. Take it to God in prayer, over and over again, weeping in despair and anger if necessary until you can weep in gratitude. If possible, find a friend to travel with you to the depths, bringing his or her own hope alongside to carry you through.

See Meeting God in Prayer

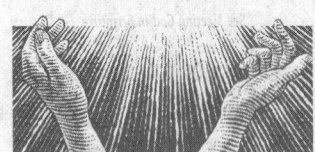

still living?" But his brothers were not able to answer him, because they were terrified at his presence.

⁴Then Joseph said to his brothers, "Come close to me." When they had done so, he said, "I am your brother Joseph, the one you sold into Egypt! ⁵And now, do not be distressed and do not be angry with yourselves for selling me here, because it was to save lives that God sent me ahead of you. ⁶For two years now there has been famine in the land, and for the next five years there will not be plowing and reaping. ⁷But God sent me ahead of you to preserve for you a remnant on earth and to save your lives by a great deliverance.ᵃ

⁸"So then, it was not you who sent me here, but God. He made me father to Pharaoh, lord of his entire household and ruler of all Egypt. ⁹Now hurry back to my father and say to him, 'This is what your son Joseph says: God has made me lord of all Egypt. Come down to me; don't delay. ¹⁰You shall live in the region of Goshen and be near me— you, your children and grandchildren, your flocks and herds, and all you have. ¹¹I will provide for you there, because five years of famine are still to come. Otherwise you and your household and all who belong to you will become destitute.'

¹²"You can see for yourselves, and so can my brother Benjamin, that it is really I who am speaking to you. ¹³Tell my father about all the honor accorded me in Egypt and about everything you have seen. And bring my father down here quickly."

¹⁴Then he threw his arms around his brother Benjamin and wept, and Benjamin embraced him, weeping. ¹⁵And he kissed all his brothers and wept over them. Afterward his brothers talked with him.

¹⁶When the news reached Pharaoh's palace that Joseph's brothers had come, Pharaoh and all his officials were pleased. ¹⁷Pharaoh said to Joseph, "Tell your brothers, 'Do this: Load your animals and return to the land of Canaan, ¹⁸and bring your father and your families back to me. I will give you the best of the land of Egypt and you can enjoy the fat of the land.'

¹⁹"You are also directed to tell them, 'Do this: Take some carts from Egypt for your children and your wives, and get your father and come. ²⁰Never mind about your belongings, because the best of all Egypt will be yours.' "

²¹So the sons of Israel did this. Joseph gave them carts, as Pharaoh had commanded, and he also gave them provisions for their journey. ²²To each of them he gave new clothing, but to Benjamin he gave three hundred shekelsᵇ of silver and five sets of clothes. ²³And this is what he sent to his father: ten donkeys loaded with the best things of Egypt, and ten female donkeys loaded with grain and bread and other provisions for his journey. ²⁴Then he sent his brothers away, and as they were leaving he said to them, "Don't quarrel on the way!"

²⁵So they went up out of Egypt and came to their father Jacob in the land of Canaan. ²⁶They told him, "Joseph is still alive! In fact, he is ruler of all Egypt." Jacob was stunned; he did not believe them. ²⁷But when they told him everything Joseph had said to them, and when he saw the

ᵃ 7 Or *save you as a great band of survivors*   ᵇ 22 That is, about 7 1/2 pounds (about 3.5 kilograms)

carts Joseph had sent to carry him back, the spirit of their father Jacob revived. ²⁸And Israel said, "I'm convinced! My son Joseph is still alive. I will go and see him before I die."

Jacob Goes to Egypt

46 So Israel set out with all that was his, and when he reached Beersheba, he offered sacrifices to the God of his father Isaac.

²And God spoke to Israel in a vision at night and said, "Jacob! Jacob!"

"Here I am," he replied.

³"I am God, the God of your father," he said. "Do not be afraid to go down to Egypt, for I will make you into a great nation there. ⁴I will go down to Egypt with you, and I will surely bring you back again. And Joseph's own hand will close your eyes."

⁵Then Jacob left Beersheba, and Israel's sons took their father Jacob and their children and their wives in the carts that Pharaoh had sent to transport him. ⁶They also took with them their livestock and the possessions they had acquired in Canaan, and Jacob and all his offspring went to Egypt. ⁷He took with him to Egypt his sons and grandsons and his daughters and granddaughters—all his offspring.

⁸These are the names of the sons of Israel (Jacob and his descendants) who went to Egypt:

Reuben the firstborn of Jacob.
⁹The sons of Reuben:
Hanoch, Pallu, Hezron and Carmi.
¹⁰The sons of Simeon:
Jemuel, Jamin, Ohad, Jakin, Zohar and Shaul the son of a Canaanite woman.
¹¹The sons of Levi:
Gershon, Kohath and Merari.
¹²The sons of Judah:
Er, Onan, Shelah, Perez and Zerah (but Er and Onan had died in the land of Canaan).
The sons of Perez:
Hezron and Hamul.
¹³The sons of Issachar:
Tola, Puah,ᵃ Jashubᵇ and Shimron.
¹⁴The sons of Zebulun:
Sered, Elon and Jahleel.
¹⁵These were the sons Leah bore to Jacob in Paddan Aram,ᶜ besides his daughter Dinah. These sons and daughters of his were thirty-three in all.

¹⁶The sons of Gad:
Zephon,ᵈ Haggi, Shuni, Ezbon, Eri, Arodi and Areli.
¹⁷The sons of Asher:
Imnah, Ishvah, Ishvi and Beriah.
Their sister was Serah.
The sons of Beriah:
Heber and Malkiel.
¹⁸These were the children born to Jacob by Zilpah, whom Laban had given to his daughter Leah—sixteen in all.

ᵃ 13 Samaritan Pentateuch and Syriac (see also 1 Chron. 7:1); Masoretic Text *Puvah*   ᵇ 13 Samaritan Pentateuch and some Septuagint manuscripts (see also Num. 26:24 and 1 Chron. 7:1); Masoretic Text *Iob*   ᶜ 15 That is, Northwest Mesopotamia   ᵈ 16 Samaritan Pentateuch and Septuagint (see also Num. 26:15); Masoretic Text *Ziphion*

I'm Convinced!

GENESIS 45:26–28

At first Israel is disbelieving, but when he sees the full carts he believes. Perhaps there are some small parts within yourself that even today are "holdouts"; you're not yet willing to trust in God's care—you're waiting for a "sign" like the carts or Jesus' wounded hands and side. But seldom can anything important be proven with certainty: How can you prove that you love someone? There is always a place for faith beside reason. Think back on times when your God has strengthened your faith. Recall what was going on in your life beforehand, what actually happened, and what occurred afterward. Based on those experiences, how can you create a more receptive climate within yourself for deepening faith today?

See Meeting God in Everyday Life

Reconciled and Restored

GENESIS 46:29

In a grand sweep of God's divine love, Joseph is restored to his beloved father Jacob. God's generosity is astounding. Through a remarkable chain of events, God's people are saved from famine, and a family, split apart by jealousy, is reconciled and restored.

God is concerned for your family as well. Has your family experienced a rift or an estrangement that seems irreconcilable? Keeping the story of Joseph and his family in mind, write a prayer that lays all the complicated emotions and issues before God. Make that prayer your ministry to your family by repeating it often.

See Meeting God in Prayer

¹⁹The sons of Jacob's wife Rachel:

Joseph and Benjamin. ²⁰In Egypt, Manasseh and Ephraim were born to Joseph by Asenath daughter of Potiphera, priest of On.[a]

²¹The sons of Benjamin:

Bela, Beker, Ashbel, Gera, Naaman, Ehi, Rosh, Muppim, Huppim and Ard.

²²These were the sons of Rachel who were born to Jacob—fourteen in all.

²³The son of Dan:

Hushim.

²⁴The sons of Naphtali:

Jahziel, Guni, Jezer and Shillem.

²⁵These were the sons born to Jacob by Bilhah, whom Laban had given to his daughter Rachel—seven in all.

²⁶All those who went to Egypt with Jacob—those who were his direct descendants, not counting his sons' wives—numbered sixty-six persons. ²⁷With the two sons[b] who had been born to Joseph in Egypt, the members of Jacob's family, which went to Egypt, were seventy[c] in all.

²⁸Now Jacob sent Judah ahead of him to Joseph to get directions to Goshen. When they arrived in the region of Goshen, ²⁹Joseph had his chariot made ready and went to Goshen to meet his father Israel. As soon as Joseph appeared before him, he threw his arms around his father[d] and wept for a long time.

³⁰Israel said to Joseph, "Now I am ready to die, since I have seen for myself that you are still alive."

³¹Then Joseph said to his brothers and to his father's household, "I will go up and speak to Pharaoh and will say to him, 'My brothers and my father's household, who were living in the land of Canaan, have come to me. ³²The men are shepherds; they tend livestock, and they have brought along their flocks and herds and everything they own.' ³³When Pharaoh calls you in and asks, 'What is your occupation?' ³⁴you should answer, 'Your servants have tended livestock from our boyhood on, just as our fathers did.' Then you will be allowed to settle in the region of Goshen, for all shepherds are detestable to the Egyptians."

47 Joseph went and told Pharaoh, "My father and brothers, with their flocks and herds and everything they own, have come from the land of Canaan and are now in Goshen." ²He chose five of his brothers and presented them before Pharaoh.

³Pharaoh asked the brothers, "What is your occupation?"

"Your servants are shepherds," they replied to Pharaoh, "just as our fathers were." ⁴They also said to him, "We have come to live here awhile, because the famine is severe in Canaan and your servants' flocks have no pasture. So now, please let your servants settle in Goshen."

⁵Pharaoh said to Joseph, "Your father and your brothers have come to you, ⁶and the land of Egypt is before you; settle your father and your brothers in the best part of the land. Let them live in Goshen. And if you know of any among them with special ability, put them in charge of my own livestock."

a 20 That is, Heliopolis   b 27 Hebrew; Septuagint *the nine children*
c 27 Hebrew (see also Exodus 1:5 and footnote); Septuagint (see also Acts 7:14) *seventy-five*   d 29 Hebrew *around him*

⁷Then Joseph brought his father Jacob in and presented him before Pharaoh. After Jacob blessed*a* Pharaoh, ⁸Pharaoh asked him, "How old are you?"

⁹And Jacob said to Pharaoh, "The years of my pilgrimage are a hundred and thirty. My years have been few and difficult, and they do not equal the years of the pilgrimage of my fathers." ¹⁰Then Jacob blessed*b* Pharaoh and went out from his presence.

¹¹So Joseph settled his father and his brothers in Egypt and gave them property in the best part of the land, the district of Rameses, as Pharaoh directed. ¹²Joseph also provided his father and his brothers and all his father's household with food, according to the number of their children.

Joseph and the Famine

¹³There was no food, however, in the whole region because the famine was severe; both Egypt and Canaan wasted away because of the famine. ¹⁴Joseph collected all the money that was to be found in Egypt and Canaan in payment for the grain they were buying, and he brought it to Pharaoh's palace. ¹⁵When the money of the people of Egypt and Canaan was gone, all Egypt came to Joseph and said, "Give us food. Why should we die before your eyes? Our money is used up."

¹⁶"Then bring your livestock," said Joseph. "I will sell you food in exchange for your livestock, since your money is gone." ¹⁷So they brought their livestock to Joseph, and he gave them food in exchange for their horses, their sheep and goats, their cattle and donkeys. And he brought them through that year with food in exchange for all their livestock.

¹⁸When that year was over, they came to him the following year and said, "We cannot hide from our lord the fact that since our money is gone and our livestock belongs to you, there is nothing left for our lord except our bodies and our land. ¹⁹Why should we perish before your eyes—we and our land as well? Buy us and our land in exchange for food, and we with our land will be in bondage to Pharaoh. Give us seed so that we may live and not die, and that the land may not become desolate."

²⁰So Joseph bought all the land in Egypt for Pharaoh. The Egyptians, one and all, sold their fields, because the famine was too severe for them. The land became Pharaoh's, ²¹and Joseph reduced the people to servitude,*c* from one end of Egypt to the other. ²²However, he did not buy the land of the priests, because they received a regular allotment from Pharaoh and had food enough from the allotment Pharaoh gave them. That is why they did not sell their land.

²³Joseph said to the people, "Now that I have bought you and your land today for Pharaoh, here is seed for you so you can plant the ground. ²⁴But when the crop comes in, give a fifth of it to Pharaoh. The other four-fifths you may keep as seed for the fields and as food for yourselves and your households and your children."

²⁵"You have saved our lives," they said. "May we find favor in the eyes of our lord; we will be in bondage to Pharaoh."

Jacob Blessed Pharaoh

GENESIS 47:7–10

How moving to see the dignified old patriarch blessing the pharaoh of all Egypt! Contrast this picture with that of the younger Jacob, conniving for his brother's birthright. Jacob has walked with God all the days of his life, and he bears the mark of God's shaping. His spiritual transformation is almost imperceptible as it is happening; yet at the end of his life God's glory shines through him. Every one of us is invited to the same deepening, loving relationship with God. It may involve difficulties; certainly it will involve counting ourselves as part of the whole people of God. Today, in the midst of all the practical matters of your life, how can you best cooperate with God in your transformation?

See Meeting God in Everyday Life

---

a 7 Or *greeted*   *b 10* Or *said farewell to*   *c 21* Samaritan Pentateuch and Septuagint (see also Vulgate); Masoretic Text *and he moved the people into the cities*

God Blessed Me

GENESIS 48:3–4

We bless others because we have been blessed. At life's end, we gratefully recall moments when we felt God's presence and blessing. Such moments may be intangible and incommunicable, yet they are the most real events of our lives. God gives us these "moments of meeting" for our joy, for our formation into his likeness. God's blessings are formative for us when we recall them often, ponder them and allow grace to enlarge our hearts. Think back over your experience of God and remember several sacred times of encounter with him. Begin a regular discipline of dwelling within those cherished moments. If you do not remember such times, watch attentively for the way God is trying to reach you even now.

See Meeting God in Prayer

²⁶So Joseph established it as a law concerning land in Egypt—still in force today—that a fifth of the produce belongs to Pharaoh. It was only the land of the priests that did not become Pharaoh's.

²⁷Now the Israelites settled in Egypt in the region of Goshen. They acquired property there and were fruitful and increased greatly in number.

²⁸Jacob lived in Egypt seventeen years, and the years of his life were a hundred and forty-seven. ²⁹When the time drew near for Israel to die, he called for his son Joseph and said to him, "If I have found favor in your eyes, put your hand under my thigh and promise that you will show me kindness and faithfulness. Do not bury me in Egypt, ³⁰but when I rest with my fathers, carry me out of Egypt and bury me where they are buried."

"I will do as you say," he said.

³¹"Swear to me," he said. Then Joseph swore to him, and Israel worshiped as he leaned on the top of his staff.ᵃ

Manasseh and Ephraim

48 Some time later Joseph was told, "Your father is ill." So he took his two sons Manasseh and Ephraim along with him. ²When Jacob was told, "Your son Joseph has come to you," Israel rallied his strength and sat up on the bed.

³Jacob said to Joseph, "God Almightyᵇ appeared to me at Luz in the land of Canaan, and there he blessed me ⁴and said to me, 'I am going to make you fruitful and will increase your numbers. I will make you a community of peoples, and I will give this land as an everlasting possession to your descendants after you.'

⁵"Now then, your two sons born to you in Egypt before I came to you here will be reckoned as mine; Ephraim and Manasseh will be mine, just as Reuben and Simeon are mine. ⁶Any children born to you after them will be yours; in the territory they inherit they will be reckoned under the names of their brothers. ⁷As I was returning from Paddan,ᶜ to my sorrow Rachel died in the land of Canaan while we were still on the way, a little distance from Ephrath. So I buried her there beside the road to Ephrath" (that is, Bethlehem).

⁸When Israel saw the sons of Joseph, he asked, "Who are these?"

⁹"They are the sons God has given me here," Joseph said to his father.

Then Israel said, "Bring them to me so I may bless them."

¹⁰Now Israel's eyes were failing because of old age, and he could hardly see. So Joseph brought his sons close to him, and his father kissed them and embraced them.

¹¹Israel said to Joseph, "I never expected to see your face again, and now God has allowed me to see your children too."

¹²Then Joseph removed them from Israel's knees and bowed down with his face to the ground. ¹³And Joseph took both of them, Ephraim on his right toward Israel's left hand and Manasseh on his left toward Israel's right hand, and brought them close to him. ¹⁴But Israel reached out his

---

ᵃ 31 Or *Israel bowed down at the head of his bed*   ᵇ 3 Hebrew *El-Shaddai*
ᶜ 7 That is, Northwest Mesopotamia

right hand and put it on Ephraim's head, though he was the younger, and crossing his arms, he put his left hand on Manasseh's head, even though Manasseh was the firstborn. [15]Then he blessed Joseph and said,

"May the God before whom my fathers
Abraham and Isaac walked,
the God who has been my shepherd
all my life to this day,
[16]the Angel who has delivered me from all harm
—may he bless these boys.
May they be called by my name
and the names of my fathers Abraham and
Isaac,
and may they increase greatly
upon the earth."

[17]When Joseph saw his father placing his right hand on Ephraim's head he was displeased; so he took hold of his father's hand to move it from Ephraim's head to Manasseh's head. [18]Joseph said to him, "No, my father, this one is the firstborn; put your right hand on his head."

[19]But his father refused and said, "I know, my son, I know. He too will become a people, and he too will become great. Nevertheless, his younger brother will be greater than he, and his descendants will become a group of nations." [20]He blessed them that day and said,

"In your[a] name will Israel pronounce this
blessing:
'May God make you like Ephraim and
Manasseh.'"

So he put Ephraim ahead of Manasseh.

[21]Then Israel said to Joseph, "I am about to die, but God will be with you[b] and take you[b] back to the land of your[b] fathers. [22]And to you, as one who is over your brothers, I give the ridge of land[c] I took from the Amorites with my sword and my bow."

Jacob Blesses His Sons

49 Then Jacob called for his sons and said: "Gather around so I can tell you what will happen to you in days to come.

[2]"Assemble and listen, sons of Jacob;
listen to your father Israel.

[3]"Reuben, you are my firstborn,
my might, the first sign of my strength,
excelling in honor, excelling in power.
[4]Turbulent as the waters, you will no longer excel,
for you went up onto your father's bed,
onto my couch and defiled it.

[5]"Simeon and Levi are brothers—
their swords[d] are weapons of violence.
[6]Let me not enter their council,
let me not join their assembly,
for they have killed men in their anger
and hamstrung oxen as they pleased.

God Who is My Shepherd

GENESIS 48:15–16

"Loving, tender Lord! My mind has from the earliest days of my childhood sought something with an earnest thirst of longing, Lord, and what that is I have not yet perfectly apprehended. Lord, I have now for many a year been in hot pursuit of it, and never yet have I been able to succeed, for I know not aright what it is. And yet it is something that draws my heart and my soul after it, and without which I can never attain full repose."

—HENRY SUSO,
Works

---

[a]20 The Hebrew is singular.   [b]21 The Hebrew is plural.   [c]22 Or *And to you I give one portion more than to your brothers—the portion*   [d]5 The meaning of the Hebrew for this word is uncertain.

God of the Future As Well As the Past

GENESIS 49:8–12

Judah is probably the most promising of Leah's sons, and Jacob is generous in blessing him. He remembers the past as he did in blessing his other sons, but here Jacob, in his blessing, looks also to Judah's future, as God does. Our God has been with us in all that is completed, but God also draws us toward the "not yet," the promised fulfillment both of his reign and of our place in it. Can you envision God standing in the future, calling you forth to your very best, unfolding the potential he has given you? Does that possibility change the way you think about the present? Write a poem expressing what you feel and imagine about God's calling and blessing of what is yet to be.

7 Cursed be their anger, so fierce,
    and their fury, so cruel!
I will scatter them in Jacob
    and disperse them in Israel.

8 "Judah,*a* your brothers will praise you;
    your hand will be on the neck of your enemies;
    your father's sons will bow down to you.
9 You are a lion's cub, O Judah;
    you return from the prey, my son.
Like a lion he crouches and lies down,
    like a lioness—who dares to rouse him?
10 The scepter will not depart from Judah,
    nor the ruler's staff from between his feet,
until he comes to whom it belongs*b*
    and the obedience of the nations is his.
11 He will tether his donkey to a vine,
    his colt to the choicest branch;
he will wash his garments in wine,
    his robes in the blood of grapes.
12 His eyes will be darker than wine,
    his teeth whiter than milk.*c*

13 "Zebulun will live by the seashore
    and become a haven for ships;
    his border will extend toward Sidon.

14 "Issachar is a rawboned*d* donkey
    lying down between two saddlebags.*e*
15 When he sees how good is his resting place
    and how pleasant is his land,
he will bend his shoulder to the burden
    and submit to forced labor.

16 "Dan*f* will provide justice for his people
    as one of the tribes of Israel.
17 Dan will be a serpent by the roadside,
    a viper along the path,
that bites the horse's heels
    so that its rider tumbles backward.

18 "I look for your deliverance, O LORD.

19 "Gad*g* will be attacked by a band of raiders,
    but he will attack them at their heels.

20 "Asher's food will be rich;
    he will provide delicacies fit for a king.

21 "Naphtali is a doe set free
    that bears beautiful fawns.*h*

22 "Joseph is a fruitful vine,
    a fruitful vine near a spring,
    whose branches climb over a wall.*i*
23 With bitterness archers attacked him;
    they shot at him with hostility.
24 But his bow remained steady,

a 8 Judah sounds like and may be derived from the Hebrew for praise.
b 10 Or until Shiloh comes; or until he comes to whom tribute belongs
c 12 Or will be dull from wine, / his teeth white from milk   *d 14 Or strong*
e 14 Or campfires   *f 16 Dan here means he provides justice.*   *g 19 Gad can*
mean attack and band of raiders.   *h 21 Or free; / he utters beautiful words*
i 22 Or Joseph is a wild colt, / a wild colt near a spring, / a wild donkey on a
terraced hill

his strong arms stayed[a] limber,
    because of the hand of the Mighty One of Jacob,
    because of the Shepherd, the Rock of Israel,
25 because of your father's God, who helps you,
    because of the Almighty,[b] who blesses you
with blessings of the heavens above,
    blessings of the deep that lies below,
    blessings of the breast and womb.
26 Your father's blessings are greater
    than the blessings of the ancient mountains,
    than[c] the bounty of the age-old hills.
Let all these rest on the head of Joseph,
    on the brow of the prince among[d] his brothers.

27 "Benjamin is a ravenous wolf;
    in the morning he devours the prey,
    in the evening he divides the plunder."

28 All these are the twelve tribes of Israel, and this is what their father said to them when he blessed them, giving each the blessing appropriate to him.

The Death of Jacob

29 Then he gave them these instructions: "I am about to be gathered to my people. Bury me with my fathers in the cave in the field of Ephron the Hittite, 30 the cave in the field of Machpelah, near Mamre in Canaan, which Abraham bought as a burial place from Ephron the Hittite, along with the field. 31 There Abraham and his wife Sarah were buried, there Isaac and his wife Rebekah were buried, and there I buried Leah. 32 The field and the cave in it were bought from the Hittites.[e]"

33 When Jacob had finished giving instructions to his sons, he drew his feet up into the bed, breathed his last and was gathered to his people.

50 Joseph threw himself upon his father and wept over him and kissed him. 2 Then Joseph directed the physicians in his service to embalm his father Israel. So the physicians embalmed him, 3 taking a full forty days, for that was the time required for embalming. And the Egyptians mourned for him seventy days.

4 When the days of mourning had passed, Joseph said to Pharaoh's court, "If I have found favor in your eyes, speak to Pharaoh for me. Tell him, 5 'My father made me swear an oath and said, "I am about to die; bury me in the tomb I dug for myself in the land of Canaan." Now let me go up and bury my father; then I will return.' "

6 Pharaoh said, "Go up and bury your father, as he made you swear to do."

7 So Joseph went up to bury his father. All Pharaoh's officials accompanied him—the dignitaries of his court and all the dignitaries of Egypt— 8 besides all the members of Joseph's household and his brothers and those belonging to his father's household. Only their children and their flocks and herds were left in Goshen. 9 Chariots and horsemen[f] also went up with him. It was a very large company.

10 When they reached the threshing floor of Atad, near the Jordan, they lamented loudly and bitterly; and there Jo-

The Almighty Who Blesses

GENESIS 49:24-25

We bless God and God blesses us and that is everything. But what *is* blessing? The essence of blessing is to be in relationship with Almighty God, to be dedicated to him and encouraged by him. Apart from that relationship, blessing makes no sense. If you were to describe blessing to someone who did not speak English, could you communicate its meaning with gestures or signs? Decide on a nonverbal "explanation" and see whether your best friend can understand it. How about developing a game of "holy charades" in which each team tries to identify words of faith as they are wordlessly acted out by the other team?

See *Meeting God in Everyday Life*

---

a 23,24 Or *archers will attack . . . will shoot . . . will remain . . . will stay*
b 25 Hebrew *Shaddai*   c 26 Or *of my progenitors, / as great as*   d 26 Or the *one separated from*   e 32 Or *the sons of Heth*   f 9 Or *charioteers*

He Reassured Them

GENESIS 50:21

"To conclude your meditation
. . . you must gather a little devotional bouquet. I explain my
meaning. People who have been
walking about in a beautiful
garden do not like to leave
without gathering in their
hands four or five flowers to
smell and keep for the rest of
the day. In the same way, when
our soul has carefully considered by meditation a certain
mystery, we should select one,
two, or three points that we
liked best and that are most
adapted to our improvement,
think frequently about them,
and smell them spiritually during the rest of the day."

—FRANCIS DE SALES,
Introduction to the Devout Life

See Meeting God in Prayer

seph observed a seven-day period of mourning for his fa-
ther. [11]When the Canaanites who lived there saw the
mourning at the threshing floor of Atad, they said, "The
Egyptians are holding a solemn ceremony of mourning."
That is why that place near the Jordan is called Abel
Mizraim.[a]

[12]So Jacob's sons did as he had commanded them:
[13]They carried him to the land of Canaan and buried him in
the cave in the field of Machpelah, near Mamre, which
Abraham had bought as a burial place from Ephron the Hittite, along with the field. [14]After burying his father, Joseph
returned to Egypt, together with his brothers and all the
others who had gone with him to bury his father.

Joseph Reassures His Brothers

[15]When Joseph's brothers saw that their father was dead,
they said, "What if Joseph holds a grudge against us and
pays us back for all the wrongs we did to him?" [16]So they
sent word to Joseph, saying, "Your father left these instructions before he died: [17]'This is what you are to say to Joseph: I ask you to forgive your brothers the sins and the
wrongs they committed in treating you so badly.' Now
please forgive the sins of the servants of the God of your father." When their message came to him, Joseph wept.

[18]His brothers then came and threw themselves down
before him. "We are your slaves," they said.

[19]But Joseph said to them, "Don't be afraid. Am I in the
place of God? [20]You intended to harm me, but God intended it for good to accomplish what is now being done, the
saving of many lives. [21]So then, don't be afraid. I will provide for you and your children." And he reassured them
and spoke kindly to them.

The Death of Joseph

[22]Joseph stayed in Egypt, along with all his father's family. He lived a hundred and ten years [23]and saw the third
generation of Ephraim's children. Also the children of
Makir son of Manasseh were placed at birth on Joseph's
knees.[b]

[24]Then Joseph said to his brothers, "I am about to die. But
God will surely come to your aid and take you up out of this
land to the land he promised on oath to Abraham, Isaac
and Jacob." [25]And Joseph made the sons of Israel swear an
oath and said, "God will surely come to your aid, and then
you must carry my bones up from this place."

[26]So Joseph died at the age of a hundred and ten. And
after they embalmed him, he was placed in a coffin in
Egypt.

---

[a] 11 *Abel Mizraim* means *mourning of the Egyptians.*   [b] 23 That is, were
counted as his

EXODUS
Journey From Bondage to Liberation

KEY VERSE:

The LORD said, "I have indeed seen the misery of my people in Egypt. I have heard them crying out because of their slave drivers, and I am concerned about their suffering."—Exodus 3:7

Among all the books of the canon, Biblical writers quote or refer to Exodus more often than any other book. Though numerically second in the vast collection of the Hebrew Scriptures, it has played a foundational role in the development of both Hebrew and Christian traditions. The earliest Christian writers carefully probed this book as they gave expression to the message and meaning of the life of Jesus.

Exodus abounds with themes of profound relevance to the Christian life. As you prayerfully read this book, give special attention to the symbols and images (such as the sacrificial lamb) that resurface in the Gospels. Try to identify with the new nation of Israel as they experience God's hand in their corporate life. Be alert especially to these events and images: the giving of the manna or bread of life, the guiding presence of fire and cloud, the centrality of the tabernacle and tent, and the mountain as a meeting place with God.

Don't read Exodus as a spectator! Watch for opportunities to put yourself in the story, to interact with the narrative. In what ways can you identify with Moses? His self-doubt? His hesitancy to answer God's call to take responsibility for others? His frustration? Or, as you follow Moses up the mountain to converse with God as a "man speaks with his friend" (Exodus 33:11), do you find yourself hungering for intimacy with God? The Exodus story is ultimately the story of all God's people from age to age, and it can become your story too.

> "Lord God, in the new covenant you shed light on the miracles you worked in ancient times: the Red Sea is a symbol of our baptism, and the nation you freed from slavery is a sign of your Christian people."
>
> —Roman Missal, "Prayer at Easter Vigil"

Transitions

EXODUS 1:1–12

"Then a new king, who did not know about Joseph, came to power in Egypt." In one chilling sentence the fate of a people is sealed. The comforts and certainties they have known will be shattered. Who of us cannot look back on our own lives and recall a loss that seemed to mark the end of our world: a divorce, a downsizing, the death of a child? What spiritual truths do you cling to when you believe you have lost everything? Or what wise and holy person do you trust to say the helpful thing? Do you have a group of people, a spiritual family, that sustains you during dark periods? If you have these aids in your life, thank God for them; if not, ask for God's presence to sustain you and to help you find other divine solutions.

See Meeting God in Everyday Life

The Israelites Oppressed

1 These are the names of the sons of Israel who went to Egypt with Jacob, each with his family: ²Reuben, Simeon, Levi and Judah; ³Issachar, Zebulun and Benjamin; ⁴Dan and Naphtali; Gad and Asher. ⁵The descendants of Jacob numbered seventy[a] in all; Joseph was already in Egypt.

⁶Now Joseph and all his brothers and all that generation died, ⁷but the Israelites were fruitful and multiplied greatly and became exceedingly numerous, so that the land was filled with them.

⁸Then a new king, who did not know about Joseph, came to power in Egypt. ⁹"Look," he said to his people, "the Israelites have become much too numerous for us. ¹⁰Come, we must deal shrewdly with them or they will become even more numerous and, if war breaks out, will join our enemies, fight against us and leave the country."

¹¹So they put slave masters over them to oppress them with forced labor, and they built Pithom and Rameses as store cities for Pharaoh. ¹²But the more they were oppressed, the more they multiplied and spread; so the Egyptians came to dread the Israelites ¹³and worked them ruthlessly. ¹⁴They made their lives bitter with hard labor in brick and mortar and with all kinds of work in the fields; in all their hard labor the Egyptians used them ruthlessly.

¹⁵The king of Egypt said to the Hebrew midwives, whose names were Shiphrah and Puah, ¹⁶"When you help the Hebrew women in childbirth and observe them on the delivery stool, if it is a boy, kill him; but if it is a girl, let her live." ¹⁷The midwives, however, feared God and did not do what the king of Egypt had told them to do; they let the boys live. ¹⁸Then the king of Egypt summoned the midwives and asked them, "Why have you done this? Why have you let the boys live?"

¹⁹The midwives answered Pharaoh, "Hebrew women are not like Egyptian women; they are vigorous and give birth before the midwives arrive."

²⁰So God was kind to the midwives and the people increased and became even more numerous. ²¹And because the midwives feared God, he gave them families of their own.

²²Then Pharaoh gave this order to all his people: "Every boy that is born[b] you must throw into the Nile, but let every girl live."

The Birth of Moses

2 Now a man of the house of Levi married a Levite woman, ²and she became pregnant and gave birth to a son. When she saw that he was a fine child, she hid him for three months. ³But when she could hide him no longer, she got a papyrus basket for him and coated it with tar and pitch. Then she placed the child in it and put it among the reeds along the bank of the Nile. ⁴His sister stood at a distance to see what would happen to him.

⁵Then Pharaoh's daughter went down to the Nile to bathe, and her attendants were walking along the river bank. She saw the basket among the reeds and sent her slave girl to get it. ⁶She opened it and saw the baby. He was

a 5 Masoretic Text (see also Gen. 46:27); Dead Sea Scrolls and Septuagint (see also Acts 7:14 and note at Gen. 46:27) *seventy-five* *b 22* Masoretic Text; Samaritan Pentateuch, Septuagint and Targums *born to the Hebrews*

crying, and she felt sorry for him. "This is one of the He-brew babies," she said.

⁷Then his sister asked Pharaoh's daughter, "Shall I go and get one of the Hebrew women to nurse the baby for you?"

⁸"Yes, go," she answered. And the girl went and got the baby's mother. ⁹Pharaoh's daughter said to her, "Take this baby and nurse him for me, and I will pay you." So the woman took the baby and nursed him. ¹⁰When the child grew older, she took him to Pharaoh's daughter and he be-came her son. She named him Moses,ᵃ saying, "I drew him out of the water."

Moses Flees to Midian

¹¹One day, after Moses had grown up, he went out to where his own people were and watched them at their hard labor. He saw an Egyptian beating a Hebrew, one of his own people. ¹²Glancing this way and that and seeing no one, he killed the Egyptian and hid him in the sand. ¹³The next day he went out and saw two Hebrews fighting. He asked the one in the wrong, "Why are you hitting your fel-low Hebrew?"

¹⁴The man said, "Who made you ruler and judge over us? Are you thinking of killing me as you killed the Egyp-tian?" Then Moses was afraid and thought, "What I did must have become known."

¹⁵When Pharaoh heard of this, he tried to kill Moses, but Moses fled from Pharaoh and went to live in Midian, where he sat down by a well. ¹⁶Now a priest of Midian had seven daughters, and they came to draw water and fill the troughs to water their father's flock. ¹⁷Some shepherds came along and drove them away, but Moses got up and came to their rescue and watered their flock.

¹⁸When the girls returned to Reuel their father, he asked them, "Why have you returned so early today?"

¹⁹They answered, "An Egyptian rescued us from the shepherds. He even drew water for us and watered the flock."

²⁰"And where is he?" he asked his daughters. "Why did you leave him? Invite him to have something to eat."

²¹Moses agreed to stay with the man, who gave his daughter Zipporah to Moses in marriage. ²²Zipporah gave birth to a son, and Moses named him Gershom,ᵇ saying, "I have become an alien in a foreign land."

²³During that long period, the king of Egypt died. The Is-raelites groaned in their slavery and cried out, and their cry for help because of their slavery went up to God. ²⁴God heard their groaning and he remembered his covenant with Abraham, with Isaac and with Jacob. ²⁵So God looked on the Israelites and was concerned about them.

Moses and the Burning Bush

3 Now Moses was tending the flock of Jethro his father-in-law, the priest of Midian, and he led the flock to the far side of the desert and came to Horeb, the mountain of God. ²There the angel of the Lord appeared to him in flames of fire from within a bush. Moses saw that though the bush was on fire it did not burn up. ³So Moses thought,

Baby in a Basket

EXODUS 2:6–14

The story of the baby Moses in the basket reveals a strange paradox: Pharaoh's power is threatened by the weakness of an infant. How can this be? In a way, the baby's salvation lies in his helplessness, in the fact that what happens next hinges on God's intervention. The little baby floats quietly in a basket right into the halls of power.

When we are humble, we learn to depend on a power be-yond ourselves. Reflect on how you handle the threatening and troubling situations in your life. The next time you find yourself a basket case, think of Moses floating in his little ark. Let go. Let God.

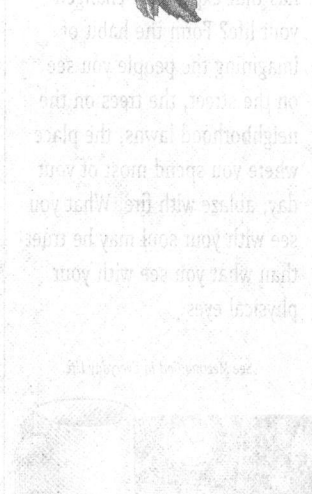

ᵃ 10 *Moses* sounds like the Hebrew for *draw out.*   ᵇ 22 *Gershom* sounds like the Hebrew for *an alien there.*

Burning Bushes

EXODUS 3:1–12

The burning bush can be seen as a metaphor for all of creation—it is afire with God. This story illustrates that any place can become a meeting place with God and that God can break into our lives when we least expect it. Who would have thought simply going to work in the morning (as Moses did) could lead to an experience that would turn one's whole life around? When we encounter God we come to a deeper level of awareness of the Presence that is around us, within us and yet beyond us.

Have you ever had a "burning bush" experience? Think back on a person or event that gave you a special sense of encounter with the Holy One. How has that experience changed your life? Form the habit of imagining the people you see on the street, the trees on the neighborhood lawns, the place where you spend most of your day, ablaze with fire. What you see with your soul may be truer than what you see with your physical eyes.

See Meeting God in Everyday Life

"I will go over and see this strange sight—why the bush does not burn up."

⁴When the LORD saw that he had gone over to look, God called to him from within the bush, "Moses! Moses!"

And Moses said, "Here I am."

⁵"Do not come any closer," God said. "Take off your sandals, for the place where you are standing is holy ground." ⁶Then he said, "I am the God of your father, the God of Abraham, the God of Isaac and the God of Jacob." At this, Moses hid his face, because he was afraid to look at God.

⁷The LORD said, "I have indeed seen the misery of my people in Egypt. I have heard them crying out because of their slave drivers, and I am concerned about their suffering. ⁸So I have come down to rescue them from the hand of the Egyptians and to bring them up out of that land into a good and spacious land, a land flowing with milk and honey—the home of the Canaanites, Hittites, Amorites, Perizzites, Hivites and Jebusites. ⁹And now the cry of the Israelites has reached me, and I have seen the way the Egyptians are oppressing them. ¹⁰So now, go. I am sending you to Pharaoh to bring my people the Israelites out of Egypt."

¹¹But Moses said to God, "Who am I, that I should go to Pharaoh and bring the Israelites out of Egypt?"

¹²And God said, "I will be with you. And this will be the sign to you that it is I who have sent you: When you have brought the people out of Egypt, you*ᵃ* will worship God on this mountain."

¹³Moses said to God, "Suppose I go to the Israelites and say to them, 'The God of your fathers has sent me to you,' and they ask me, 'What is his name?' Then what shall I tell them?"

¹⁴God said to Moses, "I AM WHO I AM.*ᵇ* This is what you are to say to the Israelites: 'I AM has sent me to you.' "

¹⁵God also said to Moses, "Say to the Israelites, 'The LORD,*ᶜ* the God of your fathers—the God of Abraham, the God of Isaac and the God of Jacob—has sent me to you.' This is my name forever, the name by which I am to be remembered from generation to generation.

¹⁶"Go, assemble the elders of Israel and say to them, 'The LORD, the God of your fathers—the God of Abraham, Isaac and Jacob—appeared to me and said: I have watched over you and have seen what has been done to you in Egypt. ¹⁷And I have promised to bring you up out of your misery in Egypt into the land of the Canaanites, Hittites, Amorites, Perizzites, Hivites and Jebusites—a land flowing with milk and honey.'

¹⁸"The elders of Israel will listen to you. Then you and the elders are to go to the king of Egypt and say to him, 'The LORD, the God of the Hebrews, has met with us. Let us take a three-day journey into the desert to offer sacrifices to the LORD our God.' ¹⁹But I know that the king of Egypt will not let you go unless a mighty hand compels him. ²⁰So I will stretch out my hand and strike the Egyptians with all the wonders that I will perform among them. After that, he will let you go.

²¹"And I will make the Egyptians favorably disposed toward this people, so that when you leave you will not go

---

ᵃ 12 The Hebrew is plural.   *ᵇ 14* Or *I WILL BE WHAT I WILL BE*   *ᶜ 15* The Hebrew for LORD sounds like and may be derived from the Hebrew for *I AM* in verse 14.

empty-handed. ²²Every woman is to ask her neighbor and any woman living in her house for articles of silver and gold and for clothing, which you will put on your sons and daughters. And so you will plunder the Egyptians."

Signs for Moses

4 Moses answered, "What if they do not believe me or listen to me and say, 'The LORD did not appear to you'?"

²Then the LORD said to him, "What is that in your hand?"

"A staff," he replied.

³The LORD said, "Throw it on the ground."

Moses threw it on the ground and it became a snake, and he ran from it. ⁴Then the LORD said to him, "Reach out your hand and take it by the tail." So Moses reached out and took hold of the snake and it turned back into a staff in his hand. ⁵"This," said the LORD, "is so that they may believe that the LORD, the God of their fathers—the God of Abraham, the God of Isaac and the God of Jacob—has appeared to you."

⁶Then the LORD said, "Put your hand inside your cloak." So Moses put his hand into his cloak, and when he took it out, it was leprous,ᵃ like snow.

⁷"Now put it back into your cloak," he said. So Moses put his hand back into his cloak, and when he took it out, it was restored, like the rest of his flesh.

⁸Then the LORD said, "If they do not believe you or pay attention to the first miraculous sign, they may believe the second. ⁹But if they do not believe these two signs or listen to you, take some water from the Nile and pour it on the dry ground. The water you take from the river will become blood on the ground."

¹⁰Moses said to the LORD, "O Lord, I have never been eloquent, neither in the past nor since you have spoken to your servant. I am slow of speech and tongue."

¹¹The LORD said to him, "Who gave man his mouth? Who makes him deaf or mute? Who gives him sight or makes him blind? Is it not I, the LORD? ¹²Now go; I will help you speak and will teach you what to say."

¹³But Moses said, "O Lord, please send someone else to do it."

¹⁴Then the LORD's anger burned against Moses and he said, "What about your brother, Aaron the Levite? I know he can speak well. He is already on his way to meet you, and his heart will be glad when he sees you. ¹⁵You shall speak to him and put words in his mouth; I will help both of you speak and will teach you what to do. ¹⁶He will speak to the people for you, and it will be as if he were your mouth and as if you were God to him. ¹⁷But take this staff in your hand so you can perform miraculous signs with it."

Moses Returns to Egypt

¹⁸Then Moses went back to Jethro his father-in-law and said to him, "Let me go back to my own people in Egypt to see if any of them are still alive."

Jethro said, "Go, and I wish you well."

¹⁹Now the LORD had said to Moses in Midian, "Go back to Egypt, for all the men who wanted to kill you are dead." ²⁰So Moses took his wife and sons, put them on a donkey

---

Closing the Credibility Gap

EXODUS 4:1-17

What if they do not believe me or listen to me? This is the question that haunts the soul of every preacher and minister and teacher. The same question should haunt the mind of every Christian. What sign shall we give to the people we speak to? What proof shall we offer today to convince others that we speak in the name of God? We want to offer a sign of credibility to those with whom we work, to our families, to friends, and even to our enemies. God speaks to us as he spoke to Moses: "I will help you speak and will teach you what to say." Today, before you speak, ask yourself: "Is what I am about to say necessary? And if it is necessary, is God in it?"

See *Meeting God in Community*

ᵃ 6 The Hebrew word was used for various diseases affecting the skin—not necessarily leprosy.

The Sign That Convinces

EXODUS 4:21–31

"Even if it is perhaps possible for doctors to cure patients even when the doctors hardly believe in the value of life, Christian ministers will never be able to minister if their own most personal faith and insight into life do not form the core of their pastoral work. So ministry and spirituality never can be separated. Ministry is not an eight-to-five job but primarily a way of life, which is for others to see and understand so that liberation can become a possibility."

—HENRI J. M. NOUWEN,
Creative Ministry

and started back to Egypt. And he took the staff of God in his hand.

²¹The LORD said to Moses, "When you return to Egypt, see that you perform before Pharaoh all the wonders I have given you the power to do. But I will harden his heart so that he will not let the people go. ²²Then say to Pharaoh, 'This is what the LORD says: Israel is my firstborn son, ²³and I told you, "Let my son go, so he may worship me." But you refused to let him go; so I will kill your firstborn son.' "

²⁴At a lodging place on the way, the LORD met ⌊Moses⌋ᵃ and was about to kill him. ²⁵But Zipporah took a flint knife, cut off her son's foreskin and touched ⌊Moses'⌋ feet with it.ᵇ "Surely you are a bridegroom of blood to me," she said. ²⁶So the LORD let him alone. (At that time she said "bridegroom of blood," referring to circumcision.)

²⁷The LORD said to Aaron, "Go into the desert to meet Moses." So he met Moses at the mountain of God and kissed him. ²⁸Then Moses told Aaron everything the LORD had sent him to say, and also about all the miraculous signs he had commanded him to perform.

²⁹Moses and Aaron brought together all the elders of the Israelites, ³⁰and Aaron told them everything the LORD had said to Moses. He also performed the signs before the people, ³¹and they believed. And when they heard that the LORD was concerned about them and had seen their misery, they bowed down and worshiped.

Bricks Without Straw

5 Afterward Moses and Aaron went to Pharaoh and said, "This is what the LORD, the God of Israel, says: 'Let my people go, so that they may hold a festival to me in the desert.' "

²Pharaoh said, "Who is the LORD, that I should obey him and let Israel go? I do not know the LORD and I will not let Israel go."

³Then they said, "The God of the Hebrews has met with us. Now let us take a three-day journey into the desert to offer sacrifices to the LORD our God, or he may strike us with plagues or with the sword."

⁴But the king of Egypt said, "Moses and Aaron, why are you taking the people away from their labor? Get back to your work!" ⁵Then Pharaoh said, "Look, the people of the land are now numerous, and you are stopping them from working."

⁶That same day Pharaoh gave this order to the slave drivers and foremen in charge of the people: ⁷"You are no longer to supply the people with straw for making bricks; let them go and gather their own straw. ⁸But require them to make the same number of bricks as before; don't reduce the quota. They are lazy; that is why they are crying out, 'Let us go and sacrifice to our God.' ⁹Make the work harder for the men so that they keep working and pay no attention to lies."

¹⁰Then the slave drivers and the foremen went out and said to the people, "This is what Pharaoh says: 'I will not give you any more straw. ¹¹Go and get your own straw wherever you can find it, but your work will not be reduced at all.' " ¹²So the people scattered all over Egypt to gather stubble to use for straw. ¹³The slave drivers kept pressing

ᵃ 24 Or ⌊Moses' son⌋; Hebrew *him*   ᵇ 25 Or *and drew near* ⌊Moses'⌋ *feet* them, saying, "Complete the work required of you for each day, just as when you had straw." ¹⁴The Israelite foremen appointed by Pharaoh's slave drivers were beaten and were asked, "Why didn't you meet your quota of bricks yesterday or today, as before?"

¹⁵Then the Israelite foremen went and appealed to Pharaoh: "Why have you treated your servants this way? ¹⁶Your servants are given no straw, yet we are told, 'Make bricks!' Your servants are being beaten, but the fault is with your own people."

¹⁷Pharaoh said, "Lazy, that's what you are—lazy! That is why you keep saying, 'Let us go and sacrifice to the LORD.' ¹⁸Now get to work. You will not be given any straw, yet you must produce your full quota of bricks."

¹⁹The Israelite foremen realized they were in trouble when they were told, "You are not to reduce the number of bricks required of you for each day." ²⁰When they left Pharaoh, they found Moses and Aaron waiting to meet them, ²¹and they said, "May the LORD look upon you and judge you! You have made us a stench to Pharaoh and his officials and have put a sword in their hand to kill us."

God Promises Deliverance

²²Moses returned to the LORD and said, "O Lord, why have you brought trouble upon this people? Is this why you sent me? ²³Ever since I went to Pharaoh to speak in your name, he has brought trouble upon this people, and you have not rescued your people at all."

6 Then the LORD said to Moses, "Now you will see what I will do to Pharaoh: Because of my mighty hand he will let them go; because of my mighty hand he will drive them out of his country."

²God also said to Moses, "I am the LORD. ³I appeared to Abraham, to Isaac and to Jacob as God Almighty,ᵃ but by my name the LORDᵇ I did not make myself known to them.ᶜ ⁴I also established my covenant with them to give them the land of Canaan, where they lived as aliens. ⁵Moreover, I have heard the groaning of the Israelites, whom the Egyptians are enslaving, and I have remembered my covenant.

⁶"Therefore, say to the Israelites: 'I am the LORD, and I will bring you out from under the yoke of the Egyptians. I will free you from being slaves to them, and I will redeem you with an outstretched arm and with mighty acts of judgment. ⁷I will take you as my own people, and I will be your God. Then you will know that I am the LORD your God, who brought you out from under the yoke of the Egyptians. ⁸And I will bring you to the land I swore with uplifted hand to give to Abraham, to Isaac and to Jacob. I will give it to you as a possession. I am the LORD.' "

⁹Moses reported this to the Israelites, but they did not listen to him because of their discouragement and cruel bondage.

¹⁰Then the LORD said to Moses, ¹¹"Go, tell Pharaoh king of Egypt to let the Israelites go out of his country."

¹²But Moses said to the LORD, "If the Israelites will not listen to me, why would Pharaoh listen to me, since I speak with faltering lipsᵈ?"

ᵃ 3 Hebrew El-Shaddai   ᵇ 3 See note at Exodus 3:15.   ᶜ 3 Or Almighty, and by my name the LORD did I not let myself be known to them?
ᵈ 12 Hebrew I am uncircumcised of lips; also in verse 30

Remember the Covenant

EXODUS 6:2–8

God tells Moses that the groans of the enslaved Hebrew people were heard and that "I have remembered my covenant." With words that echo throughout the Bible as the very definition of this covenant, God says, "I will take you as my own people, and I will be your God."

There comes a time when every faithful person wonders if God has heard them in their distress. Take time today to find or create some symbol of God's covenant with you so that you will remember that God hears you. Make it as durable as possible to remind you of the permanency of God's plans. Perhaps you can write it on official-looking paper as if it were a law passed by Congress: "Be it resolved, I am your God and you are my people." Or have a stone mason engrave these words on a large piece of masonry, or have them written on a bracelet of some fine metal. Ask God in prayer to help you keep this covenant ever before your eyes.

See Meeting God in Scripture

Fulfilling the Dream

EXODUS 6:12–13

As believers, we are the privileged recipients of divine revelation. But we also discover that, like Moses, we are commissioned to carry that revelation to others, even when it means controversy, even when we address issues that may upset others, even when it means breaking through the barriers of discouragement. Where do we find the courage to do so? Make a list of the controversial issues that divide people in your family or community today. What issues need to be addressed? How can you prepare to say the things that need to be said? (See 2 Timothy 4:2 for guidelines.) Like Moses, ask God to prepare the way for you.

See Meeting God in Community

Family Record of Moses and Aaron

¹³Now the LORD spoke to Moses and Aaron about the Israelites and Pharaoh king of Egypt, and he commanded them to bring the Israelites out of Egypt.

¹⁴These were the heads of their families*ᵃ*:

The sons of Reuben the firstborn son of Israel were Hanoch and Pallu, Hezron and Carmi. These were the clans of Reuben.

¹⁵The sons of Simeon were Jemuel, Jamin, Ohad, Jakin, Zohar and Shaul the son of a Canaanite woman. These were the clans of Simeon.

¹⁶These were the names of the sons of Levi according to their records: Gershon, Kohath and Merari. Levi lived 137 years.

¹⁷The sons of Gershon, by clans, were Libni and Shimei.

¹⁸The sons of Kohath were Amram, Izhar, Hebron and Uzziel. Kohath lived 133 years.

¹⁹The sons of Merari were Mahli and Mushi.

These were the clans of Levi according to their records.

²⁰Amram married his father's sister Jochebed, who bore him Aaron and Moses. Amram lived 137 years.

²¹The sons of Izhar were Korah, Nepheg and Zicri.

²²The sons of Uzziel were Mishael, Elzaphan and Sithri.

²³Aaron married Elisheba, daughter of Amminadab and sister of Nahshon, and she bore him Nadab and Abihu, Eleazar and Ithamar.

²⁴The sons of Korah were Assir, Elkanah and Abiasaph. These were the Korahite clans.

²⁵Eleazar son of Aaron married one of the daughters of Putiel, and she bore him Phinehas.

These were the heads of the Levite families, clan by clan.

²⁶It was this same Aaron and Moses to whom the LORD said, "Bring the Israelites out of Egypt by their divisions." ²⁷They were the ones who spoke to Pharaoh king of Egypt about bringing the Israelites out of Egypt. It was the same Moses and Aaron.

Aaron to Speak for Moses

²⁸Now when the LORD spoke to Moses in Egypt, ²⁹he said to him, "I am the LORD. Tell Pharaoh king of Egypt everything I tell you."

³⁰But Moses said to the LORD, "Since I speak with faltering lips, why would Pharaoh listen to me?"

7 Then the LORD said to Moses, "See, I have made you like God to Pharaoh, and your brother Aaron will be your prophet. ²You are to say everything I command you, and your brother Aaron is to tell Pharaoh to let the Israelites go out of his country. ³But I will harden Pharaoh's heart, and though I multiply my miraculous signs and wonders in Egypt, ⁴he will not listen to you. Then I will lay my hand on Egypt and with mighty acts of judgment I will bring out my

ᵃ 14 The Hebrew for *families* here and in verse 25 refers to units larger than clans.

divisions, my people the Israelites. ⁵And the Egyptians will know that I am the LORD when I stretch out my hand against Egypt and bring the Israelites out of it."

⁶Moses and Aaron did just as the LORD commanded them. ⁷Moses was eighty years old and Aaron eighty-three when they spoke to Pharaoh.

Aaron's Staff Becomes a Snake

⁸The LORD said to Moses and Aaron, ⁹"When Pharaoh says to you, 'Perform a miracle,' then say to Aaron, 'Take your staff and throw it down before Pharaoh,' and it will become a snake."

¹⁰So Moses and Aaron went to Pharaoh and did just as the LORD commanded. Aaron threw his staff down in front of Pharaoh and his officials, and it became a snake. ¹¹Pharaoh then summoned wise men and sorcerers, and the Egyptian magicians also did the same things by their secret arts: ¹²Each one threw down his staff and it became a snake. But Aaron's staff swallowed up their staffs. ¹³Yet Pharaoh's heart became hard and he would not listen to them, just as the LORD had said.

The Plague of Blood

¹⁴Then the LORD said to Moses, "Pharaoh's heart is unyielding; he refuses to let the people go. ¹⁵Go to Pharaoh in the morning as he goes out to the water. Wait on the bank of the Nile to meet him, and take in your hand the staff that was changed into a snake. ¹⁶Then say to him, 'The LORD, the God of the Hebrews, has sent me to say to you: Let my people go, so that they may worship me in the desert. But until now you have not listened. ¹⁷This is what the LORD says: By this you will know that I am the LORD: With the staff that is in my hand I will strike the water of the Nile, and it will be changed into blood. ¹⁸The fish in the Nile will die, and the river will stink; the Egyptians will not be able to drink its water.' "

¹⁹The LORD said to Moses, "Tell Aaron, 'Take your staff and stretch out your hand over the waters of Egypt—over the streams and canals, over the ponds and all the reservoirs'—and they will turn to blood. Blood will be everywhere in Egypt, even in the wooden buckets and stone jars."

²⁰Moses and Aaron did just as the LORD had commanded. He raised his staff in the presence of Pharaoh and his officials and struck the water of the Nile, and all the water was changed into blood. ²¹The fish in the Nile died, and the river smelled so bad that the Egyptians could not drink its water. Blood was everywhere in Egypt.

²²But the Egyptian magicians did the same things by their secret arts, and Pharaoh's heart became hard; he would not listen to Moses and Aaron, just as the LORD had said. ²³Instead, he turned and went into his palace, and did not take even this to heart. ²⁴And all the Egyptians dug along the Nile to get drinking water, because they could not drink the water of the river.

The Plague of Frogs

8 ²⁵Seven days passed after the LORD struck the Nile. ¹Then the LORD said to Moses, "Go to Pharaoh and say to him, 'This is what the LORD says: Let my people go, so

Turning Rivers to Blood

EXODUS 7:14–25

Whole rivers turned into blood? At first sight this miracle seems beyond belief. Yet it issues a powerful statement that commands our attention: God speaks to us through the signs and forces of nature. Sometimes it is not hard to hear. We willingly listen to God speaking to us through the beauty of a sunrise or a rushing, foaming waterfall. But do we listen as carefully when God speaks to us through a calamity such as a hurricane or tornado?

By using Moses to change rivers into blood, God gave Pharaoh a strong message: God, the creator of all, was not to be trifled with. Spend time now contemplating the awesome power of God, who sees the nations as "a drop in the bucket," who "weighs the islands as though they were fine dust" (Isaiah 40:15). Draw a picture of a tornado, volcano, sunrise or waterfall, or find a picture in a magazine. Place it on your refrigerator or at your work station to remind you of God's awesome power.

See Meeting God in the Created Order

Frogs, Gnats and Flies

EXODUS 8:1–24

Frogs, gnats and flies do not ordinarily claim much of our attention. They are nuisances we merely tolerate—at least until they get in our soup or crawl up our pants, or climb our walls, or burrow their way under our bed sheets. Pharaoh, too, took these creatures for granted until they became God's means to get his attention. Then Pharaoh listened—for a while. When relief came in answer to Moses' prayer, Pharaoh went back to his old ways.

Reflect now on ways petty annoyances such as heavy traffic, cold symptoms and lost keys can become occasions for turning to God. Ask God to help you be spiritually sensitive to what you can learn from the daily nuisances and irritations of life.

See Meeting God in Everyday Life

that they may worship me. ²If you refuse to let them go, I will plague your whole country with frogs. ³The Nile will teem with frogs. They will come up into your palace and your bedroom and onto your bed, into the houses of your officials and on your people, and into your ovens and kneading troughs. ⁴The frogs will go up on you and your people and all your officials.' "

⁵Then the LORD said to Moses, "Tell Aaron, 'Stretch out your hand with your staff over the streams and canals and ponds, and make frogs come up on the land of Egypt.' "

⁶So Aaron stretched out his hand over the waters of Egypt, and the frogs came up and covered the land. ⁷But the magicians did the same things by their secret arts; they also made frogs come up on the land of Egypt.

⁸Pharaoh summoned Moses and Aaron and said, "Pray to the LORD to take the frogs away from me and my people, and I will let your people go to offer sacrifices to the LORD."

⁹Moses said to Pharaoh, "I leave to you the honor of setting the time for me to pray for you and your officials and your people that you and your houses may be rid of the frogs, except for those that remain in the Nile."

¹⁰"Tomorrow," Pharaoh said.

Moses replied, "It will be as you say, so that you may know there is no one like the LORD our God. ¹¹The frogs will leave you and your houses, your officials and your people; they will remain only in the Nile."

¹²After Moses and Aaron left Pharaoh, Moses cried out to the LORD about the frogs he had brought on Pharaoh. ¹³And the LORD did what Moses asked. The frogs died in the houses, in the courtyards and in the fields. ¹⁴They were piled into heaps, and the land reeked of them. ¹⁵But when Pharaoh saw that there was relief, he hardened his heart and would not listen to Moses and Aaron, just as the LORD had said.

The Plague of Gnats

¹⁶Then the LORD said to Moses, "Tell Aaron, 'Stretch out your staff and strike the dust of the ground,' and throughout the land of Egypt the dust will become gnats." ¹⁷They did this, and when Aaron stretched out his hand with the staff and struck the dust of the ground, gnats came upon men and animals. All the dust throughout the land of Egypt became gnats. ¹⁸But when the magicians tried to produce gnats by their secret arts, they could not. And the gnats were on men and animals.

¹⁹The magicians said to Pharaoh, "This is the finger of God." But Pharaoh's heart was hard and he would not listen, just as the LORD had said.

The Plague of Flies

²⁰Then the LORD said to Moses, "Get up early in the morning and confront Pharaoh as he goes to the water and say to him, 'This is what the LORD says: Let my people go, so that they may worship me. ²¹If you do not let my people go, I will send swarms of flies on you and your officials, on your people and into your houses. The houses of the Egyptians will be full of flies, and even the ground where they are.

²²" 'But on that day I will deal differently with the land of Goshen, where my people live; no swarms of flies will be

there, so that you will know that I, the LORD, am in this land. ²³I will make a distinction[a] between my people and your people. This miraculous sign will occur tomorrow.' "

²⁴And the LORD did this. Dense swarms of flies poured into Pharaoh's palace and into the houses of his officials, and throughout Egypt the land was ruined by the flies.

²⁵Then Pharaoh summoned Moses and Aaron and said, "Go, sacrifice to your God here in the land."

²⁶But Moses said, "That would not be right. The sacrifices we offer the LORD our God would be detestable to the Egyptians. And if we offer sacrifices that are detestable in their eyes, will they not stone us? ²⁷We must take a three-day journey into the desert to offer sacrifices to the LORD our God, as he commands us."

²⁸Pharaoh said, "I will let you go to offer sacrifices to the LORD your God in the desert, but you must not go very far. Now pray for me."

²⁹Moses answered, "As soon as I leave you, I will pray to the LORD, and tomorrow the flies will leave Pharaoh and his officials and his people. Only be sure that Pharaoh does not act deceitfully again by not letting the people go to offer sacrifices to the LORD."

³⁰Then Moses left Pharaoh and prayed to the LORD, ³¹and the LORD did what Moses asked: The flies left Pharaoh and his officials and his people; not a fly remained. ³²But this time also Pharaoh hardened his heart and would not let the people go.

The Plague on Livestock

9 Then the LORD said to Moses, "Go to Pharaoh and say to him, 'This is what the LORD, the God of the Hebrews, says: "Let my people go, so that they may worship me." ²If you refuse to let them go and continue to hold them back, ³the hand of the LORD will bring a terrible plague on your livestock in the field—on your horses and donkeys and camels and on your cattle and sheep and goats. ⁴But the LORD will make a distinction between the livestock of Israel and that of Egypt, so that no animal belonging to the Israelites will die.' "

⁵The LORD set a time and said, "Tomorrow the LORD will do this in the land." ⁶And the next day the LORD did it: All the livestock of the Egyptians died, but not one animal belonging to the Israelites died. ⁷Pharaoh sent men to investigate and found that not even one of the animals of the Israelites had died. Yet his heart was unyielding and he would not let the people go.

The Plague of Boils

⁸Then the LORD said to Moses and Aaron, "Take handfuls of soot from a furnace and have Moses toss it into the air in the presence of Pharaoh. ⁹It will become fine dust over the whole land of Egypt, and festering boils will break out on men and animals throughout the land."

¹⁰So they took soot from a furnace and stood before Pharaoh. Moses tossed it into the air, and festering boils broke out on men and animals. ¹¹The magicians could not stand before Moses because of the boils that were on them and on all the Egyptians. ¹²But the LORD hardened Phar-

A Temporary Peace

EXODUS 8:25–31

Because of Israel's faithfulness, God stops the plague of flies. Moses' prayer restores calm to the land once again. Peace, said Augustine, is "the order of tranquillity." In this case peace is restored when Israel—and even Pharaoh—are in harmony with the will of God. In Pharaoh's case, however, the submission to God's "order of tranquillity" never becomes more than a short-lived intention.

How do you come to know the will of God? What are the means God uses to get across a message to you? How can you make hearing God's will more than a temporary project? In what ways might God come alongside you to help you remain faithful?

---

[a] 23 Septuagint and Vulgate; Hebrew *will put a deliverance*

Hailstones and Stonewalling

EXODUS 9:13–26

The story seems to go around and around in circles. Moses uses his big stick. Pharaoh backs off. Moses relents. Pharaoh reneges. Moses calls down hailstones. Pharaoh stonewalls. Moses looks weak. Pharaoh looks strong. But Pharaoh's strength is not strength of character, but the brick-wall stubbornness of entrenched attitudes that keep him in bondage. Being in control is the only mode of operation Pharaoh has known. Giving it up seems more threatening to him than having stars fall down around him. In contrast, Moses can afford to take short-term losses because he knows who is ultimately in control.

Ask yourself whose behavior your behavior most resembles. In which areas in your life do you insist on having control? What would happen if you turned control over to God?

See Meeting God in Scripture

The Plague of Hail

aoh's heart and he would not listen to Moses and Aaron, just as the LORD had said to Moses.

¹³Then the LORD said to Moses, "Get up early in the morning, confront Pharaoh and say to him, 'This is what the LORD, the God of the Hebrews, says: Let my people go, so that they may worship me, ¹⁴or this time I will send the full force of my plagues against you and against your officials and your people, so you may know that there is no one like me in all the earth. ¹⁵For by now I could have stretched out my hand and struck you and your people with a plague that would have wiped you off the earth. ¹⁶But I have raised you up[a] for this very purpose, that I might show you my power and that my name might be proclaimed in all the earth. ¹⁷You still set yourself against my people and will not let them go. ¹⁸Therefore, at this time tomorrow I will send the worst hailstorm that has ever fallen on Egypt, from the day it was founded till now. ¹⁹Give an order now to bring your livestock and everything you have in the field to a place of shelter, because the hail will fall on every man and animal that has not been brought in and is still out in the field, and they will die.' "

²⁰Those officials of Pharaoh who feared the word of the LORD hurried to bring their slaves and their livestock inside. ²¹But those who ignored the word of the LORD left their slaves and livestock in the field.

²²Then the LORD said to Moses, "Stretch out your hand toward the sky so that hail will fall all over Egypt—on men and animals and on everything growing in the fields of Egypt." ²³When Moses stretched out his staff toward the sky, the LORD sent thunder and hail, and lightning flashed down to the ground. So the LORD rained hail on the land of Egypt; ²⁴hail fell and lightning flashed back and forth. It was the worst storm in all the land of Egypt since it had become a nation. ²⁵Throughout Egypt hail struck everything in the fields—both men and animals; it beat down everything growing in the fields and stripped every tree. ²⁶The only place it did not hail was the land of Goshen, where the Israelites were.

²⁷Then Pharaoh summoned Moses and Aaron. "This time I have sinned," he said to them. "The LORD is in the right, and I and my people are in the wrong. ²⁸Pray to the LORD, for we have had enough thunder and hail. I will let you go; you don't have to stay any longer."

²⁹Moses replied, "When I have gone out of the city, I will spread out my hands in prayer to the LORD. The thunder will stop and there will be no more hail, so you may know that the earth is the LORD's. ³⁰But I know that you and your officials still do not fear the LORD God."

³¹(The flax and barley were destroyed, since the barley had headed and the flax was in bloom. ³²The wheat and spelt, however, were not destroyed, because they ripen later.)

³³Then Moses left Pharaoh and went out of the city. He spread out his hands toward the LORD; the thunder and hail stopped, and the rain no longer poured down on the land. ³⁴When Pharaoh saw that the rain and hail and thunder had stopped, he sinned again: He and his officials hard-

a 16 Or have spared you

ened their hearts. ³⁵So Pharaoh's heart was hard and he would not let the Israelites go, just as the LORD had said through Moses.

The Plague of Locusts

10 Then the LORD said to Moses, "Go to Pharaoh, for I have hardened his heart and the hearts of his officials so that I may perform these miraculous signs of mine among them ²that you may tell your children and grandchildren how I dealt harshly with the Egyptians and how I performed my signs among them, and that you may know that I am the LORD."

³So Moses and Aaron went to Pharaoh and said to him, "This is what the LORD, the God of the Hebrews, says: 'How long will you refuse to humble yourself before me? Let my people go, so that they may worship me. ⁴If you refuse to let them go, I will bring locusts into your country tomorrow. ⁵They will cover the face of the ground so that it cannot be seen. They will devour what little you have left after the hail, including every tree that is growing in your fields. ⁶They will fill your houses and those of all your officials and all the Egyptians—something neither your fathers nor your forefathers have ever seen from the day they settled in this land till now.' " Then Moses turned and left Pharaoh.

⁷Pharaoh's officials said to him, "How long will this man be a snare to us? Let the people go, so that they may worship the LORD their God. Do you not yet realize that Egypt is ruined?"

⁸Then Moses and Aaron were brought back to Pharaoh. "Go, worship the LORD your God," he said. "But just who will be going?"

⁹Moses answered, "We will go with our young and old, with our sons and daughters, and with our flocks and herds, because we are to celebrate a festival to the LORD."

¹⁰Pharaoh said, "The LORD be with you—if I let you go, along with your women and children! Clearly you are bent on evil.ᵃ ¹¹No! Have only the men go; and worship the LORD, since that's what you have been asking for." Then Moses and Aaron were driven out of Pharaoh's presence.

¹²And the LORD said to Moses, "Stretch out your hand over Egypt so that locusts will swarm over the land and devour everything growing in the fields, everything left by the hail."

¹³So Moses stretched out his staff over Egypt, and the LORD made an east wind blow across the land all that day and all that night. By morning the wind had brought the locusts; ¹⁴they invaded all Egypt and settled down in every area of the country in great numbers. Never before had there been such a plague of locusts, nor will there ever be again. ¹⁵They covered all the ground until it was black. They devoured all that was left after the hail—everything growing in the fields and the fruit on the trees. Nothing green remained on tree or plant in all the land of Egypt.

¹⁶Pharaoh quickly summoned Moses and Aaron and said, "I have sinned against the LORD your God and against you. ¹⁷Now forgive my sin once more and pray to the LORD your God to take this deadly plague away from me."

¹⁸Moses then left Pharaoh and prayed to the LORD. ¹⁹And the LORD changed the wind to a very strong west wind,

Pharaoh's Dilemma

EXODUS 10:7–19

Pharaoh faced a troubling dilemma. If he let the Israelites go it would devastate the economy. He needed the Hebrew slaves to maintain and continue capital expansion. In the same way, much resistance to ending slavery in the United States came from economic fears in a region dependent on slave labor.

There may be areas in our lives that need to be yielded to God but that, if done, would cause some troubling dislocation. Perhaps your job does not glorify God, but to consider leaving it creates economic fears. Maybe you have long been feuding with someone, and to make amends would be a painful process. Ask God in prayer to reveal these areas to you—perhaps some you have been unwilling to think about. Next ask God for the strength to face them and then follow the Lord's will in everything.

See Meeting God in Prayer

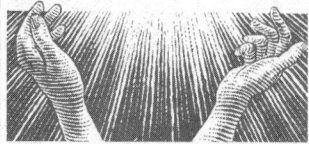

ᵃ 10 Or *Be careful, trouble is in store for you!*

Zero Hour: Midnight

EXODUS 11:4

The standoff between Moses and Pharaoh is coming to a climax. The hour is set: Midnight is the turning point. It is an hour of deep darkness—the hour when all is still. It is the hour of expectation and decision—marking both an end and a new beginning. This story invites us to see the midnight hour both as a symbol of death and of liberation. Set your alarm tonight for midnight. Once awake, sit in complete silence for fifteen minutes in an attitude of expectation toward God before going back to sleep.

See Meeting God in Scripture

which caught up the locusts and carried them into the Red Sea.[a] Not a locust was left anywhere in Egypt. [20]But the LORD hardened Pharaoh's heart, and he would not let the Israelites go.

The Plague of Darkness

[21]Then the LORD said to Moses, "Stretch out your hand toward the sky so that darkness will spread over Egypt—darkness that can be felt." [22]So Moses stretched out his hand toward the sky, and total darkness covered all Egypt for three days. [23]No one could see anyone else or leave his place for three days. Yet all the Israelites had light in the places where they lived.

[24]Then Pharaoh summoned Moses and said, "Go, worship the LORD. Even your women and children may go with you; only leave your flocks and herds behind."

[25]But Moses said, "You must allow us to have sacrifices and burnt offerings to present to the LORD our God. [26]Our livestock too must go with us; not a hoof is to be left behind. We have to use some of them in worshiping the LORD our God, and until we get there we will not know what we are to use to worship the LORD."

[27]But the LORD hardened Pharaoh's heart, and he was not willing to let them go. [28]Pharaoh said to Moses, "Get out of my sight! Make sure you do not appear before me again! The day you see my face you will die."

[29]"Just as you say," Moses replied, "I will never appear before you again."

The Plague on the Firstborn

11 Now the LORD had said to Moses, "I will bring one more plague on Pharaoh and on Egypt. After that, he will let you go from here, and when he does, he will drive you out completely. [2]Tell the people that men and women alike are to ask their neighbors for articles of silver and gold." [3](The LORD made the Egyptians favorably disposed toward the people, and Moses himself was highly regarded in Egypt by Pharaoh's officials and by the people.)

[4]So Moses said, "This is what the LORD says: 'About midnight I will go throughout Egypt. [5]Every firstborn son in Egypt will die, from the firstborn son of Pharaoh, who sits on the throne, to the firstborn son of the slave girl, who is at her hand mill, and all the firstborn of the cattle as well. [6]There will be loud wailing throughout Egypt—worse than there has ever been or ever will be again. [7]But among the Israelites not a dog will bark at any man or animal.' Then you will know that the LORD makes a distinction between Egypt and Israel. [8]All these officials of yours will come to me, bowing down before me and saying, 'Go, you and all the people who follow you!' After that I will leave." Then Moses, hot with anger, left Pharaoh.

[9]The LORD had said to Moses, "Pharaoh will refuse to listen to you—so that my wonders may be multiplied in Egypt." [10]Moses and Aaron performed all these wonders before Pharaoh, but the LORD hardened Pharaoh's heart, and he would not let the Israelites go out of his country.

[a] 19 Hebrew *Yam Suph*; that is, Sea of Reeds

The Passover

12 The Lord said to Moses and Aaron in Egypt, ²"This month is to be for you the first month, the first month of your year. ³Tell the whole community of Israel that on the tenth day of this month each man is to take a lamb[a] for his family, one for each household. ⁴If any household is too small for a whole lamb, they must share one with their nearest neighbor, having taken into account the number of people there are. You are to determine the amount of lamb needed in accordance with what each person will eat. ⁵The animals you choose must be year-old males without defect, and you may take them from the sheep or the goats. ⁶Take care of them until the fourteenth day of the month, when all the people of the community of Israel must slaughter them at twilight. ⁷Then they are to take some of the blood and put it on the sides and tops of the doorframes of the houses where they eat the lambs. ⁸That same night they are to eat the meat roasted over the fire, along with bitter herbs, and bread made without yeast. ⁹Do not eat the meat raw or cooked in water, but roast it over the fire—head, legs and inner parts. ¹⁰Do not leave any of it till morning; if some is left till morning, you must burn it. ¹¹This is how you are to eat it: with your cloak tucked into your belt, your sandals on your feet and your staff in your hand. Eat it in haste; it is the Lord's Passover.

¹²"On that same night I will pass through Egypt and strike down every firstborn—both men and animals—and I will bring judgment on all the gods of Egypt. I am the Lord. ¹³The blood will be a sign for you on the houses where you are; and when I see the blood, I will pass over you. No destructive plague will touch you when I strike Egypt.

¹⁴"This is a day you are to commemorate; for the generations to come you shall celebrate it as a festival to the Lord—a lasting ordinance. ¹⁵For seven days you are to eat bread made without yeast. On the first day remove the yeast from your houses, for whoever eats anything with yeast in it from the first day through the seventh must be cut off from Israel. ¹⁶On the first day hold a sacred assembly, and another one on the seventh day. Do no work at all on these days, except to prepare food for everyone to eat—that is all you may do.

¹⁷"Celebrate the Feast of Unleavened Bread, because it was on this very day that I brought your divisions out of Egypt. Celebrate this day as a lasting ordinance for the generations to come. ¹⁸In the first month you are to eat bread made without yeast, from the evening of the fourteenth day until the evening of the twenty-first day. ¹⁹For seven days no yeast is to be found in your houses. And whoever eats anything with yeast in it must be cut off from the community of Israel, whether he is an alien or native-born. ²⁰Eat nothing made with yeast. Wherever you live, you must eat unleavened bread."

²¹Then Moses summoned all the elders of Israel and said to them, "Go at once and select the animals for your families and slaughter the Passover lamb. ²²Take a bunch of hyssop, dip it into the blood in the basin and put some of the blood on the top and on both sides of the doorframe. Not

---

Passover

EXODUS 12:3–13

Here we read of a departure made in haste, but this is not a story to be read in haste. It holds the key to the meaning of many symbols that will resurface in New Testament writings. It should be read with one finger holding your place in Exodus and another holding your place in the Gospels and related New Testament writings. Note the parallel: John the Baptist refers to Jesus as the "Lamb of God" (John 1:36); and the Evangelist John fixes the hour of Jesus' sentencing at noon, the hour at which priests began to slaughter Passover lambs in the temple (John 19:14). Let the symbol of the paschal lamb in Exodus shed light on your reading whenever you turn to the four Gospels and other New Testament passages.

See *Meeting God in Scripture*

---

[a] 3 The Hebrew word can mean *lamb* or *kid*; also in verse 4.

Death of the Firstborn

EXODUS 12:29

Midnight has come. Pharaoh, who has turned a deaf ear to the voice of Moses, listens to the booming voice of Death. Henceforth the symbol of the firstborn as a sign of liberation becomes deeply etched in the communal memory of the Hebrew people. So much so that the coming of the Messiah is heralded with the words: "And she gave birth to her firstborn son" (Luke 2:7).

Identify those people, events or objects in your life—the ones that seem to give you a new freedom, fresh strength or renewed joy—that you might label "firstborn." Can you see them as gifts from God? How do you offer these back to God in thanksgiving and gratitude?

See Meeting God in Community

one of you shall go out the door of his house until morning. ²³When the Lord goes through the land to strike down the Egyptians, he will see the blood on the top and sides of the doorframe and will pass over that doorway, and he will not permit the destroyer to enter your houses and strike you down.

²⁴"Obey these instructions as a lasting ordinance for you and your descendants. ²⁵When you enter the land that the Lord will give you as he promised, observe this ceremony. ²⁶And when your children ask you, 'What does this ceremony mean to you?' ²⁷then tell them, 'It is the Passover sacrifice to the Lord, who passed over the houses of the Israelites in Egypt and spared our homes when he struck down the Egyptians.' " Then the people bowed down and worshiped. ²⁸The Israelites did just what the Lord commanded Moses and Aaron.

²⁹At midnight the Lord struck down all the firstborn in Egypt, from the firstborn of Pharaoh, who sat on the throne, to the firstborn of the prisoner, who was in the dungeon, and the firstborn of all the livestock as well. ³⁰Pharaoh and all his officials and all the Egyptians got up during the night, and there was loud wailing in Egypt, for there was not a house without someone dead.

The Exodus

³¹During the night Pharaoh summoned Moses and Aaron and said, "Up! Leave my people, you and the Israelites! Go, worship the Lord as you have requested. ³²Take your flocks and herds, as you have said, and go. And also bless me."

³³The Egyptians urged the people to hurry and leave the country. "For otherwise," they said, "we will all die!" ³⁴So the people took their dough before the yeast was added, and carried it on their shoulders in kneading troughs wrapped in clothing. ³⁵The Israelites did as Moses instructed and asked the Egyptians for articles of silver and gold and for clothing. ³⁶The Lord had made the Egyptians favorably disposed toward the people, and they gave them what they asked for; so they plundered the Egyptians.

³⁷The Israelites journeyed from Rameses to Succoth. There were about six hundred thousand men on foot, besides women and children. ³⁸Many other people went up with them, as well as large droves of livestock, both flocks and herds. ³⁹With the dough they had brought from Egypt, they baked cakes of unleavened bread. The dough was without yeast because they had been driven out of Egypt and did not have time to prepare food for themselves.

⁴⁰Now the length of time the Israelite people lived in Egypt[a] was 430 years. ⁴¹At the end of the 430 years, to the very day, all the Lord's divisions left Egypt. ⁴²Because the Lord kept vigil that night to bring them out of Egypt, on this night all the Israelites are to keep vigil to honor the Lord for the generations to come.

Passover Restrictions

⁴³The Lord said to Moses and Aaron, "These are the regulations for the Passover:

"No foreigner is to eat of it. ⁴⁴Any slave you have bought may eat of it after you have circumcised him, ⁴⁵but a temporary resident and a hired worker may not eat of it.

ᵃ *40* Masoretic Text; Samaritan Pentateuch and Septuagint *Egypt and Canaan*

⁴⁶"It must be eaten inside one house; take none of the meat outside the house. Do not break any of the bones. ⁴⁷The whole community of Israel must celebrate it.

⁴⁸"An alien living among you who wants to celebrate the LORD's Passover must have all the males in his household circumcised; then he may take part like one born in the land. No uncircumcised male may eat of it. ⁴⁹The same law applies to the native-born and to the alien living among you."

⁵⁰All the Israelites did just what the LORD had command- ed Moses and Aaron. ⁵¹And on that very day the LORD brought the Israelites out of Egypt by their divisions.

Consecration of the Firstborn

13 The LORD said to Moses, ²"Consecrate to me every firstborn male. The first offspring of every womb among the Israelites belongs to me, whether man or animal."

³Then Moses said to the people, "Commemorate this day, the day you came out of Egypt, out of the land of slav- ery, because the LORD brought you out of it with a mighty hand. Eat nothing containing yeast. ⁴Today, in the month of Abib, you are leaving. ⁵When the LORD brings you into the land of the Canaanites, Hittites, Amorites, Hivites and Je- busites—the land he swore to your forefathers to give you, a land flowing with milk and honey—you are to observe this ceremony in this month: ⁶For seven days eat bread made without yeast and on the seventh day hold a festival to the LORD. ⁷Eat unleavened bread during those seven days; nothing with yeast in it is to be seen among you, nor shall any yeast be seen anywhere within your borders. ⁸On that day tell your son, 'I do this because of what the LORD did for me when I came out of Egypt.' ⁹This observance will be for you like a sign on your hand and a reminder on your forehead that the law of the LORD is to be on your lips. For the LORD brought you out of Egypt with his mighty hand. ¹⁰You must keep this ordinance at the appointed time year after year.

¹¹"After the LORD brings you into the land of the Canaan- ites and gives it to you, as he promised on oath to you and your forefathers, ¹²you are to give over to the LORD the first offspring of every womb. All the firstborn males of your livestock belong to the LORD. ¹³Redeem with a lamb every firstborn donkey, but if you do not redeem it, break its neck. Redeem every firstborn among your sons.

¹⁴"In days to come, when your son asks you, 'What does this mean?' say to him, 'With a mighty hand the LORD brought us out of Egypt, out of the land of slavery. ¹⁵When Pharaoh stubbornly refused to let us go, the LORD killed every firstborn in Egypt, both man and animal. This is why I sacrifice to the LORD the first male offspring of every womb and redeem each of my firstborn sons.' ¹⁶And it will be like a sign on your hand and a symbol on your forehead that the LORD brought us out of Egypt with his mighty hand."

Crossing the Sea

¹⁷When Pharaoh let the people go, God did not lead them on the road through the Philistine country, though that was shorter. For God said, "If they face war, they might change

The First Commandment

EXODUS 13:3

Before ever reaching Mount Sinai Moses gives his people a commandment: *Remember.* If we do remember then every- thing else falls into place. These exhortations to remember should not be left to fossilize in their original context, but should be lifted out and con- verted into the context of our own lives. We are all busy. That is why we must set aside specif- ic times that belong to God alone, times we call to mind or "re-collect" what God has said or done.

What events have been im- portant in your personal jour- ney, bringing you to where you are today? What signposts or "memory points" have you built into your day to remind you of the presence of God?

See Meeting God in Everyday Life

Exodus

EXODUS 14:1-14

This chapter contains one of the most repeated, most passed-along stories of God's people. God's leading of Israel out of captivity provides a central metaphor for both the Old and New Testaments. Its almost universal appeal has to do not only with the drama and power of the story itself, but also its meaning for our own journeys of faith.

Let Moses' uplifted staff provide you with an image of God's caring power in your life. The army of the Egyptians chasing you might represent the dangers you face. As God parts the waters, see his intervention in your life—things he has done to save you. Look back and see the miracles, the parted waters you have passed through, the shore of safety to which a loving God has brought you.

their minds and return to Egypt." [18]So God led the people around by the desert road toward the Red Sea.[a] The Israelites went up out of Egypt armed for battle.

[19]Moses took the bones of Joseph with him because Joseph had made the sons of Israel swear an oath. He had said, "God will surely come to your aid, and then you must carry my bones up with you from this place."[b]

[20]After leaving Succoth they camped at Etham on the edge of the desert. [21]By day the LORD went ahead of them in a pillar of cloud to guide them on their way and by night in a pillar of fire to give them light, so that they could travel by day or night. [22]Neither the pillar of cloud by day nor the pillar of fire by night left its place in front of the people.

14 Then the LORD said to Moses, [2]"Tell the Israelites to turn back and encamp near Pi Hahiroth, between Migdol and the sea. They are to encamp by the sea, directly opposite Baal Zephon. [3]Pharaoh will think, 'The Israelites are wandering around the land in confusion, hemmed in by the desert.' [4]And I will harden Pharaoh's heart, and he will pursue them. But I will gain glory for myself through Pharaoh and all his army, and the Egyptians will know that I am the LORD." So the Israelites did this.

[5]When the king of Egypt was told that the people had fled, Pharaoh and his officials changed their minds about them and said, "What have we done? We have let the Israelites go and have lost their services!" [6]So he had his chariot made ready and took his army with him. [7]He took six hundred of the best chariots, along with all the other chariots of Egypt, with officers over all of them. [8]The LORD hardened the heart of Pharaoh king of Egypt, so that he pursued the Israelites, who were marching out boldly. [9]The Egyptians—all Pharaoh's horses and chariots, horsemen[c] and troops—pursued the Israelites and overtook them as they camped by the sea near Pi Hahiroth, opposite Baal Zephon.

[10]As Pharaoh approached, the Israelites looked up, and there were the Egyptians, marching after them. They were terrified and cried out to the LORD. [11]They said to Moses, "Was it because there were no graves in Egypt that you brought us to the desert to die? What have you done to us by bringing us out of Egypt? [12]Didn't we say to you in Egypt, 'Leave us alone; let us serve the Egyptians'? It would have been better for us to serve the Egyptians than to die in the desert!"

[13]Moses answered the people, "Do not be afraid. Stand firm and you will see the deliverance the LORD will bring you today. The Egyptians you see today you will never see again. [14]The LORD will fight for you; you need only to be still."

[15]Then the LORD said to Moses, "Why are you crying out to me? Tell the Israelites to move on. [16]Raise your staff and stretch out your hand over the sea to divide the water so that the Israelites can go through the sea on dry ground. [17]I will harden the hearts of the Egyptians so that they will go in after them. And I will gain glory through Pharaoh and all his army, through his chariots and his horsemen. [18]The Egyptians will know that I am the LORD when I gain glory through Pharaoh, his chariots and his horsemen."

[19]Then the angel of God, who had been traveling in front

---

[a] 18 Hebrew *Yam Suph*; that is, Sea of Reeds   [b] 19 See Gen. 50:25.
[c] 9 Or *charioteers*; also in verses 17, 18, 23, 26 and 28

of Israel's army, withdrew and went behind them. The pillar of cloud also moved from in front and stood behind them, ²⁰coming between the armies of Egypt and Israel. Throughout the night the cloud brought darkness to the one side and light to the other side; so neither went near the other all night long.

²¹Then Moses stretched out his hand over the sea, and all that night the LORD drove the sea back with a strong east wind and turned it into dry land. The waters were divided, ²²and the Israelites went through the sea on dry ground, with a wall of water on their right and on their left.

²³The Egyptians pursued them, and all Pharaoh's horses and chariots and horsemen followed them into the sea. ²⁴During the last watch of the night the LORD looked down from the pillar of fire and cloud at the Egyptian army and threw it into confusion. ²⁵He made the wheels of their chariots come off ᵃ so that they had difficulty driving. And the Egyptians said, "Let's get away from the Israelites! The LORD is fighting for them against Egypt."

²⁶Then the LORD said to Moses, "Stretch out your hand over the sea so that the waters may flow back over the Egyptians and their chariots and horsemen." ²⁷Moses stretched out his hand over the sea, and at daybreak the sea went back to its place. The Egyptians were fleeing toward ᵇ it, and the LORD swept them into the sea. ²⁸The water flowed back and covered the chariots and horsemen—the entire army of Pharaoh that had followed the Israelites into the sea. Not one of them survived.

²⁹But the Israelites went through the sea on dry ground, with a wall of water on their right and on their left. ³⁰That day the LORD saved Israel from the hands of the Egyptians, and Israel saw the Egyptians lying dead on the shore. ³¹And when the Israelites saw the great power the LORD displayed against the Egyptians, the people feared the LORD and put their trust in him and in Moses his servant.

The Song of Moses and Miriam

15 Then Moses and the Israelites sang this song to the LORD:

> "I will sing to the LORD,
>   for he is highly exalted.
> The horse and its rider
>   he has hurled into the sea.
> ²The LORD is my strength and my song;
>   he has become my salvation.
> He is my God, and I will praise him,
>   my father's God, and I will exalt him.
> ³The LORD is a warrior;
>   the LORD is his name.
> ⁴Pharaoh's chariots and his army
>   he has hurled into the sea.
> The best of Pharaoh's officers
>   are drowned in the Red Sea.ᶜ
> ⁵The deep waters have covered them;
>   they sank to the depths like a stone.
>
> ⁶"Your right hand, O LORD,

Following God's Ways

EXODUS 14:21-31

"God wants to lead us. Not all the ways of humans are God's leading. For a long time we can walk our own paths. On those we are pawns of coincidence, whether they bring good luck or misfortune. Our own ways always lead in a circle back to ourselves. But when God leads our ways, they guide us to him. God's ways guide us to God. God leads us through happiness and unhappiness always and only towards God. In this we recognize God's ways."

—DIETRICH BONHOEFFER,
"The Mystery of Easter"

ᵃ 25 Or *He jammed the wheels of their chariots* (see Samaritan Pentateuch, Septuagint and Syriac)   ᵇ 27 Or *from*   ᶜ 4 Hebrew *Yam Suph*; that is, Sea of Reeds; also in verse 22

Something to Sing About

EXODUS 15:1–18

This is one of many great songs found throughout the Bible. Many of the psalms are written as songs. There are also songs in Isaiah at 12:1–6, 55:6–11 and elsewhere. In the New Testament we think of the Song of Mary (Luke 1:46–55), the Song of Simeon (Luke 2:29–32), the Song of Christ Jesus (Philippians 2:6–11) and many others. Then, like now, certain occasions seem to call for music and singing, songs like "Happy Birthday" and The National Anthem.

Try to think now of songs that are especially appropriate at important times. Perhaps you have favorite hymns or songs that are particularly meaningful. Find recordings to play or write down the words of the songs. Then offer these tunes or words to God when you pray. Or you may play or hum the music alone as prayers without words. Thank God for the meaning and beauty of music.

See *Meeting God in Worship*

was majestic in power.
Your right hand, O LORD,
  shattered the enemy.
[7] In the greatness of your majesty
  you threw down those who opposed you.
You unleashed your burning anger;
  it consumed them like stubble.
[8] By the blast of your nostrils
  the waters piled up.
The surging waters stood firm like a wall;
  the deep waters congealed in the heart of the
    sea.
[9] "The enemy boasted,
  'I will pursue, I will overtake them.
I will divide the spoils;
  I will gorge myself on them.
I will draw my sword
  and my hand will destroy them.'
[10] But you blew with your breath,
  and the sea covered them.
They sank like lead
  in the mighty waters.
[11] "Who among the gods is like you, O LORD?
  Who is like you—
    majestic in holiness,
    awesome in glory,
    working wonders?
[12] You stretched out your right hand
  and the earth swallowed them.
[13] "In your unfailing love you will lead
  the people you have redeemed.
In your strength you will guide them
  to your holy dwelling.
[14] The nations will hear and tremble;
  anguish will grip the people of Philistia.
[15] The chiefs of Edom will be terrified,
  the leaders of Moab will be seized with
    trembling,
the people[a] of Canaan will melt away;
[16]   terror and dread will fall upon them.
By the power of your arm
  they will be as still as a stone—
until your people pass by, O LORD,
  until the people you bought[b] pass by.
[17] You will bring them in and plant them
  on the mountain of your inheritance—
the place, O LORD, you made for your dwelling,
  the sanctuary, O Lord, your hands established.
[18] The LORD will reign
  for ever and ever."

[19] When Pharaoh's horses, chariots and horsemen[c] went into the sea, the LORD brought the waters of the sea back over them, but the Israelites walked through the sea on dry ground. [20] Then Miriam the prophetess, Aaron's sister, took a tambourine in her hand, and all the women followed her, with tambourines and dancing. [21] Miriam sang to them:

a 15 Or rulers   *b 16 Or created*   *c 19 Or charioteers*

"Sing to the LORD,
  for he is highly exalted.
The horse and its rider
  he has hurled into the sea."

The Waters of Marah and Elim

²²Then Moses led Israel from the Red Sea and they went into the Desert of Shur. For three days they traveled in the desert without finding water. ²³When they came to Marah, they could not drink its water because it was bitter. (That is why the place is called Marah.*ᵃ*) ²⁴So the people grumbled against Moses, saying, "What are we to drink?"

²⁵Then Moses cried out to the LORD, and the LORD showed him a piece of wood. He threw it into the water, and the water became sweet.

There the LORD made a decree and a law for them, and there he tested them. ²⁶He said, "If you listen carefully to the voice of the LORD your God and do what is right in his eyes, if you pay attention to his commands and keep all his decrees, I will not bring on you any of the diseases I brought on the Egyptians, for I am the LORD, who heals you."

²⁷Then they came to Elim, where there were twelve springs and seventy palm trees, and they camped there near the water.

Manna and Quail

16 The whole Israelite community set out from Elim and came to the Desert of Sin, which is between Elim and Sinai, on the fifteenth day of the second month after they had come out of Egypt. ²In the desert the whole community grumbled against Moses and Aaron. ³The Israelites said to them, "If only we had died by the LORD's hand in Egypt! There we sat around pots of meat and ate all the food we wanted, but you have brought us out into this desert to starve this entire assembly to death."

⁴Then the LORD said to Moses, "I will rain down bread from heaven for you. The people are to go out each day and gather enough for that day. In this way I will test them and see whether they will follow my instructions. ⁵On the sixth day they are to prepare what they bring in, and that is to be twice as much as they gather on the other days."

⁶So Moses and Aaron said to all the Israelites, "In the evening you will know that it was the LORD who brought you out of Egypt, ⁷and in the morning you will see the glory of the LORD, because he has heard your grumbling against him. Who are we, that you should grumble against us?" ⁸Moses also said, "You will know that it was the LORD when he gives you meat to eat in the evening and all the bread you want in the morning, because he has heard your grumbling against him. Who are we? You are not grumbling against us, but against the LORD."

⁹Then Moses told Aaron, "Say to the entire Israelite community, 'Come before the LORD, for he has heard your grumbling.' "

¹⁰While Aaron was speaking to the whole Israelite community, they looked toward the desert, and there was the glory of the LORD appearing in the cloud.

¹¹The LORD said to Moses, ¹²"I have heard the grumbling

Manna and Quail

EXODUS 16:4–12

Perhaps we can best appreciate the story of bread from heaven by getting in touch with bread from the kitchen table. Pick up a fresh loaf of homemade bread or one you have just brought home from the store. Hold it in your hands. Feel the weight of it. Inhale the aroma of baked grain. Compare your experience of bread from the kitchen with the Israelites' search for manna in the desert. How is it that while the desert wanderers complained in the midst of dire necessity, we complain today in the midst of abundance? What do you find yourself complaining about most? Turn it around and say a prayer of thanksgiving for the person, experience or challenge you are taking for granted. Make a list of the sustaining, life-giving things in your life that might be symbolized by bread and thank God for each of them. Be thankful for all the things God provides for your sustenance.

See Meeting God in Everyday Life

Freedom From Want

EXODUS 16:13–36

"It is not God's will that we should remain in need. He would fulfill all our needs by delivering us from all possessions and giving us Himself in exchange. If we would belong to His love, we must remain always empty of everything else, not in order to be in need, but precisely because possessions make us needy."

—THOMAS MERTON,
No Man Is an Island

of the Israelites. Tell them, 'At twilight you will eat meat, and in the morning you will be filled with bread. Then you will know that I am the LORD your God.' "

¹³That evening quail came and covered the camp, and in the morning there was a layer of dew around the camp. ¹⁴When the dew was gone, thin flakes like frost on the ground appeared on the desert floor. ¹⁵When the Israelites saw it, they said to each other, "What is it?" For they did not know what it was.

Moses said to them, "It is the bread the LORD has given you to eat. ¹⁶This is what the LORD has commanded: 'Each one is to gather as much as he needs. Take an omer*a* for each person you have in your tent.' "

¹⁷The Israelites did as they were told; some gathered much, some little. ¹⁸And when they measured it by the omer, he who gathered much did not have too much, and he who gathered little did not have too little. Each one gathered as much as he needed.

¹⁹Then Moses said to them, "No one is to keep any of it until morning."

²⁰However, some of them paid no attention to Moses; they kept part of it until morning, but it was full of maggots and began to smell. So Moses was angry with them.

²¹Each morning everyone gathered as much as he needed, and when the sun grew hot, it melted away. ²²On the sixth day, they gathered twice as much—two omers*b* for each person—and the leaders of the community came and reported this to Moses. ²³He said to them, "This is what the LORD commanded: 'Tomorrow is to be a day of rest, a holy Sabbath to the LORD. So bake what you want to bake and boil what you want to boil. Save whatever is left and keep it until morning.' "

²⁴So they saved it until morning, as Moses commanded, and it did not stink or get maggots in it. ²⁵"Eat it today," Moses said, "because today is a Sabbath to the LORD. You will not find any of it on the ground today. ²⁶Six days you are to gather it, but on the seventh day, the Sabbath, there will not be any."

²⁷Nevertheless, some of the people went out on the seventh day to gather it, but they found none. ²⁸Then the LORD said to Moses, "How long will you*c* refuse to keep my commands and my instructions? ²⁹Bear in mind that the LORD has given you the Sabbath; that is why on the sixth day he gives you bread for two days. Everyone is to stay where he is on the seventh day; no one is to go out." ³⁰So the people rested on the seventh day.

³¹The people of Israel called the bread manna.*d* It was white like coriander seed and tasted like wafers made with honey. ³²Moses said, "This is what the LORD has commanded: 'Take an omer of manna and keep it for the generations to come, so they can see the bread I gave you to eat in the desert when I brought you out of Egypt.' "

³³So Moses said to Aaron, "Take a jar and put an omer of manna in it. Then place it before the LORD to be kept for the generations to come."

³⁴As the LORD commanded Moses, Aaron put the manna in front of the Testimony, that it might be kept. ³⁵The Isra-

a 16 That is, probably about 2 quarts (about 2 liters); also in verses 18, 32, 33 and 36   *b 22* That is, probably about 4 quarts (about 4.5 liters)
c 28 The Hebrew is plural.   *d 31* *Manna* means *What is it?* (see verse 15).

elites ate manna forty years, until they came to a land that was settled; they ate manna until they reached the border of Canaan. ³⁶(An omer is one tenth of an ephah.)

Water From the Rock

17 The whole Israelite community set out from the Desert of Sin, traveling from place to place as the LORD commanded. They camped at Rephidim, but there was no water for the people to drink. ²So they quarreled with Moses and said, "Give us water to drink."

Moses replied, "Why do you quarrel with me? Why do you put the LORD to the test?"

³But the people were thirsty for water there, and they grumbled against Moses. They said, "Why did you bring us up out of Egypt to make us and our children and livestock die of thirst?"

⁴Then Moses cried out to the LORD, "What am I to do with these people? They are almost ready to stone me."

⁵The LORD answered Moses, "Walk on ahead of the people. Take with you some of the elders of Israel and take in your hand the staff with which you struck the Nile, and go. ⁶I will stand there before you by the rock at Horeb. Strike the rock, and water will come out of it for the people to drink." So Moses did this in the sight of the elders of Israel. ⁷And he called the place Massah^a and Meribah^b because the Israelites quarreled and because they tested the LORD saying, "Is the LORD among us or not?"

The Amalekites Defeated

⁸The Amalekites came and attacked the Israelites at Rephidim. ⁹Moses said to Joshua, "Choose some of our men and go out to fight the Amalekites. Tomorrow I will stand on top of the hill with the staff of God in my hands."

¹⁰So Joshua fought the Amalekites as Moses had ordered, and Moses, Aaron and Hur went to the top of the hill. ¹¹As long as Moses held up his hands, the Israelites were winning, but whenever he lowered his hands, the Amalekites were winning. ¹²When Moses' hands grew tired, they took a stone and put it under him and he sat on it. Aaron and Hur held his hands up—one on one side, one on the other—so that his hands remained steady till sunset. ¹³So Joshua overcame the Amalekite army with the sword.

¹⁴Then the LORD said to Moses, "Write this on a scroll as something to be remembered and make sure that Joshua hears it, because I will completely blot out the memory of Amalek from under heaven."

¹⁵Moses built an altar and called it The LORD is my Banner. ¹⁶He said, "For hands were lifted up to the throne of the LORD. The^c LORD will be at war against the Amalekites from generation to generation."

Jethro Visits Moses

18 Now Jethro, the priest of Midian and father-in-law of Moses, heard of everything God had done for Moses and for his people Israel, and how the LORD had brought Israel out of Egypt.

²After Moses had sent away his wife Zipporah, his father-

Water From the Rock

EXODUS 17:6

Moses got water the hard way. First, he risked being stoned by the impatient people he led. Second, he found himself driven to seek divine intervention. Third, he had to search for a rock. Finally, he had to strike the rock with a very special stick. Finding water was an act of faith.

All most of us have to do to find water is turn on the faucet. Most of us have never lived in an area where water—the basis of life—is scarce, a subject for daily concern.

Think of a day, perhaps a hot one, when you grew very thirsty. Remember the very moment the first sip of cool water hit your mouth. Recall the sense of relief, of refreshment. Can you recall a spiritual experience that felt like a cool drink of water? Perhaps it was an answered prayer, an insight into Scripture, a real sense of God's presence. Give thanks for all the ways God slakes our spiritual thirst.

See Meeting God in the Created Order

---

^{a} 7 *Massah* means *testing*. ^{b} 7 *Meribah* means *quarreling*. ^{c} 16 Or "Because a hand was against the throne of the LORD, the

The Leader's Burden

EXODUS 18:13–19

Jethro offers good advice to Moses. Like so many of us, Moses' idea is to do everything himself. Jethro knows this allows for no weakness or failure and that it is unrealistic. In a sentence that must have rung in Moses' ear, Jethro said to him, "You must be the people's representative before God."

Can you remember a time when someone represented you before God? Perhaps you felt dry spiritually and found it difficult to pray. Give God great thanks if you have friends like that. If not, ask God to help you find the sort of person who can pray for you when you need it and for whom you can pray as well.

See Meeting God in Prayer

in-law Jethro received her ³and her two sons. One son was named Gershom,ᵃ for Moses said, "I have become an alien in a foreign land"; ⁴and the other was named Eliezer,ᵇ for he said, "My father's God was my helper; he saved me from the sword of Pharaoh."

⁵Jethro, Moses' father-in-law, together with Moses' sons and wife, came to him in the desert, where he was camped near the mountain of God. ⁶Jethro had sent word to him, "I, your father-in-law Jethro, am coming to you with your wife and her two sons."

⁷So Moses went out to meet his father-in-law and bowed down and kissed him. They greeted each other and then went into the tent. ⁸Moses told his father-in-law about everything the LORD had done to Pharaoh and the Egyptians for Israel's sake and about all the hardships they had met along the way and how the LORD had saved them.

⁹Jethro was delighted to hear about all the good things the LORD had done for Israel in rescuing them from the hand of the Egyptians. ¹⁰He said, "Praise be to the LORD, who rescued you from the hand of the Egyptians and of Pharaoh, and who rescued the people from the hand of the Egyptians. ¹¹Now I know that the LORD is greater than all other gods, for he did this to those who had treated Israel arrogantly." ¹²Then Jethro, Moses' father-in-law, brought a burnt offering and other sacrifices to God, and Aaron came with all the elders of Israel to eat bread with Moses' father-in-law in the presence of God.

¹³The next day Moses took his seat to serve as judge for the people, and they stood around him from morning till evening. ¹⁴When his father-in-law saw all that Moses was doing for the people, he said, "What is this you are doing for the people? Why do you alone sit as judge, while all these people stand around you from morning till evening?"

¹⁵Moses answered him, "Because the people come to me to seek God's will. ¹⁶Whenever they have a dispute, it is brought to me, and I decide between the parties and inform them of God's decrees and laws."

¹⁷Moses' father-in-law replied, "What you are doing is not good. ¹⁸You and these people who come to you will only wear yourselves out. The work is too heavy for you; you cannot handle it alone. ¹⁹Listen now to me and I will give you some advice, and may God be with you. You must be the people's representative before God and bring their disputes to him. ²⁰Teach them the decrees and laws, and show them the way to live and the duties they are to perform. ²¹But select capable men from all the people—men who fear God, trustworthy men who hate dishonest gain—and appoint them as officials over thousands, hundreds, fifties and tens. ²²Have them serve as judges for the people at all times, but have them bring every difficult case to you; the simple cases they can decide themselves. That will make your load lighter, because they will share it with you. ²³If you do this and God so commands, you will be able to stand the strain, and all these people will go home satisfied."

²⁴Moses listened to his father-in-law and did everything he said. ²⁵He chose capable men from all Israel and made them leaders of the people, officials over thousands, hun-

ᵃ 3 *Gershom* sounds like the Hebrew for *an alien there.*   ᵇ 4 *Eliezer* means *my God is helper.*

dreds, fifties and tens. ²⁶They served as judges for the people at all times. The difficult cases they brought to Moses, but the simple ones they decided themselves.

²⁷Then Moses sent his father-in-law on his way, and Jethro returned to his own country.

At Mount Sinai

19 In the third month after the Israelites left Egypt—on the very day—they came to the Desert of Sinai. ²After they set out from Rephidim, they entered the Desert of Sinai, and Israel camped there in the desert in front of the mountain.

³Then Moses went up to God, and the LORD called to him from the mountain and said, "This is what you are to say to the house of Jacob and what you are to tell the people of Israel: ⁴'You yourselves have seen what I did to Egypt, and how I carried you on eagles' wings and brought you to myself. ⁵Now if you obey me fully and keep my covenant, then out of all nations you will be my treasured possession. Although the whole earth is mine, ⁶you*a* will be for me a kingdom of priests and a holy nation.' These are the words you are to speak to the Israelites."

⁷So Moses went back and summoned the elders of the people and set before them all the words the LORD had commanded him to speak. ⁸The people all responded together, "We will do everything the LORD has said." So Moses brought their answer back to the LORD.

⁹The LORD said to Moses, "I am going to come to you in a dense cloud, so that the people will hear me speaking with you and will always put their trust in you." Then Moses told the LORD what the people had said.

¹⁰And the LORD said to Moses, "Go to the people and consecrate them today and tomorrow. Have them wash their clothes ¹¹and be ready by the third day, because on that day the LORD will come down on Mount Sinai in the sight of all the people. ¹²Put limits for the people around the mountain and tell them, 'Be careful that you do not go up the mountain or touch the foot of it. Whoever touches the mountain shall surely be put to death. ¹³He shall surely be stoned or shot with arrows; not a hand is to be laid on him. Whether man or animal, he shall not be permitted to live.' Only when the ram's horn sounds a long blast may they go up to the mountain."

¹⁴After Moses had gone down the mountain to the people, he consecrated them, and they washed their clothes. ¹⁵Then he said to the people, "Prepare yourselves for the third day. Abstain from sexual relations."

¹⁶On the morning of the third day there was thunder and lightning, with a thick cloud over the mountain, and a very loud trumpet blast. Everyone in the camp trembled. ¹⁷Then Moses led the people out of the camp to meet with God, and they stood at the foot of the mountain. ¹⁸Mount Sinai was covered with smoke, because the LORD descended on it in fire. The smoke billowed up from it like smoke from a furnace, the whole mountain*b* trembled violently, ¹⁹and the sound of the trumpet grew louder and louder. Then Moses spoke and the voice of God answered him.*c*

---

a 5,6 Or *possession, for the whole earth is mine.* *6You*   *b 18* Most Hebrew manuscripts; a few Hebrew manuscripts and Septuagint *all the people*
c 19 Or *and God answered him with thunder*

Peak Experience

EXODUS 19:1

Chapters 19 and 20 are the very heart of the book of Exodus, the dramatic climax. These pages are more to be "dwelt in" than analyzed or studied. In this chapter, we are ushered into the Presence of the Holy One. Here we remove our shoes. Place yourself in the scene. Look. Listen. Allow yourself to stand with the community in the Presence. Stay here. Forget the clock. After you have left the scene, take the memory of it with you. Dwell on it. Return to the mountain, again and again.

See *Meeting God in Worship*

The Ten Commandments

EXODUS 20:1–17

Kathleen Norris, author of the award-winning *Cloister Walk*, decided one day to search through the four Gospels to sift out a set of "imperatives" that might be juxtaposed to the commandments of the Old Testament. The result was a poem she published under the title "Imperatives":

"Look at the birds
Consider the lilies
Drink ye all of it
Ask
Seek
Knock
Enter by the narrow gate

"Do not be anxious
Judge not; do not give dogs
what is holy
Go: be it done for you
Do not be afraid
Maiden, arise
Young man, I say arise

"Stretch out your hand
Stand up, be still

"Rise, let us be going . . .
Love
Forgive
Remember me."

—KATHLEEN NORRIS,
"Little Girls In Church"

20 The LORD descended to the top of Mount Sinai and called Moses to the top of the mountain. So Moses went up **21** and the LORD said to him, "Go down and warn the people so they do not force their way through to see the LORD and many of them perish. **22** Even the priests, who approach the LORD, must consecrate themselves, or the LORD will break out against them."

23 Moses said to the LORD, "The people cannot come up Mount Sinai, because you yourself warned us, 'Put limits around the mountain and set it apart as holy.' "

24 The LORD replied, "Go down and bring Aaron up with you. But the priests and the people must not force their way through to come up to the LORD, or he will break out against them."

25 So Moses went down to the people and told them.

The Ten Commandments

20 And God spoke all these words:

2 "I am the LORD your God, who brought you out of Egypt, out of the land of slavery.

3 "You shall have no other gods before*a* me.

4 "You shall not make for yourself an idol in the form of anything in heaven above or on the earth beneath or in the waters below. **5** You shall not bow down to them or worship them; for I, the LORD your God, am a jealous God, punishing the children for the sin of the fathers to the third and fourth generation of those who hate me, **6** but showing love to a thousand ˪generations˺ of those who love me and keep my commandments.

7 "You shall not misuse the name of the LORD your God, for the LORD will not hold anyone guiltless who misuses his name.

8 "Remember the Sabbath day by keeping it holy. **9** Six days you shall labor and do all your work, **10** but the seventh day is a Sabbath to the LORD your God. On it you shall not do any work, neither you, nor your son or daughter, nor your manservant or maidservant, nor your animals, nor the alien within your gates. **11** For in six days the LORD made the heavens and the earth, the sea, and all that is in them, but he rested on the seventh day. Therefore the LORD blessed the Sabbath day and made it holy.

12 "Honor your father and your mother, so that you may live long in the land the LORD your God is giving you.

13 "You shall not murder.

14 "You shall not commit adultery.

15 "You shall not steal.

16 "You shall not give false testimony against your neighbor.

17 "You shall not covet your neighbor's house. You shall not covet your neighbor's wife, or his manservant or maidservant, his ox or donkey, or anything that belongs to your neighbor."

18 When the people saw the thunder and lightning and

a 3 Or besides

heard the trumpet and saw the mountain in smoke, they trembled with fear. They stayed at a distance ¹⁹and said to Moses, "Speak to us yourself and we will listen. But do not have God speak to us or we will die."

²⁰Moses said to the people, "Do not be afraid. God has come to test you, so that the fear of God will be with you to keep you from sinning."

²¹The people remained at a distance, while Moses approached the thick darkness where God was.

Idols and Altars

²²Then the LORD said to Moses, "Tell the Israelites this: 'You have seen for yourselves that I have spoken to you from heaven: ²³Do not make any gods to be alongside me; do not make for yourselves gods of silver or gods of gold.

²⁴" 'Make an altar of earth for me and sacrifice on it your burnt offerings and fellowship offerings,ᵃ your sheep and goats and your cattle. Wherever I cause my name to be honored, I will come to you and bless you. ²⁵If you make an altar of stones for me, do not build it with dressed stones, for you will defile it if you use a tool on it. ²⁶And do not go up to my altar on steps, lest your nakedness be exposed on it.'

21

"These are the laws you are to set before them:

Hebrew Servants

²"If you buy a Hebrew servant, he is to serve you for six years. But in the seventh year, he shall go free, without paying anything. ³If he comes alone, he is to go free alone; but if he has a wife when he comes, she is to go with him. ⁴If his master gives him a wife and she bears him sons or daughters, the woman and her children shall belong to her master, and only the man shall go free.

⁵"But if the servant declares, 'I love my master and my wife and children and do not want to go free,' ⁶then his master must take him before the judges.ᵇ He shall take him to the door or the doorpost and pierce his ear with an awl. Then he will be his servant for life.

⁷"If a man sells his daughter as a servant, she is not to go free as menservants do. ⁸If she does not please the master who has selected her for himself,ᶜ he must let her be redeemed. He has no right to sell her to foreigners, because he has broken faith with her. ⁹If he selects her for his son, he must grant her the rights of a daughter. ¹⁰If he marries another woman, he must not deprive the first one of her food, clothing and marital rights. ¹¹If he does not provide her with these three things, she is to go free, without any payment of money.

Personal Injuries

¹²"Anyone who strikes a man and kills him shall surely be put to death. ¹³However, if he does not do it intentionally, but God lets it happen, he is to flee to a place I will designate. ¹⁴But if a man schemes and kills another man deliberately, take him away from my altar and put him to death.

ᵃ 24 Traditionally *peace offerings*   ᵇ 6 Or *before God*   ᶜ 8 Or *master so that he does not choose her*

Sinai and Our Life Together

EXODUS 21:1–18

God sets a lengthy series of laws before Moses and the people. As we read through them, we can see an amazing thing—a nation is brought into being. For in the end, this is a purpose of the laws: They define how the people will live together in health and righteousness to the glory of God.

On a sheet of paper, make a list of the rules that govern the life of your family, your smaller community of faith or your church. What are the unspoken rules? Is it taken for granted, for instance, that if someone asks for prayers, you will all pray for that person? Do you honor confidences and refuse to gossip? If someone is in need, do you take what actions you can to help? Perhaps there are other things you can do as a family or as a church that will glorify God and promote loving relationships.

See Meeting God in Community

An Eye for an Eye?

EXODUS 21:23–25

What are we to make of this well-known law of retaliation? It helps to remember that its balanced approach represented a great advance among ancient legal systems, a softening influence among a people sometimes known for casual cruelty and escalating retribution. Later, Jesus was to go even further with the law of love, insisting that believers turn the other cheek and go the extra mile (see Matthew 5:38–42).

When have you been tempted to take revenge? Think about people against whom you may harbor hard or harsh feelings. Write down their names. One by one, pray about the hurt each one has caused you. Seek God's help for the difficult process of forgiveness and reconciliation. Ask God if there is anything you need to do to make something right, or if you need to take the risk of confronting someone.

See Meeting God in Community

15 "Anyone who attacks[a] his father or his mother must be put to death.

16 "Anyone who kidnaps another and either sells him or still has him when he is caught must be put to death.

17 "Anyone who curses his father or mother must be put to death.

18 "If men quarrel and one hits the other with a stone or with his fist[b] and he does not die but is confined to bed, 19 the one who struck the blow will not be held responsible if the other gets up and walks around outside with his staff; however, he must pay the injured man for the loss of his time and see that he is completely healed.

20 "If a man beats his male or female slave with a rod and the slave dies as a direct result, he must be punished, 21 but he is not to be punished if the slave gets up after a day or two, since the slave is his property.

22 "If men who are fighting hit a pregnant woman and she gives birth prematurely[c] but there is no serious injury, the offender must be fined whatever the woman's husband demands and the court allows. 23 But if there is serious injury, you are to take life for life, 24 eye for eye, tooth for tooth, hand for hand, foot for foot, 25 burn for burn, wound for wound, bruise for bruise.

26 "If a man hits a manservant or maidservant in the eye and destroys it, he must let the servant go free to compensate for the eye. 27 And if he knocks out the tooth of a manservant or maidservant, he must let the servant go free to compensate for the tooth.

28 "If a bull gores a man or a woman to death, the bull must be stoned to death, and its meat must not be eaten. But the owner of the bull will not be held responsible. 29 If, however, the bull has had the habit of goring and the owner has been warned but has not kept it penned up and it kills a man or woman, the bull must be stoned and the owner also must be put to death. 30 However, if payment is demanded of him, he may redeem his life by paying whatever is demanded. 31 This law also applies if the bull gores a son or daughter. 32 If the bull gores a male or female slave, the owner must pay thirty shekels[d] of silver to the master of the slave, and the bull must be stoned.

33 "If a man uncovers a pit or digs one and fails to cover it and an ox or a donkey falls into it, 34 the owner of the pit must pay for the loss; he must pay its owner, and the dead animal will be his.

35 "If a man's bull injures the bull of another and it dies, they are to sell the live one and divide both the money and the dead animal equally. 36 However, if it was known that the bull had the habit of goring, yet the owner did not keep it penned up, the owner must pay, animal for animal, and the dead animal will be his.

Protection of Property

22 "If a man steals an ox or a sheep and slaughters it or sells it, he must pay back five head of cattle for the ox and four sheep for the sheep.

2 "If a thief is caught breaking in and is struck so that he dies, the defender is not guilty of bloodshed; 3 but if it happens[e] after sunrise, he is guilty of bloodshed.

---

a 15 Or *kills*　　b 18 Or *with a tool*　　c 22 Or *she has a miscarriage*
d 32 That is, about 12 ounces (about 0.3 kilogram)　　e 3 Or *if he strikes him*

"A thief must certainly make restitution, but if he has nothing, he must be sold to pay for his theft.

[4] "If the stolen animal is found alive in his possession—whether ox or donkey or sheep—he must pay back double.

[5] "If a man grazes his livestock in a field or vineyard and lets them stray and they graze in another man's field, he must make restitution from the best of his own field or vineyard.

[6] "If a fire breaks out and spreads into thornbushes so that it burns shocks of grain or standing grain or the whole field, the one who started the fire must make restitution.

[7] "If a man gives his neighbor silver or goods for safekeeping and they are stolen from the neighbor's house, the thief, if he is caught, must pay back double. [8] But if the thief is not found, the owner of the house must appear before the judges[a] to determine whether he has laid his hands on the other man's property. [9] In all cases of illegal possession of an ox, a donkey, a sheep, a garment, or any other lost property about which somebody says, 'This is mine,' both parties are to bring their cases before the judges. The one whom the judges declare[b] guilty must pay back double to his neighbor.

[10] "If a man gives a donkey, an ox, a sheep or any other animal to his neighbor for safekeeping and it dies or is injured or is taken away while no one is looking, [11] the issue between them will be settled by the taking of an oath before the LORD that the neighbor did not lay hands on the other person's property. The owner is to accept this, and no restitution is required. [12] But if the animal was stolen from the neighbor, he must make restitution to the owner. [13] If it was torn to pieces by a wild animal, he shall bring in the remains as evidence and he will not be required to pay for the torn animal.

[14] "If a man borrows an animal from his neighbor and it is injured or dies while the owner is not present, he must make restitution. [15] But if the owner is with the animal, the borrower will not have to pay. If the animal was hired, the money paid for the hire covers the loss.

Social Responsibility

[16] "If a man seduces a virgin who is not pledged to be married and sleeps with her, he must pay the bride-price, and she shall be his wife. [17] If her father absolutely refuses to give her to him, he must still pay the bride-price for virgins.

[18] "Do not allow a sorceress to live.

[19] "Anyone who has sexual relations with an animal must be put to death.

[20] "Whoever sacrifices to any god other than the LORD must be destroyed.[c]

[21] "Do not mistreat an alien or oppress him, for you were aliens in Egypt.

[22] "Do not take advantage of a widow or an orphan. [23] If you do and they cry out to me, I will certainly hear their cry. [24] My anger will be aroused, and I will kill you with the sword; your wives will become widows and your children fatherless.

Whatsoever You Do . . .

EXODUS 22:5–9

"Keep in mind that each of you has your own vineyard. But every one is joined to your neighbors' vineyards without any dividing lines. They are so joined together, in fact, that you cannot do good or evil for yourself without doing the same for your neighbors."

—CATHERINE OF SIENA,
The Dialogue

See *Meeting God in Community*

---

[a] 8 Or *before God*; also in verse 9   [b] 9 Or *whom God declares*   [c] 20 The Hebrew term refers to the irrevocable giving over of things or persons to the LORD, often by totally destroying them.

Enemy Love

EXODUS 23:4–5

Here we find a highly refined sensitivity to fairness in legal justice and even an expansive benevolence toward one's enemy: "If you come across your enemy's ox or donkey wandering off, be sure to take it back to him." These are challenging directives even for Christians today. It is sometimes difficult to remember, in the middle of all our own concerns, that God also expects us to concern ourselves with the lives of others, including those who are a source of pain or irritation. The next time you find yourself ready to give a sharp response, recall God's directive in this Scripture passage to show compassion even to those you find difficult. Surprise your enemy with a soft word or an act of kindness.

See Meeting God in Community

[25]"If you lend money to one of my people among you who is needy, do not be like a moneylender; charge him no interest.[a] [26]If you take your neighbor's cloak as a pledge, return it to him by sunset, [27]because his cloak is the only covering he has for his body. What else will he sleep in? When he cries out to me, I will hear, for I am compassionate.

[28]"Do not blaspheme God[b] or curse the ruler of your people.

[29]"Do not hold back offerings from your granaries or your vats.[c]

"You must give me the firstborn of your sons. [30]Do the same with your cattle and your sheep. Let them stay with their mothers for seven days, but give them to me on the eighth day.

[31]"You are to be my holy people. So do not eat the meat of an animal torn by wild beasts; throw it to the dogs.

Laws of Justice and Mercy

23 "Do not spread false reports. Do not help a wicked man by being a malicious witness.

[2]"Do not follow the crowd in doing wrong. When you give testimony in a lawsuit, do not pervert justice by siding with the crowd, [3]and do not show favoritism to a poor man in his lawsuit.

[4]"If you come across your enemy's ox or donkey wandering off, be sure to take it back to him. [5]If you see the donkey of someone who hates you fallen down under its load, do not leave it there; be sure you help him with it.

[6]"Do not deny justice to your poor people in their lawsuits. [7]Have nothing to do with a false charge and do not put an innocent or honest person to death, for I will not acquit the guilty.

[8]"Do not accept a bribe, for a bribe blinds those who see and twists the words of the righteous.

[9]"Do not oppress an alien; you yourselves know how it feels to be aliens, because you were aliens in Egypt.

Sabbath Laws

[10]"For six years you are to sow your fields and harvest the crops, [11]but during the seventh year let the land lie unplowed and unused. Then the poor among your people may get food from it, and the wild animals may eat what they leave. Do the same with your vineyard and your olive grove.

[12]"Six days do your work, but on the seventh day do not work, so that your ox and your donkey may rest and the slave born in your household, and the alien as well, may be refreshed.

[13]"Be careful to do everything I have said to you. Do not invoke the names of other gods; do not let them be heard on your lips.

The Three Annual Festivals

[14]"Three times a year you are to celebrate a festival to me.

[15]"Celebrate the Feast of Unleavened Bread; for seven days eat bread made without yeast, as I commanded you.

a 25 Or *excessive interest*   *b 28* Or *Do not revile the judges*   *c 29* The meaning of the Hebrew for this phrase is uncertain.

Do this at the appointed time in the month of Abib, for in that month you came out of Egypt.

"No one is to appear before me empty-handed.

¹⁶"Celebrate the Feast of Harvest with the firstfruits of the crops you sow in your field.

"Celebrate the Feast of Ingathering at the end of the year, when you gather in your crops from the field.

¹⁷"Three times a year all the men are to appear before the Sovereign LORD.

¹⁸"Do not offer the blood of a sacrifice to me along with anything containing yeast.

"The fat of my festival offerings must not be kept until morning.

¹⁹"Bring the best of the firstfruits of your soil to the house of the LORD your God.

"Do not cook a young goat in its mother's milk.

God's Angel to Prepare the Way

²⁰"See, I am sending an angel ahead of you to guard you along the way and to bring you to the place I have prepared. ²¹Pay attention to him and listen to what he says. Do not rebel against him; he will not forgive your rebellion, since my Name is in him. ²²If you listen carefully to what he says and do all that I say, I will be an enemy to your enemies and will oppose those who oppose you. ²³My angel will go ahead of you and bring you into the land of the Amorites, Hittites, Perizzites, Canaanites, Hivites and Jebusites, and I will wipe them out. ²⁴Do not bow down before their gods or worship them or follow their practices. You must demolish them and break their sacred stones to pieces. ²⁵Worship the LORD your God, and his blessing will be on your food and water. I will take away sickness from among you, ²⁶and none will miscarry or be barren in your land. I will give you a full life span.

²⁷"I will send my terror ahead of you and throw into confusion every nation you encounter. I will make all your enemies turn their backs and run. ²⁸I will send the hornet ahead of you to drive the Hivites, Canaanites and Hittites out of your way. ²⁹But I will not drive them out in a single year, because the land would become desolate and the wild animals too numerous for you. ³⁰Little by little I will drive them out before you, until you have increased enough to take possession of the land.

³¹"I will establish your borders from the Red Sea[a] to the Sea of the Philistines,[b] and from the desert to the River.[c] I will hand over to you the people who live in the land and you will drive them out before you. ³²Do not make a covenant with them or with their gods. ³³Do not let them live in your land, or they will cause you to sin against me, because the worship of their gods will certainly be a snare to you."

The Covenant Confirmed

24 Then he said to Moses, "Come up to the LORD, you and Aaron, Nadab and Abihu, and seventy of the elders of Israel. You are to worship at a distance, ²but Moses alone is to approach the LORD; the others must not come near. And the people may not come up with him."

Remember Your Angel

EXODUS 23:20

God sends an angel in front of the people to guard them and to bring them "to the place I have prepared." Even though they trekked through a desert, they knew they were not alone.

These words invite your personal response. Hear them as though they are spoken to you. Think back to earlier stages in your own journey when it seemed difficult, if not impossible, to go on. Remember how, in spite of overwhelming problems, emotional or financial struggles, perhaps even moral lapses, God walked with you and assisted you. You made it after all. Make this promise of presence and protection the basis of grateful prayer.

See Meeting God in Everyday Life

Entering the Cloud

There is a Moses inside every one of us, hungering to break away from the ordinary and everyday, to explore frontiers, to ascend the heights, to get close to the heart of God.

When was the last time you set apart a time and a place to be alone with God, to allow God to speak to you? Explore the possibilities of finding a monastic or lay retreat center that offers weekend or extended retreats. And don't overlook the resources nearest you: a solitary walk in the park, a place at the water's edge to watch a sunrise or sunset. The glory of the Lord awaits you.

See Meeting God in Prayer

³When Moses went and told the people all the Lord's words and laws, they responded with one voice, "Everything the Lord has said we will do." ⁴Moses then wrote down everything the Lord had said.

He got up early the next morning and built an altar at the foot of the mountain and set up twelve stone pillars representing the twelve tribes of Israel. ⁵Then he sent young Israelite men, and they offered burnt offerings and sacrificed young bulls as fellowship offerings[a] to the Lord. ⁶Moses took half of the blood and put it in bowls, and the other half he sprinkled on the altar. ⁷Then he took the Book of the Covenant and read it to the people. They responded, "We will do everything the Lord has said; we will obey."

⁸Moses then took the blood, sprinkled it on the people and said, "This is the blood of the covenant that the Lord has made with you in accordance with all these words."

⁹Moses and Aaron, Nadab and Abihu, and the seventy elders of Israel went up ¹⁰and saw the God of Israel. Under his feet was something like a pavement made of sapphire,[b] clear as the sky itself. ¹¹But God did not raise his hand against these leaders of the Israelites; they saw God, and they ate and drank.

¹²The Lord said to Moses, "Come up to me on the mountain and stay here, and I will give you the tablets of stone, with the law and commands I have written for their instruction."

¹³Then Moses set out with Joshua his aide, and Moses went up on the mountain of God. ¹⁴He said to the elders, "Wait here for us until we come back to you. Aaron and Hur are with you, and anyone involved in a dispute can go to them."

¹⁵When Moses went up on the mountain, the cloud covered it, ¹⁶and the glory of the Lord settled on Mount Sinai. For six days the cloud covered the mountain, and on the seventh day the Lord called to Moses from within the cloud. ¹⁷To the Israelites the glory of the Lord looked like a consuming fire on top of the mountain. ¹⁸Then Moses entered the cloud as he went on up the mountain. And he stayed on the mountain forty days and forty nights.

Offerings for the Tabernacle

25 The Lord said to Moses, ²"Tell the Israelites to bring me an offering. You are to receive the offering for me from each man whose heart prompts him to give. ³These are the offerings you are to receive from them: gold, silver and bronze; ⁴blue, purple and scarlet yarn and fine linen; goat hair; ⁵ram skins dyed red and hides of sea cows[c]; acacia wood; ⁶olive oil for the light; spices for the anointing oil and for the fragrant incense; ⁷and onyx stones and other gems to be mounted on the ephod and breastpiece.

⁸"Then have them make a sanctuary for me, and I will dwell among them. ⁹Make this tabernacle and all its furnishings exactly like the pattern I will show you.

The Ark

¹⁰"Have them make a chest of acacia wood—two and a half cubits long, a cubit and a half wide, and a cubit and a

half high.*ª* ¹¹Overlay it with pure gold, both inside and out, and make a gold molding around it. ¹²Cast four gold rings for it and fasten them to its four feet, with two rings on one side and two rings on the other. ¹³Then make poles of acacia wood and overlay them with gold. ¹⁴Insert the poles into the rings on the sides of the chest to carry it. ¹⁵The poles are to remain in the rings of this ark; they are not to be removed. ¹⁶Then put in the ark the Testimony, which I will give you.

¹⁷"Make an atonement cover*ᵇ* of pure gold—two and a half cubits long and a cubit and a half wide.*ᶜ* ¹⁸And make two cherubim out of hammered gold at the ends of the cover. ¹⁹Make one cherub on one end and the second cherub on the other; make the cherubim of one piece with the cover, at the two ends. ²⁰The cherubim are to have their wings spread upward, overshadowing the cover with them. The cherubim are to face each other, looking toward the cover. ²¹Place the cover on top of the ark and put in the ark the Testimony, which I will give you. ²²There, above the cover between the two cherubim that are over the ark of the Testimony, I will meet with you and give you all my commands for the Israelites.

The Table

²³"Make a table of acacia wood—two cubits long, a cubit wide and a cubit and a half high.*ᵈ* ²⁴Overlay it with pure gold and make a gold molding around it. ²⁵Also make around it a rim a handbreadth*ᵉ* wide and put a gold molding on the rim. ²⁶Make four gold rings for the table and fasten them to the four corners, where the four legs are. ²⁷The rings are to be close to the rim to hold the poles used in carrying the table. ²⁸Make the poles of acacia wood, overlay them with gold and carry the table with them. ²⁹And make its plates and dishes of pure gold, as well as its pitchers and bowls for the pouring out of offerings. ³⁰Put the bread of the Presence on this table to be before me at all times.

The Lampstand

³¹"Make a lampstand of pure gold and hammer it out, base and shaft; its flowerlike cups, buds and blossoms shall be of one piece with it. ³²Six branches are to extend from the sides of the lampstand—three on one side and three on the other. ³³Three cups shaped like almond flowers with buds and blossoms are to be on one branch, three on the next branch, and the same for all six branches extending from the lampstand. ³⁴And on the lampstand there are to be four cups shaped like almond flowers with buds and blossoms. ³⁵One bud shall be under the first pair of branches extending from the lampstand, a second bud under the second pair, and a third bud under the third pair—six branches in all. ³⁶The buds and branches shall all be of one piece with the lampstand, hammered out of pure gold.

³⁷"Then make its seven lamps and set them up on it so that they light the space in front of it. ³⁸Its wick trimmers and trays are to be of pure gold. ³⁹A talent*ᶠ* of pure gold is

---

ª 10 That is, about 3 3/4 feet (about 1.1 meters) long and 2 1/4 feet (about 0.7 meter) wide and high   *ᵇ 17* Traditionally *a mercy seat*   *ᶜ 17* That is, about 3 3/4 feet (about 1.1 meters) long and 2 1/4 feet (about 0.7 meter) wide   *ᵈ 23* That is, about 3 feet (about 0.9 meter) long and 1 1/2 feet (about 0.5 meter) wide and 2 1/4 feet (about 0.7 meter) high   *ᵉ 25* That is, about 3 inches (about 8 centimeters)   *ᶠ 39* That is, about 75 pounds (about 34 kilograms)

A Matter of the Heart

EXODUS 25:10–30

Moses was not commanded to build the tabernacle by himself. It was to be a community effort. Building resources were to come "from each man whose heart prompt[ed]him to give" (v. 2). Likewise, religious leaders are facilitators at the service of the community, not independent entities. Community worship is meant to provide a way for everyone in the body of Christ to participate.

Take time now to reflect on the role you fill in your worshiping community. What personal contribution can you make to public worship? Prayerfully think about volunteering to work as an usher, Scripture reader, minister of the bread or cup, hospitality helper, or whatever gift your heart prompts you to give.

See Meeting God in Service

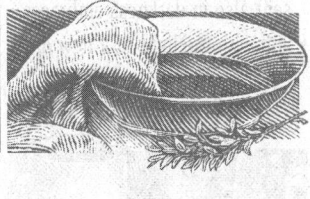

Curtains and Light

EXODUS 26: 1–14

As you read the details of God's instructions to Moses for the furnishings of the tabernacle, you may be struck by the importance given to curtains. Stop and reflect on the role curtains play in ordinary home life. Closed, they provide privacy, a space where we can be alone. Open, they invite rays of golden sunlight. Curtains in the tabernacle can speak to us powerfully as symbols of God's nearness, but also of God's hiddenness. Recall the experiences in your life when God seemed most present. Next recall when God seemed most hidden.

Set your alarm and get up a few minutes before dawn. Go to a window and open the curtains. In the quiet of early morning, experience the transition from darkness to light. Greet the dawn with the prayer of your heart as the God present also in darkness embraces you with the light of a new day.

See Meeting God in Everyday Life

to be used for the lampstand and all these accessories. [40]See that you make them according to the pattern shown you on the mountain.

The Tabernacle

26 "Make the tabernacle with ten curtains of finely twisted linen and blue, purple and scarlet yarn, with cherubim worked into them by a skilled craftsman. [2]All the curtains are to be the same size—twenty-eight cubits long and four cubits wide.[a] [3]Join five of the curtains together, and do the same with the other five. [4]Make loops of blue material along the edge of the end curtain in one set, and do the same with the end curtain in the other set. [5]Make fifty loops on one curtain and fifty loops on the end curtain of the other set, with the loops opposite each other. [6]Then make fifty gold clasps and use them to fasten the curtains together so that the tabernacle is a unit.

[7]"Make curtains of goat hair for the tent over the tabernacle—eleven altogether. [8]All eleven curtains are to be the same size—thirty cubits long and four cubits wide.[b] [9]Join five of the curtains together into one set and the other six into another set. Fold the sixth curtain double at the front of the tent. [10]Make fifty loops along the edge of the end curtain in one set and also along the edge of the end curtain in the other set. [11]Then make fifty bronze clasps and put them in the loops to fasten the tent together as a unit. [12]As for the additional length of the tent curtains, the half curtain that is left over is to hang down at the rear of the tabernacle. [13]The tent curtains will be a cubit[c] longer on both sides; what is left will hang over the sides of the tabernacle so as to cover it. [14]Make for the tent a covering of ram skins dyed red, and over that a covering of hides of sea cows.[d]

[15]"Make upright frames of acacia wood for the tabernacle. [16]Each frame is to be ten cubits long and a cubit and a half wide,[e] [17]with two projections set parallel to each other. Make all the frames of the tabernacle in this way. [18]Make twenty frames for the south side of the tabernacle [19]and make forty silver bases to go under them—two bases for each frame, one under each projection. [20]For the other side, the north side of the tabernacle, make twenty frames [21]and forty silver bases—two under each frame. [22]Make six frames for the far end, that is, the west end of the tabernacle, [23]and make two frames for the corners at the far end. [24]At these two corners they must be double from the bottom all the way to the top, and fitted into a single ring; both shall be like that. [25]So there will be eight frames and sixteen silver bases—two under each frame.

[26]"Also make crossbars of acacia wood: five for the frames on one side of the tabernacle, [27]five for those on the other side, and five for the frames on the west, at the far end of the tabernacle. [28]The center crossbar is to extend from end to end at the middle of the frames. [29]Overlay the frames with gold and make gold rings to hold the crossbars. Also overlay the crossbars with gold.

a 2 That is, about 42 feet (about 12.5 meters) long and 6 feet (about 1.8 meters) wide   *b 8* That is, about 45 feet (about 13.5 meters) long and 6 feet (about 1.8 meters) wide   *c 13* That is, about 1 1/2 feet (about 0.5 meter)   *d 14* That is, dugongs   *e 16* That is, about 15 feet (about 4.5 meters) long and 2 1/4 feet (about 0.7 meter) wide

30"Set up the tabernacle according to the plan shown you on the mountain.

31"Make a curtain of blue, purple and scarlet yarn and finely twisted linen, with cherubim worked into it by a skilled craftsman. 32Hang it with gold hooks on four posts of acacia wood overlaid with gold and standing on four silver bases. 33Hang the curtain from the clasps and place the ark of the Testimony behind the curtain. The curtain will separate the Holy Place from the Most Holy Place. 34Put the atonement cover on the ark of the Testimony in the Most Holy Place. 35Place the table outside the curtain on the north side of the tabernacle and put the lampstand opposite it on the south side.

36"For the entrance to the tent make a curtain of blue, purple and scarlet yarn and finely twisted linen—the work of an embroiderer. 37Make gold hooks for this curtain and five posts of acacia wood overlaid with gold. And cast five bronze bases for them.

The Altar of Burnt Offering

27 "Build an altar of acacia wood, three cubits*a* high; it is to be square, five cubits long and five cubits wide.*b* 2Make a horn at each of the four corners, so that the horns and the altar are of one piece, and overlay the altar with bronze. 3Make all its utensils of bronze—its pots to remove the ashes, and its shovels, sprinkling bowls, meat forks and firepans. 4Make a grating for it, a bronze network, and make a bronze ring at each of the four corners of the network. 5Put it under the ledge of the altar so that it is halfway up the altar. 6Make poles of acacia wood for the altar and overlay them with bronze. 7The poles are to be inserted into the rings so they will be on two sides of the altar when it is carried. 8Make the altar hollow, out of boards. It is to be made just as you were shown on the mountain.

The Courtyard

9"Make a courtyard for the tabernacle. The south side shall be a hundred cubits*c* long and is to have curtains of finely twisted linen, 10with twenty posts and twenty bronze bases and with silver hooks and bands on the posts. 11The north side shall also be a hundred cubits long and is to have curtains, with twenty posts and twenty bronze bases and with silver hooks and bands on the posts.

12"The west end of the courtyard shall be fifty cubits*d* wide and have curtains, with ten posts and ten bases. 13On the east end, toward the sunrise, the courtyard shall also be fifty cubits wide. 14Curtains fifteen cubits*e* long are to be on one side of the entrance, with three posts and three bases, 15and curtains fifteen cubits long are to be on the other side, with three posts and three bases.

16"For the entrance to the courtyard, provide a curtain twenty cubits*f* long, of blue, purple and scarlet yarn and finely twisted linen—the work of an embroiderer—with four posts and four bases. 17All the posts around the courtyard are to have silver bands and hooks, and bronze bases.

---

a 1 That is, about 4 1/2 feet (about 1.3 meters)   *b 1* That is, about 7 1/2 feet (about 2.3 meters) long and wide   *c 9* That is, about 150 feet (about 46 meters); also in verse 11   *d 12* That is, about 75 feet (about 23 meters); also in verse 13   *e 14* That is, about 22 1/2 feet (about 6.9 meters); also in verse 15   *f 16* That is, about 30 feet (about 9 meters)

Making a Sanctuary

EXODUS 26:26–37

"God wishes . . . . that we make a sanctuary for him. For he promises that if we make a sanctuary for him, he can be seen by us . . . . This, therefore, is the sanctuary which the Lord wishes to be constructed . . . knowing without doubt that he who makes a sanctuary for the Lord by the purity of his own heart and body will himself see God. Let us, therefore, also make a sanctuary for the Lord both collectively and individually."

—ORIGEN OF ALEXANDRIA,
Homilies On Exodus

A Lamp to Burn Regularly

EXODUS 27:20–21

Note the importance placed on keeping a lamp burning at all times. Candlelight has always had a special place in both religious and civil festive celebration. Lighting a candle before a meal or before saying a prayer can be an effective way to instill in those gathered a sense of the sacred. Let candles light the family table or the places where you pray. Consider lighting a candle now, letting the light remind you of Jesus, the light of the world.

[18]The courtyard shall be a hundred cubits long and fifty cubits wide,[a] with curtains of finely twisted linen five cubits[b] high, and with bronze bases. [19]All the other articles used in the service of the tabernacle, whatever their function, including all the tent pegs for it and those for the courtyard, are to be of bronze.

Oil for the Lampstand

[20]"Command the Israelites to bring you clear oil of pressed olives for the light so that the lamps may be kept burning. [21]In the Tent of Meeting, outside the curtain that is in front of the Testimony, Aaron and his sons are to keep the lamps burning before the LORD from evening till morning. This is to be a lasting ordinance among the Israelites for the generations to come.

The Priestly Garments

28 "Have Aaron your brother brought to you from among the Israelites, along with his sons Nadab and Abihu, Eleazar and Ithamar, so they may serve me as priests. [2]Make sacred garments for your brother Aaron, to give him dignity and honor. [3]Tell all the skilled men to whom I have given wisdom in such matters that they are to make garments for Aaron, for his consecration, so he may serve me as priest. [4]These are the garments they are to make: a breastpiece, an ephod, a robe, a woven tunic, a turban and a sash. They are to make these sacred garments for your brother Aaron and his sons, so they may serve me as priests. [5]Have them use gold, and blue, purple and scarlet yarn, and fine linen.

The Ephod

[6]"Make the ephod of gold, and of blue, purple and scarlet yarn, and of finely twisted linen—the work of a skilled craftsman. [7]It is to have two shoulder pieces attached to two of its corners, so it can be fastened. [8]Its skillfully woven waistband is to be like it—of one piece with the ephod and made with gold, and with blue, purple and scarlet yarn, and with finely twisted linen.

[9]"Take two onyx stones and engrave on them the names of the sons of Israel [10]in the order of their birth—six names on one stone and the remaining six on the other. [11]Engrave the names of the sons of Israel on the two stones the way a gem cutter engraves a seal. Then mount the stones in gold filigree settings [12]and fasten them on the shoulder pieces of the ephod as memorial stones for the sons of Israel. Aaron is to bear the names on his shoulders as a memorial before the LORD. [13]Make gold filigree settings [14]and two braided chains of pure gold, like a rope, and attach the chains to the settings.

The Breastpiece

[15]"Fashion a breastpiece for making decisions—the work of a skilled craftsman. Make it like the ephod: of gold, and of blue, purple and scarlet yarn, and of finely twisted linen. [16]It is to be square—a span[c] long and a span wide—and folded double. [17]Then mount four rows of precious stones

---

[a] 18 That is, about 150 feet (about 46 meters) long and 75 feet (about 23 meters) wide   [b] 18 That is, about 7 1/2 feet (about 2.3 meters)   [c] 16 That is, about 9 inches (about 22 centimeters)

on it. In the first row there shall be a ruby, a topaz and a beryl; [18]in the second row a turquoise, a sapphire[a] and an emerald; [19]in the third row a jacinth, an agate and an amethyst; [20]in the fourth row a chrysolite, an onyx and a jasper.[b] Mount them in gold filigree settings. [21]There are to be twelve stones, one for each of the names of the sons of Israel, each engraved like a seal with the name of one of the twelve tribes.

[22]"For the breastpiece make braided chains of pure gold, like a rope. [23]Make two gold rings for it and fasten them to two corners of the breastpiece. [24]Fasten the two gold chains to the rings at the corners of the breastpiece, [25]and the other ends of the chains to the two settings, attaching them to the shoulder pieces of the ephod at the front. [26]Make two gold rings and attach them to the other two corners of the breastpiece on the inside edge next to the ephod. [27]Make two more gold rings and attach them to the bottom of the shoulder pieces on the front of the ephod, close to the seam just above the waistband of the ephod. [28]The rings of the breastpiece are to be tied to the rings of the ephod with blue cord, connecting it to the waistband, so that the breastpiece will not swing out from the ephod.

[29]"Whenever Aaron enters the Holy Place, he will bear the names of the sons of Israel over his heart on the breastpiece of decision as a continuing memorial before the LORD. [30]Also put the Urim and the Thummim in the breastpiece, so they may be over Aaron's heart whenever he enters the presence of the LORD. Thus Aaron will always bear the means of making decisions for the Israelites over his heart before the LORD.

Other Priestly Garments

[31]"Make the robe of the ephod entirely of blue cloth, [32]with an opening for the head in its center. There shall be a woven edge like a collar[c] around this opening, so that it will not tear. [33]Make pomegranates of blue, purple and scarlet yarn around the hem of the robe, with gold bells between them. [34]The gold bells and the pomegranates are to alternate around the hem of the robe. [35]Aaron must wear it when he ministers. The sound of the bells will be heard when he enters the Holy Place before the LORD and when he comes out, so that he will not die.

[36]"Make a plate of pure gold and engrave on it as on a seal: HOLY TO THE LORD. [37]Fasten a blue cord to it to attach it to the turban; it is to be on the front of the turban. [38]It will be on Aaron's forehead, and he will bear the guilt involved in the sacred gifts the Israelites consecrate, whatever their gifts may be. It will be on Aaron's forehead continually so that they will be acceptable to the LORD.

[39]"Weave the tunic of fine linen and make the turban of fine linen. The sash is to be the work of an embroiderer. [40]Make tunics, sashes and headbands for Aaron's sons, to give them dignity and honor. [41]After you put these clothes on your brother Aaron and his sons, anoint and ordain them. Consecrate them so they may serve me as priests.

[42]"Make linen undergarments as a covering for the body, reaching from the waist to the thigh. [43]Aaron and his sons

---

Living to Make Intercession

EXODUS 28:29–40

Notice that Aaron, when approaching the holy place, is directed to "bear the names of the sons of Israel over his heart." With this passage in mind, notice how the New Testament letter to the Hebrews refers to the risen Christ entering the heavenly sanctuary: "He is able to save completely those who come to God through him, because he always lives to intercede for them" (Hebrews 7:25). Reflect on the implications of knowing that the risen Jesus enters the heavenly sanctuary bearing your name in his heart. In what ways do you find encouragement in your praying from knowing that Jesus intercedes for you?

See Meeting God in Prayer

---

[a]18 Or *lapis lazuli*   [b]20 The precise identification of some of these precious stones is uncertain.   [c]32 The meaning of the Hebrew for this word is uncertain.

Ritual Sacrifices: A Contemporary Reading

EXODUS 29:1–14

Trying to understand the religious rituals of ancient times can be a challenge to modern believers. While we no longer slaughter cattle and burn livestock in our houses of worship, the vividness of Old Testament animal sacrifice still reminds us of the seriousness with which God views wrongdoing; restoration of what is broken by sin is never a casual affair.

Now that Jesus has come, abolishing forever the need for animal sacrifices, reflect prayerfully on God's costly, forgiving grace. What areas do you need to bring to God for an assurance of forgiveness? If it helps, write them down. Lift them up to God, reminding yourself that his love overcomes what separates you from him.

See Meeting God in Scripture

must wear them whenever they enter the Tent of Meeting or approach the altar to minister in the Holy Place, so that they will not incur guilt and die.

"This is to be a lasting ordinance for Aaron and his descendants.

Consecration of the Priests

29 "This is what you are to do to consecrate them, so they may serve me as priests: Take a young bull and two rams without defect. ²And from fine wheat flour, without yeast, make bread, and cakes mixed with oil, and wafers spread with oil. ³Put them in a basket and present them in it—along with the bull and the two rams. ⁴Then bring Aaron and his sons to the entrance to the Tent of Meeting and wash them with water. ⁵Take the garments and dress Aaron with the tunic, the robe of the ephod, the ephod itself and the breastpiece. Fasten the ephod on him by its skillfully woven waistband. ⁶Put the turban on his head and attach the sacred diadem to the turban. ⁷Take the anointing oil and anoint him by pouring it on his head. ⁸Bring his sons and dress them in tunics ⁹and put headbands on them. Then tie sashes on Aaron and his sons.ᵃ The priesthood is theirs by a lasting ordinance. In this way you shall ordain Aaron and his sons.

¹⁰"Bring the bull to the front of the Tent of Meeting, and Aaron and his sons shall lay their hands on its head. ¹¹Slaughter it in the LORD's presence at the entrance to the Tent of Meeting. ¹²Take some of the bull's blood and put it on the horns of the altar with your finger, and pour out the rest of it at the base of the altar. ¹³Then take all the fat around the inner parts, the covering of the liver, and both kidneys with the fat on them, and burn them on the altar. ¹⁴But burn the bull's flesh and its hide and its offal outside the camp. It is a sin offering.

¹⁵"Take one of the rams, and Aaron and his sons shall lay their hands on its head. ¹⁶Slaughter it and take the blood and sprinkle it against the altar on all sides. ¹⁷Cut the ram into pieces and wash the inner parts and the legs, putting them with the head and the other pieces. ¹⁸Then burn the entire ram on the altar. It is a burnt offering to the LORD, a pleasing aroma, an offering made to the LORD by fire.

¹⁹"Take the other ram, and Aaron and his sons shall lay their hands on its head. ²⁰Slaughter it, take some of its blood and put it on the lobes of the right ears of Aaron and his sons, on the thumbs of their right hands, and on the big toes of their right feet. Then sprinkle blood against the altar on all sides. ²¹And take some of the blood on the altar and some of the anointing oil and sprinkle it on Aaron and his garments and on his sons and their garments. Then he and his sons and their garments will be consecrated.

²²"Take from this ram the fat, the fat tail, the fat around the inner parts, the covering of the liver, both kidneys with the fat on them, and the right thigh. (This is the ram for the ordination.) ²³From the basket of bread made without yeast, which is before the LORD, take a loaf, and a cake made with oil, and a wafer. ²⁴Put all these in the hands of Aaron and his sons and wave them before the LORD as a wave offering. ²⁵Then take them from their hands and burn them on the altar along with the burnt offering for a pleas-

ᵃ9 Hebrew; Septuagint *on them*

ing aroma to the LORD, an offering made to the LORD by fire. ²⁶After you take the breast of the ram for Aaron's ordination, wave it before the LORD as a wave offering, and it will be your share.

²⁷"Consecrate those parts of the ordination ram that belong to Aaron and his sons: the breast that was waved and the thigh that was presented. ²⁸This is always to be the regular share from the Israelites for Aaron and his sons. It is the contribution the Israelites are to make to the LORD from their fellowship offerings.ᵃ

²⁹"Aaron's sacred garments will belong to his descendants so that they can be anointed and ordained in them. ³⁰The son who succeeds him as priest and comes to the Tent of Meeting to minister in the Holy Place is to wear them seven days.

³¹"Take the ram for the ordination and cook the meat in a sacred place. ³²At the entrance to the Tent of Meeting, Aaron and his sons are to eat the meat of the ram and the bread that is in the basket. ³³They are to eat these offerings by which atonement was made for their ordination and consecration. But no one else may eat them, because they are sacred. ³⁴And if any of the meat of the ordination ram or any bread is left over till morning, burn it up. It must not be eaten, because it is sacred.

³⁵"Do for Aaron and his sons everything I have commanded you, taking seven days to ordain them. ³⁶Sacrifice a bull each day as a sin offering to make atonement. Purify the altar by making atonement for it, and anoint it to consecrate it. ³⁷For seven days make atonement for the altar and consecrate it. Then the altar will be most holy, and whatever touches it will be holy.

³⁸"This is what you are to offer on the altar regularly each day: two lambs a year old. ³⁹Offer one in the morning and the other at twilight. ⁴⁰With the first lamb offer a tenth of an ephahᵇ of fine flour mixed with a quarter of a hinᶜ of oil from pressed olives, and a quarter of a hin of wine as a drink offering. ⁴¹Sacrifice the other lamb at twilight with the same grain offering and its drink offering as in the morning—a pleasing aroma, an offering made to the LORD by fire.

⁴²"For the generations to come this burnt offering is to be made regularly at the entrance to the Tent of Meeting before the LORD. There I will meet you and speak to you; ⁴³there also I will meet with the Israelites, and the place will be consecrated by my glory.

⁴⁴"So I will consecrate the Tent of Meeting and the altar and will consecrate Aaron and his sons to serve me as priests. ⁴⁵Then I will dwell among the Israelites and be their God. ⁴⁶They will know that I am the LORD their God, who brought them out of Egypt so that I might dwell among them. I am the LORD their God.

The Altar of Incense

30 "Make an altar of acacia wood for burning incense. ²It is to be square, a cubit long and a cubit wide, and two cubits highᵈ—its horns of one piece with it. ³Overlay the top and all the sides and the horns with pure gold, and

---

ᵃ28 Traditionally *peace offerings*   ᵇ40 That is, probably about 2 quarts (about 2 liters)   ᶜ40 That is, probably about 1 quart (about 1 liter)
ᵈ2 That is, about 1 1/2 feet (about 0.5 meter) long and wide and about 3 feet (about 0.9 meter) high

Ritual and Daily Life

EXODUS 29:29–46

What we do regularly has a way of seeping into our minds and influencing our daily behavior. Rituals such as those described in these verses, far from being irrelevant, can form a kind of backbone of religious life. Referring to the Tent of Meeting where offerings were made, God tells Moses, "There I will meet you and speak to you."

What role do rituals or spiritual habits play in your experience of faith and worship? Do they ever get in the way of your experience of God? Can you think of ways in which habitual practices enhance your worship? Pray about your participation in worship. How can it continue to keep your faith vital and growing?

See Meeting God in Worship

Precious Oils

EXODUS 30:22–38

Moses is commanded here to prepare oil for anointing with the rarest and most precious spices and perfumes. The oil is to be used only for sacred purposes in the sanctuary. What is marked with oil is thus declared holy and consecrated to God. Moses is to anoint not only Aaron and his sons, but practically everything!

Make a precious ointment yourself with mineral or baby oil and add your favorite fragrances to it. Today, or on some significant occasion, anoint your spouse, your children and your home. Use some appropriate words like, "You are set aside for God's work," or "You are sealed with this oil in the royal priesthood of Jesus Christ." Like another Moses you will be proclaiming their true worth in the Lord's eyes, and giving new sight to your own.

See Meeting God in Everyday Life

make a gold molding around it. ⁴Make two gold rings for the altar below the molding—two on opposite sides—to hold the poles used to carry it. ⁵Make the poles of acacia wood and overlay them with gold. ⁶Put the altar in front of the curtain that is before the ark of the Testimony—before the atonement cover that is over the Testimony—where I will meet with you.

⁷"Aaron must burn fragrant incense on the altar every morning when he tends the lamps. ⁸He must burn incense again when he lights the lamps at twilight so incense will burn regularly before the LORD for the generations to come. ⁹Do not offer on this altar any other incense or any burnt offering or grain offering, and do not pour a drink offering on it. ¹⁰Once a year Aaron shall make atonement on its horns. This annual atonement must be made with the blood of the atoning sin offering for the generations to come. It is most holy to the LORD."

Atonement Money

¹¹Then the LORD said to Moses, ¹²"When you take a census of the Israelites to count them, each one must pay the LORD a ransom for his life at the time he is counted. Then no plague will come on them when you number them. ¹³Each one who crosses over to those already counted is to give a half shekel,ᵃ according to the sanctuary shekel, which weighs twenty gerahs. This half shekel is an offering to the LORD. ¹⁴All who cross over, those twenty years old or more, are to give an offering to the LORD. ¹⁵The rich are not to give more than a half shekel and the poor are not to give less when you make the offering to the LORD to atone for your lives. ¹⁶Receive the atonement money from the Israelites and use it for the service of the Tent of Meeting. It will be a memorial for the Israelites before the LORD, making atonement for your lives."

Basin for Washing

¹⁷Then the LORD said to Moses, ¹⁸"Make a bronze basin, with its bronze stand, for washing. Place it between the Tent of Meeting and the altar, and put water in it. ¹⁹Aaron and his sons are to wash their hands and feet with water from it. ²⁰Whenever they enter the Tent of Meeting, they shall wash with water so that they will not die. Also, when they approach the altar to minister by presenting an offering made to the LORD by fire, ²¹they shall wash their hands and feet so that they will not die. This is to be a lasting ordinance for Aaron and his descendants for the generations to come."

Anointing Oil

²²Then the LORD said to Moses, ²³"Take the following fine spices: 500 shekelsᵇ of liquid myrrh, half as much (that is, 250 shekels) of fragrant cinnamon, 250 shekels of fragrant cane, ²⁴500 shekels of cassia—all according to the sanctuary shekel—and a hinᶜ of olive oil. ²⁵Make these into a sacred anointing oil, a fragrant blend, the work of a perfumer. It will be the sacred anointing oil. ²⁶Then use it to anoint the Tent of Meeting, the ark of the Testimony, ²⁷the table and all its articles, the lampstand and its accessories, the

---

ᵃ 13 That is, about 1/5 ounce (about 6 grams); also in verse 15   ᵇ 23 That is, about 12 1/2 pounds (about 6 kilograms)   ᶜ 24 That is, probably about 4 quarts (about 4 liters)

[18]Moses replied:

"It is not the sound of victory,
 it is not the sound of defeat;
 it is the sound of singing that I hear."

[19]When Moses approached the camp and saw the calf and the dancing, his anger burned and he threw the tablets out of his hands, breaking them to pieces at the foot of the mountain. [20]And he took the calf they had made and burned it in the fire; then he ground it to powder, scattered it on the water and made the Israelites drink it.

[21]He said to Aaron, "What did these people do to you, that you led them into such great sin?"

[22]"Do not be angry, my lord," Aaron answered. "You know how prone these people are to evil. [23]They said to me, 'Make us gods who will go before us. As for this fellow Moses who brought us up out of Egypt, we don't know what has happened to him.' [24]So I told them, 'Whoever has any gold jewelry, take it off.' Then they gave me the gold, and I threw it into the fire, and out came this calf!"

[25]Moses saw that the people were running wild and that Aaron had let them get out of control and so become a laughingstock to their enemies. [26]So he stood at the entrance to the camp and said, "Whoever is for the LORD, come to me." And all the Levites rallied to him.

[27]Then he said to them, "This is what the LORD, the God of Israel, says: 'Each man strap a sword to his side. Go back and forth through the camp from one end to the other, each killing his brother and friend and neighbor.'" [28]The Levites did as Moses commanded, and that day about three thousand of the people died. [29]Then Moses said, "You have been set apart to the LORD today, for you were against your own sons and brothers, and he has blessed you this day."

[30]The next day Moses said to the people, "You have committed a great sin. But now I will go up to the LORD; perhaps I can make atonement for your sin."

[31]So Moses went back to the LORD and said, "Oh, what a great sin these people have committed! They have made themselves gods of gold. [32]But now, please forgive their sin—but if not, then blot me out of the book you have written."

[33]The LORD replied to Moses, "Whoever has sinned against me I will blot out of my book. [34]Now go, lead the people to the place I spoke of, and my angel will go before you. However, when the time comes for me to punish, I will punish them for their sin."

[35]And the LORD struck the people with a plague because of what they did with the calf Aaron had made.

33 Then the LORD said to Moses, "Leave this place, you and the people you brought up out of Egypt, and go up to the land I promised on oath to Abraham, Isaac and Jacob, saying, 'I will give it to your descendants.' [2]I will send an angel before you and drive out the Canaanites, Amorites, Hittites, Perizzites, Hivites and Jebusites. [3]Go up to the land flowing with milk and honey. But I will not go with you, because you are a stiff-necked people and I might destroy you on the way."

[4]When the people heard these distressing words, they began to mourn and no one put on any ornaments. [5]For the LORD had said to Moses, "Tell the Israelites, 'You are a

From Administration to Contemplation

EXODUS 33:1–11

While we have been given glimpses in preceding chapters of Moses' privileged access to conversations with God, for the greater part we've seen Moses in his role as leader or administrator. Here we tiptoe, as it were, into the most private chamber of his dwelling, the place where we discover that the Lord speaks to Moses "face to face, as a man speaks with his friend." This story contains one of the most sublime passages in all the inspired Scriptures—a passage that invites attentive reading and deep reflection. It bids us to enter quietly into the scene, bringing with us our own hunger for intimate communion with God.

See *Meeting God in Prayer*

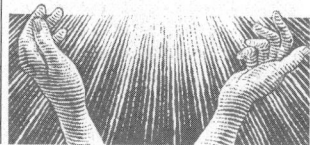

"When My Glory Passes By"

"Moses, who eagerly seeks to behold God, is now taught how he can behold him: to follow God wherever he might lead is to behold God. His passing by signifies his guiding the one who follows, for someone who does not know the way cannot complete his journey safely in any other way than by following behind his guide. He who leads, then, by guidance shows the way to the one following. He who follows will not turn aside from the right way if he always keeps the back of his leader in view."

—GREGORY OF NYSSA,
The Life of Moses

stiff-necked people. If I were to go with you even for a moment, I might destroy you. Now take off your ornaments and I will decide what to do with you.' " ⁶So the Israelites stripped off their ornaments at Mount Horeb.

The Tent of Meeting

⁷Now Moses used to take a tent and pitch it outside the camp some distance away, calling it the "tent of meeting." Anyone inquiring of the LORD would go to the tent of meeting outside the camp. ⁸And whenever Moses went out to the tent, all the people rose and stood at the entrances to their tents, watching Moses until he entered the tent. ⁹As Moses went into the tent, the pillar of cloud would come down and stay at the entrance, while the LORD spoke with Moses. ¹⁰Whenever the people saw the pillar of cloud standing at the entrance to the tent, they all stood and worshiped, each at the entrance to his tent. ¹¹The LORD would speak to Moses face to face, as a man speaks with his friend. Then Moses would return to the camp, but his young aide Joshua son of Nun did not leave the tent.

Moses and the Glory of the LORD

¹²Moses said to the LORD, "You have been telling me, 'Lead these people,' but you have not let me know whom you will send with me. You have said, 'I know you by name and you have found favor with me.' ¹³If you are pleased with me, teach me your ways so I may know you and continue to find favor with you. Remember that this nation is your people."

¹⁴The LORD replied, "My Presence will go with you, and I will give you rest."

¹⁵Then Moses said to him, "If your Presence does not go with us, do not send us up from here. ¹⁶How will anyone know that you are pleased with me and with your people unless you go with us? What else will distinguish me and your people from all the other people on the face of the earth?"

¹⁷And the LORD said to Moses, "I will do the very thing you have asked, because I am pleased with you and I know you by name."

¹⁸Then Moses said, "Now show me your glory."

¹⁹And the LORD said, "I will cause all my goodness to pass in front of you, and I will proclaim my name, the LORD, in your presence. I will have mercy on whom I will have mercy, and I will have compassion on whom I will have compassion. ²⁰But," he said, "you cannot see my face, for no one may see me and live."

²¹Then the LORD said, "There is a place near me where you may stand on a rock. ²²When my glory passes by, I will put you in a cleft in the rock and cover you with my hand until I have passed by. ²³Then I will remove my hand and you will see my back; but my face must not be seen."

The New Stone Tablets

34 The LORD said to Moses, "Chisel out two stone tablets like the first ones, and I will write on them the words that were on the first tablets, which you broke. ²Be ready in the morning, and then come up on Mount Sinai. Present yourself to me there on top of the mountain. ³No one is to come with you or be seen anywhere on the mountain; not even the flocks and herds may graze in front of the mountain."

⁴So Moses chiseled out two stone tablets like the first ones and went up Mount Sinai early in the morning, as the LORD had commanded him; and he carried the two stone tablets in his hands. ⁵Then the LORD came down in the cloud and stood there with him and proclaimed his name, the LORD. ⁶And he passed in front of Moses, proclaiming, "The LORD, the LORD, the compassionate and gracious God, slow to anger, abounding in love and faithfulness, ⁷maintaining love to thousands, and forgiving wickedness, rebellion and sin. Yet he does not leave the guilty unpunished; he punishes the children and their children for the sin of the fathers to the third and fourth generation."

⁸Moses bowed to the ground at once and worshiped. ⁹"O Lord, if I have found favor in your eyes," he said, "then let the Lord go with us. Although this is a stiff-necked people, forgive our wickedness and our sin, and take us as your inheritance."

¹⁰Then the LORD said: "I am making a covenant with you. Before all your people I will do wonders never before done in any nation in all the world. The people you live among will see how awesome is the work that I, the LORD, will do for you. ¹¹Obey what I command you today. I will drive out before you the Amorites, Canaanites, Hittites, Perizzites, Hivites and Jebusites. ¹²Be careful not to make a treaty with those who live in the land where you are going, or they will be a snare among you. ¹³Break down their altars, smash their sacred stones and cut down their Asherah poles.ᵃ ¹⁴Do not worship any other god, for the LORD, whose name is Jealous, is a jealous God.

¹⁵"Be careful not to make a treaty with those who live in the land; for when they prostitute themselves to their gods and sacrifice to them, they will invite you and you will eat their sacrifices. ¹⁶And when you choose some of their daughters as wives for your sons and those daughters prostitute themselves to their gods, they will lead your sons to do the same.

¹⁷"Do not make cast idols.

¹⁸"Celebrate the Feast of Unleavened Bread. For seven days eat bread made without yeast, as I commanded you. Do this at the appointed time in the month of Abib, for in that month you came out of Egypt.

¹⁹"The first offspring of every womb belongs to me, including all the firstborn males of your livestock, whether from herd or flock. ²⁰Redeem the firstborn donkey with a lamb, but if you do not redeem it, break its neck. Redeem all your firstborn sons.

"No one is to appear before me empty-handed.

²¹"Six days you shall labor, but on the seventh day you shall rest; even during the plowing season and harvest you must rest.

²²"Celebrate the Feast of Weeks with the firstfruits of the wheat harvest, and the Feast of Ingathering at the turn of the year.ᵇ ²³Three times a year all your men are to appear before the Sovereign LORD, the God of Israel. ²⁴I will drive out nations before you and enlarge your territory, and no one will covet your land when you go up three times each year to appear before the LORD your God.

The Compassionate and Gracious God

EXODUS 34:4–14

Through this passage we have the privilege of going with Moses to Mount Sinai. Begin by thinking about the laborious work of chiseling two stone tablets, a task that could take days. Imagine that you are carrying them up the mist-shrouded mountain—the exertion robbing you of breath. Now you are at the pinnacle, gripped by a sense of expectancy and uncertainty. Suddenly—dramatically—God appears in front of you and declares himself, "The LORD, the LORD, the compassionate and gracious God, slow to anger, abounding in love and faithfulness, maintaining love to thousands and forgiving wickedness, rebellion and sin."

Be still before God for a while. Let God's words sink into your soul. What is your response? How is it like or unlike Moses' response? What is God saying to you personally in this passage?

See Meeting God in Scripture

ᵃ 13 That is, symbols of the goddess Asherah   ᵇ 22 That is, in the fall

The Face of Moses

EXODUS 34:27–35

Inevitably our faces mirror our inner disposition to others. Moses was so intensely present with God, and God with Moses, that God's presence radiated from his face.

Sometimes a face turned resolutely and lovingly to God will finally be the most powerful word we can utter. Think about your own facial expressions and demeanor. Do they reflect the indwelling presence of God? In your preparation for ministry and service, what role does spending time in God's presence play? How does it show? Reflect on these words of an old theology professor who enjoyed saying to his students: "By the time you reach the age of forty, you are responsible for your face."

See Meeting God in Worship

25"Do not offer the blood of a sacrifice to me along with anything containing yeast, and do not let any of the sacrifice from the Passover Feast remain until morning.

26"Bring the best of the firstfruits of your soil to the house of the LORD your God.

"Do not cook a young goat in its mother's milk."

27Then the LORD said to Moses, "Write down these words, for in accordance with these words I have made a covenant with you and with Israel." 28Moses was there with the LORD forty days and forty nights without eating bread or drinking water. And he wrote on the tablets the words of the covenant—the Ten Commandments.

The Radiant Face of Moses

29When Moses came down from Mount Sinai with the two tablets of the Testimony in his hands, he was not aware that his face was radiant because he had spoken with the LORD. 30When Aaron and all the Israelites saw Moses, his face was radiant, and they were afraid to come near him. 31But Moses called to them; so Aaron and all the leaders of the community came back to him, and he spoke to them. 32Afterward all the Israelites came near him, and he gave them all the commands the LORD had given him on Mount Sinai.

33When Moses finished speaking to them, he put a veil over his face. 34But whenever he entered the LORD's presence to speak with him, he removed the veil until he came out. And when he came out and told the Israelites what he had been commanded, 35they saw that his face was radiant. Then Moses would put the veil back over his face until he went in to speak with the LORD.

Sabbath Regulations

35 Moses assembled the whole Israelite community and said to them, "These are the things the LORD has commanded you to do: 2For six days, work is to be done, but the seventh day shall be your holy day, a Sabbath of rest to the LORD. Whoever does any work on it must be put to death. 3Do not light a fire in any of your dwellings on the Sabbath day."

Materials for the Tabernacle

4Moses said to the whole Israelite community, "This is what the LORD has commanded: 5From what you have, take an offering for the LORD. Everyone who is willing is to bring to the LORD an offering of gold, silver and bronze; 6blue, purple and scarlet yarn and fine linen; goat hair; 7ram skins dyed red and hides of sea cows*a*; acacia wood; 8olive oil for the light; spices for the anointing oil and for the fragrant incense; 9and onyx stones and other gems to be mounted on the ephod and breastpiece.

10"All who are skilled among you are to come and make everything the LORD has commanded: 11the tabernacle with its tent and its covering, clasps, frames, crossbars, posts and bases; 12the ark with its poles and the atonement cover and the curtain that shields it; 13the table with its poles and all its articles and the bread of the Presence; 14the lampstand that is for light with its accessories, lamps and oil for the light; 15the altar of incense with its poles, the anointing

a 7 That is, dugongs; also in verse 23

oil and the fragrant incense; the curtain for the doorway at the entrance to the tabernacle; [16]the altar of burnt offering with its bronze grating, its poles and all its utensils; the bronze basin with its stand; [17]the curtains of the courtyard with its posts and bases, and the curtain for the entrance to the courtyard; [18]the tent pegs for the tabernacle and for the courtyard, and their ropes; [19]the woven garments worn for ministering in the sanctuary—both the sacred garments for Aaron the priest and the garments for his sons when they serve as priests."

[20]Then the whole Israelite community withdrew from Moses' presence, [21]and everyone who was willing and whose heart moved him came and brought an offering to the LORD for the work on the Tent of Meeting, for all its service, and for the sacred garments. [22]All who were willing, men and women alike, came and brought gold jewelry of all kinds: brooches, earrings, rings and ornaments. They all presented their gold as a wave offering to the LORD. [23]Everyone who had blue, purple or scarlet yarn or fine linen, or goat hair, ram skins dyed red or hides of sea cows brought them. [24]Those presenting an offering of silver or bronze brought it as an offering to the LORD, and everyone who had acacia wood for any part of the work brought it. [25]Every skilled woman spun with her hands and brought what she had spun—blue, purple or scarlet yarn or fine linen. [26]And all the women who were willing and had the skill spun the goat hair. [27]The leaders brought onyx stones and other gems to be mounted on the ephod and breastpiece. [28]They also brought spices and olive oil for the light and for the anointing oil and for the fragrant incense. [29]All the Israelite men and women who were willing brought to the LORD freewill offerings for all the work the LORD through Moses had commanded them to do.

Bezalel and Oholiab

[30]Then Moses said to the Israelites, "See, the LORD has chosen Bezalel son of Uri, the son of Hur, of the tribe of Judah, [31]and he has filled him with the Spirit of God, with skill, ability and knowledge in all kinds of crafts— [32]to make artistic designs for work in gold, silver and bronze, [33]to cut and set stones, to work in wood and to engage in all kinds of artistic craftsmanship. [34]And he has given both him and Oholiab son of Ahisamach, of the tribe of Dan, the ability to teach others. [35]He has filled them with skill to do all kinds of work as craftsmen, designers, embroiderers in blue, purple and scarlet yarn and fine linen, and weavers—all of them master craftsmen and designers.

36 [1]So Bezalel, Oholiab and every skilled person to whom the LORD has given skill and ability to know how to carry out all the work of constructing the sanctuary are to do the work just as the LORD has commanded."

[2]Then Moses summoned Bezalel and Oholiab and every skilled person to whom the LORD had given ability and who was willing to come and do the work. [3]They received from Moses all the offerings the Israelites had brought to carry out the work of constructing the sanctuary. And the people continued to bring freewill offerings morning after morning. [4]So all the skilled craftsmen who were doing all the work on the sanctuary left their work [5]and said to Moses,

The Spirituality of Art

EXODUS 35:30

Bezalel could be a kind of patron saint to artists and other creative types. His name figures prominently, and his craftsmanship is celebrated, in the following verses. While due credit is given to his coworker Oholiab, Moses obviously gives his highest praise to Bezalel. Bezalel challenges our cultural tendency to separate the secular from the sacred in the artistic realm. He is obviously gifted in arts and crafts; his example teaches us that we can pray not only with folded hands, but with busy hands. Hands that carve wood or sweep a paintbrush or cut stone give glory to God also. What worthwhile things do you do with your hands? Ask God to use your creative talents to bring good to others and honor to him.

See Meeting God in Everyday Life

Curtains, Rings, Pegs and Frames

EXODUS 36:10–19

It is hard to read passages like this that give meticulous attention to detail and not wonder why. Why so much attention to the minute details of the furnishings of the tabernacle? Attention to detail, however, can be an indication of excitement and enthusiasm. Listen to new homeowners talk about the house they have just had built! No detail is spared!

The next time you attend worship or join in a small-group Bible study, pay careful attention to details: the chair you sit in, the walls and windows that surround you, any objects with liturgical or spiritual significance. Especially pay attention to those things that remind you of the presence of God in your midst. Ask God to open your eyes and allow the experience to become an expedition of visual discovery.

See Meeting God in Everyday Life

"The people are bringing more than enough for doing the work the LORD commanded to be done."

⁶Then Moses gave an order and they sent this word throughout the camp: "No man or woman is to make anything else as an offering for the sanctuary." And so the people were restrained from bringing more, ⁷because what they already had was more than enough to do all the work.

The Tabernacle

⁸All the skilled men among the workmen made the tabernacle with ten curtains of finely twisted linen and blue, purple and scarlet yarn, with cherubim worked into them by a skilled craftsman. ⁹All the curtains were the same size—twenty-eight cubits long and four cubits wide.ᵃ ¹⁰They joined five of the curtains together and did the same with the other five. ¹¹Then they made loops of blue material along the edge of the end curtain in one set, and the same was done with the end curtain in the other set. ¹²They also made fifty loops on one curtain and fifty loops on the end curtain of the other set, with the loops opposite each other. ¹³Then they made fifty gold clasps and used them to fasten the two sets of curtains together so that the tabernacle was a unit.

¹⁴They made curtains of goat hair for the tent over the tabernacle—eleven altogether. ¹⁵All eleven curtains were the same size—thirty cubits long and four cubits wide.ᵇ ¹⁶They joined five of the curtains into one set and the other six into another set. ¹⁷Then they made fifty loops along the edge of the end curtain in one set and also along the edge of the end curtain in the other set. ¹⁸They made fifty bronze clasps to fasten the tent together as a unit. ¹⁹Then they made for the tent a covering of ram skins dyed red, and over that a covering of hides of sea cows.ᶜ

²⁰They made upright frames of acacia wood for the tabernacle. ²¹Each frame was ten cubits long and a cubit and a half wide,ᵈ ²²with two projections set parallel to each other. They made all the frames of the tabernacle in this way. ²³They made twenty frames for the south side of the tabernacle ²⁴and made forty silver bases to go under them—two bases for each frame, one under each projection. ²⁵For the other side, the north side of the tabernacle, they made twenty frames ²⁶and forty silver bases—two under each frame. ²⁷They made six frames for the far end, that is, the west end of the tabernacle, ²⁸and two frames were made for the corners of the tabernacle at the far end. ²⁹At these two corners the frames were double from the bottom all the way to the top and fitted into a single ring; both were made alike. ³⁰So there were eight frames and sixteen silver bases—two under each frame.

³¹They also made crossbars of acacia wood: five for the frames on one side of the tabernacle, ³²five for those on the other side, and five for the frames on the west, at the far end of the tabernacle. ³³They made the center crossbar so that it extended from end to end at the middle of the frames. ³⁴They overlaid the frames with gold and made

ᵃ9 That is, about 42 feet (about 12.5 meters) long and 6 feet (about 1.8 meters) wide   ᵇ15 That is, about 45 feet (about 13.5 meters) long and 6 feet (about 1.8 meters) wide   ᶜ19 That is, dugongs   ᵈ21 That is, about 15 feet (about 4.5 meters) long and 2 1/4 feet (about 0.7 meter) wide

gold rings to hold the crossbars. They also overlaid the crossbars with gold.

³⁵They made the curtain of blue, purple and scarlet yarn and finely twisted linen, with cherubim worked into it by a skilled craftsman. ³⁶They made four posts of acacia wood for it and overlaid them with gold. They made gold hooks for them and cast their four silver bases. ³⁷For the entrance to the tent they made a curtain of blue, purple and scarlet yarn and finely twisted linen—the work of an embroiderer; ³⁸and they made five posts with hooks for them. They overlaid the tops of the posts and their bands with gold and made their five bases of bronze.

The Ark

37 Bezalel made the ark of acacia wood—two and a half cubits long, a cubit and a half wide, and a cubit and a half high.ᵃ ²He overlaid it with pure gold, both inside and out, and made a gold molding around it. ³He cast four gold rings for it and fastened them to its four feet, with two rings on one side and two rings on the other. ⁴Then he made poles of acacia wood and overlaid them with gold. ⁵And he inserted the poles into the rings on the sides of the ark to carry it.

⁶He made the atonement cover of pure gold—two and a half cubits long and a cubit and a half wide.ᵇ ⁷Then he made two cherubim out of hammered gold at the ends of the cover. ⁸He made one cherub on one end and the second cherub on the other; at the two ends he made them of one piece with the cover. ⁹The cherubim had their wings spread upward, overshadowing the cover with them. The cherubim faced each other, looking toward the cover.

The Table

¹⁰Theyᶜ made the table of acacia wood—two cubits long, a cubit wide, and a cubit and a half high.ᵈ ¹¹Then they overlaid it with pure gold and made a gold molding around it. ¹²They also made around it a rim a handbreadthᵉ wide and put a gold molding on the rim. ¹³They cast four gold rings for the table and fastened them to the four corners, where the four legs were. ¹⁴The rings were put close to the rim to hold the poles used in carrying the table. ¹⁵The poles for carrying the table were made of acacia wood and were overlaid with gold. ¹⁶And they made from pure gold the articles for the table—its plates and dishes and bowls and its pitchers for the pouring out of drink offerings.

The Lampstand

¹⁷They made the lampstand of pure gold and hammered it out, base and shaft; its flowerlike cups, buds and blossoms were of one piece with it. ¹⁸Six branches extended from the sides of the lampstand—three on one side and three on the other. ¹⁹Three cups shaped like almond flowers with buds and blossoms were on one branch, three on the next branch and the same for all six branches extending from the lampstand. ²⁰And on the lampstand were four

---

The Angels on the Ark

EXODUS 37:6–9

The cherubim mentioned in these verses are heavenly beings often depicted in Scripture in mysterious fashion. Descriptions of cherubim are always tantalizingly brief, just as is the spare, simple picture painted here. We could wish for more details, for a peek into vast heavenly realities, but here we content ourselves with knowing that the gold representations of cherubim are to remind the people of the holiness and sanctity of the ark and its contents.

What do you think it means that the cherubim are shown with wings "spread upward"? In what ways might angels have served as a reminder to the people of a God of glory and grace? Find a picture of an angel—or sketch your own. How can pondering God's heavenly realm invest your thoughts and actions with greater reverence?

See Meeting God in Scripture

ᵃ*1* That is, about 3 3/4 feet (about 1.1 meters) long and 2 1/4 feet (about 0.7 meter) wide and high   ᵇ*6* That is, about 3 3/4 feet (about 1.1 meters) long and 2 1/4 feet (about 0.7 meter) wide   ᶜ*10* Or *He;* also in verses 11–29
ᵈ*10* That is, about 3 feet (about 0.9 meter) long, 1 1/2 feet (about 0.5 meter) wide, and 2 1/4 feet (about 0.7 meter) high   ᵉ*12* That is, about 3 inches (about 8 centimeters)

Preparing for Worship

EXODUS 37:25—38:17

"Why, then, do I not long more ardently for your adorable presence? Why do I not prepare myself with greater care to receive your sacred gifts, since those holy patriarchs and prophets of old, as well as kings and princes with all their people, have shown such affectionate devotion for the worship of God?"

—THOMAS À KEMPIS,
The Imitation of Christ

See *Meeting God in Worship*

cups shaped like almond flowers with buds and blossoms. [21]One bud was under the first pair of branches extending from the lampstand, a second bud under the second pair, and a third bud under the third pair—six branches in all. [22]The buds and the branches were all of one piece with the lampstand, hammered out of pure gold.

[23]They made its seven lamps, as well as its wick trimmers and trays, of pure gold. [24]They made the lampstand and all its accessories from one talent[a] of pure gold.

The Altar of Incense

[25]They made the altar of incense out of acacia wood. It was square, a cubit long and a cubit wide, and two cubits high[b]—its horns of one piece with it. [26]They overlaid the top and all the sides and the horns with pure gold, and made a gold molding around it. [27]They made two gold rings below the molding—two on opposite sides—to hold the poles used to carry it. [28]They made the poles of acacia wood and overlaid them with gold.

[29]They also made the sacred anointing oil and the pure, fragrant incense—the work of a perfumer.

The Altar of Burnt Offering

38 They[c] built the altar of burnt offering of acacia wood, three cubits[d] high; it was square, five cubits long and five cubits wide.[e] [2]They made a horn at each of the four corners, so that the horns and the altar were of one piece, and they overlaid the altar with bronze. [3]They made all its utensils of bronze—its pots, shovels, sprinkling bowls, meat forks and firepans. [4]They made a grating for the altar, a bronze network, to be under its ledge, halfway up the altar. [5]They cast bronze rings to hold the poles for the four corners of the bronze grating. [6]They made the poles of acacia wood and overlaid them with bronze. [7]They inserted the poles into the rings so they would be on the sides of the altar for carrying it. They made it hollow, out of boards.

Basin for Washing

[8]They made the bronze basin and its bronze stand from the mirrors of the women who served at the entrance to the Tent of Meeting.

The Courtyard

[9]Next they made the courtyard. The south side was a hundred cubits[f] long and had curtains of finely twisted linen, [10]with twenty posts and twenty bronze bases, and with silver hooks and bands on the posts. [11]The north side was also a hundred cubits long and had twenty posts and twenty bronze bases, with silver hooks and bands on the posts.

[12]The west end was fifty cubits[g] wide and had curtains, with ten posts and ten bases, with silver hooks and bands on the posts. [13]The east end, toward the sunrise, was also fifty cubits wide. [14]Curtains fifteen cubits[h] long were on one

---

[a] 24 That is, about 75 pounds (about 34 kilograms)   [b] 25 That is, about 1 1/2 feet (about 0.5 meter) long and wide, and about 3 feet (about 0.9 meter) high   [c] 1 Or *He*; also in verses 2–9   [d] 1 That is, about 4 1/2 feet (about 1.3 meters)   [e] 1 That is, about 7 1/2 feet (about 2.3 meters) long and wide   [f] 9 That is, about 150 feet (about 46 meters)   [g] 12 That is, about 75 feet (about 23 meters)   [h] 14 That is, about 22 1/2 feet (about 6.9 meters)

side of the entrance, with three posts and three bases, ¹⁵and curtains fifteen cubits long were on the other side of the entrance to the courtyard, with three posts and three bases. ¹⁶All the curtains around the courtyard were of finely twisted linen. ¹⁷The bases for the posts were bronze. The hooks and bands on the posts were silver, and their tops were overlaid with silver; so all the posts of the courtyard had silver bands.

¹⁸The curtain for the entrance to the courtyard was of blue, purple and scarlet yarn and finely twisted linen—the work of an embroiderer. It was twenty cubits*a* long and, like the curtains of the courtyard, five cubits*b* high, ¹⁹with four posts and four bronze bases. Their hooks and bands were silver, and their tops were overlaid with silver. ²⁰All the tent pegs of the tabernacle and of the surrounding courtyard were bronze.

The Materials Used

²¹These are the amounts of the materials used for the tabernacle, the tabernacle of the Testimony, which were recorded at Moses' command by the Levites under the direction of Ithamar son of Aaron, the priest. ²²(Bezalel son of Uri, the son of Hur, of the tribe of Judah, made everything the LORD commanded Moses; ²³with him was Oholiab son of Ahisamach, of the tribe of Dan—a craftsman and designer, and an embroiderer in blue, purple and scarlet yarn and fine linen.) ²⁴The total amount of the gold from the wave offering used for all the work on the sanctuary was 29 talents and 730 shekels,*c* according to the sanctuary shekel.

²⁵The silver obtained from those of the community who were counted in the census was 100 talents and 1,775 shekels,*d* according to the sanctuary shekel— ²⁶one beka per person, that is, half a shekel,*e* according to the sanctuary shekel, from everyone who had crossed over to those counted, twenty years old or more, a total of 603,550 men. ²⁷The 100 talents*f* of silver were used to cast the bases for the sanctuary and for the curtain—100 bases from the 100 talents, one talent for each base. ²⁸They used the 1,775 shekels*g* to make the hooks for the posts, to overlay the tops of the posts, and to make their bands.

²⁹The bronze from the wave offering was 70 talents and 2,400 shekels.*h* ³⁰They used it to make the bases for the entrance to the Tent of Meeting, the bronze altar with its bronze grating and all its utensils, ³¹the bases for the surrounding courtyard and those for its entrance and all the tent pegs for the tabernacle and those for the surrounding courtyard.

The Priestly Garments

39 From the blue, purple and scarlet yarn they made woven garments for ministering in the sanctuary. They also made sacred garments for Aaron, as the LORD commanded Moses.

---

a 18 That is, about 30 feet (about 9 meters) *b 18* That is, about 7 1/2 feet (about 2.3 meters) *c 24* The weight of the gold was a little over one ton (about 1 metric ton). *d 25* The weight of the silver was a little over 3 3/4 tons (about 3.4 metric tons). *e 26* That is, about 1/5 ounce (about 5.5 grams) *f 27* That is, about 3 3/4 tons (about 3.4 metric tons) *g 28* That is, about 45 pounds (about 20 kilograms) *h 29* The weight of the bronze was about 2 1/2 tons (about 2.4 metric tons).

Unstinting Preparation

EXODUS 38:18–39:4

These verses reveal the great care and expense the people of Israel invested in the worship of God. There was to be no scrimping! Even the curtain for the entrance to the temple courtyard used the best: blue, purple and scarlet yarn, and finely twisted linen.

In what ways can you make your worship this coming Sabbath a matter of careful preparation and unstinting self-offering? Begin, even now, to prepare to meet and worship God. Make yourself a small card or note with the word *worship* on it to carry around with you. Pull it out occasionally or post it in a prominent place so it can remind you to get ready for heartfelt participation in your Lord's Day celebration.

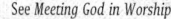
See Meeting God in Worship

The Work of a Skilled Craftsman

EXODUS 39:2–7

The priestly garments were carefully and elaborately constructed to signify to the people that worshiping God was an awesome privilege and not to be undertaken carelessly or casually—God is honored by the work of a skilled craftsman.

Think about your talents and gifts. What can you offer God in worship today? Might it be a song played or sung with all your heart? A few moments of your undivided attention spent in prayer? A poem that expresses your gratitude to God or a sketch that shows your appreciation for God's creation? Whatever you offer to God in worship, offer your best.

See *Meeting God in Worship*

The Ephod

²They[a] made the ephod of gold, and of blue, purple and scarlet yarn, and of finely twisted linen. ³They hammered out thin sheets of gold and cut strands to be worked into the blue, purple and scarlet yarn and fine linen—the work of a skilled craftsman. ⁴They made shoulder pieces for the ephod, which were attached to two of its corners, so it could be fastened. ⁵Its skillfully woven waistband was like it—of one piece with the ephod and made with gold, and with blue, purple and scarlet yarn, and with finely twisted linen, as the LORD commanded Moses.

⁶They mounted the onyx stones in gold filigree settings and engraved them like a seal with the names of the sons of Israel. ⁷Then they fastened them on the shoulder pieces of the ephod as memorial stones for the sons of Israel, as the LORD commanded Moses.

The Breastpiece

⁸They fashioned the breastpiece—the work of a skilled craftsman. They made it like the ephod: of gold, and of blue, purple and scarlet yarn, and of finely twisted linen. ⁹It was square—a span[b] long and a span wide—and folded double. ¹⁰Then they mounted four rows of precious stones on it. In the first row there was a ruby, a topaz and a beryl; ¹¹in the second row a turquoise, a sapphire[c] and an emerald; ¹²in the third row a jacinth, an agate and an amethyst; ¹³in the fourth row a chrysolite, an onyx and a jasper.[d] They were mounted in gold filigree settings. ¹⁴There were twelve stones, one for each of the names of the sons of Israel, each engraved like a seal with the name of one of the twelve tribes.

¹⁵For the breastpiece they made braided chains of pure gold, like a rope. ¹⁶They made two gold filigree settings and two gold rings, and fastened the rings to two of the corners of the breastpiece. ¹⁷They fastened the two gold chains to the rings at the corners of the breastpiece, ¹⁸and the other ends of the chains to the two settings, attaching them to the shoulder pieces of the ephod at the front. ¹⁹They made two gold rings and attached them to the other two corners of the breastpiece on the inside edge next to the ephod. ²⁰Then they made two more gold rings and attached them to the bottom of the shoulder pieces on the front of the ephod, close to the seam just above the waistband of the ephod. ²¹They tied the rings of the breastpiece to the rings of the ephod with blue cord, connecting it to the waistband so that the breastpiece would not swing out from the ephod—as the LORD commanded Moses.

Other Priestly Garments

²²They made the robe of the ephod entirely of blue cloth—the work of a weaver— ²³with an opening in the center of the robe like the opening of a collar,[e] and a band around this opening, so that it would not tear. ²⁴They made pomegranates of blue, purple and scarlet yarn and finely twisted linen around the hem of the robe. ²⁵And they made bells of pure gold and attached them around the hem be-

---

[a] *2* Or *He*; also in verses 7, 8 and 22   [b] *9* That is, about 9 inches (about 22 centimeters)   [c] *11* Or *lapis lazuli*   [d] *13* The precise identification of some of these precious stones is uncertain.   [e] *23* The meaning of the Hebrew for this word is uncertain.

tween the pomegranates. ²⁶The bells and pomegranates alternated around the hem of the robe to be worn for ministering, as the LORD commanded Moses.

²⁷For Aaron and his sons, they made tunics of fine linen—the work of a weaver— ²⁸and the turban of fine linen, the linen headbands and the undergarments of finely twisted linen. ²⁹The sash was of finely twisted linen and blue, purple and scarlet yarn—the work of an embroiderer—as the LORD commanded Moses.

³⁰They made the plate, the sacred diadem, out of pure gold and engraved on it, like an inscription on a seal: HOLY TO THE LORD. ³¹Then they fastened a blue cord to it to attach it to the turban, as the LORD commanded Moses.

Moses Inspects the Tabernacle

³²So all the work on the tabernacle, the Tent of Meeting, was completed. The Israelites did everything just as the LORD commanded Moses. ³³Then they brought the tabernacle to Moses: the tent and all its furnishings, its clasps, frames, crossbars, posts and bases; ³⁴the covering of ram skins dyed red, the covering of hides of sea cows[a] and the shielding curtain; ³⁵the ark of the Testimony with its poles and the atonement cover; ³⁶the table with all its articles and the bread of the Presence; ³⁷the pure gold lampstand with its row of lamps and all its accessories, and the oil for the light; ³⁸the gold altar, the anointing oil, the fragrant incense, and the curtain for the entrance to the tent; ³⁹the bronze altar with its bronze grating, its poles and all its utensils; the basin with its stand; ⁴⁰the curtains of the courtyard with its posts and bases, and the curtain for the entrance to the courtyard; the ropes and tent pegs for the courtyard; all the furnishings for the tabernacle, the Tent of Meeting; ⁴¹and the woven garments worn for ministering in the sanctuary, both the sacred garments for Aaron the priest and the garments for his sons when serving as priests.

⁴²The Israelites had done all the work just as the LORD had commanded Moses. ⁴³Moses inspected the work and saw that they had done it just as the LORD had commanded. So Moses blessed them.

Setting Up the Tabernacle

40 Then the LORD said to Moses: ²"Set up the tabernacle, the Tent of Meeting, on the first day of the first month. ³Place the ark of the Testimony in it and shield the ark with the curtain. ⁴Bring in the table and set out what belongs on it. Then bring in the lampstand and set up its lamps. ⁵Place the gold altar of incense in front of the ark of the Testimony and put the curtain at the entrance to the tabernacle.

⁶"Place the altar of burnt offering in front of the entrance to the tabernacle, the Tent of Meeting; ⁷place the basin between the Tent of Meeting and the altar and put water in it. ⁸Set up the courtyard around it and put the curtain at the entrance to the courtyard.

⁹"Take the anointing oil and anoint the tabernacle and everything in it; consecrate it and all its furnishings, and it will be holy. ¹⁰Then anoint the altar of burnt offering and all its utensils; consecrate the altar, and it will be most holy. ¹¹Anoint the basin and its stand and consecrate them.

Just as the Lord Had Commanded

EXODUS 39:32–40:16

In the space of these two chapters alone the phrase "as the LORD commanded Moses" is repeated eighteen times with only minor variations. In each case, Moses and the people completed some work that God had commanded them to do. Most significant of all is the completion of the tabernacle (the Tent of Meeting), which is henceforth a sacred sign to the people of the God who dwells in their midst.

What symbolizes God's presence to you? For some, it is the people they love most of all. For others it may be a beautiful picture, a family Bible, some family heirloom. Find or make some object that reminds you of the place where you most frequently worship God. Put it in some important place in your home. Or if it is portable, keep it in your wallet or purse all the time. Each time you see or touch this object, remind yourself that God is in this place, indeed in every place.

See Meeting God in Everyday Life

God's Sweet and Awesome Presence

EXODUS 40:34–38

"As the soul goes ever after God with love so true, imbued with the spirit of suffering for His sake, God's majesty often and regularly grants it joy, and visits it sweetly and delectably in the spirit; for the boundless love of Christ, the Word, cannot see the afflictions of his lover without comforting him or her."

—JOHN OF THE CROSS,
The Dark Night of the Soul

12"Bring Aaron and his sons to the entrance to the Tent of Meeting and wash them with water. 13Then dress Aaron in the sacred garments, anoint him and consecrate him so he may serve me as priest. 14Bring his sons and dress them in tunics. 15Anoint them just as you anointed their father, so they may serve me as priests. Their anointing will be to a priesthood that will continue for all generations to come." 16Moses did everything just as the LORD commanded him.

17So the tabernacle was set up on the first day of the first month in the second year. 18When Moses set up the tabernacle, he put the bases in place, erected the frames, inserted the crossbars and set up the posts. 19Then he spread the tent over the tabernacle and put the covering over the tent, as the LORD commanded him.

20He took the Testimony and placed it in the ark, attached the poles to the ark and put the atonement cover over it. 21Then he brought the ark into the tabernacle and hung the shielding curtain and shielded the ark of the Testimony, as the LORD commanded him.

22Moses placed the table in the Tent of Meeting on the north side of the tabernacle outside the curtain 23and set out the bread on it before the LORD, as the LORD commanded him.

24He placed the lampstand in the Tent of Meeting opposite the table on the south side of the tabernacle 25and set up the lamps before the LORD, as the LORD commanded him.

26Moses placed the gold altar in the Tent of Meeting in front of the curtain 27and burned fragrant incense on it, as the LORD commanded him. 28Then he put up the curtain at the entrance to the tabernacle.

29He set the altar of burnt offering near the entrance to the tabernacle, the Tent of Meeting, and offered on it burnt offerings and grain offerings, as the LORD commanded him.

30He placed the basin between the Tent of Meeting and the altar and put water in it for washing, 31and Moses and Aaron and his sons used it to wash their hands and feet. 32They washed whenever they entered the Tent of Meeting or approached the altar, as the LORD commanded Moses.

33Then Moses set up the courtyard around the tabernacle and altar and put up the curtain at the entrance to the courtyard. And so Moses finished the work.

The Glory of the LORD

34Then the cloud covered the Tent of Meeting, and the glory of the LORD filled the tabernacle. 35Moses could not enter the Tent of Meeting because the cloud had settled upon it, and the glory of the LORD filled the tabernacle.

36In all the travels of the Israelites, whenever the cloud lifted from above the tabernacle, they would set out; 37but if the cloud did not lift, they did not set out—until the day it lifted. 38So the cloud of the LORD was over the tabernacle by day, and fire was in the cloud by night, in the sight of all the house of Israel during all their travels.

LEVITICUS

For the Common Good

KEY VERSE:

"Be holy because I, the Lord your God, am holy."—Leviticus 19:2

For many Christians, Leviticus is perhaps the most difficult book of the Bible from which to draw spiritual guidance. We wonder, "What do all these ancient laws about sacrifice have to do with me, anyhow? And haven't they all been nullified in the death and resurrection of Jesus?"

Yet if you have ever struggled with working out the complex connections among grace, obedience, repentance and forgiveness then Leviticus has a great deal to say. The book of Leviticus demonstrates how the people of Israel, as a nation and as individuals, could maintain a righteous relationship with God and receive the blessings that accompany that relationship.

Leviticus teaches us that the proper response to God's saving grace is to live holy lives, lives that are an imitation of God's holiness. In addition, Leviticus demonstrates that God understood that the ancient Israelites, like all humans, were not perfect and so provided a way for them to atone for their sins. Finally, Leviticus shows that empty ritual and blind compliance are not true worship. As Jesus and the prophets so clearly recognized and preached, and as the laws of Leviticus make clear, the most ornate worship services are no substitute for the ultimate requirements of God's instruction, or Torah: "Love the Lord your God with all your heart and with all your soul and with all your strength," and " love your neighbor as yourself" (Deuteronomy 6:5; Leviticus 19:18).

As you read Leviticus, be open to experiencing God's forgiveness even as you seek to live out these great commandments.

"Christ came provided with the Holy Spirit after a peculiar manner . . . that he might separate us from the world, and unite us in the hope of an eternal inheritance."

—JOHN CALVIN,
Institutes of the Christian Religion

Offering God Our Best

LEVITICUS 1:2,14; 2:1–3

Livestock, poultry and grain were important sources of wealth and security in the era before hard currency. Leviticus begins by describing proper sacrifices, outlining those things the Israelites could give to God from their abundance in recognition that everything was a gift.

Compose a mental checklist of your physical possessions. Suppose that you could no longer offer monetary gifts to God but were required to offer something from your non-monetary possessions. What do you own that would be a worthy gift for the Lord? Would you be willing to part with it? What are some non-material ways that you can offer gifts to the Giver of Life?

See *Meeting God in Service*

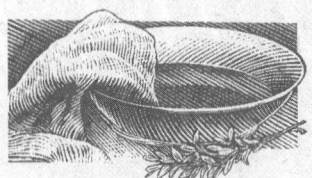

The Burnt Offering

1 The LORD called to Moses and spoke to him from the Tent of Meeting. He said, ²"Speak to the Israelites and say to them: 'When any of you brings an offering to the LORD, bring as your offering an animal from either the herd or the flock.

³" 'If the offering is a burnt offering from the herd, he is to offer a male without defect. He must present it at the entrance to the Tent of Meeting so that it*a* will be acceptable to the LORD. ⁴He is to lay his hand on the head of the burnt offering, and it will be accepted on his behalf to make atonement for him. ⁵He is to slaughter the young bull before the LORD, and then Aaron's sons the priests shall bring the blood and sprinkle it against the altar on all sides at the entrance to the Tent of Meeting. ⁶He is to skin the burnt offering and cut it into pieces. ⁷The sons of Aaron the priest are to put fire on the altar and arrange wood on the fire. ⁸Then Aaron's sons the priests shall arrange the pieces, including the head and the fat, on the burning wood that is on the altar. ⁹He is to wash the inner parts and the legs with water, and the priest is to burn all of it on the altar. It is a burnt offering, an offering made by fire, an aroma pleasing to the LORD.

¹⁰" 'If the offering is a burnt offering from the flock, from either the sheep or the goats, he is to offer a male without defect. ¹¹He is to slaughter it at the north side of the altar before the LORD, and Aaron's sons the priests shall sprinkle its blood against the altar on all sides. ¹²He is to cut it into pieces, and the priest shall arrange them, including the head and the fat, on the burning wood that is on the altar. ¹³He is to wash the inner parts and the legs with water, and the priest is to bring all of it and burn it on the altar. It is a burnt offering, an offering made by fire, an aroma pleasing to the LORD.

¹⁴" 'If the offering to the LORD is a burnt offering of birds, he is to offer a dove or a young pigeon. ¹⁵The priest shall bring it to the altar, wring off the head and burn it on the altar; its blood shall be drained out on the side of the altar. ¹⁶He is to remove the crop with its contents*b* and throw it to the east side of the altar, where the ashes are. ¹⁷He shall tear it open by the wings, not severing it completely, and then the priest shall burn it on the wood that is on the fire on the altar. It is a burnt offering, an offering made by fire, an aroma pleasing to the LORD.

The Grain Offering

2 " 'When someone brings a grain offering to the LORD, his offering is to be of fine flour. He is to pour oil on it, put incense on it ²and take it to Aaron's sons the priests. The priest shall take a handful of the fine flour and oil, together with all the incense, and burn this as a memorial portion on the altar, an offering made by fire, an aroma pleasing to the LORD. ³The rest of the grain offering belongs to Aaron and his sons; it is a most holy part of the offerings made to the LORD by fire.

⁴" 'If you bring a grain offering baked in an oven, it is to consist of fine flour: cakes made without yeast and mixed

a 3 Or *he*   *b 16* Or *crop and the feathers*; the meaning of the Hebrew for this word is uncertain.

with oil, or*a* wafers made without yeast and spread with oil. ⁵If your grain offering is prepared on a griddle, it is to be made of fine flour mixed with oil, and without yeast. ⁶Crumble it and pour oil on it; it is a grain offering. ⁷If your grain offering is cooked in a pan, it is to be made of fine flour and oil. ⁸Bring the grain offering made of these things to the LORD; present it to the priest, who shall take it to the altar. ⁹He shall take out the memorial portion from the grain offering and burn it on the altar as an offering made by fire, an aroma pleasing to the LORD. ¹⁰The rest of the grain offering belongs to Aaron and his sons; it is a most holy part of the offerings made to the LORD by fire.

¹¹" 'Every grain offering you bring to the LORD must be made without yeast, for you are not to burn any yeast or honey in an offering made to the LORD by fire. ¹²You may bring them to the LORD as an offering of the firstfruits, but they are not to be offered on the altar as a pleasing aroma. ¹³Season all your grain offerings with salt. Do not leave the salt of the covenant of your God out of your grain offerings; add salt to all your offerings.

¹⁴" 'If you bring a grain offering of firstfruits to the LORD, offer crushed heads of new grain roasted in the fire. ¹⁵Put oil and incense on it; it is a grain offering. ¹⁶The priest shall burn the memorial portion of the crushed grain and the oil, together with all the incense, as an offering made to the LORD by fire.

The Fellowship Offering

3 " 'If someone's offering is a fellowship offering,*b* and he offers an animal from the herd, whether male or female, he is to present before the LORD an animal without defect. ²He is to lay his hand on the head of his offering and slaughter it at the entrance to the Tent of Meeting. Then Aaron's sons the priests shall sprinkle the blood against the altar on all sides. ³From the fellowship offering he is to bring a sacrifice made to the LORD by fire: all the fat that covers the inner parts or is connected to them, ⁴both kidneys with the fat on them near the loins, and the covering of the liver, which he will remove with the kidneys. ⁵Then Aaron's sons are to burn it on the altar on top of the burnt offering that is on the burning wood, as an offering made by fire, an aroma pleasing to the LORD.

⁶" 'If he offers an animal from the flock as a fellowship offering to the LORD, he is to offer a male or female without defect. ⁷If he offers a lamb, he is to present it before the LORD. ⁸He is to lay his hand on the head of his offering and slaughter it in front of the Tent of Meeting. Then Aaron's sons shall sprinkle its blood against the altar on all sides. ⁹From the fellowship offering he is to bring a sacrifice made to the LORD by fire: its fat, the entire fat tail cut off close to the backbone, all the fat that covers the inner parts or is connected to them, ¹⁰both kidneys with the fat on them near the loins, and the covering of the liver, which he will remove with the kidneys. ¹¹The priest shall burn them on the altar as food, an offering made to the LORD by fire.

¹²" 'If his offering is a goat, he is to present it before the LORD. ¹³He is to lay his hand on its head and slaughter it in front of the Tent of Meeting. Then Aaron's sons shall sprinkle its blood against the altar on all sides. ¹⁴From what he

Celebrating God's Kingdom

LEVITICUS 3:1–17

"Fellowship offerings" were only offered in part on the altar. The meat from these animals was shared with God and the priests, but the bulk of the meat was used to provide a feast for the donor's family in celebration of the goodness of creation and God's generosity. Fellowship meals, which included even prostitutes and other social outcasts, were also a primary feature of Jesus' earthly mission.

What role do communal meals serve in your church and family? What are other ways that you or your faith community celebrate the presence of God and God's blessings? How does your celebration include those who are less fortunate?

See Meeting God in Community

---

a 4 Or *and*   *b* 1 Traditionally *peace offering*; also in verses 3, 6 and 9

This Is My Body, Broken for You

LEVITICUS 4:1–21

Sin offerings allowed an individual or the community the opportunity to repent and reestablish their relationship with God. Failing to do so placed the community in grave danger.

Imagine yourself as an ancient Israelite: You are choosing a sacrificial animal, standing at the entrance to the tabernacle or temple and watching the priests attend to your sacrifice. There are meat and fat burning on the altar, and blood is being sprinkled around. What do you see, smell, hear and feel?

Recall Jesus' words at the Last Supper: "This is my body . . . this is my blood." Remember his death on the cross. Ancient Israelites offered sacrifices when they sinned. In what ways does Jesus' death on the cross parallel (and so replace) a sin offering? In what ways does it transcend it? In what ways (rites or prayers) do you and your community confess your sin and appropriate Jesus' once-and-for-all sacrifice?

See Meeting God in Worship

offers he is to make this offering to the LORD by fire: all the fat that covers the inner parts or is connected to them, ¹⁵both kidneys with the fat on them near the loins, and the covering of the liver, which he will remove with the kidneys. ¹⁶The priest shall burn them on the altar as food, an offering made by fire, a pleasing aroma. All the fat is the LORD's.

¹⁷" 'This is a lasting ordinance for the generations to come, wherever you live: You must not eat any fat or any blood.' "

The Sin Offering

4 The LORD said to Moses, ²"Say to the Israelites: 'When anyone sins unintentionally and does what is forbidden in any of the LORD's commands—

³" 'If the anointed priest sins, bringing guilt on the people, he must bring to the LORD a young bull without defect as a sin offering for the sin he has committed. ⁴He is to present the bull at the entrance to the Tent of Meeting before the LORD. He is to lay his hand on its head and slaughter it before the LORD. ⁵Then the anointed priest shall take some of the bull's blood and carry it into the Tent of Meeting. ⁶He is to dip his finger into the blood and sprinkle some of it seven times before the LORD, in front of the curtain of the sanctuary. ⁷The priest shall then put some of the blood on the horns of the altar of fragrant incense that is before the LORD in the Tent of Meeting. The rest of the bull's blood he shall pour out at the base of the altar of burnt offering at the entrance to the Tent of Meeting. ⁸He shall remove all the fat from the bull of the sin offering—the fat that covers the inner parts or is connected to them, ⁹both kidneys with the fat on them near the loins, and the covering of the liver, which he will remove with the kidneys— ¹⁰just as the fat is removed from the ox*ᵃ* sacrificed as a fellowship offering.*ᵇ* Then the priest shall burn them on the altar of burnt offering. ¹¹But the hide of the bull and all its flesh, as well as the head and legs, the inner parts and offal— ¹²that is, all the rest of the bull—he must take outside the camp to a place ceremonially clean, where the ashes are thrown, and burn it in a wood fire on the ash heap.

¹³" 'If the whole Israelite community sins unintentionally and does what is forbidden in any of the LORD's commands, even though the community is unaware of the matter, they are guilty. ¹⁴When they become aware of the sin they committed, the assembly must bring a young bull as a sin offering and present it before the Tent of Meeting. ¹⁵The elders of the community are to lay their hands on the bull's head before the LORD, and the bull shall be slaughtered before the LORD. ¹⁶Then the anointed priest is to take some of the bull's blood into the Tent of Meeting. ¹⁷He shall dip his finger into the blood and sprinkle it before the LORD seven times in front of the curtain. ¹⁸He is to put some of the blood on the horns of the altar that is before the LORD in the Tent of Meeting. The rest of the blood he shall pour out at the base of the altar of burnt offering at the entrance to the Tent of Meeting. ¹⁹He shall remove all the fat from it

---

ᵃ 10 The Hebrew word can include both male and female.
ᵇ 10 Traditionally *peace offering*; also in verses 26, 31 and 35

[5]or whatever it was he swore falsely about. He must make restitution in full, add a fifth of the value to it and give it all to the owner on the day he presents his guilt offering. [6]And as a penalty he must bring to the priest, that is, to the LORD, his guilt offering, a ram from the flock, one without defect and of the proper value. [7]In this way the priest will make atonement for him before the LORD, and he will be forgiven for any of these things he did that made him guilty."

The Burnt Offering

[8]The LORD said to Moses: [9]"Give Aaron and his sons this command: 'These are the regulations for the burnt offering: The burnt offering is to remain on the altar hearth throughout the night, till morning, and the fire must be kept burning on the altar. [10]The priest shall then put on his linen clothes, with linen undergarments next to his body, and shall remove the ashes of the burnt offering that the fire has consumed on the altar and place them beside the altar. [11]Then he is to take off these clothes and put on others, and carry the ashes outside the camp to a place that is ceremonially clean. [12]The fire on the altar must be kept burning; it must not go out. Every morning the priest is to add firewood and arrange the burnt offering on the fire and burn the fat of the fellowship offerings[a] on it. [13]The fire must be kept burning on the altar continuously; it must not go out.

The Grain Offering

[14]" 'These are the regulations for the grain offering: Aaron's sons are to bring it before the LORD, in front of the altar. [15]The priest is to take a handful of fine flour and oil, together with all the incense on the grain offering, and burn the memorial portion on the altar as an aroma pleasing to the LORD. [16]Aaron and his sons shall eat the rest of it, but it is to be eaten without yeast in a holy place; they are to eat it in the courtyard of the Tent of Meeting. [17]It must not be baked with yeast; I have given it as their share of the offerings made to me by fire. Like the sin offering and the guilt offering, it is most holy. [18]Any male descendant of Aaron may eat it. It is his regular share of the offerings made to the LORD by fire for the generations to come. Whatever touches them will become holy.[b] ' "

[19]The LORD also said to Moses, [20]"This is the offering Aaron and his sons are to bring to the LORD on the day he[c] is anointed: a tenth of an ephah[d] of fine flour as a regular grain offering, half of it in the morning and half in the evening. [21]Prepare it with oil on a griddle; bring it well-mixed and present the grain offering broken[e] in pieces as an aroma pleasing to the LORD. [22]The son who is to succeed him as anointed priest shall prepare it. It is the LORD's regular share and is to be burned completely. [23]Every grain offering of a priest shall be burned completely; it must not be eaten."

The Sin Offering

[24]The LORD said to Moses, [25]"Say to Aaron and his sons: 'These are the regulations for the sin offering: The sin of-

---

Keep a Fire Burning

LEVITICUS 6:13

Light a candle and watch it burn for several minutes. Time (or estimate) how long it takes to burn down. Calculate the number of candles that would be required to keep the same flame burning uninterrupted for a week, a year.

Imagine that you live in the time of Jeremiah and you are going to worship at the temple in Jerusalem. You watch the priest lay your sacrifice on the altar. What might your feelings be when you realize that the fire that is burning on the altar is the same fire that has burned uninterrupted for over seven hundred years—the same fire that burned before Aaron and Moses (see 9:24)? As you watch the portion of your sacrifice being burned on the altar, ponder what it means to say that God is a consuming fire.

See Meeting God in Worship

---

[a] 12 Traditionally *peace offerings*   [b] 18 Or *Whoever touches them must be holy*; similarly in verse 27   [c] 20 Or *each*   [d] 20 That is, probably about 2 quarts (about 2 liters)   [e] 21 The meaning of the Hebrew for this word is uncertain.

Keeping the Community Pure

LEVITICUS 7:20–21

Because the covenant with God defines the nation, being cut off or separated from it is a terrible event. It is just the opposite of what God intends for his people—to be partakers of the covenant. In ancient Israel the priests would decide whether a person should be cut off from the community.

Picture an occasion (real or hypothetical) when this passage would be applicable to your spiritual community. What might be your response toward someone who has been "cut off"? Jesus specifically charges us "Do not judge, or you too will be judged" (Matthew 7:1). Does this command negate the requirement to exclude known sinners from the church (see also 1 Corinthians 5:1–5; Ephesians 5:3)? Who would make that decision in your community? When have you been tempted to usurp God's role as judge? Was someone "cut off" from your faith community as a result? What effects might this have on the community as a whole?

See Meeting God in Community

fering is to be slaughtered before the LORD in the place the burnt offering is slaughtered; it is most holy. [26]The priest who offers it shall eat it; it is to be eaten in a holy place, in the courtyard of the Tent of Meeting. [27]Whatever touches any of the flesh will become holy, and if any of the blood is spattered on a garment, you must wash it in a holy place. [28]The clay pot the meat is cooked in must be broken; but if it is cooked in a bronze pot, the pot is to be scoured and rinsed with water. [29]Any male in a priest's family may eat it; it is most holy. [30]But any sin offering whose blood is brought into the Tent of Meeting to make atonement in the Holy Place must not be eaten; it must be burned.

The Guilt Offering

7 " 'These are the regulations for the guilt offering, which is most holy: [2]The guilt offering is to be slaughtered in the place where the burnt offering is slaughtered, and its blood is to be sprinkled against the altar on all sides. [3]All its fat shall be offered: the fat tail and the fat that covers the inner parts, [4]both kidneys with the fat on them near the loins, and the covering of the liver, which is to be removed with the kidneys. [5]The priest shall burn them on the altar as an offering made to the LORD by fire. It is a guilt offering. [6]Any male in a priest's family may eat it, but it must be eaten in a holy place; it is most holy.

[7]" 'The same law applies to both the sin offering and the guilt offering: They belong to the priest who makes atonement with them. [8]The priest who offers a burnt offering for anyone may keep its hide for himself. [9]Every grain offering baked in an oven or cooked in a pan or on a griddle belongs to the priest who offers it, [10]and every grain offering, whether mixed with oil or dry, belongs equally to all the sons of Aaron.

The Fellowship Offering

[11]" 'These are the regulations for the fellowship offering[a] a person may present to the LORD:

[12]" 'If he offers it as an expression of thankfulness, then along with this thank offering he is to offer cakes of bread made without yeast and mixed with oil, wafers made without yeast and spread with oil, and cakes of fine flour well-kneaded and mixed with oil. [13]Along with his fellowship offering of thanksgiving he is to present an offering with cakes of bread made with yeast. [14]He is to bring one of each kind as an offering, a contribution to the LORD; it belongs to the priest who sprinkles the blood of the fellowship offerings. [15]The meat of his fellowship offering of thanksgiving must be eaten on the day it is offered; he must leave none of it till morning.

[16]" 'If, however, his offering is the result of a vow or is a freewill offering, the sacrifice shall be eaten on the day he offers it, but anything left over may be eaten on the next day. [17]Any meat of the sacrifice left over till the third day must be burned up. [18]If any meat of the fellowship offering is eaten on the third day, it will not be accepted. It will not be credited to the one who offered it, for it is impure; the person who eats any of it will be held responsible.

[19]" 'Meat that touches anything ceremonially unclean must not be eaten; it must be burned up. As for other

a 11 Traditionally peace offering; also in verses 13–37

meat, anyone ceremonially clean may eat it. [20]But if anyone who is unclean eats any meat of the fellowship offering belonging to the LORD, that person must be cut off from his people. [21]If anyone touches something unclean—whether human uncleanness or an unclean animal or any unclean, detestable thing—and then eats any of the meat of the fellowship offering belonging to the LORD, that person must be cut off from his people.' "

Eating Fat and Blood Forbidden

[22]The LORD said to Moses, [23]"Say to the Israelites: 'Do not eat any of the fat of cattle, sheep or goats. [24]The fat of an animal found dead or torn by wild animals may be used for any other purpose, but you must not eat it. [25]Anyone who eats the fat of an animal from which an offering by fire may be[a] made to the LORD must be cut off from his people. [26]And wherever you live, you must not eat the blood of any bird or animal. [27]If anyone eats blood, that person must be cut off from his people.' "

The Priests' Share

[28]The LORD said to Moses, [29]"Say to the Israelites: 'Anyone who brings a fellowship offering to the LORD is to bring part of it as his sacrifice to the LORD. [30]With his own hands he is to bring the offering made to the LORD by fire; he is to bring the fat, together with the breast, and wave the breast before the LORD as a wave offering. [31]The priest shall burn the fat on the altar, but the breast belongs to Aaron and his sons. [32]You are to give the right thigh of your fellowship offerings to the priest as a contribution. [33]The son of Aaron who offers the blood and the fat of the fellowship offering shall have the right thigh as his share. [34]From the fellowship offerings of the Israelites, I have taken the breast that is waved and the thigh that is presented and have given them to Aaron the priest and his sons as their regular share from the Israelites.' "

[35]This is the portion of the offerings made to the LORD by fire that were allotted to Aaron and his sons on the day they were presented to serve the LORD as priests. [36]On the day they were anointed, the LORD commanded that the Israelites give this to them as their regular share for the generations to come.

[37]These, then, are the regulations for the burnt offering, the grain offering, the sin offering, the guilt offering, the ordination offering and the fellowship offering, [38]which the LORD gave Moses on Mount Sinai on the day he commanded the Israelites to bring their offerings to the LORD, in the Desert of Sinai.

The Ordination of Aaron and His Sons

8 The LORD said to Moses, [2]"Bring Aaron and his sons, their garments, the anointing oil, the bull for the sin offering, the two rams and the basket containing bread made without yeast, [3]and gather the entire assembly at the entrance to the Tent of Meeting." [4]Moses did as the LORD commanded him, and the assembly gathered at the entrance to the Tent of Meeting.

[5]Moses said to the assembly, "This is what the LORD has

God's Portion

LEVITICUS 7:22–27

Blood is forbidden because it contains life (see 17:11) and effects atonement (by substituting one life for another). Fat is forbidden because it is God's portion (see 3:16). Thus, all blood and fat are holy and, in some sense, a part of every meal becomes an offering to God.

Ancient Israelites offered their sacrificial portions from food and animals that they had raised in their own gardens and herds. Because they had to work hard, often under adverse conditions, just to survive, giving away food was a hardship, truly a sacrifice. Grill a piece of prepackaged meat on a barbecue. Experience the aroma and smoke. Imagine what it must have been like to be in the temple compound where sacrifices were continually burning.

What is the spiritual cost to a society such as ours that eats prepackaged food as opposed to raising it?

See Meeting God in the Created Order

Rites of Ordination

LEVITICUS 8:10–13

In the sight of all the community, Moses anoints and consecrates the tabernacle and Aaron and his sons, fulfilling the command of God (see Exodus 30:22–33). From this point on, the tabernacle, all its furnishings, and Aaron and his sons are set apart for service to God.

Christians are called to be "separated" from the world in which they live. Make a list of five ways that your Christian faith distinguishes you and your faith community from the culture around you. Make a second list of ways that you and your faith community are more like the culture than you might wish to be. Take your lists before God, asking God to strengthen you in your attempts to be faithfully set apart.

See Meeting God in Community

commanded to be done." ⁶Then Moses brought Aaron and his sons forward and washed them with water. ⁷He put the tunic on Aaron, tied the sash around him, clothed him with the robe and put the ephod on him. He also tied the ephod to him by its skillfully woven waistband; so it was fastened on him. ⁸He placed the breastpiece on him and put the Urim and Thummim in the breastpiece. ⁹Then he placed the turban on Aaron's head and set the gold plate, the sacred diadem, on the front of it, as the LORD commanded Moses.

¹⁰Then Moses took the anointing oil and anointed the tabernacle and everything in it, and so consecrated them. ¹¹He sprinkled some of the oil on the altar seven times, anointing the altar and all its utensils and the basin with its stand, to consecrate them. ¹²He poured some of the anointing oil on Aaron's head and anointed him to consecrate him. ¹³Then he brought Aaron's sons forward, put tunics on them, tied sashes around them and put headbands on them, as the LORD commanded Moses.

¹⁴He then presented the bull for the sin offering, and Aaron and his sons laid their hands on its head. ¹⁵Moses slaughtered the bull and took some of the blood, and with his finger he put it on all the horns of the altar to purify the altar. He poured out the rest of the blood at the base of the altar. So he consecrated it to make atonement for it. ¹⁶Moses also took all the fat around the inner parts, the covering of the liver, and both kidneys and their fat, and burned it on the altar. ¹⁷But the bull with its hide and its flesh and its offal he burned up outside the camp, as the LORD commanded Moses.

¹⁸He then presented the ram for the burnt offering, and Aaron and his sons laid their hands on its head. ¹⁹Then Moses slaughtered the ram and sprinkled the blood against the altar on all sides. ²⁰He cut the ram into pieces and burned the head, the pieces and the fat. ²¹He washed the inner parts and the legs with water and burned the whole ram on the altar as a burnt offering, a pleasing aroma, an offering made to the LORD by fire, as the LORD commanded Moses.

²²He then presented the other ram, the ram for the ordination, and Aaron and his sons laid their hands on its head. ²³Moses slaughtered the ram and took some of its blood and put it on the lobe of Aaron's right ear, on the thumb of his right hand and on the big toe of his right foot. ²⁴Moses also brought Aaron's sons forward and put some of the blood on the lobes of their right ears, on the thumbs of their right hands and on the big toes of their right feet. Then he sprinkled blood against the altar on all sides. ²⁵He took the fat, the fat tail, all the fat around the inner parts, the covering of the liver, both kidneys and their fat and the right thigh. ²⁶Then from the basket of bread made without yeast, which was before the LORD, he took a cake of bread, and one made with oil, and a wafer; he put these on the fat portions and on the right thigh. ²⁷He put all these in the hands of Aaron and his sons and waved them before the LORD as a wave offering. ²⁸Then Moses took them from their hands and burned them on the altar on top of the burnt offering as an ordination offering, a pleasing aroma, an offering made to the LORD by fire. ²⁹He also took the breast—Moses' share of the ordination ram—and waved it

before the LORD as a wave offering, as the LORD commanded Moses.

³⁰Then Moses took some of the anointing oil and some of the blood from the altar and sprinkled them on Aaron and his garments and on his sons and their garments. So he consecrated Aaron and his garments and his sons and their garments.

³¹Moses then said to Aaron and his sons, "Cook the meat at the entrance to the Tent of Meeting and eat it there with the bread from the basket of ordination offerings, as I commanded, saying,ᵃ 'Aaron and his sons are to eat it.' ³²Then burn up the rest of the meat and the bread. ³³Do not leave the entrance to the Tent of Meeting for seven days, until the days of your ordination are completed, for your ordination will last seven days. ³⁴What has been done today was commanded by the LORD to make atonement for you. ³⁵You must stay at the entrance to the Tent of Meeting day and night for seven days and do what the LORD requires, so you will not die; for that is what I have been commanded." ³⁶So Aaron and his sons did everything the LORD commanded through Moses.

The Priests Begin Their Ministry

9 On the eighth day Moses summoned Aaron and his sons and the elders of Israel. ²He said to Aaron, "Take a bull calf for your sin offering and a ram for your burnt offering, both without defect, and present them before the LORD. ³Then say to the Israelites: 'Take a male goat for a sin offering, a calf and a lamb—both a year old and without defect—for a burnt offering, ⁴and an oxᵇ and a ram for a fellowship offeringᶜ to sacrifice before the LORD, together with a grain offering mixed with oil. For today the LORD will appear to you.' "

⁵They took the things Moses commanded to the front of the Tent of Meeting, and the entire assembly came near and stood before the LORD. ⁶Then Moses said, "This is what the LORD has commanded you to do, so that the glory of the LORD may appear to you."

⁷Moses said to Aaron, "Come to the altar and sacrifice your sin offering and your burnt offering and make atonement for yourself and the people; sacrifice the offering that is for the people and make atonement for them, as the LORD has commanded."

⁸So Aaron came to the altar and slaughtered the calf as a sin offering for himself. ⁹His sons brought the blood to him, and he dipped his finger into the blood and put it on the horns of the altar; the rest of the blood he poured out at the base of the altar. ¹⁰On the altar he burned the fat, the kidneys and the covering of the liver from the sin offering, as the LORD commanded Moses; ¹¹the flesh and the hide he burned up outside the camp.

¹²Then he slaughtered the burnt offering. His sons handed him the blood, and he sprinkled it against the altar on all sides. ¹³They handed him the burnt offering piece by piece, including the head, and he burned them on the altar. ¹⁴He washed the inner parts and the legs and burned them on top of the burnt offering on the altar.

Completely Burned

LEVITICUS 8:31—9:17

By Levitical law, a whole burnt offering was to be completely burned up and the ashes properly disposed of, removing the guilt from the person offering the sacrifice.

On a piece of paper, record some past sins that have separated you from others and from God. Now contemplate any current sins that may be standing between you and God and record them as well. Offer the paper as your sacrifice to God and burn it. Take the ashes outside and blow them into the wind.

See Meeting God in Scripture

ᵃ 31 Or *I was commanded:*   ᵇ 4 The Hebrew word can include both male and female; also in verses 18 and 19.   ᶜ 4 Traditionally *peace offering;* also in verses 18 and 22

Fire From the Lord

LEVITICUS 9:23–24

Imagine yourself watching as Aaron lays the sacrificial portions on the altar; the fire suddenly shoots out from the presence of the LORD and consumes them. What are you feeling—awe, fear, joy, excitement?

Recall a time in your life when you suddenly and unexpectedly experienced the presence of God. Where were you? In worship? In private meditation? What emotions did you experience then? What are some of the ways you experience God's presence today?

See *Meeting God in Scripture*

¹⁵Aaron then brought the offering that was for the people. He took the goat for the people's sin offering and slaughtered it and offered it for a sin offering as he did with the first one.

¹⁶He brought the burnt offering and offered it in the prescribed way. ¹⁷He also brought the grain offering, took a handful of it and burned it on the altar in addition to the morning's burnt offering.

¹⁸He slaughtered the ox and the ram as the fellowship offering for the people. His sons handed him the blood, and he sprinkled it against the altar on all sides. ¹⁹But the fat portions of the ox and the ram—the fat tail, the layer of fat, the kidneys and the covering of the liver— ²⁰these they laid on the breasts, and then Aaron burned the fat on the altar. ²¹Aaron waved the breasts and the right thigh before the LORD as a wave offering, as Moses commanded.

²²Then Aaron lifted his hands toward the people and blessed them. And having sacrificed the sin offering, the burnt offering and the fellowship offering, he stepped down.

²³Moses and Aaron then went into the Tent of Meeting. When they came out, they blessed the people; and the glory of the LORD appeared to all the people. ²⁴Fire came out from the presence of the LORD and consumed the burnt offering and the fat portions on the altar. And when all the people saw it, they shouted for joy and fell facedown.

The Death of Nadab and Abihu

10 Aaron's sons Nadab and Abihu took their censers, put fire in them and added incense; and they offered unauthorized fire before the LORD, contrary to his command. ²So fire came out from the presence of the LORD and consumed them, and they died before the LORD. ³Moses then said to Aaron, "This is what the LORD spoke of when he said:

" 'Among those who approach me
I will show myself holy;
in the sight of all the people
I will be honored.' "

Aaron remained silent.

⁴Moses summoned Mishael and Elzaphan, sons of Aaron's uncle Uzziel, and said to them, "Come here; carry your cousins outside the camp, away from the front of the sanctuary." ⁵So they came and carried them, still in their tunics, outside the camp, as Moses ordered.

⁶Then Moses said to Aaron and his sons Eleazar and Ithamar, "Do not let your hair become unkempt,ᵃ and do not tear your clothes, or you will die and the LORD will be angry with the whole community. But your relatives, all the house of Israel, may mourn for those the LORD has destroyed by fire. ⁷Do not leave the entrance to the Tent of Meeting or you will die, because the LORD's anointing oil is on you." So they did as Moses said.

⁸Then the LORD said to Aaron, ⁹"You and your sons are not to drink wine or other fermented drink whenever you go into the Tent of Meeting, or you will die. This is a lasting ordinance for the generations to come. ¹⁰You must distinguish between the holy and the common, between the un-

ᵃ 6 Or *Do not uncover your heads*

clean and the clean, ¹¹and you must teach the Israelites all the decrees the Lᴏʀᴅ has given them through Moses."

¹²Moses said to Aaron and his remaining sons, Eleazar and Ithamar, "Take the grain offering left over from the offerings made to the Lᴏʀᴅ by fire and eat it prepared without yeast beside the altar, for it is most holy. ¹³Eat it in a holy place, because it is your share and your sons' share of the offerings made to the Lᴏʀᴅ by fire; for so I have been commanded. ¹⁴But you and your sons and your daughters may eat the breast that was waved and the thigh that was presented. Eat them in a ceremonially clean place; they have been given to you and your children as your share of the Israelites' fellowship offerings.ᵃ ¹⁵The thigh that was presented and the breast that was waved must be brought with the fat portions of the offerings made by fire, to be waved before the Lᴏʀᴅ as a wave offering. This will be the regular share for you and your children, as the Lᴏʀᴅ has commanded."

¹⁶When Moses inquired about the goat of the sin offering and found that it had been burned up, he was angry with Eleazar and Ithamar, Aaron's remaining sons, and asked, ¹⁷"Why didn't you eat the sin offering in the sanctuary area? It is most holy; it was given to you to take away the guilt of the community by making atonement for them before the Lᴏʀᴅ. ¹⁸Since its blood was not taken into the Holy Place, you should have eaten the goat in the sanctuary area, as I commanded."

¹⁹Aaron replied to Moses, "Today they sacrificed their sin offering and their burnt offering before the Lᴏʀᴅ, but such things as this have happened to me. Would the Lᴏʀᴅ have been pleased if I had eaten the sin offering today?" ²⁰When Moses heard this, he was satisfied.

Clean and Unclean Food

11 The Lᴏʀᴅ said to Moses and Aaron, ²"Say to the Israelites: 'Of all the animals that live on land, these are the ones you may eat: ³You may eat any animal that has a split hoof completely divided and that chews the cud.

⁴" 'There are some that only chew the cud or only have a split hoof, but you must not eat them. The camel, though it chews the cud, does not have a split hoof; it is ceremonially unclean for you. ⁵The coney,ᵇ though it chews the cud, does not have a split hoof; it is unclean for you. ⁶The rabbit, though it chews the cud, does not have a split hoof; it is unclean for you. ⁷And the pig, though it has a split hoof completely divided, does not chew the cud; it is unclean for you. ⁸You must not eat their meat or touch their carcasses; they are unclean for you.

⁹" 'Of all the creatures living in the water of the seas and the streams, you may eat any that have fins and scales. ¹⁰But all creatures in the seas or streams that do not have fins and scales—whether among all the swarming things or among all the other living creatures in the water—you are to detest. ¹¹And since you are to detest them, you must not eat their meat and you must detest their carcasses. ¹²Anything living in the water that does not have fins and scales is to be detestable to you.

¹³" 'These are the birds you are to detest and not eat because they are detestable: the eagle, the vulture, the black

Removing the Guilt

LEVITICUS 10:17

The New Testament builds on this verse to describe Jesus' role in removing our sin (1 Peter 2:24; John 1:29). God has placed all of our sin on the cross with Jesus and has removed it.

God has removed our sin. Explore the implications of what that means. Does this include only our past misdeeds or also any sins we may commit in the future? If future sins are included, does that mean Christians have no restrictions placed on their actions? What is the meaning of salvation if there is no punishment for sin? If future sins are not automatically included, what rituals are available for Christians to confess their sin and once again be at peace with God?

Clean and Unclean

LEVITICUS 11:22—12:1

"Moses . . . describes the clean and unclean beasts, and says that all beasts which are not cloven-footed and chew their cud, shall be unclean. This refers to people who are not cloven-hoofed, that is, those who rush aimlessly into life, and snatch up whatever crosses their path and follow it. But the clean beasts are they who act with the discrimination of the spirit in external matters and in things relating to doctrine. They retain what they observe to be in harmony with the Scriptures, but whatever has no basis in the Scriptures and is a valueless human trifle, they reject."

—MARTIN LUTHER,
Sermons

See *Meeting God in Scripture*

vulture, [14]the red kite, any kind of black kite, [15]any kind of raven, [16]the horned owl, the screech owl, the gull, any kind of hawk, [17]the little owl, the cormorant, the great owl, [18]the white owl, the desert owl, the osprey, [19]the stork, any kind of heron, the hoopoe and the bat.[a]

[20]" 'All flying insects that walk on all fours are to be detestable to you. [21]There are, however, some winged creatures that walk on all fours that you may eat: those that have jointed legs for hopping on the ground. [22]Of these you may eat any kind of locust, katydid, cricket or grasshopper. [23]But all other winged creatures that have four legs you are to detest.

[24]" 'You will make yourselves unclean by these; whoever touches their carcasses will be unclean till evening. [25]Whoever picks up one of their carcasses must wash his clothes, and he will be unclean till evening.

[26]" 'Every animal that has a split hoof not completely divided or that does not chew the cud is unclean for you; whoever touches the carcass of any of them will be unclean. [27]Of all the animals that walk on all fours, those that walk on their paws are unclean for you; whoever touches their carcasses will be unclean till evening. [28]Anyone who picks up their carcasses must wash his clothes, and he will be unclean till evening. They are unclean for you.

[29]" 'Of the animals that move about on the ground, these are unclean for you: the weasel, the rat, any kind of great lizard, [30]the gecko, the monitor lizard, the wall lizard, the skink and the chameleon. [31]Of all those that move along the ground, these are unclean for you. Whoever touches them when they are dead will be unclean till evening. [32]When one of them dies and falls on something, that article, whatever its use, will be unclean, whether it is made of wood, cloth, hide or sackcloth. Put it in water; it will be unclean till evening, and then it will be clean. [33]If one of them falls into a clay pot, everything in it will be unclean, and you must break the pot. [34]Any food that could be eaten but has water on it from such a pot is unclean, and any liquid that could be drunk from it is unclean. [35]Anything that one of their carcasses falls on becomes unclean; an oven or cooking pot must be broken up. They are unclean, and you are to regard them as unclean. [36]A spring, however, or a cistern for collecting water remains clean, but anyone who touches one of these carcasses is unclean. [37]If a carcass falls on any seeds that are to be planted, they remain clean. [38]But if water has been put on the seed and a carcass falls on it, it is unclean for you.

[39]" 'If an animal that you are allowed to eat dies, anyone who touches the carcass will be unclean till evening. [40]Anyone who eats some of the carcass must wash his clothes, and he will be unclean till evening. Anyone who picks up the carcass must wash his clothes, and he will be unclean till evening.

[41]" 'Every creature that moves about on the ground is detestable; it is not to be eaten. [42]You are not to eat any creature that moves about on the ground, whether it moves on its belly or walks on all fours or on many feet; it is detestable. [43]Do not defile yourselves by any of these creatures. Do not make yourselves unclean by means of them

---

[a] *19* The precise identification of some of the birds, insects and animals in this chapter is uncertain.

or be made unclean by them. ⁴⁴I am the LORD your God; consecrate yourselves and be holy, because I am holy. Do not make yourselves unclean by any creature that moves about on the ground. ⁴⁵I am the LORD who brought you up out of Egypt to be your God; therefore be holy, because I am holy.

⁴⁶ " 'These are the regulations concerning animals, birds, every living thing that moves in the water and every creature that moves about on the ground. ⁴⁷You must distinguish between the unclean and the clean, between living creatures that may be eaten and those that may not be eaten.' "

Purification After Childbirth

12 The LORD said to Moses, ²"Say to the Israelites: 'A woman who becomes pregnant and gives birth to a son will be ceremonially unclean for seven days, just as she is unclean during her monthly period. ³On the eighth day the boy is to be circumcised. ⁴Then the woman must wait thirty-three days to be purified from her bleeding. She must not touch anything sacred or go to the sanctuary until the days of her purification are over. ⁵If she gives birth to a daughter, for two weeks the woman will be unclean, as during her period. Then she must wait sixty-six days to be purified from her bleeding.

⁶ " 'When the days of her purification for a son or daughter are over, she is to bring to the priest at the entrance to the Tent of Meeting a year-old lamb for a burnt offering and a young pigeon or a dove for a sin offering. ⁷He shall offer them before the LORD to make atonement for her, and then she will be ceremonially clean from her flow of blood.

" 'These are the regulations for the woman who gives birth to a boy or a girl. ⁸If she cannot afford a lamb, she is to bring two doves or two young pigeons, one for a burnt offering and the other for a sin offering. In this way the priest will make atonement for her, and she will be clean.' "

Regulations About Infectious Skin Diseases

13 The LORD said to Moses and Aaron, ²"When anyone has a swelling or a rash or a bright spot on his skin that may become an infectious skin disease,ᵃ he must be brought to Aaron the priest or to one of his sonsᵇ who is a priest. ³The priest is to examine the sore on his skin, and if the hair in the sore has turned white and the sore appears to be more than skin deep,ᶜ it is an infectious skin disease. When the priest examines him, he shall pronounce him ceremonially unclean. ⁴If the spot on his skin is white but does not appear to be more than skin deep and the hair in it has not turned white, the priest is to put the infected person in isolation for seven days. ⁵On the seventh day the priest is to examine him, and if he sees that the sore is unchanged and has not spread in the skin, he is to keep him in isolation another seven days. ⁶On the seventh day the priest is to examine him again, and if the sore has faded and has not spread in the skin, the priest shall pronounce him clean; it is only a rash. The man must wash his clothes,

---

Purification

LEVITICUS 12:1–8

According to Levitical law, childbirth is a milestone in a woman's life that is marked by a special religious observance. It is meant to be a holy occasion, a time to bring a family closer to God, and is not meant to be a burden to those who are not well-off. The offering Joseph and Mary offered when they brought Jesus to the temple was the offering mandated for the poor (see Luke 2:24). What does the fact that our Savior was born to a poor family rather than to a wealthy, powerful one signify to us? What does this tell us about God's nature? Why do you think we are surprised that God appeared to humans in so humble a form? What does that tell us about human nature?

Examine your own actions and feelings: Do you show deference or respect for wealth and power? How might you react when you encounter a homeless person asking for help?

See Meeting God in Community

ᵃ2 Traditionally *leprosy*; the Hebrew word was used for various diseases affecting the skin—not necessarily leprosy; also elsewhere in this chapter.
ᵇ2 Or *descendants* ᶜ3 Or *be lower than the rest of the skin*; also elsewhere in this chapter

Prayer of Thanks

"Thanks, thanks to thee,
O Eternal Father, for thou hast
not despised me, the work of
thy hands, nor turned thy face
from me, nor despised my desires; thou, the Light, hast not
regarded my darkness; thou,
true Life, has not regarded my
living death; thou, the Physician, hast not been repelled by
my grave infirmities; thou, the
Eternal Purity, hast not considered the many miseries of
which I am full; thou, who art
the Infinite, hast overlooked
that I am finite; thou, who are
Wisdom, but overlooked my
folly; thy wisdom, thy goodness, thy clemency, thy infinite
good, have overlooked these infinite evils and sins, and the
many others which are in me."
—CATHERINE OF SIENA,
The Dialogue

See Meeting God in Prayer

and he will be clean. ⁷But if the rash does spread in his skin after he has shown himself to the priest to be pronounced clean, he must appear before the priest again. ⁸The priest is to examine him, and if the rash has spread in the skin, he shall pronounce him unclean; it is an infectious disease.

⁹"When anyone has an infectious skin disease, he must be brought to the priest. ¹⁰The priest is to examine him, and if there is a white swelling in the skin that has turned the hair white and if there is raw flesh in the swelling, ¹¹it is a chronic skin disease and the priest shall pronounce him unclean. He is not to put him in isolation, because he is already unclean.

¹²"If the disease breaks out all over his skin and, so far as the priest can see, it covers all the skin of the infected person from head to foot, ¹³the priest is to examine him, and if the disease has covered his whole body, he shall pronounce that person clean. Since it has all turned white, he is clean. ¹⁴But whenever raw flesh appears on him, he will be unclean. ¹⁵When the priest sees the raw flesh, he shall pronounce him unclean. The raw flesh is unclean; he has an infectious disease. ¹⁶Should the raw flesh change and turn white, he must go to the priest. ¹⁷The priest is to examine him, and if the sores have turned white, the priest shall pronounce the infected person clean; then he will be clean.

¹⁸"When someone has a boil on his skin and it heals, ¹⁹and in the place where the boil was, a white swelling or reddish-white spot appears, he must present himself to the priest. ²⁰The priest is to examine it, and if it appears to be more than skin deep and the hair in it has turned white, the priest shall pronounce him unclean. It is an infectious skin disease that has broken out where the boil was. ²¹But if, when the priest examines it, there is no white hair in it and it is not more than skin deep and has faded, then the priest is to put him in isolation for seven days. ²²If it is spreading in the skin, the priest shall pronounce him unclean; it is infectious. ²³But if the spot is unchanged and has not spread, it is only a scar from the boil, and the priest shall pronounce him clean.

²⁴"When someone has a burn on his skin and a reddish-white or white spot appears in the raw flesh of the burn, ²⁵the priest is to examine the spot, and if the hair in it has turned white, and it appears to be more than skin deep, it is an infectious disease that has broken out in the burn. The priest shall pronounce him unclean; it is an infectious skin disease. ²⁶But if the priest examines it and there is no white hair in the spot and if it is not more than skin deep and has faded, then the priest is to put him in isolation for seven days. ²⁷On the seventh day the priest is to examine him, and if it is spreading in the skin, the priest shall pronounce him unclean; it is an infectious skin disease. ²⁸If, however, the spot is unchanged and has not spread in the skin but has faded, it is a swelling from the burn, and the priest shall pronounce him clean; it is only a scar from the burn.

²⁹"If a man or woman has a sore on the head or on the chin, ³⁰the priest is to examine the sore, and if it appears to be more than skin deep and the hair in it is yellow and thin, the priest shall pronounce that person unclean; it is an itch, an infectious disease of the head or chin. ³¹But if, when the

priest examines this kind of sore, it does not seem to be more than skin deep and there is no black hair in it, then the priest is to put the infected person in isolation for seven days. [32]On the seventh day the priest is to examine the sore, and if the itch has not spread and there is no yellow hair in it and it does not appear to be more than skin deep, [33]he must be shaved except for the diseased area, and the priest is to keep him in isolation another seven days. [34]On the seventh day the priest is to examine the itch, and if it has not spread in the skin and appears to be no more than skin deep, the priest shall pronounce him clean. He must wash his clothes, and he will be clean. [35]But if the itch does spread in the skin after he is pronounced clean, [36]the priest is to examine him, and if the itch has spread in the skin, the priest does not need to look for yellow hair; the person is unclean. [37]If, however, in his judgment it is unchanged and black hair has grown in it, the itch is healed. He is clean, and the priest shall pronounce him clean.

[38]"When a man or woman has white spots on the skin, [39]the priest is to examine them, and if the spots are dull white, it is a harmless rash that has broken out on the skin; that person is clean.

[40]"When a man has lost his hair and is bald, he is clean. [41]If he has lost his hair from the front of his scalp and has a bald forehead, he is clean. [42]But if he has a reddish-white sore on his bald head or forehead, it is an infectious disease breaking out on his head or forehead. [43]The priest is to examine him, and if the swollen sore on his head or forehead is reddish-white like an infectious skin disease, [44]the man is diseased and is unclean. The priest shall pronounce him unclean because of the sore on his head.

[45]"The person with such an infectious disease must wear torn clothes, let his hair be unkempt,[a] cover the lower part of his face and cry out, 'Unclean! Unclean!' [46]As long as he has the infection he remains unclean. He must live alone; he must live outside the camp.

Regulations About Mildew

[47]"If any clothing is contaminated with mildew—any woolen or linen clothing, [48]any woven or knitted material of linen or wool, any leather or anything made of leather— [49]and if the contamination in the clothing, or leather, or woven or knitted material, or any leather article, is greenish or reddish, it is a spreading mildew and must be shown to the priest. [50]The priest is to examine the mildew and isolate the affected article for seven days. [51]On the seventh day he is to examine it, and if the mildew has spread in the clothing, or the woven or knitted material, or the leather, whatever its use, it is a destructive mildew; the article is unclean. [52]He must burn up the clothing, or the woven or knitted material of wool or linen, or any leather article that has the contamination in it, because the mildew is destructive; the article must be burned up.

[53]"But if, when the priest examines it, the mildew has not spread in the clothing, or the woven or knitted material, or the leather article, [54]he shall order that the contaminated article be washed. Then he is to isolate it for another seven days. [55]After the affected article has been washed, the priest is to examine it, and if the mildew has not

---

Unclean, Unclean!

LEVITICUS 13:45–46

To protect the other members of the community, those with "leprous diseases" are forced to live separately, wear special clothes and warn others to stay away.

In our society, certain groups are treated as if they were lepers and forced into virtual isolation. Can you think of people whom you or your immediate circle of friends treat as if they were lepers? What is it about them that makes you uncomfortable? What types of things have you or others done to make them feel unwanted? How do you suppose they feel? Share your thoughts with God and pray for those people.

See *Meeting God in Service*

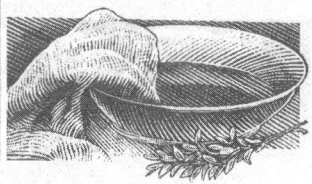

---

[a] 45 Or *clothes, uncover his head*

Coming Home

LEVITICUS 13:59—14:19

The term translated "guilt offering" in this passage is sometimes called a "purification offering." It signifies that the individual is ready to return to active participation in the community.

Recall a time when you or someone you know has been ill or injured and absent from your faith community for an extended period. In what ways was your community diminished by the absence? Write or perform an act of praise or a prayer (perhaps based on a familiar Scriptural passage) to welcome someone back into normal communion with the community after a prolonged absence.

See Meeting God in Community

changed its appearance, even though it has not spread, it is unclean. Burn it with fire, whether the mildew has affected one side or the other. ⁵⁶If, when the priest examines it, the mildew has faded after the article has been washed, he is to tear the contaminated part out of the clothing, or the leather, or the woven or knitted material. ⁵⁷But if it reappears in the clothing, or in the woven or knitted material, or in the leather article, it is spreading, and whatever has the mildew must be burned with fire. ⁵⁸The clothing, or the woven or knitted material, or any leather article that has been washed and is rid of the mildew, must be washed again, and it will be clean."

⁵⁹These are the regulations concerning contamination by mildew in woolen or linen clothing, woven or knitted material, or any leather article, for pronouncing them clean or unclean.

Cleansing From Infectious Skin Diseases

14 The LORD said to Moses, ²"These are the regulations for the diseased person at the time of his ceremonial cleansing, when he is brought to the priest: ³The priest is to go outside the camp and examine him. If the person has been healed of his infectious skin disease,ᵃ ⁴the priest shall order that two live clean birds and some cedar wood, scarlet yarn and hyssop be brought for the one to be cleansed. ⁵Then the priest shall order that one of the birds be killed over fresh water in a clay pot. ⁶He is then to take the live bird and dip it, together with the cedar wood, the scarlet yarn and the hyssop, into the blood of the bird that was killed over the fresh water. ⁷Seven times he shall sprinkle the one to be cleansed of the infectious disease and pronounce him clean. Then he is to release the live bird in the open fields.

⁸"The person to be cleansed must wash his clothes, shave off all his hair and bathe with water; then he will be ceremonially clean. After this he may come into the camp, but he must stay outside his tent for seven days. ⁹On the seventh day he must shave off all his hair; he must shave his head, his beard, his eyebrows and the rest of his hair. He must wash his clothes and bathe himself with water, and he will be clean.

¹⁰"On the eighth day he must bring two male lambs and one ewe lamb a year old, each without defect, along with three-tenths of an ephahᵇ of fine flour mixed with oil for a grain offering, and one logᶜ of oil. ¹¹The priest who pronounces him clean shall present both the one to be cleansed and his offerings before the LORD at the entrance to the Tent of Meeting.

¹²"Then the priest is to take one of the male lambs and offer it as a guilt offering, along with the log of oil; he shall wave them before the LORD as a wave offering. ¹³He is to slaughter the lamb in the holy place where the sin offering and the burnt offering are slaughtered. Like the sin offering, the guilt offering belongs to the priest; it is most holy. ¹⁴The priest is to take some of the blood of the guilt offering and put it on the lobe of the right ear of the one to be

---

ᵃ 3 Traditionally *leprosy*; the Hebrew word was used for various diseases affecting the skin—not necessarily leprosy; also elsewhere in this chapter. ᵇ 10 That is, probably about 6 quarts (about 6.5 liters)   ᶜ 10 That is, probably about 2/3 pint (about 0.3 liter); also in verses 12, 15, 21 and 24

cleansed, on the thumb of his right hand and on the big toe of his right foot. ¹⁵The priest shall then take some of the log of oil, pour it in the palm of his own left hand, ¹⁶dip his right forefinger into the oil in his palm, and with his finger sprinkle some of it before the LORD seven times. ¹⁷The priest is to put some of the oil remaining in his palm on the lobe of the right ear of the one to be cleansed, on the thumb of his right hand and on the big toe of his right foot, on top of the blood of the guilt offering. ¹⁸The rest of the oil in his palm the priest shall put on the head of the one to be cleansed and make atonement for him before the LORD.

¹⁹"Then the priest is to sacrifice the sin offering and make atonement for the one to be cleansed from his uncleanness. After that, the priest shall slaughter the burnt offering ²⁰and offer it on the altar, together with the grain offering, and make atonement for him, and he will be clean.

²¹"If, however, he is poor and cannot afford these, he must take one male lamb as a guilt offering to be waved to make atonement for him, together with a tenth of an ephah*a* of fine flour mixed with oil for a grain offering, a log of oil, ²²and two doves or two young pigeons, which he can afford, one for a sin offering and the other for a burnt offering.

²³"On the eighth day he must bring them for his cleansing to the priest at the entrance to the Tent of Meeting, before the LORD. ²⁴The priest is to take the lamb for the guilt offering, together with the log of oil, and wave them before the LORD as a wave offering. ²⁵He shall slaughter the lamb for the guilt offering and take some of its blood and put it on the lobe of the right ear of the one to be cleansed, on the thumb of his right hand and on the big toe of his right foot. ²⁶The priest is to pour some of the oil into the palm of his own left hand, ²⁷and with his right forefinger sprinkle some of the oil from his palm seven times before the LORD. ²⁸Some of the oil in his palm he is to put on the same places he put the blood of the guilt offering—on the lobe of the right ear of the one to be cleansed, on the thumb of his right hand and on the big toe of his right foot. ²⁹The rest of the oil in his palm the priest shall put on the head of the one to be cleansed, to make atonement for him before the LORD. ³⁰Then he shall sacrifice the doves or the young pigeons, which the person can afford, ³¹one*b* as a sin offering and the other as a burnt offering, together with the grain offering. In this way the priest will make atonement before the LORD on behalf of the one to be cleansed."

³²These are the regulations for anyone who has an infectious skin disease and who cannot afford the regular offerings for his cleansing.

Cleansing From Mildew

³³The LORD said to Moses and Aaron, ³⁴"When you enter the land of Canaan, which I am giving you as your possession, and I put a spreading mildew in a house in that land, ³⁵the owner of the house must go and tell the priest, 'I have seen something that looks like mildew in my house.' ³⁶The priest is to order the house to be emptied before he goes in to examine the mildew, so that nothing in the house will be

Infectious Houses

LEVITICUS 14:34–42

Buildings as well as people can be "infectious" and contaminate the community. As you read this passage, identify "houses" or neighborhoods that might be considered "unclean" in your own community, perhaps due to illegal or immoral activity. What are ways that they "infect" your community and the individuals comprising it? As a Christian, what are things that, based on the ministry of Jesus, you feel called to do to help "purify" your community?

See Meeting God in Service

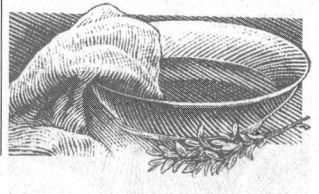

---

a 21 That is, probably about 2 quarts (about 2 liters)   *b 31* Septuagint and Syriac; Hebrew *³¹such as the person can afford, one*

Cleaning House

LEVITICUS 14:43–53

These rituals for removing mildew from a dwelling may seem rather strange to us today. Yet left untreated, mildew could spread and destroy the dwelling. The Israelites' homes were to conform to God's standards of holiness and cleanliness.

When Jesus Christ comes into our lives, he sweeps our sins out the door. Choose some area of your house or apartment to clean or organize today. As you do so, meditate with gratitude on how Jesus has destroyed the power of sin—and continues to cleanse and transform you.

See Meeting God in Prayer

pronounced unclean. After this the priest is to go in and inspect the house. ³⁷He is to examine the mildew on the walls, and if it has greenish or reddish depressions that appear to be deeper than the surface of the wall, ³⁸the priest shall go out the doorway of the house and close it up for seven days. ³⁹On the seventh day the priest shall return to inspect the house. If the mildew has spread on the walls, ⁴⁰he is to order that the contaminated stones be torn out and thrown into an unclean place outside the town. ⁴¹He must have all the inside walls of the house scraped and the material that is scraped off dumped into an unclean place outside the town. ⁴²Then they are to take other stones to replace these and take new clay and plaster the house.

⁴³"If the mildew reappears in the house after the stones have been torn out and the house scraped and plastered, ⁴⁴the priest is to go and examine it and, if the mildew has spread in the house, it is a destructive mildew; the house is unclean. ⁴⁵It must be torn down—its stones, timbers and all the plaster—and taken out of the town to an unclean place.

⁴⁶"Anyone who goes into the house while it is closed up will be unclean till evening. ⁴⁷Anyone who sleeps or eats in the house must wash his clothes.

⁴⁸"But if the priest comes to examine it and the mildew has not spread after the house has been plastered, he shall pronounce the house clean, because the mildew is gone. ⁴⁹To purify the house he is to take two birds and some cedar wood, scarlet yarn and hyssop. ⁵⁰He shall kill one of the birds over fresh water in a clay pot. ⁵¹Then he is to take the cedar wood, the hyssop, the scarlet yarn and the live bird, dip them into the blood of the dead bird and the fresh water, and sprinkle the house seven times. ⁵²He shall purify the house with the bird's blood, the fresh water, the live bird, the cedar wood, the hyssop and the scarlet yarn. ⁵³Then he is to release the live bird in the open fields outside the town. In this way he will make atonement for the house, and it will be clean."

⁵⁴These are the regulations for any infectious skin disease, for an itch, ⁵⁵for mildew in clothing or in a house, ⁵⁶and for a swelling, a rash or a bright spot, ⁵⁷to determine when something is clean or unclean.

These are the regulations for infectious skin diseases and mildew.

Discharges Causing Uncleanness

15 The Lord said to Moses and Aaron, ²"Speak to the Israelites and say to them: 'When any man has a bodily discharge, the discharge is unclean. ³Whether it continues flowing from his body or is blocked, it will make him unclean. This is how his discharge will bring about uncleanness:

⁴" 'Any bed the man with a discharge lies on will be unclean, and anything he sits on will be unclean. ⁵Anyone who touches his bed must wash his clothes and bathe with water, and he will be unclean till evening. ⁶Whoever sits on anything that the man with a discharge sat on must wash his clothes and bathe with water, and he will be unclean till evening.

⁷" 'Whoever touches the man who has a discharge must wash his clothes and bathe with water, and he will be unclean till evening.

⁸" 'If the man with the discharge spits on someone who is clean, that person must wash his clothes and bathe with water, and he will be unclean till evening.

⁹" 'Everything the man sits on when riding will be unclean, ¹⁰and whoever touches any of the things that were under him will be unclean till evening; whoever picks up those things must wash his clothes and bathe with water, and he will be unclean till evening.

¹¹" 'Anyone the man with a discharge touches without rinsing his hands with water must wash his clothes and bathe with water, and he will be unclean till evening.

¹²" 'A clay pot that the man touches must be broken, and any wooden article is to be rinsed with water.

¹³" 'When a man is cleansed from his discharge, he is to count off seven days for his ceremonial cleansing; he must wash his clothes and bathe himself with fresh water, and he will be clean. ¹⁴On the eighth day he must take two doves or two young pigeons and come before the LORD to the entrance to the Tent of Meeting and give them to the priest. ¹⁵The priest is to sacrifice them, the one for a sin offering and the other for a burnt offering. In this way he will make atonement before the LORD for the man because of his discharge.

¹⁶" 'When a man has an emission of semen, he must bathe his whole body with water, and he will be unclean till evening. ¹⁷Any clothing or leather that has semen on it must be washed with water, and it will be unclean till evening. ¹⁸When a man lies with a woman and there is an emission of semen, both must bathe with water, and they will be unclean till evening.

¹⁹" 'When a woman has her regular flow of blood, the impurity of her monthly period will last seven days, and anyone who touches her will be unclean till evening.

²⁰" 'Anything she lies on during her period will be unclean, and anything she sits on will be unclean. ²¹Whoever touches her bed must wash his clothes and bathe with water, and he will be unclean till evening. ²²Whoever touches anything she sits on must wash his clothes and bathe with water, and he will be unclean till evening. ²³Whether it is the bed or anything she was sitting on, when anyone touches it, he will be unclean till evening.

²⁴" 'If a man lies with her and her monthly flow touches him, he will be unclean for seven days; any bed he lies on will be unclean.

²⁵" 'When a woman has a discharge of blood for many days at a time other than her monthly period or has a discharge that continues beyond her period, she will be unclean as long as she has the discharge, just as in the days of her period. ²⁶Any bed she lies on while her discharge continues will be unclean, as is her bed during her monthly period, and anything she sits on will be unclean, as during her period. ²⁷Whoever touches them will be unclean; he must wash his clothes and bathe with water, and he will be unclean till evening.

²⁸" 'When she is cleansed from her discharge, she must count off seven days, and after that she will be ceremonially clean. ²⁹On the eighth day she must take two doves or two young pigeons and bring them to the priest at the entrance to the Tent of Meeting. ³⁰The priest is to sacrifice one for a sin offering and the other for a burnt offering. In

Separate from Uncleanness

LEVITICUS 15:1-31

Make a list of the people with whom you come into contact on a normal workday. Now, assuming everyone on your list comes into contact with approximately the same number of people daily, calculate how many people's lives you might affect, directly or indirectly, in a single day.

Suppose that you "infected" each person you encountered by your attitude, either positive or negative. Would you infect them with joy, apathy, indifference, concern, anger? Write a statement: "Today I will infect people with my

_____." List five ways you can accomplish this goal.

See Meeting God in Everyday Life

The Day of Atonement

LEVITICUS 16:2–20

Read this passage aloud slowly, imagining yourself as a member of the crowd watching Aaron performing these rites on the very first Day of Atonement. Listen for words that appeal to your senses, and let them help you to become part of the story itself. Then ponder this question: How important is it to have a set, yearly ritual to purify both the people and their place of worship? Other passages, such as Joshua 24:1–27, indicate that yearly renewal included a recitation of God's saving acts and a reaffirmation of the people's commitment to God. Why are these elements important? Which elements speak most strongly to you at this moment? Share your feelings with God.

See Meeting God in Worship

this way he will make atonement for her before the LORD for the uncleanness of her discharge.

³¹ " 'You must keep the Israelites separate from things that make them unclean, so they will not die in their uncleanness for defiling my dwelling place,ᵃ which is among them.' "

³²These are the regulations for a man with a discharge, for anyone made unclean by an emission of semen, ³³for a woman in her monthly period, for a man or a woman with a discharge, and for a man who lies with a woman who is ceremonially unclean.

The Day of Atonement

16 The LORD spoke to Moses after the death of the two sons of Aaron who died when they approached the LORD. ²The LORD said to Moses: "Tell your brother Aaron not to come whenever he chooses into the Most Holy Place behind the curtain in front of the atonement cover on the ark, or else he will die, because I appear in the cloud over the atonement cover.

³"This is how Aaron is to enter the sanctuary area: with a young bull for a sin offering and a ram for a burnt offering. ⁴He is to put on the sacred linen tunic, with linen undergarments next to his body; he is to tie the linen sash around him and put on the linen turban. These are sacred garments; so he must bathe himself with water before he puts them on. ⁵From the Israelite community he is to take two male goats for a sin offering and a ram for a burnt offering.

⁶"Aaron is to offer the bull for his own sin offering to make atonement for himself and his household. ⁷Then he is to take the two goats and present them before the LORD at the entrance to the Tent of Meeting. ⁸He is to cast lots for the two goats—one lot for the LORD and the other for the scapegoat.ᵇ ⁹Aaron shall bring the goat whose lot falls to the LORD and sacrifice it for a sin offering. ¹⁰But the goat chosen by lot as the scapegoat shall be presented alive before the LORD to be used for making atonement by sending it into the desert as a scapegoat.

¹¹"Aaron shall bring the bull for his own sin offering to make atonement for himself and his household, and he is to slaughter the bull for his own sin offering. ¹²He is to take a censer full of burning coals from the altar before the LORD and two handfuls of finely ground fragrant incense and take them behind the curtain. ¹³He is to put the incense on the fire before the LORD, and the smoke of the incense will conceal the atonement cover above the Testimony, so that he will not die. ¹⁴He is to take some of the bull's blood and with his finger sprinkle it on the front of the atonement cover; then he shall sprinkle some of it with his finger seven times before the atonement cover.

¹⁵"He shall then slaughter the goat for the sin offering for the people and take its blood behind the curtain and do with it as he did with the bull's blood: He shall sprinkle it on the atonement cover and in front of it. ¹⁶In this way he will make atonement for the Most Holy Place because of the uncleanness and rebellion of the Israelites, whatever their sins have been. He is to do the same for the Tent of Meet-

---

ᵃ 31 Or *my tabernacle*   ᵇ 8 That is, the goat of removal; Hebrew *azazel*; also in verses 10 and 26

ing, which is among them in the midst of their uncleanness. ¹⁷No one is to be in the Tent of Meeting from the time Aaron goes in to make atonement in the Most Holy Place until he comes out, having made atonement for himself, his household and the whole community of Israel.

¹⁸"Then he shall come out to the altar that is before the LORD and make atonement for it. He shall take some of the bull's blood and some of the goat's blood and put it on all the horns of the altar. ¹⁹He shall sprinkle some of the blood on it with his finger seven times to cleanse it and to consecrate it from the uncleanness of the Israelites.

²⁰"When Aaron has finished making atonement for the Most Holy Place, the Tent of Meeting and the altar, he shall bring forward the live goat. ²¹He is to lay both hands on the head of the live goat and confess over it all the wickedness and rebellion of the Israelites—all their sins—and put them on the goat's head. He shall send the goat away into the desert in the care of a man appointed for the task. ²²The goat will carry on itself all their sins to a solitary place; and the man shall release it in the desert.

²³"Then Aaron is to go into the Tent of Meeting and take off the linen garments he put on before he entered the Most Holy Place, and he is to leave them there. ²⁴He shall bathe himself with water in a holy place and put on his regular garments. Then he shall come out and sacrifice the burnt offering for himself and the burnt offering for the people, to make atonement for himself and for the people. ²⁵He shall also burn the fat of the sin offering on the altar.

²⁶"The man who releases the goat as a scapegoat must wash his clothes and bathe himself with water; afterward he may come into the camp. ²⁷The bull and the goat for the sin offerings, whose blood was brought into the Most Holy Place to make atonement, must be taken outside the camp; their hides, flesh and offal are to be burned up. ²⁸The man who burns them must wash his clothes and bathe himself with water; afterward he may come into the camp.

²⁹"This is to be a lasting ordinance for you: On the tenth day of the seventh month you must deny yourselves^a and not do any work—whether native-born or an alien living among you— ³⁰because on this day atonement will be made for you, to cleanse you. Then, before the LORD, you will be clean from all your sins. ³¹It is a sabbath of rest, and you must deny yourselves; it is a lasting ordinance. ³²The priest who is anointed and ordained to succeed his father as high priest is to make atonement. He is to put on the sacred linen garments ³³and make atonement for the Most Holy Place, for the Tent of Meeting and the altar, and for the priests and all the people of the community.

³⁴"This is to be a lasting ordinance for you: Atonement is to be made once a year for all the sins of the Israelites."

And it was done, as the LORD commanded Moses.

Eating Blood Forbidden

17 The LORD said to Moses, ²"Speak to Aaron and his sons and to all the Israelites and say to them: 'This is what the LORD has commanded: ³Any Israelite who sacrifices an ox,^b a lamb or a goat in the camp or outside of it ⁴instead of bringing it to the entrance to the Tent of Meet-

The Scapegoat

LEVITICUS 16:21–22

As you read these two verses, meditate on the actions taking place and their underlying meaning. Given that all other animal sacrifices are slaughtered, why do you suppose this sacrifice is not? What is the symbolic meaning of laying hands on the goat and then sending it into the desert?

Find a stuffed animal. As you read this passage again, place your hands on the animal and imagine that your sins are being transferred to it. What feelings does this action arouse in you? How has Jesus replaced the scapegoat? Offer a prayer to God describing your feelings.

See *Meeting God in Scripture*

---

^a29 Or *must fast*; also in verse 31   ^b3 The Hebrew word can include both male and female.

The Law and Grace

LEVITICUS 17:8—18:17

"The Lord Himself not only shows us the evil we are to avoid and the good we are to do (which is all that the letter of the law can do), but also helps us to avoid evil and to do good—things that are impossible without the spirit of grace. If grace is lacking, the law is there simply to make culprits and to slay; for this reason, the Apostle said: "The letter kills, but the Spirit gives life" (2 Corinthians 3:6). He, therefore, who uses the law according to the law learns from it good and evil, and, trusting not in his own strength, has recourse to grace, which enable[s] him to avoid evil and to do good. But when has a [person] recourse to grace, except when the steps of [that person] are directed by the Lord and he delighteth in His way? Therefore, even the desire for the help of grace is itself the beginning of grace."

—AUGUSTINE,
"Admonition and Grace"

ing to present it as an offering to the LORD in front of the tabernacle of the LORD—that man shall be considered guilty of bloodshed; he has shed blood and must be cut off from his people. ⁵This is so the Israelites will bring to the LORD the sacrifices they are now making in the open fields. They must bring them to the priest, that is, to the LORD, at the entrance to the Tent of Meeting and sacrifice them as fellowship offerings.ᵃ ⁶The priest is to sprinkle the blood against the altar of the LORD at the entrance to the Tent of Meeting and burn the fat as an aroma pleasing to the LORD. ⁷They must no longer offer any of their sacrifices to the goat idolsᵇ to whom they prostitute themselves. This is to be a lasting ordinance for them and for the generations to come.'

⁸"Say to them: 'Any Israelite or any alien living among them who offers a burnt offering or sacrifice ⁹and does not bring it to the entrance to the Tent of Meeting to sacrifice it to the LORD—that man must be cut off from his people.

¹⁰"'Any Israelite or any alien living among them who eats any blood—I will set my face against that person who eats blood and will cut him off from his people. ¹¹For the life of a creature is in the blood, and I have given it to you to make atonement for yourselves on the altar; it is the blood that makes atonement for one's life. ¹²Therefore I say to the Israelites, "None of you may eat blood, nor may an alien living among you eat blood."

¹³"'Any Israelite or any alien living among you who hunts any animal or bird that may be eaten must drain out the blood and cover it with earth, ¹⁴because the life of every creature is its blood. That is why I have said to the Israelites, "You must not eat the blood of any creature, because the life of every creature is its blood; anyone who eats it must be cut off."

¹⁵"'Anyone, whether native-born or alien, who eats anything found dead or torn by wild animals must wash his clothes and bathe with water, and he will be ceremonially unclean till evening; then he will be clean. ¹⁶But if he does not wash his clothes and bathe himself, he will be held responsible.' "

Unlawful Sexual Relations

18 The LORD said to Moses, ²"Speak to the Israelites and say to them: 'I am the LORD your God. ³You must not do as they do in Egypt, where you used to live, and you must not do as they do in the land of Canaan, where I am bringing you. Do not follow their practices. ⁴You must obey my laws and be careful to follow my decrees. I am the LORD your God. ⁵Keep my decrees and laws, for the man who obeys them will live by them. I am the LORD.

⁶"'No one is to approach any close relative to have sexual relations. I am the LORD.

⁷"'Do not dishonor your father by having sexual relations with your mother. She is your mother; do not have relations with her.

⁸"'Do not have sexual relations with your father's wife; that would dishonor your father.

⁹"'Do not have sexual relations with your sister, either

ᵃ5 Traditionally *peace offerings*   ᵇ7 Or *demons*

your father's daughter or your mother's daughter, whether she was born in the same home or elsewhere.

¹⁰ " 'Do not have sexual relations with your son's daughter or your daughter's daughter; that would dishonor you.

¹¹ " 'Do not have sexual relations with the daughter of your father's wife, born to your father; she is your sister.

¹² " 'Do not have sexual relations with your father's sister; she is your father's close relative.

¹³ " 'Do not have sexual relations with your mother's sister, because she is your mother's close relative.

¹⁴ " 'Do not dishonor your father's brother by approaching his wife to have sexual relations; she is your aunt.

¹⁵ " 'Do not have sexual relations with your daughter-in-law. She is your son's wife; do not have relations with her.

¹⁶ " 'Do not have sexual relations with your brother's wife; that would dishonor your brother.

¹⁷ " 'Do not have sexual relations with both a woman and her daughter. Do not have sexual relations with either her son's daughter or her daughter's daughter; they are her close relatives. That is wickedness.

¹⁸ " 'Do not take your wife's sister as a rival wife and have sexual relations with her while your wife is living.

¹⁹ " 'Do not approach a woman to have sexual relations during the uncleanness of her monthly period.

²⁰ " 'Do not have sexual relations with your neighbor's wife and defile yourself with her.

²¹ " 'Do not give any of your children to be sacrificed*ᵃ* to Molech, for you must not profane the name of your God. I am the LORD.

²² " 'Do not lie with a man as one lies with a woman; that is detestable.

²³ " 'Do not have sexual relations with an animal and defile yourself with it. A woman must not present herself to an animal to have sexual relations with it; that is a perversion.

²⁴ " 'Do not defile yourselves in any of these ways, because this is how the nations that I am going to drive out before you became defiled. ²⁵Even the land was defiled; so I punished it for its sin, and the land vomited out its inhabitants. ²⁶But you must keep my decrees and my laws. The native-born and the aliens living among you must not do any of these detestable things, ²⁷for all these things were done by the people who lived in the land before you, and the land became defiled. ²⁸And if you defile the land, it will vomit you out as it vomited out the nations that were before you.

²⁹ " 'Everyone who does any of these detestable things— such persons must be cut off from their people. ³⁰Keep my requirements and do not follow any of the detestable customs that were practiced before you came and do not defile yourselves with them. I am the LORD your God.' "

Various Laws

19 The LORD said to Moses, ²"Speak to the entire assembly of Israel and say to them: 'Be holy because I, the LORD your God, am holy.

³ " 'Each of you must respect his mother and father, and you must observe my Sabbaths. I am the LORD your God.

ᵃ 21 Or to be passed through ⌊the fire⌋

Be Holy, for I Am Holy

LEVITICUS 19:1–2

Read verses 1–2, then read 18:1–5. At the heart of these verses lies the major presupposition that forms the basis of all of God's charges against human sin, namely, that God's values are not human values (see Isaiah 55:6–9).

Write the headings "God's Values" and "Human Values" on a piece of paper. Read chapters 18 and 19 all the way through more slowly, making lists under the columns based on what you read. Compare and contrast them. What do these passages tell you about God's nature, as compared to human nature? What changes are you called to make in your life after looking at these passages?

See Meeting God in Scripture

Love Your Neighbor as Yourself

LEVITICUS 19:18

Does it surprise you that the rule of life that Christians equate so strongly with the New Testament—where it is quoted by Jesus (see Matthew 22:37–39), Paul (see Galatians 5:14) and James (see James 2:8)—is actually the core of the Old Testament's call to obedience?

Jesus quoted the Torah (the body of Jewish law) to condemn the self-righteous Pharisees, who were considered "experts" at interpreting and living it. Pharisees had turned this command into a way of excluding others by narrowing the definition of neighbor so much that it was practically meaningless. They twisted God's intent—to build up the community—into its exact opposite. What does the command to "Love your neighbor as yourself" mean to you? Within your understanding of grace, what does it require of you?

See Meeting God in Community

4 " 'Do not turn to idols or make gods of cast metal for yourselves. I am the LORD your God.

5 " 'When you sacrifice a fellowship offering[a] to the LORD, sacrifice it in such a way that it will be accepted on your behalf. 6It shall be eaten on the day you sacrifice it or on the next day; anything left over until the third day must be burned up. 7If any of it is eaten on the third day, it is impure and will not be accepted. 8Whoever eats it will be held responsible because he has desecrated what is holy to the LORD; that person must be cut off from his people.

9 " 'When you reap the harvest of your land, do not reap to the very edges of your field or gather the gleanings of your harvest. 10Do not go over your vineyard a second time or pick up the grapes that have fallen. Leave them for the poor and the alien. I am the LORD your God.

11 " 'Do not steal.

" 'Do not lie.

" 'Do not deceive one another.

12 " 'Do not swear falsely by my name and so profane the name of your God. I am the LORD.

13 " 'Do not defraud your neighbor or rob him.

" 'Do not hold back the wages of a hired man overnight.

14 " 'Do not curse the deaf or put a stumbling block in front of the blind, but fear your God. I am the LORD.

15 " 'Do not pervert justice; do not show partiality to the poor or favoritism to the great, but judge your neighbor fairly.

16 " 'Do not go about spreading slander among your people.

" 'Do not do anything that endangers your neighbor's life. I am the LORD.

17 " 'Do not hate your brother in your heart. Rebuke your neighbor frankly so you will not share in his guilt.

18 " 'Do not seek revenge or bear a grudge against one of your people, but love your neighbor as yourself. I am the LORD.

19 " 'Keep my decrees.

" 'Do not mate different kinds of animals.

" 'Do not plant your field with two kinds of seed.

" 'Do not wear clothing woven of two kinds of material.

20 " 'If a man sleeps with a woman who is a slave girl promised to another man but who has not been ransomed or given her freedom, there must be due punishment. Yet they are not to be put to death, because she had not been freed. 21The man, however, must bring a ram to the entrance to the Tent of Meeting for a guilt offering to the LORD. 22With the ram of the guilt offering the priest is to make atonement for him before the LORD for the sin he has committed, and his sin will be forgiven.

23 " 'When you enter the land and plant any kind of fruit tree, regard its fruit as forbidden.[b] For three years you are to consider it forbidden[b]; it must not be eaten. 24In the fourth year all its fruit will be holy, an offering of praise to the LORD. 25But in the fifth year you may eat its fruit. In this way your harvest will be increased. I am the LORD your God.

26 " 'Do not eat any meat with the blood still in it.

" 'Do not practice divination or sorcery.

a 5 Traditionally peace offering   b 23 Hebrew uncircumcised

²⁷" 'Do not cut the hair at the sides of your head or clip off the edges of your beard.

²⁸" 'Do not cut your bodies for the dead or put tattoo marks on yourselves. I am the LORD.

²⁹" 'Do not degrade your daughter by making her a prostitute, or the land will turn to prostitution and be filled with wickedness.

³⁰" 'Observe my Sabbaths and have reverence for my sanctuary. I am the LORD.

³¹" 'Do not turn to mediums or seek out spiritists, for you will be defiled by them. I am the LORD your God.

³²" 'Rise in the presence of the aged, show respect for the elderly and revere your God. I am the LORD.

³³" 'When an alien lives with you in your land, do not mistreat him. ³⁴The alien living with you must be treated as one of your native-born. Love him as yourself, for you were aliens in Egypt. I am the LORD your God.

³⁵" 'Do not use dishonest standards when measuring length, weight or quantity. ³⁶Use honest scales and honest weights, an honest ephah*ᵃ* and an honest hin.*ᵇ* I am the LORD your God, who brought you out of Egypt.

³⁷" 'Keep all my decrees and all my laws and follow them. I am the LORD.' "

Punishments for Sin

20 The LORD said to Moses, ²"Say to the Israelites: 'Any Israelite or any alien living in Israel who gives*ᶜ* any of his children to Molech must be put to death. The people of the community are to stone him. ³I will set my face against that man and I will cut him off from his people; for by giving his children to Molech, he has defiled my sanctuary and profaned my holy name. ⁴If the people of the community close their eyes when that man gives one of his children to Molech and they fail to put him to death, ⁵I will set my face against that man and his family and will cut off from their people both him and all who follow him in prostituting themselves to Molech.

⁶" 'I will set my face against the person who turns to mediums and spiritists to prostitute himself by following them, and I will cut him off from his people.

⁷" 'Consecrate yourselves and be holy, because I am the LORD your God. ⁸Keep my decrees and follow them. I am the LORD, who makes you holy.*ᵈ*

⁹" 'If anyone curses his father or mother, he must be put to death. He has cursed his father or his mother, and his blood will be on his own head.

¹⁰" 'If a man commits adultery with another man's wife—with the wife of his neighbor—both the adulterer and the adulteress must be put to death.

¹¹" 'If a man sleeps with his father's wife, he has dishonored his father. Both the man and the woman must be put to death; their blood will be on their own heads.

¹²" 'If a man sleeps with his daughter-in-law, both of them must be put to death. What they have done is a perversion; their blood will be on their own heads.

¹³" 'If a man lies with a man as one lies with a woman,

I Am the Lord Your God

LEVITICUS 20:1–5

Chapter 20 is similar to chapter 18 in many ways. The harsh punishments called for in this chapter may be difficult for us to comprehend and accept. Even more difficult is to draw spiritual guidance from them. Most of the actions described in chapters 18 and 20, however, are not only violations against God, but are also actions that threaten the fabric of society itself. Passages such as these teach us just how society's values differ from God's.

Verse 4 warns that "If the people of the community close their eyes [to the worship of Molech]," God will personally step in and punish the evildoers. In addition, the nation itself will be punished for disobedience (see verses 22–26). Make a list of ways that our society has "closed its eyes" to things that are an "abomination" to God. Are there ways that you, personally, are guilty of "closing your eyes" by being part of a society based on oppression?

See Meeting God in Community

ᵃ 36 An ephah was a dry measure. *ᵇ 36* A hin was a liquid measure.
ᶜ 2 Or *sacrifices*; also in verses 3 and 4   *ᵈ 8* Or *who sanctifies you*; or *who sets you apart as holy*

The Conduct of Leaders

LEVITICUS 21:1–14

Priests are held to a stricter standard than the average Israelite; the standard for the high priest is even more so. Similarly, the standard for overseers and deacons is high in the New Testament church (see 1 Timothy 3).

How important is it for a community that its leaders, whether religious or secular, be held to a stricter code of behavior than its lay people? Some Christian denominations choose their leaders by lot from a pool of qualified candidates, believing that God's Spirit will determine the final choice. What are some arguments for and against this procedure?

See *Meeting God in Community*

both of them have done what is detestable. They must be put to death; their blood will be on their own heads.

¹⁴ " 'If a man marries both a woman and her mother, it is wicked. Both he and they must be burned in the fire, so that no wickedness will be among you.

¹⁵ " 'If a man has sexual relations with an animal, he must be put to death, and you must kill the animal.

¹⁶ " 'If a woman approaches an animal to have sexual relations with it, kill both the woman and the animal. They must be put to death; their blood will be on their own heads.

¹⁷ " 'If a man marries his sister, the daughter of either his father or his mother, and they have sexual relations, it is a disgrace. They must be cut off before the eyes of their people. He has dishonored his sister and will be held responsible.

¹⁸ " 'If a man lies with a woman during her monthly period and has sexual relations with her, he has exposed the source of her flow, and she has also uncovered it. Both of them must be cut off from their people.

¹⁹ " 'Do not have sexual relations with the sister of either your mother or your father, for that would dishonor a close relative; both of you would be held responsible.

²⁰ " 'If a man sleeps with his aunt, he has dishonored his uncle. They will be held responsible; they will die childless.

²¹ " 'If a man marries his brother's wife, it is an act of impurity; he has dishonored his brother. They will be childless.

²² " 'Keep all my decrees and laws and follow them, so that the land where I am bringing you to live may not vomit you out. ²³ You must not live according to the customs of the nations I am going to drive out before you. Because they did all these things, I abhorred them. ²⁴ But I said to you, "You will possess their land; I will give it to you as an inheritance, a land flowing with milk and honey." I am the LORD your God, who has set you apart from the nations.

²⁵ " 'You must therefore make a distinction between clean and unclean animals and between unclean and clean birds. Do not defile yourselves by any animal or bird or anything that moves along the ground—those which I have set apart as unclean for you. ²⁶ You are to be holy to me*a* because I, the LORD, am holy, and I have set you apart from the nations to be my own.

²⁷ " 'A man or woman who is a medium or spiritist among you must be put to death. You are to stone them; their blood will be on their own heads.' "

Rules for Priests

21 The LORD said to Moses, "Speak to the priests, the sons of Aaron, and say to them: 'A priest must not make himself ceremonially unclean for any of his people who die, ²except for a close relative, such as his mother or father, his son or daughter, his brother, ³or an unmarried sister who is dependent on him since she has no husband—for her he may make himself unclean. ⁴He must not make himself unclean for people related to him by marriage,*b* and so defile himself.

⁵ " 'Priests must not shave their heads or shave off the edges of their beards or cut their bodies. ⁶They must be

a 26 Or *be my holy ones* *b 4* Or *unclean as a leader among his people* holy to their God and must not profane the name of their God. Because they present the offerings made to the LORD by fire, the food of their God, they are to be holy.

⁷" 'They must not marry women defiled by prostitution or divorced from their husbands, because priests are holy to their God. ⁸Regard them as holy, because they offer up the food of your God. Consider them holy, because I the LORD am holy—I who make you holy.ᵃ

⁹" 'If a priest's daughter defiles herself by becoming a prostitute, she disgraces her father; she must be burned in the fire.

¹⁰" 'The high priest, the one among his brothers who has had the anointing oil poured on his head and who has been ordained to wear the priestly garments, must not let his hair become unkemptᵇ or tear his clothes. ¹¹He must not enter a place where there is a dead body. He must not make himself unclean, even for his father or mother, ¹²nor leave the sanctuary of his God or desecrate it, because he has been dedicated by the anointing oil of his God. I am the LORD.

¹³" 'The woman he marries must be a virgin. ¹⁴He must not marry a widow, a divorced woman, or a woman defiled by prostitution, but only a virgin from his own people, ¹⁵so he will not defile his offspring among his people. I am the LORD, who makes him holy.ᶜ' "

¹⁶The LORD said to Moses, ¹⁷"Say to Aaron: 'For the generations to come none of your descendants who has a defect may come near to offer the food of his God. ¹⁸No man who has any defect may come near: no man who is blind or lame, disfigured or deformed; ¹⁹no man with a crippled foot or hand, ²⁰or who is hunchbacked or dwarfed, or who has any eye defect, or who has festering or running sores or damaged testicles. ²¹No descendant of Aaron the priest who has any defect is to come near to present the offerings made to the LORD by fire. He has a defect; he must not come near to offer the food of his God. ²²He may eat the most holy food of his God, as well as the holy food; ²³yet because of his defect, he must not go near the curtain or approach the altar, and so desecrate my sanctuary. I am the LORD, who makes them holy.ᵈ' "

²⁴So Moses told this to Aaron and his sons and to all the Israelites.

22 The LORD said to Moses, ²"Tell Aaron and his sons to treat with respect the sacred offerings the Israelites consecrate to me, so they will not profane my holy name. I am the LORD.

³"Say to them: 'For the generations to come, if any of your descendants is ceremonially unclean and yet comes near the sacred offerings that the Israelites consecrate to the LORD, that person must be cut off from my presence. I am the LORD.

⁴" 'If a descendant of Aaron has an infectious skin diseaseᵉ or a bodily discharge, he may not eat the sacred offerings until he is cleansed. He will also be unclean if he touches something defiled by a corpse or by anyone who

Sacred Offerings

LEVITICUS 22:1–13

The "sacred offerings" mentioned in this chapter are the portions of sacrificial animals received by the priests, and to some extent these portions represent their wages. Even so, the priests were not allowed to use them as they pleased.

Try to rewrite Leviticus 22:1–13 in your own words. Contemplate why the demands for obedience and penalties for disobedience were so much stricter for priests. What might be the effect on a society if it fails to hold its leadership accountable? What might be the effect if leadership is held to too strict a standard?

See Meeting God in Community

ᵃ 8 Or *who sanctify you*; or *who set you apart as holy*   ᵇ 10 Or *not uncover his head*   ᶜ 15 Or *who sanctifies him*; or *who sets him apart as holy*   ᵈ 23 Or *who sanctifies them*; or *who sets them apart as holy*   ᵉ 4 Traditionally *leprosy*; the Hebrew word was used for various diseases affecting the skin—not necessarily leprosy.

Acceptable Offerings

LEVITICUS 22:19,29

Read these verses aloud. What does it mean to offer a sacrifice "in such a way that it will be accepted on your behalf"? What are ways that one might offer a sacrifice that would make it unacceptable?

While Christians believe that Jesus was *the* offering for our sin, we are also told by the apostle Paul to offer our bodies as "living sacrifices." In what ways might we try to offer our lives with wrong or mixed motives?

Think about your own worship practices and those of the congregation you are part of. Are there aspects about your worship that might make it unacceptable? Offer these things in prayer to God.

See Meeting God in Worship

has an emission of semen, ⁵or if he touches any crawling thing that makes him unclean, or any person who makes him unclean, whatever the uncleanness may be. ⁶The one who touches any such thing will be unclean till evening. He must not eat any of the sacred offerings unless he has bathed himself with water. ⁷When the sun goes down, he will be clean, and after that he may eat the sacred offerings, for they are his food. ⁸He must not eat anything found dead or torn by wild animals, and so become unclean through it. I am the LORD.

⁹" 'The priests are to keep my requirements so that they do not become guilty and die for treating them with contempt. I am the LORD, who makes them holy.ᵃ

¹⁰" 'No one outside a priest's family may eat the sacred offering, nor may the guest of a priest or his hired worker eat it. ¹¹But if a priest buys a slave with money, or if a slave is born in his household, that slave may eat his food. ¹²If a priest's daughter marries anyone other than a priest, she may not eat any of the sacred contributions. ¹³But if a priest's daughter becomes a widow or is divorced, yet has no children, and she returns to live in her father's house as in her youth, she may eat of her father's food. No unauthorized person, however, may eat any of it.

¹⁴" 'If anyone eats a sacred offering by mistake, he must make restitution to the priest for the offering and add a fifth of the value to it. ¹⁵The priests must not desecrate the sacred offerings the Israelites present to the LORD ¹⁶by allowing them to eat the sacred offerings and so bring upon them guilt requiring payment. I am the LORD, who makes them holy.' "

Unacceptable Sacrifices

¹⁷The LORD said to Moses, ¹⁸"Speak to Aaron and his sons and to all the Israelites and say to them: 'If any of you—either an Israelite or an alien living in Israel—presents a gift for a burnt offering to the LORD, either to fulfill a vow or as a freewill offering, ¹⁹you must present a male without defect from the cattle, sheep or goats in order that it may be accepted on your behalf. ²⁰Do not bring anything with a defect, because it will not be accepted on your behalf. ²¹When anyone brings from the herd or flock a fellowship offeringᵇ to the LORD to fulfill a special vow or as a freewill offering, it must be without defect or blemish to be acceptable. ²²Do not offer to the LORD the blind, the injured or the maimed, or anything with warts or festering or running sores. Do not place any of these on the altar as an offering made to the LORD by fire. ²³You may, however, present as a freewill offering an oxᶜ or a sheep that is deformed or stunted, but it will not be accepted in fulfillment of a vow. ²⁴You must not offer to the LORD an animal whose testicles are bruised, crushed, torn or cut. You must not do this in your own land, ²⁵and you must not accept such animals from the hand of a foreigner and offer them as the food of your God. They will not be accepted on your behalf, because they are deformed and have defects.' "

²⁶The LORD said to Moses, ²⁷"When a calf, a lamb or a goat is born, it is to remain with its mother for seven days.

ᵃ9 Or *who sanctifies them*; or *who sets them apart as holy*; also in verse 16   ᵇ21 Traditionally *peace offering*   ᶜ23 The Hebrew word can include both male and female.

From the eighth day on, it will be acceptable as an offering made to the LORD by fire. ²⁸Do not slaughter a cow or a sheep and its young on the same day.

²⁹"When you sacrifice a thank offering to the LORD, sacrifice it in such a way that it will be accepted on your behalf. ³⁰It must be eaten that same day; leave none of it till morning. I am the LORD.

³¹"Keep my commands and follow them. I am the LORD. ³²Do not profane my holy name. I must be acknowledged as holy by the Israelites. I am the LORD, who makes*a* you holy*b* ³³and who brought you out of Egypt to be your God. I am the LORD."

23 The LORD said to Moses, ²"Speak to the Israelites and say to them: 'These are my appointed feasts, the appointed feasts of the LORD, which you are to proclaim as sacred assemblies.

The Sabbath

³" 'There are six days when you may work, but the seventh day is a Sabbath of rest, a day of sacred assembly. You are not to do any work; wherever you live, it is a Sabbath to the LORD.

The Passover and Unleavened Bread

⁴" 'These are the LORD's appointed feasts, the sacred assemblies you are to proclaim at their appointed times: ⁵The LORD's Passover begins at twilight on the fourteenth day of the first month. ⁶On the fifteenth day of that month the LORD's Feast of Unleavened Bread begins; for seven days you must eat bread made without yeast. ⁷On the first day hold a sacred assembly and do no regular work. ⁸For seven days present an offering made to the LORD by fire. And on the seventh day hold a sacred assembly and do no regular work.' "

Firstfruits

⁹The LORD said to Moses, ¹⁰"Speak to the Israelites and say to them: 'When you enter the land I am going to give you and you reap its harvest, bring to the priest a sheaf of the first grain you harvest. ¹¹He is to wave the sheaf before the LORD so it will be accepted on your behalf; the priest is to wave it on the day after the Sabbath. ¹²On the day you wave the sheaf, you must sacrifice as a burnt offering to the LORD a lamb a year old without defect, ¹³together with its grain offering of two-tenths of an ephah*c* of fine flour mixed with oil—an offering made to the LORD by fire, a pleasing aroma—and its drink offering of a quarter of a hin*d* of wine. ¹⁴You must not eat any bread, or roasted or new grain, until the very day you bring this offering to your God. This is to be a lasting ordinance for the generations to come, wherever you live.

Feast of Weeks

¹⁵" 'From the day after the Sabbath, the day you brought the sheaf of the wave offering, count off seven full weeks. ¹⁶Count off fifty days up to the day after the seventh Sab-

Remember the Sabbath

LEVITICUS 23:3

The Hebrew word *Sabbath* comes from the root word "to stop." God delivered the Israelites from harsh slavery and required that for one day out of every seven everyone should rest from the daily routine. Jesus taught that the Sabbath was created for humans, and not vice versa. Given this background, what are the implications of the Sabbath regulations?

What is your view of the Sabbath? Does your weekly routine include a "Sabbath"? Consider celebrating the Sabbath as an act of faith, a way of letting go of your normal routine and your worldly concerns, and trusting God to provide what you need.

See Meeting God in Worship

---

a 32 Or *made*   *b 32* Or *who sanctifies you; or who sets you apart as holy*
c 13 That is, probably about 4 quarts (about 4.5 liters); also in verse 17
d 13 That is, probably about 1 quart (about 1 liter)

The Earth Is the Lord's

LEVITICUS 23:37–38

The largest part of the offerings the Hebrew people brought were the fruits of the field. If you have a vegetable or flower garden, arrange an offering from it in a basket. If you don't have a garden, prepare an offering basket using produce you buy (or use canned goods). Place the basket in a prominent place in your home. Write a special prayer of thanksgiving to use as a blessing at meals (or read Psalm 67). After a week, use the food to prepare a special meal of thanks, or give the food (or a monetary donation) to a food bank or other organization that helps to feed the poor.

See Meeting God in Service

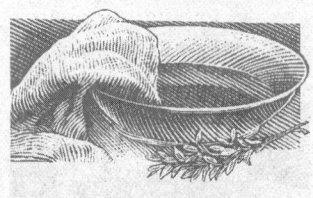

bath, and then present an offering of new grain to the LORD. [17] From wherever you live, bring two loaves made of two-tenths of an ephah of fine flour, baked with yeast, as a wave offering of firstfruits to the LORD. [18] Present with this bread seven male lambs, each a year old and without defect, one young bull and two rams. They will be a burnt offering to the LORD, together with their grain offerings and drink offerings—an offering made by fire, an aroma pleasing to the LORD. [19] Then sacrifice one male goat for a sin offering and two lambs, each a year old, for a fellowship offering.[a] [20] The priest is to wave the two lambs before the LORD as a wave offering, together with the bread of the firstfruits. They are a sacred offering to the LORD for the priest. [21] On that same day you are to proclaim a sacred assembly and do no regular work. This is to be a lasting ordinance for the generations to come, wherever you live.

[22] " 'When you reap the harvest of your land, do not reap to the very edges of your field or gather the gleanings of your harvest. Leave them for the poor and the alien. I am the LORD your God.' "

Feast of Trumpets

[23] The LORD said to Moses, [24] "Say to the Israelites: 'On the first day of the seventh month you are to have a day of rest, a sacred assembly commemorated with trumpet blasts. [25] Do no regular work, but present an offering made to the LORD by fire.' "

Day of Atonement

[26] The LORD said to Moses, [27] "The tenth day of this seventh month is the Day of Atonement. Hold a sacred assembly and deny yourselves,[b] and present an offering made to the LORD by fire. [28] Do no work on that day, because it is the Day of Atonement, when atonement is made for you before the LORD your God. [29] Anyone who does not deny himself on that day must be cut off from his people. [30] I will destroy from among his people anyone who does any work on that day. [31] You shall do no work at all. This is to be a lasting ordinance for the generations to come, wherever you live. [32] It is a sabbath of rest for you, and you must deny yourselves. From the evening of the ninth day of the month until the following evening you are to observe your sabbath."

Feast of Tabernacles

[33] The LORD said to Moses, [34] "Say to the Israelites: 'On the fifteenth day of the seventh month the LORD's Feast of Tabernacles begins, and it lasts for seven days. [35] The first day is a sacred assembly; do no regular work. [36] For seven days present offerings made to the LORD by fire, and on the eighth day hold a sacred assembly and present an offering made to the LORD by fire. It is the closing assembly; do no regular work.

[37] (" 'These are the LORD's appointed feasts, which you are to proclaim as sacred assemblies for bringing offerings made to the LORD by fire—the burnt offerings and grain offerings, sacrifices and drink offerings required for each day. [38] These offerings are in addition to those for the LORD's Sabbaths and[c] in addition to your gifts and whatever you have vowed and all the freewill offerings you give to the LORD.)

a 19 Traditionally *peace offering*   b 27 Or *and fast*; also in verses 29 and 32
c 38 Or *These feasts are in addition to the LORD's Sabbaths, and these offerings are*

³⁹" 'So beginning with the fifteenth day of the seventh month, after you have gathered the crops of the land, celebrate the festival to the LORD for seven days; the first day is a day of rest, and the eighth day also is a day of rest. ⁴⁰On the first day you are to take choice fruit from the trees, and palm fronds, leafy branches and poplars, and rejoice before the LORD your God for seven days. ⁴¹Celebrate this as a festival to the LORD for seven days each year. This is to be a lasting ordinance for the generations to come; celebrate it in the seventh month. ⁴²Live in booths for seven days: All native-born Israelites are to live in booths ⁴³so your descendants will know that I had the Israelites live in booths when I brought them out of Egypt. I am the LORD your God.' "

⁴⁴So Moses announced to the Israelites the appointed feasts of the LORD.

Oil and Bread Set Before the LORD

24 The LORD said to Moses, ²"Command the Israelites to bring you clear oil of pressed olives for the light so that the lamps may be kept burning continually. ³Outside the curtain of the Testimony in the Tent of Meeting, Aaron is to tend the lamps before the LORD from evening till morning, continually. This is to be a lasting ordinance for the generations to come. ⁴The lamps on the pure gold lampstand before the LORD must be tended continually.

⁵"Take fine flour and bake twelve loaves of bread, using two-tenths of an ephah^a for each loaf. ⁶Set them in two rows, six in each row, on the table of pure gold before the LORD. ⁷Along each row put some pure incense as a memorial portion to represent the bread and to be an offering made to the LORD by fire. ⁸This bread is to be set out before the LORD regularly, Sabbath after Sabbath, on behalf of the Israelites, as a lasting covenant. ⁹It belongs to Aaron and his sons, who are to eat it in a holy place, because it is a most holy part of their regular share of the offerings made to the LORD by fire."

A Blasphemer Stoned

¹⁰Now the son of an Israelite mother and an Egyptian father went out among the Israelites, and a fight broke out in the camp between him and an Israelite. ¹¹The son of the Israelite woman blasphemed the Name with a curse; so they brought him to Moses. (His mother's name was Shelomith, the daughter of Dibri the Danite.) ¹²They put him in custody until the will of the LORD should be made clear to them.

¹³Then the LORD said to Moses: ¹⁴"Take the blasphemer outside the camp. All those who heard him are to lay their hands on his head, and the entire assembly is to stone him. ¹⁵Say to the Israelites: 'If anyone curses his God, he will be held responsible; ¹⁶anyone who blasphemes the name of the LORD must be put to death. The entire assembly must stone him. Whether an alien or native-born, when he blasphemes the Name, he must be put to death.

¹⁷" 'If anyone takes the life of a human being, he must be put to death. ¹⁸Anyone who takes the life of someone's animal must make restitution—life for life. ¹⁹If anyone injures his neighbor, whatever he has done must be done to him: ²⁰fracture for fracture, eye for eye, tooth for tooth. As he

Eye for Eye, Tooth for Tooth

LEVITICUS 24:17–21

This so-called "law of retaliation," which for many people symbolizes the harshness of the Old Testament law, is actually an attempt to prevent a punishment from exceeding the crime. Rather than retribution, the major purpose of the law codes is to restore the community to its original state. What is more, this law was rarely interpreted literally. With the exception of murder, crimes of bodily injury were normally settled by paying the injured person a fine.

When does our society still demand "eye for eye, tooth for tooth"? Read Matthew 5:38–42. How does Jesus' interpretation counter traditional thinking? Are his demands practical? What might the effect be on an individual or on a society that strictly follows this command without exception?

See Meeting God in Community

---

^a5 That is, probably about 4 quarts (about 4.5 liters)

The Year of Jubilee

LEVITICUS 25:1–55

The Year of Jubilee was a year when the slate was wiped clean and Israel returned to its original state: All debts were forgiven, all Israelite slaves were freed, all land was returned to its original owners (and owners to their land!) and the land was to lie fallow.

Imagine yourself as a wealthy Israelite, and read this passage again. Imagine yourself as a poor Israelite. How do your emotions change?

For Isaiah, the Year of Jubilee symbolized God's coming reign on earth (Isaiah 62:1–4); for Jesus, it symbolized his ministry and the kingdom of God (Luke 4:18–21). Write your own description of God's reign with Leviticus 25 as a model. What would be the result of a Jubilee year (or even a sabbatical year) on our economy?

See Meeting God in Community

has injured the other, so he is to be injured. ²¹Whoever kills an animal must make restitution, but whoever kills a man must be put to death. ²²You are to have the same law for the alien and the native-born. I am the LORD your God.' "

²³Then Moses spoke to the Israelites, and they took the blasphemer outside the camp and stoned him. The Israelites did as the LORD commanded Moses.

The Sabbath Year

25 The LORD said to Moses on Mount Sinai, ²"Speak to the Israelites and say to them: 'When you enter the land I am going to give you, the land itself must observe a sabbath to the LORD. ³For six years sow your fields, and for six years prune your vineyards and gather their crops. ⁴But in the seventh year the land is to have a sabbath of rest, a sabbath to the LORD. Do not sow your fields or prune your vineyards. ⁵Do not reap what grows of itself or harvest the grapes of your untended vines. The land is to have a year of rest. ⁶Whatever the land yields during the sabbath year will be food for you—for yourself, your manservant and maidservant, and the hired worker and temporary resident who live among you, ⁷as well as for your livestock and the wild animals in your land. Whatever the land produces may be eaten.

The Year of Jubilee

⁸" 'Count off seven sabbaths of years—seven times seven years—so that the seven sabbaths of years amount to a period of forty-nine years. ⁹Then have the trumpet sounded everywhere on the tenth day of the seventh month; on the Day of Atonement sound the trumpet throughout your land. ¹⁰Consecrate the fiftieth year and proclaim liberty throughout the land to all its inhabitants. It shall be a jubilee for you; each one of you is to return to his family property and each to his own clan. ¹¹The fiftieth year shall be a jubilee for you; do not sow and do not reap what grows of itself or harvest the untended vines. ¹²For it is a jubilee and is to be holy for you; eat only what is taken directly from the fields.

¹³" 'In this Year of Jubilee everyone is to return to his own property.

¹⁴" 'If you sell land to one of your countrymen or buy any from him, do not take advantage of each other. ¹⁵You are to buy from your countryman on the basis of the number of years since the Jubilee. And he is to sell to you on the basis of the number of years left for harvesting crops. ¹⁶When the years are many, you are to increase the price, and when the years are few, you are to decrease the price, because what he is really selling you is the number of crops. ¹⁷Do not take advantage of each other, but fear your God. I am the LORD your God.

¹⁸" 'Follow my decrees and be careful to obey my laws, and you will live safely in the land. ¹⁹Then the land will yield its fruit, and you will eat your fill and live there in safety. ²⁰You may ask, "What will we eat in the seventh year if we do not plant or harvest our crops?" ²¹I will send you such a blessing in the sixth year that the land will yield enough for three years. ²²While you plant during the eighth year, you will eat from the old crop and will continue to eat from it until the harvest of the ninth year comes in.

23 " 'The land must not be sold permanently, because the land is mine and you are but aliens and my tenants. 24Throughout the country that you hold as a possession, you must provide for the redemption of the land.

25 " 'If one of your countrymen becomes poor and sells some of his property, his nearest relative is to come and redeem what his countryman has sold. 26If, however, a man has no one to redeem it for him but he himself prospers and acquires sufficient means to redeem it, 27he is to determine the value for the years since he sold it and refund the balance to the man to whom he sold it; he can then go back to his own property. 28But if he does not acquire the means to repay him, what he sold will remain in the possession of the buyer until the Year of Jubilee. It will be returned in the Jubilee, and he can then go back to his property.

29 " 'If a man sells a house in a walled city, he retains the right of redemption a full year after its sale. During that time he may redeem it. 30If it is not redeemed before a full year has passed, the house in the walled city shall belong permanently to the buyer and his descendants. It is not to be returned in the Jubilee. 31But houses in villages without walls around them are to be considered as open country. They can be redeemed, and they are to be returned in the Jubilee.

32 " 'The Levites always have the right to redeem their houses in the Levitical towns, which they possess. 33So the property of the Levites is redeemable—that is, a house sold in any town they hold—and is to be returned in the Jubilee, because the houses in the towns of the Levites are their property among the Israelites. 34But the pastureland belonging to their towns must not be sold; it is their permanent possession.

35 " 'If one of your countrymen becomes poor and is unable to support himself among you, help him as you would an alien or a temporary resident, so he can continue to live among you. 36Do not take interest of any kind[a] from him, but fear your God, so that your countryman may continue to live among you. 37You must not lend him money at interest or sell him food at a profit. 38I am the LORD your God, who brought you out of Egypt to give you the land of Canaan and to be your God.

39 " 'If one of your countrymen becomes poor among you and sells himself to you, do not make him work as a slave. 40He is to be treated as a hired worker or a temporary resident among you; he is to work for you until the Year of Jubilee. 41Then he and his children are to be released, and he will go back to his own clan and to the property of his forefathers. 42Because the Israelites are my servants, whom I brought out of Egypt, they must not be sold as slaves. 43Do not rule over them ruthlessly, but fear your God.

44 " 'Your male and female slaves are to come from the nations around you; from them you may buy slaves. 45You may also buy some of the temporary residents living among you and members of their clans born in your country, and they will become your property. 46You can will them to your children as inherited property and can make them slaves for life, but you must not rule over your fellow Israelites ruthlessly.

But Fear Your God

LEVITICUS 25:36–37

Throughout chapters 24 and 25, these guidelines about property ownership and monetary ethics are accented with the phrase, "I am the LORD your God" (24:22; 25:17,37). Verse 36 of chapter 25 underlines the principle that determines all financial and business dealings—indeed, all of life, with the phrase: "but fear your God." Write out each of these phrases. In a few words or a paragraph, write down what each one means to you. Why would God be interested in your financial transactions? Make it personal. Think of some of the financial and business dealings you may have carried out in the last month or some of the interactions you may have had at work or school. How does each one appear when scrutinized in the light of these two phrases?

See Meeting God in Everyday Life

The Fruit of Obedience

LEVITICUS 26:3–13

We are saved by God's grace. Our obedience is to be a joyous response to God's saving acts (in the case of Israel, this was deliverance from slavery in Egypt; for Christians, it is deliverance from the bondage of sin through Jesus' death and resurrection). But God has also promised further blessings for obedient individuals and communities.

Read these verses slowly, as if God were speaking directly to you and your faith community. What emotions do these verses prompt within you? Share them with God in prayer. Contemplate the difference between honest obedience as a joyous response to both God's past saving acts and your anticipation of future blessings, and obedience based primarily on the hope of reward. Could you, like Job, lose everything and still praise God (see Job 13:15)? Contemplate whether your obedience is motivated by joy, hope of reward or fear of punishment. Offer your response to God.

See Meeting God in Scripture

47 " 'If an alien or a temporary resident among you becomes rich and one of your countrymen becomes poor and sells himself to the alien living among you or to a member of the alien's clan, 48he retains the right of redemption after he has sold himself. One of his relatives may redeem him: 49An uncle or a cousin or any blood relative in his clan may redeem him. Or if he prospers, he may redeem himself. 50He and his buyer are to count the time from the year he sold himself up to the Year of Jubilee. The price for his release is to be based on the rate paid to a hired man for that number of years. 51If many years remain, he must pay for his redemption a larger share of the price paid for him. 52If only a few years remain until the Year of Jubilee, he is to compute that and pay for his redemption accordingly. 53He is to be treated as a man hired from year to year; you must see to it that his owner does not rule over him ruthlessly.

54 " 'Even if he is not redeemed in any of these ways, he and his children are to be released in the Year of Jubilee, 55for the Israelites belong to me as servants. They are my servants, whom I brought out of Egypt. I am the LORD your God.

Reward for Obedience

26 " 'Do not make idols or set up an image or a sacred stone for yourselves, and do not place a carved stone in your land to bow down before it. I am the LORD your God.

2 " 'Observe my Sabbaths and have reverence for my sanctuary. I am the LORD.

3 " 'If you follow my decrees and are careful to obey my commands, 4I will send you rain in its season, and the ground will yield its crops and the trees of the field their fruit. 5Your threshing will continue until grape harvest and the grape harvest will continue until planting, and you will eat all the food you want and live in safety in your land.

6 " 'I will grant peace in the land, and you will lie down and no one will make you afraid. I will remove savage beasts from the land, and the sword will not pass through your country. 7You will pursue your enemies, and they will fall by the sword before you. 8Five of you will chase a hundred, and a hundred of you will chase ten thousand, and your enemies will fall by the sword before you.

9 " 'I will look on you with favor and make you fruitful and increase your numbers, and I will keep my covenant with you. 10You will still be eating last year's harvest when you will have to move it out to make room for the new. 11I will put my dwelling place*a* among you, and I will not abhor you. 12I will walk among you and be your God, and you will be my people. 13I am the LORD your God, who brought you out of Egypt so that you would no longer be slaves to the Egyptians; I broke the bars of your yoke and enabled you to walk with heads held high.

Punishment for Disobedience

14 " 'But if you will not listen to me and carry out all these commands, 15and if you reject my decrees and abhor my laws and fail to carry out all my commands and so violate my covenant, 16then I will do this to you: I will bring upon you sudden terror, wasting diseases and fever that will de-

a 11 Or my tabernacle

stroy your sight and drain away your life. You will plant seed in vain, because your enemies will eat it. ¹⁷I will set my face against you so that you will be defeated by your enemies; those who hate you will rule over you, and you will flee even when no one is pursuing you.

¹⁸ 'If after all this you will not listen to me, I will punish you for your sins seven times over. ¹⁹I will break down your stubborn pride and make the sky above you like iron and the ground beneath you like bronze. ²⁰Your strength will be spent in vain, because your soil will not yield its crops, nor will the trees of the land yield their fruit.

²¹ 'If you remain hostile toward me and refuse to listen to me, I will multiply your afflictions seven times over, as your sins deserve. ²²I will send wild animals against you, and they will rob you of your children, destroy your cattle and make you so few in number that your roads will be deserted.

²³ 'If in spite of these things you do not accept my correction but continue to be hostile toward me, ²⁴I myself will be hostile toward you and will afflict you for your sins seven times over. ²⁵And I will bring the sword upon you to avenge the breaking of the covenant. When you withdraw into your cities, I will send a plague among you, and you will be given into enemy hands. ²⁶When I cut off your supply of bread, ten women will be able to bake your bread in one oven, and they will dole out the bread by weight. You will eat, but you will not be satisfied.

²⁷ 'If in spite of this you still do not listen to me but continue to be hostile toward me, ²⁸then in my anger I will be hostile toward you, and I myself will punish you for your sins seven times over. ²⁹You will eat the flesh of your sons and the flesh of your daughters. ³⁰I will destroy your high places, cut down your incense altars and pile your dead bodies on the lifeless forms of your idols, and I will abhor you. ³¹I will turn your cities into ruins and lay waste your sanctuaries, and I will take no delight in the pleasing aroma of your offerings. ³²I will lay waste the land, so that your enemies who live there will be appalled. ³³I will scatter you among the nations and will draw out my sword and pursue you. Your land will be laid waste, and your cities will lie in ruins. ³⁴Then the land will enjoy its sabbath years all the time that it lies desolate and you are in the country of your enemies; then the land will rest and enjoy its sabbaths. ³⁵All the time that it lies desolate, the land will have the rest it did not have during the sabbaths you lived in it.

³⁶ 'As for those of you who are left, I will make their hearts so fearful in the lands of their enemies that the sound of a windblown leaf will put them to flight. They will run as though fleeing from the sword, and they will fall, even though no one is pursuing them. ³⁷They will stumble over one another as though fleeing from the sword, even though no one is pursuing them. So you will not be able to stand before your enemies. ³⁸You will perish among the nations; the land of your enemies will devour you. ³⁹Those of you who are left will waste away in the lands of their enemies because of their sins; also because of their fathers' sins they will waste away.

⁴⁰ 'But if they will confess their sins and the sins of their fathers—their treachery against me and their hostility toward me, ⁴¹which made me hostile toward them so that I

The Land Must Rest

LEVITICUS 26:23–26

As God declared the day of Sabbath rest for men and women to be renewed and to rest from labor, so he declared a year of Sabbath rest for the land. Why do you think God wanted the land to rest? How might the people have survived without cultivating the land? How might they have prepared for the Sabbath year? What is God saying to you about creation through this passage? What might you do in response?

See *Meeting God in Scripture*

And to God, the Things That Are God's

LEVITICUS 27:2–23

Chapter 27 deals with the payment of vows, which were offerings usually given as expressions of thanks in special circumstances. Items themselves, or their value (plus twenty percent), could be donated.

When you have unexpected windfalls or times of joy, is your first reaction to thank God and make a special offering? Think of times when it might be appropriate for you or your faith community to make a special donation to God. Some churches include a budget line in capital improvements as a special donation to serve as a reminder that all things come from God. What are other ways that we can go beyond our normal requirement to honor God?

Put a jar or bank in a conspicuous place in your home. Then, whenever you buy a gift for a friend or something for yourself, make a donation to God as well. Decide ahead of time which charity will receive the money.

See Meeting God in Service

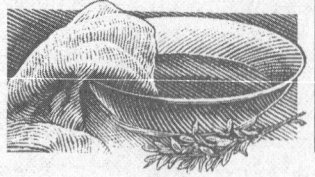

162

sent them into the land of their enemies—then when their uncircumcised hearts are humbled and they pay for their sin, ⁴²I will remember my covenant with Jacob and my covenant with Isaac and my covenant with Abraham, and I will remember the land. ⁴³For the land will be deserted by them and will enjoy its sabbaths while it lies desolate without them. They will pay for their sins because they rejected my laws and abhorred my decrees. ⁴⁴Yet in spite of this, when they are in the land of their enemies, I will not reject them or abhor them so as to destroy them completely, breaking my covenant with them. I am the LORD their God. ⁴⁵But for their sake I will remember the covenant with their ancestors whom I brought out of Egypt in the sight of the nations to be their God. I am the LORD.' "

⁴⁶These are the decrees, the laws and the regulations that the LORD established on Mount Sinai between himself and the Israelites through Moses.

Redeeming What Is the LORD's

27 The LORD said to Moses, ²"Speak to the Israelites and say to them: 'If anyone makes a special vow to dedicate persons to the LORD by giving equivalent values, ³set the value of a male between the ages of twenty and sixty at fifty shekels*ᵃ* of silver, according to the sanctuary shekel*ᵇ*; ⁴and if it is a female, set her value at thirty shekels.*ᶜ* ⁵If it is a person between the ages of five and twenty, set the value of a male at twenty shekels*ᵈ* and of a female at ten shekels.*ᵉ* ⁶If it is a person between one month and five years, set the value of a male at five shekels*ᶠ* of silver and that of a female at three shekels*ᵍ* of silver. ⁷If it is a person sixty years old or more, set the value of a male at fifteen shekels*ʰ* and of a female at ten shekels. ⁸If anyone making the vow is too poor to pay the specified amount, he is to present the person to the priest, who will set the value for him according to what the man making the vow can afford.

⁹" 'If what he vowed is an animal that is acceptable as an offering to the LORD, such an animal given to the LORD becomes holy. ¹⁰He must not exchange it or substitute a good one for a bad one, or a bad one for a good one; if he should substitute one animal for another, both it and the substitute become holy. ¹¹If what he vowed is a ceremonially unclean animal—one that is not acceptable as an offering to the LORD—the animal must be presented to the priest, ¹²who will judge its quality as good or bad. Whatever value the priest then sets, that is what it will be. ¹³If the owner wishes to redeem the animal, he must add a fifth to its value.

¹⁴" 'If a man dedicates his house as something holy to the LORD, the priest will judge its quality as good or bad. Whatever value the priest then sets, so it will remain. ¹⁵If the man who dedicates his house redeems it, he must add a fifth to its value, and the house will again become his.

¹⁶" 'If a man dedicates to the LORD part of his family land, its value is to be set according to the amount of seed required for it—fifty shekels of silver to a homer*ⁱ* of barley

---

ᵃ3 That is, about 1 1/4 pounds (about 0.6 kilogram); also in verse 16   *ᵇ3* That is, about 2/5 ounce (about 11.5 grams); also in verse 25   *ᶜ4* That is, about 12 ounces (about 0.3 kilogram)   *ᵈ5* That is, about 8 ounces (about 0.2 kilogram)   *ᵉ5* That is, about 4 ounces (about 110 grams); also in verse 7   *ᶠ6* That is, about 2 ounces (about 55 grams)   *ᵍ6* That is, about 1 1/4 ounces (about 35 grams)   *ʰ7* That is, about 6 ounces (about 170 grams)   *ⁱ16* That is, probably about 6 bushels (about 220 liters)

seed. ¹⁷If he dedicates his field during the Year of Jubilee, the value that has been set remains. ¹⁸But if he dedicates his field after the Jubilee, the priest will determine the value according to the number of years that remain until the next Year of Jubilee, and its set value will be reduced. ¹⁹If the man who dedicates the field wishes to redeem it, he must add a fifth to its value, and the field will again become his. ²⁰If, however, he does not redeem the field, or if he has sold it to someone else, it can never be redeemed. ²¹When the field is released in the Jubilee, it will become holy, like a field devoted to the Lord; it will become the property of the priests.^a

²²" 'If a man dedicates to the Lord a field he has bought, which is not part of his family land, ²³the priest will determine its value up to the Year of Jubilee, and the man must pay its value on that day as something holy to the Lord. ²⁴In the Year of Jubilee the field will revert to the person from whom he bought it, the one whose land it was. ²⁵Every value is to be set according to the sanctuary shekel, twenty gerahs to the shekel.

²⁶" 'No one, however, may dedicate the firstborn of an animal, since the firstborn already belongs to the Lord; whether an ox^b or a sheep, it is the Lord's. ²⁷If it is one of the unclean animals, he may buy it back at its set value, adding a fifth of the value to it. If he does not redeem it, it is to be sold at its set value.

²⁸" 'But nothing that a man owns and devotes^c to the Lord—whether man or animal or family land—may be sold or redeemed; everything so devoted is most holy to the Lord.

²⁹" 'No person devoted to destruction^d may be ransomed; he must be put to death.

³⁰" 'A tithe of everything from the land, whether grain from the soil or fruit from the trees, belongs to the Lord; it is holy to the Lord. ³¹If a man redeems any of his tithe, he must add a fifth of the value to it. ³²The entire tithe of the herd and flock—every tenth animal that passes under the shepherd's rod—will be holy to the Lord. ³³He must not pick out the good from the bad or make any substitution. If he does make a substitution, both the animal and its substitute become holy and cannot be redeemed.' "

³⁴These are the commands the Lord gave Moses on Mount Sinai for the Israelites.

What Belongs to the Lord

LEVITICUS 27:26

Suppose you were to take an article of clothing from your spouse's closet, wrap it up and give it to him or her for Christmas. What kind of response might you expect?

Giving to God what already belongs to him is not a gift. What can you give to God that goes beyond your normal tithe or usual offering? Such a gift is voluntary, but not to be entered into lightly or casually. Consider giving a special gift of devotion to God today. Will it be monetary? A gift of service?

See *Meeting God in Worship*

^a21 Or *priest*   ^b26 The Hebrew word can include both male and female.
^c28 The Hebrew term refers to the irrevocable giving over of things or persons to the Lord.   ^d29 The Hebrew term refers to the irrevocable giving over of things or persons to the Lord, often by totally destroying them.

163

WAYS of MEETING GOD

Meeting God in Prayer

Many Christians suffer under the assumption that they should automatically know how to pray. If someone has a real relationship with God, the reasoning goes, prayer should flow spontaneously from the heart. And it often does.

Sometimes, however, we need guidance—we need to learn to pray. Prayer grows out of a relationship with God that is permeated by grace and love and is therefore preeminently communion—wordless, spirit-to-spirit oneness with God.

> The Lord's Prayer is not just a prayer to *say* but, more significantly, a *way* to pray.

But prayer is also conversation with God. And just as toddlers learn to talk by listening and mimicking the words of their parents, so we learn to pray by using the words God has given us. In the pages of the Bible we discover not only teaching about prayer but ancient prayers that help us dialogue with God today. "Repeating God's words after [God]," wrote Dietrich Bonhoeffer, "we begin to pray to [God]."

The Lord's Prayer. One very meaningful way to "repeat God's words" in our prayers is through the prayer Jesus gave his disciples—the Lord's Prayer. In Luke 11:1–13 an anonymous disciple comes to Jesus saying, "Lord, teach us to pray, just as John taught his disciples." The man is making an understandable request; a Jewish rabbi in that time often gave his followers an outline for prayer that expressed the unique characteristics of his teaching, an exercise that brought the group together around a common identity. But behind the disciple's request lies a deeper need. He wants to know how to both *commune* and *communicate* with God. Many of us still make the same request as this disciple. Jesus' response can enrich and transform our praying. In fact, many consider the "discovery" of this prayer as a turning point in their prayer life. The Lord's Prayer is not just a prayer to *say* but, more significantly, a *way* to pray. More than a formula to recite, the Lord's Prayer guides us through three successive movements of opening ourselves to God.

Adoration. "Father, hallowed be your name, your kingdom come." Adoration celebrates our communion with God. It brings us into conscious awareness of the reality of God with us. Adoration focuses our attention on God, liberating us from focusing on ourselves and setting the context for all true prayer. In adoration we align our lives with God's purposes; we gladly let go of lesser attachments and give God's love full control of our hearts and minds. We respond with gratitude to the God who first called us into a loving relationship.

An act of adoration may consist of slowly repeating the words, "Father, holy and honored be your name", for a period of time, letting Jesus' name for God give expression to our love and praise as God's children. We may build on these trusted words with psalms of praise or familiar hymns that come to mind. Our prayer may give way to improvisation: words of our own, images, songs and other spontaneous expressions of praise and thanksgiving that we verbalize or write. Adoration may consist of quiet reading and reflection on Scripture verses and spiritual classics that bring us into God's presence.

Petition. "Give us each day our daily bread . . . and lead us not into temptation." Petition is asking God for what we need, especially for those things we need in order to continue in our communion with him. When adoration has set the proper context for prayer—a focus on God and his kingdom—no need or concern is too small to bring to him. Jesus said, "Ask and it will be given to you; seek and you will find; knock and the door will be opened to you" (Matthew 7:7). In doing so, we daily acknowledge this all-embracing truth about our lives: We are creatures who are utterly dependent on our loving Creator. Petition is the expression of our total dependence on God for everything: our existence, bread and water, relationships and community, grace and destiny.

Petition invites us to bring to God no less than the totality of our daily lives: our joys and struggles, hopes and hurts, desires and disappointments, loves and hates, pleas and resentments, and our need for healing and for change. By opening ourselves fully to God, we allow God to meet our true needs; God may also kindle in us a desire to question some of our perceived needs. By presenting to God every desire and request, we allow God to bless worthy dreams, to expose not-so-worthy dreams and to give us a passion for God's own dreams. Far from being self-centered, petition is the avenue through which God sustains us in grace and transforms our daily lives. It expresses our faith that God is committed to giving us all we truly need in order to grow in grace and truth.

Contrition. "Forgive us our sins, for we also forgive everyone who sins against us." Contrition seeks grace to restore our communion with God. It is acknowledging the relationships that exist between God and ourselves and ourselves and our neighbor. It is admitting that there are areas in which we have failed. Contri
the inner chamber of decision and transformation where sin and c-
where, with Jesus, we die to sin and rise with him to new life. In t

allow God's love to melt our hate, his forgiveness to wash away our guilt and his Spirit to move us to change. "If we claim to be without sin, we deceive ourselves and the truth is not in us," John writes. "If we confess our sins, he is faithful and just and will forgive us our sins and purify us from all unrighteousness" (1 John 1:8–9).

Contrition is also opening to God those parts of our lives that have been closed to him. We humbly confess our unfaithfulness and surrender the sin at work within us to the mercy of God. We receive God's forgiveness and take steps to turn around and live in grateful cooperation with the redeeming love of God. We pray for the sort of world God wants and for the ability to be the sort of people God desires us to be. The prayer Jesus taught us is a pattern for opening ourselves up to God—for transforming our lives.

The Lord's Prayer, then, is both a prayer and a formula for prayer. Dietrich Bonhoeffer says of it, "Every prayer is contained in it . . . . All the prayers of Holy Scripture are summarized in the Lord's Prayer, and are contained in its immeasurable breadth."

> The prayer Jesus taught us is a pattern for opening ourselves up to God —for transforming our lives.

Praying the Bible. Notwithstanding the centrality of the Lord's Prayer, there is much to be learned about praying other prayers of the Bible. Perhaps no other book of the Bible has been prayed more frequently than the book of Psalms. Of the Psalter, the collection of psalms, Martin Luther once wrote, "It penetrates the Lord's Prayer and the Lord's Prayer penetrates it, so that it is possible to understand one on the basis of the other and to bring them into joyful harmony." No wonder some call Psalms the "prayer book of the Bible." The psalms can help us find prayerful expression for all of our life before God: from lamentations to praises, from doubt to joy. For example, "The LORD is my shepherd, I shall not be in want" (Psalm 23:1) may serve to lead us into actual conversation with God. "You are my shepherd, Lord," we might say. "Thank you for promising to provide what I need."

Any Biblical passage that speaks to us can be woven into our praying. This is a powerful way to enter into the heart of Scripture. Praying through the Ten Commandments can become a prayer of self-examination. Praying through the parables helps us understand God's values. Praying through 1 Corinthians 13 aligns us with God's heart of love for others.

In a liturgy in which the prayers of adoration, confession and petition are from Scripture—whether in the form of readings, hymns or canticles—the body of

Christ, past and present, prays with one voice. Even in our private prayers we are, in one sense, never alone when we pray using the words and phrases of the Bible; we are praying the book common to God's people everywhere and in every time—the whole family of God. We pray with the same words that God's people have prayed throughout the ages.

In praying from Scripture, the passage often suggests what form the prayer should take. For example, Scriptural prayers are often preparatory to silent prayer. Prayers of intercession—based, perhaps, on one of Paul's letters—in which we vocalize our love and longings for others, are especially fitted to spoken, public prayer. Passages that express adoration, when prayed aloud, impress our minds and hearts with God's majesty and goodness.

Being Quiet Before God. Learning to be quiet and to rest with God is essential in prayer. Silence is the discipline of pushing aside words, busyness and noise in order to create space within for God. Someone once asked a spiritual adviser, "What should I do when I pray?" "Don't do anything," was the response. "Just love." The experience of stillness provides a space within which we can, unhurried, recognize God's presence. Some find "centering prayer," the repetition of a single word or phrase, to be an aid to this kind of quiet communion. In what some have called "contemplative prayer," the words and forms recede altogether. Prayer becomes a simple, restful experience of basking in the Lord's presence. Rich silences—not of our own making—allow us to commune with God. Our prayers may even alternate between articulated words and these quieter, less verbal times.

Whether we pray with the depth and breadth of the Lord's Prayer or recite a verse of a psalm, whether our words are many or few, whether we actively intercede or simply rest in God's presence, prayer is an intimate meeting with God.

See Page 304 for the next Ways of Meeting God *article.*

NUMBERS

Wandering in the Desert

KEY VERSE:

[The people] spoke against God and against Moses, and said, "Why have you brought us up out of Egypt to die in the desert? There is no bread! There is no water! And we detest this miserable food!"

—*Numbers 21:5*

"The people in the wilderness deserved reproof, not because they desired meat, but because in their desire they murmured against the Lord."

—AUGUSTINE,
Confessions

The book of Numbers portrays God's people at what may be their worst—ungrateful and inattentive. Traveling toward the promised land, they do not seem to make much real progress. Though they have left Egypt physically, they have not left it behind emotionally and spiritually. Every time something goes wrong or they become unhappy, they criticize Moses and, by association, God. They complain about the manna and water God miraculously gives them. The Israelites harbor jealousy, fight among themselves, offer "unauthorized fire" before the Lord, intermarry with women God tells them to avoid, and publicly criticize one another. They appear to learn their lessons—but then turn and make the same mistakes again. God becomes angry with the people, but still loves them and repeatedly forgives them.

In short, the book of Numbers shows us a portrait of the relationship between imperfect people and the Holy One who loves and guides them in spite of their stubbornness. The Israelites are shown God's glory in unmistakable ways; when they listen and obey, they move toward the good life that God offers.

Our journey today, like that of the Israelites—from bondage to what God has promised us—is often anything but a straight line or smooth sailing. But we journey with a patient and faithful God. Perhaps the greatest lesson from the book of Numbers is that when we are willing to listen and follow, God is always ready to speak to us and guide us.

The Census

1 The LORD spoke to Moses in the Tent of Meeting in the Desert of Sinai on the first day of the second month of the second year after the Israelites came out of Egypt. He said: ²"Take a census of the whole Israelite community by their clans and families, listing every man by name, one by one. ³You and Aaron are to number by their divisions all the men in Israel twenty years old or more who are able to serve in the army. ⁴One man from each tribe, each the head of his family, is to help you. ⁵These are the names of the men who are to assist you:

from Reuben, Elizur son of Shedeur;
⁶from Simeon, Shelumiel son of Zurishaddai;
⁷from Judah, Nahshon son of Amminadab;
⁸from Issachar, Nethanel son of Zuar;
⁹from Zebulun, Eliab son of Helon;
¹⁰from the sons of Joseph:
    from Ephraim, Elishama son of Ammihud;
    from Manasseh, Gamaliel son of Pedahzur;
¹¹from Benjamin, Abidan son of Gideoni;
¹²from Dan, Ahiezer son of Ammishaddai;
¹³from Asher, Pagiel son of Ocran;
¹⁴from Gad, Eliasaph son of Deuel;
¹⁵from Naphtali, Ahira son of Enan."

¹⁶These were the men appointed from the community, the leaders of their ancestral tribes. They were the heads of the clans of Israel.

¹⁷Moses and Aaron took these men whose names had been given, ¹⁸and they called the whole community together on the first day of the second month. The people indicated their ancestry by their clans and families, and the men twenty years old or more were listed by name, one by one, ¹⁹as the LORD commanded Moses. And so he counted them in the Desert of Sinai:

²⁰From the descendants of Reuben the firstborn son of Israel:
    All the men twenty years old or more who were able to serve in the army were listed by name, one by one, according to the records of their clans and families. ²¹The number from the tribe of Reuben was 46,500.

²²From the descendants of Simeon:
    All the men twenty years old or more who were able to serve in the army were counted and listed by name, one by one, according to the records of their clans and families. ²³The number from the tribe of Simeon was 59,300.

²⁴From the descendants of Gad:
    All the men twenty years old or more who were able to serve in the army were listed by name, according to the records of their clans and families. ²⁵The number from the tribe of Gad was 45,650.

²⁶From the descendants of Judah:
    All the men twenty years old or more who were able to serve in the army were listed by name, according to the records of their clans and families. ²⁷The number from the tribe of Judah was 74,600.

A Big Job

NUMBERS 1:2–5

Moses is given charge of the whole congregation of Israelites. Imagine over six hundred thousand able-bodied men; the women, children and men not able to fight were not even counted! The crowd must have stretched as far as the eye could see! But Moses does a very sensible thing—he subdivides the group by tribe, by clan, by houses, by age and by gender, and then he chooses people to help him govern.

Consider a task, group or project God has given into your charge. The task may look overwhelming or the goal seem unreachable. Following Moses' example, divide the task into smaller components. Ask God for insight into what you can do today and whom you should ask to help you. What do you need strength for immediately, and what can you place in God's keeping until another time?

See Meeting God in Everyday Life

Unapproachably Holy

NUMBERS 1:48–53

The tabernacle of the Testimony was a holy place, so holy that ordinary people could not come close to it. The Levites encamped around the tabernacle as a sort of buffer between the incredible power of God's holiness and the people.

Think about a time when you had a strong sense of the holiness of God. Where were you? What did you feel? Envision God's holy presence surrounding you now, perhaps as light or warmth. If there is a lamp near you, hold your hand in the light. As you move your hand closer to the light, what do you see? How does what you see change as you get nearer to the light? What do you see about yourself as you contemplate God's holiness?

See Meeting God in Worship

28From the descendants of Issachar:
All the men twenty years old or more who were able to serve in the army were listed by name, according to the records of their clans and families. 29The number from the tribe of Issachar was 54,400.

30From the descendants of Zebulun:
All the men twenty years old or more who were able to serve in the army were listed by name, according to the records of their clans and families. 31The number from the tribe of Zebulun was 57,400.

32From the sons of Joseph:
From the descendants of Ephraim:
All the men twenty years old or more who were able to serve in the army were listed by name, according to the records of their clans and families. 33The number from the tribe of Ephraim was 40,500.

34From the descendants of Manasseh:
All the men twenty years old or more who were able to serve in the army were listed by name, according to the records of their clans and families. 35The number from the tribe of Manasseh was 32,200.

36From the descendants of Benjamin:
All the men twenty years old or more who were able to serve in the army were listed by name, according to the records of their clans and families. 37The number from the tribe of Benjamin was 35,400.

38From the descendants of Dan:
All the men twenty years old or more who were able to serve in the army were listed by name, according to the records of their clans and families. 39The number from the tribe of Dan was 62,700.

40From the descendants of Asher:
All the men twenty years old or more who were able to serve in the army were listed by name, according to the records of their clans and families. 41The number from the tribe of Asher was 41,500.

42From the descendants of Naphtali:
All the men twenty years old or more who were able to serve in the army were listed by name, according to the records of their clans and families. 43The number from the tribe of Naphtali was 53,400.

44These were the men counted by Moses and Aaron and the twelve leaders of Israel, each one representing his family. 45All the Israelites twenty years old or more who were able to serve in Israel's army were counted according to their families. 46The total number was 603,550.

47The families of the tribe of Levi, however, were not counted along with the others. 48The LORD had said to Moses: 49"You must not count the tribe of Levi or include them in the census of the other Israelites. 50Instead, appoint the Levites to be in charge of the tabernacle of the Testimony—over all its furnishings and everything belonging to it. They are to carry the tabernacle and all its furnishings; they are to take care of it and encamp around it. 51Whenever the tabernacle is to move, the Levites are to take it down, and whenever the tabernacle is to be set up, the Levites shall do it. Anyone else who goes near it shall be put to death. ⁵²The Israelites are to set up their tents by divisions, each man in his own camp under his own standard. ⁵³The Levites, however, are to set up their tents around the tabernacle of the Testimony so that wrath will not fall on the Israelite community. The Levites are to be responsible for the care of the tabernacle of the Testimony."

⁵⁴The Israelites did all this just as the LORD commanded Moses.

The Arrangement of the Tribal Camps

2 The LORD said to Moses and Aaron: ²"The Israelites are to camp around the Tent of Meeting some distance from it, each man under his standard with the banners of his family."

³On the east, toward the sunrise, the divisions of the camp of Judah are to encamp under their standard. The leader of the people of Judah is Nahshon son of Amminadab. ⁴His division numbers 74,600.

⁵The tribe of Issachar will camp next to them. The leader of the people of Issachar is Nethanel son of Zuar. ⁶His division numbers 54,400.

⁷The tribe of Zebulun will be next. The leader of the people of Zebulun is Eliab son of Helon. ⁸His division numbers 57,400.

⁹All the men assigned to the camp of Judah, according to their divisions, number 186,400. They will set out first.

¹⁰On the south will be the divisions of the camp of Reuben under their standard. The leader of the people of Reuben is Elizur son of Shedeur. ¹¹His division numbers 46,500.

¹²The tribe of Simeon will camp next to them. The leader of the people of Simeon is Shelumiel son of Zurishaddai. ¹³His division numbers 59,300.

¹⁴The tribe of Gad will be next. The leader of the people of Gad is Eliasaph son of Deuel.ᵃ ¹⁵His division numbers 45,650.

¹⁶All the men assigned to the camp of Reuben, according to their divisions, number 151,450. They will set out second.

¹⁷Then the Tent of Meeting and the camp of the Levites will set out in the middle of the camps. They will set out in the same order as they encamp, each in his own place under his standard.

¹⁸On the west will be the divisions of the camp of Ephraim under their standard. The leader of the people of Ephraim is Elishama son of Ammihud. ¹⁹His division numbers 40,500.

²⁰The tribe of Manasseh will be next to them. The leader of the people of Manasseh is Gamaliel son of Pedahzur. ²¹His division numbers 32,200.

²²The tribe of Benjamin will be next. The leader of the people of Benjamin is Abidan son of Gideoni. ²³His division numbers 35,400.

²⁴All the men assigned to the camp of Ephraim, ac-

The Center of the Circle

NUMBERS 2:2,17–34

The Tent of Meeting, where the people meet God, is placed in the center of their camp; God's dwelling is at the center of their lives.

What is at the center of your life? Draw a circle to represent your waking hours on a typical day and subdivide it to represent how you spend your time. Does the picture created by the circle reflect what you want to be most important in your life? Do you see changes that you want to make?

See Meeting God in Everyday Life

ᵃ 14 Many manuscripts of the Masoretic Text, Samaritan Pentateuch and Vulgate (see also Num. 1:14); most manuscripts of the Masoretic Text *Reuel*

171

Children Gone Wrong

NUMBERS 3:2–4

Two of Aaron's sons serve faithfully with him as priests, but two of them make unacceptable offerings to God. This "unauthorized fire" is an affront to God, and the two men die.

Picture Aaron grieving for his disobedient sons, perhaps for some time even before they died. The difficulties that led to their death probably began long before this moment.

Many faithful parents have some children who follow God's way and others who do not. Do you know parents who are in pain because of difficulties with troubled children, children whose actions may even be life-threatening? In your prayers, hold them and their children before God. What kind of help and support can you offer them?

See Meeting God in Service

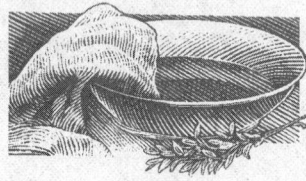

cording to their divisions, number 108,100. They will set out third.

²⁵On the north will be the divisions of the camp of Dan, under their standard. The leader of the people of Dan is Ahiezer son of Ammishaddai. ²⁶His division numbers 62,700.

²⁷The tribe of Asher will camp next to them. The leader of the people of Asher is Pagiel son of Ocran. ²⁸His division numbers 41,500.

²⁹The tribe of Naphtali will be next. The leader of the people of Naphtali is Ahira son of Enan. ³⁰His division numbers 53,400.

³¹All the men assigned to the camp of Dan number 157,600. They will set out last, under their standards.

³²These are the Israelites, counted according to their families. All those in the camps, by their divisions, number 603,550. ³³The Levites, however, were not counted along with the other Israelites, as the LORD commanded Moses.

³⁴So the Israelites did everything the LORD commanded Moses; that is the way they encamped under their standards, and that is the way they set out, each with his clan and family.

The Levites

3 This is the account of the family of Aaron and Moses at the time the LORD talked with Moses on Mount Sinai.

²The names of the sons of Aaron were Nadab the firstborn and Abihu, Eleazar and Ithamar. ³Those were the names of Aaron's sons, the anointed priests, who were ordained to serve as priests. ⁴Nadab and Abihu, however, fell dead before the LORD when they made an offering with unauthorized fire before him in the Desert of Sinai. They had no sons; so only Eleazar and Ithamar served as priests during the lifetime of their father Aaron.

⁵The LORD said to Moses, ⁶"Bring the tribe of Levi and present them to Aaron the priest to assist him. ⁷They are to perform duties for him and for the whole community at the Tent of Meeting by doing the work of the tabernacle. ⁸They are to take care of all the furnishings of the Tent of Meeting, fulfilling the obligations of the Israelites by doing the work of the tabernacle. ⁹Give the Levites to Aaron and his sons; they are the Israelites who are to be given wholly to him.ᵃ ¹⁰Appoint Aaron and his sons to serve as priests; anyone else who approaches the sanctuary must be put to death."

¹¹The LORD also said to Moses, ¹²"I have taken the Levites from among the Israelites in place of the first male offspring of every Israelite woman. The Levites are mine, ¹³for all the firstborn are mine. When I struck down all the firstborn in Egypt, I set apart for myself every firstborn in Israel, whether man or animal. They are to be mine. I am the LORD."

¹⁴The LORD said to Moses in the Desert of Sinai, ¹⁵"Count the Levites by their families and clans. Count every male a

ᵃ9 Most manuscripts of the Masoretic Text; some manuscripts of the Masoretic Text, Samaritan Pentateuch and Septuagint (see also Num. 8:16) *to me*

month old or more." ¹⁶So Moses counted them, as he was commanded by the word of the LORD.
¹⁷These were the names of the sons of Levi:
Gershon, Kohath and Merari.
¹⁸These were the names of the Gershonite clans:
Libni and Shimei.
¹⁹The Kohathite clans:
Amram, Izhar, Hebron and Uzziel.
²⁰The Merarite clans:
Mahli and Mushi.
These were the Levite clans, according to their families.

²¹To Gershon belonged the clans of the Libnites and Shimeites; these were the Gershonite clans. ²²The number of all the males a month old or more who were counted was 7,500. ²³The Gershonite clans were to camp on the west, behind the tabernacle. ²⁴The leader of the families of the Gershonites was Eliasaph son of Lael. ²⁵At the Tent of Meeting the Gershonites were responsible for the care of the tabernacle and tent, its coverings, the curtain at the entrance to the Tent of Meeting, ²⁶the curtains of the courtyard, the curtain at the entrance to the courtyard surrounding the tabernacle and altar, and the ropes—and everything related to their use.

²⁷To Kohath belonged the clans of the Amramites, Izharites, Hebronites and Uzzielites; these were the Kohathite clans. ²⁸The number of all the males a month old or more was 8,600.ᵃ The Kohathites were responsible for the care of the sanctuary. ²⁹The Kohathite clans were to camp on the south side of the tabernacle. ³⁰The leader of the families of the Kohathite clans was Elizaphan son of Uzziel. ³¹They were responsible for the care of the ark, the table, the lampstand, the altars, the articles of the sanctuary used in ministering, the curtain, and everything related to their use. ³²The chief leader of the Levites was Eleazar son of Aaron, the priest. He was appointed over those who were responsible for the care of the sanctuary.

³³To Merari belonged the clans of the Mahlites and the Mushites; these were the Merarite clans. ³⁴The number of all the males a month old or more who were counted was 6,200. ³⁵The leader of the families of the Merarite clans was Zuriel son of Abihail; they were to camp on the north side of the tabernacle. ³⁶The Merarites were appointed to take care of the frames of the tabernacle, its crossbars, posts, bases, all its equipment, and everything related to their use, ³⁷as well as the posts of the surrounding courtyard with their bases, tent pegs and ropes.

³⁸Moses and Aaron and his sons were to camp to the east of the tabernacle, toward the sunrise, in front of the Tent of Meeting. They were responsible for the care of the sanctuary on behalf of the Israelites. Anyone else who approached the sanctuary was to be put to death.

³⁹The total number of Levites counted at the LORD's command by Moses and Aaron according to their clans, including every male a month old or more, was 22,000.

ᵃ 28 Hebrew; some Septuagint manuscripts 8,300

Family Expectations

NUMBERS 3:25–27,31–32,36–37

The clans are assigned specific duties. Picture the adults training the children to polish the tabernacle furnishings or roll up the cords that held the curtains at the tabernacle entrance. From generation to generation, they know what their work will be.

In your family, are there traditions of faith that are carried on from one generation to another? Does your family voice expectations about faith or other behavior for its members? Do you have expectations—expressed or unexpressed—of those you care about? Consider what your response would be if God were to call you or someone you care about to an unexpected place of service.

See Meeting God in Everyday Life

A Clear Claim

NUMBERS 3:44–45

"I am the LORD," God said. The Levites are to be set apart for God. God is sovereign, and God's claim is absolute.

Today's culture promotes individualism that encourages us to think we are autonomous, self-contained, free to determine our own way. What absolute claims does God make on your life? Is your list different today than it was at some point in the past? Do you feel resistance to the idea that God is sovereign and has claim on you? In what areas do you try to bargain with God to ask less of you?

40The LORD said to Moses, "Count all the firstborn Israelite males who are a month old or more and make a list of their names. 41Take the Levites for me in place of all the firstborn of the Israelites, and the livestock of the Levites in place of all the firstborn of the livestock of the Israelites. I am the LORD."

42So Moses counted all the firstborn of the Israelites, as the LORD commanded him. 43The total number of firstborn males a month old or more, listed by name, was 22,273.

44The LORD also said to Moses, 45"Take the Levites in place of all the firstborn of Israel, and the livestock of the Levites in place of their livestock. The Levites are to be mine. I am the LORD. 46To redeem the 273 firstborn Israelites who exceed the number of the Levites, 47collect five shekels[a] for each one, according to the sanctuary shekel, which weighs twenty gerahs. 48Give the money for the redemption of the additional Israelites to Aaron and his sons."

49So Moses collected the redemption money from those who exceeded the number redeemed by the Levites. 50From the firstborn of the Israelites he collected silver weighing 1,365 shekels,[b] according to the sanctuary shekel. 51Moses gave the redemption money to Aaron and his sons, as he was commanded by the word of the LORD.

The Kohathites

4 The LORD said to Moses and Aaron: 2"Take a census of the Kohathite branch of the Levites by their clans and families. 3Count all the men from thirty to fifty years of age who come to serve in the work in the Tent of Meeting.

4"This is the work of the Kohathites in the Tent of Meeting: the care of the most holy things. 5When the camp is to move, Aaron and his sons are to go in and take down the shielding curtain and cover the ark of the Testimony with it. 6Then they are to cover this with hides of sea cows,[c] spread a cloth of solid blue over that and put the poles in place.

7"Over the table of the Presence they are to spread a blue cloth and put on it the plates, dishes and bowls, and the jars for drink offerings; the bread that is continually there is to remain on it. 8Over these they are to spread a scarlet cloth, cover that with hides of sea cows and put its poles in place.

9"They are to take a blue cloth and cover the lampstand that is for light, together with its lamps, its wick trimmers and trays, and all its jars for the oil used to supply it. 10Then they are to wrap it and all its accessories in a covering of hides of sea cows and put it on a carrying frame.

11"Over the gold altar they are to spread a blue cloth and cover that with hides of sea cows and put its poles in place.

12"They are to take all the articles used for ministering in the sanctuary, wrap them in a blue cloth, cover that with hides of sea cows and put them on a carrying frame.

13"They are to remove the ashes from the bronze altar and spread a purple cloth over it. 14Then they are to place on it all the utensils used for ministering at the altar, including the firepans, meat forks, shovels and sprinkling bowls. Over it they are to spread a covering of hides of sea cows and put its poles in place.

a 47 That is, about 2 ounces (about 55 grams)   b 50 That is, about 35 pounds (about 15.5 kilograms)   c 6 That is, dugongs; also in verses 8, 10, 11, 12, 14 and 25

[15]"After Aaron and his sons have finished covering the holy furnishings and all the holy articles, and when the camp is ready to move, the Kohathites are to come to do the carrying. But they must not touch the holy things or they will die. The Kohathites are to carry those things that are in the Tent of Meeting.

[16]"Eleazar son of Aaron, the priest, is to have charge of the oil for the light, the fragrant incense, the regular grain offering and the anointing oil. He is to be in charge of the entire tabernacle and everything in it, including its holy furnishings and articles."

[17]The LORD said to Moses and Aaron, [18]"See that the Kohathite tribal clans are not cut off from the Levites. [19]So that they may live and not die when they come near the most holy things, do this for them: Aaron and his sons are to go into the sanctuary and assign to each man his work and what he is to carry. [20]But the Kohathites must not go in to look at the holy things, even for a moment, or they will die."

The Gershonites

[21]The LORD said to Moses, [22]"Take a census also of the Gershonites by their families and clans. [23]Count all the men from thirty to fifty years of age who come to serve in the work at the Tent of Meeting.

[24]"This is the service of the Gershonite clans as they work and carry burdens: [25]They are to carry the curtains of the tabernacle, the Tent of Meeting, its covering and the outer covering of hides of sea cows, the curtains for the entrance to the Tent of Meeting, [26]the curtains of the courtyard surrounding the tabernacle and altar, the curtain for the entrance, the ropes and all the equipment used in its service. The Gershonites are to do all that needs to be done with these things. [27]All their service, whether carrying or doing other work, is to be done under the direction of Aaron and his sons. You shall assign to them as their responsibility all they are to carry. [28]This is the service of the Gershonite clans at the Tent of Meeting. Their duties are to be under the direction of Ithamar son of Aaron, the priest.

The Merarites

[29]"Count the Merarites by their clans and families. [30]Count all the men from thirty to fifty years of age who come to serve in the work at the Tent of Meeting. [31]This is their duty as they perform service at the Tent of Meeting: to carry the frames of the tabernacle, its crossbars, posts and bases, [32]as well as the posts of the surrounding courtyard with their bases, tent pegs, ropes, all their equipment and everything related to their use. Assign to each man the specific things he is to carry. [33]This is the service of the Merarite clans as they work at the Tent of Meeting under the direction of Ithamar son of Aaron, the priest."

The Numbering of the Levite Clans

[34]Moses, Aaron and the leaders of the community counted the Kohathites by their clans and families. [35]All the men from thirty to fifty years of age who came to serve in the work in the Tent of Meeting, [36]counted by clans, were 2,750. [37]This was the total of all those in the Kohathite clans who served in the Tent of Meeting. Moses and Aaron

Special Moments

NUMBERS 4:5–15

The vessels and supplies for the sanctuary are revered and handled in specific ways because they represent contact with God. The people's manner with them is evidence that they have a profound sense of God's holiness.

Sacraments and rituals of worship such as Holy Communion, the wedding ceremony, or praying the Lord's Prayer aloud with other believers, call us to step aside from our routines. The extraordinary language and symbolic movements make these moments different from others, to remind us that God is present in a special way for a special purpose. We may feel comforted, welcomed, challenged by other believers and bound to them. Think about a ritual that holds power for you. What does it show you about God? How can you prepare to approach that ritual with deeper attentiveness?

See *Meeting God in Worship*

Strong Backs, Servant Hearts

NUMBERS 4:46–49

The Levites served according to their individual abilities. For instance, only those who were physically strong were expected to carry heavy loads.

Likewise, God calls us according to our unique aptitudes. But we often overlook our more "everyday" human attributes like having a strong back or being able to repair machines or grow flowers. Some of us can organize; some can do accounting; some can greet people warmly and make them feel welcome; some can make plants grow. Think about such abilities and how God might use them. Which of your natural aptitudes and interests do you use to serve God? What skills and aptitudes are you working to develop for God's use in the future?

See Meeting God in Everyday Life

counted them according to the Lord's command through Moses.

³⁸The Gershonites were counted by their clans and families. ³⁹All the men from thirty to fifty years of age who came to serve in the work at the Tent of Meeting, ⁴⁰counted by their clans and families, were 2,630. ⁴¹This was the total of those in the Gershonite clans who served at the Tent of Meeting. Moses and Aaron counted them according to the Lord's command.

⁴²The Merarites were counted by their clans and families. ⁴³All the men from thirty to fifty years of age who came to serve in the work at the Tent of Meeting, ⁴⁴counted by their clans, were 3,200. ⁴⁵This was the total of those in the Merarite clans. Moses and Aaron counted them according to the Lord's command through Moses.

⁴⁶So Moses, Aaron and the leaders of Israel counted all the Levites by their clans and families. ⁴⁷All the men from thirty to fifty years of age who came to do the work of serving and carrying the Tent of Meeting ⁴⁸numbered 8,580. ⁴⁹At the Lord's command through Moses, each was assigned his work and told what to carry.

Thus they were counted, as the Lord commanded Moses.

The Purity of the Camp

5 The Lord said to Moses, ²"Command the Israelites to send away from the camp anyone who has an infectious skin disease[a] or a discharge of any kind, or who is ceremonially unclean because of a dead body. ³Send away male and female alike; send them outside the camp so they will not defile their camp, where I dwell among them." ⁴The Israelites did this; they sent them outside the camp. They did just as the Lord had instructed Moses.

Restitution for Wrongs

⁵The Lord said to Moses, ⁶"Say to the Israelites: 'When a man or woman wrongs another in any way[b] and so is unfaithful to the Lord, that person is guilty ⁷and must confess the sin he has committed. He must make full restitution for his wrong, add one fifth to it and give it all to the person he has wronged. ⁸But if that person has no close relative to whom restitution can be made for the wrong, the restitution belongs to the Lord and must be given to the priest, along with the ram with which atonement is made for him. ⁹All the sacred contributions the Israelites bring to a priest will belong to him. ¹⁰Each man's sacred gifts are his own, but what he gives to the priest will belong to the priest.' "

The Test for an Unfaithful Wife

¹¹Then the Lord said to Moses, ¹²"Speak to the Israelites and say to them: 'If a man's wife goes astray and is unfaithful to him ¹³by sleeping with another man, and this is hidden from her husband and her impurity is undetected (since there is no witness against her and she has not been caught in the act), ¹⁴and if feelings of jealousy come over her husband and he suspects his wife and she is impure—or if he is jealous and suspects his wife even though she is not

---

[a] 2 Traditionally *leprosy*; the Hebrew word was used for various diseases affecting the skin—not necessarily leprosy.   [b] 6 Or *woman commits any wrong common to mankind*

impure— ¹⁵then he is to take his wife to the priest. He must also take an offering of a tenth of an ephah*a* of barley flour on her behalf. He must not pour oil on it or put incense on it, because it is a grain offering for jealousy, a reminder offering to draw attention to guilt.

¹⁶" 'The priest shall bring her and have her stand before the LORD. ¹⁷Then he shall take some holy water in a clay jar and put some dust from the tabernacle floor into the water. ¹⁸After the priest has had the woman stand before the LORD, he shall loosen her hair and place in her hands the reminder offering, the grain offering for jealousy, while he himself holds the bitter water that brings a curse. ¹⁹Then the priest shall put the woman under oath and say to her, "If no other man has slept with you and you have not gone astray and become impure while married to your husband, may this bitter water that brings a curse not harm you. ²⁰But if you have gone astray while married to your husband and you have defiled yourself by sleeping with a man other than your husband"— ²¹here the priest is to put the woman under this curse of the oath—"may the LORD cause your people to curse and denounce you when he causes your thigh to waste away and your abdomen to swell.*b* ²²May this water that brings a curse enter your body so that your abdomen swells and your thigh wastes away.*c*"

" 'Then the woman is to say, "Amen. So be it."

²³" 'The priest is to write these curses on a scroll and then wash them off into the bitter water. ²⁴He shall have the woman drink the bitter water that brings a curse, and this water will enter her and cause bitter suffering. ²⁵The priest is to take from her hands the grain offering for jealousy, wave it before the LORD and bring it to the altar. ²⁶The priest is then to take a handful of the grain offering as a memorial offering and burn it on the altar; after that, he is to have the woman drink the water. ²⁷If she has defiled herself and been unfaithful to her husband, then when she is made to drink the water that brings a curse, it will go into her and cause bitter suffering; her abdomen will swell and her thigh waste away,*d* and she will become accursed among her people. ²⁸If, however, the woman has not defiled herself and is free from impurity, she will be cleared of guilt and will be able to have children.

²⁹" 'This, then, is the law of jealousy when a woman goes astray and defiles herself while married to her husband, ³⁰or when feelings of jealousy come over a man because he suspects his wife. The priest is to have her stand before the LORD and is to apply this entire law to her. ³¹The husband will be innocent of any wrongdoing, but the woman will bear the consequences of her sin.' "

The Nazirite

6 The LORD said to Moses, ²"Speak to the Israelites and say to them: 'If a man or woman wants to make a special vow, a vow of separation to the LORD as a Nazirite, ³he must abstain from wine and other fermented drink and must not drink vinegar made from wine or from other fermented drink. He must not drink grape juice or eat grapes

---

Broken Threads

NUMBERS 5:5–15

God's rules about their life together protected the Israelites and reinforced the importance of community.

God's Word indicates to us that what we do affects others (see Romans 12:5–21; Ephesians 2:19–22). Our relationships with God and with other people are part of a single piece of fabric. Pick up a piece of fabric and examine it. What would happen if you broke some threads? What happens if several threads are cut or torn? Now turn your mind to the fabric of relationships in your life. Are there torn places? Are the edges fraying? Picture yourself going to someone with whom you have some difficulty. What do you need to say? What do you need to do?

See *Meeting God in Community*

---

a 15 That is, probably about 2 quarts (about 2 liters)   *b 21* Or *causes you to have a miscarrying womb and barrenness*   *c 22* Or *body and cause you to be barren and have a miscarrying womb*   *d 27* Or *suffering; she will have barrenness and a miscarrying womb*

Vows and Gestures

NUMBERS 6:1–8

Some people make special commitments to God to live by particular disciplines. They may engage in special activities such as daily, structured times of prayer or Bible reading. Or they may abstain from food or from some activity. Nazirites neither cut their hair nor ate or drank any product of the vine. What marks you as someone who serves God? What is the evidence in your life that proves you a believer? What value do you see in special vows?

or raisins. ⁴As long as he is a Nazirite, he must not eat anything that comes from the grapevine, not even the seeds or skins.

⁵" 'During the entire period of his vow of separation no razor may be used on his head. He must be holy until the period of his separation to the LORD is over; he must let the hair of his head grow long. ⁶Throughout the period of his separation to the LORD he must not go near a dead body. ⁷Even if his own father or mother or brother or sister dies, he must not make himself ceremonially unclean on account of them, because the symbol of his separation to God is on his head. ⁸Throughout the period of his separation he is consecrated to the LORD.

⁹" 'If someone dies suddenly in his presence, thus defiling the hair he has dedicated, he must shave his head on the day of his cleansing—the seventh day. ¹⁰Then on the eighth day he must bring two doves or two young pigeons to the priest at the entrance to the Tent of Meeting. ¹¹The priest is to offer one as a sin offering and the other as a burnt offering to make atonement for him because he sinned by being in the presence of the dead body. That same day he is to consecrate his head. ¹²He must dedicate himself to the LORD for the period of his separation and must bring a year-old male lamb as a guilt offering. The previous days do not count, because he became defiled during his separation.

¹³" 'Now this is the law for the Nazirite when the period of his separation is over. He is to be brought to the entrance to the Tent of Meeting. ¹⁴There he is to present his offerings to the LORD: a year-old male lamb without defect for a burnt offering, a year-old ewe lamb without defect for a sin offering, a ram without defect for a fellowship offering,ᵃ ¹⁵together with their grain offerings and drink offerings, and a basket of bread made without yeast—cakes made of fine flour mixed with oil, and wafers spread with oil.

¹⁶" 'The priest is to present them before the LORD and make the sin offering and the burnt offering. ¹⁷He is to present the basket of unleavened bread and is to sacrifice the ram as a fellowship offering to the LORD, together with its grain offering and drink offering.

¹⁸" 'Then at the entrance to the Tent of Meeting, the Nazirite must shave off the hair that he dedicated. He is to take the hair and put it in the fire that is under the sacrifice of the fellowship offering.

¹⁹" 'After the Nazirite has shaved off the hair of his dedication, the priest is to place in his hands a boiled shoulder of the ram, and a cake and a wafer from the basket, both made without yeast. ²⁰The priest shall then wave them before the LORD as a wave offering; they are holy and belong to the priest, together with the breast that was waved and the thigh that was presented. After that, the Nazirite may drink wine.

²¹" 'This is the law of the Nazirite who vows his offering to the LORD in accordance with his separation, in addition to whatever else he can afford. He must fulfill the vow he has made, according to the law of the Nazirite.' "

ᵃ 14 Traditionally *peace offering*; also in verses 17 and 18

The Priestly Blessing

²²The LORD said to Moses, ²³"Tell Aaron and his sons, 'This is how you are to bless the Israelites. Say to them:

²⁴" ' "The LORD bless you
and keep you;
²⁵the LORD make his face shine upon you
and be gracious to you;
²⁶the LORD turn his face toward you
and give you peace." '

²⁷"So they will put my name on the Israelites, and I will bless them."

Offerings at the Dedication of the Tabernacle

7 When Moses finished setting up the tabernacle, he anointed it and consecrated it and all its furnishings. He also anointed and consecrated the altar and all its utensils. ²Then the leaders of Israel, the heads of families who were the tribal leaders in charge of those who were counted, made offerings. ³They brought as their gifts before the LORD six covered carts and twelve oxen—an ox from each leader and a cart from every two. These they presented before the tabernacle.

⁴The LORD said to Moses, ⁵"Accept these from them, that they may be used in the work at the Tent of Meeting. Give them to the Levites as each man's work requires."

⁶So Moses took the carts and oxen and gave them to the Levites. ⁷He gave two carts and four oxen to the Gershonites, as their work required, ⁸and he gave four carts and eight oxen to the Merarites, as their work required. They were all under the direction of Ithamar son of Aaron, the priest. ⁹But Moses did not give any to the Kohathites, because they were to carry on their shoulders the holy things, for which they were responsible.

¹⁰When the altar was anointed, the leaders brought their offerings for its dedication and presented them before the altar. ¹¹For the LORD had said to Moses, "Each day one leader is to bring his offering for the dedication of the altar."

¹²The one who brought his offering on the first day was Nahshon son of Amminadab of the tribe of Judah.

¹³His offering was one silver plate weighing a hundred and thirty shekels,ᵃ and one silver sprinkling bowl weighing seventy shekels,ᵇ both according to the sanctuary shekel, each filled with fine flour mixed with oil as a grain offering; ¹⁴one gold dish weighing ten shekels,ᶜ filled with incense; ¹⁵one young bull, one ram and one male lamb a year old, for a burnt offering; ¹⁶one male goat for a sin offering; ¹⁷and two oxen, five rams, five male goats and five male lambs a year old, to be sacrificed as a fellowship offering.ᵈ This was the offering of Nahshon son of Amminadab.

¹⁸On the second day Nethanel son of Zuar, the leader of Issachar, brought his offering.

ᵃ *13* That is, about 3 1/4 pounds (about 1.5 kilograms); also elsewhere in this chapter   ᵇ *13* That is, about 1 3/4 pounds (about 0.8 kilogram); also elsewhere in this chapter   ᶜ *14* That is, about 4 ounces (about 110 grams); also elsewhere in this chapter   ᵈ *17* Traditionally *peace offering*; also elsewhere in this chapter

The Power to Bless

NUMBERS 6:22–27

Blessing another in the name of God is a powerful act. Bidding God's face to "shine upon" someone is asking God to turn toward them and work for their good. When we "put [God's] name on" someone, we do something important. Think of those you know who need God's help. In your mind, envision God's power surrounding them. Hold them in the light that shines from God's face. Bless them in the name of God.

See Meeting God in Prayer

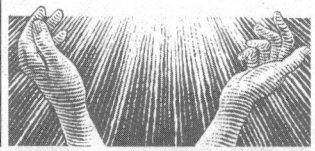

Ordinary Gifts

NUMBERS 7:23,29,35,41,47

The fellowship offering signifies thanksgiving for the day-by-day sustenance God provides. We too can mark our gratitude daily for God's ordinary gifts. Practices such as giving thanks at mealtime, praying for those we love, and keeping a journal record of where we see God at work can become our "fellowship offering." What are you grateful for? What "ordinary" gifts from God make your life better, day by day? How does your gratitude show in your words and actions?

See Meeting God in Everyday Life

¹⁹The offering he brought was one silver plate weighing a hundred and thirty shekels, and one silver sprinkling bowl weighing seventy shekels, both according to the sanctuary shekel, each filled with fine flour mixed with oil as a grain offering; ²⁰one gold dish weighing ten shekels, filled with incense; ²¹one young bull, one ram and one male lamb a year old, for a burnt offering; ²²one male goat for a sin offering; ²³and two oxen, five rams, five male goats and five male lambs a year old, to be sacrificed as a fellowship offering. This was the offering of Nethanel son of Zuar.

²⁴On the third day, Eliab son of Helon, the leader of the people of Zebulun, brought his offering.
²⁵His offering was one silver plate weighing a hundred and thirty shekels, and one silver sprinkling bowl weighing seventy shekels, both according to the sanctuary shekel, each filled with fine flour mixed with oil as a grain offering; ²⁶one gold dish weighing ten shekels, filled with incense; ²⁷one young bull, one ram and one male lamb a year old, for a burnt offering; ²⁸one male goat for a sin offering; ²⁹and two oxen, five rams, five male goats and five male lambs a year old, to be sacrificed as a fellowship offering. This was the offering of Eliab son of Helon.

³⁰On the fourth day Elizur son of Shedeur, the leader of the people of Reuben, brought his offering.
³¹His offering was one silver plate weighing a hundred and thirty shekels, and one silver sprinkling bowl weighing seventy shekels, both according to the sanctuary shekel, each filled with fine flour mixed with oil as a grain offering; ³²one gold dish weighing ten shekels, filled with incense; ³³one young bull, one ram and one male lamb a year old, for a burnt offering; ³⁴one male goat for a sin offering; ³⁵and two oxen, five rams, five male goats and five male lambs a year old, to be sacrificed as a fellowship offering. This was the offering of Elizur son of Shedeur.

³⁶On the fifth day Shelumiel son of Zurishaddai, the leader of the people of Simeon, brought his offering.
³⁷His offering was one silver plate weighing a hundred and thirty shekels, and one silver sprinkling bowl weighing seventy shekels, both according to the sanctuary shekel, each filled with fine flour mixed with oil as a grain offering; ³⁸one gold dish weighing ten shekels, filled with incense; ³⁹one young bull, one ram and one male lamb a year old, for a burnt offering; ⁴⁰one male goat for a sin offering; ⁴¹and two oxen, five rams, five male goats and five male lambs a year old, to be sacrificed as a fellowship offering. This was the offering of Shelumiel son of Zurishaddai.

⁴²On the sixth day Eliasaph son of Deuel, the leader of the people of Gad, brought his offering.
⁴³His offering was one silver plate weighing a hundred and thirty shekels, and one silver sprinkling bowl weighing seventy shekels, both according to the sanctuary shekel, each filled with fine flour mixed with oil as a grain offering; ⁴⁴one gold dish weighing ten shekels, filled with incense; ⁴⁵one young bull, one ram

and one male lamb a year old, for a burnt offering; ⁴⁶one male goat for a sin offering; ⁴⁷and two oxen, five rams, five male goats and five male lambs a year old, to be sacrificed as a fellowship offering. This was the offering of Eliasaph son of Deuel.

⁴⁸On the seventh day Elishama son of Ammihud, the leader of the people of Ephraim, brought his offering.

⁴⁹His offering was one silver plate weighing a hundred and thirty shekels, and one silver sprinkling bowl weighing seventy shekels, both according to the sanctuary shekel, each filled with fine flour mixed with oil as a grain offering; ⁵⁰one gold dish weighing ten shekels, filled with incense; ⁵¹one young bull, one ram and one male lamb a year old, for a burnt offering; ⁵²one male goat for a sin offering; ⁵³and two oxen, five rams, five male goats and five male lambs a year old, to be sacrificed as a fellowship offering. This was the offering of Elishama son of Ammihud.

⁵⁴On the eighth day Gamaliel son of Pedahzur, the leader of the people of Manasseh, brought his offering.

⁵⁵His offering was one silver plate weighing a hundred and thirty shekels, and one silver sprinkling bowl weighing seventy shekels, both according to the sanctuary shekel, each filled with fine flour mixed with oil as a grain offering; ⁵⁶one gold dish weighing ten shekels, filled with incense; ⁵⁷one young bull, one ram and one male lamb a year old, for a burnt offering; ⁵⁸one male goat for a sin offering; ⁵⁹and two oxen, five rams, five male goats and five male lambs a year old, to be sacrificed as a fellowship offering. This was the offering of Gamaliel son of Pedahzur.

⁶⁰On the ninth day Abidan son of Gideoni, the leader of the people of Benjamin, brought his offering.

⁶¹His offering was one silver plate weighing a hundred and thirty shekels, and one silver sprinkling bowl weighing seventy shekels, both according to the sanctuary shekel, each filled with fine flour mixed with oil as a grain offering; ⁶²one gold dish weighing ten shekels, filled with incense; ⁶³one young bull, one ram and one male lamb a year old, for a burnt offering; ⁶⁴one male goat for a sin offering; ⁶⁵and two oxen, five rams, five male goats and five male lambs a year old, to be sacrificed as a fellowship offering. This was the offering of Abidan son of Gideoni.

⁶⁶On the tenth day Ahiezer son of Ammishaddai, the leader of the people of Dan, brought his offering.

⁶⁷His offering was one silver plate weighing a hundred and thirty shekels, and one silver sprinkling bowl weighing seventy shekels, both according to the sanctuary shekel, each filled with fine flour mixed with oil as a grain offering; ⁶⁸one gold dish weighing ten shekels, filled with incense; ⁶⁹one young bull, one ram and one male lamb a year old, for a burnt offering; ⁷⁰one male goat for a sin offering; ⁷¹and two oxen, five rams, five male goats and five male lambs a year old, to be sacrificed as a fellowship offering. This was the offering of Ahiezer son of Ammishaddai.

Majestic Procession

NUMBERS 7:12–83

The measured cadence of this account suggests the magnificence of the ceremony of the dedication of the altar. Envision yourself among the watchers as each leader brings the tribe's finest goods in offering. See the sheen of the gold and silver and fine clothing you have helped carry from Egypt. Sense the air of celebration and excitement building more and more each day. With Moses' blessing from God echoing in your heart (vv. 24–26), feel the anticipation as the altar is readied for the presence of the Lord. What is happening within you?

See Meeting God in Scripture

A Place to Meet God

NUMBERS 7:89

After many days of setting up, anointing and preparing the altar and the Tent of Meeting with the finest the tribes had to offer, the climactic moment arrives. Moses enters the Tent of Meeting and hears the voice of God. "And he spoke with him."

Where do you speak with the Lord? Do you have a special place reserved for prayer and reflection? Consider clearing a corner of your house or apartment for just this holy use. Furnish it with objects that represent the finest things you own—a beautiful candle, flowers, a picture, a lovely tablecloth. Find time every day to go to your special place to listen to God.

See *Meeting God in Worship*

72On the eleventh day Pagiel son of Ocran, the leader of the people of Asher, brought his offering. 73His offering was one silver plate weighing a hundred and thirty shekels, and one silver sprinkling bowl weighing seventy shekels, both according to the sanctuary shekel, each filled with fine flour mixed with oil as a grain offering; 74one gold dish weighing ten shekels, filled with incense; 75one young bull, one ram and one male lamb a year old, for a burnt offering; 76one male goat for a sin offering; 77and two oxen, five rams, five male goats and five male lambs a year old, to be sacrificed as a fellowship offering. This was the offering of Pagiel son of Ocran.

78On the twelfth day Ahira son of Enan, the leader of the people of Naphtali, brought his offering. 79His offering was one silver plate weighing a hundred and thirty shekels, and one silver sprinkling bowl weighing seventy shekels, both according to the sanctuary shekel, each filled with fine flour mixed with oil as a grain offering; 80one gold dish weighing ten shekels, filled with incense; 81one young bull, one ram and one male lamb a year old, for a burnt offering; 82one male goat for a sin offering; 83and two oxen, five rams, five male goats and five male lambs a year old, to be sacrificed as a fellowship offering. This was the offering of Ahira son of Enan.

84These were the offerings of the Israelite leaders for the dedication of the altar when it was anointed: twelve silver plates, twelve silver sprinkling bowls and twelve gold dishes. 85Each silver plate weighed a hundred and thirty shekels, and each sprinkling bowl seventy shekels. Altogether, the silver dishes weighed two thousand four hundred shekels,*a* according to the sanctuary shekel. 86The twelve gold dishes filled with incense weighed ten shekels each, according to the sanctuary shekel. Altogether, the gold dishes weighed a hundred and twenty shekels.*b* 87The total number of animals for the burnt offering came to twelve young bulls, twelve rams and twelve male lambs a year old, together with their grain offering. Twelve male goats were used for the sin offering. 88The total number of animals for the sacrifice of the fellowship offering came to twenty-four oxen, sixty rams, sixty male goats and sixty male lambs a year old. These were the offerings for the dedication of the altar after it was anointed.

89When Moses entered the Tent of Meeting to speak with the Lord, he heard the voice speaking to him from between the two cherubim above the atonement cover on the ark of the Testimony. And he spoke with him.

Setting Up the Lamps

8 The Lord said to Moses, 2"Speak to Aaron and say to him, 'When you set up the seven lamps, they are to light the area in front of the lampstand.' "

3Aaron did so; he set up the lamps so that they faced forward on the lampstand, just as the Lord commanded Moses. 4This is how the lampstand was made: It was made of hammered gold—from its base to its blossoms. The

a 85 That is, about 60 pounds (about 28 kilograms)   *b 86* That is, about 3 pounds (about 1.4 kilograms)

lampstand was made exactly like the pattern the LORD had shown Moses.

The Setting Apart of the Levites

⁵The LORD said to Moses: ⁶"Take the Levites from among the other Israelites and make them ceremonially clean. ⁷To purify them, do this: Sprinkle the water of cleansing on them; then have them shave their whole bodies and wash their clothes, and so purify themselves. ⁸Have them take a young bull with its grain offering of fine flour mixed with oil; then you are to take a second young bull for a sin offering. ⁹Bring the Levites to the front of the Tent of Meeting and assemble the whole Israelite community. ¹⁰You are to bring the Levites before the LORD, and the Israelites are to lay their hands on them. ¹¹Aaron is to present the Levites before the LORD as a wave offering from the Israelites, so that they may be ready to do the work of the LORD.

¹²"After the Levites lay their hands on the heads of the bulls, use the one for a sin offering to the LORD and the other for a burnt offering, to make atonement for the Levites. ¹³Have the Levites stand in front of Aaron and his sons and then present them as a wave offering to the LORD. ¹⁴In this way you are to set the Levites apart from the other Israelites, and the Levites will be mine.

¹⁵"After you have purified the Levites and presented them as a wave offering, they are to come to do their work at the Tent of Meeting. ¹⁶They are the Israelites who are to be given wholly to me. I have taken them as my own in place of the firstborn, the first male offspring from every Israelite woman. ¹⁷Every firstborn male in Israel, whether man or animal, is mine. When I struck down all the firstborn in Egypt, I set them apart for myself. ¹⁸And I have taken the Levites in place of all the firstborn sons in Israel. ¹⁹Of all the Israelites, I have given the Levites as gifts to Aaron and his sons to do the work at the Tent of Meeting on behalf of the Israelites and to make atonement for them so that no plague will strike the Israelites when they go near the sanctuary."

²⁰Moses, Aaron and the whole Israelite community did with the Levites just as the LORD commanded Moses. ²¹The Levites purified themselves and washed their clothes. Then Aaron presented them as a wave offering before the LORD and made atonement for them to purify them. ²²After that, the Levites came to do their work at the Tent of Meeting under the supervision of Aaron and his sons. They did with the Levites just as the LORD commanded Moses.

²³The LORD said to Moses, ²⁴"This applies to the Levites: Men twenty-five years old or more shall come to take part in the work at the Tent of Meeting, ²⁵but at the age of fifty, they must retire from their regular service and work no longer. ²⁶They may assist their brothers in performing their duties at the Tent of Meeting, but they themselves must not do the work. This, then, is how you are to assign the responsibilities of the Levites."

The Passover

9 The LORD spoke to Moses in the Desert of Sinai in the first month of the second year after they came out of Egypt. He said, ²"Have the Israelites celebrate the Passover at the appointed time. ³Celebrate it at the appointed time,

Time to Remember

NUMBERS 9:1–2

Even though the people are in the desert, they are to keep the Passover as a reminder of what God has done for them.

When you are in a "desert"—a spiritually dry place—what practices keep you in touch with God? Can you think of a practice such as attending worship, reading the Bible, writing in your journal, receiving Holy Communion, or some other discipline that may have begun as a duty but has become a window to God's grace? Make work of learning about one new regular discipline you may not have tried before.

See *Meeting God in Worship*

Traffic Control

NUMBERS 9:15–18

The Israelites are visibly directed by God regarding when to move and when to stay put. God's directions to us are seldom this dramatic and clear, yet most of us feel that God does guide us. How does God's guidance usually come to you? Does it come as an inner nudge? As an idea? Through reading or remembering Scripture? Look around you and consider through whom or through what circumstances God may be speaking to you today.

See Meeting God in Prayer

at twilight on the fourteenth day of this month, in accordance with all its rules and regulations."

⁴So Moses told the Israelites to celebrate the Passover, ⁵and they did so in the Desert of Sinai at twilight on the fourteenth day of the first month. The Israelites did everything just as the LORD commanded Moses.

⁶But some of them could not celebrate the Passover on that day because they were ceremonially unclean on account of a dead body. So they came to Moses and Aaron that same day ⁷and said to Moses, "We have become unclean because of a dead body, but why should we be kept from presenting the LORD's offering with the other Israelites at the appointed time?"

⁸Moses answered them, "Wait until I find out what the LORD commands concerning you."

⁹Then the LORD said to Moses, ¹⁰"Tell the Israelites: 'When any of you or your descendants are unclean because of a dead body or are away on a journey, they may still celebrate the LORD's Passover. ¹¹They are to celebrate it on the fourteenth day of the second month at twilight. They are to eat the lamb, together with unleavened bread and bitter herbs. ¹²They must not leave any of it till morning or break any of its bones. When they celebrate the Passover, they must follow all the regulations. ¹³But if a man who is ceremonially clean and not on a journey fails to celebrate the Passover, that person must be cut off from his people because he did not present the LORD's offering at the appointed time. That man will bear the consequences of his sin.

¹⁴"'An alien living among you who wants to celebrate the LORD's Passover must do so in accordance with its rules and regulations. You must have the same regulations for the alien and the native-born.'"

The Cloud Above the Tabernacle

¹⁵On the day the tabernacle, the Tent of the Testimony, was set up, the cloud covered it. From evening till morning the cloud above the tabernacle looked like fire. ¹⁶That is how it continued to be; the cloud covered it, and at night it looked like fire. ¹⁷Whenever the cloud lifted from above the Tent, the Israelites set out; wherever the cloud settled, the Israelites encamped. ¹⁸At the LORD's command the Israelites set out, and at his command they encamped. As long as the cloud stayed over the tabernacle, they remained in camp. ¹⁹When the cloud remained over the tabernacle a long time, the Israelites obeyed the LORD's order and did not set out. ²⁰Sometimes the cloud was over the tabernacle only a few days; at the LORD's command they would encamp, and then at his command they would set out. ²¹Sometimes the cloud stayed only from evening till morning, and when it lifted in the morning, they set out. Whether by day or by night, whenever the cloud lifted, they set out. ²²Whether the cloud stayed over the tabernacle for two days or a month or a year, the Israelites would remain in camp and not set out; but when it lifted, they would set out. ²³At the LORD's command they encamped, and at the LORD's command they set out. They obeyed the LORD's order, in accordance with his command through Moses.

The Silver Trumpets

10 The LORD said to Moses: ²"Make two trumpets of hammered silver, and use them for calling the community together and for having the camps set out. ³When both are sounded, the whole community is to assemble before you at the entrance to the Tent of Meeting. ⁴If only one is sounded, the leaders—the heads of the clans of Israel—are to assemble before you. ⁵When a trumpet blast is sounded, the tribes camping on the east are to set out. ⁶At the sounding of a second blast, the camps on the south are to set out. The blast will be the signal for setting out. ⁷To gather the assembly, blow the trumpets, but not with the same signal.

⁸"The sons of Aaron, the priests, are to blow the trumpets. This is to be a lasting ordinance for you and the generations to come. ⁹When you go into battle in your own land against an enemy who is oppressing you, sound a blast on the trumpets. Then you will be remembered by the LORD your God and rescued from your enemies. ¹⁰Also at your times of rejoicing—your appointed feasts and New Moon festivals—you are to sound the trumpets over your burnt offerings and fellowship offerings,ᵃ and they will be a memorial for you before your God. I am the LORD your God."

The Israelites Leave Sinai

¹¹On the twentieth day of the second month of the second year, the cloud lifted from above the tabernacle of the Testimony. ¹²Then the Israelites set out from the Desert of Sinai and traveled from place to place until the cloud came to rest in the Desert of Paran. ¹³They set out, this first time, at the LORD's command through Moses.

¹⁴The divisions of the camp of Judah went first, under their standard. Nahshon son of Amminadab was in command. ¹⁵Nethanel son of Zuar was over the division of the tribe of Issachar, ¹⁶and Eliab son of Helon was over the division of the tribe of Zebulun. ¹⁷Then the tabernacle was taken down, and the Gershonites and Merarites, who carried it, set out.

¹⁸The divisions of the camp of Reuben went next, under their standard. Elizur son of Shedeur was in command. ¹⁹Shelumiel son of Zurishaddai was over the division of the tribe of Simeon, ²⁰and Eliasaph son of Deuel was over the division of the tribe of Gad. ²¹Then the Kohathites set out, carrying the holy things. The tabernacle was to be set up before they arrived.

²²The divisions of the camp of Ephraim went next, under their standard. Elishama son of Ammihud was in command. ²³Gamaliel son of Pedahzur was over the division of the tribe of Manasseh, ²⁴and Abidan son of Gideoni was over the division of the tribe of Benjamin. ²⁵Finally, as the rear guard for all the units, the divisions of the camp of Dan set out, under their standard. Ahiezer son of Ammishaddai was in command. ²⁶Pagiel son of Ocran was over the division of the tribe of Asher, ²⁷and Ahira son of Enan was over the division of the tribe of Naphtali. ²⁸This was the order of march for the Israelite divisions as they set out.

Desert, Mountains, Plain?

NUMBERS 10:12

Look back over your life. Consider your spiritual journey and the terrain through which you have passed. Close your eyes and consider the terrain of your life right now. What picture comes to mind? Are you in a desert? Are you camping at an oasis, a place of refreshment? Are you living in a fruitful plain and enjoying its abundance? Are you struggling to scale mountains? Are you living in the middle of a bustling city? Through what people and experiences is God present for you in your situation? Give thanks for the ways God has been with you in those places and is with you now.

ᵃ 10 Traditionally *peace offerings*

An Experienced Guide

NUMBERS 10:29–32

We know people like Hobab—those who know "the lay of the land" and can guide us. Who functions in your life as a spiritual guide? Who has helped you in the past to see important things and to find your way through difficulties?

We can also be like Hobab for others. What help can you offer someone you know who is going through spiritual, emotional or vocational terrain with which you are familiar?

See Meeting God in Community

29 Now Moses said to Hobab son of Reuel the Midianite, Moses' father-in-law, "We are setting out for the place about which the LORD said, 'I will give it to you.' Come with us and we will treat you well, for the LORD has promised good things to Israel."

30 He answered, "No, I will not go; I am going back to my own land and my own people."

31 But Moses said, "Please do not leave us. You know where we should camp in the desert, and you can be our eyes. 32 If you come with us, we will share with you whatever good things the LORD gives us."

33 So they set out from the mountain of the LORD and traveled for three days. The ark of the covenant of the LORD went before them during those three days to find them a place to rest. 34 The cloud of the LORD was over them by day when they set out from the camp.

35 Whenever the ark set out, Moses said,

"Rise up, O LORD!
May your enemies be scattered;
may your foes flee before you."

36 Whenever it came to rest, he said,

"Return, O LORD,
to the countless thousands of Israel."

Fire From the LORD

11 Now the people complained about their hardships in the hearing of the LORD, and when he heard them his anger was aroused. Then fire from the LORD burned among them and consumed some of the outskirts of the camp. 2 When the people cried out to Moses, he prayed to the LORD and the fire died down. 3 So that place was called Taberah,*a* because fire from the LORD had burned among them.

Quail From the LORD

4 The rabble with them began to crave other food, and again the Israelites started wailing and said, "If only we had meat to eat! 5 We remember the fish we ate in Egypt at no cost—also the cucumbers, melons, leeks, onions and garlic. 6 But now we have lost our appetite; we never see anything but this manna!"

7 The manna was like coriander seed and looked like resin. 8 The people went around gathering it, and then ground it in a handmill or crushed it in a mortar. They cooked it in a pot or made it into cakes. And it tasted like something made with olive oil. 9 When the dew settled on the camp at night, the manna also came down.

10 Moses heard the people of every family wailing, each at the entrance to his tent. The LORD became exceedingly angry, and Moses was troubled. 11 He asked the LORD, "Why have you brought this trouble on your servant? What have I done to displease you that you put the burden of all these people on me? 12 Did I conceive all these people? Did I give them birth? Why do you tell me to carry them in my arms, as a nurse carries an infant, to the land you promised on oath to their forefathers? 13 Where can I get meat for all these people? They keep wailing to me, 'Give us meat to

a 3 Taberah means burning.

eat!' ¹⁴I cannot carry all these people by myself; the burden is too heavy for me. ¹⁵If this is how you are going to treat me, put me to death right now—if I have found favor in your eyes—and do not let me face my own ruin."

¹⁶The LORD said to Moses: "Bring me seventy of Israel's elders who are known to you as leaders and officials among the people. Have them come to the Tent of Meeting, that they may stand there with you. ¹⁷I will come down and speak with you there, and I will take of the Spirit that is on you and put the Spirit on them. They will help you carry the burden of the people so that you will not have to carry it alone.

¹⁸"Tell the people: 'Consecrate yourselves in preparation for tomorrow, when you will eat meat. The LORD heard you when you wailed, "If only we had meat to eat! We were better off in Egypt!" Now the LORD will give you meat, and you will eat it. ¹⁹You will not eat it for just one day, or two days, or five, ten or twenty days, ²⁰but for a whole month—until it comes out of your nostrils and you loathe it—because you have rejected the LORD, who is among you, and have wailed before him, saying, "Why did we ever leave Egypt?" ' "

²¹But Moses said, "Here I am among six hundred thousand men on foot, and you say, 'I will give them meat to eat for a whole month!' ²²Would they have enough if flocks and herds were slaughtered for them? Would they have enough if all the fish in the sea were caught for them?"

²³The LORD answered Moses, "Is the LORD's arm too short? You will now see whether or not what I say will come true for you."

²⁴So Moses went out and told the people what the LORD had said. He brought together seventy of their elders and had them stand around the Tent. ²⁵Then the LORD came down in the cloud and spoke with him, and he took of the Spirit that was on him and put the Spirit on the seventy elders. When the Spirit rested on them, they prophesied, but they did not do so again.ᵃ

²⁶However, two men, whose names were Eldad and Medad, had remained in the camp. They were listed among the elders, but did not go out to the Tent. Yet the Spirit also rested on them, and they prophesied in the camp. ²⁷A young man ran and told Moses, "Eldad and Medad are prophesying in the camp."

²⁸Joshua son of Nun, who had been Moses' aide since youth, spoke up and said, "Moses, my lord, stop them!"

²⁹But Moses replied, "Are you jealous for my sake? I wish that all the LORD's people were prophets and that the LORD would put his Spirit on them!" ³⁰Then Moses and the elders of Israel returned to the camp.

³¹Now a wind went out from the LORD and drove quail in from the sea. It brought themᵇ down all around the camp to about three feetᶜ above the ground, as far as a day's walk in any direction. ³²All that day and night and all the next day the people went out and gathered quail. No one gathered less than ten homers.ᵈ Then they spread them out all around the camp. ³³But while the meat was still between their teeth and before it could be consumed, the anger of

A Weary Leader

NUMBERS 11:10–17

Moses was so overwhelmed by the task of leading the people that he asked God to put him to death. God's solution was less spectacular but considerably healthier. God told Moses to gather helpers.

Our leaders are often overworked, and they often feel unappreciated. Pray for the leaders in your community, both the public leaders and those who work behind the scenes. In addition to praying for them, consider what else you can do to lighten their load.

See Meeting God in Community

ᵃ 25 Or *prophesied and continued to do so*   ᵇ 31 Or *They flew*   ᶜ 31 Hebrew *two cubits* (about 1 meter)   ᵈ 32 That is, probably about 60 bushels (about 2.2 kiloliters)

Open Rebellion

NUMBERS 12:1–13

Aaron and Miriam rebel against Moses' leadership. They are jealous of his close relationship with God and criticize him. Yet when Miriam is stricken with leprosy Moses prays fervently for her healing.

Imagine yourself in Moses' shoes, facing two people who oppose you. What emotions do you experience? What do you want to do? Do you respond with compassion? What resources help you do so? How can you draw on these resources when coping with some difficult relationship you are facing now?

See Meeting God in Community

the LORD burned against the people, and he struck them with a severe plague. ³⁴Therefore the place was named Kibroth Hattaavah,^a because there they buried the people who had craved other food.

³⁵From Kibroth Hattaavah the people traveled to Hazeroth and stayed there.

Miriam and Aaron Oppose Moses

12 Miriam and Aaron began to talk against Moses because of his Cushite wife, for he had married a Cushite. ²"Has the LORD spoken only through Moses?" they asked. "Hasn't he also spoken through us?" And the LORD heard this.

³(Now Moses was a very humble man, more humble than anyone else on the face of the earth.)

⁴At once the LORD said to Moses, Aaron and Miriam, "Come out to the Tent of Meeting, all three of you." So the three of them came out. ⁵Then the LORD came down in a pillar of cloud; he stood at the entrance to the Tent and summoned Aaron and Miriam. When both of them stepped forward, ⁶he said, "Listen to my words:

"When a prophet of the LORD is among you,
  I reveal myself to him in visions,
  I speak to him in dreams.
⁷But this is not true of my servant Moses;
  he is faithful in all my house.
⁸With him I speak face to face,
  clearly and not in riddles;
  he sees the form of the LORD.
Why then were you not afraid
  to speak against my servant Moses?"

⁹The anger of the LORD burned against them, and he left them.

¹⁰When the cloud lifted from above the Tent, there stood Miriam—leprous,^b like snow. Aaron turned toward her and saw that she had leprosy; ¹¹and he said to Moses, "Please, my lord, do not hold against us the sin we have so foolishly committed. ¹²Do not let her be like a stillborn infant coming from its mother's womb with its flesh half eaten away."

¹³So Moses cried out to the LORD, "O God, please heal her!"

¹⁴The LORD replied to Moses, "If her father had spit in her face, would she not have been in disgrace for seven days? Confine her outside the camp for seven days; after that she can be brought back." ¹⁵So Miriam was confined outside the camp for seven days, and the people did not move on till she was brought back.

¹⁶After that, the people left Hazeroth and encamped in the Desert of Paran.

Exploring Canaan

13 The LORD said to Moses, ²"Send some men to explore the land of Canaan, which I am giving to the Israelites. From each ancestral tribe send one of its leaders."

³So at the LORD's command Moses sent them out from

^a *34 Kibroth Hattaavah* means *graves of craving.*   ^b *10* The Hebrew word was used for various diseases affecting the skin—not necessarily leprosy.

the Desert of Paran. All of them were leaders of the Israelites. ⁴These are their names:

from the tribe of Reuben, Shammua son of Zaccur;
⁵from the tribe of Simeon, Shaphat son of Hori;
⁶from the tribe of Judah, Caleb son of Jephunneh;
⁷from the tribe of Issachar, Igal son of Joseph;
⁸from the tribe of Ephraim, Hoshea son of Nun;
⁹from the tribe of Benjamin, Palti son of Raphu;
¹⁰from the tribe of Zebulun, Gaddiel son of Sodi;
¹¹from the tribe of Manasseh (a tribe of Joseph), Gaddi son of Susi;
¹²from the tribe of Dan, Ammiel son of Gemalli;
¹³from the tribe of Asher, Sethur son of Michael;
¹⁴from the tribe of Naphtali, Nahbi son of Vophsi;
¹⁵from the tribe of Gad, Geuel son of Maki.

¹⁶These are the names of the men Moses sent to explore the land. (Moses gave Hoshea son of Nun the name Joshua.)

¹⁷When Moses sent them to explore Canaan, he said, "Go up through the Negev and on into the hill country. ¹⁸See what the land is like and whether the people who live there are strong or weak, few or many. ¹⁹What kind of land do they live in? Is it good or bad? What kind of towns do they live in? Are they unwalled or fortified? ²⁰How is the soil? Is it fertile or poor? Are there trees on it or not? Do your best to bring back some of the fruit of the land." (It was the season for the first ripe grapes.)

²¹So they went up and explored the land from the Desert of Zin as far as Rehob, toward Lebo^a Hamath. ²²They went up through the Negev and came to Hebron, where Ahiman, Sheshai and Talmai, the descendants of Anak, lived. (Hebron had been built seven years before Zoan in Egypt.) ²³When they reached the Valley of Eshcol,^b they cut off a branch bearing a single cluster of grapes. Two of them carried it on a pole between them, along with some pomegranates and figs. ²⁴That place was called the Valley of Eshcol because of the cluster of grapes the Israelites cut off there. ²⁵At the end of forty days they returned from exploring the land.

Report on the Exploration

²⁶They came back to Moses and Aaron and the whole Israelite community at Kadesh in the Desert of Paran. There they reported to them and to the whole assembly and showed them the fruit of the land. ²⁷They gave Moses this account: "We went into the land to which you sent us, and it does flow with milk and honey! Here is its fruit. ²⁸But the people who live there are powerful, and the cities are fortified and very large. We even saw descendants of Anak there. ²⁹The Amalekites live in the Negev; the Hittites, Jebusites and Amorites live in the hill country; and the Canaanites live near the sea and along the Jordan."

³⁰Then Caleb silenced the people before Moses and said, "We should go up and take possession of the land, for we can certainly do it."

³¹But the men who had gone up with him said, "We can't attack those people; they are stronger than we are." ³²And they spread among the Israelites a bad report about the

---

No More Than Grasshoppers!

NUMBERS 13:25–33

The scouts come back to report that the inhabitants of the land are like giants. Alongside them the Israelite scouts feel no bigger than grasshoppers.

The way we perceive reality depends on the frame of reference we use when we look at problems. Relying on our human perceptions can make us feel overwhelmed. Take a magnifying glass and hold it above this page. Move the glass and notice how the print seems to grow and shrink. Does the size of the print actually change? Of course it doesn't, but the lens changes our perception. Think about a time when you faced a task that seemed impossible. How did you see yourself? Do you see yourself and the task differently now? What demanding tasks are you facing today, and how can you find a godly perspective on them?

See *Meeting God in Everyday Life*

---

^a 21 Or *toward the entrance to*   ^b 23 *Eshcol* means *cluster*; also in verse 24.

Facing the Consequences

NUMBERS 14:18–23

The kind of fruit we grow depends on the kind of seeds we sow. Our behavior has consequences. If we overeat, we gain weight. If we don't exercise, our muscles become weak. If we mistreat others, relationships deteriorate. And the consequences may affect others, even across generations. What patterns of behavior in your life have had negative consequences for you or for those you love? In what areas do you need God's help in changing those patterns? What patterns have had good consequences? What practices such as daily prayer or Bible study have been especially helpful to you in your faith?

See Meeting God in Community

land they had explored. They said, "The land we explored devours those living in it. All the people we saw there are of great size. ³³We saw the Nephilim there (the descendants of Anak come from the Nephilim). We seemed like grasshoppers in our own eyes, and we looked the same to them."

The People Rebel

14 That night all the people of the community raised their voices and wept aloud. ²All the Israelites grumbled against Moses and Aaron, and the whole assembly said to them, "If only we had died in Egypt! Or in this desert! ³Why is the LORD bringing us to this land only to let us fall by the sword? Our wives and children will be taken as plunder. Wouldn't it be better for us to go back to Egypt?" ⁴And they said to each other, "We should choose a leader and go back to Egypt."

⁵Then Moses and Aaron fell facedown in front of the whole Israelite assembly gathered there. ⁶Joshua son of Nun and Caleb son of Jephunneh, who were among those who had explored the land, tore their clothes ⁷and said to the entire Israelite assembly, "The land we passed through and explored is exceedingly good. ⁸If the LORD is pleased with us, he will lead us into that land, a land flowing with milk and honey, and will give it to us. ⁹Only do not rebel against the LORD. And do not be afraid of the people of the land, because we will swallow them up. Their protection is gone, but the LORD is with us. Do not be afraid of them."

¹⁰But the whole assembly talked about stoning them. Then the glory of the LORD appeared at the Tent of Meeting to all the Israelites. ¹¹The LORD said to Moses, "How long will these people treat me with contempt? How long will they refuse to believe in me, in spite of all the miraculous signs I have performed among them? ¹²I will strike them down with a plague and destroy them, but I will make you into a nation greater and stronger than they."

¹³Moses said to the LORD, "Then the Egyptians will hear about it! By your power you brought these people up from among them. ¹⁴And they will tell the inhabitants of this land about it. They have already heard that you, O LORD, are with these people and that you, O LORD, have been seen face to face, that your cloud stays over them, and that you go before them in a pillar of cloud by day and a pillar of fire by night. ¹⁵If you put these people to death all at one time, the nations who have heard this report about you will say, ¹⁶'The LORD was not able to bring these people into the land he promised them on oath; so he slaughtered them in the desert.'

¹⁷"Now may the Lord's strength be displayed, just as you have declared: ¹⁸'The LORD is slow to anger, abounding in love and forgiving sin and rebellion. Yet he does not leave the guilty unpunished; he punishes the children for the sin of the fathers to the third and fourth generation.' ¹⁹In accordance with your great love, forgive the sin of these people, just as you have pardoned them from the time they left Egypt until now."

²⁰The LORD replied, "I have forgiven them, as you asked. ²¹Nevertheless, as surely as I live and as surely as the glory of the LORD fills the whole earth, ²²not one of the men who saw my glory and the miraculous signs I performed in Egypt and in the desert but who disobeyed me and tested

me ten times— ²³not one of them will ever see the land I promised on oath to their forefathers. No one who has treated me with contempt will ever see it. ²⁴But because my servant Caleb has a different spirit and follows me wholeheartedly, I will bring him into the land he went to, and his descendants will inherit it. ²⁵Since the Amalekites and Canaanites are living in the valleys, turn back tomorrow and set out toward the desert along the route to the Red Sea.ᵃ"

²⁶The LORD said to Moses and Aaron: ²⁷"How long will this wicked community grumble against me? I have heard the complaints of these grumbling Israelites. ²⁸So tell them, 'As surely as I live, declares the LORD, I will do to you the very things I heard you say: ²⁹In this desert your bodies will fall—every one of you twenty years old or more who was counted in the census and who has grumbled against me. ³⁰Not one of you will enter the land I swore with uplifted hand to make your home, except Caleb son of Jephunneh and Joshua son of Nun. ³¹As for your children that you said would be taken as plunder, I will bring them in to enjoy the land you have rejected. ³²But you—your bodies will fall in this desert. ³³Your children will be shepherds here for forty years, suffering for your unfaithfulness, until the last of your bodies lies in the desert. ³⁴For forty years—one year for each of the forty days you explored the land—you will suffer for your sins and know what it is like to have me against you.' ³⁵I, the LORD, have spoken, and I will surely do these things to this whole wicked community, which has banded together against me. They will meet their end in this desert; here they will die."

³⁶So the men Moses had sent to explore the land, who returned and made the whole community grumble against him by spreading a bad report about it— ³⁷these men responsible for spreading the bad report about the land were struck down and died of a plague before the LORD. ³⁸Of the men who went to explore the land, only Joshua son of Nun and Caleb son of Jephunneh survived.

³⁹When Moses reported this to all the Israelites, they mourned bitterly. ⁴⁰Early the next morning they went up toward the high hill country. "We have sinned," they said. "We will go up to the place the LORD promised."

⁴¹But Moses said, "Why are you disobeying the LORD's command? This will not succeed! ⁴²Do not go up, because the LORD is not with you. You will be defeated by your enemies, ⁴³for the Amalekites and Canaanites will face you there. Because you have turned away from the LORD, he will not be with you and you will fall by the sword."

⁴⁴Nevertheless, in their presumption they went up toward the high hill country, though neither Moses nor the ark of the LORD's covenant moved from the camp. ⁴⁵Then the Amalekites and Canaanites who lived in that hill country came down and attacked them and beat them down all the way to Hormah.

Supplementary Offerings

15 The LORD said to Moses, ²"Speak to the Israelites and say to them: 'After you enter the land I am giving you as a home ³and you present to the LORD offerings made by fire, from the herd or the flock, as an aroma pleas-

Without Reservation

NUMBERS 14:24

Think about what it would mean to give yourself to God wholly, without reservation. What images come to mind? What would your life look like if you completely depended on God and allowed God into every part of it? What do you feel as you consider the idea? Consider whether there are areas that you want to open more fully to God and areas that you are withholding from God. What can you do to entrust yourself more completely to the love that sustains you and carries you along?

New in Town?

NUMBERS 15:14–16

God's people are commanded to include outsiders in their worship. Visualize your community of faith at a typical gathering. Are the people all of the same ethnic background or social class? If your community is diverse, what does the diversity add to your life together? If it isn't diverse, what can you do to make your worship setting more welcoming? Consider also how you can better incorporate new people into the life of your church, communicating your values and history to the new members even as you learn from them in turn.

See Meeting God in Community

ing to the LORD—whether burnt offerings or sacrifices, for special vows or freewill offerings or festival offerings— ⁴then the one who brings his offering shall present to the LORD a grain offering of a tenth of an ephah*ᵃ* of fine flour mixed with a quarter of a hin*ᵇ* of oil. ⁵With each lamb for the burnt offering or the sacrifice, prepare a quarter of a hin of wine as a drink offering.

⁶" 'With a ram prepare a grain offering of two-tenths of an ephah*ᶜ* of fine flour mixed with a third of a hin*ᵈ* of oil, ⁷and a third of a hin of wine as a drink offering. Offer it as an aroma pleasing to the LORD.

⁸" 'When you prepare a young bull as a burnt offering or sacrifice, for a special vow or a fellowship offering*ᵉ* to the LORD, ⁹bring with the bull a grain offering of three-tenths of an ephah*ᶠ* of fine flour mixed with half a hin*ᵍ* of oil. ¹⁰Also bring half a hin of wine as a drink offering. It will be an offering made by fire, an aroma pleasing to the LORD. ¹¹Each bull or ram, each lamb or young goat, is to be prepared in this manner. ¹²Do this for each one, for as many as you prepare.

¹³" 'Everyone who is native-born must do these things in this way when he brings an offering made by fire as an aroma pleasing to the LORD. ¹⁴For the generations to come, whenever an alien or anyone else living among you presents an offering made by fire as an aroma pleasing to the LORD, he must do exactly as you do. ¹⁵The community is to have the same rules for you and for the alien living among you; this is a lasting ordinance for the generations to come. You and the alien shall be the same before the LORD: ¹⁶The same laws and regulations will apply both to you and to the alien living among you.' "

¹⁷The LORD said to Moses, ¹⁸"Speak to the Israelites and say to them: 'When you enter the land to which I am taking you ¹⁹and you eat the food of the land, present a portion as an offering to the LORD. ²⁰Present a cake from the first of your ground meal and present it as an offering from the threshing floor. ²¹Throughout the generations to come you are to give this offering to the LORD from the first of your ground meal.

Offerings for Unintentional Sins

²²" 'Now if you unintentionally fail to keep any of these commands the LORD gave Moses— ²³any of the LORD's commands to you through him, from the day the LORD gave them and continuing through the generations to come— ²⁴and if this is done unintentionally without the community being aware of it, then the whole community is to offer a young bull for a burnt offering as an aroma pleasing to the LORD, along with its prescribed grain offering and drink offering, and a male goat for a sin offering. ²⁵The priest is to make atonement for the whole Israelite community, and they will be forgiven, for it was not intentional and they have brought to the LORD for their wrong an offering made by fire and a sin offering. ²⁶The whole Israelite community

---

ᵃ 4 That is, probably about 2 quarts (about 2 liters)   *ᵇ 4* That is, probably about 1 quart (about 1 liter); also in verse 5   *ᶜ 6* That is, probably about 4 quarts (about 4.5 liters)   *ᵈ 6* That is, probably about 1 1/4 quarts (about 1.2 liters); also in verse 7   *ᵉ 8* Traditionally *peace offering*   *ᶠ 9* That is, probably about 6 quarts (about 6.5 liters)   *ᵍ 9* That is, probably about 2 quarts (about 2 liters); also in verse 10

and the aliens living among them will be forgiven, because all the people were involved in the unintentional wrong.

²⁷" 'But if just one person sins unintentionally, he must bring a year-old female goat for a sin offering. ²⁸The priest is to make atonement before the LORD for the one who erred by sinning unintentionally, and when atonement has been made for him, he will be forgiven. ²⁹One and the same law applies to everyone who sins unintentionally, whether he is a native-born Israelite or an alien.

³⁰" 'But anyone who sins defiantly, whether native-born or alien, blasphemes the LORD, and that person must be cut off from his people. ³¹Because he has despised the LORD's word and broken his commands, that person must surely be cut off; his guilt remains on him.' "

The Sabbath-Breaker Put to Death

³²While the Israelites were in the desert, a man was found gathering wood on the Sabbath day. ³³Those who found him gathering wood brought him to Moses and Aaron and the whole assembly, ³⁴and they kept him in custody, because it was not clear what should be done to him. ³⁵Then the LORD said to Moses, "The man must die. The whole assembly must stone him outside the camp." ³⁶So the assembly took him outside the camp and stoned him to death, as the LORD commanded Moses.

Tassels on Garments

³⁷The LORD said to Moses, ³⁸"Speak to the Israelites and say to them: 'Throughout the generations to come you are to make tassels on the corners of your garments, with a blue cord on each tassel. ³⁹You will have these tassels to look at and so you will remember all the commands of the LORD, that you may obey them and not prostitute yourselves by going after the lusts of your own hearts and eyes. ⁴⁰Then you will remember to obey all my commands and will be consecrated to your God. ⁴¹I am the LORD your God, who brought you out of Egypt to be your God. I am the LORD your God.' "

Korah, Dathan and Abiram

16 Korah son of Izhar, the son of Kohath, the son of Levi, and certain Reubenites—Dathan and Abiram, sons of Eliab, and On son of Peleth—became insolent*ᵃ* ²and rose up against Moses. With them were 250 Israelite men, well-known community leaders who had been appointed members of the council. ³They came as a group to oppose Moses and Aaron and said to them, "You have gone too far! The whole community is holy, every one of them, and the LORD is with them. Why then do you set yourselves above the LORD's assembly?"

⁴When Moses heard this, he fell facedown. ⁵Then he said to Korah and all his followers: "In the morning the LORD will show who belongs to him and who is holy, and he will have that person come near him. The man he chooses he will cause to come near him. ⁶You, Korah, and all your followers are to do this: Take censers ⁷and tomorrow put fire and incense in them before the LORD. The man the LORD chooses will be the one who is holy. You Levites have gone too far!"

Your Calls to Prayer

NUMBERS 15:37–41

The blue cords are to remind the Israelites of what God has done for them. For many Christian believers throughout the centuries, the chiming of a clock on the hour has signified a reminder—a call to prayer that bids them pause momentarily, recognize God's presence and give thanks. Sounds, objects or experiences can be a personal call to prayer still today. Seeing objects that remind us of a favorite friend or relative can become a call to pray for them; waiting for a phone to be answered can remind us to pray for willingness to listen to God. For the next twenty-four hours pay attention to small reminders of people and situations, and consider how each of them may become your call to prayer.

See Meeting God in Everyday Life

ᵃ 1 Or Peleth—took ⸤men⸥

Fierce Holiness

NUMBERS 16:19–34

Moses warned the people to stay away from Korah and his followers. Then the ground opened and swallowed up those who were unholy! Put yourself in the place of one of those watching. What do you see and hear? What do you feel? What does this scene convey to you about God's call to be holy? Does this scene suggest to you how to pray?

See Meeting God in Scripture

⁸Moses also said to Korah, "Now listen, you Levites! ⁹Isn't it enough for you that the God of Israel has separated you from the rest of the Israelite community and brought you near himself to do the work at the Lord's tabernacle and to stand before the community and minister to them? ¹⁰He has brought you and all your fellow Levites near himself, but now you are trying to get the priesthood too. ¹¹It is against the Lord that you and all your followers have banded together. Who is Aaron that you should grumble against him?"

¹²Then Moses summoned Dathan and Abiram, the sons of Eliab. But they said, "We will not come! ¹³Isn't it enough that you have brought us up out of a land flowing with milk and honey to kill us in the desert? And now you also want to lord it over us? ¹⁴Moreover, you haven't brought us into a land flowing with milk and honey or given us an inheritance of fields and vineyards. Will you gouge out the eyes of*ᵃ* these men? No, we will not come!"

¹⁵Then Moses became very angry and said to the Lord, "Do not accept their offering. I have not taken so much as a donkey from them, nor have I wronged any of them."

¹⁶Moses said to Korah, "You and all your followers are to appear before the Lord tomorrow—you and they and Aaron. ¹⁷Each man is to take his censer and put incense in it—250 censers in all—and present it before the Lord. You and Aaron are to present your censers also." ¹⁸So each man took his censer, put fire and incense in it, and stood with Moses and Aaron at the entrance to the Tent of Meeting. ¹⁹When Korah had gathered all his followers in opposition to them at the entrance to the Tent of Meeting, the glory of the Lord appeared to the entire assembly. ²⁰The Lord said to Moses and Aaron, ²¹"Separate yourselves from this assembly so I can put an end to them at once."

²²But Moses and Aaron fell facedown and cried out, "O God, God of the spirits of all mankind, will you be angry with the entire assembly when only one man sins?"

²³Then the Lord said to Moses, ²⁴"Say to the assembly, 'Move away from the tents of Korah, Dathan and Abiram.' "

²⁵Moses got up and went to Dathan and Abiram, and the elders of Israel followed him. ²⁶He warned the assembly, "Move back from the tents of these wicked men! Do not touch anything belonging to them, or you will be swept away because of all their sins." ²⁷So they moved away from the tents of Korah, Dathan and Abiram. Dathan and Abiram had come out and were standing with their wives, children and little ones at the entrances to their tents.

²⁸Then Moses said, "This is how you will know that the Lord has sent me to do all these things and that it was not my idea: ²⁹If these men die a natural death and experience only what usually happens to men, then the Lord has not sent me. ³⁰But if the Lord brings about something totally new, and the earth opens its mouth and swallows them, with everything that belongs to them, and they go down alive into the grave,ᵇ then you will know that these men have treated the Lord with contempt."

³¹As soon as he finished saying all this, the ground under them split apart ³²and the earth opened its mouth and swallowed them, with their households and all Korah's men and all their possessions. ³³They went down alive into

ᵃ 14 Or you make slaves of; or you deceive   ᵇ 30 Hebrew Sheol; also in verse 33

the grave, with everything they owned; the earth closed over them, and they perished and were gone from the community. ³⁴At their cries, all the Israelites around them fled, shouting, "The earth is going to swallow us too!"

³⁵And fire came out from the LORD and consumed the 250 men who were offering the incense.

³⁶The LORD said to Moses, ³⁷"Tell Eleazar son of Aaron, the priest, to take the censers out of the smoldering remains and scatter the coals some distance away, for the censers are holy— ³⁸the censers of the men who sinned at the cost of their lives. Hammer the censers into sheets to overlay the altar, for they were presented before the LORD and have become holy. Let them be a sign to the Israelites."

³⁹So Eleazar the priest collected the bronze censers brought by those who had been burned up, and he had them hammered out to overlay the altar, ⁴⁰as the LORD directed him through Moses. This was to remind the Israelites that no one except a descendant of Aaron should come to burn incense before the LORD, or he would become like Korah and his followers.

⁴¹The next day the whole Israelite community grumbled against Moses and Aaron. "You have killed the LORD's people," they said.

⁴²But when the assembly gathered in opposition to Moses and Aaron and turned toward the Tent of Meeting, suddenly the cloud covered it and the glory of the LORD appeared. ⁴³Then Moses and Aaron went to the front of the Tent of Meeting, ⁴⁴and the LORD said to Moses, ⁴⁵"Get away from this assembly so I can put an end to them at once." And they fell facedown.

⁴⁶Then Moses said to Aaron, "Take your censer and put incense in it, along with fire from the altar, and hurry to the assembly to make atonement for them. Wrath has come out from the LORD; the plague has started." ⁴⁷So Aaron did as Moses said, and ran into the midst of the assembly. The plague had already started among the people, but Aaron offered the incense and made atonement for them. ⁴⁸He stood between the living and the dead, and the plague stopped. ⁴⁹But 14,700 people died from the plague, in addition to those who had died because of Korah. ⁵⁰Then Aaron returned to Moses at the entrance to the Tent of Meeting, for the plague had stopped.

The Budding of Aaron's Staff

17 The LORD said to Moses, ²"Speak to the Israelites and get twelve staffs from them, one from the leader of each of their ancestral tribes. Write the name of each man on his staff. ³On the staff of Levi write Aaron's name, for there must be one staff for the head of each ancestral tribe. ⁴Place them in the Tent of Meeting in front of the Testimony, where I meet with you. ⁵The staff belonging to the man I choose will sprout, and I will rid myself of this constant grumbling against you by the Israelites."

⁶So Moses spoke to the Israelites, and their leaders gave him twelve staffs, one for the leader of each of their ancestral tribes, and Aaron's staff was among them. ⁷Moses placed the staffs before the LORD in the Tent of the Testimony.

⁸The next day Moses entered the Tent of the Testimony and saw that Aaron's staff, which represented the house of

The Fragrance of Mercy

NUMBERS 16:46–48

Imagine yourself in this scene. Breathe deeply. Inhale the burning incense that Aaron is carrying in the censer. What does mercy "smell" like? Aaron could condemn these rebellious people to suffer for their sin. Instead, he walks among them, effecting reconciliation, bringing healing.

Do you know people who need someone to "burn incense for them," someone to represent God's mercy and love in a way that they can recognize? What can you carry with you as a reminder to burn the incense of grace and mercy for others?

See Meeting God in Community

195

A Dangerous Gift

NUMBERS 17:8; 18:6–8

Overnight, Aaron's staff buds, blossoms and bears fruit. His priesthood is a God-given gift, a special calling. What evidence might you see that God has called someone for a special role? What gifts do leaders need in order to care for God's people effectively? What are your leadership gifts, and in what ways are you exercising them for God's kingdom?

See Meeting God in Community

Levi, had not only sprouted but had budded, blossomed and produced almonds. ⁹Then Moses brought out all the staffs from the LORD's presence to all the Israelites. They looked at them, and each man took his own staff.

¹⁰The LORD said to Moses, "Put back Aaron's staff in front of the Testimony, to be kept as a sign to the rebellious. This will put an end to their grumbling against me, so that they will not die." ¹¹Moses did just as the LORD commanded him.

¹²The Israelites said to Moses, "We will die! We are lost, we are all lost! ¹³Anyone who even comes near the tabernacle of the LORD will die. Are we all going to die?"

Duties of Priests and Levites

18 The LORD said to Aaron, "You, your sons and your father's family are to bear the responsibility for offenses against the sanctuary, and you and your sons alone are to bear the responsibility for offenses against the priesthood. ²Bring your fellow Levites from your ancestral tribe to join you and assist you when you and your sons minister before the Tent of the Testimony. ³They are to be responsible to you and are to perform all the duties of the Tent, but they must not go near the furnishings of the sanctuary or the altar, or both they and you will die. ⁴They are to join you and be responsible for the care of the Tent of Meeting—all the work at the Tent—and no one else may come near where you are.

⁵"You are to be responsible for the care of the sanctuary and the altar, so that wrath will not fall on the Israelites again. ⁶I myself have selected your fellow Levites from among the Israelites as a gift to you, dedicated to the LORD to do the work at the Tent of Meeting. ⁷But only you and your sons may serve as priests in connection with everything at the altar and inside the curtain. I am giving you the service of the priesthood as a gift. Anyone else who comes near the sanctuary must be put to death."

Offerings for Priests and Levites

⁸Then the LORD said to Aaron, "I myself have put you in charge of the offerings presented to me; all the holy offerings the Israelites give me I give to you and your sons as your portion and regular share. ⁹You are to have the part of the most holy offerings that is kept from the fire. From all the gifts they bring me as most holy offerings, whether grain or sin or guilt offerings, that part belongs to you and your sons. ¹⁰Eat it as something most holy; every male shall eat it. You must regard it as holy.

¹¹"This also is yours: whatever is set aside from the gifts of all the wave offerings of the Israelites. I give this to you and your sons and daughters as your regular share. Everyone in your household who is ceremonially clean may eat it.

¹²"I give you all the finest olive oil and all the finest new wine and grain they give the LORD as the firstfruits of their harvest. ¹³All the land's firstfruits that they bring to the LORD will be yours. Everyone in your household who is ceremonially clean may eat it.

¹⁴"Everything in Israel that is devoted*ᵃ* to the LORD is yours. ¹⁵The first offspring of every womb, both man and

---

ᵃ 14 The Hebrew term refers to the irrevocable giving over of things or persons to the LORD.

animal, that is offered to the LORD is yours. But you must redeem every firstborn son and every firstborn male of unclean animals. ¹⁶When they are a month old, you must redeem them at the redemption price set at five shekels*a* of silver, according to the sanctuary shekel, which weighs twenty gerahs.

¹⁷"But you must not redeem the firstborn of an ox, a sheep or a goat; they are holy. Sprinkle their blood on the altar and burn their fat as an offering made by fire, an aroma pleasing to the LORD. ¹⁸Their meat is to be yours, just as the breast of the wave offering and the right thigh are yours. ¹⁹Whatever is set aside from the holy offerings the Israelites present to the LORD I give to you and your sons and daughters as your regular share. It is an everlasting covenant of salt before the LORD for both you and your offspring."

²⁰The LORD said to Aaron, "You will have no inheritance in their land, nor will you have any share among them; I am your share and your inheritance among the Israelites.

²¹"I give to the Levites all the tithes in Israel as their inheritance in return for the work they do while serving at the Tent of Meeting. ²²From now on the Israelites must not go near the Tent of Meeting, or they will bear the consequences of their sin and will die. ²³It is the Levites who are to do the work at the Tent of Meeting and bear the responsibility for offenses against it. This is a lasting ordinance for the generations to come. They will receive no inheritance among the Israelites. ²⁴Instead, I give to the Levites as their inheritance the tithes that the Israelites present as an offering to the LORD. That is why I said concerning them: 'They will have no inheritance among the Israelites.' "

²⁵The LORD said to Moses, ²⁶"Speak to the Levites and say to them: 'When you receive from the Israelites the tithe I give you as your inheritance, you must present a tenth of that tithe as the LORD's offering. ²⁷Your offering will be reckoned to you as grain from the threshing floor or juice from the winepress. ²⁸In this way you also will present an offering to the LORD from all the tithes you receive from the Israelites. From these tithes you must give the LORD's portion to Aaron the priest. ²⁹You must present as the LORD's portion the best and holiest part of everything given to you.'

³⁰"Say to the Levites: 'When you present the best part, it will be reckoned to you as the product of the threshing floor or the winepress. ³¹You and your households may eat the rest of it anywhere, for it is your wages for your work at the Tent of Meeting. ³²By presenting the best part of it you will not be guilty in this matter; then you will not defile the holy offerings of the Israelites, and you will not die.' "

The Water of Cleansing

19 The LORD said to Moses and Aaron: ²"This is a requirement of the law that the LORD has commanded: Tell the Israelites to bring you a red heifer without defect or blemish and that has never been under a yoke. ³Give it to Eleazar the priest; it is to be taken outside the camp and slaughtered in his presence. ⁴Then Eleazar the priest is to take some of its blood on his finger and sprinkle it seven times toward the front of the Tent of Meeting. ⁵While he watches, the heifer is to be burned—its hide,

A Secure Possession

NUMBERS 18:20

Listen as God communicates to you, "I am your share and your inheritance." Mull over that thought. What does it mean to you? Think about your dearest possession. How do you care for it? How do you care for your most important relationships? Consider what you can do to show your gratitude for the gift of God's presence in your life.

---

a 16 That is, about 2 ounces (about 55 grams)

Made Pure

NUMBERS 19:7–8

Water is a recurring, powerful symbol of cleansing in the Bible. The next time you bathe or shower, pour water over yourself or stand still under the running water. As the water flows over you, imagine that it is God's grace washing you, cleansing you inwardly as you bathe outwardly. In what area of your mind and emotions do you need cleansing? In what ways do you want God to wipe the slate clean and give you a fresh start? What do you need to let go of and allow to drain away? Whatever it is, picture it being washed away by God's cleansing love.

See Meeting God in the Created Order

flesh, blood and offal. ⁶The priest is to take some cedar wood, hyssop and scarlet wool and throw them onto the burning heifer. ⁷After that, the priest must wash his clothes and bathe himself with water. He may then come into the camp, but he will be ceremonially unclean till evening. ⁸The man who burns it must also wash his clothes and bathe with water, and he too will be unclean till evening.

⁹"A man who is clean shall gather up the ashes of the heifer and put them in a ceremonially clean place outside the camp. They shall be kept by the Israelite community for use in the water of cleansing; it is for purification from sin. ¹⁰The man who gathers up the ashes of the heifer must also wash his clothes, and he too will be unclean till evening. This will be a lasting ordinance both for the Israelites and for the aliens living among them.

¹¹"Whoever touches the dead body of anyone will be unclean for seven days. ¹²He must purify himself with the water on the third day and on the seventh day; then he will be clean. But if he does not purify himself on the third and seventh days, he will not be clean. ¹³Whoever touches the dead body of anyone and fails to purify himself defiles the LORD's tabernacle. That person must be cut off from Israel. Because the water of cleansing has not been sprinkled on him, he is unclean; his uncleanness remains on him.

¹⁴"This is the law that applies when a person dies in a tent: Anyone who enters the tent and anyone who is in it will be unclean for seven days, ¹⁵and every open container without a lid fastened on it will be unclean.

¹⁶"Anyone out in the open who touches someone who has been killed with a sword or someone who has died a natural death, or anyone who touches a human bone or a grave, will be unclean for seven days.

¹⁷"For the unclean person, put some ashes from the burned purification offering into a jar and pour fresh water over them. ¹⁸Then a man who is ceremonially clean is to take some hyssop, dip it in the water and sprinkle the tent and all the furnishings and the people who were there. He must also sprinkle anyone who has touched a human bone or a grave or someone who has been killed or someone who has died a natural death. ¹⁹The man who is clean is to sprinkle the unclean person on the third and seventh days, and on the seventh day he is to purify him. The person being cleansed must wash his clothes and bathe with water, and that evening he will be clean. ²⁰But if a person who is unclean does not purify himself, he must be cut off from the community, because he has defiled the sanctuary of the LORD. The water of cleansing has not been sprinkled on him, and he is unclean. ²¹This is a lasting ordinance for them.

"The man who sprinkles the water of cleansing must also wash his clothes, and anyone who touches the water of cleansing will be unclean till evening. ²²Anything that an unclean person touches becomes unclean, and anyone who touches it becomes unclean till evening."

Water From the Rock

20 In the first month the whole Israelite community arrived at the Desert of Zin, and they stayed at Kadesh. There Miriam died and was buried.

²Now there was no water for the community, and the

people gathered in opposition to Moses and Aaron. ³They quarreled with Moses and said, "If only we had died when our brothers fell dead before the LORD! ⁴Why did you bring the LORD's community into this desert, that we and our livestock should die here? ⁵Why did you bring us up out of Egypt to this terrible place? It has no grain or figs, grapevines or pomegranates. And there is no water to drink!"

⁶Moses and Aaron went from the assembly to the entrance to the Tent of Meeting and fell facedown, and the glory of the LORD appeared to them. ⁷The LORD said to Moses, ⁸"Take the staff, and you and your brother Aaron gather the assembly together. Speak to that rock before their eyes and it will pour out its water. You will bring water out of the rock for the community so they and their livestock can drink."

⁹So Moses took the staff from the LORD's presence, just as he commanded him. ¹⁰He and Aaron gathered the assembly together in front of the rock and Moses said to them, "Listen, you rebels, must we bring you water out of this rock?" ¹¹Then Moses raised his arm and struck the rock twice with his staff. Water gushed out, and the community and their livestock drank.

¹²But the LORD said to Moses and Aaron, "Because you did not trust in me enough to honor me as holy in the sight of the Israelites, you will not bring this community into the land I give them."

¹³These were the waters of Meribah,ᵃ where the Israelites quarreled with the LORD and where he showed himself holy among them.

Edom Denies Israel Passage

¹⁴Moses sent messengers from Kadesh to the king of Edom, saying:

"This is what your brother Israel says: You know about all the hardships that have come upon us. ¹⁵Our forefathers went down into Egypt, and we lived there many years. The Egyptians mistreated us and our fathers, ¹⁶but when we cried out to the LORD, he heard our cry and sent an angel and brought us out of Egypt.

"Now we are here at Kadesh, a town on the edge of your territory. ¹⁷Please let us pass through your country. We will not go through any field or vineyard, or drink water from any well. We will travel along the king's highway and not turn to the right or to the left until we have passed through your territory."

¹⁸But Edom answered:

"You may not pass through here; if you try, we will march out and attack you with the sword."

¹⁹The Israelites replied:

"We will go along the main road, and if we or our livestock drink any of your water, we will pay for it. We only want to pass through on foot—nothing else."

²⁰Again they answered:

"You may not pass through."

Again? Again?

NUMBERS 20:1–12

The Israelites witness many miracles and are sustained daily by heaven-sent manna, yet they still fail to trust God and to rely on his goodness. We may wonder how they remain so stubborn, but think for a moment. Most of us have an arena of continuing struggle in our spiritual life, some fear or area of worry that we wrestle with year after year, some attitude in which we resist God's grace. What is your arena of continuing challenge? Where do you struggle to be faithful? How have you experienced God's grace in the times you have failed? What progress have you made and where do you still need to grow in faithfulness?

ᵃ *13 Meribah* means *quarreling.*

Looking at the Snake

NUMBERS 21:4–9

God's people are healed when they turn to look directly at the bronze snake—a symbol of what is harming them—their rebellion against God's grace. Sometimes we don't want to face what harms us or has harmed us in the past. We may find it easier to ignore our own faults and failures than to admit there's a problem, name it and deal with it. Facing problems honestly can be the key to healing. Are there areas in your life where you need help with this? What trusted person could help you to face your "snakes"?

Then Edom came out against them with a large and powerful army. ²¹Since Edom refused to let them go through their territory, Israel turned away from them.

The Death of Aaron

²²The whole Israelite community set out from Kadesh and came to Mount Hor. ²³At Mount Hor, near the border of Edom, the LORD said to Moses and Aaron, ²⁴"Aaron will be gathered to his people. He will not enter the land I give the Israelites, because both of you rebelled against my command at the waters of Meribah. ²⁵Get Aaron and his son Eleazar and take them up Mount Hor. ²⁶Remove Aaron's garments and put them on his son Eleazar, for Aaron will be gathered to his people; he will die there."

²⁷Moses did as the LORD commanded: They went up Mount Hor in the sight of the whole community. ²⁸Moses removed Aaron's garments and put them on his son Eleazar. And Aaron died there on top of the mountain. Then Moses and Eleazar came down from the mountain, ²⁹and when the whole community learned that Aaron had died, the entire house of Israel mourned for him thirty days.

Arad Destroyed

21 When the Canaanite king of Arad, who lived in the Negev, heard that Israel was coming along the road to Atharim, he attacked the Israelites and captured some of them. ²Then Israel made this vow to the LORD: "If you will deliver these people into our hands, we will totally destroy*ª* their cities." ³The LORD listened to Israel's plea and gave the Canaanites over to them. They completely destroyed them and their towns; so the place was named Hormah.*ᵇ*

The Bronze Snake

⁴They traveled from Mount Hor along the route to the Red Sea,*ᶜ* to go around Edom. But the people grew impatient on the way; ⁵they spoke against God and against Moses, and said, "Why have you brought us up out of Egypt to die in the desert? There is no bread! There is no water! And we detest this miserable food!"

⁶Then the LORD sent venomous snakes among them; they bit the people and many Israelites died. ⁷The people came to Moses and said, "We sinned when we spoke against the LORD and against you. Pray that the LORD will take the snakes away from us." So Moses prayed for the people.

⁸The LORD said to Moses, "Make a snake and put it up on a pole; anyone who is bitten can look at it and live." ⁹So Moses made a bronze snake and put it up on a pole. Then when anyone was bitten by a snake and looked at the bronze snake, he lived.

The Journey to Moab

¹⁰The Israelites moved on and camped at Oboth. ¹¹Then they set out from Oboth and camped in Iye Abarim, in the desert that faces Moab toward the sunrise. ¹²From there they moved on and camped in the Zered Valley. ¹³They set out from there and camped alongside the Arnon, which is

---

ª 2 The Hebrew term refers to the irrevocable giving over of things or persons to the LORD, often by totally destroying them; also in verse 3.
ᵇ 3 Hormah means *destruction.*   *ᶜ 4* Hebrew *Yam Suph*; that is, Sea of Reeds

in the desert extending into Amorite territory. The Arnon is the border of Moab, between Moab and the Amorites. [14]That is why the Book of the Wars of the LORD says:

> ". . . Waheb in Suphah[a] and the ravines,
>   the Arnon [15]and[b] the slopes of the ravines
> that lead to the site of Ar
>   and lie along the border of Moab."

[16]From there they continued on to Beer, the well where the LORD said to Moses, "Gather the people together and I will give them water."

[17]Then Israel sang this song:

> "Spring up, O well!
>   Sing about it,
> [18]about the well that the princes dug,
>   that the nobles of the people sank—
>   the nobles with scepters and staffs."

Then they went from the desert to Mattanah, [19]from Mattanah to Nahaliel, from Nahaliel to Bamoth, [20]and from Bamoth to the valley in Moab where the top of Pisgah overlooks the wasteland.

Defeat of Sihon and Og

[21]Israel sent messengers to say to Sihon king of the Amorites:

[22]"Let us pass through your country. We will not turn aside into any field or vineyard, or drink water from any well. We will travel along the king's highway until we have passed through your territory."

[23]But Sihon would not let Israel pass through his territory. He mustered his entire army and marched out into the desert against Israel. When he reached Jahaz, he fought with Israel. [24]Israel, however, put him to the sword and took over his land from the Arnon to the Jabbok, but only as far as the Ammonites, because their border was fortified. [25]Israel captured all the cities of the Amorites and occupied them, including Heshbon and all its surrounding settlements. [26]Heshbon was the city of Sihon king of the Amorites, who had fought against the former king of Moab and had taken from him all his land as far as the Arnon.

[27]That is why the poets say:

> "Come to Heshbon and let it be rebuilt;
>   let Sihon's city be restored.
> [28]"Fire went out from Heshbon,
>   a blaze from the city of Sihon.
> It consumed Ar of Moab,
>   the citizens of Arnon's heights.
> [29]Woe to you, O Moab!
>   You are destroyed, O people of Chemosh!
> He has given up his sons as fugitives
>   and his daughters as captives
> to Sihon king of the Amorites.
> [30]"But we have overthrown them;
>   Heshbon is destroyed all the way to Dibon.

Your Song of Praise

NUMBERS 21:17–18

God provides water in the desert, and in response the people sing a song of praise. Make a list of good things God has done for you—things that you can celebrate today. Think of a familiar hymn of praise and thanksgiving, or compose your own. Sing it aloud, adding items from your list as part of the song. It doesn't matter if you don't sing well or can't carry a tune. Just make a "joyful noise" before God.

See Meeting God in Worship

---

a 14 The meaning of the Hebrew for this phrase is uncertain.   *b 14,15* Or *"I have been given from Suphah and the ravines / of the Arnon* [15]*to*

Making War

NUMBERS 21:32–35

"Briefly, in this tempest, there is no help for it but to wait upon the mercy of God, Who suddenly, at the most un-looked-for hour, with a single word, or on some chance occasion, lifts the whole of this burden from the soul, so that it seems as if it has never been clouded over, but is full of sunshine and far happier than it was before. Then, like one who has escaped from a perilous battle and gained the victory, the soul keeps praising Our Lord, for it is He Who has fought and enabled it to conquer. It knows very well that it did not itself do the fighting. For it saw that all the weapons with which it could defend itself were in the hands of the enemy, and it was thus clearly aware of its misery and realized how little we can do of ourselves if the Lord should forsake us."

—TERESA OF AVILA,
The Interior Castle

We have demolished them as far as Nophah,
which extends to Medeba."

³¹So Israel settled in the land of the Amorites.
³²After Moses had sent spies to Jazer, the Israelites captured its surrounding settlements and drove out the Amorites who were there. ³³Then they turned and went up along the road toward Bashan, and Og king of Bashan and his whole army marched out to meet them in battle at Edrei.

³⁴The LORD said to Moses, "Do not be afraid of him, for I have handed him over to you, with his whole army and his land. Do to him what you did to Sihon king of the Amorites, who reigned in Heshbon."

³⁵So they struck him down, together with his sons and his whole army, leaving them no survivors. And they took possession of his land.

Balak Summons Balaam

22 Then the Israelites traveled to the plains of Moab and camped along the Jordan across from Jericho.ᵃ
²Now Balak son of Zippor saw all that Israel had done to the Amorites, ³and Moab was terrified because there were so many people. Indeed, Moab was filled with dread because of the Israelites.

⁴The Moabites said to the elders of Midian, "This horde is going to lick up everything around us, as an ox licks up the grass of the field."

So Balak son of Zippor, who was king of Moab at that time, ⁵sent messengers to summon Balaam son of Beor, who was at Pethor, near the River,ᵇ in his native land. Balak said:

"A people has come out of Egypt; they cover the face of the land and have settled next to me. ⁶Now come and put a curse on these people, because they are too powerful for me. Perhaps then I will be able to defeat them and drive them out of the country. For I know that those you bless are blessed, and those you curse are cursed."

⁷The elders of Moab and Midian left, taking with them the fee for divination. When they came to Balaam, they told him what Balak had said.

⁸"Spend the night here," Balaam said to them, "and I will bring you back the answer the LORD gives me." So the Moabite princes stayed with him.

⁹God came to Balaam and asked, "Who are these men with you?"

¹⁰Balaam said to God, "Balak son of Zippor, king of Moab, sent me this message: ¹¹'A people that has come out of Egypt covers the face of the land. Now come and put a curse on them for me. Perhaps then I will be able to fight them and drive them away.'"

¹²But God said to Balaam, "Do not go with them. You must not put a curse on those people, because they are blessed."

¹³The next morning Balaam got up and said to Balak's

ᵃ 1 Hebrew *Jordan of Jericho*; possibly an ancient name for the Jordan River
ᵇ 5 That is, the Euphrates

princes, "Go back to your own country, for the LORD has refused to let me go with you."

¹⁴So the Moabite princes returned to Balak and said, "Balaam refused to come with us."

¹⁵Then Balak sent other princes, more numerous and more distinguished than the first. ¹⁶They came to Balaam and said:

> "This is what Balak son of Zippor says: Do not let anything keep you from coming to me, ¹⁷because I will reward you handsomely and do whatever you say. Come and put a curse on these people for me."

¹⁸But Balaam answered them, "Even if Balak gave me his palace filled with silver and gold, I could not do anything great or small to go beyond the command of the LORD my God. ¹⁹Now stay here tonight as the others did, and I will find out what else the LORD will tell me."

²⁰That night God came to Balaam and said, "Since these men have come to summon you, go with them, but do only what I tell you."

Balaam's Donkey

²¹Balaam got up in the morning, saddled his donkey and went with the princes of Moab. ²²But God was very angry when he went, and the angel of the LORD stood in the road to oppose him. Balaam was riding on his donkey, and his two servants were with him. ²³When the donkey saw the angel of the LORD standing in the road with a drawn sword in his hand, she turned off the road into a field. Balaam beat her to get her back on the road.

²⁴Then the angel of the LORD stood in a narrow path between two vineyards, with walls on both sides. ²⁵When the donkey saw the angel of the LORD, she pressed close to the wall, crushing Balaam's foot against it. So he beat her again.

²⁶Then the angel of the LORD moved on ahead and stood in a narrow place where there was no room to turn, either to the right or to the left. ²⁷When the donkey saw the angel of the LORD, she lay down under Balaam, and he was angry and beat her with his staff. ²⁸Then the LORD opened the donkey's mouth, and she said to Balaam, "What have I done to you to make you beat me these three times?"

²⁹Balaam answered the donkey, "You have made a fool of me! If I had a sword in my hand, I would kill you right now."

³⁰The donkey said to Balaam, "Am I not your own donkey, which you have always ridden, to this day? Have I been in the habit of doing this to you?"

"No," he said.

³¹Then the LORD opened Balaam's eyes, and he saw the angel of the LORD standing in the road with his sword drawn. So he bowed low and fell facedown.

³²The angel of the LORD asked him, "Why have you beaten your donkey these three times? I have come here to oppose you because your path is a reckless one before me.ᵃ ³³The donkey saw me and turned away from me these three times. If she had not turned away, I would certainly have killed you by now, but I would have spared her."

³⁴Balaam said to the angel of the LORD, "I have sinned. I

Pressured to Speak

NUMBERS 22:38

Balaam and Balak are engaged in a tug of war over words—but not just any words. Balak wants Balaam to curse God's people. Each time Balaam consults his oracle he is told not to curse them, but Balak keeps asking him to do it anyway, trying to get him to compromise.

Think of a time when you have felt pressured to do or say something that you felt was wrong. Perhaps something like this is going on in your life right now. At such times, in what ways can you ask for help and guidance from God and others?

See Meeting God in Everyday Life

ᵃ 32 The meaning of the Hebrew for this clause is uncertain.

Must I Not Speak?

NUMBERS 23:12

Balaam seems an unlikely candidate for a prophet of God, yet God uses him to utter the truth to Balak, a mission Balaam cannot resist: "Must I not speak what the Lord puts in my mouth?"

We sometimes find ourselves with a word from God in our mouth—a word of truth, encouragement or comfort—yet we hold back because we're afraid we might sound overly pious, or because we just don't want to deal with the emotions such words might invoke. Can you think of occasions when you held back from speaking a word from the Lord? When you did speak up? What was the result? How does this passage give you courage to speak up next time?

did not realize you were standing in the road to oppose me. Now if you are displeased, I will go back."

³⁵The angel of the LORD said to Balaam, "Go with the men, but speak only what I tell you." So Balaam went with the princes of Balak.

³⁶When Balak heard that Balaam was coming, he went out to meet him at the Moabite town on the Arnon border, at the edge of his territory. ³⁷Balak said to Balaam, "Did I not send you an urgent summons? Why didn't you come to me? Am I really not able to reward you?"

³⁸"Well, I have come to you now," Balaam replied. "But can I say just anything? I must speak only what God puts in my mouth."

³⁹Then Balaam went with Balak to Kiriath Huzoth. ⁴⁰Balak sacrificed cattle and sheep, and gave some to Balaam and the princes who were with him. ⁴¹The next morning Balak took Balaam up to Bamoth Baal, and from there he saw part of the people.

Balaam's First Oracle

23 Balaam said, "Build me seven altars here, and prepare seven bulls and seven rams for me." ²Balak did as Balaam said, and the two of them offered a bull and a ram on each altar.

³Then Balaam said to Balak, "Stay here beside your offering while I go aside. Perhaps the LORD will come to meet with me. Whatever he reveals to me I will tell you." Then he went off to a barren height.

⁴God met with him, and Balaam said, "I have prepared seven altars, and on each altar I have offered a bull and a ram."

⁵The LORD put a message in Balaam's mouth and said, "Go back to Balak and give him this message."

⁶So he went back to him and found him standing beside his offering, with all the princes of Moab. ⁷Then Balaam uttered his oracle:

"Balak brought me from Aram,
    the king of Moab from the eastern mountains.
'Come,' he said, 'curse Jacob for me;
    come, denounce Israel.'
⁸How can I curse
    those whom God has not cursed?
How can I denounce
    those whom the LORD has not denounced?
⁹From the rocky peaks I see them,
    from the heights I view them.
I see a people who live apart
    and do not consider themselves one of the
        nations.
¹⁰Who can count the dust of Jacob
    or number the fourth part of Israel?
Let me die the death of the righteous,
    and may my end be like theirs!"

¹¹Balak said to Balaam, "What have you done to me? I brought you to curse my enemies, but you have done nothing but bless them!"

¹²He answered, "Must I not speak what the LORD puts in my mouth?"

Balaam's Second Oracle

¹³Then Balak said to him, "Come with me to another place where you can see them; you will see only a part but not all of them. And from there, curse them for me." ¹⁴So he took him to the field of Zophim on the top of Pisgah, and there he built seven altars and offered a bull and a ram on each altar.

¹⁵Balaam said to Balak, "Stay here beside your offering while I meet with him over there."

¹⁶The LORD met with Balaam and put a message in his mouth and said, "Go back to Balak and give him this message."

¹⁷So he went to him and found him standing beside his offering, with the princes of Moab. Balak asked him, "What did the LORD say?"

¹⁸Then he uttered his oracle:

> "Arise, Balak, and listen;
>   hear me, son of Zippor.
> ¹⁹God is not a man, that he should lie,
>   nor a son of man, that he should change his
>   mind.
> Does he speak and then not act?
>   Does he promise and not fulfill?
> ²⁰I have received a command to bless;
>   he has blessed, and I cannot change it.
>
> ²¹ "No misfortune is seen in Jacob,
>   no misery observed in Israel.ᵃ
> The LORD their God is with them;
>   the shout of the King is among them.
> ²²God brought them out of Egypt;
>   they have the strength of a wild ox.
> ²³There is no sorcery against Jacob,
>   no divination against Israel.
> It will now be said of Jacob
>   and of Israel, 'See what God has done!'
> ²⁴The people rise like a lioness;
>   they rouse themselves like a lion
> that does not rest till he devours his prey
>   and drinks the blood of his victims."

²⁵Then Balak said to Balaam, "Neither curse them at all nor bless them at all!"

²⁶Balaam answered, "Did I not tell you I must do whatever the LORD says?"

Balaam's Third Oracle

²⁷Then Balak said to Balaam, "Come, let me take you to another place. Perhaps it will please God to let you curse them for me from there." ²⁸And Balak took Balaam to the top of Peor, overlooking the wasteland.

²⁹Balaam said, "Build me seven altars here, and prepare seven bulls and seven rams for me." ³⁰Balak did as Balaam had said, and offered a bull and a ram on each altar.

24 Now when Balaam saw that it pleased the LORD to bless Israel, he did not resort to sorcery as at other times, but turned his face toward the desert. ²When Balaam looked out and saw Israel encamped tribe by tribe, the Spirit of God came upon him ³and he uttered his oracle:

A Beautiful Vision

NUMBERS 24:3–7

As the Spirit of God comes upon him, Balaam describes the abundance and verdancy of the new land in which the Israelites will dwell. What does the kingdom of heaven look like from where you stand? What does it smell and feel like? What do you hear? Using paint, pencil, words, music or whatever creative medium you wish, create a representation of your vision of the kingdom of heaven.

ᵃ 21 Or *He has not looked on Jacob's offenses / or on the wrongs found in Israel.*

A Word From God

NUMBERS 24:12–14

Think about a dilemma or a decision you are facing. Ask God to show you what you should do in the situation. Wait quietly. If you do not receive immediate guidance, can you wait and do nothing until God gives you direction? Balaam waited for God's leading and obeyed; then he told Balak that he would not go beyond what God said.

As you read and think about this Scripture passage, listen for God's guidance. Ask for strength to do what God tells you to do, even if it is to do nothing.

See Meeting God in Everyday Life

"The oracle of Balaam son of Beor,
　　the oracle of one whose eye sees clearly,
⁴ the oracle of one who hears the words of God,
　　who sees a vision from the Almighty,ᵃ
　　who falls prostrate, and whose eyes are
　　　　opened:

⁵ "How beautiful are your tents, O Jacob,
　　your dwelling places, O Israel!

⁶ "Like valleys they spread out,
　　like gardens beside a river,
like aloes planted by the LORD,
　　like cedars beside the waters.
⁷ Water will flow from their buckets;
　　their seed will have abundant water.

"Their king will be greater than Agag;
　　their kingdom will be exalted.

⁸ "God brought them out of Egypt;
　　they have the strength of a wild ox.
They devour hostile nations
　　and break their bones in pieces;
　　with their arrows they pierce them.
⁹ Like a lion they crouch and lie down,
　　like a lioness—who dares to rouse them?

"May those who bless you be blessed
　　and those who curse you be cursed!"

¹⁰Then Balak's anger burned against Balaam. He struck his hands together and said to him, "I summoned you to curse my enemies, but you have blessed them these three times. ¹¹Now leave at once and go home! I said I would reward you handsomely, but the LORD has kept you from being rewarded."

¹²Balaam answered Balak, "Did I not tell the messengers you sent me, ¹³'Even if Balak gave me his palace filled with silver and gold, I could not do anything of my own accord, good or bad, to go beyond the command of the LORD—and I must say only what the LORD says'? ¹⁴Now I am going back to my people, but come, let me warn you of what this people will do to your people in days to come."

Balaam's Fourth Oracle

¹⁵Then he uttered his oracle:

"The oracle of Balaam son of Beor,
　　the oracle of one whose eye sees clearly,
¹⁶ the oracle of one who hears the words of God,
　　who has knowledge from the Most High,
　　who sees a vision from the Almighty,
　　who falls prostrate, and whose eyes are
　　　　opened:

¹⁷ "I see him, but not now;
　　I behold him, but not near.
A star will come out of Jacob;
　　a scepter will rise out of Israel.
He will crush the foreheads of Moab,

　　　　ᵃ 4 Hebrew *Shaddai*; also in verse 16

the skulls[a] of[b] all the sons of Sheth.[c]
18 Edom will be conquered;
  Seir, his enemy, will be conquered,
    but Israel will grow strong.
19 A ruler will come out of Jacob
  and destroy the survivors of the city."

Balaam's Final Oracles

20 Then Balaam saw Amalek and uttered his oracle:

  "Amalek was first among the nations,
    but he will come to ruin at last."

21 Then he saw the Kenites and uttered his oracle:

  "Your dwelling place is secure,
    your nest is set in a rock;
22 yet you Kenites will be destroyed
    when Asshur takes you captive."

23 Then he uttered his oracle:

  "Ah, who can live when God does this?[d]
24   · Ships will come from the shores of Kittim;
  they will subdue Asshur and Eber,
    but they too will come to ruin."

25 Then Balaam got up and returned home and Balak
went his own way.

Moab Seduces Israel

25 While Israel was staying in Shittim, the men began to indulge in sexual immorality with Moabite women, 2 who invited them to the sacrifices to their gods. The people ate and bowed down before these gods. 3 So Israel joined in worshiping the Baal of Peor. And the LORD's anger burned against them.

4 The LORD said to Moses, "Take all the leaders of these people, kill them and expose them in broad daylight before the LORD, so that the LORD's fierce anger may turn away from Israel."

5 So Moses said to Israel's judges, "Each of you must put to death those of your men who have joined in worshiping the Baal of Peor."

6 Then an Israelite man brought to his family a Midianite woman right before the eyes of Moses and the whole assembly of Israel while they were weeping at the entrance to the Tent of Meeting. 7 When Phinehas son of Eleazar, the son of Aaron, the priest, saw this, he left the assembly, took a spear in his hand 8 and followed the Israelite into the tent. He drove the spear through both of them—through the Israelite and into the woman's body. Then the plague against the Israelites was stopped; 9 but those who died in the plague numbered 24,000.

10 The LORD said to Moses, 11 "Phinehas son of Eleazar, the son of Aaron, the priest, has turned my anger away from the Israelites; for he was as zealous as I am for my honor among them, so that in my zeal I did not put an end to them. 12 Therefore tell him I am making my covenant of

Purging the Camp

NUMBERS 25:1–5

Alliances with the Moabites were pulling the Israelites away from God. They were allowing themselves to be "yoked with unbelievers" (2 Corinthians 6:14). Sharing a yoke requires the bearers to go in the same direction. Physical yokes like those used on oxen are not familiar in our urban culture, but we have various other kinds of yokes—marriage, legal contracts, relationships with employers or employees—that directly influence us. Think about the "yokes" you share with others right now. Are they helping you to walk in the direction God wants for you? In what ways might you be yoked to people or activities from which you need to be free?

Think about someone who supports you in growing toward being the person God wants you to be. List the traits that make your alliance with that person healthy and beneficial.

See Meeting God in Community

---

[a] 17 Samaritan Pentateuch (see also Jer. 48:45); the meaning of the word in the Masoretic Text is uncertain.   [b] 17 Or possibly *Moab, / batter*   [c] 17 Or *all the noisy boasters*   [d] 23 Masoretic Text; with a different word division of the Hebrew *A people will gather from the north.*

The People of God

NUMBERS 26:3–18

Some of the names here are slightly familiar—perhaps the names of the twelve tribes. But most of these names are unfamiliar. Yet these people are important to us because they passed their faith from generation to generation. Picture in your mind the generations of believers that stretch back through the centuries, crossing continents and oceans. Whom do you see? What sacrifices did they make for the faith? What do you feel? Which of the gifts they gave us do you especially value today?

See Meeting God in Community

peace with him. ¹³He and his descendants will have a covenant of a lasting priesthood, because he was zealous for the honor of his God and made atonement for the Israelites."

¹⁴The name of the Israelite who was killed with the Midianite woman was Zimri son of Salu, the leader of a Simeonite family. ¹⁵And the name of the Midianite woman who was put to death was Cozbi daughter of Zur, a tribal chief of a Midianite family.

¹⁶The LORD said to Moses, ¹⁷"Treat the Midianites as enemies and kill them, ¹⁸because they treated you as enemies when they deceived you in the affair of Peor and their sister Cozbi, the daughter of a Midianite leader, the woman who was killed when the plague came as a result of Peor."

The Second Census

26 After the plague the LORD said to Moses and Eleazar son of Aaron, the priest, ²"Take a census of the whole Israelite community by families—all those twenty years old or more who are able to serve in the army of Israel." ³So on the plains of Moab by the Jordan across from Jericho,ᵃ Moses and Eleazar the priest spoke with them and said, ⁴"Take a census of the men twenty years old or more, as the LORD commanded Moses."

These were the Israelites who came out of Egypt:

⁵The descendants of Reuben, the firstborn son of Israel, were:

through Hanoch, the Hanochite clan;
through Pallu, the Palluite clan;
⁶through Hezron, the Hezronite clan;
through Carmi, the Carmite clan.
⁷These were the clans of Reuben; those numbered were 43,730.

⁸The son of Pallu was Eliab, ⁹and the sons of Eliab were Nemuel, Dathan and Abiram. The same Dathan and Abiram were the community officials who rebelled against Moses and Aaron and were among Korah's followers when they rebelled against the LORD. ¹⁰The earth opened its mouth and swallowed them along with Korah, whose followers died when the fire devoured the 250 men. And they served as a warning sign. ¹¹The line of Korah, however, did not die out.

¹²The descendants of Simeon by their clans were:
through Nemuel, the Nemuelite clan;
through Jamin, the Jaminite clan;
through Jakin, the Jakinite clan;
¹³through Zerah, the Zerahite clan;
through Shaul, the Shaulite clan.
¹⁴These were the clans of Simeon; there were 22,200 men.

¹⁵The descendants of Gad by their clans were:
through Zephon, the Zephonite clan;
through Haggi, the Haggite clan;
through Shuni, the Shunite clan;
¹⁶through Ozni, the Oznite clan;
through Eri, the Erite clan;
¹⁷through Arodi,ᵇ the Arodite clan;

ᵃ 3 Hebrew *Jordan of Jericho*; possibly an ancient name for the Jordan River; also in verse 63   ᵇ 17 Samaritan Pentateuch and Syriac (see also Gen. 46:16); Masoretic Text *Arod* through Areli, the Arelite clan.

[18] These were the clans of Gad; those numbered were 40,500.

[19] Er and Onan were sons of Judah, but they died in Canaan.
[20] The descendants of Judah by their clans were:
through Shelah, the Shelanite clan;
through Perez, the Perezite clan;
through Zerah, the Zerahite clan.
[21] The descendants of Perez were:
through Hezron, the Hezronite clan;
through Hamul, the Hamulite clan.

[22] These were the clans of Judah; those numbered were 76,500.

[23] The descendants of Issachar by their clans were:
through Tola, the Tolaite clan;
through Puah, the Puite[a] clan;
[24] through Jashub, the Jashubite clan;
through Shimron, the Shimronite clan.
[25] These were the clans of Issachar; those numbered were 64,300.

[26] The descendants of Zebulun by their clans were:
through Sered, the Seredite clan;
through Elon, the Elonite clan;
through Jahleel, the Jahleelite clan.
[27] These were the clans of Zebulun; those numbered were 60,500.

[28] The descendants of Joseph by their clans through Manasseh and Ephraim were:

[29] The descendants of Manasseh:
through Makir, the Makirite clan (Makir was the father of Gilead);
through Gilead, the Gileadite clan.
[30] These were the descendants of Gilead:
through Iezer, the Iezerite clan;
through Helek, the Helekite clan;
[31] through Asriel, the Asrielite clan;
through Shechem, the Shechemite clan;
[32] through Shemida, the Shemidaite clan;
through Hepher, the Hepherite clan.
[33] (Zelophehad son of Hepher had no sons; he had only daughters, whose names were Mahlah, Noah, Hoglah, Milcah and Tirzah.)
[34] These were the clans of Manasseh; those numbered were 52,700.

[35] These were the descendants of Ephraim by their clans:
through Shuthelah, the Shuthelahite clan;
through Beker, the Bekerite clan;
through Tahan, the Tahanite clan.
[36] These were the descendants of Shuthelah:
through Eran, the Eranite clan.
[37] These were the clans of Ephraim; those numbered were 32,500.

These were the descendants of Joseph by their clans.

[38] The descendants of Benjamin by their clans were:

A Faith Family Tree

NUMBERS 26:28–34

Look at your ancestors in your personal faith heritage and lineage. What faith traditions shaped the lives of your parents, grandparents, great-grandparents? Can you trace more than one faith among your biological kin? Beyond family, who are your faith ancestors? What relationships, writers, artists or places have shaped your ways of believing and worshiping?

Draw a "faith family tree," placing yourself at its base. On the branches and trunk nearest you, write in the strongest influences in your spiritual life. On other branches, place names or descriptions of other such influences. As you remember and realize more, add branches to your "tree of faith" picture.

See Meeting God in Community

---

a 23 Samaritan Pentateuch, Septuagint, Vulgate and Syriac (see also 1 Chron. 7:1); Masoretic Text *through Puvah, the Punite*

According to Need

NUMBERS 26:52–56

The land is apportioned to the tribes according to their size and how much each tribe needs to survive. Larger tribes with more people are given more land, and smaller tribes are given less land. Many of us are accustomed to abundance in many areas of our lives, and we tend to think in terms of what we want rather than what we need. Examine your closets. How many coats do you have? How many pairs of shoes? How many changes of clothes? Do you have more than you need? In what other areas of your life do you have abundance—in education, money, specialized skills, energy and physical stamina? Think of at least one way you can share what you have in abundance with those who need it, then do it.

See Meeting God in Service

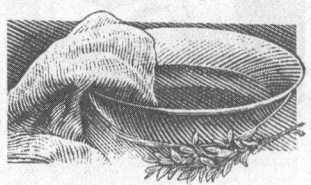

through Bela, the Belaite clan;
through Ashbel, the Ashbelite clan;
through Ahiram, the Ahiramite clan;
³⁹through Shupham,ᵃ the Shuphamite clan;
through Hupham, the Huphamite clan.
⁴⁰The descendants of Bela through Ard and Naaman were:
through Ard,ᵇ the Ardite clan;
through Naaman, the Naamite clan.
⁴¹These were the clans of Benjamin; those numbered were 45,600.

⁴²These were the descendants of Dan by their clans:
through Shuham, the Shuhamite clan.
These were the clans of Dan: ⁴³All of them were Shuhamite clans; and those numbered were 64,400.

⁴⁴The descendants of Asher by their clans were:
through Imnah, the Imnite clan;
through Ishvi, the Ishvite clan;
through Beriah, the Beriite clan;
⁴⁵and through the descendants of Beriah:
through Heber, the Heberite clan;
through Malkiel, the Malkielite clan.
⁴⁶(Asher had a daughter named Serah.)
⁴⁷These were the clans of Asher; those numbered were 53,400.

⁴⁸The descendants of Naphtali by their clans were:
through Jahzeel, the Jahzeelite clan;
through Guni, the Gunite clan;
⁴⁹through Jezer, the Jezerite clan;
through Shillem, the Shillemite clan.
⁵⁰These were the clans of Naphtali; those numbered were 45,400.

⁵¹The total number of the men of Israel was 601,730.

⁵²The LORD said to Moses, ⁵³"The land is to be allotted to them as an inheritance based on the number of names. ⁵⁴To a larger group give a larger inheritance, and to a smaller group a smaller one; each is to receive its inheritance according to the number of those listed. ⁵⁵Be sure that the land is distributed by lot. What each group inherits will be according to the names for its ancestral tribe. ⁵⁶Each inheritance is to be distributed by lot among the larger and smaller groups."

⁵⁷These were the Levites who were counted by their clans:
through Gershon, the Gershonite clan;
through Kohath, the Kohathite clan;
through Merari, the Merarite clan.
⁵⁸These also were Levite clans:
the Libnite clan,
the Hebronite clan,
the Mahlite clan,
the Mushite clan,
the Korahite clan.

ᵃ 39 A few manuscripts of the Masoretic Text, Samaritan Pentateuch, Vulgate and Syriac (see also Septuagint); most manuscripts of the Masoretic Text *Shephupham*   ᵇ 40 Samaritan Pentateuch and Vulgate (see also Septuagint); Masoretic Text does not have *through Ard*.

(Kohath was the forefather of Amram; ⁵⁹the name of Amram's wife was Jochebed, a descendant of Levi, who was born to the Levites*a* in Egypt. To Amram she bore Aaron, Moses and their sister Miriam. ⁶⁰Aaron was the father of Nadab and Abihu, Eleazar and Ithamar. ⁶¹But Nadab and Abihu died when they made an offering before the LORD with unauthorized fire.)

⁶²All the male Levites a month old or more numbered 23,000. They were not counted along with the other Israelites because they received no inheritance among them.

⁶³These are the ones counted by Moses and Eleazar the priest when they counted the Israelites on the plains of Moab by the Jordan across from Jericho. ⁶⁴Not one of them was among those counted by Moses and Aaron the priest when they counted the Israelites in the Desert of Sinai. ⁶⁵For the LORD had told those Israelites they would surely die in the desert, and not one of them was left except Caleb son of Jephunneh and Joshua son of Nun.

Zelophehad's Daughters

27 The daughters of Zelophehad son of Hepher, the son of Gilead, the son of Makir, the son of Manasseh, belonged to the clans of Manasseh son of Joseph. The names of the daughters were Mahlah, Noah, Hoglah, Milcah and Tirzah. They approached ²the entrance to the Tent of Meeting and stood before Moses, Eleazar the priest, the leaders and the whole assembly, and said, ³"Our father died in the desert. He was not among Korah's followers, who banded together against the LORD, but he died for his own sin and left no sons. ⁴Why should our father's name disappear from his clan because he had no son? Give us property among our father's relatives."

⁵So Moses brought their case before the LORD ⁶and the LORD said to him, ⁷"What Zelophehad's daughters are saying is right. You must certainly give them property as an inheritance among their father's relatives and turn their father's inheritance over to them.

⁸"Say to the Israelites, 'If a man dies and leaves no son, turn his inheritance over to his daughter. ⁹If he has no daughter, give his inheritance to his brothers. ¹⁰If he has no brothers, give his inheritance to his father's brothers. ¹¹If his father had no brothers, give his inheritance to the nearest relative in his clan, that he may possess it. This is to be a legal requirement for the Israelites, as the LORD commanded Moses.' "

Joshua to Succeed Moses

¹²Then the LORD said to Moses, "Go up this mountain in the Abarim range and see the land I have given the Israelites. ¹³After you have seen it, you too will be gathered to your people, as your brother Aaron was, ¹⁴for when the community rebelled at the waters in the Desert of Zin, both of you disobeyed my command to honor me as holy before their eyes." (These were the waters of Meribah Kadesh, in the Desert of Zin.)

¹⁵Moses said to the LORD, ¹⁶"May the LORD, the God of the spirits of all mankind, appoint a man over this community ¹⁷to go out and come in before them, one who will lead

Stand Up and Speak

NUMBERS 27:1–5

Mahlah and her sisters join together and speak out for their rights. Imagine standing up in the assembly before all the people, asking Moses to change the rules. Would you be quaking inwardly, outwardly or both? What kinds of issues might be serious enough to call for such action? These women feel they are being treated unfairly, and they say so. Moses listens. This is a new situation, and it calls for new ways of dealing with people.

Have you ever spoken out when you saw someone being treated unfairly? When you are being treated unfairly, do you tend to speak up, or do you avoid confrontation? What situations in our time call for new rules, new ways of dealing with people? What does this model offer us for these situations?

See *Meeting God in Community*

A Pleasing Aroma

NUMBERS 28:6,8

The sacrifices carefully prepared and offered are a "pleasing aroma" to God. Similarly, God is pleased with the fragrant offering of Christ's sacrifice (Ephesians 5:2). The image helps us understand that God is pleased with offerings made with an honest and righteous heart.

Try the practice of using fragrance in your worship time. Bring a scented candle, a bundle of fresh herbs, spices or potpourri to your prayer place. Let the fragrance represent your wholehearted and obedient offering of worship, prayer and repentance before God.

See Meeting God in Worship

them out and bring them in, so the LORD's people will not be like sheep without a shepherd."

¹⁸So the LORD said to Moses, "Take Joshua son of Nun, a man in whom is the spirit,ᵃ and lay your hand on him. ¹⁹Have him stand before Eleazar the priest and the entire assembly and commission him in their presence. ²⁰Give him some of your authority so the whole Israelite community will obey him. ²¹He is to stand before Eleazar the priest, who will obtain decisions for him by inquiring of the Urim before the LORD. At his command he and the entire community of the Israelites will go out, and at his command they will come in."

²²Moses did as the LORD commanded him. He took Joshua and had him stand before Eleazar the priest and the whole assembly. ²³Then he laid his hands on him and commissioned him, as the LORD instructed through Moses.

Daily Offerings

28 The LORD said to Moses, ²"Give this command to the Israelites and say to them: 'See that you present to me at the appointed time the food for my offerings made by fire, as an aroma pleasing to me.' ³Say to them: 'This is the offering made by fire that you are to present to the LORD: two lambs a year old without defect, as a regular burnt offering each day. ⁴Prepare one lamb in the morning and the other at twilight, ⁵together with a grain offering of a tenth of an ephahᵇ of fine flour mixed with a quarter of a hinᶜ of oil from pressed olives. ⁶This is the regular burnt offering instituted at Mount Sinai as a pleasing aroma, an offering made to the LORD by fire. ⁷The accompanying drink offering is to be a quarter of a hin of fermented drink with each lamb. Pour out the drink offering to the LORD at the sanctuary. ⁸Prepare the second lamb at twilight, along with the same kind of grain offering and drink offering that you prepare in the morning. This is an offering made by fire, an aroma pleasing to the LORD.

Sabbath Offerings

⁹" 'On the Sabbath day, make an offering of two lambs a year old without defect, together with its drink offering and a grain offering of two-tenths of an ephahᵈ of fine flour mixed with oil. ¹⁰This is the burnt offering for every Sabbath, in addition to the regular burnt offering and its drink offering.

Monthly Offerings

¹¹" 'On the first of every month, present to the LORD a burnt offering of two young bulls, one ram and seven male lambs a year old, all without defect. ¹²With each bull there is to be a grain offering of three-tenths of an ephahᵉ of fine flour mixed with oil; with the ram, a grain offering of two-tenths of an ephah of fine flour mixed with oil; ¹³and with each lamb, a grain offering of a tenth of an ephah of fine flour mixed with oil. This is for a burnt offering, a pleasing aroma, an offering made to the LORD by fire. ¹⁴With each

---

a 18 Or *Spirit*   *b 5* That is, probably about 2 quarts (about 2 liters); also in verses 13, 21 and 29   *c 5* That is, probably about 1 quart (about 1 liter); also in verses 7 and 14   *d 9* That is, probably about 4 quarts (about 4.5 liters); also in verses 12, 20 and 28   *e 12* That is, probably about 6 quarts (about 6.5 liters); also in verses 20 and 28

bull there is to be a drink offering of half a hin[a] of wine; with the ram, a third of a hin[b]; and with each lamb, a quarter of a hin. This is the monthly burnt offering to be made at each new moon during the year. [15]Besides the regular burnt offering with its drink offering, one male goat is to be presented to the LORD as a sin offering.

The Passover

[16]" 'On the fourteenth day of the first month the LORD's Passover is to be held. [17]On the fifteenth day of this month there is to be a festival; for seven days eat bread made without yeast. [18]On the first day hold a sacred assembly and do no regular work. [19]Present to the LORD an offering made by fire, a burnt offering of two young bulls, one ram and seven male lambs a year old, all without defect. [20]With each bull prepare a grain offering of three-tenths of an ephah of fine flour mixed with oil; with the ram, two-tenths; [21]and with each of the seven lambs, one-tenth. [22]Include one male goat as a sin offering to make atonement for you. [23]Prepare these in addition to the regular morning burnt offering. [24]In this way prepare the food for the offering made by fire every day for seven days as an aroma pleasing to the LORD; it is to be prepared in addition to the regular burnt offering and its drink offering. [25]On the seventh day hold a sacred assembly and do no regular work.

Feast of Weeks

[26]" 'On the day of firstfruits, when you present to the LORD an offering of new grain during the Feast of Weeks, hold a sacred assembly and do no regular work. [27]Present a burnt offering of two young bulls, one ram and seven male lambs a year old as an aroma pleasing to the LORD. [28]With each bull there is to be a grain offering of three-tenths of an ephah of fine flour mixed with oil; with the ram, two-tenths; [29]and with each of the seven lambs, one-tenth. [30]Include one male goat to make atonement for you. [31]Prepare these together with their drink offerings, in addition to the regular burnt offering and its grain offering. Be sure the animals are without defect.

Feast of Trumpets

29

" 'On the first day of the seventh month hold a sacred assembly and do no regular work. It is a day for you to sound the trumpets. [2]As an aroma pleasing to the LORD, prepare a burnt offering of one young bull, one ram and seven male lambs a year old, all without defect. [3]With the bull prepare a grain offering of three-tenths of an ephah[c] of fine flour mixed with oil; with the ram, two-tenths[d]; [4]and with each of the seven lambs, one-tenth.[e] [5]Include one male goat as a sin offering to make atonement for you. [6]These are in addition to the monthly and daily burnt offerings with their grain offerings and drink offerings as specified. They are offerings made to the LORD by fire—a pleasing aroma.

---

[a]14 That is, probably about 2 quarts (about 2 liters)   [b]14 That is, probably about 1 1/4 quarts (about 1.2 liters)   [c]3 That is, probably about 6 quarts (about 6.5 liters); also in verses 9 and 14   [d]3 That is, probably about 4 quarts (about 4.5 liters); also in verses 9 and 14   [e]4 That is, probably about 2 quarts (about 2 liters); also in verses 10 and 15

Set the Date

NUMBERS 28:25–26; 29:1

The Israelites set aside a special time to hold a "sacred assembly and do no regular work." Think about your calendar. When can you set aside some time to spend with God, a special time for prayer, Bible study, spiritual reading and simply resting in God's presence, in addition to your usual worship or service? Perhaps you can participate in a retreat alone or with others. If you cannot take an entire day or weekend, consider setting aside a few hours on Saturday mornings or a few afternoons this month. God longs for time with you as loved ones long for time with their beloved. God will meet you whenever and wherever you make a meeting place. Make an appointment to meet with God.

See Meeting God in Prayer

Do What Is Right

NUMBERS 29:12–38

"It is the duty of every one to be firm in that which they certainly know is right for them."
—JOHN WOOLMAN,
The Journal of John Woolman

Day of Atonement

⁷" 'On the tenth day of this seventh month hold a sacred assembly. You must deny yourselves*ᵃ* and do no work. ⁸Present as an aroma pleasing to the Lᴏʀᴅ a burnt offering of one young bull, one ram and seven male lambs a year old, all without defect. ⁹With the bull prepare a grain offering of three-tenths of an ephah of fine flour mixed with oil; with the ram, two-tenths; ¹⁰and with each of the seven lambs, one-tenth. ¹¹Include one male goat as a sin offering, in addition to the sin offering for atonement and the regular burnt offering with its grain offering, and their drink offerings.

Feast of Tabernacles

¹²" 'On the fifteenth day of the seventh month, hold a sacred assembly and do no regular work. Celebrate a festival to the Lᴏʀᴅ for seven days. ¹³Present an offering made by fire as an aroma pleasing to the Lᴏʀᴅ, a burnt offering of thirteen young bulls, two rams and fourteen male lambs a year old, all without defect. ¹⁴With each of the thirteen bulls prepare a grain offering of three-tenths of an ephah of fine flour mixed with oil; with each of the two rams, two-tenths; ¹⁵and with each of the fourteen lambs, one-tenth. ¹⁶Include one male goat as a sin offering, in addition to the regular burnt offering with its grain offering and drink offering.

¹⁷" 'On the second day prepare twelve young bulls, two rams and fourteen male lambs a year old, all without defect. ¹⁸With the bulls, rams and lambs, prepare their grain offerings and drink offerings according to the number specified. ¹⁹Include one male goat as a sin offering, in addition to the regular burnt offering with its grain offering, and their drink offerings.

²⁰" 'On the third day prepare eleven bulls, two rams and fourteen male lambs a year old, all without defect. ²¹With the bulls, rams and lambs, prepare their grain offerings and drink offerings according to the number specified. ²²Include one male goat as a sin offering, in addition to the regular burnt offering with its grain offering and drink offering.

²³" 'On the fourth day prepare ten bulls, two rams and fourteen male lambs a year old, all without defect. ²⁴With the bulls, rams and lambs, prepare their grain offerings and drink offerings according to the number specified. ²⁵Include one male goat as a sin offering, in addition to the regular burnt offering with its grain offering and drink offering.

²⁶" 'On the fifth day prepare nine bulls, two rams and fourteen male lambs a year old, all without defect. ²⁷With the bulls, rams and lambs, prepare their grain offerings and drink offerings according to the number specified. ²⁸Include one male goat as a sin offering, in addition to the regular burnt offering with its grain offering and drink offering.

²⁹" 'On the sixth day prepare eight bulls, two rams and fourteen male lambs a year old, all without defect. ³⁰With the bulls, rams and lambs, prepare their grain offerings and drink offerings according to the number specified. ³¹Include one male goat as a sin offering, in addition to the reg-

ᵃ 7 Or must fast

ular burnt offering with its grain offering and drink offering.

³²" 'On the seventh day prepare seven bulls, two rams and fourteen male lambs a year old, all without defect. ³³With the bulls, rams and lambs, prepare their grain offerings and drink offerings according to the number specified. ³⁴Include one male goat as a sin offering, in addition to the regular burnt offering with its grain offering and drink offering.

³⁵" 'On the eighth day hold an assembly and do no regular work. ³⁶Present an offering made by fire as an aroma pleasing to the LORD, a burnt offering of one bull, one ram and seven male lambs a year old, all without defect. ³⁷With the bull, the ram and the lambs, prepare their grain offerings and drink offerings according to the number specified. ³⁸Include one male goat as a sin offering, in addition to the regular burnt offering with its grain offering and drink offering.

³⁹" 'In addition to what you vow and your freewill offerings, prepare these for the LORD at your appointed feasts: your burnt offerings, grain offerings, drink offerings and fellowship offerings.ᵃ' "

⁴⁰Moses told the Israelites all that the LORD commanded him.

Vows

30 Moses said to the heads of the tribes of Israel: "This is what the LORD commands: ²When a man makes a vow to the LORD or takes an oath to obligate himself by a pledge, he must not break his word but must do everything he said.

³"When a young woman still living in her father's house makes a vow to the LORD or obligates herself by a pledge ⁴and her father hears about her vow or pledge but says nothing to her, then all her vows and every pledge by which she obligated herself will stand. ⁵But if her father forbids her when he hears about it, none of her vows or the pledges by which she obligated herself will stand; the LORD will release her because her father has forbidden her.

⁶"If she marries after she makes a vow or after her lips utter a rash promise by which she obligates herself ⁷and her husband hears about it but says nothing to her, then her vows or the pledges by which she obligated herself will stand. ⁸But if her husband forbids her when he hears about it, he nullifies the vow that obligates her or the rash promise by which she obligates herself, and the LORD will release her.

⁹"Any vow or obligation taken by a widow or divorced woman will be binding on her.

¹⁰"If a woman living with her husband makes a vow or obligates herself by a pledge under oath ¹¹and her husband hears about it but says nothing to her and does not forbid her, then all her vows or the pledges by which she obligated herself will stand. ¹²But if her husband nullifies them when he hears about them, then none of the vows or pledges that came from her lips will stand. Her husband has nullified them, and the LORD will release her. ¹³Her husband may confirm or nullify any vow she makes or any sworn pledge to deny herself. ¹⁴But if her husband says

Supporting the Vows

NUMBERS 30:1–15

This passage describes the role the Israelites assumed, by their verbal or tacit assent, in vows made by others. A similar principle is invoked in the traditional marriage ceremony when the officiant asks the gathered witnesses to assent to the lawfulness of the marriage, "If anyone knows any reason why this man and this woman may not be lawfully joined, let them speak now or forever hold their peace."

We can learn from this passage that we are not to hinder others in keeping their vows. We have a responsibility to uphold those close to us in keeping their commitments to God. Who supports you in your faith? What can you do to support those you care about in living their faith?

See *Meeting God in Community*

Purity of Heart

"Be exceedingly quick to turn aside from the slightest thing leading to impurity, for it is an evil that approaches stealthily and in which the very smallest beginnings are apt to grow rapidly."

—FRANCIS DE SALES,
Introduction to the Devout Life

nothing to her about it from day to day, then he confirms all her vows or the pledges binding on her. He confirms them by saying nothing to her when he hears about them. ¹⁵If, however, he nullifies them some time after he hears about them, then he is responsible for her guilt."

¹⁶These are the regulations the LORD gave Moses concerning relationships between a man and his wife, and between a father and his young daughter still living in his house.

Vengeance on the Midianites

31 The LORD said to Moses, ²"Take vengeance on the Midianites for the Israelites. After that, you will be gathered to your people."

³So Moses said to the people, "Arm some of your men to go to war against the Midianites and to carry out the LORD's vengeance on them. ⁴Send into battle a thousand men from each of the tribes of Israel." ⁵So twelve thousand men armed for battle, a thousand from each tribe, were supplied from the clans of Israel. ⁶Moses sent them into battle, a thousand from each tribe, along with Phinehas son of Eleazar, the priest, who took with him articles from the sanctuary and the trumpets for signaling.

⁷They fought against Midian, as the LORD commanded Moses, and killed every man. ⁸Among their victims were Evi, Rekem, Zur, Hur and Reba—the five kings of Midian. They also killed Balaam son of Beor with the sword. ⁹The Israelites captured the Midianite women and children and took all the Midianite herds, flocks and goods as plunder. ¹⁰They burned all the towns where the Midianites had settled, as well as all their camps. ¹¹They took all the plunder and spoils, including the people and animals, ¹²and brought the captives, spoils and plunder to Moses and Eleazar the priest and the Israelite assembly at their camp on the plains of Moab, by the Jordan across from Jericho.ᵃ

¹³Moses, Eleazar the priest and all the leaders of the community went to meet them outside the camp. ¹⁴Moses was angry with the officers of the army—the commanders of thousands and commanders of hundreds—who returned from the battle.

¹⁵"Have you allowed all the women to live?" he asked them. ¹⁶"They were the ones who followed Balaam's advice and were the means of turning the Israelites away from the LORD in what happened at Peor, so that a plague struck the LORD's people. ¹⁷Now kill all the boys. And kill every woman who has slept with a man, ¹⁸but save for yourselves every girl who has never slept with a man.

¹⁹"All of you who have killed anyone or touched anyone who was killed must stay outside the camp seven days. On the third and seventh days you must purify yourselves and your captives. ²⁰Purify every garment as well as everything made of leather, goat hair or wood."

²¹Then Eleazar the priest said to the soldiers who had gone into battle, "This is the requirement of the law that the LORD gave Moses: ²²Gold, silver, bronze, iron, tin, lead ²³and anything else that can withstand fire must be put through the fire, and then it will be clean. But it must also be purified with the water of cleansing. And whatever cannot withstand fire must be put through that water. ²⁴On the sev-

ᵃ 12 Hebrew *Jordan of Jericho*; possibly an ancient name for the Jordan River

enth day wash your clothes and you will be clean. Then you may come into the camp."

Dividing the Spoils

²⁵The LORD said to Moses, ²⁶"You and Eleazar the priest and the family heads of the community are to count all the people and animals that were captured. ²⁷Divide the spoils between the soldiers who took part in the battle and the rest of the community. ²⁸From the soldiers who fought in the battle, set apart as tribute for the LORD one out of every five hundred, whether persons, cattle, donkeys, sheep or goats. ²⁹Take this tribute from their half share and give it to Eleazar the priest as the LORD's part. ³⁰From the Israelites' half, select one out of every fifty, whether persons, cattle, donkeys, sheep, goats or other animals. Give them to the Levites, who are responsible for the care of the LORD's tabernacle." ³¹So Moses and Eleazar the priest did as the LORD commanded Moses.

³²The plunder remaining from the spoils that the soldiers took was 675,000 sheep, ³³72,000 cattle, ³⁴61,000 donkeys ³⁵and 32,000 women who had never slept with a man.

³⁶The half share of those who fought in the battle was:

337,500 sheep, ³⁷of which the tribute for the LORD was 675;

³⁸36,000 cattle, of which the tribute for the LORD was 72;

³⁹30,500 donkeys, of which the tribute for the LORD was 61;

⁴⁰16,000 people, of which the tribute for the LORD was 32.

⁴¹Moses gave the tribute to Eleazar the priest as the LORD's part, as the LORD commanded Moses.

⁴²The half belonging to the Israelites, which Moses set apart from that of the fighting men— ⁴³the community's half—was 337,500 sheep, ⁴⁴36,000 cattle, ⁴⁵30,500 donkeys ⁴⁶and 16,000 people. ⁴⁷From the Israelites' half, Moses selected one out of every fifty persons and animals, as the LORD commanded him, and gave them to the Levites, who were responsible for the care of the LORD's tabernacle.

⁴⁸Then the officers who were over the units of the army—the commanders of thousands and commanders of hundreds—went to Moses ⁴⁹and said to him, "Your servants have counted the soldiers under our command, and not one is missing. ⁵⁰So we have brought as an offering to the LORD the gold articles each of us acquired—armlets, bracelets, signet rings, earrings and necklaces—to make atonement for ourselves before the LORD."

⁵¹Moses and Eleazar the priest accepted from them the gold—all the crafted articles. ⁵²All the gold from the commanders of thousands and commanders of hundreds that Moses and Eleazar presented as a gift to the LORD weighed 16,750 shekels.ᵃ ⁵³Each soldier had taken plunder for himself. ⁵⁴Moses and Eleazar the priest accepted the gold from the commanders of thousands and commanders of hundreds and brought it into the Tent of Meeting as a memorial for the Israelites before the LORD.

ᵃ 52 That is, about 420 pounds (about 190 kilograms)

Dividing the Spoils

NUMBERS 31:25–51

Not only was God giving the Israelites the land of the Midianites, he also allowed them to gather the spoils of war to give them the wealth to establish themselves in the land. The spoils of war were to be divided according to strict guidelines, however, with a certain percentage going to the Levites. All the gold the commanders of the army had collected was to be brought into the Tent of Meeting as a memorial before the Lord.

What would you do with a sudden windfall of wealth? How would you divide the "spoils" if you won a sweepstakes or received a bonus or an unexpected tax refund? Set up a new business? Buy a new house? Pay off your mortgage? What would be an appropriate way to thank God? What is the first thing you think of when you contemplate such a situation? Use this scenario to think through your values and priorities.

See Meeting God in Everyday Life

Cause and Effect

NUMBERS 32:15,20,29

Moses repeats the "if, then" pattern several times in this passage, making sure that the Reubenites and Gadites understand that their choices will have clear consequences and that turning away from God will have an undesirable result.

Though God forgives us when we make selfish and stubborn choices, he does sometimes let us suffer the consequences for our decisions. Many of our difficulties are consequences of our own acts. What consequences have taught you valuable lessons? What consequences are you struggling with now and what are you learning in the process?

See Meeting God in Everyday Life

The Transjordan Tribes

32 The Reubenites and Gadites, who had very large herds and flocks, saw that the lands of Jazer and Gilead were suitable for livestock. ²So they came to Moses and Eleazar the priest and to the leaders of the community, and said, ³"Ataroth, Dibon, Jazer, Nimrah, Heshbon, Elealeh, Sebam, Nebo and Beon— ⁴the land the LORD subdued before the people of Israel—are suitable for livestock, and your servants have livestock. ⁵If we have found favor in your eyes," they said, "let this land be given to your servants as our possession. Do not make us cross the Jordan."

⁶Moses said to the Gadites and Reubenites, "Shall your countrymen go to war while you sit here? ⁷Why do you discourage the Israelites from going over into the land the LORD has given them? ⁸This is what your fathers did when I sent them from Kadesh Barnea to look over the land. ⁹After they went up to the Valley of Eshcol and viewed the land, they discouraged the Israelites from entering the land the LORD had given them. ¹⁰The LORD's anger was aroused that day and he swore this oath: ¹¹'Because they have not followed me wholeheartedly, not one of the men twenty years old or more who came up out of Egypt will see the land I promised on oath to Abraham, Isaac and Jacob— ¹²not one except Caleb son of Jephunneh the Kenizzite and Joshua son of Nun, for they followed the LORD wholeheartedly.' ¹³The LORD's anger burned against Israel and he made them wander in the desert forty years, until the whole generation of those who had done evil in his sight was gone.

¹⁴"And here you are, a brood of sinners, standing in the place of your fathers and making the LORD even more angry with Israel. ¹⁵If you turn away from following him, he will again leave all this people in the desert, and you will be the cause of their destruction."

¹⁶Then they came up to him and said, "We would like to build pens here for our livestock and cities for our women and children. ¹⁷But we are ready to arm ourselves and go ahead of the Israelites until we have brought them to their place. Meanwhile our women and children will live in fortified cities, for protection from the inhabitants of the land. ¹⁸We will not return to our homes until every Israelite has received his inheritance. ¹⁹We will not receive any inheritance with them on the other side of the Jordan, because our inheritance has come to us on the east side of the Jordan."

²⁰Then Moses said to them, "If you will do this—if you will arm yourselves before the LORD for battle, ²¹and if all of you will go armed over the Jordan before the LORD until he has driven his enemies out before him— ²²then when the land is subdued before the LORD, you may return and be free from your obligation to the LORD and to Israel. And this land will be your possession before the LORD.

²³"But if you fail to do this, you will be sinning against the LORD; and you may be sure that your sin will find you out. ²⁴Build cities for your women and children, and pens for your flocks, but do what you have promised."

²⁵The Gadites and Reubenites said to Moses, "We your servants will do as our lord commands. ²⁶Our children and wives, our flocks and herds will remain here in the cities of Gilead. ²⁷But your servants, every man armed for battle, will cross over to fight before the LORD, just as our lord says."

²⁸Then Moses gave orders about them to Eleazar the priest and Joshua son of Nun and to the family heads of the Israelite tribes. ²⁹He said to them, "If the Gadites and Reubenites, every man armed for battle, cross over the Jordan with you before the LORD, then when the land is subdued before you, give them the land of Gilead as their possession. ³⁰But if they do not cross over with you armed, they must accept their possession with you in Canaan."

³¹The Gadites and Reubenites answered, "Your servants will do what the LORD has said. ³²We will cross over before the LORD into Canaan armed, but the property we inherit will be on this side of the Jordan."

³³Then Moses gave to the Gadites, the Reubenites and the half-tribe of Manasseh son of Joseph the kingdom of Sihon king of the Amorites and the kingdom of Og king of Bashan—the whole land with its cities and the territory around them.

³⁴The Gadites built up Dibon, Ataroth, Aroer, ³⁵Atroth Shophan, Jazer, Jogbehah, ³⁶Beth Nimrah and Beth Haran as fortified cities, and built pens for their flocks. ³⁷And the Reubenites rebuilt Heshbon, Elealeh and Kiriathaim, ³⁸as well as Nebo and Baal Meon (these names were changed) and Sibmah. They gave names to the cities they rebuilt.

³⁹The descendants of Makir son of Manasseh went to Gilead, captured it and drove out the Amorites who were there. ⁴⁰So Moses gave Gilead to the Makirites, the descendants of Manasseh, and they settled there. ⁴¹Jair, a descendant of Manasseh, captured their settlements and called them Havvoth Jair.ᵃ ⁴²And Nobah captured Kenath and its surrounding settlements and called it Nobah after himself.

Stages in Israel's Journey

33 Here are the stages in the journey of the Israelites when they came out of Egypt by divisions under the leadership of Moses and Aaron. ²At the LORD's command Moses recorded the stages in their journey. This is their journey by stages:

³The Israelites set out from Rameses on the fifteenth day of the first month, the day after the Passover. They marched out boldly in full view of all the Egyptians, ⁴who were burying all their firstborn, whom the LORD had struck down among them; for the LORD had brought judgment on their gods.

⁵The Israelites left Rameses and camped at Succoth. ⁶They left Succoth and camped at Etham, on the edge of the desert. ⁷They left Etham, turned back to Pi Hahiroth, to the east of Baal Zephon, and camped near Migdol. ⁸They left Pi Hahirothᵇ and passed through the sea into the desert, and when they had traveled for three days in the Desert of Etham, they camped at Marah. ⁹They left Marah and went to Elim, where there were twelve springs and seventy palm trees, and they camped there.

¹⁰They left Elim and camped by the Red Sea.ᶜ

ᵃ 41 Or *them the settlements of Jair*   ᵇ 8 Many manuscripts of the Masoretic Text, Samaritan Pentateuch and Vulgate; most manuscripts of the Masoretic Text *left from before Hahiroth*   ᶜ 10 Hebrew *Yam Suph*; that is, Sea of Reeds; also in verse 11

Your Lifeline

NUMBERS 33:1–2

Record the stages of your journey, as Moses recorded the journey of the Israelites. (If you keep a spiritual journal, you may want to record this.) Draw a horizontal line to represent your life. Beginning with your birth year, mark off five- or ten-year sections on the line. Above the line, list significant events within each time span. Below the line, list spiritual milestones or some wisdom you have gained from each period. Did you spend time wandering in the desert? If you were writing a book about your life, what would the chapter titles be? What would the title of the last chapter be? Do you see any patterns in your journey so far? Take some time to reflect on where you started and where you are today.

See Meeting God in Everyday Life

Vestiges of the Old Life

NUMBERS 33:51–55

Moderation is not necessarily a Biblical ideal, it seems. Again in this passage, the Israelites hear that it must be all or nothing. Moses demands that the people demolish all the "high places," every vestige of idols and idol worship. If they allow any trace to remain, these will become "barbs" in their eyes and "thorns" in their sides.

Though we say we want to follow God, we may try to keep some of our old ways, perhaps some old relationships. In what ways are your past actions like a barb to you? What bad habit is like a thorn in your side? Are there areas in which you still need to let go of habits or activities that keep you from serving God with all your heart? What do you need to do in order to be free of them?

See Meeting God in Everyday Life

[11] They left the Red Sea and camped in the Desert of Sin.

[12] They left the Desert of Sin and camped at Dophkah.

[13] They left Dophkah and camped at Alush.

[14] They left Alush and camped at Rephidim, where there was no water for the people to drink.

[15] They left Rephidim and camped in the Desert of Sinai.

[16] They left the Desert of Sinai and camped at Kibroth Hattaavah.

[17] They left Kibroth Hattaavah and camped at Hazeroth.

[18] They left Hazeroth and camped at Rithmah.

[19] They left Rithmah and camped at Rimmon Perez.

[20] They left Rimmon Perez and camped at Libnah.

[21] They left Libnah and camped at Rissah.

[22] They left Rissah and camped at Kehelathah.

[23] They left Kehelathah and camped at Mount Shepher.

[24] They left Mount Shepher and camped at Haradah.

[25] They left Haradah and camped at Makheloth.

[26] They left Makheloth and camped at Tahath.

[27] They left Tahath and camped at Terah.

[28] They left Terah and camped at Mithcah.

[29] They left Mithcah and camped at Hashmonah.

[30] They left Hashmonah and camped at Moseroth.

[31] They left Moseroth and camped at Bene Jaakan.

[32] They left Bene Jaakan and camped at Hor Haggidgad.

[33] They left Hor Haggidgad and camped at Jotbathah.

[34] They left Jotbathah and camped at Abronah.

[35] They left Abronah and camped at Ezion Geber.

[36] They left Ezion Geber and camped at Kadesh, in the Desert of Zin.

[37] They left Kadesh and camped at Mount Hor, on the border of Edom. [38] At the LORD's command Aaron the priest went up Mount Hor, where he died on the first day of the fifth month of the fortieth year after the Israelites came out of Egypt. [39] Aaron was a hundred and twenty-three years old when he died on Mount Hor.

[40] The Canaanite king of Arad, who lived in the Negev of Canaan, heard that the Israelites were coming.

[41] They left Mount Hor and camped at Zalmonah.

[42] They left Zalmonah and camped at Punon.

[43] They left Punon and camped at Oboth.

[44] They left Oboth and camped at Iye Abarim, on the border of Moab.

[45] They left Iyim[a] and camped at Dibon Gad.

[46] They left Dibon Gad and camped at Almon Diblathaim.

[47] They left Almon Diblathaim and camped in the mountains of Abarim, near Nebo.

[48] They left the mountains of Abarim and camped on the plains of Moab by the Jordan across from Jericho.[b]

[49] There on the plains of Moab they camped along the Jordan from Beth Jeshimoth to Abel Shittim.

---

a 45 That is, Iye Abarim   *b 48* Hebrew *Jordan of Jericho*; possibly an ancient name for the Jordan River; also in verse 50

⁵⁰On the plains of Moab by the Jordan across from Jericho the Lord said to Moses, ⁵¹"Speak to the Israelites and say to them: 'When you cross the Jordan into Canaan, ⁵²drive out all the inhabitants of the land before you. Destroy all their carved images and their cast idols, and demolish all their high places. ⁵³Take possession of the land and settle in it, for I have given you the land to possess. ⁵⁴Distribute the land by lot, according to your clans. To a larger group give a larger inheritance, and to a smaller group a smaller one. Whatever falls to them by lot will be theirs. Distribute it according to your ancestral tribes.

⁵⁵ 'But if you do not drive out the inhabitants of the land, those you allow to remain will become barbs in your eyes and thorns in your sides. They will give you trouble in the land where you will live. ⁵⁶And then I will do to you what I plan to do to them.' "

Boundaries of Canaan

34 The Lord said to Moses, ²"Command the Israelites and say to them: 'When you enter Canaan, the land that will be allotted to you as an inheritance will have these boundaries:

³" 'Your southern side will include some of the Desert of Zin along the border of Edom. On the east, your southern boundary will start from the end of the Salt Sea,ᵃ ⁴cross south of Scorpionᵇ Pass, continue on to Zin and go south of Kadesh Barnea. Then it will go to Hazar Addar and over to Azmon, ⁵where it will turn, join the Wadi of Egypt and end at the Sea.ᶜ

⁶" 'Your western boundary will be the coast of the Great Sea. This will be your boundary on the west.

⁷" 'For your northern boundary, run a line from the Great Sea to Mount Hor ⁸and from Mount Hor to Leboᵈ Hamath. Then the boundary will go to Zedad, ⁹continue to Ziphron and end at Hazar Enan. This will be your boundary on the north.

¹⁰" 'For your eastern boundary, run a line from Hazar Enan to Shepham. ¹¹The boundary will go down from Shepham to Riblah on the east side of Ain and continue along the slopes east of the Sea of Kinnereth.ᵉ ¹²Then the boundary will go down along the Jordan and end at the Salt Sea.

" 'This will be your land, with its boundaries on every side.' "

¹³Moses commanded the Israelites: "Assign this land by lot as an inheritance. The Lord has ordered that it be given to the nine and a half tribes, ¹⁴because the families of the tribe of Reuben, the tribe of Gad and the half-tribe of Manasseh have received their inheritance. ¹⁵These two and a half tribes have received their inheritance on the east side of the Jordan of Jericho,ᶠ toward the sunrise."

¹⁶The Lord said to Moses, ¹⁷"These are the names of the men who are to assign the land for you as an inheritance: Eleazar the priest and Joshua son of Nun. ¹⁸And appoint one leader from each tribe to help assign the land. ¹⁹These are their names:

Your Boundaries

NUMBERS 34:1–15

God gave the Israelites a specific area as their domain; God gives us opportunities and responsibilities. The outline of the modern country of Israel looks roughly like a wide, shortened necktie. Draw this shape to represent your life and what God has given you. Subdivide the shape into portions, labeling the parts to show the things on which you spend time, energy and care. Put your major concerns in the center of your "country," as Jerusalem is in the center of Israel. Draw the same shape again and label it to show what you want to be spending time, energy and care on five years from now.

ᵃ3 That is, the Dead Sea; also in verse 12   ᵇ4 Hebrew *Akrabbim*
ᶜ5 That is, the Mediterranean; also in verses 6 and 7   ᵈ8 Or *to the entrance to*   ᵉ11 That is, Galilee   ᶠ15 *Jordan of Jericho* was possibly an ancient name for the Jordan River.

Cities of Refuge

NUMBERS 35:9–15

This passage invites us to consider our attitudes toward mercy. Recall a death that has touched your community. Perhaps someone driving under the influence of alchohol has caused the deaths of an entire family, or someone playing a prank has caused a young person to be killed. Would your church be willing to be a "city of refuge" for the person or persons who caused the death(s)? What would people's reactions be if the person who caused a death were to stand up in your worship service and ask for help? What if the family of the victim were also a part of your congregation? How can we respond to both perpetrator and victim with mercy? God calls for mercy. How can you extend mercy in these and other less serious everyday situations?

See *Meeting God in Community*

Caleb son of Jephunneh,
from the tribe of Judah;
²⁰Shemuel son of Ammihud,
from the tribe of Simeon;
²¹Elidad son of Kislon,
from the tribe of Benjamin;
²²Bukki son of Jogli,
the leader from the tribe of Dan;
²³Hanniel son of Ephod,
the leader from the tribe of Manasseh son of Joseph;
²⁴Kemuel son of Shiphtan,
the leader from the tribe of Ephraim son of Joseph;
²⁵Elizaphan son of Parnach,
the leader from the tribe of Zebulun;
²⁶Paltiel son of Azzan,
the leader from the tribe of Issachar;
²⁷Ahihud son of Shelomi,
the leader from the tribe of Asher;
²⁸Pedahel son of Ammihud,
the leader from the tribe of Naphtali."
²⁹These are the men the LORD commanded to assign the inheritance to the Israelites in the land of Canaan.

Towns for the Levites

35 On the plains of Moab by the Jordan across from Jericho,ᵃ the LORD said to Moses, ²"Command the Israelites to give the Levites towns to live in from the inheritance the Israelites will possess. And give them pasturelands around the towns. ³Then they will have towns to live in and pasturelands for their cattle, flocks and all their other livestock.

⁴"The pasturelands around the towns that you give the Levites will extend out fifteen hundred feetᵇ from the town wall. ⁵Outside the town, measure three thousand feetᶜ on the east side, three thousand on the south side, three thousand on the west and three thousand on the north, with the town in the center. They will have this area as pastureland for the towns.

Cities of Refuge

⁶"Six of the towns you give the Levites will be cities of refuge, to which a person who has killed someone may flee. In addition, give them forty-two other towns. ⁷In all you must give the Levites forty-eight towns, together with their pasturelands. ⁸The towns you give the Levites from the land the Israelites possess are to be given in proportion to the inheritance of each tribe: Take many towns from a tribe that has many, but few from one that has few."

⁹Then the LORD said to Moses: ¹⁰"Speak to the Israelites and say to them: 'When you cross the Jordan into Canaan, ¹¹select some towns to be your cities of refuge, to which a person who has killed someone accidentally may flee. ¹²They will be places of refuge from the avenger, so that a person accused of murder may not die before he stands trial before the assembly. ¹³These six towns you give will be your cities of refuge. ¹⁴Give three on this side of the Jordan and three in Canaan as cities of refuge. ¹⁵These six towns

ᵃ 1 Hebrew *Jordan of Jericho*; possibly an ancient name for the Jordan River   ᵇ 4 Hebrew *a thousand cubits* (about 450 meters)   ᶜ 5 Hebrew *two thousand cubits* (about 900 meters)

will be a place of refuge for Israelites, aliens and any other people living among them, so that anyone who has killed another accidentally can flee there.

16" 'If a man strikes someone with an iron object so that he dies, he is a murderer; the murderer shall be put to death. 17Or if anyone has a stone in his hand that could kill, and he strikes someone so that he dies, he is a murderer; the murderer shall be put to death. 18Or if anyone has a wooden object in his hand that could kill, and he hits someone so that he dies, he is a murderer; the murderer shall be put to death. 19The avenger of blood shall put the murderer to death; when he meets him, he shall put him to death. 20If anyone with malice aforethought shoves another or throws something at him intentionally so that he dies 21or if in hostility he hits him with his fist so that he dies, that person shall be put to death; he is a murderer. The avenger of blood shall put the murderer to death when he meets him.

22" 'But if without hostility someone suddenly shoves another or throws something at him unintentionally 23or, without seeing him, drops a stone on him that could kill him, and he dies, then since he was not his enemy and he did not intend to harm him, 24the assembly must judge between him and the avenger of blood according to these regulations. 25The assembly must protect the one accused of murder from the avenger of blood and send him back to the city of refuge to which he fled. He must stay there until the death of the high priest, who was anointed with the holy oil.

26" 'But if the accused ever goes outside the limits of the city of refuge to which he has fled 27and the avenger of blood finds him outside the city, the avenger of blood may kill the accused without being guilty of murder. 28The accused must stay in his city of refuge until the death of the high priest; only after the death of the high priest may he return to his own property.

29" 'These are to be legal requirements for you throughout the generations to come, wherever you live.

30" 'Anyone who kills a person is to be put to death as a murderer only on the testimony of witnesses. But no one is to be put to death on the testimony of only one witness.

31" 'Do not accept a ransom for the life of a murderer, who deserves to die. He must surely be put to death.

32" 'Do not accept a ransom for anyone who has fled to a city of refuge and so allow him to go back and live on his own land before the death of the high priest.

33" 'Do not pollute the land where you are. Bloodshed pollutes the land, and atonement cannot be made for the land on which blood has been shed, except by the blood of the one who shed it. 34Do not defile the land where you live and where I dwell, for I, the LORD, dwell among the Israelites.' "

Inheritance of Zelophehad's Daughters

36 The family heads of the clan of Gilead son of Makir, the son of Manasseh, who were from the clans of the descendants of Joseph, came and spoke before Moses and the leaders, the heads of the Israelite families. 2They said, "When the LORD commanded my lord to give the land as an inheritance to the Israelites by lot, he ordered you to

God's Dwelling

NUMBERS 35:22-34

Violence "pollutes" the land, and pollution is unacceptable because God dwells with the Israelites. The passage suggests that we seek justice as a way of honoring God, who dwells among us. How might we deal with violence to make our communities places that reflect the presence of God? If violence pollutes the places where it occurs, how can we pray and act to cleanse our surroundings of violence? What can you do to help victims of violence?

See Meeting God in Service

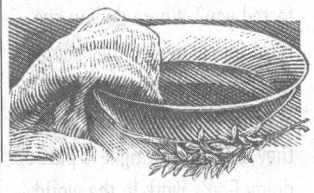

Women's Rights?

NUMBERS 36:1–7

The women of Israel had not been allowed to inherit property, but Moses changed the rules in order to give these women an inheritance—because it was the just, fair thing to do.

In modern times, changes in written and unwritten "rules" have allowed women to be employed, vote for candidates for political office, be educated, hold political office and be ordained as clergy. Think about your life. What changes in society's "rules" about ethnic groups, social class, gender roles and occupations have affected you? Where do you see need for change so that people may be treated more fairly? Making such changes because they are just and right is part of doing God's work in the world. How are you seeking God's justice in the community?

See Meeting God in Community

give the inheritance of our brother Zelophehad to his daughters. ³Now suppose they marry men from other Israelite tribes; then their inheritance will be taken from our ancestral inheritance and added to that of the tribe they marry into. And so part of the inheritance allotted to us will be taken away. ⁴When the Year of Jubilee for the Israelites comes, their inheritance will be added to that of the tribe into which they marry, and their property will be taken from the tribal inheritance of our forefathers."

⁵Then at the LORD's command Moses gave this order to the Israelites: "What the tribe of the descendants of Joseph is saying is right. ⁶This is what the LORD commands for Zelophehad's daughters: They may marry anyone they please as long as they marry within the tribal clan of their father. ⁷No inheritance in Israel is to pass from tribe to tribe, for every Israelite shall keep the tribal land inherited from his forefathers. ⁸Every daughter who inherits land in any Israelite tribe must marry someone in her father's tribal clan, so that every Israelite will possess the inheritance of his fathers. ⁹No inheritance may pass from tribe to tribe, for each Israelite tribe is to keep the land it inherits."

¹⁰So Zelophehad's daughters did as the LORD commanded Moses. ¹¹Zelophehad's daughters—Mahlah, Tirzah, Hoglah, Milcah and Noah—married their cousins on their father's side. ¹²They married within the clans of the descendants of Manasseh son of Joseph, and their inheritance remained in their father's clan and tribe.

¹³These are the commands and regulations the LORD gave through Moses to the Israelites on the plains of Moab by the Jordan across from Jericho.ᵃ

ᵃ 13 Hebrew *Jordan of Jericho*; possibly an ancient name for the Jordan River

DEUTERONOMY

Remember to Remember

KEY VERSES:

"Acknowledge and take to heart this day that the LORD is God in heaven above and on the earth below. There is no other. Keep his decrees and commands, which I am giving you today, so that it may go well with you and your children after you and that you may live long in the land the LORD your God gives you for all time."—Deuteronomy 4:39–40

Have you ever given a farewell address? Imagine Moses' situation. In the process of transferring the leadership of Israel to Joshua, he delivers this address to prepare God's people to enter the promised land. God had performed many miracles during the previous years, but almost everyone who had witnessed his mighty works had died in the desert. And yet, somehow, Moses must make known all that God has done, direct the people with various laws and decrees, and show them a vision of the future that they might experience—depending on whether the people remember their relationship with God or go their own way.

The key theme in Deuteronomy is "remembering to remember." And as the book of Deuteronomy opens, Moses is obviously intent on embedding the memory of God's faithfulness to Israel into the hearts of his listeners. Israel is urged to remember the past, remember the present obligations and remember the future that the people might build.

In his classic work *Letters and Papers from Prison,* the Christian martyr Dietrich Bonhoeffer called forgetfulness "the great problem of Christian ministry." In what ways do you think this might be so? As you read this foundational book of the Old Testament, ask God to open your heart to the past, to make you sensitive to God's claim on your life today and to help you anticipate your vivid future with the Lord of your life. See if you don't agree that your memories and your faith are inextricably entwined as you walk with God.

> "Turning myself towards my most gracious and merciful God, I desire, purpose, and am irrevocably resolved to serve and love him now and forever; and to this end, I give and consecrate to him my soul with all its powers, my heart with all its affections, and my body with all its senses . . . to be forever his loyal, obedient, and faithful creature."
>
> —FRANCIS DE SALES,
> *Introduction to the Devout Life*

A Corporate Challenge

DEUTERONOMY 1:3–6

Imagine that you are present when Moses calls the Israelites together after forty years of wandering and says, "Okay, now it's time to go in and take the promised land." Listen in on some of the conversations that are taking place among your neighbors. What are some of their worries? Fears? Hopes?

If Moses showed up at your church with a similar call to action—not to war, certainly, but to a risky, corporate challenge—how do you think you would respond? How would other church members respond?

See Meeting God in Scripture

The Command to Leave Horeb

1 These are the words Moses spoke to all Israel in the desert east of the Jordan—that is, in the Arabah—opposite Suph, between Paran and Tophel, Laban, Hazeroth and Dizahab. ²(It takes eleven days to go from Horeb to Kadesh Barnea by the Mount Seir road.)

³In the fortieth year, on the first day of the eleventh month, Moses proclaimed to the Israelites all that the LORD had commanded him concerning them. ⁴This was after he had defeated Sihon king of the Amorites, who reigned in Heshbon, and at Edrei had defeated Og king of Bashan, who reigned in Ashtaroth.

⁵East of the Jordan in the territory of Moab, Moses began to expound this law, saying:

⁶The LORD our God said to us at Horeb, "You have stayed long enough at this mountain. ⁷Break camp and advance into the hill country of the Amorites; go to all the neighboring peoples in the Arabah, in the mountains, in the western foothills, in the Negev and along the coast, to the land of the Canaanites and to Lebanon, as far as the great river, the Euphrates. ⁸See, I have given you this land. Go in and take possession of the land that the LORD swore he would give to your fathers—to Abraham, Isaac and Jacob—and to their descendants after them."

The Appointment of Leaders

⁹At that time I said to you, "You are too heavy a burden for me to carry alone. ¹⁰The LORD your God has increased your numbers so that today you are as many as the stars in the sky. ¹¹May the LORD, the God of your fathers, increase you a thousand times and bless you as he has promised! ¹²But how can I bear your problems and your burdens and your disputes all by myself? ¹³Choose some wise, understanding and respected men from each of your tribes, and I will set them over you."

¹⁴You answered me, "What you propose to do is good."

¹⁵So I took the leading men of your tribes, wise and respected men, and appointed them to have authority over you—as commanders of thousands, of hundreds, of fifties and of tens and as tribal officials. ¹⁶And I charged your judges at that time: Hear the disputes between your brothers and judge fairly, whether the case is between brother Israelites or between one of them and an alien. ¹⁷Do not show partiality in judging; hear both small and great alike. Do not be afraid of any man, for judgment belongs to God. Bring me any case too hard for you, and I will hear it. ¹⁸And at that time I told you everything you were to do.

Spies Sent Out

¹⁹Then, as the LORD our God commanded us, we set out from Horeb and went toward the hill country of the Amorites through all that vast and dreadful desert that you have seen, and so we reached Kadesh Barnea. ²⁰Then I said to you, "You have reached the hill country of the Amorites, which the LORD our God is giving us. ²¹See, the LORD your God has given you the land. Go up and take possession of it as the LORD, the God of your fathers, told you. Do not be afraid; do not be discouraged."

²²Then all of you came to me and said, "Let us send men

ahead to spy out the land for us and bring back a report about the route we are to take and the towns we will come to."

²³The idea seemed good to me; so I selected twelve of you, one man from each tribe. ²⁴They left and went up into the hill country, and came to the Valley of Eshcol and explored it. ²⁵Taking with them some of the fruit of the land, they brought it down to us and reported, "It is a good land that the LORD our God is giving us."

Rebellion Against the LORD

²⁶But you were unwilling to go up; you rebelled against the command of the LORD your God. ²⁷You grumbled in your tents and said, "The LORD hates us; so he brought us out of Egypt to deliver us into the hands of the Amorites to destroy us. ²⁸Where can we go? Our brothers have made us lose heart. They say, 'The people are stronger and taller than we are; the cities are large, with walls up to the sky. We even saw the Anakites there.' "

²⁹Then I said to you, "Do not be terrified; do not be afraid of them. ³⁰The LORD your God, who is going before you, will fight for you, as he did for you in Egypt, before your very eyes, ³¹and in the desert. There you saw how the LORD your God carried you, as a father carries his son, all the way you went until you reached this place."

³²In spite of this, you did not trust in the LORD your God, ³³who went ahead of you on your journey, in fire by night and in a cloud by day, to search out places for you to camp and to show you the way you should go.

³⁴When the LORD heard what you said, he was angry and solemnly swore: ³⁵"Not a man of this evil generation shall see the good land I swore to give your forefathers, ³⁶except Caleb son of Jephunneh. He will see it, and I will give him and his descendants the land he set his feet on, because he followed the LORD wholeheartedly."

³⁷Because of you the LORD became angry with me also and said, "You shall not enter it, either. ³⁸But your assistant, Joshua son of Nun, will enter it. Encourage him, because he will lead Israel to inherit it. ³⁹And the little ones that you said would be taken captive, your children who do not yet know good from bad—they will enter the land. I will give it to them and they will take possession of it. ⁴⁰But as for you, turn around and set out toward the desert along the route to the Red Sea.ᵃ"

⁴¹Then you replied, "We have sinned against the LORD. We will go up and fight, as the LORD our God commanded us." So every one of you put on his weapons, thinking it easy to go up into the hill country.

⁴²But the LORD said to me, "Tell them, 'Do not go up and fight, because I will not be with you. You will be defeated by your enemies.' "

⁴³So I told you, but you would not listen. You rebelled against the LORD's command and in your arrogance you marched up into the hill country. ⁴⁴The Amorites who lived in those hills came out against you; they chased you like a swarm of bees and beat you down from Seir all the way to Hormah. ⁴⁵You came back and wept before the LORD, but he paid no attention to your weeping and turned a deaf ear

---

A Father's Burden

DEUTERONOMY 1:31

If you have a young child, take her for a walk around the block, praying as you carry her. Use this experience to imagine how the Lord might carry a nation as a father carries his son or daughter. If you don't have a young child, go to a mall and study the expressions of children and the expressions of their parents. Try to enter into the experience from both perspectives—the emotions and challenges of the parent, and the security and needs of the child. Now imagine God carrying your church as a parent would carry a child. How might this affect your church's leadership, relationships and mission if the church were to picture itself this way?

ᵃ 40 Hebrew *Yam Suph*; that is, Sea of Reeds

Walking Through Others' Blessings

DEUTERONOMY 2:4–5,9,19

Place yourself in the sandals of an Israelite. You have been wandering for forty years and most of your life is behind you. Now you pass through land belonging to Esau's descendants—the Moabites and the Ammonites. You're hungry for your own land, but God makes you walk through somebody else's land as you wait. Describe the envy you might feel. How hard is it to wait? Does someone else's good fortune make it even more difficult to wait for your own land?

In your present life, do you see anything owned or experienced by your neighbor or fellow church member that makes it hard for you to be content with what you have? What can you learn from the experience of the Israelites?

See Meeting God in Community

to you. ⁴⁶And so you stayed in Kadesh many days—all the time you spent there.

Wanderings in the Desert

2 Then we turned back and set out toward the desert along the route to the Red Sea,ᵃ as the LORD had directed me. For a long time we made our way around the hill country of Seir.

²Then the LORD said to me, ³"You have made your way around this hill country long enough; now turn north. ⁴Give the people these orders: 'You are about to pass through the territory of your brothers the descendants of Esau, who live in Seir. They will be afraid of you, but be very careful. ⁵Do not provoke them to war, for I will not give you any of their land, not even enough to put your foot on. I have given Esau the hill country of Seir as his own. ⁶You are to pay them in silver for the food you eat and the water you drink.' "

⁷The LORD your God has blessed you in all the work of your hands. He has watched over your journey through this vast desert. These forty years the LORD your God has been with you, and you have not lacked anything.

⁸So we went on past our brothers the descendants of Esau, who live in Seir. We turned from the Arabah road, which comes up from Elath and Ezion Geber, and traveled along the desert road of Moab.

⁹Then the LORD said to me, "Do not harass the Moabites or provoke them to war, for I will not give you any part of their land. I have given Ar to the descendants of Lot as a possession."

¹⁰(The Emites used to live there—a people strong and numerous, and as tall as the Anakites. ¹¹Like the Anakites, they too were considered Rephaites, but the Moabites called them Emites. ¹²Horites used to live in Seir, but the descendants of Esau drove them out. They destroyed the Horites from before them and settled in their place, just as Israel did in the land the LORD gave them as their possession.)

¹³And the LORD said, "Now get up and cross the Zered Valley." So we crossed the valley.

¹⁴Thirty-eight years passed from the time we left Kadesh Barnea until we crossed the Zered Valley. By then, that entire generation of fighting men had perished from the camp, as the LORD had sworn to them. ¹⁵The LORD's hand was against them until he had completely eliminated them from the camp.

¹⁶Now when the last of these fighting men among the people had died, ¹⁷the LORD said to me, ¹⁸"Today you are to pass by the region of Moab at Ar. ¹⁹When you come to the Ammonites, do not harass them or provoke them to war, for I will not give you possession of any land belonging to the Ammonites. I have given it as a possession to the descendants of Lot."

²⁰(That too was considered a land of the Rephaites, who used to live there; but the Ammonites called them Zamzummites. ²¹They were a people strong and numerous, and as tall as the Anakites. The LORD destroyed them from before the Ammonites, who drove them out and settled in their place. ²²The LORD had done the same for the descendants of Esau, who lived in Seir, when he destroyed the Horites from before them. They drove them out and have

ᵃ 1 Hebrew *Yam Suph*; that is, Sea of Reeds

lived in their place to this day. ²³And as for the Avvites who lived in villages as far as Gaza, the Caphtorites coming out from Caphtor*ᵃ* destroyed them and settled in their place.)

Defeat of Sihon King of Heshbon

²⁴"Set out now and cross the Arnon Gorge. See, I have given into your hand Sihon the Amorite, king of Heshbon, and his country. Begin to take possession of it and engage him in battle. ²⁵This very day I will begin to put the terror and fear of you on all the nations under heaven. They will hear reports of you and will tremble and be in anguish because of you."

²⁶From the desert of Kedemoth I sent messengers to Sihon king of Heshbon offering peace and saying, ²⁷"Let us pass through your country. We will stay on the main road; we will not turn aside to the right or to the left. ²⁸Sell us food to eat and water to drink for their price in silver. Only let us pass through on foot— ²⁹as the descendants of Esau, who live in Seir, and the Moabites, who live in Ar, did for us—until we cross the Jordan into the land the LORD our God is giving us." ³⁰But Sihon king of Heshbon refused to let us pass through. For the LORD your God had made his spirit stubborn and his heart obstinate in order to give him into your hands, as he has now done.

³¹The LORD said to me, "See, I have begun to deliver Sihon and his country over to you. Now begin to conquer and possess his land."

³²When Sihon and all his army came out to meet us in battle at Jahaz, ³³the LORD our God delivered him over to us and we struck him down, together with his sons and his whole army. ³⁴At that time we took all his towns and completely destroyed*ᵇ* them—men, women and children. We left no survivors. ³⁵But the livestock and the plunder from the towns we had captured we carried off for ourselves. ³⁶From Aroer on the rim of the Arnon Gorge, and from the town in the gorge, even as far as Gilead, not one town was too strong for us. The LORD our God gave us all of them. ³⁷But in accordance with the command of the LORD our God, you did not encroach on any of the land of the Ammonites, neither the land along the course of the Jabbok nor that around the towns in the hills.

Defeat of Og King of Bashan

3 Next we turned and went up along the road toward Bashan, and Og king of Bashan with his whole army marched out to meet us in battle at Edrei. ²The LORD said to me, "Do not be afraid of him, for I have handed him over to you with his whole army and his land. Do to him what you did to Sihon king of the Amorites, who reigned in Heshbon."

³So the LORD our God also gave into our hands Og king of Bashan and all his army. We struck them down, leaving no survivors. ⁴At that time we took all his cities. There was not one of the sixty cities that we did not take from them—the whole region of Argob, Og's kingdom in Bashan. ⁵All these cities were fortified with high walls and with gates and bars, and there were also a great many unwalled villages. ⁶We completely destroyed*ᵇ* them, as we had done with Sihon king of Heshbon, destroying*ᵇ* every city—men,

A Masked Entrance

DEUTERONOMY 2:30–32

The Israelites are out in the desert; they need food to eat, water to drink and a road to travel on. The local king brings his army out to "greet" them. Things couldn't look worse, but then God says, "See, I have begun to deliver Sihon and his country over to you. Now begin to conquer and possess his land." In the midst of what looks like certain disaster, God tells Moses to go on the offensive, because God has already begun to deliver the Israelites.

Is there a bleak situation in your life that God might look at differently from the way you do? Can you recall a moment that looked ominous but proved instead to be a prelude to God's redeeming entrance?

See Meeting God in Everyday Life

ᵃ 23 That is, Crete *ᵇ* 34,6 The Hebrew term refers to the irrevocable giving over of things or persons to the LORD, often by totally destroying them.

Sacrificial Service

DEUTERONOMY 3:19–20

Have you ever missed time with your family because you were helping someone else? What did that teach you about unselfishness? Service? Godly love? To more fully experience this passage, go out on an unusually cold or hot day, leave the shelter of your heated or air-conditioned house and perform a service out-of-doors for someone else. As you do this, prayerfully consider the self-denial the Reubenites and Gadites must have endured to fight their brothers' battles when their own land was already won. What temptations must they have faced? How might their hearts have changed after they returned home?

See *Meeting God in Community*

women and children. [7]But all the livestock and the plunder from their cities we carried off for ourselves.

[8]So at that time we took from these two kings of the Amorites the territory east of the Jordan, from the Arnon Gorge as far as Mount Hermon. [9](Hermon is called Sirion by the Sidonians; the Amorites call it Senir.) [10]We took all the towns on the plateau, and all Gilead, and all Bashan as far as Salecah and Edrei, towns of Og's kingdom in Bashan. [11](Only Og king of Bashan was left of the remnant of the Rephaites. His bed[a] was made of iron and was more than thirteen feet long and six feet wide.[b] It is still in Rabbah of the Ammonites.)

Division of the Land

[12]Of the land that we took over at that time, I gave the Reubenites and the Gadites the territory north of Aroer by the Arnon Gorge, including half the hill country of Gilead, together with its towns. [13]The rest of Gilead and also all of Bashan, the kingdom of Og, I gave to the half tribe of Manasseh. (The whole region of Argob in Bashan used to be known as a land of the Rephaites. [14]Jair, a descendant of Manasseh, took the whole region of Argob as far as the border of the Geshurites and the Maacathites; it was named after him, so that to this day Bashan is called Havvoth Jair.[c]) [15]And I gave Gilead to Makir. [16]But to the Reubenites and the Gadites I gave the territory extending from Gilead down to the Arnon Gorge (the middle of the gorge being the border) and out to the Jabbok River, which is the border of the Ammonites. [17]Its western border was the Jordan in the Arabah, from Kinnereth to the Sea of the Arabah (the Salt Sea[d]), below the slopes of Pisgah.

[18]I commanded you at that time: "The LORD your God has given you this land to take possession of it. But all your able-bodied men, armed for battle, must cross over ahead of your brother Israelites. [19]However, your wives, your children and your livestock (I know you have much livestock) may stay in the towns I have given you, [20]until the LORD gives rest to your brothers as he has to you, and they too have taken over the land that the LORD your God is giving them, across the Jordan. After that, each of you may go back to the possession I have given you."

Moses Forbidden to Cross the Jordan

[21]At that time I commanded Joshua: "You have seen with your own eyes all that the LORD your God has done to these two kings. The LORD will do the same to all the kingdoms over there where you are going. [22]Do not be afraid of them; the LORD your God himself will fight for you."

[23]At that time I pleaded with the LORD: [24]"O Sovereign LORD, you have begun to show to your servant your greatness and your strong hand. For what god is there in heaven or on earth who can do the deeds and mighty works you do? [25]Let me go over and see the good land beyond the Jordan—that fine hill country and Lebanon."

[26]But because of you the LORD was angry with me and would not listen to me. "That is enough," the LORD said. "Do not speak to me anymore about this matter. [27]Go up to

---

[a] 11 Or *sarcophagus*   [b] 11 Hebrew *nine cubits long and four cubits wide* (about 4 meters long and 1.8 meters wide)   [c] 14 Or *called the settlements of Jair*   [d] 17 That is, the Dead Sea

the top of Pisgah and look west and north and south and east. Look at the land with your own eyes, since you are not going to cross this Jordan. ²⁸But commission Joshua, and encourage and strengthen him, for he will lead this people across and will cause them to inherit the land that you will see." ²⁹So we stayed in the valley near Beth Peor.

Obedience Commanded

4 Hear now, O Israel, the decrees and laws I am about to teach you. Follow them so that you may live and may go in and take possession of the land that the LORD, the God of your fathers, is giving you. ²Do not add to what I command you and do not subtract from it, but keep the commands of the LORD your God that I give you.

³You saw with your own eyes what the LORD did at Baal Peor. The LORD your God destroyed from among you everyone who followed the Baal of Peor, ⁴but all of you who held fast to the LORD your God are still alive today.

⁵See, I have taught you decrees and laws as the LORD my God commanded me, so that you may follow them in the land you are entering to take possession of it. ⁶Observe them carefully, for this will show your wisdom and understanding to the nations, who will hear about all these decrees and say, "Surely this great nation is a wise and understanding people." ⁷What other nation is so great as to have their gods near them the way the LORD our God is near us whenever we pray to him? ⁸And what other nation is so great as to have such righteous decrees and laws as this body of laws I am setting before you today?

⁹Only be careful, and watch yourselves closely so that you do not forget the things your eyes have seen or let them slip from your heart as long as you live. Teach them to your children and to their children after them. ¹⁰Remember the day you stood before the LORD your God at Horeb, when he said to me, "Assemble the people before me to hear my words so that they may learn to revere me as long as they live in the land and may teach them to their children." ¹¹You came near and stood at the foot of the mountain while it blazed with fire to the very heavens, with black clouds and deep darkness. ¹²Then the LORD spoke to you out of the fire. You heard the sound of words but saw no form; there was only a voice. ¹³He declared to you his covenant, the Ten Commandments, which he commanded you to follow and then wrote them on two stone tablets. ¹⁴And the LORD directed me at that time to teach you the decrees and laws you are to follow in the land that you are crossing the Jordan to possess.

Idolatry Forbidden

¹⁵You saw no form of any kind the day the LORD spoke to you at Horeb out of the fire. Therefore watch yourselves very carefully, ¹⁶so that you do not become corrupt and make for yourselves an idol, an image of any shape, whether formed like a man or a woman, ¹⁷or like any animal on earth or any bird that flies in the air, ¹⁸or like any creature that moves along the ground or any fish in the waters below. ¹⁹And when you look up to the sky and see the sun, the moon and the stars—all the heavenly array—do not be enticed into bowing down to them and worshiping things the LORD your God has apportioned to all the nations

---

Close Watch

DEUTERONOMY 4:9

"If thou canst not continually recollect thyself, yet do it sometimes, at least once a day, namely, in the morning or at night. In the morning fix thy good purpose; and at night examine thyself what thou hast done, how thou hast behaved thyself in word, deed, and thought; for in these perhaps thou hast oftentimes offended both God and thy neighbor. Gird up thy loins like a man against the evil assaults of the devil; bridle thy riotous appetite, and thou shalt be the better able to keep under all the unruly desires of the flesh."

—THOMAS À KEMPIS,
The Imitation of Christ

Remember to Remember

DEUTERONOMY 4:23

Can you remember your 16th birthday? How about your 21st? What about a less momentous one, say, your 19th? Read Deuteronomy 6:6–9; 8:10–14; 9:7. How does God encourage Israel to remember important events? Can you think of any ways you can create contemporary equivalents that will help you "remember to remember"? To what holidays might you pay particular attention? What has happened in your life that you want to remember? What memories do you want to pass on to your children? How might you make that happen? Reflect on the many ways that remembering is important to our faith.

See Meeting God in Everyday Life

under heaven. **20**But as for you, the LORD took you and brought you out of the iron-smelting furnace, out of Egypt, to be the people of his inheritance, as you now are.

21The LORD was angry with me because of you, and he solemnly swore that I would not cross the Jordan and enter the good land the LORD your God is giving you as your inheritance. **22**I will die in this land; I will not cross the Jordan; but you are about to cross over and take possession of that good land. **23**Be careful not to forget the covenant of the LORD your God that he made with you; do not make for yourselves an idol in the form of anything the LORD your God has forbidden. **24**For the LORD your God is a consuming fire, a jealous God.

25After you have had children and grandchildren and have lived in the land a long time—if you then become corrupt and make any kind of idol, doing evil in the eyes of the LORD your God and provoking him to anger, **26**I call heaven and earth as witnesses against you this day that you will quickly perish from the land that you are crossing the Jordan to possess. You will not live there long but will certainly be destroyed. **27**The LORD will scatter you among the peoples, and only a few of you will survive among the nations to which the LORD will drive you. **28**There you will worship man-made gods of wood and stone, which cannot see or hear or eat or smell. **29**But if from there you seek the LORD your God, you will find him if you look for him with all your heart and with all your soul. **30**When you are in distress and all these things have happened to you, then in later days you will return to the LORD your God and obey him. **31**For the LORD your God is a merciful God; he will not abandon or destroy you or forget the covenant with your forefathers, which he confirmed to them by oath.

The LORD Is God

32Ask now about the former days, long before your time, from the day God created man on the earth; ask from one end of the heavens to the other. Has anything so great as this ever happened, or has anything like it ever been heard of? **33**Has any other people heard the voice of God*a* speaking out of fire, as you have, and lived? **34**Has any god ever tried to take for himself one nation out of another nation, by testings, by miraculous signs and wonders, by war, by a mighty hand and an outstretched arm, or by great and awesome deeds, like all the things the LORD your God did for you in Egypt before your very eyes?

35You were shown these things so that you might know that the LORD is God; besides him there is no other. **36**From heaven he made you hear his voice to discipline you. On earth he showed you his great fire, and you heard his words from out of the fire. **37**Because he loved your forefathers and chose their descendants after them, he brought you out of Egypt by his Presence and his great strength, **38**to drive out before you nations greater and stronger than you and to bring you into their land to give it to you for your inheritance, as it is today.

39Acknowledge and take to heart this day that the LORD is God in heaven above and on the earth below. There is no other. **40**Keep his decrees and commands, which I am giving you today, so that it may go well with you and your chil-

a 33 Or of a god

dren after you and that you may live long in the land the LORD your God gives you for all time.

Cities of Refuge

⁴¹Then Moses set aside three cities east of the Jordan, ⁴²to which anyone who had killed a person could flee if he had unintentionally killed his neighbor without malice aforethought. He could flee into one of these cities and save his life. ⁴³The cities were these: Bezer in the desert plateau, for the Reubenites; Ramoth in Gilead, for the Gadites; and Golan in Bashan, for the Manassites.

Introduction to the Law

⁴⁴This is the law Moses set before the Israelites. ⁴⁵These are the stipulations, decrees and laws Moses gave them when they came out of Egypt ⁴⁶and were in the valley near Beth Peor east of the Jordan, in the land of Sihon king of the Amorites, who reigned in Heshbon and was defeated by Moses and the Israelites as they came out of Egypt. ⁴⁷They took possession of his land and the land of Og king of Bashan, the two Amorite kings east of the Jordan. ⁴⁸This land extended from Aroer on the rim of the Arnon Gorge to Mount Siyon[a] (that is, Hermon), ⁴⁹and included all the Arabah east of the Jordan, as far as the Sea of the Arabah,[b] below the slopes of Pisgah.

The Ten Commandments

5 Moses summoned all Israel and said:

Hear, O Israel, the decrees and laws I declare in your hearing today. Learn them and be sure to follow them. ²The LORD our God made a covenant with us at Horeb. ³It was not with our fathers that the LORD made this covenant, but with us, with all of us who are alive here today. ⁴The LORD spoke to you face to face out of the fire on the mountain. ⁵(At that time I stood between the LORD and you to declare to you the word of the LORD, because you were afraid of the fire and did not go up the mountain.) And he said:

> ⁶"I am the LORD your God, who brought you out of Egypt, out of the land of slavery.
> ⁷"You shall have no other gods before[c] me.
> ⁸"You shall not make for yourself an idol in the form of anything in heaven above or on the earth beneath or in the waters below. ⁹You shall not bow down to them or worship them; for I, the LORD your God, am a jealous God, punishing the children for the sin of the fathers to the third and fourth generation of those who hate me, ¹⁰but showing love to a thousand ₍generations₎ of those who love me and keep my commandments.
> ¹¹"You shall not misuse the name of the LORD your God, for the LORD will not hold anyone guiltless who misuses his name.
> ¹²"Observe the Sabbath day by keeping it holy, as the LORD your God has commanded you. ¹³Six days you shall labor and do all your work, ¹⁴but the seventh day is a Sabbath to the LORD your God. On it you shall not do any work, neither you, nor your

The Ten Evaluations

DEUTERONOMY 5:6–21

Martin Luther encouraged Christians to pray through the Ten Commandments each day as a form of spiritual evaluation. Christians are to look at each commandment both positively and negatively: that is, the negative commandment not to steal leads to reflection on the positive virtue of giving; the positive commandment to honor our parents invites reflection on how we might have dishonored them. Using this framework, pray through each commandment. Allow God time to speak to your heart about the positive and negative elements of each one. This will be an evaluative prayer, so have pen and paper handy in case the Lord brings to mind someone with whom you need to set things right.

See Meeting God in Prayer

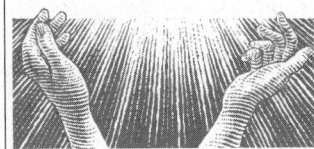

A Dramatic Entrance

DEUTERONOMY 5:22–23

Get out some drawing materials and, based on these two verses, try to re-create (in symbolic form) the encounter between God and Israel. How will you depict the loud voice, the fire, the cloud, the deep darkness? Next, draw a symbolic representation of how God has met you recently. Think about the images you chose. What might they tell you about your prayer life? How does God most often approach you? How would you react if God were to approach you as he did the Israelites?

See Meeting God in Scripture

son or daughter, nor your manservant or maidservant, nor your ox, your donkey or any of your animals, nor the alien within your gates, so that your manservant and maidservant may rest, as you do. ¹⁵Remember that you were slaves in Egypt and that the LORD your God brought you out of there with a mighty hand and an outstretched arm. Therefore the LORD your God has commanded you to observe the Sabbath day.

¹⁶"Honor your father and your mother, as the LORD your God has commanded you, so that you may live long and that it may go well with you in the land the LORD your God is giving you.

¹⁷"You shall not murder.

¹⁸"You shall not commit adultery.

¹⁹"You shall not steal.

²⁰"You shall not give false testimony against your neighbor.

²¹"You shall not covet your neighbor's wife. You shall not set your desire on your neighbor's house or land, his manservant or maidservant, his ox or donkey, or anything that belongs to your neighbor."

²²These are the commandments the LORD proclaimed in a loud voice to your whole assembly there on the mountain from out of the fire, the cloud and the deep darkness; and he added nothing more. Then he wrote them on two stone tablets and gave them to me.

²³When you heard the voice out of the darkness, while the mountain was ablaze with fire, all the leading men of your tribes and your elders came to me. ²⁴And you said, "The LORD our God has shown us his glory and his majesty, and we have heard his voice from the fire. Today we have seen that a man can live even if God speaks with him. ²⁵But now, why should we die? This great fire will consume us, and we will die if we hear the voice of the LORD our God any longer. ²⁶For what mortal man has ever heard the voice of the living God speaking out of fire, as we have, and survived? ²⁷Go near and listen to all that the LORD our God says. Then tell us whatever the LORD our God tells you. We will listen and obey."

²⁸The LORD heard you when you spoke to me and the LORD said to me, "I have heard what this people said to you. Everything they said was good. ²⁹Oh, that their hearts would be inclined to fear me and keep all my commands always, so that it might go well with them and their children forever!

³⁰"Go, tell them to return to their tents. ³¹But you stay here with me so that I may give you all the commands, decrees and laws you are to teach them to follow in the land I am giving them to possess."

³²So be careful to do what the LORD your God has commanded you; do not turn aside to the right or to the left. ³³Walk in all the way that the LORD your God has commanded you, so that you may live and prosper and prolong your days in the land that you will possess.

Love the LORD Your God

6 These are the commands, decrees and laws the LORD your God directed me to teach you to observe in the land that you are crossing the Jordan to possess, ²so that you, your children and their children after them may fear the LORD your God as long as you live by keeping all his decrees and commands that I give you, and so that you may enjoy long life. ³Hear, O Israel, and be careful to obey so that it may go well with you and that you may increase greatly in a land flowing with milk and honey, just as the LORD, the God of your fathers, promised you.

⁴Hear, O Israel: The LORD our God, the LORD is one.ᵃ ⁵Love the LORD your God with all your heart and with all your soul and with all your strength. ⁶These commandments that I give you today are to be upon your hearts. ⁷Impress them on your children. Talk about them when you sit at home and when you walk along the road, when you lie down and when you get up. ⁸Tie them as symbols on your hands and bind them on your foreheads. ⁹Write them on the doorframes of your houses and on your gates.

¹⁰When the LORD your God brings you into the land he swore to your fathers, to Abraham, Isaac and Jacob, to give you—a land with large, flourishing cities you did not build, ¹¹houses filled with all kinds of good things you did not provide, wells you did not dig, and vineyards and olive groves you did not plant—then when you eat and are satisfied, ¹²be careful that you do not forget the LORD, who brought you out of Egypt, out of the land of slavery.

¹³Fear the LORD your God, serve him only and take your oaths in his name. ¹⁴Do not follow other gods, the gods of the peoples around you; ¹⁵for the LORD your God, who is among you, is a jealous God and his anger will burn against you, and he will destroy you from the face of the land. ¹⁶Do not test the LORD your God as you did at Massah. ¹⁷Be sure to keep the commands of the LORD your God and the stipulations and decrees he has given you. ¹⁸Do what is right and good in the LORD's sight, so that it may go well with you and you may go in and take over the good land that the LORD promised on oath to your forefathers, ¹⁹thrusting out all your enemies before you, as the LORD said.

²⁰In the future, when your son asks you, "What is the meaning of the stipulations, decrees and laws the LORD our God has commanded you?" ²¹tell him: "We were slaves of Pharaoh in Egypt, but the LORD brought us out of Egypt with a mighty hand. ²²Before our eyes the LORD sent miraculous signs and wonders—great and terrible—upon Egypt and Pharaoh and his whole household. ²³But he brought us out from there to bring us in and give us the land that he promised on oath to our forefathers. ²⁴The LORD commanded us to obey all these decrees and to fear the LORD our God, so that we might always prosper and be kept alive, as is the case today. ²⁵And if we are careful to obey all this law before the LORD our God, as he has commanded us, that will be our righteousness."

Driving Out the Nations

7 When the LORD your God brings you into the land you are entering to possess and drives out before you many nations—the Hittites, Girgashites, Amorites, Canaanites, Perizzites, Hivites and Jebusites, seven nations larger and stronger than you— ²and when the LORD your God has delivered them over to you and you have defeated them, then

Milk and Honey

DEUTERONOMY 6:3

Invite some friends over, take them into your kitchen, and sample some milk and honey. Think about (and discuss) the qualities of milk, particularly its life-giving nutrients. Also consider the nature of honey, particularly its sweet flavor. Reflect on the larger implications of God's promise to bring Israel into a land "flowing" with these two elements. Look at your current situation: How has God provided you with nourishing "milk"? Do you see any evidence of sweet "honey"? Why do you think God chose these two food items to describe the promised land?

See *Meeting God in Everyday Life*

ᵃ 4 Or *The LORD our God is one LORD*; or *The LORD is our God, the LORD is one*; or *The LORD is our God, the LORD alone*

Sweet, Happy Devotion

DEUTERONOMY 7:17

"They who discouraged the Israelites from going into the
land of promise told them it
was a country which devoured
its inhabitants . . . It is in this
manner . . . that the world de-
fames holy devotion, representing devout persons as a
peevish, gloomy, and sullen
race of men, pretending that
devotion begets melancholy and
insupportable humors. But as
Joshua and Caleb protested that
the promised land was not only
good and fair, but also that the
possession of it would be sweet
and agreeable, so the Holy
Ghost . . . and our Savior . . .
assure us that a devout life is a
life of all others the most
sweet, happy, and amiable."

—FRANCIS DE SALES,
Introduction to the Devout Life

you must destroy them totally.[a] Make no treaty with them,
and show them no mercy. ³Do not intermarry with them.
Do not give your daughters to their sons or take their
daughters for your sons, ⁴for they will turn your sons away
from following me to serve other gods, and the LORD's
anger will burn against you and will quickly destroy you.
⁵This is what you are to do to them: Break down their altars, smash their sacred stones, cut down their Asherah
poles[b] and burn their idols in the fire. ⁶For you are a people
holy to the LORD your God. The LORD your God has chosen
you out of all the peoples on the face of the earth to be his
people, his treasured possession.

⁷The LORD did not set his affection on you and choose
you because you were more numerous than other peoples,
for you were the fewest of all peoples. ⁸But it was because
the LORD loved you and kept the oath he swore to your forefathers that he brought you out with a mighty hand and redeemed you from the land of slavery, from the power of
Pharaoh king of Egypt. ⁹Know therefore that the LORD your
God is God; he is the faithful God, keeping his covenant of
love to a thousand generations of those who love him and
keep his commands. ¹⁰But

those who hate him he will repay to their face by
    destruction;
  he will not be slow to repay to their face those
    who hate him.

¹¹Therefore, take care to follow the commands, decrees and
laws I give you today.

¹²If you pay attention to these laws and are careful to follow them, then the LORD your God will keep his covenant of
love with you, as he swore to your forefathers. ¹³He will love
you and bless you and increase your numbers. He will bless
the fruit of your womb, the crops of your land—your grain,
new wine and oil—the calves of your herds and the lambs
of your flocks in the land that he swore to your forefathers
to give you. ¹⁴You will be blessed more than any other people; none of your men or women will be childless, nor any
of your livestock without young. ¹⁵The LORD will keep you
free from every disease. He will not inflict on you the horrible diseases you knew in Egypt, but he will inflict them on
all who hate you. ¹⁶You must destroy all the peoples the
LORD your God gives over to you. Do not look on them with
pity and do not serve their gods, for that will be a snare to
you.

¹⁷You may say to yourselves, "These nations are stronger
than we are. How can we drive them out?" ¹⁸But do not be
afraid of them; remember well what the LORD your God did
to Pharaoh and to all Egypt. ¹⁹You saw with your own eyes
the great trials, the miraculous signs and wonders, the
mighty hand and outstretched arm, with which the LORD
your God brought you out. The LORD your God will do the
same to all the peoples you now fear. ²⁰Moreover, the LORD
your God will send the hornet among them until even the
survivors who hide from you have perished. ²¹Do not be
terrified by them, for the LORD your God, who is among

---

[a] 2 The Hebrew term refers to the irrevocable giving over of things or
persons to the LORD, often by totally destroying them; also in verse 26.
[b] 5 That is, symbols of the goddess Asherah; here and elsewhere in
Deuteronomy

you, is a great and awesome God. ²²The LORD your God will drive out those nations before you, little by little. You will not be allowed to eliminate them all at once, or the wild animals will multiply around you. ²³But the LORD your God will deliver them over to you, throwing them into great confusion until they are destroyed. ²⁴He will give their kings into your hand, and you will wipe out their names from under heaven. No one will be able to stand up against you; you will destroy them. ²⁵The images of their gods you are to burn in the fire. Do not covet the silver and gold on them, and do not take it for yourselves, or you will be ensnared by it, for it is detestable to the LORD your God. ²⁶Do not bring a detestable thing into your house or you, like it, will be set apart for destruction. Utterly abhor and detest it, for it is set apart for destruction.

Do Not Forget the LORD

8 Be careful to follow every command I am giving you today, so that you may live and increase and may enter and possess the land that the LORD promised on oath to your forefathers. ²Remember how the LORD your God led you all the way in the desert these forty years, to humble you and to test you in order to know what was in your heart, whether or not you would keep his commands. ³He humbled you, causing you to hunger and then feeding you with manna, which neither you nor your fathers had known, to teach you that man does not live on bread alone but on every word that comes from the mouth of the LORD. ⁴Your clothes did not wear out and your feet did not swell during these forty years. ⁵Know then in your heart that as a man disciplines his son, so the LORD your God disciplines you.

⁶Observe the commands of the LORD your God, walking in his ways and revering him. ⁷For the LORD your God is bringing you into a good land—a land with streams and pools of water, with springs flowing in the valleys and hills; ⁸a land with wheat and barley, vines and fig trees, pomegranates, olive oil and honey; ⁹a land where bread will not be scarce and you will lack nothing; a land where the rocks are iron and you can dig copper out of the hills.

¹⁰When you have eaten and are satisfied, praise the LORD your God for the good land he has given you. ¹¹Be careful that you do not forget the LORD your God, failing to observe his commands, his laws and his decrees that I am giving you this day. ¹²Otherwise, when you eat and are satisfied, when you build fine houses and settle down, ¹³and when your herds and flocks grow large and your silver and gold increase and all you have is multiplied, ¹⁴then your heart will become proud and you will forget the LORD your God, who brought you out of Egypt, out of the land of slavery. ¹⁵He led you through the vast and dreadful desert, that thirsty and waterless land, with its venomous snakes and scorpions. He brought you water out of hard rock. ¹⁶He gave you manna to eat in the desert, something your fathers had never known, to humble and to test you so that in the end it might go well with you. ¹⁷You may say to yourself, "My power and the strength of my hands have produced this wealth for me." ¹⁸But remember the LORD your God, for it is he who gives you the ability to produce wealth,

Don't Forget

DEUTERONOMY 8:1–20

Moses declares to the Israelites that God is eager to bless them. Go through chapter 8 and write down the types of blessings Moses promises in the future (particularly vv.7–10, 12–13). Next, go back through this chapter and compare the future blessings with the past sojourn in the desert (particularly vv.4,14–16).

Consider your own life before and after you began actively following God. Have any blessings tempted you to forget your need for God? Have you forgotten what life was like without God? How can your memory of God's deliverance in the past enhance your thankfulness today? How can you fully enjoy God's blessings without losing sight of the One who provided them?

A Devouring Fire

DEUTERONOMY 9:3,15

Twice in this chapter, Moses uses the image of fire to describe God's dealings with people. Build a fire in a fireplace, and burn several different items—newspaper, a piece of wood, and one or two other items of your choosing. As you see the items consumed, reflect on how God will go before you as "a devouring fire." Notice how quickly the paper burns compared to the wood. What comfort can you take from the thought that God precedes his people as a devouring fire? What challenges are you facing that you wish God would destroy?

See Meeting God in Everyday Life

and so confirms his covenant, which he swore to your forefathers, as it is today.

¹⁹If you ever forget the LORD your God and follow other gods and worship and bow down to them, I testify against you today that you will surely be destroyed. ²⁰Like the nations the LORD destroyed before you, so you will be destroyed for not obeying the LORD your God.

Not Because of Israel's Righteousness

9 Hear, O Israel. You are now about to cross the Jordan to go in and dispossess nations greater and stronger than you, with large cities that have walls up to the sky. ²The people are strong and tall—Anakites! You know about them and have heard it said: "Who can stand up against the Anakites?" ³But be assured today that the LORD your God is the one who goes across ahead of you like a devouring fire. He will destroy them; he will subdue them before you. And you will drive them out and annihilate them quickly, as the LORD has promised you.

⁴After the LORD your God has driven them out before you, do not say to yourself, "The LORD has brought me here to take possession of this land because of my righteousness." No, it is on account of the wickedness of these nations that the LORD is going to drive them out before you. ⁵It is not because of your righteousness or your integrity that you are going in to take possession of their land; but on account of the wickedness of these nations, the LORD your God will drive them out before you, to accomplish what he swore to your fathers, to Abraham, Isaac and Jacob. ⁶Understand, then, that it is not because of your righteousness that the LORD your God is giving you this good land to possess, for you are a stiff-necked people.

The Golden Calf

⁷Remember this and never forget how you provoked the LORD your God to anger in the desert. From the day you left Egypt until you arrived here, you have been rebellious against the LORD. ⁸At Horeb you aroused the LORD's wrath so that he was angry enough to destroy you. ⁹When I went up on the mountain to receive the tablets of stone, the tablets of the covenant that the LORD had made with you, I stayed on the mountain forty days and forty nights; I ate no bread and drank no water. ¹⁰The LORD gave me two stone tablets inscribed by the finger of God. On them were all the commandments the LORD proclaimed to you on the mountain out of the fire, on the day of the assembly.

¹¹At the end of the forty days and forty nights, the LORD gave me the two stone tablets, the tablets of the covenant. ¹²Then the LORD told me, "Go down from here at once, because your people whom you brought out of Egypt have become corrupt. They have turned away quickly from what I commanded them and have made a cast idol for themselves."

¹³And the LORD said to me, "I have seen this people, and they are a stiff-necked people indeed! ¹⁴Let me alone, so that I may destroy them and blot out their name from under heaven. And I will make you into a nation stronger and more numerous than they."

¹⁵So I turned and went down from the mountain while it was ablaze with fire. And the two tablets of the covenant

were in my hands.[a] ¹⁶When I looked, I saw that you had sinned against the LORD your God; you had made for yourselves an idol cast in the shape of a calf. You had turned aside quickly from the way that the LORD had commanded you. ¹⁷So I took the two tablets and threw them out of my hands, breaking them to pieces before your eyes.

¹⁸Then once again I fell prostrate before the LORD for forty days and forty nights; I ate no bread and drank no water, because of all the sin you had committed, doing what was evil in the LORD's sight and so provoking him to anger. ¹⁹I feared the anger and wrath of the LORD, for he was angry enough with you to destroy you. But again the LORD listened to me. ²⁰And the LORD was angry enough with Aaron to destroy him, but at that time I prayed for Aaron too. ²¹Also I took that sinful thing of yours, the calf you had made, and burned it in the fire. Then I crushed it and ground it to powder as fine as dust and threw the dust into a stream that flowed down the mountain.

²²You also made the LORD angry at Taberah, at Massah and at Kibroth Hattaavah.

²³And when the LORD sent you out from Kadesh Barnea, he said, "Go up and take possession of the land I have given you." But you rebelled against the command of the LORD your God. You did not trust him or obey him. ²⁴You have been rebellious against the LORD ever since I have known you.

²⁵I lay prostrate before the LORD those forty days and forty nights because the LORD had said he would destroy you. ²⁶I prayed to the LORD and said, "O Sovereign LORD, do not destroy your people, your own inheritance that you redeemed by your great power and brought out of Egypt with a mighty hand. ²⁷Remember your servants Abraham, Isaac and Jacob. Overlook the stubbornness of this people, their wickedness and their sin. ²⁸Otherwise, the country from which you brought us will say, 'Because the LORD was not able to take them into the land he had promised them, and because he hated them, he brought them out to put them to death in the desert.' ²⁹But they are your people, your inheritance that you brought out by your great power and your outstretched arm."

Tablets Like the First Ones

10 At that time the LORD said to me, "Chisel out two stone tablets like the first ones and come up to me on the mountain. Also make a wooden chest.[b] ²I will write on the tablets the words that were on the first tablets, which you broke. Then you are to put them in the chest."

³So I made the ark out of acacia wood and chiseled out two stone tablets like the first ones, and I went up on the mountain with the two tablets in my hands. ⁴The LORD wrote on these tablets what he had written before, the Ten Commandments he had proclaimed to you on the mountain, out of the fire, on the day of the assembly. And the LORD gave them to me. ⁵Then I came back down the mountain and put the tablets in the ark I had made, as the LORD commanded me, and they are there now.

⁶(The Israelites traveled from the wells of the Jaakanites to Moserah. There Aaron died and was buried, and Eleazar

Hunger and Thirst

DEUTERONOMY 9:18

Have you ever responded to a spiritual challenge by fasting? Why do you think so many people in the Bible regularly engaged in fasting? What can we learn spiritually from our hunger and thirst? How might fasting help us to focus on God? How does fasting promote true contrition and repentance? If you've never fasted, consider skipping one or two meals, and devote to prayer the time that you'd normally spend preparing the food, eating it and cleaning up afterwards.

See *Meeting God in Prayer*

---

[a] 15 Or *And I had the two tablets of the covenant with me, one in each hand*
[b] 1 That is, an ark

Pure Love for God

"Whosoever seeketh of God anything besides God, doth not love God purely. If a wife loved her husband because he is rich, she is not pure, for she loveth not her husband, but the gold of her husband . . . Who so seeks from God any other reward but God, and for it would serve God, esteems what he wishes to receive, more than Him from whom he would receive it. What then? Hath God no reward? None, save Himself. The reward of God is God Himself."

—AUGUSTINE,
Sermons, 137

his son succeeded him as priest. [7]From there they traveled to Gudgodah and on to Jotbathah, a land with streams of water. [8]At that time the LORD set apart the tribe of Levi to carry the ark of the covenant of the LORD, to stand before the LORD to minister and to pronounce blessings in his name, as they still do today. [9]That is why the Levites have no share or inheritance among their brothers; the LORD is their inheritance, as the LORD your God told them.)

[10]Now I had stayed on the mountain forty days and nights, as I did the first time, and the LORD listened to me at this time also. It was not his will to destroy you. [11]"Go," the LORD said to me, "and lead the people on their way, so that they may enter and possess the land that I swore to their fathers to give them."

Fear the LORD

[12]And now, O Israel, what does the LORD your God ask of you but to fear the LORD your God, to walk in all his ways, to love him, to serve the LORD your God with all your heart and with all your soul, [13]and to observe the LORD's commands and decrees that I am giving you today for your own good?

[14]To the LORD your God belong the heavens, even the highest heavens, the earth and everything in it. [15]Yet the LORD set his affection on your forefathers and loved them, and he chose you, their descendants, above all the nations, as it is today. [16]Circumcise your hearts, therefore, and do not be stiff-necked any longer. [17]For the LORD your God is God of gods and Lord of lords, the great God, mighty and awesome, who shows no partiality and accepts no bribes. [18]He defends the cause of the fatherless and the widow, and loves the alien, giving him food and clothing. [19]And you are to love those who are aliens, for you yourselves were aliens in Egypt. [20]Fear the LORD your God and serve him. Hold fast to him and take your oaths in his name. [21]He is your praise; he is your God, who performed for you those great and awesome wonders you saw with your own eyes. [22]Your forefathers who went down into Egypt were seventy in all, and now the LORD your God has made you as numerous as the stars in the sky.

Love and Obey the LORD

11 Love the LORD your God and keep his requirements, his decrees, his laws and his commands always. [2]Remember today that your children were not the ones who saw and experienced the discipline of the LORD your God: his majesty, his mighty hand, his outstretched arm; [3]the signs he performed and the things he did in the heart of Egypt, both to Pharaoh king of Egypt and to his whole country; [4]what he did to the Egyptian army, to its horses and chariots, how he overwhelmed them with the waters of the Red Sea[a] as they were pursuing you, and how the LORD brought lasting ruin on them. [5]It was not your children who saw what he did for you in the desert until you arrived at this place, [6]and what he did to Dathan and Abiram, sons of Eliab the Reubenite, when the earth opened its mouth right in the middle of all Israel and swallowed them up with their households, their tents and every living thing that belonged

a 4 Hebrew *Yam Suph*; that is, Sea of Reeds

to them. [7]But it was your own eyes that saw all these great things the LORD has done.

[8]Observe therefore all the commands I am giving you today, so that you may have the strength to go in and take over the land that you are crossing the Jordan to possess, [9]and so that you may live long in the land that the LORD swore to your forefathers to give to them and their descendants, a land flowing with milk and honey. [10]The land you are entering to take over is not like the land of Egypt, from which you have come, where you planted your seed and irrigated it by foot as in a vegetable garden. [11]But the land you are crossing the Jordan to take possession of is a land of mountains and valleys that drinks rain from heaven. [12]It is a land the LORD your God cares for; the eyes of the LORD your God are continually on it from the beginning of the year to its end.

[13]So if you faithfully obey the commands I am giving you today—to love the LORD your God and to serve him with all your heart and with all your soul— [14]then I will send rain on your land in its season, both autumn and spring rains, so that you may gather in your grain, new wine and oil. [15]I will provide grass in the fields for your cattle, and you will eat and be satisfied.

[16]Be careful, or you will be enticed to turn away and worship other gods and bow down to them. [17]Then the LORD's anger will burn against you, and he will shut the heavens so that it will not rain and the ground will yield no produce, and you will soon perish from the good land the LORD is giving you. [18]Fix these words of mine in your hearts and minds; tie them as symbols on your hands and bind them on your foreheads. [19]Teach them to your children, talking about them when you sit at home and when you walk along the road, when you lie down and when you get up. [20]Write them on the doorframes of your houses and on your gates, [21]so that your days and the days of your children may be many in the land that the LORD swore to give your forefathers, as many as the days that the heavens are above the earth.

[22]If you carefully observe all these commands I am giving you to follow—to love the LORD your God, to walk in all his ways and to hold fast to him— [23]then the LORD will drive out all these nations before you, and you will dispossess nations larger and stronger than you. [24]Every place where you set your foot will be yours: Your territory will extend from the desert to Lebanon, and from the Euphrates River to the western sea.[a] [25]No man will be able to stand against you. The LORD your God, as he promised you, will put the terror and fear of you on the whole land, wherever you go.

[26]See, I am setting before you today a blessing and a curse— [27]the blessing if you obey the commands of the LORD your God that I am giving you today; [28]the curse if you disobey the commands of the LORD your God and turn from the way that I command you today by following other gods, which you have not known. [29]When the LORD your God has brought you into the land you are entering to possess, you are to proclaim on Mount Gerizim the blessings, and on Mount Ebal the curses. [30]As you know, these mountains are across the Jordan, west of the road,[b] toward the setting sun, near the great trees of Moreh, in the territory of those

Remembering With Symbols

DEUTERONOMY 11:18

The Christian church has often made elaborate use of symbols to help its adherents "remember to remember." Byzantine churches, for example, were frequently designed in the shape of a cross. In art, the Holy Spirit was often symbolized as fire or a dove; the Trinity has been symbolized by a triangle or three interlocking circles. Some branches of the church have used colors to mark the seasons of the church year: white for Easter and Christmas, red for Pentecost, purple for Lent and Advent. Think about some ways you might incorporate symbols into your life to help you remember eternal truths. Think of a symbol you can carry with you—perhaps while you drive in your car—or one you can put on the main entrance of your home. (See Numbers 15:37–40.)

See Meeting God in Everyday Life

---

[a] 24 That is, the Mediterranean   [b] 30 Or *Jordan, westward*

Remembering With Gifts

DEUTERONOMY 12:6,11

God has ordained the tithe—giving a portion of our goods and resources to his work—as one of the ways to help us remember that the Lord is the source of all blessings. Instead of mindlessly dropping a check in the offering plate or the mail, try to make your giving a spiritually enriching experience, an expression of a worshipful and grateful heart. The next time you write out a check to a favorite charity or ministry, consciously connect it with a blessing God has given you: "Lord, this is in honor of the health you've given us"; "Lord, thank you for providing us with our children"; "Lord, thank you for keeping us warm and well fed."

See Meeting God in Community

Canaanites living in the Arabah in the vicinity of Gilgal. [31]You are about to cross the Jordan to enter and take possession of the land the LORD your God is giving you. When you have taken it over and are living there, [32]be sure that you obey all the decrees and laws I am setting before you today.

The One Place of Worship

12 These are the decrees and laws you must be careful to follow in the land that the LORD, the God of your fathers, has given you to possess—as long as you live in the land. [2]Destroy completely all the places on the high mountains and on the hills and under every spreading tree where the nations you are dispossessing worship their gods. [3]Break down their altars, smash their sacred stones and burn their Asherah poles in the fire; cut down the idols of their gods and wipe out their names from those places.

[4]You must not worship the LORD your God in their way. [5]But you are to seek the place the LORD your God will choose from among all your tribes to put his Name there for his dwelling. To that place you must go; [6]there bring your burnt offerings and sacrifices, your tithes and special gifts, what you have vowed to give and your freewill offerings, and the firstborn of your herds and flocks. [7]There, in the presence of the LORD your God, you and your families shall eat and shall rejoice in everything you have put your hand to, because the LORD your God has blessed you.

[8]You are not to do as we do here today, everyone as he sees fit, [9]since you have not yet reached the resting place and the inheritance the LORD your God is giving you. [10]But you will cross the Jordan and settle in the land the LORD your God is giving you as an inheritance, and he will give you rest from all your enemies around you so that you will live in safety. [11]Then to the place the LORD your God will choose as a dwelling for his Name—there you are to bring everything I command you: your burnt offerings and sacrifices, your tithes and special gifts, and all the choice possessions you have vowed to the LORD. [12]And there rejoice before the LORD your God, you, your sons and daughters, your menservants and maidservants, and the Levites from your towns, who have no allotment or inheritance of their own. [13]Be careful not to sacrifice your burnt offerings anywhere you please. [14]Offer them only at the place the LORD will choose in one of your tribes, and there observe everything I command you.

[15]Nevertheless, you may slaughter your animals in any of your towns and eat as much of the meat as you want, as if it were gazelle or deer, according to the blessing the LORD your God gives you. Both the ceremonially unclean and the clean may eat it. [16]But you must not eat the blood; pour it out on the ground like water. [17]You must not eat in your own towns the tithe of your grain and new wine and oil, or the firstborn of your herds and flocks, or whatever you have vowed to give, or your freewill offerings or special gifts. [18]Instead, you are to eat them in the presence of the LORD your God at the place the LORD your God will choose—you, your sons and daughters, your menservants and maidservants, and the Levites from your towns—and you are to rejoice before the LORD your God in everything you put your

hand to. ¹⁹Be careful not to neglect the Levites as long as you live in your land.

²⁰When the LORD your God has enlarged your territory as he promised you, and you crave meat and say, "I would like some meat," then you may eat as much of it as you want. ²¹If the place where the LORD your God chooses to put his Name is too far away from you, you may slaughter animals from the herds and flocks the LORD has given you, as I have commanded you, and in your own towns you may eat as much of them as you want. ²²Eat them as you would gazelle or deer. Both the ceremonially unclean and the clean may eat. ²³But be sure you do not eat the blood, because the blood is the life, and you must not eat the life with the meat. ²⁴You must not eat the blood; pour it out on the ground like water. ²⁵Do not eat it, so that it may go well with you and your children after you, because you will be doing what is right in the eyes of the LORD.

²⁶But take your consecrated things and whatever you have vowed to give, and go to the place the LORD will choose. ²⁷Present your burnt offerings on the altar of the LORD your God, both the meat and the blood. The blood of your sacrifices must be poured beside the altar of the LORD your God, but you may eat the meat. ²⁸Be careful to obey all these regulations I am giving you, so that it may always go well with you and your children after you, because you will be doing what is good and right in the eyes of the LORD your God.

²⁹The LORD your God will cut off before you the nations you are about to invade and dispossess. But when you have driven them out and settled in their land, ³⁰and after they have been destroyed before you, be careful not to be ensnared by inquiring about their gods, saying, "How do these nations serve their gods? We will do the same." ³¹You must not worship the LORD your God in their way, because in worshiping their gods, they do all kinds of detestable things the LORD hates. They even burn their sons and daughters in the fire as sacrifices to their gods. ³²See that you do all I command you; do not add to it or take away from it.

Worshiping Other Gods

13 If a prophet, or one who foretells by dreams, appears among you and announces to you a miraculous sign or wonder, ²and if the sign or wonder of which he has spoken takes place, and he says, "Let us follow other gods" (gods you have not known) "and let us worship them," ³you must not listen to the words of that prophet or dreamer. The LORD your God is testing you to find out whether you love him with all your heart and with all your soul. ⁴It is the LORD your God you must follow, and him you must revere. Keep his commands and obey him; serve him and hold fast to him. ⁵That prophet or dreamer must be put to death, because he preached rebellion against the LORD your God, who brought you out of Egypt and redeemed you from the land of slavery; he has tried to turn you from the way the LORD your God commanded you to follow. You must purge the evil from among you.

⁶If your very own brother, or your son or daughter, or the wife you love, or your closest friend secretly entices you, saying, "Let us go and worship other gods" (gods that nei-

Hold Fast

DEUTERONOMY 13:4

Have you ever climbed rocks and mountains, or gone waterskiing? If you have, you know the importance of "holding fast" to something. Imagine that a rope is the only thing keeping you from falling hundreds of feet. How tightly would you clasp it?

What are some of the ways we can "hold fast" to God? Moses mentions two ways in this verse—keeping God's commands and serving him—but can you think of any others? Picture yourself holding tightly to a rope. What insights come to mind as you meditate on this passage?

See Meeting God in Scripture

Health and Remembering

DEUTERONOMY 14:1–3

"For the love of God, therefore, regulate yourself prudently both in body and in soul and secure your health as much as you can. And if beyond your power sickness does come to you, be patient and await God's mercy with meekness. At such times, everything is good enough. In fact, it is often true that patience in sickness and in other kinds of trouble is much more pleasing to God than any other devotion you might make when you have your health."

ANONYMOUS,
The Cloud of Unknowing

ther you nor your fathers have known, [7]gods of the peoples around you, whether near or far, from one end of the land to the other), [8]do not yield to him or listen to him. Show him no pity. Do not spare him or shield him. [9]You must certainly put him to death. Your hand must be the first in putting him to death, and then the hands of all the people. [10]Stone him to death, because he tried to turn you away from the LORD your God, who brought you out of Egypt, out of the land of slavery. [11]Then all Israel will hear and be afraid, and no one among you will do such an evil thing again.

[12]If you hear it said about one of the towns the LORD your God is giving you to live in [13]that wicked men have arisen among you and have led the people of their town astray, saying, "Let us go and worship other gods" (gods you have not known), [14]then you must inquire, probe and investigate it thoroughly. And if it is true and it has been proved that this detestable thing has been done among you, [15]you must certainly put to the sword all who live in that town. Destroy it completely,[a] both its people and its livestock. [16]Gather all the plunder of the town into the middle of the public square and completely burn the town and all its plunder as a whole burnt offering to the LORD your God. It is to remain a ruin forever, never to be rebuilt. [17]None of those condemned things[a] shall be found in your hands, so that the LORD will turn from his fierce anger; he will show you mercy, have compassion on you, and increase your numbers, as he promised on oath to your forefathers, [18]because you obey the LORD your God, keeping all his commands that I am giving you today and doing what is right in his eyes.

Clean and Unclean Food

14 You are the children of the LORD your God. Do not cut yourselves or shave the front of your heads for the dead, [2]for you are a people holy to the LORD your God. Out of all the peoples on the face of the earth, the LORD has chosen you to be his treasured possession.

[3]Do not eat any detestable thing. [4]These are the animals you may eat: the ox, the sheep, the goat, [5]the deer, the gazelle, the roe deer, the wild goat, the ibex, the antelope and the mountain sheep.[b] [6]You may eat any animal that has a split hoof divided in two and that chews the cud. [7]However, of those that chew the cud or that have a split hoof completely divided you may not eat the camel, the rabbit or the coney.[c] Although they chew the cud, they do not have a split hoof; they are ceremonially unclean for you. [8]The pig is also unclean; although it has a split hoof, it does not chew the cud. You are not to eat their meat or touch their carcasses.

[9]Of all the creatures living in the water, you may eat any that has fins and scales. [10]But anything that does not have fins and scales you may not eat; for you it is unclean.

[11]You may eat any clean bird. [12]But these you may not eat: the eagle, the vulture, the black vulture, [13]the red kite, the black kite, any kind of falcon, [14]any kind of raven, [15]the

---

[a] *15,17* The Hebrew term refers to the irrevocable giving over of things or persons to the LORD, often by totally destroying them,   [b] *5* The precise identification of some of the birds and animals in this chapter is uncertain.
[c] *7* That is, the hyrax or rock badger

horned owl, the screech owl, the gull, any kind of hawk, ¹⁶the little owl, the great owl, the white owl, ¹⁷the desert owl, the osprey, the cormorant, ¹⁸the stork, any kind of heron, the hoopoe and the bat.

¹⁹All flying insects that swarm are unclean to you; do not eat them. ²⁰But any winged creature that is clean you may eat.

²¹Do not eat anything you find already dead. You may give it to an alien living in any of your towns, and he may eat it, or you may sell it to a foreigner. But you are a people holy to the LORD your God.

Do not cook a young goat in its mother's milk.

Tithes

²²Be sure to set aside a tenth of all that your fields produce each year. ²³Eat the tithe of your grain, new wine and oil, and the firstborn of your herds and flocks in the presence of the LORD your God at the place he will choose as a dwelling for his Name, so that you may learn to revere the LORD your God always. ²⁴But if that place is too distant and you have been blessed by the LORD your God and cannot carry your tithe (because the place where the LORD will choose to put his Name is so far away), ²⁵then exchange your tithe for silver, and take the silver with you and go to the place the LORD your God will choose. ²⁶Use the silver to buy whatever you like: cattle, sheep, wine or other fermented drink, or anything you wish. Then you and your household shall eat there in the presence of the LORD your God and rejoice. ²⁷And do not neglect the Levites living in your towns, for they have no allotment or inheritance of their own.

²⁸At the end of every three years, bring all the tithes of that year's produce and store it in your towns, ²⁹so that the Levites (who have no allotment or inheritance of their own) and the aliens, the fatherless and the widows who live in your towns may come and eat and be satisfied, and so that the LORD your God may bless you in all the work of your hands.

The Year for Canceling Debts

15 At the end of every seven years you must cancel debts. ²This is how it is to be done: Every creditor shall cancel the loan he has made to his fellow Israelite. He shall not require payment from his fellow Israelite or brother, because the LORD's time for canceling debts has been proclaimed. ³You may require payment from a foreigner, but you must cancel any debt your brother owes you. ⁴However, there should be no poor among you, for in the land the LORD your God is giving you to possess as your inheritance, he will richly bless you, ⁵if only you fully obey the LORD your God and are careful to follow all these commands I am giving you today. ⁶For the LORD your God will bless you as he has promised, and you will lend to many nations but will borrow from none. You will rule over many nations but none will rule over you.

⁷If there is a poor man among your brothers in any of the towns of the land that the LORD your God is giving you, do not be hardhearted or tightfisted toward your poor brother. ⁸Rather be openhanded and freely lend him whatever he needs. ⁹Be careful not to harbor this wicked thought: "The

Remember With a Party

DEUTERONOMY 14:26

Have you ever thought of organizing a party specifically to celebrate God's goodness? Here the Israelites are commanded to take some of the money they have set aside and buy their favorite food and drink so that they can celebrate the Lord's presence. Consider planning such an affair. Whom would you invite (see 15:11)? What would you serve? What activities would you want to organize? On what would the celebration focus? As an act of worship, take the next step and actually hold such a party. Celebrate God!

See Meeting God in Worship

Remember With Food

DEUTERONOMY 16:1–3

To enter into the spirit of the verse, make a list of foods that will help you remember God's work in history. We often bake Christmas cookies, for example, but what can you do during the rest of the year? What foods might you prepare around Easter or Pentecost to help you commemorate those days? A number of books are available to tell you how to cook a Passover meal and organize a seder table. Your family might remember God's work through Esther and Mordecai by making *Hamantashen,* triangular-shaped cookies resembling the hat that Haman wore. Get creative and "pray with your oven." How can you help your family remember God with food?

See Meeting God in Everyday Life

seventh year, the year for canceling debts, is near," so that you do not show ill will toward your needy brother and give him nothing. He may then appeal to the LORD against you, and you will be found guilty of sin. [10]Give generously to him and do so without a grudging heart; then because of this the LORD your God will bless you in all your work and in everything you put your hand to. [11]There will always be poor people in the land. Therefore I command you to be openhanded toward your brothers and toward the poor and needy in your land.

Freeing Servants

[12]If a fellow Hebrew, a man or a woman, sells himself to you and serves you six years, in the seventh year you must let him go free. [13]And when you release him, do not send him away empty-handed. [14]Supply him liberally from your flock, your threshing floor and your winepress. Give to him as the LORD your God has blessed you. [15]Remember that you were slaves in Egypt and the LORD your God redeemed you. That is why I give you this command today.

[16]But if your servant says to you, "I do not want to leave you," because he loves you and your family and is well off with you, [17]then take an awl and push it through his ear lobe into the door, and he will become your servant for life. Do the same for your maidservant.

[18]Do not consider it a hardship to set your servant free, because his service to you these six years has been worth twice as much as that of a hired hand. And the LORD your God will bless you in everything you do.

The Firstborn Animals

[19]Set apart for the LORD your God every firstborn male of your herds and flocks. Do not put the firstborn of your oxen to work, and do not shear the firstborn of your sheep. [20]Each year you and your family are to eat them in the presence of the LORD your God at the place he will choose. [21]If an animal has a defect, is lame or blind, or has any serious flaw, you must not sacrifice it to the LORD your God. [22]You are to eat it in your own towns. Both the ceremonially unclean and the clean may eat it, as if it were gazelle or deer. [23]But you must not eat the blood; pour it out on the ground like water.

Passover

16 Observe the month of Abib and celebrate the Passover of the LORD your God, because in the month of Abib he brought you out of Egypt by night. [2]Sacrifice as the Passover to the LORD your God an animal from your flock or herd at the place the LORD will choose as a dwelling for his Name. [3]Do not eat it with bread made with yeast, but for seven days eat unleavened bread, the bread of affliction, because you left Egypt in haste—so that all the days of your life you may remember the time of your departure from Egypt. [4]Let no yeast be found in your possession in all your land for seven days. Do not let any of the meat you sacrifice on the evening of the first day remain until morning.

[5]You must not sacrifice the Passover in any town the LORD your God gives you [6]except in the place he will choose as a dwelling for his Name. There you must sacrifice the

Passover in the evening, when the sun goes down, on the anniversary[a] of your departure from Egypt. [7]Roast it and eat it at the place the LORD your God will choose. Then in the morning return to your tents. [8]For six days eat unleavened bread and on the seventh day hold an assembly to the LORD your God and do no work.

Feast of Weeks

[9]Count off seven weeks from the time you begin to put the sickle to the standing grain. [10]Then celebrate the Feast of Weeks to the LORD your God by giving a freewill offering in proportion to the blessings the LORD your God has given you. [11]And rejoice before the LORD your God at the place he will choose as a dwelling for his Name—you, your sons and daughters, your menservants and maidservants, the Levites in your towns, and the aliens, the fatherless and the widows living among you. [12]Remember that you were slaves in Egypt, and follow carefully these decrees.

Feast of Tabernacles

[13]Celebrate the Feast of Tabernacles for seven days after you have gathered the produce of your threshing floor and your winepress. [14]Be joyful at your Feast—you, your sons and daughters, your menservants and maidservants, and the Levites, the aliens, the fatherless and the widows who live in your towns. [15]For seven days celebrate the Feast to the LORD your God at the place the LORD will choose. For the LORD your God will bless you in all your harvest and in all the work of your hands, and your joy will be complete.

[16]Three times a year all your men must appear before the LORD your God at the place he will choose: at the Feast of Unleavened Bread, the Feast of Weeks and the Feast of Tabernacles. No man should appear before the LORD empty-handed: [17]Each of you must bring a gift in proportion to the way the LORD your God has blessed you.

Judges

[18]Appoint judges and officials for each of your tribes in every town the LORD your God is giving you, and they shall judge the people fairly. [19]Do not pervert justice or show partiality. Do not accept a bribe, for a bribe blinds the eyes of the wise and twists the words of the righteous. [20]Follow justice and justice alone, so that you may live and possess the land the LORD your God is giving you.

Worshiping Other Gods

[21]Do not set up any wooden Asherah pole[b] beside the altar you build to the LORD your God, [22]and do not erect a sacred stone, for these the LORD your God hates.

17 Do not sacrifice to the LORD your God an ox or a sheep that has any defect or flaw in it, for that would be detestable to him.

[2]If a man or woman living among you in one of the towns the LORD gives you is found doing evil in the eyes of the LORD your God in violation of his covenant, [3]and contrary to my command has worshiped other gods, bowing down to them or to the sun or the moon or the stars of the sky, [4]and this has been brought to your attention, then you

A House of Mirrors

DEUTERONOMY 16:18–20

Have you ever walked through a carnival "house of mirrors"? Try to imagine what it would be like to walk through a dark place where you've never been before, to look into mirrors that distort your image into funny or grotesque shapes and to walk on planks that move so that you're unsure of your footing. Imagine what it would be like *living* in that world. Now compare that with living in the world as we know it—defined shapes, solid ground, well-lit corridors. According to Moses, doing business and making laws according to greed, bribery and unfairness distort our world. How would you describe the way *you* do business or approach the law? Do others feel as if they are in a house of mirrors when they do business with you? Write down a code of ethics for the way you do business. What "laws" are the basis for your actions?

See Meeting God in Everyday Life

---

[a] 6 Or *down, at the time of day*   [b] 21 Or *Do not plant any tree dedicated to Asherah*

Leading Under Authority

DEUTERONOMY 17:18–20

Why do you think it is important for the king to consciously place himself under God's authority? What might happen if he considers himself autonomous, the final word for how the kingdom is to be run? What types of authority has God placed in your hands? How do God's laws, commands and Scriptures direct you to behave in these situations? How might your leadership be shaped by remembering not to consider yourself better than those you lead? Is there a symbol you can develop (a facsimile of the scrolled copy of the law the king was to make, for example) to help you remember God's authority over you?

See Meeting God in Community

must investigate it thoroughly. If it is true and it has been proved that this detestable thing has been done in Israel, ⁵take the man or woman who has done this evil deed to your city gate and stone that person to death. ⁶On the testimony of two or three witnesses a man shall be put to death, but no one shall be put to death on the testimony of only one witness. ⁷The hands of the witnesses must be the first in putting him to death, and then the hands of all the people. You must purge the evil from among you.

Law Courts

⁸If cases come before your courts that are too difficult for you to judge—whether bloodshed, lawsuits or assaults—take them to the place the LORD your God will choose. ⁹Go to the priests, who are Levites, and to the judge who is in office at that time. Inquire of them and they will give you the verdict. ¹⁰You must act according to the decisions they give you at the place the LORD will choose. Be careful to do everything they direct you to do. ¹¹Act according to the law they teach you and the decisions they give you. Do not turn aside from what they tell you, to the right or to the left. ¹²The man who shows contempt for the judge or for the priest who stands ministering there to the LORD your God must be put to death. You must purge the evil from Israel. ¹³All the people will hear and be afraid, and will not be contemptuous again.

The King

¹⁴When you enter the land the LORD your God is giving you and have taken possession of it and settled in it, and you say, "Let us set a king over us like all the nations around us," ¹⁵be sure to appoint over you the king the LORD your God chooses. He must be from among your own brothers. Do not place a foreigner over you, one who is not a brother Israelite. ¹⁶The king, moreover, must not acquire great numbers of horses for himself or make the people return to Egypt to get more of them, for the LORD has told you, "You are not to go back that way again." ¹⁷He must not take many wives, or his heart will be led astray. He must not accumulate large amounts of silver and gold.

¹⁸When he takes the throne of his kingdom, he is to write for himself on a scroll a copy of this law, taken from that of the priests, who are Levites. ¹⁹It is to be with him, and he is to read it all the days of his life so that he may learn to revere the LORD his God and follow carefully all the words of this law and these decrees ²⁰and not consider himself better than his brothers and turn from the law to the right or to the left. Then he and his descendants will reign a long time over his kingdom in Israel.

Offerings for Priests and Levites

18 The priests, who are Levites—indeed the whole tribe of Levi—are to have no allotment or inheritance with Israel. They shall live on the offerings made to the LORD by fire, for that is their inheritance. ²They shall have no inheritance among their brothers; the LORD is their inheritance, as he promised them.

³This is the share due the priests from the people who sacrifice a bull or a sheep: the shoulder, the jowls and the inner parts. ⁴You are to give them the firstfruits of your

grain, new wine and oil, and the first wool from the shearing of your sheep, ⁵for the LORD your God has chosen them and their descendants out of all your tribes to stand and minister in the LORD's name always.

⁶If a Levite moves from one of your towns anywhere in Israel where he is living, and comes in all earnestness to the place the LORD will choose, ⁷he may minister in the name of the LORD his God like all his fellow Levites who serve there in the presence of the LORD. ⁸He is to share equally in their benefits, even though he has received money from the sale of family possessions.

Detestable Practices

⁹When you enter the land the LORD your God is giving you, do not learn to imitate the detestable ways of the nations there. ¹⁰Let no one be found among you who sacrifices his son or daughter in*a* the fire, who practices divination or sorcery, interprets omens, engages in witchcraft, ¹¹or casts spells, or who is a medium or spiritist or who consults the dead. ¹²Anyone who does these things is detestable to the LORD, and because of these detestable practices the LORD your God will drive out those nations before you. ¹³You must be blameless before the LORD your God.

The Prophet

¹⁴The nations you will dispossess listen to those who practice sorcery or divination. But as for you, the LORD your God has not permitted you to do so. ¹⁵The LORD your God will raise up for you a prophet like me from among your own brothers. You must listen to him. ¹⁶For this is what you asked of the LORD your God at Horeb on the day of the assembly when you said, "Let us not hear the voice of the LORD our God nor see this great fire anymore, or we will die."

¹⁷The LORD said to me: "What they say is good. ¹⁸I will raise up for them a prophet like you from among their brothers; I will put my words in his mouth, and he will tell them everything I command him. ¹⁹If anyone does not listen to my words that the prophet speaks in my name, I myself will call him to account. ²⁰But a prophet who presumes to speak in my name anything I have not commanded him to say, or a prophet who speaks in the name of other gods, must be put to death."

²¹You may say to yourselves, "How can we know when a message has not been spoken by the LORD?" ²²If what a prophet proclaims in the name of the LORD does not take place or come true, that is a message the LORD has not spoken. That prophet has spoken presumptuously. Do not be afraid of him.

Cities of Refuge

19 When the LORD your God has destroyed the nations whose land he is giving you, and when you have driven them out and settled in their towns and houses, ²then set aside for yourselves three cities centrally located in the land the LORD your God is giving you to possess. ³Build roads to them and divide into three parts the land

Refuge and Mercy

DEUTERONOMY 19:1–7

Have you ever unintentionally harmed someone? Imagine yourself in a situation such as the one described in verse 5. You are cutting wood with a good friend when an accident occurs and your friend is killed. What goes through your mind? Now remember that the friend's family is obligated to kill you in order to honor its relative. What are you feeling now? Map out in your mind (or on paper) how God specifically instructed the cities of refuge to be made accessible. What does this attention to detail say about God's mercy? In what ways do you or someone you know need "refuge" today?

See *Meeting God in Community*

---

a 10 Or *who makes his son or daughter pass through*

Strength From the Past

DEUTERONOMY 20:1

Moses tells the Israelites to overcome their fear by remembering God's provision in the past—the same God who brought them out of Egypt would continue to fight their battles in the future. Spend some time writing a history of God's provision in your life. You might want to write it in the form of a poem, a song, a list or a short narrative that consists of the key moments in your life—moments when God delivered you from trials or provided strength to handle them. What will you title this work of remembering? Is there a general theme that flows throughout? Are you going through a current trial in which you need to remember how God has helped you in the past?

See *Meeting God in Everyday Life*

the LORD your God is giving you as an inheritance, so that anyone who kills a man may flee there.

⁴This is the rule concerning the man who kills another and flees there to save his life—one who kills his neighbor unintentionally, without malice aforethought. ⁵For instance, a man may go into the forest with his neighbor to cut wood, and as he swings his ax to fell a tree, the head may fly off and hit his neighbor and kill him. That man may flee to one of these cities and save his life. ⁶Otherwise, the avenger of blood might pursue him in a rage, overtake him if the distance is too great, and kill him even though he is not deserving of death, since he did it to his neighbor without malice aforethought. ⁷This is why I command you to set aside for yourselves three cities.

⁸If the LORD your God enlarges your territory, as he promised on oath to your forefathers, and gives you the whole land he promised them, ⁹because you carefully follow all these laws I command you today—to love the LORD your God and to walk always in his ways—then you are to set aside three more cities. ¹⁰Do this so that innocent blood will not be shed in your land, which the LORD your God is giving you as your inheritance, and so that you will not be guilty of bloodshed.

¹¹But if a man hates his neighbor and lies in wait for him, assaults and kills him, and then flees to one of these cities, ¹²the elders of his town shall send for him, bring him back from the city, and hand him over to the avenger of blood to die. ¹³Show him no pity. You must purge from Israel the guilt of shedding innocent blood, so that it may go well with you.

¹⁴Do not move your neighbor's boundary stone set up by your predecessors in the inheritance you receive in the land the LORD your God is giving you to possess.

Witnesses

¹⁵One witness is not enough to convict a man accused of any crime or offense he may have committed. A matter must be established by the testimony of two or three witnesses.

¹⁶If a malicious witness takes the stand to accuse a man of a crime, ¹⁷the two men involved in the dispute must stand in the presence of the LORD before the priests and the judges who are in office at the time. ¹⁸The judges must make a thorough investigation, and if the witness proves to be a liar, giving false testimony against his brother, ¹⁹then do to him as he intended to do to his brother. You must purge the evil from among you. ²⁰The rest of the people will hear of this and be afraid, and never again will such an evil thing be done among you. ²¹Show no pity: life for life, eye for eye, tooth for tooth, hand for hand, foot for foot.

Going to War

20 When you go to war against your enemies and see horses and chariots and an army greater than yours, do not be afraid of them, because the LORD your God, who brought you up out of Egypt, will be with you. ²When you are about to go into battle, the priest shall come forward and address the army. ³He shall say: "Hear, O Israel, today you are going into battle against your enemies. Do not be fainthearted or afraid; do not be terrified or give way to

panic before them. ⁴For the LORD your God is the one who goes with you to fight for you against your enemies to give you victory."

⁵The officers shall say to the army: "Has anyone built a new house and not dedicated it? Let him go home, or he may die in battle and someone else may dedicate it. ⁶Has anyone planted a vineyard and not begun to enjoy it? Let him go home, or he may die in battle and someone else enjoy it. ⁷Has anyone become pledged to a woman and not married her? Let him go home, or he may die in battle and someone else marry her." ⁸Then the officers shall add, "Is any man afraid or fainthearted? Let him go home so that his brothers will not become disheartened too." ⁹When the officers have finished speaking to the army, they shall appoint commanders over it.

¹⁰When you march up to attack a city, make its people an offer of peace. ¹¹If they accept and open their gates, all the people in it shall be subject to forced labor and shall work for you. ¹²If they refuse to make peace and they engage you in battle, lay siege to that city. ¹³When the LORD your God delivers it into your hand, put to the sword all the men in it. ¹⁴As for the women, the children, the livestock and everything else in the city, you may take these as plunder for yourselves. And you may use the plunder the LORD your God gives you from your enemies. ¹⁵This is how you are to treat all the cities that are at a distance from you and do not belong to the nations nearby.

¹⁶However, in the cities of the nations the LORD your God is giving you as an inheritance, do not leave alive anything that breathes. ¹⁷Completely destroy*a* them—the Hittites, Amorites, Canaanites, Perizzites, Hivites and Jebusites—as the LORD your God has commanded you. ¹⁸Otherwise, they will teach you to follow all the detestable things they do in worshiping their gods, and you will sin against the LORD your God.

¹⁹When you lay siege to a city for a long time, fighting against it to capture it, do not destroy its trees by putting an ax to them, because you can eat their fruit. Do not cut them down. Are the trees of the field people, that you should besiege them?*b* ²⁰However, you may cut down trees that you know are not fruit trees and use them to build siege works until the city at war with you falls.

Atonement for an Unsolved Murder

21 If a man is found slain, lying in a field in the land the LORD your God is giving you to possess, and it is not known who killed him, ²your elders and judges shall go out and measure the distance from the body to the neighboring towns. ³Then the elders of the town nearest the body shall take a heifer that has never been worked and has never worn a yoke ⁴and lead her down to a valley that has not been plowed or planted and where there is a flowing stream. There in the valley they are to break the heifer's neck. ⁵The priests, the sons of Levi, shall step forward, for the LORD your God has chosen them to minister and to pronounce blessings in the name of the LORD and to decide all cases of dispute and assault. ⁶Then all the elders of the

Loving God's Creation

DEUTERONOMY 20:19-20

Whether this command has to do with the humane treatment of wildlife or with preservation of the food supply, it calls for a gentle concern for the natural world. Christians have a long tradition of appreciating the beauty of creation and caring for nature. How might your care and stewardship of creation be considered a form of prayer, worship and service toward God? Reflect on ways that you might show your allegiance to the Creator by caring for the earth.

See Meeting God in the Created Order

---

a 17 The Hebrew term refers to the irrevocable giving over of things or persons to the LORD, often by totally destroying them.   *b 19* Or *down to use in the siege, for the fruit trees are for the benefit of man.*

A New Start

DEUTERONOMY 21:10–14

When a captive woman shaved her head, cut her nails and discarded her clothes, her actions could be rituals of mourning or symbolic of her subjugation. One commentator suggests that such actions may have been symbolic of initiation into a new way of life: "It is with new hair, nails and clothes that she enters on her new life as a married woman in Israel." Have you ever considered changing your outward appearance to reflect an inner, spiritual change —shaving your beard, cutting your hair, choosing a new style of clothing? What change in appearance would be most appropriate in your life? How might it symbolize or direct your prayers throughout the day?

See Meeting God in Everyday Life

town nearest the body shall wash their hands over the heifer whose neck was broken in the valley, ⁷and they shall declare: "Our hands did not shed this blood, nor did our eyes see it done. ⁸Accept this atonement for your people Israel, whom you have redeemed, O LORD, and do not hold your people guilty of the blood of an innocent man." And the bloodshed will be atoned for. ⁹So you will purge from yourselves the guilt of shedding innocent blood, since you have done what is right in the eyes of the LORD.

Marrying a Captive Woman

¹⁰When you go to war against your enemies and the LORD your God delivers them into your hands and you take captives, ¹¹if you notice among the captives a beautiful woman and are attracted to her, you may take her as your wife. ¹²Bring her into your home and have her shave her head, trim her nails ¹³and put aside the clothes she was wearing when captured. After she has lived in your house and mourned her father and mother for a full month, then you may go to her and be her husband and she shall be your wife. ¹⁴If you are not pleased with her, let her go wherever she wishes. You must not sell her or treat her as a slave, since you have dishonored her.

The Right of the Firstborn

¹⁵If a man has two wives, and he loves one but not the other, and both bear him sons but the firstborn is the son of the wife he does not love, ¹⁶when he wills his property to his sons, he must not give the rights of the firstborn to the son of the wife he loves in preference to his actual firstborn, the son of the wife he does not love. ¹⁷He must acknowledge the son of his unloved wife as the firstborn by giving him a double share of all he has. That son is the first sign of his father's strength. The right of the firstborn belongs to him.

A Rebellious Son

¹⁸If a man has a stubborn and rebellious son who does not obey his father and mother and will not listen to them when they discipline him, ¹⁹his father and mother shall take hold of him and bring him to the elders at the gate of his town. ²⁰They shall say to the elders, "This son of ours is stubborn and rebellious. He will not obey us. He is a profligate and a drunkard." ²¹Then all the men of his town shall stone him to death. You must purge the evil from among you. All Israel will hear of it and be afraid.

Various Laws

²²If a man guilty of a capital offense is put to death and his body is hung on a tree, ²³you must not leave his body on the tree overnight. Be sure to bury him that same day, because anyone who is hung on a tree is under God's curse. You must not desecrate the land the LORD your God is giving you as an inheritance.

22 If you see your brother's ox or sheep straying, do not ignore it but be sure to take it back to him. ²If the brother does not live near you or if you do not know who he is, take it home with you and keep it until he comes looking for it. Then give it back to him. ³Do the same if you

find your brother's donkey or his cloak or anything he loses. Do not ignore it.

⁴If you see your brother's donkey or his ox fallen on the road, do not ignore it. Help him get it to its feet.

⁵A woman must not wear men's clothing, nor a man wear women's clothing, for the LORD your God detests anyone who does this.

⁶If you come across a bird's nest beside the road, either in a tree or on the ground, and the mother is sitting on the young or on the eggs, do not take the mother with the young. ⁷You may take the young, but be sure to let the mother go, so that it may go well with you and you may have a long life.

⁸When you build a new house, make a parapet around your roof so that you may not bring the guilt of bloodshed on your house if someone falls from the roof.

⁹Do not plant two kinds of seed in your vineyard; if you do, not only the crops you plant but also the fruit of the vineyard will be defiled.ᵃ

¹⁰Do not plow with an ox and a donkey yoked together.

¹¹Do not wear clothes of wool and linen woven together.

¹²Make tassels on the four corners of the cloak you wear.

Marriage Violations

¹³If a man takes a wife and, after lying with her, dislikes her ¹⁴and slanders her and gives her a bad name, saying, "I married this woman, but when I approached her, I did not find proof of her virginity," ¹⁵then the girl's father and mother shall bring proof that she was a virgin to the town elders at the gate. ¹⁶The girl's father will say to the elders, "I gave my daughter in marriage to this man, but he dislikes her. ¹⁷Now he has slandered her and said, 'I did not find your daughter to be a virgin.' But here is the proof of my daughter's virginity." Then her parents shall display the cloth before the elders of the town, ¹⁸and the elders shall take the man and punish him. ¹⁹They shall fine him a hundred shekels of silverᵇ and give them to the girl's father, because this man has given an Israelite virgin a bad name. She shall continue to be his wife; he must not divorce her as long as he lives.

²⁰If, however, the charge is true and no proof of the girl's virginity can be found, ²¹she shall be brought to the door of her father's house and there the men of her town shall stone her to death. She has done a disgraceful thing in Israel by being promiscuous while still in her father's house. You must purge the evil from among you.

²²If a man is found sleeping with another man's wife, both the man who slept with her and the woman must die. You must purge the evil from Israel.

²³If a man happens to meet in a town a virgin pledged to be married and he sleeps with her, ²⁴you shall take both of them to the gate of that town and stone them to death—the girl because she was in a town and did not scream for help, and the man because he violated another man's wife. You must purge the evil from among you.

²⁵But if out in the country a man happens to meet a girl pledged to be married and rapes her, only the man who has done this shall die. ²⁶Do nothing to the girl; she has

Right Desires

DEUTERONOMY 22:13–30

"Desire not that which is at a great distance, nor that which cannot happen for a long time, as many do, who, by this means, weary and distract their hearts unprofitably. If a married woman desires to be a nun, to what purpose? If I desire to buy my neighbor's goods before he is willing to sell them, is it not a loss of time to entertain this desire? . . . I can by no means approve that persons should desire to amuse themselves in any other kind of life than that in which they are already engaged; nor in any exercises that are incompatible with their present condition; for this dissipates the heart, and makes it unfit for its necessary occupations."

—FRANCIS DE SALES,
Introduction to the Devout Life

ᵃ 9 Or *be forfeited to the sanctuary*   ᵇ 19 That is, about 2 1/2 pounds (about 1 kilogram)

Holy Business

DEUTERONOMY 23:19–20

Many people compartmentalize their lives, relegating religion and faith to a weekly worship service; Deuteronomy, however, contains many passages that stress the practical, everyday nature of true faith and worship. Imagine that you are the CEO of a major corporation, or perhaps a land developer, banker, landlord or small-business owner. How would remembering God daily affect the way you do business? Now reflect on your vocational calling. If Moses were writing about what you do, what changes in your daily routine might he suggest?

See *Meeting God in Everyday Life*

committed no sin deserving death. This case is like that of someone who attacks and murders his neighbor, ²⁷for the man found the girl out in the country, and though the betrothed girl screamed, there was no one to rescue her.

²⁸If a man happens to meet a virgin who is not pledged to be married and rapes her and they are discovered, ²⁹he shall pay the girl's father fifty shekels of silver.*ᵃ* He must marry the girl, for he has violated her. He can never divorce her as long as he lives.

³⁰A man is not to marry his father's wife; he must not dishonor his father's bed.

Exclusion From the Assembly

23 No one who has been emasculated by crushing or cutting may enter the assembly of the LORD.

²No one born of a forbidden marriage*ᵇ* nor any of his descendants may enter the assembly of the LORD, even down to the tenth generation.

³No Ammonite or Moabite or any of his descendants may enter the assembly of the LORD, even down to the tenth generation. ⁴For they did not come to meet you with bread and water on your way when you came out of Egypt, and they hired Balaam son of Beor from Pethor in Aram Naharaim*ᶜ* to pronounce a curse on you. ⁵However, the LORD your God would not listen to Balaam but turned the curse into a blessing for you, because the LORD your God loves you. ⁶Do not seek a treaty of friendship with them as long as you live.

⁷Do not abhor an Edomite, for he is your brother. Do not abhor an Egyptian, because you lived as an alien in his country. ⁸The third generation of children born to them may enter the assembly of the LORD.

Uncleanness in the Camp

⁹When you are encamped against your enemies, keep away from everything impure. ¹⁰If one of your men is unclean because of a nocturnal emission, he is to go outside the camp and stay there. ¹¹But as evening approaches he is to wash himself, and at sunset he may return to the camp.

¹²Designate a place outside the camp where you can go to relieve yourself. ¹³As part of your equipment have something to dig with, and when you relieve yourself, dig a hole and cover up your excrement. ¹⁴For the LORD your God moves about in your camp to protect you and to deliver your enemies to you. Your camp must be holy, so that he will not see among you anything indecent and turn away from you.

Miscellaneous Laws

¹⁵If a slave has taken refuge with you, do not hand him over to his master. ¹⁶Let him live among you wherever he likes and in whatever town he chooses. Do not oppress him.

¹⁷No Israelite man or woman is to become a shrine prostitute. ¹⁸You must not bring the earnings of a female prostitute or of a male prostitute*ᵈ* into the house of the LORD your God to pay any vow, because the LORD your God detests them both.

¹⁹Do not charge your brother interest, whether on money

---

*ᶜ29 That is, about 1 1/4 pounds (about 0.6 kilogram) *ᵇ2 Or *one of illegitimate birth* *ᶜ4 That is, Northwest Mesopotamia *ᵈ18 Hebrew *of a dog*

or food or anything else that may earn interest. ²⁰You may charge a foreigner interest, but not a brother Israelite, so that the LORD your God may bless you in everything you put your hand to in the land you are entering to possess.

²¹If you make a vow to the LORD your God, do not be slow to pay it, for the LORD your God will certainly demand it of you and you will be guilty of sin. ²²But if you refrain from making a vow, you will not be guilty. ²³Whatever your lips utter you must be sure to do, because you made your vow freely to the LORD your God with your own mouth.

²⁴If you enter your neighbor's vineyard, you may eat all the grapes you want, but do not put any in your basket. ²⁵If you enter your neighbor's grainfield, you may pick kernels with your hands, but you must not put a sickle to his standing grain.

24 If a man marries a woman who becomes displeasing to him because he finds something indecent about her, and he writes her a certificate of divorce, gives it to her and sends her from his house, ²and if after she leaves his house she becomes the wife of another man, ³and her second husband dislikes her and writes her a certificate of divorce, gives it to her and sends her from his house, or if he dies, ⁴then her first husband, who divorced her, is not allowed to marry her again after she has been defiled. That would be detestable in the eyes of the LORD. Do not bring sin upon the land the LORD your God is giving you as an inheritance.

⁵If a man has recently married, he must not be sent to war or have any other duty laid on him. For one year he is to be free to stay at home and bring happiness to the wife he has married.

⁶Do not take a pair of millstones—not even the upper one—as security for a debt, because that would be taking a man's livelihood as security.

⁷If a man is caught kidnapping one of his brother Israelites and treats him as a slave or sells him, the kidnapper must die. You must purge the evil from among you.

⁸In cases of leprous[a] diseases be very careful to do exactly as the priests, who are Levites, instruct you. You must follow carefully what I have commanded them. ⁹Remember what the LORD your God did to Miriam along the way after you came out of Egypt.

¹⁰When you make a loan of any kind to your neighbor, do not go into his house to get what he is offering as a pledge. ¹¹Stay outside and let the man to whom you are making the loan bring the pledge out to you. ¹²If the man is poor, do not go to sleep with his pledge in your possession. ¹³Return his cloak to him by sunset so that he may sleep in it. Then he will thank you, and it will be regarded as a righteous act in the sight of the LORD your God.

¹⁴Do not take advantage of a hired man who is poor and needy, whether he is a brother Israelite or an alien living in one of your towns. ¹⁵Pay him his wages each day before sunset, because he is poor and is counting on it. Otherwise he may cry to the LORD against you, and you will be guilty of sin.

¹⁶Fathers shall not be put to death for their children, nor children put to death for their fathers; each is to die for his own sin.

---

a 8 The Hebrew word was used for various diseases affecting the skin—not necessarily leprosy.

Holy Happiness

DEUTERONOMY 24:5

Does it surprise you that serving God might require you to take time off to focus on making someone else happy? Why do you think this pleases God? What sort of limits might be placed on this form of remembering God? Reflect on how it would touch you emotionally if someone were to go out of his or her way to please one of your close family members. What might this reveal about God? Given your life circumstances, how can you remember God today by making someone else happy?

See Meeting God in Service

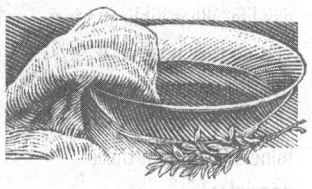

Holy Living

DEUTERONOMY 23:15—25:19

This passage offers the Israelites guidelines for many aspects of life—covering everything from eating too much from a neighbor's garden to paying wages on time to honest weights and measures. As varied as these laws are, the principles underlying them are familiar and simple: justice, honesty, compassion and so forth.

As you read through this list of laws, see whether you can discern the Biblical principle that each law upholds. Beside each law, jot down this principle in the margin of your Bible. Think of some of the laws and mores that govern our day-to-day life. What Biblical principles do they uphold, if any? How do common sense, self-control, courtesy and thoughtfulness grow from these principles?

Use this exercise as a springboard for examining your own behavior. What principles govern your actions as you drive your car, shop for groceries, write out your monthly bills or gather with others in the lunchroom?

See Meeting God in Everyday Life

256

¹⁷Do not deprive the alien or the fatherless of justice, or take the cloak of the widow as a pledge. ¹⁸Remember that you were slaves in Egypt and the LORD your God redeemed you from there. That is why I command you to do this.

¹⁹When you are harvesting in your field and you overlook a sheaf, do not go back to get it. Leave it for the alien, the fatherless and the widow, so that the LORD your God may bless you in all the work of your hands. ²⁰When you beat the olives from your trees, do not go over the branches a second time. Leave what remains for the alien, the fatherless and the widow. ²¹When you harvest the grapes in your vineyard, do not go over the vines again. Leave what remains for the alien, the fatherless and the widow. ²²Remember that you were slaves in Egypt. That is why I command you to do this.

25 When men have a dispute, they are to take it to court and the judges will decide the case, acquitting the innocent and condemning the guilty. ²If the guilty man deserves to be beaten, the judge shall make him lie down and have him flogged in his presence with the number of lashes his crime deserves, ³but he must not give him more than forty lashes. If he is flogged more than that, your brother will be degraded in your eyes.

⁴Do not muzzle an ox while it is treading out the grain.

⁵If brothers are living together and one of them dies without a son, his widow must not marry outside the family. Her husband's brother shall take her and marry her and fulfill the duty of a brother-in-law to her. ⁶The first son she bears shall carry on the name of the dead brother so that his name will not be blotted out from Israel.

⁷However, if a man does not want to marry his brother's wife, she shall go to the elders at the town gate and say, "My husband's brother refuses to carry on his brother's name in Israel. He will not fulfill the duty of a brother-in-law to me." ⁸Then the elders of his town shall summon him and talk to him. If he persists in saying, "I do not want to marry her," ⁹his brother's widow shall go up to him in the presence of the elders, take off one of his sandals, spit in his face and say, "This is what is done to the man who will not build up his brother's family line." ¹⁰That man's line shall be known in Israel as The Family of the Unsandaled.

¹¹If two men are fighting and the wife of one of them comes to rescue her husband from his assailant, and she reaches out and seizes him by his private parts, ¹²you shall cut off her hand. Show her no pity.

¹³Do not have two differing weights in your bag—one heavy, one light. ¹⁴Do not have two differing measures in your house—one large, one small. ¹⁵You must have accurate and honest weights and measures, so that you may live long in the land the LORD your God is giving you. ¹⁶For the LORD your God detests anyone who does these things, anyone who deals dishonestly.

¹⁷Remember what the Amalekites did to you along the way when you came out of Egypt. ¹⁸When you were weary and worn out, they met you on your journey and cut off all who were lagging behind; they had no fear of God. ¹⁹When the LORD your God gives you rest from all the enemies around you in the land he is giving you to possess as an inheritance, you shall blot out the memory of Amalek from under heaven. Do not forget!

Firstfruits and Tithes

26 When you have entered the land the LORD your God is giving you as an inheritance and have taken possession of it and settled in it, ²take some of the firstfruits of all that you produce from the soil of the land the LORD your God is giving you and put them in a basket. Then go to the place the LORD your God will choose as a dwelling for his Name ³and say to the priest in office at the time, "I declare today to the LORD your God that I have come to the land the LORD swore to our forefathers to give us." ⁴The priest shall take the basket from your hands and set it down in front of the altar of the LORD your God. ⁵Then you shall declare before the LORD your God: "My father was a wandering Aramean, and he went down into Egypt with a few people and lived there and became a great nation, powerful and numerous. ⁶But the Egyptians mistreated us and made us suffer, putting us to hard labor. ⁷Then we cried out to the LORD, the God of our fathers, and the LORD heard our voice and saw our misery, toil and oppression. ⁸So the LORD brought us out of Egypt with a mighty hand and an outstretched arm, with great terror and with miraculous signs and wonders. ⁹He brought us to this place and gave us this land, a land flowing with milk and honey; ¹⁰and now I bring the firstfruits of the soil that you, O LORD, have given me." Place the basket before the LORD your God and bow down before him. ¹¹And you and the Levites and the aliens among you shall rejoice in all the good things the LORD your God has given to you and your household.

¹²When you have finished setting aside a tenth of all your produce in the third year, the year of the tithe, you shall give it to the Levite, the alien, the fatherless and the widow, so that they may eat in your towns and be satisfied. ¹³Then say to the LORD your God: "I have removed from my house the sacred portion and have given it to the Levite, the alien, the fatherless and the widow, according to all you commanded. I have not turned aside from your commands nor have I forgotten any of them. ¹⁴I have not eaten any of the sacred portion while I was in mourning, nor have I removed any of it while I was unclean, nor have I offered any of it to the dead. I have obeyed the LORD my God; I have done everything you commanded me. ¹⁵Look down from heaven, your holy dwelling place, and bless your people Israel and the land you have given us as you promised on oath to our forefathers, a land flowing with milk and honey."

Follow the LORD's Commands

¹⁶The LORD your God commands you this day to follow these decrees and laws; carefully observe them with all your heart and with all your soul. ¹⁷You have declared this day that the LORD is your God and that you will walk in his ways, that you will keep his decrees, commands and laws, and that you will obey him. ¹⁸And the LORD has declared this day that you are his people, his treasured possession as he promised, and that you are to keep all his commands. ¹⁹He has declared that he will set you in praise, fame and honor high above all the nations he has made and that you will be a people holy to the LORD your God, as he promised.

Holy History

DEUTERONOMY 26:1–11

The Israelites are commanded to give the firstfruits of their labor and their tithes as a way of remembering God's provision throughout the generations. In this way, remembering becomes a spiritual discipline. Reflect on (or even better, write out) your "spiritual autobiography." How many generations does your family's faith go back? Or perhaps you are the first person in your family to come to faith. Either way, in this autobiography recount the moment when your faith became a personal matter. Tell how God has nurtured you spiritually through the years. How does your history ultimately connect with that of the nation of Israel? With the early church? With the advent of your denomination or congregation? What kind of response does such remembering elicit from you?

See Meeting God in Community

A Visible Reminder

DEUTERONOMY 27:1–8

Moses and the people of Israel built an altar of stone to remind them of the presence of the Lord with them. How might such an altar help them remember God's commandments and laws? Gather your family or roommates together and discuss how you might create such a visible reminder in your home of God's claim on your life. Is there a work of calligraphy, a piece of art or a symbol you can think of? Where will you place it?

See Meeting God in Everyday Life

The Altar on Mount Ebal

27 Moses and the elders of Israel commanded the people: "Keep all these commands that I give you today. ²When you have crossed the Jordan into the land the LORD your God is giving you, set up some large stones and coat them with plaster. ³Write on them all the words of this law when you have crossed over to enter the land the LORD your God is giving you, a land flowing with milk and honey, just as the LORD, the God of your fathers, promised you. ⁴And when you have crossed the Jordan, set up these stones on Mount Ebal, as I command you today, and coat them with plaster. ⁵Build there an altar to the LORD your God, an altar of stones. Do not use any iron tool upon them. ⁶Build the altar of the LORD your God with fieldstones and offer burnt offerings on it to the LORD your God. ⁷Sacrifice fellowship offerings[a] there, eating them and rejoicing in the presence of the LORD your God. ⁸And you shall write very clearly all the words of this law on these stones you have set up."

Curses From Mount Ebal

⁹Then Moses and the priests, who are Levites, said to all Israel, "Be silent, O Israel, and listen! You have now become the people of the LORD your God. ¹⁰Obey the LORD your God and follow his commands and decrees that I give you today."

¹¹On the same day Moses commanded the people:

¹²When you have crossed the Jordan, these tribes shall stand on Mount Gerizim to bless the people: Simeon, Levi, Judah, Issachar, Joseph and Benjamin. ¹³And these tribes shall stand on Mount Ebal to pronounce curses: Reuben, Gad, Asher, Zebulun, Dan and Naphtali.

¹⁴The Levites shall recite to all the people of Israel in a loud voice:

¹⁵"Cursed is the man who carves an image or casts an idol—a thing detestable to the LORD, the work of the craftsman's hands—and sets it up in secret."

Then all the people shall say, "Amen!"

¹⁶"Cursed is the man who dishonors his father or his mother."

Then all the people shall say, "Amen!"

¹⁷"Cursed is the man who moves his neighbor's boundary stone."

Then all the people shall say, "Amen!"

¹⁸"Cursed is the man who leads the blind astray on the road."

Then all the people shall say, "Amen!"

¹⁹"Cursed is the man who withholds justice from the alien, the fatherless or the widow."

Then all the people shall say, "Amen!"

²⁰"Cursed is the man who sleeps with his father's wife, for he dishonors his father's bed."

Then all the people shall say, "Amen!"

²¹"Cursed is the man who has sexual relations with any animal."

Then all the people shall say, "Amen!"

²²"Cursed is the man who sleeps with his sister, the daughter of his father or the daughter of his mother."

Then all the people shall say, "Amen!"

a 7 Traditionally *peace offerings*

²³"Cursed is the man who sleeps with his mother-in-law."

Then all the people shall say, "Amen!"

²⁴"Cursed is the man who kills his neighbor secretly."

Then all the people shall say, "Amen!"

²⁵"Cursed is the man who accepts a bribe to kill an innocent person."

Then all the people shall say, "Amen!"

²⁶"Cursed is the man who does not uphold the words of this law by carrying them out."

Then all the people shall say, "Amen!"

Blessings for Obedience

28 If you fully obey the LORD your God and carefully follow all his commands I give you today, the LORD your God will set you high above all the nations on earth. ²All these blessings will come upon you and accompany you if you obey the LORD your God:

³You will be blessed in the city and blessed in the country.

⁴The fruit of your womb will be blessed, and the crops of your land and the young of your livestock—the calves of your herds and the lambs of your flocks.

⁵Your basket and your kneading trough will be blessed.

⁶You will be blessed when you come in and blessed when you go out.

⁷The LORD will grant that the enemies who rise up against you will be defeated before you. They will come at you from one direction but flee from you in seven.

⁸The LORD will send a blessing on your barns and on everything you put your hand to. The LORD your God will bless you in the land he is giving you.

⁹The LORD will establish you as his holy people, as he promised you on oath, if you keep the commands of the LORD your God and walk in his ways. ¹⁰Then all the peoples on earth will see that you are called by the name of the LORD, and they will fear you. ¹¹The LORD will grant you abundant prosperity—in the fruit of your womb, the young of your livestock and the crops of your ground—in the land he swore to your forefathers to give you.

¹²The LORD will open the heavens, the storehouse of his bounty, to send rain on your land in season and to bless all the work of your hands. You will lend to many nations but will borrow from none. ¹³The LORD will make you the head, not the tail. If you pay attention to the commands of the LORD your God that I give you this day and carefully follow them, you will always be at the top, never at the bottom. ¹⁴Do not turn aside from any of the commands I give you today, to the right or to the left, following other gods and serving them.

Curses for Disobedience

¹⁵However, if you do not obey the LORD your God and do not carefully follow all his commands and decrees I am giving you today, all these curses will come upon you and overtake you:

¹⁶You will be cursed in the city and cursed in the country.

Abundant Blessings

DEUTERONOMY 28:2–15

Write a poem about God's blessings using this passage as a starting point. Moses dwells on blessings within an agrarian society, but what might be some of the modern, especially urban, equivalents? Now go through the curses beginning in 28:16, also thinking of modern-day examples. What are some of the worst misfortunes you can imagine? Have you experienced any of these blessings or curses? How do they draw you into God's presence? How do they create questions and doubts, or perhaps anger, in your mind? How does your understanding of the death and resurrection of Jesus affect the way you read this passage in Deuteronomy?

See Meeting God in Scripture

Remembering Through Adversity

DEUTERONOMY 28:32–35

Have you ever been in a situation where, regardless of how hard you worked, you just couldn't seem to meet all your financial obligations? What did you do with the frustration? Have you ever faced persistent medical problems, or even a severe case of the flu that lingered too long? How have these difficult moments pointed you toward eternity? What is your greatest difficulty today? How can you use it to remember God rather than grow bitter toward him?

See *Meeting God in Everyday Life*

¹⁷Your basket and your kneading trough will be cursed.

¹⁸The fruit of your womb will be cursed, and the crops of your land, and the calves of your herds and the lambs of your flocks.

¹⁹You will be cursed when you come in and cursed when you go out.

²⁰The LORD will send on you curses, confusion and rebuke in everything you put your hand to, until you are destroyed and come to sudden ruin because of the evil you have done in forsaking him.[a] ²¹The LORD will plague you with diseases until he has destroyed you from the land you are entering to possess. ²²The LORD will strike you with wasting disease, with fever and inflammation, with scorching heat and drought, with blight and mildew, which will plague you until you perish. ²³The sky over your head will be bronze, the ground beneath you iron. ²⁴The LORD will turn the rain of your country into dust and powder; it will come down from the skies until you are destroyed.

²⁵The LORD will cause you to be defeated before your enemies. You will come at them from one direction but flee from them in seven, and you will become a thing of horror to all the kingdoms on earth. ²⁶Your carcasses will be food for all the birds of the air and the beasts of the earth, and there will be no one to frighten them away. ²⁷The LORD will afflict you with the boils of Egypt and with tumors, festering sores and the itch, from which you cannot be cured. ²⁸The LORD will afflict you with madness, blindness and confusion of mind. ²⁹At midday you will grope about like a blind man in the dark. You will be unsuccessful in everything you do; day after day you will be oppressed and robbed, with no one to rescue you.

³⁰You will be pledged to be married to a woman, but another will take her and ravish her. You will build a house, but you will not live in it. You will plant a vineyard, but you will not even begin to enjoy its fruit. ³¹Your ox will be slaughtered before your eyes, but you will eat none of it. Your donkey will be forcibly taken from you and will not be returned. Your sheep will be given to your enemies, and no one will rescue them. ³²Your sons and daughters will be given to another nation, and you will wear out your eyes watching for them day after day, powerless to lift a hand. ³³A people that you do not know will eat what your land and labor produce, and you will have nothing but cruel oppression all your days. ³⁴The sights you see will drive you mad. ³⁵The LORD will afflict your knees and legs with painful boils that cannot be cured, spreading from the soles of your feet to the top of your head.

³⁶The LORD will drive you and the king you set over you to a nation unknown to you or your fathers. There you will worship other gods, gods of wood and stone. ³⁷You will become a thing of horror and an object of scorn and ridicule to all the nations where the LORD will drive you.

³⁸You will sow much seed in the field but you will harvest little, because locusts will devour it. ³⁹You will plant vineyards and cultivate them but you will not drink the wine or gather the grapes, because worms will eat them. ⁴⁰You will have olive trees throughout your country but you will not

a 20 Hebrew *me*

use the oil, because the olives will drop off. ⁴¹You will have sons and daughters but you will not keep them, because they will go into captivity. ⁴²Swarms of locusts will take over all your trees and the crops of your land.

⁴³The alien who lives among you will rise above you higher and higher, but you will sink lower and lower. ⁴⁴He will lend to you, but you will not lend to him. He will be the head, but you will be the tail.

⁴⁵All these curses will come upon you. They will pursue you and overtake you until you are destroyed, because you did not obey the LORD your God and observe the commands and decrees he gave you. ⁴⁶They will be a sign and a wonder to you and your descendants forever. ⁴⁷Because you did not serve the LORD your God joyfully and gladly in the time of prosperity, ⁴⁸therefore in hunger and thirst, in nakedness and dire poverty, you will serve the enemies the LORD sends against you. He will put an iron yoke on your neck until he has destroyed you.

⁴⁹The LORD will bring a nation against you from far away, from the ends of the earth, like an eagle swooping down, a nation whose language you will not understand, ⁵⁰a fierce-looking nation without respect for the old or pity for the young. ⁵¹They will devour the young of your livestock and the crops of your land until you are destroyed. They will leave you no grain, new wine or oil, nor any calves of your herds or lambs of your flocks until you are ruined. ⁵²They will lay siege to all the cities throughout your land until the high fortified walls in which you trust fall down. They will besiege all the cities throughout the land the LORD your God is giving you.

⁵³Because of the suffering that your enemy will inflict on you during the siege, you will eat the fruit of the womb, the flesh of the sons and daughters the LORD your God has given you. ⁵⁴Even the most gentle and sensitive man among you will have no compassion on his own brother or the wife he loves or his surviving children, ⁵⁵and he will not give to one of them any of the flesh of his children that he is eating. It will be all he has left because of the suffering your enemy will inflict on you during the siege of all your cities. ⁵⁶The most gentle and sensitive woman among you—so sensitive and gentle that she would not venture to touch the ground with the sole of her foot—will begrudge the husband she loves and her own son or daughter ⁵⁷the afterbirth from her womb and the children she bears. For she intends to eat them secretly during the siege and in the distress that your enemy will inflict on you in your cities.

⁵⁸If you do not carefully follow all the words of this law, which are written in this book, and do not revere this glorious and awesome name—the LORD your God— ⁵⁹the LORD will send fearful plagues on you and your descendants, harsh and prolonged disasters, and severe and lingering illnesses. ⁶⁰He will bring upon you all the diseases of Egypt that you dreaded, and they will cling to you. ⁶¹The LORD will also bring on you every kind of sickness and disaster not recorded in this Book of the Law, until you are destroyed. ⁶²You who were as numerous as the stars in the sky will be left but few in number, because you did not obey the LORD your God. ⁶³Just as it pleased the LORD to make you prosper and increase in number, so it will please him to ruin and destroy you. You will be uprooted from the land you are entering to possess.

Living in the Present

DEUTERONOMY 28:58–67

"Let each of us examine his thoughts; he will find them wholly concerned with the past or the future. We almost never think of the present, and if we do think of it, it is only to see what light it throws on our plans for the future. The present is never our end. The past and the present are our means, the future alone our end. Thus we never actually live, but hope to live, and since we are always planning how to be happy, it is inevitable that we should never be so."

—BLAISE PASCAL,
Pensees

Covenant Keeper

DEUTERONOMY 29:9–15

Have you ever signed a contract when buying a house or car? What kind of thought did you give it beforehand? How did you feel as you signed your name on the dotted line? Have you ever signed a contract that you didn't read first? Keeping in mind the death and resurrection of Jesus Christ, and using Scripture (see 2 Corinthians 3:6; Hebrews 8—9) as a guide, write out an agreement between yourself and God. What does God expect of you, and what does he promise in return? How willing are you to sign this covenant? How might reflecting on its terms help you to mature spiritually?

See *Meeting God in Scripture*

⁶⁴Then the LORD will scatter you among all nations, from one end of the earth to the other. There you will worship other gods—gods of wood and stone, which neither you nor your fathers have known. ⁶⁵Among those nations you will find no repose, no resting place for the sole of your foot. There the LORD will give you an anxious mind, eyes weary with longing, and a despairing heart. ⁶⁶You will live in constant suspense, filled with dread both night and day, never sure of your life. ⁶⁷In the morning you will say, "If only it were evening!" and in the evening, "If only it were morning!"—because of the terror that will fill your hearts and the sights that your eyes will see. ⁶⁸The LORD will send you back in ships to Egypt on a journey I said you should never make again. There you will offer yourselves for sale to your enemies as male and female slaves, but no one will buy you.

Renewal of the Covenant

29 These are the terms of the covenant the LORD commanded Moses to make with the Israelites in Moab, in addition to the covenant he had made with them at Horeb.

²Moses summoned all the Israelites and said to them:

Your eyes have seen all that the LORD did in Egypt to Pharaoh, to all his officials and to all his land. ³With your own eyes you saw those great trials, those miraculous signs and great wonders. ⁴But to this day the LORD has not given you a mind that understands or eyes that see or ears that hear. ⁵During the forty years that I led you through the desert, your clothes did not wear out, nor did the sandals on your feet. ⁶You ate no bread and drank no wine or other fermented drink. I did this so that you might know that I am the LORD your God.

⁷When you reached this place, Sihon king of Heshbon and Og king of Bashan came out to fight against us, but we defeated them. ⁸We took their land and gave it as an inheritance to the Reubenites, the Gadites and the half-tribe of Manasseh.

⁹Carefully follow the terms of this covenant, so that you may prosper in everything you do. ¹⁰All of you are standing today in the presence of the LORD your God—your leaders and chief men, your elders and officials, and all the other men of Israel, ¹¹together with your children and your wives, and the aliens living in your camps who chop your wood and carry your water. ¹²You are standing here in order to enter into a covenant with the LORD your God, a covenant the LORD is making with you this day and sealing with an oath, ¹³to confirm you this day as his people, that he may be your God as he promised you and as he swore to your fathers, Abraham, Isaac and Jacob. ¹⁴I am making this covenant, with its oath, not only with you ¹⁵who are standing here with us today in the presence of the LORD our God but also with those who are not here today.

¹⁶You yourselves know how we lived in Egypt and how we passed through the countries on the way here. ¹⁷You saw among them their detestable images and idols of wood and stone, of silver and gold. ¹⁸Make sure there is no man or woman, clan or tribe among you today whose heart turns away from the LORD our God to go and worship the gods of those nations; make sure there is no root among you that produces such bitter poison.

¹⁹When such a person hears the words of this oath, he in-

vokes a blessing on himself and therefore thinks, "I will be safe, even though I persist in going my own way." This will bring disaster on the watered land as well as the dry.[a] 20 The LORD will never be willing to forgive him; his wrath and zeal will burn against that man. All the curses written in this book will fall upon him, and the LORD will blot out his name from under heaven. 21 The LORD will single him out from all the tribes of Israel for disaster, according to all the curses of the covenant written in this Book of the Law.

22 Your children who follow you in later generations and foreigners who come from distant lands will see the calamities that have fallen on the land and the diseases with which the LORD has afflicted it. 23 The whole land will be a burning waste of salt and sulfur—nothing planted, nothing sprouting, no vegetation growing on it. It will be like the destruction of Sodom and Gomorrah, Admah and Zeboiim, which the LORD overthrew in fierce anger. 24 All the nations will ask: "Why has the LORD done this to this land? Why this fierce, burning anger?"

25 And the answer will be: "It is because this people abandoned the covenant of the LORD, the God of their fathers, the covenant he made with them when he brought them out of Egypt. 26 They went off and worshiped other gods and bowed down to them, gods they did not know, gods he had not given them. 27 Therefore the LORD's anger burned against this land, so that he brought on it all the curses written in this book. 28 In furious anger and in great wrath the LORD uprooted them from their land and thrust them into another land, as it is now."

29 The secret things belong to the LORD our God, but the things revealed belong to us and to our children forever, that we may follow all the words of this law.

Prosperity After Turning to the LORD

30 When all these blessings and curses I have set before you come upon you and you take them to heart wherever the LORD your God disperses you among the nations, 2 and when you and your children return to the LORD your God and obey him with all your heart and with all your soul according to everything I command you today, 3 then the LORD your God will restore your fortunes[b] and have compassion on you and gather you again from all the nations where he scattered you. 4 Even if you have been banished to the most distant land under the heavens, from there the LORD your God will gather you and bring you back. 5 He will bring you to the land that belonged to your fathers, and you will take possession of it. He will make you more prosperous and numerous than your fathers. 6 The LORD your God will circumcise your hearts and the hearts of your descendants, so that you may love him with all your heart and with all your soul, and live. 7 The LORD your God will put all these curses on your enemies who hate and persecute you. 8 You will again obey the LORD and follow all his commands I am giving you today. 9 Then the LORD your God will make you most prosperous in all the work of your hands and in the fruit of your womb, the young of your livestock and the crops of your land. The LORD will again delight in you and make you prosperous, just as he delighted

An Angry Enemy

DEUTERONOMY 29:18–38

Although at times Scripture urges us to take comfort in God, other passages remind us of how terrible a foe God could be. The next time you're in a small group—at a dinner or a Bible study—ask the provocative question, "What would it be like to have God for an enemy?" Consider all the ways that an angry, all-seeing, all-powerful, ever-present God could make someone's life absolutely miserable. Discuss how God could make war on his enemy physically as well as emotionally and spiritually. How might this discussion affect how you choose to respond to God? How might this reality affect your relationship with Jesus Christ?

---

[a] 19 Or way, in order to add drunkenness to thirst."   [b] 3 Or will bring you back from captivity

Within Reach

What if following God's way required you to climb to the top of Mount Everest or cross an ocean in a rowboat? How would you assess the risks and the rewards? Moses here says that doing God's will is not impossible or even as difficult as one of these challenges. What does it mean to you that God's Word is not far away, but "in your mouth and in your heart"?

See Meeting God in Scripture

in your fathers, [10]if you obey the Lord your God and keep his commands and decrees that are written in this Book of the Law and turn to the Lord your God with all your heart and with all your soul.

The Offer of Life or Death

[11]Now what I am commanding you today is not too difficult for you or beyond your reach. [12]It is not up in heaven, so that you have to ask, "Who will ascend into heaven to get it and proclaim it to us so we may obey it?" [13]Nor is it beyond the sea, so that you have to ask, "Who will cross the sea to get it and proclaim it to us so we may obey it?" [14]No, the word is very near you; it is in your mouth and in your heart so you may obey it.

[15]See, I set before you today life and prosperity, death and destruction. [16]For I command you today to love the Lord your God, to walk in his ways, and to keep his commands, decrees and laws; then you will live and increase, and the Lord your God will bless you in the land you are entering to possess.

[17]But if your heart turns away and you are not obedient, and if you are drawn away to bow down to other gods and worship them, [18]I declare to you this day that you will certainly be destroyed. You will not live long in the land you are crossing the Jordan to enter and possess.

[19]This day I call heaven and earth as witnesses against you that I have set before you life and death, blessings and curses. Now choose life, so that you and your children may live [20]and that you may love the Lord your God, listen to his voice, and hold fast to him. For the Lord is your life, and he will give you many years in the land he swore to give to your fathers, Abraham, Isaac and Jacob.

Joshua to Succeed Moses

31 Then Moses went out and spoke these words to all Israel: [2]"I am now a hundred and twenty years old and I am no longer able to lead you. The Lord has said to me, 'You shall not cross the Jordan.' [3]The Lord your God himself will cross over ahead of you. He will destroy these nations before you, and you will take possession of their land. Joshua also will cross over ahead of you, as the Lord said. [4]And the Lord will do to them what he did to Sihon and Og, the kings of the Amorites, whom he destroyed along with their land. [5]The Lord will deliver them to you, and you must do to them all that I have commanded you. [6]Be strong and courageous. Do not be afraid or terrified because of them, for the Lord your God goes with you; he will never leave you nor forsake you."

[7]Then Moses summoned Joshua and said to him in the presence of all Israel, "Be strong and courageous, for you must go with this people into the land that the Lord swore to their forefathers to give them, and you must divide it among them as their inheritance. [8]The Lord himself goes before you and will be with you; he will never leave you nor forsake you. Do not be afraid; do not be discouraged."

The Reading of the Law

[9]So Moses wrote down this law and gave it to the priests, the sons of Levi, who carried the ark of the covenant of the Lord, and to all the elders of Israel. [10]Then Moses com-

manded them: "At the end of every seven years, in the year for canceling debts, during the Feast of Tabernacles, [11]when all Israel comes to appear before the LORD your God at the place he will choose, you shall read this law before them in their hearing. [12]Assemble the people—men, women and children, and the aliens living in your towns—so they can listen and learn to fear the LORD your God and follow carefully all the words of this law. [13]Their children, who do not know this law, must hear it and learn to fear the LORD your God as long as you live in the land you are crossing the Jordan to possess."

Israel's Rebellion Predicted

[14]The LORD said to Moses, "Now the day of your death is near. Call Joshua and present yourselves at the Tent of Meeting, where I will commission him." So Moses and Joshua came and presented themselves at the Tent of Meeting.

[15]Then the LORD appeared at the Tent in a pillar of cloud, and the cloud stood over the entrance to the Tent. [16]And the LORD said to Moses: "You are going to rest with your fathers, and these people will soon prostitute themselves to the foreign gods of the land they are entering. They will forsake me and break the covenant I made with them. [17]On that day I will become angry with them and forsake them; I will hide my face from them, and they will be destroyed. Many disasters and difficulties will come upon them, and on that day they will ask, 'Have not these disasters come upon us because our God is not with us?' [18]And I will certainly hide my face on that day because of all their wickedness in turning to other gods.

[19]"Now write down for yourselves this song and teach it to the Israelites and have them sing it, so that it may be a witness for me against them. [20]When I have brought them into the land flowing with milk and honey, the land I promised on oath to their forefathers, and when they eat their fill and thrive, they will turn to other gods and worship them, rejecting me and breaking my covenant. [21]And when many disasters and difficulties come upon them, this song will testify against them, because it will not be forgotten by their descendants. I know what they are disposed to do, even before I bring them into the land I promised them on oath." [22]So Moses wrote down this song that day and taught it to the Israelites.

[23]The LORD gave this command to Joshua son of Nun: "Be strong and courageous, for you will bring the Israelites into the land I promised them on oath, and I myself will be with you."

[24]After Moses finished writing in a book the words of this law from beginning to end, [25]he gave this command to the Levites who carried the ark of the covenant of the LORD: [26]"Take this Book of the Law and place it beside the ark of the covenant of the LORD your God. There it will remain as a witness against you. [27]For I know how rebellious and stiffnecked you are. If you have been rebellious against the LORD while I am still alive and with you, how much more will you rebel after I die! [28]Assemble before me all the elders of your tribes and all your officials, so that I can speak these words in their hearing and call heaven and earth to testify against them. [29]For I know that after my death you

Last Words

DEUTERONOMY 31:14

Moses is given an opportunity that many of us will never have—he knows that his death is at hand. If God were to tell you that you had just one year left to live, how would you spend it? What relationships would you need to address? On what form of ministry would you focus? How would you reprioritize your life? Whom would you want to train or to whom would you want to give special instructions before you died?

Natural Insights

DEUTERONOMY 32:2,4

Moses uses natural images to capture the beauty of God's truth. Meditate on these images: God's teaching falling like rain, descending like dew or like abundant rain on tender plants. Next spend some time on the image of God as the Rock. What security does this thought provide for you? Can you find any other natural images in Scripture that especially appeal to you? What natural image (or images) would *you* use to describe God's teaching and protection?

See Meeting God in the Created Order

are sure to become utterly corrupt and to turn from the way I have commanded you. In days to come, disaster will fall upon you because you will do evil in the sight of the LORD and provoke him to anger by what your hands have made."

The Song of Moses

³⁰And Moses recited the words of this song from beginning to end in the hearing of the whole assembly of Israel:

32 Listen, O heavens, and I will speak;
      hear, O earth, the words of my mouth.
² Let my teaching fall like rain
      and my words descend like dew,
   like showers on new grass,
      like abundant rain on tender plants.

³ I will proclaim the name of the LORD.
      Oh, praise the greatness of our God!
⁴ He is the Rock, his works are perfect,
      and all his ways are just.
   A faithful God who does no wrong,
      upright and just is he.

⁵ They have acted corruptly toward him;
      to their shame they are no longer his children,
      but a warped and crooked generation.ᵃ
⁶ Is this the way you repay the LORD,
      O foolish and unwise people?
   Is he not your Father, your Creator,ᵇ
      who made you and formed you?

⁷ Remember the days of old;
      consider the generations long past.
   Ask your father and he will tell you,
      your elders, and they will explain to you.
⁸ When the Most High gave the nations their
         inheritance,
      when he divided all mankind,
   he set up boundaries for the peoples
      according to the number of the sons of Israel.ᶜ
⁹ For the LORD's portion is his people,
      Jacob his allotted inheritance.

¹⁰ In a desert land he found him,
      in a barren and howling waste.
   He shielded him and cared for him;
      he guarded him as the apple of his eye,
¹¹ like an eagle that stirs up its nest
      and hovers over its young,
   that spreads its wings to catch them
      and carries them on its pinions.
¹² The LORD alone led him;
      no foreign god was with him.

¹³ He made him ride on the heights of the land
      and fed him with the fruit of the fields.
   He nourished him with honey from the rock,
      and with oil from the flinty crag,
¹⁴ with curds and milk from herd and flock

ᵃ5 Or *Corrupt are they and not his children, / a generation warped and twisted to their shame*   ᵇ6 Or *Father, who bought you*   ᶜ8 Masoretic Text; Dead Sea Scrolls (see also Septuagint) *sons of God*

and with fattened lambs and goats,
with choice rams of Bashan
and the finest kernels of wheat.
You drank the foaming blood of the grape.

¹⁵ Jeshurun*ᵃ* grew fat and kicked;
filled with food, he became heavy and sleek.
He abandoned the God who made him
and rejected the Rock his Savior.
¹⁶ They made him jealous with their foreign gods
and angered him with their detestable idols.
¹⁷ They sacrificed to demons, which are not God—
gods they had not known,
gods that recently appeared,
gods your fathers did not fear.
¹⁸ You deserted the Rock, who fathered you;
you forgot the God who gave you birth.

¹⁹ The LORD saw this and rejected them
because he was angered by his sons and
daughters.
²⁰ "I will hide my face from them," he said,
"and see what their end will be;
for they are a perverse generation,
children who are unfaithful.
²¹ They made me jealous by what is no god
and angered me with their worthless idols.
I will make them envious by those who are not a
people;
I will make them angry by a nation that has no
understanding.
²² For a fire has been kindled by my wrath,
one that burns to the realm of death*ᵇ* below.
It will devour the earth and its harvests
and set afire the foundations of the mountains.

²³ "I will heap calamities upon them
and spend my arrows against them.
²⁴ I will send wasting famine against them,
consuming pestilence and deadly plague;
I will send against them the fangs of wild beasts,
the venom of vipers that glide in the dust.
²⁵ In the street the sword will make them childless;
in their homes terror will reign.
Young men and young women will perish,
infants and gray-haired men.
²⁶ I said I would scatter them
and blot out their memory from mankind,
²⁷ but I dreaded the taunt of the enemy,
lest the adversary misunderstand
and say, 'Our hand has triumphed;
the LORD has not done all this.' "

²⁸ They are a nation without sense,
there is no discernment in them.
²⁹ If only they were wise and would understand this
and discern what their end will be!
³⁰ How could one man chase a thousand,
or two put ten thousand to flight,
unless their Rock had sold them,
unless the LORD had given them up?

Relational Insights

DEUTERONOMY 32:6,8,18

How might thinking about God as Father create a different understanding from meditating on God as Creator? What insights might you gain by reflecting on other names for God used in these verses, including Most High, Savior, and Rock? List some of the other names for God (see Exodus 17:15; Daniel 7:9) mentioned in the Bible. Which image is most meaningful to you? Which image is most difficult for you to relate to? Why do you think Scripture describes God with many metaphors rather than just one?

See *Meeting God in Scripture*

ᵃ 15 Jeshurun means *the upright one,* that is, Israel.   *ᵇ 22* Hebrew *to Sheol*

A Final Denial

DEUTERONOMY 32:48–52

What might Moses' emotions have been as he looked out over the promised land and knew that he would not enter it? If you were in Moses' situation, would seeing the land make it harder or easier to accept God's denial? Is there anything in your life that God seems to be denying you? Do you think God is denying you because you have disobeyed, or is there another reason? Imagine having a conversation with Moses on Mount Nebo. What might he say to encourage you as you struggle to accept God's denial of what you desire?

See *Meeting God in Scripture*

³¹ For their rock is not like our Rock,
   as even our enemies concede.
³² Their vine comes from the vine of Sodom
   and from the fields of Gomorrah.
Their grapes are filled with poison,
   and their clusters with bitterness.
³³ Their wine is the venom of serpents,
   the deadly poison of cobras.

³⁴ "Have I not kept this in reserve
   and sealed it in my vaults?
³⁵ It is mine to avenge; I will repay.
   In due time their foot will slip;
their day of disaster is near
   and their doom rushes upon them."

³⁶ The LORD will judge his people
   and have compassion on his servants
when he sees their strength is gone
   and no one is left, slave or free.
³⁷ He will say: "Now where are their gods,
   the rock they took refuge in,
³⁸ the gods who ate the fat of their sacrifices
   and drank the wine of their drink offerings?
Let them rise up to help you!
   Let them give you shelter!

³⁹ "See now that I myself am He!
   There is no god besides me.
I put to death and I bring to life,
   I have wounded and I will heal,
   and no one can deliver out of my hand.
⁴⁰ I lift my hand to heaven and declare:
   As surely as I live forever,
⁴¹ when I sharpen my flashing sword
   and my hand grasps it in judgment,
I will take vengeance on my adversaries
   and repay those who hate me.
⁴² I will make my arrows drunk with blood,
   while my sword devours flesh:
the blood of the slain and the captives,
   the heads of the enemy leaders."

⁴³ Rejoice, O nations, with his people,ᵃ,ᵇ
   for he will avenge the blood of his servants;
he will take vengeance on his enemies
   and make atonement for his land and people.

⁴⁴ Moses came with Joshuaᶜ son of Nun and spoke all the words of this song in the hearing of the people. ⁴⁵ When Moses finished reciting all these words to all Israel, ⁴⁶ he said to them, "Take to heart all the words I have solemnly declared to you this day, so that you may command your children to obey carefully all the words of this law. ⁴⁷ They are not just idle words for you—they are your life. By them you will live long in the land you are crossing the Jordan to possess."

Moses to Die on Mount Nebo

⁴⁸ On that same day the LORD told Moses, ⁴⁹ "Go up into

ᵃ 43 Or *Make his people rejoice, O nations*   ᵇ 43 Masoretic Text; Dead Sea Scrolls (see also Septuagint) *people, / and let all the angels worship him /*   ᶜ 44 Hebrew *Hoshea*, a variant of *Joshua*

the Abarim Range to Mount Nebo in Moab, across from Jericho, and view Canaan, the land I am giving the Israelites as their own possession. ⁵⁰There on the mountain that you have climbed you will die and be gathered to your people, just as your brother Aaron died on Mount Hor and was gathered to his people. ⁵¹This is because both of you broke faith with me in the presence of the Israelites at the waters of Meribah Kadesh in the Desert of Zin and because you did not uphold my holiness among the Israelites. ⁵²Therefore, you will see the land only from a distance; you will not enter the land I am giving to the people of Israel."

Moses Blesses the Tribes

33 This is the blessing that Moses the man of God pronounced on the Israelites before his death. ²He said:

"The LORD came from Sinai
 and dawned over them from Seir;
 he shone forth from Mount Paran.
He came with*ᵃ* myriads of holy ones
 from the south, from his mountain slopes.*ᵇ*
³Surely it is you who love the people;
 all the holy ones are in your hand.
At your feet they all bow down,
 and from you receive instruction,
⁴the law that Moses gave us,
 the possession of the assembly of Jacob.
⁵He was king over Jeshurun*ᶜ*
 when the leaders of the people assembled,
 along with the tribes of Israel.

⁶"Let Reuben live and not die,
 nor*ᵈ* his men be few."

⁷And this he said about Judah:

"Hear, O LORD, the cry of Judah;
 bring him to his people.
With his own hands he defends his cause.
 Oh, be his help against his foes!"

⁸About Levi he said:

"Your Thummim and Urim belong
 to the man you favored.
You tested him at Massah;
 you contended with him at the waters of
 Meribah.
⁹He said of his father and mother,
 'I have no regard for them.'
He did not recognize his brothers
 or acknowledge his own children,
but he watched over your word
 and guarded your covenant.
¹⁰He teaches your precepts to Jacob
 and your law to Israel.
He offers incense before you
 and whole burnt offerings on your altar.
¹¹Bless all his skills, O LORD,
 and be pleased with the work of his hands.

The Lord's Beloved

DEUTERONOMY 33:1–12

"Blessed is he that understandeth what it is to love Jesus, and to despise himself for Jesus' sake. Thou oughtest to leave thy beloved, for thy Beloved; for Jesus will be loved alone above all things. The love of things created is deceitful and inconstant; the love of Jesus is faithful and lasting. He that cleaveth unto creatures, shall fall with that which is frail; he that embraceth Jesus, shall stand firmly for ever. Love Him and keep Him for thy friend, who, when all go away, will not forsake thee, nor suffer thee to perish in the end."

—THOMAS À KEMPIS,
The Imitation of Christ

ᵃ2 Or *from*   *ᵇ2* The meaning of the Hebrew for this phrase is uncertain.
ᶜ5 *Jeshurun* means *the upright one*, that is, Israel; also in verse 26.
ᵈ6 Or *but let*

269

A Secure Shelter

DEUTERONOMY 33:26–29

This is Moses' final address to Israel. He has led this people through an astounding, perilous and miracle-laden journey, and now he is about to leave them with a final portrait of the God they know, love and serve. Moses wants Israel to remember a God who "rides on the heavens" and the clouds, an "eternal" God of refuge who drives out enemies, who provides basic needs even to the point of abundance and who acts as a shield, help and sword. Spend a few minutes meditating on each image. How can you personally draw security from such a God? What aspect of God's shelter and care is most precious and meaningful to you? Drawing from your own experience and vocabulary, how would you describe God to someone else?

See *Meeting God in Scripture*

Smite the loins of those who rise up against him;
    strike his foes till they rise no more."

¹² About Benjamin he said:

"Let the beloved of the LORD rest secure in him,
    for he shields him all day long,
    and the one the LORD loves rests between his
        shoulders."

¹³ About Joseph he said:

"May the LORD bless his land
    with the precious dew from heaven above
    and with the deep waters that lie below;
¹⁴ with the best the sun brings forth
    and the finest the moon can yield;
¹⁵ with the choicest gifts of the ancient mountains
    and the fruitfulness of the everlasting hills;
¹⁶ with the best gifts of the earth and its fullness
    and the favor of him who dwelt in the burning
        bush.
Let all these rest on the head of Joseph,
    on the brow of the prince among*ᵃ* his brothers.
¹⁷ In majesty he is like a firstborn bull;
    his horns are the horns of a wild ox.
With them he will gore the nations,
    even those at the ends of the earth.
Such are the ten thousands of Ephraim;
    such are the thousands of Manasseh."

¹⁸ About Zebulun he said:

"Rejoice, Zebulun, in your going out,
    and you, Issachar, in your tents.
¹⁹ They will summon peoples to the mountain
    and there offer sacrifices of righteousness;
they will feast on the abundance of the seas,
    on the treasures hidden in the sand."

²⁰ About Gad he said:

"Blessed is he who enlarges Gad's domain!
    Gad lives there like a lion,
    tearing at arm or head.
²¹ He chose the best land for himself;
    the leader's portion was kept for him.
When the heads of the people assembled,
    he carried out the LORD's righteous will,
    and his judgments concerning Israel."

²² About Dan he said:

"Dan is a lion's cub,
    springing out of Bashan."

²³ About Naphtali he said:

"Naphtali is abounding with the favor of the LORD
    and is full of his blessing;
    he will inherit southward to the lake."

²⁴ About Asher he said:

"Most blessed of sons is Asher;
    let him be favored by his brothers,

ᵃ *16 Or of the one separated from*

and let him bathe his feet in oil.
²⁵ The bolts of your gates will be iron and bronze,
and your strength will equal your days.

²⁶ "There is no one like the God of Jeshurun,
who rides on the heavens to help you
and on the clouds in his majesty.
²⁷ The eternal God is your refuge,
and underneath are the everlasting arms.
He will drive out your enemy before you,
saying, 'Destroy him!'
²⁸ So Israel will live in safety alone;
Jacob's spring is secure
in a land of grain and new wine,
where the heavens drop dew.
²⁹ Blessed are you, O Israel!
Who is like you,
a people saved by the LORD?
He is your shield and helper
and your glorious sword.
Your enemies will cower before you,
and you will trample down their high places.ᵃ"

The Death of Moses

34 Then Moses climbed Mount Nebo from the plains of Moab to the top of Pisgah, across from Jericho. There the LORD showed him the whole land—from Gilead to Dan, ²all of Naphtali, the territory of Ephraim and Manasseh, all the land of Judah as far as the western sea,ᵇ ³the Negev and the whole region from the Valley of Jericho, the City of Palms, as far as Zoar. ⁴Then the LORD said to him, "This is the land I promised on oath to Abraham, Isaac and Jacob when I said, 'I will give it to your descendants.' I have let you see it with your eyes, but you will not cross over into it."

⁵And Moses the servant of the LORD died there in Moab, as the LORD had said. ⁶He buried himᶜ in Moab, in the valley opposite Beth Peor, but to this day no one knows where his grave is. ⁷Moses was a hundred and twenty years old when he died, yet his eyes were not weak nor his strength gone. ⁸The Israelites grieved for Moses in the plains of Moab thirty days, until the time of weeping and mourning was over.

⁹Now Joshua son of Nun was filled with the spiritᵈ of wisdom because Moses had laid his hands on him. So the Israelites listened to him and did what the LORD had commanded Moses.

¹⁰Since then, no prophet has risen in Israel like Moses, whom the LORD knew face to face, ¹¹who did all those miraculous signs and wonders the LORD sent him to do in Egypt—to Pharaoh and to all his officials and to his whole land. ¹²For no one has ever shown the mighty power or performed the awesome deeds that Moses did in the sight of all Israel.

Passing of the Spiritual Guard

DEUTERONOMY 34:8–10

Has someone who was very influential in your spiritual life passed away? How did this loss affect your faith? What do you think it was like for the Israelites to grieve over Moses? What comfort did God provide them? Moses was a singular character (see 34:12), but now that the Holy Spirit has come, how might we approach the death of an influential person differently from the way the Israelites did?

ᵃ 29 Or *will tread upon their bodies* ᵇ 2 That is, the Mediterranean
ᶜ 6 Or *He was buried* ᵈ 9 Or *Spirit*

JOSHUA
Good News of Second Chances

KEY VERSE:

"No one will be able to stand up against you all the days of your life. As I was with Moses, so I will be with you; I will never leave you nor forsake you."—Joshua 1:5

"If you and I are to be made by God into people for God's purposes, it will depend largely on the courage with which we respond to God. It won't be worked by God's action alone . . . It works through our brave and willing cooperation, our active acceptance and use of all the material we are offered, even everything that damages our vanity and opposes our self-will."

—EVELYN UNDERHILL,
The Ways of the Spirit

When the book of Joshua opens, Israel is still journeying to the promised land. Though God knows Israel's rebellious history, he gives the people another chance to possess the land promised them. Under Joshua's leadership (and with God's intervention) they finally cross the Jordan River and take control of Canaan. Though God's goals for them have not changed, entering and possessing the land requires of them renewed courage, perseverance and faith. The Israelites face a difficult task—to conquer and settle the land. The good news is that God is with them every step of the way.

As spiritual pilgrims in quest of our own land of promise, we can be encouraged by this story of renewed faith as the Israelites finally take possession of God's gift. The book of Joshua suggests abundant parallels between conquering a geographic Canaan and a spiritual Canaan. How are we called to exercise courage when facing the enemies of our souls? What does perseverance in daily spiritual practice look like in our lives? What do we allow to hinder us from possessing our inheritance? How is God giving us a second chance to renew our relationship with him? How is God giving us opportunity to cover new spiritual ground?

The LORD Commands Joshua

1 After the death of Moses the servant of the LORD, the LORD said to Joshua son of Nun, Moses' aide: ²"Moses my servant is dead. Now then, you and all these people, get ready to cross the Jordan River into the land I am about to give to them—to the Israelites. ³I will give you every place where you set your foot, as I promised Moses. ⁴Your territory will extend from the desert to Lebanon, and from the great river, the Euphrates—all the Hittite country—to the Great Sea*ᵃ* on the west. ⁵No one will be able to stand up against you all the days of your life. As I was with Moses, so I will be with you; I will never leave you nor forsake you.

⁶"Be strong and courageous, because you will lead these people to inherit the land I swore to their forefathers to give them. ⁷Be strong and very courageous. Be careful to obey all the law my servant Moses gave you; do not turn from it to the right or to the left, that you may be successful wherever you go. ⁸Do not let this Book of the Law depart from your mouth; meditate on it day and night, so that you may be careful to do everything written in it. Then you will be prosperous and successful. ⁹Have I not commanded you? Be strong and courageous. Do not be terrified; do not be discouraged, for the LORD your God will be with you wherever you go."

¹⁰So Joshua ordered the officers of the people: ¹¹"Go through the camp and tell the people, 'Get your supplies ready. Three days from now you will cross the Jordan here to go in and take possession of the land the LORD your God is giving you for your own.' "

¹²But to the Reubenites, the Gadites and the half-tribe of Manasseh, Joshua said, ¹³"Remember the command that Moses the servant of the LORD gave you: 'The LORD your God is giving you rest and has granted you this land.' ¹⁴Your wives, your children and your livestock may stay in the land that Moses gave you east of the Jordan, but all your fighting men, fully armed, must cross over ahead of your brothers. You are to help your brothers ¹⁵until the LORD gives them rest, as he has done for you, and until they too have taken possession of the land that the LORD your God is giving them. After that, you may go back and occupy your own land, which Moses the servant of the LORD gave you east of the Jordan toward the sunrise."

¹⁶Then they answered Joshua, "Whatever you have commanded us we will do, and wherever you send us we will go. ¹⁷Just as we fully obeyed Moses, so we will obey you. Only may the LORD your God be with you as he was with Moses. ¹⁸Whoever rebels against your word and does not obey your words, whatever you may command them, will be put to death. Only be strong and courageous!"

Rahab and the Spies

2 Then Joshua son of Nun secretly sent two spies from Shittim. "Go, look over the land," he said, "especially Jericho." So they went and entered the house of a prostitute*ᵇ* named Rahab and stayed there.

²The king of Jericho was told, "Look! Some of the Israelites have come here tonight to spy out the land." ³So the king of Jericho sent this message to Rahab: "Bring out the

---

Fighting and Faith

JOSHUA 1:1–9

God suggests to the people through Joshua that taking Canaan will require faith, courage and great effort. Is there a parallel to our spiritual lives today? Do we have to fight to possess what God has already promised? How do we wage such a fight? In what ways are we strengthened in our inner being by exercising faith in possessing the promises of God? In what areas of your life is God calling you to fight? This is God's word to you: "Be strong and courageous . . . for the LORD your God will be with you wherever you go" (v.9).

ᵃ 4 That is, the Mediterranean   *ᵇ 1* Or possibly *an innkeeper*

Spies for the Lord

JOSHUA 2:1–7

"The soul, then, touched with the love of Christ the Spouse, and longing to attain to his grace and gain his goodwill, goes forth here disguised with that disguise which most vividly represents the affections of its spirit and which will protect it most securely on its journey from its adversaries and enemies, which are the devil, the world and the flesh."

—JOHN OF THE CROSS,
The Dark Night of the Soul

men who came to you and entered your house, because they have come to spy out the whole land."

⁴But the woman had taken the two men and hidden them. She said, "Yes, the men came to me, but I did not know where they had come from. ⁵At dusk, when it was time to close the city gate, the men left. I don't know which way they went. Go after them quickly. You may catch up with them." ⁶(But she had taken them up to the roof and hidden them under the stalks of flax she had laid out on the roof.) ⁷So the men set out in pursuit of the spies on the road that leads to the fords of the Jordan, and as soon as the pursuers had gone out, the gate was shut.

⁸Before the spies lay down for the night, she went up on the roof ⁹and said to them, "I know that the LORD has given this land to you and that a great fear of you has fallen on us, so that all who live in this country are melting in fear because of you. ¹⁰We have heard how the LORD dried up the water of the Red Sea[a] for you when you came out of Egypt, and what you did to Sihon and Og, the two kings of the Amorites east of the Jordan, whom you completely destroyed.[b] ¹¹When we heard of it, our hearts melted and everyone's courage failed because of you, for the LORD your God is God in heaven above and on the earth below. ¹²Now then, please swear to me by the LORD that you will show kindness to my family, because I have shown kindness to you. Give me a sure sign ¹³that you will spare the lives of my father and mother, my brothers and sisters, and all who belong to them, and that you will save us from death."

¹⁴"Our lives for your lives!" the men assured her. "If you don't tell what we are doing, we will treat you kindly and faithfully when the LORD gives us the land."

¹⁵So she let them down by a rope through the window, for the house she lived in was part of the city wall. ¹⁶Now she had said to them, "Go to the hills so the pursuers will not find you. Hide yourselves there three days until they return, and then go on your way."

¹⁷The men said to her, "This oath you made us swear will not be binding on us ¹⁸unless, when we enter the land, you have tied this scarlet cord in the window through which you let us down, and unless you have brought your father and mother, your brothers and all your family into your house. ¹⁹If anyone goes outside your house into the street, his blood will be on his own head; we will not be responsible. As for anyone who is in the house with you, his blood will be on our head if a hand is laid on him. ²⁰But if you tell what we are doing, we will be released from the oath you made us swear."

²¹"Agreed," she replied. "Let it be as you say." So she sent them away and they departed. And she tied the scarlet cord in the window.

²²When they left, they went into the hills and stayed there three days, until the pursuers had searched all along the road and returned without finding them. ²³Then the two men started back. They went down out of the hills, forded the river and came to Joshua son of Nun and told him everything that had happened to them. ²⁴They said to

---

ᵃ 10 Hebrew *Yam Suph*; that is, Sea of Reeds   ᵇ 10 The Hebrew term refers to the irrevocable giving over of things or persons to the LORD, often by totally destroying them.

Joshua, "The LORD has surely given the whole land into our hands; all the people are melting in fear because of us."

Crossing the Jordan

3 Early in the morning Joshua and all the Israelites set out from Shittim and went to the Jordan, where they camped before crossing over. ²After three days the officers went throughout the camp, ³giving orders to the people: "When you see the ark of the covenant of the LORD your God, and the priests, who are Levites, carrying it, you are to move out from your positions and follow it. ⁴Then you will know which way to go, since you have never been this way before. But keep a distance of about a thousand yards° between you and the ark; do not go near it."

⁵Joshua told the people, "Consecrate yourselves, for tomorrow the LORD will do amazing things among you."

⁶Joshua said to the priests, "Take up the ark of the covenant and pass on ahead of the people." So they took it up and went ahead of them.

⁷And the LORD said to Joshua, "Today I will begin to exalt you in the eyes of all Israel, so they may know that I am with you as I was with Moses. ⁸Tell the priests who carry the ark of the covenant: 'When you reach the edge of the Jordan's waters, go and stand in the river.' "

⁹Joshua said to the Israelites, "Come here and listen to the words of the LORD your God. ¹⁰This is how you will know that the living God is among you and that he will certainly drive out before you the Canaanites, Hittites, Hivites, Perizzites, Girgashites, Amorites and Jebusites. ¹¹See, the ark of the covenant of the Lord of all the earth will go into the Jordan ahead of you. ¹²Now then, choose twelve men from the tribes of Israel, one from each tribe. ¹³And as soon as the priests who carry the ark of the LORD—the Lord of all the earth—set foot in the Jordan, its waters flowing downstream will be cut off and stand up in a heap."

¹⁴So when the people broke camp to cross the Jordan, the priests carrying the ark of the covenant went ahead of them. ¹⁵Now the Jordan is at flood stage all during harvest. Yet as soon as the priests who carried the ark reached the Jordan and their feet touched the water's edge, ¹⁶the water from upstream stopped flowing. It piled up in a heap a great distance away, at a town called Adam in the vicinity of Zarethan, while the water flowing down to the Sea of the Arabah (the Salt Sea°) was completely cut off. So the people crossed over opposite Jericho. ¹⁷The priests who carried the ark of the covenant of the LORD stood firm on dry ground in the middle of the Jordan, while all Israel passed by until the whole nation had completed the crossing on dry ground.

4 When the whole nation had finished crossing the Jordan, the LORD said to Joshua, ²"Choose twelve men from among the people, one from each tribe, ³and tell them to take up twelve stones from the middle of the Jordan from right where the priests stood and to carry them over with you and put them down at the place where you stay tonight."

⁴So Joshua called together the twelve men he had appointed from the Israelites, one from each tribe, ⁵and said

Wet Feet

JOSHUA 3:1–17

The waters of the Jordan River part, but not until the feet of the priests touch the water. How is God calling you to get your feet "wet" through actions of faith? What waters are waiting to roll back in response to your steps? Meditate on God's challenge to step in and walk forward. What might be the outcome of your boldness?

See Meeting God in Everyday Life

° 4 Hebrew *about two thousand cubits* (about 900 meters)   ° 16 That is, the Dead Sea

275

Stones of Memory

JOSHUA 4:5–7

The people of Israel set up a memorial of stones from the bed of the river to commemorate the miraculous crossing. Find a stone you can hold in your hands. As you hold it, think about times when God has brought you through the raging waters of trouble and confusion. Remember times when God's presence and touch seemed especially real. As you thank God for those times, put the stone in a place where you will be able to see it. Let it serve as a "memorial" of God's love and grace.

See Meeting God in Everyday Life

to them, "Go over before the ark of the LORD your God into the middle of the Jordan. Each of you is to take up a stone on his shoulder, according to the number of the tribes of the Israelites, ⁶to serve as a sign among you. In the future, when your children ask you, 'What do these stones mean?' ⁷tell them that the flow of the Jordan was cut off before the ark of the covenant of the LORD. When it crossed the Jordan, the waters of the Jordan were cut off. These stones are to be a memorial to the people of Israel forever."

⁸So the Israelites did as Joshua commanded them. They took twelve stones from the middle of the Jordan, according to the number of the tribes of the Israelites, as the LORD had told Joshua; and they carried them over with them to their camp, where they put them down. ⁹Joshua set up the twelve stones that had been*ᵃ* in the middle of the Jordan at the spot where the priests who carried the ark of the covenant had stood. And they are there to this day.

¹⁰Now the priests who carried the ark remained standing in the middle of the Jordan until everything the LORD had commanded Joshua was done by the people, just as Moses had directed Joshua. The people hurried over, ¹¹and as soon as all of them had crossed, the ark of the LORD and the priests came to the other side while the people watched. ¹²The men of Reuben, Gad and the half-tribe of Manasseh crossed over, armed, in front of the Israelites, as Moses had directed them. ¹³About forty thousand armed for battle crossed over before the LORD to the plains of Jericho for war.

¹⁴That day the LORD exalted Joshua in the sight of all Israel; and they revered him all the days of his life, just as they had revered Moses.

¹⁵Then the LORD said to Joshua, ¹⁶"Command the priests carrying the ark of the Testimony to come up out of the Jordan."

¹⁷So Joshua commanded the priests, "Come up out of the Jordan."

¹⁸And the priests came up out of the river carrying the ark of the covenant of the LORD. No sooner had they set their feet on the dry ground than the waters of the Jordan returned to their place and ran at flood stage as before.

¹⁹On the tenth day of the first month the people went up from the Jordan and camped at Gilgal on the eastern border of Jericho. ²⁰And Joshua set up at Gilgal the twelve stones they had taken out of the Jordan. ²¹He said to the Israelites, "In the future when your descendants ask their fathers, 'What do these stones mean?' ²²tell them, 'Israel crossed the Jordan on dry ground.' ²³For the LORD your God dried up the Jordan before you until you had crossed over. The LORD your God did to the Jordan just what he had done to the Red Sea*ᵇ* when he dried it up before us until we had crossed over. ²⁴He did this so that all the peoples of the earth might know that the hand of the LORD is powerful and so that you might always fear the LORD your God."

Circumcision at Gilgal

5 Now when all the Amorite kings west of the Jordan and all the Canaanite kings along the coast heard how the LORD had dried up the Jordan before the Israelites until we

ᵃ 9 Or Joshua also set up twelve stones   ᵇ 23 Hebrew Yam Suph; that is, Sea of Reeds had crossed over, their hearts melted and they no longer had the courage to face the Israelites.

²At that time the LORD said to Joshua, "Make flint knives and circumcise the Israelites again." ³So Joshua made flint knives and circumcised the Israelites at Gibeath Haaraloth.ᵃ

⁴Now this is why he did so: All those who came out of Egypt—all the men of military age—died in the desert on the way after leaving Egypt. ⁵All the people that came out had been circumcised, but all the people born in the desert during the journey from Egypt had not. ⁶The Israelites had moved about in the desert forty years until all the men who were of military age when they left Egypt had died, since they had not obeyed the LORD. For the LORD had sworn to them that they would not see the land that he had solemnly promised their fathers to give us, a land flowing with milk and honey. ⁷So he raised up their sons in their place, and these were the ones Joshua circumcised. They were still uncircumcised because they had not been circumcised on the way. ⁸And after the whole nation had been circumcised, they remained where they were in camp until they were healed.

⁹Then the LORD said to Joshua, "Today I have rolled away the reproach of Egypt from you." So the place has been called Gilgalᵇ to this day.

¹⁰On the evening of the fourteenth day of the month, while camped at Gilgal on the plains of Jericho, the Israelites celebrated the Passover. ¹¹The day after the Passover, that very day, they ate some of the produce of the land: unleavened bread and roasted grain. ¹²The manna stopped the day afterᶜ they ate this food from the land; there was no longer any manna for the Israelites, but that year they ate of the produce of Canaan.

The Fall of Jericho

¹³Now when Joshua was near Jericho, he looked up and saw a man standing in front of him with a drawn sword in his hand. Joshua went up to him and asked, "Are you for us or for our enemies?"

¹⁴"Neither," he replied, "but as commander of the army of the LORD I have now come." Then Joshua fell facedown to the ground in reverence, and asked him, "What message does my Lordᵈ have for his servant?"

¹⁵The commander of the LORD's army replied, "Take off your sandals, for the place where you are standing is holy." And Joshua did so.

6 Now Jericho was tightly shut up because of the Israelites. No one went out and no one came in.

²Then the LORD said to Joshua, "See, I have delivered Jericho into your hands, along with its king and its fighting men. ³March around the city once with all the armed men. Do this for six days. ⁴Have seven priests carry trumpets of rams' horns in front of the ark. On the seventh day, march around the city seven times, with the priests blowing the trumpets. ⁵When you hear them sound a long blast on the trumpets, have all the people give a loud shout; then the wall of the city will collapse and the people will go up, every man straight in."

⁶So Joshua son of Nun called the priests and said to

Manna No More

JOSHUA 5:10–12

"O most blessed grace, which makes the poor in spirit rich in virtues, which renders one who is rich in many good things humble of heart, come, descend upon me, fill me quickly with your consolation lest my soul faint with weariness and dryness of mind. Let me find grace in your sight, I beg, Lord, for your grace is enough for me, even though I obtain none of the things which nature desires."

—THOMAS À KEMPIS,
The Imitation of Christ

ᵃ 3 *Gibeath Haaraloth* means *hill of foreskins.*   ᵇ 9 *Gilgal* sounds like the Hebrew for *roll.*   ᶜ 12 Or *the day*   ᵈ 14 Or *lord*

Do Not Raise Your Voices

JOSHUA 6:8–11

God gives explicit instructions to Joshua on how to take Jericho. There is a time for the army to march in silence and a time to shout—and take the city.

Can silence and shouting have their places in the spiritual life? How might silence be an act of obedience (see Psalm 46:10)? How might shouting initiate an act of power (see Mark 10:47)? In what way is God calling you to be silent or to speak out?

See Meeting God in Service

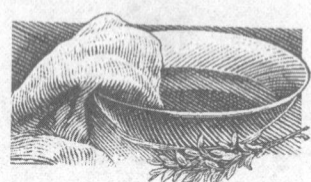

them, "Take up the ark of the covenant of the LORD and have seven priests carry trumpets in front of it." ⁷And he ordered the people, "Advance! March around the city, with the armed guard going ahead of the ark of the LORD."

⁸When Joshua had spoken to the people, the seven priests carrying the seven trumpets before the LORD went forward, blowing their trumpets, and the ark of the LORD's covenant followed them. ⁹The armed guard marched ahead of the priests who blew the trumpets, and the rear guard followed the ark. All this time the trumpets were sounding. ¹⁰But Joshua had commanded the people, "Do not give a war cry, do not raise your voices, do not say a word until the day I tell you to shout. Then shout!" ¹¹So he had the ark of the LORD carried around the city, circling it once. Then the people returned to camp and spent the night there.

¹²Joshua got up early the next morning and the priests took up the ark of the LORD. ¹³The seven priests carrying the seven trumpets went forward, marching before the ark of the LORD and blowing the trumpets. The armed men went ahead of them and the rear guard followed the ark of the LORD, while the trumpets kept sounding. ¹⁴So on the second day they marched around the city once and returned to the camp. They did this for six days.

¹⁵On the seventh day, they got up at daybreak and marched around the city seven times in the same manner, except that on that day they circled the city seven times. ¹⁶The seventh time around, when the priests sounded the trumpet blast, Joshua commanded the people, "Shout! For the LORD has given you the city! ¹⁷The city and all that is in it are to be devoted^a to the LORD. Only Rahab the prostitute^b and all who are with her in her house shall be spared, because she hid the spies we sent. ¹⁸But keep away from the devoted things, so that you will not bring about your own destruction by taking any of them. Otherwise you will make the camp of Israel liable to destruction and bring trouble on it. ¹⁹All the silver and gold and the articles of bronze and iron are sacred to the LORD and must go into his treasury."

²⁰When the trumpets sounded, the people shouted, and at the sound of the trumpet, when the people gave a loud shout, the wall collapsed; so every man charged straight in, and they took the city. ²¹They devoted the city to the LORD and destroyed with the sword every living thing in it—men and women, young and old, cattle, sheep and donkeys.

²²Joshua said to the two men who had spied out the land, "Go into the prostitute's house and bring her out and all who belong to her, in accordance with your oath to her." ²³So the young men who had done the spying went in and brought out Rahab, her father and mother and brothers and all who belonged to her. They brought out her entire family and put them in a place outside the camp of Israel.

²⁴Then they burned the whole city and everything in it, but they put the silver and gold and the articles of bronze and iron into the treasury of the LORD's house. ²⁵But Joshua spared Rahab the prostitute, with her family and all who belonged to her, because she hid the men Joshua had sent

---

^a 17 The Hebrew term refers to the irrevocable giving over of things or persons to the LORD, often by totally destroying them; also in verses 18 and 21.   ^b 17 Or possibly *innkeeper*; also in verses 22 and 25

as spies to Jericho—and she lives among the Israelites to this day.

²⁶At that time Joshua pronounced this solemn oath: "Cursed before the LORD is the man who undertakes to rebuild this city, Jericho:

"At the cost of his firstborn son
　　will he lay its foundations;
　at the cost of his youngest
　　will he set up its gates."

²⁷So the LORD was with Joshua, and his fame spread throughout the land.

Achan's Sin

7 But the Israelites acted unfaithfully in regard to the devoted things*a*; Achan son of Carmi, the son of Zimri,*b* the son of Zerah, of the tribe of Judah, took some of them. So the LORD's anger burned against Israel.

²Now Joshua sent men from Jericho to Ai, which is near Beth Aven to the east of Bethel, and told them, "Go up and spy out the region." So the men went up and spied out Ai. ³When they returned to Joshua, they said, "Not all the people will have to go up against Ai. Send two or three thousand men to take it and do not weary all the people, for only a few men are there." ⁴So about three thousand men went up; but they were routed by the men of Ai, ⁵who killed about thirty-six of them. They chased the Israelites from the city gate as far as the stone quarries*c* and struck them down on the slopes. At this the hearts of the people melted and became like water.

⁶Then Joshua tore his clothes and fell facedown to the ground before the ark of the LORD, remaining there till evening. The elders of Israel did the same, and sprinkled dust on their heads. ⁷And Joshua said, "Ah, Sovereign LORD, why did you ever bring this people across the Jordan to deliver us into the hands of the Amorites to destroy us? If only we had been content to stay on the other side of the Jordan! ⁸O Lord, what can I say, now that Israel has been routed by its enemies? ⁹The Canaanites and the other people of the country will hear about this and they will surround us and wipe out our name from the earth. What then will you do for your own great name?"

¹⁰The LORD said to Joshua, "Stand up! What are you doing down on your face? ¹¹Israel has sinned; they have violated my covenant, which I commanded them to keep. They have taken some of the devoted things; they have stolen, they have lied, they have put them with their own possessions. ¹²That is why the Israelites cannot stand against their enemies; they turn their backs and run because they have been made liable to destruction. I will not be with you anymore unless you destroy whatever among you is devoted to destruction.

¹³"Go, consecrate the people. Tell them, 'Consecrate yourselves in preparation for tomorrow; for this is what the LORD, the God of Israel, says: That which is devoted is

---

Small Sins, Big Consequences

JOSHUA 7:1–5

Achan takes some of the gold and silver set apart for God from the spoils of Jericho. It seems to be only a little thing. Yet in God's eyes his action counts as the whole people breaking faith. It brings disaster as God withdraws his help from the army of Israel.

Can you recall an occasion when your "private" actions had consequences for a larger group—your family, your friends, your church, your company? Did it seem like a "little thing" at first? When did you realize that your actions had consequences for others? What did you learn from the experience? Ask God to help you see the big picture as you look at your own life.

See Meeting God in Community

---

a 1 The Hebrew term refers to the irrevocable giving over of things or persons to the LORD, often by totally destroying them; also in verses 11, 12, 13 and 15.　*b 1* See Septuagint and 1 Chron. 2:6; Hebrew *Zabdi*; also in verses 17 and 18.　*c 5* Or *as far as Shebarim*

Hidden Things

JOSHUA 7:13–15

Achan tries to hide his dishonest actions, yet God still knows all about them. In what ways do you try to hide from God? At what point does hiding your sin become exhausting enough to bring you to confession and repentance before the Lord? Why does the all-seeing God want us to open the door to our own hidden things? If you are able, invite God into the "hidden" places of your heart. Offer them to God; ask God to bring healing and cleansing. If you cannot yet make the invitation, ask for the grace to be more open and honest.

See Meeting God in Prayer

among you, O Israel. You cannot stand against your enemies until you remove it.

¹⁴" 'In the morning, present yourselves tribe by tribe. The tribe that the LORD takes shall come forward clan by clan; the clan that the LORD takes shall come forward family by family; and the family that the LORD takes shall come forward man by man. ¹⁵He who is caught with the devoted things shall be destroyed by fire, along with all that belongs to him. He has violated the covenant of the LORD and has done a disgraceful thing in Israel!' "

¹⁶Early the next morning Joshua had Israel come forward by tribes, and Judah was taken. ¹⁷The clans of Judah came forward, and he took the Zerahites. He had the clan of the Zerahites come forward by families, and Zimri was taken. ¹⁸Joshua had his family come forward man by man, and Achan son of Carmi, the son of Zimri, the son of Zerah, of the tribe of Judah, was taken.

¹⁹Then Joshua said to Achan, "My son, give glory to the LORD,ᵃ the God of Israel, and give him the praise.ᵇ Tell me what you have done; do not hide it from me."

²⁰Achan replied, "It is true! I have sinned against the LORD, the God of Israel. This is what I have done: ²¹When I saw in the plunder a beautiful robe from Babylonia,ᶜ two hundred shekelsᵈ of silver and a wedge of gold weighing fifty shekels,ᵉ I coveted them and took them. They are hidden in the ground inside my tent, with the silver underneath."

²²So Joshua sent messengers, and they ran to the tent, and there it was, hidden in his tent, with the silver underneath. ²³They took the things from the tent, brought them to Joshua and all the Israelites and spread them out before the LORD.

²⁴Then Joshua, together with all Israel, took Achan son of Zerah, the silver, the robe, the gold wedge, his sons and daughters, his cattle, donkeys and sheep, his tent and all that he had, to the Valley of Achor. ²⁵Joshua said, "Why have you brought this trouble on us? The LORD will bring trouble on you today."

Then all Israel stoned him, and after they had stoned the rest, they burned them. ²⁶Over Achan they heaped up a large pile of rocks, which remains to this day. Then the LORD turned from his fierce anger. Therefore that place has been called the Valley of Achorᶠ ever since.

Ai Destroyed

8 Then the LORD said to Joshua, "Do not be afraid; do not be discouraged. Take the whole army with you, and go up and attack Ai. For I have delivered into your hands the king of Ai, his people, his city and his land. ²You shall do to Ai and its king as you did to Jericho and its king, except that you may carry off their plunder and livestock for yourselves. Set an ambush behind the city."

³So Joshua and the whole army moved out to attack Ai. He chose thirty thousand of his best fighting men and sent them out at night ⁴with these orders: "Listen carefully. You are to set an ambush behind the city. Don't go very far

---

ᵃ *19* A solemn charge to tell the truth   ᵇ *19* Or *and confess to him*
ᶜ *21* Hebrew *Shinar*   ᵈ *21* That is, about 5 pounds (about 2.3 kilograms)
ᵉ *21* That is, about 1 1/4 pounds (about 0.6 kilogram)   ᶠ *26 Achor* means *trouble.*

from it. All of you be on the alert. ⁵I and all those with me will advance on the city, and when the men come out against us, as they did before, we will flee from them. ⁶They will pursue us until we have lured them away from the city, for they will say, 'They are running away from us as they did before.' So when we flee from them, ⁷you are to rise up from ambush and take the city. The LORD your God will give it into your hand. ⁸When you have taken the city, set it on fire. Do what the LORD has commanded. See to it; you have my orders."

⁹Then Joshua sent them off, and they went to the place of ambush and lay in wait between Bethel and Ai, to the west of Ai—but Joshua spent that night with the people.

¹⁰Early the next morning Joshua mustered his men, and he and the leaders of Israel marched before them to Ai. ¹¹The entire force that was with him marched up and approached the city and arrived in front of it. They set up camp north of Ai, with the valley between them and the city. ¹²Joshua had taken about five thousand men and set them in ambush between Bethel and Ai, to the west of the city. ¹³They had the soldiers take up their positions—all those in the camp to the north of the city and the ambush to the west of it. That night Joshua went into the valley.

¹⁴When the king of Ai saw this, he and all the men of the city hurried out early in the morning to meet Israel in battle at a certain place overlooking the Arabah. But he did not know that an ambush had been set against him behind the city. ¹⁵Joshua and all Israel let themselves be driven back before them, and they fled toward the desert. ¹⁶All the men of Ai were called to pursue them, and they pursued Joshua and were lured away from the city. ¹⁷Not a man remained in Ai or Bethel who did not go after Israel. They left the city open and went in pursuit of Israel.

¹⁸Then the LORD said to Joshua, "Hold out toward Ai the javelin that is in your hand, for into your hand I will deliver the city." So Joshua held out his javelin toward Ai. ¹⁹As soon as he did this, the men in the ambush rose quickly from their position and rushed forward. They entered the city and captured it and quickly set it on fire.

²⁰The men of Ai looked back and saw the smoke of the city rising against the sky, but they had no chance to escape in any direction, for the Israelites who had been fleeing toward the desert had turned back against their pursuers. ²¹For when Joshua and all Israel saw that the ambush had taken the city and that smoke was going up from the city, they turned around and attacked the men of Ai. ²²The men of the ambush also came out of the city against them, so that they were caught in the middle, with Israelites on both sides. Israel cut them down, leaving them neither survivors nor fugitives. ²³But they took the king of Ai alive and brought him to Joshua.

²⁴When Israel had finished killing all the men of Ai in the fields and in the desert where they had chased them, and when every one of them had been put to the sword, all the Israelites returned to Ai and killed those who were in it. ²⁵Twelve thousand men and women fell that day—all the people of Ai. ²⁶For Joshua did not draw back the hand that held out his javelin until he had destroyed*ᵃ* all who lived in

---

Conquest a Different Way

JOSHUA 8:3–23

Though Ai, like Jericho, is Joshua's to conquer, God's strategy for defeating Ai is very different than the strategy used in defeating Jericho. Joshua and his army draw all the inhabitants of Ai completely outside the city walls, with the gates standing open.

What diverse ways and means has God used to defeat the enemies of your soul? How do Israel's experiences encourage you? What enemy do you face now? Ask God for guidance in developing a plan to defeat this enemy. Be open to new ways of defeating spiritual enemies.

ᵃ 26 The Hebrew term refers to the irrevocable giving over of things or persons to the LORD, often by totally destroying them.

Including the Strangers

JOSHUA 8:30–35

In triumph Joshua reads the Book of the Law to all the people, including the strangers who lived among the citizens of the land. God's Word was for all the people. God's Word addresses all areas of our lives, including those we haven't yet yielded to God. Write a journal page identifying areas you have surrendered to God and areas you haven't submitted to the authority of God's Word. Write a conversation between these varied aspects of your life. What is God saying to you through this exercise?

See Meeting God in Scripture

Ai. [27]But Israel did carry off for themselves the livestock and plunder of this city, as the LORD had instructed Joshua.

[28]So Joshua burned Ai and made it a permanent heap of ruins, a desolate place to this day. [29]He hung the king of Ai on a tree and left him there until evening. At sunset, Joshua ordered them to take his body from the tree and throw it down at the entrance of the city gate. And they raised a large pile of rocks over it, which remains to this day.

The Covenant Renewed at Mount Ebal

[30]Then Joshua built on Mount Ebal an altar to the LORD, the God of Israel, [31]as Moses the servant of the LORD had commanded the Israelites. He built it according to what is written in the Book of the Law of Moses—an altar of uncut stones, on which no iron tool had been used. On it they offered to the LORD burnt offerings and sacrificed fellowship offerings.[a] [32]There, in the presence of the Israelites, Joshua copied on stones the law of Moses, which he had written. [33]All Israel, aliens and citizens alike, with their elders, officials and judges, were standing on both sides of the ark of the covenant of the LORD, facing those who carried it—the priests, who were Levites. Half of the people stood in front of Mount Gerizim and half of them in front of Mount Ebal, as Moses the servant of the LORD had formerly commanded when he gave instructions to bless the people of Israel.

[34]Afterward, Joshua read all the words of the law—the blessings and the curses—just as it is written in the Book of the Law. [35]There was not a word of all that Moses had commanded that Joshua did not read to the whole assembly of Israel, including the women and children, and the aliens who lived among them.

The Gibeonite Deception

9 Now when all the kings west of the Jordan heard about these things—those in the hill country, in the western foothills, and along the entire coast of the Great Sea[b] as far as Lebanon (the kings of the Hittites, Amorites, Canaanites, Perizzites, Hivites and Jebusites)— [2]they came together to make war against Joshua and Israel.

[3]However, when the people of Gibeon heard what Joshua had done to Jericho and Ai, [4]they resorted to a ruse: They went as a delegation whose donkeys were loaded[c] with worn-out sacks and old wineskins, cracked and mended. [5]The men put worn and patched sandals on their feet and wore old clothes. All the bread of their food supply was dry and moldy. [6]Then they went to Joshua in the camp at Gilgal and said to him and the men of Israel, "We have come from a distant country; make a treaty with us."

[7]The men of Israel said to the Hivites, "But perhaps you live near us. How then can we make a treaty with you?"

[8]"We are your servants," they said to Joshua.

But Joshua asked, "Who are you and where do you come from?"

[9]They answered: "Your servants have come from a very distant country because of the fame of the LORD your God. For we have heard reports of him: all that he did in Egypt, [10]and all that he did to the two kings of the Amorites east

a 31 Traditionally *peace offerings*   *b 1* That is, the Mediterranean
c 4 Most Hebrew manuscripts; some Hebrew manuscripts, Vulgate and Syriac (see also Septuagint) *They prepared provisions and loaded their donkeys*

282

of the Jordan—Sihon king of Heshbon, and Og king of Bashan, who reigned in Ashtaroth. ¹¹And our elders and all those living in our country said to us, 'Take provisions for your journey; go and meet them and say to them, "We are your servants; make a treaty with us." ' ¹²This bread of ours was warm when we packed it at home on the day we left to come to you. But now see how dry and moldy it is. ¹³And these wineskins that we filled were new, but see how cracked they are. And our clothes and sandals are worn out by the very long journey."

¹⁴The men of Israel sampled their provisions but did not inquire of the LORD. ¹⁵Then Joshua made a treaty of peace with them to let them live, and the leaders of the assembly ratified it by oath.

¹⁶Three days after they made the treaty with the Gibeonites, the Israelites heard that they were neighbors, living near them. ¹⁷So the Israelites set out and on the third day came to their cities: Gibeon, Kephirah, Beeroth and Kiriath Jearim. ¹⁸But the Israelites did not attack them, because the leaders of the assembly had sworn an oath to them by the LORD, the God of Israel.

The whole assembly grumbled against the leaders, ¹⁹but all the leaders answered, "We have given them our oath by the LORD, the God of Israel, and we cannot touch them now. ²⁰This is what we will do to them: We will let them live, so that wrath will not fall on us for breaking the oath we swore to them." ²¹They continued, "Let them live, but let them be woodcutters and water carriers for the entire community." So the leaders' promise to them was kept.

²²Then Joshua summoned the Gibeonites and said, "Why did you deceive us by saying, 'We live a long way from you,' while actually you live near us? ²³You are now under a curse: You will never cease to serve as woodcutters and water carriers for the house of my God."

²⁴They answered Joshua, "Your servants were clearly told how the LORD your God had commanded his servant Moses to give you the whole land and to wipe out all its inhabitants from before you. So we feared for our lives because of you, and that is why we did this. ²⁵We are now in your hands. Do to us whatever seems good and right to you."

²⁶So Joshua saved them from the Israelites, and they did not kill them. ²⁷That day he made the Gibeonites woodcutters and water carriers for the community and for the altar of the LORD at the place the LORD would choose. And that is what they are to this day.

The Sun Stands Still

10 Now Adoni-Zedek king of Jerusalem heard that Joshua had taken Ai and totally destroyed*ᵃ* it, doing to Ai and its king as he had done to Jericho and its king, and that the people of Gibeon had made a treaty of peace with Israel and were living near them. ²He and his people were very much alarmed at this, because Gibeon was an important city, like one of the royal cities; it was larger than Ai, and all its men were good fighters. ³So Adoni-Zedek king of Jerusalem appealed to Hoham king of Hebron, Piram king of Jarmuth, Japhia king of Lachish and Debir king of Eglon.

ᵃ 1 The Hebrew term refers to the irrevocable giving over of things or persons to the LORD, often by totally destroying them; also in verses 28, 35, 37, 39 and 40.

Inquire First

JOSHUA 9:3–15

When the people of Gibeon come to Joshua, he judges them by their appearance and makes a hasty alliance without bothering to consult God. Joshua finds himself trapped by his shortsightedness.

Meeting deadlines, responding to the demands of family life, coping with fatigue or feeling "stressed" often tempt us to go ahead with plans without inquiring about God's will in the situation. In what ways does failing to inquire of the Lord make you vulnerable to attack, difficulty, failure, damage? What kinds of pressures cause you to step out with your own power of reasoning and make assumptions without consulting God directly? What issue needs prayerful consultation right now, before you rush into action?

See Meeting God in Everyday Life

When God Listens to Humans

JOSHUA 10:6–14

Envision yourself in Joshua's army of the Lord. You have fought all day. You are tired but exhilarated. Feel the heat of the sun, smell the parched earth and trampled grass, hear the buzzing of insects attracted to the sweat running down your neck. Hear Joshua's voice as he addresses the troops. How do you feel as you hear him command the sun and moon to stand still? What do you see in the sky?

In what extraordinary ways has God answered Joshua's prayer and given victory to Israel? What will you tell your children about this day? What is God saying to you through this drama?

See Meeting God in Scripture

⁴"Come up and help me attack Gibeon," he said, "because it has made peace with Joshua and the Israelites."

⁵Then the five kings of the Amorites—the kings of Jerusalem, Hebron, Jarmuth, Lachish and Eglon—joined forces. They moved up with all their troops and took up positions against Gibeon and attacked it.

⁶The Gibeonites then sent word to Joshua in the camp at Gilgal: "Do not abandon your servants. Come up to us quickly and save us! Help us, because all the Amorite kings from the hill country have joined forces against us."

⁷So Joshua marched up from Gilgal with his entire army, including all the best fighting men. ⁸The Lord said to Joshua, "Do not be afraid of them; I have given them into your hand. Not one of them will be able to withstand you."

⁹After an all-night march from Gilgal, Joshua took them by surprise. ¹⁰The Lord threw them into confusion before Israel, who defeated them in a great victory at Gibeon. Israel pursued them along the road going up to Beth Horon and cut them down all the way to Azekah and Makkedah. ¹¹As they fled before Israel on the road down from Beth Horon to Azekah, the Lord hurled large hailstones down on them from the sky, and more of them died from the hailstones than were killed by the swords of the Israelites.

¹²On the day the Lord gave the Amorites over to Israel, Joshua said to the Lord in the presence of Israel:

"O sun, stand still over Gibeon,
O moon, over the Valley of Aijalon."
¹³So the sun stood still,
and the moon stopped,
till the nation avenged itself on*ᵃ* its enemies,

as it is written in the Book of Jashar.

The sun stopped in the middle of the sky and delayed going down about a full day. ¹⁴There has never been a day like it before or since, a day when the Lord listened to a man. Surely the Lord was fighting for Israel!

¹⁵Then Joshua returned with all Israel to the camp at Gilgal.

Five Amorite Kings Killed

¹⁶Now the five kings had fled and hidden in the cave at Makkedah. ¹⁷When Joshua was told that the five kings had been found hiding in the cave at Makkedah, ¹⁸he said, "Roll large rocks up to the mouth of the cave, and post some men there to guard it. ¹⁹But don't stop! Pursue your enemies, attack them from the rear and don't let them reach their cities, for the Lord your God has given them into your hand."

²⁰So Joshua and the Israelites destroyed them completely—almost to a man—but the few who were left reached their fortified cities. ²¹The whole army then returned safely to Joshua in the camp at Makkedah, and no one uttered a word against the Israelites.

²²Joshua said, "Open the mouth of the cave and bring those five kings out to me." ²³So they brought the five kings out of the cave—the kings of Jerusalem, Hebron, Jarmuth, Lachish and Eglon. ²⁴When they had brought these kings to Joshua, he summoned all the men of Israel and said to the army commanders who had come with him, "Come here

ᵃ 13 Or nation triumphed over

and put your feet on the necks of these kings." So they came forward and placed their feet on their necks.

²⁵Joshua said to them, "Do not be afraid; do not be discouraged. Be strong and courageous. This is what the LORD will do to all the enemies you are going to fight." ²⁶Then Joshua struck and killed the kings and hung them on five trees, and they were left hanging on the trees until evening.

²⁷At sunset Joshua gave the order and they took them down from the trees and threw them into the cave where they had been hiding. At the mouth of the cave they placed large rocks, which are there to this day.

²⁸That day Joshua took Makkedah. He put the city and its king to the sword and totally destroyed everyone in it. He left no survivors. And he did to the king of Makkedah as he had done to the king of Jericho.

Southern Cities Conquered

²⁹Then Joshua and all Israel with him moved on from Makkedah to Libnah and attacked it. ³⁰The LORD also gave that city and its king into Israel's hand. The city and everyone in it Joshua put to the sword. He left no survivors there. And he did to its king as he had done to the king of Jericho.

³¹Then Joshua and all Israel with him moved on from Libnah to Lachish; he took up positions against it and attacked it. ³²The LORD handed Lachish over to Israel, and Joshua took it on the second day. The city and everyone in it he put to the sword, just as he had done to Libnah. ³³Meanwhile, Horam king of Gezer had come up to help Lachish, but Joshua defeated him and his army—until no survivors were left.

³⁴Then Joshua and all Israel with him moved on from Lachish to Eglon; they took up positions against it and attacked it. ³⁵They captured it that same day and put it to the sword and totally destroyed everyone in it, just as they had done to Lachish.

³⁶Then Joshua and all Israel with him went up from Eglon to Hebron and attacked it. ³⁷They took the city and put it to the sword, together with its king, its villages and everyone in it. They left no survivors. Just as at Eglon, they totally destroyed it and everyone in it.

³⁸Then Joshua and all Israel with him turned around and attacked Debir. ³⁹They took the city, its king and its villages, and put them to the sword. Everyone in it they totally destroyed. They left no survivors. They did to Debir and its king as they had done to Libnah and its king and to Hebron.

⁴⁰So Joshua subdued the whole region, including the hill country, the Negev, the western foothills and the mountain slopes, together with all their kings. He left no survivors. He totally destroyed all who breathed, just as the LORD, the God of Israel, had commanded. ⁴¹Joshua subdued them from Kadesh Barnea to Gaza and from the whole region of Goshen to Gibeon. ⁴²All these kings and their lands Joshua conquered in one campaign, because the LORD, the God of Israel, fought for Israel.

⁴³Then Joshua returned with all Israel to the camp at Gilgal.

God's Rx—Strength and Courage

JOSHUA 10:24–26

Write a litany, naming to the Lord the "spiritual enemies" you face, enemies such as negative attitudes, unbelief, self-absorption and broken relationships. After each "enemy" write, "Be strong and courageous." Make this a litany of prayer, praying it each day as an act of "putting your feet on the necks" of your spiritual foes.

See *Meeting God in Prayer*

Conquering With Burning Passion

JOSHUA 11:10–11

"When God calls . . . God bids us to come and burn—burn with a new love, a new desire, that will take all the mixed and muddled desires and ambitions and burn till it has refined all that was God-given in them and purged out all that was going in other directions."

—N. T. WRIGHT,
The Crown and the Fire

Northern Kings Defeated

11 When Jabin king of Hazor heard of this, he sent word to Jobab king of Madon, to the kings of Shimron and Acshaph, ²and to the northern kings who were in the mountains, in the Arabah south of Kinnereth, in the western foothills and in Naphoth Dor*ᵃ* on the west; ³to the Canaanites in the east and west; to the Amorites, Hittites, Perizzites and Jebusites in the hill country; and to the Hivites below Hermon in the region of Mizpah. ⁴They came out with all their troops and a large number of horses and chariots—a huge army, as numerous as the sand on the seashore. ⁵All these kings joined forces and made camp together at the Waters of Merom, to fight against Israel.

⁶The LORD said to Joshua, "Do not be afraid of them, because by this time tomorrow I will hand all of them over to Israel, slain. You are to hamstring their horses and burn their chariots."

⁷So Joshua and his whole army came against them suddenly at the Waters of Merom and attacked them, ⁸and the LORD gave them into the hand of Israel. They defeated them and pursued them all the way to Greater Sidon, to Misrephoth Maim, and to the Valley of Mizpah on the east, until no survivors were left. ⁹Joshua did to them as the LORD had directed: He hamstrung their horses and burned their chariots.

¹⁰At that time Joshua turned back and captured Hazor and put its king to the sword. (Hazor had been the head of all these kingdoms.) ¹¹Everyone in it they put to the sword. They totally destroyed*ᵇ* them, not sparing anything that breathed, and he burned up Hazor itself.

¹²Joshua took all these royal cities and their kings and put them to the sword. He totally destroyed them, as Moses the servant of the LORD had commanded. ¹³Yet Israel did not burn any of the cities built on their mounds—except Hazor, which Joshua burned. ¹⁴The Israelites carried off for themselves all the plunder and livestock of these cities, but all the people they put to the sword until they completely destroyed them, not sparing anyone that breathed. ¹⁵As the LORD commanded his servant Moses, so Moses commanded Joshua, and Joshua did it; he left nothing undone of all that the LORD commanded Moses.

¹⁶So Joshua took this entire land: the hill country, all the Negev, the whole region of Goshen, the western foothills, the Arabah and the mountains of Israel with their foothills, ¹⁷from Mount Halak, which rises toward Seir, to Baal Gad in the Valley of Lebanon below Mount Hermon. He captured all their kings and struck them down, putting them to death. ¹⁸Joshua waged war against all these kings for a long time. ¹⁹Except for the Hivites living in Gibeon, not one city made a treaty of peace with the Israelites, who took them all in battle. ²⁰For it was the LORD himself who hardened their hearts to wage war against Israel, so that he might destroy them totally, exterminating them without mercy, as the LORD had commanded Moses.

²¹At that time Joshua went and destroyed the Anakites from the hill country: from Hebron, Debir and Anab, from all the hill country of Judah, and from all the hill country of

---

ᵃ 2 Or *in the heights of Dor*   *ᵇ 11* The Hebrew term refers to the irrevocable giving over of things or persons to the LORD, often by totally destroying them; also in verses 12, 20 and 21.

Let no day

pass by without reading

some portion of the

sacred Scriptures

and giving some space to

meditation;

for **nothing** feeds the soul

so well as those sacred studies do.

THEONAS OF ALEXANDRIA (C. 300)

The Epistle of Theonas

Scripture
is like a river,
broad and deep,
shallow enough here
for the lamb to go wading,
but deep enough there
for the elephant to swim.

GREGORY THE GREAT (540-604)
Moralia in Iob, Book I

Even when carrying out needful tasks, keep meditating inwardly and praying. Thus you can grasp the depths of divine Scripture and the power hidden in it, and "pray without ceasing."

ABBA PHILIMON (LATE SIXTH CENTURY?)
The Philokalia (Volume Two)

Reading
seeks for the sweetness
of a blessed life,
meditation perceives it,
prayer asks for it,
contemplation tastes it.

GUIGO II (D. 1188)
The Ladder of Monks

Israel. Joshua totally destroyed them and their towns. ²²No Anakites were left in Israelite territory; only in Gaza, Gath and Ashdod did any survive. ²³So Joshua took the entire land, just as the LORD had directed Moses, and he gave it as an inheritance to Israel according to their tribal divisions.

Then the land had rest from war.

List of Defeated Kings

12 These are the kings of the land whom the Israelites had defeated and whose territory they took over east of the Jordan, from the Arnon Gorge to Mount Hermon, including all the eastern side of the Arabah:

²Sihon king of the Amorites,
who reigned in Heshbon. He ruled from Aroer on the rim of the Arnon Gorge—from the middle of the gorge—to the Jabbok River, which is the border of the Ammonites. This included half of Gilead. ³He also ruled over the eastern Arabah from the Sea of Kinnereth[a] to the Sea of the Arabah (the Salt Sea[b]), to Beth Jeshimoth, and then southward below the slopes of Pisgah.

⁴And the territory of Og king of Bashan,
one of the last of the Rephaites, who reigned in Ashtaroth and Edrei. ⁵He ruled over Mount Hermon, Salecah, all of Bashan to the border of the people of Geshur and Maacah, and half of Gilead to the border of Sihon king of Heshbon.

⁶Moses, the servant of the LORD, and the Israelites conquered them. And Moses the servant of the LORD gave their land to the Reubenites, the Gadites and the half-tribe of Manasseh to be their possession.

⁷These are the kings of the land that Joshua and the Israelites conquered on the west side of the Jordan, from Baal Gad in the Valley of Lebanon to Mount Halak, which rises toward Seir (their lands Joshua gave as an inheritance to the tribes of Israel according to their tribal divisions— ⁸the hill country, the western foothills, the Arabah, the mountain slopes, the desert and the Negev—the lands of the Hittites, Amorites, Canaanites, Perizzites, Hivites and Jebusites):

⁹the king of Jericho	one
the king of Ai (near Bethel)	one
¹⁰the king of Jerusalem	one
the king of Hebron	one
¹¹the king of Jarmuth	one
the king of Lachish	one
¹²the king of Eglon	one
the king of Gezer	one
¹³the king of Debir	one
the king of Geder	one
¹⁴the king of Hormah	one
the king of Arad	one
¹⁵the king of Libnah	one
the king of Adullam	one
¹⁶the king of Makkedah	one
the king of Bethel	one
¹⁷the king of Tappuah	one
the king of Hepher	one

Resting From War

JOSHUA 11:21–23

Even when God required much warfare from the Israelites so that they could possess the land, there did come a time of rest and distribution of the fruits of victory.

In what ways are you enjoying the fruits of your obedience to God? When do you know you are experiencing God-ordained rest? How can you tell when it is time to do spiritual battle? How do you know when it is time to rest? What time is it now?

See Meeting God in the Created Order

God At All Ages and Stages

JOSHUA 13:1–7

Although Joshua is now very old, there is more land yet to be taken. In spite of Joshua's age, God wants to use him.

We are never too old to be used by God and to exercise our faith in obedience. To what new challenge is God calling you? Do you feel too old, too tired? What will be the source of your strength to continue to actively obey God?

See *Meeting God in Service*

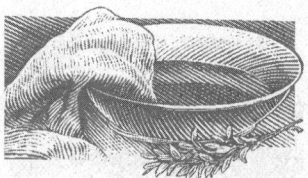

---

¹⁸ the king of Aphek   one
the king of Lasharon   one
¹⁹ the king of Madon   one
the king of Hazor   one
²⁰ the king of Shimron Meron   one
the king of Acshaph   one
²¹ the king of Taanach   one
the king of Megiddo   one
²² the king of Kedesh   one
the king of Jokneam in Carmel   one
²³ the king of Dor (in Naphoth Dor[a])   one
the king of Goyim in Gilgal   one
²⁴ the king of Tirzah   one
thirty-one kings in all.

Land Still to Be Taken

13 When Joshua was old and well advanced in years, the LORD said to him, "You are very old, and there are still very large areas of land to be taken over.

² "This is the land that remains: all the regions of the Philistines and Geshurites: ³ from the Shihor River on the east of Egypt to the territory of Ekron on the north, all of it counted as Canaanite (the territory of the five Philistine rulers in Gaza, Ashdod, Ashkelon, Gath and Ekron—that of the Avvites); ⁴ from the south, all the land of the Canaanites, from Arah of the Sidonians as far as Aphek, the region of the Amorites, ⁵ the area of the Gebalites[b]; and all Lebanon to the east, from Baal Gad below Mount Hermon to Lebo[c] Hamath.

⁶ "As for all the inhabitants of the mountain regions from Lebanon to Misrephoth Maim, that is, all the Sidonians, I myself will drive them out before the Israelites. Be sure to allocate this land to Israel for an inheritance, as I have instructed you, ⁷ and divide it as an inheritance among the nine tribes and half of the tribe of Manasseh."

Division of the Land East of the Jordan

⁸ The other half of Manasseh,[d] the Reubenites and the Gadites had received the inheritance that Moses had given them east of the Jordan, as he, the servant of the LORD, had assigned it to them.

⁹ It extended from Aroer on the rim of the Arnon Gorge, and from the town in the middle of the gorge, and included the whole plateau of Medeba as far as Dibon, ¹⁰ and all the towns of Sihon king of the Amorites, who ruled in Heshbon, out to the border of the Ammonites. ¹¹ It also included Gilead, the territory of the people of Geshur and Maacah, all of Mount Hermon and all Bashan as far as Salecah— ¹² that is, the whole kingdom of Og in Bashan, who had reigned in Ashtaroth and Edrei and had survived as one of the last of the Rephaites. Moses had defeated them and taken over their land. ¹³ But the Israelites did not drive out the people of Geshur and Maacah, so they continue to live among the Israelites to this day.

¹⁴ But to the tribe of Levi he gave no inheritance, since the

---

^a 23 Or *in the heights of Dor*   ^b 5 That is, the area of Byblos   ^c 5 Or *to the entrance to*   ^d 8 Hebrew *With it* (that is, with the other half of Manasseh)

offerings made by fire to the LORD, the God of Israel, are their inheritance, as he promised them.

¹⁵This is what Moses had given to the tribe of Reuben, clan by clan:

¹⁶The territory from Aroer on the rim of the Arnon Gorge, and from the town in the middle of the gorge, and the whole plateau past Medeba ¹⁷to Heshbon and all its towns on the plateau, including Dibon, Bamoth Baal, Beth Baal Meon, ¹⁸Jahaz, Kedemoth, Mephaath, ¹⁹Kiriathaim, Sibmah, Zereth Shahar on the hill in the valley, ²⁰Beth Peor, the slopes of Pisgah, and Beth Jeshimoth ²¹—all the towns on the plateau and the entire realm of Sihon king of the Amorites, who ruled at Heshbon. Moses had defeated him and the Midianite chiefs, Evi, Rekem, Zur, Hur and Reba—princes allied with Sihon—who lived in that country. ²²In addition to those slain in battle, the Israelites had put to the sword Balaam son of Beor, who practiced divination. ²³The boundary of the Reubenites was the bank of the Jordan. These towns and their villages were the inheritance of the Reubenites, clan by clan.

²⁴This is what Moses had given to the tribe of Gad, clan by clan:

²⁵The territory of Jazer, all the towns of Gilead and half the Ammonite country as far as Aroer, near Rabbah; ²⁶and from Heshbon to Ramath Mizpah and Betonim, and from Mahanaim to the territory of Debir; ²⁷and in the valley, Beth Haram, Beth Nimrah, Succoth and Zaphon with the rest of the realm of Sihon king of Heshbon (the east side of the Jordan, the territory up to the end of the Sea of Kinnereth[a]). ²⁸These towns and their villages were the inheritance of the Gadites, clan by clan.

²⁹This is what Moses had given to the half-tribe of Manasseh, that is, to half the family of the descendants of Manasseh, clan by clan:

³⁰The territory extending from Mahanaim and including all of Bashan, the entire realm of Og king of Bashan—all the settlements of Jair in Bashan, sixty towns, ³¹half of Gilead, and Ashtaroth and Edrei (the royal cities of Og in Bashan). This was for the descendants of Makir son of Manasseh—for half of the sons of Makir, clan by clan.

³²This is the inheritance Moses had given when he was in the plains of Moab across the Jordan east of Jericho. ³³But to the tribe of Levi, Moses had given no inheritance; the LORD, the God of Israel, is their inheritance, as he promised them.

Division of the Land West of the Jordan

14 Now these are the areas the Israelites received as an inheritance in the land of Canaan, which Eleazar the priest, Joshua son of Nun and the heads of the tribal clans of Israel allotted to them. ²Their inheritances were assigned by lot to the nine-and-a-half tribes, as the LORD had com-

---

Our Divine Inheritance

JOSHUA 13:32–33

"This divine king, full of mercy and goodness, far from chastising me, embraces me with love, makes me eat at his table, serves me with his own hands, gives me the key of his treasures; God converses and delights himself with me incessantly, in a thousand and a thousand ways . . . It is thus I consider myself from time to time in God's holy presence."

—BROTHER LAWRENCE,
The Practice of the Presence of God

Testimony of an Explorer

JOSHUA 14:6–12

Caleb recounts his life of service to God and God's people. Now, at eighty-five, he asks not for retirement, but for a new challenge—a territory to conquer and make his own for God's sake.

Give some thought to your own aging. Do you fear it or welcome it? "You have made my days a mere handbreath," confesses the psalmist (Psalm 39:5). What plans can you make now to ensure that you live vigorously in the Lord in your later years? What spiritual habits can you form now to prepare you for faithful service even when you are old?

See Meeting God in Service

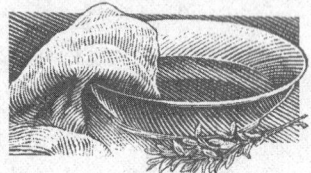

manded through Moses. ³Moses had granted the two-and-a-half tribes their inheritance east of the Jordan but had not granted the Levites an inheritance among the rest, ⁴for the sons of Joseph had become two tribes—Manasseh and Ephraim. The Levites received no share of the land but only towns to live in, with pasturelands for their flocks and herds. ⁵So the Israelites divided the land, just as the LORD had commanded Moses.

Hebron Given to Caleb

⁶Now the men of Judah approached Joshua at Gilgal, and Caleb son of Jephunneh the Kenizzite said to him, "You know what the LORD said to Moses the man of God at Kadesh Barnea about you and me. ⁷I was forty years old when Moses the servant of the LORD sent me from Kadesh Barnea to explore the land. And I brought him back a report according to my convictions, ⁸but my brothers who went up with me made the hearts of the people melt with fear. I, however, followed the LORD my God wholeheartedly. ⁹So on that day Moses swore to me, 'The land on which your feet have walked will be your inheritance and that of your children forever, because you have followed the LORD my God wholeheartedly.'ᵃ

¹⁰"Now then, just as the LORD promised, he has kept me alive for forty-five years since the time he said this to Moses, while Israel moved about in the desert. So here I am today, eighty-five years old! ¹¹I am still as strong today as the day Moses sent me out; I'm just as vigorous to go out to battle now as I was then. ¹²Now give me this hill country that the LORD promised me that day. You yourself heard then that the Anakites were there and their cities were large and fortified, but, the LORD helping me, I will drive them out just as he said."

¹³Then Joshua blessed Caleb son of Jephunneh and gave him Hebron as his inheritance. ¹⁴So Hebron has belonged to Caleb son of Jephunneh the Kenizzite ever since, because he followed the LORD, the God of Israel, wholeheartedly. ¹⁵(Hebron used to be called Kiriath Arba after Arba, who was the greatest man among the Anakites.)

Then the land had rest from war.

Allotment for Judah

15 The allotment for the tribe of Judah, clan by clan, extended down to the territory of Edom, to the Desert of Zin in the extreme south.

²Their southern boundary started from the bay at the southern end of the Salt Sea,ᵇ ³crossed south of Scorpionᶜ Pass, continued on to Zin and went over to the south of Kadesh Barnea. Then it ran past Hezron up to Addar and curved around to Karka. ⁴It then passed along to Azmon and joined the Wadi of Egypt, ending at the sea. This is theirᵈ southern boundary.

⁵The eastern boundary is the Salt Sea as far as the mouth of the Jordan.

The northern boundary started from the bay of the sea at the mouth of the Jordan, ⁶went up to Beth Hoglah and continued north of Beth Arabah to the Stone of Bohan son of Reuben. ⁷The boundary then went up to

---

ᵃ9 Deut. 1:36   ᵇ2 That is, the Dead Sea; also in verse 5   ᶜ3 Hebrew *Akrabbim*   ᵈ4 Hebrew *your*

Debir from the Valley of Achor and turned north to Gilgal, which faces the Pass of Adummim south of the gorge. It continued along to the waters of En Shemesh and came out at En Rogel. [8]Then it ran up the Valley of Ben Hinnom along the southern slope of the Jebusite city (that is, Jerusalem). From there it climbed to the top of the hill west of the Hinnom Valley at the northern end of the Valley of Rephaim. [9]From the hilltop the boundary headed toward the spring of the waters of Nephtoah, came out at the towns of Mount Ephron and went down toward Baalah (that is, Kiriath Jearim). [10]Then it curved westward from Baalah to Mount Seir, ran along the northern slope of Mount Jearim (that is, Kesalon), continued down to Beth Shemesh and crossed to Timnah. [11]It went to the northern slope of Ekron, turned toward Shikkeron, passed along to Mount Baalah and reached Jabneel. The boundary ended at the sea.

[12]The western boundary is the coastline of the Great Sea.[a]

These are the boundaries around the people of Judah by their clans.

[13]In accordance with the LORD's command to him, Joshua gave to Caleb son of Jephunneh a portion in Judah—Kiriath Arba, that is, Hebron. (Arba was the forefather of Anak.) [14]From Hebron Caleb drove out the three Anakites—Sheshai, Ahiman and Talmai—descendants of Anak. [15]From there he marched against the people living in Debir (formerly called Kiriath Sepher). [16]And Caleb said, "I will give my daughter Acsah in marriage to the man who attacks and captures Kiriath Sepher." [17]Othniel son of Kenaz, Caleb's brother, took it; so Caleb gave his daughter Acsah to him in marriage.

[18]One day when she came to Othniel, she urged him[b] to ask her father for a field. When she got off her donkey, Caleb asked her, "What can I do for you?"

[19]She replied, "Do me a special favor. Since you have given me land in the Negev, give me also springs of water." So Caleb gave her the upper and lower springs.

[20]This is the inheritance of the tribe of Judah, clan by clan:

[21]The southernmost towns of the tribe of Judah in the Negev toward the boundary of Edom were:

Kabzeel, Eder, Jagur, [22]Kinah, Dimonah, Adadah, [23]Kedesh, Hazor, Ithnan, [24]Ziph, Telem, Bealoth, [25]Hazor Hadattah, Kerioth Hezron (that is, Hazor), [26]Amam, Shema, Moladah, [27]Hazar Gaddah, Heshmon, Beth Pelet, [28]Hazar Shual, Beersheba, Biziothiah, [29]Baalah, Iim, Ezem, [30]Eltolad, Kesil, Hormah, [31]Ziklag, Madmannah, Sansannah, [32]Lebaoth, Shilhim, Ain and Rimmon—a total of twenty-nine towns and their villages.

[33]In the western foothills:

Eshtaol, Zorah, Ashnah, [34]Zanoah, En Gannim, Tappuah, Enam, [35]Jarmuth, Adullam, Socoh, Azekah,

Give Me Springs of Water

JOSHUA 15:15–19

Caleb's daughter, Acsah, is a reward for a conqueror. Not only does her husband receive land along with his bride, but, at Acsah's request, also receives springs of water. This bride knows that the land must have a source of water to keep it fruitful, to make things grow and to nourish it.

What images come to mind when you think of springs of waters? What do these images convey to you about your source of spiritual nourishment and sustenance? Spend some time sitting quietly, picturing God's love—God's Spirit—welling up in your heart, nurturing your spirit and overflowing to those around you.

See *Meeting God in the Created Order*

[a] 12 That is, the Mediterranean; also in verse 47   [b] 18 Hebrew and some Septuagint manuscripts; other Septuagint manuscripts (see also note at Judges 1:14) *Othniel, he urged her*

The Deserts and Hills of Life

JOSHUA 16:1–3

This passage outlines the allotment of land to Ephraim and Manasseh. This allotment encompasses both hill country and desert. While that geography has a very physical significance for the people, it also carries spiritual meaning.

Throughout Scripture, hills and deserts have symbolic as well as literal significance. Walk in memory through the spiritual "deserts" of your life. Feel again the dryness of those times when spiritual refreshment seemed meager and experience again the heat of pressure to "look" Christian even though you didn't "feel" Christian; recollect the disappointment in the mirage of ritual without meaning. Recall also the climb up hills of spiritual challenge. How did God beckon you onward up the hill or across the desert? How have you learned to dwell both in the hills and in the desert as you respond to God's direction?

See Meeting God in Everyday Life

³⁶Shaaraim, Adithaim and Gederah (or Gederothaim)ᵃ—fourteen towns and their villages.

³⁷Zenan, Hadashah, Migdal Gad, ³⁸Dilean, Mizpah, Joktheel, ³⁹Lachish, Bozkath, Eglon, ⁴⁰Cabbon, Lahmas, Kitlish, ⁴¹Gederoth, Beth Dagon, Naamah and Makkedah—sixteen towns and their villages.

⁴²Libnah, Ether, Ashan, ⁴³Iphtah, Ashnah, Nezib, ⁴⁴Keilah, Aczib and Mareshah—nine towns and their villages.

⁴⁵Ekron, with its surrounding settlements and villages; ⁴⁶west of Ekron, all that were in the vicinity of Ashdod, together with their villages; ⁴⁷Ashdod, its surrounding settlements and villages; and Gaza, its settlements and villages, as far as the Wadi of Egypt and the coastline of the Great Sea.

⁴⁸In the hill country:

Shamir, Jattir, Socoh, ⁴⁹Dannah, Kiriath Sannah (that is, Debir), ⁵⁰Anab, Eshtemoh, Anim, ⁵¹Goshen, Holon and Giloh—eleven towns and their villages.

⁵²Arab, Dumah, Eshan, ⁵³Janim, Beth Tappuah, Aphekah, ⁵⁴Humtah, Kiriath Arba (that is, Hebron) and Zior—nine towns and their villages.

⁵⁵Maon, Carmel, Ziph, Juttah, ⁵⁶Jezreel, Jokdeam, Zanoah, ⁵⁷Kain, Gibeah and Timnah—ten towns and their villages.

⁵⁸Halhul, Beth Zur, Gedor, ⁵⁹Maarath, Beth Anoth and Eltekon—six towns and their villages.

⁶⁰Kiriath Baal (that is, Kiriath Jearim) and Rabbah—two towns and their villages.

⁶¹In the desert:

Beth Arabah, Middin, Secacah, ⁶²Nibshan, the City of Salt and En Gedi—six towns and their villages.

⁶³Judah could not dislodge the Jebusites, who were living in Jerusalem; to this day the Jebusites live there with the people of Judah.

Allotment for Ephraim and Manasseh

16 The allotment for Joseph began at the Jordan of Jericho,ᵇ east of the waters of Jericho, and went up from there through the desert into the hill country of Bethel. ²It went on from Bethel (that is, Luz),ᶜ crossed over to the territory of the Arkites in Ataroth, ³descended westward to the territory of the Japhletites as far as the region of Lower Beth Horon and on to Gezer, ending at the sea.

⁴So Manasseh and Ephraim, the descendants of Joseph, received their inheritance.

⁵This was the territory of Ephraim, clan by clan:

The boundary of their inheritance went from Ataroth Addar in the east to Upper Beth Horon ⁶and continued to the sea. From Micmethath on the north it curved eastward to Taanath Shiloh, passing by it to Janoah on the east. ⁷Then it went down from Janoah to Ataroth and Naarah, touched Jericho and came out at the Jordan. ⁸From Tappuah the border went west to the Kanah Ravine and ended at the sea. This was the in-

---

ᵃ 36 Or *Gederah and Gederothaim*   ᵇ 1 *Jordan of Jericho* was possibly an ancient name for the Jordan River.   ᶜ 2 Septuagint; Hebrew *Bethel to Luz*

heritance of the tribe of the Ephraimites, clan by clan. [9]It also included all the towns and their villages that were set aside for the Ephraimites within the inheritance of the Manassites.

[10]They did not dislodge the Canaanites living in Gezer; to this day the Canaanites live among the people of Ephraim but are required to do forced labor.

[17] This was the allotment for the tribe of Manasseh as Joseph's firstborn, that is, for Makir, Manasseh's firstborn. Makir was the ancestor of the Gileadites, who had received Gilead and Bashan because the Makirites were great soldiers. [2]So this allotment was for the rest of the people of Manasseh—the clans of Abiezer, Helek, Asriel, Shechem, Hepher and Shemida. These are the other male descendants of Manasseh son of Joseph by their clans.

[3]Now Zelophehad son of Hepher, the son of Gilead, the son of Makir, the son of Manasseh, had no sons but only daughters, whose names were Mahlah, Noah, Hoglah, Milcah and Tirzah. [4]They went to Eleazar the priest, Joshua son of Nun, and the leaders and said, "The LORD commanded Moses to give us an inheritance among our brothers." So Joshua gave them an inheritance along with the brothers of their father, according to the LORD's command. [5]Manasseh's share consisted of ten tracts of land besides Gilead and Bashan east of the Jordan, [6]because the daughters of the tribe of Manasseh received an inheritance among the sons. The land of Gilead belonged to the rest of the descendants of Manasseh.

[7]The territory of Manasseh extended from Asher to Micmethath east of Shechem. The boundary ran southward from there to include the people living at En Tappuah. [8](Manasseh had the land of Tappuah, but Tappuah itself, on the boundary of Manasseh, belonged to the Ephraimites.) [9]Then the boundary continued south to the Kanah Ravine. There were towns belonging to Ephraim lying among the towns of Manasseh, but the boundary of Manasseh was the northern side of the ravine and ended at the sea. [10]On the south the land belonged to Ephraim, on the north to Manasseh. The territory of Manasseh reached the sea and bordered Asher on the north and Issachar on the east.

[11]Within Issachar and Asher, Manasseh also had Beth Shan, Ibleam and the people of Dor, Endor, Taanach and Megiddo, together with their surrounding settlements (the third in the list is Naphoth[a]).

[12]Yet the Manassites were not able to occupy these towns, for the Canaanites were determined to live in that region. [13]However, when the Israelites grew stronger, they subjected the Canaanites to forced labor but did not drive them out completely.

[14]The people of Joseph said to Joshua, "Why have you given us only one allotment and one portion for an inheritance? We are a numerous people and the LORD has blessed us abundantly."

[15]"If you are so numerous," Joshua answered, "and if the hill country of Ephraim is too small for you, go up into the forest and clear land for yourselves there in the land of the Perizzites and Rephaites."

Stand Up and Be Counted

JOSHUA 17:3–6

What amazing women these daughters of Zelophehad must have been to stand up and demand their right to be counted along with the male heirs of Manasseh! They got what they asked for—their own portion of the promised land.

Can you think of an occasion when you were overlooked because of your gender or age or race or some other aspect of your identity? Did you have the courage to stand up and insist on being counted? How has God encouraged you to do so? In what ways do you need to remind others that you, too, are one of God's people?

See Meeting God in Community

---

[a] 11 That is, Naphoth Dor

When Will You Possess the Land?

JOSHUA 18:3

"When I say 'Yes' to God, I am taking the first step along that road which is as direct as the air path of the migratory bird . . . My every moment, my every fiber and sinew must be coordinated to the purposes of God. Words aren't enough; they often darken knowledge. Deeds aren't enough; they often hide God. My whole nature must be God's to use as God will. Results are not my concern."

—MURIEL LESTER,
Dare We Face Facts

[16]The people of Joseph replied, "The hill country is not enough for us, and all the Canaanites who live in the plain have iron chariots, both those in Beth Shan and its settlements and those in the Valley of Jezreel."

[17]But Joshua said to the house of Joseph—to Ephraim and Manasseh—"You are numerous and very powerful. You will have not only one allotment [18]but the forested hill country as well. Clear it, and its farthest limits will be yours; though the Canaanites have iron chariots and though they are strong, you can drive them out."

Division of the Rest of the Land

18 The whole assembly of the Israelites gathered at Shiloh and set up the Tent of Meeting there. The country was brought under their control, [2]but there were still seven Israelite tribes who had not yet received their inheritance.

[3]So Joshua said to the Israelites: "How long will you wait before you begin to take possession of the land that the LORD, the God of your fathers, has given you? [4]Appoint three men from each tribe. I will send them out to make a survey of the land and to write a description of it, according to the inheritance of each. Then they will return to me. [5]You are to divide the land into seven parts. Judah is to remain in its territory on the south and the house of Joseph in its territory on the north. [6]After you have written descriptions of the seven parts of the land, bring them here to me and I will cast lots for you in the presence of the LORD our God. [7]The Levites, however, do not get a portion among you, because the priestly service of the LORD is their inheritance. And Gad, Reuben and the half-tribe of Manasseh have already received their inheritance on the east side of the Jordan. Moses the servant of the LORD gave it to them."

[8]As the men started on their way to map out the land, Joshua instructed them, "Go and make a survey of the land and write a description of it. Then return to me, and I will cast lots for you here at Shiloh in the presence of the LORD." [9]So the men left and went through the land. They wrote its description on a scroll, town by town, in seven parts, and returned to Joshua in the camp at Shiloh. [10]Joshua then cast lots for them in Shiloh in the presence of the LORD, and there he distributed the land to the Israelites according to their tribal divisions.

Allotment for Benjamin

[11]The lot came up for the tribe of Benjamin, clan by clan. Their allotted territory lay between the tribes of Judah and Joseph:

[12]On the north side their boundary began at the Jordan, passed the northern slope of Jericho and headed west into the hill country, coming out at the desert of Beth Aven. [13]From there it crossed to the south slope of Luz (that is, Bethel) and went down to Ataroth Addar on the hill south of Lower Beth Horon.

[14]From the hill facing Beth Horon on the south the boundary turned south along the western side and came out at Kiriath Baal (that is, Kiriath Jearim), a town of the people of Judah. This was the western side.

[15]The southern side began at the outskirts of Kiriath Jearim on the west, and the boundary came out at the

spring of the waters of Nephtoah. ¹⁶The boundary went down to the foot of the hill facing the Valley of Ben Hinnom, north of the Valley of Rephaim. It continued down the Hinnom Valley along the southern slope of the Jebusite city and so to En Rogel. ¹⁷It then curved north, went to En Shemesh, continued to Geliloth, which faces the Pass of Adummim, and ran down to the Stone of Bohan son of Reuben. ¹⁸It continued to the northern slope of Beth Arabah[a] and on down into the Arabah. ¹⁹It then went to the northern slope of Beth Hoglah and came out at the northern bay of the Salt Sea,[b] at the mouth of the Jordan in the south. This was the southern boundary.

²⁰The Jordan formed the boundary on the eastern side.

These were the boundaries that marked out the inheritance of the clans of Benjamin on all sides.

²¹The tribe of Benjamin, clan by clan, had the following cities:

Jericho, Beth Hoglah, Emek Keziz, ²²Beth Arabah, Zemaraim, Bethel, ²³Avvim, Parah, Ophrah, ²⁴Kephar Ammoni, Ophni and Geba—twelve towns and their villages.

²⁵Gibeon, Ramah, Beeroth, ²⁶Mizpah, Kephirah, Mozah, ²⁷Rekem, Irpeel, Taralah, ²⁸Zelah, Haeleph, the Jebusite city (that is, Jerusalem), Gibeah and Kiriath—fourteen towns and their villages.

This was the inheritance of Benjamin for its clans.

Allotment for Simeon

19 The second lot came out for the tribe of Simeon, clan by clan. Their inheritance lay within the territory of Judah. ²It included:

Beersheba (or Sheba),[c] Moladah, ³Hazar Shual, Balah, Ezem, ⁴Eltolad, Bethul, Hormah, ⁵Ziklag, Beth Marcaboth, Hazar Susah, ⁶Beth Lebaoth and Sharuhen—thirteen towns and their villages;

⁷Ain, Rimmon, Ether and Ashan—four towns and their villages— ⁸and all the villages around these towns as far as Baalath Beer (Ramah in the Negev).

This was the inheritance of the tribe of the Simeonites, clan by clan. ⁹The inheritance of the Simeonites was taken from the share of Judah, because Judah's portion was more than they needed. So the Simeonites received their inheritance within the territory of Judah.

Allotment for Zebulun

¹⁰The third lot came up for Zebulun, clan by clan:

The boundary of their inheritance went as far as Sarid. ¹¹Going west it ran to Maralah, touched Dabbesheth, and extended to the ravine near Jokneam. ¹²It turned east from Sarid toward the sunrise to the territory of Kisloth Tabor and went on to Daberath and up to Japhia. ¹³Then it continued eastward to Gath Hepher and Eth Kazin; it came out at Rimmon and turned toward Neah. ¹⁴There the boundary went around on the north to Hannathon and ended at the

Your Lot in Life

JOSHUA 19:1–9

The leaders of Israel draw lots to decide the homeland for each tribe. The tribe of Simeon doesn't get a homeland of its own—just some towns in the territory of Judah.

What is your lot in life? What are the givens into which you were born? Some may have nothing to do with accomplishments and choices—family, nation, religion, social status. Others may be chosen or earned. What do you do with your givens? Do you wish they were different, wondering, "If only . . ."? Or do you accept them as a starting point and move on? Do you proudly embrace them as your heritage? How have they had a part in forming you? Spend some time thanking God for your lot in life.

See Meeting God in Everyday Life

ᵃ 18 Septuagint; Hebrew *slope facing the Arabah*   ᵇ 19 That is, the Dead Sea
ᶜ 2 Or *Beersheba, Sheba*; 1 Chron. 4:28 does not have *Sheba.*

295

Boundaries of Inheritance

JOSHUA 19:24–31

The lists of boundaries occupy substantial space in this chapter. Why is it important to know one's boundaries geographically? Why might it be important to know them emotionally and spiritually?

Our spiritual boundaries define our very character, the sort of person we are, just like the boundaries of a baseball field define the game. Boundaries also define what we may and may not do. What are the boundaries that God asks you to observe? Do you feel fenced in by such boundaries or liberated to enjoy the extent of them? Do you focus more on the "don'ts" of your spiritual life or on the freedoms of living in obedience to God?

See Meeting God in the Created Order

Valley of Iphtah El. ¹⁵Included were Kattath, Nahalal, Shimron, Idalah and Bethlehem. There were twelve towns and their villages.

¹⁶These towns and their villages were the inheritance of Zebulun, clan by clan.

Allotment for Issachar

¹⁷The fourth lot came out for Issachar, clan by clan. ¹⁸Their territory included:

Jezreel, Kesulloth, Shunem, ¹⁹Hapharaim, Shion, Anaharath, ²⁰Rabbith, Kishion, Ebez, ²¹Remeth, En Gannim, En Haddah and Beth Pazzez. ²²The boundary touched Tabor, Shahazumah and Beth Shemesh, and ended at the Jordan. There were sixteen towns and their villages.

²³These towns and their villages were the inheritance of the tribe of Issachar, clan by clan.

Allotment for Asher

²⁴The fifth lot came out for the tribe of Asher, clan by clan. ²⁵Their territory included:

Helkath, Hali, Beten, Acshaph, ²⁶Allammelech, Amad and Mishal. On the west the boundary touched Carmel and Shihor Libnath. ²⁷It then turned east toward Beth Dagon, touched Zebulun and the Valley of Iphtah El, and went north to Beth Emek and Neiel, passing Cabul on the left. ²⁸It went to Abdon,ᵃ Rehob, Hammon and Kanah, as far as Greater Sidon. ²⁹The boundary then turned back toward Ramah and went to the fortified city of Tyre, turned toward Hosah and came out at the sea in the region of Aczib, ³⁰Ummah, Aphek and Rehob. There were twenty-two towns and their villages.

³¹These towns and their villages were the inheritance of the tribe of Asher, clan by clan.

Allotment for Naphtali

³²The sixth lot came out for Naphtali, clan by clan:

³³Their boundary went from Heleph and the large tree in Zaanannim, passing Adami Nekeb and Jabneel to Lakkum and ending at the Jordan. ³⁴The boundary ran west through Aznoth Tabor and came out at Hukkok. It touched Zebulun on the south, Asher on the west and the Jordanᵇ on the east. ³⁵The fortified cities were Ziddim, Zer, Hammath, Rakkath, Kinnereth, ³⁶Adamah, Ramah, Hazor, ³⁷Kedesh, Edrei, En Hazor, ³⁸Iron, Migdal El, Horem, Beth Anath and Beth Shemesh. There were nineteen towns and their villages.

³⁹These towns and their villages were the inheritance of the tribe of Naphtali, clan by clan.

Allotment for Dan

⁴⁰The seventh lot came out for the tribe of Dan, clan by clan. ⁴¹The territory of their inheritance included:

Zorah, Eshtaol, Ir Shemesh, ⁴²Shaalabbin, Aijalon, Ithlah, ⁴³Elon, Timnah, Ekron, ⁴⁴Eltekeh, Gibbethon, Baalath, ⁴⁵Jehud, Bene Berak, Gath Rimmon, ⁴⁶Me Jarkon and Rakkon, with the area facing Joppa.

ᵃ 28 Some Hebrew manuscripts (see also Joshua 21:30); most Hebrew manuscripts *Ebron*   ᵇ 34 Septuagint; Hebrew *west, and Judah, the Jordan.*

⁴⁷(But the Danites had difficulty taking possession of their territory, so they went up and attacked Leshem, took it, put it to the sword and occupied it. They settled in Leshem and named it Dan after their forefather.) ⁴⁸These towns and their villages were the inheritance of the tribe of Dan, clan by clan.

Allotment for Joshua

⁴⁹When they had finished dividing the land into its allotted portions, the Israelites gave Joshua son of Nun an inheritance among them, ⁵⁰as the LORD had commanded. They gave him the town he asked for—Timnath Serah*ᵃ* in the hill country of Ephraim. And he built up the town and settled there.

⁵¹These are the territories that Eleazar the priest, Joshua son of Nun and the heads of the tribal clans of Israel assigned by lot at Shiloh in the presence of the LORD at the entrance to the Tent of Meeting. And so they finished dividing the land.

Cities of Refuge

20 Then the LORD said to Joshua: ²"Tell the Israelites to designate the cities of refuge, as I instructed you through Moses, ³so that anyone who kills a person accidentally and unintentionally may flee there and find protection from the avenger of blood.

⁴"When he flees to one of these cities, he is to stand in the entrance of the city gate and state his case before the elders of that city. Then they are to admit him into their city and give him a place to live with them. ⁵If the avenger of blood pursues him, they must not surrender the one accused, because he killed his neighbor unintentionally and without malice aforethought. ⁶He is to stay in that city until he has stood trial before the assembly and until the death of the high priest who is serving at that time. Then he may go back to his own home in the town from which he fled."

⁷So they set apart Kedesh in Galilee in the hill country of Naphtali, Shechem in the hill country of Ephraim, and Kiriath Arba (that is, Hebron) in the hill country of Judah. ⁸On the east side of the Jordan of Jericho*ᵇ* they designated Bezer in the desert on the plateau in the tribe of Reuben, Ramoth in Gilead in the tribe of Gad, and Golan in Bashan in the tribe of Manasseh. ⁹Any of the Israelites or any alien living among them who killed someone accidentally could flee to these designated cities and not be killed by the avenger of blood prior to standing trial before the assembly.

Towns for the Levites

21 Now the family heads of the Levites approached Eleazar the priest, Joshua son of Nun, and the heads of the other tribal families of Israel ²at Shiloh in Canaan and said to them, "The LORD commanded through Moses that you give us towns to live in, with pasturelands for our livestock." ³So, as the LORD had commanded, the Israelites gave the Levites the following towns and pasturelands out of their own inheritance:

⁴The first lot came out for the Kohathites, clan by clan. The Levites who were descendants of Aaron the priest were

---

Cities of Refuge

JOSHUA 20:1–9

God provides places of refuge for those in need of protection and shelter, especially for the unjustly accused. Can you think of people and places that God has placed in your life that function as places of refuge for you? How and when do you make use of them? In what ways can friends, family or fellow church members give you refuge? How has the Word of God been your refuge? You might close by singing and meditating on a hymn of refuge, such as "A Mighty Fortress Is Our God" or "Rock of Ages" or "O God, Our Help in Ages Past."

See Meeting God in Community

ᵃ 50 Also known as *Timnath Heres* (see Judges 2:9)   *ᵇ 8 Jordan of Jericho* was possibly an ancient name for the Jordan River.

297

Open Hands to Receive Inheritance

JOSHUA 21:4–8

The Levites have no territory of their own but rather receive towns scattered throughout the promised land. Like many who devote themselves to God's service today, they were open to going wherever God sent them. Open and close your hands. Notice how these gestures hinder or assist your power to receive. How does the power to receive depend on the willingness to be open? What is the power of the open hand? Of the closed hand? What does God want you to receive? What is hindering you?

allotted thirteen towns from the tribes of Judah, Simeon and Benjamin. ⁵The rest of Kohath's descendants were allotted ten towns from the clans of the tribes of Ephraim, Dan and half of Manasseh.

⁶The descendants of Gershon were allotted thirteen towns from the clans of the tribes of Issachar, Asher, Naphtali and the half-tribe of Manasseh in Bashan.

⁷The descendants of Merari, clan by clan, received twelve towns from the tribes of Reuben, Gad and Zebulun.

⁸So the Israelites allotted to the Levites these towns and their pasturelands, as the Lᴏʀᴅ had commanded through Moses.

⁹From the tribes of Judah and Simeon they allotted the following towns by name ¹⁰(these towns were assigned to the descendants of Aaron who were from the Kohathite clans of the Levites, because the first lot fell to them):

¹¹They gave them Kiriath Arba (that is, Hebron), with its surrounding pastureland, in the hill country of Judah. (Arba was the forefather of Anak.) ¹²But the fields and villages around the city they had given to Caleb son of Jephunneh as his possession.

¹³So to the descendants of Aaron the priest they gave Hebron (a city of refuge for one accused of murder), Libnah, ¹⁴Jattir, Eshtemoa, ¹⁵Holon, Debir, ¹⁶Ain, Juttah and Beth Shemesh, together with their pasturelands—nine towns from these two tribes.

¹⁷And from the tribe of Benjamin they gave them Gibeon, Geba, ¹⁸Anathoth and Almon, together with their pasturelands—four towns.

¹⁹All the towns for the priests, the descendants of Aaron, were thirteen, together with their pasturelands.

²⁰The rest of the Kohathite clans of the Levites were allotted towns from the tribe of Ephraim:

²¹In the hill country of Ephraim they were given Shechem (a city of refuge for one accused of murder) and Gezer, ²²Kibzaim and Beth Horon, together with their pasturelands—four towns.

²³Also from the tribe of Dan they received Eltekeh, Gibbethon, ²⁴Aijalon and Gath Rimmon, together with their pasturelands—four towns.

²⁵From half the tribe of Manasseh they received Taanach and Gath Rimmon, together with their pasturelands—two towns.

²⁶All these ten towns and their pasturelands were given to the rest of the Kohathite clans.

²⁷The Levite clans of the Gershonites were given:
from the half-tribe of Manasseh,
Golan in Bashan (a city of refuge for one accused of murder) and Be Eshtarah, together with their pasturelands—two towns;
²⁸from the tribe of Issachar,
Kishion, Daberath, ²⁹Jarmuth and En Gannim, together with their pasturelands—four towns;
³⁰from the tribe of Asher,
Mishal, Abdon, ³¹Helkath and Rehob, together with their pasturelands—four towns;
³²from the tribe of Naphtali,
Kedesh in Galilee (a city of refuge for one accused of

murder), Hammoth Dor and Kartan, together with their pasturelands—three towns.

³³All the towns of the Gershonite clans were thirteen, together with their pasturelands.

³⁴The Merarite clans (the rest of the Levites) were given:
from the tribe of Zebulun,
Jokneam, Kartah, ³⁵Dimnah and Nahalal, together with their pasturelands—four towns;
³⁶from the tribe of Reuben,
Bezer, Jahaz, ³⁷Kedemoth and Mephaath, together with their pasturelands—four towns;
³⁸from the tribe of Gad,
Ramoth in Gilead (a city of refuge for one accused of murder), Mahanaim, ³⁹Heshbon and Jazer, together with their pasturelands—four towns in all.

⁴⁰All the towns allotted to the Merarite clans, who were the rest of the Levites, were twelve.

⁴¹The towns of the Levites in the territory held by the Israelites were forty-eight in all, together with their pasturelands. ⁴²Each of these towns had pasturelands surrounding it; this was true for all these towns.

⁴³So the LORD gave Israel all the land he had sworn to give their forefathers, and they took possession of it and settled there. ⁴⁴The LORD gave them rest on every side, just as he had sworn to their forefathers. Not one of their enemies withstood them; the LORD handed all their enemies over to them. ⁴⁵Not one of all the LORD's good promises to the house of Israel failed; every one was fulfilled.

Eastern Tribes Return Home

22 Then Joshua summoned the Reubenites, the Gadites and the half-tribe of Manasseh ²and said to them, "You have done all that Moses the servant of the LORD commanded, and you have obeyed me in everything I commanded. ³For a long time now—to this very day—you have not deserted your brothers but have carried out the mission the LORD your God gave you. ⁴Now that the LORD your God has given your brothers rest as he promised, return to your homes in the land that Moses the servant of the LORD gave you on the other side of the Jordan. ⁵But be very careful to keep the commandment and the law that Moses the servant of the LORD gave you: to love the LORD your God, to walk in all his ways, to obey his commands, to hold fast to him and to serve him with all your heart and all your soul."

⁶Then Joshua blessed them and sent them away, and they went to their homes. ⁷(To the half-tribe of Manasseh Moses had given land in Bashan, and to the other half of the tribe Joshua gave land on the west side of the Jordan with their brothers.) When Joshua sent them home, he blessed them, ⁸saying, "Return to your homes with your great wealth—with large herds of livestock, with silver, gold, bronze and iron, and a great quantity of clothing—and divide with your brothers the plunder from your enemies."

⁹So the Reubenites, the Gadites and the half-tribe of Manasseh left the Israelites at Shiloh in Canaan to return to Gilead, their own land, which they had acquired in accordance with the command of the LORD through Moses.

Loving the Destination

JOSHUA 22:1–6

"A sense of inward division fosters within us a longing for heaven. It is not that we hate the world and want nothing more to do with it . . . Rather there develops within us a nostalgia for a 'homeland' . . . Our life is a journey that makes sense only on the supposition that we are going somewhere."
—MICHAEL CASEY,
Toward God

Come Over to the Lord's Land

JOSHUA 22:16–19

The tribes who had land east of the Jordan are settled and comfortable. Yet they fear being left out of the blessings God seems to promise to the tribes to the west. Rather than remain part of the whole people of God and join those in the west, where the war of conquest continued, some in the eastern tribes set up their own temple.

Are you settled and comfortable in your spiritual life? What choices must you make in order to move from your "comfort zone" to God's land of blessing? What must you leave behind? What concrete things can you do this day, this week, to make this move? How might your personal obedience to God affect your spiritual community as a whole? How do the spiritual choices of others affect you? How does your life extend the invitation, "Come over to the Lord's land"? (v.19).

See Meeting God in Community

¹⁰When they came to Geliloth near the Jordan in the land of Canaan, the Reubenites, the Gadites and the half-tribe of Manasseh built an imposing altar there by the Jordan. ¹¹And when the Israelites heard that they had built the altar on the border of Canaan at Geliloth near the Jordan on the Israelite side, ¹²the whole assembly of Israel gathered at Shiloh to go to war against them.

¹³So the Israelites sent Phinehas son of Eleazar, the priest, to the land of Gilead—to Reuben, Gad and the half-tribe of Manasseh. ¹⁴With him they sent ten of the chief men, one for each of the tribes of Israel, each the head of a family division among the Israelite clans.

¹⁵When they went to Gilead—to Reuben, Gad and the half-tribe of Manasseh—they said to them: ¹⁶"The whole assembly of the LORD says: 'How could you break faith with the God of Israel like this? How could you turn away from the LORD and build yourselves an altar in rebellion against him now? ¹⁷Was not the sin of Peor enough for us? Up to this very day we have not cleansed ourselves from that sin, even though a plague fell on the community of the LORD! ¹⁸And are you now turning away from the LORD?

" 'If you rebel against the LORD today, tomorrow he will be angry with the whole community of Israel. ¹⁹If the land you possess is defiled, come over to the LORD's land, where the LORD's tabernacle stands, and share the land with us. But do not rebel against the LORD or against us by building an altar for yourselves, other than the altar of the LORD our God. ²⁰When Achan son of Zerah acted unfaithfully regarding the devoted things,[a] did not wrath come upon the whole community of Israel? He was not the only one who died for his sin.' "

²¹Then Reuben, Gad and the half-tribe of Manasseh replied to the heads of the clans of Israel: ²²"The Mighty One, God, the LORD! The Mighty One, God, the LORD! He knows! And let Israel know! If this has been in rebellion or disobedience to the LORD, do not spare us this day. ²³If we have built our own altar to turn away from the LORD and to offer burnt offerings and grain offerings, or to sacrifice fellowship offerings[b] on it, may the LORD himself call us to account.

²⁴"No! We did it for fear that some day your descendants might say to ours, 'What do you have to do with the LORD, the God of Israel? ²⁵The LORD has made the Jordan a boundary between us and you—you Reubenites and Gadites! You have no share in the LORD.' So your descendants might cause ours to stop fearing the LORD.

²⁶"That is why we said, 'Let us get ready and build an altar—but not for burnt offerings or sacrifices.' ²⁷On the contrary, it is to be a witness between us and you and the generations that follow, that we will worship the LORD at his sanctuary with our burnt offerings, sacrifices and fellowship offerings. Then in the future your descendants will not be able to say to ours, 'You have no share in the LORD.'

²⁸"And we said, 'If they ever say this to us, or to our descendants, we will answer: Look at the replica of the LORD's altar, which our fathers built, not for burnt offerings and sacrifices, but as a witness between us and you.'

---

a 20 The Hebrew term refers to the irrevocable giving over of things or persons to the LORD, often by totally destroying them.   *b 23* Traditionally *peace offerings*; also in verse 27

²⁹"Far be it from us to rebel against the LORD and turn away from him today by building an altar for burnt offerings, grain offerings and sacrifices, other than the altar of the LORD our God that stands before his tabernacle."

³⁰When Phinehas the priest and the leaders of the community—the heads of the clans of the Israelites—heard what Reuben, Gad and Manasseh had to say, they were pleased. ³¹And Phinehas son of Eleazar, the priest, said to Reuben, Gad and Manasseh, "Today we know that the LORD is with us, because you have not acted unfaithfully toward the LORD in this matter. Now you have rescued the Israelites from the LORD's hand."

³²Then Phinehas son of Eleazar, the priest, and the leaders returned to Canaan from their meeting with the Reubenites and Gadites in Gilead and reported to the Israelites. ³³They were glad to hear the report and praised God. And they talked no more about going to war against them to devastate the country where the Reubenites and the Gadites lived.

³⁴And the Reubenites and the Gadites gave the altar this name: A Witness Between Us that the LORD is God.

Joshua's Farewell to the Leaders

23 After a long time had passed and the LORD had given Israel rest from all their enemies around them, Joshua, by then old and well advanced in years, ²summoned all Israel—their elders, leaders, judges and officials—and said to them: "I am old and well advanced in years. ³You yourselves have seen everything the LORD your God has done to all these nations for your sake; it was the LORD your God who fought for you. ⁴Remember how I have allotted as an inheritance for your tribes all the land of the nations that remain—the nations I conquered—between the Jordan and the Great Sea*ᵃ* in the west. ⁵The LORD your God himself will drive them out of your way. He will push them out before you, and you will take possession of their land, as the LORD your God promised you.

⁶"Be very strong; be careful to obey all that is written in the Book of the Law of Moses, without turning aside to the right or to the left. ⁷Do not associate with these nations that remain among you; do not invoke the names of their gods or swear by them. You must not serve them or bow down to them. ⁸But you are to hold fast to the LORD your God, as you have until now.

⁹"The LORD has driven out before you great and powerful nations; to this day no one has been able to withstand you. ¹⁰One of you routs a thousand, because the LORD your God fights for you, just as he promised. ¹¹So be very careful to love the LORD your God.

¹²"But if you turn away and ally yourselves with the survivors of these nations that remain among you and if you intermarry with them and associate with them, ¹³then you may be sure that the LORD your God will no longer drive out these nations before you. Instead, they will become snares and traps for you, whips on your backs and thorns in your eyes, until you perish from this good land, which the LORD your God has given you.

¹⁴"Now I am about to go the way of all the earth. You know with all your heart and soul that not one of all the

---

Remembering to Remember

JOSHUA 23:2–11

"When would there be enough time to recount all thy great blessings that you bestow on us . . . especially as I am hastening on to still greater mercies? For my memory recalls them to me and it is pleasant to confess them to you, O Lord: the inward goads by which you subdued me and how you brought me low, leveling the mountains and hills of my thoughts, straightening my crookedness, and smoothing my rough ways."

—AUGUSTINE,
Confessions

Enjoying the Plantings of Others

JOSHUA 24:13

What vineyards and gardens—spiritual benefits—have you enjoyed, which you neither planted nor cultivated? Bring God into the scene with you as you walk in these lush places. What is God saying to you about your inheritance?

Give praise to God for what has come your way in the spiritual journey without effort on your part. Examine your heart to see if you have ever taken this effortless abundance for granted. Offer your repentance to God if there are ways in which you have not lived in gratitude for the plantings of others.

Contemplate the images of fruition, plenty, provision—all unearned bounty. How do these images speak of the nature of God? Are you content to admire the beauty rather than taste the fruit? Wait and listen in God's presence.

See Meeting God in Prayer

good promises the LORD your God gave you has failed. Every promise has been fulfilled; not one has failed. [15]But just as every good promise of the LORD your God has come true, so the LORD will bring on you all the evil he has threatened, until he has destroyed you from this good land he has given you. [16]If you violate the covenant of the LORD your God, which he commanded you, and go and serve other gods and bow down to them, the LORD's anger will burn against you, and you will quickly perish from the good land he has given you."

The Covenant Renewed at Shechem

24 Then Joshua assembled all the tribes of Israel at Shechem. He summoned the elders, leaders, judges and officials of Israel, and they presented themselves before God.

[2]Joshua said to all the people, "This is what the LORD, the God of Israel, says: 'Long ago your forefathers, including Terah the father of Abraham and Nahor, lived beyond the River[a] and worshiped other gods. [3]But I took your father Abraham from the land beyond the River and led him throughout Canaan and gave him many descendants. I gave him Isaac, [4]and to Isaac I gave Jacob and Esau. I assigned the hill country of Seir to Esau, but Jacob and his sons went down to Egypt.

[5]" 'Then I sent Moses and Aaron, and I afflicted the Egyptians by what I did there, and I brought you out. [6]When I brought your fathers out of Egypt, you came to the sea, and the Egyptians pursued them with chariots and horsemen[b] as far as the Red Sea.[c] [7]But they cried to the LORD for help, and he put darkness between you and the Egyptians; he brought the sea over them and covered them. You saw with your own eyes what I did to the Egyptians. Then you lived in the desert for a long time.

[8]" 'I brought you to the land of the Amorites who lived east of the Jordan. They fought against you, but I gave them into your hands. I destroyed them from before you, and you took possession of their land. [9]When Balak son of Zippor, the king of Moab, prepared to fight against Israel, he sent for Balaam son of Beor to put a curse on you. [10]But I would not listen to Balaam, so he blessed you again and again, and I delivered you out of his hand.

[11]" 'Then you crossed the Jordan and came to Jericho. The citizens of Jericho fought against you, as did also the Amorites, Perizzites, Canaanites, Hittites, Girgashites, Hivites and Jebusites, but I gave them into your hands. [12]I sent the hornet ahead of you, which drove them out before you—also the two Amorite kings. You did not do it with your own sword and bow. [13]So I gave you a land on which you did not toil and cities you did not build; and you live in them and eat from vineyards and olive groves that you did not plant.'

[14]"Now fear the LORD and serve him with all faithfulness. Throw away the gods your forefathers worshiped beyond the River and in Egypt, and serve the LORD. [15]But if serving the LORD seems undesirable to you, then choose for yourselves this day whom you will serve, whether the gods your forefathers served beyond the River, or the gods of the Am-

[a]2 That is, the Euphrates; also in verses 3, 14 and 15   [b]6 Or *charioteers*
[c]6 Hebrew *Yam Suph*; that is, Sea of Reeds

orites, in whose land you are living. But as for me and my household, we will serve the LORD."

¹⁶Then the people answered, "Far be it from us to forsake the LORD to serve other gods! ¹⁷It was the LORD our God himself who brought us and our fathers up out of Egypt, from that land of slavery, and performed those great signs before our eyes. He protected us on our entire journey and among all the nations through which we traveled. ¹⁸And the LORD drove out before us all the nations, including the Amorites, who lived in the land. We too will serve the LORD, because he is our God."

¹⁹Joshua said to the people, "You are not able to serve the LORD. He is a holy God; he is a jealous God. He will not forgive your rebellion and your sins. ²⁰If you forsake the LORD and serve foreign gods, he will turn and bring disaster on you and make an end of you, after he has been good to you."

²¹But the people said to Joshua, "No! We will serve the LORD."

²²Then Joshua said, "You are witnesses against yourselves that you have chosen to serve the LORD."

"Yes, we are witnesses," they replied.

²³"Now then," said Joshua, "throw away the foreign gods that are among you and yield your hearts to the LORD, the God of Israel."

²⁴And the people said to Joshua, "We will serve the LORD our God and obey him."

²⁵On that day Joshua made a covenant for the people, and there at Shechem he drew up for them decrees and laws. ²⁶And Joshua recorded these things in the Book of the Law of God. Then he took a large stone and set it up there under the oak near the holy place of the LORD.

²⁷"See!" he said to all the people. "This stone will be a witness against us. It has heard all the words the LORD has said to us. It will be a witness against you if you are untrue to your God."

Buried in the Promised Land

²⁸Then Joshua sent the people away, each to his own inheritance.

²⁹After these things, Joshua son of Nun, the servant of the LORD, died at the age of a hundred and ten. ³⁰And they buried him in the land of his inheritance, at Timnath Serah[a] in the hill country of Ephraim, north of Mount Gaash.

³¹Israel served the LORD throughout the lifetime of Joshua and of the elders who outlived him and who had experienced everything the LORD had done for Israel.

³²And Joseph's bones, which the Israelites had brought up from Egypt, were buried at Shechem in the tract of land that Jacob bought for a hundred pieces of silver[b] from the sons of Hamor, the father of Shechem. This became the inheritance of Joseph's descendants.

³³And Eleazar son of Aaron died and was buried at Gibeah, which had been allotted to his son Phinehas in the hill country of Ephraim.

Choosing Faithfulness to the End

JOSHUA 24:29–31

"My Lord God, I have no idea where I am going. I do not see the road ahead of me, I cannot know for certain where it will end. Nor do I really know myself, and the fact that I think I am following your will does not mean that I am actually doing so. But I believe that the desire to please you does in fact please you. And I hope I have that desire in all that I am doing. I hope that I will never do anything apart from that desire. And I know that if I do this you will lead me by the right road, though I may know nothing about it. Therefore I will trust you always though I may seem to be lost and in the shadow of death. I will not fear, for you are ever with me, and you will never leave me to face my perils alone."

—THOMAS MERTON,
Thoughts in Solitude

---

a 30 Also known as *Timnath Heres* (see Judges 2:9)   b 32 Hebrew *hundred kesitahs*; a kesitah was a unit of money of unknown weight and value.

303

WAYS of MEETING GOD

Meeting God in Service

Ten chairs were pulled closely together in a circle, but we were all leaning forward to catch Mary Jean's words. She seldom spoke during our small-group meetings, yet this week she seemed eager to talk. She described the time she had spent working in a community center and the relentless problems of poverty, addiction and abuse she had encountered there. Tears came to her eyes as she concluded, "I feel helpless as I look at these families and see their suffering. What does God expect of me? How can I make a difference?"

Like Mary Jean, we may struggle to see just how God acts in a world of great suffering. And when it comes to our own role, we often don't know where to begin or what God might be asking of us. We sometimes feel overwhelmed or we want to turn away from the realities that surround us. Yet as we begin to serve others, we often find our hesitations fading. We discover that when we help others we encounter God. We meet God in the midst of our efforts. This can happen in several ways.

> *We learn to see God by opening our eyes and actively looking for opportunities to serve others.*

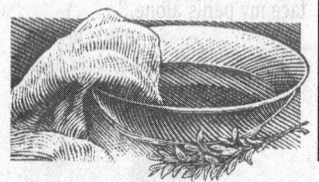

Learning to Look. We learn to see God by opening our eyes and actively looking for opportunities to serve others. From the beginning of his ministry, Jesus constantly stayed alert to people and their needs. It was one reason why he came. Jesus read from the book of Isaiah in the synagogue at Nazareth, applying these words to himself:

> "The Spirit of the Lord is on me,
>   because he has anointed me
>   to preach good news to the poor.
> He has sent me to proclaim freedom for the prisoners
>   and recovery of sight for the blind,
> to release the oppressed,
>   to proclaim the year of the Lord's favor."—Luke 4:18–19

Every day as he traveled with his disciples Jesus healed and fed and loved people. A number of stories in the Gospels tell us that Jesus acted because he was moved with compassion. As painful as it must have been sometimes, he did not turn aside from seeing people suffer.

Jesus not only saw the sufferings of human beings but also became involved in people's suffering to heal and bring new life. The story of the widow of Nain in Luke 7:11–17 illustrates this. As Jesus travels with his disciples and a crowd of followers, he encounters a funeral procession. The widow, he discovers, has lost her only son. Jesus sees her grief with eyes of compassion, knowing that as a widow she has been completely dependent on her son. Now she has no one—and nothing. Jesus says to her, "Don't cry," and raises the young man back to life. Then we find the words, "Jesus gave him back to his mother" (v.15). What compassion and mercy are captured in those words!

Again and again Jesus actively seeks the sick and needy. He goes directly to them; he notices their pain and suffering and responds with divine grace and love. The common activities of his life—travels, conversations, seemingly chance meetings with people—become the settings for expressions of his caring alertness. He appropriately perceives himself as a servant of God, and in serving God he ministers to those God loves.

Learning to Listen. In the Gospel of John, Jesus demonstrates that this open-eyed attitude of caring was not to be confined only to his own ministry but was to characterize the lives of his followers as well. Jesus washed the disciples' feet as they gathered to celebrate the Feast of the Passover, in part to remind us of our proper posture before others: "You call me 'Teacher' and 'Lord,' and rightly so, for that is what I am. Now that I, your Lord and Teacher, have washed your feet, you also should wash one another's feet" (John 13:13–14). Not only do we open our eyes to need; we also listen to those we serve. We cannot know how to help others if we simply barge in to "fix" a list of problems we think we see in them. We must serve others with gentle openness to them and with a willingness to relinquish our own agenda. We listen to their ideas and hopes and longings.

To listen requires a quieting of our own interests and experiences so that we can become open not only in that particular relationship but also to the ways in which God is present in the relationship. Henri J. M. Nouwen writes, "Real training for service asks for a hard and often painful process of self-emptying. The main problem of service is to be the way without being 'in the way.' "

Learning to become more open to others teaches us many things. Openness cultivates in us an attitude of honesty. We see ourselves, as well as others, more clearly. Then we are able to open ourselves to God—to let him have those parts of us that are wounded and in need of healing and forgiveness. Just as we speak of God's love for and forgiveness of others, so we can claim that healing in our own lives.

Our lives may be deeply changed as we serve others. As those we serve share their own pilgrimages, we see how God has been a part of their experiences. Their vision of God may enlarge ours. Their words, feelings and desires may challenge us in surprising ways. When twentieth-century spiritual writer Evelyn Underhill went to Baron von Hÿgel for guidance about her relationship with God, he recommended that she spend a designated amount of time each week directly serving the poor so as to break open her heart to the needs of people and open her up more fully to experience God's grace. As a result she met a woman named Laura Rose, the beginning of a relationship that was to become deeply significant for Underhill's spiritual growth.

Learning to Love. To looking and listening we add loving—of the most radical, sacrificial kind. It is easy to be captured by our own special interests and by self-absorption. When we follow Jesus, however, normal priorities get turned upside down. We confront what German pastor and theologian Dietrich Bonhoeffer called "the cost of discipleship."

God thereby transforms our self-interest into a new awareness of our interdependence. We identify the ways in which we need one another in order to grow in faithfulness. We find a new identity by centering our lives in the One who is the light of the world and who calls us to let our lights "shine before [others], that they may see [our] good deeds and praise [our] Father in heaven" (Matthew 5:16). We realize that nothing matters more than bringing people to Jesus for healing and salvation.

The radical call to service does not pose for us an impossible duty . . . God promises to give us the power and resources we need through the indwelling Spirit of Jesus.

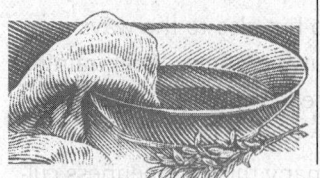

Little by little our hearts, which can so easily become hardened to the needs of others, are changed into caring and compassionate hearts. Thomas Kelly, in his book, *A Testament of Devotion*, captures this phenomenon in these words: "God plucks the world out of our hearts, loosening the chains of attachment. And He hurls the world into our hearts, where we and He together carry it in infinitely tender love."

Resources to Get Us Through. The radical call to service does not pose for us an impossible duty, however. God promises to give us the power and resources we need through the indwelling Spirit of Jesus. Paul wrote to the new converts in the first-century church in Corinth to remind them of their calling. Paul pointed out that he had come to them in weakness, fear and trembling, but that God had used him to demonstrate the power of the Spirit (see 1 Corinthians 1:18–31; 2:6–13). What freedom there is in knowing that God can use us in spite of our weaknesses!

Indeed, power is released through our vulnerability. It is through our vulnerabilities that we learn the nature of God's sufficiency. The only way in which we can confront head-on the pain of a suffering world is through utter reliance on God's grace. We can take to heart God's word to Paul, "My grace is sufficient for you, for my power is made perfect in weakness" (2 Corinthians 12:9).

Jesus is inviting us to love the world as he loves. Paul encouraged a congregation of Christians who were undergoing much struggle by reminding them that they were a letter of Christ, written not with ink but with the Spirit of the living God (2 Corinthians 3:2–3). What a word of promise for today! We go in the power of the Spirit. The Spirit speaks in and through what we do.

"Christian ministry," writes James Fenhagen, "is more than doing good. Ministry is an act of service performed either consciously or unconsciously in the name of Christ. Ministry is Jesus Christ expressing his life through us." When we are tempted to run and hide because the needs of the world are overwhelming and we feel helpless to make a difference, we can remember that we do not go alone. We venture out boldly, not because we underestimate or devalue the needs and woundedness of others, but because we trust in the steadfast and abiding love of God.

In serving the needs of others in society, we meet God. We find joy, as Brother Lawrence found centuries ago, "doing little things for the love of God." And as we grow, we learn more about the love of Jesus and what it means to share it with others. This prayer in Ephesians describes what it means to mature in our relationship with Jesus: "I pray that out of his glorious riches [God] may strengthen you with power through his Spirit in your inner being, so that Christ may dwell in your hearts through faith . . . that you [may be] rooted and established in love" (Ephesians 3:16–17).

See Page 556 for the next Ways of Meeting God *article.*

JUDGES

God's Imperfect People

KEY VERSE:

Whenever the LORD raised up a judge for them, he was with the judge and saved them out of the hands of their enemies as long as the judge lived; for the LORD had compassion on them as they groaned under those who oppressed and afflicted them.—Judges 2:18

"The worst things that happen do not happen because a few people are monstrously wicked, but because most people are like us. When we grasp that, we begin to realize that our need is not merely for moving quietly on in the way we are going; our need is for radical change, to find a power that is going to turn us into somebody else."

—WILLIAM TEMPLE,
Christian Faith and Life

Within this Bible designed to help you listen to God, you are reading a book that shows what happens when people listen mostly to themselves. The book of Judges presents an account of twelve military heroes who deliver Israel from its oppressors. Not all of these judges are heroes in every sense—one is an assassin (Ehud) and another is sexually promiscuous (Samson). Yet God has raised them up to carry out his will in Israel and, for the most part, the judges are willing to follow the will of the Lord.

The judges' interest in doing God's will is significant because the Israelites are mostly interested in doing their own will; "everyone did as he saw fit" (17:6; 21:25) because "Israel had no king" (17:6; 18:1).The Israelites lived to please themselves and experienced this cycle six times in three centuries: apostasy (wandering from God); oppression (domination by other things and other nations); renewal and repentance (returning to God); deliverance by a dynamic leader (freedom based on God-provided human help).

The book of Judges drives home the truth that people who lose their spiritual commitment wander into idolatry and anarchy. This book may be disturbing to read, for it recounts massive civil war, violence, abuse of women, and power-grabbing leaders. But allow God to use this book to help you grow in wisdom. Imagine how differently this book would read if the Israelites had sought God more consistently. Perhaps reading Judges will help you ponder possible cycles in your own spiritual life and prompt you to examine your willingness to listen to God.

Israel Fights the Remaining Canaanites

1 After the death of Joshua, the Israelites asked the LORD, "Who will be the first to go up and fight for us against the Canaanites?"

²The LORD answered, "Judah is to go; I have given the land into their hands."

³Then the men of Judah said to the Simeonites their brothers, "Come up with us into the territory allotted to us, to fight against the Canaanites. We in turn will go with you into yours." So the Simeonites went with them.

⁴When Judah attacked, the LORD gave the Canaanites and Perizzites into their hands and they struck down ten thousand men at Bezek. ⁵It was there that they found Adoni-Bezek and fought against him, putting to rout the Canaanites and Perizzites. ⁶Adoni-Bezek fled, but they chased him and caught him, and cut off his thumbs and big toes.

⁷Then Adoni-Bezek said, "Seventy kings with their thumbs and big toes cut off have picked up scraps under my table. Now God has paid me back for what I did to them." They brought him to Jerusalem, and he died there.

⁸The men of Judah attacked Jerusalem also and took it. They put the city to the sword and set it on fire.

⁹After that, the men of Judah went down to fight against the Canaanites living in the hill country, the Negev and the western foothills. ¹⁰They advanced against the Canaanites living in Hebron (formerly called Kiriath Arba) and defeated Sheshai, Ahiman and Talmai.

¹¹From there they advanced against the people living in Debir (formerly called Kiriath Sepher). ¹²And Caleb said, "I will give my daughter Acsah in marriage to the man who attacks and captures Kiriath Sepher." ¹³Othniel son of Kenaz, Caleb's younger brother, took it; so Caleb gave his daughter Acsah to him in marriage.

¹⁴One day when she came to Othniel, she urged him[a] to ask her father for a field. When she got off her donkey, Caleb asked her, "What can I do for you?"

¹⁵She replied, "Do me a special favor. Since you have given me land in the Negev, give me also springs of water." Then Caleb gave her the upper and lower springs.

¹⁶The descendants of Moses' father-in-law, the Kenite, went up from the City of Palms[b] with the men of Judah to live among the people of the Desert of Judah in the Negev near Arad.

¹⁷Then the men of Judah went with the Simeonites their brothers and attacked the Canaanites living in Zephath, and they totally destroyed[c] the city. Therefore it was called Hormah.[d] ¹⁸The men of Judah also took[e] Gaza, Ashkelon and Ekron—each city with its territory.

¹⁹The LORD was with the men of Judah. They took possession of the hill country, but they were unable to drive the people from the plains, because they had iron chariots. ²⁰As Moses had promised, Hebron was given to Caleb, who drove from it the three sons of Anak. ²¹The Benjamites, however, failed to dislodge the Jebusites, who were living in

---

Willing to Give

JUDGES 1:14–15

Although Acsah has to abide by the customary way of being married off as a daughter, she enjoys an unusually generous relationship with her father Caleb. He asks her a question that stands out: "What can I do for you?" We often hear these words used in a customer service context, but why not let them help us develop a giving heart?

Picture the people to whom you could easily say, "What can I do for you?" How does it feel to be so open and vulnerable with them? Imagine yourself answering their request as Caleb did (giving Acsah both the upper and lower springs of water). How do you feel about being so generous?

See Meeting God in Community

---

a 14 Hebrew; Septuagint and Vulgate *Othniel, he urged her*   *b 16* That is, Jericho   *c 17* The Hebrew term refers to the irrevocable giving over of things or persons to the LORD, often by totally destroying them.   *d 17 Hormah* means *destruction.*   *e 18* Hebrew; Septuagint *Judah did not take*

Divine Confrontation

JUDGES 2:1–5

The confrontational words of the angel make the Israelites weep. Ponder how the angel of the Lord goes out of the way to make a personal appearance, driving home to the Israelites the real consequences of their behavior.

Reread Judges 2:1–5, absorbing the words and phrases of the angel of the Lord. Pick a word or phrase on which to reflect. Why is this important for you? Rest in silence, staying open for any impressions from God. How does this passage touch your life today?

See Meeting God in Scripture

Jerusalem; to this day the Jebusites live there with the Benjamites.

²²Now the house of Joseph attacked Bethel, and the Lord was with them. ²³When they sent men to spy out Bethel (formerly called Luz), ²⁴the spies saw a man coming out of the city and they said to him, "Show us how to get into the city and we will see that you are treated well." ²⁵So he showed them, and they put the city to the sword but spared the man and his whole family. ²⁶He then went to the land of the Hittites, where he built a city and called it Luz, which is its name to this day.

²⁷But Manasseh did not drive out the people of Beth Shan or Taanach or Dor or Ibleam or Megiddo and their surrounding settlements, for the Canaanites were determined to live in that land. ²⁸When Israel became strong, they pressed the Canaanites into forced labor but never drove them out completely. ²⁹Nor did Ephraim drive out the Canaanites living in Gezer, but the Canaanites continued to live there among them. ³⁰Neither did Zebulun drive out the Canaanites living in Kitron or Nahalol, who remained among them; but they did subject them to forced labor. ³¹Nor did Asher drive out those living in Acco or Sidon or Ahlab or Aczib or Helbah or Aphek or Rehob, ³²and because of this the people of Asher lived among the Canaanite inhabitants of the land. ³³Neither did Naphtali drive out those living in Beth Shemesh or Beth Anath; but the Naphtalites too lived among the Canaanite inhabitants of the land, and those living in Beth Shemesh and Beth Anath became forced laborers for them. ³⁴The Amorites confined the Danites to the hill country, not allowing them to come down into the plain. ³⁵And the Amorites were determined also to hold out in Mount Heres, Aijalon and Shaalbim, but when the power of the house of Joseph increased, they too were pressed into forced labor. ³⁶The boundary of the Amorites was from Scorpionᵃ Pass to Sela and beyond.

The Angel of the Lord at Bokim

2 The angel of the Lord went up from Gilgal to Bokim and said, "I brought you up out of Egypt and led you into the land that I swore to give to your forefathers. I said, 'I will never break my covenant with you, ²and you shall not make a covenant with the people of this land, but you shall break down their altars.' Yet you have disobeyed me. Why have you done this? ³Now therefore I tell you that I will not drive them out before you; they will be ⌊thorns⌋ in your sides and their gods will be a snare to you."

⁴When the angel of the Lord had spoken these things to all the Israelites, the people wept aloud, ⁵and they called that place Bokim.ᵇ There they offered sacrifices to the Lord.

Disobedience and Defeat

⁶After Joshua had dismissed the Israelites, they went to take possession of the land, each to his own inheritance. ⁷The people served the Lord throughout the lifetime of Joshua and of the elders who outlived him and who had seen all the great things the Lord had done for Israel.

⁸Joshua son of Nun, the servant of the Lord, died at the age of a hundred and ten. ⁹And they buried him in the land

ᵃ 36 Hebrew *Akrabbim*   ᵇ 5 *Bokim* means *weepers*.

of his inheritance, at Timnath Heres[a] in the hill country of Ephraim, north of Mount Gaash.

[10]After that whole generation had been gathered to their fathers, another generation grew up, who knew neither the LORD nor what he had done for Israel. [11]Then the Israelites did evil in the eyes of the LORD and served the Baals. [12]They forsook the LORD, the God of their fathers, who had brought them out of Egypt. They followed and worshiped various gods of the peoples around them. They provoked the LORD to anger [13]because they forsook him and served Baal and the Ashtoreths. [14]In his anger against Israel the LORD handed them over to raiders who plundered them. He sold them to their enemies all around, whom they were no longer able to resist. [15]Whenever Israel went out to fight, the hand of the LORD was against them to defeat them, just as he had sworn to them. They were in great distress.

[16]Then the LORD raised up judges,[b] who saved them out of the hands of these raiders. [17]Yet they would not listen to their judges but prostituted themselves to other gods and worshiped them. Unlike their fathers, they quickly turned from the way in which their fathers had walked, the way of obedience to the LORD's commands. [18]Whenever the LORD raised up a judge for them, he was with the judge and saved them out of the hands of their enemies as long as the judge lived; for the LORD had compassion on them as they groaned under those who oppressed and afflicted them. [19]But when the judge died, the people returned to ways even more corrupt than those of their fathers, following other gods and serving and worshiping them. They refused to give up their evil practices and stubborn ways.

[20]Therefore the LORD was very angry with Israel and said, "Because this nation has violated the covenant that I laid down for their forefathers and has not listened to me, [21]I will no longer drive out before them any of the nations Joshua left when he died. [22]I will use them to test Israel and see whether they will keep the way of the LORD and walk in it as their forefathers did." [23]The LORD had allowed those nations to remain; he did not drive them out at once by giving them into the hands of Joshua.

3 These are the nations the LORD left to test all those Israelites who had not experienced any of the wars in Canaan [2](he did this only to teach warfare to the descendants of the Israelites who had not had previous battle experience): [3]the five rulers of the Philistines, all the Canaanites, the Sidonians, and the Hivites living in the Lebanon mountains from Mount Baal Hermon to Lebo[c] Hamath. [4]They were left to test the Israelites to see whether they would obey the LORD's commands, which he had given their forefathers through Moses.

[5]The Israelites lived among the Canaanites, Hittites, Amorites, Perizzites, Hivites and Jebusites. [6]They took their daughters in marriage and gave their own daughters to their sons, and served their gods.

Othniel

[7]The Israelites did evil in the eyes of the LORD; they forgot the LORD their God and served the Baals and the Asherahs. [8]The anger of the LORD burned against Israel so that he sold

Leaning Too Hard

JUDGES 2:16–19

Just as the Israelites rely too much on the judges to inspire them to obey, we in our celebrity-driven society often rely excessively on others to inspire, instruct and comfort us. What does this passage say about the way God works in people's lives? What does it say about the way humans behave in relation to leaders? What does this passage suggest to you as a leader? As a follower? What do you most need to say to God regarding this passage?

See Meeting God in Community

---

[a]9 Also known as *Timnath Serah* (see Joshua 19:50 and 24:30)   [b]16 Or *leaders*; similarly in verses 17–19   [c]3 Or *to the entrance to*

Your Deliverer

JUDGES 3:12–15

The Israelites' behavior forms a pattern through the book of Judges: The Israelites wander from God; they are captured; God provides a deliverer. Ponder the word "deliverer." Consider times in your life when you have wandered and God provided a deliverer—perhaps the deliverer was a person or an event or a group of people. If you could have a deliverer now, from what would you want to be delivered? What possible forms could that deliverer take?

them into the hands of Cushan-Rishathaim king of Aram Naharaim,[a] to whom the Israelites were subject for eight years. [9]But when they cried out to the LORD, he raised up for them a deliverer, Othniel son of Kenaz, Caleb's younger brother, who saved them. [10]The Spirit of the LORD came upon him, so that he became Israel's judge[b] and went to war. The LORD gave Cushan-Rishathaim king of Aram into the hands of Othniel, who overpowered him. [11]So the land had peace for forty years, until Othniel son of Kenaz died.

Ehud

[12]Once again the Israelites did evil in the eyes of the LORD, and because they did this evil the LORD gave Eglon king of Moab power over Israel. [13]Getting the Ammonites and Amalekites to join him, Eglon came and attacked Israel, and they took possession of the City of Palms.[c] [14]The Israelites were subject to Eglon king of Moab for eighteen years.

[15]Again the Israelites cried out to the LORD, and he gave them a deliverer—Ehud, a left-handed man, the son of Gera the Benjamite. The Israelites sent him with tribute to Eglon king of Moab. [16]Now Ehud had made a double-edged sword about a foot and a half[d] long, which he strapped to his right thigh under his clothing. [17]He presented the tribute to Eglon king of Moab, who was a very fat man. [18]After Ehud had presented the tribute, he sent on their way the men who had carried it. [19]At the idols[e] near Gilgal he himself turned back and said, "I have a secret message for you, O king."

The king said, "Quiet!" And all his attendants left him.

[20]Ehud then approached him while he was sitting alone in the upper room of his summer palace[f] and said, "I have a message from God for you." As the king rose from his seat, [21]Ehud reached with his left hand, drew the sword from his right thigh and plunged it into the king's belly. [22]Even the handle sank in after the blade, which came out his back. Ehud did not pull the sword out, and the fat closed in over it. [23]Then Ehud went out to the porch[g]; he shut the doors of the upper room behind him and locked them.

[24]After he had gone, the servants came and found the doors of the upper room locked. They said, "He must be relieving himself in the inner room of the house." [25]They waited to the point of embarrassment, but when he did not open the doors of the room, they took a key and unlocked them. There they saw their lord fallen to the floor, dead.

[26]While they waited, Ehud got away. He passed by the idols and escaped to Seirah. [27]When he arrived there, he blew a trumpet in the hill country of Ephraim, and the Israelites went down with him from the hills, with him leading them.

[28]"Follow me," he ordered, "for the LORD has given Moab, your enemy, into your hands." So they followed him down and, taking possession of the fords of the Jordan that led to Moab, they allowed no one to cross over. [29]At that time they struck down about ten thousand Moabites, all vigorous and

[a]8 That is, Northwest Mesopotamia [b]10 Or leader [c]13 That is, Jericho [d]16 Hebrew a cubit (about 0.5 meter) [e]19 Or the stone quarries; also in verse 26 [f]20 The meaning of the Hebrew for this phrase is uncertain. [g]23 The meaning of the Hebrew for this word is uncertain.

strong; not a man escaped. ³⁰That day Moab was made subject to Israel, and the land had peace for eighty years.

Shamgar

³¹After Ehud came Shamgar son of Anath, who struck down six hundred Philistines with an oxgoad. He too saved Israel.

Deborah

4 After Ehud died, the Israelites once again did evil in the eyes of the LORD. ²So the LORD sold them into the hands of Jabin, a king of Canaan, who reigned in Hazor. The commander of his army was Sisera, who lived in Harosheth Haggoyim. ³Because he had nine hundred iron chariots and had cruelly oppressed the Israelites for twenty years, they cried to the LORD for help.

⁴Deborah, a prophetess, the wife of Lappidoth, was leading[a] Israel at that time. ⁵She held court under the Palm of Deborah between Ramah and Bethel in the hill country of Ephraim, and the Israelites came to her to have their disputes decided. ⁶She sent for Barak son of Abinoam from Kedesh in Naphtali and said to him, "The LORD, the God of Israel, commands you: 'Go, take with you ten thousand men of Naphtali and Zebulun and lead the way to Mount Tabor. ⁷I will lure Sisera, the commander of Jabin's army, with his chariots and his troops to the Kishon River and give him into your hands.' "

⁸Barak said to her, "If you go with me, I will go; but if you don't go with me, I won't go."

⁹"Very well," Deborah said, "I will go with you. But because of the way you are going about this,[b] the honor will not be yours, for the LORD will hand Sisera over to a woman." So Deborah went with Barak to Kedesh, ¹⁰where he summoned Zebulun and Naphtali. Ten thousand men followed him, and Deborah also went with him.

¹¹Now Heber the Kenite had left the other Kenites, the descendants of Hobab, Moses' brother-in-law,[c] and pitched his tent by the great tree in Zaanannim near Kedesh.

¹²When they told Sisera that Barak son of Abinoam had gone up to Mount Tabor, ¹³Sisera gathered together his nine hundred iron chariots and all the men with him, from Harosheth Haggoyim to the Kishon River.

¹⁴Then Deborah said to Barak, "Go! This is the day the LORD has given Sisera into your hands. Has not the LORD gone ahead of you?" So Barak went down Mount Tabor, followed by ten thousand men. ¹⁵At Barak's advance, the LORD routed Sisera and all his chariots and army by the sword, and Sisera abandoned his chariot and fled on foot. ¹⁶But Barak pursued the chariots and army as far as Harosheth Haggoyim. All the troops of Sisera fell by the sword; not a man was left.

¹⁷Sisera, however, fled on foot to the tent of Jael, the wife of Heber the Kenite, because there were friendly relations between Jabin king of Hazor and the clan of Heber the Kenite.

¹⁸Jael went out to meet Sisera and said to him, "Come, my lord, come right in. Don't be afraid." So he entered her tent, and she put a covering over him.

God Goes Ahead of You

JUDGES 4:14

Deborah's wisdom leads her to expect God to go before the Israelites and to do the hard work ahead of time.

Get out your calendar of things to do this week or month. Pick an item and pray that God will go ahead of you. How does it change the way you approach an activity when you understand that God goes ahead of you? How does it change the way you think or feel about it and about the people involved in it?

See Meeting God in Everyday Life

ᵃ 4 Traditionally *judging*   ᵇ 9 Or *But on the expedition you are undertaking*
ᶜ 11 Or *father-in-law*

Making Music

JUDGES 5:1–3

Occasionally things go well in the nation. Deborah and Barak burst into song when the Israelites offer themselves in service. They thank God because they realize that the people's willingness to serve the Lord is a sign of spiritual wholeness.

Consider your favorite way to "make music"—whistling, humming, or singing in the shower. For whom are you willing to offer yourself? Whom would you love to see praising God and "making music" because you willingly served them?

See *Meeting God in Worship*

19"I'm thirsty," he said. "Please give me some water." She opened a skin of milk, gave him a drink, and covered him up.

20"Stand in the doorway of the tent," he told her. "If someone comes by and asks you, 'Is anyone here?' say 'No.' "

21But Jael, Heber's wife, picked up a tent peg and a hammer and went quietly to him while he lay fast asleep, exhausted. She drove the peg through his temple into the ground, and he died.

22Barak came by in pursuit of Sisera, and Jael went out to meet him. "Come," she said, "I will show you the man you're looking for." So he went in with her, and there lay Sisera with the tent peg through his temple—dead.

23On that day God subdued Jabin, the Canaanite king, before the Israelites. 24And the hand of the Israelites grew stronger and stronger against Jabin, the Canaanite king, until they destroyed him.

The Song of Deborah

5 On that day Deborah and Barak son of Abinoam sang this song:

2"When the princes in Israel take the lead,
    when the people willingly offer themselves—
    praise the LORD!

3"Hear this, you kings! Listen, you rulers!
    I will sing to*a* the LORD, I will sing;
    I will make music to*b* the LORD, the God of
        Israel.

4"O LORD, when you went out from Seir,
    when you marched from the land of Edom,
the earth shook, the heavens poured,
    the clouds poured down water.
5The mountains quaked before the LORD, the One
        of Sinai,
    before the LORD, the God of Israel.

6"In the days of Shamgar son of Anath,
    in the days of Jael, the roads were abandoned;
    travelers took to winding paths.
7Village life*c* in Israel ceased,
    ceased until I,*d* Deborah, arose,
    arose a mother in Israel.
8When they chose new gods,
    war came to the city gates,
and not a shield or spear was seen
    among forty thousand in Israel.
9My heart is with Israel's princes,
    with the willing volunteers among the people.
    Praise the LORD!

10"You who ride on white donkeys,
    sitting on your saddle blankets,
    and you who walk along the road,
    consider 11the voice of the singers*e* at the
        watering places.

a 3 Or *of*   *b 3* Or *I with song I will praise*   *c 7* Or *Warriors*   *d 7* Or *you*
e 11 Or *archers*; the meaning of the Hebrew for this word is uncertain.

314

They recite the righteous acts of the Lord,
   the righteous acts of his warriors*a* in Israel.

"Then the people of the Lord
   went down to the city gates.
¹² 'Wake up, wake up, Deborah!
   Wake up, wake up, break out in song!
   Arise, O Barak!
   Take captive your captives, O son of Abinoam.'

¹³ "Then the men who were left
   came down to the nobles;
the people of the Lord
   came to me with the mighty.
¹⁴ Some came from Ephraim, whose roots were in
   Amalek;
   Benjamin was with the people who followed you.
From Makir captains came down,
   from Zebulun those who bear a commander's
   staff.
¹⁵ The princes of Issachar were with Deborah;
   yes, Issachar was with Barak,
   rushing after him into the valley.
In the districts of Reuben
   there was much searching of heart.
¹⁶ Why did you stay among the campfires*b*
   to hear the whistling for the flocks?
In the districts of Reuben
   there was much searching of heart.
¹⁷ Gilead stayed beyond the Jordan.
   And Dan, why did he linger by the ships?
Asher remained on the coast
   and stayed in his coves.
¹⁸ The people of Zebulun risked their very lives;
   so did Naphtali on the heights of the field.

¹⁹ "Kings came, they fought;
   the kings of Canaan fought
at Taanach by the waters of Megiddo,
   but they carried off no silver, no plunder.
²⁰ From the heavens the stars fought,
   from their courses they fought against Sisera.
²¹ The river Kishon swept them away,
   the age-old river, the river Kishon.
March on, my soul; be strong!
²² Then thundered the horses' hoofs—
   galloping, galloping go his mighty steeds.
²³ 'Curse Meroz,' said the angel of the Lord.
   'Curse its people bitterly,
because they did not come to help the Lord,
   to help the Lord against the mighty.'

²⁴ "Most blessed of women be Jael,
   the wife of Heber the Kenite,
   most blessed of tent-dwelling women.
²⁵ He asked for water, and she gave him milk;
   in a bowl fit for nobles she brought him curdled
   milk.
²⁶ Her hand reached for the tent peg,
   her right hand for the workman's hammer.

Searching the Heart

JUDGES 5:15–18

The tribes of Reuben, Dan, Gilead and Asher stay behind, probably because they live some distance from the threat of violence, yet "there [is] much searching of heart" while others risk their lives rushing into the valley with Deborah and Barak.

Consider a skirmish taking place in your life—a family disagreement, a work conflict or a church squabble. What are you called to do—to "stay at the campfire" away from the clash of words, or to "rush into the valley" and contribute what you can? In either case, what does it mean to "search your heart"? How can you behave with integrity and mercy toward the people involved? How is God calling you to make the best of an imperfect situation?

See Meeting God in Community

Protesting to the Angel

JUDGES 6:11–14

How would you behave if an angel appeared to you? Would you have some protest to offer as Gideon does: "If the LORD is with us . . ."?

Let God address you in this passage as you read it aloud. Then shut your eyes and listen for the words or phrases that echo in your heart. Slowly turn the words over in your heart without trying too hard to turn them into a "message." Sitting quietly, offering protests if you need to, listen for a word from God.

See Meeting God in Scripture

She struck Sisera, she crushed his head,
    she shattered and pierced his temple.
[27] At her feet he sank,
    he fell; there he lay.
At her feet he sank, he fell;
    where he sank, there he fell—dead.

[28] "Through the window peered Sisera's mother;
    behind the lattice she cried out,
'Why is his chariot so long in coming?
    Why is the clatter of his chariots delayed?'
[29] The wisest of her ladies answer her;
    indeed, she keeps saying to herself,
[30] 'Are they not finding and dividing the spoils:
    a girl or two for each man,
    colorful garments as plunder for Sisera,
    colorful garments embroidered,
    highly embroidered garments for my neck—
all this as plunder?'

[31] "So may all your enemies perish, O LORD!
    But may they who love you be like the sun
    when it rises in its strength."

Then the land had peace forty years.

Gideon

6 Again the Israelites did evil in the eyes of the LORD, and for seven years he gave them into the hands of the Midianites. [2] Because the power of Midian was so oppressive, the Israelites prepared shelters for themselves in mountain clefts, caves and strongholds. [3] Whenever the Israelites planted their crops, the Midianites, Amalekites and other eastern peoples invaded the country. [4] They camped on the land and ruined the crops all the way to Gaza and did not spare a living thing for Israel, neither sheep nor cattle nor donkeys. [5] They came up with their livestock and their tents like swarms of locusts. It was impossible to count the men and their camels; they invaded the land to ravage it. [6] Midian so impoverished the Israelites that they cried out to the LORD for help.

[7] When the Israelites cried to the LORD because of Midian, [8] he sent them a prophet, who said, "This is what the LORD, the God of Israel, says: I brought you up out of Egypt, out of the land of slavery. [9] I snatched you from the power of Egypt and from the hand of all your oppressors. I drove them from before you and gave you their land. [10] I said to you, 'I am the LORD your God; do not worship the gods of the Amorites, in whose land you live.' But you have not listened to me."

[11] The angel of the LORD came and sat down under the oak in Ophrah that belonged to Joash the Abiezrite, where his son Gideon was threshing wheat in a winepress to keep it from the Midianites. [12] When the angel of the LORD appeared to Gideon, he said, "The LORD is with you, mighty warrior."

[13] "But sir," Gideon replied, "if the LORD is with us, why has all this happened to us? Where are all his wonders that our fathers told us about when they said, 'Did not the LORD bring us up out of Egypt?' But now the LORD has abandoned us and put us into the hand of Midian."

¹⁴The Lord turned to him and said, "Go in the strength you have and save Israel out of Midian's hand. Am I not sending you?"

¹⁵"But Lord,ᵃ" Gideon asked, "how can I save Israel? My clan is the weakest in Manasseh, and I am the least in my family."

¹⁶The Lord answered, "I will be with you, and you will strike down all the Midianites together."

¹⁷Gideon replied, "If now I have found favor in your eyes, give me a sign that it is really you talking to me. ¹⁸Please do not go away until I come back and bring my offering and set it before you."

And the Lord said, "I will wait until you return."

¹⁹Gideon went in, prepared a young goat, and from an ephahᵇ of flour he made bread without yeast. Putting the meat in a basket and its broth in a pot, he brought them out and offered them to him under the oak.

²⁰The angel of God said to him, "Take the meat and the unleavened bread, place them on this rock, and pour out the broth." And Gideon did so. ²¹With the tip of the staff that was in his hand, the angel of the Lord touched the meat and the unleavened bread. Fire flared from the rock, consuming the meat and the bread. And the angel of the Lord disappeared. ²²When Gideon realized that it was the angel of the Lord, he exclaimed, "Ah, Sovereign Lord! I have seen the angel of the Lord face to face!"

²³But the Lord said to him, "Peace! Do not be afraid. You are not going to die."

²⁴So Gideon built an altar to the Lord there and called it The Lord is Peace. To this day it stands in Ophrah of the Abiezrites.

²⁵That same night the Lord said to him, "Take the second bull from your father's herd, the one seven years old.ᶜ Tear down your father's altar to Baal and cut down the Asherah poleᵈ beside it. ²⁶Then build a proper kind ofᵉ altar to the Lord your God on the top of this height. Using the wood of the Asherah pole that you cut down, offer the secondᶠ bull as a burnt offering."

²⁷So Gideon took ten of his servants and did as the Lord told him. But because he was afraid of his family and the men of the town, he did it at night rather than in the daytime.

²⁸In the morning when the men of the town got up, there was Baal's altar, demolished, with the Asherah pole beside it cut down and the second bull sacrificed on the newly built altar!

²⁹They asked each other, "Who did this?"

When they carefully investigated, they were told, "Gideon son of Joash did it."

³⁰The men of the town demanded of Joash, "Bring out your son. He must die, because he has broken down Baal's altar and cut down the Asherah pole beside it."

³¹But Joash replied to the hostile crowd around him, "Are you going to plead Baal's cause? Are you trying to save him? Whoever fights for him shall be put to death by morning! If Baal really is a god, he can defend himself when

Holy Moments

JUDGES 6:22–24

Gideon converses with an angel and lives to tell about it (although we don't know if he actually told anyone). What does this passage tell us about God? That God is quick to declare peace and calm Gideon's fears?

Consider a situation in which you may frighten, intimidate or confuse someone. Picture the person's face for a moment. How could you communicate to the person the peace God speaks to Gideon? With what gesture or facial expression could you communicate: "Peace! Do not be afraid"?

ᵃ 15 Or sir   ᵇ 19 That is, probably about 3/5 bushel (about 22 liters)
ᶜ 25 Or Take a full-grown, mature bull from your father's herd   ᵈ 25 That is, a symbol of the goddess Asherah; here and elsewhere in Judges   ᵉ 26 Or build with layers of stone an   ᶠ 26 Or full-grown; also in verse 28

In God's Strength

JUDGES 7:2

Gideon's role as judge is about more than driving out Israel's enemies. If the people pay attention, both Israel and Gideon may discover greater trust in God.

Ponder the words God speaks to Gideon. Let God fill in the blanks for you: "You have too many _____ for me to _____."
Look at your personal belongings—your books, your personal telephone book, your clothes closet, maybe even your kitchen cabinet. What strengths have you relied on? Have you gathered too much and worked too hard?

If nothing comes to mind, turn that statement over to your subconscious in an effort to hear God. Check back in a few days to see if you've heard anything.

See Meeting God in Everyday Life

someone breaks down his altar." ³²So that day they called Gideon "Jerub-Baal,ᵃ" saying, "Let Baal contend with him," because he broke down Baal's altar.

³³Now all the Midianites, Amalekites and other eastern peoples joined forces and crossed over the Jordan and camped in the Valley of Jezreel. ³⁴Then the Spirit of the LORD came upon Gideon, and he blew a trumpet, summoning the Abiezrites to follow him. ³⁵He sent messengers throughout Manasseh, calling them to arms, and also into Asher, Zebulun and Naphtali, so that they too went up to meet them.

³⁶Gideon said to God, "If you will save Israel by my hand as you have promised— ³⁷look, I will place a wool fleece on the threshing floor. If there is dew only on the fleece and all the ground is dry, then I will know that you will save Israel by my hand, as you said." ³⁸And that is what happened. Gideon rose early the next day; he squeezed the fleece and wrung out the dew—a bowlful of water.

³⁹Then Gideon said to God, "Do not be angry with me. Let me make just one more request. Allow me one more test with the fleece. This time make the fleece dry and the ground covered with dew." ⁴⁰That night God did so. Only the fleece was dry; all the ground was covered with dew.

Gideon Defeats the Midianites

7 Early in the morning, Jerub-Baal (that is, Gideon) and all his men camped at the spring of Harod. The camp of Midian was north of them in the valley near the hill of Moreh. ²The LORD said to Gideon, "You have too many men for me to deliver Midian into their hands. In order that Israel may not boast against me that her own strength has saved her, ³announce now to the people, 'Anyone who trembles with fear may turn back and leave Mount Gilead.' " So twenty-two thousand men left, while ten thousand remained.

⁴But the LORD said to Gideon, "There are still too many men. Take them down to the water, and I will sift them for you there. If I say, 'This one shall go with you,' he shall go; but if I say, 'This one shall not go with you,' he shall not go."

⁵So Gideon took the men down to the water. There the LORD told him, "Separate those who lap the water with their tongues like a dog from those who kneel down to drink." ⁶Three hundred men lapped with their hands to their mouths. All the rest got down on their knees to drink.

⁷The LORD said to Gideon, "With the three hundred men that lapped I will save you and give the Midianites into your hands. Let all the other men go, each to his own place." ⁸So Gideon sent the rest of the Israelites to their tents but kept the three hundred, who took over the provisions and trumpets of the others.

Now the camp of Midian lay below him in the valley. ⁹During that night the LORD said to Gideon, "Get up, go down against the camp, because I am going to give it into your hands. ¹⁰If you are afraid to attack, go down to the camp with your servant Purah ¹¹and listen to what they are saying. Afterward, you will be encouraged to attack the camp." So he and Purah his servant went down to the outposts of the camp. ¹²The Midianites, the Amalekites and all the other eastern peoples had settled in the valley, thick as

ᵃ 32 *Jerub-Baal* means *let Baal contend.*

locusts. Their camels could no more be counted than the sand on the seashore.

¹³Gideon arrived just as a man was telling a friend his dream. "I had a dream," he was saying. "A round loaf of barley bread came tumbling into the Midianite camp. It struck the tent with such force that the tent overturned and collapsed."

¹⁴His friend responded, "This can be nothing other than the sword of Gideon son of Joash, the Israelite. God has given the Midianites and the whole camp into his hands."

¹⁵When Gideon heard the dream and its interpretation, he worshiped God. He returned to the camp of Israel and called out, "Get up! The LORD has given the Midianite camp into your hands." ¹⁶Dividing the three hundred men into three companies, he placed trumpets and empty jars in the hands of all of them, with torches inside.

¹⁷"Watch me," he told them. "Follow my lead. When I get to the edge of the camp, do exactly as I do. ¹⁸When I and all who are with me blow our trumpets, then from all around the camp blow yours and shout, 'For the LORD and for Gideon.'"

¹⁹Gideon and the hundred men with him reached the edge of the camp at the beginning of the middle watch, just after they had changed the guard. They blew their trumpets and broke the jars that were in their hands. ²⁰The three companies blew the trumpets and smashed the jars. Grasping the torches in their left hands and holding in their right hands the trumpets they were to blow, they shouted, "A sword for the LORD and for Gideon!" ²¹While each man held his position around the camp, all the Midianites ran, crying out as they fled.

²²When the three hundred trumpets sounded, the LORD caused the men throughout the camp to turn on each other with their swords. The army fled to Beth Shittah toward Zererah as far as the border of Abel Meholah near Tabbath. ²³Israelites from Naphtali, Asher and all Manasseh were called out, and they pursued the Midianites. ²⁴Gideon sent messengers throughout the hill country of Ephraim, saying, "Come down against the Midianites and seize the waters of the Jordan ahead of them as far as Beth Barah."

So all the men of Ephraim were called out and they took the waters of the Jordan as far as Beth Barah. ²⁵They also captured two of the Midianite leaders, Oreb and Zeeb. They killed Oreb at the rock of Oreb, and Zeeb at the winepress of Zeeb. They pursued the Midianites and brought the heads of Oreb and Zeeb to Gideon, who was by the Jordan.

Zebah and Zalmunna

8 Now the Ephraimites asked Gideon, "Why have you treated us like this? Why didn't you call us when you went to fight Midian?" And they criticized him sharply.

²But he answered them, "What have I accomplished compared to you? Aren't the gleanings of Ephraim's grapes better than the full grape harvest of Abiezer? ³God gave Oreb and Zeeb, the Midianite leaders, into your hands. What was I able to do compared to you?" At this, their resentment against him subsided.

⁴Gideon and his three hundred men, exhausted yet keeping up the pursuit, came to the Jordan and crossed it. ⁵He said to the men of Succoth, "Give my troops some bread;

Dreaming of God's Will

JUDGES 7:13–15

Gideon takes dreams seriously. Even though both the dreamer and the interpreter are non-Israelites, Gideon recognizes the voice of God and acts upon what God says.

Do you listen to your dreams? Your friends' dreams? How open are you to hear God speaking in ways that seem unconventional?

Reread these three verses. See if you can sense the excitement of the two friends who hear God. Pick a word or phrase from the passage on which to reflect. Why is this important for you? Rest in silence, being open for any impressions from God. What might God be saying to you?

See *Meeting God in Prayer*

Power Plays

JUDGES 8:22–23

After Gideon frees Israel from its oppressors, he is asked to rule over Israel—to be a king, if not in name then at least in practice. It would be a natural position for Gideon to accept if he wanted to grab the power, but instead he insists that Israel must be governed by God alone.

Would such an offer—to be ruler over a country—entice you? If not that, what sort of power does attract you? Ask God what you need to know today about acquiring power and giving him sovereignty. In what ways do you grab for power?

See Meeting God in Community

they are worn out, and I am still pursuing Zebah and Zalmunna, the kings of Midian."

⁶But the officials of Succoth said, "Do you already have the hands of Zebah and Zalmunna in your possession? Why should we give bread to your troops?"

⁷Then Gideon replied, "Just for that, when the LORD has given Zebah and Zalmunna into my hand, I will tear your flesh with desert thorns and briers."

⁸From there he went up to Peniel*a* and made the same request of them, but they answered as the men of Succoth had. ⁹So he said to the men of Peniel, "When I return in triumph, I will tear down this tower."

¹⁰Now Zebah and Zalmunna were in Karkor with a force of about fifteen thousand men, all that were left of the armies of the eastern peoples; a hundred and twenty thousand swordsmen had fallen. ¹¹Gideon went up by the route of the nomads east of Nobah and Jogbehah and fell upon the unsuspecting army. ¹²Zebah and Zalmunna, the two kings of Midian, fled, but he pursued them and captured them, routing their entire army.

¹³Gideon son of Joash then returned from the battle by the Pass of Heres. ¹⁴He caught a young man of Succoth and questioned him, and the young man wrote down for him the names of the seventy-seven officials of Succoth, the elders of the town. ¹⁵Then Gideon came and said to the men of Succoth, "Here are Zebah and Zalmunna, about whom you taunted me by saying, 'Do you already have the hands of Zebah and Zalmunna in your possession? Why should we give bread to your exhausted men?' " ¹⁶He took the elders of the town and taught the men of Succoth a lesson by punishing them with desert thorns and briers. ¹⁷He also pulled down the tower of Peniel and killed the men of the town.

¹⁸Then he asked Zebah and Zalmunna, "What kind of men did you kill at Tabor?"

"Men like you," they answered, "each one with the bearing of a prince."

¹⁹Gideon replied, "Those were my brothers, the sons of my own mother. As surely as the LORD lives, if you had spared their lives, I would not kill you." ²⁰Turning to Jether, his oldest son, he said, "Kill them!" But Jether did not draw his sword, because he was only a boy and was afraid.

²¹Zebah and Zalmunna said, "Come, do it yourself. 'As is the man, so is his strength.' " So Gideon stepped forward and killed them, and took the ornaments off their camels' necks.

Gideon's Ephod

²²The Israelites said to Gideon, "Rule over us—you, your son and your grandson—because you have saved us out of the hand of Midian."

²³But Gideon told them, "I will not rule over you, nor will my son rule over you. The LORD will rule over you." ²⁴And he said, "I do have one request, that each of you give me an earring from your share of the plunder." (It was the custom of the Ishmaelites to wear gold earrings.)

²⁵They answered, "We'll be glad to give them." So they spread out a garment, and each man threw a ring from his plunder onto it. ²⁶The weight of the gold rings he asked for

a 8 Hebrew Penuel, a variant of Peniel; also in verses 9 and 17

came to seventeen hundred shekels,[a] not counting the ornaments, the pendants and the purple garments worn by the kings of Midian or the chains that were on their camels' necks. 27Gideon made the gold into an ephod, which he placed in Ophrah, his town. All Israel prostituted themselves by worshiping it there, and it became a snare to Gideon and his family.

Gideon's Death

28Thus Midian was subdued before the Israelites and did not raise its head again. During Gideon's lifetime, the land enjoyed peace forty years.

29Jerub-Baal son of Joash went back home to live. 30He had seventy sons of his own, for he had many wives. 31His concubine, who lived in Shechem, also bore him a son, whom he named Abimelech. 32Gideon son of Joash died at a good old age and was buried in the tomb of his father Joash in Ophrah of the Abiezrites.

33No sooner had Gideon died than the Israelites again prostituted themselves to the Baals. They set up Baal-Berith as their god and 34did not remember the LORD their God, who had rescued them from the hands of all their enemies on every side. 35They also failed to show kindness to the family of Jerub-Baal (that is, Gideon) for all the good things he had done for them.

Abimelech

9 Abimelech son of Jerub-Baal went to his mother's brothers in Shechem and said to them and to all his mother's clan, 2"Ask all the citizens of Shechem, 'Which is better for you: to have all seventy of Jerub-Baal's sons rule over you, or just one man?' Remember, I am your flesh and blood."

3When the brothers repeated all this to the citizens of Shechem, they were inclined to follow Abimelech, for they said, "He is our brother." 4They gave him seventy shekels[b] of silver from the temple of Baal-Berith, and Abimelech used it to hire reckless adventurers, who became his followers. 5He went to his father's home in Ophrah and on one stone murdered his seventy brothers, the sons of Jerub-Baal. But Jotham, the youngest son of Jerub-Baal, escaped by hiding. 6Then all the citizens of Shechem and Beth Millo gathered beside the great tree at the pillar in Shechem to crown Abimelech king.

7When Jotham was told about this, he climbed up on the top of Mount Gerizim and shouted to them, "Listen to me, citizens of Shechem, so that God may listen to you. 8One day the trees went out to anoint a king for themselves. They said to the olive tree, 'Be our king.'

9"But the olive tree answered, 'Should I give up my oil, by which both gods and men are honored, to hold sway over the trees?'

10"Next, the trees said to the fig tree, 'Come and be our king.'

11"But the fig tree replied, 'Should I give up my fruit, so good and sweet, to hold sway over the trees?'

12"Then the trees said to the vine, 'Come and be our king.'

Speaking Up Against Injustice

JUDGES 9:1–22

After Abimelech slaughters the seventy (minus one) sons of Jerub-Baal, Jotham risks his life by speaking out against this injustice. It's interesting how Jotham does so by using an allegory about an olive tree, a fig tree, a vine and a thornbush—everyday objects to his listeners.

Consider an injustice you've witnessed recently—an unfair law, a group unjustly punished, a helpless person oppressed. Write a few sentences to describe what needs to be said about this situation. Is there possibly a story to be told? How could you use everyday objects to make the dilemma more understandable to people who could do something to alleviate the situation? Write out your story or draw an illustrated version of it.

See Meeting God in Community

---

[a] 26 That is, about 43 pounds (about 19.5 kilograms)   [b] 4 That is, about 1 3/4 pounds (about 0.8 kilogram)

A Relationship Rooted in Treachery

JUDGES 9:23–24

The author of Judges declares that God sent the evil spirit between Abimelech and the citizens of Shechem. Ponder: Was the spirit a supernatural being, or was it the attitude of bitterness and distrust that had permeated the relationship from its inception, rooted as it was in the murder of Jerub-Baal's (Gideon's) sons?

Is there a troubling relationship in your experience—a relationship that has "gone sour"? Can you trace the present problems to earlier ones? Ask God to show you how you might have done wrong. Ask God for the grace to heal the mistakes of the past and mend the relationship. Take whatever action God suggests to you.

See Meeting God in Community

13"But the vine answered, 'Should I give up my wine, which cheers both gods and men, to hold sway over the trees?'

14"Finally all the trees said to the thornbush, 'Come and be our king.'

15"The thornbush said to the trees, 'If you really want to anoint me king over you, come and take refuge in my shade; but if not, then let fire come out of the thornbush and consume the cedars of Lebanon!'

16"Now if you have acted honorably and in good faith when you made Abimelech king, and if you have been fair to Jerub-Baal and his family, and if you have treated him as he deserves— 17and to think that my father fought for you, risked his life to rescue you from the hand of Midian 18(but today you have revolted against my father's family, murdered his seventy sons on a single stone, and made Abimelech, the son of his slave girl, king over the citizens of Shechem because he is your brother)— 19if then you have acted honorably and in good faith toward Jerub-Baal and his family today, may Abimelech be your joy, and may you be his, too! 20But if you have not, let fire come out from Abimelech and consume you, citizens of Shechem and Beth Millo, and let fire come out from you, citizens of Shechem and Beth Millo, and consume Abimelech!"

21Then Jotham fled, escaping to Beer, and he lived there because he was afraid of his brother Abimelech.

22After Abimelech had governed Israel three years, 23God sent an evil spirit between Abimelech and the citizens of Shechem, who acted treacherously against Abimelech. 24God did this in order that the crime against Jerub-Baal's seventy sons, the shedding of their blood, might be avenged on their brother Abimelech and on the citizens of Shechem, who had helped him murder his brothers. 25In opposition to him these citizens of Shechem set men on the hilltops to ambush and rob everyone who passed by, and this was reported to Abimelech.

26Now Gaal son of Ebed moved with his brothers into Shechem, and its citizens put their confidence in him. 27After they had gone out into the fields and gathered the grapes and trodden them, they held a festival in the temple of their god. While they were eating and drinking, they cursed Abimelech. 28Then Gaal son of Ebed said, "Who is Abimelech, and who is Shechem, that we should be subject to him? Isn't he Jerub-Baal's son, and isn't Zebul his deputy? Serve the men of Hamor, Shechem's father! Why should we serve Abimelech? 29If only this people were under my command! Then I would get rid of him. I would say to Abimelech, 'Call out your whole army!' "[a]

30When Zebul the governor of the city heard what Gaal son of Ebed said, he was very angry. 31Under cover he sent messengers to Abimelech, saying, "Gaal son of Ebed and his brothers have come to Shechem and are stirring up the city against you. 32Now then, during the night you and your men should come and lie in wait in the fields. 33In the morning at sunrise, advance against the city. When Gaal and his men come out against you, do whatever your hand finds to do."

34So Abimelech and all his troops set out by night and

---

^a29 Septuagint; Hebrew *him."* Then he said to Abimelech, *"Call out your whole army!"*

took up concealed positions near Shechem in four companies. ³⁵Now Gaal son of Ebed had gone out and was standing at the entrance to the city gate just as Abimelech and his soldiers came out from their hiding place.

³⁶When Gaal saw them, he said to Zebul, "Look, people are coming down from the tops of the mountains!"

Zebul replied, "You mistake the shadows of the mountains for men."

³⁷But Gaal spoke up again: "Look, people are coming down from the center of the land, and a company is coming from the direction of the soothsayers' tree."

³⁸Then Zebul said to him, "Where is your big talk now, you who said, 'Who is Abimelech that we should be subject to him?' Aren't these the men you ridiculed? Go out and fight them!"

³⁹So Gaal led out^a the citizens of Shechem and fought Abimelech. ⁴⁰Abimelech chased him, and many fell wounded in the flight—all the way to the entrance to the gate. ⁴¹Abimelech stayed in Arumah, and Zebul drove Gaal and his brothers out of Shechem.

⁴²The next day the people of Shechem went out to the fields, and this was reported to Abimelech. ⁴³So he took his men, divided them into three companies and set an ambush in the fields. When he saw the people coming out of the city, he rose to attack them. ⁴⁴Abimelech and the companies with him rushed forward to a position at the entrance to the city gate. Then two companies rushed upon those in the fields and struck them down. ⁴⁵All that day Abimelech pressed his attack against the city until he had captured it and killed its people. Then he destroyed the city and scattered salt over it.

⁴⁶On hearing this, the citizens in the tower of Shechem went into the stronghold of the temple of El-Berith. ⁴⁷When Abimelech heard that they had assembled there, ⁴⁸he and all his men went up Mount Zalmon. He took an ax and cut off some branches, which he lifted to his shoulders. He ordered the men with him, "Quick! Do what you have seen me do!" ⁴⁹So all the men cut branches and followed Abimelech. They piled them against the stronghold and set it on fire over the people inside. So all the people in the tower of Shechem, about a thousand men and women, also died.

⁵⁰Next Abimelech went to Thebez and besieged it and captured it. ⁵¹Inside the city, however, was a strong tower, to which all the men and women—all the people of the city—fled. They locked themselves in and climbed up on the tower roof. ⁵²Abimelech went to the tower and stormed it. But as he approached the entrance to the tower to set it on fire, ⁵³a woman dropped an upper millstone on his head and cracked his skull.

⁵⁴Hurriedly he called to his armor-bearer, "Draw your sword and kill me, so that they can't say, 'A woman killed him.'" So his servant ran him through, and he died. ⁵⁵When the Israelites saw that Abimelech was dead, they went home.

⁵⁶Thus God repaid the wickedness that Abimelech had done to his father by murdering his seventy brothers. ⁵⁷God also made the men of Shechem pay for all their wickedness. The curse of Jotham son of Jerub-Baal came on them.

^a 39 Or Gaal went out in the sight of

God in the News

JUDGES 9:56–57

When we read the newspaper, many events seem to randomly occur, but the eyes of God do not stray from human affairs. Abimelech, a bloodthirsty man, is not allowed to rage on indefinitely but is instead brought to a quick and shameful end. The newspapers of that day would have claimed that the woman dropped the stone on him and that Abimelech then asked his armor-bearer to kill him. But the truth is that God intervened.

Pick up a newspaper and peruse the stories. What situations are full of injustice? In which situation is God likely to intervene? How is God calling you to intercede so that justice and mercy prevail?

See Meeting God in Community

Cry for Rescue

JUDGES 10:10-15

Many people today would question your sanity if you said you regularly hold dialogues with God, but that's what is happening between Israel and God. Israel cries out; God answers, identifying its wrong behavior; then Israel confesses its sin.

Notice the rhythm of the conversation between God and Israel. Pick a word or phrase that resonates with you. Why is it important for you? Rest in silence, being open to whatever conversation you may need to have with God. What do you believe God is trying to communicate to you today?

See Meeting God in Scripture

Tola

10 After the time of Abimelech a man of Issachar, Tola son of Puah, the son of Dodo, rose to save Israel. He lived in Shamir, in the hill country of Ephraim. ²He led[a] Israel twenty-three years; then he died, and was buried in Shamir.

Jair

³He was followed by Jair of Gilead, who led Israel twenty-two years. ⁴He had thirty sons, who rode thirty donkeys. They controlled thirty towns in Gilead, which to this day are called Havvoth Jair.[b] ⁵When Jair died, he was buried in Kamon.

Jephthah

⁶Again the Israelites did evil in the eyes of the LORD. They served the Baals and the Ashtoreths, and the gods of Aram, the gods of Sidon, the gods of Moab, the gods of the Ammonites and the gods of the Philistines. And because the Israelites forsook the LORD and no longer served him, ⁷he became angry with them. He sold them into the hands of the Philistines and the Ammonites, ⁸who that year shattered and crushed them. For eighteen years they oppressed all the Israelites on the east side of the Jordan in Gilead, the land of the Amorites. ⁹The Ammonites also crossed the Jordan to fight against Judah, Benjamin and the house of Ephraim; and Israel was in great distress. ¹⁰Then the Israelites cried out to the LORD, "We have sinned against you, forsaking our God and serving the Baals."

¹¹The LORD replied, "When the Egyptians, the Amorites, the Ammonites, the Philistines, ¹²the Sidonians, the Amalekites and the Maonites[c] oppressed you and you cried to me for help, did I not save you from their hands? ¹³But you have forsaken me and served other gods, so I will no longer save you. ¹⁴Go and cry out to the gods you have chosen. Let them save you when you are in trouble!"

¹⁵But the Israelites said to the LORD, "We have sinned. Do with us whatever you think best, but please rescue us now." ¹⁶Then they got rid of the foreign gods among them and served the LORD. And he could bear Israel's misery no longer.

¹⁷When the Ammonites were called to arms and camped in Gilead, the Israelites assembled and camped at Mizpah. ¹⁸The leaders of the people of Gilead said to each other, "Whoever will launch the attack against the Ammonites will be the head of all those living in Gilead."

11 Jephthah the Gileadite was a mighty warrior. His father was Gilead; his mother was a prostitute. ²Gilead's wife also bore him sons, and when they were grown up, they drove Jephthah away. "You are not going to get any inheritance in our family," they said, "because you are the son of another woman." ³So Jephthah fled from his brothers and settled in the land of Tob, where a group of adventurers gathered around him and followed him.

⁴Some time later, when the Ammonites made war on Israel, ⁵the elders of Gilead went to get Jephthah from the

---

a 2 Traditionally *judged;* also in verse 3   *b 4* Or *called the settlements of Jair*
c 12 Hebrew; some Septuagint manuscripts *Midianites*

land of Tob. **6**"Come," they said, "be our commander, so we can fight the Ammonites."

7Jephthah said to them, "Didn't you hate me and drive me from my father's house? Why do you come to me now, when you're in trouble?"

8The elders of Gilead said to him, "Nevertheless, we are turning to you now; come with us to fight the Ammonites, and you will be our head over all who live in Gilead."

9Jephthah answered, "Suppose you take me back to fight the Ammonites and the LORD gives them to me—will I really be your head?"

10The elders of Gilead replied, "The LORD is our witness; we will certainly do as you say." **11**So Jephthah went with the elders of Gilead, and the people made him head and commander over them. And he repeated all his words before the LORD in Mizpah.

12Then Jephthah sent messengers to the Ammonite king with the question: "What do you have against us that you have attacked our country?"

13The king of the Ammonites answered Jephthah's messengers, "When Israel came up out of Egypt, they took away my land from the Arnon to the Jabbok, all the way to the Jordan. Now give it back peaceably."

14Jephthah sent back messengers to the Ammonite king, **15**saying:

"This is what Jephthah says: Israel did not take the land of Moab or the land of the Ammonites. **16**But when they came up out of Egypt, Israel went through the desert to the Red Sea*a* and on to Kadesh. **17**Then Israel sent messengers to the king of Edom, saying, 'Give us permission to go through your country,' but the king of Edom would not listen. They sent also to the king of Moab, and he refused. So Israel stayed at Kadesh.

18"Next they traveled through the desert, skirted the lands of Edom and Moab, passed along the eastern side of the country of Moab, and camped on the other side of the Arnon. They did not enter the territory of Moab, for the Arnon was its border.

19"Then Israel sent messengers to Sihon king of the Amorites, who ruled in Heshbon, and said to him, 'Let us pass through your country to our own place.' **20**Sihon, however, did not trust Israel*b* to pass through his territory. He mustered all his men and encamped at Jahaz and fought with Israel.

21"Then the LORD, the God of Israel, gave Sihon and all his men into Israel's hands, and they defeated them. Israel took over all the land of the Amorites who lived in that country, **22**capturing all of it from the Arnon to the Jabbok and from the desert to the Jordan.

23"Now since the LORD, the God of Israel, has driven the Amorites out before his people Israel, what right have you to take it over? **24**Will you not take what your god Chemosh gives you? Likewise, whatever the LORD our God has given us, we will possess. **25**Are you better than Balak son of Zippor, king of Moab? Did he ever quarrel with Israel or fight with them? **26**For three hun-

---

Grace to Pass Through

JUDGES 11:17–19

Israel asks permission to pass through Edom, Moab and the land of the Amorites on the way to the promised land, but these nations do not give it. They may feel threatened by the possibility of aggression, sabotage or intermarriage.

Who is passing through your life? A new coworker, a new in-law, a new neighbor? You might consider this person bothersome or even threatening, but take a moment to pray for this person, asking God to show you what you need to know about him or her.

See *Meeting God in Community*

---

a 16 Hebrew *Yam Suph*; that is, Sea of Reeds   *b 20* Or *however, would not make an agreement for Israel*

An Acceptable Sacrifice

JUDGES 11:37–40

"And when a deep consideration had from the secret bottom of my soul drawn together and heaped up all my misery in the sight of my heart, there arose a mighty storm, bringing a shower of tears . . . I cast myself down I know not how, under a certain fig tree, giving full vent to my tears; and the floods of mine eyes gushed out an acceptable sacrifice to Thee."

—AUGUSTINE,
Confessions

dred years Israel occupied Heshbon, Aroer, the surrounding settlements and all the towns along the Arnon. Why didn't you retake them during that time? ²⁷I have not wronged you, but you are doing me wrong by waging war against me. Let the LORD, the Judge,*^a* decide the dispute this day between the Israelites and the Ammonites."

²⁸The king of Ammon, however, paid no attention to the message Jephthah sent him.

²⁹Then the Spirit of the LORD came upon Jephthah. He crossed Gilead and Manasseh, passed through Mizpah of Gilead, and from there he advanced against the Ammonites. ³⁰And Jephthah made a vow to the LORD: "If you give the Ammonites into my hands, ³¹whatever comes out of the door of my house to meet me when I return in triumph from the Ammonites will be the LORD's, and I will sacrifice it as a burnt offering."

³²Then Jephthah went over to fight the Ammonites, and the LORD gave them into his hands. ³³He devastated twenty towns from Aroer to the vicinity of Minnith, as far as Abel Keramim. Thus Israel subdued Ammon.

³⁴When Jephthah returned to his home in Mizpah, who should come out to meet him but his daughter, dancing to the sound of tambourines! She was an only child. Except for her he had neither son nor daughter. ³⁵When he saw her, he tore his clothes and cried, "Oh! My daughter! You have made me miserable and wretched, because I have made a vow to the LORD that I cannot break."

³⁶"My father," she replied, "you have given your word to the LORD. Do to me just as you promised, now that the LORD has avenged you of your enemies, the Ammonites. ³⁷But grant me this one request," she said. "Give me two months to roam the hills and weep with my friends, because I will never marry."

³⁸"You may go," he said. And he let her go for two months. She and the girls went into the hills and wept because she would never marry. ³⁹After the two months, she returned to her father and he did to her as he had vowed. And she was a virgin.

From this comes the Israelite custom ⁴⁰that each year the young women of Israel go out for four days to commemorate the daughter of Jephthah the Gileadite.

Jephthah and Ephraim

12 The men of Ephraim called out their forces, crossed over to Zaphon and said to Jephthah, "Why did you go to fight the Ammonites without calling us to go with you? We're going to burn down your house over your head."

²Jephthah answered, "I and my people were engaged in a great struggle with the Ammonites, and although I called, you didn't save me out of their hands. ³When I saw that you wouldn't help, I took my life in my hands and crossed over to fight the Ammonites, and the LORD gave me the victory over them. Now why have you come up today to fight me?"

⁴Jephthah then called together the men of Gilead and fought against Ephraim. The Gileadites struck them down

a 27 Or Ruler

because the Ephraimites had said, "You Gileadites are renegades from Ephraim and Manasseh." ⁵The Gileadites captured the fords of the Jordan leading to Ephraim, and whenever a survivor of Ephraim said, "Let me cross over," the men of Gilead asked him, "Are you an Ephraimite?" If he replied, "No," ⁶they said, "All right, say 'Shibboleth.' " If he said, "Sibboleth," because he could not pronounce the word correctly, they seized him and killed him at the fords of the Jordan. Forty-two thousand Ephraimites were killed at that time.

⁷Jephthah led*ᵃ* Israel six years. Then Jephthah the Gileadite died, and was buried in a town in Gilead.

Ibzan, Elon and Abdon

⁸After him, Ibzan of Bethlehem led Israel. ⁹He had thirty sons and thirty daughters. He gave his daughters away in marriage to those outside his clan, and for his sons he brought in thirty young women as wives from outside his clan. Ibzan led Israel seven years. ¹⁰Then Ibzan died, and was buried in Bethlehem.

¹¹After him, Elon the Zebulunite led Israel ten years. ¹²Then Elon died, and was buried in Aijalon in the land of Zebulun.

¹³After him, Abdon son of Hillel, from Pirathon, led Israel. ¹⁴He had forty sons and thirty grandsons, who rode on seventy donkeys. He led Israel eight years. ¹⁵Then Abdon son of Hillel died, and was buried at Pirathon in Ephraim, in the hill country of the Amalekites.

The Birth of Samson

13 Again the Israelites did evil in the eyes of the Lord, so the Lord delivered them into the hands of the Philistines for forty years.

²A certain man of Zorah, named Manoah, from the clan of the Danites, had a wife who was sterile and remained childless. ³The angel of the Lord appeared to her and said, "You are sterile and childless, but you are going to conceive and have a son. ⁴Now see to it that you drink no wine or other fermented drink and that you do not eat anything unclean, ⁵because you will conceive and give birth to a son. No razor may be used on his head, because the boy is to be a Nazirite, set apart to God from birth, and he will begin the deliverance of Israel from the hands of the Philistines."

⁶Then the woman went to her husband and told him, "A man of God came to me. He looked like an angel of God, very awesome. I didn't ask him where he came from, and he didn't tell me his name. ⁷But he said to me, 'You will conceive and give birth to a son. Now then, drink no wine or other fermented drink and do not eat anything unclean, because the boy will be a Nazirite of God from birth until the day of his death.' "

⁸Then Manoah prayed to the Lord: "O Lord, I beg you, let the man of God you sent to us come again to teach us how to bring up the boy who is to be born."

⁹God heard Manoah, and the angel of God came again to the woman while she was out in the field; but her husband Manoah was not with her. ¹⁰The woman hurried to tell her husband, "He's here! The man who appeared to me the other day!"

Asking for Further Instructions

JUDGES 13:2–16

Put yourself in the place of Manoah and his wife. You are being granted a request you've probably despaired of ever receiving. A stranger—actually an angel—promises you a child. This angel instructs you to bring up the boy as a Nazirite, so you ask the angel to teach you how to do that.

What great gifts has God given to you, in the sense of having "the desires of your heart" granted? (Psalm 37:4). What do you need God to teach you further about those gifts?

See Meeting God in Prayer

ᵃ 7 Traditionally *judged*; also in verses 8–14

Faces to the Ground

JUDGES 13:17–21

Imagine yourself and someone close to you experiencing the things Manoah and his wife experience: They are told they are speaking to a person with a name "beyond understanding," and they watch an angel ascend in a flame. In awe they lie down with their faces to the ground.

What would cause you to be that awestruck? Consider praying in that face-to-the-ground position or some other position you rarely use, such as kneeling or bowing. What sort of prayers come out of your mouth in that position? Are they words of human humility or a testament to God's majesty? What do you need to say to God?

See *Meeting God in Worship*

¹¹Manoah got up and followed his wife. When he came to the man, he said, "Are you the one who talked to my wife?"

"I am," he said.

¹²So Manoah asked him, "When your words are fulfilled, what is to be the rule for the boy's life and work?"

¹³The angel of the LORD answered, "Your wife must do all that I have told her. ¹⁴She must not eat anything that comes from the grapevine, nor drink any wine or other fermented drink nor eat anything unclean. She must do everything I have commanded her."

¹⁵Manoah said to the angel of the LORD, "We would like you to stay until we prepare a young goat for you."

¹⁶The angel of the LORD replied, "Even though you detain me, I will not eat any of your food. But if you prepare a burnt offering, offer it to the LORD." (Manoah did not realize that it was the angel of the LORD.)

¹⁷Then Manoah inquired of the angel of the LORD, "What is your name, so that we may honor you when your word comes true?"

¹⁸He replied, "Why do you ask my name? It is beyond understanding.[a]" ¹⁹Then Manoah took a young goat, together with the grain offering, and sacrificed it on a rock to the LORD. And the LORD did an amazing thing while Manoah and his wife watched: ²⁰As the flame blazed up from the altar toward heaven, the angel of the LORD ascended in the flame. Seeing this, Manoah and his wife fell with their faces to the ground. ²¹When the angel of the LORD did not show himself again to Manoah and his wife, Manoah realized that it was the angel of the LORD.

²²"We are doomed to die!" he said to his wife. "We have seen God!"

²³But his wife answered, "If the LORD had meant to kill us, he would not have accepted a burnt offering and grain offering from our hands, nor shown us all these things or now told us this."

²⁴The woman gave birth to a boy and named him Samson. He grew and the LORD blessed him, ²⁵and the Spirit of the LORD began to stir him while he was in Mahaneh Dan, between Zorah and Eshtaol.

Samson's Marriage

14 Samson went down to Timnah and saw there a young Philistine woman. ²When he returned, he said to his father and mother, "I have seen a Philistine woman in Timnah; now get her for me as my wife."

³His father and mother replied, "Isn't there an acceptable woman among your relatives or among all our people? Must you go to the uncircumcised Philistines to get a wife?"

But Samson said to his father, "Get her for me. She's the right one for me." ⁴(His parents did not know that this was from the LORD, who was seeking an occasion to confront the Philistines; for at that time they were ruling over Israel.) ⁵Samson went down to Timnah together with his father and mother. As they approached the vineyards of Timnah, suddenly a young lion came roaring toward him. ⁶The Spirit of the LORD came upon him in power so that he tore the lion apart with his bare hands as he might have torn a young goat. But he told neither his father nor his mother

ᵃ 18 Or *is wonderful*

what he had done. ⁷Then he went down and talked with the woman, and he liked her.

⁸Some time later, when he went back to marry her, he turned aside to look at the lion's carcass. In it was a swarm of bees and some honey, ⁹which he scooped out with his hands and ate as he went along. When he rejoined his parents, he gave them some, and they too ate it. But he did not tell them that he had taken the honey from the lion's carcass.

¹⁰Now his father went down to see the woman. And Samson made a feast there, as was customary for bridegrooms. ¹¹When he appeared, he was given thirty companions.

¹²"Let me tell you a riddle," Samson said to them. "If you can give me the answer within the seven days of the feast, I will give you thirty linen garments and thirty sets of clothes. ¹³If you can't tell me the answer, you must give me thirty linen garments and thirty sets of clothes."

"Tell us your riddle," they said. "Let's hear it."

¹⁴He replied,

> "Out of the eater, something to eat;
>   out of the strong, something sweet."

For three days they could not give the answer.

¹⁵On the fourth[a] day, they said to Samson's wife, "Coax your husband into explaining the riddle for us, or we will burn you and your father's household to death. Did you invite us here to rob us?"

¹⁶Then Samson's wife threw herself on him, sobbing, "You hate me! You don't really love me. You've given my people a riddle, but you haven't told me the answer."

"I haven't even explained it to my father or mother," he replied, "so why should I explain it to you?" ¹⁷She cried the whole seven days of the feast. So on the seventh day he finally told her, because she continued to press him. She in turn explained the riddle to her people.

¹⁸Before sunset on the seventh day the men of the town said to him,

> "What is sweeter than honey?
>   What is stronger than a lion?"

Samson said to them,

> "If you had not plowed with my heifer,
>   you would not have solved my riddle."

¹⁹Then the Spirit of the LORD came upon him in power. He went down to Ashkelon, struck down thirty of their men, stripped them of their belongings and gave their clothes to those who had explained the riddle. Burning with anger, he went up to his father's house. ²⁰And Samson's wife was given to the friend who had attended him at his wedding.

Samson's Vengeance on the Philistines

15 Later on, at the time of wheat harvest, Samson took a young goat and went to visit his wife. He said, "I'm going to my wife's room." But her father would not let him go in.

²"I was so sure you thoroughly hated her," he said, "that

Tales of Manipulation

JUDGES 14:13–20

Samson's wife manipulates him with tears and accusations. Enter this story for a moment from the perspective of God's unseen heart. How does it feel to watch a man whom you've set aside for special service being manipulated? How does it feel to watch him respond?

Take a few minutes to grieve with God over the people in this world who are being manipulated. Include yourself as one who has been manipulated. Include others whom you have manipulated.

See Meeting God in Community

---

a 15 Some Septuagint manuscripts and Syriac; Hebrew *seventh*

Power of the Spirit

JUDGES 15:14

When the Spirit comes over Samson, Samson has great physical power to free himself from the Philistines. What important work is God calling you to do—work that is important in God's eyes, but perhaps not in society's? What sort of power of the Spirit do you need in order to do this work? What are the ropes binding your hands at this time—ropes that God's Spirit can rip away?

See Meeting God in Service

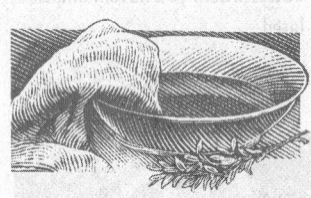

I gave her to your friend. Isn't her younger sister more attractive? Take her instead."

³Samson said to them, "This time I have a right to get even with the Philistines; I will really harm them." ⁴So he went out and caught three hundred foxes and tied them tail to tail in pairs. He then fastened a torch to every pair of tails, ⁵lit the torches and let the foxes loose in the standing grain of the Philistines. He burned up the shocks and standing grain, together with the vineyards and olive groves.

⁶When the Philistines asked, "Who did this?" they were told, "Samson, the Timnite's son-in-law, because his wife was given to his friend."

So the Philistines went up and burned her and her father to death. ⁷Samson said to them, "Since you've acted like this, I won't stop until I get my revenge on you." ⁸He attacked them viciously and slaughtered many of them. Then he went down and stayed in a cave in the rock of Etam.

⁹The Philistines went up and camped in Judah, spreading out near Lehi. ¹⁰The men of Judah asked, "Why have you come to fight us?"

"We have come to take Samson prisoner," they answered, "to do to him as he did to us."

¹¹Then three thousand men from Judah went down to the cave in the rock of Etam and said to Samson, "Don't you realize that the Philistines are rulers over us? What have you done to us?"

He answered, "I merely did to them what they did to me."

¹²They said to him, "We've come to tie you up and hand you over to the Philistines."

Samson said, "Swear to me that you won't kill me yourselves."

¹³"Agreed," they answered. "We will only tie you up and hand you over to them. We will not kill you." So they bound him with two new ropes and led him up from the rock. ¹⁴As he approached Lehi, the Philistines came toward him shouting. The Spirit of the LORD came upon him in power. The ropes on his arms became like charred flax, and the bindings dropped from his hands. ¹⁵Finding a fresh jawbone of a donkey, he grabbed it and struck down a thousand men.

¹⁶Then Samson said,

> "With a donkey's jawbone
> I have made donkeys of them.ᵃ
> With a donkey's jawbone
> I have killed a thousand men."

¹⁷When he finished speaking, he threw away the jawbone; and the place was called Ramath Lehi.ᵇ

¹⁸Because he was very thirsty, he cried out to the LORD, "You have given your servant this great victory. Must I now die of thirst and fall into the hands of the uncircumcised?" ¹⁹Then God opened up the hollow place in Lehi, and water came out of it. When Samson drank, his strength returned and he revived. So the spring was called En Hakkore,ᶜ and it is still there in Lehi.

²⁰Samson ledᵈ Israel for twenty years in the days of the Philistines.

ᵃ 16 Or *made a heap or two*; the Hebrew for *donkey* sounds like the Hebrew for *heap*. ᵇ 17 *Ramath Lehi* means *jawbone hill*. ᶜ 19 *En Hakkore* means *caller's spring*. ᵈ 20 Traditionally *judged*

Samson and Delilah

16 One day Samson went to Gaza, where he saw a prostitute. He went in to spend the night with her. ²The people of Gaza were told, "Samson is here!" So they surrounded the place and lay in wait for him all night at the city gate. They made no move during the night, saying, "At dawn we'll kill him."

³But Samson lay there only until the middle of the night. Then he got up and took hold of the doors of the city gate, together with the two posts, and tore them loose, bar and all. He lifted them to his shoulders and carried them to the top of the hill that faces Hebron.

⁴Some time later, he fell in love with a woman in the Valley of Sorek whose name was Delilah. ⁵The rulers of the Philistines went to her and said, "See if you can lure him into showing you the secret of his great strength and how we can overpower him so we may tie him up and subdue him. Each one of us will give you eleven hundred shekels*ᵃ* of silver."

⁶So Delilah said to Samson, "Tell me the secret of your great strength and how you can be tied up and subdued."

⁷Samson answered her, "If anyone ties me with seven fresh thongs*ᵇ* that have not been dried, I'll become as weak as any other man."

⁸Then the rulers of the Philistines brought her seven fresh thongs that had not been dried, and she tied him with them. ⁹With men hidden in the room, she called to him, "Samson, the Philistines are upon you!" But he snapped the thongs as easily as a piece of string snaps when it comes close to a flame. So the secret of his strength was not discovered.

¹⁰Then Delilah said to Samson, "You have made a fool of me; you lied to me. Come now, tell me how you can be tied."

¹¹He said, "If anyone ties me securely with new ropes that have never been used, I'll become as weak as any other man."

¹²So Delilah took new ropes and tied him with them. Then, with men hidden in the room, she called to him, "Samson, the Philistines are upon you!" But he snapped the ropes off his arms as if they were threads.

¹³Delilah then said to Samson, "Until now, you have been making a fool of me and lying to me. Tell me how you can be tied."

He replied, "If you weave the seven braids of my head into the fabric ⌊on the loom⌋ and tighten it with the pin, I'll become as weak as any other man." So while he was sleeping, Delilah took the seven braids of his head, wove them into the fabric ¹⁴and*ᶜ* tightened it with the pin.

Again she called to him, "Samson, the Philistines are upon you!" He awoke from his sleep and pulled up the pin and the loom, with the fabric.

¹⁵Then she said to him, "How can you say, 'I love you,' when you won't confide in me? This is the third time you have made a fool of me and haven't told me the secret of your great strength." ¹⁶With such nagging she prodded him day after day until he was tired to death.

ᵃ 5 That is, about 28 pounds (about 13 kilograms)   *ᵇ 7* Or *bowstrings*; also in verses 8 and 9   *ᶜ 13,14* Some Septuagint manuscripts; Hebrew *"I can, if you weave the seven braids of my head into the fabric ⌊on the loom⌋." ¹⁴So she*

Failing—in Spite of Advantages

JUDGES 16:15–20

Samson, divinely appointed by God to save Israel, is allowed to fail. What does this passage say about the nature of God in relation to human failure? What does it say about human nature that Samson, so blessed with loving parents and Nazirite righteousness, can fail so miserably? How does this passage lead you to pray? In what areas have you failed? How do you feel about those failures? How do you think God sees your failures? After you ponder these questions, read Ephesians 1:1–8.

See Meeting God in Everyday Life

The Destruction of a Soul

JUDGES 16:26–31

"A man will have a great and long struggle with himself, before he fully learns to master self and to turn his whole affection towards God. When a man relies on himself, he easily turns aside to human consolations. But a true lover of Christ, and a diligent pursuer of virtue, does not fall back upon consolations, nor seek such sensible sweetnesses; he prefers hard trials and would wish to undergo severe labours for Christ. The devil sleeps not, neither is the flesh yet dead; therefore you must not cease to prepare yourself for the battle; for on the right hand and on the left are enemies that never rest."

—THOMAS À KEMPIS,
The Imitation of Christ

[17]So he told her everything. "No razor has ever been used on my head," he said, "because I have been a Nazirite set apart to God since birth. If my head were shaved, my strength would leave me, and I would become as weak as any other man."

[18]When Delilah saw that he had told her everything, she sent word to the rulers of the Philistines, "Come back once more; he has told me everything." So the rulers of the Philistines returned with the silver in their hands. [19]Having put him to sleep on her lap, she called a man to shave off the seven braids of his hair, and so began to subdue him.[a] And his strength left him.

[20]Then she called, "Samson, the Philistines are upon you!"

He awoke from his sleep and thought, "I'll go out as before and shake myself free." But he did not know that the LORD had left him.

[21]Then the Philistines seized him, gouged out his eyes and took him down to Gaza. Binding him with bronze shackles, they set him to grinding in the prison. [22]But the hair on his head began to grow again after it had been shaved.

The Death of Samson

[23]Now the rulers of the Philistines assembled to offer a great sacrifice to Dagon their god and to celebrate, saying, "Our god has delivered Samson, our enemy, into our hands."

[24]When the people saw him, they praised their god, saying,

> "Our god has delivered our enemy
> into our hands,
> the one who laid waste our land
> and multiplied our slain."

[25]While they were in high spirits, they shouted, "Bring out Samson to entertain us." So they called Samson out of the prison, and he performed for them.

When they stood him among the pillars, [26]Samson said to the servant who held his hand, "Put me where I can feel the pillars that support the temple, so that I may lean against them." [27]Now the temple was crowded with men and women; all the rulers of the Philistines were there, and on the roof were about three thousand men and women watching Samson perform. [28]Then Samson prayed to the LORD, "O Sovereign LORD, remember me. O God, please strengthen me just once more, and let me with one blow get revenge on the Philistines for my two eyes." [29]Then Samson reached toward the two central pillars on which the temple stood. Bracing himself against them, his right hand on the one and his left hand on the other, [30]Samson said, "Let me die with the Philistines!" Then he pushed with all his might, and down came the temple on the rulers and all the people in it. Thus he killed many more when he died than while he lived.

[31]Then his brothers and his father's whole family went down to get him. They brought him back and buried him between Zorah and Eshtaol in the tomb of Manoah his father. He had led[b] Israel twenty years.

[a] 19 Hebrew; some Septuagint manuscripts *and he began to weaken*
[b] 31 Traditionally *judged*

Micah's Idols

17 Now a man named Micah from the hill country of Ephraim ²said to his mother, "The eleven hundred shekels*ᵃ* of silver that were taken from you and about which I heard you utter a curse—I have that silver with me; I took it."

Then his mother said, "The LORD bless you, my son!"

³When he returned the eleven hundred shekels of silver to his mother, she said, "I solemnly consecrate my silver to the LORD for my son to make a carved image and a cast idol. I will give it back to you."

⁴So he returned the silver to his mother, and she took two hundred shekels*ᵇ* of silver and gave them to a silversmith, who made them into the image and the idol. And they were put in Micah's house.

⁵Now this man Micah had a shrine, and he made an ephod and some idols and installed one of his sons as his priest. ⁶In those days Israel had no king; everyone did as he saw fit.

⁷A young Levite from Bethlehem in Judah, who had been living within the clan of Judah, ⁸left that town in search of some other place to stay. On his way*ᶜ* he came to Micah's house in the hill country of Ephraim.

⁹Micah asked him, "Where are you from?"

"I'm a Levite from Bethlehem in Judah," he said, "and I'm looking for a place to stay."

¹⁰Then Micah said to him, "Live with me and be my father and priest, and I'll give you ten shekels*ᵈ* of silver a year, your clothes and your food." ¹¹So the Levite agreed to live with him, and the young man was to him like one of his sons. ¹²Then Micah installed the Levite, and the young man became his priest and lived in his house. ¹³And Micah said, "Now I know that the LORD will be good to me, since this Levite has become my priest."

Danites Settle in Laish

18 In those days Israel had no king.
And in those days the tribe of the Danites was seeking a place of their own where they might settle, because they had not yet come into an inheritance among the tribes of Israel. ²So the Danites sent five warriors from Zorah and Eshtaol to spy out the land and explore it. These men represented all their clans. They told them, "Go, explore the land."

The men entered the hill country of Ephraim and came to the house of Micah, where they spent the night. ³When they were near Micah's house, they recognized the voice of the young Levite; so they turned in there and asked him, "Who brought you here? What are you doing in this place? Why are you here?"

⁴He told them what Micah had done for him, and said, "He has hired me and I am his priest."

⁵Then they said to him, "Please inquire of God to learn whether our journey will be successful."

⁶The priest answered them, "Go in peace. Your journey has the LORD's approval."

⁷So the five men left and came to Laish, where they saw

Minding My Own Business

JUDGES 18:7

The people of Laish live an ideal life of safety, security and prosperity. God's imperfect people, the Danites, decide to conquer the people of Laish, who are without help because they have "no relationship with anyone else." What does the unwitting isolation of this content, prosperous people say about human nature? What does this passage say about how isolation can make you vulnerable to ruthless people? What does it suggest about how you might pray? What does it suggest about what you need to do?

See Meeting God in Community

ᵃ2 That is, about 28 pounds (about 13 kilograms)   *ᵇ4* That is, about 5 pounds (about 2.3 kilograms)   *ᶜ8* Or *To carry on his profession*   *ᵈ10* That is, about 4 ounces (about 110 grams)

Because "I Can"

JUDGES 18:18–26

The Danites steal from Micah and later subdue Laish with no thought of whether doing these things is consistent with God's will or morally right. They do them because they want to do them; they have the power to do them. They give in to the human inclination to treat the powerless in any way they choose.

Imagine for a moment that the Danite men seek God in the matter. What possible solutions might God suggest to escape their dilemma (which is that "they had not yet come into an inheritance among the tribes of Israel" [18:1])?

See Meeting God in Scripture

that the people were living in safety, like the Sidonians, unsuspecting and secure. And since their land lacked nothing, they were prosperous.*ᵃ* Also, they lived a long way from the Sidonians and had no relationship with anyone else.*ᵇ*

⁸When they returned to Zorah and Eshtaol, their brothers asked them, "How did you find things?"

⁹They answered, "Come on, let's attack them! We have seen that the land is very good. Aren't you going to do something? Don't hesitate to go there and take it over. ¹⁰When you get there, you will find an unsuspecting people and a spacious land that God has put into your hands, a land that lacks nothing whatever."

¹¹Then six hundred men from the clan of the Danites, armed for battle, set out from Zorah and Eshtaol. ¹²On their way they set up camp near Kiriath Jearim in Judah. This is why the place west of Kiriath Jearim is called Mahaneh Dan*ᶜ* to this day. ¹³From there they went on to the hill country of Ephraim and came to Micah's house.

¹⁴Then the five men who had spied out the land of Laish said to their brothers, "Do you know that one of these houses has an ephod, other household gods, a carved image and a cast idol? Now you know what to do." ¹⁵So they turned in there and went to the house of the young Levite at Micah's place and greeted him. ¹⁶The six hundred Danites, armed for battle, stood at the entrance to the gate. ¹⁷The five men who had spied out the land went inside and took the carved image, the ephod, the other household gods and the cast idol while the priest and the six hundred armed men stood at the entrance to the gate.

¹⁸When these men went into Micah's house and took the carved image, the ephod, the other household gods and the cast idol, the priest said to them, "What are you doing?"

¹⁹They answered him, "Be quiet! Don't say a word. Come with us, and be our father and priest. Isn't it better that you serve a tribe and clan in Israel as priest rather than just one man's household?" ²⁰Then the priest was glad. He took the ephod, the other household gods and the carved image and went along with the people. ²¹Putting their little children, their livestock and their possessions in front of them, they turned away and left.

²²When they had gone some distance from Micah's house, the men who lived near Micah were called together and overtook the Danites. ²³As they shouted after them, the Danites turned and said to Micah, "What's the matter with you that you called out your men to fight?"

²⁴He replied, "You took the gods I made, and my priest, and went away. What else do I have? How can you ask, 'What's the matter with you?' "

²⁵The Danites answered, "Don't argue with us, or some hot-tempered men will attack you, and you and your family will lose your lives." ²⁶So the Danites went their way, and Micah, seeing that they were too strong for him, turned around and went back home.

²⁷Then they took what Micah had made, and his priest, and went on to Laish, against a peaceful and unsuspecting people. They attacked them with the sword and burned

ᵃ 7 The meaning of the Hebrew for this clause is uncertain. *ᵇ 7 Hebrew; some Septuagint manuscripts with the Arameans* *ᶜ 12 Mahaneh Dan means Dan's camp.*

down their city. [28]There was no one to rescue them because they lived a long way from Sidon and had no relationship with anyone else. The city was in a valley near Beth Rehob.

The Danites rebuilt the city and settled there. [29]They named it Dan after their forefather Dan, who was born to Israel—though the city used to be called Laish. [30]There the Danites set up for themselves the idols, and Jonathan son of Gershom, the son of Moses,[a] and his sons were priests for the tribe of Dan until the time of the captivity of the land. [31]They continued to use the idols Micah had made, all the time the house of God was in Shiloh.

A Levite and His Concubine

19 In those days Israel had no king.
Now a Levite who lived in a remote area in the hill country of Ephraim took a concubine from Bethlehem in Judah. [2]But she was unfaithful to him. She left him and went back to her father's house in Bethlehem, Judah. After she had been there four months, [3]her husband went to her to persuade her to return. He had with him his servant and two donkeys. She took him into her father's house, and when her father saw him, he gladly welcomed him. [4]His father-in-law, the girl's father, prevailed upon him to stay; so he remained with him three days, eating and drinking, and sleeping there.

[5]On the fourth day they got up early and he prepared to leave, but the girl's father said to his son-in-law, "Refresh yourself with something to eat; then you can go." [6]So the two of them sat down to eat and drink together. Afterward the girl's father said, "Please stay tonight and enjoy yourself." [7]And when the man got up to go, his father-in-law persuaded him, so he stayed there that night. [8]On the morning of the fifth day, when he rose to go, the girl's father said, "Refresh yourself. Wait till afternoon!" So the two of them ate together.

[9]Then when the man, with his concubine and his servant, got up to leave, his father-in-law, the girl's father, said, "Now look, it's almost evening. Spend the night here; the day is nearly over. Stay and enjoy yourself. Early tomorrow morning you can get up and be on your way home." [10]But, unwilling to stay another night, the man left and went toward Jebus (that is, Jerusalem), with his two saddled donkeys and his concubine.

[11]When they were near Jebus and the day was almost gone, the servant said to his master, "Come, let's stop at this city of the Jebusites and spend the night."

[12]His master replied, "No. We won't go into an alien city, whose people are not Israelites. We will go on to Gibeah." [13]He added, "Come, let's try to reach Gibeah or Ramah and spend the night in one of those places." [14]So they went on, and the sun set as they neared Gibeah in Benjamin. [15]There they stopped to spend the night. They went and sat in the city square, but no one took them into his home for the night.

[16]That evening an old man from the hill country of Ephraim, who was living in Gibeah (the men of the place were Benjamites), came in from his work in the fields. [17]When he looked and saw the traveler in the city square, the old man asked, "Where are you going? Where did you come from?"

[18]He answered, "We are on our way from Bethlehem in

Sin on Sin, Sorrow on Sorrow

JUDGES 19–20

One sin leads to another in these disquieting passages, and each sinful choice—each decision made without calling on God—is compounded until the tragic conflict mushrooms into widespread death and destruction.

Are you involved in a conflict today? A small difference of opinion? A seemingly minor personality conflict? How can you stop it from mushrooming? By saying a quick prayer before you reply to criticism or a sharp word? By choosing words of reconciliation rather than retort? By choosing humility and offering an apology rather than striking out in defensiveness? By asking God how the conflict might be resolved with fairness and justice?

See Meeting God in Community

---

[a]30 An ancient Hebrew scribal tradition, some Septuagint manuscripts and Vulgate; Masoretic Text *Manasseh*

Paying Attention to Tragedy

JUDGES 19:29-30

Why does the Levite do such a shocking thing? Apparently he wants to get the twelve tribes' attention and knows that sending body parts will serve just that purpose. Sometimes God will allow us to be alarmed and appalled.

In the face of our dulled sensitivity, others may feel the need to be overly dramatic in order to get our attention. Consider the requests your coworkers and children have made of you today. What would it take for you to consider them seriously? Or even better, as you open your mail today, open and read the pleas for donations you receive. Ask God, "What would it take to cultivate an inner person that is readily sensitive to others?"

See Meeting God in Community

Judah to a remote area in the hill country of Ephraim where I live. I have been to Bethlehem in Judah and now I am going to the house of the LORD. No one has taken me into his house. ¹⁹We have both straw and fodder for our donkeys and bread and wine for ourselves your servants—me, your maidservant, and the young man with us. We don't need anything."

²⁰"You are welcome at my house," the old man said. "Let me supply whatever you need. Only don't spend the night in the square." ²¹So he took him into his house and fed his donkeys. After they had washed their feet, they had something to eat and drink.

²²While they were enjoying themselves, some of the wicked men of the city surrounded the house. Pounding on the door, they shouted to the old man who owned the house, "Bring out the man who came to your house so we can have sex with him."

²³The owner of the house went outside and said to them, "No, my friends, don't be so vile. Since this man is my guest, don't do this disgraceful thing. ²⁴Look, here is my virgin daughter, and his concubine. I will bring them out to you now, and you can use them and do to them whatever you wish. But to this man, don't do such a disgraceful thing."

²⁵But the men would not listen to him. So the man took his concubine and sent her outside to them, and they raped her and abused her throughout the night, and at dawn they let her go. ²⁶At daybreak the woman went back to the house where her master was staying, fell down at the door and lay there until daylight.

²⁷When her master got up in the morning and opened the door of the house and stepped out to continue on his way, there lay his concubine, fallen in the doorway of the house, with her hands on the threshold. ²⁸He said to her, "Get up; let's go." But there was no answer. Then the man put her on his donkey and set out for home.

²⁹When he reached home, he took a knife and cut up his concubine, limb by limb, into twelve parts and sent them into all the areas of Israel. ³⁰Everyone who saw it said, "Such a thing has never been seen or done, not since the day the Israelites came up out of Egypt. Think about it! Consider it! Tell us what to do!"

Israelites Fight the Benjamites

20 Then all the Israelites from Dan to Beersheba and from the land of Gilead came out as one man and assembled before the LORD in Mizpah. ²The leaders of all the people of the tribes of Israel took their places in the assembly of the people of God, four hundred thousand soldiers armed with swords. ³(The Benjamites heard that the Israelites had gone up to Mizpah.) Then the Israelites said, "Tell us how this awful thing happened."

⁴So the Levite, the husband of the murdered woman, said, "I and my concubine came to Gibeah in Benjamin to spend the night. ⁵During the night the men of Gibeah came after me and surrounded the house, intending to kill me. They raped my concubine, and she died. ⁶I took my concubine, cut her into pieces and sent one piece to each region of Israel's inheritance, because they committed this lewd and disgraceful act in Israel. ⁷Now, all you Israelites, speak up and give your verdict."

⁸All the people rose as one man, saying, "None of us will

go home. No, not one of us will return to his house. ⁹But now this is what we'll do to Gibeah: We'll go up against it as the lot directs. ¹⁰We'll take ten men out of every hundred from all the tribes of Israel, and a hundred from a thousand, and a thousand from ten thousand, to get provisions for the army. Then, when the army arrives at Gibeah*a* in Benjamin, it can give them what they deserve for all this vileness done in Israel." ¹¹So all the men of Israel got together and united as one man against the city.

¹²The tribes of Israel sent men throughout the tribe of Benjamin, saying, "What about this awful crime that was committed among you? ¹³Now surrender those wicked men of Gibeah so that we may put them to death and purge the evil from Israel."

But the Benjamites would not listen to their fellow Israelites. ¹⁴From their towns they came together at Gibeah to fight against the Israelites. ¹⁵At once the Benjamites mobilized twenty-six thousand swordsmen from their towns, in addition to seven hundred chosen men from those living in Gibeah. ¹⁶Among all these soldiers there were seven hundred chosen men who were left-handed, each of whom could sling a stone at a hair and not miss.

¹⁷Israel, apart from Benjamin, mustered four hundred thousand swordsmen, all of them fighting men.

¹⁸The Israelites went up to Bethel*b* and inquired of God. They said, "Who of us shall go first to fight against the Benjamites?"

The LORD replied, "Judah shall go first."

¹⁹The next morning the Israelites got up and pitched camp near Gibeah. ²⁰The men of Israel went out to fight the Benjamites and took up battle positions against them at Gibeah. ²¹The Benjamites came out of Gibeah and cut down twenty-two thousand Israelites on the battlefield that day. ²²But the men of Israel encouraged one another and again took up their positions where they had stationed themselves the first day. ²³The Israelites went up and wept before the LORD until evening, and they inquired of the LORD. They said, "Shall we go up again to battle against the Benjamites, our brothers?"

The LORD answered, "Go up against them."

²⁴Then the Israelites drew near to Benjamin the second day. ²⁵This time, when the Benjamites came out from Gibeah to oppose them, they cut down another eighteen thousand Israelites, all of them armed with swords.

²⁶Then the Israelites, all the people, went up to Bethel, and there they sat weeping before the LORD. They fasted that day until evening and presented burnt offerings and fellowship offerings*c* to the LORD. ²⁷And the Israelites inquired of the LORD. (In those days the ark of the covenant of God was there, ²⁸with Phinehas son of Eleazar, the son of Aaron, ministering before it.) They asked, "Shall we go up again to battle with Benjamin our brother, or not?"

The LORD responded, "Go, for tomorrow I will give them into your hands."

²⁹Then Israel set an ambush around Gibeah. ³⁰They went up against the Benjamites on the third day and took up positions against Gibeah as they had done before. ³¹The Ben-

Righteous Anger Is Never Enough

JUDGES 20:26–28

Shocked by the evil committed by the city of Gibeah, Israel comes against the city and its tribe. Being on the right side isn't enough, and appropriately they seek God—weeping, fasting, inquiring and offering themselves to God.

Notice the many outward ways Israel worships God. Pick a word, phrase or movement described in this passage that impresses you. Why is it important for you? To what service is God calling you? In what ways do you need to worship before you begin to serve?

See Meeting God in Worship

---

a 10 One Hebrew manuscript; most Hebrew manuscripts *Geba,* a variant of *Gibeah*   *b 18* Or *to the house of God;* also in verse 26   *c 26* Traditionally *peace offerings*

Mercy for the Wicked

JUDGES 21:1–5

The first hint of mercy for the tribe of Benjamin occurs in the writer's description of their fighters: "valiant" (20:44,46). Suddenly Israel—a country made up of distant but related tribes—realizes that it has been fighting its own people and that it must take steps to preserve the nation.

If you have pictures of your family or friends in your wallet or hanging on the wall of your home, look at these pictures. Whom, if anyone, have you declared war on? Whom would you like to declare war on? Whom would you judge to be unredeemable? What can you do to restore them to the family? Pray that they be restored.

See *Meeting God in Community*

jamites came out to meet them and were drawn away from the city. They began to inflict casualties on the Israelites as before, so that about thirty men fell in the open field and on the roads—the one leading to Bethel and the other to Gibeah.

³²While the Benjamites were saying, "We are defeating them as before," the Israelites were saying, "Let's retreat and draw them away from the city to the roads."

³³All the men of Israel moved from their places and took up positions at Baal Tamar, and the Israelite ambush charged out of its place on the west*ᵃ* of Gibeah.*ᵇ* ³⁴Then ten thousand of Israel's finest men made a frontal attack on Gibeah. The fighting was so heavy that the Benjamites did not realize how near disaster was. ³⁵The LORD defeated Benjamin before Israel, and on that day the Israelites struck down 25,100 Benjamites, all armed with swords. ³⁶Then the Benjamites saw that they were beaten.

Now the men of Israel had given way before Benjamin, because they relied on the ambush they had set near Gibeah. ³⁷The men who had been in ambush made a sudden dash into Gibeah, spread out and put the whole city to the sword. ³⁸The men of Israel had arranged with the ambush that they should send up a great cloud of smoke from the city, ³⁹and then the men of Israel would turn in the battle.

The Benjamites had begun to inflict casualties on the men of Israel (about thirty), and they said, "We are defeating them as in the first battle." ⁴⁰But when the column of smoke began to rise from the city, the Benjamites turned and saw the smoke of the whole city going up into the sky. ⁴¹Then the men of Israel turned on them, and the men of Benjamin were terrified, because they realized that disaster had come upon them. ⁴²So they fled before the Israelites in the direction of the desert, but they could not escape the battle. And the men of Israel who came out of the towns cut them down there. ⁴³They surrounded the Benjamites, chased them and easily*ᶜ* overran them in the vicinity of Gibeah on the east. ⁴⁴Eighteen thousand Benjamites fell, all of them valiant fighters. ⁴⁵As they turned and fled toward the desert to the rock of Rimmon, the Israelites cut down five thousand men along the roads. They kept pressing after the Benjamites as far as Gidom and struck down two thousand more.

⁴⁶On that day twenty-five thousand Benjamite swordsmen fell, all of them valiant fighters. ⁴⁷But six hundred men turned and fled into the desert to the rock of Rimmon, where they stayed four months. ⁴⁸The men of Israel went back to Benjamin and put all the towns to the sword, including the animals and everything else they found. All the towns they came across they set on fire.

Wives for the Benjamites

21 The men of Israel had taken an oath at Mizpah: "Not one of us will give his daughter in marriage to a Benjamite."

²The people went to Bethel,*ᵈ* where they sat before God until evening, raising their voices and weeping bitterly. ³"O LORD, the God of Israel," they cried, "why has this hap-

---

ᵃ 33 Some Septuagint manuscripts and Vulgate; the meaning of the Hebrew for this word is uncertain.   *ᵇ 33* Hebrew *Geba*, a variant of *Gibeah*
ᶜ 43 The meaning of the Hebrew for this word is uncertain.   *ᵈ 2* Or *to the house of God*

pened to Israel? Why should one tribe be missing from Israel today?"

⁴Early the next day the people built an altar and presented burnt offerings and fellowship offerings.ᵃ

⁵Then the Israelites asked, "Who from all the tribes of Israel has failed to assemble before the LORD?" For they had taken a solemn oath that anyone who failed to assemble before the LORD at Mizpah should certainly be put to death.

⁶Now the Israelites grieved for their brothers, the Benjamites. "Today one tribe is cut off from Israel," they said. ⁷"How can we provide wives for those who are left, since we have taken an oath by the LORD not to give them any of our daughters in marriage?" ⁸Then they asked, "Which one of the tribes of Israel failed to assemble before the LORD at Mizpah?" They discovered that no one from Jabesh Gilead had come to the camp for the assembly. ⁹For when they counted the people, they found that none of the people of Jabesh Gilead were there.

¹⁰So the assembly sent twelve thousand fighting men with instructions to go to Jabesh Gilead and put to the sword those living there, including the women and children. ¹¹"This is what you are to do," they said. "Kill every male and every woman who is not a virgin." ¹²They found among the people living in Jabesh Gilead four hundred young women who had never slept with a man, and they took them to the camp at Shiloh in Canaan.

¹³Then the whole assembly sent an offer of peace to the Benjamites at the rock of Rimmon. ¹⁴So the Benjamites returned at that time and were given the women of Jabesh Gilead who had been spared. But there were not enough for all of them.

¹⁵The people grieved for Benjamin, because the LORD had made a gap in the tribes of Israel. ¹⁶And the elders of the assembly said, "With the women of Benjamin destroyed, how shall we provide wives for the men who are left? ¹⁷The Benjamite survivors must have heirs," they said, "so that a tribe of Israel will not be wiped out. ¹⁸We can't give them our daughters as wives, since we Israelites have taken this oath: 'Cursed be anyone who gives a wife to a Benjamite.' ¹⁹But look, there is the annual festival of the LORD in Shiloh, to the north of Bethel, and east of the road that goes from Bethel to Shechem, and to the south of Lebonah."

²⁰So they instructed the Benjamites, saying, "Go and hide in the vineyards ²¹and watch. When the girls of Shiloh come out to join in the dancing, then rush from the vineyards and each of you seize a wife from the girls of Shiloh and go to the land of Benjamin. ²²When their fathers or brothers complain to us, we will say to them, 'Do us a kindness by helping them, because we did not get wives for them during the war, and you are innocent, since you did not give your daughters to them.' "

²³So that is what the Benjamites did. While the girls were dancing, each man caught one and carried her off to be his wife. Then they returned to their inheritance and rebuilt the towns and settled in them.

²⁴At that time the Israelites left that place and went home to their tribes and clans, each to his own inheritance.

²⁵In those days Israel had no king; everyone did as he saw fit.

ᵃ 4 Traditionally *peace offerings*

Conscience

JUDGES 21:25

"Some people even say that so long as a man follows his conscience he cannot be committing sin. Certainly a man should follow his conscience; but that is not the whole of his duty. Still more important is it to enlighten the conscience itself, lest 'your whole body . . . be full of darkness' (Matthew 6:23) . . . But we shall not set ourselves that standard, to say nothing of attaining it, if we are left to our own resource. And we do not know what the perfection of God is until we have seen it in Christ."

—WILLIAM TEMPLE,
Christus Veritas

RUTH
The Power of Relationships

KEY VERSE:

"Where you go I will go, and where you stay I will stay. Your people will be my people and your God my God."—Ruth 1:16

"All . . . are to be welcomed as Christ, for he himself will say: 'I was a stranger and you welcomed me' " (Matthew 25:35).
—The Rule of St. Benedict, Chapter 53:1

Set squarely within the daily life of common people, the book of Ruth tells a story about people who need God and how God responds. The story demonstrates that, though mysterious and unpredictable, God's provision can be sought confidently in the midst of ordinary human problems. The enduring power of the story of Ruth and Naomi rests in the fact that two outcast women—one a foreigner and one an elderly widow—become significant links in the family line of the Christ child. God's grace often comes in surprising ways.

This story also reminds us that God uses people from unexpected places in unexpected ways. Ruth is not a Hebrew; she cannot inherit a claim to the promises of God to Israel, yet God blesses her with compassion, resourcefulness and courage. Her faith and love transform a tragic situation into a joyous one.

Redemption—rescuing and reclaiming one apart or adrift—is the central theme of the book of Ruth. The focus is on the management of the land and family obligations, but the story teaches us a more profound meaning of redemption: God gives new life in abundance where only death and emptiness are expected. And while God is easing Naomi's and Ruth's need, he is also bringing about his purposes for the whole nation.

Ask yourself where you least expect to find God at work, and give new attention to that place or those people. If you feel like an "outcast," ask God what he might be seeking from you and ask him to bring about transformation. Expect to be surprised!

Naomi and Ruth

1 In the days when the judges ruled,*ª* there was a famine in the land, and a man from Bethlehem in Judah, together with his wife and two sons, went to live for a while in the country of Moab. ²The man's name was Elimelech, his wife's name Naomi, and the names of his two sons were Mahlon and Kilion. They were Ephrathites from Bethlehem, Judah. And they went to Moab and lived there.

³Now Elimelech, Naomi's husband, died, and she was left with her two sons. ⁴They married Moabite women, one named Orpah and the other Ruth. After they had lived there about ten years, ⁵both Mahlon and Kilion also died, and Naomi was left without her two sons and her husband.

⁶When she heard in Moab that the LORD had come to the aid of his people by providing food for them, Naomi and her daughters-in-law prepared to return home from there. ⁷With her two daughters-in-law she left the place where she had been living and set out on the road that would take them back to the land of Judah.

⁸Then Naomi said to her two daughters-in-law, "Go back, each of you, to your mother's home. May the LORD show kindness to you, as you have shown to your dead and to me. ⁹May the LORD grant that each of you will find rest in the home of another husband."

Then she kissed them and they wept aloud ¹⁰and said to her, "We will go back with you to your people."

¹¹But Naomi said, "Return home, my daughters. Why would you come with me? Am I going to have any more sons, who could become your husbands? ¹²Return home, my daughters; I am too old to have another husband. Even if I thought there was still hope for me—even if I had a husband tonight and then gave birth to sons— ¹³would you wait until they grew up? Would you remain unmarried for them? No, my daughters. It is more bitter for me than for you, because the LORD's hand has gone out against me!"

¹⁴At this they wept again. Then Orpah kissed her mother-in-law good-by, but Ruth clung to her.

¹⁵"Look," said Naomi, "your sister-in-law is going back to her people and her gods. Go back with her."

¹⁶But Ruth replied, "Don't urge me to leave you or to turn back from you. Where you go I will go, and where you stay I will stay. Your people will be my people and your God my God. ¹⁷Where you die I will die, and there I will be buried. May the LORD deal with me, be it ever so severely, if anything but death separates you and me." ¹⁸When Naomi realized that Ruth was determined to go with her, she stopped urging her.

¹⁹So the two women went on until they came to Bethlehem. When they arrived in Bethlehem, the whole town was stirred because of them, and the women exclaimed, "Can this be Naomi?"

²⁰"Don't call me Naomi,*ᵇ*" she told them. "Call me Mara,*ᶜ* because the Almighty*ᵈ* has made my life very bitter. ²¹I went away full, but the LORD has brought me back empty. Why call me Naomi? The LORD has afflicted*ᵉ* me; the Almighty has brought misfortune upon me."

²²So Naomi returned from Moab accompanied by Ruth

How Bitter to Be Alone!

RUTH 1:20–21

Naomi's life had been full of family love, even in the midst of famine. But she now feels empty and bitter, and she blames God. Enter Ruth, her daughter-in-law, a Moabite "outsider" whose kindness moves her to share Naomi's isolation rather than return to "her own" people. Do the situations of either of these women remind you of an important time in your own life—when loss and grief, and even bitterness, threatened to overwhelm you? Or when love called you to do something others considered foolish or risky? Recall such a time, remembering how despair and hope mingled with one another. What happened to change your sense of emptiness?

See Meeting God in Community

ª 1 Traditionally judged   *ᵇ 20 Naomi means pleasant; also in verse 21.*
ᶜ 20 Mara means bitter.   *ᵈ 20 Hebrew Shaddai; also in verse 21*   *ᵉ 21 Or has testified against*

A Place of Safety

God's care is like the wings of a mother bird, gently covering her baby chicks, keeping them warm and safe from harm. The image of shelter under wings is repeated later in the story when Ruth asks Boaz to spread the corner of his garment over her (see 3:9). What image comes to your mind when you think of safety, security and generous care? Perhaps you think of a hearth fire, or a cozy old chair, or a childhood treehouse. Imagine yourself now sheltered in this way within God's loving embrace. Explore what you feel in that secure and welcoming place.

the Moabitess, her daughter-in-law, arriving in Bethlehem as the barley harvest was beginning.

Ruth Meets Boaz

2 Now Naomi had a relative on her husband's side, from the clan of Elimelech, a man of standing, whose name was Boaz.

²And Ruth the Moabitess said to Naomi, "Let me go to the fields and pick up the leftover grain behind anyone in whose eyes I find favor."

Naomi said to her, "Go ahead, my daughter." ³So she went out and began to glean in the fields behind the harvesters. As it turned out, she found herself working in a field belonging to Boaz, who was from the clan of Elimelech.

⁴Just then Boaz arrived from Bethlehem and greeted the harvesters, "The LORD be with you!"

"The LORD bless you!" they called back.

⁵Boaz asked the foreman of his harvesters, "Whose young woman is that?"

⁶The foreman replied, "She is the Moabitess who came back from Moab with Naomi. ⁷She said, 'Please let me glean and gather among the sheaves behind the harvesters.' She went into the field and has worked steadily from morning till now, except for a short rest in the shelter."

⁸So Boaz said to Ruth, "My daughter, listen to me. Don't go and glean in another field and don't go away from here. Stay here with my servant girls. ⁹Watch the field where the men are harvesting, and follow along after the girls. I have told the men not to touch you. And whenever you are thirsty, go and get a drink from the water jars the men have filled."

¹⁰At this, she bowed down with her face to the ground. She exclaimed, "Why have I found such favor in your eyes that you notice me—a foreigner?"

¹¹Boaz replied, "I've been told all about what you have done for your mother-in-law since the death of your husband—how you left your father and mother and your homeland and came to live with a people you did not know before. ¹²May the LORD repay you for what you have done. May you be richly rewarded by the LORD, the God of Israel, under whose wings you have come to take refuge."

¹³"May I continue to find favor in your eyes, my lord," she said. "You have given me comfort and have spoken kindly to your servant—though I do not have the standing of one of your servant girls."

¹⁴At mealtime Boaz said to her, "Come over here. Have some bread and dip it in the wine vinegar."

When she sat down with the harvesters, he offered her some roasted grain. She ate all she wanted and had some left over. ¹⁵As she got up to glean, Boaz gave orders to his men, "Even if she gathers among the sheaves, don't embarrass her. ¹⁶Rather, pull out some stalks for her from the bundles and leave them for her to pick up, and don't rebuke her."

¹⁷So Ruth gleaned in the field until evening. Then she threshed the barley she had gathered, and it amounted to about an ephah.ᵃ ¹⁸She carried it back to town, and her

ᵃ 17 That is, probably about 3/5 bushel (about 22 liters)

mother-in-law saw how much she had gathered. Ruth also brought out and gave her what she had left over after she had eaten enough.

¹⁹Her mother-in-law asked her, "Where did you glean today? Where did you work? Blessed be the man who took notice of you!"

Then Ruth told her mother-in-law about the one at whose place she had been working. "The name of the man I worked with today is Boaz," she said.

²⁰"The LORD bless him!" Naomi said to her daughter-in-law. "He has not stopped showing his kindness to the living and the dead." She added, "That man is our close relative; he is one of our kinsman-redeemers."

²¹Then Ruth the Moabitess said, "He even said to me, 'Stay with my workers until they finish harvesting all my grain.'"

²²Naomi said to Ruth her daughter-in-law, "It will be good for you, my daughter, to go with his girls, because in someone else's field you might be harmed."

²³So Ruth stayed close to the servant girls of Boaz to glean until the barley and wheat harvests were finished. And she lived with her mother-in-law.

Ruth and Boaz at the Threshing Floor

3 One day Naomi her mother-in-law said to her, "My daughter, should I not try to find a home*a* for you, where you will be well provided for? ²Is not Boaz, with whose servant girls you have been, a kinsman of ours? Tonight he will be winnowing barley on the threshing floor. ³Wash and perfume yourself, and put on your best clothes. Then go down to the threshing floor, but don't let him know you are there until he has finished eating and drinking. ⁴When he lies down, note the place where he is lying. Then go and uncover his feet and lie down. He will tell you what to do."

⁵"I will do whatever you say," Ruth answered. ⁶So she went down to the threshing floor and did everything her mother-in-law told her to do.

⁷When Boaz had finished eating and drinking and was in good spirits, he went over to lie down at the far end of the grain pile. Ruth approached quietly, uncovered his feet and lay down. ⁸In the middle of the night something startled the man, and he turned and discovered a woman lying at his feet.

⁹"Who are you?" he asked.

"I am your servant Ruth," she said. "Spread the corner of your garment over me, since you are a kinsman-redeemer."

¹⁰"The LORD bless you, my daughter," he replied. "This kindness is greater than that which you showed earlier: You have not run after the younger men, whether rich or poor. ¹¹And now, my daughter, don't be afraid. I will do for you all you ask. All my fellow townsmen know that you are a woman of noble character. ¹²Although it is true that I am near of kin, there is a kinsman-redeemer nearer than I. ¹³Stay here for the night, and in the morning if he wants to redeem, good; let him redeem. But if he is not willing, as surely as the LORD lives I will do it. Lie here until morning."

¹⁴So she lay at his feet until morning, but got up before

Who Is My Mother and Brother and Sister?

RUTH 3:10–12

Naomi calls Ruth "daughter" (v.1), as does Boaz (v.11). Neither Naomi nor Boaz can mean the word literally, yet the term highlights the meaning of kinship in this story about "strangers." Despite the differences of their backgrounds, a deep bond develops among Naomi, Ruth and Boaz, the essence of which is kindness. When you think of kindness, what feelings arise? Can you imagine a smell or a taste that evokes feelings of kindness in you, such as hot milk and cookies before jumping into a warm bed? Do you find it easier to be kind to a stranger or to a family member? What is the difference between your response when you expect kindness from another and your response when kindness comes "out of the blue"?

See Meeting God in Service

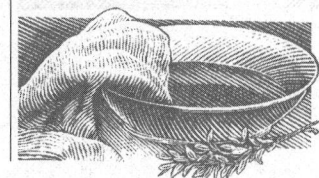

A Tender Interlude

RUTH 3:1–18

Having met Boaz and experienced his kindness and generosity, Ruth goes to the threshing floor at night to make a discreet request for marriage. As you read this tender interlude between Boaz and Ruth, enter the scene for yourself. Sense Ruth's excitement and nervousness as she dresses and perfumes herself to visit Boaz. Feel the damp coolness of the night air as she walks toward the threshing floor. Smell the dusty fragrance of the grain piles in the threshing shed. Imagine Boaz's sleepy surprise as he wakes to find Ruth at his feet and feel the emotion of their quiet talk in the predawn. How is God's tender care for us reflected in this story?

See Meeting God in Scripture

anyone could be recognized; and he said, "Don't let it be known that a woman came to the threshing floor."

¹⁵He also said, "Bring me the shawl you are wearing and hold it out." When she did so, he poured into it six measures of barley and put it on her. Then he*a* went back to town.

¹⁶When Ruth came to her mother-in-law, Naomi asked, "How did it go, my daughter?"

Then she told her everything Boaz had done for her ¹⁷and added, "He gave me these six measures of barley, saying, 'Don't go back to your mother-in-law empty-handed.' "

¹⁸Then Naomi said, "Wait, my daughter, until you find out what happens. For the man will not rest until the matter is settled today."

Boaz Marries Ruth

4 Meanwhile Boaz went up to the town gate and sat there. When the kinsman-redeemer he had mentioned came along, Boaz said, "Come over here, my friend, and sit down." So he went over and sat down. ²Boaz took ten of the elders of the town and said, "Sit here," and they did so. ³Then he said to the kinsman-redeemer, "Naomi, who has come back from Moab, is selling the piece of land that belonged to our brother Elimelech. ⁴I thought I should bring the matter to your attention and suggest that you buy it in the presence of these seated here and in the presence of the elders of my people. If you will redeem it, do so. But if you*b* will not, tell me, so I will know. For no one has the right to do it except you, and I am next in line."

"I will redeem it," he said.

⁵Then Boaz said, "On the day you buy the land from Naomi and from Ruth the Moabitess, you acquire*c* the dead man's widow, in order to maintain the name of the dead with his property."

⁶At this, the kinsman-redeemer said, "Then I cannot redeem it because I might endanger my own estate. You redeem it yourself. I cannot do it."

⁷(Now in earlier times in Israel, for the redemption and transfer of property to become final, one party took off his sandal and gave it to the other. This was the method of legalizing transactions in Israel.)

⁸So the kinsman-redeemer said to Boaz, "Buy it yourself." And he removed his sandal.

⁹Then Boaz announced to the elders and all the people, "Today you are witnesses that I have bought from Naomi all the property of Elimelech, Kilion and Mahlon. ¹⁰I have also acquired Ruth the Moabitess, Mahlon's widow, as my wife, in order to maintain the name of the dead with his property, so that his name will not disappear from among his family or from the town records. Today you are witnesses!"

¹¹Then the elders and all those at the gate said, "We are witnesses. May the LORD make the woman who is coming into your home like Rachel and Leah, who together built up the house of Israel. May you have standing in Ephrathah

<hr />

a 15 Most Hebrew manuscripts; many Hebrew manuscripts, Vulgate and Syriac *she*   *b 4* Many Hebrew manuscripts, Septuagint, Vulgate and Syriac; most Hebrew manuscripts *he*   *c 5* Hebrew; Vulgate and Syriac *Naomi, you acquire Ruth the Moabitess,* and be famous in Bethlehem. ¹²Through the offspring the LORD gives you by this young woman, may your family be like that of Perez, whom Tamar bore to Judah."

The Genealogy of David

¹³So Boaz took Ruth and she became his wife. Then he went to her, and the LORD enabled her to conceive, and she gave birth to a son. ¹⁴The women said to Naomi: "Praise be to the LORD, who this day has not left you without a kinsman-redeemer. May he become famous throughout Israel! ¹⁵He will renew your life and sustain you in your old age. For your daughter-in-law, who loves you and who is better to you than seven sons, has given him birth."

¹⁶Then Naomi took the child, laid him in her lap and cared for him. ¹⁷The women living there said, "Naomi has a son." And they named him Obed. He was the father of Jesse, the father of David.

¹⁸This, then, is the family line of Perez:

Perez was the father of Hezron,
¹⁹Hezron the father of Ram,
Ram the father of Amminadab,
²⁰Amminadab the father of Nahshon,
Nahshon the father of Salmon,[a]
²¹Salmon the father of Boaz,
Boaz the father of Obed,
²²Obed the father of Jesse,
and Jesse the father of David.

God's Mysterious Ways

RUTH 4:17

The son of Ruth and Boaz will be Jesse's father and David's grandfather. What an unexpected surprise that this family's troubles should culminate in the kingship of David, and later the birth of the Lord Jesus Christ! If you were to tell this story with puppets, how would you show the special qualities of this family? They had no status or wealth; why would God choose them? What sort of a puppet would you make for God? Or would God be offstage all the time? What action scene could convey how God is working in this story to bring about such a wonderful outcome?

See Meeting God in Scripture

---

a 20 A few Hebrew manuscripts, some Septuagint manuscripts and Vulgate (see also verse 21 and Septuagint of 1 Chron. 2:11); most Hebrew manuscripts *Salma*

1 SAMUEL

Learning to Listen

KEY VERSE:

"Speak, LORD, for your servant is listening."—1 Samuel 3:9

"Listen carefully, my son, to the master's instructions, and attend to them with the ear of your heart. This is the advice from a father who loves you; welcome it, and faithfully put it into practice. The labor of obedience will bring you back to him from whom you had drifted through the sloth of disobedience. This message of mine is for you, then, if you are ready to give up your own will, once for all, and armed with the strong and noble weapons of obedience to do battle for the true King, Christ the Lord."

—Prologue,
The Rule of Saint Benedict

The book of 1 Samuel unfolds like a historical novel, interweaving the lives of the prophet Samuel, King Saul and his family, and David, the God-appointed heir to the throne of Israel. The nation of Israel is struggling to remain loyal to God as its only supreme Ruler and still survive among surrounding nations that boast superior technology, military organization and government. Israel, by contrast, relies on a loose tribal confederacy rooted in ancient, sacred law and a faith in God's intervention to save.

We can profitably approach the book of 1 Samuel by praying the words of one of its early characters: "Speak, LORD, for your servant is listening." Just as the boy Samuel learned early in life to listen deeply (3:1–10), so can we. We can hear God's voice in this story telling us of his own character and his actions among humans. We can hear about our own struggles; we too are sometimes pulled between obedient loyalty to God and the temptation to put our trust in self-chosen causes, ideas and preferences. We can listen for what it means to be a person after God's own heart and see how God blesses those who listen. We can claim the promise that God directs and changes human lives today as he did long ago.

Prepare yourself to realize that promise for yourself as you absorb yourself in the reflections and activities suggested in each entry point. As you read ancient words about God's anointed leaders—the kings and prophets—let them guide you into a deeper relationship with God's Anointed, Jesus the Christ.

The Birth of Samuel

1 There was a certain man from Ramathaim, a Zuphite[a] from the hill country of Ephraim, whose name was Elkanah son of Jeroham, the son of Elihu, the son of Tohu, the son of Zuph, an Ephraimite. ²He had two wives; one was called Hannah and the other Peninnah. Peninnah had children, but Hannah had none.

³Year after year this man went up from his town to worship and sacrifice to the LORD Almighty at Shiloh, where Hophni and Phinehas, the two sons of Eli, were priests of the LORD. ⁴Whenever the day came for Elkanah to sacrifice, he would give portions of the meat to his wife Peninnah and to all her sons and daughters. ⁵But to Hannah he gave a double portion because he loved her, and the LORD had closed her womb. ⁶And because the LORD had closed her womb, her rival kept provoking her in order to irritate her. ⁷This went on year after year. Whenever Hannah went up to the house of the LORD, her rival provoked her till she wept and would not eat. ⁸Elkanah her husband would say to her, "Hannah, why are you weeping? Why don't you eat? Why are you downhearted? Don't I mean more to you than ten sons?"

⁹Once when they had finished eating and drinking in Shiloh, Hannah stood up. Now Eli the priest was sitting on a chair by the doorpost of the LORD's temple.[b] ¹⁰In bitterness of soul Hannah wept much and prayed to the LORD. ¹¹And she made a vow, saying, "O LORD Almighty, if you will only look upon your servant's misery and remember me, and not forget your servant but give her a son, then I will give him to the LORD for all the days of his life, and no razor will ever be used on his head."

¹²As she kept on praying to the LORD, Eli observed her mouth. ¹³Hannah was praying in her heart, and her lips were moving but her voice was not heard. Eli thought she was drunk ¹⁴and said to her, "How long will you keep on getting drunk? Get rid of your wine."

¹⁵"Not so, my lord," Hannah replied, "I am a woman who is deeply troubled. I have not been drinking wine or beer; I was pouring out my soul to the LORD. ¹⁶Do not take your servant for a wicked woman; I have been praying here out of my great anguish and grief."

¹⁷Eli answered, "Go in peace, and may the God of Israel grant you what you have asked of him."

¹⁸She said, "May your servant find favor in your eyes." Then she went her way and ate something, and her face was no longer downcast.

¹⁹Early the next morning they arose and worshiped before the LORD and then went back to their home at Ramah. Elkanah lay with Hannah his wife, and the LORD remembered her. ²⁰So in the course of time Hannah conceived and gave birth to a son. She named him Samuel,[c] saying, "Because I asked the LORD for him."

Hannah Dedicates Samuel

²¹When the man Elkanah went up with all his family to offer the annual sacrifice to the LORD and to fulfill his vow, ²²Hannah did not go. She said to her husband, "After the

---

"If You . . . Then I Will"

1 SAMUEL 1:3–11

Hannah's inability to have a child has affected her deeply. She weeps, loses her appetite, endures taunts from a rival and receives tender treatment from her understanding husband. But Hannah's prayers are not for her own benefit. Hannah promises God that she will offer back the very gift she asks for: the child for whom she yearns.

Take stock of at least one of the gifts God has given you. Now act out the offering of that gift: if it is singing, sing now; if writing, jot down the nucleus of an idea to expand; if caring for others, plan a specific caring action for another, then embrace yourself as a rehearsal for that action. Use your talent imaginatively, expressively and thankfully.

See Meeting God in Service

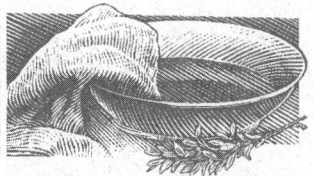

Given Over to the Lord

1 SAMUEL 1:27–28

"I am sometimes almost terrified at the scope of the demands made upon me, at the perfection of the self-abandonment required of me; yet outside of such absoluteness can be no salvation. In God we live every commonplace as well as most exalted moment of our being. To trust *in Him* when no need is pressing, when things seem going right of themselves, may be harder than when things seem going wrong."

—GEORGE MACDONALD,
as quoted in C.S. Lewis's
George MacDonald: 365 Readings

boy is weaned, I will take him and present him before the LORD, and he will live there always."

[23] "Do what seems best to you," Elkanah her husband told her. "Stay here until you have weaned him; only may the LORD make good his[a] word." So the woman stayed at home and nursed her son until she had weaned him. [24] After he was weaned, she took the boy with her, young as he was, along with a three-year-old bull,[b] an ephah[c] of flour and a skin of wine, and brought him to the house of the LORD at Shiloh. [25] When they had slaughtered the bull, they brought the boy to Eli, [26] and she said to him, "As surely as you live, my lord, I am the woman who stood here beside you praying to the LORD. [27] I prayed for this child, and the LORD has granted me what I asked of him. [28] So now I give him to the LORD. For his whole life he will be given over to the LORD." And he worshiped the LORD there.

Hannah's Prayer

2 Then Hannah prayed and said:

"My heart rejoices in the LORD;
   in the LORD my horn[d] is lifted high.
My mouth boasts over my enemies,
   for I delight in your deliverance.

[2] "There is no one holy[e] like the LORD;
   there is no one besides you;
   there is no Rock like our God.

[3] "Do not keep talking so proudly
   or let your mouth speak such arrogance,
for the LORD is a God who knows,
   and by him deeds are weighed.

[4] "The bows of the warriors are broken,
   but those who stumbled are armed with
      strength.
[5] Those who were full hire themselves out for food,
   but those who were hungry hunger no more.
She who was barren has borne seven children,
   but she who has had many sons pines away.

[6] "The LORD brings death and makes alive;
   he brings down to the grave[f] and raises up.
[7] The LORD sends poverty and wealth;
   he humbles and he exalts.
[8] He raises the poor from the dust
   and lifts the needy from the ash heap;
he seats them with princes
   and has them inherit a throne of honor.

"For the foundations of the earth are the LORD's;
   upon them he has set the world.
[9] He will guard the feet of his saints,
   but the wicked will be silenced in darkness.

"It is not by strength that one prevails;
[10]   those who oppose the LORD will be shattered.
He will thunder against them from heaven;

a 23 Masoretic Text; Dead Sea Scrolls, Septuagint and Syriac *your*   *b 24* Dead Sea Scrolls, Septuagint and Syriac; Masoretic Text *with three bulls*   *c 24* That is, probably about 3/5 bushel (about 22 liters)   *d 1* *Horn* here symbolizes strength; also in verse 10.   *e 2* Or *no Holy One*   *f 6* Hebrew *Sheol*

the LORD will judge the ends of the earth.

"He will give strength to his king
and exalt the horn of his anointed."

[11]Then Elkanah went home to Ramah, but the boy ministered before the LORD under Eli the priest.

Eli's Wicked Sons

[12]Eli's sons were wicked men; they had no regard for the LORD. [13]Now it was the practice of the priests with the people that whenever anyone offered a sacrifice and while the meat was being boiled, the servant of the priest would come with a three-pronged fork in his hand. [14]He would plunge it into the pan or kettle or caldron or pot, and the priest would take for himself whatever the fork brought up. This is how they treated all the Israelites who came to Shiloh. [15]But even before the fat was burned, the servant of the priest would come and say to the man who was sacrificing, "Give the priest some meat to roast; he won't accept boiled meat from you, but only raw."

[16]If the man said to him, "Let the fat be burned up first, and then take whatever you want," the servant would then answer, "No, hand it over now; if you don't, I'll take it by force."

[17]This sin of the young men was very great in the LORD's sight, for they[a] were treating the LORD's offering with contempt.

[18]But Samuel was ministering before the LORD—a boy wearing a linen ephod. [19]Each year his mother made him a little robe and took it to him when she went up with her husband to offer the annual sacrifice. [20]Eli would bless Elkanah and his wife, saying, "May the LORD give you children by this woman to take the place of the one she prayed for and gave to the LORD." Then they would go home. [21]And the LORD was gracious to Hannah; she conceived and gave birth to three sons and two daughters. Meanwhile, the boy Samuel grew up in the presence of the LORD.

[22]Now Eli, who was very old, heard about everything his sons were doing to all Israel and how they slept with the women who served at the entrance to the Tent of Meeting. [23]So he said to them, "Why do you do such things? I hear from all the people about these wicked deeds of yours. [24]No, my sons; it is not a good report that I hear spreading among the LORD's people. [25]If a man sins against another man, God[b] may mediate for him; but if a man sins against the LORD, who will intercede for him?" His sons, however, did not listen to their father's rebuke, for it was the LORD's will to put them to death.

[26]And the boy Samuel continued to grow in stature and in favor with the LORD and with men.

Prophecy Against the House of Eli

[27]Now a man of God came to Eli and said to him, "This is what the LORD says: 'Did I not clearly reveal myself to your father's house when they were in Egypt under Pharaoh? [28]I chose your father out of all the tribes of Israel to be my priest, to go up to my altar, to burn incense, and to wear an ephod in my presence. I also gave your father's house all the offerings made with fire by the Israelites. [29]Why do you[c]

Growing in the Presence of the Lord

1 SAMUEL 2:21

Samuel grew up in the presence of God, the writer tells us. In what ways might that be said about your life?

Prayerfully recall how God has been quietly present in your life in times of distress or loneliness as well as in times of progress and achievement. Do you picture a judgmental or a loving Presence, an intimate or a somewhat distant God? Recall your responses to God during and after the crises, and in the midst of the successes. Make a simple drawing expressing how you have grown through these periods. Then stand up to your full stature as you offer the drawing to God in thankfulness for that abiding presence.

See Meeting God in Prayer

Called a Third Time

1 SAMUEL 3:10

With old Eli's advice, young Samuel realizes that it is God who calls in the night. Then Eli tells Samuel how to listen and respond.

Participants in the monastic tradition take a vow "to hear," which moves them beyond mere obedience. Those who listen deeply for God's voice—and hear it—act in spiritual agreement with one another rather than simply obey a rule.

Practice your listening skills. Walk to a window, look outside for thirty seconds or so, then close your eyes for several minutes. Attend to whatever comes to your ears—traffic noise, birds, playing children, the sounds of your own movements. Return to your chair and think about what or whom you listen to most regularly: family members, television, your work supervisor or someone else. How might you hear God speaking through these things? How might you listen more carefully to what God has to tell you?

See Meeting God in Prayer

scorn my sacrifice and offering that I prescribed for my dwelling? Why do you honor your sons more than me by fattening yourselves on the choice parts of every offering made by my people Israel?'

³⁰"Therefore the LORD, the God of Israel, declares: 'I promised that your house and your father's house would minister before me forever.' But now the LORD declares: 'Far be it from me! Those who honor me I will honor, but those who despise me will be disdained. ³¹The time is coming when I will cut short your strength and the strength of your father's house, so that there will not be an old man in your family line ³²and you will see distress in my dwelling. Although good will be done to Israel, in your family line there will never be an old man. ³³Every one of you that I do not cut off from my altar will be spared only to blind your eyes with tears and to grieve your heart, and all your descendants will die in the prime of life.

³⁴" 'And what happens to your two sons, Hophni and Phinehas, will be a sign to you—they will both die on the same day. ³⁵I will raise up for myself a faithful priest, who will do according to what is in my heart and mind. I will firmly establish his house, and he will minister before my anointed one always. ³⁶Then everyone left in your family line will come and bow down before him for a piece of silver and a crust of bread and plead, "Appoint me to some priestly office so I can have food to eat." ' "

The LORD Calls Samuel

3 The boy Samuel ministered before the LORD under Eli. In those days the word of the LORD was rare; there were not many visions.

²One night Eli, whose eyes were becoming so weak that he could barely see, was lying down in his usual place. ³The lamp of God had not yet gone out, and Samuel was lying down in the temple*ᵃ* of the LORD, where the ark of God was. ⁴Then the LORD called Samuel.

Samuel answered, "Here I am." ⁵And he ran to Eli and said, "Here I am; you called me."

But Eli said, "I did not call; go back and lie down." So he went and lay down.

⁶Again the LORD called, "Samuel!" And Samuel got up and went to Eli and said, "Here I am; you called me."

"My son," Eli said, "I did not call; go back and lie down."

⁷Now Samuel did not yet know the LORD: The word of the LORD had not yet been revealed to him.

⁸The LORD called Samuel a third time, and Samuel got up and went to Eli and said, "Here I am; you called me."

Then Eli realized that the LORD was calling the boy. ⁹So Eli told Samuel, "Go and lie down, and if he calls you, say, 'Speak, LORD, for your servant is listening.' " So Samuel went and lay down in his place.

¹⁰The LORD came and stood there, calling as at the other times, "Samuel! Samuel!"

Then Samuel said, "Speak, for your servant is listening."

¹¹And the LORD said to Samuel: "See, I am about to do something in Israel that will make the ears of everyone who hears of it tingle. ¹²At that time I will carry out against Eli everything I spoke against his family—from beginning to end. ¹³For I told him that I would judge his family forev-

ᵃ 3 That is, tabernacle

er because of the sin he knew about; his sons made themselves contemptible,[a] and he failed to restrain them. [14]Therefore, I swore to the house of Eli, 'The guilt of Eli's house will never be atoned for by sacrifice or offering.' "

[15]Samuel lay down until morning and then opened the doors of the house of the LORD. He was afraid to tell Eli the vision, [16]but Eli called him and said, "Samuel, my son."

Samuel answered, "Here I am."

[17]"What was it he said to you?" Eli asked. "Do not hide it from me. May God deal with you, be it ever so severely, if you hide from me anything he told you." [18]So Samuel told him everything, hiding nothing from him. Then Eli said, "He is the LORD; let him do what is good in his eyes."

[19]The LORD was with Samuel as he grew up, and he let none of his words fall to the ground. [20]And all Israel from Dan to Beersheba recognized that Samuel was attested as a prophet of the LORD. [21]The LORD continued to appear at Shiloh, and there he revealed himself to Samuel through his word.

4 And Samuel's word came to all Israel.

The Philistines Capture the Ark

Now the Israelites went out to fight against the Philistines. The Israelites camped at Ebenezer, and the Philistines at Aphek. [2]The Philistines deployed their forces to meet Israel, and as the battle spread, Israel was defeated by the Philistines, who killed about four thousand of them on the battlefield. [3]When the soldiers returned to camp, the elders of Israel asked, "Why did the LORD bring defeat upon us today before the Philistines? Let us bring the ark of the LORD's covenant from Shiloh, so that it[b] may go with us and save us from the hand of our enemies."

[4]So the people sent men to Shiloh, and they brought back the ark of the covenant of the LORD Almighty, who is enthroned between the cherubim. And Eli's two sons, Hophni and Phinehas, were there with the ark of the covenant of God.

[5]When the ark of the LORD's covenant came into the camp, all Israel raised such a great shout that the ground shook. [6]Hearing the uproar, the Philistines asked, "What's all this shouting in the Hebrew camp?"

When they learned that the ark of the LORD had come into the camp, [7]the Philistines were afraid. "A god has come into the camp," they said. "We're in trouble! Nothing like this has happened before. [8]Woe to us! Who will deliver us from the hand of these mighty gods? They are the gods who struck the Egyptians with all kinds of plagues in the desert. [9]Be strong, Philistines! Be men, or you will be subject to the Hebrews, as they have been to you. Be men, and fight!"

[10]So the Philistines fought, and the Israelites were defeated and every man fled to his tent. The slaughter was very great; Israel lost thirty thousand foot soldiers. [11]The ark of God was captured, and Eli's two sons, Hophni and Phinehas, died.

A God Too Small?

1 SAMUEL 4:3

In crisis, Israel turns to the ways they have known God in the past, fetching the neglected ark of the covenant to lead them into a battle. But the symbol of God's presence in the past cannot help them unless they have a living relationship with God in the present.

Sometimes our ideas about God grow more meaningful through the years while others restrict our faith. On paper, draw sketches of at least two ways you thought about God during your childhood and your teen years; or describe in writing how you perceived God during those years. Now sketch or describe some of the ways you have held God at a distance. Finally, draw or write about a way in which you can now let God's Spirit move recognizably in your life. Leave your Bible open until your next reading to signify that you do not want to limit God's presence in your life.

---

[a]13 Masoretic Text; an ancient Hebrew scribal tradition and Septuagint *sons blasphemed God*   [b]3 Or *he*

News of Loss

1 SAMUEL 4:21

How awful it is to be the one at home wondering about the safety of loved ones in wartime! Loss can strike unexpectedly at any moment. Old Eli, receiving the news that both his sons have perished and that the ark is captured, dies. His daughter-in-law, in grief, names his grandson Ichabod as she mourns the loss of the divine presence and the nation's glory.

In times of loss—of a loved one, a job, health, confidence, hope, even of a precious object—we might feel deep pain, perhaps perceiving our loss as abandonment by God. Bring to mind two or more such losses of the past; then acknowledge what pain may remain, and ask God now to help you deal with the hurt. Resolve to reach out within the next three days to someone who is struggling with a loss and try to listen to that person rather than advise him or her. Write down the name of that person now.

See Meeting God in Community

Death of Eli

12That same day a Benjamite ran from the battle line and went to Shiloh, his clothes torn and dust on his head. **13**When he arrived, there was Eli sitting on his chair by the side of the road, watching, because his heart feared for the ark of God. When the man entered the town and told what had happened, the whole town sent up a cry.

14Eli heard the outcry and asked, "What is the meaning of this uproar?"

The man hurried over to Eli, **15**who was ninety-eight years old and whose eyes were set so that he could not see. **16**He told Eli, "I have just come from the battle line; I fled from it this very day."

Eli asked, "What happened, my son?"

17The man who brought the news replied, "Israel fled before the Philistines, and the army has suffered heavy losses. Also your two sons, Hophni and Phinehas, are dead, and the ark of God has been captured."

18When he mentioned the ark of God, Eli fell backward off his chair by the side of the gate. His neck was broken and he died, for he was an old man and heavy. He had led*a* Israel forty years.

19His daughter-in-law, the wife of Phinehas, was pregnant and near the time of delivery. When she heard the news that the ark of God had been captured and that her father-in-law and her husband were dead, she went into labor and gave birth, but was overcome by her labor pains. **20**As she was dying, the women attending her said, "Don't despair; you have given birth to a son." But she did not respond or pay any attention.

21She named the boy Ichabod,*b* saying, "The glory has departed from Israel"—because of the capture of the ark of God and the deaths of her father-in-law and her husband. **22**She said, "The glory has departed from Israel, for the ark of God has been captured."

The Ark in Ashdod and Ekron

5 After the Philistines had captured the ark of God, they took it from Ebenezer to Ashdod. **2**Then they carried the ark into Dagon's temple and set it beside Dagon. **3**When the people of Ashdod rose early the next day, there was Dagon, fallen on his face on the ground before the ark of the LORD! They took Dagon and put him back in his place. **4**But the following morning when they rose, there was Dagon, fallen on his face on the ground before the ark of the LORD! His head and hands had been broken off and were lying on the threshold; only his body remained. **5**That is why to this day neither the priests of Dagon nor any others who enter Dagon's temple at Ashdod step on the threshold.

6The LORD's hand was heavy upon the people of Ashdod and its vicinity; he brought devastation upon them and afflicted them with tumors.*c* **7**When the men of Ashdod saw what was happening, they said, "The ark of the god of Israel must not stay here with us, because his hand is heavy upon us and upon Dagon our god." **8**So they called togeth-

a 18 Traditionally judged   b 21 Ichabod means no glory.   c 6 Hebrew; Septuagint and Vulgate tumors. And rats appeared in their land, and death and destruction were throughout the city

er all the rulers of the Philistines and asked them, "What shall we do with the ark of the god of Israel?"

They answered, "Have the ark of the god of Israel moved to Gath." So they moved the ark of the God of Israel.

⁹But after they had moved it, the LORD's hand was against that city, throwing it into a great panic. He afflicted the people of the city, both young and old, with an outbreak of tumors.ᵃ ¹⁰So they sent the ark of God to Ekron.

As the ark of God was entering Ekron, the people of Ekron cried out, "They have brought the ark of the god of Israel around to us to kill us and our people." ¹¹So they called together all the rulers of the Philistines and said, "Send the ark of the god of Israel away; let it go back to its own place, or itᵇ will kill us and our people." For death had filled the city with panic; God's hand was very heavy upon it. ¹²Those who did not die were afflicted with tumors, and the outcry of the city went up to heaven.

The Ark Returned to Israel

6 When the ark of the LORD had been in Philistine territory seven months, ²the Philistines called for the priests and the diviners and said, "What shall we do with the ark of the LORD? Tell us how we should send it back to its place."

³They answered, "If you return the ark of the god of Israel, do not send it away empty, but by all means send a guilt offering to him. Then you will be healed, and you will know why his hand has not been lifted from you."

⁴The Philistines asked, "What guilt offering should we send to him?"

They replied, "Five gold tumors and five gold rats, according to the number of the Philistine rulers, because the same plague has struck both you and your rulers. ⁵Make models of the tumors and of the rats that are destroying the country, and pay honor to Israel's god. Perhaps he will lift his hand from you and your gods and your land. ⁶Why do you harden your hearts as the Egyptians and Pharaoh did? When heᶜ treated them harshly, did they not send the Israelites out so they could go on their way?

⁷"Now then, get a new cart ready, with two cows that have calved and have never been yoked. Hitch the cows to the cart, but take their calves away and pen them up. ⁸Take the ark of the LORD and put it on the cart, and in a chest beside it put the gold objects you are sending back to him as a guilt offering. Send it on its way, ⁹but keep watching it. If it goes up to its own territory, toward Beth Shemesh, then the LORD has brought this great disaster on us. But if it does not, then we will know that it was not his hand that struck us and that it happened to us by chance."

¹⁰So they did this. They took two such cows and hitched them to the cart and penned up their calves. ¹¹They placed the ark of the LORD on the cart and along with it the chest containing the gold rats and the models of the tumors. ¹²Then the cows went straight up toward Beth Shemesh, keeping on the road and lowing all the way; they did not turn to the right or to the left. The rulers of the Philistines followed them as far as the border of Beth Shemesh.

¹³Now the people of Beth Shemesh were harvesting their wheat in the valley, and when they looked up and saw the

The Most Important Occasions

1 SAMUEL 5:8–9

Rather than return the ark empty, the Philistines place highly symbolic objects in a chest beside it. Mainly they intended to mollify the Israelites' God. But perhaps they also knew that such important events must be accompanied by something purely ceremonial. Even today, the life of the nation and the community is marked by times of ceremony: the Fourth of July, Thanksgiving Day, a presidential inauguration.

What celebrations do you observe? Which ones mean the most to you? What important events do you like to remember by planning something special? What moments in your journey of faith do you celebrate? Look back over your life and the life of your family and choose four or five of the most important events. Do you observe these events with some sort of ceremony? If not, perhaps with your closest family and friends, you can plan ways to remember the turning points in your life and the life of your family.

See *Meeting God in Everyday Life*

Water, Water

1 SAMUEL 7:6

As part of its ritual of repentance, Israel pours out water, the most common, essential, life-sustaining resource on earth. We can survive without food for weeks but without water for only a short while. How we regard and use water is representative of how we treat the gift of life itself.

Our water usually comes from faucets and bottle dispensers, but what would be the nearest natural source supplying your home if these modern systems failed? Enjoy the gift of water now, giving thanks in several ways. Hold up a glass filled with water and look through it at the sky. Taste the water, sipping it very slowly, as you continue your thanksgiving. Pour the water back and forth between two glasses, enjoying the sound. Pour out the water, perhaps over your hands and down your arms, recalling your baptism (or what you have been told about it). Ponder and repent of the ways you may squander water or use it without gratitude, then dedicate your hands to handle water gratefully.

See Meeting God in the Created Order

ark, they rejoiced at the sight. [14]The cart came to the field of Joshua of Beth Shemesh, and there it stopped beside a large rock. The people chopped up the wood of the cart and sacrificed the cows as a burnt offering to the LORD. [15]The Levites took down the ark of the LORD, together with the chest containing the gold objects, and placed them on the large rock. On that day the people of Beth Shemesh offered burnt offerings and made sacrifices to the LORD. [16]The five rulers of the Philistines saw all this and then returned that same day to Ekron.

[17]These are the gold tumors the Philistines sent as a guilt offering to the LORD—one each for Ashdod, Gaza, Ashkelon, Gath and Ekron. [18]And the number of the gold rats was according to the number of Philistine towns belonging to the five rulers—the fortified towns with their country villages. The large rock, on which[a] they set the ark of the LORD, is a witness to this day in the field of Joshua of Beth Shemesh.

[19]But God struck down some of the men of Beth Shemesh, putting seventy[b] of them to death because they had looked into the ark of the LORD. The people mourned because of the heavy blow the LORD had dealt them, [20]and the men of Beth Shemesh asked, "Who can stand in the presence of the LORD, this holy God? To whom will the ark go up from here?"

[21]Then they sent messengers to the people of Kiriath Jearim, saying, "The Philistines have returned the ark of the LORD. Come down and take it up to your place." 7 [1]So the men of Kiriath Jearim came and took up the ark of the LORD. They took it to Abinadab's house on the hill and consecrated Eleazar his son to guard the ark of the LORD.

Samuel Subdues the Philistines at Mizpah

[2]It was a long time, twenty years in all, that the ark remained at Kiriath Jearim, and all the people of Israel mourned and sought after the LORD. [3]And Samuel said to the whole house of Israel, "If you are returning to the LORD with all your hearts, then rid yourselves of the foreign gods and the Ashtoreths and commit yourselves to the LORD and serve him only, and he will deliver you out of the hand of the Philistines." [4]So the Israelites put away their Baals and Ashtoreths, and served the LORD only.

[5]Then Samuel said, "Assemble all Israel at Mizpah and I will intercede with the LORD for you." [6]When they had assembled at Mizpah, they drew water and poured it out before the LORD. On that day they fasted and there they confessed, "We have sinned against the LORD." And Samuel was leader[c] of Israel at Mizpah.

[7]When the Philistines heard that Israel had assembled at Mizpah, the rulers of the Philistines came up to attack them. And when the Israelites heard of it, they were afraid because of the Philistines. [8]They said to Samuel, "Do not stop crying out to the LORD our God for us, that he may rescue us from the hand of the Philistines." [9]Then Samuel took a suckling lamb and offered it up as a whole burnt offering

---

[a] 18 A few Hebrew manuscripts (see also Septuagint); most Hebrew manuscripts *villages as far as Greater Abel, where* [b] 19 A few Hebrew manuscripts; most Hebrew manuscripts and Septuagint *50,070* [c] 6 Traditionally *judge*

to the LORD. He cried out to the LORD on Israel's behalf, and the LORD answered him.

¹⁰While Samuel was sacrificing the burnt offering, the Philistines drew near to engage Israel in battle. But that day the LORD thundered with loud thunder against the Philistines and threw them into such a panic that they were routed before the Israelites. ¹¹The men of Israel rushed out of Mizpah and pursued the Philistines, slaughtering them along the way to a point below Beth Car.

¹²Then Samuel took a stone and set it up between Mizpah and Shen. He named it Ebenezer,ᵃ saying, "Thus far has the LORD helped us." ¹³So the Philistines were subdued and did not invade Israelite territory again.

Throughout Samuel's lifetime, the hand of the LORD was against the Philistines. ¹⁴The towns from Ekron to Gath that the Philistines had captured from Israel were restored to her, and Israel delivered the neighboring territory from the power of the Philistines. And there was peace between Israel and the Amorites.

¹⁵Samuel continued as judge over Israel all the days of his life. ¹⁶From year to year he went on a circuit from Bethel to Gilgal to Mizpah, judging Israel in all those places. ¹⁷But he always went back to Ramah, where his home was, and there he also judged Israel. And he built an altar there to the LORD.

Israel Asks for a King

8 When Samuel grew old, he appointed his sons as judges for Israel. ²The name of his firstborn was Joel and the name of his second was Abijah, and they served at Beersheba. ³But his sons did not walk in his ways. They turned aside after dishonest gain and accepted bribes and perverted justice.

⁴So all the elders of Israel gathered together and came to Samuel at Ramah. ⁵They said to him, "You are old, and your sons do not walk in your ways; now appoint a king to leadᵇ us, such as all the other nations have."

⁶But when they said, "Give us a king to lead us," this displeased Samuel; so he prayed to the LORD. ⁷And the LORD told him: "Listen to all that the people are saying to you; it is not you they have rejected, but they have rejected me as their king. ⁸As they have done from the day I brought them up out of Egypt until this day, forsaking me and serving other gods, so they are doing to you. ⁹Now listen to them; but warn them solemnly and let them know what the king who will reign over them will do."

¹⁰Samuel told all the words of the LORD to the people who were asking him for a king. ¹¹He said, "This is what the king who will reign over you will do: He will take your sons and make them serve with his chariots and horses, and they will run in front of his chariots. ¹²Some he will assign to be commanders of thousands and commanders of fifties, and others to plow his ground and reap his harvest, and still others to make weapons of war and equipment for his chariots. ¹³He will take your daughters to be perfumers and cooks and bakers. ¹⁴He will take the best of your fields and vineyards and olive groves and give them to his attendants. ¹⁵He will take a tenth of your grain and of your vintage and

---

O God, Help!

1 SAMUEL 7:2–17

"[Each service of daily prayer begins with] 'O God, make speed to save me: O Lord, make haste to help me' [see Psalm 40:13]. This verse has rightly been selected from the whole Bible for this purpose. It fits every mood and temper of human nature, every temptation, every circumstance. It contains an invocation of God, a humble confession of faith, a reverent watchfulness, a meditation upon our frailty, a confidence in God's answer, an assurance of ever-present support."

—JOHN CASSIAN,
Conference X on Prayer

See *Meeting God in Prayer*

ᵃ 12 *Ebenezer* means *stone of help.*   ᵇ 5 Traditionally *judge*; also in verses 6 and 20

Keeping Up With the Neighbors

1 SAMUEL 8:19–20

The Israelites shout, "We want a king," bypassing God as their promised leader, the only dependable source of certainty amidst hostile forces. The people's motives are clear: They covet the political securities their neighbors seem to enjoy. Their insistence takes precedence over God's ways. How like a basic human inclination: "I want to be true to myself and God's ways, but I don't want to miss out on the advantages others enjoy." What is it about the lives of those who may not follow God that makes you less willing to trust God's pattern for your life? In what ways are you willing to compromise your values to be like that other person, or to fit into another group? Can you trust God to guide you? Pray for assistance in following the path God has set before you.

See Meeting God in Everyday Life

give it to his officials and attendants. [16]Your menservants and maidservants and the best of your cattle[a] and donkeys he will take for his own use. [17]He will take a tenth of your flocks, and you yourselves will become his slaves. [18]When that day comes, you will cry out for relief from the king you have chosen, and the LORD will not answer you in that day."

[19]But the people refused to listen to Samuel. "No!" they said. "We want a king over us. [20]Then we will be like all the other nations, with a king to lead us and to go out before us and fight our battles."

[21]When Samuel heard all that the people said, he repeated it before the LORD. [22]The LORD answered, "Listen to them and give them a king."

Then Samuel said to the men of Israel, "Everyone go back to his town."

Samuel Anoints Saul

9 There was a Benjamite, a man of standing, whose name was Kish son of Abiel, the son of Zeror, the son of Becorath, the son of Aphiah of Benjamin. [2]He had a son named Saul, an impressive young man without equal among the Israelites—a head taller than any of the others.

[3]Now the donkeys belonging to Saul's father Kish were lost, and Kish said to his son Saul, "Take one of the servants with you and go and look for the donkeys." [4]So he passed through the hill country of Ephraim and through the area around Shalisha, but they did not find them. They went on into the district of Shaalim, but the donkeys were not there. Then he passed through the territory of Benjamin, but they did not find them.

[5]When they reached the district of Zuph, Saul said to the servant who was with him, "Come, let's go back, or my father will stop thinking about the donkeys and start worrying about us."

[6]But the servant replied, "Look, in this town there is a man of God; he is highly respected, and everything he says comes true. Let's go there now. Perhaps he will tell us what way to take."

[7]Saul said to his servant, "If we go, what can we give the man? The food in our sacks is gone. We have no gift to take to the man of God. What do we have?"

[8]The servant answered him again. "Look," he said, "I have a quarter of a shekel[b] of silver. I will give it to the man of God so that he will tell us what way to take." [9](Formerly in Israel, if a man went to inquire of God, he would say, "Come, let us go to the seer," because the prophet of today used to be called a seer.)

[10]"Good," Saul said to his servant. "Come, let's go." So they set out for the town where the man of God was.

[11]As they were going up the hill to the town, they met some girls coming out to draw water, and they asked them, "Is the seer here?"

[12]"He is," they answered. "He's ahead of you. Hurry now; he has just come to our town today, for the people have a sacrifice at the high place. [13]As soon as you enter the town, you will find him before he goes up to the high place to eat. The people will not begin eating until he comes, because he

[a] 16 Septuagint; Hebrew *young men*   [b] 8 That is, about 1/10 ounce (about 3 grams)

must bless the sacrifice; afterward, those who are invited will eat. Go up now; you should find him about this time."

¹⁴They went up to the town, and as they were entering it, there was Samuel, coming toward them on his way up to the high place.

¹⁵Now the day before Saul came, the LORD had revealed this to Samuel: ¹⁶"About this time tomorrow I will send you a man from the land of Benjamin. Anoint him leader over my people Israel; he will deliver my people from the hand of the Philistines. I have looked upon my people, for their cry has reached me."

¹⁷When Samuel caught sight of Saul, the LORD said to him, "This is the man I spoke to you about; he will govern my people."

¹⁸Saul approached Samuel in the gateway and asked, "Would you please tell me where the seer's house is?"

¹⁹"I am the seer," Samuel replied. "Go up ahead of me to the high place, for today you are to eat with me, and in the morning I will let you go and will tell you all that is in your heart. ²⁰As for the donkeys you lost three days ago, do not worry about them; they have been found. And to whom is all the desire of Israel turned, if not to you and all your father's family?"

²¹Saul answered, "But am I not a Benjamite, from the smallest tribe of Israel, and is not my clan the least of all the clans of the tribe of Benjamin? Why do you say such a thing to me?"

²²Then Samuel brought Saul and his servant into the hall and seated them at the head of those who were invited—about thirty in number. ²³Samuel said to the cook, "Bring the piece of meat I gave you, the one I told you to lay aside."

²⁴So the cook took up the leg with what was on it and set it in front of Saul. Samuel said, "Here is what has been kept for you. Eat, because it was set aside for you for this occasion, from the time I said, 'I have invited guests.' " And Saul dined with Samuel that day.

²⁵After they came down from the high place to the town, Samuel talked with Saul on the roof of his house. ²⁶They rose about daybreak and Samuel called to Saul on the roof, "Get ready, and I will send you on your way." When Saul got ready, he and Samuel went outside together. ²⁷As they were going down to the edge of the town, Samuel said to Saul, "Tell the servant to go on ahead of us"—and the servant did so—"but you stay here awhile, so that I may give you a message from God."

10 Then Samuel took a flask of oil and poured it on Saul's head and kissed him, saying, "Has not the LORD anointed you leader over his inheritance?ᵃ ²When you leave me today, you will meet two men near Rachel's tomb, at Zelzah on the border of Benjamin. They will say to you, 'The donkeys you set out to look for have been found. And now your father has stopped thinking about them and is worried about you. He is asking, "What shall I do about my son?" '

³"Then you will go on from there until you reach the

Sacred Meals

1 SAMUEL 9:11–14

Sacred meals such as the Sabbath dinner, Passover and the Eucharist play a large part in religious observance to this day. But making mealtime an opportunity for holiness is also something you can do in daily life.

Look at the room where you usually eat meals. In what way is it conducive to creating a sacred space for a sacred meal? What might you change or add? You may wish to add candles or a lamp to remind you of the inner light God imparts. A small picture, flowers, or a souvenir from a place which once brought you contentment also helps create a reflective and meaningful environment.

Prayer, heartfelt conversation, laughter, singing, and mindfulness at meals can all contribute to a sense of the sacred. Sharing a meal with others is a powerful reminder of community, but even dining alone can be an entryway to grace.

See Meeting God in Everyday Life

ᵃ 1 Hebrew; Septuagint and Vulgate *over his people Israel? You will reign over the* LORD's *people and save them from the power of their enemies round about. And this will be a sign to you that the* LORD *has anointed you leader over his inheritance:*

A Spiritual Overhaul

1 SAMUEL 10:6

Clever Samuel! He has already anointed Saul as the new king, yet he has made no public announcement. There is much political intrigue here, but the real life-changing act is God's, as Samuel prophesies: "The Spirit of the LORD will come upon you in power . . . , you will be changed into a different person."

How unsettling, that the person you know best will be changed! Can you trust God—really trust—if your life is significantly changed? Try taking a threefold inventory of the state of your soul: Very specifically, what do you think God would really like to change in you? What will you relinquish to make room for the change? What decision or action will you make at this moment to invite God to initiate the change?

See *Meeting God in Everyday Life*

great tree of Tabor. Three men going up to God at Bethel will meet you there. One will be carrying three young goats, another three loaves of bread, and another a skin of wine. ⁴They will greet you and offer you two loaves of bread, which you will accept from them.

⁵"After that you will go to Gibeah of God, where there is a Philistine outpost. As you approach the town, you will meet a procession of prophets coming down from the high place with lyres, tambourines, flutes and harps being played before them, and they will be prophesying. ⁶The Spirit of the LORD will come upon you in power, and you will prophesy with them; and you will be changed into a different person. ⁷Once these signs are fulfilled, do whatever your hand finds to do, for God is with you.

⁸"Go down ahead of me to Gilgal. I will surely come down to you to sacrifice burnt offerings and fellowship offerings,ᵃ but you must wait seven days until I come to you and tell you what you are to do."

Saul Made King

⁹As Saul turned to leave Samuel, God changed Saul's heart, and all these signs were fulfilled that day. ¹⁰When they arrived at Gibeah, a procession of prophets met him; the Spirit of God came upon him in power, and he joined in their prophesying. ¹¹When all those who had formerly known him saw him prophesying with the prophets, they asked each other, "What is this that has happened to the son of Kish? Is Saul also among the prophets?"

¹²A man who lived there answered, "And who is their father?" So it became a saying: "Is Saul also among the prophets?" ¹³After Saul stopped prophesying, he went to the high place.

¹⁴Now Saul's uncle asked him and his servant, "Where have you been?"

"Looking for the donkeys," he said. "But when we saw they were not to be found, we went to Samuel."

¹⁵Saul's uncle said, "Tell me what Samuel said to you."

¹⁶Saul replied, "He assured us that the donkeys had been found." But he did not tell his uncle what Samuel had said about the kingship.

¹⁷Samuel summoned the people of Israel to the LORD at Mizpah ¹⁸and said to them, "This is what the LORD, the God of Israel, says: 'I brought Israel up out of Egypt, and I delivered you from the power of Egypt and all the kingdoms that oppressed you.' ¹⁹But you have now rejected your God, who saves you out of all your calamities and distresses. And you have said, 'No, set a king over us.' So now present yourselves before the LORD by your tribes and clans."

²⁰When Samuel brought all the tribes of Israel near, the tribe of Benjamin was chosen. ²¹Then he brought forward the tribe of Benjamin, clan by clan, and Matri's clan was chosen. Finally Saul son of Kish was chosen. But when they looked for him, he was not to be found. ²²So they inquired further of the LORD, "Has the man come here yet?"

And the LORD said, "Yes, he has hidden himself among the baggage."

²³They ran and brought him out, and as he stood among the people he was a head taller than any of the others. ²⁴Samuel said to all the people, "Do you see the man the

ᵃ 8 Traditionally *peace offerings*

LORD has chosen? There is no one like him among all the people."

Then the people shouted, "Long live the king!"

²⁵Samuel explained to the people the regulations of the kingship. He wrote them down on a scroll and deposited it before the LORD. Then Samuel dismissed the people, each to his own home.

²⁶Saul also went to his home in Gibeah, accompanied by valiant men whose hearts God had touched. ²⁷But some troublemakers said, "How can this fellow save us?" They despised him and brought him no gifts. But Saul kept silent.

Saul Rescues the City of Jabesh

11 Nahash the Ammonite went up and besieged Jabesh Gilead. And all the men of Jabesh said to him, "Make a treaty with us, and we will be subject to you."

²But Nahash the Ammonite replied, "I will make a treaty with you only on the condition that I gouge out the right eye of every one of you and so bring disgrace on all Israel."

³The elders of Jabesh said to him, "Give us seven days so we can send messengers throughout Israel; if no one comes to rescue us, we will surrender to you."

⁴When the messengers came to Gibeah of Saul and reported these terms to the people, they all wept aloud. ⁵Just then Saul was returning from the fields, behind his oxen, and he asked, "What is wrong with the people? Why are they weeping?" Then they repeated to him what the men of Jabesh had said.

⁶When Saul heard their words, the Spirit of God came upon him in power, and he burned with anger. ⁷He took a pair of oxen, cut them into pieces, and sent the pieces by messengers throughout Israel, proclaiming, "This is what will be done to the oxen of anyone who does not follow Saul and Samuel." Then the terror of the LORD fell on the people, and they turned out as one man. ⁸When Saul mustered them at Bezek, the men of Israel numbered three hundred thousand and the men of Judah thirty thousand.

⁹They told the messengers who had come, "Say to the men of Jabesh Gilead, 'By the time the sun is hot tomorrow, you will be delivered.' " When the messengers went and reported this to the men of Jabesh, they were elated. ¹⁰They said to the Ammonites, "Tomorrow we will surrender to you, and you can do to us whatever seems good to you."

¹¹The next day Saul separated his men into three divisions; during the last watch of the night they broke into the camp of the Ammonites and slaughtered them until the heat of the day. Those who survived were scattered, so that no two of them were left together.

Saul Confirmed as King

¹²The people then said to Samuel, "Who was it that asked, 'Shall Saul reign over us?' Bring these men to us and we will put them to death."

¹³But Saul said, "No one shall be put to death today, for this day the LORD has rescued Israel."

¹⁴Then Samuel said to the people, "Come, let us go to Gilgal and there reaffirm the kingship." ¹⁵So all the people went to Gilgal and confirmed Saul as king in the presence of the LORD. There they sacrificed fellowship offerings[a] be-

---

a 15 Traditionally *peace offerings*

Fellowship Offerings

1 SAMUEL 11:15

Saul is on the throne as king. Even those who initially objected are convinced after a military victory won against high odds. (Affirmation seems to come easily after victories!) This time they are united in ratifying his kingship "in the presence of the LORD." They act out this renewal with a fellowship offering

(Another name for a ritual of acceptance is "fellowship offering.") You can make a "fellowship offering" today in a note to or in conversation with a friend, in which you express how important they are to you and how you value their friendship. If you plan to write a note, at least outline it now; if you plan to make a telephone call, at least write down the number and the time when you plan to call.

See Meeting God in Community

Stop Doing; Take Stock

1 SAMUEL 12:15–16

How often we hear, "Don't just stand there; do something!" In his farewell speech to his people, Samuel reverses the clauses: "Don't just keep doing; stand still, and pay attention." After sketching the history of the people, and warning of the risks of giving up God's primary guidance in exchange for a king who is an able warrior, Samuel calls rain down upon the very day of the wheat harvest. The people are stopped in their tracks, both literally and emotionally, and called to reflect on their relationship with God.

In silence, take stock of your relationship with God. Recall the times, if you can, when God caught your attention or changed the direction of your life. How did it happen? What means or circumstances did God use to catch your attention? How did you respond? Slowly? Right away? In what ways might God be calling you today to trust his guidance more completely?

See Meeting God in Everyday Life

fore the LORD, and Saul and all the Israelites held a great celebration.

Samuel's Farewell Speech

12 Samuel said to all Israel, "I have listened to everything you said to me and have set a king over you. ²Now you have a king as your leader. As for me, I am old and gray, and my sons are here with you. I have been your leader from my youth until this day. ³Here I stand. Testify against me in the presence of the LORD and his anointed. Whose ox have I taken? Whose donkey have I taken? Whom have I cheated? Whom have I oppressed? From whose hand have I accepted a bribe to make me shut my eyes? If I have done any of these, I will make it right."

⁴"You have not cheated or oppressed us," they replied. "You have not taken anything from anyone's hand."

⁵Samuel said to them, "The LORD is witness against you, and also his anointed is witness this day, that you have not found anything in my hand."

"He is witness," they said.

⁶Then Samuel said to the people, "It is the LORD who appointed Moses and Aaron and brought your forefathers up out of Egypt. ⁷Now then, stand here, because I am going to confront you with evidence before the LORD as to all the righteous acts performed by the LORD for you and your fathers.

⁸"After Jacob entered Egypt, they cried to the LORD for help, and the LORD sent Moses and Aaron, who brought your forefathers out of Egypt and settled them in this place.

⁹"But they forgot the LORD their God; so he sold them into the hand of Sisera, the commander of the army of Hazor, and into the hands of the Philistines and the king of Moab, who fought against them. ¹⁰They cried out to the LORD and said, 'We have sinned; we have forsaken the LORD and served the Baals and the Ashtoreths. But now deliver us from the hands of our enemies, and we will serve you.' ¹¹Then the LORD sent Jerub-Baal,ᵃ Barak,ᵇ Jephthah and Samuel,ᶜ and he delivered you from the hands of your enemies on every side, so that you lived securely.

¹²"But when you saw that Nahash king of the Ammonites was moving against you, you said to me, 'No, we want a king to rule over us'—even though the LORD your God was your king. ¹³Now here is the king you have chosen, the one you asked for; see, the LORD has set a king over you. ¹⁴If you fear the LORD and serve and obey him and do not rebel against his commands, and if both you and the king who reigns over you follow the LORD your God—good! ¹⁵But if you do not obey the LORD, and if you rebel against his commands, his hand will be against you, as it was against your fathers.

¹⁶"Now then, stand still and see this great thing the LORD is about to do before your eyes! ¹⁷Is it not wheat harvest now? I will call upon the LORD to send thunder and rain. And you will realize what an evil thing you did in the eyes of the LORD when you asked for a king."

¹⁸Then Samuel called upon the LORD, and that same day

ᵃ 11 Also called *Gideon*   ᵇ 11 Some Septuagint manuscripts and Syriac; Hebrew *Bedan*   ᶜ 11 Hebrew; some Septuagint manuscripts and Syriac *Samson*

the LORD sent thunder and rain. So all the people stood in awe of the LORD and of Samuel.

[19]The people all said to Samuel, "Pray to the LORD your God for your servants so that we will not die, for we have added to all our other sins the evil of asking for a king."

[20]"Do not be afraid," Samuel replied. "You have done all this evil; yet do not turn away from the LORD, but serve the LORD with all your heart. [21]Do not turn away after useless idols. They can do you no good, nor can they rescue you, because they are useless. [22]For the sake of his great name the LORD will not reject his people, because the LORD was pleased to make you his own. [23]As for me, far be it from me that I should sin against the LORD by failing to pray for you. And I will teach you the way that is good and right. [24]But be sure to fear the LORD and serve him faithfully with all your heart; consider what great things he has done for you. [25]Yet if you persist in doing evil, both you and your king will be swept away."

Samuel Rebukes Saul

13 Saul was ⌊thirty⌋[a] years old when he became king, and he reigned over Israel ⌊forty-⌋[b] two years.

[2]Saul[c] chose three thousand men from Israel; two thousand were with him at Micmash and in the hill country of Bethel, and a thousand were with Jonathan at Gibeah in Benjamin. The rest of the men he sent back to their homes.

[3]Jonathan attacked the Philistine outpost at Geba, and the Philistines heard about it. Then Saul had the trumpet blown throughout the land and said, "Let the Hebrews hear!" [4]So all Israel heard the news: "Saul has attacked the Philistine outpost, and now Israel has become a stench to the Philistines." And the people were summoned to join Saul at Gilgal.

[5]The Philistines assembled to fight Israel, with three thousand[d] chariots, six thousand charioteers, and soldiers as numerous as the sand on the seashore. They went up and camped at Micmash, east of Beth Aven. [6]When the men of Israel saw that their situation was critical and that their army was hard pressed, they hid in caves and thickets, among the rocks, and in pits and cisterns. [7]Some Hebrews even crossed the Jordan to the land of Gad and Gilead.

Saul remained at Gilgal, and all the troops with him were quaking with fear. [8]He waited seven days, the time set by Samuel; but Samuel did not come to Gilgal, and Saul's men began to scatter. [9]So he said, "Bring me the burnt offering and the fellowship offerings.[e]" And Saul offered up the burnt offering. [10]Just as he finished making the offering, Samuel arrived, and Saul went out to greet him.

[11]"What have you done?" asked Samuel.

Saul replied, "When I saw that the men were scattering, and that you did not come at the set time, and that the Philistines were assembling at Micmash, [12]I thought, 'Now the Philistines will come down against me at Gilgal, and I have

---

Halfway Is Not Wholehearted

1 SAMUEL 12:20

"Meister Eckhart wrote: 'There are plenty to follow our Lord half-way, but not the other half. They will give up possessions, friends and honors, but it touches them too closely to disown themselves.' It is just this astonishing life which is willing to follow Him the other half, sincerely to disown itself, this life which intends complete obedience, without any reservations, that I would propose to you in all humility, in all boldness, in all seriousness."

—THOMAS KELLY,
A Testament of Devotion

See Meeting God in Service

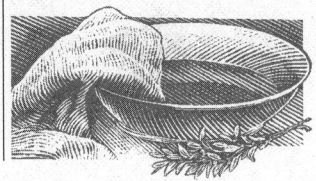

---

[a] *1* A few late manuscripts of the Septuagint; Hebrew does not have *thirty.*
[b] *1* See the round number in Acts 13:21; Hebrew does not have *forty-*.
[c] *1,2* Or *and when he had reigned over Israel two years,* [2]*he*   [d] *5* Some Septuagint manuscripts and Syriac; Hebrew *thirty thousand*
[e] *9* Traditionally *peace offerings*

Unarmed–but Prepared

1 SAMUEL 13:22

What a challenge for military leadership: The new warrior-king Saul has troops but no weapons with which to arm them! Yet God will give them victory.

Recall a time when you felt totally unprepared for an important meeting or duty, yet things turned out because something intervened: a sudden inspiration, a coincidence, a lead from an understanding person who helped you. Consider how this unexpected help equipped you for your task. In what ways did it represent God-given strength or ability? Take time now to thank God for a specific instance when divine help made the difference.

not sought the LORD's favor.' So I felt compelled to offer the burnt offering."

¹³"You acted foolishly," Samuel said. "You have not kept the command the LORD your God gave you; if you had, he would have established your kingdom over Israel for all time. ¹⁴But now your kingdom will not endure; the LORD has sought out a man after his own heart and appointed him leader of his people, because you have not kept the LORD's command."

¹⁵Then Samuel left Gilgal[a] and went up to Gibeah in Benjamin, and Saul counted the men who were with him. They numbered about six hundred.

Israel Without Weapons

¹⁶Saul and his son Jonathan and the men with them were staying in Gibeah[b] in Benjamin, while the Philistines camped at Micmash. ¹⁷Raiding parties went out from the Philistine camp in three detachments. One turned toward Ophrah in the vicinity of Shual, ¹⁸another toward Beth Horon, and the third toward the borderland overlooking the Valley of Zeboim facing the desert.

¹⁹Not a blacksmith could be found in the whole land of Israel, because the Philistines had said, "Otherwise the Hebrews will make swords or spears!" ²⁰So all Israel went down to the Philistines to have their plowshares, mattocks, axes and sickles[c] sharpened. ²¹The price was two thirds of a shekel[d] for sharpening plowshares and mattocks, and a third of a shekel[e] for sharpening forks and axes and for re-pointing goads.

²²So on the day of the battle not a soldier with Saul and Jonathan had a sword or spear in his hand; only Saul and his son Jonathan had them.

Jonathan Attacks the Philistines

²³Now a detachment of Philistines had gone out to the pass at Micmash. ¹One day Jonathan son of Saul said to the young man bearing his armor, "Come, let's go over to the Philistine outpost on the other side." But he did not tell his father.

²Saul was staying on the outskirts of Gibeah under a pomegranate tree in Migron. With him were about six hundred men, ³among whom was Ahijah, who was wearing an ephod. He was a son of Ichabod's brother Ahitub son of Phinehas, the son of Eli, the LORD's priest in Shiloh. No one was aware that Jonathan had left.

⁴On each side of the pass that Jonathan intended to cross to reach the Philistine outpost was a cliff; one was called Bozez, and the other Seneh. ⁵One cliff stood to the north toward Micmash, the other to the south toward Geba.

⁶Jonathan said to his young armor-bearer, "Come, let's go over to the outpost of those uncircumcised fellows. Perhaps the LORD will act in our behalf. Nothing can hinder the LORD from saving, whether by many or by few."

⁷"Do all that you have in mind," his armor-bearer said. "Go ahead; I am with you heart and soul."

⁸Jonathan said, "Come, then; we will cross over toward

---

a 15 Hebrew; Septuagint *Gilgal and went his way; the rest of the people went after Saul to meet the army, and they went out of Gilgal*   *b 16* Two Hebrew manuscripts; most Hebrew manuscripts *Geba,* a variant of *Gibeah*
c 20 Septuagint; Hebrew *plowshares*   *d 21* Hebrew *pim;* that is, about 1/4 ounce (about 8 grams)   *e 21* That is, about 1/8 ounce (about 4 grams)

the men and let them see us. [9]If they say to us, 'Wait there until we come to you,' we will stay where we are and not go up to them. [10]But if they say, 'Come up to us,' we will climb up, because that will be our sign that the LORD has given them into our hands."

[11]So both of them showed themselves to the Philistine outpost. "Look!" said the Philistines. "The Hebrews are crawling out of the holes they were hiding in." [12]The men of the outpost shouted to Jonathan and his armor-bearer, "Come up to us and we'll teach you a lesson."

So Jonathan said to his armor-bearer, "Climb up after me; the LORD has given them into the hand of Israel."

[13]Jonathan climbed up, using his hands and feet, with his armor-bearer right behind him. The Philistines fell before Jonathan, and his armor-bearer followed and killed behind him. [14]In that first attack Jonathan and his armor-bearer killed some twenty men in an area of about half an acre.[a]

Israel Routs the Philistines

[15]Then panic struck the whole army—those in the camp and field, and those in the outposts and raiding parties—and the ground shook. It was a panic sent by God.[b]

[16]Saul's lookouts at Gibeah in Benjamin saw the army melting away in all directions. [17]Then Saul said to the men who were with him, "Muster the forces and see who has left us." When they did, it was Jonathan and his armor-bearer who were not there.

[18]Saul said to Ahijah, "Bring the ark of God." (At that time it was with the Israelites.)[c] [19]While Saul was talking to the priest, the tumult in the Philistine camp increased more and more. So Saul said to the priest, "Withdraw your hand."

[20]Then Saul and all his men assembled and went to the battle. They found the Philistines in total confusion, striking each other with their swords. [21]Those Hebrews who had previously been with the Philistines and had gone up with them to their camp went over to the Israelites who were with Saul and Jonathan. [22]When all the Israelites who had hidden in the hill country of Ephraim heard that the Philistines were on the run, they joined the battle in hot pursuit. [23]So the LORD rescued Israel that day, and the battle moved on beyond Beth Aven.

Jonathan Eats Honey

[24]Now the men of Israel were in distress that day, because Saul had bound the people under an oath, saying, "Cursed be any man who eats food before evening comes, before I have avenged myself on my enemies!" So none of the troops tasted food.

[25]The entire army[d] entered the woods, and there was honey on the ground. [26]When they went into the woods, they saw the honey oozing out, yet no one put his hand to his mouth, because they feared the oath. [27]But Jonathan had not heard that his father had bound the people with the oath, so he reached out the end of the staff that was in his hand and dipped it into the honeycomb. He raised his hand to his mouth, and his eyes brightened.[e] [28]Then one of

---

Heroism or Imprudence?

> 1 SAMUEL 14:8–14

Visualize Jonathan and his armor-bearer as they struggle up a very steep ascent, exposing themselves to great risk yet dispatching many enemies in the process. For a similar accomplishment today they might well be awarded Medals of Honor!

Take five minutes to reflect on these verses. Listen for a word or short phrase that attracts you and repeat it silently ten or more times. Imagine yourself in the scene and dwell there for a minute or more. How does what you experience or feel relate to your life? For the next two or three days, listen for an invitation from God as revealed through that word or phrase.

See Meeting God in Scripture

---

[a] 14 Hebrew *half a yoke*; a "yoke" was the land plowed by a yoke of oxen in one day.   [b] 15 Or *a terrible panic*   [c] 18 Hebrew; Septuagint *"Bring the ephod." (At that time he wore the ephod before the Israelites.)*   [d] 25 Or *Now all the people of the land*   [e] 27 Or *his strength was renewed*

Rescued by the Crowd

1 SAMUEL 14:45

A crowd challenges the king about what they consider the unfair treatment of Jonathan, who is threatened with death because he did something he didn't know was banned. Their argument is not simply that Jonathan has delivered them from defeat, but that he did so with God's help.

Recall a time when you defended someone unjustly accused. Or remember a time when you joined, or wanted to join, a group protest against what you considered to be an injustice upheld by law or custom. What led you to take this stand? How did it feel to behave counter to prevailing opinion or law? How much of your action was prompted by a sense of God's call? Ask God for courage to stand firm when justice requires it.

See Meeting God in Community

the soldiers told him, "Your father bound the army under a strict oath, saying, 'Cursed be any man who eats food today!' That is why the men are faint."

²⁹Jonathan said, "My father has made trouble for the country. See how my eyes brightened*a* when I tasted a little of this honey. ³⁰How much better it would have been if the men had eaten today some of the plunder they took from their enemies. Would not the slaughter of the Philistines have been even greater?"

³¹That day, after the Israelites had struck down the Philistines from Micmash to Aijalon, they were exhausted. ³²They pounced on the plunder and, taking sheep, cattle and calves, they butchered them on the ground and ate them, together with the blood. ³³Then someone said to Saul, "Look, the men are sinning against the LORD by eating meat that has blood in it."

"You have broken faith," he said. "Roll a large stone over here at once." ³⁴Then he said, "Go out among the men and tell them, 'Each of you bring me your cattle and sheep, and slaughter them here and eat them. Do not sin against the LORD by eating meat with blood still in it.'"

So everyone brought his ox that night and slaughtered it there. ³⁵Then Saul built an altar to the LORD; it was the first time he had done this.

³⁶Saul said, "Let us go down after the Philistines by night and plunder them till dawn, and let us not leave one of them alive."

"Do whatever seems best to you," they replied.

But the priest said, "Let us inquire of God here."

³⁷So Saul asked God, "Shall I go down after the Philistines? Will you give them into Israel's hand?" But God did not answer him that day.

³⁸Saul therefore said, "Come here, all you who are leaders of the army, and let us find out what sin has been committed today. ³⁹As surely as the LORD who rescues Israel lives, even if it lies with my son Jonathan, he must die." But not one of the men said a word.

⁴⁰Saul then said to all the Israelites, "You stand over there; I and Jonathan my son will stand over here."

"Do what seems best to you," the men replied.

⁴¹Then Saul prayed to the LORD, the God of Israel, "Give me the right answer."*b* And Jonathan and Saul were taken by lot, and the men were cleared. ⁴²Saul said, "Cast the lot between me and Jonathan my son." And Jonathan was taken.

⁴³Then Saul said to Jonathan, "Tell me what you have done."

So Jonathan told him, "I merely tasted a little honey with the end of my staff. And now must I die?"

⁴⁴Saul said, "May God deal with me, be it ever so severely, if you do not die, Jonathan."

⁴⁵But the men said to Saul, "Should Jonathan die—he who has brought about this great deliverance in Israel? Never! As surely as the LORD lives, not a hair of his head will fall to the ground, for he did this today with God's help." So the men rescued Jonathan, and he was not put to death.

a 29 Or *my strength was renewed*   *b 41* Hebrew; Septuagint *"Why have you not answered your servant today? If the fault is in me or my son Jonathan, respond with Urim, but if the men of Israel are at fault, respond with Thummim."*

46Then Saul stopped pursuing the Philistines, and they withdrew to their own land.

47After Saul had assumed rule over Israel, he fought against their enemies on every side: Moab, the Ammonites, Edom, the kings[a] of Zobah, and the Philistines. Wherever he turned, he inflicted punishment on them.[b] **48**He fought valiantly and defeated the Amalekites, delivering Israel from the hands of those who had plundered them.

Saul's Family

49Saul's sons were Jonathan, Ishvi and Malki-Shua. The name of his older daughter was Merab, and that of the younger was Michal. **50**His wife's name was Ahinoam daughter of Ahimaaz. The name of the commander of Saul's army was Abner son of Ner, and Ner was Saul's uncle. **51**Saul's father Kish and Abner's father Ner were sons of Abiel.

52All the days of Saul there was bitter war with the Philistines, and whenever Saul saw a mighty or brave man, he took him into his service.

The LORD Rejects Saul as King

15 Samuel said to Saul, "I am the one the LORD sent to anoint you king over his people Israel; so listen now to the message from the LORD. **2**This is what the LORD Almighty says: 'I will punish the Amalekites for what they did to Israel when they waylaid them as they came up from Egypt. **3**Now go, attack the Amalekites and totally destroy[c] everything that belongs to them. Do not spare them; put to death men and women, children and infants, cattle and sheep, camels and donkeys.' "

4So Saul summoned the men and mustered them at Telaim—two hundred thousand foot soldiers and ten thousand men from Judah. **5**Saul went to the city of Amalek and set an ambush in the ravine. **6**Then he said to the Kenites, "Go away, leave the Amalekites so that I do not destroy you along with them; for you showed kindness to all the Israelites when they came up out of Egypt." So the Kenites moved away from the Amalekites.

7Then Saul attacked the Amalekites all the way from Havilah to Shur, to the east of Egypt. **8**He took Agag king of the Amalekites alive, and all his people he totally destroyed with the sword. **9**But Saul and the army spared Agag and the best of the sheep and cattle, the fat calves[d] and lambs—everything that was good. These they were unwilling to destroy completely, but everything that was despised and weak they totally destroyed.

10Then the word of the LORD came to Samuel: **11**"I am grieved that I have made Saul king, because he has turned away from me and has not carried out my instructions." Samuel was troubled, and he cried out to the LORD all that night.

12Early in the morning Samuel got up and went to meet Saul, but he was told, "Saul has gone to Carmel. There he has set up a monument in his own honor and has turned and gone on down to Gilgal."

Recruiting for the Lord's Service

1 SAMUEL 14:52

"If a person would gain spiritual freedom and not be continually troubled, let him begin by not being afraid of the Cross and he will find that the Lord will help him to bear it; he will then advance happily and find profit in everything. It is now clear that, if no water is coming from the well, we ourselves can put none into it. But of course we must not be careless: water must always be drawn when there is any there, for at such a time God's will is that we should use it so that He may multiply our virtues."

—TERESA OF AVILA,
The Life of Teresa of Jesus

See *Meeting God in Service*

---

a 47 Masoretic Text; Dead Sea Scrolls and Septuagint *king*   *b 47* Hebrew; Septuagint *he was victorious*   *c 3* The Hebrew term refers to the irrevocable giving over of things or persons to the LORD, often by totally destroying them; also in verses 8, 9, 15, 18, 20 and 21.   *d 9* Or *the grown bulls*; the meaning of the Hebrew for this phrase is uncertain.

Holding and Releasing

1 SAMUEL 15:24–27

Like Saul, hunger for acceptance by others can weaken our resolve to "[speak] the truth in love (Ephesians 4:15)." It can even lead us to compromise our standards.

Consider ways in which you may be hesitating to speak honestly to someone involved in destructive behavior because you fear their response—or lack of response. As you pray about the matter, grip tightly some part of your clothing as a symbol of any insistence on your part to control or change the other person. Signify letting go of your need for control by releasing your garment. Commend that person to God's life-changing power. Prayerfully consider how to wait for receptivity in that person, and how to speak to him or her.

See Meeting God in Community

[13] When Samuel reached him, Saul said, "The LORD bless you! I have carried out the LORD's instructions."

[14] But Samuel said, "What then is this bleating of sheep in my ears? What is this lowing of cattle that I hear?"

[15] Saul answered, "The soldiers brought them from the Amalekites; they spared the best of the sheep and cattle to sacrifice to the LORD your God, but we totally destroyed the rest."

[16] "Stop!" Samuel said to Saul. "Let me tell you what the LORD said to me last night."

"Tell me," Saul replied.

[17] Samuel said, "Although you were once small in your own eyes, did you not become the head of the tribes of Israel? The LORD anointed you king over Israel. [18] And he sent you on a mission, saying, 'Go and completely destroy those wicked people, the Amalekites; make war on them until you have wiped them out.' [19] Why did you not obey the LORD? Why did you pounce on the plunder and do evil in the eyes of the LORD?"

[20] "But I did obey the LORD," Saul said. "I went on the mission the LORD assigned me. I completely destroyed the Amalekites and brought back Agag their king. [21] The soldiers took sheep and cattle from the plunder, the best of what was devoted to God, in order to sacrifice them to the LORD your God at Gilgal."

[22] But Samuel replied:

"Does the LORD delight in burnt offerings and
        sacrifices
    as much as in obeying the voice of the LORD?
To obey is better than sacrifice,
    and to heed is better than the fat of rams.
[23] For rebellion is like the sin of divination,
    and arrogance like the evil of idolatry.
Because you have rejected the word of the LORD,
    he has rejected you as king."

[24] Then Saul said to Samuel, "I have sinned. I violated the LORD's command and your instructions. I was afraid of the people and so I gave in to them. [25] Now I beg you, forgive my sin and come back with me, so that I may worship the LORD."

[26] But Samuel said to him, "I will not go back with you. You have rejected the word of the LORD, and the LORD has rejected you as king over Israel!"

[27] As Samuel turned to leave, Saul caught hold of the hem of his robe, and it tore. [28] Samuel said to him, "The LORD has torn the kingdom of Israel from you today and has given it to one of your neighbors—to one better than you. [29] He who is the Glory of Israel does not lie or change his mind; for he is not a man, that he should change his mind."

[30] Saul replied, "I have sinned. But please honor me before the elders of my people and before Israel; come back with me, so that I may worship the LORD your God." [31] So Samuel went back with Saul, and Saul worshiped the LORD.

[32] Then Samuel said, "Bring me Agag king of the Amalekites."

Agag came to him confidently,[a] thinking, "Surely the bitterness of death is past."

[33] But Samuel said,

a 32 Or *him trembling, yet*

"As your sword has made women childless,
so will your mother be childless among
women."

And Samuel put Agag to death before the Lord at Gilgal.

³⁴Then Samuel left for Ramah, but Saul went up to his home in Gibeah of Saul. ³⁵Until the day Samuel died, he did not go to see Saul again, though Samuel mourned for him. And the Lord was grieved that he had made Saul king over Israel.

Samuel Anoints David

16 The Lord said to Samuel, "How long will you mourn for Saul, since I have rejected him as king over Israel? Fill your horn with oil and be on your way; I am sending you to Jesse of Bethlehem. I have chosen one of his sons to be king."

²But Samuel said, "How can I go? Saul will hear about it and kill me."

The Lord said, "Take a heifer with you and say, 'I have come to sacrifice to the Lord.' ³Invite Jesse to the sacrifice, and I will show you what to do. You are to anoint for me the one I indicate."

⁴Samuel did what the Lord said. When he arrived at Bethlehem, the elders of the town trembled when they met him. They asked, "Do you come in peace?"

⁵Samuel replied, "Yes, in peace; I have come to sacrifice to the Lord. Consecrate yourselves and come to the sacrifice with me." Then he consecrated Jesse and his sons and invited them to the sacrifice.

⁶When they arrived, Samuel saw Eliab and thought, "Surely the Lord's anointed stands here before the Lord."

⁷But the Lord said to Samuel, "Do not consider his appearance or his height, for I have rejected him. The Lord does not look at the things man looks at. Man looks at the outward appearance, but the Lord looks at the heart."

⁸Then Jesse called Abinadab and had him pass in front of Samuel. But Samuel said, "The Lord has not chosen this one either." ⁹Jesse then had Shammah pass by, but Samuel said, "Nor has the Lord chosen this one." ¹⁰Jesse had seven of his sons pass before Samuel, but Samuel said to him, "The Lord has not chosen these." ¹¹So he asked Jesse, "Are these all the sons you have?"

"There is still the youngest," Jesse answered, "but he is tending the sheep."

Samuel said, "Send for him; we will not sit down*ᵃ* until he arrives."

¹²So he sent and had him brought in. He was ruddy, with a fine appearance and handsome features.

Then the Lord said, "Rise and anoint him; he is the one."

¹³So Samuel took the horn of oil and anointed him in the presence of his brothers, and from that day on the Spirit of the Lord came upon David in power. Samuel then went to Ramah.

David in Saul's Service

¹⁴Now the Spirit of the Lord had departed from Saul, and an evil*ᵇ* spirit from the Lord tormented him.

Looking at the Heart

1 SAMUEL 16:7

Samuel has warned Saul (see 13:13–14) that the Lord will remove him as king in favor of one "after [the Lord's] own heart." Samuel is guided by the Lord in his search for the new king, learning that "man looks at the outward appearance, but the Lord looks at the heart," the core of one's being.

Recall a time when your evaluation of a person's character or suitability for service relied mainly on outward appearance. Did this prove to be misleading or cause problems later? Consider now how God can help you look at people rightly, as the Lord sees them. Pray about a relationship with someone in which having new eyes might make all the difference.

See Meeting God in Service

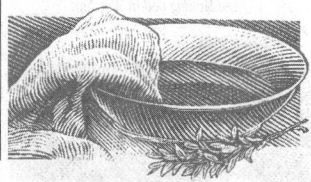

ᵃ 11 Some Septuagint manuscripts; Hebrew *not gather around*
ᵇ 14 Or *injurious*; also in verses 15, 16 and 23

Sweet Music

1 SAMUEL 16:23

Shakespeare often gets the credit, but William Congreve actually wrote the words: "Music has charms to soothe a savage breast, to soften rocks, or bend a knotted oak." When Saul is beset by an evil spirit, David's music brings him tenderness and peace.

What music soothes your "savage breast"? What hymns or sacred songs draw you toward a calm and peaceful trust in God? Sing such a hymn to yourself, or turn on background music as you read or reread this passage. What phrases or Bible verses deepen your trust in God's peace-giving power? Recite prayerfully a phrase or Bible verse, either on a single note or in a simple melody, as music of praise from your heart.

See *Meeting God in Worship*

¹⁵Saul's attendants said to him, "See, an evil spirit from God is tormenting you. ¹⁶Let our lord command his servants here to search for someone who can play the harp. He will play when the evil spirit from God comes upon you, and you will feel better."

¹⁷So Saul said to his attendants, "Find someone who plays well and bring him to me."

¹⁸One of the servants answered, "I have seen a son of Jesse of Bethlehem who knows how to play the harp. He is a brave man and a warrior. He speaks well and is a fine-looking man. And the Lord is with him."

¹⁹Then Saul sent messengers to Jesse and said, "Send me your son David, who is with the sheep." ²⁰So Jesse took a donkey loaded with bread, a skin of wine and a young goat and sent them with his son David to Saul.

²¹David came to Saul and entered his service. Saul liked him very much, and David became one of his armor-bearers. ²²Then Saul sent word to Jesse, saying, "Allow David to remain in my service, for I am pleased with him."

²³Whenever the spirit from God came upon Saul, David would take his harp and play. Then relief would come to Saul; he would feel better, and the evil spirit would leave him.

David and Goliath

17 Now the Philistines gathered their forces for war and assembled at Socoh in Judah. They pitched camp at Ephes Dammim, between Socoh and Azekah. ²Saul and the Israelites assembled and camped in the Valley of Elah and drew up their battle line to meet the Philistines. ³The Philistines occupied one hill and the Israelites another, with the valley between them.

⁴A champion named Goliath, who was from Gath, came out of the Philistine camp. He was over nine feet^a tall. ⁵He had a bronze helmet on his head and wore a coat of scale armor of bronze weighing five thousand shekels^b; ⁶on his legs he wore bronze greaves, and a bronze javelin was slung on his back. ⁷His spear shaft was like a weaver's rod, and its iron point weighed six hundred shekels.^c His shield bearer went ahead of him.

⁸Goliath stood and shouted to the ranks of Israel, "Why do you come out and line up for battle? Am I not a Philistine, and are you not the servants of Saul? Choose a man and have him come down to me. ⁹If he is able to fight and kill me, we will become your subjects; but if I overcome him and kill him, you will become our subjects and serve us." ¹⁰Then the Philistine said, "This day I defy the ranks of Israel! Give me a man and let us fight each other." ¹¹On hearing the Philistine's words, Saul and all the Israelites were dismayed and terrified.

¹²Now David was the son of an Ephrathite named Jesse, who was from Bethlehem in Judah. Jesse had eight sons, and in Saul's time he was old and well advanced in years. ¹³Jesse's three oldest sons had followed Saul to the war: The firstborn was Eliab; the second, Abinadab; and the third, Shammah. ¹⁴David was the youngest. The three oldest fol-

---

^a4 Hebrew *was six cubits and a span* (about 3 meters)   ^b5 That is, about 125 pounds (about 57 kilograms)   ^c7 That is, about 15 pounds (about 7 kilograms)

lowed Saul, ¹⁵but David went back and forth from Saul to tend his father's sheep at Bethlehem.

¹⁶For forty days the Philistine came forward every morning and evening and took his stand.

¹⁷Now Jesse said to his son David, "Take this ephah*ᵃ* of roasted grain and these ten loaves of bread for your brothers and hurry to their camp. ¹⁸Take along these ten cheeses to the commander of their unit.*ᵇ* See how your brothers are and bring back some assurance*ᶜ* from them. ¹⁹They are with Saul and all the men of Israel in the Valley of Elah, fighting against the Philistines."

²⁰Early in the morning David left the flock with a shepherd, loaded up and set out, as Jesse had directed. He reached the camp as the army was going out to its battle positions, shouting the war cry. ²¹Israel and the Philistines were drawing up their lines facing each other. ²²David left his things with the keeper of supplies, ran to the battle lines and greeted his brothers. ²³As he was talking with them, Goliath, the Philistine champion from Gath, stepped out from his lines and shouted his usual defiance, and David heard it. ²⁴When the Israelites saw the man, they all ran from him in great fear.

²⁵Now the Israelites had been saying, "Do you see how this man keeps coming out? He comes out to defy Israel. The king will give great wealth to the man who kills him. He will also give him his daughter in marriage and will exempt his father's family from taxes in Israel."

²⁶David asked the men standing near him, "What will be done for the man who kills this Philistine and removes this disgrace from Israel? Who is this uncircumcised Philistine that he should defy the armies of the living God?"

²⁷They repeated to him what they had been saying and told him, "This is what will be done for the man who kills him."

²⁸When Eliab, David's oldest brother, heard him speaking with the men, he burned with anger at him and asked, "Why have you come down here? And with whom did you leave those few sheep in the desert? I know how conceited you are and how wicked your heart is; you came down only to watch the battle."

²⁹"Now what have I done?" said David. "Can't I even speak?" ³⁰He then turned away to someone else and brought up the same matter, and the men answered him as before. ³¹What David said was overheard and reported to Saul, and Saul sent for him.

³²David said to Saul, "Let no one lose heart on account of this Philistine; your servant will go and fight him."

³³Saul replied, "You are not able to go out against this Philistine and fight him; you are only a boy, and he has been a fighting man from his youth."

³⁴But David said to Saul, "Your servant has been keeping his father's sheep. When a lion or a bear came and carried off a sheep from the flock, ³⁵I went after it, struck it and rescued the sheep from its mouth. When it turned on me, I seized it by its hair, struck it and killed it. ³⁶Your servant has killed both the lion and the bear; this uncircumcised Philistine will be like one of them, because he has defied the armies of the living God. ³⁷The LORD who delivered me

God's Plans

1 SAMUEL 17:17–37

This well-known passage describes the most significant turning point in young David's life. Imagine that you are David, given a perfectly ordinary task by your father. Think of the long—and perhaps monotonous—walk to the battlefront. When you arrive, you sense the tension in the air. You smell campfires all around you, hear the sounds of an army, see soldiers everywhere. When you ask a few questions, your brothers tell you about Goliath and his challenge; you hear fear in everyone's voice. You feel the weight of adult armor and know you can hardly move under it. You feel small and weak.

Suddenly you know that God intends for you to take the lead and confront the Philistine giant. Despite all evidence to the contrary, you still are certain that God has work for you to do in this situation.

In your own life today, pray that God will allow you this same certainty of divine guidance when you need it, even in the most unlikely of situations.

See Meeting God in Service

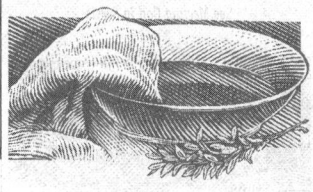

ᵃ 17 That is, probably about 3/5 bushel (about 22 liters)   *ᵇ 18* Hebrew *thousand*   *ᶜ 18* Or *some token*; or *some pledge of spoils*

369

One Smooth Stone Is Enough

1 SAMUEL 17:49

One small stone doesn't seem potent enough to slay a giant, but David's aim is good, and the sling sends the missile at high velocity. Just as a knife with the sharpest possible edge cuts best, the smallest stone, with all of David's prayer-driven energy behind it—sinks into the body of the Philistines' strongest champion.

Take a moment now to think about your weaknesses—not your sins, but those areas in your life where you may not be especially gifted. Perhaps you don't speak well in public (like Moses) or you suffer some physical affliction (like Paul). Think of areas in your life where you feel inadequate. Read 2 Corinthians 12:7–9 where God says to Paul: "My grace is sufficient for you, for my power is made perfect in weakness." If it helps, write down the list of weaknesses. Read each one and try to imagine how the power of God can shine through, not merely *despite* that weakness but *because* of it. Offer those weaknesses to God. Ask God to use your weaknesses as well as your strengths.

See Meeting God in Service

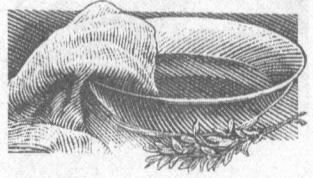

from the paw of the lion and the paw of the bear will deliver me from the hand of this Philistine."

Saul said to David, "Go, and the LORD be with you."

³⁸Then Saul dressed David in his own tunic. He put a coat of armor on him and a bronze helmet on his head. ³⁹David fastened on his sword over the tunic and tried walking around, because he was not used to them.

"I cannot go in these," he said to Saul, "because I am not used to them." So he took them off. ⁴⁰Then he took his staff in his hand, chose five smooth stones from the stream, put them in the pouch of his shepherd's bag and, with his sling in his hand, approached the Philistine.

⁴¹Meanwhile, the Philistine, with his shield bearer in front of him, kept coming closer to David. ⁴²He looked David over and saw that he was only a boy, ruddy and handsome, and he despised him. ⁴³He said to David, "Am I a dog, that you come at me with sticks?" And the Philistine cursed David by his gods. ⁴⁴"Come here," he said, "and I'll give your flesh to the birds of the air and the beasts of the field!"

⁴⁵David said to the Philistine, "You come against me with sword and spear and javelin, but I come against you in the name of the LORD Almighty, the God of the armies of Israel, whom you have defied. ⁴⁶This day the LORD will hand you over to me, and I'll strike you down and cut off your head. Today I will give the carcasses of the Philistine army to the birds of the air and the beasts of the earth, and the whole world will know that there is a God in Israel. ⁴⁷All those gathered here will know that it is not by sword or spear that the LORD saves; for the battle is the LORD's, and he will give all of you into our hands."

⁴⁸As the Philistine moved closer to attack him, David ran quickly toward the battle line to meet him. ⁴⁹Reaching into his bag and taking out a stone, he slung it and struck the Philistine on the forehead. The stone sank into his forehead, and he fell facedown on the ground.

⁵⁰So David triumphed over the Philistine with a sling and a stone; without a sword in his hand he struck down the Philistine and killed him.

⁵¹David ran and stood over him. He took hold of the Philistine's sword and drew it from the scabbard. After he killed him, he cut off his head with the sword.

When the Philistines saw that their hero was dead, they turned and ran. ⁵²Then the men of Israel and Judah surged forward with a shout and pursued the Philistines to the entrance of Gath^a and to the gates of Ekron. Their dead were strewn along the Shaaraim road to Gath and Ekron. ⁵³When the Israelites returned from chasing the Philistines, they plundered their camp. ⁵⁴David took the Philistine's head and brought it to Jerusalem, and he put the Philistine's weapons in his own tent.

⁵⁵As Saul watched David going out to meet the Philistine, he said to Abner, commander of the army, "Abner, whose son is that young man?"

Abner replied, "As surely as you live, O king, I don't know."

⁵⁶The king said, "Find out whose son this young man is."

⁵⁷As soon as David returned from killing the Philistine, Abner took him and brought him before Saul, with David still holding the Philistine's head.

^a 52 Some Septuagint manuscripts; Hebrew *a valley*

⁵⁸"Whose son are you, young man?" Saul asked him.

David said, "I am the son of your servant Jesse of Bethlehem."

Saul's Jealousy of David

18 After David had finished talking with Saul, Jonathan became one in spirit with David, and he loved him as himself. ²From that day Saul kept David with him and did not let him return to his father's house. ³And Jonathan made a covenant with David because he loved him as himself. ⁴Jonathan took off the robe he was wearing and gave it to David, along with his tunic, and even his sword, his bow and his belt.

⁵Whatever Saul sent him to do, David did it so successfully[a] that Saul gave him a high rank in the army. This pleased all the people, and Saul's officers as well.

⁶When the men were returning home after David had killed the Philistine, the women came out from all the towns of Israel to meet King Saul with singing and dancing, with joyful songs and with tambourines and lutes. ⁷As they danced, they sang:

"Saul has slain his thousands,
    and David his tens of thousands."

⁸Saul was very angry; this refrain galled him. "They have credited David with tens of thousands," he thought, "but me with only thousands. What more can he get but the kingdom?" ⁹And from that time on Saul kept a jealous eye on David.

¹⁰The next day an evil[b] spirit from God came forcefully upon Saul. He was prophesying in his house, while David was playing the harp, as he usually did. Saul had a spear in his hand ¹¹and he hurled it, saying to himself, "I'll pin David to the wall." But David eluded him twice.

¹²Saul was afraid of David, because the Lᴏʀᴅ was with David but had left Saul. ¹³So he sent David away from him and gave him command over a thousand men, and David led the troops in their campaigns. ¹⁴In everything he did he had great success,[c] because the Lᴏʀᴅ was with him. ¹⁵When Saul saw how successful[d] he was, he was afraid of him. ¹⁶But all Israel and Judah loved David, because he led them in their campaigns.

¹⁷Saul said to David, "Here is my older daughter Merab. I will give her to you in marriage; only serve me bravely and fight the battles of the Lᴏʀᴅ." For Saul said to himself, "I will not raise a hand against him. Let the Philistines do that!"

¹⁸But David said to Saul, "Who am I, and what is my family or my father's clan in Israel, that I should become the king's son-in-law?" ¹⁹So[e] when the time came for Merab, Saul's daughter, to be given to David, she was given in marriage to Adriel of Meholah.

²⁰Now Saul's daughter Michal was in love with David, and when they told Saul about it, he was pleased. ²¹"I will give her to him," he thought, "so that she may be a snare to him and so that the hand of the Philistines may be against him." So Saul said to David, "Now you have a second opportunity to become my son-in-law."

²²Then Saul ordered his attendants: "Speak to David pri-

Friendship

1 SAMUEL 18:1

"What happiness, what security, what joy to have someone to whom you dare to speak on terms of equality as to another self; one to whom you need have no fear to confess your failings; one to whom you can unblushingly make known what progress you have made in the spiritual life; one to whom you can entrust all the secrets of your heart and before whom you can place all your plans!"

—AELRED OF RIEVAULX,
Spiritual Friendship

See *Meeting God in Community*

ᵃ 5 Or *wisely*   ᵇ 10 Or *injurious*   ᶜ 14 Or *he was very wise*   ᵈ 15 Or *wise*
ᵉ 19 Or *However,*

The Corrosiveness of Envy

1 SAMUEL 19:9–10

For Saul, what may have begun as competition now spins out of control on a slippery slope, downhill from envy to attempted murder.

Competition, like many words in English that refer to human relationships, begins with the Latin prefix *com*, meaning "together with." In competition, the "together with" can be wholesome or unhealthy. Make a list, using a dictionary if need be, of a number of relational words beginning with *com*—comrade, compassion and companionable, for example. Consider how each of these words apply to your relationships with several people. Then prayerfully consider how Jesus Christ would view each of these people. How can God help you to keep these relationships free of envy and competitiveness?

See Meeting God in Community

vately and say, 'Look, the king is pleased with you, and his attendants all like you; now become his son-in-law.' "

²³They repeated these words to David. But David said, "Do you think it is a small matter to become the king's son-in-law? I'm only a poor man and little known."

²⁴When Saul's servants told him what David had said, ²⁵Saul replied, "Say to David, 'The king wants no other price for the bride than a hundred Philistine foreskins, to take revenge on his enemies.' " Saul's plan was to have David fall by the hands of the Philistines.

²⁶When the attendants told David these things, he was pleased to become the king's son-in-law. So before the allotted time elapsed, ²⁷David and his men went out and killed two hundred Philistines. He brought their foreskins and presented the full number to the king so that he might become the king's son-in-law. Then Saul gave him his daughter Michal in marriage.

²⁸When Saul realized that the LORD was with David and that his daughter Michal loved David, ²⁹Saul became still more afraid of him, and he remained his enemy the rest of his days.

³⁰The Philistine commanders continued to go out to battle, and as often as they did, David met with more success[a] than the rest of Saul's officers, and his name became well known.

Saul Tries to Kill David

19 Saul told his son Jonathan and all the attendants to kill David. But Jonathan was very fond of David ²and warned him, "My father Saul is looking for a chance to kill you. Be on your guard tomorrow morning; go into hiding and stay there. ³I will go out and stand with my father in the field where you are. I'll speak to him about you and will tell you what I find out."

⁴Jonathan spoke well of David to Saul his father and said to him, "Let not the king do wrong to his servant David; he has not wronged you, and what he has done has benefited you greatly. ⁵He took his life in his hands when he killed the Philistine. The LORD won a great victory for all Israel, and you saw it and were glad. Why then would you do wrong to an innocent man like David by killing him for no reason?"

⁶Saul listened to Jonathan and took this oath: "As surely as the LORD lives, David will not be put to death."

⁷So Jonathan called David and told him the whole conversation. He brought him to Saul, and David was with Saul as before.

⁸Once more war broke out, and David went out and fought the Philistines. He struck them with such force that they fled before him.

⁹But an evil[b] spirit from the LORD came upon Saul as he was sitting in his house with his spear in his hand. While David was playing the harp, ¹⁰Saul tried to pin him to the wall with his spear, but David eluded him as Saul drove the spear into the wall. That night David made good his escape.

¹¹Saul sent men to David's house to watch it and to kill him in the morning. But Michal, David's wife, warned him, "If you don't run for your life tonight, tomorrow you'll be killed." ¹²So Michal let David down through a window, and he fled and escaped. ¹³Then Michal took an idol[c] and laid it

---

a 30 Or *David acted more wisely*   *b 9* Or *injurious*   *c 13* Hebrew *teraphim*; also in verse 16

on the bed, covering it with a garment and putting some goats' hair at the head.

¹⁴When Saul sent the men to capture David, Michal said, "He is ill."

¹⁵Then Saul sent the men back to see David and told them, "Bring him up to me in his bed so that I may kill him." ¹⁶But when the men entered, there was the idol in the bed, and at the head was some goats' hair.

¹⁷Saul said to Michal, "Why did you deceive me like this and send my enemy away so that he escaped?"

Michal told him, "He said to me, 'Let me get away. Why should I kill you?' "

¹⁸When David had fled and made his escape, he went to Samuel at Ramah and told him all that Saul had done to him. Then he and Samuel went to Naioth and stayed there. ¹⁹Word came to Saul: "David is in Naioth at Ramah"; ²⁰so he sent men to capture him. But when they saw a group of prophets prophesying, with Samuel standing there as their leader, the Spirit of God came upon Saul's men and they also prophesied. ²¹Saul was told about it, and he sent more men, and they prophesied too. Saul sent men a third time, and they also prophesied. ²²Finally, he himself left for Ramah and went to the great cistern at Secu. And he asked, "Where are Samuel and David?"

"Over in Naioth at Ramah," they said.

²³So Saul went to Naioth at Ramah. But the Spirit of God came even upon him, and he walked along prophesying until he came to Naioth. ²⁴He stripped off his robes and also prophesied in Samuel's presence. He lay that way all that day and night. This is why people say, "Is Saul also among the prophets?"

David and Jonathan

20 Then David fled from Naioth at Ramah and went to Jonathan and asked, "What have I done? What is my crime? How have I wronged your father, that he is trying to take my life?"

²"Never!" Jonathan replied. "You are not going to die! Look, my father doesn't do anything, great or small, without confiding in me. Why would he hide this from me? It's not so!"

³But David took an oath and said, "Your father knows very well that I have found favor in your eyes, and he has said to himself, 'Jonathan must not know this or he will be grieved.' Yet as surely as the LORD lives and as you live, there is only a step between me and death."

⁴Jonathan said to David, "Whatever you want me to do, I'll do for you."

⁵So David said, "Look, tomorrow is the New Moon festival, and I am supposed to dine with the king; but let me go and hide in the field until the evening of the day after tomorrow. ⁶If your father misses me at all, tell him, 'David earnestly asked my permission to hurry to Bethlehem, his hometown, because an annual sacrifice is being made there for his whole clan.' ⁷If he says, 'Very well,' then your servant is safe. But if he loses his temper, you can be sure that he is determined to harm me. ⁸As for you, show kindness to your servant, for you have brought him into a covenant with you before the LORD. If I am guilty, then kill me yourself! Why hand me over to your father?"

The Spirit's Power

1 SAMUEL 19:23

Soldiers sent to capture David fail in their assignment, but the Spirit of God invades their hearts. So it is with two other groups, and finally Saul himself ventures to handle the matter—and he too is caught up in the Spirit power.

Recall the feelings that accompanied a profound spiritual experience you may have had—an awakening to God, a sense of God's call, your conversion to Jesus Christ as your Savior and Lord. What commitments did you make in such a moment? Did you share your excitement with others? How long did you keep reminding yourself that something special had occurred? How have those feelings and commitments changed since then? In what ways do you now seek the Spirit's refreshment?

See Meeting God in Everyday Life

Spiritual Murder

"It may be infinitely less evil to murder a man than to refuse to forgive him. The former may be an act of a moment of passion: the latter is the heart's choice. It is spiritual murder, the worst, to hate, to brood over the feeling that excludes, that, in our microcosm, kills the image, the idea of the hated."

—GEORGE MACDONALD
quoted in C. S. Lewis's
George MacDonald, 365 Readings

[9]"Never!" Jonathan said. "If I had the least inkling that my father was determined to harm you, wouldn't I tell you?"

[10]David asked, "Who will tell me if your father answers you harshly?"

[11]"Come," Jonathan said, "let's go out into the field." So they went there together.

[12]Then Jonathan said to David: "By the LORD, the God of Israel, I will surely sound out my father by this time the day after tomorrow! If he is favorably disposed toward you, will I not send you word and let you know? [13]But if my father is inclined to harm you, may the LORD deal with me, be it ever so severely, if I do not let you know and send you away safely. May the LORD be with you as he has been with my father. [14]But show me unfailing kindness like that of the LORD as long as I live, so that I may not be killed, [15]and do not ever cut off your kindness from my family—not even when the LORD has cut off every one of David's enemies from the face of the earth."

[16]So Jonathan made a covenant with the house of David, saying, "May the LORD call David's enemies to account." [17]And Jonathan had David reaffirm his oath out of love for him, because he loved him as he loved himself.

[18]Then Jonathan said to David: "Tomorrow is the New Moon festival. You will be missed, because your seat will be empty. [19]The day after tomorrow, toward evening, go to the place where you hid when this trouble began, and wait by the stone Ezel. [20]I will shoot three arrows to the side of it, as though I were shooting at a target. [21]Then I will send a boy and say, 'Go, find the arrows.' If I say to him, 'Look, the arrows are on this side of you; bring them here,' then come, because, as surely as the LORD lives, you are safe; there is no danger. [22]But if I say to the boy, 'Look, the arrows are beyond you,' then you must go, because the LORD has sent you away. [23]And about the matter you and I discussed—remember, the LORD is witness between you and me forever."

[24]So David hid in the field, and when the New Moon festival came, the king sat down to eat. [25]He sat in his customary place by the wall, opposite Jonathan,[a] and Abner sat next to Saul, but David's place was empty. [26]Saul said nothing that day, for he thought, "Something must have happened to David to make him ceremonially unclean—surely he is unclean." [27]But the next day, the second day of the month, David's place was empty again. Then Saul said to his son Jonathan, "Why hasn't the son of Jesse come to the meal, either yesterday or today?"

[28]Jonathan answered, "David earnestly asked me for permission to go to Bethlehem. [29]He said, 'Let me go, because our family is observing a sacrifice in the town and my brother has ordered me to be there. If I have found favor in your eyes, let me get away to see my brothers.' That is why he has not come to the king's table."

[30]Saul's anger flared up at Jonathan and he said to him, "You son of a perverse and rebellious woman! Don't I know that you have sided with the son of Jesse to your own shame and to the shame of the mother who bore you? [31]As long as the son of Jesse lives on this earth, neither you nor your kingdom will be established. Now send and bring him to me, for he must die!"

a 25 Septuagint; Hebrew *wall. Jonathan arose*

³²"Why should he be put to death? What has he done?" Jonathan asked his father. ³³But Saul hurled his spear at him to kill him. Then Jonathan knew that his father intended to kill David.

³⁴Jonathan got up from the table in fierce anger; on that second day of the month he did not eat, because he was grieved at his father's shameful treatment of David.

³⁵In the morning Jonathan went out to the field for his meeting with David. He had a small boy with him, ³⁶and he said to the boy, "Run and find the arrows I shoot." As the boy ran, he shot an arrow beyond him. ³⁷When the boy came to the place where Jonathan's arrow had fallen, Jonathan called out after him, "Isn't the arrow beyond you?" ³⁸Then he shouted, "Hurry! Go quickly! Don't stop!" The boy picked up the arrow and returned to his master. ³⁹(The boy knew nothing of all this; only Jonathan and David knew.) ⁴⁰Then Jonathan gave his weapons to the boy and said, "Go, carry them back to town."

⁴¹After the boy had gone, David got up from the south side ⌊of the stone⌋ and bowed down before Jonathan three times, with his face to the ground. Then they kissed each other and wept together—but David wept the most.

⁴²Jonathan said to David, "Go in peace, for we have sworn friendship with each other in the name of the Lord, saying, 'The Lord is witness between you and me, and between your descendants and my descendants forever.' " Then David left, and Jonathan went back to the town.

David at Nob

21 David went to Nob, to Ahimelech the priest. Ahimelech trembled when he met him, and asked, "Why are you alone? Why is no one with you?"

²David answered Ahimelech the priest, "The king charged me with a certain matter and said to me, 'No one is to know anything about your mission and your instructions.' As for my men, I have told them to meet me at a certain place. ³Now then, what do you have on hand? Give me five loaves of bread, or whatever you can find."

⁴But the priest answered David, "I don't have any ordinary bread on hand; however, there is some consecrated bread here—provided the men have kept themselves from women."

⁵David replied, "Indeed women have been kept from us, as usual whenever* I set out. The men's things* are holy even on missions that are not holy. How much more so today!" ⁶So the priest gave him the consecrated bread, since there was no bread there except the bread of the Presence that had been removed from before the Lord and replaced by hot bread on the day it was taken away.

⁷Now one of Saul's servants was there that day, detained before the Lord; he was Doeg the Edomite, Saul's head shepherd.

⁸David asked Ahimelech, "Don't you have a spear or a sword here? I haven't brought my sword or any other weapon, because the king's business was urgent."

⁹The priest replied, "The sword of Goliath the Philistine, whom you killed in the Valley of Elah, is here; it is wrapped in a cloth behind the ephod. If you want it, take it; there is no sword here but that one."

The Gift of Hospitality

1 SAMUEL 21:4–6

The priest gave David the "bread of the Presence" to feed his hungry men. This bread was a sign of hospitality, presented as a meal to a God who did not eat! Hospitality to hungry humans took precedence over symbolic hospitality to God when the priest had validated David's motives and honesty. Just so, *The Rule of Saint Benedict*, for centuries the basis of monastic life, reads, "All guests . . . are to be welcomed as Christ" (chapter 53). What physical signs around your home convey to others that they are truly welcomed? Do you have a clear address number, a door ornament, color around your entryway, a doormat announcing "Welcome" or your family name, a doorbell that works? How do you express welcome and hospitality? Is there a cordial answering of the telephone, a courteous greeting of even unexpected arrivals, a welcoming refreshment? Consider what more you might do to welcome all guests as Christ.

See Meeting God in Community

Really Together

1 SAMUEL 22:2

David gathered about him "all those who were in distress or in debt or discontented . . . and he became their leader. About four hundred men were with him." Another great leader, Martin Luther King, Jr., in a speech on August 28, 1963, saw a similar gathering: "I have a dream that one day on the red hills of Georgia the sons of former slaves and the sons of former slave owners will be able to sit down together at the table of brotherhood." Thank God for the ways in which common needs or common causes draw you and others together.

See Meeting God in Community

David said, "There is none like it; give it to me."

David at Gath

[10]That day David fled from Saul and went to Achish king of Gath. [11]But the servants of Achish said to him, "Isn't this David, the king of the land? Isn't he the one they sing about in their dances:

> " 'Saul has slain his thousands,
> and David his tens of thousands'?"

[12]David took these words to heart and was very much afraid of Achish king of Gath. [13]So he pretended to be insane in their presence; and while he was in their hands he acted like a madman, making marks on the doors of the gate and letting saliva run down his beard.

[14]Achish said to his servants, "Look at the man! He is insane! Why bring him to me? [15]Am I so short of madmen that you have to bring this fellow here to carry on like this in front of me? Must this man come into my house?"

David at Adullam and Mizpah

22 David left Gath and escaped to the cave of Adullam. When his brothers and his father's household heard about it, they went down to him there. [2]All those who were in distress or in debt or discontented gathered around him, and he became their leader. About four hundred men were with him.

[3]From there David went to Mizpah in Moab and said to the king of Moab, "Would you let my father and mother come and stay with you until I learn what God will do for me?" [4]So he left them with the king of Moab, and they stayed with him as long as David was in the stronghold.

[5]But the prophet Gad said to David, "Do not stay in the stronghold. Go into the land of Judah." So David left and went to the forest of Hereth.

Saul Kills the Priests of Nob

[6]Now Saul heard that David and his men had been discovered. And Saul, spear in hand, was seated under the tamarisk tree on the hill at Gibeah, with all his officials standing around him. [7]Saul said to them, "Listen, men of Benjamin! Will the son of Jesse give all of you fields and vineyards? Will he make all of you commanders of thousands and commanders of hundreds? [8]Is that why you have all conspired against me? No one tells me when my son makes a covenant with the son of Jesse. None of you is concerned about me or tells me that my son has incited my servant to lie in wait for me, as he does today."

[9]But Doeg the Edomite, who was standing with Saul's officials, said, "I saw the son of Jesse come to Ahimelech son of Ahitub at Nob. [10]Ahimelech inquired of the LORD for him; he also gave him provisions and the sword of Goliath the Philistine."

[11]Then the king sent for the priest Ahimelech son of Ahitub and his father's whole family, who were the priests at Nob, and they all came to the king. [12]Saul said, "Listen now, son of Ahitub."

"Yes, my lord," he answered.

[13]Saul said to him, "Why have you conspired against me, you and the son of Jesse, giving him bread and a sword

and inquiring of God for him, so that he has rebelled against me and lies in wait for me, as he does today?"

¹⁴Ahimelech answered the king, "Who of all your servants is as loyal as David, the king's son-in-law, captain of your bodyguard and highly respected in your household? ¹⁵Was that day the first time I inquired of God for him? Of course not! Let not the king accuse your servant or any of his father's family, for your servant knows nothing at all about this whole affair."

¹⁶But the king said, "You will surely die, Ahimelech, you and your father's whole family."

¹⁷Then the king ordered the guards at his side: "Turn and kill the priests of the LORD, because they too have sided with David. They knew he was fleeing, yet they did not tell me."

But the king's officials were not willing to raise a hand to strike the priests of the LORD.

¹⁸The king then ordered Doeg, "You turn and strike down the priests." So Doeg the Edomite turned and struck them down. That day he killed eighty-five men who wore the linen ephod. ¹⁹He also put to the sword Nob, the town of the priests, with its men and women, its children and infants, and its cattle, donkeys and sheep.

²⁰But Abiathar, a son of Ahimelech son of Ahitub, escaped and fled to join David. ²¹He told David that Saul had killed the priests of the LORD. ²²Then David said to Abiathar: "That day, when Doeg the Edomite was there, I knew he would be sure to tell Saul. I am responsible for the death of your father's whole family. ²³Stay with me; don't be afraid; the man who is seeking your life is seeking mine also. You will be safe with me."

David Saves Keilah

23 When David was told, "Look, the Philistines are fighting against Keilah and are looting the threshing floors," ²he inquired of the LORD, saying, "Shall I go and attack these Philistines?"

The LORD answered him, "Go, attack the Philistines and save Keilah."

³But David's men said to him, "Here in Judah we are afraid. How much more, then, if we go to Keilah against the Philistine forces!"

⁴Once again David inquired of the LORD, and the LORD answered him, "Go down to Keilah, for I am going to give the Philistines into your hand." ⁵So David and his men went to Keilah, fought the Philistines and carried off their livestock. He inflicted heavy losses on the Philistines and saved the people of Keilah. ⁶(Now Abiathar son of Ahimelech had brought the ephod down with him when he fled to David at Keilah.)

Saul Pursues David

⁷Saul was told that David had gone to Keilah, and he said, "God has handed him over to me, for David has imprisoned himself by entering a town with gates and bars." ⁸And Saul called up all his forces for battle, to go down to Keilah to besiege David and his men.

⁹When David learned that Saul was plotting against him, he said to Abiathar the priest, "Bring the ephod." ¹⁰David said, "O LORD, God of Israel, your servant has heard defi-

Timely Guidance

1 SAMUEL 23:9

When David seeks guidance from God by means of the mysterious ephod about what Saul will do next, he is rewarded with clear answers. Have you ever had an experience where you seemed clearly guided by the Spirit about a situation in your life? How did the guidance come—through an idea, dream, feeling, friend or passage of Scripture? When you are in difficulty or in a quandary, what or whom do you consult to find trustworthy guidance? Make a list of the ways you feel God provides guidance to human beings, and notice which ones you have experienced yourself.

Guides for the Soul

1 SAMUEL 23:16–18

"In the Book of Proverbs it says, 'Those who have no guidance fall like leaves but there is safety in much counsel' [see Proverbs 11:14]. Take a good look at this saying. Brothers, look at what Scripture is teaching us. It assures us that we should not set ourselves up as guide posts, that we should not consider ourselves sagacious, that we should not believe we can direct ourselves. We need assistance, we need guidance in addition to God's grace. No one is more wretched, no one is more easily caught unawares, than a man who has no one to guide him along the road to God."

—DOROTHEOS OF GAZA,
Discourses and Sayings

See *Meeting God in Community*

nitely that Saul plans to come to Keilah and destroy the town on account of me. ¹¹Will the citizens of Keilah surrender me to him? Will Saul come down, as your servant has heard? O Lᴏʀᴅ, God of Israel, tell your servant."

And the Lᴏʀᴅ said, "He will."

¹²Again David asked, "Will the citizens of Keilah surrender me and my men to Saul?"

And the Lᴏʀᴅ said, "They will."

¹³So David and his men, about six hundred in number, left Keilah and kept moving from place to place. When Saul was told that David had escaped from Keilah, he did not go there.

¹⁴David stayed in the desert strongholds and in the hills of the Desert of Ziph. Day after day Saul searched for him, but God did not give David into his hands.

¹⁵While David was at Horesh in the Desert of Ziph, he learned that Saul had come out to take his life. ¹⁶And Saul's son Jonathan went to David at Horesh and helped him find strength in God. ¹⁷"Don't be afraid," he said. "My father Saul will not lay a hand on you. You will be king over Israel, and I will be second to you. Even my father Saul knows this." ¹⁸The two of them made a covenant before the Lᴏʀᴅ. Then Jonathan went home, but David remained at Horesh.

¹⁹The Ziphites went up to Saul at Gibeah and said, "Is not David hiding among us in the strongholds at Horesh, on the hill of Hakilah, south of Jeshimon? ²⁰Now, O king, come down whenever it pleases you to do so, and we will be responsible for handing him over to the king."

²¹Saul replied, "The Lᴏʀᴅ bless you for your concern for me. ²²Go and make further preparation. Find out where David usually goes and who has seen him there. They tell me he is very crafty. ²³Find out about all the hiding places he uses and come back to me with definite information.ᵃ Then I will go with you; if he is in the area, I will track him down among all the clans of Judah."

²⁴So they set out and went to Ziph ahead of Saul. Now David and his men were in the Desert of Maon, in the Arabah south of Jeshimon. ²⁵Saul and his men began the search, and when David was told about it, he went down to the rock and stayed in the Desert of Maon. When Saul heard this, he went into the Desert of Maon in pursuit of David.

²⁶Saul was going along one side of the mountain, and David and his men were on the other side, hurrying to get away from Saul. As Saul and his forces were closing in on David and his men to capture them, ²⁷a messenger came to Saul, saying, "Come quickly! The Philistines are raiding the land." ²⁸Then Saul broke off his pursuit of David and went to meet the Philistines. That is why they call this place Sela Hammahlekoth.ᵇ ²⁹And David went up from there and lived in the strongholds of En Gedi.

David Spares Saul's Life

24 After Saul returned from pursuing the Philistines, he was told, "David is in the Desert of En Gedi." ²So Saul took three thousand chosen men from all Israel and set out to look for David and his men near the Crags of the Wild Goats.

³He came to the sheep pens along the way; a cave was

ᵃ 23 Or *me at Nacon*   ᵇ 28 *Sela Hammahlekoth* means *rock of parting.*

there, and Saul went in to relieve himself. David and his men were far back in the cave. [4]The men said, "This is the day the LORD spoke of when he said[a] to you, 'I will give your enemy into your hands for you to deal with as you wish.' " Then David crept up unnoticed and cut off a corner of Saul's robe.

[5]Afterward, David was conscience-stricken for having cut off a corner of his robe. [6]He said to his men, "The LORD forbid that I should do such a thing to my master, the LORD's anointed, or lift my hand against him; for he is the anointed of the LORD." [7]With these words David rebuked his men and did not allow them to attack Saul. And Saul left the cave and went his way.

[8]Then David went out of the cave and called out to Saul, "My lord the king!" When Saul looked behind him, David bowed down and prostrated himself with his face to the ground. [9]He said to Saul, "Why do you listen when men say, 'David is bent on harming you'? [10]This day you have seen with your own eyes how the LORD delivered you into my hands in the cave. Some urged me to kill you, but I spared you; I said, 'I will not lift my hand against my master, because he is the LORD's anointed.' [11]See, my father, look at this piece of your robe in my hand! I cut off the corner of your robe but did not kill you. Now understand and recognize that I am not guilty of wrongdoing or rebellion. I have not wronged you, but you are hunting me down to take my life. [12]May the LORD judge between you and me. And may the LORD avenge the wrongs you have done to me, but my hand will not touch you. [13]As the old saying goes, 'From evildoers come evil deeds,' so my hand will not touch you.

[14]"Against whom has the king of Israel come out? Whom are you pursuing? A dead dog? A flea? [15]May the LORD be our judge and decide between us. May he consider my cause and uphold it; may he vindicate me by delivering me from your hand."

[16]When David finished saying this, Saul asked, "Is that your voice, David my son?" And he wept aloud. [17]"You are more righteous than I," he said. "You have treated me well, but I have treated you badly. [18]You have just now told me of the good you did to me; the LORD delivered me into your hands, but you did not kill me. [19]When a man finds his enemy, does he let him get away unharmed? May the LORD reward you well for the way you treated me today. [20]I know that you will surely be king and that the kingdom of Israel will be established in your hands. [21]Now swear to me by the LORD that you will not cut off my descendants or wipe out my name from my father's family."

[22]So David gave his oath to Saul. Then Saul returned home, but David and his men went up to the stronghold.

David, Nabal and Abigail

25 Now Samuel died, and all Israel assembled and mourned for him; and they buried him at his home in Ramah.

Then David moved down into the Desert of Maon.[b] [2]A certain man in Maon, who had property there at Carmel, was very wealthy. He had a thousand goats and three thou-

---

God's Judgment in Relationships

1 SAMUEL 24:15

David, not swayed by his troops who want him to dispatch the erratic King Saul (see 24:4), leaves the judgment up to God, saying "May the LORD be the judge and decide between us." He expects God to act decisively to vindicate him in the face of Saul's attack.

How do you think God's judgment works in day-to-day life? How, and for what reasons, does God "judge and decide" between people? How is that judgment made manifest? Through arguments and disagreements? In court decisions? By the Spirit's work in the innermost conscience? In what ways does God's judgment feel hard and painful to you? In what ways is God's judgment constructive? Make a list of the ways judgment from God can be constructive and life-giving.

See Meeting God in Community

Intercession That Makes for Peace

1 SAMUEL 25:23–25

"O God, you made us in your own image and redeemed us through Jesus your Son: Look with compassion on the whole human family; take away the arrogance and hatred which infect our hearts; break down the walls that separate us; unite us in bonds of love; and work through our struggle and confusion to accomplish your purposes on earth; that, in your good time, all nations and races may serve you in harmony around your heavenly throne; through Jesus Christ our Lord."

—"Prayer for the Human Family,"
The Episcopal *Book of Common Prayer*

sand sheep, which he was shearing in Carmel. ³His name was Nabal and his wife's name was Abigail. She was an intelligent and beautiful woman, but her husband, a Calebite, was surly and mean in his dealings.

⁴While David was in the desert, he heard that Nabal was shearing sheep. ⁵So he sent ten young men and said to them, "Go up to Nabal at Carmel and greet him in my name. ⁶Say to him: 'Long life to you! Good health to you and your household! And good health to all that is yours!

⁷" 'Now I hear that it is sheep-shearing time. When your shepherds were with us, we did not mistreat them, and the whole time they were at Carmel nothing of theirs was missing. ⁸Ask your own servants and they will tell you. Therefore be favorable toward my young men, since we come at a festive time. Please give your servants and your son David whatever you can find for them.' "

⁹When David's men arrived, they gave Nabal this message in David's name. Then they waited.

¹⁰Nabal answered David's servants, "Who is this David? Who is this son of Jesse? Many servants are breaking away from their masters these days. ¹¹Why should I take my bread and water, and the meat I have slaughtered for my shearers, and give it to men coming from who knows where?"

¹²David's men turned around and went back. When they arrived, they reported every word. ¹³David said to his men, "Put on your swords!" So they put on their swords, and David put on his. About four hundred men went up with David, while two hundred stayed with the supplies.

¹⁴One of the servants told Nabal's wife Abigail: "David sent messengers from the desert to give our master his greetings, but he hurled insults at them. ¹⁵Yet these men were very good to us. They did not mistreat us, and the whole time we were out in the fields near them nothing was missing. ¹⁶Night and day they were a wall around us all the time we were herding our sheep near them. ¹⁷Now think it over and see what you can do, because disaster is hanging over our master and his whole household. He is such a wicked man that no one can talk to him."

¹⁸Abigail lost no time. She took two hundred loaves of bread, two skins of wine, five dressed sheep, five seahs[a] of roasted grain, a hundred cakes of raisins and two hundred cakes of pressed figs, and loaded them on donkeys. ¹⁹Then she told her servants, "Go on ahead; I'll follow you." But she did not tell her husband Nabal.

²⁰As she came riding her donkey into a mountain ravine, there were David and his men descending toward her, and she met them. ²¹David had just said, "It's been useless—all my watching over this fellow's property in the desert so that nothing of his was missing. He has paid me back evil for good. ²²May God deal with David,[b] be it ever so severely, if by morning I leave alive one male of all who belong to him!"

²³When Abigail saw David, she quickly got off her donkey and bowed down before David with her face to the ground. ²⁴She fell at his feet and said: "My lord, let the blame be on me alone. Please let your servant speak to you; hear what your servant has to say. ²⁵May my lord pay

---

a 18 That is, probably about a bushel (about 37 liters)   *b 22* Some Septuagint manuscripts; Hebrew *with David's enemies*

no attention to that wicked man Nabal. He is just like his name—his name is Fool, and folly goes with him. But as for me, your servant, I did not see the men my master sent.

²⁶"Now since the LORD has kept you, my master, from bloodshed and from avenging yourself with your own hands, as surely as the LORD lives and as you live, may your enemies and all who intend to harm my master be like Nabal. ²⁷And let this gift, which your servant has brought to my master, be given to the men who follow you. ²⁸Please forgive your servant's offense, for the LORD will certainly make a lasting dynasty for my master, because he fights the LORD's battles. Let no wrongdoing be found in you as long as you live. ²⁹Even though someone is pursuing you to take your life, the life of my master will be bound securely in the bundle of the living by the LORD your God. But the lives of your enemies he will hurl away as from the pocket of a sling. ³⁰When the LORD has done for my master every good thing he promised concerning him and has appointed him leader over Israel, ³¹my master will not have on his conscience the staggering burden of needless bloodshed or of having avenged himself. And when the LORD has brought my master success, remember your servant."

³²David said to Abigail, "Praise be to the LORD, the God of Israel, who has sent you today to meet me. ³³May you be blessed for your good judgment and for keeping me from bloodshed this day and from avenging myself with my own hands. ³⁴Otherwise, as surely as the LORD, the God of Israel, lives, who has kept me from harming you, if you had not come quickly to meet me, not one male belonging to Nabal would have been left alive by daybreak."

³⁵Then David accepted from her hand what she had brought him and said, "Go home in peace. I have heard your words and granted your request."

³⁶When Abigail went to Nabal, he was in the house holding a banquet like that of a king. He was in high spirits and very drunk. So she told him nothing until daybreak. ³⁷Then in the morning, when Nabal was sober, his wife told him all these things, and his heart failed him and he became like a stone. ³⁸About ten days later, the LORD struck Nabal and he died.

³⁹When David heard that Nabal was dead, he said, "Praise be to the LORD, who has upheld my cause against Nabal for treating me with contempt. He has kept his servant from doing wrong and has brought Nabal's wrongdoing down on his own head."

Then David sent word to Abigail, asking her to become his wife. ⁴⁰His servants went to Carmel and said to Abigail, "David has sent us to you to take you to become his wife."

⁴¹She bowed down with her face to the ground and said, "Here is your maidservant, ready to serve you and wash the feet of my master's servants." ⁴²Abigail quickly got on a donkey and, attended by her five maids, went with David's messengers and became his wife. ⁴³David had also married Ahinoam of Jezreel, and they both were his wives. ⁴⁴But Saul had given his daughter Michal, David's wife, to Paltiel*ᵃ* son of Laish, who was from Gallim.

ᵃ 44 Hebrew Palti, a variant of Paltiel

The Power of Goodness

1 SAMUEL 25:32–33

Reinhold Niebuhr wrote in *Beyond Tragedy*: "Goodness, armed with power, is corrupted; and pure love without power is destroyed." Abigail's sensible intercession saves David from misusing his power by launching a bloodbath. As his temper subsides, David realizes that Abigail's transparent goodness has brought about this change of heart.

Recall one or more persons who have brought such goodness into your life, perhaps saving you from an unwise or destructive course of action. Calling upon this lived experience, make a list of the attributes of a "good person." Prudence might be one, and gentleness another; try to think of at least ten other qualities. Prayerfully consider how you might cultivate such virtues.

See Meeting God in Community

Holy Reading

Slowly read the story of David's encounter with Saul and Abner, looking for a word or phrase that attracts you. Then close your eyes and repeat it silently. Be open to what comes into your mind—other words, feelings, images, even sensations of touch and smell—in association with the word or phrase. What might the Spirit be trying to bring to your mind by guiding you to this word or phrase? For the next few days, be receptive to an invitation from God about how you might live or what you might do.

See Meeting God in Scripture

David Again Spares Saul's Life

26 The Ziphites went to Saul at Gibeah and said, "Is not David hiding on the hill of Hakilah, which faces Jeshimon?"

²So Saul went down to the Desert of Ziph, with his three thousand chosen men of Israel, to search there for David. ³Saul made his camp beside the road on the hill of Hakilah facing Jeshimon, but David stayed in the desert. When he saw that Saul had followed him there, ⁴he sent out scouts and learned that Saul had definitely arrived.*ᵃ*

⁵Then David set out and went to the place where Saul had camped. He saw where Saul and Abner son of Ner, the commander of the army, had lain down. Saul was lying inside the camp, with the army encamped around him.

⁶David then asked Ahimelech the Hittite and Abishai son of Zeruiah, Joab's brother, "Who will go down into the camp with me to Saul?"

"I'll go with you," said Abishai.

⁷So David and Abishai went to the army by night, and there was Saul, lying asleep inside the camp with his spear stuck in the ground near his head. Abner and the soldiers were lying around him.

⁸Abishai said to David, "Today God has delivered your enemy into your hands. Now let me pin him to the ground with one thrust of my spear; I won't strike him twice."

⁹But David said to Abishai, "Don't destroy him! Who can lay a hand on the Lord's anointed and be guiltless? ¹⁰As surely as the Lord lives," he said, "the Lord himself will strike him; either his time will come and he will die, or he will go into battle and perish. ¹¹But the Lord forbid that I should lay a hand on the Lord's anointed. Now get the spear and water jug that are near his head, and let's go."

¹²So David took the spear and water jug near Saul's head, and they left. No one saw or knew about it, nor did anyone wake up. They were all sleeping, because the Lord had put them into a deep sleep.

¹³Then David crossed over to the other side and stood on top of the hill some distance away; there was a wide space between them. ¹⁴He called out to the army and to Abner son of Ner, "Aren't you going to answer me, Abner?"

Abner replied, "Who are you who calls to the king?"

¹⁵David said, "You're a man, aren't you? And who is like you in Israel? Why didn't you guard your lord the king? Someone came to destroy your lord the king. ¹⁶What you have done is not good. As surely as the Lord lives, you and your men deserve to die, because you did not guard your master, the Lord's anointed. Look around you. Where are the king's spear and water jug that were near his head?"

¹⁷Saul recognized David's voice and said, "Is that your voice, David my son?"

David replied, "Yes it is, my lord the king." ¹⁸And he added, "Why is my lord pursuing his servant? What have I done, and what wrong am I guilty of? ¹⁹Now let my lord the king listen to his servant's words. If the Lord has incited you against me, then may he accept an offering. If, however, men have done it, may they be cursed before the Lord! They have now driven me from my share in the Lord's inheritance and have said, 'Go, serve other gods.' ²⁰Now do

ᵃ 4 Or had come to Nacon

not let my blood fall to the ground far from the presence of the LORD. The king of Israel has come out to look for a flea—as one hunts a partridge in the mountains."

²¹Then Saul said, "I have sinned. Come back, David my son. Because you considered my life precious today, I will not try to harm you again. Surely I have acted like a fool and have erred greatly."

²²"Here is the king's spear," David answered. "Let one of your young men come over and get it. ²³The LORD rewards every man for his righteousness and faithfulness. The LORD delivered you into my hands today, but I would not lay a hand on the LORD's anointed. ²⁴As surely as I valued your life today, so may the LORD value my life and deliver me from all trouble."

²⁵Then Saul said to David, "May you be blessed, my son David; you will do great things and surely triumph."

So David went on his way, and Saul returned home.

David Among the Philistines

27 But David thought to himself, "One of these days I will be destroyed by the hand of Saul. The best thing I can do is to escape to the land of the Philistines. Then Saul will give up searching for me anywhere in Israel, and I will slip out of his hand."

²So David and the six hundred men with him left and went over to Achish son of Maoch king of Gath. ³David and his men settled in Gath with Achish. Each man had his family with him, and David had his two wives: Ahinoam of Jezreel and Abigail of Carmel, the widow of Nabal. ⁴When Saul was told that David had fled to Gath, he no longer searched for him.

⁵Then David said to Achish, "If I have found favor in your eyes, let a place be assigned to me in one of the country towns, that I may live there. Why should your servant live in the royal city with you?"

⁶So on that day Achish gave him Ziklag, and it has belonged to the kings of Judah ever since. ⁷David lived in Philistine territory a year and four months.

⁸Now David and his men went up and raided the Geshurites, the Girzites and the Amalekites. (From ancient times these peoples had lived in the land extending to Shur and Egypt.) ⁹Whenever David attacked an area, he did not leave a man or woman alive, but took sheep and cattle, donkeys and camels, and clothes. Then he returned to Achish.

¹⁰When Achish asked, "Where did you go raiding today?" David would say, "Against the Negev of Judah" or "Against the Negev of Jerahmeel" or "Against the Negev of the Kenites." ¹¹He did not leave a man or woman alive to be brought to Gath, for he thought, "They might inform on us and say, 'This is what David did.'" And such was his practice as long as he lived in Philistine territory. ¹²Achish trusted David and said to himself, "He has become so odious to his people, the Israelites, that he will be my servant forever."

Saul and the Witch of Endor

28 In those days the Philistines gathered their forces to fight against Israel. Achish said to David, "You must understand that you and your men will accompany me in the army."

To Whom Vengeance Belongs

1 SAMUEL 26:21–25

Saul responds, although only temporarily, with insight when David consistently refrains from vengeance, even when opportunity puts Saul at his mercy. David's respect, even kindness, touches Saul's heart. Have you ever received mercy when vengeance might have been an understandable response? How did it feel? Did it change your behavior? Have you ever felt such grace from God—a generous goodness in the face of your hostile or heedless behavior? Bring a person who has hurt you, or sought to harm you, into your heart and mind now. Consider that person in the light of God's mercy to you, and shed that light on him or her.

See Meeting God in Prayer

Abandoned by God?

1 SAMUEL 28:5–15

Saul, knowing that God has abandoned him, is desperate enough to disturb the departed Samuel by consulting a medium. Lonely and afraid, he tells Samuel, "God has turned away from me. He no longer answers me, either by prophets or by dreams."

How do you feel when God seems absent? What's missing when God seems far away? What is your understanding of such a situation? Do you feel God has actually left you, or do you assume that arid periods are a natural part of the ups and downs of any spiritual journey? What do you do to continue your relationship with God when you feel out of touch?

See Meeting God in Prayer

²David said, "Then you will see for yourself what your servant can do."

Achish replied, "Very well, I will make you my bodyguard for life."

³Now Samuel was dead, and all Israel had mourned for him and buried him in his own town of Ramah. Saul had expelled the mediums and spiritists from the land.

⁴The Philistines assembled and came and set up camp at Shunem, while Saul gathered all the Israelites and set up camp at Gilboa. ⁵When Saul saw the Philistine army, he was afraid; terror filled his heart. ⁶He inquired of the LORD, but the LORD did not answer him by dreams or Urim or prophets. ⁷Saul then said to his attendants, "Find me a woman who is a medium, so I may go and inquire of her."

"There is one in Endor," they said.

⁸So Saul disguised himself, putting on other clothes, and at night he and two men went to the woman. "Consult a spirit for me," he said, "and bring up for me the one I name."

⁹But the woman said to him, "Surely you know what Saul has done. He has cut off the mediums and spiritists from the land. Why have you set a trap for my life to bring about my death?"

¹⁰Saul swore to her by the LORD, "As surely as the LORD lives, you will not be punished for this."

¹¹Then the woman asked, "Whom shall I bring up for you?"

"Bring up Samuel," he said.

¹²When the woman saw Samuel, she cried out at the top of her voice and said to Saul, "Why have you deceived me? You are Saul!"

¹³The king said to her, "Don't be afraid. What do you see?"

The woman said, "I see a spirit*ᵃ* coming up out of the ground."

¹⁴"What does he look like?" he asked.

"An old man wearing a robe is coming up," she said.

Then Saul knew it was Samuel, and he bowed down and prostrated himself with his face to the ground.

¹⁵Samuel said to Saul, "Why have you disturbed me by bringing me up?"

"I am in great distress," Saul said. "The Philistines are fighting against me, and God has turned away from me. He no longer answers me, either by prophets or by dreams. So I have called on you to tell me what to do."

¹⁶Samuel said, "Why do you consult me, now that the LORD has turned away from you and become your enemy? ¹⁷The LORD has done what he predicted through me. The LORD has torn the kingdom out of your hands and given it to one of your neighbors—to David. ¹⁸Because you did not obey the LORD or carry out his fierce wrath against the Amalekites, the LORD has done this to you today. ¹⁹The LORD will hand over both Israel and you to the Philistines, and tomorrow you and your sons will be with me. The LORD will also hand over the army of Israel to the Philistines."

²⁰Immediately Saul fell full length on the ground, filled with fear because of Samuel's words. His strength was gone, for he had eaten nothing all that day and night.

²¹When the woman came to Saul and saw that he was

ᵃ 13 Or see spirits; or see gods

greatly shaken, she said, "Look, your maidservant has obeyed you. I took my life in my hands and did what you told me to do. ²²Now please listen to your servant and let me give you some food so you may eat and have the strength to go on your way."

²³He refused and said, "I will not eat."

But his men joined the woman in urging him, and he listened to them. He got up from the ground and sat on the couch.

²⁴The woman had a fattened calf at the house, which she butchered at once. She took some flour, kneaded it and baked bread without yeast. ²⁵Then she set it before Saul and his men, and they ate. That same night they got up and left.

Achish Sends David Back to Ziklag

29 The Philistines gathered all their forces at Aphek, and Israel camped by the spring in Jezreel. ²As the Philistine rulers marched with their units of hundreds and thousands, David and his men were marching at the rear with Achish. ³The commanders of the Philistines asked, "What about these Hebrews?"

Achish replied, "Is this not David, who was an officer of Saul king of Israel? He has already been with me for over a year, and from the day he left Saul until now, I have found no fault in him."

⁴But the Philistine commanders were angry with him and said, "Send the man back, that he may return to the place you assigned him. He must not go with us into battle, or he will turn against us during the fighting. How better could he regain his master's favor than by taking the heads of our own men? ⁵Isn't this the David they sang about in their dances:

" 'Saul has slain his thousands,
and David his tens of thousands'?"

⁶So Achish called David and said to him, "As surely as the LORD lives, you have been reliable, and I would be pleased to have you serve with me in the army. From the day you came to me until now, I have found no fault in you, but the rulers don't approve of you. ⁷Turn back and go in peace; do nothing to displease the Philistine rulers."

⁸"But what have I done?" asked David. "What have you found against your servant from the day I came to you until now? Why can't I go and fight against the enemies of my lord the king?"

⁹Achish answered, "I know that you have been as pleasing in my eyes as an angel of God; nevertheless, the Philistine commanders have said, 'He must not go up with us into battle.' ¹⁰Now get up early, along with your master's servants who have come with you, and leave in the morning as soon as it is light."

¹¹So David and his men got up early in the morning to go back to the land of the Philistines, and the Philistines went up to Jezreel.

David Destroys the Amalekites

30 David and his men reached Ziklag on the third day. Now the Amalekites had raided the Negev and Ziklag. They had attacked Ziklag and burned it, ²and had taken

Where Is Home?

1 SAMUEL 30:1–5

David, sent home from battle, finds the place sacked and deserted, the wives, children and elderly captured. How like the present time it is, when more human beings are displaced from their homelands than at any other time in history!

Pray for those refugees and prisoners. What attitudes and spiritual resources do they need? Are there ways in which you feel emotionally or spiritually displaced? Reflect on what Jesus said about himself: "Foxes have holes and birds of the air have nests, but the Son of Man has no place to lay his head" (Matthew 8:20). How might inviting Jesus into your life more deeply help you find a spiritual "home" in the universe and resources to deal with your displacement?

See Meeting God in Community

Locating Your Roots

1 SAMUEL 30:11–13

How would you answer David's question: "To whom do you belong, and where do you come from?" The Egyptian slave defines himself by his country of origin and his owner. Dietrich Bonhoeffer wrote when imprisoned by the Nazis: "Who am I? Am I then all that which other men tell of?" (*Letters and Papers from Prison*).

Am I more concerned about "who I am" in the eyes of others than "whose I am"? Draw a tree (like a family tree) of your commitments, and rank them by importance. To whom or what do you primarily belong? Who or what is at the bottom of the list? Are you satisfied with the priorities this tree illustrates? Read Psalm 139:1–14 as you ponder.

See Meeting God in Prayer

captive the women and all who were in it, both young and old. They killed none of them, but carried them off as they went on their way.

³When David and his men came to Ziklag, they found it destroyed by fire and their wives and sons and daughters taken captive. ⁴So David and his men wept aloud until they had no strength left to weep. ⁵David's two wives had been captured—Ahinoam of Jezreel and Abigail, the widow of Nabal of Carmel. ⁶David was greatly distressed because the men were talking of stoning him; each one was bitter in spirit because of his sons and daughters. But David found strength in the LORD his God.

⁷Then David said to Abiathar the priest, the son of Ahimelech, "Bring me the ephod." Abiathar brought it to him, ⁸and David inquired of the LORD, "Shall I pursue this raiding party? Will I overtake them?"

"Pursue them," he answered. "You will certainly overtake them and succeed in the rescue."

⁹David and the six hundred men with him came to the Besor Ravine, where some stayed behind, ¹⁰for two hundred men were too exhausted to cross the ravine. But David and four hundred men continued the pursuit.

¹¹They found an Egyptian in a field and brought him to David. They gave him water to drink and food to eat— ¹²part of a cake of pressed figs and two cakes of raisins. He ate and was revived, for he had not eaten any food or drunk any water for three days and three nights.

¹³David asked him, "To whom do you belong, and where do you come from?"

He said, "I am an Egyptian, the slave of an Amalekite. My master abandoned me when I became ill three days ago. ¹⁴We raided the Negev of the Kerethites and the territory belonging to Judah and the Negev of Caleb. And we burned Ziklag."

¹⁵David asked him, "Can you lead me down to this raiding party?"

He answered, "Swear to me before God that you will not kill me or hand me over to my master, and I will take you down to them."

¹⁶He led David down, and there they were, scattered over the countryside, eating, drinking and reveling because of the great amount of plunder they had taken from the land of the Philistines and from Judah. ¹⁷David fought them from dusk until the evening of the next day, and none of them got away, except four hundred young men who rode off on camels and fled. ¹⁸David recovered everything the Amalekites had taken, including his two wives. ¹⁹Nothing was missing: young or old, boy or girl, plunder or anything else they had taken. David brought everything back. ²⁰He took all the flocks and herds, and his men drove them ahead of the other livestock, saying, "This is David's plunder."

²¹Then David came to the two hundred men who had been too exhausted to follow him and who were left behind at the Besor Ravine. They came out to meet David and the people with him. As David and his men approached, he greeted them. ²²But all the evil men and troublemakers among David's followers said, "Because they did not go out with us, we will not share with them the plunder we recov-

ered. However, each man may take his wife and children and go."

²³David replied, "No, my brothers, you must not do that with what the LORD has given us. He has protected us and handed over to us the forces that came against us. ²⁴Who will listen to what you say? The share of the man who stayed with the supplies is to be the same as that of him who went down to the battle. All will share alike." ²⁵David made this a statute and ordinance for Israel from that day to this.

²⁶When David arrived in Ziklag, he sent some of the plunder to the elders of Judah, who were his friends, saying, "Here is a present for you from the plunder of the LORD's enemies."

²⁷He sent it to those who were in Bethel, Ramoth Negev and Jattir; ²⁸to those in Aroer, Siphmoth, Eshtemoa ²⁹and Racal; to those in the towns of the Jerahmeelites and the Kenites; ³⁰to those in Hormah, Bor Ashan, Athach ³¹and Hebron; and to those in all the other places where David and his men had roamed.

Saul Takes His Life

31 Now the Philistines fought against Israel; the Israelites fled before them, and many fell slain on Mount Gilboa. ²The Philistines pressed hard after Saul and his sons, and they killed his sons Jonathan, Abinadab and Malki-Shua. ³The fighting grew fierce around Saul, and when the archers overtook him, they wounded him critically.

⁴Saul said to his armor-bearer, "Draw your sword and run me through, or these uncircumcised fellows will come and run me through and abuse me."

But his armor-bearer was terrified and would not do it; so Saul took his own sword and fell on it. ⁵When the armor-bearer saw that Saul was dead, he too fell on his sword and died with him. ⁶So Saul and his three sons and his armor-bearer and all his men died together that same day.

⁷When the Israelites along the valley and those across the Jordan saw that the Israelite army had fled and that Saul and his sons had died, they abandoned their towns and fled. And the Philistines came and occupied them.

⁸The next day, when the Philistines came to strip the dead, they found Saul and his three sons fallen on Mount Gilboa. ⁹They cut off his head and stripped off his armor, and they sent messengers throughout the land of the Philistines to proclaim the news in the temple of their idols and among their people. ¹⁰They put his armor in the temple of the Ashtoreths and fastened his body to the wall of Beth Shan.

¹¹When the people of Jabesh Gilead heard of what the Philistines had done to Saul, ¹²all their valiant men journeyed through the night to Beth Shan. They took down the bodies of Saul and his sons from the wall of Beth Shan and went to Jabesh, where they burned them. ¹³Then they took their bones and buried them under a tamarisk tree at Jabesh, and they fasted seven days.

Losing the Vision

1 SAMUEL 31:1–4

Saul has fallen from being a visionary, charismatic leader to a lost and despairing wreck of a man. Imaginatively review the tale of his fall, perhaps drawing a diagram of his downward spiral. How did he lose the call that raised him up to service? What did he allow to isolate him from those who could have been most helpful, especially the God who had called him? In what ways did he try to manage alone instead of listening and obeying?

Do you have a "community of faith"—companions in the faith with whom you can be open and honest and who can do the same with you? Make a list of the most important "spiritual friends" in your life. Pray for them individually and ask God that all of you together may help keep one another faithful. Talk to your spiritual friends and share this resolution openly with them; ask them for their prayers for you.

See *Meeting God in Community*

2 SAMUEL

Seduced by Power

KEY VERSE:

And David knew that the LORD had established him as king over Israel and had exalted his kingdom for the sake of his people Israel. —2 Samuel 5:12

"The battle you are to fight is within you . . . Your enemy comes out of your own heart. We shall not fight, as the men of former times . . . against men on earth, but against principalities and authorities, against the cosmic powers of this dark world . . . We also arm ourselves and bestir ourselves to do battle, but against those enemies which come forth from our own hearts, evil thoughts, thefts, lies about other people, blasphemies, and all other enemies of our soul that are like them . . . For if we prevail against these enemies, we shall lay hold on the spiritual forces well enough and throw them out of that kingdom which they have set up within us."

—ORIGEN OF ALEXANDRIA,
Homily on Joshua

In 2 Samuel, the young King David comes into his own. His story is full of power struggles, duplicity, tragedy and the violence of war. Presented as "the LORD's anointed," David evokes both admiration and dislike. A musician and a soldier, brave and passionate, he dances with joy, sings praises to God and mourns his sons—all with his whole heart. But personal ambition causes David to trample on other people's lives, and his actions illustrate Lord Acton's maxim: "Power corrupts and absolute power corrupts absolutely." David, however, is remarkable in that, having surrounded himself with advisers unafraid to confront his hypocrisy, he *listens*—to them, to his own conscience and to the God he loves. His imperfect life is lived in constant relationship with the Divine One who is the true sovereign and Israel's only security.

The book of 2 Samuel can be read quickly as a compelling story or contemplated slowly. You may identify with the Lord's call to missions—a call that is both daunting and inspiring. You may mourn with David at the tragedies involving his children, reflecting on the difficulties and ambiguities of parenting. You may find yourself pondering the similarities between these ancient characters and events and some of today's public figures and media headlines. But be sure to look through the windows of this story into your own soul—in the ways you deal with the temptations inherent in power and influence. Like David, stay aware of the real, enduring power that reposes in God and is lived out in the Lord's Anointed, "great David's greater Son."

David Hears of Saul's Death

1 After the death of Saul, David returned from defeating the Amalekites and stayed in Ziklag two days. ²On the third day a man arrived from Saul's camp, with his clothes torn and with dust on his head. When he came to David, he fell to the ground to pay him honor.

³"Where have you come from?" David asked him.

He answered, "I have escaped from the Israelite camp."

⁴"What happened?" David asked. "Tell me."

He said, "The men fled from the battle. Many of them fell and died. And Saul and his son Jonathan are dead."

⁵Then David said to the young man who brought him the report, "How do you know that Saul and his son Jonathan are dead?"

⁶"I happened to be on Mount Gilboa," the young man said, "and there was Saul, leaning on his spear, with the chariots and riders almost upon him. ⁷When he turned around and saw me, he called out to me, and I said, 'What can I do?'

⁸"He asked me, 'Who are you?'

" 'An Amalekite,' I answered.

⁹"Then he said to me, 'Stand over me and kill me! I am in the throes of death, but I'm still alive.'

¹⁰"So I stood over him and killed him, because I knew that after he had fallen he could not survive. And I took the crown that was on his head and the band on his arm and have brought them here to my lord."

¹¹Then David and all the men with him took hold of their clothes and tore them. ¹²They mourned and wept and fasted till evening for Saul and his son Jonathan, and for the army of the LORD and the house of Israel, because they had fallen by the sword.

¹³David said to the young man who brought him the report, "Where are you from?"

"I am the son of an alien, an Amalekite," he answered.

¹⁴David asked him, "Why were you not afraid to lift your hand to destroy the LORD's anointed?"

¹⁵Then David called one of his men and said, "Go, strike him down!" So he struck him down, and he died. ¹⁶For David had said to him, "Your blood be on your own head. Your own mouth testified against you when you said, 'I killed the LORD's anointed.' "

David's Lament for Saul and Jonathan

¹⁷David took up this lament concerning Saul and his son Jonathan, ¹⁸and ordered that the men of Judah be taught this lament of the bow (it is written in the Book of Jashar):

¹⁹"Your glory, O Israel, lies slain on your heights.
　　How the mighty have fallen!

²⁰"Tell it not in Gath,
　　proclaim it not in the streets of Ashkelon,
　lest the daughters of the Philistines be glad,
　　lest the daughters of the uncircumcised rejoice.

²¹"O mountains of Gilboa,
　　may you have neither dew nor rain,
　　nor fields that yield offerings ⌊of grain⌋.
　For there the shield of the mighty was defiled,
　　the shield of Saul—no longer rubbed with oil.

Ancient Enemies

2 SAMUEL 1:13–16

The Amalekites, Israel's enemy from the time of Moses, have been part of Saul's downfall (see 1 Samuel 15:18–19). Now David gives orders to execute the young Amalekite who claimed to slay King Saul, for he has "lift[ed his] hand to destroy the LORD's anointed." What do you suppose God thinks of David's act of revenge? Do you believe that God takes sides in the conflicts of history, especially when one of the parties to the conflict, like the Amalekites, engages in especially vicious, unjust or destructive behavior? What emotions arise in you when you encounter, or read about, people who belong to such an unjust group or nation? What temptations toward revenge have you felt in your conflicts with other people? How would you pray for those other people; what might you need to ask God for in order to help you relate justly to them?

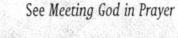
See *Meeting God in Prayer*

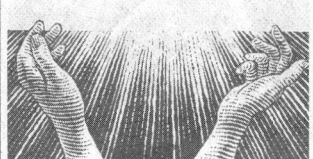

389

The Mighty Are Fallen

2 SAMUEL 1:25–26

Quietly reflect on any relationships you may have had in your life that have affected you deeply—perhaps a relationship that has bound you to the soul of the other person, as David and Jonathan were bound together (see 1 Samuel 18:1). What was it about that other person that you loved, respected, and admired? What gifts does that friendship still give you? Remember what it was like to lose that person—or imagine what it might be like to lose him or her. Enter into the emotions of David's lament over the deaths of Saul and Jonathan by reading the text two or three times, aloud; in each repetition, vary the emotion expressed: anger, quiet mourning, bitterness or gentle affection, for instance. Then thank God for that friendship and its enduring effect in your life.

See *Meeting God in Community*

22 From the blood of the slain,
　　from the flesh of the mighty,
　the bow of Jonathan did not turn back,
　　the sword of Saul did not return unsatisfied.

23 "Saul and Jonathan—
　　in life they were loved and gracious,
　　and in death they were not parted.
　They were swifter than eagles,
　　they were stronger than lions.

24 "O daughters of Israel,
　　weep for Saul,
　who clothed you in scarlet and finery,
　　who adorned your garments with ornaments of
　　　gold.

25 "How the mighty have fallen in battle!
　　Jonathan lies slain on your heights.
26 I grieve for you, Jonathan my brother;
　　you were very dear to me.
　Your love for me was wonderful,
　　more wonderful than that of women.

27 "How the mighty have fallen!
　　The weapons of war have perished!"

David Anointed King Over Judah

2 In the course of time, David inquired of the LORD. "Shall I go up to one of the towns of Judah?" he asked.
The LORD said, "Go up."
David asked, "Where shall I go?"
"To Hebron," the LORD answered. ²So David went up there with his two wives, Ahinoam of Jezreel and Abigail, the widow of Nabal of Carmel. ³David also took the men who were with him, each with his family, and they settled in Hebron and its towns. ⁴Then the men of Judah came to Hebron and there they anointed David king over the house of Judah.

When David was told that it was the men of Jabesh Gilead who had buried Saul, ⁵he sent messengers to the men of Jabesh Gilead to say to them, "The LORD bless you for showing this kindness to Saul your master by burying him. ⁶May the LORD now show you kindness and faithfulness, and I too will show you the same favor because you have done this. ⁷Now then, be strong and brave, for Saul your master is dead, and the house of Judah has anointed me king over them."

War Between the Houses of David and Saul

⁸Meanwhile, Abner son of Ner, the commander of Saul's army, had taken Ish-Bosheth son of Saul and brought him over to Mahanaim. ⁹He made him king over Gilead, Ashuri*a* and Jezreel, and also over Ephraim, Benjamin and all Israel.

¹⁰Ish-Bosheth son of Saul was forty years old when he became king over Israel, and he reigned two years. The house of Judah, however, followed David. ¹¹The length of time David was king in Hebron over the house of Judah was seven years and six months.

¹²Abner son of Ner, together with the men of Ish-Bosheth son of Saul, left Mahanaim and went to Gibeon. ¹³Joab son

a 9 Or Asher

of Zeruiah and David's men went out and met them at the pool of Gibeon. One group sat down on one side of the pool and one group on the other side.

¹⁴Then Abner said to Joab, "Let's have some of the young men get up and fight hand to hand in front of us."

"All right, let them do it," Joab said.

¹⁵So they stood up and were counted off—twelve men for Benjamin and Ish-Bosheth son of Saul, and twelve for David. ¹⁶Then each man grabbed his opponent by the head and thrust his dagger into his opponent's side, and they fell down together. So that place in Gibeon was called Helkath Hazzurim.ᵃ

¹⁷The battle that day was very fierce, and Abner and the men of Israel were defeated by David's men.

¹⁸The three sons of Zeruiah were there: Joab, Abishai and Asahel. Now Asahel was as fleet-footed as a wild gazelle. ¹⁹He chased Abner, turning neither to the right nor to the left as he pursued him. ²⁰Abner looked behind him and asked, "Is that you, Asahel?"

"It is," he answered.

²¹Then Abner said to him, "Turn aside to the right or to the left; take on one of the young men and strip him of his weapons." But Asahel would not stop chasing him.

²²Again Abner warned Asahel, "Stop chasing me! Why should I strike you down? How could I look your brother Joab in the face?"

²³But Asahel refused to give up the pursuit; so Abner thrust the butt of his spear into Asahel's stomach, and the spear came out through his back. He fell there and died on the spot. And every man stopped when he came to the place where Asahel had fallen and died.

²⁴But Joab and Abishai pursued Abner, and as the sun was setting, they came to the hill of Ammah, near Giah on the way to the wasteland of Gibeon. ²⁵Then the men of Benjamin rallied behind Abner. They formed themselves into a group and took their stand on top of a hill.

²⁶Abner called out to Joab, "Must the sword devour forever? Don't you realize that this will end in bitterness? How long before you order your men to stop pursuing their brothers?"

²⁷Joab answered, "As surely as God lives, if you had not spoken, the men would have continued the pursuit of their brothers until morning.ᵇ"

²⁸So Joab blew the trumpet, and all the men came to a halt; they no longer pursued Israel, nor did they fight anymore.

²⁹All that night Abner and his men marched through the Arabah. They crossed the Jordan, continued through the whole Bithronᶜ and came to Mahanaim.

³⁰Then Joab returned from pursuing Abner and assembled all his men. Besides Asahel, nineteen of David's men were found missing. ³¹But David's men had killed three hundred and sixty Benjamites who were with Abner. ³²They took Asahel and buried him in his father's tomb at

---

Civil War Begins

2 SAMUEL 2:14–17

"Let's have the young men fight," the leaders and generals of the world say. The Civil War's General Sherman said, "War is hell! It is only those who have neither fired a shot nor heard the shrieks and groans of the wounded who cry aloud for blood, more vengeance, more desolation." Sherman's frank assessment of America's Civil War applies equally well to the dozen or more such conflicts being fought by young men and women in the world today. Bring to mind a contemporary civil conflict by reading the daily paper or a news magazine or by asking others to help you. Pray for sanity and peace in each country racked by such strife.

See Meeting God in Prayer

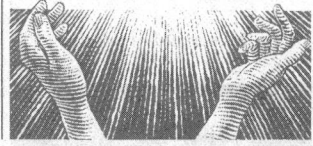

ᵃ *16 Helkath Hazzurim means field of daggers or field of hostilities.* ᵇ *27 Or spoken this morning, the men would not have taken up the pursuit of their brothers; or spoken, the men would have given up the pursuit of their brothers by morning* ᶜ *29 Or morning; or ravine; the meaning of the Hebrew for this word is uncertain.*

Victimized by the Powers That Be

2 SAMUEL 3:15–16

Paltiel follows behind his wife, weeping; Michal must remain silent because she is now "owned" as David's property. Their lives are once again fodder for the power struggle between Saul and David. In what ways are innocent lives today disrupted and destroyed by such powerful forces—institutions or individuals? What incidents have you personally witnessed when weakness or difference in age, race, gender, wealth or ability has been exploited or punished? In what ways have you participated in such exploitation—or been the object of it? How would you pray for the perpetrators of such injustices? Spend some time with a trusted friend sharing your insights, perhaps praying together about them.

See Meeting God in Community

Bethlehem. Then Joab and his men marched all night and arrived at Hebron by daybreak.

3 The war between the house of Saul and the house of David lasted a long time. David grew stronger and stronger, while the house of Saul grew weaker and weaker. ²Sons were born to David in Hebron:

His firstborn was Amnon the son of Ahinoam of Jezreel;

³his second, Kileab the son of Abigail the widow of Nabal of Carmel;

the third, Absalom the son of Maacah daughter of Talmai king of Geshur;

⁴the fourth, Adonijah the son of Haggith;

the fifth, Shephatiah the son of Abital;

⁵and the sixth, Ithream the son of David's wife Eglah.

These were born to David in Hebron.

Abner Goes Over to David

⁶During the war between the house of Saul and the house of David, Abner had been strengthening his own position in the house of Saul. ⁷Now Saul had had a concubine named Rizpah daughter of Aiah. And Ish-Bosheth said to Abner, "Why did you sleep with my father's concubine?"

⁸Abner was very angry because of what Ish-Bosheth said and he answered, "Am I a dog's head—on Judah's side? This very day I am loyal to the house of your father Saul and to his family and friends. I haven't handed you over to David. Yet now you accuse me of an offense involving this woman! ⁹May God deal with Abner, be it ever so severely, if I do not do for David what the LORD promised him on oath ¹⁰and transfer the kingdom from the house of Saul and establish David's throne over Israel and Judah from Dan to Beersheba." ¹¹Ish-Bosheth did not dare to say another word to Abner, because he was afraid of him.

¹²Then Abner sent messengers on his behalf to say to David, "Whose land is it? Make an agreement with me, and I will help you bring all Israel over to you."

¹³"Good," said David. "I will make an agreement with you. But I demand one thing of you: Do not come into my presence unless you bring Michal daughter of Saul when you come to see me." ¹⁴Then David sent messengers to Ish-Bosheth son of Saul, demanding, "Give me my wife Michal, whom I betrothed to myself for the price of a hundred Philistine foreskins."

¹⁵So Ish-Bosheth gave orders and had her taken away from her husband Paltiel son of Laish. ¹⁶Her husband, however, went with her, weeping behind her all the way to Bahurim. Then Abner said to him, "Go back home!" So he went back.

¹⁷Abner conferred with the elders of Israel and said, "For some time you have wanted to make David your king. ¹⁸Now do it! For the LORD promised David, 'By my servant David I will rescue my people Israel from the hand of the Philistines and from the hand of all their enemies.' "

¹⁹Abner also spoke to the Benjamites in person. Then he went to Hebron to tell David everything that Israel and the whole house of Benjamin wanted to do. ²⁰When Abner, who had twenty men with him, came to David at Hebron, David prepared a feast for him and his men. ²¹Then Abner said to David, "Let me go at once and assemble all Israel for

my lord the king, so that they may make a compact with you, and that you may rule over all that your heart desires." So David sent Abner away, and he went in peace.

Joab Murders Abner

²²Just then David's men and Joab returned from a raid and brought with them a great deal of plunder. But Abner was no longer with David in Hebron, because David had sent him away, and he had gone in peace. ²³When Joab and all the soldiers with him arrived, he was told that Abner son of Ner had come to the king and that the king had sent him away and that he had gone in peace.

²⁴So Joab went to the king and said, "What have you done? Look, Abner came to you. Why did you let him go? Now he is gone! ²⁵You know Abner son of Ner; he came to deceive you and observe your movements and find out everything you are doing."

²⁶Joab then left David and sent messengers after Abner, and they brought him back from the well of Sirah. But David did not know it. ²⁷Now when Abner returned to Hebron, Joab took him aside into the gateway, as though to speak with him privately. And there, to avenge the blood of his brother Asahel, Joab stabbed him in the stomach, and he died.

²⁸Later, when David heard about this, he said, "I and my kingdom are forever innocent before the LORD concerning the blood of Abner son of Ner. ²⁹May his blood fall upon the head of Joab and upon all his father's house! May Joab's house never be without someone who has a running sore or leprosy*ᵃ* or who leans on a crutch or who falls by the sword or who lacks food."

³⁰(Joab and his brother Abishai murdered Abner because he had killed their brother Asahel in the battle at Gibeon.)

³¹Then David said to Joab and all the people with him, "Tear your clothes and put on sackcloth and walk in mourning in front of Abner." King David himself walked behind the bier. ³²They buried Abner in Hebron, and the king wept aloud at Abner's tomb. All the people wept also.

³³The king sang this lament for Abner:

> "Should Abner have died as the lawless die?
> ³⁴ Your hands were not bound,
>   your feet were not fettered.
> You fell as one falls before wicked men."

And all the people wept over him again.

³⁵Then they all came and urged David to eat something while it was still day; but David took an oath, saying, "May God deal with me, be it ever so severely, if I taste bread or anything else before the sun sets!"

³⁶All the people took note and were pleased; indeed, everything the king did pleased them. ³⁷So on that day all the people and all Israel knew that the king had no part in the murder of Abner son of Ner.

³⁸Then the king said to his men, "Do you not realize that a prince and a great man has fallen in Israel this day? ³⁹And today, though I am the anointed king, I am weak, and these sons of Zeruiah are too strong for me. May the LORD repay the evildoer according to his evil deeds!"

ᵃ 29 The Hebrew word was used for various diseases affecting the skin—not necessarily leprosy.

Chief Mourner

2 SAMUEL 3:31

David's public mourning for Abner (walking behind the bier, weeping aloud at his tomb, singing a lament, fasting) was a comfort to his people: They "took note and were pleased" (3:36). All grief is deeply personal, but at moments of corporate loss, we look to our leaders to express our feelings by their words and actions. When Princess Diana was killed in a car accident in August, 1997, the British royal family was criticized for their reserved response, resulting in an uncharacteristically emotional address by Queen Elizabeth. What have been the times of grief and loss in your own life, especially those shared by others? Whose vocal lament or behavior comforted you? In what situations have you been called upon to be chief mourner, or one of the lead mourners? What words or deeds best express authentic sympathy and comfort? How does God's presence help?

See Meeting God in Community

Images of Leadership

2 SAMUEL 5:1–3

David is now king over the land, and the clans of Israel acknowledge that God has made him shepherd of the people. The pledge of loyalty springs easily to their lips because their new leader fits the image of the king they want and need. Brave and strong, David is the human representative of the God who leads them as a nation. In a few minutes of silence, consider the characteristics of righteous leadership. What makes for good leadership in a nation? A work force? A spiritual community? A family? What are the leadership qualities manifested in the God of the Bible, and in God's human manifestation in Jesus Christ, the Good Shepherd? How are these qualities reflected in your own life?

See Meeting God in Community

Ish-Bosheth Murdered

4 When Ish-Bosheth son of Saul heard that Abner had died in Hebron, he lost courage, and all Israel became alarmed. ²Now Saul's son had two men who were leaders of raiding bands. One was named Baanah and the other Recab; they were sons of Rimmon the Beerothite from the tribe of Benjamin—Beeroth is considered part of Benjamin, ³because the people of Beeroth fled to Gittaim and have lived there as aliens to this day.

⁴(Jonathan son of Saul had a son who was lame in both feet. He was five years old when the news about Saul and Jonathan came from Jezreel. His nurse picked him up and fled, but as she hurried to leave, he fell and became crippled. His name was Mephibosheth.)

⁵Now Recab and Baanah, the sons of Rimmon the Beerothite, set out for the house of Ish-Bosheth, and they arrived there in the heat of the day while he was taking his noonday rest. ⁶They went into the inner part of the house as if to get some wheat, and they stabbed him in the stomach. Then Recab and his brother Baanah slipped away.

⁷They had gone into the house while he was lying on the bed in his bedroom. After they stabbed and killed him, they cut off his head. Taking it with them, they traveled all night by way of the Arabah. ⁸They brought the head of Ish-Bosheth to David at Hebron and said to the king, "Here is the head of Ish-Bosheth son of Saul, your enemy, who tried to take your life. This day the LORD has avenged my lord the king against Saul and his offspring."

⁹David answered Recab and his brother Baanah, the sons of Rimmon the Beerothite, "As surely as the LORD lives, who has delivered me out of all trouble, ¹⁰when a man told me, 'Saul is dead,' and thought he was bringing good news, I seized him and put him to death in Ziklag. That was the reward I gave him for his news! ¹¹How much more—when wicked men have killed an innocent man in his own house and on his own bed—should I not now demand his blood from your hand and rid the earth of you!"

¹²So David gave an order to his men, and they killed them. They cut off their hands and feet and hung the bodies by the pool in Hebron. But they took the head of Ish-Bosheth and buried it in Abner's tomb at Hebron.

David Becomes King Over Israel

5 All the tribes of Israel came to David at Hebron and said, "We are your own flesh and blood. ²In the past, while Saul was king over us, you were the one who led Israel on their military campaigns. And the LORD said to you, 'You will shepherd my people Israel, and you will become their ruler.' "

³When all the elders of Israel had come to King David at Hebron, the king made a compact with them at Hebron before the LORD, and they anointed David king over Israel.

⁴David was thirty years old when he became king, and he reigned forty years. ⁵In Hebron he reigned over Judah seven years and six months, and in Jerusalem he reigned over all Israel and Judah thirty-three years.

David Conquers Jerusalem

⁶The king and his men marched to Jerusalem to attack the Jebusites, who lived there. The Jebusites said to David,

"You will not get in here; even the blind and the lame can ward you off." They thought, "David cannot get in here." [7]Nevertheless, David captured the fortress of Zion, the City of David.

[8]On that day, David said, "Anyone who conquers the Jebusites will have to use the water shaft[a] to reach those 'lame and blind' who are David's enemies.[b]" That is why they say, "The 'blind and lame' will not enter the palace."

[9]David then took up residence in the fortress and called it the City of David. He built up the area around it, from the supporting terraces[c] inward. [10]And he became more and more powerful, because the Lord God Almighty was with him.

[11]Now Hiram king of Tyre sent messengers to David, along with cedar logs and carpenters and stonemasons, and they built a palace for David. [12]And David knew that the Lord had established him as king over Israel and had exalted his kingdom for the sake of his people Israel.

[13]After he left Hebron, David took more concubines and wives in Jerusalem, and more sons and daughters were born to him. [14]These are the names of the children born to him there: Shammua, Shobab, Nathan, Solomon, [15]Ibhar, Elishua, Nepheg, Japhia, [16]Elishama, Eliada and Eliphelet.

David Defeats the Philistines

[17]When the Philistines heard that David had been anointed king over Israel, they went up in full force to search for him, but David heard about it and went down to the stronghold. [18]Now the Philistines had come and spread out in the Valley of Rephaim; [19]so David inquired of the Lord, "Shall I go and attack the Philistines? Will you hand them over to me?"

The Lord answered him, "Go, for I will surely hand the Philistines over to you."

[20]So David went to Baal Perazim, and there he defeated them. He said, "As waters break out, the Lord has broken out against my enemies before me." So that place was called Baal Perazim.[d] [21]The Philistines abandoned their idols there, and David and his men carried them off.

[22]Once more the Philistines came up and spread out in the Valley of Rephaim; [23]so David inquired of the Lord, and he answered, "Do not go straight up, but circle around behind them and attack them in front of the balsam trees. [24]As soon as you hear the sound of marching in the tops of the balsam trees, move quickly, because that will mean the Lord has gone out in front of you to strike the Philistine army." [25]So David did as the Lord commanded him, and he struck down the Philistines all the way from Gibeon[e] to Gezer.

The Ark Brought to Jerusalem

6 David again brought together out of Israel chosen men, thirty thousand in all. [2]He and all his men set out from Baalah of Judah[f] to bring up from there the ark of God, which is called by the Name,[g] the name of the Lord

---

The Constant Presence of God

2 SAMUEL 5:17–25

"Alas . . . we do not see God, who is present with us; and, though faith assures us of His presence, yet, not beholding Him with our eyes, we too often forget Him and behave ourselves as though He were at a distance from us; for, although we well know that He is present in all things, yet, not reflecting on it, we act as if we knew it not. Therefore, before prayer, we must always excite in our souls a lively apprehension of the presence of God, such as David conceived when he exclaimed: 'If I go up to the heavens, you are there; if I make my bed in the depths, you are there' [Psalm 139:8] . . . When, therefore, you come to prayer, you must say with your whole heart and in your heart, 'O my heart! Be attentive, for God is truly here.' "

—FRANCIS DE SALES,
Introduction to the Devout Life

See *Meeting God in Prayer*

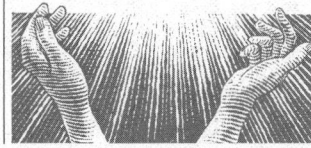

---

[a]8 Or *use scaling hooks*   [b]8 Or *are hated by David*   [c]9 Or *the Millo*
[d]20 *Baal Perazim* means *the lord who breaks out.*   [e]25 Septuagint (see also
1 Chron. 14:16); Hebrew *Geba*   [f]2 That is, Kiriath Jearim; Hebrew *Baale
Judah*, a variant of *Baalah of Judah*   [g]2 Hebrew; Septuagint and Vulgate do
not have *the Name.*

Dancing Before the Lord

2 SAMUEL 6:16

I cannot dance, O Lord
unless you lead me.
If you will
that I leap joyfully
then you must be the first
    to dance
and sing.

Then, and only then,
will I leap for love.

Then I will soar
from love to knowledge,
from knowledge to fruition
from fruition to beyond
all human sense.

And there
I will remain
and circle for evermore.
—MECHTILD OF MAGDEBURG

See *Meeting God in Worship*

Almighty, who is enthroned between the cherubim that are on the ark. ³They set the ark of God on a new cart and brought it from the house of Abinadab, which was on the hill. Uzzah and Ahio, sons of Abinadab, were guiding the new cart ⁴with the ark of God on it,ᵃ and Ahio was walking in front of it. ⁵David and the whole house of Israel were celebrating with all their might before the Lᴏʀᴅ, with songsᵇ and with harps, lyres, tambourines, sistrums and cymbals.

⁶When they came to the threshing floor of Nacon, Uzzah reached out and took hold of the ark of God, because the oxen stumbled. ⁷The Lᴏʀᴅ's anger burned against Uzzah because of his irreverent act; therefore God struck him down and he died there beside the ark of God.

⁸Then David was angry because the Lᴏʀᴅ's wrath had broken out against Uzzah, and to this day that place is called Perez Uzzah.ᶜ

⁹David was afraid of the Lᴏʀᴅ that day and said, "How can the ark of the Lᴏʀᴅ ever come to me?" ¹⁰He was not willing to take the ark of the Lᴏʀᴅ to be with him in the City of David. Instead, he took it aside to the house of Obed-Edom the Gittite. ¹¹The ark of the Lᴏʀᴅ remained in the house of Obed-Edom the Gittite for three months, and the Lᴏʀᴅ blessed him and his entire household.

¹²Now King David was told, "The Lᴏʀᴅ has blessed the household of Obed-Edom and everything he has, because of the ark of God." So David went down and brought up the ark of God from the house of Obed-Edom to the City of David with rejoicing. ¹³When those who were carrying the ark of the Lᴏʀᴅ had taken six steps, he sacrificed a bull and a fattened calf. ¹⁴David, wearing a linen ephod, danced before the Lᴏʀᴅ with all his might, ¹⁵while he and the entire house of Israel brought up the ark of the Lᴏʀᴅ with shouts and the sound of trumpets.

¹⁶As the ark of the Lᴏʀᴅ was entering the City of David, Michal daughter of Saul watched from a window. And when she saw King David leaping and dancing before the Lᴏʀᴅ, she despised him in her heart.

¹⁷They brought the ark of the Lᴏʀᴅ and set it in its place inside the tent that David had pitched for it, and David sacrificed burnt offerings and fellowship offeringsᵈ before the Lᴏʀᴅ. ¹⁸After he had finished sacrificing the burnt offerings and fellowship offerings, he blessed the people in the name of the Lᴏʀᴅ Almighty. ¹⁹Then he gave a loaf of bread, a cake of dates and a cake of raisins to each person in the whole crowd of Israelites, both men and women. And all the people went to their homes.

²⁰When David returned home to bless his household, Michal daughter of Saul came out to meet him and said, "How the king of Israel has distinguished himself today, disrobing in the sight of the slave girls of his servants as any vulgar fellow would!"

²¹David said to Michal, "It was before the Lᴏʀᴅ, who chose me rather than your father or anyone from his house when he appointed me ruler over the Lᴏʀᴅ's people Israel—I will celebrate before the Lᴏʀᴅ. ²²I will become even

---

ᵃ *3,4* Dead Sea Scrolls and some Septuagint manuscripts; Masoretic Text *cart* ⁴*and they brought it with the ark of God from the house of Abinadab, which was on the hill* ᵇ *5* See Dead Sea Scrolls, Septuagint and 1 Chronicles 13:8; Masoretic Text *celebrating before the Lᴏʀᴅ with all kinds of instruments made of pine.* ᶜ *8 Perez Uzzah* means *outbreak against Uzzah.* ᵈ *17* Traditionally *peace offerings*; also in verse 18

more undignified than this, and I will be humiliated in my own eyes. But by these slave girls you spoke of, I will be held in honor."

²³And Michal daughter of Saul had no children to the day of her death.

God's Promise to David

7 After the king was settled in his palace and the LORD had given him rest from all his enemies around him, ²he said to Nathan the prophet, "Here I am, living in a palace of cedar, while the ark of God remains in a tent."

³Nathan replied to the king, "Whatever you have in mind, go ahead and do it, for the LORD is with you."

⁴That night the word of the LORD came to Nathan, saying:

⁵"Go and tell my servant David, 'This is what the LORD says: Are you the one to build me a house to dwell in? ⁶I have not dwelt in a house from the day I brought the Israelites up out of Egypt to this day. I have been moving from place to place with a tent as my dwelling. ⁷Wherever I have moved with all the Israelites, did I ever say to any of their rulers whom I commanded to shepherd my people Israel, "Why have you not built me a house of cedar?"'

⁸"Now then, tell my servant David, 'This is what the LORD Almighty says: I took you from the pasture and from following the flock to be ruler over my people Israel. ⁹I have been with you wherever you have gone, and I have cut off all your enemies from before you. Now I will make your name great, like the names of the greatest men of the earth. ¹⁰And I will provide a place for my people Israel and will plant them so that they can have a home of their own and no longer be disturbed. Wicked people will not oppress them anymore, as they did at the beginning ¹¹and have done ever since the time I appointed leaders[a] over my people Israel. I will also give you rest from all your enemies.

"'The LORD declares to you that the LORD himself will establish a house for you: ¹²When your days are over and you rest with your fathers, I will raise up your offspring to succeed you, who will come from your own body, and I will establish his kingdom. ¹³He is the one who will build a house for my Name, and I will establish the throne of his kingdom forever. ¹⁴I will be his father, and he will be my son. When he does wrong, I will punish him with the rod of men, with floggings inflicted by men. ¹⁵But my love will never be taken away from him, as I took it away from Saul, whom I removed from before you. ¹⁶Your house and your kingdom will endure forever before me[b]; your throne will be established forever.'"

¹⁷Nathan reported to David all the words of this entire revelation.

David's Prayer

¹⁸Then King David went in and sat before the LORD, and he said:

---

11 Traditionally *judges*   16 Some Hebrew manuscripts and Septuagint; most Hebrew manuscripts *you*

I Will Give You Rest

2 SAMUEL 7:1

An ancient prayer for a service at the end of the day says, "Guide us waking, O Lord, and guard us sleeping; that awake we may watch with Christ, and asleep we may rest in peace." The purpose of resting in the Lord is not merely to relax and refresh ourselves; resting is also eliminating distractions so that we may be fully aware of the presence of God.

Before going to sleep tonight, after you turn the lights out, repeat to yourself several times, "I rest in the Lord." If you wake up before morning, lie very still and say the name of Jesus, or say again, "I rest in the Lord." Use this exercise anytime you take a break from work or stop for a period of relaxation.

See Meeting God in Everyday Life

"You Have Brought Me This Far"

2 SAMUEL 7:18–19

The expression "brought this far" suggests a journey taken with a special guide. Struck by Nathan's words, David asks God, "Is this your usual way of dealing with man?" Consider how God has brought you to this point by drawing a trail map for your own life. Imagine a hiking trail that begins with your birth and label that event on a large sheet of paper. Proceed down the imaginary trail, marking on your map the high moments, narrow ways, verdant valleys, patches, inspiration points, caves, islands and other features that describe events in your life. In what direction do you think God wishes to take you next?

See Meeting God in Everyday Life

"Who am I, O Sovereign LORD, and what is my family, that you have brought me this far? ¹⁹And as if this were not enough in your sight, O Sovereign LORD, you have also spoken about the future of the house of your servant. Is this your usual way of dealing with man, O Sovereign LORD?

²⁰"What more can David say to you? For you know your servant, O Sovereign LORD. ²¹For the sake of your word and according to your will, you have done this great thing and made it known to your servant.

²²"How great you are, O Sovereign LORD! There is no one like you, and there is no God but you, as we have heard with our own ears. ²³And who is like your people Israel—the one nation on earth that God went out to redeem as a people for himself, and to make a name for himself, and to perform great and awesome wonders by driving out nations and their gods from before your people, whom you redeemed from Egypt?ᵃ ²⁴You have established your people Israel as your very own forever, and you, O LORD, have become their God.

²⁵"And now, LORD God, keep forever the promise you have made concerning your servant and his house. Do as you promised, ²⁶so that your name will be great forever. Then men will say, 'The LORD Almighty is God over Israel!' And the house of your servant David will be established before you.

²⁷"O LORD Almighty, God of Israel, you have revealed this to your servant, saying, 'I will build a house for you.' So your servant has found courage to offer you this prayer. ²⁸O Sovereign LORD, you are God! Your words are trustworthy, and you have promised these good things to your servant. ²⁹Now be pleased to bless the house of your servant, that it may continue forever in your sight; for you, O Sovereign LORD, have spoken, and with your blessing the house of your servant will be blessed forever."

David's Victories

8 In the course of time, David defeated the Philistines and subdued them, and he took Metheg Ammah from the control of the Philistines.

²David also defeated the Moabites. He made them lie down on the ground and measured them off with a length of cord. Every two lengths of them were put to death, and the third length was allowed to live. So the Moabites became subject to David and brought tribute.

³Moreover, David fought Hadadezer son of Rehob, king of Zobah, when he went to restore his control along the Euphrates River. ⁴David captured a thousand of his chariots, seven thousand charioteersᵇ and twenty thousand foot soldiers. He hamstrung all but a hundred of the chariot horses.

⁵When the Arameans of Damascus came to help Hadadezer king of Zobah, David struck down twenty-two thousand of them. ⁶He put garrisons in the Aramean kingdom of Damascus, and the Arameans became subject to

---

ᵃ 23 See Septuagint and 1 Chron. 17:21; Hebrew *wonders for your land and before your people, whom you redeemed from Egypt, from the nations and their gods.*   ᵇ 4 Septuagint (see also Dead Sea Scrolls and 1 Chron. 18:4); Masoretic Text *captured seventeen hundred of his charioteers*

him and brought tribute. The LORD gave David victory wherever he went.

[7]David took the gold shields that belonged to the officers of Hadadezer and brought them to Jerusalem. [8]From Tebah[a] and Berothai, towns that belonged to Hadadezer, King David took a great quantity of bronze.

[9]When Tou[b] king of Hamath heard that David had defeated the entire army of Hadadezer, [10]he sent his son Joram[c] to King David to greet him and congratulate him on his victory in battle over Hadadezer, who had been at war with Tou. Joram brought with him articles of silver and gold and bronze.

[11]King David dedicated these articles to the LORD, as he had done with the silver and gold from all the nations he had subdued: [12]Edom[d] and Moab, the Ammonites and the Philistines, and Amalek. He also dedicated the plunder taken from Hadadezer son of Rehob, king of Zobah.

[13]And David became famous after he returned from striking down eighteen thousand Edomites[e] in the Valley of Salt.

[14]He put garrisons throughout Edom, and all the Edomites became subject to David. The LORD gave David victory wherever he went.

David's Officials

[15]David reigned over all Israel, doing what was just and right for all his people. [16]Joab son of Zeruiah was over the army; Jehoshaphat son of Ahilud was recorder; [17]Zadok son of Ahitub and Ahimelech son of Abiathar were priests; Seraiah was secretary; [18]Benaiah son of Jehoiada was over the Kerethites and Pelethites; and David's sons were royal advisers.[f]

David and Mephibosheth

9 David asked, "Is there anyone still left of the house of Saul to whom I can show kindness for Jonathan's sake?"

[2]Now there was a servant of Saul's household named Ziba. They called him to appear before David, and the king said to him, "Are you Ziba?"

"Your servant," he replied.

[3]The king asked, "Is there no one still left of the house of Saul to whom I can show God's kindness?"

Ziba answered the king, "There is still a son of Jonathan; he is crippled in both feet."

[4]"Where is he?" the king asked.

Ziba answered, "He is at the house of Makir son of Ammiel in Lo Debar."

[5]So King David had him brought from Lo Debar, from the house of Makir son of Ammiel.

[6]When Mephibosheth son of Jonathan, the son of Saul, came to David, he bowed down to pay him honor.

David said, "Mephibosheth!"

"Your servant," he replied.

[7]"Don't be afraid," David said to him, "for I will surely

A Vow Fulfilled

2 SAMUEL 9:1–6

David asks, "Is there anyone . . . to whom I can show kindness?" By vowing protection for Jonathan's descendants, he turns away from a custom that permitted the slaying of all surviving members of a former dynasty; his love for Jonathan lives on in his kindly treatment of Jonathan's crippled son. We also often benefit from the affections for, and promises made to, our parents, ancestors or friends. On a small piece of paper, write the names of people who have treated you kindly "for the sake" of another person. Use the paper as a bookmark, reminding you for the next three days to look intentionally for ways to extend kindness to someone else.

See Meeting God in Service

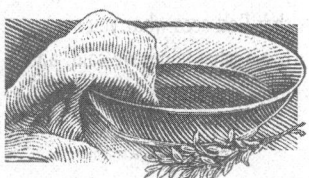

---

[a]8 See some Septuagint manuscripts (see also 1 Chron. 18:8); Hebrew *Betah*.   [b]9 Hebrew *Toi*, a variant of *Tou*; also in verse 10   [c]10 A variant of *Hadoram*   [d]12 Some Hebrew manuscripts, Septuagint and Syriac (see also 1 Chron. 18:11); most Hebrew manuscripts *Aram*   [e]13 A few Hebrew manuscripts, Septuagint and Syriac (see also 1 Chron. 18:12); most Hebrew manuscripts *Aram* (that is, Arameans)   [f]18 Or *were priests*

Humiliation and Humility

2 SAMUEL 10:4–5

Curiously, both "humiliate" and "humble" come from the Latin word *humus*, meaning soil. When we are humiliated, we may feel like "dirt," like the disgraced warriors in the story. Humility, on the other hand, connotes having one's feet on the ground of reality, being clear in one's self-assessment. As Dag Hammarskjöld wrote in *Markings*: "Humility is just as much the opposite of self-abasement as it is of self-exaltation. To be humble is [not to make comparisons]."

Recall moments when you have felt humiliated. Then, by contrast, consider what it means to see yourself humbly, simply as you are, without comparison to someone else. Go to a mirror now and describe yourself in your own words. Then imagine that God sees what you see, hears what you have said, and loves you just as you are.

See Meeting God in Prayer

show you kindness for the sake of your father Jonathan. I will restore to you all the land that belonged to your grandfather Saul, and you will always eat at my table."

⁸Mephibosheth bowed down and said, "What is your servant, that you should notice a dead dog like me?"

⁹Then the king summoned Ziba, Saul's servant, and said to him, "I have given your master's grandson everything that belonged to Saul and his family. ¹⁰You and your sons and your servants are to farm the land for him and bring in the crops, so that your master's grandson may be provided for. And Mephibosheth, grandson of your master, will always eat at my table." (Now Ziba had fifteen sons and twenty servants.)

¹¹Then Ziba said to the king, "Your servant will do whatever my lord the king commands his servant to do." So Mephibosheth ate at David's*ᵃ* table like one of the king's sons.

¹²Mephibosheth had a young son named Mica, and all the members of Ziba's household were servants of Mephibosheth. ¹³And Mephibosheth lived in Jerusalem, because he always ate at the king's table, and he was crippled in both feet.

David Defeats the Ammonites

10 In the course of time, the king of the Ammonites died, and his son Hanun succeeded him as king. ²David thought, "I will show kindness to Hanun son of Nahash, just as his father showed kindness to me." So David sent a delegation to express his sympathy to Hanun concerning his father.

When David's men came to the land of the Ammonites, ³the Ammonite nobles said to Hanun their lord, "Do you think David is honoring your father by sending men to you to express sympathy? Hasn't David sent them to you to explore the city and spy it out and overthrow it?" ⁴So Hanun seized David's men, shaved off half of each man's beard, cut off their garments in the middle at the buttocks, and sent them away.

⁵When David was told about this, he sent messengers to meet the men, for they were greatly humiliated. The king said, "Stay at Jericho till your beards have grown, and then come back."

⁶When the Ammonites realized that they had become a stench in David's nostrils, they hired twenty thousand Aramean foot soldiers from Beth Rehob and Zobah, as well as the king of Maacah with a thousand men, and also twelve thousand men from Tob.

⁷On hearing this, David sent Joab out with the entire army of fighting men. ⁸The Ammonites came out and drew up in battle formation at the entrance to their city gate, while the Arameans of Zobah and Rehob and the men of Tob and Maacah were by themselves in the open country.

⁹Joab saw that there were battle lines in front of him and behind him; so he selected some of the best troops in Israel and deployed them against the Arameans. ¹⁰He put the rest of the men under the command of Abishai his brother and deployed them against the Ammonites. ¹¹Joab said, "If the Arameans are too strong for me, then you are to come to my rescue; but if the Ammonites are too strong for you, then I will come to rescue you. ¹²Be strong and let us fight

ᵃ 11 Septuagint; Hebrew *my*

bravely for our people and the cities of our God. The LORD will do what is good in his sight."

¹³Then Joab and the troops with him advanced to fight the Arameans, and they fled before him. ¹⁴When the Ammonites saw that the Arameans were fleeing, they fled before Abishai and went inside the city. So Joab returned from fighting the Ammonites and came to Jerusalem.

¹⁵After the Arameans saw that they had been routed by Israel, they regrouped. ¹⁶Hadadezer had Arameans brought from beyond the River[a]; they went to Helam, with Shobach the commander of Hadadezer's army leading them.

¹⁷When David was told of this, he gathered all Israel, crossed the Jordan and went to Helam. The Arameans formed their battle lines to meet David and fought against him. ¹⁸But they fled before Israel, and David killed seven hundred of their charioteers and forty thousand of their foot soldiers.[b] He also struck down Shobach the commander of their army, and he died there. ¹⁹When all the kings who were vassals of Hadadezer saw that they had been defeated by Israel, they made peace with the Israelites and became subject to them.

So the Arameans were afraid to help the Ammonites anymore.

David and Bathsheba

11 In the spring, at the time when kings go off to war, David sent Joab out with the king's men and the whole Israelite army. They destroyed the Ammonites and besieged Rabbah. But David remained in Jerusalem.

²One evening David got up from his bed and walked around on the roof of the palace. From the roof he saw a woman bathing. The woman was very beautiful, ³and David sent someone to find out about her. The man said, "Isn't this Bathsheba, the daughter of Eliam and the wife of Uriah the Hittite?" ⁴Then David sent messengers to get her. She came to him, and he slept with her. (She had purified herself from her uncleanness.) Then[c] she went back home. ⁵The woman conceived and sent word to David, saying, "I am pregnant."

⁶So David sent this word to Joab: "Send me Uriah the Hittite." And Joab sent him to David. ⁷When Uriah came to him, David asked him how Joab was, how the soldiers were and how the war was going. ⁸Then David said to Uriah, "Go down to your house and wash your feet." So Uriah left the palace, and a gift from the king was sent after him. ⁹But Uriah slept at the entrance to the palace with all his master's servants and did not go down to his house.

¹⁰When David was told, "Uriah did not go home," he asked him, "Haven't you just come from a distance? Why didn't you go home?"

¹¹Uriah said to David, "The ark and Israel and Judah are staying in tents, and my master Joab and my lord's men are camped in the open fields. How could I go to my house to eat and drink and lie with my wife? As surely as you live, I will not do such a thing!"

¹²Then David said to him, "Stay here one more day, and tomorrow I will send you back." So Uriah remained in

Friends in Need

2 SAMUEL 10:11–12

How reassuring it is to have someone to depend on in times of need. And how validating to know that others are willing to call on us in their difficult periods. Think of your own times of need, recollecting two people still living who have come to your aid. Write or call to let these people know that you still treasure their past support. If you are going through a difficult time right now, ask for support from someone else. Reach out to offer help to someone who has been on your mind; tell them you have been thinking warmly of them and hope that all is well. Ask what you might do to help them.

See Meeting God in Community

Good Greed?

2 SAMUEL 11:27—12:7

In his 1986 commencement address at the University of California at Berkeley, trader Ivan Boesky asserted: "Greed is all right . . . Greed is healthy. You can be greedy and still feel good about yourself." David might have been comforted by such an adviser, but instead he had Nathan, whose rebuke helped him recognize and repent of his greediness in arranging Uriah's death and marrying Bathsheba. In what areas of your life are you greedy, taking more than you need and failing to be grateful for what you have received? Are there "Ivans" inside you or around you who encourage you to rationalize this behavior as good? Do you have a "Nathan," someone who challenges you to confront your weaknesses and helps you to be your best self?

See *Meeting God in Service*

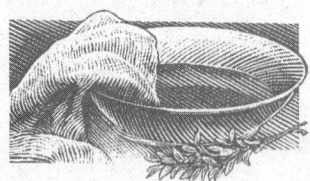

Jerusalem that day and the next. ¹³At David's invitation, he ate and drank with him, and David made him drunk. But in the evening Uriah went out to sleep on his mat among his master's servants; he did not go home.

¹⁴In the morning David wrote a letter to Joab and sent it with Uriah. ¹⁵In it he wrote, "Put Uriah in the front line where the fighting is fiercest. Then withdraw from him so he will be struck down and die."

¹⁶So while Joab had the city under siege, he put Uriah at a place where he knew the strongest defenders were. ¹⁷When the men of the city came out and fought against Joab, some of the men in David's army fell; moreover, Uriah the Hittite died.

¹⁸Joab sent David a full account of the battle. ¹⁹He instructed the messenger: "When you have finished giving the king this account of the battle, ²⁰the king's anger may flare up, and he may ask you, 'Why did you get so close to the city to fight? Didn't you know they would shoot arrows from the wall? ²¹Who killed Abimelech son of Jerub-Besheth*? Didn't a woman throw an upper millstone on him from the wall, so that he died in Thebez? Why did you get so close to the wall?' If he asks you this, then say to him, 'Also, your servant Uriah the Hittite is dead.' "

²²The messenger set out, and when he arrived he told David everything Joab had sent him to say. ²³The messenger said to David, "The men overpowered us and came out against us in the open, but we drove them back to the entrance to the city gate. ²⁴Then the archers shot arrows at your servants from the wall, and some of the king's men died. Moreover, your servant Uriah the Hittite is dead."

²⁵David told the messenger, "Say this to Joab: 'Don't let this upset you; the sword devours one as well as another. Press the attack against the city and destroy it.' Say this to encourage Joab."

²⁶When Uriah's wife heard that her husband was dead, she mourned for him. ²⁷After the time of mourning was over, David had her brought to his house, and she became his wife and bore him a son. But the thing David had done displeased the LORD.

Nathan Rebukes David

12 The LORD sent Nathan to David. When he came to him, he said, "There were two men in a certain town, one rich and the other poor. ²The rich man had a very large number of sheep and cattle, ³but the poor man had nothing except one little ewe lamb he had bought. He raised it, and it grew up with him and his children. It shared his food, drank from his cup and even slept in his arms. It was like a daughter to him.

⁴"Now a traveler came to the rich man, but the rich man refrained from taking one of his own sheep or cattle to prepare a meal for the traveler who had come to him. Instead, he took the ewe lamb that belonged to the poor man and prepared it for the one who had come to him."

⁵David burned with anger against the man and said to Nathan, "As surely as the LORD lives, the man who did this deserves to die! ⁶He must pay for that lamb four times over, because he did such a thing and had no pity."

⁷Then Nathan said to David, "You are the man! This is

*21 Also known as *Jerub-Baal* (that is, Gideon)

what the Lord, the God of Israel, says: 'I anointed you king over Israel, and I delivered you from the hand of Saul. [8]I gave your master's house to you, and your master's wives into your arms. I gave you the house of Israel and Judah. And if all this had been too little, I would have given you even more. [9]Why did you despise the word of the Lord by doing what is evil in his eyes? You struck down Uriah the Hittite with the sword and took his wife to be your own. You killed him with the sword of the Ammonites. [10]Now, therefore, the sword will never depart from your house, because you despised me and took the wife of Uriah the Hittite to be your own.'

[11]"This is what the Lord says: 'Out of your own household I am going to bring calamity upon you. Before your very eyes I will take your wives and give them to one who is close to you, and he will lie with your wives in broad daylight. [12]You did it in secret, but I will do this thing in broad daylight before all Israel.'"

[13]Then David said to Nathan, "I have sinned against the Lord."

Nathan replied, "The Lord has taken away your sin. You are not going to die. [14]But because by doing this you have made the enemies of the Lord show utter contempt,[a] the son born to you will die."

[15]After Nathan had gone home, the Lord struck the child that Uriah's wife had borne to David, and he became ill. [16]David pleaded with God for the child. He fasted and went into his house and spent the nights lying on the ground. [17]The elders of his household stood beside him to get him up from the ground, but he refused, and he would not eat any food with them.

[18]On the seventh day the child died. David's servants were afraid to tell him that the child was dead, for they thought, "While the child was still living, we spoke to David but he would not listen to us. How can we tell him the child is dead? He may do something desperate."

[19]David noticed that his servants were whispering among themselves and he realized the child was dead. "Is the child dead?" he asked.

"Yes," they replied, "he is dead."

[20]Then David got up from the ground. After he had washed, put on lotions and changed his clothes, he went into the house of the Lord and worshiped. Then he went to his own house, and at his request they served him food, and he ate.

[21]His servants asked him, "Why are you acting this way? While the child was alive, you fasted and wept, but now that the child is dead, you get up and eat!"

[22]He answered, "While the child was still alive, I fasted and wept. I thought, 'Who knows? The Lord may be gracious to me and let the child live.' [23]But now that he is dead, why should I fast? Can I bring him back again? I will go to him, but he will not return to me."

[24]Then David comforted his wife Bathsheba, and he went to her and lay with her. She gave birth to a son, and they named him Solomon. The Lord loved him; [25]and because the Lord loved him, he sent word through Nathan the prophet to name him Jedidiah.[b]

---

[a] 14 Masoretic Text; an ancient Hebrew scribal tradition *this you have shown utter contempt for the Lord*   [b] 25 *Jedidiah* means *loved by the Lord.*

Pleading for Another

2 SAMUEL 12:16

David's pleading and fasting constitute a prayer of intercession, which in his day was a priestly act of loving identification with a suffering person.

For whom are you called to intercede today? Bring one or more persons into your heart and mind. In love, try to identify with their need or distress. Then, holding them in your heart, open yourself to God's love for them as you understand that love. Let that love flow through you toward those in need.

See Meeting God in Prayer

Good and Evil

2 SAMUEL 13:5

"Evil is changed into good when it is received in patience through the love of God; while good is changed into evil when we become attached to it through the love of self. True good lies only in detachment, and abandonment to God. You are now in the trial; put yourself confidently and without reserve into his hand. What would I not sacrifice to see you once more restored in body, but heartily sick of the love of the world! Attachment to ourselves is a thousand times more infectious than a contagious poison, for it contains the venom of self. I pray for you with all my heart."

—FRANÇOIS FÈNELON,
Spiritual Letters (Letter 7)

²⁶Meanwhile Joab fought against Rabbah of the Ammonites and captured the royal citadel. ²⁷Joab then sent messengers to David, saying, "I have fought against Rabbah and taken its water supply. ²⁸Now muster the rest of the troops and besiege the city and capture it. Otherwise I will take the city, and it will be named after me." ²⁹So David mustered the entire army and went to Rabbah, and attacked and captured it. ³⁰He took the crown from the head of their king*a*—its weight was a talent*b* of gold, and it was set with precious stones—and it was placed on David's head. He took a great quantity of plunder from the city ³¹and brought out the people who were there, consigning them to labor with saws and with iron picks and axes, and he made them work at brickmaking.*c* He did this to all the Ammonite towns. Then David and his entire army returned to Jerusalem.

Amnon and Tamar

13 In the course of time, Amnon son of David fell in love with Tamar, the beautiful sister of Absalom son of David.

²Amnon became frustrated to the point of illness on account of his sister Tamar, for she was a virgin, and it seemed impossible for him to do anything to her.

³Now Amnon had a friend named Jonadab son of Shimeah, David's brother. Jonadab was a very shrewd man. ⁴He asked Amnon, "Why do you, the king's son, look so haggard morning after morning? Won't you tell me?"

Amnon said to him, "I'm in love with Tamar, my brother Absalom's sister."

⁵"Go to bed and pretend to be ill," Jonadab said. "When your father comes to see you, say to him, 'I would like my sister Tamar to come and give me something to eat. Let her prepare the food in my sight so I may watch her and then eat it from her hand.' "

⁶So Amnon lay down and pretended to be ill. When the king came to see him, Amnon said to him, "I would like my sister Tamar to come and make some special bread in my sight, so I may eat from her hand."

⁷David sent word to Tamar at the palace: "Go to the house of your brother Amnon and prepare some food for him." ⁸So Tamar went to the house of her brother Amnon, who was lying down. She took some dough, kneaded it, made the bread in his sight and baked it. ⁹Then she took the pan and served him the bread, but he refused to eat.

"Send everyone out of here," Amnon said. So everyone left him. ¹⁰Then Amnon said to Tamar, "Bring the food here into my bedroom so I may eat from your hand." And Tamar took the bread she had prepared and brought it to her brother Amnon in his bedroom. ¹¹But when she took it to him to eat, he grabbed her and said, "Come to bed with me, my sister."

¹²"Don't, my brother!" she said to him. "Don't force me. Such a thing should not be done in Israel! Don't do this wicked thing. ¹³What about me? Where could I get rid of my disgrace? And what about you? You would be like one of the wicked fools in Israel. Please speak to the king; he

---

a 30 Or *of Milcom* (that is, Molech)   *b 30* That is, about 75 pounds (about 34 kilograms)   *c 31* The meaning of the Hebrew for this clause is uncertain.

will not keep me from being married to you." ¹⁴But he refused to listen to her, and since he was stronger than she, he raped her.

¹⁵Then Amnon hated her with intense hatred. In fact, he hated her more than he had loved her. Amnon said to her, "Get up and get out!"

¹⁶"No!" she said to him. "Sending me away would be a greater wrong than what you have already done to me."

But he refused to listen to her. ¹⁷He called his personal servant and said, "Get this woman out of here and bolt the door after her." ¹⁸So his servant put her out and bolted the door after her. She was wearing a richly ornamented*a* robe, for this was the kind of garment the virgin daughters of the king wore. ¹⁹Tamar put ashes on her head and tore the ornamented*b* robe she was wearing. She put her hand on her head and went away, weeping aloud as she went.

²⁰Her brother Absalom said to her, "Has that Amnon, your brother, been with you? Be quiet now, my sister; he is your brother. Don't take this thing to heart." And Tamar lived in her brother Absalom's house, a desolate woman.

²¹When King David heard all this, he was furious. ²²Absalom never said a word to Amnon, either good or bad; he hated Amnon because he had disgraced his sister Tamar.

Absalom Kills Amnon

²³Two years later, when Absalom's sheepshearers were at Baal Hazor near the border of Ephraim, he invited all the king's sons to come there. ²⁴Absalom went to the king and said, "Your servant has had shearers come. Will the king and his officials please join me?"

²⁵"No, my son," the king replied. "All of us should not go; we would only be a burden to you." Although Absalom urged him, he still refused to go, but gave him his blessing.

²⁶Then Absalom said, "If not, please let my brother Amnon come with us."

The king asked him, "Why should he go with you?" ²⁷But Absalom urged him, so he sent with him Amnon and the rest of the king's sons.

²⁸Absalom ordered his men, "Listen! When Amnon is in high spirits from drinking wine and I say to you, 'Strike Amnon down,' then kill him. Don't be afraid. Have not I given you this order? Be strong and brave." ²⁹So Absalom's men did to Amnon what Absalom had ordered. Then all the king's sons got up, mounted their mules and fled.

³⁰While they were on their way, the report came to David: "Absalom has struck down all the king's sons; not one of them is left." ³¹The king stood up, tore his clothes and lay down on the ground; and all his servants stood by with their clothes torn.

³²But Jonadab son of Shimeah, David's brother, said, "My lord should not think that they killed all the princes; only Amnon is dead. This has been Absalom's expressed intention ever since the day Amnon raped his sister Tamar. ³³My lord the king should not be concerned about the report that all the king's sons are dead. Only Amnon is dead."

³⁴Meanwhile, Absalom had fled.

Now the man standing watch looked up and saw many people on the road west of him, coming down the side of

---

Violent Cruelty

2 SAMUEL 13:15

The story of Tamar, Amnon and Jonadab is hard to read for it is a story of cruelty, abuse and neglect. But we may also realize through this story that God does not hide his face from the hardest things in life. Through this story we see that evil is real and that God does not gloss over this reality.

Pray today for anyone you know who is or has been abused. Set aside a special time each day this week and offer to God's care all people who suffer from violence within their families. Pray for people who are afraid. Pray for those people who try to protect the weaker and more vulnerable members of our communities.

See Meeting God in Community

---

a 18 The meaning of the Hebrew for this phrase is uncertain.   *b 19* The meaning of the Hebrew for this word is uncertain.

405

Justice

2 SAMUEL 14:4–13

Like Nathan's earlier tale of the little ewe lamb (chapter 12), Joab's hired "wise woman" spins a tale about her family's threatened clan feud and bloodbath. She, too, makes the point that the king's principles do not necessarily carry over into his concrete decisions—in this case, to call his own son Absalom out of exile. We, too, may not always practice what we preach, calling for justice for oppressed groups while avoiding contact with their members or neglecting to bring justice into our own relationships, work situation or families. Can you think of areas where your abstract principles are not practiced concretely? The Choristers' Prayer of the Royal School of Church Music asks God that "what we sing [or say] with our lips we may believe in our hearts and what we believe in our hearts, we may show forth in our lives." Let this be your prayer today.

See *Meeting God in Service*

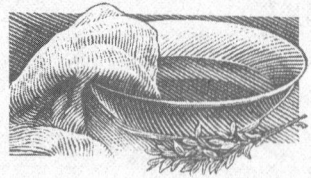

the hill. The watchman went and told the king, "I see men in the direction of Horonaim, on the side of the hill."*a*

³⁵Jonadab said to the king, "See, the king's sons are here; it has happened just as your servant said."

³⁶As he finished speaking, the king's sons came in, wailing loudly. The king, too, and all his servants wept very bitterly.

³⁷Absalom fled and went to Talmai son of Ammihud, the king of Geshur. But King David mourned for his son every day.

³⁸After Absalom fled and went to Geshur, he stayed there three years. ³⁹And the spirit of the king*b* longed to go to Absalom, for he was consoled concerning Amnon's death.

Absalom Returns to Jerusalem

14 Joab son of Zeruiah knew that the king's heart longed for Absalom. ²So Joab sent someone to Tekoa and had a wise woman brought from there. He said to her, "Pretend you are in mourning. Dress in mourning clothes, and don't use any cosmetic lotions. Act like a woman who has spent many days grieving for the dead. ³Then go to the king and speak these words to him." And Joab put the words in her mouth.

⁴When the woman from Tekoa went*c* to the king, she fell with her face to the ground to pay him honor, and she said, "Help me, O king!"

⁵The king asked her, "What is troubling you?"

She said, "I am indeed a widow; my husband is dead. ⁶I your servant had two sons. They got into a fight with each other in the field, and no one was there to separate them. One struck the other and killed him. ⁷Now the whole clan has risen up against your servant; they say, 'Hand over the one who struck his brother down, so that we may put him to death for the life of his brother whom he killed; then we will get rid of the heir as well.' They would put out the only burning coal I have left, leaving my husband neither name nor descendant on the face of the earth."

⁸The king said to the woman, "Go home, and I will issue an order in your behalf."

⁹But the woman from Tekoa said to him, "My lord the king, let the blame rest on me and on my father's family, and let the king and his throne be without guilt."

¹⁰The king replied, "If anyone says anything to you, bring him to me, and he will not bother you again."

¹¹She said, "Then let the king invoke the LORD his God to prevent the avenger of blood from adding to the destruction, so that my son will not be destroyed."

"As surely as the LORD lives," he said, "not one hair of your son's head will fall to the ground."

¹²Then the woman said, "Let your servant speak a word to my lord the king."

"Speak," he replied.

¹³The woman said, "Why then have you devised a thing like this against the people of God? When the king says this, does he not convict himself, for the king has not brought back his banished son? ¹⁴Like water spilled on the ground,

---

a 34 Septuagint; Hebrew does not have this sentence. *b 39* Dead Sea Scrolls and some Septuagint manuscripts; Masoretic Text *But ⌊the spirit of⌋ David the king* *c 4* Many Hebrew manuscripts, Septuagint, Vulgate and Syriac; most Hebrew manuscripts *spoke*

which cannot be recovered, so we must die. But God does not take away life; instead, he devises ways so that a banished person may not remain estranged from him.

¹⁵"And now I have come to say this to my lord the king because the people have made me afraid. Your servant thought, 'I will speak to the king; perhaps he will do what his servant asks. ¹⁶Perhaps the king will agree to deliver his servant from the hand of the man who is trying to cut off both me and my son from the inheritance God gave us.'

¹⁷"And now your servant says, 'May the word of my lord the king bring me rest, for my lord the king is like an angel of God in discerning good and evil. May the LORD your God be with you.'"

¹⁸Then the king said to the woman, "Do not keep from me the answer to what I am going to ask you."

"Let my lord the king speak," the woman said.

¹⁹The king asked, "Isn't the hand of Joab with you in all this?"

The woman answered, "As surely as you live, my lord the king, no one can turn to the right or to the left from anything my lord the king says. Yes, it was your servant Joab who instructed me to do this and who put all these words into the mouth of your servant. ²⁰Your servant Joab did this to change the present situation. My lord has wisdom like that of an angel of God—he knows everything that happens in the land."

²¹The king said to Joab, "Very well, I will do it. Go, bring back the young man Absalom."

²²Joab fell with his face to the ground to pay him honor, and he blessed the king. Joab said, "Today your servant knows that he has found favor in your eyes, my lord the king, because the king has granted his servant's request."

²³Then Joab went to Geshur and brought Absalom back to Jerusalem. ²⁴But the king said, "He must go to his own house; he must not see my face." So Absalom went to his own house and did not see the face of the king.

²⁵In all Israel there was not a man so highly praised for his handsome appearance as Absalom. From the top of his head to the sole of his foot there was no blemish in him. ²⁶Whenever he cut the hair of his head—he used to cut his hair from time to time when it became too heavy for him—he would weigh it, and its weight was two hundred shekels[a] by the royal standard.

²⁷Three sons and a daughter were born to Absalom. The daughter's name was Tamar, and she became a beautiful woman.

²⁸Absalom lived two years in Jerusalem without seeing the king's face. ²⁹Then Absalom sent for Joab in order to send him to the king, but Joab refused to come to him. So he sent a second time, but he refused to come. ³⁰Then he said to his servants, "Look, Joab's field is next to mine, and he has barley there. Go and set it on fire." So Absalom's servants set the field on fire.

³¹Then Joab did go to Absalom's house and he said to him, "Why have your servants set my field on fire?"

³²Absalom said to Joab, "Look, I sent word to you and said, 'Come here so I can send you to the king to ask, "Why have I come from Geshur? It would be better for me if I

Like Water Spilled

2 SAMUEL 14:14

Reflect on this verse, allowing it to illuminate your relationship with God. Respond to these questions, perhaps writing your thoughts in a journal: What does the verse say, in general, about human life? What does it say personally to you? What in your life is spilled and seems unrecoverable? Health, goodwill, opportunities, patience, personal talents? What does it say about your periodic feelings of estrangement from God? About the ways God devises to reverse your banishment?

Conspiracies of Silence

2 SAMUEL 15:10–12

"In Germany they came first for the Communists, and I didn't speak up because I wasn't a Communist. Then they came for the Jews, and I didn't speak up because I wasn't a Jew. Then they came for the trade unionists, and I didn't speak up because I wasn't a trade unionist. Then they came for the Catholics, and I didn't speak up because I was a Protestant. Then they came for me, and by that time, there was no one left to speak up."

—Attributed to Pastor Martin Niemoeller

were still there!" ' Now then, I want to see the king's face, and if I am guilty of anything, let him put me to death."

³³So Joab went to the king and told him this. Then the king summoned Absalom, and he came in and bowed down with his face to the ground before the king. And the king kissed Absalom.

Absalom's Conspiracy

15 In the course of time, Absalom provided himself with a chariot and horses and with fifty men to run ahead of him. ²He would get up early and stand by the side of the road leading to the city gate. Whenever anyone came with a complaint to be placed before the king for a decision, Absalom would call out to him, "What town are you from?" He would answer, "Your servant is from one of the tribes of Israel." ³Then Absalom would say to him, "Look, your claims are valid and proper, but there is no representative of the king to hear you." ⁴And Absalom would add, "If only I were appointed judge in the land! Then everyone who has a complaint or case could come to me and I would see that he gets justice."

⁵Also, whenever anyone approached him to bow down before him, Absalom would reach out his hand, take hold of him and kiss him. ⁶Absalom behaved in this way toward all the Israelites who came to the king asking for justice, and so he stole the hearts of the men of Israel.

⁷At the end of four[a] years, Absalom said to the king, "Let me go to Hebron and fulfill a vow I made to the Lord. ⁸While your servant was living at Geshur in Aram, I made this vow: 'If the Lord takes me back to Jerusalem, I will worship the Lord in Hebron.[b]' "

⁹The king said to him, "Go in peace." So he went to Hebron.

¹⁰Then Absalom sent secret messengers throughout the tribes of Israel to say, "As soon as you hear the sound of the trumpets, then say, 'Absalom is king in Hebron.' " ¹¹Two hundred men from Jerusalem had accompanied Absalom. They had been invited as guests and went quite innocently, knowing nothing about the matter. ¹²While Absalom was offering sacrifices, he also sent for Ahithophel the Gilonite, David's counselor, to come from Giloh, his hometown. And so the conspiracy gained strength, and Absalom's following kept on increasing.

David Flees

¹³A messenger came and told David, "The hearts of the men of Israel are with Absalom."

¹⁴Then David said to all his officials who were with him in Jerusalem, "Come! We must flee, or none of us will escape from Absalom. We must leave immediately, or he will move quickly to overtake us and bring ruin upon us and put the city to the sword."

¹⁵The king's officials answered him, "Your servants are ready to do whatever our lord the king chooses."

¹⁶The king set out, with his entire household following him; but he left ten concubines to take care of the palace. ¹⁷So the king set out, with all the people following him, and they halted at a place some distance away. ¹⁸All his men

---

[a] 7 Some Septuagint manuscripts, Syriac and Josephus; Hebrew *forty*
[b] 8 Some Septuagint manuscripts; Hebrew does not have *in Hebron*.

marched past him, along with all the Kerethites and Pelethites; and all the six hundred Gittites who had accompanied him from Gath marched before the king.

¹⁹The king said to Ittai the Gittite, "Why should you come along with us? Go back and stay with King Absalom. You are a foreigner, an exile from your homeland. ²⁰You came only yesterday. And today shall I make you wander about with us, when I do not know where I am going? Go back, and take your countrymen. May kindness and faithfulness be with you."

²¹But Ittai replied to the king, "As surely as the LORD lives, and as my lord the king lives, wherever my lord the king may be, whether it means life or death, there will your servant be."

²²David said to Ittai, "Go ahead, march on." So Ittai the Gittite marched on with all his men and the families that were with him.

²³The whole countryside wept aloud as all the people passed by. The king also crossed the Kidron Valley, and all the people moved on toward the desert.

²⁴Zadok was there, too, and all the Levites who were with him were carrying the ark of the covenant of God. They set down the ark of God, and Abiathar offered sacrifices*a* until all the people had finished leaving the city.

²⁵Then the king said to Zadok, "Take the ark of God back into the city. If I find favor in the LORD's eyes, he will bring me back and let me see it and his dwelling place again. ²⁶But if he says, 'I am not pleased with you,' then I am ready; let him do to me whatever seems good to him."

²⁷The king also said to Zadok the priest, "Aren't you a seer? Go back to the city in peace, with your son Ahimaaz and Jonathan son of Abiathar. You and Abiathar take your two sons with you. ²⁸I will wait at the fords in the desert until word comes from you to inform me." ²⁹So Zadok and Abiathar took the ark of God back to Jerusalem and stayed there.

³⁰But David continued up the Mount of Olives, weeping as he went; his head was covered and he was barefoot. All the people with him covered their heads too and were weeping as they went up. ³¹Now David had been told, "Ahithophel is among the conspirators with Absalom." So David prayed, "O LORD, turn Ahithophel's counsel into foolishness."

³²When David arrived at the summit, where people used to worship God, Hushai the Arkite was there to meet him, his robe torn and dust on his head. ³³David said to him, "If you go with me, you will be a burden to me. ³⁴But if you return to the city and say to Absalom, 'I will be your servant, O king; I was your father's servant in the past, but now I will be your servant,' then you can help me by frustrating Ahithophel's advice. ³⁵Won't the priests Zadok and Abiathar be there with you? Tell them anything you hear in the king's palace. ³⁶Their two sons, Ahimaaz son of Zadok and Jonathan son of Abiathar, are there with them. Send them to me with anything you hear."

³⁷So David's friend Hushai arrived at Jerusalem as Absalom was entering the city.

Fidelity

2 SAMUEL 15:21

Ittai the Gittite pledges that in life or death, "Wherever my lord the king may be . . . there will your servant be." Such fidelity is particularly striking today, when people are shifting residences, work places, relationships and church affiliations with such frequency. To what values, and to which people, do you commit yourself? What commitments have you made—to yourself, to others, to your community and to God—that involve real pledges of fidelity? How do you nurture these commitments to help them become stronger? How do you stay faithful to old commitments as you move on to new interests? Take your current commitments to prayer, being open to any ideas that come regarding how to strengthen them; be open to new commitments you may be called to make.

See Meeting God in Community

---

a 24 Or Abiathar went up

Cursing and Blessing

2 SAMUEL 16:5–7

When Shimei curses David, saying "You have come to ruin because you are a man of blood!" the refugee king does not retaliate. In what situations do you feel called to "curse" by blasting someone personally, or by sounding off about some social issue? Christians are called to bless and not curse (see Luke 6:28), a principle founded on the belief that goodness can overcome evil, and blessings can counteract curses. Consider how you might reframe your "curse" into a more positive declaration of objection or challenge—and follow up on the issue by communicating with a government official or business leader.

See Meeting God in Everyday Life

David and Ziba

16 When David had gone a short distance beyond the summit, there was Ziba, the steward of Mephibosheth, waiting to meet him. He had a string of donkeys saddled and loaded with two hundred loaves of bread, a hundred cakes of raisins, a hundred cakes of figs and a skin of wine.

²The king asked Ziba, "Why have you brought these?"

Ziba answered, "The donkeys are for the king's household to ride on, the bread and fruit are for the men to eat, and the wine is to refresh those who become exhausted in the desert."

³The king then asked, "Where is your master's grandson?"

Ziba said to him, "He is staying in Jerusalem, because he thinks, 'Today the house of Israel will give me back my grandfather's kingdom.' "

⁴Then the king said to Ziba, "All that belonged to Mephibosheth is now yours."

"I humbly bow," Ziba said. "May I find favor in your eyes, my lord the king."

Shimei Curses David

⁵As King David approached Bahurim, a man from the same clan as Saul's family came out from there. His name was Shimei son of Gera, and he cursed as he came out. ⁶He pelted David and all the king's officials with stones, though all the troops and the special guard were on David's right and left. ⁷As he cursed, Shimei said, "Get out, get out, you man of blood, you scoundrel! ⁸The LORD has repaid you for all the blood you shed in the household of Saul, in whose place you have reigned. The LORD has handed the kingdom over to your son Absalom. You have come to ruin because you are a man of blood!"

⁹Then Abishai son of Zeruiah said to the king, "Why should this dead dog curse my lord the king? Let me go over and cut off his head."

¹⁰But the king said, "What do you and I have in common, you sons of Zeruiah? If he is cursing because the LORD said to him, 'Curse David,' who can ask, 'Why do you do this?' "

¹¹David then said to Abishai and all his officials, "My son, who is of my own flesh, is trying to take my life. How much more, then, this Benjamite! Leave him alone; let him curse, for the LORD has told him to. ¹²It may be that the LORD will see my distress and repay me with good for the cursing I am receiving today."

¹³So David and his men continued along the road while Shimei was going along the hillside opposite him, cursing as he went and throwing stones at him and showering him with dirt. ¹⁴The king and all the people with him arrived at their destination exhausted. And there he refreshed himself.

The Advice of Hushai and Ahithophel

¹⁵Meanwhile, Absalom and all the men of Israel came to Jerusalem, and Ahithophel was with him. ¹⁶Then Hushai the Arkite, David's friend, went to Absalom and said to him, "Long live the king! Long live the king!"

¹⁷Absalom asked Hushai, "Is this the love you show your friend? Why didn't you go with your friend?"

¹⁸Hushai said to Absalom, "No, the one chosen by the LORD, by these people, and by all the men of Israel—his I will be, and I will remain with him. ¹⁹Furthermore, whom should I serve? Should I not serve the son? Just as I served your father, so I will serve you."

²⁰Absalom said to Ahithophel, "Give us your advice. What should we do?"

²¹Ahithophel answered, "Lie with your father's concubines whom he left to take care of the palace. Then all Israel will hear that you have made yourself a stench in your father's nostrils, and the hands of everyone with you will be strengthened." ²²So they pitched a tent for Absalom on the roof, and he lay with his father's concubines in the sight of all Israel.

²³Now in those days the advice Ahithophel gave was like that of one who inquires of God. That was how both David and Absalom regarded all of Ahithophel's advice.

17 Ahithophel said to Absalom, "I would^a choose twelve thousand men and set out tonight in pursuit of David. ²I would^b attack him while he is weary and weak. I would^b strike him with terror, and then all the people with him will flee. I would^b strike down only the king ³and bring all the people back to you. The death of the man you seek will mean the return of all; all the people will be unharmed." ⁴This plan seemed good to Absalom and to all the elders of Israel.

⁵But Absalom said, "Summon also Hushai the Arkite, so we can hear what he has to say." ⁶When Hushai came to him, Absalom said, "Ahithophel has given this advice. Should we do what he says? If not, give us your opinion."

⁷Hushai replied to Absalom, "The advice Ahithophel has given is not good this time. ⁸You know your father and his men; they are fighters, and as fierce as a wild bear robbed of her cubs. Besides, your father is an experienced fighter; he will not spend the night with the troops. ⁹Even now, he is hidden in a cave or some other place. If he should attack your troops first,^c whoever hears about it will say, 'There has been a slaughter among the troops who follow Absalom.' ¹⁰Then even the bravest soldier, whose heart is like the heart of a lion, will melt with fear, for all Israel knows that your father is a fighter and that those with him are brave.

¹¹"So I advise you: Let all Israel, from Dan to Beersheba—as numerous as the sand on the seashore—be gathered to you, with you yourself leading them into battle. ¹²Then we will attack him wherever he may be found, and we will fall on him as dew settles on the ground. Neither he nor any of his men will be left alive. ¹³If he withdraws into a city, then all Israel will bring ropes to that city, and we will drag it down to the valley until not even a piece of it can be found."

¹⁴Absalom and all the men of Israel said, "The advice of Hushai the Arkite is better than that of Ahithophel." For the LORD had determined to frustrate the good advice of Ahithophel in order to bring disaster on Absalom.

¹⁵Hushai told Zadok and Abiathar, the priests, "Ahithophel has advised Absalom and the elders of Israel to do such and such, but I have advised them to do so and so. ¹⁶Now send a message immediately and tell David, 'Do not spend the night at the fords in the desert; cross over without fail, or the king and all the people with him will be swallowed up.' "

Advice Is Easily Given

2 SAMUEL 17:7

Absalom rejects Ahithophel's sage advice for a bold strike against David in favor of the more cautious counsel of Hushai, thus dooming his cause. On what occasions in your life have you rejected the advice of wise and experienced souls in favor of more comforting counsel? When have you chosen, unwisely, the cautious and careful course when the bold, decisive one would have been more fruitful? What qualities make for a good adviser? Who have been your most trusted advisers—the people whose counsel has proven most accurate and helpful? Are there occasions when you have felt that the counsel you received through another was, in truth, the guidance of God?

See Meeting God in Community

Leadership and Authority

2 SAMUEL 18:3

"You are worth ten thousand of us," the men tell David, recognizing the innate authority of inspiring leadership on the battlefield and firm discipline applied well. The Gospels describe Jesus, the Son of David, as one who speaks with authority.

Such authority arises from how one conducts oneself, not merely from appointment or election. Who are the people you look up to as having authentic authority? What characteristics do they have?

What is the main source of your authority: age, size, assertiveness, hierarchy at work, parental status? How much of your authority comes from your status, and how much comes from your character and actions? In what ways do you use your authority for the good of others? How is your exercise of authority Christlike?

See Meeting God in Service

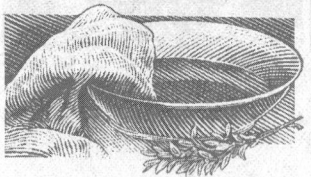

¹⁷Jonathan and Ahimaaz were staying at En Rogel. A servant girl was to go and inform them, and they were to go and tell King David, for they could not risk being seen entering the city. ¹⁸But a young man saw them and told Absalom. So the two of them left quickly and went to the house of a man in Bahurim. He had a well in his courtyard, and they climbed down into it. ¹⁹His wife took a covering and spread it out over the opening of the well and scattered grain over it. No one knew anything about it.

²⁰When Absalom's men came to the woman at the house, they asked, "Where are Ahimaaz and Jonathan?"

The woman answered them, "They crossed over the brook."ᵃ The men searched but found no one, so they returned to Jerusalem.

²¹After the men had gone, the two climbed out of the well and went to inform King David. They said to him, "Set out and cross the river at once; Ahithophel has advised such and such against you." ²²So David and all the people with him set out and crossed the Jordan. By daybreak, no one was left who had not crossed the Jordan.

²³When Ahithophel saw that his advice had not been followed, he saddled his donkey and set out for his house in his hometown. He put his house in order and then hanged himself. So he died and was buried in his father's tomb.

²⁴David went to Mahanaim, and Absalom crossed the Jordan with all the men of Israel. ²⁵Absalom had appointed Amasa over the army in place of Joab. Amasa was the son of a man named Jether,ᵇ an Israeliteᶜ who had married Abigail,ᵈ the daughter of Nahash and sister of Zeruiah the mother of Joab. ²⁶The Israelites and Absalom camped in the land of Gilead.

²⁷When David came to Mahanaim, Shobi son of Nahash from Rabbah of the Ammonites, and Makir son of Ammiel from Lo Debar, and Barzillai the Gileadite from Rogelim ²⁸brought bedding and bowls and articles of pottery. They also brought wheat and barley, flour and roasted grain, beans and lentils,ᵉ ²⁹honey and curds, sheep, and cheese from cows' milk for David and his people to eat. For they said, "The people have become hungry and tired and thirsty in the desert."

Absalom's Death

18 David mustered the men who were with him and appointed over them commanders of thousands and commanders of hundreds. ²David sent the troops out—a third under the command of Joab, a third under Joab's brother Abishai son of Zeruiah, and a third under Ittai the Gittite. The king told the troops, "I myself will surely march out with you."

³But the men said, "You must not go out; if we are forced to flee, they won't care about us. Even if half of us die, they won't care; but you are worth ten thousand of us.ʲ It would be better now for you to give us support from the city."

ᵃ 20 Or *"They passed by the sheep pen toward the water."* ᵇ 25 Hebrew *Ithra,* a variant of *Jether* ᶜ 25 Hebrew and some Septuagint manuscripts; other Septuagint manuscripts (see also 1 Chron. 2:17) *Ishmaelite* or *Jezreelite* ᵈ 25 Hebrew *Abigal,* a variant of *Abigail* ᵉ 28 Most Septuagint manuscripts and Syriac; Hebrew *lentils, and roasted grain* ʲ 3 Two Hebrew manuscripts, some Septuagint manuscripts and Vulgate; most Hebrew manuscripts *care; for now there are ten thousand like us*

⁴The king answered, "I will do whatever seems best to you."

So the king stood beside the gate while all the men marched out in units of hundreds and of thousands. ⁵The king commanded Joab, Abishai and Ittai, "Be gentle with the young man Absalom for my sake." And all the troops heard the king giving orders concerning Absalom to each of the commanders.

⁶The army marched into the field to fight Israel, and the battle took place in the forest of Ephraim. ⁷There the army of Israel was defeated by David's men, and the casualties that day were great—twenty thousand men. ⁸The battle spread out over the whole countryside, and the forest claimed more lives that day than the sword.

⁹Now Absalom happened to meet David's men. He was riding his mule, and as the mule went under the thick branches of a large oak, Absalom's head got caught in the tree. He was left hanging in midair, while the mule he was riding kept on going.

¹⁰When one of the men saw this, he told Joab, "I just saw Absalom hanging in an oak tree."

¹¹Joab said to the man who had told him this, "What! You saw him? Why didn't you strike him to the ground right there? Then I would have had to give you ten shekels*ᵃ* of silver and a warrior's belt."

¹²But the man replied, "Even if a thousand shekels*ᵇ* were weighed out into my hands, I would not lift my hand against the king's son. In our hearing the king commanded you and Abishai and Ittai, 'Protect the young man Absalom for my sake.'*ᶜ* ¹³And if I had put my life in jeopardy*ᵈ*—and nothing is hidden from the king—you would have kept your distance from me."

¹⁴Joab said, "I'm not going to wait like this for you." So he took three javelins in his hand and plunged them into Absalom's heart while Absalom was still alive in the oak tree. ¹⁵And ten of Joab's armor-bearers surrounded Absalom, struck him and killed him.

¹⁶Then Joab sounded the trumpet, and the troops stopped pursuing Israel, for Joab halted them. ¹⁷They took Absalom, threw him into a big pit in the forest and piled up a large heap of rocks over him. Meanwhile, all the Israelites fled to their homes.

¹⁸During his lifetime Absalom had taken a pillar and erected it in the King's Valley as a monument to himself, for he thought, "I have no son to carry on the memory of my name." He named the pillar after himself, and it is called Absalom's Monument to this day.

David Mourns

¹⁹Now Ahimaaz son of Zadok said, "Let me run and take the news to the king that the LORD has delivered him from the hand of his enemies."

²⁰"You are not the one to take the news today," Joab told him. "You may take the news another time, but you must not do so today, because the king's son is dead."

Remembrance

2 SAMUEL 18:18

Very likely there was little or no writing on Absalom's monument. Even today, our gravestones often list only a name and the dates of birth and death. Draw the outline of a tombstone, or a pillar like Absalom's, and write on it what you would like to be remembered for: your accomplishments, relationships with God and others, aspirations, commitments, enduring loves. Then consider, in prayer, what sort of monument you are erecting with your life, and what God might wish to say about it.

See Meeting God in Everyday Life

Deep Love

2 SAMUEL 18:33

"O my son Absalom! . . . If only I had died instead of you!" David's indulgent fondness for Absalom, though rooted in genuine, parental love, has led to this tragedy. Now his loud grieving demoralizes the very troops who have saved his kingship. Yet his capacity to give his whole heart to others and to God lies at the center of David's greatness.

Ponder the mystery of such love in your own life. Have your mistakes sometimes been overlooked or forgiven because of another's fondness for you? Have you treated other people close to your heart over-generously, even indulgently? What are some of the warning signs that fondness is leading to indulgence that ought to be challenged? How do you think God seeks to challenge our behavior while still loving us deeply?

21Then Joab said to a Cushite, "Go, tell the king what you have seen." The Cushite bowed down before Joab and ran off.

22Ahimaaz son of Zadok again said to Joab, "Come what may, please let me run behind the Cushite."

But Joab replied, "My son, why do you want to go? You don't have any news that will bring you a reward."

23He said, "Come what may, I want to run."

So Joab said, "Run!" Then Ahimaaz ran by way of the plain*a* and outran the Cushite.

24While David was sitting between the inner and outer gates, the watchman went up to the roof of the gateway by the wall. As he looked out, he saw a man running alone. 25The watchman called out to the king and reported it.

The king said, "If he is alone, he must have good news." And the man came closer and closer.

26Then the watchman saw another man running, and he called down to the gatekeeper, "Look, another man running alone!"

The king said, "He must be bringing good news, too."

27The watchman said, "It seems to me that the first one runs like Ahimaaz son of Zadok."

"He's a good man," the king said. "He comes with good news."

28Then Ahimaaz called out to the king, "All is well!" He bowed down before the king with his face to the ground and said, "Praise be to the Lord your God! He has delivered up the men who lifted their hands against my lord the king."

29The king asked, "Is the young man Absalom safe?"

Ahimaaz answered, "I saw great confusion just as Joab was about to send the king's servant and me, your servant, but I don't know what it was."

30The king said, "Stand aside and wait here." So he stepped aside and stood there.

31Then the Cushite arrived and said, "My lord the king, hear the good news! The Lord has delivered you today from all who rose up against you."

32The king asked the Cushite, "Is the young man Absalom safe?"

The Cushite replied, "May the enemies of my lord the king and all who rise up to harm you be like that young man."

33The king was shaken. He went up to the room over the gateway and wept. As he went, he said: "O my son Absalom! My son, my son Absalom! If only I had died instead of you—O Absalom, my son, my son!"

19 Joab was told, "The king is weeping and mourning for Absalom." 2And for the whole army the victory that day was turned into mourning, because on that day the troops heard it said, "The king is grieving for his son." 3The men stole into the city that day as men steal in who are ashamed when they flee from battle. 4The king covered his face and cried aloud, "O my son Absalom! O Absalom, my son, my son!"

5Then Joab went into the house to the king and said, "Today you have humiliated all your men, who have just saved your life and the lives of your sons and daughters and the lives of your wives and concubines. 6You love those

*a 23 That is, the plain of the Jordan

who hate you and hate those who love you. You have made it clear today that the commanders and their men mean nothing to you. I see that you would be pleased if Absalom were alive today and all of us were dead. ⁷Now go out and encourage your men. I swear by the LORD that if you don't go out, not a man will be left with you by nightfall. This will be worse for you than all the calamities that have come upon you from your youth till now."

⁸So the king got up and took his seat in the gateway. When the men were told, "The king is sitting in the gateway," they all came before him.

David Returns to Jerusalem

Meanwhile, the Israelites had fled to their homes. ⁹Throughout the tribes of Israel, the people were all arguing with each other, saying, "The king delivered us from the hand of our enemies; he is the one who rescued us from the hand of the Philistines. But now he has fled the country because of Absalom; ¹⁰and Absalom, whom we anointed to rule over us, has died in battle. So why do you say nothing about bringing the king back?"

¹¹King David sent this message to Zadok and Abiathar, the priests: "Ask the elders of Judah, 'Why should you be the last to bring the king back to his palace, since what is being said throughout Israel has reached the king at his quarters? ¹²You are my brothers, my own flesh and blood. So why should you be the last to bring back the king?' ¹³And say to Amasa, 'Are you not my own flesh and blood? May God deal with me, be it ever so severely, if from now on you are not the commander of my army in place of Joab.'"

¹⁴He won over the hearts of all the men of Judah as though they were one man. They sent word to the king, "Return, you and all your men." ¹⁵Then the king returned and went as far as the Jordan.

Now the men of Judah had come to Gilgal to go out and meet the king and bring him across the Jordan. ¹⁶Shimei son of Gera, the Benjamite from Bahurim, hurried down with the men of Judah to meet King David. ¹⁷With him were a thousand Benjamites, along with Ziba, the steward of Saul's household, and his fifteen sons and twenty servants. They rushed to the Jordan, where the king was. ¹⁸They crossed at the ford to take the king's household over and to do whatever he wished.

When Shimei son of Gera crossed the Jordan, he fell prostrate before the king ¹⁹and said to him, "May my lord not hold me guilty. Do not remember how your servant did wrong on the day my lord the king left Jerusalem. May the king put it out of his mind. ²⁰For I your servant know that I have sinned, but today I have come here as the first of the whole house of Joseph to come down and meet my lord the king."

²¹Then Abishai son of Zeruiah said, "Shouldn't Shimei be put to death for this? He cursed the LORD's anointed."

²²David replied, "What do you and I have in common, you sons of Zeruiah? This day you have become my adversaries! Should anyone be put to death in Israel today? Do I not know that today I am king over Israel?" ²³So the king said to Shimei, "You shall not die." And the king promised him on oath.

Returning Home

2 SAMUEL 19:14–18

David returns to Judah and Jerusalem in a humble, grateful and forgiving spirit. Consider the many "returns" you have made in your life: to important places, to relationships with people, to a lapsed discipline, to a belief or moral behavior. In each act of return, what have you had to be grateful for? What might you have had to forgive in others, or in yourself? As a token of several possible returns in your life, make a point of pausing as you approach your residence or place of work the next few times. Be aware of your first glimpse of the building and its surroundings, of what you treasure there, of the spirit that characterizes your life there, of things that need forgiving, and of how God's abiding presence is manifested to you there.

See Meeting God in Everyday Life

Age and Beauty

2 SAMUEL 19:35

Our youth-glorifying society is often ready to agree with Barzillai's characterization of the aged as an "added burden" because of perceived diminished capabilities. But David accords him the respect he deserves. First, enter into Barzillai's self-estimation: Imagine how it must feel to no longer be able to "tell the difference between what is good and what is not," to lose the sensations of taste and hearing? Second, say aloud Augustine's lament, "Too late I loved you, O Beauty ever ancient and ever new! . . . Behold, you were within me" (*Confessions* X.27). Take David's place in the story, and ponder how this "Beauty" is made manifest in those of advanced age. Then begin today, before it is "too late," to use all your senses (inner and outer) to find specific examples of God's beauty in yourself, in others and in the world.

See Meeting God in the Created Order

24Mephibosheth, Saul's grandson, also went down to meet the king. He had not taken care of his feet or trimmed his mustache or washed his clothes from the day the king left until the day he returned safely. 25When he came from Jerusalem to meet the king, the king asked him, "Why didn't you go with me, Mephibosheth?"

26He said, "My lord the king, since I your servant am lame, I said, 'I will have my donkey saddled and will ride on it, so I can go with the king.' But Ziba my servant betrayed me. 27And he has slandered your servant to my lord the king. My lord the king is like an angel of God; so do whatever pleases you. 28All my grandfather's descendants deserved nothing but death from my lord the king, but you gave your servant a place among those who eat at your table. So what right do I have to make any more appeals to the king?"

29The king said to him, "Why say more? I order you and Ziba to divide the fields."

30Mephibosheth said to the king, "Let him take everything, now that my lord the king has arrived home safely."

31Barzillai the Gileadite also came down from Rogelim to cross the Jordan with the king and to send him on his way from there. 32Now Barzillai was a very old man, eighty years of age. He had provided for the king during his stay in Mahanaim, for he was a very wealthy man. 33The king said to Barzillai, "Cross over with me and stay with me in Jerusalem, and I will provide for you."

34But Barzillai answered the king, "How many more years will I live, that I should go up to Jerusalem with the king? 35I am now eighty years old. Can I tell the difference between what is good and what is not? Can your servant taste what he eats and drinks? Can I still hear the voices of men and women singers? Why should your servant be an added burden to my lord the king? 36Your servant will cross over the Jordan with the king for a short distance, but why should the king reward me in this way? 37Let your servant return, that I may die in my own town near the tomb of my father and mother. But here is your servant Kimham. Let him cross over with my lord the king. Do for him whatever pleases you."

38The king said, "Kimham shall cross over with me, and I will do for him whatever pleases you. And anything you desire from me I will do for you."

39So all the people crossed the Jordan, and then the king crossed over. The king kissed Barzillai and gave him his blessing, and Barzillai returned to his home.

40When the king crossed over to Gilgal, Kimham crossed with him. All the troops of Judah and half the troops of Israel had taken the king over.

41Soon all the men of Israel were coming to the king and saying to him, "Why did our brothers, the men of Judah, steal the king away and bring him and his household across the Jordan, together with all his men?"

42All the men of Judah answered the men of Israel, "We did this because the king is closely related to us. Why are you angry about it? Have we eaten any of the king's provisions? Have we taken anything for ourselves?"

43Then the men of Israel answered the men of Judah, "We have ten shares in the king; and besides, we have a greater claim on David than you have. So why do you treat us with contempt? Were we not the first to speak of bringing back our king?"

But the men of Judah responded even more harshly than the men of Israel.

Sheba Rebels Against David

20 Now a troublemaker named Sheba son of Bicri, a Benjamite, happened to be there. He sounded the trumpet and shouted,

"We have no share in David,
no part in Jesse's son!
Every man to his tent, O Israel!"

²So all the men of Israel deserted David to follow Sheba son of Bicri. But the men of Judah stayed by their king all the way from the Jordan to Jerusalem.

³When David returned to his palace in Jerusalem, he took the ten concubines he had left to take care of the palace and put them in a house under guard. He provided for them, but did not lie with them. They were kept in confinement till the day of their death, living as widows.

⁴Then the king said to Amasa, "Summon the men of Judah to come to me within three days, and be here yourself." ⁵But when Amasa went to summon Judah, he took longer than the time the king had set for him.

⁶David said to Abishai, "Now Sheba son of Bicri will do us more harm than Absalom did. Take your master's men and pursue him, or he will find fortified cities and escape from us." ⁷So Joab's men and the Kerethites and Pelethites and all the mighty warriors went out under the command of Abishai. They marched out from Jerusalem to pursue Sheba son of Bicri.

⁸While they were at the great rock in Gibeon, Amasa came to meet them. Joab was wearing his military tunic, and strapped over it at his waist was a belt with a dagger in its sheath. As he stepped forward, it dropped out of its sheath.

⁹Joab said to Amasa, "How are you, my brother?" Then Joab took Amasa by the beard with his right hand to kiss him. ¹⁰Amasa was not on his guard against the dagger in Joab's hand, and Joab plunged it into his belly, and his intestines spilled out on the ground. Without being stabbed again, Amasa died. Then Joab and his brother Abishai pursued Sheba son of Bicri.

¹¹One of Joab's men stood beside Amasa and said, "Whoever favors Joab, and whoever is for David, let him follow Joab!" ¹²Amasa lay wallowing in his blood in the middle of the road, and the man saw that all the troops came to a halt there. When he realized that everyone who came up to Amasa stopped, he dragged him from the road into a field and threw a garment over him. ¹³After Amasa had been removed from the road, all the men went on with Joab to pursue Sheba son of Bicri.

¹⁴Sheba passed through all the tribes of Israel to Abel Beth Maacah*a* and through the entire region of the Berites, who gathered together and followed him. ¹⁵All the troops with Joab came and besieged Sheba in Abel Beth Maacah. They built a siege ramp up to the city, and it stood against the outer fortifications. While they were battering the wall

---

Going Along With the Crowd

2 SAMUEL 20:2

The fickleness of David's troops is no surprise to us, tugged about by instant fads and rising and falling tides of popular opinion. The desire to be "in" is a nonviolent expression of mob mentality. Take a paper and make three columns on it. In the first column, list the messages you are receiving daily from the media and other people about what's "in" and "essential" right now. Then make a list of the core values on the basis of which you decide what is really worthwhile among these many choices. Finally, list ways in which you can resist this cultural pressure and find the strength to be steadfast, like the men of Judah who "stayed by their king."

See Meeting God in Everyday Life

---

a 14 Or Abel, even Beth Maacah; also in verse 15

Famine

2 SAMUEL 21:1

Hunger is as near to us as the newspaper headlines—and not just in far-off deserts but in our own communities. Pray at one meal each day this week, "O Lord, help me truly to know how my rich diet affects scarce resources that feed my sisters and brothers around your abundant earth." Keep a list of your discoveries and use it to consider ways to simplify your diet, contributing any monetary savings to hunger-fighting organizations. Explore ways to share your time, talent or treasure with food banks and soup kitchens in your community; you will then become part of the solution rather than part of the problem.

See *Meeting God in the Created Order*

to bring it down, [16]a wise woman called from the city, "Listen! Listen! Tell Joab to come here so I can speak to him." [17]He went toward her, and she asked, "Are you Joab?"

"I am," he answered.

She said, "Listen to what your servant has to say."

"I'm listening," he said.

[18]She continued, "Long ago they used to say, 'Get your answer at Abel,' and that settled it. [19]We are the peaceful and faithful in Israel. You are trying to destroy a city that is a mother in Israel. Why do you want to swallow up the Lord's inheritance?"

[20]"Far be it from me!" Joab replied, "Far be it from me to swallow up or destroy! [21]That is not the case. A man named Sheba son of Bicri, from the hill country of Ephraim, has lifted up his hand against the king, against David. Hand over this one man, and I'll withdraw from the city."

The woman said to Joab, "His head will be thrown to you from the wall."

[22]Then the woman went to all the people with her wise advice, and they cut off the head of Sheba son of Bicri and threw it to Joab. So he sounded the trumpet, and his men dispersed from the city, each returning to his home. And Joab went back to the king in Jerusalem.

[23]Joab was over Israel's entire army; Benaiah son of Jehoiada was over the Kerethites and Pelethites; [24]Adoniram[a] was in charge of forced labor; Jehoshaphat son of Ahilud was recorder; [25]Sheva was secretary; Zadok and Abiathar were priests; [26]and Ira the Jairite was David's priest.

The Gibeonites Avenged

21 During the reign of David, there was a famine for three successive years; so David sought the face of the Lord. The Lord said, "It is on account of Saul and his blood-stained house; it is because he put the Gibeonites to death."

[2]The king summoned the Gibeonites and spoke to them. (Now the Gibeonites were not a part of Israel but were survivors of the Amorites; the Israelites had sworn to ⌊spare⌋ them, but Saul in his zeal for Israel and Judah had tried to annihilate them.) [3]David asked the Gibeonites, "What shall I do for you? How shall I make amends so that you will bless the Lord's inheritance?"

[4]The Gibeonites answered him, "We have no right to demand silver or gold from Saul or his family, nor do we have the right to put anyone in Israel to death."

"What do you want me to do for you?" David asked.

[5]They answered the king, "As for the man who destroyed us and plotted against us so that we have been decimated and have no place anywhere in Israel, [6]let seven of his male descendants be given to us to be killed and exposed before the Lord at Gibeah of Saul—the Lord's chosen one."

So the king said, "I will give them to you."

[7]The king spared Mephibosheth son of Jonathan, the son of Saul, because of the oath before the Lord between David and Jonathan son of Saul. [8]But the king took Armoni and Mephibosheth, the two sons of Aiah's daughter Rizpah, whom she had borne to Saul, together with the five sons of

---

[a] 24 Some Septuagint manuscripts (see also 1 Kings 4:6 and 5:14); Hebrew *Adoram*

Saul's daughter Merab,[a] whom she had borne to Adriel son of Barzillai the Meholathite. [9]He handed them over to the Gibeonites, who killed and exposed them on a hill before the LORD. All seven of them fell together; they were put to death during the first days of the harvest, just as the barley harvest was beginning.

[10]Rizpah daughter of Aiah took sackcloth and spread it out for herself on a rock. From the beginning of the harvest till the rain poured down from the heavens on the bodies, she did not let the birds of the air touch them by day or the wild animals by night. [11]When David was told what Aiah's daughter Rizpah, Saul's concubine, had done, [12]he went and took the bones of Saul and his son Jonathan from the citizens of Jabesh Gilead. (They had taken them secretly from the public square at Beth Shan, where the Philistines had hung them after they struck Saul down on Gilboa.) [13]David brought the bones of Saul and his son Jonathan from there, and the bones of those who had been killed and exposed were gathered up.

[14]They buried the bones of Saul and his son Jonathan in the tomb of Saul's father Kish, at Zela in Benjamin, and did everything the king commanded. After that, God answered prayer in behalf of the land.

Wars Against the Philistines

[15]Once again there was a battle between the Philistines and Israel. David went down with his men to fight against the Philistines, and he became exhausted. [16]And Ishbi-Benob, one of the descendants of Rapha, whose bronze spearhead weighed three hundred shekels[b] and who was armed with a new ⌊sword⌋, said he would kill David. [17]But Abishai son of Zeruiah came to David's rescue; he struck the Philistine down and killed him. Then David's men swore to him, saying, "Never again will you go out with us to battle, so that the lamp of Israel will not be extinguished."

[18]In the course of time, there was another battle with the Philistines, at Gob. At that time Sibbecai the Hushathite killed Saph, one of the descendants of Rapha.

[19]In another battle with the Philistines at Gob, Elhanan son of Jaare-Oregim[c] the Bethlehemite killed Goliath[d] the Gittite, who had a spear with a shaft like a weaver's rod.

[20]In still another battle, which took place at Gath, there was a huge man with six fingers on each hand and six toes on each foot—twenty-four in all. He also was descended from Rapha. [21]When he taunted Israel, Jonathan son of Shimeah, David's brother, killed him.

[22]These four were descendants of Rapha in Gath, and they fell at the hands of David and his men.

David's Song of Praise

22 David sang to the LORD the words of this song when the LORD delivered him from the hand of all his enemies and from the hand of Saul. [2]He said:

---

a 8 Two Hebrew manuscripts, some Septuagint manuscripts and Syriac (see also 1 Samuel 18:19); most Hebrew and Septuagint manuscripts *Michal* b 16 That is, about 7 1/2 pounds (about 3.5 kilograms) c 19 Or *son of Jair the weaver* d 19 Hebrew and Septuagint; 1 Chron. 20:5 *son of Jair killed Lahmi the brother of Goliath*

A Psalm of Praise: *Lectio Divina*

2 SAMUEL 22:1–19

After endless war, David thanks God in a song, recorded both here and in Psalm 18. Read through a portion of this dramatic and jubilant poem slowly and meditatively, keeping in mind the events in David's life recorded in 1 and 2 Samuel. Then read it again, looking for words or phrases that remind you of events in your own life. Select one phrase that connects with such a memory, and sing it to a simple tune of your own devising, repeating the phrase again and again as a prayer. Memorize the phrase and repeat it to yourself periodically throughout the day, remembering with thanksgiving the situation it recalls for you.

See *Meeting God in Worship*

God's Delight

2 SAMUEL 22:20

Why didn't the Lord leave David and his fighters to fend for themselves? God's love is often difficult to accept, perhaps because it seems too good to be true, especially for "just plain me!" The "spacious place" of God's love for us is unfamiliar at first, accustomed as we are to the narrowness of self-deprecation. To the mirror you look into most frequently, attach a piece of paper or card bearing these words: "God delights in me; I am loved eternally." Read those words aloud now and daily for as many days or months as the paper remains intact.

See Meeting God in Everyday Life

"The LORD is my rock, my fortress and my
    deliverer;
³   my God is my rock, in whom I take refuge,
    my shield and the horn*a* of my salvation.
He is my stronghold, my refuge and my savior—
    from violent men you save me.
⁴I call to the LORD, who is worthy of praise,
    and I am saved from my enemies.

⁵"The waves of death swirled about me;
    the torrents of destruction overwhelmed me.
⁶The cords of the grave*b* coiled around me;
    the snares of death confronted me.
⁷In my distress I called to the LORD;
    I called out to my God.
From his temple he heard my voice;
    my cry came to his ears.

⁸"The earth trembled and quaked,
    the foundations of the heavens*c* shook;
    they trembled because he was angry.
⁹Smoke rose from his nostrils;
    consuming fire came from his mouth,
    burning coals blazed out of it.
¹⁰He parted the heavens and came down;
    dark clouds were under his feet.
¹¹He mounted the cherubim and flew;
    he soared*d* on the wings of the wind.
¹²He made darkness his canopy around him—
    the dark*e* rain clouds of the sky.
¹³Out of the brightness of his presence
    bolts of lightning blazed forth.
¹⁴The LORD thundered from heaven;
    the voice of the Most High resounded.
¹⁵He shot arrows and scattered ⌊the enemies⌋,
    bolts of lightning and routed them.
¹⁶The valleys of the sea were exposed
    and the foundations of the earth laid bare
at the rebuke of the LORD,
    at the blast of breath from his nostrils.

¹⁷"He reached down from on high and took hold
    of me;
    he drew me out of deep waters.
¹⁸He rescued me from my powerful enemy,
    from my foes, who were too strong for me.
¹⁹They confronted me in the day of my disaster,
    but the LORD was my support.
²⁰He brought me out into a spacious place;
    he rescued me because he delighted in me.

²¹"The LORD has dealt with me according to my
    righteousness;
    according to the cleanness of my hands he has
        rewarded me.
²²For I have kept the ways of the LORD;
    I have not done evil by turning from my God.
²³All his laws are before me;

---

a 3 Horn here symbolizes strength.   *b 6* Hebrew *Sheol*   *c 8* Hebrew;
Vulgate and Syriac (see also Psalm 18:7) *mountains*   *d 11* Many Hebrew
manuscripts (see also Psalm 18:10); most Hebrew manuscripts *appeared*
e 12 Septuagint and Vulgate (see also Psalm 18:11); Hebrew *massed*

I have not turned away from his decrees.
24 I have been blameless before him
    and have kept myself from sin.
25 The LORD has rewarded me according to my
    righteousness,
    according to my cleanness*a* in his sight.

26 "To the faithful you show yourself faithful,
    to the blameless you show yourself blameless,
27 to the pure you show yourself pure,
    but to the crooked you show yourself shrewd.
28 You save the humble,
    but your eyes are on the haughty to bring them
    low.
29 You are my lamp, O LORD;
    the LORD turns my darkness into light.
30 With your help I can advance against a troop*b*;
    with my God I can scale a wall.

31 "As for God, his way is perfect;
    the word of the LORD is flawless.
    He is a shield
    for all who take refuge in him.
32 For who is God besides the LORD?
    And who is the Rock except our God?
33 It is God who arms me with strength*c*
    and makes my way perfect.
34 He makes my feet like the feet of a deer;
    he enables me to stand on the heights.
35 He trains my hands for battle;
    my arms can bend a bow of bronze.
36 You give me your shield of victory;
    you stoop down to make me great.
37 You broaden the path beneath me,
    so that my ankles do not turn.

38 "I pursued my enemies and crushed them;
    I did not turn back till they were destroyed.
39 I crushed them completely, and they could not
    rise;
    they fell beneath my feet.
40 You armed me with strength for battle;
    you made my adversaries bow at my feet.
41 You made my enemies turn their backs in flight,
    and I destroyed my foes.
42 They cried for help, but there was no one to save
    them—
    to the LORD, but he did not answer.
43 I beat them as fine as the dust of the earth;
    I pounded and trampled them like mud in the
    streets.

44 "You have delivered me from the attacks of my
    people;
    you have preserved me as the head of nations.
    People I did not know are subject to me,
45   and foreigners come cringing to me;
    as soon as they hear me, they obey me.

---

a 25 Hebrew; Septuagint and Vulgate (see also Psalm 18:24) *to the cleanness
of my hands*   *b 30* Or *can run through a barricade*   *c 33* Dead Sea Scrolls,
some Septuagint manuscripts, Vulgate and Syriac (see also Psalm 18:32);
Masoretic Text *who is my strong refuge*

Darkness Into Light

2 SAMUEL 22:29

The beautiful light of God's presence in art and nature is one of the best antidotes to the darkness of "worldly cares." As Johann von Goethe said, "A person should hear a little music, read a little poetry and see a fine picture every day in order that worldly cares may not obliterate the sense of the beautiful which God has implanted in the human soul." Revise your schedule today to include at least fifteen minutes to listen to peaceful music, read poetry about nature, meditate before a painting or reflect on a photograph that reminds you of your relationship with God. Or, weather permitting, go outdoors to admire the sunrise or sunset. Let your immersion in beauty end with a prayer of thanksgiving to the One who is the source of beauty.

See Meeting God in the Created Order

I Will Sing Praises

2 SAMUEL 22:48–50

William Wordsworth viewed poetry as the "spontaneous overflow of powerful feelings; it takes its origins from emotion recollected in tranquillity." Sit quietly and focus on your breathing for a few moments, preparing to write a psalm about an experience of powerful emotion in your life. Recall a difficult situation in which you feel God came to your aid. Revisit the emotions you experienced before and after God's assistance became evident. Write your own psalm in three or four verses, expressing how difficulty gave way to deliverance and how your feelings in the midst of difficulty yielded to feelings of gratitude and praise.

See Meeting God in Worship

⁴⁶They all lose heart;
  they come trembling*ᵃ* from their strongholds.
⁴⁷ "The LORD lives! Praise be to my Rock!
  Exalted be God, the Rock, my Savior!
⁴⁸ He is the God who avenges me,
  who puts the nations under me,
⁴⁹   who sets me free from my enemies.
You exalted me above my foes;
  from violent men you rescued me.
⁵⁰ Therefore I will praise you, O LORD, among the nations;
  I will sing praises to your name.
⁵¹ He gives his king great victories;
  he shows unfailing kindness to his anointed,
  to David and his descendants forever."

The Last Words of David

23 These are the last words of David:

"The oracle of David son of Jesse,
  the oracle of the man exalted by the Most High,
the man anointed by the God of Jacob,
  Israel's singer of songs*ᵇ*:

² "The Spirit of the LORD spoke through me;
  his word was on my tongue.
³ The God of Israel spoke,
  the Rock of Israel said to me:
'When one rules over men in righteousness,
  when he rules in the fear of God,
⁴ he is like the light of morning at sunrise
  on a cloudless morning,
like the brightness after rain
  that brings the grass from the earth.'

⁵ "Is not my house right with God?
  Has he not made with me an everlasting covenant,
  arranged and secured in every part?
Will he not bring to fruition my salvation
  and grant me my every desire?
⁶ But evil men are all to be cast aside like thorns,
  which are not gathered with the hand.
⁷ Whoever touches thorns
  uses a tool of iron or the shaft of a spear;
  they are burned up where they lie."

David's Mighty Men

⁸These are the names of David's mighty men:

Josheb-Basshebeth,*ᶜ* a Tahkemonite,*ᵈ* was chief of the Three; he raised his spear against eight hundred men, whom he killed*ᵉ* in one encounter.

⁹Next to him was Eleazar son of Dodai the Ahohite. As one of the three mighty men, he was with David when they

---

ᵃ46 Some Septuagint manuscripts and Vulgate (see also Psalm 18:45); Masoretic Text *they arm themselves.*   *ᵇ1* Or *Israel's beloved singer*
ᶜ8 Hebrew; some Septuagint manuscripts suggest *Ish-Bosheth, that is, Esh-Baal* (see also 1 Chron. 11:11 *Jashobeam*).   *ᵈ8* Probably a variant of *Hacmonite* (see 1 Chron. 11:11)   *ᵉ8* Some Septuagint manuscripts (see also 1 Chron. 11:11); Hebrew and other Septuagint manuscripts *Three; it was Adino the Eznite who killed eight hundred men*

taunted the Philistines gathered ⌊at Pas Dammim⌋ᵃ for battle. Then the men of Israel retreated, ¹⁰but he stood his ground and struck down the Philistines till his hand grew tired and froze to the sword. The Lᴏʀᴅ brought about a great victory that day. The troops returned to Eleazar, but only to strip the dead.

¹¹Next to him was Shammah son of Agee the Hararite. When the Philistines banded together at a place where there was a field full of lentils, Israel's troops fled from them. ¹²But Shammah took his stand in the middle of the field. He defended it and struck the Philistines down, and the Lᴏʀᴅ brought about a great victory.

¹³During harvest time, three of the thirty chief men came down to David at the cave of Adullam, while a band of Philistines was encamped in the Valley of Rephaim. ¹⁴At that time David was in the stronghold, and the Philistine garrison was at Bethlehem. ¹⁵David longed for water and said, "Oh, that someone would get me a drink of water from the well near the gate of Bethlehem!" ¹⁶So the three mighty men broke through the Philistine lines, drew water from the well near the gate of Bethlehem and carried it back to David. But he refused to drink it; instead, he poured it out before the Lᴏʀᴅ. ¹⁷"Far be it from me, O Lᴏʀᴅ, to do this!" he said. "Is it not the blood of men who went at the risk of their lives?" And David would not drink it.

Such were the exploits of the three mighty men.

¹⁸Abishai the brother of Joab son of Zeruiah was chief of the Three.ᵇ He raised his spear against three hundred men, whom he killed, and so he became as famous as the Three. ¹⁹Was he not held in greater honor than the Three? He became their commander, even though he was not included among them.

²⁰Benaiah son of Jehoiada was a valiant fighter from Kabzeel, who performed great exploits. He struck down two of Moab's best men. He also went down into a pit on a snowy day and killed a lion. ²¹And he struck down a huge Egyptian. Although the Egyptian had a spear in his hand, Benaiah went against him with a club. He snatched the spear from the Egyptian's hand and killed him with his own spear. ²²Such were the exploits of Benaiah son of Jehoiada; he too was as famous as the three mighty men. ²³He was held in greater honor than any of the Thirty, but he was not included among the Three. And David put him in charge of his bodyguard.

²⁴Among the Thirty were:
    Asahel the brother of Joab,
    Elhanan son of Dodo from Bethlehem,
  ²⁵Shammah the Harodite,
    Elika the Harodite,
  ²⁶Helez the Paltite,
    Ira son of Ikkesh from Tekoa,
  ²⁷Abiezer from Anathoth,
    Mebunnaiᶜ the Hushathite,
  ²⁸Zalmon the Ahohite,
    Maharai the Netophathite,

In the Pits

2 SAMUEL 23:20–22

Imaginatively place yourself in this one-paragraph story, seeing yourself as Benaiah. Imagine the sensations of your feet on the snow, the rush of adrenaline as you struggle with the lion. Then begin to invite memories of your own struggles with "lions" or in "pits" in your life. Perhaps you recall an incident when you found yourself in an awkward and hostile situation. Or maybe you recall being "in the pits" emotionally. Especially recall how you vanquished the lion or got out of the pit, whether by your own mental discipline, through strength or guidance gained in prayer, or by another person's assistance.

Say a prayer of thanksgiving to God, or write a grateful note to your "rescuer," expressing gratitude for this deliverance.

See Meeting God in Scripture

ᵃ9 See 1 Chron. 11:13; Hebrew *gathered there.*   ᵇ18 Most Hebrew manuscripts (see also 1 Chron. 11:20); two Hebrew manuscripts and Syriac *Thirty* ᶜ27 Hebrew; some Septuagint manuscripts (see also 1 Chron. 11:29) *Sibbecai*

423

Your Hall of Fame

2 SAMUEL 23:8–39

Who are some of the top thirty "mighty men" and women in your life? Make a list of five persons whom you have admired during the course of your life, and recount their exploits. Then write a second list of five characters in the Bible whom you have admired or perhaps tried to emulate. Pair up people from your admiration list with people from your Biblical list by noting similar characteristics. Imagine yourself speaking to each one in turn about what they mean to you, then thank God for what their presence or inspiration has meant in your life.

See Meeting God in Scripture

29 Heled*a* son of Baanah the Netophathite,
    Ithai son of Ribai from Gibeah in Benjamin,
30 Benaiah the Pirathonite,
    Hiddai*b* from the ravines of Gaash,
31 Abi-Albon the Arbathite,
    Azmaveth the Barhumite,
32 Eliahba the Shaalbonite,
    the sons of Jashen,
    Jonathan **33** son of*c* Shammah the Hararite,
    Ahiam son of Sharar*d* the Hararite,
34 Eliphelet son of Ahasbai the Maacathite,
    Eliam son of Ahithophel the Gilonite,
35 Hezro the Carmelite,
    Paarai the Arbite,
36 Igal son of Nathan from Zobah,
    the son of Hagri,*e*
37 Zelek the Ammonite,
    Naharai the Beerothite, the armor-bearer of Joab son of Zeruiah,
38 Ira the Ithrite,
    Gareb the Ithrite
39 and Uriah the Hittite.
    There were thirty-seven in all.

David Counts the Fighting Men

24 Again the anger of the LORD burned against Israel, and he incited David against them, saying, "Go and take a census of Israel and Judah."

2 So the king said to Joab and the army commanders*f* with him, "Go throughout the tribes of Israel from Dan to Beersheba and enroll the fighting men, so that I may know how many there are."

3 But Joab replied to the king, "May the LORD your God multiply the troops a hundred times over, and may the eyes of my lord the king see it. But why does my lord the king want to do such a thing?"

4 The king's word, however, overruled Joab and the army commanders; so they left the presence of the king to enroll the fighting men of Israel.

5 After crossing the Jordan, they camped near Aroer, south of the town in the gorge, and then went through Gad and on to Jazer. **6** They went to Gilead and the region of Tahtim Hodshi, and on to Dan Jaan and around toward Sidon. **7** Then they went toward the fortress of Tyre and all the towns of the Hivites and Canaanites. Finally, they went on to Beersheba in the Negev of Judah.

8 After they had gone through the entire land, they came back to Jerusalem at the end of nine months and twenty days.

9 Joab reported the number of the fighting men to the king: In Israel there were eight hundred thousand able-bodied men who could handle a sword, and in Judah five hundred thousand.

a 29 Some Hebrew manuscripts and Vulgate (see also 1 Chron. 11:30); most Hebrew manuscripts *Heleb*   *b 30* Hebrew; some Septuagint manuscripts (see also 1 Chron. 11:32) *Hurai*   *c 33* Some Septuagint manuscripts (see also 1 Chron. 11:34); Hebrew does not have *son of.*   *d 33* Hebrew; some Septuagint manuscripts (see also 1 Chron. 11:35) *Sacar*   *e 36* Some Septuagint manuscripts (see also 1 Chron. 11:38); Hebrew *Haggadi*   *f 2* Septuagint (see also verse 4 and 1 Chron. 21:2); Hebrew *Joab the army commander*

[10]David was conscience-stricken after he had counted the fighting men, and he said to the LORD, "I have sinned greatly in what I have done. Now, O LORD, I beg you, take away the guilt of your servant. I have done a very foolish thing."

[11]Before David got up the next morning, the word of the LORD had come to Gad the prophet, David's seer: [12]"Go and tell David, 'This is what the LORD says: I am giving you three options. Choose one of them for me to carry out against you.'"

[13]So Gad went to David and said to him, "Shall there come upon you three[a] years of famine in your land? Or three months of fleeing from your enemies while they pursue you? Or three days of plague in your land? Now then, think it over and decide how I should answer the one who sent me."

[14]David said to Gad, "I am in deep distress. Let us fall into the hands of the LORD, for his mercy is great; but do not let me fall into the hands of men."

[15]So the LORD sent a plague on Israel from that morning until the end of the time designated, and seventy thousand of the people from Dan to Beersheba died. [16]When the angel stretched out his hand to destroy Jerusalem, the LORD was grieved because of the calamity and said to the angel who was afflicting the people, "Enough! Withdraw your hand." The angel of the LORD was then at the threshing floor of Araunah the Jebusite.

[17]When David saw the angel who was striking down the people, he said to the LORD, "I am the one who has sinned and done wrong. These are but sheep. What have they done? Let your hand fall upon me and my family."

David Builds an Altar

[18]On that day Gad went to David and said to him, "Go up and build an altar to the LORD on the threshing floor of Araunah the Jebusite." [19]So David went up, as the LORD had commanded through Gad. [20]When Araunah looked and saw the king and his men coming toward him, he went out and bowed down before the king with his face to the ground.

[21]Araunah said, "Why has my lord the king come to his servant?"

"To buy your threshing floor," David answered, "so I can build an altar to the LORD, that the plague on the people may be stopped."

[22]Araunah said to David, "Let my lord the king take whatever pleases him and offer it up. Here are oxen for the burnt offering, and here are threshing sledges and ox yokes for the wood. [23]O king, Araunah gives all this to the king." Araunah also said to him, "May the LORD your God accept you."

[24]But the king replied to Araunah, "No, I insist on paying you for it. I will not sacrifice to the LORD my God burnt offerings that cost me nothing."

So David bought the threshing floor and the oxen and paid fifty shekels[b] of silver for them. [25]David built an altar to the LORD there and sacrificed burnt offerings and fellowship offerings.[c] Then the LORD answered prayer in behalf of the land, and the plague on Israel was stopped.

---

[a] 13 Septuagint (see also 1 Chron. 21:12); Hebrew *seven*   [b] 24 That is, about 1 1/4 pounds (about 0.6 kilogram)   [c] 25 Traditionally *peace offerings*

Conscience: Nag or Friend?

> 2 SAMUEL 24:10

After the census, David came to his senses, "conscience-stricken," recognizing that he had done "a very foolish thing." Conscience can remind us of the persons we really are when we are not "on camera." Such reminders from the heart can sometimes be upsetting and persistent, often because we have not completed the work that conscience reveals is still undone. Acknowledge a continuing discomfort traceable to something you have done or left undone. Ask yourself why you have not dealt with the issue that continues to overshadow you. Resolve to take corrective action when that becomes possible. At this moment, write words that clearly describe what is troubling you, say these words in confession to God, and pray for help in releasing the burden and making all possible amends.

See Meeting God in Prayer

1 KINGS

Making Room for God

KEY VERSES:

"As for you, if you walk before me in integrity of heart and uprightness, as David your father did, and do all I command and observe my decrees and laws, I will establish your royal throne over Israel forever, as I promised David your father when I said, 'You shall never fail to have a man on the throne of Israel.'" —1 Kings 9:4–5

"God hates evil because it deprives man of the highest joy of which he is capable and the fullness of life for which he was designed. But His attitude to the sinner is unvarying love and compassion, a longing that he may 'turn from his wickedness and live.'"

—LESLIE D. WEATHERHEAD,
Time for God

The book of 1 Kings can be read as the history of a nation on a collision course with itself.

The harsh judgment of history turns a glaring spotlight on the deeds of its kings. The ancient Israelites are learning life's lessons the hard way. The people of Israel have sought the counsel of God and the wisdom of the prophets, but they do not heed, hear or respond to the call to wholeness.

The account in 1 Kings tells a harsh tale of national tragedy and spiritual bankruptcy. Ignorance and pride battle with wisdom; greed and lust diminish prosperity. The people call on prophets—such as the great Elijah—for counsel, then ignore, persecute or even kill them. The ancient Israelite kingdom is divided into two rival nations, north and south, because the nation has lost sight of its spiritual source, the Lord God.

As you read 1 Kings, meditate on how the cycle of sin, repentance and restoration repeats itself. Consider how that same cycle occurs in your own life. As you read and study 1 Kings, look at your life and see where the call to act *now* for change strikes home.

Disobedience, evil, hatred, racism and indifference have been around since the earliest days of humankind. Countless others have already endured many of the personal and national struggles we experience today, yet the presence and love of our forgiving God is not new either! At the heart of the story in 1 Kings is the gracious One who promises to be faithful to us in love regardless of the chaos we create.

Adonijah Sets Himself Up as King

1 When King David was old and well advanced in years, he could not keep warm even when they put covers over him. ²So his servants said to him, "Let us look for a young virgin to attend the king and take care of him. She can lie beside him so that our lord the king may keep warm."

³Then they searched throughout Israel for a beautiful girl and found Abishag, a Shunammite, and brought her to the king. ⁴The girl was very beautiful; she took care of the king and waited on him, but the king had no intimate relations with her.

⁵Now Adonijah, whose mother was Haggith, put himself forward and said, "I will be king." So he got chariots and horses*a* ready, with fifty men to run ahead of him. ⁶(His father had never interfered with him by asking, "Why do you behave as you do?" He was also very handsome and was born next after Absalom.)

⁷Adonijah conferred with Joab son of Zeruiah and with Abiathar the priest, and they gave him their support. ⁸But Zadok the priest, Benaiah son of Jehoiada, Nathan the prophet, Shimei and Rei*b* and David's special guard did not join Adonijah.

⁹Adonijah then sacrificed sheep, cattle and fattened calves at the Stone of Zoheleth near En Rogel. He invited all his brothers, the king's sons, and all the men of Judah who were royal officials, ¹⁰but he did not invite Nathan the prophet or Benaiah or the special guard or his brother Solomon.

¹¹Then Nathan asked Bathsheba, Solomon's mother, "Have you not heard that Adonijah, the son of Haggith, has become king without our lord David's knowing it? ¹²Now then, let me advise you how you can save your own life and the life of your son Solomon. ¹³Go in to King David and say to him, 'My lord the king, did you not swear to me your servant: "Surely Solomon your son shall be king after me, and he will sit on my throne"? Why then has Adonijah become king?' ¹⁴While you are still there talking to the king, I will come in and confirm what you have said."

¹⁵So Bathsheba went to see the aged king in his room, where Abishag the Shunammite was attending him. ¹⁶Bathsheba bowed low and knelt before the king.

"What is it you want?" the king asked.

¹⁷She said to him, "My lord, you yourself swore to me your servant by the LORD your God: 'Solomon your son shall be king after me, and he will sit on my throne.' ¹⁸But now Adonijah has become king, and you, my lord the king, do not know about it. ¹⁹He has sacrificed great numbers of cattle, fattened calves, and sheep, and has invited all the king's sons, Abiathar the priest and Joab the commander of the army, but he has not invited Solomon your servant. ²⁰My lord the king, the eyes of all Israel are on you, to learn from you who will sit on the throne of my lord the king after him. ²¹Otherwise, as soon as my lord the king is laid to rest with his fathers, I and my son Solomon will be treated as criminals."

²²While she was still speaking with the king, Nathan the prophet arrived. ²³And they told the king, "Nathan the

Legacy

1 KINGS 1:5–11

Even as King David nears death, the legacy of his dysfunctional family and rocky marriages catches up with him. His son Adonijah connives to become king as Absalom had done before him.

Prayerfully consider the legacy, both for good and ill, that previous generations have given to you. What recurrent patterns of behavior of previous generations do you see in your family life today? What major influences for good shaped you in childhood (consider the habits of parents, grandparents, and other close family and friends)? What influences were less helpful, or even harmful? In prayer, hold the image of each family member in your mind as you pray God's blessing on him or her.

See Meeting God in Everyday Life

---

a 5 Or *charioteers*   *b 8* Or *and his friends*

Getting Ahead

1 KINGS 1:23–27

It is hard to blame Adonijah for wanting to get ahead. After all, don't we encourage our sons and daughters to do the same? To be ambitious is not necessarily sinful. But ambition is too often blind and driven, and it leads to a costly downfall. As you reflect on your life, pray that you will be able to discern the fine line between healthy ambition and sin. As you go through the day, be prayerfully aware of how ambition is at work in your encounters. Ponder what desires fuel these ambitions—and note when the ambition leads you to behave in destructive ways. Take note of how you are climbing the ladder of success and ask God to help you view your actions through his eyes.

prophet is here." So he went before the king and bowed with his face to the ground.

²⁴Nathan said, "Have you, my lord the king, declared that Adonijah shall be king after you, and that he will sit on your throne? ²⁵Today he has gone down and sacrificed great numbers of cattle, fattened calves, and sheep. He has invited all the king's sons, the commanders of the army and Abiathar the priest. Right now they are eating and drinking with him and saying, 'Long live King Adonijah!' ²⁶But me your servant, and Zadok the priest, and Benaiah son of Jehoiada, and your servant Solomon he did not invite. ²⁷Is this something my lord the king has done without letting his servants know who should sit on the throne of my lord the king after him?"

David Makes Solomon King

²⁸Then King David said, "Call in Bathsheba." So she came into the king's presence and stood before him. ²⁹The king then took an oath: "As surely as the LORD lives, who has delivered me out of every trouble, ³⁰I will surely carry out today what I swore to you by the LORD, the God of Israel: Solomon your son shall be king after me, and he will sit on my throne in my place." ³¹Then Bathsheba bowed low with her face to the ground and, kneeling before the king, said, "May my lord King David live forever!"

³²King David said, "Call in Zadok the priest, Nathan the prophet and Benaiah son of Jehoiada." When they came before the king, ³³he said to them: "Take your lord's servants with you and set Solomon my son on my own mule and take him down to Gihon. ³⁴There have Zadok the priest and Nathan the prophet anoint him king over Israel. Blow the trumpet and shout, 'Long live King Solomon!' ³⁵Then you are to go up with him, and he is to come and sit on my throne and reign in my place. I have appointed him ruler over Israel and Judah."

³⁶Benaiah son of Jehoiada answered the king, "Amen! May the LORD, the God of my lord the king, so declare it. ³⁷As the LORD was with my lord the king, so may he be with Solomon to make his throne even greater than the throne of my lord King David!"

³⁸So Zadok the priest, Nathan the prophet, Benaiah son of Jehoiada, the Kerethites and the Pelethites went down and put Solomon on King David's mule and escorted him to Gihon. ³⁹Zadok the priest took the horn of oil from the sacred tent and anointed Solomon. Then they sounded the trumpet and all the people shouted, "Long live King Solomon!" ⁴⁰And all the people went up after him, playing flutes and rejoicing greatly, so that the ground shook with the sound.

⁴¹Adonijah and all the guests who were with him heard it as they were finishing their feast. On hearing the sound of the trumpet, Joab asked, "What's the meaning of all the noise in the city?"

⁴²Even as he was speaking, Jonathan son of Abiathar the priest arrived. Adonijah said, "Come in. A worthy man like you must be bringing good news."

⁴³"Not at all!" Jonathan answered. "Our lord King David has made Solomon king. ⁴⁴The king has sent with him Zadok the priest, Nathan the prophet, Benaiah son of Je-

hoiada, the Kerethites and the Pelethites, and they have put him on the king's mule, ⁴⁵and Zadok the priest and Nathan the prophet have anointed him king at Gihon. From there they have gone up cheering, and the city resounds with it. That's the noise you hear. ⁴⁶Moreover, Solomon has taken his seat on the royal throne. ⁴⁷Also, the royal officials have come to congratulate our lord King David, saying, 'May your God make Solomon's name more famous than yours and his throne greater than yours!' And the king bowed in worship on his bed ⁴⁸and said, 'Praise be to the LORD, the God of Israel, who has allowed my eyes to see a successor on my throne today.' "

⁴⁹At this, all Adonijah's guests rose in alarm and dispersed. ⁵⁰But Adonijah, in fear of Solomon, went and took hold of the horns of the altar. ⁵¹Then Solomon was told, "Adonijah is afraid of King Solomon and is clinging to the horns of the altar. He says, 'Let King Solomon swear to me today that he will not put his servant to death with the sword.' "

⁵²Solomon replied, "If he shows himself to be a worthy man, not a hair of his head will fall to the ground; but if evil is found in him, he will die." ⁵³Then King Solomon sent men, and they brought him down from the altar. And Adonijah came and bowed down to King Solomon, and Solomon said, "Go to your home."

David's Charge to Solomon

2 When the time drew near for David to die, he gave a charge to Solomon his son.

²"I am about to go the way of all the earth," he said. "So be strong, show yourself a man, ³and observe what the LORD your God requires: Walk in his ways, and keep his decrees and commands, his laws and requirements, as written in the Law of Moses, so that you may prosper in all you do and wherever you go, ⁴and that the LORD may keep his promise to me: 'If your descendants watch how they live, and if they walk faithfully before me with all their heart and soul, you will never fail to have a man on the throne of Israel.'

⁵"Now you yourself know what Joab son of Zeruiah did to me—what he did to the two commanders of Israel's armies, Abner son of Ner and Amasa son of Jether. He killed them, shedding their blood in peacetime as if in battle, and with that blood stained the belt around his waist and the sandals on his feet. ⁶Deal with him according to your wisdom, but do not let his gray head go down to the grave[a] in peace.

⁷"But show kindness to the sons of Barzillai of Gilead and let them be among those who eat at your table. They stood by me when I fled from your brother Absalom.

⁸"And remember, you have with you Shimei son of Gera, the Benjamite from Bahurim, who called down bitter curses on me the day I went to Mahanaim. When he came down to meet me at the Jordan, I swore to him by the LORD: 'I will not put you to death by the sword.' ⁹But now, do not consider him innocent. You are a man of wisdom; you will know what to do to him. Bring his gray head down to the grave in blood."

¹⁰Then David rested with his fathers and was buried in

A Father and His Son

1 KINGS 2:1–4

David charges his son Solomon to be a wise ruler. Each generation wants "the best" for the next. Think about the children you know—within your sphere of influence—whether you are a parent, a relative, a teacher or a member of a community with children. What hopes do you have for these children? What hopes do you think God may have for them? What blessings or struggles have children brought into your life? How have these children affected your relationship with God? How would you pray today for them?

See Meeting God in Community

---

a 6 Hebrew Sheol; also in verse 9

Solomon Consolidates His Reign

1 KINGS 2:12–29

"David's kingdom was established into the hands of Solomon. How Solomon ruled and lived personally remained to be seen. We may feel established in our lives, our marriage, spiritual journey, or career. There is a danger that we can get too comfortable. We must reflect daily on how we are living before the Lord. God is present. The purpose of spiritual discipline is to help us recognize what is already a fact and to open us up to the reality of God in human life. The best life we can live is a life oriented toward God. To live any other way is to rebel against our Creator and to destroy what we were made to be."

—WILLIAM O. PAULSELL,
Taste and See

the City of David. ¹¹He had reigned forty years over Israel—seven years in Hebron and thirty-three in Jerusalem. ¹²So Solomon sat on the throne of his father David, and his rule was firmly established.

Solomon's Throne Established

¹³Now Adonijah, the son of Haggith, went to Bathsheba, Solomon's mother. Bathsheba asked him, "Do you come peacefully?"

He answered, "Yes, peacefully." ¹⁴Then he added, "I have something to say to you."

"You may say it," she replied.

¹⁵"As you know," he said, "the kingdom was mine. All Israel looked to me as their king. But things changed, and the kingdom has gone to my brother; for it has come to him from the LORD. ¹⁶Now I have one request to make of you. Do not refuse me."

"You may make it," she said.

¹⁷So he continued, "Please ask King Solomon—he will not refuse you—to give me Abishag the Shunammite as my wife."

¹⁸"Very well," Bathsheba replied, "I will speak to the king for you."

¹⁹When Bathsheba went to King Solomon to speak to him for Adonijah, the king stood up to meet her, bowed down to her and sat down on his throne. He had a throne brought for the king's mother, and she sat down at his right hand.

²⁰"I have one small request to make of you," she said. "Do not refuse me."

The king replied, "Make it, my mother; I will not refuse you."

²¹So she said, "Let Abishag the Shunammite be given in marriage to your brother Adonijah."

²²King Solomon answered his mother, "Why do you request Abishag the Shunammite for Adonijah? You might as well request the kingdom for him—after all, he is my older brother—yes, for him and for Abiathar the priest and Joab son of Zeruiah!"

²³Then King Solomon swore by the LORD: "May God deal with me, be it ever so severely, if Adonijah does not pay with his life for this request! ²⁴And now, as surely as the LORD lives—he who has established me securely on the throne of my father David and has founded a dynasty for me as he promised—Adonijah shall be put to death today!" ²⁵So King Solomon gave orders to Benaiah son of Jehoiada, and he struck down Adonijah and he died.

²⁶To Abiathar the priest the king said, "Go back to your fields in Anathoth. You deserve to die, but I will not put you to death now, because you carried the ark of the Sovereign LORD before my father David and shared all my father's hardships." ²⁷So Solomon removed Abiathar from the priesthood of the LORD, fulfilling the word the LORD had spoken at Shiloh about the house of Eli.

²⁸When the news reached Joab, who had conspired with Adonijah though not with Absalom, he fled to the tent of the LORD and took hold of the horns of the altar. ²⁹King Solomon was told that Joab had fled to the tent of the LORD and was beside the altar. Then Solomon ordered Benaiah son of Jehoiada, "Go, strike him down!"

³⁰So Benaiah entered the tent of the LORD and said to Joab, "The king says, 'Come out!' "

But he answered, "No, I will die here."

Benaiah reported to the king, "This is how Joab answered me."

³¹Then the king commanded Benaiah, "Do as he says. Strike him down and bury him, and so clear me and my father's house of the guilt of the innocent blood that Joab shed. ³²The LORD will repay him for the blood he shed, because without the knowledge of my father David he attacked two men and killed them with the sword. Both of them—Abner son of Ner, commander of Israel's army, and Amasa son of Jether, commander of Judah's army—were better men and more upright than he. ³³May the guilt of their blood rest on the head of Joab and his descendants forever. But on David and his descendants, his house and his throne, may there be the LORD's peace forever."

³⁴So Benaiah son of Jehoiada went up and struck down Joab and killed him, and he was buried on his own land*a* in the desert. ³⁵The king put Benaiah son of Jehoiada over the army in Joab's position and replaced Abiathar with Zadok the priest.

³⁶Then the king sent for Shimei and said to him, "Build yourself a house in Jerusalem and live there, but do not go anywhere else. ³⁷The day you leave and cross the Kidron Valley, you can be sure you will die; your blood will be on your own head."

³⁸Shimei answered the king, "What you say is good. Your servant will do as my lord the king has said." And Shimei stayed in Jerusalem for a long time.

³⁹But three years later, two of Shimei's slaves ran off to Achish son of Maacah, king of Gath, and Shimei was told, "Your slaves are in Gath." ⁴⁰At this, he saddled his donkey and went to Achish at Gath in search of his slaves. So Shimei went away and brought the slaves back from Gath.

⁴¹When Solomon was told that Shimei had gone from Jerusalem to Gath and had returned, ⁴²the king summoned Shimei and said to him, "Did I not make you swear by the LORD and warn you, 'On the day you leave to go anywhere else, you can be sure you will die'? At that time you said to me, 'What you say is good. I will obey.' ⁴³Why then did you not keep your oath to the LORD and obey the command I gave you?"

⁴⁴The king also said to Shimei, "You know in your heart all the wrong you did to my father David. Now the LORD will repay you for your wrongdoing. ⁴⁵But King Solomon will be blessed, and David's throne will remain secure before the LORD forever."

⁴⁶Then the king gave the order to Benaiah son of Jehoiada, and he went out and struck Shimei down and killed him.

The kingdom was now firmly established in Solomon's hands.

Solomon Asks for Wisdom

3 Solomon made an alliance with Pharaoh king of Egypt and married his daughter. He brought her to the City of David until he finished building his palace and the temple of the LORD, and the wall around Jerusalem. ²The people,

---

Joab's Fate

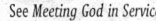

1 KINGS 2:31–34

Personal characteristics and traits can be strengths in one phase of our lives and become our undoing in another phase. Joab, King David's general, is struck down for plotting with Adonijah for the throne of King David.

A strong and confident commander, warrior, strategist and leader, Joab has been overconfident in deciding what is best for David. That self-confident, commanding style now leads him to disaster.

What are your primary strengths, talents and gifts? How have they changed over time? Have the same talents been used for both good and ill? In what areas is God calling you to grow? In which situations are you relying on your own confidence rather than seeking God's will?

See Meeting God in Service

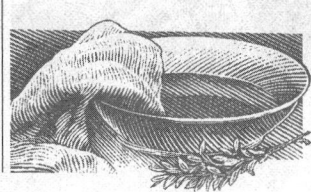

---

a 34 Or buried in his tomb

Solomon's Wisdom

1 KINGS 3:9–14

Solomon is given a "wise and discerning heart." In the Bible, wisdom is the exercise of sound and reverent judgment. The test of true wisdom is how well it is applied in day-to-day practice. The wise are those who, through faithfulness to the commandments of God, live well. Through spiritual knowledge, combined with practical experience, they are able to give astute counsel about navigating life's pitfalls.

Reflect with gratitude on your own life: Who are some of the wise mentors you have known? When have you called upon them for their wisdom? In what areas of your own life are you blessed with wisdom? When do others call upon you for that wisdom?

See Meeting God in Community

however, were still sacrificing at the high places, because a temple had not yet been built for the Name of the LORD. ³Solomon showed his love for the LORD by walking according to the statutes of his father David, except that he offered sacrifices and burned incense on the high places.

⁴The king went to Gibeon to offer sacrifices, for that was the most important high place, and Solomon offered a thousand burnt offerings on that altar. ⁵At Gibeon the LORD appeared to Solomon during the night in a dream, and God said, "Ask for whatever you want me to give you."

⁶Solomon answered, "You have shown great kindness to your servant, my father David, because he was faithful to you and righteous and upright in heart. You have continued this great kindness to him and have given him a son to sit on his throne this very day.

⁷"Now, O LORD my God, you have made your servant king in place of my father David. But I am only a little child and do not know how to carry out my duties. ⁸Your servant is here among the people you have chosen, a great people, too numerous to count or number. ⁹So give your servant a discerning heart to govern your people and to distinguish between right and wrong. For who is able to govern this great people of yours?"

¹⁰The Lord was pleased that Solomon had asked for this. ¹¹So God said to him, "Since you have asked for this and not for long life or wealth for yourself, nor have asked for the death of your enemies but for discernment in administering justice, ¹²I will do what you have asked. I will give you a wise and discerning heart, so that there will never have been anyone like you, nor will there ever be. ¹³Moreover, I will give you what you have not asked for—both riches and honor—so that in your lifetime you will have no equal among kings. ¹⁴And if you walk in my ways and obey my statutes and commands as David your father did, I will give you a long life." ¹⁵Then Solomon awoke—and he realized it had been a dream.

He returned to Jerusalem, stood before the ark of the Lord's covenant and sacrificed burnt offerings and fellowship offerings.ᵃ Then he gave a feast for all his court.

A Wise Ruling

¹⁶Now two prostitutes came to the king and stood before him. ¹⁷One of them said, "My lord, this woman and I live in the same house. I had a baby while she was there with me. ¹⁸The third day after my child was born, this woman also had a baby. We were alone; there was no one in the house but the two of us.

¹⁹"During the night this woman's son died because she lay on him. ²⁰So she got up in the middle of the night and took my son from my side while I your servant was asleep. She put him by her breast and put her dead son by my breast. ²¹The next morning, I got up to nurse my son—and he was dead! But when I looked at him closely in the morning light, I saw that it wasn't the son I had borne."

²²The other woman said, "No! The living one is my son; the dead one is yours."

But the first one insisted, "No! The dead one is yours; the living one is mine." And so they argued before the king.

²³The king said, "This one says, 'My son is alive and your

ᵃ 15 Traditionally peace offerings

son is dead,' while that one says, 'No! Your son is dead and mine is alive.' "

²⁴Then the king said, "Bring me a sword." So they brought a sword for the king. ²⁵He then gave an order: "Cut the living child in two and give half to one and half to the other."

²⁶The woman whose son was alive was filled with compassion for her son and said to the king, "Please, my lord, give her the living baby! Don't kill him!"

But the other said, "Neither I nor you shall have him. Cut him in two!"

²⁷Then the king gave his ruling: "Give the living baby to the first woman. Do not kill him; she is his mother."

²⁸When all Israel heard the verdict the king had given, they held the king in awe, because they saw that he had wisdom from God to administer justice.

Solomon's Officials and Governors

4 So King Solomon ruled over all Israel. ²And these were his chief officials:

Azariah son of Zadok—the priest;
³Elihoreph and Ahijah, sons of Shisha—secretaries;
Jehoshaphat son of Ahilud—recorder;
⁴Benaiah son of Jehoiada—commander in chief;
Zadok and Abiathar—priests;
⁵Azariah son of Nathan—in charge of the district officers;
Zabud son of Nathan—a priest and personal adviser to the king;
⁶Ahishar—in charge of the palace;
Adoniram son of Abda—in charge of forced labor.

⁷Solomon also had twelve district governors over all Israel, who supplied provisions for the king and the royal household. Each one had to provide supplies for one month in the year. ⁸These are their names:

Ben-Hur—in the hill country of Ephraim;
⁹Ben-Deker—in Makaz, Shaalbim, Beth Shemesh and Elon Bethhanan;
¹⁰Ben-Hesed—in Arubboth (Socoh and all the land of Hepher were his);
¹¹Ben-Abinadab—in Naphoth Dor*ᵃ* (he was married to Taphath daughter of Solomon);
¹²Baana son of Ahilud—in Taanach and Megiddo, and in all of Beth Shan next to Zarethan below Jezreel, from Beth Shan to Abel Meholah across to Jokmeam;
¹³Ben-Geber—in Ramoth Gilead (the settlements of Jair son of Manasseh in Gilead were his, as well as the district of Argob in Bashan and its sixty large walled cities with bronze gate bars);
¹⁴Ahinadab son of Iddo—in Mahanaim;
¹⁵Ahimaaz—in Naphtali (he had married Basemath daughter of Solomon);
¹⁶Baana son of Hushai—in Asher and in Aloth;
¹⁷Jehoshaphat son of Paruah—in Issachar;
¹⁸Shimei son of Ela—in Benjamin;
¹⁹Geber son of Uri—in Gilead (the country of Sihon king

The Path to Wisdom

1 KINGS 3:28

"If one is to have true wisdom, it is not enough merely to have a handbook in one's hands, it is also necessary that a great zeal be kindled in one's heart."

—AUGUSTINE, *Enchiridion*

David's Dream Deferred

1 KINGS 5:1–4

David's fondest dream was to build a temple for the Lord, but his dream was put on hold—permanently. Regardless, dreaming is not a luxury for the child of God. Dreams are what form our spirits and lives. What happens to us when dreams are deferred? Do our dreams just go away and become forgotten pieces of our lives? Do we hang on to them in hopes of future fulfillment? What dreams do you have? Which ones are alive and active? Which dreams have been deferred? Pray for discernment about which dreams to hold on to, and about which dreams to let go.

See Meeting God in Prayer

of the Amorites and the country of Og king of Bashan). He was the only governor over the district.

Solomon's Daily Provisions

[20]The people of Judah and Israel were as numerous as the sand on the seashore; they ate, they drank and they were happy. [21]And Solomon ruled over all the kingdoms from the River[a] to the land of the Philistines, as far as the border of Egypt. These countries brought tribute and were Solomon's subjects all his life.

[22]Solomon's daily provisions were thirty cors[b] of fine flour and sixty cors[c] of meal, [23]ten head of stall-fed cattle, twenty of pasture-fed cattle and a hundred sheep and goats, as well as deer, gazelles, roebucks and choice fowl. [24]For he ruled over all the kingdoms west of the River, from Tiphsah to Gaza, and had peace on all sides. [25]During Solomon's lifetime Judah and Israel, from Dan to Beersheba, lived in safety, each man under his own vine and fig tree.

[26]Solomon had four[d] thousand stalls for chariot horses, and twelve thousand horses.[e]

[27]The district officers, each in his month, supplied provisions for King Solomon and all who came to the king's table. They saw to it that nothing was lacking. [28]They also brought to the proper place their quotas of barley and straw for the chariot horses and the other horses.

Solomon's Wisdom

[29]God gave Solomon wisdom and very great insight, and a breadth of understanding as measureless as the sand on the seashore. [30]Solomon's wisdom was greater than the wisdom of all the men of the East, and greater than all the wisdom of Egypt. [31]He was wiser than any other man, including Ethan the Ezrahite—wiser than Heman, Calcol and Darda, the sons of Mahol. And his fame spread to all the surrounding nations. [32]He spoke three thousand proverbs and his songs numbered a thousand and five. [33]He described plant life, from the cedar of Lebanon to the hyssop that grows out of walls. He also taught about animals and birds, reptiles and fish. [34]Men of all nations came to listen to Solomon's wisdom, sent by all the kings of the world, who had heard of his wisdom.

Preparations for Building the Temple

5 When Hiram king of Tyre heard that Solomon had been anointed king to succeed his father David, he sent his envoys to Solomon, because he had always been on friendly terms with David. [2]Solomon sent back this message to Hiram:

> [3]"You know that because of the wars waged against my father David from all sides, he could not build a temple for the Name of the LORD his God until the LORD put his enemies under his feet. [4]But now the LORD my God has given me rest on every side, and there is no adversary or disaster. [5]I intend, therefore, to build a temple for the Name of the LORD my God, as the LORD

a 21 That is, the Euphrates; also in verse 24   *b 22* That is, probably about 185 bushels (about 6.6 kiloliters)   *c 22* That is, probably about 375 bushels (about 13.2 kiloliters)   *d 26* Some Septuagint manuscripts (see also 2 Chron. 9:25); Hebrew *forty*   *e 26* Or *charioteers*

told my father David, when he said, 'Your son whom I will put on the throne in your place will build the temple for my Name.'

⁶"So give orders that cedars of Lebanon be cut for me. My men will work with yours, and I will pay you for your men whatever wages you set. You know that we have no one so skilled in felling timber as the Sidonians."

⁷When Hiram heard Solomon's message, he was greatly pleased and said, "Praise be to the LORD today, for he has given David a wise son to rule over this great nation."

⁸So Hiram sent word to Solomon:

"I have received the message you sent me and will do all you want in providing the cedar and pine logs. ⁹My men will haul them down from Lebanon to the sea, and I will float them in rafts by sea to the place you specify. There I will separate them and you can take them away. And you are to grant my wish by providing food for my royal household."

¹⁰In this way Hiram kept Solomon supplied with all the cedar and pine logs he wanted, ¹¹and Solomon gave Hiram twenty thousand cors*ᵃ* of wheat as food for his household, in addition to twenty thousand baths*ᵇ,ᶜ* of pressed olive oil. Solomon continued to do this for Hiram year after year. ¹²The LORD gave Solomon wisdom, just as he had promised him. There were peaceful relations between Hiram and Solomon, and the two of them made a treaty.

¹³King Solomon conscripted laborers from all Israel—thirty thousand men. ¹⁴He sent them off to Lebanon in shifts of ten thousand a month, so that they spent one month in Lebanon and two months at home. Adoniram was in charge of the forced labor. ¹⁵Solomon had seventy thousand carriers and eighty thousand stonecutters in the hills, ¹⁶as well as thirty-three hundred*ᵈ* foremen who supervised the project and directed the workmen. ¹⁷At the king's command they removed from the quarry large blocks of quality stone to provide a foundation of dressed stone for the temple. ¹⁸The craftsmen of Solomon and Hiram and the men of Gebal*ᵉ* cut and prepared the timber and stone for the building of the temple.

Solomon Builds the Temple

6 In the four hundred and eightieth*ᶠ* year after the Israelites had come out of Egypt, in the fourth year of Solomon's reign over Israel, in the month of Ziv, the second month, he began to build the temple of the LORD.

²The temple that King Solomon built for the LORD was sixty cubits long, twenty wide and thirty high.*ᵍ* ³The portico at the front of the main hall of the temple extended the width of the temple, that is twenty cubits,*ʰ* and projected ten cubits*ⁱ* from the front of the temple. ⁴He made narrow clerestory windows in the temple. ⁵Against the walls of the

---

When God Answers Yes or No

1 KINGS 5:5

God does not always say "yes" to all our hopes and dreams. God said "no" to David's aspiration to build the temple. Because God wanted a peacemaker and not a warrior to build the temple, he said "yes" to Solomon instead. Our hopes, dreams and possibilities are often unfulfilled because God says, "No, not now." Do Solomon's and David's experiences resemble your own experiences? What is your prayer for the dreams of your life? When have you yearned to accomplish something personal only to hear that clear "no"? How did that "no" affect your relationship with God?

ᵃ 11 That is, probably about 125,000 bushels (about 4,400 kiloliters)
ᵇ 11 Septuagint (see also 2 Chron. 2:10); Hebrew *twenty cors*   *ᶜ 11* That is, about 115,000 gallons (about 440 kiloliters)   *ᵈ 16* Hebrew; some Septuagint manuscripts (see also 2 Chron. 2:2, 18) *thirty-six hundred*
ᵉ 18 That is, Byblos   *ᶠ 1* Hebrew; Septuagint *four hundred and fortieth*
ᵍ 2 That is, about 90 feet (about 27 meters) long and 30 feet (about 9 meters) wide and 45 feet (about 13.5 meters) high   *ʰ 3* That is, about 30 feet (about 9 meters)   *ⁱ 3* That is, about 15 feet (about 4.5 meters)

An Eternal Presence

1 KINGS 6:14

The temple is a sign of God's presence in the lives of his people. Through such signs and symbols God reaches out to embrace us in relationship. Prayerfully recall from your experience some of the signs of the presence of God. It may be a building, a community of faith, a relationship or a specific occasion. Bring it into focus in your memory, recalling sights, colors, smells, sounds, emotions and conversations that mark the sign in your memory. Remember the particular spiritual quality of your "sign"—a spirit of love, peace, hope, comfort, encouragement or challenge. Now, in that living recollection of your "temple," give thanks to God and store that memory in your heart for future thanksgiving.

See *Meeting God in Worship*

main hall and inner sanctuary he built a structure around the building, in which there were side rooms. ⁶The lowest floor was five cubits*ᵃ* wide, the middle floor six cubits*ᵇ* and the third floor seven.*ᶜ* He made offset ledges around the outside of the temple so that nothing would be inserted into the temple walls.

⁷In building the temple, only blocks dressed at the quarry were used, and no hammer, chisel or any other iron tool was heard at the temple site while it was being built.

⁸The entrance to the lowest*ᵈ* floor was on the south side of the temple; a stairway led up to the middle level and from there to the third. ⁹So he built the temple and completed it, roofing it with beams and cedar planks. ¹⁰And he built the side rooms all along the temple. The height of each was five cubits, and they were attached to the temple by beams of cedar.

¹¹The word of the LORD came to Solomon: ¹²"As for this temple you are building, if you follow my decrees, carry out my regulations and keep all my commands and obey them, I will fulfill through you the promise I gave to David your father. ¹³And I will live among the Israelites and will not abandon my people Israel."

¹⁴So Solomon built the temple and completed it. ¹⁵He lined its interior walls with cedar boards, paneling them from the floor of the temple to the ceiling, and covered the floor of the temple with planks of pine. ¹⁶He partitioned off twenty cubits*ᵉ* at the rear of the temple with cedar boards from floor to ceiling to form within the temple an inner sanctuary, the Most Holy Place. ¹⁷The main hall in front of this room was forty cubits*ᶠ* long. ¹⁸The inside of the temple was cedar, carved with gourds and open flowers. Everything was cedar; no stone was to be seen.

¹⁹He prepared the inner sanctuary within the temple to set the ark of the covenant of the LORD there. ²⁰The inner sanctuary was twenty cubits long, twenty wide and twenty high.*ᵍ* He overlaid the inside with pure gold, and he also overlaid the altar of cedar. ²¹Solomon covered the inside of the temple with pure gold, and he extended gold chains across the front of the inner sanctuary, which was overlaid with gold. ²²So he overlaid the whole interior with gold. He also overlaid with gold the altar that belonged to the inner sanctuary.

²³In the inner sanctuary he made a pair of cherubim of olive wood, each ten cubits*ʰ* high. ²⁴One wing of the first cherub was five cubits long, and the other wing five cubits—ten cubits from wing tip to wing tip. ²⁵The second cherub also measured ten cubits, for the two cherubim were identical in size and shape. ²⁶The height of each cherub was ten cubits. ²⁷He placed the cherubim inside the innermost room of the temple, with their wings spread out. The wing of one cherub touched one wall, while the wing of the other touched the other wall, and their wings touched each other in the middle of the room. ²⁸He overlaid the cherubim with gold.

²⁹On the walls all around the temple, in both the inner

ᵃ6 That is, about 7 1/2 feet (about 2.3 meters); also in verses 10 and 24   *ᵇ6* That is, about 9 feet (about 2.7 meters)   *ᶜ6* That is, about 10 1/2 feet (about 3.1 meters)   *ᵈ8* Septuagint; Hebrew *middle*   *ᵉ16* That is, about 30 feet (about 9 meters)   *ᶠ17* That is, about 60 feet (about 18 meters)   *ᵍ20* That is, about 30 feet (about 9 meters) long, wide and high   *ʰ23* That is, about 15 feet (about 4.5 meters)

and outer rooms, he carved cherubim, palm trees and open flowers. ³⁰He also covered the floors of both the inner and outer rooms of the temple with gold.

³¹For the entrance of the inner sanctuary he made doors of olive wood with five-sided jambs. ³²And on the two olive wood doors he carved cherubim, palm trees and open flowers, and overlaid the cherubim and palm trees with beaten gold. ³³In the same way he made four-sided jambs of olive wood for the entrance to the main hall. ³⁴He also made two pine doors, each having two leaves that turned in sockets. ³⁵He carved cherubim, palm trees and open flowers on them and overlaid them with gold hammered evenly over the carvings.

³⁶And he built the inner courtyard of three courses of dressed stone and one course of trimmed cedar beams.

³⁷The foundation of the temple of the LORD was laid in the fourth year, in the month of Ziv. ³⁸In the eleventh year in the month of Bul, the eighth month, the temple was finished in all its details according to its specifications. He had spent seven years building it.

Solomon Builds His Palace

7 It took Solomon thirteen years, however, to complete the construction of his palace. ²He built the Palace of the Forest of Lebanon a hundred cubits long, fifty wide and thirty high,ᵃ with four rows of cedar columns supporting trimmed cedar beams. ³It was roofed with cedar above the beams that rested on the columns—forty-five beams, fifteen to a row. ⁴Its windows were placed high in sets of three, facing each other. ⁵All the doorways had rectangular frames; they were in the front part in sets of three, facing each other.ᵇ

⁶He made a colonnade fifty cubits long and thirty wide.ᶜ In front of it was a portico, and in front of that were pillars and an overhanging roof.

⁷He built the throne hall, the Hall of Justice, where he was to judge, and he covered it with cedar from floor to ceiling.ᵈ ⁸And the palace in which he was to live, set farther back, was similar in design. Solomon also made a palace like this hall for Pharaoh's daughter, whom he had married.

⁹All these structures, from the outside to the great courtyard and from foundation to eaves, were made of blocks of high-grade stone cut to size and trimmed with a saw on their inner and outer faces. ¹⁰The foundations were laid with large stones of good quality, some measuring ten cubitsᵉ and some eight.ᶠ ¹¹Above were high-grade stones, cut to size, and cedar beams. ¹²The great courtyard was surrounded by a wall of three courses of dressed stone and one course of trimmed cedar beams, as was the inner courtyard of the temple of the LORD with its portico.

The Temple's Furnishings

¹³King Solomon sent to Tyre and brought Huram,ᵍ ¹⁴whose mother was a widow from the tribe of Naphtali

Building Our Life for God

1 KINGS 6:38–7:1

Solomon spent seven years building the house of God and thirteen years building his own palace. What does this say about Solomon's priorities? What can we learn from them? Examine your priorities. How have you been building your life and career? Name a foundational principle (for example, integrity, love, creativity) for each area of your life (for example, career, family, avocation). What are some of the things you have accomplished in each area? What are your goals and priorities for each? How have these priorities come into conflict with each other? With your life of the spirit?

See Meeting God in Everyday Life

ᵃ2 That is, about 150 feet (about 46 meters) long, 75 feet (about 23 meters) wide and 45 feet (about 13.5 meters) high   ᵇ5 The meaning of the Hebrew for this verse is uncertain.   ᶜ6 That is, about 75 feet (about 23 meters) long and 45 feet (about 13.5 meters) wide   ᵈ7 Vulgate and Syriac; Hebrew *floor*   ᵉ10 That is, about 15 feet (about 4.5 meters)   ᶠ10 That is, about 12 feet (about 3.6 meters)   ᵍ13 Hebrew *Hiram*, a variant of *Huram*; also in verses 40 and 45

Articles of Worship

1 KINGS 7:13–30

Our modern articles of worship are different than those used in Solomon's temple, but the purpose of sacred things remains the same. The Israelites used iron and bronze, fire and priests, sacrificial offerings and basins. Our hymnals, altars, stained glass windows and pulpits look different, but their purpose is still to lead hearts and minds to give honor and glory to God.

How do you prepare yourself to enter into worship? What elements of the building or the order of service most help you to worship God? What inward and outward obstacles impede your worship? How is your daily and weekly journey affected by missed opportunities for worship?

See Meeting God in Worship

and whose father was a man of Tyre and a craftsman in bronze. Huram was highly skilled and experienced in all kinds of bronze work. He came to King Solomon and did all the work assigned to him.

[15]He cast two bronze pillars, each eighteen cubits high and twelve cubits around,[a] by line. [16]He also made two capitals of cast bronze to set on the tops of the pillars; each capital was five cubits[b] high. [17]A network of interwoven chains festooned the capitals on top of the pillars, seven for each capital. [18]He made pomegranates in two rows[c] encircling each network to decorate the capitals on top of the pillars.[d] He did the same for each capital. [19]The capitals on top of the pillars in the portico were in the shape of lilies, four cubits[e] high. [20]On the capitals of both pillars, above the bowl-shaped part next to the network, were the two hundred pomegranates in rows all around. [21]He erected the pillars at the portico of the temple. The pillar to the south he named Jakin[f] and the one to the north Boaz.[g] [22]The capitals on top were in the shape of lilies. And so the work on the pillars was completed.

[23]He made the Sea of cast metal, circular in shape, measuring ten cubits[h] from rim to rim and five cubits high. It took a line of thirty cubits[i] to measure around it. [24]Below the rim, gourds encircled it—ten to a cubit. The gourds were cast in two rows in one piece with the Sea.

[25]The Sea stood on twelve bulls, three facing north, three facing west, three facing south and three facing east. The Sea rested on top of them, and their hindquarters were toward the center. [26]It was a handbreadth[j] in thickness, and its rim was like the rim of a cup, like a lily blossom. It held two thousand baths.[k]

[27]He also made ten movable stands of bronze; each was four cubits long, four wide and three high.[l] [28]This is how the stands were made: They had side panels attached to uprights. [29]On the panels between the uprights were lions, bulls and cherubim—and on the uprights as well. Above and below the lions and bulls were wreaths of hammered work. [30]Each stand had four bronze wheels with bronze axles, and each had a basin resting on four supports, cast with wreaths on each side. [31]On the inside of the stand there was an opening that had a circular frame one cubit[m] deep. This opening was round, and with its basework it measured a cubit and a half.[n] Around its opening there was engraving. The panels of the stands were square, not round. [32]The four wheels were under the panels, and the axles of the wheels were attached to the stand. The diameter of each wheel was a cubit and a half. [33]The wheels were made like chariot wheels; the axles, rims, spokes and hubs were all of cast metal.

[a] 15 That is, about 27 feet (about 8.1 meters) high and 18 feet (about 5.4 meters) around   [b] 16 That is, about 7 1/2 feet (about 2.3 meters); also in verse 23   [c] 18 Two Hebrew manuscripts and Septuagint; most Hebrew manuscripts *made the pillars, and there were two rows*   [d] 18 Many Hebrew manuscripts and Syriac; most Hebrew manuscripts *pomegranates*   [e] 19 That is, about 6 feet (about 1.8 meters); also in verse 38   [f] 21 *Jakin* probably means *he establishes.*   [g] 21 *Boaz* probably means *in him is strength.*   [h] 23 That is, about 15 feet (about 4.5 meters)   [i] 23 That is, about 45 feet (about 13.5 meters)   [j] 26 That is, about 3 inches (about 8 centimeters)   [k] 26 That is, probably about 11,500 gallons (about 44 kiloliters); the Septuagint does not have this sentence.   [l] 27 That is, about 6 feet (about 1.8 meters) long and wide and about 4 1/2 feet (about 1.3 meters) high   [m] 31 That is, about 1 1/2 feet (about 0.5 meter)   [n] 31 That is, about 2 1/4 feet (about 0.7 meter); also in verse 32

³⁴Each stand had four handles, one on each corner, projecting from the stand. ³⁵At the top of the stand there was a circular band half a cubit*ᵃ* deep. The supports and panels were attached to the top of the stand. ³⁶He engraved cherubim, lions and palm trees on the surfaces of the supports and on the panels, in every available space, with wreaths all around. ³⁷This is the way he made the ten stands. They were all cast in the same molds and were identical in size and shape.

³⁸He then made ten bronze basins, each holding forty baths*ᵇ* and measuring four cubits across, one basin to go on each of the ten stands. ³⁹He placed five of the stands on the south side of the temple and five on the north. He placed the Sea on the south side, at the southeast corner of the temple. ⁴⁰He also made the basins and shovels and sprinkling bowls.

So Huram finished all the work he had undertaken for King Solomon in the temple of the LORD:

⁴¹the two pillars;
the two bowl-shaped capitals on top of the pillars;
the two sets of network decorating the two bowl-shaped capitals on top of the pillars;
⁴²the four hundred pomegranates for the two sets of network (two rows of pomegranates for each network, decorating the bowl-shaped capitals on top of the pillars);
⁴³the ten stands with their ten basins;
⁴⁴the Sea and the twelve bulls under it;
⁴⁵the pots, shovels and sprinkling bowls.

All these objects that Huram made for King Solomon for the temple of the LORD were of burnished bronze. ⁴⁶The king had them cast in clay molds in the plain of the Jordan between Succoth and Zarethan. ⁴⁷Solomon left all these things unweighed, because there were so many; the weight of the bronze was not determined.

⁴⁸Solomon also made all the furnishings that were in the LORD's temple:

the golden altar;
the golden table on which was the bread of the Presence;
⁴⁹the lampstands of pure gold (five on the right and five on the left, in front of the inner sanctuary);
the gold floral work and lamps and tongs;
⁵⁰the pure gold basins, wick trimmers, sprinkling bowls, dishes and censers;
and the gold sockets for the doors of the innermost room, the Most Holy Place, and also for the doors of the main hall of the temple.

⁵¹When all the work King Solomon had done for the temple of the LORD was finished, he brought in the things his father David had dedicated—the silver and gold and the furnishings—and he placed them in the treasuries of the LORD's temple.

ᵃ 35 That is, about 3/4 foot (about 0.2 meter)   *ᵇ 38* That is, about 230 gallons (about 880 liters)

Dedicated Contributions

1 KINGS 7:50

Solomon goes to great lengths to build the temple; he makes fine vessels for the temple. There are far simpler contributions that we can make to the places in which we worship. Such an act can be a response to God's love for us.

Have you ever thought about what you contribute to your place of worship? Do you sew, bake bread, arrange flowers, read or sing? Can you make banners or altar cloths? Your worshiping community can use your gifts and skills to draw people closer to God. Pray about what contributions you could make to help your worship community draw closer to God.

See Meeting God in Worship

God's Dwelling Place

1 KINGS 8:12–21

"God, who is wholly present everywhere, [dwells] in those whom he has made into His most blessed temple or temples, delivering them from the power of darkness and translating them into the Kingdom of the Son of his Love [see Colossians 1:13]. God dwells within each one singly as in His temples, and in all of them gathered together as His temple . . . But in his indwelling, he is received more fully by some, less by others."

—AUGUSTINE,
"On the Presence of God," Letter 187

The Ark Brought to the Temple

8 Then King Solomon summoned into his presence at Jerusalem the elders of Israel, all the heads of the tribes and the chiefs of the Israelite families, to bring up the ark of the LORD's covenant from Zion, the City of David. ²All the men of Israel came together to King Solomon at the time of the festival in the month of Ethanim, the seventh month.

³When all the elders of Israel had arrived, the priests took up the ark, ⁴and they brought up the ark of the LORD and the Tent of Meeting and all the sacred furnishings in it. The priests and Levites carried them up, ⁵and King Solomon and the entire assembly of Israel that had gathered about him were before the ark, sacrificing so many sheep and cattle that they could not be recorded or counted.

⁶The priests then brought the ark of the LORD's covenant to its place in the inner sanctuary of the temple, the Most Holy Place, and put it beneath the wings of the cherubim. ⁷The cherubim spread their wings over the place of the ark and overshadowed the ark and its carrying poles. ⁸These poles were so long that their ends could be seen from the Holy Place in front of the inner sanctuary, but not from outside the Holy Place; and they are still there today. ⁹There was nothing in the ark except the two stone tablets that Moses had placed in it at Horeb, where the LORD made a covenant with the Israelites after they came out of Egypt.

¹⁰When the priests withdrew from the Holy Place, the cloud filled the temple of the LORD. ¹¹And the priests could not perform their service because of the cloud, for the glory of the LORD filled his temple.

¹²Then Solomon said, "The LORD has said that he would dwell in a dark cloud; ¹³I have indeed built a magnificent temple for you, a place for you to dwell forever."

¹⁴While the whole assembly of Israel was standing there, the king turned around and blessed them. ¹⁵Then he said:

"Praise be to the LORD, the God of Israel, who with his own hand has fulfilled what he promised with his own mouth to my father David. For he said, ¹⁶'Since the day I brought my people Israel out of Egypt, I have not chosen a city in any tribe of Israel to have a temple built for my Name to be there, but I have chosen David to rule my people Israel.'

¹⁷"My father David had it in his heart to build a temple for the Name of the LORD, the God of Israel. ¹⁸But the LORD said to my father David, 'Because it was in your heart to build a temple for my Name, you did well to have this in your heart. ¹⁹Nevertheless, you are not the one to build the temple, but your son, who is your own flesh and blood—he is the one who will build the temple for my Name.'

²⁰"The LORD has kept the promise he made: I have succeeded David my father and now I sit on the throne of Israel, just as the LORD promised, and I have built the temple for the Name of the LORD, the God of Israel. ²¹I have provided a place there for the ark, in which is the covenant of the LORD that he made with our fathers when he brought them out of Egypt."

Solomon's Prayer of Dedication

²²Then Solomon stood before the altar of the LORD in

front of the whole assembly of Israel, spread out his hands toward heaven ²³and said:

"O LORD, God of Israel, there is no God like you in heaven above or on earth below—you who keep your covenant of love with your servants who continue wholeheartedly in your way. ²⁴You have kept your promise to your servant David my father; with your mouth you have promised and with your hand you have fulfilled it—as it is today.

²⁵"Now LORD, God of Israel, keep for your servant David my father the promises you made to him when you said, 'You shall never fail to have a man to sit before me on the throne of Israel, if only your sons are careful in all they do to walk before me as you have done.' ²⁶And now, O God of Israel, let your word that you promised your servant David my father come true.

²⁷"But will God really dwell on earth? The heavens, even the highest heaven, cannot contain you. How much less this temple I have built! ²⁸Yet give attention to your servant's prayer and his plea for mercy, O LORD my God. Hear the cry and the prayer that your servant is praying in your presence this day. ²⁹May your eyes be open toward this temple night and day, this place of which you said, 'My Name shall be there,' so that you will hear the prayer your servant prays toward this place. ³⁰Hear the supplication of your servant and of your people Israel when they pray toward this place. Hear from heaven, your dwelling place, and when you hear, forgive.

³¹"When a man wrongs his neighbor and is required to take an oath and he comes and swears the oath before your altar in this temple, ³²then hear from heaven and act. Judge between your servants, condemning the guilty and bringing down on his own head what he has done. Declare the innocent not guilty, and so establish his innocence.

³³"When your people Israel have been defeated by an enemy because they have sinned against you, and when they turn back to you and confess your name, praying and making supplication to you in this temple, ³⁴then hear from heaven and forgive the sin of your people Israel and bring them back to the land you gave to their fathers.

³⁵"When the heavens are shut up and there is no rain because your people have sinned against you, and when they pray toward this place and confess your name and turn from their sin because you have afflicted them, ³⁶then hear from heaven and forgive the sin of your servants, your people Israel. Teach them the right way to live, and send rain on the land you gave your people for an inheritance.

³⁷"When famine or plague comes to the land, or blight or mildew, locusts or grasshoppers, or when an enemy besieges them in any of their cities, whatever disaster or disease may come, ³⁸and when a prayer or plea is made by any of your people Israel—each one aware of the afflictions of his own heart, and spreading out his hands toward this temple— ³⁹then hear from heaven, your dwelling place. Forgive and act; deal with each man according to all he does, since you know his

Prayer of Dedication

1 KINGS 8:20–25

Solomon dedicates the temple for "the Name of the LORD"; God's name represents every aspect of his being. Look through your house, home and family. Walk about your own house, considering how it, and the activities that take place within it, can be more deeply consecrated to God. In each place, frame a prayer of dedication. Where in your house are reminders of God's glory and presence? In what rooms have forgiveness and reconciliation been sought and received? Where are the places of hospitality and prayer? How is the frailty of the humans residing there in evidence? You might pray this prayer: "Day by day, week by week, help us to make our home a sacred place dedicated to you, a place where we may dwell in harmony, peace and joy. Amen."

See Meeting God in Everyday Life

When God's People Repent

1 KINGS 8:46–53

Sometimes defeat or frustration is a sign that we are on the wrong track. We realize we have missed opportunities and blundered and blown more chances than we care to admit. Sometimes the darkness of despair covers the light of hope. Somehow, though, life goes on; miraculously, so does God's forgiveness. Like ancient Israel, we can start over with each new day. Turning toward God from wherever we are, confessing all before our loving God, we can let go of the past and embrace the future. What are your unforgiven blunders and mistakes? How is the past holding you down? What is God calling you to do and to become? Trusting God, tell all to God and accept the new, clean slate he offers.

See Meeting God in Prayer

heart (for you alone know the hearts of all men), ⁴⁰so that they will fear you all the time they live in the land you gave our fathers.

⁴¹"As for the foreigner who does not belong to your people Israel but has come from a distant land because of your name— ⁴²for men will hear of your great name and your mighty hand and your outstretched arm—when he comes and prays toward this temple, ⁴³then hear from heaven, your dwelling place, and do whatever the foreigner asks of you, so that all the peoples of the earth may know your name and fear you, as do your own people Israel, and may know that this house I have built bears your Name.

⁴⁴"When your people go to war against their enemies, wherever you send them, and when they pray to the LORD toward the city you have chosen and the temple I have built for your Name, ⁴⁵then hear from heaven their prayer and their plea, and uphold their cause.

⁴⁶"When they sin against you—for there is no one who does not sin—and you become angry with them and give them over to the enemy, who takes them captive to his own land, far away or near; ⁴⁷and if they have a change of heart in the land where they are held captive, and repent and plead with you in the land of their conquerors and say, 'We have sinned, we have done wrong, we have acted wickedly'; ⁴⁸and if they turn back to you with all their heart and soul in the land of their enemies who took them captive, and pray to you toward the land you gave their fathers, toward the city you have chosen and the temple I have built for your Name; ⁴⁹then from heaven, your dwelling place, hear their prayer and their plea, and uphold their cause. ⁵⁰And forgive your people, who have sinned against you; forgive all the offenses they have committed against you, and cause their conquerors to show them mercy; ⁵¹for they are your people and your inheritance, whom you brought out of Egypt, out of that iron-smelting furnace.

⁵²"May your eyes be open to your servant's plea and to the plea of your people Israel, and may you listen to them whenever they cry out to you. ⁵³For you singled them out from all the nations of the world to be your own inheritance, just as you declared through your servant Moses when you, O Sovereign LORD, brought our fathers out of Egypt."

⁵⁴When Solomon had finished all these prayers and supplications to the LORD, he rose from before the altar of the LORD, where he had been kneeling with his hands spread out toward heaven. ⁵⁵He stood and blessed the whole assembly of Israel in a loud voice, saying:

⁵⁶"Praise be to the LORD, who has given rest to his people Israel just as he promised. Not one word has failed of all the good promises he gave through his servant Moses. ⁵⁷May the LORD our God be with us as he was with our fathers; may he never leave us nor forsake us. ⁵⁸May he turn our hearts to him, to walk in all his ways and to keep the commands, decrees and regulations he gave our fathers. ⁵⁹And may these words of mine, which I have prayed before the LORD, be near to

the LORD our God day and night, that he may uphold the cause of his servant and the cause of his people Israel according to each day's need, [60]so that all the peoples of the earth may know that the LORD is God and that there is no other. [61]But your hearts must be fully committed to the LORD our God, to live by his decrees and obey his commands, as at this time."

The Dedication of the Temple

[62]Then the king and all Israel with him offered sacrifices before the LORD. [63]Solomon offered a sacrifice of fellowship offerings[a] to the LORD: twenty-two thousand cattle and a hundred and twenty thousand sheep and goats. So the king and all the Israelites dedicated the temple of the LORD.

[64]On that same day the king consecrated the middle part of the courtyard in front of the temple of the LORD, and there he offered burnt offerings, grain offerings and the fat of the fellowship offerings, because the bronze altar before the LORD was too small to hold the burnt offerings, the grain offerings and the fat of the fellowship offerings.

[65]So Solomon observed the festival at that time, and all Israel with him—a vast assembly, people from Lebo[b] Hamath to the Wadi of Egypt. They celebrated it before the LORD our God for seven days and seven days more, fourteen days in all. [66]On the following day he sent the people away. They blessed the king and then went home, joyful and glad in heart for all the good things the LORD had done for his servant David and his people Israel.

The LORD Appears to Solomon

9 When Solomon had finished building the temple of the LORD and the royal palace, and had achieved all he had desired to do, [2]the LORD appeared to him a second time, as he had appeared to him at Gibeon. [3]The LORD said to him:

"I have heard the prayer and plea you have made before me; I have consecrated this temple, which you have built, by putting my Name there forever. My eyes and my heart will always be there.

[4]"As for you, if you walk before me in integrity of heart and uprightness, as David your father did, and do all I command and observe my decrees and laws, [5]I will establish your royal throne over Israel forever, as I promised David your father when I said, 'You shall never fail to have a man on the throne of Israel.'

[6]"But if you[c] or your sons turn away from me and do not observe the commands and decrees I have given you[c] and go off to serve other gods and worship them, [7]then I will cut off Israel from the land I have given them and will reject this temple I have consecrated for my Name. Israel will then become a byword and an object of ridicule among all peoples. [8]And though this temple is now imposing, all who pass by will be appalled and will scoff and say, 'Why has the LORD done such a thing to this land and to this temple?' [9]People will answer, 'Because they have forsaken the LORD their God, who brought their fathers out of Egypt, and have embraced other gods, worshiping and serving them—

---

[a] 63 Traditionally *peace offerings*; also in verse 64   [b] 65 Or *from the entrance to*   [c] 6 The Hebrew is plural.

Praying for the Basics

1 KINGS 8:56–61

Solomon's blessing concludes with the simple plea that God "may uphold the cause of his servant and the cause of his people Israel according to each day's need" and that the people will be devoted to God in their daily lives. Suppose you were to ask for such a blessing on your life. Envision the day ahead and imagine God's blessing pouring forth on all the events you anticipate. Craft a prayer, in your mind or on paper, for this day. Include the simple basics you really require *today* to "uphold [your] cause" in service to God's purposes, to your family's essential needs, and to the most urgent needs of your community and nation. Pray your prayer two or three times during the day.

See *Meeting God in Everyday Life*

Wandering Away From Real Relationship

1 KINGS 9:15–26

Amid all the building projects Solomon launched (the temple, his own palace, the supporting terraces and the wall) he still "fulfilled the temple obligations."

When life's duties press in on you, how well do you maintain your spiritual disciplines? When is busyness most likely to crowd out your times of practicing the presence of God? Ask God to help you cultivate your spiritual life despite the demands on your time. How can you practice God's presence even amid the busyness of life?

See Meeting God in Everyday Life

that is why the LORD brought all this disaster on them.'"

Solomon's Other Activities

¹⁰At the end of twenty years, during which Solomon built these two buildings—the temple of the LORD and the royal palace— ¹¹King Solomon gave twenty towns in Galilee to Hiram king of Tyre, because Hiram had supplied him with all the cedar and pine and gold he wanted. ¹²But when Hiram went from Tyre to see the towns that Solomon had given him, he was not pleased with them. ¹³"What kind of towns are these you have given me, my brother?" he asked. And he called them the Land of Cabul,ᵃ a name they have to this day. ¹⁴Now Hiram had sent to the king 120 talentsᵇ of gold.

¹⁵Here is the account of the forced labor King Solomon conscripted to build the LORD's temple, his own palace, the supporting terraces,ᶜ the wall of Jerusalem, and Hazor, Megiddo and Gezer. ¹⁶(Pharaoh king of Egypt had attacked and captured Gezer. He had set it on fire. He killed its Canaanite inhabitants and then gave it as a wedding gift to his daughter, Solomon's wife. ¹⁷And Solomon rebuilt Gezer.) He built up Lower Beth Horon, ¹⁸Baalath, and Tadmorᵈ in the desert, within his land, ¹⁹as well as all his store cities and the towns for his chariots and for his horsesᵉ—whatever he desired to build in Jerusalem, in Lebanon and throughout all the territory he ruled.

²⁰All the people left from the Amorites, Hittites, Perizzites, Hivites and Jebusites (these peoples were not Israelites), ²¹that is, their descendants remaining in the land, whom the Israelites could not exterminateᶠ—these Solomon conscripted for his slave labor force, as it is to this day. ²²But Solomon did not make slaves of any of the Israelites; they were his fighting men, his government officials, his officers, his captains, and the commanders of his chariots and charioteers. ²³They were also the chief officials in charge of Solomon's projects—550 officials supervising the men who did the work.

²⁴After Pharaoh's daughter had come up from the City of David to the palace Solomon had built for her, he constructed the supporting terraces.

²⁵Three times a year Solomon sacrificed burnt offerings and fellowship offeringsᵍ on the altar he had built for the LORD, burning incense before the LORD along with them, and so fulfilled the temple obligations.

²⁶King Solomon also built ships at Ezion Geber, which is near Elath in Edom, on the shore of the Red Sea.ʰ ²⁷And Hiram sent his men—sailors who knew the sea—to serve in the fleet with Solomon's men. ²⁸They sailed to Ophir and brought back 420 talentsⁱ of gold, which they delivered to King Solomon.

ᵃ 13 *Cabul* sounds like the Hebrew for *good-for-nothing.*   ᵇ 14 That is, about 4 1/2 tons (about 4 metric tons)   ᶜ 15 Or *the Millo*; also in verse 24   ᵈ 18 The Hebrew may also be read *Tamar.*   ᵉ 19 Or *charioteers*   ᶠ 21 The Hebrew term refers to the irrevocable giving over of things or persons to the LORD, often by totally destroying them.   ᵍ 25 Traditionally *peace offerings*   ʰ 26 Hebrew *Yam Suph*; that is, Sea of Reeds   ⁱ 28 That is, about 16 tons (about 14.5 metric tons)

The Queen of Sheba Visits Solomon

10 When the queen of Sheba heard about the fame of Solomon and his relation to the name of the LORD, she came to test him with hard questions. ²Arriving at Jerusalem with a very great caravan—with camels carrying spices, large quantities of gold, and precious stones—she came to Solomon and talked with him about all that she had on her mind. ³Solomon answered all her questions; nothing was too hard for the king to explain to her. ⁴When the queen of Sheba saw all the wisdom of Solomon and the palace he had built, ⁵the food on his table, the seating of his officials, the attending servants in their robes, his cupbearers, and the burnt offerings he made at*ᵃ* the temple of the LORD, she was overwhelmed.

⁶She said to the king, "The report I heard in my own country about your achievements and your wisdom is true. ⁷But I did not believe these things until I came and saw with my own eyes. Indeed, not even half was told me; in wisdom and wealth you have far exceeded the report I heard. ⁸How happy your men must be! How happy your officials, who continually stand before you and hear your wisdom! ⁹Praise be to the LORD your God, who has delighted in you and placed you on the throne of Israel. Because of the LORD's eternal love for Israel, he has made you king, to maintain justice and righteousness."

¹⁰And she gave the king 120 talents*ᵇ* of gold, large quantities of spices, and precious stones. Never again were so many spices brought in as those the queen of Sheba gave to King Solomon.

¹¹(Hiram's ships brought gold from Ophir; and from there they brought great cargoes of almugwood*ᶜ* and precious stones. ¹²The king used the almugwood to make supports for the temple of the LORD and for the royal palace, and to make harps and lyres for the musicians. So much almugwood has never been imported or seen since that day.)

¹³King Solomon gave the queen of Sheba all she desired and asked for, besides what he had given her out of his royal bounty. Then she left and returned with her retinue to her own country.

Solomon's Splendor

¹⁴The weight of the gold that Solomon received yearly was 666 talents,*ᵈ* ¹⁵not including the revenues from merchants and traders and from all the Arabian kings and the governors of the land.

¹⁶King Solomon made two hundred large shields of hammered gold; six hundred bekas*ᵉ* of gold went into each shield. ¹⁷He also made three hundred small shields of hammered gold, with three minas*ᶠ* of gold in each shield. The king put them in the Palace of the Forest of Lebanon.

¹⁸Then the king made a great throne inlaid with ivory and overlaid with fine gold. ¹⁹The throne had six steps, and its back had a rounded top. On both sides of the seat were armrests, with a lion standing beside each of them. ²⁰Twelve lions stood on the six steps, one at either end of

---

ᵃ 5 Or *the ascent by which he went up to*   *ᵇ 10* That is, about 4 1/2 tons (about 4 metric tons)   *ᶜ 11* Probably a variant of *algumwood*; also in verse 12   *ᵈ 14* That is, about 25 tons (about 23 metric tons)   *ᵉ 16* That is, about 7 1/2 pounds (about 3.5 kilograms)   *ᶠ 17* That is, about 3 3/4 pounds (about 1.7 kilograms)

Hard Questions for a Famous King

1 KINGS 10:1–9

After a contest and a series of riddles, proverbs and quizzes, the queen of Sheba decides that Solomon is indeed as wise as she had been told. The queen leaves in awe of him. Imagine that you are talking with Solomon, the wisest man who ever lived. What questions would you ask him about the source of his wisdom? What would you want to learn from him? What would you want to glean from an encounter with him? How might his answers help you lead a more faithful life?

A Marriage of Convenience

1 KINGS 11:1–10

Solomon's wisdom in public affairs was not reflected in his personal life. If Solomon knew the right way to live, what pressures might have caused him to make "marriages of convenience" with lesser gods?

What choices of convenience have you made that conflict with your real values? What pressures and inner weaknesses led you to such choices? When have you chosen to resist convenient choices for the sake of God's way? What gave you the strength to resist? What consequences in your spiritual life have these choices led to?

See Meeting God in Community

each step. Nothing like it had ever been made for any other kingdom. ²¹All King Solomon's goblets were gold, and all the household articles in the Palace of the Forest of Lebanon were pure gold. Nothing was made of silver, because silver was considered of little value in Solomon's days. ²²The king had a fleet of trading ships[a] at sea along with the ships of Hiram. Once every three years it returned, carrying gold, silver and ivory, and apes and baboons.

²³King Solomon was greater in riches and wisdom than all the other kings of the earth. ²⁴The whole world sought audience with Solomon to hear the wisdom God had put in his heart. ²⁵Year after year, everyone who came brought a gift—articles of silver and gold, robes, weapons and spices, and horses and mules.

²⁶Solomon accumulated chariots and horses; he had fourteen hundred chariots and twelve thousand horses,[b] which he kept in the chariot cities and also with him in Jerusalem. ²⁷The king made silver as common in Jerusalem as stones, and cedar as plentiful as sycamore-fig trees in the foothills. ²⁸Solomon's horses were imported from Egypt[c] and from Kue[d]—the royal merchants purchased them from Kue. ²⁹They imported a chariot from Egypt for six hundred shekels[e] of silver, and a horse for a hundred and fifty.[f] They also exported them to all the kings of the Hittites and of the Arameans.

Solomon's Wives

11 King Solomon, however, loved many foreign women besides Pharaoh's daughter—Moabites, Ammonites, Edomites, Sidonians and Hittites. ²They were from nations about which the LORD had told the Israelites, "You must not intermarry with them, because they will surely turn your hearts after their gods." Nevertheless, Solomon held fast to them in love. ³He had seven hundred wives of royal birth and three hundred concubines, and his wives led him astray. ⁴As Solomon grew old, his wives turned his heart after other gods, and his heart was not fully devoted to the LORD his God, as the heart of David his father had been. ⁵He followed Ashtoreth the goddess of the Sidonians, and Molech[g] the detestable god of the Ammonites. ⁶So Solomon did evil in the eyes of the LORD; he did not follow the LORD completely, as David his father had done.

⁷On a hill east of Jerusalem, Solomon built a high place for Chemosh the detestable god of Moab, and for Molech the detestable god of the Ammonites. ⁸He did the same for all his foreign wives, who burned incense and offered sacrifices to their gods.

⁹The LORD became angry with Solomon because his heart had turned away from the LORD, the God of Israel, who had appeared to him twice. ¹⁰Although he had forbidden Solomon to follow other gods, Solomon did not keep the LORD's command. ¹¹So the LORD said to Solomon, "Since this is your attitude and you have not kept my covenant and my decrees, which I commanded you, I will most certainly tear the kingdom away from you and give it to one of your subordinates. ¹²Nevertheless, for the sake of

a 22 Hebrew *of ships of Tarshish*   *b 26* Or *charioteers*   *c 28* Or possibly *Muzur,* a region in Cilicia; also in verse 29   *d 28* Probably *Cilicia*   *e 29* That is, about 15 pounds (about 7 kilograms)   *f 29* That is, about 3 3/4 pounds (about 1.7 kilograms)   *g 5* Hebrew *Milcom*; also in verse 33

David your father, I will not do it during your lifetime. I will tear it out of the hand of your son. ¹³Yet I will not tear the whole kingdom from him, but will give him one tribe for the sake of David my servant and for the sake of Jerusalem, which I have chosen."

Solomon's Adversaries

¹⁴Then the LORD raised up against Solomon an adversary, Hadad the Edomite, from the royal line of Edom. ¹⁵Earlier when David was fighting with Edom, Joab the commander of the army, who had gone up to bury the dead, had struck down all the men in Edom. ¹⁶Joab and all the Israelites stayed there for six months, until they had destroyed all the men in Edom. ¹⁷But Hadad, still only a boy, fled to Egypt with some Edomite officials who had served his father. ¹⁸They set out from Midian and went to Paran. Then taking men from Paran with them, they went to Egypt, to Pharaoh king of Egypt, who gave Hadad a house and land and provided him with food.

¹⁹Pharaoh was so pleased with Hadad that he gave him a sister of his own wife, Queen Tahpenes, in marriage. ²⁰The sister of Tahpenes bore him a son named Genubath, whom Tahpenes brought up in the royal palace. There Genubath lived with Pharaoh's own children.

²¹While he was in Egypt, Hadad heard that David rested with his fathers and that Joab the commander of the army was also dead. Then Hadad said to Pharaoh, "Let me go, that I may return to my own country."

²²"What have you lacked here that you want to go back to your own country?" Pharaoh asked.

"Nothing," Hadad replied, "but do let me go!"

²³And God raised up against Solomon another adversary, Rezon son of Eliada, who had fled from his master, Hadadezer king of Zobah. ²⁴He gathered men around him and became the leader of a band of rebels when David destroyed the forces*ᵃ* ⌊of Zobah⌋; the rebels went to Damascus, where they settled and took control. ²⁵Rezon was Israel's adversary as long as Solomon lived, adding to the trouble caused by Hadad. So Rezon ruled in Aram and was hostile toward Israel.

Jeroboam Rebels Against Solomon

²⁶Also, Jeroboam son of Nebat rebelled against the king. He was one of Solomon's officials, an Ephraimite from Zeredah, and his mother was a widow named Zeruah.

²⁷Here is the account of how he rebelled against the king: Solomon had built the supporting terraces*ᵇ* and had filled in the gap in the wall of the city of David his father. ²⁸Now Jeroboam was a man of standing, and when Solomon saw how well the young man did his work, he put him in charge of the whole labor force of the house of Joseph.

²⁹About that time Jeroboam was going out of Jerusalem, and Ahijah the prophet of Shiloh met him on the way, wearing a new cloak. The two of them were alone out in the country, ³⁰and Ahijah took hold of the new cloak he was wearing and tore it into twelve pieces. ³¹Then he said to Jeroboam, "Take ten pieces for yourself, for this is what the LORD, the God of Israel, says: 'See, I am going to tear the kingdom out of Solomon's hand and give you ten tribes.

ᵃ 24 Hebrew destroyed them   *ᵇ 27 Or the Millo*

Death of the King

1 KINGS 11:41–43

Solomon "rested with his fathers"; his passing was no doubt noted with elaborate funeral rituals. Funerals can be routine and impersonal or genuine celebrations of the life of one of God's children. Planning your own funeral rites can be both a great help to your family and a testimony of faith. Spend some time envisioning your own funeral, not just the service but the events surrounding it. Should it be small and quiet or more of a celebration? What hymns would you like sung? What readings—from Scripture, poetry or books—are especially meaningful to you? How do you want your faith in God to be exemplified in this celebration?

See Meeting God in Everyday Life

32But for the sake of my servant David and the city of Jerusalem, which I have chosen out of all the tribes of Israel, he will have one tribe. 33I will do this because they have*a* forsaken me and worshiped Ashtoreth the goddess of the Sidonians, Chemosh the god of the Moabites, and Molech the god of the Ammonites, and have not walked in my ways, nor done what is right in my eyes, nor kept my statutes and laws as David, Solomon's father, did.

34" 'But I will not take the whole kingdom out of Solomon's hand; I have made him ruler all the days of his life for the sake of David my servant, whom I chose and who observed my commands and statutes. 35I will take the kingdom from his son's hands and give you ten tribes. 36I will give one tribe to his son so that David my servant may always have a lamp before me in Jerusalem, the city where I chose to put my Name. 37However, as for you, I will take you, and you will rule over all that your heart desires; you will be king over Israel. 38If you do whatever I command you and walk in my ways and do what is right in my eyes by keeping my statutes and commands, as David my servant did, I will be with you. I will build you a dynasty as enduring as the one I built for David and will give Israel to you. 39I will humble David's descendants because of this, but not forever.' "

40Solomon tried to kill Jeroboam, but Jeroboam fled to Egypt, to Shishak the king, and stayed there until Solomon's death.

Solomon's Death

41As for the other events of Solomon's reign—all he did and the wisdom he displayed—are they not written in the book of the annals of Solomon? 42Solomon reigned in Jerusalem over all Israel forty years. 43Then he rested with his fathers and was buried in the city of David his father. And Rehoboam his son succeeded him as king.

Israel Rebels Against Rehoboam

12 Rehoboam went to Shechem, for all the Israelites had gone there to make him king. 2When Jeroboam son of Nebat heard this (he was still in Egypt, where he had fled from King Solomon), he returned from*b* Egypt. 3So they sent for Jeroboam, and he and the whole assembly of Israel went to Rehoboam and said to him: 4"Your father put a heavy yoke on us, but now lighten the harsh labor and the heavy yoke he put on us, and we will serve you."

5Rehoboam answered, "Go away for three days and then come back to me." So the people went away.

6Then King Rehoboam consulted the elders who had served his father Solomon during his lifetime. "How would you advise me to answer these people?" he asked.

7They replied, "If today you will be a servant to these people and serve them and give them a favorable answer, they will always be your servants."

8But Rehoboam rejected the advice the elders gave him and consulted the young men who had grown up with him and were serving him. 9He asked them, "What is your advice? How should we answer these people who say to me, 'Lighten the yoke your father put on us'?"

---

a 33 Hebrew; Septuagint, Vulgate and Syriac *because he has remained in*   *b 2* Or *he remained in*

[10]The young men who had grown up with him replied, "Tell these people who have said to you, 'Your father put a heavy yoke on us, but make our yoke lighter'—tell them, 'My little finger is thicker than my father's waist. [11]My father laid on you a heavy yoke; I will make it even heavier. My father scourged you with whips; I will scourge you with scorpions.' "

[12]Three days later Jeroboam and all the people returned to Rehoboam, as the king had said, "Come back to me in three days." [13]The king answered the people harshly. Rejecting the advice given him by the elders, [14]he followed the advice of the young men and said, "My father made your yoke heavy; I will make it even heavier. My father scourged you with whips; I will scourge you with scorpions." [15]So the king did not listen to the people, for this turn of events was from the LORD, to fulfill the word the LORD had spoken to Jeroboam son of Nebat through Ahijah the Shilonite.

[16]When all Israel saw that the king refused to listen to them, they answered the king:

"What share do we have in David,
    what part in Jesse's son?
To your tents, O Israel!
    Look after your own house, O David!"

So the Israelites went home. [17]But as for the Israelites who were living in the towns of Judah, Rehoboam still ruled over them.

[18]King Rehoboam sent out Adoniram,[a] who was in charge of forced labor, but all Israel stoned him to death. King Rehoboam, however, managed to get into his chariot and escape to Jerusalem. [19]So Israel has been in rebellion against the house of David to this day.

[20]When all the Israelites heard that Jeroboam had returned, they sent and called him to the assembly and made him king over all Israel. Only the tribe of Judah remained loyal to the house of David.

[21]When Rehoboam arrived in Jerusalem, he mustered the whole house of Judah and the tribe of Benjamin—a hundred and eighty thousand fighting men—to make war against the house of Israel and to regain the kingdom for Rehoboam son of Solomon.

[22]But this word of God came to Shemaiah the man of God: [23]"Say to Rehoboam son of Solomon king of Judah, to the whole house of Judah and Benjamin, and to the rest of the people, [24]'This is what the LORD says: Do not go up to fight against your brothers, the Israelites. Go home, every one of you, for this is my doing.' " So they obeyed the word of the LORD and went home again, as the LORD had ordered.

Golden Calves at Bethel and Dan

[25]Then Jeroboam fortified Shechem in the hill country of Ephraim and lived there. From there he went out and built up Peniel.[b]

[26]Jeroboam thought to himself, "The kingdom will now likely revert to the house of David. [27]If these people go up to offer sacrifices at the temple of the LORD in Jerusalem, they will again give their allegiance to their lord, Rehoboam

Hard Consequences of Wrong Choices

1 KINGS 12:1–15

Picture yourself as the new leader of all Israel. The people are assembled before you with one request: that the harsh conditions of forced labor imposed by the previous leader be lightened. You have two choices. You can listen to your elders and follow their advice to lighten the load of the people; or you can listen to the voices of your peers, who have their own ideas about how you should rule. Bring to mind the times when your own unwise decisions may have caused harm—times when you have heeded the wrong advice. How have you handled the consequences that came with making such mistakes? What did you learn? How did you relate to God in such situations?

See Meeting God in Prayer

---

[a] 18 Some Septuagint manuscripts and Syriac (see also 1 Kings 4:6 and 5:14); Hebrew *Adoram*   [b] 25 Hebrew *Penuel*, a variant of *Peniel*

Disrupting Worship

1 KINGS 13:1–10

After reading the narrative of this passage, imagine this incident step by step. Notice how beautiful the sanctuary is. Listen to the reactions of the priests and King Jeroboam. Hear the tone of the prophet's voice and see his facial expression. Is his voice soft or loud, harsh or compassionate? Now imagine a similar scene happening in a contemporary house of worship, perhaps your own. What judgments would the prophet make about the worship of your congregation. What would he say about the people's lives? Let the prophet now turn to you and tell you what you may need to hear about the way you worship God.

See *Meeting God in Worship*

king of Judah. They will kill me and return to King Rehoboam."

²⁸After seeking advice, the king made two golden calves. He said to the people, "It is too much for you to go up to Jerusalem. Here are your gods, O Israel, who brought you up out of Egypt." ²⁹One he set up in Bethel, and the other in Dan. ³⁰And this thing became a sin; the people went even as far as Dan to worship the one there.

³¹Jeroboam built shrines on high places and appointed priests from all sorts of people, even though they were not Levites. ³²He instituted a festival on the fifteenth day of the eighth month, like the festival held in Judah, and offered sacrifices on the altar. This he did in Bethel, sacrificing to the calves he had made. And at Bethel he also installed priests at the high places he had made. ³³On the fifteenth day of the eighth month, a month of his own choosing, he offered sacrifices on the altar he had built at Bethel. So he instituted the festival for the Israelites and went up to the altar to make offerings.

The Man of God From Judah

13 By the word of the Lord a man of God came from Judah to Bethel, as Jeroboam was standing by the altar to make an offering. ²He cried out against the altar by the word of the Lord: "O altar, altar! This is what the Lord says: 'A son named Josiah will be born to the house of David. On you he will sacrifice the priests of the high places who now make offerings here, and human bones will be burned on you.'" ³That same day the man of God gave a sign: "This is the sign the Lord has declared: The altar will be split apart and the ashes on it will be poured out."

⁴When King Jeroboam heard what the man of God cried out against the altar at Bethel, he stretched out his hand from the altar and said, "Seize him!" But the hand he stretched out toward the man shriveled up, so that he could not pull it back. ⁵Also, the altar was split apart and its ashes poured out according to the sign given by the man of God by the word of the Lord.

⁶Then the king said to the man of God, "Intercede with the Lord your God and pray for me that my hand may be restored." So the man of God interceded with the Lord, and the king's hand was restored and became as it was before.

⁷The king said to the man of God, "Come home with me and have something to eat, and I will give you a gift."

⁸But the man of God answered the king, "Even if you were to give me half your possessions, I would not go with you, nor would I eat bread or drink water here. ⁹For I was commanded by the word of the Lord: 'You must not eat bread or drink water or return by the way you came.'" ¹⁰So he took another road and did not return by the way he had come to Bethel.

¹¹Now there was a certain old prophet living in Bethel, whose sons came and told him all that the man of God had done there that day. They also told their father what he had said to the king. ¹²Their father asked them, "Which way did he go?" And his sons showed him which road the man of God from Judah had taken. ¹³So he said to his sons, "Saddle the donkey for me." And when they had saddled the donkey for him, he mounted it ¹⁴and rode after the man of

God. He found him sitting under an oak tree and asked, "Are you the man of God who came from Judah?"

"I am," he replied.

¹⁵So the prophet said to him, "Come home with me and eat."

¹⁶The man of God said, "I cannot turn back and go with you, nor can I eat bread or drink water with you in this place. ¹⁷I have been told by the word of the LORD: 'You must not eat bread or drink water there or return by the way you came.' "

¹⁸The old prophet answered, "I too am a prophet, as you are. And an angel said to me by the word of the LORD: 'Bring him back with you to your house so that he may eat bread and drink water.' " (But he was lying to him.) ¹⁹So the man of God returned with him and ate and drank in his house.

²⁰While they were sitting at the table, the word of the LORD came to the old prophet who had brought him back. ²¹He cried out to the man of God who had come from Judah, "This is what the LORD says: 'You have defied the word of the LORD and have not kept the command the LORD your God gave you. ²²You came back and ate bread and drank water in the place where he told you not to eat or drink. Therefore your body will not be buried in the tomb of your fathers.' "

²³When the man of God had finished eating and drinking, the prophet who had brought him back saddled his donkey for him. ²⁴As he went on his way, a lion met him on the road and killed him, and his body was thrown down on the road, with both the donkey and the lion standing beside it. ²⁵Some people who passed by saw the body thrown down there, with the lion standing beside the body, and they went and reported it in the city where the old prophet lived.

²⁶When the prophet who had brought him back from his journey heard of it, he said, "It is the man of God who defied the word of the LORD. The LORD has given him over to the lion, which has mauled him and killed him, as the word of the LORD had warned him."

²⁷The prophet said to his sons, "Saddle the donkey for me," and they did so. ²⁸Then he went out and found the body thrown down on the road, with the donkey and the lion standing beside it. The lion had neither eaten the body nor mauled the donkey. ²⁹So the prophet picked up the body of the man of God, laid it on the donkey, and brought it back to his own city to mourn for him and bury him. ³⁰Then he laid the body in his own tomb, and they mourned over him and said, "Oh, my brother!"

³¹After burying him, he said to his sons, "When I die, bury me in the grave where the man of God is buried; lay my bones beside his bones. ³²For the message he declared by the word of the LORD against the altar in Bethel and against all the shrines on the high places in the towns of Samaria will certainly come true."

³³Even after this, Jeroboam did not change his evil ways, but once more appointed priests for the high places from all sorts of people. Anyone who wanted to become a priest he consecrated for the high places. ³⁴This was the sin of the house of Jeroboam that led to its downfall and to its destruction from the face of the earth.

Facing Lions

1 KINGS 13:20–25

In the Old Testament, stories about David, Samson and Daniel all include lions. In ancient times lions were a common threat to flocks and occasionally to people, attacking and destroying without warning.

Attacks in this life come from many places and take many forms—physical illness, financial loss or spiritual struggles. Think back on the various attacks you have experienced. When were you attacked without warning? What form did the lion take? In what ways was God present with you through the experience? How did this experience change your relationship with God?

See Meeting God in Everyday Life

Justice and the Unjust King

1 KINGS 14:1–18

"Do not sneer at justice, for it is one of the three feet of the world, for the sages taught that the world stands on three things: justice, truth and peace. Therefore reflect that if you pervert justice, you shake the world . . . It is written, 'To do justice and righteousness is better than sacrifice' [Proverbs 21:3]. For . . . sacrifices can occur only in this world, but righteousness and justice are for this world and the world to come." (Rabbi Simeon, b. Gamaliel, 2nd century B.C.)

—*THE TALMUD,*
Deuteronomy Rabba, Shofetim, V, 1 and 3

Ahijah's Prophecy Against Jeroboam

14 At that time Abijah son of Jeroboam became ill, ²and Jeroboam said to his wife, "Go, disguise yourself, so you won't be recognized as the wife of Jeroboam. Then go to Shiloh. Ahijah the prophet is there—the one who told me I would be king over this people. ³Take ten loaves of bread with you, some cakes and a jar of honey, and go to him. He will tell you what will happen to the boy." ⁴So Jeroboam's wife did what he said and went to Ahijah's house in Shiloh.

Now Ahijah could not see; his sight was gone because of his age. ⁵But the LORD had told Ahijah, "Jeroboam's wife is coming to ask you about her son, for he is ill, and you are to give her such and such an answer. When she arrives, she will pretend to be someone else."

⁶So when Ahijah heard the sound of her footsteps at the door, he said, "Come in, wife of Jeroboam. Why this pretense? I have been sent to you with bad news. ⁷Go, tell Jeroboam that this is what the LORD, the God of Israel, says: 'I raised you up from among the people and made you a leader over my people Israel. ⁸I tore the kingdom away from the house of David and gave it to you, but you have not been like my servant David, who kept my commands and followed me with all his heart, doing only what was right in my eyes. ⁹You have done more evil than all who lived before you. You have made for yourself other gods, idols made of metal; you have provoked me to anger and thrust me behind your back.

¹⁰" 'Because of this, I am going to bring disaster on the house of Jeroboam. I will cut off from Jeroboam every last male in Israel—slave or free. I will burn up the house of Jeroboam as one burns dung, until it is all gone. ¹¹Dogs will eat those belonging to Jeroboam who die in the city, and the birds of the air will feed on those who die in the country. The LORD has spoken!'

¹²"As for you, go back home. When you set foot in your city, the boy will die. ¹³All Israel will mourn for him and bury him. He is the only one belonging to Jeroboam who will be buried, because he is the only one in the house of Jeroboam in whom the LORD, the God of Israel, has found anything good.

¹⁴"The LORD will raise up for himself a king over Israel who will cut off the family of Jeroboam. This is the day! What? Yes, even now.ᵃ ¹⁵And the LORD will strike Israel, so that it will be like a reed swaying in the water. He will uproot Israel from this good land that he gave to their forefathers and scatter them beyond the River,ᵇ because they provoked the LORD to anger by making Asherah poles.ᶜ ¹⁶And he will give Israel up because of the sins Jeroboam has committed and has caused Israel to commit."

¹⁷Then Jeroboam's wife got up and left and went to Tirzah. As soon as she stepped over the threshold of the house, the boy died. ¹⁸They buried him, and all Israel mourned for him, as the LORD had said through his servant the prophet Ahijah.

¹⁹The other events of Jeroboam's reign, his wars and how he ruled, are written in the book of the annals of the kings

---

ᵃ*14* The meaning of the Hebrew for this sentence is uncertain.   ᵇ*15* That is, the Euphrates   ᶜ*15* That is, symbols of the goddess Asherah; here and elsewhere in 1 Kings

of Israel. ²⁰He reigned for twenty-two years and then rested with his fathers. And Nadab his son succeeded him as king.

Rehoboam King of Judah

²¹Rehoboam son of Solomon was king in Judah. He was forty-one years old when he became king, and he reigned seventeen years in Jerusalem, the city the LORD had chosen out of all the tribes of Israel in which to put his Name. His mother's name was Naamah; she was an Ammonite. ²²Judah did evil in the eyes of the LORD. By the sins they committed they stirred up his jealous anger more than their fathers had done. ²³They also set up for themselves high places, sacred stones and Asherah poles on every high hill and under every spreading tree. ²⁴There were even male shrine prostitutes in the land; the people engaged in all the detestable practices of the nations the LORD had driven out before the Israelites.

²⁵In the fifth year of King Rehoboam, Shishak king of Egypt attacked Jerusalem. ²⁶He carried off the treasures of the temple of the LORD and the treasures of the royal palace. He took everything, including all the gold shields Solomon had made. ²⁷So King Rehoboam made bronze shields to replace them and assigned these to the commanders of the guard on duty at the entrance to the royal palace. ²⁸Whenever the king went to the LORD's temple, the guards bore the shields, and afterward they returned them to the guardroom.

²⁹As for the other events of Rehoboam's reign, and all he did, are they not written in the book of the annals of the kings of Judah? ³⁰There was continual warfare between Rehoboam and Jeroboam. ³¹And Rehoboam rested with his fathers and was buried with them in the City of David. His mother's name was Naamah; she was an Ammonite. And Abijah[a] his son succeeded him as king.

Abijah King of Judah

15 In the eighteenth year of the reign of Jeroboam son of Nebat, Abijah[b] became king of Judah, ²and he reigned in Jerusalem three years. His mother's name was Maacah daughter of Abishalom.[c]

³He committed all the sins his father had done before him; his heart was not fully devoted to the LORD his God, as the heart of David his forefather had been. ⁴Nevertheless, for David's sake the LORD his God gave him a lamp in Jerusalem by raising up a son to succeed him and by making Jerusalem strong. ⁵For David had done what was right in the eyes of the LORD and had not failed to keep any of the LORD's commands all the days of his life—except in the case of Uriah the Hittite.

⁶There was war between Rehoboam[d] and Jeroboam throughout ⌊Abijah's⌋ lifetime. ⁷As for the other events of Abijah's reign, and all he did, are they not written in the book of the annals of the kings of Judah? There was war between Abijah and Jeroboam. ⁸And Abijah rested with his fa-

---

a 31 Some Hebrew manuscripts and Septuagint (see also 2 Chron. 12:16); most Hebrew manuscripts *Abijam*   *b 1* Some Hebrew manuscripts and Septuagint (see also 2 Chron. 12:16); most Hebrew manuscripts *Abijam*; also in verses 7 and 8   *c 2* A variant of *Absalom*; also in verse 10   *d 6* Most Hebrew manuscripts; some Hebrew manuscripts and Syriac *Abijam* (that is, Abijah)

The Temple and Palace Plundered

1 KINGS 14:25–26

God's judgment on the people's idolatry, evil and sin is executed by foreign armies. Riches that took years to accumulate are plundered overnight, initiating a time of great social, political and religious change.

How are the "riches" of your own community or nation being "plundered" because of individual or communal sin? How have decisions made by our leaders, local and national, diminished the moral and spiritual quality of life? What changes in the nation upset or encourage you? What leaders attract your attention by their stands for or against what you consider God's values? Consider these concerns as your call to specific prayer; spend time praying for the nation and its leaders.

See Meeting God in Community

Return to the Sovereign God

1 KINGS 15:9–15

"If God is indeed sovereign, it is utter foolishness to ignore the One who is in complete control. Our lives cannot possibly be what they were intended to be apart from the Source of life. The folly of resisting the Power that transcends all powers of men is so obvious it is difficult to understand why we do it. Quite clearly, life can be what it should be only when it is lived in a conscious relationship with God."

—WILLIAM O. PAULSELL,
Taste and See

thers and was buried in the City of David. And Asa his son succeeded him as king.

Asa King of Judah

⁹In the twentieth year of Jeroboam king of Israel, Asa became king of Judah, ¹⁰and he reigned in Jerusalem forty-one years. His grandmother's name was Maacah daughter of Abishalom.

¹¹Asa did what was right in the eyes of the Lord, as his father David had done. ¹²He expelled the male shrine prostitutes from the land and got rid of all the idols his fathers had made. ¹³He even deposed his grandmother Maacah from her position as queen mother, because she had made a repulsive Asherah pole. Asa cut the pole down and burned it in the Kidron Valley. ¹⁴Although he did not remove the high places, Asa's heart was fully committed to the Lord all his life. ¹⁵He brought into the temple of the Lord the silver and gold and the articles that he and his father had dedicated.

¹⁶There was war between Asa and Baasha king of Israel throughout their reigns. ¹⁷Baasha king of Israel went up against Judah and fortified Ramah to prevent anyone from leaving or entering the territory of Asa king of Judah.

¹⁸Asa then took all the silver and gold that was left in the treasuries of the Lord's temple and of his own palace. He entrusted it to his officials and sent them to Ben-Hadad son of Tabrimmon, the son of Hezion, the king of Aram, who was ruling in Damascus. ¹⁹"Let there be a treaty between me and you," he said, "as there was between my father and your father. See, I am sending you a gift of silver and gold. Now break your treaty with Baasha king of Israel so he will withdraw from me."

²⁰Ben-Hadad agreed with King Asa and sent the commanders of his forces against the towns of Israel. He conquered Ijon, Dan, Abel Beth Maacah and all Kinnereth in addition to Naphtali. ²¹When Baasha heard this, he stopped building Ramah and withdrew to Tirzah. ²²Then King Asa issued an order to all Judah—no one was exempt—and they carried away from Ramah the stones and timber Baasha had been using there. With them King Asa built up Geba in Benjamin, and also Mizpah.

²³As for all the other events of Asa's reign, all his achievements, all he did and the cities he built, are they not written in the book of the annals of the kings of Judah? In his old age, however, his feet became diseased. ²⁴Then Asa rested with his fathers and was buried with them in the city of his father David. And Jehoshaphat his son succeeded him as king.

Nadab King of Israel

²⁵Nadab son of Jeroboam became king of Israel in the second year of Asa king of Judah, and he reigned over Israel two years. ²⁶He did evil in the eyes of the Lord, walking in the ways of his father and in his sin, which he had caused Israel to commit.

²⁷Baasha son of Ahijah of the house of Issachar plotted against him, and he struck him down at Gibbethon, a Philistine town, while Nadab and all Israel were besieging it. ²⁸Baasha killed Nadab in the third year of Asa king of Judah and succeeded him as king.

²⁹As soon as he began to reign, he killed Jeroboam's whole family. He did not leave Jeroboam anyone that breathed, but destroyed them all, according to the word of the LORD given through his servant Ahijah the Shilonite—³⁰because of the sins Jeroboam had committed and had caused Israel to commit, and because he provoked the LORD, the God of Israel, to anger.

³¹As for the other events of Nadab's reign, and all he did, are they not written in the book of the annals of the kings of Israel? ³²There was war between Asa and Baasha king of Israel throughout their reigns.

Baasha King of Israel

³³In the third year of Asa king of Judah, Baasha son of Ahijah became king of all Israel in Tirzah, and he reigned twenty-four years. ³⁴He did evil in the eyes of the LORD, walking in the ways of Jeroboam and in his sin, which he had caused Israel to commit.

16 Then the word of the LORD came to Jehu son of Hanani against Baasha: ²"I lifted you up from the dust and made you leader of my people Israel, but you walked in the ways of Jeroboam and caused my people Israel to sin and to provoke me to anger by their sins. ³So I am about to consume Baasha and his house, and I will make your house like that of Jeroboam son of Nebat. ⁴Dogs will eat those belonging to Baasha who die in the city, and the birds of the air will feed on those who die in the country."

⁵As for the other events of Baasha's reign, what he did and his achievements, are they not written in the book of the annals of the kings of Israel? ⁶Baasha rested with his fathers and was buried in Tirzah. And Elah his son succeeded him as king.

⁷Moreover, the word of the LORD came through the prophet Jehu son of Hanani to Baasha and his house, because of all the evil he had done in the eyes of the LORD, provoking him to anger by the things he did, and becoming like the house of Jeroboam—and also because he destroyed it.

Elah King of Israel

⁸In the twenty-sixth year of Asa king of Judah, Elah son of Baasha became king of Israel, and he reigned in Tirzah two years.

⁹Zimri, one of his officials, who had command of half his chariots, plotted against him. Elah was in Tirzah at the time, getting drunk in the home of Arza, the man in charge of the palace at Tirzah. ¹⁰Zimri came in, struck him down and killed him in the twenty-seventh year of Asa king of Judah. Then he succeeded him as king.

¹¹As soon as he began to reign and was seated on the throne, he killed off Baasha's whole family. He did not spare a single male, whether relative or friend. ¹²So Zimri destroyed the whole family of Baasha, in accordance with the word of the LORD spoken against Baasha through the prophet Jehu— ¹³because of all the sins Baasha and his son Elah had committed and had caused Israel to commit, so that they provoked the LORD, the God of Israel, to anger by their worthless idols.

¹⁴As for the other events of Elah's reign, and all he did,

God Alone

1 KINGS 16:1–4

Over the door of the guest house of a famous American Trappist monastery are the words "God alone." Baasha is judged severely, as are most of the kings, for not making "God alone" his aim. When we firmly and decisively decide to live for God alone, our activities, problems, anxieties and hopes begin to fit into place. Life can have new orderliness and peace.

Is this a basic value for your life? Look at your schedule for today and the rest of the week. What times are set aside for God and God alone? What occasions are available for prayer and reflection? When are there times for relationships and family? What changes do you have to make in order to make time for these things?

See Meeting God in Everyday Life

The Problem of Human Evil

1 KINGS 16:29–30

"Evil is in opposition to life. Evil, then, for the moment, is that force, residing either inside or outside human beings, that seeks to kill life or liveliness. And goodness is its opposite. Goodness promotes life and liveliness."

—M. SCOTT PECK,
People of the Lie

are they not written in the book of the annals of the kings of Israel?

Zimri King of Israel

[15]In the twenty-seventh year of Asa king of Judah, Zimri reigned in Tirzah seven days. The army was encamped near Gibbethon, a Philistine town. [16]When the Israelites in the camp heard that Zimri had plotted against the king and murdered him, they proclaimed Omri, the commander of the army, king over Israel that very day there in the camp. [17]Then Omri and all the Israelites with him withdrew from Gibbethon and laid siege to Tirzah. [18]When Zimri saw that the city was taken, he went into the citadel of the royal palace and set the palace on fire around him. So he died, [19]because of the sins he had committed, doing evil in the eyes of the LORD and walking in the ways of Jeroboam and in the sin he had committed and had caused Israel to commit.

[20]As for the other events of Zimri's reign, and the rebellion he carried out, are they not written in the book of the annals of the kings of Israel?

Omri King of Israel

[21]Then the people of Israel were split into two factions; half supported Tibni son of Ginath for king, and the other half supported Omri. [22]But Omri's followers proved stronger than those of Tibni son of Ginath. So Tibni died and Omri became king.

[23]In the thirty-first year of Asa king of Judah, Omri became king of Israel, and he reigned twelve years, six of them in Tirzah. [24]He bought the hill of Samaria from Shemer for two talents[a] of silver and built a city on the hill, calling it Samaria, after Shemer, the name of the former owner of the hill.

[25]But Omri did evil in the eyes of the LORD and sinned more than all those before him. [26]He walked in all the ways of Jeroboam son of Nebat and in his sin, which he had caused Israel to commit, so that they provoked the LORD, the God of Israel, to anger by their worthless idols.

[27]As for the other events of Omri's reign, what he did and the things he achieved, are they not written in the book of the annals of the kings of Israel? [28]Omri rested with his fathers and was buried in Samaria. And Ahab his son succeeded him as king.

Ahab Becomes King of Israel

[29]In the thirty-eighth year of Asa king of Judah, Ahab son of Omri became king of Israel, and he reigned in Samaria over Israel twenty-two years. [30]Ahab son of Omri did more evil in the eyes of the LORD than any of those before him. [31]He not only considered it trivial to commit the sins of Jeroboam son of Nebat, but he also married Jezebel daughter of Ethbaal king of the Sidonians, and began to serve Baal and worship him. [32]He set up an altar for Baal in the temple of Baal that he built in Samaria. [33]Ahab also made an Asherah pole and did more to provoke the LORD, the God of Israel, to anger than did all the kings of Israel before him.

[34]In Ahab's time, Hiel of Bethel rebuilt Jericho. He laid its foundations at the cost of his firstborn son Abiram, and he

[a] 24 That is, about 150 pounds (about 70 kilograms)

set up its gates at the cost of his youngest son Segub, in accordance with the word of the LORD spoken by Joshua son of Nun.

Elijah Fed by Ravens

17 Now Elijah the Tishbite, from Tishbe[a] in Gilead, said to Ahab, "As the LORD, the God of Israel, lives, whom I serve, there will be neither dew nor rain in the next few years except at my word."

²Then the word of the LORD came to Elijah: ³"Leave here, turn eastward and hide in the Kerith Ravine, east of the Jordan. ⁴You will drink from the brook, and I have ordered the ravens to feed you there."

⁵So he did what the LORD had told him. He went to the Kerith Ravine, east of the Jordan, and stayed there. ⁶The ravens brought him bread and meat in the morning and bread and meat in the evening, and he drank from the brook.

The Widow at Zarephath

⁷Some time later the brook dried up because there had been no rain in the land. ⁸Then the word of the LORD came to him: ⁹"Go at once to Zarephath of Sidon and stay there. I have commanded a widow in that place to supply you with food." ¹⁰So he went to Zarephath. When he came to the town gate, a widow was there gathering sticks. He called to her and asked, "Would you bring me a little water in a jar so I may have a drink?" ¹¹As she was going to get it, he called, "And bring me, please, a piece of bread."

¹²"As surely as the LORD your God lives," she replied, "I don't have any bread—only a handful of flour in a jar and a little oil in a jug. I am gathering a few sticks to take home and make a meal for myself and my son, that we may eat it—and die."

¹³Elijah said to her, "Don't be afraid. Go home and do as you have said. But first make a small cake of bread for me from what you have and bring it to me, and then make something for yourself and your son. ¹⁴For this is what the LORD, the God of Israel, says: 'The jar of flour will not be used up and the jug of oil will not run dry until the day the LORD gives rain on the land.' "

¹⁵She went away and did as Elijah had told her. So there was food every day for Elijah and for the woman and her family. ¹⁶For the jar of flour was not used up and the jug of oil did not run dry, in keeping with the word of the LORD spoken by Elijah.

¹⁷Some time later the son of the woman who owned the house became ill. He grew worse and worse, and finally stopped breathing. ¹⁸She said to Elijah, "What do you have against me, man of God? Did you come to remind me of my sin and kill my son?"

¹⁹"Give me your son," Elijah replied. He took him from her arms, carried him to the upper room where he was staying, and laid him on his bed. ²⁰Then he cried out to the LORD, "O LORD my God, have you brought tragedy also upon this widow I am staying with, by causing her son to die?" ²¹Then he stretched himself out on the boy three times and cried to the LORD, "O LORD my God, let this boy's life return to him!"

Help From Unlikely Sources

1 KINGS 17:1–16

God turned to ravens (unclean birds) and to a widow—a foreigner from Jezebel's home territory—to care for the prophet Elijah. This zealous prophet is called to go stand for the Lord against the corrupt mainstream, yet God takes care of him by means Elijah might have prejudged negatively.

God uses unexpected sources to teach us lessons. In what ways has God provided you with help from surprising sources? In what ways has God's help in the past broadened your expectations of how God may bring help in the future? When has God helped you unexpectedly? What have been some of the unexpected places where you have found God's help?

Spiritual Burnout

1 KINGS 18:1–22

Ahab and Jezebel chase Elijah. The people of Israel say nothing in response to Elijah's call to worship God. It hardly seems surprising, therefore, that Elijah would say, "I am the only one of the LORD's prophets left." Recall a time when you felt discouraged and alone and perhaps unable to see God at work in your situation. What brought your perspective back into focus? What spiritual resources can save you from spiritual depletion?

See Meeting God in Prayer

²²The LORD heard Elijah's cry, and the boy's life returned to him, and he lived. ²³Elijah picked up the child and carried him down from the room into the house. He gave him to his mother and said, "Look, your son is alive!"

²⁴Then the woman said to Elijah, "Now I know that you are a man of God and that the word of the LORD from your mouth is the truth."

Elijah and Obadiah

18 After a long time, in the third year, the word of the LORD came to Elijah: "Go and present yourself to Ahab, and I will send rain on the land." ²So Elijah went to present himself to Ahab.

Now the famine was severe in Samaria, ³and Ahab had summoned Obadiah, who was in charge of his palace. (Obadiah was a devout believer in the LORD. ⁴While Jezebel was killing off the LORD's prophets, Obadiah had taken a hundred prophets and hidden them in two caves, fifty in each, and had supplied them with food and water.) ⁵Ahab had said to Obadiah, "Go through the land to all the springs and valleys. Maybe we can find some grass to keep the horses and mules alive so we will not have to kill any of our animals." ⁶So they divided the land they were to cover, Ahab going in one direction and Obadiah in another.

⁷As Obadiah was walking along, Elijah met him. Obadiah recognized him, bowed down to the ground, and said, "Is it really you, my lord Elijah?"

⁸"Yes," he replied. "Go tell your master, 'Elijah is here.' "

⁹"What have I done wrong," asked Obadiah, "that you are handing your servant over to Ahab to be put to death? ¹⁰As surely as the LORD your God lives, there is not a nation or kingdom where my master has not sent someone to look for you. And whenever a nation or kingdom claimed you were not there, he made them swear they could not find you. ¹¹But now you tell me to go to my master and say, 'Elijah is here.' ¹²I don't know where the Spirit of the LORD may carry you when I leave you. If I go and tell Ahab and he doesn't find you, he will kill me. Yet I your servant have worshiped the LORD since my youth. ¹³Haven't you heard, my lord, what I did while Jezebel was killing the prophets of the LORD? I hid a hundred of the LORD's prophets in two caves, fifty in each, and supplied them with food and water. ¹⁴And now you tell me to go to my master and say, 'Elijah is here.' He will kill me!"

¹⁵Elijah said, "As the LORD Almighty lives, whom I serve, I will surely present myself to Ahab today."

Elijah on Mount Carmel

¹⁶So Obadiah went to meet Ahab and told him, and Ahab went to meet Elijah. ¹⁷When he saw Elijah, he said to him, "Is that you, you troubler of Israel?"

¹⁸"I have not made trouble for Israel," Elijah replied. "But you and your father's family have. You have abandoned the LORD's commands and have followed the Baals. ¹⁹Now summon the people from all over Israel to meet me on Mount Carmel. And bring the four hundred and fifty prophets of Baal and the four hundred prophets of Asherah, who eat at Jezebel's table."

²⁰So Ahab sent word throughout all Israel and assembled the prophets on Mount Carmel. ²¹Elijah went before the

people and said, "How long will you waver between two opinions? If the LORD is God, follow him; but if Baal is God, follow him."

But the people said nothing.

²²Then Elijah said to them, "I am the only one of the LORD's prophets left, but Baal has four hundred and fifty prophets. ²³Get two bulls for us. Let them choose one for themselves, and let them cut it into pieces and put it on the wood but not set fire to it. I will prepare the other bull and put it on the wood but not set fire to it. ²⁴Then you call on the name of your god, and I will call on the name of the LORD. The god who answers by fire—he is God."

Then all the people said, "What you say is good."

²⁵Elijah said to the prophets of Baal, "Choose one of the bulls and prepare it first, since there are so many of you. Call on the name of your god, but do not light the fire." ²⁶So they took the bull given them and prepared it.

Then they called on the name of Baal from morning till noon. "O Baal, answer us!" they shouted. But there was no response; no one answered. And they danced around the altar they had made.

²⁷At noon Elijah began to taunt them. "Shout louder!" he said. "Surely he is a god! Perhaps he is deep in thought, or busy, or traveling. Maybe he is sleeping and must be awakened." ²⁸So they shouted louder and slashed themselves with swords and spears, as was their custom, until their blood flowed. ²⁹Midday passed, and they continued their frantic prophesying until the time for the evening sacrifice. But there was no response, no one answered, no one paid attention.

³⁰Then Elijah said to all the people, "Come here to me." They came to him, and he repaired the altar of the LORD, which was in ruins. ³¹Elijah took twelve stones, one for each of the tribes descended from Jacob, to whom the word of the LORD had come, saying, "Your name shall be Israel." ³²With the stones he built an altar in the name of the LORD, and he dug a trench around it large enough to hold two seahs^a of seed. ³³He arranged the wood, cut the bull into pieces and laid it on the wood. Then he said to them, "Fill four large jars with water and pour it on the offering and on the wood."

³⁴"Do it again," he said, and they did it again.

"Do it a third time," he ordered, and they did it the third time. ³⁵The water ran down around the altar and even filled the trench.

³⁶At the time of sacrifice, the prophet Elijah stepped forward and prayed: "O LORD, God of Abraham, Isaac and Israel, let it be known today that you are God in Israel and that I am your servant and have done all these things at your command. ³⁷Answer me, O LORD, answer me, so these people will know that you, O LORD, are God, and that you are turning their hearts back again."

³⁸Then the fire of the LORD fell and burned up the sacrifice, the wood, the stones and the soil, and also licked up the water in the trench.

³⁹When all the people saw this, they fell prostrate and cried, "The LORD—he is God! The LORD—he is God!"

⁴⁰Then Elijah commanded them, "Seize the prophets of Baal. Don't let anyone get away!" They seized them, and

Elijah and the Priests of Baal

1 KINGS 18:20–40

Read the dramatic narrative of Elijah's confrontation with the priests of Baal, and their defeat. Then pray that you may be open to God's living word for you in this text. Now read the passage again more slowly. Look for any word, phrase or scene that seems to leap off the page at you, or that calls to you for further thought. Write down each notable phrase as you read through the passage, then choose one phrase or scene to spend time with. Let it fill your mind and heart. Be open to the living voice of the Spirit to show you how this might apply to your life today.

See Meeting God in Scripture

---

^a 32 That is, probably about 13 quarts (about 15 liters)

Victory, Exhaustion and Restoration

1 KINGS 19:1–18

Imagine that you are the prophet Elijah. After your stunning victory, you suddenly have to flee for your life. You are alone in the battle for righteousness. God leads you into the desert, providing you with shelter and sending an angel to deliver food. Experience the wind, the earthquake and the fire, then, "a gentle whisper." Listen as God reminds you that you are not alone, that he is still with you and that you have more work to do. As you step back out onto the road and continue the journey, how are you different? Note your emotions and give thanks to God.

See Meeting God in Scripture

Elijah had them brought down to the Kishon Valley and slaughtered there.

⁴¹ And Elijah said to Ahab, "Go, eat and drink, for there is the sound of a heavy rain." ⁴² So Ahab went off to eat and drink, but Elijah climbed to the top of Carmel, bent down to the ground and put his face between his knees.

⁴³ "Go and look toward the sea," he told his servant. And he went up and looked.

"There is nothing there," he said.

Seven times Elijah said, "Go back."

⁴⁴ The seventh time the servant reported, "A cloud as small as a man's hand is rising from the sea."

So Elijah said, "Go and tell Ahab, 'Hitch up your chariot and go down before the rain stops you.'"

⁴⁵ Meanwhile, the sky grew black with clouds, the wind rose, a heavy rain came on and Ahab rode off to Jezreel. ⁴⁶ The power of the LORD came upon Elijah and, tucking his cloak into his belt, he ran ahead of Ahab all the way to Jezreel.

Elijah Flees to Horeb

19 Now Ahab told Jezebel everything Elijah had done and how he had killed all the prophets with the sword. ² So Jezebel sent a messenger to Elijah to say, "May the gods deal with me, be it ever so severely, if by this time tomorrow I do not make your life like that of one of them."

³ Elijah was afraid[a] and ran for his life. When he came to Beersheba in Judah, he left his servant there, ⁴ while he himself went a day's journey into the desert. He came to a broom tree, sat down under it and prayed that he might die. "I have had enough, LORD," he said. "Take my life; I am no better than my ancestors." ⁵ Then he lay down under the tree and fell asleep.

All at once an angel touched him and said, "Get up and eat." ⁶ He looked around, and there by his head was a cake of bread baked over hot coals, and a jar of water. He ate and drank and then lay down again.

⁷ The angel of the LORD came back a second time and touched him and said, "Get up and eat, for the journey is too much for you." ⁸ So he got up and ate and drank. Strengthened by that food, he traveled forty days and forty nights until he reached Horeb, the mountain of God. ⁹ There he went into a cave and spent the night.

The LORD Appears to Elijah

And the word of the LORD came to him: "What are you doing here, Elijah?"

¹⁰ He replied, "I have been very zealous for the LORD God Almighty. The Israelites have rejected your covenant, broken down your altars, and put your prophets to death with the sword. I am the only one left, and now they are trying to kill me too."

¹¹ The LORD said, "Go out and stand on the mountain in the presence of the LORD, for the LORD is about to pass by."

Then a great and powerful wind tore the mountains apart and shattered the rocks before the LORD, but the LORD was not in the wind. After the wind there was an earthquake, but the LORD was not in the earthquake. ¹² After the earthquake came a fire, but the LORD was not in the fire. And

a 3 Or Elijah saw

after the fire came a gentle whisper. ¹³When Elijah heard it, he pulled his cloak over his face and went out and stood at the mouth of the cave.

Then a voice said to him, "What are you doing here, Elijah?"

¹⁴He replied, "I have been very zealous for the LORD God Almighty. The Israelites have rejected your covenant, broken down your altars, and put your prophets to death with the sword. I am the only one left, and now they are trying to kill me too."

¹⁵The LORD said to him, "Go back the way you came, and go to the Desert of Damascus. When you get there, anoint Hazael king over Aram. ¹⁶Also, anoint Jehu son of Nimshi king over Israel, and anoint Elisha son of Shaphat from Abel Meholah to succeed you as prophet. ¹⁷Jehu will put to death any who escape the sword of Hazael, and Elisha will put to death any who escape the sword of Jehu. ¹⁸Yet I reserve seven thousand in Israel—all whose knees have not bowed down to Baal and all whose mouths have not kissed him."

The Call of Elisha

¹⁹So Elijah went from there and found Elisha son of Shaphat. He was plowing with twelve yoke of oxen, and he himself was driving the twelfth pair. Elijah went up to him and threw his cloak around him. ²⁰Elisha then left his oxen and ran after Elijah. "Let me kiss my father and mother good-by," he said, "and then I will come with you."

"Go back," Elijah replied. "What have I done to you?"

²¹So Elisha left him and went back. He took his yoke of oxen and slaughtered them. He burned the plowing equipment to cook the meat and gave it to the people, and they ate. Then he set out to follow Elijah and became his attendant.

Ben-Hadad Attacks Samaria

20 Now Ben-Hadad king of Aram mustered his entire army. Accompanied by thirty-two kings with their horses and chariots, he went up and besieged Samaria and attacked it. ²He sent messengers into the city to Ahab king of Israel, saying, "This is what Ben-Hadad says: ³'Your silver and gold are mine, and the best of your wives and children are mine.' "

⁴The king of Israel answered, "Just as you say, my lord the king. I and all I have are yours."

⁵The messengers came again and said, "This is what Ben-Hadad says: 'I sent to demand your silver and gold, your wives and your children. ⁶But about this time tomorrow I am going to send my officials to search your palace and the houses of your officials. They will seize everything you value and carry it away.' "

⁷The king of Israel summoned all the elders of the land and said to them, "See how this man is looking for trouble! When he sent for my wives and my children, my silver and my gold, I did not refuse him."

⁸The elders and the people all answered, "Don't listen to him or agree to his demands."

⁹So he replied to Ben-Hadad's messengers, "Tell my lord the king, 'Your servant will do all you demanded the first

Passing the Mantle

1 KINGS 19:19–21

The mantle was the prophet's most important article of clothing. An animal skin covered with hair, it served as a coat, a blanket, a satchel to carry goods and a bundle to sit on, as well as security for a debt. A prophet's mantle identified him as a man of God.

Search your photo album, house, garage and attic. What are the most important things you own? What possessions, perhaps those that have been passed down through generations, are rich with meaning? What items indicate your family's heritage and spiritual identity? Gather these things together and decide how to preserve them. How do they tell the story of your life or the story of your family and heritage?

See *Meeting God in Everyday Life*

Untapped Skill in the Young

1 KINGS 20:13–22

Israel faces a formidable challenge: Ben-Hadad and his thirty-two kings besiege Samaria. But a prophet is able to discern real hope in the situation. Victory will come from the "young officers of the provincial commanders" rather than from the old, the trusted and the experienced. What trends among those younger than yourself do you see as positive and hopeful? If you are discouraged by what you see in younger people, prayerfully ask God to show you what you may have overlooked. What young people do you know who are gifted and willing to serve God and humankind? How can you support them? Pray now for guidance in how to encourage those younger than yourself.

See Meeting God in Service

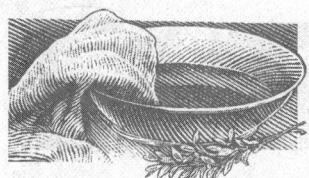

time, but this demand I cannot meet.' " They left and took the answer back to Ben-Hadad.

¹⁰Then Ben-Hadad sent another message to Ahab: "May the gods deal with me, be it ever so severely, if enough dust remains in Samaria to give each of my men a handful."

¹¹The king of Israel answered, "Tell him: 'One who puts on his armor should not boast like one who takes it off.' "

¹²Ben-Hadad heard this message while he and the kings were drinking in their tents,ᵃ and he ordered his men: "Prepare to attack." So they prepared to attack the city.

Ahab Defeats Ben-Hadad

¹³Meanwhile a prophet came to Ahab king of Israel and announced, "This is what the Lᴏʀᴅ says: 'Do you see this vast army? I will give it into your hand today, and then you will know that I am the Lᴏʀᴅ.' "

¹⁴"But who will do this?" asked Ahab.

The prophet replied, "This is what the Lᴏʀᴅ says: 'The young officers of the provincial commanders will do it.' "

"And who will start the battle?" he asked.

The prophet answered, "You will."

¹⁵So Ahab summoned the young officers of the provincial commanders, 232 men. Then he assembled the rest of the Israelites, 7,000 in all. ¹⁶They set out at noon while Ben-Hadad and the 32 kings allied with him were in their tents getting drunk. ¹⁷The young officers of the provincial commanders went out first.

Now Ben-Hadad had dispatched scouts, who reported, "Men are advancing from Samaria."

¹⁸He said, "If they have come out for peace, take them alive; if they have come out for war, take them alive."

¹⁹The young officers of the provincial commanders marched out of the city with the army behind them ²⁰and each one struck down his opponent. At that, the Arameans fled, with the Israelites in pursuit. But Ben-Hadad king of Aram escaped on horseback with some of his horsemen. ²¹The king of Israel advanced and overpowered the horses and chariots and inflicted heavy losses on the Arameans.

²²Afterward, the prophet came to the king of Israel and said, "Strengthen your position and see what must be done, because next spring the king of Aram will attack you again."

²³Meanwhile, the officials of the king of Aram advised him, "Their gods are gods of the hills. That is why they were too strong for us. But if we fight them on the plains, surely we will be stronger than they. ²⁴Do this: Remove all the kings from their commands and replace them with other officers. ²⁵You must also raise an army like the one you lost—horse for horse and chariot for chariot—so we can fight Israel on the plains. Then surely we will be stronger than they." He agreed with them and acted accordingly.

²⁶The next spring Ben-Hadad mustered the Arameans and went up to Aphek to fight against Israel. ²⁷When the Israelites were also mustered and given provisions, they marched out to meet them. The Israelites camped opposite them like two small flocks of goats, while the Arameans covered the countryside.

²⁸The man of God came up and told the king of Israel,

ᵃ 12 Or *in Succoth*; also in verse 16

"This is what the LORD says: 'Because the Arameans think the LORD is a god of the hills and not a god of the valleys, I will deliver this vast army into your hands, and you will know that I am the LORD.' "

²⁹For seven days they camped opposite each other, and on the seventh day the battle was joined. The Israelites inflicted a hundred thousand casualties on the Aramean foot soldiers in one day. ³⁰The rest of them escaped to the city of Aphek, where the wall collapsed on twenty-seven thousand of them. And Ben-Hadad fled to the city and hid in an inner room.

³¹His officials said to him, "Look, we have heard that the kings of the house of Israel are merciful. Let us go to the king of Israel with sackcloth around our waists and ropes around our heads. Perhaps he will spare your life."

³²Wearing sackcloth around their waists and ropes around their heads, they went to the king of Israel and said, "Your servant Ben-Hadad says: 'Please let me live.' "

The king answered, "Is he still alive? He is my brother."

³³The men took this as a good sign and were quick to pick up his word. "Yes, your brother Ben-Hadad!" they said.

"Go and get him," the king said. When Ben-Hadad came out, Ahab had him come up into his chariot.

³⁴"I will return the cities my father took from your father," Ben-Hadad offered. "You may set up your own market areas in Damascus, as my father did in Samaria."

⌊Ahab said,⌋ "On the basis of a treaty I will set you free." So he made a treaty with him, and let him go.

A Prophet Condemns Ahab

³⁵By the word of the LORD one of the sons of the prophets said to his companion, "Strike me with your weapon," but the man refused.

³⁶So the prophet said, "Because you have not obeyed the LORD, as soon as you leave me a lion will kill you." And after the man went away, a lion found him and killed him.

³⁷The prophet found another man and said, "Strike me, please." So the man struck him and wounded him. ³⁸Then the prophet went and stood by the road waiting for the king. He disguised himself with his headband down over his eyes. ³⁹As the king passed by, the prophet called out to him, "Your servant went into the thick of the battle, and someone came to me with a captive and said, 'Guard this man. If he is missing, it will be your life for his life, or you must pay a talent*ᵃ* of silver.' ⁴⁰While your servant was busy here and there, the man disappeared."

"That is your sentence," the king of Israel said. "You have pronounced it yourself."

⁴¹Then the prophet quickly removed the headband from his eyes, and the king of Israel recognized him as one of the prophets. ⁴²He said to the king, "This is what the LORD says: 'You have set free a man I had determined should die.*ᵇ* Therefore it is your life for his life, your people for his people.' " ⁴³Sullen and angry, the king of Israel went to his palace in Samaria.

Wavering Between Obedience and Disobedience

1 KINGS 20:30–31

This book's litany continues, tale after tale, of people who waver between doing right and doing evil—between following God and following their own way. While God presents them with countless opportunities to return to him and pursue order and justice, they refuse to repent and to accept God's forgiveness. The results are devastating. Ponder this: Repentance is an act of change, restoration and grace. Remember times when you have repented or accepted the repentance of others.

How has repentance and forgiveness been a part of your journey with God? What role has forgiveness played in your relationships? How do you express your repentance to God and others? How do you express forgiveness?

At this time, is there any situation that requires you to repent? Is there anyone who needs your forgiveness? Ask God to give you courage to remedy this situation. Ask how you might do so.

See Meeting God in Prayer

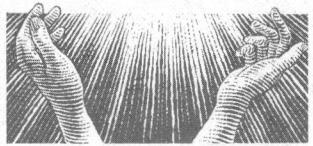

ᵃ 39 That is, about 75 pounds (about 34 kilograms)   *ᵇ 42* The Hebrew term refers to the irrevocable giving over of things or persons to the LORD, often by totally destroying them.

King Ahab's Greed

1 KINGS 21:4–7

"Then [Jesus] said to them, 'Watch out! Be on your guard against all kinds of greed; a man's life does not consist in the abundance of his possessions . . . The ground of a certain rich man produced a good crop. He thought to himself, "What shall I do? I have no place to store my crops." Then he said, "This is what I'll do. I will tear down my barns and build bigger ones, and there I will store all my grain and my goods. And I'll say to myself, 'You have plenty of good things laid up for many years. Take life easy; eat, drink, and be merry.' " But God said to him, "You fool! This very night your life will be demanded from you. Then who will get what you have prepared for yourself?" This is how it will be with anyone who stores up things for himself but is not rich toward God.' "

—Luke 12:15–21

Naboth's Vineyard

21 Some time later there was an incident involving a vineyard belonging to Naboth the Jezreelite. The vineyard was in Jezreel, close to the palace of Ahab king of Samaria. ²Ahab said to Naboth, "Let me have your vineyard to use for a vegetable garden, since it is close to my palace. In exchange I will give you a better vineyard or, if you prefer, I will pay you whatever it is worth."

³But Naboth replied, "The Lord forbid that I should give you the inheritance of my fathers."

⁴So Ahab went home, sullen and angry because Naboth the Jezreelite had said, "I will not give you the inheritance of my fathers." He lay on his bed sulking and refused to eat.

⁵His wife Jezebel came in and asked him, "Why are you so sullen? Why won't you eat?"

⁶He answered her, "Because I said to Naboth the Jezreelite, 'Sell me your vineyard; or if you prefer, I will give you another vineyard in its place.' But he said, 'I will not give you my vineyard.' "

⁷Jezebel his wife said, "Is this how you act as king over Israel? Get up and eat! Cheer up. I'll get you the vineyard of Naboth the Jezreelite."

⁸So she wrote letters in Ahab's name, placed his seal on them, and sent them to the elders and nobles who lived in Naboth's city with him. ⁹In those letters she wrote:

> "Proclaim a day of fasting and seat Naboth in a prominent place among the people. ¹⁰But seat two scoundrels opposite him and have them testify that he has cursed both God and the king. Then take him out and stone him to death."

¹¹So the elders and nobles who lived in Naboth's city did as Jezebel directed in the letters she had written to them. ¹²They proclaimed a fast and seated Naboth in a prominent place among the people. ¹³Then two scoundrels came and sat opposite him and brought charges against Naboth before the people, saying, "Naboth has cursed both God and the king." So they took him outside the city and stoned him to death. ¹⁴Then they sent word to Jezebel: "Naboth has been stoned and is dead."

¹⁵As soon as Jezebel heard that Naboth had been stoned to death, she said to Ahab, "Get up and take possession of the vineyard of Naboth the Jezreelite that he refused to sell you. He is no longer alive, but dead." ¹⁶When Ahab heard that Naboth was dead, he got up and went down to take possession of Naboth's vineyard.

¹⁷Then the word of the Lord came to Elijah the Tishbite: ¹⁸"Go down to meet Ahab king of Israel, who rules in Samaria. He is now in Naboth's vineyard, where he has gone to take possession of it. ¹⁹Say to him, 'This is what the Lord says: Have you not murdered a man and seized his property?' Then say to him, 'This is what the Lord says: In the place where dogs licked up Naboth's blood, dogs will lick up your blood—yes, yours!' "

²⁰Ahab said to Elijah, "So you have found me, my enemy!"

"I have found you," he answered, "because you have sold yourself to do evil in the eyes of the Lord. ²¹I am going to bring disaster on you. I will consume your descendants and cut off from Ahab every last male in Israel—slave or free. ²²I will make your house like that of Jeroboam son of Nebat and that of Baasha son of Ahijah, because you have provoked me to anger and have caused Israel to sin.'

23"And also concerning Jezebel the LORD says: 'Dogs will devour Jezebel by the wall of*a* Jezreel.'

24"Dogs will eat those belonging to Ahab who die in the city, and the birds of the air will feed on those who die in the country."

25(There was never a man like Ahab, who sold himself to do evil in the eyes of the LORD, urged on by Jezebel his wife. 26He behaved in the vilest manner by going after idols, like the Amorites the LORD drove out before Israel.)

27When Ahab heard these words, he tore his clothes, put on sackcloth and fasted. He lay in sackcloth and went around meekly.

28Then the word of the LORD came to Elijah the Tishbite: 29"Have you noticed how Ahab has humbled himself before me? Because he has humbled himself, I will not bring this disaster in his day, but I will bring it on his house in the days of his son."

Micaiah Prophesies Against Ahab

22 For three years there was no war between Aram and Israel. 2But in the third year Jehoshaphat king of Judah went down to see the king of Israel. 3The king of Israel had said to his officials, "Don't you know that Ramoth Gilead belongs to us and yet we are doing nothing to retake it from the king of Aram?"

4So he asked Jehoshaphat, "Will you go with me to fight against Ramoth Gilead?"

Jehoshaphat replied to the king of Israel, "I am as you are, my people as your people, my horses as your horses." 5But Jehoshaphat also said to the king of Israel, "First seek the counsel of the LORD."

6So the king of Israel brought together the prophets— about four hundred men—and asked them, "Shall I go to war against Ramoth Gilead, or shall I refrain?"

"Go," they answered, "for the Lord will give it into the king's hand."

7But Jehoshaphat asked, "Is there not a prophet of the LORD here whom we can inquire of?"

8The king of Israel answered Jehoshaphat, "There is still one man through whom we can inquire of the LORD, but I hate him because he never prophesies anything good about me, but always bad. He is Micaiah son of Imlah."

"The king should not say that," Jehoshaphat replied.

9So the king of Israel called one of his officials and said, "Bring Micaiah son of Imlah at once."

10Dressed in their royal robes, the king of Israel and Jehoshaphat king of Judah were sitting on their thrones at the threshing floor by the entrance of the gate of Samaria, with all the prophets prophesying before them. 11Now Zedekiah son of Kenaanah had made iron horns and he declared, "This is what the LORD says: 'With these you will gore the Arameans until they are destroyed.' "

12All the other prophets were prophesying the same thing. "Attack Ramoth Gilead and be victorious," they said, "for the LORD will give it into the king's hand."

a 23 Most Hebrew manuscripts; a few Hebrew manuscripts, Vulgate and Syriac (see also 2 Kings 9:26) *the plot of ground at*

King Ahab's Repentance

1 KINGS 21:25-29

According to this report, Ahab "behaved in the vilest manner by going after idols." But because he repented in deep humility, God spared him from full and immediate punishment for his deeds. Often we think that the guilt for the worst things we have done will be with us forever. The same God who forgave Ahab forgives us today. Make a list of the idols in your life or sketch a picture of each one. You might want to construct a model of an idol from materials you have at hand. Which of your senses led you to these idols—touch, smell, taste, sight or hearing? Ask God to give you the grace you need to be freed from the power of these idols so that you can worship the one true God. As a symbol of your repentance, destroy the idols or burn the list as you offer a prayer of rededication.

See Meeting God in Prayer

Micaiah's Prophecy

1 KINGS 22:17–18

Micaiah is a man of conviction and forthright speech and the courage to go against the easy words of the false prophets. We may sometimes wonder whether anyone is speaking for God in the midst of all of the easy speeches, comforting lies and destructive forces in our culture. Can you name anyone who speaks the uncomfortable truth to kings, presidents and other leaders about their false sense of security in power, weapons or each other? Imagine that you are the prophet Micaiah. Write a prayer for your nation and its leaders from Micaiah's perspective. Use it in your daily devotions this week. What do you need and what do our leaders need? What should be the church's role in speaking out against injustice? How is God calling you to be a voice such as Micaiah's?

See Meeting God in Service

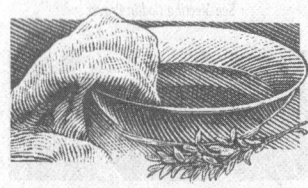

¹³The messenger who had gone to summon Micaiah said to him, "Look, as one man the other prophets are predicting success for the king. Let your word agree with theirs, and speak favorably."

¹⁴But Micaiah said, "As surely as the LORD lives, I can tell him only what the LORD tells me."

¹⁵When he arrived, the king asked him, "Micaiah, shall we go to war against Ramoth Gilead, or shall I refrain?"

"Attack and be victorious," he answered, "for the LORD will give it into the king's hand."

¹⁶The king said to him, "How many times must I make you swear to tell me nothing but the truth in the name of the LORD?"

¹⁷Then Micaiah answered, "I saw all Israel scattered on the hills like sheep without a shepherd, and the LORD said, 'These people have no master. Let each one go home in peace.' "

¹⁸The king of Israel said to Jehoshaphat, "Didn't I tell you that he never prophesies anything good about me, but only bad?"

¹⁹Micaiah continued, "Therefore hear the word of the LORD: I saw the LORD sitting on his throne with all the host of heaven standing around him on his right and on his left. ²⁰And the LORD said, 'Who will entice Ahab into attacking Ramoth Gilead and going to his death there?'

"One suggested this, and another that. ²¹Finally, a spirit came forward, stood before the LORD and said, 'I will entice him.'

²²" 'By what means?' the LORD asked.

" 'I will go out and be a lying spirit in the mouths of all his prophets,' he said.

" 'You will succeed in enticing him,' said the LORD. 'Go and do it.'

²³"So now the LORD has put a lying spirit in the mouths of all these prophets of yours. The LORD has decreed disaster for you."

²⁴Then Zedekiah son of Kenaanah went up and slapped Micaiah in the face. "Which way did the spirit from*ᵃ* the LORD go when he went from me to speak to you?" he asked.

²⁵Micaiah replied, "You will find out on the day you go to hide in an inner room."

²⁶The king of Israel then ordered, "Take Micaiah and send him back to Amon the ruler of the city and to Joash the king's son ²⁷and say, 'This is what the king says: Put this fellow in prison and give him nothing but bread and water until I return safely.' "

²⁸Micaiah declared, "If you ever return safely, the LORD has not spoken through me." Then he added, "Mark my words, all you people!"

Ahab Killed at Ramoth Gilead

²⁹So the king of Israel and Jehoshaphat king of Judah went up to Ramoth Gilead. ³⁰The king of Israel said to Jehoshaphat, "I will enter the battle in disguise, but you wear your royal robes." So the king of Israel disguised himself and went into battle.

³¹Now the king of Aram had ordered his thirty-two chariot commanders, "Do not fight with anyone, small or great, except the king of Israel." ³²When the chariot commanders

ᵃ 24 Or Spirit of

saw Jehoshaphat, they thought, "Surely this is the king of Israel." So they turned to attack him, but when Jehoshaphat cried out, ³³the chariot commanders saw that he was not the king of Israel and stopped pursuing him.

³⁴But someone drew his bow at random and hit the king of Israel between the sections of his armor. The king told his chariot driver, "Wheel around and get me out of the fighting. I've been wounded." ³⁵All day long the battle raged, and the king was propped up in his chariot facing the Arameans. The blood from his wound ran onto the floor of the chariot, and that evening he died. ³⁶As the sun was setting, a cry spread through the army: "Every man to his town; everyone to his land!"

³⁷So the king died and was brought to Samaria, and they buried him there. ³⁸They washed the chariot at a pool in Samaria (where the prostitutes bathed),ᵃ and the dogs licked up his blood, as the word of the LORD had declared.

³⁹As for the other events of Ahab's reign, including all he did, the palace he built and inlaid with ivory, and the cities he fortified, are they not written in the book of the annals of the kings of Israel? ⁴⁰Ahab rested with his fathers. And Ahaziah his son succeeded him as king.

Jehoshaphat King of Judah

⁴¹Jehoshaphat son of Asa became king of Judah in the fourth year of Ahab king of Israel. ⁴²Jehoshaphat was thirty-five years old when he became king, and he reigned in Jerusalem twenty-five years. His mother's name was Azubah daughter of Shilhi. ⁴³In everything he walked in the ways of his father Asa and did not stray from them; he did what was right in the eyes of the LORD. The high places, however, were not removed, and the people continued to offer sacrifices and burn incense there. ⁴⁴Jehoshaphat was also at peace with the king of Israel.

⁴⁵As for the other events of Jehoshaphat's reign, the things he achieved and his military exploits, are they not written in the book of the annals of the kings of Judah? ⁴⁶He rid the land of the rest of the male shrine prostitutes who remained there even after the reign of his father Asa. ⁴⁷There was then no king in Edom; a deputy ruled.

⁴⁸Now Jehoshaphat built a fleet of trading shipsᵇ to go to Ophir for gold, but they never set sail—they were wrecked at Ezion Geber. ⁴⁹At that time Ahaziah son of Ahab said to Jehoshaphat, "Let my men sail with your men," but Jehoshaphat refused.

⁵⁰Then Jehoshaphat rested with his fathers and was buried with them in the city of David his father. And Jehoram his son succeeded him.

Ahaziah King of Israel

⁵¹Ahaziah son of Ahab became king of Israel in Samaria in the seventeenth year of Jehoshaphat king of Judah, and he reigned over Israel two years. ⁵²He did evil in the eyes of the LORD, because he walked in the ways of his father and mother and in the ways of Jeroboam son of Nebat, who caused Israel to sin. ⁵³He served and worshiped Baal and provoked the LORD, the God of Israel, to anger, just as his father had done.

Final Judgment

1 KINGS 22:37–40

Review this national tragedy by drawing a simple time line of the events in 1 Kings. Make a list of the major national mistakes in this tale of disobedience, and note the instances of righteousness and obedience. Note on the time line the leaders who ignore God and whose wrongdoing leads to lifestyles of blatant wickedness. Note God's prophets and others who call the people to return to God. Conclude by praying for the present-day: "Gracious God, may we never forget that you are the source of life and hope. May we acknowledge you as the guide and inspiration for our living. May we, your people, always be light, hope and peace to all people. Amen."

2 KINGS
Our Weakness, God's Power

KEY VERSES:

The LORD warned Israel and Judah through all his prophets and seers: "Turn from your evil ways. Observe my commands and decrees, in accordance with the entire Law that I commanded your fathers to obey and that I delivered to you through my servants the prophets." But they would not listen and were as stiff-necked as their fathers, who did not trust in the LORD their God.—2 Kings 17:13–14

"Most of our conflicts and difficulties come from trying to deal with the spiritual and practical aspects of life separately instead of realizing them as parts of a whole. If our practical life is centered on our own interests, cluttered up by our possessions, distracted by ambitions, passions, wants and worries, beset by a sense of our own rights and importance, or anxieties for our own future, or longings for our own success, we need not expect that our spiritual life will be a contrast to all of this."

—EVELYN UNDERHILL,
The Spiritual Life

The book of 2 Kings continues the saga of the dearth of God-centered leadership among Israel's kings. It describes Israel's downward slide away from God and into idolatry and immorality—an era of kings who do "evil in the eyes of the LORD" by imitating the sins of other nations. Once a great nation built by David, Israel is now divided and surrounded by powerful enemies and teeters on the verge of complete destruction.

Thirty prophets, most notably Elijah and Elisha, call the alarm using signs, miracles, warnings and proclamations—to no avail. Both kingdoms continue to turn from God and are ultimately exiled. Is there any word from the Lord in this desperate and lost situation? The book of 2 Kings demonstrates all too clearly the fate of those who stubbornly refuse to follow God's commandments. There is hope however. The God of the covenant always offers hope and restoration. A remnant is taken to Babylon to be called into new faithfulness and to receive God's blessings.

Consider how some of these destructive patterns may be at work in our own day. What are some of the unwise choices and destructive actions that undermine the health and spirit of the nation? How might we be "exiled" from the blessings we enjoy today if we do not face our own behavior squarely?

God still needs faithful and courageous people who are willing to proclaim the truth. As you read, search your own heart for how you can be part of God's remnant of faithful people today.

The LORD's Judgment on Ahaziah

1 After Ahab's death, Moab rebelled against Israel. ²Now Ahaziah had fallen through the lattice of his upper room in Samaria and injured himself. So he sent messengers, saying to them, "Go and consult Baal-Zebub, the god of Ekron, to see if I will recover from this injury."

³But the angel of the LORD said to Elijah the Tishbite, "Go up and meet the messengers of the king of Samaria and ask them, 'Is it because there is no God in Israel that you are going off to consult Baal-Zebub, the god of Ekron?' ⁴Therefore this is what the LORD says: 'You will not leave the bed you are lying on. You will certainly die!' " So Elijah went.

⁵When the messengers returned to the king, he asked them, "Why have you come back?"

⁶"A man came to meet us," they replied. "And he said to us, 'Go back to the king who sent you and tell him, "This is what the LORD says: Is it because there is no God in Israel that you are sending men to consult Baal-Zebub, the god of Ekron? Therefore you will not leave the bed you are lying on. You will certainly die!" ' "

⁷The king asked them, "What kind of man was it who came to meet you and told you this?"

⁸They replied, "He was a man with a garment of hair and with a leather belt around his waist."

The king said, "That was Elijah the Tishbite."

⁹Then he sent to Elijah a captain with his company of fifty men. The captain went up to Elijah, who was sitting on the top of a hill, and said to him, "Man of God, the king says, 'Come down!' "

¹⁰Elijah answered the captain, "If I am a man of God, may fire come down from heaven and consume you and your fifty men!" Then fire fell from heaven and consumed the captain and his men.

¹¹At this the king sent to Elijah another captain with his fifty men. The captain said to him, "Man of God, this is what the king says, 'Come down at once!' "

¹²"If I am a man of God," Elijah replied, "may fire come down from heaven and consume you and your fifty men!" Then the fire of God fell from heaven and consumed him and his fifty men.

¹³So the king sent a third captain with his fifty men. This third captain went up and fell on his knees before Elijah. "Man of God," he begged, "please have respect for my life and the lives of these fifty men, your servants! ¹⁴See, fire has fallen from heaven and consumed the first two captains and all their men. But now have respect for my life!"

¹⁵The angel of the LORD said to Elijah, "Go down with him; do not be afraid of him." So Elijah got up and went down with him to the king.

¹⁶He told the king, "This is what the LORD says: Is it because there is no God in Israel for you to consult that you have sent messengers to consult Baal-Zebub, the god of Ekron? Because you have done this, you will never leave the bed you are lying on. You will certainly die!" ¹⁷So he died, according to the word of the LORD that Elijah had spoken.

Because Ahaziah had no son, Joram*ᵃ* succeeded him as

ᵃ 17 Hebrew *Jehoram,* a variant of *Joram*

Pictures of a Troubled World

2 KINGS 1:1–8

Leaf through some favorite magazines and periodicals. List the characteristics of the culture these publications represent. In what ways does our world look much like the world in the opening chapters of 2 Kings? What false gods does contemporary culture worship? What aspects of that culture allure you to wander from what is good and true? What is your hope for God's people in these times? What role might you play in proclaiming truth and hope? Make a collage, if you wish, of both the good and evil of our society, using pages from the publications; then spend time praying for God's Spirit to work among us.

See Meeting God in Prayer

Elijah's Ascension

2 KINGS 2:1–16

Like Enoch before him (Genesis 5:24) and Jesus after him (Luke 24:51), Elijah "went up" into God's heavenly presence. Read the passage, then imagine that you can craft your own cinematic version of this dramatic event. Find your own role as a participant. Are you Elisha? One of the company of the prophets? As you imagine the poignant parting from your master, let your God-given imagination give life to the fiery horses and chariot. What happens within you as Elijah bestows the Spirit on you? You may choose to imagine the story more than once, taking different roles each time, in order to write this story deeply in your heart.

See *Meeting God in Scripture*

king in the second year of Jehoram son of Jehoshaphat king of Judah. ¹⁸As for all the other events of Ahaziah's reign, and what he did, are they not written in the book of the annals of the kings of Israel?

Elijah Taken Up to Heaven

2 When the LORD was about to take Elijah up to heaven in a whirlwind, Elijah and Elisha were on their way from Gilgal. ²Elijah said to Elisha, "Stay here; the LORD has sent me to Bethel."

But Elisha said, "As surely as the LORD lives and as you live, I will not leave you." So they went down to Bethel.

³The company of the prophets at Bethel came out to Elisha and asked, "Do you know that the LORD is going to take your master from you today?"

"Yes, I know," Elisha replied, "but do not speak of it."

⁴Then Elijah said to him, "Stay here, Elisha; the LORD has sent me to Jericho."

And he replied, "As surely as the LORD lives and as you live, I will not leave you." So they went to Jericho.

⁵The company of the prophets at Jericho went up to Elisha and asked him, "Do you know that the LORD is going to take your master from you today?"

"Yes, I know," he replied, "but do not speak of it."

⁶Then Elijah said to him, "Stay here; the LORD has sent me to the Jordan."

And he replied, "As surely as the LORD lives and as you live, I will not leave you." So the two of them walked on.

⁷Fifty men of the company of the prophets went and stood at a distance, facing the place where Elijah and Elisha had stopped at the Jordan. ⁸Elijah took his cloak, rolled it up and struck the water with it. The water divided to the right and to the left, and the two of them crossed over on dry ground.

⁹When they had crossed, Elijah said to Elisha, "Tell me, what can I do for you before I am taken from you?"

"Let me inherit a double portion of your spirit," Elisha replied.

¹⁰"You have asked a difficult thing," Elijah said, "yet if you see me when I am taken from you, it will be yours—otherwise not."

¹¹As they were walking along and talking together, suddenly a chariot of fire and horses of fire appeared and separated the two of them, and Elijah went up to heaven in a whirlwind. ¹²Elisha saw this and cried out, "My father! My father! The chariots and horsemen of Israel!" And Elisha saw him no more. Then he took hold of his own clothes and tore them apart.

¹³He picked up the cloak that had fallen from Elijah and went back and stood on the bank of the Jordan. ¹⁴Then he took the cloak that had fallen from him and struck the water with it. "Where now is the LORD, the God of Elijah?" he asked. When he struck the water, it divided to the right and to the left, and he crossed over.

¹⁵The company of the prophets from Jericho, who were watching, said, "The spirit of Elijah is resting on Elisha." And they went to meet him and bowed to the ground before him. ¹⁶"Look," they said, "we your servants have fifty able men. Let them go and look for your master. Perhaps

the Spirit of the Lord has picked him up and set him down on some mountain or in some valley."

"No," Elisha replied, "do not send them."

[17]But they persisted until he was too ashamed to refuse. So he said, "Send them." And they sent fifty men, who searched for three days but did not find him. [18]When they returned to Elisha, who was staying in Jericho, he said to them, "Didn't I tell you not to go?"

Healing of the Water

[19]The men of the city said to Elisha, "Look, our lord, this town is well situated, as you can see, but the water is bad and the land is unproductive."

[20]"Bring me a new bowl," he said, "and put salt in it." So they brought it to him.

[21]Then he went out to the spring and threw the salt into it, saying, "This is what the Lord says: 'I have healed this water. Never again will it cause death or make the land unproductive.' " [22]And the water has remained wholesome to this day, according to the word Elisha had spoken.

Elisha Is Jeered

[23]From there Elisha went up to Bethel. As he was walking along the road, some youths came out of the town and jeered at him. "Go on up, you baldhead!" they said. "Go on up, you baldhead!" [24]He turned around, looked at them and called down a curse on them in the name of the Lord. Then two bears came out of the woods and mauled forty-two of the youths. [25]And he went on to Mount Carmel and from there returned to Samaria.

Moab Revolts

3 Joram[a] son of Ahab became king of Israel in Samaria in the eighteenth year of Jehoshaphat king of Judah, and he reigned twelve years. [2]He did evil in the eyes of the Lord, but not as his father and mother had done. He got rid of the sacred stone of Baal that his father had made. [3]Nevertheless he clung to the sins of Jeroboam son of Nebat, which he had caused Israel to commit; he did not turn away from them.

[4]Now Mesha king of Moab raised sheep, and he had to supply the king of Israel with a hundred thousand lambs and with the wool of a hundred thousand rams. [5]But after Ahab died, the king of Moab rebelled against the king of Israel. [6]So at that time King Joram set out from Samaria and mobilized all Israel. [7]He also sent this message to Jehoshaphat king of Judah: "The king of Moab has rebelled against me. Will you go with me to fight against Moab?"

"I will go with you," he replied. "I am as you are, my people as your people, my horses as your horses."

[8]"By what route shall we attack?" he asked.

"Through the Desert of Edom," he answered.

[9]So the king of Israel set out with the king of Judah and the king of Edom. After a roundabout march of seven days, the army had no more water for themselves or for the animals with them.

[10]"What!" exclaimed the king of Israel. "Has the Lord called us three kings together only to hand us over to Moab?"

[11]But Jehoshaphat asked, "Is there no prophet of the Lord here, that we may inquire of the Lord through him?"

The Simplicity of Service

2 KINGS 3:11

Elisha learned the art of service, in part, through simple acts such as pouring water on the hands of his master and teacher. Sometimes it is the simplest acts that have the greatest meaning. Look at your hands for a moment. Reflect on the many tasks that you have accomplished today with them. What would your life be without them? For which menial, but important, tasks have you used your hands today? How have you touched or served people? How can you find ways to do so tomorrow? What is your prayer for the use of your hands?

See Meeting God in Service

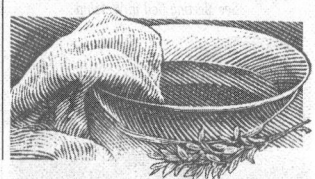

---

[a] 1 Hebrew *Jehoram*, a variant of *Joram*; also in verse 6

Music's Spiritual Power

2 KINGS 3:12—4:3

Elisha calls for a musician, knowing that music will help him be more open to the "hand of the LORD." How does music make you more receptive to God, more aware of God's presence? Make a list of your own "top ten" spiritual songs, including hymns, classical pieces and popular tunes. Take time now to find a hymnal, other printed music or a recording. Then play or sing one of these musical selections as you open your heart and mind to the presence of God here and now. Keep the list near your prayer or study space to use on other days as a prelude or postlude to your devotions.

See *Meeting God in Worship*

An officer of the king of Israel answered, "Elisha son of Shaphat is here. He used to pour water on the hands of Elijah.*ᵃ*"

¹²Jehoshaphat said, "The word of the LORD is with him." So the king of Israel and Jehoshaphat and the king of Edom went down to him.

¹³Elisha said to the king of Israel, "What do we have to do with each other? Go to the prophets of your father and the prophets of your mother."

"No," the king of Israel answered, "because it was the LORD who called us three kings together to hand us over to Moab."

¹⁴Elisha said, "As surely as the LORD Almighty lives, whom I serve, if I did not have respect for the presence of Jehoshaphat king of Judah, I would not look at you or even notice you. ¹⁵But now bring me a harpist."

While the harpist was playing, the hand of the LORD came upon Elisha ¹⁶and he said, "This is what the LORD says: Make this valley full of ditches. ¹⁷For this is what the LORD says: You will see neither wind nor rain, yet this valley will be filled with water, and you, your cattle and your other animals will drink. ¹⁸This is an easy thing in the eyes of the LORD; he will also hand Moab over to you. ¹⁹You will overthrow every fortified city and every major town. You will cut down every good tree, stop up all the springs, and ruin every good field with stones."

²⁰The next morning, about the time for offering the sacrifice, there it was—water flowing from the direction of Edom! And the land was filled with water.

²¹Now all the Moabites had heard that the kings had come to fight against them; so every man, young and old, who could bear arms was called up and stationed on the border. ²²When they got up early in the morning, the sun was shining on the water. To the Moabites across the way, the water looked red—like blood. ²³"That's blood!" they said. "Those kings must have fought and slaughtered each other. Now to the plunder, Moab!"

²⁴But when the Moabites came to the camp of Israel, the Israelites rose up and fought them until they fled. And the Israelites invaded the land and slaughtered the Moabites. ²⁵They destroyed the towns, and each man threw a stone on every good field until it was covered. They stopped up all the springs and cut down every good tree. Only Kir Hareseth was left with its stones in place, but men armed with slings surrounded it and attacked it as well.

²⁶When the king of Moab saw that the battle had gone against him, he took with him seven hundred swordsmen to break through to the king of Edom, but they failed. ²⁷Then he took his firstborn son, who was to succeed him as king, and offered him as a sacrifice on the city wall. The fury against Israel was great; they withdrew and returned to their own land.

The Widow's Oil

4 The wife of a man from the company of the prophets cried out to Elisha, "Your servant my husband is dead, and you know that he revered the LORD. But now his creditor is coming to take my two boys as his slaves."

ᵃ 11 That is, he was Elijah's personal servant.

²Elisha replied to her, "How can I help you? Tell me, what do you have in your house?"

"Your servant has nothing there at all," she said, "except a little oil."

³Elisha said, "Go around and ask all your neighbors for empty jars. Don't ask for just a few. ⁴Then go inside and shut the door behind you and your sons. Pour oil into all the jars, and as each is filled, put it to one side."

⁵She left him and afterward shut the door behind her and her sons. They brought the jars to her and she kept pouring. ⁶When all the jars were full, she said to her son, "Bring me another one."

But he replied, "There is not a jar left." Then the oil stopped flowing.

⁷She went and told the man of God, and he said, "Go, sell the oil and pay your debts. You and your sons can live on what is left."

The Shunammite's Son Restored to Life

⁸One day Elisha went to Shunem. And a well-to-do woman was there, who urged him to stay for a meal. So whenever he came by, he stopped there to eat. ⁹She said to her husband, "I know that this man who often comes our way is a holy man of God. ¹⁰Let's make a small room on the roof and put in it a bed and a table, a chair and a lamp for him. Then he can stay there whenever he comes to us."

¹¹One day when Elisha came, he went up to his room and lay down there. ¹²He said to his servant Gehazi, "Call the Shunammite." So he called her, and she stood before him. ¹³Elisha said to him, "Tell her, 'You have gone to all this trouble for us. Now what can be done for you? Can we speak on your behalf to the king or the commander of the army?'"

She replied, "I have a home among my own people."

¹⁴"What can be done for her?" Elisha asked.

Gehazi said, "Well, she has no son and her husband is old."

¹⁵Then Elisha said, "Call her." So he called her, and she stood in the doorway. ¹⁶"About this time next year," Elisha said, "you will hold a son in your arms."

"No, my lord," she objected. "Don't mislead your servant, O man of God!"

¹⁷But the woman became pregnant, and the next year about that same time she gave birth to a son, just as Elisha had told her.

¹⁸The child grew, and one day he went out to his father, who was with the reapers. ¹⁹"My head! My head!" he said to his father.

His father told a servant, "Carry him to his mother." ²⁰After the servant had lifted him up and carried him to his mother, the boy sat on her lap until noon, and then he died. ²¹She went up and laid him on the bed of the man of God, then shut the door and went out.

²²She called her husband and said, "Please send me one of the servants and a donkey so I can go to the man of God quickly and return."

²³"Why go to him today?" he asked. "It's not the New Moon or the Sabbath."

"It's all right," she said.

Pouring Out Blessings

2 KINGS 4:1–7

Even though God had ordered creditors and rich people not to take advantage of debtors in extreme need (Leviticus 25:39), this woman and her children are in danger of being sold into slavery. The compassionate prophet responds with instructions for her, which she follows in faith, and God blesses her abundantly. Review your financial history: How has your faith been tested in financial matters? Has it ever seemed as if you were at the end of your resources? Have you ever experienced receiving or offering compassion in money matters? In what other ways has God poured out blessings on you in hard times? How does the way you spend your money reflect an active compassion in your life?

See Meeting God in Everyday Life

473

A Mother's Faith

2 KINGS 4:27–44

Elisha, whose name means "God's healing and salvation," brings God's healing love to the son of a widow, in much the same way that Jesus healed the daughter of Jairus (Mark 5:35–43). Read the entire passage through once, then see the story imaginatively through the eyes of the mother. Reach out your arms and hold your afflicted son on your lap. What emotions churn within you as you search for the prophet? Imagine approaching the prophet and kneeling at his feet. You wonder what is transpiring behind the closed doors of the prophet's room; you joyfully receive your restored son. Pray that God will help grow such faith in your own heart.

See Meeting God in Scripture

²⁴She saddled the donkey and said to her servant, "Lead on; don't slow down for me unless I tell you." ²⁵So she set out and came to the man of God at Mount Carmel.

When he saw her in the distance, the man of God said to his servant Gehazi, "Look! There's the Shunammite! ²⁶Run to meet her and ask her, 'Are you all right? Is your husband all right? Is your child all right?'"

"Everything is all right," she said.

²⁷When she reached the man of God at the mountain, she took hold of his feet. Gehazi came over to push her away, but the man of God said, "Leave her alone! She is in bitter distress, but the Lord has hidden it from me and has not told me why."

²⁸"Did I ask you for a son, my lord?" she said. "Didn't I tell you, 'Don't raise my hopes'?"

²⁹Elisha said to Gehazi, "Tuck your cloak into your belt, take my staff in your hand and run. If you meet anyone, do not greet him, and if anyone greets you, do not answer. Lay my staff on the boy's face."

³⁰But the child's mother said, "As surely as the Lord lives and as you live, I will not leave you." So he got up and followed her.

³¹Gehazi went on ahead and laid the staff on the boy's face, but there was no sound or response. So Gehazi went back to meet Elisha and told him, "The boy has not awakened."

³²When Elisha reached the house, there was the boy lying dead on his couch. ³³He went in, shut the door on the two of them and prayed to the Lord. ³⁴Then he got on the bed and lay upon the boy, mouth to mouth, eyes to eyes, hands to hands. As he stretched himself out upon him, the boy's body grew warm. ³⁵Elisha turned away and walked back and forth in the room and then got on the bed and stretched out upon him once more. The boy sneezed seven times and opened his eyes.

³⁶Elisha summoned Gehazi and said, "Call the Shunammite." And he did. When she came, he said, "Take your son." ³⁷She came in, fell at his feet and bowed to the ground. Then she took her son and went out.

Death in the Pot

³⁸Elisha returned to Gilgal and there was a famine in that region. While the company of the prophets was meeting with him, he said to his servant, "Put on the large pot and cook some stew for these men."

³⁹One of them went out into the fields to gather herbs and found a wild vine. He gathered some of its gourds and filled the fold of his cloak. When he returned, he cut them up into the pot of stew, though no one knew what they were. ⁴⁰The stew was poured out for the men, but as they began to eat it, they cried out, "O man of God, there is death in the pot!" And they could not eat it.

⁴¹Elisha said, "Get some flour." He put it into the pot and said, "Serve it to the people to eat." And there was nothing harmful in the pot.

Feeding of a Hundred

⁴²A man came from Baal Shalishah, bringing the man of God twenty loaves of barley bread baked from the first ripe

grain, along with some heads of new grain. "Give it to the people to eat," Elisha said.

⁴³"How can I set this before a hundred men?" his servant asked.

But Elisha answered, "Give it to the people to eat. For this is what the LORD says: 'They will eat and have some left over.' " ⁴⁴Then he set it before them, and they ate and had some left over, according to the word of the LORD.

Naaman Healed of Leprosy

5 Now Naaman was commander of the army of the king of Aram. He was a great man in the sight of his master and highly regarded, because through him the LORD had given victory to Aram. He was a valiant soldier, but he had leprosy.ᵃ

²Now bands from Aram had gone out and had taken captive a young girl from Israel, and she served Naaman's wife. ³She said to her mistress, "If only my master would see the prophet who is in Samaria! He would cure him of his leprosy."

⁴Naaman went to his master and told him what the girl from Israel had said. ⁵"By all means, go," the king of Aram replied. "I will send a letter to the king of Israel." So Naaman left, taking with him ten talentsᵇ of silver, six thousand shekelsᶜ of gold and ten sets of clothing. ⁶The letter that he took to the king of Israel read: "With this letter I am sending my servant Naaman to you so that you may cure him of his leprosy."

⁷As soon as the king of Israel read the letter, he tore his robes and said, "Am I God? Can I kill and bring back to life? Why does this fellow send someone to me to be cured of his leprosy? See how he is trying to pick a quarrel with me!"

⁸When Elisha the man of God heard that the king of Israel had torn his robes, he sent him this message: "Why have you torn your robes? Have the man come to me and he will know that there is a prophet in Israel." ⁹So Naaman went with his horses and chariots and stopped at the door of Elisha's house. ¹⁰Elisha sent a messenger to say to him, "Go, wash yourself seven times in the Jordan, and your flesh will be restored and you will be cleansed."

¹¹But Naaman went away angry and said, "I thought that he would surely come out to me and stand and call on the name of the LORD his God, wave his hand over the spot and cure me of my leprosy. ¹²Are not Abana and Pharpar, the rivers of Damascus, better than any of the waters of Israel? Couldn't I wash in them and be cleansed?" So he turned and went off in a rage.

¹³Naaman's servants went to him and said, "My father, if the prophet had told you to do some great thing, would you not have done it? How much more, then, when he tells you, 'Wash and be cleansed'!" ¹⁴So he went down and dipped himself in the Jordan seven times, as the man of God had told him, and his flesh was restored and became clean like that of a young boy.

¹⁵Then Naaman and all his attendants went back to the man of God. He stood before him and said, "Now I know

---

Stubbornness, Foolishness and Faith

2 KINGS 5:1–14

As desperate as Naaman is to have his leprosy cured, he is furious that Elisha does not show up in person. He is more concerned about the perceived insult than about humbly following the instructions of Elisha's messenger. Pride jeopardizes Naaman's chance to be healed.

Pride has long been acknowledged as the source of many other sins. This is a good time to take stock of where sinful pride occurs in your own life. Ask someone whom you love and trust (and who loves and trusts you) for help. List two or three areas in your life where pride undermines your closeness to God. What are the sources of pride in these areas? What is the difference between pride and wholesome confidence? Ask God to show you ways to be free from sinful pride.

See *Meeting God in Community*

ᵃ 1 The Hebrew word was used for various diseases affecting the skin—not necessarily leprosy; also in verses 3, 6, 7, 11 and 27.   ᵇ 5 That is, about 750 pounds (about 340 kilograms)   ᶜ 5 That is, about 150 pounds (about 70 kilograms)

A Servant's Deceit and Greed

2 KINGS 5:19–27

"Avarice is selfishness, expressed in hoarding what we don't need, refusing to share. Covetousness is selfishness expressed in desiring what other people have that we don't, or specifically desiring something that belongs to someone else. Greed is selfishness expressed in always wanting more. Someone defined enough as 'a little more than what you have.' "

—MAXIE DUNNAM,
KIMBERLY DUNNAM REISMAN,
Workbook on the Seven Deadly Sins

that there is no God in all the world except in Israel. Please accept now a gift from your servant."

¹⁶The prophet answered, "As surely as the LORD lives, whom I serve, I will not accept a thing." And even though Naaman urged him, he refused.

¹⁷"If you will not," said Naaman, "please let me, your servant, be given as much earth as a pair of mules can carry, for your servant will never again make burnt offerings and sacrifices to any other god but the LORD. ¹⁸But may the LORD forgive your servant for this one thing: When my master enters the temple of Rimmon to bow down and he is leaning on my arm and I bow there also—when I bow down in the temple of Rimmon, may the LORD forgive your servant for this."

¹⁹"Go in peace," Elisha said.

After Naaman had traveled some distance, ²⁰Gehazi, the servant of Elisha the man of God, said to himself, "My master was too easy on Naaman, this Aramean, by not accepting from him what he brought. As surely as the LORD lives, I will run after him and get something from him."

²¹So Gehazi hurried after Naaman. When Naaman saw him running toward him, he got down from the chariot to meet him. "Is everything all right?" he asked.

²²"Everything is all right," Gehazi answered. "My master sent me to say, 'Two young men from the company of the prophets have just come to me from the hill country of Ephraim. Please give them a talent[a] of silver and two sets of clothing.' "

²³"By all means, take two talents," said Naaman. He urged Gehazi to accept them, and then tied up the two talents of silver in two bags, with two sets of clothing. He gave them to two of his servants, and they carried them ahead of Gehazi. ²⁴When Gehazi came to the hill, he took the things from the servants and put them away in the house. He sent the men away and they left. ²⁵Then he went in and stood before his master Elisha.

"Where have you been, Gehazi?" Elisha asked.

"Your servant didn't go anywhere," Gehazi answered.

²⁶But Elisha said to him, "Was not my spirit with you when the man got down from his chariot to meet you? Is this the time to take money, or to accept clothes, olive groves, vineyards, flocks, herds, or menservants and maidservants? ²⁷Naaman's leprosy will cling to you and to your descendants forever." Then Gehazi went from Elisha's presence and he was leprous, as white as snow.

An Axhead Floats

6 The company of the prophets said to Elisha, "Look, the place where we meet with you is too small for us. ²Let us go to the Jordan, where each of us can get a pole; and let us build a place there for us to live."

And he said, "Go."

³Then one of them said, "Won't you please come with your servants?"

"I will," Elisha replied. ⁴And he went with them.

They went to the Jordan and began to cut down trees. ⁵As one of them was cutting down a tree, the iron axhead fell into the water. "Oh, my lord," he cried out, "it was borrowed!"

a 22 That is, about 75 pounds (about 34 kilograms)

⁶The man of God asked, "Where did it fall?" When he showed him the place, Elisha cut a stick and threw it there, and made the iron float. ⁷"Lift it out," he said. Then the man reached out his hand and took it.

Elisha Traps Blinded Arameans

⁸Now the king of Aram was at war with Israel. After conferring with his officers, he said, "I will set up my camp in such and such a place."

⁹The man of God sent word to the king of Israel: "Beware of passing that place, because the Arameans are going down there." ¹⁰So the king of Israel checked on the place indicated by the man of God. Time and again Elisha warned the king, so that he was on his guard in such places.

¹¹This enraged the king of Aram. He summoned his officers and demanded of them, "Will you not tell me which of us is on the side of the king of Israel?"

¹²"None of us, my lord the king," said one of his officers, "but Elisha, the prophet who is in Israel, tells the king of Israel the very words you speak in your bedroom."

¹³"Go, find out where he is," the king ordered, "so I can send men and capture him." The report came back: "He is in Dothan." ¹⁴Then he sent horses and chariots and a strong force there. They went by night and surrounded the city.

¹⁵When the servant of the man of God got up and went out early the next morning, an army with horses and chariots had surrounded the city. "Oh, my lord, what shall we do?" the servant asked.

¹⁶"Don't be afraid," the prophet answered. "Those who are with us are more than those who are with them."

¹⁷And Elisha prayed, "O Lord, open his eyes so he may see." Then the Lord opened the servant's eyes, and he looked and saw the hills full of horses and chariots of fire all around Elisha.

¹⁸As the enemy came down toward him, Elisha prayed to the Lord, "Strike these people with blindness." So he struck them with blindness, as Elisha had asked.

¹⁹Elisha told them, "This is not the road and this is not the city. Follow me, and I will lead you to the man you are looking for." And he led them to Samaria.

²⁰After they entered the city, Elisha said, "Lord, open the eyes of these men so they can see." Then the Lord opened their eyes and they looked, and there they were, inside Samaria.

²¹When the king of Israel saw them, he asked Elisha, "Shall I kill them, my father? Shall I kill them?"

²²"Do not kill them," he answered. "Would you kill men you have captured with your own sword or bow? Set food and water before them so that they may eat and drink and then go back to their master." ²³So he prepared a great feast for them, and after they had finished eating and drinking, he sent them away, and they returned to their master. So the bands from Aram stopped raiding Israel's territory.

Famine in Besieged Samaria

²⁴Some time later, Ben-Hadad king of Aram mobilized his entire army and marched up and laid siege to Samaria. ²⁵There was a great famine in the city; the siege lasted so

Invisible Support

2 KINGS 6:11–17

Elisha is surrounded by enemy warriors, but he knows that "those who are with us are more than those who are with them." Imagine that you are Elisha's attendant, spiritually blind to the presence of God's invisible aid. Imagine that your eyes are opened to see that "the hills [are] full of horses and chariots of fire." Transpose this vision into your own life. Bring to mind a situation where you may feel "surrounded" by opposing or unhelpful forces. Ask God to oppose the negative powers at work in your situation. Through images, feelings or words, confirm to your mind and heart the reality of God's presence. Repeat: "There are more with me than I realize."

See Meeting God in Scripture

Don't Just Sit There!

2 KINGS 7:3–7

These four lepers are sure they are all alone and headed for certain death. No one wants these outcasts. They are faced with famine in the city and the Aramean army outside the city. They decide they might as well get up and do something—and they find that God has already acted, and their lives are spared.

Perhaps there was a time in your life when you felt you were all alone and destined to die—emotionally, spiritually or physically. In what form did rescue come? How do you see the hand of God in your predicament? Is there a situation in your life where are you just "sitting around," waiting for the worst to happen? What do you need to get up and do while trusting in God's help?

long that a donkey's head sold for eighty shekels[a] of silver, and a quarter of a cab[b] of seed pods[c] for five shekels.[d]

²⁶As the king of Israel was passing by on the wall, a woman cried to him, "Help me, my lord the king!"

²⁷The king replied, "If the LORD does not help you, where can I get help for you? From the threshing floor? From the winepress?" ²⁸Then he asked her, "What's the matter?"

She answered, "This woman said to me, 'Give up your son so we may eat him today, and tomorrow we'll eat my son.' ²⁹So we cooked my son and ate him. The next day I said to her, 'Give up your son so we may eat him,' but she had hidden him."

³⁰When the king heard the woman's words, he tore his robes. As he went along the wall, the people looked, and there, underneath, he had sackcloth on his body. ³¹He said, "May God deal with me, be it ever so severely, if the head of Elisha son of Shaphat remains on his shoulders today!"

³²Now Elisha was sitting in his house, and the elders were sitting with him. The king sent a messenger ahead, but before he arrived, Elisha said to the elders, "Don't you see how this murderer is sending someone to cut off my head? Look, when the messenger comes, shut the door and hold it shut against him. Is not the sound of his master's footsteps behind him?"

³³While he was still talking to them, the messenger came down to him. And ⌊the king⌋ said, "This disaster is from the LORD. Why should I wait for the LORD any longer?"

7 Elisha said, "Hear the word of the LORD. This is what the LORD says: About this time tomorrow, a seah[e] of flour will sell for a shekel[f] and two seahs[g] of barley for a shekel at the gate of Samaria."

²The officer on whose arm the king was leaning said to the man of God, "Look, even if the LORD should open the floodgates of the heavens, could this happen?"

"You will see it with your own eyes," answered Elisha, "but you will not eat any of it!"

The Siege Lifted

³Now there were four men with leprosy[h] at the entrance of the city gate. They said to each other, "Why stay here until we die? ⁴If we say, 'We'll go into the city'—the famine is there, and we will die. And if we stay here, we will die. So let's go over to the camp of the Arameans and surrender. If they spare us, we live; if they kill us, then we die."

⁵At dusk they got up and went to the camp of the Arameans. When they reached the edge of the camp, not a man was there, ⁶for the Lord had caused the Arameans to hear the sound of chariots and horses and a great army, so that they said to one another, "Look, the king of Israel has hired the Hittite and Egyptian kings to attack us!" ⁷So they got up and fled in the dusk and abandoned their tents and their horses and donkeys. They left the camp as it was and ran for their lives.

⁸The men who had leprosy reached the edge of the camp

---

a 25 That is, about 2 pounds (about 1 kilogram)   *b 25* That is, probably about 1/2 pint (about 0.3 liter)   *c 25* Or *of dove's dung*   *d 25* That is, about 2 ounces (about 55 grams)   *e 1* That is, probably about 7 quarts (about 7.3 liters); also in verses 16 and 18   *f 1* That is, about 2/5 ounce (about 11 grams); also in verses 16 and 18   *g 1* That is, probably about 13 quarts (about 15 liters); also in verses 16 and 18   *h 3* The Hebrew word is used for various diseases affecting the skin—not necessarily leprosy; also in verse 8.

and entered one of the tents. They ate and drank, and carried away silver, gold and clothes, and went off and hid them. They returned and entered another tent and took some things from it and hid them also.

⁹Then they said to each other, "We're not doing right. This is a day of good news and we are keeping it to ourselves. If we wait until daylight, punishment will overtake us. Let's go at once and report this to the royal palace."

¹⁰So they went and called out to the city gatekeepers and told them, "We went into the Aramean camp and not a man was there—not a sound of anyone—only tethered horses and donkeys, and the tents left just as they were." ¹¹The gatekeepers shouted the news, and it was reported within the palace.

¹²The king got up in the night and said to his officers, "I will tell you what the Arameans have done to us. They know we are starving; so they have left the camp to hide in the countryside, thinking, 'They will surely come out, and then we will take them alive and get into the city.' "

¹³One of his officers answered, "Have some men take five of the horses that are left in the city. Their plight will be like that of all the Israelites left here—yes, they will only be like all these Israelites who are doomed. So let us send them to find out what happened."

¹⁴So they selected two chariots with their horses, and the king sent them after the Aramean army. He commanded the drivers, "Go and find out what has happened." ¹⁵They followed them as far as the Jordan, and they found the whole road strewn with the clothing and equipment the Arameans had thrown away in their headlong flight. So the messengers returned and reported to the king. ¹⁶Then the people went out and plundered the camp of the Arameans. So a seah of flour sold for a shekel, and two seahs of barley sold for a shekel, as the LORD had said.

¹⁷Now the king had put the officer on whose arm he leaned in charge of the gate, and the people trampled him in the gateway, and he died, just as the man of God had foretold when the king came down to his house. ¹⁸It happened as the man of God had said to the king: "About this time tomorrow, a seah of flour will sell for a shekel and two seahs of barley for a shekel at the gate of Samaria."

¹⁹The officer had said to the man of God, "Look, even if the LORD should open the floodgates of the heavens, could this happen?" The man of God had replied, "You will see it with your own eyes, but you will not eat any of it!" ²⁰And that is exactly what happened to him, for the people trampled him in the gateway, and he died.

The Shunammite's Land Restored

8 Now Elisha had said to the woman whose son he had restored to life, "Go away with your family and stay for a while wherever you can, because the LORD has decreed a famine in the land that will last seven years." ²The woman proceeded to do as the man of God said. She and her family went away and stayed in the land of the Philistines seven years.

³At the end of the seven years she came back from the land of the Philistines and went to the king to beg for her house and land. ⁴The king was talking to Gehazi, the servant of the man of God, and had said, "Tell me about all the

A Simple Act of Kindness

2 KINGS 8:1–6

This story reflects Elisha's kindness and concern for the well-being of the widow. His ministry to her is both public and private. Read through the story, imagining the feelings and thoughts of the characters. How might it feel to be so dependent on someone else? What does Elisha's ministry teach you about God? How does the widow's need and your need reflect the needs of every human being? How do Elisha's actions reflect God's concern for others? Does this time of reflection suggest any specific actions you might take to express God's concern to the people around you?

See Meeting God in Service

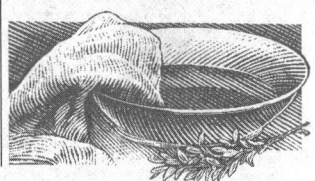

Weeping for Israel

2 KINGS 8:11–12

The prophet weeps in sorrow over the destruction Hazael will visit upon Israel. Tears can be a burden or a release, an act of joy or an act of sorrow. When someone cries in our presence, they are sharing an expression of deepest emotion. Tears lovingly received can be a blessing from God. Remember the last time you shared tears with someone. What brings tears of joy and what brings tears of sorrow? How have tears expressed your deepest emotions? How do you respond to the tears of others? When have you been in Elisha's position—knowing the necessity of harsh actions, yet sorrowful about the pain they may cause?

great things Elisha has done." ⁵Just as Gehazi was telling the king how Elisha had restored the dead to life, the woman whose son Elisha had brought back to life came to beg the king for her house and land.

Gehazi said, "This is the woman, my lord the king, and this is her son whom Elisha restored to life." ⁶The king asked the woman about it, and she told him.

Then he assigned an official to her case and said to him, "Give back everything that belonged to her, including all the income from her land from the day she left the country until now."

Hazael Murders Ben-Hadad

⁷Elisha went to Damascus, and Ben-Hadad king of Aram was ill. When the king was told, "The man of God has come all the way up here," ⁸he said to Hazael, "Take a gift with you and go to meet the man of God. Consult the LORD through him; ask him, 'Will I recover from this illness?' "

⁹Hazael went to meet Elisha, taking with him as a gift forty camel-loads of all the finest wares of Damascus. He went in and stood before him, and said, "Your son Ben-Hadad king of Aram has sent me to ask, 'Will I recover from this illness?' "

¹⁰Elisha answered, "Go and say to him, 'You will certainly recover'; but*ᵃ* the LORD has revealed to me that he will in fact die." ¹¹He stared at him with a fixed gaze until Hazael felt ashamed. Then the man of God began to weep.

¹²"Why is my lord weeping?" asked Hazael.

"Because I know the harm you will do to the Israelites," he answered. "You will set fire to their fortified places, kill their young men with the sword, dash their little children to the ground, and rip open their pregnant women."

¹³Hazael said, "How could your servant, a mere dog, accomplish such a feat?"

"The LORD has shown me that you will become king of Aram," answered Elisha.

¹⁴Then Hazael left Elisha and returned to his master. When Ben-Hadad asked, "What did Elisha say to you?" Hazael replied, "He told me that you would certainly recover." ¹⁵But the next day he took a thick cloth, soaked it in water and spread it over the king's face, so that he died. Then Hazael succeeded him as king.

Jehoram King of Judah

¹⁶In the fifth year of Joram son of Ahab king of Israel, when Jehoshaphat was king of Judah, Jehoram son of Jehoshaphat began his reign as king of Judah. ¹⁷He was thirty-two years old when he became king, and he reigned in Jerusalem eight years. ¹⁸He walked in the ways of the kings of Israel, as the house of Ahab had done, for he married a daughter of Ahab. He did evil in the eyes of the LORD. ¹⁹Nevertheless, for the sake of his servant David, the LORD was not willing to destroy Judah. He had promised to maintain a lamp for David and his descendants forever.

²⁰In the time of Jehoram, Edom rebelled against Judah and set up its own king. ²¹So Jehoram*ᵇ* went to Zair with all his chariots. The Edomites surrounded him and his chariot commanders, but he rose up and broke through by night;

ᵃ 10 The Hebrew may also be read *Go and say, 'You will certainly not recover,' for.* *ᵇ 21* Hebrew *Joram*, a variant of *Jehoram*; also in verses 23 and 24

his army, however, fled back home. ²²To this day Edom has been in rebellion against Judah. Libnah revolted at the same time.

²³As for the other events of Jehoram's reign, and all he did, are they not written in the book of the annals of the kings of Judah? ²⁴Jehoram rested with his fathers and was buried with them in the City of David. And Ahaziah his son succeeded him as king.

Ahaziah King of Judah

²⁵In the twelfth year of Joram son of Ahab king of Israel, Ahaziah son of Jehoram king of Judah began to reign. ²⁶Ahaziah was twenty-two years old when he became king, and he reigned in Jerusalem one year. His mother's name was Athaliah, a granddaughter of Omri king of Israel. ²⁷He walked in the ways of the house of Ahab and did evil in the eyes of the LORD, as the house of Ahab had done, for he was related by marriage to Ahab's family.

²⁸Ahaziah went with Joram son of Ahab to war against Hazael king of Aram at Ramoth Gilead. The Arameans wounded Joram; ²⁹so King Joram returned to Jezreel to recover from the wounds the Arameans had inflicted on him at Ramoth[a] in his battle with Hazael king of Aram.

Then Ahaziah son of Jehoram king of Judah went down to Jezreel to see Joram son of Ahab, because he had been wounded.

Jehu Anointed King of Israel

9 The prophet Elisha summoned a man from the company of the prophets and said to him, "Tuck your cloak into your belt, take this flask of oil with you and go to Ramoth Gilead. ²When you get there, look for Jehu son of Jehoshaphat, the son of Nimshi. Go to him, get him away from his companions and take him into an inner room. ³Then take the flask and pour the oil on his head and declare, 'This is what the LORD says: I anoint you king over Israel.' Then open the door and run; don't delay!"

⁴So the young man, the prophet, went to Ramoth Gilead. ⁵When he arrived, he found the army officers sitting together. "I have a message for you, commander," he said.

"For which of us?" asked Jehu.

"For you, commander," he replied.

⁶Jehu got up and went into the house. Then the prophet poured the oil on Jehu's head and declared, "This is what the LORD, the God of Israel, says: 'I anoint you king over the LORD's people Israel. ⁷You are to destroy the house of Ahab your master, and I will avenge the blood of my servants the prophets and the blood of all the LORD's servants shed by Jezebel. ⁸The whole house of Ahab will perish. I will cut off from Ahab every last male in Israel—slave or free. ⁹I will make the house of Ahab like the house of Jeroboam son of Nebat and like the house of Baasha son of Ahijah. ¹⁰As for Jezebel, dogs will devour her on the plot of ground at Jezreel, and no one will bury her.' " Then he opened the door and ran.

¹¹When Jehu went out to his fellow officers, one of them asked him, "Is everything all right? Why did this madman come to you?"

Anointed for Service

2 KINGS 9:1–3

Anointing symbolizes divine empowerment to render specific service. God raised up and anointed servants. Sometimes they were obscure and unknown before their call, sometimes they were not even from the "chosen people."

Picture in your mind the great leaders of the past century—people through whom God has judged, restored or healed others. Who will be raised up in our own day of crisis? Spend time praying for them, whomever they might be, and thanking God for their anointed service. What other situations are in need of God-inspired leadership? Spend time praying for such leaders in situations (global or local) that are close to your heart.

See Meeting God in Prayer

Jehu's Zeal

2 KINGS 9:20

Jehu "drives like a madman" as he is used as an instrument of justice for God. He is a passionate reformer, set apart to clean up the spiritual mess with the cry, "See my zeal for the LORD" (10:16).

What are the passions of your heart? What people or issues do you care about passionately? Make a list of the roles you assume every day—husband, wife, friend, parent and so forth. What passions do you express in each role? How can your passions be consecrated to the Lord? Is there a special ministry or work that may be calling you to new or deeper consecration? Ask God to redeem and sanctify your passions.

See Meeting God in Everyday Life

"You know the man and the sort of things he says," Jehu replied.

¹²"That's not true!" they said. "Tell us."

Jehu said, "Here is what he told me: 'This is what the LORD says: I anoint you king over Israel.'"

¹³They hurried and took their cloaks and spread them under him on the bare steps. Then they blew the trumpet and shouted, "Jehu is king!"

Jehu Kills Joram and Ahaziah

¹⁴So Jehu son of Jehoshaphat, the son of Nimshi, conspired against Joram. (Now Joram and all Israel had been defending Ramoth Gilead against Hazael king of Aram, ¹⁵but King Joram[a] had returned to Jezreel to recover from the wounds the Arameans had inflicted on him in the battle with Hazael king of Aram.) Jehu said, "If this is the way you feel, don't let anyone slip out of the city to go and tell the news in Jezreel." ¹⁶Then he got into his chariot and rode to Jezreel, because Joram was resting there and Ahaziah king of Judah had gone down to see him.

¹⁷When the lookout standing on the tower in Jezreel saw Jehu's troops approaching, he called out, "I see some troops coming."

"Get a horseman," Joram ordered. "Send him to meet them and ask, 'Do you come in peace?'"

¹⁸The horseman rode off to meet Jehu and said, "This is what the king says: 'Do you come in peace?'"

"What do you have to do with peace?" Jehu replied. "Fall in behind me."

The lookout reported, "The messenger has reached them, but he isn't coming back."

¹⁹So the king sent out a second horseman. When he came to them he said, "This is what the king says: 'Do you come in peace?'"

Jehu replied, "What do you have to do with peace? Fall in behind me."

²⁰The lookout reported, "He has reached them, but he isn't coming back either. The driving is like that of Jehu son of Nimshi—he drives like a madman."

²¹"Hitch up my chariot," Joram ordered. And when it was hitched up, Joram king of Israel and Ahaziah king of Judah rode out, each in his own chariot, to meet Jehu. They met him at the plot of ground that had belonged to Naboth the Jezreelite. ²²When Joram saw Jehu he asked, "Have you come in peace, Jehu?"

"How can there be peace," Jehu replied, "as long as all the idolatry and witchcraft of your mother Jezebel abound?"

²³Joram turned about and fled, calling out to Ahaziah, "Treachery, Ahaziah!"

²⁴Then Jehu drew his bow and shot Joram between the shoulders. The arrow pierced his heart and he slumped down in his chariot. ²⁵Jehu said to Bidkar, his chariot officer, "Pick him up and throw him on the field that belonged to Naboth the Jezreelite. Remember how you and I were riding together in chariots behind Ahab his father when the LORD made this prophecy about him: ²⁶'Yesterday I saw the blood of Naboth and the blood of his sons, declares the LORD, and I will surely make you pay for it on this plot of

a 15 Hebrew *Jehoram,* a variant of *Joram;* also in verses 17 and 21–24

ground, declares the LORD.'[a] Now then, pick him up and throw him on that plot, in accordance with the word of the LORD."

[27]When Ahaziah king of Judah saw what had happened, he fled up the road to Beth Haggan.[b] Jehu chased him, shouting, "Kill him too!" They wounded him in his chariot on the way up to Gur near Ibleam, but he escaped to Megiddo and died there. [28]His servants took him by chariot to Jerusalem and buried him with his fathers in his tomb in the City of David. [29](In the eleventh year of Joram son of Ahab, Ahaziah had become king of Judah.)

Jezebel Killed

[30]Then Jehu went to Jezreel. When Jezebel heard about it, she painted her eyes, arranged her hair and looked out of a window. [31]As Jehu entered the gate, she asked, "Have you come in peace, Zimri, you murderer of your master?"[c]

[32]He looked up at the window and called out, "Who is on my side? Who?" Two or three eunuchs looked down at him. [33]"Throw her down!" Jehu said. So they threw her down, and some of her blood spattered the wall and the horses as they trampled her underfoot.

[34]Jehu went in and ate and drank. "Take care of that cursed woman," he said, "and bury her, for she was a king's daughter." [35]But when they went out to bury her, they found nothing except her skull, her feet and her hands. [36]They went back and told Jehu, who said, "This is the word of the LORD that he spoke through his servant Elijah the Tishbite: On the plot of ground at Jezreel dogs will devour Jezebel's flesh.[d] [37]Jezebel's body will be like refuse on the ground in the plot at Jezreel, so that no one will be able to say, 'This is Jezebel.'"

Ahab's Family Killed

10 Now there were in Samaria seventy sons of the house of Ahab. So Jehu wrote letters and sent them to Samaria: to the officials of Jezreel,[e] to the elders and to the guardians of Ahab's children. He said, [2]"As soon as this letter reaches you, since your master's sons are with you and you have chariots and horses, a fortified city and weapons, [3]choose the best and most worthy of your master's sons and set him on his father's throne. Then fight for your master's house."

[4]But they were terrified and said, "If two kings could not resist him, how can we?"

[5]So the palace administrator, the city governor, the elders and the guardians sent this message to Jehu: "We are your servants and we will do anything you say. We will not appoint anyone as king; you do whatever you think best."

[6]Then Jehu wrote them a second letter, saying, "If you are on my side and will obey me, take the heads of your master's sons and come to me in Jezreel by this time tomorrow."

Now the royal princes, seventy of them, were with the leading men of the city, who were rearing them. [7]When the letter arrived, these men took the princes and slaughtered all seventy of them. They put their heads in baskets and

Human Brutality

2 KINGS 9:27—10:9

At times the violence and brutality detailed in Biblical accounts can seem overwhelming and puzzling; we wonder how a loving God can allow such suffering. Yet violence and death are the consequences of human evil. How do you think God feels about such violence? How are people today like the people in this passage? What is your prayer for those who suffer violence? Cultivate the habit of praying—as you listen to the news broadcast or read the newspaper—for all who suffer brutality at the hands of others.

See Meeting God in Service

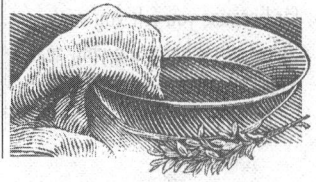

---

[a]26 See 1 Kings 21:19.   [b]27 Or *fled by way of the garden house*   [c]31 Or *"Did Zimri have peace, who murdered his master?"*   [d]36 See 1 Kings 21:23.
[e]1 Hebrew; some Septuagint manuscripts and Vulgate *of the city*

Going Too Far

2 KINGS 10:9–11

Jehu leaves no survivors, destroying Ahab's family and supporters in a bloodbath. Elijah's prophecy is fulfilled, but Jehu goes too far. He would later be punished for his excessive brutality. Sometimes personal ambition, zeal, power and cruelty become mixed with holy causes. A genuine calling to do good can become a destructive weapon if not wielded in genuine love. Where do you think people of faith go too far in a misguided zeal, even though the cause is just? When have you, or those you know, been injured by overzealous people? When have you ever gone too far because you felt you were right? What harm did your zeal cause? Is there a way, now, to make amends?

sent them to Jehu in Jezreel. ⁸When the messenger arrived, he told Jehu, "They have brought the heads of the princes."

Then Jehu ordered, "Put them in two piles at the entrance of the city gate until morning."

⁹The next morning Jehu went out. He stood before all the people and said, "You are innocent. It was I who conspired against my master and killed him, but who killed all these? ¹⁰Know then, that not a word the Lord has spoken against the house of Ahab will fail. The Lord has done what he promised through his servant Elijah." ¹¹So Jehu killed everyone in Jezreel who remained of the house of Ahab, as well as all his chief men, his close friends and his priests, leaving him no survivor.

¹²Jehu then set out and went toward Samaria. At Beth Eked of the Shepherds, ¹³he met some relatives of Ahaziah king of Judah and asked, "Who are you?"

They said, "We are relatives of Ahaziah, and we have come down to greet the families of the king and of the queen mother."

¹⁴"Take them alive!" he ordered. So they took them alive and slaughtered them by the well of Beth Eked—forty-two men. He left no survivor.

¹⁵After he left there, he came upon Jehonadab son of Recab, who was on his way to meet him. Jehu greeted him and said, "Are you in accord with me, as I am with you?"

"I am," Jehonadab answered.

"If so," said Jehu, "give me your hand." So he did, and Jehu helped him up into the chariot. ¹⁶Jehu said, "Come with me and see my zeal for the Lord." Then he had him ride along in his chariot.

¹⁷When Jehu came to Samaria, he killed all who were left there of Ahab's family; he destroyed them, according to the word of the Lord spoken to Elijah.

Ministers of Baal Killed

¹⁸Then Jehu brought all the people together and said to them, "Ahab served Baal a little; Jehu will serve him much. ¹⁹Now summon all the prophets of Baal, all his ministers and all his priests. See that no one is missing, because I am going to hold a great sacrifice for Baal. Anyone who fails to come will no longer live." But Jehu was acting deceptively in order to destroy the ministers of Baal.

²⁰Jehu said, "Call an assembly in honor of Baal." So they proclaimed it. ²¹Then he sent word throughout Israel, and all the ministers of Baal came; not one stayed away. They crowded into the temple of Baal until it was full from one end to the other. ²²And Jehu said to the keeper of the wardrobe, "Bring robes for all the ministers of Baal." So he brought out robes for them.

²³Then Jehu and Jehonadab son of Recab went into the temple of Baal. Jehu said to the ministers of Baal, "Look around and see that no servants of the Lord are here with you—only ministers of Baal." ²⁴So they went in to make sacrifices and burnt offerings. Now Jehu had posted eighty men outside with this warning: "If one of you lets any of the men I am placing in your hands escape, it will be your life for his life."

²⁵As soon as Jehu had finished making the burnt offering, he ordered the guards and officers: "Go in and kill them; let no one escape." So they cut them down with the sword.

The guards and officers threw the bodies out and then entered the inner shrine of the temple of Baal. 26They brought the sacred stone out of the temple of Baal and burned it. 27They demolished the sacred stone of Baal and tore down the temple of Baal, and people have used it for a latrine to this day.

28So Jehu destroyed Baal worship in Israel. 29However, he did not turn away from the sins of Jeroboam son of Nebat, which he had caused Israel to commit—the worship of the golden calves at Bethel and Dan.

30The LORD said to Jehu, "Because you have done well in accomplishing what is right in my eyes and have done to the house of Ahab all I had in mind to do, your descendants will sit on the throne of Israel to the fourth generation." 31Yet Jehu was not careful to keep the law of the LORD, the God of Israel, with all his heart. He did not turn away from the sins of Jeroboam, which he had caused Israel to commit.

32In those days the LORD began to reduce the size of Israel. Hazael overpowered the Israelites throughout their territory 33east of the Jordan in all the land of Gilead (the region of Gad, Reuben and Manasseh), from Aroer by the Arnon Gorge through Gilead to Bashan.

34As for the other events of Jehu's reign, all he did, and all his achievements, are they not written in the book of the annals of the kings of Israel?

35Jehu rested with his fathers and was buried in Samaria. And Jehoahaz his son succeeded him as king. 36The time that Jehu reigned over Israel in Samaria was twenty-eight years.

Athaliah and Joash

11 When Athaliah the mother of Ahaziah saw that her son was dead, she proceeded to destroy the whole royal family. 2But Jehosheba, the daughter of King Jehoram*a* and sister of Ahaziah, took Joash son of Ahaziah and stole him away from among the royal princes, who were about to be murdered. She put him and his nurse in a bedroom to hide him from Athaliah; so he was not killed. 3He remained hidden with his nurse at the temple of the LORD for six years while Athaliah ruled the land.

4In the seventh year Jehoiada sent for the commanders of units of a hundred, the Carites and the guards and had them brought to him at the temple of the LORD. He made a covenant with them and put them under oath at the temple of the LORD. Then he showed them the king's son. 5He commanded them, saying, "This is what you are to do: You who are in the three companies that are going on duty on the Sabbath—a third of you guarding the royal palace, 6a third at the Sur Gate, and a third at the gate behind the guard, who take turns guarding the temple— 7and you who are in the other two companies that normally go off Sabbath duty are all to guard the temple for the king. 8Station yourselves around the king, each man with his weapon in his hand. Anyone who approaches your ranks*b* must be put to death. Stay close to the king wherever he goes."

9The commanders of units of a hundred did just as Jehoiada the priest ordered. Each one took his men—those who were going on duty on the Sabbath and those who

Joash, a Special Baby

2 KINGS 11:1–11

The young king, hidden for six years, is finally crowned. He is another special child rescued from death, as were Moses, Isaac and Jesus. Reread the story, putting yourself in Jehosheba's shoes. Hear the call of God to save the infant prince. Experience the tension of stealing Joash and his nurse away to the hidden bedroom and the despair of knowing you cannot save all your nephews. Or put on Joash's shoes; imagine six years of hiding and fear. With relief, hear the faithful few calling you to serve God's ways; feel the excitement of your crowning. Reflect on ways in which you might hear God's call to be a Jehosheba preserving what is vulnerable, or a Joash coming out of hiding to do good.

See Meeting God in Scripture

Jehoiada, a Good Teacher

2 KINGS 11:17—12:3

Good teachers have a lasting influence on our lives. We read in this passage how the priest Jehoiada instructs both the people and the king in the ways of the Lord. Review the passage. How does Jehoiada's correct instruction lead the people toward spiritual renewal? What impact did this one man have on the religious life of the people?

Make a list of the people who have been inspirational teachers in your life. In what ways did their teaching reflect spirituality, wholeness and maturity? In what ways do you want to be like them? How can you mentor others as you have been mentored? Take time to call or write your teachers and mentors, thanking them for their inspiration.

See *Meeting God in Community*

were going off duty—and came to Jehoiada the priest. [10]Then he gave the commanders the spears and shields that had belonged to King David and that were in the temple of the LORD. [11]The guards, each with his weapon in his hand, stationed themselves around the king—near the altar and the temple, from the south side to the north side of the temple.

[12]Jehoiada brought out the king's son and put the crown on him; he presented him with a copy of the covenant and proclaimed him king. They anointed him, and the people clapped their hands and shouted, "Long live the king!"

[13]When Athaliah heard the noise made by the guards and the people, she went to the people at the temple of the LORD. [14]She looked and there was the king, standing by the pillar, as the custom was. The officers and the trumpeters were beside the king, and all the people of the land were rejoicing and blowing trumpets. Then Athaliah tore her robes and called out, "Treason! Treason!"

[15]Jehoiada the priest ordered the commanders of units of a hundred, who were in charge of the troops: "Bring her out between the ranks[a] and put to the sword anyone who follows her." For the priest had said, "She must not be put to death in the temple of the LORD." [16]So they seized her as she reached the place where the horses enter the palace grounds, and there she was put to death.

[17]Jehoiada then made a covenant between the LORD and the king and people that they would be the LORD's people. He also made a covenant between the king and the people. [18]All the people of the land went to the temple of Baal and tore it down. They smashed the altars and idols to pieces and killed Mattan the priest of Baal in front of the altars.

Then Jehoiada the priest posted guards at the temple of the LORD. [19]He took with him the commanders of hundreds, the Carites, the guards and all the people of the land, and together they brought the king down from the temple of the LORD and went into the palace, entering by way of the gate of the guards. The king then took his place on the royal throne, [20]and all the people of the land rejoiced. And the city was quiet, because Athaliah had been slain with the sword at the palace.

[21]Joash[b] was seven years old when he began to reign.

Joash Repairs the Temple

12 In the seventh year of Jehu, Joash[c] became king, and he reigned in Jerusalem forty years. His mother's name was Zibiah; she was from Beersheba. [2]Joash did what was right in the eyes of the LORD all the years Jehoiada the priest instructed him. [3]The high places, however, were not removed; the people continued to offer sacrifices and burn incense there.

[4]Joash said to the priests, "Collect all the money that is brought as sacred offerings to the temple of the LORD—the money collected in the census, the money received from personal vows and the money brought voluntarily to the temple. [5]Let every priest receive the money from one of the treasurers, and let it be used to repair whatever damage is found in the temple."

[6]But by the twenty-third year of King Joash the priests

---

[a] 15 Or *out from the precincts*   [b] 21 Hebrew *Jehoash,* a variant of *Joash*
[c] 1 Hebrew *Jehoash,* a variant of *Joash*; also in verses 2, 4, 6, 7 and 18

still had not repaired the temple. [7]Therefore King Joash summoned Jehoiada the priest and the other priests and asked them, "Why aren't you repairing the damage done to the temple? Take no more money from your treasurers, but hand it over for repairing the temple." [8]The priests agreed that they would not collect any more money from the people and that they would not repair the temple themselves.

[9]Jehoiada the priest took a chest and bored a hole in its lid. He placed it beside the altar, on the right side as one enters the temple of the LORD. The priests who guarded the entrance put into the chest all the money that was brought to the temple of the LORD. [10]Whenever they saw that there was a large amount of money in the chest, the royal secretary and the high priest came, counted the money that had been brought into the temple of the LORD and put it into bags. [11]When the amount had been determined, they gave the money to the men appointed to supervise the work on the temple. With it they paid those who worked on the temple of the LORD—the carpenters and builders, [12]the masons and stonecutters. They purchased timber and dressed stone for the repair of the temple of the LORD, and met all the other expenses of restoring the temple.

[13]The money brought into the temple was not spent for making silver basins, wick trimmers, sprinkling bowls, trumpets or any other articles of gold or silver for the temple of the LORD; [14]it was paid to the workmen, who used it to repair the temple. [15]They did not require an accounting from those to whom they gave the money to pay the workers, because they acted with complete honesty. [16]The money from the guilt offerings and sin offerings was not brought into the temple of the LORD; it belonged to the priests.

[17]About this time Hazael king of Aram went up and attacked Gath and captured it. Then he turned to attack Jerusalem. [18]But Joash king of Judah took all the sacred objects dedicated by his fathers—Jehoshaphat, Jehoram and Ahaziah, the kings of Judah—and the gifts he himself had dedicated and all the gold found in the treasuries of the temple of the LORD and of the royal palace, and he sent them to Hazael king of Aram, who then withdrew from Jerusalem.

[19]As for the other events of the reign of Joash, and all he did, are they not written in the book of the annals of the kings of Judah? [20]His officials conspired against him and assassinated him at Beth Millo, on the road down to Silla. [21]The officials who murdered him were Jozabad son of Shimeath and Jehozabad son of Shomer. He died and was buried with his fathers in the City of David. And Amaziah his son succeeded him as king.

Jehoahaz King of Israel

13 In the twenty-third year of Joash son of Ahaziah king of Judah, Jehoahaz son of Jehu became king of Israel in Samaria, and he reigned seventeen years. [2]He did evil in the eyes of the LORD by following the sins of Jeroboam son of Nebat, which he had caused Israel to commit, and he did not turn away from them. [3]So the LORD's anger burned against Israel, and for a long time he kept them under the power of Hazael king of Aram and Ben-Hadad his son.

Praying in a Crisis

2 KINGS 13:1–5

Jehoahaz is introduced by the refrain used for most of the kings of Israel and Judah: "He did evil in the eyes of the LORD." But during his reign, when King Hazael of Aram threatens, Jehoahaz calls on the Lord for help and is answered with "a deliverer," probably an Assyrian king who draws Hazael's attention away from Israel for the moment. How often have you gone along, doing your own thing, and then in a troubled moment called on the Lord to save you? Remember the times when you have been helped in such a way or have been given another chance to live more fully for God. Relive one such experience in your mind right now. How did you grow from that experience? How did you resolve to change your life? What lasting effects has it had?

See Meeting God in Everyday Life

Settling for Halfhearted Faith

2 KINGS 13:15–19

"No one is ever really at ease in facing what we call 'life' and 'death' without religious faith. The trouble with many people today is that they have not found a God big enough for modern needs. While their experience of life has grown in a score of directions, and their emotional horizons have been expanded to the point of bewilderment by world events and by scientific discoveries, their ideas of God have remained largely static."

—J. B. PHILLIPS,
Your God Is Too Small

⁴Then Jehoahaz sought the LORD's favor, and the LORD listened to him, for he saw how severely the king of Aram was oppressing Israel. ⁵The LORD provided a deliverer for Israel, and they escaped from the power of Aram. So the Israelites lived in their own homes as they had before. ⁶But they did not turn away from the sins of the house of Jeroboam, which he had caused Israel to commit; they continued in them. Also, the Asherah pole*ᵃ* remained standing in Samaria.

⁷Nothing had been left of the army of Jehoahaz except fifty horsemen, ten chariots and ten thousand foot soldiers, for the king of Aram had destroyed the rest and made them like the dust at threshing time.

⁸As for the other events of the reign of Jehoahaz, all he did and his achievements, are they not written in the book of the annals of the kings of Israel? ⁹Jehoahaz rested with his fathers and was buried in Samaria. And Jehoash*ᵇ* his son succeeded him as king.

Jehoash King of Israel

¹⁰In the thirty-seventh year of Joash king of Judah, Jehoash son of Jehoahaz became king of Israel in Samaria, and he reigned sixteen years. ¹¹He did evil in the eyes of the LORD and did not turn away from any of the sins of Jeroboam son of Nebat, which he had caused Israel to commit; he continued in them.

¹²As for the other events of the reign of Jehoash, all he did and his achievements, including his war against Amaziah king of Judah, are they not written in the book of the annals of the kings of Israel? ¹³Jehoash rested with his fathers, and Jeroboam succeeded him on the throne. Jehoash was buried in Samaria with the kings of Israel.

¹⁴Now Elisha was suffering from the illness from which he died. Jehoash king of Israel went down to see him and wept over him. "My father! My father!" he cried. "The chariots and horsemen of Israel!"

¹⁵Elisha said, "Get a bow and some arrows," and he did so. ¹⁶"Take the bow in your hands," he said to the king of Israel. When he had taken it, Elisha put his hands on the king's hands.

¹⁷"Open the east window," he said, and he opened it. "Shoot!" Elisha said, and he shot. "The LORD's arrow of victory, the arrow of victory over Aram!" Elisha declared. "You will completely destroy the Arameans at Aphek."

¹⁸Then he said, "Take the arrows," and the king took them. Elisha told him, "Strike the ground." He struck it three times and stopped. ¹⁹The man of God was angry with him and said, "You should have struck the ground five or six times; then you would have defeated Aram and completely destroyed it. But now you will defeat it only three times."

²⁰Elisha died and was buried.

Now Moabite raiders used to enter the country every spring. ²¹Once while some Israelites were burying a man, suddenly they saw a band of raiders; so they threw the man's body into Elisha's tomb. When the body touched Elisha's bones, the man came to life and stood up on his feet.

²²Hazael king of Aram oppressed Israel throughout the

ᵃ 6 That is, a symbol of the goddess Asherah; here and elsewhere in 2 Kings
ᵇ 9 Hebrew *Joash,* a variant of *Jehoash;* also in verses 12–14 and 25

reign of Jehoahaz. ²³But the LORD was gracious to them and had compassion and showed concern for them because of his covenant with Abraham, Isaac and Jacob. To this day he has been unwilling to destroy them or banish them from his presence.

²⁴Hazael king of Aram died, and Ben-Hadad his son succeeded him as king. ²⁵Then Jehoash son of Jehoahaz recaptured from Ben-Hadad son of Hazael the towns he had taken in battle from his father Jehoahaz. Three times Jehoash defeated him, and so he recovered the Israelite towns.

Amaziah King of Judah

14 In the second year of Jehoash[a] son of Jehoahaz king of Israel, Amaziah son of Joash king of Judah began to reign. ²He was twenty-five years old when he became king, and he reigned in Jerusalem twenty-nine years. His mother's name was Jehoaddin; she was from Jerusalem. ³He did what was right in the eyes of the LORD, but not as his father David had done. In everything he followed the example of his father Joash. ⁴The high places, however, were not removed; the people continued to offer sacrifices and burn incense there.

⁵After the kingdom was firmly in his grasp, he executed the officials who had murdered his father the king. ⁶Yet he did not put the sons of the assassins to death, in accordance with what is written in the Book of the Law of Moses where the LORD commanded: "Fathers shall not be put to death for their children, nor children put to death for their fathers; each is to die for his own sins."[b]

⁷He was the one who defeated ten thousand Edomites in the Valley of Salt and captured Sela in battle, calling it Joktheel, the name it has to this day.

⁸Then Amaziah sent messengers to Jehoash son of Jehoahaz, the son of Jehu, king of Israel, with the challenge: "Come, meet me face to face."

⁹But Jehoash king of Israel replied to Amaziah king of Judah: "A thistle in Lebanon sent a message to a cedar in Lebanon, 'Give your daughter to my son in marriage.' Then a wild beast in Lebanon came along and trampled the thistle underfoot. ¹⁰You have indeed defeated Edom and now you are arrogant. Glory in your victory, but stay at home! Why ask for trouble and cause your own downfall and that of Judah also?"

¹¹Amaziah, however, would not listen, so Jehoash king of Israel attacked. He and Amaziah king of Judah faced each other at Beth Shemesh in Judah. ¹²Judah was routed by Israel, and every man fled to his home. ¹³Jehoash king of Israel captured Amaziah king of Judah, the son of Joash, the son of Ahaziah, at Beth Shemesh. Then Jehoash went to Jerusalem and broke down the wall of Jerusalem from the Ephraim Gate to the Corner Gate—a section about six hundred feet long.[c] ¹⁴He took all the gold and silver and all the articles found in the temple of the LORD and in the treasuries of the royal palace. He also took hostages and returned to Samaria.

¹⁵As for the other events of the reign of Jehoash, what he did and his achievements, including his war against Amaziah king of Judah, are they not written in the book of the

A Parable of Warning

2 KINGS 14:9–11

We have all experienced times when a task seemed greater than our abilities. King Amaziah, flushed with pride in his victory over the Edomites, rejects King Jehoash's warning parable, overrates his own strength and is soundly defeated. Stepping out into life with hope, ambition and dreams is one thing; to overestimate our ability to produce is another. How often is it that you have not listened to your own inner warnings or those of others and you were soundly defeated? It has been said that defeat is not fatal, nor is it final. What does defeat do to your relationship with God? How do you respond to defeat or disappointment? What do you do to get back on your feet?

See Meeting God in Service

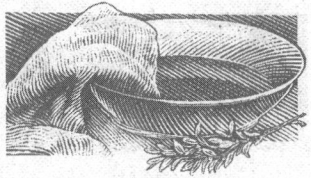

ᵃ 1 Hebrew *Joash*, a variant of *Jehoash*; also in verses 13, 23 and 27   ᵇ 6 Deut. 24:16   ᶜ 13 Hebrew *four hundred cubits* (about 180 meters)

Following the Ways of Others

2 KINGS 14:23–24

The sins of a dynasty live on in succeeding rulers. Likewise, those around us are affected by the way we treat them, live our lives and make decisions. We want the good we do today to be remembered tomorrow. Consider your own "dynasty" by gathering pictures of your own family, friends, relatives and children. How have you made a difference in their lives? Can you recall specific situations in which your influence became apparent? Holding each picture in turn, pray for those who are within your sphere of influence: "Loving God, in this world of evil, selfishness and suffering, let me live before you in such a way as to make a difference to this person. Amen."

See *Meeting God in Community*

annals of the kings of Israel? ¹⁶Jehoash rested with his fathers and was buried in Samaria with the kings of Israel. And Jeroboam his son succeeded him as king.

¹⁷Amaziah son of Joash king of Judah lived for fifteen years after the death of Jehoash son of Jehoahaz king of Israel. ¹⁸As for the other events of Amaziah's reign, are they not written in the book of the annals of the kings of Judah?

¹⁹They conspired against him in Jerusalem, and he fled to Lachish, but they sent men after him to Lachish and killed him there. ²⁰He was brought back by horse and was buried in Jerusalem with his fathers, in the City of David.

²¹Then all the people of Judah took Azariah,ᵃ who was sixteen years old, and made him king in place of his father Amaziah. ²²He was the one who rebuilt Elath and restored it to Judah after Amaziah rested with his fathers.

Jeroboam II King of Israel

²³In the fifteenth year of Amaziah son of Joash king of Judah, Jeroboam son of Jehoash king of Israel became king in Samaria, and he reigned forty-one years. ²⁴He did evil in the eyes of the LORD and did not turn away from any of the sins of Jeroboam son of Nebat, which he had caused Israel to commit. ²⁵He was the one who restored the boundaries of Israel from Leboᵇ Hamath to the Sea of the Arabah,ᶜ in accordance with the word of the LORD, the God of Israel, spoken through his servant Jonah son of Amittai, the prophet from Gath Hepher.

²⁶The LORD had seen how bitterly everyone in Israel, whether slave or free, was suffering; there was no one to help them. ²⁷And since the LORD had not said he would blot out the name of Israel from under heaven, he saved them by the hand of Jeroboam son of Jehoash.

²⁸As for the other events of Jeroboam's reign, all he did, and his military achievements, including how he recovered for Israel both Damascus and Hamath, which had belonged to Yaudi,ᵈ are they not written in the book of the annals of the kings of Israel? ²⁹Jeroboam rested with his fathers, the kings of Israel. And Zechariah his son succeeded him as king.

Azariah King of Judah

15 In the twenty-seventh year of Jeroboam king of Israel, Azariah son of Amaziah king of Judah began to reign. ²He was sixteen years old when he became king, and he reigned in Jerusalem fifty-two years. His mother's name was Jecoliah; she was from Jerusalem. ³He did what was right in the eyes of the LORD, just as his father Amaziah had done. ⁴The high places, however, were not removed; the people continued to offer sacrifices and burn incense there.

⁵The LORD afflicted the king with leprosyᵉ until the day he died, and he lived in a separate house.ᶠ Jotham the king's son had charge of the palace and governed the people of the land.

⁶As for the other events of Azariah's reign, and all he did, are they not written in the book of the annals of the kings of Judah? ⁷Azariah rested with his fathers and was buried

ᵃ 21 Also called *Uzziah*   ᵇ 25 Or *from the entrance to*   ᶜ 25 That is, the Dead Sea   ᵈ 28 Or *Judah*   ᵉ 5 The Hebrew word was used for various diseases affecting the skin—not necessarily leprosy.   ᶠ 5 Or *in a house where he was relieved of responsibility*

near them in the City of David. And Jotham his son succeeded him as king.

Zechariah King of Israel

⁸In the thirty-eighth year of Azariah king of Judah, Zechariah son of Jeroboam became king of Israel in Samaria, and he reigned six months. ⁹He did evil in the eyes of the LORD, as his fathers had done. He did not turn away from the sins of Jeroboam son of Nebat, which he had caused Israel to commit.

¹⁰Shallum son of Jabesh conspired against Zechariah. He attacked him in front of the people,ᵃ assassinated him and succeeded him as king. ¹¹The other events of Zechariah's reign are written in the book of the annals of the kings of Israel. ¹²So the word of the LORD spoken to Jehu was fulfilled: "Your descendants will sit on the throne of Israel to the fourth generation."ᵇ

Shallum King of Israel

¹³Shallum son of Jabesh became king in the thirty-ninth year of Uzziah king of Judah, and he reigned in Samaria one month. ¹⁴Then Menahem son of Gadi went from Tirzah up to Samaria. He attacked Shallum son of Jabesh in Samaria, assassinated him and succeeded him as king.

¹⁵The other events of Shallum's reign, and the conspiracy he led, are written in the book of the annals of the kings of Israel.

¹⁶At that time Menahem, starting out from Tirzah, attacked Tiphsah and everyone in the city and its vicinity, because they refused to open their gates. He sacked Tiphsah and ripped open all the pregnant women.

Menahem King of Israel

¹⁷In the thirty-ninth year of Azariah king of Judah, Menahem son of Gadi became king of Israel, and he reigned in Samaria ten years. ¹⁸He did evil in the eyes of the LORD. During his entire reign he did not turn away from the sins of Jeroboam son of Nebat, which he had caused Israel to commit.

¹⁹Then Pulᶜ king of Assyria invaded the land, and Menahem gave him a thousand talentsᵈ of silver to gain his support and strengthen his own hold on the kingdom. ²⁰Menahem exacted this money from Israel. Every wealthy man had to contribute fifty shekelsᵉ of silver to be given to the king of Assyria. So the king of Assyria withdrew and stayed in the land no longer.

²¹As for the other events of Menahem's reign, and all he did, are they not written in the book of the annals of the kings of Israel? ²²Menahem rested with his fathers. And Pekahiah his son succeeded him as king.

Pekahiah King of Israel

²³In the fiftieth year of Azariah king of Judah, Pekahiah son of Menahem became king of Israel in Samaria, and he reigned two years. ²⁴Pekahiah did evil in the eyes of the LORD. He did not turn away from the sins of Jeroboam son of Nebat, which he had caused Israel to commit. ²⁵One of

---

The Annals of the Kings

2 KINGS 15:8–26

Several times in these pages the writer refers to the annals of the kings of Israel. This was probably an official government record, which has, unfortunately, been lost. As you read these passages, try to imagine that someday you will write the annals of your own life. What characteristics would someone reading your annals see in your history? What would be the highlights of your spiritual journey? Try writing your annals for the past year, looking particularly for the times and events in which the hand of God was clearly evident.

See Meeting God in Everyday Life

ᵃ *10* Hebrew; some Septuagint manuscripts *in Ibleam*   ᵇ *12* 2 Kings 10:30
ᶜ *19* Also called *Tiglath-Pileser*   ᵈ *19* That is, about 37 tons (about 34 metric tons)   ᵉ *20* That is, about 1 1/4 pounds (about 0.6 kilogram)

Crisis, Judgment and Condemnation

2 KINGS 16:1–7

Read Isaiah 7:1–17, a passage referring to this time in Ahaz's life, in which Isaiah counsels Ahaz to stand firm and trust in God. In this 2 Kings account we see Ahaz capitulating to Assyrian domination rather than taking any such advice.

When faced with crisis, where do you turn for help first? How do you seek God's aid? In what ways have you found God's help in past crises? If the crisis is because of your own misdeeds or mistakes, how does your own spirit speak to you when you realize judgment is at hand? Is there a difference between God's judgment and God's condemnation? What does "there is now no condemnation for those who are in Christ Jesus" (Romans 8:1) mean to you?

his chief officers, Pekah son of Remaliah, conspired against him. Taking fifty men of Gilead with him, he assassinated Pekahiah, along with Argob and Arieh, in the citadel of the royal palace at Samaria. So Pekah killed Pekahiah and succeeded him as king.

²⁶The other events of Pekahiah's reign, and all he did, are written in the book of the annals of the kings of Israel.

Pekah King of Israel

²⁷In the fifty-second year of Azariah king of Judah, Pekah son of Remaliah became king of Israel in Samaria, and he reigned twenty years. ²⁸He did evil in the eyes of the LORD. He did not turn away from the sins of Jeroboam son of Nebat, which he had caused Israel to commit.

²⁹In the time of Pekah king of Israel, Tiglath-Pileser king of Assyria came and took Ijon, Abel Beth Maacah, Janoah, Kedesh and Hazor. He took Gilead and Galilee, including all the land of Naphtali, and deported the people to Assyria. ³⁰Then Hoshea son of Elah conspired against Pekah son of Remaliah. He attacked and assassinated him, and then succeeded him as king in the twentieth year of Jotham son of Uzziah.

³¹As for the other events of Pekah's reign, and all he did, are they not written in the book of the annals of the kings of Israel?

Jotham King of Judah

³²In the second year of Pekah son of Remaliah king of Israel, Jotham son of Uzziah king of Judah began to reign. ³³He was twenty-five years old when he became king, and he reigned in Jerusalem sixteen years. His mother's name was Jerusha daughter of Zadok. ³⁴He did what was right in the eyes of the LORD, just as his father Uzziah had done. ³⁵The high places, however, were not removed; the people continued to offer sacrifices and burn incense there. Jotham rebuilt the Upper Gate of the temple of the LORD.

³⁶As for the other events of Jotham's reign, and what he did, are they not written in the book of the annals of the kings of Judah? ³⁷(In those days the LORD began to send Rezin king of Aram and Pekah son of Remaliah against Judah.) ³⁸Jotham rested with his fathers and was buried with them in the City of David, the city of his father. And Ahaz his son succeeded him as king.

Ahaz King of Judah

16 In the seventeenth year of Pekah son of Remaliah, Ahaz son of Jotham king of Judah began to reign. ²Ahaz was twenty years old when he became king, and he reigned in Jerusalem sixteen years. Unlike David his father, he did not do what was right in the eyes of the LORD his God. ³He walked in the ways of the kings of Israel and even sacrificed his son in*ᵃ* the fire, following the detestable ways of the nations the LORD had driven out before the Israelites. ⁴He offered sacrifices and burned incense at the high places, on the hilltops and under every spreading tree.

⁵Then Rezin king of Aram and Pekah son of Remaliah king of Israel marched up to fight against Jerusalem and besieged Ahaz, but they could not overpower him. ⁶At that time, Rezin king of Aram recovered Elath for Aram by driving out the

ᵃ 3 Or even made his son pass through

men of Judah. Edomites then moved into Elath and have lived there to this day.

⁷Ahaz sent messengers to say to Tiglath-Pileser king of Assyria, "I am your servant and vassal. Come up and save me out of the hand of the king of Aram and of the king of Israel, who are attacking me." ⁸And Ahaz took the silver and gold found in the temple of the Lord and in the treasuries of the royal palace and sent it as a gift to the king of Assyria. ⁹The king of Assyria complied by attacking Damascus and capturing it. He deported its inhabitants to Kir and put Rezin to death.

¹⁰Then King Ahaz went to Damascus to meet Tiglath-Pileser king of Assyria. He saw an altar in Damascus and sent to Uriah the priest a sketch of the altar, with detailed plans for its construction. ¹¹So Uriah the priest built an altar in accordance with all the plans that King Ahaz had sent from Damascus and finished it before King Ahaz returned. ¹²When the king came back from Damascus and saw the altar, he approached it and presented offerings*a* on it. ¹³He offered up his burnt offering and grain offering, poured out his drink offering, and sprinkled the blood of his fellowship offerings*b* on the altar. ¹⁴The bronze altar that stood before the Lord he brought from the front of the temple—from between the new altar and the temple of the Lord—and put it on the north side of the new altar.

¹⁵King Ahaz then gave these orders to Uriah the priest: "On the large new altar, offer the morning burnt offering and the evening grain offering, the king's burnt offering and his grain offering, and the burnt offering of all the people of the land, and their grain offering and their drink offering. Sprinkle on the altar all the blood of the burnt offerings and sacrifices. But I will use the bronze altar for seeking guidance." ¹⁶And Uriah the priest did just as King Ahaz had ordered.

¹⁷King Ahaz took away the side panels and removed the basins from the movable stands. He removed the Sea from the bronze bulls that supported it and set it on a stone base. ¹⁸He took away the Sabbath canopy*c* that had been built at the temple and removed the royal entryway outside the temple of the Lord, in deference to the king of Assyria.

¹⁹As for the other events of the reign of Ahaz, and what he did, are they not written in the book of the annals of the kings of Judah? ²⁰Ahaz rested with his fathers and was buried with them in the City of David. And Hezekiah his son succeeded him as king.

Hoshea Last King of Israel

17 In the twelfth year of Ahaz king of Judah, Hoshea son of Elah became king of Israel in Samaria, and he reigned nine years. ²He did evil in the eyes of the Lord, but not like the kings of Israel who preceded him.

³Shalmaneser king of Assyria came up to attack Hoshea, who had been Shalmaneser's vassal and had paid him tribute. ⁴But the king of Assyria discovered that Hoshea was a traitor, for he had sent envoys to So*d* king of Egypt, and he no longer paid tribute to the king of Assyria, as he had done year by year. Therefore Shalmaneser seized him and

---

First Wave of Destruction

2 KINGS 17:1–7

Assyria invades, but the worst is still to come. Israel will be exiled, eventually becoming the "ten lost tribes." While this passage tells us that Israel's exile came as divine judgment, it also reminds us of the ever-present reality of international turmoil. The cost of conflict in terms of deaths, suffering, upheaval and sorrow cannot be counted. Today's world is full of slaves and refugees created by political invasions and war. Children are especially vulnerable at these times.

God can work through our prayers and deeds to bring about peace and justice. Look at a map of the world. Where are wars occurring now? From what countries are refugees fleeing? Where are they taking sanctuary? How can you become involved in giving aid to these victims? How might a nation's spiritual renewal make a difference? Use your map as a guide to prayer for governments at war and for the people who suffer.

---

a 12 Or *and went up*   *b 13* Traditionally *peace offerings*   *c 18* Or *the dais of his throne* (see Septuagint)   *d 4* Or *to Sais, to the*; *So* is possibly an abbreviation for *Osorkon.*

Conformed to God's Will

2 KINGS 17:17

The people of Israel have conformed to the destructive ways of the nations around them, bringing displeasure to God's heart. Following social norms founded on unsound principles and evil practices leads Israel to ruin.

Reflect on your actions in light of the Word of God by reading Romans 12:1–2. In what ways have you conformed to this world? What needs to be changed so that you conform to the Word and will of God? What do you need to cultivate in order to become aligned with God's love and justice? Pray daily for the grace and power to live for God.

put him in prison. ⁵The king of Assyria invaded the entire land, marched against Samaria and laid siege to it for three years. ⁶In the ninth year of Hoshea, the king of Assyria captured Samaria and deported the Israelites to Assyria. He settled them in Halah, in Gozan on the Habor River and in the towns of the Medes.

Israel Exiled Because of Sin

⁷All this took place because the Israelites had sinned against the LORD their God, who had brought them up out of Egypt from under the power of Pharaoh king of Egypt. They worshiped other gods ⁸and followed the practices of the nations the LORD had driven out before them, as well as the practices that the kings of Israel had introduced. ⁹The Israelites secretly did things against the LORD their God that were not right. From watchtower to fortified city they built themselves high places in all their towns. ¹⁰They set up sacred stones and Asherah poles on every high hill and under every spreading tree. ¹¹At every high place they burned incense, as the nations whom the LORD had driven out before them had done. They did wicked things that provoked the LORD to anger. ¹²They worshiped idols, though the LORD had said, "You shall not do this."[a] ¹³The LORD warned Israel and Judah through all his prophets and seers: "Turn from your evil ways. Observe my commands and decrees, in accordance with the entire Law that I commanded your fathers to obey and that I delivered to you through my servants the prophets."

¹⁴But they would not listen and were as stiff-necked as their fathers, who did not trust in the LORD their God. ¹⁵They rejected his decrees and the covenant he had made with their fathers and the warnings he had given them. They followed worthless idols and themselves became worthless. They imitated the nations around them although the LORD had ordered them, "Do not do as they do," and they did the things the LORD had forbidden them to do.

¹⁶They forsook all the commands of the LORD their God and made for themselves two idols cast in the shape of calves, and an Asherah pole. They bowed down to all the starry hosts, and they worshiped Baal. ¹⁷They sacrificed their sons and daughters in[b] the fire. They practiced divination and sorcery and sold themselves to do evil in the eyes of the LORD, provoking him to anger.

¹⁸So the LORD was very angry with Israel and removed them from his presence. Only the tribe of Judah was left, ¹⁹and even Judah did not keep the commands of the LORD their God. They followed the practices Israel had introduced. ²⁰Therefore the LORD rejected all the people of Israel; he afflicted them and gave them into the hands of plunderers, until he thrust them from his presence.

²¹When he tore Israel away from the house of David, they made Jeroboam son of Nebat their king. Jeroboam enticed Israel away from following the LORD and caused them to commit a great sin. ²²The Israelites persisted in all the sins of Jeroboam and did not turn away from them ²³until the LORD removed them from his presence, as he had warned through all his servants the prophets. So the people of Israel were taken from their homeland into exile in Assyria, and they are still there.

a 12 Exodus 20:4, 5   *b 17* Or *They made their sons and daughters pass through*

Samaria Resettled

²⁴The king of Assyria brought people from Babylon, Cuthah, Avva, Hamath and Sepharvaim and settled them in the towns of Samaria to replace the Israelites. They took over Samaria and lived in its towns. ²⁵When they first lived there, they did not worship the LORD; so he sent lions among them and they killed some of the people. ²⁶It was reported to the king of Assyria: "The people you deported and resettled in the towns of Samaria do not know what the god of that country requires. He has sent lions among them, which are killing them off, because the people do not know what he requires."

²⁷Then the king of Assyria gave this order: "Have one of the priests you took captive from Samaria go back to live there and teach the people what the god of the land requires." ²⁸So one of the priests who had been exiled from Samaria came to live in Bethel and taught them how to worship the LORD.

²⁹Nevertheless, each national group made its own gods in the several towns where they settled, and set them up in the shrines the people of Samaria had made at the high places. ³⁰The men from Babylon made Succoth Benoth, the men from Cuthah made Nergal, and the men from Hamath made Ashima; ³¹the Avvites made Nibhaz and Tartak, and the Sepharvites burned their children in the fire as sacrifices to Adrammelech and Anammelech, the gods of Sepharvaim. ³²They worshiped the LORD, but they also appointed all sorts of their own people to officiate for them as priests in the shrines at the high places. ³³They worshiped the LORD, but they also served their own gods in accordance with the customs of the nations from which they had been brought.

³⁴To this day they persist in their former practices. They neither worship the LORD nor adhere to the decrees and ordinances, the laws and commands that the LORD gave the descendants of Jacob, whom he named Israel. ³⁵When the LORD made a covenant with the Israelites, he commanded them: "Do not worship any other gods or bow down to them, serve them or sacrifice to them. ³⁶But the LORD, who brought you up out of Egypt with mighty power and outstretched arm, is the one you must worship. To him you shall bow down and to him offer sacrifices. ³⁷You must always be careful to keep the decrees and ordinances, the laws and commands he wrote for you. Do not worship other gods. ³⁸Do not forget the covenant I have made with you, and do not worship other gods. ³⁹Rather, worship the LORD your God; it is he who will deliver you from the hand of all your enemies."

⁴⁰They would not listen, however, but persisted in their former practices. ⁴¹Even while these people were worshiping the LORD, they were serving their idols. To this day their children and grandchildren continue to do as their fathers did.

Hezekiah King of Judah

18 In the third year of Hoshea son of Elah king of Israel, Hezekiah son of Ahaz king of Judah began to reign. ²He was twenty-five years old when he became king, and he reigned in Jerusalem twenty-nine years. His mother's name was Abijah*ᵃ* daughter of Zechariah. ³He did what

---

Spiritual Housecleaning

2 KINGS 18:1–4

Hezekiah does not hesitate to discard time-honored customs and objects that impede the people's pure worship of God. The high places and sacred poles, long beloved, are destroyed. Even Moses' bronze snake, used idolatrously, is broken into pieces. Take stock of your own practices. What habits or customs are impeding your response to God's purposes—such as aimless television watching or purposeless reading? What is one habit you can begin discarding today? What will you put in its place? Prayerfully make a decision. If actually throwing something out helps enact this decision, do so as soon as you finish your prayer.

See Meeting God in Everyday Life

ᵃ*2* Hebrew *Abi,* a variant of *Abijah*

A Good King in Hard Times

2 KINGS 18:5

Hezekiah's strong, moral, focused leadership leads to reform and revival. He is the only good king in one hundred years, and "there was no one like him among all the kings of Judah" because he followed God closely and kept God's commands. The nation's downfall was postponed.

Who are the good leaders of our day? Have you ever thought about calling them or writing a letter in support of their good efforts? Think about what you want to say to them; then call, write, fax or send an e-mail message to them. Let them know that you pray for them. Encourage them to do what is "right in the eyes of the LORD."

See Meeting God in Community

was right in the eyes of the LORD, just as his father David had done. ⁴He removed the high places, smashed the sacred stones and cut down the Asherah poles. He broke into pieces the bronze snake Moses had made, for up to that time the Israelites had been burning incense to it. (It was called*ᵃ* Nehushtan.*ᵇ*)

⁵Hezekiah trusted in the LORD, the God of Israel. There was no one like him among all the kings of Judah, either before him or after him. ⁶He held fast to the LORD and did not cease to follow him; he kept the commands the LORD had given Moses. ⁷And the LORD was with him; he was successful in whatever he undertook. He rebelled against the king of Assyria and did not serve him. ⁸From watchtower to fortified city, he defeated the Philistines, as far as Gaza and its territory.

⁹In King Hezekiah's fourth year, which was the seventh year of Hoshea son of Elah king of Israel, Shalmaneser king of Assyria marched against Samaria and laid siege to it. ¹⁰At the end of three years the Assyrians took it. So Samaria was captured in Hezekiah's sixth year, which was the ninth year of Hoshea king of Israel. ¹¹The king of Assyria deported Israel to Assyria and settled them in Halah, in Gozan on the Habor River and in towns of the Medes. ¹²This happened because they had not obeyed the LORD their God, but had violated his covenant—all that Moses the servant of the LORD commanded. They neither listened to the commands nor carried them out.

¹³In the fourteenth year of King Hezekiah's reign, Sennacherib king of Assyria attacked all the fortified cities of Judah and captured them. ¹⁴So Hezekiah king of Judah sent this message to the king of Assyria at Lachish: "I have done wrong. Withdraw from me, and I will pay whatever you demand of me." The king of Assyria exacted from Hezekiah king of Judah three hundred talents*ᶜ* of silver and thirty talents*ᵈ* of gold. ¹⁵So Hezekiah gave him all the silver that was found in the temple of the LORD and in the treasuries of the royal palace.

¹⁶At this time Hezekiah king of Judah stripped off the gold with which he had covered the doors and doorposts of the temple of the LORD, and gave it to the king of Assyria.

Sennacherib Threatens Jerusalem

¹⁷The king of Assyria sent his supreme commander, his chief officer and his field commander with a large army, from Lachish to King Hezekiah at Jerusalem. They came up to Jerusalem and stopped at the aqueduct of the Upper Pool, on the road to the Washerman's Field. ¹⁸They called for the king; and Eliakim son of Hilkiah the palace administrator, Shebna the secretary, and Joah son of Asaph the recorder went out to them.

¹⁹The field commander said to them, "Tell Hezekiah:

" 'This is what the great king, the king of Assyria, says: On what are you basing this confidence of yours? ²⁰You say you have strategy and military strength—but you speak only empty words. On whom are you depending, that you rebel against me? ²¹Look now, you are depending on Egypt, that splintered reed of a staff,

---

ᵃ 4 Or *He called it*   *ᵇ 4 Nehushtan* sounds like the Hebrew for *bronze* and *snake* and *unclean thing.*   *ᶜ 14* That is, about 11 tons (about 10 metric tons)   *ᵈ 14* That is, about 1 ton (about 1 metric ton)

which pierces a man's hand and wounds him if he leans on it! Such is Pharaoh king of Egypt to all who depend on him. ²²And if you say to me, "We are depending on the LORD our God"—isn't he the one whose high places and altars Hezekiah removed, saying to Judah and Jerusalem, "You must worship before this altar in Jerusalem"?

²³"'Come now, make a bargain with my master, the king of Assyria: I will give you two thousand horses— if you can put riders on them! ²⁴How can you repulse one officer of the least of my master's officials, even though you are depending on Egypt for chariots and horsemen*ᵃ*? ²⁵Furthermore, have I come to attack and destroy this place without word from the LORD? The LORD himself told me to march against this country and destroy it.'"

²⁶Then Eliakim son of Hilkiah, and Shebna and Joah said to the field commander, "Please speak to your servants in Aramaic, since we understand it. Don't speak to us in Hebrew in the hearing of the people on the wall."

²⁷But the commander replied, "Was it only to your master and you that my master sent me to say these things, and not to the men sitting on the wall—who, like you, will have to eat their own filth and drink their own urine?"

²⁸Then the commander stood and called out in Hebrew: "Hear the word of the great king, the king of Assyria! ²⁹This is what the king says: Do not let Hezekiah deceive you. He cannot deliver you from my hand. ³⁰Do not let Hezekiah persuade you to trust in the LORD when he says, 'The LORD will surely deliver us; this city will not be given into the hand of the king of Assyria.'

³¹"Do not listen to Hezekiah. This is what the king of Assyria says: Make peace with me and come out to me. Then every one of you will eat from his own vine and fig tree and drink water from his own cistern, ³²until I come and take you to a land like your own, a land of grain and new wine, a land of bread and vineyards, a land of olive trees and honey. Choose life and not death!

"Do not listen to Hezekiah, for he is misleading you when he says, 'The LORD will deliver us.' ³³Has the god of any nation ever delivered his land from the hand of the king of Assyria? ³⁴Where are the gods of Hamath and Arpad? Where are the gods of Sepharvaim, Hena and Ivvah? Have they rescued Samaria from my hand? ³⁵Who of all the gods of these countries has been able to save his land from me? How then can the LORD deliver Jerusalem from my hand?"

³⁶But the people remained silent and said nothing in reply, because the king had commanded, "Do not answer him."

³⁷Then Eliakim son of Hilkiah the palace administrator, Shebna the secretary and Joah son of Asaph the recorder went to Hezekiah, with their clothes torn, and told him what the field commander had said.

Jerusalem's Deliverance Foretold

19 When King Hezekiah heard this, he tore his clothes and put on sackcloth and went into the temple of

Enemies at the Gate

2 KINGS 18:17–25

Unexpected trouble arises in the midst of good times: An enemy is trying to convince Hezekiah and Judah that God is not with them. What unexpected enemies—a health problem, financial concerns, family troubles, employment issues or other matters—have you had to face that threatened to shake your faith in God's providential care? When your faith is tested, who or what helps you? Pray, "Help me, O mighty God, to see how you have helped when enemies have marched up to the gate of my life. I thank you that when I am threatened or discouraged, attacked or misunderstood, you are my help and shield. Amen."

See Meeting God in Prayer

Birthing the New

2 KINGS 19:3–7

Just as the nation is being re-born, a threat arises. Hezekiah laments, likening the situation to a woman without the "strength to deliver" her child; he turns to the Lord and his prophet Isaiah. God says, "Do not be afraid." When has opposition threatened to stop something you were trying to accomplish? When have you felt so discouraged that you did not have "the strength to deliver"? What gave you strength to carry on? Prayerfully imagine yourself in one of those past situations, or in a current dilemma; ask God to show you where "the strength to deliver" can be found. Repeat quietly, as you envision the situation, "This is what the LORD says: 'Do not be afraid.' "

See Meeting God in Prayer

the LORD. ²He sent Eliakim the palace administrator, Shebna the secretary and the leading priests, all wearing sackcloth, to the prophet Isaiah son of Amoz. ³They told him, "This is what Hezekiah says: This day is a day of distress and rebuke and disgrace, as when children come to the point of birth and there is no strength to deliver them. ⁴It may be that the LORD your God will hear all the words of the field commander, whom his master, the king of Assyria, has sent to ridicule the living God, and that he will rebuke him for the words the LORD your God has heard. Therefore pray for the remnant that still survives."

⁵When King Hezekiah's officials came to Isaiah, ⁶Isaiah said to them, "Tell your master, 'This is what the LORD says: Do not be afraid of what you have heard—those words with which the underlings of the king of Assyria have blasphemed me. ⁷Listen! I am going to put such a spirit in him that when he hears a certain report, he will return to his own country, and there I will have him cut down with the sword.' "

⁸When the field commander heard that the king of Assyria had left Lachish, he withdrew and found the king fighting against Libnah.

⁹Now Sennacherib received a report that Tirhakah, the Cushite[a] king ⌊of Egypt⌋, was marching out to fight against him. So he again sent messengers to Hezekiah with this word: ¹⁰"Say to Hezekiah king of Judah: Do not let the god you depend on deceive you when he says, 'Jerusalem will not be handed over to the king of Assyria.' ¹¹Surely you have heard what the kings of Assyria have done to all the countries, destroying them completely. And will you be delivered? ¹²Did the gods of the nations that were destroyed by my forefathers deliver them: the gods of Gozan, Haran, Rezeph and the people of Eden who were in Tel Assar? ¹³Where is the king of Hamath, the king of Arpad, the king of the city of Sepharvaim, or of Hena or Ivvah?"

Hezekiah's Prayer

¹⁴Hezekiah received the letter from the messengers and read it. Then he went up to the temple of the LORD and spread it out before the LORD. ¹⁵And Hezekiah prayed to the LORD: "O LORD, God of Israel, enthroned between the cherubim, you alone are God over all the kingdoms of the earth. You have made heaven and earth. ¹⁶Give ear, O LORD, and hear; open your eyes, O LORD, and see; listen to the words Sennacherib has sent to insult the living God.

¹⁷"It is true, O LORD, that the Assyrian kings have laid waste these nations and their lands. ¹⁸They have thrown their gods into the fire and destroyed them, for they were not gods but only wood and stone, fashioned by men's hands. ¹⁹Now, O LORD our God, deliver us from his hand, so that all kingdoms on earth may know that you alone, O LORD, are God."

Isaiah Prophesies Sennacherib's Fall

²⁰Then Isaiah son of Amoz sent a message to Hezekiah: "This is what the LORD, the God of Israel, says: I have heard your prayer concerning Sennacherib king of Assyria. ²¹This is the word that the LORD has spoken against him:

a 9 That is, from the upper Nile region

" 'The Virgin Daughter of Zion
    despises you and mocks you.
The Daughter of Jerusalem
    tosses her head as you flee.
²² Who is it you have insulted and blasphemed?
    Against whom have you raised your voice
and lifted your eyes in pride?
    Against the Holy One of Israel!
²³ By your messengers
    you have heaped insults on the Lord.
And you have said,
    "With my many chariots
I have ascended the heights of the mountains,
    the utmost heights of Lebanon.
I have cut down its tallest cedars,
    the choicest of its pines.
I have reached its remotest parts,
    the finest of its forests.
²⁴ I have dug wells in foreign lands
    and drunk the water there.
With the soles of my feet
    I have dried up all the streams of Egypt."

²⁵ " 'Have you not heard?
    Long ago I ordained it.
In days of old I planned it;
    now I have brought it to pass,
that you have turned fortified cities
    into piles of stone.
²⁶ Their people, drained of power,
    are dismayed and put to shame.
They are like plants in the field,
    like tender green shoots,
like grass sprouting on the roof,
    scorched before it grows up.

²⁷ " 'But I know where you stay
    and when you come and go
    and how you rage against me.
²⁸ Because you rage against me
    and your insolence has reached my ears,
I will put my hook in your nose
    and my bit in your mouth,
and I will make you return
    by the way you came.'

²⁹ "This will be the sign for you, O Hezekiah:

"This year you will eat what grows by itself,
    and the second year what springs from that.
But in the third year sow and reap,
    plant vineyards and eat their fruit.
³⁰ Once more a remnant of the house of Judah
    will take root below and bear fruit above.
³¹ For out of Jerusalem will come a remnant,
    and out of Mount Zion a band of survivors.

The zeal of the Lᴏʀᴅ Almighty will accomplish this.

³² "Therefore this is what the Lᴏʀᴅ says concerning the
king of Assyria:

"He will not enter this city
    or shoot an arrow here.

A Fruitful Remnant

2 KINGS 19:30–31

God promises that a small remnant will "take root" after the fall of David's kingdom, and that from the exiles he will bring new growth for the nation's future. Even a small thing, held in faith, can be the sprout of new life. God can use the bare remnants of a relationship, small hopes, simple deeds and small groups for renewal.

When you look back over your life, how have you received hope and inspiration from such small things? In what ways has God used a small remnant of faithful people to bring new life to you—to your family, church and community? Give thanks: "Loving God, help me to know how to offer small things to you so that you can use them to bring new life. I thank you that you use humble things to do great things for you."

See Meeting God in Service

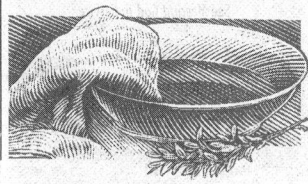

A King's Desperation and Vanity

2 KINGS 20:1–14

Hezekiah turns to God in his illness and is granted an additional fifteen years of life. Safely delivered, he now shows off his wealth to impress envoys from Babylon. How quickly he turns God's blessings into a show of vanity! He prays for healing, he gets well and then, in all-too-human fashion, Hezekiah ignores the source of all goodness!

Think back to a significant illness in your life or in the life of a loved one. Remember your journey and how you sought after, and received, spiritual or physical recovery. Perhaps you are still longing for recovery. What have you learned through your experience about your relationship to God, to your family and to your friends? What changes in outlook and behavior did you make?

See Meeting God in Service

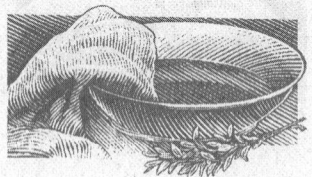

He will not come before it with shield
  or build a siege ramp against it.
33 By the way that he came he will return;
  he will not enter this city,
                              declares the LORD.
34 I will defend this city and save it,
  for my sake and for the sake of David my
    servant."

35 That night the angel of the LORD went out and put to death a hundred and eighty-five thousand men in the Assyrian camp. When the people got up the next morning—there were all the dead bodies! 36 So Sennacherib king of Assyria broke camp and withdrew. He returned to Nineveh and stayed there.

37 One day, while he was worshiping in the temple of his god Nisroch, his sons Adrammelech and Sharezer cut him down with the sword, and they escaped to the land of Ararat. And Esarhaddon his son succeeded him as king.

Hezekiah's Illness

20 In those days Hezekiah became ill and was at the point of death. The prophet Isaiah son of Amoz went to him and said, "This is what the LORD says: Put your house in order, because you are going to die; you will not recover."

2 Hezekiah turned his face to the wall and prayed to the LORD, 3 "Remember, O LORD, how I have walked before you faithfully and with wholehearted devotion and have done what is good in your eyes." And Hezekiah wept bitterly.

4 Before Isaiah had left the middle court, the word of the LORD came to him: 5 "Go back and tell Hezekiah, the leader of my people, 'This is what the LORD, the God of your father David, says: I have heard your prayer and seen your tears; I will heal you. On the third day from now you will go up to the temple of the LORD. 6 I will add fifteen years to your life. And I will deliver you and this city from the hand of the king of Assyria. I will defend this city for my sake and for the sake of my servant David.' "

7 Then Isaiah said, "Prepare a poultice of figs." They did so and applied it to the boil, and he recovered.

8 Hezekiah had asked Isaiah, "What will be the sign that the LORD will heal me and that I will go up to the temple of the LORD on the third day from now?"

9 Isaiah answered, "This is the LORD's sign to you that the LORD will do what he has promised: Shall the shadow go forward ten steps, or shall it go back ten steps?"

10 "It is a simple matter for the shadow to go forward ten steps," said Hezekiah. "Rather, have it go back ten steps."

11 Then the prophet Isaiah called upon the LORD, and the LORD made the shadow go back the ten steps it had gone down on the stairway of Ahaz.

Envoys From Babylon

12 At that time Merodach-Baladan son of Baladan king of Babylon sent Hezekiah letters and a gift, because he had heard of Hezekiah's illness. 13 Hezekiah received the messengers and showed them all that was in his storehouses—the silver, the gold, the spices and the fine oil—his armory and everything found among his treasures. There was noth-

ing in his palace or in all his kingdom that Hezekiah did not show them.

¹⁴Then Isaiah the prophet went to King Hezekiah and asked, "What did those men say, and where did they come from?"

"From a distant land," Hezekiah replied. "They came from Babylon."

¹⁵The prophet asked, "What did they see in your palace?"

"They saw everything in my palace," Hezekiah said. "There is nothing among my treasures that I did not show them."

¹⁶Then Isaiah said to Hezekiah, "Hear the word of the LORD: ¹⁷The time will surely come when everything in your palace, and all that your fathers have stored up until this day, will be carried off to Babylon. Nothing will be left, says the LORD. ¹⁸And some of your descendants, your own flesh and blood, that will be born to you, will be taken away, and they will become eunuchs in the palace of the king of Babylon."

¹⁹"The word of the LORD you have spoken is good," Hezekiah replied. For he thought, "Will there not be peace and security in my lifetime?"

²⁰As for the other events of Hezekiah's reign, all his achievements and how he made the pool and the tunnel by which he brought water into the city, are they not written in the book of the annals of the kings of Judah? ²¹Hezekiah rested with his fathers. And Manasseh his son succeeded him as king.

Manasseh King of Judah

21 Manasseh was twelve years old when he became king, and he reigned in Jerusalem fifty-five years. His mother's name was Hephzibah. ²He did evil in the eyes of the LORD, following the detestable practices of the nations the LORD had driven out before the Israelites. ³He rebuilt the high places his father Hezekiah had destroyed; he also erected altars to Baal and made an Asherah pole, as Ahab king of Israel had done. He bowed down to all the starry hosts and worshiped them. ⁴He built altars in the temple of the LORD, of which the LORD had said, "In Jerusalem I will put my Name." ⁵In both courts of the temple of the LORD, he built altars to all the starry hosts. ⁶He sacrificed his own son in^a the fire, practiced sorcery and divination, and consulted mediums and spiritists. He did much evil in the eyes of the LORD, provoking him to anger.

⁷He took the carved Asherah pole he had made and put it in the temple, of which the LORD had said to David and to his son Solomon, "In this temple and in Jerusalem, which I have chosen out of all the tribes of Israel, I will put my Name forever. ⁸I will not again make the feet of the Israelites wander from the land I gave their forefathers, if only they will be careful to do everything I commanded them and will keep the whole Law that my servant Moses gave them." ⁹But the people did not listen. Manasseh led them astray, so that they did more evil than the nations the LORD had destroyed before the Israelites.

¹⁰The LORD said through his servants the prophets: ¹¹"Manasseh king of Judah has committed these detestable sins. He has done more evil than the Amorites who preceded

---

True Treasures

2 KINGS 20:12–15

Recovered from his illness, Hezekiah takes pleasure and pride in flaunting his great treasures to the Babylonian envoys.

Prayerfully wander through your own house or around your property, noting all your treasures, giving thanks where appropriate as you remember how these objects came into your life. Then sit quietly and make a list of the less tangible treasures you possess—relationships, values, ideas, skills—that cannot be taken away by fire, flood or violence. Spend time giving thanks for all these treasures, inner and outer, and ask for guidance in how to pass them on to specific people in the next generation.

See Meeting God in Everyday Life

---

^a 6 Or *He made his own son pass through*

The Measuring Line

2 KINGS 21:13

As Manasseh reverses the good of King Hezekiah's reforms, God declares that he will measure Judah with a "measuring line." What do you think the divine measuring line is comprised of? What are the minimum standards for survival? What are the divine Judge's standards for a truly godly nation? What might be uppermost in the mind of the Shepherd of nations regarding the needs of the world today? How does God communicate his standards to the leaders and peoples of nations in our day? In what ways are God's judgments shown to a nation? As you pray for God's will to be done "on earth as it is in heaven," what is most important to pray for today? Pray that prayer now.

See Meeting God in Prayer

him and has led Judah into sin with his idols. [12]Therefore this is what the LORD, the God of Israel, says: I am going to bring such disaster on Jerusalem and Judah that the ears of everyone who hears of it will tingle. [13]I will stretch out over Jerusalem the measuring line used against Samaria and the plumb line used against the house of Ahab. I will wipe out Jerusalem as one wipes a dish, wiping it and turning it upside down. [14]I will forsake the remnant of my inheritance and hand them over to their enemies. They will be looted and plundered by all their foes, [15]because they have done evil in my eyes and have provoked me to anger from the day their forefathers came out of Egypt until this day."

[16]Moreover, Manasseh also shed so much innocent blood that he filled Jerusalem from end to end—besides the sin that he had caused Judah to commit, so that they did evil in the eyes of the LORD.

[17]As for the other events of Manasseh's reign, and all he did, including the sin he committed, are they not written in the book of the annals of the kings of Judah? [18]Manasseh rested with his fathers and was buried in his palace garden, the garden of Uzza. And Amon his son succeeded him as king.

Amon King of Judah

[19]Amon was twenty-two years old when he became king, and he reigned in Jerusalem two years. His mother's name was Meshullemeth daughter of Haruz; she was from Jotbah. [20]He did evil in the eyes of the LORD, as his father Manasseh had done. [21]He walked in all the ways of his father; he worshiped the idols his father had worshiped, and bowed down to them. [22]He forsook the LORD, the God of his fathers, and did not walk in the way of the LORD.

[23]Amon's officials conspired against him and assassinated the king in his palace. [24]Then the people of the land killed all who had plotted against King Amon, and they made Josiah his son king in his place.

[25]As for the other events of Amon's reign, and what he did, are they not written in the book of the annals of the kings of Judah? [26]He was buried in his grave in the garden of Uzza. And Josiah his son succeeded him as king.

The Book of the Law Found

22 Josiah was eight years old when he became king, and he reigned in Jerusalem thirty-one years. His mother's name was Jedidah daughter of Adaiah; she was from Bozkath. [2]He did what was right in the eyes of the LORD and walked in all the ways of his father David, not turning aside to the right or to the left.

[3]In the eighteenth year of his reign, King Josiah sent the secretary, Shaphan son of Azaliah, the son of Meshullam, to the temple of the LORD. He said: [4]"Go up to Hilkiah the high priest and have him get ready the money that has been brought into the temple of the LORD, which the doorkeepers have collected from the people. [5]Have them entrust it to the men appointed to supervise the work on the temple. And have these men pay the workers who repair the temple of the LORD— [6]the carpenters, the builders and the masons. Also have them purchase timber and dressed stone to repair the temple. [7]But they need not account for the

money entrusted to them, because they are acting faithfully."

⁸Hilkiah the high priest said to Shaphan the secretary, "I have found the Book of the Law in the temple of the LORD." He gave it to Shaphan, who read it. ⁹Then Shaphan the secretary went to the king and reported to him: "Your officials have paid out the money that was in the temple of the LORD and have entrusted it to the workers and supervisors at the temple." ¹⁰Then Shaphan the secretary informed the king, "Hilkiah the priest has given me a book." And Shaphan read from it in the presence of the king.

¹¹When the king heard the words of the Book of the Law, he tore his robes. ¹²He gave these orders to Hilkiah the priest, Ahikam son of Shaphan, Acbor son of Micaiah, Shaphan the secretary and Asaiah the king's attendant: ¹³"Go and inquire of the LORD for me and for the people and for all Judah about what is written in this book that has been found. Great is the LORD's anger that burns against us because our fathers have not obeyed the words of this book; they have not acted in accordance with all that is written there concerning us."

¹⁴Hilkiah the priest, Ahikam, Acbor, Shaphan and Asaiah went to speak to the prophetess Huldah, who was the wife of Shallum son of Tikvah, the son of Harhas, keeper of the wardrobe. She lived in Jerusalem, in the Second District.

¹⁵She said to them, "This is what the LORD, the God of Israel, says: Tell the man who sent you to me, ¹⁶'This is what the LORD says: I am going to bring disaster on this place and its people, according to everything written in the book the king of Judah has read. ¹⁷Because they have forsaken me and burned incense to other gods and provoked me to anger by all the idols their hands have made,ᵃ my anger will burn against this place and will not be quenched.' ¹⁸Tell the king of Judah, who sent you to inquire of the LORD, 'This is what the LORD, the God of Israel, says concerning the words you heard: ¹⁹Because your heart was responsive and you humbled yourself before the LORD when you heard what I have spoken against this place and its people, that they would become accursed and laid waste, and because you tore your robes and wept in my presence, I have heard you, declares the LORD. ²⁰Therefore I will gather you to your fathers, and you will be buried in peace. Your eyes will not see all the disaster I am going to bring on this place.' "

So they took her answer back to the king.

Josiah Renews the Covenant

23 Then the king called together all the elders of Judah and Jerusalem. ²He went up to the temple of the LORD with the men of Judah, the people of Jerusalem, the priests and the prophets—all the people from the least to the greatest. He read in their hearing all the words of the Book of the Covenant, which had been found in the temple of the LORD. ³The king stood by the pillar and renewed the covenant in the presence of the LORD—to follow the LORD and keep his commands, regulations and decrees with all his heart and all his soul, thus confirming the words of the covenant written in this book. Then all the people pledged themselves to the covenant.

⁴The king ordered Hilkiah the high priest, the priests next

Hearing and Response

2 KINGS 22:8–20

Josiah begins following God's way from the beginning of his reign, when he was eight years old. At age twenty-six, he reads the newly found scroll, probably the book of Deuteronomy, and responds with lament and with readiness to institute reforms. His quick repentance speaks well of his childhood spiritual formation. Think about your childhood. How did you hear about God? Were you schooled in the church? If so, what kinds of memories do you have about that experience and those who taught you? How was your spiritual life nurtured in other ways? What books or ideas have helped you grow and develop more mature ideas about God?

See Meeting God in Worship

ᵃ 17 Or *by everything they have done*

Celebrating the Passover

2 KINGS 23:21

Turn to Deuteronomy 16 and read the instructions for keeping the Passover. It had been generations since Israel celebrated this yearly feast in the manner the "lost book" demanded. God rejoices in celebration, and the Passover feast commemorates God's saving power to the people of Israel.

God wants us to live life and have life to the fullest. Which celebrations do you enjoy most? How does that day of celebration demonstrate God's goodness? What brings you joy that might deserve its own special celebration? Make a list of events you have celebrated recently. Make another list of events you want to celebrate and make specific plans to do so!

See Meeting God in Worship

in rank and the doorkeepers to remove from the temple of the LORD all the articles made for Baal and Asherah and all the starry hosts. He burned them outside Jerusalem in the fields of the Kidron Valley and took the ashes to Bethel. [5]He did away with the pagan priests appointed by the kings of Judah to burn incense on the high places of the towns of Judah and on those around Jerusalem—those who burned incense to Baal, to the sun and moon, to the constellations and to all the starry hosts. [6]He took the Asherah pole from the temple of the LORD to the Kidron Valley outside Jerusalem and burned it there. He ground it to powder and scattered the dust over the graves of the common people. [7]He also tore down the quarters of the male shrine prostitutes, which were in the temple of the LORD and where women did weaving for Asherah.

[8]Josiah brought all the priests from the towns of Judah and desecrated the high places, from Geba to Beersheba, where the priests had burned incense. He broke down the shrines[a] at the gates—at the entrance to the Gate of Joshua, the city governor, which is on the left of the city gate. [9]Although the priests of the high places did not serve at the altar of the LORD in Jerusalem, they ate unleavened bread with their fellow priests.

[10]He desecrated Topheth, which was in the Valley of Ben Hinnom, so no one could use it to sacrifice his son or daughter in[b] the fire to Molech. [11]He removed from the entrance to the temple of the LORD the horses that the kings of Judah had dedicated to the sun. They were in the court near the room of an official named Nathan-Melech. Josiah then burned the chariots dedicated to the sun.

[12]He pulled down the altars the kings of Judah had erected on the roof near the upper room of Ahaz, and the altars Manasseh had built in the two courts of the temple of the LORD. He removed them from there, smashed them to pieces and threw the rubble into the Kidron Valley. [13]The king also desecrated the high places that were east of Jerusalem on the south of the Hill of Corruption—the ones Solomon king of Israel had built for Ashtoreth the vile goddess of the Sidonians, for Chemosh the vile god of Moab, and for Molech[c] the detestable god of the people of Ammon. [14]Josiah smashed the sacred stones and cut down the Asherah poles and covered the sites with human bones.

[15]Even the altar at Bethel, the high place made by Jeroboam son of Nebat, who had caused Israel to sin—even that altar and high place he demolished. He burned the high place and ground it to powder, and burned the Asherah pole also. [16]Then Josiah looked around, and when he saw the tombs that were there on the hillside, he had the bones removed from them and burned on the altar to defile it, in accordance with the word of the LORD proclaimed by the man of God who foretold these things.

[17]The king asked, "What is that tombstone I see?"

The men of the city said, "It marks the tomb of the man of God who came from Judah and pronounced against the altar of Bethel the very things you have done to it."

[18]"Leave it alone," he said. "Don't let anyone disturb his bones." So they spared his bones and those of the prophet who had come from Samaria.

[a] 8 Or *high places*   [b] 10 Or *to make his son or daughter pass through*
[c] 13 Hebrew *Milcom*

¹⁹Just as he had done at Bethel, Josiah removed and defiled all the shrines at the high places that the kings of Israel had built in the towns of Samaria that had provoked the LORD to anger. ²⁰Josiah slaughtered all the priests of those high places on the altars and burned human bones on them. Then he went back to Jerusalem.

²¹The king gave this order to all the people: "Celebrate the Passover to the LORD your God, as it is written in this Book of the Covenant." ²²Not since the days of the judges who led Israel, nor throughout the days of the kings of Israel and the kings of Judah, had any such Passover been observed. ²³But in the eighteenth year of King Josiah, this Passover was celebrated to the LORD in Jerusalem.

²⁴Furthermore, Josiah got rid of the mediums and spiritists, the household gods, the idols and all the other detestable things seen in Judah and Jerusalem. This he did to fulfill the requirements of the law written in the book that Hilkiah the priest had discovered in the temple of the LORD. ²⁵Neither before nor after Josiah was there a king like him who turned to the LORD as he did—with all his heart and with all his soul and with all his strength, in accordance with all the Law of Moses.

²⁶Nevertheless, the LORD did not turn away from the heat of his fierce anger, which burned against Judah because of all that Manasseh had done to provoke him to anger. ²⁷So the LORD said, "I will remove Judah also from my presence as I removed Israel, and I will reject Jerusalem, the city I chose, and this temple, about which I said, 'There shall my Name be.'ᵃ"

²⁸As for the other events of Josiah's reign, and all he did, are they not written in the book of the annals of the kings of Judah?

²⁹While Josiah was king, Pharaoh Neco king of Egypt went up to the Euphrates River to help the king of Assyria. King Josiah marched out to meet him in battle, but Neco faced him and killed him at Megiddo. ³⁰Josiah's servants brought his body in a chariot from Megiddo to Jerusalem and buried him in his own tomb. And the people of the land took Jehoahaz son of Josiah and anointed him and made him king in place of his father.

Jehoahaz King of Judah

³¹Jehoahaz was twenty-three years old when he became king, and he reigned in Jerusalem three months. His mother's name was Hamutal daughter of Jeremiah; she was from Libnah. ³²He did evil in the eyes of the LORD, just as his fathers had done. ³³Pharaoh Neco put him in chains at Riblah in the land of Hamathᵇ so that he might not reign in Jerusalem, and he imposed on Judah a levy of a hundred talentsᶜ of silver and a talentᵈ of gold. ³⁴Pharaoh Neco made Eliakim son of Josiah king in place of his father Josiah and changed Eliakim's name to Jehoiakim. But he took Jehoahaz and carried him off to Egypt, and there he died. ³⁵Jehoiakim paid Pharaoh Neco the silver and gold he demanded. In order to do so, he taxed the land and exacted the silver and gold from the people of the land according to their assessments.

ᵃ27 1 Kings 8:29   ᵇ33 Hebrew; Septuagint (see also 2 Chron. 36:3) *Neco at Riblah in Hamath removed him*   ᶜ33 That is, about 3 3/4 tons (about 3.4 metric tons)   ᵈ33 That is, about 75 pounds (about 34 kilograms)

Service to God

2 KINGS 23:21–25

"Men and women, rich and poor must . . . walk before God in the same wise and holy spirit, in the same denial of all vain tempers, and in the same discipline and care of their souls; not only because they have all the same rational nature and are servants of the same God, but because they all need the same holiness to make them fit for the same happiness to which they are called. It is therefore absolutely necessary for all Christians, whether men or women, to consider themselves as persons that are devoted to holiness and so order their common ways of life by such rules of reason and piety as may turn it into continual service unto Almighty God."

—WILLIAM LAW,
A Serious Call to a Devout and Holy Life

A New World Power

2 KINGS 24:1

Now Babylon, after defeating Assyria and Egypt, reduces Judah—once triumphant—to vassal status. As this story draws to a close, its lessons are clear: Power is fleeting. Without God, no nation can endure for long. Yet nations and individuals still strive after the fleeting "number one" status, seeking temporal power rather than investing in things that last.

When have you wanted to be first? How did this desire or accomplishment affect your relationship to God—to other people? What values do you feel are more enduring than the rewards of being number one?

Jehoiakim King of Judah

³⁶Jehoiakim was twenty-five years old when he became king, and he reigned in Jerusalem eleven years. His mother's name was Zebidah daughter of Pedaiah; she was from Rumah. ³⁷And he did evil in the eyes of the LORD, just as his fathers had done.

24 During Jehoiakim's reign, Nebuchadnezzar king of Babylon invaded the land, and Jehoiakim became his vassal for three years. But then he changed his mind and rebelled against Nebuchadnezzar. ²The LORD sent Babylonian,ᵃ Aramean, Moabite and Ammonite raiders against him. He sent them to destroy Judah, in accordance with the word of the LORD proclaimed by his servants the prophets. ³Surely these things happened to Judah according to the LORD's command, in order to remove them from his presence because of the sins of Manasseh and all he had done, ⁴including the shedding of innocent blood. For he had filled Jerusalem with innocent blood, and the LORD was not willing to forgive.

⁵As for the other events of Jehoiakim's reign, and all he did, are they not written in the book of the annals of the kings of Judah? ⁶Jehoiakim rested with his fathers. And Jehoiachin his son succeeded him as king.

⁷The king of Egypt did not march out from his own country again, because the king of Babylon had taken all his territory, from the Wadi of Egypt to the Euphrates River.

Jehoiachin King of Judah

⁸Jehoiachin was eighteen years old when he became king, and he reigned in Jerusalem three months. His mother's name was Nehushta daughter of Elnathan; she was from Jerusalem. ⁹He did evil in the eyes of the LORD, just as his father had done.

¹⁰At that time the officers of Nebuchadnezzar king of Babylon advanced on Jerusalem and laid siege to it, ¹¹and Nebuchadnezzar himself came up to the city while his officers were besieging it. ¹²Jehoiachin king of Judah, his mother, his attendants, his nobles and his officials all surrendered to him.

In the eighth year of the reign of the king of Babylon, he took Jehoiachin prisoner. ¹³As the LORD had declared, Nebuchadnezzar removed all the treasures from the temple of the LORD and from the royal palace, and took away all the gold articles that Solomon king of Israel had made for the temple of the LORD. ¹⁴He carried into exile all Jerusalem: all the officers and fighting men, and all the craftsmen and artisans—a total of ten thousand. Only the poorest people of the land were left.

¹⁵Nebuchadnezzar took Jehoiachin captive to Babylon. He also took from Jerusalem to Babylon the king's mother, his wives, his officials and the leading men of the land. ¹⁶The king of Babylon also deported to Babylon the entire force of seven thousand fighting men, strong and fit for war, and a thousand craftsmen and artisans. ¹⁷He made Mattaniah, Jehoiachin's uncle, king in his place and changed his name to Zedekiah.

ᵃ 2 Or Chaldean

Zedekiah King of Judah

18Zedekiah was twenty-one years old when he became king, and he reigned in Jerusalem eleven years. His mother's name was Hamutal daughter of Jeremiah; she was from Libnah. **19**He did evil in the eyes of the LORD, just as Jehoiakim had done. **20**It was because of the LORD's anger that all this happened to Jerusalem and Judah, and in the end he thrust them from his presence.

The Fall of Jerusalem

Now Zedekiah rebelled against the king of Babylon.

25 So in the ninth year of Zedekiah's reign, on the tenth day of the tenth month, Nebuchadnezzar king of Babylon marched against Jerusalem with his whole army. He encamped outside the city and built siege works all around it. **2**The city was kept under siege until the eleventh year of King Zedekiah. **3**By the ninth day of the ₌fourth₌*a* month the famine in the city had become so severe that there was no food for the people to eat. **4**Then the city wall was broken through, and the whole army fled at night through the gate between the two walls near the king's garden, though the Babylonians*b* were surrounding the city. They fled toward the Arabah,*c* **5**but the Babylonian*d* army pursued the king and overtook him in the plains of Jericho. All his soldiers were separated from him and scattered, **6**and he was captured. He was taken to the king of Babylon at Riblah, where sentence was pronounced on him. **7**They killed the sons of Zedekiah before his eyes. Then they put out his eyes, bound him with bronze shackles and took him to Babylon.

8On the seventh day of the fifth month, in the nineteenth year of Nebuchadnezzar king of Babylon, Nebuzaradan commander of the imperial guard, an official of the king of Babylon, came to Jerusalem. **9**He set fire to the temple of the LORD, the royal palace and all the houses of Jerusalem. Every important building he burned down. **10**The whole Babylonian army, under the commander of the imperial guard, broke down the walls around Jerusalem. **11**Nebuzaradan the commander of the guard carried into exile the people who remained in the city, along with the rest of the populace and those who had gone over to the king of Babylon. **12**But the commander left behind some of the poorest people of the land to work the vineyards and fields.

13The Babylonians broke up the bronze pillars, the movable stands and the bronze Sea that were at the temple of the LORD and they carried the bronze to Babylon. **14**They also took away the pots, shovels, wick trimmers, dishes and all the bronze articles used in the temple service. **15**The commander of the imperial guard took away the censers and sprinkling bowls—all that were made of pure gold or silver.

16The bronze from the two pillars, the Sea and the movable stands, which Solomon had made for the temple of the LORD, was more than could be weighed. **17**Each pillar was twenty-seven feet*e* high. The bronze capital on top of one pillar was four and a half feet*f* high and was decorated

---

Broken Walls

2 KINGS 25:10

The enemy tears down Jerusalem's walls as a final act of humiliation. In Biblical times, a city without walls was doomed, unprotected from wild animals, marauders and enemies.

We often think of walls as being symbolic of that which protects us from harm, shelters the vulnerable aspects of our soul, and marks the emotional boundaries between people. But walls have the potential to divide us destructively.

Reflect on your key relationships with others. How does your behavior respect healthy boundaries between yourself and others? In what ways may you be trespassing those boundaries? Are there unhelpful walls that need to be torn down? After making a list of these walls, prayerfully consider how to strengthen the life-giving walls and dismantle the divisive ones.

See Meeting God in Community

---

a 3 See Jer. 52:6.   *b 4* Or *Chaldeans*; also in verses 13, 25 and 26   *c 4* Or *the Jordan Valley*   *d 5* Or *Chaldean*; also in verses 10 and 24   *e 17* Hebrew *eighteen cubits* (about 8.1 meters)   *f 17* Hebrew *three cubits* (about 1.3 meters)

Expelled From God's Presence

2 KINGS 25:27–30

After ignoring the warnings of the prophets for so long, the people of Jerusalem and Judah are carried to Babylon in exile, cast out of God's presence (see 24:20).

Exile has become a powerful symbol in Jewish liturgy and in Christian prayer of the experience of God's hiddenness. Sing or say prayerfully the hymn, "O come, O come, Emmanuel, and ransom captive Israel, that mourns in lowly exile here, until the Son of God appear." As you sing or speak the words again and again, remember situations in which God seemed hidden from you. Bring to mind similar situations in the lives of those you know. Conclude with the refrain: "Rejoice! Rejoice! Emmanuel shall come to thee, O Israel!"

See Meeting God in Worship

with a network and pomegranates of bronze all around. The other pillar, with its network, was similar.

[18]The commander of the guard took as prisoners Seraiah the chief priest, Zephaniah the priest next in rank and the three doorkeepers. [19]Of those still in the city, he took the officer in charge of the fighting men and five royal advisers. He also took the secretary who was chief officer in charge of conscripting the people of the land and sixty of his men who were found in the city. [20]Nebuzaradan the commander took them all and brought them to the king of Babylon at Riblah. [21]There at Riblah, in the land of Hamath, the king had them executed.

So Judah went into captivity, away from her land.

[22]Nebuchadnezzar king of Babylon appointed Gedaliah son of Ahikam, the son of Shaphan, to be over the people he had left behind in Judah. [23]When all the army officers and their men heard that the king of Babylon had appointed Gedaliah as governor, they came to Gedaliah at Mizpah—Ishmael son of Nethaniah, Johanan son of Kareah, Seraiah son of Tanhumeth the Netophathite, Jaazaniah the son of the Maacathite, and their men. [24]Gedaliah took an oath to reassure them and their men. "Do not be afraid of the Babylonian officials," he said. "Settle down in the land and serve the king of Babylon, and it will go well with you."

[25]In the seventh month, however, Ishmael son of Nethaniah, the son of Elishama, who was of royal blood, came with ten men and assassinated Gedaliah and also the men of Judah and the Babylonians who were with him at Mizpah. [26]At this, all the people from the least to the greatest, together with the army officers, fled to Egypt for fear of the Babylonians.

Jehoiachin Released

[27]In the thirty-seventh year of the exile of Jehoiachin king of Judah, in the year Evil-Merodach[a] became king of Babylon, he released Jehoiachin from prison on the twenty-seventh day of the twelfth month. [28]He spoke kindly to him and gave him a seat of honor higher than those of the other kings who were with him in Babylon. [29]So Jehoiachin put aside his prison clothes and for the rest of his life ate regularly at the king's table. [30]Day by day the king gave Jehoiachin a regular allowance as long as he lived.

a 27 Also called Amel-Marduk

1 CHRONICLES
The People of God

KEY VERSE:

When all the elders of Israel had come to King David at Hebron, he made a compact with them
at Hebron before the LORD, and they anointed David king over Israel, as the LORD had promised
through Samuel—1 Chronicles 11:3

I f you glance through this book, you will notice
the large number of names. Everywhere are long
lists of names: the generations from Adam to
Abraham, the many families descended from the
twelve sons of Jacob, the officials of David's court, the
priests and Levites who served before the Lord. So
many people!

Some of the names have Biblical stories connected
to them. Some we know from other references. But
most are no more than names and titles, yet each
name represents one of God's people. Each had a
unique role to play in the history of Israel. No doubt
many would be surprised that anyone remembers
them at all today, three thousand years later.

They are remembered because God still has faithful followers who know they are part of a long tradition. God's people still tell the old, old stories. As
people of God—the church—we continue to worship
God with prayer, song, musical instruments and
dance. We continue to organize and take on special
responsibilities to deal with practical matters. We continue to struggle to know how to be faithful in a confusing and often hostile world.

As you read this book, consider your place among
God's people. How are you tied into the tradition
through your family and your church? What is your
special role within your church or within the church
as a whole? To what deeper involvement is God calling you?

"At all times and in every race,
anyone who fears God and does
what is right has been acceptable to him [see Acts 10:35].
God has, however, willed to
make people holy and save
them, not as individuals without any bond or link between
them, but rather to make them
into a people who might acknowledge him and serve him
in holiness. He therefore chose
the Israelite race to be his own
people and established a covenant with it. He gradually instructed this people—in its
history manifesting both himself and the decree of his will—
and made it holy unto
himself."

—SECOND VATICAN COUNCIL,
Lumen Gentium, Chapter 2

From the Beginning

1 CHRONICLES 1:1–4

The Chronicler begins his story at the beginning, simply listing the names of generations of Adam's descendants. You might flesh out this outline by reading the stories of Adam (and why the descent is through his third son Seth) and of Noah and his three sons (see Genesis 1–9). You might even continue by reading through the accounts of Enoch or Methuselah. Can you imagine seeing your name in this list? Where do you see yourself in these ancient stories? How do they illuminate your walk with God?

Historical Records From Adam to Abraham

To Noah's Sons

1 Adam, Seth, Enosh, ²Kenan, Mahalalel, Jared, ³Enoch, Methuselah, Lamech, Noah.

⁴The sons of Noah:ᵃ
Shem, Ham and Japheth.

The Japhethites

⁵The sonsᵇ of Japheth:
Gomer, Magog, Madai, Javan, Tubal, Meshech and Tiras.
⁶The sons of Gomer:
Ashkenaz, Riphathᶜ and Togarmah.
⁷The sons of Javan:
Elishah, Tarshish, the Kittim and the Rodanim.

The Hamites

⁸The sons of Ham:
Cush, Mizraim,ᵈ Put and Canaan.
⁹The sons of Cush:
Seba, Havilah, Sabta, Raamah and Sabteca.
The sons of Raamah:
Sheba and Dedan.
¹⁰Cush was the fatherᵉ of
Nimrod, who grew to be a mighty warrior on earth.
¹¹Mizraim was the father of
the Ludites, Anamites, Lehabites, Naphtuhites, ¹²Pathrusites, Casluhites (from whom the Philistines came) and Caphtorites.
¹³Canaan was the father of
Sidon his firstborn,ᶠ and of the Hittites, ¹⁴Jebusites, Amorites, Girgashites, ¹⁵Hivites, Arkites, Sinites, ¹⁶Arvadites, Zemarites and Hamathites.

The Semites

¹⁷The sons of Shem:
Elam, Asshur, Arphaxad, Lud and Aram.
The sons of Aramᵍ:
Uz, Hul, Gether and Meshech.
¹⁸Arphaxad was the father of Shelah,
and Shelah the father of Eber.
¹⁹Two sons were born to Eber:
One was named Peleg,ʰ because in his time the earth was divided; his brother was named Joktan.
²⁰Joktan was the father of
Almodad, Sheleph, Hazarmaveth, Jerah, ²¹Hadoram, Uzal, Diklah, ²²Obal,ⁱ Abimael, Sheba, ²³Ophir, Havilah and Jobab. All these were sons of Joktan.

ᵃ4 Septuagint; Hebrew does not have The sons of Noah: ᵇ5 Sons may mean descendants or successors or nations; also in verses 6–10, 17 and 20.   ᶜ6 Many Hebrew manuscripts and Vulgate (see also Septuagint and Gen. 10:3); most Hebrew manuscripts Diphath   ᵈ8 That is, Egypt; also in verse 11   ᵉ10 Father may mean ancestor or predecessor or founder; also in verses 11, 13, 18 and 20.   ᶠ13 Or of the Sidonians, the foremost   ᵍ17 One Hebrew manuscript and some Septuagint manuscripts (see also Gen. 10:23); most Hebrew manuscripts do not have this line.   ʰ19 Peleg means division.   ⁱ22 Some Hebrew manuscripts and Syriac (see also Gen. 10:28); most Hebrew manuscripts Ebal

²⁴ Shem, Arphaxad,ᵃ Shelah,
²⁵ Eber, Peleg, Reu,
²⁶ Serug, Nahor, Terah
²⁷ and Abram (that is, Abraham).

The Family of Abraham

²⁸ The sons of Abraham:
    Isaac and Ishmael.

Descendants of Hagar

²⁹ These were their descendants:
    Nebaioth the firstborn of Ishmael, Kedar, Adbeel,
    Mibsam, ³⁰ Mishma, Dumah, Massa, Hadad, Tema,
    ³¹ Jetur, Naphish and Kedemah. These were the
    sons of Ishmael.

Descendants of Keturah

³² The sons born to Keturah, Abraham's concubine:
    Zimran, Jokshan, Medan, Midian, Ishbak and Shuah.
    The sons of Jokshan:
    Sheba and Dedan.
³³ The sons of Midian:
    Ephah, Epher, Hanoch, Abida and Eldaah.
    All these were descendants of Keturah.

Descendants of Sarah

³⁴ Abraham was the father of Isaac.
    The sons of Isaac:
    Esau and Israel.

Esau's Sons

³⁵ The sons of Esau:
    Eliphaz, Reuel, Jeush, Jalam and Korah.
³⁶ The sons of Eliphaz:
    Teman, Omar, Zepho,ᵇ Gatam and Kenaz;
    by Timna: Amalek.ᶜ
³⁷ The sons of Reuel:
    Nahath, Zerah, Shammah and Mizzah.

The People of Seir in Edom

³⁸ The sons of Seir:
    Lotan, Shobal, Zibeon, Anah, Dishon, Ezer and
    Dishan.
³⁹ The sons of Lotan:
    Hori and Homam. Timna was Lotan's sister.
⁴⁰ The sons of Shobal:
    Alvan,ᵈ Manahath, Ebal, Shepho and Onam.
    The sons of Zibeon:
    Aiah and Anah.
⁴¹ The son of Anah:
    Dishon.
    The sons of Dishon:
    Hemdan,ᵉ Eshban, Ithran and Keran.

ᵃ24 Hebrew; some Septuagint manuscripts *Arphaxad, Cainan* (see also note at
Gen. 11:10)   ᵇ36 Many Hebrew manuscripts, some Septuagint manuscripts
and Syriac (see also Gen. 36:11); most Hebrew manuscripts *Zephi*
ᶜ36 Some Septuagint manuscripts (see also Gen. 36:12); Hebrew *Gatam,
Kenaz, Timna and Amalek*   ᵈ40 Many Hebrew manuscripts and some
Septuagint manuscripts (see also Gen. 36:23); most Hebrew manuscripts
Alian   ᵉ41 Many Hebrew manuscripts and some Septuagint manuscripts
(see also Gen. 36:26); most Hebrew manuscripts *Hamran*

Children of Abraham

1 CHRONICLES 1:28

Here is a reminder that the people of God, the children of Abraham, include both the descendants of Isaac (the Jews and, by adoption, Christians) and the descendants of Ishmael (the Arabs). The same point is brought out in the Koran. The struggles in the Middle East today, then, are family quarrels. With a globe or atlas in front of you, spend some time in prayer for all the children of Abraham, that their fighting may cease and that they may rediscover their unity as Abraham's children.

See *Meeting God in Community*

Faithful Outsider

1 CHRONICLES 2:4

Tamar is only the third woman mentioned in 1 Chronicles, and the first whose story we know (see Genesis 38). She is one of many outsiders who teaches God's people about true faithfulness. Who are the "outsiders" who inspire you by their example of devotion to principles or their concern for humanity? What can they teach you about faithfulness? What can they teach you about the extent of God's reach and about the variety of people God uses? You might thank God for breaking through the human boundaries we draw and for raising up faithful people from every nation.

See Meeting God in Community

---

⁴²The sons of Ezer:

Bilhan, Zaavan and Akan.ᵃ

The sons of Dishanᵇ:

Uz and Aran.

The Rulers of Edom

⁴³These were the kings who reigned in Edom before any Israelite king reignedᶜ:

Bela son of Beor, whose city was named Dinhabah.

⁴⁴When Bela died, Jobab son of Zerah from Bozrah succeeded him as king.

⁴⁵When Jobab died, Husham from the land of the Temanites succeeded him as king.

⁴⁶When Husham died, Hadad son of Bedad, who defeated Midian in the country of Moab, succeeded him as king. His city was named Avith.

⁴⁷When Hadad died, Samlah from Masrekah succeeded him as king.

⁴⁸When Samlah died, Shaul from Rehoboth on the riverᵈ succeeded him as king.

⁴⁹When Shaul died, Baal-Hanan son of Acbor succeeded him as king.

⁵⁰When Baal-Hanan died, Hadad succeeded him as king. His city was named Pau,ᵉ and his wife's name was Mehetabel daughter of Matred, the daughter of Me-Zahab. ⁵¹Hadad also died.

The chiefs of Edom were:

Timna, Alvah, Jetheth, ⁵²Oholibamah, Elah, Pinon, ⁵³Kenaz, Teman, Mibzar, ⁵⁴Magdiel and Iram. These were the chiefs of Edom.

Israel's Sons

2 These were the sons of Israel:

Reuben, Simeon, Levi, Judah, Issachar, Zebulun, ²Dan, Joseph, Benjamin, Naphtali, Gad and Asher.

Judah

To Hezron's Sons

³The sons of Judah:

Er, Onan and Shelah. These three were born to him by a Canaanite woman, the daughter of Shua. Er, Judah's firstborn, was wicked in the LORD's sight; so the LORD put him to death. ⁴Tamar, Judah's daughter-in-law, bore him Perez and Zerah. Judah had five sons in all.

⁵The sons of Perez:

Hezron and Hamul.

⁶The sons of Zerah:

Zimri, Ethan, Heman, Calcol and Darahᶠ—five in all.

⁷The son of Carmi:

ᵃ *42* Many Hebrew and Septuagint manuscripts (see also Gen. 36:27); most Hebrew manuscripts *Zaavan, Jaakan*   ᵇ *42* Hebrew *Dishon,* a variant of *Dishan*   ᶜ *43* Or *before an Israelite king reigned over them*   ᵈ *48* Possibly the Euphrates   ᵉ *50* Many Hebrew manuscripts, some Septuagint manuscripts, Vulgate and Syriac (see also Gen. 36:39); most Hebrew manuscripts *Pai*   ᶠ *6* Many Hebrew manuscripts, some Septuagint manuscripts and Syriac (see also 1 Kings 4:31); most Hebrew manuscripts *Dara*

Achar,ᵃ who brought trouble on Israel by violating the ban on taking devoted things.ᵇ

⁸ The son of Ethan:

Azariah.

⁹ The sons born to Hezron were:

Jerahmeel, Ram and Caleb.ᶜ

From Ram Son of Hezron

¹⁰ Ram was the father of

Amminadab, and Amminadab the father of Nahshon, the leader of the people of Judah. ¹¹ Nahshon was the father of Salmon,ᵈ Salmon the father of Boaz, ¹² Boaz the father of Obed and Obed the father of Jesse.

¹³ Jesse was the father of

Eliab his firstborn; the second son was Abinadab, the third Shimea, ¹⁴ the fourth Nethanel, the fifth Raddai, ¹⁵ the sixth Ozem and the seventh David. ¹⁶ Their sisters were Zeruiah and Abigail. Zeruiah's three sons were Abishai, Joab and Asahel. ¹⁷ Abigail was the mother of Amasa, whose father was Jether the Ishmaelite.

Caleb Son of Hezron

¹⁸ Caleb son of Hezron had children by his wife Azubah (and by Jerioth). These were her sons: Jesher, Shobab and Ardon. ¹⁹ When Azubah died, Caleb married Ephrath, who bore him Hur. ²⁰ Hur was the father of Uri, and Uri the father of Bezalel.

²¹ Later, Hezron lay with the daughter of Makir the father of Gilead (he had married her when he was sixty years old), and she bore him Segub. ²² Segub was the father of Jair, who controlled twenty-three towns in Gilead. ²³ (But Geshur and Aram captured Havvoth Jair,ᵉ as well as Kenath with its surrounding settlements—sixty towns.) All these were descendants of Makir the father of Gilead.

²⁴ After Hezron died in Caleb Ephrathah, Abijah the wife of Hezron bore him Ashhur the fatherᶠ of Tekoa.

Jerahmeel Son of Hezron

²⁵ The sons of Jerahmeel the firstborn of Hezron:

Ram his firstborn, Bunah, Oren, Ozem andᵍ Ahijah. ²⁶ Jerahmeel had another wife, whose name was Atarah; she was the mother of Onam.

²⁷ The sons of Ram the firstborn of Jerahmeel:

Maaz, Jamin and Eker.

²⁸ The sons of Onam:

Shammai and Jada.

The sons of Shammai:

Nadab and Abishur.

²⁹ Abishur's wife was named Abihail, who bore him Ahban and Molid.

People of God

1 CHRONICLES 2

"The people of God are the Church made visible in the world. It is they who must convince the world of the reality of the gospel or leave it unconvinced. There can be no evasion or delegation of this responsibility; the Church is either faithful as a witnessing and serving community, or it loses its vitality and its impact on an unbelieving world."

—*The Book of Discipline of the United Methodist Church* (1992)

ᵃ 7 *Achar* means *trouble; Achar* is called *Achan* in Joshua.   ᵇ 7 The Hebrew term refers to the irrevocable giving over of things or persons to the LORD, often by totally destroying them.   ᶜ 9 Hebrew *Kelubai*, a variant of *Caleb*   ᵈ 11 Septuagint (see also Ruth 4:21); Hebrew *Salma*   ᵉ 23 Or *captured the settlements of Jair*   ᶠ 24 *Father* may mean *civic leader* or *military leader*; also in verses 42, 45, 49–52 and possibly elsewhere.   ᵍ 25 Or *Oren and Ozem, by*

Desire for Children

1 CHRONICLES 2:34–35

People have always taken extraordinary steps in order to have a child to carry on the family name. Today many couples struggle to become parents, whether through complex medical procedures or through adoption. Pray for those who seek to share their love with a child. Pray for the clinics, adoption agencies and foster care programs that help them. Pray also for all women who consider their pregnancies a problem; pray for them as they face critical choices. You might also want to thank God for the parents who gave you life or raised you or for your own children.

See Meeting God in Community

30 The sons of Nadab:
Seled and Appaim. Seled died without children.
31 The son of Appaim:
Ishi, who was the father of Sheshan.
Sheshan was the father of Ahlai.
32 The sons of Jada, Shammai's brother:
Jether and Jonathan. Jether died without children.
33 The sons of Jonathan:
Peleth and Zaza.
These were the descendants of Jerahmeel.
34 Sheshan had no sons—only daughters.
He had an Egyptian servant named Jarha. 35 Sheshan gave his daughter in marriage to his servant Jarha, and she bore him Attai.
36 Attai was the father of Nathan,
Nathan the father of Zabad,
37 Zabad the father of Ephlal,
Ephlal the father of Obed,
38 Obed the father of Jehu,
Jehu the father of Azariah,
39 Azariah the father of Helez,
Helez the father of Eleasah,
40 Eleasah the father of Sismai,
Sismai the father of Shallum,
41 Shallum the father of Jekamiah,
and Jekamiah the father of Elishama.

The Clans of Caleb

42 The sons of Caleb the brother of Jerahmeel:
Mesha his firstborn, who was the father of Ziph, and his son Mareshah,*a* who was the father of Hebron.
43 The sons of Hebron:
Korah, Tappuah, Rekem and Shema. 44 Shema was the father of Raham, and Raham the father of Jorkeam. Rekem was the father of Shammai. 45 The son of Shammai was Maon, and Maon was the father of Beth Zur.
46 Caleb's concubine Ephah was the mother of Haran, Moza and Gazez. Haran was the father of Gazez.
47 The sons of Jahdai:
Regem, Jotham, Geshan, Pelet, Ephah and Shaaph.
48 Caleb's concubine Maacah was the mother of Sheber and Tirhanah. 49 She also gave birth to Shaaph the father of Madmannah and to Sheva the father of Macbenah and Gibea. Caleb's daughter was Acsah.
50 These were the descendants of Caleb.

The sons of Hur the firstborn of Ephrathah:
Shobal the father of Kiriath Jearim, 51 Salma the father of Bethlehem, and Hareph the father of Beth Gader.
52 The descendants of Shobal the father of Kiriath Jearim were:
Haroeh, half the Manahathites, 53 and the clans of Kiriath Jearim: the Ithrites, Puthites, Shumathites and Mishraites. From these descended the Zorathites and Eshtaolites.
54 The descendants of Salma:

a 42 The meaning of the Hebrew for this phrase is uncertain.

Bethlehem, the Netophathites, Atroth Beth Joab, half the Manahathites, the Zorites, [55] and the clans of scribes[a] who lived at Jabez: the Tirathites, Shimeathites and Sucathites. These are the Kenites who came from Hammath, the father of the house of Recab.[b]

The Sons of David

3 These were the sons of David born to him in Hebron:

The firstborn was Amnon the son of Ahinoam of Jezreel;

the second, Daniel the son of Abigail of Carmel;

[2] the third, Absalom the son of Maacah daughter of Talmai king of Geshur;

the fourth, Adonijah the son of Haggith;

[3] the fifth, Shephatiah the son of Abital;

and the sixth, Ithream, by his wife Eglah.

[4] These six were born to David in Hebron, where he reigned seven years and six months.

David reigned in Jerusalem thirty-three years, [5] and these were the children born to him there:

Shammua,[c] Shobab, Nathan and Solomon. These four were by Bathsheba[d] daughter of Ammiel. [6] There were also Ibhar, Elishua,[e] Eliphelet, [7] Nogah, Nepheg, Japhia, [8] Elishama, Eliada and Eliphelet— nine in all. [9] All these were the sons of David, besides his sons by his concubines. And Tamar was their sister.

The Kings of Judah

[10] Solomon's son was Rehoboam,

Abijah his son,

Asa his son,

Jehoshaphat his son,

[11] Jehoram[f] his son,

Ahaziah his son,

Joash his son,

[12] Amaziah his son,

Azariah his son,

Jotham his son,

[13] Ahaz his son,

Hezekiah his son,

Manasseh his son,

[14] Amon his son,

Josiah his son.

[15] The sons of Josiah:

Johanan the firstborn,

Jehoiakim the second son,

Zedekiah the third,

Shallum the fourth.

[16] The successors of Jehoiakim:

Jehoiachin[g] his son,

and Zedekiah.

Into the Future

1 CHRONICLES 3:10–23

Suddenly the list of names ranges beyond David, whose story fills the bulk of 1 Chronicles, and then even beyond Zedekiah, the last king mentioned in 2 Chronicles. We are given a glimpse of the generations that extend beyond the end of this account. You might spend some time imagining the generations of progeny who will follow you—your children's children or simply generations yet to come. What will their world be like? How will your actions affect their lives? Pray for them and for the wisdom to leave them a legacy of faith.

a 55 Or of the Sopherites   b 55 Or father of Beth Recab   c 5 Hebrew Shimea, a variant of Shammua   d 5 One Hebrew manuscript and Vulgate (see also Septuagint and 2 Samuel 11:3); most Hebrew manuscripts Bathshua   e 6 Two Hebrew manuscripts (see also 2 Samuel 5:15 and 1 Chron. 14:5); most Hebrew manuscripts Elishama   f 11 Hebrew Joram, a variant of Jehoram   g 16 Hebrew Jeconiah, a variant of Jehoiachin; also in verse 17

Jabez

1 CHRONICLES 4:9–10

This is the whole story of Jabez, who is mentioned only once in the Bible. He was born; he prayed; his prayer was heard. Look at his prayer. It is quite simple: God, help me, be with me, protect me. How many of your prayers, especially short spontaneous prayers, ask simply for God's help, presence or protection? You might pray with Jabez—take time to dwell on each of his petitions. What kind of help do you most want from God? How would you like to experience God's presence with you? From what do you seek God's protection?

See Meeting God in Prayer

The Royal Line After the Exile

¹⁷The descendants of Jehoiachin the captive:

Shealtiel his son, ¹⁸Malkiram, Pedaiah, Shenazzar, Jekamiah, Hoshama and Nedabiah.

¹⁹The sons of Pedaiah:

Zerubbabel and Shimei.

The sons of Zerubbabel:

Meshullam and Hananiah.

Shelomith was their sister.

²⁰There were also five others:

Hashubah, Ohel, Berekiah, Hasadiah and Jushab-Hesed.

²¹The descendants of Hananiah:

Pelatiah and Jeshaiah, and the sons of Rephaiah, of Arnan, of Obadiah and of Shecaniah.

²²The descendants of Shecaniah:

Shemaiah and his sons:

Hattush, Igal, Bariah, Neariah and Shaphat—six in all.

²³The sons of Neariah:

Elioenai, Hizkiah and Azrikam—three in all.

²⁴The sons of Elioenai:

Hodaviah, Eliashib, Pelaiah, Akkub, Johanan, Delaiah and Anani—seven in all.

Other Clans of Judah

4 The descendants of Judah:

Perez, Hezron, Carmi, Hur and Shobal.

²Reaiah son of Shobal was the father of Jahath, and Jahath the father of Ahumai and Lahad. These were the clans of the Zorathites.

³These were the sons*ᵃ* of Etam:

Jezreel, Ishma and Idbash. Their sister was named Hazzelelponi. ⁴Penuel was the father of Gedor, and Ezer the father of Hushah.

These were the descendants of Hur, the firstborn of Ephrathah and father*ᵇ* of Bethlehem.

⁵Ashhur the father of Tekoa had two wives, Helah and Naarah.

⁶Naarah bore him Ahuzzam, Hepher, Temeni and Haahashtari. These were the descendants of Naarah.

⁷The sons of Helah:

Zereth, Zohar, Ethnan, ⁸and Koz, who was the father of Anub and Hazzobebah and of the clans of Aharhel son of Harum.

⁹Jabez was more honorable than his brothers. His mother had named him Jabez,*ᶜ* saying, "I gave birth to him in pain." ¹⁰Jabez cried out to the God of Israel, "Oh, that you would bless me and enlarge my territory! Let your hand be with me, and keep me from harm so that I will be free from pain." And God granted his request.

¹¹Kelub, Shuhah's brother, was the father of Mehir, who was the father of Eshton. ¹²Eshton was the father of Beth Rapha, Paseah and Tehinnah the father of Ir Nahash.*ᵈ* These were the men of Recah.

ᵃ 3 Some Septuagint manuscripts (see also Vulgate); Hebrew *father*
ᵇ 4 Father may mean *civic leader* or *military leader*; also in verses 12, 14, 17, 18 and possibly elsewhere.   *ᶜ 9 Jabez* sounds like the Hebrew for *pain.*
ᵈ 12 Or *of the city of Nahash*

¹³The sons of Kenaz:
   Othniel and Seraiah.
   The sons of Othniel:
   Hathath and Meonothai.ª ¹⁴Meonothai was the father of Ophrah.
   Seraiah was the father of Joab,
   the father of Ge Harashim.ᵇ It was called this because its people were craftsmen.
¹⁵The sons of Caleb son of Jephunneh:
   Iru, Elah and Naam.
   The son of Elah:
   Kenaz.
¹⁶The sons of Jehallelel:
   Ziph, Ziphah, Tiria and Asarel.
¹⁷The sons of Ezrah:
   Jether, Mered, Epher and Jalon. One of Mered's
   wives gave birth to Miriam, Shammai and Ishbah
   the father of Eshtemoa. ¹⁸(His Judean wife gave
   birth to Jered the father of Gedor, Heber the father
   of Soco, and Jekuthiel the father of Zanoah.) These
   were the children of Pharaoh's daughter Bithiah,
   whom Mered had married.
¹⁹The sons of Hodiah's wife, the sister of Naham:
   the father of Keilah the Garmite, and Eshtemoa the
   Maacathite.
²⁰The sons of Shimon:
   Amnon, Rinnah, Ben-Hanan and Tilon.
   The descendants of Ishi:
   Zoheth and Ben-Zoheth.
²¹The sons of Shelah son of Judah:
   Er the father of Lecah, Laadah the father of Mareshah and the clans of the linen workers at Beth Ash-
   bea, ²²Jokim, the men of Cozeba, and Joash and
   Saraph, who ruled in Moab and Jashubi Lehem.
   (These records are from ancient times.) ²³They were
   the potters who lived at Netaim and Gederah; they
   stayed there and worked for the king.

Simeon

²⁴The descendants of Simeon:
   Nemuel, Jamin, Jarib, Zerah and Shaul;
   ²⁵Shallum was Shaul's son, Mibsam his son and
   Mishma his son.
²⁶The descendants of Mishma:
   Hammuel his son, Zaccur his son and Shimei his
   son.
²⁷Shimei had sixteen sons and six daughters, but his
brothers did not have many children; so their entire clan
did not become as numerous as the people of Judah.
²⁸They lived in Beersheba, Moladah, Hazar Shual, ²⁹Bil-
hah, Ezem, Tolad, ³⁰Bethuel, Hormah, Ziklag, ³¹Beth Marcaboth, Hazar Susim, Beth Biri and Shaaraim. These were
their towns until the reign of David. ³²Their surrounding
villages were Etam, Ain, Rimmon, Token and Ashan—five
towns— ³³and all the villages around these towns as far as
Baalath.ᶜ These were their settlements. And they kept a
genealogical record.

ª 13 Some Septuagint manuscripts and Vulgate; Hebrew does not have *and
Meonothai*.   ᵇ 14 *Ge Harashim* means *valley of craftsmen*.   ᶜ 33 Some
Septuagint manuscripts (see also Joshua 19:8); Hebrew *Baal*

Holy Fellowship

1 CHRONICLES 4:24

"The final grounds of holy Fellowship are in God. Lives im-
mersed and drowned in God are
drowned in love, and know one
another in him, and know one
another in love. God is the medium, the matrix, the focus, the
solvent . . . Persons in the Fellowship are related to one another through him, as all
mountains go down into the
same earth. They get at one another through him. He is actively moving in all, coordinating
those who are pliant to his will
and suffusing them all with his
glory and his joy."

—THOMAS KELLY,
A Testament of Devotion

Praying a Family Tree

1 CHRONICLES 4:33–39

Genealogy is obviously important to the Chronicler and to those to whom he writes. How much do you know about your family tree, whether "family" means to you the people who gave you birth or others who chose to raise you? Who are "your people"? How have they helped make you who you are, for good or ill? You might take time to draw up your family tree. Then spend some time praying for those who are still living, thanking God for each person's contribution to your life.

See Meeting God in Community

³⁴Meshobab, Jamlech, Joshah son of Amaziah, ³⁵Joel, Jehu son of Joshibiah, the son of Seraiah, the son of Asiel, ³⁶also Elioenai, Jaakobah, Jeshohaiah, Asaiah, Adiel, Jesimiel, Benaiah, ³⁷and Ziza son of Shiphi, the son of Allon, the son of Jedaiah, the son of Shimri, the son of Shemaiah.

³⁸The men listed above by name were leaders of their clans. Their families increased greatly, ³⁹and they went to the outskirts of Gedor to the east of the valley in search of pasture for their flocks. ⁴⁰They found rich, good pasture, and the land was spacious, peaceful and quiet. Some Hamites had lived there formerly.

⁴¹The men whose names were listed came in the days of Hezekiah king of Judah. They attacked the Hamites in their dwellings and also the Meunites who were there and completely destroyed*ᵃ* them, as is evident to this day. Then they settled in their place, because there was pasture for their flocks. ⁴²And five hundred of these Simeonites, led by Pelatiah, Neariah, Rephaiah and Uzziel, the sons of Ishi, invaded the hill country of Seir. ⁴³They killed the remaining Amalekites who had escaped, and they have lived there to this day.

Reuben

5 The sons of Reuben the firstborn of Israel (he was the firstborn, but when he defiled his father's marriage bed, his rights as firstborn were given to the sons of Joseph son of Israel; so he could not be listed in the genealogical record in accordance with his birthright, ²and though Judah was the strongest of his brothers and a ruler came from him, the rights of the firstborn belonged to Joseph)— ³the sons of Reuben the firstborn of Israel:

Hanoch, Pallu, Hezron and Carmi.
⁴The descendants of Joel:
Shemaiah his son, Gog his son,
Shimei his son, ⁵Micah his son,
Reaiah his son, Baal his son,
⁶and Beerah his son, whom Tiglath-Pileser*ᵇ* king of Assyria took into exile. Beerah was a leader of the Reubenites.
⁷Their relatives by clans, listed according to their genealogical records:
Jeiel the chief, Zechariah, ⁸and Bela son of Azaz, the son of Shema, the son of Joel. They settled in the area from Aroer to Nebo and Baal Meon. ⁹To the east they occupied the land up to the edge of the desert that extends to the Euphrates River, because their livestock had increased in Gilead.
¹⁰During Saul's reign they waged war against the Hagrites, who were defeated at their hands; they occupied the dwellings of the Hagrites throughout the entire region east of Gilead.

Gad

¹¹The Gadites lived next to them in Bashan, as far as Salecah:

ᵃ 41 The Hebrew term refers to the irrevocable giving over of things or persons to the LORD, often by totally destroying them.   *ᵇ 6* Hebrew *Tilgath-Pilneser,* a variant of *Tiglath-Pileser;* also in verse 26

¹²Joel was the chief, Shapham the second, then Janai and Shaphat, in Bashan.
¹³Their relatives, by families, were:
Michael, Meshullam, Sheba, Jorai, Jacan, Zia and Eber—seven in all.
¹⁴These were the sons of Abihail son of Huri, the son of Jaroah, the son of Gilead, the son of Michael, the son of Jeshishai, the son of Jahdo, the son of Buz.
¹⁵Ahi son of Abdiel, the son of Guni, was head of their family.
¹⁶The Gadites lived in Gilead, in Bashan and its outlying villages, and on all the pasturelands of Sharon as far as they extended.
¹⁷All these were entered in the genealogical records during the reigns of Jotham king of Judah and Jeroboam king of Israel.

¹⁸The Reubenites, the Gadites and the half-tribe of Manasseh had 44,760 men ready for military service—able-bodied men who could handle shield and sword, who could use a bow, and who were trained for battle. ¹⁹They waged war against the Hagrites, Jetur, Naphish and Nodab. ²⁰They were helped in fighting them, and God handed the Hagrites and all their allies over to them, because they cried out to him during the battle. He answered their prayers, because they trusted in him. ²¹They seized the livestock of the Hagrites—fifty thousand camels, two hundred fifty thousand sheep and two thousand donkeys. They also took one hundred thousand people captive, ²²and many others fell slain, because the battle was God's. And they occupied the land until the exile.

The Half-Tribe of Manasseh

²³The people of the half-tribe of Manasseh were numerous; they settled in the land from Bashan to Baal Hermon, that is, to Senir (Mount Hermon).
²⁴These were the heads of their families: Epher, Ishi, Eliel, Azriel, Jeremiah, Hodaviah and Jahdiel. They were brave warriors, famous men, and heads of their families. ²⁵But they were unfaithful to the God of their fathers and prostituted themselves to the gods of the peoples of the land, whom God had destroyed before them. ²⁶So the God of Israel stirred up the spirit of Pul king of Assyria (that is, Tiglath-Pileser king of Assyria), who took the Reubenites, the Gadites and the half-tribe of Manasseh into exile. He took them to Halah, Habor, Hara and the river of Gozan, where they are to this day.

Levi

6 The sons of Levi:
Gershon, Kohath and Merari.
²The sons of Kohath:
Amram, Izhar, Hebron and Uzziel.
³The children of Amram:
Aaron, Moses and Miriam.
The sons of Aaron:
Nadab, Abihu, Eleazar and Ithamar.
⁴Eleazar was the father of Phinehas,
Phinehas the father of Abishua,
⁵Abishua the father of Bukki,

Fitting In

1 CHRONICLES 5:23–26

The half-tribe of Manasseh adapted to the culture they found in the land they conquered, and they eventually worshiped other gods. The result was their destruction.

We are often faced with conflicts between what God calls us to be and to do and what others do in the society around us. Where do you experience such conflicts in your own life? What are the outcomes of these conflicts? What "other gods" vie for your allegiance and your devotion? What does it cost you to resist them? What does it cost you to give in to them? Ask for God's help to remain faithful despite the temptation to fit in.

See Meeting God in Everyday Life

519

Nurturing Our Gifts

1 CHRONICLES 6:1

"A primary purpose of the Church is to help us discover our gifts and, in the face of our fears, to hold us accountable for them so that we can enter into the joy of creating. The major obligation of the Church to children is to enjoy them and to listen to them so that [they] can grow according to the design which is written into [their] being and [emerge] only under the care and warmth of another life."

—ELIZABETH O'CONNOR,
Eighth Day of Creation

Bukki the father of Uzzi,
⁶Uzzi the father of Zerahiah,
Zerahiah the father of Meraioth,
⁷Meraioth the father of Amariah,
Amariah the father of Ahitub,
⁸Ahitub the father of Zadok,
Zadok the father of Ahimaaz,
⁹Ahimaaz the father of Azariah,
Azariah the father of Johanan,
¹⁰Johanan the father of Azariah (it was he who served as priest in the temple Solomon built in Jerusalem),
¹¹Azariah the father of Amariah,
Amariah the father of Ahitub,
¹²Ahitub the father of Zadok,
Zadok the father of Shallum,
¹³Shallum the father of Hilkiah,
Hilkiah the father of Azariah,
¹⁴Azariah the father of Seraiah,
and Seraiah the father of Jehozadak.

¹⁵Jehozadak was deported when the LORD sent Judah and Jerusalem into exile by the hand of Nebuchadnezzar.

¹⁶The sons of Levi:
Gershon,ᵃ Kohath and Merari.
¹⁷These are the names of the sons of Gershon:
Libni and Shimei.
¹⁸The sons of Kohath:
Amram, Izhar, Hebron and Uzziel.
¹⁹The sons of Merari:
Mahli and Mushi.
These are the clans of the Levites listed according to their fathers:
²⁰Of Gershon:
Libni his son, Jehath his son,
Zimmah his son, ²¹Joah his son,
Iddo his son, Zerah his son
and Jeatherai his son.
²²The descendants of Kohath:
Amminadab his son, Korah his son,
Assir his son, ²³Elkanah his son,
Ebiasaph his son, Assir his son,
²⁴Tahath his son, Uriel his son,
Uzziah his son and Shaul his son.
²⁵The descendants of Elkanah:
Amasai, Ahimoth,
²⁶Elkanah his son,ᵇ Zophai his son,
Nahath his son, ²⁷Eliab his son,
Jeroham his son, Elkanah his son
and Samuel his son.ᶜ
²⁸The sons of Samuel:
Joelᵈ the firstborn
and Abijah the second son.

ᵃ16 Hebrew *Gershom*, a variant of *Gershon*; also in verses 17, 20, 43, 62 and 71   ᵇ26 Some Hebrew manuscripts, Septuagint and Syriac; most Hebrew manuscripts *Ahimoth ²⁶and Elkanah. The sons of Elkanah:*   ᶜ27 Some Septuagint manuscripts (see also 1 Samuel 1:19,20 and 1 Chron. 6:33,34); Hebrew does not have *and Samuel his son.*   ᵈ28 Some Septuagint manuscripts and Syriac (see also 1 Samuel 8:2 and 1 Chron. 6:33); Hebrew does not have *Joel.*

²⁹The descendants of Merari:
  Mahli, Libni his son,
  Shimei his son, Uzzah his son,
  ³⁰Shimea his son, Haggiah his son
  and Asaiah his son.

The Temple Musicians

³¹These are the men David put in charge of the music in the house of the LORD after the ark came to rest there. ³²They ministered with music before the tabernacle, the Tent of Meeting, until Solomon built the temple of the LORD in Jerusalem. They performed their duties according to the regulations laid down for them.

³³Here are the men who served, together with their sons:

From the Kohathites:
  Heman, the musician,
  the son of Joel, the son of Samuel,
  ³⁴the son of Elkanah, the son of Jeroham,
  the son of Eliel, the son of Toah,
  ³⁵the son of Zuph, the son of Elkanah,
  the son of Mahath, the son of Amasai,
  ³⁶the son of Elkanah, the son of Joel,
  the son of Azariah, the son of Zephaniah,
  ³⁷the son of Tahath, the son of Assir,
  the son of Ebiasaph, the son of Korah,
  ³⁸the son of Izhar, the son of Kohath,
  the son of Levi, the son of Israel;

³⁹and Heman's associate Asaph, who served at his right hand:
  Asaph son of Berekiah, the son of Shimea,
  ⁴⁰the son of Michael, the son of Baaseiah,ᵃ
  the son of Malkijah, ⁴¹the son of Ethni,
  the son of Zerah, the son of Adaiah,
  ⁴²the son of Ethan, the son of Zimmah,
  the son of Shimei, ⁴³the son of Jahath,
  the son of Gershon, the son of Levi;

⁴⁴and from their associates, the Merarites, at his left hand:
  Ethan son of Kishi, the son of Abdi,
  the son of Malluch, ⁴⁵the son of Hashabiah,
  the son of Amaziah, the son of Hilkiah,
  ⁴⁶the son of Amzi, the son of Bani,
  the son of Shemer, ⁴⁷the son of Mahli,
  the son of Mushi, the son of Merari,
  the son of Levi.

⁴⁸Their fellow Levites were assigned to all the other duties of the tabernacle, the house of God. ⁴⁹But Aaron and his descendants were the ones who presented offerings on the altar of burnt offering and on the altar of incense in connection with all that was done in the Most Holy Place, making atonement for Israel, in accordance with all that Moses the servant of God had commanded.

⁵⁰These were the descendants of Aaron:
  Eleazar his son, Phinehas his son,
  Abishua his son, ⁵¹Bukki his son,
  Uzzi his son, Zerahiah his son,

Ministering With Song

1 CHRONICLES 6:31

Here is your chance to be a Kohathite, ministering with song before the Lord. Which hymns or gospel songs particularly speak to you? Which ones lift your heart in praise? Sing one or two now, aloud if possible. You might go a step further and write your own song of praise. If coming up with words and music seems too difficult, you might try creating a tune for a favorite verse of Scripture or writing new words to a familiar tune. If all else fails, just make a joyful noise to the Lord!

See Meeting God in Worship

ᵃ 40 Most Hebrew manuscripts; some Hebrew manuscripts, one Septuagint manuscript and Syriac *Maaseiah*

Through the Ages

1 CHRONICLES 6:61

"Forward through the ages,
in unbroken line,
move the faithful spirits at
the call divine;
gifts in differing measure,
hearts of one accord,
manifold the service, one
the sure reward.
Wider grows the kingdom,
reign of love and light;
for it we must labor, till our
faith is sight.
Prophets have proclaimed it,
martyrs testified,
poets sung its glory, heroes
for it died.
Forward through the ages,
in unbroken line,
move the faithful spirits at
the call divine."

—FREDERICK LUCIAN HOSMER

52 Meraioth his son, Amariah his son,
Ahitub his son, 53 Zadok his son
and Ahimaaz his son.

54 These were the locations of their settlements allotted as their territory (they were assigned to the descendants of Aaron who were from the Kohathite clan, because the first lot was for them):

55 They were given Hebron in Judah with its surrounding pasturelands. 56 But the fields and villages around the city were given to Caleb son of Jephunneh.

57 So the descendants of Aaron were given Hebron (a city of refuge), and Libnah,*a* Jattir, Eshtemoa, 58 Hilen, Debir, 59 Ashan, Juttah*b* and Beth Shemesh, together with their pasturelands. 60 And from the tribe of Benjamin they were given Gibeon,*c* Geba, Alemeth and Anathoth, together with their pasturelands.

These towns, which were distributed among the Kohathite clans, were thirteen in all.

61 The rest of Kohath's descendants were allotted ten towns from the clans of half the tribe of Manasseh.

62 The descendants of Gershon, clan by clan, were allotted thirteen towns from the tribes of Issachar, Asher and Naphtali, and from the part of the tribe of Manasseh that is in Bashan.

63 The descendants of Merari, clan by clan, were allotted twelve towns from the tribes of Reuben, Gad and Zebulun.

64 So the Israelites gave the Levites these towns and their pasturelands. 65 From the tribes of Judah, Simeon and Benjamin they allotted the previously named towns.

66 Some of the Kohathite clans were given as their territory towns from the tribe of Ephraim.

67 In the hill country of Ephraim they were given Shechem (a city of refuge), and Gezer,*d* 68 Jokmeam, Beth Horon, 69 Aijalon and Gath Rimmon, together with their pasturelands.

70 And from half the tribe of Manasseh the Israelites gave Aner and Bileam, together with their pasturelands, to the rest of the Kohathite clans.

71 The Gershonites received the following:
From the clan of the half-tribe of Manasseh
they received Golan in Bashan and also Ashtaroth,
together with their pasturelands;
72 from the tribe of Issachar
they received Kedesh, Daberath, 73 Ramoth and
Anem, together with their pasturelands;
74 from the tribe of Asher
they received Mashal, Abdon, 75 Hukok and Rehob,
together with their pasturelands;
76 and from the tribe of Naphtali
they received Kedesh in Galilee, Hammon and Kiriathaim, together with their pasturelands.

77 The Merarites (the rest of the Levites) received the following:
From the tribe of Zebulun

a 57 See Joshua 21:13; Hebrew *given the cities of refuge: Hebron, Libnah.*
b 59 Syriac (see also Septuagint and Joshua 21:16); Hebrew does not have *Juttah.* *c 60* See Joshua 21:17; Hebrew does not have *Gibeon.* *d 67* See Joshua 21:21; Hebrew *given the cities of refuge: Shechem, Gezer.*

they received Jokneam, Kartah,[a] Rimmono and Tabor, together with their pasturelands;

78 from the tribe of Reuben across the Jordan east of Jericho
they received Bezer in the desert, Jahzah, 79 Kedemoth and Mephaath, together with their pasturelands;

80 and from the tribe of Gad
they received Ramoth in Gilead, Mahanaim, 81 Heshbon and Jazer, together with their pasturelands.

Issachar

7 The sons of Issachar:
Tola, Puah, Jashub and Shimron—four in all.

2 The sons of Tola:
Uzzi, Rephaiah, Jeriel, Jahmai, Ibsam and Samuel—heads of their families. During the reign of David, the descendants of Tola listed as fighting men in their genealogy numbered 22,600.

3 The son of Uzzi:
Izrahiah.

The sons of Izrahiah:
Michael, Obadiah, Joel and Isshiah. All five of them were chiefs. 4 According to their family genealogy, they had 36,000 men ready for battle, for they had many wives and children.

5 The relatives who were fighting men belonging to all the clans of Issachar, as listed in their genealogy, were 87,000 in all.

Benjamin

6 Three sons of Benjamin:
Bela, Beker and Jediael.

7 The sons of Bela:
Ezbon, Uzzi, Uzziel, Jerimoth and Iri, heads of families—five in all. Their genealogical record listed 22,034 fighting men.

8 The sons of Beker:
Zemirah, Joash, Eliezer, Elioenai, Omri, Jeremoth, Abijah, Anathoth and Alemeth. All these were the sons of Beker. 9 Their genealogical record listed the heads of families and 20,200 fighting men.

10 The son of Jediael:
Bilhan.

The sons of Bilhan:
Jeush, Benjamin, Ehud, Kenaanah, Zethan, Tarshish and Ahishahar. 11 All these sons of Jediael were heads of families. There were 17,200 fighting men ready to go out to war.

12 The Shuppites and Huppites were the descendants of Ir, and the Hushites the descendants of Aher.

Naphtali

13 The sons of Naphtali:
Jahziel, Guni, Jezer and Shillem[b]—the descendants of Bilhah.

---

a 77 See Septuagint and Joshua 21:34; Hebrew does not have *Jokneam, Kartah.*   b 13 Some Hebrew and Septuagint manuscripts (see also Gen. 46:24 and Num. 26:49); most Hebrew manuscripts *Shallum*

Christ's Whole Body

1 CHRONICLES 6:72–7:12

Tribe after tribe and name after name—these verses may not be the most inspiring passages of Scripture, but they can serve to remind us of the vast number of people who have worshiped God throughout the centuries, as well as the number of people around the globe who worship him today. Each name is more than a statistic—it represents a person who lived and worked, laughed and cried, and who faced challenges of life and faith.

Sometimes we can become dull to statistics about churches that are being persecuted and people who are suffering. We may tend to ignore the individuals behind those statistics. Take time to pray through your denominational list of mission locations, or pray with an atlas open before you, asking God to give you a heart for the real people—his people—who live behind the statistics.

See *Meeting God in Community*

Life From the Ashes

1 CHRONICLES 7:20–24

These verses form a curious side note to this list of allotments. They tell a sad tale of two sons who went down to their land to claim their livestock and were killed. Ephraim mourned for many days; even the birth of another son couldn't erase the pain of his family's misfortune. His daughter is mentioned though as a construction supervisor, an unusual position for a woman in this patriarchal society.

Tragedy and loss often change families forever. The pain of loss remains even though the family must "keep on keeping on." Still, through God's grace, new life can grow out of loss. Wisdom grows out of pain. Family members may find strengths they never knew they had and fill new roles. They find that their loss helps them help others. Have you and your family suffered tragedy and loss? How is God's grace helping you go on, to grow, to find new wisdom in your tragedy? Reflect on how new life can grow out of ashes.

Manasseh

14 The descendants of Manasseh:

Asriel was his descendant through his Aramean concubine. She gave birth to Makir the father of Gilead. **15** Makir took a wife from among the Huppites and Shuppites. His sister's name was Maacah.

Another descendant was named Zelophehad, who had only daughters.

16 Makir's wife Maacah gave birth to a son and named him Peresh. His brother was named Sheresh, and his sons were Ulam and Rakem.

17 The son of Ulam:

Bedan.

These were the sons of Gilead son of Makir, the son of Manasseh. **18** His sister Hammoleketh gave birth to Ishhod, Abiezer and Mahlah.

19 The sons of Shemida were:

Ahian, Shechem, Likhi and Aniam.

Ephraim

20 The descendants of Ephraim:

Shuthelah, Bered his son,

Tahath his son, Eleadah his son,

Tahath his son, **21** Zabad his son

and Shuthelah his son.

Ezer and Elead were killed by the native-born men of Gath, when they went down to seize their livestock. **22** Their father Ephraim mourned for them many days, and his relatives came to comfort him. **23** Then he lay with his wife again, and she became pregnant and gave birth to a son. He named him Beriah,[a] because there had been misfortune in his family. **24** His daughter was Sheerah, who built Lower and Upper Beth Horon as well as Uzzen Sheerah.

25 Rephah was his son, Resheph his son,[b]

Telah his son, Tahan his son,

26 Ladan his son, Ammihud his son,

Elishama his son, **27** Nun his son

and Joshua his son.

28 Their lands and settlements included Bethel and its surrounding villages, Naaran to the east, Gezer and its villages to the west, and Shechem and its villages all the way to Ayyah and its villages. **29** Along the borders of Manasseh were Beth Shan, Taanach, Megiddo and Dor, together with their villages. The descendants of Joseph son of Israel lived in these towns.

Asher

30 The sons of Asher:

Imnah, Ishvah, Ishvi and Beriah. Their sister was Serah.

31 The sons of Beriah:

Heber and Malkiel, who was the father of Birzaith.

32 Heber was the father of Japhlet, Shomer and Hotham and of their sister Shua.

33 The sons of Japhlet:

Pasach, Bimhal and Ashvath.

---

[a] 23 *Beriah* sounds like the Hebrew for *misfortune.*   [b] 25 Some Septuagint manuscripts; Hebrew does not have *his son.*

These were Japhlet's sons.

³⁴The sons of Shomer:

Ahi, Rohgah,ᵃ Hubbah and Aram.

³⁵The sons of his brother Helem:

Zophah, Imna, Shelesh and Amal.

³⁶The sons of Zophah:

Suah, Harnepher, Shual, Beri, Imrah, ³⁷Bezer, Hod, Shamma, Shilshah, Ithranᵇ and Beera.

³⁸The sons of Jether:

Jephunneh, Pispah and Ara.

³⁹The sons of Ulla:

Arah, Hanniel and Rizia.

⁴⁰All these were descendants of Asher—heads of families, choice men, brave warriors and outstanding leaders. The number of men ready for battle, as listed in their genealogy, was 26,000.

The Genealogy of Saul the Benjamite

8 Benjamin was the father of Bela his firstborn, Ashbel the second son, Aharah the third, ²Nohah the fourth and Rapha the fifth.

³The sons of Bela were:

Addar, Gera, Abihud,ᶜ ⁴Abishua, Naaman, Ahoah, ⁵Gera, Shephuphan and Huram.

⁶These were the descendants of Ehud, who were heads of families of those living in Geba and were deported to Manahath:

⁷Naaman, Ahijah, and Gera, who deported them and who was the father of Uzza and Ahihud.

⁸Sons were born to Shaharaim in Moab after he had divorced his wives Hushim and Baara. ⁹By his wife Hodesh he had Jobab, Zibia, Mesha, Malcam, ¹⁰Jeuz, Sakia and Mirmah. These were his sons, heads of families. ¹¹By Hushim he had Abitub and Elpaal.

¹²The sons of Elpaal:

Eber, Misham, Shemed (who built Ono and Lod with its surrounding villages), ¹³and Beriah and Shema, who were heads of families of those living in Aijalon and who drove out the inhabitants of Gath.

¹⁴Ahio, Shashak, Jeremoth, ¹⁵Zebadiah, Arad, Eder, ¹⁶Michael, Ishpah and Joha were the sons of Beriah.

¹⁷Zebadiah, Meshullam, Hizki, Heber, ¹⁸Ishmerai, Izliah and Jobab were the sons of Elpaal.

¹⁹Jakim, Zicri, Zabdi, ²⁰Elienai, Zillethai, Eliel, ²¹Adaiah, Beraiah and Shimrath were the sons of Shimei.

²²Ishpan, Eber, Eliel, ²³Abdon, Zicri, Hanan, ²⁴Hananiah, Elam, Anthothijah, ²⁵Iphdeiah and Penuel were the sons of Shashak.

²⁶Shamsherai, Shehariah, Athaliah, ²⁷Jaareshiah, Elijah and Zicri were the sons of Jeroham.

²⁸All these were heads of families, chiefs as listed in their genealogy, and they lived in Jerusalem.

²⁹Jeielᵈ the fatherᵉ of Gibeon lived in Gibeon.

ᵃ 34 Or of his brother Shomer: Rohgah   ᵇ 37 Possibly a variant of Jether
ᶜ 3 Or Gera the father of Ehud   ᵈ 29 Some Septuagint manuscripts (see also
1 Chron. 9:35); Hebrew does not have Jeiel.   ᵉ 29 Father may mean civic
leader or military leader.

A Living Structure

1 CHRONICLES 8:1

"The Church is a living structure, made up of live building stones. They are far from perfect; they need to be dressed and hewn if they are to fit into the building. And yet it is a perfect building. The mystery is this: the life of this building does not reside in its parts, but rather in the living, gathering Holy Spirit. Its unity does not result from assembling the parts that make it up or from an agreement of opinions. By nature the stones are spiritually dead. But the Holy Spirit awakens them to life by joining them together in a new unity."

—EBERHARD ARNOLD,
God's Revolution

Into Exile

1 CHRONICLES 9:1

For the Chronicler, the story is simple: "The people of Judah were taken captive . . . because of their unfaithfulness." It may not be so clear for us when we feel isolated, exiled, cut off from the people and places we have loved. Still, God can help bring us home. Ask for God's help in looking at your feelings of exile. What have you done to cause broken relationships? What can you do to mend them? How can God help you to return from exile? What breaks can be repaired only by God's grace? Offer God your brokenness and receive God's healing.

See Meeting God in Community

His wife's name was Maacah, ³⁰and his firstborn son was Abdon, followed by Zur, Kish, Baal, Ner,ᵃ Nadab, ³¹Gedor, Ahio, Zeker ³²and Mikloth, who was the father of Shimeah. They too lived near their relatives in Jerusalem.

³³Ner was the father of Kish, Kish the father of Saul, and Saul the father of Jonathan, Malki-Shua, Abinadab and Esh-Baal.ᵇ

³⁴The son of Jonathan:

Merib-Baal,ᶜ who was the father of Micah.

³⁵The sons of Micah:

Pithon, Melech, Tarea and Ahaz.

³⁶Ahaz was the father of Jehoaddah, Jehoaddah was the father of Alemeth, Azmaveth and Zimri, and Zimri was the father of Moza. ³⁷Moza was the father of Binea; Raphah was his son, Eleasah his son and Azel his son.

³⁸Azel had six sons, and these were their names:

Azrikam, Bokeru, Ishmael, Sheariah, Obadiah and Hanan. All these were the sons of Azel.

³⁹The sons of his brother Eshek:

Ulam his firstborn, Jeush the second son and Eliphelet the third. ⁴⁰The sons of Ulam were brave warriors who could handle the bow. They had many sons and grandsons—150 in all.

All these were the descendants of Benjamin.

9 All Israel was listed in the genealogies recorded in the book of the kings of Israel.

The People in Jerusalem

The people of Judah were taken captive to Babylon because of their unfaithfulness. ²Now the first to resettle on their own property in their own towns were some Israelites, priests, Levites and temple servants.

³Those from Judah, from Benjamin, and from Ephraim and Manasseh who lived in Jerusalem were:

⁴Uthai son of Ammihud, the son of Omri, the son of Imri, the son of Bani, a descendant of Perez son of Judah.

⁵Of the Shilonites:

Asaiah the firstborn and his sons.

⁶Of the Zerahites:

Jeuel.

The people from Judah numbered 690.

⁷Of the Benjamites:

Sallu son of Meshullam, the son of Hodaviah, the son of Hassenuah;

⁸Ibneiah son of Jeroham; Elah son of Uzzi, the son of Micri; and Meshullam son of Shephatiah, the son of Reuel, the son of Ibnijah.

⁹The people from Benjamin, as listed in their genealogy, numbered 956. All these men were heads of their families.

¹⁰Of the priests:

Jedaiah; Jehoiarib; Jakin;

¹¹Azariah son of Hilkiah, the son of Meshullam, the

ᵃ30 Some Septuagint manuscripts (see also 1 Chron. 9:36); Hebrew does not have *Ner.*   ᵇ33 Also known as *Ish-Bosheth*   ᶜ34 Also known as *Mephibosheth*

son of Zadok, the son of Meraioth, the son of Ahitub, the official in charge of the house of God;

¹²Adaiah son of Jeroham, the son of Pashhur, the son
of Malkijah; and Maasai son of Adiel, the son of
Jahzerah, the son of Meshullam, the son of Meshil-
lemith, the son of Immer.

¹³The priests, who were heads of families, numbered
1,760. They were able men, responsible for ministering in the house of God.

¹⁴Of the Levites:

Shemaiah son of Hasshub, the son of Azrikam, the
son of Hashabiah, a Merarite; ¹⁵Bakbakkar, Heresh,
Galal and Mattaniah son of Mica, the son of Zicri,
the son of Asaph; ¹⁶Obadiah son of Shemaiah, the
son of Galal, the son of Jeduthun; and Berekiah son
of Asa, the son of Elkanah, who lived in the villages
of the Netophathites.

¹⁷The gatekeepers:

Shallum, Akkub, Talmon, Ahiman and their brothers, Shallum their chief ¹⁸being stationed at the
King's Gate on the east, up to the present time.
These were the gatekeepers belonging to the camp
of the Levites. ¹⁹Shallum son of Kore, the son of
Ebiasaph, the son of Korah, and his fellow gatekeepers from his family (the Korahites) were responsible for guarding the thresholds of the Tent*ᵃ*
just as their fathers had been responsible for guarding the entrance to the dwelling of the LORD. ²⁰In
earlier times Phinehas son of Eleazar was in charge
of the gatekeepers, and the LORD was with him.
²¹Zechariah son of Meshelemiah was the gatekeeper at the entrance to the Tent of Meeting.

²²Altogether, those chosen to be gatekeepers at the
thresholds numbered 212. They were registered by genealogy in their villages. The gatekeepers had been assigned to their positions of trust by David and Samuel the
seer. ²³They and their descendants were in charge of
guarding the gates of the house of the LORD—the house
called the Tent. ²⁴The gatekeepers were on the four sides:
east, west, north and south. ²⁵Their brothers in their villages had to come from time to time and share their duties for seven-day periods. ²⁶But the four principal
gatekeepers, who were Levites, were entrusted with the
responsibility for the rooms and treasuries in the house of
God. ²⁷They would spend the night stationed around the
house of God, because they had to guard it; and they had
charge of the key for opening it each morning.

²⁸Some of them were in charge of the articles used in
the temple service; they counted them when they were
brought in and when they were taken out. ²⁹Others were
assigned to take care of the furnishings and all the other
articles of the sanctuary, as well as the flour and wine,
and the oil, incense and spices. ³⁰But some of the priests
took care of mixing the spices. ³¹A Levite named Mattithiah, the firstborn son of Shallum the Korahite, was entrusted with the responsibility for baking the offering bread.
³²Some of their Kohathite brothers were in charge of
preparing for every Sabbath the bread set out on the
table.

ᵃ *19 That is, the temple; also in verses 21 and 23*

God in the Details

1 CHRONICLES 9:28

Even counting the knives and
spoons can be a holy task if offered to the Lord. Spiritual writers call this "the sacrament of
the present moment." As you
go about your chores today—
cleaning the house, pulling the
weeds, doing the laundry, taking out the trash—invite God to
be with you. Thank God for giving you work to do and ability
to do it. At first it will take a
lot of effort to remember God,
to let God's presence light up
even the most tedious tasks.
But as you continue to "practice the presence of God" it will
become easier.

See Meeting God in Everyday Life

Good Intentions

1 CHRONICLES 10:13–14

The sins for which Saul is condemned, failing to follow God's instructions (see 1 Samuel 13:1–15) and consulting a medium (see 1 Samuel 28:3–25), represent good intentions gone bad. When have you done the wrong thing for what seemed the right reasons? How did your good reasons block you from admitting that what you did was wrong? Are there still such situations in your life that are unresolved? Ask God to help you let go of self-righteousness so that you can confess your wrongdoing both to God and to those who might have been hurt by it. Ask for forgiveness and mercy so that God's love can cleanse your heart.

See Meeting God in Prayer

33 Those who were musicians, heads of Levite families, stayed in the rooms of the temple and were exempt from other duties because they were responsible for the work day and night.

34 All these were heads of Levite families, chiefs as listed in their genealogy, and they lived in Jerusalem.

The Genealogy of Saul

35 Jeiel the father*ᵃ* of Gibeon lived in Gibeon.
His wife's name was Maacah, 36 and his firstborn son was Abdon, followed by Zur, Kish, Baal, Ner, Nadab, 37 Gedor, Ahio, Zechariah and Mikloth. 38 Mikloth was the father of Shimeam. They too lived near their relatives in Jerusalem.

39 Ner was the father of Kish, Kish the father of Saul, and Saul the father of Jonathan, Malki-Shua, Abinadab and Esh-Baal.*ᵇ*

40 The son of Jonathan:
Merib-Baal,*ᶜ* who was the father of Micah.

41 The sons of Micah:
Pithon, Melech, Tahrea and Ahaz.*ᵈ*

42 Ahaz was the father of Jadah, Jadah*ᵉ* was the father of Alemeth, Azmaveth and Zimri, and Zimri was the father of Moza. 43 Moza was the father of Binea; Rephaiah was his son, Eleasah his son and Azel his son.

44 Azel had six sons, and these were their names:
Azrikam, Bokeru, Ishmael, Sheariah, Obadiah and Hanan. These were the sons of Azel.

Saul Takes His Life

10 Now the Philistines fought against Israel; the Israelites fled before them, and many fell slain on Mount Gilboa. 2 The Philistines pressed hard after Saul and his sons, and they killed his sons Jonathan, Abinadab and Malki-Shua. 3 The fighting grew fierce around Saul, and when the archers overtook him, they wounded him.

4 Saul said to his armor-bearer, "Draw your sword and run me through, or these uncircumcised fellows will come and abuse me."

But his armor-bearer was terrified and would not do it; so Saul took his own sword and fell on it. 5 When the armor-bearer saw that Saul was dead, he too fell on his sword and died. 6 So Saul and his three sons died, and all his house died together.

7 When all the Israelites in the valley saw that the army had fled and that Saul and his sons had died, they abandoned their towns and fled. And the Philistines came and occupied them.

8 The next day, when the Philistines came to strip the dead, they found Saul and his sons fallen on Mount Gilboa. 9 They stripped him and took his head and his armor, and sent messengers throughout the land of the Philistines to proclaim the news among their idols and their

---

ᵃ 35 Father *may mean* civic leader *or* military leader. *ᵇ 39 Also known as* Ish-Bosheth *ᶜ 40 Also known as* Mephibosheth *ᵈ 41 Vulgate and Syriac (see also Septuagint and 1 Chron. 8:35); Hebrew does not have* and Ahaz. *ᵉ 42 Some Hebrew manuscripts and Septuagint (see also 1 Chron. 8:36); most Hebrew manuscripts* Jarah, Jarah

people. ¹⁰They put his armor in the temple of their gods and hung up his head in the temple of Dagon.

¹¹When all the inhabitants of Jabesh Gilead heard of everything the Philistines had done to Saul, ¹²all their valiant men went and took the bodies of Saul and his sons and brought them to Jabesh. Then they buried their bones under the great tree in Jabesh, and they fasted seven days.

¹³Saul died because he was unfaithful to the Lord; he did not keep the word of the Lord and even consulted a medium for guidance, ¹⁴and did not inquire of the Lord. So the Lord put him to death and turned the kingdom over to David son of Jesse.

David Becomes King Over Israel

11 All Israel came together to David at Hebron and said, "We are your own flesh and blood. ²In the past, even while Saul was king, you were the one who led Israel on their military campaigns. And the Lord your God said to you, 'You will shepherd my people Israel, and you will become their ruler.' "

³When all the elders of Israel had come to King David at Hebron, he made a compact with them at Hebron before the Lord, and they anointed David king over Israel, as the Lord had promised through Samuel.

David Conquers Jerusalem

⁴David and all the Israelites marched to Jerusalem (that is, Jebus). The Jebusites who lived there ⁵said to David, "You will not get in here." Nevertheless, David captured the fortress of Zion, the City of David.

⁶David had said, "Whoever leads the attack on the Jebusites will become commander-in-chief." Joab son of Zeruiah went up first, and so he received the command.

⁷David then took up residence in the fortress, and so it was called the City of David. ⁸He built up the city around it, from the supporting terraces*a* to the surrounding wall, while Joab restored the rest of the city. ⁹And David became more and more powerful, because the Lord Almighty was with him.

David's Mighty Men

¹⁰These were the chiefs of David's mighty men—they, together with all Israel, gave his kingship strong support to extend it over the whole land, as the Lord had promised— ¹¹this is the list of David's mighty men:

Jashobeam,*b* a Hacmonite, was chief of the officers*c*; he raised his spear against three hundred men, whom he killed in one encounter.

¹²Next to him was Eleazar son of Dodai the Ahohite, one of the three mighty men. ¹³He was with David at Pas Dammim when the Philistines gathered there for battle. At a place where there was a field full of barley, the troops fled from the Philistines. ¹⁴But they took their stand in the middle of the field. They defended it and struck the Philistines down, and the Lord brought about a great victory.

¹⁵Three of the thirty chiefs came down to David to the rock at the cave of Adullam, while a band of Philistines

A Gift Too Precious

1 CHRONICLES 11:10–19

Try to imagine the scene. David is hiding in a cave while the Philistines occupy his hometown of Bethlehem. See the cave, the guards on watch. Hear the commotion as three of his companions come running and gasping to David, holding aloft a water skin. It is water from the well of Bethlehem. Notice the fresh bloodstains, the bandaged wounds. David pours out the water, saying it has become their blood and can be offered only to God. How do you respond to David's action? When have you received a gift that was too precious to be kept for yourself? What was it? How did you offer it to God? What precious gift do you keep for your own use? How might you use it to glorify God?

See Meeting God in Scripture

a 8 Or *the Millo*   *b 11* Possibly a variant of *Jashob-Baal*   *c 11* Or *Thirty*; some Septuagint manuscripts *Three* (see also 2 Samuel 23:8)

Celestial Warfare

1 CHRONICLES 11:26

"Do you, however, whom the celestial warfare has enlisted in the spiritual camp, only observe a discipline uncorrupted and chastened in the virtues of religion. Be constant as well in prayer as in reading. Now speak with God, now let God speak with you. Let God instruct you in his precepts. Let God direct you. Whom God has made rich, none shall make poor. In fact, there can be no poverty to one whose breast has once been supplied with heavenly food."

—CYPRIAN OF CARTHAGE,
Letter 1

was encamped in the Valley of Rephaim. ¹⁶At that time David was in the stronghold, and the Philistine garrison was at Bethlehem. ¹⁷David longed for water and said, "Oh, that someone would get me a drink of water from the well near the gate of Bethlehem!" ¹⁸So the Three broke through the Philistine lines, drew water from the well near the gate of Bethlehem and carried it back to David. But he refused to drink it; instead, he poured it out before the LORD. ¹⁹"God forbid that I should do this!" he said. "Should I drink the blood of these men who went at the risk of their lives?" Because they risked their lives to bring it back, David would not drink it.

Such were the exploits of the three mighty men.

²⁰Abishai the brother of Joab was chief of the Three. He raised his spear against three hundred men, whom he killed, and so he became as famous as the Three. ²¹He was doubly honored above the Three and became their commander, even though he was not included among them.

²²Benaiah son of Jehoiada was a valiant fighter from Kabzeel, who performed great exploits. He struck down two of Moab's best men. He also went down into a pit on a snowy day and killed a lion. ²³And he struck down an Egyptian who was seven and a half feet^a tall. Although the Egyptian had a spear like a weaver's rod in his hand, Benaiah went against him with a club. He snatched the spear from the Egyptian's hand and killed him with his own spear. ²⁴Such were the exploits of Benaiah son of Jehoiada; he too was as famous as the three mighty men. ²⁵He was held in greater honor than any of the Thirty, but he was not included among the Three. And David put him in charge of his bodyguard.

²⁶The mighty men were:
  Asahel the brother of Joab,
  Elhanan son of Dodo from Bethlehem,
²⁷Shammoth the Harorite,
  Helez the Pelonite,
²⁸Ira son of Ikkesh from Tekoa,
  Abiezer from Anathoth,
²⁹Sibbecai the Hushathite,
  Ilai the Ahohite,
³⁰Maharai the Netophathite,
  Heled son of Baanah the Netophathite,
³¹Ithai son of Ribai from Gibeah in Benjamin,
  Benaiah the Pirathonite,
³²Hurai from the ravines of Gaash,
  Abiel the Arbathite,
³³Azmaveth the Baharumite,
  Eliahba the Shaalbonite,
³⁴the sons of Hashem the Gizonite,
  Jonathan son of Shagee the Hararite,
³⁵Ahiam son of Sacar the Hararite,
  Eliphal son of Ur,
³⁶Hepher the Mekerathite,
  Ahijah the Pelonite,
³⁷Hezro the Carmelite,
  Naarai son of Ezbai,
³⁸Joel the brother of Nathan,

^a 23 Hebrew *five cubits* (about 2.3 meters)

Mibhar son of Hagri,
³⁹ Zelek the Ammonite,
Naharai the Berothite, the armor-bearer of Joab son
of Zeruiah,
⁴⁰ Ira the Ithrite,
Gareb the Ithrite,
⁴¹ Uriah the Hittite,
Zabad son of Ahlai,
⁴² Adina son of Shiza the Reubenite, who was chief of
the Reubenites, and the thirty with him,
⁴³ Hanan son of Maacah,
Joshaphat the Mithnite,
⁴⁴ Uzzia the Ashterathite,
Shama and Jeiel the sons of Hotham the Aroerite,
⁴⁵ Jediael son of Shimri,
his brother Joha the Tizite,
⁴⁶ Eliel the Mahavite,
Jeribai and Joshaviah the sons of Elnaam,
Ithmah the Moabite,
⁴⁷ Eliel, Obed and Jaasiel the Mezobaite.

Warriors Join David

12 These were the men who came to David at Ziklag,
while he was banished from the presence of Saul
son of Kish (they were among the warriors who helped
him in battle; ²they were armed with bows and were able
to shoot arrows or to sling stones right-handed or left-
handed; they were kinsmen of Saul from the tribe of
Benjamin):

³Ahiezer their chief and Joash the sons of Shemaah
the Gibeathite; Jeziel and Pelet the sons of Azmaveth;
Beracah, Jehu the Anathothite, ⁴and Ishmaiah the
Gibeonite, a mighty man among the Thirty, who was
a leader of the Thirty; Jeremiah, Jahaziel, Johanan,
Jozabad the Gederathite, ⁵Eluzai, Jerimoth, Bealiah,
Shemariah and Shephatiah the Haruphite; ⁶Elkanah,
Isshiah, Azarel, Joezer and Jashobeam the Korahites;
⁷and Joelah and Zebadiah the sons of Jeroham from
Gedor.

⁸Some Gadites defected to David at his stronghold in
the desert. They were brave warriors, ready for battle and
able to handle the shield and spear. Their faces were the
faces of lions, and they were as swift as gazelles in the
mountains.
⁹Ezer was the chief,
Obadiah the second in command, Eliab the third,
¹⁰ Mishmannah the fourth, Jeremiah the fifth,
¹¹ Attai the sixth, Eliel the seventh,
¹² Johanan the eighth, Elzabad the ninth,
¹³ Jeremiah the tenth and Macbannai the eleventh.
¹⁴These Gadites were army commanders; the least was
a match for a hundred, and the greatest for a thousand.
¹⁵It was they who crossed the Jordan in the first month
when it was overflowing all its banks, and they put to
flight everyone living in the valleys, to the east and to the
west.
¹⁶Other Benjamites and some men from Judah also
came to David in his stronghold. ¹⁷David went out to meet
them and said to them, "If you have come to me in peace,

God Will Help

"If God is for us," asks Paul,
"who can be against us?" (Romans 8:31). Here David's companions promise him loyalty
because they know that God
will help him. Their statement
of affirmation might be a good
one to use as a breath prayer.
Sit quietly, eyes closed, and repeat to yourself: "My God will
help me." Time it to your
breathing by saying "My God"
as you breathe in and "will
help me" as you breathe out. If
you find your thoughts wandering, come back to the breath
prayer. You might close your
prayer time with the Lord's
Prayer. During the day, stop
from time to time to repeat the
prayer.

See *Meeting God in Prayer*

Discernment

1 CHRONICLES 13:2

David knows what he wants to do, but he still puts the decision before the people and before the Lord. What major decision is hanging over you? Which of your friends can you ask, "Does this seem good to you?" How can you discern what is the will of the Lord? Perhaps you could gather a few trusted friends and pray together for guidance before discussing the pros and cons of each possibility. Ask God to guide and inspire your time together.

See Meeting God in Community

to help me, I am ready to have you unite with me. But if you have come to betray me to my enemies when my hands are free from violence, may the God of our fathers see it and judge you."

¹⁸Then the Spirit came upon Amasai, chief of the Thirty, and he said:

> "We are yours, O David!
>   We are with you, O son of Jesse!
> Success, success to you,
>   and success to those who help you,
>   for your God will help you."

So David received them and made them leaders of his raiding bands.

¹⁹Some of the men of Manasseh defected to David when he went with the Philistines to fight against Saul. (He and his men did not help the Philistines because, after consultation, their rulers sent him away. They said, "It will cost us our heads if he deserts to his master Saul.") ²⁰When David went to Ziklag, these were the men of Manasseh who defected to him: Adnah, Jozabad, Jediael, Michael, Jozabad, Elihu and Zillethai, leaders of units of a thousand in Manasseh. ²¹They helped David against raiding bands, for all of them were brave warriors, and they were commanders in his army. ²²Day after day men came to help David, until he had a great army, like the army of God.*ᵃ*

Others Join David at Hebron

²³These are the numbers of the men armed for battle who came to David at Hebron to turn Saul's kingdom over to him, as the LORD had said:

²⁴men of Judah, carrying shield and spear—6,800 armed for battle;

²⁵men of Simeon, warriors ready for battle—7,100;

²⁶men of Levi—4,600, ²⁷including Jehoiada, leader of the family of Aaron, with 3,700 men, ²⁸and Zadok, a brave young warrior, with 22 officers from his family;

²⁹men of Benjamin, Saul's kinsmen—3,000, most of whom had remained loyal to Saul's house until then;

³⁰men of Ephraim, brave warriors, famous in their own clans—20,800;

³¹men of half the tribe of Manasseh, designated by name to come and make David king—18,000;

³²men of Issachar, who understood the times and knew what Israel should do—200 chiefs, with all their relatives under their command;

³³men of Zebulun, experienced soldiers prepared for battle with every type of weapon, to help David with undivided loyalty—50,000;

³⁴men of Naphtali—1,000 officers, together with 37,000 men carrying shields and spears;

³⁵men of Dan, ready for battle—28,600;

³⁶men of Asher, experienced soldiers prepared for battle—40,000;

³⁷and from east of the Jordan, men of Reuben, Gad and

ᵃ 22 Or a great and mighty army

the half-tribe of Manasseh, armed with every type of weapon—120,000.

³⁸All these were fighting men who volunteered to serve in the ranks. They came to Hebron fully determined to make David king over all Israel. All the rest of the Israelites were also of one mind to make David king. ³⁹The men spent three days there with David, eating and drinking, for their families had supplied provisions for them. ⁴⁰Also, their neighbors from as far away as Issachar, Zebulun and Naphtali came bringing food on donkeys, camels, mules and oxen. There were plentiful supplies of flour, fig cakes, raisin cakes, wine, oil, cattle and sheep, for there was joy in Israel.

Bringing Back the Ark

13 David conferred with each of his officers, the commanders of thousands and commanders of hundreds. ²He then said to the whole assembly of Israel, "If it seems good to you and if it is the will of the LORD our God, let us send word far and wide to the rest of our brothers throughout the territories of Israel, and also to the priests and Levites who are with them in their towns and pasturelands, to come and join us. ³Let us bring the ark of our God back to us, for we did not inquire of^a it^b during the reign of Saul." ⁴The whole assembly agreed to do this, because it seemed right to all the people.

⁵So David assembled all the Israelites, from the Shihor River in Egypt to Lebo^c Hamath, to bring the ark of God from Kiriath Jearim. ⁶David and all the Israelites with him went to Baalah of Judah (Kiriath Jearim) to bring up from there the ark of God the LORD, who is enthroned between the cherubim—the ark that is called by the Name.

⁷They moved the ark of God from Abinadab's house on a new cart, with Uzzah and Ahio guiding it. ⁸David and all the Israelites were celebrating with all their might before God, with songs and with harps, lyres, tambourines, cymbals and trumpets.

⁹When they came to the threshing floor of Kidon, Uzzah reached out his hand to steady the ark, because the oxen stumbled. ¹⁰The LORD's anger burned against Uzzah, and he struck him down because he had put his hand on the ark. So he died there before God.

¹¹Then David was angry because the LORD's wrath had broken out against Uzzah, and to this day that place is called Perez Uzzah.^{d}

¹²David was afraid of God that day and asked, "How can I ever bring the ark of God to me?" ¹³He did not take the ark to be with him in the City of David. Instead, he took it aside to the house of Obed-Edom the Gittite. ¹⁴The ark of God remained with the family of Obed-Edom in his house for three months, and the LORD blessed his household and everything he had.

David's House and Family

14 Now Hiram king of Tyre sent messengers to David, along with cedar logs, stonemasons and carpenters to build a palace for him. ²And David knew that the LORD had established him as king over Israel and that his

Keeping Your Distance

1 CHRONICLES 13:11–12

When David saw that God's wrath had "broken out" against Uzzah, he was afraid. The fear of getting too close to such an awesome God or the fear of drawing God's attention to our own sinfulness can be a major block to a deeper relationship. What are the fears that keep you at a distance from God? Try drawing a picture to express your fear. Then draw a second picture to express God's love for you. As you look at the two pictures, let the one depicting God's love cover over the other, overwhelming your fear. Let God's love come into your heart and banish every fear. As the apostle John writes, "Perfect love drives out fear" (1 John 4:18).

See Meeting God in Prayer

---

^{a}3 Or *we neglected* ^{b}3 Or *him* ^{c}5 Or *to the entrance to* ^{d}11 *Perez Uzzah* means *outbreak against Uzzah.*

Lover of Harmony

"Now David was a man skilled in songs, who dearly loved musical harmony, not with a vulgar delight, but with a believing disposition, and by it served his God, who is the true God, by the mystical representation of a great thing. For the rational and well-ordered concord of diverse sounds in harmonious variety suggests the compact unity of the well-ordered city."

—AUGUSTINE,
The City of God

kingdom had been highly exalted for the sake of his people Israel.

[3] In Jerusalem David took more wives and became the father of more sons and daughters. [4] These are the names of the children born to him there: Shammua, Shobab, Nathan, Solomon, [5] Ibhar, Elishua, Elpelet, [6] Nogah, Nepheg, Japhia, [7] Elishama, Beeliada[a] and Eliphelet.

David Defeats the Philistines

[8] When the Philistines heard that David had been anointed king over all Israel, they went up in full force to search for him, but David heard about it and went out to meet them. [9] Now the Philistines had come and raided the Valley of Rephaim; [10] so David inquired of God: "Shall I go and attack the Philistines? Will you hand them over to me?"

The LORD answered him, "Go, I will hand them over to you."

[11] So David and his men went up to Baal Perazim, and there he defeated them. He said, "As waters break out, God has broken out against my enemies by my hand." So that place was called Baal Perazim.[b] [12] The Philistines had abandoned their gods there, and David gave orders to burn them in the fire.

[13] Once more the Philistines raided the valley; [14] so David inquired of God again, and God answered him, "Do not go straight up, but circle around them and attack them in front of the balsam trees. [15] As soon as you hear the sound of marching in the tops of the balsam trees, move out to battle, because that will mean God has gone out in front of you to strike the Philistine army." [16] So David did as God commanded him, and they struck down the Philistine army, all the way from Gibeon to Gezer.

[17] So David's fame spread throughout every land, and the LORD made all the nations fear him.

The Ark Brought to Jerusalem

15 After David had constructed buildings for himself in the City of David, he prepared a place for the ark of God and pitched a tent for it. [2] Then David said, "No one but the Levites may carry the ark of God, because the LORD chose them to carry the ark of the LORD and to minister before him forever."

[3] David assembled all Israel in Jerusalem to bring up the ark of the LORD to the place he had prepared for it. [4] He called together the descendants of Aaron and the Levites:

[5] From the descendants of Kohath,
Uriel the leader and 120 relatives;
[6] from the descendants of Merari,
Asaiah the leader and 220 relatives;
[7] from the descendants of Gershon,[c]
Joel the leader and 130 relatives;
[8] from the descendants of Elizaphan,
Shemaiah the leader and 200 relatives;
[9] from the descendants of Hebron,
Eliel the leader and 80 relatives;
[10] from the descendants of Uzziel,
Amminadab the leader and 112 relatives.

---

[a] 7 A variant of *Eliada*   [b] 11 *Baal Perazim* means *the lord who breaks out.*
[c] 7 Hebrew *Gershom,* a variant of *Gershon*

¹¹Then David summoned Zadok and Abiathar the priests, and Uriel, Asaiah, Joel, Shemaiah, Eliel and Amminadab the Levites. ¹²He said to them, "You are the heads of the Levitical families; you and your fellow Levites are to consecrate yourselves and bring up the ark of the LORD, the God of Israel, to the place I have prepared for it. ¹³It was because you, the Levites, did not bring it up the first time that the LORD our God broke out in anger against us. We did not inquire of him about how to do it in the prescribed way." ¹⁴So the priests and Levites consecrated themselves in order to bring up the ark of the LORD, the God of Israel. ¹⁵And the Levites carried the ark of God with the poles on their shoulders, as Moses had commanded in accordance with the word of the LORD.

¹⁶David told the leaders of the Levites to appoint their brothers as singers to sing joyful songs, accompanied by musical instruments: lyres, harps and cymbals.

¹⁷So the Levites appointed Heman son of Joel; from his brothers, Asaph son of Berekiah; and from their brothers the Merarites, Ethan son of Kushaiah; ¹⁸and with them their brothers next in rank: Zechariah,[a] Jaaziel, Shemiramoth, Jehiel, Unni, Eliab, Benaiah, Maaseiah, Mattithiah, Eliphelehu, Mikneiah, Obed-Edom and Jeiel,[b] the gatekeepers.

¹⁹The musicians Heman, Asaph and Ethan were to sound the bronze cymbals; ²⁰Zechariah, Aziel, Shemiramoth, Jehiel, Unni, Eliab, Maaseiah and Benaiah were to play the lyres according to *alamoth,*[c] ²¹and Mattithiah, Eliphelehu, Mikneiah, Obed-Edom, Jeiel and Azaziah were to play the harps, directing according to *sheminith.*[c] ²²Kenaniah the head Levite was in charge of the singing; that was his responsibility because he was skillful at it.

²³Berekiah and Elkanah were to be doorkeepers for the ark. ²⁴Shebaniah, Joshaphat, Nethanel, Amasai, Zechariah, Benaiah and Eliezer the priests were to blow trumpets before the ark of God. Obed-Edom and Jehiah were also to be doorkeepers for the ark.

²⁵So David and the elders of Israel and the commanders of units of a thousand went to bring up the ark of the covenant of the LORD from the house of Obed-Edom, with rejoicing. ²⁶Because God had helped the Levites who were carrying the ark of the covenant of the LORD, seven bulls and seven rams were sacrificed. ²⁷Now David was clothed in a robe of fine linen, as were all the Levites who were carrying the ark, and as were the singers, and Kenaniah, who was in charge of the singing of the choirs. David also wore a linen ephod. ²⁸So all Israel brought up the ark of the covenant of the LORD with shouts, with the sounding of rams' horns and trumpets, and of cymbals, and the playing of lyres and harps.

²⁹As the ark of the covenant of the LORD was entering the City of David, Michal daughter of Saul watched from a window. And when she saw King David dancing and celebrating, she despised him in her heart.

Dancing Before the Lord

1 CHRONICLES 15:29

David was "dancing and celebrating" to show his love for God. What body language do you use to communicate with God? Do you come before God hunched over like a cowering slave? Do you lift your hands in praise? Do you dance? Try praising God through movement. Select some music that can lift your heart and that might help you move. Find a space where you can move freely, even if only to sway or clap your hands or spin around. Let the music flow through you to express your love for God in sound and rhythm. Let the Holy Spirit guide you. You will probably want to assure yourself of privacy when you try this. Remember Michal. Observers might not understand.

See Meeting God in Worship

---

a 18 Three Hebrew manuscripts and most Septuagint manuscripts (see also verse 20 and 1 Chron. 16:5); most Hebrew manuscripts *Zechariah son and* or *Zechariah, Ben and*   *b 18* Hebrew; Septuagint (see also verse 21) *Jeiel and Azaziah*   *c 20, 21* Probably a musical term

A Psalm of Praise

1 CHRONICLES 16:8–36

David's psalm of thanks resounds with praise for all that God has done, all that God is doing and all that God will do for his people in the future.

What has God done for you and your family? What is God doing in your life today? What is your hope for the future? Using David's psalm as a pattern, write your own psalm of thanks and pray it to the Lord today.

See Meeting God in Prayer

16 They brought the ark of God and set it inside the tent that David had pitched for it, and they presented burnt offerings and fellowship offerings[a] before God. ²After David had finished sacrificing the burnt offerings and fellowship offerings, he blessed the people in the name of the LORD. ³Then he gave a loaf of bread, a cake of dates and a cake of raisins to each Israelite man and woman.

⁴He appointed some of the Levites to minister before the ark of the LORD, to make petition, to give thanks, and to praise the LORD, the God of Israel: ⁵Asaph was the chief, Zechariah second, then Jeiel, Shemiramoth, Jehiel, Mattithiah, Eliab, Benaiah, Obed-Edom and Jeiel. They were to play the lyres and harps, Asaph was to sound the cymbals, ⁶and Benaiah and Jahaziel the priests were to blow the trumpets regularly before the ark of the covenant of God.

David's Psalm of Thanks

⁷That day David first committed to Asaph and his associates this psalm of thanks to the LORD:

⁸ Give thanks to the LORD, call on his name;
 make known among the nations what he has done.
⁹ Sing to him, sing praise to him;
 tell of all his wonderful acts.
¹⁰ Glory in his holy name;
 let the hearts of those who seek the LORD rejoice.
¹¹ Look to the LORD and his strength;
 seek his face always.
¹² Remember the wonders he has done,
 his miracles, and the judgments he pronounced,
¹³ O descendants of Israel his servant,
 O sons of Jacob, his chosen ones.

¹⁴ He is the LORD our God;
 his judgments are in all the earth.
¹⁵ He remembers[b] his covenant forever,
 the word he commanded, for a thousand generations,
¹⁶ the covenant he made with Abraham,
 the oath he swore to Isaac.
¹⁷ He confirmed it to Jacob as a decree,
 to Israel as an everlasting covenant:
¹⁸ "To you I will give the land of Canaan
 as the portion you will inherit."

¹⁹ When they were but few in number,
 few indeed, and strangers in it,
²⁰ they[c] wandered from nation to nation,
 from one kingdom to another.
²¹ He allowed no man to oppress them;
 for their sake he rebuked kings:
²² "Do not touch my anointed ones;
 do my prophets no harm."

---

a 1 Traditionally *peace offerings*; also in verse 2   *b 15* Some Septuagint manuscripts (see also Psalm 105:8); Hebrew *Remember*   *c 18–20* One Hebrew manuscript, Septuagint and Vulgate (see also Psalm 105:12); most Hebrew manuscripts *inherit,* / *¹⁹though you are but few in number,* / *few indeed, and strangers in it."* / *²⁰They*

²³ Sing to the LORD, all the earth;
  proclaim his salvation day after day.
²⁴ Declare his glory among the nations,
  his marvelous deeds among all peoples.
²⁵ For great is the LORD and most worthy of praise;
  he is to be feared above all gods.
²⁶ For all the gods of the nations are idols,
  but the LORD made the heavens.
²⁷ Splendor and majesty are before him;
  strength and joy in his dwelling place.
²⁸ Ascribe to the LORD, O families of nations,
  ascribe to the LORD glory and strength,
²⁹   ascribe to the LORD the glory due his name.
  Bring an offering and come before him;
  worship the LORD in the splendor of his[a]
  holiness.
³⁰ Tremble before him, all the earth!
  The world is firmly established; it cannot be
  moved.
³¹ Let the heavens rejoice, let the earth be glad;
  let them say among the nations, "The LORD
  reigns!"
³² Let the sea resound, and all that is in it;
  let the fields be jubilant, and everything in
  them!
³³ Then the trees of the forest will sing,
  they will sing for joy before the LORD,
  for he comes to judge the earth.

³⁴ Give thanks to the LORD, for he is good;
  his love endures forever.
³⁵ Cry out, "Save us, O God our Savior;
  gather us and deliver us from the nations,
  that we may give thanks to your holy name,
  that we may glory in your praise."
³⁶ Praise be to the LORD, the God of Israel,
  from everlasting to everlasting.

Then all the people said "Amen" and "Praise the LORD."

³⁷ David left Asaph and his associates before the ark of the covenant of the LORD to minister there regularly, according to each day's requirements. ³⁸ He also left Obed-Edom and his sixty-eight associates to minister with them. Obed-Edom son of Jeduthun, and also Hosah, were gatekeepers.

³⁹ David left Zadok the priest and his fellow priests before the tabernacle of the LORD at the high place in Gibeon ⁴⁰ to present burnt offerings to the LORD on the altar of burnt offering regularly, morning and evening, in accordance with everything written in the Law of the LORD, which he had given Israel. ⁴¹ With them were Heman and Jeduthun and the rest of those chosen and designated by name to give thanks to the LORD, "for his love endures forever." ⁴² Heman and Jeduthun were responsible for the sounding of the trumpets and cymbals and for the playing of the other instruments for sacred song. The sons of Jeduthun were stationed at the gate.

⁴³ Then all the people left, each for his own home, and David returned home to bless his family.

Glory Due God's Name

1 CHRONICLES 16:28–30

How do you ascribe glory and strength to God? What words or images come to mind when you hear the words "the glory of God" or "the power of God"? Linger over each word or image. What offering can you bring to such a God? How can you glorify God by your actions as well as by your words? Be as specific as you can, trying to name at least five things you can do today or tomorrow to give God glory.

See Meeting God in Worship

Grace Reaches Everyone

1 CHRONICLES 17:16

"Thy sovereign grace to all
extends,
Immense and unconfined;
From age to age it never
ends;
It reaches all mankind.
Throughout the world its
breadth is known,
Wide as infinity;
So wide, it never passed by
one,
Or it had passed by me."

—CHARLES WESLEY

God's Promise to David

17 After David was settled in his palace, he said to Nathan the prophet, "Here I am, living in a palace of cedar, while the ark of the covenant of the LORD is under a tent."

²Nathan replied to David, "Whatever you have in mind, do it, for God is with you."

³That night the word of God came to Nathan, saying:

⁴"Go and tell my servant David, 'This is what the LORD says: You are not the one to build me a house to dwell in. ⁵I have not dwelt in a house from the day I brought Israel up out of Egypt to this day. I have moved from one tent site to another, from one dwelling place to another. ⁶Wherever I have moved with all the Israelites, did I ever say to any of their leaders*a* whom I commanded to shepherd my people, "Why have you not built me a house of cedar?" '

⁷"Now then, tell my servant David, 'This is what the LORD Almighty says: I took you from the pasture and from following the flock, to be ruler over my people Israel. ⁸I have been with you wherever you have gone, and I have cut off all your enemies from before you. Now I will make your name like the names of the greatest men of the earth. ⁹And I will provide a place for my people Israel and will plant them so that they can have a home of their own and no longer be disturbed. Wicked people will not oppress them anymore, as they did at the beginning ¹⁰and have done ever since the time I appointed leaders over my people Israel. I will also subdue all your enemies.

" 'I declare to you that the LORD will build a house for you: ¹¹When your days are over and you go to be with your fathers, I will raise up your offspring to succeed you, one of your own sons, and I will establish his kingdom. ¹²He is the one who will build a house for me, and I will establish his throne forever. ¹³I will be his father, and he will be my son. I will never take my love away from him, as I took it away from your predecessor. ¹⁴I will set him over my house and my kingdom forever; his throne will be established forever.' "

¹⁵Nathan reported to David all the words of this entire revelation.

David's Prayer

¹⁶Then King David went in and sat before the LORD, and he said:

"Who am I, O LORD God, and what is my family, that you have brought me this far? ¹⁷And as if this were not enough in your sight, O God, you have spoken about the future of the house of your servant. You have looked on me as though I were the most exalted of men, O LORD God.

¹⁸"What more can David say to you for honoring your servant? For you know your servant, ¹⁹O LORD. For the sake of your servant and according to your

a 6 Traditionally *judges*; also in verse 10

will, you have done this great thing and made known all these great promises.

²⁰"There is no one like you, O LORD, and there is no God but you, as we have heard with our own ears. ²¹And who is like your people Israel—the one nation on earth whose God went out to redeem a people for himself, and to make a name for yourself, and to perform great and awesome wonders by driving out nations from before your people, whom you redeemed from Egypt? ²²You made your people Israel your very own forever, and you, O LORD, have become their God.

²³"And now, LORD, let the promise you have made concerning your servant and his house be established forever. Do as you promised, ²⁴so that it will be established and that your name will be great forever. Then men will say, 'The LORD Almighty, the God over Israel, is Israel's God!' And the house of your servant David will be established before you.

²⁵"You, my God, have revealed to your servant that you will build a house for him. So your servant has found courage to pray to you. ²⁶O LORD, you are God! You have promised these good things to your servant. ²⁷Now you have been pleased to bless the house of your servant, that it may continue forever in your sight; for you, O LORD, have blessed it, and it will be blessed forever."

David's Victories

18 In the course of time, David defeated the Philistines and subdued them, and he took Gath and its surrounding villages from the control of the Philistines.

²David also defeated the Moabites, and they became subject to him and brought tribute.

³Moreover, David fought Hadadezer king of Zobah, as far as Hamath, when he went to establish his control along the Euphrates River. ⁴David captured a thousand of his chariots, seven thousand charioteers and twenty thousand foot soldiers. He hamstrung all but a hundred of the chariot horses.

⁵When the Arameans of Damascus came to help Hadadezer king of Zobah, David struck down twenty-two thousand of them. ⁶He put garrisons in the Aramean kingdom of Damascus, and the Arameans became subject to him and brought tribute. The LORD gave David victory everywhere he went.

⁷David took the gold shields carried by the officers of Hadadezer and brought them to Jerusalem. ⁸From Tebah*a* and Cun, towns that belonged to Hadadezer, David took a great quantity of bronze, which Solomon used to make the bronze Sea, the pillars and various bronze articles.

⁹When Tou king of Hamath heard that David had defeated the entire army of Hadadezer king of Zobah, ¹⁰he sent his son Hadoram to King David to greet him and congratulate him on his victory in battle over Hadadezer, who had been at war with Tou. Hadoram brought all kinds of articles of gold and silver and bronze.

¹¹King David dedicated these articles to the LORD, as he had done with the silver and gold he had taken from all

---

David's Prayer

1 CHRONICLES 17:16–27

Read this passage using the method of *lectio divina*. Read the passage through twice carefully. What words or phrases strike you as meaningful? Write them down. Choose one or two and spend some time with them. Write down some of the images that come to mind. Rest in receptive silence. What is God saying to you through this word or phrase? What is your response? Pray accordingly.

---

a 8 Hebrew *Tibhath,* a variant of *Tebah*

Simple Prayer

1 CHRONICLES 19:10–15

Abba Macarius was asked, "How should one pray?" The old man said, "There is no need at all to make long discourses; it is enough to stretch out one's hands and say, 'Lord, as you will, and as you know, have mercy.' And if the conflict grows any fiercer say, 'Lord, help!' He knows very well what we need and he shows us his mercy."

—MACARIUS THE GREAT,
Sayings of the Desert Fathers

See *Meeting God in Prayer*

these nations: Edom and Moab, the Ammonites and the Philistines, and Amalek. [12]Abishai son of Zeruiah struck down eighteen thousand Edomites in the Valley of Salt. [13]He put garrisons in Edom, and all the Edomites became subject to David. The LORD gave David victory everywhere he went.

David's Officials

[14]David reigned over all Israel, doing what was just and right for all his people. [15]Joab son of Zeruiah was over the army; Jehoshaphat son of Ahilud was recorder; [16]Zadok son of Ahitub and Ahimelech[a] son of Abiathar were priests; Shavsha was secretary; [17]Benaiah son of Jehoiada was over the Kerethites and Pelethites; and David's sons were chief officials at the king's side.

The Battle Against the Ammonites

19 In the course of time, Nahash king of the Ammonites died, and his son succeeded him as king. [2]David thought, "I will show kindness to Hanun son of Nahash, because his father showed kindness to me." So David sent a delegation to express his sympathy to Hanun concerning his father.

When David's men came to Hanun in the land of the Ammonites to express sympathy to him, [3]the Ammonite nobles said to Hanun, "Do you think David is honoring your father by sending men to you to express sympathy? Haven't his men come to you to explore and spy out the country and overthrow it?" [4]So Hanun seized David's men, shaved them, cut off their garments in the middle at the buttocks, and sent them away.

[5]When someone came and told David about the men, he sent messengers to meet them, for they were greatly humiliated. The king said, "Stay at Jericho till your beards have grown, and then come back."

[6]When the Ammonites realized that they had become a stench in David's nostrils, Hanun and the Ammonites sent a thousand talents[b] of silver to hire chariots and charioteers from Aram Naharaim,[c] Aram Maacah and Zobah. [7]They hired thirty-two thousand chariots and charioteers, as well as the king of Maacah with his troops, who came and camped near Medeba, while the Ammonites were mustered from their towns and moved out for battle.

[8]On hearing this, David sent Joab out with the entire army of fighting men. [9]The Ammonites came out and drew up in battle formation at the entrance to their city, while the kings who had come were by themselves in the open country.

[10]Joab saw that there were battle lines in front of him and behind him; so he selected some of the best troops in Israel and deployed them against the Arameans. [11]He put the rest of the men under the command of Abishai his brother, and they were deployed against the Ammonites. [12]Joab said, "If the Arameans are too strong for me, then you are to rescue me; but if the Ammonites are too strong for you, then I will rescue you. [13]Be strong and let us fight

a 16 Some Hebrew manuscripts, Vulgate and Syriac (see also 2 Samuel 8:17); most Hebrew manuscripts *Abimelech*   *b 6* That is, about 37 tons (about 34 metric tons)   *c 6* That is, Northwest Mesopotamia

bravely for our people and the cities of our God. The LORD will do what is good in his sight."

¹⁴Then Joab and the troops with him advanced to fight the Arameans, and they fled before him. ¹⁵When the Ammonites saw that the Arameans were fleeing, they too fled before his brother Abishai and went inside the city. So Joab went back to Jerusalem.

¹⁶After the Arameans saw that they had been routed by Israel, they sent messengers and had Arameans brought from beyond the River,ᵃ with Shophach the commander of Hadadezer's army leading them.

¹⁷When David was told of this, he gathered all Israel and crossed the Jordan; he advanced against them and formed his battle lines opposite them. David formed his lines to meet the Arameans in battle, and they fought against him. ¹⁸But they fled before Israel, and David killed seven thousand of their charioteers and forty thousand of their foot soldiers. He also killed Shophach the commander of their army.

¹⁹When the vassals of Hadadezer saw that they had been defeated by Israel, they made peace with David and became subject to him.

So the Arameans were not willing to help the Ammonites anymore.

The Capture of Rabbah

20 In the spring, at the time when kings go off to war, Joab led out the armed forces. He laid waste the land of the Ammonites and went to Rabbah and besieged it, but David remained in Jerusalem. Joab attacked Rabbah and left it in ruins. ²David took the crown from the head of their kingᵇ—its weight was found to be a talentᶜ of gold, and it was set with precious stones—and it was placed on David's head. He took a great quantity of plunder from the city ³and brought out the people who were there, consigning them to labor with saws and with iron picks and axes. David did this to all the Ammonite towns. Then David and his entire army returned to Jerusalem.

War With the Philistines

⁴In the course of time, war broke out with the Philistines, at Gezer. At that time Sibbecai the Hushathite killed Sippai, one of the descendants of the Rephaites, and the Philistines were subjugated.

⁵In another battle with the Philistines, Elhanan son of Jair killed Lahmi the brother of Goliath the Gittite, who had a spear with a shaft like a weaver's rod.

⁶In still another battle, which took place at Gath, there was a huge man with six fingers on each hand and six toes on each foot—twenty-four in all. He also was descended from Rapha. ⁷When he taunted Israel, Jonathan son of Shimea, David's brother, killed him.

⁸These were descendants of Rapha in Gath, and they fell at the hands of David and his men.

David Numbers the Fighting Men

21 Satan rose up against Israel and incited David to take a census of Israel. ²So David said to Joab and

They Might Be Giants

1 CHRONICLES 20:4–8

The people of God still have to face giants. But today's giants are more likely to be the faceless giants of corporations, nations and social problems. What are the giants attacking you, your family, your church or your community? Do they need to be fought, or can they be engaged and redeemed? You might spend some time imagining one of these giants. What does it look like? Try talking with it. Writing out your conversation could help to keep you focused. You might want to invite God into the conversation to mediate your dispute or to advise you on how to proceed.

See Meeting God in Everyday Life

ᵃ 16 That is, the Euphrates   ᵇ 2 Or *of Milcom*, that is, Molech   ᶜ 2 That is, about 75 pounds (about 34 kilograms)

Justice or Mercy?

1 CHRONICLES 21:11–13

Human ideas of justice center on retribution. But God offers mercy even while we are in the midst of suffering the consequences of our actions. Our call is to be merciful as God is merciful (see Luke 6:36). Where in your life are you aching for someone to "fall into the hands of [people]"? Try praying for that person or persons. Ask God to break into their lives, to offer them mercy and forgiveness even if you cannot do so. You might also ask God to fill you with love so that you, too, can offer mercy. What can you do to be an agent of mercy rather than retribution?

See Meeting God in Community

the commanders of the troops, "Go and count the Israelites from Beersheba to Dan. Then report back to me so that I may know how many there are."

³But Joab replied, "May the LORD multiply his troops a hundred times over. My lord the king, are they not all my lord's subjects? Why does my lord want to do this? Why should he bring guilt on Israel?"

⁴The king's word, however, overruled Joab; so Joab left and went throughout Israel and then came back to Jerusalem. ⁵Joab reported the number of the fighting men to David: In all Israel there were one million one hundred thousand men who could handle a sword, including four hundred and seventy thousand in Judah.

⁶But Joab did not include Levi and Benjamin in the numbering, because the king's command was repulsive to him. ⁷This command was also evil in the sight of God; so he punished Israel.

⁸Then David said to God, "I have sinned greatly by doing this. Now, I beg you, take away the guilt of your servant. I have done a very foolish thing."

⁹The LORD said to Gad, David's seer, ¹⁰"Go and tell David, 'This is what the LORD says: I am giving you three options. Choose one of them for me to carry out against you.' "

¹¹So Gad went to David and said to him, "This is what the LORD says: 'Take your choice: ¹²three years of famine, three months of being swept away*ᵃ* before your enemies, with their swords overtaking you, or three days of the sword of the LORD—days of plague in the land, with the angel of the LORD ravaging every part of Israel.' Now then, decide how I should answer the one who sent me."

¹³David said to Gad, "I am in deep distress. Let me fall into the hands of the LORD, for his mercy is very great; but do not let me fall into the hands of men."

¹⁴So the LORD sent a plague on Israel, and seventy thousand men of Israel fell dead. ¹⁵And God sent an angel to destroy Jerusalem. But as the angel was doing so, the LORD saw it and was grieved because of the calamity and said to the angel who was destroying the people, "Enough! Withdraw your hand." The angel of the LORD was then standing at the threshing floor of Araunah*ᵇ* the Jebusite.

¹⁶David looked up and saw the angel of the LORD standing between heaven and earth, with a drawn sword in his hand extended over Jerusalem. Then David and the elders, clothed in sackcloth, fell facedown.

¹⁷David said to God, "Was it not I who ordered the fighting men to be counted? I am the one who has sinned and done wrong. These are but sheep. What have they done? O LORD my God, let your hand fall upon me and my family, but do not let this plague remain on your people."

¹⁸Then the angel of the LORD ordered Gad to tell David to go up and build an altar to the LORD on the threshing floor of Araunah the Jebusite. ¹⁹So David went up in obedience to the word that Gad had spoken in the name of the LORD.

²⁰While Araunah was threshing wheat, he turned and saw the angel; his four sons who were with him hid them-

---

ᵃ 12 Hebrew; Septuagint and Vulgate (see also 2 Samuel 24:13) *of fleeing*
ᵇ 15 Hebrew *Ornan,* a variant of *Araunah;* also in verses 18–28

selves. ²¹Then David approached, and when Araunah looked and saw him, he left the threshing floor and bowed down before David with his face to the ground.

²²David said to him, "Let me have the site of your threshing floor so I can build an altar to the LORD, that the plague on the people may be stopped. Sell it to me at the full price."

²³Araunah said to David, "Take it! Let my lord the king do whatever pleases him. Look, I will give the oxen for the burnt offerings, the threshing sledges for the wood, and the wheat for the grain offering. I will give all this."

²⁴But King David replied to Araunah, "No, I insist on paying the full price. I will not take for the LORD what is yours, or sacrifice a burnt offering that costs me nothing."

²⁵So David paid Araunah six hundred shekels*a* of gold for the site. ²⁶David built an altar to the LORD there and sacrificed burnt offerings and fellowship offerings.*b* He called on the LORD, and the LORD answered him with fire from heaven on the altar of burnt offering.

²⁷Then the LORD spoke to the angel, and he put his sword back into its sheath. ²⁸At that time, when David saw that the LORD had answered him on the threshing floor of Araunah the Jebusite, he offered sacrifices there. ²⁹The tabernacle of the LORD, which Moses had made in the desert, and the altar of burnt offering were at that time on the high place at Gibeon. ³⁰But David could not go before it to inquire of God, because he was afraid of the sword of the angel of the LORD.

22 Then David said, "The house of the LORD God is to be here, and also the altar of burnt offering for Israel."

Preparations for the Temple

²So David gave orders to assemble the aliens living in Israel, and from among them he appointed stonecutters to prepare dressed stone for building the house of God. ³He provided a large amount of iron to make nails for the doors of the gateways and for the fittings, and more bronze than could be weighed. ⁴He also provided more cedar logs than could be counted, for the Sidonians and Tyrians had brought large numbers of them to David.

⁵David said, "My son Solomon is young and inexperienced, and the house to be built for the LORD should be of great magnificence and fame and splendor in the sight of all the nations. Therefore I will make preparations for it." So David made extensive preparations before his death.

⁶Then he called for his son Solomon and charged him to build a house for the LORD, the God of Israel. ⁷David said to Solomon: "My son, I had it in my heart to build a house for the Name of the LORD my God. ⁸But this word of the LORD came to me: 'You have shed much blood and have fought many wars. You are not to build a house for my Name, because you have shed much blood on the earth in my sight. ⁹But you will have a son who will be a man of peace and rest, and I will give him rest from all his enemies on every side. His name will be Solomon,*c* and I will grant Israel peace and quiet during his reign. ¹⁰He is

---

Words for the Leader

1 CHRONICLES 22:6-13

David's prayer and charge to Solomon might make a good blessing for any national leader. You might use this passage as a basis for prayer for the leader of your nation. Ask God to grant him or her discretion and understanding, strength and courage, confidence and, above all, care in seeking God's will as an individual and as a leader. You might also send a note of encouragement, letting the leader know about your prayer.

See Meeting God in Service

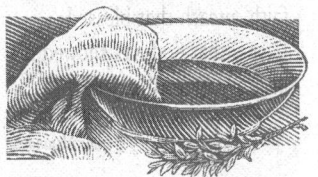

---

a 25 That is, about 15 pounds (about 7 kilograms)   *b 26* Traditionally *peace offerings*   *c 9 Solomon* sounds like and may be derived from the Hebrew for *peace.*

Gifts Are to Be Used

1 CHRONICLES 22:14–19

"I was made to see that the Holy Ghost never intended that [those] who have gifts and abilities should bury them in the earth, but rather did command and stir up such to the exercise of their gift, and also did commend those that were apt and ready so to do . . . Wherefore, though of myself of all the saints the most unworthy, yet I, but with great fear and trembling at the sight of my own weakness, did set upon the work, and did according to my gift, and the proportion of my faith, preach that blessed Gospel that God has showed me in the holy word of truth."

—JOHN BUNYAN,
Grace Abounding

the one who will build a house for my Name. He will be my son, and I will be his father. And I will establish the throne of his kingdom over Israel forever.'

¹¹"Now, my son, the LORD be with you, and may you have success and build the house of the LORD your God, as he said you would. ¹²May the LORD give you discretion and understanding when he puts you in command over Israel, so that you may keep the law of the LORD your God. ¹³Then you will have success if you are careful to observe the decrees and laws that the LORD gave Moses for Israel. Be strong and courageous. Do not be afraid or discouraged.

¹⁴"I have taken great pains to provide for the temple of the LORD a hundred thousand talents[a] of gold, a million talents[b] of silver, quantities of bronze and iron too great to be weighed, and wood and stone. And you may add to them. ¹⁵You have many workmen: stonecutters, masons and carpenters, as well as men skilled in every kind of work ¹⁶in gold and silver, bronze and iron—craftsmen beyond number. Now begin the work, and the LORD be with you."

¹⁷Then David ordered all the leaders of Israel to help his son Solomon. ¹⁸He said to them, "Is not the LORD your God with you? And has he not granted you rest on every side? For he has handed the inhabitants of the land over to me, and the land is subject to the LORD and to his people. ¹⁹Now devote your heart and soul to seeking the LORD your God. Begin to build the sanctuary of the LORD God, so that you may bring the ark of the covenant of the LORD and the sacred articles belonging to God into the temple that will be built for the Name of the LORD."

The Levites

23 When David was old and full of years, he made his son Solomon king over Israel.

²He also gathered together all the leaders of Israel, as well as the priests and Levites. ³The Levites thirty years old or more were counted, and the total number of men was thirty-eight thousand. ⁴David said, "Of these, twenty-four thousand are to supervise the work of the temple of the LORD and six thousand are to be officials and judges. ⁵Four thousand are to be gatekeepers and four thousand are to praise the LORD with the musical instruments I have provided for that purpose."

⁶David divided the Levites into groups corresponding to the sons of Levi: Gershon, Kohath and Merari.

Gershonites

⁷Belonging to the Gershonites:
    Ladan and Shimei.
⁸The sons of Ladan:
    Jehiel the first, Zetham and Joel—three in all.
⁹The sons of Shimei:
    Shelomoth, Haziel and Haran—three in all.
    These were the heads of the families of Ladan.
¹⁰And the sons of Shimei:
    Jahath, Ziza,[c] Jeush and Beriah.

---

a 14 That is, about 3,750 tons (about 3,450 metric tons) *b 14* That is, about 37,500 tons (about 34,500 metric tons) *c 10* One Hebrew manuscript, Septuagint and Vulgate (see also verse 11); most Hebrew manuscripts *Zina*

These were the sons of Shimei—four in all.
¹¹Jahath was the first and Ziza the second, but Jeush and Beriah did not have many sons; so they were counted as one family with one assignment.

Kohathites

¹²The sons of Kohath:
Amram, Izhar, Hebron and Uzziel—four in all.
¹³The sons of Amram:
Aaron and Moses.
Aaron was set apart, he and his descendants forever, to consecrate the most holy things, to offer sacrifices before the LORD, to minister before him and to pronounce blessings in his name forever. ¹⁴The sons of Moses the man of God were counted as part of the tribe of Levi.
¹⁵The sons of Moses:
Gershom and Eliezer.
¹⁶The descendants of Gershom:
Shubael was the first.
¹⁷The descendants of Eliezer:
Rehabiah was the first.
Eliezer had no other sons, but the sons of Rehabiah were very numerous.
¹⁸The sons of Izhar:
Shelomith was the first.
¹⁹The sons of Hebron:
Jeriah the first, Amariah the second, Jahaziel the third and Jekameam the fourth.
²⁰The sons of Uzziel:
Micah the first and Isshiah the second.

Merarites

²¹The sons of Merari:
Mahli and Mushi.
The sons of Mahli:
Eleazar and Kish.
²²Eleazar died without having sons: he had only daughters. Their cousins, the sons of Kish, married them.
²³The sons of Mushi:
Mahli, Eder and Jerimoth—three in all.

²⁴These were the descendants of Levi by their families—the heads of families as they were registered under their names and counted individually, that is, the workers twenty years old or more who served in the temple of the LORD. ²⁵For David had said, "Since the LORD, the God of Israel, has granted rest to his people and has come to dwell in Jerusalem forever, ²⁶the Levites no longer need to carry the tabernacle or any of the articles used in its service." ²⁷According to the last instructions of David, the Levites were counted from those twenty years old or more.
²⁸The duty of the Levites was to help Aaron's descendants in the service of the temple of the LORD: to be in charge of the courtyards, the side rooms, the purification of all sacred things and the performance of other duties at the house of God. ²⁹They were in charge of the bread set out on the table, the flour for the grain offerings, the unleavened wafers, the baking and the mixing, and all measurements of quantity and size. ³⁰They were also to stand

New Times, New Duties

1 CHRONICLES 23:25–28

With the ark of the covenant settled in Jerusalem, the traditional duty of the Levites, who tended the tabernacle, is ended. But there is still plenty for them to do. What traditional church activities have been meaningful to you but are now passing away? How do you respond to their passing? What new activities could you take part in? How can your gifts (both spiritual and natural) and your experience be used to serve the present needs of your church or your community? You might want to thank God for what has been and ask for God's help to be open to new challenges and new opportunities.

See *Meeting God in Service*

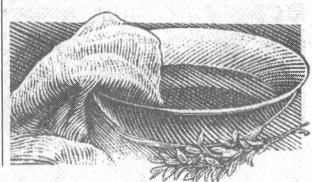

Prayer Is Communal

1 CHRONICLES 23:32–24:19

"Before all things, the Teacher of peace and the Master of unity would not have prayer to be made singly and individually, as for one who prays to pray for himself alone. For we do not say, 'My Father, which art in heaven,' nor 'Give me this day my daily bread;' nor does each one ask that only his own debt should be forgiven him; nor does he request for himself alone that he may not be led into temptation, and delivered from evil. Our prayer is public and common; and when we pray, we pray not for one, but for the whole people, because we are the whole people are one."

—CYPRIAN OF CARTHAGE,
Treatise "On the Lord's Prayer"

See Meeting God in Prayer

every morning to thank and praise the LORD. They were to do the same in the evening ³¹and whenever burnt offerings were presented to the LORD on Sabbaths and at New Moon festivals and at appointed feasts. They were to serve before the LORD regularly in the proper number and in the way prescribed for them.

³²And so the Levites carried out their responsibilities for the Tent of Meeting, for the Holy Place and, under their brothers the descendants of Aaron, for the service of the temple of the LORD.

The Divisions of Priests

24 These were the divisions of the sons of Aaron:
The sons of Aaron were Nadab, Abihu, Eleazar and Ithamar. ²But Nadab and Abihu died before their father did, and they had no sons; so Eleazar and Ithamar served as the priests. ³With the help of Zadok a descendant of Eleazar and Ahimelech a descendant of Ithamar, David separated them into divisions for their appointed order of ministering. ⁴A larger number of leaders were found among Eleazar's descendants than among Ithamar's, and they were divided accordingly: sixteen heads of families from Eleazar's descendants and eight heads of families from Ithamar's descendants. ⁵They divided them impartially by drawing lots, for there were officials of the sanctuary and officials of God among the descendants of both Eleazar and Ithamar.

⁶The scribe Shemaiah son of Nethanel, a Levite, recorded their names in the presence of the king and of the officials: Zadok the priest, Ahimelech son of Abiathar and the heads of families of the priests and of the Levites—one family being taken from Eleazar and then one from Ithamar.

⁷The first lot fell to Jehoiarib,
the second to Jedaiah,
⁸the third to Harim,
the fourth to Seorim,
⁹the fifth to Malkijah,
the sixth to Mijamin,
¹⁰the seventh to Hakkoz,
the eighth to Abijah,
¹¹the ninth to Jeshua,
the tenth to Shecaniah,
¹²the eleventh to Eliashib,
the twelfth to Jakim,
¹³the thirteenth to Huppah,
the fourteenth to Jeshebeab,
¹⁴the fifteenth to Bilgah,
the sixteenth to Immer,
¹⁵the seventeenth to Hezir,
the eighteenth to Happizzez,
¹⁶the nineteenth to Pethahiah,
the twentieth to Jehezkel,
¹⁷the twenty-first to Jakin,
the twenty-second to Gamul,
¹⁸the twenty-third to Delaiah
and the twenty-fourth to Maaziah.

¹⁹This was their appointed order of ministering when they entered the temple of the LORD, according to the reg-

ulations prescribed for them by their forefather Aaron, as the LORD, the God of Israel, had commanded him.

The Rest of the Levites

²⁰As for the rest of the descendants of Levi:
from the sons of Amram: Shubael;
from the sons of Shubael: Jehdeiah.
²¹As for Rehabiah, from his sons:
Isshiah was the first.
²²From the Izharites: Shelomoth;
from the sons of Shelomoth: Jahath.
²³The sons of Hebron: Jeriah the first,ᵃ Amariah the second, Jahaziel the third and Jekameam the fourth.
²⁴The son of Uzziel: Micah;
from the sons of Micah: Shamir.
²⁵The brother of Micah: Isshiah;
from the sons of Isshiah: Zechariah.
²⁶The sons of Merari: Mahli and Mushi.
The son of Jaaziah: Beno.
²⁷The sons of Merari:
from Jaaziah: Beno, Shoham, Zaccur and Ibri.
²⁸From Mahli: Eleazar, who had no sons.
²⁹From Kish: the son of Kish:
Jerahmeel.
³⁰And the sons of Mushi: Mahli, Eder and Jerimoth.

These were the Levites, according to their families. ³¹They also cast lots, just as their brothers the descendants of Aaron did, in the presence of King David and of Zadok, Ahimelech, and the heads of families of the priests and of the Levites. The families of the oldest brother were treated the same as those of the youngest.

The Singers

25 David, together with the commanders of the army, set apart some of the sons of Asaph, Heman and Jeduthun for the ministry of prophesying, accompanied by harps, lyres and cymbals. Here is the list of the men who performed this service:

²From the sons of Asaph:
Zaccur, Joseph, Nethaniah and Asarelah. The sons of Asaph were under the supervision of Asaph, who prophesied under the king's supervision.
³As for Jeduthun, from his sons:
Gedaliah, Zeri, Jeshaiah, Shimei,ᵇ Hashabiah and Mattithiah, six in all, under the supervision of their father Jeduthun, who prophesied, using the harp in thanking and praising the LORD.
⁴As for Heman, from his sons:
Bukkiah, Mattaniah, Uzziel, Shubael and Jerimoth; Hananiah, Hanani, Eliathah, Giddalti and Romamti-Ezer; Joshbekashah, Mallothi, Hothir and Mahazioth.
⁵All these were sons of Heman the king's seer. They were given him through the promises of God to exalt

---

God's Word Through Music

To prophesy is to speak God's message. Here are people set apart to prophesy through music. Great music has the power to lift us up and to inspire us. Try letting music carry you in prayer. Find a place where you can relax and listen undistracted. Select music that can allow your spirit to soar freely, whether it be a Bach fugue, a Beethoven symphony, a Stravinsky tone poem or some other composition that inspires you. Do not try to analyze the music. Simply offer the time to God and let the music speak. You might want to avoid music with lyrics, for words would suggest a particular direction. Allow yourself to rest in God's presence.

See Meeting God in Worship

ᵃ 23 Two Hebrew manuscripts and some Septuagint manuscripts (see also 1 Chron. 23:19); most Hebrew manuscripts *The sons of Jeriah:*   ᵇ 3 One Hebrew manuscript and some Septuagint manuscripts (see also verse 17); most Hebrew manuscripts do not have *Shimei.*

Called to a Special Place

1 CHRONICLES 25:6–31

"Each one of us has some kind of vocation. We are all called by God to share in his life and in His Kingdom. Each one of us is called to a special place in the Kingdom. If we find that place we will be happy. If we do not find it, we can never be completely happy. For each one of us, there is only one thing necessary: to fulfill our own destiny, according to God's will, to be what God wants us to be."

—THOMAS MERTON,
No Man Is an Island

him.[a] God gave Heman fourteen sons and three daughters.

[6] All these men were under the supervision of their fathers for the music of the temple of the Lord, with cymbals, lyres and harps, for the ministry at the house of God. Asaph, Jeduthun and Heman were under the supervision of the king. [7] Along with their relatives—all of them trained and skilled in music for the Lord—they numbered 288. [8] Young and old alike, teacher as well as student, cast lots for their duties.

[9] The first lot, which was for Asaph, fell to Joseph, his sons and relatives,[b]		12[c]
the second to Gedaliah, he and his relatives and sons,		12
[10] the third to Zaccur, his sons and relatives,		12
[11] the fourth to Izri,[d] his sons and relatives,		12
[12] the fifth to Nethaniah, his sons and relatives,		12
[13] the sixth to Bukkiah, his sons and relatives,		12
[14] the seventh to Jesarelah,[e] his sons and relatives,		12
[15] the eighth to Jeshaiah, his sons and relatives,		12
[16] the ninth to Mattaniah, his sons and relatives,		12
[17] the tenth to Shimei, his sons and relatives,		12
[18] the eleventh to Azarel,[f] his sons and relatives,		12
[19] the twelfth to Hashabiah, his sons and relatives,		12
[20] the thirteenth to Shubael, his sons and relatives,		12
[21] the fourteenth to Mattithiah, his sons and relatives,		12
[22] the fifteenth to Jerimoth, his sons and relatives,		12
[23] the sixteenth to Hananiah, his sons and relatives,		12
[24] the seventeenth to Joshbekashah, his sons and relatives,		12
[25] the eighteenth to Hanani, his sons and relatives,		12
[26] the nineteenth to Mallothi, his sons and relatives,		12
[27] the twentieth to Eliathah, his sons and relatives,		12
[28] the twenty-first to Hothir, his sons and relatives,		12
[29] the twenty-second to Giddalti, his sons and relatives,		12
[30] the twenty-third to Mahazioth,		

his sons and relatives, 12

31 the twenty-fourth to Romamti-Ezer,
  his sons and relatives, 12

The Gatekeepers

26

The divisions of the gatekeepers:

From the Korahites: Meshelemiah son of Kore, one of
  the sons of Asaph.
2 Meshelemiah had sons:
  Zechariah the firstborn,
  Jediael the second,
  Zebadiah the third,
  Jathniel the fourth,
  3 Elam the fifth,
  Jehohanan the sixth
  and Eliehoenai the seventh.
4 Obed-Edom also had sons:
  Shemaiah the firstborn,
  Jehozabad the second,
  Joah the third,
  Sacar the fourth,
  Nethanel the fifth,
  5 Ammiel the sixth,
  Issachar the seventh
  and Peullethai the eighth.
  (For God had blessed Obed-Edom.)

6 His son Shemaiah also had sons, who were leaders in
  their father's family because they were very capable men. 7 The sons of Shemaiah: Othni, Rephael,
  Obed and Elzabad; his relatives Elihu and Semaki-
  ah were also able men. 8 All these were descendants of Obed-Edom; they and their sons and their
  relatives were capable men with the strength to do
  the work—descendants of Obed-Edom, 62 in all.
9 Meshelemiah had sons and relatives, who were able
  men—18 in all.

10 Hosah the Merarite had sons: Shimri the first (although he was not the firstborn, his father had appointed him the first), 11 Hilkiah the second,
  Tabaliah the third and Zechariah the fourth. The
  sons and relatives of Hosah were 13 in all.
  12 These divisions of the gatekeepers, through their chief
men, had duties for ministering in the temple of the LORD,
just as their relatives had. 13 Lots were cast for each gate,
according to their families, young and old alike.
  14 The lot for the East Gate fell to Shelemiah.ᵃ Then lots
were cast for his son Zechariah, a wise counselor, and the
lot for the North Gate fell to him. 15 The lot for the South
Gate fell to Obed-Edom, and the lot for the storehouse fell
to his sons. 16 The lots for the West Gate and the
Shalleketh Gate on the upper road fell to Shuppim and
Hosah.
  Guard was alongside of guard: 17 There were six Levites
a day on the east, four a day on the north, four a day on
the south and two at a time at the storehouse. 18 As for the
court to the west, there were four at the road and two at
the court itself.

ᵃ 14 A variant of *Meshelemiah*

Gatekeepers

1 CHRONICLES 25:31–26:26

The gatekeepers guarded the
temple entrances against theft
and defilement. They also probably gathered offerings and
physically cared for the temple.
They were required to be "capable" and "able" and have "the
strength to do the work."

Who are the "gatekeepers"
of the church today? Pastors,
deacons, elders, church-school
teachers and parents? Anyone
who is a disciple of Jesus? In
what way are you a "gatekeeper" of God's truth? What makes
you able to do your job well?
How can you strengthen yourself to do the work of defending
the faith and keeping it secure?
For what do you need to ask
God in order to qualify as a
gatekeeper of the faith?

See Meeting God in Community

Seeking Ability

1 CHRONICLES 26:31

Much of this book has listed people in terms of their families and their family duties. Now we are told that some were sought out, not on the basis of the genealogical records of their families but because they were people who were "capable." What parts of your life have been determined by family roles, traditions or expectations? Where have you been able to use your unique abilities and interests? How has God called you from the "expected" and set you free to be fully yourself? To what further growth is God calling you?

See Meeting God in the Created Order

[19]These were the divisions of the gatekeepers who were descendants of Korah and Merari.

The Treasurers and Other Officials

[20]Their fellow Levites were[a] in charge of the treasuries of the house of God and the treasuries for the dedicated things.

[21]The descendants of Ladan, who were Gershonites through Ladan and who were heads of families belonging to Ladan the Gershonite, were Jehieli, [22]the sons of Jehieli, Zetham and his brother Joel. They were in charge of the treasuries of the temple of the LORD.

[23]From the Amramites, the Izharites, the Hebronites and the Uzzielites:

[24]Shubael, a descendant of Gershom son of Moses, was the officer in charge of the treasuries. [25]His relatives through Eliezer: Rehabiah his son, Jeshaiah his son, Joram his son, Zicri his son and Shelomith his son. [26]Shelomith and his relatives were in charge of all the treasuries for the things dedicated by King David, by the heads of families who were the commanders of thousands and commanders of hundreds, and by the other army commanders. [27]Some of the plunder taken in battle they dedicated for the repair of the temple of the LORD. [28]And everything dedicated by Samuel the seer and by Saul son of Kish, Abner son of Ner and Joab son of Zeruiah, and all the other dedicated things were in the care of Shelomith and his relatives.

[29]From the Izharites: Kenaniah and his sons were assigned duties away from the temple, as officials and judges over Israel.

[30]From the Hebronites: Hashabiah and his relatives—seventeen hundred able men—were responsible in Israel west of the Jordan for all the work of the LORD and for the king's service. [31]As for the Hebronites, Jeriah was their chief according to the genealogical records of their families. In the fortieth year of David's reign a search was made in the records, and capable men among the Hebronites were found at Jazer in Gilead. [32]Jeriah had twenty-seven hundred relatives, who were able men and heads of families, and King David put them in charge of the Reubenites, the Gadites and the half-tribe of Manasseh for every matter pertaining to God and for the affairs of the king.

Army Divisions

27 This is the list of the Israelites—heads of families, commanders of thousands and commanders of hundreds, and their officers, who served the king in all that concerned the army divisions that were on duty month by month throughout the year. Each division consisted of 24,000 men.

[2]In charge of the first division, for the first month, was Jashobeam son of Zabdiel. There were 24,000 men in

[a] 20 Septuagint; Hebrew *As for the Levites, Ahijah was*

his division. ³He was a descendant of Perez and chief of all the army officers for the first month.

⁴In charge of the division for the second month was Dodai the Ahohite; Mikloth was the leader of his division. There were 24,000 men in his division.

⁵The third army commander, for the third month, was Benaiah son of Jehoiada the priest. He was chief and there were 24,000 men in his division. ⁶This was the Benaiah who was a mighty man among the Thirty and was over the Thirty. His son Ammizabad was in charge of his division.

⁷The fourth, for the fourth month, was Asahel the brother of Joab; his son Zebadiah was his successor. There were 24,000 men in his division.

⁸The fifth, for the fifth month, was the commander Shamhuth the Izrahite. There were 24,000 men in his division.

⁹The sixth, for the sixth month, was Ira the son of Ikkesh the Tekoite. There were 24,000 men in his division.

¹⁰The seventh, for the seventh month, was Helez the Pelonite, an Ephraimite. There were 24,000 men in his division.

¹¹The eighth, for the eighth month, was Sibbecai the Hushathite, a Zerahite. There were 24,000 men in his division.

¹²The ninth, for the ninth month, was Abiezer the Anathothite, a Benjamite. There were 24,000 men in his division.

¹³The tenth, for the tenth month, was Maharai the Netophathite, a Zerahite. There were 24,000 men in his division.

¹⁴The eleventh, for the eleventh month, was Benaiah the Pirathonite, an Ephraimite. There were 24,000 men in his division.

¹⁵The twelfth, for the twelfth month, was Heldai the Netophathite, from the family of Othniel. There were 24,000 men in his division.

Officers of the Tribes

¹⁶The officers over the tribes of Israel:

over the Reubenites: Eliezer son of Zicri;
over the Simeonites: Shephatiah son of Maacah;
¹⁷over Levi: Hashabiah son of Kemuel;
over Aaron: Zadok;
¹⁸over Judah: Elihu, a brother of David;
over Issachar: Omri son of Michael;
¹⁹over Zebulun: Ishmaiah son of Obadiah;
over Naphtali: Jerimoth son of Azriel;
²⁰over the Ephraimites: Hoshea son of Azaziah;
over half the tribe of Manasseh: Joel son of Pedaiah;
²¹over the half-tribe of Manasseh in Gilead: Iddo son of Zechariah;
over Benjamin: Jaasiel son of Abner;
²²over Dan: Azarel son of Jeroham.
These were the officers over the tribes of Israel.

²³David did not take the number of the men twenty years old or less, because the Lord had promised to make Israel as numerous as the stars in the sky. ²⁴Joab son of Zeruiah began to count the men but did not finish. Wrath

Stewardship

1 CHRONICLES 27:23–25

One of the most thankless jobs can be caring for the finances of God's people. Spend some time in prayer for the treasurer and other financial officers of your church, or for those in similar roles in other charitable organizations. You might thank God for them and pray that they be filled with God's love. Pray similarly for those who collect the offering and those who count it. If you don't know who they are, find out! When you next see them, tell them you appreciate the work they do.

See Meeting God in Service

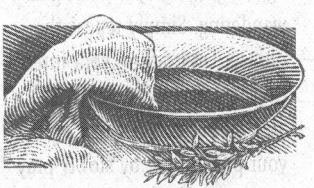

With a Willing Mind

1 CHRONICLES 28:2–10

Sometimes it is hard for us to pray "with wholehearted devotion and with a willing mind." Instead, our thoughts run in many directions: praying, thinking over the things we have to do, monitoring our devotional "temperature," listening to cars going by or to the TV playing in the next room. One way of focusing our thoughts is through a breath prayer. Try using the phrase "with wholehearted devotion and with a willing mind" as a breath prayer, repeating it to yourself slowly with each breath. Don't become discouraged if you find your thoughts wandering. Simply repeat the phrase. Let it affirm your intention to serve God completely and willingly. You might end your prayer time by slowly praying the Lord's Prayer.

See Meeting God in Prayer

came on Israel on account of this numbering, and the number was not entered in the book[a] of the annals of King David.

The King's Overseers

25Azmaveth son of Adiel was in charge of the royal storehouses.

Jonathan son of Uzziah was in charge of the storehouses in the outlying districts, in the towns, the villages and the watchtowers.

26Ezri son of Kelub was in charge of the field workers who farmed the land.

27Shimei the Ramathite was in charge of the vineyards.

Zabdi the Shiphmite was in charge of the produce of the vineyards for the wine vats.

28Baal-Hanan the Gederite was in charge of the olive and sycamore-fig trees in the western foothills.

Joash was in charge of the supplies of olive oil.

29Shitrai the Sharonite was in charge of the herds grazing in Sharon.

Shaphat son of Adlai was in charge of the herds in the valleys.

30Obil the Ishmaelite was in charge of the camels.

Jehdeiah the Meronothite was in charge of the donkeys.

31Jaziz the Hagrite was in charge of the flocks.

All these were the officials in charge of King David's property.

32Jonathan, David's uncle, was a counselor, a man of insight and a scribe. Jehiel son of Hacmoni took care of the king's sons.

33Ahithophel was the king's counselor.

Hushai the Arkite was the king's friend. 34Ahithophel was succeeded by Jehoiada son of Benaiah and by Abiathar.

Joab was the commander of the royal army.

David's Plans for the Temple

28 David summoned all the officials of Israel to assemble at Jerusalem: the officers over the tribes, the commanders of the divisions in the service of the king, the commanders of thousands and commanders of hundreds, and the officials in charge of all the property and livestock belonging to the king and his sons, together with the palace officials, the mighty men and all the brave warriors.

2King David rose to his feet and said: "Listen to me, my brothers and my people. I had it in my heart to build a house as a place of rest for the ark of the covenant of the LORD, for the footstool of our God, and I made plans to build it. 3But God said to me, 'You are not to build a house for my Name, because you are a warrior and have shed blood.'

4"Yet the LORD, the God of Israel, chose me from my whole family to be king over Israel forever. He chose Judah as leader, and from the house of Judah he chose my family, and from my father's sons he was pleased to make me king over all Israel. 5Of all my sons—and the LORD has given me many—he has chosen my son Solomon to sit on

a 24 Septuagint; Hebrew *number*

the throne of the kingdom of the LORD over Israel. ⁶He said to me: 'Solomon your son is the one who will build my house and my courts, for I have chosen him to be my son, and I will be his father. ⁷I will establish his kingdom forever if he is unswerving in carrying out my commands and laws, as is being done at this time.'

⁸"So now I charge you in the sight of all Israel and of the assembly of the LORD, and in the hearing of our God: Be careful to follow all the commands of the LORD your God, that you may possess this good land and pass it on as an inheritance to your descendants forever.

⁹"And you, my son Solomon, acknowledge the God of your father, and serve him with wholehearted devotion and with a willing mind, for the LORD searches every heart and understands every motive behind the thoughts. If you seek him, he will be found by you; but if you forsake him, he will reject you forever. ¹⁰Consider now, for the LORD has chosen you to build a temple as a sanctuary. Be strong and do the work."

¹¹Then David gave his son Solomon the plans for the portico of the temple, its buildings, its storerooms, its upper parts, its inner rooms and the place of atonement. ¹²He gave him the plans of all that the Spirit had put in his mind for the courts of the temple of the LORD and all the surrounding rooms, for the treasuries of the temple of God and for the treasuries for the dedicated things. ¹³He gave him instructions for the divisions of the priests and Levites, and for all the work of serving in the temple of the LORD, as well as for all the articles to be used in its service. ¹⁴He designated the weight of gold for all the gold articles to be used in various kinds of service, and the weight of silver for all the silver articles to be used in various kinds of service: ¹⁵the weight of gold for the gold lampstands and their lamps, with the weight for each lampstand and its lamps; and the weight of silver for each silver lampstand and its lamps, according to the use of each lampstand; ¹⁶the weight of gold for each table for consecrated bread; the weight of silver for the silver tables; ¹⁷the weight of pure gold for the forks, sprinkling bowls and pitchers; the weight of gold for each gold dish; the weight of silver for each silver dish; ¹⁸and the weight of the refined gold for the altar of incense. He also gave him the plan for the chariot, that is, the cherubim of gold that spread their wings and shelter the ark of the covenant of the LORD.

¹⁹"All this," David said, "I have in writing from the hand of the LORD upon me, and he gave me understanding in all the details of the plan."

²⁰David also said to Solomon his son, "Be strong and courageous, and do the work. Do not be afraid or discouraged, for the LORD God, my God, is with you. He will not fail you or forsake you until all the work for the service of the temple of the LORD is finished. ²¹The divisions of the priests and Levites are ready for all the work on the temple of God, and every willing man skilled in any craft will help you in all the work. The officials and all the people will obey your every command."

Not for Humankind but for God

1 CHRONICLES 28:20—29:5

Imagine walking through your church. Better yet, take a real walk through your church building. As you walk, notice all of the things you think of as yours: your pew, your choir robe, your classroom. As you come to each of them, remind yourself, "This is not for people but for the Lord God." When you find yourself resisting, stop a while to ponder what makes you feel possessive. Ask God for the wisdom to use this object or this space for God. Finally, find (or imagine) a mirror. As you look at yourself in the mirror, say again, "I am not for people but for the Lord God."

Blessing God

1 CHRONICLES 29:10–13

Read this passage slowly. Let David's prayer of praise become your own. Think of the blessings you have received and how you have experienced God's glory. If a phrase or a word claims your attention, stay with it for a while. When you reach the end of the passage, return to the beginning until the praise is echoing in your mind and you can carry thanks and praise from your prayer time into the rest of your day.

See Meeting God in Worship

Gifts for Building the Temple

29 Then King David said to the whole assembly: "My son Solomon, the one whom God has chosen, is young and inexperienced. The task is great, because this palatial structure is not for man but for the LORD God. ²With all my resources I have provided for the temple of my God—gold for the gold work, silver for the silver, bronze for the bronze, iron for the iron and wood for the wood, as well as onyx for the settings, turquoise,ᵃ stones of various colors, and all kinds of fine stone and marble— all of these in large quantities. ³Besides, in my devotion to the temple of my God I now give my personal treasures of gold and silver for the temple of my God, over and above everything I have provided for this holy temple: ⁴three thousand talentsᵇ of gold (gold of Ophir) and seven thousand talentsᶜ of refined silver, for the overlaying of the walls of the buildings, ⁵for the gold work and the silver work, and for all the work to be done by the craftsmen. Now, who is willing to consecrate himself today to the LORD?"

⁶Then the leaders of families, the officers of the tribes of Israel, the commanders of thousands and commanders of hundreds, and the officials in charge of the king's work gave willingly. ⁷They gave toward the work on the temple of God five thousand talentsᵈ and ten thousand daricsᵉ of gold, ten thousand talentsᶠ of silver, eighteen thousand talentsᵍ of bronze and a hundred thousand talentsʰ of iron. ⁸Any who had precious stones gave them to the treasury of the temple of the LORD in the custody of Jehiel the Gershonite. ⁹The people rejoiced at the willing response of their leaders, for they had given freely and wholeheartedly to the LORD. David the king also rejoiced greatly.

David's Prayer

¹⁰David praised the LORD in the presence of the whole assembly, saying,

"Praise be to you, O LORD,
    God of our father Israel,
    from everlasting to everlasting.
¹¹Yours, O LORD, is the greatness and the power
    and the glory and the majesty and the
        splendor,
    for everything in heaven and earth is yours.
Yours, O LORD, is the kingdom;
    you are exalted as head over all.
¹²Wealth and honor come from you;
    you are the ruler of all things.
In your hands are strength and power
    to exalt and give strength to all.
¹³Now, our God, we give you thanks,
    and praise your glorious name.

¹⁴"But who am I, and who are my people, that we should be able to give as generously as this? Everything

---

ᵃ 2 The meaning of the Hebrew for this word is uncertain. ᵇ 4 That is, about 110 tons (about 100 metric tons) ᶜ 4 That is, about 260 tons (about 240 metric tons) ᵈ 7 That is, about 190 tons (about 170 metric tons) ᵉ 7 That is, about 185 pounds (about 84 kilograms) ᶠ 7 That is, about 375 tons (about 345 metric tons) ᵍ 7 That is, about 675 tons (about 610 metric tons) ʰ 7 That is, about 3,750 tons (about 3,450 metric tons)

comes from you, and we have given you only what comes from your hand. ¹⁵We are aliens and strangers in your sight, as were all our forefathers. Our days on earth are like a shadow, without hope. ¹⁶O Lord our God, as for all this abundance that we have provided for building you a temple for your Holy Name, it comes from your hand, and all of it belongs to you. ¹⁷I know, my God, that you test the heart and are pleased with integrity. All these things have I given willingly and with honest intent. And now I have seen with joy how willingly your people who are here have given to you. ¹⁸O Lord, God of our fathers Abraham, Isaac and Israel, keep this desire in the hearts of your people forever, and keep their hearts loyal to you. ¹⁹And give my son Solomon the wholehearted devotion to keep your commands, requirements and decrees and to do everything to build the palatial structure for which I have provided."

²⁰Then David said to the whole assembly, "Praise the Lord your God." So they all praised the Lord, the God of their fathers; they bowed low and fell prostrate before the Lord and the king.

Solomon Acknowledged as King

²¹The next day they made sacrifices to the Lord and presented burnt offerings to him: a thousand bulls, a thousand rams and a thousand male lambs, together with their drink offerings, and other sacrifices in abundance for all Israel. ²²They ate and drank with great joy in the presence of the Lord that day.

Then they acknowledged Solomon son of David as king a second time, anointing him before the Lord to be ruler and Zadok to be priest. ²³So Solomon sat on the throne of the Lord as king in place of his father David. He prospered and all Israel obeyed him. ²⁴All the officers and mighty men, as well as all of King David's sons, pledged their submission to King Solomon.

²⁵The Lord highly exalted Solomon in the sight of all Israel and bestowed on him royal splendor such as no king over Israel ever had before.

The Death of David

²⁶David son of Jesse was king over all Israel. ²⁷He ruled over Israel forty years—seven in Hebron and thirty-three in Jerusalem. ²⁸He died at a good old age, having enjoyed long life, wealth and honor. His son Solomon succeeded him as king.

²⁹As for the events of King David's reign, from beginning to end, they are written in the records of Samuel the seer, the records of Nathan the prophet and the records of Gad the seer, ³⁰together with the details of his reign and power, and the circumstances that surrounded him and Israel and the kingdoms of all the other lands.

WAYS of MEETING GOD

Meeting God in Worship

The Bible places worship at the heart of life with God—and it is no wonder that it should do so. Over and over Scripture invites us to praise God—to "ascribe to the LORD the glory due his name. Bring an offering and come before him; worship the LORD in the splendor of his holiness" (1 Chronicles 16:29).

From the sacrificial offerings of Cain and Abel (see Genesis 4) to the expressions of the saints worshiping around the throne of God in the new Jerusalem (see Revelation 21–22), the act of worship is woven throughout Scripture like a glittering thread. Noah leaves the ark and immediately builds an altar to make an offering of thanksgiving. The Israelites escape from Pharaoh at the Red Sea and begin to dance and sing God's praise. God offers detailed instruction about the settings, times and forms of worship (Exodus 25–31; Leviticus 1–8,16,23; Numbers 28–29). The book of Psalms is the Bible's own hymnal, offering choruses of praise, cries for help, prayers of confession and songs of thanksgiving. We read of the earliest Christians devoting themselves "to the apostles' teaching and to the fellowship, to the breaking of bread and to prayer" (Acts 2:42). Paul offers advice about the conduct of worship (see 1 Corinthians 11,14) and expects that his letters will be read to the gathered community (see Colossians 4:16).

For many of us the impulse to worship seems instinctive. The human heart cries: "O God, you are my God, earnestly I seek you; my soul thirsts for you, my body longs for you" (Psalm 63:1). In one sense, at least, seeking God comes naturally; we long for God because we have been created for companionship with God. As Augustine prayed, "You move

> **W**orship begins with God reaching out to the ones he made. God floods our lives with blessing, and we give thanks: "Give thanks to the LORD, for he is good. *His love endures forever*" (Psalm 136:1).

us to delight in praising you; for you have formed us for yourself, and our hearts are restless till they find rest in you."

Worship, however, is more than the human soul reaching out to God. Worship begins with God reaching out to the ones he made. God floods our lives with blessing, and we give thanks: "Give thanks to the LORD, for he is good. *His love endures forever*" (Psalm 136:1). God utters a prophetic word of warning that cuts us to the heart, and we cry out for mercy and forgiveness, individually (see Psalm 51) or even nationally (see Jonah 3). God comes to us in Jesus Christ, saying, in effect, "See who I am, what I am like, how I love you. This is what I expect. I offer you myself and the full inheritance that is yours as my faithful children." And we fall on our knees and say, "My Lord and my God!" (John 20:28).

Worship Is Personal. Worship involves an immediate, personal response to God. In worship we remember personally how God has acted in our past. In worship we hear God's voice, silence, music, preaching and the testimony of other believers in Jesus. In worship we experience the presence of Jesus Christ and hear his life-giving word to each of us in our particular time and situation.

Worship Is Corporate. However, we cannot do without the benefits of worship in the midst of the faithful congregation (see Matthew 18:20; Acts 2:1–4,42–47). Whenever we pray the opening words of the Lord's Prayer, "Our Father," we recognize that we never really pray or worship alone. There will always be times when we must stand in God's presence together. "I rejoiced," says the psalmist, "with those who said to me, 'Let us go to the house of the LORD' " (Psalm 122:1). In corporate worship we discern ourselves more clearly as walking with other Christians, together seeking God and following Jesus. Here, bowed before God or gathered at Christ's table, we are reminded again of the equality of all God's children. For here none is excluded because of race, status, gender, health, economics, language or age. We are united in "one body and one Spirit . . . one Lord, one faith, one baptism; one God and Father of all" (Ephesians 4:4–6).

In corporate worship sisters and brothers help us to hear and interpret God's Word. Each one has truth to share, and together we can hear and see so much more of God and of the gospel than we could ever hear or see alone. The gathered community of believers not only holds us accountable to God but also holds us close to God. In those moments during which our memories or our wills fail and we would otherwise drift away from God and from the abundant life in Jesus, the rest of the body of Christ upholds us and even carries us until we are able to walk again. Acts of worship—sharing a meal, passing the peace, baptizing new Christians—allow us to practice the sharing and forgiveness of Christian love that we carry from our worship into our world.

Corporate worship pushes back the horizons of our self-centered world and reminds us of our identity as people of God. As we participate in the baptism of a child or adult, the conversion of an individual or the reception of new members into the church, we are reminded of and given opportunity to renew our own covenant with God. As we share in the Lord's Supper, we unite to "proclaim the Lord's death until he comes" (1 Corinthians 11:26). In corporate worship, it is easier to remember who we are, from where we have come and where we are going. We encounter God in ways in which we would not have met him on our own. This awareness helps us to live more faithful lives as followers of Jesus Christ.

Public worship acknowledges that our relationship with God requires a corporate expression that is rooted in tradition. The Jewish cycle of festivals and gatherings at Sabbath synagogues offered the people regular opportunities to worship, to "tell the old, old story," and to hear again God's instruction on how to live as his anointed, set-apart people. In a similar way the holy days of the church year and the weekly worship services offer Christians such opportunities. Worship becomes an occasion for meeting God. Such regular worship transforms our spirits until we become more and more like our Master, Jesus Christ.

Worship Is Biblical. Both the words and the manner of Christian worship are grounded in the Bible. This holds true for private worship, which may consist of reflecting on a passage of Scripture or praying psalms; the same holds true for public worship in which the Bible provides the lessons for the day and the basis for a sermon or homily. The Bible may also provide the basis for a call to worship, words of assurance, responsive readings and hymns. Prayers at baptism recall Biblical references to water, including the passage concerning Jesus' own baptism. Prayers at Communion refer to the actions of Jesus at the Last Supper as recorded in the Gospels and 1 Corinthians 11, particularly in verses 23–29.

Worship Is Transforming. Christian worship that is anchored in the Bible may take on a variety of forms while remaining faithful and faith-centered. But through it all God's Word is proclaimed and our lives are touched—our hearts transformed. Unfortunately, the act of worship can become routine. The truth is, we frequently attend worship services from a sense of duty or custom rather than with any hope of encountering God. If we wish to be transformed by worship—if we truly want to meet God—we must adopt three essential practices.

> Christian worship that is anchored in the Bible may take on a variety of forms while remaining faithful and faith-centered. But through it all God's Word is proclaimed and our lives are touched—our hearts transformed.

We are to worship *regularly*. We need regular times and places for personal and corporate worship. Without such regularity we are likely to forget or to allow other things to crowd out life's most important relationship. But the life given to God and lived intentionally in God's presence is always secure and sustained. Luke tells us that Jesus on the Sabbath day "went into the synagogue, as was his custom" (Luke 4:16).

We are to worship *reverently*. When we enter our church or the special place set aside for worship in our home, we need to consciously focus our minds and hearts. In worship we remember, reflect, plead, offer and receive as we come intentionally into the presence of the One who created us in love. We come not only seeking God's gifts and presence but also offering all that we are and all that we hope to become as our gift of response.

We are to worship *expectantly*. If we are not listening for God to speak to us, we are not likely to hear. In Christian community we help each other to be strong enough to hear the prophetic word calling us to righteousness and humble enough to hear the hopeful word calling us to receive the gift of God's salvation. God enables us to use the gifts of the Spirit in ways that are humble—and sometimes dramatic—in order to make hearing him possible (see Romans 12:6–8; 1 Corinthians 12:1–13; Ephesians 4:11–13). God can reach out to us not only in Scripture and sermon but also in the songs we sing, the prayers we pray and the love of those around us.

See Page 826 for the next Ways of Meeting God *article.*

2 CHRONICLES

Covenants Broken, Covenants Renewed

KEY VERSE:

The king stood by his pillar and renewed the covenant in the presence of the Lord—to follow the Lord and keep his commands, regulations and decrees with all his heart and all his soul, and to obey the words of the covenant written in this book.—2 Chronicles 34:31

"Fri. 25.[December 1747]— We met at four, and solemnly rejoiced in God our Savior. I found much revival in my own soul this day; and so did many others also. Both this and the following days, I strongly urged the wholly giving up ourselves to God, and renewing in every point our covenant, that the Lord should be our God."

—JOHN WESLEY,
Journal

Covenant is one of the key concepts in the Old Testament. A covenant is a binding agreement, a promise to behave in a particular way toward another person or group. God makes covenants with Noah (Genesis 9), Abraham (Genesis 15), the Israelites (Exodus 19—24) and David (2 Samuel 7). The prophets call the people to return to covenant faithfulness while reminding them that God is always faithful—"gracious and compassionate, slow to anger and abounding in love" (Joel 2:13). Jeremiah looks to a new day when God's covenant will be written directly on our hearts (Jeremiah 31:31–34).

In this second part of the Chronicler's account, references to covenant are myriad. Bad kings break the covenant or fail to keep it. Good kings keep the covenant with God. Great kings are reformers who restore the covenant, especially Hezekiah (chapters 29—31) and Josiah (chapters 34—35). No other measure—not peace at home or victory in battle—can measure a king's true worth.

In our baptism, God seals his amazing promise that he will forever be our gracious and forgiving God. He calls us to put our trust in Jesus and to respond in obedience. We renew this covenant in many ways throughout our lives: when we take part in the baptism of another, in confirmation and other special services of baptismal renewal, and when we gather at the Lord's Table. As you read 2 Chronicles seek to renew your own covenant with your sovereign and loving God.

Solomon Asks for Wisdom

1 Solomon son of David established himself firmly over his kingdom, for the LORD his God was with him and made him exceedingly great. ²Then Solomon spoke to all Israel—to the commanders of thousands and commanders of hundreds, to the judges and to all the leaders in Israel, the heads of families— ³and Solomon and the whole assembly went to the high place at Gibeon, for God's Tent of Meeting was there, which Moses the LORD's servant had made in the desert. ⁴Now David had brought up the ark of God from Kiriath Jearim to the place he had prepared for it, because he had pitched a tent for it in Jerusalem. ⁵But the bronze altar that Bezalel son of Uri, the son of Hur, had made was in Gibeon in front of the tabernacle of the LORD; so Solomon and the assembly inquired of him there. ⁶Solomon went up to the bronze altar before the LORD in the Tent of Meeting and offered a thousand burnt offerings on it.

⁷That night God appeared to Solomon and said to him, "Ask for whatever you want me to give you."

⁸Solomon answered God, "You have shown great kindness to David my father and have made me king in his place. ⁹Now, LORD God, let your promise to my father David be confirmed, for you have made me king over a people who are as numerous as the dust of the earth. ¹⁰Give me wisdom and knowledge, that I may lead this people, for who is able to govern this great people of yours?"

¹¹God said to Solomon, "Since this is your heart's desire and you have not asked for wealth, riches or honor, nor for the death of your enemies, and since you have not asked for a long life but for wisdom and knowledge to govern my people over whom I have made you king, ¹²therefore wisdom and knowledge will be given you. And I will also give you wealth, riches and honor, such as no king who was before you ever had and none after you will have."

¹³Then Solomon went to Jerusalem from the high place at Gibeon, from before the Tent of Meeting. And he reigned over Israel.

¹⁴Solomon accumulated chariots and horses; he had fourteen hundred chariots and twelve thousand horses,ᵃ which he kept in the chariot cities and also with him in Jerusalem. ¹⁵The king made silver and gold as common in Jerusalem as stones, and cedar as plentiful as sycamore-fig trees in the foothills. ¹⁶Solomon's horses were imported from Egyptᵇ and from Kueᶜ—the royal merchants purchased them from Kue. ¹⁷They imported a chariot from Egypt for six hundred shekelsᵈ of silver, and a horse for a hundred and fifty.ᵉ They also exported them to all the kings of the Hittites and of the Arameans.

Preparations for Building the Temple

2 Solomon gave orders to build a temple for the Name of the LORD and a royal palace for himself. ²He conscripted seventy thousand men as carriers and eighty thousand as stonecutters in the hills and thirty-six hundred as foremen over them.

A Question to Ponder

2 CHRONICLES 1:7

How would you respond if God said to you what he said to Solomon: "Ask for whatever you want me to give you"? What would you ask for? How would God respond? This might be a good question to explore in writing. Spell out the dialogue between God and yourself. When you have finished, read aloud what you have written. What have you learned from this second reading?

ᵃ *14* Or *charioteers*   ᵇ *16* Or possibly *Muzur,* a region in Cilicia; also in verse 17   ᶜ *16* Probably Cilicia   ᵈ *17* That is, about 15 pounds (about 7 kilograms)   ᵉ *17* That is, about 3 3/4 pounds (about 1.7 kilograms)

Who Am I?

2 CHRONICLES 2:6

Solomon explains that the task of building a temple for God is overwhelming, so he asks for help. What task is God calling you to perform? What is your part in building up God's people into a living temple? What can you do on your own? What kind of help do you need? Who might provide that help? Who might know where you can find help? Ask God to give you both help and helpers for the task ahead.

See Meeting God in Service

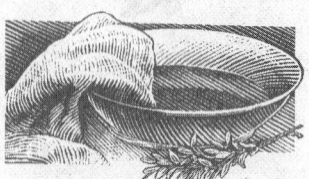

³Solomon sent this message to Hiram[a] king of Tyre:

"Send me cedar logs as you did for my father David when you sent him cedar to build a palace to live in. ⁴Now I am about to build a temple for the Name of the Lord my God and to dedicate it to him for burning fragrant incense before him, for setting out the consecrated bread regularly, and for making burnt offerings every morning and evening and on Sabbaths and New Moons and at the appointed feasts of the Lord our God. This is a lasting ordinance for Israel.

⁵"The temple I am going to build will be great, because our God is greater than all other gods. ⁶But who is able to build a temple for him, since the heavens, even the highest heavens, cannot contain him? Who then am I to build a temple for him, except as a place to burn sacrifices before him?

⁷"Send me, therefore, a man skilled to work in gold and silver, bronze and iron, and in purple, crimson and blue yarn, and experienced in the art of engraving, to work in Judah and Jerusalem with my skilled craftsmen, whom my father David provided.

⁸"Send me also cedar, pine and algum[b] logs from Lebanon, for I know that your men are skilled in cutting timber there. My men will work with yours ⁹to provide me with plenty of lumber, because the temple I build must be large and magnificent. ¹⁰I will give your servants, the woodsmen who cut the timber, twenty thousand cors[c] of ground wheat, twenty thousand cors of barley, twenty thousand baths[d] of wine and twenty thousand baths of olive oil."

¹¹Hiram king of Tyre replied by letter to Solomon:

"Because the Lord loves his people, he has made you their king."

¹²And Hiram added:

"Praise be to the Lord, the God of Israel, who made heaven and earth! He has given King David a wise son, endowed with intelligence and discernment, who will build a temple for the Lord and a palace for himself.

¹³"I am sending you Huram-Abi, a man of great skill, ¹⁴whose mother was from Dan and whose father was from Tyre. He is trained to work in gold and silver, bronze and iron, stone and wood, and with purple and blue and crimson yarn and fine linen. He is experienced in all kinds of engraving and can execute any design given to him. He will work with your craftsmen and with those of my lord, David your father.

¹⁵"Now let my lord send his servants the wheat and barley and the olive oil and wine he promised, ¹⁶and we will cut all the logs from Lebanon that you need and will float them in rafts by sea down to Joppa. You can then take them up to Jerusalem."

¹⁷Solomon took a census of all the aliens who were in Israel, after the census his father David had taken; and they

---

[a] 3 Hebrew *Huram*, a variant of *Hiram*; also in verses 11 and 12
[b] 8 Probably a variant of *almug*; possibly juniper   [c] 10 That is, probably about 125,000 bushels (about 4,400 kiloliters)   [d] 10 That is, probably about 115,000 gallons (about 440 kiloliters)

were found to be 153,600. ¹⁸He assigned 70,000 of them to be carriers and 80,000 to be stonecutters in the hills, with 3,600 foremen over them to keep the people working.

Solomon Builds the Temple

3 Then Solomon began to build the temple of the Lᴏʀᴅ in Jerusalem on Mount Moriah, where the Lᴏʀᴅ had appeared to his father David. It was on the threshing floor of Araunah*ᵃ* the Jebusite, the place provided by David. ²He began building on the second day of the second month in the fourth year of his reign.

³The foundation Solomon laid for building the temple of God was sixty cubits long and twenty cubits wide*ᵇ* (using the cubit of the old standard). ⁴The portico at the front of the temple was twenty cubits*ᶜ* long across the width of the building and twenty cubits*ᵈ* high.

He overlaid the inside with pure gold. ⁵He paneled the main hall with pine and covered it with fine gold and decorated it with palm tree and chain designs. ⁶He adorned the temple with precious stones. And the gold he used was gold of Parvaim. ⁷He overlaid the ceiling beams, doorframes, walls and doors of the temple with gold, and he carved cherubim on the walls.

⁸He built the Most Holy Place, its length corresponding to the width of the temple—twenty cubits long and twenty cubits wide. He overlaid the inside with six hundred talents*ᵉ* of fine gold. ⁹The gold nails weighed fifty shekels.*ᶠ* He also overlaid the upper parts with gold.

¹⁰In the Most Holy Place he made a pair of sculptured cherubim and overlaid them with gold. ¹¹The total wingspan of the cherubim was twenty cubits. One wing of the first cherub was five cubits*ᵍ* long and touched the temple wall, while its other wing, also five cubits long, touched the wing of the other cherub. ¹²Similarly one wing of the second cherub was five cubits long and touched the other temple wall, and its other wing, also five cubits long, touched the wing of the first cherub. ¹³The wings of these cherubim extended twenty cubits. They stood on their feet, facing the main hall.*ʰ*

¹⁴He made the curtain of blue, purple and crimson yarn and fine linen, with cherubim worked into it.

¹⁵In the front of the temple he made two pillars, which ⌊together⌋ were thirty-five cubits*ⁱ* long, each with a capital on top measuring five cubits. ¹⁶He made interwoven chains*ʲ* and put them on top of the pillars. He also made a hundred pomegranates and attached them to the chains. ¹⁷He erected the pillars in the front of the temple, one to the south and one to the north. The one to the south he named Jakin*ᵏ* and the one to the north Boaz.*ˡ*

A House of Stories

2 CHRONICLES 3:1

A church is a holy place, not only because of its use, but also because of the people who have helped to build it. In your imagination—or perhaps in reality—take a walk through your church. What are the stories it tells? Notice windows and pictures that may tell Biblical stories. What places or objects evoke memories of particular people or events? Thank God for your church as a house of stories.

See Meeting God in Worship

ᵃ 1 Hebrew *Ornan*, a variant of *Araunah*   *ᵇ 3* That is, about 90 feet (about 27 meters) long and 30 feet (about 9 meters) wide   *ᶜ 4* That is, about 30 feet (about 9 meters); also in verses 8, 11 and 13   *ᵈ 4* Some Septuagint and Syriac manuscripts; Hebrew *and a hundred and twenty*   *ᵉ 8* That is, about 23 tons (about 21 metric tons)   *ᶠ 9* That is, about 1 1/4 pounds (about 0.6 kilogram)   *ᵍ 11* That is, about 7 1/2 feet (about 2.3 meters); also in verse 15   *ʰ 13* Or *facing inward*   *ⁱ 15* That is, about 52 feet (about 16 meters)   *ʲ 16* Or possibly *made chains in the inner sanctuary*; the meaning of the Hebrew for this phrase is uncertain.   *ᵏ 17* Jakin probably means *he establishes*.   *ˡ 17* Boaz probably means *in him is strength*.

563

A House of Praise

2 CHRONICLES 4:7

Take another walk through your church. This time notice things in terms of their use in the church. There may be lampstands, special doors and basins, as in the temple of Solomon. There may be books and pews and musical instruments. How is each item a part of the worship of God? How do these items contribute to the work of God's people? How about you? What is your part in the worship and work of your church? How do you think God wants to use you?

See Meeting God in Worship

The Temple's Furnishings

4 He made a bronze altar twenty cubits long, twenty cubits wide and ten cubits high.[a] ²He made the Sea of cast metal, circular in shape, measuring ten cubits from rim to rim and five cubits[b] high. It took a line of thirty cubits[c] to measure around it. ³Below the rim, figures of bulls encircled it—ten to a cubit.[d] The bulls were cast in two rows in one piece with the Sea.

⁴The Sea stood on twelve bulls, three facing north, three facing west, three facing south and three facing east. The Sea rested on top of them, and their hindquarters were toward the center. ⁵It was a handbreadth[e] in thickness, and its rim was like the rim of a cup, like a lily blossom. It held three thousand baths.[f]

⁶He then made ten basins for washing and placed five on the south side and five on the north. In them the things to be used for the burnt offerings were rinsed, but the Sea was to be used by the priests for washing.

⁷He made ten gold lampstands according to the specifications for them and placed them in the temple, five on the south side and five on the north.

⁸He made ten tables and placed them in the temple, five on the south side and five on the north. He also made a hundred gold sprinkling bowls.

⁹He made the courtyard of the priests, and the large court and the doors for the court, and overlaid the doors with bronze. ¹⁰He placed the Sea on the south side, at the southeast corner.

¹¹He also made the pots and shovels and sprinkling bowls.

So Huram finished the work he had undertaken for King Solomon in the temple of God:

¹²the two pillars;
the two bowl-shaped capitals on top of the pillars;
the two sets of network decorating the two bowl-shaped capitals on top of the pillars;
¹³the four hundred pomegranates for the two sets of network (two rows of pomegranates for each network, decorating the bowl-shaped capitals on top of the pillars);
¹⁴the stands with their basins;
¹⁵the Sea and the twelve bulls under it;
¹⁶the pots, shovels, meat forks and all related articles.

All the objects that Huram-Abi made for King Solomon for the temple of the LORD were of polished bronze. ¹⁷The king had them cast in clay molds in the plain of the Jordan between Succoth and Zarethan.[g] ¹⁸All these things that Solomon made amounted to so much that the weight of the bronze was not determined.

¹⁹Solomon also made all the furnishings that were in God's temple:

the golden altar;
the tables on which was the bread of the Presence;

---

[a] 1 That is, about 30 feet (about 9 meters) long and wide, and about 15 feet (about 4.5 meters) high   [b] 2 That is, about 7 1/2 feet (about 2.3 meters)   [c] 2 That is, about 45 feet (about 13.5 meters)   [d] 3 That is, about 1 1/2 feet (about 0.5 meter)   [e] 5 That is, about 3 inches (about 8 centimeters)   [f] 5 That is, about 17,500 gallons (about 66 kiloliters)   [g] 17 Hebrew *Zeredatha*, a variant of *Zarethan*

20 the lampstands of pure gold with their lamps, to burn in front of the inner sanctuary as prescribed;
21 the gold floral work and lamps and tongs (they were solid gold);
22 the pure gold wick trimmers, sprinkling bowls, dishes and censers; and the gold doors of the temple: the inner doors to the Most Holy Place and the doors of the main hall.

5 When all the work Solomon had done for the temple of the LORD was finished, he brought in the things his father David had dedicated—the silver and gold and all the furnishings—and he placed them in the treasuries of God's temple.

The Ark Brought to the Temple

2 Then Solomon summoned to Jerusalem the elders of Israel, all the heads of the tribes and the chiefs of the Israelite families, to bring up the ark of the LORD's covenant from Zion, the City of David. 3 And all the men of Israel came together to the king at the time of the festival in the seventh month.

4 When all the elders of Israel had arrived, the Levites took up the ark, 5 and they brought up the ark and the Tent of Meeting and all the sacred furnishings in it. The priests, who were Levites, carried them up; 6 and King Solomon and the entire assembly of Israel that had gathered about him were before the ark, sacrificing so many sheep and cattle that they could not be recorded or counted.

7 The priests then brought the ark of the LORD's covenant to its place in the inner sanctuary of the temple, the Most Holy Place, and put it beneath the wings of the cherubim. 8 The cherubim spread their wings over the place of the ark and covered the ark and its carrying poles. 9 These poles were so long that their ends, extending from the ark, could be seen from in front of the inner sanctuary, but not from outside the Holy Place; and they are still there today. 10 There was nothing in the ark except the two tablets that Moses had placed in it at Horeb, where the LORD made a covenant with the Israelites after they came out of Egypt.

11 The priests then withdrew from the Holy Place. All the priests who were there had consecrated themselves, regardless of their divisions. 12 All the Levites who were musicians—Asaph, Heman, Jeduthun and their sons and relatives—stood on the east side of the altar, dressed in fine linen and playing cymbals, harps and lyres. They were accompanied by 120 priests sounding trumpets. 13 The trumpeters and singers joined in unison, as with one voice, to give praise and thanks to the LORD. Accompanied by trumpets, cymbals and other instruments, they raised their voices in praise to the LORD and sang:

> "He is good;
>   his love endures forever."

Then the temple of the LORD was filled with a cloud, 14 and the priests could not perform their service because of the cloud, for the glory of the LORD filled the temple of God.

6 Then Solomon said, "The LORD has said that he would dwell in a dark cloud; 2 I have built a magnificent temple for you, a place for you to dwell forever."

In the Dark Cloud

2 CHRONICLES 5:11—6:1

"Try as you might, this darkness and this cloud will remain between you and your God. You will feel frustrated, for your mind will be unable to grasp him, and your heart will not relish the delight of his love. But learn to be at home in this darkness. Return to it as often as you can, letting your spirit cry out to him whom you love. For if, in this life, you hope to feel and see God as he is in himself it must be within this darkness and this cloud."

—ANONYMOUS,
The Cloud of Unknowing

Promises Fulfilled

Think back through your life. What promises did God make to you? What promises have been proclaimed in God's name? How have you experienced promises fulfilled? You might want to write down some experiences that come to mind. You might make a litany by reading one of those experiences aloud and then repeating verse 14. What promises are still awaiting fulfillment?

[3]While the whole assembly of Israel was standing there, the king turned around and blessed them. [4]Then he said:

"Praise be to the LORD, the God of Israel, who with his hands has fulfilled what he promised with his mouth to my father David. For he said, [5]'Since the day I brought my people out of Egypt, I have not chosen a city in any tribe of Israel to have a temple built for my Name to be there, nor have I chosen anyone to be the leader over my people Israel. [6]But now I have chosen Jerusalem for my Name to be there, and I have chosen David to rule my people Israel.'

[7]"My father David had it in his heart to build a temple for the Name of the LORD, the God of Israel. [8]But the LORD said to my father David, 'Because it was in your heart to build a temple for my Name, you did well to have this in your heart. [9]Nevertheless, you are not the one to build the temple, but your son, who is your own flesh and blood—he is the one who will build the temple for my Name.'

[10]"The LORD has kept the promise he made. I have succeeded David my father and now I sit on the throne of Israel, just as the LORD promised, and I have built the temple for the Name of the LORD, the God of Israel. [11]There I have placed the ark, in which is the covenant of the LORD that he made with the people of Israel."

Solomon's Prayer of Dedication

[12]Then Solomon stood before the altar of the LORD in front of the whole assembly of Israel and spread out his hands. [13]Now he had made a bronze platform, five cubits[a] long, five cubits wide and three cubits[b] high, and had placed it in the center of the outer court. He stood on the platform and then knelt down before the whole assembly of Israel and spread out his hands toward heaven. [14]He said:

"O LORD, God of Israel, there is no God like you in heaven or on earth—you who keep your covenant of love with your servants who continue wholeheartedly in your way. [15]You have kept your promise to your servant David my father; with your mouth you have promised and with your hand you have fulfilled it—as it is today.

[16]"Now LORD, God of Israel, keep for your servant David my father the promises you made to him when you said, 'You shall never fail to have a man to sit before me on the throne of Israel, if only your sons are careful in all they do to walk before me according to my law, as you have done.' [17]And now, O LORD, God of Israel, let your word that you promised your servant David come true.

[18]"But will God really dwell on earth with men? The heavens, even the highest heavens, cannot contain you. How much less this temple I have built! [19]Yet give attention to your servant's prayer and his plea for mercy, O LORD my God. Hear the cry and the prayer that your servant is praying in your presence. [20]May your eyes be open toward this temple day and night,

---

[a] 13 That is, about 7 1/2 feet (about 2.3 meters) [b] 13 That is, about 4 1/2 feet (about 1.3 meters)

this place of which you said you would put your Name there. May you hear the prayer your servant prays toward this place. ²¹Hear the supplications of your servant and of your people Israel when they pray toward this place. Hear from heaven, your dwelling place; and when you hear, forgive.

²²"When a man wrongs his neighbor and is required to take an oath and he comes and swears the oath before your altar in this temple, ²³then hear from heaven and act. Judge between your servants, repaying the guilty by bringing down on his own head what he has done. Declare the innocent not guilty and so establish his innocence.

²⁴"When your people Israel have been defeated by an enemy because they have sinned against you and when they turn back and confess your name, praying and making supplication before you in this temple, ²⁵then hear from heaven and forgive the sin of your people Israel and bring them back to the land you gave to them and their fathers.

²⁶"When the heavens are shut up and there is no rain because your people have sinned against you, and when they pray toward this place and confess your name and turn from their sin because you have afflicted them, ²⁷then hear from heaven and forgive the sin of your servants, your people Israel. Teach them the right way to live, and send rain on the land you gave your people for an inheritance.

²⁸"When famine or plague comes to the land, or blight or mildew, locusts or grasshoppers, or when enemies besiege them in any of their cities, whatever disaster or disease may come, ²⁹and when a prayer or plea is made by any of your people Israel—each one aware of his afflictions and pains, and spreading out his hands toward this temple— ³⁰then hear from heaven, your dwelling place. Forgive, and deal with each man according to all he does, since you know his heart (for you alone know the hearts of men), ³¹so that they will fear you and walk in your ways all the time they live in the land you gave our fathers.

³²"As for the foreigner who does not belong to your people Israel but has come from a distant land because of your great name and your mighty hand and your outstretched arm—when he comes and prays toward this temple, ³³then hear from heaven, your dwelling place, and do whatever the foreigner asks of you, so that all the peoples of the earth may know your name and fear you, as do your own people Israel, and may know that this house I have built bears your Name.

³⁴"When your people go to war against their enemies, wherever you send them, and when they pray to you toward this city you have chosen and the temple I have built for your Name, ³⁵then hear from heaven their prayer and their plea, and uphold their cause.

³⁶"When they sin against you—for there is no one who does not sin—and you become angry with them and give them over to the enemy, who takes them captive to a land far away or near; ³⁷and if they have a change of heart in the land where they are held cap-

Outsiders Welcome!

2 CHRONICLES 6:32–33

What an amazing request! Solomon asks that even foreigners may find the temple to be a place where they can encounter God and receive God's blessings. How are strangers made to feel welcome at your church? How are they reminded that they are outsiders? What might be done to help them feel at home? To bring them into God's presence? How might God use you to accomplish this?

See *Meeting God in Community*

Awesome Glory

2 CHRONICLES 7:1–3

When you encounter God's glory, words just aren't enough to express what you feel. You can't even think straight. So don't try. Simply relax and give yourself over to adoration. You might try repeating the single word "glory" to provide a focus, to keep your mind from running about wildly. Or you might prefer to repeat the affirmation "God's love endures forever" as a breath prayer, that is, saying it once slowly with each breath. If you become distracted, simply return to the prayer word or breath prayer. You might end by singing the Doxology or by praying the Lord's Prayer.

See *Meeting God in Worship*

tive, and repent and plead with you in the land of their captivity and say, 'We have sinned, we have done wrong and acted wickedly'; ³⁸and if they turn back to you with all their heart and soul in the land of their captivity where they were taken, and pray toward the land you gave their fathers, toward the city you have chosen and toward the temple I have built for your Name; ³⁹then from heaven, your dwelling place, hear their prayer and their pleas, and uphold their cause. And forgive your people, who have sinned against you.

⁴⁰"Now, my God, may your eyes be open and your ears attentive to the prayers offered in this place.

⁴¹ "Now arise, O LORD God, and come to your resting place,
      you and the ark of your might.
   May your priests, O LORD God, be clothed with salvation,
      may your saints rejoice in your goodness.
⁴² O LORD God, do not reject your anointed one.
      Remember the great love promised to David your servant."

The Dedication of the Temple

7 When Solomon finished praying, fire came down from heaven and consumed the burnt offering and the sacrifices, and the glory of the LORD filled the temple. ²The priests could not enter the temple of the LORD because the glory of the LORD filled it. ³When all the Israelites saw the fire coming down and the glory of the LORD above the temple, they knelt on the pavement with their faces to the ground, and they worshiped and gave thanks to the LORD, saying,

   "He is good;
      his love endures forever."

⁴Then the king and all the people offered sacrifices before the LORD. ⁵And King Solomon offered a sacrifice of twenty-two thousand head of cattle and a hundred and twenty thousand sheep and goats. So the king and all the people dedicated the temple of God. ⁶The priests took their positions, as did the Levites with the LORD's musical instruments, which King David had made for praising the LORD and which were used when he gave thanks, saying, "His love endures forever." Opposite the Levites, the priests blew their trumpets, and all the Israelites were standing.

⁷Solomon consecrated the middle part of the courtyard in front of the temple of the LORD, and there he offered burnt offerings and the fat of the fellowship offerings,ᵃ because the bronze altar he had made could not hold the burnt offerings, the grain offerings and the fat portions.

⁸So Solomon observed the festival at that time for seven days, and all Israel with him—a vast assembly, people from Leboᵇ Hamath to the Wadi of Egypt. ⁹On the eighth day they held an assembly, for they had celebrated the dedication of the altar for seven days and the festival for seven days more. ¹⁰On the twenty-third day of the seventh month he sent the people to their homes, joyful and glad in heart

ᵃ 7 Traditionally *peace offerings*   ᵇ 8 Or *from the entrance to*

for the good things the LORD had done for David and Solomon and for his people Israel.

The LORD Appears to Solomon

[11]When Solomon had finished the temple of the LORD and the royal palace, and had succeeded in carrying out all he had in mind to do in the temple of the LORD and in his own palace, [12]the LORD appeared to him at night and said:

"I have heard your prayer and have chosen this place for myself as a temple for sacrifices.

[13]"When I shut up the heavens so that there is no rain, or command locusts to devour the land or send a plague among my people, [14]if my people, who are called by my name, will humble themselves and pray and seek my face and turn from their wicked ways, then will I hear from heaven and will forgive their sin and will heal their land. [15]Now my eyes will be open and my ears attentive to the prayers offered in this place. [16]I have chosen and consecrated this temple so that my Name may be there forever. My eyes and my heart will always be there.

[17]"As for you, if you walk before me as David your father did, and do all I command, and observe my decrees and laws, [18]I will establish your royal throne, as I covenanted with David your father when I said, 'You shall never fail to have a man to rule over Israel.'

[19]"But if you[a] turn away and forsake the decrees and commands I have given you[a] and go off to serve other gods and worship them, [20]then I will uproot Israel from my land, which I have given them, and will reject this temple I have consecrated for my Name. I will make it a byword and an object of ridicule among all peoples. [21]And though this temple is now so imposing, all who pass by will be appalled and say, 'Why has the LORD done such a thing to this land and to this temple?' [22]People will answer, 'Because they have forsaken the LORD, the God of their fathers, who brought them out of Egypt, and have embraced other gods, worshiping and serving them—that is why he brought all this disaster on them.' "

Solomon's Other Activities

8 At the end of twenty years, during which Solomon built the temple of the LORD and his own palace, [2]Solomon rebuilt the villages that Hiram[b] had given him, and settled Israelites in them. [3]Solomon then went to Hamath Zobah and captured it. [4]He also built up Tadmor in the desert and all the store cities he had built in Hamath. [5]He rebuilt Upper Beth Horon and Lower Beth Horon as fortified cities, with walls and with gates and bars, [6]as well as Baalath and all his store cities, and all the cities for his chariots and for his horses[c]—whatever he desired to build in Jerusalem, in Lebanon and throughout all the territory he ruled.

[7]All the people left from the Hittites, Amorites, Perizzites, Hivites and Jebusites (these peoples were not Israelites), [8]that is, their descendants remaining in the land, whom the Israelites had not destroyed—these Solomon conscripted

National Repentance

2 CHRONICLES 7:14

Imagine that you have been asked to lead a time of national repentance based on this verse. What national sins would you recount as part of the humbling process? What actions, symbolic or practical, would you call for? What prayer would you offer to lead the nation in seeking God's face? How would you proclaim the good news that God will forgive the nation's sin and heal the land? Now that you have all these great ideas, how will you use them?

See Meeting God in Community

---

[a] *19 The Hebrew is plural.*   [b] *2 Hebrew Huram, a variant of Hiram; also in verse 18*   [c] *6 Or charioteers*

Prayer for the King

2 CHRONICLES 9:8

The queen of Sheba, seeing all that Solomon has built and hearing his wisdom, is inspired to bless God. What qualities or actions of the leaders of your country, your state or your community inspire you? You might want to spend some time in prayer for these leaders, thanking God for the good you see in them and asking God to strengthen or inspire them where you see faults. You might also write to them to let them know you are holding them up in prayer.

See Meeting God in Community

for his slave labor force, as it is to this day. ⁹But Solomon did not make slaves of the Israelites for his work; they were his fighting men, commanders of his captains, and commanders of his chariots and charioteers. ¹⁰They were also King Solomon's chief officials—two hundred and fifty officials supervising the men.

¹¹Solomon brought Pharaoh's daughter up from the City of David to the palace he had built for her, for he said, "My wife must not live in the palace of David king of Israel, because the places the ark of the LORD has entered are holy."

¹²On the altar of the LORD that he had built in front of the portico, Solomon sacrificed burnt offerings to the LORD, ¹³according to the daily requirement for offerings commanded by Moses for Sabbaths, New Moons and the three annual feasts—the Feast of Unleavened Bread, the Feast of Weeks and the Feast of Tabernacles. ¹⁴In keeping with the ordinance of his father David, he appointed the divisions of the priests for their duties, and the Levites to lead the praise and to assist the priests according to each day's requirement. He also appointed the gatekeepers by divisions for the various gates, because this was what David the man of God had ordered. ¹⁵They did not deviate from the king's commands to the priests or to the Levites in any matter, including that of the treasuries.

¹⁶All Solomon's work was carried out, from the day the foundation of the temple of the LORD was laid until its completion. So the temple of the LORD was finished.

¹⁷Then Solomon went to Ezion Geber and Elath on the coast of Edom. ¹⁸And Hiram sent him ships commanded by his own officers, men who knew the sea. These, with Solomon's men, sailed to Ophir and brought back four hundred and fifty talents[a] of gold, which they delivered to King Solomon.

The Queen of Sheba Visits Solomon

9 When the queen of Sheba heard of Solomon's fame, she came to Jerusalem to test him with hard questions. Arriving with a very great caravan—with camels carrying spices, large quantities of gold, and precious stones—she came to Solomon and talked with him about all she had on her mind. ²Solomon answered all her questions; nothing was too hard for him to explain to her. ³When the queen of Sheba saw the wisdom of Solomon, as well as the palace he had built, ⁴the food on his table, the seating of his officials, the attending servants in their robes, the cupbearers in their robes and the burnt offerings he made at[b] the temple of the LORD, she was overwhelmed.

⁵She said to the king, "The report I heard in my own country about your achievements and your wisdom is true. ⁶But I did not believe what they said until I came and saw with my own eyes. Indeed, not even half the greatness of your wisdom was told me; you have far exceeded the report I heard. ⁷How happy your men must be! How happy your officials, who continually stand before you and hear your wisdom! ⁸Praise be to the LORD your God, who has delighted in you and placed you on his throne as king to rule for the LORD your God. Because of the love of your God for

[a] *18* That is, about 17 tons (about 16 metric tons)   [b] *4* Or *the ascent by which he went up to*

Israel and his desire to uphold them forever, he has made you king over them, to maintain justice and righteousness."

⁹Then she gave the king 120 talents*ᵃ* of gold, large quantities of spices, and precious stones. There had never been such spices as those the queen of Sheba gave to King Solomon.

¹⁰(The men of Hiram and the men of Solomon brought gold from Ophir; they also brought algumwood*ᵇ* and precious stones. ¹¹The king used the algumwood to make steps for the temple of the Lᴏʀᴅ and for the royal palace, and to make harps and lyres for the musicians. Nothing like them had ever been seen in Judah.)

¹²King Solomon gave the queen of Sheba all she desired and asked for; he gave her more than she had brought to him. Then she left and returned with her retinue to her own country.

Solomon's Splendor

¹³The weight of the gold that Solomon received yearly was 666 talents,*ᶜ* ¹⁴not including the revenues brought in by merchants and traders. Also all the kings of Arabia and the governors of the land brought gold and silver to Solomon.

¹⁵King Solomon made two hundred large shields of hammered gold; six hundred bekas*ᵈ* of hammered gold went into each shield. ¹⁶He also made three hundred small shields of hammered gold, with three hundred bekas*ᵉ* of gold in each shield. The king put them in the Palace of the Forest of Lebanon.

¹⁷Then the king made a great throne inlaid with ivory and overlaid with pure gold. ¹⁸The throne had six steps, and a footstool of gold was attached to it. On both sides of the seat were armrests, with a lion standing beside each of them. ¹⁹Twelve lions stood on the six steps, one at either end of each step. Nothing like it had ever been made for any other kingdom. ²⁰All King Solomon's goblets were gold, and all the household articles in the Palace of the Forest of Lebanon were pure gold. Nothing was made of silver, because silver was considered of little value in Solomon's day. ²¹The king had a fleet of trading ships*ᶠ* manned by Hiram's*ᵍ* men. Once every three years it returned, carrying gold, silver and ivory, and apes and baboons.

²²King Solomon was greater in riches and wisdom than all the other kings of the earth. ²³All the kings of the earth sought audience with Solomon to hear the wisdom God had put in his heart. ²⁴Year after year, everyone who came brought a gift—articles of silver and gold, and robes, weapons and spices, and horses and mules.

²⁵Solomon had four thousand stalls for horses and chariots, and twelve thousand horses,*ʰ* which he kept in the chariot cities and also with him in Jerusalem. ²⁶He ruled over all the kings from the River*ⁱ* to the land of the Philistines, as far as the border of Egypt. ²⁷The king made silver as common in Jerusalem as stones, and cedar as plentiful as sycamore-fig trees in the foothills. ²⁸Solomon's horses were imported from Egypt*ʲ* and from all other countries.

Signs of Greatness

2 CHRONICLES 9:13–28

Solomon surrounds himself with the trappings of wealth and power as signs of his greatness. What would some equivalent signs be today? Think about the lifestyles of the rich and famous or about monumental government buildings. What do you look for as indications of greatness in a person? What makes a person great in your eyes? What impression would you like to make on others? What impression do you think you do make? (You might want to discuss this with someone you can trust to be honest.) How do you need to change in order to match your standards of greatness? How do your ambitions differ from what God is calling you to be?

ᵃ 9 That is, about 4 1/2 tons (about 4 metric tons)   *ᵇ 10* Probably a variant of *almugwood*   *ᶜ 13* That is, about 25 tons (about 23 metric tons)
ᵈ 15 That is, about 7 1/2 pounds (about 3.5 kilograms)   *ᵉ 16* That is, about 3 3/4 pounds (about 1.7 kilograms)   *ᶠ 21* Hebrew *of ships that could go to Tarshish*   *ᵍ 21* Hebrew *Huram,* a variant of *Hiram*   *ʰ 25* Or *charioteers*
ⁱ 26 That is, the Euphrates   *ʲ 28* Or possibly *Muzur,* a region in Cilicia

Temptations to Evil

2 CHRONICLES 10:6–11

"Inconstancy of mind, and a weak confidence in God, are the beginning of all temptations to evil. For as a ship without a rudder is driven to and fro by the waves so those who are remiss and give up their resolution are in many ways tempted. As fire tries iron, so temptation tries the just. We often know not what we can do; but temptation reveals what we are."

—THOMAS À KEMPIS,
The Imitation of Christ

Solomon's Death

29As for the other events of Solomon's reign, from beginning to end, are they not written in the records of Nathan the prophet, in the prophecy of Ahijah the Shilonite and in the visions of Iddo the seer concerning Jeroboam son of Nebat? 30Solomon reigned in Jerusalem over all Israel forty years. 31Then he rested with his fathers and was buried in the city of David his father. And Rehoboam his son succeeded him as king.

Israel Rebels Against Rehoboam

10 Rehoboam went to Shechem, for all the Israelites had gone there to make him king. 2When Jeroboam son of Nebat heard this (he was in Egypt, where he had fled from King Solomon), he returned from Egypt. 3So they sent for Jeroboam, and he and all Israel went to Rehoboam and said to him: 4"Your father put a heavy yoke on us, but now lighten the harsh labor and the heavy yoke he put on us, and we will serve you."

5Rehoboam answered, "Come back to me in three days." So the people went away.

6Then King Rehoboam consulted the elders who had served his father Solomon during his lifetime. "How would you advise me to answer these people?" he asked.

7They replied, "If you will be kind to these people and please them and give them a favorable answer, they will always be your servants."

8But Rehoboam rejected the advice the elders gave him and consulted the young men who had grown up with him and were serving him. 9He asked them, "What is your advice? How should we answer these people who say to me, 'Lighten the yoke your father put on us'?"

10The young men who had grown up with him replied, "Tell the people who have said to you, 'Your father put a heavy yoke on us, but make our yoke lighter'—tell them, 'My little finger is thicker than my father's waist. 11My father laid on you a heavy yoke; I will make it even heavier. My father scourged you with whips; I will scourge you with scorpions.' "

12Three days later Jeroboam and all the people returned to Rehoboam, as the king had said, "Come back to me in three days." 13The king answered them harshly. Rejecting the advice of the elders, 14he followed the advice of the young men and said, "My father made your yoke heavy; I will make it even heavier. My father scourged you with whips; I will scourge you with scorpions." 15So the king did not listen to the people, for this turn of events was from God, to fulfill the word the LORD had spoken to Jeroboam son of Nebat through Ahijah the Shilonite.

16When all Israel saw that the king refused to listen to them, they answered the king:

"What share do we have in David,
    what part in Jesse's son?
To your tents, O Israel!
    Look after your own house, O David!"

So all the Israelites went home. 17But as for the Israelites who were living in the towns of Judah, Rehoboam still ruled over them.

¹⁸King Rehoboam sent out Adoniram,ᵃ who was in charge of forced labor, but the Israelites stoned him to death. King Rehoboam, however, managed to get into his chariot and escape to Jerusalem. ¹⁹So Israel has been in rebellion against the house of David to this day.

11 When Rehoboam arrived in Jerusalem, he mustered the house of Judah and Benjamin—a hundred and eighty thousand fighting men—to make war against Israel and to regain the kingdom for Rehoboam.

²But this word of the LORD came to Shemaiah the man of God: ³"Say to Rehoboam son of Solomon king of Judah and to all the Israelites in Judah and Benjamin, ⁴'This is what the LORD says: Do not go up to fight against your brothers. Go home, every one of you, for this is my doing.' " So they obeyed the words of the LORD and turned back from marching against Jeroboam.

Rehoboam Fortifies Judah

⁵Rehoboam lived in Jerusalem and built up towns for defense in Judah: ⁶Bethlehem, Etam, Tekoa, ⁷Beth Zur, Soco, Adullam, ⁸Gath, Mareshah, Ziph, ⁹Adoraim, Lachish, Azekah, ¹⁰Zorah, Aijalon and Hebron. These were fortified cities in Judah and Benjamin. ¹¹He strengthened their defenses and put commanders in them, with supplies of food, olive oil and wine. ¹²He put shields and spears in all the cities, and made them very strong. So Judah and Benjamin were his.

¹³The priests and Levites from all their districts throughout Israel sided with him. ¹⁴The Levites even abandoned their pasturelands and property, and came to Judah and Jerusalem because Jeroboam and his sons had rejected them as priests of the LORD. ¹⁵And he appointed his own priests for the high places and for the goat and calf idols he had made. ¹⁶Those from every tribe of Israel who set their hearts on seeking the LORD, the God of Israel, followed the Levites to Jerusalem to offer sacrifices to the LORD, the God of their fathers. ¹⁷They strengthened the kingdom of Judah and supported Rehoboam son of Solomon three years, walking in the ways of David and Solomon during this time.

Rehoboam's Family

¹⁸Rehoboam married Mahalath, who was the daughter of David's son Jerimoth and of Abihail, the daughter of Jesse's son Eliab. ¹⁹She bore him sons: Jeush, Shemariah and Zaham. ²⁰Then he married Maacah daughter of Absalom, who bore him Abijah, Attai, Ziza and Shelomith. ²¹Rehoboam loved Maacah daughter of Absalom more than any of his other wives and concubines. In all, he had eighteen wives and sixty concubines, twenty-eight sons and sixty daughters.

²²Rehoboam appointed Abijah son of Maacah to be the chief prince among his brothers, in order to make him king. ²³He acted wisely, dispersing some of his sons throughout the districts of Judah and Benjamin, and to all the fortified cities. He gave them abundant provisions and took many wives for them.

ᵃ 18 Hebrew *Hadoram*, a variant of *Adoniram*

An Instrument of Peace

2 CHRONICLES 11:4

"Lord, make me an instrument of your peace. Where there is hatred, let me sow love; where there is injury, pardon; where there is doubt, faith; where there is despair, hope; where there is darkness, light; where there is sadness, joy. O Divine Master, grant that I may not so much seek to be consoled as to console; to be understood, as to understand; to be loved, as to love; for it is in giving that we receive, it is in pardoning that we are pardoned, and it is in dying that we are born to eternal life."

—ANONYMOUS FRANCISCAN

Outgrowing God

2 CHRONICLES 12:1

Rehoboam seems to be like many people who feel they have outgrown their need for God. Some leave the church when they leave their parents' home. Some get so caught up in working and raising a family that it seems easy to skip attending worship services or to omit quiet times with God. Where can you see this happening in your own life? Where is your love growing cold? What former activities no longer seem important? You might ask God to fan the flame of the Spirit in your heart. You might also seek new, more mature ways of relating to God and living out your devotion to God.

See Meeting God in Prayer

Shishak Attacks Jerusalem

12 After Rehoboam's position as king was established and he had become strong, he and all Israel[a] with him abandoned the law of the LORD. [2]Because they had been unfaithful to the LORD, Shishak king of Egypt attacked Jerusalem in the fifth year of King Rehoboam. [3]With twelve hundred chariots and sixty thousand horsemen and the innumerable troops of Libyans, Sukkites and Cushites[b] that came with him from Egypt, [4]he captured the fortified cities of Judah and came as far as Jerusalem.

[5]Then the prophet Shemaiah came to Rehoboam and to the leaders of Judah who had assembled in Jerusalem for fear of Shishak, and he said to them, "This is what the LORD says, 'You have abandoned me; therefore, I now abandon you to Shishak.' "

[6]The leaders of Israel and the king humbled themselves and said, "The LORD is just."

[7]When the LORD saw that they humbled themselves, this word of the LORD came to Shemaiah: "Since they have humbled themselves, I will not destroy them but will soon give them deliverance. My wrath will not be poured out on Jerusalem through Shishak. [8]They will, however, become subject to him, so that they may learn the difference between serving me and serving the kings of other lands."

[9]When Shishak king of Egypt attacked Jerusalem, he carried off the treasures of the temple of the LORD and the treasures of the royal palace. He took everything, including the gold shields Solomon had made. [10]So King Rehoboam made bronze shields to replace them and assigned these to the commanders of the guard on duty at the entrance to the royal palace. [11]Whenever the king went to the LORD's temple, the guards went with him, bearing the shields, and afterward they returned them to the guardroom.

[12]Because Rehoboam humbled himself, the LORD's anger turned from him, and he was not totally destroyed. Indeed, there was some good in Judah.

[13]King Rehoboam established himself firmly in Jerusalem and continued as king. He was forty-one years old when he became king, and he reigned seventeen years in Jerusalem, the city the LORD had chosen out of all the tribes of Israel in which to put his Name. His mother's name was Naamah; she was an Ammonite. [14]He did evil because he had not set his heart on seeking the LORD.

[15]As for the events of Rehoboam's reign, from beginning to end, are they not written in the records of Shemaiah the prophet and of Iddo the seer that deal with genealogies? There was continual warfare between Rehoboam and Jeroboam. [16]Rehoboam rested with his fathers and was buried in the City of David. And Abijah his son succeeded him as king.

Abijah King of Judah

13 In the eighteenth year of the reign of Jeroboam, Abijah became king of Judah, [2]and he reigned in Jerusalem three years. His mother's name was Maacah,[c] a daughter[d] of Uriel of Gibeah.

---

[a]1 That is, Judah, as frequently in 2 Chronicles   [b]3 That is, people from the upper Nile region   [c]2 Most Septuagint manuscripts and Syriac (see also 2 Chron. 11:20 and 1 Kings 15:2); Hebrew *Micaiah*   [d]2 Or *granddaughter*

There was war between Abijah and Jeroboam. ³Abijah went into battle with a force of four hundred thousand able fighting men, and Jeroboam drew up a battle line against him with eight hundred thousand able troops.

⁴Abijah stood on Mount Zemaraim, in the hill country of Ephraim, and said, "Jeroboam and all Israel, listen to me! ⁵Don't you know that the LORD, the God of Israel, has given the kingship of Israel to David and his descendants forever by a covenant of salt? ⁶Yet Jeroboam son of Nebat, an official of Solomon son of David, rebelled against his master. ⁷Some worthless scoundrels gathered around him and opposed Rehoboam son of Solomon when he was young and indecisive and not strong enough to resist them.

⁸"And now you plan to resist the kingdom of the LORD, which is in the hands of David's descendants. You are indeed a vast army and have with you the golden calves that Jeroboam made to be your gods. ⁹But didn't you drive out the priests of the LORD, the sons of Aaron, and the Levites, and make priests of your own as the peoples of other lands do? Whoever comes to consecrate himself with a young bull and seven rams may become a priest of what are not gods.

¹⁰"As for us, the LORD is our God, and we have not forsaken him. The priests who serve the LORD are sons of Aaron, and the Levites assist them. ¹¹Every morning and evening they present burnt offerings and fragrant incense to the LORD. They set out the bread on the ceremonially clean table and light the lamps on the gold lampstand every evening. We are observing the requirements of the LORD our God. But you have forsaken him. ¹²God is with us; he is our leader. His priests with their trumpets will sound the battle cry against you. Men of Israel, do not fight against the LORD, the God of your fathers, for you will not succeed."

¹³Now Jeroboam had sent troops around to the rear, so that while he was in front of Judah the ambush was behind them. ¹⁴Judah turned and saw that they were being attacked at both front and rear. Then they cried out to the LORD. The priests blew their trumpets ¹⁵and the men of Judah raised the battle cry. At the sound of their battle cry, God routed Jeroboam and all Israel before Abijah and Judah. ¹⁶The Israelites fled before Judah, and God delivered them into their hands. ¹⁷Abijah and his men inflicted heavy losses on them, so that there were five hundred thousand casualties among Israel's able men. ¹⁸The men of Israel were subdued on that occasion, and the men of Judah were victorious because they relied on the LORD, the God of their fathers.

¹⁹Abijah pursued Jeroboam and took from him the towns of Bethel, Jeshanah and Ephron, with their surrounding villages. ²⁰Jeroboam did not regain power during the time of Abijah. And the LORD struck him down and he died.

²¹But Abijah grew in strength. He married fourteen wives and had twenty-two sons and sixteen daughters. ²²The other events of Abijah's reign, what he did and what he said, are written in the annotations of the prophet Iddo.

14 And Abijah rested with his fathers and was buried in the City of David. Asa his son succeeded him as king, and in his days the country was at peace for ten years.

Clever Plans

2 CHRONICLES 13:13–15

Jeroboam makes careful and clever plans for trapping the army of Judah and gaining victory. But God has other plans. When have your plans been overthrown? Do you see that as a tragedy? Or can you see it as God leading you in another direction? What have you learned from plans gone wrong? Where is God leading you today? How can you best cooperate with God's leading?

See Meeting God in Prayer

I Need Thee Every Hour

2 CHRONICLES 14:11

"I need thee every hour,
     most gracious Lord;
no tender voice like thine
     can peace afford.
I need thee, O I need thee,
     every hour I need thee;
O bless me now, my Savior,
     I come to thee.

I need thee every hour, in
     joy or pain;
come quickly and abide, or
     life is vain.
I need thee, O I need thee,
     every hour I need thee;
O bless me now, my Savior,
     I come to thee."

—ANNIE S. HAWKS

Asa King of Judah

[2] Asa did what was good and right in the eyes of the LORD his God. [3] He removed the foreign altars and the high places, smashed the sacred stones and cut down the Asherah poles.[a] [4] He commanded Judah to seek the LORD, the God of their fathers, and to obey his laws and commands. [5] He removed the high places and incense altars in every town in Judah, and the kingdom was at peace under him. [6] He built up the fortified cities of Judah, since the land was at peace. No one was at war with him during those years, for the LORD gave him rest.

[7] "Let us build up these towns," he said to Judah, "and put walls around them, with towers, gates and bars. The land is still ours, because we have sought the LORD our God; we sought him and he has given us rest on every side." So they built and prospered.

[8] Asa had an army of three hundred thousand men from Judah, equipped with large shields and with spears, and two hundred and eighty thousand from Benjamin, armed with small shields and with bows. All these were brave fighting men.

[9] Zerah the Cushite marched out against them with a vast army[b] and three hundred chariots, and came as far as Mareshah. [10] Asa went out to meet him, and they took up battle positions in the Valley of Zephathah near Mareshah.

[11] Then Asa called to the LORD his God and said, "LORD, there is no one like you to help the powerless against the mighty. Help us, O LORD our God, for we rely on you, and in your name we have come against this vast army. O LORD, you are our God; do not let man prevail against you."

[12] The LORD struck down the Cushites before Asa and Judah. The Cushites fled, [13] and Asa and his army pursued them as far as Gerar. Such a great number of Cushites fell that they could not recover; they were crushed before the LORD and his forces. The men of Judah carried off a large amount of plunder. [14] They destroyed all the villages around Gerar, for the terror of the LORD had fallen upon them. They plundered all these villages, since there was much booty there. [15] They also attacked the camps of the herdsmen and carried off droves of sheep and goats and camels. Then they returned to Jerusalem.

Asa's Reform

15 The Spirit of God came upon Azariah son of Oded. [2] He went out to meet Asa and said to him, "Listen to me, Asa and all Judah and Benjamin. The LORD is with you when you are with him. If you seek him, he will be found by you, but if you forsake him, he will forsake you. [3] For a long time Israel was without the true God, without a priest to teach and without the law. [4] But in their distress they turned to the LORD, the God of Israel, and sought him, and he was found by them. [5] In those days it was not safe to travel about, for all the inhabitants of the lands were in great turmoil. [6] One nation was being crushed by another and one city by another, because God was troubling them with every kind of distress. [7] But as for you, be strong and do not give up, for your work will be rewarded."

[a] 3 That is, symbols of the goddess Asherah; here and elsewhere in 2 Chronicles   [b] 9 Hebrew *with an army of a thousand thousands* or *with an army of thousands upon thousands*

[8] When Asa heard these words and the prophecy of Aza-riah son of[a] Oded the prophet, he took courage. He removed the detestable idols from the whole land of Judah and Benjamin and from the towns he had captured in the hills of Ephraim. He repaired the altar of the LORD that was in front of the portico of the LORD's temple.

[9] Then he assembled all Judah and Benjamin and the people from Ephraim, Manasseh and Simeon who had settled among them, for large numbers had come over to him from Israel when they saw that the LORD his God was with him.

[10] They assembled at Jerusalem in the third month of the fifteenth year of Asa's reign. [11] At that time they sacrificed to the LORD seven hundred head of cattle and seven thousand sheep and goats from the plunder they had brought back. [12] They entered into a covenant to seek the LORD, the God of their fathers, with all their heart and soul. [13] All who would not seek the LORD, the God of Israel, were to be put to death, whether small or great, man or woman. [14] They took an oath to the LORD with loud acclamation, with shouting and with trumpets and horns. [15] All Judah rejoiced about the oath because they had sworn it wholeheartedly. They sought God eagerly, and he was found by them. So the LORD gave them rest on every side.

[16] King Asa also deposed his grandmother Maacah from her position as queen mother, because she had made a repulsive Asherah pole. Asa cut the pole down, broke it up and burned it in the Kidron Valley. [17] Although he did not remove the high places from Israel, Asa's heart was fully committed ∟to the LORD⌐ all his life. [18] He brought into the temple of God the silver and gold and the articles that he and his father had dedicated.

[19] There was no more war until the thirty-fifth year of Asa's reign.

Asa's Last Years

16 In the thirty-sixth year of Asa's reign Baasha king of Israel went up against Judah and fortified Ramah to prevent anyone from leaving or entering the territory of Asa king of Judah.

[2] Asa then took the silver and gold out of the treasuries of the LORD's temple and of his own palace and sent it to Ben-Hadad king of Aram, who was ruling in Damascus. [3] "Let there be a treaty between me and you," he said, "as there was between my father and your father. See, I am sending you silver and gold. Now break your treaty with Baasha king of Israel so he will withdraw from me."

[4] Ben-Hadad agreed with King Asa and sent the commanders of his forces against the towns of Israel. They conquered Ijon, Dan, Abel Maim[b] and all the store cities of Naphtali. [5] When Baasha heard this, he stopped building Ramah and abandoned his work. [6] Then King Asa brought all the men of Judah, and they carried away from Ramah the stones and timber Baasha had been using. With them he built up Geba and Mizpah.

[7] At that time Hanani the seer came to Asa king of Judah and said to him: "Because you relied on the king of Aram and not on the LORD your God, the army of the king of

A Joyful Oath

2 CHRONICLES 15:12–15

The people of Judah find joy and rest in a renewed covenant. Spend some time remembering the promises you have already made as a Christian. What vows did you take when you joined your church? What faith have you proclaimed by reciting creeds? What private promises have you made to God? How well do your actions reflect what you have said? What steps can you take to renew the covenant you have already made? Write down a proclamation of your desire to renew your covenant with God and ask God to bless it.

See Meeting God in Prayer

[a] 8 Vulgate and Syriac (see also Septuagint and verse 1); Hebrew does not have *Azariah son of*.   [b] 4 Also known as *Abel Beth Maacah*

577

Holy Medicine

2 CHRONICLES 16:12

Asa is faulted, not for calling in the doctors, but for failing to call on God. How can you become involved in asking God for healing for yourself or for others? If your church announces, in the bulletin or during worship, the names of those who are sick, you might continue to pray for those people during the week. You might add to that list the names of friends and family members who also need prayer for healing. If your church has regularly scheduled healing services, you might attend one or more. If a healing service is not available, you might ask about starting such a healing ministry.

See Meeting God in Service

Aram has escaped from your hand. [8]Were not the Cushites[a] and Libyans a mighty army with great numbers of chariots and horsemen[b]? Yet when you relied on the LORD, he delivered them into your hand. [9]For the eyes of the LORD range throughout the earth to strengthen those whose hearts are fully committed to him. You have done a foolish thing, and from now on you will be at war."

[10]Asa was angry with the seer because of this; he was so enraged that he put him in prison. At the same time Asa brutally oppressed some of the people.

[11]The events of Asa's reign, from beginning to end, are written in the book of the kings of Judah and Israel. [12]In the thirty-ninth year of his reign Asa was afflicted with a disease in his feet. Though his disease was severe, even in his illness he did not seek help from the LORD, but only from the physicians. [13]Then in the forty-first year of his reign Asa died and rested with his fathers. [14]They buried him in the tomb that he had cut out for himself in the City of David. They laid him on a bier covered with spices and various blended perfumes, and they made a huge fire in his honor.

Jehoshaphat King of Judah

17 Jehoshaphat his son succeeded him as king and strengthened himself against Israel. [2]He stationed troops in all the fortified cities of Judah and put garrisons in Judah and in the towns of Ephraim that his father Asa had captured.

[3]The LORD was with Jehoshaphat because in his early years he walked in the ways his father David had followed. He did not consult the Baals [4]but sought the God of his father and followed his commands rather than the practices of Israel. [5]The LORD established the kingdom under his control; and all Judah brought gifts to Jehoshaphat, so that he had great wealth and honor. [6]His heart was devoted to the ways of the LORD; furthermore, he removed the high places and the Asherah poles from Judah.

[7]In the third year of his reign he sent his officials Ben-Hail, Obadiah, Zechariah, Nethanel and Micaiah to teach in the towns of Judah. [8]With them were certain Levites—Shemaiah, Nethaniah, Zebadiah, Asahel, Shemiramoth, Jehonathan, Adonijah, Tobijah and Tob-Adonijah—and the priests Elishama and Jehoram. [9]They taught throughout Judah, taking with them the Book of the Law of the LORD; they went around to all the towns of Judah and taught the people.

[10]The fear of the LORD fell on all the kingdoms of the lands surrounding Judah, so that they did not make war with Jehoshaphat. [11]Some Philistines brought Jehoshaphat gifts and silver as tribute, and the Arabs brought him flocks: seven thousand seven hundred rams and seven thousand seven hundred goats.

[12]Jehoshaphat became more and more powerful; he built forts and store cities in Judah [13]and had large supplies in the towns of Judah. He also kept experienced fighting men in Jerusalem. [14]Their enrollment by families was as follows:

From Judah, commanders of units of 1,000:
Adnah the commander, with 300,000 fighting men;
[15]next, Jehohanan the commander, with 280,000;

a 8 That is, people from the upper Nile region   *b 8* Or *charioteers*

¹⁶ next, Amasiah son of Zicri, who volunteered himself for the service of the LORD, with 200,000.
¹⁷ From Benjamin:
Eliada, a valiant soldier, with 200,000 men armed with bows and shields;
¹⁸ next, Jehozabad, with 180,000 men armed for battle.
¹⁹ These were the men who served the king, besides those he stationed in the fortified cities throughout Judah.

Micaiah Prophesies Against Ahab

18 Now Jehoshaphat had great wealth and honor, and he allied himself with Ahab by marriage. ²Some years later he went down to visit Ahab in Samaria. Ahab slaughtered many sheep and cattle for him and the people with him and urged him to attack Ramoth Gilead. ³Ahab king of Israel asked Jehoshaphat king of Judah, "Will you go with me against Ramoth Gilead?"

Jehoshaphat replied, "I am as you are, and my people as your people; we will join you in the war." ⁴But Jehoshaphat also said to the king of Israel, "First seek the counsel of the LORD."

⁵So the king of Israel brought together the prophets—four hundred men—and asked them, "Shall we go to war against Ramoth Gilead, or shall I refrain?"

"Go," they answered, "for God will give it into the king's hand."

⁶But Jehoshaphat asked, "Is there not a prophet of the LORD here whom we can inquire of?"

⁷The king of Israel answered Jehoshaphat, "There is still one man through whom we can inquire of the LORD, but I hate him because he never prophesies anything good about me, but always bad. He is Micaiah son of Imlah."

"The king should not say that," Jehoshaphat replied.

⁸So the king of Israel called one of his officials and said, "Bring Micaiah son of Imlah at once."

⁹Dressed in their royal robes, the king of Israel and Jehoshaphat king of Judah were sitting on their thrones at the threshing floor by the entrance to the gate of Samaria, with all the prophets prophesying before them. ¹⁰Now Zedekiah son of Kenaanah had made iron horns, and he declared, "This is what the LORD says: 'With these you will gore the Arameans until they are destroyed.'"

¹¹All the other prophets were prophesying the same thing. "Attack Ramoth Gilead and be victorious," they said, "for the LORD will give it into the king's hand."

¹²The messenger who had gone to summon Micaiah said to him, "Look, as one man the other prophets are predicting success for the king. Let your word agree with theirs, and speak favorably."

¹³But Micaiah said, "As surely as the LORD lives, I can tell him only what my God says."

¹⁴When he arrived, the king asked him, "Micaiah, shall we go to war against Ramoth Gilead, or shall I refrain?"

"Attack and be victorious," he answered, "for they will be given into your hand."

¹⁵The king said to him, "How many times must I make you swear to tell me nothing but the truth in the name of the LORD?"

¹⁶Then Micaiah answered, "I saw all Israel scattered on

No Bad News

2 CHRONICLES 18:7

King Ahab rejects the prophet Micaiah, not because what Micaiah says is untrue, but because what he says is unpleasant. Do you find yourself doing the same thing? What unpleasant truths do you try to ignore? What people do you avoid because they have told you things you did not want to hear? In prayer God often confronts us with deep truths about ourselves. Does unwillingness to face such truths block you from deeper prayer and from growing closer to God? It might help to talk with an intimate friend or spiritual mentor. Such conversation may encourage you to allow yourself to hear what God has to say.

How Can You Know?

2 CHRONICLES 18:25-27

Discernment is difficult. Sometimes it is not easy to know whether a word or a perceived call to action is really from God. As Ahab waffles between conflicting prophecies, Micaiah offers a suggestion: Ahab should do what he wants and see what happens. If things turn out as Micaiah predicted, he was right. What decision has stumped you, so that you cannot tell what is really God's will? Can you explore one choice, trusting God to give you greater clarity somewhere down the road? You might reaffirm your trust in God as you step out in faith.

See *Meeting God in Everyday Life*

the hills like sheep without a shepherd, and the LORD said, 'These people have no master. Let each one go home in peace.' "

¹⁷The king of Israel said to Jehoshaphat, "Didn't I tell you that he never prophesies anything good about me, but only bad?"

¹⁸Micaiah continued, "Therefore hear the word of the LORD: I saw the LORD sitting on his throne with all the host of heaven standing on his right and on his left. ¹⁹And the LORD said, 'Who will entice Ahab king of Israel into attacking Ramoth Gilead and going to his death there?'

"One suggested this, and another that. ²⁰Finally, a spirit came forward, stood before the LORD and said, 'I will entice him.'

" 'By what means?' the LORD asked.

²¹" 'I will go and be a lying spirit in the mouths of all his prophets,' he said.

" 'You will succeed in enticing him,' said the LORD. 'Go and do it.'

²²"So now the LORD has put a lying spirit in the mouths of these prophets of yours. The LORD has decreed disaster for you."

²³Then Zedekiah son of Kenaanah went up and slapped Micaiah in the face. "Which way did the spirit from*a* the LORD go when he went from me to speak to you?" he asked.

²⁴Micaiah replied, "You will find out on the day you go to hide in an inner room."

²⁵The king of Israel then ordered, "Take Micaiah and send him back to Amon the ruler of the city and to Joash the king's son, ²⁶and say, 'This is what the king says: Put this fellow in prison and give him nothing but bread and water until I return safely.' "

²⁷Micaiah declared, "If you ever return safely, the LORD has not spoken through me." Then he added, "Mark my words, all you people!"

Ahab Killed at Ramoth Gilead

²⁸So the king of Israel and Jehoshaphat king of Judah went up to Ramoth Gilead. ²⁹The king of Israel said to Jehoshaphat, "I will enter the battle in disguise, but you wear your royal robes." So the king of Israel disguised himself and went into battle.

³⁰Now the king of Aram had ordered his chariot commanders, "Do not fight with anyone, small or great, except the king of Israel." ³¹When the chariot commanders saw Jehoshaphat, they thought, "This is the king of Israel." So they turned to attack him, but Jehoshaphat cried out, and the LORD helped him. God drew them away from him, ³²for when the chariot commanders saw that he was not the king of Israel, they stopped pursuing him.

³³But someone drew his bow at random and hit the king of Israel between the sections of his armor. The king told the chariot driver, "Wheel around and get me out of the fighting. I've been wounded." ³⁴All day long the battle raged, and the king of Israel propped himself up in his chariot facing the Arameans until evening. Then at sunset he died.

19 When Jehoshaphat king of Judah returned safely to his palace in Jerusalem, ²Jehu the seer, the son of

ᵃ 23 Or Spirit of

Hanani, went out to meet him and said to the king, "Should you help the wicked and love*ᵃ* those who hate the Lord? Because of this, the wrath of the Lord is upon you. ³There is, however, some good in you, for you have rid the land of the Asherah poles and have set your heart on seeking God."

Jehoshaphat Appoints Judges

⁴Jehoshaphat lived in Jerusalem, and he went out again among the people from Beersheba to the hill country of Ephraim and turned them back to the Lord, the God of their fathers. ⁵He appointed judges in the land, in each of the fortified cities of Judah. ⁶He told them, "Consider carefully what you do, because you are not judging for man but for the Lord, who is with you whenever you give a verdict. ⁷Now let the fear of the Lord be upon you. Judge carefully, for with the Lord our God there is no injustice or partiality or bribery."

⁸In Jerusalem also, Jehoshaphat appointed some of the Levites, priests and heads of Israelite families to administer the law of the Lord and to settle disputes. And they lived in Jerusalem. ⁹He gave them these orders: "You must serve faithfully and wholeheartedly in the fear of the Lord. ¹⁰In every case that comes before you from your fellow countrymen who live in the cities—whether bloodshed or other concerns of the law, commands, decrees or ordinances—you are to warn them not to sin against the Lord; otherwise his wrath will come on you and your brothers. Do this, and you will not sin.

¹¹"Amariah the chief priest will be over you in any matter concerning the Lord, and Zebadiah son of Ishmael, the leader of the tribe of Judah, will be over you in any matter concerning the king, and the Levites will serve as officials before you. Act with courage, and may the Lord be with those who do well."

Jehoshaphat Defeats Moab and Ammon

20 After this, the Moabites and Ammonites with some of the Meunites*ᵇ* came to make war on Jehoshaphat. ²Some men came and told Jehoshaphat, "A vast army is coming against you from Edom,*ᶜ* from the other side of the Sea.*ᵈ* It is already in Hazazon Tamar" (that is, En Gedi). ³Alarmed, Jehoshaphat resolved to inquire of the Lord, and he proclaimed a fast for all Judah. ⁴The people of Judah came together to seek help from the Lord; indeed, they came from every town in Judah to seek him.

⁵Then Jehoshaphat stood up in the assembly of Judah and Jerusalem at the temple of the Lord in the front of the new courtyard ⁶and said:

"O Lord, God of our fathers, are you not the God who is in heaven? You rule over all the kingdoms of the nations. Power and might are in your hand, and no one can withstand you. ⁷O our God, did you not drive out the inhabitants of this land before your people Israel and give it forever to the descendants of Abraham your friend? ⁸They have lived in it and have built in it a sanctuary for your Name, saying, ⁹'If calamity comes upon us, whether the sword of judgment, or plague or

---

Shades of Gray

2 CHRONICLES 19:2–3

The Chronicler, like most of us, tends to see characters as either good or evil. Here, though, Jehu lifts up both the good and the evil in Jehoshaphat's actions. As a result, Jehoshaphat's good resolve is strengthened. Think of one person whom you dislike. What good points can you list about that person? How can you encourage that good? Where can you see Jesus in that person? Thank God for Jesus' presence in that person's life. These are ways of loving your enemies. You might want to repeat this exercise several times, thinking of other people whom you dislike.

See Meeting God in Community

ᵃ2 Or *and make alliances with*   *ᵇ1* Some Septuagint manuscripts; Hebrew *Ammonites*   *ᶜ2* One Hebrew manuscript; most Hebrew manuscripts, Septuagint and Vulgate *Aram*   *ᵈ2* That is, the Dead Sea

The Battle Is God's

2 CHRONICLES 20:12,15

It is not only invading armies that leave people feeling powerless. Temptations, habits and oppressive situations can all overwhelm us. What makes you feel helpless? Let God fight for you. You might pray in words similar to those used by Jehoshaphat: "Lord, I am powerless against _____. I do not know what to do. My eyes are on you." Then hear for yourself the prophet's word of hope: "Do not be afraid or discouraged . . . For the battle is not yours, but God's."

See Meeting God in Scripture

famine, we will stand in your presence before this temple that bears your Name and will cry out to you in our distress, and you will hear us and save us.'

¹⁰"But now here are men from Ammon, Moab and Mount Seir, whose territory you would not allow Israel to invade when they came from Egypt; so they turned away from them and did not destroy them. ¹¹See how they are repaying us by coming to drive us out of the possession you gave us as an inheritance. ¹²O our God, will you not judge them? For we have no power to face this vast army that is attacking us. We do not know what to do, but our eyes are upon you."

¹³All the men of Judah, with their wives and children and little ones, stood there before the LORD.

¹⁴Then the Spirit of the LORD came upon Jahaziel son of Zechariah, the son of Benaiah, the son of Jeiel, the son of Mattaniah, a Levite and descendant of Asaph, as he stood in the assembly.

¹⁵He said: "Listen, King Jehoshaphat and all who live in Judah and Jerusalem! This is what the LORD says to you: 'Do not be afraid or discouraged because of this vast army. For the battle is not yours, but God's. ¹⁶Tomorrow march down against them. They will be climbing up by the Pass of Ziz, and you will find them at the end of the gorge in the Desert of Jeruel. ¹⁷You will not have to fight this battle. Take up your positions; stand firm and see the deliverance the LORD will give you, O Judah and Jerusalem. Do not be afraid; do not be discouraged. Go out to face them tomorrow, and the LORD will be with you.' "

¹⁸Jehoshaphat bowed with his face to the ground, and all the people of Judah and Jerusalem fell down in worship before the LORD. ¹⁹Then some Levites from the Kohathites and Korahites stood up and praised the LORD, the God of Israel, with very loud voice.

²⁰Early in the morning they left for the Desert of Tekoa. As they set out, Jehoshaphat stood and said, "Listen to me, Judah and people of Jerusalem! Have faith in the LORD your God and you will be upheld; have faith in his prophets and you will be successful." ²¹After consulting the people, Jehoshaphat appointed men to sing to the LORD and to praise him for the splendor of his*a* holiness as they went out at the head of the army, saying:

"Give thanks to the LORD,
for his love endures forever."

²²As they began to sing and praise, the LORD set ambushes against the men of Ammon and Moab and Mount Seir who were invading Judah, and they were defeated. ²³The men of Ammon and Moab rose up against the men from Mount Seir to destroy and annihilate them. After they finished slaughtering the men from Seir, they helped to destroy one another.

²⁴When the men of Judah came to the place that overlooks the desert and looked toward the vast army, they saw only dead bodies lying on the ground; no one had escaped. ²⁵So Jehoshaphat and his men went to carry off their plunder, and they found among them a great amount of equip-

a 21 Or him with the splendor of

ment and clothing*a* and also articles of value—more than they could take away. There was so much plunder that it took three days to collect it. ²⁶On the fourth day they assembled in the Valley of Beracah, where they praised the Lord. This is why it is called the Valley of Beracah*b* to this day.

²⁷Then, led by Jehoshaphat, all the men of Judah and Jerusalem returned joyfully to Jerusalem, for the Lord had given them cause to rejoice over their enemies. ²⁸They entered Jerusalem and went to the temple of the Lord with harps and lutes and trumpets.

²⁹The fear of God came upon all the kingdoms of the countries when they heard how the Lord had fought against the enemies of Israel. ³⁰And the kingdom of Jehoshaphat was at peace, for his God had given him rest on every side.

The End of Jehoshaphat's Reign

³¹So Jehoshaphat reigned over Judah. He was thirty-five years old when he became king of Judah, and he reigned in Jerusalem twenty-five years. His mother's name was Azubah daughter of Shilhi. ³²He walked in the ways of his father Asa and did not stray from them; he did what was right in the eyes of the Lord. ³³The high places, however, were not removed, and the people still had not set their hearts on the God of their fathers.

³⁴The other events of Jehoshaphat's reign, from beginning to end, are written in the annals of Jehu son of Hanani, which are recorded in the book of the kings of Israel.

³⁵Later, Jehoshaphat king of Judah made an alliance with Ahaziah king of Israel, who was guilty of wickedness. ³⁶He agreed with him to construct a fleet of trading ships.*c* After these were built at Ezion Geber, ³⁷Eliezer son of Dodavahu of Mareshah prophesied against Jehoshaphat, saying, "Because you have made an alliance with Ahaziah, the Lord will destroy what you have made." The ships were wrecked and were not able to set sail to trade.*d*

21 Then Jehoshaphat rested with his fathers and was buried with them in the City of David. And Jehoram his son succeeded him as king. ²Jehoram's brothers, the sons of Jehoshaphat, were Azariah, Jehiel, Zechariah, Azariahu, Michael and Shephatiah. All these were sons of Jehoshaphat king of Israel.*e* ³Their father had given them many gifts of silver and gold and articles of value, as well as fortified cities in Judah, but he had given the kingdom to Jehoram because he was his firstborn son.

Jehoram King of Judah

⁴When Jehoram established himself firmly over his father's kingdom, he put all his brothers to the sword along with some of the princes of Israel. ⁵Jehoram was thirty-two years old when he became king, and he reigned in Jerusalem eight years. ⁶He walked in the ways of the kings of Israel, as the house of Ahab had done, for he married a daughter of Ahab. He did evil in the eyes of the Lord. ⁷Nevertheless, because of the covenant the Lord had made with

---

Great Is the Lord!

2 CHRONICLES 20:30

"Great are you, O Lord, and greatly to be praised; great is your power, and your understanding is beyond measure. And people, being a part of your creation, desire to praise you—people who bear about with them their mortality, the witness of their sin, even the witness that you oppose the proud. Nevertheless, people, this part of your creation, desire to praise you. You move us to delight in praising you; for you have formed us for yourself, and our hearts are restless until they find rest in you."

—AUGUSTINE,
Confessions

---

a 25 Some Hebrew manuscripts and Vulgate; most Hebrew manuscripts *corpses*   *b 26* Beracah means *praise*.   *c 36* Hebrew *of ships that could go to Tarshish*   *d 37* Hebrew *sail for Tarshish*   *e 2* That is, Judah, as frequently in 2 Chronicles

A Letter From a Prophet

2 CHRONICLES 21:12–15

Jehoram receives a rather convicting letter from Elijah containing a point-by-point indictment of his behavior. Imagine that God asked Elijah to write to you about the way you are walking. What would the letter say? Actually writing a letter out may be helpful; perhaps you could begin it, "This is what the Lord says." What is your response to this letter? For what do you need to ask God's forgiveness? For what do you need to make amends to others? What is God pleased with in your life?

See Meeting God in Everyday Life

David, the Lord was not willing to destroy the house of David. He had promised to maintain a lamp for him and his descendants forever.

[8]In the time of Jehoram, Edom rebelled against Judah and set up its own king. [9]So Jehoram went there with his officers and all his chariots. The Edomites surrounded him and his chariot commanders, but he rose up and broke through by night. [10]To this day Edom has been in rebellion against Judah.

Libnah revolted at the same time, because Jehoram had forsaken the Lord, the God of his fathers. [11]He had also built high places on the hills of Judah and had caused the people of Jerusalem to prostitute themselves and had led Judah astray.

[12]Jehoram received a letter from Elijah the prophet, which said:

> "This is what the Lord, the God of your father David, says: 'You have not walked in the ways of your father Jehoshaphat or of Asa king of Judah. [13]But you have walked in the ways of the kings of Israel, and you have led Judah and the people of Jerusalem to prostitute themselves, just as the house of Ahab did. You have also murdered your own brothers, members of your father's house, men who were better than you. [14]So now the Lord is about to strike your people, your sons, your wives and everything that is yours, with a heavy blow. [15]You yourself will be very ill with a lingering disease of the bowels, until the disease causes your bowels to come out.' "

[16]The Lord aroused against Jehoram the hostility of the Philistines and of the Arabs who lived near the Cushites. [17]They attacked Judah, invaded it and carried off all the goods found in the king's palace, together with his sons and wives. Not a son was left to him except Ahaziah,[a] the youngest.

[18]After all this, the Lord afflicted Jehoram with an incurable disease of the bowels. [19]In the course of time, at the end of the second year, his bowels came out because of the disease, and he died in great pain. His people made no fire in his honor, as they had for his fathers.

[20]Jehoram was thirty-two years old when he became king, and he reigned in Jerusalem eight years. He passed away, to no one's regret, and was buried in the City of David, but not in the tombs of the kings.

Ahaziah King of Judah

22 The people of Jerusalem made Ahaziah, Jehoram's youngest son, king in his place, since the raiders, who came with the Arabs into the camp, had killed all the older sons. So Ahaziah son of Jehoram king of Judah began to reign.

[2]Ahaziah was twenty-two[b] years old when he became king, and he reigned in Jerusalem one year. His mother's name was Athaliah, a granddaughter of Omri.

[3]He too walked in the ways of the house of Ahab, for his mother encouraged him in doing wrong. [4]He did evil in the eyes of the Lord, as the house of Ahab had done, for after

---

[a] 17 Hebrew *Jehoahaz,* a variant of *Ahaziah*   [b] 2 Some Septuagint manuscripts and Syriac (see also 2 Kings 8:26); Hebrew *forty-two*

his father's death they became his advisers, to his undoing. ⁵He also followed their counsel when he went with Joram*ᵃ* son of Ahab king of Israel to war against Hazael king of Aram at Ramoth Gilead. The Arameans wounded Joram; ⁶so he returned to Jezreel to recover from the wounds they had inflicted on him at Ramoth*ᵇ* in his battle with Hazael king of Aram.

Then Ahaziah*ᶜ* son of Jehoram king of Judah went down to Jezreel to see Joram son of Ahab because he had been wounded.

⁷Through Ahaziah's visit to Joram, God brought about Ahaziah's downfall. When Ahaziah arrived, he went out with Joram to meet Jehu son of Nimshi, whom the LORD had anointed to destroy the house of Ahab. ⁸While Jehu was executing judgment on the house of Ahab, he found the princes of Judah and the sons of Ahaziah's relatives, who had been attending Ahaziah, and he killed them. ⁹He then went in search of Ahaziah, and his men captured him while he was hiding in Samaria. He was brought to Jehu and put to death. They buried him, for they said, "He was a son of Jehoshaphat, who sought the LORD with all his heart." So there was no one in the house of Ahaziah powerful enough to retain the kingdom.

Athaliah and Joash

¹⁰When Athaliah the mother of Ahaziah saw that her son was dead, she proceeded to destroy the whole royal family of the house of Judah. ¹¹But Jehosheba,*ᵈ* the daughter of King Jehoram, took Joash son of Ahaziah and stole him away from among the royal princes who were about to be murdered and put him and his nurse in a bedroom. Because Jehosheba,*ᵈ* the daughter of King Jehoram and wife of the priest Jehoiada, was Ahaziah's sister, she hid the child from Athaliah so she could not kill him. ¹²He remained hidden with them at the temple of God for six years while Athaliah ruled the land.

23 In the seventh year Jehoiada showed his strength. He made a covenant with the commanders of units of a hundred: Azariah son of Jeroham, Ishmael son of Jehohanan, Azariah son of Obed, Maaseiah son of Adaiah, and Elishaphat son of Zicri. ²They went throughout Judah and gathered the Levites and the heads of Israelite families from all the towns. When they came to Jerusalem, ³the whole assembly made a covenant with the king at the temple of God.

Jehoiada said to them, "The king's son shall reign, as the LORD promised concerning the descendants of David. ⁴Now this is what you are to do: A third of you priests and Levites who are going on duty on the Sabbath are to keep watch at the doors, ⁵a third of you at the royal palace and a third at the Foundation Gate, and all the other men are to be in the courtyards of the temple of the LORD. ⁶No one is to enter the temple of the LORD except the priests and Levites on duty; they may enter because they are consecrated, but all the other men are to guard what the LORD has assigned to them.*ᵉ* ⁷The Levites are to station themselves around the

Rescuing the Persecuted

2 CHRONICLES 22:11–12

Protecting the helpless has always been a significant calling for God's people. Just as Jehosheba and the priests helped to protect Joash, so Christians have been involved in protecting escaped slaves along the Underground Railroad and in helping Jews hiding from Nazi persecution. How might you be involved in helping the helpless today? You might explore the refugee relief opportunities of your denomination or wider efforts such as those provided by Amnesty International. You might ask God if you should be more directly involved, perhaps by opening your home to a refugee family or volunteering to go to a refugee camp. As you watch or read news reports about refugees, take time to ask God, "Is there anything you want me to do?"

See Meeting God in Community

ᵃ 5 Hebrew *Jehoram,* a variant of *Joram;* also in verses 6 and 7   *ᵇ 6* Hebrew *Ramah,* a variant of *Ramoth*   *ᶜ 6* Some Hebrew manuscripts, Septuagint, Vulgate and Syriac (see also 2 Kings 8:29); most Hebrew manuscripts *Azariah*   *ᵈ 11* Hebrew *Jehoshabeath,* a variant of *Jehosheba*   *ᵉ 6* Or *to observe the LORD's command* ⌊*not to enter*⌋

Renewed Hope

2 CHRONICLES 23:1–21

Try to imagine this scene of violent revolution and restored hope. Imagine yourself in Jerusalem, listening to the series of surprising commands and announcements from Jehoiada (vv. 3–7,11,14,16). What emotions run through you? Where do you find yourself participating? Some scholars have suggested that Isaiah 9:2–7, so often associated with the birth of Jesus, may originally have been used for Joash's coronation. You might read that passage as you think about this one and the new hope that comes with the end of any oppressive regime. What oppressive powers need to be overthrown in your own life? You might ask God to come and rule in your heart, in order to restore hope, peace and joy.

See *Meeting God in Scripture*

king, each man with his weapons in his hand. Anyone who enters the temple must be put to death. Stay close to the king wherever he goes."

⁸The Levites and all the men of Judah did just as Jehoiada the priest ordered. Each one took his men—those who were going on duty on the Sabbath and those who were going off duty—for Jehoiada the priest had not released any of the divisions. ⁹Then he gave the commanders of units of a hundred the spears and the large and small shields that had belonged to King David and that were in the temple of God. ¹⁰He stationed all the men, each with his weapon in his hand, around the king—near the altar and the temple, from the south side to the north side of the temple.

¹¹Jehoiada and his sons brought out the king's son and put the crown on him; they presented him with a copy of the covenant and proclaimed him king. They anointed him and shouted, "Long live the king!"

¹²When Athaliah heard the noise of the people running and cheering the king, she went to them at the temple of the LORD. ¹³She looked, and there was the king, standing by his pillar at the entrance. The officers and the trumpeters were beside the king, and all the people of the land were rejoicing and blowing trumpets, and singers with musical instruments were leading the praises. Then Athaliah tore her robes and shouted, "Treason! Treason!"

¹⁴Jehoiada the priest sent out the commanders of units of a hundred, who were in charge of the troops, and said to them: "Bring her out between the ranks[a] and put to the sword anyone who follows her." For the priest had said, "Do not put her to death at the temple of the LORD." ¹⁵So they seized her as she reached the entrance of the Horse Gate on the palace grounds, and there they put her to death.

¹⁶Jehoiada then made a covenant that he and the people and the king[b] would be the LORD's people. ¹⁷All the people went to the temple of Baal and tore it down. They smashed the altars and idols and killed Mattan the priest of Baal in front of the altars.

¹⁸Then Jehoiada placed the oversight of the temple of the LORD in the hands of the priests, who were Levites, to whom David had made assignments in the temple, to present the burnt offerings of the LORD as written in the Law of Moses, with rejoicing and singing, as David had ordered. ¹⁹He also stationed doorkeepers at the gates of the LORD's temple so that no one who was in any way unclean might enter.

²⁰He took with him the commanders of hundreds, the nobles, the rulers of the people and all the people of the land and brought the king down from the temple of the LORD. They went into the palace through the Upper Gate and seated the king on the royal throne, ²¹and all the people of the land rejoiced. And the city was quiet, because Athaliah had been slain with the sword.

Joash Repairs the Temple

24 Joash was seven years old when he became king, and he reigned in Jerusalem forty years. His moth-

---

a 14 Or out from the precincts   b 16 Or covenant between ⸤the LORD⸥ and the people and the king that they (see 2 Kings 11:17) er's name was Zibiah; she was from Beersheba. ²Joash did what was right in the eyes of the LORD all the years of Jehoiada the priest. ³Jehoiada chose two wives for him, and he had sons and daughters.

⁴Some time later Joash decided to restore the temple of the LORD. ⁵He called together the priests and Levites and said to them, "Go to the towns of Judah and collect the money due annually from all Israel, to repair the temple of your God. Do it now." But the Levites did not act at once.

⁶Therefore the king summoned Jehoiada the chief priest and said to him, "Why haven't you required the Levites to bring in from Judah and Jerusalem the tax imposed by Moses the servant of the LORD and by the assembly of Israel for the Tent of the Testimony?"

⁷Now the sons of that wicked woman Athaliah had broken into the temple of God and had used even its sacred objects for the Baals.

⁸At the king's command, a chest was made and placed outside, at the gate of the temple of the LORD. ⁹A proclamation was then issued in Judah and Jerusalem that they should bring to the LORD the tax that Moses the servant of God had required of Israel in the desert. ¹⁰All the officials and all the people brought their contributions gladly, dropping them into the chest until it was full. ¹¹Whenever the chest was brought in by the Levites to the king's officials and they saw that there was a large amount of money, the royal secretary and the officer of the chief priest would come and empty the chest and carry it back to its place. They did this regularly and collected a great amount of money. ¹²The king and Jehoiada gave it to the men who carried out the work required for the temple of the LORD. They hired masons and carpenters to restore the LORD's temple, and also workers in iron and bronze to repair the temple.

¹³The men in charge of the work were diligent, and the repairs progressed under them. They rebuilt the temple of God according to its original design and reinforced it. ¹⁴When they had finished, they brought the rest of the money to the king and Jehoiada, and with it were made articles for the LORD's temple: articles for the service and for the burnt offerings, and also dishes and other objects of gold and silver. As long as Jehoiada lived, burnt offerings were presented continually in the temple of the LORD.

¹⁵Now Jehoiada was old and full of years, and he died at the age of a hundred and thirty. ¹⁶He was buried with the kings in the City of David, because of the good he had done in Israel for God and his temple.

The Wickedness of Joash

¹⁷After the death of Jehoiada, the officials of Judah came and paid homage to the king, and he listened to them. ¹⁸They abandoned the temple of the LORD, the God of their fathers, and worshiped Asherah poles and idols. Because of their guilt, God's anger came upon Judah and Jerusalem. ¹⁹Although the LORD sent prophets to the people to bring them back to him, and though they testified against them, they would not listen.

²⁰Then the Spirit of God came upon Zechariah son of Jehoiada the priest. He stood before the people and said, "This is what God says: 'Why do you disobey the LORD's

Take, Lord, Receive

2 CHRONICLES 24:8–9

"Take, Lord, and receive all my liberty, my memory, my understanding, and my entire will, all that I have and possess. Thou hast given all to me. To Thee, O Lord, I return it. All is Thine, dispose of it wholly according to Thy will. Give me Thy love and Thy grace, for this is sufficient for me."

—IGNATIUS OF LOYOLA,
The Spiritual Exercises, 234

Halfhearted Love

2 CHRONICLES 25:2

What a sad statement to have to make about anyone: "He did what was right . . . but not wholeheartedly." Yet all of us experience times when we are doing something we know is good, but we are just going through the motions. Our hearts aren't in it. What are those things for you? Why have they become dull, halfhearted routine? Are you burned out? Are you doing too many different things? Ask for God's guidance as you look at changes you might make in your life. What are the things you *can* do wholeheartedly? How can you build on that core?

See *Meeting God in Service*

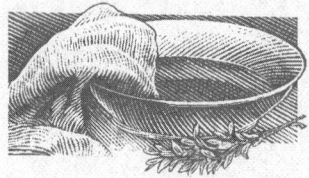

commands? You will not prosper. Because you have forsaken the LORD, he has forsaken you.' "

21But they plotted against him, and by order of the king they stoned him to death in the courtyard of the LORD's temple. 22King Joash did not remember the kindness Zechariah's father Jehoiada had shown him but killed his son, who said as he lay dying, "May the LORD see this and call you to account."

23At the turn of the year,[a] the army of Aram marched against Joash; it invaded Judah and Jerusalem and killed all the leaders of the people. They sent all the plunder to their king in Damascus. 24Although the Aramean army had come with only a few men, the LORD delivered into their hands a much larger army. Because Judah had forsaken the LORD, the God of their fathers, judgment was executed on Joash. 25When the Arameans withdrew, they left Joash severely wounded. His officials conspired against him for murdering the son of Jehoiada the priest, and they killed him in his bed. So he died and was buried in the City of David, but not in the tombs of the kings.

26Those who conspired against him were Zabad,[b] son of Shimeath an Ammonite woman, and Jehozabad, son of Shimrith[c] a Moabite woman. 27The account of his sons, the many prophecies about him, and the record of the restoration of the temple of God are written in the annotations on the book of the kings. And Amaziah his son succeeded him as king.

Amaziah King of Judah

25 Amaziah was twenty-five years old when he became king, and he reigned in Jerusalem twenty-nine years. His mother's name was Jehoaddin[d]; she was from Jerusalem. 2He did what was right in the eyes of the LORD, but not wholeheartedly. 3After the kingdom was firmly in his control, he executed the officials who had murdered his father the king. 4Yet he did not put their sons to death, but acted in accordance with what is written in the Law, in the Book of Moses, where the LORD commanded: "Fathers shall not be put to death for their children, nor children put to death for their fathers; each is to die for his own sins."[e]

5Amaziah called the people of Judah together and assigned them according to their families to commanders of thousands and commanders of hundreds for all Judah and Benjamin. He then mustered those twenty years old or more and found that there were three hundred thousand men ready for military service, able to handle the spear and shield. 6He also hired a hundred thousand fighting men from Israel for a hundred talents[f] of silver.

7But a man of God came to him and said, "O king, these troops from Israel must not march with you, for the LORD is not with Israel—not with any of the people of Ephraim. 8Even if you go and fight courageously in battle, God will overthrow you before the enemy, for God has the power to help or to overthrow."

9Amaziah asked the man of God, "But what about the hundred talents I paid for these Israelite troops?"

a 23 Probably in the spring *b 26* A variant of *Jozabad* *c 26* A variant of *Shomer* *d 1* Hebrew *Jehoaddan,* a variant of *Jehoaddin* *e 4* Deut. 24:16 *f 6* That is, about 3 3/4 tons (about 3.4 metric tons); also in verse 9

The man of God replied, "The LORD can give you much more than that."

¹⁰So Amaziah dismissed the troops who had come to him from Ephraim and sent them home. They were furious with Judah and left for home in a great rage.

¹¹Amaziah then marshaled his strength and led his army to the Valley of Salt, where he killed ten thousand men of Seir. ¹²The army of Judah also captured ten thousand men alive, took them to the top of a cliff and threw them down so that all were dashed to pieces.

¹³Meanwhile the troops that Amaziah had sent back and had not allowed to take part in the war raided Judean towns from Samaria to Beth Horon. They killed three thousand people and carried off great quantities of plunder.

¹⁴When Amaziah returned from slaughtering the Edomites, he brought back the gods of the people of Seir. He set them up as his own gods, bowed down to them and burned sacrifices to them. ¹⁵The anger of the LORD burned against Amaziah, and he sent a prophet to him, who said, "Why do you consult this people's gods, which could not save their own people from your hand?"

¹⁶While he was still speaking, the king said to him, "Have we appointed you an adviser to the king? Stop! Why be struck down?"

So the prophet stopped but said, "I know that God has determined to destroy you, because you have done this and have not listened to my counsel."

¹⁷After Amaziah king of Judah consulted his advisers, he sent this challenge to Jehoash*a* son of Jehoahaz, the son of Jehu, king of Israel: "Come, meet me face to face."

¹⁸But Jehoash king of Israel replied to Amaziah king of Judah: "A thistle in Lebanon sent a message to a cedar in Lebanon, 'Give your daughter to my son in marriage.' Then a wild beast in Lebanon came along and trampled the thistle underfoot. ¹⁹You say to yourself that you have defeated Edom, and now you are arrogant and proud. But stay at home! Why ask for trouble and cause your own downfall and that of Judah also?"

²⁰Amaziah, however, would not listen, for God so worked that he might hand them over to ⸤Jehoash⸣, because they sought the gods of Edom. ²¹So Jehoash king of Israel attacked. He and Amaziah king of Judah faced each other at Beth Shemesh in Judah. ²²Judah was routed by Israel, and every man fled to his home. ²³Jehoash king of Israel captured Amaziah king of Judah, the son of Joash, the son of Ahaziah,*b* at Beth Shemesh. Then Jehoash brought him to Jerusalem and broke down the wall of Jerusalem from the Ephraim Gate to the Corner Gate—a section about six hundred feet*c* long. ²⁴He took all the gold and silver and all the articles found in the temple of God that had been in the care of Obed-Edom, together with the palace treasures and the hostages, and returned to Samaria.

²⁵Amaziah son of Joash king of Judah lived for fifteen years after the death of Jehoash son of Jehoahaz king of Israel. ²⁶As for the other events of Amaziah's reign, from beginning to end, are they not written in the book of the kings of Judah and Israel? ²⁷From the time that Amaziah turned

Worshiping Defeated Powers

2 CHRONICLES 25:14–15

What could Amaziah have been thinking? Why, if he had defeated the Edomites, might he have wanted to make offerings to their gods? In what ways do you give honor to powers such as consumerism, nationalism, racism or sexism, powers which have already been defeated by Jesus Christ? What other powers have you set up in the temple of your heart alongside him? Why do you keep them there? You might want to invite God to cleanse your heart of such false allegiances and make a renewed covenant to have no other gods before God. The prayers "Take, Lord, Receive" and "A Covenant Prayer" (see Entry Points at 24:8–9 and 29:4) might be good models.

See Meeting God in Prayer

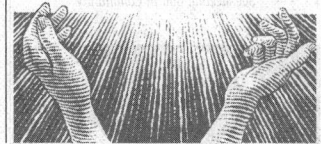

---

a 17 Hebrew *Joash,* a variant of *Jehoash*; also in verses 18, 21, 23 and 25
b 23 Hebrew *Jehoahaz,* a variant of *Ahaziah*   *c 23* Hebrew *four hundred cubits* (about 180 meters)

Pride and Presumption

2 CHRONICLES 26:16–18

It is all too easy when things are going well for us to begin to think that we have God in our back pockets. Like Uzziah, we can begin to believe we have a special status that sets us above the usual rules for God's people. When in your life has success led to presumption? Do you find yourself distracted in worship by your critical thoughts? Do you evaluate others not by how well they are using their gifts, but by how their accomplishments compare to yours? Have you tried to take over tasks assigned to others because you think you could do better? You might ask God to grant you the humility to accept your limited role in your church and community and to help you to appreciate others as they go about their tasks.

See Meeting God in Community

away from following the Lord, they conspired against him in Jerusalem and he fled to Lachish, but they sent men after him to Lachish and killed him there. [28]He was brought back by horse and was buried with his fathers in the City of Judah.

Uzziah King of Judah

26 Then all the people of Judah took Uzziah,[a] who was sixteen years old, and made him king in place of his father Amaziah. [2]He was the one who rebuilt Elath and restored it to Judah after Amaziah rested with his fathers.

[3]Uzziah was sixteen years old when he became king, and he reigned in Jerusalem fifty-two years. His mother's name was Jecoliah; she was from Jerusalem. [4]He did what was right in the eyes of the Lord, just as his father Amaziah had done. [5]He sought God during the days of Zechariah, who instructed him in the fear[b] of God. As long as he sought the Lord, God gave him success.

[6]He went to war against the Philistines and broke down the walls of Gath, Jabneh and Ashdod. He then rebuilt towns near Ashdod and elsewhere among the Philistines. [7]God helped him against the Philistines and against the Arabs who lived in Gur Baal and against the Meunites. [8]The Ammonites brought tribute to Uzziah, and his fame spread as far as the border of Egypt, because he had become very powerful.

[9]Uzziah built towers in Jerusalem at the Corner Gate, at the Valley Gate and at the angle of the wall, and he fortified them. [10]He also built towers in the desert and dug many cisterns, because he had much livestock in the foothills and in the plain. He had people working his fields and vineyards in the hills and in the fertile lands, for he loved the soil.

[11]Uzziah had a well-trained army, ready to go out by divisions according to their numbers as mustered by Jeiel the secretary and Maaseiah the officer under the direction of Hananiah, one of the royal officials. [12]The total number of family leaders over the fighting men was 2,600. [13]Under their command was an army of 307,500 men trained for war, a powerful force to support the king against his enemies. [14]Uzziah provided shields, spears, helmets, coats of armor, bows and slingstones for the entire army. [15]In Jerusalem he made machines designed by skillful men for use on the towers and on the corner defenses to shoot arrows and hurl large stones. His fame spread far and wide, for he was greatly helped until he became powerful.

[16]But after Uzziah became powerful, his pride led to his downfall. He was unfaithful to the Lord his God, and entered the temple of the Lord to burn incense on the altar of incense. [17]Azariah the priest with eighty other courageous priests of the Lord followed him in. [18]They confronted him and said, "It is not right for you, Uzziah, to burn incense to the Lord. That is for the priests, the descendants of Aaron, who have been consecrated to burn incense. Leave the sanctuary, for you have been unfaithful; and you will not be honored by the Lord God."

[19]Uzziah, who had a censer in his hand ready to burn incense, became angry. While he was raging at the priests in

[a]1 Also called *Azariah*   [b]5 Many Hebrew manuscripts, Septuagint and Syriac; other Hebrew manuscripts *vision*

their presence before the incense altar in the LORD's temple, leprosy[a] broke out on his forehead. **20**When Azariah the chief priest and all the other priests looked at him, they saw that he had leprosy on his forehead, so they hurried him out. Indeed, he himself was eager to leave, because the LORD had afflicted him.

21King Uzziah had leprosy until the day he died. He lived in a separate house[b]—leprous, and excluded from the temple of the LORD. Jotham his son had charge of the palace and governed the people of the land.

22The other events of Uzziah's reign, from beginning to end, are recorded by the prophet Isaiah son of Amoz. **23**Uzziah rested with his fathers and was buried near them in a field for burial that belonged to the kings, for people said, "He had leprosy." And Jotham his son succeeded him as king.

Jotham King of Judah

27 Jotham was twenty-five years old when he became king, and he reigned in Jerusalem sixteen years. His mother's name was Jerusha daughter of Zadok. **2**He did what was right in the eyes of the LORD, just as his father Uzziah had done, but unlike him he did not enter the temple of the LORD. The people, however, continued their corrupt practices. **3**Jotham rebuilt the Upper Gate of the temple of the LORD and did extensive work on the wall at the hill of Ophel. **4**He built towns in the Judean hills and forts and towers in the wooded areas.

5Jotham made war on the king of the Ammonites and conquered them. That year the Ammonites paid him a hundred talents[c] of silver, ten thousand cors[d] of wheat and ten thousand cors of barley. The Ammonites brought him the same amount also in the second and third years.

6Jotham grew powerful because he walked steadfastly before the LORD his God.

7The other events in Jotham's reign, including all his wars and the other things he did, are written in the book of the kings of Israel and Judah. **8**He was twenty-five years old when he became king, and he reigned in Jerusalem sixteen years. **9**Jotham rested with his fathers and was buried in the City of David. And Ahaz his son succeeded him as king.

Ahaz King of Judah

28 Ahaz was twenty years old when he became king, and he reigned in Jerusalem sixteen years. Unlike David his father, he did not do what was right in the eyes of the LORD. **2**He walked in the ways of the kings of Israel and also made cast idols for worshiping the Baals. **3**He burned sacrifices in the Valley of Ben Hinnom and sacrificed his sons in the fire, following the detestable ways of the nations the LORD had driven out before the Israelites. **4**He offered sacrifices and burned incense at the high places, on the hilltops and under every spreading tree.

5Therefore the LORD his God handed him over to the king

Followership

2 CHRONICLES 27:2

At last the people are ruled by a truly good king. But they are so stuck in old habits that they do not follow his example. Good leaders need good followers. Spend some time in prayer for your church, for your denomination and for Christians everywhere. Pray for inspired and inspiring leaders. Then pray for God to stir up hearts to follow these leaders—to catch their vision and to break old habits that harm or hinder the mission of the church. You might also ask God to show you ways in which you can be a better follower.

See Meeting God in Prayer

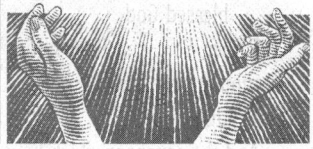

A Covenant Prayer

"I am no longer my own,
    but thine.
Put me to what thou wilt,
    rank me with whom
    thou wilt.
Put me to doing, put me to
    suffering.
Let me be employed by thee
    or laid aside for thee,
exalted for thee or brought
    low for thee.
Let me be full, let me be
    empty.
Let me have all things, let
    me have nothing.
I freely and heartily yield all
    things
to thy pleasure and
    disposal.
And now, O glorious and
    blessed God,
Father, Son, and Holy Spirit,
thou art mine, and I am
    thine. So be it.
And the covenant which I
    have made on earth,
let it be ratified in heaven.
    Amen."

—GEORGE B. ROBSON

of Aram. The Arameans defeated him and took many of his people as prisoners and brought them to Damascus.

He was also given into the hands of the king of Israel, who inflicted heavy casualties on him. [6]In one day Pekah son of Remaliah killed a hundred and twenty thousand soldiers in Judah—because Judah had forsaken the LORD, the God of their fathers. [7]Zicri, an Ephraimite warrior, killed Maaseiah the king's son, Azrikam the officer in charge of the palace, and Elkanah, second to the king. [8]The Israelites took captive from their kinsmen two hundred thousand wives, sons and daughters. They also took a great deal of plunder, which they carried back to Samaria.

[9]But a prophet of the LORD named Oded was there, and he went out to meet the army when it returned to Samaria. He said to them, "Because the LORD, the God of your fathers, was angry with Judah, he gave them into your hand. But you have slaughtered them in a rage that reaches to heaven. [10]And now you intend to make the men and women of Judah and Jerusalem your slaves. But aren't you also guilty of sins against the LORD your God? [11]Now listen to me! Send back your fellow countrymen you have taken as prisoners, for the LORD's fierce anger rests on you."

[12]Then some of the leaders in Ephraim—Azariah son of Jehohanan, Berekiah son of Meshillemoth, Jehizkiah son of Shallum, and Amasa son of Hadlai—confronted those who were arriving from the war. [13]"You must not bring those prisoners here," they said, "or we will be guilty before the LORD. Do you intend to add to our sin and guilt? For our guilt is already great, and his fierce anger rests on Israel."

[14]So the soldiers gave up the prisoners and plunder in the presence of the officials and all the assembly. [15]The men designated by name took the prisoners, and from the plunder they clothed all who were naked. They provided them with clothes and sandals, food and drink, and healing balm. All those who were weak they put on donkeys. So they took them back to their fellow countrymen at Jericho, the City of Palms, and returned to Samaria.

[16]At that time King Ahaz sent to the king[a] of Assyria for help. [17]The Edomites had again come and attacked Judah and carried away prisoners, [18]while the Philistines had raided towns in the foothills and in the Negev of Judah. They captured and occupied Beth Shemesh, Aijalon and Gederoth, as well as Soco, Timnah and Gimzo, with their surrounding villages. [19]The LORD had humbled Judah because of Ahaz king of Israel,[b] for he had promoted wickedness in Judah and had been most unfaithful to the LORD. [20]Tiglath-Pileser[c] king of Assyria came to him, but he gave him trouble instead of help. [21]Ahaz took some of the things from the temple of the LORD and from the royal palace and from the princes and presented them to the king of Assyria, but that did not help him.

[22]In his time of trouble King Ahaz became even more unfaithful to the LORD. [23]He offered sacrifices to the gods of Damascus, who had defeated him; for he thought, "Since the gods of the kings of Aram have helped them, I will sacrifice to them so they will help me." But they were his downfall and the downfall of all Israel.

[a] 16 One Hebrew manuscript, Septuagint and Vulgate (see also 2 Kings 16:7); most Hebrew manuscripts *kings*   [b] 19 That is, Judah, as frequently in 2 Chronicles   [c] 20 Hebrew *Tilgath-Pilneser*, a variant of *Tiglath-Pileser*

²⁴Ahaz gathered together the furnishings from the temple of God and took them away.ᵃ He shut the doors of the LORD's temple and set up altars at every street corner in Jerusalem. ²⁵In every town in Judah he built high places to burn sacrifices to other gods and provoked the LORD, the God of his fathers, to anger.

²⁶The other events of his reign and all his ways, from beginning to end, are written in the book of the kings of Judah and Israel. ²⁷Ahaz rested with his fathers and was buried in the city of Jerusalem, but he was not placed in the tombs of the kings of Israel. And Hezekiah his son succeeded him as king.

Hezekiah Purifies the Temple

29 Hezekiah was twenty-five years old when he became king, and he reigned in Jerusalem twenty-nine years. His mother's name was Abijah daughter of Zechariah. ²He did what was right in the eyes of the LORD, just as his father David had done.

³In the first month of the first year of his reign, he opened the doors of the temple of the LORD and repaired them. ⁴He brought in the priests and the Levites, assembled them in the square on the east side ⁵and said: "Listen to me, Levites! Consecrate yourselves now and consecrate the temple of the LORD, the God of your fathers. Remove all defilement from the sanctuary. ⁶Our fathers were unfaithful; they did evil in the eyes of the LORD our God and forsook him. They turned their faces away from the LORD's dwelling place and turned their backs on him. ⁷They also shut the doors of the portico and put out the lamps. They did not burn incense or present any burnt offerings at the sanctuary to the God of Israel. ⁸Therefore, the anger of the LORD has fallen on Judah and Jerusalem; he has made them an object of dread and horror and scorn, as you can see with your own eyes. ⁹This is why our fathers have fallen by the sword and why our sons and daughters and our wives are in captivity. ¹⁰Now I intend to make a covenant with the LORD, the God of Israel, so that his fierce anger will turn away from us. ¹¹My sons, do not be negligent now, for the LORD has chosen you to stand before him and serve him, to minister before him and to burn incense."

¹²Then these Levites set to work:
from the Kohathites,
Mahath son of Amasai and Joel son of Azariah;
from the Merarites,
Kish son of Abdi and Azariah son of Jehallelel;
from the Gershonites,
Joah son of Zimmah and Eden son of Joah;
¹³from the descendants of Elizaphan,
Shimri and Jeiel;
from the descendants of Asaph,
Zechariah and Mattaniah;
¹⁴from the descendants of Heman,
Jehiel and Shimei;
from the descendants of Jeduthun,
Shemaiah and Uzziel.
¹⁵When they had assembled their brothers and consecrated themselves, they went in to purify the temple of the LORD, as the king had ordered, following the word of the

ᵃ 24 Or and cut them up

Time of Cleansing

2 CHRONICLES 29:5–11

Try to imagine yourself present during this time of religious renewal and cleansing. See the animals being slaughtered as atoning sacrifices. Smell the blood and the smoke. Hear trumpets blaring, cymbals clashing, crowds singing. Join in the shouts of praise. Listen to the prayers and proclamations. What parts of this scene do you find particularly moving? What disturbs you? If you were to design a service of cleansing and renewal for your church, what actions, symbolic or direct, would you include?

See *Meeting God in Worship*

The Sacrifice We Can Offer

2 CHRONICLES 29:20–30

"The Lord doesn't look so much at the greatness of our works as at the love with which they are done. And if we do what we can, his Majesty will enable us each day to do more and more, provided that we do not quickly tire. But during the little while this life lasts—and perhaps it will last a shorter time than each one thinks—let us offer the Lord interiorly and exteriorly the sacrifice we can."

—TERESA OF AVILA,
The Interior Castle

LORD. [16]The priests went into the sanctuary of the LORD to purify it. They brought out to the courtyard of the LORD's temple everything unclean that they found in the temple of the LORD. The Levites took it and carried it out to the Kidron Valley. [17]They began the consecration on the first day of the first month, and by the eighth day of the month they reached the portico of the LORD. For eight more days they consecrated the temple of the LORD itself, finishing on the sixteenth day of the first month.

[18]Then they went in to King Hezekiah and reported: "We have purified the entire temple of the LORD, the altar of burnt offering with all its utensils, and the table for setting out the consecrated bread, with all its articles. [19]We have prepared and consecrated all the articles that King Ahaz removed in his unfaithfulness while he was king. They are now in front of the LORD's altar."

[20]Early the next morning King Hezekiah gathered the city officials together and went up to the temple of the LORD. [21]They brought seven bulls, seven rams, seven male lambs and seven male goats as a sin offering for the kingdom, for the sanctuary and for Judah. The king commanded the priests, the descendants of Aaron, to offer these on the altar of the LORD. [22]So they slaughtered the bulls, and the priests took the blood and sprinkled it on the altar; next they slaughtered the rams and sprinkled their blood on the altar; then they slaughtered the lambs and sprinkled their blood on the altar. [23]The goats for the sin offering were brought before the king and the assembly, and they laid their hands on them. [24]The priests then slaughtered the goats and presented their blood on the altar for a sin offering to atone for all Israel, because the king had ordered the burnt offering and the sin offering for all Israel.

[25]He stationed the Levites in the temple of the LORD with cymbals, harps and lyres in the way prescribed by David and Gad the king's seer and Nathan the prophet; this was commanded by the LORD through his prophets. [26]So the Levites stood ready with David's instruments, and the priests with their trumpets.

[27]Hezekiah gave the order to sacrifice the burnt offering on the altar. As the offering began, singing to the LORD began also, accompanied by trumpets and the instruments of David king of Israel. [28]The whole assembly bowed in worship, while the singers sang and the trumpeters played. All this continued until the sacrifice of the burnt offering was completed.

[29]When the offerings were finished, the king and everyone present with him knelt down and worshiped. [30]King Hezekiah and his officials ordered the Levites to praise the LORD with the words of David and of Asaph the seer. So they sang praises with gladness and bowed their heads and worshiped.

[31]Then Hezekiah said, "You have now dedicated yourselves to the LORD. Come and bring sacrifices and thank offerings to the temple of the LORD." So the assembly brought sacrifices and thank offerings, and all whose hearts were willing brought burnt offerings.

[32]The number of burnt offerings the assembly brought was seventy bulls, a hundred rams and two hundred male lambs—all of them for burnt offerings to the LORD. [33]The animals consecrated as sacrifices amounted to six hundred

bulls and three thousand sheep and goats. ³⁴The priests, however, were too few to skin all the burnt offerings; so their kinsmen the Levites helped them until the task was finished and until other priests had been consecrated, for the Levites had been more conscientious in consecrating themselves than the priests had been. ³⁵There were burnt offerings in abundance, together with the fat of the fellowship offerings*ᵃ* and the drink offerings that accompanied the burnt offerings.

So the service of the temple of the LORD was reestablished. ³⁶Hezekiah and all the people rejoiced at what God had brought about for his people, because it was done so quickly.

Hezekiah Celebrates the Passover

30 Hezekiah sent word to all Israel and Judah and also wrote letters to Ephraim and Manasseh, inviting them to come to the temple of the LORD in Jerusalem and celebrate the Passover to the LORD, the God of Israel. ²The king and his officials and the whole assembly in Jerusalem decided to celebrate the Passover in the second month. ³They had not been able to celebrate it at the regular time because not enough priests had consecrated themselves and the people had not assembled in Jerusalem. ⁴The plan seemed right both to the king and to the whole assembly. ⁵They decided to send a proclamation throughout Israel, from Beersheba to Dan, calling the people to come to Jerusalem and celebrate the Passover to the LORD, the God of Israel. It had not been celebrated in large numbers according to what was written.

⁶At the king's command, couriers went throughout Israel and Judah with letters from the king and from his officials, which read:

"People of Israel, return to the LORD, the God of Abraham, Isaac and Israel, that he may return to you who are left, who have escaped from the hand of the kings of Assyria. ⁷Do not be like your fathers and brothers, who were unfaithful to the LORD, the God of their fathers, so that he made them an object of horror, as you see. ⁸Do not be stiff-necked, as your fathers were; submit to the LORD. Come to the sanctuary, which he has consecrated forever. Serve the LORD your God, so that his fierce anger will turn away from you. ⁹If you return to the LORD, then your brothers and your children will be shown compassion by their captors and will come back to this land, for the LORD your God is gracious and compassionate. He will not turn his face from you if you return to him."

¹⁰The couriers went from town to town in Ephraim and Manasseh, as far as Zebulun, but the people scorned and ridiculed them. ¹¹Nevertheless, some men of Asher, Manasseh and Zebulun humbled themselves and went to Jerusalem. ¹²Also in Judah the hand of God was on the people to give them unity of mind to carry out what the king and his officials had ordered, following the word of the LORD.

¹³A very large crowd of people assembled in Jerusalem to celebrate the Feast of Unleavened Bread in the second

Prayer for Return

2 CHRONICLES 30:6–9

Carefully read this call to the people of Israel to return to God. As you read, think of people who have left their churches or become inactive. Remember them in prayer. First simply commend them to God's care. Ask God to reach out to them and gently call them to return. Then ask God to show you ways in which you might invite them to return. You might want to call them or visit them. If so, you will probably need to ask for patience to listen to grievances without becoming defensive.

See *Meeting God in Community*

Rules Aren't Everything

2 CHRONICLES 30:18–20,25–26

For one moment "business as usual" is suspended and people are invited to come to God without worrying about all the traditional rules of cleanliness. What are the special rules—mostly unwritten—that serve as barriers to people who might want to come to your church? You might try to list "rules" involving standards of dress or cleanliness, proper behavior, literacy (do people have to be able to read to participate?), social or economic status, or anything else you can think of. As you review the list, which rules are important to you personally? Why? What can you do to make your church more welcoming to all who seek to encounter God?

See Meeting God in Community

month. ¹⁴They removed the altars in Jerusalem and cleared away the incense altars and threw them into the Kidron Valley.

¹⁵They slaughtered the Passover lamb on the fourteenth day of the second month. The priests and the Levites were ashamed and consecrated themselves and brought burnt offerings to the temple of the LORD. ¹⁶Then they took up their regular positions as prescribed in the Law of Moses the man of God. The priests sprinkled the blood handed to them by the Levites. ¹⁷Since many in the crowd had not consecrated themselves, the Levites had to kill the Passover lambs for all those who were not ceremonially clean and could not consecrate ⌐their lambs⌐ to the LORD. ¹⁸Although most of the many people who came from Ephraim, Manasseh, Issachar and Zebulun had not purified themselves, yet they ate the Passover, contrary to what was written. But Hezekiah prayed for them, saying, "May the LORD, who is good, pardon everyone ¹⁹who sets his heart on seeking God—the LORD, the God of his fathers—even if he is not clean according to the rules of the sanctuary." ²⁰And the LORD heard Hezekiah and healed the people.

²¹The Israelites who were present in Jerusalem celebrated the Feast of Unleavened Bread for seven days with great rejoicing, while the Levites and priests sang to the LORD every day, accompanied by the LORD's instruments of praise.[a]

²²Hezekiah spoke encouragingly to all the Levites, who showed good understanding of the service of the LORD. For the seven days they ate their assigned portion and offered fellowship offerings[b] and praised the LORD, the God of their fathers.

²³The whole assembly then agreed to celebrate the festival seven more days; so for another seven days they celebrated joyfully. ²⁴Hezekiah king of Judah provided a thousand bulls and seven thousand sheep and goats for the assembly, and the officials provided them with a thousand bulls and ten thousand sheep and goats. A great number of priests consecrated themselves. ²⁵The entire assembly of Judah rejoiced, along with the priests and Levites and all who had assembled from Israel, including the aliens who had come from Israel and those who lived in Judah. ²⁶There was great joy in Jerusalem, for since the days of Solomon son of David king of Israel there had been nothing like this in Jerusalem. ²⁷The priests and the Levites stood to bless the people, and God heard them, for their prayer reached heaven, his holy dwelling place.

31 When all this had ended, the Israelites who were there went out to the towns of Judah, smashed the sacred stones and cut down the Asherah poles. They destroyed the high places and the altars throughout Judah and Benjamin and in Ephraim and Manasseh. After they had destroyed all of them, the Israelites returned to their own towns and to their own property.

Contributions for Worship

²Hezekiah assigned the priests and Levites to divisions—each of them according to their duties as priests or Levites—to offer burnt offerings and fellowship offerings,[b] to

a 21 Or priests praised the LORD every day with resounding instruments belonging to the LORD   b 22, 2 Traditionally peace offerings

minister, to give thanks and to sing praises at the gates of the LORD's dwelling. ³The king contributed from his own possessions for the morning and evening burnt offerings and for the burnt offerings on the Sabbaths, New Moons and appointed feasts as written in the Law of the LORD. ⁴He ordered the people living in Jerusalem to give the portion due the priests and Levites so they could devote themselves to the Law of the LORD. ⁵As soon as the order went out, the Israelites generously gave the firstfruits of their grain, new wine, oil and honey and all that the fields produced. They brought a great amount, a tithe of everything. ⁶The men of Israel and Judah who lived in the towns of Judah also brought a tithe of their herds and flocks and a tithe of the holy things dedicated to the LORD their God, and they piled them in heaps. ⁷They began doing this in the third month and finished in the seventh month. ⁸When Hezekiah and his officials came and saw the heaps, they praised the LORD and blessed his people Israel.

⁹Hezekiah asked the priests and Levites about the heaps; ¹⁰and Azariah the chief priest, from the family of Zadok, answered, "Since the people began to bring their contributions to the temple of the LORD, we have had enough to eat and plenty to spare, because the LORD has blessed his people, and this great amount is left over."

¹¹Hezekiah gave orders to prepare storerooms in the temple of the LORD, and this was done. ¹²Then they faithfully brought in the contributions, tithes and dedicated gifts. Conaniah, a Levite, was in charge of these things, and his brother Shimei was next in rank. ¹³Jehiel, Azaziah, Nahath, Asahel, Jerimoth, Jozabad, Eliel, Ismakiah, Mahath and Benaiah were supervisors under Conaniah and Shimei his brother, by appointment of King Hezekiah and Azariah the official in charge of the temple of God.

¹⁴Kore son of Imnah the Levite, keeper of the East Gate, was in charge of the freewill offerings given to God, distributing the contributions made to the LORD and also the consecrated gifts. ¹⁵Eden, Miniamin, Jeshua, Shemaiah, Amariah and Shecaniah assisted him faithfully in the towns of the priests, distributing to their fellow priests according to their divisions, old and young alike.

¹⁶In addition, they distributed to the males three years old or more whose names were in the genealogical records—all who would enter the temple of the LORD to perform the daily duties of their various tasks, according to their responsibilities and their divisions. ¹⁷And they distributed to the priests enrolled by their families in the genealogical records and likewise to the Levites twenty years old or more, according to their responsibilities and their divisions. ¹⁸They included all the little ones, the wives, and the sons and daughters of the whole community listed in these genealogical records. For they were faithful in consecrating themselves.

¹⁹As for the priests, the descendants of Aaron, who lived on the farm lands around their towns or in any other towns, men were designated by name to distribute portions to every male among them and to all who were recorded in the genealogies of the Levites.

²⁰This is what Hezekiah did throughout Judah, doing what was good and right and faithful before the LORD his God. ²¹In everything that he undertook in the service of

Thanksgiving

2 CHRONICLES 31:11

"With praise and adoration to God comes thanksgiving to him for his good gifts. In the devotional life these moods are intertwined, and we discuss them separately only for the sake of further analysis of the place of gratitude in prayer. We ought to praise God anyway for being what he is, quite regardless of our particular blessings. Otherwise, our worship is not centered in God but in ourselves. Yet praise leads normally to the mood of thanksgiving for God's bounties."

—GEORGIA HARKNESS,
Prayer and the Common Life

Trust God and Be Ready

2 CHRONICLES 32:7–8

Prayer is not an alternative to preparing for battle but an essential part of it. Hezekiah makes all the standard military preparations, but he insists that the deciding factor is that God will fight with them. What battles are you fighting or preparing to fight? Which ones are God's battles too? What preparations do you need to make? What must you surrender to God's care? You might want to turn the entire battle over to God by offering your efforts and your preparations to God's service. Repeat to yourself, "With us is the LORD our God to help us and to fight our battles."

See Meeting God in Prayer

God's temple and in obedience to the law and the commands, he sought his God and worked wholeheartedly. And so he prospered.

Sennacherib Threatens Jerusalem

32 After all that Hezekiah had so faithfully done, Sennacherib king of Assyria came and invaded Judah. He laid siege to the fortified cities, thinking to conquer them for himself. ²When Hezekiah saw that Sennacherib had come and that he intended to make war on Jerusalem, ³he consulted with his officials and military staff about blocking off the water from the springs outside the city, and they helped him. ⁴A large force of men assembled, and they blocked all the springs and the stream that flowed through the land. "Why should the kings*ᵃ* of Assyria come and find plenty of water?" they said. ⁵Then he worked hard repairing all the broken sections of the wall and building towers on it. He built another wall outside that one and reinforced the supporting terraces*ᵇ* of the City of David. He also made large numbers of weapons and shields.

⁶He appointed military officers over the people and assembled them before him in the square at the city gate and encouraged them with these words: ⁷"Be strong and courageous. Do not be afraid or discouraged because of the king of Assyria and the vast army with him, for there is a greater power with us than with him. ⁸With him is only the arm of flesh, but with us is the LORD our God to help us and to fight our battles." And the people gained confidence from what Hezekiah the king of Judah said.

⁹Later, when Sennacherib king of Assyria and all his forces were laying siege to Lachish, he sent his officers to Jerusalem with this message for Hezekiah king of Judah and for all the people of Judah who were there:

¹⁰"This is what Sennacherib king of Assyria says: On what are you basing your confidence, that you remain in Jerusalem under siege? ¹¹When Hezekiah says, 'The LORD our God will save us from the hand of the king of Assyria,' he is misleading you, to let you die of hunger and thirst. ¹²Did not Hezekiah himself remove this god's high places and altars, saying to Judah and Jerusalem, 'You must worship before one altar and burn sacrifices on it'?

¹³"Do you not know what I and my fathers have done to all the peoples of the other lands? Were the gods of those nations ever able to deliver their land from my hand? ¹⁴Who of all the gods of these nations that my fathers destroyed has been able to save his people from me? How then can your god deliver you from my hand? ¹⁵Now do not let Hezekiah deceive you and mislead you like this. Do not believe him, for no god of any nation or kingdom has been able to deliver his people from my hand or the hand of my fathers. How much less will your god deliver you from my hand!"

¹⁶Sennacherib's officers spoke further against the LORD God and against his servant Hezekiah. ¹⁷The king also wrote letters insulting the LORD, the God of Israel, and saying this against him: "Just as the gods of the peoples of the

ᵃ 4 Hebrew; Septuagint and Syriac *king*   *ᵇ 5* Or *the Millo*

other lands did not rescue their people from my hand, so the god of Hezekiah will not rescue his people from my hand." **¹⁸**Then they called out in Hebrew to the people of Jerusalem who were on the wall, to terrify them and make them afraid in order to capture the city. **¹⁹**They spoke about the God of Jerusalem as they did about the gods of the other peoples of the world—the work of men's hands.

²⁰King Hezekiah and the prophet Isaiah son of Amoz cried out in prayer to heaven about this. **²¹**And the LORD sent an angel, who annihilated all the fighting men and the leaders and officers in the camp of the Assyrian king. So he withdrew to his own land in disgrace. And when he went into the temple of his god, some of his sons cut him down with the sword.

²²So the LORD saved Hezekiah and the people of Jerusalem from the hand of Sennacherib king of Assyria and from the hand of all others. He took care of them*ª* on every side. **²³**Many brought offerings to Jerusalem to the LORD and valuable gifts for Hezekiah king of Judah. From then on he was highly regarded by all the nations.

Hezekiah's Pride, Success and Death

²⁴In those days Hezekiah became ill and was at the point of death. He prayed to the LORD, who answered him and gave him a miraculous sign. **²⁵**But Hezekiah's heart was proud and he did not respond to the kindness shown him; therefore the LORD's wrath was on him and on Judah and Jerusalem. **²⁶**Then Hezekiah repented of the pride of his heart, as did the people of Jerusalem; therefore the LORD's wrath did not come upon them during the days of Hezekiah.

²⁷Hezekiah had very great riches and honor, and he made treasuries for his silver and gold and for his precious stones, spices, shields and all kinds of valuables. **²⁸**He also made buildings to store the harvest of grain, new wine and oil; and he made stalls for various kinds of cattle, and pens for the flocks. **²⁹**He built villages and acquired great numbers of flocks and herds, for God had given him very great riches.

³⁰It was Hezekiah who blocked the upper outlet of the Gihon spring and channeled the water down to the west side of the City of David. He succeeded in everything he undertook. **³¹**But when envoys were sent by the rulers of Babylon to ask him about the miraculous sign that had occurred in the land, God left him to test him and to know everything that was in his heart.

³²The other events of Hezekiah's reign and his acts of devotion are written in the vision of the prophet Isaiah son of Amoz in the book of the kings of Judah and Israel. **³³**Hezekiah rested with his fathers and was buried on the hill where the tombs of David's descendants are. All Judah and the people of Jerusalem honored him when he died. And Manasseh his son succeeded him as king.

Manasseh King of Judah

33 Manasseh was twelve years old when he became king, and he reigned in Jerusalem fifty-five years. **²**He did evil in the eyes of the LORD, following the detestable practices of the nations the LORD had driven out before the Israelites. **³**He rebuilt the high places his father Hezekiah

ª 22 Hebrew; Septuagint and Vulgate He gave them rest

God Welcomes Repentance

2 CHRONICLES 32:24–26

A soldier asked Abba Mius if God accepted repentance. After the old man had taught him many things he said, "Tell me, my dear, if your cloak is torn, do you throw it away?" He replied, "No, I mend it and use it again." The old man said to him, "If you are so careful about your cloak, will not God be equally careful about his creature?"

—MIUS OF BELOS,
Sayings of the Desert Fathers

Never Too Late

2 CHRONICLES 33:10–13

It is never too late to repent and receive God's forgiveness and grace. Even after Manasseh has brought disaster to himself and God's people, he still can turn to God and be restored. Are there sins for which you have been afraid to ask God's forgiveness? Ask now. You might turn to God and ask for the grace of a new start. You might also take special notice (on television and in newspapers and novels) of others who have received God's gift of love after making disasters of their lives.

See Meeting God in Prayer

had demolished; he also erected altars to the Baals and made Asherah poles. He bowed down to all the starry hosts and worshiped them. [4]He built altars in the temple of the LORD, of which the LORD had said, "My Name will remain in Jerusalem forever." [5]In both courts of the temple of the LORD, he built altars to all the starry hosts. [6]He sacrificed his sons in[a] the fire in the Valley of Ben Hinnom, practiced sorcery, divination and witchcraft, and consulted mediums and spiritists. He did much evil in the eyes of the LORD, provoking him to anger.

[7]He took the carved image he had made and put it in God's temple, of which God had said to David and to his son Solomon, "In this temple and in Jerusalem, which I have chosen out of all the tribes of Israel, I will put my Name forever. [8]I will not again make the feet of the Israelites leave the land I assigned to your forefathers, if only they will be careful to do everything I commanded them concerning all the laws, decrees and ordinances given through Moses." [9]But Manasseh led Judah and the people of Jerusalem astray, so that they did more evil than the nations the LORD had destroyed before the Israelites.

[10]The LORD spoke to Manasseh and his people, but they paid no attention. [11]So the LORD brought against them the army commanders of the king of Assyria, who took Manasseh prisoner, put a hook in his nose, bound him with bronze shackles and took him to Babylon. [12]In his distress he sought the favor of the LORD his God and humbled himself greatly before the God of his fathers. [13]And when he prayed to him, the LORD was moved by his entreaty and listened to his plea; so he brought him back to Jerusalem and to his kingdom. Then Manasseh knew that the LORD is God.

[14]Afterward he rebuilt the outer wall of the City of David, west of the Gihon spring in the valley, as far as the entrance of the Fish Gate and encircling the hill of Ophel; he also made it much higher. He stationed military commanders in all the fortified cities in Judah.

[15]He got rid of the foreign gods and removed the image from the temple of the LORD, as well as all the altars he had built on the temple hill and in Jerusalem; and he threw them out of the city. [16]Then he restored the altar of the LORD and sacrificed fellowship offerings[b] and thank offerings on it, and told Judah to serve the LORD, the God of Israel. [17]The people, however, continued to sacrifice at the high places, but only to the LORD their God.

[18]The other events of Manasseh's reign, including his prayer to his God and the words the seers spoke to him in the name of the LORD, the God of Israel, are written in the annals of the kings of Israel.[c] [19]His prayer and how God was moved by his entreaty, as well as all his sins and unfaithfulness, and the sites where he built high places and set up Asherah poles and idols before he humbled himself—all are written in the records of the seers.[d] [20]Manasseh rested with his fathers and was buried in his palace. And Amon his son succeeded him as king.

Amon King of Judah

[21]Amon was twenty-two years old when he became king,

---

[a]6 Or *He made his sons pass through*   [b]16 Traditionally *peace offerings*
[c]18 That is, Judah, as frequently in 2 Chronicles   [d]19 One Hebrew manuscript and Septuagint; most Hebrew manuscripts *of Hozai*

and he reigned in Jerusalem two years. ²²He did evil in the eyes of the LORD, as his father Manasseh had done. Amon worshiped and offered sacrifices to all the idols Manasseh had made. ²³But unlike his father Manasseh, he did not humble himself before the LORD; Amon increased his guilt.

²⁴Amon's officials conspired against him and assassinated him in his palace. ²⁵Then the people of the land killed all who had plotted against King Amon, and they made Josiah his son king in his place.

Josiah's Reforms

34 Josiah was eight years old when he became king, and he reigned in Jerusalem thirty-one years. ²He did what was right in the eyes of the LORD and walked in the ways of his father David, not turning aside to the right or to the left.

³In the eighth year of his reign, while he was still young, he began to seek the God of his father David. In his twelfth year he began to purge Judah and Jerusalem of high places, Asherah poles, carved idols and cast images. ⁴Under his direction the altars of the Baals were torn down; he cut to pieces the incense altars that were above them, and smashed the Asherah poles, the idols and the images. These he broke to pieces and scattered over the graves of those who had sacrificed to them. ⁵He burned the bones of the priests on their altars, and so he purged Judah and Jerusalem. ⁶In the towns of Manasseh, Ephraim and Simeon, as far as Naphtali, and in the ruins around them, ⁷he tore down the altars and the Asherah poles and crushed the idols to powder and cut to pieces all the incense altars throughout Israel. Then he went back to Jerusalem.

⁸In the eighteenth year of Josiah's reign, to purify the land and the temple, he sent Shaphan son of Azaliah and Maaseiah the ruler of the city, with Joah son of Joahaz, the recorder, to repair the temple of the LORD his God.

⁹They went to Hilkiah the high priest and gave him the money that had been brought into the temple of God, which the Levites who were the doorkeepers had collected from the people of Manasseh, Ephraim and the entire remnant of Israel and from all the people of Judah and Benjamin and the inhabitants of Jerusalem. ¹⁰Then they entrusted it to the men appointed to supervise the work on the LORD's temple. These men paid the workers who repaired and restored the temple. ¹¹They also gave money to the carpenters and builders to purchase dressed stone, and timber for joists and beams for the buildings that the kings of Judah had allowed to fall into ruin.

¹²The men did the work faithfully. Over them to direct them were Jahath and Obadiah, Levites descended from Merari, and Zechariah and Meshullam, descended from Kohath. The Levites—all who were skilled in playing musical instruments— ¹³had charge of the laborers and supervised all the workers from job to job. Some of the Levites were secretaries, scribes and doorkeepers.

The Book of the Law Found

¹⁴While they were bringing out the money that had been taken into the temple of the LORD, Hilkiah the priest found the Book of the Law of the LORD that had been given through Moses. ¹⁵Hilkiah said to Shaphan the secretary, "I

Destroying Idols

2 CHRONICLES 34:3–7

As you read this vivid account of Josiah pulling down idols and destroying their altars, consider the idols that may be in your life. What are the possessions, organizations, places that seem to have power over you—that seem to be able to command you? You might imagine yourself pulling them from their places of honor and making dust of them. How can you bring your imagining into reality? What things need to be eliminated from your life? What can be redeemed? How can things that use you and that require your time and attention become things that you can use to serve God? You might start by offering or consecrating these things to God's service.

See *Meeting God in Everyday Life*

Discovering the Bible

2 CHRONICLES 34:29–32

Try to imagine yourself in the crowd as the newly discovered scroll is read. Because some scholars believe that this scroll was the book of Deuteronomy, you might get a sense of the occasion by reading Deuteronomy 29–30 aloud. What is your mood as you hear yourself read these words? How do these words apply to your life and to the life of your community? What response would you make? What would it mean for you to act "in accordance with the covenant of God"? What specific changes do you need to make in the way you have been living?

See Meeting God in Everyday Life

have found the Book of the Law in the temple of the LORD." He gave it to Shaphan.

¹⁶Then Shaphan took the book to the king and reported to him: "Your officials are doing everything that has been committed to them. ¹⁷They have paid out the money that was in the temple of the LORD and have entrusted it to the supervisors and workers." ¹⁸Then Shaphan the secretary informed the king, "Hilkiah the priest has given me a book." And Shaphan read from it in the presence of the king.

¹⁹When the king heard the words of the Law, he tore his robes. ²⁰He gave these orders to Hilkiah, Ahikam son of Shaphan, Abdon son of Micah,[a] Shaphan the secretary and Asaiah the king's attendant: ²¹"Go and inquire of the LORD for me and for the remnant in Israel and Judah about what is written in this book that has been found. Great is the LORD's anger that is poured out on us because our fathers have not kept the word of the LORD; they have not acted in accordance with all that is written in this book."

²²Hilkiah and those the king had sent with him[b] went to speak to the prophetess Huldah, who was the wife of Shallum son of Tokhath,[c] the son of Hasrah,[d] keeper of the wardrobe. She lived in Jerusalem, in the Second District.

²³She said to them, "This is what the LORD, the God of Israel, says: Tell the man who sent you to me, ²⁴'This is what the LORD says: I am going to bring disaster on this place and its people—all the curses written in the book that has been read in the presence of the king of Judah. ²⁵Because they have forsaken me and burned incense to other gods and provoked me to anger by all that their hands have made,[e] my anger will be poured out on this place and will not be quenched.' ²⁶Tell the king of Judah, who sent you to inquire of the LORD, 'This is what the LORD, the God of Israel, says concerning the words you heard: ²⁷Because your heart was responsive and you humbled yourself before God when you heard what he spoke against this place and its people, and because you humbled yourself before me and tore your robes and wept in my presence, I have heard you, declares the LORD. ²⁸Now I will gather you to your fathers, and you will be buried in peace. Your eyes will not see all the disaster I am going to bring on this place and on those who live here.' "

So they took her answer back to the king.

²⁹Then the king called together all the elders of Judah and Jerusalem. ³⁰He went up to the temple of the LORD with the men of Judah, the people of Jerusalem, the priests and the Levites—all the people from the least to the greatest. He read in their hearing all the words of the Book of the Covenant, which had been found in the temple of the LORD. ³¹The king stood by his pillar and renewed the covenant in the presence of the LORD—to follow the LORD and keep his commands, regulations and decrees with all his heart and all his soul, and to obey the words of the covenant written in this book.

³²Then he had everyone in Jerusalem and Benjamin pledge themselves to it; the people of Jerusalem did this in accordance with the covenant of God, the God of their fathers.

³³Josiah removed all the detestable idols from all the territory belonging to the Israelites, and he had all who were pres-

---

[a] 20 Also called *Acbor son of Micaiah*   [b] 22 One Hebrew manuscript, Vulgate and Syriac; most Hebrew manuscripts do not have *had sent with him*.   [c] 22 Also called *Tikvah*   [d] 22 Also called *Harhas*   [e] 25 Or *by everything they have done*

ent in Israel serve the LORD their God. As long as he lived, they did not fail to follow the LORD, the God of their fathers.

Josiah Celebrates the Passover

35 Josiah celebrated the Passover to the LORD in Jerusalem, and the Passover lamb was slaughtered on the fourteenth day of the first month. ²He appointed the priests to their duties and encouraged them in the service of the LORD's temple. ³He said to the Levites, who instructed all Israel and who had been consecrated to the LORD: "Put the sacred ark in the temple that Solomon son of David king of Israel built. It is not to be carried about on your shoulders. Now serve the LORD your God and his people Israel. ⁴Prepare yourselves by families in your divisions, according to the directions written by David king of Israel and by his son Solomon.

⁵"Stand in the holy place with a group of Levites for each subdivision of the families of your fellow countrymen, the lay people. ⁶Slaughter the Passover lambs, consecrate yourselves and prepare ⌊the lambs⌋ for your fellow countrymen, doing what the LORD commanded through Moses."

⁷Josiah provided for all the lay people who were there a total of thirty thousand sheep and goats for the Passover offerings, and also three thousand cattle—all from the king's own possessions.

⁸His officials also contributed voluntarily to the people and the priests and Levites. Hilkiah, Zechariah and Jehiel, the administrators of God's temple, gave the priests twenty-six hundred Passover offerings and three hundred cattle. ⁹Also Conaniah along with Shemaiah and Nethanel, his brothers, and Hashabiah, Jeiel and Jozabad, the leaders of the Levites, provided five thousand Passover offerings and five hundred head of cattle for the Levites.

¹⁰The service was arranged and the priests stood in their places with the Levites in their divisions as the king had ordered. ¹¹The Passover lambs were slaughtered, and the priests sprinkled the blood handed to them, while the Levites skinned the animals. ¹²They set aside the burnt offerings to give them to the subdivisions of the families of the people to offer to the LORD, as is written in the Book of Moses. They did the same with the cattle. ¹³They roasted the Passover animals over the fire as prescribed, and boiled the holy offerings in pots, caldrons and pans and served them quickly to all the people. ¹⁴After this, they made preparations for themselves and for the priests, because the priests, the descendants of Aaron, were sacrificing the burnt offerings and the fat portions until nightfall. So the Levites made preparations for themselves and for the Aaronic priests.

¹⁵The musicians, the descendants of Asaph, were in the places prescribed by David, Asaph, Heman and Jeduthun the king's seer. The gatekeepers at each gate did not need to leave their posts, because their fellow Levites made the preparations for them.

¹⁶So at that time the entire service of the LORD was carried out for the celebration of the Passover and the offering of burnt offerings on the altar of the LORD, as King Josiah had ordered. ¹⁷The Israelites who were present celebrated the Passover at that time and observed the Feast of Unleavened Bread for seven days. ¹⁸The Passover had not been observed like this in Israel since the days of the

In Every Generation

2 CHRONICLES 35:10–11

"In every generation, let all people look on themselves as if they came forth out of Egypt . . . It was not only our ancestors that the Holy One (blessed be he) redeemed, but he redeemed us as well along with them . . . Therefore we are bound to thank, praise, laud, glorify, exalt, honor, bless, extol, and adore God who performed all these miracles for our ancestors and for us. God has brought us forth from slavery to freedom, from sorrow to joy, from mourning to holiday, from darkness to great light, and from bondage to redemption. Therefore let us recite before God a new song: Praise the Lord!"

—*THE PASSOVER HAGGADAH,*
Traditional

Lamentation

2 CHRONICLES 35:25

Josiah's death is lamentable, not only because a righteous king is dead, but also because he represented Israel's last great hope for freedom. What are the losses in your life that are suffocating your hopes? You might offer your own lament, crying to God over destroyed plans, dashed hopes, lost friends and painful mistakes. Offer God your sorrow. If you have trouble putting your feelings into words, you might "prime the pump" by reading the book of Lamentations. As you mourn the past, be open to hearing God's gracious call to new beginnings.

See Meeting God in Everyday Life

prophet Samuel; and none of the kings of Israel had ever celebrated such a Passover as did Josiah, with the priests, the Levites and all Judah and Israel who were there with the people of Jerusalem. ¹⁹This Passover was celebrated in the eighteenth year of Josiah's reign.

The Death of Josiah

²⁰After all this, when Josiah had set the temple in order, Neco king of Egypt went up to fight at Carchemish on the Euphrates, and Josiah marched out to meet him in battle. ²¹But Neco sent messengers to him, saying, "What quarrel is there between you and me, O king of Judah? It is not you I am attacking at this time, but the house with which I am at war. God has told me to hurry; so stop opposing God, who is with me, or he will destroy you."

²²Josiah, however, would not turn away from him, but disguised himself to engage him in battle. He would not listen to what Neco had said at God's command but went to fight him on the plain of Megiddo.

²³Archers shot King Josiah, and he told his officers, "Take me away; I am badly wounded." ²⁴So they took him out of his chariot, put him in the other chariot he had and brought him to Jerusalem, where he died. He was buried in the tombs of his fathers, and all Judah and Jerusalem mourned for him.

²⁵Jeremiah composed laments for Josiah, and to this day all the men and women singers commemorate Josiah in the laments. These became a tradition in Israel and are written in the Laments.

²⁶The other events of Josiah's reign and his acts of devotion, according to what is written in the Law of the LORD— ²⁷all the events, from beginning to end, are written in the book of the kings of Israel and Judah. ¹And the people of the land took Jehoahaz son of Josiah and made him king in Jerusalem in place of his father.

36

Jehoahaz King of Judah

²Jehoahaz[a] was twenty-three years old when he became king, and he reigned in Jerusalem three months. ³The king of Egypt dethroned him in Jerusalem and imposed on Judah a levy of a hundred talents[b] of silver and a talent[c] of gold. ⁴The king of Egypt made Eliakim, a brother of Jehoahaz, king over Judah and Jerusalem and changed Eliakim's name to Jehoiakim. But Neco took Eliakim's brother Jehoahaz and carried him off to Egypt.

Jehoiakim King of Judah

⁵Jehoiakim was twenty-five years old when he became king, and he reigned in Jerusalem eleven years. He did evil in the eyes of the LORD his God. ⁶Nebuchadnezzar king of Babylon attacked him and bound him with bronze shackles to take him to Babylon. ⁷Nebuchadnezzar also took to Babylon articles from the temple of the LORD and put them in his temple[d] there.

⁸The other events of Jehoiakim's reign, the detestable things he did and all that was found against him, are written in the book of the kings of Israel and Judah. And Jehoiachin his son succeeded him as king.

a 2 Hebrew Joahaz, a variant of Jehoahaz; also in verse 4   b 3 That is, about 3 3/4 tons (about 3.4 metric tons)   c 3 That is, about 75 pounds (about 34 kilograms)   d 7 Or palace

Jehoiachin King of Judah

⁹Jehoiachin was eighteen*ᵃ* years old when he became king, and he reigned in Jerusalem three months and ten days. He did evil in the eyes of the LORD. ¹⁰In the spring, King Nebuchadnezzar sent for him and brought him to Babylon, together with articles of value from the temple of the LORD, and he made Jehoiachin's uncle,*ᵇ* Zedekiah, king over Judah and Jerusalem.

Zedekiah King of Judah

¹¹Zedekiah was twenty-one years old when he became king, and he reigned in Jerusalem eleven years. ¹²He did evil in the eyes of the LORD his God and did not humble himself before Jeremiah the prophet, who spoke the word of the LORD. ¹³He also rebelled against King Nebuchadnezzar, who had made him take an oath in God's name. He became stiff-necked and hardened his heart and would not turn to the LORD, the God of Israel. ¹⁴Furthermore, all the leaders of the priests and the people became more and more unfaithful, following all the detestable practices of the nations and defiling the temple of the LORD, which he had consecrated in Jerusalem.

The Fall of Jerusalem

¹⁵The LORD, the God of their fathers, sent word to them through his messengers again and again, because he had pity on his people and on his dwelling place. ¹⁶But they mocked God's messengers, despised his words and scoffed at his prophets until the wrath of the LORD was aroused against his people and there was no remedy. ¹⁷He brought up against them the king of the Babylonians,*ᶜ* who killed their young men with the sword in the sanctuary, and spared neither young man nor young woman, old man or aged. God handed all of them over to Nebuchadnezzar. ¹⁸He carried to Babylon all the articles from the temple of God, both large and small, and the treasures of the LORD's temple and the treasures of the king and his officials. ¹⁹They set fire to God's temple and broke down the wall of Jerusalem; they burned all the palaces and destroyed everything of value there.

²⁰He carried into exile to Babylon the remnant, who escaped from the sword, and they became servants to him and his sons until the kingdom of Persia came to power. ²¹The land enjoyed its sabbath rests; all the time of its desolation it rested, until the seventy years were completed in fulfillment of the word of the LORD spoken by Jeremiah.

²²In the first year of Cyrus king of Persia, in order to fulfill the word of the LORD spoken by Jeremiah, the LORD moved the heart of Cyrus king of Persia to make a proclamation throughout his realm and to put it in writing:

²³"This is what Cyrus king of Persia says:

" 'The LORD, the God of heaven, has given me all the kingdoms of the earth and he has appointed me to build a temple for him at Jerusalem in Judah. Anyone of his people among you—may the LORD his God be with him, and let him go up.' "

The Last Word

2 CHRONICLES 36:15–16

The book of 1 Chronicles ended with an epitaph for a king; the book of 2 Chronicles ends with an epitaph for a nation. And what a sad one it is! God's people ignored warning after warning until it was too late and disaster came. Where have you seen this pattern in your life? In your community? What warnings are you hearing now? What warnings do you need to pass on to others? How can you respond to these warnings? What actions can you take? What words of hope can you proclaim along with the words of warning?

See Meeting God in Community

ᵃ 9 One Hebrew manuscript, some Septuagint manuscripts and Syriac (see also 2 Kings 24:8); most Hebrew manuscripts *eight*   *ᵇ 10* Hebrew *brother, that is, relative* (see 2 Kings 24:17)   *ᶜ 17* Or *Chaldeans*

EZRA
Rebuilding and Reclaiming

KEY VERSE:

For seven days they celebrated with joy the Feast of Unleavened Bread, because the Lord had filled them with joy by changing the attitude of the king of Assyria, so that he assisted them in the work on the house of God, the God of Israel—Ezra 6:22

"Now my heart began to ache and fear again I might meet with disappointment at the last . . . at which point I began to consider whether one who had sinned as I have might with confidence trust the faithfulness of God . . . And as I was in a muse about this thing, that Scripture came home to me, 'Mercy triumphs over judgment!' [James 2:13]. This was a wonderment to me; yet truly I am apt to think it was of God; for the word of the law and wrath must give place to the word of life and grace."

—JOHN BUNYAN,
Grace Abounding

There are plenty of instances in history where a nation was exiled and never received its homeland back. Think, for example, of the Armenians, who have suffered massacres and who are without their ancient land; and think of the Kurdish people, now spread out in Turkey, Iraq and elsewhere. Yet, against all odds, God restored the people of Israel to Jerusalem and made provision for rebuilding the temple. Of course, Israel was not just any nation exiled and the temple was not just any temple destroyed. This nation was the chosen of the one, true God. They had worshiped God in the temple that lay in ruins: "By the rivers of Babylon we sat and wept when we remembered Zion" (Psalm 137:1).

Beneath the rather dry lists and the copies of official documents and decrees in the book of Ezra, this is a dramatic story—a resurrection story. What seems like the death of a nation is, in reality, new life. Have you ever been forced to live away from home for an extended period of time? Do you know people who are refugees from their homes? Try to place yourself in this story. Imagine the emotions God's people experience as they return to their ancient land: "The wonder of it! We never expected this! Is it too good to be true? How could we have imagined that God would forget the covenant, that God would no longer be gracious and loving toward us?" While Israel may be faithless, God is forever faithful!

Cyrus Helps the Exiles to Return

1 In the first year of Cyrus king of Persia, in order to fulfill the word of the LORD spoken by Jeremiah, the LORD moved the heart of Cyrus king of Persia to make a proclamation throughout his realm and to put it in writing:

2 "This is what Cyrus king of Persia says:

" 'The LORD, the God of heaven, has given me all the kingdoms of the earth and he has appointed me to build a temple for him at Jerusalem in Judah. ³Anyone of his people among you—may his God be with him, and let him go up to Jerusalem in Judah and build the temple of the LORD, the God of Israel, the God who is in Jerusalem. ⁴And the people of any place where survivors may now be living are to provide him with silver and gold, with goods and livestock, and with freewill offerings for the temple of God in Jerusalem.' "

5 Then the family heads of Judah and Benjamin, and the priests and Levites—everyone whose heart God had moved—prepared to go up and build the house of the LORD in Jerusalem. ⁶All their neighbors assisted them with articles of silver and gold, with goods and livestock, and with valuable gifts, in addition to all the freewill offerings. ⁷Moreover, King Cyrus brought out the articles belonging to the temple of the LORD, which Nebuchadnezzar had carried away from Jerusalem and had placed in the temple of his god.ᵃ ⁸Cyrus king of Persia had them brought by Mithredath the treasurer, who counted them out to Sheshbazzar the prince of Judah.

9 This was the inventory:

gold dishes	30
silver dishes	1,000
silver pansᵇ	29
¹⁰ gold bowls	30
matching silver bowls	410
other articles	1,000

11 In all, there were 5,400 articles of gold and of silver. Sheshbazzar brought all these along when the exiles came up from Babylon to Jerusalem.

The List of the Exiles Who Returned

2 Now these are the people of the province who came up from the captivity of the exiles, whom Nebuchadnezzar king of Babylon had taken captive to Babylon (they returned to Jerusalem and Judah, each to his own town, ²in company with Zerubbabel, Jeshua, Nehemiah, Seraiah, Reelaiah, Mordecai, Bilshan, Mispar, Bigvai, Rehum and Baanah):

The list of the men of the people of Israel:

³ the descendants of Parosh	2,172
⁴ of Shephatiah	372
⁵ of Arah	775
⁶ of Pahath-Moab (through the line of Jeshua and Joab)	2,812
⁷ of Elam	1,254
⁸ of Zattu	945

The Kingdoms of This World

EZRA 1:1,5

While we are accustomed to looking for God's hand in the details of our daily lives, we sometimes fail to see God working out his purposes among the nations of the world. Here, at the very beginning of the book, we are alerted to the fact that God "moved the heart" of a world leader.

Today, watch the news broadcast or read the newspaper and list the world leaders whose names are prominent. Keep their names before you as you pray this week and offer each of them to God's care. Pray that they will be open to God's leading. Listen for God's leading in your prayer. What does God wish for these leaders? What does God want you to pray for when you hold the nations of the world before God?

See Meeting God in Prayer

Generation to Generation

EZRA 2:36–61

Through the long years of exile, the Hebrew people did not lose their identity or forget their fathers and mothers in the faith. Their commitment to remember those who served God was especially strong. Priests, Levites, temple servants, Solomon's servants—the people recorded their names and remembered how they had served.

If you come from a family that has been faithful to God for generations, how did your family maintain that tradition? What special beliefs and understandings were prevalent in your family? Do you remember things your parents and grandparents did or said to help preserve your family's worship of God? If you are the first in your family to worship God, what can you do to establish an allegiance to God that will last for generations?

See Meeting God in Community

[9] of Zaccai	760
[10] of Bani	642
[11] of Bebai	623
[12] of Azgad	1,222
[13] of Adonikam	666
[14] of Bigvai	2,056
[15] of Adin	454
[16] of Ater (through Hezekiah)	98
[17] of Bezai	323
[18] of Jorah	112
[19] of Hashum	223
[20] of Gibbar	95
[21] the men of Bethlehem	123
[22] of Netophah	56
[23] of Anathoth	128
[24] of Azmaveth	42
[25] of Kiriath Jearim,[a] Kephirah and Beeroth	743
[26] of Ramah and Geba	621
[27] of Micmash	122
[28] of Bethel and Ai	223
[29] of Nebo	52
[30] of Magbish	156
[31] of the other Elam	1,254
[32] of Harim	320
[33] of Lod, Hadid and Ono	725
[34] of Jericho	345
[35] of Senaah	3,630

[36] The priests:

the descendants of Jedaiah (through the family of Jeshua)	973
[37] of Immer	1,052
[38] of Pashhur	1,247
[39] of Harim	1,017

[40] The Levites:

the descendants of Jeshua and Kadmiel (through the line of Hodaviah)	74

[41] The singers:

the descendants of Asaph	128

[42] The gatekeepers of the temple:

the descendants of Shallum, Ater, Talmon, Akkub, Hatita and Shobai	139

[43] The temple servants:

the descendants of
Ziha, Hasupha, Tabbaoth,
[44] Keros, Siaha, Padon,
[45] Lebanah, Hagabah, Akkub,
[46] Hagab, Shalmai, Hanan,
[47] Giddel, Gahar, Reaiah,
[48] Rezin, Nekoda, Gazzam,
[49] Uzza, Paseah, Besai,
[50] Asnah, Meunim, Nephussim,
[51] Bakbuk, Hakupha, Harhur,

[a] 25 See Septuagint (see also Neh. 7:29); Hebrew *Kiriath Arim.*

⁵²Bazluth, Mehida, Harsha,
⁵³Barkos, Sisera, Temah,
⁵⁴Neziah and Hatipha

⁵⁵The descendants of the servants of Solomon:

the descendants of
Sotai, Hassophereth, Peruda,
⁵⁶Jaala, Darkon, Giddel,
⁵⁷Shephatiah, Hattil,
Pokereth-Hazzebaim and Ami

⁵⁸The temple servants and the descendants of
the servants of Solomon   392

⁵⁹The following came up from the towns of Tel Melah, Tel Harsha, Kerub, Addon and Immer, but they could not show that their families were descended from Israel:

⁶⁰The descendants of
Delaiah, Tobiah and Nekoda   652

⁶¹And from among the priests:

The descendants of
Hobaiah, Hakkoz and Barzillai (a man who had married a daughter of Barzillai the Gileadite and was called by that name).
⁶²These searched for their family records, but they could not find them and so were excluded from the priesthood as unclean. ⁶³The governor ordered them not to eat any of the most sacred food until there was a priest ministering with the Urim and Thummim.

⁶⁴The whole company numbered 42,360, ⁶⁵besides their 7,337 menservants and maidservants; and they also had 200 men and women singers. ⁶⁶They had 736 horses, 245 mules, ⁶⁷435 camels and 6,720 donkeys.

⁶⁸When they arrived at the house of the Lᴏʀᴅ in Jerusalem, some of the heads of the families gave freewill offerings toward the rebuilding of the house of God on its site. ⁶⁹According to their ability they gave to the treasury for this work 61,000 drachmas*ᵃ* of gold, 5,000 minas*ᵇ* of silver and 100 priestly garments.
⁷⁰The priests, the Levites, the singers, the gatekeepers and the temple servants settled in their own towns, along with some of the other people, and the rest of the Israelites settled in their towns.

Rebuilding the Altar

3 When the seventh month came and the Israelites had settled in their towns, the people assembled as one man in Jerusalem. ²Then Jeshua son of Jozadak and his fellow priests and Zerubbabel son of Shealtiel and his associates began to build the altar of the God of Israel to sacrifice burnt offerings on it, in accordance with what is written in the Law of Moses the man of God. ³Despite their fear of the peoples around them, they built the altar on its foundation and sacrificed burnt offerings on it to the Lᴏʀᴅ, both the morning and evening sacrifices. ⁴Then in accordance with

---

A Great Company of Faithful People

EZRA 2:64–69

Try to picture yourself among the vast horde of people—tired and dusty—nearing the end of a very long walk from your country of exile. You stand on tiptoe to see over the heads of the people in front of you, longing for the first glimpse of Jerusalem. Word spreads through the crowd that the heads of families are to meet at the site where the temple will be built in order to contribute to its construction. Perhaps this is the very first thing you will do, even before you go to look for your ancestral home. The crowd grows quiet as, finally in Jerusalem, everyone begins to picture a new temple and how they will again worship God in Jerusalem.

Now, try to picture the people of God gathering in your church each week. Imagine that this coming Sabbath day is the first day back for all of you after a lengthy absence. What special items might you bring? How would the leaders mark this event in a special way? What songs would you sing? What sort of prayers would you pray?

See *Meeting God in Worship*

A New Beginning

EZRA 3:10–13

The people gather for a grand celebration. They never thought this would happen—a new foundation for a new temple. The shouts of joy are loud enough to be heard far away. But astonishingly, those who remember the old temple weep just as loudly as those who shout for joy.

Every new beginning is also an occasion of loss. Something old is abandoned; something new takes its place. We cannot be sure what the future will bring. Sometimes the old things should be abandoned; the new beginning is a necessary thing.

Think back on the times in which you have made a new beginning. Make a list of these on paper. In each case, what was left behind? How did you see God's hand in your new beginning? Even in retrospect, offer each new beginning to God in prayer.

See Meeting God in Everyday Life

what is written, they celebrated the Feast of Tabernacles with the required number of burnt offerings prescribed for each day. [5]After that, they presented the regular burnt offerings, the New Moon sacrifices and the sacrifices for all the appointed sacred feasts of the LORD, as well as those brought as freewill offerings to the LORD. [6]On the first day of the seventh month they began to offer burnt offerings to the LORD, though the foundation of the LORD's temple had not yet been laid.

Rebuilding the Temple

[7]Then they gave money to the masons and carpenters, and gave food and drink and oil to the people of Sidon and Tyre, so that they would bring cedar logs by sea from Lebanon to Joppa, as authorized by Cyrus king of Persia.

[8]In the second month of the second year after their arrival at the house of God in Jerusalem, Zerubbabel son of Shealtiel, Jeshua son of Jozadak and the rest of their brothers (the priests and the Levites and all who had returned from the captivity to Jerusalem) began the work, appointing Levites twenty years of age and older to supervise the building of the house of the LORD. [9]Jeshua and his sons and brothers and Kadmiel and his sons (descendants of Hodaviah[a]) and the sons of Henadad and their sons and brothers—all Levites—joined together in supervising those working on the house of God.

[10]When the builders laid the foundation of the temple of the LORD, the priests in their vestments and with trumpets, and the Levites (the sons of Asaph) with cymbals, took their places to praise the LORD, as prescribed by David king of Israel. [11]With praise and thanksgiving they sang to the LORD:

"He is good;
his love to Israel endures forever."

And all the people gave a great shout of praise to the LORD, because the foundation of the house of the LORD was laid. [12]But many of the older priests and Levites and family heads, who had seen the former temple, wept aloud when they saw the foundation of this temple being laid, while many others shouted for joy. [13]No one could distinguish the sound of the shouts of joy from the sound of weeping, because the people made so much noise. And the sound was heard far away.

Opposition to the Rebuilding

4 When the enemies of Judah and Benjamin heard that the exiles were building a temple for the LORD, the God of Israel, [2]they came to Zerubbabel and to the heads of the families and said, "Let us help you build because, like you, we seek your God and have been sacrificing to him since the time of Esarhaddon king of Assyria, who brought us here."

[3]But Zerubbabel, Jeshua and the rest of the heads of the families of Israel answered, "You have no part with us in building a temple to our God. We alone will build it for the LORD, the God of Israel, as King Cyrus, the king of Persia, commanded us."

[4]Then the peoples around them set out to discourage the people of Judah and make them afraid to go on building.[b] [5]They hired counselors to work against them and frustrate

a 9 Hebrew Yehudah, probably a variant of Hodaviah   b 4 Or and troubled them as they built their plans during the entire reign of Cyrus king of Persia and down to the reign of Darius king of Persia.

Later Opposition Under Xerxes and Artaxerxes

[6] At the beginning of the reign of Xerxes,[a] they lodged an accusation against the people of Judah and Jerusalem.

[7] And in the days of Artaxerxes king of Persia, Bishlam, Mithredath, Tabeel and the rest of his associates wrote a letter to Artaxerxes. The letter was written in Aramaic script and in the Aramaic language.[b,c]

[8] Rehum the commanding officer and Shimshai the secretary wrote a letter against Jerusalem to Artaxerxes the king as follows:

[9] Rehum the commanding officer and Shimshai the secretary, together with the rest of their associates— the judges and officials over the men from Tripolis, Persia,[d] Erech and Babylon, the Elamites of Susa, [10] and the other people whom the great and honorable Ashurbanipal[e] deported and settled in the city of Samaria and elsewhere in Trans-Euphrates.

[11] (This is a copy of the letter they sent him.)

To King Artaxerxes,

From your servants, the men of Trans-Euphrates:

[12] The king should know that the Jews who came up to us from you have gone to Jerusalem and are rebuilding that rebellious and wicked city. They are restoring the walls and repairing the foundations.

[13] Furthermore, the king should know that if this city is built and its walls are restored, no more taxes, tribute or duty will be paid, and the royal revenues will suffer. [14] Now since we are under obligation to the palace and it is not proper for us to see the king dishonored, we are sending this message to inform the king, [15] so that a search may be made in the archives of your predecessors. In these records you will find that this city is a rebellious city, troublesome to kings and provinces, a place of rebellion from ancient times. That is why this city was destroyed. [16] We inform the king that if this city is built and its walls are restored, you will be left with nothing in Trans-Euphrates.

[17] The king sent this reply:

To Rehum the commanding officer, Shimshai the secretary and the rest of their associates living in Samaria and elsewhere in Trans-Euphrates:

Greetings.

[18] The letter you sent us has been read and translated in my presence. [19] I issued an order and a search was made, and it was found that this city has a long history of revolt against kings and has been a place of rebellion and sedition. [20] Jerusalem has had powerful kings ruling over the whole of Trans-Euphrates, and

---

Discouragement and Fear

EZRA 4:6–16

No wonder the people of Judah are discouraged and afraid (v.4). The rebuilding of the temple means everything to them. This is their defining moment, the very thing they dared to hope for during the long years in exile. They might ask themselves, "Why do these people want to stop us? Will our fondest dreams never be fulfilled?"

Sometime when you are alone and quiet, stand up and close your eyes. Imagine yourself standing beside the foundation of the yet-to-be-completed temple. Imagine the fear and discouragement of the people of God. Ask yourself the despairing questions they must have asked. Reach out and touch the massive stones of the foundation. Now remember your resource in trying times— the massive strength of God upholding you. There is a small group standing near you: What can you say to them to help restore their hope?

See Meeting God in Scripture

---

[a] 6 Hebrew *Ahasuerus*, a variant of Xerxes' Persian name   [b] 7 Or *written in Aramaic and translated*   [c] 7 The text of Ezra 4:8—6:18 is in Aramaic.   [d] 9 Or *officials, magistrates and governors over the men from*   [e] 10 Aramaic *Osnappar*, a variant of *Ashurbanipal*

Servants of God

EZRA 5:11

"Invocation is made as follows: your soul, having realized God's presence, will prostrate itself with the utmost reverence, acknowledging its unworthiness to abide before God's Sovereign Majesty; and yet knowing that God of his goodness would have you come, you must ask God for grace to serve and worship him."

—FRANCIS DE SALES,
Introduction to the Devout Life

See Meeting God in Worship

taxes, tribute and duty were paid to them. [21] Now issue an order to these men to stop work, so that this city will not be rebuilt until I so order. [22] Be careful not to neglect this matter. Why let this threat grow, to the detriment of the royal interests?

[23] As soon as the copy of the letter of King Artaxerxes was read to Rehum and Shimshai the secretary and their associates, they went immediately to the Jews in Jerusalem and compelled them by force to stop.

[24] Thus the work on the house of God in Jerusalem came to a standstill until the second year of the reign of Darius king of Persia.

Tattenai's Letter to Darius

5 Now Haggai the prophet and Zechariah the prophet, a descendant of Iddo, prophesied to the Jews in Judah and Jerusalem in the name of the God of Israel, who was over them. [2] Then Zerubbabel son of Shealtiel and Jeshua son of Jozadak set to work to rebuild the house of God in Jerusalem. And the prophets of God were with them, helping them.

[3] At that time Tattenai, governor of Trans-Euphrates, and Shethar-Bozenai and their associates went to them and asked, "Who authorized you to rebuild this temple and restore this structure?" [4] They also asked, "What are the names of the men constructing this building?"[a] [5] But the eye of their God was watching over the elders of the Jews, and they were not stopped until a report could go to Darius and his written reply be received.

[6] This is a copy of the letter that Tattenai, governor of Trans-Euphrates, and Shethar-Bozenai and their associates, the officials of Trans-Euphrates, sent to King Darius. [7] The report they sent him read as follows:

To King Darius:

Cordial greetings.

[8] The king should know that we went to the district of Judah, to the temple of the great God. The people are building it with large stones and placing the timbers in the walls. The work is being carried on with diligence and is making rapid progress under their direction.

[9] We questioned the elders and asked them, "Who authorized you to rebuild this temple and restore this structure?" [10] We also asked them their names, so that we could write down the names of their leaders for your information.

[11] This is the answer they gave us:

"We are the servants of the God of heaven and earth, and we are rebuilding the temple that was built many years ago, one that a great king of Israel built and finished. [12] But because our fathers angered the God of heaven, he handed them over to Nebuchadnezzar the Chaldean, king of Babylon, who destroyed this temple and deported the people to Babylon.

[13] "However, in the first year of Cyrus king of Babylon, King Cyrus issued a decree to rebuild this house

---

[a] 4 See Septuagint; Aramaic *We told them the names of the men constructing this building.*

of God. ¹⁴He even removed from the temple*a* of Babylon the gold and silver articles of the house of God, which Nebuchadnezzar had taken from the temple in Jerusalem and brought to the temple*a* in Babylon.

"Then King Cyrus gave them to a man named Sheshbazzar, whom he had appointed governor, ¹⁵and he told him, 'Take these articles and go and deposit them in the temple in Jerusalem. And rebuild the house of God on its site.' ¹⁶So this Sheshbazzar came and laid the foundations of the house of God in Jerusalem. From that day to the present it has been under construction but is not yet finished."

¹⁷Now if it pleases the king, let a search be made in the royal archives of Babylon to see if King Cyrus did in fact issue a decree to rebuild this house of God in Jerusalem. Then let the king send us his decision in this matter.

The Decree of Darius

6 King Darius then issued an order, and they searched in the archives stored in the treasury at Babylon. ²A scroll was found in the citadel of Ecbatana in the province of Media, and this was written on it:

Memorandum:

³In the first year of King Cyrus, the king issued a decree concerning the temple of God in Jerusalem:

Let the temple be rebuilt as a place to present sacrifices, and let its foundations be laid. It is to be ninety feet*b* high and ninety feet wide, ⁴with three courses of large stones and one of timbers. The costs are to be paid by the royal treasury. ⁵Also, the gold and silver articles of the house of God, which Nebuchadnezzar took from the temple in Jerusalem and brought to Babylon, are to be returned to their places in the temple in Jerusalem; they are to be deposited in the house of God.

⁶Now then, Tattenai, governor of Trans-Euphrates, and Shethar-Bozenai and you, their fellow officials of that province, stay away from there. ⁷Do not interfere with the work on this temple of God. Let the governor of the Jews and the Jewish elders rebuild this house of God on its site.

⁸Moreover, I hereby decree what you are to do for these elders of the Jews in the construction of this house of God:

The expenses of these men are to be fully paid out of the royal treasury, from the revenues of Trans-Euphrates, so that the work will not stop. ⁹Whatever is needed—young bulls, rams, male lambs for burnt offerings to the God of heaven, and wheat, salt, wine and oil, as requested by the priests in Jerusalem—must be given them daily without fail, ¹⁰so that they may offer sacrifices pleasing to the God of heaven and pray for the well-being of the king and his sons.

¹¹Furthermore, I decree that if anyone changes this edict, a beam is to be pulled from his house and he is to be lifted up and impaled on it. And for this crime his

---

Precious Mementos

EZRA 6:5

The Hebrew people find joy, not only in rebuilding the temple, but also in seeing all the holy objects that adorn their place of worship.

Take a camera or a sketch pad to your church (or to some other place that is holy to you) when it is empty. Take pictures of the places there that are important to you, perhaps the place where you usually sit, the communion table, a church school room, the baptismal area, the pulpit area or the wall on which hangs a piece of art. Put your pictures in a scrapbook or a journal. Thank God for these representations and pray that they will be as meaningful for others as they are for you.

See Meeting God in Worship

---

a 14 Or *palace*   *b 3* Aramaic *sixty cubits* (about 27 meters)

Celebration

EZRA 6:16

The temple is finished! The house of God has been rebuilt! What joy is in the hearts of God's people. Draw a party hat and write on it what you want to celebrate today. Celebrate with joy what God is building within you. In what areas is God rebuilding and renovating you? How can you celebrate that? What areas are still unfinished? What are the "stones and mortar" God will use to build you up?

See Meeting God in Everyday Life

house is to be made a pile of rubble. ¹²May God, who has caused his Name to dwell there, overthrow any king or people who lifts a hand to change this decree or to destroy this temple in Jerusalem.

I Darius have decreed it. Let it be carried out with diligence.

Completion and Dedication of the Temple

¹³Then, because of the decree King Darius had sent, Tattenai, governor of Trans-Euphrates, and Shethar-Bozenai and their associates carried it out with diligence. ¹⁴So the elders of the Jews continued to build and prosper under the preaching of Haggai the prophet and Zechariah, a descendant of Iddo. They finished building the temple according to the command of the God of Israel and the decrees of Cyrus, Darius and Artaxerxes, kings of Persia. ¹⁵The temple was completed on the third day of the month Adar, in the sixth year of the reign of King Darius.

¹⁶Then the people of Israel—the priests, the Levites and the rest of the exiles—celebrated the dedication of the house of God with joy. ¹⁷For the dedication of this house of God they offered a hundred bulls, two hundred rams, four hundred male lambs and, as a sin offering for all Israel, twelve male goats, one for each of the tribes of Israel. ¹⁸And they installed the priests in their divisions and the Levites in their groups for the service of God at Jerusalem, according to what is written in the Book of Moses.

The Passover

¹⁹On the fourteenth day of the first month, the exiles celebrated the Passover. ²⁰The priests and Levites had purified themselves and were all ceremonially clean. The Levites slaughtered the Passover lamb for all the exiles, for their brothers the priests and for themselves. ²¹So the Israelites who had returned from the exile ate it, together with all who had separated themselves from the unclean practices of their Gentile neighbors in order to seek the LORD, the God of Israel. ²²For seven days they celebrated with joy the Feast of Unleavened Bread, because the LORD had filled them with joy by changing the attitude of the king of Assyria, so that he assisted them in the work on the house of God, the God of Israel.

Ezra Comes to Jerusalem

7 After these things, during the reign of Artaxerxes king of Persia, Ezra son of Seraiah, the son of Azariah, the son of Hilkiah, ²the son of Shallum, the son of Zadok, the son of Ahitub, ³the son of Amariah, the son of Azariah, the son of Meraioth, ⁴the son of Zerahiah, the son of Uzzi, the son of Bukki, ⁵the son of Abishua, the son of Phinehas, the son of Eleazar, the son of Aaron the chief priest— ⁶this Ezra came up from Babylon. He was a teacher well versed in the Law of Moses, which the LORD, the God of Israel, had given. The king had granted him everything he asked, for the hand of the LORD his God was on him. ⁷Some of the Israelites, including priests, Levites, singers, gatekeepers and temple servants, also came up to Jerusalem in the seventh year of King Artaxerxes.

⁸Ezra arrived in Jerusalem in the fifth month of the seventh year of the king. ⁹He had begun his journey from Bab-

ylon on the first day of the first month, and he arrived in Jerusalem on the first day of the fifth month, for the gracious hand of his God was on him. ¹⁰For Ezra had devoted himself to the study and observance of the Law of the LORD, and to teaching its decrees and laws in Israel.

King Artaxerxes' Letter to Ezra

¹¹This is a copy of the letter King Artaxerxes had given to Ezra the priest and teacher, a man learned in matters concerning the commands and decrees of the LORD for Israel:

¹²ᵃ Artaxerxes, king of kings,

To Ezra the priest, a teacher of the Law of the God of heaven:

Greetings.

¹³Now I decree that any of the Israelites in my kingdom, including priests and Levites, who wish to go to Jerusalem with you, may go. ¹⁴You are sent by the king and his seven advisers to inquire about Judah and Jerusalem with regard to the Law of your God, which is in your hand. ¹⁵Moreover, you are to take with you the silver and gold that the king and his advisers have freely given to the God of Israel, whose dwelling is in Jerusalem, ¹⁶together with all the silver and gold you may obtain from the province of Babylon, as well as the freewill offerings of the people and priests for the temple of their God in Jerusalem. ¹⁷With this money be sure to buy bulls, rams and male lambs, together with their grain offerings and drink offerings, and sacrifice them on the altar of the temple of your God in Jerusalem.

¹⁸You and your brother Jews may then do whatever seems best with the rest of the silver and gold, in accordance with the will of your God. ¹⁹Deliver to the God of Jerusalem all the articles entrusted to you for worship in the temple of your God. ²⁰And anything else needed for the temple of your God that you may have occasion to supply, you may provide from the royal treasury.

²¹Now I, King Artaxerxes, order all the treasurers of Trans-Euphrates to provide with diligence whatever Ezra the priest, a teacher of the Law of the God of heaven, may ask of you— ²²up to a hundred talentsᵇ of silver, a hundred corsᶜ of wheat, a hundred bathsᵈ of wine, a hundred bathsᵈ of olive oil, and salt without limit. ²³Whatever the God of heaven has prescribed, let it be done with diligence for the temple of the God of heaven. Why should there be wrath against the realm of the king and of his sons? ²⁴You are also to know that you have no authority to impose taxes, tribute or duty on any of the priests, Levites, singers, gatekeepers, temple servants or other workers at this house of God.

²⁵And you, Ezra, in accordance with the wisdom of your God, which you possess, appoint magistrates and judges to administer justice to all the people of Trans-Euphrates—all who know the laws of your God. And you are to teach any who do not know them. ²⁶Who-

---

A Commission From God

EZRA 7:11–20

Ezra is a fortunate man. He has in his hand a decree in which the king commissions Ezra with a specific task. Moreover, the king has given Ezra silver and gold to accomplish his task.

What has God commissioned you to do? Find a special sheet of handmade paper or one that looks like parchment. With any pen that will make bold letters, write out a decree from God to yourself. What has God decreed for your life? What specific jobs does God intend for you to perform? What means has God provided you with to accomplish his will?

See Meeting God in Service

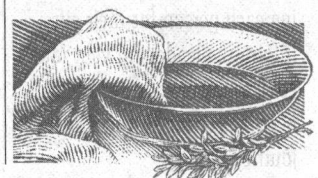

ᵃ 12 The text of Ezra 7:12–26 is in Aramaic.   ᵇ 22 That is, about 3 3/4 tons (about 3.4 metric tons)   ᶜ 22 That is, probably about 600 bushels (about 22 kiloliters)   ᵈ 22 That is, probably about 600 gallons (about 2.2 kiloliters)

Leaders of Faith

EZRA 8:16

In this recital of names we may lose sight of the real people to whom the names belong. Some are known as leaders and others are known as men of learning. In such a close-knit community, the talents of each leader and scholar are well known.

Who are the leaders in your community of faith? Who are the people others go to for advice? Are there people whose native gifts or life experiences have made them especially wise? Uphold these people in prayer. Write down their names (perhaps in a prayer journal, if you keep one) and pray for each person specifically. Make a point of encouraging and thanking each person for their gifts. Inform the leaders in your faith community of those who have been a blessing to you in your journey.

See *Meeting God in Community*

ever does not obey the law of your God and the law of the king must surely be punished by death, banishment, confiscation of property, or imprisonment.

²⁷Praise be to the LORD, the God of our fathers, who has put it into the king's heart to bring honor to the house of the LORD in Jerusalem in this way ²⁸and who has extended his good favor to me before the king and his advisers and all the king's powerful officials. Because the hand of the LORD my God was on me, I took courage and gathered leading men from Israel to go up with me.

List of the Family Heads Returning With Ezra

8 These are the family heads and those registered with them who came up with me from Babylon during the reign of King Artaxerxes:

²of the descendants of Phinehas, Gershom;
of the descendants of Ithamar, Daniel;
of the descendants of David, Hattush ³of the descendants of Shecaniah;

of the descendants of Parosh, Zechariah, and with him were registered 150 men;
⁴of the descendants of Pahath-Moab, Eliehoenai son of Zerahiah, and with him 200 men;
⁵of the descendants of Zattu,ᵃ Shecaniah son of Jahaziel, and with him 300 men;
⁶of the descendants of Adin, Ebed son of Jonathan, and with him 50 men;
⁷of the descendants of Elam, Jeshaiah son of Athaliah, and with him 70 men;
⁸of the descendants of Shephatiah, Zebadiah son of Michael, and with him 80 men;
⁹of the descendants of Joab, Obadiah son of Jehiel, and with him 218 men;
¹⁰of the descendants of Bani,ᵇ Shelomith son of Josiphiah, and with him 160 men;
¹¹of the descendants of Bebai, Zechariah son of Bebai, and with him 28 men;
¹²of the descendants of Azgad, Johanan son of Hakkatan, and with him 110 men;
¹³of the descendants of Adonikam, the last ones, whose names were Eliphelet, Jeuel and Shemaiah, and with them 60 men;
¹⁴of the descendants of Bigvai, Uthai and Zaccur, and with them 70 men.

The Return to Jerusalem

¹⁵I assembled them at the canal that flows toward Ahava, and we camped there three days. When I checked among the people and the priests, I found no Levites there. ¹⁶So I summoned Eliezer, Ariel, Shemaiah, Elnathan, Jarib, Elnathan, Nathan, Zechariah and Meshullam, who were leaders, and Joiarib and Elnathan, who were men of learning, ¹⁷and I sent them to Iddo, the leader in Casiphia. I told them what to say to Iddo and his kinsmen, the temple servants in Casiphia, so that they might bring attendants to us for the house of our God. ¹⁸Because the gracious hand of our God was on us,

ᵃ5 Some Septuagint manuscripts (also 1 Esdras 8:32); Hebrew does not have *Zattu*.   ᵇ10 Some Septuagint manuscripts (also 1 Esdras 8:36); Hebrew does not have *Bani*.

they brought us Sherebiah, a capable man, from the descendants of Mahli son of Levi, the son of Israel, and Sherebiah's sons and brothers, 18 men; ¹⁹and Hashabiah, together with Jeshaiah from the descendants of Merari, and his brothers and nephews, 20 men. ²⁰They also brought 220 of the temple servants—a body that David and the officials had established to assist the Levites. All were registered by name.

²¹There, by the Ahava Canal, I proclaimed a fast, so that we might humble ourselves before our God and ask him for a safe journey for us and our children, with all our possessions. ²²I was ashamed to ask the king for soldiers and horsemen to protect us from enemies on the road, because we had told the king, "The gracious hand of our God is on everyone who looks to him, but his great anger is against all who forsake him." ²³So we fasted and petitioned our God about this, and he answered our prayer.

²⁴Then I set apart twelve of the leading priests, together with Sherebiah, Hashabiah and ten of their brothers, ²⁵and I weighed out to them the offering of silver and gold and the articles that the king, his advisers, his officials and all Israel present there had donated for the house of our God. ²⁶I weighed out to them 650 talents*a* of silver, silver articles weighing 100 talents,*b* 100 talents*b* of gold, ²⁷20 bowls of gold valued at 1,000 darics,*c* and two fine articles of polished bronze, as precious as gold.

²⁸I said to them, "You as well as these articles are consecrated to the LORD. The silver and gold are a freewill offering to the LORD, the God of your fathers. ²⁹Guard them carefully until you weigh them out in the chambers of the house of the LORD in Jerusalem before the leading priests and the Levites and the family heads of Israel." ³⁰Then the priests and Levites received the silver and gold and sacred articles that had been weighed out to be taken to the house of our God in Jerusalem.

³¹On the twelfth day of the first month we set out from the Ahava Canal to go to Jerusalem. The hand of our God was on us, and he protected us from enemies and bandits along the way. ³²So we arrived in Jerusalem, where we rested three days.

³³On the fourth day, in the house of our God, we weighed out the silver and gold and the sacred articles into the hands of Meremoth son of Uriah, the priest. Eleazar son of Phinehas was with him, and so were the Levites Jozabad son of Jeshua and Noadiah son of Binnui. ³⁴Everything was accounted for by number and weight, and the entire weight was recorded at that time.

³⁵Then the exiles who had returned from captivity sacrificed burnt offerings to the God of Israel: twelve bulls for all Israel, ninety-six rams, seventy-seven male lambs and, as a sin offering, twelve male goats. All this was a burnt offering to the LORD. ³⁶They also delivered the king's orders to the royal satraps and to the governors of Trans-Euphrates, who then gave assistance to the people and to the house of God.

Ezra's Prayer About Intermarriage

9 After these things had been done, the leaders came to me and said, "The people of Israel, including the priests

---

A Fast Before the Lord

EZRA 8:21–23

When Ezra stops the whole procession and declares a fast, he is not initiating an unfamiliar practice. Fasting has a long tradition; for thousands of years many have found fasting to be a useful, even powerful, spiritual exercise. Fasting is an act that declares that we rely on God—not on ourselves.

Fasting need not only be abstinence from food. We may decide for a period of time to abstain from other consumer goods as an offering to God. Try to think of several things you might do without for a period of time, perhaps rich or sweet foods, television or maybe all media, some luxury items, forms of entertainment or a new item of clothing. Then plan for a period of time—perhaps a week or a month—when you will do without these things. Each day during that period, turn your attention away from yourself and toward the One who loves you.

See *Meeting God in Everyday Life*

---

a 26 That is, about 25 tons (about 22 metric tons)   *b 26* That is, about 3 3/4 tons (about 3.4 metric tons)   *c 27* That is, about 19 pounds (about 8.5 kilograms)

617

Ashamed in God's Presence

EZRA 9:5–15

Ezra uses an inclusive "we" when he confesses the people's iniquities before God. Ezra so identifies with his people that he feels complicity in their guilt. Whether our guilt is communal or individual, the common experience of humanity is the need for forgiveness.

Painful as it may be, recall a time when you felt keenly ashamed. A good time to do this is during some strenuous activity such as gardening or exercising. Let the dirt and sweat symbolize your guilt. Then take a shower or a bath and think of the soap and warm water as representative of the forgiveness of God. Experience God's cleansing love as you picture your faults and shortcomings disappearing down the drain.

See Meeting God in Everyday Life

and the Levites, have not kept themselves separate from the neighboring peoples with their detestable practices, like those of the Canaanites, Hittites, Perizzites, Jebusites, Ammonites, Moabites, Egyptians and Amorites. ²They have taken some of their daughters as wives for themselves and their sons, and have mingled the holy race with the peoples around them. And the leaders and officials have led the way in this unfaithfulness."

³When I heard this, I tore my tunic and cloak, pulled hair from my head and beard and sat down appalled. ⁴Then everyone who trembled at the words of the God of Israel gathered around me because of this unfaithfulness of the exiles. And I sat there appalled until the evening sacrifice.

⁵Then, at the evening sacrifice, I rose from my self-abasement, with my tunic and cloak torn, and fell on my knees with my hands spread out to the LORD my God ⁶and prayed:

"O my God, I am too ashamed and disgraced to lift up my face to you, my God, because our sins are higher than our heads and our guilt has reached to the heavens. ⁷From the days of our forefathers until now, our guilt has been great. Because of our sins, we and our kings and our priests have been subjected to the sword and captivity, to pillage and humiliation at the hand of foreign kings, as it is today.

⁸"But now, for a brief moment, the LORD our God has been gracious in leaving us a remnant and giving us a firm place in his sanctuary, and so our God gives light to our eyes and a little relief in our bondage. ⁹Though we are slaves, our God has not deserted us in our bondage. He has shown us kindness in the sight of the kings of Persia: He has granted us new life to rebuild the house of our God and repair its ruins, and he has given us a wall of protection in Judah and Jerusalem.

¹⁰"But now, O our God, what can we say after this? For we have disregarded the commands ¹¹you gave through your servants the prophets when you said: 'The land you are entering to possess is a land polluted by the corruption of its peoples. By their detestable practices they have filled it with their impurity from one end to the other. ¹²Therefore, do not give your daughters in marriage to their sons or take their daughters for your sons. Do not seek a treaty of friendship with them at any time, that you may be strong and eat the good things of the land and leave it to your children as an everlasting inheritance.'

¹³"What has happened to us is a result of our evil deeds and our great guilt, and yet, our God, you have punished us less than our sins have deserved and have given us a remnant like this. ¹⁴Shall we again break your commands and intermarry with the peoples who commit such detestable practices? Would you not be angry enough with us to destroy us, leaving us no remnant or survivor? ¹⁵O LORD, God of Israel, you are righteous! We are left this day as a remnant. Here we are before you in our guilt, though because of it not one of us can stand in your presence."

The People's Confession of Sin

10 While Ezra was praying and confessing, weeping and throwing himself down before the house of God, a large crowd of Israelites—men, women and children—gathered around him. They too wept bitterly. ²Then Shecaniah son of Jehiel, one of the descendants of Elam, said to Ezra, "We have been unfaithful to our God by marrying foreign women from the peoples around us. But in spite of this, there is still hope for Israel. ³Now let us make a covenant before our God to send away all these women and their children, in accordance with the counsel of my lord and of those who fear the commands of our God. Let it be done according to the Law. ⁴Rise up; this matter is in your hands. We will support you, so take courage and do it."

⁵So Ezra rose up and put the leading priests and Levites and all Israel under oath to do what had been suggested. And they took the oath. ⁶Then Ezra withdrew from before the house of God and went to the room of Jehohanan son of Eliashib. While he was there, he ate no food and drank no water, because he continued to mourn over the unfaithfulness of the exiles.

⁷A proclamation was then issued throughout Judah and Jerusalem for all the exiles to assemble in Jerusalem. ⁸Anyone who failed to appear within three days would forfeit all his property, in accordance with the decision of the officials and elders, and would himself be expelled from the assembly of the exiles.

⁹Within the three days, all the men of Judah and Benjamin had gathered in Jerusalem. And on the twentieth day of the ninth month, all the people were sitting in the square before the house of God, greatly distressed by the occasion and because of the rain. ¹⁰Then Ezra the priest stood up and said to them, "You have been unfaithful; you have married foreign women, adding to Israel's guilt. ¹¹Now make confession to the LORD, the God of your fathers, and do his will. Separate yourselves from the peoples around you and from your foreign wives."

¹²The whole assembly responded with a loud voice: "You are right! We must do as you say. ¹³But there are many people here and it is the rainy season; so we cannot stand outside. Besides, this matter cannot be taken care of in a day or two, because we have sinned greatly in this thing. ¹⁴Let our officials act for the whole assembly. Then let everyone in our towns who has married a foreign woman come at a set time, along with the elders and judges of each town, until the fierce anger of our God in this matter is turned away from us." ¹⁵Only Jonathan son of Asahel and Jahzeiah son of Tikvah, supported by Meshullam and Shabbethai the Levite, opposed this.

¹⁶So the exiles did as was proposed. Ezra the priest selected men who were family heads, one from each family division, and all of them designated by name. On the first day of the tenth month they sat down to investigate the cases, ¹⁷and by the first day of the first month they finished dealing with all the men who had married foreign women.

Those Guilty of Intermarriage

¹⁸Among the descendants of the priests, the following had married foreign women:

From the descendants of Jeshua son of Jozadak, and his brothers: Maaseiah, Eliezer, Jarib and Gedaliah. ¹⁹(They all gave their hands in pledge to put away

Grieving God's Heart

EZRA 10:6

Ezra's grief represents God's grief as the prophet mourns the self-destructive failures of the people. We all too easily slip into thinking that God is distant, unsympathetic, unemotional. Perhaps we rarely stop to think that we individually and collectively might be breaking God's heart. As you take an inner inventory, what thoughts and behaviors might break God's heart? Why do you think God grieves over them? Now consider your family, your faith community and your nation. What collective acts and assumptions of these groups might cause God grief? In both arenas, personal and public, what steps can we take to warm God's heart?

Hard Choices

EZRA 10:44

Despite the moral ambiguity of the actions described in this verse (and the preceding chapters), the fact remains that no such bitter and difficult choices would have been necessary if the Hebrew men had obeyed the law of God in the first place. The difficulty of restoring faithfulness is complicated by the snowball effect: Bad decisions lead to other bad decisions; sooner or later hard choices have to be made.

Think of three or four major decisions in your life, both good and bad. On an unlined piece of paper, draw a "family tree" for each one. Show on this diagram how your decisions resulted from earlier choices. There may be more than one line of choices leading to each decision. Try to trace this process to the present time. Now offer all this to God. For those decisions that have led to difficult times, ask God for ways to redeem the situation. For decisions that in retrospect were wise ones, thank God for wisdom and understanding.

See Meeting God in Everyday Life

their wives, and for their guilt they each presented a ram from the flock as a guilt offering.)

²⁰ From the descendants of Immer:
Hanani and Zebadiah.

²¹ From the descendants of Harim:
Maaseiah, Elijah, Shemaiah, Jehiel and Uzziah.

²² From the descendants of Pashhur:
Elioenai, Maaseiah, Ishmael, Nethanel, Jozabad and Elasah.

²³ Among the Levites:
Jozabad, Shimei, Kelaiah (that is, Kelita), Pethahiah, Judah and Eliezer.

²⁴ From the singers:
Eliashib.
From the gatekeepers:
Shallum, Telem and Uri.

²⁵ And among the other Israelites:
From the descendants of Parosh:
Ramiah, Izziah, Malkijah, Mijamin, Eleazar, Malkijah and Benaiah.

²⁶ From the descendants of Elam:
Mattaniah, Zechariah, Jehiel, Abdi, Jeremoth and Elijah.

²⁷ From the descendants of Zattu:
Elioenai, Eliashib, Mattaniah, Jeremoth, Zabad and Aziza.

²⁸ From the descendants of Bebai:
Jehohanan, Hananiah, Zabbai and Athlai.

²⁹ From the descendants of Bani:
Meshullam, Malluch, Adaiah, Jashub, Sheal and Jeremoth.

³⁰ From the descendants of Pahath-Moab:
Adna, Kelal, Benaiah, Maaseiah, Mattaniah, Bezalel, Binnui and Manasseh.

³¹ From the descendants of Harim:
Eliezer, Ishijah, Malkijah, Shemaiah, Shimeon, ³²Benjamin, Malluch and Shemariah.

³³ From the descendants of Hashum:
Mattenai, Mattattah, Zabad, Eliphelet, Jeremai, Manasseh and Shimei.

³⁴ From the descendants of Bani:
Maadai, Amram, Uel, ³⁵Benaiah, Bedeiah, Keluhi, ³⁶Vaniah, Meremoth, Eliashib, ³⁷Mattaniah, Mattenai and Jaasu.

³⁸ From the descendants of Binnui:ᵃ
Shimei, ³⁹Shelemiah, Nathan, Adaiah, ⁴⁰Macnadebai, Shashai, Sharai, ⁴¹Azarel, Shelemiah, Shemariah, ⁴²Shallum, Amariah and Joseph.

⁴³ From the descendants of Nebo:
Jeiel, Mattithiah, Zabad, Zebina, Jaddai, Joel and Benaiah.

⁴⁴ All these had married foreign women, and some of them had children by these wives.ᵇ

ᵃ 37,38 See Septuagint (also 1 Esdras 9:34); Hebrew *Jaasu* ³⁸*and Bani and Binnui.*   ᵇ 44 Or *and they sent them away with their children*

NEHEMIAH

Remember Who You Are

KEY VERSES:

Then I said to them, "You see the trouble we are in: Jerusalem lies in ruins, and its gates have been burned with fire. Come, let us rebuild the wall of Jerusalem, and we will no longer be in disgrace." I also told them about the gracious hand of my God upon me and what the king had said to me. They replied, "Let us start rebuilding." So they began this good work.—Nehemiah 2:17–18

The task that Nehemiah and his people faced was formidable. With limited resources, and in the midst of political pressure and sabotage, they began to rebuild the walls of their beloved city Jerusalem. Under the guidance of Ezra, they had reconstructed the temple, but the challenges of rebuilding had demoralized them. In this book, we see how Nehemiah's reliance on and faith in God helped him lead his people to successfully accomplish a task and restore his people's courage and renew their respect and appreciation for God's Word. Nehemiah was a man of action, but he was also a man of deep faith. Because he lived in relationship with the all-knowing God, he knew when to pray and when to act.

In the book of Nehemiah, we find more than an historical account of God's people at a certain point in time; we discover a reminder that we are partners with God. We are not exiles recently returned to our homeland. Our destroyed city walls do not need to be rebuilt. Yet we are called just as surely to be builders of faithful lives, relationships and communities. If you ever face these tasks with feelings of being overwhelmed or inadequate, you'll be able to identify with Nehemiah. Just as surely as he struggled with issues of motivation, fatigue and criticism, so too do we today. But this book also offers inspiration to lean on the living God as we go about our building tasks.

> "God is our creator. God made us in his image and likeness. Therefore we are creators. [God] gave us a garden to till and cultivate. We became co-creators by our responsible acts, whether in bringing forth children, or producing food, furniture or clothing. The joy of creativeness should be ours."
>
> —DOROTHY DAY,
> *The Long Loneliness*

On Our Knees Before God

NEHEMIAH 1:3–11

Upon hearing the "state of the union" of his beloved Jerusalem and her people, Nehemiah went into mourning. What would the future hold for those who had survived exile? Nehemiah's faith in God's loving covenant prompted him to offer a prayer of confession for himself and all the Israelites because he was sure of his future with God. Think about your own congregation or denomination. Have there been times when you fell on your knees before God, seeking corporate forgiveness or renewal? Did you feel God was attentive to your prayer? Give thanks to God, who shows us our wrongdoing but always stands ready to hear our prayers of repentance and pronounce his forgiveness.

See *Meeting God in Prayer*

Nehemiah's Prayer

1 The words of Nehemiah son of Hacaliah:

In the month of Kislev in the twentieth year, while I was in the citadel of Susa, ²Hanani, one of my brothers, came from Judah with some other men, and I questioned them about the Jewish remnant that survived the exile, and also about Jerusalem.

³They said to me, "Those who survived the exile and are back in the province are in great trouble and disgrace. The wall of Jerusalem is broken down, and its gates have been burned with fire."

⁴When I heard these things, I sat down and wept. For some days I mourned and fasted and prayed before the God of heaven. ⁵Then I said:

"O Lord, God of heaven, the great and awesome God, who keeps his covenant of love with those who love him and obey his commands, ⁶let your ear be attentive and your eyes open to hear the prayer your servant is praying before you day and night for your servants, the people of Israel. I confess the sins we Israelites, including myself and my father's house, have committed against you. ⁷We have acted very wickedly toward you. We have not obeyed the commands, decrees and laws you gave your servant Moses.

⁸"Remember the instruction you gave your servant Moses, saying, 'If you are unfaithful, I will scatter you among the nations, ⁹but if you return to me and obey my commands, then even if your exiled people are at the farthest horizon, I will gather them from there and bring them to the place I have chosen as a dwelling for my Name.'

¹⁰"They are your servants and your people, whom you redeemed by your great strength and your mighty hand. ¹¹O Lord, let your ear be attentive to the prayer of this your servant and to the prayer of your servants who delight in revering your name. Give your servant success today by granting him favor in the presence of this man."

I was cupbearer to the king.

Artaxerxes Sends Nehemiah to Jerusalem

2 In the month of Nisan in the twentieth year of King Artaxerxes, when wine was brought for him, I took the wine and gave it to the king. I had not been sad in his presence before; ²so the king asked me, "Why does your face look so sad when you are not ill? This can be nothing but sadness of heart."

I was very much afraid, ³but I said to the king, "May the king live forever! Why should my face not look sad when the city where my fathers are buried lies in ruins, and its gates have been destroyed by fire?"

⁴The king said to me, "What is it you want?"

Then I prayed to the God of heaven, ⁵and I answered the king, "If it pleases the king and if your servant has found favor in his sight, let him send me to the city in Judah where my fathers are buried so that I can rebuild it."

⁶Then the king, with the queen sitting beside him, asked

me, "How long will your journey take, and when will you get back?" It pleased the king to send me; so I set a time.

[7] I also said to him, "If it pleases the king, may I have letters to the governors of Trans-Euphrates, so that they will provide me safe-conduct until I arrive in Judah? [8] And may I have a letter to Asaph, keeper of the king's forest, so he will give me timber to make beams for the gates of the citadel by the temple and for the city wall and for the residence I will occupy?" And because the gracious hand of my God was upon me, the king granted my requests. [9] So I went to the governors of Trans-Euphrates and gave them the king's letters. The king had also sent army officers and cavalry with me.

[10] When Sanballat the Horonite and Tobiah the Ammonite official heard about this, they were very much disturbed that someone had come to promote the welfare of the Israelites.

Nehemiah Inspects Jerusalem's Walls

[11] I went to Jerusalem, and after staying there three days [12] I set out during the night with a few men. I had not told anyone what my God had put in my heart to do for Jerusalem. There were no mounts with me except the one I was riding on.

[13] By night I went out through the Valley Gate toward the Jackal[a] Well and the Dung Gate, examining the walls of Jerusalem, which had been broken down, and its gates, which had been destroyed by fire. [14] Then I moved on toward the Fountain Gate and the King's Pool, but there was not enough room for my mount to get through; [15] so I went up the valley by night, examining the wall. Finally, I turned back and reentered through the Valley Gate. [16] The officials did not know where I had gone or what I was doing, because as yet I had said nothing to the Jews or the priests or nobles or officials or any others who would be doing the work.

[17] Then I said to them, "You see the trouble we are in: Jerusalem lies in ruins, and its gates have been burned with fire. Come, let us rebuild the wall of Jerusalem, and we will no longer be in disgrace." [18] I also told them about the gracious hand of my God upon me and what the king had said to me.

They replied, "Let us start rebuilding." So they began this good work.

[19] But when Sanballat the Horonite, Tobiah the Ammonite official and Geshem the Arab heard about it, they mocked and ridiculed us. "What is this you are doing?" they asked. "Are you rebelling against the king?"

[20] I answered them by saying, "The God of heaven will give us success. We his servants will start rebuilding, but as for you, you have no share in Jerusalem or any claim or historic right to it."

Builders of the Wall

3 Eliashib the high priest and his fellow priests went to work and rebuilt the Sheep Gate. They dedicated it and set its doors in place, building as far as the Tower of the Hundred, which they dedicated, and as far as the Tower of

---

God's Gracious Hand

NEHEMIAH 2:17–18

Nehemiah's message is straightforward: We're in trouble; Jerusalem is in ruins; we need to rebuild.

We've all had times when our own lives have crumbled and fallen into ruins: A marriage has failed or a friendship has ended; we have lost a job, have had to claim bankruptcy, have moved to a new city or have lost a loved one. Using paper and markers or paints, draw a time line of your life, designating the times when you have needed to rebuild your life. Were you able to feel, as Nehemiah did, "the gracious hand of [your] God upon [you]?" On your time line, draw a small hand to note those times when you especially felt God's presence. As you look at your sketch, how often did God's healing presence coincide with rebuilding? If your life is in ruins right now, offer it to God with your palms open and your hands outstretched. Ask God to place his gracious hand upon you today.

See *Meeting God in Everyday Life*

God's Beautiful Work

NEHEMIAH 3:3–19

"There is something very beautiful in work which is well and precisely done. It is a participation in the activity of God, who makes all things well and wisely, beautiful to the last detail."
—JEAN VANIER,
Community and Growth

See *Meeting God in Everyday Life*

Hananel. [2]The men of Jericho built the adjoining section, and Zaccur son of Imri built next to them.

[3]The Fish Gate was rebuilt by the sons of Hassenaah. They laid its beams and put its doors and bolts and bars in place. [4]Meremoth son of Uriah, the son of Hakkoz, repaired the next section. Next to him Meshullam son of Berekiah, the son of Meshezabel, made repairs, and next to him Zadok son of Baana also made repairs. [5]The next section was repaired by the men of Tekoa, but their nobles would not put their shoulders to the work under their supervisors.[a]

[6]The Jeshanah[b] Gate was repaired by Joiada son of Paseah and Meshullam son of Besodeiah. They laid its beams and put its doors and bolts and bars in place. [7]Next to them, repairs were made by men from Gibeon and Mizpah—Melatiah of Gibeon and Jadon of Meronoth—places under the authority of the governor of Trans-Euphrates. [8]Uzziel son of Harhaiah, one of the goldsmiths, repaired the next section; and Hananiah, one of the perfume-makers, made repairs next to that. They restored[c] Jerusalem as far as the Broad Wall. [9]Rephaiah son of Hur, ruler of a half-district of Jerusalem, repaired the next section. [10]Adjoining this, Jedaiah son of Harumaph made repairs opposite his house, and Hattush son of Hashabneiah made repairs next to him. [11]Malkijah son of Harim and Hasshub son of Pahath-Moab repaired another section and the Tower of the Ovens. [12]Shallum son of Hallohesh, ruler of a half-district of Jerusalem, repaired the next section with the help of his daughters.

[13]The Valley Gate was repaired by Hanun and the residents of Zanoah. They rebuilt it and put its doors and bolts and bars in place. They also repaired five hundred yards[d] of the wall as far as the Dung Gate.

[14]The Dung Gate was repaired by Malkijah son of Recab, ruler of the district of Beth Hakkerem. He rebuilt it and put its doors and bolts and bars in place.

[15]The Fountain Gate was repaired by Shallun son of Col-Hozeh, ruler of the district of Mizpah. He rebuilt it, roofing it over and putting its doors and bolts and bars in place. He also repaired the wall of the Pool of Siloam,[e] by the King's Garden, as far as the steps going down from the City of David. [16]Beyond him, Nehemiah son of Azbuk, ruler of a half-district of Beth Zur, made repairs up to a point opposite the tombs[f] of David, as far as the artificial pool and the House of the Heroes. [17]Next to him, the repairs were made by the Levites under Rehum son of Bani. Beside him, Hashabiah, ruler of half the district of Keilah, carried out repairs for his district. [18]Next to him, the repairs were made by their countrymen under Binnui[g] son of Henadad, ruler of the other half-district of Keilah. [19]Next to him, Ezer son of Jeshua, ruler of Mizpah, repaired another section, from a point facing the ascent to the armory as far as the angle. [20]Next to him, Bar-

---

[a] 5 Or *their Lord* or *the governor*   [b] 6 Or *Old*   [c] 8 Or *They left out part of*
[d] 13 Hebrew *a thousand cubits* (about 450 meters)   [e] 15 Hebrew *Shelah,* a variant of *Shiloah,* that is, Siloam   [f] 16 Hebrew; Septuagint, some Vulgate manuscripts and Syriac *tomb*   [g] 18 Two Hebrew manuscripts and Syriac (see also Septuagint and verse 24); most Hebrew manuscripts *Bavvai*

uch son of Zabbai zealously repaired another section, from the angle to the entrance of the house of Eliashib the high priest. ²¹Next to him, Meremoth son of Uriah, the son of Hakkoz, repaired another section, from the entrance of Eliashib's house to the end of it.

²²The repairs next to him were made by the priests from the surrounding region. ²³Beyond them, Benjamin and Hasshub made repairs in front of their house; and next to them, Azariah son of Maaseiah, the son of Ananiah, made repairs beside his house. ²⁴Next to him, Binnui son of Henadad repaired another section, from Azariah's house to the angle and the corner, ²⁵and Palal son of Uzai worked opposite the angle and the tower projecting from the upper palace near the court of the guard. Next to him, Pedaiah son of Parosh ²⁶and the temple servants living on the hill of Ophel made repairs up to a point opposite the Water Gate toward the east and the projecting tower. ²⁷Next to them, the men of Tekoa repaired another section, from the great projecting tower to the wall of Ophel.

²⁸Above the Horse Gate, the priests made repairs, each in front of his own house. ²⁹Next to them, Zadok son of Immer made repairs opposite his house. Next to him, Shemaiah son of Shecaniah, the guard at the East Gate, made repairs. ³⁰Next to him, Hananiah son of Shelemiah, and Hanun, the sixth son of Zalaph, repaired another section. Next to them, Meshullam son of Berekiah made repairs opposite his living quarters. ³¹Next to him, Malkijah, one of the goldsmiths, made repairs as far as the house of the temple servants and the merchants, opposite the Inspection Gate, and as far as the room above the corner; ³²and between the room above the corner and the Sheep Gate the goldsmiths and merchants made repairs.

Opposition to the Rebuilding

4 When Sanballat heard that we were rebuilding the wall, he became angry and was greatly incensed. He ridiculed the Jews, ²and in the presence of his associates and the army of Samaria, he said, "What are those feeble Jews doing? Will they restore their wall? Will they offer sacrifices? Will they finish in a day? Can they bring the stones back to life from those heaps of rubble—burned as they are?"

³Tobiah the Ammonite, who was at his side, said, "What they are building—if even a fox climbed up on it, he would break down their wall of stones!"

⁴Hear us, O our God, for we are despised. Turn their insults back on their own heads. Give them over as plunder in a land of captivity. ⁵Do not cover up their guilt or blot out their sins from your sight, for they have thrown insults in the face of[a] the builders.

⁶So we rebuilt the wall till all of it reached half its height, for the people worked with all their heart.

⁷But when Sanballat, Tobiah, the Arabs, the Ammonites and the men of Ashdod heard that the repairs to Jerusalem's walls had gone ahead and that the gaps were being closed, they were very angry. ⁸They all plotted together to come and fight against Jerusalem and stir up trou-

Remembering God Brings Courage

NEHEMIAH 4:1–18

Read this story slowly and meditatively. As you read, imagine that you are a laborer or worker-guard rebuilding the wall. What do you see? What do you hear? How do the stones feel beneath your hands? How well do you work with a sword in your belt? How do you respond to the insults and threats of those who oppose the work? Do Nehemiah's words, "Remember the Lord, who is great and awesome," give you courage?

See Meeting God in Scripture

Symbols of Our Work in God

NEHEMIAH 4:19–20

When the trumpet sounds, every worker is reminded of the God who has brought them together, even though they work on separate parts of the wall. Whom do you consider your work team for God? What symbolizes the way you were brought together? Think of a sound, logo, smell or symbol of your common life in God. It might be the communion chalice, a denominational logo, the view of your church doors, a hammer and saw, or the smell of incense. When you have something in mind, take a few minutes to meditate on the image, giving thanks for the opportunity to work with others for God.

See Meeting God in Service

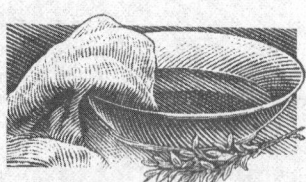

ble against it. ⁹But we prayed to our God and posted a guard day and night to meet this threat.

¹⁰Meanwhile, the people in Judah said, "The strength of the laborers is giving out, and there is so much rubble that we cannot rebuild the wall."

¹¹Also our enemies said, "Before they know it or see us, we will be right there among them and will kill them and put an end to the work."

¹²Then the Jews who lived near them came and told us ten times over, "Wherever you turn, they will attack us."

¹³Therefore I stationed some of the people behind the lowest points of the wall at the exposed places, posting them by families, with their swords, spears and bows. ¹⁴After I looked things over, I stood up and said to the nobles, the officials and the rest of the people, "Don't be afraid of them. Remember the Lord, who is great and awesome, and fight for your brothers, your sons and your daughters, your wives and your homes."

¹⁵When our enemies heard that we were aware of their plot and that God had frustrated it, we all returned to the wall, each to his own work.

¹⁶From that day on, half of my men did the work, while the other half were equipped with spears, shields, bows and armor. The officers posted themselves behind all the people of Judah ¹⁷who were building the wall. Those who carried materials did their work with one hand and held a weapon in the other, ¹⁸and each of the builders wore his sword at his side as he worked. But the man who sounded the trumpet stayed with me.

¹⁹Then I said to the nobles, the officials and the rest of the people, "The work is extensive and spread out, and we are widely separated from each other along the wall. ²⁰Wherever you hear the sound of the trumpet, join us there. Our God will fight for us!"

²¹So we continued the work with half the men holding spears, from the first light of dawn till the stars came out. ²²At that time I also said to the people, "Have every man and his helper stay inside Jerusalem at night, so they can serve us as guards by night and workmen by day." ²³Neither I nor my brothers nor my men nor the guards with me took off our clothes; each had his weapon, even when he went for water.ᵃ

Nehemiah Helps the Poor

5 Now the men and their wives raised a great outcry against their Jewish brothers. ²Some were saying, "We and our sons and daughters are numerous; in order for us to eat and stay alive, we must get grain."

³Others were saying, "We are mortgaging our fields, our vineyards and our homes to get grain during the famine."

⁴Still others were saying, "We have had to borrow money to pay the king's tax on our fields and vineyards. ⁵Although we are of the same flesh and blood as our countrymen and though our sons are as good as theirs, yet we have to subject our sons and daughters to slavery. Some of our daughters have already been enslaved, but we are powerless, because our fields and our vineyards belong to others."

⁶When I heard their outcry and these charges, I was very angry. ⁷I pondered them in my mind and then accused the

ᵃ 23 The meaning of the Hebrew for this clause is uncertain.

nobles and officials. I told them, "You are exacting usury from your own countrymen!" So I called together a large meeting to deal with them [8]and said: "As far as possible, we have bought back our Jewish brothers who were sold to the Gentiles. Now you are selling your brothers, only for them to be sold back to us!" They kept quiet, because they could find nothing to say.

[9]So I continued, "What you are doing is not right. Shouldn't you walk in the fear of our God to avoid the reproach of our Gentile enemies? [10]I and my brothers and my men are also lending the people money and grain. But let the exacting of usury stop! [11]Give back to them immediately their fields, vineyards, olive groves and houses, and also the usury you are charging them—the hundredth part of the money, grain, new wine and oil."

[12]"We will give it back," they said. "And we will not demand anything more from them. We will do as you say."

Then I summoned the priests and made the nobles and officials take an oath to do what they had promised. [13]I also shook out the folds of my robe and said, "In this way may God shake out of his house and possessions every man who does not keep this promise. So may such a man be shaken out and emptied!"

At this the whole assembly said, "Amen," and praised the LORD. And the people did as they had promised.

[14]Moreover, from the twentieth year of King Artaxerxes, when I was appointed to be their governor in the land of Judah, until his thirty-second year—twelve years—neither I nor my brothers ate the food allotted to the governor. [15]But the earlier governors—those preceding me—placed a heavy burden on the people and took forty shekels[a] of silver from them in addition to food and wine. Their assistants also lorded it over the people. But out of reverence for God I did not act like that. [16]Instead, I devoted myself to the work on this wall. All my men were assembled there for the work; we[b] did not acquire any land.

[17]Furthermore, a hundred and fifty Jews and officials ate at my table, as well as those who came to us from the surrounding nations. [18]Each day one ox, six choice sheep and some poultry were prepared for me, and every ten days an abundant supply of wine of all kinds. In spite of all this, I never demanded the food allotted to the governor, because the demands were heavy on these people.

[19]Remember me with favor, O my God, for all I have done for these people.

Further Opposition to the Rebuilding

6 When word came to Sanballat, Tobiah, Geshem the Arab and the rest of our enemies that I had rebuilt the wall and not a gap was left in it—though up to that time I had not set the doors in the gates— [2]Sanballat and Geshem sent me this message: "Come, let us meet together in one of the villages[c] on the plain of Ono."

But they were scheming to harm me; [3]so I sent messengers to them with this reply: "I am carrying on a great project and cannot go down. Why should the work stop while I leave it and go down to you?" [4]Four times they sent

---

[a] 15 That is, about 1 pound (about 0.5 kilogram)   [b] 16 Most Hebrew manuscripts; some Hebrew manuscripts, Septuagint, Vulgate and Syriac *I*
[c] 2 Or in *Kephirim*

Strengthen My Hands

NEHEMIAH 6:5–9

Stretch your hands out in front of you. Examine them closely. Notice the uniqueness of your fingernails, your veins, the shape of your fingers, the wrinkles of your knuckles, the colors of your skin. Name some of the jobs your hands have done in the past. What tasks do your hands accomplish on a daily basis? How have your hands shown mercy and compassion? If your own hands were included in a photo of many hands, how would you know which ones were yours? After you have taken time to examine your fingers and the palms and backs of your hands, meditate on the gift that your hands are. Repeat Nehemiah's prayer, "Now strengthen my hands," several times, trusting that your prayer will be answered.

See Meeting God in Service

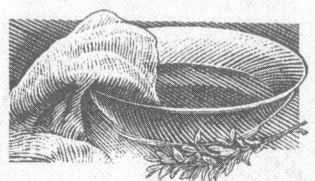

me the same message, and each time I gave them the same answer.

⁵Then, the fifth time, Sanballat sent his aide to me with the same message, and in his hand was an unsealed letter ⁶in which was written:

"It is reported among the nations—and Geshem*ᵃ* says it is true—that you and the Jews are plotting to revolt, and therefore you are building the wall. Moreover, according to these reports you are about to become their king ⁷and have even appointed prophets to make this proclamation about you in Jerusalem: 'There is a king in Judah!' Now this report will get back to the king; so come, let us confer together."

⁸I sent him this reply: "Nothing like what you are saying is happening; you are just making it up out of your head."

⁹They were all trying to frighten us, thinking, "Their hands will get too weak for the work, and it will not be completed."

But I prayed, "Now strengthen my hands."

¹⁰One day I went to the house of Shemaiah son of Delaiah, the son of Mehetabel, who was shut in at his home. He said, "Let us meet in the house of God, inside the temple, and let us close the temple doors, because men are coming to kill you—by night they are coming to kill you."

¹¹But I said, "Should a man like me run away? Or should one like me go into the temple to save his life? I will not go!" ¹²I realized that God had not sent him, but that he had prophesied against me because Tobiah and Sanballat had hired him. ¹³He had been hired to intimidate me so that I would commit a sin by doing this, and then they would give me a bad name to discredit me.

¹⁴Remember Tobiah and Sanballat, O my God, because of what they have done; remember also the prophetess Noadiah and the rest of the prophets who have been trying to intimidate me.

The Completion of the Wall

¹⁵So the wall was completed on the twenty-fifth of Elul, in fifty-two days. ¹⁶When all our enemies heard about this, all the surrounding nations were afraid and lost their self-confidence, because they realized that this work had been done with the help of our God.

¹⁷Also, in those days the nobles of Judah were sending many letters to Tobiah, and replies from Tobiah kept coming to them. ¹⁸For many in Judah were under oath to him, since he was son-in-law to Shecaniah son of Arah, and his son Jehohanan had married the daughter of Meshullam son of Berekiah. ¹⁹Moreover, they kept reporting to me his good deeds and then telling him what I said. And Tobiah sent letters to intimidate me.

7 After the wall had been rebuilt and I had set the doors in place, the gatekeepers and the singers and the Levites were appointed. ²I put in charge of Jerusalem my brother Hanani, along with*ᵇ* Hananiah the commander of the citadel, because he was a man of integrity and feared God more than most men do. ³I said to them, "The gates of Jerusalem are not to be opened until the sun is hot. While

ᵃ6 Hebrew *Gashmu*, a variant of *Geshem*   *ᵇ2* Or *Hanani, that is,* the gatekeepers are still on duty, have them shut the doors and bar them. Also appoint residents of Jerusalem as guards, some at their posts and some near their own houses."

The List of the Exiles Who Returned

⁴Now the city was large and spacious, but there were few people in it, and the houses had not yet been rebuilt. ⁵So my God put it into my heart to assemble the nobles, the officials and the common people for registration by families. I found the genealogical record of those who had been the first to return. This is what I found written there:

⁶These are the people of the province who came up from the captivity of the exiles whom Nebuchadnezzar king of Babylon had taken captive (they returned to Jerusalem and Judah, each to his own town, ⁷in company with Zerubbabel, Jeshua, Nehemiah, Azariah, Raamiah, Nahamani, Mordecai, Bilshan, Mispereth, Bigvai, Nehum and Baanah):

The list of the men of Israel:

⁸	the descendants of Parosh	2,172
⁹	of Shephatiah	372
¹⁰	of Arah	652
¹¹	of Pahath-Moab (through the line of Jeshua and Joab)	2,818
¹²	of Elam	1,254
¹³	of Zattu	845
¹⁴	of Zaccai	760
¹⁵	of Binnui	648
¹⁶	of Bebai	628
¹⁷	of Azgad	2,322
¹⁸	of Adonikam	667
¹⁹	of Bigvai	2,067
²⁰	of Adin	655
²¹	of Ater (through Hezekiah)	98
²²	of Hashum	328
²³	of Bezai	324
²⁴	of Hariph	112
²⁵	of Gibeon	95
²⁶	the men of Bethlehem and Netophah	188
²⁷	of Anathoth	128
²⁸	of Beth Azmaveth	42
²⁹	of Kiriath Jearim, Kephirah and Beeroth	743
³⁰	of Ramah and Geba	621
³¹	of Micmash	122
³²	of Bethel and Ai	123
³³	of the other Nebo	52
³⁴	of the other Elam	1,254
³⁵	of Harim	320
³⁶	of Jericho	345
³⁷	of Lod, Hadid and Ono	721
³⁸	of Senaah	3,930

³⁹The priests:

	the descendants of Jedaiah (through the family of Jeshua)	973
⁴⁰	of Immer	1,052
⁴¹	of Pashhur	1,247

Building Relationships

NEHEMIAH 7:4

Building can take many forms. Structures are constructed from brick, stucco, wood, steel—one brick, one nail, one trowel of plaster at a time. Relationships, however, are built with conversations, time spent together, common interests and goals, and a common faith—one word, one action, one gesture at a time. Each of us builds relationships on a daily basis. With whom are you presently building a new or continued relationship? What "tools" do you bring to the task? What "tools" do you need to sharpen or acquire? How do you see God as a partner in the construction effort?

See Meeting God in Community

My Spiritual Genealogy

NEHEMIAH 7:44–69

Genealogies are important in the Bible. Long passages list generation after generation and number the members of various clans and groups. The practice seems strange, in a way, to our modern minds. Most of us can name parents, grandparents, and perhaps great- and great-great-grandparents. Few of us, though, can name our ancestors back to the beginning of time or list the number of people in our extended family group.

While we do not tend to pay as much attention to family trees as the Israelites did, there is great value in thinking about people whose lives have influenced us and who have nurtured us spiritually. Who in your life has been a spiritual guide? A relative, friend, mentor or historical figure? Name some people who have helped you to know God and to live as God's beloved child.

See Meeting God in Community

⁴²of Harim   1,017

⁴³The Levites:

the descendants of Jeshua (through Kadmiel through the line of Hodaviah)   74

⁴⁴The singers:

the descendants of Asaph   148

⁴⁵The gatekeepers:

the descendants of
Shallum, Ater, Talmon, Akkub, Hatita and Shobai   138

⁴⁶The temple servants:

the descendants of
Ziha, Hasupha, Tabbaoth,
⁴⁷Keros, Sia, Padon,
⁴⁸Lebana, Hagaba, Shalmai,
⁴⁹Hanan, Giddel, Gahar,
⁵⁰Reaiah, Rezin, Nekoda,
⁵¹Gazzam, Uzza, Paseah,
⁵²Besai, Meunim, Nephussim,
⁵³Bakbuk, Hakupha, Harhur,
⁵⁴Bazluth, Mehida, Harsha,
⁵⁵Barkos, Sisera, Temah,
⁵⁶Neziah and Hatipha

⁵⁷The descendants of the servants of Solomon:

the descendants of
Sotai, Sophereth, Perida,
⁵⁸Jaala, Darkon, Giddel,
⁵⁹Shephatiah, Hattil,
Pokereth-Hazzebaim and Amon

⁶⁰The temple servants and the descendants of the servants of Solomon   392

⁶¹The following came up from the towns of Tel Melah, Tel Harsha, Kerub, Addon and Immer, but they could not show that their families were descended from Israel:

⁶²the descendants of
Delaiah, Tobiah and Nekoda   642

⁶³And from among the priests:

the descendants of
Hobaiah, Hakkoz and Barzillai (a man who had married a daughter of Barzillai the Gileadite and was called by that name).

⁶⁴These searched for their family records, but they could not find them and so were excluded from the priesthood as unclean. ⁶⁵The governor, therefore, ordered them not to eat any of the most sacred food until there should be a priest ministering with the Urim and Thummim.

⁶⁶The whole company numbered 42,360, ⁶⁷besides their 7,337 menservants and maidservants; and they also had 245 men and women singers. ⁶⁸There were

736 horses, 245 mules,*a* *69*435 camels and 6,720 donkeys.

*70*Some of the heads of the families contributed to the work. The governor gave to the treasury 1,000 drachmas*b* of gold, 50 bowls and 530 garments for priests. *71*Some of the heads of the families gave to the treasury for the work 20,000 drachmas*c* of gold and 2,200 minas*d* of silver. *72*The total given by the rest of the people was 20,000 drachmas of gold, 2,000 minas*e* of silver and 67 garments for priests.

*73*The priests, the Levites, the gatekeepers, the singers and the temple servants, along with certain of the people and the rest of the Israelites, settled in their own towns.

Ezra Reads the Law

When the seventh month came and the Israelites had settled in their towns,*1* all the people assembled as one
8 man in the square before the Water Gate. They told Ezra the scribe to bring out the Book of the Law of Moses, which the LORD had commanded for Israel.

*2*So on the first day of the seventh month Ezra the priest brought the Law before the assembly, which was made up of men and women and all who were able to understand. *3*He read it aloud from daybreak till noon as he faced the square before the Water Gate in the presence of the men, women and others who could understand. And all the people listened attentively to the Book of the Law.

*4*Ezra the scribe stood on a high wooden platform built for the occasion. Beside him on his right stood Mattithiah, Shema, Anaiah, Uriah, Hilkiah and Maaseiah; and on his left were Pedaiah, Mishael, Malkijah, Hashum, Hashbaddanah, Zechariah and Meshullam.

*5*Ezra opened the book. All the people could see him because he was standing above them; and as he opened it, the people all stood up. *6*Ezra praised the LORD, the great God; and all the people lifted their hands and responded, "Amen! Amen!" Then they bowed down and worshiped the LORD with their faces to the ground.

*7*The Levites—Jeshua, Bani, Sherebiah, Jamin, Akkub, Shabbethai, Hodiah, Maaseiah, Kelita, Azariah, Jozabad, Hanan and Pelaiah—instructed the people in the Law while the people were standing there. *8*They read from the Book of the Law of God, making it clear*f* and giving the meaning so that the people could understand what was being read.

*9*Then Nehemiah the governor, Ezra the priest and scribe, and the Levites who were instructing the people said to them all, "This day is sacred to the LORD your God. Do not mourn or weep." For all the people had been weeping as they listened to the words of the Law.

*10*Nehemiah said, "Go and enjoy choice food and sweet drinks, and send some to those who have nothing prepared. This day is sacred to our Lord. Do not grieve, for the joy of the LORD is your strength."

Joyfully Listening to God's Voice

NEHEMIAH 8:2–12

Can you imagine standing for five or six hours while Scripture is read? The people who gather in assembly before Ezra listen attentively to the Book of the Law, bow down and worship, and "[weep] as they [listen] to the words of the Law," grieving as they understand how they have not lived according to God's ways. But Nehemiah proclaims God's grace: "Do not grieve, for the joy of the LORD is your strength." Read verse 12 again. What is your response to this story? How can you relate to the emotions of the people?

What does this story say about how God relates to us? How does the experience of listening to God's Word being read differ from the experience of reading it yourself? What can you learn from these ancient believers about listening to the reading of Scripture?

See Meeting God in Scripture

---

a 68 Some Hebrew manuscripts (see also Ezra 2:66); most Hebrew manuscripts do not have this verse.   *b 70* That is, about 19 pounds (about 8.5 kilograms)   *c 71* That is, about 375 pounds (about 170 kilograms); also in verse 72   *d 71* That is, about 1 1/3 tons (about 1.2 metric tons)
e 72 That is, about 1 1/4 tons (about 1.1 metric tons)   *f 8* Or God, translating it

Time to Party!

NEHEMIAH 8:17

The Israelites have much to celebrate. The wall is complete, they are settling into their homeland and the community has heard Scripture read aloud. It is time to feast! Enjoying a long-standing tradition, they gather branches of lovely greenery and make shelters (booths) in which to celebrate once again the Feast of Booths. How does your faith community celebrate? Do you have regular times when you joyfully commemorate all the good that happens in your communal or individual lives? Consider celebrating with a springtime or summer camping trip to commemorate Paul's words from the New Testament: "Rejoice in the Lord always. I will say it again: Rejoice!" (Philippians 4:4).

See Meeting God in Community

[11]The Levites calmed all the people, saying, "Be still, for this is a sacred day. Do not grieve."

[12]Then all the people went away to eat and drink, to send portions of food and to celebrate with great joy, because they now understood the words that had been made known to them.

[13]On the second day of the month, the heads of all the families, along with the priests and the Levites, gathered around Ezra the scribe to give attention to the words of the Law. [14]They found written in the Law, which the LORD had commanded through Moses, that the Israelites were to live in booths during the feast of the seventh month [15]and that they should proclaim this word and spread it throughout their towns and in Jerusalem: "Go out into the hill country and bring back branches from olive and wild olive trees, and from myrtles, palms and shade trees, to make booths"—as it is written.[a]

[16]So the people went out and brought back branches and built themselves booths on their own roofs, in their courtyards, in the courts of the house of God and in the square by the Water Gate and the one by the Gate of Ephraim. [17]The whole company that had returned from exile built booths and lived in them. From the days of Joshua son of Nun until that day, the Israelites had not celebrated it like this. And their joy was very great.

[18]Day after day, from the first day to the last, Ezra read from the Book of the Law of God. They celebrated the feast for seven days, and on the eighth day, in accordance with the regulation, there was an assembly.

The Israelites Confess Their Sins

9 On the twenty-fourth day of the same month, the Israelites gathered together, fasting and wearing sackcloth and having dust on their heads. [2]Those of Israelite descent had separated themselves from all foreigners. They stood in their places and confessed their sins and the wickedness of their fathers. [3]They stood where they were and read from the Book of the Law of the LORD their God for a quarter of the day, and spent another quarter in confession and in worshiping the LORD their God. [4]Standing on the stairs were the Levites—Jeshua, Bani, Kadmiel, Shebaniah, Bunni, Sherebiah, Bani and Kenani—who called with loud voices to the LORD their God. [5]And the Levites—Jeshua, Kadmiel, Bani, Hashabneiah, Sherebiah, Hodiah, Shebaniah and Pethahiah—said: "Stand up and praise the LORD your God, who is from everlasting to everlasting.[b]"

"Blessed be your glorious name, and may it be exalted above all blessing and praise. [6]You alone are the LORD. You made the heavens, even the highest heavens, and all their starry host, the earth and all that is on it, the seas and all that is in them. You give life to everything, and the multitudes of heaven worship you.

[7]"You are the LORD God, who chose Abram and brought him out of Ur of the Chaldeans and named him Abraham. [8]You found his heart faithful to you, and you made a covenant with him to give to his descendants the land of the Canaanites, Hittites, Amorites,

a 15 See Lev. 23:37–40.   *b 5* Or *God for ever and ever*

Perizzites, Jebusites and Girgashites. You have kept your promise because you are righteous.

⁹"You saw the suffering of our forefathers in Egypt; you heard their cry at the Red Sea.ᵃ ¹⁰You sent miraculous signs and wonders against Pharaoh, against all his officials and all the people of his land, for you knew how arrogantly the Egyptians treated them. You made a name for yourself, which remains to this day. ¹¹You divided the sea before them, so that they passed through it on dry ground, but you hurled their pursuers into the depths, like a stone into mighty waters. ¹²By day you led them with a pillar of cloud, and by night with a pillar of fire to give them light on the way they were to take.

¹³"You came down on Mount Sinai; you spoke to them from heaven. You gave them regulations and laws that are just and right, and decrees and commands that are good. ¹⁴You made known to them your holy Sabbath and gave them commands, decrees and laws through your servant Moses. ¹⁵In their hunger you gave them bread from heaven and in their thirst you brought them water from the rock; you told them to go in and take possession of the land you had sworn with uplifted hand to give them.

¹⁶"But they, our forefathers, became arrogant and stiff-necked, and did not obey your commands. ¹⁷They refused to listen and failed to remember the miracles you performed among them. They became stiff-necked and in their rebellion appointed a leader in order to return to their slavery. But you are a forgiving God, gracious and compassionate, slow to anger and abounding in love. Therefore you did not desert them, ¹⁸even when they cast for themselves an image of a calf and said, 'This is your god, who brought you up out of Egypt,' or when they committed awful blasphemies.

¹⁹"Because of your great compassion you did not abandon them in the desert. By day the pillar of cloud did not cease to guide them on their path, nor the pillar of fire by night to shine on the way they were to take. ²⁰You gave your good Spirit to instruct them. You did not withhold your manna from their mouths, and you gave them water for their thirst. ²¹For forty years you sustained them in the desert; they lacked nothing, their clothes did not wear out nor did their feet become swollen.

²²"You gave them kingdoms and nations, allotting to them even the remotest frontiers. They took over the country of Sihonᵇ king of Heshbon and the country of Og king of Bashan. ²³You made their sons as numerous as the stars in the sky, and you brought them into the land that you told their fathers to enter and possess. ²⁴Their sons went in and took possession of the land. You subdued before them the Canaanites, who lived in the land; you handed the Canaanites over to them, along with their kings and the peoples of the land, to deal with them as they pleased. ²⁵They captured fortified cities and fertile land; they took posses-

God in the Details

NEHEMIAH 9:19–21

The Levites recite their history, recalling how, in the Desert of Sinai, God had provided pillars of cloud and fire as a constant guide, food and water, and all manner of sustenance for their survival. Focus on verse 21: "Their clothes did not wear out nor did their feet become swollen." God cared about the big picture (providing cloud and fire to show them the way) and the small details (no one can walk far with swollen or blistered feet). Most of us remember the large gifts from God— our lives, food, our families. Take time to consider the small gifts God may be giving you— the intense colors of a patch of pansies, the patience to handle a conflict with graciousness, a good night's sleep.

See Meeting God in Everyday Life

ᵃ9 Hebrew *Yam Suph*; that is, Sea of Reeds   ᵇ22 One Hebrew manuscript and Septuagint; most Hebrew manuscripts *Sihon, that is, the country of the*

633

A Binding Agreement

NEHEMIAH 9:38

Most of us operate on an "oral agreement" with God. We listen to Scripture and think about God. We attend worship and express our devotion and love in prayer and song. Take the time to write out your end of a "binding agreement" as the Israelites did. List those things you commit to (such as, I will honor you as my God, I will always tell the truth, I promise to share your love), then carefully rewrite or type your agreement on an elegant piece of stationery or paper. Date and sign it, and place it in your Bible.

sion of houses filled with all kinds of good things, wells already dug, vineyards, olive groves and fruit trees in abundance. They ate to the full and were well-nourished; they reveled in your great goodness.

²⁶"But they were disobedient and rebelled against you; they put your law behind their backs. They killed your prophets, who had admonished them in order to turn them back to you; they committed awful blasphemies. ²⁷So you handed them over to their enemies, who oppressed them. But when they were oppressed they cried out to you. From heaven you heard them, and in your great compassion you gave them deliverers, who rescued them from the hand of their enemies.

²⁸"But as soon as they were at rest, they again did what was evil in your sight. Then you abandoned them to the hand of their enemies so that they ruled over them. And when they cried out to you again, you heard from heaven, and in your compassion you delivered them time after time.

²⁹"You warned them to return to your law, but they became arrogant and disobeyed your commands. They sinned against your ordinances, by which a man will live if he obeys them. Stubbornly they turned their backs on you, became stiff-necked and refused to listen. ³⁰For many years you were patient with them. By your Spirit you admonished them through your prophets. Yet they paid no attention, so you handed them over to the neighboring peoples. ³¹But in your great mercy you did not put an end to them or abandon them, for you are a gracious and merciful God.

³²"Now therefore, O our God, the great, mighty and awesome God, who keeps his covenant of love, do not let all this hardship seem trifling in your eyes—the hardship that has come upon us, upon our kings and leaders, upon our priests and prophets, upon our fathers and all your people, from the days of the kings of Assyria until today. ³³In all that has happened to us, you have been just; you have acted faithfully, while we did wrong. ³⁴Our kings, our leaders, our priests and our fathers did not follow your law; they did not pay attention to your commands or the warnings you gave them. ³⁵Even while they were in their kingdom, enjoying your great goodness to them in the spacious and fertile land you gave them, they did not serve you or turn from their evil ways.

³⁶"But see, we are slaves today, slaves in the land you gave our forefathers so they could eat its fruit and the other good things it produces. ³⁷Because of our sins, its abundant harvest goes to the kings you have placed over us. They rule over our bodies and our cattle as they please. We are in great distress.

The Agreement of the People

³⁸"In view of all this, we are making a binding agreement, putting it in writing, and our leaders, our Levites and our priests are affixing their seals to it."

10 Those who sealed it were:

Nehemiah the governor, the son of Hacaliah.

Zedekiah, ²Seraiah, Azariah, Jeremiah,
³Pashhur, Amariah, Malkijah,
⁴Hattush, Shebaniah, Malluch,
⁵Harim, Meremoth, Obadiah,
⁶Daniel, Ginnethon, Baruch,
⁷Meshullam, Abijah, Mijamin,
⁸Maaziah, Bilgai and Shemaiah.
These were the priests.

⁹The Levites:

Jeshua son of Azaniah, Binnui of the sons of Henadad,
    Kadmiel,
¹⁰and their associates: Shebaniah,
    Hodiah, Kelita, Pelaiah, Hanan,
¹¹Mica, Rehob, Hashabiah,
¹²Zaccur, Sherebiah, Shebaniah,
¹³Hodiah, Bani and Beninu.

¹⁴The leaders of the people:

Parosh, Pahath-Moab, Elam, Zattu, Bani,
¹⁵Bunni, Azgad, Bebai,
¹⁶Adonijah, Bigvai, Adin,
¹⁷Ater, Hezekiah, Azzur,
¹⁸Hodiah, Hashum, Bezai,
¹⁹Hariph, Anathoth, Nebai,
²⁰Magpiash, Meshullam, Hezir,
²¹Meshezabel, Zadok, Jaddua,
²²Pelatiah, Hanan, Anaiah,
²³Hoshea, Hananiah, Hasshub,
²⁴Hallohesh, Pilha, Shobek,
²⁵Rehum, Hashabnah, Maaseiah,
²⁶Ahiah, Hanan, Anan,
²⁷Malluch, Harim and Baanah.

²⁸"The rest of the people—priests, Levites, gatekeepers, singers, temple servants and all who separated themselves from the neighboring peoples for the sake of the Law of God, together with their wives and all their sons and daughters who are able to understand— ²⁹all these now join their brothers the nobles, and bind themselves with a curse and an oath to follow the Law of God given through Moses the servant of God and to obey carefully all the commands, regulations and decrees of the LORD our Lord.

³⁰"We promise not to give our daughters in marriage to the peoples around us or take their daughters for our sons.

³¹"When the neighboring peoples bring merchandise or grain to sell on the Sabbath, we will not buy from them on the Sabbath or on any holy day. Every seventh year we will forgo working the land and will cancel all debts.

³²"We assume the responsibility for carrying out the commands to give a third of a shekel[a] each year for the service of the house of our God: ³³for the bread set out on the table; for the regular grain offerings and burnt offerings; for the offerings on the Sabbaths, New Moon festivals and appointed feasts; for the holy offerings;

God in All Our Work

NEHEMIAH 10:28–29

"My God, since You are with me, and since it is Your will that I should apply my mind to these outward things, I pray that You will give me the grace to remain with You and to keep company with You. But so that my work may be better, Lord, work with me; receive my work and possess all my affections. Amen."

—BROTHER LAWRENCE,
The Practice of the Presence of God

---

a 32 That is, about 1/8 ounce (about 4 grams)

Gifts for the Storeroom of God

NEHEMIAH 10:35–39

Imagine that you are sitting outside the house of God, watching the stream of people who are walking toward the temple. The people are lined up as far as you can see, their arms laden with offerings. A lamb squirms in a shepherd's arms. Two brothers bring sacks of grain carefully balanced on a cart. People holding bags of fruits and vegetables mingle with those pulling calves by leather reins. What animal sounds do you hear? Do you smell the ripeness of fresh fruit? What colors and textures illumine the gifts piled outside the door of God's house? What expressions are on the faces of those who gladly bring gifts of their firstborn and the firstfruits of their crops? And what have you brought?

See Meeting God in Worship

for sin offerings to make atonement for Israel; and for all the duties of the house of our God.

³⁴"We—the priests, the Levites and the people—have cast lots to determine when each of our families is to bring to the house of our God at set times each year a contribution of wood to burn on the altar of the LORD our God, as it is written in the Law.

³⁵"We also assume responsibility for bringing to the house of the LORD each year the firstfruits of our crops and of every fruit tree.

³⁶"As it is also written in the Law, we will bring the firstborn of our sons and of our cattle, of our herds and of our flocks to the house of our God, to the priests ministering there.

³⁷"Moreover, we will bring to the storerooms of the house of our God, to the priests, the first of our ground meal, of our ⌊grain⌋ offerings, of the fruit of all our trees and of our new wine and oil. And we will bring a tithe of our crops to the Levites, for it is the Levites who collect the tithes in all the towns where we work. ³⁸A priest descended from Aaron is to accompany the Levites when they receive the tithes, and the Levites are to bring a tenth of the tithes up to the house of our God, to the storerooms of the treasury. ³⁹The people of Israel, including the Levites, are to bring their contributions of grain, new wine and oil to the storerooms where the articles for the sanctuary are kept and where the ministering priests, the gatekeepers and the singers stay.

"We will not neglect the house of our God."

The New Residents of Jerusalem

11 Now the leaders of the people settled in Jerusalem, and the rest of the people cast lots to bring one out of every ten to live in Jerusalem, the holy city, while the remaining nine were to stay in their own towns. ²The people commended all the men who volunteered to live in Jerusalem.

³These are the provincial leaders who settled in Jerusalem (now some Israelites, priests, Levites, temple servants and descendants of Solomon's servants lived in the towns of Judah, each on his own property in the various towns, ⁴while other people from both Judah and Benjamin lived in Jerusalem):

From the descendants of Judah:

Athaiah son of Uzziah, the son of Zechariah, the son of Amariah, the son of Shephatiah, the son of Mahalalel, a descendant of Perez; ⁵and Maaseiah son of Baruch, the son of Col-Hozeh, the son of Hazaiah, the son of Adaiah, the son of Joiarib, the son of Zechariah, a descendant of Shelah. ⁶The descendants of Perez who lived in Jerusalem totaled 468 able men.

⁷From the descendants of Benjamin:

Sallu son of Meshullam, the son of Joed, the son of Pedaiah, the son of Kolaiah, the son of Maaseiah, the son of Ithiel, the son of Jeshaiah, ⁸and his followers, Gabbai and Sallai—928 men. ⁹Joel son of Zicri was their chief officer, and Judah son of Hassenuah was over the Second District of the city.

¹⁰From the priests:

Jedaiah; the son of Joiarib; Jakin; ¹¹Seraiah son of Hilkiah, the son of Meshullam, the son of Zadok, the son of Meraioth, the son of Ahitub, supervisor in the house of God, ¹²and their associates, who carried on work for the temple—822 men; Adaiah son of Jeroham, the son of Pelaliah, the son of Amzi, the son of Zechariah, the son of Pashhur, the son of Malkijah, ¹³and his associates, who were heads of families—242 men; Amashsai son of Azarel, the son of Ahzai, the son of Meshillemoth, the son of Immer, ¹⁴and his*a* associates, who were able men—128. Their chief officer was Zabdiel son of Haggedolim.

¹⁵From the Levites:

Shemaiah son of Hasshub, the son of Azrikam, the son of Hashabiah, the son of Bunni; ¹⁶Shabbethai and Jozabad, two of the heads of the Levites, who had charge of the outside work of the house of God; ¹⁷Mattaniah son of Mica, the son of Zabdi, the son of Asaph, the director who led in thanksgiving and prayer; Bakbukiah, second among his associates; and Abda son of Shammua, the son of Galal, the son of Jeduthun. ¹⁸The Levites in the holy city totaled 284.

¹⁹The gatekeepers:

Akkub, Talmon and their associates, who kept watch at the gates—172 men.

²⁰The rest of the Israelites, with the priests and Levites, were in all the towns of Judah, each on his ancestral property.

²¹The temple servants lived on the hill of Ophel, and Ziha and Gishpa were in charge of them.

²²The chief officer of the Levites in Jerusalem was Uzzi son of Bani, the son of Hashabiah, the son of Mattaniah, the son of Mica. Uzzi was one of Asaph's descendants, who were the singers responsible for the service of the house of God. ²³The singers were under the king's orders, which regulated their daily activity.

²⁴Pethahiah son of Meshezabel, one of the descendants of Zerah son of Judah, was the king's agent in all affairs relating to the people.

²⁵As for the villages with their fields, some of the people of Judah lived in Kiriath Arba and its surrounding settlements, in Dibon and its settlements, in Jekabzeel and its villages, ²⁶in Jeshua, in Moladah, in Beth Pelet, ²⁷in Hazar Shual, in Beersheba and its settlements, ²⁸in Ziklag, in Meconah and its settlements, ²⁹in En Rimmon, in Zorah, in Jarmuth, ³⁰Zanoah, Adullam and their villages, in Lachish and its fields, and in Azekah and its settlements. So they were living all the way from Beersheba to the Valley of Hinnom.

³¹The descendants of the Benjamites from Geba lived in Micmash, Aija, Bethel and its settlements, ³²in Anathoth, Nob and Ananiah, ³³in Hazor, Ramah and Gittaim, ³⁴in

God's Work of Transformation

NEHEMIAH 11:13–36

"Our whole life is to be poised on a certain glad expectancy of God; taking each moment, incident, choice and opportunity as material placed in our hand by the Creator whose whole intricate and mysterious process moved toward the triumph of Charity, and who has given each living spirit a tiny part in this vast work of transformation."

—EVELYN UNDERHILL,
The School of Charity

Meeting Through Music

NEHEMIAH 12:27

Harps, voices, flutes, lyres, trumpets, tambourines and cymbals join in joyful euphony to praise and worship God. Who can fathom the fullness of the way music communicates with God and other believers? How does music play a part in your faith? Do you love to sing hymns and praise songs? Do you play an instrument to connect with God? Is listening to religious music important in your spiritual life? Spend some time singing, playing an instrument or listening to music that brings you closer to God.

See Meeting God in Worship

Hadid, Zeboim and Neballat, [35]in Lod and Ono, and in the Valley of the Craftsmen.

[36]Some of the divisions of the Levites of Judah settled in Benjamin.

Priests and Levites

12 These were the priests and Levites who returned with Zerubbabel son of Shealtiel and with Jeshua: Seraiah, Jeremiah, Ezra,
[2]Amariah, Malluch, Hattush,
[3]Shecaniah, Rehum, Meremoth,
[4]Iddo, Ginnethon,[a] Abijah,
[5]Mijamin,[b] Moadiah, Bilgah,
[6]Shemaiah, Joiarib, Jedaiah,
[7]Sallu, Amok, Hilkiah and Jedaiah.

These were the leaders of the priests and their associates in the days of Jeshua.

[8]The Levites were Jeshua, Binnui, Kadmiel, Sherebiah, Judah, and also Mattaniah, who, together with his associates, was in charge of the songs of thanksgiving. [9]Bakbukiah and Unni, their associates, stood opposite them in the services.

[10]Jeshua was the father of Joiakim, Joiakim the father of Eliashib, Eliashib the father of Joiada, [11]Joiada the father of Jonathan, and Jonathan the father of Jaddua.

[12]In the days of Joiakim, these were the heads of the priestly families:

of Seraiah's family, Meraiah;
of Jeremiah's, Hananiah;
[13]of Ezra's, Meshullam;
of Amariah's, Jehohanan;
[14]of Malluch's, Jonathan;
of Shecaniah's,[c] Joseph;
[15]of Harim's, Adna;
of Meremoth's,[d] Helkai;
[16]of Iddo's, Zechariah;
of Ginnethon's, Meshullam;
[17]of Abijah's, Zicri;
of Miniamin's and of Moadiah's, Piltai;
[18]of Bilgah's, Shammua;
of Shemaiah's, Jehonathan;
[19]of Joiarib's, Mattenai;
of Jedaiah's, Uzzi;
[20]of Sallu's, Kallai;
of Amok's, Eber;
[21]of Hilkiah's, Hashabiah;
of Jedaiah's, Nethanel.

[22]The family heads of the Levites in the days of Eliashib, Joiada, Johanan and Jaddua, as well as those of the priests, were recorded in the reign of Darius the Persian. [23]The family heads among the descendants of Levi up to the time of Johanan son of Eliashib were recorded in the book of the annals. [24]And the leaders of the Levites were Hashabiah, Sherebiah, Jeshua son of Kadmiel, and their associates, who stood opposite them to give praise and thanksgiving,

---

a 4 Many Hebrew manuscripts and Vulgate (see also Neh. 12:16); most Hebrew manuscripts *Ginnethoi*   *b 5* A variant of *Miniamin*   *c 14* Very many Hebrew manuscripts, some Septuagint manuscripts and Syriac (see also Neh. 12:3); most Hebrew manuscripts *Shebaniah's*   *d 15* Some Septuagint manuscripts (see also Neh. 12:3); Hebrew *Meraioth's*

one section responding to the other, as prescribed by David the man of God. ²⁵Mattaniah, Bakbukiah, Obadiah, Meshullam, Talmon and Akkub were gatekeepers who guarded the storerooms at the gates. ²⁶They served in the days of Joiakim son of Jeshua, the son of Jozadak, and in the days of Nehemiah the governor and of Ezra the priest and scribe.

Dedication of the Wall of Jerusalem

²⁷At the dedication of the wall of Jerusalem, the Levites were sought out from where they lived and were brought to Jerusalem to celebrate joyfully the dedication with songs of thanksgiving and with the music of cymbals, harps and lyres. ²⁸The singers also were brought together from the region around Jerusalem—from the villages of the Netophathites, ²⁹from Beth Gilgal, and from the area of Geba and Azmaveth, for the singers had built villages for themselves around Jerusalem. ³⁰When the priests and Levites had purified themselves ceremonially, they purified the people, the gates and the wall.

³¹I had the leaders of Judah go up on top*ᵃ* of the wall. I also assigned two large choirs to give thanks. One was to proceed on top*ᵇ* of the wall to the right, toward the Dung Gate. ³²Hoshaiah and half the leaders of Judah followed them, ³³along with Azariah, Ezra, Meshullam, ³⁴Judah, Benjamin, Shemaiah, Jeremiah, ³⁵as well as some priests with trumpets, and also Zechariah son of Jonathan, the son of Shemaiah, the son of Mattaniah, the son of Micaiah, the son of Zaccur, the son of Asaph, ³⁶and his associates—Shemaiah, Azarel, Milalai, Gilalai, Maai, Nethanel, Judah and Hanani—with musical instruments ⌐prescribed by⌐ David the man of God. Ezra the scribe led the procession. ³⁷At the Fountain Gate they continued directly up the steps of the City of David on the ascent to the wall and passed above the house of David to the Water Gate on the east.

³⁸The second choir proceeded in the opposite direction. I followed them on top*ᶜ* of the wall, together with half the people—past the Tower of the Ovens to the Broad Wall, ³⁹over the Gate of Ephraim, the Jeshanah*ᵈ* Gate, the Fish Gate, the Tower of Hananel and the Tower of the Hundred, as far as the Sheep Gate. At the Gate of the Guard they stopped.

⁴⁰The two choirs that gave thanks then took their places in the house of God; so did I, together with half the officials, ⁴¹as well as the priests—Eliakim, Maaseiah, Miniamin, Micaiah, Elioenai, Zechariah and Hananiah with their trumpets— ⁴²and also Maaseiah, Shemaiah, Eleazar, Uzzi, Jehohanan, Malkijah, Elam and Ezer. The choirs sang under the direction of Jezrahiah. ⁴³And on that day they offered great sacrifices, rejoicing because God had given them great joy. The women and children also rejoiced. The sound of rejoicing in Jerusalem could be heard far away.

⁴⁴At that time men were appointed to be in charge of the storerooms for the contributions, firstfruits and tithes. From the fields around the towns they were to bring into the storerooms the portions required by the Law for the priests and the Levites, for Judah was pleased with the ministering priests and Levites. ⁴⁵They performed the service of

Thus Rejoicing

NEHEMIAH 12:43

How has God given you joy? Set a timer for two minutes. Put pen to paper and see how many joys you can list in that short time. Jot down whatever comes to you—big and little things, those that seem important and those that appear insignificant. If after writing furiously for a time you draw a blank, think about a different aspect of your life (past, present, family, friends, work, faith community, creation) to inspire new ideas. When the timer sounds, reread your list of joys and thank God for giving them to you.

See Meeting God in Prayer

Turning a Curse Into a Blessing

NEHEMIAH 13:1–2

Have you ever tried to repair a shattered vase? Worked hard to restore a relationship that had gone sour? Found yourself genuinely loving a person who had previously been difficult to even like? Has disaster or tragedy befallen you—and only later did you see blessings come from what had seemed the worst possible scenario? In the miracle of God's loving power, what seems negative can often lead to something positive, as verse 2 illustrates. Is there something in your life right now that feels as though it is unredeemable? Offer that situation to God, who can make all things new.

See Meeting God in Everyday Life

their God and the service of purification, as did also the singers and gatekeepers, according to the commands of David and his son Solomon. ⁴⁶For long ago, in the days of David and Asaph, there had been directors for the singers and for the songs of praise and thanksgiving to God. ⁴⁷So in the days of Zerubbabel and of Nehemiah, all Israel contributed the daily portions for the singers and gatekeepers. They also set aside the portion for the other Levites, and the Levites set aside the portion for the descendants of Aaron.

Nehemiah's Final Reforms

13 On that day the Book of Moses was read aloud in the hearing of the people and there it was found written that no Ammonite or Moabite should ever be admitted into the assembly of God, ²because they had not met the Israelites with food and water but had hired Balaam to call a curse down on them. (Our God, however, turned the curse into a blessing.) ³When the people heard this law, they excluded from Israel all who were of foreign descent.

⁴Before this, Eliashib the priest had been put in charge of the storerooms of the house of our God. He was closely associated with Tobiah, ⁵and he had provided him with a large room formerly used to store the grain offerings and incense and temple articles, and also the tithes of grain, new wine and oil prescribed for the Levites, singers and gatekeepers, as well as the contributions for the priests.

⁶But while all this was going on, I was not in Jerusalem, for in the thirty-second year of Artaxerxes king of Babylon I had returned to the king. Some time later I asked his permission ⁷and came back to Jerusalem. Here I learned about the evil thing Eliashib had done in providing Tobiah a room in the courts of the house of God. ⁸I was greatly displeased and threw all Tobiah's household goods out of the room. ⁹I gave orders to purify the rooms, and then I put back into them the equipment of the house of God, with the grain offerings and the incense.

¹⁰I also learned that the portions assigned to the Levites had not been given to them, and that all the Levites and singers responsible for the service had gone back to their own fields. ¹¹So I rebuked the officials and asked them, "Why is the house of God neglected?" Then I called them together and stationed them at their posts.

¹²All Judah brought the tithes of grain, new wine and oil into the storerooms. ¹³I put Shelemiah the priest, Zadok the scribe, and a Levite named Pedaiah in charge of the storerooms and made Hanan son of Zaccur, the son of Mattaniah, their assistant, because these men were considered trustworthy. They were made responsible for distributing the supplies to their brothers.

¹⁴Remember me for this, O my God, and do not blot out what I have so faithfully done for the house of my God and its services.

¹⁵In those days I saw men in Judah treading winepresses on the Sabbath and bringing in grain and loading it on donkeys, together with wine, grapes, figs and all other kinds of loads. And they were bringing all this into Jerusalem on the Sabbath. Therefore I warned them against selling food on

that day. ¹⁶Men from Tyre who lived in Jerusalem were bringing in fish and all kinds of merchandise and selling them in Jerusalem on the Sabbath to the people of Judah. ¹⁷I rebuked the nobles of Judah and said to them, "What is this wicked thing you are doing—desecrating the Sabbath day? ¹⁸Didn't your forefathers do the same things, so that our God brought all this calamity upon us and upon this city? Now you are stirring up more wrath against Israel by desecrating the Sabbath."

¹⁹When evening shadows fell on the gates of Jerusalem before the Sabbath, I ordered the doors to be shut and not opened until the Sabbath was over. I stationed some of my own men at the gates so that no load could be brought in on the Sabbath day. ²⁰Once or twice the merchants and sellers of all kinds of goods spent the night outside Jerusalem. ²¹But I warned them and said, "Why do you spend the night by the wall? If you do this again, I will lay hands on you." From that time on they no longer came on the Sabbath. ²²Then I commanded the Levites to purify themselves and go and guard the gates in order to keep the Sabbath day holy.

Remember me for this also, O my God, and show mercy to me according to your great love.

²³Moreover, in those days I saw men of Judah who had married women from Ashdod, Ammon and Moab. ²⁴Half of their children spoke the language of Ashdod or the language of one of the other peoples, and did not know how to speak the language of Judah. ²⁵I rebuked them and called curses down on them. I beat some of the men and pulled out their hair. I made them take an oath in God's name and said: "You are not to give your daughters in marriage to their sons, nor are you to take their daughters in marriage for your sons or for yourselves. ²⁶Was it not because of marriages like these that Solomon king of Israel sinned? Among the many nations there was no king like him. He was loved by his God, and God made him king over all Israel, but even he was led into sin by foreign women. ²⁷Must we hear now that you too are doing all this terrible wickedness and are being unfaithful to our God by marrying foreign women?"

²⁸One of the sons of Joiada son of Eliashib the high priest was son-in-law to Sanballat the Horonite. And I drove him away from me.

²⁹Remember them, O my God, because they defiled the priestly office and the covenant of the priesthood and of the Levites.

³⁰So I purified the priests and the Levites of everything foreign, and assigned them duties, each to his own task. ³¹I also made provision for contributions of wood at designated times, and for the firstfruits.

Remember me with favor, O my God.

Serving God Faithfully

NEHEMIAH 13:31

Nehemiah served God throughout his life. Sometimes he had success (the wall was rebuilt) and sometimes, when his people did not follow God's laws, he felt frustrated. This last chapter of Nehemiah ends with the plaintive statement, "Remember me with favor." When have you felt that your endeavors for God were not successful despite your best efforts? When did you simply have to trust that God knew you well enough to understand both the highs and the lows of your circumstances? Offer your own "Remember me with favor" prayer in the belief that God will acknowledge all you do and deem you faithful.

See Meeting God in Prayer

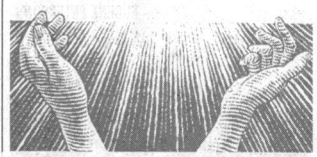

ESTHER

Courage to Be Faithful

KEY VERSE:

"And who knows but that you have come to royal position for such a time as this?" —Esther 4:14

> "Most of the time we are not living in a crisis in which we are conscious of our need of God, yet everything we do is critical to our faith, and God is critically involved in it. All day long we are doing eternally important things without knowing it. All through the day we inadvertently speak words that enter people's lives and change them in minor or major ways, and we never know it."
>
> —EUGENE PETERSON,
> *Reversed Thunder*

Every year in late winter Jews celebrate the Feast of Purim to commemorate their deliverance from those in a position to destroy them. This book is the story of how that feast came into being. The Jews living in exile in Persia are first threatened with extermination and then granted the sort of vindication the psalmists continually pleaded with God to pursue on their behalf.

This is also a story of irony, a dark comedy that reveals the posturing of the proud as foolishness. First, the ruler of the entire Middle East is thwarted by his wife when he tries to display her as a trophy at a feast. Then the scheming Haman, jealous of another's reward, ends up being hanged on his own gallows.

How is this reversal accomplished? By militia groups and palace coups? No. By an orphan girl isolated in the Persian harem. Counseled by her uncle, Mordecai, she first hides her identity as a Jew, revealing it only when her privileged position allows her to intercede on behalf of her people. She risks her life, yet fulfills her true destiny—one greater than she had ever dreamed.

Stuck in our everyday routine, we may find it difficult to remember our deepest identity as members of the body of Christ. To revive your awareness of that identity, consider carefully how much of your energy you expend on personal advancement. Compare that to your concern for the community of faith that sustains you. What risks do you take on behalf of that body?

Consider your destiny. Ask yourself, "Who knows for what purpose I have been brought to this time and place?"

Queen Vashti Deposed

1 This is what happened during the time of Xerxes,[a] the Xerxes who ruled over 127 provinces stretching from India to Cush[b]: ²At that time King Xerxes reigned from his royal throne in the citadel of Susa, ³and in the third year of his reign he gave a banquet for all his nobles and officials. The military leaders of Persia and Media, the princes, and the nobles of the provinces were present.

⁴For a full 180 days he displayed the vast wealth of his kingdom and the splendor and glory of his majesty. ⁵When these days were over, the king gave a banquet, lasting seven days, in the enclosed garden of the king's palace, for all the people from the least to the greatest, who were in the citadel of Susa. ⁶The garden had hangings of white and blue linen, fastened with cords of white linen and purple material to silver rings on marble pillars. There were couches of gold and silver on a mosaic pavement of porphyry, marble, mother-of-pearl and other costly stones. ⁷Wine was served in goblets of gold, each one different from the other, and the royal wine was abundant, in keeping with the king's liberality. ⁸By the king's command each guest was allowed to drink in his own way, for the king instructed all the wine stewards to serve each man what he wished.

⁹Queen Vashti also gave a banquet for the women in the royal palace of King Xerxes.

¹⁰On the seventh day, when King Xerxes was in high spirits from wine, he commanded the seven eunuchs who served him—Mehuman, Biztha, Harbona, Bigtha, Abagtha, Zethar and Carcas— ¹¹to bring before him Queen Vashti, wearing her royal crown, in order to display her beauty to the people and nobles, for she was lovely to look at. ¹²But when the attendants delivered the king's command, Queen Vashti refused to come. Then the king became furious and burned with anger.

¹³Since it was customary for the king to consult experts in matters of law and justice, he spoke with the wise men who understood the times ¹⁴and were closest to the king— Carshena, Shethar, Admatha, Tarshish, Meres, Marsena and Memucan, the seven nobles of Persia and Media who had special access to the king and were highest in the kingdom.

¹⁵"According to law, what must be done to Queen Vashti?" he asked. "She has not obeyed the command of King Xerxes that the eunuchs have taken to her."

¹⁶Then Memucan replied in the presence of the king and the nobles, "Queen Vashti has done wrong, not only against the king but also against all the nobles and the peoples of all the provinces of King Xerxes. ¹⁷For the queen's conduct will become known to all the women, and so they will despise their husbands and say, 'King Xerxes commanded Queen Vashti to be brought before him, but she would not come.' ¹⁸This very day the Persian and Median women of the nobility who have heard about the queen's conduct will respond to all the king's nobles in the same way. There will be no end of disrespect and discord.

¹⁹"Therefore, if it pleases the king, let him issue a royal decree and let it be written in the laws of Persia and Media,

---

People and Prizes

ESTHER 1:4–12

Conspicuous consumption often goes beyond acquiring a beautifully furnished home and entertaining royally. The process can become addictive. Intoxicated with ownership, we seek to enlarge our identities by adding to our possessions. Sometimes we even seek to possess and control other people.

Look around your house—in the closets, the living room, the garage. Which objects were acquired for their beauty or usefulness? Were any bought to impress others with your importance?

Look at the people you love. Do you ever use them to feel good about yourself? If your child brings home a report card with poor grades, do you respond in anger because you believe it reflects badly on you?

See Meeting God in Everyday Life

---

a 1 Hebrew *Ahasuerus,* a variant of Xerxes' Persian name; here and throughout Esther   *b 1* That is, the upper Nile region

643

The Need for Mentors

ESTHER 2:10–11

A true mentor not only encourages another to reach his or her potential and instructs his or her student but also actively seeks the student's advancement. Every athlete needs a coach who can continue to guide and counsel, even after the athlete's abilities and fame surpass the teacher's. We need experienced spiritual tutors to track our progress.

Imagine yourself in Esther's predicament full of unfamiliar people and bizarre circumstances. God brings to you a person, full of wisdom and deep concern, who paces back and forth waiting to see you and help you. How would this make you feel?

Consider any strange circumstances you are now encountering. Whom might you ask to become your mentor?

See Meeting God in Community

which cannot be repealed, that Vashti is never again to enter the presence of King Xerxes. Also let the king give her royal position to someone else who is better than she. ²⁰Then when the king's edict is proclaimed throughout all his vast realm, all the women will respect their husbands, from the least to the greatest."

²¹The king and his nobles were pleased with this advice, so the king did as Memucan proposed. ²²He sent dispatches to all parts of the kingdom, to each province in its own script and to each people in its own language, proclaiming in each people's tongue that every man should be ruler over his own household.

Esther Made Queen

2 Later when the anger of King Xerxes had subsided, he remembered Vashti and what she had done and what he had decreed about her. ²Then the king's personal attendants proposed, "Let a search be made for beautiful young virgins for the king. ³Let the king appoint commissioners in every province of his realm to bring all these beautiful girls into the harem at the citadel of Susa. Let them be placed under the care of Hegai, the king's eunuch, who is in charge of the women; and let beauty treatments be given to them. ⁴Then let the girl who pleases the king be queen instead of Vashti." This advice appealed to the king, and he followed it.

⁵Now there was in the citadel of Susa a Jew of the tribe of Benjamin, named Mordecai son of Jair, the son of Shimei, the son of Kish, ⁶who had been carried into exile from Jerusalem by Nebuchadnezzar king of Babylon, among those taken captive with Jehoiachin*a* king of Judah. ⁷Mordecai had a cousin named Hadassah, whom he had brought up because she had neither father nor mother. This girl, who was also known as Esther, was lovely in form and features, and Mordecai had taken her as his own daughter when her father and mother died.

⁸When the king's order and edict had been proclaimed, many girls were brought to the citadel of Susa and put under the care of Hegai. Esther also was taken to the king's palace and entrusted to Hegai, who had charge of the harem. ⁹The girl pleased him and won his favor. Immediately he provided her with her beauty treatments and special food. He assigned to her seven maids selected from the king's palace and moved her and her maids into the best place in the harem.

¹⁰Esther had not revealed her nationality and family background, because Mordecai had forbidden her to do so. ¹¹Every day he walked back and forth near the courtyard of the harem to find out how Esther was and what was happening to her.

¹²Before a girl's turn came to go in to King Xerxes, she had to complete twelve months of beauty treatments prescribed for the women, six months with oil of myrrh and six with perfumes and cosmetics. ¹³And this is how she would go to the king: Anything she wanted was given her to take with her from the harem to the king's palace. ¹⁴In the evening she would go there and in the morning return to another part of the harem to the care of Shaashgaz, the king's eunuch who was in charge of the concubines. She

a 6 Hebrew *Jeconiah*, a variant of *Jehoiachin*

would not return to the king unless he was pleased with her and summoned her by name.

¹⁵When the turn came for Esther (the girl Mordecai had adopted, the daughter of his uncle Abihail) to go to the king, she asked for nothing other than what Hegai, the king's eunuch who was in charge of the harem, suggested. And Esther won the favor of everyone who saw her. ¹⁶She was taken to King Xerxes in the royal residence in the tenth month, the month of Tebeth, in the seventh year of his reign.

¹⁷Now the king was attracted to Esther more than to any of the other women, and she won his favor and approval more than any of the other virgins. So he set a royal crown on her head and made her queen instead of Vashti. ¹⁸And the king gave a great banquet, Esther's banquet, for all his nobles and officials. He proclaimed a holiday throughout the provinces and distributed gifts with royal liberality.

Mordecai Uncovers a Conspiracy

¹⁹When the virgins were assembled a second time, Mordecai was sitting at the king's gate. ²⁰But Esther had kept secret her family background and nationality just as Mordecai had told her to do, for she continued to follow Mordecai's instructions as she had done when he was bringing her up.

²¹During the time Mordecai was sitting at the king's gate, Bigthana*ᵃ* and Teresh, two of the king's officers who guarded the doorway, became angry and conspired to assassinate King Xerxes. ²²But Mordecai found out about the plot and told Queen Esther, who in turn reported it to the king, giving credit to Mordecai. ²³And when the report was investigated and found to be true, the two officials were hanged on a gallows.*ᵇ* All this was recorded in the book of the annals in the presence of the king.

Haman's Plot to Destroy the Jews

3 After these events, King Xerxes honored Haman son of Hammedatha, the Agagite, elevating him and giving him a seat of honor higher than that of all the other nobles. ²All the royal officials at the king's gate knelt down and paid honor to Haman, for the king had commanded this concerning him. But Mordecai would not kneel down or pay him honor.

³Then the royal officials at the king's gate asked Mordecai, "Why do you disobey the king's command?" ⁴Day after day they spoke to him but he refused to comply. Therefore they told Haman about it to see whether Mordecai's behavior would be tolerated, for he had told them he was a Jew.

⁵When Haman saw that Mordecai would not kneel down or pay him honor, he was enraged. ⁶Yet having learned who Mordecai's people were, he scorned the idea of killing only Mordecai. Instead Haman looked for a way to destroy all Mordecai's people, the Jews, throughout the whole kingdom of Xerxes.

⁷In the twelfth year of King Xerxes, in the first month, the month of Nisan, they cast the *pur* (that is, the lot) in the

Refusing to Kneel

ESTHER 3:2–4

Being a Jew meant acknowledging that only God is worthy of worship. Much as Mordecai did in Persia, Christians today live both as citizens and as strangers in this world. We are surrounded by people whose values we may not share and with whom we may disagree on numerous issues.

Reread Esther 3:2–4. Notice what word or phrase or action attracts your attention. Reflect on this word or phrase or action. Why is it meaningful to you?

Remain silent and open for insight from God—perhaps about divided loyalties or frustrating disagreements. In what way does this passage touch your life today?

See *Meeting God in Scripture*

Sharing Suffering

ESTHER 4:1,5

Compassion means, literally, to "suffer with." The ancient world had active means of portraying this shared anguish and showing solidarity with sufferers. Esther makes an effort to discover the cause of Mordecai's grief.

Do you seek to discover the cause of suffering even if it does not affect you directly? Do you try to guard against hearing such unpleasant information? What means do we have at our disposal for suffering with other parts of the body of Christ? How is grief expressed publicly in your church?

See Meeting God in Community

presence of Haman to select a day and month. And the lot fell on*a* the twelfth month, the month of Adar. *8*Then Haman said to King Xerxes, "There is a certain people dispersed and scattered among the peoples in all the provinces of your kingdom whose customs are different from those of all other people and who do not obey the king's laws; it is not in the king's best interest to tolerate them. *9*If it pleases the king, let a decree be issued to destroy them, and I will put ten thousand talents*b* of silver into the royal treasury for the men who carry out this business."

*10*So the king took his signet ring from his finger and gave it to Haman son of Hammedatha, the Agagite, the enemy of the Jews. *11*"Keep the money," the king said to Haman, "and do with the people as you please."

*12*Then on the thirteenth day of the first month the royal secretaries were summoned. They wrote out in the script of each province and in the language of each people all Haman's orders to the king's satraps, the governors of the various provinces and the nobles of the various peoples. These were written in the name of King Xerxes himself and sealed with his own ring. *13*Dispatches were sent by couriers to all the king's provinces with the order to destroy, kill and annihilate all the Jews—young and old, women and little children—on a single day, the thirteenth day of the twelfth month, the month of Adar, and to plunder their goods. *14*A copy of the text of the edict was to be issued as law in every province and made known to the people of every nationality so they would be ready for that day.

*15*Spurred on by the king's command, the couriers went out, and the edict was issued in the citadel of Susa. The king and Haman sat down to drink, but the city of Susa was bewildered.

Mordecai Persuades Esther to Help

4 When Mordecai learned of all that had been done, he tore his clothes, put on sackcloth and ashes, and went out into the city, wailing loudly and bitterly. *2*But he went only as far as the king's gate, because no one clothed in sackcloth was allowed to enter it. *3*In every province to which the edict and order of the king came, there was great mourning among the Jews, with fasting, weeping and wailing. Many lay in sackcloth and ashes.

*4*When Esther's maids and eunuchs came and told her about Mordecai, she was in great distress. She sent clothes for him to put on instead of his sackcloth, but he would not accept them. *5*Then Esther summoned Hathach, one of the king's eunuchs assigned to attend her, and ordered him to find out what was troubling Mordecai and why.

*6*So Hathach went out to Mordecai in the open square of the city in front of the king's gate. *7*Mordecai told him everything that had happened to him, including the exact amount of money Haman had promised to pay into the royal treasury for the destruction of the Jews. *8*He also gave him a copy of the text of the edict for their annihilation, which had been published in Susa, to show to Esther and explain it to her, and he told him to urge her to go into the

a 7 Septuagint; Hebrew does not have *And the lot fell on.*   *b* 9 That is, about 375 tons (about 345 metric tons)

king's presence to beg for mercy and plead with him for her people.

⁹Hathach went back and reported to Esther what Mordecai had said. ¹⁰Then she instructed him to say to Mordecai, ¹¹"All the king's officials and the people of the royal provinces know that for any man or woman who approaches the king in the inner court without being summoned the king has but one law: that he be put to death. The only exception to this is for the king to extend the gold scepter to him and spare his life. But thirty days have passed since I was called to go to the king."

¹²When Esther's words were reported to Mordecai, ¹³he sent back this answer: "Do not think that because you are in the king's house you alone of all the Jews will escape. ¹⁴For if you remain silent at this time, relief and deliverance for the Jews will arise from another place, but you and your father's family will perish. And who knows but that you have come to royal position for such a time as this?"

¹⁵Then Esther sent this reply to Mordecai: ¹⁶"Go, gather together all the Jews who are in Susa, and fast for me. Do not eat or drink for three days, night or day. I and my maids will fast as you do. When this is done, I will go to the king, even though it is against the law. And if I perish, I perish."

¹⁷So Mordecai went away and carried out all of Esther's instructions.

Esther's Request to the King

5 On the third day Esther put on her royal robes and stood in the inner court of the palace, in front of the king's hall. The king was sitting on his royal throne in the hall, facing the entrance. ²When he saw Queen Esther standing in the court, he was pleased with her and held out to her the gold scepter that was in his hand. So Esther approached and touched the tip of the scepter.

³Then the king asked, "What is it, Queen Esther? What is your request? Even up to half the kingdom, it will be given you."

⁴"If it pleases the king," replied Esther, "let the king, together with Haman, come today to a banquet I have prepared for him."

⁵"Bring Haman at once," the king said, "so that we may do what Esther asks."

So the king and Haman went to the banquet Esther had prepared. ⁶As they were drinking wine, the king again asked Esther, "Now what is your petition? It will be given you. And what is your request? Even up to half the kingdom, it will be granted."

⁷Esther replied, "My petition and my request is this: ⁸If the king regards me with favor and if it pleases the king to grant my petition and fulfill my request, let the king and Haman come tomorrow to the banquet I will prepare for them. Then I will answer the king's question."

Haman's Rage Against Mordecai

⁹Haman went out that day happy and in high spirits. But when he saw Mordecai at the king's gate and observed that he neither rose nor showed fear in his presence, he was filled with rage against Mordecai. ¹⁰Nevertheless, Haman restrained himself and went home.

Calling together his friends and Zeresh, his wife,

On the Way to Freedom

ESTHER 4:14

"Do and dare what is right, not swayed by the whim of the moment. Bravely take hold of the real, not dallying now with what might be. Not in the flight of ideas but only in action is freedom. Make up your mind and come out into the tempest of living. God's command is enough and your faith in him to sustain you. Then at last freedom will welcome your spirit among great rejoicing."

—DIETRICH BONHOEFFER,
Ethics

The Rival's Reward

ESTHER 6:6

In a twist of irony, the proud Haman puts the noose around his own neck as he mistakes "the man the king delights to honor" for himself. The wonderful reward he dreams up for himself turns into his worst nightmare when the reward goes to his enemy instead.

Write down ways you secretly dream of being recognized for your worth—perhaps by winning a marathon, getting a raise or graduating *magna cum laude*. Then think of someone with whom you feel competitive—a sibling, a coworker or even a spouse. Now imagine that person receiving the rewards on your list instead of you. How does that feel? What would need to happen in order for you to congratulate him or her with a pure heart?

See Meeting God in Everyday Life

11Haman boasted to them about his vast wealth, his many sons, and all the ways the king had honored him and how he had elevated him above the other nobles and officials. 12"And that's not all," Haman added. "I'm the only person Queen Esther invited to accompany the king to the banquet she gave. And she has invited me along with the king tomorrow. 13But all this gives me no satisfaction as long as I see that Jew Mordecai sitting at the king's gate."

14His wife Zeresh and all his friends said to him, "Have a gallows built, seventy-five feet*a* high, and ask the king in the morning to have Mordecai hanged on it. Then go with the king to the dinner and be happy." This suggestion delighted Haman, and he had the gallows built.

Mordecai Honored

6 That night the king could not sleep; so he ordered the book of the chronicles, the record of his reign, to be brought in and read to him. 2It was found recorded there that Mordecai had exposed Bigthana and Teresh, two of the king's officers who guarded the doorway, who had conspired to assassinate King Xerxes.

3"What honor and recognition has Mordecai received for this?" the king asked.

"Nothing has been done for him," his attendants answered.

4The king said, "Who is in the court?" Now Haman had just entered the outer court of the palace to speak to the king about hanging Mordecai on the gallows he had erected for him.

5His attendants answered, "Haman is standing in the court."

"Bring him in," the king ordered.

6When Haman entered, the king asked him, "What should be done for the man the king delights to honor?"

Now Haman thought to himself, "Who is there that the king would rather honor than me?" 7So he answered the king, "For the man the king delights to honor, 8have them bring a royal robe the king has worn and a horse the king has ridden, one with a royal crest placed on its head. 9Then let the robe and horse be entrusted to one of the king's most noble princes. Let them robe the man the king delights to honor, and lead him on the horse through the city streets, proclaiming before him, 'This is what is done for the man the king delights to honor!' "

10"Go at once," the king commanded Haman. "Get the robe and the horse and do just as you have suggested for Mordecai the Jew, who sits at the king's gate. Do not neglect anything you have recommended."

11So Haman got the robe and the horse. He robed Mordecai, and led him on horseback through the city streets, proclaiming before him, "This is what is done for the man the king delights to honor!"

12Afterward Mordecai returned to the king's gate. But Haman rushed home, with his head covered in grief, 13and told Zeresh his wife and all his friends everything that had happened to him.

His advisers and his wife Zeresh said to him, "Since Mordecai, before whom your downfall has started, is of Jewish origin, you cannot stand against him—you will surely come

a 14 Hebrew *fifty cubits* (about 23 meters)

to ruin!" ¹⁴While they were still talking with him, the king's eunuchs arrived and hurried Haman away to the banquet Esther had prepared.

Haman Hanged

7 So the king and Haman went to dine with Queen Esther, ²and as they were drinking wine on that second day, the king again asked, "Queen Esther, what is your petition? It will be given you. What is your request? Even up to half the kingdom, it will be granted."

³Then Queen Esther answered, "If I have found favor with you, O king, and if it pleases your majesty, grant me my life—this is my petition. And spare my people—this is my request. ⁴For I and my people have been sold for destruction and slaughter and annihilation. If we had merely been sold as male and female slaves, I would have kept quiet, because no such distress would justify disturbing the king.ᵃ"

⁵King Xerxes asked Queen Esther, "Who is he? Where is the man who has dared to do such a thing?"

⁶Esther said, "The adversary and enemy is this vile Haman."

Then Haman was terrified before the king and queen. ⁷The king got up in a rage, left his wine and went out into the palace garden. But Haman, realizing that the king had already decided his fate, stayed behind to beg Queen Esther for his life.

⁸Just as the king returned from the palace garden to the banquet hall, Haman was falling on the couch where Esther was reclining.

The king exclaimed, "Will he even molest the queen while she is with me in the house?"

As soon as the word left the king's mouth, they covered Haman's face. ⁹Then Harbona, one of the eunuchs attending the king, said, "A gallows seventy-five feetᵇ high stands by Haman's house. He had it made for Mordecai, who spoke up to help the king."

The king said, "Hang him on it!" ¹⁰So they hanged Haman on the gallows he had prepared for Mordecai. Then the king's fury subsided.

The King's Edict in Behalf of the Jews

8 That same day King Xerxes gave Queen Esther the estate of Haman, the enemy of the Jews. And Mordecai came into the presence of the king, for Esther had told how he was related to her. ²The king took off his signet ring, which he had reclaimed from Haman, and presented it to Mordecai. And Esther appointed him over Haman's estate.

³Esther again pleaded with the king, falling at his feet and weeping. She begged him to put an end to the evil plan of Haman the Agagite, which he had devised against the Jews. ⁴Then the king extended the gold scepter to Esther and she arose and stood before him.

⁵"If it pleases the king," she said, "and if he regards me with favor and thinks it the right thing to do, and if he is pleased with me, let an order be written overruling the dispatches that Haman son of Hammedatha, the Agagite, devised and wrote to destroy the Jews in all the king's

---

Risking Revelation

ESTHER 7:3–4

Knowing how much is at stake, Esther does not undertake her mission without preparation and planning. First, she asks the Jews to fast and pray for her (see 4:16). Then she waits for the proper moment. Only then does she reveal her true identity as a Jew and appeal to the king for mercy for her people.

Have you had to reveal some secret from your own life to another person? Were you fearful of the outcome? What was at stake? How did you prepare for that moment? What truth about yourself do you wish to be known now? How might its revelation change your life? Take a few days to pray about this or about another major decision in your life.

See Meeting God in Prayer

ᵃ 4 Or *quiet, but the compensation our adversary offers cannot be compared with the loss the king would suffer*   ᵇ 9 Hebrew *fifty cubits* (about 23 meters)

Rescue and Rejoicing

ESTHER 8:16–17

The Jews' prayers are answered when the king grants them rights of assembly and self-protection. Mourning turns to joy as the Jews feast in celebration of their rescue.

Celebrating times of deliverance is important. Consider the problems or situations from which God has delivered you in the last year. Take a few minutes to celebrate one or two of them by writing about them, by allowing yourself a treat or by thinking about your deliverance as you perform an appropriate action, such as rocking your now-healthy baby, driving in your repaired car or holding the letter that welcomes you to your new job.

See *Meeting God in Everyday Life*

provinces. **6**For how can I bear to see disaster fall on my people? How can I bear to see the destruction of my family?"

7King Xerxes replied to Queen Esther and to Mordecai the Jew, "Because Haman attacked the Jews, I have given his estate to Esther, and they have hanged him on the gallows. **8**Now write another decree in the king's name in behalf of the Jews as seems best to you, and seal it with the king's signet ring—for no document written in the king's name and sealed with his ring can be revoked."

9At once the royal secretaries were summoned—on the twenty-third day of the third month, the month of Sivan. They wrote out all Mordecai's orders to the Jews, and to the satraps, governors and nobles of the 127 provinces stretching from India to Cush.*ᵃ* These orders were written in the script of each province and the language of each people and also to the Jews in their own script and language. **10**Mordecai wrote in the name of King Xerxes, sealed the dispatches with the king's signet ring, and sent them by mounted couriers, who rode fast horses especially bred for the king.

11The king's edict granted the Jews in every city the right to assemble and protect themselves; to destroy, kill and annihilate any armed force of any nationality or province that might attack them and their women and children; and to plunder the property of their enemies. **12**The day appointed for the Jews to do this in all the provinces of King Xerxes was the thirteenth day of the twelfth month, the month of Adar. **13**A copy of the text of the edict was to be issued as law in every province and made known to the people of every nationality so that the Jews would be ready on that day to avenge themselves on their enemies.

14The couriers, riding the royal horses, raced out, spurred on by the king's command. And the edict was also issued in the citadel of Susa.

15Mordecai left the king's presence wearing royal garments of blue and white, a large crown of gold and a purple robe of fine linen. And the city of Susa held a joyous celebration. **16**For the Jews it was a time of happiness and joy, gladness and honor. **17**In every province and in every city, wherever the edict of the king went, there was joy and gladness among the Jews, with feasting and celebrating. And many people of other nationalities became Jews because fear of the Jews had seized them.

Triumph of the Jews

9 On the thirteenth day of the twelfth month, the month of Adar, the edict commanded by the king was to be carried out. On this day the enemies of the Jews had hoped to overpower them, but now the tables were turned and the Jews got the upper hand over those who hated them. **2**The Jews assembled in their cities in all the provinces of King Xerxes to attack those seeking their destruction. No one could stand against them, because the people of all the other nationalities were afraid of them. **3**And all the nobles of the provinces, the satraps, the governors and the king's administrators helped the Jews, because fear of Mordecai had seized them. **4**Mordecai was prominent in the palace;

ᵃ 9 That is, the upper Nile region

his reputation spread throughout the provinces, and he became more and more powerful.

⁵The Jews struck down all their enemies with the sword, killing and destroying them, and they did what they pleased to those who hated them. ⁶In the citadel of Susa, the Jews killed and destroyed five hundred men. ⁷They also killed Parshandatha, Dalphon, Aspatha, ⁸Poratha, Adalia, Aridatha, ⁹Parmashta, Arisai, Aridai and Vaizatha, ¹⁰the ten sons of Haman son of Hammedatha, the enemy of the Jews. But they did not lay their hands on the plunder.

¹¹The number of those slain in the citadel of Susa was reported to the king that same day. ¹²The king said to Queen Esther, "The Jews have killed and destroyed five hundred men and the ten sons of Haman in the citadel of Susa. What have they done in the rest of the king's provinces? Now what is your petition? It will be given you. What is your request? It will also be granted."

¹³"If it pleases the king," Esther answered, "give the Jews in Susa permission to carry out this day's edict tomorrow also, and let Haman's ten sons be hanged on gallows."

¹⁴So the king commanded that this be done. An edict was issued in Susa, and they hanged the ten sons of Haman. ¹⁵The Jews in Susa came together on the fourteenth day of the month of Adar, and they put to death in Susa three hundred men, but they did not lay their hands on the plunder.

¹⁶Meanwhile, the remainder of the Jews who were in the king's provinces also assembled to protect themselves and get relief from their enemies. They killed seventy-five thousand of them but did not lay their hands on the plunder. ¹⁷This happened on the thirteenth day of the month of Adar, and on the fourteenth they rested and made it a day of feasting and joy.

Purim Celebrated

¹⁸The Jews in Susa, however, had assembled on the thirteenth and fourteenth, and then on the fifteenth they rested and made it a day of feasting and joy.

¹⁹That is why rural Jews—those living in villages—observe the fourteenth of the month of Adar as a day of joy and feasting, a day for giving presents to each other.

²⁰Mordecai recorded these events, and he sent letters to all the Jews throughout the provinces of King Xerxes, near and far, ²¹to have them celebrate annually the fourteenth and fifteenth days of the month of Adar ²²as the time when the Jews got relief from their enemies, and as the month when their sorrow was turned into joy and their mourning into a day of celebration. He wrote them to observe the days as days of feasting and joy and giving presents of food to one another and gifts to the poor.

²³So the Jews agreed to continue the celebration they had begun, doing what Mordecai had written to them. ²⁴For Haman son of Hammedatha, the Agagite, the enemy of all the Jews, had plotted against the Jews to destroy them and had cast the *pur* (that is, the lot) for their ruin and destruction. ²⁵But when the plot came to the king's attention,ᵃ he issued written orders that the evil scheme Haman had devised against the Jews should come back onto his own head, and that he and his sons should be hanged on the

---

The Widening Circle

ESTHER 9:20–22

Mordecai sends instructions to the Jews in all the provinces to celebrate their deliverance by sharing food with others and showering the poor with gifts. This celebration ensures that no one is left out and it further deepens the exiled people's sense of community.

Read the passage again slowly. Listen for a word or phrase that draws your attention. Wait for something to happen apart from yourself. Reflect on this word or phrase. What comes to you as you turn it over in your mind? Pray that phrase back to God. How does it sound as a prayer? Rest in silence, letting the text work its way throughout the layers of who you are.

See Meeting God in Scripture

ᵃ 25 Or *when Esther came before the king*

Commemoration

ESTHER 9:28

"Lest we forget" marks many a soldier's tombstone. "Remember!" begins every Passover celebration. We remember the Lord's death in every celebration of the Lord's Supper. Memory is essential to being human. Commemoration acknowledges and honors God's saving acts among us. The past is not obsolete or irrelevant. We do not invent the life of faith; we come to a dynamic and personal faith within the context of the traditions our spiritual ancestors have shaped and preserved for us. What have you inherited from your spiritual forebears? Thank God for their faithfulness. Make a list of what you would like your children or some future generation to remember about your spiritual life.

See Meeting God in Community

gallows. ²⁶(Therefore these days were called Purim, from the word *pur*.) Because of everything written in this letter and because of what they had seen and what had happened to them, ²⁷the Jews took it upon themselves to establish the custom that they and their descendants and all who join them should without fail observe these two days every year, in the way prescribed and at the time appointed. ²⁸These days should be remembered and observed in every generation by every family, and in every province and in every city. And these days of Purim should never cease to be celebrated by the Jews, nor should the memory of them die out among their descendants.

²⁹So Queen Esther, daughter of Abihail, along with Mordecai the Jew, wrote with full authority to confirm this second letter concerning Purim. ³⁰And Mordecai sent letters to all the Jews in the 127 provinces of the kingdom of Xerxes—words of goodwill and assurance— ³¹to establish these days of Purim at their designated times, as Mordecai the Jew and Queen Esther had decreed for them, and as they had established for themselves and their descendants in regard to their times of fasting and lamentation. ³²Esther's decree confirmed these regulations about Purim, and it was written down in the records.

The Greatness of Mordecai

10 King Xerxes imposed tribute throughout the empire, to its distant shores. ²And all his acts of power and might, together with a full account of the greatness of Mordecai to which the king had raised him, are they not written in the book of the annals of the kings of Media and Persia? ³Mordecai the Jew was second in rank to King Xerxes, preeminent among the Jews, and held in high esteem by his many fellow Jews, because he worked for the good of his people and spoke up for the welfare of all the Jews.

JOB
When Bad Things Happen

KEY VERSE:

"My ears had heard of you but now my eyes have seen you."—Job 42:5

Read the book of Job as a drama being played out on a stage. Act I begins with Job living in happiness and prosperity. Then, through one calamity after another, Job loses everything—his livestock, his servants, his children, his health. In Act II Job converses with his friends, who try to help him make sense of his suffering. In Act III Job speaks directly with God, and Job grasps—apparently for the first time—the depth of God's power and love. Job knows he has personally encountered the Eternal God: "My ears had heard of you but now my eyes have seen you" (42:5).

The book of Job endures as a drama because it addresses the reality of suffering. Not surprisingly, Job struggles more with the crisis of faith going on within himself than he does with what has happened to him externally. But Job persists in loving God—refusing to curse God—in spite of all his deeply felt losses. He never abandons his own honest, relentless and tormented pursuit of God.

All of us eventually travel the way of suffering. As we journey into its darkness, we may find ourselves tempted to doubt God's goodness, mercy and love. But Job gives us the courage to face honestly our hard questions and to wrestle with God. Like Job, we may meet God face-to-face at a depth we have not known before. Like Job, we can come to know that when all we have is taken away, God is enough.

"It is well for those who find themselves in the dark night of the soul to persevere in patience . . . Let them trust in God, who does not abandon those who seek God with a simple and right heart, and will not fail to give them what is needful for the road, until he brings them into the clear and pure light of love."

—JOHN OF THE CROSS,
The Dark Night of the Soul

When Hardship Overtakes the Upright

JOB 1:1

From the first few words of the book we learn that Job is blameless and upright. This is the point on which the whole of the book of Job turns: He does not deserve the various calamities that befall him. He has done nothing wrong, though his friends later argue the contrary. The book of Job shows us that bad things happen to good people, and that we may have to struggle to be faithful when things seem unfair.

Perhaps you, like Job, are experiencing pain or distress. What questions do you bring to God? If you or someone you love is enduring great pain or loss, hold yourself or that other person in silence before God. Simply be still. Wait patiently.

Prologue

1 In the land of Uz there lived a man whose name was Job. This man was blameless and upright; he feared God and shunned evil. ²He had seven sons and three daughters, ³and he owned seven thousand sheep, three thousand camels, five hundred yoke of oxen and five hundred donkeys, and had a large number of servants. He was the greatest man among all the people of the East.

⁴His sons used to take turns holding feasts in their homes, and they would invite their three sisters to eat and drink with them. ⁵When a period of feasting had run its course, Job would send and have them purified. Early in the morning he would sacrifice a burnt offering for each of them, thinking, "Perhaps my children have sinned and cursed God in their hearts." This was Job's regular custom.

Job's First Test

⁶One day the angels^a came to present themselves before the LORD, and Satan^b also came with them. ⁷The LORD said to Satan, "Where have you come from?"

Satan answered the LORD, "From roaming through the earth and going back and forth in it."

⁸Then the LORD said to Satan, "Have you considered my servant Job? There is no one on earth like him; he is blameless and upright, a man who fears God and shuns evil."

⁹"Does Job fear God for nothing?" Satan replied. ¹⁰"Have you not put a hedge around him and his household and everything he has? You have blessed the work of his hands, so that his flocks and herds are spread throughout the land. ¹¹But stretch out your hand and strike everything he has, and he will surely curse you to your face."

¹²The LORD said to Satan, "Very well, then, everything he has is in your hands, but on the man himself do not lay a finger."

Then Satan went out from the presence of the LORD.

¹³One day when Job's sons and daughters were feasting and drinking wine at the oldest brother's house, ¹⁴a messenger came to Job and said, "The oxen were plowing and the donkeys were grazing nearby, ¹⁵and the Sabeans attacked and carried them off. They put the servants to the sword, and I am the only one who has escaped to tell you!"

¹⁶While he was still speaking, another messenger came and said, "The fire of God fell from the sky and burned up the sheep and the servants, and I am the only one who has escaped to tell you!"

¹⁷While he was still speaking, another messenger came and said, "The Chaldeans formed three raiding parties and swept down on your camels and carried them off. They put the servants to the sword, and I am the only one who has escaped to tell you!"

¹⁸While he was still speaking, yet another messenger came and said, "Your sons and daughters were feasting and drinking wine at the oldest brother's house, ¹⁹when suddenly a mighty wind swept in from the desert and struck the four corners of the house. It collapsed on them and they are dead, and I am the only one who has escaped to tell you!"

^a 6 Hebrew *the sons of God*   ^b 6 *Satan* means *accuser.*

²⁰At this, Job got up and tore his robe and shaved his head. Then he fell to the ground in worship ²¹and said:

"Naked I came from my mother's womb,
   and naked I will depart.ᵃ
The Lᴏʀᴅ gave and the Lᴏʀᴅ has taken away;
   may the name of the Lᴏʀᴅ be praised."

²²In all this, Job did not sin by charging God with wrongdoing.

Job's Second Test

2 On another day the angelsᵇ came to present themselves before the Lᴏʀᴅ, and Satan also came with them to present himself before him. ²And the Lᴏʀᴅ said to Satan, "Where have you come from?"

Satan answered the Lᴏʀᴅ, "From roaming through the earth and going back and forth in it."

³Then the Lᴏʀᴅ said to Satan, "Have you considered my servant Job? There is no one on earth like him; he is blameless and upright, a man who fears God and shuns evil. And he still maintains his integrity, though you incited me against him to ruin him without any reason."

⁴"Skin for skin!" Satan replied. "A man will give all he has for his own life. ⁵But stretch out your hand and strike his flesh and bones, and he will surely curse you to your face."

⁶The Lᴏʀᴅ said to Satan, "Very well, then, he is in your hands; but you must spare his life."

⁷So Satan went out from the presence of the Lᴏʀᴅ and afflicted Job with painful sores from the soles of his feet to the top of his head. ⁸Then Job took a piece of broken pottery and scraped himself with it as he sat among the ashes.

⁹His wife said to him, "Are you still holding on to your integrity? Curse God and die!"

¹⁰He replied, "You are talking like a foolishᶜ woman. Shall we accept good from God, and not trouble?"

In all this, Job did not sin in what he said.

Job's Three Friends

¹¹When Job's three friends, Eliphaz the Temanite, Bildad the Shuhite and Zophar the Naamathite, heard about all the troubles that had come upon him, they set out from their homes and met together by agreement to go and sympathize with him and comfort him. ¹²When they saw him from a distance, they could hardly recognize him; they began to weep aloud, and they tore their robes and sprinkled dust on their heads. ¹³Then they sat on the ground with him for seven days and seven nights. No one said a word to him, because they saw how great his suffering was.

Job Speaks

3 After this, Job opened his mouth and cursed the day of his birth. ²He said:

³ "May the day of my birth perish,
   and the night it was said, 'A boy is born!'
⁴That day—may it turn to darkness;
   may God above not care about it;
   may no light shine upon it.

Wordless Comfort

JOB 2:11–13

Job's friends come to Job to "sympathize with him and comfort him." For seven days they throw dust on their heads (a sign of grieving) and sit with him; no one says a word. At this point, Job's friends model compassionate friendship—patient presence with someone in a difficult situation.

When have you experienced such wordless comfort? Do you have friends with whom no words are necessary? Give thanks for those who understand you and stand with you emotionally, especially when you grieve. Consider whether there is someone who needs your presence and support. How can you indicate your concern and support if you are not able to be physically present with someone you care about during his or her hard times?

See *Meeting God in Service*

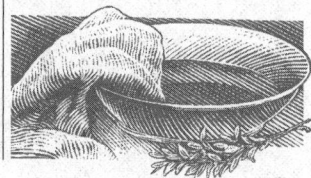

ᵃ 21 Or *will return there*   ᵇ 1 Hebrew *the sons of God*   ᶜ 10 The Hebrew word rendered *foolish* denotes moral deficiency.

655

Honest With God

JOB 3:1–15

In strong language, Job wishes that he had died at birth and compares death to release and freedom. This is not a picture of someone tiptoeing into God's presence, whispering mild displeasure. Job rails at God, expressing his anguish in complete openness and honesty.

Following Job's example, offer to God your honest feelings, whatever they are. What do you want to say to God? Express the deepest pain or the deepest joy in your heart. God listens to us and welcomes the open expression of all of our emotions.

See Meeting God in Prayer

⁵May darkness and deep shadow*ᵃ* claim it once
more;
may a cloud settle over it;
may blackness overwhelm its light.
⁶That night—may thick darkness seize it;
may it not be included among the days of the
year
nor be entered in any of the months.
⁷May that night be barren;
may no shout of joy be heard in it.
⁸May those who curse days*ᵇ* curse that day,
those who are ready to rouse Leviathan.
⁹May its morning stars become dark;
may it wait for daylight in vain
and not see the first rays of dawn,
¹⁰for it did not shut the doors of the womb on me
to hide trouble from my eyes.

¹¹ "Why did I not perish at birth,
and die as I came from the womb?
¹²Why were there knees to receive me
and breasts that I might be nursed?
¹³For now I would be lying down in peace;
I would be asleep and at rest
¹⁴with kings and counselors of the earth,
who built for themselves places now lying in
ruins,
¹⁵with rulers who had gold,
who filled their houses with silver.
¹⁶Or why was I not hidden in the ground like a
stillborn child,
like an infant who never saw the light of day?
¹⁷There the wicked cease from turmoil,
and there the weary are at rest.
¹⁸Captives also enjoy their ease;
they no longer hear the slave driver's shout.
¹⁹The small and the great are there,
and the slave is freed from his master.

²⁰ "Why is light given to those in misery,
and life to the bitter of soul,
²¹to those who long for death that does not come,
who search for it more than for hidden treasure,
²²who are filled with gladness
and rejoice when they reach the grave?
²³Why is life given to a man
whose way is hidden,
whom God has hedged in?
²⁴For sighing comes to me instead of food;
my groans pour out like water.
²⁵What I feared has come upon me;
what I dreaded has happened to me.
²⁶I have no peace, no quietness;
I have no rest, but only turmoil."

Eliphaz

4 Then Eliphaz the Temanite replied:

² "If someone ventures a word with you, will you
be impatient?

ᵃ 5 Or *and the shadow of death*   *ᵇ 8* Or *the sea*

But who can keep from speaking?
³ Think how you have instructed many,
how you have strengthened feeble hands.
⁴ Your words have supported those who stumbled;
you have strengthened faltering knees.
⁵ But now trouble comes to you, and you are
discouraged;
it strikes you, and you are dismayed.
⁶ Should not your piety be your confidence
and your blameless ways your hope?

⁷ "Consider now: Who, being innocent, has ever
perished?
Where were the upright ever destroyed?
⁸ As I have observed, those who plow evil
and those who sow trouble reap it.
⁹ At the breath of God they are destroyed;
at the blast of his anger they perish.
¹⁰ The lions may roar and growl,
yet the teeth of the great lions are broken.
¹¹ The lion perishes for lack of prey,
and the cubs of the lioness are scattered.

¹² "A word was secretly brought to me,
my ears caught a whisper of it.
¹³ Amid disquieting dreams in the night,
when deep sleep falls on men,
¹⁴ fear and trembling seized me
and made all my bones shake.
¹⁵ A spirit glided past my face,
and the hair on my body stood on end.
¹⁶ It stopped,
but I could not tell what it was.
A form stood before my eyes,
and I heard a hushed voice:
¹⁷ 'Can a mortal be more righteous than God?
Can a man be more pure than his Maker?
¹⁸ If God places no trust in his servants,
if he charges his angels with error,
¹⁹ how much more those who live in houses of clay,
whose foundations are in the dust,
who are crushed more readily than a moth!
²⁰ Between dawn and dusk they are broken to
pieces;
unnoticed, they perish forever.
²¹ Are not the cords of their tent pulled up,
so that they die without wisdom?'ᵃ

5 "Call if you will, but who will answer you?
To which of the holy ones will you turn?
² Resentment kills a fool,
and envy slays the simple.
³ I myself have seen a fool taking root,
but suddenly his house was cursed.
⁴ His children are far from safety,
crushed in court without a defender.
⁵ The hungry consume his harvest,
taking it even from among thorns,
and the thirsty pant after his wealth.

Breaking the Silence

JOB 4:1–6

Eliphaz, Bildad and Zophar care about Job and have come a long way to be with him. But one of the trials Job has to bear is hearing advice from his friends. Eliphaz breaks the seven-day silence by offering Job the first of many pieces of advice: Be a good example. Job has taught others, Eliphaz says, and now has the opportunity to practice what he preaches. Though well-meaning, these words do not help Job.

When we experience difficulty, people often struggle to find something helpful to say to us. Imagine yourself in a desperate situation; someone says to you, "Be a good Christian. Show others how strong you are. People are watching." How would this make you feel? What would you want someone to say to you? What lessons does Job's friend offer you for helping those you care about?

See Meeting God in Community

ᵃ 21 Some interpreters end the quotation after verse 17.

657

More Advice

JOB 5:8,17–21

"God is disciplining you," is the next admonition. We know from Job 1:9–12 that these calamities have not come from God, though Job's friend says otherwise. Have you ever said or heard words like these: "God is trying to teach you something through this. Just pay attention and you'll see it"?

Make a point of being prepared to comfort others before you are called to do so. Perhaps you could ask a few people who have experienced loss what kinds of words and advice helped them most when they were suffering. Read a book about comforting the grieving. Collect a file of encouraging and empathetic poetry or prayers to share with someone who is grieving.

See Meeting God in Everyday Life

⁶ For hardship does not spring from the soil,
  nor does trouble sprout from the ground.
⁷ Yet man is born to trouble
  as surely as sparks fly upward.

⁸ "But if it were I, I would appeal to God;
  I would lay my cause before him.
⁹ He performs wonders that cannot be fathomed,
  miracles that cannot be counted.
¹⁰ He bestows rain on the earth;
  he sends water upon the countryside.
¹¹ The lowly he sets on high,
  and those who mourn are lifted to safety.
¹² He thwarts the plans of the crafty,
  so that their hands achieve no success.
¹³ He catches the wise in their craftiness,
  and the schemes of the wily are swept away.
¹⁴ Darkness comes upon them in the daytime;
  at noon they grope as in the night.
¹⁵ He saves the needy from the sword in their
    mouth;
  he saves them from the clutches of the
    powerful.
¹⁶ So the poor have hope,
  and injustice shuts its mouth.

¹⁷ "Blessed is the man whom God corrects;
  so do not despise the discipline of the
    Almighty.*ᵃ*
¹⁸ For he wounds, but he also binds up;
  he injures, but his hands also heal.
¹⁹ From six calamities he will rescue you;
  in seven no harm will befall you.
²⁰ In famine he will ransom you from death,
  and in battle from the stroke of the sword.
²¹ You will be protected from the lash of the tongue,
  and need not fear when destruction comes.
²² You will laugh at destruction and famine,
  and need not fear the beasts of the earth.
²³ For you will have a covenant with the stones of
    the field,
  and the wild animals will be at peace with you.
²⁴ You will know that your tent is secure;
  you will take stock of your property and find
    nothing missing.
²⁵ You will know that your children will be many,
  and your descendants like the grass of the earth.
²⁶ You will come to the grave in full vigor,
  like sheaves gathered in season.

²⁷ "We have examined this, and it is true.
  So hear it and apply it to yourself."

Job
6

Then Job replied:

² "If only my anguish could be weighed
  and all my misery be placed on the scales!
³ It would surely outweigh the sand of the seas—
  no wonder my words have been impetuous.

ᵃ 17 Hebrew *Shaddai*; here and throughout Job

4 The arrows of the Almighty are in me,
  my spirit drinks in their poison;
  God's terrors are marshaled against me.
5 Does a wild donkey bray when it has grass,
  or an ox bellow when it has fodder?
6 Is tasteless food eaten without salt,
  or is there flavor in the white of an egg*?*
7 I refuse to touch it;
  such food makes me ill.

8 "Oh, that I might have my request,
  that God would grant what I hope for,
9 that God would be willing to crush me,
  to let loose his hand and cut me off!
10 Then I would still have this consolation—
  my joy in unrelenting pain—
  that I had not denied the words of the Holy
  One.

11 "What strength do I have, that I should still hope?
  What prospects, that I should be patient?
12 Do I have the strength of stone?
  Is my flesh bronze?
13 Do I have any power to help myself,
  now that success has been driven from me?

14 "A despairing man should have the devotion of
  his friends,
  even though he forsakes the fear of the
  Almighty.
15 But my brothers are as undependable as
  intermittent streams,
  as the streams that overflow
16 when darkened by thawing ice
  and swollen with melting snow,
17 but that cease to flow in the dry season,
  and in the heat vanish from their channels.
18 Caravans turn aside from their routes;
  they go up into the wasteland and perish.
19 The caravans of Tema look for water,
  the traveling merchants of Sheba look in hope.
20 They are distressed, because they had been
  confident;
  they arrive there, only to be disappointed.
21 Now you too have proved to be of no help;
  you see something dreadful and are afraid.
22 Have I ever said, 'Give something on my behalf,
  pay a ransom for me from your wealth,
23 deliver me from the hand of the enemy,
  ransom me from the clutches of the ruthless'?

24 "Teach me, and I will be quiet;
  show me where I have been wrong.
25 How painful are honest words!
  But what do your arguments prove?
26 Do you mean to correct what I say,
  and treat the words of a despairing man as
  wind?
27 You would even cast lots for the fatherless
  and barter away your friend.

People of Flesh

JOB 6:8–17

Job compares his friends to streams that evaporate when the weather gets hot. Job's friends offer him no refreshment; they do not follow him into the darkness of his pain, grief and loss. Job says, "Is my flesh bronze?" (v.12). In other words, he cannot shut off his feelings as if he were inanimate. While he has great faith, he acknowledges that his emotions are real, and he refuses to deny them.

Are you a good listener? When someone pours out his or her feelings to you, do you minimize their emotions or deny that person's right to experience those emotions? Or do you acknowledge their feelings as real and legitimate, even if they are hard to listen to? Practice being a good listener. The next time someone expresses an emotion to you, show them you are open to hear. Reflect that emotion back to them without judging or minimizing it.

See Meeting God in Service

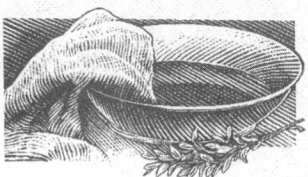

---

a 6 The meaning of the Hebrew for this phrase is uncertain.

No Sugarcoating

JOB 7:11–15

Great suffering often begets great honesty. Job doesn't sugarcoat his experience with polite distance. He complains bitterly. Job's honesty allows us to identify with him in his pain.

In spoken prayer or in your personal journal, pour out your complaints to God. God can take it. Be utterly honest about your experience. Trust that God is able to accept the full range of your emotions as he did Job's.

See Meeting God in Prayer

---

28 "But now be so kind as to look at me.
  Would I lie to your face?
29 Relent, do not be unjust;
  reconsider, for my integrity is at stake.*ª*
30 Is there any wickedness on my lips?
  Can my mouth not discern malice?

7 "Does not man have hard service on earth?
  Are not his days like those of a hired man?
2 Like a slave longing for the evening shadows,
  or a hired man waiting eagerly for his wages,
3 so I have been allotted months of futility,
  and nights of misery have been assigned to me.
4 When I lie down I think, 'How long before I get up?'
  The night drags on, and I toss till dawn.
5 My body is clothed with worms and scabs,
  my skin is broken and festering.

6 "My days are swifter than a weaver's shuttle,
  and they come to an end without hope.
7 Remember, O God, that my life is but a breath;
  my eyes will never see happiness again.
8 The eye that now sees me will see me no longer;
  you will look for me, but I will be no more.
9 As a cloud vanishes and is gone,
  so he who goes down to the grave*ᵇ* does not
    return.
10 He will never come to his house again;
  his place will know him no more.

11 "Therefore I will not keep silent;
  I will speak out in the anguish of my spirit,
  I will complain in the bitterness of my soul.
12 Am I the sea, or the monster of the deep,
  that you put me under guard?
13 When I think my bed will comfort me
  and my couch will ease my complaint,
14 even then you frighten me with dreams
  and terrify me with visions,
15 so that I prefer strangling and death,
  rather than this body of mine.
16 I despise my life; I would not live forever.
  Let me alone; my days have no meaning.

17 "What is man that you make so much of him,
  that you give him so much attention,
18 that you examine him every morning
  and test him every moment?
19 Will you never look away from me,
  or let me alone even for an instant?
20 If I have sinned, what have I done to you,
  O watcher of men?
  Why have you made me your target?
  Have I become a burden to you?*ᶜ*
21 Why do you not pardon my offenses
  and forgive my sins?
  For I will soon lie down in the dust;
  you will search for me, but I will be no more."

ª 29 Or *my righteousness still stands*   *ᵇ 9* Hebrew *Sheol*   *ᶜ 20* A few manuscripts of the Masoretic Text, an ancient Hebrew scribal tradition and Septuagint; most manuscripts of the Masoretic Text *I have become a burden to myself.*

Bildad

8 Then Bildad the Shuhite replied:

² "How long will you say such things?
  Your words are a blustering wind.
³ Does God pervert justice?
  Does the Almighty pervert what is right?
⁴ When your children sinned against him,
  he gave them over to the penalty of their sin.
⁵ But if you will look to God
  and plead with the Almighty,
⁶ if you are pure and upright,
  even now he will rouse himself on your behalf
  and restore you to your rightful place.
⁷ Your beginnings will seem humble,
  so prosperous will your future be.

⁸ "Ask the former generations
  and find out what their fathers learned,
⁹ for we were born only yesterday and know
    nothing,
  and our days on earth are but a shadow.
¹⁰ Will they not instruct you and tell you?
  Will they not bring forth words from their
    understanding?
¹¹ Can papyrus grow tall where there is no marsh?
  Can reeds thrive without water?
¹² While still growing and uncut,
  they wither more quickly than grass.
¹³ Such is the destiny of all who forget God;
  so perishes the hope of the godless.
¹⁴ What he trusts in is fragile[a];
  what he relies on is a spider's web.
¹⁵ He leans on his web, but it gives way;
  he clings to it, but it does not hold.
¹⁶ He is like a well-watered plant in the sunshine,
  spreading its shoots over the garden;
¹⁷ it entwines its roots around a pile of rocks
  and looks for a place among the stones.
¹⁸ But when it is torn from its spot,
  that place disowns it and says, 'I never saw you.'
¹⁹ Surely its life withers away,
  and[b] from the soil other plants grow.

²⁰ "Surely God does not reject a blameless man
  or strengthen the hands of evildoers.
²¹ He will yet fill your mouth with laughter
  and your lips with shouts of joy.
²² Your enemies will be clothed in shame,
  and the tents of the wicked will be no more."

Job

9 Then Job replied:

² "Indeed, I know that this is true.
  But how can a mortal be righteous before God?
³ Though one wished to dispute with him,

Another Strategy

JOB 8:1–7

Bildad offers another bit of advice: Take action. Repent. Do something. Job has the power to end his suffering if he'll just admit his sin, and then God will restore all that he has lost. Bildad's words are an attempt to protect his belief that he has power over what happens to himself. If Bildad were to admit that Job is innocent and righteous, then he would have to admit that his own good behavior is not a shield for himself either. But the truth is that loss, suffering and pain often strike for reasons that are not apparent. There is no defense against disaster.

Looking for reasons for suffering tempts us to think that we can control what happens to us. For example, we think that if we eat right, we won't ever get cancer. If we save money, we will always have financial security. Such rationalization tempts us to ignore our fears and hide from them. What are some of the thought processes you use to insulate yourself from fear? After you identify them, acknowledge them and offer your need to rationalize suffering, and your fear of suffering, to God.

ª 14 The meaning of the Hebrew for this word is uncertain.   ᵇ 19 Or *Surely all the joy it has / is that*

Innocent!

JOB 9:14–22

Job knows his suffering is not caused by anything he has done or left undone. Yet he also acknowledges God's power—and is mystified that there seems to be no justice; calamity comes to "both the blameless and the wicked." This shakes Job's concept of God, but the examination is part of Job's wrestling with what has happened to him.

Life often forces us to rethink what we believe. How have your beliefs changed over time as you have journeyed with God? What do you affirm in your heart as true about God? Write a creed that you can say with honesty and conviction: "I believe that God . . ." or "I believe in a God who . . ." Include several statements. Repeat your creed as a way to begin your times of prayer.

See Meeting God in Prayer

he could not answer him one time out of a thousand.
⁴His wisdom is profound, his power is vast.
Who has resisted him and come out unscathed?
⁵He moves mountains without their knowing it
and overturns them in his anger.
⁶He shakes the earth from its place
and makes its pillars tremble.
⁷He speaks to the sun and it does not shine;
he seals off the light of the stars.
⁸He alone stretches out the heavens
and treads on the waves of the sea.
⁹He is the Maker of the Bear and Orion,
the Pleiades and the constellations of the south.
¹⁰He performs wonders that cannot be fathomed,
miracles that cannot be counted.
¹¹When he passes me, I cannot see him;
when he goes by, I cannot perceive him.
¹²If he snatches away, who can stop him?
Who can say to him, 'What are you doing?'
¹³God does not restrain his anger;
even the cohorts of Rahab cowered at his feet.

¹⁴"How then can I dispute with him?
How can I find words to argue with him?
¹⁵Though I were innocent, I could not answer him;
I could only plead with my Judge for mercy.
¹⁶Even if I summoned him and he responded,
I do not believe he would give me a hearing.
¹⁷He would crush me with a storm
and multiply my wounds for no reason.
¹⁸He would not let me regain my breath
but would overwhelm me with misery.
¹⁹If it is a matter of strength, he is mighty!
And if it is a matter of justice, who will summon him*ᵃ*?
²⁰Even if I were innocent, my mouth would condemn me;
if I were blameless, it would pronounce me guilty.

²¹"Although I am blameless,
I have no concern for myself;
I despise my own life.
²²It is all the same; that is why I say,
'He destroys both the blameless and the wicked.'
²³When a scourge brings sudden death,
he mocks the despair of the innocent.
²⁴When a land falls into the hands of the wicked,
he blindfolds its judges.
If it is not he, then who is it?

²⁵"My days are swifter than a runner;
they fly away without a glimpse of joy.
²⁶They skim past like boats of papyrus,
like eagles swooping down on their prey.
²⁷If I say, 'I will forget my complaint,

ᵃ 19 See Septuagint; Hebrew *me.*

I will change my expression, and smile,'
²⁸ I still dread all my sufferings,
for I know you will not hold me innocent.
²⁹ Since I am already found guilty,
why should I struggle in vain?
³⁰ Even if I washed myself with soap[a]
and my hands with washing soda,
³¹ you would plunge me into a slime pit
so that even my clothes would detest me.

³² "He is not a man like me that I might answer him,
that we might confront each other in court.
³³ If only there were someone to arbitrate between us,
to lay his hand upon us both,
³⁴ someone to remove God's rod from me,
so that his terror would frighten me no more.
³⁵ Then I would speak up without fear of him,
but as it now stands with me, I cannot.

10 "I loathe my very life;
therefore I will give free rein to my complaint
and speak out in the bitterness of my soul.
² I will say to God: Do not condemn me,
but tell me what charges you have against me.
³ Does it please you to oppress me,
to spurn the work of your hands,
while you smile on the schemes of the wicked?
⁴ Do you have eyes of flesh?
Do you see as a mortal sees?
⁵ Are your days like those of a mortal
or your years like those of a man,
⁶ that you must search out my faults
and probe after my sin—
⁷ though you know that I am not guilty
and that no one can rescue me from your hand?

⁸ "Your hands shaped me and made me.
Will you now turn and destroy me?
⁹ Remember that you molded me like clay.
Will you now turn me to dust again?
¹⁰ Did you not pour me out like milk
and curdle me like cheese,
¹¹ clothe me with skin and flesh
and knit me together with bones and sinews?
¹² You gave me life and showed me kindness,
and in your providence watched over my spirit.

¹³ "But this is what you concealed in your heart,
and I know that this was in your mind:
¹⁴ If I sinned, you would be watching me
and would not let my offense go unpunished.
¹⁵ If I am guilty—woe to me!
Even if I am innocent, I cannot lift my head,
for I am full of shame
and drowned in[b] my affliction.
¹⁶ If I hold my head high, you stalk me like a lion
and again display your awesome power against me.

Put on a Happy Face

JOB 9:27

Job tells his friends that he could put his questions and struggles out of his mind and "forget [his] complaint . . . and smile." But that would not be honest, and Job is an honest man. He refuses to run from his questions and struggles. He relentlessly pursues God.

Sometimes it *is* necessary to do what Job suggests—to temporarily set aside our pain and struggles. We have to go to work or to school or take care of daily responsibilities. But we also need a safe place and non-threatening, open relationships in which to deal with our concerns. What people or places offer you the opportunity to be completely honest without hiding your feelings? Thank God for these people, times and places. How can you offer such an opportunity and place of hospitality to others?

See Meeting God in Service

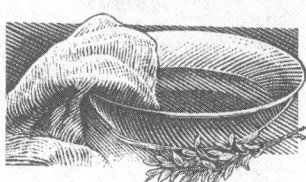

---

^a 30 Or *snow*   ^b 15 Or *and aware of*

Pushing Away

JOB 10:18–22

"Let me die," Job says in despair. He says that being alone would be better than being with his friends. Job pushes away his comforters; it seems as if he is even pushing God away. Do you sometimes prefer solitude to being with others? Do you experience God's presence more in solitude or more when you are with other believers? How does God call to you when life seems pointless and dark? Through Scripture? Through relationships with others? Through music? Consider how you can reach out to someone who feels as Job does here. How can you accept their desire for privacy and still support them?

See *Meeting God in Service*

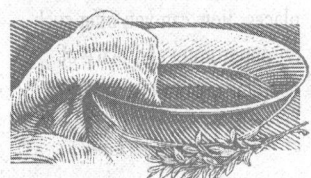

17 You bring new witnesses against me
    and increase your anger toward me;
    your forces come against me wave upon wave.
18 "Why then did you bring me out of the womb?
    I wish I had died before any eye saw me.
19 If only I had never come into being,
    or had been carried straight from the womb to
        the grave!
20 Are not my few days almost over?
    Turn away from me so I can have a moment's
        joy
21 before I go to the place of no return,
    to the land of gloom and deep shadow,[a]
22 to the land of deepest night,
    of deep shadow and disorder,
    where even the light is like darkness."

Zophar

11 Then Zophar the Naamathite replied:

2 "Are all these words to go unanswered?
    Is this talker to be vindicated?
3 Will your idle talk reduce men to silence?
    Will no one rebuke you when you mock?
4 You say to God, 'My beliefs are flawless
    and I am pure in your sight.'
5 Oh, how I wish that God would speak,
    that he would open his lips against you
6 and disclose to you the secrets of wisdom,
    for true wisdom has two sides.
    Know this: God has even forgotten some of
        your sin.

7 "Can you fathom the mysteries of God?
    Can you probe the limits of the Almighty?
8 They are higher than the heavens—what can you
        do?
    They are deeper than the depths of the
        grave[b]—what can you know?
9 Their measure is longer than the earth
    and wider than the sea.

10 "If he comes along and confines you in prison
    and convenes a court, who can oppose him?
11 Surely he recognizes deceitful men;
    and when he sees evil, does he not take note?
12 But a witless man can no more become wise
    than a wild donkey's colt can be born a man.[c]

13 "Yet if you devote your heart to him
    and stretch out your hands to him,
14 if you put away the sin that is in your hand
    and allow no evil to dwell in your tent,
15 then you will lift up your face without shame;
    you will stand firm and without fear.
16 You will surely forget your trouble,
    recalling it only as waters gone by.
17 Life will be brighter than noonday,
    and darkness will become like morning.

---

a 21 Or *and the shadow of death*; also in verse 22   b 8 Hebrew *than Sheol*
c 12 Or *wild donkey can be born tame*

¹⁸ You will be secure, because there is hope;
    you will look about you and take your rest in
      safety.
¹⁹ You will lie down, with no one to make you
    afraid,
    and many will court your favor.
²⁰ But the eyes of the wicked will fail,
    and escape will elude them;
    their hope will become a dying gasp."

Job 12

Then Job replied:

² "Doubtless you are the people,
    and wisdom will die with you!
³ But I have a mind as well as you;
    I am not inferior to you.
    Who does not know all these things?

⁴ "I have become a laughingstock to my friends,
    though I called upon God and he answered—
    a mere laughingstock, though righteous and
      blameless!
⁵ Men at ease have contempt for misfortune
    as the fate of those whose feet are slipping.
⁶ The tents of marauders are undisturbed,
    and those who provoke God are secure—
    those who carry their god in their hands.ᵃ

⁷ "But ask the animals, and they will teach you,
    or the birds of the air, and they will tell you;
⁸ or speak to the earth, and it will teach you,
    or let the fish of the sea inform you.
⁹ Which of all these does not know
    that the hand of the Lord has done this?
¹⁰ In his hand is the life of every creature
    and the breath of all mankind.
¹¹ Does not the ear test words
    as the tongue tastes food?
¹² Is not wisdom found among the aged?
    Does not long life bring understanding?

¹³ "To God belong wisdom and power;
    counsel and understanding are his.
¹⁴ What he tears down cannot be rebuilt;
    the man he imprisons cannot be released.
¹⁵ If he holds back the waters, there is drought;
    if he lets them loose, they devastate the land.
¹⁶ To him belong strength and victory;
    both deceived and deceiver are his.
¹⁷ He leads counselors away stripped
    and makes fools of judges.
¹⁸ He takes off the shackles put on by kings
    and ties a loinclothᵇ around their waist.
¹⁹ He leads priests away stripped
    and overthrows men long established.
²⁰ He silences the lips of trusted advisers
    and takes away the discernment of elders.
²¹ He pours contempt on nobles

Right Thinking

JOB 11:13–18

If you devote your heart to him, argues Zophar, God will reward you. What a seductive argument this is! If we believe a particular way and do particular things, God will make us successful. Have you heard people say things like this?

We may broaden this way of thinking even more to say that we can influence the way God treats us by becoming better people. Are you tempted to believe that you earn God's love when you do certain things or when you refrain from doing other things? Pray for the faith to believe that God loves you and embraces you just as you are. Ask God for the grace to demonstrate the same kind of acceptance to the people you love.

See Meeting God in Prayer

ᵃ 6 Or *secure / in what God's hand brings them*   ᵇ 18 Or *shackles of kings / and ties a belt*

Without a Word

JOB 13:4–5

Sometimes speaking is the wrong way to try to help someone in pain, as Job so vividly demonstrates here. Recall a time when someone helped you without saying a word, and give thanks. What did that person do that helped you? For the next twenty-four hours, challenge yourself to find ways to support, encourage, and comfort others without offering advice or even without speaking.

See Meeting God in Service

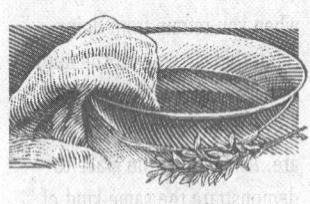

and disarms the mighty.
²² He reveals the deep things of darkness
  and brings deep shadows into the light.
²³ He makes nations great, and destroys them;
  he enlarges nations, and disperses them.
²⁴ He deprives the leaders of the earth of their
    reason;
  he sends them wandering through a trackless
    waste.
²⁵ They grope in darkness with no light;
  he makes them stagger like drunkards.

13 "My eyes have seen all this,
  my ears have heard and understood it.
² What you know, I also know;
  I am not inferior to you.
³ But I desire to speak to the Almighty
  and to argue my case with God.
⁴ You, however, smear me with lies;
  you are worthless physicians, all of you!
⁵ If only you would be altogether silent!
  For you, that would be wisdom.
⁶ Hear now my argument;
  listen to the plea of my lips.
⁷ Will you speak wickedly on God's behalf?
  Will you speak deceitfully for him?
⁸ Will you show him partiality?
  Will you argue the case for God?
⁹ Would it turn out well if he examined you?
  Could you deceive him as you might deceive
    men?
¹⁰ He would surely rebuke you
  if you secretly showed partiality.
¹¹ Would not his splendor terrify you?
  Would not the dread of him fall on you?
¹² Your maxims are proverbs of ashes;
  your defenses are defenses of clay.

¹³ "Keep silent and let me speak;
  then let come to me what may.
¹⁴ Why do I put myself in jeopardy
  and take my life in my hands?
¹⁵ Though he slay me, yet will I hope in him;
  I will surely[a] defend my ways to his face.
¹⁶ Indeed, this will turn out for my deliverance,
  for no godless man would dare come before
    him!
¹⁷ Listen carefully to my words;
  let your ears take in what I say.
¹⁸ Now that I have prepared my case,
  I know I will be vindicated.
¹⁹ Can anyone bring charges against me?
  If so, I will be silent and die.

²⁰ "Only grant me these two things, O God,
  and then I will not hide from you:
²¹ Withdraw your hand far from me,
  and stop frightening me with your terrors.
²² Then summon me and I will answer,
  or let me speak, and you reply.

a 15 Or He will surely slay me; I have no hope — / yet I will

²³ How many wrongs and sins have I committed?
  Show me my offense and my sin.
²⁴ Why do you hide your face
  and consider me your enemy?
²⁵ Will you torment a windblown leaf?
  Will you chase after dry chaff?
²⁶ For you write down bitter things against me
  and make me inherit the sins of my youth.
²⁷ You fasten my feet in shackles;
  you keep close watch on all my paths
  by putting marks on the soles of my feet.

²⁸ "So man wastes away like something rotten,
  like a garment eaten by moths.

14 "Man born of woman
  is of few days and full of trouble.
² He springs up like a flower and withers away;
  like a fleeting shadow, he does not endure.
³ Do you fix your eye on such a one?
  Will you bring him*ᵃ* before you for judgment?
⁴ Who can bring what is pure from the impure?
  No one!
⁵ Man's days are determined;
  you have decreed the number of his months
  and have set limits he cannot exceed.
⁶ So look away from him and let him alone,
  till he has put in his time like a hired man.

⁷ "At least there is hope for a tree:
  If it is cut down, it will sprout again,
  and its new shoots will not fail.
⁸ Its roots may grow old in the ground
  and its stump die in the soil,
⁹ yet at the scent of water it will bud
  and put forth shoots like a plant.
¹⁰ But man dies and is laid low;
  he breathes his last and is no more.
¹¹ As water disappears from the sea
  or a riverbed becomes parched and dry,
¹² so man lies down and does not rise;
  till the heavens are no more, men will not
    awake
  or be roused from their sleep.

¹³ "If only you would hide me in the grave*ᵇ*
  and conceal me till your anger has passed!
  If only you would set me a time
  and then remember me!
¹⁴ If a man dies, will he live again?
  All the days of my hard service
  I will wait for my renewal*ᶜ* to come.
¹⁵ You will call and I will answer you;
  you will long for the creature your hands have
    made.
¹⁶ Surely then you will count my steps
  but not keep track of my sin.
¹⁷ My offenses will be sealed up in a bag;
  you will cover over my sin.

Any One of Us

JOB 13:22–24

Reading the book of Job can make us feel very vulnerable. If such disasters can happen to a good man like Job, we must consider that tragedy can strike any one of us.

Here Job cries out in prayer, remaining vulnerable and reaching out to God even in his terrible situation. Job clings to God and will not let go. What ways of worshiping or praying help you to cling to God during difficult times? What are some of the hymns you might sing when you are down? Think of some music CDs you might use as "music therapy" the next time you are tense, anxious or depressed—music that will help calm you and help you focus on God in prayer. Set them aside for just such an occasion.

See Meeting God in Worship

ᵃ *3* Septuagint, Vulgate and Syriac; Hebrew *me*   ᵇ *13* Hebrew *Sheol*
ᶜ *14* Or *release*

Protecting God's Reputation

JOB 15:4–5

Eliphaz offers another painful comment: Job is calling the faith into question, undermining religion and interfering with others' devotion to God by his response to his tragedy. Job's friend seems more interested in protecting his perception of "the faith" than in helping Job. Job is alone.

Have you ever felt completely alone before God—when it seemed as if "religion" had nothing to offer you? Have you ever been abruptly counseled to put aside your needs and your pain and to think of others first? Or have you felt pressured to keep your struggles quiet in order to be a "good witness"? In prayer, sit alone in a dark room. Ask God to hold on to you when others leave you.

See Meeting God in Prayer

---

¹⁸ "But as a mountain erodes and crumbles
    and as a rock is moved from its place,
¹⁹ as water wears away stones
    and torrents wash away the soil,
    so you destroy man's hope.
²⁰ You overpower him once for all, and he is gone;
    you change his countenance and send him away.
²¹ If his sons are honored, he does not know it;
    if they are brought low, he does not see it.
²² He feels but the pain of his own body
    and mourns only for himself."

Eliphaz

15 Then Eliphaz the Temanite replied:

² "Would a wise man answer with empty notions
    or fill his belly with the hot east wind?
³ Would he argue with useless words,
    with speeches that have no value?
⁴ But you even undermine piety
    and hinder devotion to God.
⁵ Your sin prompts your mouth;
    you adopt the tongue of the crafty.
⁶ Your own mouth condemns you, not mine;
    your own lips testify against you.

⁷ "Are you the first man ever born?
    Were you brought forth before the hills?
⁸ Do you listen in on God's council?
    Do you limit wisdom to yourself?
⁹ What do you know that we do not know?
    What insights do you have that we do not have?
¹⁰ The gray-haired and the aged are on our side,
    men even older than your father.
¹¹ Are God's consolations not enough for you,
    words spoken gently to you?
¹² Why has your heart carried you away,
    and why do your eyes flash,
¹³ so that you vent your rage against God
    and pour out such words from your mouth?

¹⁴ "What is man, that he could be pure,
    or one born of woman, that he could be righteous?
¹⁵ If God places no trust in his holy ones,
    if even the heavens are not pure in his eyes,
¹⁶ how much less man, who is vile and corrupt,
    who drinks up evil like water!

¹⁷ "Listen to me and I will explain to you;
    let me tell you what I have seen,
¹⁸ what wise men have declared,
    hiding nothing received from their fathers
¹⁹ (to whom alone the land was given
    when no alien passed among them):
²⁰ All his days the wicked man suffers torment,
    the ruthless through all the years stored up for him.
²¹ Terrifying sounds fill his ears;
    when all seems well, marauders attack him.

22 He despairs of escaping the darkness;
   he is marked for the sword.
23 He wanders about—food for vultures[a];
   he knows the day of darkness is at hand.
24 Distress and anguish fill him with terror;
   they overwhelm him, like a king poised to
      attack,
25 because he shakes his fist at God
   and vaunts himself against the Almighty,
26 defiantly charging against him
   with a thick, strong shield.

27 "Though his face is covered with fat
   and his waist bulges with flesh,
28 he will inhabit ruined towns
   and houses where no one lives,
   houses crumbling to rubble.
29 He will no longer be rich and his wealth will not
      endure,
   nor will his possessions spread over the land.
30 He will not escape the darkness;
   a flame will wither his shoots,
   and the breath of God's mouth will carry him
      away.
31 Let him not deceive himself by trusting what is
      worthless,
   for he will get nothing in return.
32 Before his time he will be paid in full,
   and his branches will not flourish.
33 He will be like a vine stripped of its unripe
      grapes,
   like an olive tree shedding its blossoms.
34 For the company of the godless will be barren,
   and fire will consume the tents of those who
      love bribes.
35 They conceive trouble and give birth to evil;
   their womb fashions deceit."

Job

16

Then Job replied:

2 "I have heard many things like these;
   miserable comforters are you all!
3 Will your long-winded speeches never end?
   What ails you that you keep on arguing?
4 I also could speak like you,
   if you were in my place;
   I could make fine speeches against you
   and shake my head at you.
5 But my mouth would encourage you;
   comfort from my lips would bring you relief.

6 "Yet if I speak, my pain is not relieved;
   and if I refrain, it does not go away.
7 Surely, O God, you have worn me out;
   you have devastated my entire household.
8 You have bound me—and it has become a
      witness;
   my gauntness rises up and testifies against me.
9 God assails me and tears me in his anger

Naked and Alone

JOB 16:1–4

Job sits naked in the dirt; his family, possessions and health are all gone. He has nothing and is nothing; his friends don't understand the depth of his emotions.

Friends cannot always understand; sometimes, because of their own fears and doubts, they fail to be able or available to help us when we most need them. Think of a friend who has failed you, someone you counted on for help but who did not deliver. Pray for that friend and for your relationship. Think of another time when this same friend helped you and showed faithful care; express your thanks in whatever way would be meaningful to you. How does that friend's faithfulness provide an image of God's reliable and loving presence?

See Meeting God in Community

a 23 Or *about, looking for food*

Injury or Heartache?

JOB 16:11-17

Job feels assaulted. He expresses his inner pain in graphic metaphors, using images of injury to his body. His physical pain is difficult, but his heartache is even more bruising.

Think about times of anguish and upheaval when you feel assaulted by life. Much is made these days of the ways our emotions affect our bodies. Do you have headaches, an upset stomach, backaches, chest pains, a stiff neck or muscle aches? In difficult times, what would help you pay attention to the signals of distress that your body sends? Sit in God's presence and open your hands with palms upward as a way of opening yourself to God. What emotional, spiritual or physical pain do you offer to God?

See Meeting God in Prayer

and gnashes his teeth at me;
my opponent fastens on me his piercing eyes.
¹⁰Men open their mouths to jeer at me;
they strike my cheek in scorn
and unite together against me.
¹¹God has turned me over to evil men
and thrown me into the clutches of the wicked.
¹²All was well with me, but he shattered me;
he seized me by the neck and crushed me.
He has made me his target;
¹³ his archers surround me.
Without pity, he pierces my kidneys
and spills my gall on the ground.
¹⁴Again and again he bursts upon me;
he rushes at me like a warrior.

¹⁵"I have sewed sackcloth over my skin
and buried my brow in the dust.
¹⁶My face is red with weeping,
deep shadows ring my eyes;
¹⁷yet my hands have been free of violence
and my prayer is pure.

¹⁸"O earth, do not cover my blood;
may my cry never be laid to rest!
¹⁹Even now my witness is in heaven;
my advocate is on high.
²⁰My intercessor is my friend*a*
as my eyes pour out tears to God;
²¹on behalf of a man he pleads with God
as a man pleads for his friend.

²²"Only a few years will pass
before I go on the journey of no return.

17 ¹My spirit is broken,
my days are cut short,
the grave awaits me.
²Surely mockers surround me;
my eyes must dwell on their hostility.

³"Give me, O God, the pledge you demand.
Who else will put up security for me?
⁴You have closed their minds to understanding;
therefore you will not let them triumph.
⁵If a man denounces his friends for reward,
the eyes of his children will fail.

⁶"God has made me a byword to everyone,
a man in whose face people spit.
⁷My eyes have grown dim with grief;
my whole frame is but a shadow.
⁸Upright men are appalled at this;
the innocent are aroused against the ungodly.
⁹Nevertheless, the righteous will hold to their
ways,
and those with clean hands will grow stronger.

¹⁰"But come on, all of you, try again!
I will not find a wise man among you.
¹¹My days have passed, my plans are shattered,
and so are the desires of my heart.

a 20 Or *My friends treat me with scorn*

It is easy to see that the sacred Scriptures, which so far surpass all **gifts** and **graces** of human endeavor, breathe something *divine*.

JOHN CALVIN (1509-1564)

Institutes of Christian Religion, Book One

We pray

to see life as it is,
to understand it and to
make it better than it was.
We pray so that reality
can break into our souls
and give us back our
awareness of the
Divine Presence in life.

JOAN CHITTISTER, O.S.B.
Wisdom Distilled from the Daily

If God's word is so full of consolations, what overflowing springs shall we find in God himself? If the promise is so sweet, what will the performance be?

RICHARD BAXTER (1615-1691)

The Saints' Everlasting Rest

When in reading

Scripture you meet with a *passage* that seems to give your **heart** a new motion toward *God,* turn it into the form of a *petition,* and give it a place in your **prayers.**

WILLIAM LAW (1686-1761)

A Serious Call to a Devout and Holy Life

¹²These men turn night into day;
in the face of darkness they say, 'Light is near.'
¹³If the only home I hope for is the grave,ᵃ
if I spread out my bed in darkness,
¹⁴if I say to corruption, 'You are my father,'
and to the worm, 'My mother' or 'My sister,'
¹⁵where then is my hope?
Who can see any hope for me?
¹⁶Will it go down to the gates of deathᵃ?
Will we descend together into the dust?"

Bildad

18

Then Bildad the Shuhite replied:

²"When will you end these speeches?
Be sensible, and then we can talk.
³Why are we regarded as cattle
and considered stupid in your sight?
⁴You who tear yourself to pieces in your anger,
is the earth to be abandoned for your sake?
Or must the rocks be moved from their place?

⁵"The lamp of the wicked is snuffed out;
the flame of his fire stops burning.
⁶The light in his tent becomes dark;
the lamp beside him goes out.
⁷The vigor of his step is weakened;
his own schemes throw him down.
⁸His feet thrust him into a net
and he wanders into its mesh.
⁹A trap seizes him by the heel;
a snare holds him fast.
¹⁰A noose is hidden for him on the ground;
a trap lies in his path.
¹¹Terrors startle him on every side
and dog his every step.
¹²Calamity is hungry for him;
disaster is ready for him when he falls.
¹³It eats away parts of his skin;
death's firstborn devours his limbs.
¹⁴He is torn from the security of his tent
and marched off to the king of terrors.
¹⁵Fire residesᵇ in his tent;
burning sulfur is scattered over his dwelling.
¹⁶His roots dry up below
and his branches wither above.
¹⁷The memory of him perishes from the earth;
he has no name in the land.
¹⁸He is driven from light into darkness
and is banished from the world.
¹⁹He has no offspring or descendants among his
people,
no survivor where once he lived.
²⁰Men of the west are appalled at his fate;
men of the east are seized with horror.
²¹Surely such is the dwelling of an evil man;
such is the place of one who knows not God."

Where Hope Is Found

JOB 17:15

"This is the first and principal benefit caused by [the] arid and dark night of [the soul]: the knowledge of oneself and of one's misery . . . These aridities and this emptiness of the faculties, compared with the abundance which the soul experienced before and the difficulty it now finds in good works, make it recognize its own lowliness . . . which in the time of its prosperity it was unable to see."

—JOHN OF THE CROSS,
The Dark Night of the Soul

To Hurt or To Heal?

JOB 19:1–5

Job cries out for mercy. His friends torment him and "crush [him] with words."

Words have power both to hurt and to heal. Words spoken to us by others shape our perceptions of ourselves; with our words we influence the perceptions others have of themselves. Looking back over your life, think of incidents where negative or hurtful words have been spoken to you. Think of negative or hurtful words you have spoken to others. Now ask God to mend the negative effects those words have had. Then think of life-giving words spoken to you, perhaps when you were a child, which may have helped you to feel loved or capable or deeply valued by God. Give thanks for those who have spoken such words to you. Reflect on how you can speak healing and life to those you encounter day by day.

See *Meeting God in Everyday Life*

Job

19

Then Job replied:

2 "How long will you torment me
   and crush me with words?
3 Ten times now you have reproached me;
   shamelessly you attack me.
4 If it is true that I have gone astray,
   my error remains my concern alone.
5 If indeed you would exalt yourselves above me
   and use my humiliation against me,
6 then know that God has wronged me
   and drawn his net around me.

7 "Though I cry, 'I've been wronged!' I get no response;
   though I call for help, there is no justice.
8 He has blocked my way so I cannot pass;
   he has shrouded my paths in darkness.
9 He has stripped me of my honor
   and removed the crown from my head.
10 He tears me down on every side till I am gone;
   he uproots my hope like a tree.
11 His anger burns against me;
   he counts me among his enemies.
12 His troops advance in force;
   they build a siege ramp against me
   and encamp around my tent.

13 "He has alienated my brothers from me;
   my acquaintances are completely estranged from me.
14 My kinsmen have gone away;
   my friends have forgotten me.
15 My guests and my maidservants count me a stranger;
   they look upon me as an alien.
16 I summon my servant, but he does not answer,
   though I beg him with my own mouth.
17 My breath is offensive to my wife;
   I am loathsome to my own brothers.
18 Even the little boys scorn me;
   when I appear, they ridicule me.
19 All my intimate friends detest me;
   those I love have turned against me.
20 I am nothing but skin and bones;
   I have escaped with only the skin of my teeth.[a]

21 "Have pity on me, my friends, have pity,
   for the hand of God has struck me.
22 Why do you pursue me as God does?
   Will you never get enough of my flesh?

23 "Oh, that my words were recorded,
   that they were written on a scroll,
24 that they were inscribed with an iron tool on[b] lead,
   or engraved in rock forever!
25 I know that my Redeemer[c] lives,

a 20 Or *only my gums*   *b 24* Or *and*   *c 25* Or *defender*

and that in the end he will stand upon the
    earth.*ᵃ*
²⁶And after my skin has been destroyed,
    yet*ᵇ* in*ᶜ* my flesh I will see God;
²⁷I myself will see him
    with my own eyes—I, and not another.
    How my heart yearns within me!

²⁸"If you say, 'How we will hound him,
    since the root of the trouble lies in him,*ᵈ*'
²⁹you should fear the sword yourselves;
    for wrath will bring punishment by the sword,
    and then you will know that there is
    judgment.*ᵉ*"

Zophar

20

Then Zophar the Naamathite replied:

²"My troubled thoughts prompt me to answer
    because I am greatly disturbed.
³I hear a rebuke that dishonors me,
    and my understanding inspires me to reply.

⁴"Surely you know how it has been from of old,
    ever since man*ᶠ* was placed on the earth,
⁵that the mirth of the wicked is brief,
    the joy of the godless lasts but a moment.
⁶Though his pride reaches to the heavens
    and his head touches the clouds,
⁷he will perish forever, like his own dung;
    those who have seen him will say, 'Where is
    he?'
⁸Like a dream he flies away, no more to be found,
    banished like a vision of the night.
⁹The eye that saw him will not see him again;
    his place will look on him no more.
¹⁰His children must make amends to the poor;
    his own hands must give back his wealth.
¹¹The youthful vigor that fills his bones
    will lie with him in the dust.

¹²"Though evil is sweet in his mouth
    and he hides it under his tongue,
¹³though he cannot bear to let it go
    and keeps it in his mouth,
¹⁴yet his food will turn sour in his stomach;
    it will become the venom of serpents within
    him.
¹⁵He will spit out the riches he swallowed;
    God will make his stomach vomit them up.
¹⁶He will suck the poison of serpents;
    the fangs of an adder will kill him.
¹⁷He will not enjoy the streams,
    the rivers flowing with honey and cream.
¹⁸What he toiled for he must give back uneaten;
    he will not enjoy the profit from his trading.
¹⁹For he has oppressed the poor and left them
    destitute;

My Redeemer Lives

JOB 19:25–27

These famous verses contain the central truth of the book of Job: In the darkness of suffering, Job affirms that he will see God—if not in this life, then in eternity. He refuses to give up on God, remaining in relationship even when no comfort comes and his questions are unanswered.

Why do you continue to pray despite trouble and suffering? If you have ceased to pray, what is it about God that keeps you from abandoning God altogether? Close your eyes. Imagine yourself in a dark place, looking for God. What do you see? Can you see the road on which you travel or what surrounds you? Can you see God? If darkness is all you can see right now, as an expression of your faith and desire to see God, repeat Job's words in your heart: "I know that my Redeemer lives."

See Meeting God in Prayer

ᵃ 25 Or *upon my grave*   *ᵇ 26* Or *And after I awake, / though this body has been destroyed, / then*   *ᶜ 26* Or */ apart from*   *ᵈ 28* Many Hebrew manuscripts, Septuagint and Vulgate; most Hebrew manuscripts *me*
ᵉ 29 Or */ that you may come to know the Almighty*   *ᶠ 4* Or *Adam*

What They Deserve

JOB 21:7–12

Zophar has said that the wicked are punished and that Job's problems are proof of his wickedness. Job challenges this, pointing out that the wicked often prosper.

That often seems to be the case. Drug dealers get rich. Tax evaders send their children to exclusive and expensive schools. People who hurt others for pleasure sleep at night and continue their tortures in the light of day. On a smaller scale, those who cheat and lie are promoted while honest and diligent workers go unnoticed and without reward. Alongside Job, we ask God for explanations.

If you have been harmed by wickedness, or if your life has been limited by wounds and scars, place the offender in God's hands as you pray. Ask for the willingness and grace to forgive that person and to trust God to uphold justice. Or reflect on recent news stories of cruelty and suffering, and hold the people involved before God in prayer.

See Meeting God in Prayer

he has seized houses he did not build.
20 "Surely he will have no respite from his craving;
   he cannot save himself by his treasure.
21 Nothing is left for him to devour;
   his prosperity will not endure.
22 In the midst of his plenty, distress will overtake him;
   the full force of misery will come upon him.
23 When he has filled his belly,
   God will vent his burning anger against him
   and rain down his blows upon him.
24 Though he flees from an iron weapon,
   a bronze-tipped arrow pierces him.
25 He pulls it out of his back,
   the gleaming point out of his liver.
   Terrors will come over him;
26   total darkness lies in wait for his treasures.
   A fire unfanned will consume him
   and devour what is left in his tent.
27 The heavens will expose his guilt;
   the earth will rise up against him.
28 A flood will carry off his house,
   rushing waters*a* on the day of God's wrath.
29 Such is the fate God allots the wicked,
   the heritage appointed for them by God."

Job
21

Then Job replied:

2 "Listen carefully to my words;
   let this be the consolation you give me.
3 Bear with me while I speak,
   and after I have spoken, mock on.

4 "Is my complaint directed to man?
   Why should I not be impatient?
5 Look at me and be astonished;
   clap your hand over your mouth.
6 When I think about this, I am terrified;
   trembling seizes my body.
7 Why do the wicked live on,
   growing old and increasing in power?
8 They see their children established around them,
   their offspring before their eyes.
9 Their homes are safe and free from fear;
   the rod of God is not upon them.
10 Their bulls never fail to breed;
   their cows calve and do not miscarry.
11 They send forth their children as a flock;
   their little ones dance about.
12 They sing to the music of tambourine and harp;
   they make merry to the sound of the flute.
13 They spend their years in prosperity
   and go down to the grave*b* in peace.*c*
14 Yet they say to God, 'Leave us alone!
   We have no desire to know your ways.
15 Who is the Almighty, that we should serve him?
   What would we gain by praying to him?'

---

a 28 Or *The possessions in his house will be carried off, / washed away*
b 13 Hebrew *Sheol*   *c 13* Or *in an instant*

16 But their prosperity is not in their own hands,
so I stand aloof from the counsel of the wicked.

17 "Yet how often is the lamp of the wicked snuffed
out?
How often does calamity come upon them,
the fate God allots in his anger?
18 How often are they like straw before the wind,
like chaff swept away by a gale?
19 It is said,* 'God stores up a man's punishment for
his sons.'
Let him repay the man himself, so that he will
know it!
20 Let his own eyes see his destruction;
let him drink of the wrath of the Almighty.*
21 For what does he care about the family he leaves
behind
when his allotted months come to an end?

22 "Can anyone teach knowledge to God,
since he judges even the highest?
23 One man dies in full vigor,
completely secure and at ease,
24 his body* well nourished,
his bones rich with marrow.
25 Another man dies in bitterness of soul,
never having enjoyed anything good.
26 Side by side they lie in the dust,
and worms cover them both.

27 "I know full well what you are thinking,
the schemes by which you would wrong me.
28 You say, 'Where now is the great man's house,
the tents where wicked men lived?'
29 Have you never questioned those who travel?
Have you paid no regard to their accounts—
30 that the evil man is spared from the day of
calamity,
that he is delivered from* the day of wrath?
31 Who denounces his conduct to his face?
Who repays him for what he has done?
32 He is carried to the grave,
and watch is kept over his tomb.
33 The soil in the valley is sweet to him;
all men follow after him,
and a countless throng goes* before him.

34 "So how can you console me with your
nonsense?
Nothing is left of your answers but falsehood!"

Eliphaz

22

Then Eliphaz the Temanite replied:

2 "Can a man be of benefit to God?
Can even a wise man benefit him?
3 What pleasure would it give the Almighty if you
were righteous?

The Road of Pain

JOB 21:34

Once again, Job tells his friends
that he takes no comfort in
their useless, empty talk.

Often in traveling the road
of suffering, we find ourselves
without comfort—with no map
to guide us. There are no easy
answers, and even those who
want to help seem unable to do
so. Their actions may even in-
tensify our anguish.

Walk in God's presence on
behalf of someone who is traveling the dark road of pain. Picture God walking in silence and
love alongside you and that
person, present though unseen.
Walk with God in the silence.

See *Meeting God in Community*

a 17–20 Verses 17 and 18 may be taken as exclamations and 19 and 20 as
declarations.   *b 24* The meaning of the Hebrew for this word is uncertain.
c 30 Or *man is reserved for the day of calamity, / that he is brought forth to*
d 33 Or *| as a countless throng went*

A New Reason

JOB 22:21–22

Job's friends have apparently given up on getting Job to admit that he has done wrong. Now Eliphaz takes another tack, saying that Job is suffering because he hasn't done enough that is right. If he had done more good things, he would not be in this mess. Believing that doing good can insulate us from pain and loss is a trap, but Job's friends are still struggling to find a way to assure themselves that what has happened to Job will not happen to them.

What do you cling to for security—as your assurance that nothing bad is going to happen to you? What do you fear losing? Talk honestly with God in prayer about this. What does God say to you?

See Meeting God in Prayer

What would he gain if your ways were
blameless?
4 "Is it for your piety that he rebukes you
and brings charges against you?
5 Is not your wickedness great?
Are not your sins endless?
6 You demanded security from your brothers for no
reason;
you stripped men of their clothing, leaving
them naked.
7 You gave no water to the weary
and you withheld food from the hungry,
8 though you were a powerful man, owning land—
an honored man, living on it.
9 And you sent widows away empty-handed
and broke the strength of the fatherless.
10 That is why snares are all around you,
why sudden peril terrifies you,
11 why it is so dark you cannot see,
and why a flood of water covers you.

12 "Is not God in the heights of heaven?
And see how lofty are the highest stars!
13 Yet you say, 'What does God know?
Does he judge through such darkness?
14 Thick clouds veil him, so he does not see us
as he goes about in the vaulted heavens.'
15 Will you keep to the old path
that evil men have trod?
16 They were carried off before their time,
their foundations washed away by a flood.
17 They said to God, 'Leave us alone!
What can the Almighty do to us?'
18 Yet it was he who filled their houses with good
things,
so I stand aloof from the counsel of the wicked.

19 "The righteous see their ruin and rejoice;
the innocent mock them, saying,
20 'Surely our foes are destroyed,
and fire devours their wealth.'

21 "Submit to God and be at peace with him;
in this way prosperity will come to you.
22 Accept instruction from his mouth
and lay up his words in your heart.
23 If you return to the Almighty, you will be restored:
If you remove wickedness far from your tent
24 and assign your nuggets to the dust,
your gold of Ophir to the rocks in the ravines,
25 then the Almighty will be your gold,
the choicest silver for you.
26 Surely then you will find delight in the Almighty
and will lift up your face to God.
27 You will pray to him, and he will hear you,
and you will fulfill your vows.
28 What you decide on will be done,
and light will shine on your ways.
29 When men are brought low and you say, 'Lift
them up!'
then he will save the downcast.

³⁰ He will deliver even one who is not innocent,
who will be delivered through the cleanness of
your hands."

Job
23

Then Job replied:

² "Even today my complaint is bitter;
his hand*ᵃ* is heavy in spite of*ᵇ* my groaning.
³ If only I knew where to find him;
if only I could go to his dwelling!
⁴ I would state my case before him
and fill my mouth with arguments.
⁵ I would find out what he would answer me,
and consider what he would say.
⁶ Would he oppose me with great power?
No, he would not press charges against me.
⁷ There an upright man could present his case
before him,
and I would be delivered forever from my
judge.

⁸ "But if I go to the east, he is not there;
if I go to the west, I do not find him.
⁹ When he is at work in the north, I do not see
him;
when he turns to the south, I catch no glimpse
of him.
¹⁰ But he knows the way that I take;
when he has tested me, I will come forth as
gold.
¹¹ My feet have closely followed his steps;
I have kept to his way without turning aside.
¹² I have not departed from the commands of his
lips;
I have treasured the words of his mouth more
than my daily bread.

¹³ "But he stands alone, and who can oppose him?
He does whatever he pleases.
¹⁴ He carries out his decree against me,
and many such plans he still has in store.
¹⁵ That is why I am terrified before him;
when I think of all this, I fear him.
¹⁶ God has made my heart faint;
the Almighty has terrified me.
¹⁷ Yet I am not silenced by the darkness,
by the thick darkness that covers my face.

24

"Why does the Almighty not set times for judgment?
Why must those who know him look in vain for
such days?
² Men move boundary stones;
they pasture flocks they have stolen.
³ They drive away the orphan's donkey
and take the widow's ox in pledge.
⁴ They thrust the needy from the path
and force all the poor of the land into hiding.
⁵ Like wild donkeys in the desert,
the poor go about their labor of foraging food;

Traveling Blind

JOB 23:8–11

"You may find a kind of darkness around your mind, as it were a cloud of unknowing. You seem to feel nothing in your will except a naked intent toward God. However hard you try to do something about it, this darkness and this cloud remain between you and God. It seems as though you neither see God by the light of understanding nor feel God in the sweetness of love and affection. But learn to live with this darkness, crying out always to him whom you love."

—ANONYMOUS,
The Cloud of Unknowing

Souls That Cry Out

JOB 24:9–12

This passage sounds like a recap of the evening news: baby selling, homelessness, hunger, adultery, violence in the city—and yet God seems to do nothing. Job laments God's lack of response.

Think about the community in which you live. Through whom is God working to help the hungry, the homeless and the victims of violence? In what way is God using you now to respond to these situations? In what ways is God calling you to respond on his behalf to those in need?

See Meeting God in Service

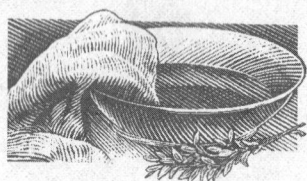

the wasteland provides food for their children.
⁶ They gather fodder in the fields
  and glean in the vineyards of the wicked.
⁷ Lacking clothes, they spend the night naked;
  they have nothing to cover themselves in the cold.
⁸ They are drenched by mountain rains
  and hug the rocks for lack of shelter.
⁹ The fatherless child is snatched from the breast;
  the infant of the poor is seized for a debt.
¹⁰ Lacking clothes, they go about naked;
  they carry the sheaves, but still go hungry.
¹¹ They crush olives among the terraces[a];
  they tread the winepresses, yet suffer thirst.
¹² The groans of the dying rise from the city,
  and the souls of the wounded cry out for help.
  But God charges no one with wrongdoing.

¹³ "There are those who rebel against the light,
  who do not know its ways
  or stay in its paths.
¹⁴ When daylight is gone, the murderer rises up
  and kills the poor and needy;
  in the night he steals forth like a thief.
¹⁵ The eye of the adulterer watches for dusk;
  he thinks, 'No eye will see me,'
  and he keeps his face concealed.
¹⁶ In the dark, men break into houses,
  but by day they shut themselves in;
  they want nothing to do with the light.
¹⁷ For all of them, deep darkness is their morning[b];
  they make friends with the terrors of darkness.[c]

¹⁸ "Yet they are foam on the surface of the water;
  their portion of the land is cursed,
  so that no one goes to the vineyards.
¹⁹ As heat and drought snatch away the melted snow,
  so the grave[d] snatches away those who have sinned.
²⁰ The womb forgets them,
  the worm feasts on them;
  evil men are no longer remembered
  but are broken like a tree.
²¹ They prey on the barren and childless woman,
  and to the widow show no kindness.
²² But God drags away the mighty by his power;
  though they become established, they have no assurance of life.
²³ He may let them rest in a feeling of security,
  but his eyes are on their ways.
²⁴ For a little while they are exalted, and then they are gone;
  they are brought low and gathered up like all others;
  they are cut off like heads of grain.

²⁵ "If this is not so, who can prove me false
  and reduce my words to nothing?"

---

[a] 11 Or *olives between the millstones*; the meaning of the Hebrew for this word is uncertain.   [b] 17 Or *them, their morning is like the shadow of death*   [c] 17 Or *of the shadow of death*   [d] 19 Hebrew *Sheol*

Bildad

25

Then Bildad the Shuhite replied:

2 "Dominion and awe belong to God;
   he establishes order in the heights of heaven.
3 Can his forces be numbered?
   Upon whom does his light not rise?
4 How then can a man be righteous before God?
   How can one born of woman be pure?
5 If even the moon is not bright
   and the stars are not pure in his eyes,
6 how much less man, who is but a maggot—
   a son of man, who is only a worm!"

Job

26

Then Job replied:

2 "How you have helped the powerless!
   How you have saved the arm that is feeble!
3 What advice you have offered to one without
      wisdom!
   And what great insight you have displayed!
4 Who has helped you utter these words?
   And whose spirit spoke from your mouth?

5 "The dead are in deep anguish,
   those beneath the waters and all that live in
      them.
6 Death*ᵃ* is naked before God;
   Destruction*ᵇ* lies uncovered.
7 He spreads out the northern ⌊skies⌋ over empty
      space;
   he suspends the earth over nothing.
8 He wraps up the waters in his clouds,
   yet the clouds do not burst under their weight.
9 He covers the face of the full moon,
   spreading his clouds over it.
10 He marks out the horizon on the face of the
      waters
   for a boundary between light and darkness.
11 The pillars of the heavens quake,
   aghast at his rebuke.
12 By his power he churned up the sea;
   by his wisdom he cut Rahab to pieces.
13 By his breath the skies became fair;
   his hand pierced the gliding serpent.
14 And these are but the outer fringe of his works;
   how faint the whisper we hear of him!
   Who then can understand the thunder of his
      power?"

27

And Job continued his discourse:

2 "As surely as God lives, who has denied me
      justice,
   the Almighty, who has made me taste
      bitterness of soul,
3 as long as I have life within me,
   the breath of God in my nostrils,

Awesome—and Out There?

JOB 25:2–6

Bildad speaks reverently, almost fearfully, of God's holiness and power—an awesome, unreachable God. In contrast, we flawed humans are "maggots" and "worms." Bildad cannot understand the give-and-take, confrontational intimacy that characterizes Job's relationship with God. Job's closeness to God seems arrogant to him.

Some of us have a reverence for God's holiness but cannot, or do not, embrace the image of God as our loving Father who desires intimacy with us. Such perceptions keep God at a distance. Are you able to speak to God openly about your anger and disappointments, as you would to a trusted family member, or do you see God as a cool, immovable judge? Do you picture yourself standing with head down before God's throne or sitting on God's lap? Consider where your images of God come from and whether your relationship with God is more like Bildad's or Job's.

See Meeting God in Scripture

Where Is Hope?

JOB 27:7–12

Job here declares that he must proclaim the power and the ways of the Almighty to those who do not know him so that they may have hope of delight and deliverance.

The world today suffers from a chronic shortage of hope. Even though many cannot identify or articulate their hopelessness, it's easy to see on faces in crowds, easy to hear on talk shows, apparent in the tough speech of children who have lost their innocence too early in life. What can we do but be ready to respond, as Job does, with words of faith? Be prepared to offer words of encouragement and hope—that God will hear, save, love and rescue them. Write out a paragraph or two articulating what God has done in your life recently so that you can share your hope with others. Update it from time to time to keep it fresh and current.

See Meeting God in Service

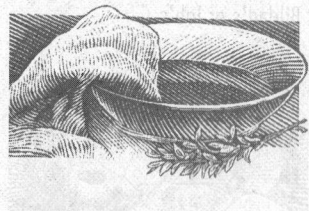

4 my lips will not speak wickedness,
   and my tongue will utter no deceit.
5 I will never admit you are in the right;
   till I die, I will not deny my integrity.
6 I will maintain my righteousness and never let go of it;
   my conscience will not reproach me as long as I live.

7 "May my enemies be like the wicked,
   my adversaries like the unjust!
8 For what hope has the godless when he is cut off,
   when God takes away his life?
9 Does God listen to his cry
   when distress comes upon him?
10 Will he find delight in the Almighty?
   Will he call upon God at all times?

11 "I will teach you about the power of God;
   the ways of the Almighty I will not conceal.
12 You have all seen this yourselves.
   Why then this meaningless talk?

13 "Here is the fate God allots to the wicked,
   the heritage a ruthless man receives from the Almighty:
14 However many his children, their fate is the sword;
   his offspring will never have enough to eat.
15 The plague will bury those who survive him,
   and their widows will not weep for them.
16 Though he heaps up silver like dust
   and clothes like piles of clay,
17 what he lays up the righteous will wear,
   and the innocent will divide his silver.
18 The house he builds is like a moth's cocoon,
   like a hut made by a watchman.
19 He lies down wealthy, but will do so no more;
   when he opens his eyes, all is gone.
20 Terrors overtake him like a flood;
   a tempest snatches him away in the night.
21 The east wind carries him off, and he is gone;
   it sweeps him out of his place.
22 It hurls itself against him without mercy
   as he flees headlong from its power.
23 It claps its hands in derision
   and hisses him out of his place.

28 "There is a mine for silver
   and a place where gold is refined.
2 Iron is taken from the earth,
   and copper is smelted from ore.
3 Man puts an end to the darkness;
   he searches the farthest recesses
   for ore in the blackest darkness.
4 Far from where people dwell he cuts a shaft,
   in places forgotten by the foot of man;
   far from men he dangles and sways.
5 The earth, from which food comes,
   is transformed below as by fire;
6 sapphires[a] come from its rocks,

a 6 Or *lapis lazuli*; also in verse 16

and its dust contains nuggets of gold.
7 No bird of prey knows that hidden path,
no falcon's eye has seen it.
8 Proud beasts do not set foot on it,
and no lion prowls there.
9 Man's hand assaults the flinty rock
and lays bare the roots of the mountains.
10 He tunnels through the rock;
his eyes see all its treasures.
11 He searches*a* the sources of the rivers
and brings hidden things to light.

12 "But where can wisdom be found?
Where does understanding dwell?
13 Man does not comprehend its worth;
it cannot be found in the land of the living.
14 The deep says, 'It is not in me';
the sea says, 'It is not with me.'
15 It cannot be bought with the finest gold,
nor can its price be weighed in silver.
16 It cannot be bought with the gold of Ophir,
with precious onyx or sapphires.
17 Neither gold nor crystal can compare with it,
nor can it be had for jewels of gold.
18 Coral and jasper are not worthy of mention;
the price of wisdom is beyond rubies.
19 The topaz of Cush cannot compare with it;
it cannot be bought with pure gold.

20 "Where then does wisdom come from?
Where does understanding dwell?
21 It is hidden from the eyes of every living thing,
concealed even from the birds of the air.
22 Destruction*b* and Death say,
'Only a rumor of it has reached our ears.'
23 God understands the way to it
and he alone knows where it dwells,
24 for he views the ends of the earth
and sees everything under the heavens.
25 When he established the force of the wind
and measured out the waters,
26 when he made a decree for the rain
and a path for the thunderstorm,
27 then he looked at wisdom and appraised it;
he confirmed it and tested it.
28 And he said to man,
'The fear of the Lord—that is wisdom,
and to shun evil is understanding.' "

29

Job continued his discourse:

2 "How I long for the months gone by,
for the days when God watched over me,
3 when his lamp shone upon my head
and by his light I walked through darkness!
4 Oh, for the days when I was in my prime,
when God's intimate friendship blessed my
house,
5 when the Almighty was still with me

Sapphire Mines

JOB 28:1–13

Truly precious, priceless things are often mined from deep, dark places. This hymn to wisdom tells us that wisdom is more priceless than sapphires or gold.

What nuggets of wisdom have you discovered in unexpected places? As you have struggled with life's challenges, what "precious stones" have you uncovered? Find an object to symbolize something you have discovered about God or yourself. Put this object in a place where you can see it when you pray to remind you to prospect for wisdom in dark days.

---

a 11 Septuagint, Aquila and Vulgate; Hebrew *He dams up*   *b 22* Hebrew
Abaddon

The "Good Old Days"

JOB 29:2–6

The memory of better days of honor and prosperity stands in poignant relief against the dark backdrop of Job's suffering. For a time, Job revels in what used to be.

Do you wistfully remember an easy, pleasant time in your life, the "good old days," when life was easier for you than it is now? Pull out some old photos and spend time thinking about what was going on in your life at the time the photos were taken, or pull out and reread your journal from that time—perhaps even an old checkbook register. What people and situations come to mind as you do so? What made those "good old days" good? How do those memories enrich your life? How can you express gratitude to God for those times now?

See Meeting God in Everyday Life

and my children were around me,
⁶ when my path was drenched with cream
and the rock poured out for me streams of olive oil.

⁷ "When I went to the gate of the city
and took my seat in the public square,
⁸ the young men saw me and stepped aside
and the old men rose to their feet;
⁹ the chief men refrained from speaking
and covered their mouths with their hands;
¹⁰ the voices of the nobles were hushed,
and their tongues stuck to the roof of their mouths.
¹¹ Whoever heard me spoke well of me,
and those who saw me commended me,
¹² because I rescued the poor who cried for help,
and the fatherless who had none to assist him.
¹³ The man who was dying blessed me;
I made the widow's heart sing.
¹⁴ I put on righteousness as my clothing;
justice was my robe and my turban.
¹⁵ I was eyes to the blind
and feet to the lame.
¹⁶ I was a father to the needy;
I took up the case of the stranger.
¹⁷ I broke the fangs of the wicked
and snatched the victims from their teeth.

¹⁸ "I thought, 'I will die in my own house,
my days as numerous as the grains of sand.
¹⁹ My roots will reach to the water,
and the dew will lie all night on my branches.
²⁰ My glory will remain fresh in me,
the bow ever new in my hand.'

²¹ "Men listened to me expectantly,
waiting in silence for my counsel.
²² After I had spoken, they spoke no more;
my words fell gently on their ears.
²³ They waited for me as for showers
and drank in my words as the spring rain.
²⁴ When I smiled at them, they scarcely believed it;
the light of my face was precious to them.ᵃ
²⁵ I chose the way for them and sat as their chief;
I dwelt as a king among his troops;
I was like one who comforts mourners.

30 "But now they mock me,
men younger than I,
whose fathers I would have disdained
to put with my sheep dogs.
² Of what use was the strength of their hands to me,
since their vigor had gone from them?
³ Haggard from want and hunger,
they roamedᵇ the parched land
in desolate wastelands at night.
⁴ In the brush they gathered salt herbs,
and their foodᶜ was the root of the broom tree.

ᵃ24 The meaning of the Hebrew for this clause is uncertain.   ᵇ3 Or *gnawed*   ᶜ4 Or *fuel*

5 They were banished from their fellow men,
  shouted at as if they were thieves.
6 They were forced to live in the dry stream beds,
  among the rocks and in holes in the ground.
7 They brayed among the bushes
  and huddled in the undergrowth.
8 A base and nameless brood,
  they were driven out of the land.

9 "And now their sons mock me in song;
  I have become a byword among them.
10 They detest me and keep their distance;
  they do not hesitate to spit in my face.
11 Now that God has unstrung my bow and afflicted
  me,
  they throw off restraint in my presence.
12 On my right the tribe[a] attacks;
  they lay snares for my feet,
  they build their siege ramps against me.
13 They break up my road;
  they succeed in destroying me—
  without anyone's helping them.[b]
14 They advance as through a gaping breach;
  amid the ruins they come rolling in.
15 Terrors overwhelm me;
  my dignity is driven away as by the wind,
  my safety vanishes like a cloud.

16 "And now my life ebbs away;
  days of suffering grip me.
17 Night pierces my bones;
  my gnawing pains never rest.
18 In his great power ⌊God⌋ becomes like clothing to
  me[c];
  he binds me like the neck of my garment.
19 He throws me into the mud,
  and I am reduced to dust and ashes.

20 "I cry out to you, O God, but you do not answer;
  I stand up, but you merely look at me.
21 You turn on me ruthlessly;
  with the might of your hand you attack me.
22 You snatch me up and drive me before the wind;
  you toss me about in the storm.
23 I know you will bring me down to death,
  to the place appointed for all the living.

24 "Surely no one lays a hand on a broken man
  when he cries for help in his distress.
25 Have I not wept for those in trouble?
  Has not my soul grieved for the poor?
26 Yet when I hoped for good, evil came;
  when I looked for light, then came darkness.
27 The churning inside me never stops;
  days of suffering confront me.
28 I go about blackened, but not by the sun;
  I stand up in the assembly and cry for help.
29 I have become a brother of jackals,
  a companion of owls.

Tossing and Turning

JOB 30:16–17

Job's days are full of affliction, and his nights provide him with little rest. He cannot sleep. What are the signs of distress when your soul is not at ease? Do you, like Job, toss and turn through the night? Are your patterns of eating and working disturbed? Do you find yourself irritable with those near you?

When you go to bed tonight, take inventory of your cares and worries—even the small irritations in your life. Acknowledge and admit them, and then commit them to God's care. Write a bedtime prayer committing your worries to God and keep it on your nightstand.

See Meeting God in Prayer

---

a 12 The meaning of the Hebrew for this word is uncertain.   *b 13* Or me. / 'No one can help him,' ⌊they say⌋.   *c 18* Hebrew; Septuagint ⌊God⌋ grasps my clothing

Areas of Discipleship

JOB 31:1–23

Job offers us a pattern for examining our conscience regarding relationships as he looks at himself in relation to God, his family, his slaves and the helpless. If we put that in modern terms, we might examine our relationship to God, our family relationships, our work relationships and our ministry to the needy in the community.

Examine yourself in these areas. In which area is your discipleship strongest? Which area needs more attention and diligence? This examination could be done regularly or during a spiritual retreat. In each category, list the persons and situations that come to mind, asking God to show you what action to take in each area and how to pray regarding that area.

See Meeting God in Everyday Life

30 My skin grows black and peels;
  my body burns with fever.
31 My harp is tuned to mourning,
  and my flute to the sound of wailing.

31 "I made a covenant with my eyes
  not to look lustfully at a girl.
2 For what is man's lot from God above,
  his heritage from the Almighty on high?
3 Is it not ruin for the wicked,
  disaster for those who do wrong?
4 Does he not see my ways
  and count my every step?

5 "If I have walked in falsehood
  or my foot has hurried after deceit—
6 let God weigh me in honest scales
  and he will know that I am blameless—
7 if my steps have turned from the path,
  if my heart has been led by my eyes,
  or if my hands have been defiled,
8 then may others eat what I have sown,
  and may my crops be uprooted.

9 "If my heart has been enticed by a woman,
  or if I have lurked at my neighbor's door,
10 then may my wife grind another man's grain,
  and may other men sleep with her.
11 For that would have been shameful,
  a sin to be judged.
12 It is a fire that burns to Destruction[a];
  it would have uprooted my harvest.

13 "If I have denied justice to my menservants and
    maidservants
  when they had a grievance against me,
14 what will I do when God confronts me?
  What will I answer when called to account?
15 Did not he who made me in the womb make
    them?
  Did not the same one form us both within our
    mothers?

16 "If I have denied the desires of the poor
  or let the eyes of the widow grow weary,
17 if I have kept my bread to myself,
  not sharing it with the fatherless—
18 but from my youth I reared him as would a father,
  and from my birth I guided the widow—
19 if I have seen anyone perishing for lack of
    clothing,
  or a needy man without a garment,
20 and his heart did not bless me
  for warming him with the fleece from my
    sheep,
21 if I have raised my hand against the fatherless,
  knowing that I had influence in court,
22 then let my arm fall from the shoulder,
  let it be broken off at the joint.
23 For I dreaded destruction from God,

a 12 Hebrew Abaddon

and for fear of his splendor I could not do such
things.

24 "If I have put my trust in gold
    or said to pure gold, 'You are my security,'
25 if I have rejoiced over my great wealth,
    the fortune my hands had gained,
26 if I have regarded the sun in its radiance
    or the moon moving in splendor,
27 so that my heart was secretly enticed
    and my hand offered them a kiss of homage,
28 then these also would be sins to be judged,
    for I would have been unfaithful to God on
    high.

29 "If I have rejoiced at my enemy's misfortune
    or gloated over the trouble that came to him—
30 I have not allowed my mouth to sin
    by invoking a curse against his life—
31 if the men of my household have never said,
    'Who has not had his fill of Job's meat?'—
32 but no stranger had to spend the night in the
    street,
    for my door was always open to the traveler—
33 if I have concealed my sin as men do,[a]
    by hiding my guilt in my heart
34 because I so feared the crowd
    and so dreaded the contempt of the clans
    that I kept silent and would not go outside

35 ("Oh, that I had someone to hear me!
    I sign now my defense—let the Almighty
        answer me;
    let my accuser put his indictment in writing.
36 Surely I would wear it on my shoulder,
    I would put it on like a crown.
37 I would give him an account of my every step;
    like a prince I would approach him.)—

38 "if my land cries out against me
    and all its furrows are wet with tears,
39 if I have devoured its yield without payment
    or broken the spirit of its tenants,
40 then let briers come up instead of wheat
    and weeds instead of barley."

The words of Job are ended.

Elihu

32 So these three men stopped answering Job, because
he was righteous in his own eyes. ²But Elihu son of
Barakel the Buzite, of the family of Ram, became very
angry with Job for justifying himself rather than God. ³He
was also angry with the three friends, because they had
found no way to refute Job, and yet had condemned him.[b]
⁴Now Elihu had waited before speaking to Job because they
were older than he. ⁵But when he saw that the three men
had nothing more to say, his anger was aroused. ⁶So Elihu son of Barakel the Buzite said:

    "I am young in years,

Looking at Values

JOB 31:24–40

Job's self-examination continues. After looking at his behavior toward God and other people, Job looks at his attitudes, ethics and values. He has not trusted in his wealth; he has wished good even for his enemies; he has shown hospitality to strangers; he has been responsible in the use of the land God has given him.

Job offers us a pattern for examination of our values and attitudes. In what do you place your trust—your abilities and achievements, or God's faithfulness? Do the attitudes of your heart mirror God's love, justice and mercy? How are you contributing to your community by upholding values God has set? How are you seeking to be a faithful steward of the resources God has given you, including your body and the earth itself? Give thanks for God's help where you are doing well, and ask for help in areas where you are not doing as well.

See Meeting God in Community

---

a 33 Or *as Adam did*   *b 3* Masoretic Text; an ancient Hebrew scribal
tradition *Job, and so had condemned God*

Lessons in Suffering

JOB 33:6–20

Elihu is right—God does sometimes teach us through suffering to live more fully in his presence. Yet those lessons may not become apparent to us until the pain has subsided and the wounds have healed. We may not be able to perceive suffering's teaching until we gain the perspective of time.

Look back over times of suffering and darkness in your life. What life lessons did God teach you? How have those times changed and matured you? How has your faith blossomed as a result of those times?

See Meeting God in Everyday Life

and you are old;
that is why I was fearful,
not daring to tell you what I know.
⁷ I thought, 'Age should speak;
advanced years should teach wisdom.'
⁸ But it is the spirit*ᵃ* in a man,
the breath of the Almighty, that gives him
understanding.
⁹ It is not only the old*ᵇ* who are wise,
not only the aged who understand what is
right.

¹⁰ "Therefore I say: Listen to me;
I too will tell you what I know.
¹¹ I waited while you spoke,
I listened to your reasoning;
while you were searching for words,
¹²   I gave you my full attention.
But not one of you has proved Job wrong;
none of you has answered his arguments.
¹³ Do not say, 'We have found wisdom;
let God refute him, not man.'
¹⁴ But Job has not marshaled his words against me,
and I will not answer him with your arguments.

¹⁵ "They are dismayed and have no more to say;
words have failed them.
¹⁶ Must I wait, now that they are silent,
now that they stand there with no reply?
¹⁷ I too will have my say;
I too will tell what I know.
¹⁸ For I am full of words,
and the spirit within me compels me;
¹⁹ inside I am like bottled-up wine,
like new wineskins ready to burst.
²⁰ I must speak and find relief;
I must open my lips and reply.
²¹ I will show partiality to no one,
nor will I flatter any man;
²² for if I were skilled in flattery,
my Maker would soon take me away.

33 "But now, Job, listen to my words;
pay attention to everything I say.
² I am about to open my mouth;
my words are on the tip of my tongue.
³ My words come from an upright heart;
my lips sincerely speak what I know.
⁴ The Spirit of God has made me;
the breath of the Almighty gives me life.
⁵ Answer me then, if you can;
prepare yourself and confront me.
⁶ I am just like you before God;
I too have been taken from clay.
⁷ No fear of me should alarm you,
nor should my hand be heavy upon you.

⁸ "But you have said in my hearing—
I heard the very words—
⁹ 'I am pure and without sin;
I am clean and free from guilt.

ᵃ 8 Or Spirit; also in verse 18   ᵇ 9 Or many; or great

10 Yet God has found fault with me;
  he considers me his enemy.
11 He fastens my feet in shackles;
  he keeps close watch on all my paths.'

12 "But I tell you, in this you are not right,
  for God is greater than man.
13 Why do you complain to him
  that he answers none of man's words*a*?
14 For God does speak—now one way, now another—
  though man may not perceive it.
15 In a dream, in a vision of the night,
  when deep sleep falls on men
  as they slumber in their beds,
16 he may speak in their ears
  and terrify them with warnings,
17 to turn man from wrongdoing
  and keep him from pride,
18 to preserve his soul from the pit,*b*
  his life from perishing by the sword.*c*
19 Or a man may be chastened on a bed of pain
  with constant distress in his bones,
20 so that his very being finds food repulsive
  and his soul loathes the choicest meal.
21 His flesh wastes away to nothing,
  and his bones, once hidden, now stick out.
22 His soul draws near to the pit,*d*
  and his life to the messengers of death.*e*

23 "Yet if there is an angel on his side
  as a mediator, one out of a thousand,
  to tell a man what is right for him,
24 to be gracious to him and say,
  'Spare him from going down to the pit*f*;
  I have found a ransom for him'—
25 then his flesh is renewed like a child's;
  it is restored as in the days of his youth.
26 He prays to God and finds favor with him,
  he sees God's face and shouts for joy;
  he is restored by God to his righteous state.
27 Then he comes to men and says,
  'I sinned, and perverted what was right,
  but I did not get what I deserved.
28 He redeemed my soul from going down to the
  pit,*g*
  and I will live to enjoy the light.'

29 "God does all these things to a man—
  twice, even three times—
30 to turn back his soul from the pit,*h*
  that the light of life may shine on him.

31 "Pay attention, Job, and listen to me;
  be silent, and I will speak.
32 If you have anything to say, answer me;
  speak up, for I want you to be cleared.
33 But if not, then listen to me;
  be silent, and I will teach you wisdom."

God's Persistence

JOB 33:29–30

Elihu proclaims that God is not a silent God who is far removed. On the contrary, God keeps coming to us, calling to us, rescuing us and turning us away from our sin. God takes the initiative in seeking us.

How has God sought you repeatedly? Through whom has God reached out to you? Consider how God wants to reach out through you to those who are in pain or are searching for meaning and joy in their lives. Give thanks for God's persistence in your life and in the lives of those who have not yet realized that God is seeking them.

See Meeting God in Service

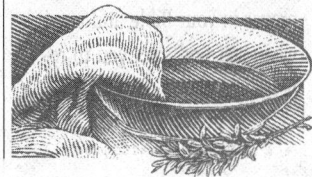

a 13 Or *that he does not answer for any of his actions*   b 18 Or *preserve him from the grave*   c 18 Or *from crossing the River*   d 22 Or *He draws near to the grave*   e 22 Or *to the dead*   f 24 Or *grave*   g 28 Or *redeemed me from going down to the grave*   h 30 Or *turn him back from the grave*

Teach Me What I Cannot See

JOB 34:16–32

Although Elihu is mistakenly telling Job to repent, he rightly indicates that the first step of repentance is to acknowledge sin. That can be difficult because we are often blind to our faults and weaknesses. The psalmist, in Psalm 139, asks God to illumine the sinfulness of his heart: "Search me, O God, and know my heart . . . See if there is any offensive way in me, and lead me in the way everlasting" (Psalm 139:23–24).

Using these verses in Job and in Psalm 139 as a starting point, write a prayer of repentance, asking God to illuminate your heart and show you what you need to confess. Keep this prayer in your Bible and use it whenever God calls you to repentance.

See *Meeting God in Scripture*

34 Then Elihu said:

2 "Hear my words, you wise men;
   listen to me, you men of learning.
3 For the ear tests words
   as the tongue tastes food.
4 Let us discern for ourselves what is right;
   let us learn together what is good.

5 "Job says, 'I am innocent,
   but God denies me justice.
6 Although I am right,
   I am considered a liar;
   although I am guiltless,
   his arrow inflicts an incurable wound.'
7 What man is like Job,
   who drinks scorn like water?
8 He keeps company with evildoers;
   he associates with wicked men.
9 For he says, 'It profits a man nothing
   when he tries to please God.'

10 "So listen to me, you men of understanding.
    Far be it from God to do evil,
    from the Almighty to do wrong.
11 He repays a man for what he has done;
    he brings upon him what his conduct deserves.
12 It is unthinkable that God would do wrong,
    that the Almighty would pervert justice.
13 Who appointed him over the earth?
    Who put him in charge of the whole world?
14 If it were his intention
    and he withdrew his spirit[a] and breath,
15 all mankind would perish together
    and man would return to the dust.

16 "If you have understanding, hear this;
    listen to what I say.
17 Can he who hates justice govern?
    Will you condemn the just and mighty One?
18 Is he not the One who says to kings, 'You are worthless,'
    and to nobles, 'You are wicked,'
19 who shows no partiality to princes
    and does not favor the rich over the poor,
    for they are all the work of his hands?
20 They die in an instant, in the middle of the night;
    the people are shaken and they pass away;
    the mighty are removed without human hand.

21 "His eyes are on the ways of men;
    he sees their every step.
22 There is no dark place, no deep shadow,
    where evildoers can hide.
23 God has no need to examine men further,
    that they should come before him for judgment.
24 Without inquiry he shatters the mighty
    and sets up others in their place.
25 Because he takes note of their deeds,

a 14 Or Spirit

he overthrows them in the night and they are
crushed.
²⁶ He punishes them for their wickedness
where everyone can see them,
²⁷ because they turned from following him
and had no regard for any of his ways.
²⁸ They caused the cry of the poor to come before
him,
so that he heard the cry of the needy.
²⁹ But if he remains silent, who can condemn him?
If he hides his face, who can see him?
Yet he is over man and nation alike,
³⁰   to keep a godless man from ruling,
from laying snares for the people.

³¹ "Suppose a man says to God,
'I am guilty but will offend no more.
³² Teach me what I cannot see;
if I have done wrong, I will not do so again.'
³³ Should God then reward you on your terms,
when you refuse to repent?
You must decide, not I;
so tell me what you know.

³⁴ "Men of understanding declare,
wise men who hear me say to me,
³⁵ 'Job speaks without knowledge;
his words lack insight.'
³⁶ Oh, that Job might be tested to the utmost
for answering like a wicked man!
³⁷ To his sin he adds rebellion;
scornfully he claps his hands among us
and multiplies his words against God."

35 Then Elihu said:

² "Do you think this is just?
You say, 'I will be cleared by God.'ᵃ
³ Yet you ask him, 'What profit is it to me,ᵇ
and what do I gain by not sinning?'

⁴ "I would like to reply to you
and to your friends with you.
⁵ Look up at the heavens and see;
gaze at the clouds so high above you.
⁶ If you sin, how does that affect him?
If your sins are many, what does that do to him?
⁷ If you are righteous, what do you give to him,
or what does he receive from your hand?
⁸ Your wickedness affects only a man like yourself,
and your righteousness only the sons of men.

⁹ "Men cry out under a load of oppression;
they plead for relief from the arm of the
powerful.
¹⁰ But no one says, 'Where is God my Maker,
who gives songs in the night,
¹¹ who teaches more to us than toᶜ the beasts of the
earth
and makes us wiser thanᵈ the birds of the air?'

The God Above

JOB 35:6–12

"In this universe, even what is called evil, when it is rightly ordered and kept in its place, commends the good more eminently, since good things yield greater pleasure and praise when compared to the bad things. For the Omnipotent God, whom even the heathen acknowledge as the Supreme Power over all, would not allow any evil in his works, unless in his omnipotence and goodness, as the Supreme Good, he is able to bring forth good out of evil."

—AUGUSTINE,
Enchiridion

ᵃ 2 Or *My righteousness is more than God's*   ᵇ 3 Or *you*   ᶜ 11 Or *teaches us by*
ᵈ 11 Or *us wise by*

My Favorite Obsession

JOB 36:17

Elihu points out that Job is obsessed with the question of whether life is fair—that Job spends too much time worrying about whether the wicked will be punished and the righteous rewarded. Elihu says that this preoccupation keeps Job from hearing God and seeing God at work in his life.

It's true we can spend so much time intellectualizing about God that we have little time to spend with God. Or we can become so busy working for God that we forget to look to him. Or we can become so caught up in our own compelling interests, even positive ones such as staying healthy or doing a good job, that we cannot sense God's nearness. What do you spend most of your time thinking about? Make a list of what has occupied your thoughts and taken up your time over the last twenty-four hours. Do these thoughts and activities reflect attention to God?

See Meeting God in Everyday Life

12 He does not answer when men cry out
   because of the arrogance of the wicked.
13 Indeed, God does not listen to their empty plea;
   the Almighty pays no attention to it.
14 How much less, then, will he listen
   when you say that you do not see him,
 that your case is before him
   and you must wait for him,
15 and further, that his anger never punishes
   and he does not take the least notice of
     wickedness.*a*
16 So Job opens his mouth with empty talk;
   without knowledge he multiplies words."

36

Elihu continued:

2 "Bear with me a little longer and I will show you
   that there is more to be said in God's behalf.
3 I get my knowledge from afar;
   I will ascribe justice to my Maker.
4 Be assured that my words are not false;
   one perfect in knowledge is with you.

5 "God is mighty, but does not despise men;
   he is mighty, and firm in his purpose.
6 He does not keep the wicked alive
   but gives the afflicted their rights.
7 He does not take his eyes off the righteous;
   he enthrones them with kings
   and exalts them forever.
8 But if men are bound in chains,
   held fast by cords of affliction,
9 he tells them what they have done—
   that they have sinned arrogantly.
10 He makes them listen to correction
   and commands them to repent of their evil.
11 If they obey and serve him,
   they will spend the rest of their days in
       prosperity
   and their years in contentment.
12 But if they do not listen,
   they will perish by the sword*b*
   and die without knowledge.

13 "The godless in heart harbor resentment;
   even when he fetters them, they do not cry for
     help.
14 They die in their youth,
   among male prostitutes of the shrines.
15 But those who suffer he delivers in their suffering;
   he speaks to them in their affliction.

16 "He is wooing you from the jaws of distress
   to a spacious place free from restriction,
   to the comfort of your table laden with choice
     food.
17 But now you are laden with the judgment due the
     wicked;
   judgment and justice have taken hold of you.

a 15 Symmachus, Theodotion and Vulgate; the meaning of the Hebrew for this word is uncertain.   b 12 Or will cross the River

¹⁸ Be careful that no one entices you by riches;
  do not let a large bribe turn you aside.
¹⁹ Would your wealth
  or even all your mighty efforts
  sustain you so you would not be in distress?
²⁰ Do not long for the night,
  to drag people away from their homes.ᵃ
²¹ Beware of turning to evil,
  which you seem to prefer to affliction.

²² "God is exalted in his power.
  Who is a teacher like him?
²³ Who has prescribed his ways for him,
  or said to him, 'You have done wrong'?
²⁴ Remember to extol his work,
  which men have praised in song.
²⁵ All mankind has seen it;
  men gaze on it from afar.
²⁶ How great is God—beyond our understanding!
  The number of his years is past finding out.

²⁷ "He draws up the drops of water,
  which distill as rain to the streamsᵇ;
²⁸ the clouds pour down their moisture
  and abundant showers fall on mankind.
²⁹ Who can understand how he spreads out the
      clouds,
  how he thunders from his pavilion?
³⁰ See how he scatters his lightning about him,
  bathing the depths of the sea.
³¹ This is the way he governsᶜ the nations
  and provides food in abundance.
³² He fills his hands with lightning
  and commands it to strike its mark.
³³ His thunder announces the coming storm;
  even the cattle make known its approach.ᵈ

37 "At this my heart pounds
  and leaps from its place.
² Listen! Listen to the roar of his voice,
  to the rumbling that comes from his mouth.
³ He unleashes his lightning beneath the whole
      heaven
  and sends it to the ends of the earth.
⁴ After that comes the sound of his roar;
  he thunders with his majestic voice.
  When his voice resounds,
  he holds nothing back.
⁵ God's voice thunders in marvelous ways;
  he does great things beyond our understanding.
⁶ He says to the snow, 'Fall on the earth,'
  and to the rain shower, 'Be a mighty downpour.'
⁷ So that all men he has made may know his work,
  he stops every man from his labor.ᵉ
⁸ The animals take cover;
  they remain in their dens.
⁹ The tempest comes out from its chamber,
  the cold from the driving winds.

God Speaks Through Pain

JOB 36:22-33

"God whispers to us in our pleasures, speaks to us in our conscience, but shouts in our pains."

—C. S. LEWIS,
The Problem of Pain

ᵃ20 The meaning of the Hebrew for verses 18–20 is uncertain.   ᵇ27 Or
distill from the mist as rain   ᶜ31 Or *nourishes*   ᵈ33 Or *announces his
coming— / the One zealous against evil*   ᵉ7 Or / *he fills all men with fear by
his power*

Amazing!

JOB 37:1–18

Elihu trembles as he considers the wondrous works of God's hand. He lists some of the wonders that awe him: thunder and lightning, snow and rain, the heavens.

What is the most awe-inspiring sight you have ever seen? Do natural wonders turn your mind toward God? Become a psalmist; choose some natural wonder and write a psalm about how it reveals God to you, or sing a hymn (one already published or one you make up) about the power of God.

See Meeting God in the Created Order

¹⁰ The breath of God produces ice,
    and the broad waters become frozen.
¹¹ He loads the clouds with moisture;
    he scatters his lightning through them.
¹² At his direction they swirl around
    over the face of the whole earth
    to do whatever he commands them.
¹³ He brings the clouds to punish men,
    or to water his earth*ᵃ* and show his love.

¹⁴ "Listen to this, Job;
    stop and consider God's wonders.
¹⁵ Do you know how God controls the clouds
    and makes his lightning flash?
¹⁶ Do you know how the clouds hang poised,
    those wonders of him who is perfect in
      knowledge?
¹⁷ You who swelter in your clothes
    when the land lies hushed under the south
      wind,
¹⁸ can you join him in spreading out the skies,
    hard as a mirror of cast bronze?

¹⁹ "Tell us what we should say to him;
    we cannot draw up our case because of our
      darkness.
²⁰ Should he be told that I want to speak?
    Would any man ask to be swallowed up?
²¹ Now no one can look at the sun,
    bright as it is in the skies
    after the wind has swept them clean.
²² Out of the north he comes in golden splendor;
    God comes in awesome majesty.
²³ The Almighty is beyond our reach and exalted in
      power;
    in his justice and great righteousness, he does
      not oppress.
²⁴ Therefore, men revere him,
    for does he not have regard for all the wise in
      heart?*ᵇ*"

The Lord Speaks

38 Then the Lord answered Job out of the storm. He said:

² "Who is this that darkens my counsel
    with words without knowledge?
³ Brace yourself like a man;
    I will question you,
    and you shall answer me.

⁴ "Where were you when I laid the earth's
      foundation?
    Tell me, if you understand.
⁵ Who marked off its dimensions? Surely you
      know!
    Who stretched a measuring line across it?
⁶ On what were its footings set,
    or who laid its cornerstone—
⁷ while the morning stars sang together

ᵃ 13 Or to favor them   ᵇ 24 Or for he does not have regard for any who think they are wise.

and all the angels[a] shouted for joy?

8 "Who shut up the sea behind doors
    when it burst forth from the womb,
9 when I made the clouds its garment
    and wrapped it in thick darkness,
10 when I fixed limits for it
    and set its doors and bars in place,
11 when I said, 'This far you may come and no
    farther;
    here is where your proud waves halt'?

12 "Have you ever given orders to the morning,
    or shown the dawn its place,
13 that it might take the earth by the edges
    and shake the wicked out of it?
14 The earth takes shape like clay under a seal;
    its features stand out like those of a garment.
15 The wicked are denied their light,
    and their upraised arm is broken.

16 "Have you journeyed to the springs of the sea
    or walked in the recesses of the deep?
17 Have the gates of death been shown to you?
    Have you seen the gates of the shadow of
    death[b]?
18 Have you comprehended the vast expanses of the
    earth?
    Tell me, if you know all this.

19 "What is the way to the abode of light?
    And where does darkness reside?
20 Can you take them to their places?
    Do you know the paths to their dwellings?
21 Surely you know, for you were already born!
    You have lived so many years!

22 "Have you entered the storehouses of the snow
    or seen the storehouses of the hail,
23 which I reserve for times of trouble,
    for days of war and battle?
24 What is the way to the place where the lightning
    is dispersed,
    or the place where the east winds are scattered
    over the earth?
25 Who cuts a channel for the torrents of rain,
    and a path for the thunderstorm,
26 to water a land where no man lives,
    a desert with no one in it,
27 to satisfy a desolate wasteland
    and make it sprout with grass?
28 Does the rain have a father?
    Who fathers the drops of dew?
29 From whose womb comes the ice?
    Who gives birth to the frost from the heavens
30 when the waters become hard as stone,
    when the surface of the deep is frozen?

31 "Can you bind the beautiful[c] Pleiades?
    Can you loose the cords of Orion?

Good Morning, Lord

JOB 38:12–21

God challenges Job to consider how little Job knows of what God has made. God sounds a bit sarcastic: "Surely you know, for you were already born [when light and darkness were created]."

Some morning soon, set your alarm to go off before dawn and rise early. Go outside or sit where you can see the sky as it becomes light and consider how the landscape changes as morning comes. What feelings rise up within you? Give thanks for God's love that is renewed with each new day. Some night soon when the sky is clear, go outside and look at the stars. Lie on your back and try to count the stars. Identify the constellations that are visible. If you don't know their names, find out.

See Meeting God in the Created Order

Where Wisdom Resides

JOB 38:36

Who bestows wisdom and understanding? God alone. Where does wisdom reside? In God alone.

On a piece of paper, write down some of the things that you "just don't understand." After you have made your list, present it as an offering to God: set the paper in a dish or bowl and burn it by lighting a match to it. As the smoke rises, allow it to represent your struggles and lack of understanding. Release them to God and trust that God knows what you do not know and is at work to carry out his plans.

See Meeting God in Prayer

---

³²Can you bring forth the constellations in their seasons*ᵃ*
or lead out the Bear*ᵇ* with its cubs?
³³Do you know the laws of the heavens?
Can you set up ⌞God's⌟*ᶜ* dominion over the earth?

³⁴"Can you raise your voice to the clouds
and cover yourself with a flood of water?
³⁵Do you send the lightning bolts on their way?
Do they report to you, 'Here we are'?
³⁶Who endowed the heart*ᵈ* with wisdom
or gave understanding to the mind*ᵈ*?
³⁷Who has the wisdom to count the clouds?
Who can tip over the water jars of the heavens
³⁸when the dust becomes hard
and the clods of earth stick together?

³⁹"Do you hunt the prey for the lioness
and satisfy the hunger of the lions
⁴⁰when they crouch in their dens
or lie in wait in a thicket?
⁴¹Who provides food for the raven
when its young cry out to God
and wander about for lack of food?

39 "Do you know when the mountain goats give birth?
Do you watch when the doe bears her fawn?
²Do you count the months till they bear?
Do you know the time they give birth?
³They crouch down and bring forth their young;
their labor pains are ended.
⁴Their young thrive and grow strong in the wilds;
they leave and do not return.

⁵"Who let the wild donkey go free?
Who untied his ropes?
⁶I gave him the wasteland as his home,
the salt flats as his habitat.
⁷He laughs at the commotion in the town;
he does not hear a driver's shout.
⁸He ranges the hills for his pasture
and searches for any green thing.

⁹"Will the wild ox consent to serve you?
Will he stay by your manger at night?
¹⁰Can you hold him to the furrow with a harness?
Will he till the valleys behind you?
¹¹Will you rely on him for his great strength?
Will you leave your heavy work to him?
¹²Can you trust him to bring in your grain
and gather it to your threshing floor?

¹³"The wings of the ostrich flap joyfully,
but they cannot compare with the pinions and feathers of the stork.
¹⁴She lays her eggs on the ground
and lets them warm in the sand,
¹⁵unmindful that a foot may crush them,
that some wild animal may trample them.

ᵃ 32 Or the morning star in its season   ᵇ 32 Or out Leo   ᶜ 33 Or his; or their   ᵈ 36 The meaning of the Hebrew for this word is uncertain.

¹⁶ She treats her young harshly, as if they were not
hers;
    she cares not that her labor was in vain,
¹⁷ for God did not endow her with wisdom
    or give her a share of good sense.
¹⁸ Yet when she spreads her feathers to run,
    she laughs at horse and rider.

¹⁹ "Do you give the horse his strength
    or clothe his neck with a flowing mane?
²⁰ Do you make him leap like a locust,
    striking terror with his proud snorting?
²¹ He paws fiercely, rejoicing in his strength,
    and charges into the fray.
²² He laughs at fear, afraid of nothing;
    he does not shy away from the sword.
²³ The quiver rattles against his side,
    along with the flashing spear and lance.
²⁴ In frenzied excitement he eats up the ground;
    he cannot stand still when the trumpet sounds.
²⁵ At the blast of the trumpet he snorts, 'Aha!'
    He catches the scent of battle from afar,
    the shout of commanders and the battle cry.

²⁶ "Does the hawk take flight by your wisdom
    and spread his wings toward the south?
²⁷ Does the eagle soar at your command
    and build his nest on high?
²⁸ He dwells on a cliff and stays there at night;
    a rocky crag is his stronghold.
²⁹ From there he seeks out his food;
    his eyes detect it from afar.
³⁰ His young ones feast on blood,
    and where the slain are, there is he."

40 The Lord said to Job:

² "Will the one who contends with the Almighty
    correct him?
    Let him who accuses God answer him!"

³ Then Job answered the Lord:

⁴ "I am unworthy—how can I reply to you?
    I put my hand over my mouth.
⁵ I spoke once, but I have no answer—
    twice, but I will say no more."

⁶ Then the Lord spoke to Job out of the storm:

⁷ "Brace yourself like a man;
    I will question you,
    and you shall answer me.

⁸ "Would you discredit my justice?
    Would you condemn me to justify yourself?
⁹ Do you have an arm like God's,
    and can your voice thunder like his?
¹⁰ Then adorn yourself with glory and splendor,
    and clothe yourself in honor and majesty.
¹¹ Unleash the fury of your wrath,
    look at every proud man and bring him low,
¹² look at every proud man and humble him,
    crush the wicked where they stand.

Evidences of God

JOB 39:19–29

"God's essence, indeed, is incomprehensible, utterly transcending all human thought; but on each of God's works his glory is engraven in characters so bright, so distinct, and so illustrious, that none, however dull and illiterate, can plead ignorance as their excuse. Hence, with perfect truth, the Psalmist exclaims, 'He wraps himself with light as with a garment,' (Psalm 104:2); as if he had said that God for the first time was arrayed in visible attire when, in the creation of the world, he displayed those glorious banners, on which, to whatever side we turn, we behold his perfections visibly portrayed."

—JOHN CALVIN,
Institutes of the Christian Religion

In Silence

JOB 40:1-14

God demands a response from Job. Job answers by not answering. Job is silent before the whirlwind out of which God speaks.

In the end, words cannot adequately express our suffering and trials and pain and darkness. Nor can words adequately express to God our awe and praise. We come in silence before a powerful, all-knowing God. Make it a priority to set aside an hour to spend in silence. Avoid conversation. Turn off the television, stereo or computer. Put aside books and magazines. Be silent before the Creator of the behemoth and the leviathan.

See Meeting God in Worship

13 Bury them all in the dust together;
    shroud their faces in the grave.
14 Then I myself will admit to you
    that your own right hand can save you.

15 "Look at the behemoth,[a]
    which I made along with you
    and which feeds on grass like an ox.
16 What strength he has in his loins,
    what power in the muscles of his belly!
17 His tail[b] sways like a cedar;
    the sinews of his thighs are close-knit.
18 His bones are tubes of bronze,
    his limbs like rods of iron.
19 He ranks first among the works of God,
    yet his Maker can approach him with his
        sword.
20 The hills bring him their produce,
    and all the wild animals play nearby.
21 Under the lotus plants he lies,
    hidden among the reeds in the marsh.
22 The lotuses conceal him in their shadow;
    the poplars by the stream surround him.
23 When the river rages, he is not alarmed;
    he is secure, though the Jordan should surge
        against his mouth.
24 Can anyone capture him by the eyes,[c]
    or trap him and pierce his nose?

41 "Can you pull in the leviathan[d] with a fishhook
    or tie down his tongue with a rope?
2 Can you put a cord through his nose
    or pierce his jaw with a hook?
3 Will he keep begging you for mercy?
    Will he speak to you with gentle words?
4 Will he make an agreement with you
    for you to take him as your slave for life?
5 Can you make a pet of him like a bird
    or put him on a leash for your girls?
6 Will traders barter for him?
    Will they divide him up among the merchants?
7 Can you fill his hide with harpoons
    or his head with fishing spears?
8 If you lay a hand on him,
    you will remember the struggle and never do it
        again!
9 Any hope of subduing him is false;
    the mere sight of him is overpowering.
10 No one is fierce enough to rouse him.
    Who then is able to stand against me?
11 Who has a claim against me that I must pay?
    Everything under heaven belongs to me.

12 "I will not fail to speak of his limbs,
    his strength and his graceful form.
13 Who can strip off his outer coat?
    Who would approach him with a bridle?
14 Who dares open the doors of his mouth,
    ringed about with his fearsome teeth?

---

[a] 15 Possibly the hippopotamus or the elephant   [b] 17 Possibly trunk
[c] 24 Or *by a water hole*   [d] 1 Possibly the crocodile

¹⁵His back has*ᵃ* rows of shields
  tightly sealed together;
¹⁶each is so close to the next
  that no air can pass between.
¹⁷They are joined fast to one another;
  they cling together and cannot be parted.
¹⁸His snorting throws out flashes of light;
  his eyes are like the rays of dawn.
¹⁹Firebrands stream from his mouth;
  sparks of fire shoot out.
²⁰Smoke pours from his nostrils
  as from a boiling pot over a fire of reeds.
²¹His breath sets coals ablaze,
  and flames dart from his mouth.
²²Strength resides in his neck;
  dismay goes before him.
²³The folds of his flesh are tightly joined;
  they are firm and immovable.
²⁴His chest is hard as rock,
  hard as a lower millstone.
²⁵When he rises up, the mighty are terrified;
  they retreat before his thrashing.
²⁶The sword that reaches him has no effect,
  nor does the spear or the dart or the javelin.
²⁷Iron he treats like straw
  and bronze like rotten wood.
²⁸Arrows do not make him flee;
  slingstones are like chaff to him.
²⁹A club seems to him but a piece of straw;
  he laughs at the rattling of the lance.
³⁰His undersides are jagged potsherds,
  leaving a trail in the mud like a threshing
    sledge.
³¹He makes the depths churn like a boiling caldron
  and stirs up the sea like a pot of ointment.
³²Behind him he leaves a glistening wake;
  one would think the deep had white hair.
³³Nothing on earth is his equal—
  a creature without fear.
³⁴He looks down on all that are haughty;
  he is king over all that are proud."

Job
42
Then Job replied to the Lᴏʀᴅ:

²"I know that you can do all things;
  no plan of yours can be thwarted.
³ᴌYou asked,ᴊ 'Who is this that obscures my
    counsel without knowledge?'
  Surely I spoke of things I did not understand,
  things too wonderful for me to know.

⁴ᴌ"You said,ᴊ 'Listen now, and I will speak;
  I will question you,
  and you shall answer me.'
⁵My ears had heard of you
  but now my eyes have seen you.
⁶Therefore I despise myself
  and repent in dust and ashes."

The Mighty Beast

JOB 41:12–34

This picture of the leviathan, the great monster of the deep, is like the loud, triumphant ending of a great symphony—intended to leave us in awe, to stop us in our tracks. What music comes to mind as you think of this picture? Listen to Haydn's oratorio *Creation*, to Grofé's *Grand Canyon Suite*, to Dvořák's symphony *From the New World* or to some exultant song of praise. What emotions does the music evoke? Then read again the poetry of 41:12–34. Compare your reactions to the music with your reactions to the words of this passage. How can you express your awe and wonder at all God has done? What moves you to praise God?

See Meeting God in Worship

ᵃ 15 Or *His pride is his*

Beyond the Questions

JOB 42:5

The affirmation that Job makes shows how he has moved from thinking and talking about God to encountering God personally —one of the greatest leaps in the spiritual life. Job has grown beyond discussing theology with his friends. He has grown beyond wanting God to answer him. Now, hearing God's voice, he sees that the goal is not an exchange of ideas but a relationship. Being with God is more important than understanding God.

Can you point to a moment when God became real to you in a way that caused you to put aside all your questions and simply rest in him? Sit in God's presence now and put aside your thoughts. Open yourself to receive God. Welcome God, even when you do not understand and even when your questions go unanswered.

See *Meeting God in Prayer*

Epilogue

⁷After the Lord had said these things to Job, he said to Eliphaz the Temanite, "I am angry with you and your two friends, because you have not spoken of me what is right, as my servant Job has. ⁸So now take seven bulls and seven rams and go to my servant Job and sacrifice a burnt offering for yourselves. My servant Job will pray for you, and I will accept his prayer and not deal with you according to your folly. You have not spoken of me what is right, as my servant Job has." ⁹So Eliphaz the Temanite, Bildad the Shuhite and Zophar the Naamathite did what the Lord told them; and the Lord accepted Job's prayer.

¹⁰After Job had prayed for his friends, the Lord made him prosperous again and gave him twice as much as he had before. ¹¹All his brothers and sisters and everyone who had known him before came and ate with him in his house. They comforted and consoled him over all the trouble the Lord had brought upon him, and each one gave him a piece of silver*ᵃ* and a gold ring.

¹²The Lord blessed the latter part of Job's life more than the first. He had fourteen thousand sheep, six thousand camels, a thousand yoke of oxen and a thousand donkeys. ¹³And he also had seven sons and three daughters. ¹⁴The first daughter he named Jemimah, the second Keziah and the third Keren-Happuch. ¹⁵Nowhere in all the land were there found women as beautiful as Job's daughters, and their father granted them an inheritance along with their brothers.

¹⁶After this, Job lived a hundred and forty years; he saw his children and their children to the fourth generation. ¹⁷And so he died, old and full of years.

ᵃ 11 Hebrew *him a kesitah*; a kesitah was a unit of money of unknown weight and value.

PSALMS

Honest to God

KEY VERSE:

Your word is a lamp to my feet and a light for my path.—Psalm 119:105

The life of prayer, like life itself, is not always happy and peaceful. Into prayer we take our anxieties, loneliness and discouragement along with our joy, awe and celebration. In order to deepen any intimate relationship, we must be honest about our feelings. Relating to the God of the universe is no different. In fact, God knows us better than we know ourselves and always desires "truth in the inner parts" (Psalm 51:6).

The book of Psalms demonstrates such honest prayer. It contains songs of praise and prayers of lament, hymns celebrating God's steadfast love and prayers for vindication against enemies. The psalmists recall God's faithful love to his people and extol the marvels of his created order. As we read we share the psalmists' loneliness, sickness, grief and dread. We experience with them the ups and downs of their genuine spiritual journeys.

Perhaps no other book in the Bible has been read and meditated on as much as the book of Psalms. In most monasteries, the psalms are recited from morning until night. Through prayerful repetition, the psalms reach deeper and deeper into our hearts. When we "pray the psalms," we find new dimensions in our relationship with God. The psalms are a sanctuary of prayer to which we may daily retreat and find crucial nourishment for our hearts.

"The psalms are more than language. They contain within themselves the silence of high mountains and the silence of heaven . . . [and] become the Tabernacle of God in which we are protected forever from the rage of the city of business, from the racket of human opinions."

—THOMAS MERTON,
Bread in the Wilderness

Deeply Rooted

PSALM 1:1–3

One legacy we receive from the Old Testament writers is their dedication to the "law of the LORD" and to its significance in daily life. By meditating on Scripture over and over, this psalmist grows roots "like a tree planted by streams of water." The practice of *lectio divina*, or divine reading, is a way to become "rooted" in Scripture. Choose a verse and repeat it silently to yourself a few times. Listen to what God may be saying to you. You may hear the Spirit ask, "How strong are your roots? Are you planting yourself by streams of water? What are those streams?"

See Meeting God in Prayer

BOOK I

Psalms 1–41

Psalm 1

[1] Blessed is the man
who does not walk in the counsel of the wicked
or stand in the way of sinners
or sit in the seat of mockers.
[2] But his delight is in the law of the LORD,
and on his law he meditates day and night.
[3] He is like a tree planted by streams of water,
which yields its fruit in season
and whose leaf does not wither.
Whatever he does prospers.

[4] Not so the wicked!
They are like chaff
that the wind blows away.
[5] Therefore the wicked will not stand in the judgment,
nor sinners in the assembly of the righteous.

[6] For the LORD watches over the way of the righteous,
but the way of the wicked will perish.

Psalm 2

[1] Why do the nations conspire[a]
and the peoples plot in vain?
[2] The kings of the earth take their stand
and the rulers gather together
against the LORD
and against his Anointed One.[b]
[3] "Let us break their chains," they say,
"and throw off their fetters."

[4] The One enthroned in heaven laughs;
the Lord scoffs at them.
[5] Then he rebukes them in his anger
and terrifies them in his wrath, saying,
[6] "I have installed my King[c]
on Zion, my holy hill."

[7] I will proclaim the decree of the LORD:

He said to me, "You are my Son[d];
today I have become your Father.[e]
[8] Ask of me,
and I will make the nations your inheritance,
the ends of the earth your possession.
[9] You will rule them with an iron scepter[f];
you will dash them to pieces like pottery."

[10] Therefore, you kings, be wise;
be warned, you rulers of the earth.
[11] Serve the LORD with fear

---

a 1 Hebrew; Septuagint *rage*   *b 2* Or *anointed one*   *c 6* Or *king*   *d 7* Or *son*; also in verse 12   *e 7* Or *have begotten you*   *f 9* Or *will break them with a rod of iron*

and rejoice with trembling.
¹²Kiss the Son, lest he be angry
  and you be destroyed in your way,
for his wrath can flare up in a moment.
  Blessed are all who take refuge in him.

Psalm 3

A psalm of David. When he fled from his son Absalom.

¹O LORD, how many are my foes!
  How many rise up against me!
²Many are saying of me,
  "God will not deliver him."   *Selah*[a]

³But you are a shield around me, O LORD;
  you bestow glory on me and lift[b] up my head.
⁴To the LORD I cry aloud,
  and he answers me from his holy hill.   *Selah*

⁵I lie down and sleep;
  I wake again, because the LORD sustains me.
⁶I will not fear the tens of thousands
  drawn up against me on every side.

⁷Arise, O LORD!
  Deliver me, O my God!
Strike all my enemies on the jaw;
  break the teeth of the wicked.

⁸From the LORD comes deliverance.
  May your blessing be on your people.   *Selah*

Psalm 4

For the director of music. With stringed instruments.
A psalm of David.

¹Answer me when I call to you,
  O my righteous God.
Give me relief from my distress;
  be merciful to me and hear my prayer.

²How long, O men, will you turn my glory into
    shame[c]?
  How long will you love delusions and seek false
    gods[d]?   *Selah*
³Know that the LORD has set apart the godly for
    himself;
  the LORD will hear when I call to him.

⁴In your anger do not sin;
  when you are on your beds,
  search your hearts and be silent.   *Selah*
⁵Offer right sacrifices
  and trust in the LORD.

⁶Many are asking, "Who can show us any good?"
  Let the light of your face shine upon us,
    O LORD.
⁷You have filled my heart with greater joy

A Constant Source of Help

PSALM 3:3–5

The psalmist faces danger and adversity but reminds himself that the Lord is a shield surrounding him; he sleeps and awakes in the assurance that God is sustaining him. What images of God's presence comfort you and remind you of your Lord's steadfast care? In the Psalms, metaphors for God's nearness include shepherd, light, rock and shield. English mystic Julian of Norwich envisioned all creation as a hazelnut carried in the palm of the divine hand. As you go to sleep this night and wake up in the morning, meditate for a few minutes on a favorite image of God's protection.

See Meeting God in Worship

---

[a]2 A word of uncertain meaning, occurring frequently in the Psalms; possibly a musical term   [b]3 Or LORD, / my Glorious One, who lifts   [c]2 Or you dishonor my Glorious One   [d]2 Or seek lies

Morning With God

PSALM 5:1–3

How easy it is to begin the day in a mad rush of getting ready—finding missing socks and eating burnt toast—and forget to begin the day in God's presence. By beginning the day in prayer, if only for several minutes, we join the psalmist in "waiting" for God. We offer our sighs, hopes, worries and dreams on the altar of our hearts before our daily concerns distract us. God desires that we wait in humble expectancy.

In your journal or with a close friend, consider practical ways that you might begin your day with God. Perhaps, for a week, you might set your alarm twenty minutes earlier than you usually do; use that extra time to meditate on a psalm, read a devotional book or offer your prayer before God in silence.

See Meeting God in Prayer

than when their grain and new wine abound.
8 I will lie down and sleep in peace,
for you alone, O Lord,
make me dwell in safety.

Psalm 5

For the director of music. For flutes. A psalm of David.

1 Give ear to my words, O Lord,
consider my sighing.
2 Listen to my cry for help,
my King and my God,
for to you I pray.
3 In the morning, O Lord, you hear my voice;
in the morning I lay my requests before you
and wait in expectation.

4 You are not a God who takes pleasure in evil;
with you the wicked cannot dwell.
5 The arrogant cannot stand in your presence;
you hate all who do wrong.
6 You destroy those who tell lies;
bloodthirsty and deceitful men
the Lord abhors.

7 But I, by your great mercy,
will come into your house;
in reverence will I bow down
toward your holy temple.
8 Lead me, O Lord, in your righteousness
because of my enemies—
make straight your way before me.

9 Not a word from their mouth can be trusted;
their heart is filled with destruction.
Their throat is an open grave;
with their tongue they speak deceit.
10 Declare them guilty, O God!
Let their intrigues be their downfall.
Banish them for their many sins,
for they have rebelled against you.

11 But let all who take refuge in you be glad;
let them ever sing for joy.
Spread your protection over them,
that those who love your name may rejoice in
you.
12 For surely, O Lord, you bless the righteous;
you surround them with your favor as with a
shield.

Psalm 6

For the director of music. With stringed instruments.
According to *sheminith.*[a] A psalm of David.

1 O Lord, do not rebuke me in your anger
or discipline me in your wrath.
2 Be merciful to me, Lord, for I am faint;
O Lord, heal me, for my bones are in agony.

[a] Title: Probably a musical term

³My soul is in anguish.
How long, O LORD, how long?

⁴Turn, O LORD, and deliver me;
save me because of your unfailing love.
⁵No one remembers you when he is dead.
Who praises you from the grave*ᵃ*?

⁶I am worn out from groaning;
all night long I flood my bed with weeping
and drench my couch with tears.
⁷My eyes grow weak with sorrow;
they fail because of all my foes.

⁸Away from me, all you who do evil,
for the LORD has heard my weeping.
⁹The LORD has heard my cry for mercy;
the LORD accepts my prayer.
¹⁰All my enemies will be ashamed and dismayed;
they will turn back in sudden disgrace.

Psalm 7

A *shiggaion*ᵇ of David, which he sang to the LORD concerning Cush, a Benjamite.

¹O LORD my God, I take refuge in you;
save and deliver me from all who pursue me,
²or they will tear me like a lion
and rip me to pieces with no one to rescue me.

³O LORD my God, if I have done this
and there is guilt on my hands—
⁴if I have done evil to him who is at peace with me
or without cause have robbed my foe—
⁵then let my enemy pursue and overtake me;
let him trample my life to the ground
and make me sleep in the dust.   *Selah*

⁶Arise, O LORD, in your anger;
rise up against the rage of my enemies.
Awake, my God; decree justice.
⁷Let the assembled peoples gather around you.
Rule over them from on high;
⁸ let the LORD judge the peoples.
Judge me, O LORD, according to my righteousness,
according to my integrity, O Most High.
⁹O righteous God,
who searches minds and hearts,
bring to an end the violence of the wicked
and make the righteous secure.

¹⁰My shieldᶜ is God Most High,
who saves the upright in heart.
¹¹God is a righteous judge,
a God who expresses his wrath every day.
¹²If he does not relent,
heᵈ will sharpen his sword;
he will bend and string his bow.

How Long?

PSALM 6:6–8

The constant pain of chronic illness and the utter loneliness of deep grief—these are realities the psalmist deals with openly before God. "Where are you, God? Why is it taking so long?" he cries out, groaning in his weariness before God. Jesus himself felt a sense of abandonment at the cross, saying "Why have you forsaken me?" (Matthew 27:46). These feelings are natural; there is no need to withhold them in prayer, for God already knows what is yet unspoken. What feelings are you trying to hide from God—anguish, despair, fear? Are you angry with God about something? On a small piece of paper, list one or more of your hidden feelings, and hold the list in your hand as you pray a prayer of waiting.

See *Meeting God in Prayer*

ᵃ5 Hebrew *Sheol*   ᵇTitle: Probably a literary or musical term   ᶜ10 Or *sovereign*   ᵈ12 Or *If a man does not repent, / God*

God's Ordering

PSALM 8:3–6

One way to understand the meaning of "ruler" is to liken it to the loving care of a parent for a child. It is remarkable that God entrusts human beings with a major role in the care of the earth. Following the Franciscan model of faithfulness in action, write down in your journal five things you can do this week to lovingly care for your home and garden, your town or city and the earth and sky. As modern mystic Pierre Teilhard de Chardin invites: "Try, with God's help, to perceive the connection—even physical and natural—which binds your labor with the building of the kingdom of heaven."

See Meeting God in the Created Order

13 He has prepared his deadly weapons;
   he makes ready his flaming arrows.

14 He who is pregnant with evil
   and conceives trouble gives birth to
      disillusionment.
15 He who digs a hole and scoops it out
   falls into the pit he has made.
16 The trouble he causes recoils on himself;
   his violence comes down on his own head.

17 I will give thanks to the LORD because of his
      righteousness
   and will sing praise to the name of the LORD
      Most High.

Psalm 8

For the director of music. According to *gittith*.[a]
A psalm of David.

1 O LORD, our Lord,
   how majestic is your name in all the earth!

You have set your glory
   above the heavens.
2 From the lips of children and infants
   you have ordained praise[b]
because of your enemies,
   to silence the foe and the avenger.

3 When I consider your heavens,
   the work of your fingers,
the moon and the stars,
   which you have set in place,
4 what is man that you are mindful of him,
   the son of man that you care for him?
5 You made him a little lower than the heavenly
      beings[c]
   and crowned him with glory and honor.

6 You made him ruler over the works of your
      hands;
   you put everything under his feet:
7 all flocks and herds,
   and the beasts of the field,
8 the birds of the air,
   and the fish of the sea,
   all that swim the paths of the seas.

9 O LORD, our Lord,
   how majestic is your name in all the earth!

Psalm 9[d]

For the director of music. To ⌊the tune of⌋ "The Death
of the Son." A psalm of David.

1 I will praise you, O LORD, with all my heart;
   I will tell of all your wonders.

[a] Title: Probably a musical term   [b] 2 Or *strength*   [c] 5 Or *than God*
[d] Psalms 9 and 10 may have been originally a single acrostic poem, the stanzas of which begin with the successive letters of the Hebrew alphabet. In the Septuagint they constitute one psalm.

²I will be glad and rejoice in you;
  I will sing praise to your name, O Most High.

³My enemies turn back;
  they stumble and perish before you.
⁴For you have upheld my right and my cause;
  you have sat on your throne, judging righteously.
⁵You have rebuked the nations and destroyed the
    wicked;
  you have blotted out their name for ever and
    ever.
⁶Endless ruin has overtaken the enemy,
  you have uprooted their cities;
  even the memory of them has perished.

⁷The LORD reigns forever;
  he has established his throne for judgment.
⁸He will judge the world in righteousness;
  he will govern the peoples with justice.
⁹The LORD is a refuge for the oppressed,
  a stronghold in times of trouble.
¹⁰Those who know your name will trust in you,
  for you, LORD, have never forsaken those who
    seek you.

¹¹Sing praises to the LORD, enthroned in Zion;
  proclaim among the nations what he has
    done.
¹²For he who avenges blood remembers;
  he does not ignore the cry of the afflicted.

¹³O LORD, see how my enemies persecute me!
  Have mercy and lift me up from the gates of
    death,
¹⁴that I may declare your praises
  in the gates of the Daughter of Zion
  and there rejoice in your salvation.
¹⁵The nations have fallen into the pit they have dug;
  their feet are caught in the net they have hidden.
¹⁶The LORD is known by his justice;
  the wicked are ensnared by the work of their
    hands.   *Higgaion.ᵃ Selah*
¹⁷The wicked return to the grave,ᵇ
  all the nations that forget God.
¹⁸But the needy will not always be forgotten,
  nor the hope of the afflicted ever perish.

¹⁹Arise, O LORD, let not man triumph;
  let the nations be judged in your presence.
²⁰Strike them with terror, O LORD;
  let the nations know they are but men.   *Selah*

Psalm 10ᶜ

¹Why, O LORD, do you stand far off?
  Why do you hide yourself in times of trouble?
²In his arrogance the wicked man hunts down the
    weak,

ᵃ 16 Or *Meditation*; possibly a musical notation   ᵇ 17 Hebrew *Sheol*
ᶜ Psalms 9 and 10 may have been originally a single acrostic poem, the
stanzas of which begin with the successive letters of the Hebrew alphabet. In
the Septuagint they constitute one psalm.

Knowing God's Name

PSALM 9:10

Think of the name of someone
you love. Whom do you picture
when you hear that name? Perhaps you see a favorite aunt
who cared for you when you
were small or a dear friend who
always makes you laugh. When
you "know" a name, you know
the person behind the name;
when we know the name of
Jesus Christ, we know God's infinite love and saving grace.
Take five minutes to meditate
on the name for God that reminds you of God's steadfast
love. Close your eyes, say the
name quietly to yourself and
reflect on the images that
emerge.

See Meeting God in Worship

Hope for the Hopeless

PSALM 10:17–18

In Matthew 5:5, Jesus makes the startling proclamation: "Blessed are the meek, for they will inherit the earth." The meek are "the fatherless and the oppressed" of this psalm, and the psalmist expresses his feelings of hopelessness on their behalf. God seems far away, while the "wicked" crush the poor. Yet as Jesus called the meek "blessed," so also there is a note of hope in the last verses of this psalm.

We may feel that "God has forgotten" when we read headlines about a baby being drowned in a bathtub by an abusive parent or about children dying of hunger by the tens of thousands every day. Today choose one newspaper headline about a troubling incident and pray in hopeful intercession for that situation.

See Meeting God in Service

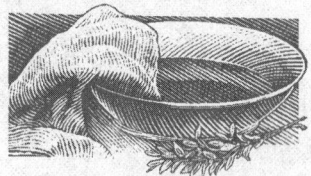

who are caught in the schemes he devises.
3 He boasts of the cravings of his heart;
 he blesses the greedy and reviles the LORD.
4 In his pride the wicked does not seek him;
 in all his thoughts there is no room for God.
5 His ways are always prosperous;
 he is haughty and your laws are far from him;
 he sneers at all his enemies.
6 He says to himself, "Nothing will shake me;
 I'll always be happy and never have trouble."
7 His mouth is full of curses and lies and threats;
 trouble and evil are under his tongue.
8 He lies in wait near the villages;
 from ambush he murders the innocent,
 watching in secret for his victims.
9 He lies in wait like a lion in cover;
 he lies in wait to catch the helpless;
 he catches the helpless and drags them off in
  his net.
10 His victims are crushed, they collapse;
 they fall under his strength.
11 He says to himself, "God has forgotten;
 he covers his face and never sees."

12 Arise, LORD! Lift up your hand, O God.
 Do not forget the helpless.
13 Why does the wicked man revile God?
 Why does he say to himself,
 "He won't call me to account"?
14 But you, O God, do see trouble and grief;
 you consider it to take it in hand.
 The victim commits himself to you;
 you are the helper of the fatherless.
15 Break the arm of the wicked and evil man;
 call him to account for his wickedness
 that would not be found out.

16 The LORD is King for ever and ever;
 the nations will perish from his land.
17 You hear, O LORD, the desire of the afflicted;
 you encourage them, and you listen to their
  cry,
18 defending the fatherless and the oppressed,
 in order that man, who is of the earth, may
  terrify no more.

Psalm 11

For the director of music. Of David.

1 In the LORD I take refuge.
 How then can you say to me:
 "Flee like a bird to your mountain.
2 For look, the wicked bend their bows;
 they set their arrows against the strings
 to shoot from the shadows
 at the upright in heart.
3 When the foundations are being destroyed,
 what can the righteous do*a*?"

a 3 Or *what is the Righteous One doing*

⁴The LORD is in his holy temple;
    the LORD is on his heavenly throne.
He observes the sons of men;
    his eyes examine them.
⁵The LORD examines the righteous,
    but the wicked*a* and those who love violence
    his soul hates.
⁶On the wicked he will rain
    fiery coals and burning sulfur;
    a scorching wind will be their lot.

⁷For the LORD is righteous,
    he loves justice;
    upright men will see his face.

Psalm 12

For the director of music. According to *sheminith.*ᵇ
A psalm of David.

¹Help, LORD, for the godly are no more;
    the faithful have vanished from among men.
²Everyone lies to his neighbor;
    their flattering lips speak with deception.

³May the LORD cut off all flattering lips
    and every boastful tongue
⁴that says, "We will triumph with our tongues;
    we own our lips*c*—who is our master?"

⁵"Because of the oppression of the weak
    and the groaning of the needy,
I will now arise," says the LORD.
    "I will protect them from those who malign
      them."
⁶And the words of the LORD are flawless,
    like silver refined in a furnace of clay,
    purified seven times.

⁷O LORD, you will keep us safe
    and protect us from such people forever.
⁸The wicked freely strut about
    when what is vile is honored among men.

Psalm 13

For the director of music. A psalm of David.

¹How long, O LORD? Will you forget me forever?
    How long will you hide your face from me?
²How long must I wrestle with my thoughts
    and every day have sorrow in my heart?
    How long will my enemy triumph over me?

³Look on me and answer, O LORD my God.
    Give light to my eyes, or I will sleep in death;
⁴my enemy will say, "I have overcome him,"
    and my foes will rejoice when I fall.

⁵But I trust in your unfailing love;
    my heart rejoices in your salvation.

God's Faithfulness in Despair

PSALM 13:1–6

Mystic Simone Weil wrote, "At the bottom of the heart of every human being, from earliest infancy until the tomb, there is something that goes on indomitably expecting, in the teeth of all experience of crimes committed, suffered, and witnessed, that good and not evil will be done to him. It is this above all that is sacred in every human being." The psalmist also "expects" God's loving faithfulness. He even believes one day he will "sing to the LORD, for [God] has been good to me." In your journal, reflect on one of your deepest hopes about a difficult situation. Find or make an object to symbolize it. Offer that hope to God in a prayer of expectancy.

a 5 Or *The LORD, the Righteous One, examines the wicked, /*   *b* Title: Probably
a musical term   *c 4* Or */ our lips are our plowshares*

707

Worship: The Heart's Examination

PSALM 15:1–5

Theologian Karl Barth tells a story of a professor who would often ask his students, "How are things with your heart?" When we worship God, we face the same question. In coming to God's "sanctuary," the psalmist asks himself the hard questions about whether he has been faithful to God's law: "Have I been honest? Have I honored God even though it might have hurt me? Have I benefited from the distress of the disadvantaged or weak?" As you prepare for worship this week, consider these questions in personal prayer, in your journal or with a close friend.

See Meeting God in Worship

⁶I will sing to the LORD,
for he has been good to me.

Psalm 14

For the director of music. Of David.

¹The fool*ᵃ* says in his heart,
"There is no God."
They are corrupt, their deeds are vile;
there is no one who does good.

²The LORD looks down from heaven
on the sons of men
to see if there are any who understand,
any who seek God.
³All have turned aside,
they have together become corrupt;
there is no one who does good,
not even one.

⁴Will evildoers never learn—
those who devour my people as men eat bread
and who do not call on the LORD?
⁵There they are, overwhelmed with dread,
for God is present in the company of the righteous.
⁶You evildoers frustrate the plans of the poor,
but the LORD is their refuge.

⁷Oh, that salvation for Israel would come out of Zion!
When the LORD restores the fortunes of his people,
let Jacob rejoice and Israel be glad!

Psalm 15

A psalm of David.

¹LORD, who may dwell in your sanctuary?
Who may live on your holy hill?

²He whose walk is blameless
and who does what is righteous,
who speaks the truth from his heart
³ and has no slander on his tongue,
who does his neighbor no wrong
and casts no slur on his fellowman,
⁴who despises a vile man
but honors those who fear the LORD,
who keeps his oath
even when it hurts,
⁵who lends his money without usury
and does not accept a bribe against the innocent.

He who does these things
will never be shaken.

ᵃ 1 The Hebrew words rendered *fool* in Psalms denote one who is morally deficient.

Psalm 16

A miktam[a] of David.

¹ Keep me safe, O God,
  for in you I take refuge.

² I said to the LORD, "You are my Lord;
  apart from you I have no good thing."
³ As for the saints who are in the land,
  they are the glorious ones in whom is all my
    delight.[b]
⁴ The sorrows of those will increase
  who run after other gods.
  I will not pour out their libations of blood
  or take up their names on my lips.

⁵ LORD, you have assigned me my portion and my
    cup;
  you have made my lot secure.
⁶ The boundary lines have fallen for me in pleasant
    places;
  surely I have a delightful inheritance.

⁷ I will praise the LORD, who counsels me;
  even at night my heart instructs me.
⁸ I have set the LORD always before me.
  Because he is at my right hand,
  I will not be shaken.

⁹ Therefore my heart is glad and my tongue
    rejoices;
  my body also will rest secure,
¹⁰ because you will not abandon me to the grave,[c]
  nor will you let your Holy One[d] see decay.
¹¹ You have made[e] known to me the path of life;
  you will fill me with joy in your presence,
  with eternal pleasures at your right hand.

Psalm 17

A prayer of David.

¹ Hear, O LORD, my righteous plea;
  listen to my cry.
  Give ear to my prayer—
  it does not rise from deceitful lips.
² May my vindication come from you;
  may your eyes see what is right.

³ Though you probe my heart and examine me at
    night,
  though you test me, you will find nothing;
  I have resolved that my mouth will not sin.
⁴ As for the deeds of men—
  by the word of your lips
  I have kept myself
  from the ways of the violent.
⁵ My steps have held to your paths;
  my feet have not slipped.

The Path of Life: Fullness of Joy

PSALM 16:11

One of the recurring themes in the Psalms is that God's path is a way of life. In the old favorite, Psalm 23, the psalmist claims God's mercy and goodness all along this path of life. The delights along the path with God are not material, but spiritual. What are the spiritual gifts you have found along your path? What moments in the last twenty-four hours do you feel grateful for? How have you experienced grace in this past week? Reflect on ways you have known God's presence in your life.

See Meeting God in Everyday Life

---

[a] Title: Probably a literary or musical term   [b] 3 Or *As for the pagan priests who are in the land / and the nobles in whom all delight, I said:*   [c] 10 Hebrew *Sheol*   [d] 10 Or *your faithful one*   [e] 11 Or *You will make*

The Apple of God's Eye

PSALM 17:7–8

The psalmist is by no means timid when he prays, "Keep me as the apple of your eye." Indeed, if we look into God's eyes deeply enough, we will find more and more love, but it is a love that is not always easy for us to accept. "The great spiritual call of the Beloved Children of God," Henri Nouwen writes, "is to pull their brokenness away from the shadow of the curse and put it under the light of the blessing."

On your bathroom mirror or the dashboard of your car, affix a Scripture passage that expresses God's blessing, such as "You are precious and honored in my sight, and . . . I love you" (Isaiah 43:4), or "I have loved you with an everlasting love; I have drawn you with loving-kindness" (Jeremiah 31:3).

See Meeting God in Scripture

⁶I call on you, O God, for you will answer me;
give ear to me and hear my prayer.
⁷Show the wonder of your great love,
you who save by your right hand
those who take refuge in you from their foes.
⁸Keep me as the apple of your eye;
hide me in the shadow of your wings
⁹from the wicked who assail me,
from my mortal enemies who surround me.

¹⁰They close up their callous hearts,
and their mouths speak with arrogance.
¹¹They have tracked me down, they now surround me,
with eyes alert, to throw me to the ground.
¹²They are like a lion hungry for prey,
like a great lion crouching in cover.

¹³Rise up, O LORD, confront them, bring them down;
rescue me from the wicked by your sword.
¹⁴O LORD, by your hand save me from such men,
from men of this world whose reward is in this life.

You still the hunger of those you cherish;
their sons have plenty,
and they store up wealth for their children.
¹⁵And I—in righteousness I will see your face;
when I awake, I will be satisfied with seeing your likeness.

Psalm 18

For the director of music. Of David the servant of the LORD. He sang to the LORD the words of this song when the LORD delivered him from the hand of all his enemies and from the hand of Saul. He said:

¹I love you, O LORD, my strength.

²The LORD is my rock, my fortress and my deliverer;
my God is my rock, in whom I take refuge.
He is my shield and the horn*ᵃ* of my salvation,
my stronghold.
³I call to the LORD, who is worthy of praise,
and I am saved from my enemies.

⁴The cords of death entangled me;
the torrents of destruction overwhelmed me.
⁵The cords of the grave*ᵇ* coiled around me;
the snares of death confronted me.
⁶In my distress I called to the LORD;
I cried to my God for help.
From his temple he heard my voice;
my cry came before him, into his ears.

⁷The earth trembled and quaked,
and the foundations of the mountains shook;
they trembled because he was angry.
⁸Smoke rose from his nostrils;

ᵃ 2 Horn here symbolizes strength.   *ᵇ 5* Hebrew *Sheol*

consuming fire came from his mouth,
burning coals blazed out of it.
9 He parted the heavens and came down;
dark clouds were under his feet.
10 He mounted the cherubim and flew;
he soared on the wings of the wind.
11 He made darkness his covering, his canopy
around him—
the dark rain clouds of the sky.
12 Out of the brightness of his presence clouds
advanced,
with hailstones and bolts of lightning.
13 The LORD thundered from heaven;
the voice of the Most High resounded.*a*
14 He shot his arrows and scattered ⌊the enemies⌋,
great bolts of lightning and routed them.
15 The valleys of the sea were exposed
and the foundations of the earth laid bare
at your rebuke, O LORD,
at the blast of breath from your nostrils.

16 He reached down from on high and took hold of
me;
he drew me out of deep waters.
17 He rescued me from my powerful enemy,
from my foes, who were too strong for me.
18 They confronted me in the day of my disaster,
but the LORD was my support.
19 He brought me out into a spacious place;
he rescued me because he delighted in me.

20 The LORD has dealt with me according to my
righteousness;
according to the cleanness of my hands he has
rewarded me.
21 For I have kept the ways of the LORD;
I have not done evil by turning from my God.
22 All his laws are before me;
I have not turned away from his decrees.
23 I have been blameless before him
and have kept myself from sin.
24 The LORD has rewarded me according to my
righteousness,
according to the cleanness of my hands in his
sight.

25 To the faithful you show yourself faithful,
to the blameless you show yourself blameless,
26 to the pure you show yourself pure,
but to the crooked you show yourself shrewd.
27 You save the humble
but bring low those whose eyes are haughty.
28 You, O LORD, keep my lamp burning;
my God turns my darkness into light.
29 With your help I can advance against a troop*b*;
with my God I can scale a wall.

30 As for God, his way is perfect;

The Lamp of God

PSALM 18:28

Light is often used as a metaphor for Jesus Christ. The Gospel of John points out that through Jesus Christ we are able to see and to understand what is true. As we read this psalm, we see vivid images of the Christ-light guiding us out of darkness. What is the light of Christ inviting you to see in your heart and life? Do you need God to illuminate an area in your life currently obstructed by "clouds"? As you go through your day, picture this divine light surrounding you and ask God for insights about this cloudy situation.

See Meeting God in Everyday Life

---

a 13 Some Hebrew manuscripts and Septuagint (see also 2 Samuel 22:14);
most Hebrew manuscripts *resounded, / amid hailstones and bolts of lightning*
b 29 Or *can run through a barricade*

711

God's Saving Presence

PSALM 18:35-36

The psalmist is not distant and polite in his devotional life. With fiery honesty the psalmist prays for victory over his enemies. We may feel uncomfortable with the violence of the psalmist's emotion and with God's intervention in the battle scenario; it seems primitive and strange to our twentieth-century minds.

There are no doubt moments in your life when God seems to have broadened the place for your steps in unseen and inexplicable ways. In your journal or on a piece of paper, mark off periods of your life in ten-year increments (i.e., 1–10, 10–20, 20–30, and so forth). For each time period, recall a special moment of God's inspiration or intervention.

See Meeting God in Everyday Life

the word of the LORD is flawless.
  He is a shield
    for all who take refuge in him.
³¹ For who is God besides the LORD?
    And who is the Rock except our God?
³² It is God who arms me with strength
    and makes my way perfect.
³³ He makes my feet like the feet of a deer;
    he enables me to stand on the heights.
³⁴ He trains my hands for battle;
    my arms can bend a bow of bronze.
³⁵ You give me your shield of victory,
    and your right hand sustains me;
    you stoop down to make me great.
³⁶ You broaden the path beneath me,
    so that my ankles do not turn.

³⁷ I pursued my enemies and overtook them;
    I did not turn back till they were destroyed.
³⁸ I crushed them so that they could not rise;
    they fell beneath my feet.
³⁹ You armed me with strength for battle;
    you made my adversaries bow at my feet.
⁴⁰ You made my enemies turn their backs in flight,
    and I destroyed my foes.
⁴¹ They cried for help, but there was no one to save
    them—
    to the LORD, but he did not answer.
⁴² I beat them as fine as dust borne on the wind;
    I poured them out like mud in the streets.

⁴³ You have delivered me from the attacks of the
    people;
    you have made me the head of nations;
    people I did not know are subject to me.
⁴⁴ As soon as they hear me, they obey me;
    foreigners cringe before me.
⁴⁵ They all lose heart;
    they come trembling from their strongholds.

⁴⁶ The LORD lives! Praise be to my Rock!
    Exalted be God my Savior!
⁴⁷ He is the God who avenges me,
    who subdues nations under me,
⁴⁸   who saves me from my enemies.
  You exalted me above my foes;
    from violent men you rescued me.
⁴⁹ Therefore I will praise you among the nations,
    O LORD;
    I will sing praises to your name.
⁵⁰ He gives his king great victories;
    he shows unfailing kindness to his anointed,
    to David and his descendants forever.

Psalm 19

For the director of music. A psalm of David.

¹ The heavens declare the glory of God;
    the skies proclaim the work of his hands.
² Day after day they pour forth speech;

night after night they display knowledge.
³There is no speech or language
  where their voice is not heard.ᵃ
⁴Their voiceᵇ goes out into all the earth,
  their words to the ends of the world.

In the heavens he has pitched a tent for the sun,
⁵ which is like a bridegroom coming forth from
    his pavilion,
  like a champion rejoicing to run his course.
⁶It rises at one end of the heavens
  and makes its circuit to the other;
  nothing is hidden from its heat.

⁷The law of the LORD is perfect,
  reviving the soul.
The statutes of the LORD are trustworthy,
  making wise the simple.
⁸The precepts of the LORD are right,
  giving joy to the heart.
The commands of the LORD are radiant,
  giving light to the eyes.
⁹The fear of the LORD is pure,
  enduring forever.
The ordinances of the LORD are sure
  and altogether righteous.
¹⁰They are more precious than gold,
  than much pure gold;
they are sweeter than honey,
  than honey from the comb.
¹¹By them is your servant warned;
  in keeping them there is great reward.

¹²Who can discern his errors?
  Forgive my hidden faults.
¹³Keep your servant also from willful sins;
  may they not rule over me.
Then will I be blameless,
  innocent of great transgression.

¹⁴May the words of my mouth and the meditation
    of my heart
  be pleasing in your sight,
  O LORD, my Rock and my Redeemer.

Psalm 20

For the director of music. A psalm of David.

¹May the LORD answer you when you are in
    distress;
  may the name of the God of Jacob protect you.
²May he send you help from the sanctuary
  and grant you support from Zion.
³May he remember all your sacrifices
  and accept your burnt offerings.   *Selah*
⁴May he give you the desire of your heart
  and make all your plans succeed.
⁵We will shout for joy when you are victorious

Sweeter Than Honey

PSALM 19:7–10

The Torah, or the Law of Moses, is central to the spirituality of the Hebrew people. The "law of the LORD," the psalmist reflects here, offers wisdom more valuable than riches and more satisfying than any sweetness. Why do we neglect Scripture, the centerpiece of our Christian lives? And when the words become all too familiar and we know the stories by heart, how are we to listen afresh to God's words?

Try reading this psalm as you would a love letter. What gifts do you receive from Scripture? What do you desire from God's truth?

See Meeting God in Scripture

ᵃ 3 Or *They have no speech, there are no words; / no sound is heard from them*
ᵇ 4 Septuagint, Jerome and Syriac; Hebrew *line*

Feeling Forsaken

PSALM 22:1

These familiar words, echoed by Jesus on the cross (Matthew 27:46; Mark 15:34), convey the utter loneliness of desperate suffering. Jesus suffered physically from torturous nails and from the pain of suffocation, but he also suffered psychologically. Abandoned by the One he loved most, Jesus cried out in terror.

You may also be waiting for God in loneliness or despairing grief, feeling you cannot find a way to hope. Cry out—as Jesus did—to the heavenly Father. God invites your honest emotions.

See Meeting God in Prayer

and will lift up our banners in the name of our God.
May the LORD grant all your requests.

⁶ Now I know that the LORD saves his anointed;
   he answers him from his holy heaven
   with the saving power of his right hand.
⁷ Some trust in chariots and some in horses,
   but we trust in the name of the LORD our God.
⁸ They are brought to their knees and fall,
   but we rise up and stand firm.

⁹ O LORD, save the king!
   Answer*ᵃ* us when we call!

Psalm 21

For the director of music. A psalm of David.

¹ O LORD, the king rejoices in your strength.
   How great is his joy in the victories you give!
² You have granted him the desire of his heart
   and have not withheld the request of his lips.
                                        Selah
³ You welcomed him with rich blessings
   and placed a crown of pure gold on his head.
⁴ He asked you for life, and you gave it to him—
   length of days, for ever and ever.
⁵ Through the victories you gave, his glory is great;
   you have bestowed on him splendor and majesty.
⁶ Surely you have granted him eternal blessings
   and made him glad with the joy of your presence.
⁷ For the king trusts in the LORD;
   through the unfailing love of the Most High
   he will not be shaken.

⁸ Your hand will lay hold on all your enemies;
   your right hand will seize your foes.
⁹ At the time of your appearing
   you will make them like a fiery furnace.
  In his wrath the LORD will swallow them up,
   and his fire will consume them.
¹⁰ You will destroy their descendants from the earth,
   their posterity from mankind.
¹¹ Though they plot evil against you
   and devise wicked schemes, they cannot succeed;
¹² for you will make them turn their backs
   when you aim at them with drawn bow.

¹³ Be exalted, O LORD, in your strength;
   we will sing and praise your might.

Psalm 22

For the director of music. To the tune of, "The Doe of the Morning." A psalm of David.

¹ My God, my God, why have you forsaken me?
   Why are you so far from saving me,

ᵃ 9 Or save! / O King, answer

so far from the words of my groaning?
²O my God, I cry out by day, but you do not
    answer,
  by night, and am not silent.

³Yet you are enthroned as the Holy One;
  you are the praise of Israel.[a]
⁴In you our fathers put their trust;
  they trusted and you delivered them.
⁵They cried to you and were saved;
  in you they trusted and were not
    disappointed.

⁶But I am a worm and not a man,
  scorned by men and despised by the people.
⁷All who see me mock me;
  they hurl insults, shaking their heads:
⁸"He trusts in the LORD;
  let the LORD rescue him.
Let him deliver him,
  since he delights in him."

⁹Yet you brought me out of the womb;
  you made me trust in you
  even at my mother's breast.
¹⁰From birth I was cast upon you;
  from my mother's womb you have been my
    God.
¹¹Do not be far from me,
  for trouble is near
  and there is no one to help.

¹²Many bulls surround me;
  strong bulls of Bashan encircle me.
¹³Roaring lions tearing their prey
  open their mouths wide against me.
¹⁴I am poured out like water,
  and all my bones are out of joint.
My heart has turned to wax;
  it has melted away within me.
¹⁵My strength is dried up like a potsherd,
  and my tongue sticks to the roof of my
    mouth;
  you lay me[b] in the dust of death.
¹⁶Dogs have surrounded me;
  a band of evil men has encircled me,
  they have pierced[c] my hands and my feet.
¹⁷I can count all my bones;
  people stare and gloat over me.
¹⁸They divide my garments among them
  and cast lots for my clothing.

¹⁹But you, O LORD, be not far off;
  O my Strength, come quickly to help me.
²⁰Deliver my life from the sword,
  my precious life from the power of the dogs.
²¹Rescue me from the mouth of the lions;
  save[d] me from the horns of the wild oxen.

Loved From Birth

PSALM 22:9–10

In the middle of this psalm about terrible suffering and forsakenness, the psalmist remembers that even in the womb he was protected by an unseen hand. We don't have to ask God to be present, for he is always with us; rather, we need to ask for an *awareness* of God's eternal presence. The mystic Meister Eckhart says, "You do not need to seek him here or there, he is no further off than the door of your heart."

What helps you to stay conscious of God's presence during the day? Find an object, such as a seashell or a picture from nature, that you can put on your desk or a table to remind you of God's nearness.

See Meeting God in the Created Order

---

^a 3 Or *Yet you are holy, / enthroned on the praises of Israel* ^b 15 Or */ I am laid* ^c 16 Some Hebrew manuscripts, Septuagint and Syriac; most Hebrew manuscripts */ like the lion.* ^d 21 Or */ you have heard*

The Lord, My Shepherd

PSALM 23:1–6

Because this beautiful, comforting psalm is very familiar, you may be inclined to rush past it. Instead, try to savor the words through the practice of divine reading—reading Scripture slowly and listening for what speaks to you. Read the psalm; then close your Bible and try to recite it from memory. Pause after each verse. Listen for a word or phrase that seems to speak to you. Perhaps "my shepherd" or "quiet waters" or "my cup overflows" catches your attention. Let the images or feelings that emerge rest gently on your heart. What is God inviting you to think or pray about today?

See Meeting God in Scripture

22 I will declare your name to my brothers;
    in the congregation I will praise you.
23 You who fear the LORD, praise him!
    All you descendants of Jacob, honor him!
    Revere him, all you descendants of Israel!
24 For he has not despised or disdained
    the suffering of the afflicted one;
  he has not hidden his face from him
    but has listened to his cry for help.

25 From you comes the theme of my praise in the
        great assembly;
    before those who fear you*a* will I fulfill my
        vows.
26 The poor will eat and be satisfied;
    they who seek the LORD will praise him—
    may your hearts live forever!
27 All the ends of the earth
    will remember and turn to the LORD,
  and all the families of the nations
    will bow down before him,
28 for dominion belongs to the LORD
    and he rules over the nations.

29 All the rich of the earth will feast and worship;
    all who go down to the dust will kneel before
        him—
    those who cannot keep themselves alive.
30 Posterity will serve him;
    future generations will be told about the Lord.
31 They will proclaim his righteousness
    to a people yet unborn—
    for he has done it.

Psalm 23

A psalm of David.

1 The LORD is my shepherd, I shall not be in want.
2   He makes me lie down in green pastures,
  he leads me beside quiet waters,
3   he restores my soul.
  He guides me in paths of righteousness
    for his name's sake.
4 Even though I walk
    through the valley of the shadow of death,*b*
  I will fear no evil,
    for you are with me;
  your rod and your staff,
    they comfort me.

5 You prepare a table before me
    in the presence of my enemies.
  You anoint my head with oil;
    my cup overflows.
6 Surely goodness and love will follow me
    all the days of my life,
  and I will dwell in the house of the LORD
    forever.

a 25 Hebrew *him*   *b 4* Or *through the darkest valley*

Psalm 24

Of David. A psalm.

¹ The earth is the LORD's, and everything in it,
  the world, and all who live in it;
² for he founded it upon the seas
  and established it upon the waters.

³ Who may ascend the hill of the LORD?
  Who may stand in his holy place?
⁴ He who has clean hands and a pure heart,
  who does not lift up his soul to an idol
  or swear by what is false.ᵃ
⁵ He will receive blessing from the LORD
  and vindication from God his Savior.
⁶ Such is the generation of those who seek him,
  who seek your face, O God of Jacob.ᵇ   *Selah*

⁷ Lift up your heads, O you gates;
  be lifted up, you ancient doors,
  that the King of glory may come in.
⁸ Who is this King of glory?
  The LORD strong and mighty,
  the LORD mighty in battle.
⁹ Lift up your heads, O you gates;
  lift them up, you ancient doors,
  that the King of glory may come in.
¹⁰ Who is he, this King of glory?
  The LORD Almighty—
  he is the King of glory.   *Selah*

Psalm 25ᶜ

Of David.

¹ To you, O LORD, I lift up my soul;
²   in you I trust, O my God.
  Do not let me be put to shame,
  nor let my enemies triumph over me.
³ No one whose hope is in you
  will ever be put to shame,
  but they will be put to shame
  who are treacherous without excuse.

⁴ Show me your ways, O LORD,
  teach me your paths;
⁵ guide me in your truth and teach me,
  for you are God my Savior,
  and my hope is in you all day long.
⁶ Remember, O LORD, your great mercy and love,
  for they are from of old.
⁷ Remember not the sins of my youth
  and my rebellious ways;
  according to your love remember me,
  for you are good, O LORD.

⁸ Good and upright is the LORD;
  therefore he instructs sinners in his ways.

ᵃ 4 Or *swear falsely*   ᵇ 6 Two Hebrew manuscripts and Syriac (see also
Septuagint); most Hebrew manuscripts *face, Jacob*   ᶜ This psalm is an
acrostic poem, the verses of which begin with the successive letters of the
Hebrew alphabet.

Our Precious Earth

PSALM 24:1–2

The earth is precious because it belongs to God, who designed an orderly and beautiful home for all creatures. Francis of Assisi lived daily in this knowledge—his image graces many gardens today because he loved the Creator and the creation. Consider which aspects of God's creation speak to you as you read a few verses from Francis's *The Canticle of Brother Sun:*

Praised be You, my Lord,
    through Brother Wind,
and through the air, cloudy
    and serene, and every
    kind of weather
through which You give
    sustenance to Your
    creatures.
Praised be You, my Lord,
    through Sister Water,
which is very useful and
    humble and precious
    and chaste.

Try writing a verse or two of your own.

See *Meeting God in the Created Order*

Humility Before God

PSALM 25:9–10

The psalmist says that God "guides the humble in what is right." When we become humble, we discover that God's ways are "loving and faithful." In what ways may God be calling you to humility in your daily life? In what ways does your schedule demand anxious efficiency rather than humble availability to God in every moment? How are you treating others you meet in your busy day?

See Meeting God in Everyday Life

9 He guides the humble in what is right
  and teaches them his way.
10 All the ways of the LORD are loving and faithful
  for those who keep the demands of his covenant.
11 For the sake of your name, O LORD,
  forgive my iniquity, though it is great.
12 Who, then, is the man that fears the LORD?
  He will instruct him in the way chosen for him.
13 He will spend his days in prosperity,
  and his descendants will inherit the land.
14 The LORD confides in those who fear him;
  he makes his covenant known to them.
15 My eyes are ever on the LORD,
  for only he will release my feet from the snare.

16 Turn to me and be gracious to me,
  for I am lonely and afflicted.
17 The troubles of my heart have multiplied;
  free me from my anguish.
18 Look upon my affliction and my distress
  and take away all my sins.
19 See how my enemies have increased
  and how fiercely they hate me!
20 Guard my life and rescue me;
  let me not be put to shame,
  for I take refuge in you.
21 May integrity and uprightness protect me,
  because my hope is in you.

22 Redeem Israel, O God,
  from all their troubles!

Psalm 26

Of David.

1 Vindicate me, O LORD,
  for I have led a blameless life;
  I have trusted in the LORD
  without wavering.
2 Test me, O LORD, and try me,
  examine my heart and my mind;
3 for your love is ever before me,
  and I walk continually in your truth.
4 I do not sit with deceitful men,
  nor do I consort with hypocrites;
5 I abhor the assembly of evildoers
  and refuse to sit with the wicked.
6 I wash my hands in innocence,
  and go about your altar, O LORD,
7 proclaiming aloud your praise
  and telling of all your wonderful deeds.
8 I love the house where you live, O LORD,
  the place where your glory dwells.

9 Do not take away my soul along with sinners,
  my life with bloodthirsty men,
10 in whose hands are wicked schemes,
  whose right hands are full of bribes.
11 But I lead a blameless life;
  redeem me and be merciful to me.

12 My feet stand on level ground;
 in the great assembly I will praise the LORD.

Psalm 27

Of David.

1 The LORD is my light and my salvation—
 whom shall I fear?
The LORD is the stronghold of my life—
 of whom shall I be afraid?
2 When evil men advance against me
 to devour my flesh,[a]
when my enemies and my foes attack me,
 they will stumble and fall.
3 Though an army besiege me,
 my heart will not fear;
though war break out against me,
 even then will I be confident.

4 One thing I ask of the LORD,
 this is what I seek:
that I may dwell in the house of the LORD
 all the days of my life,
to gaze upon the beauty of the LORD
 and to seek him in his temple.
5 For in the day of trouble
 he will keep me safe in his dwelling;
he will hide me in the shelter of his tabernacle
 and set me high upon a rock.
6 Then my head will be exalted
 above the enemies who surround me;
at his tabernacle will I sacrifice with shouts of joy;
 I will sing and make music to the LORD.

7 Hear my voice when I call, O LORD;
 be merciful to me and answer me.
8 My heart says of you, "Seek his[b] face!"
 Your face, LORD, I will seek.
9 Do not hide your face from me,
 do not turn your servant away in anger;
 you have been my helper.
Do not reject me or forsake me,
 O God my Savior.
10 Though my father and mother forsake me,
 the LORD will receive me.
11 Teach me your way, O LORD;
 lead me in a straight path
 because of my oppressors.
12 Do not turn me over to the desire of my foes,
 for false witnesses rise up against me,
 breathing out violence.

13 I am still confident of this:
 I will see the goodness of the LORD
 in the land of the living.
14 Wait for the LORD;
 be strong and take heart
 and wait for the LORD.

Waiting for God

PSALM 27:14

Waiting is difficult, especially in our age of high-speed technology. We tend to think that change should be instantaneous in ourselves, in others and in our situations. Yet again and again the psalmist admonishes us to wait for the Lord (Psalms 37:7; 62:5; 130:5). God's vision of time is much keener than ours. What problem is causing you to feel anxious or impatient? Can you surrender it to the Lord? You may choose to write all of your concerns about the situation in your journal or on a piece of paper. In silence, lay these concerns before God.

See Meeting God in Prayer

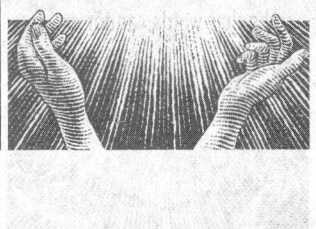

---

a 2 Or *to slander me*   b 8 Or *To you, O my heart, he has said, "Seek my*

Beyond Words

PSALM 28:1–2

In *Praying the Psalms*, Walter Brueggemann describes the pit as a "powerless, gray existence where one is removed from joy and discourse with God." Sometimes we feel, as the psalmist does, that we are in the pit, that God won't—or can't—hear our cries. In a gesture beyond words, the psalmist lifts up his hands in petition toward God's sanctuary.

Recall a time when you have felt you were in the pit. How do you express your pain and loneliness to God? What gesture or words might express your anguish to God? If you seem to be in a pit right now, remember the One who hears even your sighs that words cannot express.

See Meeting God in Prayer

Psalm 28

Of David.

¹ To you I call, O LORD my Rock;
    do not turn a deaf ear to me.
For if you remain silent,
    I will be like those who have gone down to the
        pit.
² Hear my cry for mercy
    as I call to you for help,
as I lift up my hands
    toward your Most Holy Place.

³ Do not drag me away with the wicked,
    with those who do evil,
who speak cordially with their neighbors
    but harbor malice in their hearts.
⁴ Repay them for their deeds
    and for their evil work;
repay them for what their hands have done
    and bring back upon them what they deserve.
⁵ Since they show no regard for the works of the
        LORD
    and what his hands have done,
he will tear them down
    and never build them up again.

⁶ Praise be to the LORD,
    for he has heard my cry for mercy.
⁷ The LORD is my strength and my shield;
    my heart trusts in him, and I am helped.
My heart leaps for joy
    and I will give thanks to him in song.

⁸ The LORD is the strength of his people,
    a fortress of salvation for his anointed one.
⁹ Save your people and bless your inheritance;
    be their shepherd and carry them forever.

Psalm 29

A psalm of David.

¹ Ascribe to the LORD, O mighty ones,
    ascribe to the LORD glory and strength.
² Ascribe to the LORD the glory due his name;
    worship the LORD in the splendor of his*a*
        holiness.

³ The voice of the LORD is over the waters;
    the God of glory thunders,
    the LORD thunders over the mighty waters.
⁴ The voice of the LORD is powerful;
    the voice of the LORD is majestic.
⁵ The voice of the LORD breaks the cedars;
    the LORD breaks in pieces the cedars of
        Lebanon.
⁶ He makes Lebanon skip like a calf,
    Sirion*b* like a young wild ox.
⁷ The voice of the LORD strikes

a 2 Or LORD with the splendor of   *b 6 That is, Mount Hermon*

with flashes of lightning.
⁸The voice of the LORD shakes the desert;
   the LORD shakes the Desert of Kadesh.
⁹The voice of the LORD twists the oaks*ᵃ*
   and strips the forests bare.
And in his temple all cry, "Glory!"

¹⁰The LORD sits*ᵇ* enthroned over the flood;
   the LORD is enthroned as King forever.
¹¹The LORD gives strength to his people;
   the LORD blesses his people with peace.

Psalm 30

A psalm. A song. For the dedication of the temple.*ᶜ* Of David.

¹I will exalt you, O LORD,
   for you lifted me out of the depths
   and did not let my enemies gloat over me.
²O LORD my God, I called to you for help
   and you healed me.
³O LORD, you brought me up from the grave*ᵈ*;
   you spared me from going down into the pit.

⁴Sing to the LORD, you saints of his;
   praise his holy name.
⁵For his anger lasts only a moment,
   but his favor lasts a lifetime;
weeping may remain for a night,
   but rejoicing comes in the morning.

⁶When I felt secure, I said,
   "I will never be shaken."
⁷O LORD, when you favored me,
   you made my mountain*ᵉ* stand firm;
but when you hid your face,
   I was dismayed.

⁸To you, O LORD, I called;
   to the Lord I cried for mercy:
⁹"What gain is there in my destruction,*ᶠ*
   in my going down into the pit?
Will the dust praise you?
   Will it proclaim your faithfulness?
¹⁰Hear, O LORD, and be merciful to me;
   O LORD, be my help."

¹¹You turned my wailing into dancing;
   you removed my sackcloth and clothed me
      with joy,
¹²that my heart may sing to you and not be silent.
   O LORD my God, I will give you thanks forever.

Psalm 31

For the director of music. A psalm of David.

¹In you, O LORD, I have taken refuge;
   let me never be put to shame;
   deliver me in your righteousness.
²Turn your ear to me,

Joy in God's Morning

PSALM 30:4–5

We human beings are sometimes reluctant to accept forgiveness. We continue to recall our sins and failures, unable to forgive ourselves even when God has forgiven us. We know that nothing will separate us from the love of God in Christ Jesus (see Romans 8:39), but we often act as if we are unforgivable—disbelieving that God's anger "lasts only a moment, but his favor lasts a lifetime." Are you holding a particular sin against yourself? Have you done something that you believe God can't forgive? What burden are you carrying needlessly into God's joy-filled morning?

See Meeting God in Prayer

ᵃ 9 Or *LORD makes the deer give birth*   *ᵇ 10* Or *sat*   *ᶜ* Title: Or *palace*
ᵈ 3 Hebrew *Sheol*   *ᵉ 7* Or *hill country*   *ᶠ 9* Or *there if I am silenced*

In God's Hand

PSALM 31:5

"As the life of prayer deepens it brings a gradual realization . . . . Through all the vicissitudes of trial, sin and conflict, the ground of the soul is rooted in [God's] life; that country from which we are exiled, yet which is our home . . . The ultimate humble trust of the little creature which first dared to say Abba! Father! is placed in the Absolute love; and finds in the simple return to God the Un-changing, that personal and permanent relation which is the ground of prayer."

—EVELYN UNDERHILL,
Abba

come quickly to my rescue;
be my rock of refuge,
   a strong fortress to save me.
³ Since you are my rock and my fortress,
   for the sake of your name lead and guide me.
⁴ Free me from the trap that is set for me,
   for you are my refuge.
⁵ Into your hands I commit my spirit;
   redeem me, O LORD, the God of truth.

⁶ I hate those who cling to worthless idols;
   I trust in the LORD.
⁷ I will be glad and rejoice in your love,
   for you saw my affliction
   and knew the anguish of my soul.
⁸ You have not handed me over to the enemy
   but have set my feet in a spacious place.

⁹ Be merciful to me, O LORD, for I am in distress;
   my eyes grow weak with sorrow,
   my soul and my body with grief.
¹⁰ My life is consumed by anguish
   and my years by groaning;
   my strength fails because of my affliction,ᵃ
   and my bones grow weak.
¹¹ Because of all my enemies,
   I am the utter contempt of my neighbors;
   I am a dread to my friends—
   those who see me on the street flee from me.
¹² I am forgotten by them as though I were dead;
   I have become like broken pottery.
¹³ For I hear the slander of many;
   there is terror on every side;
   they conspire against me
   and plot to take my life.

¹⁴ But I trust in you, O LORD;
   I say, "You are my God."
¹⁵ My times are in your hands;
   deliver me from my enemies
   and from those who pursue me.
¹⁶ Let your face shine on your servant;
   save me in your unfailing love.
¹⁷ Let me not be put to shame, O LORD,
   for I have cried out to you;
   but let the wicked be put to shame
   and lie silent in the grave.ᵇ
¹⁸ Let their lying lips be silenced,
   for with pride and contempt
   they speak arrogantly against the righteous.

¹⁹ How great is your goodness,
   which you have stored up for those who fear
      you,
   which you bestow in the sight of men
   on those who take refuge in you.
²⁰ In the shelter of your presence you hide them
   from the intrigues of men;

ᵃ *10* Or *guilt*   ᵇ *17* Hebrew *Sheol*

in your dwelling you keep them safe
    from accusing tongues.
21 Praise be to the LORD,
    for he showed his wonderful love to me
    when I was in a besieged city.
22 In my alarm I said,
    "I am cut off from your sight!"
    Yet you heard my cry for mercy
    when I called to you for help.

23 Love the LORD, all his saints!
    The LORD preserves the faithful,
    but the proud he pays back in full.
24 Be strong and take heart,
    all you who hope in the LORD.

Psalm 32

Of David. A *maskil.*ᵃ

1 Blessed is he
    whose transgressions are forgiven,
    whose sins are covered.
2 Blessed is the man
    whose sin the LORD does not count against him
    and in whose spirit is no deceit.

3 When I kept silent,
    my bones wasted away
    through my groaning all day long.
4 For day and night
    your hand was heavy upon me;
my strength was sapped
    as in the heat of summer.   *Selah*
5 Then I acknowledged my sin to you
    and did not cover up my iniquity.
I said, "I will confess
    my transgressions to the LORD"—
and you forgave
    the guilt of my sin.   *Selah*

6 Therefore let everyone who is godly pray to you
    while you may be found;
surely when the mighty waters rise,
    they will not reach him.
7 You are my hiding place;
    you will protect me from trouble
    and surround me with songs of deliverance.   *Selah*

8 I will instruct you and teach you in the way you
        should go;
    I will counsel you and watch over you.
9 Do not be like the horse or the mule,
    which have no understanding
but must be controlled by bit and bridle
    or they will not come to you.
10 Many are the woes of the wicked,
    but the LORD's unfailing love
    surrounds the man who trusts in him.

ᵃ Title: Probably a literary or musical term

The Call to Confession

PSALM 32:3–5

God's hand is "heavy" upon the psalmist; the writer feels the weight of guilt until he openly acknowledges his sin before God. Often it is hard to admit our sins and our failures to do what is right. Yet we know that when we confess, "he is faithful and just and will forgive us our sins and purify us from all unrighteousness" (1 John 1:9). Julian of Norwich declared that wrath is an earthly problem, but heaven is founded on mercy: "For the ground of mercy is in love; and the working of mercy is our being kept in love." Confession, oral or written, can help to free you from guilt. Is there a trusted soul friend you might share with? Or perhaps you could write a letter to God.

See *Meeting God in Community*

Celebrating God's Goodness

PSALM 33:1–5

Because the psalms are so often read without music, we may forget that many of them were *songs* of praise. The psalmist calls his hearers to "sing to [God] a new song; play skillfully and shout for joy." Praise declares God's goodness, reminds us of God's love and compassion, and opens our souls to hope. Reflect on your last twenty-four hours. When did you feel thankful? Did you gratefully witness an act of kindness? Did you stand breathless before a sunset? Did you feel God's grace in a stranger's smile? Offer these moments to God in praise.

See Meeting God in Worship

¹¹ Rejoice in the LORD and be glad, you righteous;
  sing, all you who are upright in heart!

Psalm 33

¹ Sing joyfully to the LORD, you righteous;
  it is fitting for the upright to praise him.
² Praise the LORD with the harp;
  make music to him on the ten-stringed lyre.
³ Sing to him a new song;
  play skillfully, and shout for joy.

⁴ For the word of the LORD is right and true;
  he is faithful in all he does.
⁵ The LORD loves righteousness and justice;
  the earth is full of his unfailing love.

⁶ By the word of the LORD were the heavens made,
  their starry host by the breath of his mouth.
⁷ He gathers the waters of the sea into jars[a];
  he puts the deep into storehouses.
⁸ Let all the earth fear the LORD;
  let all the people of the world revere him.
⁹ For he spoke, and it came to be;
  he commanded, and it stood firm.
¹⁰ The LORD foils the plans of the nations;
  he thwarts the purposes of the peoples.
¹¹ But the plans of the LORD stand firm forever,
  the purposes of his heart through all
    generations.

¹² Blessed is the nation whose God is the LORD,
  the people he chose for his inheritance.
¹³ From heaven the LORD looks down
  and sees all mankind;
¹⁴ from his dwelling place he watches
  all who live on earth—
¹⁵ he who forms the hearts of all,
  who considers everything they do.
¹⁶ No king is saved by the size of his army;
  no warrior escapes by his great strength.
¹⁷ A horse is a vain hope for deliverance;
  despite all its great strength it cannot save.
¹⁸ But the eyes of the LORD are on those who fear
    him,
  on those whose hope is in his unfailing love,
¹⁹ to deliver them from death
  and keep them alive in famine.

²⁰ We wait in hope for the LORD;
  he is our help and our shield.
²¹ In him our hearts rejoice,
  for we trust in his holy name.
²² May your unfailing love rest upon us, O LORD,
  even as we put our hope in you.

a 7 Or sea as into a heap

Psalm 34[a]

Of David. When he pretended to be insane before Abimelech, who drove him away, and he left.

[1] I will extol the LORD at all times;
　his praise will always be on my lips.
[2] My soul will boast in the LORD;
　let the afflicted hear and rejoice.
[3] Glorify the LORD with me;
　let us exalt his name together.

[4] I sought the LORD, and he answered me;
　he delivered me from all my fears.
[5] Those who look to him are radiant;
　their faces are never covered with shame.
[6] This poor man called, and the LORD heard him;
　he saved him out of all his troubles.
[7] The angel of the LORD encamps around those who
　　fear him,
　and he delivers them.

[8] Taste and see that the LORD is good;
　blessed is the man who takes refuge in him.
[9] Fear the LORD, you his saints,
　for those who fear him lack nothing.
[10] The lions may grow weak and hungry,
　but those who seek the LORD lack no good
　　thing.

[11] Come, my children, listen to me;
　I will teach you the fear of the LORD.
[12] Whoever of you loves life
　and desires to see many good days,
[13] keep your tongue from evil
　and your lips from speaking lies.
[14] Turn from evil and do good;
　seek peace and pursue it.

[15] The eyes of the LORD are on the righteous
　and his ears are attentive to their cry;
[16] the face of the LORD is against those who do evil,
　to cut off the memory of them from the earth.

[17] The righteous cry out, and the LORD hears them;
　he delivers them from all their troubles.
[18] The LORD is close to the brokenhearted
　and saves those who are crushed in spirit.

[19] A righteous man may have many troubles,
　but the LORD delivers him from them all;
[20] he protects all his bones,
　not one of them will be broken.

[21] Evil will slay the wicked;
　the foes of the righteous will be condemned.
[22] The LORD redeems his servants;
　no one will be condemned who takes refuge in
　　him.

A Recipe for Life

PSALM 34:11–14

The psalmist explains that to live in "the fear of the LORD" is to live fully within God's design. This recipe is uncomplicated: Speak the truth, do good and pursue peace. As you consider the week ahead, what activities in your life reflect God's intentions? Think of a person to whom you need to speak the truth in love. Perhaps you could call or visit someone who is homebound. Perhaps you could support a conflict resolution program at a local school. How do you pray and live according to God's "recipe"?

See Meeting God in Service

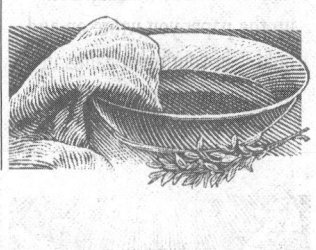

---

[a] This psalm is an acrostic poem, the verses of which begin with the successive letters of the Hebrew alphabet.

Cleansing Honesty

PSALM 35:4–8

The desire for vengeance is readily apparent in the book of Psalms. Walter Brueggemann points out that the yearning for vengeance "is not only *there* in the Psalms, but it is *here* in the human heart" as well. Though we may not be as blunt as the psalmist, we too carry grudges. By hiding them and staying silent, we hold on to them, but in naming our resentments and offering them to God, we receive freedom and grace. When we "pray" our feelings to God, those feelings lose their power over us. Take some time to write about any bitterness you may be secretly nursing. Fold up the paper you wrote on and hold it in your open palms in a prayer of relinquishment.

See Meeting God in Prayer

Psalm 35

Of David.

¹ Contend, O Lᴏʀᴅ, with those who contend with
me;
fight against those who fight against me.
² Take up shield and buckler;
arise and come to my aid.
³ Brandish spear and javelin*ᵃ*
against those who pursue me.
Say to my soul,
"I am your salvation."

⁴ May those who seek my life
be disgraced and put to shame;
may those who plot my ruin
be turned back in dismay.
⁵ May they be like chaff before the wind,
with the angel of the Lᴏʀᴅ driving them away;
⁶ may their path be dark and slippery,
with the angel of the Lᴏʀᴅ pursuing them.
⁷ Since they hid their net for me without cause
and without cause dug a pit for me,
⁸ may ruin overtake them by surprise—
may the net they hid entangle them,
may they fall into the pit, to their ruin.
⁹ Then my soul will rejoice in the Lᴏʀᴅ
and delight in his salvation.
¹⁰ My whole being will exclaim,
"Who is like you, O Lᴏʀᴅ?
You rescue the poor from those too strong for
them,
the poor and needy from those who rob them."

¹¹ Ruthless witnesses come forward;
they question me on things I know nothing
about.
¹² They repay me evil for good
and leave my soul forlorn.
¹³ Yet when they were ill, I put on sackcloth
and humbled myself with fasting.
When my prayers returned to me unanswered,
¹⁴   I went about mourning
as though for my friend or brother.
I bowed my head in grief
as though weeping for my mother.
¹⁵ But when I stumbled, they gathered in glee;
attackers gathered against me when I was
unaware.
They slandered me without ceasing.
¹⁶ Like the ungodly they maliciously mocked*ᵇ*;
they gnashed their teeth at me.
¹⁷ O Lord, how long will you look on?
Rescue my life from their ravages,
my precious life from these lions.
¹⁸ I will give you thanks in the great assembly;
among throngs of people I will praise you.

ᵃ 3 Or and block the way   ᵇ 16 Septuagint; Hebrew may mean ungodly circle of mockers.

¹⁹ Let not those gloat over me
  who are my enemies without cause;
 let not those who hate me without reason
  maliciously wink the eye.
²⁰ They do not speak peaceably,
  but devise false accusations
 against those who live quietly in the land.
²¹ They gape at me and say, "Aha! Aha!
  With our own eyes we have seen it."

²² O LORD, you have seen this; be not silent.
  Do not be far from me, O Lord.
²³ Awake, and rise to my defense!
  Contend for me, my God and Lord.
²⁴ Vindicate me in your righteousness, O LORD my
  God;
 do not let them gloat over me.
²⁵ Do not let them think, "Aha, just what we
  wanted!"
 or say, "We have swallowed him up."

²⁶ May all who gloat over my distress
  be put to shame and confusion;
 may all who exalt themselves over me
  be clothed with shame and disgrace.
²⁷ May those who delight in my vindication
  shout for joy and gladness;
 may they always say, "The LORD be exalted,
  who delights in the well-being of his servant."
²⁸ My tongue will speak of your righteousness
  and of your praises all day long.

Psalm 36

*For the director of music. Of David
the servant of the LORD.*

¹ An oracle is within my heart
  concerning the sinfulness of the wicked:*ᵃ*
 There is no fear of God
  before his eyes.
² For in his own eyes he flatters himself
  too much to detect or hate his sin.
³ The words of his mouth are wicked and deceitful;
  he has ceased to be wise and to do good.
⁴ Even on his bed he plots evil;
  he commits himself to a sinful course
  and does not reject what is wrong.

⁵ Your love, O LORD, reaches to the heavens,
  your faithfulness to the skies.
⁶ Your righteousness is like the mighty mountains,
  your justice like the great deep.
 O LORD, you preserve both man and beast.
⁷ How priceless is your unfailing love!
 Both high and low among men
  find*ᵇ* refuge in the shadow of your wings.
⁸ They feast on the abundance of your house;
  you give them drink from your river of delights.

ᵃ 1 Or heart: / Sin proceeds from the wicked. *ᵇ 7 Or love, O God! / Men find;
or love! / Both heavenly beings and men / find*

Feasting on God's Abundance

PSALM 36:7–9

Here the psalmist celebrates the abundance of God's house—its "river of delights." Once we have tasted of God's presence in prayer, we desire more and more. John Ruusbroec writes, "At each new touch our spirit falls into a state of hunger and thirst and wishes in this storm of love thoroughly to savor [it]." The prayer of silence—like centering prayer—is one way to "savor" God's abundance. For the next five minutes, sit in silent openness before God with your eyes closed or focused on a simple object.

See Meeting God in Prayer

Delight and Desire

PSALM 37:4

Delight is a word that is often used for children. Children delight in doing somersaults or watching a cat chase a bug. They possess the innocent joy of discovery and the willingness to give their whole being to that joy. When we delight in God, our deepest desires for love, significance and justice are met in God. What are the desires of your heart? How do you pray about them? Where is God in your deepest longing? Do you sense God's delight in the dreams of your heart? Reflect in a time of quiet prayer or in your journal.

See *Meeting God in Prayer*

9 For with you is the fountain of life;
   in your light we see light.

10 Continue your love to those who know you,
   your righteousness to the upright in heart.
11 May the foot of the proud not come against me,
   nor the hand of the wicked drive me away.
12 See how the evildoers lie fallen—
   thrown down, not able to rise!

Psalm 37[a]

Of David.

1 Do not fret because of evil men
   or be envious of those who do wrong;
2 for like the grass they will soon wither,
   like green plants they will soon die away.

3 Trust in the LORD and do good;
   dwell in the land and enjoy safe pasture.
4 Delight yourself in the LORD
   and he will give you the desires of your heart.

5 Commit your way to the LORD;
   trust in him and he will do this:
6 He will make your righteousness shine like the
      dawn,
   the justice of your cause like the noonday sun.

7 Be still before the LORD and wait patiently for him;
   do not fret when men succeed in their ways,
   when they carry out their wicked schemes.

8 Refrain from anger and turn from wrath;
   do not fret—it leads only to evil.
9 For evil men will be cut off,
   but those who hope in the LORD will inherit the
      land.

10 A little while, and the wicked will be no more;
   though you look for them, they will not be
      found.
11 But the meek will inherit the land
   and enjoy great peace.

12 The wicked plot against the righteous
   and gnash their teeth at them;
13 but the Lord laughs at the wicked,
   for he knows their day is coming.

14 The wicked draw the sword
   and bend the bow
to bring down the poor and needy,
   to slay those whose ways are upright.
15 But their swords will pierce their own hearts,
   and their bows will be broken.

16 Better the little that the righteous have
   than the wealth of many wicked;
17 for the power of the wicked will be broken,
   but the LORD upholds the righteous.

a This psalm is an acrostic poem, the stanzas of which begin with the successive letters of the Hebrew alphabet.

¹⁸ The days of the blameless are known to the LORD,
    and their inheritance will endure forever.
¹⁹ In times of disaster they will not wither;
    in days of famine they will enjoy plenty.

²⁰ But the wicked will perish:
    The LORD's enemies will be like the beauty of
        the fields,
    they will vanish—vanish like smoke.

²¹ The wicked borrow and do not repay,
    but the righteous give generously;
²² those the LORD blesses will inherit the land,
    but those he curses will be cut off.

²³ If the LORD delights in a man's way,
    he makes his steps firm;
²⁴ though he stumble, he will not fall,
    for the LORD upholds him with his hand.

²⁵ I was young and now I am old,
    yet I have never seen the righteous forsaken
    or their children begging bread.
²⁶ They are always generous and lend freely;
    their children will be blessed.

²⁷ Turn from evil and do good;
    then you will dwell in the land forever.
²⁸ For the LORD loves the just
    and will not forsake his faithful ones.

They will be protected forever,
    but the offspring of the wicked will be cut off;
²⁹ the righteous will inherit the land
    and dwell in it forever.

³⁰ The mouth of the righteous man utters wisdom,
    and his tongue speaks what is just.
³¹ The law of his God is in his heart;
    his feet do not slip.

³² The wicked lie in wait for the righteous,
    seeking their very lives;
³³ but the LORD will not leave them in their power
    or let them be condemned when brought to
        trial.

³⁴ Wait for the LORD
    and keep his way.
He will exalt you to inherit the land;
    when the wicked are cut off, you will see it.

³⁵ I have seen a wicked and ruthless man
    flourishing like a green tree in its native soil,
³⁶ but he soon passed away and was no more;
    though I looked for him, he could not be found.

³⁷ Consider the blameless, observe the upright;
    there is a future ᵃ for the man of peace.
³⁸ But all sinners will be destroyed;
    the future ᵇ of the wicked will be cut off.

God Enjoys Us

PSALM 37:23–24

God delights in those who walk in kindness and justice. In our faithful actions, large and small, we add to God's joy. According to Julian of Norwich, God enjoys us as a parent does a small child. Even our stumbling—our sin—does not lessen God's tender, enduring love for us. "And when we fall, quickly he raises us by the clasping of his love and touching of his grace." Consider God's delight in you, and in the personality and gifts that are unique to you. Imagine God doting on you as a loving parent, treating you as one would treat a toddler who falls and scrapes a knee.

ᵃ 37 Or *there will be posterity*   ᵇ 38 Or *posterity*

God's Presence in Loneliness

PSALM 38:9–11

The psalmist is honest about the pain of his loneliness. Friends seem to have forgotten him, or they don't know how to respond to his terrible sickness. He fights feelings of deep depression—"even the light has gone from my eyes." Yet he is also aware of the presence of the Lord who sees his hurt and hears his sighs. God is near to the lonely, healing the brokenhearted (Psalm 34:18). How do you experience God in times of loneliness or depression? What might God be saying to you in your pain? How do you talk to God in such desperate moments? Explore these questions with a close friend.

See Meeting God in Community

39 The salvation of the righteous comes from the
    LORD;
    he is their stronghold in time of trouble.
40 The LORD helps them and delivers them;
    he delivers them from the wicked and saves
        them,
    because they take refuge in him.

Psalm 38

A psalm of David. A petition.

1 O LORD, do not rebuke me in your anger
    or discipline me in your wrath.
2 For your arrows have pierced me,
    and your hand has come down upon me.
3 Because of your wrath there is no health in my
        body;
    my bones have no soundness because of my
        sin.
4 My guilt has overwhelmed me
    like a burden too heavy to bear.

5 My wounds fester and are loathsome
    because of my sinful folly.
6 I am bowed down and brought very low;
    all day long I go about mourning.
7 My back is filled with searing pain;
    there is no health in my body.
8 I am feeble and utterly crushed;
    I groan in anguish of heart.

9 All my longings lie open before you, O Lord;
    my sighing is not hidden from you.
10 My heart pounds, my strength fails me;
    even the light has gone from my eyes.
11 My friends and companions avoid me because of
        my wounds;
    my neighbors stay far away.
12 Those who seek my life set their traps,
    those who would harm me talk of my ruin;
    all day long they plot deception.

13 I am like a deaf man, who cannot hear,
    like a mute, who cannot open his mouth;
14 I have become like a man who does not hear,
    whose mouth can offer no reply.
15 I wait for you, O LORD;
    you will answer, O Lord my God.
16 For I said, "Do not let them gloat
    or exalt themselves over me when my foot
        slips."

17 For I am about to fall,
    and my pain is ever with me.
18 I confess my iniquity;
    I am troubled by my sin.
19 Many are those who are my vigorous enemies;
    those who hate me without reason are
        numerous.
20 Those who repay my good with evil
    slander me when I pursue what is good.

21 O LORD, do not forsake me;
   be not far from me, O my God.
22 Come quickly to help me,
   O Lord my Savior.

Psalm 39

*For the director of music. For Jeduthun.
A psalm of David.*

1 I said, "I will watch my ways
   and keep my tongue from sin;
 I will put a muzzle on my mouth
   as long as the wicked are in my presence."
2 But when I was silent and still,
   not even saying anything good,
   my anguish increased.
3 My heart grew hot within me,
   and as I meditated, the fire burned;
   then I spoke with my tongue:

4 "Show me, O LORD, my life's end
   and the number of my days;
   let me know how fleeting is my life.
5 You have made my days a mere handbreadth;
   the span of my years is as nothing before you.
   Each man's life is but a breath. *Selah*
6 Man is a mere phantom as he goes to and fro:
   He bustles about, but only in vain;
   he heaps up wealth, not knowing who will
      get it.

7 "But now, Lord, what do I look for?
   My hope is in you.
8 Save me from all my transgressions;
   do not make me the scorn of fools.
9 I was silent; I would not open my mouth,
   for you are the one who has done this.
10 Remove your scourge from me;
   I am overcome by the blow of your hand.
11 You rebuke and discipline men for their sin;
   you consume their wealth like a moth—
   each man is but a breath. *Selah*

12 "Hear my prayer, O LORD,
   listen to my cry for help;
   be not deaf to my weeping.
 For I dwell with you as an alien,
   a stranger, as all my fathers were.
13 Look away from me, that I may rejoice again
   before I depart and am no more."

Psalm 40

For the director of music. Of David. A psalm.

1 I waited patiently for the LORD;
   he turned to me and heard my cry.
2 He lifted me out of the slimy pit,
   out of the mud and mire;
 he set my feet on a rock
   and gave me a firm place to stand.

Why, God?

PSALM 39:7–10

"I am worn out," the psalmist cries. "Forgive me and stop punishing me." Sometimes, like the psalmist, we feel that our suffering is the result of God's chastisement. In our humanity we associate pain with punishment. Although God is not a punishing parent, we may be burdened by that mistaken image. We may secretly believe we deserve illnesses, natural catastrophes or emotional distress.

What passages can you discover that will remind you of the truth of God's tenderness in times of pain—the parable of the forgiving father and the prodigal son (see Luke 15:11–32), the simple verse that declares that "God is love" (1 John 4:8), examples of Jesus' healing compassion, or some other Biblical image? Meditate on the passage or image that speaks most vividly to you of God's tenderness.

See Meeting God in Scripture

Sharing the Good News

PSALM 40:9–10

The tradition of giving one's testimony strengthens the community of believers. Sometimes quiet people leave this responsibility to extroverts, but each of us has a unique story to tell. Reflect on your experience of community. How might you tell your story? Do you participate in a small group where sharing is encouraged? Do you meet with a soul friend? How are you witnessing to the presence of God in your life?

See *Meeting God in Community*

³ He put a new song in my mouth,
　a hymn of praise to our God.
Many will see and fear
　and put their trust in the LORD.

⁴ Blessed is the man
　who makes the LORD his trust,
who does not look to the proud,
　to those who turn aside to false gods.ᵃ
⁵ Many, O LORD my God,
　are the wonders you have done.
The things you planned for us
　no one can recount to you;
were I to speak and tell of them,
　they would be too many to declare.

⁶ Sacrifice and offering you did not desire,
　but my ears you have pierced ᵇ,ᶜ;
burnt offerings and sin offerings
　you did not require.
⁷ Then I said, "Here I am, I have come—
　it is written about me in the scroll.ᵈ
⁸ I desire to do your will, O my God;
　your law is within my heart."

⁹ I proclaim righteousness in the great assembly;
　I do not seal my lips,
　as you know, O LORD.
¹⁰ I do not hide your righteousness in my heart;
　I speak of your faithfulness and salvation.
I do not conceal your love and your truth
　from the great assembly.

¹¹ Do not withhold your mercy from me, O LORD;
　may your love and your truth always protect
　　me.
¹² For troubles without number surround me;
　my sins have overtaken me, and I cannot see.
They are more than the hairs of my head,
　and my heart fails within me.

¹³ Be pleased, O LORD, to save me;
　O LORD, come quickly to help me.
¹⁴ May all who seek to take my life
　be put to shame and confusion;
may all who desire my ruin
　be turned back in disgrace.
¹⁵ May those who say to me, "Aha! Aha!"
　be appalled at their own shame.
¹⁶ But may all who seek you
　rejoice and be glad in you;
may those who love your salvation always say,
　"The LORD be exalted!"

¹⁷ Yet I am poor and needy;
　may the Lord think of me.
You are my help and my deliverer;
　O my God, do not delay.

ᵃ 4 Or *to falsehood*　ᵇ 6 Hebrew; Septuagint *but a body you have prepared for me* (see also Symmachus and Theodotion)　ᶜ 6 Or *opened*　ᵈ 7 Or *come / with the scroll written for me*

Psalm 41

For the director of music. A psalm of David.

¹ Blessed is he who has regard for the weak;
   the Lord delivers him in times of trouble.
² The Lord will protect him and preserve his life;
   he will bless him in the land
   and not surrender him to the desire of his foes.
³ The Lord will sustain him on his sickbed
   and restore him from his bed of illness.

⁴ I said, "O Lord, have mercy on me;
   heal me, for I have sinned against you."
⁵ My enemies say of me in malice,
   "When will he die and his name perish?"
⁶ Whenever one comes to see me,
   he speaks falsely, while his heart gathers
      slander;
   then he goes out and spreads it abroad.

⁷ All my enemies whisper together against me;
   they imagine the worst for me, saying,
⁸ "A vile disease has beset him;
   he will never get up from the place where he
      lies."
⁹ Even my close friend, whom I trusted,
   he who shared my bread,
   has lifted up his heel against me.

¹⁰ But you, O Lord, have mercy on me;
   raise me up, that I may repay them.
¹¹ I know that you are pleased with me,
   for my enemy does not triumph over me.
¹² In my integrity you uphold me
   and set me in your presence forever.

¹³ Praise be to the Lord, the God of Israel,
   from everlasting to everlasting.
      Amen and Amen.

BOOK II

Psalms 42–72

Psalm 42 ᵃ

For the director of music. A *maskil* ᵇ of the Sons of Korah.

¹ As the deer pants for streams of water,
   so my soul pants for you, O God.
² My soul thirsts for God, for the living God.
   When can I go and meet with God?
³ My tears have been my food
   day and night,
   while men say to me all day long,
   "Where is your God?"
⁴ These things I remember
   as I pour out my soul:
   how I used to go with the multitude,

Thirsting for God

PSALM 42:1–2

Thirst is such a powerful longing that it displaces all others. Though the psalmist longs for God's help in the midst of physical thirst and danger, this metaphor also offers a profound spiritual image: Our relationship with God is as essential to our spiritual well-being as water is to our physical well-being.

What are you thirsty for? Is your schedule so crowded that it leaves you thirsty for time alone with God? Are you feeling dryness in your devotional habits? Are you needing a time away in retreat? Consider these questions for a few minutes and then list in your journal whatever comes to you—even half-finished sentences, images, ideas. Let your heart speak.

See Meeting God in Everyday Life

ᵃ In many Hebrew manuscripts Psalms 42 and 43 constitute one psalm.
ᵇ Title: Probably a literary or musical term

The Depth of Loving-kindness

PSALM 42:7–8

The image of a quiet stream suggests tranquillity, while a crashing wave speaks of power. Images of water can convey strength, beauty, terror or peace. The psalmist recognizes water's spiritual symbolism: God's voice is heard as "deep calls to deep in the roar of your waterfalls." Imagine with the psalmist the strong waves of God's power, the blue depths of the ocean, the sheer beauty of a waterfall. Can you feel the spray against your face? Hear the rush of the water against the rocks? Smell the moist, cool air? What are some other ways water symbolizes God's desire to refresh your spirit daily?

See Meeting God in the Created Order

leading the procession to the house of God,
    with shouts of joy and thanksgiving
        among the festive throng.
⁵ Why are you downcast, O my soul?
        Why so disturbed within me?
Put your hope in God,
    for I will yet praise him,
        my Savior and ⁶ my God.

My*ᵃ* soul is downcast within me;
    therefore I will remember you
from the land of the Jordan,
    the heights of Hermon—from Mount Mizar.
⁷ Deep calls to deep
    in the roar of your waterfalls;
all your waves and breakers
    have swept over me.

⁸ By day the LORD directs his love,
    at night his song is with me—
    a prayer to the God of my life.

⁹ I say to God my Rock,
    "Why have you forgotten me?
Why must I go about mourning,
    oppressed by the enemy?"
¹⁰ My bones suffer mortal agony
    as my foes taunt me,
saying to me all day long,
    "Where is your God?"

¹¹ Why are you downcast, O my soul?
        Why so disturbed within me?
Put your hope in God,
    for I will yet praise him,
        my Savior and my God.

Psalm 43*ᵇ*

¹ Vindicate me, O God,
    and plead my cause against an ungodly nation;
    rescue me from deceitful and wicked men.
² You are God my stronghold.
    Why have you rejected me?
Why must I go about mourning,
    oppressed by the enemy?
³ Send forth your light and your truth,
    let them guide me;
let them bring me to your holy mountain,
    to the place where you dwell.
⁴ Then will I go to the altar of God,
    to God, my joy and my delight.
I will praise you with the harp,
    O God, my God.

⁵ Why are you downcast, O my soul?
        Why so disturbed within me?
Put your hope in God,

ᵃ 5,6 A few Hebrew manuscripts, Septuagint and Syriac; most Hebrew manuscripts *praise him for his saving help.* / *⁶ O my God, my*   *ᵇ* In many Hebrew manuscripts Psalms 42 and 43 constitute one psalm.

for I will yet praise him,
    my Savior and my God.

Psalm 44

For the director of music. Of the Sons of Korah. A *maskil.*[a]

¹ We have heard with our ears, O God;
    our fathers have told us
what you did in their days,
    in days long ago.
² With your hand you drove out the nations
    and planted our fathers;
you crushed the peoples
    and made our fathers flourish.
³ It was not by their sword that they won the land,
    nor did their arm bring them victory;
it was your right hand, your arm,
    and the light of your face, for you loved them.

⁴ You are my King and my God,
    who decrees[b] victories for Jacob.
⁵ Through you we push back our enemies;
    through your name we trample our foes.
⁶ I do not trust in my bow,
    my sword does not bring me victory;
⁷ but you give us victory over our enemies,
    you put our adversaries to shame.
⁸ In God we make our boast all day long,
    and we will praise your name forever.   *Selah*

⁹ But now you have rejected and humbled us;
    you no longer go out with our armies.
¹⁰ You made us retreat before the enemy,
    and our adversaries have plundered us.
¹¹ You gave us up to be devoured like sheep
    and have scattered us among the nations.
¹² You sold your people for a pittance,
    gaining nothing from their sale.

¹³ You have made us a reproach to our neighbors,
    the scorn and derision of those around us.
¹⁴ You have made us a byword among the nations;
    the peoples shake their heads at us.
¹⁵ My disgrace is before me all day long,
    and my face is covered with shame
¹⁶ at the taunts of those who reproach and revile
    me,
because of the enemy, who is bent on revenge.

¹⁷ All this happened to us,
    though we had not forgotten you
or been false to your covenant.
¹⁸ Our hearts had not turned back;
    our feet had not strayed from your path.
¹⁹ But you crushed us and made us a haunt for
    jackals
and covered us over with deep darkness.

²⁰ If we had forgotten the name of our God

Remembering Our Story

PSALM 44:1–3

The psalmist begins by recounting the story of Israel's birth: how the people came to the promised land. Thomas Merton observes that when we read the Psalms, "we too are leaving Egypt." For each of us also has a story to tell of spiritual roots and times of transformation and growth, as well as times of drifting. By retracing our spiritual journeys, we see God's hand in our lives. Record some highlights of your spiritual story or make descriptive notes on a time line of your life. Share your story or time line with a mentor, spiritual friend or trusted small group.

See *Meeting God in Community*

---

[a] Title: Probably a literary or musical term   [b] 4 Septuagint, Aquila and Syriac; Hebrew *King, O God; / command*

Your Own Psalm

PSALM 45:1

Spiritual writers throughout the centuries have expressed their overflowing love for God in verse and song. Augustine writes, "Thou didst send forth Thy beams and shine upon me and chase away my blindness . . . Thou didst touch me, and I have burned for Thy peace." What do you do with your heart's "overflow"? What form might your own psalm take? Do you sing, play an instrument, paint, mold clay, write poetry? Take ten or fifteen minutes to experiment. Perhaps you might compose a song, draw a picture or create a collage.

See Meeting God in Worship

or spread out our hands to a foreign god,
²¹ would not God have discovered it,
since he knows the secrets of the heart?
²² Yet for your sake we face death all day long;
we are considered as sheep to be slaughtered.

²³ Awake, O Lord! Why do you sleep?
Rouse yourself! Do not reject us forever.
²⁴ Why do you hide your face
and forget our misery and oppression?

²⁵ We are brought down to the dust;
our bodies cling to the ground.
²⁶ Rise up and help us;
redeem us because of your unfailing love.

Psalm 45

For the director of music. To ⌊the tune of⌋ "Lilies." Of the Sons of Korah. A *maskil.*ᵃ A wedding song.

¹ My heart is stirred by a noble theme
as I recite my verses for the king;
my tongue is the pen of a skillful writer.

² You are the most excellent of men
and your lips have been anointed with grace,
since God has blessed you forever.
³ Gird your sword upon your side, O mighty one;
clothe yourself with splendor and majesty.
⁴ In your majesty ride forth victoriously
in behalf of truth, humility and righteousness;
let your right hand display awesome deeds.
⁵ Let your sharp arrows pierce the hearts of the
king's enemies;
let the nations fall beneath your feet.
⁶ Your throne, O God, will last for ever and ever;
a scepter of justice will be the scepter of your
kingdom.
⁷ You love righteousness and hate wickedness;
therefore God, your God, has set you above
your companions
by anointing you with the oil of joy.
⁸ All your robes are fragrant with myrrh and aloes
and cassia;
from palaces adorned with ivory
the music of the strings makes you glad.
⁹ Daughters of kings are among your honored
women;
at your right hand is the royal bride in gold of
Ophir.

¹⁰ Listen, O daughter, consider and give ear:
Forget your people and your father's house.
¹¹ The king is enthralled by your beauty;
honor him, for he is your lord.
¹² The Daughter of Tyre will come with a gift,ᵇ
men of wealth will seek your favor.

¹³ All glorious is the princess within ⌊her chamber⌋;

ᵃ Title: Probably a literary or musical term   ᵇ 12 Or *A Tyrian robe is among the gifts*

her gown is interwoven with gold.
14 In embroidered garments she is led to the king;
    her virgin companions follow her
    and are brought to you.
15 They are led in with joy and gladness;
    they enter the palace of the king.

16 Your sons will take the place of your fathers;
    you will make them princes throughout the
    land.
17 I will perpetuate your memory through all
    generations;
    therefore the nations will praise you for ever
    and ever.

Psalm 46

For the director of music. Of the Sons of Korah.
According to *alamoth.*[a] A song.

1 God is our refuge and strength,
    an ever-present help in trouble.
2 Therefore we will not fear, though the earth give
    way
    and the mountains fall into the heart of the sea,
3 though its waters roar and foam
    and the mountains quake with their surging.
                                                Selah

4 There is a river whose streams make glad the city
    of God,
    the holy place where the Most High dwells.
5 God is within her, she will not fall;
    God will help her at break of day.
6 Nations are in uproar, kingdoms fall;
    he lifts his voice, the earth melts.

7 The LORD Almighty is with us;
    the God of Jacob is our fortress.   *Selah*

8 Come and see the works of the LORD,
    the desolations he has brought on the earth.
9 He makes wars cease to the ends of the earth;
    he breaks the bow and shatters the spear,
    he burns the shields[b] with fire.
10 "Be still, and know that I am God;
    I will be exalted among the nations,
    I will be exalted in the earth."

11 The LORD Almighty is with us;
    the God of Jacob is our fortress.   *Selah*

Psalm 47

For the director of music. Of the Sons of Korah. A psalm.

1 Clap your hands, all you nations;
    shout to God with cries of joy.
2 How awesome is the LORD Most High,
    the great King over all the earth!
3 He subdued nations under us,

Our Refuge

PSALM 46:1–3

More than a dozen times, the Psalms refer to God as a refuge—a refuge "for the oppressed" (Psalm 9:9), for "the poor" (Psalm 14:6) and "in times of trouble" (Psalm 59:16). Here in Psalm 46, God is a refuge from the ravages of earthquakes and floods. The spiritual life is also beset by "climate changes." In what specific areas of your life have you found God to be your refuge and strength? What devotional practices help you to find a spiritual center in times of stress? Draw a symbolic expression of God as your refuge.

See Meeting God in Scripture

a Title: Probably a musical term   b 9 Or *chariots*

Let Zion Be Glad

PSALM 48:1–4

The city of Zion, Jerusalem, is an actual city, but it is also a spiritual one. A longing for Zion is also a yearning for the fulfillment of the prophetic vision of a holy city of peace, justice and compassion. The kingdom of heaven that Jesus proclaims is very much like this vision. How are you living Jesus' prayer that God's kingdom come on earth as in heaven? Where might God be inviting you to give your time, energy and love in order to "let your light shine"? In what small way can you extend God's reign today?

See Meeting God in Service

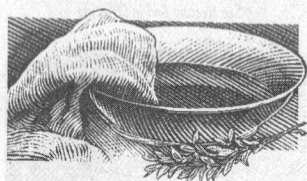

peoples under our feet.
⁴He chose our inheritance for us,
the pride of Jacob, whom he loved.   *Selah*

⁵God has ascended amid shouts of joy,
the LORD amid the sounding of trumpets.
⁶Sing praises to God, sing praises;
sing praises to our King, sing praises.

⁷For God is the King of all the earth;
sing to him a psalm[a] of praise.
⁸God reigns over the nations;
God is seated on his holy throne.
⁹The nobles of the nations assemble
as the people of the God of Abraham,
for the kings[b] of the earth belong to God;
he is greatly exalted.

Psalm 48

A song. A psalm of the Sons of Korah.

¹Great is the LORD, and most worthy of praise,
in the city of our God, his holy mountain.
²It is beautiful in its loftiness,
the joy of the whole earth.
Like the utmost heights of Zaphon[c] is Mount Zion,
the[d] city of the Great King.
³God is in her citadels;
he has shown himself to be her fortress.

⁴When the kings joined forces,
when they advanced together,
⁵they saw ⌊her⌋ and were astounded;
they fled in terror.
⁶Trembling seized them there,
pain like that of a woman in labor.
⁷You destroyed them like ships of Tarshish
shattered by an east wind.

⁸As we have heard,
so have we seen
in the city of the LORD Almighty,
in the city of our God:
God makes her secure forever.   *Selah*

⁹Within your temple, O God,
we meditate on your unfailing love.
¹⁰Like your name, O God,
your praise reaches to the ends of the earth;
your right hand is filled with righteousness.
¹¹Mount Zion rejoices,
the villages of Judah are glad
because of your judgments.

¹²Walk about Zion, go around her,
count her towers,
¹³consider well her ramparts,
view her citadels,

---

a 7 Or *a maskil* (probably a literary or musical term)   b 9 Or *shields*
c 2 *Zaphon* can refer to a sacred mountain or the direction north.   d 2 Or
earth, / Mount Zion, on the northern side / of the

that you may tell of them to the next
generation.
¹⁴ For this God is our God for ever and ever;
he will be our guide even to the end.

Psalm 49

For the director of music. Of the Sons of Korah.
A psalm.

¹ Hear this, all you peoples;
listen, all who live in this world,
² both low and high,
rich and poor alike:
³ My mouth will speak words of wisdom;
the utterance from my heart will give
understanding.
⁴ I will turn my ear to a proverb;
with the harp I will expound my riddle:

⁵ Why should I fear when evil days come,
when wicked deceivers surround me—
⁶ those who trust in their wealth
and boast of their great riches?
⁷ No man can redeem the life of another
or give to God a ransom for him—
⁸ the ransom for a life is costly,
no payment is ever enough—
⁹ that he should live on forever
and not see decay.

¹⁰ For all can see that wise men die;
the foolish and the senseless alike perish
and leave their wealth to others.
¹¹ Their tombs will remain their houses*a* forever,
their dwellings for endless generations,
though they had*b* named lands after themselves.

¹² But man, despite his riches, does not endure;
he is*c* like the beasts that perish.

¹³ This is the fate of those who trust in themselves,
and of their followers, who approve their
sayings.   *Selah*
¹⁴ Like sheep they are destined for the grave,*d*
and death will feed on them.
The upright will rule over them in the morning;
their forms will decay in the grave,*d*
far from their princely mansions.
¹⁵ But God will redeem my life*e* from the grave;
he will surely take me to himself.   *Selah*

¹⁶ Do not be overawed when a man grows rich,
when the splendor of his house increases;
¹⁷ for he will take nothing with him when he dies,
his splendor will not descend with him.
¹⁸ Though while he lived he counted himself
blessed—
and men praise you when you prosper—

A Different Perspective

PSALM 49:16–17

The psalmist speaks to an age-old issue: the power of money. As he explains, the influence of wealth is transitory, for in death we leave all possessions and all material security behind. Consider the place of money and possessions in your life. Where do you find your security? How does our culture's preoccupation with "things" affect your sense of self-worth? How might possessions be distracting you? Richard Foster, in *Freedom of Simplicity*, urges us to enjoy rather than possess. One doesn't have to own parks, beaches, country roads or blue skies in order to enjoy them. What are you enjoying in your life?

See Meeting God in Everyday Life

---

a 11 Septuagint and Syriac; Hebrew *In their thoughts their houses will remain*
b 11 Or *I for they have*   *c 12* Hebrew; Septuagint and Syriac read verse 12
the same as verse 20.   *d 14* Hebrew *Sheol*; also in verse 15   *e 15* Or *soul*

A Thanksgiving Offering

PSALM 50:14

God desires our praise. It is a simple request, but often we find it hard to comply because we come before God with our anxieties and forget to offer our gratitude. Yet praise is a natural response to God when we stop to notice the Lord's great gifts. When we see the canopy of stars on a winter night, we feel awe. When the sun peeks out after days of rain, a sense of thankfulness wells up in our hearts.

Offer God thanks for three things in the natural world that you have noticed in the last few days. As you remember each one, pause and let a mental picture take shape. Allow your joy to well up—and whisper a "thank you" to God.

See Meeting God in the Created Order

19 he will join the generation of his fathers,
    who will never see the light ⌊of life⌋.

20 A man who has riches without understanding
    is like the beasts that perish.

Psalm 50

A psalm of Asaph.

1 The Mighty One, God, the LORD,
    speaks and summons the earth
    from the rising of the sun to the place where it
        sets.
2 From Zion, perfect in beauty,
    God shines forth.
3 Our God comes and will not be silent;
    a fire devours before him,
    and around him a tempest rages.
4 He summons the heavens above,
    and the earth, that he may judge his people:
5 "Gather to me my consecrated ones,
    who made a covenant with me by sacrifice."
6 And the heavens proclaim his righteousness,
    for God himself is judge.   *Selah*

7 "Hear, O my people, and I will speak,
    O Israel, and I will testify against you:
    I am God, your God.
8 I do not rebuke you for your sacrifices
    or your burnt offerings, which are ever before me.
9 I have no need of a bull from your stall
    or of goats from your pens,
10 for every animal of the forest is mine,
    and the cattle on a thousand hills.
11 I know every bird in the mountains,
    and the creatures of the field are mine.
12 If I were hungry I would not tell you,
    for the world is mine, and all that is in it.
13 Do I eat the flesh of bulls
    or drink the blood of goats?
14 Sacrifice thank offerings to God,
    fulfill your vows to the Most High,
15 and call upon me in the day of trouble;
    I will deliver you, and you will honor me."

16 But to the wicked, God says:

"What right have you to recite my laws
    or take my covenant on your lips?
17 You hate my instruction
    and cast my words behind you.
18 When you see a thief, you join with him;
    you throw in your lot with adulterers.
19 You use your mouth for evil
    and harness your tongue to deceit.
20 You speak continually against your brother
    and slander your own mother's son.
21 These things you have done and I kept silent;
    you thought I was altogether[a] like you.

a 21 Or thought the 'I AM' was

But I will rebuke you
and accuse you to your face.

22 "Consider this, you who forget God,
or I will tear you to pieces, with none to
rescue:

23 He who sacrifices thank offerings honors me,
and he prepares the way
so that I may show him*a* the salvation of God."

Psalm 51

For the director of music. A psalm of David. When the
prophet Nathan came to him after David had committed
adultery with Bathsheba.

1 Have mercy on me, O God,
according to your unfailing love;
according to your great compassion
blot out my transgressions.

2 Wash away all my iniquity
and cleanse me from my sin.

3 For I know my transgressions,
and my sin is always before me.

4 Against you, you only, have I sinned
and done what is evil in your sight,
so that you are proved right when you speak
and justified when you judge.

5 Surely I was sinful at birth,
sinful from the time my mother conceived me.

6 Surely you desire truth in the inner parts*b*;
you teach*c* me wisdom in the inmost place.

7 Cleanse me with hyssop, and I will be clean;
wash me, and I will be whiter than snow.

8 Let me hear joy and gladness;
let the bones you have crushed rejoice.

9 Hide your face from my sins
and blot out all my iniquity.

10 Create in me a pure heart, O God,
and renew a steadfast spirit within me.

11 Do not cast me from your presence
or take your Holy Spirit from me.

12 Restore to me the joy of your salvation
and grant me a willing spirit, to sustain me.

13 Then I will teach transgressors your ways,
and sinners will turn back to you.

14 Save me from bloodguilt, O God,
the God who saves me,
and my tongue will sing of your righteousness.

15 O Lord, open my lips,
and my mouth will declare your praise.

16 You do not delight in sacrifice, or I would
bring it;
you do not take pleasure in burnt offerings.

17 The sacrifices of God are*d* a broken spirit;

A Pure Heart

PSALM 51:10

The psalmist's desire is also ours:
to be clean, whole, free from pretense. Yet opening our hearts before God can be scary. We are
careful to protect our self-images—even before God, who
knows each of us intimately.

Some spiritual writers suggest the discipline of a "daily
examen" so as to experience
God's cleansing grace. At the
end of the day, take several
minutes to review the day, recalling times you protected your
ego and times you were open. If
you remember becoming defensive, you might pray, "Lord,
have mercy." If you notice very
little self-concern, offer a word
of thanksgiving. To aid your
recollection, you might record
these insights in your journal.

See *Meeting God in Everyday Life*

---

a 23 Or *and to him who considers his way / I will show*   *b 6* The meaning of
the Hebrew for this phrase is uncertain.   *c 6* Or *you desired . . . ; / you taught*
d 17 Or *My sacrifice, O God, is*

A Flourishing Olive Tree

PSALM 52:8

Trees are visible symbols of the spiritual life. From Psalm 1 we learned that one who delights in God's way is like a "tree planted by streams of water, which yields its fruit in season" (Psalm 1:3). Rooted in the house of God, this "flourishing" olive tree also symbolizes the soul who trusts God's steadfast love. How is your spiritual life like a tree? Where are your roots finding nourishment? What source of light gives growth to your leaves? Are you withering in places? How are you tending the tree of your spirit?

See *Meeting God in Scripture*

a broken and contrite heart,
O God, you will not despise.

¹⁸ In your good pleasure make Zion prosper;
build up the walls of Jerusalem.
¹⁹ Then there will be righteous sacrifices,
whole burnt offerings to delight you;
then bulls will be offered on your altar.

Psalm 52

For the director of music. A *maskil*ᵃ of David. When Doeg the Edomite had gone to Saul and told him: "David has gone to the house of Ahimelech."

¹ Why do you boast of evil, you mighty man?
Why do you boast all day long,
you who are a disgrace in the eyes of God?
² Your tongue plots destruction;
it is like a sharpened razor,
you who practice deceit.
³ You love evil rather than good,
falsehood rather than speaking the truth. *Selah*
⁴ You love every harmful word,
O you deceitful tongue!

⁵ Surely God will bring you down to everlasting ruin:
He will snatch you up and tear you from your tent;
he will uproot you from the land of the living.
Selah
⁶ The righteous will see and fear;
they will laugh at him, saying,
⁷ "Here now is the man
who did not make God his stronghold
but trusted in his great wealth
and grew strong by destroying others!"

⁸ But I am like an olive tree
flourishing in the house of God;
I trust in God's unfailing love
for ever and ever.
⁹ I will praise you forever for what you have done;
in your name I will hope, for your name is good.
I will praise you in the presence of your saints.

Psalm 53

For the director of music. According to *mahalath*.ᵇ
A *maskil*ᵃ of David.

¹ The fool says in his heart,
"There is no God."
They are corrupt, and their ways are vile;
there is no one who does good.

² God looks down from heaven
on the sons of men
to see if there are any who understand,

ᵃ Title: Probably a literary or musical term   ᵇ Title: Probably a musical term

any who seek God.
³ Everyone has turned away,
   they have together become corrupt;
there is no one who does good,
   not even one.

⁴ Will the evildoers never learn—
   those who devour my people as men eat bread
   and who do not call on God?
⁵ There they were, overwhelmed with dread,
   where there was nothing to dread.
God scattered the bones of those who attacked
      you;
   you put them to shame, for God despised them.

⁶ Oh, that salvation for Israel would come out of
      Zion!
   When God restores the fortunes of his people,
   let Jacob rejoice and Israel be glad!

Psalm 54

For the director of music. With stringed instruments. A
*maskil*ᵃ of David. When the Ziphites had gone to Saul and
      said, "Is not David hiding among us?"

¹ Save me, O God, by your name;
   vindicate me by your might.
² Hear my prayer, O God;
   listen to the words of my mouth.

³ Strangers are attacking me;
   ruthless men seek my life—
   men without regard for God.   *Selah*

⁴ Surely God is my help;
   the Lord is the one who sustains me.

⁵ Let evil recoil on those who slander me;
   in your faithfulness destroy them.

⁶ I will sacrifice a freewill offering to you;
   I will praise your name, O LORD,
   for it is good.
⁷ For he has delivered me from all my troubles,
   and my eyes have looked in triumph on my
      foes.

Psalm 55

For the director of music. With stringed instruments.
      A *maskil*ᵃ of David.

¹ Listen to my prayer, O God,
   do not ignore my plea;
²   hear me and answer me.
My thoughts trouble me and I am distraught
³   at the voice of the enemy,
   at the stares of the wicked;
for they bring down suffering upon me
   and revile me in their anger.

⁴ My heart is in anguish within me;

A God Who Hears

PSALM 54:2

The psalmist holds nothing back from the Maker of the universe—he rejoices, complains, petitions, cries and agonizes. Even in the face of heaven's apparent silence, the psalmist waits and hopes. Over and over, stories of the Hebrew faithful demonstrate that prayer is a "two-way street." God hears, and God responds. God delivers, comforts, shields and loves steadfastly. Do you pray believing that God hears you—even your sighs, your complaints and your everyday concerns? Do you think of God as a "listener"? Reflect on this in your journal.

Letting Go of Cares

PSALM 55:22

"Cast your cares on the LORD," the psalmist urges. His charge is also a call to faith, because to let go we must trust that God will sustain us. Thus the prayer of petition is also a prayer of hope. Henri Nouwen, in *With Open Hands*, writes, "Our numerous requests simply become the concrete way of saying that we trust in the fullness of God's goodness, which he wants to share with us . . . Fear and anxiety fade away." What cares do you long to cast on the Lord? What is weighing you down? Imagine letting go of it. In what ways does your prayer of petition bring you hope?

See Meeting God in Prayer

the terrors of death assail me.
⁵ Fear and trembling have beset me;
    horror has overwhelmed me.
⁶ I said, "Oh, that I had the wings of a dove!
    I would fly away and be at rest—
⁷ I would flee far away
    and stay in the desert;   *Selah*
⁸ I would hurry to my place of shelter,
    far from the tempest and storm."

⁹ Confuse the wicked, O Lord, confound their
        speech,
    for I see violence and strife in the city.
¹⁰ Day and night they prowl about on its walls;
    malice and abuse are within it.
¹¹ Destructive forces are at work in the city;
    threats and lies never leave its streets.

¹² If an enemy were insulting me,
    I could endure it;
  if a foe were raising himself against me,
    I could hide from him.
¹³ But it is you, a man like myself,
    my companion, my close friend,
¹⁴ with whom I once enjoyed sweet fellowship
    as we walked with the throng at the house of
        God.

¹⁵ Let death take my enemies by surprise;
    let them go down alive to the grave,ᵃ
    for evil finds lodging among them.

¹⁶ But I call to God,
    and the LORD saves me.
¹⁷ Evening, morning and noon
    I cry out in distress,
    and he hears my voice.
¹⁸ He ransoms me unharmed
    from the battle waged against me,
    even though many oppose me.
¹⁹ God, who is enthroned forever,
    will hear them and afflict them—   *Selah*
  men who never change their ways
    and have no fear of God.

²⁰ My companion attacks his friends;
    he violates his covenant.
²¹ His speech is smooth as butter,
    yet war is in his heart;
  his words are more soothing than oil,
    yet they are drawn swords.

²² Cast your cares on the LORD
    and he will sustain you;
    he will never let the righteous fall.
²³ But you, O God, will bring down the wicked
    into the pit of corruption;
  bloodthirsty and deceitful men
    will not live out half their days.

  But as for me, I trust in you.

ᵃ 15 Hebrew *Sheol*

Psalm 56

For the director of music. ⌊the tune of⌋ "A Dove on Distant Oaks." Of David. A *miktam.*^a When the Philistines had seized him in Gath.

¹Be merciful to me, O God, for men hotly pursue me;
　all day long they press their attack.
²My slanderers pursue me all day long;
　many are attacking me in their pride.

³When I am afraid,
　I will trust in you.
⁴In God, whose word I praise,
　in God I trust; I will not be afraid.
　What can mortal man do to me?

⁵All day long they twist my words;
　they are always plotting to harm me.
⁶They conspire, they lurk,
　they watch my steps,
　eager to take my life.

⁷On no account let them escape;
　in your anger, O God, bring down the nations.
⁸Record my lament;
　list my tears on your scroll^b—
　are they not in your record?

⁹Then my enemies will turn back
　when I call for help.
　By this I will know that God is for me.
¹⁰In God, whose word I praise,
　in the LORD, whose word I praise—
¹¹in God I trust; I will not be afraid.
　What can man do to me?

¹²I am under vows to you, O God;
　I will present my thank offerings to you.
¹³For you have delivered me^c from death
　and my feet from stumbling,
　that I may walk before God
　in the light of life.^d

Psalm 57

For the director of music. ⌊To the tune of⌋ "Do Not Destroy." Of David. A *miktam.*^a When he had fled from Saul into the cave.

¹Have mercy on me, O God, have mercy on me,
　for in you my soul takes refuge.
　I will take refuge in the shadow of your wings
　until the disaster has passed.

²I cry out to God Most High,
　to God, who fulfills ⌊his purpose⌋ for me.
³He sends from heaven and saves me,
　rebuking those who hotly pursue me; *Selah*
　God sends his love and his faithfulness.

⁴I am in the midst of lions;

Learning to Trust

PSALM 56:3

"When I am afraid, I will trust in you" is easy to say but hard to live out. For when fear enters the heart, it often seems to take over—the mind races, the heart beats faster and a "fight or flight" reaction kicks in.

Former prisoners of war often say that verses learned from childhood helped them deal with fear. How can you prepare to combat fear before you experience it? Do you have favorite passages that you can "call up"? Try to memorize all or part of Psalm 121 or another short passage that expresses trust in God. Repeat it often as a reminder of God's care for you. Keep it as a source of spiritual comfort for difficult times.

See *Meeting God in Scripture*

---

^aTitle: Probably a literary or musical term　^b8 Or *I put my tears in your wineskin*　^c13 Or *my soul*　^d13 Or *the land of the living*

A Steadfast Heart

PSALM 57:7–10

The psalmist interrupts his litany of anxiety-ridden petitions with the exclamation, "Awake, my soul!" He reminds himself of God's steadfast love and unending faithfulness—and tells God that he, too, is trying to be faithful. Spiritual disciplines or practices are ways through which we meet God, who "awakens" our souls to faithfulness. Although methods don't make us holy, commitment to a daily devotional time, a prayer partner, small groups and worship can help us energize our spiritual lives.

In your journal, review your daily spiritual habits. What disciplines might you add or revise?

See Meeting God in Everyday Life

I lie among ravenous beasts—
men whose teeth are spears and arrows,
whose tongues are sharp swords.

⁵ Be exalted, O God, above the heavens;
let your glory be over all the earth.

⁶ They spread a net for my feet—
I was bowed down in distress.
They dug a pit in my path—
but they have fallen into it themselves. *Selah*

⁷ My heart is steadfast, O God,
my heart is steadfast;
I will sing and make music.
⁸ Awake, my soul!
Awake, harp and lyre!
I will awaken the dawn.

⁹ I will praise you, O Lord, among the nations;
I will sing of you among the peoples.
¹⁰ For great is your love, reaching to the heavens;
your faithfulness reaches to the skies.

¹¹ Be exalted, O God, above the heavens;
let your glory be over all the earth.

Psalm 58

For the director of music. ⌐To the tune of⌐ "Do Not Destroy."
Of David. A *miktam.*ᵃ

¹ Do you rulers indeed speak justly?
Do you judge uprightly among men?
² No, in your heart you devise injustice,
and your hands mete out violence on the earth.
³ Even from birth the wicked go astray;
from the womb they are wayward and speak
lies.
⁴ Their venom is like the venom of a snake,
like that of a cobra that has stopped its ears,
⁵ that will not heed the tune of the charmer,
however skillful the enchanter may be.

⁶ Break the teeth in their mouths, O God;
tear out, O Lord, the fangs of the lions!
⁷ Let them vanish like water that flows away;
when they draw the bow, let their arrows be
blunted.
⁸ Like a slug melting away as it moves along,
like a stillborn child, may they not see the sun.

⁹ Before your pots can feel ⌐the heat of⌐ the
thorns—
whether they be green or dry—the wicked will
be swept away.ᵇ
¹⁰ The righteous will be glad when they are
avenged,
when they bathe their feet in the blood of the
wicked.
¹¹ Then men will say,

ᵃ Title: Probably a literary or musical term   ᵇ 9 The meaning of the Hebrew
for this verse is uncertain.

"Surely the righteous still are rewarded;
  surely there is a God who judges the earth."

Psalm 59

For the director of music. ⌞To the tune of⌟ "Do Not Destroy."
Of David. A *miktam.* ª When Saul had sent men to watch
   David's house in order to kill him.

¹ Deliver me from my enemies, O God;
  protect me from those who rise up against me.
² Deliver me from evildoers
  and save me from bloodthirsty men.

³ See how they lie in wait for me!
  Fierce men conspire against me
  for no offense or sin of mine, O LORD.
⁴ I have done no wrong, yet they are ready to
   attack me.
  Arise to help me; look on my plight!
⁵ O LORD God Almighty, the God of Israel,
  rouse yourself to punish all the nations;
  show no mercy to wicked traitors.   *Selah*

⁶ They return at evening,
  snarling like dogs,
  and prowl about the city.
⁷ See what they spew from their mouths—
  they spew out swords from their lips,
  and they say, "Who can hear us?"
⁸ But you, O LORD, laugh at them;
  you scoff at all those nations.

⁹ O my Strength, I watch for you;
  you, O God, are my fortress, ¹⁰ my loving God.

God will go before me
  and will let me gloat over those who slander
   me.
¹¹ But do not kill them, O Lord our shield,ᵇ
  or my people will forget.
In your might make them wander about,
  and bring them down.
¹² For the sins of their mouths,
  for the words of their lips,
  let them be caught in their pride.
For the curses and lies they utter,
¹³   consume them in wrath,
  consume them till they are no more.
Then it will be known to the ends of the earth
  that God rules over Jacob.   *Selah*

¹⁴ They return at evening,
  snarling like dogs,
  and prowl about the city.
¹⁵ They wander about for food
  and howl if not satisfied.
¹⁶ But I will sing of your strength,
  in the morning I will sing of your love;
for you are my fortress,
  my refuge in times of trouble.

Consecration to God

PSALM 59:9

"O dear child! The best possible life is this: to do our utmost to content God with love, and above all to trust in him. For we come closest to him by confidence; for true prayer is nothing else than pure abandonment to him, with perfect fidelity to trust him in all that he is . . . Take care that God be honored by you and by all those whom you can help, with effort, with self-sacrifice, with counsel, and with all that you can do."

—HADEWIJCH OF ANTWERP,
The Complete Works

See *Meeting God in Service*

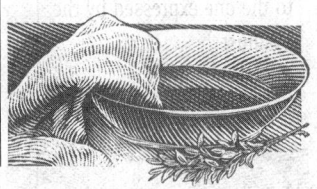

A Higher Rock

PSALM 61:1–3

There are times when, like the psalmist, we cry out to God from what seems like the "ends of the earth." We feel vulnerable and weary; we cannot see what is ahead; we don't know what to do. Reaching out to God with all of our being, we take an unseen hand and climb to a new perspective—"to the rock that is higher." Recall an experience in which you felt God's presence and help. How was God your "rock"? How did God's grace renew your soul? Record this experience in your journal, or rewrite these verses, adding your story of deliverance to the one expressed by the psalmist.

See Meeting God in Scripture

17 O my Strength, I sing praise to you;
   you, O God, are my fortress, my loving God.

Psalm 60

For the director of music. To ﹍the tune of﹚ "The Lily of the Covenant." A *miktam*[a] of David. For teaching. When he fought Aram Naharaim[b] and Aram Zobah,[c] and when Joab returned and struck down twelve thousand Edomites in the Valley of Salt.

1 You have rejected us, O God, and burst forth upon us;
   you have been angry—now restore us!
2 You have shaken the land and torn it open;
   mend its fractures, for it is quaking.
3 You have shown your people desperate times;
   you have given us wine that makes us stagger.

4 But for those who fear you, you have raised a banner
   to be unfurled against the bow.   *Selah*

5 Save us and help us with your right hand,
   that those you love may be delivered.
6 God has spoken from his sanctuary:
   "In triumph I will parcel out Shechem
   and measure off the Valley of Succoth.
7 Gilead is mine, and Manasseh is mine;
   Ephraim is my helmet,
   Judah my scepter.
8 Moab is my washbasin,
   upon Edom I toss my sandal;
   over Philistia I shout in triumph."

9 Who will bring me to the fortified city?
   Who will lead me to Edom?
10 Is it not you, O God, you who have rejected us
   and no longer go out with our armies?
11 Give us aid against the enemy,
   for the help of man is worthless.
12 With God we will gain the victory,
   and he will trample down our enemies.

Psalm 61

For the director of music. With stringed instruments. Of David.

1 Hear my cry, O God;
   listen to my prayer.

2 From the ends of the earth I call to you,
   I call as my heart grows faint;
   lead me to the rock that is higher than I.
3 For you have been my refuge,
   a strong tower against the foe.

4 I long to dwell in your tent forever
   and take refuge in the shelter of your wings.
                                              Selah

a Title: Probably a literary or musical term   b Title: That is, Arameans of Northwest Mesopotamia   c Title: That is, Arameans of central Syria

⁵For you have heard my vows, O God;
    you have given me the heritage of those who
        fear your name.

⁶Increase the days of the king's life,
    his years for many generations.
⁷May he be enthroned in God's presence forever;
    appoint your love and faithfulness to protect him.

⁸Then will I ever sing praise to your name
    and fulfill my vows day after day.

Psalm 62

For the director of music. For Jeduthun. A psalm of David.

¹My soul finds rest in God alone;
    my salvation comes from him.
²He alone is my rock and my salvation;
    he is my fortress, I will never be shaken.

³How long will you assault a man?
    Would all of you throw him down—
    this leaning wall, this tottering fence?
⁴They fully intend to topple him
    from his lofty place;
    they take delight in lies.
With their mouths they bless,
    but in their hearts they curse.   *Selah*

⁵Find rest, O my soul, in God alone;
    my hope comes from him.
⁶He alone is my rock and my salvation;
    he is my fortress, I will not be shaken.
⁷My salvation and my honor depend on God*a*;
    he is my mighty rock, my refuge.
⁸Trust in him at all times, O people;
    pour out your hearts to him,
    for God is our refuge.   *Selah*

⁹Lowborn men are but a breath,
    the highborn are but a lie;
if weighed on a balance, they are nothing;
    together they are only a breath.
¹⁰Do not trust in extortion
    or take pride in stolen goods;
though your riches increase,
    do not set your heart on them.

¹¹One thing God has spoken,
    two things have I heard:
that you, O God, are strong,
¹²   and that you, O Lord, are loving.
Surely you will reward each person
    according to what he has done.

Psalm 63

A psalm of David. When he was in the Desert of Judah.

¹O God, you are my God,
    earnestly I seek you;

A Silence Beyond Petitions

PSALM 62:5

Waiting in silence before God is hard for many of us. Although God's heart cherishes spoken prayers of petition, praise and longing, God also desires our simple, *attentive* silence. "It is in this solitude," says Henri Nouwen, "that we discover that being is more important than having, and that we are worth more than the result of our efforts." When we quiet ourselves, we become open to God's voice and leading. Try starting with a few minutes of silence. Close your eyes or focus them on an object, such as a candle or a familiar picture. Some people find that holding a coffee cup or a smooth stone is "centering." Consecrate this time of silence to God.

See Meeting God in Prayer

---

a 7 Or / *God Most High is my salvation and my honor*

The Longing for God

PSALM 63:1–8

The psalmist paints a vivid picture of his desire for God: "My body longs for you, in a dry and weary land where there is no water." Having seen God in the sanctuary, his life is saturated with love for God. Even during the night watches, he is compelled to meditate on God's comforting presence. Bernard of Clairvaux wrote that love for God is "an affection, not a contract . . . It has its reward in what it loves." How fervent is your desire for God? How do you see God in the sanctuary of your heart? God is the Beloved. In what ways do you experience this truth?

See Meeting God in Worship

my soul thirsts for you,
my body longs for you,
in a dry and weary land
where there is no water.
² I have seen you in the sanctuary
and beheld your power and your glory.
³ Because your love is better than life,
my lips will glorify you.
⁴ I will praise you as long as I live,
and in your name I will lift up my hands.
⁵ My soul will be satisfied as with the richest of
foods;
with singing lips my mouth will praise you.

⁶ On my bed I remember you;
I think of you through the watches of the night.
⁷ Because you are my help,
I sing in the shadow of your wings.
⁸ My soul clings to you;
your right hand upholds me.

⁹ They who seek my life will be destroyed;
they will go down to the depths of the earth.
¹⁰ They will be given over to the sword
and become food for jackals.

¹¹ But the king will rejoice in God;
all who swear by God's name will praise him,
while the mouths of liars will be silenced.

Psalm 64

For the director of music. A psalm of David.

¹ Hear me, O God, as I voice my complaint;
protect my life from the threat of the enemy.
² Hide me from the conspiracy of the wicked,
from that noisy crowd of evildoers.

³ They sharpen their tongues like swords
and aim their words like deadly arrows.
⁴ They shoot from ambush at the innocent man;
they shoot at him suddenly, without fear.

⁵ They encourage each other in evil plans,
they talk about hiding their snares;
they say, "Who will see them*ᵃ*?"
⁶ They plot injustice and say,
"We have devised a perfect plan!"
Surely the mind and heart of man are cunning.

⁷ But God will shoot them with arrows;
suddenly they will be struck down.
⁸ He will turn their own tongues against them
and bring them to ruin;
all who see them will shake their heads in
scorn.

⁹ All mankind will fear;
they will proclaim the works of God
and ponder what he has done.

ᵃ 5 Or us

¹⁰ Let the righteous rejoice in the LORD
    and take refuge in him;
    let all the upright in heart praise him!

Psalm 65

For the director of music. A psalm of David. A song.

¹ Praise awaits*ᵃ* you, O God, in Zion;
    to you our vows will be fulfilled.
² O you who hear prayer,
    to you all men will come.
³ When we were overwhelmed by sins,
    you forgave*ᵇ* our transgressions.
⁴ Blessed are those you choose
    and bring near to live in your courts!
We are filled with the good things of your house,
    of your holy temple.

⁵ You answer us with awesome deeds of
      righteousness,
    O God our Savior,
the hope of all the ends of the earth
    and of the farthest seas,
⁶ who formed the mountains by your power,
    having armed yourself with strength,
⁷ who stilled the roaring of the seas,
    the roaring of their waves,
    and the turmoil of the nations.
⁸ Those living far away fear your wonders;
    where morning dawns and evening fades
    you call forth songs of joy.

⁹ You care for the land and water it;
    you enrich it abundantly.
The streams of God are filled with water
    to provide the people with grain,
    for so you have ordained it.*ᶜ*
¹⁰ You drench its furrows
    and level its ridges;
you soften it with showers
    and bless its crops.
¹¹ You crown the year with your bounty,
    and your carts overflow with abundance.
¹² The grasslands of the desert overflow;
    the hills are clothed with gladness.
¹³ The meadows are covered with flocks
    and the valleys are mantled with grain;
    they shout for joy and sing.

Psalm 66

For the director of music. A song. A psalm.

¹ Shout with joy to God, all the earth!
²   Sing the glory of his name;
    make his praise glorious!
³ Say to God, "How awesome are your deeds!
    So great is your power

Hope

PSALM 65:5

Hope is a very important word in the Psalms. In the midst of this psalm about creation's beauty, we encounter the psalmist's conviction that God is "the hope of all the ends of the earth." Some days when the newspaper tells us another sad story of conflict across the ocean and the television shows us the desolate faces of hungry people, it is hard to feel that hope. An overload of bad news can numb our hearts. As a way of remaining faithful to God's undying love for the world, take a story or issue from the world news and make it a focus of intercessory prayer for the day (or perhaps for the week). Be a partner with God in hope as you pray.

See Meeting God in Prayer

ᵃ 1 Or *befits*; the meaning of the Hebrew for this word is uncertain.   *ᵇ 3* Or *made atonement for*   *ᶜ 9* Or *for that is how you prepare the land*

Worship

PSALM 67:1-4

The word *worship* means "to declare what is worthy." Here the psalmist praises God's justice and guidance. He sings about God's goodness and saving power. Through worship, we proclaim God's value to others. What do you declare is "worthy" by your worship? What are you saying about God—both to God and to others? In your conversations in the next twenty-four hours, consider how you might praise God in specific ways—through noticing something in nature, in a job situation, in a newborn baby.

See Meeting God in Worship

that your enemies cringe before you.
⁴All the earth bows down to you;
    they sing praise to you,
    they sing praise to your name."   *Selah*

⁵Come and see what God has done,
    how awesome his works in man's behalf!
⁶He turned the sea into dry land,
    they passed through the waters on foot—
    come, let us rejoice in him.
⁷He rules forever by his power,
    his eyes watch the nations—
    let not the rebellious rise up against him.   *Selah*

⁸Praise our God, O peoples,
    let the sound of his praise be heard;
⁹he has preserved our lives
    and kept our feet from slipping.
¹⁰For you, O God, tested us;
    you refined us like silver.
¹¹You brought us into prison
    and laid burdens on our backs.
¹²You let men ride over our heads;
    we went through fire and water,
    but you brought us to a place of abundance.

¹³I will come to your temple with burnt offerings
    and fulfill my vows to you—
¹⁴vows my lips promised and my mouth spoke
    when I was in trouble.
¹⁵I will sacrifice fat animals to you
    and an offering of rams;
    I will offer bulls and goats.   *Selah*

¹⁶Come and listen, all you who fear God;
    let me tell you what he has done for me.
¹⁷I cried out to him with my mouth;
    his praise was on my tongue.
¹⁸If I had cherished sin in my heart,
    the Lord would not have listened;
¹⁹but God has surely listened
    and heard my voice in prayer.
²⁰Praise be to God,
    who has not rejected my prayer
    or withheld his love from me!

Psalm 67

*For the director of music. With stringed instruments.
A psalm. A song.*

¹May God be gracious to us and bless us
    and make his face shine upon us,   *Selah*
²that your ways may be known on earth,
    your salvation among all nations.

³May the peoples praise you, O God;
    may all the peoples praise you.
⁴May the nations be glad and sing for joy,
    for you rule the peoples justly
    and guide the nations of the earth.   *Selah*

5 May the peoples praise you, O God;
   may all the peoples praise you.

6 Then the land will yield its harvest,
   and God, our God, will bless us.
7 God will bless us,
   and all the ends of the earth will fear him.

Psalm 68

For the director of music. Of David. A psalm. A song.

1 May God arise, may his enemies be scattered;
   may his foes flee before him.
2 As smoke is blown away by the wind,
   may you blow them away;
 as wax melts before the fire,
   may the wicked perish before God.
3 But may the righteous be glad
   and rejoice before God;
   may they be happy and joyful.

4 Sing to God, sing praise to his name,
   extol him who rides on the clouds*a*—
 his name is the LORD—
   and rejoice before him.
5 A father to the fatherless, a defender of widows,
   is God in his holy dwelling.
6 God sets the lonely in families,*b*
   he leads forth the prisoners with singing;
   but the rebellious live in a sun-scorched land.

7 When you went out before your people, O God,
   when you marched through the wasteland,
                                                    Selah
8 the earth shook,
   the heavens poured down rain,
 before God, the One of Sinai,
   before God, the God of Israel.
9 You gave abundant showers, O God;
   you refreshed your weary inheritance.
10 Your people settled in it,
   and from your bounty, O God, you provided for
      the poor.
11 The Lord announced the word,
   and great was the company of those who
      proclaimed it:
12 "Kings and armies flee in haste;
   in the camps men divide the plunder.
13 Even while you sleep among the campfires,*c*
   the wings of ⌐my⌐ dove are sheathed with silver,
   its feathers with shining gold."
14 When the Almighty*d* scattered the kings in the
      land,
   it was like snow fallen on Zalmon.

15 The mountains of Bashan are majestic
      mountains;
   rugged are the mountains of Bashan.

A Father's Care

PSALM 68:5–6

Although Jesus would later use "Father" as an affectionate name for God, this name for God is used only twice in the Psalms. It is significant, then, to see how it is used here. The psalmist says that God is a protective father of the orphan and a defender of the widow—the very people who were the most vulnerable in ancient times. Who are the most defenseless in your world, in your locality? In what practical ways is God leading you to help "defend" them? In Jesus' parable of the "great banquet," he extends the table to people who are poor, disabled and homeless (Luke 14:16–24). How are you extending God's table?

See Meeting God in Service

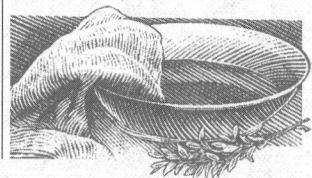

---

a 4 Or *I prepare the way for him who rides through the deserts*   *b 6* Or *the*
desolate in a homeland   *c 13* Or *saddlebags*   *d 14* Hebrew *Shaddai*

Worshiping in Body

PSALM 68:24–27

We express praise in many ways. Some of us praise God in song, others in dance, drawing, throwing pottery, playing a sport, writing, carpentry or photography. In what creative expressions, gifts or pleasures do you find yourself reaching out to God? How might you consecrate your hobbies as praise and worship? God delights in your joy, in your own particular "tambourine." Remember that God seeks the offering of your heart, not the offering of perfection.

See Meeting God in Worship

16 Why gaze in envy, O rugged mountains,
    at the mountain where God chooses to reign,
    where the LORD himself will dwell forever?
17 The chariots of God are tens of thousands
    and thousands of thousands;
    the Lord ₍has come₎ from Sinai into his
      sanctuary.
18 When you ascended on high,
    you led captives in your train;
    you received gifts from men,
  even from[a] the rebellious—
    that you,[b] O LORD God, might dwell there.

19 Praise be to the Lord, to God our Savior,
    who daily bears our burdens.   *Selah*
20 Our God is a God who saves;
    from the Sovereign LORD comes escape from
      death.

21 Surely God will crush the heads of his enemies,
    the hairy crowns of those who go on in their
      sins.
22 The Lord says, "I will bring them from Bashan;
    I will bring them from the depths of the sea,
23 that you may plunge your feet in the blood of
      your foes,
    while the tongues of your dogs have their
      share."

24 Your procession has come into view, O God,
    the procession of my God and King into the
      sanctuary.
25 In front are the singers, after them the musicians;
    with them are the maidens playing
      tambourines.
26 Praise God in the great congregation;
    praise the LORD in the assembly of Israel.
27 There is the little tribe of Benjamin, leading them,
    there the great throng of Judah's princes,
    and there the princes of Zebulun and of
      Naphtali.

28 Summon your power, O God[c];
    show us your strength, O God, as you have
      done before.
29 Because of your temple at Jerusalem
    kings will bring you gifts.
30 Rebuke the beast among the reeds,
    the herd of bulls among the calves of the
      nations.
  Humbled, may it bring bars of silver.
    Scatter the nations who delight in war.
31 Envoys will come from Egypt;
    Cush[d] will submit herself to God.

32 Sing to God, O kingdoms of the earth,
    sing praise to the Lord,   *Selah*
33 to him who rides the ancient skies above,

---

a 18 Or gifts for men, / even   b 18 Or they   c 28 Many Hebrew manuscripts, Septuagint and Syriac; most Hebrew manuscripts Your God has summoned power for you   d 31 That is, the upper Nile region

who thunders with mighty voice.
³⁴ Proclaim the power of God,
whose majesty is over Israel,
whose power is in the skies.
³⁵ You are awesome, O God, in your sanctuary;
the God of Israel gives power and strength to
his people.

Praise be to God!

Psalm 69

For the director of music. To ⌐the tune of⌐ "Lilies." Of David.

¹ Save me, O God,
for the waters have come up to my neck.
² I sink in the miry depths,
where there is no foothold.
I have come into the deep waters;
the floods engulf me.
³ I am worn out calling for help;
my throat is parched.
My eyes fail,
looking for my God.
⁴ Those who hate me without reason
outnumber the hairs of my head;
many are my enemies without cause,
those who seek to destroy me.
I am forced to restore
what I did not steal.

⁵ You know my folly, O God;
my guilt is not hidden from you.

⁶ May those who hope in you
not be disgraced because of me,
O Lord, the LORD Almighty;
may those who seek you
not be put to shame because of me,
O God of Israel.
⁷ For I endure scorn for your sake,
and shame covers my face.
⁸ I am a stranger to my brothers,
an alien to my own mother's sons;
⁹ for zeal for your house consumes me,
and the insults of those who insult you fall on me.
¹⁰ When I weep and fast,
I must endure scorn;
¹¹ when I put on sackcloth,
people make sport of me.
¹² Those who sit at the gate mock me,
and I am the song of the drunkards.

¹³ But I pray to you, O LORD,
in the time of your favor;
in your great love, O God,
answer me with your sure salvation.
¹⁴ Rescue me from the mire,
do not let me sink;
deliver me from those who hate me,
from the deep waters.
¹⁵ Do not let the floodwaters engulf me

In God's Time

PSALM 69:13–16

"The spiritual life is, first of all, a patient waiting, that is, a waiting in suffering, during which the many experiences of unfulfillment remind us of God's absence. But it also is a waiting in expectation which allows us to recognize the first signs of the coming of God in the center of our pains . . . It is in the center of our longing for the absent God that we discover his footprints."

—HENRI J.M. NOUWEN,
Reaching Out: The Three Movements
of the Spiritual Life

Giving What You Have to Give

PSALM 69:30-33

In Hebrew religious tradition, the sacrifice of one's finest livestock was highly valued, but this kind of offering was impossible for those in exile or for the poor. Yet as this psalm proclaims, God is more concerned with the heart than with any external sacrifice. We may tend to look at the talents of others and think that what we have to offer is not as good as their contribution. God desires your love, the gift of your self. What are your unique gifts? Try listing ten of your gifts on a sheet of paper (or in your journal). Which ones give you joy? Which ones are you drawn to? How could they be your offering to God?

See *Meeting God in Service*

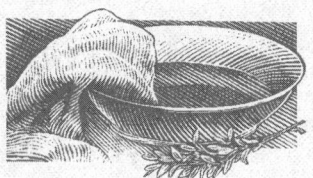

or the depths swallow me up
or the pit close its mouth over me.
¹⁶ Answer me, O LORD, out of the goodness of your
love;
in your great mercy turn to me.
¹⁷ Do not hide your face from your servant;
answer me quickly, for I am in trouble.
¹⁸ Come near and rescue me;
redeem me because of my foes.

¹⁹ You know how I am scorned, disgraced and
shamed;
all my enemies are before you.
²⁰ Scorn has broken my heart
and has left me helpless;
I looked for sympathy, but there was none,
for comforters, but I found none.
²¹ They put gall in my food
and gave me vinegar for my thirst.

²² May the table set before them become a snare;
may it become retribution and*ᵃ* a trap.
²³ May their eyes be darkened so they cannot see,
and their backs be bent forever.
²⁴ Pour out your wrath on them;
let your fierce anger overtake them.
²⁵ May their place be deserted;
let there be no one to dwell in their tents.
²⁶ For they persecute those you wound
and talk about the pain of those you hurt.
²⁷ Charge them with crime upon crime;
do not let them share in your salvation.
²⁸ May they be blotted out of the book of life
and not be listed with the righteous.

²⁹ I am in pain and distress;
may your salvation, O God, protect me.

³⁰ I will praise God's name in song
and glorify him with thanksgiving.
³¹ This will please the LORD more than an ox,
more than a bull with its horns and hoofs.
³² The poor will see and be glad—
you who seek God, may your hearts live!
³³ The LORD hears the needy
and does not despise his captive people.

³⁴ Let heaven and earth praise him,
the seas and all that move in them,
³⁵ for God will save Zion
and rebuild the cities of Judah.
Then people will settle there and possess it;
³⁶ the children of his servants will inherit it,
and those who love his name will dwell there.

Psalm 70

For the director of music. Of David. A petition.

¹ Hasten, O God, to save me;
O LORD, come quickly to help me.

ᵃ 22 Or snare / and their fellowship become

2 May those who seek my life
 be put to shame and confusion;
may all who desire my ruin
 be turned back in disgrace.
3 May those who say to me, "Aha! Aha!"
 turn back because of their shame.
4 But may all who seek you
 rejoice and be glad in you;
may those who love your salvation always say,
 "Let God be exalted!"

5 Yet I am poor and needy;
 come quickly to me, O God.
You are my help and my deliverer;
 O LORD, do not delay.

Psalm 71

1 In you, O LORD, I have taken refuge;
 let me never be put to shame.
2 Rescue me and deliver me in your righteousness;
 turn your ear to me and save me.
3 Be my rock of refuge,
 to which I can always go;
give the command to save me,
 for you are my rock and my fortress.
4 Deliver me, O my God, from the hand of the
 wicked,
 from the grasp of evil and cruel men.

5 For you have been my hope, O Sovereign LORD,
 my confidence since my youth.
6 From birth I have relied on you;
 you brought me forth from my mother's womb.
 I will ever praise you.
7 I have become like a portent to many,
 but you are my strong refuge.
8 My mouth is filled with your praise,
 declaring your splendor all day long.

9 Do not cast me away when I am old;
 do not forsake me when my strength is gone.
10 For my enemies speak against me;
 those who wait to kill me conspire together.
11 They say, "God has forsaken him;
 pursue him and seize him,
 for no one will rescue him."
12 Be not far from me, O God;
 come quickly, O my God, to help me.
13 May my accusers perish in shame;
 may those who want to harm me
 be covered with scorn and disgrace.

14 But as for me, I will always have hope;
 I will praise you more and more.
15 My mouth will tell of your righteousness,
 of your salvation all day long,
 though I know not its measure.
16 I will come and proclaim your mighty acts,
 O Sovereign LORD;
 I will proclaim your righteousness, yours alone.

Seeking God

PSALM 70:4

Jesus says that what we seek, we will find (Matthew 7:7), that where our hearts are, therein is our treasure (Matthew 6:21). To treasure the kingdom of heaven is to find God. Indeed, God is faithful to "be found" when we seek God with all of our hearts (Jeremiah 29:13). We may too easily become distracted from our heart's greatest desire. What is calling you? What distracts you from your desire for God? How do you attend to your deepest longing? Sit in silence for five minutes, then write whatever comes to you in response to these questions. God honors even your *desire* to desire him.

See *Meeting God in Prayer*

Naming Mentors

PSALM 71:18

The psalmist prays for a long life, long enough to tell "the story" to the next generation. For how do we discover our faith? We learn its truths from our parents, from teachers and ministers, and from those who have walked before us. We fathom faith's depths in the stories of Abraham, Sarah, Moses, Deborah, Peter and Paul. Our mentors may be the respected and well-known saints of the Christian tradition, teachers and writers of the present day, or the "ordinary" saints in our own families and faith communities. Think about who your mentors are. Make a list of four or five of them, and leave space to write down what each mentor has "bequeathed" to you spiritually. Then pause and offer thanksgiving for each one.

See Meeting God in Community

17 Since my youth, O God, you have taught me,
    and to this day I declare your marvelous deeds.
18 Even when I am old and gray,
    do not forsake me, O God,
till I declare your power to the next generation,
    your might to all who are to come.

19 Your righteousness reaches to the skies, O God,
    you who have done great things.
    Who, O God, is like you?
20 Though you have made me see troubles, many
    and bitter,
    you will restore my life again;
from the depths of the earth
    you will again bring me up.
21 You will increase my honor
    and comfort me once again.

22 I will praise you with the harp
    for your faithfulness, O my God;
I will sing praise to you with the lyre,
    O Holy One of Israel.
23 My lips will shout for joy
    when I sing praise to you—
    I, whom you have redeemed.
24 My tongue will tell of your righteous acts
    all day long,
for those who wanted to harm me
    have been put to shame and confusion.

Psalm 72

Of Solomon.

1 Endow the king with your justice, O God,
    the royal son with your righteousness.
2 He will*a* judge your people in righteousness,
    your afflicted ones with justice.
3 The mountains will bring prosperity to the people,
    the hills the fruit of righteousness.
4 He will defend the afflicted among the people
    and save the children of the needy;
    he will crush the oppressor.

5 He will endure*b* as long as the sun,
    as long as the moon, through all generations.
6 He will be like rain falling on a mown field,
    like showers watering the earth.
7 In his days the righteous will flourish;
    prosperity will abound till the moon is no more.

8 He will rule from sea to sea
    and from the River*c* to the ends of the earth.*d*
9 The desert tribes will bow before him
    and his enemies will lick the dust.
10 The kings of Tarshish and of distant shores
    will bring tribute to him;
the kings of Sheba and Seba
    will present him gifts.

a 2 Or May he; similarly in verses 3–11 and 17   *b 5 Septuagint; Hebrew You will be feared*   *c 8 That is, the Euphrates*   *d 8 Or the end of the land*

[11] All kings will bow down to him
and all nations will serve him.

[12] For he will deliver the needy who cry out,
the afflicted who have no one to help.
[13] He will take pity on the weak and the needy
and save the needy from death.
[14] He will rescue them from oppression and
violence,
for precious is their blood in his sight.

[15] Long may he live!
May gold from Sheba be given him.
May people ever pray for him
and bless him all day long.
[16] Let grain abound throughout the land;
on the tops of the hills may it sway.
Let its fruit flourish like Lebanon;
let it thrive like the grass of the field.
[17] May his name endure forever;
may it continue as long as the sun.

All nations will be blessed through him,
and they will call him blessed.

[18] Praise be to the LORD God, the God of Israel,
who alone does marvelous deeds.
[19] Praise be to his glorious name forever;
may the whole earth be filled with his glory.
Amen and Amen.

[20] This concludes the prayers of David son of Jesse.

BOOK III

Psalms 73–89

Psalm 73

A psalm of Asaph.

[1] Surely God is good to Israel,
to those who are pure in heart.

[2] But as for me, my feet had almost slipped;
I had nearly lost my foothold.
[3] For I envied the arrogant
when I saw the prosperity of the wicked.

[4] They have no struggles;
their bodies are healthy and strong.[a]
[5] They are free from the burdens common to man;
they are not plagued by human ills.
[6] Therefore pride is their necklace;
they clothe themselves with violence.
[7] From their callous hearts comes iniquity[b];
the evil conceits of their minds know no limits.
[8] They scoff, and speak with malice;
in their arrogance they threaten oppression.

Precious in God's Sight

PSALM 72:12–14

This psalm is sometimes entitled "The Reign of the Messiah." From our Christian perspective, we can see how Jesus fulfilled this vision. He responded to the poor and needy, healed the sick and preached a new kingdom where the first would be last and the last first. God's kingdom is based on care for the poor and the promotion of justice. Look carefully at the word *precious*. Other words such as *dear, beloved, valuable* and *cherished* come to mind. As you write a check to a charity or take food to a local shelter, offer the prayer of this psalm in thanksgiving: "God, I am grateful for these persons you so cherish."

See Meeting God in Service

---

a 4 With a different word division of the Hebrew; Masoretic Text *struggles at their death; / their bodies are healthy*   *b 7* Syriac (see also Septuagint); Hebrew *Their eyes bulge with fat*

Losing Our Way

PSALM 73:21–26

How often we wander away from God as we journey. We become distracted by anger or envy, by our individual successes or failures, and by the overcrowding of our lives. We may act, as the psalmist laments, like "a brute beast before [God]." Yet God is ever faithful—holding us, loving us, guiding us. Augustine writes, "Late have I loved Thee, O Beauty so ancient and so new; late have I loved Thee! For behold Thou wert within me, and I outside." How have you been "looking outside" for the source of your spiritual life? What areas of your life do you need to recommit to God? Make an appointment with yourself in your journal or with a spiritual adviser to consider these questions.

See Meeting God in Community

⁹Their mouths lay claim to heaven,
    and their tongues take possession of the earth.
¹⁰Therefore their people turn to them
    and drink up waters in abundance.*ᵃ*
¹¹They say, "How can God know?
    Does the Most High have knowledge?"

¹²This is what the wicked are like—
    always carefree, they increase in wealth.

¹³Surely in vain have I kept my heart pure;
    in vain have I washed my hands in innocence.
¹⁴All day long I have been plagued;
    I have been punished every morning.

¹⁵If I had said, "I will speak thus,"
    I would have betrayed your children.
¹⁶When I tried to understand all this,
    it was oppressive to me
¹⁷till I entered the sanctuary of God;
    then I understood their final destiny.

¹⁸Surely you place them on slippery ground;
    you cast them down to ruin.
¹⁹How suddenly are they destroyed,
    completely swept away by terrors!
²⁰As a dream when one awakes,
    so when you arise, O Lord,
    you will despise them as fantasies.

²¹When my heart was grieved
    and my spirit embittered,
²²I was senseless and ignorant;
    I was a brute beast before you.

²³Yet I am always with you;
    you hold me by my right hand.
²⁴You guide me with your counsel,
    and afterward you will take me into glory.
²⁵Whom have I in heaven but you?
    And earth has nothing I desire besides you.
²⁶My flesh and my heart may fail,
    but God is the strength of my heart
    and my portion forever.

²⁷Those who are far from you will perish;
    you destroy all who are unfaithful to you.
²⁸But as for me, it is good to be near God.
    I have made the Sovereign Lᴏʀᴅ my refuge;
    I will tell of all your deeds.

Psalm 74

A *maskil*ᵇ of Asaph.

¹Why have you rejected us forever, O God?
    Why does your anger smolder against the
        sheep of your pasture?
²Remember the people you purchased of old,
    the tribe of your inheritance, whom you
        redeemed—

ᵃ 10 The meaning of the Hebrew for this verse is uncertain.   *ᵇ Title:* Probably a literary or musical term

Mount Zion, where you dwelt.
³ Turn your steps toward these everlasting ruins,
all this destruction the enemy has brought on
the sanctuary.

⁴ Your foes roared in the place where you met with
us;
they set up their standards as signs.
⁵ They behaved like men wielding axes
to cut through a thicket of trees.
⁶ They smashed all the carved paneling
with their axes and hatchets.
⁷ They burned your sanctuary to the ground;
they defiled the dwelling place of your Name.
⁸ They said in their hearts, "We will crush them
completely!"
They burned every place where God was
worshiped in the land.
⁹ We are given no miraculous signs;
no prophets are left,
and none of us knows how long this will be.

¹⁰ How long will the enemy mock you, O God?
Will the foe revile your name forever?
¹¹ Why do you hold back your hand, your right
hand?
Take it from the folds of your garment and
destroy them!

¹² But you, O God, are my king from of old;
you bring salvation upon the earth.
¹³ It was you who split open the sea by your power;
you broke the heads of the monster in the
waters.
¹⁴ It was you who crushed the heads of Leviathan
and gave him as food to the creatures of the
desert.
¹⁵ It was you who opened up springs and streams;
you dried up the ever flowing rivers.
¹⁶ The day is yours, and yours also the night;
you established the sun and moon.
¹⁷ It was you who set all the boundaries of the
earth;
you made both summer and winter.

¹⁸ Remember how the enemy has mocked you,
O LORD,
how foolish people have reviled your name.
¹⁹ Do not hand over the life of your dove to wild
beasts;
do not forget the lives of your afflicted people
forever.
²⁰ Have regard for your covenant,
because haunts of violence fill the dark places
of the land.
²¹ Do not let the oppressed retreat in disgrace;
may the poor and needy praise your name.

²² Rise up, O God, and defend your cause;
remember how fools mock you all day long.
²³ Do not ignore the clamor of your adversaries,

When It Is Hard to See

PSALM 74:10–12

Even deeply committed believers sometimes feel that God is distant. A family member suffers from a life-threatening illness; the headline in the local paper announces a gruesome murder across town; a good friend seems far away. The psalmist is honest about his feelings of doubt: Where is God? Why doesn't God do something? Yet he reminds himself: God is always bringing "salvation upon the earth."

What might God be leading you to do about a discouraging situation—offer prayers of intercession, give time and energy to a local youth program, share your honest feelings of grief with a friend?

See Meeting God in Service

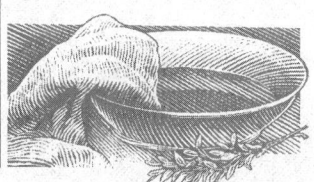

The Judgment of God

PSALM 75:6–9

As you read this psalm of judgment, you might think of Jesus' image of the Son of Man separating the "sheep" from the "goats" (Matthew 25:32). We encounter God's sifting, purifying love in our experience of inward spiritual transformation. Spiritual writers refer to this as the "death of the ego" or the "dark night of the soul." In order for God's life to grow in us, our old attitudes, prejudices and self-preoccupation must perish. In what ways have you experienced the "dark night"? How would you describe the process of "dying" to your old self and of finding new life in Jesus Christ? In what areas do you see new life? How is God still leading you to let go of your old self?

the uproar of your enemies, which rises
continually.

Psalm 75

For the director of music. ⌊To the tune of⌋ "Do Not Destroy."
A psalm of Asaph. A song.

¹ We give thanks to you, O God,
    we give thanks, for your Name is near;
    men tell of your wonderful deeds.

² You say, "I choose the appointed time;
    it is I who judge uprightly.
³ When the earth and all its people quake,
    it is I who hold its pillars firm.   *Selah*
⁴ To the arrogant I say, 'Boast no more,'
    and to the wicked, 'Do not lift up your horns.
⁵ Do not lift your horns against heaven;
    do not speak with outstretched neck.' "

⁶ No one from the east or the west
    or from the desert can exalt a man.
⁷ But it is God who judges:
    He brings one down, he exalts another.
⁸ In the hand of the LORD is a cup
    full of foaming wine mixed with spices;
  he pours it out, and all the wicked of the earth
    drink it down to its very dregs.

⁹ As for me, I will declare this forever;
    I will sing praise to the God of Jacob.
¹⁰ I will cut off the horns of all the wicked,
    but the horns of the righteous will be lifted up.

Psalm 76

For the director of music. With stringed instruments.
A psalm of Asaph. A song.

¹ In Judah God is known;
    his name is great in Israel.
² His tent is in Salem,
    his dwelling place in Zion.
³ There he broke the flashing arrows,
    the shields and the swords, the weapons of
      war.   *Selah*

⁴ You are resplendent with light,
    more majestic than mountains rich with game.
⁵ Valiant men lie plundered,
    they sleep their last sleep;
  not one of the warriors
    can lift his hands.
⁶ At your rebuke, O God of Jacob,
    both horse and chariot lie still.
⁷ You alone are to be feared.
    Who can stand before you when you are angry?
⁸ From heaven you pronounced judgment,
    and the land feared and was quiet—
⁹ when you, O God, rose up to judge,
    to save all the afflicted of the land.   *Selah*
¹⁰ Surely your wrath against men brings you praise,

and the survivors of your wrath are restrained.[a]

¹¹ Make vows to the LORD your God and fulfill them;
let all the neighboring lands
bring gifts to the One to be feared.
¹² He breaks the spirit of rulers;
he is feared by the kings of the earth.

Psalm 77

For the director of music. For Jeduthun. Of Asaph. A psalm.

¹ I cried out to God for help;
I cried out to God to hear me.
² When I was in distress, I sought the Lord;
at night I stretched out untiring hands
and my soul refused to be comforted.

³ I remembered you, O God, and I groaned;
I mused, and my spirit grew faint.   *Selah*
⁴ You kept my eyes from closing;
I was too troubled to speak.
⁵ I thought about the former days,
the years of long ago;
⁶ I remembered my songs in the night.
My heart mused and my spirit inquired:

⁷ "Will the Lord reject forever?
Will he never show his favor again?
⁸ Has his unfailing love vanished forever?
Has his promise failed for all time?
⁹ Has God forgotten to be merciful?
Has he in anger withheld his compassion?"   *Selah*

¹⁰ Then I thought, "To this I will appeal:
the years of the right hand of the Most High."
¹¹ I will remember the deeds of the LORD;
yes, I will remember your miracles of long ago.
¹² I will meditate on all your works
and consider all your mighty deeds.

¹³ Your ways, O God, are holy.
What god is so great as our God?
¹⁴ You are the God who performs miracles;
you display your power among the peoples.
¹⁵ With your mighty arm you redeemed your
people,
the descendants of Jacob and Joseph.   *Selah*

¹⁶ The waters saw you, O God,
the waters saw you and writhed;
the very depths were convulsed.
¹⁷ The clouds poured down water,
the skies resounded with thunder;
your arrows flashed back and forth.
¹⁸ Your thunder was heard in the whirlwind,
your lightning lit up the world;
the earth trembled and quaked.
¹⁹ Your path led through the sea,

Before Dawn

PSALM 77:6

Monastics typically rise while it is still dark, for in the stillness before dawn, the soul is quiet, unhurried. The day has not rushed in yet with all of its duties. In both the silence and the chanting of psalms, the monastic meditates. Meditation is a time to consecrate one's heart to God, a time of wordless communion with God. As an experiment this week, set your alarm clock ten minutes earlier than usual. Using a candle, recite the Lord's Prayer slowly or repeat a favorite psalm; rest in God's presence for several minutes of silent contemplation.

See Meeting God in Scripture

---

[a] 10 Or *Surely the wrath of men brings you praise, / and with the remainder of wrath you arm yourself*

Becoming a Mentor

PSALM 78:2–4

Each one of us in the body of Christ is called to encourage others (1 Corinthians 12:7). One important spiritual ministry is parenting—fostering faith in our children. Or we may minister to others through being in regular prayer for them, teaching or leading a small group, visiting someone who is sick or in prison, tutoring at a local school or spending time with a new Christian. Reflect on your current relationships. How might you be an encouraging presence in another person's life?

See Meeting God in Service

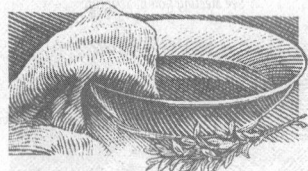

your way through the mighty waters,
    though your footprints were not seen.
20 You led your people like a flock
    by the hand of Moses and Aaron.

Psalm 78

A maskil[a] of Asaph.

1 O my people, hear my teaching;
    listen to the words of my mouth.
2 I will open my mouth in parables,
    I will utter hidden things, things from of old—
3 what we have heard and known,
    what our fathers have told us.
4 We will not hide them from their children;
    we will tell the next generation
the praiseworthy deeds of the LORD,
    his power, and the wonders he has done.
5 He decreed statutes for Jacob
    and established the law in Israel,
which he commanded our forefathers
    to teach their children,
6 so the next generation would know them,
    even the children yet to be born,
    and they in turn would tell their children.
7 Then they would put their trust in God
    and would not forget his deeds
    but would keep his commands.
8 They would not be like their forefathers—
    a stubborn and rebellious generation,
whose hearts were not loyal to God,
    whose spirits were not faithful to him.

9 The men of Ephraim, though armed with bows,
    turned back on the day of battle;
10 they did not keep God's covenant
    and refused to live by his law.
11 They forgot what he had done,
    the wonders he had shown them.
12 He did miracles in the sight of their fathers
    in the land of Egypt, in the region of Zoan.
13 He divided the sea and led them through;
    he made the water stand firm like a wall.
14 He guided them with the cloud by day
    and with light from the fire all night.
15 He split the rocks in the desert
    and gave them water as abundant as the seas;
16 he brought streams out of a rocky crag
    and made water flow down like rivers.

17 But they continued to sin against him,
    rebelling in the desert against the Most High.
18 They willfully put God to the test
    by demanding the food they craved.
19 They spoke against God, saying,
    "Can God spread a table in the desert?
20 When he struck the rock, water gushed out,
    and streams flowed abundantly.

a Title: Probably a literary or musical term

But can he also give us food?
Can he supply meat for his people?"
²¹ When the LORD heard them, he was very angry;
his fire broke out against Jacob,
and his wrath rose against Israel,
²² for they did not believe in God
or trust in his deliverance.
²³ Yet he gave a command to the skies above
and opened the doors of the heavens;
²⁴ he rained down manna for the people to eat,
he gave them the grain of heaven.
²⁵ Men ate the bread of angels;
he sent them all the food they could eat.
²⁶ He let loose the east wind from the heavens
and led forth the south wind by his power.
²⁷ He rained meat down on them like dust,
flying birds like sand on the seashore.
²⁸ He made them come down inside their camp,
all around their tents.
²⁹ They ate till they had more than enough,
for he had given them what they craved.
³⁰ But before they turned from the food they craved,
even while it was still in their mouths,
³¹ God's anger rose against them;
he put to death the sturdiest among them,
cutting down the young men of Israel.

³² In spite of all this, they kept on sinning;
in spite of his wonders, they did not believe.
³³ So he ended their days in futility
and their years in terror.
³⁴ Whenever God slew them, they would seek him;
they eagerly turned to him again.
³⁵ They remembered that God was their Rock,
that God Most High was their Redeemer.
³⁶ But then they would flatter him with their
mouths,
lying to him with their tongues;
³⁷ their hearts were not loyal to him,
they were not faithful to his covenant.
³⁸ Yet he was merciful;
he forgave their iniquities
and did not destroy them.
Time after time he restrained his anger
and did not stir up his full wrath.
³⁹ He remembered that they were but flesh,
a passing breeze that does not return.

⁴⁰ How often they rebelled against him in the desert
and grieved him in the wasteland!
⁴¹ Again and again they put God to the test;
they vexed the Holy One of Israel.
⁴² They did not remember his power—
the day he redeemed them from the oppressor,
⁴³ the day he displayed his miraculous signs in
Egypt,
his wonders in the region of Zoan.
⁴⁴ He turned their rivers to blood;
they could not drink from their streams.
⁴⁵ He sent swarms of flies that devoured them,

Being Human

PSALM 78:38–39

God is compassionate toward us—even in our frailty. As we draw closer to God, our weakness—our humanness—becomes all the more obvious. For as John of the Cross observed, "Freedom cannot abide in a heart dominated by desires, in a slave's heart. It abides in a liberated heart, in a child's heart." Although we are set free by grace, being human, we allow our hearts to become enslaved to sin over and over again. We may even think we have arrived on a higher spiritual plane, but then we realize we have taken on spiritual pride. What are some of the stumbling blocks that keep you from fully accepting God's grace? Invite God's penetrating gaze of love. How is God inviting you to embrace new freedom?

See Meeting God in Prayer

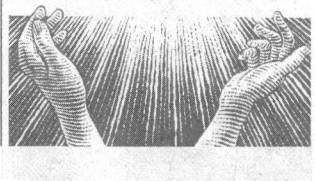

Hearing God's Voice in the Desert

PSALM 78:52–53

The psalmist remembers how, like an attentive shepherd, God faithfully led the people of Israel through the desert by means of a cloud by day and fire in the cloud by night (see Exodus 40:38). Quakers often use the metaphor of traveling in the light: By following even small signs of divine light, one finds that more and more light becomes apparent. "Travels begin at the breakings of day," Friend Isaac Pennington wrote in 1665, "wherein are but glimmerings, or little light . . . yet *there* must the traveller begin . . . and in his faithful travel the light will break in on him more and more." How do you discern God's guiding voice in your life? At what point in your day do you take time to listen, to wait for God's guidance? Perhaps you can begin right now.

See Meeting God in Everyday Life

and frogs that devastated them.
⁴⁶ He gave their crops to the grasshopper,
    their produce to the locust.
⁴⁷ He destroyed their vines with hail
    and their sycamore-figs with sleet.
⁴⁸ He gave over their cattle to the hail,
    their livestock to bolts of lightning.
⁴⁹ He unleashed against them his hot anger,
    his wrath, indignation and hostility—
    a band of destroying angels.
⁵⁰ He prepared a path for his anger;
    he did not spare them from death
    but gave them over to the plague.
⁵¹ He struck down all the firstborn of Egypt,
    the firstfruits of manhood in the tents of Ham.
⁵² But he brought his people out like a flock;
    he led them like sheep through the desert.
⁵³ He guided them safely, so they were unafraid;
    but the sea engulfed their enemies.
⁵⁴ Thus he brought them to the border of his holy
    land,
    to the hill country his right hand had taken.
⁵⁵ He drove out nations before them
    and allotted their lands to them as an
        inheritance;
    he settled the tribes of Israel in their homes.

⁵⁶ But they put God to the test
    and rebelled against the Most High;
    they did not keep his statutes.
⁵⁷ Like their fathers they were disloyal and faithless,
    as unreliable as a faulty bow.
⁵⁸ They angered him with their high places;
    they aroused his jealousy with their idols.
⁵⁹ When God heard them, he was very angry;
    he rejected Israel completely.
⁶⁰ He abandoned the tabernacle of Shiloh,
    the tent he had set up among men.
⁶¹ He sent ˻the ark of˼ his might into captivity,
    his splendor into the hands of the enemy.
⁶² He gave his people over to the sword;
    he was very angry with his inheritance.
⁶³ Fire consumed their young men,
    and their maidens had no wedding songs;
⁶⁴ their priests were put to the sword,
    and their widows could not weep.

⁶⁵ Then the Lord awoke as from sleep,
    as a man wakes from the stupor of wine.
⁶⁶ He beat back his enemies;
    he put them to everlasting shame.
⁶⁷ Then he rejected the tents of Joseph,
    he did not choose the tribe of Ephraim;
⁶⁸ but he chose the tribe of Judah,
    Mount Zion, which he loved.
⁶⁹ He built his sanctuary like the heights,
    like the earth that he established forever.
⁷⁰ He chose David his servant
    and took him from the sheep pens;

⁷¹ from tending the sheep he brought him
  to be the shepherd of his people Jacob,
  of Israel his inheritance.
⁷² And David shepherded them with integrity of
    heart;
  with skillful hands he led them.

Psalm 79

A psalm of Asaph.

¹ O God, the nations have invaded your
    inheritance;
  they have defiled your holy temple,
  they have reduced Jerusalem to rubble.
² They have given the dead bodies of your servants
    as food to the birds of the air,
  the flesh of your saints to the beasts of the
    earth.
³ They have poured out blood like water
  all around Jerusalem,
  and there is no one to bury the dead.
⁴ We are objects of reproach to our neighbors,
  of scorn and derision to those around us.

⁵ How long, O LORD? Will you be angry forever?
  How long will your jealousy burn like fire?
⁶ Pour out your wrath on the nations
    that do not acknowledge you,
  on the kingdoms
    that do not call on your name;
⁷ for they have devoured Jacob
  and destroyed his homeland.

⁸ Do not hold against us the sins of the fathers;
  may your mercy come quickly to meet us,
  for we are in desperate need.

⁹ Help us, O God our Savior,
  for the glory of your name;
  deliver us and forgive our sins
  for your name's sake.
¹⁰ Why should the nations say,
  "Where is their God?"
  Before our eyes, make known among the nations
    that you avenge the outpoured blood of your
    servants.
¹¹ May the groans of the prisoners come before you;
  by the strength of your arm
  preserve those condemned to die.

¹² Pay back into the laps of our neighbors seven
    times
  the reproach they have hurled at you, O Lord.
¹³ Then we your people, the sheep of your pasture,
  will praise you forever;
  from generation to generation
  we will recount your praise.

The Healing of the Generations

PSALM 79:8–9

The psalmist is speaking here about the destruction of Jerusalem and thus the continuing grief in Israel's spirit. In the spiritual life, we may also have concerns about how the sins of our forebears affect our souls. How have you been affected by the fears, prejudices and hurts of your parents, grandparents and great-grandparents? God's compassion can reach into our past. Take a few minutes in quiet reflection to call up in your memory one hurt you have carried as a result of someone's failure; perhaps you feel negative emotions toward God as a parent to you. Imagine God's loving concern for your pain and offer that pain to him. Feel God's unending mercy and love healing your heart.

See Meeting God in Prayer

God's Shining Face

PSALM 80:3,19

Noted psychologist Erik Erikson believes that one of our earliest experiences of the sacred occurs when we are infants. We experience what God is like through the loving face of our mother (or our primary caregiver). It is a face of love and tenderness, and we experience being loved without condition. Julian of Norwich speaks of Jesus' motherly love for us: "Thus he is our Mother in kind by the working of grace . . . And he wills that we know it. For he desires to have all of our love attached to him."

Imagine God's face turned toward you with such shining tenderness. God's eyes are full of love for you; God smiles at you and sings to you gently.

See Meeting God in Scripture

Psalm 80

For the director of music. To ⌊the tune of⌋ "The Lilies of the Covenant." Of Asaph. A psalm.

¹ Hear us, O Shepherd of Israel,
  you who lead Joseph like a flock;
 you who sit enthroned between the cherubim,
  shine forth
² before Ephraim, Benjamin and Manasseh.
 Awaken your might;
  come and save us.

³ Restore us, O God;
  make your face shine upon us,
  that we may be saved.

⁴ O LORD God Almighty,
  how long will your anger smolder
  against the prayers of your people?
⁵ You have fed them with the bread of tears;
  you have made them drink tears by the
  bowlful.
⁶ You have made us a source of contention to our
  neighbors,
  and our enemies mock us.

⁷ Restore us, O God Almighty;
  make your face shine upon us,
  that we may be saved.

⁸ You brought a vine out of Egypt;
  you drove out the nations and planted it.
⁹ You cleared the ground for it,
  and it took root and filled the land.
¹⁰ The mountains were covered with its shade,
  the mighty cedars with its branches.
¹¹ It sent out its boughs to the Sea,ᵃ
  its shoots as far as the River.ᵇ

¹² Why have you broken down its walls
  so that all who pass by pick its grapes?
¹³ Boars from the forest ravage it
  and the creatures of the field feed on it.
¹⁴ Return to us, O God Almighty!
  Look down from heaven and see!
 Watch over this vine,
¹⁵ the root your right hand has planted,
  the sonᶜ you have raised up for yourself.

¹⁶ Your vine is cut down, it is burned with fire;
  at your rebuke your people perish.
¹⁷ Let your hand rest on the man at your right hand,
  the son of man you have raised up for yourself.
¹⁸ Then we will not turn away from you;
  revive us, and we will call on your name.

¹⁹ Restore us, O LORD God Almighty;
  make your face shine upon us,
  that we may be saved.

ᵃ *11* Probably the Mediterranean   ᵇ *11* That is, the Euphrates   ᶜ *15* Or branch

Psalm 81

For the director of music. According to *gittith.*[a] Of Asaph.

1 Sing for joy to God our strength;
  shout aloud to the God of Jacob!
2 Begin the music, strike the tambourine,
  play the melodious harp and lyre.

3 Sound the ram's horn at the New Moon,
  and when the moon is full, on the day of our
    Feast;
4 this is a decree for Israel,
  an ordinance of the God of Jacob.
5 He established it as a statute for Joseph
  when he went out against Egypt,
  where we heard a language we did not
    understand.[b]

6 He says, "I removed the burden from their
    shoulders;
  their hands were set free from the basket.
7 In your distress you called and I rescued you,
  I answered you out of a thundercloud;
  I tested you at the waters of Meribah.   *Selah*

8 "Hear, O my people, and I will warn you—
  if you would but listen to me, O Israel!
9 You shall have no foreign god among you;
  you shall not bow down to an alien god.
10 I am the LORD your God,
  who brought you up out of Egypt.
  Open wide your mouth and I will fill it.

11 "But my people would not listen to me;
  Israel would not submit to me.
12 So I gave them over to their stubborn hearts
  to follow their own devices.

13 "If my people would but listen to me,
  if Israel would follow my ways,
14 how quickly would I subdue their enemies
  and turn my hand against their foes!
15 Those who hate the LORD would cringe before
    him,
  and their punishment would last forever.
16 But you would be fed with the finest of wheat;
  with honey from the rock I would satisfy you."

Psalm 82

A psalm of Asaph.

1 God presides in the great assembly;
  he gives judgment among the "gods":

2 "How long will you[c] defend the unjust
  and show partiality to the wicked?   *Selah*
3 Defend the cause of the weak and fatherless;
  maintain the rights of the poor and oppressed.

The Idolatry of Attachment

PSALM 81:9–10

Most of us are not tempted to worship other deities and images. We believe, as Israel learned, that God is unseen spirit. Idolatry for us is usually more insidious; sometimes our idols are our addictions. As psychiatrist and spiritual writer Gerald May explains, addiction is the attachment of our desire for God to objects, and such attachment "can indeed deaden our responsiveness to grace." Typically, we can name addictions to pornography or nicotine while overlooking more "acceptable" ones, such as addictions to approval, neatness, television, revenge or the Internet! What are your attachments? Study one of your "addictions" over the course of a week. How does it distract you from trusting the Spirit of God in your life? Offer your addictions by name to God and ask him to free you and fill you with himself.

---

[a] Title: Probably a musical term   [b] 5 Or *I and we heard a voice we had not known*   [c] 2 The Hebrew is plural.

A Just Judge

PSALM 82:5,8

In this psalm, God's justice and compassion are integral to the "foundations of the earth"; all of God's creation is founded on righteousness. Meditate on the nature of God. What signs do you see of God's order in creation, in our system of laws, in the caring community of the church? What does it mean to "defend the cause of the weak" and "maintain the rights of the poor and oppressed" (v.3) in our world today? In what ways might God be leading you to build justice in your community? Share your reflections with a friend.

See Meeting God in Service

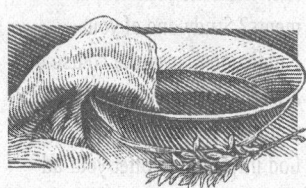

4 Rescue the weak and needy;
  deliver them from the hand of the wicked.

5 "They know nothing, they understand nothing.
  They walk about in darkness;
  all the foundations of the earth are shaken.

6 "I said, 'You are "gods";
  you are all sons of the Most High.'
7 But you will die like mere men;
  you will fall like every other ruler."

8 Rise up, O God, judge the earth,
  for all the nations are your inheritance.

Psalm 83

A song. A psalm of Asaph.

1 O God, do not keep silent;
  be not quiet, O God, be not still.
2 See how your enemies are astir,
  how your foes rear their heads.
3 With cunning they conspire against your people;
  they plot against those you cherish.
4 "Come," they say, "let us destroy them as a
    nation,
  that the name of Israel be remembered no
    more."

5 With one mind they plot together;
  they form an alliance against you—
6 the tents of Edom and the Ishmaelites,
  of Moab and the Hagrites,
7 Gebal,*a* Ammon and Amalek,
  Philistia, with the people of Tyre.
8 Even Assyria has joined them
  to lend strength to the descendants of Lot. *Selah*

9 Do to them as you did to Midian,
  as you did to Sisera and Jabin at the river
    Kishon,
10 who perished at Endor
  and became like refuse on the ground.
11 Make their nobles like Oreb and Zeeb,
  all their princes like Zebah and Zalmunna,
12 who said, "Let us take possession
  of the pasturelands of God."

13 Make them like tumbleweed, O my God,
  like chaff before the wind.
14 As fire consumes the forest
  or a flame sets the mountains ablaze,
15 so pursue them with your tempest
  and terrify them with your storm.
16 Cover their faces with shame
  so that men will seek your name, O LORD.

17 May they ever be ashamed and dismayed;
  may they perish in disgrace.
18 Let them know that you, whose name is the
  LORD—

a 7 That is, Byblos

that you alone are the Most High over all the
earth.

Psalm 84

For the director of music. According to *gittith*.[a] Of the Sons
of Korah. A psalm.

1 How lovely is your dwelling place,
  O LORD Almighty!
2 My soul yearns, even faints,
   for the courts of the LORD;
  my heart and my flesh cry out
  for the living God.

3 Even the sparrow has found a home,
   and the swallow a nest for herself,
   where she may have her young—
  a place near your altar,
  O LORD Almighty, my King and my God.
4 Blessed are those who dwell in your house;
   they are ever praising you.   *Selah*

5 Blessed are those whose strength is in you,
   who have set their hearts on pilgrimage.
6 As they pass through the Valley of Baca,
   they make it a place of springs;
   the autumn rains also cover it with pools.[b]
7 They go from strength to strength,
   till each appears before God in Zion.

8 Hear my prayer, O LORD God Almighty;
   listen to me, O God of Jacob.   *Selah*
9 Look upon our shield,[c] O God;
   look with favor on your anointed one.

10 Better is one day in your courts
   than a thousand elsewhere;
  I would rather be a doorkeeper in the house of
   my God
   than dwell in the tents of the wicked.
11 For the LORD God is a sun and shield;
   the LORD bestows favor and honor;
  no good thing does he withhold
   from those whose walk is blameless.

12 O LORD Almighty,
   blessed is the man who trusts in you.

Psalm 85

For the director of music. Of the Sons of Korah. A psalm.

1 You showed favor to your land, O LORD;
   you restored the fortunes of Jacob.
2 You forgave the iniquity of your people
   and covered all their sins.   *Selah*
3 You set aside all your wrath
   and turned from your fierce anger.

4 Restore us again, O God our Savior,
   and put away your displeasure toward us.

Water in the Desert

PSALM 84:5–7

The Valley of Baca is an arid,
desert-like place on the way to
Jerusalem. In our hearts, we
may also find a desert—a desert
of grief and loneliness or of dryness in prayer. In her dry times,
Teresa of Avila found nourishment in God's gracious
"springs": "[God] produces
this delight with the greatest
peace and quiet and sweetness
in the very interior part of our
selves . . . This water overflows
through all the dwelling places
[of the soul]." Recall a time
when you felt God's love "watering you" in a desert experience. What does it mean to rest
in God's provision rather than
in your own efforts? In your
journal, recall a recent situation in which you experienced
a "spring" of spiritual
refreshment.

See Meeting God in Everyday Life

---

[a] Title: Probably a musical term   [b] 6 Or *blessings*   [c] 9 Or *sovereign*

Spiritual Fulfillment

PSALM 85:8–13

"Then God shall be all our love, all we desire and seek and follow, all we think, all our life and speech and breath. The unity which now is between Father and Son shall be poured into our feelings and our minds: and as he loves us with a pure, sincere, unbreakable charity we on our side shall be linked to him by a lasting affection that nothing can spoil."

—JOHN CASSIAN,
The Conferences of Cassian

⁵ Will you be angry with us forever?
　Will you prolong your anger through all
　　generations?
⁶ Will you not revive us again,
　that your people may rejoice in you?
⁷ Show us your unfailing love, O LORD,
　and grant us your salvation.

⁸ I will listen to what God the LORD will say;
　he promises peace to his people, his saints—
　　but let them not return to folly.
⁹ Surely his salvation is near those who fear him,
　that his glory may dwell in our land.

¹⁰ Love and faithfulness meet together;
　righteousness and peace kiss each other.
¹¹ Faithfulness springs forth from the earth,
　and righteousness looks down from heaven.
¹² The LORD will indeed give what is good,
　and our land will yield its harvest.
¹³ Righteousness goes before him
　and prepares the way for his steps.

Psalm 86

A prayer of David.

¹ Hear, O LORD, and answer me,
　for I am poor and needy.
² Guard my life, for I am devoted to you.
　You are my God; save your servant
　who trusts in you.
³ Have mercy on me, O Lord,
　for I call to you all day long.
⁴ Bring joy to your servant,
　for to you, O Lord,
　I lift up my soul.

⁵ You are forgiving and good, O Lord,
　abounding in love to all who call to you.
⁶ Hear my prayer, O LORD;
　listen to my cry for mercy.
⁷ In the day of my trouble I will call to you,
　for you will answer me.

⁸ Among the gods there is none like you, O Lord;
　no deeds can compare with yours.
⁹ All the nations you have made
　will come and worship before you, O Lord;
　they will bring glory to your name.
¹⁰ For you are great and do marvelous deeds;
　you alone are God.

¹¹ Teach me your way, O LORD,
　and I will walk in your truth;
give me an undivided heart,
　that I may fear your name.
¹² I will praise you, O Lord my God, with all my
　　heart;
　I will glorify your name forever.
¹³ For great is your love toward me;

you have delivered me from the depths of the grave.[a]

¹⁴The arrogant are attacking me, O God;
 a band of ruthless men seeks my life—
 men without regard for you.
¹⁵But you, O Lord, are a compassionate and gracious God,
 slow to anger, abounding in love and faithfulness.
¹⁶Turn to me and have mercy on me;
 grant your strength to your servant
 and save the son of your maidservant.[b]
¹⁷Give me a sign of your goodness,
 that my enemies may see it and be put to shame,
 for you, O Lord, have helped me and comforted me.

Psalm 87

Of the Sons of Korah. A psalm. A song.

¹He has set his foundation on the holy mountain;
² the Lord loves the gates of Zion
 more than all the dwellings of Jacob.
³Glorious things are said of you,
 O city of God: *Selah*
⁴"I will record Rahab[c] and Babylon
 among those who acknowledge me—
Philistia too, and Tyre, along with Cush[d]—
 and will say, 'This[e] one was born in Zion.' "
⁵Indeed, of Zion it will be said,
 "This one and that one were born in her,
 and the Most High himself will establish her."
⁶The Lord will write in the register of the peoples:
 "This one was born in Zion." *Selah*
⁷As they make music they will sing,
 "All my fountains are in you."

Psalm 88

A song. A psalm of the Sons of Korah. For the director of music. According to mahalath leannoth.[f] A maskil[g] of Heman the Ezrahite.

¹O Lord, the God who saves me,
 day and night I cry out before you.
²May my prayer come before you;
 turn your ear to my cry.
³For my soul is full of trouble
 and my life draws near the grave.[a]
⁴I am counted among those who go down to the pit;
 I am like a man without strength.
⁵I am set apart with the dead,

The Steadfast Mercy of God

PSALM 86:15

Thomas Merton wrote that in God there is "mercy within mercy within mercy." God's mercy and compassion are greater than we could ever imagine. Jesus told many parables to help us "grasp how wide and long and high and deep" God's love is (Ephesians 3:18): The shepherd leaves his flock in search of one lost sheep, a father welcomes home a son who has disgraced the family name, the outsider rescues a dying traveler. Reflect on the word *mercy* and what it means to you. When have you felt God's mercy? What image, symbol or piece of music expresses mercy to you? In your devotions throughout the coming week, use this symbol or musical piece as a way to focus on God's merciful love.

See Meeting God in Scripture

---

a 13,3 Hebrew *Sheol* b 16 Or *save your faithful son* c 4 A poetic name for Egypt d 4 That is, the upper Nile region e 4 Or *"O Rahab and Babylon, / Philistia, Tyre and Cush, / I will record concerning those who acknowledge me: / 'This* f Title: Possibly a tune, "The Suffering of Affliction" g Title: Probably a literary or musical term

Complaining to God

PSALM 88:8–9

Laments and complaints express feelings of depression, frustration and weariness. We want so much to show the Lord only our gratitude and faith that we may feel uncomfortable speaking to God with such honesty. Yet the psalmist does not soften his negative feelings. For God knows our thoughts and remembers our human vulnerability. How do you express your honest feelings to God? Do you write in a journal, share with a spiritual mentor or friend, pray with upstretched hands toward a starlit sky or with a quiet sigh when you are alone? God hears the cry of your heart. What feelings might you be hiding from God?

See Meeting God in Prayer

like the slain who lie in the grave,
   whom you remember no more,
      who are cut off from your care.
⁶ You have put me in the lowest pit,
   in the darkest depths.
⁷ Your wrath lies heavily upon me;
   you have overwhelmed me with all your waves.
                                        Selah

⁸ You have taken from me my closest friends
   and have made me repulsive to them.
I am confined and cannot escape;
⁹   my eyes are dim with grief.

I call to you, O LORD, every day;
   I spread out my hands to you.
¹⁰ Do you show your wonders to the dead?
   Do those who are dead rise up and praise you?
                                        Selah

¹¹ Is your love declared in the grave,
   your faithfulness in Destruction*a*?
¹² Are your wonders known in the place of
      darkness,
   or your righteous deeds in the land of oblivion?

¹³ But I cry to you for help, O LORD;
   in the morning my prayer comes before you.
¹⁴ Why, O LORD, do you reject me
   and hide your face from me?

¹⁵ From my youth I have been afflicted and close to
      death;
   I have suffered your terrors and am in despair.
¹⁶ Your wrath has swept over me;
   your terrors have destroyed me.
¹⁷ All day long they surround me like a flood;
   they have completely engulfed me.
¹⁸ You have taken my companions and loved ones
      from me;
   the darkness is my closest friend.

Psalm 89

A maskilᵇ of Ethan the Ezrahite.

¹ I will sing of the LORD's great love forever;
   with my mouth I will make your faithfulness
      known through all generations.
² I will declare that your love stands firm forever,
   that you established your faithfulness in heaven
      itself.

³ You said, "I have made a covenant with my
      chosen one,
   I have sworn to David my servant,
⁴ 'I will establish your line forever
   and make your throne firm through all
      generations.' "   *Selah*

⁵ The heavens praise your wonders, O LORD,

a 11 Hebrew *Abaddon*   *b* Title: Probably a literary or musical term

your faithfulness too, in the assembly of the
holy ones.
⁶ For who in the skies above can compare with the
Lord?
Who is like the Lord among the heavenly
beings?
⁷ In the council of the holy ones God is greatly
feared;
he is more awesome than all who surround
him.
⁸ O Lord God Almighty, who is like you?
You are mighty, O Lord, and your faithfulness
surrounds you.

⁹ You rule over the surging sea;
when its waves mount up, you still them.
¹⁰ You crushed Rahab like one of the slain;
with your strong arm you scattered your
enemies.
¹¹ The heavens are yours, and yours also the earth;
you founded the world and all that is in it.
¹² You created the north and the south;
Tabor and Hermon sing for joy at your name.
¹³ Your arm is endued with power;
your hand is strong, your right hand exalted.

¹⁴ Righteousness and justice are the foundation of
your throne;
love and faithfulness go before you.
¹⁵ Blessed are those who have learned to acclaim
you,
who walk in the light of your presence, O Lord.
¹⁶ They rejoice in your name all day long;
they exult in your righteousness.
¹⁷ For you are their glory and strength,
and by your favor you exalt our horn.ᵃ
¹⁸ Indeed, our shieldᵇ belongs to the Lord,
our king to the Holy One of Israel.

¹⁹ Once you spoke in a vision,
to your faithful people you said:
"I have bestowed strength on a warrior;
I have exalted a young man from among the
people.
²⁰ I have found David my servant;
with my sacred oil I have anointed him.
²¹ My hand will sustain him;
surely my arm will strengthen him.
²² No enemy will subject him to tribute;
no wicked man will oppress him.
²³ I will crush his foes before him
and strike down his adversaries.
²⁴ My faithful love will be with him,
and through my name his hornᶜ will be exalted.
²⁵ I will set his hand over the sea,
his right hand over the rivers.
²⁶ He will call out to me, 'You are my Father,
my God, the Rock my Savior.'

Incomparable

PSALM 89:6–8

Isaiah had a heavenly vision in which he saw angels calling to one another, "Holy, holy, holy is the Lord Almighty" (Isaiah 6:3). Awe is our natural response to the majesty and holiness of God; worship is the natural expression we use to extol God's immanence, his indwelling presence in the world. Although God oversees galaxy upon galaxy in a vast, intricate universe, he faithfully offers mercy and love to us small, and often wayward, human beings. Reflect on your expression of awe toward God. What is a favorite hymn that expresses it? Recite the words or sing it on the way to work this week.

See Meeting God in Worship

ᵃ *17 Horn* here symbolizes strong one. ᵇ *18 Or sovereign* ᶜ *24 Horn* here
symbolizes strength.

God's Steadfast Love

PSALM 89:33

"Maybe we still do not fully believe that God's Spirit is, indeed, the Spirit of love, always leading us deeper into love. Maybe we still distrust the Spirit, afraid to be led to places where our freedom is taken away. Maybe we still think of God's Spirit as an enemy who wants something of us that is not good for us. But God is love, only love, and God's Spirit is the Spirit of love longing to guide us to the place where the deepest desires of our heart can be fulfilled."

—HENRI J.M. NOUWEN,
Here and Now

²⁷ I will also appoint him my firstborn,
    the most exalted of the kings of the earth.
²⁸ I will maintain my love to him forever,
    and my covenant with him will never fail.
²⁹ I will establish his line forever,
    his throne as long as the heavens endure.

³⁰ "If his sons forsake my law
    and do not follow my statutes,
³¹ if they violate my decrees
    and fail to keep my commands,
³² I will punish their sin with the rod,
    their iniquity with flogging;
³³ but I will not take my love from him,
    nor will I ever betray my faithfulness.
³⁴ I will not violate my covenant
    or alter what my lips have uttered.
³⁵ Once for all, I have sworn by my holiness—
    and I will not lie to David—
³⁶ that his line will continue forever
    and his throne endure before me like the sun;
³⁷ it will be established forever like the moon,
    the faithful witness in the sky."   *Selah*

³⁸ But you have rejected, you have spurned,
    you have been very angry with your anointed
    one.
³⁹ You have renounced the covenant with your
    servant
    and have defiled his crown in the dust.
⁴⁰ You have broken through all his walls
    and reduced his strongholds to ruins.
⁴¹ All who pass by have plundered him;
    he has become the scorn of his neighbors.
⁴² You have exalted the right hand of his foes;
    you have made all his enemies rejoice.
⁴³ You have turned back the edge of his sword
    and have not supported him in battle.
⁴⁴ You have put an end to his splendor
    and cast his throne to the ground.
⁴⁵ You have cut short the days of his youth;
    you have covered him with a mantle of shame.
       Selah

⁴⁶ How long, O LORD? Will you hide yourself forever?
    How long will your wrath burn like fire?
⁴⁷ Remember how fleeting is my life.
    For what futility you have created all men!
⁴⁸ What man can live and not see death,
    or save himself from the power of the grave*ᵃ*?
       Selah

⁴⁹ O Lord, where is your former great love,
    which in your faithfulness you swore to David?
⁵⁰ Remember, Lord, how your servant has*ᵇ* been
    mocked,
    how I bear in my heart the taunts of all the
    nations,
⁵¹ the taunts with which your enemies have
    mocked, O LORD,

with which they have mocked every step of
   your anointed one.

⁵²Praise be to the LORD forever!
   Amen and Amen.

BOOK IV

Psalms 90–106

Psalm 90

A prayer of Moses the man of God.

¹Lord, you have been our dwelling place
   throughout all generations.
²Before the mountains were born
   or you brought forth the earth and the world,
   from everlasting to everlasting you are God.

³You turn men back to dust,
   saying, "Return to dust, O sons of men."
⁴For a thousand years in your sight
   are like a day that has just gone by,
   or like a watch in the night.
⁵You sweep men away in the sleep of death;
   they are like the new grass of the morning—
⁶though in the morning it springs up new,
   by evening it is dry and withered.

⁷We are consumed by your anger
   and terrified by your indignation.
⁸You have set our iniquities before you,
   our secret sins in the light of your presence.
⁹All our days pass away under your wrath;
   we finish our years with a moan.
¹⁰The length of our days is seventy years—
   or eighty, if we have the strength;
   yet their span*ᵃ* is but trouble and sorrow,
   for they quickly pass, and we fly away.

¹¹Who knows the power of your anger?
   For your wrath is as great as the fear that is due
      you.
¹²Teach us to number our days aright,
   that we may gain a heart of wisdom.

¹³Relent, O LORD! How long will it be?
   Have compassion on your servants.
¹⁴Satisfy us in the morning with your unfailing love,
   that we may sing for joy and be glad all our
      days.
¹⁵Make us glad for as many days as you have
      afflicted us,
   for as many years as we have seen trouble.
¹⁶May your deeds be shown to your servants,
   your splendor to their children.

¹⁷May the favor*ᵇ* of the Lord our God rest upon us;
   establish the work of our hands for us—
   yes, establish the work of our hands.

In God's Time

PSALM 90:1–4

The eternal nature of God is
hard for us to grasp because we
measure our lives in terms of
past and present. Yet God, who
has an infinite understanding of
the future, suggests to our
hearts a vision we cannot begin
to fathom. We try to control
our lives, but God invites us to
open our hearts to what spiritual writer Thomas Kelly calls the
"Eternal Now," God's eternal
plan in each and every second.
What aspects of your life are
you trying to control? In what
areas do you need to "let go
and let God"? Offer these areas
in a brief prayer of surrender
throughout the day.

See Meeting God in Everyday Life

ᵃ 10 Or *yet the best of them*   *ᵇ 17* Or *beauty*

God's Shelter

PSALM 91:1–4

Fear abounds in us. Rightly, we are concerned about the rise of violence, about the dim prospect for peace in many areas of the world and about the world our grandchildren will inherit. The psalmist feels danger too, but he controls his fear by calling to mind these powerful and comforting images of God. With the psalmist, imagine this experience of protection. As your enemies pursue you, you are swept up in the warm, strong, soft wings and borne up, up, away from your enemies and into a high shelter of safety. You relax and lie down, knowing that you are resting near the heart of the Almighty God. Pray with a sense of God's love surrounding you.

Psalm 91

¹ He who dwells in the shelter of the Most High
   will rest in the shadow of the Almighty.ᵃ
² I will sayᵇ of the Lᴏʀᴅ, "He is my refuge and my fortress,
   my God, in whom I trust."

³ Surely he will save you from the fowler's snare
   and from the deadly pestilence.
⁴ He will cover you with his feathers,
   and under his wings you will find refuge;
   his faithfulness will be your shield and rampart.
⁵ You will not fear the terror of night,
   nor the arrow that flies by day,
⁶ nor the pestilence that stalks in the darkness,
   nor the plague that destroys at midday.
⁷ A thousand may fall at your side,
   ten thousand at your right hand,
   but it will not come near you.
⁸ You will only observe with your eyes
   and see the punishment of the wicked.

⁹ If you make the Most High your dwelling—
   even the Lᴏʀᴅ, who is my refuge—
¹⁰ then no harm will befall you,
   no disaster will come near your tent.
¹¹ For he will command his angels concerning you
   to guard you in all your ways;
¹² they will lift you up in their hands,
   so that you will not strike your foot against a stone.
¹³ You will tread upon the lion and the cobra;
   you will trample the great lion and the serpent.

¹⁴ "Because he loves me," says the Lᴏʀᴅ, "I will rescue him;
   I will protect him, for he acknowledges my name.
¹⁵ He will call upon me, and I will answer him;
   I will be with him in trouble,
   I will deliver him and honor him.
¹⁶ With long life will I satisfy him
   and show him my salvation."

Psalm 92

A psalm. A song. For the Sabbath day.

¹ It is good to praise the Lᴏʀᴅ
   and make music to your name, O Most High,
² to proclaim your love in the morning
   and your faithfulness at night,
³ to the music of the ten-stringed lyre
   and the melody of the harp.

⁴ For you make me glad by your deeds, O Lᴏʀᴅ;
   I sing for joy at the works of your hands.
⁵ How great are your works, O Lᴏʀᴅ,
   how profound your thoughts!
⁶ The senseless man does not know,

ᵃ 1 Hebrew *Shaddai*   ᵇ 2 Or *He says*

fools do not understand,
⁷that though the wicked spring up like grass
and all evildoers flourish,
they will be forever destroyed.

⁸But you, O LORD, are exalted forever.

⁹For surely your enemies, O LORD,
surely your enemies will perish;
all evildoers will be scattered.
¹⁰You have exalted my horn[a] like that of a wild ox;
fine oils have been poured upon me.
¹¹My eyes have seen the defeat of my adversaries;
my ears have heard the rout of my wicked foes.

¹²The righteous will flourish like a palm tree,
they will grow like a cedar of Lebanon;
¹³planted in the house of the LORD,
they will flourish in the courts of our God.
¹⁴They will still bear fruit in old age,
they will stay fresh and green,
¹⁵proclaiming, "The LORD is upright;
he is my Rock, and there is no wickedness in
him."

Psalm 93

¹The LORD reigns, he is robed in majesty;
the LORD is robed in majesty
and is armed with strength.
The world is firmly established;
it cannot be moved.
²Your throne was established long ago;
you are from all eternity.

³The seas have lifted up, O LORD,
the seas have lifted up their voice;
the seas have lifted up their pounding waves.
⁴Mightier than the thunder of the great waters,
mightier than the breakers of the sea—
the LORD on high is mighty.

⁵Your statutes stand firm;
holiness adorns your house
for endless days, O LORD.

Psalm 94

¹O LORD, the God who avenges,
O God who avenges, shine forth.
²Rise up, O Judge of the earth;
pay back to the proud what they deserve.
³How long will the wicked, O LORD,
how long will the wicked be jubilant?

⁴They pour out arrogant words;
all the evildoers are full of boasting.
⁵They crush your people, O LORD;
they oppress your inheritance.
⁶They slay the widow and the alien;
they murder the fatherless.

Longevity in the Spirit

PSALM 92:12-15

The palm tree and the cedars of Lebanon are symbols of longevity. As the psalmist proclaims, those who are rooted in God's ways flourish into old age; "they will stay fresh and green." We live in a culture obsessed with looking young, but this "green" about which the psalmist writes is not external. It is a vibrancy cultivated through a life of prayer, devotion and worship. Think of people you know who continue to "bloom" in old age. What signs do you see of their spiritual lives? How have they handled the loss of physical youth? What habits of the heart do they encourage in you?

See *Meeting God in Community*

---

[a] *10 Horn* here symbolizes strength.

Remembering

PSALM 94:17–19

We may easily remember the negative experiences of our lives; and rightly, we should be honest with God about those past hurts. But how good are we at remembering our experiences of grace and life-giving joy? Praise is a spiritual discipline, a choice of the heart. Like the psalmist, we can *choose* to remember God's grace. Take ten minutes to pause and consider God's gifts in your life. When have you experienced God in unexpected places? How have people in your life shown you love? What natural beauty have you enjoyed? What opportunities or lessons have come out of your struggles? You might write your responses in your journal or compose a collage of pictures and symbols of God's gifts.

See *Meeting God in Everyday Life*

7 They say, "The LORD does not see;
  the God of Jacob pays no heed."
8 Take heed, you senseless ones among the people;
  you fools, when will you become wise?
9 Does he who implanted the ear not hear?
  Does he who formed the eye not see?
10 Does he who disciplines nations not punish?
  Does he who teaches man lack knowledge?
11 The LORD knows the thoughts of man;
  he knows that they are futile.

12 Blessed is the man you discipline, O LORD,
  the man you teach from your law;
13 you grant him relief from days of trouble,
  till a pit is dug for the wicked.
14 For the LORD will not reject his people;
  he will never forsake his inheritance.
15 Judgment will again be founded on righteousness,
  and all the upright in heart will follow it.

16 Who will rise up for me against the wicked?
  Who will take a stand for me against evildoers?
17 Unless the LORD had given me help,
  I would soon have dwelt in the silence of death.
18 When I said, "My foot is slipping,"
  your love, O LORD, supported me.
19 When anxiety was great within me,
  your consolation brought joy to my soul.

20 Can a corrupt throne be allied with you—
  one that brings on misery by its decrees?
21 They band together against the righteous
  and condemn the innocent to death.
22 But the LORD has become my fortress,
  and my God the rock in whom I take refuge.
23 He will repay them for their sins
  and destroy them for their wickedness;
  the LORD our God will destroy them.

Psalm 95

1 Come, let us sing for joy to the LORD;
  let us shout aloud to the Rock of our salvation.
2 Let us come before him with thanksgiving
  and extol him with music and song.

3 For the LORD is the great God,
  the great King above all gods.
4 In his hand are the depths of the earth,
  and the mountain peaks belong to him.
5 The sea is his, for he made it,
  and his hands formed the dry land.

6 Come, let us bow down in worship,
  let us kneel before the LORD our Maker;
7 for he is our God
  and we are the people of his pasture,
  the flock under his care.

Today, if you hear his voice,

⁸ do not harden your hearts as you did at
  Meribah,ᵃ
  as you did that day at Massahᵇ in the desert,
⁹ where your fathers tested and tried me,
  though they had seen what I did.
¹⁰ For forty years I was angry with that generation;
  I said, "They are a people whose hearts go
  astray,
  and they have not known my ways."
¹¹ So I declared on oath in my anger,
  "They shall never enter my rest."

Psalm 96

¹ Sing to the LORD a new song;
  sing to the LORD, all the earth.
² Sing to the LORD, praise his name;
  proclaim his salvation day after day.
³ Declare his glory among the nations,
  his marvelous deeds among all peoples.

⁴ For great is the LORD and most worthy of praise;
  he is to be feared above all gods.
⁵ For all the gods of the nations are idols,
  but the LORD made the heavens.
⁶ Splendor and majesty are before him;
  strength and glory are in his sanctuary.

⁷ Ascribe to the LORD, O families of nations,
  ascribe to the LORD glory and strength.
⁸ Ascribe to the LORD the glory due his name;
  bring an offering and come into his courts.
⁹ Worship the LORD in the splendor of hisᶜ holiness;
  tremble before him, all the earth.

¹⁰ Say among the nations, "The LORD reigns."
  The world is firmly established, it cannot be
  moved;
  he will judge the peoples with equity.
¹¹ Let the heavens rejoice, let the earth be glad;
  let the sea resound, and all that is in it;
¹² let the fields be jubilant, and everything in
  them.
  Then all the trees of the forest will sing for joy;
¹³ they will sing before the LORD, for he comes,
  he comes to judge the earth.
  He will judge the world in righteousness
  and the peoples in his truth.

Psalm 97

¹ The LORD reigns, let the earth be glad;
  let the distant shores rejoice.

² Clouds and thick darkness surround him;
  righteousness and justice are the foundation of
  his throne.
³ Fire goes before him
  and consumes his foes on every side.

Hearing or Hardening?

PSALM 95:7–8

The Biblical metaphor of "hardening one's heart" aptly describes the gradual process that takes place in a relationship when we stop listening, turn away or become self-absorbed. This may happen in our relationship with God, as it did for the Hebrew people. Quakers use the word *tender* to describe the opposite spiritual process of becoming more sensitive to God's voice. How do you keep your heart tender before God? Find an object from nature, perhaps a stone or a feather, that you can put on your desk or nightstand as a reminder to remain open to God.

ᵃ 8 Meribah means *quarreling*. ᵇ 8 Massah means *testing*. ᶜ 9 Or LORD
with the splendor of

Joy Throughout the Earth

PSALM 98:4–9

Praise is not limited to human creatures. While the psalmist utters praise with his mouth, the earth raises a "shout for joy" in countless ways. God enjoys the brilliant color of a wildflower in the middle of a deserted field, a young lion running in tall grass and an ocean with its panoply of life. Our praise is not isolated from the rest of creation's. Make an appointment with nature to sit in awe or take a walk, joining your thanks to the praise of God throughout the earth.

See Meeting God in the Created Order

⁴His lightning lights up the world;
   the earth sees and trembles.
⁵The mountains melt like wax before the Lord,
   before the Lord of all the earth.
⁶The heavens proclaim his righteousness,
   and all the peoples see his glory.

⁷All who worship images are put to shame,
   those who boast in idols—
   worship him, all you gods!

⁸Zion hears and rejoices
   and the villages of Judah are glad
   because of your judgments, O Lord.
⁹For you, O Lord, are the Most High over all the
      earth;
   you are exalted far above all gods.

¹⁰Let those who love the Lord hate evil,
   for he guards the lives of his faithful ones
   and delivers them from the hand of the wicked.
¹¹Light is shed upon the righteous
   and joy on the upright in heart.
¹²Rejoice in the Lord, you who are righteous,
   and praise his holy name.

Psalm 98

A psalm.

¹Sing to the Lord a new song,
   for he has done marvelous things;
his right hand and his holy arm
   have worked salvation for him.
²The Lord has made his salvation known
   and revealed his righteousness to the nations.
³He has remembered his love
   and his faithfulness to the house of Israel;
all the ends of the earth have seen
   the salvation of our God.

⁴Shout for joy to the Lord, all the earth,
   burst into jubilant song with music;
⁵make music to the Lord with the harp,
   with the harp and the sound of singing,
⁶with trumpets and the blast of the ram's horn—
   shout for joy before the Lord, the King.

⁷Let the sea resound, and everything in it,
   the world, and all who live in it.
⁸Let the rivers clap their hands,
   let the mountains sing together for joy;
⁹let them sing before the Lord,
   for he comes to judge the earth.
He will judge the world in righteousness
   and the peoples with equity.

Psalm 99

¹The Lord reigns,
   let the nations tremble;
he sits enthroned between the cherubim,

let the earth shake.
2 Great is the LORD in Zion;
   he is exalted over all the nations.
3 Let them praise your great and awesome name—
   he is holy.

4 The King is mighty, he loves justice—
   you have established equity;
 in Jacob you have done
   what is just and right.
5 Exalt the LORD our God
   and worship at his footstool;
   he is holy.

6 Moses and Aaron were among his priests,
   Samuel was among those who called on his
      name;
 they called on the LORD
   and he answered them.
7 He spoke to them from the pillar of cloud;
   they kept his statutes and the decrees he gave
      them.

8 O LORD our God,
   you answered them;
 you were to Israel*a* a forgiving God,
   though you punished their misdeeds.*b*
9 Exalt the LORD our God
   and worship at his holy mountain,
   for the LORD our God is holy.

Psalm 100

A psalm. For giving thanks.

1 Shout for joy to the LORD, all the earth.
2   Worship the LORD with gladness;
   come before him with joyful songs.
3 Know that the LORD is God.
   It is he who made us, and we are his*c*;
   we are his people, the sheep of his pasture.

4 Enter his gates with thanksgiving
   and his courts with praise;
   give thanks to him and praise his name.
5 For the LORD is good and his love endures forever;
   his faithfulness continues through all
      generations.

Psalm 101

Of David. A psalm.

1 I will sing of your love and justice;
   to you, O LORD, I will sing praise.
2 I will be careful to lead a blameless life—
   when will you come to me?

 I will walk in my house
   with blameless heart.

Belonging to God

PSALM 100:3

We belong to God. It is a profound truth, yet one that we easily forget. The image of God as an attentive shepherd abounds in Scripture. Belonging to this loving Shepherd, we are watched and cared for with infinite tenderness. What reminds you that you belong to God? What images, songs or Bible verses remind you of God's constancy and care? How might you live today in that reality? Consider how beloved you are in God's eyes.

See *Meeting God in Scripture*

---

a 8 Hebrew *them*   *b* 8 Or *I an avenger of the wrongs done to them*   *c* 3 Or
and not we ourselves

³ I will set before my eyes
    no vile thing.

The deeds of faithless men I hate;
    they will not cling to me.
⁴ Men of perverse heart shall be far from me;
    I will have nothing to do with evil.

⁵ Whoever slanders his neighbor in secret,
    him will I put to silence;
whoever has haughty eyes and a proud heart,
    him will I not endure.

⁶ My eyes will be on the faithful in the land,
    that they may dwell with me;
he whose walk is blameless
    will minister to me.

⁷ No one who practices deceit
    will dwell in my house;
no one who speaks falsely
    will stand in my presence.

⁸ Every morning I will put to silence
    all the wicked in the land;
I will cut off every evildoer
    from the city of the LORD.

Psalm 102

*A prayer of an afflicted man. When he is faint and pours
out his lament before the LORD.*

¹ Hear my prayer, O LORD;
    let my cry for help come to you.
² Do not hide your face from me
    when I am in distress.
Turn your ear to me;
    when I call, answer me quickly.

³ For my days vanish like smoke;
    my bones burn like glowing embers.
⁴ My heart is blighted and withered like grass;
    I forget to eat my food.
⁵ Because of my loud groaning
    I am reduced to skin and bones.
⁶ I am like a desert owl,
    like an owl among the ruins.
⁷ I lie awake; I have become
    like a bird alone on a roof.
⁸ All day long my enemies taunt me;
    those who rail against me use my name as a
        curse.
⁹ For I eat ashes as my food
    and mingle my drink with tears
¹⁰ because of your great wrath,
    for you have taken me up and thrown me
        aside.
¹¹ My days are like the evening shadow;
    I wither away like grass.

¹² But you, O LORD, sit enthroned forever;
    your renown endures through all generations.

Facing Despair

PSALM 102:1–7

The psalmist's words poignantly illustrate the ache of the human heart in its pain and grief. Persons facing a life-threatening illness know what it is like to be too depleted to eat. Those who know the loss of a loved one have felt like the "owl among the ruins"—lying awake at night, tossing and turning.

God is intimately aware of our deepest heartaches. When have you felt such hopelessness? How was God with you in that despair? Is someone in your life facing this kind of pain? How might you enable that person to feel God's nearness—sitting with him or her, offering an intercessory prayer, writing a note?

See Meeting God in Service

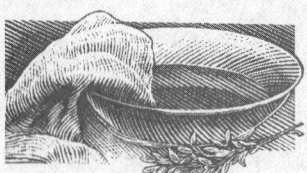

¹³ You will arise and have compassion on Zion,
  for it is time to show favor to her;
  the appointed time has come.
¹⁴ For her stones are dear to your servants;
  her very dust moves them to pity.
¹⁵ The nations will fear the name of the LORD,
  all the kings of the earth will revere your glory.
¹⁶ For the LORD will rebuild Zion
  and appear in his glory.
¹⁷ He will respond to the prayer of the destitute;
  he will not despise their plea.

¹⁸ Let this be written for a future generation,
  that a people not yet created may praise the
    LORD:
¹⁹ "The LORD looked down from his sanctuary on
    high,
  from heaven he viewed the earth,
²⁰ to hear the groans of the prisoners
  and release those condemned to death."
²¹ So the name of the LORD will be declared in Zion
  and his praise in Jerusalem
²² when the peoples and the kingdoms
  assemble to worship the LORD.

²³ In the course of my life[a] he broke my strength;
  he cut short my days.
²⁴ So I said:
  "Do not take me away, O my God, in the midst
      of my days;
  your years go on through all generations.
²⁵ In the beginning you laid the foundations of the
      earth,
  and the heavens are the work of your hands.
²⁶ They will perish, but you remain;
  they will all wear out like a garment.
  Like clothing you will change them
  and they will be discarded.
²⁷ But you remain the same,
  and your years will never end.
²⁸ The children of your servants will live in your
      presence;
  their descendants will be established before
      you."

Psalm 103

Of David.

¹ Praise the LORD, O my soul;
  all my inmost being, praise his holy name.
² Praise the LORD, O my soul,
  and forget not all his benefits—
³ who forgives all your sins
  and heals all your diseases,
⁴ who redeems your life from the pit
  and crowns you with love and compassion,
⁵ who satisfies your desires with good things
  so that your youth is renewed like the eagle's.

Praise the Lord, O My Soul

PSALM 103:1–5

What does it mean to praise the Lord with "all my inmost being"? It means that with our whole hearts, we celebrate God's goodness and rejoice in his steadfast love and mercy. Read the passage slowly, and as you come across a word or phrase that strikes you, pause there. Close your eyes and say the word or phrase to yourself. What associations do you make with these words? What touches you? What do you sense God inviting you to consider in response?

See Meeting God in Scripture

God's Compassion

PSALM 103:11–13

We cannot imagine the immensity of God's love for us. It is as high as the endless sky and as tender as a father's compassion for his children. Evelyn Underhill writes, "When we look out towards this Love that moves the stars and stirs in the child's heart . . . we see our human situation from a fresh angle; and [we] perceive that it is both more humble and dependent, and more splendid, than we had dreamed." What fresh perspective does God's extraordinary love stir in you? On a small piece of paper, write your response to this question. Tape it in the front of your Bible, and read it frequently throughout the next month.

6 The LORD works righteousness
   and justice for all the oppressed.

7 He made known his ways to Moses,
   his deeds to the people of Israel:
8 The LORD is compassionate and gracious,
   slow to anger, abounding in love.
9 He will not always accuse,
   nor will he harbor his anger forever;
10 he does not treat us as our sins deserve
   or repay us according to our iniquities.
11 For as high as the heavens are above the earth,
   so great is his love for those who fear him;
12 as far as the east is from the west,
   so far has he removed our transgressions from
   us.
13 As a father has compassion on his children,
   so the LORD has compassion on those who fear
   him;
14 for he knows how we are formed,
   he remembers that we are dust.
15 As for man, his days are like grass,
   he flourishes like a flower of the field;
16 the wind blows over it and it is gone,
   and its place remembers it no more.
17 But from everlasting to everlasting
   the LORD's love is with those who fear him,
   and his righteousness with their children's
   children—
18 with those who keep his covenant
   and remember to obey his precepts.

19 The LORD has established his throne in heaven,
   and his kingdom rules over all.

20 Praise the LORD, you his angels,
   you mighty ones who do his bidding,
   who obey his word.
21 Praise the LORD, all his heavenly hosts,
   you his servants who do his will.
22 Praise the LORD, all his works
   everywhere in his dominion.

   Praise the LORD, O my soul.

Psalm 104

1 Praise the LORD, O my soul.

   O LORD my God, you are very great;
   you are clothed with splendor and majesty.
2 He wraps himself in light as with a garment;
   he stretches out the heavens like a tent
3   and lays the beams of his upper chambers on
      their waters.
   He makes the clouds his chariot
   and rides on the wings of the wind.
4 He makes winds his messengers,[a]
   flames of fire his servants.

a 4 Or angels

⁵He set the earth on its foundations;
 it can never be moved.
⁶You covered it with the deep as with a garment;
 the waters stood above the mountains.
⁷But at your rebuke the waters fled,
 at the sound of your thunder they took to flight;
⁸they flowed over the mountains,
 they went down into the valleys,
 to the place you assigned for them.
⁹You set a boundary they cannot cross;
 never again will they cover the earth.

¹⁰He makes springs pour water into the ravines;
 it flows between the mountains.
¹¹They give water to all the beasts of the field;
 the wild donkeys quench their thirst.
¹²The birds of the air nest by the waters;
 they sing among the branches.
¹³He waters the mountains from his upper
   chambers;
 the earth is satisfied by the fruit of his work.
¹⁴He makes grass grow for the cattle,
 and plants for man to cultivate—
 bringing forth food from the earth:
¹⁵wine that gladdens the heart of man,
 oil to make his face shine,
 and bread that sustains his heart.
¹⁶The trees of the LORD are well watered,
 the cedars of Lebanon that he planted.
¹⁷There the birds make their nests;
 the stork has its home in the pine trees.
¹⁸The high mountains belong to the wild goats;
 the crags are a refuge for the coneys.ᵃ

¹⁹The moon marks off the seasons,
 and the sun knows when to go down.
²⁰You bring darkness, it becomes night,
 and all the beasts of the forest prowl.
²¹The lions roar for their prey
 and seek their food from God.
²²The sun rises, and they steal away;
 they return and lie down in their dens.
²³Then man goes out to his work,
 to his labor until evening.

²⁴How many are your works, O LORD!
 In wisdom you made them all;
 the earth is full of your creatures.
²⁵There is the sea, vast and spacious,
 teeming with creatures beyond number—
 living things both large and small.
²⁶There the ships go to and fro,
 and the leviathan, which you formed to frolic
   there.

²⁷These all look to you
 to give them their food at the proper time.
²⁸When you give it to them,
 they gather it up;

Wisdom in the Created Order

PSALM 104:24

Psalm 104 is a celebration of God as the Creator. The psalmist praises God's marvelous, ingenious ordering. Everything—from the sun that gives us light to the grass the cattle feed on—is intricately connected. Scientific knowledge only enhances the wonder of God's wisdom in this design. In your neighborhood, contemplate God's wisdom in creation. What birds frequent your backyard? What trees line your street? If you see a lot of concrete and not much green, where might you go to enjoy God's creation? Praise God *in specifics* this day for the divine wisdom displayed in creation.

See Meeting God in the Created Order

ᵃ *18* That is, the hyrax or rock badger

Seeking God Always

PSALM 105:4

"Love knows no measure, but is fervent without measure . . . He who is thus a spiritual lover knows well what that voice means which says: 'You, Lord God, are my whole love and my desire. You are all mine, and I all Yours. Dissolve my heart into Your love so that I may know how sweet it is to serve You and how joyful it is to praise You.' "

—THOMAS À KEMPIS,
The Imitation of Christ

when you open your hand,
    they are satisfied with good things.
²⁹ When you hide your face,
    they are terrified;
when you take away their breath,
    they die and return to the dust.
³⁰ When you send your Spirit,
    they are created,
    and you renew the face of the earth.

³¹ May the glory of the LORD endure forever;
    may the LORD rejoice in his works—
³² he who looks at the earth, and it trembles,
    who touches the mountains, and they smoke.

³³ I will sing to the LORD all my life;
    I will sing praise to my God as long as I live.
³⁴ May my meditation be pleasing to him,
    as I rejoice in the LORD.
³⁵ But may sinners vanish from the earth
    and the wicked be no more.

Praise the LORD, O my soul.

Praise the LORD.ᵃ

Psalm 105

¹ Give thanks to the LORD, call on his name;
    make known among the nations what he has
      done.
² Sing to him, sing praise to him;
    tell of all his wonderful acts.
³ Glory in his holy name;
    let the hearts of those who seek the LORD
      rejoice.
⁴ Look to the LORD and his strength;
    seek his face always.

⁵ Remember the wonders he has done,
    his miracles, and the judgments he
      pronounced,
⁶ O descendants of Abraham his servant,
    O sons of Jacob, his chosen ones.
⁷ He is the LORD our God;
    his judgments are in all the earth.

⁸ He remembers his covenant forever,
    the word he commanded, for a thousand
      generations,
⁹ the covenant he made with Abraham,
    the oath he swore to Isaac.
¹⁰ He confirmed it to Jacob as a decree,
    to Israel as an everlasting covenant:
¹¹ "To you I will give the land of Canaan
    as the portion you will inherit."

¹² When they were but few in number,
    few indeed, and strangers in it,
¹³ they wandered from nation to nation,

ᵃ 35 Hebrew *Hallelu Yah*; in the Septuagint this line stands at the beginning of Psalm 105.

from one kingdom to another.
¹⁴ He allowed no one to oppress them;
   for their sake he rebuked kings:
¹⁵ "Do not touch my anointed ones;
   do my prophets no harm."

¹⁶ He called down famine on the land
   and destroyed all their supplies of food;
¹⁷ and he sent a man before them—
   Joseph, sold as a slave.
¹⁸ They bruised his feet with shackles,
   his neck was put in irons,
¹⁹ till what he foretold came to pass,
   till the word of the LORD proved him true.
²⁰ The king sent and released him,
   the ruler of peoples set him free.
²¹ He made him master of his household,
   ruler over all he possessed,
²² to instruct his princes as he pleased
   and teach his elders wisdom.

²³ Then Israel entered Egypt;
   Jacob lived as an alien in the land of Ham.
²⁴ The LORD made his people very fruitful;
   he made them too numerous for their foes,
²⁵ whose hearts he turned to hate his people,
   to conspire against his servants.
²⁶ He sent Moses his servant,
   and Aaron, whom he had chosen.
²⁷ They performed his miraculous signs among
      them,
   his wonders in the land of Ham.
²⁸ He sent darkness and made the land dark—
   for had they not rebelled against his words?
²⁹ He turned their waters into blood,
   causing their fish to die.
³⁰ Their land teemed with frogs,
   which went up into the bedrooms of their
      rulers.
³¹ He spoke, and there came swarms of flies,
   and gnats throughout their country.
³² He turned their rain into hail,
   with lightning throughout their land;
³³ he struck down their vines and fig trees
   and shattered the trees of their country.
³⁴ He spoke, and the locusts came,
   grasshoppers without number;
³⁵ they ate up every green thing in their land,
   ate up the produce of their soil.
³⁶ Then he struck down all the firstborn in their
      land,
   the firstfruits of all their manhood.

³⁷ He brought out Israel, laden with silver and gold,
   and from among their tribes no one faltered.
³⁸ Egypt was glad when they left,
   because dread of Israel had fallen on them.
³⁹ He spread out a cloud as a covering,
   and a fire to give light at night.
⁴⁰ They asked, and he brought them quail
   and satisfied them with the bread of heaven.

Exodus Faith

PSALM 105:37–41

The psalmist recalls the miraculous exodus and how God led the Hebrew people out of Egypt. Their ordeal, a long walk through the rugged desert, required trust in God's grace. Often our lives require God's grace too. We cannot know ahead of time how God will lead us. We cannot imagine the grace-bearing manna that God will provide. What is your exodus story? How has God delivered you? Where is God making a way for you in "the desert"? With a spiritual mentor or close friend, or in your journal, reflect on your journey of exodus.

See Meeting God in Everyday Life

Facing Our Sin

PSALM 106:6–7

In Psalm 105, we remembered the Hebrews' joy in the exodus, but here we face the darkness of human sin in the same story. How often we are like the Hebrew people! Amidst the joy of our new salvation, or on the heels of intimate communion with God, we turn away from God's voice. We coldly ignore a coworker, we yell at our children or we don't bring our whole hearts to the devotional life. What does obedience to God mean to you? Do you detect coldness within yourself toward God or others? With a trusted mentor or friend, examine your heart thoughtfully.

See Meeting God in Prayer

---

⁴¹ He opened the rock, and water gushed out;
  like a river it flowed in the desert.
⁴² For he remembered his holy promise
  given to his servant Abraham.
⁴³ He brought out his people with rejoicing,
  his chosen ones with shouts of joy;
⁴⁴ he gave them the lands of the nations,
  and they fell heir to what others had toiled
    for—
⁴⁵ that they might keep his precepts
  and observe his laws.

Praise the LORD. [a]

Psalm 106

¹ Praise the LORD. [b]

Give thanks to the LORD, for he is good;
  his love endures forever.
² Who can proclaim the mighty acts of the LORD
  or fully declare his praise?
³ Blessed are they who maintain justice,
  who constantly do what is right.
⁴ Remember me, O LORD, when you show favor to
    your people,
  come to my aid when you save them,
⁵ that I may enjoy the prosperity of your chosen
    ones,
  that I may share in the joy of your nation
  and join your inheritance in giving praise.

⁶ We have sinned, even as our fathers did;
  we have done wrong and acted wickedly.
⁷ When our fathers were in Egypt,
  they gave no thought to your miracles;
  they did not remember your many kindnesses,
  and they rebelled by the sea, the Red Sea. [c]
⁸ Yet he saved them for his name's sake,
  to make his mighty power known.
⁹ He rebuked the Red Sea, and it dried up;
  he led them through the depths as through a
    desert.
¹⁰ He saved them from the hand of the foe;
  from the hand of the enemy he redeemed
    them.
¹¹ The waters covered their adversaries;
  not one of them survived.
¹² Then they believed his promises
  and sang his praise.

¹³ But they soon forgot what he had done
  and did not wait for his counsel.
¹⁴ In the desert they gave in to their craving;
  in the wasteland they put God to the test.
¹⁵ So he gave them what they asked for,
  but sent a wasting disease upon them.

¹⁶ In the camp they grew envious of Moses

---

a 45 Hebrew *Hallelu Yah*   b 1 Hebrew *Hallelu Yah*; also in verse 48
c 7 Hebrew *Yam Suph*; that is, Sea of Reeds; also in verses 9 and 22

and of Aaron, who was consecrated to the
LORD.
[17] The earth opened up and swallowed Dathan;
it buried the company of Abiram.
[18] Fire blazed among their followers;
a flame consumed the wicked.

[19] At Horeb they made a calf
and worshiped an idol cast from metal.
[20] They exchanged their Glory
for an image of a bull, which eats grass.
[21] They forgot the God who saved them,
who had done great things in Egypt,
[22] miracles in the land of Ham
and awesome deeds by the Red Sea.
[23] So he said he would destroy them—
had not Moses, his chosen one,
stood in the breach before him
to keep his wrath from destroying them.

[24] Then they despised the pleasant land;
they did not believe his promise.
[25] They grumbled in their tents
and did not obey the LORD.
[26] So he swore to them with uplifted hand
that he would make them fall in the desert,
[27] make their descendants fall among the nations
and scatter them throughout the lands.

[28] They yoked themselves to the Baal of Peor
and ate sacrifices offered to lifeless gods;
[29] they provoked the LORD to anger by their wicked
deeds,
and a plague broke out among them.
[30] But Phinehas stood up and intervened,
and the plague was checked.
[31] This was credited to him as righteousness
for endless generations to come.

[32] By the waters of Meribah they angered the LORD,
and trouble came to Moses because of them;
[33] for they rebelled against the Spirit of God,
and rash words came from Moses' lips. [a]

[34] They did not destroy the peoples
as the LORD had commanded them,
[35] but they mingled with the nations
and adopted their customs.
[36] They worshiped their idols,
which became a snare to them.
[37] They sacrificed their sons
and their daughters to demons.
[38] They shed innocent blood,
the blood of their sons and daughters,
whom they sacrificed to the idols of Canaan,
and the land was desecrated by their blood.
[39] They defiled themselves by what they did;
by their deeds they prostituted themselves.

[40] Therefore the LORD was angry with his people

A New Way to Love

PSALM 106:43–45

God does not vacillate when it comes to righteousness, nor is God devoid of anger. Yet in responding to human sin, God is ever compassionate, which, explains scholar Walter Brueggemann, is "possible only because God bears the pain of vengeance." Jesus proclaims this radical way of loving when he revises the "eye for an eye" version of justice: "If someone strikes you on the right cheek, turn to him the other also" (Matthew 5:39). How do you deal with the natural feelings of vengeance that rise up within you? Is there an old bitterness or vendetta that you feed? How might you offer these old hurts to God?

See Meeting God in Prayer

Let the Redeemed Say So

PSALM 107:1–16

The psalmist praises God's deliverance of the Hebrew people from exile, from the perils of the desert and from the chains of their oppressors. Likewise, Jesus Christ's death and resurrection are the means of God's deliverance for believers: We pass through a "Red Sea" of transformation, arriving to find new life on the other side. Following the model provided by verses 4–9 and 10–15, write a short psalm of praise or, using colored pencils or crayons, draw a symbolic picture illustrating God's merciful love in your life.

See Meeting God in Scripture

and abhorred his inheritance.
41 He handed them over to the nations,
    and their foes ruled over them.
42 Their enemies oppressed them
    and subjected them to their power.
43 Many times he delivered them,
    but they were bent on rebellion
    and they wasted away in their sin.

44 But he took note of their distress
    when he heard their cry;
45 for their sake he remembered his covenant
    and out of his great love he relented.
46 He caused them to be pitied
    by all who held them captive.

47 Save us, O LORD our God,
    and gather us from the nations,
    that we may give thanks to your holy name
    and glory in your praise.

48 Praise be to the LORD, the God of Israel,
    from everlasting to everlasting.
    Let all the people say, "Amen!"

    Praise the LORD.

BOOK V
Psalms 107–150

Psalm 107

1 Give thanks to the LORD, for he is good;
    his love endures forever.
2 Let the redeemed of the LORD say this—
    those he redeemed from the hand of the foe,
3 those he gathered from the lands,
    from east and west, from north and south. *a*

4 Some wandered in desert wastelands,
    finding no way to a city where they could
        settle.
5 They were hungry and thirsty,
    and their lives ebbed away.
6 Then they cried out to the LORD in their trouble,
    and he delivered them from their distress.
7 He led them by a straight way
    to a city where they could settle.
8 Let them give thanks to the LORD for his unfailing
        love
    and his wonderful deeds for men,
9 for he satisfies the thirsty
    and fills the hungry with good things.

10 Some sat in darkness and the deepest gloom,
    prisoners suffering in iron chains,
11 for they had rebelled against the words of God
    and despised the counsel of the Most High.
12 So he subjected them to bitter labor;
    they stumbled, and there was no one to help.

a 3 Hebrew *north and the sea*

¹³ Then they cried to the LORD in their trouble,
  and he saved them from their distress.
¹⁴ He brought them out of darkness and the deepest
  gloom
  and broke away their chains.
¹⁵ Let them give thanks to the LORD for his unfailing
  love
  and his wonderful deeds for men,
¹⁶ for he breaks down gates of bronze
  and cuts through bars of iron.

¹⁷ Some became fools through their rebellious ways
  and suffered affliction because of their
  iniquities.
¹⁸ They loathed all food
  and drew near the gates of death.
¹⁹ Then they cried to the LORD in their trouble,
  and he saved them from their distress.
²⁰ He sent forth his word and healed them;
  he rescued them from the grave.
²¹ Let them give thanks to the LORD for his unfailing
  love
  and his wonderful deeds for men.
²² Let them sacrifice thank offerings
  and tell of his works with songs of joy.

²³ Others went out on the sea in ships;
  they were merchants on the mighty waters.
²⁴ They saw the works of the LORD,
  his wonderful deeds in the deep.
²⁵ For he spoke and stirred up a tempest
  that lifted high the waves.
²⁶ They mounted up to the heavens and went down
  to the depths;
  in their peril their courage melted away.
²⁷ They reeled and staggered like drunken men;
  they were at their wits' end.
²⁸ Then they cried out to the LORD in their trouble,
  and he brought them out of their distress.
²⁹ He stilled the storm to a whisper;
  the waves of the sea were hushed.
³⁰ They were glad when it grew calm,
  and he guided them to their desired haven.
³¹ Let them give thanks to the LORD for his unfailing
  love
  and his wonderful deeds for men.
³² Let them exalt him in the assembly of the people
  and praise him in the council of the elders.

³³ He turned rivers into a desert,
  flowing springs into thirsty ground,
³⁴ and fruitful land into a salt waste,
  because of the wickedness of those who lived
  there.
³⁵ He turned the desert into pools of water
  and the parched ground into flowing springs;
³⁶ there he brought the hungry to live,
  and they founded a city where they could
  settle.
³⁷ They sowed fields and planted vineyards
  that yielded a fruitful harvest;

The Call to Unending Worship

PSALM 107:31–32

"This flowing forth of God constantly demands a flowing back again, for God is a flowing and ebbing sea which ceaselessly flows out into all his beloved . . . To this end, all spirits ceaselessly come together and produce a burning flame of love, so that they might bring to fulfillment the work of loving God according to his nobility. The power of reason shows clearly that this is impossible for creatures, but love constantly wishes to bring its love to fulfillment."

—JOHN RUUSBROEC,
The Spiritual Espousals

A Prayer for God's Kingdom

PSALM 108:5

In the Lord's Prayer, Jesus prays in simple but powerful words: "Your kingdom come, your will be done on earth as it is in heaven" (Matthew 6:10). Jesus, as well as the psalmist, reveals that prayer is not a private matter but a vocation that touches the whole world! Our prayers of intercession for world hunger, for peace and for the spread of Christian faith have an impact. In prayer we join in partnership with God in healing the world. In what ways might God be inviting you to a deeper life of intercessory prayer for the world? In a church school class or small group, you might offer this question for discussion.

See Meeting God in Prayer

³⁸ he blessed them, and their numbers greatly
      increased,
    and he did not let their herds diminish.

³⁹ Then their numbers decreased, and they were
      humbled
    by oppression, calamity and sorrow;
⁴⁰ he who pours contempt on nobles
    made them wander in a trackless waste.
⁴¹ But he lifted the needy out of their affliction
    and increased their families like flocks.
⁴² The upright see and rejoice,
    but all the wicked shut their mouths.

⁴³ Whoever is wise, let him heed these things
    and consider the great love of the LORD.

Psalm 108

A song. A psalm of David.

¹ My heart is steadfast, O God;
    I will sing and make music with all my soul.
² Awake, harp and lyre!
    I will awaken the dawn.
³ I will praise you, O LORD, among the nations;
    I will sing of you among the peoples.
⁴ For great is your love, higher than the heavens;
    your faithfulness reaches to the skies.
⁵ Be exalted, O God, above the heavens,
    and let your glory be over all the earth.

⁶ Save us and help us with your right hand,
    that those you love may be delivered.
⁷ God has spoken from his sanctuary:
    "In triumph I will parcel out Shechem
    and measure off the Valley of Succoth.
⁸ Gilead is mine, Manasseh is mine;
    Ephraim is my helmet,
    Judah my scepter.
⁹ Moab is my washbasin,
    upon Edom I toss my sandal;
    over Philistia I shout in triumph."

¹⁰ Who will bring me to the fortified city?
    Who will lead me to Edom?
¹¹ Is it not you, O God, you who have rejected us
    and no longer go out with our armies?
¹² Give us aid against the enemy,
    for the help of man is worthless.
¹³ With God we will gain the victory,
    and he will trample down our enemies.

Psalm 109

For the director of music. Of David. A psalm.

¹ O God, whom I praise,
    do not remain silent,
² for wicked and deceitful men
    have opened their mouths against me;

they have spoken against me with lying
   tongues.
³ With words of hatred they surround me;
   they attack me without cause.
⁴ In return for my friendship they accuse me,
   but I am a man of prayer.
⁵ They repay me evil for good,
   and hatred for my friendship.

⁶ Appoint*ᵃ* an evil man*ᵇ* to oppose him;
   let an accuser*ᶜ* stand at his right hand.
⁷ When he is tried, let him be found guilty,
   and may his prayers condemn him.
⁸ May his days be few;
   may another take his place of leadership.
⁹ May his children be fatherless
   and his wife a widow.
¹⁰ May his children be wandering beggars;
   may they be driven*ᵈ* from their ruined homes.
¹¹ May a creditor seize all he has;
   may strangers plunder the fruits of his labor.
¹² May no one extend kindness to him
   or take pity on his fatherless children.
¹³ May his descendants be cut off,
   their names blotted out from the next
      generation.
¹⁴ May the iniquity of his fathers be remembered
      before the LORD;
   may the sin of his mother never be blotted out.
¹⁵ May their sins always remain before the LORD,
   that he may cut off the memory of them from
      the earth.

¹⁶ For he never thought of doing a kindness,
   but hounded to death the poor
   and the needy and the brokenhearted.
¹⁷ He loved to pronounce a curse—
   may it*ᵉ* come on him;
   he found no pleasure in blessing—
   may it be*ᶠ* far from him.
¹⁸ He wore cursing as his garment;
   it entered into his body like water,
   into his bones like oil.
¹⁹ May it be like a cloak wrapped about him,
   like a belt tied forever around him.
²⁰ May this be the LORD's payment to my accusers,
   to those who speak evil of me.

²¹ But you, O Sovereign LORD,
   deal well with me for your name's sake;
   out of the goodness of your love, deliver me.
²² For I am poor and needy,
   and my heart is wounded within me.
²³ I fade away like an evening shadow;
   I am shaken off like a locust.
²⁴ My knees give way from fasting;
   my body is thin and gaunt.

The Cry of the Poor

PSALM 109:21–24

The psalmist trusts that God hears the cries of people who are poor, sick and needy. Indeed, throughout the Bible it is clear that God has a special love for the poor. Jesus spoke out frequently and unmistakably on their behalf and often blessed them. Who are the needy in your community? How do you treat the poor? Perhaps you can discover a literacy program needing volunteers or an older person who cannot pay his or her utility bills. Look at the year ahead. What is one spiritual habit you could acquire that would extend God's love to "the least of these" (see Matthew 25:40)?

See Meeting God in Service

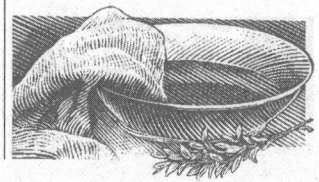

ᵃ 6 Or *They say:* "*Appoint* (with quotation marks at the end of verse 19)
ᵇ 6 Or *the Evil One*   *ᶜ 6* Or *let Satan*   *ᵈ 10* Septuagint; Hebrew *sought*
ᵉ 17 Or *curse, / and it has*   *ᶠ 17* Or *blessing, / and it is*

795

Trustworthy Precepts

PSALM 111:7–10

Just as God is a wise Creator
(Psalm 104), so he is a discerning Teacher. God's instruction
is eternally trustworthy. We
truly "fear" the Lord when we
value God's wisdom above that
of our culture and even that of
our own best intentions. How
do you discern God's wisdom?
In what areas do you need to
begin to practice what you
know to be wise and true? In
your journal, or on a piece of
paper, consider the ways you
acquire wisdom from God: your
prayer life, your experience of
Scripture, spiritual mentors,
community worship. What are
you learning in each of these
areas?

See Meeting God in Community

²⁵ I am an object of scorn to my accusers;
  when they see me, they shake their heads.

²⁶ Help me, O Lord my God;
  save me in accordance with your love.
²⁷ Let them know that it is your hand,
  that you, O Lord, have done it.
²⁸ They may curse, but you will bless;
  when they attack they will be put to shame,
  but your servant will rejoice.
²⁹ My accusers will be clothed with disgrace
  and wrapped in shame as in a cloak.

³⁰ With my mouth I will greatly extol the Lord;
  in the great throng I will praise him.
³¹ For he stands at the right hand of the needy one,
  to save his life from those who condemn him.

Psalm 110

Of David. A psalm.

¹ The Lord says to my Lord:
  "Sit at my right hand
until I make your enemies
  a footstool for your feet."

² The Lord will extend your mighty scepter from
    Zion;
  you will rule in the midst of your enemies.
³ Your troops will be willing
  on your day of battle.
Arrayed in holy majesty,
  from the womb of the dawn
  you will receive the dew of your youth.ᵃ

⁴ The Lord has sworn
  and will not change his mind:
"You are a priest forever,
  in the order of Melchizedek."

⁵ The Lord is at your right hand;
  he will crush kings on the day of his wrath.
⁶ He will judge the nations, heaping up the dead
  and crushing the rulers of the whole earth.
⁷ He will drink from a brook beside the wayᵇ;
  therefore he will lift up his head.

Psalm 111ᶜ

¹ Praise the Lord.ᵈ

I will extol the Lord with all my heart
  in the council of the upright and in the
    assembly.

² Great are the works of the Lord;
  they are pondered by all who delight in them.
³ Glorious and majestic are his deeds,

ᵃ 3 Or / your young men will come to you like the dew   ᵇ 7 Or / The One who
grants succession will set him in authority   ᶜ This psalm is an acrostic poem,
the lines of which begin with the successive letters of the Hebrew alphabet.
ᵈ 1 Hebrew *Hallelu Yah*

and his righteousness endures forever.
[4] He has caused his wonders to be remembered;
the LORD is gracious and compassionate.
[5] He provides food for those who fear him;
he remembers his covenant forever.
[6] He has shown his people the power of his works,
giving them the lands of other nations.
[7] The works of his hands are faithful and just;
all his precepts are trustworthy.
[8] They are steadfast for ever and ever,
done in faithfulness and uprightness.
[9] He provided redemption for his people;
he ordained his covenant forever—
holy and awesome is his name.

[10] The fear of the LORD is the beginning of wisdom;
all who follow his precepts have good
understanding.
To him belongs eternal praise.

Psalm 112[a]

[1] Praise the LORD.[b]

Blessed is the man who fears the LORD,
who finds great delight in his commands.

[2] His children will be mighty in the land;
the generation of the upright will be blessed.
[3] Wealth and riches are in his house,
and his righteousness endures forever.
[4] Even in darkness light dawns for the upright,
for the gracious and compassionate and
righteous man.[c]
[5] Good will come to him who is generous and lends
freely,
who conducts his affairs with justice.
[6] Surely he will never be shaken;
a righteous man will be remembered forever.
[7] He will have no fear of bad news;
his heart is steadfast, trusting in the LORD.
[8] His heart is secure, he will have no fear;
in the end he will look in triumph on his foes.
[9] He has scattered abroad his gifts to the poor,
his righteousness endures forever;
his horn[d] will be lifted high in honor.

[10] The wicked man will see and be vexed,
he will gnash his teeth and waste away;
the longings of the wicked will come to
nothing.

Psalm 113

[1] Praise the LORD.[e]

Praise, O servants of the LORD,
praise the name of the LORD.

The Fear of the Lord

PSALM 112:1–9

In the Psalms, the "fear of the LORD" (111:10) refers to awe and worship and then to the practice of obedience. If our words mean something to us, then our lives will reflect them. What are the characteristics of those who fear God? The psalmist says that daily they "delight" in God's ways, are kind to others, are not anxious and are generous to the poor. How do you worship God with your life? How might you consciously consecrate your daily activities to God? Perhaps, as you walk to a business meeting, you might pray for the persons involved. When you pause at traffic lights, pray for persons you will meet during the day.

See *Meeting God in Worship*

---

[a] This psalm is an acrostic poem, the lines of which begin with the successive letters of the Hebrew alphabet.   [b] 1 Hebrew *Hallelu Yah*
[c] 4 Or *l for the LORD is gracious and compassionate and righteous*   [d] 9 *Horn* here symbolizes dignity.   [e] 1 Hebrew *Hallelu Yah*; also in verse 9

The Answer to Modern Idolatry

PSALM 115:3–7

"The living God, the God Who is God and not a philosopher's abstraction, lies infinitely beyond the reach of anything our eyes can see or our minds can understand . . . If nothing that can be seen can either be God or represent him to us as he is, then to find God we must pass beyond everything that can be seen and enter into darkness. Since nothing that can be heard is God, to find him we must enter into silence."

—THOMAS MERTON,
New Seeds of Contemplation

² Let the name of the LORD be praised,
  both now and forevermore.
³ From the rising of the sun to the place where it sets,
  the name of the LORD is to be praised.

⁴ The LORD is exalted over all the nations,
  his glory above the heavens.
⁵ Who is like the LORD our God,
  the One who sits enthroned on high,
⁶ who stoops down to look
  on the heavens and the earth?

⁷ He raises the poor from the dust
  and lifts the needy from the ash heap;
⁸ he seats them with princes,
  with the princes of their people.
⁹ He settles the barren woman in her home
  as a happy mother of children.

Praise the LORD.

Psalm 114

¹ When Israel came out of Egypt,
  the house of Jacob from a people of foreign tongue,
² Judah became God's sanctuary,
  Israel his dominion.

³ The sea looked and fled,
  the Jordan turned back;
⁴ the mountains skipped like rams,
  the hills like lambs.

⁵ Why was it, O sea, that you fled,
  O Jordan, that you turned back,
⁶ you mountains, that you skipped like rams,
  you hills, like lambs?

⁷ Tremble, O earth, at the presence of the Lord,
  at the presence of the God of Jacob,
⁸ who turned the rock into a pool,
  the hard rock into springs of water.

Psalm 115

¹ Not to us, O LORD, not to us
  but to your name be the glory,
  because of your love and faithfulness.

² Why do the nations say,
  "Where is their God?"
³ Our God is in heaven;
  he does whatever pleases him.
⁴ But their idols are silver and gold,
  made by the hands of men.
⁵ They have mouths, but cannot speak,
  eyes, but they cannot see;
⁶ they have ears, but cannot hear,
  noses, but they cannot smell;
⁷ they have hands, but cannot feel,
  feet, but they cannot walk;

nor can they utter a sound with their throats.
8 Those who make them will be like them,
   and so will all who trust in them.

9 O house of Israel, trust in the LORD—
   he is their help and shield.
10 O house of Aaron, trust in the LORD—
   he is their help and shield.
11 You who fear him, trust in the LORD—
   he is their help and shield.

12 The LORD remembers us and will bless us:
   He will bless the house of Israel,
   he will bless the house of Aaron,
13 he will bless those who fear the LORD—
   small and great alike.

14 May the LORD make you increase,
   both you and your children.
15 May you be blessed by the LORD,
   the Maker of heaven and earth.

16 The highest heavens belong to the LORD,
   but the earth he has given to man.
17 It is not the dead who praise the LORD,
   those who go down to silence;
18 it is we who extol the LORD,
   both now and forevermore.

   Praise the LORD.[a]

Psalm 116

1 I love the LORD, for he heard my voice;
   he heard my cry for mercy.
2 Because he turned his ear to me,
   I will call on him as long as I live.

3 The cords of death entangled me,
   the anguish of the grave[b] came upon me;
   I was overcome by trouble and sorrow.
4 Then I called on the name of the LORD:
   "O LORD, save me!"

5 The LORD is gracious and righteous;
   our God is full of compassion.
6 The LORD protects the simplehearted;
   when I was in great need, he saved me.

7 Be at rest once more, O my soul,
   for the LORD has been good to you.

8 For you, O LORD, have delivered my soul from
      death,
   my eyes from tears,
   my feet from stumbling,
9 that I may walk before the LORD
   in the land of the living.
10 I believed; therefore[c] I said,
   "I am greatly afflicted."
11 And in my dismay I said,
   "All men are liars."

Resting in God

PSALM 116:5–7

Worry and stress have become constant companions for many of us in our busy culture. We might not be facing "the cords of death" (v.3), but we often live anxiously—bombarded by activities, information, appointments and debts. We find it hard to "rest" in God's mercy and bounty. What are some ways you might practice resting in God? Try sitting in silence for fifteen minutes before others in the household get up, taking a prayerful walk during a lunch break, or putting on the headphones and listening to meditative music for twenty minutes when you get home in the afternoon. Try one new "habit" of rest for three weeks.

See Meeting God in Everyday Life

Echoes of Praise

PSALM 118:1–4

In this litany of thanksgiving, we can almost hear the cantor calling to the people, priests and those who fear God to praise God's unending love. Consider the echoes of the liturgy that you hear in Sabbath worship: the call to worship, the hymn choruses, the Scripture readings. Repeating litanies of praise and thanksgiving are like saying "I love you" over and over—it reinforces that truth in our hearts and minds. How do you carry the reverberations from Sabbath worship into your daily life? Instead of throwing away the bulletin, use it. Choose a Biblical passage, a hymn or a call to worship, and make it your daily devotion over the course of a week.

See Meeting God in Worship

¹² How can I repay the LORD
for all his goodness to me?
¹³ I will lift up the cup of salvation
and call on the name of the LORD.
¹⁴ I will fulfill my vows to the LORD
in the presence of all his people.

¹⁵ Precious in the sight of the LORD
is the death of his saints.
¹⁶ O LORD, truly I am your servant;
I am your servant, the son of your
maidservant*ᵃ*;
you have freed me from my chains.

¹⁷ I will sacrifice a thank offering to you
and call on the name of the LORD.
¹⁸ I will fulfill my vows to the LORD
in the presence of all his people,
¹⁹ in the courts of the house of the LORD—
in your midst, O Jerusalem.

Praise the LORD.*ᵇ*

Psalm 117

¹ Praise the LORD, all you nations;
extol him, all you peoples.
² For great is his love toward us,
and the faithfulness of the LORD endures
forever.

Praise the LORD.*ᵇ*

Psalm 118

¹ Give thanks to the LORD, for he is good;
his love endures forever.

² Let Israel say:
"His love endures forever."
³ Let the house of Aaron say:
"His love endures forever."
⁴ Let those who fear the LORD say:
"His love endures forever."

⁵ In my anguish I cried to the LORD,
and he answered by setting me free.
⁶ The LORD is with me; I will not be afraid.
What can man do to me?
⁷ The LORD is with me; he is my helper.
I will look in triumph on my enemies.

⁸ It is better to take refuge in the LORD
than to trust in man.
⁹ It is better to take refuge in the LORD
than to trust in princes.

¹⁰ All the nations surrounded me,
but in the name of the LORD I cut them off.
¹¹ They surrounded me on every side,
but in the name of the LORD I cut them off.
¹² They swarmed around me like bees,

ᵃ 16 Or servant, your faithful son   ᵇ 19,2 Hebrew Hallelu Yah

but they died out as quickly as burning thorns;
in the name of the LORD I cut them off.
¹³ I was pushed back and about to fall,
but the LORD helped me.
¹⁴ The LORD is my strength and my song;
he has become my salvation.

¹⁵ Shouts of joy and victory
resound in the tents of the righteous:
"The LORD's right hand has done mighty things!
¹⁶   The LORD's right hand is lifted high;
the LORD's right hand has done mighty things!"

¹⁷ I will not die but live,
and will proclaim what the LORD has done.
¹⁸ The LORD has chastened me severely,
but he has not given me over to death.

¹⁹ Open for me the gates of righteousness;
I will enter and give thanks to the LORD.
²⁰ This is the gate of the LORD
through which the righteous may enter.
²¹ I will give you thanks, for you answered me;
you have become my salvation.

²² The stone the builders rejected
has become the capstone;
²³ the LORD has done this,
and it is marvelous in our eyes.
²⁴ This is the day the LORD has made;
let us rejoice and be glad in it.

²⁵ O LORD, save us;
O LORD, grant us success.
²⁶ Blessed is he who comes in the name of the
LORD.
From the house of the LORD we bless you.ᵃ
²⁷ The LORD is God,
and he has made his light shine upon us.
With boughs in hand, join in the festal procession
upᵇ to the horns of the altar.

²⁸ You are my God, and I will give you thanks;
you are my God, and I will exalt you.

²⁹ Give thanks to the LORD, for he is good;
his love endures forever.

Psalm 119ᶜ

א Aleph

¹ Blessed are they whose ways are blameless,
who walk according to the law of the LORD.
² Blessed are they who keep his statutes
and seek him with all their heart.
³ They do nothing wrong;
they walk in his ways.
⁴ You have laid down precepts

The Rejected Stone

PSALM 118:22–24

These verses, particularly 22 and 23, are often quoted in the New Testament (Matthew 21:42; 1 Peter 2:7) as a reference to the coming of Jesus Christ, for the rejected One has become what is most precious. This is often true for our inner spiritual selves as well. We may reject a part of ourselves because it seems weak but later realize that it is a strength. Perhaps it causes us to rely on God more. Or perhaps we discover that our "weakness" is a diamond in the rough that needs to be honed and shaped. In your journal or with a soul friend, reflect on what you reject in yourself: a tendency to talk too much or too little, a certain compulsivity. What might God be showing you through it?

ᵃ 26 The Hebrew is plural.   ᵇ 27 Or *Bind the festal sacrifice with ropes / and take it*   ᶜ This psalm is an acrostic poem; the verses of each stanza begin with the same letter of the Hebrew alphabet.

Running in God's Way

PSALM 119:30–35

The law is celebrated throughout Psalm 119. The psalmist delights in the law, for he has found that it is his source of strength and understanding. He feeds there. In monastic life, all 150 psalms are chanted each week. There is wisdom in nourishing the heart continuously with God's instruction in Scripture. How do you nourish your soul with Scripture? Have you cultivated a daily habit? One way to begin is to select one of the Gospels and read it meditatively (not more than ten to fifteen verses each day) or read a psalm every morning as part of a devotion or choose a favorite passage and spend a week memorizing it.

See Meeting God in Scripture

that are to be fully obeyed.
⁵ Oh, that my ways were steadfast
  in obeying your decrees!
⁶ Then I would not be put to shame
  when I consider all your commands.
⁷ I will praise you with an upright heart
  as I learn your righteous laws.
⁸ I will obey your decrees;
  do not utterly forsake me.

ב Beth

⁹ How can a young man keep his way pure?
  By living according to your word.
¹⁰ I seek you with all my heart;
  do not let me stray from your commands.
¹¹ I have hidden your word in my heart
  that I might not sin against you.
¹² Praise be to you, O LORD;
  teach me your decrees.
¹³ With my lips I recount
  all the laws that come from your mouth.
¹⁴ I rejoice in following your statutes
  as one rejoices in great riches.
¹⁵ I meditate on your precepts
  and consider your ways.
¹⁶ I delight in your decrees;
  I will not neglect your word.

ג Gimel

¹⁷ Do good to your servant, and I will live;
  I will obey your word.
¹⁸ Open my eyes that I may see
  wonderful things in your law.
¹⁹ I am a stranger on earth;
  do not hide your commands from me.
²⁰ My soul is consumed with longing
  for your laws at all times.
²¹ You rebuke the arrogant, who are cursed
  and who stray from your commands.
²² Remove from me scorn and contempt,
  for I keep your statutes.
²³ Though rulers sit together and slander me,
  your servant will meditate on your decrees.
²⁴ Your statutes are my delight;
  they are my counselors.

ד Daleth

²⁵ I am laid low in the dust;
  preserve my life according to your word.
²⁶ I recounted my ways and you answered me;
  teach me your decrees.
²⁷ Let me understand the teaching of your precepts;
  then I will meditate on your wonders.
²⁸ My soul is weary with sorrow;
  strengthen me according to your word.
²⁹ Keep me from deceitful ways;
  be gracious to me through your law.
³⁰ I have chosen the way of truth;
  I have set my heart on your laws.

³¹ I hold fast to your statutes, O Lord;
   do not let me be put to shame.
³² I run in the path of your commands,
   for you have set my heart free.

ה He

³³ Teach me, O Lord, to follow your decrees;
   then I will keep them to the end.
³⁴ Give me understanding, and I will keep your law
   and obey it with all my heart.
³⁵ Direct me in the path of your commands,
   for there I find delight.
³⁶ Turn my heart toward your statutes
   and not toward selfish gain.
³⁷ Turn my eyes away from worthless things;
   preserve my life according to your word.ᵃ
³⁸ Fulfill your promise to your servant,
   so that you may be feared.
³⁹ Take away the disgrace I dread,
   for your laws are good.
⁴⁰ How I long for your precepts!
   Preserve my life in your righteousness.

ו Waw

⁴¹ May your unfailing love come to me, O Lord,
   your salvation according to your promise;
⁴² then I will answer the one who taunts me,
   for I trust in your word.
⁴³ Do not snatch the word of truth from my mouth,
   for I have put my hope in your laws.
⁴⁴ I will always obey your law,
   for ever and ever.
⁴⁵ I will walk about in freedom,
   for I have sought out your precepts.
⁴⁶ I will speak of your statutes before kings
   and will not be put to shame,
⁴⁷ for I delight in your commands
   because I love them.
⁴⁸ I lift up my hands toᵇ your commands, which I love,
   and I meditate on your decrees.

ז Zayin

⁴⁹ Remember your word to your servant,
   for you have given me hope.
⁵⁰ My comfort in my suffering is this:
   Your promise preserves my life.
⁵¹ The arrogant mock me without restraint,
   but I do not turn from your law.
⁵² I remember your ancient laws, O Lord,
   and I find comfort in them.
⁵³ Indignation grips me because of the wicked,
   who have forsaken your law.
⁵⁴ Your decrees are the theme of my song
   wherever I lodge.
⁵⁵ In the night I remember your name, O Lord,
   and I will keep your law.

True Freedom

PSALM 119:45

Here the psalmist declares the spiritual freedom found in seeking God's ways. Freedom is something to be treasured. Prisoners, slaves and day laborers understand its preciousness; one who is shackled by an addiction longs for liberty. Often in the world today, a self-centered materialism parades as freedom. Yet Jesus calls us to a much different freedom when he says, "Seek first [God's] kingdom and his righteousness, and all these things will be given to you as well" (Matthew 6:33). Where is God calling you to detachment? In what practical ways do you give priority to God's ways in your life?

See Meeting God in Everyday Life

ᵃ 37 Two manuscripts of the Masoretic Text and Dead Sea Scrolls; most manuscripts of the Masoretic Text *life in your way*   ᵇ 48 Or *for*

Humility

PSALM 119:67

The word in this verse translated "afflicted" can also mean "humbled." The psalmist reminds us that good can come out of difficult, humbling circumstances. Reflect on a time in your life in which you went "astray" and found some painful event the catalyst for a renewed, more faithful walk with God. Ask God to allow the lesson or renewal to be an ongoing part of your life.

See Meeting God in Everyday Life

---

56 This has been my practice:
    I obey your precepts.

ח Heth

57 You are my portion, O LORD;
    I have promised to obey your words.
58 I have sought your face with all my heart;
    be gracious to me according to your promise.
59 I have considered my ways
    and have turned my steps to your statutes.
60 I will hasten and not delay
    to obey your commands.
61 Though the wicked bind me with ropes,
    I will not forget your law.
62 At midnight I rise to give you thanks
    for your righteous laws.
63 I am a friend to all who fear you,
    to all who follow your precepts.
64 The earth is filled with your love, O LORD;
    teach me your decrees.

ט Teth

65 Do good to your servant
    according to your word, O LORD.
66 Teach me knowledge and good judgment,
    for I believe in your commands.
67 Before I was afflicted I went astray,
    but now I obey your word.
68 You are good, and what you do is good;
    teach me your decrees.
69 Though the arrogant have smeared me with lies,
    I keep your precepts with all my heart.
70 Their hearts are callous and unfeeling,
    but I delight in your law.
71 It was good for me to be afflicted
    so that I might learn your decrees.
72 The law from your mouth is more precious to me
    than thousands of pieces of silver and gold.

י Yodh

73 Your hands made me and formed me;
    give me understanding to learn your
        commands.
74 May those who fear you rejoice when they see
        me,
    for I have put my hope in your word.
75 I know, O LORD, that your laws are righteous,
    and in faithfulness you have afflicted me.
76 May your unfailing love be my comfort,
    according to your promise to your servant.
77 Let your compassion come to me that I may live,
    for your law is my delight.
78 May the arrogant be put to shame for wronging
        me without cause;
    but I will meditate on your precepts.
79 May those who fear you turn to me,
    those who understand your statutes.
80 May my heart be blameless toward your decrees,
    that I may not be put to shame.

 כ Kaph

81 My soul faints with longing for your salvation,
   but I have put my hope in your word.
82 My eyes fail, looking for your promise;
   I say, "When will you comfort me?"
83 Though I am like a wineskin in the smoke,
   I do not forget your decrees.
84 How long must your servant wait?
   When will you punish my persecutors?
85 The arrogant dig pitfalls for me,
   contrary to your law.
86 All your commands are trustworthy;
   help me, for men persecute me without cause.
87 They almost wiped me from the earth,
   but I have not forsaken your precepts.
88 Preserve my life according to your love,
   and I will obey the statutes of your mouth.

ל Lamedh

89 Your word, O Lord, is eternal;
   it stands firm in the heavens.
90 Your faithfulness continues through all
      generations;
   you established the earth, and it endures.
91 Your laws endure to this day,
   for all things serve you.
92 If your law had not been my delight,
   I would have perished in my affliction.
93 I will never forget your precepts,
   for by them you have preserved my life.
94 Save me, for I am yours;
   I have sought out your precepts.
95 The wicked are waiting to destroy me,
   but I will ponder your statutes.
96 To all perfection I see a limit;
   but your commands are boundless.

מ Mem

97 Oh, how I love your law!
   I meditate on it all day long.
98 Your commands make me wiser than my
      enemies,
   for they are ever with me.
99 I have more insight than all my teachers,
   for I meditate on your statutes.
100 I have more understanding than the elders,
   for I obey your precepts.
101 I have kept my feet from every evil path
   so that I might obey your word.
102 I have not departed from your laws,
   for you yourself have taught me.
103 How sweet are your words to my taste,
   sweeter than honey to my mouth!
104 I gain understanding from your precepts;
   therefore I hate every wrong path.

נ Nun

105 Your word is a lamp to my feet
   and a light for my path.

Heart Wisdom

PSALM 119:97–100

Meditation is a word that is used in many ways today. A person may meditate in silence, meditate on a new idea or even meditate on what to eat at a favorite restaurant. But here the psalmist describes meditation as bringing Scripture into the heart. He says, "They are ever with me." How do you keep Scripture "ever" with you? Try reading slowly through the Bible, memorizing verses that touch you, and taking part in a small group where Scripture is shared (not necessarily studied). This week, commit (or recommit) to an approach of "dwelling in" Scripture.

See *Meeting God in Scripture*

Discernment

PSALM 119:130

The psalmist beautifully reminds us that the "unfolding" of Scripture offers guidance for our lives. There are times when we do not know what to do next or when we are making a difficult choice between two "goods." Through the reflective reading of a psalm, a Gospel passage or a chapter of an epistle, "light" and "understanding" may come through a word or phrase at that very moment or perhaps even later during the day. When you face a difficult decision, take a few moments to surrender it to God in prayer, and then prayerfully read a chosen passage. See what wisdom emerges.

See Meeting God in Scripture

¹⁰⁶ I have taken an oath and confirmed it,
　that I will follow your righteous laws.
¹⁰⁷ I have suffered much;
　preserve my life, O LORD, according to your
　word.
¹⁰⁸ Accept, O LORD, the willing praise of my mouth,
　and teach me your laws.
¹⁰⁹ Though I constantly take my life in my hands,
　I will not forget your law.
¹¹⁰ The wicked have set a snare for me,
　but I have not strayed from your precepts.
¹¹¹ Your statutes are my heritage forever;
　they are the joy of my heart.
¹¹² My heart is set on keeping your decrees
　to the very end.

ס Samekh

¹¹³ I hate double-minded men,
　but I love your law.
¹¹⁴ You are my refuge and my shield;
　I have put my hope in your word.
¹¹⁵ Away from me, you evildoers,
　that I may keep the commands of my God!
¹¹⁶ Sustain me according to your promise, and I will
　live;
　do not let my hopes be dashed.
¹¹⁷ Uphold me, and I will be delivered;
　I will always have regard for your decrees.
¹¹⁸ You reject all who stray from your decrees,
　for their deceitfulness is in vain.
¹¹⁹ All the wicked of the earth you discard like dross;
　therefore I love your statutes.
¹²⁰ My flesh trembles in fear of you;
　I stand in awe of your laws.

ע Ayin

¹²¹ I have done what is righteous and just;
　do not leave me to my oppressors.
¹²² Ensure your servant's well-being;
　let not the arrogant oppress me.
¹²³ My eyes fail, looking for your salvation,
　looking for your righteous promise.
¹²⁴ Deal with your servant according to your love
　and teach me your decrees.
¹²⁵ I am your servant; give me discernment
　that I may understand your statutes.
¹²⁶ It is time for you to act, O LORD;
　your law is being broken.
¹²⁷ Because I love your commands
　more than gold, more than pure gold,
¹²⁸ and because I consider all your precepts right,
　I hate every wrong path.

פ Pe

¹²⁹ Your statutes are wonderful;
　therefore I obey them.
¹³⁰ The unfolding of your words gives light;
　it gives understanding to the simple.
¹³¹ I open my mouth and pant,

longing for your commands.
¹³² Turn to me and have mercy on me,
as you always do to those who love your name.
¹³³ Direct my footsteps according to your word;
let no sin rule over me.
¹³⁴ Redeem me from the oppression of men,
that I may obey your precepts.
¹³⁵ Make your face shine upon your servant
and teach me your decrees.
¹³⁶ Streams of tears flow from my eyes,
for your law is not obeyed.

צ Tsadhe

¹³⁷ Righteous are you, O Lord,
and your laws are right.
¹³⁸ The statutes you have laid down are righteous;
they are fully trustworthy.
¹³⁹ My zeal wears me out,
for my enemies ignore your words.
¹⁴⁰ Your promises have been thoroughly tested,
and your servant loves them.
¹⁴¹ Though I am lowly and despised,
I do not forget your precepts.
¹⁴² Your righteousness is everlasting
and your law is true.
¹⁴³ Trouble and distress have come upon me,
but your commands are my delight.
¹⁴⁴ Your statutes are forever right;
give me understanding that I may live.

ק Qoph

¹⁴⁵ I call with all my heart; answer me, O Lord,
and I will obey your decrees.
¹⁴⁶ I call out to you; save me
and I will keep your statutes.
¹⁴⁷ I rise before dawn and cry for help;
I have put my hope in your word.
¹⁴⁸ My eyes stay open through the watches of the
night,
that I may meditate on your promises.
¹⁴⁹ Hear my voice in accordance with your love;
preserve my life, O Lord, according to your
laws.
¹⁵⁰ Those who devise wicked schemes are near,
but they are far from your law.
¹⁵¹ Yet you are near, O Lord,
and all your commands are true.
¹⁵² Long ago I learned from your statutes
that you established them to last forever.

ר Resh

¹⁵³ Look upon my suffering and deliver me,
for I have not forgotten your law.
¹⁵⁴ Defend my cause and redeem me;
preserve my life according to your promise.
¹⁵⁵ Salvation is far from the wicked,
for they do not seek out your decrees.
¹⁵⁶ Your compassion is great, O Lord;
preserve my life according to your laws.

Praying the Psalter

PSALM 119:147–148

"The more deeply we grow into the psalms and the more often we pray them as our own, the more simple and rich will our prayer become."

—DIETRICH BONHOEFFER,
Life Together

See *Meeting God in Prayer*

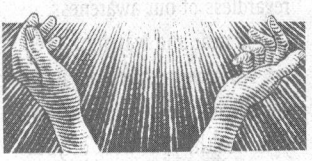

Always There

PSALM 121:1–4

This psalm speaks peace to our deepest fears. Every night, each of us must abandon consciousness for several hours. Our surrender to sleep—while God neither slumbers nor sleeps—symbolizes the truth that we are always held in God's presence regardless of our awareness. God is near and watching over us. What worries or fears make you anxious about your safety, your health, your work or your children? Make a list of three of your concerns. In the same way that you "let go" for sleep, offer these worries to God. If you think it may be helpful, put your list where you can see it and offer these concerns to God throughout the day.

See Meeting God in Everyday Life

157 Many are the foes who persecute me,
　　but I have not turned from your statutes.
158 I look on the faithless with loathing,
　　for they do not obey your word.
159 See how I love your precepts;
　　preserve my life, O LORD, according to your love.
160 All your words are true;
　　all your righteous laws are eternal.

ש Sin and Shin

161 Rulers persecute me without cause,
　　but my heart trembles at your word.
162 I rejoice in your promise
　　like one who finds great spoil.
163 I hate and abhor falsehood
　　but I love your law.
164 Seven times a day I praise you
　　for your righteous laws.
165 Great peace have they who love your law,
　　and nothing can make them stumble.
166 I wait for your salvation, O LORD,
　　and I follow your commands.
167 I obey your statutes,
　　for I love them greatly.
168 I obey your precepts and your statutes,
　　for all my ways are known to you.

ת Taw

169 May my cry come before you, O LORD;
　　give me understanding according to your word.
170 May my supplication come before you;
　　deliver me according to your promise.
171 May my lips overflow with praise,
　　for you teach me your decrees.
172 May my tongue sing of your word,
　　for all your commands are righteous.
173 May your hand be ready to help me,
　　for I have chosen your precepts.
174 I long for your salvation, O LORD,
　　and your law is my delight.
175 Let me live that I may praise you,
　　and may your laws sustain me.
176 I have strayed like a lost sheep.
　　Seek your servant,
　　for I have not forgotten your commands.

Psalm 120

A song of ascents.

1 I call on the LORD in my distress,
　　and he answers me.
2 Save me, O LORD, from lying lips
　　and from deceitful tongues.

3 What will he do to you,
　　and what more besides, O deceitful tongue?
4 He will punish you with a warrior's sharp arrows,
　　with burning coals of the broom tree.

5 Woe to me that I dwell in Meshech,
  that I live among the tents of Kedar!
6 Too long have I lived
  among those who hate peace.
7 I am a man of peace;
  but when I speak, they are for war.

Psalm 121

A song of ascents.

1 I lift up my eyes to the hills—
  where does my help come from?
2 My help comes from the LORD,
  the Maker of heaven and earth.

3 He will not let your foot slip—
  he who watches over you will not slumber;
4 indeed, he who watches over Israel
  will neither slumber nor sleep.

5 The LORD watches over you—
  the LORD is your shade at your right hand;
6 the sun will not harm you by day,
  nor the moon by night.

7 The LORD will keep you from all harm—
  he will watch over your life;
8 the LORD will watch over your coming and going
  both now and forevermore.

Psalm 122

A song of ascents. Of David.

1 I rejoiced with those who said to me,
  "Let us go to the house of the LORD."
2 Our feet are standing
  in your gates, O Jerusalem.

3 Jerusalem is built like a city
  that is closely compacted together.
4 That is where the tribes go up,
  the tribes of the LORD,
 to praise the name of the LORD
  according to the statute given to Israel.
5 There the thrones for judgment stand,
  the thrones of the house of David.

6 Pray for the peace of Jerusalem:
  "May those who love you be secure.
7 May there be peace within your walls
  and security within your citadels."
8 For the sake of my brothers and friends,
  I will say, "Peace be within you."
9 For the sake of the house of the LORD our God,
  I will seek your prosperity.

Psalm 123

A song of ascents.

1 I lift up my eyes to you,
  to you whose throne is in heaven.

Pilgrimage

PSALM 122:1–2

We are hearing about pilgrimages more and more frequently. People are making pilgrimages to Israel, to Assisi, to Ireland and to Scotland. Walking the streets where Jesus walked, worshiping "with" Francis and recovering the roots of Celtic Christian faith enrich the soul. Visiting an old family home or the church of your childhood may also be a "pilgrimage." Even if you cannot travel physically, you may do so in spirit. Using colored pencils, markers or paints, draw a picture of a "sacred place" from your childhood. Below your picture, write a word that comes to mind as you recall this place.

See Meeting God in Everyday Life

809

Returning Home

PSALM 126:1–3

Can you remember coming home after being gone for a long period of time or after enduring a terrible experience? How glad you were to see the familiar sights of home and the faces of those you love! Here the psalmist is recalling such a return from exile: "Our mouths were filled with laughter." So, too, God is always welcoming us "home." In each moment of every day, we are invited to remember that God is ever near. God's steadfast love always surrounds us, even when we don't recognize it. As you pray during the day, take a moment in silence to rest in the "home" of God's presence.

See Meeting God in Everyday Life

² As the eyes of slaves look to the hand of their
master,
as the eyes of a maid look to the hand of her
mistress,
so our eyes look to the LORD our God,
till he shows us his mercy.

³ Have mercy on us, O LORD, have mercy on us,
for we have endured much contempt.
⁴ We have endured much ridicule from the proud,
much contempt from the arrogant.

Psalm 124

A song of ascents. Of David.

¹ If the LORD had not been on our side—
let Israel say—
² if the LORD had not been on our side
when men attacked us,
³ when their anger flared against us,
they would have swallowed us alive;
⁴ the flood would have engulfed us,
the torrent would have swept over us,
⁵ the raging waters
would have swept us away.

⁶ Praise be to the LORD,
who has not let us be torn by their teeth.
⁷ We have escaped like a bird
out of the fowler's snare;
the snare has been broken,
and we have escaped.
⁸ Our help is in the name of the LORD,
the Maker of heaven and earth.

Psalm 125

A song of ascents.

¹ Those who trust in the LORD are like Mount
Zion,
which cannot be shaken but endures forever.
² As the mountains surround Jerusalem,
so the LORD surrounds his people
both now and forevermore.

³ The scepter of the wicked will not remain
over the land allotted to the righteous,
for then the righteous might use
their hands to do evil.

⁴ Do good, O LORD, to those who are good,
to those who are upright in heart.
⁵ But those who turn to crooked ways
the LORD will banish with the evildoers.

Peace be upon Israel.

Psalm 126

A song of ascents.

¹ When the LORD brought back the captives to*ᵃ*
Zion,
  we were like men who dreamed.*ᵇ*
² Our mouths were filled with laughter,
  our tongues with songs of joy.
Then it was said among the nations,
  "The LORD has done great things for them."
³ The LORD has done great things for us,
  and we are filled with joy.

⁴ Restore our fortunes,*ᶜ* O LORD,
  like streams in the Negev.
⁵ Those who sow in tears
  will reap with songs of joy.
⁶ He who goes out weeping,
  carrying seed to sow,
will return with songs of joy,
  carrying sheaves with him.

Psalm 127

A song of ascents. Of Solomon.

¹ Unless the LORD builds the house,
  its builders labor in vain.
Unless the LORD watches over the city,
  the watchmen stand guard in vain.
² In vain you rise early
  and stay up late,
toiling for food to eat—
  for he grants sleep to*ᵈ* those he loves.

³ Sons are a heritage from the LORD,
  children a reward from him.
⁴ Like arrows in the hands of a warrior
  are sons born in one's youth.
⁵ Blessed is the man
  whose quiver is full of them.
They will not be put to shame
  when they contend with their enemies in the
    gate.

Psalm 128

A song of ascents.

¹ Blessed are all who fear the LORD,
  who walk in his ways.
² You will eat the fruit of your labor;
  blessings and prosperity will be yours.
³ Your wife will be like a fruitful vine
  within your house;
your sons will be like olive shoots
  around your table.
⁴ Thus is the man blessed
  who fears the LORD.

The Problem With Vanity

PSALM 127:1–2

Vanity is an old-fashioned word, but full of meaning. It can refer to "egotism" and "self-concern," but it can also mean "futility" and "hollowness." In *vain* we do things on our own and for our own benefit—we "build our houses" without the Lord. Our culture values independence and such self-sufficiency, but the spiritual life calls us to nourish ourselves by putting down deeper roots. Daily immersion in Scripture, prayer and community (spiritual friends and mentors) helps us check our tendency toward vanity. In what areas of your life are you trying to do things under your own steam? Where is God inviting you to let go of control and learn humility?

See Meeting God in Community

ᵃ 1 Or *LORD restored the fortunes of*   *ᵇ 1* Or *men restored to health*   *ᶜ 4* Or
Bring back our captives   *ᵈ 2* Or *eat—/ for while they sleep he provides for*

811

More Than Those Who Wait for the Morning

PSALM 130:5–6

Security officers and night shift workers know how hard it is to stay awake in the hours just before dawn. Drowsiness may overcome even the strongest will. Yet the psalmist desires God with all of himself, even more than the one struggling to stay awake until morning. Ignatius shares the psalmist's commitment: "Take, O Lord, and receive all my liberty, my memory, my understanding, and my entire will, all that I have and possess." How often do you consecrate your attention and intentions to God? What simple prayer of consecration might you offer to God as you go through this day?

See Meeting God in Prayer

⁵May the LORD bless you from Zion
　all the days of your life;
may you see the prosperity of Jerusalem,
⁶　and may you live to see your children's children.

Peace be upon Israel.

Psalm 129

A song of ascents.

¹They have greatly oppressed me from my
　youth—
　let Israel say—
²they have greatly oppressed me from my youth,
　but they have not gained the victory over me.
³Plowmen have plowed my back
　and made their furrows long.
⁴But the LORD is righteous;
　he has cut me free from the cords of the wicked.

⁵May all who hate Zion
　be turned back in shame.
⁶May they be like grass on the roof,
　which withers before it can grow;
⁷with it the reaper cannot fill his hands,
　nor the one who gathers fill his arms.
⁸May those who pass by not say,
　"The blessing of the LORD be upon you;
　we bless you in the name of the LORD."

Psalm 130

A song of ascents.

¹Out of the depths I cry to you, O LORD;
²　O Lord, hear my voice.
Let your ears be attentive
　to my cry for mercy.

³If you, O LORD, kept a record of sins,
　O Lord, who could stand?
⁴But with you there is forgiveness;
　therefore you are feared.

⁵I wait for the LORD, my soul waits,
　and in his word I put my hope.
⁶My soul waits for the Lord
　more than watchmen wait for the morning,
　more than watchmen wait for the morning.

⁷O Israel, put your hope in the LORD,
　for with the LORD is unfailing love
　and with him is full redemption.
⁸He himself will redeem Israel
　from all their sins.

Psalm 131

A song of ascents. Of David.

¹My heart is not proud, O LORD,
　my eyes are not haughty;
I do not concern myself with great matters

or things too wonderful for me.
² But I have stilled and quieted my soul;
    like a weaned child with its mother,
    like a weaned child is my soul within me.

³ O Israel, put your hope in the LORD
    both now and forevermore.

Psalm 132

A song of ascents.

¹ O LORD, remember David
    and all the hardships he endured.

² He swore an oath to the LORD
    and made a vow to the Mighty One of Jacob:
³ "I will not enter my house
    or go to my bed—
⁴ I will allow no sleep to my eyes,
    no slumber to my eyelids,
⁵ till I find a place for the LORD,
    a dwelling for the Mighty One of Jacob."

⁶ We heard it in Ephrathah,
    we came upon it in the fields of Jaar*ᵃ˸ᵇ*
⁷ "Let us go to his dwelling place;
    let us worship at his footstool—
⁸ arise, O LORD, and come to your resting place,
    you and the ark of your might.
⁹ May your priests be clothed with righteousness;
    may your saints sing for joy."

¹⁰ For the sake of David your servant,
    do not reject your anointed one.

¹¹ The LORD swore an oath to David,
    a sure oath that he will not revoke:
  "One of your own descendants
    I will place on your throne—
¹² if your sons keep my covenant
    and the statutes I teach them,
  then their sons will sit
    on your throne for ever and ever."

¹³ For the LORD has chosen Zion,
    he has desired it for his dwelling:
¹⁴ "This is my resting place for ever and ever;
    here I will sit enthroned, for I have desired it—
¹⁵ I will bless her with abundant provisions;
    her poor will I satisfy with food.
¹⁶ I will clothe her priests with salvation,
    and her saints will ever sing for joy.

¹⁷ "Here I will make a horn*ᶜ* grow for David
    and set up a lamp for my anointed one.
¹⁸ I will clothe his enemies with shame,
    but the crown on his head will be resplendent."

ᵃ 6 That is, Kiriath Jearim   *ᵇ 6* Or *heard of it in Ephrathah, / we found it in the fields of Jaar.* (And no quotes around verses 7–9)   *ᶜ 17 Horn* here symbolizes strong one, that is, king.

God's Footstool

PSALM 132:7

Where is God's "dwelling place" for you? How can you go there to worship at God's footstool? What position might you take while doing so? This passage might bring to mind how Mary sat at Jesus' feet listening to him (see Luke 10:38). What attitudes does this image prompt you to assume? Is there a small footstool or step stool in your home? Consider sitting or kneeling on this small piece of furniture for a time of worship. Or is there a rock at your favorite woods or park? Let it become a "footstool" where you worship God in humility and submission.

See Meeting God in Worship

Unity: The Precious Gift

PSALM 133:1–3

The psalmist writes about how precious unity is, especially in families and communities. Yet how hard it is for us to achieve. Disagreements, hurts, indifference and self-concern divide us. Unity requires that we work continually at forgiving one another. Brother Roger of the ecumenical Taizé community writes, "A conversion takes place in the very depths of our being when, even though we are rejected or humiliated, we entrust to God, at once, those who have wounded us." What hurts or wounds are separating you from another person or community? What act of reconciliation might God be leading you to do?

See Meeting God in Community

Psalm 133

A song of ascents. Of David.

¹ How good and pleasant it is
    when brothers live together in unity!
² It is like precious oil poured on the head,
    running down on the beard,
running down on Aaron's beard,
    down upon the collar of his robes.
³ It is as if the dew of Hermon
    were falling on Mount Zion.
For there the LORD bestows his blessing,
    even life forevermore.

Psalm 134

A song of ascents.

¹ Praise the LORD, all you servants of the LORD
    who minister by night in the house of the LORD.
² Lift up your hands in the sanctuary
    and praise the LORD.

³ May the LORD, the Maker of heaven and earth,
    bless you from Zion.

Psalm 135

¹ Praise the LORD. [a]

Praise the name of the LORD;
    praise him, you servants of the LORD,
² you who minister in the house of the LORD,
    in the courts of the house of our God.

³ Praise the LORD, for the LORD is good;
    sing praise to his name, for that is pleasant.
⁴ For the LORD has chosen Jacob to be his own,
    Israel to be his treasured possession.

⁵ I know that the LORD is great,
    that our Lord is greater than all gods.
⁶ The LORD does whatever pleases him,
    in the heavens and on the earth,
    in the seas and all their depths.
⁷ He makes clouds rise from the ends of the earth;
    he sends lightning with the rain
    and brings out the wind from his storehouses.

⁸ He struck down the firstborn of Egypt,
    the firstborn of men and animals.
⁹ He sent his signs and wonders into your midst,
        O Egypt,
    against Pharaoh and all his servants.
¹⁰ He struck down many nations
    and killed mighty kings—
¹¹ Sihon king of the Amorites,
    Og king of Bashan
    and all the kings of Canaan—
¹² and he gave their land as an inheritance,
    an inheritance to his people Israel.

a 1 Hebrew *Hallelu Yah;* also in verses 3 and 21

¹³ Your name, O LORD, endures forever,
  your renown, O LORD, through all generations.
¹⁴ For the LORD will vindicate his people
  and have compassion on his servants.

¹⁵ The idols of the nations are silver and gold,
  made by the hands of men.
¹⁶ They have mouths, but cannot speak,
  eyes, but they cannot see;
¹⁷ they have ears, but cannot hear,
  nor is there breath in their mouths.
¹⁸ Those who make them will be like them,
  and so will all who trust in them.

¹⁹ O house of Israel, praise the LORD;
  O house of Aaron, praise the LORD;
²⁰ O house of Levi, praise the LORD;
  you who fear him, praise the LORD.
²¹ Praise be to the LORD from Zion,
  to him who dwells in Jerusalem.

  Praise the LORD.

Psalm 136

¹ Give thanks to the LORD, for he is good.
  His love endures forever.
² Give thanks to the God of gods.
  His love endures forever.
³ Give thanks to the Lord of lords:
  His love endures forever.

⁴ to him who alone does great wonders,
  His love endures forever.
⁵ who by his understanding made the heavens,
  His love endures forever.
⁶ who spread out the earth upon the waters,
  His love endures forever.
⁷ who made the great lights—
  His love endures forever.
⁸ the sun to govern the day,
  His love endures forever.
⁹ the moon and stars to govern the night;
  His love endures forever.

¹⁰ to him who struck down the firstborn of Egypt
  His love endures forever.
¹¹ and brought Israel out from among them
  His love endures forever.
¹² with a mighty hand and outstretched arm;
  His love endures forever.

¹³ to him who divided the Red Sea^a asunder
  His love endures forever.
¹⁴ and brought Israel through the midst of it,
  His love endures forever.
¹⁵ but swept Pharaoh and his army into the Red Sea;
  His love endures forever.

¹⁶ to him who led his people through the desert,
  His love endures forever.

The Echo of Love

PSALM 136:2–9

Throughout this hymn of praise, the psalmist sings of God's faithful, enduring love. Divine love is the echo throughout the narratives of creation, the account of the exodus from Egypt and the stories of Hebrew nationhood. Love is the echo in your story as well: You are born, and God loves you. You take your first steps, and God delights in you. You enjoy a sunset, and God smiles with you. Think back through the events of the last twenty-four hours. As you remember each event, speak this echoing refrain to yourself: "And God loves me." Reflect on the sense of God's love and presence that this meditation fosters.

See Meeting God in Scripture

---

^a 13 Hebrew *Yam Suph*; that is, Sea of Reeds; also in verse 15

With a Whole Heart

PSALM 138:1–2

The psalmist reiterates what Jesus called the greatest commandment of all: Love God with all of your heart, soul and mind (See Matthew 22:37; Deuteronomy 6:5). Yet we often worship God with divided hearts and disinterested minds. We tune out the Scripture passages that are read, we mouth the words to the hymns and we leave the worship service without a rekindled heart. How do we keep our first love vital and growing? Worship requires attention. At the next worship service you attend, consecrate your heart to God as you enter the sanctuary. Close your eyes for a few minutes as you listen to the music. Pay attention to your heart.

See Meeting God in Worship

17 who struck down great kings,
> *His love endures forever.*
18 and killed mighty kings—
> *His love endures forever.*
19 Sihon king of the Amorites
> *His love endures forever.*
20 and Og king of Bashan—
> *His love endures forever.*
21 and gave their land as an inheritance,
> *His love endures forever.*
22 an inheritance to his servant Israel;
> *His love endures forever.*
23 to the One who remembered us in our low estate
> *His love endures forever.*
24 and freed us from our enemies,
> *His love endures forever.*
25 and who gives food to every creature.
> *His love endures forever.*
26 Give thanks to the God of heaven.
> *His love endures forever.*

Psalm 137

1 By the rivers of Babylon we sat and wept
    when we remembered Zion.
2 There on the poplars
    we hung our harps,
3 for there our captors asked us for songs,
    our tormentors demanded songs of joy;
    they said, "Sing us one of the songs of Zion!"

4 How can we sing the songs of the LORD
    while in a foreign land?
5 If I forget you, O Jerusalem,
    may my right hand forget its skill.
6 May my tongue cling to the roof of my mouth
    if I do not remember you,
  if I do not consider Jerusalem
    my highest joy.

7 Remember, O LORD, what the Edomites did
    on the day Jerusalem fell.
  "Tear it down," they cried,
    "tear it down to its foundations!"

8 O Daughter of Babylon, doomed to destruction,
    happy is he who repays you
    for what you have done to us—
9 he who seizes your infants
    and dashes them against the rocks.

Psalm 138

Of David.

1 I will praise you, O LORD, with all my heart;
    before the "gods" I will sing your praise.
2 I will bow down toward your holy temple
    and will praise your name
    for your love and your faithfulness,

for you have exalted above all things
    your name and your word.
³ When I called, you answered me;
    you made me bold and stouthearted.

⁴ May all the kings of the earth praise you, O LORD,
    when they hear the words of your mouth.
⁵ May they sing of the ways of the LORD,
    for the glory of the LORD is great.

⁶ Though the LORD is on high, he looks upon the
    lowly,
    but the proud he knows from afar.
⁷ Though I walk in the midst of trouble,
    you preserve my life;
you stretch out your hand against the anger of
    my foes,
    with your right hand you save me.
⁸ The LORD will fulfill his purpose for me;
    your love, O LORD, endures forever—
    do not abandon the works of your hands.

Psalm 139

For the director of music. Of David. A psalm.

¹ O LORD, you have searched me
    and you know me.
² You know when I sit and when I rise;
    you perceive my thoughts from afar.
³ You discern my going out and my lying down;
    you are familiar with all my ways.
⁴ Before a word is on my tongue
    you know it completely, O LORD.

⁵ You hem me in—behind and before;
    you have laid your hand upon me.
⁶ Such knowledge is too wonderful for me,
    too lofty for me to attain.

⁷ Where can I go from your Spirit?
    Where can I flee from your presence?
⁸ If I go up to the heavens, you are there;
    if I make my bed in the depths,ᵃ you are there.
⁹ If I rise on the wings of the dawn,
    if I settle on the far side of the sea,
¹⁰ even there your hand will guide me,
    your right hand will hold me fast.

¹¹ If I say, "Surely the darkness will hide me
    and the light become night around me,"
¹² even the darkness will not be dark to you;
    the night will shine like the day,
    for darkness is as light to you.

¹³ For you created my inmost being;
    you knit me together in my mother's womb.
¹⁴ I praise you because I am fearfully and
     wonderfully made;
    your works are wonderful,
    I know that full well.

ᵃ 8 Hebrew *Sheol*

Search Me, O God

PSALM 139

The psalmist David exhibits an extraordinary sensitivity to God's presence even to the point of knowing that God has been intimately involved in every day of the singer's life. David's whole life span has been orchestrated by the Master Composer.

Are you aware of God's design for your life? Ask God to help you write a life mission statement, whether you're in the early stages of your life or you have many years behind you. What did God have in mind for you when your body was still being formed? How is God forming you spiritually now? Who does God want you to become? What are your dreams, your goals, your special abilities, your spiritual gifts? How does God want to use them? Dare to pray boldly. Dare to dream boldly.

See Meeting God in Prayer

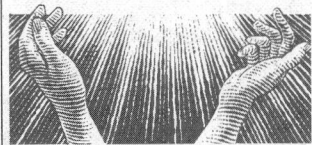

The Unruly Tongue

PSALM 141:3

The image of the psalmist is quite vivid. He prays to God to "keep watch over the door" of his lips. In the letter of James, the tongue is compared to a small fire that can set a vast forest ablaze (James 3:5–6)! Most of us have had the experience of thoughtlessly saying the wrong thing and hurting someone. Gossip and idle speculation are even more insidious. As you go through the day, listen to yourself speak. Are you speaking unfairly, rashly and thoughtlessly? If you hear yourself speaking in one of these ways, say to yourself, "Lord, have mercy." Begin anew in the next moment.

See Meeting God in Everyday Life

¹⁵ My frame was not hidden from you
  when I was made in the secret place.
When I was woven together in the depths of the
    earth,
¹⁶   your eyes saw my unformed body.
All the days ordained for me
  were written in your book
  before one of them came to be.

¹⁷ How precious to*a* me are your thoughts, O God!
  How vast is the sum of them!
¹⁸ Were I to count them,
  they would outnumber the grains of sand.
When I awake,
  I am still with you.

¹⁹ If only you would slay the wicked, O God!
  Away from me, you bloodthirsty men!
²⁰ They speak of you with evil intent;
  your adversaries misuse your name.
²¹ Do I not hate those who hate you, O Lᴏʀᴅ,
  and abhor those who rise up against you?
²² I have nothing but hatred for them;
  I count them my enemies.

²³ Search me, O God, and know my heart;
  test me and know my anxious thoughts.
²⁴ See if there is any offensive way in me,
  and lead me in the way everlasting.

Psalm 140

For the director of music. A psalm of David.

¹ Rescue me, O Lᴏʀᴅ, from evil men;
  protect me from men of violence,
² who devise evil plans in their hearts
  and stir up war every day.
³ They make their tongues as sharp as a serpent's;
  the poison of vipers is on their lips.   *Selah*

⁴ Keep me, O Lᴏʀᴅ, from the hands of the wicked;
  protect me from men of violence
  who plan to trip my feet.
⁵ Proud men have hidden a snare for me;
  they have spread out the cords of their net
  and have set traps for me along my path. *Selah*

⁶ O Lᴏʀᴅ, I say to you, "You are my God."
  Hear, O Lᴏʀᴅ, my cry for mercy.
⁷ O Sovereign Lᴏʀᴅ, my strong deliverer,
  who shields my head in the day of battle—
⁸ do not grant the wicked their desires, O Lᴏʀᴅ;
  do not let their plans succeed,
  or they will become proud.   *Selah*

⁹ Let the heads of those who surround me
  be covered with the trouble their lips have
    caused.
¹⁰ Let burning coals fall upon them;
  may they be thrown into the fire,

b 17 Or concerning

into miry pits, never to rise.
¹¹ Let slanderers not be established in the land;
may disaster hunt down men of violence.

¹² I know that the LORD secures justice for the poor
and upholds the cause of the needy.
¹³ Surely the righteous will praise your name
and the upright will live before you.

Psalm 141

A psalm of David.

¹ O LORD, I call to you; come quickly to me.
Hear my voice when I call to you.
² May my prayer be set before you like incense;
may the lifting up of my hands be like the
evening sacrifice.

³ Set a guard over my mouth, O LORD;
keep watch over the door of my lips.
⁴ Let not my heart be drawn to what is evil,
to take part in wicked deeds
with men who are evildoers;
let me not eat of their delicacies.

⁵ Let a righteous man*a* strike me—it is a kindness;
let him rebuke me—it is oil on my head.
My head will not refuse it.

Yet my prayer is ever against the deeds of
evildoers;
⁶ their rulers will be thrown down from the cliffs,
and the wicked will learn that my words were
well spoken.
⁷ ⌊They will say,⌋ "As one plows and breaks up the
earth,
so our bones have been scattered at the mouth
of the grave.*b*"

⁸ But my eyes are fixed on you, O Sovereign LORD;
in you I take refuge—do not give me over to
death.
⁹ Keep me from the snares they have laid for me,
from the traps set by evildoers.
¹⁰ Let the wicked fall into their own nets,
while I pass by in safety.

Psalm 142

A *maskil*c of David. When he was in the cave. A prayer.

¹ I cry aloud to the LORD;
I lift up my voice to the LORD for mercy.
² I pour out my complaint before him;
before him I tell my trouble.

³ When my spirit grows faint within me,
it is you who know my way.
In the path where I walk

God Knows the Way

PSALM 142:1–3

The psalmist remembers God's faithfulness to the weak: "When my spirit grows faint within me, it is you who know my way." We see our own weakness every day—a stubborn habit we cannot seem to change, a relationship that is not working despite our best efforts. We experience situations that we cannot fix; we cannot even see solutions, let alone work them out. Nevertheless we are reluctant to acknowledge that we are lost and need to wait for God. Yet in the moment we surrender to God, we find new strength, new insight, new hope. In your journal, or on a piece of paper, reflect on the situations and weaknesses that discourage you. What are you trying to control? What might God be gracefully inviting you to risk?

See Meeting God in Everyday Life

Beginning With God

PSALM 143:8

With each new day, we have a fresh beginning in God's love and faithfulness. Here, the psalmist seeks God's presence from the first light of day. Although each of us has a unique body clock, there is something significant about beginning and ending the day with God. You do not need to be a "morning person" to consecrate the start of your day to God. Perhaps as you drink your coffee, tea or juice, you could close your eyes and offer your day to God. Or when you take your shower, you could thank God for the gift of water and a new day. As you drive to work, you could offer intercessory prayer for persons on your list.

See Meeting God in Everyday Life

men have hidden a snare for me.
⁴ Look to my right and see;
  no one is concerned for me.
I have no refuge;
  no one cares for my life.

⁵ I cry to you, O LORD;
  I say, "You are my refuge,
  my portion in the land of the living."
⁶ Listen to my cry,
  for I am in desperate need;
rescue me from those who pursue me,
  for they are too strong for me.
⁷ Set me free from my prison,
  that I may praise your name.
Then the righteous will gather about me
  because of your goodness to me.

Psalm 143

A psalm of David.

¹ O LORD, hear my prayer,
  listen to my cry for mercy;
in your faithfulness and righteousness
  come to my relief.
² Do not bring your servant into judgment,
  for no one living is righteous before you.

³ The enemy pursues me,
  he crushes me to the ground;
he makes me dwell in darkness
  like those long dead.
⁴ So my spirit grows faint within me;
  my heart within me is dismayed.

⁵ I remember the days of long ago;
  I meditate on all your works
  and consider what your hands have done.
⁶ I spread out my hands to you;
  my soul thirsts for you like a parched land.
Selah

⁷ Answer me quickly, O LORD;
  my spirit fails.
Do not hide your face from me
  or I will be like those who go down to the pit.
⁸ Let the morning bring me word of your unfailing
    love,
  for I have put my trust in you.
Show me the way I should go,
  for to you I lift up my soul.
⁹ Rescue me from my enemies, O LORD,
  for I hide myself in you.
¹⁰ Teach me to do your will,
  for you are my God;
may your good Spirit
  lead me on level ground.

¹¹ For your name's sake, O LORD, preserve my life;
  in your righteousness, bring me out of trouble.
¹² In your unfailing love, silence my enemies;

destroy all my foes,
for I am your servant.

Psalm 144

Of David.

¹ Praise be to the LORD my Rock,
    who trains my hands for war,
    my fingers for battle.
² He is my loving God and my fortress,
    my stronghold and my deliverer,
    my shield, in whom I take refuge,
    who subdues peoples*ᵃ* under me.

³ O LORD, what is man that you care for him,
    the son of man that you think of him?
⁴ Man is like a breath;
    his days are like a fleeting shadow.

⁵ Part your heavens, O LORD, and come down;
    touch the mountains, so that they smoke.
⁶ Send forth lightning and scatter ⌐the enemies⌐;
    shoot your arrows and rout them.
⁷ Reach down your hand from on high;
    deliver me and rescue me
from the mighty waters,
    from the hands of foreigners
⁸ whose mouths are full of lies,
    whose right hands are deceitful.

⁹ I will sing a new song to you, O God;
    on the ten-stringed lyre I will make music to
        you,
¹⁰ to the One who gives victory to kings,
    who delivers his servant David from the deadly
        sword.

¹¹ Deliver me and rescue me
    from the hands of foreigners
whose mouths are full of lies,
    whose right hands are deceitful.

¹² Then our sons in their youth
    will be like well-nurtured plants,
and our daughters will be like pillars
    carved to adorn a palace.
¹³ Our barns will be filled
    with every kind of provision.
Our sheep will increase by thousands,
    by tens of thousands in our fields;
¹⁴   our oxen will draw heavy loads.*ᵇ*
There will be no breaching of walls,
    no going into captivity,
    no cry of distress in our streets.

¹⁵ Blessed are the people of whom this is true;
    blessed are the people whose God is the LORD.

ᵃ 2 Many manuscripts of the Masoretic Text, Dead Sea Scrolls, Aquila,
Jerome and Syriac; most manuscripts of the Masoretic Text *subdues my
people   ᵇ 14* Or *our chieftains will be firmly established*

The Spiritual Life

PSALM 144

"[A] spiritual life is a life which
is controlled by a gradually developing sense of the Eternal, of
God and his transcendent reality: an increasing capacity for
him, so that our relation to God
becomes the chief thing about
us, exceeding and also condi-
tioning our relationship with
each other . . . For, what it
means for us is surely this: that
we are meant, beyond the physical, to contribute to, indeed
collaborate in, God's spiritual
creation."

—EVELYN UNDERHILL,
The Spiritual Life

Across the Generations

PSALM 145:3–6

A gift from our Jewish spiritual heritage is its rich oral tradition. Grandparents tell their grandchildren the stories of creation, of the exodus, of God's provision in the desert and of God's continuing faithfulness. Likewise, the church has grown spiritually through telling and retelling the stories of Jesus. However, too often in our very own families we neglect to tell the meaningful stories of our own spiritual journeys. What stories of God's grace do you need to tell to someone in your family? What moments of awe at God's majesty and love in the past week do you need to share? How do you talk about your faith with loved ones?

See Meeting God in Everyday Life

Psalm 145[a]

A psalm of praise. Of David.

¹ I will exalt you, my God the King;
  I will praise your name for ever and ever.
² Every day I will praise you
  and extol your name for ever and ever.

³ Great is the LORD and most worthy of praise;
  his greatness no one can fathom.
⁴ One generation will commend your works to another;
  they will tell of your mighty acts.
⁵ They will speak of the glorious splendor of your majesty,
  and I will meditate on your wonderful works.[b]
⁶ They will tell of the power of your awesome works,
  and I will proclaim your great deeds.
⁷ They will celebrate your abundant goodness
  and joyfully sing of your righteousness.

⁸ The LORD is gracious and compassionate,
  slow to anger and rich in love.
⁹ The LORD is good to all;
  he has compassion on all he has made.
¹⁰ All you have made will praise you, O LORD;
  your saints will extol you.
¹¹ They will tell of the glory of your kingdom
  and speak of your might,
¹² so that all men may know of your mighty acts
  and the glorious splendor of your kingdom.
¹³ Your kingdom is an everlasting kingdom,
  and your dominion endures through all generations.

  The LORD is faithful to all his promises
  and loving toward all he has made.[c]
¹⁴ The LORD upholds all those who fall
  and lifts up all who are bowed down.
¹⁵ The eyes of all look to you,
  and you give them their food at the proper time.
¹⁶ You open your hand
  and satisfy the desires of every living thing.

¹⁷ The LORD is righteous in all his ways
  and loving toward all he has made.
¹⁸ The LORD is near to all who call on him,
  to all who call on him in truth.
¹⁹ He fulfills the desires of those who fear him;
  he hears their cry and saves them.
²⁰ The LORD watches over all who love him,
  but all the wicked he will destroy.

²¹ My mouth will speak in praise of the LORD.

---

[a] This psalm is an acrostic poem, the verses of which (including verse 13b) begin with the successive letters of the Hebrew alphabet. [b] 5 Dead Sea Scrolls and Syriac (see also Septuagint); Masoretic Text *On the glorious splendor of your majesty / and on your wonderful works I will meditate*
[c] 13 One manuscript of the Masoretic Text, Dead Sea Scrolls and Syriac (see also Septuagint); most manuscripts of the Masoretic Text do not have the last two lines of verse 13.

Let every creature praise his holy name
for ever and ever.

Psalm 146

¹ Praise the LORD.*a*

Praise the LORD, O my soul.
²   I will praise the LORD all my life;
    I will sing praise to my God as long as I live.

³ Do not put your trust in princes,
    in mortal men, who cannot save.
⁴ When their spirit departs, they return to the
      ground;
    on that very day their plans come to nothing.

⁵ Blessed is he whose help is the God of Jacob,
    whose hope is in the LORD his God,
⁶ the Maker of heaven and earth,
    the sea, and everything in them—
    the LORD, who remains faithful forever.
⁷ He upholds the cause of the oppressed
    and gives food to the hungry.
  The LORD sets prisoners free,
⁸   the LORD gives sight to the blind,
  the LORD lifts up those who are bowed down,
    the LORD loves the righteous.
⁹ The LORD watches over the alien
    and sustains the fatherless and the widow,
    but he frustrates the ways of the wicked.

¹⁰ The LORD reigns forever,
    your God, O Zion, for all generations.

Praise the LORD.

Psalm 147

¹ Praise the LORD.*b*

How good it is to sing praises to our God,
    how pleasant and fitting to praise him!

² The LORD builds up Jerusalem;
    he gathers the exiles of Israel.
³ He heals the brokenhearted
    and binds up their wounds.
⁴ He determines the number of the stars
    and calls them each by name.
⁵ Great is our Lord and mighty in power;
    his understanding has no limit.
⁶ The LORD sustains the humble
    but casts the wicked to the ground.

⁷ Sing to the LORD with thanksgiving;
    make music to our God on the harp.
⁸ He covers the sky with clouds;
    he supplies the earth with rain
    and makes grass grow on the hills.

A Godly Balance

PSALM 147:3–6

The psalmist reflects on the amazing paradox: The God of the universe, who names the stars and has an understanding that "has no limit," is also concerned with each unique person, poor and grief-stricken as each may be. Even though there are billions of stars in the divine purview, God calls each one of us tenderly. God "heals the brokenhearted." What does this say about God's nature? What is the image of God that you see in your mind's eye? Take five minutes to reflect on this image, then share your thoughts and feelings in your journal or on a sheet of paper.

See Meeting God in the Created Order

---

a 1 Hebrew *Hallelu Yah*; also in verse 10   *b 1* Hebrew *Hallelu Yah*; also in
verse 20

It All Comes Down to Praise

PSALM 148:1–12

Praise is a refrain in the psalms from beginning to end. Here, the psalmist calls all creation— animate and inanimate—to join a universal chorus of thanksgiving. Even "sea creatures," "stormy winds" and "small creatures" are invited to sing along. The Psalms reveal that praise is a natural response to God's Word. Think of concrete ways by which you might praise God. Could you set aside a small table in a quiet room of your house where you place symbols of God's presence? Could you plant your garden as an act of worship? What creative offering of praise can you make?

See Meeting God in the Created Order

9 He provides food for the cattle
    and for the young ravens when they call.

10 His pleasure is not in the strength of the horse,
    nor his delight in the legs of a man;
11 the LORD delights in those who fear him,
    who put their hope in his unfailing love.

12 Extol the LORD, O Jerusalem;
    praise your God, O Zion,
13 for he strengthens the bars of your gates
    and blesses your people within you.
14 He grants peace to your borders
    and satisfies you with the finest of wheat.

15 He sends his command to the earth;
    his word runs swiftly.
16 He spreads the snow like wool
    and scatters the frost like ashes.
17 He hurls down his hail like pebbles.
    Who can withstand his icy blast?
18 He sends his word and melts them;
    he stirs up his breezes, and the waters flow.

19 He has revealed his word to Jacob,
    his laws and decrees to Israel.
20 He has done this for no other nation;
    they do not know his laws.

Praise the LORD.

Psalm 148

1 Praise the LORD.[a]

Praise the LORD from the heavens,
    praise him in the heights above.
2 Praise him, all his angels,
    praise him, all his heavenly hosts.
3 Praise him, sun and moon,
    praise him, all you shining stars.
4 Praise him, you highest heavens
    and you waters above the skies.
5 Let them praise the name of the LORD,
    for he commanded and they were created.
6 He set them in place for ever and ever;
    he gave a decree that will never pass away.

7 Praise the LORD from the earth,
    you great sea creatures and all ocean depths,
8 lightning and hail, snow and clouds,
    stormy winds that do his bidding,
9 you mountains and all hills,
    fruit trees and all cedars,
10 wild animals and all cattle,
    small creatures and flying birds,
11 kings of the earth and all nations,
    you princes and all rulers on earth,
12 young men and maidens,
    old men and children.

a 1 Hebrew *Hallelu Yah*; also in verse 14

¹³Let them praise the name of the LORD,
　　for his name alone is exalted;
　　his splendor is above the earth and the
　　　heavens.
¹⁴He has raised up for his people a horn,[a]
　　the praise of all his saints,
　　of Israel, the people close to his heart.

Praise the LORD.

Psalm 149

¹Praise the LORD.[b]

Sing to the LORD a new song,
　　his praise in the assembly of the saints.

²Let Israel rejoice in their Maker;
　　let the people of Zion be glad in their King.
³Let them praise his name with dancing
　　and make music to him with tambourine and
　　　harp.
⁴For the LORD takes delight in his people;
　　he crowns the humble with salvation.
⁵Let the saints rejoice in this honor
　　and sing for joy on their beds.

⁶May the praise of God be in their mouths
　　and a double-edged sword in their hands,
⁷to inflict vengeance on the nations
　　and punishment on the peoples,
⁸to bind their kings with fetters,
　　their nobles with shackles of iron,
⁹to carry out the sentence written against them.
　　This is the glory of all his saints.

Praise the LORD.

Psalm 150

¹Praise the LORD.[c]

Praise God in his sanctuary;
　　praise him in his mighty heavens.
²Praise him for his acts of power;
　　praise him for his surpassing greatness.
³Praise him with the sounding of the trumpet,
　　praise him with the harp and lyre,
⁴praise him with tambourine and dancing,
　　praise him with the strings and flute,
⁵praise him with the clash of cymbals,
　　praise him with resounding cymbals.

⁶Let everything that has breath praise the LORD.

Praise the LORD.

Clanging Cymbals

PSALM 150:1–6

Noise pollution is a growing problem today. Airplanes fly over residential neighborhoods, music blares from open car windows and even our Saturday morning quiet is broken by buzzing power tools. But loud sounds can also be offered to God in worship. To rejoice with your whole heart may take your loudest voice and your brassiest instruments—trumpets, tambourines and loud clashing cymbals. How do you "make music" to the God of the universe? How do you declare your praise? During a period of time when you can be alone, or perhaps together with a few close friends, experiment with loud worship.

ᵃ 14 Horn here symbolizes strong one, that is, king.　ᵇ 1 Hebrew Hallelu Yah; also in verse 9　ᶜ 1 Hebrew Hallelu Yah; also in verse 6

WAYS of MEETING GOD

Meeting God in the Created Order

A man, weary with responsibilities, slips out of his front door and makes his way to a neighborhood park. Walking through dappled sunlight and shade and breathing deeply of the fresh air, he begins to relax. He thinks about all of his obligations and commitments and begins to gain perspective on his schedule. He senses God's Spirit refreshing him.

A child who lives in a difficult family situation finds refuge and solace in a backyard garden. Jesus is her companion. The quiet beauty of the flowers and the pungency of the herbs assure her of his presence. She tells him about her confusion and pain and knows that he understands.

A woman wakes up at dawn. Hearing birds calling, she opens the tent flap to gaze at a vista she hiked eight miles to see. Rose-gold streaks of light glance off mountain peaks and are mirrored in the still lake before her. The sheer extravagance of the beauty she beholds so grips her that words melt away. She finds herself drawn into wordless, awestruck communion with God.

Have you experienced something similar? From the dawn of civilization, human beings have encountered God's divine presence in the natural world. Poets and mystics of every age have seen God in the orderliness, splendor and mystery of creation. The wonders of earth and sky reminded them—as they remind us—of God's transcendence and holiness. "Earth's crammed with heaven," wrote the poet Elizabeth Barrett Browning, "and every common bush afire with God."

Scripture offers an abundance of insight into the practice of meeting God in the created order. Our un-

> **P**oets and mystics of every age have seen God in the orderliness, splendor and mystery of creation. The wonders of earth and sky reminded them—as they remind us—of God's transcendence and holiness.

826

derstanding grows from the Biblical teachings concerning God's creation of the universe, humankind's fall from grace, Jesus' saving work and the restoration of all things at the end of time.

The Order of Creation. This world is the theater for the display of God's majesty and holiness. The psalmist wrote,

> The heavens declare the glory of God;
> the skies proclaim the work of his hands.
> Day after day they pour forth speech;
> night after night they display knowledge.
> There is no speech or language
> where their voice is not heard.
> Their voice goes out into all the earth,
> their words to the ends of the world.—Psalm 19:1–4

The psalmist David knew well that the creation communicates volumes about the Creator, for everything God has made bears the stamp of divine wisdom, power and love. The God who is "unsearchable" (see Romans 11:33) becomes known in part through "the work of his hands." Writes the apostle Paul, "Since the creation of the world God's invisible qualities—his eternal power and divine nature—have been clearly seen" (Romans 1:20).

Time and again the Christian church has affirmed this intimate relationship between the Creator and creation. Eastern Orthodox churches teach that God made all matter to be "Spirit-bearing"; it can therefore communicate God's grace and presence. The Celtic Christianity of the British Isles developed a spiritual path known for earthiness—praying while kindling a hearth fire, milking a cow or tilling the ground. The early monk Benedict viewed life from a similar perspective. Benedictines (as his followers are called) encouraged people to see God in and through the ordinariness of daily work. Francis of Assisi in the thirteenth century is renowned for his love of every creature, each of whom he counted as a brother or sister. Francis preached to birds and animals, believing that the whole of creation was subject to redemption. Centuries later the Swiss Protestant reformer John Calvin wrote, "Wherever you cast your eyes, there is no spot in the universe wherein you cannot discern at least some sparks of [God's] glory." All of these diverse Christian traditions suggest an earth that is truly "crammed with heaven." The nineteenth-century Jesuit poet Gerard Manley Hopkins expressed this idea: "The earth is filled with the grandeur of God. It will flame out, like shining from shook foil."

One of the simplest ways to meet God is to contemplate his creation. Looking out of a window, taking a walk under the stars or going for a leisurely drive reminds us that the hand of the Artist is revealed in the art. Sea lions and hyacinths, volcanoes and hummingbirds speak volumes about the creative imagination of the God who made them. Contemplating the wonder of creation can move us to pray more deeply: "Through every grass blade in the thousand, thousand grasses . . . . through the song-notes and the marked feathers of the birds . . . through the soft warm air, the flecks of clouds dissolving—I used them all for prayer" wrote Richard Jefferies.

The more we see God's character and purpose revealed in each living creature, the greater our wonder and gratitude. Indeed, it seems as though everything exists to praise God. Angels and all heavenly beings; sun, moon and stars; mountains and waters; birds, beasts and sea creatures; every kind of weather; women and men, young and old—all are fashioned to praise the Creator we see in creation (see Psalm 148).

The Crown of Creation. The creation stories in Genesis show how God gives preeminence to human beings in the created order. Indeed, we were fashioned as the final act of the drama of creation—the crown of creation that bears the stamp of God's own image and likeness. We do not comprehend fully what it means to be made in the divine image, but we do know that God confers extraordinary dignity on us. In Psalm 8, David muses on the wonderful fact that human beings, seemingly so insignificant in comparison to the vast marvels of this universe, should have been made but "a little lower than the heavenly beings" (Psalm 8:5). Truly we are "fearfully and wonderfully made" (Psalm 139:14).

Looking out a window, taking a walk under the stars or going for a leisurely drive reminds us that the hand of the Artist is revealed in the art.

Yet while we were created to reflect the very goodness of God, we know that human beings have lost the ability to reflect anything but a distorted image of him. The Bible states clearly that human sin has tragic consequences for the whole of creation:

The earth dries up and withers,
  the world languishes . . .
The earth is defiled by its people;
  they have disobeyed the laws . . .
  and broken the everlasting covenant.
Therefore a curse consumes the earth;
  its people must bear their guilt.—Isaiah 24:4–6

No century has demonstrated this reality more clearly than the twentieth. Greed and injustice have brought the earth's ecosystems to the edge of peril.

Just as we can reflect on what creation may reveal to us of *God's* character, so we can ask what God may reveal to us through creation about *our* character. Are we wisely using the resources we have been given? Do we really believe that creation reflects God's glory—enough to preserve its beauty so that all people can see God? Should we interpret the earth's distress signals as a call to repentance?

Because the order of creation has been fractured by sin, we look to the order of salvation for its healing. Jesus Christ is God's answer to the groans of a creation subjected to the "bondage [of] decay" (Romans 8:21). Jesus "is the image of the invisible God, the firstborn over all creation" (Colossians 1:15). In him the clarity and purity of the image of God are restored to us. But Jesus embodies more than merely our true humanity in God. He is also the One in whom "all things were created: things in heaven and on earth" (v.16) and in whom "all things hold together" (v.17). As Paul declares, "through him [God was pleased] to reconcile to himself all things, whether things on earth or things in heaven" (v.20). And Jesus' coming points to the future restoration of the entire created order. Our salvation in Jesus Christ includes a promise whose full flower we cannot yet see. By hope we believe the seed of redemption will bear fruit in the transfiguration of all that we know and experience. God's creation will one day become what it was intended to be.

The Bodies God Has Made. We must take seriously another implication of the miracle of incarnation—that Jesus took on the form and body of a human being. God's Word "became flesh and made his dwelling among us" (John 1:14). This event makes the human body—bones, tendons, blood cells, heart, brain—a chosen instrument of salvation. God sees it as a worthy vehicle for the completion of divine purposes. We may not, then, dismiss or denigrate our bodies. Indeed, Jesus speaks of his own body as the temple of God (see John 2:21). Paul tells the Corinthians that they, too, are God's temple because God's Spirit dwells in them (see 1 Corinthians 3:16–17). Therefore, we must think of our bodies and spirits as an integrated being, and we must care for our whole self. How we treat our physical selves—eating a balanced diet, exercising regularly, getting enough sleep—has spiritual implications. We honor God in our bodies when we keep the Sabbath holy, taking a day each week to cease from labor and to worship and enjoy God's gifts. In our hard driving, stress-filled culture in which we tend to value ourselves and others on the basis of what we produce, rest becomes all the more essential; the wisdom of the Sabbath commandment becomes more readily apparent.

The fact that we sometimes find it hard to draw back from our frantic schedules only makes it more necessary to ensure that we set aside a time for rest. Place your cares in God's capable hands, then take time to pray and to play. Enjoy your most precious relationships.

Even more, rest in God and contemplate the beauty and mystery of life. Allow yourself to be absorbed by the innocent delight of a toddler's face, the quiet of an evening sky, the brilliant hues of an autumn leaf. God's creation is to be enjoyed as we let it point us back in reverence to the glorious mystery of the One who brought it into being.

See Page 1094 for the next Ways of Meeting God *article.*

PROVERBS
Wisdom Day by Day

KEY VERSE:

Wisdom is supreme; therefore get wisdom. Though it cost all you have,
get understanding.—Proverbs 4:7

"My soul's house is cramped. Expand it, so that you may enter in. It is in ruins. Restore it. It must offend your eyes. I confess and know it, but who will cleanse it? To whom shall I cry but to you? Clear me from hidden faults, O Lord, and keep back your servant also from those of others."

—AUGUSTINE,
Confessions

Proverbs is perhaps the most practical book in the Bible. These words of wisdom grew out of the common experiences of human life. The teachers of ancient times were eager to share what they had learned about life. Their insights helped them in their daily living and in their relationships. The reward of wisdom is a better and happier life. Thus, this "treasure" is more precious than silver or gold and worthy of passing on. The sayings here cover a variety of themes: love, friendship, marriage, poverty, wealth, and others.

Individual proverbs summarize wisdom that has been proven true in varied situations. But they are not absolute or applicable in every circumstance. If not taken in proper context, some may even contradict each other: "Too many cooks spoil the broth," but "Many hands make light work." True wisdom is not simply knowing the sayings of the wise but also knowing when and how to apply them.

Some proverbs may trouble us. The question of why evil besets innocent people, for example, may continue to baffle and disturb us as we meditate on some adages in this book. Nevertheless, the wisdom we find here can help us walk in the Spirit in the midst of our doubts and all that life offers—good or bad. Remember that getting insight does not mean finding quick answers. As you read and ponder, allow your soul, heart and mind to wrestle with the sages and, like Jacob wrestling with an angel, to hold on until you receive a blessing.

Prologue: Purpose and Theme

1 The proverbs of Solomon son of David, king of Israel:

² for attaining wisdom and discipline;
　　for understanding words of insight;
³ for acquiring a disciplined and prudent life,
　　doing what is right and just and fair;
⁴ for giving prudence to the simple,
　　knowledge and discretion to the young—
⁵ let the wise listen and add to their learning,
　　and let the discerning get guidance—
⁶ for understanding proverbs and parables,
　　the sayings and riddles of the wise.

⁷ The fear of the LORD is the beginning of
　　knowledge,
　　but fools*ᵃ* despise wisdom and discipline.

Exhortations to Embrace Wisdom

Warning Against Enticement

⁸ Listen, my son, to your father's instruction
　　and do not forsake your mother's teaching.
⁹ They will be a garland to grace your head
　　and a chain to adorn your neck.

¹⁰ My son, if sinners entice you,
　　do not give in to them.
¹¹ If they say, "Come along with us;
　　let's lie in wait for someone's blood,
　　let's waylay some harmless soul;
¹² let's swallow them alive, like the grave,*ᵇ*
　　and whole, like those who go down to the pit;
¹³ we will get all sorts of valuable things
　　and fill our houses with plunder;
¹⁴ throw in your lot with us,
　　and we will share a common purse"—
¹⁵ my son, do not go along with them,
　　do not set foot on their paths;
¹⁶ for their feet rush into sin,
　　they are swift to shed blood.
¹⁷ How useless to spread a net
　　in full view of all the birds!
¹⁸ These men lie in wait for their own blood;
　　they waylay only themselves!
¹⁹ Such is the end of all who go after ill-gotten gain;
　　it takes away the lives of those who get it.

Warning Against Rejecting Wisdom

²⁰ Wisdom calls aloud in the street,
　　she raises her voice in the public squares;
²¹ at the head of the noisy streets*ᶜ* she cries out,
　　in the gateways of the city she makes her
　　speech:

²² "How long will you simple ones*ᵈ* love your simple
　　ways?

Parental Teaching

PROVERBS 1:8–9

For good or for ill, much of who we are—how we think and behave—comes from our parents or others who raised us. In the midst of a conversation we may think, "I sound just like my mother." We may try to clinch an argument with, "Well, that's what my father always said."

Think of recent times when you have "heard" your parents' voices guiding you. What are some of the bits of wisdom you have received from them? Some "parental proverbs" may be sources of great strength or steadiness. Take time to give God thanks for these gifts. Other parental "teachings" may have trained you for prejudice or fearfulness. Ask God for help in discerning the difference. Ask God to let the wisdom of Proverbs become a source of insight and delight.

See Meeting God in Everyday Life

ᵃ 7 The Hebrew words rendered *fool* in Proverbs, and often elsewhere in the Old Testament, denote one who is morally deficient.　*ᵇ 12* Hebrew *Sheol*
ᶜ 21 Hebrew; Septuagint / *on the tops of the walls*　*ᵈ 22* The Hebrew word rendered *simple* in Proverbs generally denotes one without moral direction and inclined to evil.

Wisdom's Invitation

PROVERBS 1:20–23

Wisdom (a feminine noun in Hebrew) is depicted as a woman so eager to attract listeners that she raises her voice out on the streets. Imagine yourself there, listening to her call as she offers you the gift of God's wisdom. In what areas of your life are you particularly in need of wisdom? What is holding you back from seeking God's help? The simple would rather not waste the energy required to think deeply. Scoffers turn their backs on God. Fools prefer to live by their own wits. Why do you hesitate to accept wisdom's offer? Ask God for help in employing wisdom in the choices you will face today.

See Meeting God in Scripture

How long will mockers delight in mockery
and fools hate knowledge?
²³ If you had responded to my rebuke,
I would have poured out my heart to you
and made my thoughts known to you.
²⁴ But since you rejected me when I called
and no one gave heed when I stretched out my hand,
²⁵ since you ignored all my advice
and would not accept my rebuke,
²⁶ I in turn will laugh at your disaster;
I will mock when calamity overtakes you—
²⁷ when calamity overtakes you like a storm,
when disaster sweeps over you like a whirlwind,
when distress and trouble overwhelm you.

²⁸ "Then they will call to me but I will not answer;
they will look for me but will not find me.
²⁹ Since they hated knowledge
and did not choose to fear the LORD,
³⁰ since they would not accept my advice
and spurned my rebuke,
³¹ they will eat the fruit of their ways
and be filled with the fruit of their schemes.
³² For the waywardness of the simple will kill them,
and the complacency of fools will destroy them;
³³ but whoever listens to me will live in safety
and be at ease, without fear of harm."

Moral Benefits of Wisdom

2 My son, if you accept my words
and store up my commands within you,
² turning your ear to wisdom
and applying your heart to understanding,
³ and if you call out for insight
and cry aloud for understanding,
⁴ and if you look for it as for silver
and search for it as for hidden treasure,
⁵ then you will understand the fear of the LORD
and find the knowledge of God.
⁶ For the LORD gives wisdom,
and from his mouth come knowledge and understanding.
⁷ He holds victory in store for the upright,
he is a shield to those whose walk is blameless,
⁸ for he guards the course of the just
and protects the way of his faithful ones.

⁹ Then you will understand what is right and just
and fair—every good path.
¹⁰ For wisdom will enter your heart,
and knowledge will be pleasant to your soul.
¹¹ Discretion will protect you,
and understanding will guard you.

¹² Wisdom will save you from the ways of wicked men,
from men whose words are perverse,
¹³ who leave the straight paths
to walk in dark ways,

¹⁴who delight in doing wrong
　　and rejoice in the perverseness of evil,
¹⁵whose paths are crooked
　　and who are devious in their ways.

¹⁶It will save you also from the adulteress,
　　from the wayward wife with her seductive
　　　words,
¹⁷who has left the partner of her youth
　　and ignored the covenant she made before
　　　God.ᵃ
¹⁸For her house leads down to death
　　and her paths to the spirits of the dead.
¹⁹None who go to her return
　　or attain the paths of life.

²⁰Thus you will walk in the ways of good men
　　and keep to the paths of the righteous.
²¹For the upright will live in the land,
　　and the blameless will remain in it;
²²but the wicked will be cut off from the land,
　　and the unfaithful will be torn from it.

Further Benefits of Wisdom

3 My son, do not forget my teaching,
　　but keep my commands in your heart,
²for they will prolong your life many years
　　and bring you prosperity.

³Let love and faithfulness never leave you;
　　bind them around your neck,
　　write them on the tablet of your heart.
⁴Then you will win favor and a good name
　　in the sight of God and man.

⁵Trust in the LORD with all your heart
　　and lean not on your own understanding;
⁶in all your ways acknowledge him,
　　and he will make your paths straight.ᵇ

⁷Do not be wise in your own eyes;
　　fear the LORD and shun evil.
⁸This will bring health to your body
　　and nourishment to your bones.

⁹Honor the LORD with your wealth,
　　with the firstfruits of all your crops;
¹⁰then your barns will be filled to overflowing,
　　and your vats will brim over with new wine.

¹¹My son, do not despise the LORD's discipline
　　and do not resent his rebuke,
¹²because the LORD disciplines those he loves,
　　as a fatherᶜ the son he delights in.

¹³Blessed is the man who finds wisdom,
　　the man who gains understanding,
¹⁴for she is more profitable than silver
　　and yields better returns than gold.
¹⁵She is more precious than rubies;
　　nothing you desire can compare with her.
¹⁶Long life is in her right hand;

Trust and Obey

PROVERBS 3:5–7

"If a faithful soul accepts God's
will and purpose in all simplicity, he will reach perfection
without ever realizing it, just as
a sick person who swallows his
medicine obediently will be
cured, although he neither
knows nor cares about
medicine."

—JEAN-PIERRE DE CAUSSADE,
Abandonment to Divine Providence

ᵃ 17 Or *covenant of her God*　ᵇ 6 Or *will direct your paths*　ᶜ 12 Hebrew;
Septuagint / *and he punishes*

Being a Good Neighbor

PROVERBS 3:27–30

Proverbs can be extremely practical and down-to-earth. Take these proverbs about how to deal with neighbors. They tell us to help when we can, not when we want, and according to our neighbors' needs, not according to our feeling of generosity. In short, we should love our neighbors. Yet in our mobile, busy society, we often do not even know who our neighbors are.

Who are your neighbors? Do you know them well enough to name them before God? To lift up their concerns and needs? You might draw a small map of your immediate neighborhood, labeling other houses (or neighboring apartments) as well as you can. What steps do you need to take to be able to fill it in more completely? Post the map where it will remind you to pray for your neighbors regularly. Ask God to let this discipline guide you in being a better neighbor to them.

See Meeting God in Service

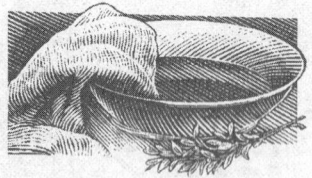

in her left hand are riches and honor.
¹⁷Her ways are pleasant ways,
and all her paths are peace.
¹⁸She is a tree of life to those who embrace her;
those who lay hold of her will be blessed.

¹⁹By wisdom the LORD laid the earth's foundations,
by understanding he set the heavens in place;
²⁰by his knowledge the deeps were divided,
and the clouds let drop the dew.

²¹My son, preserve sound judgment and discernment,
do not let them out of your sight;
²²they will be life for you,
an ornament to grace your neck.
²³Then you will go on your way in safety,
and your foot will not stumble;
²⁴when you lie down, you will not be afraid;
when you lie down, your sleep will be sweet.
²⁵Have no fear of sudden disaster
or of the ruin that overtakes the wicked,
²⁶for the LORD will be your confidence
and will keep your foot from being snared.

²⁷Do not withhold good from those who deserve it,
when it is in your power to act.
²⁸Do not say to your neighbor,
"Come back later; I'll give it tomorrow"—
when you now have it with you.

²⁹Do not plot harm against your neighbor,
who lives trustfully near you.
³⁰Do not accuse a man for no reason—
when he has done you no harm.

³¹Do not envy a violent man
or choose any of his ways,
³²for the LORD detests a perverse man
but takes the upright into his confidence.

³³The LORD's curse is on the house of the wicked,
but he blesses the home of the righteous.
³⁴He mocks proud mockers
but gives grace to the humble.
³⁵The wise inherit honor,
but fools he holds up to shame.

Wisdom Is Supreme

4 Listen, my sons, to a father's instruction;
pay attention and gain understanding.
²I give you sound learning,
so do not forsake my teaching.
³When I was a boy in my father's house,
still tender, and an only child of my mother,
⁴he taught me and said,
"Lay hold of my words with all your heart;
keep my commands and you will live.
⁵Get wisdom, get understanding;
do not forget my words or swerve from them.
⁶Do not forsake wisdom, and she will protect you;
love her, and she will watch over you.
⁷Wisdom is supreme; therefore get wisdom.

Though it cost all you have,[a] get understanding.
⁸Esteem her, and she will exalt you;
   embrace her, and she will honor you.
⁹She will set a garland of grace on your head
   and present you with a crown of splendor."

¹⁰Listen, my son, accept what I say,
   and the years of your life will be many.
¹¹I guide you in the way of wisdom
   and lead you along straight paths.
¹²When you walk, your steps will not be hampered;
   when you run, you will not stumble.
¹³Hold on to instruction, do not let it go;
   guard it well, for it is your life.
¹⁴Do not set foot on the path of the wicked
   or walk in the way of evil men.
¹⁵Avoid it, do not travel on it;
   turn from it and go on your way.
¹⁶For they cannot sleep till they do evil;
   they are robbed of slumber till they make
     someone fall.
¹⁷They eat the bread of wickedness
   and drink the wine of violence.

¹⁸The path of the righteous is like the first gleam of
   dawn,
   shining ever brighter till the full light of day.
¹⁹But the way of the wicked is like deep darkness;
   they do not know what makes them stumble.

²⁰My son, pay attention to what I say;
   listen closely to my words.
²¹Do not let them out of your sight,
   keep them within your heart;
²²for they are life to those who find them
   and health to a man's whole body.
²³Above all else, guard your heart,
   for it is the wellspring of life.
²⁴Put away perversity from your mouth;
   keep corrupt talk far from your lips.
²⁵Let your eyes look straight ahead,
   fix your gaze directly before you.
²⁶Make level[b] paths for your feet
   and take only ways that are firm.
²⁷Do not swerve to the right or the left;
   keep your foot from evil.

Warning Against Adultery

5 My son, pay attention to my wisdom,
   listen well to my words of insight,
²that you may maintain discretion
   and your lips may preserve knowledge.
³For the lips of an adulteress drip honey,
   and her speech is smoother than oil;
⁴but in the end she is bitter as gall,
   sharp as a double-edged sword.
⁵Her feet go down to death;
   her steps lead straight to the grave.[c]
⁶She gives no thought to the way of life;
   her paths are crooked, but she knows it not.

Succeeding in God's Way

PROVERBS 4:24–27

Throughout life we have been given much advice about what to do and what not to do. Much of it is aimed at helping us succeed in life. But life is more than being successful. The wise teacher knows there is a better way. Read this passage again, slowly and reflectively. What words or phrases are most meaningful to you? Write down three key words or phrases on a small piece of paper. Fold it and put it in your pocket or keep it handy so that throughout the day you may take it out and read it. Make the words or phrases your own. Begin now to succeed in God's way.

See Meeting God in Scripture

---

[a] 7 Or *Whatever else you get*   [b] 26 Or *Consider the*   [c] 5 Hebrew *Sheol*

Attractive Foolishness

PROVERBS 5:7–14

These proverbs pull no punches. Foolishness, they freely admit, can be very attractive, even seductive. Furthermore, it seems so much easier, so much less demanding. Clearly, foolishness has much more advertising potential than wisdom.

Ask God to let wisdom walk with you today, pointing out the ways foolishness calls to you. Pay attention to the seductive claims of advertisements. Which ones do you find particularly tempting? Let wisdom lead you away. Listen to her reproof when you give in to temptation. Try to take no action today without first seeking God's wisdom.

See Meeting God in Everyday Life

7 Now then, my sons, listen to me;
  do not turn aside from what I say.
8 Keep to a path far from her,
  do not go near the door of her house,
9 lest you give your best strength to others
  and your years to one who is cruel,
10 lest strangers feast on your wealth
  and your toil enrich another man's house.
11 At the end of your life you will groan,
  when your flesh and body are spent.
12 You will say, "How I hated discipline!
  How my heart spurned correction!
13 I would not obey my teachers
  or listen to my instructors.
14 I have come to the brink of utter ruin
  in the midst of the whole assembly."

15 Drink water from your own cistern,
  running water from your own well.
16 Should your springs overflow in the streets,
  your streams of water in the public squares?
17 Let them be yours alone,
  never to be shared with strangers.
18 May your fountain be blessed,
  and may you rejoice in the wife of your youth.
19 A loving doe, a graceful deer—
  may her breasts satisfy you always,
  may you ever be captivated by her love.
20 Why be captivated, my son, by an adulteress?
  Why embrace the bosom of another man's
    wife?

21 For a man's ways are in full view of the LORD,
  and he examines all his paths.
22 The evil deeds of a wicked man ensnare him;
  the cords of his sin hold him fast.
23 He will die for lack of discipline,
  led astray by his own great folly.

Warnings Against Folly

6 My son, if you have put up security for your neighbor,
  if you have struck hands in pledge for another,
2 if you have been trapped by what you said,
  ensnared by the words of your mouth,
3 then do this, my son, to free yourself,
  since you have fallen into your neighbor's
    hands:
  Go and humble yourself;
  press your plea with your neighbor!
4 Allow no sleep to your eyes,
  no slumber to your eyelids.
5 Free yourself, like a gazelle from the hand of the
    hunter,
  like a bird from the snare of the fowler.

6 Go to the ant, you sluggard;
  consider its ways and be wise!
7 It has no commander,
  no overseer or ruler,
8 yet it stores its provisions in summer
  and gathers its food at harvest.

⁹How long will you lie there, you sluggard?
  When will you get up from your sleep?
¹⁰A little sleep, a little slumber,
  a little folding of the hands to rest—
¹¹and poverty will come on you like a bandit
  and scarcity like an armed man.ᵃ

¹²A scoundrel and villain,
  who goes about with a corrupt mouth,
¹³ who winks with his eye,
  signals with his feet
  and motions with his fingers,
¹⁴ who plots evil with deceit in his heart—
  he always stirs up dissension.
¹⁵Therefore disaster will overtake him in an instant;
  he will suddenly be destroyed—without
    remedy.

¹⁶There are six things the LORD hates,
  seven that are detestable to him:
¹⁷   haughty eyes,
    a lying tongue,
    hands that shed innocent blood,
¹⁸   a heart that devises wicked schemes,
    feet that are quick to rush into evil,
¹⁹   a false witness who pours out lies
    and a man who stirs up dissension among
      brothers.

Warning Against Adultery

²⁰My son, keep your father's commands
  and do not forsake your mother's teaching.
²¹Bind them upon your heart forever;
  fasten them around your neck.
²²When you walk, they will guide you;
  when you sleep, they will watch over you;
  when you awake, they will speak to you.
²³For these commands are a lamp,
  this teaching is a light,
  and the corrections of discipline
  are the way to life,
²⁴keeping you from the immoral woman,
  from the smooth tongue of the wayward wife.
²⁵Do not lust in your heart after her beauty
  or let her captivate you with her eyes,
²⁶for the prostitute reduces you to a loaf of bread,
  and the adulteress preys upon your very life.
²⁷Can a man scoop fire into his lap
  without his clothes being burned?
²⁸Can a man walk on hot coals
  without his feet being scorched?
²⁹So is he who sleeps with another man's wife;
  no one who touches her will go unpunished.

³⁰Men do not despise a thief if he steals
  to satisfy his hunger when he is starving.
³¹Yet if he is caught, he must pay sevenfold,
  though it costs him all the wealth of his house.
³²But a man who commits adultery lacks judgment;
  whoever does so destroys himself.

A Look Inward

PROVERBS 6:16–19

To take an honest look at one's life can be uncomfortable. Scripture has a way of touching a sensitive nerve and making one feel vulnerable. These verses list actions that are offensive to God. They point out exactly what the Lord hates. The teachers of wisdom want to help their listeners take an honest look inward and to discover for themselves if there is anything in them that is causing Almighty God pain.

After reading these verses, sit quietly. Let God hold you as you take stock of each of the seven behaviors. In what ways do you see them in your own actions? In what ways do you need to seek God's forgiveness? In what ways do you need to ask forgiveness from others? Allow yourself to experience God's love, forgiveness and transforming grace.

Seeking Wisdom

PROVERBS 7:1–4

The beginning of wisdom is
the most sincere desire
for instruction,
and concern for instruction
is love of her,
and love of her is the keeping of her laws,
and giving heed to her laws
is assurance of immor-
tality,
and immortality brings one
near to God;
so the desire for wisdom
leads to a kingdom.

—*Wisdom of Solomon*,
Old Testament Apocrypha, NRSV

³³ Blows and disgrace are his lot,
    and his shame will never be wiped away;
³⁴ for jealousy arouses a husband's fury,
    and he will show no mercy when he takes
        revenge.
³⁵ He will not accept any compensation;
    he will refuse the bribe, however great it is.

Warning Against the Adulteress

7 My son, keep my words
    and store up my commands within you.
² Keep my commands and you will live;
    guard my teachings as the apple of your eye.
³ Bind them on your fingers;
    write them on the tablet of your heart.
⁴ Say to wisdom, "You are my sister,"
    and call understanding your kinsman;
⁵ they will keep you from the adulteress,
    from the wayward wife with her seductive
        words.

⁶ At the window of my house
    I looked out through the lattice.
⁷ I saw among the simple,
    I noticed among the young men,
    a youth who lacked judgment.
⁸ He was going down the street near her corner,
    walking along in the direction of her house
⁹ at twilight, as the day was fading,
    as the dark of night set in.

¹⁰ Then out came a woman to meet him,
    dressed like a prostitute and with crafty intent.
¹¹ (She is loud and defiant,
    her feet never stay at home;
¹² now in the street, now in the squares,
    at every corner she lurks.)
¹³ She took hold of him and kissed him
    and with a brazen face she said:

¹⁴ "I have fellowship offerings[a] at home;
    today I fulfilled my vows.
¹⁵ So I came out to meet you;
    I looked for you and have found you!
¹⁶ I have covered my bed
    with colored linens from Egypt.
¹⁷ I have perfumed my bed
    with myrrh, aloes and cinnamon.
¹⁸ Come, let's drink deep of love till morning;
    let's enjoy ourselves with love!
¹⁹ My husband is not at home;
    he has gone on a long journey.
²⁰ He took his purse filled with money
    and will not be home till full moon."

²¹ With persuasive words she led him astray;
    she seduced him with her smooth talk.
²² All at once he followed her
    like an ox going to the slaughter,
    like a deer[b] stepping into a noose[c]

a 14 Traditionally *peace offerings*   *b 22* Syriac (see also Septuagint); Hebrew
fool   *c 22* The meaning of the Hebrew for this line is uncertain.

23 till an arrow pierces his liver,
     like a bird darting into a snare,
        little knowing it will cost him his life.

24 Now then, my sons, listen to me;
        pay attention to what I say.
25 Do not let your heart turn to her ways
        or stray into her paths.
26 Many are the victims she has brought down;
        her slain are a mighty throng.
27 Her house is a highway to the grave,[a]
        leading down to the chambers of death.

Wisdom's Call

8 Does not wisdom call out?
        Does not understanding raise her voice?
  2 On the heights along the way,
        where the paths meet, she takes her stand;
  3 beside the gates leading into the city,
        at the entrances, she cries aloud:
  4 "To you, O men, I call out;
        I raise my voice to all mankind.
  5 You who are simple, gain prudence;
        you who are foolish, gain understanding.
  6 Listen, for I have worthy things to say;
        I open my lips to speak what is right.
  7 My mouth speaks what is true,
        for my lips detest wickedness.
  8 All the words of my mouth are just;
        none of them is crooked or perverse.
  9 To the discerning all of them are right;
        they are faultless to those who have knowledge.
10 Choose my instruction instead of silver,
        knowledge rather than choice gold,
11 for wisdom is more precious than rubies,
        and nothing you desire can compare with her.

12 "I, wisdom, dwell together with prudence;
        I possess knowledge and discretion.
13 To fear the LORD is to hate evil;
        I hate pride and arrogance,
        evil behavior and perverse speech.
14 Counsel and sound judgment are mine;
        I have understanding and power.
15 By me kings reign
        and rulers make laws that are just;
16 by me princes govern,
        and all nobles who rule on earth.[b]
17 I love those who love me,
        and those who seek me find me.
18 With me are riches and honor,
        enduring wealth and prosperity.
19 My fruit is better than fine gold;
        what I yield surpasses choice silver.
20 I walk in the way of righteousness,
        along the paths of justice,
21 bestowing wealth on those who love me
        and making their treasuries full.

An Evening Review

PROVERBS 8:5–8

This passage might be a good starting place for a review of the day. Think back over the last twenty-four hours. What have you learned? What wisdom have you gained? Now think about the things you have said, the conversations you have had. Have you spoken "worthy things" and uttered truth? Or has wickedness come from your lips? Listen to yourself and let God's wisdom comment on what you hear yourself saying. Where do you need forgiveness or guidance? You might conclude with the psalmist's plea, "May the words of my mouth and the meditation of my heart be pleasing in your sight, O LORD, my Rock and my Redeemer" (Psalm 19:14).

See Meeting God in Scripture

---

[a] 27 Hebrew *Sheol*   [b] 16 Many Hebrew manuscripts and Septuagint; most Hebrew manuscripts *and nobles—all righteous rulers*

839

Wisdom at Creation

PROVERBS 8:22–31

Use your imagination to enter into this passage. Picture the earth, fresh and new. Imagine God looking out upon this world and pronouncing each and every aspect "Good!" Now see wisdom dancing with delight at the wonder of the world. (It might help to know that the word translated *craftsman* might also mean "little child" or "darling.") Join in that dance of delight, at least in your imagination, echoing wisdom's praise of God's goodness in making the world and the people in it. You might want to get up and dance or spin with a small child's enthusiasm. God delights in your rejoicing.

See Meeting God in Scripture

> 22 "The Lord brought me forth as the first of his
>   works,*a,b*
>   before his deeds of old;
> 23 I was appointed*c* from eternity,
>   from the beginning, before the world began.
> 24 When there were no oceans, I was given birth,
>   when there were no springs abounding with
>   water;
> 25 before the mountains were settled in place,
>   before the hills, I was given birth,
> 26 before he made the earth or its fields
>   or any of the dust of the world.
> 27 I was there when he set the heavens in place,
>   when he marked out the horizon on the face of
>   the deep,
> 28 when he established the clouds above
>   and fixed securely the fountains of the deep,
> 29 when he gave the sea its boundary
>   so the waters would not overstep his
>   command,
> and when he marked out the foundations of the
>   earth.
> 30 Then I was the craftsman at his side.
> I was filled with delight day after day,
>   rejoicing always in his presence,
> 31 rejoicing in his whole world
>   and delighting in mankind.
>
> 32 "Now then, my sons, listen to me;
>   blessed are those who keep my ways.
> 33 Listen to my instruction and be wise;
>   do not ignore it.
> 34 Blessed is the man who listens to me,
>   watching daily at my doors,
>   waiting at my doorway.
> 35 For whoever finds me finds life
>   and receives favor from the Lord.
> 36 But whoever fails to find me harms himself;
>   all who hate me love death."

Invitations of Wisdom and of Folly

9 Wisdom has built her house;
     she has hewn out its seven pillars.
> 2 She has prepared her meat and mixed her wine;
>   she has also set her table.
> 3 She has sent out her maids, and she calls
>   from the highest point of the city.
> 4 "Let all who are simple come in here!"
>   she says to those who lack judgment.
> 5 "Come, eat my food
>   and drink the wine I have mixed.
> 6 Leave your simple ways and you will live;
>   walk in the way of understanding.
>
> 7 "Whoever corrects a mocker invites insult;
>   whoever rebukes a wicked man incurs abuse.
> 8 Do not rebuke a mocker or he will hate you;
>   rebuke a wise man and he will love you.

*a 22 Or way; or dominion   b 22 Or The Lord possessed me at the beginning
of his work; or The Lord brought me forth at the beginning of his work
c 23 Or fashioned*

⁹Instruct a wise man and he will be wiser still;
    teach a righteous man and he will add to his
        learning.
¹⁰"The fear of the LORD is the beginning of wisdom,
    and knowledge of the Holy One is
        understanding.
¹¹For through me your days will be many,
    and years will be added to your life.
¹²If you are wise, your wisdom will reward you;
    if you are a mocker, you alone will suffer."

¹³The woman Folly is loud;
    she is undisciplined and without knowledge.
¹⁴She sits at the door of her house,
    on a seat at the highest point of the city,
¹⁵calling out to those who pass by,
    who go straight on their way.
¹⁶"Let all who are simple come in here!"
    she says to those who lack judgment.
¹⁷"Stolen water is sweet;
    food eaten in secret is delicious!"
¹⁸But little do they know that the dead are there,
    that her guests are in the depths of the grave.ᵃ

Proverbs of Solomon

10 The proverbs of Solomon:

A wise son brings joy to his father,
    but a foolish son grief to his mother.

²Ill-gotten treasures are of no value,
    but righteousness delivers from death.

³The LORD does not let the righteous go hungry
    but he thwarts the craving of the wicked.

⁴Lazy hands make a man poor,
    but diligent hands bring wealth.

⁵He who gathers crops in summer is a wise son,
    but he who sleeps during harvest is a
        disgraceful son.

⁶Blessings crown the head of the righteous,
    but violence overwhelms the mouth of the
        wicked.ᵇ

⁷The memory of the righteous will be a blessing,
    but the name of the wicked will rot.

⁸The wise in heart accept commands,
    but a chattering fool comes to ruin.

⁹The man of integrity walks securely,
    but he who takes crooked paths will be found
        out.

¹⁰He who winks maliciously causes grief,
    and a chattering fool comes to ruin.

¹¹The mouth of the righteous is a fountain of life,
    but violence overwhelms the mouth of the
        wicked.

Walking by Insight

PROVERBS 9:6

Many magazines from time to time print self-assessment questionnaires to help readers gauge their level of maturity. We may choose to ponder the results and gain some insights about ourselves from them or we may decide to ignore them. The problem is not so much knowing what we need to do but rather choosing to do it. The sages of old counseled their hearers to lay aside immaturity lest it negatively affect their way of living.

What immature ways of thinking and living do you cling to? What is one thing you can begin to do today to think and behave in a more mature fashion? Ask for God's help. You might use the following brief prayer: "I need God's sense of order. I need God's sense. I need God." Copy this prayer and keep it to use when habits of immaturity creep back into your life.

See Meeting God in Everyday Life

ᵃ 18 Hebrew *Sheol*   ᵇ 6 Or *but the mouth of the wicked conceals violence;*
also in verse 11

Hatred and Love

PROVERBS 10:12

Picture a kettle boiling over a fire. Let the kettle represent your soul, the fire your anger. As the contents boil, what old hurts or resentments bubble up to the surface? How long have they been there? Imagine putting a cover on the pot and holding it firmly in place. The contents boil even more furiously. Simply covering the pot is not enough; you have to put out the fire. Now ask God to pour his love over the kettle and the fire. At first you may see only steam, but gradually God's love quenches the fire, and the contents of the kettle stops boiling furiously. Let God's love pour into your heart, quenching your anger and healing old wounds. Thank God for loving you, forgiving you and healing you.

See Meeting God in Scripture

12 Hatred stirs up dissension,
    but love covers over all wrongs.

13 Wisdom is found on the lips of the discerning,
    but a rod is for the back of him who lacks
        judgment.

14 Wise men store up knowledge,
    but the mouth of a fool invites ruin.

15 The wealth of the rich is their fortified city,
    but poverty is the ruin of the poor.

16 The wages of the righteous bring them life,
    but the income of the wicked brings them
        punishment.

17 He who heeds discipline shows the way to life,
    but whoever ignores correction leads others
        astray.

18 He who conceals his hatred has lying lips,
    and whoever spreads slander is a fool.

19 When words are many, sin is not absent,
    but he who holds his tongue is wise.

20 The tongue of the righteous is choice silver,
    but the heart of the wicked is of little value.

21 The lips of the righteous nourish many,
    but fools die for lack of judgment.

22 The blessing of the LORD brings wealth,
    and he adds no trouble to it.

23 A fool finds pleasure in evil conduct,
    but a man of understanding delights in
        wisdom.

24 What the wicked dreads will overtake him;
    what the righteous desire will be granted.

25 When the storm has swept by, the wicked are
        gone,
    but the righteous stand firm forever.

26 As vinegar to the teeth and smoke to the eyes,
    so is a sluggard to those who send him.

27 The fear of the LORD adds length to life,
    but the years of the wicked are cut short.

28 The prospect of the righteous is joy,
    but the hopes of the wicked come to nothing.

29 The way of the LORD is a refuge for the righteous,
    but it is the ruin of those who do evil.

30 The righteous will never be uprooted,
    but the wicked will not remain in the land.

31 The mouth of the righteous brings forth wisdom,
    but a perverse tongue will be cut out.

32 The lips of the righteous know what is fitting,
    but the mouth of the wicked only what is
        perverse.

11 The LORD abhors dishonest scales,
    but accurate weights are his delight.

² When pride comes, then comes disgrace,
    but with humility comes wisdom.

³ The integrity of the upright guides them,
    but the unfaithful are destroyed by their
      duplicity.

⁴ Wealth is worthless in the day of wrath,
    but righteousness delivers from death.

⁵ The righteousness of the blameless makes a
      straight way for them,
    but the wicked are brought down by their own
      wickedness.

⁶ The righteousness of the upright delivers them,
    but the unfaithful are trapped by evil desires.

⁷ When a wicked man dies, his hope perishes;
    all he expected from his power comes to
      nothing.

⁸ The righteous man is rescued from trouble,
    and it comes on the wicked instead.

⁹ With his mouth the godless destroys his neighbor,
    but through knowledge the righteous escape.

¹⁰ When the righteous prosper, the city rejoices;
    when the wicked perish, there are shouts of joy.

¹¹ Through the blessing of the upright a city is
      exalted,
    but by the mouth of the wicked it is destroyed.

¹² A man who lacks judgment derides his neighbor,
    but a man of understanding holds his tongue.

¹³ A gossip betrays a confidence,
    but a trustworthy man keeps a secret.

¹⁴ For lack of guidance a nation falls,
    but many advisers make victory sure.

¹⁵ He who puts up security for another will surely
      suffer,
    but whoever refuses to strike hands in pledge is
      safe.

¹⁶ A kindhearted woman gains respect,
    but ruthless men gain only wealth.

¹⁷ A kind man benefits himself,
    but a cruel man brings trouble on himself.

¹⁸ The wicked man earns deceptive wages,
    but he who sows righteousness reaps a sure
      reward.

¹⁹ The truly righteous man attains life,
    but he who pursues evil goes to his death.

²⁰ The Lord detests men of perverse heart
    but he delights in those whose ways are
      blameless.

²¹ Be sure of this: The wicked will not go
      unpunished,
    but those who are righteous will go free.

Wise Business Practices

PROVERBS 11:1–4

The sages remind us that wisdom is not only applicable to how we live our personal, private lives. Wisdom also informs our public conduct. Here the sages speak about business practices. How does your business look when held up to the bright light of wisdom? What are the ways you, or those at the company you work for, cut corners? Are there problems that you can correct? You might invite God to be present with you as you work today and to review your conduct with you. What does God see? Is it "an abomination" or "a delight"?

See Meeting God in Everyday Life

Generosity

PROVERBS 11:24–26

The generous, says Solomon, are blessed. The miserly end up miserable. And in these proverbs, generosity is defined not only as giving freely but also as making goods available at a fair price to those who need them. Spend some time making out two lists. In the first list include examples of your generosity; on the second list write down some ways in which you hold back from giving. Go beyond money and other things to the ways you share or hold back your time, your affection, your presence, your skills. Dig as deeply as you can in making these lists. Then invite God to review them with you. What does God applaud? What does God criticize? What do you want to change? Ask God to help you learn the wisdom of generosity.

See Meeting God in Service

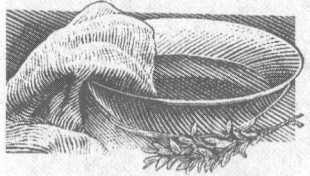

²²Like a gold ring in a pig's snout
   is a beautiful woman who shows no discretion.

²³The desire of the righteous ends only in good,
   but the hope of the wicked only in wrath.

²⁴One man gives freely, yet gains even more;
   another withholds unduly, but comes to poverty.

²⁵A generous man will prosper;
   he who refreshes others will himself be refreshed.

²⁶People curse the man who hoards grain,
   but blessing crowns him who is willing to sell.

²⁷He who seeks good finds goodwill,
   but evil comes to him who searches for it.

²⁸Whoever trusts in his riches will fall,
   but the righteous will thrive like a green leaf.

²⁹He who brings trouble on his family will inherit only wind,
   and the fool will be servant to the wise.

³⁰The fruit of the righteous is a tree of life,
   and he who wins souls is wise.

³¹If the righteous receive their due on earth,
   how much more the ungodly and the sinner!

12 Whoever loves discipline loves knowledge,
   but he who hates correction is stupid.

²A good man obtains favor from the LORD,
   but the LORD condemns a crafty man.

³A man cannot be established through wickedness,
   but the righteous cannot be uprooted.

⁴A wife of noble character is her husband's crown,
   but a disgraceful wife is like decay in his bones.

⁵The plans of the righteous are just,
   but the advice of the wicked is deceitful.

⁶The words of the wicked lie in wait for blood,
   but the speech of the upright rescues them.

⁷Wicked men are overthrown and are no more,
   but the house of the righteous stands firm.

⁸A man is praised according to his wisdom,
   but men with warped minds are despised.

⁹Better to be a nobody and yet have a servant
   than pretend to be somebody and have no food.

¹⁰A righteous man cares for the needs of his animal,
   but the kindest acts of the wicked are cruel.

¹¹He who works his land will have abundant food,
   but he who chases fantasies lacks judgment.

¹²The wicked desire the plunder of evil men,
   but the root of the righteous flourishes.

¹³ An evil man is trapped by his sinful talk,
  but a righteous man escapes trouble.

¹⁴ From the fruit of his lips a man is filled with good
    things
  as surely as the work of his hands rewards him.

¹⁵ The way of a fool seems right to him,
  but a wise man listens to advice.

¹⁶ A fool shows his annoyance at once,
  but a prudent man overlooks an insult.

¹⁷ A truthful witness gives honest testimony,
  but a false witness tells lies.

¹⁸ Reckless words pierce like a sword,
  but the tongue of the wise brings healing.

¹⁹ Truthful lips endure forever,
  but a lying tongue lasts only a moment.

²⁰ There is deceit in the hearts of those who plot
    evil,
  but joy for those who promote peace.

²¹ No harm befalls the righteous,
  but the wicked have their fill of trouble.

²² The LORD detests lying lips,
  but he delights in men who are truthful.

²³ A prudent man keeps his knowledge to himself,
  but the heart of fools blurts out folly.

²⁴ Diligent hands will rule,
  but laziness ends in slave labor.

²⁵ An anxious heart weighs a man down,
  but a kind word cheers him up.

²⁶ A righteous man is cautious in friendship,ᵃ
  but the way of the wicked leads them astray.

²⁷ The lazy man does not roastᵇ his game,
  but the diligent man prizes his possessions.

²⁸ In the way of righteousness there is life;
  along that path is immortality.

13

¹ A wise son heeds his father's instruction,
  but a mocker does not listen to rebuke.

² From the fruit of his lips a man enjoys good
    things,
  but the unfaithful have a craving for violence.

³ He who guards his lips guards his life,
  but he who speaks rashly will come to ruin.

⁴ The sluggard craves and gets nothing,
  but the desires of the diligent are fully satisfied.

⁵ The righteous hate what is false,
  but the wicked bring shame and disgrace.

⁶ Righteousness guards the man of integrity,
  but wickedness overthrows the sinner.

Prayer for God's Wisdom in All We Do

PROVERBS 12:15–20

God be in my head, and in
  my understanding;
God be in my eyes, and in
  my looking;
God be in my mouth, and in
  my speaking;
God be in my heart, and in
  my thinking;
God be at my end, and at
  my departing.
—*The Sarum Primer*

ᵃ 26 Or *man is a guide to his neighbor*   ᵇ 27 The meaning of the Hebrew for
this word is uncertain.

Hope Deferred

PROVERBS 13:12

Look at your life in the light of this proverb. What fulfilled longings have helped you feel alive and strong? What are the deferred hopes that make your heart sick? You might want to write two lists—one of fulfilled longings and one of deferred hopes—so you can consider them more fully. Do you need to let go of any of these deferred hopes so that healing can begin? What actions can you take to bring others closer to fulfillment? What help do you need from God in order to carry out these actions? What cooperation do you need from other people? What hopes can you turn over to God, to let him fulfill them or not fulfill them in his own time and according to his will? Finish your prayer time by returning to the fulfilled desires that have been a tree of life for you. Thank God for them.

See *Meeting God in Service*

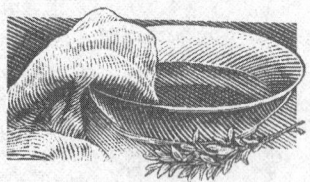

7 One man pretends to be rich, yet has nothing;
  another pretends to be poor, yet has great
  wealth.

8 A man's riches may ransom his life,
  but a poor man hears no threat.

9 The light of the righteous shines brightly,
  but the lamp of the wicked is snuffed out.

10 Pride only breeds quarrels,
  but wisdom is found in those who take advice.

11 Dishonest money dwindles away,
  but he who gathers money little by little makes
  it grow.

12 Hope deferred makes the heart sick,
  but a longing fulfilled is a tree of life.

13 He who scorns instruction will pay for it,
  but he who respects a command is rewarded.

14 The teaching of the wise is a fountain of life,
  turning a man from the snares of death.

15 Good understanding wins favor,
  but the way of the unfaithful is hard.[a]

16 Every prudent man acts out of knowledge,
  but a fool exposes his folly.

17 A wicked messenger falls into trouble,
  but a trustworthy envoy brings healing.

18 He who ignores discipline comes to poverty and
  shame,
  but whoever heeds correction is honored.

19 A longing fulfilled is sweet to the soul,
  but fools detest turning from evil.

20 He who walks with the wise grows wise,
  but a companion of fools suffers harm.

21 Misfortune pursues the sinner,
  but prosperity is the reward of the righteous.

22 A good man leaves an inheritance for his
  children's children,
  but a sinner's wealth is stored up for the
  righteous.

23 A poor man's field may produce abundant food,
  but injustice sweeps it away.

24 He who spares the rod hates his son,
  but he who loves him is careful to discipline
  him.

25 The righteous eat to their hearts' content,
  but the stomach of the wicked goes hungry.

14 The wise woman builds her house,
  but with her own hands the foolish one tears hers
  down.

2 He whose walk is upright fears the LORD,
  but he whose ways are devious despises him.

a 15 Or *unfaithful does not endure*

³ A fool's talk brings a rod to his back,
   but the lips of the wise protect them.

⁴ Where there are no oxen, the manger is empty,
   but from the strength of an ox comes an
      abundant harvest.

⁵ A truthful witness does not deceive,
   but a false witness pours out lies.

⁶ The mocker seeks wisdom and finds none,
   but knowledge comes easily to the discerning.

⁷ Stay away from a foolish man,
   for you will not find knowledge on his lips.

⁸ The wisdom of the prudent is to give thought to
      their ways,
   but the folly of fools is deception.

⁹ Fools mock at making amends for sin,
   but goodwill is found among the upright.

¹⁰ Each heart knows its own bitterness,
   and no one else can share its joy.

¹¹ The house of the wicked will be destroyed,
   but the tent of the upright will flourish.

¹² There is a way that seems right to a man,
   but in the end it leads to death.

¹³ Even in laughter the heart may ache,
   and joy may end in grief.

¹⁴ The faithless will be fully repaid for their ways,
   and the good man rewarded for his.

¹⁵ A simple man believes anything,
   but a prudent man gives thought to his steps.

¹⁶ A wise man fears the LORD and shuns evil,
   but a fool is hotheaded and reckless.

¹⁷ A quick-tempered man does foolish things,
   and a crafty man is hated.

¹⁸ The simple inherit folly,
   but the prudent are crowned with knowledge.

¹⁹ Evil men will bow down in the presence of the
      good,
   and the wicked at the gates of the righteous.

²⁰ The poor are shunned even by their neighbors,
   but the rich have many friends.

²¹ He who despises his neighbor sins,
   but blessed is he who is kind to the needy.

²² Do not those who plot evil go astray?
   But those who plan what is good find*ᵃ* love and
      faithfulness.

²³ All hard work brings a profit,
   but mere talk leads only to poverty.

²⁴ The wealth of the wise is their crown,
   but the folly of fools yields folly.

Systemic Injustice

PROVERBS 13:23

Although the sages encouraged hard work, diligence and thrift, they knew that the poor could still lose everything through the injustice of the rich or powerful. Spend some time in intercessory prayer for those who are the victims of injustice or oppression. You might let the newspaper or television news reports guide you to specific cases. Or you might think of individuals or groups you have known personally who have been crushed by circumstances beyond their control. You might also ask God to show you any ways in which you have been part of oppressive systems or in which your prosperity is the result of the poor being "swept away." What can you change in your life to help break the power of systemic injustice?

See Meeting God in Prayer

Serenity

PROVERBS 14:29–30

"God, give us grace to accept with serenity the things that cannot be changed, courage to change the things that should be changed, and the wisdom to distinguish the one from the other."

—REINHOLD NIEBUHR,
Justice and Mercy

²⁵ A truthful witness saves lives,
but a false witness is deceitful.

²⁶ He who fears the LORD has a secure fortress,
and for his children it will be a refuge.

²⁷ The fear of the LORD is a fountain of life,
turning a man from the snares of death.

²⁸ A large population is a king's glory,
but without subjects a prince is ruined.

²⁹ A patient man has great understanding,
but a quick-tempered man displays folly.

³⁰ A heart at peace gives life to the body,
but envy rots the bones.

³¹ He who oppresses the poor shows contempt for
their Maker,
but whoever is kind to the needy honors God.

³² When calamity comes, the wicked are brought
down,
but even in death the righteous have a refuge.

³³ Wisdom reposes in the heart of the discerning
and even among fools she lets herself be
known. *ᵃ*

³⁴ Righteousness exalts a nation,
but sin is a disgrace to any people.

³⁵ A king delights in a wise servant,
but a shameful servant incurs his wrath.

15 A gentle answer turns away wrath,
but a harsh word stirs up anger.

² The tongue of the wise commends knowledge,
but the mouth of the fool gushes folly.

³ The eyes of the LORD are everywhere,
keeping watch on the wicked and the good.

⁴ The tongue that brings healing is a tree of life,
but a deceitful tongue crushes the spirit.

⁵ A fool spurns his father's discipline,
but whoever heeds correction shows prudence.

⁶ The house of the righteous contains great
treasure,
but the income of the wicked brings them
trouble.

⁷ The lips of the wise spread knowledge;
not so the hearts of fools.

⁸ The LORD detests the sacrifice of the wicked,
but the prayer of the upright pleases him.

⁹ The LORD detests the way of the wicked
but he loves those who pursue righteousness.

¹⁰ Stern discipline awaits him who leaves the path;
he who hates correction will die.

ᵃ 33 Hebrew; Septuagint and Syriac / *but in the heart of fools she is not known*

¹¹ Death and Destruction[a] lie open before the
LORD—
how much more the hearts of men!

¹² A mocker resents correction;
he will not consult the wise.

¹³ A happy heart makes the face cheerful,
but heartache crushes the spirit.

¹⁴ The discerning heart seeks knowledge,
but the mouth of a fool feeds on folly.

¹⁵ All the days of the oppressed are wretched,
but the cheerful heart has a continual feast.

¹⁶ Better a little with the fear of the LORD
than great wealth with turmoil.

¹⁷ Better a meal of vegetables where there is love
than a fattened calf with hatred.

¹⁸ A hot-tempered man stirs up dissension,
but a patient man calms a quarrel.

¹⁹ The way of the sluggard is blocked with thorns,
but the path of the upright is a highway.

²⁰ A wise son brings joy to his father,
but a foolish man despises his mother.

²¹ Folly delights a man who lacks judgment,
but a man of understanding keeps a straight
course.

²² Plans fail for lack of counsel,
but with many advisers they succeed.

²³ A man finds joy in giving an apt reply—
and how good is a timely word!

²⁴ The path of life leads upward for the wise
to keep him from going down to the grave.[b]

²⁵ The LORD tears down the proud man's house
but he keeps the widow's boundaries intact.

²⁶ The LORD detests the thoughts of the wicked,
but those of the pure are pleasing to him.

²⁷ A greedy man brings trouble to his family,
but he who hates bribes will live.

²⁸ The heart of the righteous weighs its answers,
but the mouth of the wicked gushes evil.

²⁹ The LORD is far from the wicked
but he hears the prayer of the righteous.

³⁰ A cheerful look brings joy to the heart,
and good news gives health to the bones.

³¹ He who listens to a life-giving rebuke
will be at home among the wise.

³² He who ignores discipline despises himself,
but whoever heeds correction gains
understanding.

Simplicity

PROVERBS 15:16–17

Setting priorities can be extremely difficult with so many people, things and events clamoring for our attention. These proverbs suggest that two things are primary: loving God and having loving relationships with family and friends. Take a look at your life in light of these proverbs. Look at your appointment calendar (if you have one) or make a list of your scheduled activities. How do God, family and friends fit into your schedule? What activities might you give up to allow more time for your most important relationships? Simplifying your life can require painful choices. You might ask God for help in making decisions that can lead to a simpler and richer life and for strength to follow through on the decisions you have made.

See Meeting God in Everyday Life

Gaining Understanding

PROVERBS 15:32–33

Opportunities to listen to wise thinkers or to ignore life-giving advice abound. In our search for transformation, we can ask God to help us evaluate what is precious and what is offensive in the Lord's eyes. But to want instruction and to seek instruction do not necessarily imply that we will heed instruction. In our fast-moving society, few of us take time to listen to instruction unless we find it absolutely necessary.

Think back over the last few days. What good advice or thoughtful criticism has been offered to you? What have you chosen to ignore? Try to write down a few specific examples. Consider each one as you ask yourself, "Why did I ignore this? How would I have to change if I paid attention to this? Is God calling to me through this offer of wisdom? What do I need to do?" Ask God to guide you in being more open to instruction in the coming days.

See Meeting God in Community

³³ The fear of the Lord teaches a man wisdom,^a
and humility comes before honor.

16 To man belong the plans of the heart,
but from the Lord comes the reply of the tongue.

² All a man's ways seem innocent to him,
but motives are weighed by the Lord.

³ Commit to the Lord whatever you do,
and your plans will succeed.

⁴ The Lord works out everything for his own ends—
even the wicked for a day of disaster.

⁵ The Lord detests all the proud of heart.
Be sure of this: They will not go unpunished.

⁶ Through love and faithfulness sin is atoned for;
through the fear of the Lord a man avoids evil.

⁷ When a man's ways are pleasing to the Lord,
he makes even his enemies live at peace with him.

⁸ Better a little with righteousness
than much gain with injustice.

⁹ In his heart a man plans his course,
but the Lord determines his steps.

¹⁰ The lips of a king speak as an oracle,
and his mouth should not betray justice.

¹¹ Honest scales and balances are from the Lord;
all the weights in the bag are of his making.

¹² Kings detest wrongdoing,
for a throne is established through righteousness.

¹³ Kings take pleasure in honest lips;
they value a man who speaks the truth.

¹⁴ A king's wrath is a messenger of death,
but a wise man will appease it.

¹⁵ When a king's face brightens, it means life;
his favor is like a rain cloud in spring.

¹⁶ How much better to get wisdom than gold,
to choose understanding rather than silver!

¹⁷ The highway of the upright avoids evil;
he who guards his way guards his life.

¹⁸ Pride goes before destruction,
a haughty spirit before a fall.

¹⁹ Better to be lowly in spirit and among the oppressed
than to share plunder with the proud.

²⁰ Whoever gives heed to instruction prospers,
and blessed is he who trusts in the Lord.

²¹ The wise in heart are called discerning,
and pleasant words promote instruction.^b

---

a 33 Or Wisdom teaches the fear of the Lord   b 21 Or words make a man persuasive

²²Understanding is a fountain of life to those who
   have it,
   but folly brings punishment to fools.

²³A wise man's heart guides his mouth,
   and his lips promote instruction.ᵃ

²⁴Pleasant words are a honeycomb,
   sweet to the soul and healing to the bones.

²⁵There is a way that seems right to a man,
   but in the end it leads to death.

²⁶The laborer's appetite works for him;
   his hunger drives him on.

²⁷A scoundrel plots evil,
   and his speech is like a scorching fire.

²⁸A perverse man stirs up dissension,
   and a gossip separates close friends.

²⁹A violent man entices his neighbor
   and leads him down a path that is not good.

³⁰He who winks with his eye is plotting perversity;
   he who purses his lips is bent on evil.

³¹Gray hair is a crown of splendor;
   it is attained by a righteous life.

³²Better a patient man than a warrior,
   a man who controls his temper than one who
   takes a city.

³³The lot is cast into the lap,
   but its every decision is from the LORD.

17 Better a dry crust with peace and quiet
   than a house full of feasting,ᵇ with strife.

²A wise servant will rule over a disgraceful son,
   and will share the inheritance as one of the
   brothers.

³The crucible for silver and the furnace for gold,
   but the LORD tests the heart.

⁴A wicked man listens to evil lips;
   a liar pays attention to a malicious tongue.

⁵He who mocks the poor shows contempt for their
   Maker;
   whoever gloats over disaster will not go
   unpunished.

⁶Children's children are a crown to the aged,
   and parents are the pride of their children.

⁷Arrogantᶜ lips are unsuited to a fool—
   how much worse lying lips to a ruler!

⁸A bribe is a charm to the one who gives it;
   wherever he turns, he succeeds.

⁹He who covers over an offense promotes love,
   but whoever repeats the matter separates close
   friends.

Better Than Silver or Gold

PROVERBS 16:16–17

"As all wisdom, love, and
goodness proceed from God, so
nothing but love, wisdom, and
goodness can lead to God.
When you love that which God
loves, you act with God, you
join yourself to God. When you
love what God dislikes, then
you oppose God and separate
yourself from God. This is the
true and right way: think what
God loves and love it yourself
with all your heart."

—WILLIAM LAW,
A Serious Call to a Devout and Holy Life

ᵃ 23 Or *mouth / and makes his lips persuasive*   ᵇ 1 Hebrew *sacrifices*
ᶜ 7 Or *Eloquent*

Projects

PROVERBS 17:12

Today's English Version of the Bible renders the last half of this verse, ". . . than to meet some fool busy with a stupid project." Even the most in-spired idea can become a "stu-pid project" when it becomes our project and not God's inspi-ration. What are the current projects in your life? (Working your way through this Bible might be one project, for exam-ple.) When have you become so intent on a project that you have snapped at anyone who interrupted you—when have you become like the "bear robbed of her cubs"? You might spend some time offering your projects back to God, reconse-crating them to God's service. Such a prayer time might in-clude thanksgiving for what you have accomplished or learned as well as confession for times in which you have wandered away from the original inspira-tion.

See Meeting God in Service

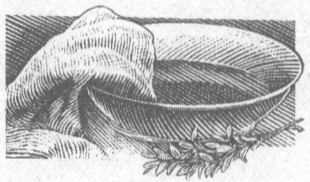

10 A rebuke impresses a man of discernment
more than a hundred lashes a fool.

11 An evil man is bent only on rebellion;
a merciless official will be sent against him.

12 Better to meet a bear robbed of her cubs
than a fool in his folly.

13 If a man pays back evil for good,
evil will never leave his house.

14 Starting a quarrel is like breaching a dam;
so drop the matter before a dispute breaks out.

15 Acquitting the guilty and condemning the
innocent—
the LORD detests them both.

16 Of what use is money in the hand of a fool,
since he has no desire to get wisdom?

17 A friend loves at all times,
and a brother is born for adversity.

18 A man lacking in judgment strikes hands in
pledge
and puts up security for his neighbor.

19 He who loves a quarrel loves sin;
he who builds a high gate invites destruction.

20 A man of perverse heart does not prosper;
he whose tongue is deceitful falls into trouble.

21 To have a fool for a son brings grief;
there is no joy for the father of a fool.

22 A cheerful heart is good medicine,
but a crushed spirit dries up the bones.

23 A wicked man accepts a bribe in secret
to pervert the course of justice.

24 A discerning man keeps wisdom in view,
but a fool's eyes wander to the ends of the
earth.

25 A foolish son brings grief to his father
and bitterness to the one who bore him.

26 It is not good to punish an innocent man,
or to flog officials for their integrity.

27 A man of knowledge uses words with restraint,
and a man of understanding is even-tempered.

28 Even a fool is thought wise if he keeps silent,
and discerning if he holds his tongue.

18 An unfriendly man pursues selfish ends;
he defies all sound judgment.

2 A fool finds no pleasure in understanding
but delights in airing his own opinions.

3 When wickedness comes, so does contempt,
and with shame comes disgrace.

4 The words of a man's mouth are deep waters,
but the fountain of wisdom is a bubbling brook.

⁵ It is not good to be partial to the wicked
   or to deprive the innocent of justice.

⁶ A fool's lips bring him strife,
   and his mouth invites a beating.

⁷ A fool's mouth is his undoing,
   and his lips are a snare to his soul.

⁸ The words of a gossip are like choice morsels;
   they go down to a man's inmost parts.

⁹ One who is slack in his work
   is brother to one who destroys.

¹⁰ The name of the LORD is a strong tower;
   the righteous run to it and are safe.

¹¹ The wealth of the rich is their fortified city;
   they imagine it an unscalable wall.

¹² Before his downfall a man's heart is proud,
   but humility comes before honor.

¹³ He who answers before listening—
   that is his folly and his shame.

¹⁴ A man's spirit sustains him in sickness,
   but a crushed spirit who can bear?

¹⁵ The heart of the discerning acquires knowledge;
   the ears of the wise seek it out.

¹⁶ A gift opens the way for the giver
   and ushers him into the presence of the great.

¹⁷ The first to present his case seems right,
   till another comes forward and questions him.

¹⁸ Casting the lot settles disputes
   and keeps strong opponents apart.

¹⁹ An offended brother is more unyielding than a
      fortified city,
   and disputes are like the barred gates of a
      citadel.

²⁰ From the fruit of his mouth a man's stomach is
      filled;
   with the harvest from his lips he is satisfied.

²¹ The tongue has the power of life and death,
   and those who love it will eat its fruit.

²² He who finds a wife finds what is good
   and receives favor from the LORD.

²³ A poor man pleads for mercy,
   but a rich man answers harshly.

²⁴ A man of many companions may come to ruin,
   but there is a friend who sticks closer than a
      brother.

19 Better a poor man whose walk is blameless
   than a fool whose lips are perverse.

² It is not good to have zeal without knowledge,
   nor to be hasty and miss the way.

The Name of the Lord

PROVERBS 18:10

Let your imagination play with the image in this verse. Picture a strong tower, a place of safety for you. Imagine that you are outside the tower, under attack. What is attacking you? As you are driven back toward the tower, you call on the name of the Lord. At once the tower gate opens and you can run inside to safety. Your enemy can no longer reach you. You are safe in the tower of the Lord's strength and goodness.

You might want to draw or paint a picture of yourself safe within the tower while enemies lurk outside. You might conclude your prayer time by singing a hymn such as "A Mighty Fortress Is Our God" or "Rock of Ages" or "The Rock That is Higher Than I."

See Meeting God in Scripture

Living or Dying

PROVERBS 19:16

The word *commandment* frightens many people because they think of something very rigid and binding. Using the word instruction instead may ease some of the tension. The author of this proverb feels strongly enough about what his beliefs are that he promises life to those who obey instructions (commandments). This saying is not a warranty for a long life but a guarantee for a more meaningful life regardless of the number of years. Choosing not to listen to instruction or to the commandments leads to death—a joyless life of angst, a despotic posture toward others, a defiant spirit toward God.

God's Word becomes flesh only when we know it, love it and live it. Spend some time reviewing the Ten Commandments (Exodus 20:1–17) and Jesus' Great Commandment (Matthew 22:34–40). How well does your life reflect God's instructions?

See Meeting God in Prayer

³ A man's own folly ruins his life,
    yet his heart rages against the LORD.

⁴ Wealth brings many friends,
    but a poor man's friend deserts him.

⁵ A false witness will not go unpunished,
    and he who pours out lies will not go free.

⁶ Many curry favor with a ruler,
    and everyone is the friend of a man who gives
        gifts.

⁷ A poor man is shunned by all his relatives—
    how much more do his friends avoid him!
  Though he pursues them with pleading,
    they are nowhere to be found.ᵃ

⁸ He who gets wisdom loves his own soul;
    he who cherishes understanding prospers.

⁹ A false witness will not go unpunished,
    and he who pours out lies will perish.

¹⁰ It is not fitting for a fool to live in luxury—
    how much worse for a slave to rule over
        princes!

¹¹ A man's wisdom gives him patience;
    it is to his glory to overlook an offense.

¹² A king's rage is like the roar of a lion,
    but his favor is like dew on the grass.

¹³ A foolish son is his father's ruin,
    and a quarrelsome wife is like a constant
        dripping.

¹⁴ Houses and wealth are inherited from parents,
    but a prudent wife is from the LORD.

¹⁵ Laziness brings on deep sleep,
    and the shiftless man goes hungry.

¹⁶ He who obeys instructions guards his life,
    but he who is contemptuous of his ways will
        die.

¹⁷ He who is kind to the poor lends to the LORD,
    and he will reward him for what he has done.

¹⁸ Discipline your son, for in that there is hope;
    do not be a willing party to his death.

¹⁹ A hot-tempered man must pay the penalty;
    if you rescue him, you will have to do it again.

²⁰ Listen to advice and accept instruction,
    and in the end you will be wise.

²¹ Many are the plans in a man's heart,
    but it is the LORD's purpose that prevails.

²² What a man desires is unfailing loveᵇ;
    better to be poor than a liar.

²³ The fear of the LORD leads to life:
    Then one rests content, untouched by trouble.

ᵃ 7 The meaning of the Hebrew for this sentence is uncertain.   ᵇ 22 Or *A man's greed is his shame*

²⁴ The sluggard buries his hand in the dish;
he will not even bring it back to his mouth!

²⁵ Flog a mocker, and the simple will learn
prudence;
rebuke a discerning man, and he will gain
knowledge.

²⁶ He who robs his father and drives out his mother
is a son who brings shame and disgrace.

²⁷ Stop listening to instruction, my son,
and you will stray from the words of
knowledge.

²⁸ A corrupt witness mocks at justice,
and the mouth of the wicked gulps down evil.

²⁹ Penalties are prepared for mockers,
and beatings for the backs of fools.

20 Wine is a mocker and beer a brawler;
whoever is led astray by them is not wise.

² A king's wrath is like the roar of a lion;
he who angers him forfeits his life.

³ It is to a man's honor to avoid strife,
but every fool is quick to quarrel.

⁴ A sluggard does not plow in season;
so at harvest time he looks but finds nothing.

⁵ The purposes of a man's heart are deep waters,
but a man of understanding draws them out.

⁶ Many a man claims to have unfailing love,
but a faithful man who can find?

⁷ The righteous man leads a blameless life;
blessed are his children after him.

⁸ When a king sits on his throne to judge,
he winnows out all evil with his eyes.

⁹ Who can say, "I have kept my heart pure;
I am clean and without sin"?

¹⁰ Differing weights and differing measures—
the LORD detests them both.

¹¹ Even a child is known by his actions,
by whether his conduct is pure and right.

¹² Ears that hear and eyes that see—
the LORD has made them both.

¹³ Do not love sleep or you will grow poor;
stay awake and you will have food to spare.

¹⁴ "It's no good, it's no good!" says the buyer;
then off he goes and boasts about his purchase.

¹⁵ Gold there is, and rubies in abundance,
but lips that speak knowledge are a rare jewel.

¹⁶ Take the garment of one who puts up security for
a stranger;
hold it in pledge if he does it for a wayward
woman.

Anger and Hatred

PROVERBS 20:3

"When anger tries to burn up my tabernacle, I will look to the goodness of God, whom anger never touched; and thus I will be sweeter than the air, which in its gentleness moistens the earth, and have spiritual joy because virtues are beginning to show themselves in me. And thus I will feel God's goodness.

"And when hatred tries to darken me, I will look to the mercy and the martyrdom of the Son of God, and so restrain my flesh, and in faithful memory receive the sweet fragrance of the roses that spring from thorns. And so I will acknowledge my Redeemer."

—HILDEGARD OF BINGEN,
Scivias

Waiting for the Lord

PROVERBS 20:22

Waiting for the Lord often makes us nervous because we do not know when or how God will respond. When evil touches our lives, we want immediate action. The silence and the waiting cause us to wonder if God really values us or cares at all. Often our impatience pushes us to take control away from God. The Lord is well aware of all that happens to us. Our instructions are not to repay evil ourselves but to wait for the Lord's help.

When do you find yourself eager to repay evil? What longing for revenge festers in your soul? Sit quietly in God's presence. Imagine plucking that longing from your heart and offering it to God. You might say, "Here, God, I will let you manage this for me. Take it from my heart. Teach me to wait in patience for your help."

See Meeting God in Prayer

¹⁷ Food gained by fraud tastes sweet to a man,
    but he ends up with a mouth full of gravel.

¹⁸ Make plans by seeking advice;
    if you wage war, obtain guidance.

¹⁹ A gossip betrays a confidence;
    so avoid a man who talks too much.

²⁰ If a man curses his father or mother,
    his lamp will be snuffed out in pitch darkness.

²¹ An inheritance quickly gained at the beginning
    will not be blessed at the end.

²² Do not say, "I'll pay you back for this wrong!"
    Wait for the LORD, and he will deliver you.

²³ The LORD detests differing weights,
    and dishonest scales do not please him.

²⁴ A man's steps are directed by the LORD.
    How then can anyone understand his own way?

²⁵ It is a trap for a man to dedicate something rashly
    and only later to consider his vows.

²⁶ A wise king winnows out the wicked;
    he drives the threshing wheel over them.

²⁷ The lamp of the LORD searches the spirit of a man*;
    it searches out his inmost being.

²⁸ Love and faithfulness keep a king safe;
    through love his throne is made secure.

²⁹ The glory of young men is their strength,
    gray hair the splendor of the old.

³⁰ Blows and wounds cleanse away evil,
    and beatings purge the inmost being.

21 The king's heart is in the hand of the LORD;
    he directs it like a watercourse wherever he pleases.

² All a man's ways seem right to him,
    but the LORD weighs the heart.

³ To do what is right and just
    is more acceptable to the LORD than sacrifice.

⁴ Haughty eyes and a proud heart,
    the lamp of the wicked, are sin!

⁵ The plans of the diligent lead to profit
    as surely as haste leads to poverty.

⁶ A fortune made by a lying tongue
    is a fleeting vapor and a deadly snare.*

⁷ The violence of the wicked will drag them away,
    for they refuse to do what is right.

⁸ The way of the guilty is devious,
    but the conduct of the innocent is upright.

---

a 27 Or *The spirit of man is the LORD's lamp*   *b 6* Some Hebrew manuscripts, Septuagint and Vulgate; most Hebrew manuscripts *vapor for those who seek death*

⁹ Better to live on a corner of the roof
  than share a house with a quarrelsome wife.

¹⁰ The wicked man craves evil;
  his neighbor gets no mercy from him.

¹¹ When a mocker is punished, the simple gain
  wisdom;
  when a wise man is instructed, he gets
  knowledge.

¹² The Righteous One[a] takes note of the house of
  the wicked
  and brings the wicked to ruin.

¹³ If a man shuts his ears to the cry of the poor,
  he too will cry out and not be answered.

¹⁴ A gift given in secret soothes anger,
  and a bribe concealed in the cloak pacifies
  great wrath.

¹⁵ When justice is done, it brings joy to the righteous
  but terror to evildoers.

¹⁶ A man who strays from the path of understanding
  comes to rest in the company of the dead.

¹⁷ He who loves pleasure will become poor;
  whoever loves wine and oil will never be rich.

¹⁸ The wicked become a ransom for the righteous,
  and the unfaithful for the upright.

¹⁹ Better to live in a desert
  than with a quarrelsome and ill-tempered wife.

²⁰ In the house of the wise are stores of choice food
  and oil,
  but a foolish man devours all he has.

²¹ He who pursues righteousness and love
  finds life, prosperity[b] and honor.

²² A wise man attacks the city of the mighty
  and pulls down the stronghold in which they
  trust.

²³ He who guards his mouth and his tongue
  keeps himself from calamity.

²⁴ The proud and arrogant man—"Mocker" is his
  name;
  he behaves with overweening pride.

²⁵ The sluggard's craving will be the death of him,
  because his hands refuse to work.
²⁶ All day long he craves for more,
  but the righteous give without sparing.

²⁷ The sacrifice of the wicked is detestable—
  how much more so when brought with evil
  intent!

²⁸ A false witness will perish,
  and whoever listens to him will be destroyed
  forever.[c]

The Lord Weighs the Heart

PROVERBS 21:2

Those of us who have gone to church most of our lives know what the better way is if we have listened well. We may consider ourselves wise in our own eyes, but outward actions form the true test of wisdom. We may fool ourselves or be blind to our inmost motives, but God looks at the heart and knows what our real purpose is.

You might ask God for the gift of insight so that you can see yourself as God sees you. What would you do if you knew what God sees and how God weighs your heart? One way to begin might be to write a dialogue between yourself and God. Begin with the question, "God, what do you see when you look at me?" Write out what you think God might answer. How do you respond?

See Meeting God in Everyday Life

---

a 12 Or *The righteous man*   *b 21* Or *righteousness*   *c 28* Or / *but the words
of an obedient man will live on*

857

Precious in God's Sight

PROVERBS 22:2

It is so easy to notice what makes us different from those around us and to zero in on those differences. Here the sage reminds us of what we have in common with all others: God made us all. As you go through your day, take time to notice the people around you. Say to yourself, "This person is God's creation and precious in God's sight." If you know the person's name, use it. When you find yourself in conflict with someone, say again, "This person is God's creation and precious in God's sight." As you look back over the day, thank God for the many different and precious gifts God has given you in the people you have encountered.

See Meeting God in Everyday Life

²⁹ A wicked man puts up a bold front,
but an upright man gives thought to his ways.

³⁰ There is no wisdom, no insight, no plan
that can succeed against the LORD.

³¹ The horse is made ready for the day of battle,
but victory rests with the LORD.

22

A good name is more desirable than great riches;
to be esteemed is better than silver or gold.

² Rich and poor have this in common:
The LORD is the Maker of them all.

³ A prudent man sees danger and takes refuge,
but the simple keep going and suffer for it.

⁴ Humility and the fear of the LORD
bring wealth and honor and life.

⁵ In the paths of the wicked lie thorns and snares,
but he who guards his soul stays far from them.

⁶ Train[a] a child in the way he should go,
and when he is old he will not turn from it.

⁷ The rich rule over the poor,
and the borrower is servant to the lender.

⁸ He who sows wickedness reaps trouble,
and the rod of his fury will be destroyed.

⁹ A generous man will himself be blessed,
for he shares his food with the poor.

¹⁰ Drive out the mocker, and out goes strife;
quarrels and insults are ended.

¹¹ He who loves a pure heart and whose speech is gracious
will have the king for his friend.

¹² The eyes of the LORD keep watch over knowledge,
but he frustrates the words of the unfaithful.

¹³ The sluggard says, "There is a lion outside!"
or, "I will be murdered in the streets!"

¹⁴ The mouth of an adulteress is a deep pit;
he who is under the LORD's wrath will fall
into it.

¹⁵ Folly is bound up in the heart of a child,
but the rod of discipline will drive it far from
him.

¹⁶ He who oppresses the poor to increase his wealth
and he who gives gifts to the rich—both come
to poverty.

Sayings of the Wise

¹⁷ Pay attention and listen to the sayings of the
wise;
apply your heart to what I teach,
¹⁸ for it is pleasing when you keep them in your
heart
and have all of them ready on your lips.

^a 6 Or *Start*

¹⁹ So that your trust may be in the LORD,
    I teach you today, even you.
²⁰ Have I not written thirty*a* sayings for you,
    sayings of counsel and knowledge,
²¹ teaching you true and reliable words,
    so that you can give sound answers
    to him who sent you?

²² Do not exploit the poor because they are poor
    and do not crush the needy in court,
²³ for the LORD will take up their case
    and will plunder those who plunder them.

²⁴ Do not make friends with a hot-tempered man,
    do not associate with one easily angered,
²⁵ or you may learn his ways
    and get yourself ensnared.

²⁶ Do not be a man who strikes hands in pledge
    or puts up security for debts;
²⁷ if you lack the means to pay,
    your very bed will be snatched from under you.

²⁸ Do not move an ancient boundary stone
    set up by your forefathers.

²⁹ Do you see a man skilled in his work?
    He will serve before kings;
    he will not serve before obscure men.

23 When you sit to dine with a ruler,
    note well what*b* is before you,
² and put a knife to your throat
    if you are given to gluttony.
³ Do not crave his delicacies,
    for that food is deceptive.

⁴ Do not wear yourself out to get rich;
    have the wisdom to show restraint.
⁵ Cast but a glance at riches, and they are gone,
    for they will surely sprout wings
    and fly off to the sky like an eagle.

⁶ Do not eat the food of a stingy man,
    do not crave his delicacies;
⁷ for he is the kind of man
    who is always thinking about the cost.*c*
    "Eat and drink," he says to you,
    but his heart is not with you.
⁸ You will vomit up the little you have eaten
    and will have wasted your compliments.

⁹ Do not speak to a fool,
    for he will scorn the wisdom of your words.

¹⁰ Do not move an ancient boundary stone
    or encroach on the fields of the fatherless,
¹¹ for their Defender is strong;
    he will take up their case against you.

¹² Apply your heart to instruction
    and your ears to words of knowledge.

Ancient Wisdom

PROVERBS 22:17–23:11

These "words of the wise" closely parallel the teachings of Amenemope, an Egyptian sage from several centuries before the time of Solomon. But they have been reworked in light of Israel's understanding of God. Read through these sayings slowly. When one in particular seems to speak to you, stay with it for a while. Why did it intrigue you? What does it have to say to you? What changes does it suggest for the way you live? You might write out your reflections.

Another approach is to try rewording these ancient sayings to fit your own time and situation. What sayings would you adapt? What sayings do you find hard to apply to your life? Where do you find yourself in full agreement with these ancient bits of wisdom?

See Meeting God in Scripture

---

a 20 Or not formerly written; or not written excellent   b 1 Or who   c 7 Or
for as he thinks within himself, / so he is; or for as he puts on a feast, / so he is

Building Houses

PROVERBS 24:1–7

What does your dream house look like? Picture it mentally. You have the land, the plans, all the necessary financial resources, and you will have the last word on every single detail. It is your house, built to your own liking—but not in one day.

You also have a spiritual house, which you are constructing from day to day. Let the foundation be wisdom, instruction, discipline and understanding. The rooms of your spiritual home need to be filled. What will go into each room? Here, too, you have the final word. But transformation does not happen overnight. It is not that God needs more time to accomplish the task. Rather, you need space from day to day to adjust to the construction process. It takes a lifetime to grow in godliness. How can God, the Master Builder, help you?

See Meeting God in Worship

13 Do not withhold discipline from a child;
      if you punish him with the rod, he will not
         die.
14 Punish him with the rod
      and save his soul from death.[a]

15 My son, if your heart is wise,
      then my heart will be glad;
16 my inmost being will rejoice
      when your lips speak what is right.

17 Do not let your heart envy sinners,
      but always be zealous for the fear of the LORD.
18 There is surely a future hope for you,
      and your hope will not be cut off.

19 Listen, my son, and be wise,
      and keep your heart on the right path.
20 Do not join those who drink too much wine
      or gorge themselves on meat,
21 for drunkards and gluttons become poor,
      and drowsiness clothes them in rags.

22 Listen to your father, who gave you life,
      and do not despise your mother when she is
         old.
23 Buy the truth and do not sell it;
      get wisdom, discipline and understanding.
24 The father of a righteous man has great joy;
      he who has a wise son delights in him.
25 May your father and mother be glad;
      may she who gave you birth rejoice!

26 My son, give me your heart
      and let your eyes keep to my ways,
27 for a prostitute is a deep pit
      and a wayward wife is a narrow well.
28 Like a bandit she lies in wait,
      and multiplies the unfaithful among men.

29 Who has woe? Who has sorrow?
      Who has strife? Who has complaints?
      Who has needless bruises? Who has bloodshot
         eyes?
30 Those who linger over wine,
      who go to sample bowls of mixed wine.
31 Do not gaze at wine when it is red,
      when it sparkles in the cup,
      when it goes down smoothly!
32 In the end it bites like a snake
      and poisons like a viper.
33 Your eyes will see strange sights
      and your mind imagine confusing things.
34 You will be like one sleeping on the high seas,
      lying on top of the rigging.
35 "They hit me," you will say, "but I'm not hurt!
      They beat me, but I don't feel it!
   When will I wake up
      so I can find another drink?"

24 Do not envy wicked men,
      do not desire their company;

a 14 Hebrew *Sheol*

² for their hearts plot violence,
and their lips talk about making trouble.

³ By wisdom a house is built,
and through understanding it is established;
⁴ through knowledge its rooms are filled
with rare and beautiful treasures.

⁵ A wise man has great power,
and a man of knowledge increases strength;
⁶ for waging war you need guidance,
and for victory many advisers.

⁷ Wisdom is too high for a fool;
in the assembly at the gate he has nothing to
say.

⁸ He who plots evil
will be known as a schemer.
⁹ The schemes of folly are sin,
and men detest a mocker.

¹⁰ If you falter in times of trouble,
how small is your strength!

¹¹ Rescue those being led away to death;
hold back those staggering toward slaughter.
¹² If you say, "But we knew nothing about this,"
does not he who weighs the heart perceive it?
Does not he who guards your life know it?
Will he not repay each person according to
what he has done?

¹³ Eat honey, my son, for it is good;
honey from the comb is sweet to your taste.
¹⁴ Know also that wisdom is sweet to your soul;
if you find it, there is a future hope for you,
and your hope will not be cut off.

¹⁵ Do not lie in wait like an outlaw against a
righteous man's house,
do not raid his dwelling place;
¹⁶ for though a righteous man falls seven times, he
rises again,
but the wicked are brought down by calamity.

¹⁷ Do not gloat when your enemy falls;
when he stumbles, do not let your heart
rejoice,
¹⁸ or the LORD will see and disapprove
and turn his wrath away from him.

¹⁹ Do not fret because of evil men
or be envious of the wicked,
²⁰ for the evil man has no future hope,
and the lamp of the wicked will be snuffed
out.

²¹ Fear the LORD and the king, my son,
and do not join with the rebellious,
²² for those two will send sudden destruction upon
them,
and who knows what calamities they can
bring?

Schadenfreude

PROVERBS 24:17–18

Schadenfreude is a rather imposing German word that means "injury joy." It refers to the glee that comes over us when someone we don't like suffers harm: We laugh when a pompous person slips on a banana peel; we cheer when the villain is blown to pieces in a movie. But Proverbs tells us not to rejoice when enemies fall, even if that fall is the result of God's wrath!

Who are your enemies? If that word seems too strong, who are the people you find yourself opposed to at work or in your church? Try praying for them, asking God for their conversion rather than their destruction. After all, if they are destroyed, you may feel a moment's *schadenfreude*. But if they repent, there will be true joy in heaven.

See Meeting God in Prayer

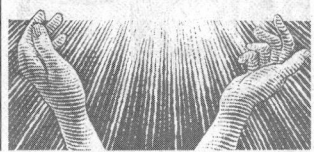

Words Aptly Spoken or Written

PROVERBS 25:11–12

The tongue and the pen are powerful weapons. We can use them to bless or to curse, to praise or to insult, to encourage or to destroy. Here, words aptly spoken are compared to apples of gold in silver settings.

Try to pay attention throughout the day to the words you speak. Do your words offer wisdom or sarcasm? Do they build up or cut down? What proverbs do you quote to others? What are your favorite sayings? What do they say about you and your values?

At the end of the day, review with God what you have said. What words have been fitly spoken? What words do you regret? Ask for God's help to speak more wisely in the future.

See Meeting God in Everyday Life

Further Sayings of the Wise

²³These also are sayings of the wise:

To show partiality in judging is not good:
²⁴Whoever says to the guilty, "You are innocent"—
    peoples will curse him and nations denounce him.
²⁵But it will go well with those who convict the guilty,
    and rich blessing will come upon them.

²⁶An honest answer
    is like a kiss on the lips.

²⁷Finish your outdoor work
    and get your fields ready;
    after that, build your house.

²⁸Do not testify against your neighbor without cause,
    or use your lips to deceive.
²⁹Do not say, "I'll do to him as he has done to me;
    I'll pay that man back for what he did."

³⁰I went past the field of the sluggard,
    past the vineyard of the man who lacks judgment;
³¹thorns had come up everywhere,
    the ground was covered with weeds,
    and the stone wall was in ruins.
³²I applied my heart to what I observed
    and learned a lesson from what I saw:
³³A little sleep, a little slumber,
    a little folding of the hands to rest—
³⁴and poverty will come on you like a bandit
    and scarcity like an armed man. *a*

More Proverbs of Solomon

25 These are more proverbs of Solomon, copied by the men of Hezekiah king of Judah:

²It is the glory of God to conceal a matter;
    to search out a matter is the glory of kings.

³As the heavens are high and the earth is deep,
    so the hearts of kings are unsearchable.

⁴Remove the dross from the silver,
    and out comes material for *b* the silversmith;
⁵remove the wicked from the king's presence,
    and his throne will be established through righteousness.

⁶Do not exalt yourself in the king's presence,
    and do not claim a place among great men;
⁷it is better for him to say to you, "Come up here,"
    than for him to humiliate you before a nobleman.

What you have seen with your eyes
⁸   do not bring *c* hastily to court,

*a 34 Or like a vagrant / and scarcity like a beggar   b 4 Or comes a vessel from
c 7,8 Or nobleman / on whom you had set your eyes. / ⁸Do not go*

for what will you do in the end
 if your neighbor puts you to shame?

⁹ If you argue your case with a neighbor,
 do not betray another man's confidence,
¹⁰ or he who hears it may shame you
 and you will never lose your bad reputation.

¹¹ A word aptly spoken
 is like apples of gold in settings of silver.

¹² Like an earring of gold or an ornament of fine
 gold
 is a wise man's rebuke to a listening ear.

¹³ Like the coolness of snow at harvest time
 is a trustworthy messenger to those who send
 him;
 he refreshes the spirit of his masters.

¹⁴ Like clouds and wind without rain
 is a man who boasts of gifts he does not give.

¹⁵ Through patience a ruler can be persuaded,
 and a gentle tongue can break a bone.

¹⁶ If you find honey, eat just enough—
 too much of it, and you will vomit.
¹⁷ Seldom set foot in your neighbor's house—
 too much of you, and he will hate you.

¹⁸ Like a club or a sword or a sharp arrow
 is the man who gives false testimony against
 his neighbor.

¹⁹ Like a bad tooth or a lame foot
 is reliance on the unfaithful in times of
 trouble.

²⁰ Like one who takes away a garment on a cold
 day,
 or like vinegar poured on soda,
 is one who sings songs to a heavy heart.

²¹ If your enemy is hungry, give him food to eat;
 if he is thirsty, give him water to drink.
²² In doing this, you will heap burning coals on his
 head,
 and the Lord will reward you.

²³ As a north wind brings rain,
 so a sly tongue brings angry looks.

²⁴ Better to live on a corner of the roof
 than share a house with a quarrelsome wife.

²⁵ Like cold water to a weary soul
 is good news from a distant land.

²⁶ Like a muddied spring or a polluted well
 is a righteous man who gives way to the
 wicked.

²⁷ It is not good to eat too much honey,
 nor is it honorable to seek one's own honor.

²⁸ Like a city whose walls are broken down
 is a man who lacks self-control.

Love of Enemies

PROVERBS 25:21–22

When the wise teacher tells us to do good to our enemies and thereby heap burning coals on them, the point is that acts of kindness, not revenge, will prick their consciences. Revenge or "getting even" only perpetuates the cycle of violence and harm.

Try to remember someone who has actively wished you harm. Perhaps this is a present situation. Offer this situation to God in prayer. How do you suppose God reacts to this conflict? What might God say to your adversary? What might God say to you? Ask God to help you as you probe the attitudes and inclinations of your heart.

See Meeting God in Prayer

Today, Tomorrow or Never

PROVERBS 27:1

Sometimes even the best-laid plans can tumble to pieces around us. We do not really know what tomorrow may bring. If we listen, though, we can hear God's voice in the midst of disaster or failure, calling us to a new direction or a new start.

Ask for God's help to be open to his plan for your future. One way to do this is to dwell on each of the petitions in the Lord's Prayer as a request for God's help and guidance for the here-and-now. For instance, you might pray, "Not my will but yours be done in me, now, here on earth, as your will is eternally fulfilled in heaven." Take as much time as you need with each line before moving on. If you don't have time to finish the whole Lord's Prayer, come back to it another day.

See Meeting God in Prayer

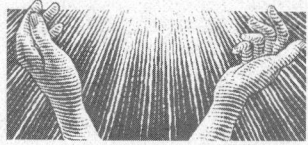

26 Like snow in summer or rain in harvest,
   honor is not fitting for a fool.

2 Like a fluttering sparrow or a darting swallow,
   an undeserved curse does not come to rest.

3 A whip for the horse, a halter for the donkey,
   and a rod for the backs of fools!

4 Do not answer a fool according to his folly,
   or you will be like him yourself.

5 Answer a fool according to his folly,
   or he will be wise in his own eyes.

6 Like cutting off one's feet or drinking violence
   is the sending of a message by the hand of a fool.

7 Like a lame man's legs that hang limp
   is a proverb in the mouth of a fool.

8 Like tying a stone in a sling
   is the giving of honor to a fool.

9 Like a thornbush in a drunkard's hand
   is a proverb in the mouth of a fool.

10 Like an archer who wounds at random
   is he who hires a fool or any passer-by.

11 As a dog returns to its vomit,
   so a fool repeats his folly.

12 Do you see a man wise in his own eyes?
   There is more hope for a fool than for him.

13 The sluggard says, "There is a lion in the road,
   a fierce lion roaming the streets!"

14 As a door turns on its hinges,
   so a sluggard turns on his bed.

15 The sluggard buries his hand in the dish;
   he is too lazy to bring it back to his mouth.

16 The sluggard is wiser in his own eyes
   than seven men who answer discreetly.

17 Like one who seizes a dog by the ears
   is a passer-by who meddles in a quarrel not his own.

18 Like a madman shooting
   firebrands or deadly arrows
19 is a man who deceives his neighbor
   and says, "I was only joking!"

20 Without wood a fire goes out;
   without gossip a quarrel dies down.

21 As charcoal to embers and as wood to fire,
   so is a quarrelsome man for kindling strife.

22 The words of a gossip are like choice morsels;
   they go down to a man's inmost parts.

23 Like a coating of glaze*a* over earthenware
   are fervent lips with an evil heart.

a 23 With a different word division of the Hebrew; Masoretic Text *of silver dross*

²⁴A malicious man disguises himself with his lips,
　　but in his heart he harbors deceit.
²⁵Though his speech is charming, do not believe
　　him,
　　for seven abominations fill his heart.
²⁶His malice may be concealed by deception,
　　but his wickedness will be exposed in the
　　assembly.

²⁷If a man digs a pit, he will fall into it;
　　if a man rolls a stone, it will roll back on him.

²⁸A lying tongue hates those it hurts,
　　and a flattering mouth works ruin.

27 Do not boast about tomorrow,
　　for you do not know what a day may bring forth.

²Let another praise you, and not your own mouth;
　　someone else, and not your own lips.

³Stone is heavy and sand a burden,
　　but provocation by a fool is heavier than both.

⁴Anger is cruel and fury overwhelming,
　　but who can stand before jealousy?

⁵Better is open rebuke
　　than hidden love.

⁶Wounds from a friend can be trusted,
　　but an enemy multiplies kisses.

⁷He who is full loathes honey,
　　but to the hungry even what is bitter tastes
　　sweet.

⁸Like a bird that strays from its nest
　　is a man who strays from his home.

⁹Perfume and incense bring joy to the heart,
　　and the pleasantness of one's friend springs
　　from his earnest counsel.

¹⁰Do not forsake your friend and the friend of your
　　father,
　　and do not go to your brother's house when
　　disaster strikes you—
　　better a neighbor nearby than a brother far
　　away.

¹¹Be wise, my son, and bring joy to my heart;
　　then I can answer anyone who treats me with
　　contempt.

¹²The prudent see danger and take refuge,
　　but the simple keep going and suffer for it.

¹³Take the garment of one who puts up security for
　　a stranger;
　　hold it in pledge if he does it for a wayward
　　woman.

¹⁴If a man loudly blesses his neighbor early in the
　　morning,
　　it will be taken as a curse.

¹⁵A quarrelsome wife is like
　　a constant dripping on a rainy day;

Unhelpful Help

PROVERBS 27:14

Which kind of help do you give to others? Ask God to help you look honestly at the help you offer. In particular, look at whether you offer your help more to meet your own needs or to meet the needs of the one you are helping. Is the assistance you offer what that person really needs or what you think he or she needs? Have you asked? What more can you do? How can you ensure that your help is a blessing rather than an annoyance or a hindrance? Where does God call you to reach out to others? You might conclude by offering whatever efforts you make to the glory of God alone.

See Meeting God in Service

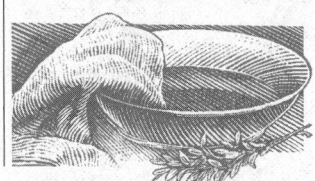

The Mark of Holiness

PROVERBS 28:4–8

"Holiness is a state of soul in which all the powers of the body and mind are consciously given up to God; and the witness of holiness is that testimony which the Holy Spirit bears with our spirit that the offering is accepted through Christ. The work is accomplished the moment we lay our all upon the altar."

—PHOEBE PALMER,
Entire Devotion to God

¹⁶restraining her is like restraining the wind
    or grasping oil with the hand.

¹⁷As iron sharpens iron,
    so one man sharpens another.

¹⁸He who tends a fig tree will eat its fruit,
    and he who looks after his master will be
        honored.

¹⁹As water reflects a face,
    so a man's heart reflects the man.

²⁰Death and Destruction[a] are never satisfied,
    and neither are the eyes of man.

²¹The crucible for silver and the furnace for gold,
    but man is tested by the praise he receives.

²²Though you grind a fool in a mortar,
    grinding him like grain with a pestle,
    you will not remove his folly from him.

²³Be sure you know the condition of your flocks,
    give careful attention to your herds;
²⁴for riches do not endure forever,
    and a crown is not secure for all generations.
²⁵When the hay is removed and new growth
        appears
    and the grass from the hills is gathered in,
²⁶the lambs will provide you with clothing,
    and the goats with the price of a field.
²⁷You will have plenty of goats' milk
    to feed you and your family
    and to nourish your servant girls.

28

The wicked man flees though no one pursues,
    but the righteous are as bold as a lion.

²When a country is rebellious, it has many rulers,
    but a man of understanding and knowledge
        maintains order.

³A ruler[b] who oppresses the poor
    is like a driving rain that leaves no crops.

⁴Those who forsake the law praise the wicked,
    but those who keep the law resist them.

⁵Evil men do not understand justice,
    but those who seek the LORD understand it fully.

⁶Better a poor man whose walk is blameless
    than a rich man whose ways are perverse.

⁷He who keeps the law is a discerning son,
    but a companion of gluttons disgraces his
        father.

⁸He who increases his wealth by exorbitant
        interest
    amasses it for another, who will be kind to the
        poor.

⁹If anyone turns a deaf ear to the law,
    even his prayers are detestable.

^a20 Hebrew *Sheol and Abaddon*   ^b3 Or *A poor man*

¹⁰ He who leads the upright along an evil path
will fall into his own trap,
but the blameless will receive a good
inheritance.

¹¹ A rich man may be wise in his own eyes,
but a poor man who has discernment sees
through him.

¹² When the righteous triumph, there is great
elation;
but when the wicked rise to power, men go into
hiding.

¹³ He who conceals his sins does not prosper,
but whoever confesses and renounces them
finds mercy.

¹⁴ Blessed is the man who always fears the Lord,
but he who hardens his heart falls into
trouble.

¹⁵ Like a roaring lion or a charging bear
is a wicked man ruling over a helpless people.

¹⁶ A tyrannical ruler lacks judgment,
but he who hates ill-gotten gain will enjoy a
long life.

¹⁷ A man tormented by the guilt of murder
will be a fugitive till death;
let no one support him.

¹⁸ He whose walk is blameless is kept safe,
but he whose ways are perverse will suddenly
fall.

¹⁹ He who works his land will have abundant food,
but the one who chases fantasies will have his
fill of poverty.

²⁰ A faithful man will be richly blessed,
but one eager to get rich will not go
unpunished.

²¹ To show partiality is not good—
yet a man will do wrong for a piece of bread.

²² A stingy man is eager to get rich
and is unaware that poverty awaits him.

²³ He who rebukes a man will in the end gain more
favor
than he who has a flattering tongue.

²⁴ He who robs his father or mother
and says, "It's not wrong"—
he is partner to him who destroys.

²⁵ A greedy man stirs up dissension,
but he who trusts in the Lord will prosper.

²⁶ He who trusts in himself is a fool,
but he who walks in wisdom is kept safe.

²⁷ He who gives to the poor will lack nothing,
but he who closes his eyes to them receives
many curses.

On the Way

PROVERBS 28:13

It is not easy for anyone to confess wrongdoing. Eve and Adam couldn't. Neither could the snake. The proverbs claim that if we conceal our transgressions, we will not prosper. More agonizing than that, perhaps, is living in fear that someone will find out. So our first impulse usually is to hide and to pretend that all is well. Confession can be a freeing spiritual experience. When we recognize our condition before God, we are reminded of our helplessness and God's grace.

Place yourself in God's presence and unburden your heart in confession. You might use a formal prayer of confession from a hymnal or prayer book, or you might use Psalm 51 as a starting point. Say to yourself and believe, "I have a covenant relationship with God. I will trust God's mercy as I confess."

See Meeting God in Prayer

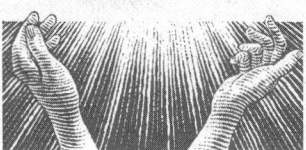

The Rights of the Poor

PROVERBS 29:7

The belief that the poor will always be around prevents some people from looking seriously at the issue of poverty and justice. The wicked have no understanding of the rights of the poor; they can always list reasons why the poor deserve their poverty.

Being faithful leads us beyond mere belief in the one true God. How would you respond if someone told you that you share responsibility before God for the plight of all of God's children? Overwhelming, isn't it? What concrete action can you take to help at least some of the poor? Listen for God's call. What is the first step you can take in response?

See *Meeting God in Service*

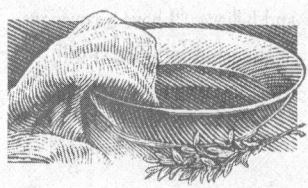

28 When the wicked rise to power, people go into hiding;
but when the wicked perish, the righteous thrive.

29 A man who remains stiff-necked after many rebukes
will suddenly be destroyed—without remedy.

2 When the righteous thrive, the people rejoice;
when the wicked rule, the people groan.

3 A man who loves wisdom brings joy to his father,
but a companion of prostitutes squanders his wealth.

4 By justice a king gives a country stability,
but one who is greedy for bribes tears it down.

5 Whoever flatters his neighbor
is spreading a net for his feet.

6 An evil man is snared by his own sin,
but a righteous one can sing and be glad.

7 The righteous care about justice for the poor,
but the wicked have no such concern.

8 Mockers stir up a city,
but wise men turn away anger.

9 If a wise man goes to court with a fool,
the fool rages and scoffs, and there is no peace.

10 Bloodthirsty men hate a man of integrity
and seek to kill the upright.

11 A fool gives full vent to his anger,
but a wise man keeps himself under control.

12 If a ruler listens to lies,
all his officials become wicked.

13 The poor man and the oppressor have this in common:
The LORD gives sight to the eyes of both.

14 If a king judges the poor with fairness,
his throne will always be secure.

15 The rod of correction imparts wisdom,
but a child left to himself disgraces his mother.

16 When the wicked thrive, so does sin,
but the righteous will see their downfall.

17 Discipline your son, and he will give you peace;
he will bring delight to your soul.

18 Where there is no revelation, the people cast off restraint;
but blessed is he who keeps the law.

19 A servant cannot be corrected by mere words;
though he understands, he will not respond.

20 Do you see a man who speaks in haste?
There is more hope for a fool than for him.

21 If a man pampers his servant from youth,
he will bring grief[a] in the end.

a 21 The meaning of the Hebrew for this word is uncertain.

22 An angry man stirs up dissension,
and a hot-tempered one commits many sins.

23 A man's pride brings him low,
but a man of lowly spirit gains honor.

24 The accomplice of a thief is his own enemy;
he is put under oath and dare not testify.

25 Fear of man will prove to be a snare,
but whoever trusts in the LORD is kept safe.

26 Many seek an audience with a ruler,
but it is from the LORD that man gets justice.

27 The righteous detest the dishonest;
the wicked detest the upright.

Sayings of Agur

30 The sayings of Agur son of Jakeh—an oracle[a]:

This man declared to Ithiel,
to Ithiel and to Ucal:[b]

2 "I am the most ignorant of men;
I do not have a man's understanding.
3 I have not learned wisdom,
nor have I knowledge of the Holy One.
4 Who has gone up to heaven and come down?
Who has gathered up the wind in the hollow of
his hands?
Who has wrapped up the waters in his cloak?
Who has established all the ends of the earth?
What is his name, and the name of his son?
Tell me if you know!

5 "Every word of God is flawless;
he is a shield to those who take refuge in him.
6 Do not add to his words,
or he will rebuke you and prove you a liar.

7 "Two things I ask of you, O LORD;
do not refuse me before I die:
8 Keep falsehood and lies far from me;
give me neither poverty nor riches,
but give me only my daily bread.
9 Otherwise, I may have too much and disown you
and say, 'Who is the LORD?'
Or I may become poor and steal,
and so dishonor the name of my God.

10 "Do not slander a servant to his master,
or he will curse you, and you will pay for it.

11 "There are those who curse their fathers
and do not bless their mothers;
12 those who are pure in their own eyes
and yet are not cleansed of their filth;
13 those whose eyes are ever so haughty,
whose glances are so disdainful;
14 those whose teeth are swords
and whose jaws are set with knives

Taking Time

PROVERBS 29:20

Often we pride ourselves on being quick to speak, on always having a ready answer. We know, though, that speaking too quickly often gets us into trouble. Cutting remarks, careless comments and poor advice tumble out of our mouths.

Try for one day to be slow to speak. Take a deep breath before replying to a question or commenting on something you see. During that breath, you might offer a silent prayer such as, "God grant me wisdom when I speak," breathing in over the first four syllables and out over the last four.

One way to prepare for a day of slow and careful speech would be to sit quietly for several minutes. As you sit, breathe slowly and repeat that prayer with each breath. This might also be a good way to prepare for a meeting.

See Meeting God in Prayer

---

a 1 Or *Jakeh of Massa*   b 1 Masoretic Text; with a different word division of
the Hebrew declared, "I am weary, O God; / I am weary, O God, and faint.

869

Playing the Fool With God's Word

PROVERBS 30:5–6,32

"No one is more foolish than one who forces the meaning of the Scriptures or finds fault with them so as to demonstrate his own knowledge—or, rather, his own ignorance. What kind of knowledge can result from adapting the meaning of the Scriptures to suit one's own likes and from daring to alter their words? The true sage is one who regards the text as authoritative and discovers, through the wisdom of the Spirit, the hidden mysteries to which the divine Scriptures bear witness."

—PETER OF DAMASKOS,
The Philokalia, Volume III

to devour the poor from the earth,
the needy from among mankind.

¹⁵ "The leech has two daughters.
'Give! Give!' they cry.

"There are three things that are never satisfied,
four that never say, 'Enough!':
¹⁶ the grave,ᵃ the barren womb,
land, which is never satisfied with water,
and fire, which never says, 'Enough!'

¹⁷ "The eye that mocks a father,
that scorns obedience to a mother,
will be pecked out by the ravens of the valley,
will be eaten by the vultures.

¹⁸ "There are three things that are too amazing for me,
four that I do not understand:
¹⁹ the way of an eagle in the sky,
the way of a snake on a rock,
the way of a ship on the high seas,
and the way of a man with a maiden.

²⁰ "This is the way of an adulteress:
She eats and wipes her mouth
and says, 'I've done nothing wrong.'

²¹ "Under three things the earth trembles,
under four it cannot bear up:
²² a servant who becomes king,
a fool who is full of food,
²³ an unloved woman who is married,
and a maidservant who displaces her mistress.

²⁴ "Four things on earth are small,
yet they are extremely wise:
²⁵ Ants are creatures of little strength,
yet they store up their food in the summer;
²⁶ coneysᵇ are creatures of little power,
yet they make their home in the crags;
²⁷ locusts have no king,
yet they advance together in ranks;
²⁸ a lizard can be caught with the hand,
yet it is found in kings' palaces.

²⁹ "There are three things that are stately in their stride,
four that move with stately bearing:
³⁰ a lion, mighty among beasts,
who retreats before nothing;
³¹ a strutting rooster, a he-goat,
and a king with his army around him.ᶜ

³² "If you have played the fool and exalted yourself,
or if you have planned evil,
clap your hand over your mouth!
³³ For as churning the milk produces butter,
and as twisting the nose produces blood,
so stirring up anger produces strife."

ᵃ 16 Hebrew *Sheol*   ᵇ 26 That is, the hyrax or rock badger   ᶜ 31 Or *king secure against revolt*

Sayings of King Lemuel

31 The sayings of King Lemuel—an oracle[a] his mother taught him:

2 "O my son, O son of my womb,
O son of my vows,[b]
3 do not spend your strength on women,
your vigor on those who ruin kings.

4 "It is not for kings, O Lemuel—
not for kings to drink wine,
not for rulers to crave beer,
5 lest they drink and forget what the law decrees,
and deprive all the oppressed of their rights.
6 Give beer to those who are perishing,
wine to those who are in anguish;
7 let them drink and forget their poverty
and remember their misery no more.

8 "Speak up for those who cannot speak for
themselves,
for the rights of all who are destitute.
9 Speak up and judge fairly;
defend the rights of the poor and needy."

Epilogue: The Wife of Noble Character

10 [c] A wife of noble character who can find?
She is worth far more than rubies.
11 Her husband has full confidence in her
and lacks nothing of value.
12 She brings him good, not harm,
all the days of her life.
13 She selects wool and flax
and works with eager hands.
14 She is like the merchant ships,
bringing her food from afar.
15 She gets up while it is still dark;
she provides food for her family
and portions for her servant girls.
16 She considers a field and buys it;
out of her earnings she plants a vineyard.
17 She sets about her work vigorously;
her arms are strong for her tasks.
18 She sees that her trading is profitable,
and her lamp does not go out at night.
19 In her hand she holds the distaff
and grasps the spindle with her fingers.
20 She opens her arms to the poor
and extends her hands to the needy.
21 When it snows, she has no fear for her
household;
for all of them are clothed in scarlet.
22 She makes coverings for her bed;
she is clothed in fine linen and purple.
23 Her husband is respected at the city gate,
where he takes his seat among the elders of the
land.
24 She makes linen garments and sells them,

A Voice for the Voiceless

PROVERBS 31:8–9

The sage challenges us to speak out and defend the powerless, whose voice is not heard; the poor, who struggle to survive; and the destitute, who have nothing. Some of life's defining moments come as we are invited and challenged to speak out for the voiceless. Henri J. M. Nouwen said, "Compassion without confrontation fades quickly into fruitless sentimental commiseration." What is he trying to tell us? If we are called to speak for the oppressed, how can we live this out? Ask God to keep you alert for surprising encounters that offer you opportunities to be a voice for the voiceless. Ask for the courage to accept such opportunities. You might conclude your prayer time by singing Frances R. Havergal's hymn "Lord, Speak to Me, That I May Speak" or S. Ralph Harlow's "O Young and Fearless Prophet."

See Meeting God in Service

---

a 1 Or *of Lemuel king of Massa, which*   b 2 Or / *the answer to my prayers*
c 10 Verses 10–31 are an acrostic, each verse beginning with a successive letter of the Hebrew alphabet.

A Working Mother

PROVERBS 31:10–31

This poem in praise of a working mother is an acrostic; each verse begins with a different letter of the Hebrew alphabet, in order from *Aleph* to *Taw*. This woman is the embodiment of wisdom in action, doing everything she does with forethought and excellence and enabling others in her family to do their best as well.

Who has been an embodiment of wisdom in your life? You might try to create an acrostic in praise of that person, listing qualities that make him or her praiseworthy or that exemplify wisdom in action. You might use the person's name, title or their relationship to you as a basis for the acrostic. (For example, think of the song "MOTHER," which begins, "M is for the million things she gave me.") If the person is still living, make a good copy of the poem and give it to him or her. In any case, thank God for the gift of this person in your life.

See *Meeting God in Everyday Life*

and supplies the merchants with sashes.
²⁵ She is clothed with strength and dignity;
   she can laugh at the days to come.
²⁶ She speaks with wisdom,
   and faithful instruction is on her tongue.
²⁷ She watches over the affairs of her household
   and does not eat the bread of idleness.
²⁸ Her children arise and call her blessed;
   her husband also, and he praises her:
²⁹ "Many women do noble things,
   but you surpass them all."
³⁰ Charm is deceptive, and beauty is fleeting;
   but a woman who fears the LORD is to be
      praised.
³¹ Give her the reward she has earned,
   and let her works bring her praise at the city
      gate.

ECCLESIASTES
A Search for Meaning

KEY VERSE:

He has also set eternity in the hearts of men; yet they cannot fathom what God has done from beginning to end.—Ecclesiastes 3:11

Ecclesiastes explores the meaning of life, and its words often seem to reflect Thoreau's famous quotation, "The mass of men lead lives of quiet desperation." The author, called "the Teacher," is not as conclusive in his exploration as we would like him to be; at times he seems uncertain about God's ways. We might wonder why he sends all of these mixed messages. He confesses that his past choices have included the pursuit of pleasure, achievement and riches (2:1–11; 4:13–16; 5:1—6:12). Even though the Teacher has found all three, he struggles with disillusionment. In contrast, his parting words seem sure of the purpose of life: "Fear God and keep his commandments, for this is the whole ⌐duty⌐ of man." We identify with his struggle to find meaning in the weariness of everyday life, a universal struggle to this day; yet beyond the recitation of troubles, his words soar with hope : "[God] has made everything beautiful in its time" (3:11).

As you read this book of wisdom, take time to ponder the "big picture"—the meaning and purpose of life—but don't forget to make a daily effort to look with wonder at God's creation and remember that it is "beautiful in its time." Learn from the Teacher about the meaninglessness of acquisition, knowledge and work in and of themselves—but also learn that your ultimate purpose in everything you do is to know, love and serve God. Even as you acknowledge the ambiguities of life, remain open to the rich and mysterious ways in which God will reveal its meaning to you.

> "The present moment holds infinite riches beyond your wildest dreams but you will only enjoy them to the extent of your faith and love. The more a soul loves, the more it longs, the more it hopes, the more it finds."
>
> —JEAN-PIERRE DE CAUSSADE,
> *The Sacrament of the Present*

Summarized

ECCLESIASTES 1:1–18

Your first response might be to think that the Teacher should have developed a rosier outlook on life. Take time to reflect on your life with some one-word summaries. What one word would you use in place of "meaningless" or "vanity" to summarize your life at present? What words best describe your search for meaning and purpose? What sort of picture do these words suggest?

See Meeting God in Scripture

Everything Is Meaningless

1 The words of the Teacher,*a* son of David, king in Jerusalem:

² "Meaningless! Meaningless!"
  says the Teacher.
"Utterly meaningless!
  Everything is meaningless."

³ What does man gain from all his labor
  at which he toils under the sun?
⁴ Generations come and generations go,
  but the earth remains forever.
⁵ The sun rises and the sun sets,
  and hurries back to where it rises.
⁶ The wind blows to the south
  and turns to the north;
round and round it goes,
  ever returning on its course.
⁷ All streams flow into the sea,
  yet the sea is never full.
To the place the streams come from,
  there they return again.
⁸ All things are wearisome,
  more than one can say.
The eye never has enough of seeing,
  nor the ear its fill of hearing.
⁹ What has been will be again,
  what has been done will be done again;
  there is nothing new under the sun.
¹⁰ Is there anything of which one can say,
  "Look! This is something new"?
It was here already, long ago;
  it was here before our time.
¹¹ There is no remembrance of men of old,
  and even those who are yet to come
will not be remembered
  by those who follow.

Wisdom Is Meaningless

¹²I, the Teacher, was king over Israel in Jerusalem. ¹³I devoted myself to study and to explore by wisdom all that is done under heaven. What a heavy burden God has laid on men! ¹⁴I have seen all the things that are done under the sun; all of them are meaningless, a chasing after the wind.

¹⁵ What is twisted cannot be straightened;
  what is lacking cannot be counted.

¹⁶I thought to myself, "Look, I have grown and increased in wisdom more than anyone who has ruled over Jerusalem before me; I have experienced much of wisdom and knowledge." ¹⁷Then I applied myself to the understanding of wisdom, and also of madness and folly, but I learned that this, too, is a chasing after the wind.

¹⁸ For with much wisdom comes much sorrow;
  the more knowledge, the more grief.

a 1 Or *leader of the assembly*; also in verses 2 and 12

Pleasures Are Meaningless

2 I thought in my heart, "Come now, I will test you with pleasure to find out what is good." But that also proved to be meaningless. [2]"Laughter," I said, "is foolish. And what does pleasure accomplish?" [3]I tried cheering myself with wine, and embracing folly—my mind still guiding me with wisdom. I wanted to see what was worthwhile for men to do under heaven during the few days of their lives.

[4]I undertook great projects: I built houses for myself and planted vineyards. [5]I made gardens and parks and planted all kinds of fruit trees in them. [6]I made reservoirs to water groves of flourishing trees. [7]I bought male and female slaves and had other slaves who were born in my house. I also owned more herds and flocks than anyone in Jerusalem before me. [8]I amassed silver and gold for myself, and the treasure of kings and provinces. I acquired men and women singers, and a harem[a] as well—the delights of the heart of man. [9]I became greater by far than anyone in Jerusalem before me. In all this my wisdom stayed with me.

[10]I denied myself nothing my eyes desired;
    I refused my heart no pleasure.
My heart took delight in all my work,
    and this was the reward for all my labor.
[11]Yet when I surveyed all that my hands had done
    and what I had toiled to achieve,
everything was meaningless, a chasing after the
    wind;
    nothing was gained under the sun.

Wisdom and Folly Are Meaningless

[12]Then I turned my thoughts to consider wisdom,
    and also madness and folly.
What more can the king's successor do
    than what has already been done?
[13]I saw that wisdom is better than folly,
    just as light is better than darkness.
[14]The wise man has eyes in his head,
    while the fool walks in the darkness;
but I came to realize
    that the same fate overtakes them both.

[15]Then I thought in my heart,

"The fate of the fool will overtake me also.
    What then do I gain by being wise?"
I said in my heart,
    "This too is meaningless."
[16]For the wise man, like the fool, will not be long
    remembered;
in days to come both will be forgotten.
Like the fool, the wise man too must die!

Toil Is Meaningless

[17]So I hated life, because the work that is done under the sun was grievous to me. All of it is meaningless, a chasing after the wind. [18]I hated all the things I had toiled for under the sun, because I must leave them to the one who comes after me. [19]And who knows whether he will be a wise man

---

Testing What Is Good

ECCLESIASTES 2:1

How like a teacher to suggest another test, but so far the Teacher has limited the scope of his tests to pleasure and achievements! Today's culture also seems bent on testing the meaning of achievement, pleasure and materialism. But why not test the meaningfulness of relationships? Apply this test to your encounter with God. In what ways do you find meaning in God's presence? What "achievements" is God accomplishing through you? How are you "relating" to God? Which areas of your life with God need a tune-up? Which area seems like a good place for God and you to begin that work?

---

[a]8 The meaning of the Hebrew for this phrase is uncertain.

A Present Shaped by the Future

ECCLESIASTES 3:11

God has given us a sense of past and future—even putting eternity in our hearts. Our present is affected not only by our past but also by the future to which God is calling us. On one half of a sheet of paper make a list of some things God might be calling you to do. Then, on the other half, list the things that you may need to relinquish to make time for responding to God's call. As you review it, ask yourself if you see signs that this "making room" has already begun.

See Meeting God in Everyday Life

or a fool? Yet he will have control over all the work into which I have poured my effort and skill under the sun. This too is meaningless. ²⁰So my heart began to despair over all my toilsome labor under the sun. ²¹For a man may do his work with wisdom, knowledge and skill, and then he must leave all he owns to someone who has not worked for it. This too is meaningless and a great misfortune. ²²What does a man get for all the toil and anxious striving with which he labors under the sun? ²³All his days his work is pain and grief; even at night his mind does not rest. This too is meaningless.

²⁴A man can do nothing better than to eat and drink and find satisfaction in his work. This too, I see, is from the hand of God, ²⁵for without him, who can eat or find enjoyment? ²⁶To the man who pleases him, God gives wisdom, knowledge and happiness, but to the sinner he gives the task of gathering and storing up wealth to hand it over to the one who pleases God. This too is meaningless, a chasing after the wind.

A Time for Everything

3 There is a time for everything,
and a season for every activity under heaven:

² a time to be born and a time to die,
a time to plant and a time to uproot,
³ a time to kill and a time to heal,
a time to tear down and a time to build,
⁴ a time to weep and a time to laugh,
a time to mourn and a time to dance,
⁵ a time to scatter stones and a time to gather
them,
a time to embrace and a time to refrain,
⁶ a time to search and a time to give up,
a time to keep and a time to throw away,
⁷ a time to tear and a time to mend,
a time to be silent and a time to speak,
⁸ a time to love and a time to hate,
a time for war and a time for peace.

⁹What does the worker gain from his toil? ¹⁰I have seen the burden God has laid on men. ¹¹He has made everything beautiful in its time. He has also set eternity in the hearts of men; yet they cannot fathom what God has done from beginning to end. ¹²I know that there is nothing better for men than to be happy and do good while they live. ¹³That everyone may eat and drink, and find satisfaction in all his toil—this is the gift of God. ¹⁴I know that everything God does will endure forever; nothing can be added to it and nothing taken from it. God does it so that men will revere him.

¹⁵ Whatever is has already been,
and what will be has been before;
and God will call the past to account.ᵃ

¹⁶And I saw something else under the sun:

In the place of judgment—wickedness was there,
in the place of justice—wickedness was there.

¹⁷I thought in my heart,

ᵃ 15 Or *God calls back the past*

"God will bring to judgment
both the righteous and the wicked,
for there will be a time for every activity,
a time for every deed."

[18]I also thought, "As for men, God tests them so that they may see that they are like the animals. [19]Man's fate is like that of the animals; the same fate awaits them both: As one dies, so dies the other. All have the same breath[a]; man has no advantage over the animal. Everything is meaningless. [20]All go to the same place; all come from dust, and to dust all return. [21]Who knows if the spirit of man rises upward and if the spirit of the animal[b] goes down into the earth?"

[22]So I saw that there is nothing better for a man than to enjoy his work, because that is his lot. For who can bring him to see what will happen after him?

Oppression, Toil, Friendlessness

4 Again I looked and saw all the oppression that was taking place under the sun:

I saw the tears of the oppressed—
and they have no comforter;
power was on the side of their oppressors—
and they have no comforter.
[2]And I declared that the dead,
who had already died,
are happier than the living,
who are still alive.
[3]But better than both
is he who has not yet been,
who has not seen the evil
that is done under the sun.

[4]And I saw that all labor and all achievement spring from man's envy of his neighbor. This too is meaningless, a chasing after the wind.

[5]The fool folds his hands
and ruins himself.
[6]Better one handful with tranquillity
than two handfuls with toil
and chasing after the wind.

[7]Again I saw something meaningless under the sun:

[8]There was a man all alone;
he had neither son nor brother.
There was no end to his toil,
yet his eyes were not content with his wealth.
"For whom am I toiling," he asked,
"and why am I depriving myself of
enjoyment?"
This too is meaningless—
a miserable business!

[9]Two are better than one,
because they have a good return for their work:
[10]If one falls down,
his friend can help him up.

Motivated by Envy

ECCLESIASTES 4:4

The Teacher offers a startling insight: Envy may be at the root of our hard work and achievement. Envy shifts our focus from what God has given us to what has been given to others. It estranges us from others and causes discontent with ourselves and our lot in life. Think of a few people you envy or have envied, and write their names in your journal or on a piece of paper. Add a few words describing what you envy about them. Finally, for each point make note of something God has given you. Carry the list with you until you read again from this book. Express your thanks to God.

See Meeting God in Community

---

[a] 19 Or *spirit*   [b] 21 Or *Who knows the spirit of man, which rises upward, or the spirit of the animal, which*

How Much Is Enough?

ECCLESIASTES 5:10–14

One of the Teacher's key questions in his struggle with meaninglessness seems to be "How much is enough?"

Quiz yourself for a few minutes on "enough-ness." Make a list down the side of a sheet of paper, including such things as love, money, rest, food, clothing, entertainment, exercise, spiritual self-examination, assurance of God's presence and so forth. Mark "yes" after those of which you believe you have enough. For the others, write a sentence describing your current needs. Pray for God's assistance in your appraisal; discern the difference between your desires and your needs. Finish by asking God, "What do I need to know about having enough?"

See *Meeting God in Prayer*

But pity the man who falls
and has no one to help him up!
¹¹ Also, if two lie down together, they will keep warm.
But how can one keep warm alone?
¹² Though one may be overpowered,
two can defend themselves.
A cord of three strands is not quickly broken.

Advancement Is Meaningless

¹³ Better a poor but wise youth than an old but foolish king who no longer knows how to take warning. ¹⁴ The youth may have come from prison to the kingship, or he may have been born in poverty within his kingdom. ¹⁵ I saw that all who lived and walked under the sun followed the youth, the king's successor. ¹⁶ There was no end to all the people who were before them. But those who came later were not pleased with the successor. This too is meaningless, a chasing after the wind.

Stand in Awe of God

5 Guard your steps when you go to the house of God. Go near to listen rather than to offer the sacrifice of fools, who do not know that they do wrong.

² Do not be quick with your mouth,
do not be hasty in your heart
to utter anything before God.
God is in heaven
and you are on earth,
so let your words be few.
³ As a dream comes when there are many cares,
so the speech of a fool when there are many words.

⁴ When you make a vow to God, do not delay in fulfilling it. He has no pleasure in fools; fulfill your vow. ⁵ It is better not to vow than to make a vow and not fulfill it. ⁶ Do not let your mouth lead you into sin. And do not protest to the ₍temple₎ messenger, "My vow was a mistake." Why should God be angry at what you say and destroy the work of your hands? ⁷ Much dreaming and many words are meaningless. Therefore stand in awe of God.

Riches Are Meaningless

⁸ If you see the poor oppressed in a district, and justice and rights denied, do not be surprised at such things; for one official is eyed by a higher one, and over them both are others higher still. ⁹ The increase from the land is taken by all; the king himself profits from the fields.

¹⁰ Whoever loves money never has money enough;
whoever loves wealth is never satisfied with his income.
This too is meaningless.

¹¹ As goods increase,
so do those who consume them.
And what benefit are they to the owner
except to feast his eyes on them?

¹² The sleep of a laborer is sweet,
whether he eats little or much,

but the abundance of a rich man
    permits him no sleep.

[13] I have seen a grievous evil under the sun:

wealth hoarded to the harm of its owner,
[14]   or wealth lost through some misfortune,
so that when he has a son
    there is nothing left for him.
[15] Naked a man comes from his mother's womb,
    and as he comes, so he departs.
He takes nothing from his labor
    that he can carry in his hand.

[16] This too is a grievous evil:

As a man comes, so he departs,
    and what does he gain,
    since he toils for the wind?
[17] All his days he eats in darkness,
    with great frustration, affliction and anger.

[18] Then I realized that it is good and proper for a man to eat and drink, and to find satisfaction in his toilsome labor under the sun during the few days of life God has given him—for this is his lot. [19] Moreover, when God gives any man wealth and possessions, and enables him to enjoy them, to accept his lot and be happy in his work—this is a gift of God. [20] He seldom reflects on the days of his life, because God keeps him occupied with gladness of heart.

6 I have seen another evil under the sun, and it weighs heavily on men: [2] God gives a man wealth, possessions and honor, so that he lacks nothing his heart desires, but God does not enable him to enjoy them, and a stranger enjoys them instead. This is meaningless, a grievous evil.
[3] A man may have a hundred children and live many years; yet no matter how long he lives, if he cannot enjoy his prosperity and does not receive proper burial, I say that a stillborn child is better off than he. [4] It comes without meaning, it departs in darkness, and in darkness its name is shrouded. [5] Though it never saw the sun or knew anything, it has more rest than does that man— [6] even if he lives a thousand years twice over but fails to enjoy his prosperity. Do not all go to the same place?

[7] All man's efforts are for his mouth,
    yet his appetite is never satisfied.
[8] What advantage has a wise man
    over a fool?
What does a poor man gain
    by knowing how to conduct himself before
      others?
[9] Better what the eye sees
    than the roving of the appetite.
This too is meaningless,
    a chasing after the wind.

[10] Whatever exists has already been named,
    and what man is has been known;
no man can contend
    with one who is stronger than he.
[11] The more the words,
    the less the meaning,
    and how does that profit anyone?

The Inability to Enjoy

ECCLESIASTES 6:2

Put yourself in the place of this great teacher. Look at the wealth, possessions and honor God has given you. Stand in the Teacher's shoes and feel his dissatisfaction. What prevents you from enjoying what God has given you? What incredible gifts do you have that other people (even strangers!) enjoy more than you enjoy? What do you need to hear from God about your inability to enjoy what God has given you?

Wise Person or Cynic?

ECCLESIASTES 7:10–14

Jesus is known for how he asked questions. He was inquisitive, but not cynical. How would he have reacted to the questions the Teacher asks and discusses here? With what attitude would Jesus have asked them? Reread Ecclesiastes 7:10–12. What word or phrase or action attracts your attention? Reflect on this word or phrase or action. Why is it meaningful to you? Write down the key words such as *shelter*, *money* and *wisdom*. Reflect on each of them. What questions might you ask God? Remain silent and open to receive insight from God.

See Meeting God in Scripture

¹²For who knows what is good for a man in life, during the few and meaningless days he passes through like a shadow? Who can tell him what will happen under the sun after he is gone?

Wisdom

7 A good name is better than fine perfume,
and the day of death better than the day of birth.
²It is better to go to a house of mourning
than to go to a house of feasting,
for death is the destiny of every man;
the living should take this to heart.
³Sorrow is better than laughter,
because a sad face is good for the heart.
⁴The heart of the wise is in the house of mourning,
but the heart of fools is in the house of
pleasure.
⁵It is better to heed a wise man's rebuke
than to listen to the song of fools.
⁶Like the crackling of thorns under the pot,
so is the laughter of fools.
This too is meaningless.

⁷Extortion turns a wise man into a fool,
and a bribe corrupts the heart.
⁸The end of a matter is better than its beginning,
and patience is better than pride.
⁹Do not be quickly provoked in your spirit,
for anger resides in the lap of fools.

¹⁰Do not say, "Why were the old days better than
these?"
For it is not wise to ask such questions.
¹¹Wisdom, like an inheritance, is a good thing
and benefits those who see the sun.
¹²Wisdom is a shelter
as money is a shelter,
but the advantage of knowledge is this:
that wisdom preserves the life of its possessor.

¹³Consider what God has done:

Who can straighten
what he has made crooked?
¹⁴When times are good, be happy;
but when times are bad, consider:
God has made the one
as well as the other.
Therefore, a man cannot discover
anything about his future.

¹⁵In this meaningless life of mine I have seen both of
these:

a righteous man perishing in his righteousness,
and a wicked man living long in his
wickedness.
¹⁶Do not be overrighteous,
neither be overwise—
why destroy yourself?
¹⁷Do not be overwicked,
and do not be a fool—

why die before your time?
¹⁸ It is good to grasp the one
  and not let go of the other.
  The man who fears God will avoid all
    ⌊extremes⌋.ᵃ

¹⁹ Wisdom makes one wise man more powerful
  than ten rulers in a city.

²⁰ There is not a righteous man on earth
  who does what is right and never sins.

²¹ Do not pay attention to every word people say,
  or you may hear your servant cursing you—
²² for you know in your heart
  that many times you yourself have cursed
    others.

²³ All this I tested by wisdom and I said,

  "I am determined to be wise"—
  but this was beyond me.
²⁴ Whatever wisdom may be,
  it is far off and most profound—
  who can discover it?
²⁵ So I turned my mind to understand,
  to investigate and to search out wisdom and
    the scheme of things
  and to understand the stupidity of wickedness
    and the madness of folly.

²⁶ I find more bitter than death
  the woman who is a snare,
  whose heart is a trap
  and whose hands are chains.
  The man who pleases God will escape her,
  but the sinner she will ensnare.

²⁷ "Look," says the Teacher,ᵇ "this is what I have
discovered:

  "Adding one thing to another to discover the
    scheme of things—
²⁸ while I was still searching
    but not finding—
  I found one ⌊upright⌋ man among a thousand,
    but not one ⌊upright⌋ woman among them all.
²⁹ This only have I found:
  God made mankind upright,
  but men have gone in search of many
    schemes."

8   Who is like the wise man?
    Who knows the explanation of things?
    Wisdom brightens a man's face
    and changes its hard appearance.

Obey the King

² Obey the king's command, I say, because you took an
oath before God. ³ Do not be in a hurry to leave the king's
presence. Do not stand up for a bad cause, for he will do
whatever he pleases. ⁴ Since a king's word is supreme, who
can say to him, "What are you doing?"

Wisdom Brings Light

ECCLESIASTES 8:1

"We have hints that there is a
way of life vastly richer and
deeper than all this hurried existence, a life of unhurried
serenity and peace and power.
We have known some people
who have found this deep Center of living. We've seen such
lives, integrated, unworried by
the tangles of close decisions,
unhurried, cheery, fresh, positive. These are not people of
dallying idleness nor of obviously mooning meditation; they
are busy carrying their full load
as well as we are, but without
any chafing of the shoulders
with the burden, with quiet joy
and springing step. They are
poised and at peace."

—THOMAS KELLY,
A Testament of Devotion

Content With Mystery

ECCLESIASTES 8:16–17

The Teacher seems to be accepting the idea that God is unsearchable: "Then I saw all that God has done. No one can comprehend what goes on under the sun." Make a list of the things you don't know and understand about God, humanity, science and relationships. (If you wish, walk around your house or apartment and touch things that represent them—a musical instrument, a box of bleach, a book, a wedding photo.)

Consider offering a prayer of acknowledgment to God that you don't understand these things and don't need to understand them. Let your acknowledgment of unknowing become an act of worship of the God who knows what you don't know.

See Meeting God in Prayer

[5] Whoever obeys his command will come to no harm,
and the wise heart will know the proper time and procedure.
[6] For there is a proper time and procedure for every matter,
though a man's misery weighs heavily upon him.

[7] Since no man knows the future,
who can tell him what is to come?
[8] No man has power over the wind to contain it[a];
so no one has power over the day of his death.
As no one is discharged in time of war,
so wickedness will not release those who practice it.

[9] All this I saw, as I applied my mind to everything done under the sun. There is a time when a man lords it over others to his own[b] hurt. [10] Then too, I saw the wicked buried—those who used to come and go from the holy place and receive praise[c] in the city where they did this. This too is meaningless.
[11] When the sentence for a crime is not quickly carried out, the hearts of the people are filled with schemes to do wrong. [12] Although a wicked man commits a hundred crimes and still lives a long time, I know that it will go better with God-fearing men, who are reverent before God. [13] Yet because the wicked do not fear God, it will not go well with them, and their days will not lengthen like a shadow.
[14] There is something else meaningless that occurs on earth: righteous men who get what the wicked deserve, and wicked men who get what the righteous deserve. This too, I say, is meaningless. [15] So I commend the enjoyment of life, because nothing is better for a man under the sun than to eat and drink and be glad. Then joy will accompany him in his work all the days of the life God has given him under the sun.
[16] When I applied my mind to know wisdom and to observe man's labor on earth—his eyes not seeing sleep day or night— [17] then I saw all that God has done. No one can comprehend what goes on under the sun. Despite all his efforts to search it out, man cannot discover its meaning. Even if a wise man claims he knows, he cannot really comprehend it.

A Common Destiny for All

9 So I reflected on all this and concluded that the righteous and the wise and what they do are in God's hands, but no man knows whether love or hate awaits him. [2] All share a common destiny—the righteous and the wicked, the good and the bad,[d] the clean and the unclean, those who offer sacrifices and those who do not.

As it is with the good man,
so with the sinner;
as it is with those who take oaths,
so with those who are afraid to take them.

---

[a] 8 Or *over his spirit to retain it*   [b] 9 Or *to their*   [c] 10 Some Hebrew manuscripts and Septuagint (Aquila); most Hebrew manuscripts *and are forgotten*   [d] 2 Septuagint (Aquila), Vulgate and Syriac; Hebrew does not have *and the bad.*

³This is the evil in everything that happens under the sun: The same destiny overtakes all. The hearts of men, moreover, are full of evil and there is madness in their hearts while they live, and afterward they join the dead. ⁴Anyone who is among the living has hope*ᵃ*—even a live dog is better off than a dead lion!

⁵For the living know that they will die,
    but the dead know nothing;
they have no further reward,
    and even the memory of them is forgotten.
⁶Their love, their hate
    and their jealousy have long since vanished;
never again will they have a part
    in anything that happens under the sun.

⁷Go, eat your food with gladness, and drink your wine with a joyful heart, for it is now that God favors what you do. ⁸Always be clothed in white, and always anoint your head with oil. ⁹Enjoy life with your wife, whom you love, all the days of this meaningless life that God has given you under the sun— all your meaningless days. For this is your lot in life and in your toilsome labor under the sun. ¹⁰Whatever your hand finds to do, do it with all your might, for in the grave,*ᵇ* where you are going, there is neither working nor planning nor knowledge nor wisdom.

¹¹I have seen something else under the sun:

The race is not to the swift
    or the battle to the strong,
nor does food come to the wise
    or wealth to the brilliant
    or favor to the learned;
but time and chance happen to them all.

¹²Moreover, no man knows when his hour will come:

As fish are caught in a cruel net,
    or birds are taken in a snare,
so men are trapped by evil times
    that fall unexpectedly upon them.

Wisdom Better Than Folly

¹³I also saw under the sun this example of wisdom that greatly impressed me: ¹⁴There was once a small city with only a few people in it. And a powerful king came against it, surrounded it and built huge siegeworks against it. ¹⁵Now there lived in that city a man poor but wise, and he saved the city by his wisdom. But nobody remembered that poor man. ¹⁶So I said, "Wisdom is better than strength." But the poor man's wisdom is despised, and his words are no longer heeded.

¹⁷The quiet words of the wise are more to be
        heeded
    than the shouts of a ruler of fools.
¹⁸Wisdom is better than weapons of war,
    but one sinner destroys much good.

10 As dead flies give perfume a bad smell,
    so a little folly outweighs wisdom and honor.

A Little Folly

ECCLESIASTES 10:1

Why do we sometimes beat ourselves up over "a little folly" of the past? Perhaps you carry within yourself a pesky burden from the past—a regret, a remnant of guilt, a nagging memory? Ponder it for a moment in silence before God: What do I have invested in this foible that prompts me to hold on to it? What is God calling me to do to rid myself of this memory? An admission to a friend or mentor? A small act of restitution? A selfless act that proves I intend to travel a different road from now on?

ᵃ 4 Or *What then is to be chosen? With all who live, there is hope*
ᵇ 10 Hebrew *Sheol*

Serenity in the Face of Anger

ECCLESIASTES 10:4

How can you remain serene as you face a powerful, angry person? Alfred, Lord Tennyson wrote, "Self-reverence, self-knowledge, self-control, these three alone lead to sovereign power." As you consider this advice for expressing power and responding to it, reflect on how a respectful self-awareness can open the way for a deepened relationship with God, the supreme Ruler. Do you treasure yourself as God does? Can you see yourself remaining serene in the knowledge of God's supreme rule in the presence of that powerful, angry person?

² The heart of the wise inclines to the right,
　　but the heart of the fool to the left.
³ Even as he walks along the road,
　　the fool lacks sense
　　and shows everyone how stupid he is.

⁴ If a ruler's anger rises against you,
　　do not leave your post;
　　calmness can lay great errors to rest.

⁵ There is an evil I have seen under the sun,
　　the sort of error that arises from a ruler:
⁶ Fools are put in many high positions,
　　while the rich occupy the low ones.
⁷ I have seen slaves on horseback,
　　while princes go on foot like slaves.

⁸ Whoever digs a pit may fall into it;
　　whoever breaks through a wall may be bitten
　　　by a snake.
⁹ Whoever quarries stones may be injured by
　　　them;
　　whoever splits logs may be endangered by
　　　them.

¹⁰ If the ax is dull
　　and its edge unsharpened,
　　more strength is needed
　　but skill will bring success.

¹¹ If a snake bites before it is charmed,
　　there is no profit for the charmer.

¹² Words from a wise man's mouth are gracious,
　　but a fool is consumed by his own lips.
¹³ At the beginning his words are folly;
　　at the end they are wicked madness—
¹⁴ 　and the fool multiplies words.

No one knows what is coming—
　　who can tell him what will happen after him?

¹⁵ A fool's work wearies him;
　　he does not know the way to town.

¹⁶ Woe to you, O land whose king was a servant[a]
　　and whose princes feast in the morning.
¹⁷ Blessed are you, O land whose king is of noble
　　　birth
　　and whose princes eat at a proper time—
　　for strength and not for drunkenness.

¹⁸ If a man is lazy, the rafters sag;
　　if his hands are idle, the house leaks.

¹⁹ A feast is made for laughter,
　　and wine makes life merry,
　　but money is the answer for everything.

²⁰ Do not revile the king even in your thoughts,
　　or curse the rich in your bedroom,
　　because a bird of the air may carry your words,
　　and a bird on the wing may report what you
　　　say.

a 16 Or king is a child

Bread Upon the Waters

11 Cast your bread upon the waters,
for after many days you will find it again.
² Give portions to seven, yes to eight,
for you do not know what disaster may come
upon the land.

³ If clouds are full of water,
they pour rain upon the earth.
Whether a tree falls to the south or to the north,
in the place where it falls, there will it lie.
⁴ Whoever watches the wind will not plant;
whoever looks at the clouds will not reap.

⁵ As you do not know the path of the wind,
or how the body is formed^a in a mother's
womb,
so you cannot understand the work of God,
the Maker of all things.

⁶ Sow your seed in the morning,
and at evening let not your hands be idle,
for you do not know which will succeed,
whether this or that,
or whether both will do equally well.

Remember Your Creator While Young

⁷ Light is sweet,
and it pleases the eyes to see the sun.
⁸ However many years a man may live,
let him enjoy them all.
But let him remember the days of darkness,
for they will be many.
Everything to come is meaningless.

⁹ Be happy, young man, while you are young,
and let your heart give you joy in the days of
your youth.
Follow the ways of your heart
and whatever your eyes see,
but know that for all these things
God will bring you to judgment.
¹⁰ So then, banish anxiety from your heart
and cast off the troubles of your body,
for youth and vigor are meaningless.

12 Remember your Creator
in the days of your youth,
before the days of trouble come
and the years approach when you will say,
"I find no pleasure in them"—
² before the sun and the light
and the moon and the stars grow dark,
and the clouds return after the rain;
³ when the keepers of the house tremble,
and the strong men stoop,
when the grinders cease because they are few,
and those looking through the windows grow
dim;
⁴ when the doors to the street are closed
and the sound of grinding fades;

Enjoy the Day

ECCLESIASTES 11:9

Ponder the seemingly paradoxical message of this passage: Be happy, but plan on facing judgment. Does this resonate with any situations you face today?

Try this exercise: Read the text slowly—reading it twice is preferable. Listen for a word or phrase that stands out—but don't rush to claim the first thing that comes to mind. Use that word or phrase to pray back to God the truth God has given you. Be quiet before God, being attentive to anything God may say to you about plans for the future.

See Meeting God in Everyday Life

---

^a 5 Or *know how life* (or *the spirit*) *enters the body being formed*

The Days of Your Youth

ECCLESIASTES 12:1–7

The Teacher writes a moving poem describing an old age of growing infirmity and perhaps bitterness. He probably uses "youth" to mean the days of good health. Honor God when things are well with you, he says, because should poor health and discouragement come, God may seem far away and uncaring. Cultivate your relationship with God now so that you may rely on it in times of trial.

Suppose the day comes when the power of your memory is fading. Yet placed in a prominent place where you live is a card or a nice sheet of paper (perhaps framed). On that card you wrote years before (today), you will read ten things you wanted most to remember throughout your life. What will you read on that card?

when men rise up at the sound of birds,
  but all their songs grow faint;
⁵ when men are afraid of heights
  and of dangers in the streets;
when the almond tree blossoms
  and the grasshopper drags himself along
  and desire no longer is stirred.
Then man goes to his eternal home
  and mourners go about the streets.

⁶ Remember him—before the silver cord is severed,
  or the golden bowl is broken;
before the pitcher is shattered at the spring,
  or the wheel broken at the well,
⁷ and the dust returns to the ground it came from,
  and the spirit returns to God who gave it.

⁸ "Meaningless! Meaningless!" says the Teacher.ᵃ
  "Everything is meaningless!"

The Conclusion of the Matter

⁹Not only was the Teacher wise, but also he imparted knowledge to the people. He pondered and searched out and set in order many proverbs. ¹⁰The Teacher searched to find just the right words, and what he wrote was upright and true.

¹¹The words of the wise are like goads, their collected sayings like firmly embedded nails—given by one Shepherd. ¹²Be warned, my son, of anything in addition to them.

Of making many books there is no end, and much study wearies the body.

¹³ Now all has been heard;
  here is the conclusion of the matter:
Fear God and keep his commandments,
  for this is the whole ⌊duty⌋ of man.
¹⁴ For God will bring every deed into judgment,
  including every hidden thing,
  whether it is good or evil.

ᵃ 8 Or *the leader of the assembly*; also in verses 9 and 10

SONG OF SONGS
The Lover and the Beloved

KEY VERSE:

Let him kiss me with the kisses of his mouth.—Song of Songs 1:2

Song of Songs, thought to be written by Solomon, is an exquisite piece of Hebrew poetry that communicates two themes interwoven in a love song. On one level, it is an evocative depiction of the love between a woman and a man. On another level, it is a parable portraying the love between God and God's people. There are a number of references in the Old Testament in which human love is used to describe our relationship with God, and Song of Songs is part of that poetic tradition.

The Song of Songs is frankly sensual. But it is also meant to be a hymn describing the rapture and mystery of the covenant relationship between God and his people. The language points to the love that is the root of all our loves—the love that is the source of our beings. This breathtaking poem is about longing—God's longing for us and our longing for God in return—a longing signified by a kiss.

As you read Song of Songs, sense—in the ardent desire of these lovers for each other—God's longing for you and your longing for God. Can you fully take in how passionately God loves you? Do you long for God as deeply as God longs for you? As you read and meditate on Song of Songs, begin to understand God's ardent desire for a relationship with you. Let it make all the difference in the way you worship and pray.

"Love then the Lord thy God with the entire and full affection of the heart; love him with all the vigilance and foresight of the reason, love him with the full strength and vigor of the soul, so that for his love you would not fear even to die; as it is written in a . . . verse of this Canticle: Love is strong as death . . ."

—BERNARD OF CLAIRVAUX,
Sermon XX on The Song of Songs

A Lover's Kiss

SONG OF SONGS 1:2

There is within each of us a restless yearning, a longing for more, a desire to be met, to be embraced, to be surrendered to Love's keeping. We may have known God as Creator, as guide, even as friend. But there is in each heart also an insistent, underlying longing to know and be known even more intimately. What aspects of yourself do you tend to withhold from God? Can you make a list of your thoughts, hopes, yearnings, ideas or activities that seem to exist apart from God's knowledge or attention? For each one, try to think of some small steps that you might take, literally or symbolically, to offer God access to them.

See *Meeting God in Prayer*

1 Solomon's Song of Songs.

Beloved[a]

² Let him kiss me with the kisses of his mouth—
  for your love is more delightful than wine.
³ Pleasing is the fragrance of your perfumes;
  your name is like perfume poured out.
  No wonder the maidens love you!
⁴ Take me away with you—let us hurry!
  Let the king bring me into his chambers.

Friends

We rejoice and delight in you[b];
  we will praise your love more than wine.

Beloved

How right they are to adore you!

⁵ Dark am I, yet lovely,
  O daughters of Jerusalem,
  dark like the tents of Kedar,
  like the tent curtains of Solomon.[c]
⁶ Do not stare at me because I am dark,
  because I am darkened by the sun.
My mother's sons were angry with me
  and made me take care of the vineyards;
  my own vineyard I have neglected.
⁷ Tell me, you whom I love, where you graze your
    flock
  and where you rest your sheep at midday.
Why should I be like a veiled woman
  beside the flocks of your friends?

Friends

⁸ If you do not know, most beautiful of women,
    follow the tracks of the sheep
  and graze your young goats
    by the tents of the shepherds.

Lover

⁹ I liken you, my darling, to a mare
  harnessed to one of the chariots of Pharaoh.
¹⁰ Your cheeks are beautiful with earrings,
  your neck with strings of jewels.
¹¹ We will make you earrings of gold,
  studded with silver.

Beloved

¹² While the king was at his table,
  my perfume spread its fragrance.
¹³ My lover is to me a sachet of myrrh
  resting between my breasts.
¹⁴ My lover is to me a cluster of henna blossoms
  from the vineyards of En Gedi.

a Primarily on the basis of the gender of the Hebrew pronouns used, male and female speakers are indicated in the margins by the captions *Lover* and *Beloved* respectively. The words of others are marked *Friends*. In some instances the divisions and their captions are debatable.   *b 4* The Hebrew is masculine singular.   *c 5* Or *Salma*

Lover

15 How beautiful you are, my darling!
   Oh, how beautiful!
   Your eyes are doves.

Beloved

16 How handsome you are, my lover!
   Oh, how charming!
   And our bed is verdant.

Lover

17 The beams of our house are cedars;
   our rafters are firs.

Beloved[a]

2 I am a rose[b] of Sharon,
   a lily of the valleys.

Lover

2 Like a lily among thorns
   is my darling among the maidens.

Beloved

3 Like an apple tree among the trees of the forest
   is my lover among the young men.
   I delight to sit in his shade,
   and his fruit is sweet to my taste.
4 He has taken me to the banquet hall,
   and his banner over me is love.
5 Strengthen me with raisins,
   refresh me with apples,
   for I am faint with love.
6 His left arm is under my head,
   and his right arm embraces me.
7 Daughters of Jerusalem, I charge you
   by the gazelles and by the does of the field:
   Do not arouse or awaken love
   until it so desires.

8 Listen! My lover!
   Look! Here he comes,
   leaping across the mountains,
   bounding over the hills.
9 My lover is like a gazelle or a young stag.
   Look! There he stands behind our wall,
   gazing through the windows,
   peering through the lattice.
10 My lover spoke and said to me,
   "Arise, my darling,
   my beautiful one, and come with me.
11 See! The winter is past;
   the rains are over and gone.
12 Flowers appear on the earth;
   the season of singing has come,
   the cooing of doves
   is heard in our land.
13 The fig tree forms its early fruit;
   the blossoming vines spread their
   fragrance.

The Soul's Springtime

SONG OF SONGS 2:10–13

Can you recall your delight at the first sign of spring, when the early crocuses first push their way through the last icy crust of snow? Similarly, God's love has a way of breaking through our times of trial and exile and waking us from lethargy and despair.

Do you sense something within yourself that is dormant or frozen? Is there a broken relationship, a sin that you cannot seem to put behind you, or an indifference to God's love for you? Whatever it is, in prayer ask that you will be open to God breaking through with the sweet, fresh growth of his presence in you.

See Meeting God in Prayer

---

a 1 Or Lover   b 1 Possibly a member of the crocus family

Lovers Seek One Another

SONG OF SONGS 3:1–5

Sometimes we feel as if we are chasing God when we approach him in prayer, so desperate are we to be near him and to express ourselves to him, much like the beloved searches everywhere for her lover in order to hold him. The next time you pray, be aware of the postures you assume and what they might mean. If you kneel and rest your head on your hands or bow your head or bend over and fold your hands—these may be signs of reverence or sometimes self-protection. Try new positions as you pray. One time-honored way is the *orans* position, standing with arms outstretched and face lifted. Another possibility is to sit with an open posture, arms extended and palms upward in a more vulnerable posture. Another is to stand as if you are just about to meet someone you love deeply. Experiment with other postures that express the way you feel.

See Meeting God in Worship

Arise, come, my darling;
 my beautiful one, come with me."

Lover
¹⁴ My dove in the clefts of the rock,
 in the hiding places on the mountainside,
show me your face,
 let me hear your voice;
for your voice is sweet,
 and your face is lovely.
¹⁵ Catch for us the foxes,
 the little foxes
that ruin the vineyards,
 our vineyards that are in bloom.

Beloved
¹⁶ My lover is mine and I am his;
 he browses among the lilies.
¹⁷ Until the day breaks
 and the shadows flee,
turn, my lover,
 and be like a gazelle
or like a young stag
 on the rugged hills.ᵃ

3 All night long on my bed
 I looked for the one my heart loves;
 I looked for him but did not find him.
² I will get up now and go about the city,
 through its streets and squares;
I will search for the one my heart loves.
 So I looked for him but did not find him.
³ The watchmen found me
 as they made their rounds in the city.
 "Have you seen the one my heart loves?"
⁴ Scarcely had I passed them
 when I found the one my heart loves.
I held him and would not let him go
 till I had brought him to my mother's house,
 to the room of the one who conceived me.
⁵ Daughters of Jerusalem, I charge you
 by the gazelles and by the does of the field:
Do not arouse or awaken love
 until it so desires.

⁶ Who is this coming up from the desert
 like a column of smoke,
perfumed with myrrh and incense
 made from all the spices of the merchant?
⁷ Look! It is Solomon's carriage,
 escorted by sixty warriors,
 the noblest of Israel,
⁸ all of them wearing the sword,
 all experienced in battle,
each with his sword at his side,
 prepared for the terrors of the night.
⁹ King Solomon made for himself the carriage;
 he made it of wood from Lebanon.
¹⁰ Its posts he made of silver,
 its base of gold.

ᵃ 17 Or *the hills of Bether*

Its seat was upholstered with purple,
　　its interior lovingly inlaid
　　by[a] the daughters of Jerusalem.
¹¹ Come out, you daughters of Zion,
　　and look at King Solomon wearing the crown,
　　the crown with which his mother crowned him
on the day of his wedding,
　　the day his heart rejoiced.

Lover

4

How beautiful you are, my darling!
　　Oh, how beautiful!
　　Your eyes behind your veil are doves.
Your hair is like a flock of goats
　　descending from Mount Gilead.
² Your teeth are like a flock of sheep just shorn,
　　coming up from the washing.
Each has its twin;
　　not one of them is alone.
³ Your lips are like a scarlet ribbon;
　　your mouth is lovely.
Your temples behind your veil
　　are like the halves of a pomegranate.
⁴ Your neck is like the tower of David,
　　built with elegance[b];
on it hang a thousand shields,
　　all of them shields of warriors.
⁵ Your two breasts are like two fawns,
　　like twin fawns of a gazelle
　　that browse among the lilies.
⁶ Until the day breaks
　　and the shadows flee,
I will go to the mountain of myrrh
　　and to the hill of incense.
⁷ All beautiful you are, my darling;
　　there is no flaw in you.
⁸ Come with me from Lebanon, my bride,
　　come with me from Lebanon.
Descend from the crest of Amana,
　　from the top of Senir, the summit of Hermon,
from the lions' dens
　　and the mountain haunts of the leopards.
⁹ You have stolen my heart, my sister, my bride;
　　you have stolen my heart
with one glance of your eyes,
　　with one jewel of your necklace.
¹⁰ How delightful is your love, my sister, my bride!
　　How much more pleasing is your love than wine,
　　and the fragrance of your perfume than any
　　　　spice!
¹¹ Your lips drop sweetness as the honeycomb, my
　　　　bride;
　　milk and honey are under your tongue.
The fragrance of your garments is like that of
　　　　Lebanon.
¹² You are a garden locked up, my sister, my bride;
　　you are a spring enclosed, a sealed fountain.

Seen Through God's Eyes

SONG OF SONGS 4:10

"Can it be? Am I really beautiful?" you ask. Indeed, God greatly delights in you. You probably are well aware of the ways your spirit tends to become disfigured by the pressures of the world—made smaller, greedier, more defensive, haughty, judgmental, bitter or frightened. But can you see yourself through God's eyes, created in God's image and likeness? Ask the One who made you to open your eyes to the beauty of your life. How might God describe your best characteristics? Can you imagine the words God might use to sing your praises to someone else?

See Meeting God in the Created Order

---

a 10 Or *its inlaid interior a gift of love / from*　*b 4* The meaning of the Hebrew for this word is uncertain.

891

Called by God

SONG OF SONGS 5:2–5

God's call to us is a call that woos us, just like the knock at the door and the quiet call of the beloved. In what ways do you sometimes find it hard to open yourself to God? What emotions do you feel when you make yourself vulnerable to God? Sit quietly and become aware of your body. Do you feel tension or resistance as you think about God? Breathe deeply and relax. Draw, paint, or sculpt an image that portrays trust and openness before God.

See Meeting God in Worship

¹³ Your plants are an orchard of pomegranates
   with choice fruits,
   with henna and nard,
¹⁴   nard and saffron,
   calamus and cinnamon,
   with every kind of incense tree,
   with myrrh and aloes
   and all the finest spices.
¹⁵ You are*a* a garden fountain,
   a well of flowing water
   streaming down from Lebanon.

Beloved

¹⁶ Awake, north wind,
   and come, south wind!
Blow on my garden,
   that its fragrance may spread abroad.
Let my lover come into his garden
   and taste its choice fruits.

Lover

5 I have come into my garden, my sister, my bride;
   I have gathered my myrrh with my spice.
I have eaten my honeycomb and my honey;
   I have drunk my wine and my milk.

Friends

   Eat, O friends, and drink;
   drink your fill, O lovers.

Beloved

² I slept but my heart was awake.
   Listen! My lover is knocking:
"Open to me, my sister, my darling,
   my dove, my flawless one.
My head is drenched with dew,
   my hair with the dampness of the night."
³ I have taken off my robe—
   must I put it on again?
I have washed my feet—
   must I soil them again?
⁴ My lover thrust his hand through the latch-
   opening;
   my heart began to pound for him.
⁵ I arose to open for my lover,
   and my hands dripped with myrrh,
my fingers with flowing myrrh,
   on the handles of the lock.
⁶ I opened for my lover,
   but my lover had left; he was gone.
   My heart sank at his departure.*b*
I looked for him but did not find him.
   I called him but he did not answer.
⁷ The watchmen found me
   as they made their rounds in the city.
They beat me, they bruised me;
   they took away my cloak,
   those watchmen of the walls!

a 15 Or *I am* (spoken by the *Beloved*)   *b 6* Or *heart had gone out to him when he spoke*

⁸ O daughters of Jerusalem, I charge you—
   if you find my lover,
what will you tell him?
   Tell him I am faint with love.

Friends

⁹ How is your beloved better than others,
   most beautiful of women?
How is your beloved better than others,
   that you charge us so?

Beloved

¹⁰ My lover is radiant and ruddy,
   outstanding among ten thousand.
¹¹ His head is purest gold;
   his hair is wavy
   and black as a raven.
¹² His eyes are like doves
   by the water streams,
   washed in milk,
   mounted like jewels.
¹³ His cheeks are like beds of spice
   yielding perfume.
His lips are like lilies
   dripping with myrrh.
¹⁴ His arms are rods of gold
   set with chrysolite.
His body is like polished ivory
   decorated with sapphires.ᵃ
¹⁵ His legs are pillars of marble
   set on bases of pure gold.
His appearance is like Lebanon,
   choice as its cedars.
¹⁶ His mouth is sweetness itself;
   he is altogether lovely.
This is my lover, this my friend,
   O daughters of Jerusalem.

Friends

6 Where has your lover gone,
   most beautiful of women?
Which way did your lover turn,
   that we may look for him with you?

Beloved

² My lover has gone down to his garden,
   to the beds of spices,
to browse in the gardens
   and to gather lilies.
³ I am my lover's and my lover is mine;
   he browses among the lilies.

Lover

⁴ You are beautiful, my darling, as Tirzah,
   lovely as Jerusalem,
   majestic as troops with banners.
⁵ Turn your eyes from me;
   they overwhelm me.
Your hair is like a flock of goats

Belonging

SONG OF SONGS 6:3

The maiden's beloved has gone to his favorite spot, a spot where he feels most accepted, safe, loved and valued. Remember a time of romance in your own life. Perhaps it was a walk on the beach or a stroll through the park, a quiet dinner with lively and intimate conversation. Do you remember how you felt at one of those moments? Relaxed and available? Open to being known deeply by the other? This is the attitude God wishes to foster in us as we pray.

Try to imagine an ideal place to meet God. Picture in your mind's eye the details of the setting. Where are you? Is it cool or warm? Outdoors or inside? What might God say to you that would lead you into a time together in which you are fully trusting and fully vulnerable? What might you and God rejoice in together, celebrate together?

See Meeting God in Prayer

ᵃ *14 Or lapis lazuli*

A Unique Love

SONG OF SONGS 6:9

The lover gives the beloved a wonderful compliment: She is unique, one-of-a-kind, and therefore, her perfect self. There is no other standard.

God loves us uniquely because he created us that way—unique and incomparable. We don't have to compete for his love or push anyone aside to find intimacy with him. The psalmist seemed to sense this: "For you created my inmost being . . . I praise you because I am fearfully and wonderfully made . . . All the days ordained for me were written in your book" (Psalm 139:13,14,16). Use these three lines from Psalm 139 as an outline for your prayer today. Pray each of these lines in turn, sharing your thoughts and feelings with the One who created you—uniquely.

descending from Gilead.
⁶ Your teeth are like a flock of sheep
    coming up from the washing.
Each has its twin,
    not one of them is alone.
⁷ Your temples behind your veil
    are like the halves of a pomegranate.
⁸ Sixty queens there may be,
    and eighty concubines,
    and virgins beyond number;
⁹ but my dove, my perfect one, is unique,
    the only daughter of her mother,
    the favorite of the one who bore her.
The maidens saw her and called her blessed;
    the queens and concubines praised her.

Friends

¹⁰ Who is this that appears like the dawn,
    fair as the moon, bright as the sun,
    majestic as the stars in procession?

Lover

¹¹ I went down to the grove of nut trees
    to look at the new growth in the valley,
to see if the vines had budded
    or the pomegranates were in bloom.
¹² Before I realized it,
    my desire set me among the royal chariots of
        my people.ᵃ

Friends

¹³ Come back, come back, O Shulammite;
    come back, come back, that we may gaze on
        you!

Lover

Why would you gaze on the Shulammite
    as on the dance of Mahanaim?

7 How beautiful your sandaled feet,
    O prince's daughter!
Your graceful legs are like jewels,
    the work of a craftsman's hands.
² Your navel is a rounded goblet
    that never lacks blended wine.
Your waist is a mound of wheat
    encircled by lilies.
³ Your breasts are like two fawns,
    twins of a gazelle.
⁴ Your neck is like an ivory tower.
Your eyes are the pools of Heshbon
    by the gate of Bath Rabbim.
Your nose is like the tower of Lebanon
    looking toward Damascus.
⁵ Your head crowns you like Mount Carmel.
    Your hair is like royal tapestry;
    the king is held captive by its tresses.
⁶ How beautiful you are and how pleasing,

ᵃ 12 Or *among the chariots of Amminadab;* or *among the chariots of the people of the prince*

O love, with your delights!
[7] Your stature is like that of the palm,
and your breasts like clusters of fruit.
[8] I said, "I will climb the palm tree;
I will take hold of its fruit."
May your breasts be like the clusters of the vine,
the fragrance of your breath like apples,
[9] and your mouth like the best wine.

Beloved

May the wine go straight to my lover,
flowing gently over lips and teeth.[a]
[10] I belong to my lover,
and his desire is for me.
[11] Come, my lover, let us go to the countryside,
let us spend the night in the villages.[b]
[12] Let us go early to the vineyards
to see if the vines have budded,
if their blossoms have opened,
and if the pomegranates are in bloom—
there I will give you my love.
[13] The mandrakes send out their fragrance,
and at our door is every delicacy,
both new and old,
that I have stored up for you, my lover.

8 If only you were to me like a brother,
who was nursed at my mother's breasts!
Then, if I found you outside,
I would kiss you,
and no one would despise me.
[2] I would lead you
and bring you to my mother's house—
she who has taught me.
I would give you spiced wine to drink,
the nectar of my pomegranates.
[3] His left arm is under my head
and his right arm embraces me.
[4] Daughters of Jerusalem, I charge you:
Do not arouse or awaken love
until it so desires.

Friends

[5] Who is this coming up from the desert
leaning on her lover?

Beloved

Under the apple tree I roused you;
there your mother conceived you,
there she who was in labor gave you birth.
[6] Place me like a seal over your heart,
like a seal on your arm;
for love is as strong as death,
its jealousy[c] unyielding as the grave.[d]
It burns like blazing fire,
like a mighty flame.[e]
[7] Many waters cannot quench love;
rivers cannot wash it away.

Awakening

SONG OF SONGS 8:5–6

"Passage from shadow to light, from the obscure light of the faith to the illumination of the spirit and heart's eyes. Astonished awakening of the Bride, whose eyes open in wonder on the dawn of the new creation . . . this is the very word of the Resurrection; the song of the new Easter that Paul will teach to the Ephesians: 'Wake up, O sleeper, rise from the dead, and Christ will shine on you' [Ephesians 5:14]."

—BLAISE ARMINJON,
The Cantata of Love

---

a 9 Septuagint, Aquila, Vulgate and Syriac; Hebrew *lips of sleepers* *b 11* Or
henna bushes *c 6* Or *ardor* *d 6* Hebrew *Sheol* *e 6* Or / *like the very
flame of the* LORD

Drawn by Love

SONG OF SONGS 8:14

People who truly share a deep love are often impatient during times of separation. Sometimes they can hardly wait to be together, and they, in effect, call out to one another to "Hurry!" Thus the Shulammite cries to her beloved to be as swift as a gazelle.

If God asked you, "Will you follow me anywhere?"—how would you respond? Would you answer immediately and gladly with a resounding yes? Or would you have to think about it awhile, turning the question over in your mind before you reply? How would God view your response? What does your response say about the level of intimacy and trust between you and God?

See Meeting God in Prayer

If one were to give
all the wealth of his house for love,
it[a] would be utterly scorned.

Friends

⁸ We have a young sister,
and her breasts are not yet grown.
What shall we do for our sister
for the day she is spoken for?
⁹ If she is a wall,
we will build towers of silver on her.
If she is a door,
we will enclose her with panels of cedar.

Beloved

¹⁰ I am a wall,
and my breasts are like towers.
Thus I have become in his eyes
like one bringing contentment.
¹¹ Solomon had a vineyard in Baal Hamon;
he let out his vineyard to tenants.
Each was to bring for its fruit
a thousand shekels[b] of silver.
¹² But my own vineyard is mine to give;
the thousand shekels are for you, O Solomon,
and two hundred[c] are for those who tend its
fruit.

Lover

¹³ You who dwell in the gardens
with friends in attendance,
let me hear your voice!

Beloved

¹⁴ Come away, my lover,
and be like a gazelle
or like a young stag
on the spice-laden mountains.

a 7 Or *he*   *b 11* That is, about 25 pounds (about 11.5 kilograms); also in
verse 12   *c 12* That is, about 5 pounds (about 2.3 kilograms)

ISAIAH
Faithful Response to God's Glory

KEY VERSE:

"Holy, holy, holy is the LORD Almighty; the whole earth is full of his glory."—Isaiah 6:3

The prophet Isaiah has a message for God's people who are "defying his glorious presence" (3:8). Isaiah is called (6:9–10) to confront the people with the dire consequences of their rebellion against their God who nonetheless remains faithful to them.

Chapters 1—39 are dominated by dark and vivid pictures of the devastation that human beings invite by defying the Lord's presence and purposes. When they stubbornly refuse to respect the fabric of creation, they experience the power of God in creation as a terror. When they do not live in the holiness that God calls them to, they ultimately experience God's holiness as wrath and judgment. The people are challenged to purify themselves and give up their persistent reliance on ritual magic and political maneuvering.

Such purifying change opens God's people to the Spirit's illumination of new insight into God's loving design for Israel. Chapters 40—66 overflow with promises of divine comfort and restoration. In the new era, the Israelites are called to be a servant people who will cooperate with God's purposes for the whole of humanity—purposes greater than any they could imagine.

You can glimpse, through Isaiah's poetry, some of the very specific social situations and highly personal emotions that God's people experience. The book abounds in pathos, terror, sorrow, compassion and exultation. As you read, be alert to parallels in your own life. Pay attention to how God may be working in you—judging, purifying and filling you with a wider vision of the "glorious presence." Consider how God is calling you to cooperate with his redeeming love in the world today.

> "The world is charged with the grandeur of God.
> It will flame out, like shining from shook foil . . .
> Oh, morning at the brown brink eastward springs—
> Because the Holy Ghost over the bent
> World broods with warm breast and with ah! bright wings."
> —GERARD MANLEY HOPKINS, "God's Grandeur"

Knowing God

ISAIAH 1:2–4

The people of Israel have "turned their backs on" the Holy One who dwells in their midst. They've resisted the teaching and holy practices that could have enabled them to recognize and respond to God in the intimate way in which children know their parents and domestic animals know their masters. What are the primary ways in which God becomes known to human beings? Through what experiences have you seen God's glory displayed in the world and in your own life? What are the habits that estrange you from God's divine presence in the world? Write a simple prayer of thanks to God for the ways the Lord shows himself in your life, even as you acknowledge the ways in which you have been blind to them.

See Meeting God in the Created Order

1 The vision concerning Judah and Jerusalem that Isaiah son of Amoz saw during the reigns of Uzziah, Jotham, Ahaz and Hezekiah, kings of Judah.

A Rebellious Nation

² Hear, O heavens! Listen, O earth!
    For the Lord has spoken:
"I reared children and brought them up,
    but they have rebelled against me.
³ The ox knows his master,
    the donkey his owner's manger,
but Israel does not know,
    my people do not understand."

⁴ Ah, sinful nation,
    a people loaded with guilt,
a brood of evildoers,
    children given to corruption!
They have forsaken the Lord;
    they have spurned the Holy One of Israel
    and turned their backs on him.

⁵ Why should you be beaten anymore?
    Why do you persist in rebellion?
Your whole head is injured,
    your whole heart afflicted.
⁶ From the sole of your foot to the top of your head
    there is no soundness—
only wounds and welts
    and open sores,
not cleansed or bandaged
    or soothed with oil.

⁷ Your country is desolate,
    your cities burned with fire;
your fields are being stripped by foreigners
    right before you,
    laid waste as when overthrown by strangers.
⁸ The Daughter of Zion is left
    like a shelter in a vineyard,
like a hut in a field of melons,
    like a city under siege.
⁹ Unless the Lord Almighty
    had left us some survivors,
we would have become like Sodom,
    we would have been like Gomorrah.

¹⁰ Hear the word of the Lord,
    you rulers of Sodom;
listen to the law of our God,
    you people of Gomorrah!
¹¹ "The multitude of your sacrifices—
    what are they to me?" says the Lord.
"I have more than enough of burnt offerings,
    of rams and the fat of fattened animals;
I have no pleasure
    in the blood of bulls and lambs and goats.
¹² When you come to appear before me,
    who has asked this of you,
    this trampling of my courts?
¹³ Stop bringing meaningless offerings!
    Your incense is detestable to me.

New Moons, Sabbaths and convocations—
   I cannot bear your evil assemblies.
¹⁴ Your New Moon festivals and your appointed
      feasts
   my soul hates.
They have become a burden to me;
   I am weary of bearing them.
¹⁵ When you spread out your hands in prayer,
   I will hide my eyes from you;
even if you offer many prayers,
   I will not listen.
Your hands are full of blood;
¹⁶   wash and make yourselves clean.
Take your evil deeds
      out of my sight!
Stop doing wrong,
¹⁷   learn to do right!
Seek justice,
   encourage the oppressed.ᵃ
Defend the cause of the fatherless,
   plead the case of the widow.

¹⁸ "Come now, let us reason together,"
   says the LORD.
"Though your sins are like scarlet,
   they shall be as white as snow;
though they are red as crimson,
   they shall be like wool.
¹⁹ If you are willing and obedient,
   you will eat the best from the land;
²⁰ but if you resist and rebel,
   you will be devoured by the sword."
            For the mouth of the LORD has spoken.

²¹ See how the faithful city
   has become a harlot!
She once was full of justice;
   righteousness used to dwell in her—
   but now murderers!
²² Your silver has become dross,
   your choice wine is diluted with water.
²³ Your rulers are rebels,
   companions of thieves;
they all love bribes
   and chase after gifts.
They do not defend the cause of the fatherless;
   the widow's case does not come before them.
²⁴ Therefore the Lord, the LORD Almighty,
   the Mighty One of Israel, declares:
"Ah, I will get relief from my foes
   and avenge myself on my enemies.
²⁵ I will turn my hand against you;
   I will thoroughly purge away your dross
   and remove all your impurities.
²⁶ I will restore your judges as in days of old,
   your counselors as at the beginning.
Afterward you will be called
   the City of Righteousness,
   the Faithful City."

God: Against Us?

ISAIAH 1:25

"If God is for us" (Romans 8:31), in what sense does God say, "I will turn my hand against you"? How does God respond when humans, including yourself, go against his desires for the well-being of his creatures? Have you ever experienced God being "against" you in some way? Are you being called to take the same stance—that is, *against* yourself in order to be *for* yourself—in some area of your life? Or against another's behavior for the sake of that person's well-being? What are you called to pray for in these situations?

See Meeting God in Everyday Life

ᵃ 17 Or / rebuke the oppressor

A Vision of God's Kingdom

ISAIAH 2:1–4

Using the classic "spiritual reading" approach, read slowly, one or more times, Isaiah's vision of the last days. Let your heart and mind be open to words, phrases and images that seem especially vital. You might practice repeating a few of them until your heart settles on just one. Turn it over in your mind, inviting it to become part of you so that you share this vision of God's kingdom fulfilled. Let a prayer arise in response to this small jewel from the Word. End your prayer with a time of silence.

See Meeting God in Scripture

27 Zion will be redeemed with justice,
    her penitent ones with righteousness.
28 But rebels and sinners will both be broken,
    and those who forsake the LORD will perish.

29 "You will be ashamed because of the sacred oaks
    in which you have delighted;
  you will be disgraced because of the gardens
    that you have chosen.
30 You will be like an oak with fading leaves,
    like a garden without water.
31 The mighty man will become tinder
    and his work a spark;
  both will burn together,
    with no one to quench the fire."

The Mountain of the LORD

2 This is what Isaiah son of Amoz saw concerning Judah and Jerusalem:

2 In the last days

  the mountain of the LORD's temple will be
      established
    as chief among the mountains;
  it will be raised above the hills,
    and all nations will stream to it.

3 Many peoples will come and say,

  "Come, let us go up to the mountain of the LORD,
    to the house of the God of Jacob.
  He will teach us his ways,
    so that we may walk in his paths."
  The law will go out from Zion,
    the word of the LORD from Jerusalem.
4 He will judge between the nations
    and will settle disputes for many peoples.
  They will beat their swords into plowshares
    and their spears into pruning hooks.
  Nation will not take up sword against nation,
    nor will they train for war anymore.

5 Come, O house of Jacob,
    let us walk in the light of the LORD.

The Day of the LORD

6 You have abandoned your people,
    the house of Jacob.
  They are full of superstitions from the East;
    they practice divination like the Philistines
    and clasp hands with pagans.
7 Their land is full of silver and gold;
    there is no end to their treasures.
  Their land is full of horses;
    there is no end to their chariots.
8 Their land is full of idols;
    they bow down to the work of their hands,
    to what their fingers have made.
9 So man will be brought low
    and mankind humbled—

a 9 Or not raise them up

do not forgive them.[a]

¹⁰ Go into the rocks,
  hide in the ground
from dread of the LORD
  and the splendor of his majesty!
¹¹ The eyes of the arrogant man will be humbled
  and the pride of men brought low;
the LORD alone will be exalted in that day.

¹² The LORD Almighty has a day in store
  for all the proud and lofty,
  for all that is exalted
  (and they will be humbled),
¹³ for all the cedars of Lebanon, tall and lofty,
  and all the oaks of Bashan,
¹⁴ for all the towering mountains
  and all the high hills,
¹⁵ for every lofty tower
  and every fortified wall,
¹⁶ for every trading ship[a]
  and every stately vessel.
¹⁷ The arrogance of man will be brought low
  and the pride of men humbled;
the LORD alone will be exalted in that day,
¹⁸   and the idols will totally disappear.

¹⁹ Men will flee to caves in the rocks
  and to holes in the ground
from dread of the LORD
  and the splendor of his majesty,
  when he rises to shake the earth.
²⁰ In that day men will throw away
  to the rodents and bats
their idols of silver and idols of gold,
  which they made to worship.
²¹ They will flee to caverns in the rocks
  and to the overhanging crags
from dread of the LORD
  and the splendor of his majesty,
  when he rises to shake the earth.

²² Stop trusting in man,
  who has but a breath in his nostrils.
Of what account is he?

Judgment on Jerusalem and Judah

3 See now, the Lord,
    the LORD Almighty,
  is about to take from Jerusalem and Judah
    both supply and support:
  all supplies of food and all supplies of water,
²   the hero and warrior,
  the judge and prophet,
    the soothsayer and elder,
³ the captain of fifty and man of rank,
    the counselor, skilled craftsman and clever
      enchanter.

⁴ I will make boys their officials;
  mere children will govern them.
⁵ People will oppress each other—

Real Humility

ISAIAH 2:11–17

A common theme throughout Scripture is that God humbles the proud. The pride Isaiah admonishes God's people for is crucially different from genuine self-esteem, which is based on a realistic acceptance of God's gifts to us and our ability to use them. Lofty haughtiness is an exaggerated confidence in our ability to control our destiny, even if that pride conceals an underlying poor self-esteem. Make a list of some of your gifts and abilities and also a list of exaggerated opinions about yourself. Offer these lists in prayer, giving thanks for those gifts and asking for God's merciful help in letting go of the exaggerations. Prayerfully ponder how best to base your self-esteem on God's gracious gift—your real abilities.

See *Meeting God in Prayer*

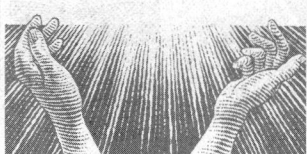

God Confronts the Leaders

ISAIAH 3:14–15

How would the God of nations make a "judgment against the elders and leaders of his people" today? Imagine Isaiah speaking to one or more leadership groups: the United Nations, the leaders of your nation, town or city government, your denomination or congregation (even yourself in any position of responsibility). What kinds of behavior would warrant the prophet's call for repentance? What attitudes would the prophet call under scrutiny? What vision of God's purposes would the prophet share with them? Pray for the Spirit to challenge, illuminate and empower those people: "May your will be done through _____."

See Meeting God in Service

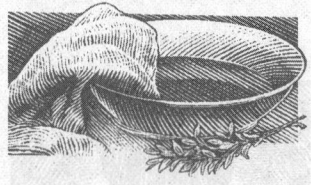

man against man, neighbor against neighbor.
The young will rise up against the old,
    the base against the honorable.

⁶A man will seize one of his brothers
    at his father's home, and say,
"You have a cloak, you be our leader;
    take charge of this heap of ruins!"
⁷But in that day he will cry out,
    "I have no remedy.
I have no food or clothing in my house;
    do not make me the leader of the people."

⁸Jerusalem staggers,
    Judah is falling;
their words and deeds are against the LORD,
    defying his glorious presence.
⁹The look on their faces testifies against them;
    they parade their sin like Sodom;
    they do not hide it.
Woe to them!
    They have brought disaster upon themselves.

¹⁰Tell the righteous it will be well with them,
    for they will enjoy the fruit of their deeds.
¹¹Woe to the wicked! Disaster is upon them!
They will be paid back for what their hands have
    done.

¹²Youths oppress my people,
    women rule over them.
O my people, your guides lead you astray;
    they turn you from the path.

¹³The LORD takes his place in court;
    he rises to judge the people.
¹⁴The LORD enters into judgment
    against the elders and leaders of his people:
"It is you who have ruined my vineyard;
    the plunder from the poor is in your houses.
¹⁵What do you mean by crushing my people
    and grinding the faces of the poor?"
          declares the Lord, the LORD Almighty.

¹⁶The LORD says,
    "The women of Zion are haughty,
walking along with outstretched necks,
    flirting with their eyes,
tripping along with mincing steps,
    with ornaments jingling on their ankles.
¹⁷Therefore the Lord will bring sores on the heads
    of the women of Zion;
    the LORD will make their scalps bald."

¹⁸In that day the Lord will snatch away their finery: the bangles and headbands and crescent necklaces, ¹⁹the earrings and bracelets and veils, ²⁰the headdresses and ankle chains and sashes, the perfume bottles and charms, ²¹the signet rings and nose rings, ²²the fine robes and the capes and cloaks, the purses ²³and mirrors, and the linen garments and tiaras and shawls.

²⁴Instead of fragrance there will be a stench;
    instead of a sash, a rope;

instead of well-dressed hair, baldness;
  instead of fine clothing, sackcloth;
  instead of beauty, branding.
²⁵ Your men will fall by the sword,
  your warriors in battle.
²⁶ The gates of Zion will lament and mourn;
  destitute, she will sit on the ground.

4 In that day seven women
  will take hold of one man
and say, "We will eat our own food
  and provide our own clothes;
only let us be called by your name.
  Take away our disgrace!"

The Branch of the LORD

²In that day the Branch of the LORD will be beautiful and glorious, and the fruit of the land will be the pride and glory of the survivors in Israel. ³Those who are left in Zion, who remain in Jerusalem, will be called holy, all who are recorded among the living in Jerusalem. ⁴The Lord will wash away the filth of the women of Zion; he will cleanse the bloodstains from Jerusalem by a spirit*ᵃ* of judgment and a spirit*ᵃ* of fire. ⁵Then the LORD will create over all of Mount Zion and over those who assemble there a cloud of smoke by day and a glow of flaming fire by night; over all the glory will be a canopy. ⁶It will be a shelter and shade from the heat of the day, and a refuge and hiding place from the storm and rain.

The Song of the Vineyard

5 I will sing for the one I love
  a song about his vineyard:
My loved one had a vineyard
  on a fertile hillside.
² He dug it up and cleared it of stones
  and planted it with the choicest vines.
He built a watchtower in it
  and cut out a winepress as well.
Then he looked for a crop of good grapes,
  but it yielded only bad fruit.

³ "Now you dwellers in Jerusalem and men of
    Judah,
  judge between me and my vineyard.
⁴ What more could have been done for my
    vineyard
  than I have done for it?
When I looked for good grapes,
  why did it yield only bad?
⁵ Now I will tell you
  what I am going to do to my vineyard:
I will take away its hedge,
  and it will be destroyed;
I will break down its wall,
  and it will be trampled.
⁶ I will make it a wasteland,
  neither pruned nor cultivated,
  and briers and thorns will grow there.
I will command the clouds

The Beloved's Vineyard

ISAIAH 5:1–2

The garden is a recurring image of human life under God's providence. How has God cleared away the stones, prepared the soil and planted good things in your life as if it were a vineyard? Draw or color a picture of your vineyard, identifying all the good things—the choice vines—that are flourishing in your life by the grace of God. Give thanks for each in turn and savor the goodness of each. Now sketch in the "bad fruit" of resistance to God's gifts and calls. As you identify each in turn, ask God to show you the nature of your resistance. Pray for the Spirit to help you let go of that resistance.

See Meeting God in Everyday Life

ᵃ 4 Or the Spirit

God as Adversary

ISAIAH 5:7–19

"The Word of God is thine adversary . . . It is the adversary of thy will till it becomes the author of thy salvation . . . It is our adversary as long as we are our own adversaries. O how goodly, how useful an 'adversary.' It does not seek our will, but our advantage. As long as thou art thine own enemy, thou hast the Word of God thine enemy; be thine own friend, and thou art in agreement with it."

—AUGUSTINE,
Sermon LIX:3

not to rain on it."
⁷The vineyard of the LORD Almighty
is the house of Israel,
and the men of Judah
are the garden of his delight.
And he looked for justice, but saw bloodshed;
for righteousness, but heard cries of distress.

Woes and Judgments

⁸Woe to you who add house to house
and join field to field
till no space is left
and you live alone in the land.

⁹The LORD Almighty has declared in my hearing:

"Surely the great houses will become desolate,
the fine mansions left without occupants.
¹⁰A ten-acre*ᵃ* vineyard will produce only a bath*ᵇ* of wine,
a homer*ᶜ* of seed only an ephah*ᵈ* of grain."

¹¹Woe to those who rise early in the morning
to run after their drinks,
who stay up late at night
till they are inflamed with wine.
¹²They have harps and lyres at their banquets,
tambourines and flutes and wine,
but they have no regard for the deeds of the LORD,
no respect for the work of his hands.
¹³Therefore my people will go into exile
for lack of understanding;
their men of rank will die of hunger
and their masses will be parched with thirst.
¹⁴Therefore the grave*ᵉ* enlarges its appetite
and opens its mouth without limit;
into it will descend their nobles and masses
with all their brawlers and revelers.
¹⁵So man will be brought low
and mankind humbled,
the eyes of the arrogant humbled.
¹⁶But the LORD Almighty will be exalted by his justice,
and the holy God will show himself holy by his righteousness.
¹⁷Then sheep will graze as in their own pasture;
lambs will feed*ᶠ* among the ruins of the rich.

¹⁸Woe to those who draw sin along with cords of deceit,
and wickedness as with cart ropes,
¹⁹to those who say, "Let God hurry,
let him hasten his work
so we may see it.
Let it approach,
let the plan of the Holy One of Israel come,
so we may know it."

ᵃ 10 Hebrew *ten-yoke,* that is, the land plowed by 10 yoke of oxen in one day
ᵇ 10 That is, probably about 6 gallons (about 22 liters)   *ᶜ 10* That is, probably about 6 bushels (about 220 liters)   *ᵈ 10* That is, probably about 3/5 bushel (about 22 liters)   *ᵉ 14* Hebrew *Sheol*   *ᶠ 17* Septuagint; Hebrew *strangers will eat*

²⁰ Woe to those who call evil good
    and good evil,
who put darkness for light
    and light for darkness,
who put bitter for sweet
    and sweet for bitter.

²¹ Woe to those who are wise in their own eyes
    and clever in their own sight.

²² Woe to those who are heroes at drinking wine
    and champions at mixing drinks,
²³ who acquit the guilty for a bribe,
    but deny justice to the innocent.

²⁴ Therefore, as tongues of fire lick up straw
    and as dry grass sinks down in the flames,
so their roots will decay
    and their flowers blow away like dust;
for they have rejected the law of the LORD
        Almighty
    and spurned the word of the Holy One of Israel.

²⁵ Therefore the LORD's anger burns against his
        people;
    his hand is raised and he strikes them down.
The mountains shake,
    and the dead bodies are like refuse in the
        streets.

Yet for all this, his anger is not turned away,
    his hand is still upraised.

²⁶ He lifts up a banner for the distant nations,
    he whistles for those at the ends of the earth.
Here they come,
    swiftly and speedily!
²⁷ Not one of them grows tired or stumbles,
    not one slumbers or sleeps;
not a belt is loosened at the waist,
    not a sandal thong is broken.
²⁸ Their arrows are sharp,
    all their bows are strung;
their horses' hoofs seem like flint,
    their chariot wheels like a whirlwind.
²⁹ Their roar is like that of the lion,
    they roar like young lions;
they growl as they seize their prey
    and carry it off with no one to rescue.
³⁰ In that day they will roar over it
    like the roaring of the sea.
And if one looks at the land,
    he will see darkness and distress;
    even the light will be darkened by the clouds.

Isaiah's Commission

6 In the year that King Uzziah died, I saw the Lord seated on a throne, high and exalted, and the train of his robe filled the temple. ²Above him were seraphs, each with six wings: With two wings they covered their faces, with two they covered their feet, and with two they were flying. ³And they were calling to one another:

"Holy, holy, holy is the LORD Almighty;
    the whole earth is full of his glory."

Filled With Glory

ISAIAH 6:1–3

The glory about which the seraphim sing hovers all about us, filling heaven and earth—shining through nature and through human beings who are open to God's goodness. Prayerfully remember a person, place or event in which you have seen or felt the glory of God. Use all your inner senses to remember the sights, sounds, feelings and smells. Allow yourself to be touched and filled with God's goodness as you repeat a prayer phrase such as, "Heaven and earth are full of your glory." Repeat this prayer exercise often, varying the recollections and building a growing collection of impressions that increase your sensitivity to God's immediate presence in the world.

See Meeting God in the Created Order

God Calling

ISAIAH 6:5–8

Most "calls" aren't as dramatic as Isaiah's. Often a call is simply what is "called for" in any situation. Prayerfully imagine or recall some situation in your life—work, family, congregation. Vividly envision the setting, noting the forces at work and your thoughts and feelings in response. Imagine the possible actions. Ask the Spirit to show you what's called for, letting possible actions emerge imaginatively. Let yourself be open to God's guidance by repeating, as a prayer phrase with each breath, "Here am I"—the repeated prayer of God's servants in Scripture. Prayerfully review the possibilities, seeking the one that seems closest to the Spirit of Christ. If you choose to act on this, end your prayer with "Send me!"

See *Meeting God in Service*

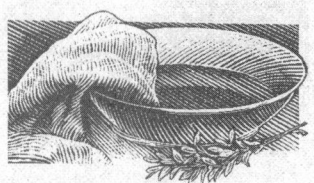

4At the sound of their voices the doorposts and thresholds shook[b] and the temple was filled with smoke.

5"Woe to me!" I cried. "I am ruined! For I am a man of unclean lips, and I live among a people of unclean lips, and my eyes have seen the King, the LORD Almighty."

6Then one of the seraphs flew to me with a live coal in his hand, which he had taken with tongs from the altar. 7With it he touched my mouth and said, "See, this has touched your lips; your guilt is taken away and your sin atoned for."

8Then I heard the voice of the Lord saying, "Whom shall I send? And who will go for us?"

And I said, "Here am I. Send me!"

9He said, "Go and tell this people:

" 'Be ever hearing, but never understanding;
        be ever seeing, but never perceiving.'
10 Make the heart of this people calloused;
        make their ears dull
        and close their eyes.[a]
Otherwise they might see with their eyes,
        hear with their ears,
        understand with their hearts,
and turn and be healed."

11Then I said, "For how long, O Lord?"
And he answered:

"Until the cities lie ruined
        and without inhabitant,
until the houses are left deserted
        and the fields ruined and ravaged,
12 until the LORD has sent everyone far away
        and the land is utterly forsaken.
13 And though a tenth remains in the land,
        it will again be laid waste.
But as the terebinth and oak
        leave stumps when they are cut down,
        so the holy seed will be the stump in the land."

The Sign of Immanuel

7 When Ahaz son of Jotham, the son of Uzziah, was king of Judah, King Rezin of Aram and Pekah son of Remaliah king of Israel marched up to fight against Jerusalem, but they could not overpower it.

2Now the house of David was told, "Aram has allied itself with[b] Ephraim"; so the hearts of Ahaz and his people were shaken, as the trees of the forest are shaken by the wind.

3Then the LORD said to Isaiah, "Go out, you and your son Shear-Jashub,[c] to meet Ahaz at the end of the aqueduct of the Upper Pool, on the road to the Washerman's Field. 4Say to him, 'Be careful, keep calm and don't be afraid. Do not lose heart because of these two smoldering stubs of firewood—because of the fierce anger of Rezin and Aram and of the son of Remaliah. 5Aram, Ephraim and Remaliah's son have plotted your ruin, saying, 6"Let us invade Judah; let us tear it apart and divide it among ourselves, and make

---

a 9,10 Hebrew; Septuagint *'You will be ever hearing, but never understanding; / you will be ever seeing, but never perceiving.' / 10This people's heart has become calloused; / they hardly hear with their ears, / and they have closed their eyes*
b 2 Or *has set up camp in*   c 3 *Shear-Jashub* means *a remnant will return.*

the son of Tabeel king over it." ⁷Yet this is what the Sovereign LORD says:

" 'It will not take place,
    it will not happen,
⁸for the head of Aram is Damascus,
    and the head of Damascus is only Rezin.
Within sixty-five years
    Ephraim will be too shattered to be a people.
⁹The head of Ephraim is Samaria,
    and the head of Samaria is only Remaliah's
        son.
If you do not stand firm in your faith,
    you will not stand at all.' "

¹⁰Again the LORD spoke to Ahaz, ¹¹"Ask the LORD your God for a sign, whether in the deepest depths or in the highest heights."

¹²But Ahaz said, "I will not ask; I will not put the LORD to the test."

¹³Then Isaiah said, "Hear now, you house of David! Is it not enough to try the patience of men? Will you try the patience of my God also? ¹⁴Therefore the Lord himself will give you*a* a sign: The virgin will be with child and will give birth to a son, and*b* will call him Immanuel.*c* ¹⁵He will eat curds and honey when he knows enough to reject the wrong and choose the right. ¹⁶But before the boy knows enough to reject the wrong and choose the right, the land of the two kings you dread will be laid waste. ¹⁷The LORD will bring on you and on your people and on the house of your father a time unlike any since Ephraim broke away from Judah—he will bring the king of Assyria."

¹⁸In that day the LORD will whistle for flies from the distant streams of Egypt and for bees from the land of Assyria. ¹⁹They will all come and settle in the steep ravines and in the crevices in the rocks, on all the thornbushes and at all the water holes. ²⁰In that day the Lord will use a razor hired from beyond the River*d*—the king of Assyria—to shave your head and the hair of your legs, and to take off your beards also. ²¹In that day, a man will keep alive a young cow and two goats. ²²And because of the abundance of the milk they give, he will have curds to eat. All who remain in the land will eat curds and honey. ²³In that day, in every place where there were a thousand vines worth a thousand silver shekels,*e* there will be only briers and thorns. ²⁴Men will go there with bow and arrow, for the land will be covered with briers and thorns. ²⁵As for all the hills once cultivated by the hoe, you will no longer go there for fear of the briers and thorns; they will become places where cattle are turned loose and where sheep run.

Assyria, the LORD's Instrument

8 The LORD said to me, "Take a large scroll and write on it with an ordinary pen: Maher-Shalal-Hash-Baz.*f* ²And I will call in Uriah the priest and Zechariah son of Jeberekiah as reliable witnesses for me."

³Then I went to the prophetess, and she conceived and

God With Us

ISAIAH 7:14

The sign of "Immanuel" is intended to give Ahaz and the people courage in spite of their shaking hearts (7:2). What makes your heart shake? Prayerfully imagine a situation or person that has brought you fear. Now let some tangible sign of Immanuel—God with you—become part of the scene. It may be the light of the Spirit in or around you, the presence of Jesus beside you or an affirmative phrase on your lips. Let the sense of that presence strengthen you as you continue to face what you fear. Consider imaginatively how you might act differently in the face of your fear, claiming God's abiding presence.

See Meeting God in Scripture

---

a 14 The Hebrew is plural.   *b 14* Masoretic Text; Dead Sea Scrolls *and he* or *and they*   *c 14 Immanuel* means *God with us.*   *d 20* That is, the Euphrates
e 23 That is, about 25 pounds (about 11.5 kilograms)   *f 1 Maher-Shalal-Hash-Baz* means *quick to the plunder, swift to the spoil*; also in verse 3.

Fearing God

ISAIAH 8:13–17

"We know that if there does exist an absolute goodness, it must hate most of what we do. That is the terrible fix we are in . . . We cannot do without it and we cannot do with it. God is the only comfort, He is also the supreme terror: the thing we need most and the thing we most want to hide from. He is our only possible ally, and we have made ourselves His enemies. Goodness is either the great safety or the great danger—depending on the way you react to it. And we have reacted the wrong way . . . If you know you are sick, you will listen to the doctor."

—C. S. LEWIS,
Mere Christianity

gave birth to a son. And the LORD said to me, "Name him Maher-Shalal-Hash-Baz. [4]Before the boy knows how to say 'My father' or 'My mother,' the wealth of Damascus and the plunder of Samaria will be carried off by the king of Assyria."

[5]The LORD spoke to me again:

[6]"Because this people has rejected
   the gently flowing waters of Shiloah
and rejoices over Rezin
   and the son of Remaliah,
[7]therefore the Lord is about to bring against them
   the mighty floodwaters of the River[a]—
   the king of Assyria with all his pomp.
It will overflow all its channels,
   run over all its banks
[8]and sweep on into Judah, swirling over it,
   passing through it and reaching up to the neck.
Its outspread wings will cover the breadth of your
      land,
   O Immanuel[b]!"

[9]Raise the war cry,[c] you nations, and be shattered!
   Listen, all you distant lands.
Prepare for battle, and be shattered!
   Prepare for battle, and be shattered!
[10]Devise your strategy, but it will be thwarted;
   propose your plan, but it will not stand,
   for God is with us.[d]

Fear God

[11]The LORD spoke to me with his strong hand upon me, warning me not to follow the way of this people. He said:

[12]"Do not call conspiracy
   everything that these people call conspiracy[e];
   do not fear what they fear,
      and do not dread it.
[13]The LORD Almighty is the one you are to regard as
      holy,
   he is the one you are to fear,
   he is the one you are to dread,
[14]and he will be a sanctuary;
   but for both houses of Israel he will be
a stone that causes men to stumble
   and a rock that makes them fall.
And for the people of Jerusalem he will be
   a trap and a snare.
[15]Many of them will stumble;
   they will fall and be broken,
   they will be snared and captured."

[16]Bind up the testimony
   and seal up the law among my disciples.
[17]I will wait for the LORD,
   who is hiding his face from the house of Jacob.
   I will put my trust in him.

[18]Here am I, and the children the LORD has given me. We

---

a 7 That is, the Euphrates   b 8 Immanuel means God with us.   c 9 Or Do your worst   d 10 Hebrew Immanuel   e 12 Or Do not call for a treaty / every time these people call for a treaty

are signs and symbols in Israel from the Lord Almighty, who dwells on Mount Zion.

¹⁹When men tell you to consult mediums and spiritists, who whisper and mutter, should not a people inquire of their God? Why consult the dead on behalf of the living? ²⁰To the law and to the testimony! If they do not speak according to this word, they have no light of dawn. ²¹Distressed and hungry, they will roam through the land; when they are famished, they will become enraged and, looking upward, will curse their king and their God. ²²Then they will look toward the earth and see only distress and darkness and fearful gloom, and they will be thrust into utter darkness.

To Us a Child Is Born

9 Nevertheless, there will be no more gloom for those who were in distress. In the past he humbled the land of Zebulun and the land of Naphtali, but in the future he will honor Galilee of the Gentiles, by the way of the sea, along the Jordan—

> ²The people walking in darkness
> have seen a great light;
> on those living in the land of the shadow of
> death[a]
> a light has dawned.
> ³You have enlarged the nation
> and increased their joy;
> they rejoice before you
> as people rejoice at the harvest,
> as men rejoice
> when dividing the plunder.
> ⁴For as in the day of Midian's defeat,
> you have shattered
> the yoke that burdens them,
> the bar across their shoulders,
> the rod of their oppressor.
> ⁵Every warrior's boot used in battle
> and every garment rolled in blood
> will be destined for burning,
> will be fuel for the fire.
> ⁶For to us a child is born,
> to us a son is given,
> and the government will be on his shoulders.
> And he will be called
> Wonderful Counselor,[b] Mighty God,
> Everlasting Father, Prince of Peace.
> ⁷Of the increase of his government and peace
> there will be no end.
> He will reign on David's throne
> and over his kingdom,
> establishing and upholding it
> with justice and righteousness
> from that time on and forever.
> The zeal of the Lord Almighty
> will accomplish this.

The Lord's Anger Against Israel

> ⁸The Lord has sent a message against Jacob;

The Royal Child

ISAIAH 9:1–7

Take time to enter deeply into this vision about the coming of the royal child by reading the passage aloud to yourself and then prayerfully allowing your imagination to give life to the sequence of images in the text. Envision the light dawning on people who live in great darkness; the breaking of the bar of oppression; the stilling of the fever of war; the appearance of the divinely given Child who brings the time of justice and peace. Let yourself see the child vividly; perhaps the child is shining with God's light. Imagine that light touching your life. Imagine the light bringing light to the darkness in the world. You might accompany your meditation with selections from Handel's *Messiah*.

See Meeting God in Scripture

---

a 2 Or *land of darkness*   *b 6* Or *Wonderful, Counselor*

The Wrath of God

ISAIAH 9:12–21

"We speak, indeed, of the 'wrath' of God . . . it is something which is assumed in order to discipline by stern means those sinners who have committed many and grievous sins. The language used regarding the wrath of God is to be understood figuratively . . . for it is as if one were to call the words of a physician 'threats,' when he tells his patients, 'I will have to use the knife, and apply cauteries, if you do not obey my prescriptions, and regulate your diet and mode of life in such a way as I direct you.' "

—ORIGEN OF ALEXANDRIA,
Contra Celsus

See *Meeting God in Scripture*

it will fall on Israel.
⁹ All the people will know it—
Ephraim and the inhabitants of Samaria—
who say with pride
and arrogance of heart,
¹⁰ "The bricks have fallen down,
but we will rebuild with dressed stone;
the fig trees have been felled,
but we will replace them with cedars."
¹¹ But the LORD has strengthened Rezin's foes
against them
and has spurred their enemies on.
¹² Arameans from the east and Philistines from the west
have devoured Israel with open mouth.

Yet for all this, his anger is not turned away,
his hand is still upraised.

¹³ But the people have not returned to him who struck them,
nor have they sought the LORD Almighty.
¹⁴ So the LORD will cut off from Israel both head and tail,
both palm branch and reed in a single day;
¹⁵ the elders and prominent men are the head,
the prophets who teach lies are the tail.
¹⁶ Those who guide this people mislead them,
and those who are guided are led astray.
¹⁷ Therefore the Lord will take no pleasure in the young men,
nor will he pity the fatherless and widows,
for everyone is ungodly and wicked,
every mouth speaks vileness.

Yet for all this, his anger is not turned away,
his hand is still upraised.

¹⁸ Surely wickedness burns like a fire;
it consumes briers and thorns,
it sets the forest thickets ablaze,
so that it rolls upward in a column of smoke.
¹⁹ By the wrath of the LORD Almighty
the land will be scorched
and the people will be fuel for the fire;
no one will spare his brother.
²⁰ On the right they will devour,
but still be hungry;
on the left they will eat,
but not be satisfied.
Each will feed on the flesh of his own offspring*ᵃ*:
²¹ Manasseh will feed on Ephraim, and Ephraim on Manasseh;
together they will turn against Judah.

Yet for all this, his anger is not turned away,
his hand is still upraised.

10 Woe to those who make unjust laws,
to those who issue oppressive decrees,
² to deprive the poor of their rights

ᵃ 20 Or *arm*

and withhold justice from the oppressed of my
people,
making widows their prey
and robbing the fatherless.
³What will you do on the day of reckoning,
when disaster comes from afar?
To whom will you run for help?
Where will you leave your riches?
⁴Nothing will remain but to cringe among the
captives
or fall among the slain.

Yet for all this, his anger is not turned away,
his hand is still upraised.

God's Judgment on Assyria

⁵"Woe to the Assyrian, the rod of my anger,
in whose hand is the club of my wrath!
⁶I send him against a godless nation,
I dispatch him against a people who anger me,
to seize loot and snatch plunder,
and to trample them down like mud in the
streets.
⁷But this is not what he intends,
this is not what he has in mind;
his purpose is to destroy,
to put an end to many nations.
⁸'Are not my commanders all kings?' he says.
⁹ 'Has not Calno fared like Carchemish?
Is not Hamath like Arpad,
and Samaria like Damascus?
¹⁰As my hand seized the kingdoms of the idols,
kingdoms whose images excelled those of
Jerusalem and Samaria—
¹¹shall I not deal with Jerusalem and her images
as I dealt with Samaria and her idols?' "

¹²When the Lord has finished all his work against Mount
Zion and Jerusalem, he will say, "I will punish the king of
Assyria for the willful pride of his heart and the haughty
look in his eyes. ¹³For he says:

" 'By the strength of my hand I have done this,
and by my wisdom, because I have
understanding.
I removed the boundaries of nations,
I plundered their treasures;
like a mighty one I subdued*a* their kings.
¹⁴As one reaches into a nest,
so my hand reached for the wealth of the
nations;
as men gather abandoned eggs,
so I gathered all the countries;
not one flapped a wing,
or opened its mouth to chirp.' "

¹⁵Does the ax raise itself above him who swings it,
or the saw boast against him who uses it?
As if a rod were to wield him who lifts it up,
or a club brandish him who is not wood!
¹⁶Therefore, the Lord, the LORD Almighty,

The Boastful Servant

ISAIAH 10:13

The king of Assyria boasts that
he is a self-made man, succeeding "by the strength of [his
own] hand," when he is actually being an unwitting servant of
God. Is there any accomplishment for which any human can
take real credit? Take time to
review, in a spirit of openness
to God, one or more achievements you feel proud to have
accomplished. What factors, in
addition to your effort, contributed to your success? What
about inborn talents? Past mentors and teachers? Current
sources of financial, emotional
or spiritual support? Are there
any specific gifts or graces you
can attribute directly to God?
Frame a short prayer of thanks.
Consider writing a thank-you
note to someone who has supported you in some way.

See Meeting God in Community

Enemies and God

ISAIAH 10:15–19

God punishes Assyria for its arrogance after using this brutal nation to execute divine judgment on Israel (see 10:5). Do you think God actually raises up the enemy, or rather, does he work to bring some good out of the enemy's evil actions? How does God's judgment against our enemies work in everyday life? In your experiences, has an enemy, opponent or opposing force ever been an important catalyst for good—or the occasion for learning some important lessons? Who are your current opponents, and what might you be able to learn from these relationships? How might you act on Jesus' command to "Love your enemies, do good to those who hate you, bless those who curse you, pray for those who mistreat you" (Luke 6:27–28)?

See Meeting God in Community

will send a wasting disease upon his sturdy
warriors;
under his pomp a fire will be kindled
like a blazing flame.
¹⁷ The Light of Israel will become a fire,
their Holy One a flame;
in a single day it will burn and consume
his thorns and his briers.
¹⁸ The splendor of his forests and fertile fields
it will completely destroy,
as when a sick man wastes away.
¹⁹ And the remaining trees of his forests will be so
few
that a child could write them down.

The Remnant of Israel

²⁰ In that day the remnant of Israel,
the survivors of the house of Jacob,
will no longer rely on him
who struck them down
but will truly rely on the LORD,
the Holy One of Israel.
²¹ A remnant will return,[a] a remnant of Jacob
will return to the Mighty God.
²² Though your people, O Israel, be like the sand by
the sea,
only a remnant will return.
Destruction has been decreed,
overwhelming and righteous.
²³ The Lord, the LORD Almighty, will carry out
the destruction decreed upon the whole land.

²⁴ Therefore, this is what the Lord, the LORD Almighty,
says:

"O my people who live in Zion,
do not be afraid of the Assyrians,
who beat you with a rod
and lift up a club against you, as Egypt did.
²⁵ Very soon my anger against you will end
and my wrath will be directed to their
destruction."

²⁶ The LORD Almighty will lash them with a whip,
as when he struck down Midian at the rock of
Oreb;
and he will raise his staff over the waters,
as he did in Egypt.
²⁷ In that day their burden will be lifted from your
shoulders,
their yoke from your neck;
the yoke will be broken
because you have grown so fat.[b]

²⁸ They enter Aiath;
they pass through Migron;
they store supplies at Micmash.
²⁹ They go over the pass, and say,
"We will camp overnight at Geba."
Ramah trembles;

a 21 Hebrew *shear-jashub*; also in verse 22   *b 27* Hebrew; Septuagint
broken / from your shoulders

Gibeah of Saul flees.
³⁰ Cry out, O Daughter of Gallim!
   Listen, O Laishah!
   Poor Anathoth!
³¹ Madmenah is in flight;
   the people of Gebim take cover.
³² This day they will halt at Nob;
   they will shake their fist
   at the mount of the Daughter of Zion,
   at the hill of Jerusalem.

³³ See, the Lord, the LORD Almighty,
   will lop off the boughs with great power.
   The lofty trees will be felled,
   the tall ones will be brought low.
³⁴ He will cut down the forest thickets with an ax;
   Lebanon will fall before the Mighty One.

The Branch From Jesse

11 A shoot will come up from the stump of Jesse;
   from his roots a Branch will bear fruit.
² The Spirit of the LORD will rest on him—
   the Spirit of wisdom and of understanding,
   the Spirit of counsel and of power,
   the Spirit of knowledge and of the fear of the
      LORD—
³ and he will delight in the fear of the LORD.

He will not judge by what he sees with his eyes,
   or decide by what he hears with his ears;
⁴ but with righteousness he will judge the needy,
   with justice he will give decisions for the poor
      of the earth.
He will strike the earth with the rod of his mouth;
   with the breath of his lips he will slay the
      wicked.
⁵ Righteousness will be his belt
   and faithfulness the sash around his waist.

⁶ The wolf will live with the lamb,
   the leopard will lie down with the goat,
   the calf and the lion and the yearling*ᵃ* together;
   and a little child will lead them.
⁷ The cow will feed with the bear,
   their young will lie down together,
   and the lion will eat straw like the ox.
⁸ The infant will play near the hole of the cobra,
   and the young child put his hand into the
      viper's nest.
⁹ They will neither harm nor destroy
   on all my holy mountain,
   for the earth will be full of the knowledge of the
      LORD
   as the waters cover the sea.

¹⁰ In that day the Root of Jesse will stand as a banner for the peoples; the nations will rally to him, and his place of rest will be glorious. ¹¹ In that day the Lord will reach out his hand a second time to reclaim the remnant that is left of his people from Assyria, from Lower Egypt, from Upper

---

Peace With Animals

ISAIAH 11:6–9

"Out of devotion a fisherman offered [Francis] a waterfowl. He took it gladly and opened his hands to let it go, but it did not want to. He prayed for a long time with his eyes turned to heaven. After more than an hour, he came back to himself as if from another realm, and gently told the bird again to go away and praise God. Having received his permission with a blessing, the bird expressed its joy in the movements of its body and flew away."

—BONAVENTURA,
The Life of St. Francis

Song of Salvation

ISAIAH 12:1–6

This exultant passage is traditionally used in Jewish prayer as part of the *havdalah*, a ceremony that marks the end of the Sabbath, because it looks ahead to the final redemption God promises to Israel and the nations. Recite this song of praise or chant it in a monotone or to a simple melody. Let your heart be open to one phrase that particularly draws your attention. Let that phrase become a breath prayer—a short phrase repeated for a period of time aloud, then continued silently. If you find your mind wandering, simply return to the inner repetition of the phrase, letting it turn your heart and mind toward a sense of God's goodness.

See Meeting God in Scripture

Egypt,[a] from Cush,[b] from Elam, from Babylonia,[c] from Hamath and from the islands of the sea.

12 He will raise a banner for the nations
    and gather the exiles of Israel;
  he will assemble the scattered people of Judah
    from the four quarters of the earth.
13 Ephraim's jealousy will vanish,
    and Judah's enemies[d] will be cut off;
  Ephraim will not be jealous of Judah,
    nor Judah hostile toward Ephraim.
14 They will swoop down on the slopes of Philistia to
      the west;
    together they will plunder the people to the
      east.
  They will lay hands on Edom and Moab,
    and the Ammonites will be subject to them.
15 The LORD will dry up
    the gulf of the Egyptian sea;
  with a scorching wind he will sweep his hand
    over the Euphrates River.[e]
  He will break it up into seven streams
    so that men can cross over in sandals.
16 There will be a highway for the remnant of his
      people
    that is left from Assyria,
  as there was for Israel
    when they came up from Egypt.

Songs of Praise

12 In that day you will say:

"I will praise you, O LORD.
  Although you were angry with me,
your anger has turned away
  and you have comforted me.
2 Surely God is my salvation;
  I will trust and not be afraid.
The LORD, the LORD, is my strength and my song;
  he has become my salvation."
3 With joy you will draw water
  from the wells of salvation.

4 In that day you will say:

"Give thanks to the LORD, call on his name;
  make known among the nations what he has
    done,
  and proclaim that his name is exalted.
5 Sing to the LORD, for he has done glorious things;
  let this be known to all the world.
6 Shout aloud and sing for joy, people of Zion,
  for great is the Holy One of Israel among you."

A Prophecy Against Babylon

13 An oracle concerning Babylon that Isaiah son of
    Amoz saw:

2 Raise a banner on a bare hilltop,
  shout to them;

a 11 Hebrew *from Pathros*   *b 11* That is, the upper Nile region
c 11 Hebrew *Shinar*   *d 13* Or *hostility*   *e 15* Hebrew *the River*

beckon to them
  to enter the gates of the nobles.
[3] I have commanded my holy ones;
  I have summoned my warriors to carry out my
     wrath—
  those who rejoice in my triumph.

[4] Listen, a noise on the mountains,
  like that of a great multitude!
Listen, an uproar among the kingdoms,
  like nations massing together!
The LORD Almighty is mustering
  an army for war.
[5] They come from faraway lands,
  from the ends of the heavens—
the LORD and the weapons of his wrath—
  to destroy the whole country.

[6] Wail, for the day of the LORD is near;
  it will come like destruction from the
    Almighty.[a]
[7] Because of this, all hands will go limp,
  every man's heart will melt.
[8] Terror will seize them,
  pain and anguish will grip them;
  they will writhe like a woman in labor.
They will look aghast at each other,
  their faces aflame.

[9] See, the day of the LORD is coming
  —a cruel day, with wrath and fierce anger—
to make the land desolate
  and destroy the sinners within it.
[10] The stars of heaven and their constellations
  will not show their light.
The rising sun will be darkened
  and the moon will not give its light.
[11] I will punish the world for its evil,
  the wicked for their sins.
I will put an end to the arrogance of the haughty
  and will humble the pride of the ruthless.
[12] I will make man scarcer than pure gold,
  more rare than the gold of Ophir.
[13] Therefore I will make the heavens tremble;
  and the earth will shake from its place
at the wrath of the LORD Almighty,
  in the day of his burning anger.

[14] Like a hunted gazelle,
  like sheep without a shepherd,
each will return to his own people,
  each will flee to his native land.
[15] Whoever is captured will be thrust through;
  all who are caught will fall by the sword.
[16] Their infants will be dashed to pieces before their
    eyes;
  their houses will be looted and their wives
    ravished.

[17] See, I will stir up against them the Medes,
  who do not care for silver

[a] 6 Hebrew *Shaddai*

Prayer Sounds

ISAIAH 13:6

Wailing, chanting, shouting and "noise"—joyful or otherwise—were common parts of ancient prayer. Experiment with sounds in your prayers: a loud repeated "hallelujah!" or a repeated sound of wonder and praise such as "ah!" Try a simple singsong chant as a prayer, such as "Here am I." You might offer your feelings about some difficulty you face—or that someone close to you faces—toward God with a low moan such as "ohhhh" or whatever sound comes naturally to you. Such sounds are the nonverbal expression of powerful feelings, even when they accompany words. Allow them to express feelings "that words cannot express" (Romans 8:26) as well. By such "groanings" the Spirit may speak through you.

See *Meeting God in Prayer*

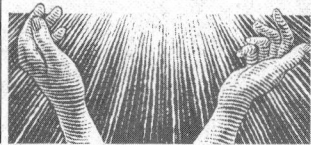

Divine Compassion

ISAIAH 14:1

"The ground of compassion is love and the working of compassion keeps us in love. Compassion is a sweet gracious working in love, mingled with abundant kindness: for compassion works at taking care of us and makes all things become good. Compassion allows us to fail measurably and in as much as we fail in so much we fall . . . our failing is fearful, and our falling is shameful, but in all this the sweet eye of kindness and love never leaves us, nor does the working of compassion cease."

—JULIAN OF NORWICH,
Revelations of Divine Love

and have no delight in gold.
18 Their bows will strike down the young men;
    they will have no mercy on infants
    nor will they look with compassion on children.
19 Babylon, the jewel of kingdoms,
    the glory of the Babylonians'[a] pride,
    will be overthrown by God
    like Sodom and Gomorrah.
20 She will never be inhabited
    or lived in through all generations;
    no Arab will pitch his tent there,
    no shepherd will rest his flocks there.
21 But desert creatures will lie there,
    jackals will fill her houses;
    there the owls will dwell,
    and there the wild goats will leap about.
22 Hyenas will howl in her strongholds,
    jackals in her luxurious palaces.
Her time is at hand,
    and her days will not be prolonged.

14 The LORD will have compassion on Jacob;
    once again he will choose Israel
    and will settle them in their own land.
Aliens will join them
    and unite with the house of Jacob.
2 Nations will take them
    and bring them to their own place.
And the house of Israel will possess the nations
    as menservants and maidservants in the LORD's land.
They will make captives of their captors
    and rule over their oppressors.

3 On the day the LORD gives you relief from suffering and turmoil and cruel bondage, 4 you will take up this taunt against the king of Babylon:

How the oppressor has come to an end!
    How his fury[b] has ended!
5 The LORD has broken the rod of the wicked,
    the scepter of the rulers,
6 which in anger struck down peoples
    with unceasing blows,
and in fury subdued nations
    with relentless aggression.
7 All the lands are at rest and at peace;
    they break into singing.
8 Even the pine trees and the cedars of Lebanon
    exult over you and say,
"Now that you have been laid low,
    no woodsman comes to cut us down."

9 The grave[c] below is all astir
    to meet you at your coming;
it rouses the spirits of the departed to greet you—
    all those who were leaders in the world;
it makes them rise from their thrones—
    all those who were kings over the nations.

---

a 19 Or *Chaldeans'*   b 4 Dead Sea Scrolls, Septuagint and Syriac; the meaning of the word in the Masoretic Text is uncertain.   c 9 Hebrew *Sheol*; also in verses 11 and 15

¹⁰ They will all respond,
they will say to you,
"You also have become weak, as we are;
you have become like us."
¹¹ All your pomp has been brought down to the grave,
along with the noise of your harps;
maggots are spread out beneath you
and worms cover you.

¹² How you have fallen from heaven,
O morning star, son of the dawn!
You have been cast down to the earth,
you who once laid low the nations!
¹³ You said in your heart,
"I will ascend to heaven;
I will raise my throne
above the stars of God;
I will sit enthroned on the mount of assembly,
on the utmost heights of the sacred mountain.ᵃ
¹⁴ I will ascend above the tops of the clouds;
I will make myself like the Most High."
¹⁵ But you are brought down to the grave,
to the depths of the pit.

¹⁶ Those who see you stare at you,
they ponder your fate:
"Is this the man who shook the earth
and made kingdoms tremble,
¹⁷ the man who made the world a desert,
who overthrew its cities
and would not let his captives go home?"

¹⁸ All the kings of the nations lie in state,
each in his own tomb.
¹⁹ But you are cast out of your tomb
like a rejected branch;
you are covered with the slain,
with those pierced by the sword,
those who descend to the stones of the pit.
Like a corpse trampled underfoot,
²⁰ you will not join them in burial,
for you have destroyed your land
and killed your people.

The offspring of the wicked
will never be mentioned again.
²¹ Prepare a place to slaughter his sons
for the sins of their forefathers;
they are not to rise to inherit the land
and cover the earth with their cities.

²² "I will rise up against them,"
declares the Lᴏʀᴅ Almighty.
"I will cut off from Babylon her name and
survivors,
her offspring and descendants,"
declares the Lᴏʀᴅ.
²³ "I will turn her into a place for owls
and into swampland;
I will sweep her with the broom of destruction,"
declares the Lᴏʀᴅ Almighty.

Dark Images

ISAIAH 14:9–21

Slowly read Israel's taunt of rejoicing over Babylon's downfall (which actually begins in 14:4). Pay attention especially to the images of destruction typical of many passages in these prophetic writings. What emotions does this vivid poetry arouse in you? Spend some time journaling about them, or use crayons to draw a picture of your emotions about this passage. Then ponder: How do you think God feels about the fall of such a violent, oppressive civilization? The same as ancient Israel does? What questions do you have about similar passages of such destruction? Take your questions into prayer and ponder them in God's presence.

See Meeting God in Scripture

ᵃ 13 Or *the north*; Hebrew *Zaphon*

God's Hand Over the Nations

ISAIAH 14:26

Pray for the nations of the world by opening your heart and mind to the Spirit's working and by envisioning the whole planet as if you were seeing it from a satellite. Behold the deep blue seas, the rusty, greenish continents, the dazzling swirl of clouds. Imagine the planet surrounded by the light of God's compassionate justice, seeing "the whole world in his hands." Offer your own love for the world to God. Bring specific concerns for world situations into your prayer by asking God to illuminate that section of the world with the light of his love and the touch of his hand. Listen for God calling you to specific action.

See Meeting God in the Created Order

A Prophecy Against Assyria

²⁴The LORD Almighty has sworn,

> "Surely, as I have planned, so it will be,
> and as I have purposed, so it will stand.
> ²⁵I will crush the Assyrian in my land;
> on my mountains I will trample him down.
> His yoke will be taken from my people,
> and his burden removed from their shoulders."

> ²⁶This is the plan determined for the whole world;
> this is the hand stretched out over all nations.
> ²⁷For the LORD Almighty has purposed, and who
> can thwart him?
> His hand is stretched out, and who can turn it
> back?

A Prophecy Against the Philistines

²⁸This oracle came in the year King Ahaz died:

> ²⁹Do not rejoice, all you Philistines,
> that the rod that struck you is broken;
> from the root of that snake will spring up a viper,
> its fruit will be a darting, venomous serpent.
> ³⁰The poorest of the poor will find pasture,
> and the needy will lie down in safety.
> But your root I will destroy by famine;
> it will slay your survivors.

> ³¹Wail, O gate! Howl, O city!
> Melt away, all you Philistines!
> A cloud of smoke comes from the north,
> and there is not a straggler in its ranks.
> ³²What answer shall be given
> to the envoys of that nation?
> "The LORD has established Zion,
> and in her his afflicted people will find refuge."

A Prophecy Against Moab

15 An oracle concerning Moab:

> Ar in Moab is ruined,
> destroyed in a night!
> Kir in Moab is ruined,
> destroyed in a night!
> ²Dibon goes up to its temple,
> to its high places to weep;
> Moab wails over Nebo and Medeba.
> Every head is shaved
> and every beard cut off.
> ³In the streets they wear sackcloth;
> on the roofs and in the public squares
> they all wail,
> prostrate with weeping.
> ⁴Heshbon and Elealeh cry out,
> their voices are heard all the way to Jahaz.
> Therefore the armed men of Moab cry out,
> and their hearts are faint.

> ⁵My heart cries out over Moab;
> her fugitives flee as far as Zoar,
> as far as Eglath Shelishiyah.

They go up the way to Luhith,
      weeping as they go;
on the road to Horonaim
      they lament their destruction.
⁶ The waters of Nimrim are dried up
      and the grass is withered;
the vegetation is gone
      and nothing green is left.
⁷ So the wealth they have acquired and stored up
      they carry away over the Ravine of the Poplars.
⁸ Their outcry echoes along the border of Moab;
      their wailing reaches as far as Eglaim,
      their lamentation as far as Beer Elim.
⁹ Dimon'sᵃ waters are full of blood,
      but I will bring still more upon Dimonᵃ—
a lion upon the fugitives of Moab
      and upon those who remain in the land.

16 Send lambs as tribute
      to the ruler of the land,
from Sela, across the desert,
      to the mount of the Daughter of Zion.
² Like fluttering birds
      pushed from the nest,
so are the women of Moab
      at the fords of the Arnon.

³ "Give us counsel,
      render a decision.
Make your shadow like night—
      at high noon.
Hide the fugitives,
      do not betray the refugees.
⁴ Let the Moabite fugitives stay with you;
      be their shelter from the destroyer."

The oppressor will come to an end,
      and destruction will cease;
the aggressor will vanish from the land.
⁵ In love a throne will be established;
      in faithfulness a man will sit on it—
      one from the houseᵇ of David—
one who in judging seeks justice
      and speeds the cause of righteousness.

⁶ We have heard of Moab's pride—
      her overweening pride and conceit,
her pride and her insolence—
      but her boasts are empty.
⁷ Therefore the Moabites wail,
      they wail together for Moab.
Lament and grieve
      for the menᶜ of Kir Hareseth.
⁸ The fields of Heshbon wither,
      the vines of Sibmah also.
The rulers of the nations
      have trampled down the choicest vines,
which once reached Jazer
      and spread toward the desert.
Their shoots spread out

Interceding for Sinners

ISAIAH 15:1–9

The prophet not only thunders against sin, his "heart cries out" over the sinner as well. This vivid portrait (15:1—16:14) of the distress of Israel's enemy Moab shows how deeply the prophet shares God's compassionate grief for those who suffer, even if their suffering is a result of their own destructive behavior. Intercede today for people caught in a web of destruction— trapped, perhaps, by a harmful relationship or an addiction. Bring to mind anyone you know personally. Spend a few minutes surrounding each one in prayer for God's compassionate help—asking God to awaken and heal each of them.

See Meeting God in Prayer

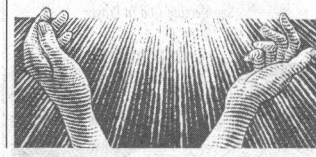

ᵃ9 Masoretic Text; Dead Sea Scrolls, some Septuagint manuscripts and Vulgate *Dibon*   ᵇ5 Hebrew *tent*   ᶜ7 Or *"raisin cakes,"* a wordplay

919

Looking to the Maker

ISAIAH 17:7

"I don't say anything," said an old Irish peasant about his quiet, solitary visits to the church. "I just look at God, and God looks at me." He was practicing the ancient, contemplative Prayer of Simple Regard (also known as centering prayer) by turning his heart and soul toward God.

Sit quietly. Spend some time becoming aware of the miracle of your breathing, which helps you focus your attention on the moment. Frame within your mind a word or an image that turns you toward God. As you become more focused and still, you will become aware of God's presence with you—beyond all words and images.

See Meeting God in Prayer

and went as far as the sea.
⁹ So I weep, as Jazer weeps,
    for the vines of Sibmah.
O Heshbon, O Elealeh,
    I drench you with tears!
The shouts of joy over your ripened fruit
    and over your harvests have been stilled.
¹⁰ Joy and gladness are taken away from the
        orchards;
    no one sings or shouts in the vineyards;
no one treads out wine at the presses,
    for I have put an end to the shouting.
¹¹ My heart laments for Moab like a harp,
    my inmost being for Kir Hareseth.
¹² When Moab appears at her high place,
    she only wears herself out;
when she goes to her shrine to pray,
    it is to no avail.

¹³ This is the word the LORD has already spoken concerning Moab. ¹⁴ But now the LORD says: "Within three years, as a servant bound by contract would count them, Moab's splendor and all her many people will be despised, and her survivors will be very few and feeble."

An Oracle Against Damascus

17 An oracle concerning Damascus:

"See, Damascus will no longer be a city
    but will become a heap of ruins.
² The cities of Aroer will be deserted
    and left to flocks, which will lie down,
    with no one to make them afraid.
³ The fortified city will disappear from Ephraim,
    and royal power from Damascus;
the remnant of Aram will be
    like the glory of the Israelites,"
                declares the LORD Almighty.

⁴ "In that day the glory of Jacob will fade;
    the fat of his body will waste away.
⁵ It will be as when a reaper gathers the standing
        grain
    and harvests the grain with his arm—
as when a man gleans heads of grain
    in the Valley of Rephaim.
⁶ Yet some gleanings will remain,
    as when an olive tree is beaten,
leaving two or three olives on the topmost
        branches,
    four or five on the fruitful boughs,"
                declares the LORD, the God of Israel.

⁷ In that day men will look to their Maker
    and turn their eyes to the Holy One of Israel.
⁸ They will not look to the altars,
    the work of their hands,
and they will have no regard for the Asherah
        poles*a*
    and the incense altars their fingers have made.

a 8 That is, symbols of the goddess Asherah

⁹In that day their strong cities, which they left because of the Israelites, will be like places abandoned to thickets and undergrowth. And all will be desolation.

¹⁰ You have forgotten God your Savior;
　　you have not remembered the Rock, your
　　　　fortress.
　Therefore, though you set out the finest plants
　　and plant imported vines,
¹¹ though on the day you set them out, you make
　　　them grow,
　　and on the morning when you plant them, you
　　　bring them to bud,
　yet the harvest will be as nothing
　　in the day of disease and incurable pain.

¹² Oh, the raging of many nations—
　　they rage like the raging sea!
　Oh, the uproar of the peoples—
　　they roar like the roaring of great waters!
¹³ Although the peoples roar like the roar of surging
　　　waters,
　　when he rebukes them they flee far away,
　driven before the wind like chaff on the hills,
　　like tumbleweed before a gale.
¹⁴ In the evening, sudden terror!
　　Before the morning, they are gone!
　This is the portion of those who loot us,
　　the lot of those who plunder us.

A Prophecy Against Cush

18 Woe to the land of whirring wings[a]
　　along the rivers of Cush,[b]
² which sends envoys by sea
　　in papyrus boats over the water.

　Go, swift messengers,
　to a people tall and smooth-skinned,
　　to a people feared far and wide,
　an aggressive nation of strange speech,
　　whose land is divided by rivers.

³ All you people of the world,
　　you who live on the earth,
　when a banner is raised on the mountains,
　　you will see it,
　and when a trumpet sounds,
　　you will hear it.
⁴ This is what the LORD says to me:
　　"I will remain quiet and will look on from my
　　　dwelling place,
　like shimmering heat in the sunshine,
　　like a cloud of dew in the heat of harvest."
⁵ For, before the harvest, when the blossom is gone
　　and the flower becomes a ripening grape,
　he will cut off the shoots with pruning knives,
　　and cut down and take away the spreading
　　　branches.
⁶ They will all be left to the mountain birds of prey
　　and to the wild animals;

God's Sunshine

ISAIAH 18:4

"I live in the sunshine of God's presence . . . I just let God shine upon me, without words or images or thoughts. I think all that matters in prayer is that we should want God to take possession of us. And if that wanting is deep enough, then anything we feel we want to do in prayer will work . . . I feel it's God's process . . . and that what goes on is God's business. My business is just to be attentive to Him, just to be waiting for God, for God to be what He wants . . . The spiritual is not there for use. The spiritual is there for blessing. You just . . . hold out your hands to receive it."

—SISTER WENDY BECKETT,
Sister Wendy in Conversation with Bill Moyers

ᵃ 1 Or *of locusts*　　ᵇ 1 That is, the upper Nile region

What Is Wisdom?

ISAIAH 19:11–15

For hundreds of years, the intellect of Egyptian wise men has been the nation's pride. But their knowledge does not save them from destruction.

The wisdom that we have from God is unlike human wisdom (see 1 Corinthians 1:20–31). It goes beyond any worldly knowledge—beyond intellectual understanding; it leads to salvation. What does godly wisdom mean to you? In what ways do you seek it? How do you depend on human wisdom to make your decisions? In what ways does it shape your lifestyle? How do you discern between God's wisdom and human wisdom? How can they become integrated? How can you filter intellectual knowledge through the lens of God's wisdom?

the birds will feed on them all summer,
  the wild animals all winter.

⁷At that time gifts will be brought to the LORD Almighty

from a people tall and smooth-skinned,
  from a people feared far and wide,
an aggressive nation of strange speech,
  whose land is divided by rivers—

the gifts will be brought to Mount Zion, the place of the Name of the LORD Almighty.

A Prophecy About Egypt

19 An oracle concerning Egypt:

See, the LORD rides on a swift cloud
  and is coming to Egypt.
The idols of Egypt tremble before him,
  and the hearts of the Egyptians melt within
    them.

²"I will stir up Egyptian against Egyptian—
  brother will fight against brother,
  neighbor against neighbor,
  city against city,
  kingdom against kingdom.
³The Egyptians will lose heart,
  and I will bring their plans to nothing;
they will consult the idols and the spirits of the
    dead,
  the mediums and the spiritists.
⁴I will hand the Egyptians over
  to the power of a cruel master,
and a fierce king will rule over them,"
  declares the Lord, the LORD Almighty.

⁵The waters of the river will dry up,
  and the riverbed will be parched and dry.
⁶The canals will stink;
  the streams of Egypt will dwindle and dry up.
The reeds and rushes will wither,
⁷ also the plants along the Nile,
  at the mouth of the river.
Every sown field along the Nile
  will become parched, will blow away and be no
    more.
⁸The fishermen will groan and lament,
  all who cast hooks into the Nile;
those who throw nets on the water
  will pine away.
⁹Those who work with combed flax will despair,
  the weavers of fine linen will lose hope.
¹⁰The workers in cloth will be dejected,
  and all the wage earners will be sick at heart.

¹¹The officials of Zoan are nothing but fools;
  the wise counselors of Pharaoh give senseless
    advice.
How can you say to Pharaoh,
  "I am one of the wise men,
  a disciple of the ancient kings"?

¹²Where are your wise men now?
    Let them show you and make known
  what the LORD Almighty
      has planned against Egypt.
¹³The officials of Zoan have become fools,
      the leaders of Memphis*ᵃ* are deceived;
  the cornerstones of her peoples
      have led Egypt astray.
¹⁴The LORD has poured into them
      a spirit of dizziness;
  they make Egypt stagger in all that she does,
      as a drunkard staggers around in his vomit.
¹⁵There is nothing Egypt can do—
      head or tail, palm branch or reed.

¹⁶In that day the Egyptians will be like women. They will shudder with fear at the uplifted hand that the LORD Almighty raises against them. ¹⁷And the land of Judah will bring terror to the Egyptians; everyone to whom Judah is mentioned will be terrified, because of what the LORD Almighty is planning against them.

¹⁸In that day five cities in Egypt will speak the language of Canaan and swear allegiance to the LORD Almighty. One of them will be called the City of Destruction.*ᵇ*

¹⁹In that day there will be an altar to the LORD in the heart of Egypt, and a monument to the LORD at its border. ²⁰It will be a sign and witness to the LORD Almighty in the land of Egypt. When they cry out to the LORD because of their oppressors, he will send them a savior and defender, and he will rescue them. ²¹So the LORD will make himself known to the Egyptians, and in that day they will acknowledge the LORD. They will worship with sacrifices and grain offerings; they will make vows to the LORD and keep them. ²²The LORD will strike Egypt with a plague; he will strike them and heal them. They will turn to the LORD, and he will respond to their pleas and heal them.

²³In that day there will be a highway from Egypt to Assyria. The Assyrians will go to Egypt and the Egyptians to Assyria. The Egyptians and Assyrians will worship together. ²⁴In that day Israel will be the third, along with Egypt and Assyria, a blessing on the earth. ²⁵The LORD Almighty will bless them, saying, "Blessed be Egypt my people, Assyria my handiwork, and Israel my inheritance."

A Prophecy Against Egypt and Cush

20 In the year that the supreme commander, sent by Sargon king of Assyria, came to Ashdod and attacked and captured it— ²at that time the LORD spoke through Isaiah son of Amoz. He said to him, "Take off the sackcloth from your body and the sandals from your feet." And he did so, going around stripped and barefoot.

³Then the LORD said, "Just as my servant Isaiah has gone stripped and barefoot for three years, as a sign and portent against Egypt and Cush,*ᶜ* ⁴so the king of Assyria will lead away stripped and barefoot the Egyptian captives and Cushite exiles, young and old, with buttocks bared—to Egypt's shame. ⁵Those who trusted in Cush and boasted in Egypt will be afraid and put to shame. ⁶In that day the peo-

---

The Hope of Reconciliation

ISAIAH 19:21–25

Isaiah envisions a vast reconciliation occurring among ancient enemy nations; God will strike and heal them, and they will respond. You might consider transforming your newspaper reading in these ways: Stop reading at the end of an article about conflict and hold the people in this situation before the light of God's judging, saving grace. As you encounter a story about troubled or warring nations, imagine the light of God's Spirit enfolding them and penetrating their difficulties. Affirm the power of God's grace to soften their hardened hearts and assist them in difficult times. After reading a story about a particular nation say, "Your will be done in [*name of nation*]!" Cut out articles regarding a variety of situations and commit yourself to continued prayer for each situation.

See Meeting God in Service

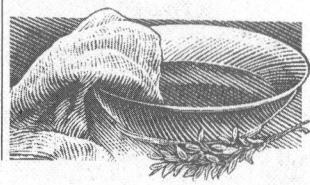

ᵃ 13 Hebrew *Noph*   *ᵇ 18* Most manuscripts of the Masoretic Text; some manuscripts of the Masoretic Text, Dead Sea Scrolls and Vulgate *City of the Sun* (that is, Heliopolis)   *ᶜ 3* That is, the upper Nile region; also in verse 5

Interior Pain

ISAIAH 21:3–8

"How the poor heart is afflicted when, as though abandoned by love, she looks everywhere, and does not find it as it seems to her. She does not find it in the exterior senses . . . nor in the imagination . . . nor in the understanding; and although at last she finds in the summit and supreme point of the spirit where the divine love resides, still she does not recognize it and does not think that it is what it is, for the greatness of the distress and darkness prevents her from experiencing its sweetness . . . But what can the soul in this case do? . . . She . . . has only the power to let herself die in the hands of the will of God."

—FRANCIS DE SALES,
Treatise on the Love of God

ple who live on this coast will say, 'See what has happened to those we relied on, those we fled to for help and deliverance from the king of Assyria! How then can we escape?' "

A Prophecy Against Babylon

21 An oracle concerning the Desert by the Sea:

Like whirlwinds sweeping through the southland,
an invader comes from the desert,
from a land of terror.

² A dire vision has been shown to me:
The traitor betrays, the looter takes loot.
Elam, attack! Media, lay siege!
I will bring to an end all the groaning she
caused.

³ At this my body is racked with pain,
pangs seize me, like those of a woman in labor;
I am staggered by what I hear,
I am bewildered by what I see.
⁴ My heart falters,
fear makes me tremble;
the twilight I longed for
has become a horror to me.

⁵ They set the tables,
they spread the rugs,
they eat, they drink!
Get up, you officers,
oil the shields!

⁶ This is what the Lord says to me:

"Go, post a lookout
and have him report what he sees.
⁷ When he sees chariots
with teams of horses,
riders on donkeys
or riders on camels,
let him be alert,
fully alert."

⁸ And the lookout[a] shouted,

"Day after day, my lord, I stand on the
watchtower;
every night I stay at my post.
⁹ Look, here comes a man in a chariot
with a team of horses.
And he gives back the answer:
'Babylon has fallen, has fallen!
All the images of its gods
lie shattered on the ground!' "

¹⁰ O my people, crushed on the threshing floor,
I tell you what I have heard
from the LORD Almighty,
from the God of Israel.

A Prophecy Against Edom

¹¹ An oracle concerning Dumah[b]:

---

a 8 Dead Sea Scrolls and Syriac; Masoretic Text *A lion*   *b 11 Dumah* means *silence* or *stillness,* a wordplay on *Edom.*

Someone calls to me from Seir,
"Watchman, what is left of the night?
Watchman, what is left of the night?"
¹²The watchman replies,
"Morning is coming, but also the night.
If you would ask, then ask;
and come back yet again."

A Prophecy Against Arabia

¹³An oracle concerning Arabia:

You caravans of Dedanites,
who camp in the thickets of Arabia,
¹⁴ bring water for the thirsty;
you who live in Tema,
bring food for the fugitives.
¹⁵They flee from the sword,
from the drawn sword,
from the bent bow
and from the heat of battle.

¹⁶This is what the Lord says to me: "Within one year, as a servant bound by contract would count it, all the pomp of Kedar will come to an end. ¹⁷The survivors of the bowmen, the warriors of Kedar, will be few." The LORD, the God of Israel, has spoken.

A Prophecy About Jerusalem

22 An oracle concerning the Valley of Vision:

What troubles you now,
that you have all gone up on the roofs,
²O town full of commotion,
O city of tumult and revelry?
Your slain were not killed by the sword,
nor did they die in battle.
³All your leaders have fled together;
they have been captured without using the
bow.
All you who were caught were taken prisoner
together,
having fled while the enemy was still far away.
⁴Therefore I said, "Turn away from me;
let me weep bitterly.
Do not try to console me
over the destruction of my people."

⁵The Lord, the LORD Almighty, has a day
of tumult and trampling and terror
in the Valley of Vision,
a day of battering down walls
and of crying out to the mountains.
⁶Elam takes up the quiver,
with her charioteers and horses;
Kir uncovers the shield.
⁷Your choicest valleys are full of chariots,
and horsemen are posted at the city gates;
⁸ the defenses of Judah are stripped away.

And you looked in that day
to the weapons in the Palace of the Forest;
⁹you saw that the City of David

The Watchman

ISAIAH 21:11–12

Isaiah's images of the lookout and the watchman represent those who remain alert to report oncoming trouble. In our day, whom is God calling to make us aware of possible threats to our communal well-being—potential difficulties that we might otherwise overlook? How does their prophetic concern reflect God's loving mindfulness of our good? Have any of these "watchmen" influenced your attitudes, actions or prayers? Have your own eyes been opened to a problem others do not see? How does this awareness affect your living and your praying?

See Meeting God in Community

Good Grief

ISAIAH 22:11–13

Jerusalem disregards the Lord Almighty's call for weeping and mourning, exhibiting instead a revelry inappropriate to the city's dire situation.

When are tears not only appropriate, but virtually demanded? What kinds of things does God call us to mourn about—in the world and in our own lives? What price do we pay for suppressing real responses of mourning and grief? Why are the mourners called "blessed" (Matthew 5:4)? Is there anything in your life, or in the world, that you are currently being called to mourn? What good can come out of such mourning? Place any grief or sorrow you feel into God's hands, asking the Spirit to work through it for good and sustain you in the midst of it.

See Meeting God in Prayer

had many breaches in its defenses;
  you stored up water
    in the Lower Pool.
¹⁰ You counted the buildings in Jerusalem
    and tore down houses to strengthen the wall.
¹¹ You built a reservoir between the two walls
    for the water of the Old Pool,
  but you did not look to the One who made it,
    or have regard for the One who planned it long
      ago.

¹² The Lord, the LORD Almighty,
    called you on that day
  to weep and to wail,
    to tear out your hair and put on sackcloth.
¹³ But see, there is joy and revelry,
    slaughtering of cattle and killing of sheep,
    eating of meat and drinking of wine!
  "Let us eat and drink," you say,
    "for tomorrow we die!"

¹⁴ The LORD Almighty has revealed this in my hearing: "Till your dying day this sin will not be atoned for," says the Lord, the LORD Almighty.

¹⁵ This is what the Lord, the LORD Almighty, says:

  "Go, say to this steward,
    to Shebna, who is in charge of the palace:
¹⁶ What are you doing here and who gave you
      permission
    to cut out a grave for yourself here,
  hewing your grave on the height
    and chiseling your resting place in the rock?

¹⁷ "Beware, the LORD is about to take firm hold of
      you
    and hurl you away, O you mighty man.
¹⁸ He will roll you up tightly like a ball
    and throw you into a large country.
  There you will die
    and there your splendid chariots will remain—
    you disgrace to your master's house!
¹⁹ I will depose you from your office,
    and you will be ousted from your position.

²⁰ "In that day I will summon my servant, Eliakim son of Hilkiah. ²¹ I will clothe him with your robe and fasten your sash around him and hand your authority over to him. He will be a father to those who live in Jerusalem and to the house of Judah. ²² I will place on his shoulder the key to the house of David; what he opens no one can shut, and what he shuts no one can open. ²³ I will drive him like a peg into a firm place; he will be a seat*ᵃ* of honor for the house of his father. ²⁴ All the glory of his family will hang on him: its offspring and offshoots—all its lesser vessels, from the bowls to all the jars.

²⁵ "In that day," declares the LORD Almighty, "the peg driven into the firm place will give way; it will be sheared off and will fall, and the load hanging on it will be cut down." The LORD has spoken.

ᵃ 23 Or throne

We are to pray during our reading so that God might enable us to properly understand himself and his will and open to us one door after the other into his Word.

PHILIPP JAKOB SPENER (1635-1705)

The Necessary and Useful Reading of the Holy Scriptures

Come before the Lord and begin to read. Stop reading when you feel the Lord drawing you inwardly to himself. Now, simply remain in stillness. Stay there for a while.

JEANNE GUYON (1648-1717)

Experiencing the Depths of Jesus Christ

Our own curiosity

often binders us in reading the Scriptures, because we wish to understand and argue when we should simply read on with humility, simplicity and faith.

THOMAS À KEMPIS (c. 1380-1471)

Imitation of Christ

Where the Spirit
does not open
the Scripture,
the Scripture is not
understood even
though it is read.

Martin Luther (1483-1546)

A Prophecy About Tyre

23 An oracle concerning Tyre:

Wail, O ships of Tarshish!
    For Tyre is destroyed
    and left without house or harbor.
From the land of Cyprus[a]
    word has come to them.

[2] Be silent, you people of the island
    and you merchants of Sidon,
    whom the seafarers have enriched.
[3] On the great waters
    came the grain of the Shihor;
the harvest of the Nile[b] was the revenue of Tyre,
    and she became the marketplace of the
        nations.

[4] Be ashamed, O Sidon, and you, O fortress of the
        sea,
    for the sea has spoken:
"I have neither been in labor nor given birth;
    I have neither reared sons nor brought up
        daughters."
[5] When word comes to Egypt,
    they will be in anguish at the report from Tyre.

[6] Cross over to Tarshish;
    wail, you people of the island.
[7] Is this your city of revelry,
    the old, old city,
whose feet have taken her
    to settle in far-off lands?
[8] Who planned this against Tyre,
    the bestower of crowns,
whose merchants are princes,
    whose traders are renowned in the earth?
[9] The LORD Almighty planned it,
    to bring low the pride of all glory
    and to humble all who are renowned on the
        earth.

[10] Till[c] your land as along the Nile,
    O Daughter of Tarshish,
    for you no longer have a harbor.
[11] The LORD has stretched out his hand over the sea
    and made its kingdoms tremble.
He has given an order concerning Phoenicia[d]
    that her fortresses be destroyed.
[12] He said, "No more of your reveling,
    O Virgin Daughter of Sidon, now crushed!

"Up, cross over to Cyprus[a];
    even there you will find no rest."
[13] Look at the land of the Babylonians,[e]
    this people that is now of no account!
The Assyrians have made it
    a place for desert creatures;

---

[a] 1,12 Hebrew *Kittim*   [b] 2,3 Masoretic Text; one Dead Sea Scroll *Sidon, /
who cross over the sea; / your envoys [3]are on the great waters. / The grain of the
Shihor, / the harvest of the Nile.*   [c] 10 Dead Sea Scrolls and some Septuagint
manuscripts; Masoretic Text *Go through*   [d] 11 Hebrew *Canaan*   [e] 13 Or
Chaldeans

The Key of David

ISAIAH 22:22

The key is a powerful symbol of
access to resources, abilities
and powers. Take your set of
keys and, holding each key in
turn, think about the door it
opens. How is each area—
house, file cabinet, car, office—
beneficial (or dangerous) to
your soul? What opportunities
to serve God does each area afford? How do the blessings you
experience in each area prompt
thanksgiving within you? As
you hold each key, bring any
desires or needs connected with
its meaning into the light of
God's loving concern.

See Meeting God in Everyday Life

A Defiled Earth

ISAIAH 24:1–5

Violation of God's intentions for creation has resulted in a planet "defiled" by humans who are seemingly bent on its devastation. How is God concerned for creation and its creatures? How are we called to care for creation and to carry out God's plan for it? How can you, in prayer, join in creation's "eager expectation" of the full disclosure of God's kingdom (Romans 8:19)? What is one activity in your life that honors God as Creator? Give thanks for that activity. Also name one activity that ignores God's role as Creator and offer contrition for it.

See Meeting God in the Created Order

they raised up their siege towers,
   they stripped its fortresses bare
   and turned it into a ruin.

¹⁴Wail, you ships of Tarshish;
   your fortress is destroyed!

¹⁵At that time Tyre will be forgotten for seventy years, the span of a king's life. But at the end of these seventy years, it will happen to Tyre as in the song of the prostitute:

¹⁶"Take up a harp, walk through the city,
   O prostitute forgotten;
play the harp well, sing many a song,
   so that you will be remembered."

¹⁷At the end of seventy years, the Lᴏʀᴅ will deal with Tyre. She will return to her hire as a prostitute and will ply her trade with all the kingdoms on the face of the earth. ¹⁸Yet her profit and her earnings will be set apart for the Lᴏʀᴅ; they will not be stored up or hoarded. Her profits will go to those who live before the Lᴏʀᴅ, for abundant food and fine clothes.

The Lᴏʀᴅ's Devastation of the Earth

24 See, the Lᴏʀᴅ is going to lay waste the earth
   and devastate it;
   he will ruin its face
   and scatter its inhabitants—
²it will be the same
   for priest as for people,
   for master as for servant,
   for mistress as for maid,
   for seller as for buyer,
   for borrower as for lender,
   for debtor as for creditor.
³The earth will be completely laid waste
   and totally plundered.
      The Lᴏʀᴅ has spoken this word.

⁴The earth dries up and withers,
   the world languishes and withers,
   the exalted of the earth languish.
⁵The earth is defiled by its people;
   they have disobeyed the laws,
 violated the statutes
   and broken the everlasting covenant.
⁶Therefore a curse consumes the earth;
   its people must bear their guilt.
Therefore earth's inhabitants are burned up,
   and very few are left.
⁷The new wine dries up and the vine withers;
   all the merrymakers groan.
⁸The gaiety of the tambourines is stilled,
   the noise of the revelers has stopped,
   the joyful harp is silent.
⁹No longer do they drink wine with a song;
   the beer is bitter to its drinkers.
¹⁰The ruined city lies desolate;
   the entrance to every house is barred.
¹¹In the streets they cry out for wine;
   all joy turns to gloom,
   all gaiety is banished from the earth.

¹²The city is left in ruins,
    its gate is battered to pieces.
¹³So will it be on the earth
    and among the nations,
  as when an olive tree is beaten,
    or as when gleanings are left after the grape
      harvest.

¹⁴They raise their voices, they shout for joy;
    from the west they acclaim the LORD's majesty.
¹⁵Therefore in the east give glory to the LORD;
    exalt the name of the LORD, the God of Israel,
    in the islands of the sea.
¹⁶From the ends of the earth we hear singing:
    "Glory to the Righteous One."

  But I said, "I waste away, I waste away!
    Woe to me!
  The treacherous betray!
    With treachery the treacherous betray!"
¹⁷Terror and pit and snare await you,
    O people of the earth.
¹⁸Whoever flees at the sound of terror
    will fall into a pit;
  whoever climbs out of the pit
    will be caught in a snare.

  The floodgates of the heavens are opened,
    the foundations of the earth shake.
¹⁹The earth is broken up,
    the earth is split asunder,
    the earth is thoroughly shaken.
²⁰The earth reels like a drunkard,
    it sways like a hut in the wind;
  so heavy upon it is the guilt of its rebellion
    that it falls—never to rise again.

²¹In that day the LORD will punish
    the powers in the heavens above
    and the kings on the earth below.
²²They will be herded together
    like prisoners bound in a dungeon;
  they will be shut up in prison
    and be punished[a] after many days.
²³The moon will be abashed, the sun ashamed;
    for the LORD Almighty will reign
  on Mount Zion and in Jerusalem,
    and before its elders, gloriously.

Praise to the LORD

25 O LORD, you are my God;
    I will exalt you and praise your name,
  for in perfect faithfulness
    you have done marvelous things,
    things planned long ago.
²You have made the city a heap of rubble,
    the fortified town a ruin,
  the foreigners' stronghold a city no more;
    it will never be rebuilt.
³Therefore strong peoples will honor you;
    cities of ruthless nations will revere you.

We Hear Singing

ISAIAH 24:16

"Holy, holy, holy
is the Lord God Almighty,
who was, and is, and is to
    come . . .
You are worthy, our Lord
    and God,
to receive glory and honor
    and power,
for you created all things,
and by your will they were
    created
and have their being."

—Revelation 4:8,11

---

a 22 Or released

"A Feast of Rich Food"

ISAIAH 25:6–7

In this image of gracious abundance, God prepares a "feast of rich food for all peoples." God's will for us is that we "may have life, and have it to the full" (John 10:10). But God's will is often hidden from us by the "shroud," an effect of sin. What activities or spiritual practices help you to delight in God's abundant goodness? Does such delight come through nature? Through other people? From deep within your soul? From Scripture and sacred writings? What creates a "shroud" that keeps you from such nourishing delight? Take some time to remember a delightful moment and relive it. Store it in your heart as a liberating remembrance when the "shroud" exerts power over you.

See Meeting God in Everyday Life

⁴ You have been a refuge for the poor,
   a refuge for the needy in his distress,
a shelter from the storm
   and a shade from the heat.
For the breath of the ruthless
   is like a storm driving against a wall
⁵   and like the heat of the desert.
You silence the uproar of foreigners;
   as heat is reduced by the shadow of a cloud,
   so the song of the ruthless is stilled.

⁶ On this mountain the LORD Almighty will prepare
   a feast of rich food for all peoples,
a banquet of aged wine—
   the best of meats and the finest of wines.
⁷ On this mountain he will destroy
   the shroud that enfolds all peoples,
the sheet that covers all nations;
⁸   he will swallow up death forever.
The Sovereign LORD will wipe away the tears
   from all faces;
he will remove the disgrace of his people
   from all the earth.
                              The LORD has spoken.

⁹ In that day they will say,

"Surely this is our God;
   we trusted in him, and he saved us.
This is the LORD, we trusted in him;
   let us rejoice and be glad in his salvation."

¹⁰ The hand of the LORD will rest on this mountain;
   but Moab will be trampled under him
   as straw is trampled down in the manure.
¹¹ They will spread out their hands in it,
   as a swimmer spreads out his hands to swim.
God will bring down their pride
   despite the cleverness*a* of their hands.
¹² He will bring down your high fortified walls
   and lay them low;
he will bring them down to the ground,
   to the very dust.

A Song of Praise

26 In that day this song will be sung in the land of Judah:

We have a strong city;
   God makes salvation
   its walls and ramparts.
² Open the gates
   that the righteous nation may enter,
   the nation that keeps faith.
³ You will keep in perfect peace
   him whose mind is steadfast,
   because he trusts in you.
⁴ Trust in the LORD forever,
   for the LORD, the LORD, is the Rock eternal.
⁵ He humbles those who dwell on high,
   he lays the lofty city low;

a 11 The meaning of the Hebrew for this word is uncertain.

he levels it to the ground
    and casts it down to the dust.
⁶ Feet trample it down—
    the feet of the oppressed,
    the footsteps of the poor.

⁷ The path of the righteous is level;
    O upright One, you make the way of the
      righteous smooth.
⁸ Yes, Lord, walking in the way of your laws,ᵃ
    we wait for you;
    your name and renown
    are the desire of our hearts.
⁹ My soul yearns for you in the night;
    in the morning my spirit longs for you.
When your judgments come upon the earth,
    the people of the world learn righteousness.
¹⁰ Though grace is shown to the wicked,
    they do not learn righteousness;
even in a land of uprightness they go on doing evil
    and regard not the majesty of the Lord.
¹¹ O Lord, your hand is lifted high,
    but they do not see it.
Let them see your zeal for your people and be put
    to shame;
    let the fire reserved for your enemies consume
      them.

¹² Lord, you establish peace for us;
    all that we have accomplished you have done
      for us.
¹³ O Lord, our God, other lords besides you have
    ruled over us,
    but your name alone do we honor.
¹⁴ They are now dead, they live no more;
    those departed spirits do not rise.
You punished them and brought them to ruin;
    you wiped out all memory of them.
¹⁵ You have enlarged the nation, O Lord;
    you have enlarged the nation.
You have gained glory for yourself;
    you have extended all the borders of the land.

¹⁶ Lord, they came to you in their distress;
    when you disciplined them,
    they could barely whisper a prayer.ᵇ
¹⁷ As a woman with child and about to give birth
    writhes and cries out in her pain,
    so were we in your presence, O Lord.
¹⁸ We were with child, we writhed in pain,
    but we gave birth to wind.
We have not brought salvation to the earth;
    we have not given birth to people of the world.

¹⁹ But your dead will live;
    their bodies will rise.
You who dwell in the dust,
    wake up and shout for joy.
Your dew is like the dew of the morning;
    the earth will give birth to her dead.

Rooted in Peace

ISAIAH 26:3

"Thou wilt keep him in perfect peace, whose mind is stayed on thee," reads the King James Version, hugging the shape of the original Hebrew metaphor. The image is that of a tent rope "stayed," or tied, to a long peg in the ground, securing the tent in the windy desert. That image was key to the Desert Fathers' practice of repeating a prayer phrase "in the heart" with each breath. The mind is trained to be "stayed" in God-awareness, rooted in God's peace. Choose a short phrase or a single word from this passage. Practice repeating that word or phrase for a few minutes and again whenever you remember it today. Return to it often in the days and weeks ahead.

See Meeting God in Prayer

ᵃ 8 Or *judgments*   ᵇ 16 The meaning of the Hebrew for this clause is uncertain.

The Dead Will Live

ISAIAH 26:19–21

"The soul comes from the dereliction and self-naughting of Calvary—from that unimaginable darkness of mind and loneliness of heart—into the world of . . . reality ablaze with God, which here and now awaits us . . . He shall roll back the heavy stone that shut us in that Cave of Illusion, the sepulchre of earthly imagination. Then we amazed and exultant shall come out to see before us a world renewed and yet the same: lit by that new colour known to those who see Creation with the eyes of God . . . Because [the soul] was not afraid to enter His darkness, lit only by the faint lantern of humble and self-giving love, now it is inundated with the Uncreated Light."

—EVELYN UNDERHILL,
The Spiral Way

²⁰Go, my people, enter your rooms
    and shut the doors behind you;
hide yourselves for a little while
    until his wrath has passed by.
²¹See, the LORD is coming out of his dwelling
    to punish the people of the earth for their sins.
The earth will disclose the blood shed upon her;
    she will conceal her slain no longer.

Deliverance of Israel

27 In that day,

the LORD will punish with his sword,
    his fierce, great and powerful sword,
Leviathan the gliding serpent,
    Leviathan the coiling serpent;
he will slay the monster of the sea.

²In that day—

"Sing about a fruitful vineyard:
³   I, the LORD, watch over it;
    I water it continually.
I guard it day and night
    so that no one may harm it.
⁴   I am not angry.
If only there were briers and thorns confronting
        me!
    I would march against them in battle;
    I would set them all on fire.
⁵Or else let them come to me for refuge;
    let them make peace with me,
    yes, let them make peace with me."

⁶In days to come Jacob will take root,
    Israel will bud and blossom
    and fill all the world with fruit.

⁷Has ⌊the LORD⌋ struck her
    as he struck down those who struck her?
Has she been killed
    as those were killed who killed her?
⁸By warfare^a and exile you contend with her—
    with his fierce blast he drives her out,
    as on a day the east wind blows.
⁹By this, then, will Jacob's guilt be atoned for,
    and this will be the full fruitage of the removal
        of his sin:
When he makes all the altar stones
    to be like chalk stones crushed to pieces,
no Asherah poles^b or incense altars
    will be left standing.
¹⁰The fortified city stands desolate,
    an abandoned settlement, forsaken like the
        desert;
there the calves graze,
    there they lie down;
    they strip its branches bare.
¹¹When its twigs are dry, they are broken off
    and women come and make fires with them.

---

^a 8 See Septuagint; the meaning of the Hebrew for this word is uncertain.
^b 9 That is, symbols of the goddess Asherah

For this is a people without understanding;
   so their Maker has no compassion on them,
   and their Creator shows them no favor.

¹²In that day the LORD will thresh from the flowing Euphrates*a* to the Wadi of Egypt, and you, O Israelites, will be gathered up one by one. ¹³And in that day a great trumpet will sound. Those who were perishing in Assyria and those who were exiled in Egypt will come and worship the LORD on the holy mountain in Jerusalem.

Woe to Ephraim

28 Woe to that wreath, the pride of Ephraim's drunkards,
   to the fading flower, his glorious beauty,
set on the head of a fertile valley—
   to that city, the pride of those laid low by wine!
² See, the Lord has one who is powerful and strong.
   Like a hailstorm and a destructive wind,
like a driving rain and a flooding downpour,
   he will throw it forcefully to the ground.
³ That wreath, the pride of Ephraim's drunkards,
   will be trampled underfoot.
⁴ That fading flower, his glorious beauty,
   set on the head of a fertile valley,
will be like a fig ripe before harvest—
   as soon as someone sees it and takes it in his
      hand,
   he swallows it.

⁵ In that day the LORD Almighty
   will be a glorious crown,
a beautiful wreath
   for the remnant of his people.
⁶ He will be a spirit of justice
   to him who sits in judgment,
a source of strength
   to those who turn back the battle at the gate.

⁷ And these also stagger from wine
   and reel from beer:
Priests and prophets stagger from beer
   and are befuddled with wine;
they reel from beer,
   they stagger when seeing visions,
   they stumble when rendering decisions.
⁸ All the tables are covered with vomit
   and there is not a spot without filth.

⁹ "Who is it he is trying to teach?
   To whom is he explaining his message?
To children weaned from their milk,
   to those just taken from the breast?
¹⁰ For it is:
   Do and do, do and do,
   rule on rule, rule on rule*b*;
   a little here, a little there."

¹¹ Very well then, with foreign lips and strange
      tongues
   God will speak to this people,

Divine Attributes

ISAIAH 28:5–6

In this passage, Isaiah ponders the attributes of God: glory, beauty, justice, love and strength. What aspects of God are especially important to you? Make your own list. Then consider where you see any of these attributes at work in people you know or in yourself. Say a short prayer of thanks such as, "I thank you for the spirit of glory at work in Brad's poetry." Use a one-sentence expression of thanksgiving, on the spot, when you encounter this aspect of God throughout the day.

See Meeting God in Everyday Life

---

a 12 Hebrew *River*   *b* 10 Hebrew / *sav lasav sav lasav / kav lakav kav lakav* (possibly meaningless sounds; perhaps a mimicking of the prophet's words); also in verse 13

Trust: The Sure Foundation

ISAIAH 28:16

Much more than a continuous state of mind, trusting is a repeated choice of risk in a relationship. What characteristics in others invite you to trust them? To distrust? What do you know, or hope, about God that calls you to trust the Lord in daily life? Name some experiences in which you trusted God. What were the results? Are there areas of your life where your trust in God is not very sure? Write a personal prayer to express your trust—and your need for more trust—in God: "O God, I trust you because _____. O God, I'm not sure how to trust you for _____." Keep adding, from time to time, to this prayer.

See Meeting God in Everyday Life

¹²to whom he said,
    "This is the resting place, let the weary rest";
and, "This is the place of repose"—
    but they would not listen.
¹³So then, the word of the LORD to them will become:
    Do and do, do and do,
    rule on rule, rule on rule;
    a little here, a little there—
so that they will go and fall backward,
    be injured and snared and captured.

¹⁴Therefore hear the word of the LORD, you scoffers
    who rule this people in Jerusalem.
¹⁵You boast, "We have entered into a covenant with death,
    with the grave*ᵃ* we have made an agreement.
When an overwhelming scourge sweeps by,
    it cannot touch us,
for we have made a lie our refuge
    and falsehood*ᵇ* our hiding place."

¹⁶So this is what the Sovereign LORD says:

"See, I lay a stone in Zion,
    a tested stone,
a precious cornerstone for a sure foundation;
    the one who trusts will never be dismayed.
¹⁷I will make justice the measuring line
    and righteousness the plumb line;
hail will sweep away your refuge, the lie,
    and water will overflow your hiding place.
¹⁸Your covenant with death will be annulled;
    your agreement with the grave will not stand.
When the overwhelming scourge sweeps by,
    you will be beaten down by it.
¹⁹As often as it comes it will carry you away;
    morning after morning, by day and by night,
    it will sweep through."

The understanding of this message
    will bring sheer terror.
²⁰The bed is too short to stretch out on,
    the blanket too narrow to wrap around you.
²¹The LORD will rise up as he did at Mount Perazim,
    he will rouse himself as in the Valley of Gibeon—
to do his work, his strange work,
    and perform his task, his alien task.
²²Now stop your mocking,
    or your chains will become heavier;
the Lord, the LORD Almighty, has told me
    of the destruction decreed against the whole land.

²³Listen and hear my voice;
    pay attention and hear what I say.
²⁴When a farmer plows for planting, does he plow continually?
    Does he keep on breaking up and harrowing the soil?

ᵃ 15 Hebrew *Sheol*; also in verse 18   *ᵇ 15* Or *false gods*

²⁵ When he has leveled the surface,
  does he not sow caraway and scatter cummin?
Does he not plant wheat in its place,ᵃ
  barley in its plot,ᵃ
  and spelt in its field?
²⁶ His God instructs him
  and teaches him the right way.

²⁷ Caraway is not threshed with a sledge,
  nor is a cartwheel rolled over cummin;
caraway is beaten out with a rod,
  and cummin with a stick.
²⁸ Grain must be ground to make bread;
  so one does not go on threshing it forever.
Though he drives the wheels of his threshing cart
    over it,
  his horses do not grind it.
²⁹ All this also comes from the Lᴏʀᴅ Almighty,
  wonderful in counsel and magnificent in
    wisdom.

Woe to David's City

29 Woe to you, Ariel, Ariel,
  the city where David settled!
Add year to year
  and let your cycle of festivals go on.
² Yet I will besiege Ariel;
  she will mourn and lament,
  she will be to me like an altar hearth.ᵇ
³ I will encamp against you all around;
  I will encircle you with towers
  and set up my siege works against you.
⁴ Brought low, you will speak from the ground;
  your speech will mumble out of the dust.
Your voice will come ghostlike from the earth;
  out of the dust your speech will whisper.

⁵ But your many enemies will become like fine
    dust,
  the ruthless hordes like blown chaff.
Suddenly, in an instant,
⁶ the Lᴏʀᴅ Almighty will come
with thunder and earthquake and great noise,
  with windstorm and tempest and flames of a
    devouring fire.
⁷ Then the hordes of all the nations that fight
    against Ariel,
  that attack her and her fortress and besiege
    her,
will be as it is with a dream,
  with a vision in the night—
⁸ as when a hungry man dreams that he is eating,
  but he awakens, and his hunger remains;
as when a thirsty man dreams that he is drinking,
  but he awakens faint, with his thirst
    unquenched.
So will it be with the hordes of all the nations
  that fight against Mount Zion.

God's Rebuke

ISAIAH 28:19–29

"When thou for sin rebukest
    man,
Forthwith he waxeth woe
    and wan:
Bitterness fills our bowels;
  all our hearts
  Pine, and decay,
  And drop away,
And carry with them
  th' other parts.

"But thou wilt sin and grief
    destroy;
That so the broken bones
    may joy,
And tune together in a well
    set song,
  Full of his praises,
  Who dead men raises,
Fractures well cur'd make us
  more strong."
            —GEORGE HERBERT,
                "Repentance"

ᵃ 25 The meaning of the Hebrew for this word is uncertain. ᵇ 2 The
Hebrew for *altar hearth* sounds like the Hebrew for *Ariel*.

The Prayer of the Heart

ISAIAH 29:13

Our hearts are the vital center of both desire and will and the wellspring of action. We often rationalize the truth in our hearts by creating false self-images with our "lips." "Putting the mind into the heart" is a traditional Eastern Orthodox practice meant to heal this split. Sit quietly, focusing in the very center of your chest, imagining an inner space or heart-cave. You may find it helpful to imagine this area filled with the light of God. Or with each breath, repeat a name of God. Imagine that your conscious awareness settles down inside this heart-space, surrounded by God's light or the sacred divine name. Practice letting your prayers come from this heart-space.

See *Meeting God in Prayer*

⁹ Be stunned and amazed,
    blind yourselves and be sightless;
be drunk, but not from wine,
    stagger, but not from beer.
¹⁰ The LORD has brought over you a deep sleep:
    He has sealed your eyes (the prophets);
    he has covered your heads (the seers).

¹¹ For you this whole vision is nothing but words sealed in a scroll. And if you give the scroll to someone who can read, and say to him, "Read this, please," he will answer, "I can't; it is sealed." ¹² Or if you give the scroll to someone who cannot read, and say, "Read this, please," he will answer, "I don't know how to read."

¹³ The Lord says:

"These people come near to me with their mouth
    and honor me with their lips,
    but their hearts are far from me.
Their worship of me
    is made up only of rules taught by men.ᵃ
¹⁴ Therefore once more I will astound these people
    with wonder upon wonder;
    the wisdom of the wise will perish,
    the intelligence of the intelligent will vanish."
¹⁵ Woe to those who go to great depths
    to hide their plans from the LORD,
who do their work in darkness and think,
    "Who sees us? Who will know?"
¹⁶ You turn things upside down,
    as if the potter were thought to be like the clay!
Shall what is formed say to him who formed it,
    "He did not make me"?
Can the pot say of the potter,
    "He knows nothing"?

¹⁷ In a very short time, will not Lebanon be turned
        into a fertile field
    and the fertile field seem like a forest?
¹⁸ In that day the deaf will hear the words of the
        scroll,
    and out of gloom and darkness
    the eyes of the blind will see.
¹⁹ Once more the humble will rejoice in the LORD;
    the needy will rejoice in the Holy One of Israel.
²⁰ The ruthless will vanish,
    the mockers will disappear,
    and all who have an eye for evil will be cut
        down—
²¹ those who with a word make a man out to be
        guilty,
    who ensnare the defender in court
    and with false testimony deprive the innocent
        of justice.

²² Therefore this is what the LORD, who redeemed Abraham, says to the house of Jacob:

"No longer will Jacob be ashamed;
    no longer will their faces grow pale.

ᵃ 13 Hebrew; Septuagint *They worship me in vain; / their teachings are but rules taught by men*

²³ When they see among them their children,
　　the work of my hands,
　they will keep my name holy;
　　they will acknowledge the holiness of the Holy
　　　　One of Jacob,
　　and will stand in awe of the God of Israel.
²⁴ Those who are wayward in spirit will gain
　　　understanding;
　　those who complain will accept instruction."

Woe to the Obstinate Nation

30 "Woe to the obstinate children,"
　　declares the LORD,
　"to those who carry out plans that are not mine,
　　forming an alliance, but not by my Spirit,
　　heaping sin upon sin;
² who go down to Egypt
　　without consulting me;
　who look for help to Pharaoh's protection,
　　to Egypt's shade for refuge.
³ But Pharaoh's protection will be to your shame,
　　Egypt's shade will bring you disgrace.
⁴ Though they have officials in Zoan
　　and their envoys have arrived in Hanes,
⁵ everyone will be put to shame
　　because of a people useless to them,
　who bring neither help nor advantage,
　　but only shame and disgrace."

⁶ An oracle concerning the animals of the Negev:

　Through a land of hardship and distress,
　　of lions and lionesses,
　　of adders and darting snakes,
　the envoys carry their riches on donkeys' backs,
　　their treasures on the humps of camels,
　to that unprofitable nation,
⁷ 　to Egypt, whose help is utterly useless.
　Therefore I call her
　　Rahab the Do-Nothing.

⁸ Go now, write it on a tablet for them,
　　inscribe it on a scroll,
　that for the days to come
　　it may be an everlasting witness.
⁹ These are rebellious people, deceitful children,
　　children unwilling to listen to the LORD's
　　　instruction.
¹⁰ They say to the seers,
　　"See no more visions!"
　and to the prophets,
　　"Give us no more visions of what is right!
　Tell us pleasant things,
　　prophesy illusions.
¹¹ Leave this way,
　　get off this path,
　and stop confronting us
　　with the Holy One of Israel!"

¹² Therefore, this is what the Holy One of Israel says:

　"Because you have rejected this message,
　　relied on oppression

We Are the Clay

ISAIAH 29:16

Clay is more than merely inert matter. It often seems to have a life and integrity all its own. All potters know that they must form a relationship with the pliable, crystalline clay to shape it into durable, strong vessels. Find some real clay and practice feeling both its innate integrity and your ability to mold it into various shapes. Notice how the clay becomes more pliable and "alive" the more you work with it. Ponder how this relationship is like the one you have with the divine potter. Consider the various means or tools God uses to shape your spiritual life. How do those means change you and bring out the best aspects of your God-given nature?

See Meeting God in Scripture

937

Remembering to Trust

ISAIAH 30:15

Israel refuses to cultivate the habit of trusting in God's faithful presence in all circumstances. Trust can be strengthened by the practice of "remembering God" in the midst of new or difficult situations. Personalizing a sacred phrase and committing it to heart can be such a reminder. Introduce one of these phrases—"In repentance and rest is your salvation" or "In quietness and trust is your strength"—into a quiet time of meditative prayer, repeating the phrase several times. As you pray, review any situation you might face that challenges your ability to trust in God, in your God-given abilities or in other people.

See Meeting God in Everyday Life

and depended on deceit,
¹³this sin will become for you
    like a high wall, cracked and bulging,
    that collapses suddenly, in an instant.
¹⁴It will break in pieces like pottery,
    shattered so mercilessly
that among its pieces not a fragment will be
        found
    for taking coals from a hearth
    or scooping water out of a cistern."

¹⁵This is what the Sovereign Lord, the Holy One of Israel, says:

"In repentance and rest is your salvation,
    in quietness and trust is your strength,
    but you would have none of it.
¹⁶You said, 'No, we will flee on horses.'
    Therefore you will flee!
You said, 'We will ride off on swift horses.'
    Therefore your pursuers will be swift!
¹⁷A thousand will flee
    at the threat of one;
at the threat of five
    you will all flee away,
till you are left
    like a flagstaff on a mountaintop,
    like a banner on a hill."

¹⁸Yet the Lord longs to be gracious to you;
    he rises to show you compassion.
For the Lord is a God of justice.
    Blessed are all who wait for him!

¹⁹O people of Zion, who live in Jerusalem, you will weep no more. How gracious he will be when you cry for help! As soon as he hears, he will answer you. ²⁰Although the Lord gives you the bread of adversity and the water of affliction, your teachers will be hidden no more; with your own eyes you will see them. ²¹Whether you turn to the right or to the left, your ears will hear a voice behind you, saying, "This is the way; walk in it." ²²Then you will defile your idols overlaid with silver and your images covered with gold; you will throw them away like a menstrual cloth and say to them, "Away with you!"

²³He will also send you rain for the seed you sow in the ground, and the food that comes from the land will be rich and plentiful. In that day your cattle will graze in broad meadows. ²⁴The oxen and donkeys that work the soil will eat fodder and mash, spread out with fork and shovel. ²⁵In the day of great slaughter, when the towers fall, streams of water will flow on every high mountain and every lofty hill. ²⁶The moon will shine like the sun, and the sunlight will be seven times brighter, like the light of seven full days, when the Lord binds up the bruises of his people and heals the wounds he inflicted.

²⁷See, the Name of the Lord comes from afar,
    with burning anger and dense clouds of smoke;
his lips are full of wrath,
    and his tongue is a consuming fire.
²⁸His breath is like a rushing torrent,

rising up to the neck.
He shakes the nations in the sieve of destruction;
   he places in the jaws of the peoples
   a bit that leads them astray.
²⁹ And you will sing
   as on the night you celebrate a holy festival;
your hearts will rejoice
   as when people go up with flutes
to the mountain of the Lord,
   to the Rock of Israel.
³⁰ The Lord will cause men to hear his majestic voice
   and will make them see his arm coming down
with raging anger and consuming fire,
   with cloudburst, thunderstorm and hail.
³¹ The voice of the Lord will shatter Assyria;
   with his scepter he will strike them down.
³² Every stroke the Lord lays on them
   with his punishing rod
will be to the music of tambourines and harps,
   as he fights them in battle with the blows of his
     arm.
³³ Topheth has long been prepared;
   it has been made ready for the king.
Its fire pit has been made deep and wide,
   with an abundance of fire and wood;
the breath of the Lord,
   like a stream of burning sulfur,
   sets it ablaze.

Woe to Those Who Rely on Egypt

31 Woe to those who go down to Egypt for help,
   who rely on horses,
who trust in the multitude of their chariots
   and in the great strength of their horsemen,
but do not look to the Holy One of Israel,
   or seek help from the Lord.
² Yet he too is wise and can bring disaster;
   he does not take back his words.
He will rise up against the house of the wicked,
   against those who help evildoers.
³ But the Egyptians are men and not God;
   their horses are flesh and not spirit.
When the Lord stretches out his hand,
   he who helps will stumble,
   he who is helped will fall;
   both will perish together.

⁴ This is what the Lord says to me:

"As a lion growls,
   a great lion over his prey—
and though a whole band of shepherds
   is called together against him,
he is not frightened by their shouts
   or disturbed by their clamor—
so the Lord Almighty will come down
   to do battle on Mount Zion and on its heights.
⁵ Like birds hovering overhead,
   the Lord Almighty will shield Jerusalem;
he will shield it and deliver it,
   he will 'pass over' it and will rescue it."

The Divine Teacher

ISAIAH 30:19–30

God is our ultimate teacher and guide who uses many methods to instruct us. Are there lessons God seems to be repeating so that you would learn them well? How is God instructing you right now, in this period of your life? Take time to remember, with love and with thanksgiving, some of the people who have been God's agents in teaching you. Consider also those who have taught you by the difficulty or opposition they have brought into your life, thereby helping you clarify your values and find new strength in dealing with those difficulties. Can you give thanks for these occasions of learning too? Consider writing a note of thanks as soon as possible to one of the people God has used to teach you.

See *Meeting God in Community*

God Is Like . . .

ISAIAH 31:4–9

Animal similes are often used in Scripture to communicate God's character and qualities. God is compared to an eagle (Deuteronomy 32:11), a lamb (John 1:29), and even the snake of healing and wisdom (Numbers 21:9; John 3:14). Isaiah uses the simile of a lion to describe God's fearlessness and power as the defender of Israel and that of a great bird to describe God's soaring and overarching protection. Choose one of these images to ponder. Draw or find a picture of this animal, observing the qualities that characterize it. Imagine that God is with you, embodying one of these qualities. Ask God to help you manifest this quality toward others.

See Meeting God in the Created Order

⁶Return to him you have so greatly revolted against, O Israelites. ⁷For in that day every one of you will reject the idols of silver and gold your sinful hands have made.

⁸"Assyria will fall by a sword that is not of man;
    a sword, not of mortals, will devour them.
They will flee before the sword
    and their young men will be put to forced labor.
⁹Their stronghold will fall because of terror;
    at sight of the battle standard their
        commanders will panic,"
declares the LORD,
    whose fire is in Zion,
    whose furnace is in Jerusalem.

The Kingdom of Righteousness

32 See, a king will reign in righteousness
    and rulers will rule with justice.
²Each man will be like a shelter from the wind
    and a refuge from the storm,
like streams of water in the desert
    and the shadow of a great rock in a thirsty
        land.
³Then the eyes of those who see will no longer be
        closed,
    and the ears of those who hear will listen.
⁴The mind of the rash will know and understand,
    and the stammering tongue will be fluent and
        clear.
⁵No longer will the fool be called noble
    nor the scoundrel be highly respected.
⁶For the fool speaks folly,
    his mind is busy with evil:
He practices ungodliness
    and spreads error concerning the LORD;
the hungry he leaves empty
    and from the thirsty he withholds water.
⁷The scoundrel's methods are wicked,
    he makes up evil schemes
to destroy the poor with lies,
    even when the plea of the needy is just.
⁸But the noble man makes noble plans,
    and by noble deeds he stands.

The Women of Jerusalem

⁹You women who are so complacent,
    rise up and listen to me;
you daughters who feel secure,
    hear what I have to say!
¹⁰In little more than a year
    you who feel secure will tremble;
the grape harvest will fail,
    and the harvest of fruit will not come.
¹¹Tremble, you complacent women;
    shudder, you daughters who feel secure!
Strip off your clothes,
    put sackcloth around your waists.
¹²Beat your breasts for the pleasant fields,
    for the fruitful vines
¹³and for the land of my people,

a land overgrown with thorns and briers—
yes, mourn for all houses of merriment
and for this city of revelry.
¹⁴ The fortress will be abandoned,
the noisy city deserted;
citadel and watchtower will become a wasteland
forever,
the delight of donkeys, a pasture for flocks,
¹⁵ till the Spirit is poured upon us from on high,
and the desert becomes a fertile field,
and the fertile field seems like a forest.
¹⁶ Justice will dwell in the desert
and righteousness live in the fertile field.
¹⁷ The fruit of righteousness will be peace;
the effect of righteousness will be quietness
and confidence forever.
¹⁸ My people will live in peaceful dwelling places,
in secure homes,
in undisturbed places of rest.
¹⁹ Though hail flattens the forest
and the city is leveled completely,
²⁰ how blessed you will be,
sowing your seed by every stream,
and letting your cattle and donkeys range free.

Distress and Help

33 Woe to you, O destroyer,
you who have not been destroyed!
Woe to you, O traitor,
you who have not been betrayed!
When you stop destroying,
you will be destroyed;
when you stop betraying,
you will be betrayed.

² O LORD, be gracious to us;
we long for you.
Be our strength every morning,
our salvation in time of distress.
³ At the thunder of your voice, the peoples flee;
when you rise up, the nations scatter.
⁴ Your plunder, O nations, is harvested as by young
locusts;
like a swarm of locusts men pounce on it.

⁵ The LORD is exalted, for he dwells on high;
he will fill Zion with justice and righteousness.
⁶ He will be the sure foundation for your times,
a rich store of salvation and wisdom and
knowledge;
the fear of the LORD is the key to this treasure.ᵃ

⁷ Look, their brave men cry aloud in the streets;
the envoys of peace weep bitterly.
⁸ The highways are deserted,
no travelers are on the roads.
The treaty is broken,
its witnessesᵇ are despised,
no one is respected.

"Peaceful Dwelling Places"

ISAIAH 32:14–20

The prophet envisions how
God's people will return to a
life of a renewed connection to
creation and to the Spirit—a return that leads them to "quietness and confidence." What
natural landscape helps you
shed the stress of an overbur-
dened life, renew the wholeness
of your soul and body, and find
a renewed sense of the presence of God's glory? Visit that
place now in your heart, imagining its sights and sounds with
all your inner senses. Rest in
this remembered landscape,
opening heart and mind to God
in trustful prayer. Know that
this place—your sanctuary—is
always available.

"The King in His Beauty"

ISAIAH 33:17

"But still I lay awake, and then our Lord opened my spiritual eyes, and showed me my soul in the midst of my heart. I saw my soul as wide as if it were a kingdom, and from the state which I saw in it, it seemed to me as if it were a fine city. In the midst of this city sits our Lord Jesus, true God and true man, a handsome person and tall, honourable, the greatest lord. And I saw him splendidly clad in honours. He sits erect there in the soul, in peace and rest . . . And my soul is bless-edly occupied by the divinity, sovereign power, sovereign wis-dom, sovereign goodness."

—JULIAN OF NORWICH,
Showings

9 The land mourns[a] and wastes away,
 Lebanon is ashamed and withers;
 Sharon is like the Arabah,
 and Bashan and Carmel drop their leaves.

10 "Now will I arise," says the LORD.
 "Now will I be exalted;
 now will I be lifted up.
11 You conceive chaff,
 you give birth to straw;
 your breath is a fire that consumes you.
12 The peoples will be burned as if to lime;
 like cut thornbushes they will be set ablaze."

13 You who are far away, hear what I have done;
 you who are near, acknowledge my power!
14 The sinners in Zion are terrified;
 trembling grips the godless:
 "Who of us can dwell with the consuming fire?
 Who of us can dwell with everlasting burning?"
15 He who walks righteously
 and speaks what is right,
 who rejects gain from extortion
 and keeps his hand from accepting bribes,
 who stops his ears against plots of murder
 and shuts his eyes against contemplating evil—
16 this is the man who will dwell on the heights,
 whose refuge will be the mountain fortress.
 His bread will be supplied,
 and water will not fail him.

17 Your eyes will see the king in his beauty
 and view a land that stretches afar.
18 In your thoughts you will ponder the former
 terror:
 "Where is that chief officer?
 Where is the one who took the revenue?
 Where is the officer in charge of the towers?"
19 You will see those arrogant people no more,
 those people of an obscure speech,
 with their strange, incomprehensible tongue.

20 Look upon Zion, the city of our festivals;
 your eyes will see Jerusalem,
 a peaceful abode, a tent that will not be moved;
 its stakes will never be pulled up,
 nor any of its ropes broken.
21 There the LORD will be our Mighty One.
 It will be like a place of broad rivers and
 streams.
 No galley with oars will ride them,
 no mighty ship will sail them.
22 For the LORD is our judge,
 the LORD is our lawgiver,
 the LORD is our king;
 it is he who will save us.

23 Your rigging hangs loose:
 The mast is not held secure,
 the sail is not spread.
 Then an abundance of spoils will be divided

a 9 Or *dries up*

and even the lame will carry off plunder.
²⁴ No one living in Zion will say, "I am ill";
    and the sins of those who dwell there will be
      forgiven.

Judgment Against the Nations

34 Come near, you nations, and listen;
    pay attention, you peoples!
Let the earth hear, and all that is in it,
    the world, and all that comes out of it!
² The LORD is angry with all nations;
    his wrath is upon all their armies.
He will totally destroy[a] them,
    he will give them over to slaughter.
³ Their slain will be thrown out,
    their dead bodies will send up a stench;
    the mountains will be soaked with their blood.
⁴ All the stars of the heavens will be dissolved
    and the sky rolled up like a scroll;
all the starry host will fall
    like withered leaves from the vine,
    like shriveled figs from the fig tree.

⁵ My sword has drunk its fill in the heavens;
    see, it descends in judgment on Edom,
    the people I have totally destroyed.
⁶ The sword of the LORD is bathed in blood,
    it is covered with fat—
the blood of lambs and goats,
    fat from the kidneys of rams.
For the LORD has a sacrifice in Bozrah
    and a great slaughter in Edom.
⁷ And the wild oxen will fall with them,
    the bull calves and the great bulls.
Their land will be drenched with blood,
    and the dust will be soaked with fat.

⁸ For the LORD has a day of vengeance,
    a year of retribution, to uphold Zion's cause.
⁹ Edom's streams will be turned into pitch,
    her dust into burning sulfur;
    her land will become blazing pitch!
¹⁰ It will not be quenched night and day;
    its smoke will rise forever.
From generation to generation it will lie desolate;
    no one will ever pass through it again.
¹¹ The desert owl[b] and screech owl[b] will possess it;
    the great owl[b] and the raven will nest there.
God will stretch out over Edom
    the measuring line of chaos
    and the plumb line of desolation.
¹² Her nobles will have nothing there to be called a
      kingdom,
    all her princes will vanish away.
¹³ Thorns will overrun her citadels,
    nettles and brambles her strongholds.
She will become a haunt for jackals,
    a home for owls.

The Place

ISAIAH 33:21–24

In Judaism, "the Place" is one of God's names, for God is seen as the Place in which everything else lives: "In him we live and move and have our being" (Acts 17:28). Try this traditional meditation: As you sit quietly, become aware of the space immediately around you. Become aware of your breathing as a gift of God. Now imaginatively expand your awareness beyond the confines of this space—imagine breathing in the air from the rest of the building. From the outside environment. From the city or town. From the surrounding countryside. Then breathe in from the whole region, country, planet—and then from God's infinite space. Breathe in the breath of God, "the Place" of all existence.

See Meeting God in Prayer

---

[a] 2 The Hebrew term refers to the irrevocable giving over of things or persons to the LORD, often by totally destroying them; also in verse 5.
[b] 11 The precise identification of these birds is uncertain.

The Place of the Wild

ISAIAH 34:11–17

Oppressive humanity, symbolized by Edom, gives way to an entire ecosystem filled with wildlife. In this passage, which contains one of Scripture's most extensive lists of animals, that ecosystem symbolizes the purification of the land from human sin—and the land subsequently brims with new life.

What are your attitudes toward the animals God has created? Do you view them as a blessed wonder or a cursed nuisance? What place is given to wild birds and animals in your neighborhood? What can you do to provide for them and offer them protection? Take a walk with keen eyes and an awakened heart, noticing with thanksgiving each of God's creatures you encounter. Look at them as God's creatures. Let your prayers include all creatures imperiled by human heedlessness and greed.

See Meeting God in the Created Order

¹⁴ Desert creatures will meet with hyenas,
　　and wild goats will bleat to each other;
　there the night creatures will also repose
　　and find for themselves places of rest.
¹⁵ The owl will nest there and lay eggs,
　　she will hatch them, and care for her young
　　　under the shadow of her wings;
　there also the falcons will gather,
　　each with its mate.

¹⁶ Look in the scroll of the LORD and read:

　None of these will be missing,
　　not one will lack her mate.
　For it is his mouth that has given the order,
　　and his Spirit will gather them together.
¹⁷ He allots their portions;
　　his hand distributes them by measure.
　They will possess it forever
　　and dwell there from generation to generation.

Joy of the Redeemed

35 The desert and the parched land will be glad;
　　the wilderness will rejoice and blossom.
　Like the crocus, ²it will burst into bloom;
　　it will rejoice greatly and shout for joy.
　The glory of Lebanon will be given to it,
　　the splendor of Carmel and Sharon;
　they will see the glory of the LORD,
　　the splendor of our God.

³ Strengthen the feeble hands,
　　steady the knees that give way;
⁴ say to those with fearful hearts,
　　"Be strong, do not fear;
　your God will come,
　　he will come with vengeance;
　with divine retribution
　　he will come to save you."

⁵ Then will the eyes of the blind be opened
　　and the ears of the deaf unstopped.
⁶ Then will the lame leap like a deer,
　　and the mute tongue shout for joy.
　Water will gush forth in the wilderness
　　and streams in the desert.
⁷ The burning sand will become a pool,
　　the thirsty ground bubbling springs.
　In the haunts where jackals once lay,
　　grass and reeds and papyrus will grow.

⁸ And a highway will be there;
　　it will be called the Way of Holiness.
　The unclean will not journey on it;
　　it will be for those who walk in that Way;
　　wicked fools will not go about on it.ᵃ
⁹ No lion will be there,
　　nor will any ferocious beast get up on it;
　　they will not be found there.
　But only the redeemed will walk there,
¹⁰　and the ransomed of the LORD will return.

ᵃ 8 Or / the simple will not stray from it

They will enter Zion with singing;
> everlasting joy will crown their heads.
Gladness and joy will overtake them,
> and sorrow and sighing will flee away.

Sennacherib Threatens Jerusalem

36 In the fourteenth year of King Hezekiah's reign, Sennacherib king of Assyria attacked all the fortified cities of Judah and captured them. ²Then the king of Assyria sent his field commander with a large army from Lachish to King Hezekiah at Jerusalem. When the commander stopped at the aqueduct of the Upper Pool, on the road to the Washerman's Field, ³Eliakim son of Hilkiah the palace administrator, Shebna the secretary, and Joah son of Asaph the recorder went out to him.

⁴The field commander said to them, "Tell Hezekiah,

" 'This is what the great king, the king of Assyria, says: On what are you basing this confidence of yours? ⁵You say you have strategy and military strength—but you speak only empty words. On whom are you depending, that you rebel against me? ⁶Look now, you are depending on Egypt, that splintered reed of a staff, which pierces a man's hand and wounds him if he leans on it! Such is Pharaoh king of Egypt to all who depend on him. ⁷And if you say to me, "We are depending on the LORD our God"—isn't he the one whose high places and altars Hezekiah removed, saying to Judah and Jerusalem, "You must worship before this altar"?

⁸" 'Come now, make a bargain with my master, the king of Assyria: I will give you two thousand horses—if you can put riders on them! ⁹How then can you repulse one officer of the least of my master's officials, even though you are depending on Egypt for chariots and horsemen? ¹⁰Furthermore, have I come to attack and destroy this land without the LORD? The LORD himself told me to march against this country and destroy it.' "

¹¹Then Eliakim, Shebna and Joah said to the field commander, "Please speak to your servants in Aramaic, since we understand it. Don't speak to us in Hebrew in the hearing of the people on the wall."

¹²But the commander replied, "Was it only to your master and you that my master sent me to say these things, and not to the men sitting on the wall—who, like you, will have to eat their own filth and drink their own urine?"

¹³Then the commander stood and called out in Hebrew, "Hear the words of the great king, the king of Assyria! ¹⁴This is what the king says: Do not let Hezekiah deceive you. He cannot deliver you! ¹⁵Do not let Hezekiah persuade you to trust in the LORD when he says, 'The LORD will surely deliver us; this city will not be given into the hand of the king of Assyria.'

¹⁶"Do not listen to Hezekiah. This is what the king of Assyria says: Make peace with me and come out to me. Then every one of you will eat from his own vine and fig tree and drink water from his own cistern, ¹⁷until I come and take you to a land like your own—a land of grain and new wine, a land of bread and vineyards.

Restoration and Healing

ISAIAH 35:4–10

Practice *lectio divina* ("divine reading") with this picture of God's saving activity. What words or phrases seem to need emphasis as you slowly read the entire section aloud? What comes to mind as you choose one word or phrase and spend some time brooding on it? What thoughts, feelings, memories or associations emerge? What might God be trying to say to you through this cluster of associations? Express in prayer your heartfelt response to what you have seen.

See Meeting God in Scripture

The Field Commander

ISAIAH 36:11–22

Who are the "field commanders" in your life—people who by their words or behavior threaten to undermine your trust in God? Who is enticing you to compromise your values? What are the situations where trust in God seems to elude you? In what areas do doubts arise about divine grace? Health? Money? Personal confrontations? As you ponder one or more of these situations, repeat Isaiah's words: "This is what the LORD says: Do not be afraid" (37:6). Ask the Spirit to show you ways to trust God in these encounters.

See Meeting God in Everyday Life

¹⁸"Do not let Hezekiah mislead you when he says, 'The LORD will deliver us.' Has the god of any nation ever delivered his land from the hand of the king of Assyria? ¹⁹Where are the gods of Hamath and Arpad? Where are the gods of Sepharvaim? Have they rescued Samaria from my hand? ²⁰Who of all the gods of these countries has been able to save his land from me? How then can the LORD deliver Jerusalem from my hand?"

²¹But the people remained silent and said nothing in reply, because the king had commanded, "Do not answer him."

²²Then Eliakim son of Hilkiah the palace administrator, Shebna the secretary, and Joah son of Asaph the recorder went to Hezekiah, with their clothes torn, and told him what the field commander had said.

Jerusalem's Deliverance Foretold

37 When King Hezekiah heard this, he tore his clothes and put on sackcloth and went into the temple of the LORD. ²He sent Eliakim the palace administrator, Shebna the secretary, and the leading priests, all wearing sackcloth, to the prophet Isaiah son of Amoz. ³They told him, "This is what Hezekiah says: This day is a day of distress and rebuke and disgrace, as when children come to the point of birth and there is no strength to deliver them. ⁴It may be that the LORD your God will hear the words of the field commander, whom his master, the king of Assyria, has sent to ridicule the living God, and that he will rebuke him for the words the LORD your God has heard. Therefore pray for the remnant that still survives."

⁵When King Hezekiah's officials came to Isaiah, ⁶Isaiah said to them, "Tell your master, 'This is what the LORD says: Do not be afraid of what you have heard—those words with which the underlings of the king of Assyria have blasphemed me. ⁷Listen! I am going to put a spirit in him so that when he hears a certain report, he will return to his own country, and there I will have him cut down with the sword.'"

⁸When the field commander heard that the king of Assyria had left Lachish, he withdrew and found the king fighting against Libnah.

⁹Now Sennacherib received a report that Tirhakah, the Cushite[a] king ⌊of Egypt⌋, was marching out to fight against him. When he heard it, he sent messengers to Hezekiah with this word: ¹⁰"Say to Hezekiah king of Judah: Do not let the god you depend on deceive you when he says, 'Jerusalem will not be handed over to the king of Assyria.' ¹¹Surely you have heard what the kings of Assyria have done to all the countries, destroying them completely. And will you be delivered? ¹²Did the gods of the nations that were destroyed by my forefathers deliver them—the gods of Gozan, Haran, Rezeph and the people of Eden who were in Tel Assar? ¹³Where is the king of Hamath, the king of Arpad, the king of the city of Sepharvaim, or of Hena or Ivvah?"

Hezekiah's Prayer

¹⁴Hezekiah received the letter from the messengers and read it. Then he went up to the temple of the LORD and

a 9 That is, from the upper Nile region

spread it out before the LORD. [15]And Hezekiah prayed to the LORD: [16]"O LORD Almighty, God of Israel, enthroned between the cherubim, you alone are God over all the kingdoms of the earth. You have made heaven and earth. [17]Give ear, O LORD, and hear; open your eyes, O LORD, and see; listen to all the words Sennacherib has sent to insult the living God.

[18]"It is true, O LORD, that the Assyrian kings have laid waste all these peoples and their lands. [19]They have thrown their gods into the fire and destroyed them, for they were not gods but only wood and stone, fashioned by human hands. [20]Now, O LORD our God, deliver us from his hand, so that all kingdoms on earth may know that you alone, O LORD, are God.[a]"

Sennacherib's Fall

[21]Then Isaiah son of Amoz sent a message to Hezekiah: "This is what the LORD, the God of Israel, says: Because you have prayed to me concerning Sennacherib king of Assyria, [22]this is the word the LORD has spoken against him:

"The Virgin Daughter of Zion
    despises and mocks you.
The Daughter of Jerusalem
    tosses her head as you flee.
[23]Who is it you have insulted and blasphemed?
    Against whom have you raised your voice
and lifted your eyes in pride?
    Against the Holy One of Israel!
[24]By your messengers
    you have heaped insults on the Lord.
And you have said,
    'With my many chariots
I have ascended the heights of the mountains,
    the utmost heights of Lebanon.
I have cut down its tallest cedars,
    the choicest of its pines.
I have reached its remotest heights,
    the finest of its forests.
[25]I have dug wells in foreign lands[b]
    and drunk the water there.
With the soles of my feet
    I have dried up all the streams of Egypt.'

[26]"Have you not heard?
    Long ago I ordained it.
In days of old I planned it;
    now I have brought it to pass,
that you have turned fortified cities
    into piles of stone.
[27]Their people, drained of power,
    are dismayed and put to shame.
They are like plants in the field,
    like tender green shoots,
like grass sprouting on the roof,
    scorched[c] before it grows up.

The Heavenly Hosts

ISAIAH 37:16

"O glorious living light,
    which lives in Divinity!
Angels who fix your eyes
    with ardent desire . . .
On him with Whom your
    desires can never be
    sated!
O glorious joy to live in
    your form and nature!

"O angels with shining faces
    who guard the people,
O ye archangels, who take
    just souls into Heaven,
And you, O virtues and
    powers, O principalities,
. . . dominions and
    thrones . . .

"And you, cherubim and
    seraphim, seal of God's
    secrets,
Praise be to you all, who
    behold the heart of the
    Father,
And see the Ancient of Days
    spring forth in the
    fountain,
And His inner power appear
    like a face from His
    heart."

—HILDEGARD OF BINGEN,
"Symphony of the Blessed"

See *Meeting God in Worship*

---

[a] 20 Dead Sea Scrolls (see also 2 Kings 19:19); Masoretic Text *alone are the LORD*   [b] 25 Dead Sea Scrolls (see also 2 Kings 19:24); Masoretic Text does not have *in foreign lands.*   [c] 27 Some manuscripts of the Masoretic Text, Dead Sea Scrolls and some Septuagint manuscripts (see also 2 Kings 19:26); most manuscripts of the Masoretic Text *roof / and terraced fields*

"For the Sake of . . ."

ISAIAH 37:35

Scripture says that God performs deeds "for the sake of David" or "for the sake of Christ" or "for the sake of God's own mercy" or "name" or "praise," showing us that God is moved to do good for the well-being of another or for the glory of his own attributes.

Think of three or four good things, however small, you have done recently. Why did you perform those actions? For whose sake? What might you have done for the sake of someone's good opinion of you? Which attributes of God awaken your sense of praise? What deed can you perform today for the sake of that facet of God?

See Meeting God in Service

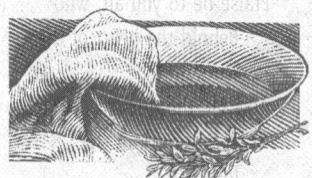

²⁸ "But I know where you stay
and when you come and go
and how you rage against me.
²⁹ Because you rage against me
and because your insolence has reached my
ears,
I will put my hook in your nose
and my bit in your mouth,
and I will make you return
by the way you came.

³⁰ "This will be the sign for you, O Hezekiah:

"This year you will eat what grows by itself,
and the second year what springs from that.
But in the third year sow and reap,
plant vineyards and eat their fruit.
³¹ Once more a remnant of the house of Judah
will take root below and bear fruit above.
³² For out of Jerusalem will come a remnant,
and out of Mount Zion a band of survivors.
The zeal of the LORD Almighty
will accomplish this.

³³ "Therefore this is what the LORD says concerning the king of Assyria:

"He will not enter this city
or shoot an arrow here.
He will not come before it with shield
or build a siege ramp against it.
³⁴ By the way that he came he will return;
he will not enter this city,"

declares the LORD.

³⁵ "I will defend this city and save it,
for my sake and for the sake of David my
servant!"

³⁶ Then the angel of the LORD went out and put to death a hundred and eighty-five thousand men in the Assyrian camp. When the people got up the next morning—there were all the dead bodies! ³⁷ So Sennacherib king of Assyria broke camp and withdrew. He returned to Nineveh and stayed there.

³⁸ One day, while he was worshiping in the temple of his god Nisroch, his sons Adrammelech and Sharezer cut him down with the sword, and they escaped to the land of Ararat. And Esarhaddon his son succeeded him as king.

Hezekiah's Illness

38 In those days Hezekiah became ill and was at the point of death. The prophet Isaiah son of Amoz went to him and said, "This is what the LORD says: Put your house in order, because you are going to die; you will not recover."

² Hezekiah turned his face to the wall and prayed to the LORD, ³ "Remember, O LORD, how I have walked before you faithfully and with wholehearted devotion and have done what is good in your eyes." And Hezekiah wept bitterly.

⁴ Then the word of the LORD came to Isaiah: ⁵ "Go and tell Hezekiah, 'This is what the LORD, the God of your father David, says: I have heard your prayer and seen your tears; I will add fifteen years to your life. ⁶ And I will deliver you

and this city from the hand of the king of Assyria. I will defend this city.

⁷" 'This is the LORD's sign to you that the LORD will do what he has promised: ⁸I will make the shadow cast by the sun go back the ten steps it has gone down on the stairway of Ahaz.' " So the sunlight went back the ten steps it had gone down.

⁹A writing of Hezekiah king of Judah after his illness and recovery:

¹⁰I said, "In the prime of my life
    must I go through the gates of death*ᵃ*
    and be robbed of the rest of my years?"
¹¹I said, "I will not again see the LORD,
    the LORD, in the land of the living;
no longer will I look on mankind,
    or be with those who now dwell in this
      world.*ᵇ*
¹²Like a shepherd's tent my house
    has been pulled down and taken from me.
Like a weaver I have rolled up my life,
    and he has cut me off from the loom;
    day and night you made an end of me.
¹³I waited patiently till dawn,
    but like a lion he broke all my bones;
    day and night you made an end of me.
¹⁴I cried like a swift or thrush,
    I moaned like a mourning dove.
My eyes grew weak as I looked to the heavens.
    I am troubled; O Lord, come to my aid!"

¹⁵But what can I say?
    He has spoken to me, and he himself has done
      this.
I will walk humbly all my years
    because of this anguish of my soul.
¹⁶Lord, by such things men live;
    and my spirit finds life in them too.
You restored me to health
    and let me live.
¹⁷Surely it was for my benefit
    that I suffered such anguish.
In your love you kept me
    from the pit of destruction;
you have put all my sins
    behind your back.
¹⁸For the grave*ᵃ* cannot praise you,
    death cannot sing your praise;
those who go down to the pit
    cannot hope for your faithfulness.
¹⁹The living, the living—they praise you,
    as I am doing today;
fathers tell their children
    about your faithfulness.

²⁰The LORD will save me,
    and we will sing with stringed instruments
all the days of our lives
    in the temple of the LORD.

ᵃ 10, 18 Hebrew *Sheol*   *ᵇ 11* A few Hebrew manuscripts; most Hebrew manuscripts *in the place of cessation*

"Put Your House in Order"

ISAIAH 38:1–16

Memento mori, the remembrance of death, is a long-neglected Christian practice designed to increase a sense of the importance of living well here and now. If you knew that you had only one more day to live, what three things would you do? How do these three things highlight the most important things in your life? How do they relate to God's values? Prayerfully consider beginning to do one or more of these things in the next twenty-four hours.

See Meeting God in Everyday Life

The Advantage of Pain

ISAIAH 38:17–22

Hezekiah gives thanks for the difficulties he faces. God can use challenges, tragedies, diseases and other difficulties, whatever their cause, to strengthen and purify us. Prayerfully recall some of the occasions when you have been able to say, "It was for my benefit that I suffered such anguish." Recall the gifts—perhaps of strength, endurance, patience, increased faith, deeper wisdom—that came from your experience, and give God thanks. Today, remember people who may be facing difficulty and surround them in your prayer with God's supportive care.

See Meeting God in Everyday Life

[21] Isaiah had said, "Prepare a poultice of figs and apply it to the boil, and he will recover."

[22] Hezekiah had asked, "What will be the sign that I will go up to the temple of the LORD?"

Envoys From Babylon

39 At that time Merodach-Baladan son of Baladan king of Babylon sent Hezekiah letters and a gift, because he had heard of his illness and recovery. [2] Hezekiah received the envoys gladly and showed them what was in his storehouses—the silver, the gold, the spices, the fine oil, his entire armory and everything found among his treasures. There was nothing in his palace or in all his kingdom that Hezekiah did not show them.

[3] Then Isaiah the prophet went to King Hezekiah and asked, "What did those men say, and where did they come from?"

"From a distant land," Hezekiah replied. "They came to me from Babylon."

[4] The prophet asked, "What did they see in your palace?"

"They saw everything in my palace," Hezekiah said. "There is nothing among my treasures that I did not show them."

[5] Then Isaiah said to Hezekiah, "Hear the word of the LORD Almighty: [6] The time will surely come when everything in your palace, and all that your fathers have stored up until this day, will be carried off to Babylon. Nothing will be left, says the LORD. [7] And some of your descendants, your own flesh and blood who will be born to you, will be taken away, and they will become eunuchs in the palace of the king of Babylon."

[8] "The word of the LORD you have spoken is good," Hezekiah replied. For he thought, "There will be peace and security in my lifetime."

Comfort for God's People

40 Comfort, comfort my people,
    says your God.
  [2] Speak tenderly to Jerusalem,
      and proclaim to her
    that her hard service has been completed,
      that her sin has been paid for,
    that she has received from the LORD's hand
      double for all her sins.

  [3] A voice of one calling:
  "In the desert prepare
      the way for the LORD[a];
    make straight in the wilderness
      a highway for our God.[b]
  [4] Every valley shall be raised up,
      every mountain and hill made low;
    the rough ground shall become level,
      the rugged places a plain.
  [5] And the glory of the LORD will be revealed,
      and all mankind together will see it.
        For the mouth of the LORD has spoken."

---

[a] 3 Or *A voice of one calling in the desert: / "Prepare the way for the LORD*
[b] 3 Hebrew; Septuagint *make straight the paths of our God*

⁶A voice says, "Cry out."
  And I said, "What shall I cry?"

"All men are like grass,
  and all their glory is like the flowers of the field.
⁷The grass withers and the flowers fall,
  because the breath of the LORD blows on them.
  Surely the people are grass.
⁸The grass withers and the flowers fall,
  but the word of our God stands forever."

⁹You who bring good tidings to Zion,
  go up on a high mountain.
You who bring good tidings to Jerusalem,ᵃ
  lift up your voice with a shout,
lift it up, do not be afraid;
  say to the towns of Judah,
  "Here is your God!"
¹⁰See, the Sovereign LORD comes with power,
  and his arm rules for him.
See, his reward is with him,
  and his recompense accompanies him.
¹¹He tends his flock like a shepherd:
  He gathers the lambs in his arms
and carries them close to his heart;
  he gently leads those that have young.

¹²Who has measured the waters in the hollow of
    his hand,
  or with the breadth of his hand marked off the
    heavens?
Who has held the dust of the earth in a basket,
  or weighed the mountains on the scales
  and the hills in a balance?
¹³Who has understood the mindᵇ of the LORD,
  or instructed him as his counselor?
¹⁴Whom did the LORD consult to enlighten him,
  and who taught him the right way?
Who was it that taught him knowledge
  or showed him the path of understanding?

¹⁵Surely the nations are like a drop in a bucket;
  they are regarded as dust on the scales;
  he weighs the islands as though they were fine
    dust.
¹⁶Lebanon is not sufficient for altar fires,
  nor its animals enough for burnt offerings.
¹⁷Before him all the nations are as nothing;
  they are regarded by him as worthless
  and less than nothing.

¹⁸To whom, then, will you compare God?
  What image will you compare him to?
¹⁹As for an idol, a craftsman casts it,
  and a goldsmith overlays it with gold
  and fashions silver chains for it.
²⁰A man too poor to present such an offering
  selects wood that will not rot.
He looks for a skilled craftsman
  to set up an idol that will not topple.

Good News of Comfort

ISAIAH 40:1–11

Slowly read this famous and familiar passage, which was so important to the writers of the New Testament. Open your heart and mind to the words or phrases that seem to leap off the page at you. Circle them or write them on another sheet of paper. Slowly reread the passage, paying attention to the emotions named in the text or that the text evokes in you. Spend time pondering this cluster of words and feelings, seeing if you can discern a particular pattern or theme in your response to the passage. What might the Spirit be trying to show you through the patterns in your response to the Word?

See Meeting God in Scripture

ᵃ 9 Or *O Zion, bringer of good tidings, / go up on a high mountain. / O Jerusalem, bringer of good tidings*   ᵇ 13 Or *Spirit;* or *spirit*

"To Whom . . . Will You Compare God?"

ISAIAH 40:18–31

The Hebrews reject idols in favor of the Holy One, whom they describe in conceptual images such as lord, light, wind, fire—metaphors and symbols of a reality that no one image can capture. Drawing from Scripture, spiritual reading and your own experience, think of some significant metaphors for God—those that are the most meaningful to you. See how many times you can complete the phrase "God is like . . ." Express those metaphors in prayer, such as: "O Living One, you are a refreshing breeze cooling the heat of my agitation." As you read the rest of Isaiah, find other images and metaphors for God and make them into brief sentence prayers.

See Meeting God in Prayer

21 Do you not know?
   Have you not heard?
Has it not been told you from the beginning?
   Have you not understood since the earth was
      founded?
22 He sits enthroned above the circle of the earth,
   and its people are like grasshoppers.
He stretches out the heavens like a canopy,
   and spreads them out like a tent to live in.
23 He brings princes to naught
   and reduces the rulers of this world to nothing.
24 No sooner are they planted,
   no sooner are they sown,
   no sooner do they take root in the ground,
than he blows on them and they wither,
   and a whirlwind sweeps them away like chaff.

25 "To whom will you compare me?
   Or who is my equal?" says the Holy One.
26 Lift your eyes and look to the heavens:
   Who created all these?
He who brings out the starry host one by one,
   and calls them each by name.
Because of his great power and mighty strength,
   not one of them is missing.

27 Why do you say, O Jacob,
   and complain, O Israel,
"My way is hidden from the LORD;
   my cause is disregarded by my God"?
28 Do you not know?
   Have you not heard?
The LORD is the everlasting God,
   the Creator of the ends of the earth.
He will not grow tired or weary,
   and his understanding no one can fathom.
29 He gives strength to the weary
   and increases the power of the weak.
30 Even youths grow tired and weary,
   and young men stumble and fall;
31 but those who hope in the LORD
   will renew their strength.
They will soar on wings like eagles;
   they will run and not grow weary,
   they will walk and not be faint.

The Helper of Israel

41 "Be silent before me, you islands!
   Let the nations renew their strength!
Let them come forward and speak;
   let us meet together at the place of judgment.

2 "Who has stirred up one from the east,
   calling him in righteousness to his service*a*?
He hands nations over to him
   and subdues kings before him.
He turns them to dust with his sword,
   to windblown chaff with his bow.
3 He pursues them and moves on unscathed,
   by a path his feet have not traveled before.

a 2 Or / whom victory meets at every step

⁴Who has done this and carried it through,
   calling forth the generations from the
      beginning?
   I, the LORD—with the first of them
   and with the last—I am he."

⁵The islands have seen it and fear;
   the ends of the earth tremble.
   They approach and come forward;
⁶   each helps the other
   and says to his brother, "Be strong!"
⁷The craftsman encourages the goldsmith,
   and he who smooths with the hammer
      spurs on him who strikes the anvil.
   He says of the welding, "It is good."
   He nails down the idol so it will not topple.

⁸"But you, O Israel, my servant,
   Jacob, whom I have chosen,
   you descendants of Abraham my friend,
⁹I took you from the ends of the earth,
   from its farthest corners I called you.
   I said, 'You are my servant';
   I have chosen you and have not rejected you.
¹⁰So do not fear, for I am with you;
   do not be dismayed, for I am your God.
   I will strengthen you and help you;
   I will uphold you with my righteous right hand.

¹¹"All who rage against you
   will surely be ashamed and disgraced;
   those who oppose you
   will be as nothing and perish.
¹²Though you search for your enemies,
   you will not find them.
   Those who wage war against you
   will be as nothing at all.
¹³For I am the LORD, your God,
   who takes hold of your right hand
   and says to you, Do not fear;
   I will help you.
¹⁴Do not be afraid, O worm Jacob,
   O little Israel,
   for I myself will help you," declares the LORD,
   your Redeemer, the Holy One of Israel.
¹⁵"See, I will make you into a threshing sledge,
   new and sharp, with many teeth.
   You will thresh the mountains and crush them,
   and reduce the hills to chaff.
¹⁶You will winnow them, the wind will pick them
      up,
   and a gale will blow them away.
   But you will rejoice in the LORD
   and glory in the Holy One of Israel.

¹⁷"The poor and needy search for water,
   but there is none;
   their tongues are parched with thirst.
   But I the LORD will answer them;
   I, the God of Israel, will not forsake them.
¹⁸I will make rivers flow on barren heights,
   and springs within the valleys.

God's Friend

ISAIAH 41:8–16

Abraham and Moses were God's "friends." Jeremiah prayed to God as an intimate, lifelong friend as well: "My Father, my friend from my youth" (Jeremiah 3:4).

What are the "seeds" of relationship—the elements that create a human friendship? What elements nurture a friendship? Bring to mind the friends you enjoy and give thanks for them. How can your human friendships help you cultivate a deeper friendship with God? What does God's desire for friendship with us show us about him? Why does God want friends? Why would God want your friendship?

See Meeting God in Community

"The Poor and Needy"

ISAIAH 41:17–20

"The human righteousness required by God . . . has necessarily the character of a vindication of right in favour of the threatened innocent, the oppressed poor, widows, orphans and aliens . . . God always takes his stand unconditionally and passionately on this side, and on this side alone: against the lofty, and on behalf of the lowly; against those who already enjoy right and privilege, and on behalf of those who are denied and deprived of it."

—KARL BARTH,
Church Dogmatics

I will turn the desert into pools of water,
and the parched ground into springs.
¹⁹ I will put in the desert
the cedar and the acacia, the myrtle and the
olive.
I will set pines in the wasteland,
the fir and the cypress together,
²⁰ so that people may see and know,
may consider and understand,
that the hand of the LORD has done this,
that the Holy One of Israel has created it.

²¹ "Present your case," says the LORD.
"Set forth your arguments," says Jacob's King.
²² "Bring in ʟ your idols⌋ to tell us
what is going to happen.
Tell us what the former things were,
so that we may consider them
and know their final outcome.
Or declare to us the things to come,
²³ tell us what the future holds,
so we may know that you are gods.
Do something, whether good or bad,
so that we will be dismayed and filled with fear.
²⁴ But you are less than nothing
and your works are utterly worthless;
he who chooses you is detestable.

²⁵ "I have stirred up one from the north, and he
comes—
one from the rising sun who calls on my name.
He treads on rulers as if they were mortar,
as if he were a potter treading the clay.
²⁶ Who told of this from the beginning, so we could
know,
or beforehand, so we could say, 'He was right'?
No one told of this,
no one foretold it,
no one heard any words from you.
²⁷ I was the first to tell Zion, 'Look, here they are!'
I gave to Jerusalem a messenger of good
tidings.
²⁸ I look but there is no one—
no one among them to give counsel,
no one to give answer when I ask them.
²⁹ See, they are all false!
Their deeds amount to nothing;
their images are but wind and confusion.

The Servant of the LORD

42 "Here is my servant, whom I uphold,
my chosen one in whom I delight;
I will put my Spirit on him
and he will bring justice to the nations.
² He will not shout or cry out,
or raise his voice in the streets.
³ A bruised reed he will not break,
and a smoldering wick he will not snuff out.
In faithfulness he will bring forth justice;
⁴ he will not falter or be discouraged
till he establishes justice on earth.

In his law the islands will put their hope."

⁵This is what God the LORD says—
he who created the heavens and stretched them
out,
who spread out the earth and all that comes
out of it,
who gives breath to its people,
and life to those who walk on it:
⁶"I, the LORD, have called you in righteousness;
I will take hold of your hand.
I will keep you and will make you
to be a covenant for the people
and a light for the Gentiles,
⁷to open eyes that are blind,
to free captives from prison
and to release from the dungeon those who sit
in darkness.

⁸"I am the LORD; that is my name!
I will not give my glory to another
or my praise to idols.
⁹See, the former things have taken place,
and new things I declare;
before they spring into being
I announce them to you."

Song of Praise to the LORD

¹⁰Sing to the LORD a new song,
his praise from the ends of the earth,
you who go down to the sea, and all that is in it,
you islands, and all who live in them.
¹¹Let the desert and its towns raise their voices;
let the settlements where Kedar lives rejoice.
Let the people of Sela sing for joy;
let them shout from the mountaintops.
¹²Let them give glory to the LORD
and proclaim his praise in the islands.
¹³The LORD will march out like a mighty man,
like a warrior he will stir up his zeal;
with a shout he will raise the battle cry
and will triumph over his enemies.

¹⁴"For a long time I have kept silent,
I have been quiet and held myself back.
But now, like a woman in childbirth,
I cry out, I gasp and pant.
¹⁵I will lay waste the mountains and hills
and dry up all their vegetation;
I will turn rivers into islands
and dry up the pools.
¹⁶I will lead the blind by ways they have not
known,
along unfamiliar paths I will guide them;
I will turn the darkness into light before them
and make the rough places smooth.
These are the things I will do;
I will not forsake them.
¹⁷But those who trust in idols,
who say to images, 'You are our gods,'
will be turned back in utter shame.

"A Smoldering Wick"

ISAIAH 42:3–9

God's strong servant of justice is compassionate and gentle with the "bruised reeds" and the "smoldering wicks"—the broken and the weak. Opening yourself to the Spirit, let God's compassionate presence surround you. Ask yourself: Is there a part of myself that is bruised or just dimly burning? An ability or interest that I am hesitant to pursue or express? Feelings I don't want to face? Let any hesitant or injured aspect of yourself come out into the accepting, enabling love of the servant, which is like a gentle breath on a dimly burning wick. Then receive back this aspect of yourself with compassion. Let the servant's love strengthen and heal the tentative, weak part of yourself.

Blinded Servants

Although Israel is God's designated messenger to the nations, it is blind and deaf to the Spirit's work in the world. How have you been blind to God's work in your life—in ways that kept you from cooperating with that work? What, or who, opened your eyes to the grace at work in that situation? In what ways do you see God at work in your religious community, even though the community may be blind to them? Pray for wisdom. How might you communicate what you see to those who do not see it? In what spirit would you best do that sharing?

See Meeting God in Community

Israel Blind and Deaf

18 "Hear, you deaf;
   look, you blind, and see!
19 Who is blind but my servant,
   and deaf like the messenger I send?
Who is blind like the one committed to me,
   blind like the servant of the LORD?
20 You have seen many things, but have paid no attention;
   your ears are open, but you hear nothing."
21 It pleased the LORD
   for the sake of his righteousness
   to make his law great and glorious.
22 But this is a people plundered and looted,
   all of them trapped in pits
   or hidden away in prisons.
They have become plunder,
   with no one to rescue them;
they have been made loot,
   with no one to say, "Send them back."

23 Which of you will listen to this
   or pay close attention in time to come?
24 Who handed Jacob over to become loot,
   and Israel to the plunderers?
Was it not the LORD,
   against whom we have sinned?
For they would not follow his ways;
   they did not obey his law.
25 So he poured out on them his burning anger,
   the violence of war.
It enveloped them in flames, yet they did not understand;
   it consumed them, but they did not take it to heart.

Israel's Only Savior

43 But now, this is what the LORD says—
   he who created you, O Jacob,
   he who formed you, O Israel:
"Fear not, for I have redeemed you;
   I have summoned you by name; you are mine.
2 When you pass through the waters,
   I will be with you;
and when you pass through the rivers,
   they will not sweep over you.
When you walk through the fire,
   you will not be burned;
   the flames will not set you ablaze.
3 For I am the LORD, your God,
   the Holy One of Israel, your Savior;
I give Egypt for your ransom,
   Cush*a* and Seba in your stead.
4 Since you are precious and honored in my sight,
   and because I love you,
I will give men in exchange for you,
   and people in exchange for your life.
5 Do not be afraid, for I am with you;
   I will bring your children from the east

a 3 That is, the upper Nile region

and gather you from the west.
[6] I will say to the north, 'Give them up!'
    and to the south, 'Do not hold them back.'
  Bring my sons from afar
    and my daughters from the ends of the earth—
[7] everyone who is called by my name,
    whom I created for my glory,
    whom I formed and made."

[8] Lead out those who have eyes but are blind,
    who have ears but are deaf.
[9] All the nations gather together
    and the peoples assemble.
  Which of them foretold this
    and proclaimed to us the former things?
  Let them bring in their witnesses to prove they
          were right,
    so that others may hear and say, "It is true."
[10] "You are my witnesses," declares the LORD,
    "and my servant whom I have chosen,
  so that you may know and believe me
    and understand that I am he.
  Before me no god was formed,
    nor will there be one after me.
[11] I, even I, am the LORD,
    and apart from me there is no savior.
[12] I have revealed and saved and proclaimed—
    I, and not some foreign god among you.
  You are my witnesses," declares the LORD, "that I
          am God.
[13]   Yes, and from ancient days I am he.
  No one can deliver out of my hand.
    When I act, who can reverse it?"

God's Mercy and Israel's Unfaithfulness

[14] This is what the LORD says—
    your Redeemer, the Holy One of Israel:
  "For your sake I will send to Babylon
    and bring down as fugitives all the
          Babylonians,*a*
    in the ships in which they took pride.
[15] I am the LORD, your Holy One,
    Israel's Creator, your King."

[16] This is what the LORD says—
    he who made a way through the sea,
    a path through the mighty waters,
[17] who drew out the chariots and horses,
    the army and reinforcements together,
  and they lay there, never to rise again,
    extinguished, snuffed out like a wick:
[18] "Forget the former things;
    do not dwell on the past.
[19] See, I am doing a new thing!
    Now it springs up; do you not perceive it?
  I am making a way in the desert
    and streams in the wasteland.
[20] The wild animals honor me,
    the jackals and the owls,
  because I provide water in the desert

"You Are My Witnesses"

ISAIAH 43:10–13

Witnessing is, simply, reporting one's encounter with the holy. More personal than giving speeches about doctrinal principles, witnessing is simply telling what you have seen and heard. Be on the lookout for the holy today. How do you see God, God's glory, God's mercy at work? How have you witnessed God's grace in action? Rehearse in your mind how you might share this with someone you love. Then share it simply and naturally, without undue drama, before the week is out: "I want to share something I saw . . . ."

See Meeting God in Community

The Redeeming God

ISAIAH 43:14–28

After a time of silent openness before God, read this passage, keeping in mind the essence of redemption—God's rescuing and rehabilitating love. Write down phrases or images that show God bringing his people out of bondage, sin and limitation into new life. Savor one or two of the phrases that seem to resonate most deeply with you. Let one phrase become a repetitive prayer, such as, "O Redeemer, break down all the bars that hold me back from loving more." Wait receptively in silence. Be receptive to any ways that God's redeeming grace, for which you have prayed might show itself in your life. Be ready to perform any actions on your part that might help you welcome it.

See *Meeting God in Scripture*

and streams in the wasteland,
to give drink to my people, my chosen,
²¹ the people I formed for myself
that they may proclaim my praise.

²² "Yet you have not called upon me, O Jacob,
you have not wearied yourselves for me,
O Israel.
²³ You have not brought me sheep for burnt offerings,
nor honored me with your sacrifices.
I have not burdened you with grain offerings
nor wearied you with demands for incense.
²⁴ You have not bought any fragrant calamus for me,
or lavished on me the fat of your sacrifices.
But you have burdened me with your sins
and wearied me with your offenses.

²⁵ "I, even I, am he who blots out
your transgressions, for my own sake,
and remembers your sins no more.
²⁶ Review the past for me,
let us argue the matter together;
state the case for your innocence.
²⁷ Your first father sinned;
your spokesmen rebelled against me.
²⁸ So I will disgrace the dignitaries of your temple,
and I will consign Jacob to destruction*a*
and Israel to scorn.

Israel the Chosen

44 "But now listen, O Jacob, my servant,
Israel, whom I have chosen.
² This is what the LORD says—
he who made you, who formed you in the womb,
and who will help you:
Do not be afraid, O Jacob, my servant,
Jeshurun, whom I have chosen.
³ For I will pour water on the thirsty land,
and streams on the dry ground;
I will pour out my Spirit on your offspring,
and my blessing on your descendants.
⁴ They will spring up like grass in a meadow,
like poplar trees by flowing streams.
⁵ One will say, 'I belong to the LORD';
another will call himself by the name of Jacob;
still another will write on his hand, 'The LORD's,'
and will take the name Israel.

The LORD, Not Idols

⁶ "This is what the LORD says—
Israel's King and Redeemer, the LORD Almighty:
I am the first and I am the last;
apart from me there is no God.
⁷ Who then is like me? Let him proclaim it.
Let him declare and lay out before me
what has happened since I established my ancient people,

---

a 28 The Hebrew term refers to the irrevocable giving over of things or persons to the LORD, often by totally destroying them.

and what is yet to come—
yes, let him foretell what will come.
⁸Do not tremble, do not be afraid.
Did I not proclaim this and foretell it long ago?
You are my witnesses. Is there any God besides
me?
No, there is no other Rock; I know not one."

⁹All who make idols are nothing,
and the things they treasure are worthless.
Those who would speak up for them are blind;
they are ignorant, to their own shame.
¹⁰Who shapes a god and casts an idol,
which can profit him nothing?
¹¹He and his kind will be put to shame;
craftsmen are nothing but men.
Let them all come together and take their stand;
they will be brought down to terror and infamy.

¹²The blacksmith takes a tool
and works with it in the coals;
he shapes an idol with hammers,
he forges it with the might of his arm.
He gets hungry and loses his strength;
he drinks no water and grows faint.
¹³The carpenter measures with a line
and makes an outline with a marker;
he roughs it out with chisels
and marks it with compasses.
He shapes it in the form of man,
of man in all his glory,
that it may dwell in a shrine.
¹⁴He cut down cedars,
or perhaps took a cypress or oak.
He let it grow among the trees of the forest,
or planted a pine, and the rain made it grow.
¹⁵It is man's fuel for burning;
some of it he takes and warms himself,
he kindles a fire and bakes bread.
But he also fashions a god and worships it;
he makes an idol and bows down to it.
¹⁶Half of the wood he burns in the fire;
over it he prepares his meal,
he roasts his meat and eats his fill.
He also warms himself and says,
"Ah! I am warm; I see the fire."
¹⁷From the rest he makes a god, his idol;
he bows down to it and worships.
He prays to it and says,
"Save me; you are my god."
¹⁸They know nothing, they understand nothing;
their eyes are plastered over so they cannot
see,
and their minds closed so they cannot
understand.
¹⁹No one stops to think,
no one has the knowledge or understanding to
say,
"Half of it I used for fuel;
I even baked bread over its coals,
I roasted meat and I ate.

God the Rock

ISAIAH 44:8–22

God is not only "above" us but also "beneath" us, firm as rock. This image of God as Rock appears more than thirty times in Scripture. God, the Rock, is often pictured as a huge, craggy refuge indented with caves where one can hide from a threat or find shelter from the scorching desert sun. Sit quietly, eyes closed, allowing your breathing to center your attention and calm your mind. Call on God as your Rock. Envision yourself settling into just such a "cleft" of the Rock. With each breath, entrust yourself more deeply to the abiding stability of the Almighty God. Hide yourself in the deep, warm shelter of the bedrock, the Savior. Sing, "The Cleft of the Rock."

See Meeting God in Scripture

959

The Song of Creation

ISAIAH 44:23

Hebrew poetry, such as that announcing Isaiah's commissioning vision (see chapter 6), is filled with the songs that pour forth from angels, creatures and the earth in praise of God.

Go for a prayerful walk in your neighborhood or in a nearby natural area. Practice listening to the sounds of creation—the breeze in the trees, the call of birds, the rustle of animals! Hear them as music. Experiment with your humming, mimicking a bird, finding the note in a machine's drone—offering these sounds as praise. End by singing a familiar hymn or repeating the refrain, "Praise the LORD, all his works" (Psalm 103:22).

See Meeting God in the Created Order

Shall I make a detestable thing from what is left?
Shall I bow down to a block of wood?"
²⁰ He feeds on ashes, a deluded heart misleads him;
he cannot save himself, or say,
"Is not this thing in my right hand a lie?"

²¹ "Remember these things, O Jacob,
for you are my servant, O Israel.
I have made you, you are my servant;
O Israel, I will not forget you.
²² I have swept away your offenses like a cloud,
your sins like the morning mist.
Return to me,
for I have redeemed you."

²³ Sing for joy, O heavens, for the LORD has done this;
shout aloud, O earth beneath.
Burst into song, you mountains,
you forests and all your trees,
for the LORD has redeemed Jacob,
he displays his glory in Israel.

Jerusalem to Be Inhabited

²⁴ "This is what the LORD says—
your Redeemer, who formed you in the womb:

I am the LORD,
who has made all things,
who alone stretched out the heavens,
who spread out the earth by myself,

²⁵ who foils the signs of false prophets
and makes fools of diviners,
who overthrows the learning of the wise
and turns it into nonsense,
²⁶ who carries out the words of his servants
and fulfills the predictions of his messengers,

who says of Jerusalem, 'It shall be inhabited,'
of the towns of Judah, 'They shall be built,'
and of their ruins, 'I will restore them,'
²⁷ who says to the watery deep, 'Be dry,
and I will dry up your streams,'
²⁸ who says of Cyrus, 'He is my shepherd
and will accomplish all that I please;
he will say of Jerusalem, "Let it be rebuilt,"
and of the temple, "Let its foundations be laid."'

45 "This is what the LORD says to his anointed,
to Cyrus, whose right hand I take hold of
to subdue nations before him
and to strip kings of their armor,
to open doors before him
so that gates will not be shut:
² I will go before you
and will level the mountains*a*;
I will break down gates of bronze
and cut through bars of iron.
³ I will give you the treasures of darkness,

---

a 2 Dead Sea Scrolls and Septuagint; the meaning of the word in the Masoretic Text is uncertain.

riches stored in secret places,
 so that you may know that I am the LORD,
  the God of Israel, who summons you by name.
⁴ For the sake of Jacob my servant,
 of Israel my chosen,
I summon you by name
 and bestow on you a title of honor,
 though you do not acknowledge me.
⁵ I am the LORD, and there is no other;
 apart from me there is no God.
I will strengthen you,
 though you have not acknowledged me,
⁶ so that from the rising of the sun
 to the place of its setting
men may know there is none besides me.
 I am the LORD, and there is no other.
⁷ I form the light and create darkness,
 I bring prosperity and create disaster;
 I, the LORD, do all these things.

⁸ "You heavens above, rain down righteousness;
 let the clouds shower it down.
Let the earth open wide,
 let salvation spring up,
let righteousness grow with it;
 I, the LORD, have created it.

⁹ "Woe to him who quarrels with his Maker,
 to him who is but a potsherd among the
  potsherds on the ground.
Does the clay say to the potter,
 'What are you making?'
Does your work say,
 'He has no hands'?
¹⁰ Woe to him who says to his father,
 'What have you begotten?'
or to his mother,
 'What have you brought to birth?'

¹¹ "This is what the LORD says—
 the Holy One of Israel, and its Maker:
Concerning things to come,
 do you question me about my children,
 or give me orders about the work of my hands?
¹² It is I who made the earth
 and created mankind upon it.
My own hands stretched out the heavens;
 I marshaled their starry hosts.
¹³ I will raise up Cyrus[a] in my righteousness:
 I will make all his ways straight.
He will rebuild my city
 and set my exiles free,
but not for a price or reward,
 says the LORD Almighty."

¹⁴ This is what the LORD says:

"The products of Egypt and the merchandise of
 Cush,[b]
and those tall Sabeans—
 they will come over to you

The Giver of Light and Darkness

ISAIAH 45:7

"Blessed art thou,
O Lord our God,
King of the universe,
who formest light
and createst darkness,
who makest peace,
and createst all things:

"In mercy thou bringest
light to the earth and to
 those who dwell thereon,
and in Thy goodness
renewest continually each
 day
the miracle of creation . . .

"O Lord of our strength,
sheltering Rock,
Shield of our salvation!
Thou art a stronghold
unto us.

"All Thy hosts in heaven
continually declare
Thy high praises . . .
for the bright luminaries
which Thou hast made;
all shall glorify Thee."
—*Jewish Morning Prayer*

See Meeting God in Worship

When God Hides

ISAIAH 45:15

Is it in the nature of the Holy One to hide or is God's hiddenness the result of our ignorance and misperceptions? Is God's grace always present in the same way for us, or does God change the way grace appears—including in the situations where it seems there is no grace visible? How do you respond when God seems hidden to you? What means have you discovered to help you through such periods? What advice would you give to another person undergoing a period of divine hiddenness?

See Meeting God in Community

and will be yours;
they will trudge behind you,
coming over to you in chains.
They will bow down before you
and plead with you, saying,
'Surely God is with you, and there is no other;
there is no other god.' "

¹⁵ Truly you are a God who hides himself,
O God and Savior of Israel.
¹⁶ All the makers of idols will be put to shame and
disgraced;
they will go off into disgrace together.
¹⁷ But Israel will be saved by the LORD
with an everlasting salvation;
you will never be put to shame or disgraced,
to ages everlasting.

¹⁸ For this is what the LORD says—
he who created the heavens,
he is God;
he who fashioned and made the earth,
he founded it;
he did not create it to be empty,
but formed it to be inhabited—
he says:
"I am the LORD,
and there is no other.
¹⁹ I have not spoken in secret,
from somewhere in a land of darkness;
I have not said to Jacob's descendants,
'Seek me in vain.'
I, the LORD, speak the truth;
I declare what is right.

²⁰ "Gather together and come;
assemble, you fugitives from the nations.
Ignorant are those who carry about idols of wood,
who pray to gods that cannot save.
²¹ Declare what is to be, present it—
let them take counsel together.
Who foretold this long ago,
who declared it from the distant past?
Was it not I, the LORD?
And there is no God apart from me,
a righteous God and a Savior;
there is none but me.

²² "Turn to me and be saved,
all you ends of the earth;
for I am God, and there is no other.
²³ By myself I have sworn,
my mouth has uttered in all integrity
a word that will not be revoked:
Before me every knee will bow;
by me every tongue will swear.
²⁴ They will say of me, 'In the LORD alone
are righteousness and strength.' "
All who have raged against him
will come to him and be put to shame.
²⁵ But in the LORD all the descendants of Israel
will be found righteous and will exult.

Gods of Babylon

46 Bel bows down, Nebo stoops low;
　　their idols are borne by beasts of burden.*ᵃ*
The images that are carried about are
　　　burdensome,
　　a burden for the weary.
² They stoop and bow down together;
　　unable to rescue the burden,
　　they themselves go off into captivity.

³ "Listen to me, O house of Jacob,
　　all you who remain of the house of Israel,
　　you whom I have upheld since you were
　　　conceived,
　　and have carried since your birth.
⁴ Even to your old age and gray hairs
　　I am he, I am he who will sustain you.
I have made you and I will carry you;
　　I will sustain you and I will rescue you.

⁵ "To whom will you compare me or count me
　　　equal?
　　To whom will you liken me that we may be
　　　compared?
⁶ Some pour out gold from their bags
　　and weigh out silver on the scales;
they hire a goldsmith to make it into a god,
　　and they bow down and worship it.
⁷ They lift it to their shoulders and carry it;
　　they set it up in its place, and there it stands.
　　From that spot it cannot move.
Though one cries out to it, it does not answer;
　　it cannot save him from his troubles.

⁸ "Remember this, fix it in mind,
　　take it to heart, you rebels.
⁹ Remember the former things, those of long ago;
　　I am God, and there is no other;
　　I am God, and there is none like me.
¹⁰ I make known the end from the beginning,
　　from ancient times, what is still to come.
I say: My purpose will stand,
　　and I will do all that I please.
¹¹ From the east I summon a bird of prey;
　　from a far-off land, a man to fulfill my purpose.
What I have said, that will I bring about;
　　what I have planned, that will I do.
¹² Listen to me, you stubborn-hearted,
　　you who are far from righteousness.
¹³ I am bringing my righteousness near,
　　it is not far away;
　　and my salvation will not be delayed.
I will grant salvation to Zion,
　　my splendor to Israel.

The Fall of Babylon

47 "Go down, sit in the dust,
　　Virgin Daughter of Babylon;
sit on the ground without a throne,
　　Daughter of the Babylonians.*ᵇ*

Aging Into God

ISAIAH 46:4

In the depths of our souls, we are ageless. The child we once were who remains within, as well as the old sage we might become, emerge sometimes with thoughts or words that surprise us with their wisdom. Prayerfully review the various periods of your life—infancy, childhood, adolescence, adulthood. For each period, bring to mind an image of yourself. Invite the Spirit to show you ways God showed grace to you then. Let this self-portrait continue through your aging. Envision yourself growing in grace and affirming your trust in the God who continues to "carry you."

See Meeting God in Everyday Life

ᵃ 1 Or *are but beasts and cattle*　*ᵇ 1* Or *Chaldeans;* also in verse 5

Sit in Silence

ISAIAH 47:4–5

This passage constitutes God's scathing indictment of Babylon, which had placed all of its trust in human knowledge, in sorcery and magic, and in its own self-sufficiency. The nation is sent into silence and darkness to ponder its refusal to acknowledge the "Lord Almighty . . . the Holy One of Israel."

How are silence and darkness conducive to repentance? Consider spending some time sitting alone in a darkened, silent room. Ask God to show you the ways in which you rely on other people and other things. Listen to God in the silence and darkness. End your session in a prayer of repentance. Ask God for his forgiveness in Christ Jesus and for the grace to renew your trust in God alone.

See Meeting God in Prayer

No more will you be called
    tender or delicate.
² Take millstones and grind flour;
    take off your veil.
Lift up your skirts, bare your legs,
    and wade through the streams.
³ Your nakedness will be exposed
    and your shame uncovered.
I will take vengeance;
    I will spare no one."

⁴ Our Redeemer—the Lord Almighty is his name—
    is the Holy One of Israel.

⁵ "Sit in silence, go into darkness,
    Daughter of the Babylonians;
no more will you be called
    queen of kingdoms.
⁶ I was angry with my people
    and desecrated my inheritance;
I gave them into your hand,
    and you showed them no mercy.
Even on the aged
    you laid a very heavy yoke.
⁷ You said, 'I will continue forever—
    the eternal queen!'
But you did not consider these things
    or reflect on what might happen.

⁸ "Now then, listen, you wanton creature,
    lounging in your security
and saying to yourself,
    'I am, and there is none besides me.
I will never be a widow
    or suffer the loss of children.'
⁹ Both of these will overtake you
    in a moment, on a single day:
    loss of children and widowhood.
They will come upon you in full measure,
    in spite of your many sorceries
    and all your potent spells.
¹⁰ You have trusted in your wickedness
    and have said, 'No one sees me.'
Your wisdom and knowledge mislead you
    when you say to yourself,
    'I am, and there is none besides me.'
¹¹ Disaster will come upon you,
    and you will not know how to conjure it away.
A calamity will fall upon you
    that you cannot ward off with a ransom;
a catastrophe you cannot foresee
    will suddenly come upon you.

¹² "Keep on, then, with your magic spells
    and with your many sorceries,
    which you have labored at since childhood.
Perhaps you will succeed,
    perhaps you will cause terror.
¹³ All the counsel you have received has only worn
      you out!
Let your astrologers come forward,

those stargazers who make predictions month by
      month,
   let them save you from what is coming upon
      you.
¹⁴ Surely they are like stubble;
   the fire will burn them up.
They cannot even save themselves
   from the power of the flame.
Here are no coals to warm anyone;
   here is no fire to sit by.
¹⁵ That is all they can do for you—
   these you have labored with
   and trafficked with since childhood.
Each of them goes on in his error;
   there is not one that can save you.

Stubborn Israel

48 "Listen to this, O house of Jacob,
   you who are called by the name of Israel
   and come from the line of Judah,
you who take oaths in the name of the LORD
   and invoke the God of Israel—
   but not in truth or righteousness—
² you who call yourselves citizens of the holy city
   and rely on the God of Israel—
   the LORD Almighty is his name:
³ I foretold the former things long ago,
   my mouth announced them and I made them
      known;
   then suddenly I acted, and they came to pass.
⁴ For I knew how stubborn you were;
   the sinews of your neck were iron,
   your forehead was bronze.
⁵ Therefore I told you these things long ago;
   before they happened I announced them to you
so that you could not say,
   'My idols did them;
   my wooden image and metal god ordained
      them.'
⁶ You have heard these things; look at them all.
   Will you not admit them?

"From now on I will tell you of new things,
   of hidden things unknown to you.
⁷ They are created now, and not long ago;
   you have not heard of them before today.
So you cannot say,
   'Yes, I knew of them.'
⁸ You have neither heard nor understood;
   from of old your ear has not been open.
Well do I know how treacherous you are;
   you were called a rebel from birth.
⁹ For my own name's sake I delay my wrath;
   for the sake of my praise I hold it back from
      you,
   so as not to cut you off.
¹⁰ See, I have refined you, though not as silver;
   I have tested you in the furnace of affliction.
¹¹ For my own sake, for my own sake, I do this.
   How can I let myself be defamed?
   I will not yield my glory to another.

True Invocation

ISAIAH 48:1

Babylon's "sorceries" (47:12) are not the practice Israel is called to. Rather, Israel is called to invoke the "God of Israel" in truth and righteousness. Invocation involves calling on God to be present and to act according to one or more of his divine roles or attributes. Choose a name or attribute of God such as holiness, justice, truth, love, compassion, beauty or peace. Or use one of the ancient names of God in Hebrew or Greek, such as *Adonai* or *Kyrios* (Lord), *El Elyon* (God Most High), *Hokhma* (Wisdom). Add to this name a prayer phrase of need or desire: "Hear my prayer . . . I need you!" Gently, fervently, play this prayer over in your mind throughout the day.

See *Meeting God in Worship*

Like a River

ISAIAH 48:17–18

Through Isaiah God declares that he is the Israelites' loving teacher who directs and teaches them what is best for them. If only they had paid attention to him, their peace would have been like a river.

Ponder that simile. The image of peace like a river is commonly used in songs and sermons, but what does it really mean to you? Picture a flowing river, perhaps one near your home or one farther away. What does it sound like? What kinds of things grow within it and on its banks? Think about how it continues to flow while you are sleeping, working, playing. Find a picture of a river, or draw or paint one yourself. Place it where you can see it from time to time. Let it remind you of the peace that flows from knowing and paying attention to God.

See Meeting God in the Created Order

Israel Freed

12 "Listen to me, O Jacob,
   Israel, whom I have called:
I am he;
   I am the first and I am the last.
13 My own hand laid the foundations of the earth,
   and my right hand spread out the heavens;
when I summon them,
   they all stand up together.
14 "Come together, all of you, and listen:
   Which of ⸤the idols⸥ has foretold these things?
The LORD's chosen ally
   will carry out his purpose against Babylon;
   his arm will be against the Babylonians.*ᵃ*
15 I, even I, have spoken;
   yes, I have called him.
I will bring him,
   and he will succeed in his mission.

16 "Come near me and listen to this:

"From the first announcement I have not spoken
   in secret;
   at the time it happens, I am there."

And now the Sovereign LORD has sent me,
   with his Spirit.

17 This is what the LORD says—
   your Redeemer, the Holy One of Israel:
"I am the LORD your God,
   who teaches you what is best for you,
   who directs you in the way you should go.
18 If only you had paid attention to my commands,
   your peace would have been like a river,
   your righteousness like the waves of the sea.
19 Your descendants would have been like the sand,
   your children like its numberless grains;
their name would never be cut off
   nor destroyed from before me."

20 Leave Babylon,
   flee from the Babylonians!
Announce this with shouts of joy
   and proclaim it.
Send it out to the ends of the earth;
   say, "The LORD has redeemed his servant
   Jacob."
21 They did not thirst when he led them through the
   deserts;
   he made water flow for them from the rock;
he split the rock
   and water gushed out.

22 "There is no peace," says the LORD, "for the
   wicked."

The Servant of the LORD

49 Listen to me, you islands;
   hear this, you distant nations:
Before I was born the LORD called me;

ᵃ 14 Or Chaldeans; also in verse 20

from my birth he has made mention of my
name.
²He made my mouth like a sharpened sword,
in the shadow of his hand he hid me;
he made me into a polished arrow
and concealed me in his quiver.
³He said to me, "You are my servant,
Israel, in whom I will display my splendor."
⁴But I said, "I have labored to no purpose;
I have spent my strength in vain and for
nothing.
Yet what is due me is in the LORD's hand,
and my reward is with my God."

⁵And now the LORD says—
he who formed me in the womb to be his
servant
to bring Jacob back to him
and gather Israel to himself,
for I am honored in the eyes of the LORD
and my God has been my strength—
⁶he says:
"It is too small a thing for you to be my servant
to restore the tribes of Jacob
and bring back those of Israel I have kept.
I will also make you a light for the Gentiles,
that you may bring my salvation to the ends of
the earth."

⁷This is what the LORD says—
the Redeemer and Holy One of Israel—
to him who was despised and abhorred by the
nation,
to the servant of rulers:
"Kings will see you and rise up,
princes will see and bow down,
because of the LORD, who is faithful,
the Holy One of Israel, who has chosen you."

Restoration of Israel

⁸This is what the LORD says:

"In the time of my favor I will answer you,
and in the day of salvation I will help you;
I will keep you and will make you
to be a covenant for the people,
to restore the land
and to reassign its desolate inheritances,
⁹to say to the captives, 'Come out,'
and to those in darkness, 'Be free!'

"They will feed beside the roads
and find pasture on every barren hill.
¹⁰They will neither hunger nor thirst,
nor will the desert heat or the sun beat upon
them.
He who has compassion on them will guide
them
and lead them beside springs of water.
¹¹I will turn all my mountains into roads,
and my highways will be raised up.
¹²See, they will come from afar—

Named Before Birth

ISAIAH 49:1–6

God has known, named and gifted his servant from before his birth: "You knit me together in my mother's womb" (Psalm 139:13). The servant's gifts are shaped for God's special purposes.

God has given each of us such native talents that can be developed for service. What unique, inborn qualities and talents do you possess? What have you always had a knack for? What activities do you feel naturally less equipped to do? How can you offer your innate abilities for carrying on God's work in the world? What native talents need further development? Give thanks for the qualities or talents that have shown themselves in your life. Pray for guidance, and let the Spirit show you one way to use a developed ability, however modest, to do God's will today—or one way to further develop a neglected talent.

See *Meeting God in Service*

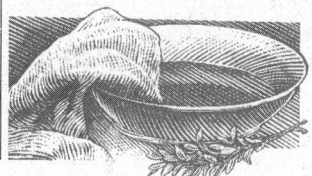

God's Mothering Love

ISAIAH 49:15

"I know not where I came from, when I came into this life-in-death . . . I only know that the gifts Your mercy provided sustained me from the first moment . . . Thus, for my sustenance and my delight I had woman's milk; yet it was not my mother or my nurses who stored their breasts for me: it was Yourself, using them to give me the food of my infancy, according to Your ordinance and the riches set by You at every level of creation . . . For it was by the love implanted in them by You that they gave so willingly that milk which by Your gift flowed in the breasts . . . All good things are from You, O God."

—AUGUSTINE,
Confessions

some from the north, some from the west,
   some from the region of Aswan.*ᵃ*"

¹³Shout for joy, O heavens;
   rejoice, O earth;
   burst into song, O mountains!
For the LORD comforts his people
   and will have compassion on his afflicted
      ones.

¹⁴But Zion said, "The LORD has forsaken me,
   the Lord has forgotten me."

¹⁵"Can a mother forget the baby at her breast
   and have no compassion on the child she has
      borne?
Though she may forget,
   I will not forget you!
¹⁶See, I have engraved you on the palms of my
      hands;
   your walls are ever before me.
¹⁷Your sons hasten back,
   and those who laid you waste depart from
      you.
¹⁸Lift up your eyes and look around;
   all your sons gather and come to you.
As surely as I live," declares the LORD,
   "you will wear them all as ornaments;
   you will put them on, like a bride.

¹⁹"Though you were ruined and made desolate
   and your land laid waste,
now you will be too small for your people,
   and those who devoured you will be far away.
²⁰The children born during your bereavement
   will yet say in your hearing,
'This place is too small for us;
   give us more space to live in.'
²¹Then you will say in your heart,
   'Who bore me these?
I was bereaved and barren;
   I was exiled and rejected.
Who brought these up?
I was left all alone,
   but these—where have they come from?' "

²²This is what the Sovereign LORD says:

"See, I will beckon to the Gentiles,
   I will lift up my banner to the peoples;
they will bring your sons in their arms
   and carry your daughters on their shoulders.
²³Kings will be your foster fathers,
   and their queens your nursing mothers.
They will bow down before you with their faces to
      the ground;
   they will lick the dust at your feet.
Then you will know that I am the LORD;
   those who hope in me will not be
      disappointed."

ᵃ 12 Dead Sea Scrolls; Masoretic Text *Sinim*

²⁴Can plunder be taken from warriors,
    or captives rescued from the fierce*ᵃ*?
²⁵But this is what the Lᴏʀᴅ says:

"Yes, captives will be taken from warriors,
    and plunder retrieved from the fierce;
I will contend with those who contend with you,
    and your children I will save.
²⁶I will make your oppressors eat their own flesh;
    they will be drunk on their own blood, as with
    wine.
Then all mankind will know
    that I, the Lᴏʀᴅ, am your Savior,
    your Redeemer, the Mighty One of Jacob."

Israel's Sin and the Servant's Obedience

50 This is what the Lᴏʀᴅ says:

"Where is your mother's certificate of divorce
    with which I sent her away?
Or to which of my creditors
    did I sell you?
Because of your sins you were sold;
    because of your transgressions your mother
    was sent away.
²When I came, why was there no one?
    When I called, why was there no one to
    answer?
Was my arm too short to ransom you?
    Do I lack the strength to rescue you?
By a mere rebuke I dry up the sea,
    I turn rivers into a desert;
their fish rot for lack of water
    and die of thirst.
³I clothe the sky with darkness
    and make sackcloth its covering."

⁴The Sovereign Lᴏʀᴅ has given me an instructed
    tongue,
to know the word that sustains the weary.
He wakens me morning by morning,
    wakens my ear to listen like one being taught.
⁵The Sovereign Lᴏʀᴅ has opened my ears,
    and I have not been rebellious;
    I have not drawn back.
⁶I offered my back to those who beat me,
    my cheeks to those who pulled out my beard;
I did not hide my face
    from mocking and spitting.
⁷Because the Sovereign Lᴏʀᴅ helps me,
    I will not be disgraced.
Therefore have I set my face like flint,
    and I know I will not be put to shame.
⁸He who vindicates me is near.
    Who then will bring charges against me?
    Let us face each other!
Who is my accuser?
    Let him confront me!

Partnership With God

ISAIAH 50:1

Isaiah uses the image of the marriage commitment to describe our partnership with God, and divorce as an image for the breakdown of that covenant of fidelity. Write down, in your journal or on a sheet of paper, the nature of your covenant with God. What do you believe God has promised to do for you, with you and through you? In what specific ways have you committed yourself to be in relationship with God? Note anything that may be interfering with your faithfulness to this covenant or any areas of relationship that may need more attention. Pray for guidance about how to grow more deeply into your partnership with God.

See Meeting God in Prayer

ᵃ 24 Dead Sea Scrolls, Vulgate and Syriac (see also Septuagint and verse 25);
Masoretic Text *righteous*

"Morning by Morning"

ISAIAH 50:4–10

What is your wake-up routine? In what ways do you intentionally turn your heart and mind to God at the beginning of your day? Experiment with ways to practice the divine presence of God at waking, such as placing a sacred symbol or picture on the wall opposite your bed; keeping a Bible or devotional manual at your bedside; using a journal to jot down significant dreams or capture ideas that may come to you in the twilight between sleeping and waking. Choose an "awakening prayer" that can rise easily to your lips, such as, "O God, you are my God, earnestly I seek you" (Psalm 63:1).

See Meeting God in Worship

[9] It is the Sovereign LORD who helps me.
  Who is he that will condemn me?
They will all wear out like a garment;
  the moths will eat them up.

[10] Who among you fears the LORD
  and obeys the word of his servant?
Let him who walks in the dark,
  who has no light,
trust in the name of the LORD
  and rely on his God.
[11] But now, all you who light fires
  and provide yourselves with flaming torches,
go, walk in the light of your fires
  and of the torches you have set ablaze.
This is what you shall receive from my hand:
  You will lie down in torment.

Everlasting Salvation for Zion

51 "Listen to me, you who pursue righteousness
  and who seek the LORD:
Look to the rock from which you were cut
  and to the quarry from which you were hewn;
[2] look to Abraham, your father,
  and to Sarah, who gave you birth.
When I called him he was but one,
  and I blessed him and made him many.
[3] The LORD will surely comfort Zion
  and will look with compassion on all her
    ruins;
he will make her deserts like Eden,
  her wastelands like the garden of the LORD.
Joy and gladness will be found in her,
  thanksgiving and the sound of singing.

[4] "Listen to me, my people;
  hear me, my nation:
The law will go out from me;
  my justice will become a light to the nations.
[5] My righteousness draws near speedily,
  my salvation is on the way,
  and my arm will bring justice to the nations.
The islands will look to me
  and wait in hope for my arm.
[6] Lift up your eyes to the heavens,
  look at the earth beneath;
the heavens will vanish like smoke,
  the earth will wear out like a garment
  and its inhabitants die like flies.
But my salvation will last forever,
  my righteousness will never fail.

[7] "Hear me, you who know what is right,
  you people who have my law in your hearts:
Do not fear the reproach of men
  or be terrified by their insults.
[8] For the moth will eat them up like a garment;
  the worm will devour them like wool.
But my righteousness will last forever,
  my salvation through all generations."

[9] Awake, awake! Clothe yourself with strength,
O arm of the LORD;
awake, as in days gone by,
as in generations of old.
Was it not you who cut Rahab to pieces,
who pierced that monster through?
[10] Was it not you who dried up the sea,
the waters of the great deep,
who made a road in the depths of the sea
so that the redeemed might cross over?
[11] The ransomed of the LORD will return.
They will enter Zion with singing;
everlasting joy will crown their heads.
Gladness and joy will overtake them,
and sorrow and sighing will flee away.

[12] "I, even I, am he who comforts you.
Who are you that you fear mortal men,
the sons of men, who are but grass,
[13] that you forget the LORD your Maker,
who stretched out the heavens
and laid the foundations of the earth,
that you live in constant terror every day
because of the wrath of the oppressor,
who is bent on destruction?
For where is the wrath of the oppressor?
[14]   The cowering prisoners will soon be set free;
they will not die in their dungeon,
nor will they lack bread.
[15] For I am the LORD your God,
who churns up the sea so that its waves
roar—
the LORD Almighty is his name.
[16] I have put my words in your mouth
and covered you with the shadow of my
hand—
I who set the heavens in place,
who laid the foundations of the earth,
and who say to Zion, 'You are my people.' "

The Cup of the LORD's Wrath

[17] Awake, awake!
Rise up, O Jerusalem,
you who have drunk from the hand of the LORD
the cup of his wrath,
you who have drained to its dregs
the goblet that makes men stagger.
[18] Of all the sons she bore
there was none to guide her;
of all the sons she reared
there was none to take her by the hand.
[19] These double calamities have come upon you—
who can comfort you?—
ruin and destruction, famine and sword—
who can[a] console you?
[20] Your sons have fainted;
they lie at the head of every street,
like antelope caught in a net.

"My Law in Your Hearts"

ISAIAH 51:7–16

Memorization of key Bible passages and wise sayings has traditionally been part of "learning by heart." Our actions are influenced by what we have stored in our hearts and carry with us into each encounter and situation we face. The ancient meanings of "read" include "learn, mark and inwardly digest" (Episcopal *Book of Common Prayer*) as well. How much of God's teaching is stored in your heart? Take pencil and paper and prayerfully recall all the Scripture passages you can remember without consulting a written text. Write until you cannot remember more. Place an asterisk next to the passage that is most important to you. Decide on a verse, perhaps from this chapter, that you wish to commit to your heart today, and take it as your prayer for the day.

See Meeting God in Scripture

"Garments of Splendor"

ISAIAH 52:1

In Scripture, garments are often symbolic of the state of one's soul. As you close your eyes, become aware of the vitality of all your present emotions, named and unnamed. If this emotional energy could express itself as a costume of some sort, what might it be? Let it appear spontaneously in your imagination. Savor the sensations of being dressed this way. Name your emotions to God in prayer. Now ask the Spirit to decorate, augment or transform your garments, however it will, to your good. Note any new emotions or attitudes that emerge as change proceeds.

See Meeting God in Scripture

They are filled with the wrath of the LORD
  and the rebuke of your God.
21 Therefore hear this, you afflicted one,
  made drunk, but not with wine.
22 This is what your Sovereign LORD says,
  your God, who defends his people:
"See, I have taken out of your hand
  the cup that made you stagger;
from that cup, the goblet of my wrath,
  you will never drink again.
23 I will put it into the hands of your tormentors,
  who said to you,
  'Fall prostrate that we may walk over you.'
And you made your back like the ground,
  like a street to be walked over."

52 Awake, awake, O Zion,
  clothe yourself with strength.
Put on your garments of splendor,
  O Jerusalem, the holy city.
The uncircumcised and defiled
  will not enter you again.
2 Shake off your dust;
  rise up, sit enthroned, O Jerusalem.
Free yourself from the chains on your neck,
  O captive Daughter of Zion.

3 For this is what the LORD says:

"You were sold for nothing,
  and without money you will be redeemed."

4 For this is what the Sovereign LORD says:

"At first my people went down to Egypt to live;
  lately, Assyria has oppressed them.

5 "And now what do I have here?" declares the LORD.

"For my people have been taken away for
    nothing,
  and those who rule them mock,*"
                    declares the LORD.
"And all day long
  my name is constantly blasphemed.
6 Therefore my people will know my name;
  therefore in that day they will know
that it is I who foretold it.
  Yes, it is I."

7 How beautiful on the mountains
  are the feet of those who bring good news,
who proclaim peace,
  who bring good tidings,
  who proclaim salvation,
who say to Zion,
  "Your God reigns!"
8 Listen! Your watchmen lift up their voices;
  together they shout for joy.
When the LORD returns to Zion,
  they will see it with their own eyes.

a 5 Dead Sea Scrolls and Vulgate; Masoretic Text *wail*

9 Burst into songs of joy together,
   you ruins of Jerusalem,
for the LORD has comforted his people,
   he has redeemed Jerusalem.
10 The LORD will lay bare his holy arm
   in the sight of all the nations,
and all the ends of the earth will see
   the salvation of our God.
11 Depart, depart, go out from there!
   Touch no unclean thing!
Come out from it and be pure,
   you who carry the vessels of the LORD.
12 But you will not leave in haste
   or go in flight;
for the LORD will go before you,
   the God of Israel will be your rear guard.

The Suffering and Glory of the Servant

13 See, my servant will act wisely[a];
   he will be raised and lifted up and highly
      exalted.
14 Just as there were many who were appalled at
      him[b]—
   his appearance was so disfigured beyond that
      of any man
   and his form marred beyond human
      likeness—
15 so will he sprinkle many nations,[c]
   and kings will shut their mouths because of
      him.
For what they were not told, they will see,
   and what they have not heard, they will
      understand.

53 Who has believed our message
      and to whom has the arm of the LORD been
         revealed?
2 He grew up before him like a tender shoot,
   and like a root out of dry ground.
He had no beauty or majesty to attract us to him,
   nothing in his appearance that we should
      desire him.
3 He was despised and rejected by men,
   a man of sorrows, and familiar with suffering.
Like one from whom men hide their faces
   he was despised, and we esteemed him not.

4 Surely he took up our infirmities
   and carried our sorrows,
yet we considered him stricken by God,
   smitten by him, and afflicted.
5 But he was pierced for our transgressions,
   he was crushed for our iniquities;
the punishment that brought us peace was upon
      him,
   and by his wounds we are healed.
6 We all, like sheep, have gone astray,
   each of us has turned to his own way;

God Before and Behind

ISAIAH 52:12

Before setting out on your next errand, or before going to bed tonight, use this traditional invocation of God's protective presence, symbolized by the four great archangels of Jewish and Christian tradition. As you say, "May God 'give his angels charge over [me], to keep [me] in all [my] ways,' " imagine that strong Michael, the captain of the heavenly hosts, stands behind you; that beautiful Gabriel, herald of good tidings, is at your right hand; that compassionate Raphael, angel of healing, is at your left; and that Uriel, angel of light, stands before you. Pray aloud if you wish, "May strong Michael stand behind me."

See Meeting God in Scripture

---

a 13 Or *will prosper*   b 14 Hebrew *you*   c 15 Hebrew; Septuagint *so will many nations marvel at him*

The Suffering Servant

ISAIAH 53:1–12

This passage is the very heart of Isaiah, for it turns our attention to the One who bore the price of the redemption of Israel—and of humankind—on his shoulders. Read this passage slowly and meditatively. What phrases or images capture your heart? Let that word or phrase bring you face to face with Jesus Christ, who alone can heal you and bring you peace. Rest in silence before him, and let him surround you with his gracious, redeeming love.

See Meeting God in Scripture

and the LORD has laid on him
   the iniquity of us all.

7 He was oppressed and afflicted,
   yet he did not open his mouth;
he was led like a lamb to the slaughter,
   and as a sheep before her shearers is silent,
   so he did not open his mouth.
8 By oppression*a* and judgment he was taken away.
   And who can speak of his descendants?
For he was cut off from the land of the living;
   for the transgression of my people he was stricken.*b*
9 He was assigned a grave with the wicked,
   and with the rich in his death,
though he had done no violence,
   nor was any deceit in his mouth.

10 Yet it was the LORD's will to crush him and cause him to suffer,
   and though the LORD makes*c* his life a guilt offering,
he will see his offspring and prolong his days,
   and the will of the LORD will prosper in his hand.
11 After the suffering of his soul,
   he will see the light ⌊of life⌋*d* and be satisfied*e*;
by his knowledge*f* my righteous servant will justify many,
   and he will bear their iniquities.
12 Therefore I will give him a portion among the great,*g*
   and he will divide the spoils with the strong,*h*
because he poured out his life unto death,
   and was numbered with the transgressors.
For he bore the sin of many,
   and made intercession for the transgressors.

The Future Glory of Zion

54 "Sing, O barren woman,
   you who never bore a child;
burst into song, shout for joy,
   you who were never in labor;
because more are the children of the desolate woman
   than of her who has a husband,"
            says the LORD.
2 "Enlarge the place of your tent,
   stretch your tent curtains wide,
   do not hold back;
lengthen your cords,
   strengthen your stakes.

---

a 8 Or *From arrest*   *b 8* Or *away. / Yet who of his generation considered / that he was cut off from the land of the living / for the transgression of my people, / to whom the blow was due?*   *c 10* Hebrew *though you make*   *d 11* Dead Sea Scrolls (see also Septuagint); Masoretic Text does not have *the light ⌊of life⌋.*   *e 11* Or (with Masoretic Text) *11He will see the result of the suffering of his soul / and be satisfied*   *f 11* Or *by knowledge of him*   *g 12* Or *many*   *h 12* Or *numerous*

³ For you will spread out to the right and to the left;
  your descendants will dispossess nations
  and settle in their desolate cities.

⁴ "Do not be afraid; you will not suffer shame.
  Do not fear disgrace; you will not be humiliated.
  You will forget the shame of your youth
  and remember no more the reproach of your widowhood.
⁵ For your Maker is your husband—
  the Lᴏʀᴅ Almighty is his name—
  the Holy One of Israel is your Redeemer;
  he is called the God of all the earth.
⁶ The Lᴏʀᴅ will call you back
  as if you were a wife deserted and distressed in spirit—
  a wife who married young,
  only to be rejected," says your God.
⁷ "For a brief moment I abandoned you,
  but with deep compassion I will bring you back.
⁸ In a surge of anger
  I hid my face from you for a moment,
  but with everlasting kindness
  I will have compassion on you,"
  says the Lᴏʀᴅ your Redeemer.

⁹ "To me this is like the days of Noah,
  when I swore that the waters of Noah would
  never again cover the earth.
  So now I have sworn not to be angry with you,
  never to rebuke you again.
¹⁰ Though the mountains be shaken
  and the hills be removed,
  yet my unfailing love for you will not be shaken
  nor my covenant of peace be removed,"
  says the Lᴏʀᴅ, who has compassion on you.

¹¹ "O afflicted city, lashed by storms and not comforted,
  I will build you with stones of turquoise,ᵃ
  your foundations with sapphires.ᵇ
¹² I will make your battlements of rubies,
  your gates of sparkling jewels,
  and all your walls of precious stones.
¹³ All your sons will be taught by the Lᴏʀᴅ,
  and great will be your children's peace.
¹⁴ In righteousness you will be established:
  Tyranny will be far from you;
  you will have nothing to fear.
  Terror will be far removed;
  it will not come near you.
¹⁵ If anyone does attack you, it will not be my doing;
  whoever attacks you will surrender to you.

¹⁶ "See, it is I who created the blacksmith
  who fans the coals into flame

After Suffering, Light

ISAIAH 53:11—54:10

"If you but gently persevere through [the stress of dryness and darkness], you will come out at the other end of the gloom, sooner or later, into even deeper, tenderer day . . . There is each time one crucial point—to make no decisions, to change nothing during such crises . . . The crisis goes by, thus, with much fruit. What is a sense of God worth which would be at your disposal, capable of being comfortably elicited when and where you please? It is far, far more God who must hold us, than we who must hold Him. And we get trained in these darknesses into that sense of our impotence without which the very presence of God becomes a snare."

—FRIEDRICH VON HÜGEL,
Letters to a Niece

Misspent Money?

ISAIAH 55:1–3

Ask the Spirit to be with you and to open your eyes as you review your expenditures over the last month or two or more. How does the way you spend your money demonstrate your values and commitments? Ponder how each expenditure may or may not conform to God's desires for your own good and the good of the community. What money is being spent for "what does not satisfy"? During this time period, what gifts of sustenance, nourishment and empowerment have appeared in your life? Consider prayerfully how you may need to alter your expenditures so that they will bring you satisfaction as you offer them in God's service.

See Meeting God in Service

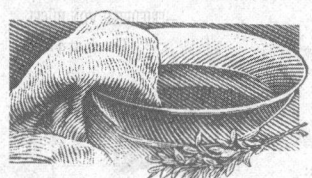

and forges a weapon fit for its work.
And it is I who have created the destroyer to work
    havoc;
¹⁷ no weapon forged against you will prevail,
    and you will refute every tongue that accuses
        you.
This is the heritage of the servants of the LORD,
    and this is their vindication from me,"
                        declares the LORD.

Invitation to the Thirsty

55 "Come, all you who are thirsty,
    come to the waters;
and you who have no money,
    come, buy and eat!
Come, buy wine and milk
    without money and without cost.
² Why spend money on what is not bread,
    and your labor on what does not satisfy?
Listen, listen to me, and eat what is good,
    and your soul will delight in the richest of
        fare.
³ Give ear and come to me;
    hear me, that your soul may live.
I will make an everlasting covenant with you,
    my faithful love promised to David.
⁴ See, I have made him a witness to the peoples,
    a leader and commander of the peoples.
⁵ Surely you will summon nations you know not,
    and nations that do not know you will hasten
        to you,
because of the LORD your God,
    the Holy One of Israel,
    for he has endowed you with splendor."

⁶ Seek the LORD while he may be found;
    call on him while he is near.
⁷ Let the wicked forsake his way
    and the evil man his thoughts.
Let him turn to the LORD, and he will have mercy
        on him,
    and to our God, for he will freely pardon.

⁸ "For my thoughts are not your thoughts,
    neither are your ways my ways,"
                        declares the LORD.
⁹ "As the heavens are higher than the earth,
    so are my ways higher than your ways
    and my thoughts than your thoughts.
¹⁰ As the rain and the snow
    come down from heaven,
and do not return to it
    without watering the earth
and making it bud and flourish,
    so that it yields seed for the sower and bread
        for the eater,
¹¹ so is my word that goes out from my mouth:
    It will not return to me empty,
but will accomplish what I desire
    and achieve the purpose for which I sent it.

¹²You will go out in joy
and be led forth in peace;
the mountains and hills
will burst into song before you,
and all the trees of the field
will clap their hands.
¹³Instead of the thornbush will grow the pine tree,
and instead of briers the myrtle will grow.
This will be for the LORD's renown,
for an everlasting sign,
which will not be destroyed."

Salvation for Others

56 This is what the LORD says:

"Maintain justice
and do what is right,
for my salvation is close at hand
and my righteousness will soon be revealed.
²Blessed is the man who does this,
the man who holds it fast,
who keeps the Sabbath without desecrating it,
and keeps his hand from doing any evil."

³Let no foreigner who has bound himself to the
LORD say,
"The LORD will surely exclude me from his
people."
And let not any eunuch complain,
"I am only a dry tree."

⁴For this is what the LORD says:

"To the eunuchs who keep my Sabbaths,
who choose what pleases me
and hold fast to my covenant—
⁵to them I will give within my temple and its walls
a memorial and a name
better than sons and daughters;
I will give them an everlasting name
that will not be cut off.
⁶And foreigners who bind themselves to the LORD
to serve him,
to love the name of the LORD,
and to worship him,
all who keep the Sabbath without desecrating it
and who hold fast to my covenant—
⁷these I will bring to my holy mountain
and give them joy in my house of prayer.
Their burnt offerings and sacrifices
will be accepted on my altar;
for my house will be called
a house of prayer for all nations."
⁸The Sovereign LORD declares—
he who gathers the exiles of Israel:
"I will gather still others to them
besides those already gathered."

God's Accusation Against the Wicked

⁹Come, all you beasts of the field,
come and devour, all you beasts of the forest!

Mercy Like Rain

ISAIAH 55:7–13

Prayerfully read this passage about God's restorative mercy toward Israel. Let yourself be open to the richness of the metaphors and phrases, perhaps envisioning the drama: God's restorative word showers down from heaven like the rain, bringing healing and fertility to the earth. As you read it a second time, notice which images or phrases seem to call for deeper attention. Ponder one or two in turn, being open to associations you might make with your memories, your current life situation or from other parts of Scripture. How does God's mercy show itself in these associations? Express these ideas and feelings in a short prayer, followed by a period of silently "soaking" in God's mercy.

See *Meeting God in Scripture*

977

Pondering in the Heart

ISAIAH 57:1

"The heart is stretched through suffering and enlarged. But O the agony of this enlarging of the heart, that one may be prepared to enter into the anguish of others! Yet the way of holy obedience leads out from the heart of God and extends through the Valley of the Shadow . . . He, more powerfully, speaks with you and me, to our truest selves, in our truest moments, and disquiets us with the world's needs. By inner persuasions He draws us to a few very definite tasks, our tasks, God's burdened heart particularizing His burdens in us . . . This my task matters for me and for my fellow men and for Eternity."

—THOMAS KELLY,
A Testament of Devotion

¹⁰ Israel's watchmen are blind,
    they all lack knowledge;
they are all mute dogs,
    they cannot bark;
they lie around and dream,
    they love to sleep.
¹¹ They are dogs with mighty appetites;
    they never have enough.
They are shepherds who lack understanding;
    they all turn to their own way,
    each seeks his own gain.
¹² "Come," each one cries, "let me get wine!
    Let us drink our fill of beer!
And tomorrow will be like today,
    or even far better."

57 The righteous perish,
    and no one ponders it in his heart;
devout men are taken away,
    and no one understands
that the righteous are taken away
    to be spared from evil.
² Those who walk uprightly
    enter into peace;
    they find rest as they lie in death.

³ "But you—come here, you sons of a sorceress,
    you offspring of adulterers and prostitutes!
⁴ Whom are you mocking?
    At whom do you sneer
    and stick out your tongue?
Are you not a brood of rebels,
    the offspring of liars?
⁵ You burn with lust among the oaks
    and under every spreading tree;
you sacrifice your children in the ravines
    and under the overhanging crags.
⁶ ⌊The idols⌋ among the smooth stones of the
        ravines are your portion;
    they, they are your lot.
Yes, to them you have poured out drink offerings
    and offered grain offerings.
    In the light of these things, should I relent?
⁷ You have made your bed on a high and lofty
        hill;
    there you went up to offer your sacrifices.
⁸ Behind your doors and your doorposts
    you have put your pagan symbols.
Forsaking me, you uncovered your bed,
    you climbed into it and opened it wide;
you made a pact with those whose beds you
        love,
    and you looked on their nakedness.
⁹ You went to Molech*ᵃ* with olive oil
    and increased your perfumes.
You sent your ambassadors*ᵇ* far away;
    you descended to the grave*ᶜ* itself!
¹⁰ You were wearied by all your ways,
    but you would not say, 'It is hopeless.'

ᵃ9 Or to the king   *ᵇ9 Or idols*   *ᶜ9 Hebrew Sheol*

You found renewal of your strength,
and so you did not faint.

11 "Whom have you so dreaded and feared
that you have been false to me,
and have neither remembered me
nor pondered this in your hearts?
Is it not because I have long been silent
that you do not fear me?
12 I will expose your righteousness and your
works,
and they will not benefit you.
13 When you cry out for help,
let your collection ⌊of idols⌋ save you!
The wind will carry all of them off,
a mere breath will blow them away.
But the man who makes me his refuge
will inherit the land
and possess my holy mountain."

Comfort for the Contrite
14 And it will be said:

"Build up, build up, prepare the road!
Remove the obstacles out of the way of my
people."
15 For this is what the high and lofty One says—
he who lives forever, whose name is holy:
"I live in a high and holy place,
but also with him who is contrite and lowly in
spirit,
to revive the spirit of the lowly
and to revive the heart of the contrite.
16 I will not accuse forever,
nor will I always be angry,
for then the spirit of man would grow faint before
me—
the breath of man that I have created.
17 I was enraged by his sinful greed;
I punished him, and hid my face in anger,
yet he kept on in his willful ways.
18 I have seen his ways, but I will heal him;
I will guide him and restore comfort to him,
19 creating praise on the lips of the mourners in
Israel.
Peace, peace, to those far and near,"
says the LORD. "And I will heal them."
20 But the wicked are like the tossing sea,
which cannot rest,
whose waves cast up mire and mud.
21 "There is no peace," says my God, "for the
wicked."

True Fasting

58 "Shout it aloud, do not hold back.
Raise your voice like a trumpet.
Declare to my people their rebellion
and to the house of Jacob their sins.
2 For day after day they seek me out;
they seem eager to know my ways,

"Your Collection of Idols"

ISAIAH 57:13

Idols are the ego's security system. An idol is anything we become dependent on to allay our anxiety and to comfort us. Our idol might be an insatiable desire to seek control or power instead of a humble willingness to use our gifts, trust in God, and live in healthy interdependence with others.

In what do you seek comfort and safety, power or control? Money? Attractiveness? Intellect? Self-righteousness? Doctrinal correctness? In what ways do you substitute those things for grace-filled, authentic relationships with God and others? Let your idols become visible "graven images" by listing them, sketching or drawing them with crayon or pastel, or by finding magazine pictures to make a collage of the "idols" in your life. Offer this picture to God for transformation, perhaps by burning it as you pray that all your idol-substitutes may be purified in the fire of God's love.

"The Kind of Fasting I Have Chosen"

ISAIAH 58:6–8

Fasting in order to cleanse heart and mind for deep prayer has been, traditionally, an integral part of Jewish and Christian practice. If one also offers the money saved in food expense, the practice can be a step toward the kind of fast described in this passage. What partial or total fast from certain foods or luxuries might you undertake today and in the coming week, so that you could make an additional donation of money to support God's work? From what amusements might you fast in order to devote the time to helping others? Prayerfully consider beginning today.

See Meeting God in Service

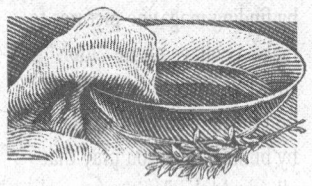

as if they were a nation that does what is right
　　and has not forsaken the commands of its
　　　God.
They ask me for just decisions
　　and seem eager for God to come near them.
³ 'Why have we fasted,' they say,
　　'and you have not seen it?
Why have we humbled ourselves,
　　and you have not noticed?'

"Yet on the day of your fasting, you do as you
　　　please
　　and exploit all your workers.
⁴ Your fasting ends in quarreling and strife,
　　and in striking each other with wicked fists.
You cannot fast as you do today
　　and expect your voice to be heard on high.
⁵ Is this the kind of fast I have chosen,
　　only a day for a man to humble himself?
Is it only for bowing one's head like a reed
　　and for lying on sackcloth and ashes?
Is that what you call a fast,
　　a day acceptable to the LORD?

⁶ "Is not this the kind of fasting I have chosen:
to loose the chains of injustice
　　and untie the cords of the yoke,
to set the oppressed free
　　and break every yoke?
⁷ Is it not to share your food with the hungry
　　and to provide the poor wanderer with
　　　shelter—
when you see the naked, to clothe him,
　　and not to turn away from your own flesh and
　　　blood?
⁸ Then your light will break forth like the dawn,
　　and your healing will quickly appear;
then your righteousness*a* will go before you,
　　and the glory of the LORD will be your rear
　　　guard.
⁹ Then you will call, and the LORD will answer;
　　you will cry for help, and he will say: Here
　　　am I.

"If you do away with the yoke of oppression,
　　with the pointing finger and malicious talk,
¹⁰ and if you spend yourselves in behalf of the
　　　hungry
　　and satisfy the needs of the oppressed,
then your light will rise in the darkness,
　　and your night will become like the noonday.
¹¹ The LORD will guide you always;
　　he will satisfy your needs in a sun-scorched
　　　land
　　and will strengthen your frame.
You will be like a well-watered garden,
　　like a spring whose waters never fail.
¹² Your people will rebuild the ancient ruins
　　and will raise up the age-old foundations;

a 8 Or your righteous One

you will be called Repairer of Broken Walls,
  Restorer of Streets with Dwellings.

[13] "If you keep your feet from breaking the
    Sabbath
  and from doing as you please on my holy day,
if you call the Sabbath a delight
  and the LORD's holy day honorable,
and if you honor it by not going your own way
  and not doing as you please or speaking idle
    words,
[14] then you will find your joy in the LORD,
  and I will cause you to ride on the heights of
    the land
  and to feast on the inheritance of your father
    Jacob."
        The mouth of the LORD has spoken.

Sin, Confession and Redemption

59 Surely the arm of the LORD is not too short to save,
    nor his ear too dull to hear.
[2] But your iniquities have separated
    you from your God;
  your sins have hidden his face from you,
    so that he will not hear.
[3] For your hands are stained with blood,
    your fingers with guilt.
  Your lips have spoken lies,
    and your tongue mutters wicked things.
[4] No one calls for justice;
    no one pleads his case with integrity.
  They rely on empty arguments and speak lies;
    they conceive trouble and give birth to evil.
[5] They hatch the eggs of vipers
    and spin a spider's web.
  Whoever eats their eggs will die,
    and when one is broken, an adder is hatched.
[6] Their cobwebs are useless for clothing;
    they cannot cover themselves with what they
      make.
  Their deeds are evil deeds,
    and acts of violence are in their hands.
[7] Their feet rush into sin;
    they are swift to shed innocent blood.
  Their thoughts are evil thoughts;
    ruin and destruction mark their ways.
[8] The way of peace they do not know;
    there is no justice in their paths.
  They have turned them into crooked roads;
    no one who walks in them will know peace.

[9] So justice is far from us,
    and righteousness does not reach us.
  We look for light, but all is darkness;
    for brightness, but we walk in deep shadows.
[10] Like the blind we grope along the wall,
    feeling our way like men without eyes.
  At midday we stumble as if it were twilight;
    among the strong, we are like the dead.
[11] We all growl like bears;
    we moan mournfully like doves.

The Sabbath—A Delight

ISAIAH 58:13

God commands us to set aside as holy a day of rest each week. What does this command reveal about God's design for human life? What might be the benefit of a hiatus from "doing as you please" for one full day, especially abstinence from working at business or home tasks? What would you do with the available time? What might be the effect on relationships with family and friends? How might this "rest" affect your relationship with the Spirit? Make a plan for some Sabbath time this week. Practice by taking an hour or so today to do something in a Sabbath spirit.

See Meeting God in the Created Order

Society Awry

ISAIAH 59:1–21

Ponder Isaiah's vivid images of a society far gone from the "way of peace." Read the entire chapter slowly, noting and perhaps writing down words and phrases that stand out. Consider each image in turn, staying open to whatever associations from current affairs—local, national, international—come to your mind as illustrations of such social patterns. Pray that God's justice-making Spirit will enter into each situation. Ask God to show you any specific way you can contribute to the "way of peace" today. Listen for an answer.

See Meeting God in Service

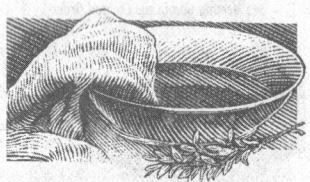

We look for justice, but find none;
    for deliverance, but it is far away.
¹²For our offenses are many in your sight,
    and our sins testify against us.
Our offenses are ever with us,
    and we acknowledge our iniquities:
¹³rebellion and treachery against the LORD,
    turning our backs on our God,
fomenting oppression and revolt,
    uttering lies our hearts have conceived.
¹⁴So justice is driven back,
    and righteousness stands at a distance;
truth has stumbled in the streets,
    honesty cannot enter.
¹⁵Truth is nowhere to be found,
    and whoever shuns evil becomes a prey.

The LORD looked and was displeased
    that there was no justice.
¹⁶He saw that there was no one,
    he was appalled that there was no one to
      intervene;
so his own arm worked salvation for him,
    and his own righteousness sustained him.
¹⁷He put on righteousness as his breastplate,
    and the helmet of salvation on his head;
he put on the garments of vengeance
    and wrapped himself in zeal as in a cloak.
¹⁸According to what they have done,
    so will he repay
wrath to his enemies
    and retribution to his foes;
    he will repay the islands their due.
¹⁹From the west, men will fear the name of the
    LORD,
    and from the rising of the sun, they will revere
      his glory.
For he will come like a pent-up flood
    that the breath of the LORD drives along.ᵃ

²⁰"The Redeemer will come to Zion,
    to those in Jacob who repent of their sins,"
               declares the LORD.

²¹"As for me, this is my covenant with them," says the LORD. "My Spirit, who is on you, and my words that I have put in your mouth will not depart from your mouth, or from the mouths of your children, or from the mouths of their descendants from this time on and forever," says the LORD.

The Glory of Zion

60 "Arise, shine, for your light has come,
    and the glory of the LORD rises upon you.
²See, darkness covers the earth
    and thick darkness is over the peoples,
but the LORD rises upon you
    and his glory appears over you.

ᵃ 19 Or *When the enemy comes in like a flood, / the Spirit of the LORD will put him to flight*

³Nations will come to your light,
  and kings to the brightness of your dawn.

⁴"Lift up your eyes and look about you:
  All assemble and come to you;
 your sons come from afar,
  and your daughters are carried on the arm.
⁵Then you will look and be radiant,
  your heart will throb and swell with joy;
 the wealth on the seas will be brought to you,
  to you the riches of the nations will come.
⁶Herds of camels will cover your land,
  young camels of Midian and Ephah.
 And all from Sheba will come,
  bearing gold and incense
  and proclaiming the praise of the LORD.
⁷All Kedar's flocks will be gathered to you,
  the rams of Nebaioth will serve you;
 they will be accepted as offerings on my altar,
  and I will adorn my glorious temple.

⁸"Who are these that fly along like clouds,
  like doves to their nests?
⁹Surely the islands look to me;
  in the lead are the ships of Tarshish,ᵃ
 bringing your sons from afar,
  with their silver and gold,
 to the honor of the LORD your God,
  the Holy One of Israel,
 for he has endowed you with splendor.

¹⁰"Foreigners will rebuild your walls,
  and their kings will serve you.
 Though in anger I struck you,
  in favor I will show you compassion.
¹¹Your gates will always stand open,
  they will never be shut, day or night,
 so that men may bring you the wealth of the
    nations—
  their kings led in triumphal procession.
¹²For the nation or kingdom that will not serve you
    will perish;
  it will be utterly ruined.

¹³"The glory of Lebanon will come to you,
  the pine, the fir and the cypress together,
 to adorn the place of my sanctuary;
  and I will glorify the place of my feet.
¹⁴The sons of your oppressors will come bowing
    before you;
  all who despise you will bow down at your
    feet
 and will call you the City of the LORD,
  Zion of the Holy One of Israel.

¹⁵"Although you have been forsaken and hated,
  with no one traveling through,
 I will make you the everlasting pride
  and the joy of all generations.
¹⁶You will drink the milk of nations
  and be nursed at royal breasts.

"The Riches of the Nations"

ISAIAH 60:5–11

Isaiah declares that God's intention is to bless all nations. What does this reveal about God's nature? What are the "riches of the nations" that are to be brought into the kingdom—beyond the material riches of silver and gold? Ponder the cultural richness of a nation you may have studied or visited, especially one different from the one that looms large in your heritage and experience. What might delight God's heart about some aspect of that culture? How does it reveal the image of God reflected in human nature? What can you learn from that culture that will help you reflect God's image in your life more fully? What in that nation's life calls for intercessory prayer today?

ᵃ 9 Or *the trading ships*

"The Spirit of the Sovereign Lord Is on Me"

ISAIAH 61:1–3

According to Isaiah, what good things does God desire for his people in this proclamation of good news? How are these values apparent in Israel's best moments and in Judaism's continued witness to the one true God? How are they visible in the life of Jesus of Nazareth, who used this passage to announce his own ministry (see Luke 4:16–19)? In what ways are they at work—or missing—in the life of your spiritual community? In what ways does your life exemplify these values? Which phrase in particular calls you to express a value in action? Ask God to show you how to participate in this aspect of the Spirit's work.

See Meeting God in Community

Then you will know that I, the LORD, am your
    Savior,
    your Redeemer, the Mighty One of Jacob.
[17] Instead of bronze I will bring you gold,
    and silver in place of iron.
Instead of wood I will bring you bronze,
    and iron in place of stones.
I will make peace your governor
    and righteousness your ruler.
[18] No longer will violence be heard in your land,
    nor ruin or destruction within your borders,
but you will call your walls Salvation
    and your gates Praise.
[19] The sun will no more be your light by day,
    nor will the brightness of the moon shine on
        you,
for the LORD will be your everlasting light,
    and your God will be your glory.
[20] Your sun will never set again,
    and your moon will wane no more;
the LORD will be your everlasting light,
    and your days of sorrow will end.
[21] Then will all your people be righteous
    and they will possess the land forever.
They are the shoot I have planted,
    the work of my hands,
    for the display of my splendor.
[22] The least of you will become a thousand,
    the smallest a mighty nation.
I am the LORD;
    in its time I will do this swiftly."

The Year of the LORD's Favor

61 The Spirit of the Sovereign LORD is on me,
    because the LORD has anointed me
    to preach good news to the poor.
He has sent me to bind up the brokenhearted,
    to proclaim freedom for the captives
    and release from darkness for the prisoners,[a]
[2] to proclaim the year of the LORD's favor
    and the day of vengeance of our God,
to comfort all who mourn,
[3]   and provide for those who grieve in Zion—
to bestow on them a crown of beauty
    instead of ashes,
the oil of gladness
    instead of mourning,
and a garment of praise
    instead of a spirit of despair.
They will be called oaks of righteousness,
    a planting of the LORD
    for the display of his splendor.

[4] They will rebuild the ancient ruins
    and restore the places long devastated;
they will renew the ruined cities
    that have been devastated for generations.
[5] Aliens will shepherd your flocks;
    foreigners will work your fields and vineyards.

⁶And you will be called priests of the Lord,
  you will be named ministers of our God.
You will feed on the wealth of nations,
  and in their riches you will boast.

⁷Instead of their shame
  my people will receive a double portion,
and instead of disgrace
  they will rejoice in their inheritance;
and so they will inherit a double portion in their
    land,
  and everlasting joy will be theirs.

⁸"For I, the Lord, love justice;
  I hate robbery and iniquity.
In my faithfulness I will reward them
  and make an everlasting covenant with them.
⁹Their descendants will be known among the
    nations
  and their offspring among the peoples.
All who see them will acknowledge
  that they are a people the Lord has blessed."

¹⁰I delight greatly in the Lord;
  my soul rejoices in my God.
For he has clothed me with garments of
    salvation
  and arrayed me in a robe of righteousness,
as a bridegroom adorns his head like a priest,
  and as a bride adorns herself with her jewels.
¹¹For as the soil makes the sprout come up
  and a garden causes seeds to grow,
so the Sovereign Lord will make righteousness
    and praise
  spring up before all nations.

Zion's New Name

62 For Zion's sake I will not keep silent,
  for Jerusalem's sake I will not remain quiet,
till her righteousness shines out like the dawn,
  her salvation like a blazing torch.
²The nations will see your righteousness,
  and all kings your glory;
you will be called by a new name
  that the mouth of the Lord will bestow.
³You will be a crown of splendor in the Lord's
    hand,
  a royal diadem in the hand of your God.
⁴No longer will they call you Deserted,
  or name your land Desolate.
But you will be called Hephzibah,ᵃ
  and your land Beulahᵇ;
for the Lord will take delight in you,
  and your land will be married.
⁵As a young man marries a maiden,
  so will your sonsᶜ marry you;
as a bridegroom rejoices over his bride,
  so will your God rejoice over you.

Clothed by God

ISAIAH 61:10–62:5

"Let your bodies—which are
  your clothing—shine out,
for they bound in fetters
    that man whose body
    was stained. Lord, do
    you
whiten my stains
at Your banquet
with Your radiance.

"Whosoever
  puts on the robe of glory
from the water and the
    Spirit, will destroy with
    its burning the thorny
    growth of his sins.

"Among the saints none is
  naked for they have put
  on glory;
nor is there any clad in fig
    leaves,
or stained in shame,
for they have found,
through our Lord,
the robe that belonged
to Adam and Eve."
—ST. EPHREM OF SYRIA

ᵃ 4 *Hephzibah* means *my delight is in her.*   ᵇ 4 *Beulah* means *married.*
ᶜ 5 Or *Builder*

Intercessors

ISAIAH 62:6–12

The watchmen "call on the LORD"—that is, they pray continually—for the needs of the people. Intercessory prayer is a channel through which God's comforting and guiding Spirit flows. Prayerfully imagine that you are just such a watchman, posted high on the city wall, atop a tall building or on a high hill where you can view your family, community, congregation, nation or world. What do you see that needs to be offered to God in intercessory prayer? Let those needs enter your heart. Offer to join your thoughts and concerns with God's compassionate and powerful love so that God's love will illuminate, surround and permeate the situation for which you are praying.

See Meeting God in Prayer

986

⁶ I have posted watchmen on your walls,
    O Jerusalem;
  they will never be silent day or night.
  You who call on the LORD,
    give yourselves no rest,
⁷ and give him no rest till he establishes
    Jerusalem
  and makes her the praise of the earth.

⁸ The LORD has sworn by his right hand
    and by his mighty arm:
  "Never again will I give your grain
    as food for your enemies,
  and never again will foreigners drink the new
    wine
  for which you have toiled;
⁹ but those who harvest it will eat it
    and praise the LORD,
  and those who gather the grapes will drink it
    in the courts of my sanctuary."

¹⁰ Pass through, pass through the gates!
    Prepare the way for the people.
  Build up, build up the highway!
    Remove the stones.
  Raise a banner for the nations.

¹¹ The LORD has made proclamation
    to the ends of the earth:
  "Say to the Daughter of Zion,
    'See, your Savior comes!
  See, his reward is with him,
    and his recompense accompanies him.' "
¹² They will be called the Holy People,
    the Redeemed of the LORD;
  and you will be called Sought After,
    the City No Longer Deserted.

God's Day of Vengeance and Redemption

63 Who is this coming from Edom,
    from Bozrah, with his garments stained crimson?
  Who is this, robed in splendor,
    striding forward in the greatness of his
      strength?

  "It is I, speaking in righteousness,
    mighty to save."

² Why are your garments red,
    like those of one treading the winepress?

³ "I have trodden the winepress alone;
    from the nations no one was with me.
  I trampled them in my anger
    and trod them down in my wrath;
  their blood spattered my garments,
    and I stained all my clothing.
⁴ For the day of vengeance was in my heart,
    and the year of my redemption has come.
⁵ I looked, but there was no one to help,
    I was appalled that no one gave support;
  so my own arm worked salvation for me,
    and my own wrath sustained me.

⁶I trampled the nations in my anger;
    in my wrath I made them drunk
    and poured their blood on the ground."

Praise and Prayer

⁷I will tell of the kindnesses of the LORD,
    the deeds for which he is to be praised,
    according to all the LORD has done for us—
    yes, the many good things he has done
      for the house of Israel,
    according to his compassion and many
      kindnesses.
⁸He said, "Surely they are my people,
    sons who will not be false to me";
    and so he became their Savior.
⁹In all their distress he too was distressed,
    and the angel of his presence saved them.
In his love and mercy he redeemed them;
    he lifted them up and carried them
    all the days of old.
¹⁰Yet they rebelled
    and grieved his Holy Spirit.
So he turned and became their enemy
    and he himself fought against them.

¹¹Then his people recalled[a] the days of old,
    the days of Moses and his people—
    where is he who brought them through the sea,
    with the shepherd of his flock?
Where is he who set
    his Holy Spirit among them,
¹²who sent his glorious arm of power
    to be at Moses' right hand,
who divided the waters before them,
    to gain for himself everlasting renown,
¹³who led them through the depths?
Like a horse in open country,
    they did not stumble;
¹⁴like cattle that go down to the plain,
    they were given rest by the Spirit of the LORD.
This is how you guided your people
    to make for yourself a glorious name.

¹⁵Look down from heaven and see
    from your lofty throne, holy and glorious.
Where are your zeal and your might?
    Your tenderness and compassion are withheld
      from us.
¹⁶But you are our Father,
    though Abraham does not know us
    or Israel acknowledge us;
you, O LORD, are our Father,
    our Redeemer from of old is your name.
¹⁷Why, O LORD, do you make us wander from your
      ways
    and harden our hearts so we do not revere you?
Return for the sake of your servants,
    the tribes that are your inheritance.
¹⁸For a little while your people possessed your holy
      place,

The Divine Warrior

ISAIAH 63:1–6

"By the hand of thy
    prophets . . . thou has
    imaged forth the . . .
glory of thy majesty.
They saw . . . . thee . . . .
as a Man of War;
he striveth with his hands.

"With dew of light
his head is filled and his
    locks with drops of the
    night . . .
His black locks
were flowing in curls.
He is bright
and ruddy in red apparel,
when he cometh from
    treading the winepresses
    of Edom.

"His glory resteth upon me,
and mine upon him; he is
    nigh unto me when I call
    upon him.
May his treasured people
be a crown in his hand!"

      —"The Hymn of Glory,"
      Hebrew Prayer Book

---

[a] 11 Or *But may he recall*

God, Our Father

ISAIAH 63:16; 64:8

These verses are among the few places in the Hebrew Bible that God is called "Father." The emphasis here is on the father's function of judging and correcting behavior. What other facets of fatherliness does God exhibit? Which of these qualities have you seen modeled by your father or other father figures in your life? Do you have any special "fathers in God" (of any age) who have helped you develop your relationship with God? What aspect of being "fatherly" might you need to explore or deepen in your character (whether you are male or female)? Who are the fathers that may need your prayers today?

See Meeting God in Scripture

but now our enemies have trampled down your sanctuary.
¹⁹ We are yours from of old;
but you have not ruled over them,
they have not been called by your name. *ᵃ*

64 Oh, that you would rend the heavens and come down,
that the mountains would tremble before you!
² As when fire sets twigs ablaze
and causes water to boil,
come down to make your name known to your enemies
and cause the nations to quake before you!
³ For when you did awesome things that we did not expect,
you came down, and the mountains trembled before you.
⁴ Since ancient times no one has heard,
no ear has perceived,
no eye has seen any God besides you,
who acts on behalf of those who wait for him.
⁵ You come to the help of those who gladly do right,
who remember your ways.
But when we continued to sin against them,
you were angry.
How then can we be saved?
⁶ All of us have become like one who is unclean,
and all our righteous acts are like filthy rags;
we all shrivel up like a leaf,
and like the wind our sins sweep us away.
⁷ No one calls on your name
or strives to lay hold of you;
for you have hidden your face from us
and made us waste away because of our sins.

⁸ Yet, O Lord, you are our Father.
We are the clay, you are the potter;
we are all the work of your hand.
⁹ Do not be angry beyond measure, O Lord;
do not remember our sins forever.
Oh, look upon us, we pray,
for we are all your people.
¹⁰ Your sacred cities have become a desert;
even Zion is a desert, Jerusalem a desolation.
¹¹ Our holy and glorious temple, where our fathers praised you,
has been burned with fire,
and all that we treasured lies in ruins.
¹² After all this, O Lord, will you hold yourself back?
Will you keep silent and punish us beyond measure?

Judgment and Salvation

65 "I revealed myself to those who did not ask for me;
I was found by those who did not seek me.
To a nation that did not call on my name,

ᵃ 19 Or *We are like those you have never ruled, / like those never called by your name*

I said, 'Here am I, here am I.'
² All day long I have held out my hands
      to an obstinate people,
who walk in ways not good,
      pursuing their own imaginations—
³ a people who continually provoke me
      to my very face,
offering sacrifices in gardens
      and burning incense on altars of brick;
⁴ who sit among the graves
      and spend their nights keeping secret vigil;
who eat the flesh of pigs,
      and whose pots hold broth of unclean meat;
⁵ who say, 'Keep away; don't come near me,
      for I am too sacred for you!'
Such people are smoke in my nostrils,
      a fire that keeps burning all day.

⁶ "See, it stands written before me:
      I will not keep silent but will pay back in full;
      I will pay it back into their laps—
⁷ both your sins and the sins of your fathers,"
      says the LORD.
"Because they burned sacrifices on the
            mountains
      and defied me on the hills,
I will measure into their laps
      the full payment for their former deeds."

⁸ This is what the LORD says:

"As when juice is still found in a cluster of grapes
      and men say, 'Don't destroy it,
      there is yet some good in it,'
so will I do in behalf of my servants;
      I will not destroy them all.
⁹ I will bring forth descendants from Jacob,
      and from Judah those who will possess my
            mountains;
my chosen people will inherit them,
      and there will my servants live.
¹⁰ Sharon will become a pasture for flocks,
      and the Valley of Achor a resting place for
            herds,
      for my people who seek me.

¹¹ "But as for you who forsake the LORD
      and forget my holy mountain,
who spread a table for Fortune
      and fill bowls of mixed wine for Destiny,
¹² I will destine you for the sword,
      and you will all bend down for the slaughter;
for I called but you did not answer,
      I spoke but you did not listen.
You did evil in my sight
      and chose what displeases me."

¹³ Therefore this is what the Sovereign LORD says:

"My servants will eat,
      but you will go hungry;

The Unnoticed Presence

ISAIAH 65:1–2

God is always pressing in on our lives, whether we heed God or not, whether we ask for God or not. God is often present incognito—without drama—in and through natural events. In what places, situations or relationships has God called out to you? In what ways might God have been saying, "Here am I" to you lately? Review the last twenty-four hours of your life for glimpses of such moments. Revisit them with a greater openness to God, "turning up the volume" of your spiritual sensitivity. Be open to what God is teaching you. This exercise can be an especially fitting way to end your day.

See Meeting God in Everyday Life

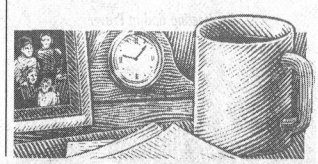

Invoking a Blessing

ISAIAH 65:16

Invoking a blessing means calling upon "the God of truth" to pour out his grace for a particular purpose. Invoking a blessing is an act of faith; it is confidently claiming a promise inherent in an attribute of God's revealed character, as in "May the God of hope fill you with all joy" (Romans 15:13). To do so connects a particular name or attribute of God with a specific human need. What blessing do you need as you face the coming day? Who in your circle of care is in need of a particular blessing? Choose an appropriate attribute of God for each blessing, and invoke the Spirit's aid: "May the God of _____ grant _____."

See Meeting God in Prayer

my servants will drink,
  but you will go thirsty;
my servants will rejoice,
  but you will be put to shame.
¹⁴ My servants will sing
  out of the joy of their hearts,
but you will cry out
  from anguish of heart
  and wail in brokenness of spirit.
¹⁵ You will leave your name
  to my chosen ones as a curse;
the Sovereign Lord will put you to death,
  but to his servants he will give another name.
¹⁶ Whoever invokes a blessing in the land
  will do so by the God of truth;
he who takes an oath in the land
  will swear by the God of truth.
For the past troubles will be forgotten
  and hidden from my eyes.

New Heavens and a New Earth

¹⁷ "Behold, I will create
  new heavens and a new earth.
The former things will not be remembered,
  nor will they come to mind.
¹⁸ But be glad and rejoice forever
  in what I will create,
for I will create Jerusalem to be a delight
  and its people a joy.
¹⁹ I will rejoice over Jerusalem
  and take delight in my people;
the sound of weeping and of crying
  will be heard in it no more.

²⁰ "Never again will there be in it
  an infant who lives but a few days,
  or an old man who does not live out his
    years;
he who dies at a hundred
  will be thought a mere youth;
he who fails to reach*ᵃ* a hundred
  will be considered accursed.
²¹ They will build houses and dwell in them;
  they will plant vineyards and eat their fruit.
²² No longer will they build houses and others live in
    them,
  or plant and others eat.
For as the days of a tree,
  so will be the days of my people;
my chosen ones will long enjoy
  the works of their hands.
²³ They will not toil in vain
  or bear children doomed to misfortune;
for they will be a people blessed by the Lord,
  they and their descendants with them.
²⁴ Before they call I will answer;
  while they are still speaking I will hear.
²⁵ The wolf and the lamb will feed together,
  and the lion will eat straw like the ox,

ᵃ 20 Or I the sinner who reaches

but dust will be the serpent's food.
They will neither harm nor destroy
on all my holy mountain,"

says the LORD.

Judgment and Hope

66 This is what the LORD says:

"Heaven is my throne,
and the earth is my footstool.
Where is the house you will build for me?
Where will my resting place be?
² Has not my hand made all these things,
and so they came into being?"

declares the LORD.

"This is the one I esteem:
he who is humble and contrite in spirit,
and trembles at my word.
³ But whoever sacrifices a bull
is like one who kills a man,
and whoever offers a lamb,
like one who breaks a dog's neck;
whoever makes a grain offering
is like one who presents pig's blood,
and whoever burns memorial incense,
like one who worships an idol.
They have chosen their own ways,
and their souls delight in their abominations;
⁴ so I also will choose harsh treatment for them
and will bring upon them what they dread.
For when I called, no one answered,
when I spoke, no one listened.
They did evil in my sight
and chose what displeases me."

⁵ Hear the word of the LORD,
you who tremble at his word:
"Your brothers who hate you,
and exclude you because of my name, have
said,
'Let the LORD be glorified,
that we may see your joy!'
Yet they will be put to shame.
⁶ Hear that uproar from the city,
hear that noise from the temple!
It is the sound of the LORD
repaying his enemies all they deserve.

⁷ "Before she goes into labor,
she gives birth;
before the pains come upon her,
she delivers a son.
⁸ Who has ever heard of such a thing?
Who has ever seen such things?
Can a country be born in a day
or a nation be brought forth in a moment?
Yet no sooner is Zion in labor
than she gives birth to her children.
⁹ Do I bring to the moment of birth
and not give delivery?" says the LORD.

"Living Sacrifices"

ISAIAH 66:1–4

Our "sacrifices" or offerings are our daily actions and habits of mind, rather than the ineffective and odious sacrifices that Isaiah pictures; God desires that his people offer righteous actions and attitudes.

Recall your day so far. What qualities and attitudes in yourself does God have to work with today? Offer yourself as a "living sacrifice" (Romans 12:1), saying, "Here I am being calm . . . loving someone . . . I offer my actions for your purposes." Offer whatever seems unworthy for transformation: "Here I am disgruntled . . . or afraid . . ." Practice pausing periodically throughout the day to make an offering of what you have just been doing, asking the Spirit to help you craft a day worthy of God's desires for your life.

See Meeting God in Worship

The Nourishing Mother

ISAIAH 66:10–14

God likens himself and the holy city Jerusalem to a generous, nourishing mother, whose overflowing grace and glory renew the bodies and hearts of her children. What do such feminine images tell us about the nature of God? How is this aspect of God manifest in men and women you know? How might you address this facet of God in prayer? Where, in your daily life, is God's nurturing care most clearly evident? What spiritual practices help you open yourself to "drink deeply and delight" in such grace? How can you embody such divine generosity in your behavior?

See Meeting God in Scripture

"Do I close up the womb
　when I bring to delivery?" says your God.
¹⁰ "Rejoice with Jerusalem and be glad for her,
　all you who love her;
rejoice greatly with her,
　all you who mourn over her.
¹¹ For you will nurse and be satisfied
　at her comforting breasts;
you will drink deeply
　and delight in her overflowing abundance."

¹²For this is what the LORD says:

"I will extend peace to her like a river,
　and the wealth of nations like a flooding
　　stream;
you will nurse and be carried on her arm
　and dandled on her knees.
¹³As a mother comforts her child,
　so will I comfort you;
and you will be comforted over Jerusalem."

¹⁴When you see this, your heart will rejoice
　and you will flourish like grass;
the hand of the LORD will be made known to his
　　servants,
　but his fury will be shown to his foes.
¹⁵See, the LORD is coming with fire,
　and his chariots are like a whirlwind;
he will bring down his anger with fury,
　and his rebuke with flames of fire.
¹⁶For with fire and with his sword
　the LORD will execute judgment upon all men,
　and many will be those slain by the LORD.

¹⁷"Those who consecrate and purify themselves to go into the gardens, following the one in the midst of*ᵃ* those who eat the flesh of pigs and rats and other abominable things—they will meet their end together," declares the LORD.

¹⁸"And I, because of their actions and their imaginations, am about to come*ᵇ* and gather all nations and tongues, and they will come and see my glory.

¹⁹"I will set a sign among them, and I will send some of those who survive to the nations—to Tarshish, to the Libyans*ᶜ* and Lydians (famous as archers), to Tubal and Greece, and to the distant islands that have not heard of my fame or seen my glory. They will proclaim my glory among the nations. ²⁰And they will bring all your brothers, from all the nations, to my holy mountain in Jerusalem as an offering to the LORD—on horses, in chariots and wagons, and on mules and camels," says the LORD. "They will bring them, as the Israelites bring their grain offerings, to the temple of the LORD in ceremonially clean vessels. ²¹And I will select some of them also to be priests and Levites," says the LORD.

²²"As the new heavens and the new earth that I make will endure before me," declares the LORD, "so will your name and descendants endure. ²³From one New Moon to

ᵃ 17 Or gardens behind one of your temples, and　*ᵇ 18 The meaning of the Hebrew for this clause is uncertain.*　*ᶜ 19 Some Septuagint manuscripts Put (Libyans); Hebrew Pul*

another and from one Sabbath to another, all mankind will come and bow down before me," says the LORD. ²⁴"And they will go out and look upon the dead bodies of those who rebelled against me; their worm will not die, nor will their fire be quenched, and they will be loathsome to all mankind."

In the End, Praise

ISAIAH 66:22–23

In synagogue reading as well as in printed texts, Jews traditionally end the book of Isaiah by repeating verse 23, so that they finish the reading with God's gracious goals rather than God's temporary wrath: " 'From one New Moon to another and from one Sabbath to another, all mankind will come and bow down before me,' says the LORD." God's goals for humanity are restoration, community, communion and praise. Prayerfully envision "the end" or fulfillment—for yourself, for humanity, for the creation. How is your hope of this glorious end encouraged and strengthened? What passages in Scripture support your hope? Describe in writing or draw a representation of your vision of the fulfillment that God intends for us. Pray that all people will come to worship God.

See *Meeting God in Worship*

JEREMIAH

Hope in Times of Weeping

KEY VERSE:

*"Is not Ephraim my dear son, the child in whom I delight? Though I often speak against him,
I still remember him. Therefore my heart yearns for him; I have great compassion for him,"
declares the* LORD.*—Jeremiah 31:20*

"Batter my heart, three-
personed God, for you
As yet but knock, breathe,
shine and seek to mend;
That I may rise and stand,
o'erthrow me and bend
your force to break, blow,
burn, and make me
new."

—JOHN DONNE,
Holy Sonnets 5

"Who am I called to be?" "How does God intend to use my gifts?" Jeremiah wrestles with such questions and finds that God has rich purposes for his life.

Jeremiah the *prophet* is a passionate man who grieves with God for a wayward people.

Jeremiah the *proclaimer* of God's word is a man of enormous courage—speaking at great personal cost in a climate of hostility and rejection. Jeremiah the *poet* is a man of such transparency of soul that he hears God and weeps with God. Jeremiah declares to his listeners that God is a Father who wants good things for his children, such as "a desirable land, the most beautiful inheritance of any nation" (3:19); God so deeply loves "[his] dear son . . . the child in whom [he] delight[s]" (31:20), that even though his children reject and deny him, he continues to show mercy. Jeremiah the *servant of God* is a man of great integrity who calls the people of God to integrity so that they might not lose their true identity as God's children.

From his perspective in the sixth century B.C., Jeremiah shows us a God who yearns for us, a God who has wonderful things in store for us, a God who grieves when we turn away. Jeremiah calls us to repent and to grieve when we fail to respond to a love that passionately desires our good. And as we respond, we discover the compassion of God, who alone can restore us.

1

The words of Jeremiah son of Hilkiah, one of the priests at Anathoth in the territory of Benjamin. ²The word of the LORD came to him in the thirteenth year of the reign of Josiah son of Amon king of Judah, ³and through the reign of Jehoiakim son of Josiah king of Judah, down to the fifth month of the eleventh year of Zedekiah son of Josiah king of Judah, when the people of Jerusalem went into exile.

The Call of Jeremiah

⁴The word of the LORD came to me, saying,

⁵ "Before I formed you in the womb I knew^a you,
before you were born I set you apart;
I appointed you as a prophet to the nations."

⁶"Ah, Sovereign LORD," I said, "I do not know how to speak; I am only a child."

⁷But the LORD said to me, "Do not say, 'I am only a child.' You must go to everyone I send you to and say whatever I command you. ⁸Do not be afraid of them, for I am with you and will rescue you," declares the LORD.

⁹Then the LORD reached out his hand and touched my mouth and said to me, "Now, I have put my words in your mouth. ¹⁰See, today I appoint you over nations and kingdoms to uproot and tear down, to destroy and overthrow, to build and to plant."

¹¹The word of the LORD came to me: "What do you see, Jeremiah?"

"I see the branch of an almond tree," I replied.

¹²The LORD said to me, "You have seen correctly, for I am watching^b to see that my word is fulfilled."

¹³The word of the LORD came to me again: "What do you see?"

"I see a boiling pot, tilting away from the north," I answered.

¹⁴The LORD said to me, "From the north disaster will be poured out on all who live in the land. ¹⁵I am about to summon all the peoples of the northern kingdoms," declares the LORD.

"Their kings will come and set up their thrones
in the entrance of the gates of Jerusalem;
they will come against all her surrounding walls
and against all the towns of Judah.
¹⁶I will pronounce my judgments on my people
because of their wickedness in forsaking me,
in burning incense to other gods
and in worshiping what their hands have made.

¹⁷"Get yourself ready! Stand up and say to them whatever I command you. Do not be terrified by them, or I will terrify you before them. ¹⁸Today I have made you a fortified city, an iron pillar and a bronze wall to stand against the whole land—against the kings of Judah, its officials, its priests and the people of the land. ¹⁹They will fight against you but will not overcome you, for I am with you and will rescue you," declares the LORD.

^a 5 Or *chose*   ^b 12 The Hebrew for *watching* sounds like the Hebrew for *almond tree.*

The Call

JEREMIAH 1:4–5

"Before I formed you in the womb I knew you, before you were born I set you apart," God tells Jeremiah. Imagine yourself being received into heaven. Your life is under review—and you are told that you have achieved that for which you were sent. You did it! You were faithful! How would you respond to the news? What is it that God has made *you* for? What awakens your passion, your creativity and your sense of being true to yourself? In other words, what is your calling? Now, ask yourself what you need to do in order to fully cooperate with that calling. Bring the matter to Jesus and ask him to guide you in your vocation.

See Meeting God in Prayer

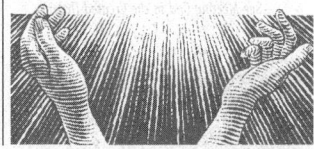

Where Is the Lord?

JEREMIAH 2:1–13

Shut your eyes and on the wide screen of your mind gaze at the spring of living water that Jeremiah mentions. What does "living water" feel like on your hands, on your face and in your mouth? In the power of your imagination, enjoy it. Return to your "big screen" and look at some still water that oozes out of a leaky pit or a stagnant cistern in the ground! What is this water like? What would it be like to touch or drink?

Letting water be an image of your relationship with God, ask yourself, "What kind of water best represents my relationship with God at the moment?" Be still. Be honest. Ask with the prophet, "Where is the Lord?" and come to God with a prayer of response.

See *Meeting God in the Created Order*

Israel Forsakes God

2 The word of the Lord came to me: [2]"Go and proclaim in the hearing of Jerusalem:

> " 'I remember the devotion of your youth,
>   how as a bride you loved me
> and followed me through the desert,
>   through a land not sown.
> [3] Israel was holy to the Lord,
>   the firstfruits of his harvest;
> all who devoured her were held guilty,
>   and disaster overtook them,' "

> declares the Lord.

[4] Hear the word of the Lord, O house of Jacob,
    all you clans of the house of Israel.

[5] This is what the Lord says:

> "What fault did your fathers find in me,
>   that they strayed so far from me?
> They followed worthless idols
>   and became worthless themselves.
> [6] They did not ask, 'Where is the Lord,
>   who brought us up out of Egypt
> and led us through the barren wilderness,
>   through a land of deserts and rifts,
> a land of drought and darkness,[a]
>   a land where no one travels and no one lives?'
> [7] I brought you into a fertile land
>   to eat its fruit and rich produce.
> But you came and defiled my land
>   and made my inheritance detestable.
> [8] The priests did not ask,
>   'Where is the Lord?'
> Those who deal with the law did not know me;
>   the leaders rebelled against me.
> The prophets prophesied by Baal,
>   following worthless idols.

[9] "Therefore I bring charges against you again,"

> declares the Lord.

> "And I will bring charges against your children's
>   children.
> [10] Cross over to the coasts of Kittim[b] and look,
>   send to Kedar[c] and observe closely;
>   see if there has ever been anything like this:
> [11] Has a nation ever changed its gods?
>   (Yet they are not gods at all.)
> But my people have exchanged their[d] Glory
>   for worthless idols.
> [12] Be appalled at this, O heavens,
>   and shudder with great horror,"

> declares the Lord.

> [13] "My people have committed two sins:
> They have forsaken me,
>   the spring of living water,
> and have dug their own cisterns,
>   broken cisterns that cannot hold water.

---

[a] 6 Or *and the shadow of death*   [b] 10 That is, Cyprus and western coastlands   [c] 10 The home of Bedouin tribes in the Syro-Arabian desert   [d] 11 Masoretic Text; an ancient Hebrew scribal tradition *my*

¹⁴ Is Israel a servant, a slave by birth?
 Why then has he become plunder?
¹⁵ Lions have roared;
 they have growled at him.
They have laid waste his land;
 his towns are burned and deserted.
¹⁶ Also, the men of Memphis*ᵃ* and Tahpanhes
 have shaved the crown of your head.*ᵇ*
¹⁷ Have you not brought this on yourselves
 by forsaking the LORD your God
 when he led you in the way?
¹⁸ Now why go to Egypt
 to drink water from the Shihor*ᶜ*?
And why go to Assyria
 to drink water from the River*ᵈ*?
¹⁹ Your wickedness will punish you;
 your backsliding will rebuke you.
Consider then and realize
 how evil and bitter it is for you
when you forsake the LORD your God
 and have no awe of me,"
 declares the Lord, the LORD Almighty.

²⁰ "Long ago you broke off your yoke
 and tore off your bonds;
 you said, 'I will not serve you!'
Indeed, on every high hill
 and under every spreading tree
 you lay down as a prostitute.
²¹ I had planted you like a choice vine
 of sound and reliable stock.
How then did you turn against me
 into a corrupt, wild vine?
²² Although you wash yourself with soda
 and use an abundance of soap,
 the stain of your guilt is still before me,"
 declares the Sovereign LORD.
²³ "How can you say, 'I am not defiled;
 I have not run after the Baals'?
See how you behaved in the valley;
 consider what you have done.
You are a swift she-camel
 running here and there,
²⁴ a wild donkey accustomed to the desert,
 sniffing the wind in her craving—
 in her heat who can restrain her?
Any males that pursue her need not tire
 themselves;
 at mating time they will find her.
²⁵ Do not run until your feet are bare
 and your throat is dry.
But you said, 'It's no use!
I love foreign gods,
 and I must go after them.'

²⁶ "As a thief is disgraced when he is caught,
 so the house of Israel is disgraced—
they, their kings and their officials,
 their priests and their prophets.

A Prodigal Departure

JEREMIAH 2:14–18

Like a defiant youth, Israel has left home and has forsaken God for what the neighbors can offer. And like a rebellious daughter, Israel has scorned the wealth of her inheritance and the love of her home and has sold herself like a whore. The stain of guilt is indelible.

In the company of God, the faithful One, consider how you have forsaken him. What appetites lure you away? What stain do you still bear? Abandon yourself to the mercy of God, in whom you will not be ashamed (see Psalm 25:20). Fast for at least one meal. When you begin to feel hungry, let your desire for food stir your desire for God, who alone can satisfy (see Psalm 16:11).

See Meeting God in Everyday Life

ᵃ 16 Hebrew *Noph* *ᵇ 16* Or *have cracked your skull* *ᶜ 18* That is, a branch
of the Nile *ᵈ 18* That is, the Euphrates

997

I've Done Nothing Wrong!

JEREMIAH 2:29–35

Israel is in denial. God has clear evidence of unfaithfulness, yet Israel insists, "I am innocent." Israel has pursued her own fancies and put her trust in things other than God.

Make a list of things of which you are allegedly "innocent." Now ask the Holy Spirit to give you freedom from denial so that you might see things God's way. Confess those sins that need confessing. Burn your list as you pray that the acknowledgment of your sins will become the seed for the planting of new life.

See Meeting God in Prayer

27 They say to wood, 'You are my father,'
    and to stone, 'You gave me birth.'
They have turned their backs to me
    and not their faces;
yet when they are in trouble, they say,
    'Come and save us!'
28 Where then are the gods you made for
        yourselves?
    Let them come if they can save you
    when you are in trouble!
For you have as many gods
    as you have towns, O Judah.

29 "Why do you bring charges against me?
    You have all rebelled against me,"

declares the LORD.

30 "In vain I punished your people;
    they did not respond to correction.
Your sword has devoured your prophets
    like a ravening lion.

31 "You of this generation, consider the word of the LORD:

"Have I been a desert to Israel
    or a land of great darkness?
Why do my people say, 'We are free to roam;
    we will come to you no more'?
32 Does a maiden forget her jewelry,
    a bride her wedding ornaments?
Yet my people have forgotten me,
    days without number.
33 How skilled you are at pursuing love!
    Even the worst of women can learn from your
        ways.
34 On your clothes men find
    the lifeblood of the innocent poor,
    though you did not catch them breaking in.
Yet in spite of all this
35   you say, 'I am innocent;
    he is not angry with me.'
But I will pass judgment on you
    because you say, 'I have not sinned.'
36 Why do you go about so much,
    changing your ways?
You will be disappointed by Egypt
    as you were by Assyria.
37 You will also leave that place
    with your hands on your head,
for the LORD has rejected those you trust;
    you will not be helped by them.

3 "If a man divorces his wife
    and she leaves him and marries another man,
should he return to her again?
    Would not the land be completely defiled?
But you have lived as a prostitute with many
        lovers—
    would you now return to me?"

declares the LORD.

2 "Look up to the barren heights and see.
    Is there any place where you have not been
        ravished?

By the roadside you sat waiting for lovers,
    sat like a nomad[a] in the desert.
You have defiled the land
    with your prostitution and wickedness.
³ Therefore the showers have been withheld,
    and no spring rains have fallen.
Yet you have the brazen look of a prostitute;
    you refuse to blush with shame.
⁴ Have you not just called to me:
    'My Father, my friend from my youth,
⁵ will you always be angry?
    Will your wrath continue forever?'
This is how you talk,
    but you do all the evil you can."

Unfaithful Israel

⁶ During the reign of King Josiah, the LORD said to me, "Have you seen what faithless Israel has done? She has gone up on every high hill and under every spreading tree and has committed adultery there. ⁷ I thought that after she had done all this she would return to me but she did not, and her unfaithful sister Judah saw it. ⁸ I gave faithless Israel her certificate of divorce and sent her away because of all her adulteries. Yet I saw that her unfaithful sister Judah had no fear; she also went out and committed adultery. ⁹ Because Israel's immorality mattered so little to her, she defiled the land and committed adultery with stone and wood. ¹⁰ In spite of all this, her unfaithful sister Judah did not return to me with all her heart, but only in pretense," declares the LORD.

¹¹ The LORD said to me, "Faithless Israel is more righteous than unfaithful Judah. ¹² Go, proclaim this message toward the north:

" 'Return, faithless Israel,' declares the LORD,
    'I will frown on you no longer,
for I am merciful,' declares the LORD,
    'I will not be angry forever.
¹³ Only acknowledge your guilt—
    you have rebelled against the LORD your God,
you have scattered your favors to foreign gods
    under every spreading tree,
    and have not obeyed me,' "
                            declares the LORD.

¹⁴ "Return, faithless people," declares the LORD, "for I am your husband. I will choose you—one from a town and two from a clan—and bring you to Zion. ¹⁵ Then I will give you shepherds after my own heart, who will lead you with knowledge and understanding. ¹⁶ In those days, when your numbers have increased greatly in the land," declares the LORD, "men will no longer say, 'The ark of the covenant of the LORD.' It will never enter their minds or be remembered; it will not be missed, nor will another one be made. ¹⁷ At that time they will call Jerusalem The Throne of the LORD, and all nations will gather in Jerusalem to honor the name of the LORD. No longer will they follow the stubbornness of their evil hearts. ¹⁸ In those days the house of Judah will join the house of Israel, and together they will come from a northern land to the land I gave your forefathers as an inheritance.

¹⁹ "I myself said,

Self-Examination

JEREMIAH 3:11–18

"Help me, O Holy Spirit, to
   search and question
   myself, and honestly to
   answer:
Am I single-minded in
   seeking my God? in
   serving him? even in
   praying to him?
Do I put God first in deed?
   in intention? or even in
   desire? in hope?
What reserves do I always
   maintain against him?
   What other loves cling
   to? . . .
Search me thyself, O God,
   seek the grounds of my
   heart;
Look well if there be any
   way of wickedness in
   me,
any subservience to mine
   own ease,
any hungering and playing
   for mine own
   honour . . .
O Saviour of the world,
   who by thy cross and
   precious Blood hast
   redeemed us,
save me and help me, I
   humbly beseech thee,
   O Lord."

—ERIC MILNER-WHITE,
My God My Glory

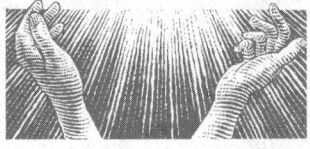

Return to God!

JEREMIAH 4:1–4

Recall an experience of returning home or being reunited with someone. What were you returning from? How were you received? What emotions from that experience remain?

Today God says, "Return!" What does it mean for you to "return to God"? Write a response in your journal or on a piece of paper. Discuss your ideas with your spiritual adviser, your pastor or a companion in faith. Take whatever action is necessary for you to "return to God."

See Meeting God in Worship

" 'How gladly would I treat you like sons
and give you a desirable land,
the most beautiful inheritance of any nation.'
I thought you would call me 'Father'
and not turn away from following me.
²⁰ But like a woman unfaithful to her husband,
so you have been unfaithful to me, O house of
Israel,"

declares the LORD.

²¹ A cry is heard on the barren heights,
the weeping and pleading of the people of Israel,
because they have perverted their ways
and have forgotten the LORD their God.

²² "Return, faithless people;
I will cure you of backsliding."

"Yes, we will come to you,
for you are the LORD our God.
²³ Surely the ⌞idolatrous⌟ commotion on the hills
and mountains is a deception;
surely in the LORD our God
is the salvation of Israel.
²⁴ From our youth shameful gods have consumed
the fruits of our fathers' labor—
their flocks and herds,
their sons and daughters.
²⁵ Let us lie down in our shame,
and let our disgrace cover us.
We have sinned against the LORD our God,
both we and our fathers;
from our youth till this day
we have not obeyed the LORD our God."

4 "If you will return, O Israel,
return to me,"

declares the LORD.
"If you put your detestable idols out of my sight
and no longer go astray,
² and if in a truthful, just and righteous way
you swear, 'As surely as the LORD lives,'
then the nations will be blessed by him
and in him they will glory."

³ This is what the LORD says to the men of Judah and to Jerusalem:

"Break up your unplowed ground
and do not sow among thorns.
⁴ Circumcise yourselves to the LORD,
circumcise your hearts,
you men of Judah and people of Jerusalem,
or my wrath will break out and burn like fire
because of the evil you have done—
burn with no one to quench it.

Disaster From the North

⁵ "Announce in Judah and proclaim in Jerusalem
and say:
'Sound the trumpet throughout the land!'
Cry aloud and say:

'Gather together!
Let us flee to the fortified cities!'
⁶ Raise the signal to go to Zion!
Flee for safety without delay!
For I am bringing disaster from the north,
even terrible destruction."

⁷ A lion has come out of his lair;
a destroyer of nations has set out.
He has left his place
to lay waste your land.
Your towns will lie in ruins
without inhabitant.
⁸ So put on sackcloth,
lament and wail,
for the fierce anger of the LORD
has not turned away from us.

⁹ "In that day," declares the LORD,
"the king and the officials will lose heart,
the priests will be horrified,
and the prophets will be appalled."

¹⁰ Then I said, "Ah, Sovereign LORD, how completely you have deceived this people and Jerusalem by saying, 'You will have peace,' when the sword is at our throats."

¹¹ At that time this people and Jerusalem will be told, "A scorching wind from the barren heights in the desert blows toward my people, but not to winnow or cleanse; ¹² a wind too strong for that comes from me.ᵃ Now I pronounce my judgments against them."

¹³ Look! He advances like the clouds,
his chariots come like a whirlwind,
his horses are swifter than eagles.
Woe to us! We are ruined!
¹⁴ O Jerusalem, wash the evil from your heart and
be saved.
How long will you harbor wicked thoughts?
¹⁵ A voice is announcing from Dan,
proclaiming disaster from the hills of Ephraim.
¹⁶ "Tell this to the nations,
proclaim it to Jerusalem:
'A besieging army is coming from a distant land,
raising a war cry against the cities of Judah.
¹⁷ They surround her like men guarding a field,
because she has rebelled against me,' "
declares the LORD.
¹⁸ "Your own conduct and actions
have brought this upon you.
This is your punishment.
How bitter it is!
How it pierces to the heart!"

¹⁹ Oh, my anguish, my anguish!
I writhe in pain.
Oh, the agony of my heart!
My heart pounds within me,
I cannot keep silent.
For I have heard the sound of the trumpet;
I have heard the battle cry.

Listen!

JEREMIAH 4:5–8

The trumpets are sounding! Disaster is on its way—as violent and terrifying as a lion in pursuit of prey. And all the signs are being ignored!

Are you listening? What is God saying to you that you are screening out? What issue have you registered but filed in the "must look at one day" box?

Bring your calendar and a bowl of cold water to your prayer place. Pray that the Holy Spirit will deliver you from illusion. Wash your hands and feel the cleansing, refreshing cold water. Pray that God will cleanse your heart. Take out your calendar and make an appointment with God to start dealing with this issue. Leave your time of prayer saying along with Paul the apostle, "I can do everything through [Christ] who gives me strength" (Philippians 4:13)!

See Meeting God in Prayer

ᵃ 12 Or *comes at my command*

Disaster

JEREMIAH 4:20–28

The prophet envisions disaster after disaster for Israel. The land is desolate. The towns are deserted. The nation groans as if in the throes of death.

As you look back over the past years of your life, what private or public disaster has most affected you? What did you learn about yourself through it? What did you learn about God?

In the center of a blank page, write what you have learned about God from the experience. In the other space write down any associated thoughts; then, with paints or crayons, fill in the page with the colors you associate with the emotions that you have. Offer your work to God and pray about whatever change in attitude or behavior it has prompted in you.

See Meeting God in Prayer

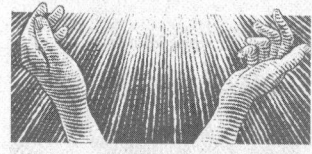

²⁰ Disaster follows disaster;
    the whole land lies in ruins.
In an instant my tents are destroyed,
    my shelter in a moment.
²¹ How long must I see the battle standard
    and hear the sound of the trumpet?

²² "My people are fools;
    they do not know me.
They are senseless children;
    they have no understanding.
They are skilled in doing evil;
    they know not how to do good."

²³ I looked at the earth,
    and it was formless and empty;
and at the heavens,
    and their light was gone.
²⁴ I looked at the mountains,
    and they were quaking;
    all the hills were swaying.
²⁵ I looked, and there were no people;
    every bird in the sky had flown away.
²⁶ I looked, and the fruitful land was a desert;
    all its towns lay in ruins
    before the Lord, before his fierce anger.

²⁷ This is what the Lord says:

"The whole land will be ruined,
    though I will not destroy it completely.
²⁸ Therefore the earth will mourn
    and the heavens above grow dark,
because I have spoken and will not relent,
    I have decided and will not turn back."

²⁹ At the sound of horsemen and archers
    every town takes to flight.
Some go into the thickets;
    some climb up among the rocks.
All the towns are deserted;
    no one lives in them.

³⁰ What are you doing, O devastated one?
    Why dress yourself in scarlet
    and put on jewels of gold?
Why shade your eyes with paint?
    You adorn yourself in vain.
Your lovers despise you;
    they seek your life.

³¹ I hear a cry as of a woman in labor,
    a groan as of one bearing her first child—
the cry of the Daughter of Zion gasping for breath,
    stretching out her hands and saying,
"Alas! I am fainting;
    my life is given over to murderers."

Not One Is Upright

5 "Go up and down the streets of Jerusalem,
    look around and consider,
    search through her squares.
If you can find but one person
    who deals honestly and seeks the truth,

I will forgive this city.
² Although they say, 'As surely as the LORD lives,'
    still they are swearing falsely."

³ O LORD, do not your eyes look for truth?
    You struck them, but they felt no pain;
    you crushed them, but they refused correction.
They made their faces harder than stone
    and refused to repent.
⁴ I thought, "These are only the poor;
    they are foolish,
for they do not know the way of the LORD,
    the requirements of their God.
⁵ So I will go to the leaders
    and speak to them;
surely they know the way of the LORD,
    the requirements of their God."
But with one accord they too had broken off the
        yoke
    and torn off the bonds.
⁶ Therefore a lion from the forest will attack them,
    a wolf from the desert will ravage them,
a leopard will lie in wait near their towns
    to tear to pieces any who venture out,
for their rebellion is great
    and their backslidings many.

⁷ "Why should I forgive you?
    Your children have forsaken me
    and sworn by gods that are not gods.
I supplied all their needs,
    yet they committed adultery
    and thronged to the houses of prostitutes.
⁸ They are well-fed, lusty stallions,
    each neighing for another man's wife.
⁹ Should I not punish them for this?"
    declares the LORD.
    "Should I not avenge myself
    on such a nation as this?

¹⁰ "Go through her vineyards and ravage them,
    but do not destroy them completely.
Strip off her branches,
    for these people do not belong to the LORD.
¹¹ The house of Israel and the house of Judah
    have been utterly unfaithful to me,"
                        declares the LORD.

¹² They have lied about the LORD;
    they said, "He will do nothing!
No harm will come to us;
    we will never see sword or famine.
¹³ The prophets are but wind
    and the word is not in them;
    so let what they say be done to them."

¹⁴ Therefore this is what the LORD God Almighty says:

"Because the people have spoken these words,
    I will make my words in your mouth a fire
    and these people the wood it consumes.
¹⁵ O house of Israel," declares the LORD,
    "I am bringing a distant nation against you—

Denial

JEREMIAH 5:12–15

"[The Lord] will do nothing" says Israel. "No harm will come to us." Are there attitudes or circumstances or situations in your own life, or in the life of your family or community, about which you might say dismissively, "God will do nothing!"? Are you prone to think God doesn't care about how you spend money, how you use the authority he has given you, what you eat and drink, or how you spend your time? Do you hear yourself saying, "It doesn't matter. No harm will come to me" in any of these areas?

Take all of the things about which you say "it doesn't matter" to God, and ask God if they matter. Is there something God wants you to attend to? Check it out with a prayer partner or trusted friend who will help you avoid denial or oversensitivity.

See Meeting God in Everyday Life

Boundaries

JEREMIAH 5:17–31

In defiance of the boundaries God has ordained for safety, the Israelites cross the boundaries and trust in military defense, not God (v.17). They serve "foreign gods," not Yahweh (v.19). They commit theft rather than trust God's provision (v.26). They are not just, nor do they defend the orphan and the needy (v.28). The prophets lie and the priests rule by their own authority (v.31). And worse still, the people have no problem with it!

What boundaries do you place around relationships, time, work and money? In what instances are you transgressing your own boundaries? In what ways are your boundaries in danger of being transgressed by others? Name some key areas in your life, and ask the Spirit for a gift of honesty and integrity as you look at your boundaries. Drawing on Scripture and your own common sense, define new boundaries, if necessary, that are appropriate for each issue. Pray about them and refer to them at least once a month.

See Meeting God in Everyday Life

an ancient and enduring nation,
    a people whose language you do not know,
    whose speech you do not understand.
16 Their quivers are like an open grave;
    all of them are mighty warriors.
17 They will devour your harvests and food,
    devour your sons and daughters;
they will devour your flocks and herds,
    devour your vines and fig trees.
With the sword they will destroy
    the fortified cities in which you trust.

18 "Yet even in those days," declares the LORD, "I will not destroy you completely. 19 And when the people ask, 'Why has the LORD our God done all this to us?' you will tell them, 'As you have forsaken me and served foreign gods in your own land, so now you will serve foreigners in a land not your own.'

20 "Announce this to the house of Jacob
    and proclaim it in Judah:
21 Hear this, you foolish and senseless people,
    who have eyes but do not see,
    who have ears but do not hear:
22 Should you not fear me?" declares the LORD.
    "Should you not tremble in my presence?
I made the sand a boundary for the sea,
    an everlasting barrier it cannot cross.
The waves may roll, but they cannot prevail;
    they may roar, but they cannot cross it.
23 But these people have stubborn and rebellious
      hearts;
    they have turned aside and gone away.
24 They do not say to themselves,
    'Let us fear the LORD our God,
who gives autumn and spring rains in season,
    who assures us of the regular weeks of harvest.'
25 Your wrongdoings have kept these away;
    your sins have deprived you of good.

26 "Among my people are wicked men
    who lie in wait like men who snare birds
    and like those who set traps to catch men.
27 Like cages full of birds,
    their houses are full of deceit;
they have become rich and powerful
28   and have grown fat and sleek.
Their evil deeds have no limit;
    they do not plead the case of the fatherless to
      win it,
    they do not defend the rights of the poor.
29 Should I not punish them for this?"
    declares the LORD.
"Should I not avenge myself
    on such a nation as this?

30 "A horrible and shocking thing
    has happened in the land:
31 The prophets prophesy lies,
    the priests rule by their own authority,
and my people love it this way.
    But what will you do in the end?

Jerusalem Under Siege

6 "Flee for safety, people of Benjamin!
Flee from Jerusalem!
Sound the trumpet in Tekoa!
Raise the signal over Beth Hakkerem!
For disaster looms out of the north,
even terrible destruction.
² I will destroy the Daughter of Zion,
so beautiful and delicate.
³ Shepherds with their flocks will come against her;
they will pitch their tents around her,
each tending his own portion."

⁴ "Prepare for battle against her!
Arise, let us attack at noon!
But, alas, the daylight is fading,
and the shadows of evening grow long.
⁵ So arise, let us attack at night
and destroy her fortresses!"

⁶ This is what the LORD Almighty says:

"Cut down the trees
and build siege ramps against Jerusalem.
This city must be punished;
it is filled with oppression.
⁷ As a well pours out its water,
so she pours out her wickedness.
Violence and destruction resound in her;
her sickness and wounds are ever before me.
⁸ Take warning, O Jerusalem,
or I will turn away from you
and make your land desolate
so no one can live in it."

⁹ This is what the LORD Almighty says:

"Let them glean the remnant of Israel
as thoroughly as a vine;
pass your hand over the branches again,
like one gathering grapes."

¹⁰ To whom can I speak and give warning?
Who will listen to me?
Their ears are closed*a*
so they cannot hear.
The word of the LORD is offensive to them;
they find no pleasure in it.
¹¹ But I am full of the wrath of the LORD,
and I cannot hold it in.

"Pour it out on the children in the street
and on the young men gathered together;
both husband and wife will be caught in it,
and the old, those weighed down with years.
¹² Their houses will be turned over to others,
together with their fields and their wives,
when I stretch out my hand
against those who live in the land,"

declares the LORD.

¹³ "From the least to the greatest,
all are greedy for gain;

Anybody Listening?

JEREMIAH 6:9–10

"To whom can I speak?" Jeremiah laments. No one is listening. The ears of Israel's people are closed to the "offense" of God's word. But the word persists, calling the people to change their minds, to see things differently—God's way—to see that there *is* sin in the land, that God *is not* honored and that judgment *is* inevitable.

Turn to a section of Scripture that you usually edit out of your consciousness. Read something that "offends" you—something that just doesn't seem fair or understandable to you. In what way does it offend you? How might God use it to speak to you? Talk it over with someone in your faith community and pray about it.

See Meeting God in Scripture

Which Way?

JEREMIAH 6:13–16

Imagine you are at a crossroads. You can travel either of two ways. One way is God's way. Through both its green pastures and dark valleys, you can be assured of God's companionship (see Psalm 23). The other way is not God's way, but it is attractive. What is attractive about it? What entices you to step toward it?

Paint or draw a picture of your crossroads, using color and shape to represent what your imagination has seen. Draw the Good Shepherd into the picture. Talk with him about the two ways you could go. Draw yourself on the road you really want to travel. Ask Jesus to lead you in the way that is truth and life.

See Meeting God in Everyday Life

prophets and priests alike,
all practice deceit.
¹⁴ They dress the wound of my people
as though it were not serious.
'Peace, peace,' they say,
when there is no peace.
¹⁵ Are they ashamed of their loathsome conduct?
No, they have no shame at all;
they do not even know how to blush.
So they will fall among the fallen;
they will be brought down when I punish
them,"

says the LORD.

¹⁶ This is what the LORD says:

"Stand at the crossroads and look;
ask for the ancient paths,
ask where the good way is, and walk in it,
and you will find rest for your souls.
But you said, 'We will not walk in it.'
¹⁷ I appointed watchmen over you and said,
'Listen to the sound of the trumpet!'
But you said, 'We will not listen.'
¹⁸ Therefore hear, O nations;
observe, O witnesses,
what will happen to them.
¹⁹ Hear, O earth:
I am bringing disaster on this people,
the fruit of their schemes,
because they have not listened to my words
and have rejected my law.
²⁰ What do I care about incense from Sheba
or sweet calamus from a distant land?
Your burnt offerings are not acceptable;
your sacrifices do not please me."

²¹ Therefore this is what the LORD says:

"I will put obstacles before this people.
Fathers and sons alike will stumble over them;
neighbors and friends will perish."

²² This is what the LORD says:

"Look, an army is coming
from the land of the north;
a great nation is being stirred up
from the ends of the earth.
²³ They are armed with bow and spear;
they are cruel and show no mercy.
They sound like the roaring sea
as they ride on their horses;
they come like men in battle formation
to attack you, O Daughter of Zion."

²⁴ We have heard reports about them,
and our hands hang limp.
Anguish has gripped us,
pain like that of a woman in labor.
²⁵ Do not go out to the fields
or walk on the roads,
for the enemy has a sword,
and there is terror on every side.

26 O my people, put on sackcloth
    and roll in ashes;
mourn with bitter wailing
    as for an only son,
for suddenly the destroyer
    will come upon us.

27 "I have made you a tester of metals
    and my people the ore,
that you may observe
    and test their ways.
28 They are all hardened rebels,
    going about to slander.
They are bronze and iron;
    they all act corruptly.
29 The bellows blow fiercely
    to burn away the lead with fire,
but the refining goes on in vain;
    the wicked are not purged out.
30 They are called rejected silver,
    because the LORD has rejected them."

False Religion Worthless

7 This is the word that came to Jeremiah from the LORD: 2 "Stand at the gate of the LORD's house and there proclaim this message:

" 'Hear the word of the LORD, all you people of Judah who come through these gates to worship the LORD. 3 This is what the LORD Almighty, the God of Israel, says: Reform your ways and your actions, and I will let you live in this place. 4 Do not trust in deceptive words and say, "This is the temple of the LORD, the temple of the LORD, the temple of the LORD!" 5 If you really change your ways and your actions and deal with each other justly, 6 if you do not oppress the alien, the fatherless or the widow and do not shed innocent blood in this place, and if you do not follow other gods to your own harm, 7 then I will let you live in this place, in the land I gave your forefathers for ever and ever. 8 But look, you are trusting in deceptive words that are worthless.

9 " 'Will you steal and murder, commit adultery and perjury,[a] burn incense to Baal and follow other gods you have not known, 10 and then come and stand before me in this house, which bears my Name, and say, "We are safe"—safe to do all these detestable things? 11 Has this house, which bears my Name, become a den of robbers to you? But I have been watching! declares the LORD.

12 " 'Go now to the place in Shiloh where I first made a dwelling for my Name, and see what I did to it because of the wickedness of my people Israel. 13 While you were doing all these things, declares the LORD, I spoke to you again and again, but you did not listen; I called you, but you did not answer. 14 Therefore, what I did to Shiloh I will now do to the house that bears my Name, the temple you trust in, the place I gave to you and your fathers. 15 I will thrust you from my presence, just as I did all your brothers, the people of Ephraim.'

16 "So do not pray for this people nor offer any plea or petition for them; do not plead with me, for I will not listen to you. 17 Do you not see what they are doing in the towns of

Deceptive Words

JEREMIAH 7:1–10

"This is the temple of the LORD!" says Israel, believing that somehow, by saying it, its "magic" will protect them from the reality of God's judgment.

What are the common phrases used in the liturgies and worship services of your faith community? Do you or your friends use any religious catchphrases? Ask someone to tell you what your common phrases are. Make a list of them. Give them a "reality check." Talk to your friends and to a worship leader in your church about any that you feel mask the reality of God. Pray that your speech may be authentic and free of jargon and that it may "set an example for the believers in speech" (1 Timothy 4:12).

See *Meeting God in Everyday Life*

---

a 9 Or *and swear by false gods*

What Is Your Guiding Light—Really?

JEREMIAH 7:21–26

Israel continues to ignore God. The people follow their own inclinations and their own counsel, and they do not turn to God. In their wayward attempts to find guidance, meaning and blessing, they sacrifice their children (32:35) and consult and worship the sun, moon and stars (8:2).

Whom or what do you unthinkingly consult before you consult God? What do you sacrifice (such as money, time or energy) without going to God first? What influences guide you—the share index, the weather, the "stars," the wills of other people? Each morning for the next week, intentionally pray for God's guidance—each moment, each day—in what you do in the situations and relationships you encounter. For each day of the week, write in your calendar, "Your word is a lamp to my feet and a light for my path" (Psalm 119:105).

See Meeting God in Everyday Life

Judah and in the streets of Jerusalem? ¹⁸The children gather wood, the fathers light the fire, and the women knead the dough and make cakes of bread for the Queen of Heaven. They pour out drink offerings to other gods to provoke me to anger. ¹⁹But am I the one they are provoking? declares the LORD. Are they not rather harming themselves, to their own shame?

²⁰" 'Therefore this is what the Sovereign LORD says: My anger and my wrath will be poured out on this place, on man and beast, on the trees of the field and on the fruit of the ground, and it will burn and not be quenched.

²¹" 'This is what the LORD Almighty, the God of Israel, says: Go ahead, add your burnt offerings to your other sacrifices and eat the meat yourselves! ²²For when I brought your forefathers out of Egypt and spoke to them, I did not just give them commands about burnt offerings and sacrifices, ²³but I gave them this command: Obey me, and I will be your God and you will be my people. Walk in all the ways I command you, that it may go well with you. ²⁴But they did not listen or pay attention; instead, they followed the stubborn inclinations of their evil hearts. They went backward and not forward. ²⁵From the time your forefathers left Egypt until now, day after day, again and again I sent you my servants the prophets. ²⁶But they did not listen to me or pay attention. They were stiff-necked and did more evil than their forefathers.'

²⁷"When you tell them all this, they will not listen to you; when you call to them, they will not answer. ²⁸Therefore say to them, 'This is the nation that has not obeyed the LORD its God or responded to correction. Truth has perished; it has vanished from their lips. ²⁹Cut off your hair and throw it away; take up a lament on the barren heights, for the LORD has rejected and abandoned this generation that is under his wrath.

The Valley of Slaughter

³⁰" 'The people of Judah have done evil in my eyes, declares the LORD. They have set up their detestable idols in the house that bears my Name and have defiled it. ³¹They have built the high places of Topheth in the Valley of Ben Hinnom to burn their sons and daughters in the fire—something I did not command, nor did it enter my mind. ³²So beware, the days are coming, declares the LORD, when people will no longer call it Topheth or the Valley of Ben Hinnom, but the Valley of Slaughter, for they will bury the dead in Topheth until there is no more room. ³³Then the carcasses of this people will become food for the birds of the air and the beasts of the earth, and there will be no one to frighten them away. ³⁴I will bring an end to the sounds of joy and gladness and to the voices of bride and bridegroom in the towns of Judah and the streets of Jerusalem, for the land will become desolate.

8 " 'At that time, declares the LORD, the bones of the kings and officials of Judah, the bones of the priests and prophets, and the bones of the people of Jerusalem will be removed from their graves. ²They will be exposed to the sun and the moon and all the stars of the heavens, which they have loved and served and which they have followed and consulted and worshiped. They will not be gathered up or buried, but will be like refuse lying on the ground.

³Wherever I banish them, all the survivors of this evil nation will prefer death to life, declares the LORD Almighty.'

Sin and Punishment

⁴"Say to them, 'This is what the LORD says:

" 'When men fall down, do they not get up?
  When a man turns away, does he not return?
⁵Why then have these people turned away?
  Why does Jerusalem always turn away?
They cling to deceit;
  they refuse to return.
⁶I have listened attentively,
  but they do not say what is right.
No one repents of his wickedness,
  saying, "What have I done?"
Each pursues his own course
  like a horse charging into battle.
⁷Even the stork in the sky
  knows her appointed seasons,
and the dove, the swift and the thrush
  observe the time of their migration.
But my people do not know
  the requirements of the LORD.

⁸" 'How can you say, "We are wise,
  for we have the law of the LORD,"
when actually the lying pen of the scribes
  has handled it falsely?
⁹The wise will be put to shame;
  they will be dismayed and trapped.
Since they have rejected the word of the LORD,
  what kind of wisdom do they have?
¹⁰Therefore I will give their wives to other men
  and their fields to new owners.
From the least to the greatest,
  all are greedy for gain;
prophets and priests alike,
  all practice deceit.
¹¹They dress the wound of my people
  as though it were not serious.
"Peace, peace," they say,
  when there is no peace.
¹²Are they ashamed of their loathsome conduct?
  No, they have no shame at all;
  they do not even know how to blush.
So they will fall among the fallen;
  they will be brought down when they are
    punished,
                              says the LORD.

¹³" 'I will take away their harvest,
                        declares the LORD.
There will be no grapes on the vine.
There will be no figs on the tree,
  and their leaves will wither.
What I have given them
  will be taken from them.ᵃ' "

¹⁴"Why are we sitting here?
  Gather together!

ᵃ 13 The meaning of the Hebrew for this sentence is uncertain.

At What Cost?

JEREMIAH 8:4–7

God grieves that while even the birds know how to regulate their lives, people don't do what they should naturally do—they don't get up when they fall down, nor do they turn back when they have turned away.

While in your prayer space, sketch a history of your life with God, focusing on the times you have turned away from God. Write down key words that summarize what it cost you to do so. Put yourself at God's mercy, confess your rejection of him and ask God to "quiet you with his love" (Zephaniah 3:17). Put a small "stone of memorial" in a special place to remind you daily to turn back to God.

See Meeting God in Everyday Life

Where Is the Healing?

JEREMIAH 8:18–22

Jeremiah weeps for his people. He loves his country. At great personal cost he has declared the hard word, and no one has paid any attention. And yet the people are hurting as a result of their rejection of God! Joy is gone and grief prevails. Where is healing? Has Gilead no balm?

Do you know someone who loves people and grieves about the suffering of others? Who is a supplier of "balm" in your community? Lest their eyes be a "fountain of tears" (9:1), write them a simple letter of encouragement and offer any practical support that you can give them.

See Meeting God in Community

Let us flee to the fortified cities
  and perish there!
For the LORD our God has doomed us to perish
  and given us poisoned water to drink,
  because we have sinned against him.
¹⁵ We hoped for peace
  but no good has come,
for a time of healing
  but there was only terror.
¹⁶ The snorting of the enemy's horses
  is heard from Dan;
at the neighing of their stallions
  the whole land trembles.
They have come to devour
  the land and everything in it,
  the city and all who live there."

¹⁷ "See, I will send venomous snakes among you,
  vipers that cannot be charmed,
  and they will bite you,"
                              declares the LORD.

¹⁸ O my Comforter[a] in sorrow,
  my heart is faint within me.
¹⁹ Listen to the cry of my people
  from a land far away:
"Is the LORD not in Zion?
  Is her King no longer there?"

"Why have they provoked me to anger with their
      images,
  with their worthless foreign idols?"

²⁰ "The harvest is past,
  the summer has ended,
  and we are not saved."

²¹ Since my people are crushed, I am crushed;
  I mourn, and horror grips me.
²² Is there no balm in Gilead?
  Is there no physician there?
Why then is there no healing
  for the wound of my people?

9 ¹ Oh, that my head were a spring of water
  and my eyes a fountain of tears!
I would weep day and night
  for the slain of my people.
² Oh, that I had in the desert
  a lodging place for travelers,
so that I might leave my people
  and go away from them;
for they are all adulterers,
  a crowd of unfaithful people.

³ "They make ready their tongue
  like a bow, to shoot lies;
it is not by truth
  that they triumph[b] in the land.
They go from one sin to another;
  they do not acknowledge me,"
                              declares the LORD.

---

⁴"Beware of your friends;
　　do not trust your brothers.
For every brother is a deceiver,ᵃ
　　and every friend a slanderer.
⁵Friend deceives friend,
　　and no one speaks the truth.
They have taught their tongues to lie;
　　they weary themselves with sinning.
⁶Youᵇ live in the midst of deception;
　　in their deceit they refuse to acknowledge me,"
　　　　　　　　　　declares the LORD.

⁷Therefore this is what the LORD Almighty says:

"See, I will refine and test them,
　　for what else can I do
　　because of the sin of my people?
⁸Their tongue is a deadly arrow;
　　it speaks with deceit.
With his mouth each speaks cordially to his
　　　　neighbor,
　　but in his heart he sets a trap for him.
⁹Should I not punish them for this?"
　　declares the LORD.
"Should I not avenge myself
　　on such a nation as this?"

¹⁰I will weep and wail for the mountains
　　and take up a lament concerning the desert
　　　　pastures.
They are desolate and untraveled,
　　and the lowing of cattle is not heard.
The birds of the air have fled
　　and the animals are gone.

¹¹"I will make Jerusalem a heap of ruins,
　　a haunt of jackals;
and I will lay waste the towns of Judah
　　so no one can live there."

¹²What man is wise enough to understand this? Who has been instructed by the LORD and can explain it? Why has the land been ruined and laid waste like a desert that no one can cross?

¹³The LORD said, "It is because they have forsaken my law, which I set before them; they have not obeyed me or followed my law. ¹⁴Instead, they have followed the stubbornness of their hearts; they have followed the Baals, as their fathers taught them." ¹⁵Therefore, this is what the LORD Almighty, the God of Israel, says: "See, I will make this people eat bitter food and drink poisoned water. ¹⁶I will scatter them among nations that neither they nor their fathers have known, and I will pursue them with the sword until I have destroyed them."

¹⁷This is what the LORD Almighty says:

"Consider now! Call for the wailing women to
　　　　come;
　　send for the most skillful of them.
¹⁸Let them come quickly
　　and wail over us

What More Can Be Done?

JEREMIAH 9:5–9

In Israel no one was safe. Because the people consistently rejected God and God's ways, they have created a society in which no one trusts or honors others. The result is abuse, and abuse leads to the breakdown of society.

And what of your community? How safe is it? What about it makes you weep? Meet with a friend and walk some streets in your neighborhood—drive through your community if it is rural. Bless the houses, the people you see and the ground you are on by calling on the name of the Lord and being a bearer of God's presence into places where God may not normally be welcomed.

See Meeting God in Service

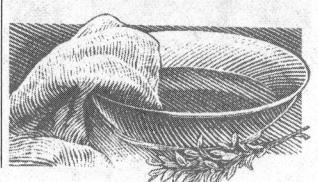

Boast Boldly

JEREMIAH 9:23–24

Gather some friends. Go around the group and talk about things each person is grateful for. In particular mention ways in which God has helped each of you. Make notes of what is said or encourage each person to keep mental notes of what is said. In prayer together give thanks for one another and what each one can, in God's grace, "boast of." Considering all the good things God has done for each of you, let your soul "boast in the LORD" (Psalm 34:2). Talk together and find some tangible way of "boasting" in God.

See Meeting God in Community

till our eyes overflow with tears
  and water streams from our eyelids.
¹⁹ The sound of wailing is heard from Zion:
  'How ruined we are!
  How great is our shame!
We must leave our land
  because our houses are in ruins.' "

²⁰ Now, O women, hear the word of the LORD;
  open your ears to the words of his mouth.
Teach your daughters how to wail;
  teach one another a lament.
²¹ Death has climbed in through our windows
  and has entered our fortresses;
it has cut off the children from the streets
  and the young men from the public squares.

²²Say, "This is what the LORD declares:

" 'The dead bodies of men will lie
  like refuse on the open field,
like cut grain behind the reaper,
  with no one to gather them.' "

²³This is what the LORD says:

"Let not the wise man boast of his wisdom
  or the strong man boast of his strength
  or the rich man boast of his riches,
²⁴ but let him who boasts boast about this:
  that he understands and knows me,
that I am the LORD, who exercises kindness,
  justice and righteousness on earth,
  for in these I delight,"
          declares the LORD.

²⁵"The days are coming," declares the LORD, "when I will punish all who are circumcised only in the flesh— ²⁶Egypt, Judah, Edom, Ammon, Moab and all who live in the desert in distant places.[a] For all these nations are really uncircumcised, and even the whole house of Israel is uncircumcised in heart."

God and Idols

10 Hear what the LORD says to you, O house of Israel. ²This is what the LORD says:

"Do not learn the ways of the nations
  or be terrified by signs in the sky,
  though the nations are terrified by them.
³ For the customs of the peoples are worthless;
  they cut a tree out of the forest,
  and a craftsman shapes it with his chisel.
⁴ They adorn it with silver and gold;
  they fasten it with hammer and nails
  so it will not totter.
⁵ Like a scarecrow in a melon patch,
  their idols cannot speak;
they must be carried
  because they cannot walk.
Do not fear them;
  they can do no harm
  nor can they do any good."

a 26 Or desert and who clip the hair by their foreheads

⁶No one is like you, O Lᴏʀᴅ;
　　you are great,
　　and your name is mighty in power.
⁷Who should not revere you,
　　O King of the nations?
　　This is your due.
　Among all the wise men of the nations
　　and in all their kingdoms,
　　there is no one like you.
⁸They are all senseless and foolish;
　　they are taught by worthless wooden idols.
⁹Hammered silver is brought from Tarshish
　　and gold from Uphaz.
　What the craftsman and goldsmith have made
　　is then dressed in blue and purple—
　　all made by skilled workers.
¹⁰But the Lᴏʀᴅ is the true God;
　　he is the living God, the eternal King.
　When he is angry, the earth trembles;
　　the nations cannot endure his wrath.

¹¹"Tell them this: 'These gods, who did not make the heavens and the earth, will perish from the earth and from under the heavens.' "ᵃ

¹²But God made the earth by his power;
　　he founded the world by his wisdom
　　and stretched out the heavens by his
　　　understanding.
¹³When he thunders, the waters in the heavens
　　　roar;
　　he makes clouds rise from the ends of the
　　　earth.
　He sends lightning with the rain
　　and brings out the wind from his storehouses.
¹⁴Everyone is senseless and without knowledge;
　　every goldsmith is shamed by his idols.
　His images are a fraud;
　　they have no breath in them.
¹⁵They are worthless, the objects of mockery;
　　when their judgment comes, they will perish.
¹⁶He who is the Portion of Jacob is not like these,
　　for he is the Maker of all things,
　including Israel, the tribe of his inheritance—
　　the Lᴏʀᴅ Almighty is his name.

Coming Destruction

¹⁷Gather up your belongings to leave the land,
　　you who live under siege.
¹⁸For this is what the Lᴏʀᴅ says:
　　"At this time I will hurl out
　　those who live in this land;
　I will bring distress on them
　　so that they may be captured."

¹⁹Woe to me because of my injury!
　　My wound is incurable!
　Yet I said to myself,
　　"This is my sickness, and I must endure it."
²⁰My tent is destroyed;

The Lord Is God!

JEREMIAH 10:7–10

"No man ever saw God and lived; and yet I shall not live till I see God, and when I have seen him I shall never die. What have I ever seen in this world that hath been truly the same thing that it seemed to me? . . . As he that fears God fears nothing else, so he that sees God sees everything else. When we shall see God as he is, we shall see all things as they are, for that is their essence, as they conduce to his glory. We shall be no more deluded with outward appearances, for when this sight which we intend here comes, there will be no delusory things to be seen. All that we have made as though we saw in this world will be vanished, and I shall see nothing but God and what is in him, and I shall see him in the flesh."

　　　　　　　　　　—JOHN DONNE,
　　　　　　　　　　Easter Day Sermon

See Meeting God in Worship

Covenant Keeping

JEREMIAH 11:1–8

Because promises can be easier to make than to keep, consider the covenants you have made. Make a list of them and write down the vows you made in each case. What vows were made to you? Choose some symbolic object to represent each covenant and place them before you in your prayer space. Hold each object in turn and pray for yourself in relation to each covenant. Pray for others involved. Now reflect on God's faithfulness and sing or recite:

"Great is your faithfulness,
    O God my Father,
you have fulfilled all your
    promise to me;
you never fail and your love
    is unchanging
all you have been you
    forever will be.
Great is your faithfulness."
—T. O. CHISHOLM

See Meeting God in Community

all its ropes are snapped.
My sons are gone from me and are no more;
    no one is left now to pitch my tent
    or to set up my shelter.
²¹ The shepherds are senseless
    and do not inquire of the LORD;
so they do not prosper
    and all their flock is scattered.
²² Listen! The report is coming—
    a great commotion from the land of the north!
It will make the towns of Judah desolate,
    a haunt of jackals.

Jeremiah's Prayer

²³ I know, O LORD, that a man's life is not his own;
    it is not for man to direct his steps.
²⁴ Correct me, LORD, but only with justice—
    not in your anger,
    lest you reduce me to nothing.
²⁵ Pour out your wrath on the nations
    that do not acknowledge you,
    on the peoples who do not call on your name.
For they have devoured Jacob;
    they have devoured him completely
    and destroyed his homeland.

The Covenant Is Broken

11 This is the word that came to Jeremiah from the LORD: ²"Listen to the terms of this covenant and tell them to the people of Judah and to those who live in Jerusalem. ³Tell them that this is what the LORD, the God of Israel, says: 'Cursed is the man who does not obey the terms of this covenant— ⁴the terms I commanded your forefathers when I brought them out of Egypt, out of the iron-smelting furnace.' I said, 'Obey me and do everything I command you, and you will be my people, and I will be your God. ⁵Then I will fulfill the oath I swore to your forefathers, to give them a land flowing with milk and honey'— the land you possess today."

I answered, "Amen, LORD."

⁶The LORD said to me, "Proclaim all these words in the towns of Judah and in the streets of Jerusalem: 'Listen to the terms of this covenant and follow them. ⁷From the time I brought your forefathers up from Egypt until today, I warned them again and again, saying, "Obey me." ⁸But they did not listen or pay attention; instead, they followed the stubbornness of their evil hearts. So I brought on them all the curses of the covenant I had commanded them to follow but that they did not keep.' "

⁹Then the LORD said to me, "There is a conspiracy among the people of Judah and those who live in Jerusalem. ¹⁰They have returned to the sins of their forefathers, who refused to listen to my words. They have followed other gods to serve them. Both the house of Israel and the house of Judah have broken the covenant I made with their forefathers. ¹¹Therefore this is what the LORD says: 'I will bring on them a disaster they cannot escape. Although they cry out to me, I will not listen to them. ¹²The towns of Judah and the people of Jerusalem will go and cry out to the gods to whom they burn incense, but they will not help them at all when disas-

ter strikes. ¹³You have as many gods as you have towns, O Judah; and the altars you have set up to burn incense to that shameful god Baal are as many as the streets of Jerusalem.'

¹⁴"Do not pray for this people nor offer any plea or petition for them, because I will not listen when they call to me in the time of their distress.

¹⁵"What is my beloved doing in my temple
　　as she works out her evil schemes with many?
　Can consecrated meat avert ᴸ your punishment ?
When you engage in your wickedness,
　　then you rejoice.ᵃ"

¹⁶The Lᴏʀᴅ called you a thriving olive tree
　　with fruit beautiful in form.
But with the roar of a mighty storm
　　he will set it on fire,
　　and its branches will be broken.

¹⁷The Lᴏʀᴅ Almighty, who planted you, has decreed disaster for you, because the house of Israel and the house of Judah have done evil and provoked me to anger by burning incense to Baal.

Plot Against Jeremiah

¹⁸Because the Lᴏʀᴅ revealed their plot to me, I knew it, for at that time he showed me what they were doing. ¹⁹I had been like a gentle lamb led to the slaughter; I did not realize that they had plotted against me, saying,

"Let us destroy the tree and its fruit;
　　let us cut him off from the land of the living,
　　that his name be remembered no more."
²⁰But, O Lᴏʀᴅ Almighty, you who judge righteously
　　and test the heart and mind,
let me see your vengeance upon them,
　　for to you I have committed my cause.

²¹"Therefore this is what the Lᴏʀᴅ says about the men of Anathoth who are seeking your life and saying, 'Do not prophesy in the name of the Lᴏʀᴅ or you will die by our hands'— ²²therefore this is what the Lᴏʀᴅ Almighty says: 'I will punish them. Their young men will die by the sword, their sons and daughters by famine. ²³Not even a remnant will be left to them, because I will bring disaster on the men of Anathoth in the year of their punishment.' "

Jeremiah's Complaint

12 You are always righteous, O Lᴏʀᴅ,
　　when I bring a case before you.
Yet I would speak with you about your justice:
　　Why does the way of the wicked prosper?
　　Why do all the faithless live at ease?
²You have planted them, and they have taken root;
　　they grow and bear fruit.
You are always on their lips
　　but far from their hearts.
³Yet you know me, O Lᴏʀᴅ;
　　you see me and test my thoughts about you.
Drag them off like sheep to be butchered!
　　Set them apart for the day of slaughter!

Those Who Are Not "for" You

JEREMIAH 11:18–23

People from Jeremiah's hometown were so incensed by his words that they wanted to end his life. Ask yourself, "Who is against me?" See their faces. Name their names aloud. What are your feelings about them? Listen to the internal dialogue you might be having with them. Sense your own vulnerability—and your power to hurt them. Breathe several slow, deep breaths and welcome God into your thoughts. Slowly name each person before God, asking, "Lord, what do you think of _____?" Confess your fears and your complaints against them. Pray for God's justice and mercy to deal with them. With God's Spirit renewing yours, what unobtrusive act of kindness can you do for someone who is not "for" you?

See Meeting God in Prayer

ᵃ *15 Or Could consecrated meat avert your punishment? / Then you would rejoice*

Reaping Thorns

JEREMIAH 12:7–13

In 1944, while World War II was raging, preacher William Bower Black of St. David's Church, Auckland, New Zealand, proclaimed these words: "We must not dare lightly to assume that everything will come out all right. God does let His children wreck their boats, and our whole modern civilization may wreck itself. If it refuses to give God His rightful place, and is contemptuous of His holy law, that very law will be its destruction . . . Have we any right to believe that God will say anything less to us than he said to Israel long ago: 'You only have I known of all the families of the earth, *therefore* will I punish you for all your iniquities'?" (William Bower Black, *Thy Steadfast Hills*).

Beginning with the prayer "Lord, teach us to pray" (Luke 11:1), pray for our modern civilization. Pray for the leaders of the nation. Pray for its corporations and institutions. Pray for its citizens that we may not be abandoned "into the hands of [our] enemies."

See Meeting God in Prayer

⁴How long will the land lie parched*a*
  and the grass in every field be withered?
Because those who live in it are wicked,
  the animals and birds have perished.
Moreover, the people are saying,
  "He will not see what happens to us."

God's Answer

⁵"If you have raced with men on foot
  and they have worn you out,
  how can you compete with horses?
If you stumble in safe country,*b*
  how will you manage in the thickets by*c* the
    Jordan?
⁶Your brothers, your own family—
  even they have betrayed you;
  they have raised a loud cry against you.
Do not trust them,
  though they speak well of you.

⁷"I will forsake my house,
  abandon my inheritance;
I will give the one I love
  into the hands of her enemies.
⁸My inheritance has become to me
  like a lion in the forest.
She roars at me;
  therefore I hate her.
⁹Has not my inheritance become to me
  like a speckled bird of prey
  that other birds of prey surround and attack?
Go and gather all the wild beasts;
  bring them to devour.
¹⁰Many shepherds will ruin my vineyard
  and trample down my field;
they will turn my pleasant field
  into a desolate wasteland.
¹¹It will be made a wasteland,
  parched and desolate before me;
the whole land will be laid waste
  because there is no one who cares.
¹²Over all the barren heights in the desert
  destroyers will swarm,
for the sword of the LORD will devour
  from one end of the land to the other;
  no one will be safe.
¹³They will sow wheat but reap thorns;
  they will wear themselves out but gain nothing.
So bear the shame of your harvest
  because of the LORD's fierce anger."

¹⁴This is what the LORD says: "As for all my wicked neighbors who seize the inheritance I gave my people Israel, I will uproot them from their lands and I will uproot the house of Judah from among them. ¹⁵But after I uproot them, I will again have compassion and will bring each of them back to his own inheritance and his own country. ¹⁶And if they learn well the ways of my people and swear by my name, saying, 'As surely as the LORD lives'—even as

a 4 Or *land mourn*   *b* 5 Or *If you put your trust in a land of safety*   *c* 5 Or *the flooding of*

they once taught my people to swear by Baal—then they will be established among my people. ¹⁷But if any nation does not listen, I will completely uproot and destroy it," declares the LORD.

A Linen Belt

13 This is what the LORD said to me: "Go and buy a linen belt and put it around your waist, but do not let it touch water." ²So I bought a belt, as the LORD directed, and put it around my waist.

³Then the word of the LORD came to me a second time: ⁴"Take the belt you bought and are wearing around your waist, and go now to Perath*a* and hide it there in a crevice in the rocks." ⁵So I went and hid it at Perath, as the LORD told me.

⁶Many days later the LORD said to me, "Go now to Perath and get the belt I told you to hide there." ⁷So I went to Perath and dug up the belt and took it from the place where I had hidden it, but now it was ruined and completely useless.

⁸Then the word of the LORD came to me: ⁹"This is what the LORD says: 'In the same way I will ruin the pride of Judah and the great pride of Jerusalem. ¹⁰These wicked people, who refuse to listen to my words, who follow the stubbornness of their hearts and go after other gods to serve and worship them, will be like this belt—completely useless! ¹¹For as a belt is bound around a man's waist, so I bound the whole house of Israel and the whole house of Judah to me,' declares the LORD, 'to be my people for my renown and praise and honor. But they have not listened.'

Wineskins

¹²"Say to them: 'This is what the LORD, the God of Israel, says: Every wineskin should be filled with wine.' And if they say to you, 'Don't we know that every wineskin should be filled with wine?' ¹³then tell them, 'This is what the LORD says: I am going to fill with drunkenness all who live in this land, including the kings who sit on David's throne, the priests, the prophets and all those living in Jerusalem. ¹⁴I will smash them one against the other, fathers and sons alike, declares the LORD. I will allow no pity or mercy or compassion to keep me from destroying them.' "

Threat of Captivity

¹⁵Hear and pay attention,
    do not be arrogant,
    for the LORD has spoken.
¹⁶Give glory to the LORD your God
    before he brings the darkness,
before your feet stumble
    on the darkening hills.
You hope for light,
    but he will turn it to thick darkness
    and change it to deep gloom.
¹⁷But if you do not listen,
    I will weep in secret
    because of your pride;
my eyes will weep bitterly,
    overflowing with tears,
    because the LORD's flock will be taken captive.

Linen Belt

JEREMIAH 13:1–11

How close are you to God today? As close as your clothing is to you? God says, "I bound the whole house of Israel and the whole house of Judah to me . . . to be my people for my renown and praise and honor."

As a reminder of God's presence and God's desire to be close to you, select an article of close-fitting clothing. You might lift it before God and pray aloud, asking God to bless it. Wear it for the day as a reminder of God's desire to stay close to you. When you take it off, thank God for staying close.

See *Meeting God in Everyday Life*

---

a 4 Or possibly *the Euphrates*; also in verses 5–7

The Mark of Forgiveness

JEREMIAH 14:1–9

Every action has consequences. Through both indifference and active choice, Israel has ignored God and now faces the consequences. Jerusalem will be devastated, its citizens exiled and the land left to perish in drought.

How do you react to this passage in light of Jesus' words to a paralyzed man, "Friend, your sins are forgiven" (Luke 5:20)? The apostle Paul says to us, "Therefore, there is now no condemnation for those who are in Christ Jesus" (Romans 8:1). What have been the consequences of your less-than-honorable actions? Place a bowl of water before you. Bring to Jesus any guilt or shame that you feel. Ask for forgiveness—and for the grace to forgive yourself. As a reminder of your baptism, put some water on your head and say, "I belong to Jesus Christ." Mark the inside of your palm with a small cross. For the rest of the day let it be a reminder of the mark of Jesus' forgiveness.

See Meeting God in Worship

¹⁸ Say to the king and to the queen mother,
"Come down from your thrones,
for your glorious crowns
will fall from your heads."
¹⁹ The cities in the Negev will be shut up,
and there will be no one to open them.
All Judah will be carried into exile,
carried completely away.

²⁰ Lift up your eyes and see
those who are coming from the north.
Where is the flock that was entrusted to you,
the sheep of which you boasted?
²¹ What will you say when ⌊the Lord⌋ sets over you
those you cultivated as your special allies?
Will not pain grip you
like that of a woman in labor?
²² And if you ask yourself,
"Why has this happened to me?"—
it is because of your many sins
that your skirts have been torn off
and your body mistreated.
²³ Can the Ethiopianª change his skin
or the leopard its spots?
Neither can you do good
who are accustomed to doing evil.

²⁴ "I will scatter you like chaff
driven by the desert wind.
²⁵ This is your lot,
the portion I have decreed for you,"
                    declares the Lord,
"because you have forgotten me
and trusted in false gods.
²⁶ I will pull up your skirts over your face
that your shame may be seen—
²⁷ your adulteries and lustful neighings,
your shameless prostitution!
I have seen your detestable acts
on the hills and in the fields.
Woe to you, O Jerusalem!
How long will you be unclean?"

Drought, Famine, Sword

14 This is the word of the Lord to Jeremiah concerning the drought:

² "Judah mourns,
her cities languish;
they wail for the land,
and a cry goes up from Jerusalem.
³ The nobles send their servants for water;
they go to the cisterns
but find no water.
They return with their jars unfilled;
dismayed and despairing,
they cover their heads.
⁴ The ground is cracked
because there is no rain in the land;

ª 23 Hebrew *Cushite* (probably a person from the upper Nile region)

the farmers are dismayed
and cover their heads.
⁵Even the doe in the field
deserts her newborn fawn
because there is no grass.
⁶Wild donkeys stand on the barren heights
and pant like jackals;
their eyesight fails
for lack of pasture."

⁷Although our sins testify against us,
O Lord, do something for the sake of your
name.
For our backsliding is great;
we have sinned against you.
⁸O Hope of Israel,
its Savior in times of distress,
why are you like a stranger in the land,
like a traveler who stays only a night?
⁹Why are you like a man taken by surprise,
like a warrior powerless to save?
You are among us, O Lord,
and we bear your name;
do not forsake us!

¹⁰This is what the Lord says about this people:

"They greatly love to wander;
they do not restrain their feet.
So the Lord does not accept them;
he will now remember their wickedness
and punish them for their sins."

¹¹Then the Lord said to me, "Do not pray for the well-being of this people. ¹²Although they fast, I will not listen to their cry; though they offer burnt offerings and grain offerings, I will not accept them. Instead, I will destroy them with the sword, famine and plague."

¹³But I said, "Ah, Sovereign Lord, the prophets keep telling them, 'You will not see the sword or suffer famine. Indeed, I will give you lasting peace in this place.' "

¹⁴Then the Lord said to me, "The prophets are prophesying lies in my name. I have not sent them or appointed them or spoken to them. They are prophesying to you false visions, divinations, idolatries[a] and the delusions of their own minds. ¹⁵Therefore, this is what the Lord says about the prophets who are prophesying in my name: I did not send them, yet they are saying, 'No sword or famine will touch this land.' Those same prophets will perish by sword and famine. ¹⁶And the people they are prophesying to will be thrown out into the streets of Jerusalem because of the famine and sword. There will be no one to bury them or their wives, their sons or their daughters. I will pour out on them the calamity they deserve.

¹⁷"Speak this word to them:

" 'Let my eyes overflow with tears
night and day without ceasing,
for my virgin daughter—my people—
has suffered a grievous wound,
a crushing blow.

Where Are You?

JEREMIAH 14:7–9

"So when we think of the absence of God, is it not worthwhile to ask ourselves whom we blame for it? We always blame God, we always accuse Him, either straight to His face or in front of people, of being absent, of never being there when He is needed, never answering when He is addressed. At times we are more 'pious' (very much in quotes), and we say piously 'God is testing my patience, my faith, my humility.' We find all sorts of ways of turning God's judgment on us into a new way of pleasing ourselves. We are so patient that we can put up even with God!"

—ARCHBISHOP ANTHONY BLOOM,
A School for Prayer

See Meeting God in Worship

Congruence

"O LORD, we acknowledge our wickedness." *That* sounds like a genuine repentance. "Do any of the worthless idols of the nations bring rain? . . . No, it is you, O LORD our God." And *that* sounds like a genuine statement of faith. But where is the change in behavior? "Send them away from my presence! Let them go!" says God.

Are your prayers and your statements about faith congruent with your behavior? To help close the gap between your faith and your behavior, ask God to fill you with his Spirit. In each of the next nine days, focus on living one aspect of the fruit of the Spirit mentioned in Galatians 5:22–23. At the end of each day, review and journal your experience of seeking to live the fruit of the Spirit.

See *Meeting God in Everyday Life*

---

¹⁸ If I go into the country,
  I see those slain by the sword;
if I go into the city,
  I see the ravages of famine.
Both prophet and priest
  have gone to a land they know not.' "

¹⁹ Have you rejected Judah completely?
  Do you despise Zion?
Why have you afflicted us
  so that we cannot be healed?
We hoped for peace
  but no good has come,
for a time of healing
  but there is only terror.
²⁰ O LORD, we acknowledge our wickedness
  and the guilt of our fathers;
  we have indeed sinned against you.
²¹ For the sake of your name do not despise us;
  do not dishonor your glorious throne.
Remember your covenant with us
  and do not break it.
²² Do any of the worthless idols of the nations bring rain?
  Do the skies themselves send down showers?
No, it is you, O LORD our God.
  Therefore our hope is in you,
  for you are the one who does all this.

15 Then the LORD said to me: "Even if Moses and Samuel were to stand before me, my heart would not go out to this people. Send them away from my presence! Let them go! ²And if they ask you, 'Where shall we go?' tell them, 'This is what the LORD says:

" 'Those destined for death, to death;
  those for the sword, to the sword;
  those for starvation, to starvation;
  those for captivity, to captivity.'

³ "I will send four kinds of destroyers against them," declares the LORD, "the sword to kill and the dogs to drag away and the birds of the air and the beasts of the earth to devour and destroy. ⁴I will make them abhorrent to all the kingdoms of the earth because of what Manasseh son of Hezekiah king of Judah did in Jerusalem.

⁵ "Who will have pity on you, O Jerusalem?
  Who will mourn for you?
  Who will stop to ask how you are?
⁶ You have rejected me," declares the LORD.
  "You keep on backsliding.
So I will lay hands on you and destroy you;
  I can no longer show compassion.
⁷ I will winnow them with a winnowing fork
  at the city gates of the land.
I will bring bereavement and destruction on my people,
  for they have not changed their ways.
⁸ I will make their widows more numerous
  than the sand of the sea.
At midday I will bring a destroyer
  against the mothers of their young men;

suddenly I will bring down on them
  anguish and terror.
⁹The mother of seven will grow faint
  and breathe her last.
Her sun will set while it is still day;
  she will be disgraced and humiliated.
I will put the survivors to the sword
  before their enemies,"
                              declares the LORD.

¹⁰Alas, my mother, that you gave me birth,
  a man with whom the whole land strives and
    contends!
I have neither lent nor borrowed,
  yet everyone curses me.

¹¹The LORD said,

"Surely I will deliver you for a good purpose;
  surely I will make your enemies plead with you
  in times of disaster and times of distress.

¹²"Can a man break iron—
  iron from the north—or bronze?

¹³Your wealth and your treasures
  I will give as plunder, without charge,
because of all your sins
  throughout your country.
¹⁴I will enslave you to your enemies
  in*a* a land you do not know,
for my anger will kindle a fire
  that will burn against you."

¹⁵You understand, O LORD;
  remember me and care for me.
  Avenge me on my persecutors.
You are long-suffering—do not take me away;
  think of how I suffer reproach for your sake.
¹⁶When your words came, I ate them;
  they were my joy and my heart's delight,
for I bear your name,
  O LORD God Almighty.
¹⁷I never sat in the company of revelers,
  never made merry with them;
I sat alone because your hand was on me
  and you had filled me with indignation.
¹⁸Why is my pain unending
  and my wound grievous and incurable?
Will you be to me like a deceptive brook,
  like a spring that fails?

¹⁹Therefore this is what the LORD says:

"If you repent, I will restore you
  that you may serve me;
if you utter worthy, not worthless, words,
  you will be my spokesman.
Let this people turn to you,
  but you must not turn to them.
²⁰I will make you a wall to this people,
  a fortified wall of bronze;

The Cost of a Call

JEREMIAH 15:15–18

Jeremiah is experiencing a "Gethsemane." Watch and pray with him. Identify with his anguish. What "cup" would you rather not drink from? What task would you rather let pass? In what ways does your vocation seem too costly at times?

Find a place to write down your responses to the book of Jeremiah, articulating that which is "worthy" (v.19), honest and real. Discuss any relevant issues with someone you trust and pray together about them.

See Meeting God in Service

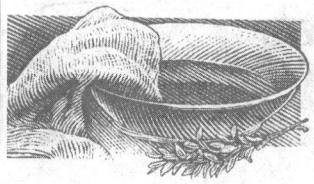

---

a 14 Some Hebrew manuscripts, Septuagint and Syriac (see also Jer. 17:4); most Hebrew manuscripts *I will cause your enemies to bring you / into*

1021

I Don't Deserve This!

JEREMIAH 16:10–13

When things go wrong—from minor irritations to total disasters—a voice within you protests, "I don't understand! I don't deserve this!"

What has happened to you that leads you to protest like the people of Israel did (v.10)? Has someone done you an injustice? Write about the circumstances. Do you feel you are being punished? That God has looked the other way? How will you react to the situation? Find someone you trust and discuss your thoughts and feelings.

See Meeting God in Everyday Life

they will fight against you
    but will not overcome you,
for I am with you
    to rescue and save you,"
                    declares the LORD.
²¹ "I will save you from the hands of the wicked
    and redeem you from the grasp of the cruel."

Day of Disaster

16 Then the word of the LORD came to me: ²"You must not marry and have sons or daughters in this place." ³For this is what the LORD says about the sons and daughters born in this land and about the women who are their mothers and the men who are their fathers: ⁴"They will die of deadly diseases. They will not be mourned or buried but will be like refuse lying on the ground. They will perish by sword and famine, and their dead bodies will become food for the birds of the air and the beasts of the earth."

⁵For this is what the LORD says: "Do not enter a house where there is a funeral meal; do not go to mourn or show sympathy, because I have withdrawn my blessing, my love and my pity from this people," declares the LORD. ⁶"Both high and low will die in this land. They will not be buried or mourned, and no one will cut himself or shave his head for them. ⁷No one will offer food to comfort those who mourn for the dead—not even for a father or a mother—nor will anyone give them a drink to console them.

⁸"And do not enter a house where there is feasting and sit down to eat and drink. ⁹For this is what the LORD Almighty, the God of Israel, says: Before your eyes and in your days I will bring an end to the sounds of joy and gladness and to the voices of bride and bridegroom in this place.

¹⁰"When you tell these people all this and they ask you, 'Why has the LORD decreed such a great disaster against us? What wrong have we done? What sin have we committed against the LORD our God?' ¹¹then say to them, 'It is because your fathers forsook me,' declares the LORD, 'and followed other gods and served and worshiped them. They forsook me and did not keep my law. ¹²But you have behaved more wickedly than your fathers. See how each of you is following the stubbornness of his evil heart instead of obeying me. ¹³So I will throw you out of this land into a land neither you nor your fathers have known, and there you will serve other gods day and night, for I will show you no favor.'

¹⁴"However, the days are coming," declares the LORD, "when men will no longer say, 'As surely as the LORD lives, who brought the Israelites up out of Egypt,' ¹⁵but they will say, 'As surely as the LORD lives, who brought the Israelites up out of the land of the north and out of all the countries where he had banished them.' For I will restore them to the land I gave their forefathers.

¹⁶"But now I will send for many fishermen," declares the LORD, "and they will catch them. After that I will send for many hunters, and they will hunt them down on every mountain and hill and from the crevices of the rocks. ¹⁷My eyes are on all their ways; they are not hidden from me, nor is their sin concealed from my eyes. ¹⁸I will repay them double for their wickedness and their sin, because they have defiled my land with the lifeless forms of their vile images and have filled my inheritance with their detestable idols."

¹⁹O Lord, my strength and my fortress,
my refuge in time of distress,
to you the nations will come
from the ends of the earth and say,
"Our fathers possessed nothing but false gods,
worthless idols that did them no good.
²⁰Do men make their own gods?
Yes, but they are not gods!"

²¹"Therefore I will teach them—
this time I will teach them
my power and might.
Then they will know
that my name is the Lord.

17 "Judah's sin is engraved with an iron tool,
inscribed with a flint point,
on the tablets of their hearts
and on the horns of their altars.
²Even their children remember
their altars and Asherah poles[a]
beside the spreading trees
and on the high hills.
³My mountain in the land
and your[b] wealth and all your treasures
I will give away as plunder,
together with your high places,
because of sin throughout your country.
⁴Through your own fault you will lose
the inheritance I gave you.
I will enslave you to your enemies
in a land you do not know,
for you have kindled my anger,
and it will burn forever."

⁵This is what the Lord says:

"Cursed is the one who trusts in man,
who depends on flesh for his strength
and whose heart turns away from the Lord.
⁶He will be like a bush in the wastelands;
he will not see prosperity when it comes.
He will dwell in the parched places of the desert,
in a salt land where no one lives.

⁷"But blessed is the man who trusts in the Lord,
whose confidence is in him.
⁸He will be like a tree planted by the water
that sends out its roots by the stream.
It does not fear when heat comes;
its leaves are always green.
It has no worries in a year of drought
and never fails to bear fruit."

⁹The heart is deceitful above all things
and beyond cure.
Who can understand it?
¹⁰"I the Lord search the heart
and examine the mind,

Seek God's Blessing

JEREMIAH 17:5–8

Whose advice do you seek when the going gets tough—a friend, a counselor, a financial consultant, a self-help book? Make a list of your resources of "flesh"—people that you might call on. Rank them according to their usefulness. Now imagine what might happen if you took your tough issue to God and trusted him to help you. What might you expect of God? Pray about it. Keep praying about it. Write down your discoveries in your journal. Watch for the fruit of your prayer—changes within yourself and any evidence of God's action.

See Meeting God in Prayer

ᵃ 2 That is, symbols of the goddess Asherah   ᵇ 2,3 Or *hills* / ³*and the mountains of the land.* / *Your*

Sabbath

JEREMIAH 17:19–27

The Lord instructed Jeremiah to stand by the gate and proclaim the holiness of the Sabbath. The people were not to bring loads through the gates of Jerusalem or out of their houses.

What does the Sabbath mean to you? Do you ever carry loads into your Sabbath time—mental or emotional burdens that might disrupt your time with God? How can you let Jesus Christ carry them for you so that you can worship without distraction (see Matthew 11:28–30)?

See Meeting God in Worship

to reward a man according to his conduct,
  according to what his deeds deserve."

¹¹ Like a partridge that hatches eggs it did not lay
  is the man who gains riches by unjust means.
When his life is half gone, they will desert him,
  and in the end he will prove to be a fool.

¹² A glorious throne, exalted from the beginning,
  is the place of our sanctuary.
¹³ O LORD, the hope of Israel,
  all who forsake you will be put to shame.
Those who turn away from you will be written in
    the dust
  because they have forsaken the LORD,
  the spring of living water.

¹⁴ Heal me, O LORD, and I will be healed;
  save me and I will be saved,
  for you are the one I praise.
¹⁵ They keep saying to me,
  "Where is the word of the LORD?
  Let it now be fulfilled!"
¹⁶ I have not run away from being your shepherd;
  you know I have not desired the day of despair.
  What passes my lips is open before you.
¹⁷ Do not be a terror to me;
  you are my refuge in the day of disaster.
¹⁸ Let my persecutors be put to shame,
  but keep me from shame;
let them be terrified,
  but keep me from terror.
Bring on them the day of disaster;
  destroy them with double destruction.

Keeping the Sabbath Holy

¹⁹This is what the LORD said to me: "Go and stand at the gate of the people, through which the kings of Judah go in and out; stand also at all the other gates of Jerusalem. ²⁰Say to them, 'Hear the word of the LORD, O kings of Judah and all people of Judah and everyone living in Jerusalem who come through these gates. ²¹This is what the LORD says: Be careful not to carry a load on the Sabbath day or bring it through the gates of Jerusalem. ²²Do not bring a load out of your houses or do any work on the Sabbath, but keep the Sabbath day holy, as I commanded your forefathers. ²³Yet they did not listen or pay attention; they were stiff-necked and would not listen or respond to discipline. ²⁴But if you are careful to obey me, declares the LORD, and bring no load through the gates of this city on the Sabbath, but keep the Sabbath day holy by not doing any work on it, ²⁵then kings who sit on David's throne will come through the gates of this city with their officials. They and their officials will come riding in chariots and on horses, accompanied by the men of Judah and those living in Jerusalem, and this city will be inhabited forever. ²⁶People will come from the towns of Judah and the villages around Jerusalem, from the territory of Benjamin and the western foothills, from the hill country and the Negev, bringing burnt offerings and sacrifices, grain offerings, incense and thank offerings to the house of the LORD. ²⁷But if you do not obey me to keep the Sabbath day holy by not carrying any load as you come through the gates of Jerusalem on the

Sabbath day, then I will kindle an unquenchable fire in the gates of Jerusalem that will consume her fortresses.' "

At the Potter's House

18 This is the word that came to Jeremiah from the LORD: ²"Go down to the potter's house, and there I will give you my message." ³So I went down to the potter's house, and I saw him working at the wheel. ⁴But the pot he was shaping from the clay was marred in his hands; so the potter formed it into another pot, shaping it as seemed best to him.

⁵Then the word of the LORD came to me: ⁶"O house of Israel, can I not do with you as this potter does?" declares the LORD. "Like clay in the hand of the potter, so are you in my hand, O house of Israel. ⁷If at any time I announce that a nation or kingdom is to be uprooted, torn down and destroyed, ⁸and if that nation I warned repents of its evil, then I will relent and not inflict on it the disaster I had planned. ⁹And if at another time I announce that a nation or kingdom is to be built up and planted, ¹⁰and if it does evil in my sight and does not obey me, then I will reconsider the good I had intended to do for it.

¹¹"Now therefore say to the people of Judah and those living in Jerusalem, 'This is what the LORD says: Look! I am preparing a disaster for you and devising a plan against you. So turn from your evil ways, each one of you, and reform your ways and your actions.' ¹²But they will reply, 'It's no use. We will continue with our own plans; each of us will follow the stubbornness of his evil heart.' "

¹³Therefore this is what the LORD says:

> "Inquire among the nations:
>   Who has ever heard anything like this?
> A most horrible thing has been done
>   by Virgin Israel.
> ¹⁴Does the snow of Lebanon
>   ever vanish from its rocky slopes?
> Do its cool waters from distant sources
>   ever cease to flow?ᵃ
> ¹⁵Yet my people have forgotten me;
>   they burn incense to worthless idols,
> which made them stumble in their ways
>   and in the ancient paths.
> They made them walk in bypaths
>   and on roads not built up.
> ¹⁶Their land will be laid waste,
>   an object of lasting scorn;
> all who pass by will be appalled
>   and will shake their heads.
> ¹⁷Like a wind from the east,
>   I will scatter them before their enemies;
> I will show them my back and not my face
>   in the day of their disaster."

¹⁸They said, "Come, let's make plans against Jeremiah; for the teaching of the law by the priest will not be lost, nor will counsel from the wise, nor the word from the prophets. So come, let's attack him with our tongues and pay no attention to anything he says."

The Nation

JEREMIAH 18:1–11

If possible, invite a friend to share this exercise with you. Find some potter's clay or other malleable substance. Hold it and warm it in your hands. Let your fingers and your heart—not your brain—shape a symbol of your nation at its worst. Place it before God and ask God to show mercy to your nation. Crush your clay symbol. Ask the Spirit to anoint your hands and then make a symbol of how God desires your nation to be. Place it before God and ask God to bless your nation. Let your molding medium harden so that it will become your reminder to pray for your nation and the forces that shape it.

See Meeting God in Prayer

ᵃ 14 The meaning of the Hebrew for this sentence is uncertain.

My Enemies

JEREMIAH 18:19–23

Who comes to mind under the heading "My Enemies"? What kind of "pit" have they dug for you? Draw a picture of it. Draw yourself in it. Under God's caring eye, write some key words beside your picture that describe what—in your rawest anger—you would like to happen to your "enemies." Do not ignore your honest feelings. When they are fully present, frame them within your mind as you read Luke 6:22–23,27–28. What is Jesus asking of you with regard to your "enemies"? Pray for them as you are able, trying to see them from God's perspective. What action does your prayer require of you?

See Meeting God in Prayer

¹⁹ Listen to me, O LORD;
  hear what my accusers are saying!
²⁰ Should good be repaid with evil?
  Yet they have dug a pit for me.
Remember that I stood before you
  and spoke in their behalf
  to turn your wrath away from them.
²¹ So give their children over to famine;
  hand them over to the power of the sword.
Let their wives be made childless and widows;
  let their men be put to death,
  their young men slain by the sword in battle.
²² Let a cry be heard from their houses
  when you suddenly bring invaders against
    them,
for they have dug a pit to capture me
  and have hidden snares for my feet.
²³ But you know, O LORD,
  all their plots to kill me.
Do not forgive their crimes
  or blot out their sins from your sight.
Let them be overthrown before you;
  deal with them in the time of your anger.

19 This is what the LORD says: "Go and buy a clay jar from a potter. Take along some of the elders of the people and of the priests ²and go out to the Valley of Ben Hinnom, near the entrance of the Potsherd Gate. There proclaim the words I tell you, ³and say, 'Hear the word of the LORD, O kings of Judah and people of Jerusalem. This is what the LORD Almighty, the God of Israel, says: Listen! I am going to bring a disaster on this place that will make the ears of everyone who hears of it tingle. ⁴For they have forsaken me and made this a place of foreign gods; they have burned sacrifices in it to gods that neither they nor their fathers nor the kings of Judah ever knew, and they have filled this place with the blood of the innocent. ⁵They have built the high places of Baal to burn their sons in the fire as offerings to Baal—something I did not command or mention, nor did it enter my mind. ⁶So beware, the days are coming, declares the LORD, when people will no longer call this place Topheth or the Valley of Ben Hinnom, but the Valley of Slaughter.

⁷" 'In this place I will ruin*ᵃ* the plans of Judah and Jerusalem. I will make them fall by the sword before their enemies, at the hands of those who seek their lives, and I will give their carcasses as food to the birds of the air and the beasts of the earth. ⁸I will devastate this city and make it an object of scorn; all who pass by will be appalled and will scoff because of all its wounds. ⁹I will make them eat the flesh of their sons and daughters, and they will eat one another's flesh during the stress of the siege imposed on them by the enemies who seek their lives.'

¹⁰"Then break the jar while those who go with you are watching, ¹¹and say to them, 'This is what the LORD Almighty says: I will smash this nation and this city just as this potter's jar is smashed and cannot be repaired. They will bury the dead in Topheth until there is no more room. ¹²This is what I will do to this place and to those who live here, declares the LORD. I will make this city like Topheth.

ᵃ 7 The Hebrew for ruin *sounds like the Hebrew for* jar *(see verses 1 and 10).*

¹³The houses in Jerusalem and those of the kings of Judah will be defiled like this place, Topheth—all the houses where they burned incense on the roofs to all the starry hosts and poured out drink offerings to other gods.' "

¹⁴Jeremiah then returned from Topheth, where the LORD had sent him to prophesy, and stood in the court of the LORD's temple and said to all the people, ¹⁵"This is what the LORD Almighty, the God of Israel, says: 'Listen! I am going to bring on this city and the villages around it every disaster I pronounced against them, because they were stiff-necked and would not listen to my words.' "

Jeremiah and Pashhur

20 When the priest Pashhur son of Immer, the chief officer in the temple of the LORD, heard Jeremiah prophesying these things, ²he had Jeremiah the prophet beaten and put in the stocks at the Upper Gate of Benjamin at the LORD's temple. ³The next day, when Pashhur released him from the stocks, Jeremiah said to him, "The LORD's name for you is not Pashhur, but Magor-Missabib.ᵃ ⁴For this is what the LORD says: 'I will make you a terror to yourself and to all your friends; with your own eyes you will see them fall by the sword of their enemies. I will hand all Judah over to the king of Babylon, who will carry them away to Babylon or put them to the sword. ⁵I will hand over to their enemies all the wealth of this city—all its products, all its valuables and all the treasures of the kings of Judah. They will take it away as plunder and carry it off to Babylon. ⁶And you, Pashhur, and all who live in your house will go into exile to Babylon. There you will die and be buried, you and all your friends to whom you have prophesied lies.' "

Jeremiah's Complaint

⁷O LORD, you deceivedᵇ me, and I was deceivedᵇ;
  you overpowered me and prevailed.
I am ridiculed all day long;
  everyone mocks me.
⁸Whenever I speak, I cry out
  proclaiming violence and destruction.
So the word of the LORD has brought me
  insult and reproach all day long.
⁹But if I say, "I will not mention him
  or speak any more in his name,"
his word is in my heart like a fire,
  a fire shut up in my bones.
I am weary of holding it in;
  indeed, I cannot.
¹⁰I hear many whispering,
  "Terror on every side!
  Report him! Let's report him!"
All my friends
  are waiting for me to slip, saying,
"Perhaps he will be deceived;
  then we will prevail over him
  and take our revenge on him."

¹¹But the LORD is with me like a mighty warrior;
  so my persecutors will stumble and not prevail.
They will fail and be thoroughly disgraced;

Terror on Every Side

JEREMIAH 20:1–6

Be seated in a place that feels safe and comfortable. Using the phrase "deliver us from evil" (from the Lord's Prayer), pray for God's protection for yourself and those close to you. In the company of Jesus, your Protector, name your terrors and your greatest fears. Write them down. Focus not on them, but on Jesus, and pray for deliverance from them. Memorize: "The Lord is my helper; I will not be afraid" (Hebrews 13:6). Share with your spiritual adviser, faith companion or a counselor what has happened.

See Meeting God in Prayer

ᵃ 3 *Magor-Missabib* means *terror on every side.*   ᵇ 7 Or *persuaded*

The Pits

JEREMIAH 20:7–18

Jeremiah is experiencing more than a blue mood. He feels that God has "deceived" him. He wrestles with inner voices that would have him question everything.

Seated in your prayer place, write an honest response to this question: "What do I say to myself when I am 'in the pits'?" Note the dominant themes of your "self-talk" at such times. Now consider what effect your melancholy has on your relationships (you might ask someone), your work, your behavior and your prayer life. What does it mean to be able to declare with Jeremiah, "The LORD is with me like a mighty warrior"? How does it help to reaffirm that God can, and will, defend us?

See Meeting God in Everyday Life

> their dishonor will never be forgotten.
> ¹²O LORD Almighty, you who examine the righteous
>   and probe the heart and mind,
>   let me see your vengeance upon them,
>   for to you I have committed my cause.
>
> ¹³Sing to the LORD!
>   Give praise to the LORD!
>   He rescues the life of the needy
>   from the hands of the wicked.
>
> ¹⁴Cursed be the day I was born!
>   May the day my mother bore me not be
>   blessed!
> ¹⁵Cursed be the man who brought my father the
>   news,
>   who made him very glad, saying,
>   "A child is born to you—a son!"
> ¹⁶May that man be like the towns
>   the LORD overthrew without pity.
>   May he hear wailing in the morning,
>   a battle cry at noon,
> ¹⁷For he did not kill me in the womb,
>   with my mother as my grave,
>   her womb enlarged forever.
> ¹⁸Why did I ever come out of the womb
>   to see trouble and sorrow
>   and to end my days in shame?

God Rejects Zedekiah's Request

21 The word came to Jeremiah from the LORD when King Zedekiah sent to him Pashhur son of Malkijah and the priest Zephaniah son of Maaseiah. They said: ²"Inquire now of the LORD for us because Nebuchadnezzar*ᵃ* king of Babylon is attacking us. Perhaps the LORD will perform wonders for us as in times past so that he will withdraw from us."

³But Jeremiah answered them, "Tell Zedekiah, ⁴'This is what the LORD, the God of Israel, says: I am about to turn against you the weapons of war that are in your hands, which you are using to fight the king of Babylon and the Babylonians*ᵇ* who are outside the wall besieging you. And I will gather them inside this city. ⁵I myself will fight against you with an outstretched hand and a mighty arm in anger and fury and great wrath. ⁶I will strike down those who live in this city—both men and animals—and they will die of a terrible plague. ⁷After that, declares the LORD, I will hand over Zedekiah king of Judah, his officials and the people in this city who survive the plague, sword and famine, to Nebuchadnezzar king of Babylon and to their enemies who seek their lives. He will put them to the sword; he will show them no mercy or pity or compassion.'

⁸"Furthermore, tell the people, 'This is what the LORD says: See, I am setting before you the way of life and the way of death. ⁹Whoever stays in this city will die by the sword, famine or plague. But whoever goes out and surrenders to the Babylonians who are besieging you will live; he will escape with his life. ¹⁰I have determined to do this city harm and not good, declares the LORD. It will be given into the hands of the king of Babylon, and he will destroy it with fire.'

ᵃ 2 Hebrew *Nebuchadrezzar,* of which *Nebuchadnezzar* is a variant; here and often in Jeremiah and Ezekiel   *ᵇ 4* Or *Chaldeans*; also in verse 9

[11] "Moreover, say to the royal house of Judah, 'Hear the word of the LORD; [12] O house of David, this is what the LORD says:

> " 'Administer justice every morning;
> rescue from the hand of his oppressor
> the one who has been robbed,
> or my wrath will break out and burn like fire
> because of the evil you have done—
> burn with no one to quench it.
> [13] I am against you, ⌊ Jerusalem,⌋
> you who live above this valley
> on the rocky plateau,
> declares the LORD—
> you who say, "Who can come against us?
> Who can enter our refuge?"
> [14] I will punish you as your deeds deserve,
> declares the LORD.
> I will kindle a fire in your forests
> that will consume everything around you.' "

Judgment Against Evil Kings

22 This is what the LORD says: "Go down to the palace of the king of Judah and proclaim this message there: [2] 'Hear the word of the LORD, O king of Judah, you who sit on David's throne—you, your officials and your people who come through these gates. [3] This is what the LORD says: Do what is just and right. Rescue from the hand of his oppressor the one who has been robbed. Do no wrong or violence to the alien, the fatherless or the widow, and do not shed innocent blood in this place. [4] For if you are careful to carry out these commands, then kings who sit on David's throne will come through the gates of this palace, riding in chariots and on horses, accompanied by their officials and their people. [5] But if you do not obey these commands, declares the LORD, I swear by myself that this palace will become a ruin.' "

[6] For this is what the LORD says about the palace of the king of Judah:

> "Though you are like Gilead to me,
> like the summit of Lebanon,
> I will surely make you like a desert,
> like towns not inhabited.
> [7] I will send destroyers against you,
> each man with his weapons,
> and they will cut up your fine cedar beams
> and throw them into the fire.

[8] "People from many nations will pass by this city and will ask one another, 'Why has the LORD done such a thing to this great city?' [9] And the answer will be: 'Because they have forsaken the covenant of the LORD their God and have worshiped and served other gods.' "

> [10] Do not weep for the dead ⌊king⌋ or mourn his loss;
> rather, weep bitterly for him who is exiled,
> because he will never return
> nor see his native land again.

[11] For this is what the LORD says about Shallum[a] son of Josi-

---

Act With Justice and Righteousness!

JEREMIAH 21:11-14

"Every plan, which aims at the welfare of a nation, in defiance of [God's] authority and laws, however apparently wise, will prove to be essentially defective, and, if persisted in, ruinous. The righteous Lord loveth righteousness, and he has engaged to plead the cause and vindicate the wrongs of the oppressed. It is righteousness that exalteth a nation; and wickedness is the present reproach, and will, sooner or later, unless repentance intervene, prove the ruin of any people . . . God forbid that any supposed profit or advantage which we derive from the groans, and agonies, and blood of the poor Africans, should draw down his heavy curse upon all that we might, otherwise, honourably and comfortably possess."

—JOHN NEWTON,
Thoughts Upon the African Slave Trade

See Meeting God in Community

Your Legacy

JEREMIAH 22:14–17

What is the legacy of a "great" national leader? A noble building named for that person—or greater justice and righteousness within the nation? What will be your legacy? Visible achievements—or quiet acts of compassion, fairness and honor?

Imagine you are a journalist. Write your own obituary. Do not write anything negative. Write the kind of obituary you would really love to have written about you—affirming all the good you want to be remembered for. Do not analyze or try to think it through logically. Under the grace of God's smile, just write. Reread it from time to time to see if there is anything you want to change or add. Pray that God will make your remaining years "fruitful."

See Meeting God in Everyday Life

ah, who succeeded his father as king of Judah but has gone from this place: "He will never return. ¹²He will die in the place where they have led him captive; he will not see this land again."

¹³ "Woe to him who builds his palace by
    unrighteousness,
  his upper rooms by injustice,
making his countrymen work for nothing,
  not paying them for their labor.
¹⁴He says, 'I will build myself a great palace
  with spacious upper rooms.'
So he makes large windows in it,
  panels it with cedar
  and decorates it in red.

¹⁵ "Does it make you a king
  to have more and more cedar?
Did not your father have food and drink?
  He did what was right and just,
  so all went well with him.
¹⁶He defended the cause of the poor and needy,
  and so all went well.
Is that not what it means to know me?"
  declares the LORD.
¹⁷ "But your eyes and your heart
  are set only on dishonest gain,
on shedding innocent blood
  and on oppression and extortion."

¹⁸Therefore this is what the LORD says about Jehoiakim son of Josiah king of Judah:

"They will not mourn for him:
  'Alas, my brother! Alas, my sister!'
They will not mourn for him:
  'Alas, my master! Alas, his splendor!'
¹⁹He will have the burial of a donkey—
  dragged away and thrown
  outside the gates of Jerusalem."

²⁰ "Go up to Lebanon and cry out,
  let your voice be heard in Bashan,
cry out from Abarim,
  for all your allies are crushed.
²¹I warned you when you felt secure,
  but you said, 'I will not listen!'
This has been your way from your youth;
  you have not obeyed me.
²²The wind will drive all your shepherds away,
  and your allies will go into exile.
Then you will be ashamed and disgraced
  because of all your wickedness.
²³You who live in 'Lebanon,'ᵃ
  who are nestled in cedar buildings,
how you will groan when pangs come upon you,
  pain like that of a woman in labor!

²⁴"As surely as I live," declares the LORD, "even if you, Jehoiachinᵇ son of Jehoiakim king of Judah, were a signet ring on my right hand, I would still pull you off. ²⁵I will hand you

ᵃ 23 That is, the palace in Jerusalem (see 1 Kings 7:2)   ᵇ 24 Hebrew *Coniah,* a variant of *Jehoiachin;* also in verse 28

over to those who seek your life, those you fear—to Nebuchadnezzar king of Babylon and to the Babylonians.ᵃ ²⁶I will hurl you and the mother who gave you birth into another country, where neither of you was born, and there you both will die. ²⁷You will never come back to the land you long to return to."

²⁸ Is this man Jehoiachin a despised, broken pot,
      an object no one wants?
   Why will he and his children be hurled out,
      cast into a land they do not know?
²⁹ O land, land, land,
      hear the word of the LORD!
³⁰ This is what the LORD says:
   "Record this man as if childless,
      a man who will not prosper in his lifetime,
   for none of his offspring will prosper,
      none will sit on the throne of David
      or rule anymore in Judah."

The Righteous Branch

23 "Woe to the shepherds who are destroying and scattering the sheep of my pasture!" declares the LORD. ²Therefore this is what the LORD, the God of Israel, says to the shepherds who tend my people: "Because you have scattered my flock and driven them away and have not bestowed care on them, I will bestow punishment on you for the evil you have done," declares the LORD. ³"I myself will gather the remnant of my flock out of all the countries where I have driven them and will bring them back to their pasture, where they will be fruitful and increase in number. ⁴I will place shepherds over them who will tend them, and they will no longer be afraid or terrified, nor will any be missing," declares the LORD.

⁵ "The days are coming," declares the LORD,
      "when I will raise up to Davidᵇ a righteous
         Branch,
   a King who will reign wisely
      and do what is just and right in the land.
⁶ In his days Judah will be saved
      and Israel will live in safety.
   This is the name by which he will be called:
      The LORD Our Righteousness.

⁷"So then, the days are coming," declares the LORD, "when people will no longer say, 'As surely as the LORD lives, who brought the Israelites up out of Egypt,' ⁸but they will say, 'As surely as the LORD lives, who brought the descendants of Israel up out of the land of the north and out of all the countries where he had banished them.' Then they will live in their own land."

Lying Prophets

⁹Concerning the prophets:

   My heart is broken within me;
      all my bones tremble.
   I am like a drunken man,
      like a man overcome by wine,
   because of the LORD

Exile

JEREMIAH 22:24–30

King Jehoiachin and his mother will be handed over to their enemies and exiled.

What is your experience of "exile"? Recall a time when you found yourself among people whose values, culture, way of life and worship were different from your own. Did you wonder if you would ever get "home" again? Write out what you learned about yourself and God through that experience.

See Meeting God in Community

Godly Leadership

JEREMIAH 23:9–19

What grieves you about the church? What has disturbed you about its leadership? What experience have you had of feeling "crushed" by those in authority?

Take these questions to your prayer place. Pray for awareness of the presence of the Good Shepherd. Pray for a particular church leader for a week, that he or she will be characterized by faithfulness to the Lord. Pray that you will be a worthy servant of God in whatever position of power you serve.

See Meeting God in Service

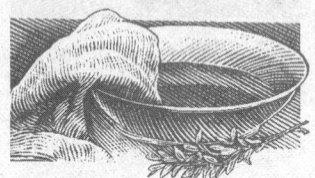

and his holy words.

¹⁰ The land is full of adulterers;
because of the curse*a* the land lies parched*b*
and the pastures in the desert are withered.
The ⌊prophets⌋ follow an evil course
and use their power unjustly.

¹¹ "Both prophet and priest are godless;
even in my temple I find their wickedness,"
declares the LORD.

¹² "Therefore their path will become slippery;
they will be banished to darkness
and there they will fall.
I will bring disaster on them
in the year they are punished,"
declares the LORD.

¹³ "Among the prophets of Samaria
I saw this repulsive thing:
They prophesied by Baal
and led my people Israel astray.

¹⁴ And among the prophets of Jerusalem
I have seen something horrible:
They commit adultery and live a lie.
They strengthen the hands of evildoers,
so that no one turns from his wickedness.
They are all like Sodom to me;
the people of Jerusalem are like Gomorrah."

¹⁵ Therefore, this is what the LORD Almighty says concerning the prophets:

"I will make them eat bitter food
and drink poisoned water,
because from the prophets of Jerusalem
ungodliness has spread throughout the land."

¹⁶ This is what the LORD Almighty says:

"Do not listen to what the prophets are
prophesying to you;
they fill you with false hopes.
They speak visions from their own minds,
not from the mouth of the LORD.

¹⁷ They keep saying to those who despise me,
'The LORD says: You will have peace.'
And to all who follow the stubbornness of their
hearts
they say, 'No harm will come to you.'

¹⁸ But which of them has stood in the council of the
LORD
to see or to hear his word?
Who has listened and heard his word?

¹⁹ See, the storm of the LORD
will burst out in wrath,
a whirlwind swirling down
on the heads of the wicked.

²⁰ The anger of the LORD will not turn back
until he fully accomplishes
the purposes of his heart.
In days to come
you will understand it clearly.

a 10 Or *because of these things* *b 10* Or *land mourns*

²¹ I did not send these prophets,
  yet they have run with their message;
 I did not speak to them,
  yet they have prophesied.
²² But if they had stood in my council,
  they would have proclaimed my words to my
   people
 and would have turned them from their evil ways
  and from their evil deeds.

²³ "Am I only a God nearby,"
                          declares the LORD,
 "and not a God far away?
²⁴ Can anyone hide in secret places
  so that I cannot see him?"
                          declares the LORD.
 "Do not I fill heaven and earth?"
                          declares the LORD.

²⁵ "I have heard what the prophets say who prophesy lies in my name. They say, 'I had a dream! I had a dream!' ²⁶ How long will this continue in the hearts of these lying prophets, who prophesy the delusions of their own minds? ²⁷ They think the dreams they tell one another will make my people forget my name, just as their fathers forgot my name through Baal worship. ²⁸ Let the prophet who has a dream tell his dream, but let the one who has my word speak it faithfully. For what has straw to do with grain?" declares the LORD. ²⁹ "Is not my word like fire," declares the LORD, "and like a hammer that breaks a rock in pieces?

³⁰ "Therefore," declares the LORD, "I am against the prophets who steal from one another words supposedly from me. ³¹ Yes," declares the LORD, "I am against the prophets who wag their own tongues and yet declare, 'The LORD declares.' ³² Indeed, I am against those who prophesy false dreams," declares the LORD. "They tell them and lead my people astray with their reckless lies, yet I did not send or appoint them. They do not benefit these people in the least," declares the LORD.

False Oracles and False Prophets

³³ "When these people, or a prophet or a priest, ask you, 'What is the oracle*ᵃ* of the LORD?' say to them, 'What oracle?*ᵇ* I will forsake you, declares the LORD.' ³⁴ If a prophet or a priest or anyone else claims, 'This is the oracle of the LORD,' I will punish that man and his household. ³⁵ This is what each of you keeps on saying to his friend or relative: 'What is the LORD's answer?' or 'What has the LORD spoken?' ³⁶ But you must not mention 'the oracle of the LORD' again, because every man's own word becomes his oracle and so you distort the words of the living God, the LORD Almighty, our God. ³⁷ This is what you keep saying to a prophet: 'What is the LORD's answer to you?' or 'What has the LORD spoken?' ³⁸ Although you claim, 'This is the oracle of the LORD,' this is what the LORD says: You used the words, 'This is the oracle of the LORD,' even though I told you that you must not claim, 'This is the oracle of the LORD.' ³⁹ Therefore, I will surely forget you and cast you out of my presence along with the city I gave to you and your fathers. ⁴⁰ I

What's God Got to Do With This Anyway?

JEREMIAH 23:20–37

"A Christian who was in a great deal of trouble was recounting to another the various efforts he had made to find deliverance, and concluded by saying, 'But it has all been in vain, and there is literally nothing left for me to do now but to trust the Lord.'

" 'Alas!' exclaimed his friend in a tone of the deepest commiseration, as though no greater risk were possible,— 'Alas! has it come to *that!*' "

—HANNAH WHITALL SMITH,
The Christian's Secret of a Happy Life

ᵃ 33 Or *burden* (see Septuagint and Vulgate)   ᵇ 33 Hebrew; Septuagint and
Vulgate *'You are the burden.* (The Hebrew for *oracle* and *burden* is the same.)

Abide in Me and Bear Much Fruit

JEREMIAH 24:1–10

Find two pieces of ripe fruit. Put one in the refrigerator and the other in a warm place and leave them until the one in the warm place starts to decay. Place them in front of you and spend some time looking at their particular details, feeling and smelling them and thinking of all the associations they evoke for you. Ask the Spirit to guide you. Write in your journal your response to the question: "What is God saying to me through each of these pieces of fruit?" Pray about the ideas and feelings you have. Plan how you will act if you see that an action is required. Ask God to make your life fruitful. Eat the good fruit and dispose of the bad piece of fruit.

See *Meeting God in the Created Order*

will bring upon you everlasting disgrace—everlasting shame that will not be forgotten."

Two Baskets of Figs

24 After Jehoiachin[a] son of Jehoiakim king of Judah and the officials, the craftsmen and the artisans of Judah were carried into exile from Jerusalem to Babylon by Nebuchadnezzar king of Babylon, the LORD showed me two baskets of figs placed in front of the temple of the LORD. ²One basket had very good figs, like those that ripen early; the other basket had very poor figs, so bad they could not be eaten.

³Then the LORD asked me, "What do you see, Jeremiah?"

"Figs," I answered. "The good ones are very good, but the poor ones are so bad they cannot be eaten."

⁴Then the word of the LORD came to me: ⁵"This is what the LORD, the God of Israel, says: 'Like these good figs, I regard as good the exiles from Judah, whom I sent away from this place to the land of the Babylonians.[b] ⁶My eyes will watch over them for their good, and I will bring them back to this land. I will build them up and not tear them down; I will plant them and not uproot them. ⁷I will give them a heart to know me, that I am the LORD. They will be my people, and I will be their God, for they will return to me with all their heart.

⁸" 'But like the poor figs, which are so bad they cannot be eaten,' says the LORD, 'so will I deal with Zedekiah king of Judah, his officials and the survivors from Jerusalem, whether they remain in this land or live in Egypt. ⁹I will make them abhorrent and an offense to all the kingdoms of the earth, a reproach and a byword, an object of ridicule and cursing, wherever I banish them. ¹⁰I will send the sword, famine and plague against them until they are destroyed from the land I gave to them and their fathers.' "

Seventy Years of Captivity

25 The word came to Jeremiah concerning all the people of Judah in the fourth year of Jehoiakim son of Josiah king of Judah, which was the first year of Nebuchadnezzar king of Babylon. ²So Jeremiah the prophet said to all the people of Judah and to all those living in Jerusalem: ³For twenty-three years—from the thirteenth year of Josiah son of Amon king of Judah until this very day—the word of the LORD has come to me and I have spoken to you again and again, but you have not listened.

⁴And though the LORD has sent all his servants the prophets to you again and again, you have not listened or paid any attention. ⁵They said, "Turn now, each of you, from your evil ways and your evil practices, and you can stay in the land the LORD gave to you and your fathers for ever and ever. ⁶Do not follow other gods to serve and worship them; do not provoke me to anger with what your hands have made. Then I will not harm you."

⁷"But you did not listen to me," declares the LORD, "and you have provoked me with what your hands have made, and you have brought harm to yourselves."

⁸Therefore the LORD Almighty says this: "Because you have not listened to my words, ⁹I will summon all the peoples of the north and my servant Nebuchadnezzar king of

a 1 Hebrew *Jeconiah*, a variant of *Jehoiachin*   *b* 5 Or *Chaldeans*

Babylon," declares the LORD, "and I will bring them against this land and its inhabitants and against all the surrounding nations. I will completely destroy[a] them and make them an object of horror and scorn, and an everlasting ruin. [10]I will banish from them the sounds of joy and gladness, the voices of bride and bridegroom, the sound of millstones and the light of the lamp. [11]This whole country will become a desolate wasteland, and these nations will serve the king of Babylon seventy years.

[12]"But when the seventy years are fulfilled, I will punish the king of Babylon and his nation, the land of the Babylonians,[b] for their guilt," declares the LORD, "and will make it desolate forever. [13]I will bring upon that land all the things I have spoken against it, all that are written in this book and prophesied by Jeremiah against all the nations. [14]They themselves will be enslaved by many nations and great kings; I will repay them according to their deeds and the work of their hands."

The Cup of God's Wrath

[15]This is what the LORD, the God of Israel, said to me: "Take from my hand this cup filled with the wine of my wrath and make all the nations to whom I send you drink it. [16]When they drink it, they will stagger and go mad because of the sword I will send among them."

[17]So I took the cup from the LORD's hand and made all the nations to whom he sent me drink it: [18]Jerusalem and the towns of Judah, its kings and officials, to make them a ruin and an object of horror and scorn and cursing, as they are today; [19]Pharaoh king of Egypt, his attendants, his officials and all his people, [20]and all the foreign people there; all the kings of Uz; all the kings of the Philistines (those of Ashkelon, Gaza, Ekron, and the people left at Ashdod); [21]Edom, Moab and Ammon; [22]all the kings of Tyre and Sidon; the kings of the coastlands across the sea; [23]Dedan, Tema, Buz and all who are in distant places[c]; [24]all the kings of Arabia and all the kings of the foreign people who live in the desert; [25]all the kings of Zimri, Elam and Media; [26]and all the kings of the north, near and far, one after the other—all the kingdoms on the face of the earth. And after all of them, the king of Sheshach[d] will drink it too.

[27]"Then tell them, 'This is what the LORD Almighty, the God of Israel, says: Drink, get drunk and vomit, and fall to rise no more because of the sword I will send among you.' [28]But if they refuse to take the cup from your hand and drink, tell them, 'This is what the LORD Almighty says: You must drink it! [29]See, I am beginning to bring disaster on the city that bears my Name, and will you indeed go unpunished? You will not go unpunished, for I am calling down a sword upon all who live on the earth, declares the LORD Almighty.'

[30]"Now prophesy all these words against them and say to them:

> " 'The LORD will roar from on high;
>   he will thunder from his holy dwelling
>   and roar mightily against his land.

The Grapes of Wrath

JEREMIAH 25:8–14

"Outrageous!" we think. How could God call Nebuchadnezzar—a pagan emperor—"my servant"? How could God bring disaster on Jerusalem, the city that bears his name? At first glance both of these actions are difficult to comprehend, even contradictory; but sometimes God uses unpredictable means to accomplish great ends.

Identify a "godless" force in your life (or in the life of your church or nation) that God used to bring about change. When change occurred, what sacred things in your life seemed threatened? What are you saying to yourself about it now? What are you feeling? Take it to God in prayer.

See Meeting God in Everyday Life

---

[a]9 The Hebrew term refers to the irrevocable giving over of things or persons to the LORD, often by totally destroying them.   [b]12 Or *Chaldeans*   [c]23 Or *who clip the hair by their foreheads*   [d]26 *Sheshach* is a cryptogram for Babylon.

Spreading Disaster

JEREMIAH 25:32–38

The prophet is to say to the nations, "Disaster is spreading from nation to nation." What disasters do you see spreading "from nation to nation" in today's world? Is your typical response, "Too hard! Forget it!"? Is it a response of despair? Turn to the God of nations. Bring your usual response and ask God what he thinks of it. Ask God to give you direction about a "disaster" you can pray for. Whom can you invite to pray with you?

See Meeting God in Everyday Life

He will shout like those who tread the grapes,
  shout against all who live on the earth.
³¹ The tumult will resound to the ends of the earth,
  for the LORD will bring charges against the
    nations;
he will bring judgment on all mankind
  and put the wicked to the sword,' "

  declares the LORD.

³² This is what the LORD Almighty says:

"Look! Disaster is spreading
  from nation to nation;
a mighty storm is rising
  from the ends of the earth."

³³ At that time those slain by the LORD will be everywhere—from one end of the earth to the other. They will not be mourned or gathered up or buried, but will be like refuse lying on the ground.

³⁴ Weep and wail, you shepherds;
  roll in the dust, you leaders of the flock.
For your time to be slaughtered has come;
  you will fall and be shattered like fine pottery.
³⁵ The shepherds will have nowhere to flee,
  the leaders of the flock no place to escape.
³⁶ Hear the cry of the shepherds,
  the wailing of the leaders of the flock,
  for the LORD is destroying their pasture.
³⁷ The peaceful meadows will be laid waste
  because of the fierce anger of the LORD.
³⁸ Like a lion he will leave his lair,
  and their land will become desolate
because of the sword[a] of the oppressor
  and because of the LORD's fierce anger.

Jeremiah Threatened With Death

26 Early in the reign of Jehoiakim son of Josiah king of Judah, this word came from the LORD: ²"This is what the LORD says: Stand in the courtyard of the LORD's house and speak to all the people of the towns of Judah who come to worship in the house of the LORD. Tell them everything I command you; do not omit a word. ³Perhaps they will listen and each will turn from his evil way. Then I will relent and not bring on them the disaster I was planning because of the evil they have done. ⁴Say to them, 'This is what the LORD says: If you do not listen to me and follow my law, which I have set before you, ⁵and if you do not listen to the words of my servants the prophets, whom I have sent to you again and again (though you have not listened), ⁶then I will make this house like Shiloh and this city an object of cursing among all the nations of the earth.' "

⁷The priests, the prophets and all the people heard Jeremiah speak these words in the house of the LORD. ⁸But as soon as Jeremiah finished telling all the people everything the LORD had commanded him to say, the priests, the prophets and all the people seized him and said, "You must die! ⁹Why do you prophesy in the LORD's name that this house will be like Shiloh and this city will be desolate and

---

a 38 Some Hebrew manuscripts and Septuagint (see also Jer. 46:16 and 50:16); most Hebrew manuscripts *anger*

deserted?" And all the people crowded around Jeremiah in the house of the LORD.

[10]When the officials of Judah heard about these things, they went up from the royal palace to the house of the LORD and took their places at the entrance of the New Gate of the LORD's house. [11]Then the priests and the prophets said to the officials and all the people, "This man should be sentenced to death because he has prophesied against this city. You have heard it with your own ears!"

[12]Then Jeremiah said to all the officials and all the people: "The LORD sent me to prophesy against this house and this city all the things you have heard. [13]Now reform your ways and your actions and obey the LORD your God. Then the LORD will relent and not bring the disaster he has pronounced against you. [14]As for me, I am in your hands; do with me whatever you think is good and right. [15]Be assured, however, that if you put me to death, you will bring the guilt of innocent blood on yourselves and on this city and on those who live in it, for in truth the LORD has sent me to you to speak all these words in your hearing."

[16]Then the officials and all the people said to the priests and the prophets, "This man should not be sentenced to death! He has spoken to us in the name of the LORD our God."

[17]Some of the elders of the land stepped forward and said to the entire assembly of people, [18]"Micah of Moresheth prophesied in the days of Hezekiah king of Judah. He told all the people of Judah, 'This is what the LORD Almighty says:

" 'Zion will be plowed like a field,
    Jerusalem will become a heap of rubble,
    the temple hill a mound overgrown with
        thickets.'[a]

[19]"Did Hezekiah king of Judah or anyone else in Judah put him to death? Did not Hezekiah fear the LORD and seek his favor? And did not the LORD relent, so that he did not bring the disaster he pronounced against them? We are about to bring a terrible disaster on ourselves!"

[20](Now Uriah son of Shemaiah from Kiriath Jearim was another man who prophesied in the name of the LORD; he prophesied the same things against this city and this land as Jeremiah did. [21]When King Jehoiakim and all his officers and officials heard his words, the king sought to put him to death. But Uriah heard of it and fled in fear to Egypt. [22]King Jehoiakim, however, sent Elnathan son of Acbor to Egypt, along with some other men. [23]They brought Uriah out of Egypt and took him to King Jehoiakim, who had him struck down with a sword and his body thrown into the burial place of the common people.)

[24]Furthermore, Ahikam son of Shaphan supported Jeremiah, and so he was not handed over to the people to be put to death.

Judah to Serve Nebuchadnezzar

27 Early in the reign of Zedekiah[b] son of Josiah king of Judah, this word came to Jeremiah from the LORD:

---

[a]18 Micah 3:12   [b]1 A few Hebrew manuscripts and Syriac (see also Jer. 27:3, 12 and 28:1); most Hebrew manuscripts *Jehoiakim* (Most Septuagint manuscripts do not have this verse.)

Integrity at What Cost?

JEREMIAH 26:12–15

Bill died at age 81, after a life of loving and serving God with great faithfulness. As you read this prayer found in Bill's Bible, note both your resistance and your affinity to these lines:

"Lord, I am willing
    to receive what you give
    to lack what you withhold
    to relinquish what you take
    to suffer what you inflict
    to be what you require."

Write out this prayer and use it as a bookmark.

See *Meeting God in Worship*

Can This Be God?

JEREMIAH 27:12–15

Does God really counsel sub-mission to a foreign power? Is God really saying, "Do not lis-ten to encouragement from your leaders"? Through the words of the prophet, God is giving unex-pected direction.

Sometimes God smashes our assumptions and bypasses our neatly packaged definitions of who he is and what he will say to us. In the quiet of your prayer space, ask yourself what God is saying to you that is dif-ferent from what you would ex-pect. Ask God to confirm what you hear, and check it with the counsel of your spiritual advis-er, pastor or faith companion.

See Meeting God in Scripture

²This is what the LORD said to me: "Make a yoke out of straps and crossbars and put it on your neck. ³Then send word to the kings of Edom, Moab, Ammon, Tyre and Sidon through the envoys who have come to Jerusalem to Zede-kiah king of Judah. ⁴Give them a message for their masters and say, 'This is what the LORD Almighty, the God of Israel, says: "Tell this to your masters: ⁵With my great power and outstretched arm I made the earth and its people and the animals that are on it, and I give it to anyone I please. ⁶Now I will hand all your countries over to my servant Nebu-chadnezzar king of Babylon; I will make even the wild ani-mals subject to him. ⁷All nations will serve him and his son and his grandson until the time for his land comes; then many nations and great kings will subjugate him.

⁸" ' "If, however, any nation or kingdom will not serve Nebuchadnezzar king of Babylon or bow its neck under his yoke, I will punish that nation with the sword, famine and plague, declares the LORD, until I destroy it by his hand. ⁹So do not listen to your prophets, your diviners, your inter-preters of dreams, your mediums or your sorcerers who tell you, 'You will not serve the king of Babylon.' ¹⁰They proph-esy lies to you that will only serve to remove you far from your lands; I will banish you and you will perish. ¹¹But if any nation will bow its neck under the yoke of the king of Babylon and serve him, I will let that nation remain in its own land to till it and to live there, declares the LORD." ' "

¹²I gave the same message to Zedekiah king of Judah. I said, "Bow your neck under the yoke of the king of Bab-ylon; serve him and his people, and you will live. ¹³Why will you and your people die by the sword, famine and plague with which the LORD has threatened any nation that will not serve the king of Babylon? ¹⁴Do not listen to the words of the prophets who say to you, 'You will not serve the king of Babylon,' for they are prophesying lies to you. ¹⁵'I have not sent them,' declares the LORD. 'They are prophesying lies in my name. Therefore, I will banish you and you will perish, both you and the prophets who prophesy to you.' "

¹⁶Then I said to the priests and all these people, "This is what the LORD says: Do not listen to the prophets who say, 'Very soon now the articles from the LORD's house will be brought back from Babylon.' They are prophesying lies to you. ¹⁷Do not listen to them. Serve the king of Babylon, and you will live. Why should this city become a ruin? ¹⁸If they are prophets and have the word of the LORD, let them plead with the LORD Almighty that the furnishings remaining in the house of the LORD and in the palace of the king of Judah and in Jerusalem not be taken to Babylon. ¹⁹For this is what the LORD Almighty says about the pillars, the Sea, the mov-able stands and the other furnishings that are left in this city, ²⁰which Nebuchadnezzar king of Babylon did not take away when he carried Jehoiachin*ᵃ* son of Jehoiakim king of Judah into exile from Jerusalem to Babylon, along with all the nobles of Judah and Jerusalem— ²¹yes, this is what the LORD Almighty, the God of Israel, says about the things that are left in the house of the LORD and in the palace of the king of Judah and in Jerusalem: ²²'They will be taken to Babylon and there they will remain until the day I come for them,' declares the LORD. 'Then I will bring them back and restore them to this place.' "

ᵃ 20 Hebrew *Jeconiah*, a variant of *Jehoiachin*

The False Prophet Hananiah

28 In the fifth month of that same year, the fourth year, early in the reign of Zedekiah king of Judah, the prophet Hananiah son of Azzur, who was from Gibeon, said to me in the house of the LORD in the presence of the priests and all the people: [2]"This is what the LORD Almighty, the God of Israel, says: 'I will break the yoke of the king of Babylon. [3]Within two years I will bring back to this place all the articles of the LORD's house that Nebuchadnezzar king of Babylon removed from here and took to Babylon. [4]I will also bring back to this place Jehoiachin[a] son of Jehoiakim king of Judah and all the other exiles from Judah who went to Babylon,' declares the LORD, 'for I will break the yoke of the king of Babylon.' "

[5]Then the prophet Jeremiah replied to the prophet Hananiah before the priests and all the people who were standing in the house of the LORD. [6]He said, "Amen! May the LORD do so! May the LORD fulfill the words you have prophesied by bringing the articles of the LORD's house and all the exiles back to this place from Babylon. [7]Nevertheless, listen to what I have to say in your hearing and in the hearing of all the people: [8]From early times the prophets who preceded you and me have prophesied war, disaster and plague against many countries and great kingdoms. [9]But the prophet who prophesies peace will be recognized as one truly sent by the LORD only if his prediction comes true."

[10]Then the prophet Hananiah took the yoke off the neck of the prophet Jeremiah and broke it, [11]and he said before all the people, "This is what the LORD says: 'In the same way will I break the yoke of Nebuchadnezzar king of Babylon off the neck of all the nations within two years.' " At this, the prophet Jeremiah went on his way.

[12]Shortly after the prophet Hananiah had broken the yoke off the neck of the prophet Jeremiah, the word of the LORD came to Jeremiah: [13]"Go and tell Hananiah, 'This is what the LORD says: You have broken a wooden yoke, but in its place you will get a yoke of iron. [14]This is what the LORD Almighty, the God of Israel, says: I will put an iron yoke on the necks of all these nations to make them serve Nebuchadnezzar king of Babylon, and they will serve him. I will even give him control over the wild animals.' "

[15]Then the prophet Jeremiah said to Hananiah the prophet, "Listen, Hananiah! The LORD has not sent you, yet you have persuaded this nation to trust in lies. [16]Therefore, this is what the LORD says: 'I am about to remove you from the face of the earth. This very year you are going to die, because you have preached rebellion against the LORD.' "

[17]In the seventh month of that same year, Hananiah the prophet died.

A Letter to the Exiles

29 This is the text of the letter that the prophet Jeremiah sent from Jerusalem to the surviving elders among the exiles and to the priests, the prophets and all the other people Nebuchadnezzar had carried into exile from Jerusalem to Babylon. [2](This was after King Jehoiachin[a] and the queen mother, the court officials and the leaders of Judah and Jerusalem, the craftsmen and the arti-

---

Peace in Our Time

JEREMIAH 28:1–9

No one wanted to face the facts. "Peace in our time," announced British Prime Minister Neville Chamberlain after signing the Munich Pact with Hitler in September 1938. And the popular press had its clairvoyants and "stars" predicting there would be no war. Events soon proved otherwise.

What is God doing that you don't want to know about? What issue would you rather not hear about from God? Ask for the double-edged sword of the Spirit to help you discern truth from wishful thinking, and write a journal entry under the heading "What I Don't Want to Hear From God." Discuss it with a trusted friend and take your answer with you the next time you go to worship. During the prayers or hymns, lift up your hesitation again before God.

See Meeting God in Worship

A Future With Hope

JEREMIAH 29:4–7,10–14

God is gracious! The steadfast love of the Lord never ceases (see Lamentations 3:22). Regardless of the data that might cause you to despair, God wills your well-being. So what does it mean for you to build and plant and eat? What does it mean for you to increase your family? What mental paradigm shift would allow you to be content with the provision that God has made for you? Spend the next several days giving thanks to God for all that you have. Dream of what God might yet provide. Seek God with all your heart, singing an appropriate song or hymn.

See Meeting God in Service

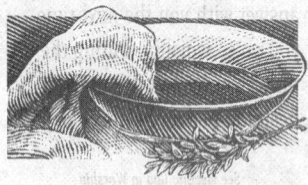

sans had gone into exile from Jerusalem.) ³He entrusted the letter to Elasah son of Shaphan and to Gemariah son of Hilkiah, whom Zedekiah king of Judah sent to King Nebuchadnezzar in Babylon. It said:

⁴This is what the LORD Almighty, the God of Israel, says to all those I carried into exile from Jerusalem to Babylon: ⁵"Build houses and settle down; plant gardens and eat what they produce. ⁶Marry and have sons and daughters; find wives for your sons and give your daughters in marriage, so that they too may have sons and daughters. Increase in number there; do not decrease. ⁷Also, seek the peace and prosperity of the city to which I have carried you into exile. Pray to the LORD for it, because if it prospers, you too will prosper." ⁸Yes, this is what the LORD Almighty, the God of Israel, says: "Do not let the prophets and diviners among you deceive you. Do not listen to the dreams you encourage them to have. ⁹They are prophesying lies to you in my name. I have not sent them," declares the LORD.

¹⁰This is what the LORD says: "When seventy years are completed for Babylon, I will come to you and fulfill my gracious promise to bring you back to this place. ¹¹For I know the plans I have for you," declares the LORD, "plans to prosper you and not to harm you, plans to give you hope and a future. ¹²Then you will call upon me and come and pray to me, and I will listen to you. ¹³You will seek me and find me when you seek me with all your heart. ¹⁴I will be found by you," declares the LORD, "and will bring you back from captivity.ᵃ I will gather you from all the nations and places where I have banished you," declares the LORD, "and will bring you back to the place from which I carried you into exile."

¹⁵You may say, "The LORD has raised up prophets for us in Babylon," ¹⁶but this is what the LORD says about the king who sits on David's throne and all the people who remain in this city, your countrymen who did not go with you into exile— ¹⁷yes, this is what the LORD Almighty says: "I will send the sword, famine and plague against them and I will make them like poor figs that are so bad they cannot be eaten. ¹⁸I will pursue them with the sword, famine and plague and will make them abhorrent to all the kingdoms of the earth and an object of cursing and horror, of scorn and reproach, among all the nations where I drive them. ¹⁹For they have not listened to my words," declares the LORD, "words that I sent to them again and again by my servants the prophets. And you exiles have not listened either," declares the LORD.

²⁰Therefore, hear the word of the LORD, all you exiles whom I have sent away from Jerusalem to Babylon. ²¹This is what the LORD Almighty, the God of Israel, says about Ahab son of Kolaiah and Zedekiah son of Maaseiah, who are prophesying lies to you in my name: "I will hand them over to Nebuchadnezzar king of Babylon, and he will put them to death before your very eyes. ²²Because of them, all the exiles from Judah who are in Babylon will use this curse: 'The LORD treat

ᵃ 14 Or *will restore your fortunes*

you like Zedekiah and Ahab, whom the king of Babylon burned in the fire.' ²³For they have done outrageous things in Israel; they have committed adultery with their neighbors' wives and in my name have spoken lies, which I did not tell them to do. I know it and am a witness to it," declares the LORD.

Message to Shemaiah

²⁴Tell Shemaiah the Nehelamite, ²⁵"This is what the LORD Almighty, the God of Israel, says: You sent letters in your own name to all the people in Jerusalem, to Zephaniah son of Maaseiah the priest, and to all the other priests. You said to Zephaniah, ²⁶'The LORD has appointed you priest in place of Jehoiada to be in charge of the house of the LORD; you should put any madman who acts like a prophet into the stocks and neck-irons. ²⁷So why have you not reprimanded Jeremiah from Anathoth, who poses as a prophet among you? ²⁸He has sent this message to us in Babylon: It will be a long time. Therefore build houses and settle down; plant gardens and eat what they produce.' "

²⁹Zephaniah the priest, however, read the letter to Jeremiah the prophet. ³⁰Then the word of the LORD came to Jeremiah: ³¹"Send this message to all the exiles: 'This is what the LORD says about Shemaiah the Nehelamite: Because Shemaiah has prophesied to you, even though I did not send him, and has led you to believe a lie, ³²this is what the LORD says: I will surely punish Shemaiah the Nehelamite and his descendants. He will have no one left among this people, nor will he see the good things I will do for my people, declares the LORD, because he has preached rebellion against me.' "

Restoration of Israel

30 This is the word that came to Jeremiah from the LORD: ²"This is what the LORD, the God of Israel, says: 'Write in a book all the words I have spoken to you. ³The days are coming,' declares the LORD, 'when I will bring my people Israel and Judah back from captivity*ᵃ* and restore them to the land I gave their forefathers to possess,' says the LORD."

⁴These are the words the LORD spoke concerning Israel and Judah: ⁵"This is what the LORD says:

" 'Cries of fear are heard—
    terror, not peace.
⁶Ask and see:
    Can a man bear children?
Then why do I see every strong man
    with his hands on his stomach like a woman in
      labor,
    every face turned deathly pale?
⁷How awful that day will be!
    None will be like it.
It will be a time of trouble for Jacob,
    but he will be saved out of it.

⁸" 'In that day,' declares the LORD Almighty,
    'I will break the yoke off their necks
and will tear off their bonds;
    no longer will foreigners enslave them.
⁹Instead, they will serve the LORD their God

ᵃ 3 Or *will restore the fortunes of my people Israel and Judah*

God Will Restore

JEREMIAH 30:12–17

Whom do you know who has a wound that is grievous and "incurable"? A family member? A friend? Yourself? Your nation? Journal your response to God's words: "I will restore you to health and heal your wounds."

What do you feel as you listen to these words? What do you think? What images come to your mind? What action is asked of you? What will you do, and when will you do it? Make yourself accountable to a faith companion for your response.

See Meeting God in Scripture

and David their king,
 whom I will raise up for them.

10 " 'So do not fear, O Jacob my servant;
 do not be dismayed, O Israel,'
 declares the LORD.
'I will surely save you out of a distant place,
 your descendants from the land of their exile.
Jacob will again have peace and security,
 and no one will make him afraid.
11 I am with you and will save you,'
 declares the LORD.
'Though I completely destroy all the nations
 among which I scatter you,
 I will not completely destroy you.
I will discipline you but only with justice;
 I will not let you go entirely unpunished.'

12 "This is what the LORD says:

 " 'Your wound is incurable,
 your injury beyond healing.
13 There is no one to plead your cause,
 no remedy for your sore,
 no healing for you.
14 All your allies have forgotten you;
 they care nothing for you.
I have struck you as an enemy would
 and punished you as would the cruel,
because your guilt is so great
 and your sins so many.
15 Why do you cry out over your wound,
 your pain that has no cure?
Because of your great guilt and many sins
 I have done these things to you.

16 " 'But all who devour you will be devoured;
 all your enemies will go into exile.
Those who plunder you will be plundered;
 all who make spoil of you I will despoil.
17 But I will restore you to health
 and heal your wounds,'
 declares the LORD,
'because you are called an outcast,
 Zion for whom no one cares.'

18 "This is what the LORD says:

 " 'I will restore the fortunes of Jacob's tents
 and have compassion on his dwellings;
the city will be rebuilt on her ruins,
 and the palace will stand in its proper place.
19 From them will come songs of thanksgiving
 and the sound of rejoicing.
I will add to their numbers,
 and they will not be decreased;
I will bring them honor,
 and they will not be disdained.
20 Their children will be as in days of old,
 and their community will be established before
 me;
 I will punish all who oppress them.

21 Their leader will be one of their own;
  their ruler will arise from among them.
I will bring him near and he will come close to me,
  for who is he who will devote himself
  to be close to me?'
                              declares the LORD.
22 " 'So you will be my people,
  and I will be your God.' "

23 See, the storm of the LORD
  will burst out in wrath,
a driving wind swirling down
  on the heads of the wicked.
24 The fierce anger of the LORD will not turn back
  until he fully accomplishes
  the purposes of his heart.
In days to come
  you will understand this.

31 "At that time," declares the LORD, "I will be the God of all the clans of Israel, and they will be my people."
2 This is what the LORD says:

  "The people who survive the sword
    will find favor in the desert;
  I will come to give rest to Israel."

3 The LORD appeared to us in the past,*a* saying:

  "I have loved you with an everlasting love;
    I have drawn you with loving-kindness.
4 I will build you up again
    and you will be rebuilt, O Virgin Israel.
  Again you will take up your tambourines
    and go out to dance with the joyful.
5 Again you will plant vineyards
    on the hills of Samaria;
  the farmers will plant them
    and enjoy their fruit.
6 There will be a day when watchmen cry out
    on the hills of Ephraim,
  'Come, let us go up to Zion,
    to the LORD our God.' "

7 This is what the LORD says:

  "Sing with joy for Jacob;
    shout for the foremost of the nations.
  Make your praises heard, and say,
    'O LORD, save your people,
    the remnant of Israel.'
8 See, I will bring them from the land of the north
    and gather them from the ends of the earth.
  Among them will be the blind and the lame,
    expectant mothers and women in labor;
    a great throng will return.
9 They will come with weeping;
    they will pray as I bring them back.
  I will lead them beside streams of water
    on a level path where they will not stumble,
  because I am Israel's father,
    and Ephraim is my firstborn son.

"With an Everlasting Love"

JEREMIAH 31:2–6

Virgin Israel? How can God call Israel "virgin" when the nation's shameful unfaithfulness has been exposed in detail by the prophet? Yet it seems that God intends the word "virgin" to mean "virgin"!

Remember that God is greater than your past. Be seated in a quiet place and listen to Jesus saying, "I am making everything new" (Revelation 21:5). Listen to the apostle Paul saying, "If anyone is in Christ, he is a new creation" (2 Corinthians 5:17). How, in the light of this, do you view yourself? Are you more aware of what is in your file of sins or are you one whom God has loved "with an everlasting love"? One spiritual adviser writes, "Say to yourself very often about everything that happens, 'God loves me! What a joy!' and reply boldly, 'And truly I love him too!' " (Abbé de Tourville).

See *Meeting God in Scripture*

---

a 3 Or LORD *has appeared to us from afar*

Ransomed, Healed, Restored, Forgiven!

JEREMIAH 31:10–14

"The texts express two anticipations about human life restored. On the one hand, there is anticipation of the restoration of public life, safe cities, caring communities, and secure streets. On the other hand, there is anticipation of the restoration of personal and interpersonal life, happy families, domestic well-being and joy, shared food and delighted relationships. Both public and interpersonal life depend on the self-giving action of God who makes newness possible. This alternative life comes from the self-giving act of atonement wrought only by God."

—WALTER BRUEGGEMANN,
Finally Comes the Poet

See Meeting God in Everyday Life

10 "Hear the word of the Lord, O nations;
    proclaim it in distant coastlands:
'He who scattered Israel will gather them
    and will watch over his flock like a shepherd.'
11 For the Lord will ransom Jacob
    and redeem them from the hand of those
        stronger than they.
12 They will come and shout for joy on the heights
        of Zion;
    they will rejoice in the bounty of the Lord—
the grain, the new wine and the oil,
    the young of the flocks and herds.
They will be like a well-watered garden,
    and they will sorrow no more.
13 Then maidens will dance and be glad,
    young men and old as well.
I will turn their mourning into gladness;
    I will give them comfort and joy instead of
        sorrow.
14 I will satisfy the priests with abundance,
    and my people will be filled with my bounty,"
                    declares the Lord.

15 This is what the Lord says:

"A voice is heard in Ramah,
    mourning and great weeping,
Rachel weeping for her children
    and refusing to be comforted,
    because her children are no more."

16 This is what the Lord says:

"Restrain your voice from weeping
    and your eyes from tears,
for your work will be rewarded,"
                    declares the Lord.
    "They will return from the land of the enemy.
17 So there is hope for your future,"
                    declares the Lord.
    "Your children will return to their own land.

18 "I have surely heard Ephraim's moaning:
    'You disciplined me like an unruly calf,
    and I have been disciplined.
Restore me, and I will return,
    because you are the Lord my God.
19 After I strayed,
    I repented;
after I came to understand,
    I beat my breast.
I was ashamed and humiliated
    because I bore the disgrace of my youth.'
20 Is not Ephraim my dear son,
    the child in whom I delight?
Though I often speak against him,
    I still remember him.
Therefore my heart yearns for him;
    I have great compassion for him,"
                    declares the Lord.

21 "Set up road signs;
    put up guideposts.

Take note of the highway,
  the road that you take.
Return, O Virgin Israel,
  return to your towns.
²² How long will you wander,
  O unfaithful daughter?
The LORD will create a new thing on earth—
  a woman will surround*a* a man.' "

²³This is what the LORD Almighty, the God of Israel, says: "When I bring them back from captivity,*b* the people in the land of Judah and in its towns will once again use these words: 'The LORD bless you, O righteous dwelling, O sacred mountain.' ²⁴People will live together in Judah and all its towns—farmers and those who move about with their flocks. ²⁵I will refresh the weary and satisfy the faint."

²⁶At this I awoke and looked around. My sleep had been pleasant to me.

²⁷"The days are coming," declares the LORD, "when I will plant the house of Israel and the house of Judah with the offspring of men and of animals. ²⁸Just as I watched over them to uproot and tear down, and to overthrow, destroy and bring disaster, so I will watch over them to build and to plant," declares the LORD. ²⁹"In those days people will no longer say,

'The fathers have eaten sour grapes,
  and the children's teeth are set on edge.'

³⁰Instead, everyone will die for his own sin; whoever eats sour grapes—his own teeth will be set on edge.

³¹ "The time is coming," declares the LORD,
  "when I will make a new covenant
with the house of Israel
  and with the house of Judah.
³² It will not be like the covenant
  I made with their forefathers
when I took them by the hand
  to lead them out of Egypt,
because they broke my covenant,
  though I was a husband to*c* them,*d*"
      declares the LORD.
³³ "This is the covenant I will make with the house
      of Israel
  after that time," declares the LORD.
"I will put my law in their minds
  and write it on their hearts.
I will be their God,
  and they will be my people.
³⁴ No longer will a man teach his neighbor,
  or a man his brother, saying, 'Know the LORD,'
because they will all know me,
  from the least of them to the greatest,"
      declares the LORD.
"For I will forgive their wickedness
  and will remember their sins no more."

³⁵This is what the LORD says,

Road Signs and Guideposts

JEREMIAH 31:21,31–34

God has embraced you in a new covenant in Jesus Christ that is built on a relationship rather than rules. God has written "I love you" on your heart.

What is the history of your covenant relationship with God? Use your journal (or any suitable paper) to write a concise history of your relationship with God. What are the key experiences and moments of insight and decision that stand out as road signs and guideposts? As best you can, remember the dates of watershed events and put them in your calendar for the year ahead. Be sure to celebrate your anniversaries with God.

See Meeting God in Everyday Life

a 22 Or *will go about* ⌊*seeking*⌋; or *will protect*   *b 23* Or *I restore their fortunes*   *c 32* Hebrew; Septuagint and Syriac / *and I turned away from*
d 32 Or *was their master*

Free to Know the Lord

JEREMIAH 31:34

What sin, if any, stands between you and God? How big is this sin within you? So that you may know the Lord in full measure, bring your sin to God and confess it, believing that God will remember your sin no more. Give your fullest attention (rather than your intention) to God. If sin continues to block your way, confess it before a trusted friend, your spiritual adviser or your pastor (see James 5:16) and listen to the authoritative word of Jesus Christ's forgiveness that that person proclaims.

See *Meeting God in Worship*

he who appoints the sun
    to shine by day,
who decrees the moon and stars
    to shine by night,
who stirs up the sea
    so that its waves roar—
    the LORD Almighty is his name:
³⁶ "Only if these decrees vanish from my sight,"
    declares the LORD,
"will the descendants of Israel ever cease
    to be a nation before me."

³⁷ This is what the LORD says:

"Only if the heavens above can be measured
    and the foundations of the earth below be
      searched out
will I reject all the descendants of Israel
    because of all they have done,"
                declares the LORD.

³⁸ "The days are coming," declares the LORD, "when this city will be rebuilt for me from the Tower of Hananel to the Corner Gate. ³⁹ The measuring line will stretch from there straight to the hill of Gareb and then turn to Goah. ⁴⁰ The whole valley where dead bodies and ashes are thrown, and all the terraces out to the Kidron Valley on the east as far as the corner of the Horse Gate, will be holy to the LORD. The city will never again be uprooted or demolished."

Jeremiah Buys a Field

32 This is the word that came to Jeremiah from the LORD in the tenth year of Zedekiah king of Judah, which was the eighteenth year of Nebuchadnezzar. ²The army of the king of Babylon was then besieging Jerusalem, and Jeremiah the prophet was confined in the courtyard of the guard in the royal palace of Judah.

³Now Zedekiah king of Judah had imprisoned him there, saying, "Why do you prophesy as you do? You say, 'This is what the LORD says: I am about to hand this city over to the king of Babylon, and he will capture it. ⁴Zedekiah king of Judah will not escape out of the hands of the Babylonians*ᵃ* but will certainly be handed over to the king of Babylon, and will speak with him face to face and see him with his own eyes. ⁵He will take Zedekiah to Babylon, where he will remain until I deal with him, declares the LORD. If you fight against the Babylonians, you will not succeed.' "

⁶Jeremiah said, "The word of the LORD came to me: ⁷Hanamel son of Shallum your uncle is going to come to you and say, 'Buy my field at Anathoth, because as nearest relative it is your right and duty to buy it.'

⁸"Then, just as the LORD had said, my cousin Hanamel came to me in the courtyard of the guard and said, 'Buy my field at Anathoth in the territory of Benjamin. Since it is your right to redeem it and possess it, buy it for yourself.'

"I knew that this was the word of the LORD; ⁹so I bought the field at Anathoth from my cousin Hanamel and weighed out for him seventeen shekels*ᵇ* of silver. ¹⁰I signed and sealed the deed, had it witnessed, and weighed out the

ᵃ4 Or *Chaldeans*; also in verses 5, 24, 25, 28, 29 and 43   *ᵇ9* That is, about 7 ounces (about 200 grams) silver on the scales. ¹¹I took the deed of purchase—the sealed copy containing the terms and conditions, as well as the unsealed copy— ¹²and I gave this deed to Baruch son of Neriah, the son of Mahseiah, in the presence of my cousin Hanamel and of the witnesses who had signed the deed and of all the Jews sitting in the courtyard of the guard.

¹³"In their presence I gave Baruch these instructions: ¹⁴'This is what the Lᴏʀᴅ Almighty, the God of Israel, says: Take these documents, both the sealed and unsealed copies of the deed of purchase, and put them in a clay jar so they will last a long time. ¹⁵For this is what the Lᴏʀᴅ Almighty, the God of Israel, says: Houses, fields and vineyards will again be bought in this land.'

¹⁶"After I had given the deed of purchase to Baruch son of Neriah, I prayed to the Lᴏʀᴅ:

¹⁷"Ah, Sovereign Lᴏʀᴅ, you have made the heavens and the earth by your great power and outstretched arm. Nothing is too hard for you. ¹⁸You show love to thousands but bring the punishment for the fathers' sins into the laps of their children after them. O great and powerful God, whose name is the Lᴏʀᴅ Almighty, ¹⁹great are your purposes and mighty are your deeds. Your eyes are open to all the ways of men; you reward everyone according to his conduct and as his deeds deserve. ²⁰You performed miraculous signs and wonders in Egypt and have continued them to this day, both in Israel and among all mankind, and have gained the renown that is still yours. ²¹You brought your people Israel out of Egypt with signs and wonders, by a mighty hand and an outstretched arm and with great terror. ²²You gave them this land you had sworn to give their forefathers, a land flowing with milk and honey. ²³They came in and took possession of it, but they did not obey you or follow your law; they did not do what you commanded them to do. So you brought all this disaster upon them.

²⁴"See how the siege ramps are built up to take the city. Because of the sword, famine and plague, the city will be handed over to the Babylonians who are attacking it. What you said has happened, as you now see. ²⁵And though the city will be handed over to the Babylonians, you, O Sovereign Lᴏʀᴅ, say to me, 'Buy the field with silver and have the transaction witnessed.' "

²⁶Then the word of the Lᴏʀᴅ came to Jeremiah: ²⁷"I am the Lᴏʀᴅ, the God of all mankind. Is anything too hard for me? ²⁸Therefore, this is what the Lᴏʀᴅ says: I am about to hand this city over to the Babylonians and to Nebuchadnezzar king of Babylon, who will capture it. ²⁹The Babylonians who are attacking this city will come in and set it on fire; they will burn it down, along with the houses where the people provoked me to anger by burning incense on the roofs to Baal and by pouring out drink offerings to other gods.

³⁰"The people of Israel and Judah have done nothing but evil in my sight from their youth; indeed, the people of Israel have done nothing but provoke me with what their hands have made, declares the Lᴏʀᴅ. ³¹From the day it was built until now, this city has so aroused my anger and wrath that I must remove it from my sight. ³²The people of Israel and Judah have provoked me by all the evil they have

Witnesses

JEREMIAH 32:9–15

Witnesses to Jeremiah's land purchase included "all the Jews sitting in the courtyard of the guard" (v.12).

Do you spend money freely, or are you cautious with money? Who witnesses what you buy? Take someone with you the next time you shop. When you return, file the receipt at this page in the book of Jeremiah. Pray with your companion for all those involved in the production and sale of your purchase. What is it like for those who cannot afford what you bought? Pray for them. And from a tithe of your purchase, give to someone in need.

See Meeting God in Service

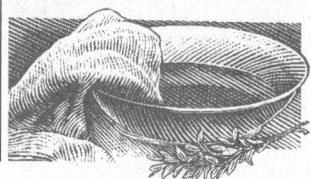

All Shall Be Well

JEREMIAH 32:42–44

"Because of our good Lord's tender love to all those who shall be saved, he quickly comforts them saying, 'The cause of this pain is sin. But all shall be well, and all shall be well, and all manner of thing shall be well.' These words were said so kindly and without a hint of blame, to me or to any who shall be saved."

—JULIAN OF NORWICH,
Enfolded in Love

See *Meeting God in Worship*

done—they, their kings and officials, their priests and prophets, the men of Judah and the people of Jerusalem. [33]They turned their backs to me and not their faces; though I taught them again and again, they would not listen or respond to discipline. [34]They set up their abominable idols in the house that bears my Name and defiled it. [35]They built high places for Baal in the Valley of Ben Hinnom to sacrifice their sons and daughters[a] to Molech, though I never commanded, nor did it enter my mind, that they should do such a detestable thing and so make Judah sin.

[36]"You are saying about this city, 'By the sword, famine and plague it will be handed over to the king of Babylon'; but this is what the LORD, the God of Israel, says: [37]I will surely gather them from all the lands where I banish them in my furious anger and great wrath; I will bring them back to this place and let them live in safety. [38]They will be my people, and I will be their God. [39]I will give them singleness of heart and action, so that they will always fear me for their own good and the good of their children after them. [40]I will make an everlasting covenant with them: I will never stop doing good to them, and I will inspire them to fear me, so that they will never turn away from me. [41]I will rejoice in doing them good and will assuredly plant them in this land with all my heart and soul.

[42]"This is what the LORD says: As I have brought all this great calamity on this people, so I will give them all the prosperity I have promised them. [43]Once more fields will be bought in this land of which you say, 'It is a desolate waste, without men or animals, for it has been handed over to the Babylonians.' [44]Fields will be bought for silver, and deeds will be signed, sealed and witnessed in the territory of Benjamin, in the villages around Jerusalem, in the towns of Judah and in the towns of the hill country, of the western foothills and of the Negev, because I will restore their fortunes,[b] declares the LORD."

Promise of Restoration

33 While Jeremiah was still confined in the courtyard of the guard, the word of the LORD came to him a second time: [2]"This is what the LORD says, he who made the earth, the LORD who formed it and established it—the LORD is his name: [3]'Call to me and I will answer you and tell you great and unsearchable things you do not know.' [4]For this is what the LORD, the God of Israel, says about the houses in this city and the royal palaces of Judah that have been torn down to be used against the siege ramps and the sword [5]in the fight with the Babylonians[c]: 'They will be filled with the dead bodies of the men I will slay in my anger and wrath. I will hide my face from this city because of all its wickedness.

[6]" 'Nevertheless, I will bring health and healing to it; I will heal my people and will let them enjoy abundant peace and security. [7]I will bring Judah and Israel back from captivity[d] and will rebuild them as they were before. [8]I will cleanse them from all the sin they have committed against me and will forgive all their sins of rebellion against me. [9]Then this city will bring me renown, joy, praise and honor

---

a 35 Or *to make their sons and daughters pass through* (*the fire*)   *b 44* Or *will bring them back from captivity*   *c 5* Or *Chaldeans*   *d 7* Or *will restore the fortunes of Judah and Israel*

before all nations on earth that hear of all the good things I do for it; and they will be in awe and will tremble at the abundant prosperity and peace I provide for it.'

¹⁰ "This is what the Lord says: 'You say about this place, "It is a desolate waste, without men or animals." Yet in the towns of Judah and the streets of Jerusalem that are deserted, inhabited by neither men nor animals, there will be heard once more ¹¹the sounds of joy and gladness, the voices of bride and bridegroom, and the voices of those who bring thank offerings to the house of the Lord, saying,

"Give thanks to the Lord Almighty,
    for the Lord is good;
    his love endures forever."

For I will restore the fortunes of the land as they were before,' says the Lord.

¹² "This is what the Lord Almighty says: 'In this place, desolate and without men or animals—in all its towns there will again be pastures for shepherds to rest their flocks. ¹³In the towns of the hill country, of the western foothills and of the Negev, in the territory of Benjamin, in the villages around Jerusalem and in the towns of Judah, flocks will again pass under the hand of the one who counts them,' says the Lord.

¹⁴ " 'The days are coming,' declares the Lord, 'when I will fulfill the gracious promise I made to the house of Israel and to the house of Judah.

¹⁵ " 'In those days and at that time
    I will make a righteous Branch sprout from
        David's line;
    he will do what is just and right in the land.
¹⁶In those days Judah will be saved
    and Jerusalem will live in safety.
This is the name by which it^a will be called:
    The Lord Our Righteousness.'

¹⁷For this is what the Lord says: 'David will never fail to have a man to sit on the throne of the house of Israel, ¹⁸nor will the priests, who are Levites, ever fail to have a man to stand before me continually to offer burnt offerings, to burn grain offerings and to present sacrifices.' "

¹⁹The word of the Lord came to Jeremiah: ²⁰ "This is what the Lord says: 'If you can break my covenant with the day and my covenant with the night, so that day and night no longer come at their appointed time, ²¹then my covenant with David my servant—and my covenant with the Levites who are priests ministering before me—can be broken and David will no longer have a descendant to reign on his throne. ²²I will make the descendants of David my servant and the Levites who minister before me as countless as the stars of the sky and as measureless as the sand on the seashore.' "

²³The word of the Lord came to Jeremiah: ²⁴ "Have you not noticed that these people are saying, 'The Lord has rejected the two kingdoms^b he chose'? So they despise my people and no longer regard them as a nation. ²⁵This is what the Lord says: 'If I have not established my covenant with day and night and the fixed laws of heaven and earth, ²⁶then I will reject the descendants of Jacob and David my

This City

JEREMIAH 33:10–16

Talk with a companion (or dialogue with God) about the ways in which your community could be described as a "desolate waste" (v.10). In what way is justice and righteousness needed? What needs to be "saved" and what issues of safety need to be addressed? Sit in a public place and observe the people and animals. What are they doing? What can you learn about them by just watching them? What spirit can you feel in your community today? As you watch and question, silently invite both the people and the animals to "Give thanks to the Lord Almighty, for the Lord is good; his love endures forever."

See Meeting God in Everyday Life

Free the Slaves!

JEREMIAH 34:8–16

The Hebrews who owned other Hebrews as slaves freed them, but later they changed their minds because it was expedient! What an irony—when God's action in freeing the Hebrew people from slavery was the heart of their national identity! But before you "throw stones," listen to God's voice in this passage proclaiming justice. Who is enslaved because of our own society's economic systems? Who is in bondage because of our society's lifestyle preferences? Who, beyond your conscious awareness, might be in bondage to serve your needs and wants? Contact an aid agency and find out. See what you can do to make a difference. Share what you learn with others in your faith community and take some specific group action.

See Meeting God in Service

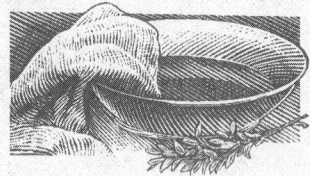

servant and will not choose one of his sons to rule over the descendants of Abraham, Isaac and Jacob. For I will restore their fortunes*a* and have compassion on them.' "

Warning to Zedekiah

34 While Nebuchadnezzar king of Babylon and all his army and all the kingdoms and peoples in the empire he ruled were fighting against Jerusalem and all its surrounding towns, this word came to Jeremiah from the Lord: ²"This is what the Lord, the God of Israel, says: Go to Zedekiah king of Judah and tell him, 'This is what the Lord says: I am about to hand this city over to the king of Babylon, and he will burn it down. ³You will not escape from his grasp but will surely be captured and handed over to him. You will see the king of Babylon with your own eyes, and he will speak with you face to face. And you will go to Babylon.

⁴" 'Yet hear the promise of the Lord, O Zedekiah king of Judah. This is what the Lord says concerning you: You will not die by the sword; ⁵you will die peacefully. As people made a funeral fire in honor of your fathers, the former kings who preceded you, so they will make a fire in your honor and lament, "Alas, O master!" I myself make this promise, declares the Lord.' "

⁶Then Jeremiah the prophet told all this to Zedekiah king of Judah, in Jerusalem, ⁷while the army of the king of Babylon was fighting against Jerusalem and the other cities of Judah that were still holding out—Lachish and Azekah. These were the only fortified cities left in Judah.

Freedom for Slaves

⁸The word came to Jeremiah from the Lord after King Zedekiah had made a covenant with all the people in Jerusalem to proclaim freedom for the slaves. ⁹Everyone was to free his Hebrew slaves, both male and female; no one was to hold a fellow Jew in bondage. ¹⁰So all the officials and people who entered into this covenant agreed that they would free their male and female slaves and no longer hold them in bondage. They agreed, and set them free. ¹¹But afterward they changed their minds and took back the slaves they had freed and enslaved them again.

¹²Then the word of the Lord came to Jeremiah: ¹³"This is what the Lord, the God of Israel, says: I made a covenant with your forefathers when I brought them out of Egypt, out of the land of slavery. I said, ¹⁴'Every seventh year each of you must free any fellow Hebrew who has sold himself to you. After he has served you six years, you must let him go free.'*b* Your fathers, however, did not listen to me or pay attention to me. ¹⁵Recently you repented and did what is right in my sight: Each of you proclaimed freedom to his countrymen. You even made a covenant before me in the house that bears my Name. ¹⁶But now you have turned around and profaned my name; each of you has taken back the male and female slaves you had set free to go where they wished. You have forced them to become your slaves again.

¹⁷"Therefore, this is what the Lord says: You have not obeyed me; you have not proclaimed freedom for your fellow countrymen. So I now proclaim 'freedom' for you, declares the Lord—'freedom' to fall by the sword, plague and famine. I will make you abhorrent to all the kingdoms of

a 26 Or *will bring them back from captivity*   *b 14* Deut. 15:12

the earth. ¹⁸The men who have violated my covenant and have not fulfilled the terms of the covenant they made before me, I will treat like the calf they cut in two and then walked between its pieces. ¹⁹The leaders of Judah and Jerusalem, the court officials, the priests and all the people of the land who walked between the pieces of the calf, ²⁰I will hand over to their enemies who seek their lives. Their dead bodies will become food for the birds of the air and the beasts of the earth.

²¹"I will hand Zedekiah king of Judah and his officials over to their enemies who seek their lives, to the army of the king of Babylon, which has withdrawn from you. ²²I am going to give the order, declares the Lord, and I will bring them back to this city. They will fight against it, take it and burn it down. And I will lay waste the towns of Judah so no one can live there."

The Recabites

35 This is the word that came to Jeremiah from the Lord during the reign of Jehoiakim son of Josiah king of Judah: ²"Go to the Recabite family and invite them to come to one of the side rooms of the house of the Lord and give them wine to drink."

³So I went to get Jaazaniah son of Jeremiah, the son of Habazziniah, and his brothers and all his sons—the whole family of the Recabites. ⁴I brought them into the house of the Lord, into the room of the sons of Hanan son of Igdaliah the man of God. It was next to the room of the officials, which was over that of Maaseiah son of Shallum the doorkeeper. ⁵Then I set bowls full of wine and some cups before the men of the Recabite family and said to them, "Drink some wine."

⁶But they replied, "We do not drink wine, because our forefather Jonadab son of Recab gave us this command: 'Neither you nor your descendants must ever drink wine. ⁷Also you must never build houses, sow seed or plant vineyards; you must never have any of these things, but must always live in tents. Then you will live a long time in the land where you are nomads.' ⁸We have obeyed everything our forefather Jonadab son of Recab commanded us. Neither we nor our wives nor our sons and daughters have ever drunk wine ⁹or built houses to live in or had vineyards, fields or crops. ¹⁰We have lived in tents and have fully obeyed everything our forefather Jonadab commanded us. ¹¹But when Nebuchadnezzar king of Babylon invaded this land, we said, 'Come, we must go to Jerusalem to escape the Babylonian*ᵃ* and Aramean armies.' So we have remained in Jerusalem."

¹²Then the word of the Lord came to Jeremiah, saying: ¹³"This is what the Lord Almighty, the God of Israel, says: Go and tell the men of Judah and the people of Jerusalem, 'Will you not learn a lesson and obey my words?' declares the Lord. ¹⁴'Jonadab son of Recab ordered his sons not to drink wine and this command has been kept. To this day they do not drink wine, because they obey their forefather's command. But I have spoken to you again and again, yet you have not obeyed me. ¹⁵Again and again I sent all my servants the prophets to you. They said, "Each of you must turn from your wicked ways and reform your

The Different

JEREMIAH 35:1–11

The Recabites were different. They chose to live in tents, work as shepherds and abstain from wine, shunning the more sophisticated, settled ways of some of God's people. God made them an example of obedience and faithfulness.

Think about committed Christians you may know who practice their faith differently than you do. Choose someone you trust and respect, and talk to that person about his or her most important convictions. Ask them honest questions and list the differences between you and that person. With this passage before you, pray over your list, asking God for new insights or reaffirmation of your own convictions.

See Meeting God in Community

Attending to the Word

JEREMIAH 36:4–8

When you hear the Word of God read publicly, are you attentive or does your mind tend to wander? To sharpen your hearing make a pact with some friends to fast for at least one meal, praying that your appetite for God's Word would be sharpened. Select a passage of Scripture and then meet together. Choose a good reader. Listen to God's Word as it is read aloud. Follow the reading with times of silent reflection, prayer and discussion about what you have heard. Finish with a simple meal commemorating the fact that together you live by both bread and the Word (see Deuteronomy 8:3).

See Meeting God in Scripture

actions; do not follow other gods to serve them. Then you will live in the land I have given to you and your fathers." But you have not paid attention or listened to me. ¹⁶The descendants of Jonadab son of Recab have carried out the command their forefather gave them, but these people have not obeyed me.'

¹⁷"Therefore, this is what the LORD God Almighty, the God of Israel, says: 'Listen! I am going to bring on Judah and on everyone living in Jerusalem every disaster I pronounced against them. I spoke to them, but they did not listen; I called to them, but they did not answer.' "

¹⁸Then Jeremiah said to the family of the Recabites, "This is what the LORD Almighty, the God of Israel, says: 'You have obeyed the command of your forefather Jonadab and have followed all his instructions and have done everything he ordered.' ¹⁹Therefore, this is what the LORD Almighty, the God of Israel, says: 'Jonadab son of Recab will never fail to have a man to serve me.' "

Jehoiakim Burns Jeremiah's Scroll

36 In the fourth year of Jehoiakim son of Josiah king of Judah, this word came to Jeremiah from the LORD: ²"Take a scroll and write on it all the words I have spoken to you concerning Israel, Judah and all the other nations from the time I began speaking to you in the reign of Josiah till now. ³Perhaps when the people of Judah hear about every disaster I plan to inflict on them, each of them will turn from his wicked way; then I will forgive their wickedness and their sin."

⁴So Jeremiah called Baruch son of Neriah, and while Jeremiah dictated all the words the LORD had spoken to him, Baruch wrote them on the scroll. ⁵Then Jeremiah told Baruch, "I am restricted; I cannot go to the LORD's temple. ⁶So you go to the house of the LORD on a day of fasting and read to the people from the scroll the words of the LORD that you wrote as I dictated. Read them to all the people of Judah who come in from their towns. ⁷Perhaps they will bring their petition before the LORD, and each will turn from his wicked ways, for the anger and wrath pronounced against this people by the LORD are great."

⁸Baruch son of Neriah did everything Jeremiah the prophet told him to do; at the LORD's temple he read the words of the LORD from the scroll. ⁹In the ninth month of the fifth year of Jehoiakim son of Josiah king of Judah, a time of fasting before the LORD was proclaimed for all the people in Jerusalem and those who had come from the towns of Judah. ¹⁰From the room of Gemariah son of Shaphan the secretary, which was in the upper courtyard at the entrance of the New Gate of the temple, Baruch read to all the people at the LORD's temple the words of Jeremiah from the scroll.

¹¹When Micaiah son of Gemariah, the son of Shaphan, heard all the words of the LORD from the scroll, ¹²he went down to the secretary's room in the royal palace, where all the officials were sitting: Elishama the secretary, Delaiah son of Shemaiah, Elnathan son of Acbor, Gemariah son of Shaphan, Zedekiah son of Hananiah, and all the other officials. ¹³After Micaiah told them everything he had heard Baruch read to the people from the scroll, ¹⁴all the officials sent Jehudi son of Nethaniah, the son of Shelemiah, the

son of Cushi, to say to Baruch, "Bring the scroll from which you have read to the people and come." So Baruch son of Neriah went to them with the scroll in his hand. [15]They said to him, "Sit down, please, and read it to us."

So Baruch read it to them. [16]When they heard all these words, they looked at each other in fear and said to Baruch, "We must report all these words to the king." [17]Then they asked Baruch, "Tell us, how did you come to write all this? Did Jeremiah dictate it?"

[18]"Yes," Baruch replied, "he dictated all these words to me, and I wrote them in ink on the scroll."

[19]Then the officials said to Baruch, "You and Jeremiah, go and hide. Don't let anyone know where you are."

[20]After they put the scroll in the room of Elishama the secretary, they went to the king in the courtyard and reported everything to him. [21]The king sent Jehudi to get the scroll, and Jehudi brought it from the room of Elishama the secretary and read it to the king and all the officials standing beside him. [22]It was the ninth month and the king was sitting in the winter apartment, with a fire burning in the firepot in front of him. [23]Whenever Jehudi had read three or four columns of the scroll, the king cut them off with a scribe's knife and threw them into the firepot, until the entire scroll was burned in the fire. [24]The king and all his attendants who heard all these words showed no fear, nor did they tear their clothes. [25]Even though Elnathan, Delaiah and Gemariah urged the king not to burn the scroll, he would not listen to them. [26]Instead, the king commanded Jerahmeel, a son of the king, Seraiah son of Azriel and Shelemiah son of Abdeel to arrest Baruch the scribe and Jeremiah the prophet. But the LORD had hidden them.

[27]After the king burned the scroll containing the words that Baruch had written at Jeremiah's dictation, the word of the LORD came to Jeremiah: [28]"Take another scroll and write on it all the words that were on the first scroll, which Jehoiakim king of Judah burned up. [29]Also tell Jehoiakim king of Judah, 'This is what the LORD says: You burned that scroll and said, "Why did you write on it that the king of Babylon would certainly come and destroy this land and cut off both men and animals from it?" [30]Therefore, this is what the LORD says about Jehoiakim king of Judah: He will have no one to sit on the throne of David; his body will be thrown out and exposed to the heat by day and the frost by night. [31]I will punish him and his children and his attendants for their wickedness; I will bring on them and those living in Jerusalem and the people of Judah every disaster I pronounced against them, because they have not listened.' "

[32]So Jeremiah took another scroll and gave it to the scribe Baruch son of Neriah, and as Jeremiah dictated, Baruch wrote on it all the words of the scroll that Jehoiakim king of Judah had burned in the fire. And many similar words were added to them.

Jeremiah in Prison

37 Zedekiah son of Josiah was made king of Judah by Nebuchadnezzar king of Babylon; he reigned in place of Jehoiachin[a] son of Jehoiakim. [2]Neither he nor his attendants nor the people of the land paid any attention to

---

What Fire Will Not Destroy

JEREMIAH 36:20–26

You may have never burned a Bible as King Jehoiakim contemptuously burned Jeremiah's manuscript, but have you neglected God's Word? Neglect can nullify the Word as effectively as fire.

Place a Bible before you. Light a candle so that it shines on it. Ask God to give you a burning desire to hear what the Word is saying. Read a familiar passage as if for the first time. Dwell on it so that you might hear something new. Fire could not destroy what God had spoken to Jeremiah, and death could not destroy God's Word spoken in Jesus; pray that you and your faith community experience new life in your desire to listen to, and act on, God's Word.

See Meeting God in Scripture

Jerusalem! Jerusalem!

JEREMIAH 37:8–10

"O Jerusalem, Jerusalem, you who kill the prophets and stone those sent to you, how often I have longed to gather your children together, as a hen gathers her chicks under her wings, but you were not willing. Look, your house is left to you desolate."

—Matthew 23:37–38

See Meeting God in Service

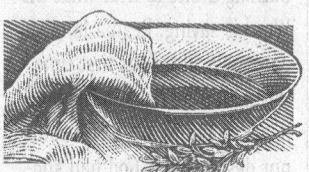

the words the LORD had spoken through Jeremiah the prophet.

[3] King Zedekiah, however, sent Jehucal son of Shelemiah with the priest Zephaniah son of Maaseiah to Jeremiah the prophet with this message: "Please pray to the LORD our God for us."

[4] Now Jeremiah was free to come and go among the people, for he had not yet been put in prison. [5] Pharaoh's army had marched out of Egypt, and when the Babylonians[a] who were besieging Jerusalem heard the report about them, they withdrew from Jerusalem.

[6] Then the word of the LORD came to Jeremiah the prophet: [7] "This is what the LORD, the God of Israel, says: Tell the king of Judah, who sent you to inquire of me, 'Pharaoh's army, which has marched out to support you, will go back to its own land, to Egypt. [8] Then the Babylonians will return and attack this city; they will capture it and burn it down.'

[9] "This is what the LORD says: Do not deceive yourselves, thinking, 'The Babylonians will surely leave us.' They will not! [10] Even if you were to defeat the entire Babylonian[b] army that is attacking you and only wounded men were left in their tents, they would come out and burn this city down."

[11] After the Babylonian army had withdrawn from Jerusalem because of Pharaoh's army, [12] Jeremiah started to leave the city to go to the territory of Benjamin to get his share of the property among the people there. [13] But when he reached the Benjamin Gate, the captain of the guard, whose name was Irijah son of Shelemiah, the son of Hananiah, arrested him and said, "You are deserting to the Babylonians!"

[14] "That's not true!" Jeremiah said. "I am not deserting to the Babylonians." But Irijah would not listen to him; instead, he arrested Jeremiah and brought him to the officials. [15] They were angry with Jeremiah and had him beaten and imprisoned in the house of Jonathan the secretary, which they had made into a prison.

[16] Jeremiah was put into a vaulted cell in a dungeon, where he remained a long time. [17] Then King Zedekiah sent for him and had him brought to the palace, where he asked him privately, "Is there any word from the LORD?"

"Yes," Jeremiah replied, "you will be handed over to the king of Babylon."

[18] Then Jeremiah said to King Zedekiah, "What crime have I committed against you or your officials or this people, that you have put me in prison? [19] Where are your prophets who prophesied to you, 'The king of Babylon will not attack you or this land'? [20] But now, my lord the king, please listen. Let me bring my petition before you: Do not send me back to the house of Jonathan the secretary, or I will die there."

[21] King Zedekiah then gave orders for Jeremiah to be placed in the courtyard of the guard and given bread from the street of the bakers each day until all the bread in the city was gone. So Jeremiah remained in the courtyard of the guard.

[a] 5 Or *Chaldeans*; also in verses 8, 9, 13 and 14   [b] 10 Or *Chaldean*; also in verse 11

Jeremiah Thrown Into a Cistern

38 Shephatiah son of Mattan, Gedaliah son of Pashhur, Jehucal[a] son of Shelemiah, and Pashhur son of Malkijah heard what Jeremiah was telling all the people when he said, [2]"This is what the LORD says: 'Whoever stays in this city will die by the sword, famine or plague, but whoever goes over to the Babylonians[b] will live. He will escape with his life; he will live.' [3]And this is what the LORD says: 'This city will certainly be handed over to the army of the king of Babylon, who will capture it.' "

[4]Then the officials said to the king, "This man should be put to death. He is discouraging the soldiers who are left in this city, as well as all the people, by the things he is saying to them. This man is not seeking the good of these people but their ruin."

[5]"He is in your hands," King Zedekiah answered. "The king can do nothing to oppose you."

[6]So they took Jeremiah and put him into the cistern of Malkijah, the king's son, which was in the courtyard of the guard. They lowered Jeremiah by ropes into the cistern; it had no water in it, only mud, and Jeremiah sank down into the mud.

[7]But Ebed-Melech, a Cushite,[c] an official[d] in the royal palace, heard that they had put Jeremiah into the cistern. While the king was sitting in the Benjamin Gate, [8]Ebed-Melech went out of the palace and said to him, [9]"My lord the king, these men have acted wickedly in all they have done to Jeremiah the prophet. They have thrown him into a cistern, where he will starve to death when there is no longer any bread in the city."

[10]Then the king commanded Ebed-Melech the Cushite, "Take thirty men from here with you and lift Jeremiah the prophet out of the cistern before he dies."

[11]So Ebed-Melech took the men with him and went to a room under the treasury in the palace. He took some old rags and worn-out clothes from there and let them down with ropes to Jeremiah in the cistern. [12]Ebed-Melech the Cushite said to Jeremiah, "Put these old rags and worn-out clothes under your arms to pad the ropes." Jeremiah did so, [13]and they pulled him up with the ropes and lifted him out of the cistern. And Jeremiah remained in the courtyard of the guard.

Zedekiah Questions Jeremiah Again

[14]Then King Zedekiah sent for Jeremiah the prophet and had him brought to the third entrance to the temple of the LORD. "I am going to ask you something," the king said to Jeremiah. "Do not hide anything from me."

[15]Jeremiah said to Zedekiah, "If I give you an answer, will you not kill me? Even if I did give you counsel, you would not listen to me."

[16]But King Zedekiah swore this oath secretly to Jeremiah: "As surely as the LORD lives, who has given us breath, I will neither kill you nor hand you over to those who are seeking your life."

[17]Then Jeremiah said to Zedekiah, "This is what the LORD God Almighty, the God of Israel, says: 'If you surrender to

---

Telling the Truth

JEREMIAH 38:1–13

Though his life is constantly at risk, Jeremiah continues to proclaim the unwelcome truth that those who leave Jerusalem and surrender to Nebuchadnezzar will live. As a reward for his persistence and faithfulness, he is dropped into a cistern and left to die in the mud—all with the passive consent of King Zedekiah. But Ebed-Melech, the foreign eunuch, takes action to rescue Jeremiah.

Who is an "Ebed-Melech" in your life? Whom do you know who is different from yourself but who is a just and compassionate person? Find some way of saying to that person, "Thank you for being you."

See Meeting God in Community

---

a 1 Hebrew *Jucal*, a variant of *Jehucal*   b 2 Or *Chaldeans*; also in verses 18, 19 and 23   c 7 Probably from the upper Nile region   d 7 Or *a eunuch*

Deliverance From Denial and Disaster

JEREMIAH 38:14–16

We ask to hear the truth, but if we do not like what we hear, can we choose to ignore it? And if we do ignore the truth, what is the cost?

Ask the Spirit to bless your imagination and guide you as you explore the truth. Imagine you are having a conversation with Jeremiah and that you are writing as you talk together. Jeremiah asks you a question about some matter that you do not want anyone else to know about at this stage. Write his question down. On the next line write your response—whatever comes to mind. Ignoring any inner voices that say, "This is silly. You're just inventing this," keep writing until your conversation is finished. Read what you have written. Take it to the Lord and ask for deliverance from denial, delusion and disaster. If it seems right, share what has happened to you with a trusted person such as your spiritual adviser, faith companion or pastor.

See Meeting God in Worship

the officers of the king of Babylon, your life will be spared and this city will not be burned down; you and your family will live. ¹⁸But if you will not surrender to the officers of the king of Babylon, this city will be handed over to the Babylonians and they will burn it down; you yourself will not escape from their hands.' "

¹⁹King Zedekiah said to Jeremiah, "I am afraid of the Jews who have gone over to the Babylonians, for the Babylonians may hand me over to them and they will mistreat me."

²⁰"They will not hand you over," Jeremiah replied. "Obey the Lord by doing what I tell you. Then it will go well with you, and your life will be spared. ²¹But if you refuse to surrender, this is what the Lord has revealed to me: ²²All the women left in the palace of the king of Judah will be brought out to the officials of the king of Babylon. Those women will say to you:

" 'They misled you and overcame you—
    those trusted friends of yours.
Your feet are sunk in the mud;
    your friends have deserted you.'

²³"All your wives and children will be brought out to the Babylonians. You yourself will not escape from their hands but will be captured by the king of Babylon; and this city will[a] be burned down."

²⁴Then Zedekiah said to Jeremiah, "Do not let anyone know about this conversation, or you may die. ²⁵If the officials hear that I talked with you, and they come to you and say, 'Tell us what you said to the king and what the king said to you; do not hide it from us or we will kill you,' ²⁶then tell them, 'I was pleading with the king not to send me back to Jonathan's house to die there.' "

²⁷All the officials did come to Jeremiah and question him, and he told them everything the king had ordered him to say. So they said no more to him, for no one had heard his conversation with the king.

²⁸And Jeremiah remained in the courtyard of the guard until the day Jerusalem was captured.

The Fall of Jerusalem

39 This is how Jerusalem was taken: ¹In the ninth year of Zedekiah king of Judah, in the tenth month, Nebuchadnezzar king of Babylon marched against Jerusalem with his whole army and laid siege to it. ²And on the ninth day of the fourth month of Zedekiah's eleventh year, the city wall was broken through. ³Then all the officials of the king of Babylon came and took seats in the Middle Gate: Nergal-Sharezer of Samgar, Nebo-Sarsekim[b] a chief officer, Nergal-Sharezer a high official and all the other officials of the king of Babylon. ⁴When Zedekiah king of Judah and all the soldiers saw them, they fled; they left the city at night by way of the king's garden, through the gate between the two walls, and headed toward the Arabah.[c]

⁵But the Babylonian[d] army pursued them and overtook Zedekiah in the plains of Jericho. They captured him and took him to Nebuchadnezzar king of Babylon at Riblah in the land of Hamath, where he pronounced sentence on him. ⁶There at Riblah the king of Babylon slaughtered the

a 23 Or *and you will cause this city to*   b 3 Or *Nergal-Sharezer, Samgar-Nebo,*
Sarsekim   c 4 Or *the Jordan Valley*   d 5 Or *Chaldean*

sons of Zedekiah before his eyes and also killed all the nobles of Judah. [7]Then he put out Zedekiah's eyes and bound him with bronze shackles to take him to Babylon.

[8]The Babylonians[a] set fire to the royal palace and the houses of the people and broke down the walls of Jerusalem. [9]Nebuzaradan commander of the imperial guard carried into exile to Babylon the people who remained in the city, along with those who had gone over to him, and the rest of the people. [10]But Nebuzaradan the commander of the guard left behind in the land of Judah some of the poor people, who owned nothing; and at that time he gave them vineyards and fields.

[11]Now Nebuchadnezzar king of Babylon had given these orders about Jeremiah through Nebuzaradan commander of the imperial guard: [12]"Take him and look after him; don't harm him but do for him whatever he asks." [13]So Nebuzaradan the commander of the guard, Nebushazban a chief officer, Nergal-Sharezer a high official and all the other officers of the king of Babylon [14]sent and had Jeremiah taken out of the courtyard of the guard. They turned him over to Gedaliah son of Ahikam, the son of Shaphan, to take him back to his home. So he remained among his own people.

[15]While Jeremiah had been confined in the courtyard of the guard, the word of the LORD came to him: [16]"Go and tell Ebed-Melech the Cushite, 'This is what the LORD Almighty, the God of Israel, says: I am about to fulfill my words against this city through disaster, not prosperity. At that time they will be fulfilled before your eyes. [17]But I will rescue you on that day, declares the LORD; you will not be handed over to those you fear. [18]I will save you; you will not fall by the sword but will escape with your life, because you trust in me, declares the LORD.' "

Jeremiah Freed

40 The word came to Jeremiah from the LORD after Nebuzaradan commander of the imperial guard had released him at Ramah. He had found Jeremiah bound in chains among all the captives from Jerusalem and Judah who were being carried into exile to Babylon. [2]When the commander of the guard found Jeremiah, he said to him, "The LORD your God decreed this disaster for this place. [3]And now the LORD has brought it about; he has done just as he said he would. All this happened because you people sinned against the LORD and did not obey him. [4]But today I am freeing you from the chains on your wrists. Come with me to Babylon, if you like, and I will look after you; but if you do not want to, then don't come. Look, the whole country lies before you; go wherever you please." [5]However, before Jeremiah turned to go,[b] Nebuzaradan added, "Go back to Gedaliah son of Ahikam, the son of Shaphan, whom the king of Babylon has appointed over the towns of Judah, and live with him among the people, or go anywhere else you please."

Then the commander gave him provisions and a present and let him go. [6]So Jeremiah went to Gedaliah son of Ahikam at Mizpah and stayed with him among the people who were left behind in the land.

Why Do the Wicked Prosper?

JEREMIAH 41:1–3

Gedaliah is a generous man who is prepared to believe the best. He dismisses Ishmael's threat, but Ishmael treacherously murders him as they eat together.

Look at some current news sources and political commentaries and find someone who might be an "Ishmael" in our era. Place a newspaper clipping about that person before you in your prayer place. (If you do not have a clipping, write his or her name in large print on a sheet of paper and place that before you.) Pray that the love of God will touch that person. Pray that those within his or her sphere of influence will be delivered from evil.

See Meeting God in Everyday Life

Gedaliah Assassinated

⁷When all the army officers and their men who were still in the open country heard that the king of Babylon had appointed Gedaliah son of Ahikam as governor over the land and had put him in charge of the men, women and children who were the poorest in the land and who had not been carried into exile to Babylon, ⁸they came to Gedaliah at Mizpah—Ishmael son of Nethaniah, Johanan and Jonathan the sons of Kareah, Seraiah son of Tanhumeth, the sons of Ephai the Netophathite, and Jaazaniah*a* the son of the Maacathite, and their men. ⁹Gedaliah son of Ahikam, the son of Shaphan, took an oath to reassure them and their men. "Do not be afraid to serve the Babylonians,*b*" he said. "Settle down in the land and serve the king of Babylon, and it will go well with you. ¹⁰I myself will stay at Mizpah to represent you before the Babylonians who come to us, but you are to harvest the wine, summer fruit and oil, and put them in your storage jars, and live in the towns you have taken over."

¹¹When all the Jews in Moab, Ammon, Edom and all the other countries heard that the king of Babylon had left a remnant in Judah and had appointed Gedaliah son of Ahikam, the son of Shaphan, as governor over them, ¹²they all came back to the land of Judah, to Gedaliah at Mizpah, from all the countries where they had been scattered. And they harvested an abundance of wine and summer fruit.

¹³Johanan son of Kareah and all the army officers still in the open country came to Gedaliah at Mizpah ¹⁴and said to him, "Don't you know that Baalis king of the Ammonites has sent Ishmael son of Nethaniah to take your life?" But Gedaliah son of Ahikam did not believe them.

¹⁵Then Johanan son of Kareah said privately to Gedaliah in Mizpah, "Let me go and kill Ishmael son of Nethaniah, and no one will know it. Why should he take your life and cause all the Jews who are gathered around you to be scattered and the remnant of Judah to perish?"

¹⁶But Gedaliah son of Ahikam said to Johanan son of Kareah, "Don't do such a thing! What you are saying about Ishmael is not true."

41 In the seventh month Ishmael son of Nethaniah, the son of Elishama, who was of royal blood and had been one of the king's officers, came with ten men to Gedaliah son of Ahikam at Mizpah. While they were eating together there, ²Ishmael son of Nethaniah and the ten men who were with him got up and struck down Gedaliah son of Ahikam, the son of Shaphan, with the sword, killing the one whom the king of Babylon had appointed as governor over the land. ³Ishmael also killed all the Jews who were with Gedaliah at Mizpah, as well as the Babylonian*c* soldiers who were there.

⁴The day after Gedaliah's assassination, before anyone knew about it, ⁵eighty men who had shaved off their beards, torn their clothes and cut themselves came from Shechem, Shiloh and Samaria, bringing grain offerings and incense with them to the house of the LORD. ⁶Ishmael son of Nethaniah went out from Mizpah to meet them, weeping as he went. When he met them, he said, "Come to Gedali-

a 8 Hebrew *Jezaniah,* a variant of *Jaazaniah*   *b 9* Or *Chaldeans;* also in verse 10   *c 3* Or *Chaldean*

ah son of Ahikam." ⁷When they went into the city, Ishmael son of Nethaniah and the men who were with him slaughtered them and threw them into a cistern. ⁸But ten of them said to Ishmael, "Don't kill us! We have wheat and barley, oil and honey, hidden in a field." So he let them alone and did not kill them with the others. ⁹Now the cistern where he threw all the bodies of the men he had killed along with Gedaliah was the one King Asa had made as part of his defense against Baasha king of Israel. Ishmael son of Nethaniah filled it with the dead.

¹⁰Ishmael made captives of all the rest of the people who were in Mizpah—the king's daughters along with all the others who were left there, over whom Nebuzaradan commander of the imperial guard had appointed Gedaliah son of Ahikam. Ishmael son of Nethaniah took them captive and set out to cross over to the Ammonites.

¹¹When Johanan son of Kareah and all the army officers who were with him heard about all the crimes Ishmael son of Nethaniah had committed, ¹²they took all their men and went to fight Ishmael son of Nethaniah. They caught up with him near the great pool in Gibeon. ¹³When all the people Ishmael had with him saw Johanan son of Kareah and the army officers who were with him, they were glad. ¹⁴All the people Ishmael had taken captive at Mizpah turned and went over to Johanan son of Kareah. ¹⁵But Ishmael son of Nethaniah and eight of his men escaped from Johanan and fled to the Ammonites.

Flight to Egypt

¹⁶Then Johanan son of Kareah and all the army officers who were with him led away all the survivors from Mizpah whom he had recovered from Ishmael son of Nethaniah after he had assassinated Gedaliah son of Ahikam: the soldiers, women, children and court officials he had brought from Gibeon. ¹⁷And they went on, stopping at Geruth Kimham near Bethlehem on their way to Egypt ¹⁸to escape the Babylonians.ᵃ They were afraid of them because Ishmael son of Nethaniah had killed Gedaliah son of Ahikam, whom the king of Babylon had appointed as governor over the land.

42 Then all the army officers, including Johanan son of Kareah and Jezaniahᵇ son of Hoshaiah, and all the people from the least to the greatest approached ²Jeremiah the prophet and said to him, "Please hear our petition and pray to the LORD your God for this entire remnant. For as you now see, though we were once many, now only a few are left. ³Pray that the LORD your God will tell us where we should go and what we should do."

⁴"I have heard you," replied Jeremiah the prophet. "I will certainly pray to the LORD your God as you have requested; I will tell you everything the LORD says and will keep nothing back from you."

⁵Then they said to Jeremiah, "May the LORD be a true and faithful witness against us if we do not act in accordance with everything the LORD your God sends you to tell us. ⁶Whether it is favorable or unfavorable, we will obey the LORD our God, to whom we are sending you, so that it will go well with us, for we will obey the LORD our God."

⁷Ten days later the word of the LORD came to Jeremiah.

Go Where? Do What?

JEREMIAH 42:1–6

The quandary the officers face is where to go and what to do. To stay where they are may bring reprisals from Babylon. To escape to Egypt could bring safety, but it carries with it a *de facto* admission of guilt. The people ask Jeremiah to pray to the Lord for guidance.

Whom do you ask to pray for you when you are in a quandary? What feedback do you give that person? Pray for her or him. Send a simple note of thanks. If you have asked no one to pray for you, consider who that person might be. Approach him or her. Present your request for prayer and discuss how you will stay in contact with one another.

See *Meeting God in Community*

Deceitful Heart

JEREMIAH 42:7–17

You say you believe God is with you always, but how solid is that belief in practice?

The Lord says, "Do not be afraid . . . I am with you and will save you and deliver you . . . I will show you compassion."

Do you really believe this or do your worries get the better of you? Write about an experience you have had in which you knew God's saving, rescuing compassion. Write a few lines about what you have learned about God as you have reflected on your experience. Now apply what you have learned to a present experience of difficulty. Pray that God will save you from the duplicity of a deceitful heart. Pray that you will be blessed with the gift of a trust in God that is bigger than your worries.

See Meeting God in Worship

⁸So he called together Johanan son of Kareah and all the army officers who were with him and all the people from the least to the greatest. ⁹He said to them, "This is what the LORD, the God of Israel, to whom you sent me to present your petition, says: ¹⁰'If you stay in this land, I will build you up and not tear you down; I will plant you and not uproot you, for I am grieved over the disaster I have inflicted on you. ¹¹Do not be afraid of the king of Babylon, whom you now fear. Do not be afraid of him, declares the LORD, for I am with you and will save you and deliver you from his hands. ¹²I will show you compassion so that he will have compassion on you and restore you to your land.'

¹³"However, if you say, 'We will not stay in this land,' and so disobey the LORD your God, ¹⁴and if you say, 'No, we will go and live in Egypt, where we will not see war or hear the trumpet or be hungry for bread,' ¹⁵then hear the word of the LORD, O remnant of Judah. This is what the LORD Almighty, the God of Israel, says: 'If you are determined to go to Egypt and you do go to settle there, ¹⁶then the sword you fear will overtake you there, and the famine you dread will follow you into Egypt, and there you will die. ¹⁷Indeed, all who are determined to go to Egypt to settle there will die by the sword, famine and plague; not one of them will survive or escape the disaster I will bring on them.' ¹⁸This is what the LORD Almighty, the God of Israel, says: 'As my anger and wrath have been poured out on those who lived in Jerusalem, so will my wrath be poured out on you when you go to Egypt. You will be an object of cursing and horror, of condemnation and reproach; you will never see this place again.'

¹⁹"O remnant of Judah, the LORD has told you, 'Do not go to Egypt.' Be sure of this: I warn you today ²⁰that you made a fatal mistake[a] when you sent me to the LORD your God and said, 'Pray to the LORD our God for us; tell us everything he says and we will do it.' ²¹I have told you today, but you still have not obeyed the LORD your God in all he sent me to tell you. ²²So now, be sure of this: You will die by the sword, famine and plague in the place where you want to go to settle."

43 When Jeremiah finished telling the people all the words of the LORD their God—everything the LORD had sent him to tell them— ²Azariah son of Hoshaiah and Johanan son of Kareah and all the arrogant men said to Jeremiah, "You are lying! The LORD our God has not sent you to say, 'You must not go to Egypt to settle there.' ³But Baruch son of Neriah is inciting you against us to hand us over to the Babylonians,[b] so they may kill us or carry us into exile to Babylon."

⁴So Johanan son of Kareah and all the army officers and all the people disobeyed the LORD's command to stay in the land of Judah. ⁵Instead, Johanan son of Kareah and all the army officers led away all the remnant of Judah who had come back to live in the land of Judah from all the nations where they had been scattered. ⁶They also led away all the men, women and children and the king's daughters whom Nebuzaradan commander of the imperial guard had left with Gedaliah son of Ahikam, the son of Shaphan, and Jeremiah the prophet and Baruch son of Neriah. ⁷So they en-

a 20 Or you erred in your hearts   b 3 Or Chaldeans

tered Egypt in disobedience to the LORD and went as far as Tahpanhes.

⁸In Tahpanhes the word of the LORD came to Jeremiah: ⁹"While the Jews are watching, take some large stones with you and bury them in clay in the brick pavement at the entrance to Pharaoh's palace in Tahpanhes. ¹⁰Then say to them, 'This is what the LORD Almighty, the God of Israel, says: I will send for my servant Nebuchadnezzar king of Babylon, and I will set his throne over these stones I have buried here; he will spread his royal canopy above them. ¹¹He will come and attack Egypt, bringing death to those destined for death, captivity to those destined for captivity, and the sword to those destined for the sword. ¹²He*ᵃ* will set fire to the temples of the gods of Egypt; he will burn their temples and take their gods captive. As a shepherd wraps his garment around him, so will he wrap Egypt around himself and depart from there unscathed. ¹³There in the temple of the sunᵇ in Egypt he will demolish the sacred pillars and will burn down the temples of the gods of Egypt.' "

Disaster Because of Idolatry

44 This word came to Jeremiah concerning all the Jews living in Lower Egypt—in Migdol, Tahpanhes and Memphisᶜ—and in Upper Egyptᵈ: ²"This is what the LORD Almighty, the God of Israel, says: You saw the great disaster I brought on Jerusalem and on all the towns of Judah. Today they lie deserted and in ruins ³because of the evil they have done. They provoked me to anger by burning incense and by worshiping other gods that neither they nor you nor your fathers ever knew. ⁴Again and again I sent my servants the prophets, who said, 'Do not do this detestable thing that I hate!' ⁵But they did not listen or pay attention; they did not turn from their wickedness or stop burning incense to other gods. ⁶Therefore, my fierce anger was poured out; it raged against the towns of Judah and the streets of Jerusalem and made them the desolate ruins they are today.

⁷"Now this is what the LORD God Almighty, the God of Israel, says: Why bring such great disaster on yourselves by cutting off from Judah the men and women, the children and infants, and so leave yourselves without a remnant? ⁸Why provoke me to anger with what your hands have made, burning incense to other gods in Egypt, where you have come to live? You will destroy yourselves and make yourselves an object of cursing and reproach among all the nations on earth. ⁹Have you forgotten the wickedness committed by your fathers and by the kings and queens of Judah and the wickedness committed by you and your wives in the land of Judah and the streets of Jerusalem? ¹⁰To this day they have not humbled themselves or shown reverence, nor have they followed my law and the decrees I set before you and your fathers.

¹¹"Therefore, this is what the LORD Almighty, the God of Israel, says: I am determined to bring disaster on you and to destroy all Judah. ¹²I will take away the remnant of Judah who were determined to go to Egypt to settle there. They will all perish in Egypt; they will fall by the sword or die from famine. From the least to the greatest, they will die by sword or famine. They will become an object of cursing

Where Can I Flee From Your Presence?

JEREMIAH 43:8–13

Where can you run to get away from God? You can immerse yourself in the busyness of work. You can let your life be taken over by the demands of a relationship. You can fill yourself with food and drink and entertaining diversions. You can escape to any "Egypt" of your own making.

Find a small stone. Set it apart as a reminder of God's sovereign presence in your life. Put it in your pocket or wallet so that it goes where you go. Touch it at various times throughout the day and, as you do so, ask yourself if you are headed toward God or toward your "Egypt."

See *Meeting God in Everyday Life*

ᵃ 12 Or I   ᵇ 13 Or in Heliopolis   ᶜ 1 Hebrew Noph   ᵈ 1 Hebrew in Pathros

Whose Word Will Stand?

JEREMIAH 44:15–19

The world is full of words—advice from politicians, researchers, sociologists, economists, statisticians, preachers, teachers and consultants. Then there are the words of your own heart—its desires, preferences and inclinations. How does God get a word in?

Place a map of your community and a picture of yourself in front of you. Put a Bible on top of them and say a prayer for your community and for yourself. Pray that the word of God and the good that God seeks will prevail through and over the torrent of words that stream through you and your community today.

See Meeting God in Everyday Life

and horror, of condemnation and reproach. ¹³I will punish those who live in Egypt with the sword, famine and plague, as I punished Jerusalem. ¹⁴None of the remnant of Judah who have gone to live in Egypt will escape or survive to return to the land of Judah, to which they long to return and live; none will return except a few fugitives."

¹⁵Then all the men who knew that their wives were burning incense to other gods, along with all the women who were present—a large assembly—and all the people living in Lower and Upper Egypt,ᵃ said to Jeremiah, ¹⁶"We will not listen to the message you have spoken to us in the name of the LORD! ¹⁷We will certainly do everything we said we would: We will burn incense to the Queen of Heaven and will pour out drink offerings to her just as we and our fathers, our kings and our officials did in the towns of Judah and in the streets of Jerusalem. At that time we had plenty of food and were well off and suffered no harm. ¹⁸But ever since we stopped burning incense to the Queen of Heaven and pouring out drink offerings to her, we have had nothing and have been perishing by sword and famine."

¹⁹The women added, "When we burned incense to the Queen of Heaven and poured out drink offerings to her, did not our husbands know that we were making cakes like her image and pouring out drink offerings to her?"

²⁰Then Jeremiah said to all the people, both men and women, who were answering him, ²¹"Did not the LORD remember and think about the incense burned in the towns of Judah and the streets of Jerusalem by you and your fathers, your kings and your officials and the people of the land? ²²When the LORD could no longer endure your wicked actions and the detestable things you did, your land became an object of cursing and a desolate waste without inhabitants, as it is today. ²³Because you have burned incense and have sinned against the LORD and have not obeyed him or followed his law or his decrees or his stipulations, this disaster has come upon you, as you now see."

²⁴Then Jeremiah said to all the people, including the women, "Hear the word of the LORD, all you people of Judah in Egypt. ²⁵This is what the LORD Almighty, the God of Israel, says: You and your wives have shown by your actions what you promised when you said, 'We will certainly carry out the vows we made to burn incense and pour out drink offerings to the Queen of Heaven.'

"Go ahead then, do what you promised! Keep your vows! ²⁶But hear the word of the LORD, all Jews living in Egypt: 'I swear by my great name,' says the LORD, 'that no one from Judah living anywhere in Egypt will ever again invoke my name or swear, "As surely as the Sovereign LORD lives." ²⁷For I am watching over them for harm, not for good; the Jews in Egypt will perish by sword and famine until they are all destroyed. ²⁸Those who escape the sword and return to the land of Judah from Egypt will be very few. Then the whole remnant of Judah who came to live in Egypt will know whose word will stand—mine or theirs.

²⁹"'This will be the sign to you that I will punish you in this place,' declares the LORD, 'so that you will know that my threats of harm against you will surely stand.' ³⁰This is what the LORD says: 'I am going to hand Pharaoh Hophra king of Egypt over to his enemies who seek his life, just as I hand-

ᵃ *15* Hebrew *in Egypt and Pathros*

ed Zedekiah king of Judah over to Nebuchadnezzar king of Babylon, the enemy who was seeking his life.' "

A Message to Baruch

45 This is what Jeremiah the prophet told Baruch son of Neriah in the fourth year of Jehoiakim son of Josiah king of Judah, after Baruch had written on a scroll the words Jeremiah was then dictating: ²"This is what the LORD, the God of Israel, says to you, Baruch: ³You said, 'Woe to me! The LORD has added sorrow to my pain; I am worn out with groaning and find no rest.' "

⁴ₗThe LORD said,⅃ "Say this to him: 'This is what the LORD says: I will overthrow what I have built and uproot what I have planted, throughout the land. ⁵Should you then seek great things for yourself? Seek them not. For I will bring disaster on all people, declares the LORD, but wherever you go I will let you escape with your life.' "

A Message About Egypt

46 This is the word of the LORD that came to Jeremiah the prophet concerning the nations:

²Concerning Egypt:

This is the message against the army of Pharaoh Neco king of Egypt, which was defeated at Carchemish on the Euphrates River by Nebuchadnezzar king of Babylon in the fourth year of Jehoiakim son of Josiah king of Judah:

³ "Prepare your shields, both large and small,
   and march out for battle!
⁴ Harness the horses,
   mount the steeds!
Take your positions
   with helmets on!
Polish your spears,
   put on your armor!
⁵ What do I see?
   They are terrified,
they are retreating,
   their warriors are defeated.
They flee in haste
   without looking back,
   and there is terror on every side,"
                                    declares the LORD.
⁶ "The swift cannot flee
   nor the strong escape.
In the north by the River Euphrates
   they stumble and fall.

⁷ "Who is this that rises like the Nile,
   like rivers of surging waters?
⁸ Egypt rises like the Nile,
   like rivers of surging waters.
She says, 'I will rise and cover the earth;
   I will destroy cities and their people.'
⁹ Charge, O horses!
   Drive furiously, O charioteers!
March on, O warriors—
   men of Cush*ᵃ* and Put who carry shields,

You Too, Baruch!

JEREMIAH 45:1–5

What is happening to the secretary? He is getting the job done effectively—ready, willing and available to Jeremiah, taking his dictation, acting on his behalf in this great and noble service of making the word of God available to the community. But he says, "I am worn out . . ."

What is your "but"? If you were completing the sentence, "I want to serve you, God, but . . .," what would come next? What would you rather be doing with your life? What wearies you? What "great things" would you rather seek for yourself? God's word will be different from the word God had for Baruch, but God has a word for you. Write about your "but . . ." and your weariness and take them to God. Make an appointment to talk with your pastor or a trusted friend about any vocational issues that arise for you.

See Meeting God in Service

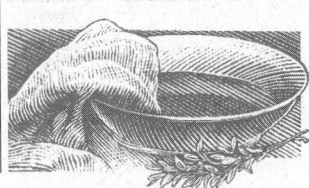

ᵃ 9 That is, the upper Nile region

Prayer for the Perishing

JEREMIAH 46:10

"I believe in the HOLY PRIEST-
HOOD OF THY SAINTS, and that
I too am a priest, with power to
appear before the Father, and
in the prayer that avails much
bring down blessing on the perishing around me.

"I believe in the POWER
OF THY PRECIOUS BLOOD to
cleanse from all sin, to give me
perfect confidence toward God,
and bring me near in the full
assurance of faith that my intercession will be heard . . .

"In this faith I yield myself
this day to God, as one of His
anointed priests, to stand before His face to intercede in behalf of sinners, and to come
out and bless in His name."

—ANDREW MURRAY,
With Christ in the School of Prayer

See Meeting God in Prayer

men of Lydia who draw the bow.
¹⁰ But that day belongs to the Lord, the LORD
Almighty—
a day of vengeance, for vengeance on his foes.
The sword will devour till it is satisfied,
till it has quenched its thirst with blood.
For the Lord, the LORD Almighty, will offer
sacrifice
in the land of the north by the River Euphrates.

¹¹ "Go up to Gilead and get balm,
O Virgin Daughter of Egypt.
But you multiply remedies in vain;
there is no healing for you.
¹² The nations will hear of your shame;
your cries will fill the earth.
One warrior will stumble over another;
both will fall down together."

¹³ This is the message the LORD spoke to Jeremiah the
prophet about the coming of Nebuchadnezzar king of Babylon to attack Egypt:

¹⁴ "Announce this in Egypt, and proclaim it in
Migdol;
proclaim it also in Memphis[a] and Tahpanhes:
'Take your positions and get ready,
for the sword devours those around you.'
¹⁵ Why will your warriors be laid low?
They cannot stand, for the LORD will push them
down.
¹⁶ They will stumble repeatedly;
they will fall over each other.
They will say, 'Get up, let us go back
to our own people and our native lands,
away from the sword of the oppressor.'
¹⁷ There they will exclaim,
'Pharaoh king of Egypt is only a loud noise;
he has missed his opportunity.'

¹⁸ "As surely as I live," declares the King,
whose name is the LORD Almighty,
"one will come who is like Tabor among the
mountains,
like Carmel by the sea.
¹⁹ Pack your belongings for exile,
you who live in Egypt,
for Memphis will be laid waste
and lie in ruins without inhabitant.

²⁰ "Egypt is a beautiful heifer,
but a gadfly is coming
against her from the north.
²¹ The mercenaries in her ranks
are like fattened calves.
They too will turn and flee together,
they will not stand their ground,
for the day of disaster is coming upon them,
the time for them to be punished.
²² Egypt will hiss like a fleeing serpent
as the enemy advances in force;

a 14 Hebrew *Noph*; also in verse 19

they will come against her with axes,
like men who cut down trees.
²³ They will chop down her forest,"

declares the LORD,

"dense though it be.
They are more numerous than locusts,
they cannot be counted.
²⁴ The Daughter of Egypt will be put to shame,
handed over to the people of the north."

²⁵ The LORD Almighty, the God of Israel, says: "I am about to bring punishment on Amon god of Thebes,ᵃ on Pharaoh, on Egypt and her gods and her kings, and on those who rely on Pharaoh. ²⁶ I will hand them over to those who seek their lives, to Nebuchadnezzar king of Babylon and his officers. Later, however, Egypt will be inhabited as in times past," declares the LORD.

²⁷ "Do not fear, O Jacob my servant;
do not be dismayed, O Israel.
I will surely save you out of a distant place,
your descendants from the land of their exile.
Jacob will again have peace and security,
and no one will make him afraid.
²⁸ Do not fear, O Jacob my servant,
for I am with you," declares the LORD.
"Though I completely destroy all the nations
among which I scatter you,
I will not completely destroy you.
I will discipline you but only with justice;
I will not let you go entirely unpunished."

A Message About the Philistines

47 This is the word of the LORD that came to Jeremiah the prophet concerning the Philistines before Pharaoh attacked Gaza:

² This is what the LORD says:

"See how the waters are rising in the north;
they will become an overflowing torrent.
They will overflow the land and everything in it,
the towns and those who live in them.
The people will cry out;
all who dwell in the land will wail
³ at the sound of the hoofs of galloping steeds,
at the noise of enemy chariots
and the rumble of their wheels.
Fathers will not turn to help their children;
their hands will hang limp.
⁴ For the day has come
to destroy all the Philistines
and to cut off all survivors
who could help Tyre and Sidon.
The LORD is about to destroy the Philistines,
the remnant from the coasts of Caphtor.ᵇ
⁵ Gaza will shave her head in mourning;
Ashkelon will be silenced.
O remnant on the plain,
how long will you cut yourselves?

Before the Floods

JEREMIAH 47:2–3

The twentieth century has been called the bloodiest century in human history. And even today terror floods into the lives of people everywhere—the terror of an invading army or a crime syndicate, the terror of a street gang or a random attacker, the terror of domestic violence or child abduction. People cry out. Parents are helpless to protect their children. Help is nowhere to be found.

What is happening within you as you consider such things? What thoughts do you have? How do you feel? How is your faith in God engaged? Drawing on your responses to these questions, write a prayer to God. Set aside some special time to plead for those who are facing terror.

See Meeting God in Prayer

God of Nations

JEREMIAH 47:6—48:7

When viewed from the inside of a sanctuary—when, from where you sit, all seems well—God's judgment, especially God's judgment on other nations, does not seem to be a matter of immediate concern. But all nations stand in judgment or in blessing before God, the One judging the "deeds and riches" in which each nation trusts. Pray for God's mercy to be showered on the nation you call your own. Pray on behalf of several other nations too.

See Meeting God in Prayer

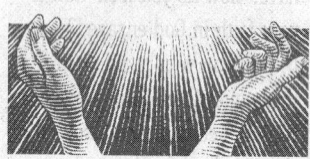

6 " 'Ah, sword of the LORD,' ⌐ you cry,⌐
'how long till you rest?
Return to your scabbard;
cease and be still.'
7 But how can it rest
when the LORD has commanded it,
when he has ordered it
to attack Ashkelon and the coast?"

A Message About Moab

48 Concerning Moab:

This is what the LORD Almighty, the God of Israel, says:

"Woe to Nebo, for it will be ruined.
Kiriathaim will be disgraced and captured;
the stronghold*a* will be disgraced and shattered.
2 Moab will be praised no more;
in Heshbon*b* men will plot her downfall:
'Come, let us put an end to that nation.'
You too, O Madmen,*c* will be silenced;
the sword will pursue you.
3 Listen to the cries from Horonaim,
cries of great havoc and destruction.
4 Moab will be broken;
her little ones will cry out.*d*
5 They go up the way to Luhith,
weeping bitterly as they go;
on the road down to Horonaim
anguished cries over the destruction are heard.
6 Flee! Run for your lives;
become like a bush*e* in the desert.
7 Since you trust in your deeds and riches,
you too will be taken captive,
and Chemosh will go into exile,
together with his priests and officials.
8 The destroyer will come against every town,
and not a town will escape.
The valley will be ruined
and the plateau destroyed,
because the LORD has spoken.
9 Put salt on Moab,
for she will be laid waste*f*;
her towns will become desolate,
with no one to live in them.

10 "A curse on him who is lax in doing the LORD's work!
A curse on him who keeps his sword from bloodshed!

11 "Moab has been at rest from youth,
like wine left on its dregs,
not poured from one jar to another—
she has not gone into exile.
So she tastes as she did,
and her aroma is unchanged.
12 But days are coming,"

---

a 1 Or / *Misgab*   *b 2* The Hebrew for *Heshbon* sounds like the Hebrew for *plot.*   *c 2* The name of the Moabite town Madmen sounds like the Hebrew for *be silenced.*   *d 4* Hebrew; Septuagint / *proclaim it to Zoar*   *e 6* Or like *Aroer*   *f 9* Or *Give wings to Moab, / for she will fly away*

declares the LORD,
"when I will send men who pour from jars,
and they will pour her out;
they will empty her jars
and smash her jugs.
¹³ Then Moab will be ashamed of Chemosh,
as the house of Israel was ashamed
when they trusted in Bethel.

¹⁴ "How can you say, 'We are warriors,
men valiant in battle'?
¹⁵ Moab will be destroyed and her towns invaded;
her finest young men will go down in the
slaughter,"
declares the King, whose name is the LORD
Almighty.
¹⁶ "The fall of Moab is at hand;
her calamity will come quickly.
¹⁷ Mourn for her, all who live around her,
all who know her fame;
say, 'How broken is the mighty scepter,
how broken the glorious staff!'

¹⁸ "Come down from your glory
and sit on the parched ground,
O inhabitants of the Daughter of Dibon,
for he who destroys Moab
will come up against you
and ruin your fortified cities.
¹⁹ Stand by the road and watch,
you who live in Aroer.
Ask the man fleeing and the woman escaping,
ask them, 'What has happened?'
²⁰ Moab is disgraced, for she is shattered.
Wail and cry out!
Announce by the Arnon
that Moab is destroyed.
²¹ Judgment has come to the plateau—
to Holon, Jahzah and Mephaath,
²² to Dibon, Nebo and Beth Diblathaim,
²³ to Kiriathaim, Beth Gamul and Beth Meon,
²⁴ to Kerioth and Bozrah—
to all the towns of Moab, far and near.
²⁵ Moab's horn[a] is cut off;
her arm is broken,"
declares the LORD.

²⁶ "Make her drunk,
for she has defied the LORD.
Let Moab wallow in her vomit;
let her be an object of ridicule.
²⁷ Was not Israel the object of your ridicule?
Was she caught among thieves,
that you shake your head in scorn
whenever you speak of her?
²⁸ Abandon your towns and dwell among the rocks,
you who live in Moab.
Be like a dove that makes its nest
at the mouth of a cave.

²⁹ "We have heard of Moab's pride—

Down From Glory

JEREMIAH 48:12–20

In the time of Augustine, the churches of North Africa were just as flourishing as the beautiful woodlands and fields that he described. Today, where is the church in North Africa? Where are the woodlands and fields? Forests become deserts, churches rise and fall like nations; individual fellowships and entire denominations come and go.

Gather with others from your church. Make a list of the glories of the tradition in which your faith community stands. What are the forces that could bring it down from glory? Agree together on how you might pray for your church and discuss what practical actions you can take to work for its health and well-being.

See *Meeting God in Community*

---

a 25 Horn here symbolizes strength.

Like a Flute

JEREMIAH 48:29–39

Pride and arrogance can be smashed as easily as a piece of pottery, for the Lord will have none of it. Yet God grieves that it should be so.

What is the pride and arrogance of your nation that may grieve God? Let a piece of crockery represent the pride and arrogance of your nation. Play some solemn music to represent the grief of God, and smash the crockery before God. Pray for the mercy of God to cover the land—its people, its institutions, governments, corporations and societies. Close by singing a prayer of contrition, using music as your accompaniment.

See Meeting God in Service

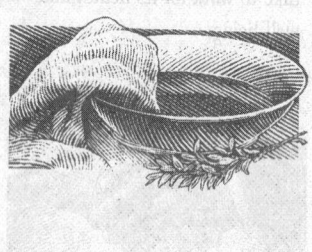

her overweening pride and conceit,
  her pride and arrogance
    and the haughtiness of her heart.
[30] I know her insolence but it is futile,"
                         declares the LORD,
  "and her boasts accomplish nothing.
[31] Therefore I wail over Moab,
  for all Moab I cry out,
  I moan for the men of Kir Hareseth.
[32] I weep for you, as Jazer weeps,
  O vines of Sibmah.
Your branches spread as far as the sea;
  they reached as far as the sea of Jazer.
The destroyer has fallen
  on your ripened fruit and grapes.
[33] Joy and gladness are gone
  from the orchards and fields of Moab.
I have stopped the flow of wine from the presses;
  no one treads them with shouts of joy.
Although there are shouts,
  they are not shouts of joy.

[34] "The sound of their cry rises
  from Heshbon to Elealeh and Jahaz,
from Zoar as far as Horonaim and Eglath
    Shelishiyah,
  for even the waters of Nimrim are dried up.
[35] In Moab I will put an end
  to those who make offerings on the high places
  and burn incense to their gods,"
                        declares the LORD.
[36] "So my heart laments for Moab like a flute;
  it laments like a flute for the men of Kir
    Hareseth.
The wealth they acquired is gone.
[37] Every head is shaved
  and every beard cut off;
every hand is slashed
  and every waist is covered with sackcloth.
[38] On all the roofs in Moab
  and in the public squares
there is nothing but mourning,
  for I have broken Moab
  like a jar that no one wants,"
                        declares the LORD.
[39] "How shattered she is! How they wail!
  How Moab turns her back in shame!
Moab has become an object of ridicule,
  an object of horror to all those around her."

[40] This is what the LORD says:

"Look! An eagle is swooping down,
  spreading its wings over Moab.
[41] Kerioth[a] will be captured
  and the strongholds taken.
In that day the hearts of Moab's warriors
  will be like the heart of a woman in labor.
[42] Moab will be destroyed as a nation
  because she defied the LORD.

a 41 Or The cities

43 Terror and pit and snare await you,
    O people of Moab,"
                            declares the LORD.
44 "Whoever flees from the terror
    will fall into a pit,
    whoever climbs out of the pit
    will be caught in a snare;
    for I will bring upon Moab
    the year of her punishment,"
                            declares the LORD.
45 "In the shadow of Heshbon
    the fugitives stand helpless,
    for a fire has gone out from Heshbon,
    a blaze from the midst of Sihon;
    it burns the foreheads of Moab,
    the skulls of the noisy boasters.
46 Woe to you, O Moab!
    The people of Chemosh are destroyed;
    your sons are taken into exile
    and your daughters into captivity.
47 "Yet I will restore the fortunes of Moab
    in days to come,"
                            declares the LORD.

Here ends the judgment on Moab.

A Message About Ammon

49
Concerning the Ammonites:

This is what the LORD says:

"Has Israel no sons?
    Has she no heirs?
Why then has Molech[a] taken possession of Gad?
    Why do his people live in its towns?
2 But the days are coming,"
    declares the LORD,
"when I will sound the battle cry
    against Rabbah of the Ammonites;
it will become a mound of ruins,
    and its surrounding villages will be set on fire.
Then Israel will drive out
    those who drove her out,"
                            says the LORD.
3 "Wail, O Heshbon, for Ai is destroyed!
    Cry out, O inhabitants of Rabbah!
Put on sackcloth and mourn;
    rush here and there inside the walls,
for Molech will go into exile,
    together with his priests and officials.
4 Why do you boast of your valleys,
    boast of your valleys so fruitful?
O unfaithful daughter,
    you trust in your riches and say,
    'Who will attack me?'
5 I will bring terror on you
    from all those around you,"
                declares the Lord, the LORD Almighty.

---

a 1 Or their king; Hebrew malcam; also in verse 3

Can Chemosh Save You?

JEREMIAH 48:45–47

Chemosh is the national god of Moab (see Judges 11:24). Chemosh cannot save anyone. His people are destroyed. His sons and daughters are taken captive.

What is the "Chemosh" in your life? What god have you been serving—your anxiety, your ambition, your property? In prayer, bring your vulnerable "Chemosh" before Yahweh, the Lord your God, in some symbolic form. Talk to God about your allegiance to false gods. And when you are ready, write a pledge of allegiance to Jesus Christ. Say it to Jesus in the presence of your "Chemosh" symbol. Tape it to your "Chemosh" symbol and begin each day of the next week with your pledge of allegiance to Jesus.

See Meeting God in Worship

Exposed!

JEREMIAH 49:7–10

Esau will be stripped! The nation is to be exposed. Who can hide from the Almighty? "For whatever is hidden is meant to be disclosed, and whatever is concealed is meant to be brought out into the open" (Mark 4:22).

What is your emotional response to Jesus' words? What would you be ashamed of if all your thoughts and actions were revealed? Before whom would you be ashamed? Confess your shame to Jesus and pray: "In you, O LORD, I have taken refuge; let me never be put to shame; deliver me in your righteousness" (Psalm 31:1).

See Meeting God in Prayer

"Every one of you will be driven away,
    and no one will gather the fugitives.
⁶ "Yet afterward, I will restore the fortunes of the Ammonites,"

                    declares the LORD.

A Message About Edom

⁷Concerning Edom:

This is what the LORD Almighty says:

"Is there no longer wisdom in Teman?
    Has counsel perished from the prudent?
    Has their wisdom decayed?
⁸ Turn and flee, hide in deep caves,
    you who live in Dedan,
for I will bring disaster on Esau
    at the time I punish him.
⁹ If grape pickers came to you,
    would they not leave a few grapes?
If thieves came during the night,
    would they not steal only as much as they
        wanted?
¹⁰ But I will strip Esau bare;
    I will uncover his hiding places,
    so that he cannot conceal himself.
His children, relatives and neighbors will perish,
    and he will be no more.
¹¹ Leave your orphans; I will protect their lives.
    Your widows too can trust in me."

¹²This is what the LORD says: "If those who do not deserve to drink the cup must drink it, why should you go unpunished? You will not go unpunished, but must drink it. ¹³I swear by myself," declares the LORD, "that Bozrah will become a ruin and an object of horror, of reproach and of cursing; and all its towns will be in ruins forever."

¹⁴ I have heard a message from the LORD:
    An envoy was sent to the nations to say,
"Assemble yourselves to attack it!
    Rise up for battle!"

¹⁵ "Now I will make you small among the nations,
    despised among men.
¹⁶ The terror you inspire
    and the pride of your heart have deceived you,
you who live in the clefts of the rocks,
    who occupy the heights of the hill.
Though you build your nest as high as the
       eagle's,
    from there I will bring you down,"

                  declares the LORD.

¹⁷ "Edom will become an object of horror;
    all who pass by will be appalled and will scoff
    because of all its wounds.
¹⁸ As Sodom and Gomorrah were overthrown,
    along with their neighboring towns,"

                  says the LORD,

"so no one will live there;
    no man will dwell in it.

¹⁹ "Like a lion coming up from Jordan's thickets
  to a rich pastureland,
I will chase Edom from its land in an instant.
  Who is the chosen one I will appoint for this?
  Who is like me and who can challenge me?
  And what shepherd can stand against me?"
²⁰ Therefore, hear what the LORD has planned
      against Edom,
  what he has purposed against those who live in
      Teman:
The young of the flock will be dragged away;
  he will completely destroy their pasture
      because of them.
²¹ At the sound of their fall the earth will tremble;
  their cry will resound to the Red Sea.ᵃ
²² Look! An eagle will soar and swoop down,
  spreading its wings over Bozrah.
In that day the hearts of Edom's warriors
  will be like the heart of a woman in labor.

A Message About Damascus

²³ Concerning Damascus:

"Hamath and Arpad are dismayed,
  for they have heard bad news.
They are disheartened,
  troubled likeᵇ the restless sea.
²⁴ Damascus has become feeble,
  she has turned to flee
  and panic has gripped her;
anguish and pain have seized her,
  pain like that of a woman in labor.
²⁵ Why has the city of renown not been abandoned,
  the town in which I delight?
²⁶ Surely, her young men will fall in the streets;
  all her soldiers will be silenced in that day,"
      declares the LORD Almighty.
²⁷ "I will set fire to the walls of Damascus;
  it will consume the fortresses of Ben-Hadad."

A Message About Kedar and Hazor

²⁸ Concerning Kedar and the kingdoms of Hazor, which
Nebuchadnezzar king of Babylon attacked:

This is what the LORD says:

"Arise, and attack Kedar
  and destroy the people of the East.
²⁹ Their tents and their flocks will be taken;
  their shelters will be carried off
  with all their goods and camels.
Men will shout to them,
  'Terror on every side!'

³⁰ "Flee quickly away!
  Stay in deep caves, you who live in Hazor,"
      declares the LORD.
"Nebuchadnezzar king of Babylon has plotted
      against you;
  he has devised a plan against you.

Alas! The Young Ones!

JEREMIAH 49:17–22

Even the young will be dragged away! How can the young ever escape what happens to their elders?

What is happening to the young people in your community? What is our society exposing them to? Young people often grow up to perpetuate the abuse that they experienced themselves. Who is there to care for them, guide them and protect them in the vulnerability of their formative years? Carefully consider a supportive action you can do for a little one this week while you pray for the young in your community, those who care for them and the agencies that exist to support them.

See *Meeting God in Service*

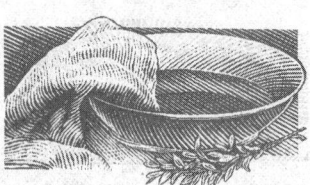

Budgeting for Defense

JEREMIAH 49:35–39

The "bow of Elam" is no defense against Yahweh, the Almighty, even though it is the mainstay of Elam's might.

What is the mainstay of your defense? Your self-defense skills? Your personality or your income? Your words, your wit or your wisdom? And against what do you need to defend yourself?

Recall an incident in which God has been your defender. In the light of that experience, meditate on Psalm 59. Memorize the verses that speak the most emphatically to you, so that when you're in danger, they may bring you to God, "the mainstay" of your defense.

See Meeting God in Scripture

³¹ "Arise and attack a nation at ease,
   which lives in confidence,"
                              declares the LORD,
  "a nation that has neither gates nor bars;
   its people live alone.
³² Their camels will become plunder,
   and their large herds will be booty.
I will scatter to the winds those who are in distant
       places*ᵃ*
   and will bring disaster on them from every side,"
                              declares the LORD.
³³ "Hazor will become a haunt of jackals,
   a desolate place forever.
No one will live there;
   no man will dwell in it."

A Message About Elam

³⁴ This is the word of the LORD that came to Jeremiah the prophet concerning Elam, early in the reign of Zedekiah king of Judah:

³⁵ This is what the LORD Almighty says:

  "See, I will break the bow of Elam,
   the mainstay of their might.
³⁶ I will bring against Elam the four winds
   from the four quarters of the heavens;
I will scatter them to the four winds,
   and there will not be a nation
   where Elam's exiles do not go.
³⁷ I will shatter Elam before their foes,
   before those who seek their lives;
I will bring disaster upon them,
   even my fierce anger,"
                              declares the LORD.
  "I will pursue them with the sword
   until I have made an end of them.
³⁸ I will set my throne in Elam
   and destroy her king and officials,"
                              declares the LORD.

³⁹ "Yet I will restore the fortunes of Elam
   in days to come,"
                              declares the LORD.

A Message About Babylon

50 This is the word the LORD spoke through Jeremiah the prophet concerning Babylon and the land of the Babylonians*ᵇ*:

² "Announce and proclaim among the nations,
   lift up a banner and proclaim it;
   keep nothing back, but say,
'Babylon will be captured;
   Bel will be put to shame,
   Marduk filled with terror.
Her images will be put to shame
   and her idols filled with terror.'
³ A nation from the north will attack her
   and lay waste her land.

ᵃ 32 Or *who clip the hair by their foreheads*   *ᵇ 1* Or *Chaldeans*; also in verses 8, 25, 35 and 45

No one will live in it;
  both men and animals will flee away.

4 "In those days, at that time,"
    declares the LORD,
"the people of Israel and the people of Judah
      together
  will go in tears to seek the LORD their God.
5 They will ask the way to Zion
    and turn their faces toward it.
They will come and bind themselves to the LORD
    in an everlasting covenant
    that will not be forgotten.

6 "My people have been lost sheep;
    their shepherds have led them astray
    and caused them to roam on the mountains.
They wandered over mountain and hill
    and forgot their own resting place.
7 Whoever found them devoured them;
    their enemies said, 'We are not guilty,
for they sinned against the LORD, their true pasture,
    the LORD, the hope of their fathers.'

8 "Flee out of Babylon;
    leave the land of the Babylonians,
    and be like the goats that lead the flock.
9 For I will stir up and bring against Babylon
    an alliance of great nations from the land of the
      north.
They will take up their positions against her,
    and from the north she will be captured.
Their arrows will be like skilled warriors
    who do not return empty-handed.
10 So Babylonia[a] will be plundered;
    all who plunder her will have their fill,"
                            declares the LORD.

11 "Because you rejoice and are glad,
    you who pillage my inheritance,
because you frolic like a heifer threshing grain
    and neigh like stallions,
12 your mother will be greatly ashamed;
    she who gave you birth will be disgraced.
She will be the least of the nations—
    a wilderness, a dry land, a desert.
13 Because of the LORD's anger she will not be
      inhabited
    but will be completely desolate.
All who pass Babylon will be horrified and scoff
    because of all her wounds.

14 "Take up your positions around Babylon,
    all you who draw the bow.
Shoot at her! Spare no arrows,
    for she has sinned against the LORD.
15 Shout against her on every side!
    She surrenders, her towers fall,
    her walls are torn down.
Since this is the vengeance of the LORD,
    take vengeance on her;
    do to her as she has done to others.

What You Give Is What You Get!

JEREMIAH 50:7–10

Babylon might well excuse herself by saying, "Not guilty! These Israelites have sinned against the Lord and have gotten what they deserve! We have acted in the service of their God anyway!" Babylon is a violent nation and the violence she inflicts will inevitably be the violence she receives.

How do you deal with violence that is directed at you? Think of a situation in which you feel you have the right to retaliate. Read Matthew 5:43–45 and think again about your desire to retaliate. What do you feel? Write your honest response and pray about it. On a card write, "A gentle answer turns away wrath" (Proverbs 15:1), and carry it with you in your wallet or purse.

See Meeting God in Scripture

---

a 10 Or Chaldea

Restoration

JEREMIAH 50:17–20

"As the word is spoken one more time, we move through the wearisome death-ridden days of our life and come back once again to Easter to be stunned into disbelief, and then beyond disbelief, to be stunned to life, now filled with fear and trembling . . . The sermon for such a time shames the Prince [of Darkness] and we become yet again more nearly human. The Author of the text laughs in delight, the way that Author has laughed only at creation and at Easter, but laughs again when the sermon carries the day against the prose of the Dark Prince who wants no new poetry in the region he thinks he governs. Where the poetry is sounded, the Prince knows a little of the territory has been lost to its true Ruler. The newly claimed territory becomes a new home of freedom, justice, peace, and abiding joy."

—WALTER BRUEGGEMANN,
Finally Comes the Poet

See *Meeting God in Worship*

¹⁶ Cut off from Babylon the sower,
  and the reaper with his sickle at harvest.
Because of the sword of the oppressor
  let everyone return to his own people,
  let everyone flee to his own land.

¹⁷ "Israel is a scattered flock
  that lions have chased away.
The first to devour him
  was the king of Assyria;
the last to crush his bones
  was Nebuchadnezzar king of Babylon."

¹⁸ Therefore this is what the LORD Almighty, the God of Israel, says:

"I will punish the king of Babylon and his land
  as I punished the king of Assyria.
¹⁹ But I will bring Israel back to his own pasture
  and he will graze on Carmel and Bashan;
his appetite will be satisfied
  on the hills of Ephraim and Gilead.
²⁰ In those days, at that time,"
  declares the LORD,
"search will be made for Israel's guilt,
  but there will be none,
and for the sins of Judah,
  but none will be found,
for I will forgive the remnant I spare.

²¹ "Attack the land of Merathaim
  and those who live in Pekod.
Pursue, kill and completely destroy*a* them,"
  declares the LORD.
"Do everything I have commanded you.
²² The noise of battle is in the land,
  the noise of great destruction!
²³ How broken and shattered
  is the hammer of the whole earth!
How desolate is Babylon
  among the nations!
²⁴ I set a trap for you, O Babylon,
  and you were caught before you knew it;
you were found and captured
  because you opposed the LORD.
²⁵ The LORD has opened his arsenal
  and brought out the weapons of his wrath,
for the Sovereign LORD Almighty has work to do
  in the land of the Babylonians.
²⁶ Come against her from afar.
  Break open her granaries;
  pile her up like heaps of grain.
Completely destroy her
  and leave her no remnant.
²⁷ Kill all her young bulls;
  let them go down to the slaughter!
Woe to them! For their day has come,
  the time for them to be punished.
²⁸ Listen to the fugitives and refugees from Babylon
  declaring in Zion

---

a 21 The Hebrew term refers to the irrevocable giving over of things or persons to the LORD, often by totally destroying them; also in verse 26.

how the LORD our God has taken vengeance,
vengeance for his temple.

29 "Summon archers against Babylon,
all those who draw the bow.
Encamp all around her;
let no one escape.
Repay her for her deeds;
do to her as she has done.
For she has defied the LORD,
the Holy One of Israel.
30 Therefore, her young men will fall in the streets;
all her soldiers will be silenced in that day,"
declares the LORD.
31 "See, I am against you, O arrogant one,"
declares the Lord, the LORD Almighty,
"for your day has come,
the time for you to be punished.
32 The arrogant one will stumble and fall
and no one will help her up;
I will kindle a fire in her towns
that will consume all who are around her."

33 This is what the LORD Almighty says:

"The people of Israel are oppressed,
and the people of Judah as well.
All their captors hold them fast,
refusing to let them go.
34 Yet their Redeemer is strong;
the LORD Almighty is his name.
He will vigorously defend their cause
so that he may bring rest to their land,
but unrest to those who live in Babylon.

35 "A sword against the Babylonians!"
declares the LORD—
"against those who live in Babylon
and against her officials and wise men!
36 A sword against her false prophets!
They will become fools.
A sword against her warriors!
They will be filled with terror.
37 A sword against her horses and chariots
and all the foreigners in her ranks!
They will become women.
A sword against her treasures!
They will be plundered.
38 A drought on^a her waters!
They will dry up.
For it is a land of idols,
idols that will go mad with terror.

39 "So desert creatures and hyenas will live there,
and there the owl will dwell.
It will never again be inhabited
or lived in from generation to generation.
40 As God overthrew Sodom and Gomorrah
along with their neighboring towns,"
declares the LORD,

Set Me Free!

JEREMIAH 50:33–34

The people of Israel and Judah are oppressed. Their captors hold them fast and refuse to let them go. Yet there is a Redeemer! "The LORD Almighty is his name."

What oppresses you? What situation, what attitude, what behavior holds you fast? What would redemption look like for you?

Take two large sheets of paper, a dinner plate and a crayon. Trace a circle around the plate on each sheet of paper. Using paint or crayons, illustrate your oppression in the first circle, paying particular attention to color. In the same way illustrate your redemption. Pray about your responses, seeking God's freedom from that which oppresses you.

See Meeting God in Worship

---

^a 38 Or A sword against

Like a Lion

JEREMIAH 50:44–46

From your awareness of the news from television, radio or the newspaper, note the people who seem to wield oppressive power today. Imagine how that person would react to a lion suddenly emerging from the thickets and bearing down on them. "Who can challenge [a lion]?" Pray for the lionlike power of Jesus, the Lion of Judah, to "challenge" the powers of this world and hold them in check.

See Meeting God in Service

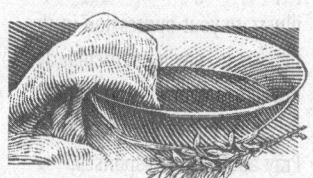

"so no one will live there;
no man will dwell in it.

41 "Look! An army is coming from the north;
a great nation and many kings
are being stirred up from the ends of the earth.
42 They are armed with bows and spears;
they are cruel and without mercy.
They sound like the roaring sea
as they ride on their horses;
they come like men in battle formation
to attack you, O Daughter of Babylon.
43 The king of Babylon has heard reports about them,
and his hands hang limp.
Anguish has gripped him,
pain like that of a woman in labor.
44 Like a lion coming up from Jordan's thickets
to a rich pastureland,
I will chase Babylon from its land in an instant.
Who is the chosen one I will appoint for this?
Who is like me and who can challenge me?
And what shepherd can stand against me?"
45 Therefore, hear what the LORD has planned
against Babylon,
what he has purposed against the land of the
Babylonians:
The young of the flock will be dragged away;
he will completely destroy their pasture
because of them.
46 At the sound of Babylon's capture the earth will
tremble;
its cry will resound among the nations.

51 This is what the LORD says:

"See, I will stir up the spirit of a destroyer
against Babylon and the people of Leb Kamai.[a]
2 I will send foreigners to Babylon
to winnow her and to devastate her land;
they will oppose her on every side
in the day of her disaster.
3 Let not the archer string his bow,
nor let him put on his armor.
Do not spare her young men;
completely destroy[b] her army.
4 They will fall down slain in Babylon,[c]
fatally wounded in her streets.
5 For Israel and Judah have not been forsaken
by their God, the LORD Almighty,
though their land[d] is full of guilt
before the Holy One of Israel.

6 "Flee from Babylon!
Run for your lives!
Do not be destroyed because of her sins.
It is time for the LORD's vengeance;
he will pay her what she deserves.

---

a 1 Leb Kamai is a cryptogram for Chaldea, that is, Babylonia.   b 3 The Hebrew term refers to the irrevocable giving over of things or persons to the LORD, often by totally destroying them.   c 4 Or Chaldea   d 5 Or I and the land of the Babylonians.

⁷Babylon was a gold cup in the Lord's hand;
　she made the whole earth drunk.
The nations drank her wine;
　therefore they have now gone mad.
⁸Babylon will suddenly fall and be broken.
　Wail over her!
Get balm for her pain;
　perhaps she can be healed.

⁹" 'We would have healed Babylon,
　but she cannot be healed;
let us leave her and each go to his own land,
　for her judgment reaches to the skies,
　it rises as high as the clouds.'

¹⁰" 'The Lord has vindicated us;
　come, let us tell in Zion
　what the Lord our God has done.'

¹¹"Sharpen the arrows,
　take up the shields!
The Lord has stirred up the kings of the Medes,
　because his purpose is to destroy Babylon.
The Lord will take vengeance,
　vengeance for his temple.
¹²Lift up a banner against the walls of Babylon!
　Reinforce the guard,
station the watchmen,
　prepare an ambush!
The Lord will carry out his purpose,
　his decree against the people of Babylon.
¹³You who live by many waters
　and are rich in treasures,
your end has come,
　the time for you to be cut off.
¹⁴The Lord Almighty has sworn by himself:
　I will surely fill you with men, as with a swarm
　　of locusts,
　and they will shout in triumph over you.

¹⁵"He made the earth by his power;
　he founded the world by his wisdom
　and stretched out the heavens by his
　　understanding.
¹⁶When he thunders, the waters in the heavens roar;
　he makes clouds rise from the ends of the
　　earth.
He sends lightning with the rain
　and brings out the wind from his storehouses.

¹⁷"Every man is senseless and without knowledge;
　every goldsmith is shamed by his idols.
His images are a fraud;
　they have no breath in them.
¹⁸They are worthless, the objects of mockery;
　when their judgment comes, they will perish.
¹⁹He who is the Portion of Jacob is not like these,
　for he is the Maker of all things,
including the tribe of his inheritance—
　the Lord Almighty is his name.

²⁰"You are my war club,
　my weapon for battle—

Freedom After the Fall!

JEREMIAH 51:7–10

How the mighty fall! Like a cup that falls and is broken—a gold cup at that—Babylon falls and is broken.

What, or who, has power over you—an organization, a person, your finances, your appetites? Compare that power with the power of God. What needs to happen in order for you to experience freedom?

Climb to the top of a hill or some small rise in your neighborhood—somewhere not too public. In a strong voice repeat the apostle Paul's words at least a dozen times: "It is for freedom that Christ has set us free. Stand firm, then, and do not let yourselves be burdened again by a yoke of slavery" (Galatians 5:1). Let your body absorb the power of the words, and assign some part of your anatomy (like your left shoulder) to hold the truth of the words for you so that, touching that part of your body later, you can remind yourself of the power of God that is setting you free.

See *Meeting God in Worship*

The Hammer of the Lord

JEREMIAH 51:20–23

Babylon was supreme. It could do as it pleased. But now its power is checked. It will no longer be an enemy but will fall under God's war club. Death, too, was once supreme. It could do as it pleased. But now it is checked. It can claim no victory and has no sting because it has fallen under the hammer of Jesus Christ's resurrection power (see 1 Corinthians 15:55–56).

Take something hard, like a walnut, and place it on a piece of wood. Pick up a hammer. Swing it around and feel its weight. Bang it onto the wood with all the strength you can manage. Now take the hard object you have selected. Imagine it as "Death." Swing the hammer high. Bring it down on the hard object and smash it in the name of the Lord! What thoughts did this experience raise? How did you feel? Pray about your responses.

See Meeting God in Everyday Life

with you I shatter nations,
    with you I destroy kingdoms,
21 with you I shatter horse and rider,
    with you I shatter chariot and driver,
22 with you I shatter man and woman,
    with you I shatter old man and youth,
    with you I shatter young man and maiden,
23 with you I shatter shepherd and flock,
    with you I shatter farmer and oxen,
    with you I shatter governors and officials.

24 "Before your eyes I will repay Babylon and all who live in Babylonia[a] for all the wrong they have done in Zion," declares the LORD.

25 "I am against you, O destroying mountain,
    you who destroy the whole earth,"
              declares the LORD.
"I will stretch out my hand against you,
    roll you off the cliffs,
    and make you a burned-out mountain.
26 No rock will be taken from you for a cornerstone,
    nor any stone for a foundation,
    for you will be desolate forever,"
              declares the LORD.

27 "Lift up a banner in the land!
    Blow the trumpet among the nations!
Prepare the nations for battle against her;
    summon against her these kingdoms:
    Ararat, Minni and Ashkenaz.
Appoint a commander against her;
    send up horses like a swarm of locusts.
28 Prepare the nations for battle against her—
    the kings of the Medes,
their governors and all their officials,
    and all the countries they rule.
29 The land trembles and writhes,
    for the LORD's purposes against Babylon
        stand—
to lay waste the land of Babylon
    so that no one will live there.
30 Babylon's warriors have stopped fighting;
    they remain in their strongholds.
Their strength is exhausted;
    they have become like women.
Her dwellings are set on fire;
    the bars of her gates are broken.
31 One courier follows another
    and messenger follows messenger
to announce to the king of Babylon
    that his entire city is captured,
32 the river crossings seized,
    the marshes set on fire,
    and the soldiers terrified."

33 This is what the LORD Almighty, the God of Israel, says:

"The Daughter of Babylon is like a threshing floor
    at the time it is trampled;
    the time to harvest her will soon come."

     a 24 Or Chaldea; also in verse 35

34 "Nebuchadnezzar king of Babylon has devoured us,
  he has thrown us into confusion,
  he has made us an empty jar.
Like a serpent he has swallowed us
  and filled his stomach with our delicacies,
  and then has spewed us out.
35 May the violence done to our flesh*a* be upon
  Babylon,"
  say the inhabitants of Zion.
"May our blood be on those who live in Babylonia,"
  says Jerusalem.

36 Therefore, this is what the LORD says:

"See, I will defend your cause
  and avenge you;
I will dry up her sea
  and make her springs dry.
37 Babylon will be a heap of ruins,
  a haunt of jackals,
an object of horror and scorn,
  a place where no one lives.
38 Her people all roar like young lions,
  they growl like lion cubs.
39 But while they are aroused,
  I will set out a feast for them
  and make them drunk,
so that they shout with laughter—
  then sleep forever and not awake,"
                                        declares the LORD.
40 "I will bring them down
  like lambs to the slaughter,
  like rams and goats.

41 "How Sheshach*b* will be captured,
  the boast of the whole earth seized!
What a horror Babylon will be
  among the nations!
42 The sea will rise over Babylon;
  its roaring waves will cover her.
43 Her towns will be desolate,
  a dry and desert land,
a land where no one lives,
  through which no man travels.
44 I will punish Bel in Babylon
  and make him spew out what he has
    swallowed.
The nations will no longer stream to him.
  And the wall of Babylon will fall.

45 "Come out of her, my people!
  Run for your lives!
  Run from the fierce anger of the LORD.
46 Do not lose heart or be afraid
  when rumors are heard in the land;
one rumor comes this year, another the next,
  rumors of violence in the land
  and of ruler against ruler.
47 For the time will surely come
  when I will punish the idols of Babylon;

a 35 Or *done to us and to our children*   *b 41 Sheshach* is a cryptogram for
Babylon.

"I Will . . . Avenge You"

JEREMIAH 51:34–37

Jerusalem has been ravished, her flesh violated and her delicacy gutted. Have you been the victim of violence—brutal or subtle? What has been the effect on your emotions, your mind, your spirit or your body? What healing have you sought? Is there still more healing to do? Meditate on the images of God's justice at work against Babylon. What redress have you sought against your abuser? Pray for strength to forgive that person and for courage not to allow continuing abuse in the future. Journal your responses and share any issues that arise within you with your pastor, spiritual adviser or counselor.

See Meeting God in Scripture

A Holy Picture

JEREMIAH 51:47–53

There is death and destruction on all sides. Babylon will be leveled. But in the face of the disaster, "Remember the LORD . . . and think on Jerusalem."

What are the central images of your faith? What "icon" of God's presence can you hold in your mind when you face nothing but calamity? Under threat of death Stephen looked to Jesus (see Acts 7:55). With paint or crayon make a holy picture that illustrates the central image of your faith.

See Meeting God in Worship

her whole land will be disgraced
    and her slain will all lie fallen within her.
⁴⁸ Then heaven and earth and all that is in them
    will shout for joy over Babylon,
for out of the north
    destroyers will attack her,"

                declares the LORD.

⁴⁹ "Babylon must fall because of Israel's slain,
    just as the slain in all the earth
    have fallen because of Babylon.
⁵⁰ You who have escaped the sword,
    leave and do not linger!
Remember the LORD in a distant land,
    and think on Jerusalem."

⁵¹ "We are disgraced,
    for we have been insulted
    and shame covers our faces,
because foreigners have entered
    the holy places of the LORD's house."

⁵² "But days are coming," declares the LORD,
    "when I will punish her idols,
and throughout her land
    the wounded will groan.
⁵³ Even if Babylon reaches the sky
    and fortifies her lofty stronghold,
    I will send destroyers against her,"

                declares the LORD.

⁵⁴ "The sound of a cry comes from Babylon,
    the sound of great destruction
    from the land of the Babylonians.ᵃ
⁵⁵ The LORD will destroy Babylon;
    he will silence her noisy din.
Waves ⌊of enemies⌋ will rage like great waters;
    the roar of their voices will resound.
⁵⁶ A destroyer will come against Babylon;
    her warriors will be captured,
    and their bows will be broken.
For the LORD is a God of retribution;
    he will repay in full.
⁵⁷ I will make her officials and wise men drunk,
    her governors, officers and warriors as well;
they will sleep forever and not awake,"
    declares the King, whose name is the LORD
    Almighty.

⁵⁸ This is what the LORD Almighty says:

"Babylon's thick wall will be leveled
    and her high gates set on fire;
the peoples exhaust themselves for nothing,
    the nations' labor is only fuel for the flames."

⁵⁹ This is the message Jeremiah gave to the staff officer Seraiah son of Neriah, the son of Mahseiah, when he went to Babylon with Zedekiah king of Judah in the fourth year of his reign. ⁶⁰ Jeremiah had written on a scroll about all the disasters that would come upon Babylon—all that had been recorded concerning Babylon. ⁶¹ He said to Seraiah, "When

ᵃ 54 Or *Chaldeans*

you get to Babylon, see that you read all these words aloud. [62]Then say, 'O LORD, you have said you will destroy this place, so that neither man nor animal will live in it; it will be desolate forever.' [63]When you finish reading this scroll, tie a stone to it and throw it into the Euphrates. [64]Then say, 'So will Babylon sink to rise no more because of the disaster I will bring upon her. And her people will fall.' "

The words of Jeremiah end here.

The Fall of Jerusalem

52 Zedekiah was twenty-one years old when he became king, and he reigned in Jerusalem eleven years. His mother's name was Hamutal daughter of Jeremiah; she was from Libnah. [2]He did evil in the eyes of the LORD, just as Jehoiakim had done. [3]It was because of the LORD's anger that all this happened to Jerusalem and Judah, and in the end he thrust them from his presence.

Now Zedekiah rebelled against the king of Babylon.

[4]So in the ninth year of Zedekiah's reign, on the tenth day of the tenth month, Nebuchadnezzar king of Babylon marched against Jerusalem with his whole army. They camped outside the city and built siege works all around it. [5]The city was kept under siege until the eleventh year of King Zedekiah.

[6]By the ninth day of the fourth month the famine in the city had become so severe that there was no food for the people to eat. [7]Then the city wall was broken through, and the whole army fled. They left the city at night through the gate between the two walls near the king's garden, though the Babylonians[a] were surrounding the city. They fled toward the Arabah,[b] [8]but the Babylonian[c] army pursued King Zedekiah and overtook him in the plains of Jericho. All his soldiers were separated from him and scattered, [9]and he was captured.

He was taken to the king of Babylon at Riblah in the land of Hamath, where he pronounced sentence on him. [10]There at Riblah the king of Babylon slaughtered the sons of Zedekiah before his eyes; he also killed all the officials of Judah. [11]Then he put out Zedekiah's eyes, bound him with bronze shackles and took him to Babylon, where he put him in prison till the day of his death.

[12]On the tenth day of the fifth month, in the nineteenth year of Nebuchadnezzar king of Babylon, Nebuzaradan commander of the imperial guard, who served the king of Babylon, came to Jerusalem. [13]He set fire to the temple of the LORD, the royal palace and all the houses of Jerusalem. Every important building he burned down. [14]The whole Babylonian army under the commander of the imperial guard broke down all the walls around Jerusalem. [15]Nebuzaradan the commander of the guard carried into exile some of the poorest people and those who remained in the city, along with the rest of the craftsmen[d] and those who had gone over to the king of Babylon. [16]But Nebuzaradan left behind the rest of the poorest people of the land to work the vineyards and fields.

[17]The Babylonians broke up the bronze pillars, the movable stands and the bronze Sea that were at the temple of

So Will Babylon Sink

JEREMIAH 51:59–64

Write on a piece of paper the name of an evil force in the world—such as domestic violence, dishonesty, pornography or embezzlement. Write some words from the Bible about this evil and what you understand to be God's perspective. Attach the paper to a stone with string or a rubber band and throw it into a pond, river or lake. Recite, "So will this evil sink to rise no more." What practical action will affirm your prayer?

See Meeting God in Scripture

---

[a] 7 Or *Chaldeans*; also in verse 17   [b] 7 Or *the Jordan Valley*   [c] 8 Or *Chaldean*; also in verse 14   [d] 15 Or *populace*

Celebrating Release

JEREMIAH 52:31–34

King Jehoiachin is free. The king of Babylon treats him kindly. His status is raised. He is invited to the king's table and treated with honor.

What is your experience of being freed by Jesus? How have you experienced his kindness? How has God raised you and honored you?

Prepare a meal fit for a king. Invite two or more of your companions in faith and share the meal with them. Intentionally talk together about your experience of God's kindness in Jesus Christ. Celebrate the goodness of God. "Taste and see that the LORD is good" (Psalm 34:8).

See Meeting God in Worship

the LORD and they carried all the bronze to Babylon. ¹⁸They also took away the pots, shovels, wick trimmers, sprinkling bowls, dishes and all the bronze articles used in the temple service. ¹⁹The commander of the imperial guard took away the basins, censers, sprinkling bowls, pots, lampstands, dishes and bowls used for drink offerings—all that were made of pure gold or silver.

²⁰The bronze from the two pillars, the Sea and the twelve bronze bulls under it, and the movable stands, which King Solomon had made for the temple of the LORD, was more than could be weighed. ²¹Each of the pillars was eighteen cubits high and twelve cubits in circumference*a*; each was four fingers thick, and hollow. ²²The bronze capital on top of the one pillar was five cubits*b* high and was decorated with a network and pomegranates of bronze all around. The other pillar, with its pomegranates, was similar. ²³There were ninety-six pomegranates on the sides; the total number of pomegranates above the surrounding network was a hundred.

²⁴The commander of the guard took as prisoners Seraiah the chief priest, Zephaniah the priest next in rank and the three doorkeepers. ²⁵Of those still in the city, he took the officer in charge of the fighting men, and seven royal advisers. He also took the secretary who was chief officer in charge of conscripting the people of the land and sixty of his men who were found in the city. ²⁶Nebuzaradan the commander took them all and brought them to the king of Babylon at Riblah. ²⁷There at Riblah, in the land of Hamath, the king had them executed.

So Judah went into captivity, away from her land. ²⁸This is the number of the people Nebuchadnezzar carried into exile:

in the seventh year, 3,023 Jews;
²⁹in Nebuchadnezzar's eighteenth year,
832 people from Jerusalem;
³⁰in his twenty-third year,
745 Jews taken into exile by Nebuzaradan the commander of the imperial guard.
There were 4,600 people in all.

Jehoiachin Released

³¹In the thirty-seventh year of the exile of Jehoiachin king of Judah, in the year Evil-Merodach*c* became king of Babylon, he released Jehoiachin king of Judah and freed him from prison on the twenty-fifth day of the twelfth month. ³²He spoke kindly to him and gave him a seat of honor higher than those of the other kings who were with him in Babylon. ³³So Jehoiachin put aside his prison clothes and for the rest of his life ate regularly at the king's table. ³⁴Day by day the king of Babylon gave Jehoiachin a regular allowance as long as he lived, till the day of his death.

---

a 21 That is, about 27 feet (about 8.1 meters) high and 18 feet (about 5.4 meters) in circumference   *b 22* That is, about 7 1/2 feet (about 2.3 meters)
c 31 Also called *Amel-Marduk*

LAMENTATIONS

Afflicted and Comforted

KEY VERSE:

Because of the LORD*'s great love we are not consumed, for his compassions never fail.*

—*Lamentations 3:22*

Although many Biblical books contain poignant expressions of grief in poetry and song, Lamentations is the only Old Testament book composed solely of such expressions. The author grieves over the destruction of Jerusalem, the Hebrew people's infidelity to God and the punishment that comes at the hands of the Babylonians when his people turned from God.

Like the author of Lamentations, we can turn to God in times of anguish and pain. We can pour out our sorrow from the depths of our souls as we look for God's healing love. Turning to God also means taking responsibility for our actions, repenting of misdeeds and accepting the new life that God offers us. No matter what our personal pain or sorrow, Lamentations tells us, God is the Rock to whom we can turn. Whatever our afflictions, God's loving arms reach out to comfort us.

"O sometimes the shadows
    are deep,
And rough seems the path
    to my goal,
And sorrows, sometimes
    how they sweep
Like tempests down over the
    soul!
O then to the Rock let me
    fly,
To the Rock that is higher
    than I!
O near to the Rock let me
    keep
If blessings or sorrows
    prevail,
Or climbing the mountain
    way steep,
Or walking the shadowy
    vale.
O then to the Rock let me
    fly,
to the Rock that is higher
    than I!"

—ERASTUS JOHNSON

A Personal Lamentation

LAMENTATIONS 1:1-4

After reading these verses, close your eyes and remember a time you felt absolutely alone and defeated. Write your own description of that anguished point in your life. Feel free to make parallels to the Scripture verses. Try to use vivid language as you detail the rejection and hopelessness you felt. Read your "lamentation" aloud and offer your words to the God who has never left you, even when you felt alone.

See Meeting God in Prayer

1 [a] How deserted lies the city,
   once so full of people!
How like a widow is she,
   who once was great among the nations!
She who was queen among the provinces
   has now become a slave.

[2] Bitterly she weeps at night,
   tears are upon her cheeks.
Among all her lovers
   there is none to comfort her.
All her friends have betrayed her;
   they have become her enemies.

[3] After affliction and harsh labor,
   Judah has gone into exile.
She dwells among the nations;
   she finds no resting place.
All who pursue her have overtaken her
   in the midst of her distress.

[4] The roads to Zion mourn,
   for no one comes to her appointed feasts.
All her gateways are desolate,
   her priests groan,
her maidens grieve,
   and she is in bitter anguish.

[5] Her foes have become her masters;
   her enemies are at ease.
The LORD has brought her grief
   because of her many sins.
Her children have gone into exile,
   captive before the foe.

[6] All the splendor has departed
   from the Daughter of Zion.
Her princes are like deer
   that find no pasture;
in weakness they have fled
   before the pursuer.

[7] In the days of her affliction and wandering
   Jerusalem remembers all the treasures
   that were hers in days of old.
When her people fell into enemy hands,
   there was no one to help her.
Her enemies looked at her
   and laughed at her destruction.

[8] Jerusalem has sinned greatly
   and so has become unclean.
All who honored her despise her,
   for they have seen her nakedness;
she herself groans
   and turns away.

[9] Her filthiness clung to her skirts;
   she did not consider her future.
Her fall was astounding;
   there was none to comfort her.
"Look, O LORD, on my affliction,
   for the enemy has triumphed."

[a] This chapter is an acrostic poem, the verses of which begin with the successive letters of the Hebrew alphabet.

¹⁰ The enemy laid hands
    on all her treasures;
she saw pagan nations
    enter her sanctuary—
those you had forbidden
    to enter your assembly.

¹¹ All her people groan
    as they search for bread;
they barter their treasures for food
    to keep themselves alive.
"Look, O Lᴏʀᴅ, and consider,
    for I am despised."

¹² "Is it nothing to you, all you who pass by?
    Look around and see.
Is any suffering like my suffering
    that was inflicted on me,
that the Lᴏʀᴅ brought on me
    in the day of his fierce anger?

¹³ "From on high he sent fire,
    sent it down into my bones.
He spread a net for my feet
    and turned me back.
He made me desolate,
    faint all the day long.

¹⁴ "My sins have been bound into a yoke*ᵃ*;
    by his hands they were woven together.
They have come upon my neck
    and the Lord has sapped my strength.
He has handed me over
    to those I cannot withstand.

¹⁵ "The Lord has rejected
    all the warriors in my midst;
he has summoned an army against me
    to*ᵇ* crush my young men.
In his winepress the Lord has trampled
    the Virgin Daughter of Judah.

¹⁶ "This is why I weep
    and my eyes overflow with tears.
No one is near to comfort me,
    no one to restore my spirit.
My children are destitute
    because the enemy has prevailed."

¹⁷ Zion stretches out her hands,
    but there is no one to comfort her.
The Lᴏʀᴅ has decreed for Jacob
    that his neighbors become his foes;
Jerusalem has become
    an unclean thing among them.

¹⁸ "The Lᴏʀᴅ is righteous,
    yet I rebelled against his command.
Listen, all you peoples;
    look upon my suffering.
My young men and maidens
    have gone into exile.

Rest for the Soul

LAMENTATIONS 1:14

Place a heavy beach towel or blanket on your shoulders, feeling the weight that is a symbol of the sins that have "come upon [your] neck." What does the weight mean to you? In what ways would such a load, pressing down on your neck and shoulders, restrict your movement? How does the weight affect how you feel inside? With your eyes closed, reach up to slowly take the weight off as you recall Jesus' words: "Come to me, all you who are weary and burdened, and I will give you rest." Give thanks that Jesus has taken the weight of your sins and promised "rest for your [soul]" (Matthew 11:28–29).

See Meeting God in Scripture

ᵃ 14 Most Hebrew manuscripts; Septuagint *He kept watch over my sins*
ᵇ 15 Or *has set a time for me / when he will*

Low As Low Can Be

LAMENTATIONS 1:20

Utterly discouraged, the author goes straight to God and pours out his distress and torment. Why is God willing to listen to his problems and complaints? Why does he feel safe in God's care?

Do you feel safe in God's care? Why or why not? How does your sense of safety influence the kinds of concerns you take to God in prayer? In those times when you feel that "inside, there is only death," how do you move on? After expressing your deepest feelings, what should you do next? In other words, how does a heart-to-heart talk with God enable you to stop complaining and start taking positive action?

See Meeting God in Prayer

19 "I called to my allies
    but they betrayed me.
My priests and my elders
    perished in the city
while they searched for food
    to keep themselves alive.

20 "See, O LORD, how distressed I am!
    I am in torment within,
and in my heart I am disturbed,
    for I have been most rebellious.
Outside, the sword bereaves;
    inside, there is only death.

21 "People have heard my groaning,
    but there is no one to comfort me.
All my enemies have heard of my distress;
    they rejoice at what you have done.
May you bring the day you have announced
    so they may become like me.

22 "Let all their wickedness come before you;
    deal with them
as you have dealt with me
    because of all my sins.
My groans are many
    and my heart is faint."

2 ᵃ How the Lord has covered the Daughter of Zion
    with the cloud of his anger ᵇ!
He has hurled down the splendor of Israel
    from heaven to earth;
he has not remembered his footstool
    in the day of his anger.

2 Without pity the Lord has swallowed up
    all the dwellings of Jacob;
in his wrath he has torn down
    the strongholds of the Daughter of Judah.
He has brought her kingdom and its princes
    down to the ground in dishonor.

3 In fierce anger he has cut off
    every horn ᶜ of Israel.
He has withdrawn his right hand
    at the approach of the enemy.
He has burned in Jacob like a flaming fire
    that consumes everything around it.

4 Like an enemy he has strung his bow;
    his right hand is ready.
Like a foe he has slain
    all who were pleasing to the eye;
he has poured out his wrath like fire
    on the tent of the Daughter of Zion.

5 The Lord is like an enemy;
    he has swallowed up Israel.
He has swallowed up all her palaces
    and destroyed her strongholds.

ᵃ This chapter is an acrostic poem, the verses of which begin with the successive letters of the Hebrew alphabet.   ᵇ 1 Or *How the Lord in his anger / has treated the Daughter of Zion with contempt*   ᶜ 3 Or / *all the strength*; or *every king*; horn here symbolizes strength.

He has multiplied mourning and lamentation
   for the Daughter of Judah.

⁶ He has laid waste his dwelling like a garden;
   he has destroyed his place of meeting.
The Lord has made Zion forget
   her appointed feasts and her Sabbaths;
in his fierce anger he has spurned
   both king and priest.

⁷ The Lord has rejected his altar
   and abandoned his sanctuary.
He has handed over to the enemy
   the walls of her palaces;
they have raised a shout in the house of the Lord
   as on the day of an appointed feast.

⁸ The Lord determined to tear down
   the wall around the Daughter of Zion.
He stretched out a measuring line
   and did not withhold his hand from destroying.
He made ramparts and walls lament;
   together they wasted away.

⁹ Her gates have sunk into the ground;
   their bars he has broken and destroyed.
Her king and her princes are exiled among the
     nations,
   the law is no more,
and her prophets no longer find
   visions from the Lord.

¹⁰ The elders of the Daughter of Zion
   sit on the ground in silence;
they have sprinkled dust on their heads
   and put on sackcloth.
The young women of Jerusalem
   have bowed their heads to the ground.

¹¹ My eyes fail from weeping,
   I am in torment within,
my heart is poured out on the ground
   because my people are destroyed,
because children and infants faint
   in the streets of the city.

¹² They say to their mothers,
   "Where is bread and wine?"
as they faint like wounded men
   in the streets of the city,
as their lives ebb away
   in their mothers' arms.

¹³ What can I say for you?
   With what can I compare you,
   O Daughter of Jerusalem?
To what can I liken you,
   that I may comfort you,
   O Virgin Daughter of Zion?
Your wound is as deep as the sea.
   Who can heal you?

¹⁴ The visions of your prophets
   were false and worthless;
they did not expose your sin

Jesus Can Heal

LAMENTATIONS 2:13

Divide a piece of paper into two columns. On the left side, make a list of those wounds that you carry—from times you have felt hurt, abandoned, misunderstood, physically injured or emotionally bruised. Be specific. On the right hand side, across from each listed hurt, write the words: "Who can heal you? Jesus can." When you feel your lists are complete, prayerfully read the lists as a litany, so that as you name each hurt, you hear the response: "Who can heal you? Jesus can."

See Meeting God in Prayer

Pour Out Your Heart

LAMENTATIONS 2:19

Fill a pitcher with water and place it on a table along with a large bowl. Sit in front of the bowl and pitcher and enter into a quiet time of prayer. Imagine yourself as the water in the pitcher, God as the bowl. Slowly pour the water into the bowl as you talk to God. Say whatever is on your mind. Follow the Scriptural directive: "Pour out your heart like water in the presence of the Lord." When all of the water is in the bowl, immerse your hands in the bowl. Let the bowl symbolize how God's love surrounds you just as the water is able to accept you as it surrounds your hands.

See Meeting God in Prayer

to ward off your captivity.
The oracles they gave you
were false and misleading.

¹⁵ All who pass your way
clap their hands at you;
they scoff and shake their heads
at the Daughter of Jerusalem:
"Is this the city that was called
the perfection of beauty,
the joy of the whole earth?"

¹⁶ All your enemies open their mouths
wide against you;
they scoff and gnash their teeth
and say, "We have swallowed her up.
This is the day we have waited for;
we have lived to see it."

¹⁷ The LORD has done what he planned;
he has fulfilled his word,
which he decreed long ago.
He has overthrown you without pity,
he has let the enemy gloat over you,
he has exalted the horn[a] of your foes.

¹⁸ The hearts of the people
cry out to the Lord.
O wall of the Daughter of Zion,
let your tears flow like a river
day and night;
give yourself no relief,
your eyes no rest.

¹⁹ Arise, cry out in the night,
as the watches of the night begin;
pour out your heart like water
in the presence of the Lord.
Lift up your hands to him
for the lives of your children,
who faint from hunger
at the head of every street.

²⁰ "Look, O LORD, and consider:
Whom have you ever treated like this?
Should women eat their offspring,
the children they have cared for?
Should priest and prophet be killed
in the sanctuary of the Lord?

²¹ "Young and old lie together
in the dust of the streets;
my young men and maidens
have fallen by the sword.
You have slain them in the day of your anger;
you have slaughtered them without pity.

²² "As you summon to a feast day,
so you summoned against me terrors on every
side.
In the day of the LORD's anger
no one escaped or survived;
those I cared for and reared,
my enemy has destroyed."

ᵃ *17 Horn* here symbolizes strength.

3[a] I am the man who has seen affliction
   by the rod of his wrath.
2 He has driven me away and made me walk
   in darkness rather than light;
3 indeed, he has turned his hand against me
   again and again, all day long.

4 He has made my skin and my flesh grow old
   and has broken my bones.
5 He has besieged me and surrounded me
   with bitterness and hardship.
6 He has made me dwell in darkness
   like those long dead.

7 He has walled me in so I cannot escape;
   he has weighed me down with chains.
8 Even when I call out or cry for help,
   he shuts out my prayer.
9 He has barred my way with blocks of stone;
   he has made my paths crooked.

10 Like a bear lying in wait,
   like a lion in hiding,
11 he dragged me from the path and mangled me
   and left me without help.
12 He drew his bow
   and made me the target for his arrows.

13 He pierced my heart
   with arrows from his quiver.
14 I became the laughingstock of all my people;
   they mock me in song all day long.
15 He has filled me with bitter herbs
   and sated me with gall.

16 He has broken my teeth with gravel;
   he has trampled me in the dust.
17 I have been deprived of peace;
   I have forgotten what prosperity is.
18 So I say, "My splendor is gone
   and all that I had hoped from the LORD."

19 I remember my affliction and my wandering,
   the bitterness and the gall.
20 I well remember them,
   and my soul is downcast within me.
21 Yet this I call to mind
   and therefore I have hope:

22 Because of the LORD's great love we are not
      consumed,
   for his compassions never fail.
23 They are new every morning;
   great is your faithfulness.
24 I say to myself, "The LORD is my portion;
   therefore I will wait for him."

25 The LORD is good to those whose hope is in him,
   to the one who seeks him;
26 it is good to wait quietly
   for the salvation of the LORD.

---

a This chapter is an acrostic poem; the verses of each stanza begin with the successive letters of the Hebrew alphabet, and the verses within each stanza begin with the same letter.

And Yet...

LAMENTATIONS 3:19–26

The author speaks on behalf of the Hebrew people who are suffering in the midst of God's discipline. In intense images, we feel with the one who says, "I remember my affliction and my wandering, the bitterness and the gall," and then continues, "Yet . . . because of the LORD's great love, we are not consumed . . ." Verses 21–26 are a turning point in this chapter. Read these verses again and again, pausing between readings to meditate on what they mean for you today. Let the words seep deep within you until you feel ready, no matter what happens in your life, to proclaim, "Yet . . . the LORD is good to those whose hope is in him."

See Meeting God in Scripture

Kept in God's Love

LAMENTATIONS 3:40–41

Thou who art—also within
us,
May all see Thee—in me
also,
May I prepare the way for
Thee,
May I thank Thee for all that
shall fall to my lot,
May I also not forget the
needs of others,
Keep me in Thy love
As Thou wouldst that all
should be kept in mine.
May everything in this my
being be directed to Thy
glory
And may I never despair
For I am under Thy hand,
And in Thee is all power
and goodness.
Give me a pure heart—that I
may see Thee,
A humble heart—that I may
hear Thee,
A heart of love—that I may
serve Thee,
A heart of faith—that I may
abide in Thee."

—DAG HAMMARSKJÖLD,
Markings

²⁷It is good for a man to bear the yoke
while he is young.
²⁸Let him sit alone in silence,
for the LORD has laid it on him.
²⁹Let him bury his face in the dust—
there may yet be hope.
³⁰Let him offer his cheek to one who would strike
him,
and let him be filled with disgrace.

³¹For men are not cast off
by the Lord forever.
³²Though he brings grief, he will show compassion,
so great is his unfailing love.
³³For he does not willingly bring affliction
or grief to the children of men.

³⁴To crush underfoot
all prisoners in the land,
³⁵to deny a man his rights
before the Most High,
³⁶to deprive a man of justice—
would not the Lord see such things?

³⁷Who can speak and have it happen
if the Lord has not decreed it?
³⁸Is it not from the mouth of the Most High
that both calamities and good things come?
³⁹Why should any living man complain
when punished for his sins?

⁴⁰Let us examine our ways and test them,
and let us return to the LORD.
⁴¹Let us lift up our hearts and our hands
to God in heaven, and say:
⁴²"We have sinned and rebelled
and you have not forgiven.

⁴³"You have covered yourself with anger and
pursued us;
you have slain without pity.
⁴⁴You have covered yourself with a cloud
so that no prayer can get through.
⁴⁵You have made us scum and refuse
among the nations.

⁴⁶"All our enemies have opened their mouths
wide against us.
⁴⁷We have suffered terror and pitfalls,
ruin and destruction."
⁴⁸Streams of tears flow from my eyes
because my people are destroyed.

⁴⁹My eyes will flow unceasingly,
without relief,
⁵⁰until the LORD looks down
from heaven and sees.
⁵¹What I see brings grief to my soul
because of all the women of my city.

⁵²Those who were my enemies without cause
hunted me like a bird.
⁵³They tried to end my life in a pit
and threw stones at me;

⁵⁴the waters closed over my head,
and I thought I was about to be cut off.

⁵⁵I called on your name, O Lᴏʀᴅ,
from the depths of the pit.

⁵⁶You heard my plea: "Do not close your ears
to my cry for relief."

⁵⁷You came near when I called you,
and you said, "Do not fear."

⁵⁸O Lord, you took up my case;
you redeemed my life.

⁵⁹You have seen, O Lᴏʀᴅ, the wrong done to me.
Uphold my cause!

⁶⁰You have seen the depth of their vengeance,
all their plots against me.

⁶¹O Lᴏʀᴅ, you have heard their insults,
all their plots against me—

⁶²what my enemies whisper and mutter
against me all day long.

⁶³Look at them! Sitting or standing,
they mock me in their songs.

⁶⁴Pay them back what they deserve, O Lᴏʀᴅ,
for what their hands have done.

⁶⁵Put a veil over their hearts,
and may your curse be on them!

⁶⁶Pursue them in anger and destroy them
from under the heavens of the Lᴏʀᴅ.

4ᵃ How the gold has lost its luster,
the fine gold become dull!
The sacred gems are scattered
at the head of every street.

²How the precious sons of Zion,
once worth their weight in gold,
are now considered as pots of clay,
the work of a potter's hands!

³Even jackals offer their breasts
to nurse their young,
but my people have become heartless
like ostriches in the desert.

⁴Because of thirst the infant's tongue
sticks to the roof of its mouth;
the children beg for bread,
but no one gives it to them.

⁵Those who once ate delicacies
are destitute in the streets.
Those nurtured in purple
now lie on ash heaps.

⁶The punishment of my people
is greater than that of Sodom,
which was overthrown in a moment
without a hand turned to help her.

⁷Their princes were brighter than snow
and whiter than milk,
their bodies more ruddy than rubies,
their appearance like sapphires.ᵇ

Help Is on the Way

LAMENTATIONS 3:55–58

Imagine yourself at the bottom of a dark, dank pit from which you can see no escape. Is anyone within earshot as you cry out in panic? Smell the mustiness; feel the dampness of the earthen walls seeping into your clothes. Goose bumps rise on your skin as you feel the cold and realize that you are all alone with no hope of escape. "Help!" you cry, and then from afar you hear a strong voice respond, "Do not fear."

How does God come to you? What help does God offer? What else does God say to you? How will you respond, both inwardly and outwardly?

See Meeting God in Scripture

ᵃThis chapter is an acrostic poem, the verses of which begin with the successive letters of the Hebrew alphabet.   ᵇ7 Or *lapis lazuli*

Content With Nothing Less

LAMENTATIONS 4:7–19

"It is too much, Lord! It is too much for me! Please give these sorts of favors and consolations to the sinners and people who do not know you at all, in order to attract them to Your service. As for me, who have the happiness of knowing You by faith, it seems to me that *that* ought to be sufficient for me. But because I ought to refuse nothing from so rich and liberal a hand as Yours, I accept, my God, the favors You do for me. Having received them, I beg You to let me return to You what You have given me, for You well know that it is not your gifts that I look for and desire but it is Yourself, and I can be content with nothing less!"

—BROTHER LAWRENCE,
The Practice of the Presence of God

⁸ But now they are blacker than soot;
    they are not recognized in the streets.
Their skin has shriveled on their bones;
    it has become as dry as a stick.

⁹ Those killed by the sword are better off
    than those who die of famine;
racked with hunger, they waste away
    for lack of food from the field.

¹⁰ With their own hands compassionate women
    have cooked their own children,
who became their food
    when my people were destroyed.

¹¹ The LORD has given full vent to his wrath;
    he has poured out his fierce anger.
He kindled a fire in Zion
    that consumed her foundations.

¹² The kings of the earth did not believe,
    nor did any of the world's people,
that enemies and foes could enter
    the gates of Jerusalem.

¹³ But it happened because of the sins of her
        prophets
    and the iniquities of her priests,
who shed within her
    the blood of the righteous.

¹⁴ Now they grope through the streets
    like men who are blind.
They are so defiled with blood
    that no one dares to touch their garments.

¹⁵ "Go away! You are unclean!" men cry to them.
    "Away! Away! Don't touch us!"
When they flee and wander about,
    people among the nations say,
    "They can stay here no longer."

¹⁶ The LORD himself has scattered them;
    he no longer watches over them.
The priests are shown no honor,
    the elders no favor.

¹⁷ Moreover, our eyes failed,
    looking in vain for help;
from our towers we watched
    for a nation that could not save us.

¹⁸ Men stalked us at every step,
    so we could not walk in our streets.
Our end was near, our days were numbered,
    for our end had come.

¹⁹ Our pursuers were swifter
    than eagles in the sky;
they chased us over the mountains
    and lay in wait for us in the desert.

²⁰ The LORD's anointed, our very life breath,
    was caught in their traps.
We thought that under his shadow
    we would live among the nations.

21 Rejoice and be glad, O Daughter of Edom,
  you who live in the land of Uz.
But to you also the cup will be passed;
  you will be drunk and stripped naked.

22 O Daughter of Zion, your punishment will end;
  he will not prolong your exile.
But, O Daughter of Edom, he will punish your sin
  and expose your wickedness.

5 Remember, O Lord, what has happened to us;
  look, and see our disgrace.
2 Our inheritance has been turned over to aliens,
  our homes to foreigners.
3 We have become orphans and fatherless,
  our mothers like widows.
4 We must buy the water we drink;
  our wood can be had only at a price.
5 Those who pursue us are at our heels;
  we are weary and find no rest.
6 We submitted to Egypt and Assyria
  to get enough bread.
7 Our fathers sinned and are no more,
  and we bear their punishment.
8 Slaves rule over us,
  and there is none to free us from their hands.
9 We get our bread at the risk of our lives
  because of the sword in the desert.
10 Our skin is hot as an oven,
  feverish from hunger.
11 Women have been ravished in Zion,
  and virgins in the towns of Judah.
12 Princes have been hung up by their hands;
  elders are shown no respect.
13 Young men toil at the millstones;
  boys stagger under loads of wood.
14 The elders are gone from the city gate;
  the young men have stopped their music.
15 Joy is gone from our hearts;
  our dancing has turned to mourning.
16 The crown has fallen from our head.
  Woe to us, for we have sinned!
17 Because of this our hearts are faint,
  because of these things our eyes grow dim
18 for Mount Zion, which lies desolate,
  with jackals prowling over it.

19 You, O Lord, reign forever;
  your throne endures from generation to
    generation.
20 Why do you always forget us?
  Why do you forsake us so long?
21 Restore us to yourself, O Lord, that we may
    return;
  renew our days as of old
22 unless you have utterly rejected us
  and are angry with us beyond measure.

A Safe Place

LAMENTATIONS 5:21

We may not have an attachment to a place as the Hebrew people did to their holy city, Jerusalem, but we know what it is to need a home. We desire a safe place where we are loved and accepted, known and cherished despite all our flaws. If we are lucky, we have family, friends or a community that provides us with nurture, acceptance and support. But even when we move to a new location and must begin again to build a loving community, God is with us, offering that home and safe place we deeply need. Copy verse 21 onto a 3x5 card and put it where you can see it often. Pray it frequently until it becomes your own personal prayer.

See Meeting God in Prayer

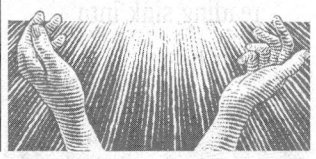

WAYS of MEETING GOD

Meeting God in Scripture

In every era, in myriad places and in all kinds of circumstances, people have testified that the Bible speaks powerfully—that the Word of God can and does change lives. But perhaps you feel that your own experience with reading the Bible pales in significance when compared to such a standard. You feel like the woman who confessed, "Surely there has to be a way to get more out of my Bible reading!" Your times with the Bible yield much of value and interest—but transformation?

That is another matter. You learn facts—places and names—but have yet to hear God's voice. As much as you value the insights gained, you long to meet God.

Christian meditation . . . is letting a special word or phrase that you discovered in the first phase of reading sink into your heart.

When you read and study Scripture it is possible to grow beyond an intellectual knowledge of the Bible to the transformation of your heart. The Bible can become "a lamp to [your] feet and a light for [your] path" (Psalm 119:105). You can go to the heart of the matter and meet the Author. The eighteenth-century bishop Tikhon of Zodonsk articulated well what can happen: "Whenever you read the Gospel," he wrote, "Christ Himself is speaking to you. And while you read, you are praying and talking to Him." Reading and studying the Bible can become more fulfilling than anything you have previously experienced.

But how? Fortunately we are heirs to several helpful approaches. The great spiritual writers of the past have given us a legacy that engages mind and heart, intellect and will. They have suggested ways that help us derive life from the text and so become agents of life for others.

Divine Reading. In the history of Christian spirituality, the oldest and best-known approach to Bible reading is called "spiritual reading" or "divine reading" (the Latin is *lectio divina*). The practice dates back to at least the fourth century, but the idea behind it is even more ancient. Spiritual reading entails a fourfold approach:

First, read slowly. Choose a relatively short passage of a Biblical book (no more than several paragraphs or a short chapter), and read meditatively, prayerfully. In this phase you are a seeker, looking for the "word within the Word." Watch for a key phrase or word that jumps out at you or promises to have special meaning for you. Concern yourself not so much with the *amount* you are reading as the *depth* with which you read. It is better to dwell profoundly on one word or phrase than to skim the surface of several chapters. Read with your own life and choices in view, recalling Paul's injunction that God's word to us is "useful for teaching, rebuking, correcting and training in righteousness" (2 Timothy 3:16).

Second, meditate. Christian meditation is not stream-of-consciousness or free association, nor is it Eastern transcendental meditation. Rather, it is letting a special word or phrase that you discovered in the first phase of reading sink into your heart. It is what the Biblical writers had in mind when they spoke of "meditating" on the Book of the Law "day and night" (Joshua 1:8, Psalm 1:2). For example, when you are reading Psalm 23, perhaps you linger at the phrase, "The LORD is my shepherd." For reasons that may not be immediately apparent, the word "my" stands out. You are struck by the idea that God can be—and wants to be—*your* shepherd. In this second phase of spiritual reading, stay with that thought. Use whatever study skills and related materials that are available to you to enrich your reflection. Bring mind, will and emotions to the enterprise. This meditative stage is comparable to walking around a great statue, viewing it from multiple vantage points. You are like Mary, Jesus' mother, who heard of the angel's announcement and "treasured up" and "pondered" what she had heard (Luke 2:19).

Third, pray the text. You have listened; now you respond—that is, you form a prayer that expresses your response to the idea. You "pray it back to God." You are, in effect, engaging God in dialogue. In the case of "The LORD is my shepherd," your response could easily be a prayer of gratitude. It might be a prolonged recollection of all of the ways that God has been present with you over the years, shepherding you through life. This phase of divine reading is in reality not separate from the other aspects but flows through all of them, so that you are continually converting the text into a prayer, a prayer formed by God's revealed will. What you have read is woven through what you tell God. You thereby acknowledge that God's Word "will not return . . . empty, but will accomplish what [God desires]" (Isaiah 55:11).

Fourth, contemplate. That is, rest. In divine reading you eventually arrive at the place at which you no longer work on the text but allow it to work itself into you. You let it soak into your deepest being. You are not straining for additional insights; you simply are savoring an encounter—with God's truth and with God himself. You enjoy the rest that Jesus promised those who come to him (see Matthew 11:28). Quietly, when ready, move toward the moment in which you ask God to show you how to live out what you have experienced.

Spiritual reading enables God to "speak and show" in ways that transform the written Word into a living Word—just for you. Then, having "[tasted] and [seen] that the LORD is good" (Psalm 34:8), you move outward in daily living to become a blessing to others.

Ignatian Reading. Attributed to Ignatius of Loyola (1491–1556) and articulated in his "Spiritual Exercises," the Ignatian method of reading the Bible likewise invites us to enter actively and fully into the text. It encourages detachment from either ego-driven success or fear-motivated anxiety, leaving the soul free to obey God's stirrings.

Generally, Ignatian reading works best with narrative material in which actual characters lived a story of faith. The idea is to place yourself into the text as a careful observer—a "fly on the wall," if you will. Ignatius commended the use of the five senses in such meditation. You taste, hear, see, smell and feel your way through the passage. Occasionally you become one of the characters, seeing the story unfold from his or her viewpoint. Most of all, the aim is to help you perceive the narrative from the viewpoint of Jesus so that you may more fully participate in his mind, heart and work.

For the sake of practice, you might like to concentrate on John 18:1–11 and spend five days reading it. Each day, imagine yourself as a different one of the characters: Judas, a soldier, Peter, the high priest's servant or Jesus. As you enter vicariously into the position of each character, ask God to teach you how to live in greater fidelity and obedience—which is the ultimate aim of the Ignatian method of reading Scripture and of Ignatian spirituality in general.

Franciscan Reading. While not a direct by-product of the teachings of Francis of Assisi, Franciscan reading exhibits primary qualities of Franciscan spirituality, such as action, spontaneity, love, praise, beauty and delight in creation. Like Ignatian reflection, Franciscan reading involves the mental process of entering personally into the text. But this method is more fluid. It allows the encounter with God to incorporate ordinary activities and daily experiences.

For example, turn in your Bible to Isaiah 53 and read through this chapter. To

Whatever method you use at any given time, . . . pray for a "Scriptural mind" that is obedient, faithful to the historic Christian tradition, Christ-centered and personal.

help you enter into its message and reflect on Jesus' sacrificial death on the cross, the Franciscan method would invite you to take actions such as these: If you have a model of a cross with Jesus on it, you might hold it in your hand, gazing at the details of the Lord's crucified body. You might sing a hymn such as "O Sacred Head, Now Wounded" or "The Old Rugged Cross." You might look through today's newspaper and identify places in the world where people are suffering. You might write a poem or paint a picture to capture what you are thinking and feeling. In the Franciscan spirit, you would allow your emotions to be expressed through an activity. You would be encouraged to "feel" something of what Jesus experienced on your behalf. You would saturate the entire experience with prayer, asking God to make you an instrument of peace in the lives of those who are suffering.

To be sure, these methods do not exhaust our options for formative reading. You might use the fruit of the Spirit described in Galatians 5:22–23 as a lens through which you read, asking yourself how a particular passage might deepen love, joy, peace, patience, kindness, goodness, gentleness, faithfulness and self-control in your life. You might use what some have called the Fivefold Question (What does this passage say about God's nature? What does it say about human nature? What does it say about how God relates to people? What does it suggest about how I might pray? What does it suggest about how I might act?).

Whatever method you use at any given time, an underlying attitude of openness to seeking truth should be adopted. We pray for a "Scriptural mind" that is obedient, faithful to the historic Christian tradition, Christ-centered and personal. We must desire to find truth and be willing to apply it to our own lives and our relationships with others. Apart from such foundational commitments, any method becomes mere technique. With them, any of the methods of reading Scripture can become a true means of grace.

See Page 1506 for the next Ways of Meeting God article.

EZEKIEL

Confronting the Holy

KEY VERSE:

"Then the nations around you that remain will know that I the Lord have rebuilt what was destroyed and have replanted what was desolate. I the Lord have spoken, and I will do it."—Ezekiel 36:36

"Brokenness and wounding do not occur in order to break human dignity but to open the heart so God can act."

—MARTIN MARTY,
A Cry of Absence

Many people know this book primarily by the author's vision of a valley of dry bones. But in these pages we also meet a priest and prophet who agonizes over the poor choices of the leaders of Israel, who bemoans the sins of the people and who condemns the desecration performed by neighboring nations.

With words and images that seem abrasive at times—yet always penetrating—Ezekiel invites us to look to the One whom we worship. He calls us to worship God with authenticity (14:6). Through his account we meet a God who is angry and disappointed (9:9), a God who laments the disasters that will come upon unjust nations (30:1–4), and a God who cares for people as a shepherd cares for a flock of sheep (34:1–24). This God holds people accountable for their actions (23:35), desires to make a new covenant of peace (34:25), and longs to put a new heart and a new spirit in them (36:26). Renewal will flow like a river to all the land (47:1).

Woven throughout the book of Ezekiel is the refrain, "Then they will know that I am the Lord." As you read Ezekiel, you may find yourself confronted and challenged, loved and renewed, and ready to sing the refrain, "Now I know that you are the Lord my God." Pray for openness to hear the words of Ezekiel and a soft heart with which to accompany him into the presence of God.

The Living Creatures and the Glory of the LORD

1 In the[a] thirtieth year, in the fourth month on the fifth day, while I was among the exiles by the Kebar River, the heavens were opened and I saw visions of God.

[2] On the fifth of the month—it was the fifth year of the exile of King Jehoiachin— [3] the word of the LORD came to Ezekiel the priest, the son of Buzi,[b] by the Kebar River in the land of the Babylonians.[c] There the hand of the LORD was upon him.

[4] I looked, and I saw a windstorm coming out of the north—an immense cloud with flashing lightning and surrounded by brilliant light. The center of the fire looked like glowing metal, [5] and in the fire was what looked like four living creatures. In appearance their form was that of a man, [6] but each of them had four faces and four wings. [7] Their legs were straight; their feet were like those of a calf and gleamed like burnished bronze. [8] Under their wings on their four sides they had the hands of a man. All four of them had faces and wings, [9] and their wings touched one another. Each one went straight ahead; they did not turn as they moved.

[10] Their faces looked like this: Each of the four had the face of a man, and on the right side each had the face of a lion, and on the left the face of an ox; each also had the face of an eagle. [11] Such were their faces. Their wings were spread out upward; each had two wings, one touching the wing of another creature on either side, and two wings covering its body. [12] Each one went straight ahead. Wherever the spirit would go, they would go, without turning as they went. [13] The appearance of the living creatures was like burning coals of fire or like torches. Fire moved back and forth among the creatures; it was bright, and lightning flashed out of it. [14] The creatures sped back and forth like flashes of lightning.

[15] As I looked at the living creatures, I saw a wheel on the ground beside each creature with its four faces. [16] This was the appearance and structure of the wheels: They sparkled like chrysolite, and all four looked alike. Each appeared to be made like a wheel intersecting a wheel. [17] As they moved, they would go in any one of the four directions the creatures faced; the wheels did not turn about[d] as the creatures went. [18] Their rims were high and awesome, and all four rims were full of eyes all around.

[19] When the living creatures moved, the wheels beside them moved; and when the living creatures rose from the ground, the wheels also rose. [20] Wherever the spirit would go, they would go, and the wheels would rise along with them, because the spirit of the living creatures was in the wheels. [21] When the creatures moved, they also moved; when the creatures stood still, they also stood still; and when the creatures rose from the ground, the wheels rose along with them, because the spirit of the living creatures was in the wheels.

[22] Spread out above the heads of the living creatures was what looked like an expanse, sparkling like ice, and awesome. [23] Under the expanse their wings were stretched out one toward the other, and each had two wings covering its

Awestruck

EZEKIEL 1:25—2:1

Carefully read this description of the "glory of the LORD." Read it again and then close your eyes and fix this image firmly in your mind. Keep it there for a period of time. What is your response to God's glory? What posture expresses your response? Is it to stand with your arms raised in praise? Or is it to lie prostrate on the floor and experience utter humility in the presence of God? Or is it to kneel in quiet adoration at the splendor of God? Repeat in prayer: "The glory of the Lord" or "Holy is God."

See Meeting God in Prayer

---

[a] 1 Or [my]   [b] 3 Or *Ezekiel son of Buzi the priest*   [c] 3 Or *Chaldeans*
[d] 17 Or *aside*

A Meal of Words

 EZEKIEL 3:1–3

The writer of Psalm 119:103 suggests that God's words are "sweeter than honey." Ezekiel carries the imagery even further by eating a scroll. Ezekiel was to let God's words fill him completely so that he could fulfill his commission to preach to Israel. Though the scroll contained words of woe and mourning, it tasted sweet to God's servant.

Spiritual teachers throughout the centuries have encouraged us to to savor the sweetness of the Word of God as we come into God's presence in prayer. What Scripture passages have you "tasted" and "digested" so that they have become part of you? What passages do you know from memory? What passages do you frequently return to for nourishment? Write out a passage that "tastes" especially sweet to you.

See Meeting God in Scripture

body. ²⁴When the creatures moved, I heard the sound of their wings, like the roar of rushing waters, like the voice of the Almighty,[a] like the tumult of an army. When they stood still, they lowered their wings.

²⁵Then there came a voice from above the expanse over their heads as they stood with lowered wings. ²⁶Above the expanse over their heads was what looked like a throne of sapphire,[b] and high above on the throne was a figure like that of a man. ²⁷I saw that from what appeared to be his waist up he looked like glowing metal, as if full of fire, and that from there down he looked like fire; and brilliant light surrounded him. ²⁸Like the appearance of a rainbow in the clouds on a rainy day, so was the radiance around him.

This was the appearance of the likeness of the glory of the LORD. When I saw it, I fell facedown, and I heard the voice of one speaking.

Ezekiel's Call

2 He said to me, "Son of man, stand up on your feet and I will speak to you." ²As he spoke, the Spirit came into me and raised me to my feet, and I heard him speaking to me.

³He said: "Son of man, I am sending you to the Israelites, to a rebellious nation that has rebelled against me; they and their fathers have been in revolt against me to this very day. ⁴The people to whom I am sending you are obstinate and stubborn. Say to them, 'This is what the Sovereign LORD says.' ⁵And whether they listen or fail to listen—for they are a rebellious house—they will know that a prophet has been among them. ⁶And you, son of man, do not be afraid of them or their words. Do not be afraid, though briers and thorns are all around you and you live among scorpions. Do not be afraid of what they say or terrified by them, though they are a rebellious house. ⁷You must speak my words to them, whether they listen or fail to listen, for they are rebellious. ⁸But you, son of man, listen to what I say to you. Do not rebel like that rebellious house; open your mouth and eat what I give you."

⁹Then I looked, and I saw a hand stretched out to me. In it was a scroll, ¹⁰which he unrolled before me. On both sides of it were written words of lament and mourning and woe.

3 And he said to me, "Son of man, eat what is before you, eat this scroll; then go and speak to the house of Israel." ²So I opened my mouth, and he gave me the scroll to eat.

³Then he said to me, "Son of man, eat this scroll I am giving you and fill your stomach with it." So I ate it, and it tasted as sweet as honey in my mouth.

⁴He then said to me: "Son of man, go now to the house of Israel and speak my words to them. ⁵You are not being sent to a people of obscure speech and difficult language, but to the house of Israel— ⁶not to many peoples of obscure speech and difficult language, whose words you cannot understand. Surely if I had sent you to them, they would have listened to you. ⁷But the house of Israel is not willing to listen to you because they are not willing to listen to me, for the whole house of Israel is hardened and obstinate. ⁸But I will make you as unyielding and hardened as

^a 24 Hebrew *Shaddai*   ^b 26 Or *lapis lazuli*

they are. 9I will make your forehead like the hardest stone, harder than flint. Do not be afraid of them or terrified by them, though they are a rebellious house."

10And he said to me, "Son of man, listen carefully and take to heart all the words I speak to you. 11Go now to your countrymen in exile and speak to them. Say to them, 'This is what the Sovereign LORD says,' whether they listen or fail to listen."

12Then the Spirit lifted me up, and I heard behind me a loud rumbling sound—May the glory of the LORD be praised in his dwelling place!— 13the sound of the wings of the living creatures brushing against each other and the sound of the wheels beside them, a loud rumbling sound. 14The Spirit then lifted me up and took me away, and I went in bitterness and in the anger of my spirit, with the strong hand of the LORD upon me. 15I came to the exiles who lived at Tel Abib near the Kebar River. And there, where they were living, I sat among them for seven days—overwhelmed.

Warning to Israel

16At the end of seven days the word of the LORD came to me: 17"Son of man, I have made you a watchman for the house of Israel; so hear the word I speak and give them warning from me. 18When I say to a wicked man, 'You will surely die,' and you do not warn him or speak out to dissuade him from his evil ways in order to save his life, that wicked man will die for[a] his sin, and I will hold you accountable for his blood. 19But if you do warn the wicked man and he does not turn from his wickedness or from his evil ways, he will die for his sin; but you will have saved yourself.

20"Again, when a righteous man turns from his righteousness and does evil, and I put a stumbling block before him, he will die. Since you did not warn him, he will die for his sin. The righteous things he did will not be remembered, and I will hold you accountable for his blood. 21But if you do warn the righteous man not to sin and he does not sin, he will surely live because he took warning, and you will have saved yourself."

22The hand of the LORD was upon me there, and he said to me, "Get up and go out to the plain, and there I will speak to you." 23So I got up and went out to the plain. And the glory of the LORD was standing there, like the glory I had seen by the Kebar River, and I fell facedown.

24Then the Spirit came into me and raised me to my feet. He spoke to me and said: "Go, shut yourself inside your house. 25And you, son of man, they will tie with ropes; you will be bound so that you cannot go out among the people. 26I will make your tongue stick to the roof of your mouth so that you will be silent and unable to rebuke them, though they are a rebellious house. 27But when I speak to you, I will open your mouth and you shall say to them, 'This is what the Sovereign LORD says.' Whoever will listen let him listen, and whoever will refuse let him refuse; for they are a rebellious house.

Siege of Jerusalem Symbolized

4 "Now, son of man, take a clay tablet, put it in front of you and draw the city of Jerusalem on it. 2Then lay

a 18 Or in; also in verses 19 and 20

An Obedient Word

EZEKIEL 3:16–17

"Even the awkwardly spoken word, if only it come out of an obedient heart, is better than a word unspoken in disobedience. Even the prayer that seems ineffectual and may perhaps be ridiculed may have left behind a seed of blessing. Indeed, even if no fruit is created in the spiritual sense, so that a soul comes nearer to God, still there is one thing that has happened: a testimony has been given in the Biblical sense. And this precisely is our task, a hard task, but a glorious task."

—ERICH SCHICK,
quoted in *A Guide to Prayer*

Days of Bread and Water

EZEKIEL 4:6–9

Ezekiel was to foreshadow the suffering of the Israelites by lying on his side for many days and eating only bread and drinking only water. He symbolically bore the sins of Israel, calling the people's attention to their sin.

There are people suffering today under poverty and oppression. Who calls our attention to the plight of the needy? What does it cost them? Offer a prayer of thanks for those who have been given a prophetic calling. Is there anyone you know in such a ministry whom you could call or to whom you could send a word of encouragement? For one meal today have bread and water, and remember the poor and hungry.

See Meeting God in Service

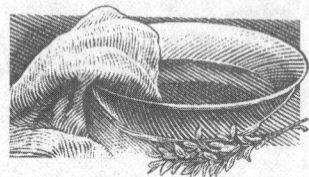

siege to it: Erect siege works against it, build a ramp up to it, set up camps against it and put battering rams around it. ³Then take an iron pan, place it as an iron wall between you and the city and turn your face toward it. It will be under siege, and you shall besiege it. This will be a sign to the house of Israel.

⁴"Then lie on your left side and put the sin of the house of Israel upon yourself.ᵃ You are to bear their sin for the number of days you lie on your side. ⁵I have assigned you the same number of days as the years of their sin. So for 390 days you will bear the sin of the house of Israel.

⁶"After you have finished this, lie down again, this time on your right side, and bear the sin of the house of Judah. I have assigned you 40 days, a day for each year. ⁷Turn your face toward the siege of Jerusalem and with bared arm prophesy against her. ⁸I will tie you up with ropes so that you cannot turn from one side to the other until you have finished the days of your siege.

⁹"Take wheat and barley, beans and lentils, millet and spelt; put them in a storage jar and use them to make bread for yourself. You are to eat it during the 390 days you lie on your side. ¹⁰Weigh out twenty shekelsᵇ of food to eat each day and eat it at set times. ¹¹Also measure out a sixth of a hinᶜ of water and drink it at set times. ¹²Eat the food as you would a barley cake; bake it in the sight of the people, using human excrement for fuel." ¹³The Lᴏʀᴅ said, "In this way the people of Israel will eat defiled food among the nations where I will drive them."

¹⁴Then I said, "Not so, Sovereign Lᴏʀᴅ! I have never defiled myself. From my youth until now I have never eaten anything found dead or torn by wild animals. No unclean meat has ever entered my mouth."

¹⁵"Very well," he said, "I will let you bake your bread over cow manure instead of human excrement."

¹⁶He then said to me: "Son of man, I will cut off the supply of food in Jerusalem. The people will eat rationed food in anxiety and drink rationed water in despair, ¹⁷for food and water will be scarce. They will be appalled at the sight of each other and will waste away because ofᵈ their sin.

5 "Now, son of man, take a sharp sword and use it as a barber's razor to shave your head and your beard. Then take a set of scales and divide up the hair. ²When the days of your siege come to an end, burn a third of the hair with fire inside the city. Take a third and strike it with the sword all around the city. And scatter a third to the wind. For I will pursue them with drawn sword. ³But take a few strands of hair and tuck them away in the folds of your garment. ⁴Again, take a few of these and throw them into the fire and burn them up. A fire will spread from there to the whole house of Israel.

⁵"This is what the Sovereign Lᴏʀᴅ says: This is Jerusalem, which I have set in the center of the nations, with countries all around her. ⁶Yet in her wickedness she has rebelled against my laws and decrees more than the nations and countries around her. She has rejected my laws and has not followed my decrees.

⁷"Therefore this is what the Sovereign Lᴏʀᴅ says: You have been more unruly than the nations around you and

ᵃ 4 Or your side   ᵇ 10 That is, about 8 ounces (about 0.2 kilogram)
ᶜ 11 That is, about 2/3 quart (about 0.6 liter)   ᵈ 17 Or away in

have not followed my decrees or kept my laws. You have not even[a] conformed to the standards of the nations around you.

8 "Therefore this is what the Sovereign LORD says: I myself am against you, Jerusalem, and I will inflict punishment on you in the sight of the nations. 9 Because of all your detestable idols, I will do to you what I have never done before and will never do again. 10 Therefore in your midst fathers will eat their children, and children will eat their fathers. I will inflict punishment on you and will scatter all your survivors to the winds. 11 Therefore as surely as I live, declares the Sovereign LORD, because you have defiled my sanctuary with all your vile images and detestable practices, I myself will withdraw my favor; I will not look on you with pity or spare you. 12 A third of your people will die of the plague or perish by famine inside you; a third will fall by the sword outside your walls; and a third I will scatter to the winds and pursue with drawn sword.

13 "Then my anger will cease and my wrath against them will subside, and I will be avenged. And when I have spent my wrath upon them, they will know that I the LORD have spoken in my zeal.

14 "I will make you a ruin and a reproach among the nations around you, in the sight of all who pass by. 15 You will be a reproach and a taunt, a warning and an object of horror to the nations around you when I inflict punishment on you in anger and in wrath and with stinging rebuke. I the LORD have spoken. 16 When I shoot at you with my deadly and destructive arrows of famine, I will shoot to destroy you. I will bring more and more famine upon you and cut off your supply of food. 17 I will send famine and wild beasts against you, and they will leave you childless. Plague and bloodshed will sweep through you, and I will bring the sword against you. I the LORD have spoken."

A Prophecy Against the Mountains of Israel

6 The word of the LORD came to me: 2 "Son of man, set your face against the mountains of Israel; prophesy against them 3 and say: 'O mountains of Israel, hear the word of the Sovereign LORD. This is what the Sovereign LORD says to the mountains and hills, to the ravines and valleys: I am about to bring a sword against you, and I will destroy your high places. 4 Your altars will be demolished and your incense altars will be smashed; and I will slay your people in front of your idols. 5 I will lay the dead bodies of the Israelites in front of their idols, and I will scatter your bones around your altars. 6 Wherever you live, the towns will be laid waste and the high places demolished, so that your altars will be laid waste and devastated, your idols smashed and ruined, your incense altars broken down, and what you have made wiped out. 7 Your people will fall slain among you, and you will know that I am the LORD.

8 " 'But I will spare some, for some of you will escape the sword when you are scattered among the lands and nations. 9 Then in the nations where they have been carried captive, those who escape will remember me—how I have been grieved by their adulterous hearts, which have turned away from me, and by their eyes, which have lusted after

On Not Choosing Idols

EZEKIEL 6:1–4

"Every time you make a choice you are turning the central part of you, the part of you that chooses, into something a little different from what it was before. And taking your life as a whole, with all your innumerable choices, all your life long you are slowly turning this central thing either into a Heavenly creature or into a hellish creature: either into a creature that is in harmony with God, with other creatures, and with itself, or else into one that is in a state of war and hatred with God, and with its fellow creatures, and with itself. To be the one kind of creature is Heaven; that is, it is joy, and peace and knowledge, and power. To be the other means madness, horror, idiocy, rage, impotence and eternal loneliness. Each of us at each moment is progressing to the one state or the other."

—C. S. LEWIS,
Mere Christianity

Dealing With the Doom

EZEKIEL 7:1–4

By this point in Ezekiel's account we have read several chapters forecasting punishment and desolations. And more hard words of doom and judgment follow in subsequent chapters. In the middle of reading such difficult words, it sometimes helps to realize that behind God's wrath is his broken heart (see 6:9). God loves the people of Jerusalem, but his heart is torn in two as the nation continues to worship idols and make unholy alliances. As a parent disciplines a child out of love, so God is forced to correct Israel. Spend a few moments meditating on how you may have broken God's heart and what might need correcting within you. Ask God for help in making amends.

See *Meeting God in Prayer*

their idols. They will loathe themselves for the evil they have done and for all their detestable practices. ¹⁰And they will know that I am the LORD; I did not threaten in vain to bring this calamity on them.

¹¹" 'This is what the Sovereign LORD says: Strike your hands together and stamp your feet and cry out "Alas!" because of all the wicked and detestable practices of the house of Israel, for they will fall by the sword, famine and plague. ¹²He that is far away will die of the plague, and he that is near will fall by the sword, and he that survives and is spared will die of famine. So will I spend my wrath upon them. ¹³And they will know that I am the LORD, when their people lie slain among their idols around their altars, on every high hill and on all the mountaintops, under every spreading tree and every leafy oak—places where they offered fragrant incense to all their idols. ¹⁴And I will stretch out my hand against them and make the land a desolate waste from the desert to Diblah[a]—wherever they live. Then they will know that I am the LORD.' "

The End Has Come

7 The word of the LORD came to me: ²"Son of man, this is what the Sovereign LORD says to the land of Israel: The end! The end has come upon the four corners of the land. ³The end is now upon you and I will unleash my anger against you. I will judge you according to your conduct and repay you for all your detestable practices. ⁴I will not look on you with pity or spare you; I will surely repay you for your conduct and the detestable practices among you. Then you will know that I am the LORD.

⁵"This is what the Sovereign LORD says: Disaster! An unheard-of[b] disaster is coming. ⁶The end has come! The end has come! It has roused itself against you. It has come! ⁷Doom has come upon you—you who dwell in the land. The time has come, the day is near; there is panic, not joy, upon the mountains. ⁸I am about to pour out my wrath on you and spend my anger against you; I will judge you according to your conduct and repay you for all your detestable practices. ⁹I will not look on you with pity or spare you; I will repay you in accordance with your conduct and the detestable practices among you. Then you will know that it is I the LORD who strikes the blow.

¹⁰"The day is here! It has come! Doom has burst forth, the rod has budded, arrogance has blossomed! ¹¹Violence has grown into[c] a rod to punish wickedness; none of the people will be left, none of that crowd—no wealth, nothing of value. ¹²The time has come, the day has arrived. Let not the buyer rejoice nor the seller grieve, for wrath is upon the whole crowd. ¹³The seller will not recover the land he has sold as long as both of them live, for the vision concerning the whole crowd will not be reversed. Because of their sins, not one of them will preserve his life. ¹⁴Though they blow the trumpet and get everything ready, no one will go into battle, for my wrath is upon the whole crowd.

¹⁵"Outside is the sword, inside are plague and famine; those in the country will die by the sword, and those in the city will be devoured by famine and plague. ¹⁶All who sur-

---

a 14 Most Hebrew manuscripts; a few Hebrew manuscripts *Riblah*
b 5 Most Hebrew manuscripts; some Hebrew manuscripts and Syriac *Disaster after*   *c 11* Or *The violent one has become*

vive and escape will be in the mountains, moaning like doves of the valleys, each because of his sins. ¹⁷Every hand will go limp, and every knee will become as weak as water. ¹⁸They will put on sackcloth and be clothed with terror. Their faces will be covered with shame and their heads will be shaved. ¹⁹They will throw their silver into the streets, and their gold will be an unclean thing. Their silver and gold will not be able to save them in the day of the LORD's wrath. They will not satisfy their hunger or fill their stomachs with it, for it has made them stumble into sin. ²⁰They were proud of their beautiful jewelry and used it to make their detestable idols and vile images. Therefore I will turn these into an unclean thing for them. ²¹I will hand it all over as plunder to foreigners and as loot to the wicked of the earth, and they will defile it. ²²I will turn my face away from them, and they will desecrate my treasured place; robbers will enter it and desecrate it.

²³"Prepare chains, because the land is full of bloodshed and the city is full of violence. ²⁴I will bring the most wicked of the nations to take possession of their houses; I will put an end to the pride of the mighty, and their sanctuaries will be desecrated. ²⁵When terror comes, they will seek peace, but there will be none. ²⁶Calamity upon calamity will come, and rumor upon rumor. They will try to get a vision from the prophet; the teaching of the law by the priest will be lost, as will the counsel of the elders. ²⁷The king will mourn, the prince will be clothed with despair, and the hands of the people of the land will tremble. I will deal with them according to their conduct, and by their own standards I will judge them. Then they will know that I am the LORD."

Idolatry in the Temple

8 In the sixth year, in the sixth month on the fifth day, while I was sitting in my house and the elders of Judah were sitting before me there, the hand of the Sovereign LORD came upon me there. ²I looked, and I saw a figure like that of a man.ᵃ From what appeared to be his waist down he was like fire, and from there up his appearance was as bright as glowing metal. ³He stretched out what looked like a hand and took me by the hair of my head. The Spirit lifted me up between earth and heaven and in visions of God he took me to Jerusalem, to the entrance to the north gate of the inner court, where the idol that provokes to jealousy stood. ⁴And there before me was the glory of the God of Israel, as in the vision I had seen in the plain.

⁵Then he said to me, "Son of man, look toward the north." So I looked, and in the entrance north of the gate of the altar I saw this idol of jealousy.

⁶And he said to me, "Son of man, do you see what they are doing—the utterly detestable things the house of Israel is doing here, things that will drive me far from my sanctuary? But you will see things that are even more detestable."

⁷Then he brought me to the entrance to the court. I looked, and I saw a hole in the wall. ⁸He said to me, "Son of man, now dig into the wall." So I dug into the wall and saw a doorway there.

⁹And he said to me, "Go in and see the wicked and detestable things they are doing here." ¹⁰So I went in and looked, and I saw portrayed all over the walls all kinds of

ᵃ 2 Or *saw a fiery figure*

Silver and Gold

EZEKIEL 7:19–20

Some people in Jerusalem turn their silver and gold into images to worship, but their idols cannot save them or satisfy their hunger.

Write down some of your thoughts and recollections about money and your relationship to it. You might address things your parents taught you about money or write about factors that influenced your attitudes about money. Think about the first money you earned, the most money you've made, or your decisions about giving or tithing. As you read what you have written, consider those attitudes and actions for which you need to ask forgiveness. What can you celebrate? In what ways do you need God's guidance?

See *Meeting God in Everyday Life*

Turning From Violence

EZEKIEL 8:17

God is already angry with the people of Jerusalem, but they provoke him even more by "fill[ing] the land with violence."

Because it is "news," violence tends to dominate the media coverage and is typically recorded in graphic and colorful detail. Therefore it is especially important to remember and support acts of peace and reconciliation. Find newspaper articles about those whose efforts bring about peace and reconciliation and pray for those efforts. Or make a list of actions that you could do to help bring about peace. Ask God to help you bring peace into troubled situations. Do something from the list each day this week.

See *Meeting God in Service*

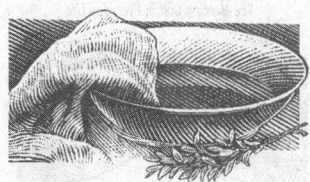

---

crawling things and detestable animals and all the idols of the house of Israel. ¹¹In front of them stood seventy elders of the house of Israel, and Jaazaniah son of Shaphan was standing among them. Each had a censer in his hand, and a fragrant cloud of incense was rising.

¹²He said to me, "Son of man, have you seen what the elders of the house of Israel are doing in the darkness, each at the shrine of his own idol? They say, 'The LORD does not see us; the LORD has forsaken the land.' " ¹³Again, he said, "You will see them doing things that are even more detestable."

¹⁴Then he brought me to the entrance to the north gate of the house of the LORD, and I saw women sitting there, mourning for Tammuz. ¹⁵He said to me, "Do you see this, son of man? You will see things that are even more detestable than this."

¹⁶He then brought me into the inner court of the house of the LORD, and there at the entrance to the temple, between the portico and the altar, were about twenty-five men. With their backs toward the temple of the LORD and their faces toward the east, they were bowing down to the sun in the east.

¹⁷He said to me, "Have you seen this, son of man? Is it a trivial matter for the house of Judah to do the detestable things they are doing here? Must they also fill the land with violence and continually provoke me to anger? Look at them putting the branch to their nose! ¹⁸Therefore I will deal with them in anger; I will not look on them with pity or spare them. Although they shout in my ears, I will not listen to them."

Idolaters Killed

9 Then I heard him call out in a loud voice, "Bring the guards of the city here, each with a weapon in his hand." ²And I saw six men coming from the direction of the upper gate, which faces north, each with a deadly weapon in his hand. With them was a man clothed in linen who had a writing kit at his side. They came in and stood beside the bronze altar.

³Now the glory of the God of Israel went up from above the cherubim, where it had been, and moved to the threshold of the temple. Then the LORD called to the man clothed in linen who had the writing kit at his side ⁴and said to him, "Go throughout the city of Jerusalem and put a mark on the foreheads of those who grieve and lament over all the detestable things that are done in it."

⁵As I listened, he said to the others, "Follow him through the city and kill, without showing pity or compassion. ⁶Slaughter old men, young men and maidens, women and children, but do not touch anyone who has the mark. Begin at my sanctuary." So they began with the elders who were in front of the temple.

⁷Then he said to them, "Defile the temple and fill the courts with the slain. Go!" So they went out and began killing throughout the city. ⁸While they were killing and I was left alone, I fell facedown, crying out, "Ah, Sovereign LORD! Are you going to destroy the entire remnant of Israel in this outpouring of your wrath on Jerusalem?"

⁹He answered me, "The sin of the house of Israel and Judah is exceedingly great; the land is full of bloodshed and

the city is full of injustice. They say, 'The LORD has forsaken the land; the LORD does not see.' [10]So I will not look on them with pity or spare them, but I will bring down on their own heads what they have done."

[11]Then the man in linen with the writing kit at his side brought back word, saying, "I have done as you commanded."

The Glory Departs From the Temple

10 I looked, and I saw the likeness of a throne of sapphire[a] above the expanse that was over the heads of the cherubim. [2]The LORD said to the man clothed in linen, "Go in among the wheels beneath the cherubim. Fill your hands with burning coals from among the cherubim and scatter them over the city." And as I watched, he went in.

[3]Now the cherubim were standing on the south side of the temple when the man went in, and a cloud filled the inner court. [4]Then the glory of the LORD rose from above the cherubim and moved to the threshold of the temple. The cloud filled the temple, and the court was full of the radiance of the glory of the LORD. [5]The sound of the wings of the cherubim could be heard as far away as the outer court, like the voice of God Almighty[b] when he speaks.

[6]When the LORD commanded the man in linen, "Take fire from among the wheels, from among the cherubim," the man went in and stood beside a wheel. [7]Then one of the cherubim reached out his hand to the fire that was among them. He took up some of it and put it into the hands of the man in linen, who took it and went out. [8](Under the wings of the cherubim could be seen what looked like the hands of a man.)

[9]I looked, and I saw beside the cherubim four wheels, one beside each of the cherubim; the wheels sparkled like chrysolite. [10]As for their appearance, the four of them looked alike; each was like a wheel intersecting a wheel. [11]As they moved, they would go in any one of the four directions the cherubim faced; the wheels did not turn about[c] as the cherubim went. The cherubim went in whatever direction the head faced, without turning as they went. [12]Their entire bodies, including their backs, their hands and their wings, were completely full of eyes, as were their four wheels. [13]I heard the wheels being called "the whirling wheels." [14]Each of the cherubim had four faces: One face was that of a cherub, the second the face of a man, the third the face of a lion, and the fourth the face of an eagle.

[15]Then the cherubim rose upward. These were the living creatures I had seen by the Kebar River. [16]When the cherubim moved, the wheels beside them moved; and when the cherubim spread their wings to rise from the ground, the wheels did not leave their side. [17]When the cherubim stood still, they also stood still; and when the cherubim rose, they rose with them, because the spirit of the living creatures was in them.

[18]Then the glory of the LORD departed from over the threshold of the temple and stopped above the cherubim. [19]While I watched, the cherubim spread their wings and rose from the ground, and as they went, the wheels went with them. They stopped at the entrance to the east gate of

The Mark of Lament

The man clothed in linen is instructed to go throughout Jerusalem and mark the foreheads of those who "grieve and lament" over the sins of the city. The mark saved them from death.

Even in times of great wrongdoing and impending judgment there are good people and good things that should be preserved, even cherished. Consider how you can become one who grieves and laments over corruption. Pray for wisdom and discernment to preserve and reinforce the good.

See Meeting God in Service

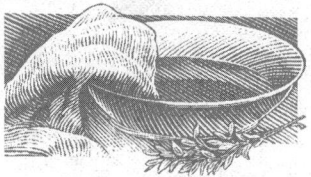

Forgiveness

EZEKIEL 11:12

"Lord, I have fallen again—
  a human clod!
Selfish I was, and heedless
  to offend,
Stood on my rights. Thy
  own child would not
  send
Away his shreds of nothing
  for the whole God!
Wretched, to thee who
  savest, low I bend:
Give me the power to let my
  rag-tag rights go
In the great wind that from
  thy gulf doth blow."
    —GEORGE MACDONALD,
      Diary of an Old Soul

the LORD's house, and the glory of the God of Israel was above them. ²⁰These were the living creatures I had seen beneath the God of Israel by the Kebar River, and I realized that they were cherubim. ²¹Each had four faces and four wings, and under their wings was what looked like the hands of a man. ²²Their faces had the same appearance as those I had seen by the Kebar River. Each one went straight ahead.

Judgment on Israel's Leaders

11 Then the Spirit lifted me up and brought me to the gate of the house of the LORD that faces east. There at the entrance to the gate were twenty-five men, and I saw among them Jaazaniah son of Azzur and Pelatiah son of Benaiah, leaders of the people. ²The LORD said to me, "Son of man, these are the men who are plotting evil and giving wicked advice in this city. ³They say, 'Will it not soon be time to build houses?[a] This city is a cooking pot, and we are the meat.' ⁴Therefore prophesy against them; prophesy, son of man."

⁵Then the Spirit of the LORD came upon me, and he told me to say: "This is what the LORD says: That is what you are saying, O house of Israel, but I know what is going through your mind. ⁶You have killed many people in this city and filled its streets with the dead.

⁷"Therefore this is what the Sovereign LORD says: The bodies you have thrown there are the meat and this city is the pot, but I will drive you out of it. ⁸You fear the sword, and the sword is what I will bring against you, declares the Sovereign LORD. ⁹I will drive you out of the city and hand you over to foreigners and inflict punishment on you. ¹⁰You will fall by the sword, and I will execute judgment on you at the borders of Israel. Then you will know that I am the LORD. ¹¹This city will not be a pot for you, nor will you be the meat in it; I will execute judgment on you at the borders of Israel. ¹²And you will know that I am the LORD, for you have not followed my decrees or kept my laws but have conformed to the standards of the nations around you."

¹³Now as I was prophesying, Pelatiah son of Benaiah died. Then I fell facedown and cried out in a loud voice, "Ah, Sovereign LORD! Will you completely destroy the remnant of Israel?"

¹⁴The word of the LORD came to me: ¹⁵"Son of man, your brothers—your brothers who are your blood relatives[b] and the whole house of Israel—are those of whom the people of Jerusalem have said, 'They are[c] far away from the LORD; this land was given to us as our possession.'

Promised Return of Israel

¹⁶"Therefore say: 'This is what the Sovereign LORD says: Although I sent them far away among the nations and scattered them among the countries, yet for a little while I have been a sanctuary for them in the countries where they have gone.'

¹⁷"Therefore say: 'This is what the Sovereign LORD says: I will gather you from the nations and bring you back from

---

a 3 Or *This is not the time to build houses.*   *b 15* Or *are in exile with you* (see Septuagint and Syriac)   *c 15* Or *those to whom the people of Jerusalem have said, 'Stay*

the countries where you have been scattered, and I will give you back the land of Israel again.'

¹⁸"They will return to it and remove all its vile images and detestable idols. ¹⁹I will give them an undivided heart and put a new spirit in them; I will remove from them their heart of stone and give them a heart of flesh. ²⁰Then they will follow my decrees and be careful to keep my laws. They will be my people, and I will be their God. ²¹But as for those whose hearts are devoted to their vile images and detestable idols, I will bring down on their own heads what they have done, declares the Sovereign LORD."

²²Then the cherubim, with the wheels beside them, spread their wings, and the glory of the God of Israel was above them. ²³The glory of the LORD went up from within the city and stopped above the mountain east of it. ²⁴The Spirit lifted me up and brought me to the exiles in Babylonia^a in the vision given by the Spirit of God.

Then the vision I had seen went up from me, ²⁵and I told the exiles everything the LORD had shown me.

The Exile Symbolized

12 The word of the LORD came to me: ²"Son of man, you are living among a rebellious people. They have eyes to see but do not see and ears to hear but do not hear, for they are a rebellious people.

³"Therefore, son of man, pack your belongings for exile and in the daytime, as they watch, set out and go from where you are to another place. Perhaps they will understand, though they are a rebellious house. ⁴During the daytime, while they watch, bring out your belongings packed for exile. Then in the evening, while they are watching, go out like those who go into exile. ⁵While they watch, dig through the wall and take your belongings out through it. ⁶Put them on your shoulder as they are watching and carry them out at dusk. Cover your face so that you cannot see the land, for I have made you a sign to the house of Israel."

⁷So I did as I was commanded. During the day I brought out my things packed for exile. Then in the evening I dug through the wall with my hands. I took my belongings out at dusk, carrying them on my shoulders while they watched.

⁸In the morning the word of the LORD came to me: ⁹"Son of man, did not that rebellious house of Israel ask you, 'What are you doing?'

¹⁰"Say to them, 'This is what the Sovereign LORD says: This oracle concerns the prince in Jerusalem and the whole house of Israel who are there.' ¹¹Say to them, 'I am a sign to you.'

"As I have done, so it will be done to them. They will go into exile as captives.

¹²"The prince among them will put his things on his shoulder at dusk and leave, and a hole will be dug in the wall for him to go through. He will cover his face so that he cannot see the land. ¹³I will spread my net for him, and he will be caught in my snare; I will bring him to Babylonia, the land of the Chaldeans, but he will not see it, and there he will die. ¹⁴I will scatter to the winds all those around him—his staff and all his troops—and I will pursue them with drawn sword.

^a 24 Or Chaldea

A New Heart

EZEKIEL 11:17–21

In the midst of pain and destruction, God speaks a word of hope. The people shall be gathered together and be given a new heart and a new spirit so they will be responsive to God's call.

A new heart is soft and resilient and responsive to God's grace.

Cut two hearts of the same size out of paper or cloth. Staple, glue or sew the two hearts together, leaving a small opening so that you can stuff the heart with tissue or cotton. Then close the opening. The heart you have made is not flat or hard, but puffed and soft and resilient. Holding the heart you have crafted, meditate on being open to God's leading today. Pray this prayer: "God, give me an open heart, a heart of flesh, a heart that is soft to your touch."

Trust the Vision

EZEKIEL 12:22–25

Will God follow through on the punishments Ezekiel has prophesied? Will he keep his promises sooner—or later? The people rationalize, saying, as humans are wont to do: It can't happen to us. This is way off in the future. We don't have to deal with this now. God follows through even if it seems to take a long time. "I the LORD will speak what I will, and it shall be fulfilled without delay." God persistently calls to us even as we ignore his still, small voice.

Just as surely, God keeps his promises as he fulfills judgment and works for good even in the midst of sorrow or despair. Recall some occasions when you wondered if God had stopped listening. Were you tempted to not bother to talk to God anymore? Or were you certain God would speak in due time? Share your times of doubt with a friend in the faith. Spend some time in prayer thinking about the times when God's promises have been fulfilled in your life.

See Meeting God in Everyday Life

¹⁵"They will know that I am the LORD, when I disperse them among the nations and scatter them through the countries. ¹⁶But I will spare a few of them from the sword, famine and plague, so that in the nations where they go they may acknowledge all their detestable practices. Then they will know that I am the LORD."

¹⁷The word of the LORD came to me: ¹⁸"Son of man, tremble as you eat your food, and shudder in fear as you drink your water. ¹⁹Say to the people of the land: 'This is what the Sovereign LORD says about those living in Jerusalem and in the land of Israel: They will eat their food in anxiety and drink their water in despair, for their land will be stripped of everything in it because of the violence of all who live there. ²⁰The inhabited towns will be laid waste and the land will be desolate. Then you will know that I am the LORD.' "

²¹The word of the LORD came to me: ²²"Son of man, what is this proverb you have in the land of Israel: 'The days go by and every vision comes to nothing'? ²³Say to them, 'This is what the Sovereign LORD says: I am going to put an end to this proverb, and they will no longer quote it in Israel.' Say to them, 'The days are near when every vision will be fulfilled. ²⁴For there will be no more false visions or flattering divinations among the people of Israel. ²⁵But I the LORD will speak what I will, and it shall be fulfilled without delay. For in your days, you rebellious house, I will fulfill whatever I say, declares the Sovereign LORD.' "

²⁶The word of the LORD came to me: ²⁷"Son of man, the house of Israel is saying, 'The vision he sees is for many years from now, and he prophesies about the distant future.'

²⁸"Therefore say to them, 'This is what the Sovereign LORD says: None of my words will be delayed any longer; whatever I say will be fulfilled, declares the Sovereign LORD.' "

False Prophets Condemned

13 The word of the LORD came to me: ²"Son of man, prophesy against the prophets of Israel who are now prophesying. Say to those who prophesy out of their own imagination: 'Hear the word of the LORD! ³This is what the Sovereign LORD says: Woe to the foolishᵃ prophets who follow their own spirit and have seen nothing! ⁴Your prophets, O Israel, are like jackals among ruins. ⁵You have not gone up to the breaks in the wall to repair it for the house of Israel so that it will stand firm in the battle on the day of the LORD. ⁶Their visions are false and their divinations a lie. They say, "The LORD declares," when the LORD has not sent them; yet they expect their words to be fulfilled. ⁷Have you not seen false visions and uttered lying divinations when you say, "The LORD declares," though I have not spoken?

⁸" 'Therefore this is what the Sovereign LORD says: Because of your false words and lying visions, I am against you, declares the Sovereign LORD. ⁹My hand will be against the prophets who see false visions and utter lying divinations. They will not belong to the council of my people or be listed in the records of the house of Israel, nor will they enter the land of Israel. Then you will know that I am the Sovereign LORD.

¹⁰" 'Because they lead my people astray, saying, "Peace,"

ᵃ 3 Or *wicked*

when there is no peace, and because, when a flimsy wall is built, they cover it with whitewash, ¹¹therefore tell those who cover it with whitewash that it is going to fall. Rain will come in torrents, and I will send hailstones hurtling down, and violent winds will burst forth. ¹²When the wall collapses, will people not ask you, "Where is the whitewash you covered it with?"

¹³ "'Therefore this is what the Sovereign LORD says: In my wrath I will unleash a violent wind, and in my anger hailstones and torrents of rain will fall with destructive fury. ¹⁴I will tear down the wall you have covered with whitewash and will level it to the ground so that its foundation will be laid bare. When it*ᵃ* falls, you will be destroyed in it; and you will know that I am the LORD. ¹⁵So I will spend my wrath against the wall and against those who covered it with whitewash. I will say to you, "The wall is gone and so are those who whitewashed it, ¹⁶those prophets of Israel who prophesied to Jerusalem and saw visions of peace for her when there was no peace, declares the Sovereign LORD."'

¹⁷"Now, son of man, set your face against the daughters of your people who prophesy out of their own imagination. Prophesy against them ¹⁸and say, 'This is what the Sovereign LORD says: Woe to the women who sew magic charms on all their wrists and make veils of various lengths for their heads in order to ensnare people. Will you ensnare the lives of my people but preserve your own? ¹⁹You have profaned me among my people for a few handfuls of barley and scraps of bread. By lying to my people, who listen to lies, you have killed those who should not have died and have spared those who should not live.

²⁰ "'Therefore this is what the Sovereign LORD says: I am against your magic charms with which you ensnare people like birds and I will tear them from your arms; I will set free the people that you ensnare like birds. ²¹I will tear off your veils and save my people from your hands, and they will no longer fall prey to your power. Then you will know that I am the LORD. ²²Because you disheartened the righteous with your lies, when I had brought them no grief, and because you encouraged the wicked not to turn from their evil ways and so save their lives, ²³therefore you will no longer see false visions or practice divination. I will save my people from your hands. And then you will know that I am the LORD.'"

Idolaters Condemned

14 Some of the elders of Israel came to me and sat down in front of me. ²Then the word of the LORD came to me: ³"Son of man, these men have set up idols in their hearts and put wicked stumbling blocks before their faces. Should I let them inquire of me at all? ⁴Therefore speak to them and tell them, 'This is what the Sovereign LORD says: When any Israelite sets up idols in his heart and puts a wicked stumbling block before his face and then goes to a prophet, I the LORD will answer him myself in keeping with his great idolatry. ⁵I will do this to recapture the hearts of the people of Israel, who have all deserted me for their idols.'

⁶"Therefore say to the house of Israel, 'This is what the

Discernment

Ezekiel prophesies against false prophets who mislead the people and proclaim peace when in fact Babylon is about to destroy Jerusalem. They are like whitewashed walls that look good but do not seal against storms and cannot stand against wind and rain. Their words and their actions deceive the people.

Are there true prophets today? Who is calling the church to reach out to the lost and care for the lonely? Whose words are reflected in their deeds? Spend a few minutes in prayer that is discerning, and ask God to help you pay heed to modern-day prophets who speak God's true words.

See Meeting God in Service

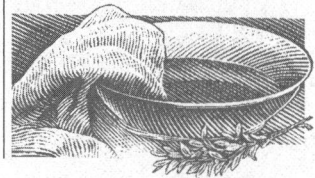

Repent and Turn

EZEKIEL 14:1–11

"To repent is to come to your senses. It is not so much something you do as something that happens. True repentance spends less time looking at the past and saying, 'I'm sorry,' than to the future and saying 'Wow!'"

—FREDERICK BUECHNER,
Wishful Thinking

Sovereign LORD says: Repent! Turn from your idols and renounce all your detestable practices!

7" 'When any Israelite or any alien living in Israel separates himself from me and sets up idols in his heart and puts a wicked stumbling block before his face and then goes to a prophet to inquire of me, I the LORD will answer him myself. 8 I will set my face against that man and make him an example and a byword. I will cut him off from my people. Then you will know that I am the LORD.

9" 'And if the prophet is enticed to utter a prophecy, I the LORD have enticed that prophet, and I will stretch out my hand against him and destroy him from among my people Israel. 10 They will bear their guilt—the prophet will be as guilty as the one who consults him. 11 Then the people of Israel will no longer stray from me, nor will they defile themselves anymore with all their sins. They will be my people, and I will be their God, declares the Sovereign LORD.' "

Judgment Inescapable

12 The word of the LORD came to me: 13 "Son of man, if a country sins against me by being unfaithful and I stretch out my hand against it to cut off its food supply and send famine upon it and kill its men and their animals, 14 even if these three men—Noah, Daniel[a] and Job—were in it, they could save only themselves by their righteousness, declares the Sovereign LORD.

15 "Or if I send wild beasts through that country and they leave it childless and it becomes desolate so that no one can pass through it because of the beasts, 16 as surely as I live, declares the Sovereign LORD, even if these three men were in it, they could not save their own sons or daughters. They alone would be saved, but the land would be desolate.

17 "Or if I bring a sword against that country and say, 'Let the sword pass throughout the land,' and I kill its men and their animals, 18 as surely as I live, declares the Sovereign LORD, even if these three men were in it, they could not save their own sons or daughters. They alone would be saved.

19 "Or if I send a plague into that land and pour out my wrath upon it through bloodshed, killing its men and their animals, 20 as surely as I live, declares the Sovereign LORD, even if Noah, Daniel and Job were in it, they could save neither son nor daughter. They would save only themselves by their righteousness.

21 "For this is what the Sovereign LORD says: How much worse will it be when I send against Jerusalem my four dreadful judgments—sword and famine and wild beasts and plague—to kill its men and their animals! 22 Yet there will be some survivors—sons and daughters who will be brought out of it. They will come to you, and when you see their conduct and their actions, you will be consoled regarding the disaster I have brought upon Jerusalem—every disaster I have brought upon it. 23 You will be consoled when you see their conduct and their actions, for you will know that I have done nothing in it without cause, declares the Sovereign LORD."

a 14 Or *Danel*; the Hebrew spelling may suggest a person other than the prophet Daniel; also in verse 20.

Jerusalem, A Useless Vine

15 The word of the Lord came to me: ²"Son of man, how is the wood of a vine better than that of a branch on any of the trees in the forest? ³Is wood ever taken from it to make anything useful? Do they make pegs from it to hang things on? ⁴And after it is thrown on the fire as fuel and the fire burns both ends and chars the middle, is it then useful for anything? ⁵If it was not useful for anything when it was whole, how much less can it be made into something useful when the fire has burned it and it is charred?

⁶"Therefore this is what the Sovereign Lord says: As I have given the wood of the vine among the trees of the forest as fuel for the fire, so will I treat the people living in Jerusalem. ⁷I will set my face against them. Although they have come out of the fire, the fire will yet consume them. And when I set my face against them, you will know that I am the Lord. ⁸I will make the land desolate because they have been unfaithful, declares the Sovereign Lord."

An Allegory of Unfaithful Jerusalem

16 The word of the Lord came to me: ²"Son of man, confront Jerusalem with her detestable practices ³and say, 'This is what the Sovereign Lord says to Jerusalem: Your ancestry and birth were in the land of the Canaanites; your father was an Amorite and your mother a Hittite. ⁴On the day you were born your cord was not cut, nor were you washed with water to make you clean, nor were you rubbed with salt or wrapped in cloths. ⁵No one looked on you with pity or had compassion enough to do any of these things for you. Rather, you were thrown out into the open field, for on the day you were born you were despised.

⁶"'Then I passed by and saw you kicking about in your blood, and as you lay there in your blood I said to you, "Live!"ᵃ ⁷I made you grow like a plant of the field. You grew up and developed and became the most beautiful of jewels.ᵇ Your breasts were formed and your hair grew, you who were naked and bare.

⁸"'Later I passed by, and when I looked at you and saw that you were old enough for love, I spread the corner of my garment over you and covered your nakedness. I gave you my solemn oath and entered into a covenant with you, declares the Sovereign Lord, and you became mine.

⁹"'I bathedᶜ you with water and washed the blood from you and put ointments on you. ¹⁰I clothed you with an embroidered dress and put leather sandals on you. I dressed you in fine linen and covered you with costly garments. ¹¹I adorned you with jewelry: I put bracelets on your arms and a necklace around your neck, ¹²and I put a ring on your nose, earrings on your ears and a beautiful crown on your head. ¹³So you were adorned with gold and silver; your clothes were of fine linen and costly fabric and embroidered cloth. Your food was fine flour, honey and olive oil. You became very beautiful and rose to be a queen. ¹⁴And your fame spread among the nations on account of your

---

The Vine

EZEKIEL 15:1–8

Ezekiel employs a harsh and bitter image to convince the people how serious their unfaithfulness is in God's eyes. He compares them to the wood of vines—wood that is of little value in making anything useful and is useless even as firewood.

Difficult as it may be, recall a time in your adult life when you were severely, but appropriately, criticized. Can you remember the guilt and shame you felt? How did you respond? Did you try to defend yourself or did you admit your mistakes? How did you seek forgiveness? Write a prayer of confession that is specific to you alone and to your own particular failings. Offer it to God in prayer. Ask God to show you in some concrete way the forgiveness he offers you.

See *Meeting God in Everyday Life*

ᵃ 6 A few Hebrew manuscripts, Septuagint and Syriac; most Hebrew manuscripts *"Live!" And as you lay there in your blood I said to you, "Live!"*
ᵇ 7 Or *became mature*   ᶜ 9 Or *I had bathed*

Looking for Love

EZEKIEL 16:26–29

God compares Jerusalem to an unfaithful bride. She is the masthead of a nation that has turned away from the loving intentions of God. She is looking for love in all the wrong places, worshiping idols and forging unholy alliances.

The apostle John refers to the New Testament church as the bride of Christ (see Revelation 19:7). Sometimes churches turn away from following their one true love. Draw a picture of your church and write "Jesus Christ" in the center of the picture. All around the outside of the building write or picture some of the temptations that may distract your church from following Jesus. Refer to your drawing as you pray.

See Meeting God in Community

beauty, because the splendor I had given you made your beauty perfect, declares the Sovereign LORD.

¹⁵ " 'But you trusted in your beauty and used your fame to become a prostitute. You lavished your favors on anyone who passed by and your beauty became his.ᵃ ¹⁶You took some of your garments to make gaudy high places, where you carried on your prostitution. Such things should not happen, nor should they ever occur. ¹⁷You also took the fine jewelry I gave you, the jewelry made of my gold and silver, and you made for yourself male idols and engaged in prostitution with them. ¹⁸And you took your embroidered clothes to put on them, and you offered my oil and incense before them. ¹⁹Also the food I provided for you—the fine flour, olive oil and honey I gave you to eat—you offered as fragrant incense before them. That is what happened, declares the Sovereign LORD.

²⁰ " 'And you took your sons and daughters whom you bore to me and sacrificed them as food to the idols. Was your prostitution not enough? ²¹You slaughtered my children and sacrificed themᵇ to the idols. ²²In all your detestable practices and your prostitution you did not remember the days of your youth, when you were naked and bare, kicking about in your blood.

²³ " 'Woe! Woe to you, declares the Sovereign LORD. In addition to all your other wickedness, ²⁴you built a mound for yourself and made a lofty shrine in every public square. ²⁵At the head of every street you built your lofty shrines and degraded your beauty, offering your body with increasing promiscuity to anyone who passed by. ²⁶You engaged in prostitution with the Egyptians, your lustful neighbors, and provoked me to anger with your increasing promiscuity. ²⁷So I stretched out my hand against you and reduced your territory; I gave you over to the greed of your enemies, the daughters of the Philistines, who were shocked by your lewd conduct. ²⁸You engaged in prostitution with the Assyrians too, because you were insatiable; and even after that, you still were not satisfied. ²⁹Then you increased your promiscuity to include Babylonia,ᶜ a land of merchants, but even with this you were not satisfied.

³⁰ " 'How weak-willed you are, declares the Sovereign LORD, when you do all these things, acting like a brazen prostitute! ³¹When you built your mounds at the head of every street and made your lofty shrines in every public square, you were unlike a prostitute, because you scorned payment.

³² " 'You adulterous wife! You prefer strangers to your own husband! ³³Every prostitute receives a fee, but you give gifts to all your lovers, bribing them to come to you from everywhere for your illicit favors. ³⁴So in your prostitution you are the opposite of others; no one runs after you for your favors. You are the very opposite, for you give payment and none is given to you.

³⁵ " 'Therefore, you prostitute, hear the word of the LORD! ³⁶This is what the Sovereign LORD says: Because you poured out your wealthᵈ and exposed your nakedness in your promiscuity with your lovers, and because of all your detestable idols, and because you gave them your children's

---

ᵃ 15 Most Hebrew manuscripts; one Hebrew manuscript (see some Septuagint manuscripts) *by. Such a thing should not happen*   ᵇ 21 Or *and made them pass through the fire*   ᶜ 29 Or *Chaldea*   ᵈ 36 Or *lust*

blood, ³⁷therefore I am going to gather all your lovers, with whom you found pleasure, those you loved as well as those you hated. I will gather them against you from all around and will strip you in front of them, and they will see all your nakedness. ³⁸I will sentence you to the punishment of women who commit adultery and who shed blood; I will bring upon you the blood vengeance of my wrath and jealous anger. ³⁹Then I will hand you over to your lovers, and they will tear down your mounds and destroy your lofty shrines. They will strip you of your clothes and take your fine jewelry and leave you naked and bare. ⁴⁰They will bring a mob against you, who will stone you and hack you to pieces with their swords. ⁴¹They will burn down your houses and inflict punishment on you in the sight of many women. I will put a stop to your prostitution, and you will no longer pay your lovers. ⁴²Then my wrath against you will subside and my jealous anger will turn away from you; I will be calm and no longer angry.

⁴³" 'Because you did not remember the days of your youth but enraged me with all these things, I will surely bring down on your head what you have done, declares the Sovereign LORD. Did you not add lewdness to all your other detestable practices?

⁴⁴" 'Everyone who quotes proverbs will quote this proverb about you: "Like mother, like daughter." ⁴⁵You are a true daughter of your mother, who despised her husband and her children; and you are a true sister of your sisters, who despised their husbands and their children. Your mother was a Hittite and your father an Amorite. ⁴⁶Your older sister was Samaria, who lived to the north of you with her daughters; and your younger sister, who lived to the south of you with her daughters, was Sodom. ⁴⁷You not only walked in their ways and copied their detestable practices, but in all your ways you soon became more depraved than they. ⁴⁸As surely as I live, declares the Sovereign LORD, your sister Sodom and her daughters never did what you and your daughters have done.

⁴⁹" 'Now this was the sin of your sister Sodom: She and her daughters were arrogant, overfed and unconcerned; they did not help the poor and needy. ⁵⁰They were haughty and did detestable things before me. Therefore I did away with them as you have seen. ⁵¹Samaria did not commit half the sins you did. You have done more detestable things than they, and have made your sisters seem righteous by all these things you have done. ⁵²Bear your disgrace, for you have furnished some justification for your sisters. Because your sins were more vile than theirs, they appear more righteous than you. So then, be ashamed and bear your disgrace, for you have made your sisters appear righteous.

⁵³" 'However, I will restore the fortunes of Sodom and her daughters and of Samaria and her daughters, and your fortunes along with them, ⁵⁴so that you may bear your disgrace and be ashamed of all you have done in giving them comfort. ⁵⁵And your sisters, Sodom with her daughters and Samaria with her daughters, will return to what they were before; and you and your daughters will return to what you were before. ⁵⁶You would not even mention your sister Sodom in the day of your pride, ⁵⁷before your wickedness was uncovered. Even so, you are now scorned by the

Hope Is Never Far Away

EZEKIEL 16:53–55

Jerusalem has been a faithless bride. Ezekiel has vividly described her behavior and condemned her ways. Yet hope is never far away and God's love is stronger than his judgment. "I will restore . . . your fortunes."

Assume a posture of disgrace or shame. You might bow your head and body, for example, or lie facedown on the floor. Now act out a gradual awakening to restoration. Is it a quiet movement of chastened confidence or a joyous prancing of great leaps? Imagine what it is like to return to your true love and be forgiven and embraced. Turn around and around. Enjoy being restored to oneness with the love of your life.

See Meeting God in Scripture

God's Memory, Our Memory

EZEKIEL 16:60–63

Some people may have agile memories, but God's capacity to remember is infinite. God remembers the covenant of love he made with Abraham and Sarah, even though Israel repeatedly breaks the covenant and runs after other gods. It is as if God is saying, "I remember my covenant. I remember my promise of love. I remember, and I forgive." Let that picture of God sink into your heart.

Our memories often bring to mind the shameful things we have done. Our memories of shame have taught us to be humble: "You will remember and be ashamed and never again open your mouth because of your humiliation." But our memories of God's faithfulness also teach us to return again and again to a God who remembers to love us. Let your memories of God's faithfulness and forgiveness move you to pray with thanksgiving. You may wish to write your prayer in your journal.

See Meeting God in Prayer

daughters of Edom[a] and all her neighbors and the daughters of the Philistines—all those around you who despise you. ⁵⁸You will bear the consequences of your lewdness and your detestable practices, declares the LORD.

⁵⁹" 'This is what the Sovereign LORD says: I will deal with you as you deserve, because you have despised my oath by breaking the covenant. ⁶⁰Yet I will remember the covenant I made with you in the days of your youth, and I will establish an everlasting covenant with you. ⁶¹Then you will remember your ways and be ashamed when you receive your sisters, both those who are older than you and those who are younger. I will give them to you as daughters, but not on the basis of my covenant with you. ⁶²So I will establish my covenant with you, and you will know that I am the LORD. ⁶³Then, when I make atonement for you for all you have done, you will remember and be ashamed and never again open your mouth because of your humiliation, declares the Sovereign LORD.' "

Two Eagles and a Vine

17 The word of the LORD came to me: ²"Son of man, set forth an allegory and tell the house of Israel a parable. ³Say to them, 'This is what the Sovereign LORD says: A great eagle with powerful wings, long feathers and full plumage of varied colors came to Lebanon. Taking hold of the top of a cedar, ⁴he broke off its topmost shoot and carried it away to a land of merchants, where he planted it in a city of traders.

⁵" 'He took some of the seed of your land and put it in fertile soil. He planted it like a willow by abundant water, ⁶and it sprouted and became a low, spreading vine. Its branches turned toward him, but its roots remained under it. So it became a vine and produced branches and put out leafy boughs.

⁷" 'But there was another great eagle with powerful wings and full plumage. The vine now sent out its roots toward him from the plot where it was planted and stretched out its branches to him for water. ⁸It had been planted in good soil by abundant water so that it would produce branches, bear fruit and become a splendid vine.'

⁹"Say to them, 'This is what the Sovereign LORD says: Will it thrive? Will it not be uprooted and stripped of its fruit so that it withers? All its new growth will wither. It will not take a strong arm or many people to pull it up by the roots. ¹⁰Even if it is transplanted, will it thrive? Will it not wither completely when the east wind strikes it—wither away in the plot where it grew?' "

¹¹Then the word of the LORD came to me: ¹²"Say to this rebellious house, 'Do you not know what these things mean?' Say to them: 'The king of Babylon went to Jerusalem and carried off her king and her nobles, bringing them back with him to Babylon. ¹³Then he took a member of the royal family and made a treaty with him, putting him under oath. He also carried away the leading men of the land, ¹⁴so that the kingdom would be brought low, unable to rise again, surviving only by keeping his treaty. ¹⁵But the king rebelled against him by sending his envoys to Egypt to get horses and a large army. Will he succeed? Will he who

---

a 57 Many Hebrew manuscripts and Syriac; most Hebrew manuscripts, Septuagint and Vulgate *Aram*

does such things escape? Will he break the treaty and yet escape?

¹⁶ " 'As surely as I live, declares the Sovereign LORD, he shall die in Babylon, in the land of the king who put him on the throne, whose oath he despised and whose treaty he broke. ¹⁷Pharaoh with his mighty army and great horde will be of no help to him in war, when ramps are built and siege works erected to destroy many lives. ¹⁸He despised the oath by breaking the covenant. Because he had given his hand in pledge and yet did all these things, he shall not escape.

¹⁹ " 'Therefore this is what the Sovereign LORD says: As surely as I live, I will bring down on his head my oath that he despised and my covenant that he broke. ²⁰I will spread my net for him, and he will be caught in my snare. I will bring him to Babylon and execute judgment upon him there because he was unfaithful to me. ²¹All his fleeing troops will fall by the sword, and the survivors will be scattered to the winds. Then you will know that I the LORD have spoken.

²² " 'This is what the Sovereign LORD says: I myself will take a shoot from the very top of a cedar and plant it; I will break off a tender sprig from its topmost shoots and plant it on a high and lofty mountain. ²³On the mountain heights of Israel I will plant it; it will produce branches and bear fruit and become a splendid cedar. Birds of every kind will nest in it; they will find shelter in the shade of its branches. ²⁴All the trees of the field will know that I the LORD bring down the tall tree and make the low tree grow tall. I dry up the green tree and make the dry tree flourish.

" 'I the LORD have spoken, and I will do it.' "

The Soul Who Sins Will Die

18 The word of the LORD came to me: ²"What do you people mean by quoting this proverb about the land of Israel:

" 'The fathers eat sour grapes,
    and the children's teeth are set on edge'?

³"As surely as I live, declares the Sovereign LORD, you will no longer quote this proverb in Israel. ⁴For every living soul belongs to me, the father as well as the son—both alike belong to me. The soul who sins is the one who will die.

⁵ "Suppose there is a righteous man
    who does what is just and right.
⁶He does not eat at the mountain shrines
    or look to the idols of the house of Israel.
He does not defile his neighbor's wife
    or lie with a woman during her period.
⁷He does not oppress anyone,
    but returns what he took in pledge for a loan.
He does not commit robbery
    but gives his food to the hungry
    and provides clothing for the naked.
⁸He does not lend at usury
    or take excessive interest.ᵃ
He withholds his hand from doing wrong
    and judges fairly between man and man.

A New Branch Bears Fruit

EZEKIEL 17:22–24

"Later the soul will bring forth fruit exactly in the measure in which the inner life is developed in it. If there is no inner life, however great may be the zeal, the high intention, the hard work, no fruit will come forth; it is like a spring that would give out sanctity to others but cannot, having none to give; one can only give that which one has. It is in solitude, in that lonely life alone with God, in profound recollection of soul, in forgetfulness of all created things, that God gives himself to the soul that thus gives itself whole and entire to him."

—CHARLES DE FOUCAULD,
Meditations of a Hermit

ᵃ8 Or *take interest*; similarly in verses 13 and 17

Bearing Our Own Responsibility

EZEKIEL 18:19–20

"It's not my fault" is a familiar refrain. We complain that our parents didn't love us enough. Our schools gave us an inadequate education. Our bosses didn't spend enough time with us, so we didn't know what was expected of us. There is always someone we can blame if we choose to.

Here in Ezekiel neither the sins nor the blessings are transferred to the next generation. There is to be no blaming others for troubles and no resting on the righteousness of someone else. This is an ethic of personal responsibility. When have you blamed others for your problems? Taken credit for another's efforts? Take some time to write in your journal about your own ethic of responsibility.

See Meeting God in Everyday Life

⁹He follows my decrees
     and faithfully keeps my laws.
That man is righteous;
     he will surely live,
                    declares the Sovereign LORD.

¹⁰"Suppose he has a violent son, who sheds blood or does any of these other things*ᵃ* ¹¹(though the father has done none of them):

"He eats at the mountain shrines.
     He defiles his neighbor's wife.
¹²He oppresses the poor and needy.
     He commits robbery.
He does not return what he took in pledge.
     He looks to the idols.
He does detestable things.
¹³He lends at usury and takes excessive interest.

Will such a man live? He will not! Because he has done all these detestable things, he will surely be put to death and his blood will be on his own head.

¹⁴"But suppose this son has a son who sees all the sins his father commits, and though he sees them, he does not do such things:

¹⁵"He does not eat at the mountain shrines
     or look to the idols of the house of Israel.
He does not defile his neighbor's wife.
¹⁶He does not oppress anyone
     or require a pledge for a loan.
He does not commit robbery
     but gives his food to the hungry
     and provides clothing for the naked.
¹⁷He withholds his hand from sin*ᵇ*
     and takes no usury or excessive interest.
He keeps my laws and follows my decrees.

He will not die for his father's sin; he will surely live. ¹⁸But his father will die for his own sin, because he practiced extortion, robbed his brother and did what was wrong among his people.

¹⁹"Yet you ask, 'Why does the son not share the guilt of his father?' Since the son has done what is just and right and has been careful to keep all my decrees, he will surely live. ²⁰The soul who sins is the one who will die. The son will not share the guilt of the father, nor will the father share the guilt of the son. The righteousness of the righteous man will be credited to him, and the wickedness of the wicked will be charged against him.

²¹"But if a wicked man turns away from all the sins he has committed and keeps all my decrees and does what is just and right, he will surely live; he will not die. ²²None of the offenses he has committed will be remembered against him. Because of the righteous things he has done, he will live. ²³Do I take any pleasure in the death of the wicked? declares the Sovereign LORD. Rather, am I not pleased when they turn from their ways and live?

²⁴"But if a righteous man turns from his righteousness and commits sin and does the same detestable things the

---

ᵃ 10 Or *things to a brother*   *ᵇ 17* Septuagint (see also verse 8); Hebrew *from the poor*

wicked man does, will he live? None of the righteous things he has done will be remembered. Because of the unfaithfulness he is guilty of and because of the sins he has committed, he will die.

25"Yet you say, 'The way of the Lord is not just.' Hear, O house of Israel: Is my way unjust? Is it not your ways that are unjust? 26If a righteous man turns from his righteousness and commits sin, he will die for it; because of the sin he has committed he will die. 27But if a wicked man turns away from the wickedness he has committed and does what is just and right, he will save his life. 28Because he considers all the offenses he has committed and turns away from them, he will surely live; he will not die. 29Yet the house of Israel says, 'The way of the Lord is not just.' Are my ways unjust, O house of Israel? Is it not your ways that are unjust?

30"Therefore, O house of Israel, I will judge you, each one according to his ways, declares the Sovereign LORD. Repent! Turn away from all your offenses; then sin will not be your downfall. 31Rid yourselves of all the offenses you have committed, and get a new heart and a new spirit. Why will you die, O house of Israel? 32For I take no pleasure in the death of anyone, declares the Sovereign LORD. Repent and live!

A Lament for Israel's Princes

19 "Take up a lament concerning the princes of Israel 2and say:

" 'What a lioness was your mother
    among the lions!
She lay down among the young lions
    and reared her cubs.
3She brought up one of her cubs,
    and he became a strong lion.
He learned to tear the prey
    and he devoured men.
4The nations heard about him,
    and he was trapped in their pit.
They led him with hooks
    to the land of Egypt.

5" 'When she saw her hope unfulfilled,
    her expectation gone,
she took another of her cubs
    and made him a strong lion.
6He prowled among the lions,
    for he was now a strong lion.
He learned to tear the prey
    and he devoured men.
7He broke down*a* their strongholds
    and devastated their towns.
The land and all who were in it
    were terrified by his roaring.
8Then the nations came against him,
    those from regions round about.
They spread their net for him,
    and he was trapped in their pit.
9With hooks they pulled him into a cage
    and brought him to the king of Babylon.
They put him in prison,

---

a 7 Targum (see Septuagint); Hebrew *He knew*

A New Heart

EZEKIEL 18:30–32

"We are speaking about a mystery for which words are inadequate. It is the mystery that the heart, which is the center of our being, is transformed by God into his own heart, a heart large enough to embrace the entire universe. Through prayer we can carry in our heart all human pain and sorrow, all conflicts and agonies, all torture and war, all hunger, loneliness, and misery, not because of some great psychological or emotional capacity, but because God's heart has become one with ours."

—HENRI J. M. NOUWEN,
The Way of the Heart

Lamentation

EZEKIEL 19:9–14

Life does not always go smoothly, even in the best of times, even for those born with seemingly everything going for them. The best-laid plans—like those for the finest youths of the Davidic dynasty—can go awry. Where does one go when disaster turns life into a dry and thirsty land? The Hebrews believed you could go to God and complain. Their prayers of lament told God in strong language what they believed to be wrong and why God should intervene. Their prayers were full of anguish but also full of faith that God would intervene.

Try writing a lament. Tell God about your concern, your anger, and why you feel God should intervene in the circumstances that trouble you. End by reaffirming your trust in God and thanking him for hearing your prayer.

See *Meeting God in Scripture*

so his roar was heard no longer
on the mountains of Israel.

¹⁰ " 'Your mother was like a vine in your vineyard*a*
planted by the water;
it was fruitful and full of branches
because of abundant water.
¹¹ Its branches were strong,
fit for a ruler's scepter.
It towered high
above the thick foliage,
conspicuous for its height
and for its many branches.
¹² But it was uprooted in fury
and thrown to the ground.
The east wind made it shrivel,
it was stripped of its fruit;
its strong branches withered
and fire consumed them.
¹³ Now it is planted in the desert,
in a dry and thirsty land.
¹⁴ Fire spread from one of its main*b* branches
and consumed its fruit.
No strong branch is left on it
fit for a ruler's scepter.'

This is a lament and is to be used as a lament."

Rebellious Israel

20 In the seventh year, in the fifth month on the tenth day, some of the elders of Israel came to inquire of the LORD, and they sat down in front of me.

²Then the word of the LORD came to me: ³"Son of man, speak to the elders of Israel and say to them, 'This is what the Sovereign LORD says: Have you come to inquire of me? As surely as I live, I will not let you inquire of me, declares the Sovereign LORD.'

⁴"Will you judge them? Will you judge them, son of man? Then confront them with the detestable practices of their fathers ⁵and say to them: 'This is what the Sovereign LORD says: On the day I chose Israel, I swore with uplifted hand to the descendants of the house of Jacob and revealed myself to them in Egypt. With uplifted hand I said to them, "I am the LORD your God." ⁶On that day I swore to them that I would bring them out of Egypt into a land I had searched out for them, a land flowing with milk and honey, the most beautiful of all lands. ⁷And I said to them, "Each of you, get rid of the vile images you have set your eyes on, and do not defile yourselves with the idols of Egypt. I am the LORD your God."

⁸" 'But they rebelled against me and would not listen to me; they did not get rid of the vile images they had set their eyes on, nor did they forsake the idols of Egypt. So I said I would pour out my wrath on them and spend my anger against them in Egypt. ⁹But for the sake of my name I did what would keep it from being profaned in the eyes of the nations they lived among and in whose sight I had revealed myself to the Israelites by bringing them out of Egypt. ¹⁰Therefore I led them out of Egypt and brought

a 10 Two Hebrew manuscripts; most Hebrew manuscripts *your blood*
b 14 Or *from under its*

them into the desert. ¹¹I gave them my decrees and made known to them my laws, for the man who obeys them will live by them. ¹²Also I gave them my Sabbaths as a sign between us, so they would know that I the LORD made them holy.

¹³" 'Yet the people of Israel rebelled against me in the desert. They did not follow my decrees but rejected my laws—although the man who obeys them will live by them—and they utterly desecrated my Sabbaths. So I said I would pour out my wrath on them and destroy them in the desert. ¹⁴But for the sake of my name I did what would keep it from being profaned in the eyes of the nations in whose sight I had brought them out. ¹⁵Also with uplifted hand I swore to them in the desert that I would not bring them into the land I had given them—a land flowing with milk and honey, most beautiful of all lands— ¹⁶because they rejected my laws and did not follow my decrees and desecrated my Sabbaths. For their hearts were devoted to their idols. ¹⁷Yet I looked on them with pity and did not destroy them or put an end to them in the desert. ¹⁸I said to their children in the desert, "Do not follow the statutes of your fathers or keep their laws or defile yourselves with their idols. ¹⁹I am the LORD your God; follow my decrees and be careful to keep my laws. ²⁰Keep my Sabbaths holy, that they may be a sign between us. Then you will know that I am the LORD your God."

²¹" 'But the children rebelled against me: They did not follow my decrees, they were not careful to keep my laws—although the man who obeys them will live by them—and they desecrated my Sabbaths. So I said I would pour out my wrath on them and spend my anger against them in the desert. ²²But I withheld my hand, and for the sake of my name I did what would keep it from being profaned in the eyes of the nations in whose sight I had brought them out. ²³Also with uplifted hand I swore to them in the desert that I would disperse them among the nations and scatter them through the countries, ²⁴because they had not obeyed my laws but had rejected my decrees and desecrated my Sabbaths, and their eyes lusted after their fathers' idols. ²⁵I also gave them over to statutes that were not good and laws they could not live by; ²⁶I let them become defiled through their gifts—the sacrifice of every firstborn*ᵃ*—that I might fill them with horror so they would know that I am the LORD.'

²⁷"Therefore, son of man, speak to the people of Israel and say to them, 'This is what the Sovereign LORD says: In this also your fathers blasphemed me by forsaking me: ²⁸When I brought them into the land I had sworn to give them and they saw any high hill or any leafy tree, there they offered their sacrifices, made offerings that provoked me to anger, presented their fragrant incense and poured out their drink offerings. ²⁹Then I said to them: What is this high place you go to?' " (It is called Bamah*ᵇ* to this day.)

Judgment and Restoration

³⁰"Therefore say to the house of Israel: 'This is what the Sovereign LORD says: Will you defile yourselves the way your fathers did and lust after their vile images? ³¹When

---

The Gift of Sabbath

EZEKIEL 20:10–13

When is your Sabbath? What day is your special time to rest in God? When do you cease being busy and just stop to acknowledge your Creator, your Savior?

In a wonderfully poignant lament, God expresses his distress at the misuse of the Sabbath: "I gave them my Sabbaths as a sign between us, so they would know that I the LORD made them holy." The Sabbath is a gift to us so that we will remember that God made us to be holy.

Take a look at your week and set aside a Sabbath time—a time and a place to focus on God. A whole day is wonderful. An hour is a start. Try to be aware during the whole period of time that God wants to be with you as much (or more!) as you want to be with God. Allow yourself to dwell in God's holy presence.

See Meeting God in the Created Order

ᵃ 26 Or —*making every firstborn pass through the fire* *ᵇ 29 Bamah* means *high place.*

Desert Journeys

EZEKIEL 20:34–37,41–44

Our lives are shaped by desert experiences. Like the Israelites in exile, we experience times and places in which we search for our authentic selves. The desert places often involve suffering, purifying, examining, wandering, correcting and remembering. God always accompanies us to the desert to help us discover our identity and lead us home.

Take a sheet of paper and draw or paint a picture of your desert. Where are you on the journey through it? Just beginning? Lost and searching for direction? Almost home? Are there any companions with you? Do you have a title for your desert picture?

See Meeting God in Scripture

you offer your gifts—the sacrifice of your sons in[a] the fire—you continue to defile yourselves with all your idols to this day. Am I to let you inquire of me, O house of Israel? As surely as I live, declares the Sovereign LORD, I will not let you inquire of me.

³²" 'You say, "We want to be like the nations, like the peoples of the world, who serve wood and stone." But what you have in mind will never happen. ³³As surely as I live, declares the Sovereign LORD, I will rule over you with a mighty hand and an outstretched arm and with outpoured wrath. ³⁴I will bring you from the nations and gather you from the countries where you have been scattered—with a mighty hand and an outstretched arm and with outpoured wrath. ³⁵I will bring you into the desert of the nations and there, face to face, I will execute judgment upon you. ³⁶As I judged your fathers in the desert of the land of Egypt, so I will judge you, declares the Sovereign LORD. ³⁷I will take note of you as you pass under my rod, and I will bring you into the bond of the covenant. ³⁸I will purge you of those who revolt and rebel against me. Although I will bring them out of the land where they are living, yet they will not enter the land of Israel. Then you will know that I am the LORD.

³⁹" 'As for you, O house of Israel, this is what the Sovereign LORD says: Go and serve your idols, every one of you! But afterward you will surely listen to me and no longer profane my holy name with your gifts and idols. ⁴⁰For on my holy mountain, the high mountain of Israel, declares the Sovereign LORD, there in the land the entire house of Israel will serve me, and there I will accept them. There I will require your offerings and your choice gifts,[b] along with all your holy sacrifices. ⁴¹I will accept you as fragrant incense when I bring you out from the nations and gather you from the countries where you have been scattered, and I will show myself holy among you in the sight of the nations. ⁴²Then you will know that I am the LORD, when I bring you into the land of Israel, the land I had sworn with uplifted hand to give to your fathers. ⁴³There you will remember your conduct and all the actions by which you have defiled yourselves, and you will loathe yourselves for all the evil you have done. ⁴⁴You will know that I am the LORD, when I deal with you for my name's sake and not according to your evil ways and your corrupt practices, O house of Israel, declares the Sovereign LORD.' "

Prophecy Against the South

⁴⁵The word of the LORD came to me: ⁴⁶"Son of man, set your face toward the south; preach against the south and prophesy against the forest of the southland. ⁴⁷Say to the southern forest: 'Hear the word of the LORD. This is what the Sovereign LORD says: I am about to set fire to you, and it will consume all your trees, both green and dry. The blazing flame will not be quenched, and every face from south to north will be scorched by it. ⁴⁸Everyone will see that I the LORD have kindled it; it will not be quenched.' "

⁴⁹Then I said, "Ah, Sovereign LORD! They are saying of me, 'Isn't he just telling parables?' "

---

[a] *31* Or *—making your sons pass through*   [b] *40* Or *and the gifts of your firstfruits*

Babylon, God's Sword of Judgment

21 The word of the LORD came to me: ²"Son of man, set your face against Jerusalem and preach against the sanctuary. Prophesy against the land of Israel ³and say to her: 'This is what the LORD says: I am against you. I will draw my sword from its scabbard and cut off from you both the righteous and the wicked. ⁴Because I am going to cut off the righteous and the wicked, my sword will be unsheathed against everyone from south to north. ⁵Then all people will know that I the LORD have drawn my sword from its scabbard; it will not return again.'

⁶"Therefore groan, son of man! Groan before them with broken heart and bitter grief. ⁷And when they ask you, 'Why are you groaning?' you shall say, 'Because of the news that is coming. Every heart will melt and every hand go limp; every spirit will become faint and every knee become as weak as water.' It is coming! It will surely take place, declares the Sovereign LORD."

⁸The word of the LORD came to me: ⁹"Son of man, prophesy and say, 'This is what the Lord says:

" 'A sword, a sword,
    sharpened and polished—
¹⁰sharpened for the slaughter,
    polished to flash like lightning!

" 'Shall we rejoice in the scepter of my son ₍Judah₎? The sword despises every such stick.

¹¹ " 'The sword is appointed to be polished,
    to be grasped with the hand;
it is sharpened and polished,
    made ready for the hand of the slayer.
¹²Cry out and wail, son of man,
    for it is against my people;
it is against all the princes of Israel.
They are thrown to the sword
    along with my people.
Therefore beat your breast.

¹³" 'Testing will surely come. And what if the scepter ₍of Judah₎, which the sword despises, does not continue? declares the Sovereign LORD.'

¹⁴"So then, son of man, prophesy
    and strike your hands together.
Let the sword strike twice,
    even three times.
It is a sword for slaughter—
    a sword for great slaughter,
    closing in on them from every side.
¹⁵So that hearts may melt
    and the fallen be many,
I have stationed the sword for slaughter[a]
    at all their gates.
Oh! It is made to flash like lightning,
    it is grasped for slaughter.
¹⁶O sword, slash to the right,
    then to the left,
    wherever your blade is turned.
¹⁷I too will strike my hands together,

---

[a] 15 Septuagint; the meaning of the Hebrew for this word is uncertain.

Song of the Sword

EZEKIEL 21:4–12

Kneeling is a posture of humility; it is the posture of a person seeking forgiveness or the prayer position of someone seeking to discern God's will.

As God calls the Israelites to repent, so might we experience a call to confess our sins. Find a comfortable place and imagine that your knees are "as weak as water" so that you have to assume a posture of kneeling. Use this posture to offer a prayer of confession. Let the image of the sword help you let go of that which limits your discipleship. Rise from your knees renewed and forgiven.

See Meeting God in Scripture

and my wrath will subside.
I the LORD have spoken."

¹⁸The word of the LORD came to me: ¹⁹"Son of man, mark out two roads for the sword of the king of Babylon to take, both starting from the same country. Make a signpost where the road branches off to the city. ²⁰Mark out one road for the sword to come against Rabbah of the Ammonites and another against Judah and fortified Jerusalem. ²¹For the king of Babylon will stop at the fork in the road, at the junction of the two roads, to seek an omen: He will cast lots with arrows, he will consult his idols, he will examine the liver. ²²Into his right hand will come the lot for Jerusalem, where he is to set up battering rams, to give the command to slaughter, to sound the battle cry, to set battering rams against the gates, to build a ramp and to erect siege works. ²³It will seem like a false omen to those who have sworn allegiance to him, but he will remind them of their guilt and take them captive.

²⁴"Therefore this is what the Sovereign LORD says: 'Because you people have brought to mind your guilt by your open rebellion, revealing your sins in all that you do—because you have done this, you will be taken captive.

²⁵" 'O profane and wicked prince of Israel, whose day has come, whose time of punishment has reached its climax, ²⁶this is what the Sovereign LORD says: Take off the turban, remove the crown. It will not be as it was: The lowly will be exalted and the exalted will be brought low. ²⁷A ruin! A ruin! I will make it a ruin! It will not be restored until he comes to whom it rightfully belongs; to him I will give it.'

²⁸"And you, son of man, prophesy and say, 'This is what the Sovereign LORD says about the Ammonites and their insults:

" 'A sword, a sword,
    drawn for the slaughter,
polished to consume
    and to flash like lightning!
²⁹Despite false visions concerning you
    and lying divinations about you,
it will be laid on the necks
    of the wicked who are to be slain,
whose day has come,
    whose time of punishment has reached its
        climax.
³⁰Return the sword to its scabbard.
    In the place where you were created,
in the land of your ancestry,
    I will judge you.
³¹I will pour out my wrath upon you
    and breathe out my fiery anger against you;
I will hand you over to brutal men,
    men skilled in destruction.
³²You will be fuel for the fire,
    your blood will be shed in your land,
you will be remembered no more;
    for I the LORD have spoken.' "

Trouble Is Coming

EZEKIEL 21:25–28

"Count each affliction,
whether light or grave,
God's messenger
sent down to thee;
do thou
with courtesy receive him."
—AUBREY THOMAS DE VERE,
"Sorrow"

Jerusalem's Sins

22 The word of the LORD came to me: ²"Son of man, will you judge her? Will you judge this city of bloodshed? Then confront her with all her detestable practices ³and say: 'This is what the Sovereign LORD says: O city that brings on herself doom by shedding blood in her midst and defiles herself by making idols, ⁴you have become guilty because of the blood you have shed and have become defiled by the idols you have made. You have brought your days to a close, and the end of your years has come. Therefore I will make you an object of scorn to the nations and a laughingstock to all the countries. ⁵Those who are near and those who are far away will mock you, O infamous city, full of turmoil.

⁶" 'See how each of the princes of Israel who are in you uses his power to shed blood. ⁷In you they have treated father and mother with contempt; in you they have oppressed the alien and mistreated the fatherless and the widow. ⁸You have despised my holy things and desecrated my Sabbaths. ⁹In you are slanderous men bent on shedding blood; in you are those who eat at the mountain shrines and commit lewd acts. ¹⁰In you are those who dishonor their fathers' bed; in you are those who violate women during their period, when they are ceremonially unclean. ¹¹In you one man commits a detestable offense with his neighbor's wife, another shamefully defiles his daughter-in-law, and another violates his sister, his own father's daughter. ¹²In you men accept bribes to shed blood; you take usury and excessive interest[a] and make unjust gain from your neighbors by extortion. And you have forgotten me, declares the Sovereign LORD.

¹³" 'I will surely strike my hands together at the unjust gain you have made and at the blood you have shed in your midst. ¹⁴Will your courage endure or your hands be strong in the day I deal with you? I the LORD have spoken, and I will do it. ¹⁵I will disperse you among the nations and scatter you through the countries; and I will put an end to your uncleanness. ¹⁶When you have been defiled[b] in the eyes of the nations, you will know that I am the LORD.' "

¹⁷Then the word of the LORD came to me: ¹⁸"Son of man, the house of Israel has become dross to me; all of them are the copper, tin, iron and lead left inside a furnace. They are but the dross of silver. ¹⁹Therefore this is what the Sovereign LORD says: 'Because you have all become dross, I will gather you into Jerusalem. ²⁰As men gather silver, copper, iron, lead and tin into a furnace to melt it with a fiery blast, so will I gather you in my anger and my wrath and put you inside the city and melt you. ²¹I will gather you and I will blow on you with my fiery wrath, and you will be melted inside her. ²²As silver is melted in a furnace, so you will be melted inside her, and you will know that I the LORD have poured out my wrath upon you.' "

²³Again the word of the LORD came to me: ²⁴"Son of man, say to the land, 'You are a land that has had no rain or showers[c] in the day of wrath.' ²⁵There is a conspiracy of her princes[d] within her like a roaring lion tearing its prey; they devour people, take treasures and precious things and

---

If We Forget

EZEKIEL 22:12

The list of sins in this chapter is overwhelming: idolatry, injustice, violence, slander, adultery, fornication, extortion. Yet perhaps the most basic sin is that the people of Judah have forgotten God. They have forgotten their key relationship with the One who would curb their wandering and sinning.

We are in deep trouble if we forget to keep our eyes on God. Make a list of the good things that you have received from God. Begin each line with, "I remember when . . ." or "I remember the time . . ." Offer a prayer of thanksgiving when you have finished the list. Add to the list as you remember other blessings. Hang the list in a prominent place to help keep your heart, mind and soul focused on God and the blessings he has given you.

See Meeting God in Everyday Life

---

[a] 12 Or *usury and interest*   [b] 16 Or *When I have allotted you your inheritance*
[c] 24 Septuagint; Hebrew *has not been cleansed or rained on*
[d] 25 Septuagint; Hebrew *prophets*

Stand in the Gap

EZEKIEL 22:29–31

Imagine walking along a riverbank; heavy rains have caused the river to rise to a dangerous level. Sandbagging efforts have contained the river thus far, but you see a trickle of water seeping through the sandbags and know that the break could bring damage to the town. You see a shovel and sandbags left over from the night before and you set to work. You discover a surge of energy that keeps you strong; your shouts bring others to help you repair the breach.

God is looking for us to "stand in the gap." What are the problems of the day? Secularism? Racism? Poverty? Violence? Greed? Abuse and addictions? How might you be called on to stand in the gap? Which of your friends might help you address these problems? Choose one problem you can respond to today.

See Meeting God in Service

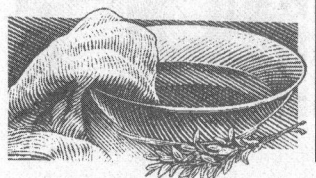

make many widows within her. ²⁶Her priests do violence to my law and profane my holy things; they do not distinguish between the holy and the common; they teach that there is no difference between the unclean and the clean; and they shut their eyes to the keeping of my Sabbaths, so that I am profaned among them. ²⁷Her officials within her are like wolves tearing their prey; they shed blood and kill people to make unjust gain. ²⁸Her prophets whitewash these deeds for them by false visions and lying divinations. They say, 'This is what the Sovereign LORD says'—when the LORD has not spoken. ²⁹The people of the land practice extortion and commit robbery; they oppress the poor and needy and mistreat the alien, denying them justice.

³⁰"I looked for a man among them who would build up the wall and stand before me in the gap on behalf of the land so I would not have to destroy it, but I found none. ³¹So I will pour out my wrath on them and consume them with my fiery anger, bringing down on their own heads all they have done, declares the Sovereign LORD."

Two Adulterous Sisters

23 The word of the LORD came to me: ²"Son of man, there were two women, daughters of the same mother. ³They became prostitutes in Egypt, engaging in prostitution from their youth. In that land their breasts were fondled and their virgin bosoms caressed. ⁴The older was named Oholah, and her sister was Oholibah. They were mine and gave birth to sons and daughters. Oholah is Samaria, and Oholibah is Jerusalem.

⁵"Oholah engaged in prostitution while she was still mine; and she lusted after her lovers, the Assyrians—warriors ⁶clothed in blue, governors and commanders, all of them handsome young men, and mounted horsemen. ⁷She gave herself as a prostitute to all the elite of the Assyrians and defiled herself with all the idols of everyone she lusted after. ⁸She did not give up the prostitution she began in Egypt, when during her youth men slept with her, caressed her virgin bosom and poured out their lust upon her.

⁹"Therefore I handed her over to her lovers, the Assyrians, for whom she lusted. ¹⁰They stripped her naked, took away her sons and daughters and killed her with the sword. She became a byword among women, and punishment was inflicted on her.

¹¹"Her sister Oholibah saw this, yet in her lust and prostitution she was more depraved than her sister. ¹²She too lusted after the Assyrians—governors and commanders, warriors in full dress, mounted horsemen, all handsome young men. ¹³I saw that she too defiled herself; both of them went the same way.

¹⁴"But she carried her prostitution still further. She saw men portrayed on a wall, figures of Chaldeans[a] portrayed in red, ¹⁵with belts around their waists and flowing turbans on their heads; all of them looked like Babylonian chariot officers, natives of Chaldea.[b] ¹⁶As soon as she saw them, she lusted after them and sent messengers to them in Chaldea. ¹⁷Then the Babylonians came to her, to the bed of love, and in their lust they defiled her. After she had been defiled by them, she turned away from them in disgust. ¹⁸When she

ᵃ 14 Or *Babylonians*   *ᵇ 15* Or *Babylonia*; also in verse 16

carried on her prostitution openly and exposed her nakedness, I turned away from her in disgust, just as I had turned away from her sister. ¹⁹Yet she became more and more promiscuous as she recalled the days of her youth, when she was a prostitute in Egypt. ²⁰There she lusted after her lovers, whose genitals were like those of donkeys and whose emission was like that of horses. ²¹So you longed for the lewdness of your youth, when in Egypt your bosom was caressed and your young breasts fondled.ᵃ

²²"Therefore, Oholibah, this is what the Sovereign LORD says: I will stir up your lovers against you, those you turned away from in disgust, and I will bring them against you from every side— ²³the Babylonians and all the Chaldeans, the men of Pekod and Shoa and Koa, and all the Assyrians with them, handsome young men, all of them governors and commanders, chariot officers and men of high rank, all mounted on horses. ²⁴They will come against you with weapons,ᵇ chariots and wagons and with a throng of people; they will take up positions against you on every side with large and small shields and with helmets. I will turn you over to them for punishment, and they will punish you according to their standards. ²⁵I will direct my jealous anger against you, and they will deal with you in fury. They will cut off your noses and your ears, and those of you who are left will fall by the sword. They will take away your sons and daughters, and those of you who are left will be consumed by fire. ²⁶They will also strip you of your clothes and take your fine jewelry. ²⁷So I will put a stop to the lewdness and prostitution you began in Egypt. You will not look on these things with longing or remember Egypt anymore.

²⁸"For this is what the Sovereign LORD says: I am about to hand you over to those you hate, to those you turned away from in disgust. ²⁹They will deal with you in hatred and take away everything you have worked for. They will leave you naked and bare, and the shame of your prostitution will be exposed. Your lewdness and promiscuity ³⁰have brought this upon you, because you lusted after the nations and defiled yourself with their idols. ³¹You have gone the way of your sister; so I will put her cup into your hand.

³²"This is what the Sovereign LORD says:

"You will drink your sister's cup,
    a cup large and deep;
it will bring scorn and derision,
    for it holds so much.
³³You will be filled with drunkenness and sorrow,
    the cup of ruin and desolation,
    the cup of your sister Samaria.
³⁴You will drink it and drain it dry;
    you will dash it to pieces
    and tear your breasts.

I have spoken, declares the Sovereign LORD.

³⁵"Therefore this is what the Sovereign LORD says: Since you have forgotten me and thrust me behind your back, you must bear the consequences of your lewdness and prostitution."

³⁶The LORD said to me: "Son of man, will you judge

Consequences

EZEKIEL 23:22–31

God is angry. The language is graphic and violent. "They will cut off your noses and your ears, and those of you who are left will fall by the sword." In the face of the Israelites' persistent sin, a loving God has become an angry God who brings punishment for their sin.

Have you angered God? Have the Christians and the churches of today angered God? Have the nations of the world angered God? Struggle with these questions. What might be the consequences of our faithlessness and our injustices? Be honest and blunt in your reflections. Ask for forgiveness in your prayer.

See Meeting God in Prayer

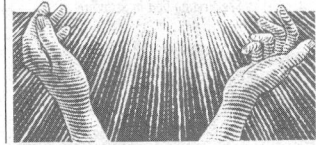

ᵃ 21 Syriac (see also verse 3); Hebrew *caressed because of your young breasts*
ᵇ 24 The meaning of the Hebrew for this word is uncertain.

A Boiling, Purifying Pot

EZEKIEL 24:1–5

Ezekiel chooses another graphic image to symbolize the trouble that Jerusalem is in. The king of Babylon has laid siege to the city; the citizens will feel like they are being roasted in a pot. The Israelites' worship of other gods, their misplaced confidence in other nations and their neglect of the poor have gotten them into deep water—hot water.

Draw a picture of a large pot and put into it your personality traits and harmful actions that need to be purified. Place into the water all the "isms" (such as racism, sexism and the like) that need to be boiled clean. In what ways does your church or country need to be purified?

See Meeting God in Scripture

Oholah and Oholibah? Then confront them with their detestable practices, [37]for they have committed adultery and blood is on their hands. They committed adultery with their idols; they even sacrificed their children, whom they bore to me,[a] as food for them. [38]They have also done this to me: At that same time they defiled my sanctuary and desecrated my Sabbaths. [39]On the very day they sacrificed their children to their idols, they entered my sanctuary and desecrated it. That is what they did in my house.

[40]"They even sent messengers for men who came from far away, and when they arrived you bathed yourself for them, painted your eyes and put on your jewelry. [41]You sat on an elegant couch, with a table spread before it on which you had placed the incense and oil that belonged to me.

[42]"The noise of a carefree crowd was around her; Sabeans[b] were brought from the desert along with men from the rabble, and they put bracelets on the arms of the woman and her sister and beautiful crowns on their heads. [43]Then I said about the one worn out by adultery, 'Now let them use her as a prostitute, for that is all she is.' [44]And they slept with her. As men sleep with a prostitute, so they slept with those lewd women, Oholah and Oholibah. [45]But righteous men will sentence them to the punishment of women who commit adultery and shed blood, because they are adulterous and blood is on their hands.

[46]"This is what the Sovereign LORD says: Bring a mob against them and give them over to terror and plunder. [47]The mob will stone them and cut them down with their swords; they will kill their sons and daughters and burn down their houses.

[48]"So I will put an end to lewdness in the land, that all women may take warning and not imitate you. [49]You will suffer the penalty for your lewdness and bear the consequences of your sins of idolatry. Then you will know that I am the Sovereign LORD."

The Cooking Pot

24 In the ninth year, in the tenth month on the tenth day, the word of the LORD came to me: [2]"Son of man, record this date, this very date, because the king of Babylon has laid siege to Jerusalem this very day. [3]Tell this rebellious house a parable and say to them: 'This is what the Sovereign LORD says:

" 'Put on the cooking pot; put it on
    and pour water into it.
[4]Put into it the pieces of meat,
    all the choice pieces—the leg and the shoulder.
Fill it with the best of these bones;
[5]   take the pick of the flock.
Pile wood beneath it for the bones;
    bring it to a boil
    and cook the bones in it.

[6]" 'For this is what the Sovereign LORD says:

" 'Woe to the city of bloodshed,

[a] 37 Or even made the children they bore to me pass through the fire
[b] 42 Or drunkards

to the pot now encrusted,
whose deposit will not go away!
Empty it piece by piece
without casting lots for them.

7 " 'For the blood she shed is in her midst:
She poured it on the bare rock;
she did not pour it on the ground,
where the dust would cover it.
8 To stir up wrath and take revenge
I put her blood on the bare rock,
so that it would not be covered.

9 " 'Therefore this is what the Sovereign LORD says:

" 'Woe to the city of bloodshed!
I, too, will pile the wood high.
10 So heap on the wood
and kindle the fire.
Cook the meat well,
mixing in the spices;
and let the bones be charred.
11 Then set the empty pot on the coals
till it becomes hot and its copper glows
so its impurities may be melted
and its deposit burned away.
12 It has frustrated all efforts;
its heavy deposit has not been removed,
not even by fire.

13 " 'Now your impurity is lewdness. Because I tried to cleanse you but you would not be cleansed from your impurity, you will not be clean again until my wrath against you has subsided.

14 " 'I the LORD have spoken. The time has come for me to act. I will not hold back; I will not have pity, nor will I relent. You will be judged according to your conduct and your actions, declares the Sovereign LORD.' "

Ezekiel's Wife Dies

15 The word of the LORD came to me: 16 "Son of man, with one blow I am about to take away from you the delight of your eyes. Yet do not lament or weep or shed any tears. 17 Groan quietly; do not mourn for the dead. Keep your turban fastened and your sandals on your feet; do not cover the lower part of your face or eat the customary food ⌊of mourners⌋."

18 So I spoke to the people in the morning, and in the evening my wife died. The next morning I did as I had been commanded.

19 Then the people asked me, "Won't you tell us what these things have to do with us?"

20 So I said to them, "The word of the LORD came to me: 21 Say to the house of Israel, 'This is what the Sovereign LORD says: I am about to desecrate my sanctuary—the stronghold in which you take pride, the delight of your eyes, the object of your affection. The sons and daughters you left behind will fall by the sword. 22 And you will do as I have done. You will not cover the lower part of your face or eat the customary food ⌊of mourners⌋. 23 You will keep your turbans on your heads and your sandals on your feet. You will not mourn or weep but will waste away because

Hold On

EZEKIEL 24:18–24

Ezekiel is instructed not to grieve for his dead wife. The traditional rites of mourning are to be dispensed with, so that the people will ask Ezekiel why he isn't grieving. This unusual behavior allows Ezekiel to pronounce a dire warning in a way so vivid that the people cannot possibly miss its meaning.

We sometimes miss warnings we should have heeded. We can often see them clearly after the fact but, unfortunately, not so clearly beforehand. Have you found a way to develop your spiritual antennae? What subtle clues do you look for as warnings regarding your actions, behaviors or relationships? What major warnings have you missed in the past? Ask God to help you see more clearly so you do not miss the signs God gives you for your benefit.

See Meeting God in Everyday Life

The Misfortune of Others

EZEKIEL 25:6–7

Some of the nations around Judah clap their hands and stamp their feet at the destruction of Jerusalem. But God will not allow his people to be mocked, so he promises that destruction will come to those jeering nations as well as to Jerusalem.

When have you taken pleasure in the misfortunes of others? Have you laughed when the butt of the joke is a vulnerable and unfortunate person? What causes this tendency in so many of us? Is it relief that the misfortune is not our own? Consider today your own vulnerability. With God's help look for an occasion to help someone who is suffering misfortune.

See Meeting God in Service

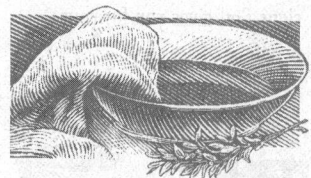

of[a] your sins and groan among yourselves. [24]Ezekiel will be a sign to you; you will do just as he has done. When this happens, you will know that I am the Sovereign Lord.'

[25]"And you, son of man, on the day I take away their stronghold, their joy and glory, the delight of their eyes, their heart's desire, and their sons and daughters as well— [26]on that day a fugitive will come to tell you the news. [27]At that time your mouth will be opened; you will speak with him and will no longer be silent. So you will be a sign to them, and they will know that I am the Lord."

A Prophecy Against Ammon

25 The word of the Lord came to me: [2]"Son of man, set your face against the Ammonites and prophesy against them. [3]Say to them, 'Hear the word of the Sovereign Lord. This is what the Sovereign Lord says: Because you said "Aha!" over my sanctuary when it was desecrated and over the land of Israel when it was laid waste and over the people of Judah when they went into exile, [4]therefore I am going to give you to the people of the East as a possession. They will set up their camps and pitch their tents among you; they will eat your fruit and drink your milk. [5]I will turn Rabbah into a pasture for camels and Ammon into a resting place for sheep. Then you will know that I am the Lord. [6]For this is what the Sovereign Lord says: Because you have clapped your hands and stamped your feet, rejoicing with all the malice of your heart against the land of Israel, [7]therefore I will stretch out my hand against you and give you as plunder to the nations. I will cut you off from the nations and exterminate you from the countries. I will destroy you, and you will know that I am the Lord.' "

A Prophecy Against Moab

[8]"This is what the Sovereign Lord says: 'Because Moab and Seir said, "Look, the house of Judah has become like all the other nations," [9]therefore I will expose the flank of Moab, beginning at its frontier towns—Beth Jeshimoth, Baal Meon and Kiriathaim—the glory of that land. [10]I will give Moab along with the Ammonites to the people of the East as a possession, so that the Ammonites will not be remembered among the nations; [11]and I will inflict punishment on Moab. Then they will know that I am the Lord.' "

A Prophecy Against Edom

[12]"This is what the Sovereign Lord says: 'Because Edom took revenge on the house of Judah and became very guilty by doing so, [13]therefore this is what the Sovereign Lord says: I will stretch out my hand against Edom and kill its men and their animals. I will lay it waste, and from Teman to Dedan they will fall by the sword. [14]I will take vengeance on Edom by the hand of my people Israel, and they will deal with Edom in accordance with my anger and my wrath; they will know my vengeance, declares the Sovereign Lord.' "

A Prophecy Against Philistia

[15]"This is what the Sovereign Lord says: 'Because the Philistines acted in vengeance and took revenge with malice in their hearts, and with ancient hostility sought to destroy

[a] 23 Or *away in*

Judah, ¹⁶therefore this is what the Sovereign LORD says: I am about to stretch out my hand against the Philistines, and I will cut off the Kerethites and destroy those remaining along the coast. ¹⁷I will carry out great vengeance on them and punish them in my wrath. Then they will know that I am the LORD, when I take vengeance on them.' "

A Prophecy Against Tyre

26 In the eleventh year, on the first day of the month, the word of the LORD came to me: ²"Son of man, because Tyre has said of Jerusalem, 'Aha! The gate to the nations is broken, and its doors have swung open to me; now that she lies in ruins I will prosper,' ³therefore this is what the Sovereign LORD says: I am against you, O Tyre, and I will bring many nations against you, like the sea casting up its waves. ⁴They will destroy the walls of Tyre and pull down her towers; I will scrape away her rubble and make her a bare rock. ⁵Out in the sea she will become a place to spread fishnets, for I have spoken, declares the Sovereign LORD. She will become plunder for the nations, ⁶and her settlements on the mainland will be ravaged by the sword. Then they will know that I am the LORD.

⁷"For this is what the Sovereign LORD says: From the north I am going to bring against Tyre Nebuchadnezzar[a] king of Babylon, king of kings, with horses and chariots, with horsemen and a great army. ⁸He will ravage your settlements on the mainland with the sword; he will set up siege works against you, build a ramp up to your walls and raise his shields against you. ⁹He will direct the blows of his battering rams against your walls and demolish your towers with his weapons. ¹⁰His horses will be so many that they will cover you with dust. Your walls will tremble at the noise of the war horses, wagons and chariots when he enters your gates as men enter a city whose walls have been broken through. ¹¹The hoofs of his horses will trample all your streets; he will kill your people with the sword, and your strong pillars will fall to the ground. ¹²They will plunder your wealth and loot your merchandise; they will break down your walls and demolish your fine houses and throw your stones, timber and rubble into the sea. ¹³I will put an end to your noisy songs, and the music of your harps will be heard no more. ¹⁴I will make you a bare rock, and you will become a place to spread fishnets. You will never be rebuilt, for I the LORD have spoken, declares the Sovereign LORD.

¹⁵"This is what the Sovereign LORD says to Tyre: Will not the coastlands tremble at the sound of your fall, when the wounded groan and the slaughter takes place in you? ¹⁶Then all the princes of the coast will step down from their thrones and lay aside their robes and take off their embroidered garments. Clothed with terror, they will sit on the ground, trembling every moment, appalled at you. ¹⁷Then they will take up a lament concerning you and say to you:

> " 'How you are destroyed, O city of renown,
>   peopled by men of the sea!
> You were a power on the seas,
>   you and your citizens;

Silence the Songs

EZEKIEL 26:13–14

A prophecy is directed against Tyre because Tyre failed to come to the aid of its ally Jerusalem. The king of Babylon will destroy the city of Tyre so completely that it will never be rebuilt. In poignant detail Ezekiel records, "I will put an end to your noisy songs, and the music of your harps will be heard no more. I will make you a bare rock, and you will become a place to spread fishnets. You will never be rebuilt." Days of sadness and lament are coming to the city of Tyre.

Sometimes it's beneficial to allow ourselves a day for sadness and lament, for grieving the loss of dreams, loved ones or other precious things. Find a passage in a novel or poem or find a piece of music that expresses the sadness you sometimes feel. Let yourself feel that sadness and ask God to be with you in that experience. Thank God for sharing your sadness.

See Meeting God in Prayer

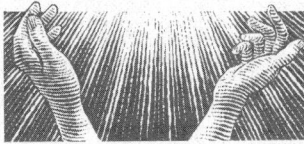

ᵃ 7 Hebrew *Nebuchadrezzar*, of which *Nebuchadnezzar* is a variant; here and often in Ezekiel and Jeremiah

A Solid Ship

EZEKIEL 27:1–9

The island city of Tyre is compared to a beautiful ship constructed of precious wood and exquisite fabrics from many nations. An exotic and cosmopolitan showplace, the city was like a lovely jewel of the sea. But the people were puffed up with pride; they thought they were invincible. And yet Ezekiel prophesies that the ship (the nation) will sink because it is built on the shaky foundation of prosperity (28:5).

What is your foundation? What are the strong planks of your faith? What experiences bind your heart and spirit into a weather-resistant craft? What Scripture passages bolt your life into a sturdy ship? Who is the wind in your sails?

See Meeting God in Scripture

you put your terror
on all who lived there.
[18] Now the coastlands tremble
on the day of your fall;
the islands in the sea
are terrified at your collapse.'

[19] "This is what the Sovereign LORD says: When I make you a desolate city, like cities no longer inhabited, and when I bring the ocean depths over you and its vast waters cover you, [20] then I will bring you down with those who go down to the pit, to the people of long ago. I will make you dwell in the earth below, as in ancient ruins, with those who go down to the pit, and you will not return or take your place[a] in the land of the living. [21] I will bring you to a horrible end and you will be no more. You will be sought, but you will never again be found, declares the Sovereign LORD."

A Lament for Tyre

27 The word of the LORD came to me: [2] "Son of man, take up a lament concerning Tyre. [3] Say to Tyre, situated at the gateway to the sea, merchant of peoples on many coasts, 'This is what the Sovereign LORD says:

" 'You say, O Tyre,
"I am perfect in beauty."
[4] Your domain was on the high seas;
your builders brought your beauty to
perfection.
[5] They made all your timbers
of pine trees from Senir[b];
they took a cedar from Lebanon
to make a mast for you.
[6] Of oaks from Bashan
they made your oars;
of cypress wood[c] from the coasts of Cyprus[d]
they made your deck, inlaid with ivory.
[7] Fine embroidered linen from Egypt was your sail
and served as your banner;
your awnings were of blue and purple
from the coasts of Elishah.
[8] Men of Sidon and Arvad were your oarsmen;
your skilled men, O Tyre, were aboard as your
seamen.
[9] Veteran craftsmen of Gebal[e] were on board
as shipwrights to caulk your seams.
All the ships of the sea and their sailors
came alongside to trade for your wares.

[10] " 'Men of Persia, Lydia and Put
served as soldiers in your army.
They hung their shields and helmets on your
walls,
bringing you splendor.
[11] Men of Arvad and Helech
manned your walls on every side;
men of Gammad
were in your towers.

---

[a] 20 Septuagint; Hebrew *return, and I will give glory*   [b] 5 That is, Hermon
[c] 6 Targum; the Masoretic Text has a different division of the consonants.
[d] 6 Hebrew *Kittim*   [e] 9 That is, Byblos

They hung their shields around your walls;
they brought your beauty to perfection.

¹²" 'Tarshish did business with you because of your great wealth of goods; they exchanged silver, iron, tin and lead for your merchandise.

¹³" 'Greece, Tubal and Meshech traded with you; they exchanged slaves and articles of bronze for your wares.

¹⁴" 'Men of Beth Togarmah exchanged work horses, war horses and mules for your merchandise.

¹⁵" 'The men of Rhodes[a] traded with you, and many coastlands were your customers; they paid you with ivory tusks and ebony.

¹⁶" 'Aram[b] did business with you because of your many products; they exchanged turquoise, purple fabric, embroidered work, fine linen, coral and rubies for your merchandise.

¹⁷" 'Judah and Israel traded with you; they exchanged wheat from Minnith and confections,[c] honey, oil and balm for your wares.

¹⁸" 'Damascus, because of your many products and great wealth of goods, did business with you in wine from Helbon and wool from Zahar.

¹⁹" 'Danites and Greeks from Uzal bought your merchandise; they exchanged wrought iron, cassia and calamus for your wares.

²⁰" 'Dedan traded in saddle blankets with you.

²¹" 'Arabia and all the princes of Kedar were your customers; they did business with you in lambs, rams and goats.

²²" 'The merchants of Sheba and Raamah traded with you; for your merchandise they exchanged the finest of all kinds of spices and precious stones, and gold.

²³" 'Haran, Canneh and Eden and merchants of Sheba, Asshur and Kilmad traded with you. ²⁴In your marketplace they traded with you beautiful garments, blue fabric, embroidered work and multicolored rugs with cords twisted and tightly knotted.

²⁵ " 'The ships of Tarshish serve
as carriers for your wares.
You are filled with heavy cargo
in the heart of the sea.
²⁶ Your oarsmen take you
out to the high seas.
But the east wind will break you to pieces
in the heart of the sea.
²⁷ Your wealth, merchandise and wares,
your mariners, seamen and shipwrights,
your merchants and all your soldiers,
and everyone else on board
will sink into the heart of the sea
on the day of your shipwreck.
²⁸ The shorelands will quake
when your seamen cry out.
²⁹ All who handle the oars
will abandon their ships;
the mariners and all the seamen

The East Wind Blows

EZEKIEL 27:26–36

The east wind has sunk Tyre. The proud nation and its mighty fleet have come to an end. Tyre's wealth and pomp cannot save the city. Its fame does not last. The lament over Tyre is a warning to us: Our plans are to be Christ-centered; our goals are to be Spirit-driven. When we ask God to direct us, we have no reason to fear the force of the east wind.

Write down three or four of the most important goals in your life. Ask tough, searching questions about these goals. What part did God play in crafting these plans? Offer your goals to God in prayer and ask the Lord to examine them. Revise them (if need be) according to God's plans for you.

See Meeting God in Everyday Life

ᵃ 15 Septuagint; Hebrew *Dedan*   ᵇ 16 Most Hebrew manuscripts; some Hebrew manuscripts and Syriac *Edom*   ᶜ 17 The meaning of the Hebrew for this word is uncertain.

Be Not Proud

EZEKIEL 28:2

"If there is any good in you, believe that there is much more in others so that you may preserve humility. It hurts you not to submit to everyone, but it hurts you most of all to prefer yourself to even one other person."

—THOMAS À KEMPIS,
The Imitation of Christ

will stand on the shore.
30 They will raise their voice
and cry bitterly over you;
they will sprinkle dust on their heads
and roll in ashes.
31 They will shave their heads because of you
and will put on sackcloth.
They will weep over you with anguish of soul
and with bitter mourning.
32 As they wail and mourn over you,
they will take up a lament concerning you:
"Who was ever silenced like Tyre,
surrounded by the sea?"
33 When your merchandise went out on the seas,
you satisfied many nations;
with your great wealth and your wares
you enriched the kings of the earth.
34 Now you are shattered by the sea
in the depths of the waters;
your wares and all your company
have gone down with you.
35 All who live in the coastlands
are appalled at you;
their kings shudder with horror
and their faces are distorted with fear.
36 The merchants among the nations hiss at you;
you have come to a horrible end
and will be no more.' "

A Prophecy Against the King of Tyre

28 The word of the LORD came to me: 2 "Son of man, say to the ruler of Tyre, 'This is what the Sovereign LORD says:

" 'In the pride of your heart
you say, "I am a god;
I sit on the throne of a god
in the heart of the seas."
But you are a man and not a god,
though you think you are as wise as a god.
3 Are you wiser than Daniel[a]?
Is no secret hidden from you?
4 By your wisdom and understanding
you have gained wealth for yourself
and amassed gold and silver
in your treasuries.
5 By your great skill in trading
you have increased your wealth,
and because of your wealth
your heart has grown proud.

6 " 'Therefore this is what the Sovereign LORD says:

" 'Because you think you are wise,
as wise as a god,
7 I am going to bring foreigners against you,
the most ruthless of nations;
they will draw their swords against your beauty
and wisdom

a 3 Or Danel; the Hebrew spelling may suggest a person other than the prophet Daniel.

and pierce your shining splendor.
⁸ They will bring you down to the pit,
and you will die a violent death
in the heart of the seas.
⁹ Will you then say, "I am a god,"
in the presence of those who kill you?
You will be but a man, not a god,
in the hands of those who slay you.
¹⁰ You will die the death of the uncircumcised
at the hands of foreigners.

I have spoken, declares the Sovereign LORD.' "

¹¹ The word of the LORD came to me: ¹² "Son of man, take up a lament concerning the king of Tyre and say to him: 'This is what the Sovereign LORD says:

" 'You were the model of perfection,
full of wisdom and perfect in beauty.
¹³ You were in Eden,
the garden of God;
every precious stone adorned you:
ruby, topaz and emerald,
chrysolite, onyx and jasper,
sapphire,ᵃ turquoise and beryl.ᵇ
Your settings and mountingsᶜ were made of gold;
on the day you were created they were
prepared.
¹⁴ You were anointed as a guardian cherub,
for so I ordained you.
You were on the holy mount of God;
you walked among the fiery stones.
¹⁵ You were blameless in your ways
from the day you were created
till wickedness was found in you.
¹⁶ Through your widespread trade
you were filled with violence,
and you sinned.
So I drove you in disgrace from the mount of
God,
and I expelled you, O guardian cherub,
from among the fiery stones.
¹⁷ Your heart became proud
on account of your beauty,
and you corrupted your wisdom
because of your splendor.
So I threw you to the earth;
I made a spectacle of you before kings.
¹⁸ By your many sins and dishonest trade
you have desecrated your sanctuaries.
So I made a fire come out from you,
and it consumed you,
and I reduced you to ashes on the ground
in the sight of all who were watching.
¹⁹ All the nations who knew you
are appalled at you;
you have come to a horrible end
and will be no more.' "

Blameless

EZEKIEL 28:15

The prophet is eloquent and comprehensive as he laments the problems in Tyre. The country and its leaders are guilty of arrogance, idolatry and injustice. There is very little that is good about Tyre. Yet, in the midst of Ezekiel's diatribe, he inserts a word of hope: "You were blameless in your ways from the day you were created till wickedness was found in you."

However far we may stray from God's chosen path for us, we carry deep within us the image of God. We are born under God's watchful eye, and we are forever in God's heart. Do you believe that you are precious in God's eyes? Can you sense that God's love has been there for you since the moment you came into being? (See Psalm 139:13–16.) Try writing a prayer of thanksgiving that expresses your joy at being loved.

See Meeting God in Scripture

ᵃ 13 Or *lapis lazuli*   ᵇ 13 The precise identification of some of these precious stones is uncertain.   ᶜ 13 The meaning of the Hebrew for this phrase is uncertain.

Gather the Scattered

EZEKIEL 28:25–26

"Hope is the primary prophetic idiom not because of the general dynamic of history or because of the signs of the times but because the prophet speaks to a people who, willy-nilly, are God's people. Hope is what this community must do because it is God's community invited to be in God's pilgrimage. And as Israel is invited to grieve God's grief over the ending, so Israel is now invited to hope in God's promises."

—WALTER BRUEGGEMANN,
The Prophetic Imagination

A Prophecy Against Sidon

²⁰The word of the LORD came to me: ²¹"Son of man, set your face against Sidon; prophesy against her ²²and say: 'This is what the Sovereign LORD says:

" 'I am against you, O Sidon,
    and I will gain glory within you.
They will know that I am the LORD,
    when I inflict punishment on her
    and show myself holy within her.
²³I will send a plague upon her
    and make blood flow in her streets.
The slain will fall within her,
    with the sword against her on every side.
Then they will know that I am the LORD.

²⁴" 'No longer will the people of Israel have malicious neighbors who are painful briers and sharp thorns. Then they will know that I am the Sovereign LORD.

²⁵" 'This is what the Sovereign LORD says: When I gather the people of Israel from the nations where they have been scattered, I will show myself holy among them in the sight of the nations. Then they will live in their own land, which I gave to my servant Jacob. ²⁶They will live there in safety and will build houses and plant vineyards; they will live in safety when I inflict punishment on all their neighbors who maligned them. Then they will know that I am the LORD their God.' "

A Prophecy Against Egypt

29 In the tenth year, in the tenth month on the twelfth day, the word of the LORD came to me: ²"Son of man, set your face against Pharaoh king of Egypt and prophesy against him and against all Egypt. ³Speak to him and say: 'This is what the Sovereign LORD says:

" 'I am against you, Pharaoh king of Egypt,
    you great monster lying among your streams.
You say, "The Nile is mine;
    I made it for myself."
⁴But I will put hooks in your jaws
    and make the fish of your streams stick to your
        scales.
I will pull you out from among your streams,
    with all the fish sticking to your scales.
⁵I will leave you in the desert,
    you and all the fish of your streams.
You will fall on the open field
    and not be gathered or picked up.
I will give you as food
    to the beasts of the earth and the birds of the
        air.

⁶Then all who live in Egypt will know that I am the LORD.

" 'You have been a staff of reed for the house of Israel. ⁷When they grasped you with their hands, you splintered and you tore open their shoulders; when they leaned on you, you broke and their backs were wrenched.[a]

⁸" 'Therefore this is what the Sovereign LORD says: I will

---

[a] 7 Syriac (see also Septuagint and Vulgate); Hebrew *and you caused their backs to stand*

bring a sword against you and kill your men and their animals. ⁹Egypt will become a desolate wasteland. Then they
will know that I am the LORD.

" 'Because you said, "The Nile is mine; I made it,"
¹⁰therefore I am against you and against your streams, and
I will make the land of Egypt a ruin and a desolate waste
from Migdol to Aswan, as far as the border of Cush.ᵃ ¹¹No
foot of man or animal will pass through it; no one will live
there for forty years. ¹²I will make the land of Egypt desolate among devastated lands, and her cities will lie desolate
forty years among ruined cities. And I will disperse the
Egyptians among the nations and scatter them through the
countries.

¹³ 'Yet this is what the Sovereign LORD says: At the end
of forty years I will gather the Egyptians from the nations
where they were scattered. ¹⁴I will bring them back from
captivity and return them to Upper Egypt,ᵇ the land of their
ancestry. There they will be a lowly kingdom. ¹⁵It will be
the lowliest of kingdoms and will never again exalt itself
above the other nations. I will make it so weak that it will
never again rule over the nations. ¹⁶Egypt will no longer be
a source of confidence for the people of Israel but will be a
reminder of their sin in turning to her for help. Then they
will know that I am the Sovereign LORD.' "

¹⁷In the twenty-seventh year, in the first month on the
first day, the word of the LORD came to me: ¹⁸"Son of man,
Nebuchadnezzar king of Babylon drove his army in a hard
campaign against Tyre; every head was rubbed bare and
every shoulder made raw. Yet he and his army got no reward from the campaign he led against Tyre. ¹⁹Therefore
this is what the Sovereign LORD says: I am going to give
Egypt to Nebuchadnezzar king of Babylon, and he will
carry off its wealth. He will loot and plunder the land as pay
for his army. ²⁰I have given him Egypt as a reward for his efforts because he and his army did it for me, declares the
Sovereign LORD.

²¹"On that day I will make a hornᶜ grow for the house of
Israel, and I will open your mouth among them. Then they
will know that I am the LORD."

A Lament for Egypt

30 The word of the LORD came to me: ²"Son of man,
prophesy and say: 'This is what the Sovereign LORD
says:

" 'Wail and say,
    "Alas for that day!"
³For the day is near,
    the day of the LORD is near—
a day of clouds,
    a time of doom for the nations.
⁴A sword will come against Egypt,
    and anguish will come upon Cush.ᵈ
When the slain fall in Egypt,
    her wealth will be carried away
    and her foundations torn down.

A Day of Clouds

EZEKIEL 30:1–3

Most often "the day of the
LORD" referred to God's judgment, though later it was associated with the day of Israel's
restoration. The "day of the
LORD" or the "day of clouds"
urges us to look out for trouble.

Imagine "a day of clouds,"
dark and threatening. The
clouds beckon you to consider
the course of your life. What
have you been putting off?
What is really important that
you want to do before the rain
comes and washes out the possibilities? The clouds are a call
to sort your priorities, to take
care of business before the
storms roll in. Let the guidance
and promises of God be a place
of shelter for your prayer and
reflection. Make some plans to
take action.

See Meeting God in Scripture

ᵃ 10 That is, the upper Nile region   ᵇ 14 Hebrew *to Pathros*   ᶜ 21 *Horn*
here symbolizes strength.   ᵈ 4 That is, the upper Nile region; also in verses
5 and 9

Idols and Images

EZEKIEL 30:13

Take a look around your house or apartment. Begin by looking at the walls. What images are most prevalent? What meaning do the pictures convey? Is there any religious art? A cross? An icon? Look at your books. Is the Bible clearly visible? What objects rest on your shelves? What magazines, newspapers or catalogs do you see? How prominent a place does the television or computer or stereo have? Do any of the things in your house tempt you to turn away from God, cause you to miss worship services, or neglect prayer or Bible study? What activities take up most of your time? Can you affirm the words of Scripture, "As for me and my household, we will serve the LORD" (Joshua 24:15)?

See Meeting God in Everyday Life

⁵Cush and Put, Lydia and all Arabia, Libya*ᵃ* and the people of the covenant land will fall by the sword along with Egypt.

⁶" 'This is what the LORD says:

" 'The allies of Egypt will fall
    and her proud strength will fail.
From Migdol to Aswan
    they will fall by the sword within her,
                    declares the Sovereign LORD.
⁷" 'They will be desolate
    among desolate lands,
and their cities will lie
    among ruined cities.
⁸Then they will know that I am the LORD,
    when I set fire to Egypt
    and all her helpers are crushed.

⁹" 'On that day messengers will go out from me in ships to frighten Cush out of her complacency. Anguish will take hold of them on the day of Egypt's doom, for it is sure to come.

¹⁰" 'This is what the Sovereign LORD says:

" 'I will put an end to the hordes of Egypt
    by the hand of Nebuchadnezzar king of
        Babylon.
¹¹He and his army—the most ruthless of nations—
    will be brought in to destroy the land.
They will draw their swords against Egypt
    and fill the land with the slain.
¹²I will dry up the streams of the Nile
    and sell the land to evil men;
by the hand of foreigners
    I will lay waste the land and everything in it.

I the LORD have spoken.

¹³" 'This is what the Sovereign LORD says:

" 'I will destroy the idols
    and put an end to the images in Memphis.*ᵇ*
No longer will there be a prince in Egypt,
    and I will spread fear throughout the land.
¹⁴I will lay waste Upper Egypt,*ᶜ*
    set fire to Zoan
    and inflict punishment on Thebes.*ᵈ*
¹⁵I will pour out my wrath on Pelusium,*ᵉ*
    the stronghold of Egypt,
    and cut off the hordes of Thebes.
¹⁶I will set fire to Egypt;
    Pelusium will writhe in agony.
Thebes will be taken by storm;
    Memphis will be in constant distress.
¹⁷The young men of Heliopolis*ᶠ* and Bubastis*ᵍ*
    will fall by the sword,
    and the cities themselves will go into captivity.
¹⁸Dark will be the day at Tahpanhes
    when I break the yoke of Egypt;
    there her proud strength will come to an end.
She will be covered with clouds,

ᵃ5 Hebrew *Cub*   *ᵇ13* Hebrew *Noph*; also in verse 16   *ᶜ14* Hebrew *waste Pathros*   *ᵈ14* Hebrew *No*; also in verses 15 and 16   *ᵉ15* Hebrew *Sin*; also in verse 16   *ᶠ17* Hebrew *Awen* (or *On*)   *ᵍ17* Hebrew *Pi Beseth*

and her villages will go into captivity.
¹⁹ So I will inflict punishment on Egypt,
  and they will know that I am the Lord.' "

²⁰ In the eleventh year, in the first month on the seventh day, the word of the Lord came to me: ²¹ "Son of man, I have broken the arm of Pharaoh king of Egypt. It has not been bound up for healing or put in a splint so as to become strong enough to hold a sword. ²² Therefore this is what the Sovereign Lord says: I am against Pharaoh king of Egypt. I will break both his arms, the good arm as well as the broken one, and make the sword fall from his hand. ²³ I will disperse the Egyptians among the nations and scatter them through the countries. ²⁴ I will strengthen the arms of the king of Babylon and put my sword in his hand, but I will break the arms of Pharaoh, and he will groan before him like a mortally wounded man. ²⁵ I will strengthen the arms of the king of Babylon, but the arms of Pharaoh will fall limp. Then they will know that I am the Lord, when I put my sword into the hand of the king of Babylon and he brandishes it against Egypt. ²⁶ I will disperse the Egyptians among the nations and scatter them through the countries. Then they will know that I am the Lord."

A Cedar in Lebanon

31 In the eleventh year, in the third month on the first day, the word of the Lord came to me: ² "Son of man, say to Pharaoh king of Egypt and to his hordes:

" 'Who can be compared with you in majesty?
³ Consider Assyria, once a cedar in Lebanon,
    with beautiful branches overshadowing the
      forest;
  it towered on high,
    its top above the thick foliage.
⁴ The waters nourished it,
    deep springs made it grow tall;
  their streams flowed
    all around its base
  and sent their channels
    to all the trees of the field.
⁵ So it towered higher
    than all the trees of the field;
  its boughs increased
    and its branches grew long,
    spreading because of abundant waters.
⁶ All the birds of the air
    nested in its boughs,
  all the beasts of the field
    gave birth under its branches;
  all the great nations
    lived in its shade.
⁷ It was majestic in beauty,
    with its spreading boughs,
  for its roots went down
    to abundant waters.
⁸ The cedars in the garden of God
    could not rival it,
  nor could the pine trees
    equal its boughs,
  nor could the plane trees

Like a Tree Planted by the Water

EZEKIEL 31:3–9

The tree image is woven throughout Scripture. There is the tree of knowledge in the Garden of Eden, the tree turned into a cross on the hill of Calvary and the tree of life in Revelation. This passage in Ezekiel presents a beautiful description of a cedar. Yet this glorious tree, with deep roots, bountiful branches and grand height, is a symbol of a nation that is infested with sinful pride. And this tree—this nation—is about to be felled because of that pride.

Pay attention today to small, humble trees. The mighty oaks and cedars may be felled in a storm in which the smaller trees remain standing. Perhaps you might sit under a small tree and pray for the gift of humility.

See *Meeting God in the Created Order*

Seeing Ourselves

EZEKIEL 32: 1–3

How do we think of ourselves? Do we see ourselves with the eyes of God? Or do we measure ourselves by the standards of the world? The lament over Egypt and its pharaoh focuses on their pride and arrogance: "You are like a lion . . . you are like a monster."

One way God measures nations, its leaders and its people is with the yardstick of compassion. Are the poor, the strangers and the hurting being taken care of? Are the people caring and loving in their attitudes and actions?

Choose a special friend whom you trust and discuss these questions with that person. Begin with your nation, your community or your church. Then ask for your friend's candid and honest help in examining yourself. Have you fallen into arrogant habits without realizing it? In what ways do you express compassion regularly?

See Meeting God in Community

compare with its branches—
no tree in the garden of God
could match its beauty.
⁹I made it beautiful
with abundant branches,
the envy of all the trees of Eden
in the garden of God.

¹⁰" 'Therefore this is what the Sovereign LORD says: Because it towered on high, lifting its top above the thick foliage, and because it was proud of its height, ¹¹I handed it over to the ruler of the nations, for him to deal with according to its wickedness. I cast it aside, ¹²and the most ruthless of foreign nations cut it down and left it. Its boughs fell on the mountains and in all the valleys; its branches lay broken in all the ravines of the land. All the nations of the earth came out from under its shade and left it. ¹³All the birds of the air settled on the fallen tree, and all the beasts of the field were among its branches. ¹⁴Therefore no other trees by the waters are ever to tower proudly on high, lifting their tops above the thick foliage. No other trees so well-watered are ever to reach such a height; they are all destined for death, for the earth below, among mortal men, with those who go down to the pit.

¹⁵" 'This is what the Sovereign LORD says: On the day it was brought down to the grave[a] I covered the deep springs with mourning for it; I held back its streams, and its abundant waters were restrained. Because of it I clothed Lebanon with gloom, and all the trees of the field withered away. ¹⁶I made the nations tremble at the sound of its fall when I brought it down to the grave with those who go down to the pit. Then all the trees of Eden, the choicest and best of Lebanon, all the trees that were well-watered, were consoled in the earth below. ¹⁷Those who lived in its shade, its allies among the nations, had also gone down to the grave with it, joining those killed by the sword.

¹⁸" 'Which of the trees of Eden can be compared with you in splendor and majesty? Yet you, too, will be brought down with the trees of Eden to the earth below; you will lie among the uncircumcised, with those killed by the sword.

" 'This is Pharaoh and all his hordes, declares the Sovereign LORD.' "

A Lament for Pharaoh

32 In the twelfth year, in the twelfth month on the first day, the word of the LORD came to me: ²"Son of man, take up a lament concerning Pharaoh king of Egypt and say to him:

" 'You are like a lion among the nations;
you are like a monster in the seas
thrashing about in your streams,
churning the water with your feet
and muddying the streams.

³" 'This is what the Sovereign LORD says:

" 'With a great throng of people
I will cast my net over you,
and they will haul you up in my net.
⁴I will throw you on the land

ᵃ 15 Hebrew *Sheol*; also in verses 16 and 17

and hurl you on the open field.
I will let all the birds of the air settle on you
    and all the beasts of the earth gorge themselves
        on you.
⁵ I will spread your flesh on the mountains
    and fill the valleys with your remains.
⁶ I will drench the land with your flowing blood
    all the way to the mountains,
    and the ravines will be filled with your flesh.
⁷ When I snuff you out, I will cover the heavens
    and darken their stars;
I will cover the sun with a cloud,
    and the moon will not give its light.
⁸ All the shining lights in the heavens
    I will darken over you;
I will bring darkness over your land,
                        declares the Sovereign LORD.
⁹ I will trouble the hearts of many peoples
    when I bring about your destruction among the
        nations,
    among*ᵃ* lands you have not known.
¹⁰ I will cause many peoples to be appalled at you,
    and their kings will shudder with horror
        because of you
    when I brandish my sword before them.
On the day of your downfall
    each of them will tremble
    every moment for his life.

¹¹ " 'For this is what the Sovereign LORD says:

" 'The sword of the king of Babylon
    will come against you.
¹² I will cause your hordes to fall
    by the swords of mighty men—
    the most ruthless of all nations.
They will shatter the pride of Egypt,
    and all her hordes will be overthrown.
¹³ I will destroy all her cattle
    from beside abundant waters
no longer to be stirred by the foot of man
    or muddied by the hoofs of cattle.
¹⁴ Then I will let her waters settle
    and make her streams flow like oil,
                        declares the Sovereign LORD.
¹⁵ When I make Egypt desolate
    and strip the land of everything in it,
when I strike down all who live there,
    then they will know that I am the LORD.'

¹⁶ "This is the lament they will chant for her. The daughters of the nations will chant it; for Egypt and all her hordes they will chant it, declares the Sovereign LORD."

¹⁷ In the twelfth year, on the fifteenth day of the month, the word of the LORD came to me: ¹⁸ "Son of man, wail for the hordes of Egypt and consign to the earth below both her and the daughters of mighty nations, with those who go down to the pit. ¹⁹ Say to them, 'Are you more favored than others? Go down and be laid among the uncircumcised.' ²⁰ They will fall among those killed by the sword. The

---

Chant

EZEKIEL 32:16

Music is a powerful force that can be used to build up or tear down, to make people happy or sad. It can articulate love or revitalize revolution or express otherwise inexpressible sadness.

In this passage, the women chant a lament for Egypt, a nation that squandered so much of its potential. What opportunities in our society are wasted through greed, addictions, violence and ignorance? Try writing a chant, a lament, over potential left unfulfilled. Sing your lament for the people and nations who waste potential and leave possibilities unexplored.

See Meeting God in Scripture

Blow the Trumpet

EZEKIEL 33:1–9

The watchman is to blow the trumpet when the enemy approaches. Likewise, the responsibility for warning the people of impending doom was squarely on the prophet Ezekiel's shoulders. In some communities today, a central siren announces that bad weather threatens or a civil threat exists. Trumpet blasts and loud sirens serve the same purpose: to alert the people who hear them to impending danger.

Are you in danger? Have you drifted away from God? Do your deeds match your words? Is your religious community in danger because it does not take God's Word seriously? Who is sounding a trumpet blast? Is the nation in trouble? Are you called to be a watchman? Is there an injustice or a wrong to which no one is paying attention? Is it time to raise your trumpet?

See *Meeting God in Community*

sword is drawn; let her be dragged off with all her hordes. [21] From within the grave[a] the mighty leaders will say of Egypt and her allies, 'They have come down and they lie with the uncircumcised, with those killed by the sword.'

[22] "Assyria is there with her whole army; she is surrounded by the graves of all her slain, all who have fallen by the sword. [23] Their graves are in the depths of the pit and her army lies around her grave. All who had spread terror in the land of the living are slain, fallen by the sword.

[24] "Elam is there, with all her hordes around her grave. All of them are slain, fallen by the sword. All who had spread terror in the land of the living went down uncircumcised to the earth below. They bear their shame with those who go down to the pit. [25] A bed is made for her among the slain, with all her hordes around her grave. All of them are uncircumcised, killed by the sword. Because their terror had spread in the land of the living, they bear their shame with those who go down to the pit; they are laid among the slain.

[26] "Meshech and Tubal are there, with all their hordes around their graves. All of them are uncircumcised, killed by the sword because they spread their terror in the land of the living. [27] Do they not lie with the other uncircumcised warriors who have fallen, who went down to the grave with their weapons of war, whose swords were placed under their heads? The punishment for their sins rested on their bones, though the terror of these warriors had stalked through the land of the living.

[28] "You too, O Pharaoh, will be broken and will lie among the uncircumcised, with those killed by the sword.

[29] "Edom is there, her kings and all her princes; despite their power, they are laid with those killed by the sword. They lie with the uncircumcised, with those who go down to the pit.

[30] "All the princes of the north and all the Sidonians are there; they went down with the slain in disgrace despite the terror caused by their power. They lie uncircumcised with those killed by the sword and bear their shame with those who go down to the pit.

[31] "Pharaoh—he and all his army—will see them and he will be consoled for all his hordes that were killed by the sword, declares the Sovereign LORD. [32] Although I had him spread terror in the land of the living, Pharaoh and all his hordes will be laid among the uncircumcised, with those killed by the sword, declares the Sovereign LORD."

Ezekiel a Watchman

33 The word of the LORD came to me: [2] "Son of man, speak to your countrymen and say to them: 'When I bring the sword against a land, and the people of the land choose one of their men and make him their watchman, [3] and he sees the sword coming against the land and blows the trumpet to warn the people, [4] then if anyone hears the trumpet but does not take warning and the sword comes and takes his life, his blood will be on his own head. [5] Since he heard the sound of the trumpet but did not take warning, his blood will be on his own head. If he had taken warning, he would have saved himself. [6] But if the watchman sees the sword coming and does not blow the trumpet

a 21 Hebrew *Sheol*; also in verse 27

to warn the people and the sword comes and takes the life of one of them, that man will be taken away because of his sin, but I will hold the watchman accountable for his blood.'

7 "Son of man, I have made you a watchman for the house of Israel; so hear the word I speak and give them warning from me. 8 When I say to the wicked, 'O wicked man, you will surely die,' and you do not speak out to dissuade him from his ways, that wicked man will die for[a] his sin, and I will hold you accountable for his blood. 9 But if you do warn the wicked man to turn from his ways and he does not do so, he will die for his sin, but you will have saved yourself.

10 "Son of man, say to the house of Israel, 'This is what you are saying: "Our offenses and sins weigh us down, and we are wasting away because of[b] them. How then can we live?" ' 11 Say to them, 'As surely as I live, declares the Sovereign LORD, I take no pleasure in the death of the wicked, but rather that they turn from their ways and live. Turn! Turn from your evil ways! Why will you die, O house of Israel?'

12 "Therefore, son of man, say to your countrymen, 'The righteousness of the righteous man will not save him when he disobeys, and the wickedness of the wicked man will not cause him to fall when he turns from it. The righteous man, if he sins, will not be allowed to live because of his former righteousness.' 13 If I tell the righteous man that he will surely live, but then he trusts in his righteousness and does evil, none of the righteous things he has done will be remembered; he will die for the evil he has done. 14 And if I say to the wicked man, 'You will surely die,' but he then turns away from his sin and does what is just and right— 15 if he gives back what he took in pledge for a loan, returns what he has stolen, follows the decrees that give life, and does no evil, he will surely live; he will not die. 16 None of the sins he has committed will be remembered against him. He has done what is just and right; he will surely live.

17 "Yet your countrymen say, 'The way of the Lord is not just.' But it is their way that is not just. 18 If a righteous man turns from his righteousness and does evil, he will die for it. 19 And if a wicked man turns away from his wickedness and does what is just and right, he will live by doing so. 20 Yet, O house of Israel, you say, 'The way of the Lord is not just.' But I will judge each of you according to his own ways."

Jerusalem's Fall Explained

21 In the twelfth year of our exile, in the tenth month on the fifth day, a man who had escaped from Jerusalem came to me and said, "The city has fallen!" 22 Now the evening before the man arrived, the hand of the LORD was upon me, and he opened my mouth before the man came to me in the morning. So my mouth was opened and I was no longer silent.

23 Then the word of the LORD came to me: 24 "Son of man, the people living in those ruins in the land of Israel are saying, 'Abraham was only one man, yet he possessed the land. But we are many; surely the land has been given to us as our possession.' 25 Therefore say to them, 'This is what the Sovereign LORD says: Since you eat meat with the blood still in it and look to your idols and shed blood, should you

---

Turn Back to God

EZEKIEL 33:11–16

"And then he showed me a little thing, the size of a hazelnut, lying in the palm of my hand, as it seemed to me. It was as round as a ball. I looked at it with the eye of my understanding and thought, *What can this be?* It was answered generally thus: 'It is all that is made.' I marveled that it could last, for it was so little that it could suddenly have become nothing. I was answered in my understanding, 'It lasts and ever shall, for God loves it.' And so everything has being by the love of God. In this little thing I saw three properties. The first is that God made it, the second that God loves it, and the third that God keeps it."

—JULIAN OF NORWICH, *Showings*

The Whole Person Obeys

EZEKIEL 33:31–33

The people of Israel are physically present at worship, but their minds and hearts are somewhere else. Although they listen to the word of God, they have no intention of obeying it.

Draw a large picture of a person. (Artistic ability not required!) Next to the mouth you have drawn, write words of flattery that you might use—that are only partially true or hollow-sounding—to praise others. Draw a heart and inside of it write words of greed you might use to express some of your attitudes about money and possessions. Lastly, near the feet write some words that define those things that draw you away from the path of discipleship. Now draw another person and put words of kindness by the mouth, words of love and compassion inside the heart, and words of service next to the feet. Offer a prayer that your whole being might be responsive to God's guidance.

See Meeting God in Prayer

1144

then possess the land? ²⁶You rely on your sword, you do detestable things, and each of you defiles his neighbor's wife. Should you then possess the land?'

²⁷"Say this to them: 'This is what the Sovereign LORD says: As surely as I live, those who are left in the ruins will fall by the sword, those out in the country I will give to the wild animals to be devoured, and those in strongholds and caves will die of a plague. ²⁸I will make the land a desolate waste, and her proud strength will come to an end, and the mountains of Israel will become desolate so that no one will cross them. ²⁹Then they will know that I am the LORD, when I have made the land a desolate waste because of all the detestable things they have done.'

³⁰"As for you, son of man, your countrymen are talking together about you by the walls and at the doors of the houses, saying to each other, 'Come and hear the message that has come from the LORD.' ³¹My people come to you, as they usually do, and sit before you to listen to your words, but they do not put them into practice. With their mouths they express devotion, but their hearts are greedy for unjust gain. ³²Indeed, to them you are nothing more than one who sings love songs with a beautiful voice and plays an instrument well, for they hear your words but do not put them into practice.

³³"When all this comes true—and it surely will—then they will know that a prophet has been among them."

Shepherds and Sheep

34 The word of the LORD came to me: ²"Son of man, prophesy against the shepherds of Israel; prophesy and say to them: 'This is what the Sovereign LORD says: Woe to the shepherds of Israel who only take care of themselves! Should not shepherds take care of the flock? ³You eat the curds, clothe yourselves with the wool and slaughter the choice animals, but you do not take care of the flock. ⁴You have not strengthened the weak or healed the sick or bound up the injured. You have not brought back the strays or searched for the lost. You have ruled them harshly and brutally. ⁵So they were scattered because there was no shepherd, and when they were scattered they became food for all the wild animals. ⁶My sheep wandered over all the mountains and on every high hill. They were scattered over the whole earth, and no one searched or looked for them.

⁷" 'Therefore, you shepherds, hear the word of the LORD: ⁸As surely as I live, declares the Sovereign LORD, because my flock lacks a shepherd and so has been plundered and has become food for all the wild animals, and because my shepherds did not search for my flock but cared for themselves rather than for my flock, ⁹therefore, O shepherds, hear the word of the LORD: ¹⁰This is what the Sovereign LORD says: I am against the shepherds and will hold them accountable for my flock. I will remove them from tending the flock so that the shepherds can no longer feed themselves. I will rescue my flock from their mouths, and it will no longer be food for them.

¹¹" 'For this is what the Sovereign LORD says: I myself will search for my sheep and look after them. ¹²As a shepherd looks after his scattered flock when he is with them, so will I look after my sheep. I will rescue them from all the places

where they were scattered on a day of clouds and darkness. ¹³I will bring them out from the nations and gather them from the countries, and I will bring them into their own land. I will pasture them on the mountains of Israel, in the ravines and in all the settlements in the land. ¹⁴I will tend them in a good pasture, and the mountain heights of Israel will be their grazing land. There they will lie down in good grazing land, and there they will feed in a rich pasture on the mountains of Israel. ¹⁵I myself will tend my sheep and have them lie down, declares the Sovereign LORD. ¹⁶I will search for the lost and bring back the strays. I will bind up the injured and strengthen the weak, but the sleek and the strong I will destroy. I will shepherd the flock with justice.

¹⁷" 'As for you, my flock, this is what the Sovereign LORD says: I will judge between one sheep and another, and between rams and goats. ¹⁸Is it not enough for you to feed on the good pasture? Must you also trample the rest of your pasture with your feet? Is it not enough for you to drink clear water? Must you also muddy the rest with your feet? ¹⁹Must my flock feed on what you have trampled and drink what you have muddied with your feet?

²⁰" 'Therefore this is what the Sovereign LORD says to them: See, I myself will judge between the fat sheep and the lean sheep. ²¹Because you shove with flank and shoulder, butting all the weak sheep with your horns until you have driven them away, ²²I will save my flock, and they will no longer be plundered. I will judge between one sheep and another. ²³I will place over them one shepherd, my servant David, and he will tend them; he will tend them and be their shepherd. ²⁴I the LORD will be their God, and my servant David will be prince among them. I the LORD have spoken.

²⁵" 'I will make a covenant of peace with them and rid the land of wild beasts so that they may live in the desert and sleep in the forests in safety. ²⁶I will bless them and the places surrounding my hill.ᵃ I will send down showers in season; there will be showers of blessing. ²⁷The trees of the field will yield their fruit and the ground will yield its crops; the people will be secure in their land. They will know that I am the LORD, when I break the bars of their yoke and rescue them from the hands of those who enslaved them. ²⁸They will no longer be plundered by the nations, nor will wild animals devour them. They will live in safety, and no one will make them afraid. ²⁹I will provide for them a land renowned for its crops, and they will no longer be victims of famine in the land or bear the scorn of the nations. ³⁰Then they will know that I, the LORD their God, am with them and that they, the house of Israel, are my people, declares the Sovereign LORD. ³¹You my sheep, the sheep of my pasture, are people, and I am your God, declares the Sovereign LORD.' "

A Prophecy Against Edom

35 The word of the LORD came to me: ²"Son of man, set your face against Mount Seir; prophesy against it ³and say: 'This is what the Sovereign LORD says: I am against you, Mount Seir, and I will stretch out my hand against you and make you a desolate waste. ⁴I will turn

---

The Good Shepherd

EZEKIEL 34:1–31

The people of Israel are like abandoned sheep. Their leaders have been poor shepherds who have not gathered them, nursed their wounds, fed them or protected them from danger. So God promises that he will lead them himself and place over them a shepherd like David, thereby promising to establish a new covenant of peace through the coming Messiah.

Turn to either Psalm 23 or John 10 (or both) and read these familiar texts that tell of the caring, guiding role of the shepherd. Reflect on ways in which you need to be cared for. Are you lost? Are you carrying wounds or resentments that get in the way of joyful living? Are you hungry for spiritual food? Has someone given you false guidance? Imagine a plentiful pasture and a gentle shepherd. Repeat as a prayer guide, "The LORD is my shepherd, I shall not be in want" (Psalm 23:1).

See Meeting God in Scripture

ᵃ26 Or *I will make them and the places surrounding my hill a blessing*

Hope and Restoration

EZEKIEL 36:8–12

After many chapters of doom and gloom, the prophet speaks a word of hope and restoration. The people will come home from exile, the towns will be rebuilt and the land will once again become fruitful. God promises them, "[I] will make you prosper more than before."

Restoration is a word of hope. Think about times of restoration in your life—a restoration to health, a renewal of your family life after an absence or separation, a restoration of prosperity after a transition or loss. Perhaps you could plant a tree or a garden as an affirmation of trust in God's ability to bring about hope and restoration.

See Meeting God in Everyday Life

your towns into ruins and you will be desolate. Then you will know that I am the LORD.

⁵" 'Because you harbored an ancient hostility and delivered the Israelites over to the sword at the time of their calamity, the time their punishment reached its climax, ⁶therefore as surely as I live, declares the Sovereign LORD, I will give you over to bloodshed and it will pursue you. Since you did not hate bloodshed, bloodshed will pursue you. ⁷I will make Mount Seir a desolate waste and cut off from it all who come and go. ⁸I will fill your mountains with the slain; those killed by the sword will fall on your hills and in your valleys and in all your ravines. ⁹I will make you desolate forever; your towns will not be inhabited. Then you will know that I am the LORD.

¹⁰" 'Because you have said, "These two nations and countries will be ours and we will take possession of them," even though I the LORD was there, ¹¹therefore as surely as I live, declares the Sovereign LORD, I will treat you in accordance with the anger and jealousy you showed in your hatred of them and I will make myself known among them when I judge you. ¹²Then you will know that I the LORD have heard all the contemptible things you have said against the mountains of Israel. You said, "They have been laid waste and have been given over to us to devour." ¹³You boasted against me and spoke against me without restraint, and I heard it. ¹⁴This is what the Sovereign LORD says: While the whole earth rejoices, I will make you desolate. ¹⁵Because you rejoiced when the inheritance of the house of Israel became desolate, that is how I will treat you. You will be desolate, O Mount Seir, you and all of Edom. Then they will know that I am the LORD.' "

A Prophecy to the Mountains of Israel

36 "Son of man, prophesy to the mountains of Israel and say, 'O mountains of Israel, hear the word of the LORD. ²This is what the Sovereign LORD says: The enemy said of you, "Aha! The ancient heights have become our possession." ' ³Therefore prophesy and say, 'This is what the Sovereign LORD says: Because they ravaged and hounded you from every side so that you became the possession of the rest of the nations and the object of people's malicious talk and slander, ⁴therefore, O mountains of Israel, hear the word of the Sovereign LORD: This is what the Sovereign LORD says to the mountains and hills, to the ravines and valleys, to the desolate ruins and the deserted towns that have been plundered and ridiculed by the rest of the nations around you— ⁵this is what the Sovereign LORD says: In my burning zeal I have spoken against the rest of the nations, and against all Edom, for with glee and with malice in their hearts they made my land their own possession so that they might plunder its pastureland.' ⁶Therefore prophesy concerning the land of Israel and say to the mountains and hills, to the ravines and valleys: 'This is what the Sovereign LORD says: I speak in my jealous wrath because you have suffered the scorn of the nations. ⁷Therefore this is what the Sovereign LORD says: I swear with uplifted hand that the nations around you will also suffer scorn.

⁸" 'But you, O mountains of Israel, will produce branches and fruit for my people Israel, for they will soon come home. ⁹I am concerned for you and will look on you with

favor; you will be plowed and sown, [10]and I will multiply the number of people upon you, even the whole house of Israel. The towns will be inhabited and the ruins rebuilt. [11]I will increase the number of men and animals upon you, and they will be fruitful and become numerous. I will settle people on you as in the past and will make you prosper more than before. Then you will know that I am the LORD. [12]I will cause people, my people Israel, to walk upon you. They will possess you, and you will be their inheritance; you will never again deprive them of their children.

[13]" 'This is what the Sovereign LORD says: Because people say to you, "You devour men and deprive your nation of its children," [14]therefore you will no longer devour men or make your nation childless, declares the Sovereign LORD. [15]No longer will I make you hear the taunts of the nations, and no longer will you suffer the scorn of the peoples or cause your nation to fall, declares the Sovereign LORD.' "

[16]Again the word of the LORD came to me: [17]"Son of man, when the people of Israel were living in their own land, they defiled it by their conduct and their actions. Their conduct was like a woman's monthly uncleanness in my sight. [18]So I poured out my wrath on them because they had shed blood in the land and because they had defiled it with their idols. [19]I dispersed them among the nations, and they were scattered through the countries; I judged them according to their conduct and their actions. [20]And wherever they went among the nations they profaned my holy name, for it was said of them, 'These are the LORD's people, and yet they had to leave his land.' [21]I had concern for my holy name, which the house of Israel profaned among the nations where they had gone.

[22]"Therefore say to the house of Israel, 'This is what the Sovereign LORD says: It is not for your sake, O house of Israel, that I am going to do these things, but for the sake of my holy name, which you have profaned among the nations where you have gone. [23]I will show the holiness of my great name, which has been profaned among the nations, the name you have profaned among them. Then the nations will know that I am the LORD, declares the Sovereign LORD, when I show myself holy through you before their eyes.

[24]" 'For I will take you out of the nations; I will gather you from all the countries and bring you back into your own land. [25]I will sprinkle clean water on you, and you will be clean; I will cleanse you from all your impurities and from all your idols. [26]I will give you a new heart and put a new spirit in you; I will remove from you your heart of stone and give you a heart of flesh. [27]And I will put my Spirit in you and move you to follow my decrees and be careful to keep my laws. [28]You will live in the land I gave your forefathers; you will be my people, and I will be your God. [29]I will save you from all your uncleanness. I will call for the grain and make it plentiful and will not bring famine upon you. [30]I will increase the fruit of the trees and the crops of the field, so that you will no longer suffer disgrace among the nations because of famine. [31]Then you will remember your evil ways and wicked deeds, and you will loathe yourselves for your sins and detestable practices. [32]I want you to know that I am not doing this for your sake, declares the Sover-

Clean and New

EZEKIEL 36:25–28

The images in this passage are like sunshine after a long, hard winter. Ezekiel declares that the nation and the people will be sprinkled with clean water and given a new spirit and a new heart. The relationship between God and Israel is to be restored.

What does this passage say about God's character? What does it say about our need for forgiveness and salvation? How might you pray to God, who is seeking you at this very moment? Sprinkle a little water on yourself and remember how God's love and forgiveness bring you the sense of being fresh and newly cleansed. Better still, "Remember your baptism and be thankful" (United Methodist "Service of Baptism Covenant I").

See Meeting God in Worship

In the Valley

EZEKIEL 37:1–14

Join Ezekiel in his visit to the valley of dry bones. Imagine you are there, looking out over the barren, dry landscape covered with bleached white bones. The smell of dust and decay is acrid in your nostrils. You wonder with Ezekiel, "How can these bones live again?"

Tell the bones to hear the word of the Lord and live. Watch and listen as the bones shake and rattle, bone meeting bone as they snap together.

Then breath comes from the four winds as you call it to come. Hear the rush of the wind and feel its breeze. See the movement of breath in the bellies and chests of the flesh. See the bones become living people and begin to dance. Now read verses 12–14. Ask God to continue to breathe life into you and your congregation.

See Meeting God in Scripture

---

eign LORD. Be ashamed and disgraced for your conduct, O house of Israel!

33 " 'This is what the Sovereign LORD says: On the day I cleanse you from all your sins, I will resettle your towns, and the ruins will be rebuilt. 34 The desolate land will be cultivated instead of lying desolate in the sight of all who pass through it. 35 They will say, "This land that was laid waste has become like the garden of Eden; the cities that were lying in ruins, desolate and destroyed, are now fortified and inhabited." 36 Then the nations around you that remain will know that I the LORD have rebuilt what was destroyed and have replanted what was desolate. I the LORD have spoken, and I will do it.'

37 "This is what the Sovereign LORD says: Once again I will yield to the plea of the house of Israel and do this for them: I will make their people as numerous as sheep, 38 as numerous as the flocks for offerings at Jerusalem during her appointed feasts. So will the ruined cities be filled with flocks of people. Then they will know that I am the LORD."

The Valley of Dry Bones

37 The hand of the LORD was upon me, and he brought me out by the Spirit of the LORD and set me in the middle of a valley; it was full of bones. 2 He led me back and forth among them, and I saw a great many bones on the floor of the valley, bones that were very dry. 3 He asked me, "Son of man, can these bones live?"

I said, "O Sovereign LORD, you alone know."

4 Then he said to me, "Prophesy to these bones and say to them, 'Dry bones, hear the word of the LORD! 5 This is what the Sovereign LORD says to these bones: I will make breath*a* enter you, and you will come to life. 6 I will attach tendons to you and make flesh come upon you and cover you with skin; I will put breath in you, and you will come to life. Then you will know that I am the LORD.' "

7 So I prophesied as I was commanded. And as I was prophesying, there was a noise, a rattling sound, and the bones came together, bone to bone. 8 I looked, and tendons and flesh appeared on them and skin covered them, but there was no breath in them.

9 Then he said to me, "Prophesy to the breath; prophesy, son of man, and say to it, 'This is what the Sovereign LORD says: Come from the four winds, O breath, and breathe into these slain, that they may live.' " 10 So I prophesied as he commanded me, and breath entered them; they came to life and stood up on their feet—a vast army.

11 Then he said to me: "Son of man, these bones are the whole house of Israel. They say, 'Our bones are dried up and our hope is gone; we are cut off.' 12 Therefore prophesy and say to them: 'This is what the Sovereign LORD says: O my people, I am going to open your graves and bring you up from them; I will bring you back to the land of Israel. 13 Then you, my people, will know that I am the LORD, when I open your graves and bring you up from them. 14 I will put my Spirit in you and you will live, and I will settle you in your own land. Then you will know that I the LORD have spoken, and I have done it, declares the LORD.' "

a 5 The Hebrew for this word can also mean *wind* or *spirit* (see verses 6–14).

One Nation Under One King

[15]The word of the LORD came to me: [16]"Son of man, take a stick of wood and write on it, 'Belonging to Judah and the Israelites associated with him.' Then take another stick of wood, and write on it, 'Ephraim's stick, belonging to Joseph and all the house of Israel associated with him.' [17]Join them together into one stick so that they will become one in your hand.

[18]"When your countrymen ask you, 'Won't you tell us what you mean by this?' [19]say to them, 'This is what the Sovereign LORD says: I am going to take the stick of Joseph—which is in Ephraim's hand—and of the Israelite tribes associated with him, and join it to Judah's stick, making them a single stick of wood, and they will become one in my hand.' [20]Hold before their eyes the sticks you have written on [21]and say to them, 'This is what the Sovereign LORD says: I will take the Israelites out of the nations where they have gone. I will gather them from all around and bring them back into their own land. [22]I will make them one nation in the land, on the mountains of Israel. There will be one king over all of them and they will never again be two nations or be divided into two kingdoms. [23]They will no longer defile themselves with their idols and vile images or with any of their offenses, for I will save them from all their sinful backsliding,[a] and I will cleanse them. They will be my people, and I will be their God.

[24]" 'My servant David will be king over them, and they will all have one shepherd. They will follow my laws and be careful to keep my decrees. [25]They will live in the land I gave to my servant Jacob, the land where your fathers lived. They and their children and their children's children will live there forever, and David my servant will be their prince forever. [26]I will make a covenant of peace with them; it will be an everlasting covenant. I will establish them and increase their numbers, and I will put my sanctuary among them forever. [27]My dwelling place will be with them; I will be their God, and they will be my people. [28]Then the nations will know that I the LORD make Israel holy, when my sanctuary is among them forever.' "

A Prophecy Against Gog

38 The word of the LORD came to me: [2]"Son of man, set your face against Gog, of the land of Magog, the chief prince of[b] Meshech and Tubal; prophesy against him [3]and say: 'This is what the Sovereign LORD says: I am against you, O Gog, chief prince of[c] Meshech and Tubal. [4]I will turn you around, put hooks in your jaws and bring you out with your whole army—your horses, your horsemen fully armed, and a great horde with large and small shields, all of them brandishing their swords. [5]Persia, Cush[d] and Put will be with them, all with shields and helmets, [6]also Gomer with all its troops, and Beth Togarmah from the far north with all its troops—the many nations with you.

[7]" 'Get ready; be prepared, you and all the hordes gathered about you, and take command of them. [8]After many days you will be called to arms. In future years you will invade a land that has recovered from war, whose people

---

---

[a]23 Many Hebrew manuscripts (see also Septuagint); most Hebrew manuscripts *all their dwelling places where they sinned*   [b]2 Or *the prince of Rosh,*   [c]3 Or *Gog, prince of Rosh,*   [d]5 That is, the upper Nile region

When What Looks Like Disaster Isn't

EZEKIEL 38:16

A nation from the north is coming like a dark cloud to crush Israel, but the ultimate defeat of that marauding nation will show that God is still in charge.

Remember a time in your life when some disaster threatened the "end" of your world. Can you remember how you felt, what you did? With the gift of hindsight, note how where you have been has brought you to where you are today. How are you a different person because of that experience? How did God bring you to a new day? Did you thank God? If not, today is a good day for a prayer of thanksgiving.

See *Meeting God in Everyday Life*

were gathered from many nations to the mountains of Israel, which had long been desolate. They had been brought out from the nations, and now all of them live in safety. ⁹You and all your troops and the many nations with you will go up, advancing like a storm; you will be like a cloud covering the land.

¹⁰" 'This is what the Sovereign LORD says: On that day thoughts will come into your mind and you will devise an evil scheme. ¹¹You will say, "I will invade a land of unwalled villages; I will attack a peaceful and unsuspecting people— all of them living without walls and without gates and bars. ¹²I will plunder and loot and turn my hand against the resettled ruins and the people gathered from the nations, rich in livestock and goods, living at the center of the land." ¹³Sheba and Dedan and the merchants of Tarshish and all her villages*a* will say to you, "Have you come to plunder? Have you gathered your hordes to loot, to carry off silver and gold, to take away livestock and goods and to seize much plunder?" '

¹⁴"Therefore, son of man, prophesy and say to Gog: 'This is what the Sovereign LORD says: In that day, when my people Israel are living in safety, will you not take notice of it? ¹⁵You will come from your place in the far north, you and many nations with you, all of them riding on horses, a great horde, a mighty army. ¹⁶You will advance against my people Israel like a cloud that covers the land. In days to come, O Gog, I will bring you against my land, so that the nations may know me when I show myself holy through you before their eyes.

¹⁷" 'This is what the Sovereign LORD says: Are you not the one I spoke of in former days by my servants the prophets of Israel? At that time they prophesied for years that I would bring you against them. ¹⁸This is what will happen in that day: When Gog attacks the land of Israel, my hot anger will be aroused, declares the Sovereign LORD. ¹⁹In my zeal and fiery wrath I declare that at that time there shall be a great earthquake in the land of Israel. ²⁰The fish of the sea, the birds of the air, the beasts of the field, every creature that moves along the ground, and all the people on the face of the earth will tremble at my presence. The mountains will be overturned, the cliffs will crumble and every wall will fall to the ground. ²¹I will summon a sword against Gog on all my mountains, declares the Sovereign LORD. Every man's sword will be against his brother. ²²I will execute judgment upon him with plague and bloodshed; I will pour down torrents of rain, hailstones and burning sulfur on him and on his troops and on the many nations with him. ²³And so I will show my greatness and my holiness, and I will make myself known in the sight of many nations. Then they will know that I am the LORD.'

39 "Son of man, prophesy against Gog and say: 'This is what the Sovereign LORD says: I am against you, O Gog, chief prince of*b* Meshech and Tubal. ²I will turn you around and drag you along. I will bring you from the far north and send you against the mountains of Israel. ³Then I will strike your bow from your left hand and make your arrows drop from your right hand. ⁴On the mountains of Israel you will fall, you and all your troops and the nations with you. I will give you as food to all kinds of carrion birds

a 13 Or *her strong lions*   *b 1* Or *Gog, prince of Rosh,* and to the wild animals. ⁵You will fall in the open field, for I have spoken, declares the Sovereign LORD. ⁶I will send fire on Magog and on those who live in safety in the coastlands, and they will know that I am the LORD.

⁷" 'I will make known my holy name among my people Israel. I will no longer let my holy name be profaned, and the nations will know that I the LORD am the Holy One in Israel. ⁸It is coming! It will surely take place, declares the Sovereign LORD. This is the day I have spoken of.

⁹" 'Then those who live in the towns of Israel will go out and use the weapons for fuel and burn them up—the small and large shields, the bows and arrows, the war clubs and spears. For seven years they will use them for fuel. ¹⁰They will not need to gather wood from the fields or cut it from the forests, because they will use the weapons for fuel. And they will plunder those who plundered them and loot those who looted them, declares the Sovereign LORD.

¹¹" 'On that day I will give Gog a burial place in Israel, in the valley of those who travel east toward*a* the Sea.*b* It will block the way of travelers, because Gog and all his hordes will be buried there. So it will be called the Valley of Hamon Gog.*c*

¹²" 'For seven months the house of Israel will be burying them in order to cleanse the land. ¹³All the people of the land will bury them, and the day I am glorified will be a memorable day for them, declares the Sovereign LORD.

¹⁴" 'Men will be regularly employed to cleanse the land. Some will go throughout the land and, in addition to them, others will bury those that remain on the ground. At the end of the seven months they will begin their search. ¹⁵As they go through the land and one of them sees a human bone, he will set up a marker beside it until the gravediggers have buried it in the Valley of Hamon Gog. ¹⁶(Also a town called Hamonah*d* will be there.) And so they will cleanse the land.'

¹⁷"Son of man, this is what the Sovereign LORD says: Call out to every kind of bird and all the wild animals: 'Assemble and come together from all around to the sacrifice I am preparing for you, the great sacrifice on the mountains of Israel. There you will eat flesh and drink blood. ¹⁸You will eat the flesh of mighty men and drink the blood of the princes of the earth as if they were rams and lambs, goats and bulls—all of them fattened animals from Bashan. ¹⁹At the sacrifice I am preparing for you, you will eat fat till you are glutted and drink blood till you are drunk. ²⁰At my table you will eat your fill of horses and riders, mighty men and soldiers of every kind,' declares the Sovereign LORD.

²¹"I will display my glory among the nations, and all the nations will see the punishment I inflict and the hand I lay upon them. ²²From that day forward the house of Israel will know that I am the LORD their God. ²³And the nations will know that the people of Israel went into exile for their sin, because they were unfaithful to me. So I hid my face from them and handed them over to their enemies, and they all fell by the sword. ²⁴I dealt with them according to their uncleanness and their offenses, and I hid my face from them.

²⁵"Therefore this is what the Sovereign LORD says: I will now bring Jacob back from captivity*e* and will have com-

Hide and Seek

EZEKIEL 39:24,29

We often think that it is we humans who hide from God and God who seeks us. But here in this passage we have the image of God hiding from humanity, or at least turning away: "I hid my face from them."

The mystics have written of experiencing these times when God seems distant or absent. Jesus experienced such a time as he hung on the cross on our behalf (see Matthew 27:46). Does God seem distant or absent from you right now? Why do you think such moments or seasons occur? What do you think is necessary for you to restore a keen awareness of God's presence? Read Psalm 51 for one answer.

See Meeting God in Prayer

---

a 11 Or *of*   *b 11* That is, the Dead Sea   *c 11* *Hamon Gog* means *hordes of Gog.*   *d 16* *Hamonah* means *horde.*   *e 25* Or *now restore the fortunes of Jacob*

1151

Visions

EZEKIEL 40:1–4

There are many kinds of sight. We speak of plain sight (seeing what is right before us) and hindsight (clarity of sight when we look back at something that has already happened). Just as important is insight, the perception of deeper layers of wisdom and meaning. Insight has an element of mystery or grace, because we can't manufacture it; it is a gift from God.

Do you have insight? How can you humbly share it with others? Have you ever had a vision? What was it about? Was it a personal vision or for the wider community? Have you shared the vision with anyone? What steps have you taken to act on this gift from God?

See Meeting God in Community

passion on all the people of Israel, and I will be zealous for my holy name. ²⁶They will forget their shame and all the unfaithfulness they showed toward me when they lived in safety in their land with no one to make them afraid. ²⁷When I have brought them back from the nations and have gathered them from the countries of their enemies, I will show myself holy through them in the sight of many nations. ²⁸Then they will know that I am the LORD their God, for though I sent them into exile among the nations, I will gather them to their own land, not leaving any behind. ²⁹I will no longer hide my face from them, for I will pour out my Spirit on the house of Israel, declares the Sovereign LORD."

The New Temple Area

40 In the twenty-fifth year of our exile, at the beginning of the year, on the tenth of the month, in the fourteenth year after the fall of the city—on that very day the hand of the LORD was upon me and he took me there. ²In visions of God he took me to the land of Israel and set me on a very high mountain, on whose south side were some buildings that looked like a city. ³He took me there, and I saw a man whose appearance was like bronze; he was standing in the gateway with a linen cord and a measuring rod in his hand. ⁴The man said to me, "Son of man, look with your eyes and hear with your ears and pay attention to everything I am going to show you, for that is why you have been brought here. Tell the house of Israel everything you see."

The East Gate to the Outer Court

⁵I saw a wall completely surrounding the temple area. The length of the measuring rod in the man's hand was six long cubits, each of which was a cubit*a* and a handbreadth.*b* He measured the wall; it was one measuring rod thick and one rod high.

⁶Then he went to the gate facing east. He climbed its steps and measured the threshold of the gate; it was one rod deep.*c* ⁷The alcoves for the guards were one rod long and one rod wide, and the projecting walls between the alcoves were five cubits thick. And the threshold of the gate next to the portico facing the temple was one rod deep.

⁸Then he measured the portico of the gateway; ⁹it*d* was eight cubits deep and its jambs were two cubits thick. The portico of the gateway faced the temple.

¹⁰Inside the east gate were three alcoves on each side; the three had the same measurements, and the faces of the projecting walls on each side had the same measurements. ¹¹Then he measured the width of the entrance to the gateway; it was ten cubits and its length was thirteen cubits. ¹²In front of each alcove was a wall one cubit high, and the alcoves were six cubits square. ¹³Then he measured the gateway from the top of the rear wall of one alcove to the top of the opposite one; the distance was twenty-five cubits from one parapet opening to the opposite one. ¹⁴He mea-

a 5 The common cubit was about 1 1/2 feet (about 0.5 meter).   *b 5* That is, about 3 inches (about 8 centimeters)   *c 6* Septuagint; Hebrew *deep, the first threshold, one rod deep*   *d 8,9* Many Hebrew manuscripts, Septuagint, Vulgate and Syriac; most Hebrew manuscripts *gateway facing the temple; it was one rod deep.* ⁹*Then he measured the portico of the gateway; it*

sured along the faces of the projecting walls all around the inside of the gateway—sixty cubits. The measurement was up to the portico[a] facing the courtyard.[b] ¹⁵The distance from the entrance of the gateway to the far end of its portico was fifty cubits. ¹⁶The alcoves and the projecting walls inside the gateway were surmounted by narrow parapet openings all around, as was the portico; the openings all around faced inward. The faces of the projecting walls were decorated with palm trees.

The Outer Court

¹⁷Then he brought me into the outer court. There I saw some rooms and a pavement that had been constructed all around the court; there were thirty rooms along the pavement. ¹⁸It abutted the sides of the gateways and was as wide as they were long; this was the lower pavement. ¹⁹Then he measured the distance from the inside of the lower gateway to the outside of the inner court; it was a hundred cubits on the east side as well as on the north.

The North Gate

²⁰Then he measured the length and width of the gate facing north, leading into the outer court. ²¹Its alcoves—three on each side—its projecting walls and its portico had the same measurements as those of the first gateway. It was fifty cubits long and twenty-five cubits wide. ²²Its openings, its portico and its palm tree decorations had the same measurements as those of the gate facing east. Seven steps led up to it, with its portico opposite them. ²³There was a gate to the inner court facing the north gate, just as there was on the east. He measured from one gate to the opposite one; it was a hundred cubits.

The South Gate

²⁴Then he led me to the south side and I saw a gate facing south. He measured its jambs and its portico, and they had the same measurements as the others. ²⁵The gateway and its portico had narrow openings all around, like the openings of the others. It was fifty cubits long and twenty-five cubits wide. ²⁶Seven steps led up to it, with its portico opposite them; it had palm tree decorations on the faces of the projecting walls on each side. ²⁷The inner court also had a gate facing south, and he measured from this gate to the outer gate on the south side; it was a hundred cubits.

Gates to the Inner Court

²⁸Then he brought me into the inner court through the south gate, and he measured the south gate; it had the same measurements as the others. ²⁹Its alcoves, its projecting walls and its portico had the same measurements as the others. The gateway and its portico had openings all around. It was fifty cubits long and twenty-five cubits wide. ³⁰(The porticoes of the gateways around the inner court were twenty-five cubits wide and five cubits deep.) ³¹Its portico faced the outer court; palm trees decorated its jambs, and eight steps led up to it.

³²Then he brought me to the inner court on the east side, and he measured the gateway; it had the same measure-

The Measure of Worship

EZEKIEL 40:20–27

"When we come to a service of worship, we should come to participate, to bring our praise and honor and thanks—as well as our needs—and lay them at God's feet in the midst of this great mixed community of the present and the past. In this act, we are lifted out of our private world into a public one, out of our personal situations into a social situation . . . The humbling, enlarging, encompassing fellowship into which the church's corporate exercise sweeps us is a part of the Christian experience that we dare not forgo if we are able to attend."

—DOUGLAS STEERE,
Dimensions of Prayer

See *Meeting God in Worship*

^a 14 Septuagint; Hebrew *projecting wall*   ^b 14 The meaning of the Hebrew for this verse is uncertain.

1153

The Most Holy Place

EZEKIEL 41:4

For the Israelites the Most Holy Place had profound significance. For most people, having a place to pray is very important. Where is your most holy place of prayer? Do you have a room or area in your home designated to use for prayer and meditation? What sets it apart? Are there special pictures or objects in the room? Do you light candles? Is there a special chair? Do you keep a Bible, journal and other spiritual books nearby? Perhaps your holy place is in a church or small chapel. Or perhaps it is outside.

God can be present anywhere, of course, but often a designated place helps us turn our hearts and minds toward God. If you do not have a special holy place for prayer, consider finding or making one. Visit your holy place as often as you can.

See Meeting God in Prayer

ments as the others. ³³Its alcoves, its projecting walls and its portico had the same measurements as the others. The gateway and its portico had openings all around. It was fifty cubits long and twenty-five cubits wide. ³⁴Its portico faced the outer court; palm trees decorated the jambs on either side, and eight steps led up to it.

³⁵Then he brought me to the north gate and measured it. It had the same measurements as the others, ³⁶as did its alcoves, its projecting walls and its portico, and it had openings all around. It was fifty cubits long and twenty-five cubits wide. ³⁷Its portico*a* faced the outer court; palm trees decorated the jambs on either side, and eight steps led up to it.

The Rooms for Preparing Sacrifices

³⁸A room with a doorway was by the portico in each of the inner gateways, where the burnt offerings were washed. ³⁹In the portico of the gateway were two tables on each side, on which the burnt offerings, sin offerings and guilt offerings were slaughtered. ⁴⁰By the outside wall of the portico of the gateway, near the steps at the entrance to the north gateway were two tables, and on the other side of the steps were two tables. ⁴¹So there were four tables on one side of the gateway and four on the other—eight tables in all—on which the sacrifices were slaughtered. ⁴²There were also four tables of dressed stone for the burnt offerings, each a cubit and a half long, a cubit and a half wide and a cubit high. On them were placed the utensils for slaughtering the burnt offerings and the other sacrifices. ⁴³And double-pronged hooks, each a handbreadth long, were attached to the wall all around. The tables were for the flesh of the offerings.

Rooms for the Priests

⁴⁴Outside the inner gate, within the inner court, were two rooms, one*b* at the side of the north gate and facing south, and another at the side of the south*c* gate and facing north. ⁴⁵He said to me, "The room facing south is for the priests who have charge of the temple, ⁴⁶and the room facing north is for the priests who have charge of the altar. These are the sons of Zadok, who are the only Levites who may draw near to the LORD to minister before him."

⁴⁷Then he measured the court: It was square—a hundred cubits long and a hundred cubits wide. And the altar was in front of the temple.

The Temple

⁴⁸He brought me to the portico of the temple and measured the jambs of the portico; they were five cubits wide on either side. The width of the entrance was fourteen cubits and its projecting walls were*d* three cubits wide on either side. ⁴⁹The portico was twenty cubits wide, and twelve*e* cubits from front to back. It was reached by a flight of stairs,*f* and there were pillars on each side of the jambs.

41 Then the man brought me to the outer sanctuary and measured the jambs; the width of the jambs

---

a 37 Septuagint (see also verses 31 and 34); Hebrew *jambs*   *b 44* Septuagint; Hebrew *were rooms for singers, which were*   *c 44* Septuagint; Hebrew *east*   *d 48* Septuagint; Hebrew *entrance was*   *e 49* Septuagint; Hebrew *eleven*   *f 49* Hebrew; Septuagint *Ten steps led up to it*

was six cubits[a] on each side.[b] ²The entrance was ten cubits wide, and the projecting walls on each side of it were five cubits wide. He also measured the outer sanctuary; it was forty cubits long and twenty cubits wide.

³Then he went into the inner sanctuary and measured the jambs of the entrance; each was two cubits wide. The entrance was six cubits wide, and the projecting walls on each side of it were seven cubits wide. ⁴And he measured the length of the inner sanctuary; it was twenty cubits, and its width was twenty cubits across the end of the outer sanctuary. He said to me, "This is the Most Holy Place."

⁵Then he measured the wall of the temple; it was six cubits thick, and each side room around the temple was four cubits wide. ⁶The side rooms were on three levels, one above another, thirty on each level. There were ledges all around the wall of the temple to serve as supports for the side rooms, so that the supports were not inserted into the wall of the temple. ⁷The side rooms all around the temple were wider at each successive level. The structure surrounding the temple was built in ascending stages, so that the rooms widened as one went upward. A stairway went up from the lowest floor to the top floor through the middle floor.

⁸I saw that the temple had a raised base all around it, forming the foundation of the side rooms. It was the length of the rod, six long cubits. ⁹The outer wall of the side rooms was five cubits thick. The open area between the side rooms of the temple ¹⁰and the ⌊priests'⌋ rooms was twenty cubits wide all around the temple. ¹¹There were entrances to the side rooms from the open area, one on the north and another on the south; and the base adjoining the open area was five cubits wide all around.

¹²The building facing the temple courtyard on the west side was seventy cubits wide. The wall of the building was five cubits thick all around, and its length was ninety cubits.

¹³Then he measured the temple; it was a hundred cubits long, and the temple courtyard and the building with its walls were also a hundred cubits long. ¹⁴The width of the temple courtyard on the east, including the front of the temple, was a hundred cubits.

¹⁵Then he measured the length of the building facing the courtyard at the rear of the temple, including its galleries on each side; it was a hundred cubits.

The outer sanctuary, the inner sanctuary and the portico facing the court, ¹⁶as well as the thresholds and the narrow windows and galleries around the three of them—everything beyond and including the threshold was covered with wood. The floor, the wall up to the windows, and the windows were covered. ¹⁷In the space above the outside of the entrance to the inner sanctuary and on the walls at regular intervals all around the inner and outer sanctuary ¹⁸were carved cherubim and palm trees. Palm trees alternated with cherubim. Each cherub had two faces: ¹⁹the face of a man toward the palm tree on one side and the face of a lion toward the palm tree on the other. They were carved all around the whole temple. ²⁰From the floor to the area

The Table of the Lord

EZEKIEL 41:15–22

"Whenever we come together around the table, take bread, bless it, break it, and give it to one another, saying, 'The Body of Christ,' we know that Jesus is among us not as a vague memory of a person who lived long ago but as a real, life-giving presence that transforms us. By eating the Body of Christ, we become the living Christ and we are enabled to discover our own chosenness and blessedness, acknowledge our brokenness, and trust that all we live we live for others. Thus, we, like Jesus himself, become food for the world."

—HENRI J. M. NOUWEN,
Bread for the Journey

See *Meeting God in Worship*

---
[a] *1* The common cubit was about 1 1/2 feet (about 0.5 meter).   [b] *1* One Hebrew manuscript and Septuagint; most Hebrew manuscripts *side, the width of the tent*

1155

Clothed With the Spirit

EZEKIEL 42:13–14

All of us think about what is appropriate clothing for worship and for work. It is even more important to think about clothing ourselves with appropriate attitudes.

Paul counsels us to clothe ourselves with "compassion, kindness, humility, gentleness and patience . . . And over all these virtues put on love" (Colossians 3:12–14). Wherever we go and whomever we meet, this attire should reveal God's presence. Each morning this week, as you dress, mentally label one item of clothing with a specifically Christian virtue—one aspect of the fruit of the Spirit perhaps (see Galatians 5:22–23). Choose a new characteristic each day. All through the day let that piece of clothing remind you of how you are growing more Christlike.

See *Meeting God in Scripture*

above the entrance, cherubim and palm trees were carved on the wall of the outer sanctuary.

²¹ The outer sanctuary had a rectangular doorframe, and the one at the front of the Most Holy Place was similar. ²² There was a wooden altar three cubits high and two cubits square*ᵃ*; its corners, its base*ᵇ* and its sides were of wood. The man said to me, "This is the table that is before the LORD." ²³ Both the outer sanctuary and the Most Holy Place had double doors. ²⁴ Each door had two leaves—two hinged leaves for each door. ²⁵ And on the doors of the outer sanctuary were carved cherubim and palm trees like those carved on the walls, and there was a wooden overhang on the front of the portico. ²⁶ On the sidewalls of the portico were narrow windows with palm trees carved on each side. The side rooms of the temple also had overhangs.

Rooms for the Priests

42 Then the man led me northward into the outer court and brought me to the rooms opposite the temple courtyard and opposite the outer wall on the north side. ² The building whose door faced north was a hundred cubits*ᶜ* long and fifty cubits wide. ³ Both in the section twenty cubits from the inner court and in the section opposite the pavement of the outer court, gallery faced gallery at the three levels. ⁴ In front of the rooms was an inner passageway ten cubits wide and a hundred cubits*ᵈ* long. Their doors were on the north. ⁵ Now the upper rooms were narrower, for the galleries took more space from them than from the rooms on the lower and middle floors of the building. ⁶ The rooms on the third floor had no pillars, as the courts had; so they were smaller in floor space than those on the lower and middle floors. ⁷ There was an outer wall parallel to the rooms and the outer court; it extended in front of the rooms for fifty cubits. ⁸ While the row of rooms on the side next to the outer court was fifty cubits long, the row on the side nearest the sanctuary was a hundred cubits long. ⁹ The lower rooms had an entrance on the east side as one enters them from the outer court.

¹⁰ On the south side*ᵉ* along the length of the wall of the outer court, adjoining the temple courtyard and opposite the outer wall, were rooms ¹¹ with a passageway in front of them. These were like the rooms on the north; they had the same length and width, with similar exits and dimensions. Similar to the doorways on the north ¹² were the doorways of the rooms on the south. There was a doorway at the beginning of the passageway that was parallel to the corresponding wall extending eastward, by which one enters the rooms.

¹³ Then he said to me, "The north and south rooms facing the temple courtyard are the priests' rooms, where the priests who approach the LORD will eat the most holy offerings. There they will put the most holy offerings—the grain offerings, the sin offerings and the guilt offerings—for the place is holy. ¹⁴ Once the priests enter the holy precincts, they are not to go into the outer court until they leave behind the garments in which they minister, for these are holy. They are to put on other clothes before they go near the places that are for the people."

ᵃ 22 Septuagint; Hebrew *long*   *ᵇ 22* Septuagint; Hebrew *length*   *ᶜ 2* The common cubit was about 1 1/2 feet (about 0.5 meter).   *ᵈ 4* Septuagint and Syriac; Hebrew *and one cubit*   *ᵉ 10* Septuagint; Hebrew *Eastward*

¹⁵When he had finished measuring what was inside the temple area, he led me out by the east gate and measured the area all around: ¹⁶He measured the east side with the measuring rod; it was five hundred cubits.ᵃ ¹⁷He measured the north side; it was five hundred cubitsᵇ by the measuring rod. ¹⁸He measured the south side; it was five hundred cubits by the measuring rod. ¹⁹He turned to the west side and measured; it was five hundred cubits by the measuring rod. ²⁰So he measured the area on all four sides. It had a wall around it, five hundred cubits long and five hundred cubits wide, to separate the holy from the common.

The Glory Returns to the Temple

43 Then the man brought me to the gate facing east, ²and I saw the glory of the God of Israel coming from the east. His voice was like the roar of rushing waters, and the land was radiant with his glory. ³The vision I saw was like the vision I had seen when heᶜ came to destroy the city and like the visions I had seen by the Kebar River, and I fell facedown. ⁴The glory of the Lord entered the temple through the gate facing east. ⁵Then the Spirit lifted me up and brought me into the inner court, and the glory of the Lord filled the temple.

⁶While the man was standing beside me, I heard someone speaking to me from inside the temple. ⁷He said: "Son of man, this is the place of my throne and the place for the soles of my feet. This is where I will live among the Israelites forever. The house of Israel will never again defile my holy name—neither they nor their kings—by their prostitutionᵈ and the lifeless idolsᵉ of their kings at their high places. ⁸When they placed their threshold next to my threshold and their doorposts beside my doorposts, with only a wall between me and them, they defiled my holy name by their detestable practices. So I destroyed them in my anger. ⁹Now let them put away from me their prostitution and the lifeless idols of their kings, and I will live among them forever.

¹⁰"Son of man, describe the temple to the people of Israel, that they may be ashamed of their sins. Let them consider the plan, ¹¹and if they are ashamed of all they have done, make known to them the design of the temple—its arrangement, its exits and entrances—its whole design and all its regulationsᶠ and laws. Write these down before them so that they may be faithful to its design and follow all its regulations.

¹²"This is the law of the temple: All the surrounding area on top of the mountain will be most holy. Such is the law of the temple.

The Altar

¹³"These are the measurements of the altar in long cubits, that cubit being a cubitᵍ and a handbreadthʰ: Its gutter is a cubit deep and a cubit wide, with a rim of one spanⁱ

ᵃ 16 See Septuagint of verse 17; Hebrew *rods*; also in verses 18 and 19.
ᵇ 17 Septuagint; Hebrew *rods*   ᶜ 3 Some Hebrew manuscripts and Vulgate; most Hebrew manuscripts *I*   ᵈ 7 Or *their spiritual adultery*; also in verse 9
ᵉ 7 Or *the corpses*; also in verse 9   ᶠ 11 Some Hebrew manuscripts and Septuagint; most Hebrew manuscripts *regulations and its whole design*
ᵍ 13 The common cubit was about 1 1/2 feet (about 0.5 meter).   ʰ 13 That is, about 3 inches (about 8 centimeters)   ⁱ 13 That is, about 9 inches (about 22 centimeters)

Preparing to Worship

EZEKIEL 43:1–5

Worship ushers us into the presence of God with sights and sounds. Encountering God may sound like the "roar of rushing waters." It may be as bright as the radiance of the sun. Ezekiel uses vivid words to describe the experience of meeting God in his vision of the temple. Not all our worship will be so dramatic, but we can always enter worship expecting to meet the holy, living God.

How do you prepare for worship? Do you have times during the week for individual prayer and worship? Do you get plenty of rest the night before? Do you give yourself time to get to worship services without having to rush? Do you pray for openness—that through the words and music you might hear the word of God? This week be ready to let "the glory of the Lord" fill your house of worship.

See Meeting God in Worship

Facedown Worship

EZEKIEL 44:4

The glory of the Lord is so awesome, so brilliant, that Ezekiel can only fall to the ground facedown. Follow Ezekiel's example and lie facedown in God's presence. As you assume this posture, think about God. How is he so awesome that you cannot look at him? What is so grand about God that you cannot approach or talk to him? Let that kind of reverence and awe sink in. Ponder God's goodness and mercy that reveals your shame. Do you find that tears come more easily as you lie prostrate?

Rest and remain in that posture for a few moments, and know that the God who is awesome is also forgiving, slow to anger, and full of compassion and kindness. Add this posture of prayer to your practice of communing with God.

See Meeting God in Prayer

around the edge. And this is the height of the altar: [14]From the gutter on the ground up to the lower ledge it is two cubits high and a cubit wide, and from the smaller ledge up to the larger ledge it is four cubits high and a cubit wide. [15]The altar hearth is four cubits high, and four horns project upward from the hearth. [16]The altar hearth is square, twelve cubits long and twelve cubits wide. [17]The upper ledge also is square, fourteen cubits long and fourteen cubits wide, with a rim of half a cubit and a gutter of a cubit all around. The steps of the altar face east."

[18]Then he said to me, "Son of man, this is what the Sovereign LORD says: These will be the regulations for sacrificing burnt offerings and sprinkling blood upon the altar when it is built: [19]You are to give a young bull as a sin offering to the priests, who are Levites, of the family of Zadok, who come near to minister before me, declares the Sovereign LORD. [20]You are to take some of its blood and put it on the four horns of the altar and on the four corners of the upper ledge and all around the rim, and so purify the altar and make atonement for it. [21]You are to take the bull for the sin offering and burn it in the designated part of the temple area outside the sanctuary.

[22]"On the second day you are to offer a male goat without defect for a sin offering, and the altar is to be purified as it was purified with the bull. [23]When you have finished purifying it, you are to offer a young bull and a ram from the flock, both without defect. [24]You are to offer them before the LORD, and the priests are to sprinkle salt on them and sacrifice them as a burnt offering to the LORD.

[25]"For seven days you are to provide a male goat daily for a sin offering; you are also to provide a young bull and a ram from the flock, both without defect. [26]For seven days they are to make atonement for the altar and cleanse it; thus they will dedicate it. [27]At the end of these days, from the eighth day on, the priests are to present your burnt offerings and fellowship offerings[a] on the altar. Then I will accept you, declares the Sovereign LORD."

The Prince, the Levites, the Priests

44 Then the man brought me back to the outer gate of the sanctuary, the one facing east, and it was shut. [2]The LORD said to me, "This gate is to remain shut. It must not be opened; no one may enter through it. It is to remain shut because the LORD, the God of Israel, has entered through it. [3]The prince himself is the only one who may sit inside the gateway to eat in the presence of the LORD. He is to enter by way of the portico of the gateway and go out the same way."

[4]Then the man brought me by way of the north gate to the front of the temple. I looked and saw the glory of the LORD filling the temple of the LORD, and I fell facedown.

[5]The LORD said to me, "Son of man, look carefully, listen closely and give attention to everything I tell you concerning all the regulations regarding the temple of the LORD. Give attention to the entrance of the temple and all the exits of the sanctuary. [6]Say to the rebellious house of Israel, 'This is what the Sovereign LORD says: Enough of your detestable practices, O house of Israel! [7]In addition to all your other detestable practices, you brought foreigners uncircumcised in heart and flesh into my sanctuary, desecrating my temple

while you offered me food, fat and blood, and you broke my covenant. ⁸Instead of carrying out your duty in regard to my holy things, you put others in charge of my sanctuary. ⁹This is what the Sovereign LORD says: No foreigner uncircumcised in heart and flesh is to enter my sanctuary, not even the foreigners who live among the Israelites.

¹⁰" 'The Levites who went far from me when Israel went astray and who wandered from me after their idols must bear the consequences of their sin. ¹¹They may serve in my sanctuary, having charge of the gates of the temple and serving in it; they may slaughter the burnt offerings and sacrifices for the people and stand before the people and serve them. ¹²But because they served them in the presence of their idols and made the house of Israel fall into sin, therefore I have sworn with uplifted hand that they must bear the consequences of their sin, declares the Sovereign LORD. ¹³They are not to come near to serve me as priests or come near any of my holy things or my most holy offerings; they must bear the shame of their detestable practices. ¹⁴Yet I will put them in charge of the duties of the temple and all the work that is to be done in it.

¹⁵" 'But the priests, who are Levites and descendants of Zadok and who faithfully carried out the duties of my sanctuary when the Israelites went astray from me, are to come near to minister before me; they are to stand before me to offer sacrifices of fat and blood, declares the Sovereign LORD. ¹⁶They alone are to enter my sanctuary; they alone are to come near my table to minister before me and perform my service.

¹⁷" 'When they enter the gates of the inner court, they are to wear linen clothes; they must not wear any woolen garment while ministering at the gates of the inner court or inside the temple. ¹⁸They are to wear linen turbans on their heads and linen undergarments around their waists. They must not wear anything that makes them perspire. ¹⁹When they go out into the outer court where the people are, they are to take off the clothes they have been ministering in and are to leave them in the sacred rooms, and put on other clothes, so that they do not consecrate the people by means of their garments.

²⁰" 'They must not shave their heads or let their hair grow long, but they are to keep the hair of their heads trimmed. ²¹No priest is to drink wine when he enters the inner court. ²²They must not marry widows or divorced women; they may marry only virgins of Israelite descent or widows of priests. ²³They are to teach my people the difference between the holy and the common and show them how to distinguish between the unclean and the clean.

²⁴" 'In any dispute, the priests are to serve as judges and decide it according to my ordinances. They are to keep my laws and my decrees for all my appointed feasts, and they are to keep my Sabbaths holy.

²⁵" 'A priest must not defile himself by going near a dead person; however, if the dead person was his father or mother, son or daughter, brother or unmarried sister, then he may defile himself. ²⁶After he is cleansed, he must wait seven days. ²⁷On the day he goes into the inner court of the sanctuary to minister in the sanctuary, he is to offer a sin offering for himself, declares the Sovereign LORD.

²⁸" 'I am to be the only inheritance the priests have. You

The Care of God's Servants

EZEKIEL 44:28–31

Ezekiel reminds the people that they are responsible for the care and support of the priests.

Call to mind those who are your shepherds (chapter 34), teachers (44:23) and priests. Who guides your spiritual life? A number of names may come to mind.

How do you care for those who minister to you? Do you remember them in your prayers each day? Do you send them a note of thanks or encouragement? Have you ever given them a gift for Easter or Christmas? Have you invited them over for a meal or taken them out to lunch? Are you honest in your praise and gentle in your criticism? Today is a good day to do something caring for your "shepherd."

See *Meeting God in Service*

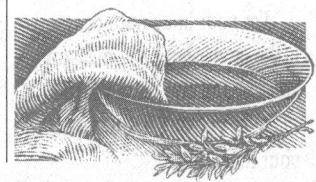

An Honest Ephah and an Honest Bath

EZEKIEL 45:10–11

An ephah was a dry measure. For a time of meditation, find a measuring cup and some measuring spoons. Hold the measuring spoons and imagine measuring some virtues as you would measure spices. Do you give your children the full tablespoon of patience? Do you pour out a full quart of joy to your spouse? Do you give your employer the full cup of an honest day's work? What else do you measure out?

Now hold the measuring cup and pour a liquid into it (a bath was a liquid measure). Pour out the oil of gladness in gratitude for your parents and the wine of compassion for those who need it. Pour out tears of sorrow and tears of joy for your friends. What would go into your cup?

Let your imagination soar a little as you hold the measuring spoons and cup. God wants to make something good out of your life.

See *Meeting God in Everyday Life*

are to give them no possession in Israel; I will be their possession. [29]They will eat the grain offerings, the sin offerings and the guilt offerings; and everything in Israel devoted[a] to the LORD will belong to them. [30]The best of all the firstfruits and of all your special gifts will belong to the priests. You are to give them the first portion of your ground meal so that a blessing may rest on your household. [31]The priests must not eat anything, bird or animal, found dead or torn by wild animals.

Division of the Land

45 " 'When you allot the land as an inheritance, you are to present to the LORD a portion of the land as a sacred district, 25,000 cubits long and 20,000[b] cubits wide; the entire area will be holy. [2]Of this, a section 500 cubits square is to be for the sanctuary, with 50 cubits around it for open land. [3]In the sacred district, measure off a section 25,000 cubits[c] long and 10,000 cubits[d] wide. In it will be the sanctuary, the Most Holy Place. [4]It will be the sacred portion of the land for the priests, who minister in the sanctuary and who draw near to minister before the LORD. It will be a place for their houses as well as a holy place for the sanctuary. [5]An area 25,000 cubits long and 10,000 cubits wide will belong to the Levites, who serve in the temple, as their possession for towns to live in.[e]

[6]" 'You are to give the city as its property an area 5,000 cubits wide and 25,000 cubits long, adjoining the sacred portion; it will belong to the whole house of Israel.

[7]" 'The prince will have the land bordering each side of the area formed by the sacred district and the property of the city. It will extend westward from the west side and eastward from the east side, running lengthwise from the western to the eastern border parallel to one of the tribal portions. [8]This land will be his possession in Israel. And my princes will no longer oppress my people but will allow the house of Israel to possess the land according to their tribes.

[9]" 'This is what the Sovereign LORD says: You have gone far enough, O princes of Israel! Give up your violence and oppression and do what is just and right. Stop dispossessing my people, declares the Sovereign LORD. [10]You are to use accurate scales, an accurate ephah[f] and an accurate bath.[g] [11]The ephah and the bath are to be the same size, the bath containing a tenth of a homer[h] and the ephah a tenth of a homer; the homer is to be the standard measure for both. [12]The shekel[i] is to consist of twenty gerahs. Twenty shekels plus twenty-five shekels plus fifteen shekels equal one mina.[j]

Offerings and Holy Days

[13]" 'This is the special gift you are to offer: a sixth of an ephah from each homer of wheat and a sixth of an ephah from each homer of barley. [14]The prescribed portion of oil, measured by the bath, is a tenth of a bath from each cor (which consists of ten baths or one homer, for ten baths are

a 29 The Hebrew term refers to the irrevocable giving over of things or persons to the LORD.   b 1 Septuagint (see also verses 3 and 5 and 48:9); Hebrew 10,000   c 3 That is, about 7 miles (about 12 kilometers)   d 3 That is, about 3 miles (about 5 kilometers)   e 5 Septuagint; Hebrew temple; they will have as their possession 20 rooms   f 10 An ephah was a dry measure.   g 10 A bath was a liquid measure.   h 11 A homer was a dry measure.   i 12 A shekel weighed about 2/5 ounce (about 11.5 grams).   j 12 That is, 60 shekels; the common mina was 50 shekels.

equivalent to a homer). ¹⁵Also one sheep is to be taken from every flock of two hundred from the well-watered pastures of Israel. These will be used for the grain offerings, burnt offerings and fellowship offerings*ᵃ* to make atonement for the people, declares the Sovereign LORD. ¹⁶All the people of the land will participate in this special gift for the use of the prince in Israel. ¹⁷It will be the duty of the prince to provide the burnt offerings, grain offerings and drink offerings at the festivals, the New Moons and the Sabbaths—at all the appointed feasts of the house of Israel. He will provide the sin offerings, grain offerings, burnt offerings and fellowship offerings to make atonement for the house of Israel.

¹⁸" 'This is what the Sovereign LORD says: In the first month on the first day you are to take a young bull without defect and purify the sanctuary. ¹⁹The priest is to take some of the blood of the sin offering and put it on the doorposts of the temple, on the four corners of the upper ledge of the altar and on the gateposts of the inner court. ²⁰You are to do the same on the seventh day of the month for anyone who sins unintentionally or through ignorance; so you are to make atonement for the temple.

²¹" 'In the first month on the fourteenth day you are to observe the Passover, a feast lasting seven days, during which you shall eat bread made without yeast. ²²On that day the prince is to provide a bull as a sin offering for himself and for all the people of the land. ²³Every day during the seven days of the Feast he is to provide seven bulls and seven rams without defect as a burnt offering to the LORD, and a male goat for a sin offering. ²⁴He is to provide as a grain offering an ephah for each bull and an ephah for each ram, along with a hin*ᵇ* of oil for each ephah.

²⁵" 'During the seven days of the Feast, which begins in the seventh month on the fifteenth day, he is to make the same provision for sin offerings, burnt offerings, grain offerings and oil.

46 " 'This is what the Sovereign LORD says: The gate of the inner court facing east is to be shut on the six working days, but on the Sabbath day and on the day of the New Moon it is to be opened. ²The prince is to enter from the outside through the portico of the gateway and stand by the gatepost. The priests are to sacrifice his burnt offering and his fellowship offerings.*ᶜ* He is to worship at the threshold of the gateway and then go out, but the gate will not be shut until evening. ³On the Sabbaths and New Moons the people of the land are to worship in the presence of the LORD at the entrance to that gateway. ⁴The burnt offering the prince brings to the LORD on the Sabbath day is to be six male lambs and a ram, all without defect. ⁵The grain offering given with the ram is to be an ephah,*ᵈ* and the grain offering with the lambs is to be as much as he pleases, along with a hin*ᵇ* of oil for each ephah. ⁶On the day of the New Moon he is to offer a young bull, six lambs and a ram, all without defect. ⁷He is to provide as a grain offering one ephah with the bull, one ephah with the ram, and with the lambs as much as he wants to give, along with a hin of oil with each ephah. ⁸When the prince enters, he is to go in through the portico of the gateway, and he is to come out the same way.

Open the Gates of Worship

EZEKIEL 46:1

"O my God, let me remember with gratitude and confess to you your mercies toward me. Let my bones be bathed in your love and let them say, 'Lord who is like unto thee? You have broken my bonds apart, I will offer to you the sacrifice of thanksgiving.' And how you broke them I will declare and all who worship you will say when they hear these things: 'Blessed be the Lord in heaven and earth, great and wonderful is his name.' "

—AUGUSTINE,
Confessions

---

*ᵃ*15 Traditionally *peace offerings*; also in verse 17   *ᵇ*24,5 That is, probably about 4 quarts (about 4 liters)   *ᶜ*2 Traditionally *peace offerings*; also in verse 12   *ᵈ*5 That is, probably about 3/5 bushel (about 22 liters)

Morning by Morning

Worship at the temple was not just for the great festivals, Sabbaths and New Moons, but each day, "morning by morning," there were to be rituals of praise and sacrifice.

Though we no longer practice animal sacrifice in worship, the instruction to worship God daily is a "lasting ordinance" for all time. "Morning by morning" is a wonderful expression of God's faithfulness in the beloved hymn: "Great is thy faithfulness! Great is thy faithfulness! Morning by morning new mercies I see; all I have needed thy hand has provided; great is thy faithfulness, Lord, unto me" (Thomas O. Chisholm, "Great Is Thy Faithfulness").

What prayer do you say or song do you sing "morning by morning" to declare your praise?

9 " 'When the people of the land come before the LORD at the appointed feasts, whoever enters by the north gate to worship is to go out the south gate; and whoever enters by the south gate is to go out the north gate. No one is to return through the gate by which he entered, but each is to go out the opposite gate. 10 The prince is to be among them, going in when they go in and going out when they go out.

11 " 'At the festivals and the appointed feasts, the grain offering is to be an ephah with a bull, an ephah with a ram, and with the lambs as much as one pleases, along with a hin of oil for each ephah. 12 When the prince provides a freewill offering to the LORD—whether a burnt offering or fellowship offerings—the gate facing east is to be opened for him. He shall offer his burnt offering or his fellowship offerings as he does on the Sabbath day. Then he shall go out, and after he has gone out, the gate will be shut.

13 " 'Every day you are to provide a year-old lamb without defect for a burnt offering to the LORD; morning by morning you shall provide it. 14 You are also to provide with it morning by morning a grain offering, consisting of a sixth of an ephah with a third of a hin of oil to moisten the flour. The presenting of this grain offering to the LORD is a lasting ordinance. 15 So the lamb and the grain offering and the oil shall be provided morning by morning for a regular burnt offering.

16 " 'This is what the Sovereign LORD says: If the prince makes a gift from his inheritance to one of his sons, it will also belong to his descendants; it is to be their property by inheritance. 17 If, however, he makes a gift from his inheritance to one of his servants, the servant may keep it until the year of freedom; then it will revert to the prince. His inheritance belongs to his sons only; it is theirs. 18 The prince must not take any of the inheritance of the people, driving them off their property. He is to give his sons their inheritance out of his own property, so that none of my people will be separated from his property.' "

19 Then the man brought me through the entrance at the side of the gate to the sacred rooms facing north, which belonged to the priests, and showed me a place at the western end. 20 He said to me, "This is the place where the priests will cook the guilt offering and the sin offering and bake the grain offering, to avoid bringing them into the outer court and consecrating the people."

21 He then brought me to the outer court and led me around to its four corners, and I saw in each corner another court. 22 In the four corners of the outer court were enclosed[a] courts, forty cubits long and thirty cubits wide; each of the courts in the four corners was the same size. 23 Around the inside of each of the four courts was a ledge of stone, with places for fire built all around under the ledge. 24 He said to me, "These are the kitchens where those who minister at the temple will cook the sacrifices of the people."

The River From the Temple

47 The man brought me back to the entrance of the temple, and I saw water coming out from under the threshold of the temple toward the east (for the temple faced east). The water was coming down from under the south side of the temple, south of the altar. 2 He then brought me out through the north gate and led me around

a 22 The meaning of the Hebrew for this word is uncertain.

the outside to the outer gate facing east, and the water was flowing from the south side.

³As the man went eastward with a measuring line in his hand, he measured off a thousand cubits*ᵃ* and then led me through water that was ankle-deep. ⁴He measured off another thousand cubits and led me through water that was knee-deep. He measured off another thousand and led me through water that was up to the waist. ⁵He measured off another thousand, but now it was a river that I could not cross, because the water had risen and was deep enough to swim in—a river that no one could cross. ⁶He asked me, "Son of man, do you see this?"

Then he led me back to the bank of the river. ⁷When I arrived there, I saw a great number of trees on each side of the river. ⁸He said to me, "This water flows toward the eastern region and goes down into the Arabah,*ᵇ* where it enters the Sea.*ᶜ* When it empties into the Sea,*ᶜ* the water there becomes fresh. ⁹Swarms of living creatures will live wherever the river flows. There will be large numbers of fish, because this water flows there and makes the salt water fresh; so where the river flows everything will live. ¹⁰Fishermen will stand along the shore; from En Gedi to En Eglaim there will be places for spreading nets. The fish will be of many kinds—like the fish of the Great Sea.*ᵈ* ¹¹But the swamps and marshes will not become fresh; they will be left for salt. ¹²Fruit trees of all kinds will grow on both banks of the river. Their leaves will not wither, nor will their fruit fail. Every month they will bear, because the water from the sanctuary flows to them. Their fruit will serve for food and their leaves for healing."

The Boundaries of the Land

¹³This is what the Sovereign LORD says: "These are the boundaries by which you are to divide the land for an inheritance among the twelve tribes of Israel, with two portions for Joseph. ¹⁴You are to divide it equally among them. Because I swore with uplifted hand to give it to your forefathers, this land will become your inheritance.

¹⁵"This is to be the boundary of the land:

"On the north side it will run from the Great Sea by the Hethlon road past Lebo*ᵉ* Hamath to Zedad, ¹⁶Berothah*ᶠ* and Sibraim (which lies on the border between Damascus and Hamath), as far as Hazer Hatticon, which is on the border of Hauran. ¹⁷The boundary will extend from the sea to Hazar Enan,*ᵍ* along the northern border of Damascus, with the border of Hamath to the north. This will be the north boundary.
¹⁸"On the east side the boundary will run between Hauran and Damascus, along the Jordan between Gilead and the land of Israel, to the eastern sea and as far as Tamar.*ʰ* This will be the east boundary.
¹⁹"On the south side it will run from Tamar as far as the waters of Meribah Kadesh, then along the Wadi ιof Egyptɹ to the Great Sea. This will be the south boundary.

ᵃ3 That is, about 1,500 feet (about 450 meters)   *ᵇ8* Or *the Jordan Valley*
ᶜ8 That is, the Dead Sea   *ᵈ10* That is, the Mediterranean; also in verses 15, 19 and 20   *ᵉ15* Or *past the entrance to*   *ᶠ15,16* See Septuagint and Ezekiel 48:1; Hebrew *road to go into Zedad,* ¹⁶*Hamath, Berothah*
ᵍ17 Hebrew *Enon,* a variant of *Enan*   *ʰ18* Septuagint and Syriac; Hebrew *Israel. You will measure to the eastern sea*

Water of Life

EZEKIEL 47:7–12

The water flows from the throne of God. From under the temple the water flows to change the salty water of the Dead Sea into a freshwater sea of life. It irrigates the desert into an orchard of fruit trees, where the fruit provides food and the leaves bring healing. Can you see this in your mind's eye?

Walk beside a stream or river. Or turn on a faucet for ten seconds. Touch the water. Listen to the sound of running water. Hold a few drops of water in your cupped hands. Marvel at such a precious gift. Drink a glass of water slowly and mindfully. Be aware of its life-giving properties as you swallow it. Imagine a stream of water flowing from God's throne to the place where you live and work. Offer thanksgiving to Almighty God.

See Meeting God in the Created Order

Compassion for the Foreigner

EZEKIEL 47:21–23

When the people of Israel return from captivity, the land is to be divided equally among the tribes. The foreigners and aliens who are living among them are also to receive an allotment. They are to be considered citizens of Israel. God's grace knows no boundaries.

Dorotheus of Gaza, a sixth-century monk, suggested that love can be viewed as a compass with God in the center. "To move toward God, then, human beings move from the circumference along the various radii of the circle to the center. But at the same time, the closer they are to God, the closer they become to one another; and the closer they are to one another, the closer they become to God." All the people you meet today, whatever the color of their skin or their station in life, are gifts to help you move closer to God.

²⁰"On the west side, the Great Sea will be the boundary to a point opposite Lebo[a] Hamath. This will be the west boundary.

²¹"You are to distribute this land among yourselves according to the tribes of Israel. ²²You are to allot it as an inheritance for yourselves and for the aliens who have settled among you and who have children. You are to consider them as native-born Israelites; along with you they are to be allotted an inheritance among the tribes of Israel. ²³In whatever tribe the alien settles, there you are to give him his inheritance," declares the Sovereign LORD.

The Division of the Land

48 "These are the tribes, listed by name: At the northern frontier, Dan will have one portion; it will follow the Hethlon road to Lebo[b] Hamath; Hazar Enan and the northern border of Damascus next to Hamath will be part of its border from the east side to the west side.

²"Asher will have one portion; it will border the territory of Dan from east to west.

³"Naphtali will have one portion; it will border the territory of Asher from east to west.

⁴"Manasseh will have one portion; it will border the territory of Naphtali from east to west.

⁵"Ephraim will have one portion; it will border the territory of Manasseh from east to west.

⁶"Reuben will have one portion; it will border the territory of Ephraim from east to west.

⁷"Judah will have one portion; it will border the territory of Reuben from east to west.

⁸"Bordering the territory of Judah from east to west will be the portion you are to present as a special gift. It will be 25,000 cubits[c] wide, and its length from east to west will equal one of the tribal portions; the sanctuary will be in the center of it.

⁹"The special portion you are to offer to the LORD will be 25,000 cubits long and 10,000 cubits[d] wide. ¹⁰This will be the sacred portion for the priests. It will be 25,000 cubits long on the north side, 10,000 cubits wide on the west side, 10,000 cubits wide on the east side and 25,000 cubits long on the south side. In the center of it will be the sanctuary of the LORD. ¹¹This will be for the consecrated priests, the Zadokites, who were faithful in serving me and did not go astray as the Levites did when the Israelites went astray. ¹²It will be a special gift to them from the sacred portion of the land, a most holy portion, bordering the territory of the Levites.

¹³"Alongside the territory of the priests, the Levites will have an allotment 25,000 cubits long and 10,000 cubits wide. Its total length will be 25,000 cubits and its width 10,000 cubits. ¹⁴They must not sell or exchange any of it. This is the best of the land and must not pass into other hands, because it is holy to the LORD.

¹⁵"The remaining area, 5,000 cubits wide and 25,000 cubits long, will be for the common use of the city, for houses and for pastureland. The city will be in the center of it ¹⁶and will have these measurements: the north side 4,500 cubits, the south side 4,500 cubits, the east side 4,500 cubits, and

a 20 Or *opposite the entrance to*   *b 1* Or *to the entrance to*   *c 8* That is, about 7 miles (about 12 kilometers)   *d 9* That is, about 3 miles (about 5 kilometers)

the west side 4,500 cubits. [17]The pastureland for the city will be 250 cubits on the north, 250 cubits on the south, 250 cubits on the east, and 250 cubits on the west. [18]What remains of the area, bordering on the sacred portion and running the length of it, will be 10,000 cubits on the east side and 10,000 cubits on the west side. Its produce will supply food for the workers of the city. [19]The workers from the city who farm it will come from all the tribes of Israel. [20]The entire portion will be a square, 25,000 cubits on each side. As a special gift you will set aside the sacred portion, along with the property of the city.

[21]"What remains on both sides of the area formed by the sacred portion and the city property will belong to the prince. It will extend eastward from the 25,000 cubits of the sacred portion to the eastern border, and westward from the 25,000 cubits to the western border. Both these areas running the length of the tribal portions will belong to the prince, and the sacred portion with the temple sanctuary will be in the center of them. [22]So the property of the Levites and the property of the city will lie in the center of the area that belongs to the prince. The area belonging to the prince will lie between the border of Judah and the border of Benjamin.

[23]"As for the rest of the tribes: Benjamin will have one portion; it will extend from the east side to the west side.

[24]"Simeon will have one portion; it will border the territory of Benjamin from east to west.

[25]"Issachar will have one portion; it will border the territory of Simeon from east to west.

[26]"Zebulun will have one portion; it will border the territory of Issachar from east to west.

[27]"Gad will have one portion; it will border the territory of Zebulun from east to west.

[28]"The southern boundary of Gad will run south from Tamar to the waters of Meribah Kadesh, then along the Wadi ⌊of Egypt⌋ to the Great Sea.[a]

[29]"This is the land you are to allot as an inheritance to the tribes of Israel, and these will be their portions," declares the Sovereign LORD.

The Gates of the City

[30]"These will be the exits of the city: Beginning on the north side, which is 4,500 cubits long, [31]the gates of the city will be named after the tribes of Israel. The three gates on the north side will be the gate of Reuben, the gate of Judah and the gate of Levi.

[32]"On the east side, which is 4,500 cubits long, will be three gates: the gate of Joseph, the gate of Benjamin and the gate of Dan.

[33]"On the south side, which measures 4,500 cubits, will be three gates: the gate of Simeon, the gate of Issachar and the gate of Zebulun.

[34]"On the west side, which is 4,500 cubits long, will be three gates: the gate of Gad, the gate of Asher and the gate of Naphtali.

[35]"The distance all around will be 18,000 cubits.

"And the name of the city from that time on will be:

THE LORD IS THERE."

The Lord is There

EZEKIEL 48:35

Ezekiel has lived through bad alliances, the destruction of Jerusalem, the captivity in Babylon. Now, at the end of his ministry, he has a vision of the new Jerusalem, which will be known as "THE LORD IS THERE." We have been on a journey with this incredible prophet and his colorful words and actions. The book ends in hope, but our journey goes on, and we know that wherever we are, "THE LORD IS THERE."

Take a moment to thank God for the prophet Ezekiel. Make some notes in your journal or in the margin of this Bible about how your life has been affected by this major prophet. Have you claimed some Sabbath time, created a holy place, tried some new prayer postures, written some prayers, become more compassionate? Remember, wherever you are, wherever you go, "THE LORD IS THERE."

See Meeting God in Prayer

DANIEL

The Power to Stand

KEY VERSE:

"We will not serve your gods or worship the image of gold you have set up."—Daniel 3:18

The book of Daniel is a story of intrigue and mystery, of dreams and visions and miracles. It is also the story of four young men who find the power to stand firm while living in a culture whose values oppose their faith.

Daniel, Hananiah, Mishael and Azariah are carried away as captives to Babylon when Jerusalem falls. They are of royal and noble lineage—four of the finest young men of Judah—and so they are chosen for special roles. They are given new names (Belteshazzar, Shadrach, Meshach and Abednego) and are to be educated and groomed for service in Nebuchadnezzar's court, learning the literature, language and customs of Babylon.

The four young men refuse to worship the image the king has set up. The advisers to the Babylonian king oppose the young men for expressing their faith, and they plot against them. The young men, however, pray for one another and stand together. Daniel rises to a place of power in the kingdom as an interpreter of the king's dreams, and he writes down his visions of how God will work in human events.

The book of Daniel shows how the faithful can triumph even in difficult situations by remaining true to God and living by God's standards despite opposition from the culture. Their reliance on one another and on the power of prayer are models that all of us can use as a pattern for our lives, whatever the difficult situations in which we find ourselves.

Daniel's Training in Babylon

1 In the third year of the reign of Jehoiakim king of Judah, Nebuchadnezzar king of Babylon came to Jerusalem and besieged it. ²And the Lord delivered Jehoiakim king of Judah into his hand, along with some of the articles from the temple of God. These he carried off to the temple of his god in Babylonia[a] and put in the treasure house of his god.

³Then the king ordered Ashpenaz, chief of his court officials, to bring in some of the Israelites from the royal family and the nobility— ⁴young men without any physical defect, handsome, showing aptitude for every kind of learning, well informed, quick to understand, and qualified to serve in the king's palace. He was to teach them the language and literature of the Babylonians.[b] ⁵The king assigned them a daily amount of food and wine from the king's table. They were to be trained for three years, and after that they were to enter the king's service.

⁶Among these were some from Judah: Daniel, Hananiah, Mishael and Azariah. ⁷The chief official gave them new names: to Daniel, the name Belteshazzar; to Hananiah, Shadrach; to Mishael, Meshach; and to Azariah, Abednego.

⁸But Daniel resolved not to defile himself with the royal food and wine, and he asked the chief official for permission not to defile himself this way. ⁹Now God had caused the official to show favor and sympathy to Daniel, ¹⁰but the official told Daniel, "I am afraid of my lord the king, who has assigned your[c] food and drink. Why should he see you looking worse than the other young men your age? The king would then have my head because of you."

¹¹Daniel then said to the guard whom the chief official had appointed over Daniel, Hananiah, Mishael and Azariah, ¹²"Please test your servants for ten days: Give us nothing but vegetables to eat and water to drink. ¹³Then compare our appearance with that of the young men who eat the royal food, and treat your servants in accordance with what you see." ¹⁴So he agreed to this and tested them for ten days.

¹⁵At the end of the ten days they looked healthier and better nourished than any of the young men who ate the royal food. ¹⁶So the guard took away their choice food and the wine they were to drink and gave them vegetables instead.

¹⁷To these four young men God gave knowledge and understanding of all kinds of literature and learning. And Daniel could understand visions and dreams of all kinds.

¹⁸At the end of the time set by the king to bring them in, the chief official presented them to Nebuchadnezzar. ¹⁹The king talked with them, and he found none equal to Daniel, Hananiah, Mishael and Azariah; so they entered the king's service. ²⁰In every matter of wisdom and understanding about which the king questioned them, he found them ten times better than all the magicians and enchanters in his whole kingdom.

²¹And Daniel remained there until the first year of King Cyrus.

---

a 2 Hebrew *Shinar*   *b 4* Or *Chaldeans*   *c 10* The Hebrew for *your* and *you* in this verse is plural.

Political Gifts

DANIEL 1:17

God gave the young Hebrews wisdom and knowledge and skill in literature and political administration. God gives all of us many ordinary gifts. Aptitudes for organization, sewing, car repair and teaching someone to read are also God-given. When we serve food to the homeless, help an elderly neighbor or speak out for mercy, we are using our gifts to do God's work. Look back over the last week to see how you have used your gifts, even ordinary ones, in ways that grow out of your faith.

See Meeting God in Service

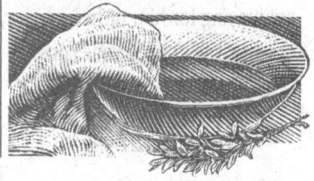

A Pact of Prayer

DANIEL 2:14–18

Daniel, Hananiah, Mishael and Azariah show us that we do something very important when we pray for one another. They were a community of faith, and when they banded together to pray, their prayers benefited others as well as themselves. To whom do you turn for support when you are in a crisis, spiritual or otherwise? In what personal crises have your prayers and the prayers of others made a difference? In what ways have you prayed for others who were not a part of your community of faith? Who needs your prayers today? Write a note to let someone know you are praying for him or her, or call them to convey your concern.

See Meeting God in Prayer

Nebuchadnezzar's Dream

2 In the second year of his reign, Nebuchadnezzar had dreams; his mind was troubled and he could not sleep. ²So the king summoned the magicians, enchanters, sorcerers and astrologers[a] to tell him what he had dreamed. When they came in and stood before the king, ³he said to them, "I have had a dream that troubles me and I want to know what it means.[b]"

⁴Then the astrologers answered the king in Aramaic,[c] "O king, live forever! Tell your servants the dream, and we will interpret it."

⁵The king replied to the astrologers, "This is what I have firmly decided: If you do not tell me what my dream was and interpret it, I will have you cut into pieces and your houses turned into piles of rubble. ⁶But if you tell me the dream and explain it, you will receive from me gifts and rewards and great honor. So tell me the dream and interpret it for me."

⁷Once more they replied, "Let the king tell his servants the dream, and we will interpret it."

⁸Then the king answered, "I am certain that you are trying to gain time, because you realize that this is what I have firmly decided: ⁹If you do not tell me the dream, there is just one penalty for you. You have conspired to tell me misleading and wicked things, hoping the situation will change. So then, tell me the dream, and I will know that you can interpret it for me."

¹⁰The astrologers answered the king, "There is not a man on earth who can do what the king asks! No king, however great and mighty, has ever asked such a thing of any magician or enchanter or astrologer. ¹¹What the king asks is too difficult. No one can reveal it to the king except the gods, and they do not live among men."

¹²This made the king so angry and furious that he ordered the execution of all the wise men of Babylon. ¹³So the decree was issued to put the wise men to death, and men were sent to look for Daniel and his friends to put them to death.

¹⁴When Arioch, the commander of the king's guard, had gone out to put to death the wise men of Babylon, Daniel spoke to him with wisdom and tact. ¹⁵He asked the king's officer, "Why did the king issue such a harsh decree?" Arioch then explained the matter to Daniel. ¹⁶At this, Daniel went in to the king and asked for time, so that he might interpret the dream for him.

¹⁷Then Daniel returned to his house and explained the matter to his friends Hananiah, Mishael and Azariah. ¹⁸He urged them to plead for mercy from the God of heaven concerning this mystery, so that he and his friends might not be executed with the rest of the wise men of Babylon. ¹⁹During the night the mystery was revealed to Daniel in a vision. Then Daniel praised the God of heaven ²⁰and said:

"Praise be to the name of God for ever and ever;
    wisdom and power are his.
²¹He changes times and seasons;
    he sets up kings and deposes them.

a 2 Or Chaldeans; also in verses 4, 5 and 10   b 3 Or was   c 4 The text from here through chapter 7 is in Aramaic.

He gives wisdom to the wise
>   and knowledge to the discerning.
> ²² He reveals deep and hidden things;
>   he knows what lies in darkness,
>   and light dwells with him.
> ²³ I thank and praise you, O God of my fathers:
>   You have given me wisdom and power,
>   you have made known to me what we asked of
>   you,
>   you have made known to us the dream of the
>   king."

Daniel Interprets the Dream

²⁴Then Daniel went to Arioch, whom the king had appointed to execute the wise men of Babylon, and said to him, "Do not execute the wise men of Babylon. Take me to the king, and I will interpret his dream for him."

²⁵Arioch took Daniel to the king at once and said, "I have found a man among the exiles from Judah who can tell the king what his dream means."

²⁶The king asked Daniel (also called Belteshazzar), "Are you able to tell me what I saw in my dream and interpret it?"

²⁷Daniel replied, "No wise man, enchanter, magician or diviner can explain to the king the mystery he has asked about, ²⁸but there is a God in heaven who reveals mysteries. He has shown King Nebuchadnezzar what will happen in days to come. Your dream and the visions that passed through your mind as you lay on your bed are these:

²⁹"As you were lying there, O king, your mind turned to things to come, and the revealer of mysteries showed you what is going to happen. ³⁰As for me, this mystery has been revealed to me, not because I have greater wisdom than other living men, but so that you, O king, may know the interpretation and that you may understand what went through your mind.

³¹"You looked, O king, and there before you stood a large statue—an enormous, dazzling statue, awesome in appearance. ³²The head of the statue was made of pure gold, its chest and arms of silver, its belly and thighs of bronze, ³³its legs of iron, its feet partly of iron and partly of baked clay. ³⁴While you were watching, a rock was cut out, but not by human hands. It struck the statue on its feet of iron and clay and smashed them. ³⁵Then the iron, the clay, the bronze, the silver and the gold were broken to pieces at the same time and became like chaff on a threshing floor in the summer. The wind swept them away without leaving a trace. But the rock that struck the statue became a huge mountain and filled the whole earth.

³⁶"This was the dream, and now we will interpret it to the king. ³⁷You, O king, are the king of kings. The God of heaven has given you dominion and power and might and glory; ³⁸in your hands he has placed mankind and the beasts of the field and the birds of the air. Wherever they live, he has made you ruler over them all. You are that head of gold.

³⁹"After you, another kingdom will rise, inferior to yours. Next, a third kingdom, one of bronze, will rule over the whole earth. ⁴⁰Finally, there will be a fourth kingdom, strong as iron—for iron breaks and smashes everything—and as

Dream Talker

DANIEL 2:20–23

God does not communicate with us only in our waking hours. Paying attention to our dreams can be a way of paying attention to God. Recurring patterns in our dreams—such as feelings of deep love or a sense of searching for something lost—can help us to understand more deeply our spiritual needs. Consider writing down your dreams when you awaken. If you record even snippets of dreams, you will gradually remember more and more of your dreams. Look for connections between your dreams and the events of your waking hours. Ask God to show you the meaning of your dreams so that you would gain understanding of them.

See Meeting God in Everyday Life

Speak Up!

DANIEL 2:46–47

Because Daniel spoke up, the king gave God credit for Daniel's wisdom. Living in a culture that is not always receptive to expressions of personal belief, we are sometimes reluctant to mention our faith. Think about how you speak in the company of nonbelievers. What subjects do you refer to? Do those you work with and enjoy leisure activities with know from your conversations that you are a believer? What conclusions about believers' interests and behavior might they draw from your example? When we mention serving God or talk with excitement about the role of faith in our lives, we may be inviting others to think about spiritual things. Like the king of Babylon, they may be moved to ponder who God is and how God is working in the world.

See Meeting God in Community

iron breaks things to pieces, so it will crush and break all the others. ⁴¹Just as you saw that the feet and toes were partly of baked clay and partly of iron, so this will be a divided kingdom; yet it will have some of the strength of iron in it, even as you saw iron mixed with clay. ⁴²As the toes were partly iron and partly clay, so this kingdom will be partly strong and partly brittle. ⁴³And just as you saw the iron mixed with baked clay, so the people will be a mixture and will not remain united, any more than iron mixes with clay.

⁴⁴"In the time of those kings, the God of heaven will set up a kingdom that will never be destroyed, nor will it be left to another people. It will crush all those kingdoms and bring them to an end, but it will itself endure forever. ⁴⁵This is the meaning of the vision of the rock cut out of a mountain, but not by human hands—a rock that broke the iron, the bronze, the clay, the silver and the gold to pieces.

"The great God has shown the king what will take place in the future. The dream is true and the interpretation is trustworthy."

⁴⁶Then King Nebuchadnezzar fell prostrate before Daniel and paid him honor and ordered that an offering and incense be presented to him. ⁴⁷The king said to Daniel, "Surely your God is the God of gods and the Lord of kings and a revealer of mysteries, for you were able to reveal this mystery."

⁴⁸Then the king placed Daniel in a high position and lavished many gifts on him. He made him ruler over the entire province of Babylon and placed him in charge of all its wise men. ⁴⁹Moreover, at Daniel's request the king appointed Shadrach, Meshach and Abednego administrators over the province of Babylon, while Daniel himself remained at the royal court.

The Image of Gold and the Fiery Furnace

3 King Nebuchadnezzar made an image of gold, ninety feet high and nine feet[a] wide, and set it up on the plain of Dura in the province of Babylon. ²He then summoned the satraps, prefects, governors, advisers, treasurers, judges, magistrates and all the other provincial officials to come to the dedication of the image he had set up. ³So the satraps, prefects, governors, advisers, treasurers, judges, magistrates and all the other provincial officials assembled for the dedication of the image that King Nebuchadnezzar had set up, and they stood before it.

⁴Then the herald loudly proclaimed, "This is what you are commanded to do, O peoples, nations and men of every language: ⁵As soon as you hear the sound of the horn, flute, zither, lyre, harp, pipes and all kinds of music, you must fall down and worship the image of gold that King Nebuchadnezzar has set up. ⁶Whoever does not fall down and worship will immediately be thrown into a blazing furnace."

⁷Therefore, as soon as they heard the sound of the horn, flute, zither, lyre, harp and all kinds of music, all the peoples, nations and men of every language fell down and worshiped the image of gold that King Nebuchadnezzar had set up.

⁸At this time some astrologers[b] came forward and denounced the Jews. ⁹They said to King Nebuchadnezzar,

---

[a] *1 Aramaic* sixty cubits high and six cubits wide *(about 27 meters high and 2.7 meters wide)*   [b] *8 Or* Chaldeans

"O king, live forever! ¹⁰You have issued a decree, O king, that everyone who hears the sound of the horn, flute, zither, lyre, harp, pipes and all kinds of music must fall down and worship the image of gold, ¹¹and that whoever does not fall down and worship will be thrown into a blazing furnace. ¹²But there are some Jews whom you have set over the affairs of the province of Babylon—Shadrach, Meshach and Abednego—who pay no attention to you, O king. They neither serve your gods nor worship the image of gold you have set up."

¹³Furious with rage, Nebuchadnezzar summoned Shadrach, Meshach and Abednego. So these men were brought before the king, ¹⁴and Nebuchadnezzar said to them, "Is it true, Shadrach, Meshach and Abednego, that you do not serve my gods or worship the image of gold I have set up? ¹⁵Now when you hear the sound of the horn, flute, zither, lyre, harp, pipes and all kinds of music, if you are ready to fall down and worship the image I made, very good. But if you do not worship it, you will be thrown immediately into a blazing furnace. Then what god will be able to rescue you from my hand?"

¹⁶Shadrach, Meshach and Abednego replied to the king, "O Nebuchadnezzar, we do not need to defend ourselves before you in this matter. ¹⁷If we are thrown into the blazing furnace, the God we serve is able to save us from it, and he will rescue us from your hand, O king. ¹⁸But even if he does not, we want you to know, O king, that we will not serve your gods or worship the image of gold you have set up."

¹⁹Then Nebuchadnezzar was furious with Shadrach, Meshach and Abednego, and his attitude toward them changed. He ordered the furnace heated seven times hotter than usual ²⁰and commanded some of the strongest soldiers in his army to tie up Shadrach, Meshach and Abednego and throw them into the blazing furnace. ²¹So these men, wearing their robes, trousers, turbans and other clothes, were bound and thrown into the blazing furnace. ²²The king's command was so urgent and the furnace so hot that the flames of the fire killed the soldiers who took up Shadrach, Meshach and Abednego, ²³and these three men, firmly tied, fell into the blazing furnace.

²⁴Then King Nebuchadnezzar leaped to his feet in amazement and asked his advisers, "Weren't there three men that we tied up and threw into the fire?"

They replied, "Certainly, O king."

²⁵He said, "Look! I see four men walking around in the fire, unbound and unharmed, and the fourth looks like a son of the gods."

²⁶Nebuchadnezzar then approached the opening of the blazing furnace and shouted, "Shadrach, Meshach and Abednego, servants of the Most High God, come out! Come here!"

So Shadrach, Meshach and Abednego came out of the fire, ²⁷and the satraps, prefects, governors and royal advisers crowded around them. They saw that the fire had not harmed their bodies, nor was a hair of their heads singed; their robes were not scorched, and there was no smell of fire on them.

²⁸Then Nebuchadnezzar said, "Praise be to the God of Shadrach, Meshach and Abednego, who has sent his angel

But If Not . . .

DANIEL 3:18

It is showdown time—pitting God against the officials who are trying to have the Hebrews killed. Shadrach, Meshach and Abednego make a stand for their faith, telling their accusers that God will deliver them, but even if God does not, they still will remain faithful.

"But if not" is a phrase we all may have occasion to use. "God will heal my friend of this disease, but if not . . ." "God will keep our business from failing, but if not . . ." Consider an area of your life where you expect or want God to do something specific, in a certain way. On a piece of paper, write down a phrase or draw a symbol that represents this area and your desire concerning it. Hold this before God in prayer. Then take a felt-tip marker or dark pen and write over your phrase or symbol, "God's will be done, no matter what might happen."

See Meeting God in Scripture

Imagine the Heat!

DANIEL 3:19–30

The Hebrews are thrown into the fiery furnace, but they are not burned. Do you believe that spectacular miracles like this happen today? On the other hand, is there such a thing as a small miracle? Anytime God intervenes in our lives, it is a miracle. Can you identify times when God intervened in your life or in the life of someone close to you? What "miracles" have you seen recently? Think of a situation in which you want God to act. Lift up this situation before God and watch for a miracle.

See *Meeting God in Prayer*

and rescued his servants! They trusted in him and defied the king's command and were willing to give up their lives rather than serve or worship any god except their own God. [29]Therefore I decree that the people of any nation or language who say anything against the God of Shadrach, Meshach and Abednego be cut into pieces and their houses be turned into piles of rubble, for no other god can save in this way."

[30]Then the king promoted Shadrach, Meshach and Abednego in the province of Babylon.

Nebuchadnezzar's Dream of a Tree

4 King Nebuchadnezzar,

To the peoples, nations and men of every language, who live in all the world:

May you prosper greatly!

[2]It is my pleasure to tell you about the miraculous signs and wonders that the Most High God has performed for me.

[3]How great are his signs,
  how mighty his wonders!
His kingdom is an eternal kingdom;
  his dominion endures from generation to
    generation.

[4]I, Nebuchadnezzar, was at home in my palace, contented and prosperous. [5]I had a dream that made me afraid. As I was lying in my bed, the images and visions that passed through my mind terrified me. [6]So I commanded that all the wise men of Babylon be brought before me to interpret the dream for me. [7]When the magicians, enchanters, astrologers[a] and diviners came, I told them the dream, but they could not interpret it for me. [8]Finally, Daniel came into my presence and I told him the dream. (He is called Belteshazzar, after the name of my god, and the spirit of the holy gods is in him.)

[9]I said, "Belteshazzar, chief of the magicians, I know that the spirit of the holy gods is in you, and no mystery is too difficult for you. Here is my dream; interpret it for me. [10]These are the visions I saw while lying in my bed: I looked, and there before me stood a tree in the middle of the land. Its height was enormous. [11]The tree grew large and strong and its top touched the sky; it was visible to the ends of the earth. [12]Its leaves were beautiful, its fruit abundant, and on it was food for all. Under it the beasts of the field found shelter, and the birds of the air lived in its branches; from it every creature was fed.

[13]"In the visions I saw while lying in my bed, I looked, and there before me was a messenger,[b] a holy one, coming down from heaven. [14]He called in a loud voice: 'Cut down the tree and trim off its branches; strip off its leaves and scatter its fruit. Let the animals flee from under it and the birds from its branches. [15]But let the stump and its roots, bound

[a]7 Or *Chaldeans*   [b]13 Or *watchman*; also in verses 17 and 23

with iron and bronze, remain in the ground, in the grass of the field.

" 'Let him be drenched with the dew of heaven, and let him live with the animals among the plants of the earth. [16]Let his mind be changed from that of a man and let him be given the mind of an animal, till seven times[a] pass by for him.

[17]" 'The decision is announced by messengers, the holy ones declare the verdict, so that the living may know that the Most High is sovereign over the kingdoms of men and gives them to anyone he wishes and sets over them the lowliest of men.'

[18]"This is the dream that I, King Nebuchadnezzar, had. Now, Belteshazzar, tell me what it means, for none of the wise men in my kingdom can interpret it for me. But you can, because the spirit of the holy gods is in you."

Daniel Interprets the Dream

[19]Then Daniel (also called Belteshazzar) was greatly perplexed for a time, and his thoughts terrified him. So the king said, "Belteshazzar, do not let the dream or its meaning alarm you."

Belteshazzar answered, "My lord, if only the dream applied to your enemies and its meaning to your adversaries! [20]The tree you saw, which grew large and strong, with its top touching the sky, visible to the whole earth, [21]with beautiful leaves and abundant fruit, providing food for all, giving shelter to the beasts of the field, and having nesting places in its branches for the birds of the air— [22]you, O king, are that tree! You have become great and strong; your greatness has grown until it reaches the sky, and your dominion extends to distant parts of the earth.

[23]"You, O king, saw a messenger, a holy one, coming down from heaven and saying, 'Cut down the tree and destroy it, but leave the stump, bound with iron and bronze, in the grass of the field, while its roots remain in the ground. Let him be drenched with the dew of heaven; let him live like the wild animals, until seven times pass by for him.'

[24]"This is the interpretation, O king, and this is the decree the Most High has issued against my lord the king: [25]You will be driven away from people and will live with the wild animals; you will eat grass like cattle and be drenched with the dew of heaven. Seven times will pass by for you until you acknowledge that the Most High is sovereign over the kingdoms of men and gives them to anyone he wishes. [26]The command to leave the stump of the tree with its roots means that your kingdom will be restored to you when you acknowledge that Heaven rules. [27]Therefore, O king, be pleased to accept my advice: Renounce your sins by doing what is right, and your wickedness by being kind to the oppressed. It may be that then your prosperity will continue."

The Dream Is Fulfilled

[28]All this happened to King Nebuchadnezzar.

Desecrating the Holy

DANIEL 5:2–4

The king desecrates the temple goblets by using them to toast idols. He takes the holy things of God and uses them to praise the unholy "gods" of Babylon.

We would never do something like this, would we? We would never use God's people or God's house for our own ends. But we all hear stories about scandals within the religious community, situations in which people misuse what belongs to God. Think about a scandal you've heard about. Does it involve money? Sexual misconduct? Abuse of power or trust? Pray for the people involved. What do you want God to do? Think about your own motives for doing what you do among God's people. Examine yourself. What do you want to say to God about this?

See *Meeting God in Prayer*

²⁹Twelve months later, as the king was walking on the roof of the royal palace of Babylon, ³⁰he said, "Is not this the great Babylon I have built as the royal residence, by my mighty power and for the glory of my majesty?"

³¹The words were still on his lips when a voice came from heaven, "This is what is decreed for you, King Nebuchadnezzar: Your royal authority has been taken from you. ³²You will be driven away from people and will live with the wild animals; you will eat grass like cattle. Seven times will pass by for you until you acknowledge that the Most High is sovereign over the kingdoms of men and gives them to anyone he wishes."

³³Immediately what had been said about Nebuchadnezzar was fulfilled. He was driven away from people and ate grass like cattle. His body was drenched with the dew of heaven until his hair grew like the feathers of an eagle and his nails like the claws of a bird.

³⁴At the end of that time, I, Nebuchadnezzar, raised my eyes toward heaven, and my sanity was restored. Then I praised the Most High; I honored and glorified him who lives forever.

His dominion is an eternal dominion;
  his kingdom endures from generation to
    generation.
³⁵All the peoples of the earth
  are regarded as nothing.
He does as he pleases
  with the powers of heaven
  and the peoples of the earth.
No one can hold back his hand
  or say to him: "What have you done?"

³⁶At the same time that my sanity was restored, my honor and splendor were returned to me for the glory of my kingdom. My advisers and nobles sought me out, and I was restored to my throne and became even greater than before. ³⁷Now I, Nebuchadnezzar, praise and exalt and glorify the King of heaven, because everything he does is right and all his ways are just. And those who walk in pride he is able to humble.

The Writing on the Wall

5 King Belshazzar gave a great banquet for a thousand of his nobles and drank wine with them. ²While Belshazzar was drinking his wine, he gave orders to bring in the gold and silver goblets that Nebuchadnezzar his father^a had taken from the temple in Jerusalem, so that the king and his nobles, his wives and his concubines might drink from them. ³So they brought in the gold goblets that had been taken from the temple of God in Jerusalem, and the king and his nobles, his wives and his concubines drank from them. ⁴As they drank the wine, they praised the gods of gold and silver, of bronze, iron, wood and stone.

⁵Suddenly the fingers of a human hand appeared and wrote on the plaster of the wall, near the lampstand in the royal palace. The king watched the hand as it wrote. ⁶His

^a2 Or *ancestor*; or *predecessor*; also in verses 11, 13 and 18

face turned pale and he was so frightened that his knees knocked together and his legs gave way.

[7] The king called out for the enchanters, astrologers[a] and diviners to be brought and said to these wise men of Babylon, "Whoever reads this writing and tells me what it means will be clothed in purple and have a gold chain placed around his neck, and he will be made the third highest ruler in the kingdom."

[8] Then all the king's wise men came in, but they could not read the writing or tell the king what it meant. [9] So King Belshazzar became even more terrified and his face grew more pale. His nobles were baffled.

[10] The queen,[b] hearing the voices of the king and his nobles, came into the banquet hall. "O king, live forever!" she said. "Don't be alarmed! Don't look so pale! [11] There is a man in your kingdom who has the spirit of the holy gods in him. In the time of your father he was found to have insight and intelligence and wisdom like that of the gods. King Nebuchadnezzar your father—your father the king, I say—appointed him chief of the magicians, enchanters, astrologers and diviners. [12] This man Daniel, whom the king called Belteshazzar, was found to have a keen mind and knowledge and understanding, and also the ability to interpret dreams, explain riddles and solve difficult problems. Call for Daniel, and he will tell you what the writing means."

[13] So Daniel was brought before the king, and the king said to him, "Are you Daniel, one of the exiles my father the king brought from Judah? [14] I have heard that the spirit of the gods is in you and that you have insight, intelligence and outstanding wisdom. [15] The wise men and enchanters were brought before me to read this writing and tell me what it means, but they could not explain it. [16] Now I have heard that you are able to give interpretations and to solve difficult problems. If you can read this writing and tell me what it means, you will be clothed in purple and have a gold chain placed around your neck, and you will be made the third highest ruler in the kingdom."

[17] Then Daniel answered the king, "You may keep your gifts for yourself and give your rewards to someone else. Nevertheless, I will read the writing for the king and tell him what it means.

[18] "O king, the Most High God gave your father Nebuchadnezzar sovereignty and greatness and glory and splendor. [19] Because of the high position he gave him, all the peoples and nations and men of every language dreaded and feared him. Those the king wanted to put to death, he put to death; those he wanted to spare, he spared; those he wanted to promote, he promoted; and those he wanted to humble, he humbled. [20] But when his heart became arrogant and hardened with pride, he was deposed from his royal throne and stripped of his glory. [21] He was driven away from people and given the mind of an animal; he lived with the wild donkeys and ate grass like cattle; and his body was drenched with the dew of heaven, until he acknowledged that the Most High God is sovereign over the kingdoms of men and sets over them anyone he wishes.

[22] "But you his son,[c] O Belshazzar, have not humbled

The Search for Meaning

DANIEL 5:5–16

Daniel helps others make sense of life's mysteries. This passage makes it clear that such a skill is a divine gift. Do you know someone who is truly wise, someone who has a gift for helping others make sense of confusion? Do you have this gift? Give thanks for those who have helped you to see the way before you in a confusing time.

See *Meeting God in Community*

In God's Hand

DANIEL 5:23

All people, even those who are not believers, are held in God's hand. Think about this. God holds each of us— even those who do not recognize that it is God who gives them breath—in his hand. Imagine yourself in God's hand, and there, right beside you, is someone whose beliefs are very different from yours. Perhaps it is someone who has done heinous things or someone you have hated for years. Yet you both are there. And God gives breath to both of you. What do you feel? What does this say to you about God?

See Meeting God in Worship

yourself, though you knew all this. [23]Instead, you have set yourself up against the Lord of heaven. You had the goblets from his temple brought to you, and you and your nobles, your wives and your concubines drank wine from them. You praised the gods of silver and gold, of bronze, iron, wood and stone, which cannot see or hear or understand. But you did not honor the God who holds in his hand your life and all your ways. [24]Therefore he sent the hand that wrote the inscription.

[25]"This is the inscription that was written:

MENE, MENE, TEKEL, PARSIN[a]

[26]"This is what these words mean:

Mene[b]: God has numbered the days of your reign and brought it to an end.
[27]*Tekel*[c]: You have been weighed on the scales and found wanting.
[28]*Peres*[d]: Your kingdom is divided and given to the Medes and Persians."

[29]Then at Belshazzar's command, Daniel was clothed in purple, a gold chain was placed around his neck, and he was proclaimed the third highest ruler in the kingdom. [30]That very night Belshazzar, king of the Babylonians,[e] was slain, [31]and Darius the Mede took over the kingdom, at the age of sixty-two.

Daniel in the Den of Lions

6 It pleased Darius to appoint 120 satraps to rule throughout the kingdom, [2]with three administrators over them, one of whom was Daniel. The satraps were made accountable to them so that the king might not suffer loss. [3]Now Daniel so distinguished himself among the administrators and the satraps by his exceptional qualities that the king planned to set him over the whole kingdom. [4]At this, the administrators and the satraps tried to find grounds for charges against Daniel in his conduct of government affairs, but they were unable to do so. They could find no corruption in him, because he was trustworthy and neither corrupt nor negligent. [5]Finally these men said, "We will never find any basis for charges against this man Daniel unless it has something to do with the law of his God."

[6]So the administrators and the satraps went as a group to the king and said: "O King Darius, live forever! [7]The royal administrators, prefects, satraps, advisers and governors have all agreed that the king should issue an edict and enforce the decree that anyone who prays to any god or man during the next thirty days, except to you, O king, shall be thrown into the lions' den. [8]Now, O king, issue the decree and put it in writing so that it cannot be altered—in accordance with the laws of the Medes and Persians, which cannot be repealed." [9]So King Darius put the decree in writing.

[10]Now when Daniel learned that the decree had been published, he went home to his upstairs room where the windows opened toward Jerusalem. Three times a day he got down on his knees and prayed, giving thanks to his

---

[a] 25 Aramaic *UPARSIN* (that is, *AND PARSIN*)   [b] 26 *Mene* can mean *numbered* or *mina* (a unit of money).   [c] 27 *Tekel* can mean *weighed* or *shekel*.   [d] 28 *Peres* (the singular of *Parsin*) can mean *divided* or *Persia* or *a half mina* or *a half shekel*.   [e] 30 Or *Chaldeans*

God, just as he had done before. ¹¹Then these men went as a group and found Daniel praying and asking God for help. ¹²So they went to the king and spoke to him about his royal decree: "Did you not publish a decree that during the next thirty days anyone who prays to any god or man except to you, O king, would be thrown into the lions' den?"

The king answered, "The decree stands—in accordance with the laws of the Medes and Persians, which cannot be repealed."

¹³Then they said to the king, "Daniel, who is one of the exiles from Judah, pays no attention to you, O king, or to the decree you put in writing. He still prays three times a day." ¹⁴When the king heard this, he was greatly distressed; he was determined to rescue Daniel and made every effort until sundown to save him.

¹⁵Then the men went as a group to the king and said to him, "Remember, O king, that according to the law of the Medes and Persians no decree or edict that the king issues can be changed."

¹⁶So the king gave the order, and they brought Daniel and threw him into the lions' den. The king said to Daniel, "May your God, whom you serve continually, rescue you!"

¹⁷A stone was brought and placed over the mouth of the den, and the king sealed it with his own signet ring and with the rings of his nobles, so that Daniel's situation might not be changed. ¹⁸Then the king returned to his palace and spent the night without eating and without any entertainment being brought to him. And he could not sleep.

¹⁹At the first light of dawn, the king got up and hurried to the lions' den. ²⁰When he came near the den, he called to Daniel in an anguished voice, "Daniel, servant of the living God, has your God, whom you serve continually, been able to rescue you from the lions?"

²¹Daniel answered, "O king, live forever! ²²My God sent his angel, and he shut the mouths of the lions. They have not hurt me, because I was found innocent in his sight. Nor have I ever done any wrong before you, O king."

²³The king was overjoyed and gave orders to lift Daniel out of the den. And when Daniel was lifted from the den, no wound was found on him, because he had trusted in his God.

²⁴At the king's command, the men who had falsely accused Daniel were brought in and thrown into the lions' den, along with their wives and children. And before they reached the floor of the den, the lions overpowered them and crushed all their bones.

²⁵Then King Darius wrote to all the peoples, nations and men of every language throughout the land:

"May you prosper greatly!

²⁶"I issue a decree that in every part of my kingdom people must fear and reverence the God of Daniel.

"For he is the living God
    and he endures forever;
his kingdom will not be destroyed,
    his dominion will never end.
²⁷He rescues and he saves;
    he performs signs and wonders
    in the heavens and on the earth.

Caught in the System

DANIEL 6:10–18

Jealous officials set up a law to force the king into throwing Daniel into the lions' den. The system assumes a life of its own; once the machinery starts, the king cannot stop it and rescue Daniel even though he wants to. But God intervenes to shut the mouths of the lions.

Think about the social systems in our society—welfare, health, corporate and political systems—that sometimes help but often hurt people (not to mention the snares of sweatshop labor and the drug culture). We feel powerless to make changes that will keep people from being ground up in the machinery of the system. In what situations might you call out to God to "shut the mouths of the lions"? What systems seem out of control—too powerful for us to make a difference? Where do you need to stand firm? What helps you to remember that God is with you?

See Meeting God in Service

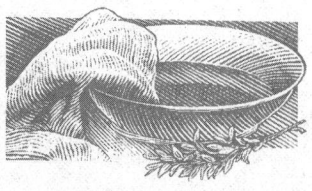

A Fearsome Vision

DANIEL 7:1–14

Like many visions of judgment, this one is full of symbols that can be interpreted many different ways. Most interpreters say the four beasts represent four kingdoms that will rise and fall. But the vision also offers hope in its picture of the "Ancient of Days," the One who will ultimately triumph over all kingdoms, good and bad. Read again verses 9 and 10 and draw a picture to represent the One who holds the victory. What colors will you use? What emotions does the picture evoke in you? What feelings would you want your picture to evoke in those who might see it?

See Meeting God in Scripture

He has rescued Daniel
from the power of the lions."

²⁸So Daniel prospered during the reign of Darius and the reign of Cyrus*a* the Persian.

Daniel's Dream of Four Beasts

7 In the first year of Belshazzar king of Babylon, Daniel had a dream, and visions passed through his mind as he was lying on his bed. He wrote down the substance of his dream.

²Daniel said: "In my vision at night I looked, and there before me were the four winds of heaven churning up the great sea. ³Four great beasts, each different from the others, came up out of the sea.

⁴"The first was like a lion, and it had the wings of an eagle. I watched until its wings were torn off and it was lifted from the ground so that it stood on two feet like a man, and the heart of a man was given to it.

⁵"And there before me was a second beast, which looked like a bear. It was raised up on one of its sides, and it had three ribs in its mouth between its teeth. It was told, 'Get up and eat your fill of flesh!'

⁶"After that, I looked, and there before me was another beast, one that looked like a leopard. And on its back it had four wings like those of a bird. This beast had four heads, and it was given authority to rule.

⁷"After that, in my vision at night I looked, and there before me was a fourth beast—terrifying and frightening and very powerful. It had large iron teeth; it crushed and devoured its victims and trampled underfoot whatever was left. It was different from all the former beasts, and it had ten horns.

⁸"While I was thinking about the horns, there before me was another horn, a little one, which came up among them; and three of the first horns were uprooted before it. This horn had eyes like the eyes of a man and a mouth that spoke boastfully.

⁹"As I looked,

"thrones were set in place,
and the Ancient of Days took his seat.
His clothing was as white as snow;
the hair of his head was white like wool.
His throne was flaming with fire,
and its wheels were all ablaze.
¹⁰A river of fire was flowing,
coming out from before him.
Thousands upon thousands attended him;
ten thousand times ten thousand stood before
him.
The court was seated,
and the books were opened.

¹¹"Then I continued to watch because of the boastful words the horn was speaking. I kept looking until the beast was slain and its body destroyed and thrown into the blazing fire. ¹²(The other beasts had been stripped of their authority, but were allowed to live for a period of time.)

¹³"In my vision at night I looked, and there before me

a 28 Or Darius, that is, the reign of Cyrus

was one like a son of man, coming with the clouds of heaven. He approached the Ancient of Days and was led into his presence. ¹⁴He was given authority, glory and sovereign power; all peoples, nations and men of every language worshiped him. His dominion is an everlasting dominion that will not pass away, and his kingdom is one that will never be destroyed.

The Interpretation of the Dream

¹⁵"I, Daniel, was troubled in spirit, and the visions that passed through my mind disturbed me. ¹⁶I approached one of those standing there and asked him the true meaning of all this.

"So he told me and gave me the interpretation of these things: ¹⁷'The four great beasts are four kingdoms that will rise from the earth. ¹⁸But the saints of the Most High will receive the kingdom and will possess it forever—yes, for ever and ever.'

¹⁹"Then I wanted to know the true meaning of the fourth beast, which was different from all the others and most terrifying, with its iron teeth and bronze claws—the beast that crushed and devoured its victims and trampled underfoot whatever was left. ²⁰I also wanted to know about the ten horns on its head and about the other horn that came up, before which three of them fell—the horn that looked more imposing than the others and that had eyes and a mouth that spoke boastfully. ²¹As I watched, this horn was waging war against the saints and defeating them, ²²until the Ancient of Days came and pronounced judgment in favor of the saints of the Most High, and the time came when they possessed the kingdom.

²³"He gave me this explanation: 'The fourth beast is a fourth kingdom that will appear on earth. It will be different from all the other kingdoms and will devour the whole earth, trampling it down and crushing it. ²⁴The ten horns are ten kings who will come from this kingdom. After them another king will arise, different from the earlier ones; he will subdue three kings. ²⁵He will speak against the Most High and oppress his saints and try to change the set times and the laws. The saints will be handed over to him for a time, times and half a time.ᵃ

²⁶" 'But the court will sit, and his power will be taken away and completely destroyed forever. ²⁷Then the sovereignty, power and greatness of the kingdoms under the whole heaven will be handed over to the saints, the people of the Most High. His kingdom will be an everlasting kingdom, and all rulers will worship and obey him.'

²⁸"This is the end of the matter. I, Daniel, was deeply troubled by my thoughts, and my face turned pale, but I kept the matter to myself."

Daniel's Vision of a Ram and a Goat

8 In the third year of King Belshazzar's reign, I, Daniel, had a vision, after the one that had already appeared to me. ²In my vision I saw myself in the citadel of Susa in the province of Elam; in the vision I was beside the Ulai Canal. ³I looked up, and there before me was a ram with two horns, standing beside the canal, and the horns were long. One of the horns was longer than the other but grew up

Faith Responds to Fear

DANIEL 7:15

Daniel's vision frightens and unsettles him, and so he asks for help. Think about your own life. What is it that you fear? Do you imagine terrible possibilities? Are there troublesome situations facing you that you need help understanding? How can you follow Daniel's example? Consider talking with a trusted friend, a counselor or a pastor if you find that fears intrude on your ability to face daily life with peace.

See Meeting God in Community

ᵃ 25 Or *for a year, two years and half a year*

Who Can Break This?

DANIEL 8:23–25

When deceit seems to prosper, Gabriel's words remind us that we are not alone and that we do not work alone to overcome evil. We must do what we can, but evil is overcome finally "not by human power" but by the power of God. This is good news for us. God will keep on working until evil is defeated.

Bring to mind a situation in which evil and deceit seem to dominate. Now envision the light of God's power flooding into that situation. Envision yourself as a torchbearer, carrying God's light on a pole. Approach the situation, praying for God's power to be with you and within you. Plant the torch in the middle of the situation and, in your mind's eye, leave it there as a reminder that God is at work.

See *Meeting God in Scripture*

later. ⁴I watched the ram as he charged toward the west and the north and the south. No animal could stand against him, and none could rescue from his power. He did as he pleased and became great.

⁵As I was thinking about this, suddenly a goat with a prominent horn between his eyes came from the west, crossing the whole earth without touching the ground. ⁶He came toward the two-horned ram I had seen standing beside the canal and charged at him in great rage. ⁷I saw him attack the ram furiously, striking the ram and shattering his two horns. The ram was powerless to stand against him; the goat knocked him to the ground and trampled on him, and none could rescue the ram from his power. ⁸The goat became very great, but at the height of his power his large horn was broken off, and in its place four prominent horns grew up toward the four winds of heaven.

⁹Out of one of them came another horn, which started small but grew in power to the south and to the east and toward the Beautiful Land. ¹⁰It grew until it reached the host of the heavens, and it threw some of the starry host down to the earth and trampled on them. ¹¹It set itself up to be as great as the Prince of the host; it took away the daily sacrifice from him, and the place of his sanctuary was brought low. ¹²Because of rebellion, the host ⌊of the saints⌋ᵃ and the daily sacrifice were given over to it. It prospered in everything it did, and truth was thrown to the ground.

¹³Then I heard a holy one speaking, and another holy one said to him, "How long will it take for the vision to be fulfilled—the vision concerning the daily sacrifice, the rebellion that causes desolation, and the surrender of the sanctuary and of the host that will be trampled underfoot?"

¹⁴He said to me, "It will take 2,300 evenings and mornings; then the sanctuary will be reconsecrated."

The Interpretation of the Vision

¹⁵While I, Daniel, was watching the vision and trying to understand it, there before me stood one who looked like a man. ¹⁶And I heard a man's voice from the Ulai calling, "Gabriel, tell this man the meaning of the vision."

¹⁷As he came near the place where I was standing, I was terrified and fell prostrate. "Son of man," he said to me, "understand that the vision concerns the time of the end."

¹⁸While he was speaking to me, I was in a deep sleep, with my face to the ground. Then he touched me and raised me to my feet.

¹⁹He said: "I am going to tell you what will happen later in the time of wrath, because the vision concerns the appointed time of the end.ᵇ ²⁰The two-horned ram that you saw represents the kings of Media and Persia. ²¹The shaggy goat is the king of Greece, and the large horn between his eyes is the first king. ²²The four horns that replaced the one that was broken off represent four kingdoms that will emerge from his nation but will not have the same power.

²³"In the latter part of their reign, when rebels have become completely wicked, a stern-faced king, a master of intrigue, will arise. ²⁴He will become very strong, but not by his own power. He will cause astounding devastation and will succeed in whatever he does. He will destroy the

---

ᵃ 12 Or *rebellion, the armies*   ᵇ 19 Or *because the end will be at the appointed time*

mighty men and the holy people. [25]He will cause deceit to prosper, and he will consider himself superior. When they feel secure, he will destroy many and take his stand against the Prince of princes. Yet he will be destroyed, but not by human power.

[26]"The vision of the evenings and mornings that has been given you is true, but seal up the vision, for it concerns the distant future."

[27]I, Daniel, was exhausted and lay ill for several days. Then I got up and went about the king's business. I was appalled by the vision; it was beyond understanding.

Daniel's Prayer

9 In the first year of Darius son of Xerxes[a] (a Mede by descent), who was made ruler over the Babylonian[b] kingdom— [2]in the first year of his reign, I, Daniel, understood from the Scriptures, according to the word of the LORD given to Jeremiah the prophet, that the desolation of Jerusalem would last seventy years. [3]So I turned to the Lord God and pleaded with him in prayer and petition, in fasting, and in sackcloth and ashes.

[4]I prayed to the LORD my God and confessed:

"O Lord, the great and awesome God, who keeps his covenant of love with all who love him and obey his commands, [5]we have sinned and done wrong. We have been wicked and have rebelled; we have turned away from your commands and laws. [6]We have not listened to your servants the prophets, who spoke in your name to our kings, our princes and our fathers, and to all the people of the land.

[7]"Lord, you are righteous, but this day we are covered with shame—the men of Judah and people of Jerusalem and all Israel, both near and far, in all the countries where you have scattered us because of our unfaithfulness to you. [8]O LORD, we and our kings, our princes and our fathers are covered with shame because we have sinned against you. [9]The Lord our God is merciful and forgiving, even though we have rebelled against him; [10]we have not obeyed the LORD our God or kept the laws he gave us through his servants the prophets. [11]All Israel has transgressed your law and turned away, refusing to obey you.

"Therefore the curses and sworn judgments written in the Law of Moses, the servant of God, have been poured out on us, because we have sinned against you. [12]You have fulfilled the words spoken against us and against our rulers by bringing upon us great disaster. Under the whole heaven nothing has ever been done like what has been done to Jerusalem. [13]Just as it is written in the Law of Moses, all this disaster has come upon us, yet we have not sought the favor of the LORD our God by turning from our sins and giving attention to your truth. [14]The LORD did not hesitate to bring the disaster upon us, for the LORD our God is righteous in everything he does; yet we have not obeyed him.

[15]"Now, O Lord our God, who brought your people out of Egypt with a mighty hand and who made for yourself a name that endures to this day, we have

God's Fidelity

DANIEL 9:4–5,9,13,18

Daniel is praying again. He begins by praising God for his steadfastness in keeping the covenant with his people. God has shown great mercy and love even though his people have not kept faith. That is the story of this people over and over again. Look back over your life for evidence of God's "great mercy" and love shown toward you. Especially look for times when your faithfulness waned but God's did not. Reflect on God's faithfulness. How has God loved you? Through whom has God loved you? Make a list of instances of God's faithfulness and carry it with you for the next several days. Each time you see the list or think of it, place your hand on your heart as an acknowledgment that God's faithfulness is as steady as the rhythm of your beating heart.

See Meeting God in Everyday Life

For the Nation

DANIEL 9:20

Daniel offers a model of confessing on behalf of a nation and praying for it. What might you confess on behalf of your nation today? What might you ask God to do for your nation? And what is your prayer for nations other than your own? Write on a small card or piece of paper something to remind you to pray for your country, and place the card near your television, radio or stack of news magazines. For the next week, "pray through the news." Pray about the people, systems and situations mentioned in the news stories.

See Meeting God in Prayer

sinned, we have done wrong. [16]O Lord, in keeping with all your righteous acts, turn away your anger and your wrath from Jerusalem, your city, your holy hill. Our sins and the iniquities of our fathers have made Jerusalem and your people an object of scorn to all those around us.

[17]"Now, our God, hear the prayers and petitions of your servant. For your sake, O Lord, look with favor on your desolate sanctuary. [18]Give ear, O God, and hear; open your eyes and see the desolation of the city that bears your Name. We do not make requests of you because we are righteous, but because of your great mercy. [19]O Lord, listen! O Lord, forgive! O Lord, hear and act! For your sake, O my God, do not delay, because your city and your people bear your Name."

The Seventy "Sevens"

[20]While I was speaking and praying, confessing my sin and the sin of my people Israel and making my request to the LORD my God for his holy hill— [21]while I was still in prayer, Gabriel, the man I had seen in the earlier vision, came to me in swift flight about the time of the evening sacrifice. [22]He instructed me and said to me, "Daniel, I have now come to give you insight and understanding. [23]As soon as you began to pray, an answer was given, which I have come to tell you, for you are highly esteemed. Therefore, consider the message and understand the vision:

[24]"Seventy 'sevens'[a] are decreed for your people and your holy city to finish[b] transgression, to put an end to sin, to atone for wickedness, to bring in everlasting righteousness, to seal up vision and prophecy and to anoint the most holy.[c]

[25]"Know and understand this: From the issuing of the decree[d] to restore and rebuild Jerusalem until the Anointed One,[e] the ruler, comes, there will be seven 'sevens,' and sixty-two 'sevens.' It will be rebuilt with streets and a trench, but in times of trouble. [26]After the sixty-two 'sevens,' the Anointed One will be cut off and will have nothing.[f] The people of the ruler who will come will destroy the city and the sanctuary. The end will come like a flood: War will continue until the end, and desolations have been decreed. [27]He will confirm a covenant with many for one 'seven.'[g] In the middle of the 'seven'[g] he will put an end to sacrifice and offering. And on a wing ⌊of the temple⌋ he will set up an abomination that causes desolation, until the end that is decreed is poured out on him.[h]"[i]

Daniel's Vision of a Man

10 In the third year of Cyrus king of Persia, a revelation was given to Daniel (who was called Belteshazzar). Its message was true and it concerned a great war.[j] The understanding of the message came to him in a vision.

[2]At that time I, Daniel, mourned for three weeks. [3]I ate no choice food; no meat or wine touched my lips; and I used no lotions at all until the three weeks were over.

---

[a] 24 Or 'weeks'; also in verses 25 and 26   [b] 24 Or restrain   [c] 24 Or Most Holy Place; or most holy One   [d] 25 Or word   [e] 25 Or an anointed one; also in verse 26   [f] 26 Or off and will have no one; or off, but not for himself   [g] 27 Or 'week'   [h] 27. Or it   [i] 27 Or And one who causes desolation will come upon the pinnacle of the abominable ⌊temple⌋, until the end that is decreed is poured out on the desolated ⌊city⌋   [j] 1 Or true and burdensome

⁴On the twenty-fourth day of the first month, as I was standing on the bank of the great river, the Tigris, ⁵I looked up and there before me was a man dressed in linen, with a belt of the finest gold around his waist. ⁶His body was like chrysolite, his face like lightning, his eyes like flaming torches, his arms and legs like the gleam of burnished bronze, and his voice like the sound of a multitude.

⁷I, Daniel, was the only one who saw the vision; the men with me did not see it, but such terror overwhelmed them that they fled and hid themselves. ⁸So I was left alone, gazing at this great vision; I had no strength left, my face turned deathly pale and I was helpless. ⁹Then I heard him speaking, and as I listened to him, I fell into a deep sleep, my face to the ground.

¹⁰A hand touched me and set me trembling on my hands and knees. ¹¹He said, "Daniel, you who are highly esteemed, consider carefully the words I am about to speak to you, and stand up, for I have now been sent to you." And when he said this to me, I stood up trembling.

¹²Then he continued, "Do not be afraid, Daniel. Since the first day that you set your mind to gain understanding and to humble yourself before your God, your words were heard, and I have come in response to them. ¹³But the prince of the Persian kingdom resisted me twenty-one days. Then Michael, one of the chief princes, came to help me, because I was detained there with the king of Persia. ¹⁴Now I have come to explain to you what will happen to your people in the future, for the vision concerns a time yet to come."

¹⁵While he was saying this to me, I bowed with my face toward the ground and was speechless. ¹⁶Then one who looked like a man*ᵃ* touched my lips, and I opened my mouth and began to speak. I said to the one standing before me, "I am overcome with anguish because of the vision, my lord, and I am helpless. ¹⁷How can I, your servant, talk with you, my lord? My strength is gone and I can hardly breathe."

¹⁸Again the one who looked like a man touched me and gave me strength. ¹⁹"Do not be afraid, O man highly esteemed," he said. "Peace! Be strong now; be strong."

When he spoke to me, I was strengthened and said, "Speak, my lord, since you have given me strength."

²⁰So he said, "Do you know why I have come to you? Soon I will return to fight against the prince of Persia, and when I go, the prince of Greece will come; ²¹but first I will tell you what is written in the Book of Truth. (No one supports me against them except Michael, your prince. ¹And in the first year of Darius the Mede, I took my stand to support and protect him.)

The Kings of the South and the North

²"Now then, I tell you the truth: Three more kings will appear in Persia, and then a fourth, who will be far richer than all the others. When he has gained power by his wealth, he will stir up everyone against the kingdom of Greece. ³Then a mighty king will appear, who will rule with great power and do as he pleases. ⁴After he has appeared, his empire

---

Answers to Prayer

DANIEL 10:10–18

Daniel has been praying and fasting for three weeks. The heavenly messenger says Daniel's words have been heard from the first day that he started to pray.

The absence of a visible answer does not mean our prayers are not heard. Some prayers are answered quickly, but sometimes we must persevere in prayer and "pray continually" (1 Thessalonians 5:17). Write down on a slip of paper the names of the persons or situations that have dominated your prayers. On the same slip of paper, write, "My words have been heard, and God is sending help." Place the paper in a place where you will see it frequently as a reminder that persistent prayer matters and that God responds to your perseverance.

See Meeting God in Prayer

ᵃ 16 Most manuscripts of the Masoretic Text; one manuscript of the Masoretic Text, Dead Sea Scrolls and Septuagint *Then something that looked like a man's hand*

1183

History Through God's Eyes

DANIEL 11:6–24

In this extended passage, God gives Daniel a gift—the ability to see his contemporary situation against the backdrop of the divine time line of the universe. No matter how bleak or dark the human story appears to be—God is ultimately in control and will bring the kingdom to fruition.

How does the knowledge that God is in control of history help give you perspective on your own situation? Find a time line of Biblical history in a Bible reference book, or look in a world historical atlas in order to envision all of human history. Or read the first three chapters of Genesis and the last three of Revelation in one sitting. What is God saying to you about your place in history?

See Meeting God in Scripture

will be broken up and parceled out toward the four winds of heaven. It will not go to his descendants, nor will it have the power he exercised, because his empire will be uprooted and given to others.

5 "The king of the South will become strong, but one of his commanders will become even stronger than he and will rule his own kingdom with great power. 6 After some years, they will become allies. The daughter of the king of the South will go to the king of the North to make an alliance, but she will not retain her power, and he and his power*a* will not last. In those days she will be handed over, together with her royal escort and her father*b* and the one who supported her.

7 "One from her family line will arise to take her place. He will attack the forces of the king of the North and enter his fortress; he will fight against them and be victorious. 8 He will also seize their gods, their metal images and their valuable articles of silver and gold and carry them off to Egypt. For some years he will leave the king of the North alone. 9 Then the king of the North will invade the realm of the king of the South but will retreat to his own country. 10 His sons will prepare for war and assemble a great army, which will sweep on like an irresistible flood and carry the battle as far as his fortress.

11 "Then the king of the South will march out in a rage and fight against the king of the North, who will raise a large army, but it will be defeated. 12 When the army is carried off, the king of the South will be filled with pride and will slaughter many thousands, yet he will not remain triumphant. 13 For the king of the North will muster another army, larger than the first; and after several years, he will advance with a huge army fully equipped.

14 "In those times many will rise against the king of the South. The violent men among your own people will rebel in fulfillment of the vision, but without success. 15 Then the king of the North will come and build up siege ramps and will capture a fortified city. The forces of the South will be powerless to resist; even their best troops will not have the strength to stand. 16 The invader will do as he pleases; no one will be able to stand against him. He will establish himself in the Beautiful Land and will have the power to destroy it. 17 He will determine to come with the might of his entire kingdom and will make an alliance with the king of the South. And he will give him a daughter in marriage in order to overthrow the kingdom, but his plans*c* will not succeed or help him. 18 Then he will turn his attention to the coastlands and will take many of them, but a commander will put an end to his insolence and will turn his insolence back upon him. 19 After this, he will turn back toward the fortresses of his own country but will stumble and fall, to be seen no more.

20 "His successor will send out a tax collector to maintain the royal splendor. In a few years, however, he will be destroyed, yet not in anger or in battle.

21 "He will be succeeded by a contemptible person who has not been given the honor of royalty. He will invade the kingdom when its people feel secure, and he will seize it through intrigue. 22 Then an overwhelming army will be swept away before him; both it and a prince of the cov-

a 6 Or *offspring*   *b 6* Or *child* (see Vulgate and Syriac)   *c 17* Or *but she* enant will be destroyed. ²³After coming to an agreement with him, he will act deceitfully, and with only a few people he will rise to power. ²⁴When the richest provinces feel secure, he will invade them and will achieve what neither his fathers nor his forefathers did. He will distribute plunder, loot and wealth among his followers. He will plot the overthrow of fortresses—but only for a time.

²⁵"With a large army he will stir up his strength and courage against the king of the South. The king of the South will wage war with a large and very powerful army, but he will not be able to stand because of the plots devised against him. ²⁶Those who eat from the king's provisions will try to destroy him; his army will be swept away, and many will fall in battle. ²⁷The two kings, with their hearts bent on evil, will sit at the same table and lie to each other, but to no avail, because an end will still come at the appointed time. ²⁸The king of the North will return to his own country with great wealth, but his heart will be set against the holy covenant. He will take action against it and then return to his own country.

²⁹"At the appointed time he will invade the South again, but this time the outcome will be different from what it was before. ³⁰Ships of the western coastlands*a* will oppose him, and he will lose heart. Then he will turn back and vent his fury against the holy covenant. He will return and show favor to those who forsake the holy covenant.

³¹"His armed forces will rise up to desecrate the temple fortress and will abolish the daily sacrifice. Then they will set up the abomination that causes desolation. ³²With flattery he will corrupt those who have violated the covenant, but the people who know their God will firmly resist him.

³³"Those who are wise will instruct many, though for a time they will fall by the sword or be burned or captured or plundered. ³⁴When they fall, they will receive a little help, and many who are not sincere will join them. ³⁵Some of the wise will stumble, so that they may be refined, purified and made spotless until the time of the end, for it will still come at the appointed time.

The King Who Exalts Himself

³⁶"The king will do as he pleases. He will exalt and magnify himself above every god and will say unheard-of things against the God of gods. He will be successful until the time of wrath is completed, for what has been determined must take place. ³⁷He will show no regard for the gods of his fathers or for the one desired by women, nor will he regard any god, but will exalt himself above them all. ³⁸Instead of them, he will honor a god of fortresses; a god unknown to his fathers he will honor with gold and silver, with precious stones and costly gifts. ³⁹He will attack the mightiest fortresses with the help of a foreign god and will greatly honor those who acknowledge him. He will make them rulers over many people and will distribute the land at a price.*b*

⁴⁰"At the time of the end the king of the South will engage him in battle, and the king of the North will storm out against him with chariots and cavalry and a great fleet of ships. He will invade many countries and sweep through them like a flood. ⁴¹He will also invade the Beautiful Land.

God in Politics

DANIEL 11:29–32

Monarchs rise and monarchs fall. Countries overcome one another and are conquered in turn. God is involved. God is not apolitical—he directs the drama of world events "at the appointed time."

Are you to be one of the players? Is it the appointed time for you to be involved in political matters? Are you being called to be God's servant in shaping the history of humankind in one way or another? Do you ask God to guide and shape your political views and help you make wise decisions at the polls?

See Meeting God in Service

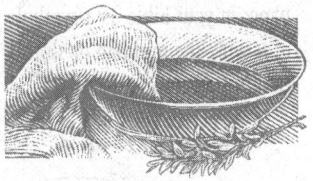

Rest in Peace

DANIEL 12:13

Rest? In the midst of receiving this confusing and troubling vision, Daniel is urged by God's messenger to do exactly that. The things that will be done, *will be done*—in God's time. Daniel cannot hurry the events or hasten his understanding of them. Until God's appointed time, he is told to rest.

Reflect on your recent prayers and isolate something you are troubled about or do not understand. Draw a picture to remind you of this situation, fold the paper and offer this concern to God. Remind yourself that you cannot hurry or slow down the resolution of some events. Place the folded paper in your Bible as a symbol of leaving the problem or situation in God's hand.

See Meeting God in Everyday Life

Many countries will fall, but Edom, Moab and the leaders of Ammon will be delivered from his hand. ⁴²He will extend his power over many countries; Egypt will not escape. ⁴³He will gain control of the treasures of gold and silver and all the riches of Egypt, with the Libyans and Nubians in submission. ⁴⁴But reports from the east and the north will alarm him, and he will set out in a great rage to destroy and annihilate many. ⁴⁵He will pitch his royal tents between the seas at*ᵃ* the beautiful holy mountain. Yet he will come to his end, and no one will help him.

The End Times

12 "At that time Michael, the great prince who protects your people, will arise. There will be a time of distress such as has not happened from the beginning of nations until then. But at that time your people—everyone whose name is found written in the book—will be delivered. ²Multitudes who sleep in the dust of the earth will awake: some to everlasting life, others to shame and everlasting contempt. ³Those who are wise*ᵇ* will shine like the brightness of the heavens, and those who lead many to righteousness, like the stars for ever and ever. ⁴But you, Daniel, close up and seal the words of the scroll until the time of the end. Many will go here and there to increase knowledge."

⁵Then I, Daniel, looked, and there before me stood two others, one on this bank of the river and one on the opposite bank. ⁶One of them said to the man clothed in linen, who was above the waters of the river, "How long will it be before these astonishing things are fulfilled?"

⁷The man clothed in linen, who was above the waters of the river, lifted his right hand and his left hand toward heaven, and I heard him swear by him who lives forever, saying, "It will be for a time, times and half a time.*ᶜ* When the power of the holy people has been finally broken, all these things will be completed."

⁸I heard, but I did not understand. So I asked, "My lord, what will the outcome of all this be?"

⁹He replied, "Go your way, Daniel, because the words are closed up and sealed until the time of the end. ¹⁰Many will be purified, made spotless and refined, but the wicked will continue to be wicked. None of the wicked will understand, but those who are wise will understand.

¹¹"From the time that the daily sacrifice is abolished and the abomination that causes desolation is set up, there will be 1,290 days. ¹²Blessed is the one who waits for and reaches the end of the 1,335 days.

¹³"As for you, go your way till the end. You will rest, and then at the end of the days you will rise to receive your allotted inheritance."

ᵃ 45 Or the sea and   ᵇ 3 Or who impart wisdom   ᶜ 7 Or a year, two years and half a year

HOSEA

Unwavering Love

KEY VERSE:

Return, O Israel, to the LORD your God.—Hosea 14:1

I n the book of Hosea, God calls, confronts and woos the people of Israel. Herein unfolds the account of a rebellious Israel—a people looking to idols rather than to God. God directs the prophet Hosea to marry Gomer, a prostitute, to be a living metaphor of God's unwavering love to his unfaithful people. Hosea marries Gomer, knowing she will be repeatedly unfaithful. God instructs Hosea to remain faithful regardless of Gomer's behavior. Hosea obeys (3:1–2), and, while the people deserve God's wrath, through the drama of his life Hosea demonstrates God's constant love for Israel.

The Israelites vacillate between clinging to idol worship and crying out to God for help. Israel's sin is so great that the people become "as vile as the thing they [love]" (9:10). Yet in a dramatic flood of compassion, God acts—not as a human being would, but as only God can (11:8–11). God chooses to forgive his people and draw them near once again.

This book has much to say about the human propensity to look anywhere but to God for meaning and comfort. Even more vividly it reminds us of the wonder of God's faithful love to persistently unfaithful people. Why does God repeatedly forgive and love a people who deserve only judgment? As passionately as anywhere in Scripture, the book of Hosea speaks of God's intention to be Israel's faithful, loving spouse. As you read Hosea let God nurture in you an intimacy with him that is the fruit of knowing and receiving him in spirit and in truth.

"O eternal Father! . . . O eternal, infinite God! O mad lover! And you have need of your creature? It seems so to me, for you act as if you could not live without her, in spite of the fact that you are Life itself, and everything has life from you and nothing can have life without you. Why then are you so mad? Because you have fallen in love with what you have made! You are pleased and delighted over her within yourself, as if you were drunk with desire for her salvation. She runs away from you and you go looking for her. She strays and you draw closer to her. You clothed yourself in our humanity, and nearer than that you could not have come."

—CATHERINE OF SIENA,
The Dialogue

A Radical Obedience

HOSEA 1:1–2:5

God calls Hosea to make a covenant with a woman identified from the beginning as a prostitute. God is asking for radical obedience from Hosea; Hosea must give up much to follow God.

How do you respond when God asks you to obey in radical ways? Think of a time when the cost of discipleship required courage and a relinquishment of your own preferences or plans. Is God asking you to follow him in a radical way right now? Write a prayer asking God to help you be willing to relinquish your will, plans and life to him.

See Meeting God in Prayer

1 The word of the LORD that came to Hosea son of Beeri during the reigns of Uzziah, Jotham, Ahaz and Hezekiah, kings of Judah, and during the reign of Jeroboam son of Jehoash*a* king of Israel:

Hosea's Wife and Children

²When the LORD began to speak through Hosea, the LORD said to him, "Go, take to yourself an adulterous wife and children of unfaithfulness, because the land is guilty of the vilest adultery in departing from the LORD." ³So he married Gomer daughter of Diblaim, and she conceived and bore him a son.

⁴Then the LORD said to Hosea, "Call him Jezreel, because I will soon punish the house of Jehu for the massacre at Jezreel, and I will put an end to the kingdom of Israel. ⁵In that day I will break Israel's bow in the Valley of Jezreel."

⁶Gomer conceived again and gave birth to a daughter. Then the LORD said to Hosea, "Call her Lo-Ruhamah,*b* for I will no longer show love to the house of Israel, that I should at all forgive them. ⁷Yet I will show love to the house of Judah; and I will save them—not by bow, sword or battle, or by horses and horsemen, but by the LORD their God."

⁸After she had weaned Lo-Ruhamah, Gomer had another son. ⁹Then the LORD said, "Call him Lo-Ammi,*c* for you are not my people, and I am not your God.

¹⁰"Yet the Israelites will be like the sand on the seashore, which cannot be measured or counted. In the place where it was said to them, 'You are not my people,' they will be called 'sons of the living God.' ¹¹The people of Judah and the people of Israel will be reunited, and they will appoint one leader and will come up out of the land, for great will be the day of Jezreel.

2 "Say of your brothers, 'My people,' and of your sisters, 'My loved one.'

Israel Punished and Restored

²"Rebuke your mother, rebuke her,
    for she is not my wife,
    and I am not her husband.
Let her remove the adulterous look from her face
    and the unfaithfulness from between her breasts.
³Otherwise I will strip her naked
    and make her as bare as on the day she was born;
I will make her like a desert,
    turn her into a parched land,
    and slay her with thirst.
⁴I will not show my love to her children,
    because they are the children of adultery.
⁵Their mother has been unfaithful
    and has conceived them in disgrace.
She said, 'I will go after my lovers,
    who give me my food and my water,
    my wool and my linen, my oil and my drink.'
⁶Therefore I will block her path with thornbushes;

*a 1 Hebrew Joash, a variant of Jehoash   b 6 Lo-Ruhamah means not loved.
c 9 Lo-Ammi means not my people.*

I will wall her in so that she cannot find her
way.
⁷She will chase after her lovers but not catch
them;
she will look for them but not find them.
Then she will say,
'I will go back to my husband as at first,
for then I was better off than now.'
⁸She has not acknowledged that I was the one
who gave her the grain, the new wine and oil,
who lavished on her the silver and gold—
which they used for Baal.
⁹"Therefore I will take away my grain when it
ripens,
and my new wine when it is ready.
I will take back my wool and my linen,
intended to cover her nakedness.
¹⁰So now I will expose her lewdness
before the eyes of her lovers;
no one will take her out of my hands.
¹¹I will stop all her celebrations:
her yearly festivals, her New Moons,
her Sabbath days—all her appointed feasts.
¹²I will ruin her vines and her fig trees,
which she said were her pay from her lovers;
I will make them a thicket,
and wild animals will devour them.
¹³I will punish her for the days
she burned incense to the Baals;
she decked herself with rings and jewelry,
and went after her lovers,
but me she forgot,"

declares the LORD.

¹⁴"Therefore I am now going to allure her;
I will lead her into the desert
and speak tenderly to her.
¹⁵There I will give her back her vineyards,
and will make the Valley of Achor*ᵃ* a door of
hope.
There she will sing*ᵇ* as in the days of her youth,
as in the day she came up out of Egypt.

¹⁶"In that day," declares the LORD,
"you will call me 'my husband';
you will no longer call me 'my master.*ᶜ*'
¹⁷I will remove the names of the Baals from her
lips;
no longer will their names be invoked.
¹⁸In that day I will make a covenant for them
with the beasts of the field and the birds of the
air
and the creatures that move along the ground.
Bow and sword and battle
I will abolish from the land,
so that all may lie down in safety.
¹⁹I will betroth you to me forever;
I will betroth you in*ᵈ* righteousness and justice,

Reality and Restoration

HOSEA 2:14–20

Imagine standing in a valley
named "Trouble" (see footnote *a*), and in the far distance
you see a doorway labeled
"Hope." What do you hope is
on the other side of that door?
From where you stand in the
valley, what lies between you
and the door? What steps must
you take to go through the Valley of Trouble and walk through
the door into renewal? How can
focusing on God's intimate,
committed love deliver, heal
and transform you? Pray
through Psalm 23, 91 or 103
for more guidance.

See *Meeting God in Scripture*

ᵃ 15 Achor *means* trouble.   *ᵇ 15 Or* respond   *ᶜ 16 Hebrew* baal   *ᵈ 19 Or*
with; *also in verse 20*

1189

Compassionate Beyond Words

HOSEA 2:19—3:5

"The thing which may for long prevent the soul from thus accepting the Lord, is that it forgets to think of Him always and above all as compassionate. Yet in everything, that is the first idea we must try to have about Him. We shall be quite differently affected by [God's] great splendor if we first realize that He to whom it belongs and who offers it to us is compassionate beyond all words. How gladly shall we then rejoice in [God's] Divine splendors! For they are the splendors of the All-Compassionate, the Intimate, and the Familiar God."

—ABBE DE TOURVILLE,
Letters of Direction

in[a] love and compassion.
²⁰ I will betroth you in faithfulness,
and you will acknowledge the LORD.

²¹ "In that day I will respond,"
declares the LORD—
"I will respond to the skies,
and they will respond to the earth;
²² and the earth will respond to the grain,
the new wine and oil,
and they will respond to Jezreel.[b]
²³ I will plant her for myself in the land;
I will show my love to the one I called 'Not my
loved one.'[c]
I will say to those called 'Not my people,[d]' 'You
are my people';
and they will say, 'You are my God.' "

Hosea's Reconciliation With His Wife

3 The LORD said to me, "Go, show your love to your wife again, though she is loved by another and is an adulteress. Love her as the LORD loves the Israelites, though they turn to other gods and love the sacred raisin cakes."

² So I bought her for fifteen shekels[e] of silver and about a homer and a lethek[f] of barley. ³ Then I told her, "You are to live with[g] me many days; you must not be a prostitute or be intimate with any man, and I will live with[g] you."

⁴ For the Israelites will live many days without king or prince, without sacrifice or sacred stones, without ephod or idol. ⁵ Afterward the Israelites will return and seek the LORD their God and David their king. They will come trembling to the LORD and to his blessings in the last days.

The Charge Against Israel

4 Hear the word of the LORD, you Israelites,
because the LORD has a charge to bring
against you who live in the land:
"There is no faithfulness, no love,
no acknowledgment of God in the land.
² There is only cursing,[h] lying and murder,
stealing and adultery;
they break all bounds,
and bloodshed follows bloodshed.
³ Because of this the land mourns,[i]
and all who live in it waste away;
the beasts of the field and the birds of the air
and the fish of the sea are dying.

⁴ "But let no man bring a charge,
let no man accuse another,
for your people are like those
who bring charges against a priest.
⁵ You stumble day and night,
and the prophets stumble with you.
So I will destroy your mother—
⁶   my people are destroyed from lack of
knowledge.

---

[a] 19 Or *with*   [b] 22 *Jezreel* means *God plants.*   [c] 23 Hebrew *Lo-Ruhamah*
[d] 23 Hebrew *Lo-Ammi*   [e] 2 That is, about 6 ounces (about 170 grams)
[f] 2 That is, probably about 10 bushels (about 330 liters)   [g] 3 Or *wait for*
[h] 2 That is, to pronounce a curse upon   [i] 3 Or *dries up*

"Because you have rejected knowledge,
    I also reject you as my priests;
because you have ignored the law of your God,
    I also will ignore your children.
7 The more the priests increased,
    the more they sinned against me;
they exchanged[a] their[b] Glory for something
        disgraceful.
8 They feed on the sins of my people
    and relish their wickedness.
9 And it will be: Like people, like priests.
    I will punish both of them for their ways
    and repay them for their deeds.

10 "They will eat but not have enough;
    they will engage in prostitution but not
        increase,
because they have deserted the LORD
    to give themselves 11 to prostitution,
to old wine and new,
    which take away the understanding 12 of my
        people.
They consult a wooden idol
    and are answered by a stick of wood.
A spirit of prostitution leads them astray;
    they are unfaithful to their God.
13 They sacrifice on the mountaintops
    and burn offerings on the hills,
under oak, poplar and terebinth,
    where the shade is pleasant.
Therefore your daughters turn to prostitution
    and your daughters-in-law to adultery.

14 "I will not punish your daughters
    when they turn to prostitution,
nor your daughters-in-law
    when they commit adultery,
because the men themselves consort with harlots
    and sacrifice with shrine prostitutes—
a people without understanding will come to
        ruin!

15 "Though you commit adultery, O Israel,
    let not Judah become guilty.

"Do not go to Gilgal;
    do not go up to Beth Aven.[c]
And do not swear, 'As surely as the LORD lives!'
16 The Israelites are stubborn,
    like a stubborn heifer.
How then can the LORD pasture them
    like lambs in a meadow?
17 Ephraim is joined to idols;
    leave him alone!
18 Even when their drinks are gone,
    they continue their prostitution;
    their rulers dearly love shameful ways.

Consulting a Wooden Idol

HOSEA 4:6–7

To worship idols is to allow something or someone (other than God) the power to appropriate our attention, steal our affections, and dictate our choices and actions. When we worship idols we tend to substitute the most paltry things for the comfort and security God provides.

Reflect on your own spiritual pilgrimage. How do you give power to paltry substitutes rather than commit to trust in God? What do you gain from such idolatry? Is it ever worth it? How have you made the choice to give God the holy place, the first place, in your life? Is God in that place today? How do you know?

See Meeting God in Prayer

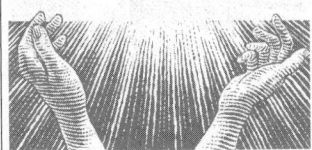

---

a 7 Syriac and an ancient Hebrew scribal tradition; Masoretic Text *I will exchange*   b 7 Masoretic Text; an ancient Hebrew scribal tradition *my*
c 15 *Beth Aven* means *house of wickedness* (a name for Bethel, which means *house of God*).

Vulnerability and Obedience

HOSEA 5:5–6

We read in these verses that when the people look for God, God has "withdrawn himself from them." What a poignant picture! To help you meditate, write these two verses from Hosea in your journal. Then, between the lines of this Hosea passage, write out this promise from Deuteronomy 4:29 with a different color pen: "If . . . you seek the LORD your God, you will find him if you look for him with all your heart and with all your soul." Turn your reflection toward God and ask him to reveal himself to you as you pray.

See Meeting God in Everyday Life

---

¹⁹ A whirlwind will sweep them away,
　and their sacrifices will bring them shame.

Judgment Against Israel

5 "Hear this, you priests!
　Pay attention, you Israelites!
Listen, O royal house!
　This judgment is against you:
You have been a snare at Mizpah,
　a net spread out on Tabor.
² The rebels are deep in slaughter.
　I will discipline all of them.
³ I know all about Ephraim;
　Israel is not hidden from me.
Ephraim, you have now turned to prostitution;
　Israel is corrupt.

⁴ "Their deeds do not permit them
　to return to their God.
A spirit of prostitution is in their heart;
　they do not acknowledge the LORD.
⁵ Israel's arrogance testifies against them;
　the Israelites, even Ephraim, stumble in their sin;
　Judah also stumbles with them.
⁶ When they go with their flocks and herds
　to seek the LORD,
they will not find him;
　he has withdrawn himself from them.
⁷ They are unfaithful to the LORD;
　they give birth to illegitimate children.
Now their New Moon festivals
　will devour them and their fields.

⁸ "Sound the trumpet in Gibeah,
　the horn in Ramah.
Raise the battle cry in Beth Aven*ᵃ*;
　lead on, O Benjamin.
⁹ Ephraim will be laid waste
　on the day of reckoning.
Among the tribes of Israel
　I proclaim what is certain.
¹⁰ Judah's leaders are like those
　who move boundary stones.
I will pour out my wrath on them
　like a flood of water.
¹¹ Ephraim is oppressed,
　trampled in judgment,
　intent on pursuing idols.*ᵇ*
¹² I am like a moth to Ephraim,
　like rot to the people of Judah.

¹³ "When Ephraim saw his sickness,
　and Judah his sores,
then Ephraim turned to Assyria,
　and sent to the great king for help.
But he is not able to cure you,
　not able to heal your sores.

ᵃ 8 *Beth Aven* means *house of wickedness* (a name for Bethel, which means *house of God*).　*ᵇ 11* The meaning of the Hebrew for this word is uncertain.

14 For I will be like a lion to Ephraim,
    like a great lion to Judah.
I will tear them to pieces and go away;
    I will carry them off, with no one to rescue
        them.
15 Then I will go back to my place
    until they admit their guilt.
And they will seek my face;
    in their misery they will earnestly seek me."

Israel Unrepentant

6 "Come, let us return to the LORD.
    He has torn us to pieces
        but he will heal us;
    he has injured us
        but he will bind up our wounds.
2 After two days he will revive us;
    on the third day he will restore us,
    that we may live in his presence.
3 Let us acknowledge the LORD;
    let us press on to acknowledge him.
As surely as the sun rises,
    he will appear;
he will come to us like the winter rains,
    like the spring rains that water the earth."

4 "What can I do with you, Ephraim?
    What can I do with you, Judah?
Your love is like the morning mist,
    like the early dew that disappears.
5 Therefore I cut you in pieces with my prophets,
    I killed you with the words of my mouth;
    my judgments flashed like lightning upon
        you.
6 For I desire mercy, not sacrifice,
    and acknowledgment of God rather than burnt
        offerings.
7 Like Adam,*a* they have broken the covenant—
    they were unfaithful to me there.
8 Gilead is a city of wicked men,
    stained with footprints of blood.
9 As marauders lie in ambush for a man,
    so do bands of priests;
they murder on the road to Shechem,
    committing shameful crimes.
10 I have seen a horrible thing
    in the house of Israel.
There Ephraim is given to prostitution
    and Israel is defiled.

11 "Also for you, Judah,
    a harvest is appointed.

"Whenever I would restore the fortunes of my
        people,

7 1   whenever I would heal Israel,
the sins of Ephraim are exposed
    and the crimes of Samaria revealed.
They practice deceit,
    thieves break into houses,

To Desire God Forever

HOSEA 6:3

"What is that sweet thing that comes sometimes to touch me at the thought of God? . . . I struggle deliciously to prevent myself [from] leaving this thing which I desire to embrace forever."

—HUGH OF ST. VICTOR

---

a 7 Or *As at Adam;* or *Like men*

What Prevents Our Return?

HOSEA 7:10–11

Despite God's judgment—despite God's repeated attempts to call the people back—Israel steadfastly refuses to turn back and seek God. Instead the Israelites turn to alliances with foreign nations to find the help they need.

When you are "stressed out" or distressed, to what or to whom do you turn first? Food? Alcohol? Television? Your credit card? Sports? Your friends? Make a list of "foreign alliances" you are tempted to turn to. Study your list. What do any of these things or people offer you that God cannot? How might God become your true source of life, contentment and health?

See Meeting God in Prayer

bandits rob in the streets;
² but they do not realize
that I remember all their evil deeds.
Their sins engulf them;
they are always before me.

³ "They delight the king with their wickedness,
the princes with their lies.
⁴ They are all adulterers,
burning like an oven
whose fire the baker need not stir
from the kneading of the dough till it rises.
⁵ On the day of the festival of our king
the princes become inflamed with wine,
and he joins hands with the mockers.
⁶ Their hearts are like an oven;
they approach him with intrigue.
Their passion smolders all night;
in the morning it blazes like a flaming fire.
⁷ All of them are hot as an oven;
they devour their rulers.
All their kings fall,
and none of them calls on me.

⁸ "Ephraim mixes with the nations;
Ephraim is a flat cake not turned over.
⁹ Foreigners sap his strength,
but he does not realize it.
His hair is sprinkled with gray,
but he does not notice.
¹⁰ Israel's arrogance testifies against him,
but despite all this
he does not return to the Lord his God
or search for him.

¹¹ "Ephraim is like a dove,
easily deceived and senseless—
now calling to Egypt,
now turning to Assyria.
¹² When they go, I will throw my net over them;
I will pull them down like birds of the air.
When I hear them flocking together,
I will catch them.
¹³ Woe to them,
because they have strayed from me!
Destruction to them,
because they have rebelled against me!
I long to redeem them
but they speak lies against me.
¹⁴ They do not cry out to me from their hearts
but wail upon their beds.
They gather together*a* for grain and new wine
but turn away from me.
¹⁵ I trained them and strengthened them,
but they plot evil against me.
¹⁶ They do not turn to the Most High;
they are like a faulty bow.
Their leaders will fall by the sword
because of their insolent words.

a 14 Most Hebrew manuscripts; some Hebrew manuscripts and Septuagint
They slash themselves

For this they will be ridiculed
in the land of Egypt.

Israel to Reap the Whirlwind

8 "Put the trumpet to your lips!
An eagle is over the house of the LORD
because the people have broken my covenant
and rebelled against my law.
[2] Israel cries out to me,
'O our God, we acknowledge you!'
[3] But Israel has rejected what is good;
an enemy will pursue him.
[4] They set up kings without my consent;
they choose princes without my approval.
With their silver and gold
they make idols for themselves
to their own destruction.
[5] Throw out your calf-idol, O Samaria!
My anger burns against them.
How long will they be incapable of purity?
[6] They are from Israel!
This calf—a craftsman has made it;
it is not God.
It will be broken in pieces,
that calf of Samaria.

[7] "They sow the wind
and reap the whirlwind.
The stalk has no head;
it will produce no flour.
Were it to yield grain,
foreigners would swallow it up.
[8] Israel is swallowed up;
now she is among the nations
like a worthless thing.
[9] For they have gone up to Assyria
like a wild donkey wandering alone.
Ephraim has sold herself to lovers.
[10] Although they have sold themselves among the
nations,
I will now gather them together.
They will begin to waste away
under the oppression of the mighty king.

[11] "Though Ephraim built many altars for sin
offerings,
these have become altars for sinning.
[12] I wrote for them the many things of my law,
but they regarded them as something alien.
[13] They offer sacrifices given to me
and they eat the meat,
but the LORD is not pleased with them.
Now he will remember their wickedness
and punish their sins:
They will return to Egypt.
[14] Israel has forgotten his Maker
and built palaces;
Judah has fortified many towns.
But I will send fire upon their cities
that will consume their fortresses."

The Way Rejected

HOSEA 8:14

Thinking themselves safe the Israelites "forget" God, preferring instead to rely on their palaces and fortified towns. Do they really think God can be so easily outmaneuvered or put off? Consider your own life. Find someone you trust with whom you can discuss your attitudes toward God. Do you gladly welcome God into the scenes of your daily life? With your mentor consider whether there are times when you tend to evade or avoid God and hide behind your accomplishments or possessions.

See Meeting God in Community

Subtle Deformation

HOSEA 9:1–4

"When it is true that the image you carry in your mind can affect your physical, mental and emotional life, then it becomes a crucial question as to which images we expose ourselves or allow ourselves to be exposed to."

—HENRI J. M. NOUWEN,
Gracias

Punishment for Israel

9 Do not rejoice, O Israel;
　　do not be jubilant like the other nations.
　For you have been unfaithful to your God;
　　you love the wages of a prostitute
　　at every threshing floor.
2 Threshing floors and winepresses will not feed
　　the people;
　　the new wine will fail them.
3 They will not remain in the LORD's land;
　　Ephraim will return to Egypt
　　and eat unclean[a] food in Assyria.
4 They will not pour out wine offerings to the LORD,
　　nor will their sacrifices please him.
　Such sacrifices will be to them like the bread of
　　mourners;
　　all who eat them will be unclean.
　This food will be for themselves;
　　it will not come into the temple of the LORD.

5 What will you do on the day of your appointed
　　feasts,
　　on the festival days of the LORD?
6 Even if they escape from destruction,
　　Egypt will gather them,
　　and Memphis will bury them.
　Their treasures of silver will be taken over by
　　briers,
　　and thorns will overrun their tents.
7 The days of punishment are coming,
　　the days of reckoning are at hand.
　　Let Israel know this.
　Because your sins are so many
　　and your hostility so great,
　the prophet is considered a fool,
　　the inspired man a maniac.
8 The prophet, along with my God,
　　is the watchman over Ephraim,[b]
　yet snares await him on all his paths,
　　and hostility in the house of his God.
9 They have sunk deep into corruption,
　　as in the days of Gibeah.
　God will remember their wickedness
　　and punish them for their sins.

10 "When I found Israel,
　　it was like finding grapes in the desert;
　when I saw your fathers,
　　it was like seeing the early fruit on the fig tree.
　But when they came to Baal Peor,
　　they consecrated themselves to that shameful
　　idol
　　and became as vile as the thing they loved.
11 Ephraim's glory will fly away like a bird—
　　no birth, no pregnancy, no conception.
12 Even if they rear children,
　　I will bereave them of every one.
　Woe to them

---

a 3 That is, ceremonially unclean　*b 8* Or *The prophet is the watchman over
Ephraim, / the people of my God*

when I turn away from them!
¹³ I have seen Ephraim, like Tyre,
    planted in a pleasant place.
But Ephraim will bring out
    their children to the slayer."

¹⁴ Give them, O LORD—
    what will you give them?
Give them wombs that miscarry
    and breasts that are dry.

¹⁵ "Because of all their wickedness in Gilgal,
    I hated them there.
Because of their sinful deeds,
    I will drive them out of my house.
I will no longer love them;
    all their leaders are rebellious.
¹⁶ Ephraim is blighted,
    their root is withered,
    they yield no fruit.
Even if they bear children,
    I will slay their cherished offspring."

¹⁷ My God will reject them
    because they have not obeyed him;
    they will be wanderers among the nations.

10 Israel was a spreading vine;
    he brought forth fruit for himself.
As his fruit increased,
    he built more altars;
as his land prospered,
    he adorned his sacred stones.
² Their heart is deceitful,
    and now they must bear their guilt.
The LORD will demolish their altars
    and destroy their sacred stones.

³ Then they will say, "We have no king
    because we did not revere the LORD.
But even if we had a king,
    what could he do for us?"
⁴ They make many promises,
    take false oaths
    and make agreements;
therefore lawsuits spring up
    like poisonous weeds in a plowed field.
⁵ The people who live in Samaria fear
    for the calf-idol of Beth Aven.ᵃ
Its people will mourn over it,
    and so will its idolatrous priests,
those who had rejoiced over its splendor,
    because it is taken from them into exile.
⁶ It will be carried to Assyria
    as tribute for the great king.
Ephraim will be disgraced;
    Israel will be ashamed of its wooden idols.ᵇ
⁷ Samaria and its king will float away
    like a twig on the surface of the waters.

The Sign of Unfruitfulness

HOSEA 9:10-16

As a new bride Israel has been ripe with promise, but she turns away from God, the very source of her fruitfulness. She consecrates herself to idols and reaps the consequences of unfaithfulness—she becomes barren and unable to sustain her children.

A fruitful life is a result of following God, yet fruitful abundance can also lead to complacency. How can you keep from taking God's blessings for granted? What keeps your zeal and your desire for God fresh and new? How can being accountable to others in the community keep you fruitful?

See Meeting God in Community

ᵃ 5 *Beth Aven* means *house of wickedness* (a name for Bethel, which means *house of God*).   ᵇ 6 Or *its counsel*

In Praise of the Gardener

HOSEA 10:12

Using the metaphor of a vine for your life in Christ Jesus, map out your history. Be creative and extend the metaphor with other horticultural illustrations from Scripture (see Matthew 13:1–23; John 15:1–8; Galatians 5:22–23). Where did God plant you? What made you grow in one direction and not another? Where did you branch off in the wrong direction? How did God prune you and discipline you? Who were the people who came along and watered and nourished you? What experiences have stimulated you to seek the light of the Lord? What fruit are you bearing?

See Meeting God in Scripture

8 The high places of wickedness*ᵃ* will be
destroyed—
it is the sin of Israel.
Thorns and thistles will grow up
and cover their altars.
Then they will say to the mountains, "Cover us!"
and to the hills, "Fall on us!"

9 "Since the days of Gibeah, you have sinned,
O Israel,
and there you have remained.*ᵇ*
Did not war overtake
the evildoers in Gibeah?
10 When I please, I will punish them;
nations will be gathered against them
to put them in bonds for their double sin.
11 Ephraim is a trained heifer
that loves to thresh;
so I will put a yoke
on her fair neck.
I will drive Ephraim,
Judah must plow,
and Jacob must break up the ground.
12 Sow for yourselves righteousness,
reap the fruit of unfailing love,
and break up your unplowed ground;
for it is time to seek the Lord,
until he comes
and showers righteousness on you.
13 But you have planted wickedness,
you have reaped evil,
you have eaten the fruit of deception.
Because you have depended on your own
strength
and on your many warriors,
14 the roar of battle will rise against your people,
so that all your fortresses will be devastated—
as Shalman devastated Beth Arbel on the day of
battle,
when mothers were dashed to the ground with
their children.
15 Thus will it happen to you, O Bethel,
because your wickedness is great.
When that day dawns,
the king of Israel will be completely destroyed.

God's Love for Israel

11 "When Israel was a child, I loved him,
and out of Egypt I called my son.
2 But the more I*ᶜ* called Israel,
the further they went from me.*ᵈ*
They sacrificed to the Baals
and they burned incense to images.
3 It was I who taught Ephraim to walk,
taking them by the arms;
but they did not realize
it was I who healed them.
4 I led them with cords of human kindness,

ᵃ 8 Hebrew *aven,* a reference to Beth Aven (a derogatory name for Bethel)
ᵇ 9 Or *there a stand was taken*   *ᶜ 2* Some Septuagint manuscripts; Hebrew
they   *ᵈ 2* Septuagint; Hebrew *them*

with ties of love;
  I lifted the yoke from their neck
    and bent down to feed them.

5 "Will they not return to Egypt
    and will not Assyria rule over them
  because they refuse to repent?
6 Swords will flash in their cities,
    will destroy the bars of their gates
    and put an end to their plans.
7 My people are determined to turn from me.
    Even if they call to the Most High,
  he will by no means exalt them.

8 "How can I give you up, Ephraim?
    How can I hand you over, Israel?
  How can I treat you like Admah?
    How can I make you like Zeboiim?
  My heart is changed within me;
    all my compassion is aroused.
9 I will not carry out my fierce anger,
    nor will I turn and devastate Ephraim.
  For I am God, and not man—
    the Holy One among you.
  I will not come in wrath.[a]
10 They will follow the Lord;
    he will roar like a lion.
  When he roars,
    his children will come trembling from the west.
11 They will come trembling
    like birds from Egypt,
    like doves from Assyria.
  I will settle them in their homes,"
    declares the Lord.

Israel's Sin

12 Ephraim has surrounded me with lies,
    the house of Israel with deceit.
  And Judah is unruly against God,
    even against the faithful Holy One.

12 1 Ephraim feeds on the wind;
    he pursues the east wind all day
    and multiplies lies and violence.
  He makes a treaty with Assyria
    and sends olive oil to Egypt.
2 The Lord has a charge to bring against Judah;
    he will punish Jacob[b] according to his ways
    and repay him according to his deeds.
3 In the womb he grasped his brother's heel;
    as a man he struggled with God.
4 He struggled with the angel and overcame him;
    he wept and begged for his favor.
  He found him at Bethel
    and talked with him there—
5 the Lord God Almighty,
    the Lord is his name of renown!
6 But you must return to your God;
    maintain love and justice,
    and wait for your God always.

Nurture in Spite of Nature

HOSEA 11:1–3

Using a tender picture of a father teaching a child to walk, Hosea relays God's nurturing love to his people. God's nature is to guide us, while our nature is to wander, much like a headstrong two-year-old in a crowded mall.

In what ways do you allow God to guide you and lead you step by step? What traits, attitudes and desires cause you to pull away from God's guiding hand? What happens when you insist on having your own way? Do you get lost among the "giants" around you? Do you fall on your face? At what point do you turn and look for God? Does God ever really lose track of his children?

See Meeting God in Everyday Life

---

a 9 Or *come against any city*   b 2 *Jacob* means *he grasps the heel* (figuratively, *he deceives*).

The Sum of What We Hold Dear

HOSEA 13:1–3

Israel offends God by sinning more and more, until the people are crafting cleverly fashioned silver idols. Do you ascribe too much worth to things, position, security or human recognition? Have they become idols? Have you started to resemble the sum of what you hold dear?

Sketch a large figure to represent yourself. Inside the head write down some of the things you are thinking about most. In the area of the heart, name three or four things that are claiming your emotional energy. On the hands name two projects or activities that are presently occupying most of your time. Repeat this process for any part of the body that applies. Does your portrait look like an idol? Or does it resemble a child of your heavenly Father? In what ways are you content with this picture? Concerned?

See Meeting God in Everyday Life

⁷The merchant uses dishonest scales;
  he loves to defraud.
⁸Ephraim boasts,
  "I am very rich; I have become wealthy.
With all my wealth they will not find in me
  any iniquity or sin."

⁹"I am the LORD your God,
  ⌊who brought you⌋ out of ᵃ Egypt;
I will make you live in tents again,
  as in the days of your appointed feasts.
¹⁰I spoke to the prophets,
  gave them many visions
  and told parables through them."

¹¹Is Gilead wicked?
  Its people are worthless!
Do they sacrifice bulls in Gilgal?
  Their altars will be like piles of stones
  on a plowed field.
¹²Jacob fled to the country of Aramᵇ;
  Israel served to get a wife,
  and to pay for her he tended sheep.
¹³The LORD used a prophet to bring Israel up from
  Egypt,
  by a prophet he cared for him.
¹⁴But Ephraim has bitterly provoked him to anger;
  his Lord will leave upon him the guilt of his
  bloodshed
  and will repay him for his contempt.

The LORD's Anger Against Israel

13 When Ephraim spoke, men trembled;
  he was exalted in Israel.
  But he became guilty of Baal worship and died.
²Now they sin more and more;
  they make idols for themselves from their
  silver,
cleverly fashioned images,
  all of them the work of craftsmen.
It is said of these people,
  "They offer human sacrifice
  and kissᶜ the calf-idols."
³Therefore they will be like the morning mist,
  like the early dew that disappears,
  like chaff swirling from a threshing floor,
  like smoke escaping through a window.

⁴"But I am the LORD your God,
  ⌊who brought you⌋ out of ᵃ Egypt.
You shall acknowledge no God but me,
  no Savior except me.
⁵I cared for you in the desert,
  in the land of burning heat.
⁶When I fed them, they were satisfied;
  when they were satisfied, they became proud;
  then they forgot me.
⁷So I will come upon them like a lion,
  like a leopard I will lurk by the path.

ᵃ 9,4 Or God / ever since you were in   ᵇ 12 That is, Northwest Mesopotamia
ᶜ 2 Or "Men who sacrifice / kiss

⁸Like a bear robbed of her cubs,
  I will attack them and rip them open.
Like a lion I will devour them;
  a wild animal will tear them apart.

⁹"You are destroyed, O Israel,
  because you are against me, against your
    helper.
¹⁰Where is your king, that he may save you?
  Where are your rulers in all your towns,
of whom you said,
  'Give me a king and princes'?
¹¹So in my anger I gave you a king,
  and in my wrath I took him away.
¹²The guilt of Ephraim is stored up,
  his sins are kept on record.
¹³Pains as of a woman in childbirth come to him,
  but he is a child without wisdom;
when the time arrives,
  he does not come to the opening of the womb.

¹⁴"I will ransom them from the power of the grave*ᵃ*;
  I will redeem them from death.
Where, O death, are your plagues?
  Where, O grave,ᵃ is your destruction?

"I will have no compassion,
¹⁵ even though he thrives among his brothers.
An east wind from the LORD will come,
  blowing in from the desert;
his spring will fail
  and his well dry up.
His storehouse will be plundered
  of all its treasures.
¹⁶The people of Samaria must bear their guilt,
  because they have rebelled against their God.
They will fall by the sword;
  their little ones will be dashed to the ground,
  their pregnant women ripped open."

Repentance to Bring Blessing

14 Return, O Israel, to the LORD your God.
  Your sins have been your downfall!
²Take words with you
  and return to the LORD.
Say to him:
  "Forgive all our sins
  and receive us graciously,
    that we may offer the fruit of our lips.ᵇ
³Assyria cannot save us;
  we will not mount war-horses.
We will never again say 'Our gods'
  to what our own hands have made,
  for in you the fatherless find compassion."

⁴"I will heal their waywardness
  and love them freely,
  for my anger has turned away from them.
⁵I will be like the dew to Israel;
  he will blossom like a lily.
Like a cedar of Lebanon

Take Words With You

HOSEA 14:1–4

Hosea advises the people of God to take this simple offering to God: "Forgive all our sins and receive us graciously, that we may offer the fruit of our lips." And God replies with gracious compassion: "I will heal their waywardness and love them freely."

What "words" do you take with you when you go into God's presence? Are they the words of confession as in verse 2? Do you offer God an exuberant, resounding YES? Do you go before God offering "a sacrifice of praise—the fruit of lips that confess his name" (Hebrews 13:15)? Be silent before God, whom no words can describe, yet who is approachable and knowable. What does God say to you in your silence?

See Meeting God in Prayer

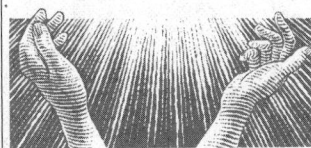

ᵃ *14* Hebrew *Sheol*   ᵇ *2* Or *offer our lips as sacrifices of bulls*

Love Triumphant

HOSEA 14:5–9

"Once I 'know' God, that is, once I experience God's love as the love in which all my human experiences are anchored, I can only desire one thing: to be in that love. 'Being' anywhere else, then, is shown to be illusory and eventually lethal . . . The great temptation is to use our many obvious failures and disappointments in our lives to convince ourselves that we are really not worth being loved . . . But for a person of faith the opposite is true. The many failures may open that place where we have nothing to brag about but everything to be loved for."

—HENRI J. M. NOUWEN,
Gracias

he will send down his roots;
6   his young shoots will grow.
His splendor will be like an olive tree,
    his fragrance like a cedar of Lebanon.
7 Men will dwell again in his shade.
    He will flourish like the grain.
He will blossom like a vine,
    and his fame will be like the wine from
        Lebanon.
8 O Ephraim, what more have I*a* to do with idols?
    I will answer him and care for him.
I am like a green pine tree;
    your fruitfulness comes from me."

9 Who is wise? He will realize these things.
    Who is discerning? He will understand them.
The ways of the LORD are right;
    the righteous walk in them,
    but the rebellious stumble in them.

a 8 Or What more has Ephraim

JOEL
The Coming Day of the Lord

KEY VERSES:

"And afterward, I will pour out my Spirit on all people. Your sons and daughters will prophesy, your old men will dream dreams, your young men will see visions . . . I will pour out my Spirit in those days . . . And everyone who calls on the name of the LORD will be saved."—Joel 2:28-29,32

I s the day of the Lord a day of judgment or a day of salvation? Is it a day of wrath or a day of restoration? As we read Joel's prophecy, we discover that it is both. God's earlier judgment against the apostasy of Judah is reversed, not by the actions of the people, but by God's loving determination to restore his people to fellowship and life. This prophecy is a debate within the very mind of God—the people of Judah deserve judgment (a plague of locusts) and yet God wants to offer the people miraculous mercy (the gift of abundant life).

God waits for each of us to rend our hearts, to repent and to receive in faith the salvation that God desires to give us. Through the prophet Joel, God invites you to listen. You will be standing on holy ground as you read, for the message of the book of Joel is that God's arms are extended to you, inviting you to return to him so that you may stand in God's presence in the day of the Lord—a day when God's Spirit would be poured out on all people.

> "Courage, then, O soul most beautiful, you now know that your Beloved, whom you long for, dwells hidden within your breast; strive, therefore, to be truly hidden with your Beloved, and then you will embrace him, and be conscious of his presence with loving affection."
>
> —JOHN OF THE CROSS,
> *A Spiritual Canticle of the Soul*

The Lament

JOEL 1:5–12

The devastation of Judah is complete. An invasion of locusts has plunged the nation into famine. Joel calls all in the land—the drunkards, the young women, the priests, the farmers, the vine growers—to lament their waywardness and repent of their sins.

Reflect: Why does the prophet refer to Judah's destruction in agricultural and ecological terms? Is it a merely figurative destruction or is it a literal one? Have you ever wept or mourned over the destruction of a land and its people? What repercussions does human sin have on creation? What repercussions might your own ignorance, carelessness or greed have on the environment? How do you think God views ecological devastation? After considering these questions respond by finding a Scripture passage that reflects God's joy in his created world and pray through it.

See Meeting God in the Created Order

1 The word of the LORD that came to Joel son of Pethuel.

An Invasion of Locusts

² Hear this, you elders;
   listen, all who live in the land.
Has anything like this ever happened in your days
   or in the days of your forefathers?
³ Tell it to your children,
   and let your children tell it to their children,
   and their children to the next generation.
⁴ What the locust swarm has left
   the great locusts have eaten;
what the great locusts have left
   the young locusts have eaten;
what the young locusts have left
   other locusts*ᵃ* have eaten.

⁵ Wake up, you drunkards, and weep!
   Wail, all you drinkers of wine;
wail because of the new wine,
   for it has been snatched from your lips.
⁶ A nation has invaded my land,
   powerful and without number;
it has the teeth of a lion,
   the fangs of a lioness.
⁷ It has laid waste my vines
   and ruined my fig trees.
It has stripped off their bark
   and thrown it away,
   leaving their branches white.

⁸ Mourn like a virgin*ᵇ* in sackcloth
   grieving for the husband*ᶜ* of her youth.
⁹ Grain offerings and drink offerings
   are cut off from the house of the LORD.
The priests are in mourning,
   those who minister before the LORD.
¹⁰ The fields are ruined,
   the ground is dried up*ᵈ*;
the grain is destroyed,
   the new wine is dried up,
   the oil fails.
¹¹ Despair, you farmers,
   wail, you vine growers;
grieve for the wheat and the barley,
   because the harvest of the field is destroyed.
¹² The vine is dried up
   and the fig tree is withered;
the pomegranate, the palm and the apple tree—
   all the trees of the field—are dried up.
Surely the joy of mankind
   is withered away.

A Call to Repentance

¹³ Put on sackcloth, O priests, and mourn;
   wail, you who minister before the altar.
Come, spend the night in sackcloth,

ᵃ 4 The precise meaning of the four Hebrew words used here for locusts is uncertain.   *ᵇ 8* Or *young woman*   *ᶜ 8* Or *betrothed*   *ᵈ 10* Or *ground mourns*

you who minister before my God;
for the grain offerings and drink offerings
    are withheld from the house of your God.
¹⁴ Declare a holy fast;
    call a sacred assembly.
Summon the elders
    and all who live in the land
to the house of the Lord your God,
    and cry out to the Lord.

¹⁵ Alas for that day!
    For the day of the Lord is near;
    it will come like destruction from the Almighty.ᵃ

¹⁶ Has not the food been cut off
    before our very eyes—
joy and gladness
    from the house of our God?
¹⁷ The seeds are shriveled
    beneath the clods.ᵇ
The storehouses are in ruins,
    the granaries have been broken down,
    for the grain has dried up.
¹⁸ How the cattle moan!
    The herds mill about
because they have no pasture;
    even the flocks of sheep are suffering.

¹⁹ To you, O Lord, I call,
    for fire has devoured the open pastures
    and flames have burned up all the trees of the
        field.
²⁰ Even the wild animals pant for you;
    the streams of water have dried up
    and fire has devoured the open pastures.

An Army of Locusts

2 Blow the trumpet in Zion;
    sound the alarm on my holy hill.
Let all who live in the land tremble,
    for the day of the Lord is coming.
It is close at hand—
² a day of darkness and gloom,
    a day of clouds and blackness.
Like dawn spreading across the mountains
    a large and mighty army comes,
such as never was of old
    nor ever will be in ages to come.

³ Before them fire devours,
    behind them a flame blazes.
Before them the land is like the garden of Eden,
    behind them, a desert waste—
    nothing escapes them.
⁴ They have the appearance of horses;
    they gallop along like cavalry.
⁵ With a noise like that of chariots
    they leap over the mountaintops,
like a crackling fire consuming stubble,
    like a mighty army drawn up for battle.

Sackcloth and Fasting

JOEL 1:13–14

Joel is calling the priests who serve at the altar in the temple to lead the people of the nation in a "sacred assembly" or special service of repentance. They are to "spend the night in sackcloth" and "declare a holy fast" as signs of their heartfelt penitence and humility before God. Their very lives and the life of the nation depend on how they respond to the prophet's call.

How can you designate a special time of confession and repentance on behalf of your nation, your family or yourself? Might it be a late-night vigil once a week? A weekend retreat during the season of Advent or Lent? A day of fasting once a month? Consider wearing a dark scarf or stole around your shoulders during your confessional prayer time as an outward sign of inward humility.

ᵃ 15 Hebrew *Shaddai*   ᵇ 17 The meaning of the Hebrew for this word is uncertain.

Rend Your Heart

JOEL 2:12–14

Tear a piece of cloth or an old garment in two. Watch what happens. What do you notice? Does it require effort to tear it? What noise does the fabric make? In this passage God commands the Judeans to rend their hearts and return to the Lord God. "The sacrifices of God are a broken spirit; a broken and contrite heart . . . [God] will not despise" (Psalm 51:17). Such a return to God is a deliberate act of will on our part. Such repentance requires effort. It may involve wrenching pain as we give up the excesses, false security and comfortable, destructive ruts we are fond of. It may leave some raw edges and cause bits of fluff to fly as the fabric of our ego rips. None of us can do this apart from the help of our gracious and compassionate God. What deliberate steps will you take to open your heart to God and walk steadfastly in God's way?

See *Meeting God in Scripture*

⁶At the sight of them, nations are in anguish;
   every face turns pale.
⁷They charge like warriors;
   they scale walls like soldiers.
They all march in line,
   not swerving from their course.
⁸They do not jostle each other;
   each marches straight ahead.
They plunge through defenses
   without breaking ranks.
⁹They rush upon the city;
   they run along the wall.
They climb into the houses;
   like thieves they enter through the windows.

¹⁰Before them the earth shakes,
   the sky trembles,
the sun and moon are darkened,
   and the stars no longer shine.
¹¹The LORD thunders
   at the head of his army;
his forces are beyond number,
   and mighty are those who obey his command.
The day of the LORD is great;
   it is dreadful.
   Who can endure it?

Rend Your Heart

¹²"Even now," declares the LORD,
   "return to me with all your heart,
   with fasting and weeping and mourning."

¹³Rend your heart
   and not your garments.
Return to the LORD your God,
   for he is gracious and compassionate,
slow to anger and abounding in love,
   and he relents from sending calamity.
¹⁴Who knows? He may turn and have pity
   and leave behind a blessing—
grain offerings and drink offerings
   for the LORD your God.

¹⁵Blow the trumpet in Zion,
   declare a holy fast,
   call a sacred assembly.
¹⁶Gather the people,
   consecrate the assembly;
bring together the elders,
   gather the children,
   those nursing at the breast.
Let the bridegroom leave his room
   and the bride her chamber.
¹⁷Let the priests, who minister before the LORD,
   weep between the temple porch and the altar.
Let them say, "Spare your people, O LORD.
   Do not make your inheritance an object of scorn,
   a byword among the nations.
Why should they say among the peoples,
   'Where is their God?' "

The LORD's Answer

18 Then the LORD will be jealous for his land
  and take pity on his people.

19 The LORD will reply[a] to them:

"I am sending you grain, new wine and oil,
  enough to satisfy you fully;
never again will I make you
  an object of scorn to the nations.

20 "I will drive the northern army far from you,
  pushing it into a parched and barren land,
with its front columns going into the eastern sea[b]
  and those in the rear into the western sea.[c]
And its stench will go up;
  its smell will rise."

Surely he has done great things.[d]
21 Be not afraid, O land;
  be glad and rejoice.
Surely the LORD has done great things.
22 Be not afraid, O wild animals,
  for the open pastures are becoming green.
The trees are bearing their fruit;
  the fig tree and the vine yield their riches.
23 Be glad, O people of Zion,
  rejoice in the LORD your God,
for he has given you
  the autumn rains in righteousness.[e]
He sends you abundant showers,
  both autumn and spring rains, as before.
24 The threshing floors will be filled with grain;
  the vats will overflow with new wine and oil.

25 "I will repay you for the years the locusts have
    eaten—
  the great locust and the young locust,
  the other locusts and the locust swarm[f]—
my great army that I sent among you.
26 You will have plenty to eat, until you are full,
  and you will praise the name of the LORD your
    God,
  who has worked wonders for you;
never again will my people be shamed.
27 Then you will know that I am in Israel,
  that I am the LORD your God,
  and that there is no other;
never again will my people be shamed.

The Day of the LORD

28 "And afterward,
  I will pour out my Spirit on all people.
Your sons and daughters will prophesy,
  your old men will dream dreams,
  your young men will see visions.
29 Even on my servants, both men and women,
  I will pour out my Spirit in those days.

---

a 18,19 Or LORD was jealous . . . / and took pity . . . / ¹⁹The LORD replied
b 20 That is, the Dead Sea   c 20 That is, the Mediterranean   d 20 Or rise.
/ Surely it has done great things."   e 23 Or / the teacher for righteousness:
f 25 The precise meaning of the four Hebrew words used here for locusts is
uncertain.

1207

God's Jealousy

JOEL 2:18–20

We generally think of jealousy as a negative trait or feeling, but have you ever thought of jealousy as redemptive? God's "jealousy" is the fountainhead of his great love for us. God is zealous to carry out his purpose of salvation for his people, even when they turn away. God's yearning for us is stronger than his anger and wrath. How is God's yearning for your attention and your companionship being expressed to you? How does God call you into communion? How does God's still, small voice whisper to you that he wants you to spend time with him? Offer thanksgiving for God's jealous, wooing, pursuing love.

See Meeting God in Prayer

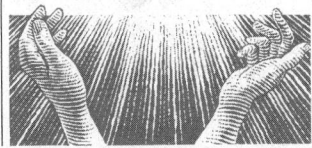

The Gift of the Spirit

JOEL 2:28–29

God promises to pour out his Spirit on all people, an event that would signify a new era in the advancement of God's kingdom. Joel's prophecy is fulfilled when the Holy Spirit is poured out on the disciples gathered in Jerusalem (see Acts 2). This wonderful gift of the Holy Spirit is given to all who "repent and [are] baptized . . . in the name of Jesus Christ" (Acts 2:38). The Holy Spirit reveals God's will, renews our energy, redeems us, restores the covenant relationship and removes our fear. Recall a Pentecost experience in your own life. How are you experiencing the gift of the Holy Spirit today?

³⁰ I will show wonders in the heavens
and on the earth,
blood and fire and billows of smoke.
³¹ The sun will be turned to darkness
and the moon to blood
before the coming of the great and dreadful
day of the LORD.
³² And everyone who calls
on the name of the LORD will be saved;
for on Mount Zion and in Jerusalem
there will be deliverance,
as the LORD has said,
among the survivors
whom the LORD calls.

The Nations Judged

3 "In those days and at that time,
when I restore the fortunes of Judah and Jerusalem,
² I will gather all nations
and bring them down to the Valley of
Jehoshaphat.^a
There I will enter into judgment against them
concerning my inheritance, my people Israel,
for they scattered my people among the nations
and divided up my land.
³ They cast lots for my people
and traded boys for prostitutes;
they sold girls for wine
that they might drink.

⁴ "Now what have you against me, O Tyre and Sidon and all you regions of Philistia? Are you repaying me for something I have done? If you are paying me back, I will swiftly and speedily return on your own heads what you have done. ⁵ For you took my silver and my gold and carried off my finest treasures to your temples. ⁶ You sold the people of Judah and Jerusalem to the Greeks, that you might send them far from their homeland.

⁷ "See, I am going to rouse them out of the places to which you sold them, and I will return on your own heads what you have done. ⁸ I will sell your sons and daughters to the people of Judah, and they will sell them to the Sabeans, a nation far away." The LORD has spoken.

⁹ Proclaim this among the nations:
Prepare for war!
Rouse the warriors!
Let all the fighting men draw near and attack.
¹⁰ Beat your plowshares into swords
and your pruning hooks into spears.
Let the weakling say,
"I am strong!"
¹¹ Come quickly, all you nations from every side,
and assemble there.

Bring down your warriors, O LORD!

¹² "Let the nations be roused;
let them advance into the Valley of Jehoshaphat,
for there I will sit
to judge all the nations on every side.

---

^a 2 *Jehoshaphat* means *the LORD judges*; also in verse 12.

¹³ Swing the sickle,
　　for the harvest is ripe.
Come, trample the grapes,
　　for the winepress is full
　　and the vats overflow—
so great is their wickedness!"

¹⁴ Multitudes, multitudes
　　in the valley of decision!
For the day of the LORD is near
　　in the valley of decision.
¹⁵ The sun and moon will be darkened,
　　and the stars no longer shine.
¹⁶ The LORD will roar from Zion
　　and thunder from Jerusalem;
　　the earth and the sky will tremble.
But the LORD will be a refuge for his people,
　　a stronghold for the people of Israel.

Blessings for God's People

¹⁷ "Then you will know that I, the LORD your God,
　　dwell in Zion, my holy hill.
Jerusalem will be holy;
　　never again will foreigners invade her.
¹⁸ "In that day the mountains will drip new wine,
　　and the hills will flow with milk;
　　all the ravines of Judah will run with water.
A fountain will flow out of the LORD's house
　　and will water the valley of acacias.ᵃ
¹⁹ But Egypt will be desolate,
　　Edom a desert waste,
because of violence done to the people of Judah,
　　in whose land they shed innocent blood.
²⁰ Judah will be inhabited forever
　　and Jerusalem through all generations.
²¹ Their bloodguilt, which I have not pardoned,
　　I will pardon."

　　　The LORD dwells in Zion!

Hills Flow With Milk

JOEL 3:17–21

After lengthy descriptions of war and judgment, the book of Joel concludes with a moving poetic description of the restoration of Judah. Destruction is not God's final word for Judah or for the people of God. The final word is unimaginable grace—grace made visible in a verdant land with plentiful water and abundant harvests. The rhythm of God's life in us, revealed in Jesus Christ, is death *and* resurrection. Nothing that happens to us is so bad that it cannot be redeemed.

Think of the low points in your life. Write descriptions of four or five of them on the left side of a piece of paper. Label that column "death." Opposite each entry, write down how God led you through "the valley," strengthened you, redeemed the situation. Label that column "resurrection."

See Meeting God in Everyday Life

ᵃ *18 Or Valley of Shittim*

AMOS

Let Justice Roll

KEY VERSE:

"Let justice roll on like a river, righteousness like a never-failing stream!"—Amos 5:24

"The Lord is gentle; the Lord is slow to anger; the Lord is gracious. But the Lord is also just. The Lord is also faithful. God gives you space for correction, but you love the delay of judgment more than the amendment of your ways."

—AUGUSTINE,
Commentary on John's Gospel, Treatise 33

Perhaps nowhere in the Bible is God's desire for justice and righteousness more explicitly proclaimed than in the book of Amos. Again and again Amos details the sins of a society that thinks it has it all together—it is prospering economically and militarily as it proclaims faith in the one true God. But Amos peers beneath the prosperous and religious surface, and what he sees spells doom for Israel.

The name *Amos* aptly means "burden bearer," and this prophet bears the burden of announcing some painful truths to errant Israel. Amos is not a prophet by trade but a herdsman and cultivator of sycamore-fig trees. This outdoorsman-tradesman declares the word of the Lord in terms familiar to him: vineyards and trees, marketplaces and caravan customs.

Amos is not an easy or comforting book to read, but its words are as relevant today as they were almost three thousand years ago. We simply cannot get around the book's hard-hitting truth: If we misuse power or have gained wealth unjustly, if we are indifferent to the suffering of the distressed and disadvantaged, we are to stop and "seek God and live." As you read this book, try to see ways in which you are similar to the people of Israel, no matter how disturbing it may be to do so.

Like any good prophet, Amos offers hope as well as reproach. There is no mistaking the kind of life God desires for us, and that life is an existence far more meaningful and fulfilling than any we could ever imagine in the midst of our comfortable complacency.

1 The words of Amos, one of the shepherds of Tekoa—
what he saw concerning Israel two years before the
earthquake, when Uzziah was king of Judah and Jeroboam
son of Jehoash[a] was king of Israel.

²He said:

"The LORD roars from Zion
    and thunders from Jerusalem;
the pastures of the shepherds dry up,[b]
    and the top of Carmel withers."

Judgment on Israel's Neighbors

³This is what the LORD says:

"For three sins of Damascus,
    even for four, I will not turn back ⌐my wrath⌐.
Because she threshed Gilead
    with sledges having iron teeth,
⁴I will send fire upon the house of Hazael
    that will consume the fortresses of Ben-Hadad.
⁵I will break down the gate of Damascus;
    I will destroy the king who is in[c] the Valley of
      Aven[d]
and the one who holds the scepter in Beth Eden.
    The people of Aram will go into exile to Kir,"
                                        says the LORD.

⁶This is what the LORD says:

"For three sins of Gaza,
    even for four, I will not turn back ⌐my wrath⌐.
Because she took captive whole communities
    and sold them to Edom,
⁷I will send fire upon the walls of Gaza
    that will consume her fortresses.
⁸I will destroy the king[e] of Ashdod
    and the one who holds the scepter in
      Ashkelon.
I will turn my hand against Ekron,
    till the last of the Philistines is dead,"
                                says the Sovereign LORD.

⁹This is what the LORD says:

"For three sins of Tyre,
    even for four, I will not turn back ⌐my wrath⌐.
Because she sold whole communities of captives
      to Edom,
    disregarding a treaty of brotherhood,
¹⁰I will send fire upon the walls of Tyre
    that will consume her fortresses."

¹¹This is what the LORD says:

"For three sins of Edom,
    even for four, I will not turn back ⌐my wrath⌐.
Because he pursued his brother with a sword,
    stifling all compassion,[f]
because his anger raged continually
    and his fury flamed unchecked,

Thus Says the Lord

AMOS 1:1–11

Amos begins by prophesying,
not about Israel's sins, but
about the sins of its neighbors.
Perhaps Israel feels pretty smug
at this point. It's always easy
to recognize the sins of others.
After all, God had chosen the
Israelites, so their nation would
always be prosperous and safe,
wouldn't it? It's those *other*
people who deserve God's judgment. Perhaps Israel is glad
that the Lord is finally going to
do something about "those
people"—the people of Damascus, Gaza, Tyre and Edom.

Who are those you might
label "those people"? What are
their sins? How do you distinguish yourself from them? Ask
God to help you identify with
them in your mutual need for
confession and repentance.

See Meeting God in Community

ᵃ 1 Hebrew *Joash*, a variant of *Jehoash*   ᵇ 2 Or *shepherds mourn*   ᶜ 5 Or
the inhabitants of   ᵈ 5 *Aven* means *wickedness*.   ᵉ 8 Or *inhabitants*
ᶠ 11 Or *sword / and destroyed his allies*

Beneath the Surface

AMOS 2:6–8

Wait! Does Amos say *Israel*? But the Lord has chosen Israel! And Israel worships the Lord. How can a God-fearing nation sell the righteous and the needy? How can such a nation trample on people who are poor and deny justice to the oppressed? Amos sees corruption and exploitation beneath the surface of Israel's society—things Israel either hasn't seen or has turned a blind eye toward.

How are nations today corrupt in similar ways? What sins do you think Amos would point out in your town? How do you participate in these sins? Offer prayers of confession on behalf of yourself and your community.

See Meeting God in Prayer

---

¹²I will send fire upon Teman
　　that will consume the fortresses of Bozrah."

¹³This is what the LORD says:

"For three sins of Ammon,
　　even for four, I will not turn back ⌊my wrath⌋.
Because he ripped open the pregnant women of
　　Gilead
　　in order to extend his borders,
¹⁴I will set fire to the walls of Rabbah
　　that will consume her fortresses
amid war cries on the day of battle,
　　amid violent winds on a stormy day.
¹⁵Her king*a* will go into exile,
　　he and his officials together,"
　　　　　　　　　　　　says the LORD.

2 This is what the LORD says:

"For three sins of Moab,
　　even for four, I will not turn back ⌊my wrath⌋.
Because he burned, as if to lime,
　　the bones of Edom's king,
²I will send fire upon Moab
　　that will consume the fortresses of Kerioth.*b*
Moab will go down in great tumult
　　amid war cries and the blast of the trumpet.
³I will destroy her ruler
　　and kill all her officials with him,"
　　　　　　　　　　　　says the LORD.

⁴This is what the LORD says:

"For three sins of Judah,
　　even for four, I will not turn back ⌊my wrath⌋.
Because they have rejected the law of the LORD
　　and have not kept his decrees,
because they have been led astray by false
　　gods,*c*
　　the gods*d* their ancestors followed,
⁵I will send fire upon Judah
　　that will consume the fortresses of Jerusalem."

Judgment on Israel

⁶This is what the LORD says:

"For three sins of Israel,
　　even for four, I will not turn back ⌊my wrath⌋.
They sell the righteous for silver,
　　and the needy for a pair of sandals.
⁷They trample on the heads of the poor
　　as upon the dust of the ground
　　and deny justice to the oppressed.
Father and son use the same girl
　　and so profane my holy name.
⁸They lie down beside every altar
　　on garments taken in pledge.
In the house of their god
　　they drink wine taken as fines.

a 15 Or *I Molech*; Hebrew *malcam*　　*b 2* Or *of her cities*　　*c 4* Or *by lies*
d 4 Or *lies*

9 "I destroyed the Amorite before them,
 though he was tall as the cedars
 and strong as the oaks.
 I destroyed his fruit above
 and his roots below.

10 "I brought you up out of Egypt,
 and I led you forty years in the desert
 to give you the land of the Amorites.
11 I also raised up prophets from among your sons
 and Nazirites from among your young men.
 Is this not true, people of Israel?"

 declares the LORD.

12 "But you made the Nazirites drink wine
 and commanded the prophets not to
 prophesy.

13 "Now then, I will crush you
 as a cart crushes when loaded with grain.
14 The swift will not escape,
 the strong will not muster their strength,
 and the warrior will not save his life.
15 The archer will not stand his ground,
 the fleet-footed soldier will not get away,
 and the horseman will not save his life.
16 Even the bravest warriors
 will flee naked on that day,"

 declares the LORD.

Witnesses Summoned Against Israel

3 Hear this word the LORD has spoken against you, O people of Israel—against the whole family I brought up out of Egypt:

2 "You only have I chosen
 of all the families of the earth;
 therefore I will punish you
 for all your sins."

3 Do two walk together
 unless they have agreed to do so?
4 Does a lion roar in the thicket
 when he has no prey?
 Does he growl in his den
 when he has caught nothing?
5 Does a bird fall into a trap on the ground
 where no snare has been set?
 Does a trap spring up from the earth
 when there is nothing to catch?
6 When a trumpet sounds in a city,
 do not the people tremble?
 When disaster comes to a city,
 has not the LORD caused it?

7 Surely the Sovereign LORD does nothing
 without revealing his plan
 to his servants the prophets.

8 The lion has roared—
 who will not fear?
 The Sovereign LORD has spoken—
 who can but prophesy?

A Covenant Broken

AMOS 3:2

How does the first half of this verse cause you to feel? Honored? Secure? Loved? What happens when you read the second half of the verse? Imagine Israel hearing these words for the first time and experiencing such a reversal of emotions. The Israelites may feel betrayed—until they remember that their relationship with God is a covenant relationship! God rescued them from Egypt, bringing them to a good place where they are to love God and keep God's commandments.

Try to remember some occasions from childhood when you were punished. Can you remember occasions when you were undeservedly punished? Can you also remember times when you deserved your punishment? Now try to recall being punished by someone you loved and who loved you. Write a short paragraph or two describing that event. What does your story reveal about love and punishment?

See Meeting God in Prayer

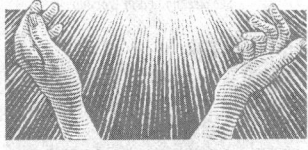

Harsh Words

AMOS 4:1–3

Imagine entering a worship service, eagerly anticipating an inspiring message from the dynamic, young preacher. But instead the message the young preacher delivers is confrontational, directive, even appalling! You are called a "cow of Bashan." You're told you have much more wealth and power than you need and that you obtained it at the expense of people who are poor and needy—that you are overly ambitious, a social climber, a corporate ladder-climber.

How do you react? Are you defensive? Do you deny everything and hope everyone else got the message that, of course, wasn't directed at you? Or do you humbly begin to examine your own conscience and ask God to illumine your heart? Do you ask: "How have I treated others to get what I have? How have I claimed credit that others deserved? Whom have I ignored in order to get ahead?" Ask God to show you how to pray regarding these situations.

See Meeting God in Worship

---

⁹ Proclaim to the fortresses of Ashdod
  and to the fortresses of Egypt:
"Assemble yourselves on the mountains of
    Samaria;
  see the great unrest within her
  and the oppression among her people."

¹⁰ "They do not know how to do right," declares the
    LORD,
  "who hoard plunder and loot in their
    fortresses."

¹¹ Therefore this is what the Sovereign LORD says:

"An enemy will overrun the land;
  he will pull down your strongholds
  and plunder your fortresses."

¹² This is what the LORD says:

"As a shepherd saves from the lion's mouth
  only two leg bones or a piece of an ear,
so will the Israelites be saved,
those who sit in Samaria
  on the edge of their beds
  and in Damascus on their couches.ᵃ"

¹³ "Hear this and testify against the house of Jacob," declares the Lord, the LORD God Almighty.

¹⁴ "On the day I punish Israel for her sins,
  I will destroy the altars of Bethel;
the horns of the altar will be cut off
  and fall to the ground.
¹⁵ I will tear down the winter house
  along with the summer house;
the houses adorned with ivory will be destroyed
  and the mansions will be demolished,"
                          declares the LORD.

Israel Has Not Returned to God

4 Hear this word, you cows of Bashan on Mount
    Samaria,
  you women who oppress the poor and crush
    the needy
  and say to your husbands, "Bring us some
    drinks!"
² The Sovereign LORD has sworn by his holiness:
  "The time will surely come
when you will be taken away with hooks,
  the last of you with fishhooks.
³ You will each go straight out
  through breaks in the wall,
  and you will be cast out toward Harmon,ᵇ"
                          declares the LORD.
⁴ "Go to Bethel and sin;
  go to Gilgal and sin yet more.
Bring your sacrifices every morning,
  your tithes every three years.ᶜ
⁵ Burn leavened bread as a thank offering
  and brag about your freewill offerings—

ᵃ 12 The meaning of the Hebrew for this line is uncertain.   ᵇ 3 Masoretic Text; with a different word division of the Hebrew (see Septuagint) *out, O mountain of oppression*   ᶜ 4 Or *tithes on the third day*

boast about them, you Israelites,
for this is what you love to do,"
declares the Sovereign Lord.

⁶"I gave you empty stomachs[a] in every city
and lack of bread in every town,
yet you have not returned to me,"
declares the Lord.

⁷"I also withheld rain from you
when the harvest was still three months away.
I sent rain on one town,
but withheld it from another.
One field had rain;
another had none and dried up.
⁸People staggered from town to town for water
but did not get enough to drink,
yet you have not returned to me,"
declares the Lord.

⁹"Many times I struck your gardens and
vineyards,
I struck them with blight and mildew.
Locusts devoured your fig and olive trees,
yet you have not returned to me,"
declares the Lord.

¹⁰"I sent plagues among you
as I did to Egypt.
I killed your young men with the sword,
along with your captured horses.
I filled your nostrils with the stench of your
camps,
yet you have not returned to me,"
declares the Lord.

¹¹"I overthrew some of you
as I[b] overthrew Sodom and Gomorrah.
You were like a burning stick snatched from the
fire,
yet you have not returned to me,"
declares the Lord.

¹²"Therefore this is what I will do to you, Israel,
and because I will do this to you,
prepare to meet your God, O Israel."

¹³He who forms the mountains,
creates the wind,
and reveals his thoughts to man,
he who turns dawn to darkness,
and treads the high places of the earth—
the Lord God Almighty is his name.

A Lament and Call to Repentance

5 Hear this word, O house of Israel, this lament I take up
concerning you:

²"Fallen is Virgin Israel,
never to rise again,
deserted in her own land,
with no one to lift her up."

You Did Not Return to Me

AMOS 4:6-13

Amos outlines each step that God has taken in order to compel his people to acknowledge his sovereignty and return to him, but Amos also demonstrates how the people thwarted (at least temporarily) God's will by exercising free will and choosing to turn away. The Israelites had encountered God during many difficult times throughout their history, yet the Lord declares to them, "You have not returned to me."

Have you encountered God's discipline? In what ways? Make a list of actions God has taken in your life in an effort to turn you back to himself. In what way do you need to return to God now? Consider this question for a moment and then paraphrase verse 13, using it as a prayer of acknowledgment of God's sovereignty in your life.

See *Meeting God in Everyday Life*

A Fulfilling Life

AMOS 5:4–6,14–15

In just four words God tells Israel what is necessary to live a life of fulfillment: "Seek me and live." But God—and therefore life—isn't to be found in showy, empty worship or in riches gained by perverting justice and exploiting the poor. We can know the true joy of God's gift of life only when justice is our rule and when righteousness, rather than evil, determines our choices.

Take the words "Seek me and live" with you into each situation and circumstance of your day. Consider what it would mean to "seek God and live" in each one of them.

See Meeting God in Scripture

³ This is what the Sovereign LORD says:

"The city that marches out a thousand strong for
  Israel
  will have only a hundred left;
the town that marches out a hundred strong
  will have only ten left."

⁴ This is what the LORD says to the house of Israel:

"Seek me and live;
⁵   do not seek Bethel,
do not go to Gilgal,
  do not journey to Beersheba.
For Gilgal will surely go into exile,
  and Bethel will be reduced to nothing.ᵃ"
⁶ Seek the LORD and live,
  or he will sweep through the house of Joseph
    like a fire;
it will devour,
  and Bethel will have no one to quench it.

⁷ You who turn justice into bitterness
  and cast righteousness to the ground
⁸ (he who made the Pleiades and Orion,
  who turns blackness into dawn
  and darkens day into night,
who calls for the waters of the sea
  and pours them out over the face of the land—
  the LORD is his name—
⁹ he flashes destruction on the stronghold
  and brings the fortified city to ruin),
¹⁰ you hate the one who reproves in court
  and despise him who tells the truth.

¹¹ You trample on the poor
  and force him to give you grain.
Therefore, though you have built stone
    mansions,
  you will not live in them;
though you have planted lush vineyards,
  you will not drink their wine.
¹² For I know how many are your offenses
  and how great your sins.

You oppress the righteous and take bribes
  and you deprive the poor of justice in the
    courts.
¹³ Therefore the prudent man keeps quiet in such
    times,
  for the times are evil.

¹⁴ Seek good, not evil,
  that you may live.
Then the LORD God Almighty will be with you,
  just as you say he is.
¹⁵ Hate evil, love good;
  maintain justice in the courts.
Perhaps the LORD God Almighty will have mercy
  on the remnant of Joseph.

ᵃ 5 Or *grief*; or *wickedness*; Hebrew *aven*, a reference to Beth Aven (a derogatory name for Bethel)

¹⁶Therefore this is what the Lord, the LORD God Almighty, says:

"There will be wailing in all the streets
    and cries of anguish in every public square.
The farmers will be summoned to weep
    and the mourners to wail.
¹⁷There will be wailing in all the vineyards,
    for I will pass through your midst,"
                                    says the LORD.

The Day of the LORD

¹⁸Woe to you who long
    for the day of the LORD!
Why do you long for the day of the LORD?
    That day will be darkness, not light.
¹⁹It will be as though a man fled from a lion
    only to meet a bear,
as though he entered his house
    and rested his hand on the wall
    only to have a snake bite him.
²⁰Will not the day of the LORD be darkness, not
        light—
    pitch-dark, without a ray of brightness?

²¹"I hate, I despise your religious feasts;
    I cannot stand your assemblies.
²²Even though you bring me burnt offerings and
        grain offerings,
    I will not accept them.
Though you bring choice fellowship offerings,ᵃ
    I will have no regard for them.
²³Away with the noise of your songs!
    I will not listen to the music of your harps.
²⁴But let justice roll on like a river,
    righteousness like a never-failing stream!

²⁵"Did you bring me sacrifices and offerings
    forty years in the desert, O house of Israel?
²⁶You have lifted up the shrine of your king,
    the pedestal of your idols,
    the star of your godᵇ—
    which you made for yourselves.
²⁷Therefore I will send you into exile beyond
        Damascus,"
    says the LORD, whose name is God Almighty.

Woe to the Complacent

6 Woe to you who are complacent in Zion,
    and to you who feel secure on Mount Samaria,
you notable men of the foremost nation,
    to whom the people of Israel come!
²Go to Calneh and look at it;
    go from there to great Hamath,
    and then go down to Gath in Philistia.
Are they better off than your two kingdoms?
    Is their land larger than yours?
³You put off the evil day
    and bring near a reign of terror.

ᵃ 22 Traditionally *peace offerings*   ᵇ 26 Or *lifted up Sakkuth your king / and Kaiwan your idols, / your star-gods;* Septuagint *lifted up the shrine of Molech / and the star of your god Rephan, / their idols*

True Worship

AMOS 5:21–24

If worshipers forget God's true nature, if they do not love justice and righteousness, then all of their worship and its accoutrements count for nothing. What place do justice and righteousness occupy in your worship? How could your worship more fully include these characteristics? What other forms of worship might you embrace in order to do so? How could you increase your love of justice and righteousness? What would that mean in your life? Would some attitudes need to change? What about your actions? Would your prayers change in any way? As you worship and pray, ask God to help you answer these questions.

See Meeting God in Worship

We've Done It!

AMOS 6:13

One of the Israelites' sins is their belief that they have accomplished great things on their own. They seem to have forgotten that God has brought them out of Egypt into a good land and has continued to protect them and provide for them.

Like the Israelites we may lapse into similar thinking, particularly when things are going well. As you go about your daily activity, make a special effort to recall how God has benefited you, and then thank God for the blessings you enjoy.

See Meeting God in Everyday Life

⁴You lie on beds inlaid with ivory
  and lounge on your couches.
You dine on choice lambs
  and fattened calves.
⁵You strum away on your harps like David
  and improvise on musical instruments.
⁶You drink wine by the bowlful
  and use the finest lotions,
  but you do not grieve over the ruin of Joseph.
⁷Therefore you will be among the first to go into
    exile;
  your feasting and lounging will end.

The Lord Abhors the Pride of Israel

⁸The Sovereign Lord has sworn by himself—the Lord God Almighty declares:

"I abhor the pride of Jacob
  and detest his fortresses;
I will deliver up the city
  and everything in it."

⁹If ten men are left in one house, they too will die. ¹⁰And if a relative who is to burn the bodies comes to carry them out of the house and asks anyone still hiding there, "Is anyone with you?" and he says, "No," then he will say, "Hush! We must not mention the name of the Lord."

¹¹For the Lord has given the command,
  and he will smash the great house into pieces
  and the small house into bits.

¹²Do horses run on the rocky crags?
  Does one plow there with oxen?
But you have turned justice into poison
  and the fruit of righteousness into bitterness—
¹³you who rejoice in the conquest of Lo Debar*a*
  and say, "Did we not take Karnaim*b* by our own
    strength?"

¹⁴For the Lord God Almighty declares,
  "I will stir up a nation against you, O house of
    Israel,
that will oppress you all the way
  from Lebo*c* Hamath to the valley of the
    Arabah."

Locusts, Fire and a Plumb Line

7 This is what the Sovereign Lord showed me: He was preparing swarms of locusts after the king's share had been harvested and just as the second crop was coming up. ²When they had stripped the land clean, I cried out, "Sovereign Lord, forgive! How can Jacob survive? He is so small!"

³So the Lord relented.

"This will not happen," the Lord said.

⁴This is what the Sovereign Lord showed me: The Sovereign Lord was calling for judgment by fire; it dried up the great deep and devoured the land. ⁵Then I cried out, "Sov-

---

a 13 Lo Debar means *nothing.*   *b 13 Karnaim* means *horns;* *horn* here symbolizes *strength.*   *c 14* Or *from the entrance to* ereign LORD, I beg you, stop! How can Jacob survive? He is so small!"

⁶So the LORD relented.

"This will not happen either," the Sovereign LORD said.

⁷This is what he showed me: The Lord was standing by a wall that had been built true to plumb, with a plumb line in his hand. ⁸And the LORD asked me, "What do you see, Amos?"

"A plumb line," I replied.

Then the Lord said, "Look, I am setting a plumb line among my people Israel; I will spare them no longer.

⁹"The high places of Isaac will be destroyed
    and the sanctuaries of Israel will be ruined;
    with my sword I will rise against the house of
        Jeroboam."

Amos and Amaziah

¹⁰Then Amaziah the priest of Bethel sent a message to Jeroboam king of Israel: "Amos is raising a conspiracy against you in the very heart of Israel. The land cannot bear all his words. ¹¹For this is what Amos is saying:

" 'Jeroboam will die by the sword,
    and Israel will surely go into exile,
    away from their native land.' "

¹²Then Amaziah said to Amos, "Get out, you seer! Go back to the land of Judah. Earn your bread there and do your prophesying there. ¹³Don't prophesy anymore at Bethel, because this is the king's sanctuary and the temple of the kingdom."

¹⁴Amos answered Amaziah, "I was neither a prophet nor a prophet's son, but I was a shepherd, and I also took care of sycamore-fig trees. ¹⁵But the LORD took me from tending the flock and said to me, 'Go, prophesy to my people Israel.' ¹⁶Now then, hear the word of the LORD. You say,

" 'Do not prophesy against Israel,
    and stop preaching against the house of Isaac.'

¹⁷"Therefore this is what the LORD says:

" 'Your wife will become a prostitute in the city,
    and your sons and daughters will fall by the
        sword.
Your land will be measured and divided up,
    and you yourself will die in a pagan[a] country.
And Israel will certainly go into exile,
    away from their native land.' "

A Basket of Ripe Fruit

8 This is what the Sovereign LORD showed me: a basket of ripe fruit. ²"What do you see, Amos?" he asked.

"A basket of ripe fruit," I answered.

Then the LORD said to me, "The time is ripe for my people Israel; I will spare them no longer.

³"In that day," declares the Sovereign LORD, "the songs in the temple will turn to wailing.[b] Many, many bodies—flung everywhere! Silence!"

Prophesy Somewhere Else!

AMOS 7:12–13

Picture this scene: Amos is being told, "Go away! Stand on another street corner! Find another pulpit! Your message doesn't please us! Go spread your gloom and doom elsewhere!" This scene seems almost comical until we ask ourselves how many times we have done the same thing in one way or another. Have you ever heard an unsettling message, which may have come from God, but responded by dismissing the prophet entirely?

Write a prayer, asking that you be able to discern God's word in the many voices around you. Use a breath prayer—such as, "Immanuel—God with us, let me be open to hearing your word"—to remind you to listen for God's word today.

See Meeting God in Worship

---

a 17 Hebrew *an unclean*   *b 3* Or *"the temple singers will wail*

Famine

AMOS 8:11–14

A famine is coming, but this famine is different. It is not food that the people will lack; they will experience a dearth of hearing the words of the Lord. Place yourself in the scenario in verse 12. You search everywhere for a word of guidance, a word of comfort, a word of redemption from the Lord, but you are unable to find it anywhere. Your need is so acute, so painful that you stagger beneath its burden. Perhaps you thought that God would always be there, patiently waiting for you to come back to him. Will you ever hear God again?

What word is God asking you to hear today? What are you waiting for? What is stopping you?

See *Meeting God in Scripture*

⁴Hear this, you who trample the needy
    and do away with the poor of the land,

⁵saying,

"When will the New Moon be over
    that we may sell grain,
and the Sabbath be ended
    that we may market wheat?"—
skimping the measure,
    boosting the price
    and cheating with dishonest scales,
⁶buying the poor with silver
    and the needy for a pair of sandals,
    selling even the sweepings with the wheat.

⁷The LORD has sworn by the Pride of Jacob: "I will never forget anything they have done.

⁸"Will not the land tremble for this,
    and all who live in it mourn?
The whole land will rise like the Nile;
    it will be stirred up and then sink
    like the river of Egypt.

⁹"In that day," declares the Sovereign LORD,

"I will make the sun go down at noon
    and darken the earth in broad daylight.
¹⁰I will turn your religious feasts into mourning
    and all your singing into weeping.
I will make all of you wear sackcloth
    and shave your heads.
I will make that time like mourning for an only son
    and the end of it like a bitter day.

¹¹"The days are coming," declares the Sovereign LORD,
    "when I will send a famine through the land—
not a famine of food or a thirst for water,
    but a famine of hearing the words of the LORD.
¹²Men will stagger from sea to sea
    and wander from north to east,
searching for the word of the LORD,
    but they will not find it.

¹³"In that day

"the lovely young women and strong young men
    will faint because of thirst.
¹⁴They who swear by the shame*a* of Samaria,
    or say, 'As surely as your god lives, O Dan,'
    or, 'As surely as the god*b* of Beersheba lives'—
they will fall,
    never to rise again."

Israel to Be Destroyed

9 I saw the Lord standing by the altar, and he said:

"Strike the tops of the pillars
    so that the thresholds shake.
Bring them down on the heads of all the people;

a 14 Or *by Ashima;* or *by the idol*   *b 14* Or *power*

those who are left I will kill with the sword.
Not one will get away,
    none will escape.
2 Though they dig down to the depths of the
        grave,ᵃ
    from there my hand will take them.
Though they climb up to the heavens,
    from there I will bring them down.
3 Though they hide themselves on the top of
        Carmel,
    there I will hunt them down and seize them.
Though they hide from me at the bottom of the
        sea,
    there I will command the serpent to bite them.
4 Though they are driven into exile by their
        enemies,
    there I will command the sword to slay them.
I will fix my eyes upon them
    for evil and not for good."

5 The Lord, the LORD Almighty,
    he who touches the earth and it melts,
    and all who live in it mourn—
the whole land rises like the Nile,
    then sinks like the river of Egypt—
6 he who builds his lofty palaceᵇ in the heavens
    and sets its foundationᶜ on the earth,
who calls for the waters of the sea
    and pours them out over the face of the land—
    the LORD is his name.

7 "Are not you Israelites
    the same to me as the Cushitesᵈ?"
                            declares the LORD.
"Did I not bring Israel up from Egypt,
    the Philistines from Caphtorᵉ
    and the Arameans from Kir?

8 "Surely the eyes of the Sovereign LORD
    are on the sinful kingdom.
I will destroy it
    from the face of the earth—
yet I will not totally destroy
    the house of Jacob,"
                            declares the LORD.
9 "For I will give the command,
    and I will shake the house of Israel
    among all the nations
as grain is shaken in a sieve,
    and not a pebble will reach the ground.
10 All the sinners among my people
    will die by the sword,
all those who say,
    'Disaster will not overtake or meet us.'

Israel's Restoration

11 "In that day I will restore
    David's fallen tent.
I will repair its broken places,

Nowhere to Hide

AMOS 9:2–10

We like to take comfort in knowing that God is always with us. We delight in the comforting proximity of God, which we read about in Psalm 139. We savor the thought that God formed us in our mother's womb and will never leave us. But in the book of Amos this inescapable God is not a comforting figure. The Israelites are told that, no matter where they might try to hide, God will find them. They have abused the covenant relationship by not accepting its accompanying responsibilities.

Why might you want to hide from God? Is there a responsibility in your relationship with God that you've refused to embrace? What do you need to pray now, so that you no longer have to hide from God? Write in your journal your anticipation of that time.

See Meeting God in Prayer

ᵃ 2 Hebrew *to Sheol*   ᵇ 6 The meaning of the Hebrew for this phrase is uncertain.   ᶜ 6 The meaning of the Hebrew for this word is uncertain.
ᵈ 7 That is, people from the upper Nile region   ᵉ 7 That is, Crete

Restoration

AMOS 9:11–15

A glimmer of hope finally appears: "I will bring back my exiled people Israel." Notice the rich lavishness of the restoration: "New wine will drip from the mountains and flow from all the hills." But until that time the people of Israel must live with the consequences of their actions. Like the Israelites we often have to live with the consequences of our wrongful actions. What consequences are you presently living with? How are you experiencing God's grace and forgiveness in spite of them? Can you imagine the lush restoration God has planned for you? How does the promise and picture of future restoration help you through your present difficulties?

See Meeting God in the Created Order

restore its ruins,
  and build it as it used to be,
¹²so that they may possess the remnant of Edom
  and all the nations that bear my name,ᵃ"
      declares the LORD, who will
          do these things.

¹³"The days are coming," declares the LORD,

"when the reaper will be overtaken by the
    plowman
  and the planter by the one treading grapes.
New wine will drip from the mountains
  and flow from all the hills.
¹⁴I will bring back my exiledᵇ people Israel;
  they will rebuild the ruined cities and live in
    them.
They will plant vineyards and drink their wine;
  they will make gardens and eat their fruit.
¹⁵I will plant Israel in their own land,
  never again to be uprooted
  from the land I have given them,"
          says the LORD your God.

OBADIAH

God's Passion for Justice

KEY VERSE:

"The day of the LORD is near for all nations. As you have done, it will be done to you; your deeds will return upon your own head."—Obadiah 15

N o one likes to be treated unfairly or see others so treated. When injustices occur, it helps to know that God is watching and will see that justice ultimately prevails.

Although the book of Obadiah gives us very little information about the prophet, it reiterates God's zeal for justice, a theme that is woven throughout the prophetic books. Therefore God pledges to bring judgment on the people of Edom, who stand by (and even cause harm) while their Israelite kinfolk are conquered (v.11). Obadiah declares that God will bring "the day of the LORD," a day of judgment for all nations (vv.15–16). God will not forget those who are treated unfairly!

In these twenty-one verses we are once again impressed with God's passion for justice. And we know that in the end all nations and people—indeed, all of life—belong to God. "And the kingdom will be the LORD'S" (v.21).

> "Truly at the day of judgment we shall not be examined on what we have read, but what we have done; not how well we have spoken, but how religiously we have lived."
>
> —THOMAS À KEMPIS,
> *The Imitation of Christ*

Standing By, Doing Nothing

OBADIAH 11

Sometimes to take no action is to act. The Edomites were guilty of ignoring the plight of God's people. They did nothing to stop the attacks on Judah; in fact they rejoiced! The Edomites even joined in the looting that followed the Babylonian capture of Judah.

Read the newspaper or listen to a news broadcast today with the goal of listening for God's call concerning some contemporary dilemma. Pray about the situation. Then perhaps write a letter, mail a check or make a phone call to express your concern. Let this be one day when you do not turn aside from the cries of the needy or oppressed. Ask God to make you aware of those who may need your help or who may need to hear your voice today.

See Meeting God in Service

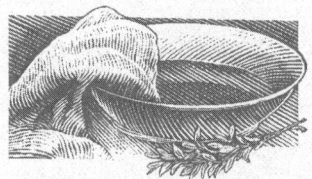

¹The vision of Obadiah.

This is what the Sovereign LORD says about Edom—

We have heard a message from the LORD:
    An envoy was sent to the nations to say,
"Rise, and let us go against her for battle"—
  ²"See, I will make you small among the nations;
    you will be utterly despised.
  ³The pride of your heart has deceived you,
    you who live in the clefts of the rocks*a*
    and make your home on the heights,
you who say to yourself,
    'Who can bring me down to the ground?'
  ⁴Though you soar like the eagle
    and make your nest among the stars,
    from there I will bring you down,"
                declares the LORD.
  ⁵"If thieves came to you,
    if robbers in the night—
Oh, what a disaster awaits you—
    would they not steal only as much as they
      wanted?
If grape pickers came to you,
    would they not leave a few grapes?
  ⁶But how Esau will be ransacked,
    his hidden treasures pillaged!
  ⁷All your allies will force you to the border;
    your friends will deceive and overpower you;
those who eat your bread will set a trap for you,*b*
    but you will not detect it.
  ⁸"In that day," declares the LORD,
    "will I not destroy the wise men of Edom,
    men of understanding in the mountains of
      Esau?
  ⁹Your warriors, O Teman, will be terrified,
    and everyone in Esau's mountains
    will be cut down in the slaughter.
  ¹⁰Because of the violence against your brother
      Jacob,
    you will be covered with shame;
    you will be destroyed forever.
  ¹¹On the day you stood aloof
    while strangers carried off his wealth
and foreigners entered his gates
    and cast lots for Jerusalem,
you were like one of them.
  ¹²You should not look down on your brother
    in the day of his misfortune,
nor rejoice over the people of Judah
    in the day of their destruction,
nor boast so much
    in the day of their trouble.
  ¹³You should not march through the gates of my
      people
    in the day of their disaster,
nor look down on them in their calamity
    in the day of their disaster,

a 3 Or *of Sela*   *b 7* The meaning of the Hebrew for this clause is uncertain.

nor seize their wealth
in the day of their disaster.
¹⁴You should not wait at the crossroads
to cut down their fugitives,
nor hand over their survivors
in the day of their trouble.

¹⁵"The day of the LORD is near
for all nations.
As you have done, it will be done to you;
your deeds will return upon your own head.
¹⁶Just as you drank on my holy hill,
so all the nations will drink continually;
they will drink and drink
and be as if they had never been.
¹⁷But on Mount Zion will be deliverance;
it will be holy,
and the house of Jacob
will possess its inheritance.
¹⁸The house of Jacob will be a fire
and the house of Joseph a flame;
the house of Esau will be stubble,
and they will set it on fire and consume it.
There will be no survivors
from the house of Esau."
The LORD has spoken.

¹⁹People from the Negev will occupy
the mountains of Esau,
and people from the foothills will possess
the land of the Philistines.
They will occupy the fields of Ephraim and
Samaria,
and Benjamin will possess Gilead.
²⁰This company of Israelite exiles who are in
Canaan
will possess ⌊the land⌋ as far as Zarephath;
the exiles from Jerusalem who are in Sepharad
will possess the towns of the Negev.
²¹Deliverers will go up on^a Mount Zion
to govern the mountains of Esau.
And the kingdom will be the LORD's.

Your Deeds Will Return

OBADIAH 15

The proverb, "You reap what you sow," is similar to these words of Obadiah. It is a word of warning: As you have treated others, so will you be treated.

Today is a good day to seek forgiveness for your actions and to make amends to anyone you may have hurt. Bring to mind anyone who may have something against you. Lift them to God in prayer and ask for forgiveness and for wisdom in seeking reconciliation. Let your prayer guide you in the steps you should take in making amends.

See Meeting God in Prayer

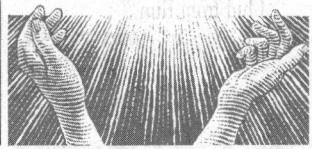

JONAH

Running From God

KEY VERSE:

"Should I not be concerned about that great city?"—Jonah 4:11

At first glance the book of Jonah is an account of the strangest two-way journey ever described: A reluctant prophet flees in fear as far away as ships could sail, only to return to land within the belly of a giant fish. But the story of Jonah's strange journey underlines a great truth about God: God can use even a stubborn and reluctant prophet to bring the truth to those who need to hear it. In spite of Jonah's ungracious willfulness, God's compassion prevails—the entire population of Nineveh repents and experiences God's healing love.

This fascinating story makes us wonder if Jonah ever clearly grasped that "the love of God is broader than the measure of the mind," as an old hymn says so well. God's compassion is so great and unwavering that we, like Jonah, struggle to believe it. We wince at the prospect of having to imitate it, particularly when we need to demonstrate it to certain people.

As you read this book, you might identify with Jonah's struggle as he first does the wrong thing and then finally does the right thing but with a wrong heart. Perhaps you have felt at odds with what God has asked you to do, and so you've offered a stiff handshake or a fake smile. You've kept people at a distance whom God would have you love. Let God penetrate the areas of your life in which you barely cooperate or even resist. Experience God's wonderfully embracing love for you—and for others—even when you feel tempted to run.

Jonah Flees From the LORD

1 The word of the LORD came to Jonah son of Amittai: ²"Go to the great city of Nineveh and preach against it, because its wickedness has come up before me."

³But Jonah ran away from the LORD and headed for Tarshish. He went down to Joppa, where he found a ship bound for that port. After paying the fare, he went aboard and sailed for Tarshish to flee from the LORD.

⁴Then the LORD sent a great wind on the sea, and such a violent storm arose that the ship threatened to break up. ⁵All the sailors were afraid and each cried out to his own god. And they threw the cargo into the sea to lighten the ship.

But Jonah had gone below deck, where he lay down and fell into a deep sleep. ⁶The captain went to him and said, "How can you sleep? Get up and call on your god! Maybe he will take notice of us, and we will not perish."

⁷Then the sailors said to each other, "Come, let us cast lots to find out who is responsible for this calamity." They cast lots and the lot fell on Jonah.

⁸So they asked him, "Tell us, who is responsible for making all this trouble for us? What do you do? Where do you come from? What is your country? From what people are you?"

⁹He answered, "I am a Hebrew and I worship the LORD, the God of heaven, who made the sea and the land."

¹⁰This terrified them and they asked, "What have you done?" (They knew he was running away from the LORD, because he had already told them so.)

¹¹The sea was getting rougher and rougher. So they asked him, "What should we do to you to make the sea calm down for us?"

¹²"Pick me up and throw me into the sea," he replied, "and it will become calm. I know that it is my fault that this great storm has come upon you."

¹³Instead, the men did their best to row back to land. But they could not, for the sea grew even wilder than before. ¹⁴Then they cried to the LORD, "O LORD, please do not let us die for taking this man's life. Do not hold us accountable for killing an innocent man, for you, O LORD, have done as you pleased." ¹⁵Then they took Jonah and threw him overboard, and the raging sea grew calm. ¹⁶At this the men greatly feared the LORD, and they offered a sacrifice to the LORD and made vows to him.

¹⁷But the LORD provided a great fish to swallow Jonah, and Jonah was inside the fish three days and three nights.

Jonah's Prayer

2 From inside the fish Jonah prayed to the LORD his God. ²He said:

> "In my distress I called to the LORD,
>   and he answered me.
> From the depths of the grave*a* I called for help,
>   and you listened to my cry.
> ³You hurled me into the deep,
>   into the very heart of the seas,
>   and the currents swirled about me;

God of *All*?

JONAH 1:2–3

Jonah and his people have a keen awareness of their relationship with God. Error creeps in when Jonah begins to consider God his exclusive possession. Jonah would rather flee from God than give up his narrow views about who deserves to know God and experience God's mercy.

Think about those whom you consider impervious to change. Are you tempted to steer clear of them? Are you trying to ignore God's clear leading to become involved? How can you let Jonah's negative example remind you that God is not willing that anyone should perish (2 Peter 3:9)? In prayer, name two or three people desperately in need of God's gracious intervention.

See Meeting God in Service

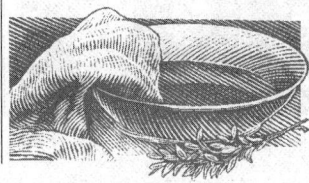

---

a 2 Hebrew *Sheol*

No Foxhole Faith

JONAH 2:4–9

The wartime expression "There are no atheists in foxholes" is illustrated well by Jonah's cry to God. It's easy to remember God when we're in trouble and forget to practice God's presence in ordinary times. Use this exercise to recall God's tender deliverance of you in the past: Recall a situation in which you were displaced or threatened in some way. How deeply into despair did you sink? What caused you to remember God and pray? What did you learn from your experience? How has that experience taught you to call on God when trouble looms? Rest in silent assurance, enjoying the steady sense of God's presence in this ordinary moment.

See Meeting God in Everyday Life

all your waves and breakers
    swept over me.
⁴I said, 'I have been banished
    from your sight;
yet I will look again
    toward your holy temple.'
⁵The engulfing waters threatened me,*a*
    the deep surrounded me;
seaweed was wrapped around my head.
⁶To the roots of the mountains I sank down;
    the earth beneath barred me in forever.
But you brought my life up from the pit,
    O Lᴏʀᴅ my God.

⁷"When my life was ebbing away,
    I remembered you, Lᴏʀᴅ,
and my prayer rose to you,
    to your holy temple.

⁸"Those who cling to worthless idols
    forfeit the grace that could be theirs.
⁹But I, with a song of thanksgiving,
    will sacrifice to you.
What I have vowed I will make good.
    Salvation comes from the Lᴏʀᴅ."

¹⁰And the Lᴏʀᴅ commanded the fish, and it vomited Jonah onto dry land.

Jonah Goes to Nineveh

3 Then the word of the Lᴏʀᴅ came to Jonah a second time: ²"Go to the great city of Nineveh and proclaim to it the message I give you."

³Jonah obeyed the word of the Lᴏʀᴅ and went to Nineveh. Now Nineveh was a very important city—a visit required three days. ⁴On the first day, Jonah started into the city. He proclaimed: "Forty more days and Nineveh will be overturned." ⁵The Ninevites believed God. They declared a fast, and all of them, from the greatest to the least, put on sackcloth.

⁶When the news reached the king of Nineveh, he rose from his throne, took off his royal robes, covered himself with sackcloth and sat down in the dust. ⁷Then he issued a proclamation in Nineveh:

"By the decree of the king and his nobles:

Do not let any man or beast, herd or flock, taste anything; do not let them eat or drink. ⁸But let man and beast be covered with sackcloth. Let everyone call urgently on God. Let them give up their evil ways and their violence. ⁹Who knows? God may yet relent and with compassion turn from his fierce anger so that we will not perish."

¹⁰When God saw what they did and how they turned from their evil ways, he had compassion and did not bring upon them the destruction he had threatened.

Jonah's Anger at the Lᴏʀᴅ's Compassion

4 But Jonah was greatly displeased and became angry. ²He prayed to the Lᴏʀᴅ, "O Lᴏʀᴅ, is this not what I said

a 5 Or waters were at my throat

when I was still at home? That is why I was so quick to flee to Tarshish. I knew that you are a gracious and compassionate God, slow to anger and abounding in love, a God who relents from sending calamity. ³Now, O Lord, take away my life, for it is better for me to die than to live."

⁴But the Lord replied, "Have you any right to be angry?"

⁵Jonah went out and sat down at a place east of the city. There he made himself a shelter, sat in its shade and waited to see what would happen to the city. ⁶Then the Lord God provided a vine and made it grow up over Jonah to give shade for his head to ease his discomfort, and Jonah was very happy about the vine. ⁷But at dawn the next day God provided a worm, which chewed the vine so that it withered. ⁸When the sun rose, God provided a scorching east wind, and the sun blazed on Jonah's head so that he grew faint. He wanted to die, and said, "It would be better for me to die than to live."

⁹But God said to Jonah, "Do you have a right to be angry about the vine?"

"I do," he said. "I am angry enough to die."

¹⁰But the Lord said, "You have been concerned about this vine, though you did not tend it or make it grow. It sprang up overnight and died overnight. ¹¹But Nineveh has more than a hundred and twenty thousand people who cannot tell their right hand from their left, and many cattle as well. Should I not be concerned about that great city?"

"Should I Not Be Concerned?"

JONAH 4:11

Jonah is pouting—dangerously close to a tantrum. And why? Because God's sweeping, inclusive love extends to even "those people" whom our protagonist has been conditioned to hold in low regard. God's ways are not Jonah's ways, and Jonah makes it known loud and clear.

Alas, when the story ends, we have not discovered how Jonah responds. But we can proceed to discover what's in our own hearts. Bring to mind someone or some group of people whom you resent—perhaps for what seem to be good reasons. Paraphrase this verse, including information about those people so that in prayer you can express concern for them by using God's own words.

See Meeting God in Prayer

MICAH
What God Requires

KEY VERSE:

He has showed you, O man, what is good. And what does the Lord require of you? To act justly and to love mercy and to walk humbly with your God.—*Micah 6:8*

"Where people let loose their minds after the love of outward things and are more engaged in pursuing the profits and seeking the friendships of this world than to be inwardly acquainted with the way of true peace, such walk in a vain shadow while the true comfort of life is wanting."

—JOHN WOOLMAN,
The Journal of John Woolman

Micah looks beneath the surface of Judah's society and sees fundamental flaws that will result in the nation's downfall. Greed and dishonesty permeate the nation, and the result is a compromised legal system, a callous disregard for the poor and an unethical business practice. Ironically all this takes place while Judah publicly professes to be faithful to the one true God and to the divine law handed down to the people during their desert wandering. They are hypocrites; their religion is a sham and God is angry.

Micah's prophetic words give us occasion to ask ourselves several questions: How can I be willing to hear all that God has to say, even when it is unpleasant? How might God be speaking to me about my thoughts and activities in light of the faith I profess? How do I need to participate in calling society to account for being less than it professes to be? How can I claim for myself Micah's hope for a time when a just and peaceful world will be God's prized possession? How open am I to acknowledging God's presence in every area of my life?

1 The word of the LORD that came to Micah of Moresheth during the reigns of Jotham, Ahaz and Hezekiah, kings of Judah—the vision he saw concerning Samaria and Jerusalem.

² Hear, O peoples, all of you,
  listen, O earth and all who are in it,
that the Sovereign LORD may witness against you,
  the Lord from his holy temple.

Judgment Against Samaria and Jerusalem

³ Look! The LORD is coming from his dwelling place;
  he comes down and treads the high places of
    the earth.
⁴ The mountains melt beneath him
  and the valleys split apart,
like wax before the fire,
  like water rushing down a slope.
⁵ All this is because of Jacob's transgression,
  because of the sins of the house of Israel.
What is Jacob's transgression?
  Is it not Samaria?
What is Judah's high place?
  Is it not Jerusalem?

⁶ "Therefore I will make Samaria a heap of rubble,
  a place for planting vineyards.
I will pour her stones into the valley
  and lay bare her foundations.
⁷ All her idols will be broken to pieces;
  all her temple gifts will be burned with fire;
  I will destroy all her images.
Since she gathered her gifts from the wages of
    prostitutes,
  as the wages of prostitutes they will again be
    used."

Weeping and Mourning

⁸ Because of this I will weep and wail;
  I will go about barefoot and naked.
I will howl like a jackal
  and moan like an owl.
⁹ For her wound is incurable;
  it has come to Judah.
It*a* has reached the very gate of my people,
  even to Jerusalem itself.
¹⁰ Tell it not in Gath*b*;
  weep not at all.*c*
In Beth Ophrah*d*
  roll in the dust.
¹¹ Pass on in nakedness and shame,
  you who live in Shaphir.*e*
Those who live in Zaanan*f*
  will not come out.
Beth Ezel is in mourning;
  its protection is taken from you.

The Lord Is Coming!

MICAH 1:1–7

What a picture Micah's words bring to mind! "The LORD is coming from his dwelling place; he comes down and treads . . . the earth." The power of God's touch on the earth is so awesome that "mountains melt beneath him and the valleys split apart."

To say that God's presence among us brings radical change is a gross understatement. When we ask God into our lives, we can expect transformation of earthshaking proportions. How would you respond to an announcement of God's presence upon the earth—a place nearby? What does it mean for God to come "from his dwelling place" and radically change you—even a part of you that you would prefer to leave undisturbed?

See Meeting God in the Created Order

---

a 9 Or *He*   *b 10 Gath* sounds like the Hebrew for *tell.*   *c 10* Hebrew; Septuagint may suggest *not in Acco.* The Hebrew for *in Acco* sounds like the Hebrew for *weep.*   *d 10 Beth Ophrah* means *house of dust.*   *e 11 Shaphir* means *pleasant.*   *f 11 Zaanan* sounds like the Hebrew for *come out.*

Plotting Evil

MICAH 2:1–6

Micah accuses the people of Judah of planning iniquity and plotting "evil on their beds!" They aren't planning heinous crimes like serial murder or mass genocide, but their night-time scheming results in the misuse of power in their day-to-day dealings with people.

How does this passage challenge you to consider what kind of thought life you might be indulging in during your leisure time? Consider what you could do or say during those restful moments instead of pondering how to acquire more or get more done to advance your agenda. How could you use those moments to connect with God and consider God's agenda?

See Meeting God in Everyday Life

¹²Those who live in Maroth[a] writhe in pain,
　　waiting for relief,
　because disaster has come from the LORD,
　　even to the gate of Jerusalem.
¹³You who live in Lachish,[b]
　　harness the team to the chariot.
　You were the beginning of sin
　　to the Daughter of Zion,
　for the transgressions of Israel
　　were found in you.
¹⁴Therefore you will give parting gifts
　　to Moresheth Gath.
　The town of Aczib[c] will prove deceptive
　　to the kings of Israel.
¹⁵I will bring a conqueror against you
　　who live in Mareshah.[d]
　He who is the glory of Israel
　　will come to Adullam.
¹⁶Shave your heads in mourning
　　for the children in whom you delight;
　make yourselves as bald as the vulture,
　　for they will go from you into exile.

Man's Plans and God's

2 Woe to those who plan iniquity,
　　to those who plot evil on their beds!
　At morning's light they carry it out
　　because it is in their power to do it.
²They covet fields and seize them,
　　and houses, and take them.
　They defraud a man of his home,
　　a fellowman of his inheritance.

³Therefore, the LORD says:

"I am planning disaster against this people,
　　from which you cannot save yourselves.
　You will no longer walk proudly,
　　for it will be a time of calamity.
⁴In that day men will ridicule you;
　　they will taunt you with this mournful song:
'We are utterly ruined;
　　my people's possession is divided up.
　He takes it from me!
　　He assigns our fields to traitors.' "

⁵Therefore you will have no one in the assembly of
　　the LORD
　to divide the land by lot.

False Prophets

⁶"Do not prophesy," their prophets say.
　　"Do not prophesy about these things;
　　disgrace will not overtake us."
⁷Should it be said, O house of Jacob:
　　"Is the Spirit of the LORD angry?
　　Does he do such things?"

---

a 12 Maroth sounds like the Hebrew for bitter.　b 13 Lachish sounds like the Hebrew for team.　c 14 Aczib means deception.　d 15 Mareshah sounds like the Hebrew for conqueror.

"Do not my words do good
to him whose ways are upright?
⁸ Lately my people have risen up
like an enemy.
You strip off the rich robe
from those who pass by without a care,
like men returning from battle.
⁹ You drive the women of my people
from their pleasant homes.
You take away my blessing
from their children forever.
¹⁰ Get up, go away!
For this is not your resting place,
because it is defiled,
it is ruined, beyond all remedy.
¹¹ If a liar and deceiver comes and says,
'I will prophesy for you plenty of wine and
beer,'
he would be just the prophet for this people!

Deliverance Promised

¹² "I will surely gather all of you, O Jacob;
I will surely bring together the remnant of
Israel.
I will bring them together like sheep in a pen,
like a flock in its pasture;
the place will throng with people.
¹³ One who breaks open the way will go up before
them;
they will break through the gate and go out.
Their king will pass through before them,
the LORD at their head."

Leaders and Prophets Rebuked

3 Then I said,

"Listen, you leaders of Jacob,
you rulers of the house of Israel.
Should you not know justice,
² you who hate good and love evil;
who tear the skin from my people
and the flesh from their bones;
³ who eat my people's flesh,
strip off their skin
and break their bones in pieces;
who chop them up like meat for the pan,
like flesh for the pot?"

⁴ Then they will cry out to the LORD,
but he will not answer them.
At that time he will hide his face from them
because of the evil they have done.

⁵ This is what the LORD says:

"As for the prophets
who lead my people astray,
if one feeds them,
they proclaim 'peace';
if he does not,
they prepare to wage war against him.

False Prophets

MICAH 2:11

Micah must not only proclaim an unpopular message, but he must also contend with false prophets whose message is that God requires only business as usual of his chosen people. Notice the sarcasm in verse 11. Write down the verse and carry it with you as you go about your day today. Be on the lookout for "a liar and deceiver." What message is being proclaimed today that seems to be just what people want to hear? What messages today are unpopular? How can you discredit the false messages and support God's true messages and messengers today?

See Meeting God in Everyday Life

An Invitation

MICAH 4:1–5

Place yourself in the midst of this text. You hear the invitation: "Come, let us go up to the mountain of the LORD . . . He will teach us his ways, so that we may walk in his paths."

What is your response to the invitation? What would beating "swords into plowshares" and "spears into pruning hooks" look like in your life? What weapons—words, facial expressions, invitation lists—that you sometimes wield could become tools of peace? Is this message a welcome word to you, or is it one you would rather not hear because it requires too much from you? Why?

See *Meeting God in Scripture*

⁶Therefore night will come over you, without visions,
    and darkness, without divination.
The sun will set for the prophets,
    and the day will go dark for them.
⁷The seers will be ashamed
    and the diviners disgraced.
They will all cover their faces
    because there is no answer from God."

⁸But as for me, I am filled with power,
    with the Spirit of the LORD,
    and with justice and might,
to declare to Jacob his transgression,
    to Israel his sin.
⁹Hear this, you leaders of the house of Jacob,
    you rulers of the house of Israel,
who despise justice
    and distort all that is right;
¹⁰who build Zion with bloodshed,
    and Jerusalem with wickedness.
¹¹Her leaders judge for a bribe,
    her priests teach for a price,
    and her prophets tell fortunes for money.
Yet they lean upon the LORD and say,
    "Is not the LORD among us?
    No disaster will come upon us."
¹²Therefore because of you,
    Zion will be plowed like a field,
Jerusalem will become a heap of rubble,
    the temple hill a mound overgrown with
        thickets.

The Mountain of the LORD

4 In the last days

the mountain of the LORD's temple will be established
    as chief among the mountains;
it will be raised above the hills,
    and peoples will stream to it.
²Many nations will come and say,

"Come, let us go up to the mountain of the
        LORD,
    to the house of the God of Jacob.
He will teach us his ways,
    so that we may walk in his paths."
The law will go out from Zion,
    the word of the LORD from Jerusalem.
³He will judge between many peoples
    and will settle disputes for strong nations far
        and wide.
They will beat their swords into plowshares
    and their spears into pruning hooks.
Nation will not take up sword against nation,
    nor will they train for war anymore.
⁴Every man will sit under his own vine
    and under his own fig tree,
and no one will make them afraid,
    for the LORD Almighty has spoken.

⁵All the nations may walk
  in the name of their gods;
we will walk in the name of the LORD
  our God for ever and ever.

The LORD's Plan

⁶"In that day," declares the LORD,

"I will gather the lame;
  I will assemble the exiles
  and those I have brought to grief.
⁷I will make the lame a remnant,
  those driven away a strong nation.
The LORD will rule over them in Mount Zion
  from that day and forever.
⁸As for you, O watchtower of the flock,
  O stronghold[a] of the Daughter of Zion,
the former dominion will be restored to you;
  kingship will come to the Daughter of
    Jerusalem."

⁹Why do you now cry aloud—
  have you no king?
Has your counselor perished,
  that pain seizes you like that of a woman in
    labor?
¹⁰Writhe in agony, O Daughter of Zion,
  like a woman in labor,
for now you must leave the city
  to camp in the open field.
You will go to Babylon;
  there you will be rescued.
There the LORD will redeem you
  out of the hand of your enemies.

¹¹But now many nations
  are gathered against you.
They say, "Let her be defiled,
  let our eyes gloat over Zion!"
¹²But they do not know
  the thoughts of the LORD;
they do not understand his plan,
  he who gathers them like sheaves to the
    threshing floor.

¹³"Rise and thresh, O Daughter of Zion,
  for I will give you horns of iron;
I will give you hoofs of bronze
  and you will break to pieces many nations."

You will devote their ill-gotten gains to the LORD,
  their wealth to the Lord of all the earth.

A Promised Ruler From Bethlehem

5 Marshal your troops, O city of troops,[b]
  for a siege is laid against us.
They will strike Israel's ruler
  on the cheek with a rod.

²"But you, Bethlehem Ephrathah,
  though you are small among the clans[c] of
    Judah,

The Other Side of Ruin–Restoration

MICAH 4:6–13

Micah's message of restoration tells us three things: (1) God will ultimately prevail in spite of the prevalence of evil; (2) it is no accident that individuals and nations suffer the consequences of the evil they do; and (3) no matter how complete individual or national ruin seems, restoration awaits beyond the ruin.

Do you hear this message with a sense of hope or doom? How have you experienced suffering as a consequence of evil? In what ways have you seen God restore people, churches, communities? How has God restored you? Make this your breath prayer (a short prayer repeated frequently) today: "O God who acts in history, restore me to a right relationship with you."

See Meeting God in Scripture

ᵃ8 Or *hill*   ᵇ1 Or *Strengthen your walls, O walled city*   ᶜ2 Or *rulers*

The One of Peace

MICAH 5:2–5

In this passage Micah describes a future deliverer who will once and for all time restore Judah to its rightful place among the nations. The source of this new leader's power is proclaimed in verses 4–5. What kind of leader do these verses describe? Think about the areas in your life where you serve in a leadership role—perhaps on your block, at work, among friends, with children. Evaluate your leadership in the light of these verses. If our nation looked for these qualities in its leaders, how would the nation be affected?

See *Meeting God in Community*

out of you will come for me
  one who will be ruler over Israel,
whose origins*a* are from of old,
  from ancient times.*b*"

³ Therefore Israel will be abandoned
  until the time when she who is in labor gives
      birth
and the rest of his brothers return
  to join the Israelites.

⁴ He will stand and shepherd his flock
  in the strength of the LORD,
  in the majesty of the name of the LORD his God.
And they will live securely, for then his greatness
  will reach to the ends of the earth.
⁵   And he will be their peace.

Deliverance and Destruction

When the Assyrian invades our land
  and marches through our fortresses,
we will raise against him seven shepherds,
  even eight leaders of men.
⁶ They will rule*c* the land of Assyria with the sword,
  the land of Nimrod with drawn sword.*d*
He will deliver us from the Assyrian
  when he invades our land
  and marches into our borders.

⁷ The remnant of Jacob will be
  in the midst of many peoples
like dew from the LORD,
  like showers on the grass,
which do not wait for man
  or linger for mankind.
⁸ The remnant of Jacob will be among the nations,
  in the midst of many peoples,
like a lion among the beasts of the forest,
  like a young lion among flocks of sheep,
which mauls and mangles as it goes,
  and no one can rescue.
⁹ Your hand will be lifted up in triumph over your
      enemies,
  and all your foes will be destroyed.

¹⁰ "In that day," declares the LORD,

"I will destroy your horses from among you
  and demolish your chariots.
¹¹ I will destroy the cities of your land
  and tear down all your strongholds.
¹² I will destroy your witchcraft
  and you will no longer cast spells.
¹³ I will destroy your carved images
  and your sacred stones from among you;
you will no longer bow down
  to the work of your hands.
¹⁴ I will uproot from among you your Asherah
      poles*e*
  and demolish your cities.

a 2 Hebrew *goings out*   *b* 2 Or *from days of eternity*   *c* 6 Or *crush*
d 6 Or *Nimrod in its gates*   *e* 14 That is, symbols of the goddess Asherah

15 I will take vengeance in anger and wrath
   upon the nations that have not obeyed me."

The Lord's Case Against Israel

6 Listen to what the Lord says:

   "Stand up, plead your case before the mountains;
      let the hills hear what you have to say.
2 Hear, O mountains, the Lord's accusation;
      listen, you everlasting foundations of the earth.
For the Lord has a case against his people;
      he is lodging a charge against Israel.

3 "My people, what have I done to you?
      How have I burdened you? Answer me.
4 I brought you up out of Egypt
      and redeemed you from the land of slavery.
I sent Moses to lead you,
      also Aaron and Miriam.
5 My people, remember
      what Balak king of Moab counseled
      and what Balaam son of Beor answered.
Remember ⌊ your journey⌋ from Shittim to Gilgal,
      that you may know the righteous acts of the
         Lord."

6 With what shall I come before the Lord
      and bow down before the exalted God?
Shall I come before him with burnt offerings,
      with calves a year old?
7 Will the Lord be pleased with thousands of rams,
      with ten thousand rivers of oil?
Shall I offer my firstborn for my transgression,
      the fruit of my body for the sin of my soul?
8 He has showed you, O man, what is good.
      And what does the Lord require of you?
To act justly and to love mercy
      and to walk humbly with your God.

Israel's Guilt and Punishment

9 Listen! The Lord is calling to the city—
      and to fear your name is wisdom—
      "Heed the rod and the One who appointed it.ᵃ
10 Am I still to forget, O wicked house,
      your ill-gotten treasures
      and the short ephah,ᵇ which is accursed?
11 Shall I acquit a man with dishonest scales,
      · with a bag of false weights?
12 Her rich men are violent;
      her people are liars
      and their tongues speak deceitfully.
13 Therefore, I have begun to destroy you,
      to ruin you because of your sins.
14 You will eat but not be satisfied;
      your stomach will still be empty.ᶜ
You will store up but save nothing,
      because what you save I will give to the
         sword.

What the Lord Requires

MICAH 6:6–8

Let this passage speak directly to you. Slowly read the passage aloud. (You may want to read it more than once.) Is there a word or phrase or image that particularly draws your attention? Reflect on that word or phrase or image. Why is it important? Wait silently, asking yourself what God might be trying to say to you in this passage. Pray that God will reveal the meaning of this passage to you and then hide the meaning deep in your heart.

See Meeting God in Scripture

ᵃ 9 The meaning of the Hebrew for this line is uncertain.   ᵇ 10 An ephah was a dry measure.   ᶜ 14 The meaning of the Hebrew for this word is uncertain.

Hopeful Waiting

MICAH 7:1–7

Read aloud verses 1–6 of Micah's lament. Can you identify with Micah's despair over a society lacking justice and mercy? Make a list of the problems of our society that cause you to despair.

Micah's lament does not end in despair however. He declares he will "watch in hope for the LORD" and "wait for" the God of his salvation. Micah's faith allows him to rise above his despair and continue to work for God. Pray through your list of our society's dilemmas. Ask God to act in these areas and to show you how it may be possible for you to address them. When you are finished, write verse 7 in red ink across your list and read it aloud.

See Meeting God in Scripture

¹⁵ You will plant but not harvest;
   you will press olives but not use the oil on yourselves,
   you will crush grapes but not drink the wine.
¹⁶ You have observed the statutes of Omri
   and all the practices of Ahab's house,
   and you have followed their traditions.
Therefore I will give you over to ruin
   and your people to derision;
   you will bear the scorn of the nations.ᵃ"

Israel's Misery

7 What misery is mine!
I am like one who gathers summer fruit
   at the gleaning of the vineyard;
there is no cluster of grapes to eat,
   none of the early figs that I crave.
² The godly have been swept from the land;
   not one upright man remains.
All men lie in wait to shed blood;
   each hunts his brother with a net.
³ Both hands are skilled in doing evil;
   the ruler demands gifts,
the judge accepts bribes,
   the powerful dictate what they desire—
   they all conspire together.
⁴ The best of them is like a brier,
   the most upright worse than a thorn hedge.
The day of your watchmen has come,
   the day God visits you.
   Now is the time of their confusion.
⁵ Do not trust a neighbor;
   put no confidence in a friend.
Even with her who lies in your embrace
   be careful of your words.
⁶ For a son dishonors his father,
   a daughter rises up against her mother,
a daughter-in-law against her mother-in-law—
   a man's enemies are the members of his own household.

⁷ But as for me, I watch in hope for the LORD,
   I wait for God my Savior;
   my God will hear me.

Israel Will Rise

⁸ Do not gloat over me, my enemy!
   Though I have fallen, I will rise.
Though I sit in darkness,
   the LORD will be my light.
⁹ Because I have sinned against him,
   I will bear the LORD's wrath,
until he pleads my case
   and establishes my right.
He will bring me out into the light;
   I will see his righteousness.
¹⁰ Then my enemy will see it
   and will be covered with shame,
she who said to me,

ᵃ 16 Septuagint; Hebrew *scorn due my people*

"Where is the LORD your God?"
My eyes will see her downfall;
even now she will be trampled underfoot
like mire in the streets.

¹¹ The day for building your walls will come,
the day for extending your boundaries.
¹² In that day people will come to you
from Assyria and the cities of Egypt,
even from Egypt to the Euphrates
and from sea to sea
and from mountain to mountain.
¹³ The earth will become desolate because of its
inhabitants,
as the result of their deeds.

Prayer and Praise

¹⁴ Shepherd your people with your staff,
the flock of your inheritance,
which lives by itself in a forest,
in fertile pasturelands.*ᵃ*
Let them feed in Bashan and Gilead
as in days long ago.

¹⁵ "As in the days when you came out of Egypt,
I will show them my wonders."

¹⁶ Nations will see and be ashamed,
deprived of all their power.
They will lay their hands on their mouths
and their ears will become deaf.
¹⁷ They will lick dust like a snake,
like creatures that crawl on the ground.
They will come trembling out of their dens;
they will turn in fear to the LORD our God
and will be afraid of you.

¹⁸ Who is a God like you,
who pardons sin and forgives the transgression
of the remnant of his inheritance?
You do not stay angry forever
but delight to show mercy.
¹⁹ You will again have compassion on us;
you will tread our sins underfoot
and hurl all our iniquities into the depths of the
sea.
²⁰ You will be true to Jacob,
and show mercy to Abraham,
as you pledged on oath to our fathers
in days long ago.

A Compassionate and Loving God

MICAH 7:18–20

The book of Micah closes with God's assurance of compassion and steadfast love: God does not "stay angry forever." In light of this passage, reflect on the state of your heart right now. In what ways do you need assurance of God's forgiveness and love? Write on a piece of paper, "[You] delight to show mercy. You will again have compassion on us." Carry this message of hope with you today, and at the end of the day reread the words and thank God for the compassion and steadfast love he offers to you. Exult in the freedom that the knowledge of your forgiveness brings.

See Meeting God in Scripture

NAHUM

Woe and Reassurance

KEY VERSE:

Look, there on the mountains, the feet of one who brings good news, who proclaims peace! Celebrate your festivals, O Judah, and fulfill your vows. No more will the wicked invade you; they will be completely destroyed.—Nahum 1:15

"And though this world,
   with devils filled,
Should threaten to undo us,
We will not fear, for God
   hath willed
His truth to triumph
   through us:
The Prince of Darkness grim,
We tremble not for him;
His rage we can endure,
For lo his doom is sure,
One little word shall fell
   him."

—MARTIN LUTHER,
"A Mighty Fortress Is Our God"

The prophet Nahum is given a vision, and with poetic passion he tells the world what he sees. His call is to announce that God opposes the arrogant Assyrian empire and will bring about the downfall of Nineveh, the proud city of Assyria. Nahum's descriptions are astonishingly powerful. "Woe to the city of blood, full of lies, full of plunder, never without victims! The crack of whips, the clatter of wheels, galloping horses and jolting chariots! Charging cavalry, flashing swords and glittering spears!" (3:1–3). The language is terse and clear: "Nothing can heal your wound; your injury is fatal" (3:19).

Among the Israelites, though, there will be rejoicing. The images of destruction also contain a word of hope for the people of Israel, long oppressed by the Assyrians: "Look, there on the mountains, the feet of one who brings good news, who proclaims peace!" (1:15). Nahum calls us to look at our own arrogance and faithlessness and welcome the herald who brings us news of peace and hope.

1

An oracle concerning Nineveh. The book of the vision of Nahum the Elkoshite.

The Lord's Anger Against Nineveh

² The LORD is a jealous and avenging God;
  the LORD takes vengeance and is filled with
    wrath.
The LORD takes vengeance on his foes
  and maintains his wrath against his enemies.
³ The LORD is slow to anger and great in power;
  the LORD will not leave the guilty unpunished.
His way is in the whirlwind and the storm,
  and clouds are the dust of his feet.
⁴ He rebukes the sea and dries it up;
  he makes all the rivers run dry.
Bashan and Carmel wither
  and the blossoms of Lebanon fade.
⁵ The mountains quake before him
  and the hills melt away.
The earth trembles at his presence,
  the world and all who live in it.
⁶ Who can withstand his indignation?
  Who can endure his fierce anger?
His wrath is poured out like fire;
  the rocks are shattered before him.

⁷ The LORD is good,
  a refuge in times of trouble.
He cares for those who trust in him,
⁸   but with an overwhelming flood
he will make an end of ⌊Nineveh⌋;
  he will pursue his foes into darkness.

⁹ Whatever they plot against the LORD
  he[a] will bring to an end;
  trouble will not come a second time.
¹⁰ They will be entangled among thorns
  and drunk from their wine;
  they will be consumed like dry stubble.[b]
¹¹ From you, ⌊O Nineveh,⌋ has one come forth
  who plots evil against the LORD
  and counsels wickedness.

¹² This is what the LORD says:

"Although they have allies and are numerous,
  they will be cut off and pass away.
Although I have afflicted you, ⌊O Judah,⌋
  I will afflict you no more.
¹³ Now I will break their yoke from your neck
  and tear your shackles away."

¹⁴ The LORD has given a command concerning you,
    ⌊Nineveh⌋:
"You will have no descendants to bear your
    name.
I will destroy the carved images and cast idols
  that are in the temple of your gods.
I will prepare your grave,
  for you are vile."

ᵃ 9 Or *What do you foes plot against the LORD? / He* ᵇ 10 The meaning of the Hebrew for this verse is uncertain.

1241

God Is Wholly Holy

NAHUM 1:3,6–7

Although our God is caring and compassionate, his holiness cannot tolerate wrongdoing and evil. They simply cannot co-exist. God's indignation at evil is consuming and complete.

God's anger with us is as-suaged in Christ Jesus, yet God asks us to be holy because he is holy (see 1 Peter 1:16). Is there anything in your life, past or present, that cannot dwell alongside God's holiness within your redeemed spirit? Is there anything for which you need to ask forgiveness? As an act of confession, list your wrongdo-ings. Confess them to the Lord who "cares for those who trust in him." Roll up that piece of paper and throw it away, or burn it. Experience the joy that comes from letting God cleanse you from all your sin.

See Meeting God in Prayer

Behold, Good News Is Coming

NAHUM 1:15

Imagine yourself a captive in a walled city. As you look out through holes in the city wall, you see hills and mountains—beautiful and green, yet inaccessible to you. You have almost given up hope of ever being free. Then you hear a trumpet sound and people shouting. Someone is coming toward the city; someone is coming with good news. Your captivity is over! You are free to go! Peace is coming to you!

You have heard the good news. What barriers have been overcome? How has your life been transformed? Who brings the word of peace to you? Who will attend a celebration with you? What will you do to celebrate? Throw a party? Write a prayer of thanksgiving?

See Meeting God in Scripture

15 Look, there on the mountains,
    the feet of one who brings good news,
    who proclaims peace!
Celebrate your festivals, O Judah,
    and fulfill your vows.
No more will the wicked invade you;
    they will be completely destroyed.

Nineveh to Fall

2 An attacker advances against you, ⌊Nineveh⌋.
    Guard the fortress,
    watch the road,
    brace yourselves,
    marshal all your strength!

2 The LORD will restore the splendor of Jacob
    like the splendor of Israel,
though destroyers have laid them waste
    and have ruined their vines.

3 The shields of his soldiers are red;
    the warriors are clad in scarlet.
The metal on the chariots flashes
    on the day they are made ready;
    the spears of pine are brandished.*a*
4 The chariots storm through the streets,
    rushing back and forth through the squares.
They look like flaming torches;
    they dart about like lightning.

5 He summons his picked troops,
    yet they stumble on their way.
They dash to the city wall;
    the protective shield is put in place.
6 The river gates are thrown open
    and the palace collapses.
7 It is decreed*b* that ⌊the city⌋
    be exiled and carried away.
Its slave girls moan like doves
    and beat upon their breasts.
8 Nineveh is like a pool,
    and its water is draining away.
"Stop! Stop!" they cry,
    but no one turns back.
9 Plunder the silver!
    Plunder the gold!
The supply is endless,
    the wealth from all its treasures!
10 She is pillaged, plundered, stripped!
    Hearts melt, knees give way,
    bodies tremble, every face grows pale.

11 Where now is the lions' den,
    the place where they fed their young,
where the lion and lioness went,
    and the cubs, with nothing to fear?
12 The lion killed enough for his cubs
    and strangled the prey for his mate,
filling his lairs with the kill
    and his dens with the prey.

a 3 Hebrew; Septuagint and Syriac / *the horsemen rush to and fro*   *b 7* The meaning of the Hebrew for this word is uncertain.

¹³ "I am against you,"
     declares the LORD Almighty.
"I will burn up your chariots in smoke,
     and the sword will devour your young lions.
I will leave you no prey on the earth.
The voices of your messengers
     will no longer be heard."

Woe to Nineveh

3 Woe to the city of blood,
     full of lies,
full of plunder,
     never without victims!
² The crack of whips,
     the clatter of wheels,
galloping horses
     and jolting chariots!
³ Charging cavalry,
     flashing swords
     and glittering spears!
Many casualties,
     piles of dead,
bodies without number,
     people stumbling over the corpses—
⁴ all because of the wanton lust of a harlot,
     alluring, the mistress of sorceries,
who enslaved nations by her prostitution
     and peoples by her witchcraft.

⁵ "I am against you," declares the LORD Almighty.
     "I will lift your skirts over your face.
I will show the nations your nakedness
     and the kingdoms your shame.
⁶ I will pelt you with filth,
     I will treat you with contempt
     and make you a spectacle.
⁷ All who see you will flee from you and say,
     'Nineveh is in ruins—who will mourn for her?'
Where can I find anyone to comfort you?"

⁸ Are you better than Thebes,ᵃ
     situated on the Nile,
     with water around her?
The river was her defense,
     the waters her wall.
⁹ Cushᵇ and Egypt were her boundless strength;
     Put and Libya were among her allies.
¹⁰ Yet she was taken captive
     and went into exile.
Her infants were dashed to pieces
     at the head of every street.
Lots were cast for her nobles,
     and all her great men were put in chains.
¹¹ You too will become drunk;
     you will go into hiding
     and seek refuge from the enemy.

¹² All your fortresses are like fig trees
     with their first ripe fruit;

Not Pride but Humility

NAHUM 3:8–11

"Let God do as He likes; consider yourself as a picture which a great master is proposing to paint; but take courage, for I foresee that it will take some time to grind and powder the colors, and then to lay them on, combine them and shade them. All you have to do is to keep the canvas ready, well-cleaned and fastened on its two motionless pivots, the one being self-humiliation . . . the other a complete self-abandonment pushed to the point of losing your will altogether in the will of God."

—JEAN-PIERRE DE CAUSSADE,
in *Living Water, An Anthology
of Letters of Direction*

ᵃ 8 Hebrew *No Amon*   ᵇ 9 That is, the upper Nile region

No Hope, New Hope

NAHUM 3:12–19

There is no hope for Nineveh. She is doomed. Sometimes we feel hopeless ourselves: when a job we count on falls through; a troubling report from the doctor changes all our plans; a relationship unravels and we are left alone and desolate. Or despair may grip us during those times when we realize our faithlessness has caused unnecessary pain to ourselves, to others, even to God. "Nothing can heal your wound; your injury is fatal." All seems hopeless.

But we must remember that although life may at times seem helpless and hopeless, there is hope for us in Jesus Christ. Light a candle. It is a simple act of faith that reaffirms that Jesus is the light of the world (John 8:12) who casts out darkness and hopelessness. Give thanks for the light.

See Meeting God in Everyday Life

when they are shaken,
    the figs fall into the mouth of the eater.
¹³ Look at your troops—
    they are all women!
The gates of your land
    are wide open to your enemies;
    fire has consumed their bars.

¹⁴ Draw water for the siege,
    strengthen your defenses!
Work the clay,
    tread the mortar,
    repair the brickwork!
¹⁵ There the fire will devour you;
    the sword will cut you down
    and, like grasshoppers, consume you.
Multiply like grasshoppers,
    multiply like locusts!
¹⁶ You have increased the number of your
        merchants
    till they are more than the stars of the sky,
but like locusts they strip the land
    and then fly away.
¹⁷ Your guards are like locusts,
    your officials like swarms of locusts
    that settle in the walls on a cold day—
but when the sun appears they fly away,
    and no one knows where.

¹⁸ O king of Assyria, your shepherds*a* slumber;
    your nobles lie down to rest.
Your people are scattered on the mountains
    with no one to gather them.
¹⁹ Nothing can heal your wound;
    your injury is fatal.
Everyone who hears the news about you
    claps his hands at your fall,
for who has not felt
    your endless cruelty?

1244   *a 18 Or rulers*

HABAKKUK

Waiting and Hoping

KEY VERSE:

"For the revelation awaits an appointed time; it speaks of the end and will not prove false. Though it linger, wait for it; it will certainly come and will not delay."—Habakkuk 2:3

Habakkuk, a seventh-century B.C. Judean prophet, is pressed between the two horns of a dilemma of faith. On one side are his people, the people of God, living as faithlessly as though they are not God's people at all. On the other side are surrounding nations whose "own strength is their god" (1:11), yet who have been given a role in punishing God's errant people. As the pressure mounts Habakkuk cries out to the Lord: "Why then do you tolerate the treacherous? Why are you silent while the wicked swallow up those more righteous than themselves?" (1:13). Habakkuk is restless, hungry for answers. The result is a prophet's narrative of waiting and hoping, hoping and waiting.

Although Habakkuk never receives complete answers to his difficult questions about justice and fairness, he does receive a word from the Lord that encourages him. A book that begins in a desperate cry ends with a song declaring that "the Sovereign LORD is my strength; he makes my feet like the feet of a deer, he enables me to go on the heights" (3:19). As the prophet waits through trouble, he has a sure and certain hope that God will save him.

As you read these three intense chapters, recall times when it seemed to you that life was unfair, that there were more questions than answers or that God was slow to reveal his purposes. When have you prayed, "How long . . .?" When have you sensed that God was telling you to "wait" for insight or resolution to a problem? Where have you found hope in such times?

> "Nothing that is worth doing can be achieved in a lifetime; therefore, we must be saved by hope. Nothing which is true or beautiful or good makes complete sense in any immediate context of history; therefore, we must be saved by faith."
> —REINHOLD NIEBUHR,
> *Justice and Mercy*

Questioning God

HABAKKUK 1:1–4

We don't readily think that questioning God is a faithful expression of prayer, but the Bible contains many instances in which prayer became an avenue for confronting or questioning God. Think of a time when you, like Habakkuk, have wanted to confront God with an experience of unfairness, an untimely death, a frustrating circumstance, an injustice, intense suffering. Have you felt that it was permissible to express those emotions in prayer? Could you find the language? Habakkuk's prayer begins, "How long, O LORD . . . ?" Based on your circumstances or perceptions of the world and its needs, how would you conclude this question with your own words?

See Meeting God in Prayer

1 The oracle that Habakkuk the prophet received.

Habakkuk's Complaint

² How long, O LORD, must I call for help,
    but you do not listen?
Or cry out to you, "Violence!"
    but you do not save?
³ Why do you make me look at injustice?
    Why do you tolerate wrong?
Destruction and violence are before me;
    there is strife, and conflict abounds.
⁴ Therefore the law is paralyzed,
    and justice never prevails.
The wicked hem in the righteous,
    so that justice is perverted.

The LORD's Answer

⁵ "Look at the nations and watch—
    and be utterly amazed.
For I am going to do something in your days
    that you would not believe,
    even if you were told.
⁶ I am raising up the Babylonians,ᵃ
    that ruthless and impetuous people,
who sweep across the whole earth
    to seize dwelling places not their own.
⁷ They are a feared and dreaded people;
    they are a law to themselves
    and promote their own honor.
⁸ Their horses are swifter than leopards,
    fiercer than wolves at dusk.
Their cavalry gallops headlong;
    their horsemen come from afar.
They fly like a vulture swooping to devour;
⁹   they all come bent on violence.
Their hordesᵇ advance like a desert wind
    and gather prisoners like sand.
¹⁰ They deride kings
    and scoff at rulers.
They laugh at all fortified cities;
    they build earthen ramps and capture them.
¹¹ Then they sweep past like the wind and go on—
    guilty men, whose own strength is their god."

Habakkuk's Second Complaint

¹² O LORD, are you not from everlasting?
    My God, my Holy One, we will not die.
O LORD, you have appointed them to execute
        judgment;
    O Rock, you have ordained them to punish.
¹³ Your eyes are too pure to look on evil;
    you cannot tolerate wrong.
Why then do you tolerate the treacherous?
    Why are you silent while the wicked
    swallow up those more righteous than
        themselves?

ᵃ 6 Or *Chaldeans*   ᵇ 9 The meaning of the Hebrew for this word is uncertain.

The actions of our Savior are so rich in meaning that every soul that ponders them finds in them its own share of spiritual food to nourish it and bring it to salvation.

CATHERINE OF SIENA (1347-1380)
The Life of Catherine of Siena

what knowledge can result from adapting the meaning of the Scriptures to suit one's own likes? The true sage discovers, through the Spirit's wisdom, the hidden mysteries to which the Scriptures bear witness.

PETER OF DAMASKOS (TWELFTH CENTURY?)

The Philokalia (Volume Three)

We should accept with simplicity whatever understanding the Lord gives us; and what he doesn't we shouldn't tire ourselves over. For one word of God's will contain within itself a thousand mysteries.

TERESA OF AVILA (1515-1582)

Meditation on the Song of Songs

If you want true knowledge of the **scriptures,** try to secure steadfast **humility** of heart, to carry you by the perfection of **love** **not to** knowledge that puffs up, but that **enlightens.**

JOHN CASSIAN (c. 365-c. 435)

Conferences, Book XIV

¹⁴You have made men like fish in the sea,
  like sea creatures that have no ruler.
¹⁵The wicked foe pulls all of them up with hooks,
  he catches them in his net,
he gathers them up in his dragnet;
  and so he rejoices and is glad.
¹⁶Therefore he sacrifices to his net
  and burns incense to his dragnet,
for by his net he lives in luxury
  and enjoys the choicest food.
¹⁷Is he to keep on emptying his net,
  destroying nations without mercy?

2 I will stand at my watch
  and station myself on the ramparts;
I will look to see what he will say to me,
  and what answer I am to give to this
    complaint.ᵃ

The Lord's Answer

²Then the Lord replied:

  "Write down the revelation
    and make it plain on tablets
    so that a heraldᵇ may run with it.
³For the revelation awaits an appointed time;
  it speaks of the end
    and will not prove false.
Though it linger, wait for it;
  itᶜ will certainly come and will not delay.

⁴"See, he is puffed up;
  his desires are not upright—
  but the righteous will live by his faithᵈ—
⁵indeed, wine betrays him;
  he is arrogant and never at rest.
Because he is as greedy as the graveᵉ
  and like death is never satisfied,
he gathers to himself all the nations
  and takes captive all the peoples.

⁶"Will not all of them taunt him with ridicule and scorn,
saying,

  " 'Woe to him who piles up stolen goods
    and makes himself wealthy by extortion!
    How long must this go on?'
⁷Will not your debtorsᶠ suddenly arise?
  Will they not wake up and make you tremble?
  Then you will become their victim.
⁸Because you have plundered many nations,
  the peoples who are left will plunder you.
For you have shed man's blood;
  you have destroyed lands and cities and
    everyone in them.

⁹"Woe to him who builds his realm by unjust gain
  to set his nest on high,
  to escape the clutches of ruin!

Waiting for God

HABAKKUK 2:1–3

The writer Anthony Padovano once observed that "we wait for everything that is really worth having . . . We even wait for God." Waiting in the Biblical tradition is not passive or forgetful, but active, eager, yearning and engaged. Habakkuk determines to wait on God for resolution of his crisis; God, in turn, bids him, "Though it linger, wait." What are you waiting for most fervently for yourself? For your loved ones? Your church? Your community? The world? Name these things before God in prayer, claiming God's promises. Wait for their fulfillment with the same attentiveness as the Bible's best "waiters."

See Meeting God in Prayer

ᵃ 1 Or *and what to answer when I am rebuked*   ᵇ 2 Or *so that whoever reads it*   ᶜ 3 Or *Though he linger, wait for him; / he*   ᵈ 4 Or *faithfulness*
ᵉ 5 Hebrew *Sheol*   ᶠ 7 Or *creditors*

The Earth Filled

HABAKKUK 2:14–17

Christians have not always associated salvation with concern for God's creation, but we are becoming more aware of how intertwined the two are. The Word of God, through the prophet Habakkuk, proclaims that the whole creation is drawn into human abuses (v.8) but that it is also subject to God's redemption (v.14). Meditate on a scene in nature you can see from where you are sitting. Or imagine yourself in a beautiful natural setting. Offer confession on behalf of all humankind for the many ways we have misused creation. Consider how God cares for the place where you are or that you are imagining, then envision in your mind's eye how the knowledge of God's glory will fill all the earth.

See Meeting God in the Created Order

¹⁰ You have plotted the ruin of many peoples,
   shaming your own house and forfeiting your life.
¹¹ The stones of the wall will cry out,
   and the beams of the woodwork will echo it.

¹² "Woe to him who builds a city with bloodshed
   and establishes a town by crime!
¹³ Has not the LORD Almighty determined
   that the people's labor is only fuel for the fire,
   that the nations exhaust themselves for nothing?
¹⁴ For the earth will be filled with the knowledge of
      the glory of the LORD,
   as the waters cover the sea.

¹⁵ "Woe to him who gives drink to his neighbors,
   pouring it from the wineskin till they are drunk,
   so that he can gaze on their naked bodies.
¹⁶ You will be filled with shame instead of glory.
   Now it is your turn! Drink and be exposed*ᵃ*!
The cup from the LORD's right hand is coming
      around to you,
   and disgrace will cover your glory.
¹⁷ The violence you have done to Lebanon will
      overwhelm you,
   and your destruction of animals will terrify you.
For you have shed man's blood;
   you have destroyed lands and cities and
      everyone in them.

¹⁸ "Of what value is an idol, since a man has carved
      it?
   Or an image that teaches lies?
For he who makes it trusts in his own creation;
   he makes idols that cannot speak.
¹⁹ Woe to him who says to wood, 'Come to life!'
   Or to lifeless stone, 'Wake up!'
Can it give guidance?
   It is covered with gold and silver;
   there is no breath in it.
²⁰ But the LORD is in his holy temple;
   let all the earth be silent before him.' "

Habakkuk's Prayer

3 A prayer of Habakkuk the prophet. On *shigionoth*.*ᵇ*

² LORD, I have heard of your fame;
   I stand in awe of your deeds, O LORD.
Renew them in our day,
   in our time make them known;
   in wrath remember mercy.

³ God came from Teman,
   the Holy One from Mount Paran.   *Selahᶜ*
His glory covered the heavens
   and his praise filled the earth.
⁴ His splendor was like the sunrise;
   rays flashed from his hand,
   where his power was hidden.

ᵃ 16 Masoretic Text; Dead Sea Scrolls, Aquila, Vulgate and Syriac (see also Septuagint) *and stagger*   *ᵇ 1* Probably a literary or musical term   *ᶜ 3* A word of uncertain meaning; possibly a musical term; also in verses 9 and 13

⁵Plague went before him;
    pestilence followed his steps.
⁶He stood, and shook the earth;
    he looked, and made the nations tremble.
The ancient mountains crumbled
    and the age-old hills collapsed.
    His ways are eternal.
⁷I saw the tents of Cushan in distress,
    the dwellings of Midian in anguish.

⁸Were you angry with the rivers, O Lord?
    Was your wrath against the streams?
Did you rage against the sea
    when you rode with your horses
    and your victorious chariots?
⁹You uncovered your bow,
    you called for many arrows.   *Selah*
You split the earth with rivers;
¹⁰   the mountains saw you and writhed.
Torrents of water swept by;
    the deep roared
    and lifted its waves on high.

¹¹Sun and moon stood still in the heavens
    at the glint of your flying arrows,
    at the lightning of your flashing spear.
¹²In wrath you strode through the earth
    and in anger you threshed the nations.
¹³You came out to deliver your people,
    to save your anointed one.
You crushed the leader of the land of wickedness,
    you stripped him from head to foot.   *Selah*
¹⁴With his own spear you pierced his head
    when his warriors stormed out to scatter us,
gloating as though about to devour
    the wretched who were in hiding.
¹⁵You trampled the sea with your horses,
    churning the great waters.

¹⁶I heard and my heart pounded,
    my lips quivered at the sound;
decay crept into my bones,
    and my legs trembled.
Yet I will wait patiently for the day of calamity
    to come on the nation invading us.
¹⁷Though the fig tree does not bud
    and there are no grapes on the vines,
though the olive crop fails
    and the fields produce no food,
though there are no sheep in the pen
    and no cattle in the stalls,
¹⁸yet I will rejoice in the Lord,
    I will be joyful in God my Savior.

¹⁹The Sovereign Lord is my strength;
    he makes my feet like the feet of a deer,
    he enables me to go on the heights.

For the director of music. On my stringed
    instruments.

The Place for *Yet*

HABAKKUK 3:17–19

The conclusion of Habakkuk could be a mourner's litany—no figs, no fruit, no food, no flocks—of all the prophet and his people have lost or fear to lose. Instead Habakkuk's list of potential or real catastrophes is turned on its head with one simple word: *yet*. That one word becomes the turning point and Habakkuk's anxiety becomes triumph; what could have been a dirge has become a dance.

Construct your own "mourner's litany," listing things you've lost or things you fear you might lose. Now add that faith word, *yet*, and borrow language from Habakkuk to express your assurance of God's provision in all circumstances.

See *Meeting God in Everyday Life*

ZEPHANIAH

Quieted by God's Love

KEY VERSE:

"The LORD your God is with you, he is mighty to save. He will take great delight in you, he will quiet you with his love, he will rejoice over you with singing."—Zephaniah 3:17

"One time, I was under very great suffering in my spirit and under the very sense of death; but when I came out of it, standing in the will of God, a heavenly breathing arose in my soul to the Lord. Then did I see the heavens opened and the glory of God shined over all."
—GEORGE FOX,
Journal

A day of judgment is coming quickly, says the prophet Zephaniah, when God is going to make a clean sweep of Judah and the nations around her. In these three chapters we learn that the priests, prophets, leaders and people are involved in idol worship (1:4–5), are complacent in doing justice while accumulating quantities of gold and silver (1:12,18), and are arrogantly rebelling against God's instructions (3:11). Yet hope and promise are woven through the predictions of darkness and gloom.

The humble and righteous will find shelter on the day of trouble and ruin (2:3), and the lowly and meek will remain as a faithful remnant (3:12–13). The greatest word of hope comes at the end of Zephaniah in a chorus of praise in which God promises to keep the nation from the impending disaster, to gather all the scattered people and bring them home, and to reestablish the Judeans as a people of honor and blessing (3:14–20).

Though we may have different idols and face different threats, the call of Zephaniah is just as important for us today—it is a call to live a life of humble obedience before God. We are to be aware of what God has done in the past and let that remembrance keep us humbly walking on the right path. There must always be room in our lives for praise, because God delights in us, quiets us with his love and rejoices over us with singing.

1

The word of the LORD that came to Zephaniah son of Cushi, the son of Gedaliah, the son of Amariah, the son of Hezekiah, during the reign of Josiah son of Amon king of Judah:

Warning of Coming Destruction

2 "I will sweep away everything
　　from the face of the earth,"
　　　　　　　　　　　　　　declares the LORD.
3 "I will sweep away both men and animals;
　　I will sweep away the birds of the air
　　and the fish of the sea.
The wicked will have only heaps of rubble[a]
　　when I cut off man from the face of the earth,"
　　　　　　　　　　　　　　declares the LORD.

Against Judah

4 "I will stretch out my hand against Judah
　　and against all who live in Jerusalem.
I will cut off from this place every remnant of
　　　Baal,
　　the names of the pagan and the idolatrous
　　　priests—
5 those who bow down on the roofs
　　to worship the starry host,
those who bow down and swear by the LORD
　　and who also swear by Molech,[b]
6 those who turn back from following the LORD
　　and neither seek the LORD nor inquire of him.
7 Be silent before the Sovereign LORD,
　　for the day of the LORD is near.
The LORD has prepared a sacrifice;
　　he has consecrated those he has invited.
8 On the day of the LORD's sacrifice
　　I will punish the princes
　　and the king's sons
　and all those clad
　　in foreign clothes.
9 On that day I will punish
　　all who avoid stepping on the threshold,[c]
who fill the temple of their gods
　　with violence and deceit.

10 "On that day," declares the LORD,
　　"a cry will go up from the Fish Gate,
　　wailing from the New Quarter,
　　and a loud crash from the hills.
11 Wail, you who live in the market district[d];
　　all your merchants will be wiped out,
　　all who trade with[e] silver will be ruined.
12 At that time I will search Jerusalem with lamps
　　and punish those who are complacent,
　　who are like wine left on its dregs,
　who think, 'The LORD will do nothing,
　　either good or bad.'
13 Their wealth will be plundered,
　　their houses demolished.

A Clean Sweep

ZEPHANIAH 1:2–4

Zephaniah cuts straight to the heart of the matter. Israel is in trouble; destruction is coming because of her idolatry. It will touch the royal court, all people, and even animals, fish and birds. God will "sweep away everything."

Find a broom and look for a place to begin sweeping. Pay attention to the sound the broom makes, the way the dirt falls into a line, how much effort and repetition it takes to get the area really clean. Give your full attention to sweeping.

You may wish to write in a journal about the experience and start reflecting on what needs to be cleaned up in your life. If God took a broom to your spiritual life, what would be swept away? Invite God to come in and begin this work.

See *Meeting God in Everyday Life*

---

a 3 The meaning of the Hebrew for this line is uncertain.　　*b 5* Hebrew *Malcam,* that is, Milcom　　*c 9* See 1 Samuel 5:5.　　*d 11* Or *the Mortar*
e 11 Or *in*

To Be Humble and Just

ZEPHANIAH 2:1–3

The great day of the Lord is coming soon, and the prophet says it will be a day of judgment and ruin. List all the abuses that Zephaniah condemns (see, for example, 1:9,11,12). Think of some injustices in our world today and add them to your list. Pray for the day when God will come to clean up all the trouble, sorrow and pain.

While these verses contain judgment, they also convey the hope that those who humble themselves and pursue righteousness will be sheltered from God's wrath. In a time of prayer, tilt your head back so your eyes focus on the heavens and then extend your arms as you would to welcome a long lost friend. In prayer give thanks that Jesus Christ has become our righteousness before God.

They will build houses
   but not live in them;
they will plant vineyards
   but not drink the wine.

The Great Day of the Lord

[14] "The great day of the Lord is near—
   near and coming quickly.
Listen! The cry on the day of the Lord will be bitter,
   the shouting of the warrior there.
[15] That day will be a day of wrath,
   a day of distress and anguish,
   a day of trouble and ruin,
   a day of darkness and gloom,
   a day of clouds and blackness,
[16] a day of trumpet and battle cry
   against the fortified cities
   and against the corner towers.
[17] I will bring distress on the people
   and they will walk like blind men,
   because they have sinned against the Lord.
Their blood will be poured out like dust
   and their entrails like filth.
[18] Neither their silver nor their gold
   will be able to save them
   on the day of the Lord's wrath.
In the fire of his jealousy
   the whole world will be consumed,
for he will make a sudden end
   of all who live in the earth."

2 Gather together, gather together,
   O shameful nation,
[2] before the appointed time arrives
   and that day sweeps on like chaff,
before the fierce anger of the Lord comes upon
   you,
   before the day of the Lord's wrath comes upon
   you.
[3] Seek the Lord, all you humble of the land,
   you who do what he commands.
Seek righteousness, seek humility;
   perhaps you will be sheltered
   on the day of the Lord's anger.

Against Philistia

[4] Gaza will be abandoned
   and Ashkelon left in ruins.
At midday Ashdod will be emptied
   and Ekron uprooted.
[5] Woe to you who live by the sea,
   O Kerethite people;
the word of the Lord is against you,
   O Canaan, land of the Philistines.

"I will destroy you,
   and none will be left."

[6] The land by the sea, where the Kerethites[a] dwell,
   will be a place for shepherds and sheep pens.

    [a] 6 The meaning of the Hebrew for this word is uncertain.

[7] It will belong to the remnant of the house of
Judah;
there they will find pasture.
In the evening they will lie down
in the houses of Ashkelon.
The LORD their God will care for them;
he will restore their fortunes.[a]

Against Moab and Ammon

[8] "I have heard the insults of Moab
and the taunts of the Ammonites,
who insulted my people
and made threats against their land.
[9] Therefore, as surely as I live,"
declares the LORD Almighty, the God of Israel,
"surely Moab will become like Sodom,
the Ammonites like Gomorrah—
a place of weeds and salt pits,
a wasteland forever.
The remnant of my people will plunder them;
the survivors of my nation will inherit their
land."

[10] This is what they will get in return for their pride,
for insulting and mocking the people of the
LORD Almighty.
[11] The LORD will be awesome to them
when he destroys all the gods of the land.
The nations on every shore will worship him,
every one in its own land.

Against Cush

[12] "You too, O Cushites,[b]
will be slain by my sword."

Against Assyria

[13] He will stretch out his hand against the north
and destroy Assyria,
leaving Nineveh utterly desolate
and dry as the desert.
[14] Flocks and herds will lie down there,
creatures of every kind.
The desert owl and the screech owl
will roost on her columns.
Their calls will echo through the windows,
rubble will be in the doorways,
the beams of cedar will be exposed.
[15] This is the carefree city
that lived in safety.
She said to herself,
"I am, and there is none besides me."
What a ruin she has become,
a lair for wild beasts!
All who pass by her scoff
and shake their fists.

Pride Goes Before a Fall

ZEPHANIAH 2:10,15

"Recollection is the only cure for your haughtiness, the sharpness of your contemptuous criticism, the sallies of your imagination, your impatience with inferiors, your love of pleasure and all your other faults. It is an excellent remedy, but it needs frequent repetition. You are like a good watch, which needs constant winding . . . Expect nothing of yourself, but all things of God. Knowledge of our own hopeless, incorrigible weakness, with unreserved confidence in God's power, are the true foundations of all spiritual life."

—FRANÇOIS FÉNELON,
in *Living Water, An Anthology
of Letters of Direction*

---

[a] 7 Or *will bring back their captives*   [b] 12 That is, people from the upper
Nile region

Look, See, Remember

ZEPHANIAH 3:7

The prophet's words convey God's anguish: "Surely you will fear me and accept correction!" *Surely* the people of Jerusalem remember how God brought them from Egypt. *Surely* they can see what has happened to other nations. *Surely* they know that God is a God of justice. But the people continue in their corrupt ways.

To help you remember what God has done, make a list of blessings and corrections that you have received from God. Give thanks for the ways that God has touched your life and kept you on the right path. Give thanks for corrections and lessons learned that you can now count as blessings.

See Meeting God in Everyday Life

The Future of Jerusalem

3 Woe to the city of oppressors,
    rebellious and defiled!
² She obeys no one,
    she accepts no correction.
She does not trust in the LORD,
    she does not draw near to her God.
³ Her officials are roaring lions,
    her rulers are evening wolves,
    who leave nothing for the morning.
⁴ Her prophets are arrogant;
    they are treacherous men.
Her priests profane the sanctuary
    and do violence to the law.
⁵ The LORD within her is righteous;
    he does no wrong.
Morning by morning he dispenses his justice,
    and every new day he does not fail,
    yet the unrighteous know no shame.

⁶ "I have cut off nations;
    their strongholds are demolished.
I have left their streets deserted,
    with no one passing through.
Their cities are destroyed;
    no one will be left—no one at all.
⁷ I said to the city,
    'Surely you will fear me
    and accept correction!'
Then her dwelling would not be cut off,
    nor all my punishments come upon her.
But they were still eager
    to act corruptly in all they did.
⁸ Therefore wait for me," declares the LORD,
    "for the day I will stand up to testify.ᵃ
I have decided to assemble the nations,
    to gather the kingdoms
and to pour out my wrath on them—
    all my fierce anger.
The whole world will be consumed
    by the fire of my jealous anger.

⁹ "Then will I purify the lips of the peoples,
    that all of them may call on the name of the
        LORD
    and serve him shoulder to shoulder.
¹⁰ From beyond the rivers of Cushᵇ
    my worshipers, my scattered people,
    will bring me offerings.
¹¹ On that day you will not be put to shame
    for all the wrongs you have done to me,
because I will remove from this city
    those who rejoice in their pride.
Never again will you be haughty
    on my holy hill.
¹² But I will leave within you
    the meek and humble,
    who trust in the name of the LORD.

ᵃ 8 Septuagint and Syriac; Hebrew *will rise up to plunder*   ᵇ 10 That is, the upper Nile region

¹³The remnant of Israel will do no wrong;
    they will speak no lies,
        nor will deceit be found in their mouths.
  They will eat and lie down
    and no one will make them afraid."

¹⁴Sing, O Daughter of Zion;
    shout aloud, O Israel!
  Be glad and rejoice with all your heart,
    O Daughter of Jerusalem!
¹⁵The LORD has taken away your punishment,
    he has turned back your enemy.
  The LORD, the King of Israel, is with you;
    never again will you fear any harm.
¹⁶On that day they will say to Jerusalem,
    "Do not fear, O Zion;
    do not let your hands hang limp.
¹⁷The LORD your God is with you,
    he is mighty to save.
  He will take great delight in you,
    he will quiet you with his love,
    he will rejoice over you with singing."

¹⁸"The sorrows for the appointed feasts
    I will remove from you;
    they are a burden and a reproach to you.[a]
¹⁹At that time I will deal
    with all who oppressed you;
  I will rescue the lame
    and gather those who have been scattered.
  I will give them praise and honor
    in every land where they were put to shame.
²⁰At that time I will gather you;
    at that time I will bring you home.
  I will give you honor and praise
    among all the peoples of the earth
  when I restore your fortunes[b]
    before your very eyes,"
                    says the LORD.

From Disaster to Celebration

ZEPHANIAH 3:14–20

In the middle of troubles and pain, there is a promise of joy. The threat of destruction is over and hope springs up once again. Using the image of a mother who comforts a child she has disciplined, God reminds his people of his great love. Reread the passage slowly, noting the words or phrases of promise that particularly speak to you. Use these words or phrases to write a prayer based on this passage. Ask God to fulfill the promises you are waiting on to be fulfilled. Praise God for making such wonderful promises.

See Meeting God in Scripture

---

a 18 Or *"I will gather you who mourn for the appointed feasts; / your reproach is a burden to you*   *b 20* Or *I bring back your captives*

1255

HAGGAI

Examine Your Ways

KEY VERSES:

Then the word of the LORD came through the prophet Haggai: "Is it a time for you yourselves to be living in your paneled houses, while this house remains a ruin?"—Haggai 1:3–4

> "During the darkest periods of history, quite often a small number of men and women, scattered throughout the world, have been able to reverse the course of historical evolutions. This was only possible because they hoped beyond all hope. What had been bound for disintegration then entered into the current of a new dynamism."
>
> —BROTHER ROGER OF TAIZÉ

Haggai encourages his listeners to anticipate that the rebuilding of the temple will set in motion a new chain of events that will reveal God's powerful presence. Haggai, a prophet in the court of King Darius (about 520 B.C.), wants to inspire the Israelites and capture their imaginations with the vision of a rebuilt Jerusalem, where God will once again be honored and praised.

Beaten down and focused on survival under alien rule, God's people are in despair. They have returned from exile physically but haven't yet returned "home" to God—they haven't begun to rebuild God's house. They can see failed crops and a government in chaos; they cannot see hope for their future.

As you read these two short chapters containing Haggai's oracles, reflect on these questions: Have you ever felt so oppressed by events in your life that you lost your focus on God? Do you in some way long for the "good old days" when things were better for you? Are you dissatisfied with the present? Have you given up on God and decided that you have to take care of things yourself? Haggai will help you put things in perspective, for his message is that hope in God is always the best option.

A Call to Build the House of the LORD

1 In the second year of King Darius, on the first day of the sixth month, the word of the LORD came through the prophet Haggai to Zerubbabel son of Shealtiel, governor of Judah, and to Joshua*ᵃ* son of Jehozadak, the high priest:

²This is what the LORD Almighty says: "These people say, 'The time has not yet come for the LORD's house to be built.' "

³Then the word of the LORD came through the prophet Haggai: ⁴"Is it a time for you yourselves to be living in your paneled houses, while this house remains a ruin?"

⁵Now this is what the LORD Almighty says: "Give careful thought to your ways. ⁶You have planted much, but have harvested little. You eat, but never have enough. You drink, but never have your fill. You put on clothes, but are not warm. You earn wages, only to put them in a purse with holes in it."

⁷This is what the LORD Almighty says: "Give careful thought to your ways. ⁸Go up into the mountains and bring down timber and build the house, so that I may take pleasure in it and be honored," says the LORD. ⁹"You expected much, but see, it turned out to be little. What you brought home, I blew away. Why?" declares the LORD Almighty. "Because of my house, which remains a ruin, while each of you is busy with his own house. ¹⁰Therefore, because of you the heavens have withheld their dew and the earth its crops. ¹¹I called for a drought on the fields and the mountains, on the grain, the new wine, the oil and whatever the ground produces, on men and cattle, and on the labor of your hands."

¹²Then Zerubbabel son of Shealtiel, Joshua son of Jehozadak, the high priest, and the whole remnant of the people obeyed the voice of the LORD their God and the message of the prophet Haggai, because the LORD their God had sent him. And the people feared the LORD.

¹³Then Haggai, the LORD's messenger, gave this message of the LORD to the people: "I am with you," declares the LORD. ¹⁴So the LORD stirred up the spirit of Zerubbabel son of Shealtiel, governor of Judah, and the spirit of Joshua son of Jehozadak, the high priest, and the spirit of the whole remnant of the people. They came and began to work on the house of the LORD Almighty, their God, ¹⁵on the twenty-fourth day of the sixth month in the second year of King Darius.

The Promised Glory of the New House

2 On the twenty-first day of the seventh month, the word of the LORD came through the prophet Haggai: ²"Speak to Zerubbabel son of Shealtiel, governor of Judah, to Joshua son of Jehozadak, the high priest, and to the remnant of the people. Ask them, ³'Who of you is left who saw this house in its former glory? How does it look to you now? Does it not seem to you like nothing? ⁴But now be strong, O Zerubbabel,' declares the LORD. 'Be strong, O Joshua son of Jehozadak, the high priest. Be strong, all you people of the land,' declares the LORD, 'and work. For I am with you,' declares the LORD Almighty. ⁵'This is what I covenanted with

---

A Personal Letter

HAGGAI 2:4–5

Scripture is our personal love letter from God, if only we can hear the voice of the One who is calling out our name. We may not be called "Zerubbabel" or "Joshua," but these verses nevertheless speak to us as they spoke to those in King Darius's court long ago.

In what way do you need courage in your life today? How do you need the strength of God's Spirit? Substitute your own name so that you hear, "But now be strong, _____, . . . for I am with you . . . My Spirit remains among you. Do not fear." Accept this personal promise; feel courage grow within you as you realize that the God who spoke through Haggai speaks to you today.

See Meeting God in Scripture

ᵃ 1 A variant of *Jeshua*; here and elsewhere in Haggai

Seed Ready to Grow

HAGGAI 2:18–19

Just as the people of God have been hurt and scarred by their long and painful exile from their native land, there are times when we too may feel that the pain of past hurts keeps us from enjoying a fruitful present. "Not so!" says God, who uses all of our experiences, positive and negative, for good. "Is there yet any seed left in the barn?" What remains within you that, with nurture, might flourish and grow into something beautiful? No matter what your past may have been, God offers you the chance to plant new seeds, nourish a new life, look toward the future with hope. What seeds are in you, ready to sprout? Hear gladly God's promise to you: "From this day on I will bless you."

See Meeting God in Everyday Life

you when you came out of Egypt. And my Spirit remains among you. Do not fear.'

⁶"This is what the LORD Almighty says: 'In a little while I will once more shake the heavens and the earth, the sea and the dry land. ⁷I will shake all nations, and the desired of all nations will come, and I will fill this house with glory,' says the LORD Almighty. ⁸'The silver is mine and the gold is mine,' declares the LORD Almighty. ⁹'The glory of this present house will be greater than the glory of the former house,' says the LORD Almighty. 'And in this place I will grant peace,' declares the LORD Almighty."

Blessings for a Defiled People

¹⁰On the twenty-fourth day of the ninth month, in the second year of Darius, the word of the LORD came to the prophet Haggai: ¹¹"This is what the LORD Almighty says: 'Ask the priests what the law says: ¹²If a person carries consecrated meat in the fold of his garment, and that fold touches some bread or stew, some wine, oil or other food, does it become consecrated?' "

The priests answered, "No."

¹³Then Haggai said, "If a person defiled by contact with a dead body touches one of these things, does it become defiled?"

"Yes," the priests replied, "it becomes defiled."

¹⁴Then Haggai said, " 'So it is with this people and this nation in my sight,' declares the LORD. 'Whatever they do and whatever they offer there is defiled.

¹⁵" 'Now give careful thought to this from this day on*a*— consider how things were before one stone was laid on another in the LORD's temple. ¹⁶When anyone came to a heap of twenty measures, there were only ten. When anyone went to a wine vat to draw fifty measures, there were only twenty. ¹⁷I struck all the work of your hands with blight, mildew and hail, yet you did not turn to me,' declares the LORD. ¹⁸'From this day on, from this twenty-fourth day of the ninth month, give careful thought to the day when the foundation of the LORD's temple was laid. Give careful thought: ¹⁹Is there yet any seed left in the barn? Until now, the vine and the fig tree, the pomegranate and the olive tree have not borne fruit.

" 'From this day on I will bless you.' "

Zerubbabel the LORD's Signet Ring

²⁰The word of the LORD came to Haggai a second time on the twenty-fourth day of the month: ²¹"Tell Zerubbabel governor of Judah that I will shake the heavens and the earth. ²²I will overturn royal thrones and shatter the power of the foreign kingdoms. I will overthrow chariots and their drivers; horses and their riders will fall, each by the sword of his brother.

²³" 'On that day,' declares the LORD Almighty, 'I will take you, my servant Zerubbabel son of Shealtiel,' declares the LORD, 'and I will make you like my signet ring, for I have chosen you,' declares the LORD Almighty."

a 15 Or to the days past

ZECHARIAH

Not By Might

KEY VERSES:

This is what the Lord Almighty says: "I will save my people from the countries of the east and the west. I will bring them back to live in Jerusalem; they will be my people, and I will be faithful and righteous to them as their God."—Zechariah 8:7–8

Zechariah seems to say, "Let's start over, refocus ourselves on God and get busy." The task at hand is the rebuilding of the temple that has lain in ruins since its destruction by the Babylonians. The focus for the future is on rebuilding the spiritual life of a people who have endured humiliation and exile. To complicate the problem, the people are apathetic about their task and indifferent to the call to restore their worship to its former glory. But the prophet reminds the returned exiles that they have a golden opportunity to renew their relationship with God—God is waiting to wrap loving arms around this people who had previously snubbed their Creator.

So too God stands ready to quiet each of us with his love if we earnestly desire to receive that love. In God's strength we can rebuild that which has been broken down. With God's vision we can look toward a future of new possibilities. What is God saying to you about your future? Are you open to this motivating, energizing, divine love—love that offers new life in this world and in eternity?

> "In this temple of God, in this divine dwelling place, God alone rejoices with the soul in the deepest silence. There is no reason for the intellect to stir or seek anything, for the Lord who created it wishes to give it repose here."
>
> —TERESA OF AVILA,
> *The Interior Castle*

Rebuilding My House

ZECHARIAH 1:2–6,16

God, speaking through Zechari-ah, extends an invitation to the people of Judah to partner with him in rebuilding the temple, "I will return to Jerusalem with mercy, and there my house will be rebuilt."

God wants to help you re-build as well. If you think of your life as your spiritual house, what might need some work? Is the substructure—your spiritual foundation—solid? Are all the rooms—the facets of your life—used for the right pur-poses? Are you conscientious about upkeep—daily spiritual practices? What about renova-tion—growing in the knowledge of Jesus Christ? When the mea-suring line of the Master Builder is laid out, how do you mea-sure up? Let Jesus come to you with mercy and build alongside you.

See Meeting God in Everyday Life

A Call to Return to the LORD

1 In the eighth month of the second year of Darius, the word of the LORD came to the prophet Zechariah son of Berekiah, the son of Iddo:

2 "The LORD was very angry with your forefathers. 3 Therefore tell the people: This is what the LORD Almighty says: 'Return to me,' declares the LORD Almighty, 'and I will return to you,' says the LORD Almighty. 4 Do not be like your forefathers, to whom the earlier prophets pro-claimed: This is what the LORD Almighty says: 'Turn from your evil ways and your evil practices.' But they would not listen or pay attention to me, declares the LORD. 5 Where are your forefathers now? And the prophets, do they live forever? 6 But did not my words and my decrees, which I commanded my servants the prophets, overtake your forefathers?

"Then they repented and said, 'The LORD Almighty has done to us what our ways and practices deserve, just as he determined to do.' "

The Man Among the Myrtle Trees

7 On the twenty-fourth day of the eleventh month, the month of Shebat, in the second year of Darius, the word of the LORD came to the prophet Zechariah son of Berekiah, the son of Iddo.

8 During the night I had a vision—and there before me was a man riding a red horse! He was standing among the myrtle trees in a ravine. Behind him were red, brown and white horses.

9 I asked, "What are these, my lord?"

The angel who was talking with me answered, "I will show you what they are."

10 Then the man standing among the myrtle trees ex-plained, "They are the ones the LORD has sent to go throughout the earth."

11 And they reported to the angel of the LORD, who was standing among the myrtle trees, "We have gone through-out the earth and found the whole world at rest and in peace."

12 Then the angel of the LORD said, "LORD Almighty, how long will you withhold mercy from Jerusalem and from the towns of Judah, which you have been angry with these sev-enty years?" 13 So the LORD spoke kind and comforting words to the angel who talked with me.

14 Then the angel who was speaking to me said, "Pro-claim this word: This is what the LORD Almighty says: 'I am very jealous for Jerusalem and Zion, 15 but I am very angry with the nations that feel secure. I was only a little angry, but they added to the calamity.'

16 "Therefore, this is what the LORD says: 'I will return to Jerusalem with mercy, and there my house will be rebuilt. And the measuring line will be stretched out over Jerusalem,' declares the LORD Almighty.

17 "Proclaim further: This is what the LORD Almighty says: 'My towns will again overflow with prosperity, and the LORD will again comfort Zion and choose Jerusalem.' "

Four Horns and Four Craftsmen

18 Then I looked up—and there before me were four

horns! ¹⁹I asked the angel who was speaking to me, "What are these?"

He answered me, "These are the horns that scattered Judah, Israel and Jerusalem."

²⁰Then the LORD showed me four craftsmen. ²¹I asked, "What are these coming to do?"

He answered, "These are the horns that scattered Judah so that no one could raise his head, but the craftsmen have come to terrify them and throw down these horns of the nations who lifted up their horns against the land of Judah to scatter its people."

A Man With a Measuring Line

2 Then I looked up—and there before me was a man with a measuring line in his hand! ²I asked, "Where are you going?"

He answered me, "To measure Jerusalem, to find out how wide and how long it is."

³Then the angel who was speaking to me left, and another angel came to meet him ⁴and said to him: "Run, tell that young man, 'Jerusalem will be a city without walls because of the great number of men and livestock in it. ⁵And I myself will be a wall of fire around it,' declares the LORD, 'and I will be its glory within.'

⁶"Come! Come! Flee from the land of the north," declares the LORD, "for I have scattered you to the four winds of heaven," declares the LORD.

⁷"Come, O Zion! Escape, you who live in the Daughter of Babylon!" ⁸For this is what the LORD Almighty says: "After he has honored me and has sent me against the nations that have plundered you—for whoever touches you touches the apple of his eye— ⁹I will surely raise my hand against them so that their slaves will plunder them.ᵃ Then you will know that the LORD Almighty has sent me.

¹⁰"Shout and be glad, O Daughter of Zion. For I am coming, and I will live among you," declares the LORD. ¹¹"Many nations will be joined with the LORD in that day and will become my people. I will live among you and you will know that the LORD Almighty has sent me to you. ¹²The LORD will inherit Judah as his portion in the holy land and will again choose Jerusalem. ¹³Be still before the LORD, all mankind, because he has roused himself from his holy dwelling."

Clean Garments for the High Priest

3 Then he showed me Joshuaᵇ the high priest standing before the angel of the LORD, and Satanᶜ standing at his right side to accuse him. ²The LORD said to Satan, "The LORD rebuke you, Satan! The LORD, who has chosen Jerusalem, rebuke you! Is not this man a burning stick snatched from the fire?"

³Now Joshua was dressed in filthy clothes as he stood before the angel. ⁴The angel said to those who were standing before him, "Take off his filthy clothes."

Then he said to Joshua, "See, I have taken away your sin, and I will put rich garments on you."

⁵Then I said, "Put a clean turban on his head." So they put a clean turban on his head and clothed him, while the angel of the LORD stood by.

ᵃ 8,9 Or *says after . . . eye:* ⁹*"I . . . plunder them."* ᵇ 1 A variant of *Jeshua*; here and elsewhere in Zechariah ᶜ 1 *Satan* means *accuser.*

Walk in My Ways

ZECHARIAH 3:3–7

Read this passage—replacing the name of Joshua with your own name—so that the story becomes your own story. Close your eyes and reenact the encounter between yourself and the angel. Pay close attention to detail. What does the angel look like? How would you describe your dirty clothes? How do you feel when the angel clothes you with a new garment and puts a clean turban on your head? What happens within you when you hear God's charge to you (v.7)? Enjoy the sense of renewal that comes when your sins are washed away and you are "clean," ready to begin again.

See Meeting God in Scripture

By My Spirit

ZECHARIAH 4:6

The definitions of "might" and "power" probably depend on one's position, culture, personality or era, yet the words of God through the angel's mouth apply to any time or place: "Not by might nor by power, but by my Spirit, says the LORD Almighty."

Along one side of a sheet of paper, write down some of the images that come to mind when you think of might and power. Do you see a soldier in full battle gear or a wealthy person who has widespread economic influence? Perhaps you see a forceful leader with a persuasive personality. On the other side of the paper, write down images that come to mind when you think of "by my Spirit." Look for other passages of Scripture that will help you develop this concept.

[6]The angel of the LORD gave this charge to Joshua: [7]"This is what the LORD Almighty says: 'If you will walk in my ways and keep my requirements, then you will govern my house and have charge of my courts, and I will give you a place among these standing here.

[8]"'Listen, O high priest Joshua and your associates seated before you, who are men symbolic of things to come: I am going to bring my servant, the Branch. [9]See, the stone I have set in front of Joshua! There are seven eyes[a] on that one stone, and I will engrave an inscription on it,' says the LORD Almighty, 'and I will remove the sin of this land in a single day.

[10]"'In that day each of you will invite his neighbor to sit under his vine and fig tree,' declares the LORD Almighty."

The Gold Lampstand and the Two Olive Trees

4 Then the angel who talked with me returned and wakened me, as a man is wakened from his sleep. [2]He asked me, "What do you see?"

I answered, "I see a solid gold lampstand with a bowl at the top and seven lights on it, with seven channels to the lights. [3]Also there are two olive trees by it, one on the right of the bowl and the other on its left."

[4]I asked the angel who talked with me, "What are these, my lord?"

[5]He answered, "Do you not know what these are?"

"No, my lord," I replied.

[6]So he said to me, "This is the word of the LORD to Zerubbabel: 'Not by might nor by power, but by my Spirit,' says the LORD Almighty.

[7]"What[b] are you, O mighty mountain? Before Zerubbabel you will become level ground. Then he will bring out the capstone to shouts of 'God bless it! God bless it!' "

[8]Then the word of the LORD came to me: [9]"The hands of Zerubbabel have laid the foundation of this temple; his hands will also complete it. Then you will know that the LORD Almighty has sent me to you.

[10]"Who despises the day of small things? Men will rejoice when they see the plumb line in the hand of Zerubbabel.

"(These seven are the eyes of the LORD, which range throughout the earth.)"

[11]Then I asked the angel, "What are these two olive trees on the right and the left of the lampstand?"

[12]Again I asked him, "What are these two olive branches beside the two gold pipes that pour out golden oil?"

[13]He replied, "Do you not know what these are?"

"No, my lord," I said.

[14]So he said, "These are the two who are anointed to[c] serve the Lord of all the earth."

The Flying Scroll

5 I looked again—and there before me was a flying scroll! [2]He asked me, "What do you see?"

I answered, "I see a flying scroll, thirty feet long and fifteen feet wide.[d]"

[3]And he said to me, "This is the curse that is going out over the whole land; for according to what it says on one

[a]9 Or *facets*   [b]7 Or *Who*   [c]14 Or *two who bring oil and*   [d]2 Hebrew *twenty cubits long and ten cubits wide* (about 9 meters long and 4.5 meters wide)

side, every thief will be banished, and according to what it says on the other, everyone who swears falsely will be banished. ⁴The LORD Almighty declares, 'I will send it out, and it will enter the house of the thief and the house of him who swears falsely by my name. It will remain in his house and destroy it, both its timbers and its stones.' "

The Woman in a Basket

⁵Then the angel who was speaking to me came forward and said to me, "Look up and see what this is that is appearing."

⁶I asked, "What is it?"

He replied, "It is a measuring basket.ᵃ" And he added, "This is the iniquityᵇ of the people throughout the land."

⁷Then the cover of lead was raised, and there in the basket sat a woman! ⁸He said, "This is wickedness," and he pushed her back into the basket and pushed the lead cover down over its mouth.

⁹Then I looked up—and there before me were two women, with the wind in their wings! They had wings like those of a stork, and they lifted up the basket between heaven and earth.

¹⁰"Where are they taking the basket?" I asked the angel who was speaking to me.

¹¹He replied, "To the country of Babyloniaᶜ to build a house for it. When it is ready, the basket will be set there in its place."

Four Chariots

6 I looked up again—and there before me were four chariots coming out from between two mountains—mountains of bronze! ²The first chariot had red horses, the second black, ³the third white, and the fourth dappled—all of them powerful. ⁴I asked the angel who was speaking to me, "What are these, my lord?"

⁵The angel answered me, "These are the four spiritsᵈ of heaven, going out from standing in the presence of the Lord of the whole world. ⁶The one with the black horses is going toward the north country, the one with the white horses toward the west,ᵉ and the one with the dappled horses toward the south."

⁷When the powerful horses went out, they were straining to go throughout the earth. And he said, "Go throughout the earth!" So they went throughout the earth.

⁸Then he called to me, "Look, those going toward the north country have given my Spiritᶠ rest in the land of the north."

A Crown for Joshua

⁹The word of the LORD came to me: ¹⁰"Take ⌊silver and gold⌋ from the exiles Heldai, Tobijah and Jedaiah, who have arrived from Babylon. Go the same day to the house of Josiah son of Zephaniah. ¹¹Take the silver and gold and make a crown, and set it on the head of the high priest, Joshua son of Jehozadak. ¹²Tell him this is what the LORD Almighty says: 'Here is the man whose name is the Branch, and he will branch out from his place and build the temple of the LORD. ¹³It is he who will build the temple of the LORD, and he will

Visions and Prophecies

ZECHARIAH 5:3—6:12

The visions that came to Zechariah contain powerful and vivid images that encourage God's people to live in anticipation of the coming of the Messiah. The prophet describes a flying scroll, a woman in a basket, and four chariots—images we are not apt to forget.

Sketch these three images or have an artistic friend draw them for you. Spend some time looking at each one and give your imagination time to absorb them. What insights do these images illustrate for you? Try describing them in your own words, as if telling a story to a friend, and use the pictures to illustrate each point you make.

See Meeting God in Scripture

ᵃ 6 Hebrew *an ephah*; also in verses 7–11   ᵇ 6 Or *appearance*   ᶜ 11 Hebrew *Shinar*   ᵈ 5 Or *winds*   ᵉ 6 Or *horses after them*   ᶠ 8 Or *spirit*

Justice, Mercy and Compassion

ZECHARIAH 7:8–10

Read these verses in Zechariah; then compare them to the following passages: Micah 6:8; Isaiah 58:6–10; Matthew 25:34–40. What do these passages have in common? To whom are we called to reach out? Think of your own life. How much contact do you have with people who are homeless, with children who need care and guidance, with people who are new in your neighborhood or with people whose basic needs are not being met? Are you ready to go out of your way to meet their needs? Talk to God about how you might be able to make a difference; then make a commitment to do acts of justice, mercy and compassion.

See Meeting God in Service

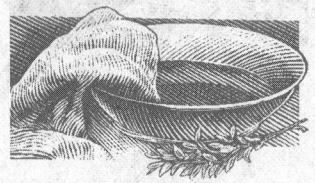

be clothed with majesty and will sit and rule on his throne. And he will be a priest on his throne. And there will be harmony between the two.' ¹⁴The crown will be given to Heldai,ᵃ Tobijah, Jedaiah and Henᵇ son of Zephaniah as a memorial in the temple of the LORD. ¹⁵Those who are far away will come and help to build the temple of the LORD, and you will know that the LORD Almighty has sent me to you. This will happen if you diligently obey the LORD your God."

Justice and Mercy, Not Fasting

7 In the fourth year of King Darius, the word of the LORD came to Zechariah on the fourth day of the ninth month, the month of Kislev. ²The people of Bethel had sent Sharezer and Regem-Melech, together with their men, to entreat the LORD ³by asking the priests of the house of the LORD Almighty and the prophets, "Should I mourn and fast in the fifth month, as I have done for so many years?"

⁴Then the word of the LORD Almighty came to me: ⁵"Ask all the people of the land and the priests, 'When you fasted and mourned in the fifth and seventh months for the past seventy years, was it really for me that you fasted? ⁶And when you were eating and drinking, were you not just feasting for yourselves? ⁷Are these not the words the LORD proclaimed through the earlier prophets when Jerusalem and its surrounding towns were at rest and prosperous, and the Negev and the western foothills were settled?' "

⁸And the word of the LORD came again to Zechariah: ⁹"This is what the LORD Almighty says: 'Administer true justice; show mercy and compassion to one another. ¹⁰Do not oppress the widow or the fatherless, the alien or the poor. In your hearts do not think evil of each other.'

¹¹"But they refused to pay attention; stubbornly they turned their backs and stopped up their ears. ¹²They made their hearts as hard as flint and would not listen to the law or to the words that the LORD Almighty had sent by his Spirit through the earlier prophets. So the LORD Almighty was very angry.

¹³" 'When I called, they did not listen; so when they called, I would not listen,' says the LORD Almighty. ¹⁴'I scattered them with a whirlwind among all the nations, where they were strangers. The land was left so desolate behind them that no one could come or go. This is how they made the pleasant land desolate.' "

The LORD Promises to Bless Jerusalem

8 Again the word of the LORD Almighty came to me. ²This is what the LORD Almighty says: "I am very jealous for Zion; I am burning with jealousy for her."

³This is what the LORD says: "I will return to Zion and dwell in Jerusalem. Then Jerusalem will be called the City of Truth, and the mountain of the LORD Almighty will be called the Holy Mountain."

⁴This is what the LORD Almighty says: "Once again men and women of ripe old age will sit in the streets of Jerusalem, each with cane in hand because of his age. ⁵The city streets will be filled with boys and girls playing there."

⁶This is what the LORD Almighty says: "It may seem marvelous to the remnant of this people at that time, but will it seem marvelous to me?" declares the LORD Almighty.

ᵃ 14 Syriac; Hebrew *Helem*   ᵇ 14 Or *and the gracious one, the*

⁷This is what the LORD Almighty says: "I will save my people from the countries of the east and the west. ⁸I will bring them back to live in Jerusalem; they will be my people, and I will be faithful and righteous to them as their God."

⁹This is what the LORD Almighty says: "You who now hear these words spoken by the prophets who were there when the foundation was laid for the house of the LORD Almighty, let your hands be strong so that the temple may be built. ¹⁰Before that time there were no wages for man or beast. No one could go about his business safely because of his enemy, for I had turned every man against his neighbor. ¹¹But now I will not deal with the remnant of this people as I did in the past," declares the LORD Almighty.

¹²"The seed will grow well, the vine will yield its fruit, the ground will produce its crops, and the heavens will drop their dew. I will give all these things as an inheritance to the remnant of this people. ¹³As you have been an object of cursing among the nations, O Judah and Israel, so will I save you, and you will be a blessing. Do not be afraid, but let your hands be strong."

¹⁴This is what the LORD Almighty says: "Just as I had determined to bring disaster upon you and showed no pity when your fathers angered me," says the LORD Almighty, ¹⁵"so now I have determined to do good again to Jerusalem and Judah. Do not be afraid. ¹⁶These are the things you are to do: Speak the truth to each other, and render true and sound judgment in your courts; ¹⁷do not plot evil against your neighbor, and do not love to swear falsely. I hate all this," declares the LORD.

¹⁸Again the word of the LORD Almighty came to me. ¹⁹This is what the LORD Almighty says: "The fasts of the fourth, fifth, seventh and tenth months will become joyful and glad occasions and happy festivals for Judah. Therefore love truth and peace."

²⁰This is what the LORD Almighty says: "Many peoples and the inhabitants of many cities will yet come, ²¹and the inhabitants of one city will go to another and say, 'Let us go at once to entreat the LORD and seek the LORD Almighty. I myself am going.' ²²And many peoples and powerful nations will come to Jerusalem to seek the LORD Almighty and to entreat him."

²³This is what the LORD Almighty says: "In those days ten men from all languages and nations will take firm hold of one Jew by the hem of his robe and say, 'Let us go with you, because we have heard that God is with you.' "

Judgment on Israel's Enemies
An Oracle

9 The word of the LORD is against the land of Hadrach
and will rest upon Damascus—
for the eyes of men and all the tribes of Israel
are on the LORD—ᵃ
²and upon Hamath too, which borders on it,
and upon Tyre and Sidon, though they are very
skillful.
³Tyre has built herself a stronghold;
she has heaped up silver like dust,

Godliness Is Attractive

ZECHARIAH 8:23

What compels ten persons from a variety of backgrounds to follow this man on his journey? What is it about this man that makes it so obvious that God is with him?

People who exhibit God's character attract others to God. Have you ever been so impressed by someone's faith that you wanted to imitate it? Can you think of anyone whose example has brought you closer to the One who made you? Can you think of a group whose love for God and each other was so contagious that you wanted to be one of them? Give thanks for the people who, by the way they lived and shared their faith, have brought you closer to God. Write them a note expressing your appreciation.

See Meeting God in Everyday Life

ᵃ1 Or *Damascus. / For the eye of the LORD is on all mankind, / as well as on the tribes of Israel.*

Clean, Ready and Worthy

ZECHARIAH 9:9–12

"We are made clean by contrition, ready by compassion, and worthy by our true desire for God. These are three means, as I understood, by which all souls come to heaven, that is to say, those who have been sinners on earth and will be saved . . . For our courteous Lord does not want his servants to despair over falling often or falling deeply. Our falling does not prevent him from loving us. Peace and love are always working in us, but we are not always in peace and love. God wants us to take heed that God is the foundation of all our whole life in love. Furthermore, God is our everlasting protector and mightily defends us against all our most dangerous and fierce enemies."

—JULIAN OF NORWICH,
Showings

and gold like the dirt of the streets.
⁴ But the Lord will take away her possessions
and destroy her power on the sea,
and she will be consumed by fire.
⁵ Ashkelon will see it and fear;
Gaza will writhe in agony,
and Ekron too, for her hope will wither.
Gaza will lose her king
and Ashkelon will be deserted.
⁶ Foreigners will occupy Ashdod,
and I will cut off the pride of the Philistines.
⁷ I will take the blood from their mouths,
the forbidden food from between their teeth.
Those who are left will belong to our God
and become leaders in Judah,
and Ekron will be like the Jebusites.
⁸ But I will defend my house
against marauding forces.
Never again will an oppressor overrun my people,
for now I am keeping watch.

The Coming of Zion's King

⁹ Rejoice greatly, O Daughter of Zion!
Shout, Daughter of Jerusalem!
See, your king*ᵃ* comes to you,
righteous and having salvation,
gentle and riding on a donkey,
on a colt, the foal of a donkey.
¹⁰ I will take away the chariots from Ephraim
and the war-horses from Jerusalem,
and the battle bow will be broken.
He will proclaim peace to the nations.
His rule will extend from sea to sea
and from the River*ᵇ* to the ends of the earth.*ᶜ*
¹¹ As for you, because of the blood of my covenant
with you,
I will free your prisoners from the waterless pit.
¹² Return to your fortress, O prisoners of hope;
even now I announce that I will restore twice as
much to you.
¹³ I will bend Judah as I bend my bow
and fill it with Ephraim.
I will rouse your sons, O Zion,
against your sons, O Greece,
and make you like a warrior's sword.

The Lord Will Appear

¹⁴ Then the Lord will appear over them;
his arrow will flash like lightning.
The Sovereign Lord will sound the trumpet;
he will march in the storms of the south,
¹⁵ and the Lord Almighty will shield them.
They will destroy
and overcome with slingstones.
They will drink and roar as with wine;
they will be full like a bowl
used for sprinkling*ᵈ* the corners of the altar.

ᵃ 9 Or *King*   *ᵇ 10* That is, the Euphrates   *ᶜ 10* Or *the end of the land*
ᵈ 15 Or *bowl, / like*

¹⁶ The Lord their God will save them on that day
  as the flock of his people.
They will sparkle in his land
  like jewels in a crown.
¹⁷ How attractive and beautiful they will be!
  Grain will make the young men thrive,
  and new wine the young women.

The Lord Will Care for Judah

10 Ask the Lord for rain in the springtime;
  it is the Lord who makes the storm clouds.
He gives showers of rain to men,
  and plants of the field to everyone.
² The idols speak deceit,
  diviners see visions that lie;
they tell dreams that are false,
  they give comfort in vain.
Therefore the people wander like sheep
  oppressed for lack of a shepherd.

³ "My anger burns against the shepherds,
  and I will punish the leaders;
for the Lord Almighty will care
  for his flock, the house of Judah,
  and make them like a proud horse in battle.
⁴ From Judah will come the cornerstone,
  from him the tent peg,
  from him the battle bow,
  from him every ruler.
⁵ Together they^a will be like mighty men
  trampling the muddy streets in battle.
Because the Lord is with them,
  they will fight and overthrow the horsemen.

⁶ "I will strengthen the house of Judah
  and save the house of Joseph.
I will restore them
  because I have compassion on them.
They will be as though
  I had not rejected them,
for I am the Lord their God
  and I will answer them.
⁷ The Ephraimites will become like mighty men,
  and their hearts will be glad as with wine.
Their children will see it and be joyful;
  their hearts will rejoice in the Lord.
⁸ I will signal for them
  and gather them in.
Surely I will redeem them;
  they will be as numerous as before.
⁹ Though I scatter them among the peoples,
  yet in distant lands they will remember me.
They and their children will survive,
  and they will return.
¹⁰ I will bring them back from Egypt
  and gather them from Assyria.
I will bring them to Gilead and Lebanon,
  and there will not be room enough for them.
¹¹ They will pass through the sea of trouble;
  the surging sea will be subdued

Give God the Credit

ZECHARIAH 9:16—10:10

The prophet Zechariah reminds his listeners that it is God, not the Canaanite god Baal, who is in charge of the weather and all things. Baal may not be our "god of choice" today, but the one true God still isn't getting credit for all he does.

In common speech today, God gets little credit: "Boy, that was lucky!" someone may say after a narrow escape from death. "Things are sure looking up for me," another may report. "Fate is smiling on me, that's for sure." How often do we hear "I've been really blessed by God" or "Thanks to God, I've made it through"? Take some quiet time to reflect on the language you use and the attitude you express when describing good things that happen to you.

See *Meeting God in Everyday Life*

---

^a 4,5 Or *ruler, all of them together.* / ⁵*They*

Gathered and Redeemed

ZECHARIAH 10:8–12

"O most blessed grace, although I be tempted and vexed with many tribulations, yet I will fear no evil, so long as thou art with me. Grace alone and by itself is my strength; this alone giveth advice and help. This is stronger than all enemies, and wiser than all the wise. Let thy grace therefore, O Lord, always follow me through thy Son Jesus Christ. Amen."

—DOUGLAS V. STEERE,
in *The Imitation of Christ (Selections)*

and all the depths of the Nile will dry up.
Assyria's pride will be brought down
and Egypt's scepter will pass away.
¹² I will strengthen them in the LORD
and in his name they will walk,"
declares the LORD.

11 Open your doors, O Lebanon,
so that fire may devour your cedars!
² Wail, O pine tree, for the cedar has fallen;
the stately trees are ruined!
Wail, oaks of Bashan;
the dense forest has been cut down!
³ Listen to the wail of the shepherds;
their rich pastures are destroyed!
Listen to the roar of the lions;
the lush thicket of the Jordan is ruined!

Two Shepherds

⁴This is what the LORD my God says: "Pasture the flock marked for slaughter. ⁵Their buyers slaughter them and go unpunished. Those who sell them say, 'Praise the LORD, I am rich!' Their own shepherds do not spare them. ⁶For I will no longer have pity on the people of the land," declares the LORD. "I will hand everyone over to his neighbor and his king. They will oppress the land, and I will not rescue them from their hands."

⁷So I pastured the flock marked for slaughter, particularly the oppressed of the flock. Then I took two staffs and called one Favor and the other Union, and I pastured the flock. ⁸In one month I got rid of the three shepherds.

The flock detested me, and I grew weary of them ⁹and said, "I will not be your shepherd. Let the dying die, and the perishing perish. Let those who are left eat one another's flesh."

¹⁰Then I took my staff called Favor and broke it, revoking the covenant I had made with all the nations. ¹¹It was revoked on that day, and so the afflicted of the flock who were watching me knew it was the word of the LORD.

¹²I told them, "If you think it best, give me my pay; but if not, keep it." So they paid me thirty pieces of silver. ¹³And the LORD said to me, "Throw it to the potter"—the handsome price at which they priced me! So I took the thirty pieces of silver and threw them into the house of the LORD to the potter.

¹⁴Then I broke my second staff called Union, breaking the brotherhood between Judah and Israel.

¹⁵Then the LORD said to me, "Take again the equipment of a foolish shepherd. ¹⁶For I am going to raise up a shepherd over the land who will not care for the lost, or seek the young, or heal the injured, or feed the healthy, but will eat the meat of the choice sheep, tearing off their hoofs.

¹⁷ "Woe to the worthless shepherd,
who deserts the flock!
May the sword strike his arm and his right eye!
May his arm be completely withered,
his right eye totally blinded!"

Jerusalem's Enemies to Be Destroyed
An Oracle

12 This is the word of the LORD concerning Israel. The LORD, who stretches out the heavens, who lays the foundation of the earth, and who forms the spirit of man within him, declares: ²"I am going to make Jerusalem a cup that sends all the surrounding peoples reeling. Judah will be besieged as well as Jerusalem. ³On that day, when all the nations of the earth are gathered against her, I will make Jerusalem an immovable rock for all the nations. All who try to move it will injure themselves. ⁴On that day I will strike every horse with panic and its rider with madness," declares the LORD. "I will keep a watchful eye over the house of Judah, but I will blind all the horses of the nations. ⁵Then the leaders of Judah will say in their hearts, 'The people of Jerusalem are strong, because the LORD Almighty is their God.'

⁶"On that day I will make the leaders of Judah like a firepot in a woodpile, like a flaming torch among sheaves. They will consume right and left all the surrounding peoples, but Jerusalem will remain intact in her place.

⁷"The LORD will save the dwellings of Judah first, so that the honor of the house of David and of Jerusalem's inhabitants may not be greater than that of Judah. ⁸On that day the LORD will shield those who live in Jerusalem, so that the feeblest among them will be like David, and the house of David will be like God, like the Angel of the LORD going before them. ⁹On that day I will set out to destroy all the nations that attack Jerusalem.

Mourning for the One They Pierced

¹⁰"And I will pour out on the house of David and the inhabitants of Jerusalem a spirit*ᵃ* of grace and supplication. They will look on*ᵇ* me, the one they have pierced, and they will mourn for him as one mourns for an only child, and grieve bitterly for him as one grieves for a firstborn son. ¹¹On that day the weeping in Jerusalem will be great, like the weeping of Hadad Rimmon in the plain of Megiddo. ¹²The land will mourn, each clan by itself, with their wives by themselves: the clan of the house of David and their wives, the clan of the house of Nathan and their wives, ¹³the clan of the house of Levi and their wives, the clan of Shimei and their wives, ¹⁴and all the rest of the clans and their wives.

Cleansing From Sin

13 "On that day a fountain will be opened to the house of David and the inhabitants of Jerusalem, to cleanse them from sin and impurity.

²"On that day, I will banish the names of the idols from the land, and they will be remembered no more," declares the LORD Almighty. "I will remove both the prophets and the spirit of impurity from the land. ³And if anyone still prophesies, his father and mother, to whom he was born, will say to him, 'You must die, because you have told lies in the LORD's name.' When he prophesies, his own parents will stab him.

⁴"On that day every prophet will be ashamed of his

ᵃ 10 Or *the Spirit*   *ᵇ 10* Or *to*

1269

God Rules

ZECHARIAH 14:9

The day will come when God is acknowledged as "king over the whole earth." What if that day was today? Write a description of what the world would be like if every living being recognized God's power and loving presence. God's Spirit would be like perfume in the air we breathe; there would be no more violence; each person would be fully conformed to the likeness of Jesus. Try to imagine what it would be like if everyone in the world lived in the fullness of faith. After you have written as many things as you can imagine, talk to God about any ways you might be part of helping to bring more of that kingdom ideal to fruition.

See Meeting God in Scripture

prophetic vision. He will not put on a prophet's garment of hair in order to deceive. [5]He will say, 'I am not a prophet. I am a farmer; the land has been my livelihood since my youth.'[a] [6]If someone asks him, 'What are these wounds on your body[b]?' he will answer, 'The wounds I was given at the house of my friends.'

The Shepherd Struck, the Sheep Scattered

[7]"Awake, O sword, against my shepherd,
    against the man who is close to me!"
    declares the LORD Almighty.
"Strike the shepherd,
    and the sheep will be scattered,
    and I will turn my hand against the little ones.
[8]In the whole land," declares the LORD,
    "two-thirds will be struck down and perish;
    yet one-third will be left in it.
[9]This third I will bring into the fire;
    I will refine them like silver
    and test them like gold.
They will call on my name
    and I will answer them;
I will say, 'They are my people,'
    and they will say, 'The LORD is our God.' "

The LORD Comes and Reigns

14 A day of the LORD is coming when your plunder will be divided among you. [2]I will gather all the nations to Jerusalem to fight against it; the city will be captured, the houses ransacked, and the women raped. Half of the city will go into exile, but the rest of the people will not be taken from the city. [3]Then the LORD will go out and fight against those nations, as he fights in the day of battle. [4]On that day his feet will stand on the Mount of Olives, east of Jerusalem, and the Mount of Olives will be split in two from east to west, forming a great valley, with half of the mountain moving north and half moving south. [5]You will flee by my mountain valley, for it will extend to Azel. You will flee as you fled from the earthquake[c] in the days of Uzziah king of Judah. Then the LORD my God will come, and all the holy ones with him.

[6]On that day there will be no light, no cold or frost. [7]It will be a unique day, without daytime or nighttime—a day known to the LORD. When evening comes, there will be light.

[8]On that day living water will flow out from Jerusalem, half to the eastern sea[d] and half to the western sea,[e] in summer and in winter.

[9]The LORD will be king over the whole earth. On that day there will be one LORD, and his name the only name.

[10]The whole land, from Geba to Rimmon, south of Jerusalem, will become like the Arabah. But Jerusalem will be raised up and remain in its place, from the Benjamin Gate to the site of the First Gate, to the Corner Gate, and from the Tower of Hananel to the royal winepresses. [11]It

---

[a]5 Or *farmer; a man sold me in my youth*   [b]6 Or *wounds between your hands*   [c]5 Or [5]*My mountain valley will be blocked and will extend to Azel. It will be blocked as it was blocked because of the earthquake*   [d]8 That is, the Dead Sea   [e]8 That is, the Mediterranean

will be inhabited; never again will it be destroyed. Jerusalem will be secure.

¹²This is the plague with which the Lord will strike all the nations that fought against Jerusalem: Their flesh will rot while they are still standing on their feet, their eyes will rot in their sockets, and their tongues will rot in their mouths. ¹³On that day men will be stricken by the Lord with great panic. Each man will seize the hand of another, and they will attack each other. ¹⁴Judah too will fight at Jerusalem. The wealth of all the surrounding nations will be collected—great quantities of gold and silver and clothing. ¹⁵A similar plague will strike the horses and mules, the camels and donkeys, and all the animals in those camps.

¹⁶Then the survivors from all the nations that have attacked Jerusalem will go up year after year to worship the King, the Lord Almighty, and to celebrate the Feast of Tabernacles. ¹⁷If any of the peoples of the earth do not go up to Jerusalem to worship the King, the Lord Almighty, they will have no rain. ¹⁸If the Egyptian people do not go up and take part, they will have no rain. The Lord[a] will bring on them the plague he inflicts on the nations that do not go up to celebrate the Feast of Tabernacles. ¹⁹This will be the punishment of Egypt and the punishment of all the nations that do not go up to celebrate the Feast of Tabernacles.

²⁰On that day HOLY TO THE LORD will be inscribed on the bells of the horses, and the cooking pots in the Lord's house will be like the sacred bowls in front of the altar. ²¹Every pot in Jerusalem and Judah will be holy to the Lord Almighty, and all who come to sacrifice will take some of the pots and cook in them. And on that day there will no longer be a Canaanite[b] in the house of the Lord Almighty.

Holy to the Lord!

ZECHARIAH 14:20

Zechariah envisions a time when even the horses have HOLY TO THE LORD engraved on their bells. Close your eyes and in your imagination take a walk through your home: HOLY TO THE LORD is written above each doorway and woven into the carpet under your feet. In each room HOLY TO THE LORD is inscribed on the furniture and objects. How does it feel to see these words on a chair, a lamp, a picture on the wall? No matter where you go, you are reminded of God's power and goodness; you are reminded that everything, no matter how ordinary, becomes holy when it is consecrated to God. As you step outside your home, you realize that the same words are invisibly written on your skin. The reminder is everywhere. HOLY TO THE LORD!

See Meeting God in Scripture

MALACHI
Keeping Promises

KEY VERSE:

"Ever since the time of your forefathers you have turned away from my decrees and have not kept them. Return to me, and I will return to you," says the LORD Almighty. "But you ask, 'How are we to return?' "—Malachi 3:7

To worship is to quicken the conscience by the holiness of God, to feed the mind with the truth of God, to purge the imagination by the beauty of God, to open the heart to the love of God, to devote the will to the purpose of God.

—WILLIAM TEMPLE

In the book of Malachi, it is the prophet's words, not his person, that demand our attention. We know next to nothing about the prophet himself, but we find in his writing a vibrant word from God (the name of the book means "my messenger").

Malachi, using a question-and-answer device, challenges the people to mend their ways. The prophet warns the priests about offering blemished sacrifices (1:8) and giving false teachings (2:8). He confronts the people about mixed marriages and divorce (2:10–16) and about not paying a full tithe (3:8–9). The day of judgment is coming, he declares, and it will be like a fire—it will burn away evil and refine what is good.

Amid Malachi's warnings and judgment, the prophet tells of some wonderful blessings that will belong to those who are faithful and obedient to God. Those who are generous and bring a full tithe to God will see God "throw open the floodgates of heaven and pour out so much blessing that [they] will not have room enough for it" (3:10). Those who revere and honor God will see the sun of righteousness "rise with healing in its wings" (4:2). Malachi calls us to return to a life of honest worship, truthful speech and generous compassion. Listen with your heart, respond with your deeds, and the Lord will come to you!

1 An oracle: The word of the LORD to Israel through Malachi.ᵃ

Jacob Loved, Esau Hated

²"I have loved you," says the LORD.

"But you ask, 'How have you loved us?'

"Was not Esau Jacob's brother?" the LORD says. "Yet I have loved Jacob, ³but Esau I have hated, and I have turned his mountains into a wasteland and left his inheritance to the desert jackals."

⁴Edom may say, "Though we have been crushed, we will rebuild the ruins."

But this is what the LORD Almighty says: "They may build, but I will demolish. They will be called the Wicked Land, a people always under the wrath of the LORD. ⁵You will see it with your own eyes and say, 'Great is the LORD— even beyond the borders of Israel!'

Blemished Sacrifices

⁶"A son honors his father, and a servant his master. If I am a father, where is the honor due me? If I am a master, where is the respect due me?" says the LORD Almighty. "It is you, O priests, who show contempt for my name.

"But you ask, 'How have we shown contempt for your name?'

⁷"You place defiled food on my altar.

"But you ask, 'How have we defiled you?'

"By saying that the LORD's table is contemptible. ⁸When you bring blind animals for sacrifice, is that not wrong? When you sacrifice crippled or diseased animals, is that not wrong? Try offering them to your governor! Would he be pleased with you? Would he accept you?" says the LORD Almighty.

⁹"Now implore God to be gracious to us. With such offerings from your hands, will he accept you?"—says the LORD Almighty.

¹⁰"Oh, that one of you would shut the temple doors, so that you would not light useless fires on my altar! I am not pleased with you," says the LORD Almighty, "and I will accept no offering from your hands. ¹¹My name will be great among the nations, from the rising to the setting of the sun. In every place incense and pure offerings will be brought to my name, because my name will be great among the nations," says the LORD Almighty.

¹²"But you profane it by saying of the Lord's table, 'It is defiled,' and of its food, 'It is contemptible.' ¹³And you say, 'What a burden!' and you sniff at it contemptuously," says the LORD Almighty.

"When you bring injured, crippled or diseased animals and offer them as sacrifices, should I accept them from your hands?" says the LORD. ¹⁴"Cursed is the cheat who has an acceptable male in his flock and vows to give it, but then sacrifices a blemished animal to the Lord. For I am a great king," says the LORD Almighty, "and my name is to be feared among the nations.

ᵃ 1 *Malachi* means *my messenger.*

Offering Less Than the Best

MALACHI 1:13–14

We may not comprehend the necessity of the animal sacrifices that were common practice in the Old Testament, but we understand all too well the prophet's disgust with offerings that were less than the best. In our spiritual life we sometimes offer God less than our best: We try to squeeze prayer in at the end of a crowded day and end up falling asleep; we go wearily to worship services after staying up too late the night before; we skip Bible study because we don't have time.

God desires our best "from the rising to the setting of the sun" (v.11), and our best is not tired prayers, halfhearted study or short-lived compassion. Review your spiritual disciplines of prayer, worship and Bible study. Write a prayer of confession for your "less than best" efforts or a prayer of thanksgiving for your ability to be faithful. Ask God to help you as you grow to be the very best he intends you to be.

See Meeting God in Prayer

The Lips and the Mouth

MALACHI 2:4–9

The prophet decries a priesthood that has become complacent and corrupt. Steady as iron, though, he upholds God's clear standards of righteousness.

Draw a picture of a mouth. On one side of the mouth write some of the words you have used to hurt, mislead or create trouble. On the other side write words you have used to comfort, guide and maintain peace. Try to speak a few words of encouragement, guidance or peace to everyone you meet today. Pray that the words you speak will be a blessing to others.

See Meeting God in Everyday Life

Admonition for the Priests

2 "And now this admonition is for you, O priests. [2]If you do not listen, and if you do not set your heart to honor my name," says the LORD Almighty, "I will send a curse upon you, and I will curse your blessings. Yes, I have already cursed them, because you have not set your heart to honor me.

[3]"Because of you I will rebuke[a] your descendants[b]; I will spread on your faces the offal from your festival sacrifices, and you will be carried off with it. [4]And you will know that I have sent you this admonition so that my covenant with Levi may continue," says the LORD Almighty. [5]"My covenant was with him, a covenant of life and peace, and I gave them to him; this called for reverence and he revered me and stood in awe of my name. [6]True instruction was in his mouth and nothing false was found on his lips. He walked with me in peace and uprightness, and turned many from sin.

[7]"For the lips of a priest ought to preserve knowledge, and from his mouth men should seek instruction—because he is the messenger of the LORD Almighty. [8]But you have turned from the way and by your teaching have caused many to stumble; you have violated the covenant with Levi," says the LORD Almighty. [9]"So I have caused you to be despised and humiliated before all the people, because you have not followed my ways but have shown partiality in matters of the law."

Judah Unfaithful

[10]Have we not all one Father[c]? Did not one God create us? Why do we profane the covenant of our fathers by breaking faith with one another?

[11]Judah has broken faith. A detestable thing has been committed in Israel and in Jerusalem: Judah has desecrated the sanctuary the LORD loves, by marrying the daughter of a foreign god. [12]As for the man who does this, whoever he may be, may the LORD cut him off from the tents of Jacob[d]—even though he brings offerings to the LORD Almighty.

[13]Another thing you do: You flood the LORD's altar with tears. You weep and wail because he no longer pays attention to your offerings or accepts them with pleasure from your hands. [14]You ask, "Why?" It is because the LORD is acting as the witness between you and the wife of your youth, because you have broken faith with her, though she is your partner, the wife of your marriage covenant.

[15]Has not ⌊the LORD⌋ made them one? In flesh and spirit they are his. And why one? Because he was seeking godly offspring.[e] So guard yourself in your spirit, and do not break faith with the wife of your youth.

[16]"I hate divorce," says the LORD God of Israel, "and I hate a man's covering himself[f] with violence as well as with his garment," says the LORD Almighty.

So guard yourself in your spirit, and do not break faith.

---

[a] 3 Or *cut off* (see Septuagint)   [b] 3 Or *will blight your grain*   [c] 10 Or *father*
[d] 12 Or [12]*May the LORD cut off from the tents of Jacob anyone who gives testimony in behalf of the man who does this*   [e] 15 Or [15]*But the one who is our father*⌋ *did not do this, not as long as life remained in him. And what was he seeking? An offspring from God*   [f] 16 Or *his wife*

The Day of Judgment

¹⁷You have wearied the LORD with your words.

"How have we wearied him?" you ask.

By saying, "All who do evil are good in the eyes of the LORD, and he is pleased with them" or "Where is the God of justice?"

3 "See, I will send my messenger, who will prepare the way before me. Then suddenly the Lord you are seeking will come to his temple; the messenger of the covenant, whom you desire, will come," says the LORD Almighty. ²But who can endure the day of his coming? Who can stand when he appears? For he will be like a refiner's fire or a launderer's soap. ³He will sit as a refiner and purifier of silver; he will purify the Levites and refine them like gold and silver. Then the LORD will have men who will bring offerings in righteousness, ⁴and the offerings of Judah and Jerusalem will be acceptable to the LORD, as in days gone by, as in former years.

⁵"So I will come near to you for judgment. I will be quick to testify against sorcerers, adulterers and perjurers, against those who defraud laborers of their wages, who oppress the widows and the fatherless, and deprive aliens of justice, but do not fear me," says the LORD Almighty.

Robbing God

⁶"I the LORD do not change. So you, O descendants of Jacob, are not destroyed. ⁷Ever since the time of your forefathers you have turned away from my decrees and have not kept them. Return to me, and I will return to you," says the LORD Almighty.

"But you ask, 'How are we to return?'

⁸"Will a man rob God? Yet you rob me.

"But you ask, 'How do we rob you?'

"In tithes and offerings. ⁹You are under a curse—the whole nation of you—because you are robbing me. ¹⁰Bring the whole tithe into the storehouse, that there may be food in my house. Test me in this," says the LORD Almighty, "and see if I will not throw open the floodgates of heaven and pour out so much blessing that you will not have room enough for it. ¹¹I will prevent pests from devouring your crops, and the vines in your fields will not cast their fruit," says the LORD Almighty. ¹²"Then all the nations will call you blessed, for yours will be a delightful land," says the LORD Almighty.

¹³"You have said harsh things against me," says the LORD.

"Yet you ask, 'What have we said against you?'

¹⁴"You have said, 'It is futile to serve God. What did we gain by carrying out his requirements and going about like mourners before the LORD Almighty? ¹⁵But now we call the arrogant blessed. Certainly the evildoers prosper, and even those who challenge God escape.' "

¹⁶Then those who feared the LORD talked with each other, and the LORD listened and heard. A scroll of remembrance was written in his presence concerning those who feared the LORD and honored his name.

¹⁷"They will be mine," says the LORD Almighty, "in the day when I make up my treasured possession.ᵃ I will spare them, just as in compassion a man spares his son who

ᵃ *17 Or Almighty, "my treasured possession, in the day when I act*

A Messenger Comes in Many Ways

MALACHI 3:1–4

"[God's] appeals come through the conversations of good people, or from sermons, or through the reading of good books; and there are many other ways . . . in which God calls. Or they come through sicknesses and trials, or by means of truths which God teaches us at times when we are engaged in prayer; however feeble such prayers may be, God values them highly. You must not despise this first favor, nor be disconsolate, even though you have not responded immediately to the Lord's call; for his majesty is quite prepared to wait for many days, and even years, especially when he sees we are persevering and have good desires."

—TERESA OF AVILA,
The Interior Castle

On That Day

MALACHI 4:1–3

Whatever judgment occurs on the day of the Lord, those who revere God will experience that day as one of rejoicing in their salvation and renewal: "You will go out and leap like calves released from the stall."

Think of the rays of the sun as white or golden birds that bring healing to your mind, body and spirit. How would those wings of healing enfold and touch you with warmth and healing? Imagine these birds flying out over your neighborhood and community. Where would they bring healing and salvation? Next see the birds winging their way over the country and around the world. Where would you ask God to send healing and renewal? Where is the sun of righteousness needed? Draw a picture of your bird of healing or write a prayer of thanksgiving.

See Meeting God in Scripture

serves him. ¹⁸And you will again see the distinction between the righteous and the wicked, between those who serve God and those who do not.

The Day of the LORD

4 "Surely the day is coming; it will burn like a furnace. All the arrogant and every evildoer will be stubble, and that day that is coming will set them on fire," says the LORD Almighty. "Not a root or a branch will be left to them. ²But for you who revere my name, the sun of righteousness will rise with healing in its wings. And you will go out and leap like calves released from the stall. ³Then you will trample down the wicked; they will be ashes under the soles of your feet on the day when I do these things," says the LORD Almighty.

⁴"Remember the law of my servant Moses, the decrees and laws I gave him at Horeb for all Israel.

⁵"See, I will send you the prophet Elijah before that great and dreadful day of the LORD comes. ⁶He will turn the hearts of the fathers to their children, and the hearts of the children to their fathers; or else I will come and strike the land with a curse."

New Testament

MATTHEW

Promises That Come True

KEY VERSE:

"Do not think that I have come to abolish the Law or the Prophets; I have not come to abolish them but to fulfill them."—Matthew 5:17

Matthew writes this Gospel in the early church period when the church is predominantly Jewish. Matthew frequently cites passages from the Old Testament that are fulfilled in the coming of Jesus the Messiah, a watershed event in the long tradition of ancient Judaism. Matthew's intent is that those who read his Gospel, whether Jews or Gentiles, will see themselves as participants in the grand sweep of God's purposes in history. The coming of Jesus, says Matthew, is the culmination of all our waiting.

Matthew almost seems astonished that God should become incarnate in Jesus Christ, that people could see and hear and touch the Almighty God. As you read Matthew's Gospel, try to imagine yourself as a Jew in Gospel times. Your people have waited a thousand years for fulfillment. You have studied and remembered all the ancient prophecies and now, for the first time, they make sense. Suddenly, Almighty God is among your people. Immanuel, *God with us*, is present and active in the day-to-day life of the people—healing, feeding, teaching—bringing the Word of God personally to the people of God.

As you read this Gospel, remember that Jesus is still *God with us*. He is God incarnate, with us in the Holy Spirit. What questions would you like to ask him? What would you like him to explain? What do you need him to do for you? What can you do for him? Make these questions the prayers of your heart.

"The Gospel is a public exhibition of the Son of God manifested in the flesh to deliver a ruined world, and to restore men from death to life. It is justly called a good and joyful message, for it contains perfect happiness. Its object is to commence the reign of God, and by means of our deliverance from the corruption of the flesh, and of our renewal by the Spirit, to conduct us to the heavenly glory."

—JOHN CALVIN,
Institutes of the Christian Religion

Your Past Doesn't Dictate Your Future

MATTHEW 1:1–17

The genealogy of Jesus is a startling testimony to God's power to overcome the sin of humankind. This is by no means a "pure" family tree: Judah visited prostitutes; Rahab was a prostitute; David committed adultery and murder; Solomon flirted with idols. Yet through these imperfect people, God was able to preserve his promises and shape earthly events to prepare the way for the Messiah. In what ways have you departed from God's will for you? How has God called you back? How do you see God working to keep you on track with his purposes, even through your times of spiritual dryness and perceived distance from God?

The Genealogy of Jesus

1 A record of the genealogy of Jesus Christ the son of David, the son of Abraham:

²Abraham was the father of Isaac,
  Isaac the father of Jacob,
  Jacob the father of Judah and his brothers,
³Judah the father of Perez and Zerah, whose mother was Tamar,
  Perez the father of Hezron,
  Hezron the father of Ram,
⁴Ram the father of Amminadab,
  Amminadab the father of Nahshon,
  Nahshon the father of Salmon,
⁵Salmon the father of Boaz, whose mother was Rahab,
  Boaz the father of Obed, whose mother was Ruth,
  Obed the father of Jesse,
⁶and Jesse the father of King David.

David was the father of Solomon, whose mother had been Uriah's wife,
⁷Solomon the father of Rehoboam,
  Rehoboam the father of Abijah,
  Abijah the father of Asa,
⁸Asa the father of Jehoshaphat,
  Jehoshaphat the father of Jehoram,
  Jehoram the father of Uzziah,
⁹Uzziah the father of Jotham,
  Jotham the father of Ahaz,
  Ahaz the father of Hezekiah,
¹⁰Hezekiah the father of Manasseh,
  Manasseh the father of Amon,
  Amon the father of Josiah,
¹¹and Josiah the father of Jeconiah*ᵃ* and his brothers at the time of the exile to Babylon.

¹²After the exile to Babylon:
  Jeconiah was the father of Shealtiel,
  Shealtiel the father of Zerubbabel,
¹³Zerubbabel the father of Abiud,
  Abiud the father of Eliakim,
  Eliakim the father of Azor,
¹⁴Azor the father of Zadok,
  Zadok the father of Akim,
  Akim the father of Eliud,
¹⁵Eliud the father of Eleazar,
  Eleazar the father of Matthan,
  Matthan the father of Jacob,
¹⁶and Jacob the father of Joseph, the husband of Mary, of whom was born Jesus, who is called Christ.

¹⁷Thus there were fourteen generations in all from Abraham to David, fourteen from David to the exile to Babylon, and fourteen from the exile to the Christ.*ᵇ*

The Birth of Jesus Christ

¹⁸This is how the birth of Jesus Christ came about: His

ᵃ 11 That is, Jehoiachin; also in verse 12   *ᵇ 17* Or *Messiah*. "The Christ" (Greek) and "the Messiah" (Hebrew) both mean "the Anointed One."

mother Mary was pledged to be married to Joseph, but before they came together, she was found to be with child through the Holy Spirit. [19]Because Joseph her husband was a righteous man and did not want to expose her to public disgrace, he had in mind to divorce her quietly.

[20]But after he had considered this, an angel of the Lord appeared to him in a dream and said, "Joseph son of David, do not be afraid to take Mary home as your wife, because what is conceived in her is from the Holy Spirit. [21]She will give birth to a son, and you are to give him the name Jesus,[a] because he will save his people from their sins."

[22]All this took place to fulfill what the Lord had said through the prophet: [23]"The virgin will be with child and will give birth to a son, and they will call him Immanuel"[b]—which means, "God with us."

[24]When Joseph woke up, he did what the angel of the Lord had commanded him and took Mary home as his wife. [25]But he had no union with her until she gave birth to a son. And he gave him the name Jesus.

The Visit of the Magi

2 After Jesus was born in Bethlehem in Judea, during the time of King Herod, Magi[c] from the east came to Jerusalem [2]and asked, "Where is the one who has been born king of the Jews? We saw his star in the east[d] and have come to worship him."

[3]When King Herod heard this he was disturbed, and all Jerusalem with him. [4]When he had called together all the people's chief priests and teachers of the law, he asked them where the Christ[e] was to be born. [5]"In Bethlehem in Judea," they replied, "for this is what the prophet has written:

[6]" 'But you, Bethlehem, in the land of Judah,
        are by no means least among the rulers of
            Judah;
    for out of you will come a ruler
        who will be the shepherd of my people Israel.'[f]"

[7]Then Herod called the Magi secretly and found out from them the exact time the star had appeared. [8]He sent them to Bethlehem and said, "Go and make a careful search for the child. As soon as you find him, report to me, so that I too may go and worship him."

[9]After they had heard the king, they went on their way, and the star they had seen in the east[g] went ahead of them until it stopped over the place where the child was. [10]When they saw the star, they were overjoyed. [11]On coming to the house, they saw the child with his mother Mary, and they bowed down and worshiped him. Then they opened their treasures and presented him with gifts of gold and of incense and of myrrh. [12]And having been warned in a dream not to go back to Herod, they returned to their country by another route.

The Escape to Egypt

[13]When they had gone, an angel of the Lord appeared to

Reasons of the Heart

MATTHEW 2:2

The Magi come to worship Jesus. Later others come to him for healing and forgiveness, to learn from him, or in hopes of gaining material blessings or power. Imagine you are a contemporary of Jesus and you have just heard about him. Who told you about Jesus? What did that person say about Jesus? What was the first thing you said? What did you think about just before falling asleep that night? What do you seek now? Ask God to help you find it. Or ask God to teach you, as you read this Gospel, what you should be seeking.

See Meeting God in Worship

---

[a] 21 *Jesus* is the Greek form of *Joshua*, which means *the LORD saves.*
[b] 23 Isaiah 7:14   [c] 1 Traditionally *Wise Men*   [d] 2 Or *star when it rose*
[e] 4 Or *Messiah*   [f] 6 Micah 5:2   [g] 9 Or *seen when it rose*

Cooperating With God

MATTHEW 2:15; 3:1

Joseph takes the young Jesus to Egypt and stays there to fulfill what God has said through the prophets. Later John the Baptist prepares the way for the Messiah by preaching repentance. Each man makes life choices that God uses to fulfill the covenant of salvation.

Take a short trip out of town; spend the night alone and reflect on how your life can be part of God's purpose. (As an alternative, take a leisurely walk some morning or afternoon.) Ask yourself: How can I cooperate with God's designs for my life? Do I have any unique qualities that might reflect a certain purpose? What promise might I help fulfill?

See Meeting God in Everyday Life

Joseph in a dream. "Get up," he said, "take the child and his mother and escape to Egypt. Stay there until I tell you, for Herod is going to search for the child to kill him."

¹⁴So he got up, took the child and his mother during the night and left for Egypt, ¹⁵where he stayed until the death of Herod. And so was fulfilled what the Lord had said through the prophet: "Out of Egypt I called my son."[a]

¹⁶When Herod realized that he had been outwitted by the Magi, he was furious, and he gave orders to kill all the boys in Bethlehem and its vicinity who were two years old and under, in accordance with the time he had learned from the Magi. ¹⁷Then what was said through the prophet Jeremiah was fulfilled:

¹⁸"A voice is heard in Ramah,
    weeping and great mourning,
Rachel weeping for her children
    and refusing to be comforted,
because they are no more."[b]

The Return to Nazareth

¹⁹After Herod died, an angel of the Lord appeared in a dream to Joseph in Egypt ²⁰and said, "Get up, take the child and his mother and go to the land of Israel, for those who were trying to take the child's life are dead."

²¹So he got up, took the child and his mother and went to the land of Israel. ²²But when he heard that Archelaus was reigning in Judea in place of his father Herod, he was afraid to go there. Having been warned in a dream, he withdrew to the district of Galilee, ²³and he went and lived in a town called Nazareth. So was fulfilled what was said through the prophets: "He will be called a Nazarene."

John the Baptist Prepares the Way

3 In those days John the Baptist came, preaching in the Desert of Judea ²and saying, "Repent, for the kingdom of heaven is near." ³This is he who was spoken of through the prophet Isaiah:

"A voice of one calling in the desert,
'Prepare the way for the Lord,
    make straight paths for him.' "[c]

⁴John's clothes were made of camel's hair, and he had a leather belt around his waist. His food was locusts and wild honey. ⁵People went out to him from Jerusalem and all Judea and the whole region of the Jordan. ⁶Confessing their sins, they were baptized by him in the Jordan River.

⁷But when he saw many of the Pharisees and Sadducees coming to where he was baptizing, he said to them: "You brood of vipers! Who warned you to flee from the coming wrath? ⁸Produce fruit in keeping with repentance. ⁹And do not think you can say to yourselves, 'We have Abraham as our father.' I tell you that out of these stones God can raise up children for Abraham. ¹⁰The ax is already at the root of the trees, and every tree that does not produce good fruit will be cut down and thrown into the fire.

¹¹"I baptize you with[d] water for repentance. But after me will come one who is more powerful than I, whose sandals I am not fit to carry. He will baptize you with the Holy Spir-

a 15 Hosea 11:1   *b 18* Jer. 31:15   *c 3* Isaiah 40:3   *d 11* Or *in*

it and with fire. ¹²His winnowing fork is in his hand, and he will clear his threshing floor, gathering his wheat into the barn and burning up the chaff with unquenchable fire."

The Baptism of Jesus

¹³Then Jesus came from Galilee to the Jordan to be baptized by John. ¹⁴But John tried to deter him, saying, "I need to be baptized by you, and do you come to me?"

¹⁵Jesus replied, "Let it be so now; it is proper for us to do this to fulfill all righteousness." Then John consented.

¹⁶As soon as Jesus was baptized, he went up out of the water. At that moment heaven was opened, and he saw the Spirit of God descending like a dove and lighting on him. ¹⁷And a voice from heaven said, "This is my Son, whom I love; with him I am well pleased."

The Temptation of Jesus

4 Then Jesus was led by the Spirit into the desert to be tempted by the devil. ²After fasting forty days and forty nights, he was hungry. ³The tempter came to him and said, "If you are the Son of God, tell these stones to become bread."

⁴Jesus answered, "It is written: 'Man does not live on bread alone, but on every word that comes from the mouth of God.'ᵃ"

⁵Then the devil took him to the holy city and had him stand on the highest point of the temple. ⁶"If you are the Son of God," he said, "throw yourself down. For it is written:

" 'He will command his angels concerning you,
    and they will lift you up in their hands,
so that you will not strike your foot against a
    stone.'ᵇ"

⁷Jesus answered him, "It is also written: 'Do not put the Lord your God to the test.'ᶜ"

⁸Again, the devil took him to a very high mountain and showed him all the kingdoms of the world and their splendor. ⁹"All this I will give you," he said, "if you will bow down and worship me."

¹⁰Jesus said to him, "Away from me, Satan! For it is written: 'Worship the Lord your God, and serve him only.'ᵈ"

¹¹Then the devil left him, and angels came and attended him.

Jesus Begins to Preach

¹²When Jesus heard that John had been put in prison, he returned to Galilee. ¹³Leaving Nazareth, he went and lived in Capernaum, which was by the lake in the area of Zebulun and Naphtali— ¹⁴to fulfill what was said through the prophet Isaiah:

¹⁵"Land of Zebulun and land of Naphtali,
    the way to the sea, along the Jordan,
        Galilee of the Gentiles—
¹⁶the people living in darkness
    have seen a great light;
on those living in the land of the shadow of death
    a light has dawned."ᵉ

The Temptation of Legitimate Needs

MATTHEW 4:1–4

After forty days of fasting, Jesus' need for food was understandably acute. Satan uses this legitimate need to tempt Jesus to "prove" his significance and power.

Temptation often results from such legitimate needs. What needs do you have in your life that aren't being met? Are you tempted to meet those needs in illegitimate ways? Put yourself in Jesus' sandals; imagine his hunger after a forty-day fast. Consider fasting for a day to more fully experience the kinds of sensations Jesus did. How can the strength Jesus exhibits and words he speaks encourage you?

ᵃ4 Deut. 8:3   ᵇ6 Psalm 91:11,12   ᶜ7 Deut. 6:16   ᵈ10 Deut. 6:13
ᵉ16 Isaiah 9:1,2

Life With Others

MATTHEW 5:3–10

If every member of your community made a concerted effort to become poor in spirit, meek, merciful, pure in heart, and prone to promoting peace, how would your community be transformed? How do these beatitudes bring people together? Reflect on this passage by looking at the harm done by the opposite attitudes. What usually follows in the wake of a haughty spirit? What happens when people become demanding? Divisive? Critical? How can God use you in your church, circle of friends, or neighborhood to reflect the character of the Spirit of Jesus?

See Meeting God in Community

[17]From that time on Jesus began to preach, "Repent, for the kingdom of heaven is near."

The Calling of the First Disciples

[18]As Jesus was walking beside the Sea of Galilee, he saw two brothers, Simon called Peter and his brother Andrew. They were casting a net into the lake, for they were fishermen. [19]"Come, follow me," Jesus said, "and I will make you fishers of men." [20]At once they left their nets and followed him.

[21]Going on from there, he saw two other brothers, James son of Zebedee and his brother John. They were in a boat with their father Zebedee, preparing their nets. Jesus called them, [22]and immediately they left the boat and their father and followed him.

Jesus Heals the Sick

[23]Jesus went throughout Galilee, teaching in their synagogues, preaching the good news of the kingdom, and healing every disease and sickness among the people. [24]News about him spread all over Syria, and people brought to him all who were ill with various diseases, those suffering severe pain, the demon-possessed, those having seizures, and the paralyzed, and he healed them. [25]Large crowds from Galilee, the Decapolis,[a] Jerusalem, Judea and the region across the Jordan followed him.

The Beatitudes

5 Now when he saw the crowds, he went up on a mountainside and sat down. His disciples came to him, [2]and he began to teach them, saying:

> [3]"Blessed are the poor in spirit,
>   for theirs is the kingdom of heaven.
> [4]Blessed are those who mourn,
>   for they will be comforted.
> [5]Blessed are the meek,
>   for they will inherit the earth.
> [6]Blessed are those who hunger and thirst for
>   righteousness,
>   for they will be filled.
> [7]Blessed are the merciful,
>   for they will be shown mercy.
> [8]Blessed are the pure in heart,
>   for they will see God.
> [9]Blessed are the peacemakers,
>   for they will be called sons of God.
> [10]Blessed are those who are persecuted because of
>   righteousness,
>   for theirs is the kingdom of heaven.

[11]"Blessed are you when people insult you, persecute you and falsely say all kinds of evil against you because of me. [12]Rejoice and be glad, because great is your reward in heaven, for in the same way they persecuted the prophets who were before you.

Salt and Light

[13]"You are the salt of the earth. But if the salt loses its saltiness, how can it be made salty again? It is no longer

[a] 25 That is, the Ten Cities

good for anything, except to be thrown out and trampled by men.

¹⁴"You are the light of the world. A city on a hill cannot be hidden. ¹⁵Neither do people light a lamp and put it under a bowl. Instead they put it on its stand, and it gives light to everyone in the house. ¹⁶In the same way, let your light shine before men, that they may see your good deeds and praise your Father in heaven.

The Fulfillment of the Law

¹⁷"Do not think that I have come to abolish the Law or the Prophets; I have not come to abolish them but to fulfill them. ¹⁸I tell you the truth, until heaven and earth disappear, not the smallest letter, not the least stroke of a pen, will by any means disappear from the Law until everything is accomplished. ¹⁹Anyone who breaks one of the least of these commandments and teaches others to do the same will be called least in the kingdom of heaven, but whoever practices and teaches these commands will be called great in the kingdom of heaven. ²⁰For I tell you that unless your righteousness surpasses that of the Pharisees and the teachers of the law, you will certainly not enter the kingdom of heaven.

Murder

²¹"You have heard that it was said to the people long ago, 'Do not murder,ᵃ and anyone who murders will be subject to judgment.' ²²But I tell you that anyone who is angry with his brotherᵇ will be subject to judgment. Again, anyone who says to his brother, 'Raca,ᶜ' is answerable to the Sanhedrin. But anyone who says, 'You fool!' will be in danger of the fire of hell.

²³"Therefore, if you are offering your gift at the altar and there remember that your brother has something against you, ²⁴leave your gift there in front of the altar. First go and be reconciled to your brother; then come and offer your gift.

²⁵"Settle matters quickly with your adversary who is taking you to court. Do it while you are still with him on the way, or he may hand you over to the judge, and the judge may hand you over to the officer, and you may be thrown into prison. ²⁶I tell you the truth, you will not get out until you have paid the last penny.ᵈ

Adultery

²⁷"You have heard that it was said, 'Do not commit adultery.'ᵉ ²⁸But I tell you that anyone who looks at a woman lustfully has already committed adultery with her in his heart. ²⁹If your right eye causes you to sin, gouge it out and throw it away. It is better for you to lose one part of your body than for your whole body to be thrown into hell. ³⁰And if your right hand causes you to sin, cut it off and throw it away. It is better for you to lose one part of your body than for your whole body to go into hell.

Divorce

³¹"It has been said, 'Anyone who divorces his wife must give her a certificate of divorce.'ᶠ ³²But I tell you that any-

---

Letting God Shine Through Us

MATTHEW 5:14

"It is said of St. Francis not merely that he prayed, but that he became a prayer. Such lives must be reborn today, if the life of the Eternal Love is to break through the heavy encrustations of our conventional church life, and apostolic life and love and power be restored to the church of God. [God] can break through any time we are really willing."

—THOMAS KELLY,
The Reality of the Spiritual World

ᵃ 21 Exodus 20:13   ᵇ 22 Some manuscripts *brother without cause*   ᶜ 22 An Aramaic term of contempt   ᵈ 26 Greek *kodrantes*   ᵉ 27 Exodus 20:14   ᶠ 31 Deut. 24:1

A Positive Ethic

MATTHEW 5:48

One thing that set Jesus' teaching so radically apart from that of the religious leaders is that the religious leaders emphasized what people *shouldn't* do while Jesus stressed the positive nature of our calling—what *we should* do. It's not enough to refrain from killing our enemies; we are called to love them and pray for them. Think about your own shortcomings and how you might counteract each one with a positive virtue. For example, instead of being critical, learn to encourage; instead of hoarding wealth, learn to be generous, and so on. Ask God to help you go beyond merely desiring change to being transformed into his likeness.

See *Meeting God in Service*

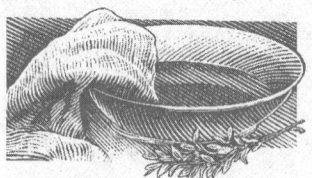

one who divorces his wife, except for marital unfaithfulness, causes her to become an adulteress, and anyone who marries the divorced woman commits adultery.

Oaths

33 "Again, you have heard that it was said to the people long ago, 'Do not break your oath, but keep the oaths you have made to the Lord.' 34 But I tell you, Do not swear at all: either by heaven, for it is God's throne; 35 or by the earth, for it is his footstool; or by Jerusalem, for it is the city of the Great King. 36 And do not swear by your head, for you cannot make even one hair white or black. 37 Simply let your 'Yes' be 'Yes,' and your 'No,' 'No'; anything beyond this comes from the evil one.

An Eye for an Eye

38 "You have heard that it was said, 'Eye for eye, and tooth for tooth.'[a] 39 But I tell you, Do not resist an evil person. If someone strikes you on the right cheek, turn to him the other also. 40 And if someone wants to sue you and take your tunic, let him have your cloak as well. 41 If someone forces you to go one mile, go with him two miles. 42 Give to the one who asks you, and do not turn away from the one who wants to borrow from you.

Love for Enemies

43 "You have heard that it was said, 'Love your neighbor[b] and hate your enemy.' 44 But I tell you: Love your enemies[c] and pray for those who persecute you, 45 that you may be sons of your Father in heaven. He causes his sun to rise on the evil and the good, and sends rain on the righteous and the unrighteous. 46 If you love those who love you, what reward will you get? Are not even the tax collectors doing that? 47 And if you greet only your brothers, what are you doing more than others? Do not even pagans do that? 48 Be perfect, therefore, as your heavenly Father is perfect.

Giving to the Needy

6 "Be careful not to do your 'acts of righteousness' before men, to be seen by them. If you do, you will have no reward from your Father in heaven.

2 "So when you give to the needy, do not announce it with trumpets, as the hypocrites do in the synagogues and on the streets, to be honored by men. I tell you the truth, they have received their reward in full. 3 But when you give to the needy, do not let your left hand know what your right hand is doing, 4 so that your giving may be in secret. Then your Father, who sees what is done in secret, will reward you.

Prayer

5 "And when you pray, do not be like the hypocrites, for they love to pray standing in the synagogues and on the street corners to be seen by men. I tell you the truth, they have received their reward in full. 6 But when you pray, go into your room, close the door and pray to your Father, who is unseen. Then your Father, who sees what is done in secret, will reward you. 7 And when you pray, do not

a 38 Exodus 21:24; Lev. 24:20; Deut. 19:21   *b 43* Lev. 19:18   *c 44* Some late manuscripts *enemies, bless those who curse you, do good to those who hate you*

keep on babbling like pagans, for they think they will be heard because of their many words. ⁸Do not be like them, for your Father knows what you need before you ask him.

⁹"This, then, is how you should pray:

> " 'Our Father in heaven,
>   hallowed be your name,
> ¹⁰your kingdom come,
>   your will be done
>   on earth as it is in heaven.
> ¹¹Give us today our daily bread.
> ¹²Forgive us our debts,
>   as we also have forgiven our debtors.
> ¹³And lead us not into temptation,
>   but deliver us from the evil one.ᵃ'

¹⁴For if you forgive men when they sin against you, your heavenly Father will also forgive you. ¹⁵But if you do not forgive men their sins, your Father will not forgive your sins.

Fasting

¹⁶"When you fast, do not look somber as the hypocrites do, for they disfigure their faces to show men they are fasting. I tell you the truth, they have received their reward in full. ¹⁷But when you fast, put oil on your head and wash your face, ¹⁸so that it will not be obvious to men that you are fasting, but only to your Father, who is unseen; and your Father, who sees what is done in secret, will reward you.

Treasures in Heaven

¹⁹"Do not store up for yourselves treasures on earth, where moth and rust destroy, and where thieves break in and steal. ²⁰But store up for yourselves treasures in heaven, where moth and rust do not destroy, and where thieves do not break in and steal. ²¹For where your treasure is, there your heart will be also.

²²"The eye is the lamp of the body. If your eyes are good, your whole body will be full of light. ²³But if your eyes are bad, your whole body will be full of darkness. If then the light within you is darkness, how great is that darkness!

²⁴"No one can serve two masters. Either he will hate the one and love the other, or he will be devoted to the one and despise the other. You cannot serve both God and Money.

Do Not Worry

²⁵"Therefore I tell you, do not worry about your life, what you will eat or drink; or about your body, what you will wear. Is not life more important than food, and the body more important than clothes? ²⁶Look at the birds of the air; they do not sow or reap or store away in barns, and yet your heavenly Father feeds them. Are you not much more valuable than they? ²⁷Who of you by worrying can add a single hour to his lifeᵇ?

²⁸"And why do you worry about clothes? See how the lilies of the field grow. They do not labor or spin. ²⁹Yet I tell

Praying Like Jesus

MATTHEW 6:9–13

Someone once approached a teacher and asked her how to cultivate a deeper prayer life. "Say the Lord's Prayer," she replied, "but take an hour to say it." Far from being a quick, rote form, this prayer Jesus taught us can become a life-giving pattern for rich communion. Take time now to slowly and meditatively pray the phrases of this prayer. Consider each clause an invitation to be specific and personal.

See Meeting God in Prayer

ᵃ 13 Or *from evil*; some late manuscripts *one, / for yours is the kingdom and the power and the glory forever. Amen.*   ᵇ 27 Or *single cubit to his height*

Cry of the Heart

MATTHEW 6:33

Righteousness doesn't come naturally or passively to us. We have to seek it. In fact it is something we're told to seek *first*, along with God's kingdom. What are your primary pursuits? What do you value most? What do you think about as you lie awake at night or drive down the road in the middle of the day? What aspect of your life occupies most of your energy? How does your life reflect your desire to seek God's kingdom and experience his righteousness?

See *Meeting God in Everyday Life*

you that not even Solomon in all his splendor was dressed like one of these. ³⁰If that is how God clothes the grass of the field, which is here today and tomorrow is thrown into the fire, will he not much more clothe you, O you of little faith? ³¹So do not worry, saying, 'What shall we eat?' or 'What shall we drink?' or 'What shall we wear?' ³²For the pagans run after all these things, and your heavenly Father knows that you need them. ³³But seek first his kingdom and his righteousness, and all these things will be given to you as well. ³⁴Therefore do not worry about tomorrow, for tomorrow will worry about itself. Each day has enough trouble of its own.

Judging Others

7 "Do not judge, or you too will be judged. ²For in the same way you judge others, you will be judged, and with the measure you use, it will be measured to you.

³"Why do you look at the speck of sawdust in your brother's eye and pay no attention to the plank in your own eye? ⁴How can you say to your brother, 'Let me take the speck out of your eye,' when all the time there is a plank in your own eye? ⁵You hypocrite, first take the plank out of your own eye, and then you will see clearly to remove the speck from your brother's eye.

⁶"Do not give dogs what is sacred; do not throw your pearls to pigs. If you do, they may trample them under their feet, and then turn and tear you to pieces.

Ask, Seek, Knock

⁷"Ask and it will be given to you; seek and you will find; knock and the door will be opened to you. ⁸For everyone who asks receives; he who seeks finds; and to him who knocks, the door will be opened.

⁹"Which of you, if his son asks for bread, will give him a stone? ¹⁰Or if he asks for a fish, will give him a snake? ¹¹If you, then, though you are evil, know how to give good gifts to your children, how much more will your Father in heaven give good gifts to those who ask him! ¹²So in everything, do to others what you would have them do to you, for this sums up the Law and the Prophets.

The Narrow and Wide Gates

¹³"Enter through the narrow gate. For wide is the gate and broad is the road that leads to destruction, and many enter through it. ¹⁴But small is the gate and narrow the road that leads to life, and only a few find it.

A Tree and Its Fruit

¹⁵"Watch out for false prophets. They come to you in sheep's clothing, but inwardly they are ferocious wolves. ¹⁶By their fruit you will recognize them. Do people pick grapes from thornbushes, or figs from thistles? ¹⁷Likewise every good tree bears good fruit, but a bad tree bears bad fruit. ¹⁸A good tree cannot bear bad fruit, and a bad tree cannot bear good fruit. ¹⁹Every tree that does not bear good fruit is cut down and thrown into the fire. ²⁰Thus, by their fruit you will recognize them.

²¹"Not everyone who says to me, 'Lord, Lord,' will enter the kingdom of heaven, but only he who does the will of my Father who is in heaven. ²²Many will say to me on that

day, 'Lord, Lord, did we not prophesy in your name, and in your name drive out demons and perform many miracles?' ²³Then I will tell them plainly, 'I never knew you. Away from me, you evildoers!'

The Wise and Foolish Builders

²⁴"Therefore everyone who hears these words of mine and puts them into practice is like a wise man who built his house on the rock. ²⁵The rain came down, the streams rose, and the winds blew and beat against that house; yet it did not fall, because it had its foundation on the rock. ²⁶But everyone who hears these words of mine and does not put them into practice is like a foolish man who built his house on sand. ²⁷The rain came down, the streams rose, and the winds blew and beat against that house, and it fell with a great crash."

²⁸When Jesus had finished saying these things, the crowds were amazed at his teaching, ²⁹because he taught as one who had authority, and not as their teachers of the law.

The Man With Leprosy

8 When he came down from the mountainside, large crowds followed him. ²A man with leprosy*a* came and knelt before him and said, "Lord, if you are willing, you can make me clean."

³Jesus reached out his hand and touched the man. "I am willing," he said. "Be clean!" Immediately he was cured*b* of his leprosy. ⁴Then Jesus said to him, "See that you don't tell anyone. But go, show yourself to the priest and offer the gift Moses commanded, as a testimony to them."

The Faith of the Centurion

⁵When Jesus had entered Capernaum, a centurion came to him, asking for help. ⁶"Lord," he said, "my servant lies at home paralyzed and in terrible suffering."

⁷Jesus said to him, "I will go and heal him."

⁸The centurion replied, "Lord, I do not deserve to have you come under my roof. But just say the word, and my servant will be healed. ⁹For I myself am a man under authority, with soldiers under me. I tell this one, 'Go,' and he goes; and that one, 'Come,' and he comes. I say to my servant, 'Do this,' and he does it."

¹⁰When Jesus heard this, he was astonished and said to those following him, "I tell you the truth, I have not found anyone in Israel with such great faith. ¹¹I say to you that many will come from the east and the west, and will take their places at the feast with Abraham, Isaac and Jacob in the kingdom of heaven. ¹²But the subjects of the kingdom will be thrown outside, into the darkness, where there will be weeping and gnashing of teeth."

¹³Then Jesus said to the centurion, "Go! It will be done just as you believed it would." And his servant was healed at that very hour.

The Solid Rock

MATTHEW 7:24-27

Picture two houses—one built on rock and one built on sand. You might recall news footage of beachfront houses tumbling into the sea as a storm surge rips the sand from their pilings. Or picture a lighthouse standing firm against pounding waves. Which of these pictures most resembles your life? Does it have characteristics of each? What storms of life are raging against you? In what way do you feel yourself tottering? How can you stand firm? What makes the difference? How can Jesus Christ become your sure foundation, your solid rock? You might crystallize this image by taking paper and colored pencils and drawing a representation of yourself as a house being battered by wind and waves.

See Meeting God in Scripture

---

a 2 The Greek word was used for various diseases affecting the skin—not necessarily leprosy.   b 3 Greek made clean

Connecting Benefits

"What is undoubtedly spoken about the impurities of the soul, Matthew applies to bodily diseases . . . [Matthew] states not merely the benefit conferred by Christ on those sick persons, but the purpose for which he healed their diseases . . . He gave sight to the blind, in order to show that he is 'the light of the world.' He restored life to the dead, to prove that he is 'the resurrection and the life.' Similar observations might be made as to those who were lame or had palsy. Following out this analogy, let us connect those benefits, which Christ bestowed on men in the flesh, with the design which is stated to us by Matthew, that he was sent by the Father, to relieve us from all evil and miseries."

—JOHN CALVIN,
Institutes of the Christian Religion

Jesus Heals Many

¹⁴When Jesus came into Peter's house, he saw Peter's mother-in-law lying in bed with a fever. ¹⁵He touched her hand and the fever left her, and she got up and began to wait on him.

¹⁶When evening came, many who were demon-possessed were brought to him, and he drove out the spirits with a word and healed all the sick. ¹⁷This was to fulfill what was spoken through the prophet Isaiah:

"He took up our infirmities
and carried our diseases."[a]

The Cost of Following Jesus

¹⁸When Jesus saw the crowd around him, he gave orders to cross to the other side of the lake. ¹⁹Then a teacher of the law came to him and said, "Teacher, I will follow you wherever you go."

²⁰Jesus replied, "Foxes have holes and birds of the air have nests, but the Son of Man has no place to lay his head."

²¹Another disciple said to him, "Lord, first let me go and bury my father."

²²But Jesus told him, "Follow me, and let the dead bury their own dead."

Jesus Calms the Storm

²³Then he got into the boat and his disciples followed him. ²⁴Without warning, a furious storm came up on the lake, so that the waves swept over the boat. But Jesus was sleeping. ²⁵The disciples went and woke him, saying, "Lord, save us! We're going to drown!"

²⁶He replied, "You of little faith, why are you so afraid?" Then he got up and rebuked the winds and the waves, and it was completely calm.

²⁷The men were amazed and asked, "What kind of man is this? Even the winds and the waves obey him!"

The Healing of Two Demon-possessed Men

²⁸When he arrived at the other side in the region of the Gadarenes,[b] two demon-possessed men coming from the tombs met him. They were so violent that no one could pass that way. ²⁹"What do you want with us, Son of God?" they shouted. "Have you come here to torture us before the appointed time?"

³⁰Some distance from them a large herd of pigs was feeding. ³¹The demons begged Jesus, "If you drive us out, send us into the herd of pigs."

³²He said to them, "Go!" So they came out and went into the pigs, and the whole herd rushed down the steep bank into the lake and died in the water. ³³Those tending the pigs ran off, went into the town and reported all this, including what had happened to the demon-possessed men. ³⁴Then the whole town went out to meet Jesus. And when they saw him, they pleaded with him to leave their region.

[a] 17 Isaiah 53:4   [b] 28 Some manuscripts *Gergesenes*; others *Gerasenes*

Jesus Heals a Paralytic

9 Jesus stepped into a boat, crossed over and came to his own town. ²Some men brought to him a paralytic, lying on a mat. When Jesus saw their faith, he said to the paralytic, "Take heart, son; your sins are forgiven."

³At this, some of the teachers of the law said to themselves, "This fellow is blaspheming!"

⁴Knowing their thoughts, Jesus said, "Why do you entertain evil thoughts in your hearts? ⁵Which is easier: to say, 'Your sins are forgiven,' or to say, 'Get up and walk'? ⁶But so that you may know that the Son of Man has authority on earth to forgive sins . . ." Then he said to the paralytic, "Get up, take your mat and go home." ⁷And the man got up and went home. ⁸When the crowd saw this, they were filled with awe; and they praised God, who had given such authority to men.

The Calling of Matthew

⁹As Jesus went on from there, he saw a man named Matthew sitting at the tax collector's booth. "Follow me," he told him, and Matthew got up and followed him.

¹⁰While Jesus was having dinner at Matthew's house, many tax collectors and "sinners" came and ate with him and his disciples. ¹¹When the Pharisees saw this, they asked his disciples, "Why does your teacher eat with tax collectors and 'sinners'?"

¹²On hearing this, Jesus said, "It is not the healthy who need a doctor, but the sick. ¹³But go and learn what this means: 'I desire mercy, not sacrifice.'ᵃ For I have not come to call the righteous, but sinners."

Jesus Questioned About Fasting

¹⁴Then John's disciples came and asked him, "How is it that we and the Pharisees fast, but your disciples do not fast?"

¹⁵Jesus answered, "How can the guests of the bridegroom mourn while he is with them? The time will come when the bridegroom will be taken from them; then they will fast.

¹⁶"No one sews a patch of unshrunk cloth on an old garment, for the patch will pull away from the garment, making the tear worse. ¹⁷Neither do men pour new wine into old wineskins. If they do, the skins will burst, the wine will run out and the wineskins will be ruined. No, they pour new wine into new wineskins, and both are preserved."

A Dead Girl and a Sick Woman

¹⁸While he was saying this, a ruler came and knelt before him and said, "My daughter has just died. But come and put your hand on her, and she will live." ¹⁹Jesus got up and went with him, and so did his disciples.

²⁰Just then a woman who had been subject to bleeding for twelve years came up behind him and touched the edge of his cloak. ²¹She said to herself, "If I only touch his cloak, I will be healed."

²²Jesus turned and saw her. "Take heart, daughter," he

Follow Me

MATTHEW 9:9

The invitation Jesus gives to Matthew is remarkably blunt and open-ended: "Follow me." Jesus offers no explanation and no incentives such as, "Follow me, and I'll do this for you. Follow me, and we'll go here and there." This is a blind call, a two-word command that comes without any promise: "Follow me." If Jesus looked into your eyes today and said, "Follow me," how would you respond? What would you have to give up? What would be most difficult to give up? Place yourself in Matthew's shoes and try to imagine the turmoil he must have felt; consider whether you're willing to give such blind allegiance to your Lord.

See Meeting God in Scripture

ᵃ 13 Hosea 6:6

Pouring Light Into Darkness

MATTHEW 9:35–38

As Jesus walks through Judea, he brings people back from the dead, heals others of long-standing diseases, frees some from demons and freely offers the wonderful news that God is at work in the world. He dismantles hell every step of the way, destroying it with the word and works of God.

Your daily passage through the streets to your office and your home may not be quite so dramatic; but how, realistically, can you help to bring God's kingdom? Start by taking notice of the people around you. Become aware of their needs for compassion and for God's love and truth. How can you bring God's light into dark situations as the Holy Spirit works through you?

See Meeting God in Service

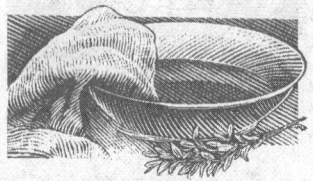

said, "your faith has healed you." And the woman was healed from that moment.

²³When Jesus entered the ruler's house and saw the flute players and the noisy crowd, ²⁴he said, "Go away. The girl is not dead but asleep." But they laughed at him. ²⁵After the crowd had been put outside, he went in and took the girl by the hand, and she got up. ²⁶News of this spread through all that region.

Jesus Heals the Blind and Mute

²⁷As Jesus went on from there, two blind men followed him, calling out, "Have mercy on us, Son of David!"

²⁸When he had gone indoors, the blind men came to him, and he asked them, "Do you believe that I am able to do this?"

"Yes, Lord," they replied.

²⁹Then he touched their eyes and said, "According to your faith will it be done to you"; ³⁰and their sight was restored. Jesus warned them sternly, "See that no one knows about this." ³¹But they went out and spread the news about him all over that region.

³²While they were going out, a man who was demon-possessed and could not talk was brought to Jesus. ³³And when the demon was driven out, the man who had been mute spoke. The crowd was amazed and said, "Nothing like this has ever been seen in Israel."

³⁴But the Pharisees said, "It is by the prince of demons that he drives out demons."

The Workers Are Few

³⁵Jesus went through all the towns and villages, teaching in their synagogues, preaching the good news of the kingdom and healing every disease and sickness. ³⁶When he saw the crowds, he had compassion on them, because they were harassed and helpless, like sheep without a shepherd. ³⁷Then he said to his disciples, "The harvest is plentiful but the workers are few. ³⁸Ask the Lord of the harvest, therefore, to send out workers into his harvest field."

Jesus Sends Out the Twelve

10 He called his twelve disciples to him and gave them authority to drive out evil*ᵃ* spirits and to heal every disease and sickness.

²These are the names of the twelve apostles: first, Simon (who is called Peter) and his brother Andrew; James son of Zebedee, and his brother John; ³Philip and Bartholomew; Thomas and Matthew the tax collector; James son of Alphaeus, and Thaddaeus; ⁴Simon the Zealot and Judas Iscariot, who betrayed him.

⁵These twelve Jesus sent out with the following instructions: "Do not go among the Gentiles or enter any town of the Samaritans. ⁶Go rather to the lost sheep of Israel. ⁷As you go, preach this message: 'The kingdom of heaven is near.' ⁸Heal the sick, raise the dead, cleanse those who have leprosy,*ᵇ* drive out demons. Freely you have received, freely give. ⁹Do not take along any gold or silver or copper

---

ᵃ 1 Greek *unclean*   *ᵇ 8* The Greek word was used for various diseases affecting the skin—not necessarily leprosy.

in your belts; ¹⁰take no bag for the journey, or extra tunic, or sandals or a staff; for the worker is worth his keep.

¹¹"Whatever town or village you enter, search for some worthy person there and stay at his house until you leave. ¹²As you enter the home, give it your greeting. ¹³If the home is deserving, let your peace rest on it; if it is not, let your peace return to you. ¹⁴If anyone will not welcome you or listen to your words, shake the dust off your feet when you leave that home or town. ¹⁵I tell you the truth, it will be more bearable for Sodom and Gomorrah on the day of judgment than for that town. ¹⁶I am sending you out like sheep among wolves. Therefore be as shrewd as snakes and as innocent as doves.

¹⁷"Be on your guard against men; they will hand you over to the local councils and flog you in their synagogues. ¹⁸On my account you will be brought before governors and kings as witnesses to them and to the Gentiles. ¹⁹But when they arrest you, do not worry about what to say or how to say it. At that time you will be given what to say, ²⁰for it will not be you speaking, but the Spirit of your Father speaking through you.

²¹"Brother will betray brother to death, and a father his child; children will rebel against their parents and have them put to death. ²²All men will hate you because of me, but he who stands firm to the end will be saved. ²³When you are persecuted in one place, flee to another. I tell you the truth, you will not finish going through the cities of Israel before the Son of Man comes.

²⁴"A student is not above his teacher, nor a servant above his master. ²⁵It is enough for the student to be like his teacher, and the servant like his master. If the head of the house has been called Beelzebub,ᵃ how much more the members of his household!

²⁶"So do not be afraid of them. There is nothing concealed that will not be disclosed, or hidden that will not be made known. ²⁷What I tell you in the dark, speak in the daylight; what is whispered in your ear, proclaim from the roofs. ²⁸Do not be afraid of those who kill the body but cannot kill the soul. Rather, be afraid of the One who can destroy both soul and body in hell. ²⁹Are not two sparrows sold for a penny ᵇ? Yet not one of them will fall to the ground apart from the will of your Father. ³⁰And even the very hairs of your head are all numbered. ³¹So don't be afraid; you are worth more than many sparrows.

³²"Whoever acknowledges me before men, I will also acknowledge him before my Father in heaven. ³³But whoever disowns me before men, I will disown him before my Father in heaven.

³⁴"Do not suppose that I have come to bring peace to the earth. I did not come to bring peace, but a sword. ³⁵For I have come to turn

> " 'a man against his father,
>   a daughter against her mother,
>   a daughter-in-law against her mother-in-law—
> ³⁶   a man's enemies will be the members of his
>   own household.'ᶜ

³⁷"Anyone who loves his father or mother more than me is not worthy of me; anyone who loves his son or

Where the Pain Comes From

MATTHEW 10:34

"It is true that there is something painful in beginning to practice piety, but this pain does not arise from the beginnings of piety within us, but from the impiety that is still there. If our senses were not opposed to penance and our corruption were not opposed to God's purity, there would be nothing painful about it. As for us, we only suffer in so far as our natural vice resists supernatural grace . . . The cruelest war that God can wage on people in this life is to leave them without the war he came to bring. 'I did not come to bring peace, but a sword.' "

—BLAISE PASCAL,
Pensees

What Do You Hear and See?

MATTHEW 11:4–6

Jesus invites John's followers to tell others what they see and hear. If you were one of them, what report would you give? What stories would you tell? What teaching would you remember? What events would lead you to fall down and worship Jesus? Is there anything about his life and teaching that would embarrass you? Is there anything that would make you want to rebel or turn away? Imagine Jesus looking into your eyes, saying, "Blessed is the one who does not fall away on account of me." How will you respond?

See Meeting God in Scripture

daughter more than me is not worthy of me; ³⁸and anyone who does not take his cross and follow me is not worthy of me. ³⁹Whoever finds his life will lose it, and whoever loses his life for my sake will find it.

⁴⁰"He who receives you receives me, and he who receives me receives the one who sent me. ⁴¹Anyone who receives a prophet because he is a prophet will receive a prophet's reward, and anyone who receives a righteous man because he is a righteous man will receive a righteous man's reward. ⁴²And if anyone gives even a cup of cold water to one of these little ones because he is my disciple, I tell you the truth, he will certainly not lose his reward."

Jesus and John the Baptist

11 After Jesus had finished instructing his twelve disciples, he went on from there to teach and preach in the towns of Galilee.*ᵃ*

²When John heard in prison what Christ was doing, he sent his disciples ³to ask him, "Are you the one who was to come, or should we expect someone else?"

⁴Jesus replied, "Go back and report to John what you hear and see: ⁵The blind receive sight, the lame walk, those who have leprosy*ᵇ* are cured, the deaf hear, the dead are raised, and the good news is preached to the poor. ⁶Blessed is the man who does not fall away on account of me."

⁷As John's disciples were leaving, Jesus began to speak to the crowd about John: "What did you go out into the desert to see? A reed swayed by the wind? ⁸If not, what did you go out to see? A man dressed in fine clothes? No, those who wear fine clothes are in kings' palaces. ⁹Then what did you go out to see? A prophet? Yes, I tell you, and more than a prophet. ¹⁰This is the one about whom it is written:

> " 'I will send my messenger ahead of you,
>   who will prepare your way before you.'*ᶜ*

¹¹I tell you the truth: Among those born of women there has not risen anyone greater than John the Baptist; yet he who is least in the kingdom of heaven is greater than he. ¹²From the days of John the Baptist until now, the kingdom of heaven has been forcefully advancing, and forceful men lay hold of it. ¹³For all the Prophets and the Law prophesied until John. ¹⁴And if you are willing to accept it, he is the Elijah who was to come. ¹⁵He who has ears, let him hear.

¹⁶"To what can I compare this generation? They are like children sitting in the marketplaces and calling out to others:

> ¹⁷" 'We played the flute for you,
>   and you did not dance;
>   we sang a dirge,
>   and you did not mourn.'

¹⁸For John came neither eating nor drinking, and they say, 'He has a demon.' ¹⁹The Son of Man came eating and drinking, and they say, 'Here is a glutton and a drunkard,

---

ᵃ 1 Greek *in their towns*   *ᵇ 5* The Greek word was used for various diseases affecting the skin—not necessarily leprosy.   *ᶜ 10* Mal. 3:1

a friend of tax collectors and "sinners." ' But wisdom is proved right by her actions."

Woe on Unrepentant Cities

²⁰Then Jesus began to denounce the cities in which most of his miracles had been performed, because they did not repent. ²¹"Woe to you, Korazin! Woe to you, Bethsaida! If the miracles that were performed in you had been performed in Tyre and Sidon, they would have repented long ago in sackcloth and ashes. ²²But I tell you, it will be more bearable for Tyre and Sidon on the day of judgment than for you. ²³And you, Capernaum, will you be lifted up to the skies? No, you will go down to the depths.ᵃ If the miracles that were performed in you had been performed in Sodom, it would have remained to this day. ²⁴But I tell you that it will be more bearable for Sodom on the day of judgment than for you."

Rest for the Weary

²⁵At that time Jesus said, "I praise you, Father, Lord of heaven and earth, because you have hidden these things from the wise and learned, and revealed them to little children. ²⁶Yes, Father, for this was your good pleasure.

²⁷"All things have been committed to me by my Father. No one knows the Son except the Father, and no one knows the Father except the Son and those to whom the Son chooses to reveal him.

²⁸"Come to me, all you who are weary and burdened, and I will give you rest. ²⁹Take my yoke upon you and learn from me, for I am gentle and humble in heart, and you will find rest for your souls. ³⁰For my yoke is easy and my burden is light."

Lord of the Sabbath

12 At that time Jesus went through the grainfields on the Sabbath. His disciples were hungry and began to pick some heads of grain and eat them. ²When the Pharisees saw this, they said to him, "Look! Your disciples are doing what is unlawful on the Sabbath."

³He answered, "Haven't you read what David did when he and his companions were hungry? ⁴He entered the house of God, and he and his companions ate the consecrated bread—which was not lawful for them to do, but only for the priests. ⁵Or haven't you read in the Law that on the Sabbath the priests in the temple desecrate the day and yet are innocent? ⁶I tell you that oneᵇ greater than the temple is here. ⁷If you had known what these words mean, 'I desire mercy, not sacrifice,'ᶜ you would not have condemned the innocent. ⁸For the Son of Man is Lord of the Sabbath."

⁹Going on from that place, he went into their synagogue, ¹⁰and a man with a shriveled hand was there. Looking for a reason to accuse Jesus, they asked him, "Is it lawful to heal on the Sabbath?"

¹¹He said to them, "If any of you has a sheep and it falls into a pit on the Sabbath, will you not take hold of it and lift it out? ¹²How much more valuable is a man than a sheep! Therefore it is lawful to do good on the Sabbath."

The Son Revealing the Father

MATTHEW 11:28–30

Imagine yourself bent low under a heavy burden. What burden are you carrying? What is weighing you down? Jesus is saying to you, "Come to me, all you who are weary and burdened, and I will give you rest." Imagine yourself joining a stream of people making their way toward Jesus. When you stand before him, he gently lifts the burden from your back. He encourages you to stand straight, and you feel the weariness leaving your body. "Take my yoke," he says. On your shoulder he places a stole or shawl, a sign of your special ministry in his name. And he hands you a certificate, your own commission from him. What does it say? Write out a copy to keep and to refer to regularly.

See Meeting God in Scripture

ᵃ 23 Greek *Hades*   ᵇ 6 Or *something*; also in verses 41 and 42
ᶜ 7 Hosea 6:6

The World's Enmity Toward God

MATTHEW 12:14

The religious leaders join in a conspiracy to destroy Jesus. They misunderstand and condemn everything he does. He heals people and the Pharisees reproach him for violating the Sabbath. He casts out a demon and his opponents accuse him of using demonic power. Those of us who have come to know Jesus as Savior, Friend and Lord may sometimes forget that the world is in enmity toward Jesus Christ. We pursue God in a world hostile to his name. We pray to a God whom other people ignore or disdain. How does the world's enmity affect your own relationship with God? How does it stifle your witness? How does the world's attitude toward God affect your behavior at home? At work? In your neighborhood? Pray for the courage to take a stand for God even in the midst of hostility.

See Meeting God in Everyday Life

13Then he said to the man, "Stretch out your hand." So he stretched it out and it was completely restored, just as sound as the other. 14But the Pharisees went out and plotted how they might kill Jesus.

God's Chosen Servant

15Aware of this, Jesus withdrew from that place. Many followed him, and he healed all their sick, 16warning them not to tell who he was. 17This was to fulfill what was spoken through the prophet Isaiah:

18"Here is my servant whom I have chosen,
    the one I love, in whom I delight;
I will put my Spirit on him,
    and he will proclaim justice to the nations.
19He will not quarrel or cry out;
    no one will hear his voice in the streets.
20A bruised reed he will not break,
    and a smoldering wick he will not snuff out,
    till he leads justice to victory.
21   In his name the nations will put their hope."[a]

Jesus and Beelzebub

22Then they brought him a demon-possessed man who was blind and mute, and Jesus healed him, so that he could both talk and see. 23All the people were astonished and said, "Could this be the Son of David?"

24But when the Pharisees heard this, they said, "It is only by Beelzebub,[b] the prince of demons, that this fellow drives out demons."

25Jesus knew their thoughts and said to them, "Every kingdom divided against itself will be ruined, and every city or household divided against itself will not stand. 26If Satan drives out Satan, he is divided against himself. How then can his kingdom stand? 27And if I drive out demons by Beelzebub, by whom do your people drive them out? So then, they will be your judges. 28But if I drive out demons by the Spirit of God, then the kingdom of God has come upon you.

29"Or again, how can anyone enter a strong man's house and carry off his possessions unless he first ties up the strong man? Then he can rob his house.

30"He who is not with me is against me, and he who does not gather with me scatters. 31And so I tell you, every sin and blasphemy will be forgiven men, but the blasphemy against the Spirit will not be forgiven. 32Anyone who speaks a word against the Son of Man will be forgiven, but anyone who speaks against the Holy Spirit will not be forgiven, either in this age or in the age to come.

33"Make a tree good and its fruit will be good, or make a tree bad and its fruit will be bad, for a tree is recognized by its fruit. 34You brood of vipers, how can you who are evil say anything good? For out of the overflow of the heart the mouth speaks. 35The good man brings good things out of the good stored up in him, and the evil man brings evil things out of the evil stored up in him. 36But I tell you that men will have to give account on the day of judgment for every careless word they have spoken. 37For by your words

a 21 Isaiah 42:1-4   *b 24* Greek *Beezeboul* or *Beelzeboul*; also in verse 27

you will be acquitted, and by your words you will be condemned."

The Sign of Jonah

³⁸Then some of the Pharisees and teachers of the law said to him, "Teacher, we want to see a miraculous sign from you."

³⁹He answered, "A wicked and adulterous generation asks for a miraculous sign! But none will be given it except the sign of the prophet Jonah. ⁴⁰For as Jonah was three days and three nights in the belly of a huge fish, so the Son of Man will be three days and three nights in the heart of the earth. ⁴¹The men of Nineveh will stand up at the judgment with this generation and condemn it; for they repented at the preaching of Jonah, and now one*a* greater than Jonah is here. ⁴²The Queen of the South will rise at the judgment with this generation and condemn it; for she came from the ends of the earth to listen to Solomon's wisdom, and now one greater than Solomon is here.

⁴³"When an evil*b* spirit comes out of a man, it goes through arid places seeking rest and does not find it. ⁴⁴Then it says, 'I will return to the house I left.' When it arrives, it finds the house unoccupied, swept clean and put in order. ⁴⁵Then it goes and takes with it seven other spirits more wicked than itself, and they go in and live there. And the final condition of that man is worse than the first. That is how it will be with this wicked generation."

Jesus' Mother and Brothers

⁴⁶While Jesus was still talking to the crowd, his mother and brothers stood outside, wanting to speak to him. ⁴⁷Someone told him, "Your mother and brothers are standing outside, wanting to speak to you."*c*

⁴⁸He replied to him, "Who is my mother, and who are my brothers?" ⁴⁹Pointing to his disciples, he said, "Here are my mother and my brothers. ⁵⁰For whoever does the will of my Father in heaven is my brother and sister and mother."

The Parable of the Sower

13 That same day Jesus went out of the house and sat by the lake. ²Such large crowds gathered around him that he got into a boat and sat in it, while all the people stood on the shore. ³Then he told them many things in parables, saying: "A farmer went out to sow his seed. ⁴As he was scattering the seed, some fell along the path, and the birds came and ate it up. ⁵Some fell on rocky places, where it did not have much soil. It sprang up quickly, because the soil was shallow. ⁶But when the sun came up, the plants were scorched, and they withered because they had no root. ⁷Other seed fell among thorns, which grew up and choked the plants. ⁸Still other seed fell on good soil, where it produced a crop—a hundred, sixty or thirty times what was sown. ⁹He who has ears, let him hear."

¹⁰The disciples came to him and asked, "Why do you speak to the people in parables?"

¹¹He replied, "The knowledge of the secrets of the kingdom of heaven has been given to you, but not to them.

The Good Soil

MATTHEW 13:3–8

If weather allows, read this parable outside—preferably near a garden—and consider the application of this parable to your own life. Consider the seeds you have planted. What will give your seeds the best chance to grow? What are the troubles that keep the seeds from growing? What has been carried off without ever growing at all? Which plants have been choked by the thorns of materialism or busyness? What has started well, but never taken root? What has flourished? What will it take to enrich the soil of your heart so that it is fertile? Draw the picture that Jesus describes, and take time to creatively depict each element.

See Meeting God in Scripture

---

a 41 Or *something*; also in verse 42   *b 43* Greek *unclean*   *c 47* Some manuscripts do not have verse 47.

A Balanced Spirituality

MATTHEW 13:18–23

Jesus says that the mark of good soil is that it produces a good crop: a hundred times what was sown, sixty times, or thirty times, but always something. Many Christians sense the tension between *being* and *doing* in the Christian life—between the contemplative life of prayer and the active life of performing good deeds. Yet it's not a matter of choosing one or the other, but of balancing the two.

Which side of the spectrum do you most readily gravitate toward? Are you "running on empty," without a foundation of prayer? Or are you so focused on the inner life that you're neglecting your social responsibility? How can you discern the unique balance of prayer and action to which God is calling you? How can you develop the element that is deficient in your life? What do you need to do to come to your own balance?

See Meeting God in Everyday Life

[12] Whoever has will be given more, and he will have an abundance. Whoever does not have, even what he has will be taken from him. [13] This is why I speak to them in parables:

> "Though seeing, they do not see;
>> though hearing, they do not hear or
>> understand.

[14] In them is fulfilled the prophecy of Isaiah:

> " 'You will be ever hearing but never
>> understanding;
>> you will be ever seeing but never perceiving.
> [15] For this people's heart has become calloused;
>> they hardly hear with their ears,
>> and they have closed their eyes.
> Otherwise they might see with their eyes,
>> hear with their ears,
>> understand with their hearts
> and turn, and I would heal them.'[a]

[16] But blessed are your eyes because they see, and your ears because they hear. [17] For I tell you the truth, many prophets and righteous men longed to see what you see but did not see it, and to hear what you hear but did not hear it.

[18] "Listen then to what the parable of the sower means: [19] When anyone hears the message about the kingdom and does not understand it, the evil one comes and snatches away what was sown in his heart. This is the seed sown along the path. [20] The one who received the seed that fell on rocky places is the man who hears the word and at once receives it with joy. [21] But since he has no root, he lasts only a short time. When trouble or persecution comes because of the word, he quickly falls away. [22] The one who received the seed that fell among the thorns is the man who hears the word, but the worries of this life and the deceitfulness of wealth choke it, making it unfruitful. [23] But the one who received the seed that fell on good soil is the man who hears the word and understands it. He produces a crop, yielding a hundred, sixty or thirty times what was sown."

The Parable of the Weeds

[24] Jesus told them another parable: "The kingdom of heaven is like a man who sowed good seed in his field. [25] But while everyone was sleeping, his enemy came and sowed weeds among the wheat, and went away. [26] When the wheat sprouted and formed heads, then the weeds also appeared.

[27] "The owner's servants came to him and said, 'Sir, didn't you sow good seed in your field? Where then did the weeds come from?'

[28] " 'An enemy did this,' he replied.

"The servants asked him, 'Do you want us to go and pull them up?'

[29] " 'No,' he answered, 'because while you are pulling the weeds, you may root up the wheat with them. [30] Let both grow together until the harvest. At that time I will tell the harvesters: First collect the weeds and tie them in bun-

a 15 Isaiah 6:9,10

dles to be burned; then gather the wheat and bring it into my barn.' "

The Parables of the Mustard Seed and the Yeast

³¹He told them another parable: "The kingdom of heaven is like a mustard seed, which a man took and planted in his field. ³²Though it is the smallest of all your seeds, yet when it grows, it is the largest of garden plants and becomes a tree, so that the birds of the air come and perch in its branches."

³³He told them still another parable: "The kingdom of heaven is like yeast that a woman took and mixed into a large amount*a* of flour until it worked all through the dough."

³⁴Jesus spoke all these things to the crowd in parables; he did not say anything to them without using a parable. ³⁵So was fulfilled what was spoken through the prophet:

> "I will open my mouth in parables,
> I will utter things hidden since the creation of
>   the world."*b*

The Parable of the Weeds Explained

³⁶Then he left the crowd and went into the house. His disciples came to him and said, "Explain to us the parable of the weeds in the field."

³⁷He answered, "The one who sowed the good seed is the Son of Man. ³⁸The field is the world, and the good seed stands for the sons of the kingdom. The weeds are the sons of the evil one, ³⁹and the enemy who sows them is the devil. The harvest is the end of the age, and the harvesters are angels.

⁴⁰"As the weeds are pulled up and burned in the fire, so it will be at the end of the age. ⁴¹The Son of Man will send out his angels, and they will weed out of his kingdom everything that causes sin and all who do evil. ⁴²They will throw them into the fiery furnace, where there will be weeping and gnashing of teeth. ⁴³Then the righteous will shine like the sun in the kingdom of their Father. He who has ears, let him hear.

The Parables of the Hidden Treasure and the Pearl

⁴⁴"The kingdom of heaven is like treasure hidden in a field. When a man found it, he hid it again, and then in his joy went and sold all he had and bought that field.

⁴⁵"Again, the kingdom of heaven is like a merchant looking for fine pearls. ⁴⁶When he found one of great value, he went away and sold everything he had and bought it.

The Parable of the Net

⁴⁷"Once again, the kingdom of heaven is like a net that was let down into the lake and caught all kinds of fish. ⁴⁸When it was full, the fishermen pulled it up on the shore. Then they sat down and collected the good fish in baskets, but threw the bad away. ⁴⁹This is how it will be at the end of the age. The angels will come and separate the wicked from the righteous ⁵⁰and throw them into the fiery

---

A Vintage Find

MATTHEW 13:44–46

An antique table, a vintage bottle of wine, or a rare first-edition book is priced according to the market demand—whatever the buyer is willing to pay for it. Jesus asserts that the kingdom of heaven is so valuable that people would gladly give all they have to possess it. Imagine God standing before you with a gift—the kingdom of heaven—just for you. What will it mean for you if you receive it? But wait, your hands are full! You cannot receive God's gift until you put down what you are holding. What is it? Are you willing to put it down to receive God's gift?

See Meeting God in Scripture

---

a 33 Greek *three satas* (probably about 1/2 bushel or 22 liters) *b 35* Psalm 78:2

Looking Up to Heaven

MATTHEW 14:13–21

The Christian life is not a matter of doing great things *for* God. That's religion. Christianity is doing great things *with* God. That's the life of Jesus Christ in us. How can you adopt a spirit of "looking up to heaven" as you go through your day? Some Christian traditions have created symbols for this purpose (a crucifix, a cross worn around the neck, a painting of a Biblical scene, and so on). If you were to create a symbol that would remind you of your dependence on God, what would it be? Where would you put it? What are some other things you could do to maintain an attitude of consistently "looking up to heaven"?

See *Meeting God in Everyday Life*

furnace, where there will be weeping and gnashing of teeth.

[51] "Have you understood all these things?" Jesus asked.

"Yes," they replied.

[52] He said to them, "Therefore every teacher of the law who has been instructed about the kingdom of heaven is like the owner of a house who brings out of his storeroom new treasures as well as old."

A Prophet Without Honor

[53] When Jesus had finished these parables, he moved on from there. [54] Coming to his hometown, he began teaching the people in their synagogue, and they were amazed. "Where did this man get this wisdom and these miraculous powers?" they asked. [55] "Isn't this the carpenter's son? Isn't his mother's name Mary, and aren't his brothers James, Joseph, Simon and Judas? [56] Aren't all his sisters with us? Where then did this man get all these things?" [57] And they took offense at him.

But Jesus said to them, "Only in his hometown and in his own house is a prophet without honor."

[58] And he did not do many miracles there because of their lack of faith.

John the Baptist Beheaded

14 At that time Herod the tetrarch heard the reports about Jesus, [2] and he said to his attendants, "This is John the Baptist; he has risen from the dead! That is why miraculous powers are at work in him."

[3] Now Herod had arrested John and bound him and put him in prison because of Herodias, his brother Philip's wife, [4] for John had been saying to him: "It is not lawful for you to have her." [5] Herod wanted to kill John, but he was afraid of the people, because they considered him a prophet.

[6] On Herod's birthday the daughter of Herodias danced for them and pleased Herod so much [7] that he promised with an oath to give her whatever she asked. [8] Prompted by her mother, she said, "Give me here on a platter the head of John the Baptist." [9] The king was distressed, but because of his oaths and his dinner guests, he ordered that her request be granted [10] and had John beheaded in the prison. [11] His head was brought in on a platter and given to the girl, who carried it to her mother. [12] John's disciples came and took his body and buried it. Then they went and told Jesus.

Jesus Feeds the Five Thousand

[13] When Jesus heard what had happened, he withdrew by boat privately to a solitary place. Hearing of this, the crowds followed him on foot from the towns. [14] When Jesus landed and saw a large crowd, he had compassion on them and healed their sick.

[15] As evening approached, the disciples came to him and said, "This is a remote place, and it's already getting late. Send the crowds away, so they can go to the villages and buy themselves some food."

[16] Jesus replied, "They do not need to go away. You give them something to eat."

¹⁷"We have here only five loaves of bread and two fish," they answered.

¹⁸"Bring them here to me," he said. ¹⁹And he directed the people to sit down on the grass. Taking the five loaves and the two fish and looking up to heaven, he gave thanks and broke the loaves. Then he gave them to the disciples, and the disciples gave them to the people. ²⁰They all ate and were satisfied, and the disciples picked up twelve basketfuls of broken pieces that were left over. ²¹The number of those who ate was about five thousand men, besides women and children.

Jesus Walks on the Water

²²Immediately Jesus made the disciples get into the boat and go on ahead of him to the other side, while he dismissed the crowd. ²³After he had dismissed them, he went up on a mountainside by himself to pray. When evening came, he was there alone, ²⁴but the boat was already a considerable distance[a] from land, buffeted by the waves because the wind was against it.

²⁵During the fourth watch of the night Jesus went out to them, walking on the lake. ²⁶When the disciples saw him walking on the lake, they were terrified. "It's a ghost," they said, and cried out in fear.

²⁷But Jesus immediately said to them: "Take courage! It is I. Don't be afraid."

²⁸"Lord, if it's you," Peter replied, "tell me to come to you on the water."

²⁹"Come," he said.

Then Peter got down out of the boat, walked on the water and came toward Jesus. ³⁰But when he saw the wind, he was afraid and, beginning to sink, cried out, "Lord, save me!"

³¹Immediately Jesus reached out his hand and caught him. "You of little faith," he said, "why did you doubt?"

³²And when they climbed into the boat, the wind died down. ³³Then those who were in the boat worshiped him, saying, "Truly you are the Son of God."

³⁴When they had crossed over, they landed at Gennesaret. ³⁵And when the men of that place recognized Jesus, they sent word to all the surrounding country. People brought all their sick to him ³⁶and begged him to let the sick just touch the edge of his cloak, and all who touched him were healed.

Clean and Unclean

15 Then some Pharisees and teachers of the law came to Jesus from Jerusalem and asked, ²"Why do your disciples break the tradition of the elders? They don't wash their hands before they eat!"

³Jesus replied, "And why do you break the command of God for the sake of your tradition? ⁴For God said, 'Honor your father and mother'[b] and 'Anyone who curses his father or mother must be put to death.'[c] ⁵But you say that if a man says to his father or mother, 'Whatever help you might otherwise have received from me is a gift devoted to God,' ⁶he is not to 'honor his father[d]' with it. Thus you nullify the word of God for the sake of your tradition. ⁷You

Full Reliance

MATTHEW 14:22–33

"The wind was actually boisterous, the waves were actually high, but Peter did not see them at first. He did not reckon with them, he simply recognized his Lord and stepped out in recognition of him, and walked on the water. Then he began to reckon with the actual things, and down he went instantly. Why could not our Lord have enabled him to walk at the bottom of the waves as well as on the top of them? . . . We step right out on God over some things, then self-consideration enters in and down we go . . . Immediately you look at [circumstances and] you are overwhelmed, you cannot recognize Jesus, and the rebuke comes: 'Wherefore didst thou doubt?' Let actual circumstances be what they may, keep recognizing Jesus, maintain complete reliance on him."

—OSWALD CHAMBERS,
My Utmost for His Highest

---

a 24 Greek *many stadia*   *b* 4 Exodus 20:12; Deut. 5:16   *c* 4 Exodus 21:17; Lev. 20:9   *d* 6 Some manuscripts *father or his mother*

Loving the Whole Person

MATTHEW 15:29–38

The physical, practical nature of Jesus' ministry is remarkable. Not only does he teach deep truths, but he also heals people who are sick or disabled and takes time to feed a crowd of hungry people.

In what ways can you minister to people—caring for the "whole person"—as Jesus did? To whom might you reach out today? While you may or may not have the gift of healing, what gifts do you have that you can use to relieve hardship and suffering? Do you share in Jesus' compassion? If not, what might be standing in your way?

See Meeting God in Service

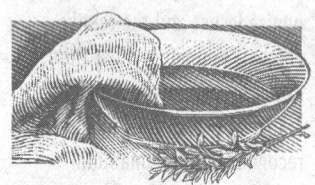

hypocrites! Isaiah was right when he prophesied about you:

> [8] " 'These people honor me with their lips,
> but their hearts are far from me.
> [9] They worship me in vain;
> their teachings are but rules taught by men.'*a*"

[10] Jesus called the crowd to him and said, "Listen and understand. [11] What goes into a man's mouth does not make him 'unclean,' but what comes out of his mouth, that is what makes him 'unclean.' "

[12] Then the disciples came to him and asked, "Do you know that the Pharisees were offended when they heard this?"

[13] He replied, "Every plant that my heavenly Father has not planted will be pulled up by the roots. [14] Leave them; they are blind guides.*b* If a blind man leads a blind man, both will fall into a pit."

[15] Peter said, "Explain the parable to us."

[16] "Are you still so dull?" Jesus asked them. [17] "Don't you see that whatever enters the mouth goes into the stomach and then out of the body? [18] But the things that come out of the mouth come from the heart, and these make a man 'unclean.' [19] For out of the heart come evil thoughts, murder, adultery, sexual immorality, theft, false testimony, slander. [20] These are what make a man 'unclean'; but eating with unwashed hands does not make him 'unclean.' "

The Faith of the Canaanite Woman

[21] Leaving that place, Jesus withdrew to the region of Tyre and Sidon. [22] A Canaanite woman from that vicinity came to him, crying out, "Lord, Son of David, have mercy on me! My daughter is suffering terribly from demon-possession."

[23] Jesus did not answer a word. So his disciples came to him and urged him, "Send her away, for she keeps crying out after us."

[24] He answered, "I was sent only to the lost sheep of Israel."

[25] The woman came and knelt before him. "Lord, help me!" she said.

[26] He replied, "It is not right to take the children's bread and toss it to their dogs."

[27] "Yes, Lord," she said, "but even the dogs eat the crumbs that fall from their masters' table."

[28] Then Jesus answered, "Woman, you have great faith! Your request is granted." And her daughter was healed from that very hour.

Jesus Feeds the Four Thousand

[29] Jesus left there and went along the Sea of Galilee. Then he went up on a mountainside and sat down. [30] Great crowds came to him, bringing the lame, the blind, the crippled, the mute and many others, and laid them at his feet; and he healed them. [31] The people were amazed when they saw the mute speaking, the crippled made well, the lame walking and the blind seeing. And they praised the God of Israel.

[32] Jesus called his disciples to him and said, "I have compassion for these people; they have already been with me

a 9 Isaiah 29:13   *b 14* Some manuscripts *guides of the blind*

three days and have nothing to eat. I do not want to send them away hungry, or they may collapse on the way."

[33]His disciples answered, "Where could we get enough bread in this remote place to feed such a crowd?"

[34]"How many loaves do you have?" Jesus asked.

"Seven," they replied, "and a few small fish."

[35]He told the crowd to sit down on the ground. [36]Then he took the seven loaves and the fish, and when he had given thanks, he broke them and gave them to the disciples, and they in turn to the people. [37]They all ate and were satisfied. Afterward the disciples picked up seven basketfuls of broken pieces that were left over. [38]The number of those who ate was four thousand, besides women and children. [39]After Jesus had sent the crowd away, he got into the boat and went to the vicinity of Magadan.

The Demand for a Sign

16 The Pharisees and Sadducees came to Jesus and tested him by asking him to show them a sign from heaven.

[2]He replied,[a] "When evening comes, you say, 'It will be fair weather, for the sky is red,' [3]and in the morning, 'Today it will be stormy, for the sky is red and overcast.' You know how to interpret the appearance of the sky, but you cannot interpret the signs of the times. [4]A wicked and adulterous generation looks for a miraculous sign, but none will be given it except the sign of Jonah." Jesus then left them and went away.

The Yeast of the Pharisees and Sadducees

[5]When they went across the lake, the disciples forgot to take bread. [6]"Be careful," Jesus said to them. "Be on your guard against the yeast of the Pharisees and Sadducees."

[7]They discussed this among themselves and said, "It is because we didn't bring any bread."

[8]Aware of their discussion, Jesus asked, "You of little faith, why are you talking among yourselves about having no bread? [9]Do you still not understand? Don't you remember the five loaves for the five thousand, and how many basketfuls you gathered? [10]Or the seven loaves for the four thousand, and how many basketfuls you gathered? [11]How is it you don't understand that I was not talking to you about bread? But be on your guard against the yeast of the Pharisees and Sadducees." [12]Then they understood that he was not telling them to guard against the yeast used in bread, but against the teaching of the Pharisees and Sadducees.

Peter's Confession of Christ

[13]When Jesus came to the region of Caesarea Philippi, he asked his disciples, "Who do people say the Son of Man is?"

[14]They replied, "Some say John the Baptist; others say Elijah; and still others, Jeremiah or one of the prophets."

[15]"But what about you?" he asked. "Who do you say I am?"

[16]Simon Peter answered, "You are the Christ,[b] the Son of the living God."

What Really Matters

MATTHEW 16:1–6

When Jesus chastises the religious leaders of his day for failing to read "the signs of the times," he's referring to their preoccupation with rules and their lack of spiritual insight. The Pharisees and Sadducees, obsessed with arguing the finer points of the law, missed seeing the very embodiment of the law, Jesus Christ himself.

What issues preoccupy you today? Do you tend to focus on central issues or peripheral ones—the big picture or the details? How does getting caught up in rules distort your faith or disrupt community life? Make a list of the actual rules you live by, not just the rules you *think* should govern your life. Do they reflect Jesus' priorities? Seek God's guidance as you reflect on them.

See Meeting God in Everyday Life

A Chance to Grow

MATTHEW 16:24–26

"Individuality is the husk of the personal life. Individuality is all elbows, it separates and isolates . . . but individuality must go in order that the personal life may come out and be brought into fellowship with God . . . God wants to bring you into union with himself, but unless you are willing to give up your right to deny yourself he cannot. 'Let him deny himself'—deny his independent right to himself, then the real life has a chance to grow."

—OSWALD CHAMBERS,
My Utmost for His Highest

17Jesus replied, "Blessed are you, Simon son of Jonah, for this was not revealed to you by man, but by my Father in heaven. 18And I tell you that you are Peter,ᵃ and on this rock I will build my church, and the gates of Hadesᵇ will not overcome it.ᶜ 19I will give you the keys of the kingdom of heaven; whatever you bind on earth will beᵈ bound in heaven, and whatever you loose on earth will beᵈ loosed in heaven." 20Then he warned his disciples not to tell anyone that he was the Christ.

Jesus Predicts His Death

21From that time on Jesus began to explain to his disciples that he must go to Jerusalem and suffer many things at the hands of the elders, chief priests and teachers of the law, and that he must be killed and on the third day be raised to life.

22Peter took him aside and began to rebuke him. "Never, Lord!" he said. "This shall never happen to you!"

23Jesus turned and said to Peter, "Get behind me, Satan! You are a stumbling block to me; you do not have in mind the things of God, but the things of men."

24Then Jesus said to his disciples, "If anyone would come after me, he must deny himself and take up his cross and follow me. 25For whoever wants to save his lifeᵉ will lose it, but whoever loses his life for me will find it. 26What good will it be for a man if he gains the whole world, yet forfeits his soul? Or what can a man give in exchange for his soul? 27For the Son of Man is going to come in his Father's glory with his angels, and then he will reward each person according to what he has done. 28I tell you the truth, some who are standing here will not taste death before they see the Son of Man coming in his kingdom."

The Transfiguration

17 After six days Jesus took with him Peter, James and John the brother of James, and led them up a high mountain by themselves. 2There he was transfigured before them. His face shone like the sun, and his clothes became as white as the light. 3Just then there appeared before them Moses and Elijah, talking with Jesus.

4Peter said to Jesus, "Lord, it is good for us to be here. If you wish, I will put up three shelters—one for you, one for Moses and one for Elijah."

5While he was still speaking, a bright cloud enveloped them, and a voice from the cloud said, "This is my Son, whom I love; with him I am well pleased. Listen to him!"

6When the disciples heard this, they fell facedown to the ground, terrified. 7But Jesus came and touched them. "Get up," he said. "Don't be afraid." 8When they looked up, they saw no one except Jesus.

9As they were coming down the mountain, Jesus instructed them, "Don't tell anyone what you have seen, until the Son of Man has been raised from the dead."

10The disciples asked him, "Why then do the teachers of the law say that Elijah must come first?"

11Jesus replied, "To be sure, Elijah comes and will re-

ᵃ *18* Peter means *rock.*   ᵇ *18* Or *hell*   ᶜ *18* Or *not prove stronger than it*
ᵈ *19* Or *have been*   ᵉ *25* The Greek word means either *life* or *soul*; also in verse 26.

store all things. ¹²But I tell you, Elijah has already come, and they did not recognize him, but have done to him everything they wished. In the same way the Son of Man is going to suffer at their hands." ¹³Then the disciples understood that he was talking to them about John the Baptist.

The Healing of a Boy With a Demon

¹⁴When they came to the crowd, a man approached Jesus and knelt before him. ¹⁵"Lord, have mercy on my son," he said. "He has seizures and is suffering greatly. He often falls into the fire or into the water. ¹⁶I brought him to your disciples, but they could not heal him."

¹⁷"O unbelieving and perverse generation," Jesus replied, "how long shall I stay with you? How long shall I put up with you? Bring the boy here to me." ¹⁸Jesus rebuked the demon, and it came out of the boy, and he was healed from that moment.

¹⁹Then the disciples came to Jesus in private and asked, "Why couldn't we drive it out?"

²⁰He replied, "Because you have so little faith. I tell you the truth, if you have faith as small as a mustard seed, you can say to this mountain, 'Move from here to there' and it will move. Nothing will be impossible for you.ᵃ"

²²When they came together in Galilee, he said to them, "The Son of Man is going to be betrayed into the hands of men. ²³They will kill him, and on the third day he will be raised to life." And the disciples were filled with grief.

The Temple Tax

²⁴After Jesus and his disciples arrived in Capernaum, the collectors of the two-drachma tax came to Peter and asked, "Doesn't your teacher pay the temple taxᵇ?"

²⁵"Yes, he does," he replied.

When Peter came into the house, Jesus was the first to speak. "What do you think, Simon?" he asked. "From whom do the kings of the earth collect duty and taxes—from their own sons or from others?"

²⁶"From others," Peter answered.

"Then the sons are exempt," Jesus said to him. ²⁷"But so that we may not offend them, go to the lake and throw out your line. Take the first fish you catch; open its mouth and you will find a four-drachma coin. Take it and give it to them for my tax and yours."

The Greatest in the Kingdom of Heaven

18 At that time the disciples came to Jesus and asked, "Who is the greatest in the kingdom of heaven?"

²He called a little child and had him stand among them. ³And he said: "I tell you the truth, unless you change and become like little children, you will never enter the kingdom of heaven. ⁴Therefore, whoever humbles himself like this child is the greatest in the kingdom of heaven.

⁵"And whoever welcomes a little child like this in my name welcomes me. ⁶But if anyone causes one of these little ones who believe in me to sin, it would be better for him to have a large millstone hung around his neck and to be drowned in the depths of the sea.

A Child's Heart

MATTHEW 18:1–5

Spend time with your children, visit a playground or volunteer to assist in a church school class. Prayerfully watch the children interact and play. What quality in children does Jesus prize so highly? How can you humble yourself like a child? What does it mean to "welcome" a child in Jesus' name? Why do you think that Jesus never said, "Unless you become like an adult . . ."? Why did he choose children to be our example? How can you become childlike without becoming childish? Pray slowly and thoughtfully through Psalm 131.

ᵃ 20 Some manuscripts *you.* ²¹*But this kind does not go out except by prayer and fasting.* ᵇ 24 Greek *the two drachmas*

The Incredible Freedom of Forgiveness

MATTHEW 18:21–34

As Christians we are to "re-flect" God's Spirit so that others will see and know God. In this passage Jesus asks us to lavish the same forgiveness on others that God has so graciously given to us. Take a few moments to put yourself in the first debtor's position: How does it feel to be forgiven such a large sum? Imagine the weight removed from your shoulders as the entire debt is canceled. Now think of those to whom you can offer the same forgiveness that you have received from God.

See Meeting God in Prayer

⁷"Woe to the world because of the things that cause people to sin! Such things must come, but woe to the man through whom they come! ⁸If your hand or your foot causes you to sin, cut it off and throw it away. It is better for you to enter life maimed or crippled than to have two hands or two feet and be thrown into eternal fire. ⁹And if your eye causes you to sin, gouge it out and throw it away. It is better for you to enter life with one eye than to have two eyes and be thrown into the fire of hell.

The Parable of the Lost Sheep

¹⁰"See that you do not look down on one of these little ones. For I tell you that their angels in heaven always see the face of my Father in heaven.ᵃ

¹²"What do you think? If a man owns a hundred sheep, and one of them wanders away, will he not leave the ninety-nine on the hills and go to look for the one that wandered off? ¹³And if he finds it, I tell you the truth, he is happier about that one sheep than about the ninety-nine that did not wander off. ¹⁴In the same way your Father in heaven is not willing that any of these little ones should be lost.

A Brother Who Sins Against You

¹⁵"If your brother sins against you,ᵇ go and show him his fault, just between the two of you. If he listens to you, you have won your brother over. ¹⁶But if he will not listen, take one or two others along, so that 'every matter may be established by the testimony of two or three witnesses.'ᶜ ¹⁷If he refuses to listen to them, tell it to the church; and if he refuses to listen even to the church, treat him as you would a pagan or a tax collector.

¹⁸"I tell you the truth, whatever you bind on earth will beᵈ bound in heaven, and whatever you loose on earth will beᵈ loosed in heaven.

¹⁹"Again, I tell you that if two of you on earth agree about anything you ask for, it will be done for you by my Father in heaven. ²⁰For where two or three come together in my name, there am I with them."

The Parable of the Unmerciful Servant

²¹Then Peter came to Jesus and asked, "Lord, how many times shall I forgive my brother when he sins against me? Up to seven times?"

²²Jesus answered, "I tell you, not seven times, but seventy-seven times.ᵉ

²³"Therefore, the kingdom of heaven is like a king who wanted to settle accounts with his servants. ²⁴As he began the settlement, a man who owed him ten thousand talentsᶠ was brought to him. ²⁵Since he was not able to pay, the master ordered that he and his wife and his children and all that he had be sold to repay the debt.

²⁶"The servant fell on his knees before him. 'Be patient with me,' he begged, 'and I will pay back everything.' ²⁷The servant's master took pity on him, canceled the debt and let him go.

²⁸"But when that servant went out, he found one of his

ᵃ 10 Some manuscripts *heaven.* ¹¹*The Son of Man came to save what was lost.*
ᵇ 15 Some manuscripts do not have *against you.*   ᶜ 16 Deut. 19:15   ᵈ 18 Or *have been*   ᵉ 22 Or *seventy times seven*   ᶠ 24 That is, millions of dollars

fellow servants who owed him a hundred denarii.ᵃ He grabbed him and began to choke him. 'Pay back what you owe me!' he demanded.

²⁹"His fellow servant fell to his knees and begged him, 'Be patient with me, and I will pay you back.'

³⁰"But he refused. Instead, he went off and had the man thrown into prison until he could pay the debt. ³¹When the other servants saw what had happened, they were greatly distressed and went and told their master everything that had happened.

³²"Then the master called the servant in. 'You wicked servant,' he said, 'I canceled all that debt of yours because you begged me to. ³³Shouldn't you have had mercy on your fellow servant just as I had on you?' ³⁴In anger his master turned him over to the jailers to be tortured, until he should pay back all he owed.

³⁵"This is how my heavenly Father will treat each of you unless you forgive your brother from your heart."

Divorce

19 When Jesus had finished saying these things, he left Galilee and went into the region of Judea to the other side of the Jordan. ²Large crowds followed him, and he healed them there.

³Some Pharisees came to him to test him. They asked, "Is it lawful for a man to divorce his wife for any and every reason?"

⁴"Haven't you read," he replied, "that at the beginning the Creator 'made them male and female,'ᵇ ⁵and said, 'For this reason a man will leave his father and mother and be united to his wife, and the two will become one flesh'ᶜ? ⁶So they are no longer two, but one. Therefore what God has joined together, let man not separate."

⁷"Why then," they asked, "did Moses command that a man give his wife a certificate of divorce and send her away?"

⁸Jesus replied, "Moses permitted you to divorce your wives because your hearts were hard. But it was not this way from the beginning. ⁹I tell you that anyone who divorces his wife, except for marital unfaithfulness, and marries another woman commits adultery."

¹⁰The disciples said to him, "If this is the situation between a husband and wife, it is better not to marry."

¹¹Jesus replied, "Not everyone can accept this word, but only those to whom it has been given. ¹²For some are eunuchs because they were born that way; others were made that way by men; and others have renounced marriageᵈ because of the kingdom of heaven. The one who can accept this should accept it."

The Little Children and Jesus

¹³Then little children were brought to Jesus for him to place his hands on them and pray for them. But the disciples rebuked those who brought them.

¹⁴Jesus said, "Let the little children come to me, and do not hinder them, for the kingdom of heaven belongs to such as these." ¹⁵When he had placed his hands on them, he went on from there.

Strong Hearts, Soft Hearts

MATTHEW 19:1–12

Moses had allowed divorce primarily to protect the vulnerable women who were put away without due cause. But Jesus goes to the heart of the matter.

After Jesus' words on marriage and divorce, we may conclude that marriage is not for the hardhearted, or as the disciples conclude, for the fainthearted (see v.10). Marriage, often the most difficult of human relationships, requires grace-filled, soft hearts to succeed, and even more important, to honor the Creator who made men and women "male and female." Make your own marriage—or those of friends or family members—a subject of your prayers today. Pray that God will give both partners strong, soft hearts for each other and a generous measure of divine grace.

See Meeting God in Community

ᵃ 28 That is, a few dollars   ᵇ 4 Gen. 1:27   ᶜ 5 Gen. 2:24   ᵈ 12 Or *have made themselves eunuchs*

The Same Reward

MATTHEW 20:1–16

How would you feel if you were one of the first workers to be hired? Imagine your excitement when you see the latecomers receiving a generous reward, and then your frustration when you receive the same amount. Now place yourself in the position of the latecomers: How do you feel receiving your reward and then hearing the early arrivals complain about how you've been treated? Next put yourself in the position of the landowner: What goes through your mind as some of the workers protest your policies? With which group do you most identify? What can you learn from the reaction of the other workers? What might you be missing by focusing only on your own perspective?

See *Meeting God in Scripture*

The Rich Young Man

¹⁶Now a man came up to Jesus and asked, "Teacher, what good thing must I do to get eternal life?"

¹⁷"Why do you ask me about what is good?" Jesus replied. "There is only One who is good. If you want to enter life, obey the commandments."

¹⁸"Which ones?" the man inquired.

Jesus replied, " 'Do not murder, do not commit adultery, do not steal, do not give false testimony, ¹⁹honor your father and mother,'*ᵃ* and 'love your neighbor as yourself.'*ᵇ*

²⁰"All these I have kept," the young man said. "What do I still lack?"

²¹Jesus answered, "If you want to be perfect, go, sell your possessions and give to the poor, and you will have treasure in heaven. Then come, follow me."

²²When the young man heard this, he went away sad, because he had great wealth.

²³Then Jesus said to his disciples, "I tell you the truth, it is hard for a rich man to enter the kingdom of heaven. ²⁴Again I tell you, it is easier for a camel to go through the eye of a needle than for a rich man to enter the kingdom of God."

²⁵When the disciples heard this, they were greatly astonished and asked, "Who then can be saved?"

²⁶Jesus looked at them and said, "With man this is impossible, but with God all things are possible."

²⁷Peter answered him, "We have left everything to follow you! What then will there be for us?"

²⁸Jesus said to them, "I tell you the truth, at the renewal of all things, when the Son of Man sits on his glorious throne, you who have followed me will also sit on twelve thrones, judging the twelve tribes of Israel. ²⁹And everyone who has left houses or brothers or sisters or father or mother*ᶜ* or children or fields for my sake will receive a hundred times as much and will inherit eternal life. ³⁰But many who are first will be last, and many who are last will be first.

The Parable of the Workers in the Vineyard

20 "For the kingdom of heaven is like a landowner who went out early in the morning to hire men to work in his vineyard. ²He agreed to pay them a denarius for the day and sent them into his vineyard.

³"About the third hour he went out and saw others standing in the marketplace doing nothing. ⁴He told them, 'You also go and work in my vineyard, and I will pay you whatever is right.' ⁵So they went.

"He went out again about the sixth hour and the ninth hour and did the same thing. ⁶About the eleventh hour he went out and found still others standing around. He asked them, 'Why have you been standing here all day long doing nothing?'

⁷" 'Because no one has hired us,' they answered.

"He said to them, 'You also go and work in my vineyard.'

⁸"When evening came, the owner of the vineyard said to his foreman, 'Call the workers and pay them their wages, beginning with the last ones hired and going on to the first.'

ᵃ19 Exodus 20:12–16; Deut. 5:16–20   *ᵇ19* Lev. 19:18   *ᶜ29* Some manuscripts *mother or wife*

⁹"The workers who were hired about the eleventh hour came and each received a denarius. ¹⁰So when those came who were hired first, they expected to receive more. But each one of them also received a denarius. ¹¹When they received it, they began to grumble against the landowner. ¹²'These men who were hired last worked only one hour,' they said, 'and you have made them equal to us who have borne the burden of the work and the heat of the day.'

¹³"But he answered one of them, 'Friend, I am not being unfair to you. Didn't you agree to work for a denarius? ¹⁴Take your pay and go. I want to give the man who was hired last the same as I gave you. ¹⁵Don't I have the right to do what I want with my own money? Or are you envious because I am generous?'

¹⁶"So the last will be first, and the first will be last."

Jesus Again Predicts His Death

¹⁷Now as Jesus was going up to Jerusalem, he took the twelve disciples aside and said to them, ¹⁸"We are going up to Jerusalem, and the Son of Man will be betrayed to the chief priests and the teachers of the law. They will condemn him to death ¹⁹and will turn him over to the Gentiles to be mocked and flogged and crucified. On the third day he will be raised to life!"

A Mother's Request

²⁰Then the mother of Zebedee's sons came to Jesus with her sons and, kneeling down, asked a favor of him.

²¹"What is it you want?" he asked.

She said, "Grant that one of these two sons of mine may sit at your right and the other at your left in your kingdom."

²²"You don't know what you are asking," Jesus said to them. "Can you drink the cup I am going to drink?"

"We can," they answered.

²³Jesus said to them, "You will indeed drink from my cup, but to sit at my right or left is not for me to grant. These places belong to those for whom they have been prepared by my Father."

²⁴When the ten heard about this, they were indignant with the two brothers. ²⁵Jesus called them together and said, "You know that the rulers of the Gentiles lord it over them, and their high officials exercise authority over them. ²⁶Not so with you. Instead, whoever wants to become great among you must be your servant, ²⁷and whoever wants to be first must be your slave— ²⁸just as the Son of Man did not come to be served, but to serve, and to give his life as a ransom for many."

Two Blind Men Receive Sight

²⁹As Jesus and his disciples were leaving Jericho, a large crowd followed him. ³⁰Two blind men were sitting by the roadside, and when they heard that Jesus was going by, they shouted, "Lord, Son of David, have mercy on us!"

³¹The crowd rebuked them and told them to be quiet, but they shouted all the louder, "Lord, Son of David, have mercy on us!"

³²Jesus stopped and called them. "What do you want me to do for you?" he asked.

³³"Lord," they answered, "we want our sight."

The Quest for Greatness

MATTHEW 20:20–28

The human quest for greatness and power has caused untold meaningless bloodshed. But ironically God's call to servanthood caused the most meaningful bloodshed of all—Jesus' own sacrifice on the cross.

If you want to know the true aim and direction of your life, ask yourself these questions: Where do I expend my greatest effort and energy? Is it to dominate others and gain control? Or is it to love and serve them? What is more important to me—taking charge, or meeting needs? Do I prefer to act in secret or do I have a burning desire to be recognized? What would Jesus say about your answers?

See Meeting God in Service

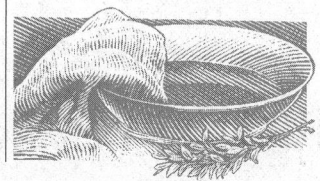

Palm Sunday

MATTHEW 21:1-11

Imagine yourself in the crowd as Jesus rides into Jerusalem. You are in the street near the city gate—a street packed with people. The shouts and cries around you are deafening. The smell of unwashed humanity mingles with the aroma of the smoke blowing down from the temple sacrifices. "What is happening?" you ask some of the others in the crowd. Why are they there? Why are they waving branches and shouting? What do you feel as Jesus rides by? What do you want to do?

See Meeting God in Scripture

34Jesus had compassion on them and touched their eyes. Immediately they received their sight and followed him.

The Triumphal Entry

21 As they approached Jerusalem and came to Bethphage on the Mount of Olives, Jesus sent two disciples, **2**saying to them, "Go to the village ahead of you, and at once you will find a donkey tied there, with her colt by her. Untie them and bring them to me. **3**If anyone says anything to you, tell him that the Lord needs them, and he will send them right away."

4This took place to fulfill what was spoken through the prophet:

5"Say to the Daughter of Zion,
  'See, your king comes to you,
gentle and riding on a donkey,
  on a colt, the foal of a donkey.' "*a*

6The disciples went and did as Jesus had instructed them. **7**They brought the donkey and the colt, placed their cloaks on them, and Jesus sat on them. **8**A very large crowd spread their cloaks on the road, while others cut branches from the trees and spread them on the road. **9**The crowds that went ahead of him and those that followed shouted,

"Hosanna*b* to the Son of David!"

"Blessed is he who comes in the name of the Lord!"*c*

"Hosanna*b* in the highest!"

10When Jesus entered Jerusalem, the whole city was stirred and asked, "Who is this?"
11The crowds answered, "This is Jesus, the prophet from Nazareth in Galilee."

Jesus at the Temple

12Jesus entered the temple area and drove out all who were buying and selling there. He overturned the tables of the money changers and the benches of those selling doves. **13**"It is written," he said to them, " 'My house will be called a house of prayer,'*d* but you are making it a 'den of robbers.'*e*"

14The blind and the lame came to him at the temple, and he healed them. **15**But when the chief priests and the teachers of the law saw the wonderful things he did and the children shouting in the temple area, "Hosanna to the Son of David," they were indignant.

16"Do you hear what these children are saying?" they asked him.

"Yes," replied Jesus, "have you never read,

" 'From the lips of children and infants
  you have ordained praise'*f*?"

17And he left them and went out of the city to Bethany, where he spent the night.

a 5 Zech. 9:9   *b 9* A Hebrew expression meaning "Save!" which became an exclamation of praise; also in verse 15   *c 9* Psalm 118:26   *d 13* Isaiah 56:7   *e 13* Jer. 7:11   *f 16* Psalm 8:2

The Fig Tree Withers

¹⁸Early in the morning, as he was on his way back to the city, he was hungry. ¹⁹Seeing a fig tree by the road, he went up to it but found nothing on it except leaves. Then he said to it, "May you never bear fruit again!" Immediately the tree withered.

²⁰When the disciples saw this, they were amazed. "How did the fig tree wither so quickly?" they asked.

²¹Jesus replied, "I tell you the truth, if you have faith and do not doubt, not only can you do what was done to the fig tree, but also you can say to this mountain, 'Go, throw yourself into the sea,' and it will be done. ²²If you believe, you will receive whatever you ask for in prayer."

The Authority of Jesus Questioned

²³Jesus entered the temple courts, and, while he was teaching, the chief priests and the elders of the people came to him. "By what authority are you doing these things?" they asked. "And who gave you this authority?"

²⁴Jesus replied, "I will also ask you one question. If you answer me, I will tell you by what authority I am doing these things. ²⁵John's baptism—where did it come from? Was it from heaven, or from men?"

They discussed it among themselves and said, "If we say, 'From heaven,' he will ask, 'Then why didn't you believe him?' ²⁶But if we say, 'From men'—we are afraid of the people, for they all hold that John was a prophet."

²⁷So they answered Jesus, "We don't know."

Then he said, "Neither will I tell you by what authority I am doing these things.

The Parable of the Two Sons

²⁸"What do you think? There was a man who had two sons. He went to the first and said, 'Son, go and work today in the vineyard.'

²⁹" 'I will not,' he answered, but later he changed his mind and went.

³⁰"Then the father went to the other son and said the same thing. He answered, 'I will, sir,' but he did not go.

³¹"Which of the two did what his father wanted?"

"The first," they answered.

Jesus said to them, "I tell you the truth, the tax collectors and the prostitutes are entering the kingdom of God ahead of you. ³²For John came to you to show you the way of righteousness, and you did not believe him, but the tax collectors and the prostitutes did. And even after you saw this, you did not repent and believe him.

The Parable of the Tenants

³³"Listen to another parable: There was a landowner who planted a vineyard. He put a wall around it, dug a winepress in it and built a watchtower. Then he rented the vineyard to some farmers and went away on a journey. ³⁴When the harvest time approached, he sent his servants to the tenants to collect his fruit.

³⁵"The tenants seized his servants; they beat one, killed another, and stoned a third. ³⁶Then he sent other servants to them, more than the first time, and the tenants treated them the same way. ³⁷Last of all, he sent his son to them. 'They will respect my son,' he said.

People-Pleasing Paralysis

MATTHEW 21:23–27

The chief priests and elders are caught—and paralyzed—by their desire to please the crowd. If they answer Jesus' question one way, they will bring shame on themselves; if they answer it the other, they may lose the people's favor. The moral vacuum created by people-pleasing destroys integrity—and reduces leadership to the emptiness of a popularity contest. Have you been in situations where you felt caught between your principles and your desire to be popular? What did you do? Where is the next conflict most likely to come from? How can you be prepared to respond with integrity?

See Meeting God in Everyday Life

A Generous Invitation

MATTHEW 22:1–14

What astonishing excuses people will give for declining the invitation to God's kingdom! Imagine God sending that invitation to you. God is throwing a party—and you are invited. But the party is occurring right now, and the invitation requires an immediate response. You'd really like to go. What is holding you back? What must you get finished before you go? What dream of your own are you pursuing? Do God's repeated calls nag at your conscience? Do they make you angry or resentful? Now imagine you see others responding—people who are homeless, young children, people who are very old. Put aside whatever you have been doing and join them. As you arrive at the party, God embraces you and says, "I'm so glad you've come!"

See Meeting God in Scripture

38 "But when the tenants saw the son, they said to each other, 'This is the heir. Come, let's kill him and take his inheritance.' 39 So they took him and threw him out of the vineyard and killed him.

40 "Therefore, when the owner of the vineyard comes, what will he do to those tenants?"

41 "He will bring those wretches to a wretched end," they replied, "and he will rent the vineyard to other tenants, who will give him his share of the crop at harvest time."

42 Jesus said to them, "Have you never read in the Scriptures:

" 'The stone the builders rejected
    has become the capstone*a*;
the Lord has done this,
    and it is marvelous in our eyes'*b*?

43 "Therefore I tell you that the kingdom of God will be taken away from you and given to a people who will produce its fruit. 44 He who falls on this stone will be broken to pieces, but he on whom it falls will be crushed."*c*

45 When the chief priests and the Pharisees heard Jesus' parables, they knew he was talking about them. 46 They looked for a way to arrest him, but they were afraid of the crowd because the people held that he was a prophet.

The Parable of the Wedding Banquet

22 Jesus spoke to them again in parables, saying: 2 "The kingdom of heaven is like a king who prepared a wedding banquet for his son. 3 He sent his servants to those who had been invited to the banquet to tell them to come, but they refused to come.

4 "Then he sent some more servants and said, 'Tell those who have been invited that I have prepared my dinner: My oxen and fattened cattle have been butchered, and everything is ready. Come to the wedding banquet.'

5 "But they paid no attention and went off—one to his field, another to his business. 6 The rest seized his servants, mistreated them and killed them. 7 The king was enraged. He sent his army and destroyed those murderers and burned their city.

8 "Then he said to his servants, 'The wedding banquet is ready, but those I invited did not deserve to come. 9 Go to the street corners and invite to the banquet anyone you find.' 10 So the servants went out into the streets and gathered all the people they could find, both good and bad, and the wedding hall was filled with guests.

11 "But when the king came in to see the guests, he noticed a man there who was not wearing wedding clothes. 12 'Friend,' he asked, 'how did you get in here without wedding clothes?' The man was speechless.

13 "Then the king told the attendants, 'Tie him hand and foot, and throw him outside, into the darkness, where there will be weeping and gnashing of teeth.'

14 "For many are invited, but few are chosen."

Paying Taxes to Caesar

15 Then the Pharisees went out and laid plans to trap him in his words. 16 They sent their disciples to him along with

---

a 42 Or *cornerstone*   *b* 42 Psalm 118:22,23   *c* 44 Some manuscripts do not have verse 44.

the Herodians. "Teacher," they said, "we know you are a man of integrity and that you teach the way of God in accordance with the truth. You aren't swayed by men, because you pay no attention to who they are. [17]Tell us then, what is your opinion? Is it right to pay taxes to Caesar or not?"

[18]But Jesus, knowing their evil intent, said, "You hypocrites, why are you trying to trap me? [19]Show me the coin used for paying the tax." They brought him a denarius, [20]and he asked them, "Whose portrait is this? And whose inscription?"

[21]"Caesar's," they replied.

Then he said to them, "Give to Caesar what is Caesar's, and to God what is God's."

[22]When they heard this, they were amazed. So they left him and went away.

Marriage at the Resurrection

[23]That same day the Sadducees, who say there is no resurrection, came to him with a question. [24]"Teacher," they said, "Moses told us that if a man dies without having children, his brother must marry the widow and have children for him. [25]Now there were seven brothers among us. The first one married and died, and since he had no children, he left his wife to his brother. [26]The same thing happened to the second and third brother, right on down to the seventh. [27]Finally, the woman died. [28]Now then, at the resurrection, whose wife will she be of the seven, since all of them were married to her?"

[29]Jesus replied, "You are in error because you do not know the Scriptures or the power of God. [30]At the resurrection people will neither marry nor be given in marriage; they will be like the angels in heaven. [31]But about the resurrection of the dead—have you not read what God said to you, [32]'I am the God of Abraham, the God of Isaac, and the God of Jacob'[a]? He is not the God of the dead but of the living."

[33]When the crowds heard this, they were astonished at his teaching.

The Greatest Commandment

[34]Hearing that Jesus had silenced the Sadducees, the Pharisees got together. [35]One of them, an expert in the law, tested him with this question: [36]"Teacher, which is the greatest commandment in the Law?"

[37]Jesus replied: " 'Love the Lord your God with all your heart and with all your soul and with all your mind.'[b] [38]This is the first and greatest commandment. [39]And the second is like it: 'Love your neighbor as yourself.'[c] [40]All the Law and the Prophets hang on these two commandments."

Whose Son Is the Christ?

[41]While the Pharisees were gathered together, Jesus asked them, [42]"What do you think about the Christ[d]? Whose son is he?"

"The son of David," they replied.

[43]He said to them, "How is it then that David, speaking by the Spirit, calls him 'Lord'? For he says,

---

To Cling to God

MATTHEW 22:34–40

"In order that we may know how to love ourselves, an end has been established for us to which we are to refer all our action, so that we may attain to bliss. For if we love ourselves, our one wish is to achieve blessedness. Now this end is to cling to God. Thus, if we know how to love ourselves, the commandment to love our neighbor bids us to do all we can to bring our neighbor to love God. This is the worship of God; this is true religion; this is the right kind of devotion; this is the service which is owed to God alone."

—AUGUSTINE,
The City of God

Whitewashed Tombs

MATTHEW 23:23–37

By using the phrase "white-washed tombs" to describe the religious leaders, Jesus evokes one of the most powerful images in literature. On the outside the religious leaders' holiness looks impressive; inside there is nothing but death and decay. Think of other instances where appearances belie reality (a tree with a rotten core, a car with no engine, a crooked judge). Ask God to help you see how your inner life contradicts your outer life. Where do they agree? How might God work to build more "holy integrity" within you?

See Meeting God in Prayer

44 " 'The Lord said to my Lord:
  "Sit at my right hand
  until I put your enemies
  under your feet." '[a]

45 If then David calls him 'Lord,' how can he be his son?" 46 No one could say a word in reply, and from that day on no one dared to ask him any more questions.

Seven Woes

23 Then Jesus said to the crowds and to his disciples: 2 "The teachers of the law and the Pharisees sit in Moses' seat. 3 So you must obey them and do everything they tell you. But do not do what they do, for they do not practice what they preach. 4 They tie up heavy loads and put them on men's shoulders, but they themselves are not willing to lift a finger to move them.

5 "Everything they do is done for men to see: They make their phylacteries[b] wide and the tassels on their garments long; 6 they love the place of honor at banquets and the most important seats in the synagogues; 7 they love to be greeted in the marketplaces and to have men call them 'Rabbi.'

8 "But you are not to be called 'Rabbi,' for you have only one Master and you are all brothers. 9 And do not call anyone on earth 'father,' for you have one Father, and he is in heaven. 10 Nor are you to be called 'teacher,' for you have one Teacher, the Christ.[c] 11 The greatest among you will be your servant. 12 For whoever exalts himself will be humbled, and whoever humbles himself will be exalted.

13 "Woe to you, teachers of the law and Pharisees, you hypocrites! You shut the kingdom of heaven in men's faces. You yourselves do not enter, nor will you let those enter who are trying to.[d]

15 "Woe to you, teachers of the law and Pharisees, you hypocrites! You travel over land and sea to win a single convert, and when he becomes one, you make him twice as much a son of hell as you are.

16 "Woe to you, blind guides! You say, 'If anyone swears by the temple, it means nothing; but if anyone swears by the gold of the temple, he is bound by his oath.' 17 You blind fools! Which is greater: the gold, or the temple that makes the gold sacred? 18 You also say, 'If anyone swears by the altar, it means nothing; but if anyone swears by the gift on it, he is bound by his oath.' 19 You blind men! Which is greater: the gift, or the altar that makes the gift sacred? 20 Therefore, he who swears by the altar swears by it and by everything on it. 21 And he who swears by the temple swears by it and by the one who dwells in it. 22 And he who swears by heaven swears by God's throne and by the one who sits on it.

23 "Woe to you, teachers of the law and Pharisees, you hypocrites! You give a tenth of your spices—mint, dill and cummin. But you have neglected the more important matters of the law—justice, mercy and faithfulness. You should have practiced the latter, without neglecting the former. 24 You blind guides! You strain out a gnat but swallow a camel.

[a] 44 Psalm 110:1   [b] 5 That is, boxes containing Scripture verses, worn on forehead and arm   [c] 10 Or *Messiah*   [d] 13 Some manuscripts *to.* 14*Woe to you, teachers of the law and Pharisees, you hypocrites! You devour widows' houses and for a show make lengthy prayers. Therefore you will be punished more severely.*

25 "Woe to you, teachers of the law and Pharisees, you hypocrites! You clean the outside of the cup and dish, but inside they are full of greed and self-indulgence. 26 Blind Pharisee! First clean the inside of the cup and dish, and then the outside also will be clean.

27 "Woe to you, teachers of the law and Pharisees, you hypocrites! You are like whitewashed tombs, which look beautiful on the outside but on the inside are full of dead men's bones and everything unclean. 28 In the same way, on the outside you appear to people as righteous but on the inside you are full of hypocrisy and wickedness.

29 "Woe to you, teachers of the law and Pharisees, you hypocrites! You build tombs for the prophets and decorate the graves of the righteous. 30 And you say, 'If we had lived in the days of our forefathers, we would not have taken part with them in shedding the blood of the prophets.' 31 So you testify against yourselves that you are the descendants of those who murdered the prophets. 32 Fill up, then, the measure of the sin of your forefathers!

33 "You snakes! You brood of vipers! How will you escape being condemned to hell? 34 Therefore I am sending you prophets and wise men and teachers. Some of them you will kill and crucify; others you will flog in your synagogues and pursue from town to town. 35 And so upon you will come all the righteous blood that has been shed on earth, from the blood of righteous Abel to the blood of Zechariah son of Berekiah, whom you murdered between the temple and the altar. 36 I tell you the truth, all this will come upon this generation.

37 "O Jerusalem, Jerusalem, you who kill the prophets and stone those sent to you, how often I have longed to gather your children together, as a hen gathers her chicks under her wings, but you were not willing. 38 Look, your house is left to you desolate. 39 For I tell you, you will not see me again until you say, 'Blessed is he who comes in the name of the Lord.' a "

Signs of the End of the Age

24 Jesus left the temple and was walking away when his disciples came up to him to call his attention to its buildings. 2 "Do you see all these things?" he asked. "I tell you the truth, not one stone here will be left on another; every one will be thrown down."

3 As Jesus was sitting on the Mount of Olives, the disciples came to him privately. "Tell us," they said, "when will this happen, and what will be the sign of your coming and of the end of the age?"

4 Jesus answered: "Watch out that no one deceives you. 5 For many will come in my name, claiming, 'I am the Christ, b ' and will deceive many. 6 You will hear of wars and rumors of wars, but see to it that you are not alarmed. Such things must happen, but the end is still to come. 7 Nation will rise against nation, and kingdom against kingdom. There will be famines and earthquakes in various places. 8 All these are the beginning of birth pains.

9 "Then you will be handed over to be persecuted and put to death, and you will be hated by all nations because of me. 10 At that time many will turn away from the faith and will betray and hate each other, 11 and many false prophets

---

A Sobering Promise

MATTHEW 24:4–14

Not many of the popular "Bible Promises" books include this promise: "You will be handed over to be persecuted and put to death, and you will be hated by all nations because of me." Is your faith such that you would be willing to face violence and ridicule—even death—rather than disown Jesus? Write down the things you do to please other people (tell jokes, succeed in business, devote attention to appearance); ask yourself how many of those things you would be willing to give up if you were called to do so. How would you cope if a number of people around you disliked or ignored you?

See Meeting God in Scripture

Expectant Living

MATTHEW 24:36–44

Jesus stresses the importance of watching vigilantly for his return. What does it mean to "keep watch"? Imagine yourself a sentry or a ship's deckhand standing a late night watch. What things might tempt you to drop your guard? Competing concerns? Fatigue? Distractions? Spend some time thinking about how believing in Jesus Christ's return, and waiting expectantly for it, can help you live the Christian life. What do you want to be doing when the Master returns? Are you doing that now? Pray this ancient prayer from *The Book of Common Prayer:* "Guide us waking, O Lord, and guard us sleeping, that awake we may watch with Christ and asleep we may rest in peace."

See Meeting God in Prayer

will appear and deceive many people. 12Because of the increase of wickedness, the love of most will grow cold, 13but he who stands firm to the end will be saved. 14And this gospel of the kingdom will be preached in the whole world as a testimony to all nations, and then the end will come.

15"So when you see standing in the holy place 'the abomination that causes desolation,'[a] spoken of through the prophet Daniel—let the reader understand— 16then let those who are in Judea flee to the mountains. 17Let no one on the roof of his house go down to take anything out of the house. 18Let no one in the field go back to get his cloak. 19How dreadful it will be in those days for pregnant women and nursing mothers! 20Pray that your flight will not take place in winter or on the Sabbath. 21For then there will be great distress, unequaled from the beginning of the world until now—and never to be equaled again. 22If those days had not been cut short, no one would survive, but for the sake of the elect those days will be shortened. 23At that time if anyone says to you, 'Look, here is the Christ!' or, 'There he is!' do not believe it. 24For false Christs and false prophets will appear and perform great signs and miracles to deceive even the elect—if that were possible. 25See, I have told you ahead of time.

26"So if anyone tells you, 'There he is, out in the desert,' do not go out; or, 'Here he is, in the inner rooms,' do not believe it. 27For as lightning that comes from the east is visible even in the west, so will be the coming of the Son of Man. 28Wherever there is a carcass, there the vultures will gather.

29"Immediately after the distress of those days

" 'the sun will be darkened,
   and the moon will not give its light;
the stars will fall from the sky,
   and the heavenly bodies will be shaken.'[b]

30"At that time the sign of the Son of Man will appear in the sky, and all the nations of the earth will mourn. They will see the Son of Man coming on the clouds of the sky, with power and great glory. 31And he will send his angels with a loud trumpet call, and they will gather his elect from the four winds, from one end of the heavens to the other.

32"Now learn this lesson from the fig tree: As soon as its twigs get tender and its leaves come out, you know that summer is near. 33Even so, when you see all these things, you know that it[c] is near, right at the door. 34I tell you the truth, this generation[d] will certainly not pass away until all these things have happened. 35Heaven and earth will pass away, but my words will never pass away.

The Day and Hour Unknown

36"No one knows about that day or hour, not even the angels in heaven, nor the Son,[e] but only the Father. 37As it was in the days of Noah, so it will be at the coming of the Son of Man. 38For in the days before the flood, people were eating and drinking, marrying and giving in marriage, up to the day Noah entered the ark; 39and they knew nothing about what would happen until the flood came and took them all away. That is how it will be at the coming of the

a 15 Daniel 9:27; 11:31; 12:11   b 29 Isaiah 13:10; 34:4   c 33 Or he
d 34 Or race   e 36 Some manuscripts do not have nor the Son.

Son of Man. ⁴⁰Two men will be in the field; one will be taken and the other left. ⁴¹Two women will be grinding with a hand mill; one will be taken and the other left.

⁴²"Therefore keep watch, because you do not know on what day your Lord will come. ⁴³But understand this: If the owner of the house had known at what time of night the thief was coming, he would have kept watch and would not have let his house be broken into. ⁴⁴So you also must be ready, because the Son of Man will come at an hour when you do not expect him.

⁴⁵"Who then is the faithful and wise servant, whom the master has put in charge of the servants in his household to give them their food at the proper time? ⁴⁶It will be good for that servant whose master finds him doing so when he returns. ⁴⁷I tell you the truth, he will put him in charge of all his possessions. ⁴⁸But suppose that servant is wicked and says to himself, 'My master is staying away a long time,' ⁴⁹and he then begins to beat his fellow servants and to eat and drink with drunkards. ⁵⁰The master of that servant will come on a day when he does not expect him and at an hour he is not aware of. ⁵¹He will cut him to pieces and assign him a place with the hypocrites, where there will be weeping and gnashing of teeth.

The Parable of the Ten Virgins

25 "At that time the kingdom of heaven will be like ten virgins who took their lamps and went out to meet the bridegroom. ²Five of them were foolish and five were wise. ³The foolish ones took their lamps but did not take any oil with them. ⁴The wise, however, took oil in jars along with their lamps. ⁵The bridegroom was a long time in coming, and they all became drowsy and fell asleep.

⁶"At midnight the cry rang out: 'Here's the bridegroom! Come out to meet him!'

⁷"Then all the virgins woke up and trimmed their lamps. ⁸The foolish ones said to the wise, 'Give us some of your oil; our lamps are going out.'

⁹" 'No,' they replied, 'there may not be enough for both us and you. Instead, go to those who sell oil and buy some for yourselves.'

¹⁰"But while they were on their way to buy the oil, the bridegroom arrived. The virgins who were ready went in with him to the wedding banquet. And the door was shut.

¹¹"Later the others also came. 'Sir! Sir!' they said. 'Open the door for us!'

¹²"But he replied, 'I tell you the truth, I don't know you.'

¹³"Therefore keep watch, because you do not know the day or the hour.

The Parable of the Talents

¹⁴"Again, it will be like a man going on a journey, who called his servants and entrusted his property to them. ¹⁵To one he gave five talents[a] of money, to another two talents, and to another one talent, each according to his ability. Then he went on his journey. ¹⁶The man who had received the five talents went at once and put his money to work and gained five more. ¹⁷So also, the one with the two talents gained two more. ¹⁸But the man who had re-

No Impossible Duty

MATTHEW 25:14–30

"There are diversities of gifts in the kingdom of God, and these gifts are divided to 'every man according to his own ability.' I may have five talents or two or only one. I may be called to do twenty things or one thing. My responsibility is simply to do that which I am called to do, and nothing more . . . Many Christians make the further mistake of looking upon every act of service as a perpetual obligation. They think because it was right for them to give a tract to one person in a railway train, for instance, that they are always to give tracts to everybody. In this way they burden themselves with an impossible duty."

—HANNAH WHITALL SMITH,
The Christian's Secret of a Happy Life

---

[a] 15 A talent was worth more than a thousand dollars.

A Heavenly Greeting

MATTHEW 25:31–46

Jesus reminds his followers that discipleship is about doing his work in his name. This parable inspired Christians of earlier times to list "works of mercy." Seven of these works deal with physical needs: feeding the hungry, giving drink to the thirsty, clothing the naked, harboring the stranger, visiting the sick, ministering to prisoners and burying the dead. Seven others deal with spiritual needs: converting the sinner, instructing the ignorant, counseling the doubtful, comforting the sorrowful, bearing wrongs patiently, forgiving injuries, and praying for others. How have these works of mercy been part of your own ministry for Jesus Christ? How could they be part of it in the future? What type of things will God commend you for when you are judged? Write out the greeting with which you hope God will meet you.

See Meeting God in Scripture

ceived the one talent went off, dug a hole in the ground and hid his master's money.

19 "After a long time the master of those servants returned and settled accounts with them. 20 The man who had received the five talents brought the other five. 'Master,' he said, 'you entrusted me with five talents. See, I have gained five more.'

21 "His master replied, 'Well done, good and faithful servant! You have been faithful with a few things; I will put you in charge of many things. Come and share your master's happiness!'

22 "The man with the two talents also came. 'Master,' he said, 'you entrusted me with two talents; see, I have gained two more.'

23 "His master replied, 'Well done, good and faithful servant! You have been faithful with a few things; I will put you in charge of many things. Come and share your master's happiness!'

24 "Then the man who had received the one talent came. 'Master,' he said, 'I knew that you are a hard man, harvesting where you have not sown and gathering where you have not scattered seed. 25 So I was afraid and went out and hid your talent in the ground. See, here is what belongs to you.'

26 "His master replied, 'You wicked, lazy servant! So you knew that I harvest where I have not sown and gather where I have not scattered seed? 27 Well then, you should have put my money on deposit with the bankers, so that when I returned I would have received it back with interest.

28 " 'Take the talent from him and give it to the one who has the ten talents. 29 For everyone who has will be given more, and he will have an abundance. Whoever does not have, even what he has will be taken from him. 30 And throw that worthless servant outside, into the darkness, where there will be weeping and gnashing of teeth.'

The Sheep and the Goats

31 "When the Son of Man comes in his glory, and all the angels with him, he will sit on his throne in heavenly glory. 32 All the nations will be gathered before him, and he will separate the people one from another as a shepherd separates the sheep from the goats. 33 He will put the sheep on his right and the goats on his left.

34 "Then the King will say to those on his right, 'Come, you who are blessed by my Father; take your inheritance, the kingdom prepared for you since the creation of the world. 35 For I was hungry and you gave me something to eat, I was thirsty and you gave me something to drink, I was a stranger and you invited me in, 36 I needed clothes and you clothed me, I was sick and you looked after me, I was in prison and you came to visit me.'

37 "Then the righteous will answer him, 'Lord, when did we see you hungry and feed you, or thirsty and give you something to drink? 38 When did we see you a stranger and invite you in, or needing clothes and clothe you? 39 When did we see you sick or in prison and go to visit you?'

40 "The King will reply, 'I tell you the truth, whatever you did for one of the least of these brothers of mine, you did for me.'

41"Then he will say to those on his left, 'Depart from me, you who are cursed, into the eternal fire prepared for the devil and his angels. 42For I was hungry and you gave me nothing to eat, I was thirsty and you gave me nothing to drink, 43I was a stranger and you did not invite me in, I needed clothes and you did not clothe me, I was sick and in prison and you did not look after me.'

44"They also will answer, 'Lord, when did we see you hungry or thirsty or a stranger or needing clothes or sick or in prison, and did not help you?'

45"He will reply, 'I tell you the truth, whatever you did not do for one of the least of these, you did not do for me.'

46"Then they will go away to eternal punishment, but the righteous to eternal life."

The Plot Against Jesus

26 When Jesus had finished saying all these things, he said to his disciples, 2"As you know, the Passover is two days away—and the Son of Man will be handed over to be crucified."

3Then the chief priests and the elders of the people assembled in the palace of the high priest, whose name was Caiaphas, 4and they plotted to arrest Jesus in some sly way and kill him. 5"But not during the Feast," they said, "or there may be a riot among the people."

Jesus Anointed at Bethany

6While Jesus was in Bethany in the home of a man known as Simon the Leper, 7a woman came to him with an alabaster jar of very expensive perfume, which she poured on his head as he was reclining at the table.

8When the disciples saw this, they were indignant. "Why this waste?" they asked. 9"This perfume could have been sold at a high price and the money given to the poor."

10Aware of this, Jesus said to them, "Why are you bothering this woman? She has done a beautiful thing to me. 11The poor you will always have with you, but you will not always have me. 12When she poured this perfume on my body, she did it to prepare me for burial. 13I tell you the truth, wherever this gospel is preached throughout the world, what she has done will also be told, in memory of her."

Judas Agrees to Betray Jesus

14Then one of the Twelve—the one called Judas Iscariot—went to the chief priests 15and asked, "What are you willing to give me if I hand him over to you?" So they counted out for him thirty silver coins. 16From then on Judas watched for an opportunity to hand him over.

The Lord's Supper

17On the first day of the Feast of Unleavened Bread, the disciples came to Jesus and asked, "Where do you want us to make preparations for you to eat the Passover?"

18He replied, "Go into the city to a certain man and tell him, 'The Teacher says: My appointed time is near. I am going to celebrate the Passover with my disciples at your house.' " 19So the disciples did as Jesus had directed them and prepared the Passover.

A Scandalous, "Wasteful" Love

MATTHEW 26:6–13

There are no "how to" books for love. When the disciples chastise the woman for "wasting" her fragrant and expensive oil, they disconnect their hearts from their heads; they can't understand the draw and depth of her passionate and holy affection.

Have you ever done something "extravagant" or "wasteful" out of love for another person? When have you done something like that out of love for God? How do you let Jesus know you love him? How can you show Jesus extravagant love today?

See Meeting God in Worship

Absolute Surrender

MATTHEW 26:39–42

Jesus' prayer—"Not as I will, but as you will"—displays a remarkable surrender to the will of his Father. Jesus knew full well the hatred, violence and separation from God that he was about to face. Try to imagine the depth of Jesus' dread. Spend some time meditating on these hardships, which Jesus eventually accepted.

Sometimes our will can come into conflict with God's will. Is there a "little" surrender you can offer to God to help build up your maturity in preparation for those times when greater conflicts arise? How might the spiritual disciplines help you in this? One beginning might be simply to contemplate Jesus' prayer for a while, slowly repeating, "Not as I will, but as you will."

See *Meeting God in Prayer*

²⁰When evening came, Jesus was reclining at the table with the Twelve. ²¹And while they were eating, he said, "I tell you the truth, one of you will betray me."

²²They were very sad and began to say to him one after the other, "Surely not I, Lord?"

²³Jesus replied, "The one who has dipped his hand into the bowl with me will betray me. ²⁴The Son of Man will go just as it is written about him. But woe to that man who betrays the Son of Man! It would be better for him if he had not been born."

²⁵Then Judas, the one who would betray him, said, "Surely not I, Rabbi?"

Jesus answered, "Yes, it is you."[a]

²⁶While they were eating, Jesus took bread, gave thanks and broke it, and gave it to his disciples, saying, "Take and eat; this is my body."

²⁷Then he took the cup, gave thanks and offered it to them, saying, "Drink from it, all of you. ²⁸This is my blood of the[b] covenant, which is poured out for many for the forgiveness of sins. ²⁹I tell you, I will not drink of this fruit of the vine from now on until that day when I drink it anew with you in my Father's kingdom."

³⁰When they had sung a hymn, they went out to the Mount of Olives.

Jesus Predicts Peter's Denial

³¹Then Jesus told them, "This very night you will all fall away on account of me, for it is written:

> " 'I will strike the shepherd,
>   and the sheep of the flock will be scattered.'[c]

³²But after I have risen, I will go ahead of you into Galilee."

³³Peter replied, "Even if all fall away on account of you, I never will."

³⁴"I tell you the truth," Jesus answered, "this very night, before the rooster crows, you will disown me three times."

³⁵But Peter declared, "Even if I have to die with you, I will never disown you." And all the other disciples said the same.

Gethsemane

³⁶Then Jesus went with his disciples to a place called Gethsemane, and he said to them, "Sit here while I go over there and pray." ³⁷He took Peter and the two sons of Zebedee along with him, and he began to be sorrowful and troubled. ³⁸Then he said to them, "My soul is overwhelmed with sorrow to the point of death. Stay here and keep watch with me."

³⁹Going a little farther, he fell with his face to the ground and prayed, "My Father, if it is possible, may this cup be taken from me. Yet not as I will, but as you will."

⁴⁰Then he returned to his disciples and found them sleeping. "Could you men not keep watch with me for one hour?" he asked Peter. ⁴¹"Watch and pray so that you will not fall into temptation. The spirit is willing, but the body is weak."

⁴²He went away a second time and prayed, "My Father,

---

a 25 Or *"You yourself have said it"*   *b 28* Some manuscripts *the new*
c 31 Zech. 13:7

if it is not possible for this cup to be taken away unless I drink it, may your will be done."

[43] When he came back, he again found them sleeping, because their eyes were heavy. [44] So he left them and went away once more and prayed the third time, saying the same thing.

[45] Then he returned to the disciples and said to them, "Are you still sleeping and resting? Look, the hour is near, and the Son of Man is betrayed into the hands of sinners. [46] Rise, let us go! Here comes my betrayer!"

Jesus Arrested

[47] While he was still speaking, Judas, one of the Twelve, arrived. With him was a large crowd armed with swords and clubs, sent from the chief priests and the elders of the people. [48] Now the betrayer had arranged a signal with them: "The one I kiss is the man; arrest him." [49] Going at once to Jesus, Judas said, "Greetings, Rabbi!" and kissed him.

[50] Jesus replied, "Friend, do what you came for."[a]

Then the men stepped forward, seized Jesus and arrested him. [51] With that, one of Jesus' companions reached for his sword, drew it out and struck the servant of the high priest, cutting off his ear.

[52] "Put your sword back in its place," Jesus said to him, "for all who draw the sword will die by the sword. [53] Do you think I cannot call on my Father, and he will at once put at my disposal more than twelve legions of angels? [54] But how then would the Scriptures be fulfilled that say it must happen in this way?"

[55] At that time Jesus said to the crowd, "Am I leading a rebellion, that you have come out with swords and clubs to capture me? Every day I sat in the temple courts teaching, and you did not arrest me. [56] But this has all taken place that the writings of the prophets might be fulfilled." Then all the disciples deserted him and fled.

Before the Sanhedrin

[57] Those who had arrested Jesus took him to Caiaphas, the high priest, where the teachers of the law and the elders had assembled. [58] But Peter followed him at a distance, right up to the courtyard of the high priest. He entered and sat down with the guards to see the outcome.

[59] The chief priests and the whole Sanhedrin were looking for false evidence against Jesus so that they could put him to death. [60] But they did not find any, though many false witnesses came forward.

Finally two came forward [61] and declared, "This fellow said, 'I am able to destroy the temple of God and rebuild it in three days.' "

[62] Then the high priest stood up and said to Jesus, "Are you not going to answer? What is this testimony that these men are bringing against you?" [63] But Jesus remained silent.

The high priest said to him, "I charge you under oath by the living God: Tell us if you are the Christ,[b] the Son of God."

[64] "Yes, it is as you say," Jesus replied. "But I say to all of you: In the future you will see the Son of Man sitting at the right hand of the Mighty One and coming on the clouds of heaven."

Holy Sense

MATTHEW 26:58

"Peter showed poor judgment in entering the high priest's court. It was, of course, an act of devotion . . . But since he had already been warned of his coming defection, he should rather have hidden himself in a corner, so as to avoid an occasion for sin. So, it happens often to believers that, while seeming to do something virtuous, they throw themselves in the way of temptation. We ought to pray to the Lord that he hold us back with the rein of his Spirit, so that we may not charge ahead on our own . . . The knowledge of our own weakness ought not so to unnerve us that we will not go when God calls us. Still, it ought to restrain our rashness, and prevent us from attempting what is beyond our calling."

—JOHN CALVIN,
Institutes of the Christian Religion

---

a 50 Or *"Friend, why have you come?"*   *b 63* Or *Messiah*; also in verse 68

Failure Times Two

MATTHEW 26:69—27:5

Each of these two disciples fails Jesus miserably. Compare and contrast their actions and reactions. Why does Peter disown Jesus? Why do you think Judas betrays Jesus? How does Peter react to his own disloyalty afterward? Judas? How might each of them have responded differently? What is the outcome of their actions? Do you think Jesus would have forgiven Judas if Judas and asked him for forgiveness? What is God saying to you through this passage? How does this passage prompt you to pray today?

See Meeting God in Scripture

[65] Then the high priest tore his clothes and said, "He has spoken blasphemy! Why do we need any more witnesses? Look, now you have heard the blasphemy. [66] What do you think?"

"He is worthy of death," they answered.

[67] Then they spit in his face and struck him with their fists. Others slapped him [68] and said, "Prophesy to us, Christ. Who hit you?"

Peter Disowns Jesus

[69] Now Peter was sitting out in the courtyard, and a servant girl came to him. "You also were with Jesus of Galilee," she said.

[70] But he denied it before them all. "I don't know what you're talking about," he said.

[71] Then he went out to the gateway, where another girl saw him and said to the people there, "This fellow was with Jesus of Nazareth."

[72] He denied it again, with an oath: "I don't know the man!"

[73] After a little while, those standing there went up to Peter and said, "Surely you are one of them, for your accent gives you away."

[74] Then he began to call down curses on himself and he swore to them, "I don't know the man!"

Immediately a rooster crowed. [75] Then Peter remembered the word Jesus had spoken: "Before the rooster crows, you will disown me three times." And he went outside and wept bitterly.

Judas Hangs Himself

27 Early in the morning, all the chief priests and the elders of the people came to the decision to put Jesus to death. [2] They bound him, led him away and handed him over to Pilate, the governor.

[3] When Judas, who had betrayed him, saw that Jesus was condemned, he was seized with remorse and returned the thirty silver coins to the chief priests and the elders. [4] "I have sinned," he said, "for I have betrayed innocent blood."

"What is that to us?" they replied. "That's your responsibility."

[5] So Judas threw the money into the temple and left. Then he went away and hanged himself.

[6] The chief priests picked up the coins and said, "It is against the law to put this into the treasury, since it is blood money." [7] So they decided to use the money to buy the potter's field as a burial place for foreigners. [8] That is why it has been called the Field of Blood to this day. [9] Then what was spoken by Jeremiah the prophet was fulfilled: "They took the thirty silver coins, the price set on him by the people of Israel, [10] and they used them to buy the potter's field, as the Lord commanded me."[a]

Jesus Before Pilate

[11] Meanwhile Jesus stood before the governor, and the governor asked him, "Are you the king of the Jews?"

"Yes, it is as you say," Jesus replied.

[12] When he was accused by the chief priests and the elders, he gave no answer. [13] Then Pilate asked him, "Don't

a 10 See Zech. 11:12,13; Jer. 19:1–13; 32:6–9.

you hear the testimony they are bringing against you?" ¹⁴But Jesus made no reply, not even to a single charge—to the great amazement of the governor.

¹⁵Now it was the governor's custom at the Feast to release a prisoner chosen by the crowd. ¹⁶At that time they had a notorious prisoner, called Barabbas. ¹⁷So when the crowd had gathered, Pilate asked them, "Which one do you want me to release to you: Barabbas, or Jesus who is called Christ?" ¹⁸For he knew it was out of envy that they had handed Jesus over to him.

¹⁹While Pilate was sitting on the judge's seat, his wife sent him this message: "Don't have anything to do with that innocent man, for I have suffered a great deal today in a dream because of him."

²⁰But the chief priests and the elders persuaded the crowd to ask for Barabbas and to have Jesus executed.

²¹"Which of the two do you want me to release to you?" asked the governor.

"Barabbas," they answered.

²²"What shall I do, then, with Jesus who is called Christ?" Pilate asked.

They all answered, "Crucify him!"

²³"Why? What crime has he committed?" asked Pilate.

But they shouted all the louder, "Crucify him!"

²⁴When Pilate saw that he was getting nowhere, but that instead an uproar was starting, he took water and washed his hands in front of the crowd. "I am innocent of this man's blood," he said. "It is your responsibility!"

²⁵All the people answered, "Let his blood be on us and on our children!"

²⁶Then he released Barabbas to them. But he had Jesus flogged, and handed him over to be crucified.

The Soldiers Mock Jesus

²⁷Then the governor's soldiers took Jesus into the Praetorium and gathered the whole company of soldiers around him. ²⁸They stripped him and put a scarlet robe on him, ²⁹and then twisted together a crown of thorns and set it on his head. They put a staff in his right hand and knelt in front of him and mocked him. "Hail, king of the Jews!" they said. ³⁰They spit on him, and took the staff and struck him on the head again and again. ³¹After they had mocked him, they took off the robe and put his own clothes on him. Then they led him away to crucify him.

The Crucifixion

³²As they were going out, they met a man from Cyrene, named Simon, and they forced him to carry the cross. ³³They came to a place called Golgotha (which means The Place of the Skull). ³⁴There they offered Jesus wine to drink, mixed with gall; but after tasting it, he refused to drink it. ³⁵When they had crucified him, they divided up his clothes by casting lots.ᵃ ³⁶And sitting down, they kept watch over him there. ³⁷Above his head they placed the written charge against him: THIS IS JESUS, THE KING OF THE JEWS. ³⁸Two robbers were crucified with him, one on his right and one on his left. ³⁹Those who passed by hurled insults at him, shaking

---

At the Cross

MATTHEW 27:32–55

Imagine that you are standing on Golgotha while Jesus is being crucified. Look around you. Listen to the sound of the hammer pounding nails into soft flesh, the thud of the cross as it is lifted into position. Look at the people there with you. Some are mocking, some weeping. What are you doing? Do you talk to others or keep to yourself? What are your thoughts and feelings as the sky grows dark and as Jesus cries out?

Sing a hymn such as "Go to Dark Gethsemane," "When I Survey the Wondrous Cross" or "Were You There?" What emotions do you experience as you sing? How have you encountered the reality of Jesus' death through these hymns?

See Meeting God in Scripture

ᵃ 35 A few late manuscripts *lots that the word spoken by the prophet might be fulfilled: "They divided my garments among themselves and cast lots for my clothing"* (Psalm 22:18)

A Promise Fulfilled

MATTHEW 28:1–10

Matthew begins his Gospel with a promise given and he ends it with a promise fulfilled. Yet nobody on earth expected the promise to be fulfilled exactly in the way it was. Have you ever doubted one of God's promises because it seemed so long in coming to fulfillment? On a sheet of paper, draw a symbol or simple representation of that time of doubt. What helped you to persevere? What can you learn from the fear, confusion and doubt of the disciples? From the attempts of the authorities to smother the hope of Jesus' followers by sealing the tomb and placing guards in front of it? From the joy of the women who first saw Jesus risen from the dead?

See Meeting God in Everyday Life

their heads [40]and saying, "You who are going to destroy the temple and build it in three days, save yourself! Come down from the cross, if you are the Son of God!"

[41]In the same way the chief priests, the teachers of the law and the elders mocked him. [42]"He saved others," they said, "but he can't save himself! He's the King of Israel! Let him come down now from the cross, and we will believe in him. [43]He trusts in God. Let God rescue him now if he wants him, for he said, 'I am the Son of God.' " [44]In the same way the robbers who were crucified with him also heaped insults on him.

The Death of Jesus

[45]From the sixth hour until the ninth hour darkness came over all the land. [46]About the ninth hour Jesus cried out in a loud voice, *"Eloi, Eloi,[a] lama sabachthani?"*—which means, "My God, my God, why have you forsaken me?"[b]

[47]When some of those standing there heard this, they said, "He's calling Elijah."

[48]Immediately one of them ran and got a sponge. He filled it with wine vinegar, put it on a stick, and offered it to Jesus to drink. [49]The rest said, "Now leave him alone. Let's see if Elijah comes to save him."

[50]And when Jesus had cried out again in a loud voice, he gave up his spirit.

[51]At that moment the curtain of the temple was torn in two from top to bottom. The earth shook and the rocks split. [52]The tombs broke open and the bodies of many holy people who had died were raised to life. [53]They came out of the tombs, and after Jesus' resurrection they went into the holy city and appeared to many people.

[54]When the centurion and those with him who were guarding Jesus saw the earthquake and all that had happened, they were terrified, and exclaimed, "Surely he was the Son[c] of God!"

[55]Many women were there, watching from a distance. They had followed Jesus from Galilee to care for his needs. [56]Among them were Mary Magdalene, Mary the mother of James and Joses, and the mother of Zebedee's sons.

The Burial of Jesus

[57]As evening approached, there came a rich man from Arimathea, named Joseph, who had himself become a disciple of Jesus. [58]Going to Pilate, he asked for Jesus' body, and Pilate ordered that it be given to him. [59]Joseph took the body, wrapped it in a clean linen cloth, [60]and placed it in his own new tomb that he had cut out of the rock. He rolled a big stone in front of the entrance to the tomb and went away. [61]Mary Magdalene and the other Mary were sitting there opposite the tomb.

The Guard at the Tomb

[62]The next day, the one after Preparation Day, the chief priests and the Pharisees went to Pilate. [63]"Sir," they said, "we remember that while he was still alive that deceiver said, 'After three days I will rise again.' [64]So give the order for the tomb to be made secure until the third day. Otherwise, his disciples may come and steal the body and tell

a 46 Some manuscripts *Eli, Eli*   *b 46* Psalm 22:1   *c 54* Or *a son* the people that he has been raised from the dead. This last deception will be worse than the first."

⁶⁵"Take a guard," Pilate answered. "Go, make the tomb as secure as you know how." ⁶⁶So they went and made the tomb secure by putting a seal on the stone and posting the guard.

The Resurrection

28 After the Sabbath, at dawn on the first day of the week, Mary Magdalene and the other Mary went to look at the tomb.

²There was a violent earthquake, for an angel of the Lord came down from heaven and, going to the tomb, rolled back the stone and sat on it. ³His appearance was like lightning, and his clothes were white as snow. ⁴The guards were so afraid of him that they shook and became like dead men.

⁵The angel said to the women, "Do not be afraid, for I know that you are looking for Jesus, who was crucified. ⁶He is not here; he has risen, just as he said. Come and see the place where he lay. ⁷Then go quickly and tell his disciples: 'He has risen from the dead and is going ahead of you into Galilee. There you will see him.' Now I have told you."

⁸So the women hurried away from the tomb, afraid yet filled with joy, and ran to tell his disciples. ⁹Suddenly Jesus met them. "Greetings," he said. They came to him, clasped his feet and worshiped him. ¹⁰Then Jesus said to them, "Do not be afraid. Go and tell my brothers to go to Galilee; there they will see me."

The Guards' Report

¹¹While the women were on their way, some of the guards went into the city and reported to the chief priests everything that had happened. ¹²When the chief priests had met with the elders and devised a plan, they gave the soldiers a large sum of money, ¹³telling them, "You are to say, 'His disciples came during the night and stole him away while we were asleep.' ¹⁴If this report gets to the governor, we will satisfy him and keep you out of trouble." ¹⁵So the soldiers took the money and did as they were instructed. And this story has been widely circulated among the Jews to this very day.

The Great Commission

¹⁶Then the eleven disciples went to Galilee, to the mountain where Jesus had told them to go. ¹⁷When they saw him, they worshiped him; but some doubted. ¹⁸Then Jesus came to them and said, "All authority in heaven and on earth has been given to me. ¹⁹Therefore go and make disciples of all nations, baptizing them in[a] the name of the Father and of the Son and of the Holy Spirit, ²⁰and teaching them to obey everything I have commanded you. And surely I am with you always, to the very end of the age."

A Great Commission

MATTHEW 28:16–20

Read the Great Commission in verses 19 and 20 as if Jesus were speaking directly to you. To what part of the world is he sending you? What is your role in making disciples? How can you extend his invitation to everyone you meet? Where will you find support in fulfilling this commission? What help do you need from God? From other people? Remember this final promise from Jesus: "And surely I am with you always, to the very end of the age."

See Meeting God in Service

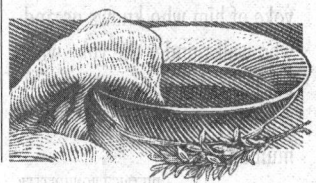

---

[a] 19 Or *into*; see Acts 8:16; 19:5; Romans 6:3; 1 Cor. 1:13; 10:2 and Gal. 3:27.

MARK

What It Costs to Follow Jesus

KEY VERSE:

*"For even the Son of Man did not come to be served, but to serve, and to give his life
as a ransom for many."*—Mark 10:45

"To go one's way under the sign of the cross is not misery and desperation, but peace and refreshment for the soul, it is the highest joy. Then we do not walk under our self-made laws and burdens, but under the yoke of him who knows us and who walks under the yoke with us. Under his yoke we are certain of his nearness and communion."

—DIETRICH BONHOEFFER,
The Cost of Discipleship

What did it cost Jesus to do the work of his Father? What will it cost you to follow Jesus? You will find the answers to both questions in the Gospel of Mark. In this fast-paced narrative the apostle Mark reveals what it cost Jesus to do this work: He was persecuted by the Pharisees (Mark 3:6); he had to address the bewilderment expressed by his family (3:21); he was rejected by his hometown crowd (6:3–4); he relinquished both his privacy (6:30–34) and material goods. When accused, he did not defend himself (14:61).

Mark also outlines the cost of following Jesus. As much as we prefer to identify ourselves with Jesus in his role of conquering king, we are also called to become like him as servants, reconciling those around us to God. Just as Jesus spoke the truth to the confused and the corrupt, so must we. Just as he addressed the physical needs of the crowds who followed him, so must we. Just as he sought to heal the broken places of people's hearts, so must we.

As you read this account, let the forward momentum of Mark's narrative instill within you a sense of urgency. The time to follow Jesus is now. As you read about Jesus' words and works, ask God what he is calling you to be and do. What do you need to know about the power of Jesus and the servant heart of Jesus in order to be conformed to his image for the sake of others?

John the Baptist Prepares the Way

1 The beginning of the gospel about Jesus Christ, the Son of God.[a]

[2] It is written in Isaiah the prophet:

> "I will send my messenger ahead of you,
> who will prepare your way"[b]—
> [3] "a voice of one calling in the desert,
> 'Prepare the way for the Lord,
> make straight paths for him.' "[c]

[4] And so John came, baptizing in the desert region and preaching a baptism of repentance for the forgiveness of sins. [5] The whole Judean countryside and all the people of Jerusalem went out to him. Confessing their sins, they were baptized by him in the Jordan River. [6] John wore clothing made of camel's hair, with a leather belt around his waist, and he ate locusts and wild honey. [7] And this was his message: "After me will come one more powerful than I, the thongs of whose sandals I am not worthy to stoop down and untie. [8] I baptize you with[d] water, but he will baptize you with the Holy Spirit."

The Baptism and Temptation of Jesus

[9] At that time Jesus came from Nazareth in Galilee and was baptized by John in the Jordan. [10] As Jesus was coming up out of the water, he saw heaven being torn open and the Spirit descending on him like a dove. [11] And a voice came from heaven: "You are my Son, whom I love; with you I am well pleased."

[12] At once the Spirit sent him out into the desert, [13] and he was in the desert forty days, being tempted by Satan. He was with the wild animals, and angels attended him.

The Calling of the First Disciples

[14] After John was put in prison, Jesus went into Galilee, proclaiming the good news of God. [15] "The time has come," he said. "The kingdom of God is near. Repent and believe the good news!"

[16] As Jesus walked beside the Sea of Galilee, he saw Simon and his brother Andrew casting a net into the lake, for they were fishermen. [17] "Come, follow me," Jesus said, "and I will make you fishers of men." [18] At once they left their nets and followed him.

[19] When he had gone a little farther, he saw James son of Zebedee and his brother John in a boat, preparing their nets. [20] Without delay he called them, and they left their father Zebedee in the boat with the hired men and followed him.

Jesus Drives Out an Evil Spirit

[21] They went to Capernaum, and when the Sabbath came, Jesus went into the synagogue and began to teach. [22] The people were amazed at his teaching, because he taught them as one who had authority, not as the teachers of the law. [23] Just then a man in their synagogue who was possessed by an evil[e] spirit cried out, [24] "What do you want

---

Grasping the Nets

MARK 1:16–18

The disciples' fishing nets represent their income, their sense of accomplishment and their identity as enterprising fish-catching businessmen. They've probably handled these nets most of their lives. No wonder they find it difficult to let go of them!

Imagine yourself clutching the tightly woven cords of the fishing nets—how familiar they feel, how secure. But Jesus is standing near you, gazing at you with a look of invitation that's somehow irresistible. He's asking you to let go of the nets and find your security in him. Jesus walks daily through your life, calling you to follow him. What is God asking you to let go of today? What do you need to relinquish in order to conform your heart to the heart of Jesus Christ?

See *Meeting God in Scripture*

---

[a] *1* Some manuscripts do not have *the Son of God.* [b] *2* Mal. 3:1
[c] *3* Isaiah 40:3 [d] *8* Or *in* [e] *23* Greek *unclean*; also in verses 26 and 27

Time Out From Service

MARK 1:29–35

On the morning after an exhausting day of healing and driving out evil spirits, it would be understandable if Jesus slept in. Although it is likely that he was tired, he got up early to go off alone to pray. What do you suppose Jesus prayed about? How do you explain the apparent longing in his heart to talk to God?

Reflect on your life. How do times of intense service affect you? In what ways do they prompt you to converse with God about them? What is God saying to you about your acts of service?

See Meeting God in Prayer

with us, Jesus of Nazareth? Have you come to destroy us? I know who you are—the Holy One of God!"

²⁵"Be quiet!" said Jesus sternly. "Come out of him!" ²⁶The evil spirit shook the man violently and came out of him with a shriek.

²⁷The people were all so amazed that they asked each other, "What is this? A new teaching—and with authority! He even gives orders to evil spirits and they obey him." ²⁸News about him spread quickly over the whole region of Galilee.

Jesus Heals Many

²⁹As soon as they left the synagogue, they went with James and John to the home of Simon and Andrew. ³⁰Simon's mother-in-law was in bed with a fever, and they told Jesus about her. ³¹So he went to her, took her hand and helped her up. The fever left her and she began to wait on them.

³²That evening after sunset the people brought to Jesus all the sick and demon-possessed. ³³The whole town gathered at the door, ³⁴and Jesus healed many who had various diseases. He also drove out many demons, but he would not let the demons speak because they knew who he was.

Jesus Prays in a Solitary Place

³⁵Very early in the morning, while it was still dark, Jesus got up, left the house and went off to a solitary place, where he prayed. ³⁶Simon and his companions went to look for him, ³⁷and when they found him, they exclaimed: "Everyone is looking for you!"

³⁸Jesus replied, "Let us go somewhere else—to the nearby villages—so I can preach there also. That is why I have come." ³⁹So he traveled throughout Galilee, preaching in their synagogues and driving out demons.

A Man With Leprosy

⁴⁰A man with leprosy*a* came to him and begged him on his knees, "If you are willing, you can make me clean."

⁴¹Filled with compassion, Jesus reached out his hand and touched the man. "I am willing," he said. "Be clean!" ⁴²Immediately the leprosy left him and he was cured.

⁴³Jesus sent him away at once with a strong warning: ⁴⁴"See that you don't tell this to anyone. But go, show yourself to the priest and offer the sacrifices that Moses commanded for your cleansing, as a testimony to them." ⁴⁵Instead he went out and began to talk freely, spreading the news. As a result, Jesus could no longer enter a town openly but stayed outside in lonely places. Yet the people still came to him from everywhere.

Jesus Heals a Paralytic

2 A few days later, when Jesus again entered Capernaum, the people heard that he had come home. ²So many gathered that there was no room left, not even outside the door, and he preached the word to them. ³Some men came, bringing to him a paralytic, carried by four of them. ⁴Since they could not get him to Jesus because of the crowd, they made an opening in the roof above Jesus

---

a 40 The Greek word was used for various diseases affecting the skin—not necessarily leprosy.

and, after digging through it, lowered the mat the paralyzed man was lying on. ⁵When Jesus saw their faith, he said to the paralytic, "Son, your sins are forgiven."

⁶Now some teachers of the law were sitting there, thinking to themselves, ⁷"Why does this fellow talk like that? He's blaspheming! Who can forgive sins but God alone?"

⁸Immediately Jesus knew in his spirit that this was what they were thinking in their hearts, and he said to them, "Why are you thinking these things? ⁹Which is easier: to say to the paralytic, 'Your sins are forgiven,' or to say, 'Get up, take your mat and walk'? ¹⁰But that you may know that the Son of Man has authority on earth to forgive sins . . ." He said to the paralytic, ¹¹"I tell you, get up, take your mat and go home." ¹²He got up, took his mat and walked out in full view of them all. This amazed everyone and they praised God, saying, "We have never seen anything like this!"

The Calling of Levi

¹³Once again Jesus went out beside the lake. A large crowd came to him, and he began to teach them. ¹⁴As he walked along, he saw Levi son of Alphaeus sitting at the tax collector's booth. "Follow me," Jesus told him, and Levi got up and followed him.

¹⁵While Jesus was having dinner at Levi's house, many tax collectors and "sinners" were eating with him and his disciples, for there were many who followed him. ¹⁶When the teachers of the law who were Pharisees saw him eating with the "sinners" and tax collectors, they asked his disciples: "Why does he eat with tax collectors and 'sinners'?"

¹⁷On hearing this, Jesus said to them, "It is not the healthy who need a doctor, but the sick. I have not come to call the righteous, but sinners."

Jesus Questioned About Fasting

¹⁸Now John's disciples and the Pharisees were fasting. Some people came and asked Jesus, "How is it that John's disciples and the disciples of the Pharisees are fasting, but yours are not?"

¹⁹Jesus answered, "How can the guests of the bridegroom fast while he is with them? They cannot, so long as they have him with them. ²⁰But the time will come when the bridegroom will be taken from them, and on that day they will fast.

²¹"No one sews a patch of unshrunk cloth on an old garment. If he does, the new piece will pull away from the old, making the tear worse. ²²And no one pours new wine into old wineskins. If he does, the wine will burst the skins, and both the wine and the wineskins will be ruined. No, he pours new wine into new wineskins."

Lord of the Sabbath

²³One Sabbath Jesus was going through the grainfields, and as his disciples walked along, they began to pick some heads of grain. ²⁴The Pharisees said to him, "Look, why are they doing what is unlawful on the Sabbath?"

²⁵He answered, "Have you never read what David did when he and his companions were hungry and in need? ²⁶In the days of Abiathar the high priest, he entered the house of God and ate the consecrated bread, which is law-

Self-Created Limits

MARK 2:15–17

"To die to our neighbors means to stop judging them, to stop evaluating them, and thus to become free to be compassionate. Compassion can never co-exist with judgment because judgment creates the distance, the distinction, which prevent us from really being with each other. Often quite unconsciously we classify people as very good, good, neutral, bad, and very bad. These judgments influence deeply the thoughts, words, and actions. These self-created limits prevent us from being available to people and shrivel up our compassion."

—HENRI J. M. NOUWEN,
The Way of the Heart

Being With Him

MARK 3:14

What are the advantages of "hanging out" with someone? Jesus must have thought this was important because he appointed the twelve so that they "might be with him." If you were to "hang out" with God all day, what would you talk about? What phrases might God use in his conversation with you? What would it be like to have an all-day companion who is intensely interested in you? How would you feel—after such a day—about going out to reflect God's concerns? How would such a day of "hanging out" with God prepare you to be sent "out to preach"?

See *Meeting God in Community*

ful only for priests to eat. And he also gave some to his companions."

²⁷Then he said to them, "The Sabbath was made for man, not man for the Sabbath. ²⁸So the Son of Man is Lord even of the Sabbath."

3 Another time he went into the synagogue, and a man with a shriveled hand was there. ²Some of them were looking for a reason to accuse Jesus, so they watched him closely to see if he would heal him on the Sabbath. ³Jesus said to the man with the shriveled hand, "Stand up in front of everyone."

⁴Then Jesus asked them, "Which is lawful on the Sabbath: to do good or to do evil, to save life or to kill?" But they remained silent.

⁵He looked around at them in anger and, deeply distressed at their stubborn hearts, said to the man, "Stretch out your hand." He stretched it out, and his hand was completely restored. ⁶Then the Pharisees went out and began to plot with the Herodians how they might kill Jesus.

Crowds Follow Jesus

⁷Jesus withdrew with his disciples to the lake, and a large crowd from Galilee followed. ⁸When they heard all he was doing, many people came to him from Judea, Jerusalem, Idumea, and the regions across the Jordan and around Tyre and Sidon. ⁹Because of the crowd he told his disciples to have a small boat ready for him, to keep the people from crowding him. ¹⁰For he had healed many, so that those with diseases were pushing forward to touch him. ¹¹Whenever the evil[a] spirits saw him, they fell down before him and cried out, "You are the Son of God." ¹²But he gave them strict orders not to tell who he was.

The Appointing of the Twelve Apostles

¹³Jesus went up on a mountainside and called to him those he wanted, and they came to him. ¹⁴He appointed twelve—designating them apostles[b]—that they might be with him and that he might send them out to preach ¹⁵and to have authority to drive out demons. ¹⁶These are the twelve he appointed: Simon (to whom he gave the name Peter); ¹⁷James son of Zebedee and his brother John (to them he gave the name Boanerges, which means Sons of Thunder); ¹⁸Andrew, Philip, Bartholomew, Matthew, Thomas, James son of Alphaeus, Thaddaeus, Simon the Zealot ¹⁹and Judas Iscariot, who betrayed him.

Jesus and Beelzebub

²⁰Then Jesus entered a house, and again a crowd gathered, so that he and his disciples were not even able to eat. ²¹When his family heard about this, they went to take charge of him, for they said, "He is out of his mind."

²²And the teachers of the law who came down from Jerusalem said, "He is possessed by Beelzebub[c]! By the prince of demons he is driving out demons."

²³So Jesus called them and spoke to them in parables: "How can Satan drive out Satan? ²⁴If a kingdom is divided against itself, that kingdom cannot stand. ²⁵If a house is divided against itself, that house cannot stand. ²⁶And if

a 11 Greek *unclean;* also in verse 30   *b 14* Some manuscripts do not have *designating them apostles.*   *c 22* Greek *Beezeboul* or *Beelzeboul*

Satan opposes himself and is divided, he cannot stand; his end has come. ²⁷In fact, no one can enter a strong man's house and carry off his possessions unless he first ties up the strong man. Then he can rob his house. ²⁸I tell you the truth, all the sins and blasphemies of men will be forgiven them. ²⁹But whoever blasphemes against the Holy Spirit will never be forgiven; he is guilty of an eternal sin."

³⁰He said this because they were saying, "He has an evil spirit."

Jesus' Mother and Brothers

³¹Then Jesus' mother and brothers arrived. Standing outside, they sent someone in to call him. ³²A crowd was sitting around him, and they told him, "Your mother and brothers are outside looking for you."

³³"Who are my mother and my brothers?" he asked.

³⁴Then he looked at those seated in a circle around him and said, "Here are my mother and my brothers! ³⁵Whoever does God's will is my brother and sister and mother."

The Parable of the Sower

4 Again Jesus began to teach by the lake. The crowd that gathered around him was so large that he got into a boat and sat in it out on the lake, while all the people were along the shore at the water's edge. ²He taught them many things by parables, and in his teaching said: ³"Listen! A farmer went out to sow his seed. ⁴As he was scattering the seed, some fell along the path, and the birds came and ate it up. ⁵Some fell on rocky places, where it did not have much soil. It sprang up quickly, because the soil was shallow. ⁶But when the sun came up, the plants were scorched, and they withered because they had no root. ⁷Other seed fell among thorns, which grew up and choked the plants, so that they did not bear grain. ⁸Still other seed fell on good soil. It came up, grew and produced a crop, multiplying thirty, sixty, or even a hundred times."

⁹Then Jesus said, "He who has ears to hear, let him hear."

¹⁰When he was alone, the Twelve and the others around him asked him about the parables. ¹¹He told them, "The secret of the kingdom of God has been given to you. But to those on the outside everything is said in parables ¹²so that,

" 'they may be ever seeing but never perceiving,
    and ever hearing but never understanding;
    otherwise they might turn and be forgiven!'ᵃ"

¹³Then Jesus said to them, "Don't you understand this parable? How then will you understand any parable? ¹⁴The farmer sows the word. ¹⁵Some people are like seed along the path, where the word is sown. As soon as they hear it, Satan comes and takes away the word that was sown in them. ¹⁶Others, like seed sown on rocky places, hear the word and at once receive it with joy. ¹⁷But since they have no root, they last only a short time. When trouble or persecution comes because of the word, they quickly fall away. ¹⁸Still others, like seed sown among thorns, hear the word; ¹⁹but the worries of this life, the deceitfulness of wealth and the desires for other things come in and choke the word, making it unfruitful. ²⁰Others, like seed sown on

Looking Inwardly With Courage

MARK 4:13–20

"Jesus doesn't take us aside and explain things to us all the time; He explains things to us as we are able to understand them. It is slow work—so slow that it takes God all of time and eternity to make a man or woman conform to His purpose. We can only be used by God after we allow Him to show us the deep, hidden areas of our own character. It is astounding how ignorant we are about ourselves! We don't even recognize the envy, laziness or pride within us when we see it. But Jesus will reveal to us everything we have held within ourselves before His grace began to work. How many of us have learned to look inwardly with courage?"

—OSWALD CHAMBERS,
My Utmost for His Highest

ᵃ 12 Isaiah 6:9,10

To Trust or Not to Trust

MARK 4:35–41

Whether it's a family estrangement, a church dispute or a national disaster, we sometimes find ourselves asking, "God, don't you care . . . ?" Imagine yourself on this life-threatening voyage. You've bailed water for hours. Your legs are bruised from being banged about the boat by the heaving waves. You are cold, wet and bone-weary. With a hoarse voice you ask, "Teacher, don't you care . . . ?"

What about this passage touches you the most? That Jesus could control an uncontrollable force? That Jesus was surprised by their fear? That the disciples expected Jesus to intervene, but then, when he did, they were astounded that he could help? What does this passage say to you about the mystery of God's presence in seemingly uncontrollable circumstances?

See Meeting God in the Created Order

good soil, hear the word, accept it, and produce a crop—thirty, sixty or even a hundred times what was sown."

A Lamp on a Stand

[21] He said to them, "Do you bring in a lamp to put it under a bowl or a bed? Instead, don't you put it on its stand? [22] For whatever is hidden is meant to be disclosed, and whatever is concealed is meant to be brought out into the open. [23] If anyone has ears to hear, let him hear."

[24] "Consider carefully what you hear," he continued. "With the measure you use, it will be measured to you—and even more. [25] Whoever has will be given more; whoever does not have, even what he has will be taken from him."

The Parable of the Growing Seed

[26] He also said, "This is what the kingdom of God is like. A man scatters seed on the ground. [27] Night and day, whether he sleeps or gets up, the seed sprouts and grows, though he does not know how. [28] All by itself the soil produces grain—first the stalk, then the head, then the full kernel in the head. [29] As soon as the grain is ripe, he puts the sickle to it, because the harvest has come."

The Parable of the Mustard Seed

[30] Again he said, "What shall we say the kingdom of God is like, or what parable shall we use to describe it? [31] It is like a mustard seed, which is the smallest seed you plant in the ground. [32] Yet when planted, it grows and becomes the largest of all garden plants, with such big branches that the birds of the air can perch in its shade."

[33] With many similar parables Jesus spoke the word to them, as much as they could understand. [34] He did not say anything to them without using a parable. But when he was alone with his own disciples, he explained everything.

Jesus Calms the Storm

[35] That day when evening came, he said to his disciples, "Let us go over to the other side." [36] Leaving the crowd behind, they took him along, just as he was, in the boat. There were also other boats with him. [37] A furious squall came up, and the waves broke over the boat, so that it was nearly swamped. [38] Jesus was in the stern, sleeping on a cushion. The disciples woke him and said to him, "Teacher, don't you care if we drown?"

[39] He got up, rebuked the wind and said to the waves, "Quiet! Be still!" Then the wind died down and it was completely calm.

[40] He said to his disciples, "Why are you so afraid? Do you still have no faith?"

[41] They were terrified and asked each other, "Who is this? Even the wind and the waves obey him!"

The Healing of a Demon-possessed Man

5 They went across the lake to the region of the Gerasenes.[a] [2] When Jesus got out of the boat, a man with an evil[b] spirit came from the tombs to meet him. [3] This man lived in the tombs, and no one could bind him any more, not even with a chain. [4] For he had often been chained

[a] 1 Some manuscripts *Gadarenes*; other manuscripts *Gergesenes* [b] 2 Greek *unclean*; also in verses 8 and 13

hand and foot, but he tore the chains apart and broke the irons on his feet. No one was strong enough to subdue him. ⁵Night and day among the tombs and in the hills he would cry out and cut himself with stones.

⁶When he saw Jesus from a distance, he ran and fell on his knees in front of him. ⁷He shouted at the top of his voice, "What do you want with me, Jesus, Son of the Most High God? Swear to God that you won't torture me!" ⁸For Jesus had said to him, "Come out of this man, you evil spirit!"

⁹Then Jesus asked him, "What is your name?"

"My name is Legion," he replied, "for we are many." ¹⁰And he begged Jesus again and again not to send them out of the area.

¹¹A large herd of pigs was feeding on the nearby hillside. ¹²The demons begged Jesus, "Send us among the pigs; allow us to go into them." ¹³He gave them permission, and the evil spirits came out and went into the pigs. The herd, about two thousand in number, rushed down the steep bank into the lake and were drowned.

¹⁴Those tending the pigs ran off and reported this in the town and countryside, and the people went out to see what had happened. ¹⁵When they came to Jesus, they saw the man who had been possessed by the legion of demons, sitting there, dressed and in his right mind; and they were afraid. ¹⁶Those who had seen it told the people what had happened to the demon-possessed man—and told about the pigs as well. ¹⁷Then the people began to plead with Jesus to leave their region.

¹⁸As Jesus was getting into the boat, the man who had been demon-possessed begged to go with him. ¹⁹Jesus did not let him, but said, "Go home to your family and tell them how much the Lord has done for you, and how he has had mercy on you." ²⁰So the man went away and began to tell in the Decapolis*ᵃ* how much Jesus had done for him. And all the people were amazed.

A Dead Girl and a Sick Woman

²¹When Jesus had again crossed over by boat to the other side of the lake, a large crowd gathered around him while he was by the lake. ²²Then one of the synagogue rulers, named Jairus, came there. Seeing Jesus, he fell at his feet ²³and pleaded earnestly with him, "My little daughter is dying. Please come and put your hands on her so that she will be healed and live." ²⁴So Jesus went with him.

A large crowd followed and pressed around him. ²⁵And a woman was there who had been subject to bleeding for twelve years. ²⁶She had suffered a great deal under the care of many doctors and had spent all she had, yet instead of getting better she grew worse. ²⁷When she heard about Jesus, she came up behind him in the crowd and touched his cloak, ²⁸because she thought, "If I just touch his clothes, I will be healed." ²⁹Immediately her bleeding stopped and she felt in her body that she was freed from her suffering.

³⁰At once Jesus realized that power had gone out from him. He turned around in the crowd and asked, "Who touched my clothes?"

When It Hurts to Stick Around

MARK 5:18–20

When we've been hurt or embarrassed by a group of people, it can be tough to sense God saying that we need to stay with those people for a while longer in order to become the person God wants us to be.

Read Mark 5:1–20, then reread verses 18–20. What word or phrase in these verses attracts your attention? Reflect on this word or phrase. What new insights come to you as you turn it over in your mind? Rest in silence, being open to anything God may want to impress on you. How does this passage touch your life today?

See Meeting God in Scripture

Telling God Where It Hurts

MARK 5:27-35

Something about Jesus captivates this woman and prompts her to appear in public, even though she has suffered from a lengthy and intensely personal disease. She recognizes his love and power and trusts him enough to touch him, even though she is ritually "unclean." Do you feel safe enough with God to trust him with everything, even the most embarrassing things? How might it contribute to your healing to tell God about your intensely personal problems, even though he is already aware of them? How might God respond to you? If you wish, paraphrase God's response from Mark 5:34: "Your faith has healed you. Go in peace and be freed from your suffering."

See Meeting God in Prayer

³¹"You see the people crowding against you," his disciples answered, "and yet you can ask, 'Who touched me?'"

³²But Jesus kept looking around to see who had done it. ³³Then the woman, knowing what had happened to her, came and fell at his feet and, trembling with fear, told him the whole truth. ³⁴He said to her, "Daughter, your faith has healed you. Go in peace and be freed from your suffering."

³⁵While Jesus was still speaking, some men came from the house of Jairus, the synagogue ruler. "Your daughter is dead," they said. "Why bother the teacher any more?"

³⁶Ignoring what they said, Jesus told the synagogue ruler, "Don't be afraid; just believe."

³⁷He did not let anyone follow him except Peter, James and John the brother of James. ³⁸When they came to the home of the synagogue ruler, Jesus saw a commotion, with people crying and wailing loudly. ³⁹He went in and said to them, "Why all this commotion and wailing? The child is not dead but asleep." ⁴⁰But they laughed at him.

After he put them all out, he took the child's father and mother and the disciples who were with him, and went in where the child was. ⁴¹He took her by the hand and said to her, *"Talitha koum!"* (which means, "Little girl, I say to you, get up!"). ⁴²Immediately the girl stood up and walked around (she was twelve years old). At this they were completely astonished. ⁴³He gave strict orders not to let anyone know about this, and told them to give her something to eat.

A Prophet Without Honor

6 Jesus left there and went to his hometown, accompanied by his disciples. ²When the Sabbath came, he began to teach in the synagogue, and many who heard him were amazed.

"Where did this man get these things?" they asked. "What's this wisdom that has been given him, that he even does miracles! ³Isn't this the carpenter? Isn't this Mary's son and the brother of James, Joseph,ᵃ Judas and Simon? Aren't his sisters here with us?" And they took offense at him.

⁴Jesus said to them, "Only in his hometown, among his relatives and in his own house is a prophet without honor." ⁵He could not do any miracles there, except lay his hands on a few sick people and heal them. ⁶And he was amazed at their lack of faith.

Jesus Sends Out the Twelve

Then Jesus went around teaching from village to village. ⁷Calling the Twelve to him, he sent them out two by two and gave them authority over evilᵇ spirits.

⁸These were his instructions: "Take nothing for the journey except a staff—no bread, no bag, no money in your belts. ⁹Wear sandals but not an extra tunic. ¹⁰Whenever you enter a house, stay there until you leave that town. ¹¹And if any place will not welcome you or listen to you, shake the dust off your feet when you leave, as a testimony against them."

¹²They went out and preached that people should repent. ¹³They drove out many demons and anointed many sick people with oil and healed them.

ᵃ 3 Greek *Joses,* a variant of *Joseph*   ᵇ 7 Greek *unclean*

John the Baptist Beheaded

¹⁴King Herod heard about this, for Jesus' name had become well known. Some were saying,[a] "John the Baptist has been raised from the dead, and that is why miraculous powers are at work in him."

¹⁵Others said, "He is Elijah."

And still others claimed, "He is a prophet, like one of the prophets of long ago."

¹⁶But when Herod heard this, he said, "John, the man I beheaded, has been raised from the dead!"

¹⁷For Herod himself had given orders to have John arrested, and he had him bound and put in prison. He did this because of Herodias, his brother Philip's wife, whom he had married. ¹⁸For John had been saying to Herod, "It is not lawful for you to have your brother's wife." ¹⁹So Herodias nursed a grudge against John and wanted to kill him. But she was not able to, ²⁰because Herod feared John and protected him, knowing him to be a righteous and holy man. When Herod heard John, he was greatly puzzled[b]; yet he liked to listen to him.

²¹Finally the opportune time came. On his birthday Herod gave a banquet for his high officials and military commanders and the leading men of Galilee. ²²When the daughter of Herodias came in and danced, she pleased Herod and his dinner guests.

The king said to the girl, "Ask me for anything you want, and I'll give it to you." ²³And he promised her with an oath, "Whatever you ask I will give you, up to half my kingdom."

²⁴She went out and said to her mother, "What shall I ask for?"

"The head of John the Baptist," she answered.

²⁵At once the girl hurried in to the king with the request: "I want you to give me right now the head of John the Baptist on a platter."

²⁶The king was greatly distressed, but because of his oaths and his dinner guests, he did not want to refuse her. ²⁷So he immediately sent an executioner with orders to bring John's head. The man went, beheaded John in the prison, ²⁸and brought back his head on a platter. He presented it to the girl, and she gave it to her mother. ²⁹On hearing of this, John's disciples came and took his body and laid it in a tomb.

Jesus Feeds the Five Thousand

³⁰The apostles gathered around Jesus and reported to him all they had done and taught. ³¹Then, because so many people were coming and going that they did not even have a chance to eat, he said to them, "Come with me by yourselves to a quiet place and get some rest."

³²So they went away by themselves in a boat to a solitary place. ³³But many who saw them leaving recognized them and ran on foot from all the towns and got there ahead of them. ³⁴When Jesus landed and saw a large crowd, he had compassion on them, because they were like sheep without a shepherd. So he began teaching them many things.

Empty and Filled

MARK 6:30–34

Jesus and the disciples give up a quiet time of fellowship because Jesus has compassion on the crowd and stops to teach and feed them. As much as we'd like to think that the Christian life will be happy and comfortable, "dying to self" often requires us to give up both our time and our personal preferences. When our service is costly, when we empty ourselves, God can fill our hearts with compassion.

Who is like that "large crowd" in your own situation? Who is like a "sheep without a shepherd"? How is God asking you to use your unique skills for a particular task? Perhaps you're not sure whether God is prompting you to go to "a quiet place and get some rest"—or compelling you to get back to work. What do you need to ask God with respect to this issue?

See Meeting God in Service

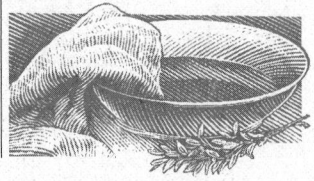

The Folly of the Distant Heart

MARK 7:1–13

Sometimes we mistakenly think that if we know facts about God and do good deeds, we're on the right track spiritually. But God wants our love to be authentic. A hypocrite, according to this Biblical definition, is a person whose heart doesn't match his or her words, actions and beliefs.

Paraphrase and personalize Mark 7:6 along these lines: "God, I honor you with my _____ (actions, words, priorities), but my heart is far from you." Confess this to God and then ask God to fill you with a genuine love that you can express with your heart, your head and your hands.

See Meeting God in Prayer

³⁵By this time it was late in the day, so his disciples came to him. "This is a remote place," they said, "and it's already very late. ³⁶Send the people away so they can go to the surrounding countryside and villages and buy themselves something to eat."

³⁷But he answered, "You give them something to eat."

They said to him, "That would take eight months of a man's wages*! Are we to go and spend that much on bread and give it to them to eat?"

³⁸"How many loaves do you have?" he asked. "Go and see."

When they found out, they said, "Five—and two fish."

³⁹Then Jesus directed them to have all the people sit down in groups on the green grass. ⁴⁰So they sat down in groups of hundreds and fifties. ⁴¹Taking the five loaves and the two fish and looking up to heaven, he gave thanks and broke the loaves. Then he gave them to his disciples to set before the people. He also divided the two fish among them all. ⁴²They all ate and were satisfied, ⁴³and the disciples picked up twelve basketfuls of broken pieces of bread and fish. ⁴⁴The number of the men who had eaten was five thousand.

Jesus Walks on the Water

⁴⁵Immediately Jesus made his disciples get into the boat and go on ahead of him to Bethsaida, while he dismissed the crowd. ⁴⁶After leaving them, he went up on a mountainside to pray.

⁴⁷When evening came, the boat was in the middle of the lake, and he was alone on land. ⁴⁸He saw the disciples straining at the oars, because the wind was against them. About the fourth watch of the night he went out to them, walking on the lake. He was about to pass by them, ⁴⁹but when they saw him walking on the lake, they thought he was a ghost. They cried out, ⁵⁰because they all saw him and were terrified.

Immediately he spoke to them and said, "Take courage! It is I. Don't be afraid." ⁵¹Then he climbed into the boat with them, and the wind died down. They were completely amazed, ⁵²for they had not understood about the loaves; their hearts were hardened.

⁵³When they had crossed over, they landed at Gennesaret and anchored there. ⁵⁴As soon as they got out of the boat, people recognized Jesus. ⁵⁵They ran throughout that whole region and carried the sick on mats to wherever they heard he was. ⁵⁶And wherever he went—into villages, towns or countryside—they placed the sick in the marketplaces. They begged him to let them touch even the edge of his cloak, and all who touched him were healed.

Clean and Unclean

7 The Pharisees and some of the teachers of the law who had come from Jerusalem gathered around Jesus and ²saw some of his disciples eating food with hands that were "unclean," that is, unwashed. ³(The Pharisees and all the Jews do not eat unless they give their hands a ceremonial washing, holding to the tradition of the elders. ⁴When they come from the marketplace they do not eat unless

a 37 Greek take two hundred denarii

they wash. And they observe many other traditions, such as the washing of cups, pitchers and kettles.[a])

[5]So the Pharisees and teachers of the law asked Jesus, "Why don't your disciples live according to the tradition of the elders instead of eating their food with 'unclean' hands?"

[6]He replied, "Isaiah was right when he prophesied about you hypocrites; as it is written:

> " 'These people honor me with their lips,
>   but their hearts are far from me.
> [7]They worship me in vain;
>   their teachings are but rules taught by men.'[b]

[8]You have let go of the commands of God and are holding on to the traditions of men."

[9]And he said to them: "You have a fine way of setting aside the commands of God in order to observe[c] your own traditions! [10]For Moses said, 'Honor your father and your mother,'[d] and, 'Anyone who curses his father or mother must be put to death.'[e] [11]But you say that if a man says to his father or mother: 'Whatever help you might otherwise have received from me is Corban' (that is, a gift devoted to God), [12]then you no longer let him do anything for his father or mother. [13]Thus you nullify the word of God by your tradition that you have handed down. And you do many things like that."

[14]Again Jesus called the crowd to him and said, "Listen to me, everyone, and understand this. [15]Nothing outside a man can make him 'unclean' by going into him. Rather, it is what comes out of a man that makes him 'unclean.'[f]"

[17]After he had left the crowd and entered the house, his disciples asked him about this parable. [18]"Are you so dull?" he asked. "Don't you see that nothing that enters a man from the outside can make him 'unclean'? [19]For it doesn't go into his heart but into his stomach, and then out of his body." (In saying this, Jesus declared all foods "clean.")

[20]He went on: "What comes out of a man is what makes him 'unclean.' [21]For from within, out of men's hearts, come evil thoughts, sexual immorality, theft, murder, adultery, [22]greed, malice, deceit, lewdness, envy, slander, arrogance and folly. [23]All these evils come from inside and make a man 'unclean.' "

The Faith of a Syrophoenician Woman

[24]Jesus left that place and went to the vicinity of Tyre.[g] He entered a house and did not want anyone to know it; yet he could not keep his presence secret. [25]In fact, as soon as she heard about him, a woman whose little daughter was possessed by an evil[h] spirit came and fell at his feet. [26]The woman was a Greek, born in Syrian Phoenicia. She begged Jesus to drive the demon out of her daughter.

[27]"First let the children eat all they want," he told her, "for it is not right to take the children's bread and toss it to their dogs."

God's Personal Touch

MARK 7:24–35

The way that Jesus heals this man requires that Jesus touch the man's head and face, perhaps even cradling the man's face in his hands. We can't help but wonder how long it has been since this person has been treated so gently.

Picture yourself face-to-face with Jesus and needing a healing touch. In what way does Jesus touch you? With a gentle pat on the back to encourage you? With his hands on your shoulders, looking you squarely in the eyes in order to get your attention? Cradling your face with compassion because you have been left out and rejected? Enjoy that image for several moments. Ask God to show you someone who needs to be touched in the same way.

See Meeting God in Service

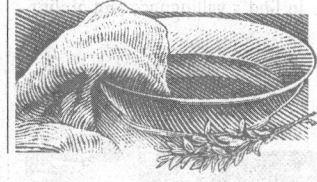

---

[a]4 Some early manuscripts *pitchers, kettles and dining couches*   [b]6,7 Isaiah 29:13   [c]9 Some manuscripts *set up*   [d]10 Exodus 20:12; Deut. 5:16   [e]10 Exodus 21:17; Lev. 20:9   [f]15 Some early manuscripts *'unclean.' 16If anyone has ears to hear, let him hear.*   [g]24 Many early manuscripts *Tyre and Sidon*   [h]25 Greek *unclean*

Remembering God's Grace

MARK 8:16–21

Hungry once again, the disciples forget that providing for their needs is Jesus' specialty. On an even deeper level, they don't understand that Jesus is the Christ, who changes water to wine and feeds five thousand people with five loaves.

Our experiences of God—the times when he has rescued, comforted, confronted and challenged us—should teach us to rely on his miraculous power. They should help us remember how he has cared for us in the past. In our human weakness, however, we forget, and our forgetfulness hardens our hearts. Recall the last time God confronted, comforted or guided you. If you wish, write about that occasion for a minute or two and place it with other reflections in a journal as a way of deepening your trust in God's willingness and ability to care for you.

See Meeting God in Everyday Life

²⁸"Yes, Lord," she replied, "but even the dogs under the table eat the children's crumbs."

²⁹Then he told her, "For such a reply, you may go; the demon has left your daughter."

³⁰She went home and found her child lying on the bed, and the demon gone.

The Healing of a Deaf and Mute Man

³¹Then Jesus left the vicinity of Tyre and went through Sidon, down to the Sea of Galilee and into the region of the Decapolis.^a ³²There some people brought to him a man who was deaf and could hardly talk, and they begged him to place his hand on the man.

³³After he took him aside, away from the crowd, Jesus put his fingers into the man's ears. Then he spit and touched the man's tongue. ³⁴He looked up to heaven and with a deep sigh said to him, *"Ephphatha!"* (which means, "Be opened!"). ³⁵At this, the man's ears were opened, his tongue was loosened and he began to speak plainly.

³⁶Jesus commanded them not to tell anyone. But the more he did so, the more they kept talking about it. ³⁷People were overwhelmed with amazement. "He has done everything well," they said. "He even makes the deaf hear and the mute speak."

Jesus Feeds the Four Thousand

8 During those days another large crowd gathered. Since they had nothing to eat, Jesus called his disciples to him and said, ²"I have compassion for these people; they have already been with me three days and have nothing to eat. ³If I send them home hungry, they will collapse on the way, because some of them have come a long distance."

⁴His disciples answered, "But where in this remote place can anyone get enough bread to feed them?"

⁵"How many loaves do you have?" Jesus asked.

"Seven," they replied.

⁶He told the crowd to sit down on the ground. When he had taken the seven loaves and given thanks, he broke them and gave them to his disciples to set before the people, and they did so. ⁷They had a few small fish as well; he gave thanks for them also and told the disciples to distribute them. ⁸The people ate and were satisfied. Afterward the disciples picked up seven basketfuls of broken pieces that were left over. ⁹About four thousand men were present. And having sent them away, ¹⁰he got into the boat with his disciples and went to the region of Dalmanutha.

¹¹The Pharisees came and began to question Jesus. To test him, they asked him for a sign from heaven. ¹²He sighed deeply and said, "Why does this generation ask for a miraculous sign? I tell you the truth, no sign will be given to it." ¹³Then he left them, got back into the boat and crossed to the other side.

The Yeast of the Pharisees and Herod

¹⁴The disciples had forgotten to bring bread, except for one loaf they had with them in the boat. ¹⁵"Be careful," Jesus warned them. "Watch out for the yeast of the Pharisees and that of Herod."

^a *31* That is, the Ten Cities

¹⁶They discussed this with one another and said, "It is because we have no bread."

¹⁷Aware of their discussion, Jesus asked them: "Why are you talking about having no bread? Do you still not see or understand? Are your hearts hardened? ¹⁸Do you have eyes but fail to see, and ears but fail to hear? And don't you remember? ¹⁹When I broke the five loaves for the five thousand, how many basketfuls of pieces did you pick up?"

"Twelve," they replied.

²⁰"And when I broke the seven loaves for the four thousand, how many basketfuls of pieces did you pick up?"

They answered, "Seven."

²¹He said to them, "Do you still not understand?"

The Healing of a Blind Man at Bethsaida

²²They came to Bethsaida, and some people brought a blind man and begged Jesus to touch him. ²³He took the blind man by the hand and led him outside the village. When he had spit on the man's eyes and put his hands on him, Jesus asked, "Do you see anything?"

²⁴He looked up and said, "I see people; they look like trees walking around."

²⁵Once more Jesus put his hands on the man's eyes. Then his eyes were opened, his sight was restored, and he saw everything clearly. ²⁶Jesus sent him home, saying, "Don't go into the village.ᵃ"

Peter's Confession of Christ

²⁷Jesus and his disciples went on to the villages around Caesarea Philippi. On the way he asked them, "Who do people say I am?"

²⁸They replied, "Some say John the Baptist; others say Elijah; and still others, one of the prophets."

²⁹"But what about you?" he asked. "Who do you say I am?"

Peter answered, "You are the Christ.ᵇ"

³⁰Jesus warned them not to tell anyone about him.

Jesus Predicts His Death

³¹He then began to teach them that the Son of Man must suffer many things and be rejected by the elders, chief priests and teachers of the law, and that he must be killed and after three days rise again. ³²He spoke plainly about this, and Peter took him aside and began to rebuke him.

³³But when Jesus turned and looked at his disciples, he rebuked Peter. "Get behind me, Satan!" he said. "You do not have in mind the things of God, but the things of men."

³⁴Then he called the crowd to him along with his disciples and said: "If anyone would come after me, he must deny himself and take up his cross and follow me. ³⁵For whoever wants to save his lifeᶜ will lose it, but whoever loses his life for me and for the gospel will save it. ³⁶What good is it for a man to gain the whole world, yet forfeit his soul? ³⁷Or what can a man give in exchange for his soul? ³⁸If anyone is ashamed of me and my words in this adulterous and sinful generation, the Son of Man will be

---

Broken Bread, Poured Out Wine

MARK 8:35

"The ecclesiastical idea of a servant of God is not Jesus Christ's idea. His idea is that we serve Him by being the servants of other [people]. The real test of the saint is not preaching the gospel, but washing disciples' feet, that is, doing the things that do not count in the actual estimate of [others] but count everything in the estimate of God. Jesus Christ's idea of a New Testament saint [is] not one who proclaims the gospel merely, but one who becomes broken bread and poured out wine in the hands of Jesus Christ for other lives."

—OSWALD CHAMBERS,
My Utmost for His Highest

ᵃ 26 Some manuscripts *Don't go and tell anyone in the village*   ᵇ 29 Or *Messiah.* "The Christ" (Greek) and "the Messiah" (Hebrew) both mean "the Anointed One."   ᶜ 35 The Greek word means either *life* or *soul*; also in verse 36.

Honest Doubt

MARK 9:24

The father of this burned and broken boy is surprisingly honest about his lack of faith. Because he wants so much for Jesus to help his son, he might have been motivated to equivocate. Jesus honors his honesty with compassion and respect.

Fold your hands with your fingers intertwined. Imagine that one hand is your belief in God's power to redeem a person or situation and that your other hand is your doubt. Ask God to help you overcome your doubts and to work in that situation to bring about renewal and healing.

See Meeting God in Prayer

ashamed of him when he comes in his Father's glory with the holy angels."

9 And he said to them, "I tell you the truth, some who are standing here will not taste death before they see the kingdom of God come with power."

The Transfiguration

²After six days Jesus took Peter, James and John with him and led them up a high mountain, where they were all alone. There he was transfigured before them. ³His clothes became dazzling white, whiter than anyone in the world could bleach them. ⁴And there appeared before them Elijah and Moses, who were talking with Jesus.

⁵Peter said to Jesus, "Rabbi, it is good for us to be here. Let us put up three shelters—one for you, one for Moses and one for Elijah." ⁶(He did not know what to say, they were so frightened.)

⁷Then a cloud appeared and enveloped them, and a voice came from the cloud: "This is my Son, whom I love. Listen to him!"

⁸Suddenly, when they looked around, they no longer saw anyone with them except Jesus.

⁹As they were coming down the mountain, Jesus gave them orders not to tell anyone what they had seen until the Son of Man had risen from the dead. ¹⁰They kept the matter to themselves, discussing what "rising from the dead" meant.

¹¹And they asked him, "Why do the teachers of the law say that Elijah must come first?"

¹²Jesus replied, "To be sure, Elijah does come first, and restores all things. Why then is it written that the Son of Man must suffer much and be rejected? ¹³But I tell you, Elijah has come, and they have done to him everything they wished, just as it is written about him."

The Healing of a Boy With an Evil Spirit

¹⁴When they came to the other disciples, they saw a large crowd around them and the teachers of the law arguing with them. ¹⁵As soon as all the people saw Jesus, they were overwhelmed with wonder and ran to greet him.

¹⁶"What are you arguing with them about?" he asked.

¹⁷A man in the crowd answered, "Teacher, I brought you my son, who is possessed by a spirit that has robbed him of speech. ¹⁸Whenever it seizes him, it throws him to the ground. He foams at the mouth, gnashes his teeth and becomes rigid. I asked your disciples to drive out the spirit, but they could not."

¹⁹"O unbelieving generation," Jesus replied, "how long shall I stay with you? How long shall I put up with you? Bring the boy to me."

²⁰So they brought him. When the spirit saw Jesus, it immediately threw the boy into a convulsion. He fell to the ground and rolled around, foaming at the mouth.

²¹Jesus asked the boy's father, "How long has he been like this?"

"From childhood," he answered. ²²"It has often thrown him into fire or water to kill him. But if you can do anything, take pity on us and help us."

²³" 'If you can'?" said Jesus. "Everything is possible for him who believes."

[24]Immediately the boy's father exclaimed, "I do believe; help me overcome my unbelief!"

[25]When Jesus saw that a crowd was running to the scene, he rebuked the evil[a] spirit. "You deaf and mute spirit," he said, "I command you, come out of him and never enter him again."

[26]The spirit shrieked, convulsed him violently and came out. The boy looked so much like a corpse that many said, "He's dead." [27]But Jesus took him by the hand and lifted him to his feet, and he stood up.

[28]After Jesus had gone indoors, his disciples asked him privately, "Why couldn't we drive it out?"

[29]He replied, "This kind can come out only by prayer.[b]"

[30]They left that place and passed through Galilee. Jesus did not want anyone to know where they were, [31]because he was teaching his disciples. He said to them, "The Son of Man is going to be betrayed into the hands of men. They will kill him, and after three days he will rise." [32]But they did not understand what he meant and were afraid to ask him about it.

Who Is the Greatest?

[33]They came to Capernaum. When he was in the house, he asked them, "What were you arguing about on the road?" [34]But they kept quiet because on the way they had argued about who was the greatest.

[35]Sitting down, Jesus called the Twelve and said, "If anyone wants to be first, he must be the very last, and the servant of all."

[36]He took a little child and had him stand among them. Taking him in his arms, he said to them, [37]"Whoever welcomes one of these little children in my name welcomes me; and whoever welcomes me does not welcome me but the one who sent me."

Whoever Is Not Against Us Is for Us

[38]"Teacher," said John, "we saw a man driving out demons in your name and we told him to stop, because he was not one of us."

[39]"Do not stop him," Jesus said. "No one who does a miracle in my name can in the next moment say anything bad about me, [40]for whoever is not against us is for us. [41]I tell you the truth, anyone who gives you a cup of water in my name because you belong to Christ will certainly not lose his reward.

Causing to Sin

[42]"And if anyone causes one of these little ones who believe in me to sin, it would be better for him to be thrown into the sea with a large millstone tied around his neck. [43]If your hand causes you to sin, cut it off. It is better for you to enter life maimed than with two hands to go into hell, where the fire never goes out.[c] [45]And if your foot causes you to sin, cut it off. It is better for you to enter life crippled than to have two feet and be thrown into hell.[d] [47]And if your eye causes you to sin, pluck it out. It is better

---

No Competition

MARK 9:38–41

Sometimes we tend to become competitive with other people, organizations or churches. When we're competitive we feel threatened. We're driven to prove we possess a special knowledge, a better method or a more honorable motive. We sometimes become territorial when someone who is not "one of us" does what we do. What if they would do it better? We want the kingdom of God to be advanced, but we want to be able to claim the credit for our corner of it.

Read this passage again and ponder these questions: What does this passage teach me about competition and God's kingdom? What can I pray for those toward whom I feel competitive?

See Meeting God in Community

---

[a] 25 Greek *unclean*   [b] 29 Some manuscripts *prayer and fasting*
[c] 43 Some manuscripts *out, [44]where / " 'their worm does not die, / and the fire is not quenched.'*   [d] 45 Some manuscripts *hell, [46]where / " 'their worm does not die, / and the fire is not quenched.'*

All Things Are Possible

MARK 10:21–27

The dashing young star of this passage is also a meticulously religious person. Jesus pierces his heart, however, by demanding that he surrender the wealth and position that he values more than God.

Imagine yourself face-to-face with Jesus. You are self-possessed, well-mannered, surrounded by your accomplishments. Your motives are honorable. Imagine Jesus looking into your eyes so that you know the depth of his love for you. Now imagine him asking you to give up something that is very precious to you. You cringe. "O Lord, not that!" Now Jesus is telling you that all things are possible with God. What do you need to say to God in response?

See *Meeting God in Scripture*

for you to enter the kingdom of God with one eye than to have two eyes and be thrown into hell, ⁴⁸where

" 'their worm does not die,
  and the fire is not quenched.'ᵃ

⁴⁹Everyone will be salted with fire.

⁵⁰"Salt is good, but if it loses its saltiness, how can you make it salty again? Have salt in yourselves, and be at peace with each other."

Divorce

10 Jesus then left that place and went into the region of Judea and across the Jordan. Again crowds of people came to him, and as was his custom, he taught them.

²Some Pharisees came and tested him by asking, "Is it lawful for a man to divorce his wife?"

³"What did Moses command you?" he replied.

⁴They said, "Moses permitted a man to write a certificate of divorce and send her away."

⁵"It was because your hearts were hard that Moses wrote you this law," Jesus replied. ⁶"But at the beginning of creation God 'made them male and female.'ᵇ ⁷'For this reason a man will leave his father and mother and be united to his wife,ᶜ ⁸and the two will become one flesh.'ᵈ So they are no longer two, but one. ⁹Therefore what God has joined together, let man not separate."

¹⁰When they were in the house again, the disciples asked Jesus about this. ¹¹He answered, "Anyone who divorces his wife and marries another woman commits adultery against her. ¹²And if she divorces her husband and marries another man, she commits adultery."

The Little Children and Jesus

¹³People were bringing little children to Jesus to have him touch them, but the disciples rebuked them. ¹⁴When Jesus saw this, he was indignant. He said to them, "Let the little children come to me, and do not hinder them, for the kingdom of God belongs to such as these. ¹⁵I tell you the truth, anyone who will not receive the kingdom of God like a little child will never enter it." ¹⁶And he took the children in his arms, put his hands on them and blessed them.

The Rich Young Man

¹⁷As Jesus started on his way, a man ran up to him and fell on his knees before him. "Good teacher," he asked, "what must I do to inherit eternal life?"

¹⁸"Why do you call me good?" Jesus answered. "No one is good—except God alone. ¹⁹You know the commandments: 'Do not murder, do not commit adultery, do not steal, do not give false testimony, do not defraud, honor your father and mother.'ᵉ"

²⁰"Teacher," he declared, "all these I have kept since I was a boy."

²¹Jesus looked at him and loved him. "One thing you lack," he said. "Go, sell everything you have and give to the poor, and you will have treasure in heaven. Then come, follow me."

ᵃ 48 Isaiah 66:24   ᵇ 6 Gen. 1:27   ᶜ 7 Some early manuscripts do not have *and be united to his wife.*   ᵈ 8 Gen. 2:24   ᵉ 19 Exodus 20:12–16; Deut. 5:16–20

²²At this the man's face fell. He went away sad, because he had great wealth.

²³Jesus looked around and said to his disciples, "How hard it is for the rich to enter the kingdom of God!"

²⁴The disciples were amazed at his words. But Jesus said again, "Children, how hard it is[a] to enter the kingdom of God! ²⁵It is easier for a camel to go through the eye of a needle than for a rich man to enter the kingdom of God."

²⁶The disciples were even more amazed, and said to each other, "Who then can be saved?"

²⁷Jesus looked at them and said, "With man this is impossible, but not with God; all things are possible with God."

²⁸Peter said to him, "We have left everything to follow you!"

²⁹"I tell you the truth," Jesus replied, "no one who has left home or brothers or sisters or mother or father or children or fields for me and the gospel ³⁰will fail to receive a hundred times as much in this present age (homes, brothers, sisters, mothers, children and fields—and with them, persecutions) and in the age to come, eternal life. ³¹But many who are first will be last, and the last first."

Jesus Again Predicts His Death

³²They were on their way up to Jerusalem, with Jesus leading the way, and the disciples were astonished, while those who followed were afraid. Again he took the Twelve aside and told them what was going to happen to him. ³³"We are going up to Jerusalem," he said, "and the Son of Man will be betrayed to the chief priests and teachers of the law. They will condemn him to death and will hand him over to the Gentiles, ³⁴who will mock him and spit on him, flog him and kill him. Three days later he will rise."

The Request of James and John

³⁵Then James and John, the sons of Zebedee, came to him. "Teacher," they said, "we want you to do for us whatever we ask."

³⁶"What do you want me to do for you?" he asked.

³⁷They replied, "Let one of us sit at your right and the other at your left in your glory."

³⁸"You don't know what you are asking," Jesus said. "Can you drink the cup I drink or be baptized with the baptism I am baptized with?"

³⁹"We can," they answered.

Jesus said to them, "You will drink the cup I drink and be baptized with the baptism I am baptized with, ⁴⁰but to sit at my right or left is not for me to grant. These places belong to those for whom they have been prepared."

⁴¹When the ten heard about this, they became indignant with James and John. ⁴²Jesus called them together and said, "You know that those who are regarded as rulers of the Gentiles lord it over them, and their high officials exercise authority over them. ⁴³Not so with you. Instead, whoever wants to become great among you must be your servant, ⁴⁴and whoever wants to be first must be slave of all. ⁴⁵For even the Son of Man did not come to be served, but to serve, and to give his life as a ransom for many."

---

a 24 Some manuscripts is for those who trust in riches

A Place of Importance

MARK 10:35–40

James and John use their friendship with Jesus in order to manipulate him into giving them a place beside him, thinking it will bring them prestige and power. It must not have seemed improper to them at the time, nor do our "order-placing" prayers look that bad to us. If we're honest, a lot of our prayers consist of politely telling God how things should be.

Think about a troublesome situation in your life. Write a prayer that tells God how you think things should be. Read it. Now write a prayer that is full of your questions rather than full of your answers.

See Meeting God in Prayer

Prayer for All Nations

MARK 11:17

Praying for people we know can be difficult—praying for people we don't know is even more challenging. Jesus said the temple was a place of prayer for all nations. The court of the Gentiles was to be a place where all people could come to God.

Try praying for other nations in one of these ways: Choose a particular nation or group of people for whom you have compassion (those who live with famine conditions in Africa, people in South America who are losing their rainforest habitat, those who live under the threat of genocide). Pray for them and their troubling situation. Or turn to the world news section of your newspaper or in a magazine and pray for the nations mentioned there. Turn to the "restaurant" category in the Yellow Pages of your telephone book and pray for the nations represented by various ethnic restaurants.

See Meeting God in Community

Blind Bartimaeus Receives His Sight

⁴⁶Then they came to Jericho. As Jesus and his disciples, together with a large crowd, were leaving the city, a blind man, Bartimaeus (that is, the Son of Timaeus), was sitting by the roadside begging. ⁴⁷When he heard that it was Jesus of Nazareth, he began to shout, "Jesus, Son of David, have mercy on me!"

⁴⁸Many rebuked him and told him to be quiet, but he shouted all the more, "Son of David, have mercy on me!"

⁴⁹Jesus stopped and said, "Call him."

So they called to the blind man, "Cheer up! On your feet! He's calling you." ⁵⁰Throwing his cloak aside, he jumped to his feet and came to Jesus.

⁵¹"What do you want me to do for you?" Jesus asked him. The blind man said, "Rabbi, I want to see."

⁵²"Go," said Jesus, "your faith has healed you." Immediately he received his sight and followed Jesus along the road.

The Triumphal Entry

11 As they approached Jerusalem and came to Bethphage and Bethany at the Mount of Olives, Jesus sent two of his disciples, ²saying to them, "Go to the village ahead of you, and just as you enter it, you will find a colt tied there, which no one has ever ridden. Untie it and bring it here. ³If anyone asks you, 'Why are you doing this?' tell him, 'The Lord needs it and will send it back here shortly.' "

⁴They went and found a colt outside in the street, tied at a doorway. As they untied it, ⁵some people standing there asked, "What are you doing, untying that colt?" ⁶They answered as Jesus had told them to, and the people let them go. ⁷When they brought the colt to Jesus and threw their cloaks over it, he sat on it. ⁸Many people spread their cloaks on the road, while others spread branches they had cut in the fields. ⁹Those who went ahead and those who followed shouted,

"Hosanna!ᵃ"

"Blessed is he who comes in the name of the Lord!"ᵇ

¹⁰"Blessed is the coming kingdom of our father David!"

"Hosanna in the highest!"

¹¹Jesus entered Jerusalem and went to the temple. He looked around at everything, but since it was already late, he went out to Bethany with the Twelve.

Jesus Clears the Temple

¹²The next day as they were leaving Bethany, Jesus was hungry. ¹³Seeing in the distance a fig tree in leaf, he went to find out if it had any fruit. When he reached it, he found nothing but leaves, because it was not the season for figs. ¹⁴Then he said to the tree, "May no one ever eat fruit from you again." And his disciples heard him say it.

¹⁵On reaching Jerusalem, Jesus entered the temple area and began driving out those who were buying and selling

---

ᵃ9 A Hebrew expression meaning "Save!" which became an exclamation of praise; also in verse 10   ᵇ9 Psalm 118:25,26

there. He overturned the tables of the money changers and the benches of those selling doves, [16]and would not allow anyone to carry merchandise through the temple courts. [17]And as he taught them, he said, "Is it not written:

" 'My house will be called
a house of prayer for all nations'[a]?

But you have made it 'a den of robbers.'[b]"

[18]The chief priests and the teachers of the law heard this and began looking for a way to kill him, for they feared him, because the whole crowd was amazed at his teaching. [19]When evening came, they[c] went out of the city.

The Withered Fig Tree

[20]In the morning, as they went along, they saw the fig tree withered from the roots. [21]Peter remembered and said to Jesus, "Rabbi, look! The fig tree you cursed has withered!"

[22]"Have[d] faith in God," Jesus answered. [23]"I tell you the truth, if anyone says to this mountain, 'Go, throw yourself into the sea,' and does not doubt in his heart but believes that what he says will happen, it will be done for him. [24]Therefore I tell you, whatever you ask for in prayer, believe that you have received it, and it will be yours. [25]And when you stand praying, if you hold anything against anyone, forgive him, so that your Father in heaven may forgive you your sins.[e]"

The Authority of Jesus Questioned

[27]They arrived again in Jerusalem, and while Jesus was walking in the temple courts, the chief priests, the teachers of the law and the elders came to him. [28]"By what authority are you doing these things?" they asked. "And who gave you authority to do this?"

[29]Jesus replied, "I will ask you one question. Answer me, and I will tell you by what authority I am doing these things. [30]John's baptism—was it from heaven, or from men? Tell me!"

[31]They discussed it among themselves and said, "If we say, 'From heaven,' he will ask, 'Then why didn't you believe him?' [32]But if we say, 'From men' . . ." (They feared the people, for everyone held that John really was a prophet.)

[33]So they answered Jesus, "We don't know."

Jesus said, "Neither will I tell you by what authority I am doing these things."

The Parable of the Tenants

12 He then began to speak to them in parables: "A man planted a vineyard. He put a wall around it, dug a pit for the winepress and built a watchtower. Then he rented the vineyard to some farmers and went away on a journey. [2]At harvest time he sent a servant to the tenants to collect from them some of the fruit of the vineyard. [3]But they seized him, beat him and sent him away empty-handed. [4]Then he sent another servant to them; they struck this man on the head and treated him shamefully.

The New Way of Faith

The fig tree is no longer bearing fruit and Jesus curses it to illustrate a point to the disciples. The old ways of the temple culture of the law and the Pharisees are past the point of being able to bear fruit. Then Jesus tells the disciples how the new covenant is characterized by faith (v.22), direct access to God through grace (v.24) and forgiveness (v.25).

Examine yourself in God's presence today. Are you bearing the fruit of faith, grace and forgiveness? How might an unforgiving spirit be causing your faith to shrivel? How can you open up the channels of God's grace so that Jesus' life-giving power can flow freely and so that you can bear fruit?

---

[a] 17 Isaiah 56:7   [b] 17 Jer. 7:11   [c] 19 Some early manuscripts he
[d] 22 Some early manuscripts If you have   [e] 25 Some manuscripts sins. [26]But if you do not forgive, neither will your Father who is in heaven forgive your sins.

A Spark of God's Love

MARK 12:28–31

"The two great commandments . . . are contained in the first two words of the Lord's Prayer, and a Christian should never say "Our Father" without feeling an awakening of the love of God and his neighbor . . . It is love which is the voice of the heart. Love God and you will be always speaking to him. Ask God to open your heart and kindle in it a spark of his love."

—JEAN NICHOLAS GROU,
How to Pray

[5]He sent still another, and that one they killed. He sent many others; some of them they beat, others they killed.

[6]"He had one left to send, a son, whom he loved. He sent him last of all, saying, 'They will respect my son.'

[7]"But the tenants said to one another, 'This is the heir. Come, let's kill him, and the inheritance will be ours.' [8]So they took him and killed him, and threw him out of the vineyard.

[9]"What then will the owner of the vineyard do? He will come and kill those tenants and give the vineyard to others. [10]Haven't you read this scripture:

> " 'The stone the builders rejected
>   has become the capstone[a];
> [11]the Lord has done this,
>   and it is marvelous in our eyes'[b]?"

[12]Then they looked for a way to arrest him because they knew he had spoken the parable against them. But they were afraid of the crowd; so they left him and went away.

Paying Taxes to Caesar

[13]Later they sent some of the Pharisees and Herodians to Jesus to catch him in his words. [14]They came to him and said, "Teacher, we know you are a man of integrity. You aren't swayed by men, because you pay no attention to who they are; but you teach the way of God in accordance with the truth. Is it right to pay taxes to Caesar or not? [15]Should we pay or shouldn't we?"

But Jesus knew their hypocrisy. "Why are you trying to trap me?" he asked. "Bring me a denarius and let me look at it." [16]They brought the coin, and he asked them, "Whose portrait is this? And whose inscription?"

"Caesar's," they replied.

[17]Then Jesus said to them, "Give to Caesar what is Caesar's and to God what is God's."

And they were amazed at him.

Marriage at the Resurrection

[18]Then the Sadducees, who say there is no resurrection, came to him with a question. [19]"Teacher," they said, "Moses wrote for us that if a man's brother dies and leaves a wife but no children, the man must marry the widow and have children for his brother. [20]Now there were seven brothers. The first one married and died without leaving any children. [21]The second one married the widow, but he also died, leaving no child. It was the same with the third. [22]In fact, none of the seven left any children. Last of all, the woman died too. [23]At the resurrection[c] whose wife will she be, since the seven were married to her?"

[24]Jesus replied, "Are you not in error because you do not know the Scriptures or the power of God? [25]When the dead rise, they will neither marry nor be given in marriage; they will be like the angels in heaven. [26]Now about the dead rising—have you not read in the book of Moses, in the account of the bush, how God said to him, 'I am the God of Abraham, the God of Isaac, and the God of Jacob'[d]? [27]He is not the God of the dead, but of the living. You are badly mistaken!"

---

[a] 10 Or *cornerstone*   [b] 11 Psalm 118:22,23   [c] 23 Some manuscripts *resurrection, when men rise from the dead,*   [d] 26 Exodus 3:6

The Greatest Commandment

²⁸One of the teachers of the law came and heard them debating. Noticing that Jesus had given them a good answer, he asked him, "Of all the commandments, which is the most important?"

²⁹"The most important one," answered Jesus, "is this: 'Hear, O Israel, the Lord our God, the Lord is one.ᵃ ³⁰Love the Lord your God with all your heart and with all your soul and with all your mind and with all your strength.'ᵇ ³¹The second is this: 'Love your neighbor as yourself.'ᶜ There is no commandment greater than these."

³²"Well said, teacher," the man replied. "You are right in saying that God is one and there is no other but him. ³³To love him with all your heart, with all your understanding and with all your strength, and to love your neighbor as yourself is more important than all burnt offerings and sacrifices."

³⁴When Jesus saw that he had answered wisely, he said to him, "You are not far from the kingdom of God." And from then on no one dared ask him any more questions.

Whose Son Is the Christ?

³⁵While Jesus was teaching in the temple courts, he asked, "How is it that the teachers of the law say that the Christᵈ is the son of David? ³⁶David himself, speaking by the Holy Spirit, declared:

" 'The Lord said to my Lord:
  "Sit at my right hand
  until I put your enemies
    under your feet." 'ᵉ

³⁷David himself calls him 'Lord.' How then can he be his son?"

The large crowd listened to him with delight.

³⁸As he taught, Jesus said, "Watch out for the teachers of the law. They like to walk around in flowing robes and be greeted in the marketplaces, ³⁹and have the most important seats in the synagogues and the places of honor at banquets. ⁴⁰They devour widows' houses and for a show make lengthy prayers. Such men will be punished most severely."

The Widow's Offering

⁴¹Jesus sat down opposite the place where the offerings were put and watched the crowd putting their money into the temple treasury. Many rich people threw in large amounts. ⁴²But a poor widow came and put in two very small copper coins,ᶠ worth only a fraction of a penny.ᵍ

⁴³Calling his disciples to him, Jesus said, "I tell you the truth, this poor widow has put more into the treasury than all the others. ⁴⁴They all gave out of their wealth; but she, out of her poverty, put in everything—all she had to live on."

Signs of the End of the Age

13 As he was leaving the temple, one of his disciples said to him, "Look, Teacher! What massive stones! What magnificent buildings!"

²"Do you see all these great buildings?" replied Jesus.

In Jesus' Eyes

MARK 12:41–44

As Jesus watches the people give their money, he interprets the scene differently than the other onlookers. He reckons the widow's two copper coins a treasure and the rich people's large offerings inconsequential. What does this tell us about the way God views what we offer? About the way God measures generosity?

Imagine that you are one of the disciples in this scene. What is God teaching you today about giving? About the state of your heart? What will you ask yourself the next time you put money into the temple treasury?

See Meeting God in Scripture

ᵃ 29 Or *the Lord our God is one Lord*   ᵇ 30 Deut. 6:4,5   ᶜ 31 Lev. 19:18
ᵈ 35 Or *Messiah*   ᵉ 36 Psalm 110:1   ᶠ 42 Greek *two lepta*   ᵍ 42 Greek *kodrantes*

1347

Be on Guard

MARK 13:9–11

Jesus tells his followers that they are to "watch themselves" so that they are not distracted by the cataclysmic events going on around them. They are to be spiritually aware and ready to proclaim the truth in tough times.

Do you ever face tough questions about your faith? Are you ready to give a passionate and compelling answer when asked why you have the hope that you have (see 1 Peter 3:15)? What can you do to prepare for such a time, even though you may not know what will be specifically asked of you? How can you be ready to let the Holy Spirit speak through you?

"Not one stone here will be left on another; every one will be thrown down."

³As Jesus was sitting on the Mount of Olives opposite the temple, Peter, James, John and Andrew asked him privately, ⁴"Tell us, when will these things happen? And what will be the sign that they are all about to be fulfilled?"

⁵Jesus said to them: "Watch out that no one deceives you. ⁶Many will come in my name, claiming, 'I am he,' and will deceive many. ⁷When you hear of wars and rumors of wars, do not be alarmed. Such things must happen, but the end is still to come. ⁸Nation will rise against nation, and kingdom against kingdom. There will be earthquakes in various places, and famines. These are the beginning of birth pains.

⁹"You must be on your guard. You will be handed over to the local councils and flogged in the synagogues. On account of me you will stand before governors and kings as witnesses to them. ¹⁰And the gospel must first be preached to all nations. ¹¹Whenever you are arrested and brought to trial, do not worry beforehand about what to say. Just say whatever is given you at the time, for it is not you speaking, but the Holy Spirit.

¹²"Brother will betray brother to death, and a father his child. Children will rebel against their parents and have them put to death. ¹³All men will hate you because of me, but he who stands firm to the end will be saved.

¹⁴"When you see 'the abomination that causes desolation'ᵃ standing where itᵇ does not belong—let the reader understand—then let those who are in Judea flee to the mountains. ¹⁵Let no one on the roof of his house go down or enter the house to take anything out. ¹⁶Let no one in the field go back to get his cloak. ¹⁷How dreadful it will be in those days for pregnant women and nursing mothers! ¹⁸Pray that this will not take place in winter, ¹⁹because those will be days of distress unequaled from the beginning, when God created the world, until now—and never to be equaled again. ²⁰If the Lord had not cut short those days, no one would survive. But for the sake of the elect, whom he has chosen, he has shortened them. ²¹At that time if anyone says to you, 'Look, here is the Christᶜ!' or, 'Look, there he is!' do not believe it. ²²For false Christs and false prophets will appear and perform signs and miracles to deceive the elect—if that were possible. ²³So be on your guard; I have told you everything ahead of time.

²⁴"But in those days, following that distress,

" 'the sun will be darkened,
    and the moon will not give its light;
²⁵the stars will fall from the sky,
    and the heavenly bodies will be shaken.'ᵈ

²⁶"At that time men will see the Son of Man coming in clouds with great power and glory. ²⁷And he will send his angels and gather his elect from the four winds, from the ends of the earth to the ends of the heavens.

²⁸"Now learn this lesson from the fig tree: As soon as its twigs get tender and its leaves come out, you know that summer is near. ²⁹Even so, when you see these things happening, you know that it is near, right at the door. ³⁰I tell you the truth, this generationᵉ will certainly not pass away

---

ᵃ14 Daniel 9:27; 11:31; 12:11   ᵇ14 Or he; also in verse 29   ᶜ21 Or Messiah   ᵈ25 Isaiah 13:10; 34:4   ᵉ30 Or race

until all these things have happened. ³¹Heaven and earth will pass away, but my words will never pass away.

The Day and Hour Unknown

³²"No one knows about that day or hour, not even the angels in heaven, nor the Son, but only the Father. ³³Be on guard! Be alert*ᵃ*! You do not know when that time will come. ³⁴It's like a man going away: He leaves his house and puts his servants in charge, each with his assigned task, and tells the one at the door to keep watch.

³⁵"Therefore keep watch because you do not know when the owner of the house will come back—whether in the evening, or at midnight, or when the rooster crows, or at dawn. ³⁶If he comes suddenly, do not let him find you sleeping. ³⁷What I say to you, I say to everyone: 'Watch!' "

Jesus Anointed at Bethany

14 Now the Passover and the Feast of Unleavened Bread were only two days away, and the chief priests and the teachers of the law were looking for some sly way to arrest Jesus and kill him. ²"But not during the Feast," they said, "or the people may riot."

³While he was in Bethany, reclining at the table in the home of a man known as Simon the Leper, a woman came with an alabaster jar of very expensive perfume, made of pure nard. She broke the jar and poured the perfume on his head.

⁴Some of those present were saying indignantly to one another, "Why this waste of perfume? ⁵It could have been sold for more than a year's wages*ᵇ* and the money given to the poor." And they rebuked her harshly.

⁶"Leave her alone," said Jesus. "Why are you bothering her? She has done a beautiful thing to me. ⁷The poor you will always have with you, and you can help them any time you want. But you will not always have me. ⁸She did what she could. She poured perfume on my body beforehand to prepare for my burial. ⁹I tell you the truth, wherever the gospel is preached throughout the world, what she has done will also be told, in memory of her."

¹⁰Then Judas Iscariot, one of the Twelve, went to the chief priests to betray Jesus to them. ¹¹They were delighted to hear this and promised to give him money. So he watched for an opportunity to hand him over.

The Lord's Supper

¹²On the first day of the Feast of Unleavened Bread, when it was customary to sacrifice the Passover lamb, Jesus' disciples asked him, "Where do you want us to go and make preparations for you to eat the Passover?"

¹³So he sent two of his disciples, telling them, "Go into the city, and a man carrying a jar of water will meet you. Follow him. ¹⁴Say to the owner of the house he enters, 'The Teacher asks: Where is my guest room, where I may eat the Passover with my disciples?' ¹⁵He will show you a large upper room, furnished and ready. Make preparations for us there."

¹⁶The disciples left, went into the city and found things just as Jesus had told them. So they prepared the Passover.

¹⁷When evening came, Jesus arrived with the Twelve. ¹⁸While they were reclining at the table eating, he said, "I

Love Poured Out

MARK 14:3–9

Jesus had told the disciples plainly that he would die (Mark 8:31–32), but only the woman in this passage seems to believe him.

Read the passage slowly, noticing the word or phrase that draws your attention. Reflect on this word or phrase. Why does it draw your attention? How does it stir your heart to pray? Rest in silence, staying open to any impressions from God. Record your impressions. Who is God inviting you to be? What is God inviting you to do?

See *Meeting God in Scripture*

ᵃ 33 Some manuscripts *alert and pray*   *ᵇ* 5 Greek *than three hundred denarii*

The Melted Will

MARK 14:35–36

Sometimes we underestimate what it cost Jesus to submit his will to the Father's. What was the price of saying yes to the Father as Jesus faced the cross?

Light a candle. Scoop up some of the melted wax as it drips down the side. Press it between your fingers and think of a situation or event that requires you to surrender your will. Sing an appropriate song such as "Have Thine Own Way, Lord," and pray that God will open your heart and make it as pliable as warm wax.

tell you the truth, one of you will betray me—one who is eating with me."

19They were saddened, and one by one they said to him, "Surely not I?"

20"It is one of the Twelve," he replied, "one who dips bread into the bowl with me. 21The Son of Man will go just as it is written about him. But woe to that man who betrays the Son of Man! It would be better for him if he had not been born."

22While they were eating, Jesus took bread, gave thanks and broke it, and gave it to his disciples, saying, "Take it; this is my body."

23Then he took the cup, gave thanks and offered it to them, and they all drank from it.

24"This is my blood of the*a* covenant, which is poured out for many," he said to them. 25"I tell you the truth, I will not drink again of the fruit of the vine until that day when I drink it anew in the kingdom of God."

26When they had sung a hymn, they went out to the Mount of Olives.

Jesus Predicts Peter's Denial

27"You will all fall away," Jesus told them, "for it is written:

" 'I will strike the shepherd,
and the sheep will be scattered.'*b*

28But after I have risen, I will go ahead of you into Galilee."

29Peter declared, "Even if all fall away, I will not."

30"I tell you the truth," Jesus answered, "today—yes, tonight—before the rooster crows twice*c* you yourself will disown me three times."

31But Peter insisted emphatically, "Even if I have to die with you, I will never disown you." And all the others said the same.

Gethsemane

32They went to a place called Gethsemane, and Jesus said to his disciples, "Sit here while I pray." 33He took Peter, James and John along with him, and he began to be deeply distressed and troubled. 34"My soul is overwhelmed with sorrow to the point of death," he said to them. "Stay here and keep watch."

35Going a little farther, he fell to the ground and prayed that if possible the hour might pass from him. 36"Abba,*d* Father," he said, "everything is possible for you. Take this cup from me. Yet not what I will, but what you will."

37Then he returned to his disciples and found them sleeping. "Simon," he said to Peter, "are you asleep? Could you not keep watch for one hour? 38Watch and pray so that you will not fall into temptation. The spirit is willing, but the body is weak."

39Once more he went away and prayed the same thing. 40When he came back, he again found them sleeping, because their eyes were heavy. They did not know what to say to him.

41Returning the third time, he said to them, "Are you still sleeping and resting? Enough! The hour has come. Look,

a 24 Some manuscripts *the new*   *b 27* Zech. 13:7   *c 30* Some early manuscripts do not have *twice.*   *d 36* Aramaic for *Father*

the Son of Man is betrayed into the hands of sinners. ⁴²Rise! Let us go! Here comes my betrayer!"

Jesus Arrested

⁴³Just as he was speaking, Judas, one of the Twelve, appeared. With him was a crowd armed with swords and clubs, sent from the chief priests, the teachers of the law, and the elders.

⁴⁴Now the betrayer had arranged a signal with them: "The one I kiss is the man; arrest him and lead him away under guard." ⁴⁵Going at once to Jesus, Judas said, "Rabbi!" and kissed him. ⁴⁶The men seized Jesus and arrested him. ⁴⁷Then one of those standing near drew his sword and struck the servant of the high priest, cutting off his ear.

⁴⁸"Am I leading a rebellion," said Jesus, "that you have come out with swords and clubs to capture me? ⁴⁹Every day I was with you, teaching in the temple courts, and you did not arrest me. But the Scriptures must be fulfilled." ⁵⁰Then everyone deserted him and fled.

⁵¹A young man, wearing nothing but a linen garment, was following Jesus. When they seized him, ⁵²he fled naked, leaving his garment behind.

Before the Sanhedrin

⁵³They took Jesus to the high priest, and all the chief priests, elders and teachers of the law came together. ⁵⁴Peter followed him at a distance, right into the courtyard of the high priest. There he sat with the guards and warmed himself at the fire.

⁵⁵The chief priests and the whole Sanhedrin were looking for evidence against Jesus so that they could put him to death, but they did not find any. ⁵⁶Many testified falsely against him, but their statements did not agree.

⁵⁷Then some stood up and gave this false testimony against him: ⁵⁸"We heard him say, 'I will destroy this man-made temple and in three days will build another, not made by man.' " ⁵⁹Yet even then their testimony did not agree.

⁶⁰Then the high priest stood up before them and asked Jesus, "Are you not going to answer? What is this testimony that these men are bringing against you?" ⁶¹But Jesus remained silent and gave no answer.

Again the high priest asked him, "Are you the Christ,ᵃ the Son of the Blessed One?"

⁶²"I am," said Jesus. "And you will see the Son of Man sitting at the right hand of the Mighty One and coming on the clouds of heaven."

⁶³The high priest tore his clothes. "Why do we need any more witnesses?" he asked. ⁶⁴"You have heard the blasphemy. What do you think?"

They all condemned him as worthy of death. ⁶⁵Then some began to spit at him; they blindfolded him, struck him with their fists, and said, "Prophesy!" And the guards took him and beat him.

Peter Disowns Jesus

⁶⁶While Peter was below in the courtyard, one of the servant girls of the high priest came by. ⁶⁷When she saw Peter warming himself, she looked closely at him.

"You also were with that Nazarene, Jesus," she said.

To Proclaim the Christ

MARK 14:61-62

At his trial Jesus, beaten and bedraggled, proclaims himself the Christ. Such a declaration must seem ridiculous to those gathered—that the man whom they are about to execute is the Messiah.

Are you called to proclaim Jesus the Christ to people to whom that reality might seem foreign or even ridiculous? To people who are sick or dying? To doubt-ridden people? To people who are destitute? To proud and self-sufficient people? In what ways might God want you to communicate divine truth? Do you have a friend with whom you could discuss this and who would pray for you?

See Meeting God in Community

ᵃ 61 Or *Messiah*

Tender, Wise and Strong

MARK 15:16–20

"It is the cup that Thou didst drink, Lord Jesus, more than ought else that renders Thee love-worthy; it is the work of our redemption that supremely claims our love. He put up with people who tried to catch Him in His talk, carped at His actions, mocked His suffering and even upbraided Him in death. This love of His is tender, wise and strong. Tender in that He took on Him our flesh; careful and wise in that He guarded against sin; and strong in that He suffered death. I trust myself entirely to Him who willed to save me, knew the way to do it, and had the power to carry out the work. He has sought me out and called me by His grace."

—BERNARD OF CLAIRVAUX,
*Selections from the Writings
of Bernard of Clairvaux*

[68]But he denied it. "I don't know or understand what you're talking about," he said, and went out into the entryway.[a]

[69]When the servant girl saw him there, she said again to those standing around, "This fellow is one of them." [70]Again he denied it.

After a little while, those standing near said to Peter, "Surely you are one of them, for you are a Galilean."

[71]He began to call down curses on himself, and he swore to them, "I don't know this man you're talking about."

[72]Immediately the rooster crowed the second time.[b] Then Peter remembered the word Jesus had spoken to him: "Before the rooster crows twice[c] you will disown me three times." And he broke down and wept.

Jesus Before Pilate

15 Very early in the morning, the chief priests, with the elders, the teachers of the law and the whole Sanhedrin, reached a decision. They bound Jesus, led him away and handed him over to Pilate.

[2]"Are you the king of the Jews?" asked Pilate.

"Yes, it is as you say," Jesus replied.

[3]The chief priests accused him of many things. [4]So again Pilate asked him, "Aren't you going to answer? See how many things they are accusing you of."

[5]But Jesus still made no reply, and Pilate was amazed.

[6]Now it was the custom at the Feast to release a prisoner whom the people requested. [7]A man called Barabbas was in prison with the insurrectionists who had committed murder in the uprising. [8]The crowd came up and asked Pilate to do for them what he usually did.

[9]"Do you want me to release to you the king of the Jews?" asked Pilate, [10]knowing it was out of envy that the chief priests had handed Jesus over to him. [11]But the chief priests stirred up the crowd to have Pilate release Barabbas instead.

[12]"What shall I do, then, with the one you call the king of the Jews?" Pilate asked them.

[13]"Crucify him!" they shouted.

[14]"Why? What crime has he committed?" asked Pilate.

But they shouted all the louder, "Crucify him!"

[15]Wanting to satisfy the crowd, Pilate released Barabbas to them. He had Jesus flogged, and handed him over to be crucified.

The Soldiers Mock Jesus

[16]The soldiers led Jesus away into the palace (that is, the Praetorium) and called together the whole company of soldiers. [17]They put a purple robe on him, then twisted together a crown of thorns and set it on him. [18]And they began to call out to him, "Hail, king of the Jews!" [19]Again and again they struck him on the head with a staff and spit on him. Falling on their knees, they paid homage to him. [20]And when they had mocked him, they took off the purple robe and put his own clothes on him. Then they led him out to crucify him.

---

[a] 68 Some early manuscripts *entryway and the rooster crowed*   [b] 72 Some early manuscripts do not have *the second time.*   [c] 72 Some early manuscripts do not have *twice.*

The Crucifixion

21 A certain man from Cyrene, Simon, the father of Alexander and Rufus, was passing by on his way in from the country, and they forced him to carry the cross. 22 They brought Jesus to the place called Golgotha (which means The Place of the Skull). 23 Then they offered him wine mixed with myrrh, but he did not take it. 24 And they crucified him. Dividing up his clothes, they cast lots to see what each would get.

25 It was the third hour when they crucified him. 26 The written notice of the charge against him read: THE KING OF THE JEWS. 27 They crucified two robbers with him, one on his right and one on his left.[a] 29 Those who passed by hurled insults at him, shaking their heads and saying, "So! You who are going to destroy the temple and build it in three days, 30 come down from the cross and save yourself!"

31 In the same way the chief priests and the teachers of the law mocked him among themselves. "He saved others," they said, "but he can't save himself! 32 Let this Christ,[b] this King of Israel, come down now from the cross, that we may see and believe." Those crucified with him also heaped insults on him.

The Death of Jesus

33 At the sixth hour darkness came over the whole land until the ninth hour. 34 And at the ninth hour Jesus cried out in a loud voice, *"Eloi, Eloi, lama sabachthani?"* —which means, "My God, my God, why have you forsaken me?"[c]

35 When some of those standing near heard this, they said, "Listen, he's calling Elijah."

36 One man ran, filled a sponge with wine vinegar, put it on a stick, and offered it to Jesus to drink. "Now leave him alone. Let's see if Elijah comes to take him down," he said.

37 With a loud cry, Jesus breathed his last.

38 The curtain of the temple was torn in two from top to bottom. 39 And when the centurion, who stood there in front of Jesus, heard his cry and[d] saw how he died, he said, "Surely this man was the Son[e] of God!"

40 Some women were watching from a distance. Among them were Mary Magdalene, Mary the mother of James the younger and of Joses, and Salome. 41 In Galilee these women had followed him and cared for his needs. Many other women who had come up with him to Jerusalem were also there.

The Burial of Jesus

42 It was Preparation Day (that is, the day before the Sabbath). So as evening approached, 43 Joseph of Arimathea, a prominent member of the Council, who was himself waiting for the kingdom of God, went boldly to Pilate and asked for Jesus' body. 44 Pilate was surprised to hear that he was already dead. Summoning the centurion, he asked him if Jesus had already died. 45 When he learned from the centurion that it was so, he gave the body to Joseph. 46 So Joseph bought some linen cloth, took down the body, wrapped it in the linen, and placed it in a tomb cut out of rock. Then he rolled a stone against the entrance of the

---

Were You There?

MARK 15:37–39

Read this passage, taking on the role of the Roman centurion. Feel the weight of the armor on your shoulders. Listen to the pathos of Jesus' loud cry. Do you see the blood and sweat drip from his body? Now he is quiet. You notice that his breathing and heartbeat have ceased. You declare: "Surely this man was the Son of God!"

Position your body in a way that expresses this phrase—facedown on the floor, standing with your hands raised or stooping over in grief. Thank Jesus the Savior for his redeeming love.

See Meeting God in Worship

---

a 27 Some manuscripts left, 28 and the scripture was fulfilled which says, "He was counted with the lawless ones" (Isaiah 53:12)   b 32 Or Messiah   c 34 Psalm 22:1   d 39 Some manuscripts do not have heard his cry and   e 39 Or a son

1353

Encountering the Unexpected

MARK 16:4–8

Meeting an angel is so shocking to this group of women that they leave the garden trembling and bewildered. Even though Jesus had told them to expect his resurrection, they are still astounded at what the angel has told them.

Read the passage slowly and sit quietly. Wait in silence, being content to enjoy God's Word. What word, phrase or image impresses you and stays with you? Reflect on this word or phrase. Why do you think it is important? What is God's message to you? How will you respond when you meet him unexpectedly? Ask God what you need to learn from this passage.

See *Meeting God in Scripture*

tomb. ⁴⁷Mary Magdalene and Mary the mother of Joses saw where he was laid.

The Resurrection

16 When the Sabbath was over, Mary Magdalene, Mary the mother of James, and Salome bought spices so that they might go to anoint Jesus' body. ²Very early on the first day of the week, just after sunrise, they were on their way to the tomb ³and they asked each other, "Who will roll the stone away from the entrance of the tomb?"

⁴But when they looked up, they saw that the stone, which was very large, had been rolled away. ⁵As they entered the tomb, they saw a young man dressed in a white robe sitting on the right side, and they were alarmed.

⁶"Don't be alarmed," he said. "You are looking for Jesus the Nazarene, who was crucified. He has risen! He is not here. See the place where they laid him. ⁷But go, tell his disciples and Peter, 'He is going ahead of you into Galilee. There you will see him, just as he told you.'"

⁸Trembling and bewildered, the women went out and fled from the tomb. They said nothing to anyone, because they were afraid.

[The earliest manuscripts and some other ancient witnesses do not have Mark 16:9–20.]

⁹When Jesus rose early on the first day of the week, he appeared first to Mary Magdalene, out of whom he had driven seven demons. ¹⁰She went and told those who had been with him and who were mourning and weeping. ¹¹When they heard that Jesus was alive and that she had seen him, they did not believe it.

¹²Afterward Jesus appeared in a different form to two of them while they were walking in the country. ¹³These returned and reported it to the rest; but they did not believe them either.

¹⁴Later Jesus appeared to the Eleven as they were eating; he rebuked them for their lack of faith and their stubborn refusal to believe those who had seen him after he had risen.

¹⁵He said to them, "Go into all the world and preach the good news to all creation. ¹⁶Whoever believes and is baptized will be saved, but whoever does not believe will be condemned. ¹⁷And these signs will accompany those who believe: In my name they will drive out demons; they will speak in new tongues; ¹⁸they will pick up snakes with their hands; and when they drink deadly poison, it will not hurt them at all; they will place their hands on sick people, and they will get well."

¹⁹After the Lord Jesus had spoken to them, he was taken up into heaven and he sat at the right hand of God. ²⁰Then the disciples went out and preached everywhere, and the Lord worked with them and confirmed his word by the signs that accompanied it.

LUKE

Life of Prayer, Life of Compassion

KEY VERSES:

"Lord, teach us to pray."—Luke 11:1

"Which of these . . . was a neighbor? . . . Go and do likewise."—Luke 10:36–37

I n the Gospel of Luke, Luke the physician draws a portrait of Jesus the Savior, who brings the love of God to earth and draws the people of God to heaven. Luke conveys his fascination with this Jesus, a man of both prayer and action, who could be continually mindful of God and yet be fully present with people as an attentive, empathetic healer. Jesus modeled perfect communication with his heavenly Father (the Lord's Prayer) and perfect compassion for those his culture considered outcasts (the parable of the Good Samaritan).

Jesus' life and teachings reconcile some of the contrasts that exist within the spiritual life, blending spiritual with physical (6:24–27), feasting with fasting (5:33–35), compassion with confrontation (6:9), and solitude with community (6:12–16).

Jesus moved beyond the restrictions of Jewish society, welcoming anyone with a seeking heart and granting the forgiveness of God to those the "righteous" Jewish leaders had rejected (6:20–26; 21:1–4). He engaged women, as well as men, in ministry (8:1–3; 23:55—24:11). For Luke, the only Gentile Gospel writer, this was good news indeed, for Jesus brought reconciliation to the Gentile world.

Let the book of Luke help you discover what it means to live an inward life of prayer and an outward life of compassion. When you struggle to balance "doing" with "being," imitate Jesus Christ, who practiced an ongoing rhythm of ministry and sabbath rest. How can you serve God in the same radical way? How can you maintain this rhythm in your personal life?

> "Let one who cannot be alone beware of community . . . Let one who is not in community beware of being alone."
>
> —DIETRICH BONHOEFFER,
> *Life Together*

Silences

LUKE 1:20–23

Like Abraham and Sarah, Zechariah expresses doubt when God promises that a child will be born to him and his wife in their old age. As a result God silences Zechariah until the child is born. What if you were to receive the most precious desire of your heart today? How would you respond? Reflect on this in a journal or notebook, using words or art. Also reflect on the times when you may have experienced periods of doubt, silence, waiting or listening. Such spiritual stillness can be a prelude to some new birth in your life, as it was for Zechariah and Elizabeth.

See Meeting God in Everyday Life

Introduction

1 Many have undertaken to draw up an account of the things that have been fulfilled[a] among us, ²just as they were handed down to us by those who from the first were eyewitnesses and servants of the word. ³Therefore, since I myself have carefully investigated everything from the beginning, it seemed good also to me to write an orderly account for you, most excellent Theophilus, ⁴so that you may know the certainty of the things you have been taught.

The Birth of John the Baptist Foretold

⁵In the time of Herod king of Judea there was a priest named Zechariah, who belonged to the priestly division of Abijah; his wife Elizabeth was also a descendant of Aaron. ⁶Both of them were upright in the sight of God, observing all the Lord's commandments and regulations blamelessly. ⁷But they had no children, because Elizabeth was barren; and they were both well along in years.

⁸Once when Zechariah's division was on duty and he was serving as priest before God, ⁹he was chosen by lot, according to the custom of the priesthood, to go into the temple of the Lord and burn incense. ¹⁰And when the time for the burning of incense came, all the assembled worshipers were praying outside.

¹¹Then an angel of the Lord appeared to him, standing at the right side of the altar of incense. ¹²When Zechariah saw him, he was startled and was gripped with fear. ¹³But the angel said to him: "Do not be afraid, Zechariah; your prayer has been heard. Your wife Elizabeth will bear you a son, and you are to give him the name John. ¹⁴He will be a joy and delight to you, and many will rejoice because of his birth, ¹⁵for he will be great in the sight of the Lord. He is never to take wine or other fermented drink, and he will be filled with the Holy Spirit even from birth.[b] ¹⁶Many of the people of Israel will he bring back to the Lord their God. ¹⁷And he will go on before the Lord, in the spirit and power of Elijah, to turn the hearts of the fathers to their children and the disobedient to the wisdom of the righteous—to make ready a people prepared for the Lord."

¹⁸Zechariah asked the angel, "How can I be sure of this? I am an old man and my wife is well along in years."

¹⁹The angel answered, "I am Gabriel. I stand in the presence of God, and I have been sent to speak to you and to tell you this good news. ²⁰And now you will be silent and not able to speak until the day this happens, because you did not believe my words, which will come true at their proper time."

²¹Meanwhile, the people were waiting for Zechariah and wondering why he stayed so long in the temple. ²²When he came out, he could not speak to them. They realized he had seen a vision in the temple, for he kept making signs to them but remained unable to speak.

²³When his time of service was completed, he returned home. ²⁴After this his wife Elizabeth became pregnant and for five months remained in seclusion. ²⁵"The Lord has done this for me," she said. "In these days he has shown his favor and taken away my disgrace among the people."

a 1 Or been surely believed   *b 15 Or from his mother's womb*

The Birth of Jesus Foretold

²⁶In the sixth month, God sent the angel Gabriel to Nazareth, a town in Galilee, ²⁷to a virgin pledged to be married to a man named Joseph, a descendant of David. The virgin's name was Mary. ²⁸The angel went to her and said, "Greetings, you who are highly favored! The Lord is with you."

²⁹Mary was greatly troubled at his words and wondered what kind of greeting this might be. ³⁰But the angel said to her, "Do not be afraid, Mary, you have found favor with God. ³¹You will be with child and give birth to a son, and you are to give him the name Jesus. ³²He will be great and will be called the Son of the Most High. The Lord God will give him the throne of his father David, ³³and he will reign over the house of Jacob forever; his kingdom will never end."

³⁴"How will this be," Mary asked the angel, "since I am a virgin?"

³⁵The angel answered, "The Holy Spirit will come upon you, and the power of the Most High will overshadow you. So the holy one to be born will be called*a* the Son of God. ³⁶Even Elizabeth your relative is going to have a child in her old age, and she who was said to be barren is in her sixth month. ³⁷For nothing is impossible with God."

³⁸"I am the Lord's servant," Mary answered. "May it be to me as you have said." Then the angel left her.

Mary Visits Elizabeth

³⁹At that time Mary got ready and hurried to a town in the hill country of Judea, ⁴⁰where she entered Zechariah's home and greeted Elizabeth. ⁴¹When Elizabeth heard Mary's greeting, the baby leaped in her womb, and Elizabeth was filled with the Holy Spirit. ⁴²In a loud voice she exclaimed: "Blessed are you among women, and blessed is the child you will bear! ⁴³But why am I so favored, that the mother of my Lord should come to me? ⁴⁴As soon as the sound of your greeting reached my ears, the baby in my womb leaped for joy. ⁴⁵Blessed is she who has believed that what the Lord has said to her will be accomplished!"

Mary's Song

⁴⁶And Mary said:

"My soul glorifies the Lord
⁴⁷ and my spirit rejoices in God my Savior,
⁴⁸for he has been mindful
    of the humble state of his servant.
From now on all generations will call me blessed,
⁴⁹ for the Mighty One has done great things for
        me—
    holy is his name.
⁵⁰His mercy extends to those who fear him,
    from generation to generation.
⁵¹He has performed mighty deeds with his arm;
    he has scattered those who are proud in their
        inmost thoughts.
⁵²He has brought down rulers from their thrones
    but has lifted up the humble.
⁵³He has filled the hungry with good things
    but has sent the rich away empty.

Spiritual Friendship

LUKE 1:39–45

"What happiness, what security, what joy to have someone to whom you dare to speak on terms of equality as to another self," wrote the twelfth-century monk Aelred of Rievaulx in *Spiritual Friendship*. What an apt description of Mary and Elizabeth's spiritual kinship as both women face unusual, yet joyous, circumstances! Recall some of the special friendships you've experienced during your lifetime. Call a friend or share a meal together, and reminisce about your friendship. Tell your friend some of the ways in which you consider him or her a blessing.

See *Meeting God in Community*

---

a 35 Or *So the child to be born will be called holy.*

Zechariah's Song

LUKE 1:67–79

Although many of our prayers tend to become "wish lists," Zechariah's prayer is full of acknowledgment of what God has done in the past and will do in the future. He worships God using the special name "Most High" and proclaims God's "tender mercy" (1:78). Try finishing these sentences: "God, I praise you because you have . . . ." "I look forward to the day when you will . . . ." "O God, I am filled with awe and wonder that you . . . ."

See Meeting God in Worship

54 He has helped his servant Israel,
    remembering to be merciful
55 to Abraham and his descendants forever,
    even as he said to our fathers."

56 Mary stayed with Elizabeth for about three months and then returned home.

The Birth of John the Baptist

57 When it was time for Elizabeth to have her baby, she gave birth to a son. 58 Her neighbors and relatives heard that the Lord had shown her great mercy, and they shared her joy.

59 On the eighth day they came to circumcise the child, and they were going to name him after his father Zechariah, 60 but his mother spoke up and said, "No! He is to be called John."

61 They said to her, "There is no one among your relatives who has that name."

62 Then they made signs to his father, to find out what he would like to name the child. 63 He asked for a writing tablet, and to everyone's astonishment he wrote, "His name is John." 64 Immediately his mouth was opened and his tongue was loosed, and he began to speak, praising God. 65 The neighbors were all filled with awe, and throughout the hill country of Judea people were talking about all these things. 66 Everyone who heard this wondered about it, asking, "What then is this child going to be?" For the Lord's hand was with him.

Zechariah's Song

67 His father Zechariah was filled with the Holy Spirit and prophesied:

68 "Praise be to the Lord, the God of Israel,
    because he has come and has redeemed his
        people.
69 He has raised up a horn[a] of salvation for us
    in the house of his servant David
70 (as he said through his holy prophets of long ago),
71 salvation from our enemies
    and from the hand of all who hate us—
72 to show mercy to our fathers
    and to remember his holy covenant,
73   the oath he swore to our father Abraham:
74 to rescue us from the hand of our enemies,
    and to enable us to serve him without fear
75   in holiness and righteousness before him all
        our days.

76 And you, my child, will be called a prophet of the
        Most High;
    for you will go on before the Lord to prepare
        the way for him,
77 to give his people the knowledge of salvation
    through the forgiveness of their sins,
78 because of the tender mercy of our God,
    by which the rising sun will come to us from
        heaven
79 to shine on those living in darkness

a 69 Horn here symbolizes strength.

and in the shadow of death,
    to guide our feet into the path of peace."

[80] And the child grew and became strong in spirit; and he lived in the desert until he appeared publicly to Israel.

The Birth of Jesus

2 In those days Caesar Augustus issued a decree that a census should be taken of the entire Roman world. [2] (This was the first census that took place while Quirinius was governor of Syria.) [3] And everyone went to his own town to register.

[4] So Joseph also went up from the town of Nazareth in Galilee to Judea, to Bethlehem the town of David, because he belonged to the house and line of David. [5] He went there to register with Mary, who was pledged to be married to him and was expecting a child. [6] While they were there, the time came for the baby to be born, [7] and she gave birth to her firstborn, a son. She wrapped him in cloths and placed him in a manger, because there was no room for them in the inn.

The Shepherds and the Angels

[8] And there were shepherds living out in the fields nearby, keeping watch over their flocks at night. [9] An angel of the Lord appeared to them, and the glory of the Lord shone around them, and they were terrified. [10] But the angel said to them, "Do not be afraid. I bring you good news of great joy that will be for all the people. [11] Today in the town of David a Savior has been born to you; he is Christ[a] the Lord. [12] This will be a sign to you: You will find a baby wrapped in cloths and lying in a manger."

[13] Suddenly a great company of the heavenly host appeared with the angel, praising God and saying,

[14] "Glory to God in the highest,
    and on earth peace to men on whom his favor
        rests."

[15] When the angels had left them and gone into heaven, the shepherds said to one another, "Let's go to Bethlehem and see this thing that has happened, which the Lord has told us about."

[16] So they hurried off and found Mary and Joseph, and the baby, who was lying in the manger. [17] When they had seen him, they spread the word concerning what had been told them about this child, [18] and all who heard it were amazed at what the shepherds said to them. [19] But Mary treasured up all these things and pondered them in her heart. [20] The shepherds returned, glorifying and praising God for all the things they had heard and seen, which were just as they had been told.

Jesus Presented in the Temple

[21] On the eighth day, when it was time to circumcise him, he was named Jesus, the name the angel had given him before he had been conceived.

[22] When the time of their purification according to the Law of Moses had been completed, Joseph and Mary took

---

Singing With Angels

LUKE 1:68; 2:14

Everyone is singing—Mary (1:46–55), Zechariah, Simeon (2:28–32), the angels! Sing a song of praise—such as "Angels We Have Heard on High" (especially the chorus)—in the shower, in the woods or in the car. Sing where no one can hear you so that you can sing exuberantly and can embellish your song of praise with worshipful gestures or movements. Experiment with the joy of worshiping God—let inward singing permeate your activities. Another option: Sing the African-American spiritual "Guide My Feet" (based on Luke 1:79).

See Meeting God in Worship

---

a 11 Or Messiah. "The Christ" (Greek) and "the Messiah" (Hebrew) both mean "the Anointed One"; also in verse 26.

Praying With Anna and Simeon

LUKE 2:22–38

An offering of doves or pigeons is a sign of poverty. Imagine the elderly Simeon and Anna holding the infant Jesus and welcoming this young, poor family. Simeon's prayer identifying Jesus as "a light for revelation . . . and for glory" indicates how much he wants to see God's penetrating light and glory displayed on earth (2:32). We can guess Anna's heart aches to see the redemption of Israel (2:38). What situations today need to be penetrated by God's light? Youth separated from older adults? Rich from poor? Try holding a symbol of these situations in your hand (a related newspaper article, a committee agenda, a child's hat, a family member's pain medication) and praying Simeon's prayer. Or write the prayer that you imagine Anna might have prayed.

See Meeting God in Community

him to Jerusalem to present him to the Lord ²³(as it is written in the Law of the Lord, "Every firstborn male is to be consecrated to the Lord"ᵃ), ²⁴and to offer a sacrifice in keeping with what is said in the Law of the Lord: "a pair of doves or two young pigeons."ᵇ

²⁵Now there was a man in Jerusalem called Simeon, who was righteous and devout. He was waiting for the consolation of Israel, and the Holy Spirit was upon him. ²⁶It had been revealed to him by the Holy Spirit that he would not die before he had seen the Lord's Christ. ²⁷Moved by the Spirit, he went into the temple courts. When the parents brought in the child Jesus to do for him what the custom of the Law required, ²⁸Simeon took him in his arms and praised God, saying:

²⁹ "Sovereign Lord, as you have promised,
    you now dismissᶜ your servant in peace.
³⁰ For my eyes have seen your salvation,
³¹   which you have prepared in the sight of all
        people,
³² a light for revelation to the Gentiles
    and for glory to your people Israel."

³³The child's father and mother marveled at what was said about him. ³⁴Then Simeon blessed them and said to Mary, his mother: "This child is destined to cause the falling and rising of many in Israel, and to be a sign that will be spoken against, ³⁵so that the thoughts of many hearts will be revealed. And a sword will pierce your own soul too."

³⁶There was also a prophetess, Anna, the daughter of Phanuel, of the tribe of Asher. She was very old; she had lived with her husband seven years after her marriage, ³⁷and then was a widow until she was eighty-four.ᵈ She never left the temple but worshiped night and day, fasting and praying. ³⁸Coming up to them at that very moment, she gave thanks to God and spoke about the child to all who were looking forward to the redemption of Jerusalem.

³⁹When Joseph and Mary had done everything required by the Law of the Lord, they returned to Galilee to their own town of Nazareth. ⁴⁰And the child grew and became strong; he was filled with wisdom, and the grace of God was upon him.

The Boy Jesus at the Temple

⁴¹Every year his parents went to Jerusalem for the Feast of the Passover. ⁴²When he was twelve years old, they went up to the Feast, according to the custom. ⁴³After the Feast was over, while his parents were returning home, the boy Jesus stayed behind in Jerusalem, but they were unaware of it. ⁴⁴Thinking he was in their company, they traveled on for a day. Then they began looking for him among their relatives and friends. ⁴⁵When they did not find him, they went back to Jerusalem to look for him. ⁴⁶After three days they found him in the temple courts, sitting among the teachers, listening to them and asking them questions. ⁴⁷Everyone who heard him was amazed at his understanding and his answers. ⁴⁸When his parents saw him, they were astonished. His mother said to him, "Son, why have

ᵃ 23 Exodus 13:2,12   ᵇ 24 Lev. 12:8   ᶜ 29 Or promised, / now dismiss
ᵈ 37 Or widow for eighty-four years

you treated us like this? Your father and I have been anxiously searching for you."

⁴⁹"Why were you searching for me?" he asked. "Didn't you know I had to be in my Father's house?" ⁵⁰But they did not understand what he was saying to them.

⁵¹Then he went down to Nazareth with them and was obedient to them. But his mother treasured all these things in her heart. ⁵²And Jesus grew in wisdom and stature, and in favor with God and men.

John the Baptist Prepares the Way

3 In the fifteenth year of the reign of Tiberius Caesar— when Pontius Pilate was governor of Judea, Herod tetrarch of Galilee, his brother Philip tetrarch of Iturea and Traconitis, and Lysanias tetrarch of Abilene— ²during the high priesthood of Annas and Caiaphas, the word of God came to John son of Zechariah in the desert. ³He went into all the country around the Jordan, preaching a baptism of repentance for the forgiveness of sins. ⁴As is written in the book of the words of Isaiah the prophet:

> "A voice of one calling in the desert,
> 'Prepare the way for the Lord,
>   make straight paths for him.
> ⁵Every valley shall be filled in,
>   every mountain and hill made low.
> The crooked roads shall become straight,
>   the rough ways smooth.
> ⁶And all mankind will see God's salvation.' "ᵃ

⁷John said to the crowds coming out to be baptized by him, "You brood of vipers! Who warned you to flee from the coming wrath? ⁸Produce fruit in keeping with repentance. And do not begin to say to yourselves, 'We have Abraham as our father.' For I tell you that out of these stones God can raise up children for Abraham. ⁹The ax is already at the root of the trees, and every tree that does not produce good fruit will be cut down and thrown into the fire."

¹⁰"What should we do then?" the crowd asked.

¹¹John answered, "The man with two tunics should share with him who has none, and the one who has food should do the same."

¹²Tax collectors also came to be baptized. "Teacher," they asked, "what should we do?"

¹³"Don't collect any more than you are required to," he told them.

¹⁴Then some soldiers asked him, "And what should we do?"

He replied, "Don't extort money and don't accuse people falsely—be content with your pay."

¹⁵The people were waiting expectantly and were all wondering in their hearts if John might possibly be the Christ.ᵇ ¹⁶John answered them all, "I baptize you withᶜ water. But one more powerful than I will come, the thongs of whose sandals I am not worthy to untie. He will baptize you with the Holy Spirit and with fire. ¹⁷His winnowing fork is in his hand to clear his threshing floor and to gather the wheat into his barn, but he will burn up the chaff with unquenchable fire." ¹⁸And with many other words John exhorted the people and preached the good news to them.

Treasuring . . .

LUKE 2:41–52

Mary reacts to crises by pondering or treasuring in her heart what God says or does. She does this when she faces the shame of becoming an unwed mother; when she responds to the shepherds' visit in a stable; and, in this passage, when she copes with the increasing independence of her twelve-year-old son (1:29; 2:19,51). How might Mary's response be an example to you? How could you respond more contemplatively and prayerfully to the events in your life? What event in your life needs more pondering instead of worrying, fixing or withdrawing?

See Meeting God in Everyday Life

ᵃ6 Isaiah 40:3–5   ᵇ15 Or *Messiah*   ᶜ16 Or *in*

Revolutionary Simplicity

LUKE 3:1–20

John the Baptist thunders a revolutionary message that costs him his life. He is imprisoned and killed by Herod for nothing less than the radical condemnation of those in power: "The ax is already at the root of the trees" (3:9; see also 3:19). Yet when the crowd asks, "What should we do then?" John suggests sharing their extra coats and food with others and living honestly. Find some extra cans of food and an extra jacket to take to a homeless shelter. Hold them in your hands. What might happen within you when you take them to the shelter? What revolution might take place within your heart if you chose to make generosity your lifestyle? What might happen to your need for security and control? Commit to one simple act at a time. Mark a date on your calendar that is a month from now; when that date arrives, assess any change you might have experienced within yourself.

See Meeting God in Community

¹⁹But when John rebuked Herod the tetrarch because of Herodias, his brother's wife, and all the other evil things he had done, ²⁰Herod added this to them all: He locked John up in prison.

The Baptism and Genealogy of Jesus

²¹When all the people were being baptized, Jesus was baptized too. And as he was praying, heaven was opened ²²and the Holy Spirit descended on him in bodily form like a dove. And a voice came from heaven: "You are my Son, whom I love; with you I am well pleased."

²³Now Jesus himself was about thirty years old when he began his ministry. He was the son, so it was thought, of Joseph,

the son of Heli, ²⁴the son of Matthat,
the son of Levi, the son of Melki,
the son of Jannai, the son of Joseph,
²⁵the son of Mattathias, the son of Amos,
the son of Nahum, the son of Esli,
the son of Naggai, ²⁶the son of Maath,
the son of Mattathias, the son of Semein,
the son of Josech, the son of Joda,
²⁷the son of Joanan, the son of Rhesa,
the son of Zerubbabel, the son of Shealtiel,
the son of Neri, ²⁸the son of Melki,
the son of Addi, the son of Cosam,
the son of Elmadam, the son of Er,
²⁹the son of Joshua, the son of Eliezer,
the son of Jorim, the son of Matthat,
the son of Levi, ³⁰the son of Simeon,
the son of Judah, the son of Joseph,
the son of Jonam, the son of Eliakim,
³¹the son of Melea, the son of Menna,
the son of Mattatha, the son of Nathan,
the son of David, ³²the son of Jesse,
the son of Obed, the son of Boaz,
the son of Salmon,ᵃ the son of Nahshon,
³³the son of Amminadab, the son of Ram,ᵇ
the son of Hezron, the son of Perez,
the son of Judah, ³⁴the son of Jacob,
the son of Isaac, the son of Abraham,
the son of Terah, the son of Nahor,
³⁵the son of Serug, the son of Reu,
the son of Peleg, the son of Eber,
the son of Shelah, ³⁶the son of Cainan,
the son of Arphaxad, the son of Shem,
the son of Noah, the son of Lamech,
³⁷the son of Methuselah, the son of Enoch,
the son of Jared, the son of Mahalalel,
the son of Kenan, ³⁸the son of Enosh,
the son of Seth, the son of Adam,
the son of God.

The Temptation of Jesus

4 Jesus, full of the Holy Spirit, returned from the Jordan and was led by the Spirit in the desert, ²where for forty

ᵃ 32 Some early manuscripts *Sala*   ᵇ 33 Some manuscripts *Amminadab, the son of Admin, the son of Arni*; other manuscripts vary widely.

days he was tempted by the devil. He ate nothing during those days, and at the end of them he was hungry.
³The devil said to him, "If you are the Son of God, tell this stone to become bread."
⁴Jesus answered, "It is written: 'Man does not live on bread alone.'[a]"
⁵The devil led him up to a high place and showed him in an instant all the kingdoms of the world. ⁶And he said to him, "I will give you all their authority and splendor, for it has been given to me, and I can give it to anyone I want to. ⁷So if you worship me, it will all be yours."
⁸Jesus answered, "It is written: 'Worship the Lord your God and serve him only.'[b]"
⁹The devil led him to Jerusalem and had him stand on the highest point of the temple. "If you are the Son of God," he said, "throw yourself down from here. ¹⁰For it is written:

" 'He will command his angels concerning you
    to guard you carefully;
¹¹they will lift you up in their hands,
    so that you will not strike your foot against a
      stone.'[c]"

¹²Jesus answered, "It says: 'Do not put the Lord your God to the test.'[d]"
¹³When the devil had finished all this tempting, he left him until an opportune time.

Jesus Rejected at Nazareth

¹⁴Jesus returned to Galilee in the power of the Spirit, and news about him spread through the whole countryside. ¹⁵He taught in their synagogues, and everyone praised him.
¹⁶He went to Nazareth, where he had been brought up, and on the Sabbath day he went into the synagogue, as was his custom. And he stood up to read. ¹⁷The scroll of the prophet Isaiah was handed to him. Unrolling it, he found the place where it is written:

¹⁸"The Spirit of the Lord is on me,
    because he has anointed me
    to preach good news to the poor.
He has sent me to proclaim freedom for the
      prisoners
    and recovery of sight for the blind,
    to release the oppressed,
¹⁹   to proclaim the year of the Lord's favor."[e]

²⁰Then he rolled up the scroll, gave it back to the attendant and sat down. The eyes of everyone in the synagogue were fastened on him, ²¹and he began by saying to them, "Today this scripture is fulfilled in your hearing."
²²All spoke well of him and were amazed at the gracious words that came from his lips. "Isn't this Joseph's son?" they asked.
²³Jesus said to them, "Surely you will quote this proverb to me: 'Physician, heal yourself! Do here in your hometown what we have heard that you did in Capernaum.' "
²⁴"I tell you the truth," he continued, "no prophet is accepted in his hometown. ²⁵I assure you that there were

The Temptations of Solitude

LUKE 4:1–15

After his baptism Jesus retreats to the desert in silence to fast and pray. In that solitude the devil tempts Jesus with pleasure and security (bread), power (the kingdoms of the world) and prestige (jumping from the highest point of the temple). How does Jesus overcome these temptations? What barriers do you face when you pursue silence and solitude in order to strengthen your spiritual life? What are some of the temptations and distractions you might face if you decided to wait on God in silence? Consider taking a significant block of time—an hour or a one-day retreat—to pray. Write about your experience in a journal.

See *Meeting God in Worship*

---

[a]4 Deut. 8:3   [b]8 Deut. 6:13   [c]11 Psalm 91:11,12   [d]12 Deut. 6:16
[e]19 Isaiah 61:1,2

Jesus Walks

LUKE 4:16–30

Picture yourself with Jesus in the hometown synagogue he attended "as was his custom." Listen as Jesus stands up to read the words of Isaiah 61:1–2 (Luke 4:18–19). Notice how the people become angry when Jesus highlights God's love for the Gentiles (Luke 4:25–27). Go along as the outraged people drive him out of town and try to hurl him from a cliff. Now picture yourself in a conflict in which you take an unpopular stand on someone's behalf. Enjoy the sense of security you feel as Jesus walks with you in the midst of a crowd of irate people. What is Jesus saying to you?

See Meeting God in Community

many widows in Israel in Elijah's time, when the sky was shut for three and a half years and there was a severe famine throughout the land. [26]Yet Elijah was not sent to any of them, but to a widow in Zarephath in the region of Sidon. [27]And there were many in Israel with leprosy[a] in the time of Elisha the prophet, yet not one of them was cleansed—only Naaman the Syrian."

[28]All the people in the synagogue were furious when they heard this. [29]They got up, drove him out of the town, and took him to the brow of the hill on which the town was built, in order to throw him down the cliff. [30]But he walked right through the crowd and went on his way.

Jesus Drives Out an Evil Spirit

[31]Then he went down to Capernaum, a town in Galilee, and on the Sabbath began to teach the people. [32]They were amazed at his teaching, because his message had authority.

[33]In the synagogue there was a man possessed by a demon, an evil[b] spirit. He cried out at the top of his voice, [34]"Ha! What do you want with us, Jesus of Nazareth? Have you come to destroy us? I know who you are—the Holy One of God!"

[35]"Be quiet!" Jesus said sternly. "Come out of him!" Then the demon threw the man down before them all and came out without injuring him.

[36]All the people were amazed and said to each other, "What is this teaching? With authority and power he gives orders to evil spirits and they come out!" [37]And the news about him spread throughout the surrounding area.

Jesus Heals Many

[38]Jesus left the synagogue and went to the home of Simon. Now Simon's mother-in-law was suffering from a high fever, and they asked Jesus to help her. [39]So he bent over her and rebuked the fever, and it left her. She got up at once and began to wait on them.

[40]When the sun was setting, the people brought to Jesus all who had various kinds of sickness, and laying his hands on each one, he healed them. [41]Moreover, demons came out of many people, shouting, "You are the Son of God!" But he rebuked them and would not allow them to speak, because they knew he was the Christ.[c]

[42]At daybreak Jesus went out to a solitary place. The people were looking for him and when they came to where he was, they tried to keep him from leaving them. [43]But he said, "I must preach the good news of the kingdom of God to the other towns also, because that is why I was sent." [44]And he kept on preaching in the synagogues of Judea.[d]

The Calling of the First Disciples

5 One day as Jesus was standing by the Lake of Gennesaret,[e] with the people crowding around him and listening to the word of God, [2]he saw at the water's edge two boats, left there by the fishermen, who were washing their nets. [3]He got into one of the boats, the one belonging to

---

[a] 27 The Greek word was used for various diseases affecting the skin—not necessarily leprosy.   [b] 33 Greek *unclean*; also in verse 36   [c] 41 Or *Messiah*   [d] 44 Or *the land of the Jews*; some manuscripts *Galilee*   [e] 1 That is, Sea of Galilee

Simon, and asked him to put out a little from shore. Then he sat down and taught the people from the boat.

⁴When he had finished speaking, he said to Simon, "Put out into deep water, and let down*ᵃ* the nets for a catch."

⁵Simon answered, "Master, we've worked hard all night and haven't caught anything. But because you say so, I will let down the nets."

⁶When they had done so, they caught such a large number of fish that their nets began to break. ⁷So they signaled their partners in the other boat to come and help them, and they came and filled both boats so full that they began to sink.

⁸When Simon Peter saw this, he fell at Jesus' knees and said, "Go away from me, Lord; I am a sinful man!" ⁹For he and all his companions were astonished at the catch of fish they had taken, ¹⁰and so were James and John, the sons of Zebedee, Simon's partners.

Then Jesus said to Simon, "Don't be afraid; from now on you will catch men." ¹¹So they pulled their boats up on shore, left everything and followed him.

The Man With Leprosy

¹²While Jesus was in one of the towns, a man came along who was covered with leprosy.*ᵇ* When he saw Jesus, he fell with his face to the ground and begged him, "Lord, if you are willing, you can make me clean."

¹³Jesus reached out his hand and touched the man. "I am willing," he said. "Be clean!" And immediately the leprosy left him.

¹⁴Then Jesus ordered him, "Don't tell anyone, but go, show yourself to the priest and offer the sacrifices that Moses commanded for your cleansing, as a testimony to them."

¹⁵Yet the news about him spread all the more, so that crowds of people came to hear him and to be healed of their sicknesses. ¹⁶But Jesus often withdrew to lonely places and prayed.

Jesus Heals a Paralytic

¹⁷One day as he was teaching, Pharisees and teachers of the law, who had come from every village of Galilee and from Judea and Jerusalem, were sitting there. And the power of the Lord was present for him to heal the sick. ¹⁸Some men came carrying a paralytic on a mat and tried to take him into the house to lay him before Jesus. ¹⁹When they could not find a way to do this because of the crowd, they went up on the roof and lowered him on his mat through the tiles into the middle of the crowd, right in front of Jesus.

²⁰When Jesus saw their faith, he said, "Friend, your sins are forgiven."

²¹The Pharisees and the teachers of the law began thinking to themselves, "Who is this fellow who speaks blasphemy? Who can forgive sins but God alone?"

²²Jesus knew what they were thinking and asked, "Why are you thinking these things in your hearts? ²³Which is easier: to say, 'Your sins are forgiven,' or to say, 'Get up and walk'? ²⁴But that you may know that the Son of Man has au-

ᵃ4 The Greek verb is plural.   *ᵇ12* The Greek word was used for various diseases affecting the skin—not necessarily leprosy.

Transforming the Beloved

LUKE 5:4–6

"We've worked hard all night and haven't caught anything." Simon's words might also describe the dark night of the soul: "The soul has to go on loving in the emptiness, or at least go on wanting to love, though it may only be with an infinitesimal part of itself. Then, one day, God will come to show himself to this soul and reveal the beauty of the world to it" (Simone Weil, *Waiting for God*). It is often in periods of seeming fruitlessness that Jesus Christ reveals his power, and in times of darkness that God sheds the greatest light. Are you enduring a period of fruitlessness or darkness? Ask Jesus to tell you where to "let down your nets" in order to see his power revealed.

See Meeting God in Everyday Life

Open to the Wonder of God

LUKE 5:26

The word *paradox* occurs only once in Scripture: "They were filled with awe and said, 'We have seen remarkable [*paradoxa*] things today' " (5:26). As onlookers watch the healing of the paralytic, they wonder that the power to heal comes not from the righteous, authoritative Pharisees, but from the peasant preacher, Jesus (5:17–26). Wonder at the unexpected, the paradoxical, often opens one's soul to God. Ponder the unexpected ways in which Jesus reveals divine power and glory. Is there anything about Jesus Christ that seems paradoxical to you? In what unconventional ways might God be speaking to you now? Close your eyes and bask in wonder at the mystery of Jesus Christ.

See Meeting God in Worship

thority on earth to forgive sins . . ." He said to the paralyzed man, "I tell you, get up, take your mat and go home." [25]Immediately he stood up in front of them, took what he had been lying on and went home praising God. [26]Everyone was amazed and gave praise to God. They were filled with awe and said, "We have seen remarkable things today."

The Calling of Levi

[27]After this, Jesus went out and saw a tax collector by the name of Levi sitting at his tax booth. "Follow me," Jesus said to him, [28]and Levi got up, left everything and followed him.

[29]Then Levi held a great banquet for Jesus at his house, and a large crowd of tax collectors and others were eating with them. [30]But the Pharisees and the teachers of the law who belonged to their sect complained to his disciples, "Why do you eat and drink with tax collectors and 'sinners'?"

[31]Jesus answered them, "It is not the healthy who need a doctor, but the sick. [32]I have not come to call the righteous, but sinners to repentance."

Jesus Questioned About Fasting

[33]They said to him, "John's disciples often fast and pray, and so do the disciples of the Pharisees, but yours go on eating and drinking."

[34]Jesus answered, "Can you make the guests of the bridegroom fast while he is with them? [35]But the time will come when the bridegroom will be taken from them; in those days they will fast."

[36]He told them this parable: "No one tears a patch from a new garment and sews it on an old one. If he does, he will have torn the new garment, and the patch from the new will not match the old. [37]And no one pours new wine into old wineskins. If he does, the new wine will burst the skins, the wine will run out and the wineskins will be ruined. [38]No, new wine must be poured into new wineskins. [39]And no one after drinking old wine wants the new, for he says, 'The old is better.' "

Lord of the Sabbath

6 One Sabbath Jesus was going through the grainfields, and his disciples began to pick some heads of grain, rub them in their hands and eat the kernels. [2]Some of the Pharisees asked, "Why are you doing what is unlawful on the Sabbath?"

[3]Jesus answered them, "Have you never read what David did when he and his companions were hungry? [4]He entered the house of God, and taking the consecrated bread, he ate what is lawful only for priests to eat. And he also gave some to his companions." [5]Then Jesus said to them, "The Son of Man is Lord of the Sabbath."

[6]On another Sabbath he went into the synagogue and was teaching, and a man was there whose right hand was shriveled. [7]The Pharisees and the teachers of the law were looking for a reason to accuse Jesus, so they watched him closely to see if he would heal on the Sabbath. [8]But Jesus knew what they were thinking and said to the man with the shriveled hand, "Get up and stand in front of everyone." So he got up and stood there.

⁹Then Jesus said to them, "I ask you, which is lawful on the Sabbath: to do good or to do evil, to save life or to destroy it?"

¹⁰He looked around at them all, and then said to the man, "Stretch out your hand." He did so, and his hand was completely restored. ¹¹But they were furious and began to discuss with one another what they might do to Jesus.

The Twelve Apostles

¹²One of those days Jesus went out to a mountainside to pray, and spent the night praying to God. ¹³When morning came, he called his disciples to him and chose twelve of them, whom he also designated apostles: ¹⁴Simon (whom he named Peter), his brother Andrew, James, John, Philip, Bartholomew, ¹⁵Matthew, Thomas, James son of Alphaeus, Simon who was called the Zealot, ¹⁶Judas son of James, and Judas Iscariot, who became a traitor.

Blessings and Woes

¹⁷He went down with them and stood on a level place. A large crowd of his disciples was there and a great number of people from all over Judea, from Jerusalem, and from the coast of Tyre and Sidon, ¹⁸who had come to hear him and to be healed of their diseases. Those troubled by evil[a] spirits were cured, ¹⁹and the people all tried to touch him, because power was coming from him and healing them all.

²⁰Looking at his disciples, he said:

"Blessed are you who are poor,
    for yours is the kingdom of God.
²¹Blessed are you who hunger now,
    for you will be satisfied.
Blessed are you who weep now,
    for you will laugh.
²²Blessed are you when men hate you,
    when they exclude you and insult you
    and reject your name as evil,
      because of the Son of Man.

²³"Rejoice in that day and leap for joy, because great is your reward in heaven. For that is how their fathers treated the prophets.

²⁴"But woe to you who are rich,
    for you have already received your comfort.
²⁵Woe to you who are well fed now,
    for you will go hungry.
Woe to you who laugh now,
    for you will mourn and weep.
²⁶Woe to you when all men speak well of you,
    for that is how their fathers treated the false
      prophets.

Love for Enemies

²⁷"But I tell you who hear me: Love your enemies, do good to those who hate you, ²⁸bless those who curse you, pray for those who mistreat you. ²⁹If someone strikes you on one cheek, turn to him the other also. If someone takes your cloak, do not stop him from taking your tunic. ³⁰Give to everyone who asks you, and if anyone takes what be-

---

[a] 18 Greek *unclean*

Divine Rhythm: Solitude and Community

LUKE 6:12–16

Jesus prays alone all night; in the morning he calls the Twelve to work alongside him. How do you balance solitude and community in your life? In what ways are your practices of solitude and community out of balance? Consider designing a pattern—called by some a "rule of life"—to maintain a rhythm of time apart for prayer and reflection and time spent with others. Consider how you can ensure neither is shortchanged. Do you spend your entire work-week with others? Your weekends entirely alone? What could you do differently? Write down some of your ideas and discuss them with a friend.

See Meeting God in Prayer

Blessing the Difficult

LUKE 6:32-36

Read this passage and then reread it slowly as you do this exercise (*lectio divina* or "divine reading"): Listen for a word or phrase that stands out—don't rush to the most obvious one first. Continue to be quiet before God. What do you think happens within you as you love your enemy? What does it teach you about yourself? Respond to whatever God is telling you through this passage.

See Meeting God in Prayer

longs to you, do not demand it back. ³¹Do to others as you would have them do to you.

³²"If you love those who love you, what credit is that to you? Even 'sinners' love those who love them. ³³And if you do good to those who are good to you, what credit is that to you? Even 'sinners' do that. ³⁴And if you lend to those from whom you expect repayment, what credit is that to you? Even 'sinners' lend to 'sinners,' expecting to be repaid in full. ³⁵But love your enemies, do good to them, and lend to them without expecting to get anything back. Then your reward will be great, and you will be sons of the Most High, because he is kind to the ungrateful and wicked. ³⁶Be merciful, just as your Father is merciful.

Judging Others

³⁷"Do not judge, and you will not be judged. Do not condemn, and you will not be condemned. Forgive, and you will be forgiven. ³⁸Give, and it will be given to you. A good measure, pressed down, shaken together and running over, will be poured into your lap. For with the measure you use, it will be measured to you."

³⁹He also told them this parable: "Can a blind man lead a blind man? Will they not both fall into a pit? ⁴⁰A student is not above his teacher, but everyone who is fully trained will be like his teacher.

⁴¹"Why do you look at the speck of sawdust in your brother's eye and pay no attention to the plank in your own eye? ⁴²How can you say to your brother, 'Brother, let me take the speck out of your eye,' when you yourself fail to see the plank in your own eye? You hypocrite, first take the plank out of your eye, and then you will see clearly to remove the speck from your brother's eye.

A Tree and Its Fruit

⁴³"No good tree bears bad fruit, nor does a bad tree bear good fruit. ⁴⁴Each tree is recognized by its own fruit. People do not pick figs from thornbushes, or grapes from briers. ⁴⁵The good man brings good things out of the good stored up in his heart, and the evil man brings evil things out of the evil stored up in his heart. For out of the overflow of his heart his mouth speaks.

The Wise and Foolish Builders

⁴⁶"Why do you call me, 'Lord, Lord,' and do not do what I say? ⁴⁷I will show you what he is like who comes to me and hears my words and puts them into practice. ⁴⁸He is like a man building a house, who dug down deep and laid the foundation on rock. When a flood came, the torrent struck that house but could not shake it, because it was well built. ⁴⁹But the one who hears my words and does not put them into practice is like a man who built a house on the ground without a foundation. The moment the torrent struck that house, it collapsed and its destruction was complete."

The Faith of the Centurion

7 When Jesus had finished saying all this in the hearing of the people, he entered Capernaum. ²There a centurion's servant, whom his master valued highly, was sick and about to die. ³The centurion heard of Jesus and sent

some elders of the Jews to him, asking him to come and heal his servant. ⁴When they came to Jesus, they pleaded earnestly with him, "This man deserves to have you do this, ⁵because he loves our nation and has built our synagogue." ⁶So Jesus went with them.

He was not far from the house when the centurion sent friends to say to him: "Lord, don't trouble yourself, for I do not deserve to have you come under my roof. ⁷That is why I did not even consider myself worthy to come to you. But say the word, and my servant will be healed. ⁸For I myself am a man under authority, with soldiers under me. I tell this one, 'Go,' and he goes; and that one, 'Come,' and he comes. I say to my servant, 'Do this,' and he does it."

⁹When Jesus heard this, he was amazed at him, and turning to the crowd following him, he said, "I tell you, I have not found such great faith even in Israel." ¹⁰Then the men who had been sent returned to the house and found the servant well.

Jesus Raises a Widow's Son

¹¹Soon afterward, Jesus went to a town called Nain, and his disciples and a large crowd went along with him. ¹²As he approached the town gate, a dead person was being carried out—the only son of his mother, and she was a widow. And a large crowd from the town was with her. ¹³When the Lord saw her, his heart went out to her and he said, "Don't cry."

¹⁴Then he went up and touched the coffin, and those carrying it stood still. He said, "Young man, I say to you, get up!" ¹⁵The dead man sat up and began to talk, and Jesus gave him back to his mother.

¹⁶They were all filled with awe and praised God. "A great prophet has appeared among us," they said. "God has come to help his people." ¹⁷This news about Jesus spread throughout Judea[a] and the surrounding country.

Jesus and John the Baptist

¹⁸John's disciples told him about all these things. Calling two of them, ¹⁹he sent them to the Lord to ask, "Are you the one who was to come, or should we expect someone else?"

²⁰When the men came to Jesus, they said, "John the Baptist sent us to you to ask, 'Are you the one who was to come, or should we expect someone else?' "

²¹At that very time Jesus cured many who had diseases, sicknesses and evil spirits, and gave sight to many who were blind. ²²So he replied to the messengers, "Go back and report to John what you have seen and heard: The blind receive sight, the lame walk, those who have leprosy[b] are cured, the deaf hear, the dead are raised, and the good news is preached to the poor. ²³Blessed is the man who does not fall away on account of me."

²⁴After John's messengers left, Jesus began to speak to the crowd about John: "What did you go out into the desert to see? A reed swayed by the wind? ²⁵If not, what did you go out to see? A man dressed in fine clothes? No, those who wear expensive clothes and indulge in luxury are in palaces. ²⁶But what did you go out to see? A prophet? Yes, I tell you, and more than a prophet. ²⁷This is the one about whom it is written:

The Journey to Belief

LUKE 7:18–23

"Perhaps it is all a mistake, this business about Christianity . . . Perhaps all this talk about God and Jesus Christ and the salvation of [human beings] is a collection of fairy tales . . . Perhaps it is a mistake to preach love in a hate-torn world, to rescue those who are in need, to teach the children, to comfort the lonely and the dying. But if it is, after all, a mistake, then it is a beautiful mistake. If Christianity should turn out, after all, to be true, then unbelief will have been a very ugly mistake."

—KAJ MUNK,
By the Rivers of Babylon

See *Meeting God in Community*

---

[a] 17 Or *the land of the Jews*   [b] 22 The Greek word was used for various diseases affecting the skin—not necessarily leprosy.

Twin Spiritual Paths

LUKE 7:33–34

Two men, two spiritual paths, two traditions exist in creative tension: the ascetic path of John the Baptist, who lived mainly in the desert, and the path of the Son of Man, who spent much of his time in cities crowded with people. These paths intersect when God calls us to retreat in order to prepare for service.

Are you being called to streamline your lifestyle so that you have more time for solitude, prayer and reflection? Or are you being called to mix more with people in the world as "a friend of sinners"? How might the cultivation of a simple, modest lifestyle better prepare you to live as Jesus did, in the world but not of the world?

See Meeting God in Community

" 'I will send my messenger ahead of you,
  who will prepare your way before you.'ᵃ

²⁸I tell you, among those born of women there is no one greater than John; yet the one who is least in the kingdom of God is greater than he."

²⁹(All the people, even the tax collectors, when they heard Jesus' words, acknowledged that God's way was right, because they had been baptized by John. ³⁰But the Pharisees and experts in the law rejected God's purpose for themselves, because they had not been baptized by John.)

³¹"To what, then, can I compare the people of this generation? What are they like? ³²They are like children sitting in the marketplace and calling out to each other:

" 'We played the flute for you,
    and you did not dance;
  we sang a dirge,
    and you did not cry.'

³³For John the Baptist came neither eating bread nor drinking wine, and you say, 'He has a demon.' ³⁴The Son of Man came eating and drinking, and you say, 'Here is a glutton and a drunkard, a friend of tax collectors and "sinners." ' ³⁵But wisdom is proved right by all her children."

Jesus Anointed by a Sinful Woman

³⁶Now one of the Pharisees invited Jesus to have dinner with him, so he went to the Pharisee's house and reclined at the table. ³⁷When a woman who had lived a sinful life in that town learned that Jesus was eating at the Pharisee's house, she brought an alabaster jar of perfume, ³⁸and as she stood behind him at his feet weeping, she began to wet his feet with her tears. Then she wiped them with her hair, kissed them and poured perfume on them.

³⁹When the Pharisee who had invited him saw this, he said to himself, "If this man were a prophet, he would know who is touching him and what kind of woman she is—that she is a sinner."

⁴⁰Jesus answered him, "Simon, I have something to tell you."

"Tell me, teacher," he said.

⁴¹"Two men owed money to a certain moneylender. One owed him five hundred denarii,ᵇ and the other fifty. ⁴²Neither of them had the money to pay him back, so he canceled the debts of both. Now which of them will love him more?"

⁴³Simon replied, "I suppose the one who had the bigger debt canceled."

"You have judged correctly," Jesus said.

⁴⁴Then he turned toward the woman and said to Simon, "Do you see this woman? I came into your house. You did not give me any water for my feet, but she wet my feet with her tears and wiped them with her hair. ⁴⁵You did not give me a kiss, but this woman, from the time I entered, has not stopped kissing my feet. ⁴⁶You did not put oil on my head, but she has poured perfume on my feet. ⁴⁷Therefore, I tell you, her many sins have been forgiven—for she loved much. But he who has been forgiven little loves little."

ᵃ 27 Mal. 3:1   ᵇ 41 A denarius was a coin worth about a day's wages.

⁴⁸Then Jesus said to her, "Your sins are forgiven."

⁴⁹The other guests began to say among themselves, "Who is this who even forgives sins?"

⁵⁰Jesus said to the woman, "Your faith has saved you; go in peace."

The Parable of the Sower

8 After this, Jesus traveled about from one town and village to another, proclaiming the good news of the kingdom of God. The Twelve were with him, ²and also some women who had been cured of evil spirits and diseases: Mary (called Magdalene) from whom seven demons had come out; ³Joanna the wife of Cuza, the manager of Herod's household; Susanna; and many others. These women were helping to support them out of their own means.

⁴While a large crowd was gathering and people were coming to Jesus from town after town, he told this parable: ⁵"A farmer went out to sow his seed. As he was scattering the seed, some fell along the path; it was trampled on, and the birds of the air ate it up. ⁶Some fell on rock, and when it came up, the plants withered because they had no moisture. ⁷Other seed fell among thorns, which grew up with it and choked the plants. ⁸Still other seed fell on good soil. It came up and yielded a crop, a hundred times more than was sown."

When he said this, he called out, "He who has ears to hear, let him hear."

⁹His disciples asked him what this parable meant. ¹⁰He said, "The knowledge of the secrets of the kingdom of God has been given to you, but to others I speak in parables, so that,

" 'though seeing, they may not see;
though hearing, they may not understand.'ᵃ

¹¹"This is the meaning of the parable: The seed is the word of God. ¹²Those along the path are the ones who hear, and then the devil comes and takes away the word from their hearts, so that they may not believe and be saved. ¹³Those on the rock are the ones who receive the word with joy when they hear it, but they have no root. They believe for a while, but in the time of testing they fall away. ¹⁴The seed that fell among thorns stands for those who hear, but as they go on their way they are choked by life's worries, riches and pleasures, and they do not mature. ¹⁵But the seed on good soil stands for those with a noble and good heart, who hear the word, retain it, and by persevering produce a crop.

A Lamp on a Stand

¹⁶"No one lights a lamp and hides it in a jar or puts it under a bed. Instead, he puts it on a stand, so that those who come in can see the light. ¹⁷For there is nothing hidden that will not be disclosed, and nothing concealed that will not be known or brought out into the open. ¹⁸Therefore consider carefully how you listen. Whoever has will be given more; whoever does not have, even what he thinks he has will be taken from him."

Letting the Word Grow

LUKE 8:11–15

Attending to God's voice requires effort. We're so unaccustomed to listening that we often let God's messages go unnoticed. Or we hear God speaking to us, but we don't let the words take root in our inner being. Pleasures and problems quickly overshadow them. What does it say about God that he continues to plant seeds even though people don't nurture them? What does it say about our human nature that we're so easily distracted? What do you want to say to God, or to ask God, about these issues? What does this passage tell you that you need to do in order to hear God better?

ᵃ *10* Isaiah 6:9

Spiritual Family

LUKE 8:19-21

Jesus provides a startling definition of his family: "those who hear God's word and put it into practice." Consider the various ages and stages of your life. Who has been that kind of "family" for you? What have these "family members" taught you? Diligence? Sensitivity? Courage? Try making a gratitude list, noting the names of people to whom you are grateful and what these people have contributed to your life. As you make your list, thank God for these people and ponder how God wants you to participate in the lives of these spiritual "family members."

See Meeting God in Community

Jesus' Mother and Brothers

¹⁹Now Jesus' mother and brothers came to see him, but they were not able to get near him because of the crowd. ²⁰Someone told him, "Your mother and brothers are standing outside, wanting to see you."

²¹He replied, "My mother and brothers are those who hear God's word and put it into practice."

Jesus Calms the Storm

²²One day Jesus said to his disciples, "Let's go over to the other side of the lake." So they got into a boat and set out. ²³As they sailed, he fell asleep. A squall came down on the lake, so that the boat was being swamped, and they were in great danger.

²⁴The disciples went and woke him, saying, "Master, Master, we're going to drown!"

He got up and rebuked the wind and the raging waters; the storm subsided, and all was calm. ²⁵"Where is your faith?" he asked his disciples.

In fear and amazement they asked one another, "Who is this? He commands even the winds and the water, and they obey him."

The Healing of a Demon-possessed Man

²⁶They sailed to the region of the Gerasenes,ᵃ which is across the lake from Galilee. ²⁷When Jesus stepped ashore, he was met by a demon-possessed man from the town. For a long time this man had not worn clothes or lived in a house, but had lived in the tombs. ²⁸When he saw Jesus, he cried out and fell at his feet, shouting at the top of his voice, "What do you want with me, Jesus, Son of the Most High God? I beg you, don't torture me!" ²⁹For Jesus had commanded the evilᵇ spirit to come out of the man. Many times it had seized him, and though he was chained hand and foot and kept under guard, he had broken his chains and had been driven by the demon into solitary places.

³⁰Jesus asked him, "What is your name?"

"Legion," he replied, because many demons had gone into him. ³¹And they begged him repeatedly not to order them to go into the Abyss.

³²A large herd of pigs was feeding there on the hillside. The demons begged Jesus to let them go into them, and he gave them permission. ³³When the demons came out of the man, they went into the pigs, and the herd rushed down the steep bank into the lake and was drowned.

³⁴When those tending the pigs saw what had happened, they ran off and reported this in the town and countryside, ³⁵and the people went out to see what had happened. When they came to Jesus, they found the man from whom the demons had gone out, sitting at Jesus' feet, dressed and in his right mind; and they were afraid. ³⁶Those who had seen it told the people how the demon-possessed man had been cured. ³⁷Then all the people of the region of the Gerasenes asked Jesus to leave them, because they were overcome with fear. So he got into the boat and left.

³⁸The man from whom the demons had gone out begged to go with him, but Jesus sent him away, saying,

ᵃ 26 Some manuscripts *Gadarenes*; other manuscripts *Gergesenes*; also in verse 37   ᵇ 29 Greek *unclean*

³⁹"Return home and tell how much God has done for you." So the man went away and told all over town how much Jesus had done for him.

A Dead Girl and a Sick Woman

⁴⁰Now when Jesus returned, a crowd welcomed him, for they were all expecting him. ⁴¹Then a man named Jairus, a ruler of the synagogue, came and fell at Jesus' feet, pleading with him to come to his house ⁴²because his only daughter, a girl of about twelve, was dying.

As Jesus was on his way, the crowds almost crushed him. ⁴³And a woman was there who had been subject to bleeding for twelve years,ᵃ but no one could heal her. ⁴⁴She came up behind him and touched the edge of his cloak, and immediately her bleeding stopped.

⁴⁵"Who touched me?" Jesus asked.

When they all denied it, Peter said, "Master, the people are crowding and pressing against you."

⁴⁶But Jesus said, "Someone touched me; I know that power has gone out from me."

⁴⁷Then the woman, seeing that she could not go unnoticed, came trembling and fell at his feet. In the presence of all the people, she told why she had touched him and how she had been instantly healed. ⁴⁸Then he said to her, "Daughter, your faith has healed you. Go in peace."

⁴⁹While Jesus was still speaking, someone came from the house of Jairus, the synagogue ruler. "Your daughter is dead," he said. "Don't bother the teacher any more."

⁵⁰Hearing this, Jesus said to Jairus, "Don't be afraid; just believe, and she will be healed."

⁵¹When he arrived at the house of Jairus, he did not let anyone go in with him except Peter, John and James, and the child's father and mother. ⁵²Meanwhile, all the people were wailing and mourning for her. "Stop wailing," Jesus said. "She is not dead but asleep."

⁵³They laughed at him, knowing that she was dead. ⁵⁴But he took her by the hand and said, "My child, get up!" ⁵⁵Her spirit returned, and at once she stood up. Then Jesus told them to give her something to eat. ⁵⁶Her parents were astonished, but he ordered them not to tell anyone what had happened.

Jesus Sends Out the Twelve

9 When Jesus had called the Twelve together, he gave them power and authority to drive out all demons and to cure diseases, ²and he sent them out to preach the kingdom of God and to heal the sick. ³He told them: "Take nothing for the journey—no staff, no bag, no bread, no money, no extra tunic. ⁴Whatever house you enter, stay there until you leave that town. ⁵If people do not welcome you, shake the dust off your feet when you leave their town, as a testimony against them." ⁶So they set out and went from village to village, preaching the gospel and healing people everywhere.

⁷Now Herod the tetrarch heard about all that was going on. And he was perplexed, because some were saying that John had been raised from the dead, ⁸others that Elijah had appeared, and still others that one of the prophets of long ago had come back to life. ⁹But Herod said, "I be-

---

When Life Is Interrupted

LUKE 8:40–56

Read this Scripture passage aloud; then reread it silently. Allow an "inner video" to play, visualizing each character and hearing each one converse with Jesus: Jairus comes to Jesus on behalf of his dying twelve-year-old daughter . . . Jesus works his way through the crowds . . . A woman who has been bleeding for twelve years touches Jesus' clothing . . . The disciples become angry . . . The woman is afraid as she is singled out . . . Jesus says, "Daughter, your faith has healed you. Go in peace." Then, to Jairus, Jesus says, "Don't be afraid; just believe." Listen to Jesus' words as if they were spoken to you: "Don't be afraid; just believe." Rest in God's presence.

See Meeting God in Scripture

ᵃ 43 Many manuscripts *years, and she had spent all she had on doctors*

Taking Inventory

LUKE 9:10–17

Imagine that you are one of the disciples, returning tired from teaching, healing and driving out demons. You have so many questions to ask Jesus. Then you hear about the execution of John the Baptist. Jesus invites you to retreat; you long to go to a quiet spot to rest and grieve. Suddenly a crowd of people arrives, asking for help. When you ask Jesus to send them away, he says, "You give them something to eat." But you protest, "I have no more than _____." In order to fill in the blank, take an inventory of the resources of your life: your personal, family, intellectual, material, physical and spiritual resources. Picture yourself placing these resources in Jesus' hands, one by one, until the last resource is yourself—resting in Jesus' arms.

See Meeting God in Community

headed John. Who, then, is this I hear such things about?" And he tried to see him.

Jesus Feeds the Five Thousand

¹⁰When the apostles returned, they reported to Jesus what they had done. Then he took them with him and they withdrew by themselves to a town called Bethsaida, ¹¹but the crowds learned about it and followed him. He welcomed them and spoke to them about the kingdom of God, and healed those who needed healing.

¹²Late in the afternoon the Twelve came to him and said, "Send the crowd away so they can go to the surrounding villages and countryside and find food and lodging, because we are in a remote place here."

¹³He replied, "You give them something to eat."

They answered, "We have only five loaves of bread and two fish—unless we go and buy food for all this crowd." ¹⁴(About five thousand men were there.)

But he said to his disciples, "Have them sit down in groups of about fifty each." ¹⁵The disciples did so, and everybody sat down. ¹⁶Taking the five loaves and the two fish and looking up to heaven, he gave thanks and broke them. Then he gave them to the disciples to set before the people. ¹⁷They all ate and were satisfied, and the disciples picked up twelve basketfuls of broken pieces that were left over.

Peter's Confession of Christ

¹⁸Once when Jesus was praying in private and his disciples were with him, he asked them, "Who do the crowds say I am?"

¹⁹They replied, "Some say John the Baptist; others say Elijah; and still others, that one of the prophets of long ago has come back to life."

²⁰"But what about you?" he asked. "Who do you say I am?"

Peter answered, "The Christ[a] of God."

²¹Jesus strictly warned them not to tell this to anyone. ²²And he said, "The Son of Man must suffer many things and be rejected by the elders, chief priests and teachers of the law, and he must be killed and on the third day be raised to life."

²³Then he said to them all: "If anyone would come after me, he must deny himself and take up his cross daily and follow me. ²⁴For whoever wants to save his life will lose it, but whoever loses his life for me will save it. ²⁵What good is it for a man to gain the whole world, and yet lose or forfeit his very self? ²⁶If anyone is ashamed of me and my words, the Son of Man will be ashamed of him when he comes in his glory and in the glory of the Father and of the holy angels. ²⁷I tell you the truth, some who are standing here will not taste death before they see the kingdom of God."

The Transfiguration

²⁸About eight days after Jesus said this, he took Peter, John and James with him and went up onto a mountain to pray. ²⁹As he was praying, the appearance of his face changed, and his clothes became as bright as a flash of lightning. ³⁰Two men, Moses and Elijah, ³¹appeared in glorious splendor, talking with Jesus. They spoke about his de-

a 20 Or Messiah

parture, which he was about to bring to fulfillment at Jerusalem. [32]Peter and his companions were very sleepy, but when they became fully awake, they saw his glory and the two men standing with him. [33]As the men were leaving Jesus, Peter said to him, "Master, it is good for us to be here. Let us put up three shelters—one for you, one for Moses and one for Elijah." (He did not know what he was saying.)

[34]While he was speaking, a cloud appeared and enveloped them, and they were afraid as they entered the cloud. [35]A voice came from the cloud, saying, "This is my Son, whom I have chosen; listen to him." [36]When the voice had spoken, they found that Jesus was alone. The disciples kept this to themselves, and told no one at that time what they had seen.

The Healing of a Boy With an Evil Spirit

[37]The next day, when they came down from the mountain, a large crowd met him. [38]A man in the crowd called out, "Teacher, I beg you to look at my son, for he is my only child. [39]A spirit seizes him and he suddenly screams; it throws him into convulsions so that he foams at the mouth. It scarcely ever leaves him and is destroying him. [40]I begged your disciples to drive it out, but they could not."

[41]"O unbelieving and perverse generation," Jesus replied, "how long shall I stay with you and put up with you? Bring your son here."

[42]Even while the boy was coming, the demon threw him to the ground in a convulsion. But Jesus rebuked the evil[a] spirit, healed the boy and gave him back to his father. [43]And they were all amazed at the greatness of God.

While everyone was marveling at all that Jesus did, he said to his disciples, [44]"Listen carefully to what I am about to tell you: The Son of Man is going to be betrayed into the hands of men." [45]But they did not understand what this meant. It was hidden from them, so that they did not grasp it, and they were afraid to ask him about it.

Who Will Be the Greatest?

[46]An argument started among the disciples as to which of them would be the greatest. [47]Jesus, knowing their thoughts, took a little child and had him stand beside him. [48]Then he said to them, "Whoever welcomes this little child in my name welcomes me; and whoever welcomes me welcomes the one who sent me. For he who is least among you all—he is the greatest."

[49]"Master," said John, "we saw a man driving out demons in your name and we tried to stop him, because he is not one of us."

[50]"Do not stop him," Jesus said, "for whoever is not against you is for you."

Samaritan Opposition

[51]As the time approached for him to be taken up to heaven, Jesus resolutely set out for Jerusalem. [52]And he sent messengers on ahead, who went into a Samaritan village to get things ready for him; [53]but the people there did not welcome him, because he was heading for Jerusalem. [54]When the disciples James and John saw this, they asked, "Lord, do you want us to call fire down from heaven to de-

[a] 42 Greek unclean

Go Forth and Travel Lightly!

LUKE 10:1–12

When Jesus sends the seventy-two out to prepare the people for his coming, he instructs them to travel lightly. They are not to attempt to control how their needs will be met or how people will respond to them. Why does God want us to serve as disciples without having control over resources or circumstances? Why do we seem to need to control these things? What do your answers suggest about how you can pray about these issues?

See Meeting God in Community

stroy them[a]?" [55]But Jesus turned and rebuked them, [56]and[b] they went to another village.

The Cost of Following Jesus

[57]As they were walking along the road, a man said to him, "I will follow you wherever you go."

[58]Jesus replied, "Foxes have holes and birds of the air have nests, but the Son of Man has no place to lay his head."

[59]He said to another man, "Follow me."

But the man replied, "Lord, first let me go and bury my father."

[60]Jesus said to him, "Let the dead bury their own dead, but you go and proclaim the kingdom of God."

[61]Still another said, "I will follow you, Lord; but first let me go back and say good-by to my family."

[62]Jesus replied, "No one who puts his hand to the plow and looks back is fit for service in the kingdom of God."

Jesus Sends Out the Seventy-two

10 After this the Lord appointed seventy-two[c] others and sent them two by two ahead of him to every town and place where he was about to go. [2]He told them, "The harvest is plentiful, but the workers are few. Ask the Lord of the harvest, therefore, to send out workers into his harvest field. [3]Go! I am sending you out like lambs among wolves. [4]Do not take a purse or bag or sandals; and do not greet anyone on the road.

[5]"When you enter a house, first say, 'Peace to this house.' [6]If a man of peace is there, your peace will rest on him; if not, it will return to you. [7]Stay in that house, eating and drinking whatever they give you, for the worker deserves his wages. Do not move around from house to house.

[8]"When you enter a town and are welcomed, eat what is set before you. [9]Heal the sick who are there and tell them, 'The kingdom of God is near you.' [10]But when you enter a town and are not welcomed, go into its streets and say, [11]'Even the dust of your town that sticks to our feet we wipe off against you. Yet be sure of this: The kingdom of God is near.' [12]I tell you, it will be more bearable on that day for Sodom than for that town.

[13]"Woe to you, Korazin! Woe to you, Bethsaida! For if the miracles that were performed in you had been performed in Tyre and Sidon, they would have repented long ago, sitting in sackcloth and ashes. [14]But it will be more bearable for Tyre and Sidon at the judgment than for you. [15]And you, Capernaum, will you be lifted up to the skies? No, you will go down to the depths.[d]

[16]"He who listens to you listens to me; he who rejects you rejects me; but he who rejects me rejects him who sent me."

[17]The seventy-two returned with joy and said, "Lord, even the demons submit to us in your name."

[18]He replied, "I saw Satan fall like lightning from heaven. [19]I have given you authority to trample on snakes and scorpions and to overcome all the power of the enemy; nothing will harm you. [20]However, do not rejoice that the

---

[a] 54 Some manuscripts *them, even as Elijah did*   [b] 55,56 Some manuscripts *them. And he said, "You do not know what kind of spirit you are of, for the Son of Man did not come to destroy men's lives, but to save them." [56]And*
[c] 1 Some manuscripts *seventy*; also in verse 17   [d] 15 Greek *Hades*

spirits submit to you, but rejoice that your names are written in heaven."

²¹At that time Jesus, full of joy through the Holy Spirit, said, "I praise you, Father, Lord of heaven and earth, because you have hidden these things from the wise and learned, and revealed them to little children. Yes, Father, for this was your good pleasure.

²²"All things have been committed to me by my Father. No one knows who the Son is except the Father, and no one knows who the Father is except the Son and those to whom the Son chooses to reveal him."

²³Then he turned to his disciples and said privately, "Blessed are the eyes that see what you see. ²⁴For I tell you that many prophets and kings wanted to see what you see but did not see it, and to hear what you hear but did not hear it."

The Parable of the Good Samaritan

²⁵On one occasion an expert in the law stood up to test Jesus. "Teacher," he asked, "what must I do to inherit eternal life?"

²⁶"What is written in the Law?" he replied. "How do you read it?"

²⁷He answered: " 'Love the Lord your God with all your heart and with all your soul and with all your strength and with all your mind'ᵃ; and, 'Love your neighbor as yourself.'ᵇ"

²⁸"You have answered correctly," Jesus replied. "Do this and you will live."

²⁹But he wanted to justify himself, so he asked Jesus, "And who is my neighbor?"

³⁰In reply Jesus said: "A man was going down from Jerusalem to Jericho, when he fell into the hands of robbers. They stripped him of his clothes, beat him and went away, leaving him half dead. ³¹A priest happened to be going down the same road, and when he saw the man, he passed by on the other side. ³²So too, a Levite, when he came to the place and saw him, passed by on the other side. ³³But a Samaritan, as he traveled, came where the man was; and when he saw him, he took pity on him. ³⁴He went to him and bandaged his wounds, pouring on oil and wine. Then he put the man on his own donkey, took him to an inn and took care of him. ³⁵The next day he took out two silver coinsᶜ and gave them to the innkeeper. 'Look after him,' he said, 'and when I return, I will reimburse you for any extra expense you may have.'

³⁶"Which of these three do you think was a neighbor to the man who fell into the hands of robbers?"

³⁷The expert in the law replied, "The one who had mercy on him."

Jesus told him, "Go and do likewise."

At the Home of Martha and Mary

³⁸As Jesus and his disciples were on their way, he came to a village where a woman named Martha opened her home to him. ³⁹She had a sister called Mary, who sat at the Lord's feet listening to what he said. ⁴⁰But Martha was distracted by all the preparations that had to be made. She came to him and asked, "Lord, don't you care that my sister has left me to do the work by myself? Tell her to help me!"

"Lord, Don't You Care?"

LUKE 10:38–42

Put yourself in Martha's place. You have worked hard to offer the Lord hospitality, using all the skills you have and providing the sumptuous feast that is fitting for your honored guest. Hot and tired, your face contorts with annoyance when you see Mary just sitting at Jesus' feet. You ask, "Lord, don't you care that my sister has left me to do the work by myself?"

Let Jesus address you lovingly, personally: "_____, you are worried and upset about many things." Tell Jesus "the many things" bothering you. Hear Jesus say to you: "_____, only one thing is needed." What is the one thing that's needed now in life? Allow a word or phrase to rise within you. Repeat it slowly, letting that word or phrase carry your concerns, one by one, into the heart of God.

See Meeting God in Prayer

The Personal Sermon

LUKE 11:1–4

"Frequently when I come to a certain part of 'Our Father' or to a petition, I land in such rich thoughts that I leave behind all set prayers. When such rich, good thoughts arrive, then one should leave the other commandments aside and offer room to those thoughts and listen in stillness and for all the world not put up obstructions. For then the Holy Spirit . . . is preaching and one word from [that] sermon is better than a thousand of our prayers. I have often learned more from one such prayer than I could have received from much reading and writing."

—MARTIN LUTHER

See *Meeting God in Worship*

"Martha, Martha," the Lord answered, "you are worried and upset about many things, [42]but only one thing is needed.[a] Mary has chosen what is better, and it will not be taken away from her."

Jesus' Teaching on Prayer

11 One day Jesus was praying in a certain place. When he finished, one of his disciples said to him, "Lord, teach us to pray, just as John taught his disciples."

[2]He said to them, "When you pray, say:

" 'Father,[b]
hallowed be your name,
your kingdom come.[c]
[3]Give us each day our daily bread.
[4]Forgive us our sins,
    for we also forgive everyone who sins against
        us.[d]
And lead us not into temptation.[e]' "

[5]Then he said to them, "Suppose one of you has a friend, and he goes to him at midnight and says, 'Friend, lend me three loaves of bread, [6]because a friend of mine on a journey has come to me, and I have nothing to set before him.'

[7]"Then the one inside answers, 'Don't bother me. The door is already locked, and my children are with me in bed. I can't get up and give you anything.' [8]I tell you, though he will not get up and give him the bread because he is his friend, yet because of the man's boldness[f] he will get up and give him as much as he needs.

[9]"So I say to you: Ask and it will be given to you; seek and you will find; knock and the door will be opened to you. [10]For everyone who asks receives; he who seeks finds; and to him who knocks, the door will be opened.

[11]"Which of you fathers, if your son asks for[g] a fish, will give him a snake instead? [12]Or if he asks for an egg, will give him a scorpion? [13]If you then, though you are evil, know how to give good gifts to your children, how much more will your Father in heaven give the Holy Spirit to those who ask him!"

Jesus and Beelzebub

[14]Jesus was driving out a demon that was mute. When the demon left, the man who had been mute spoke, and the crowd was amazed. [15]But some of them said, "By Beelzebub,[h] the prince of demons, he is driving out demons." [16]Others tested him by asking for a sign from heaven.

[17]Jesus knew their thoughts and said to them: "Any kingdom divided against itself will be ruined, and a house divided against itself will fall. [18]If Satan is divided against himself, how can his kingdom stand? I say this because you claim that I drive out demons by Beelzebub. [19]Now if I drive out demons by Beelzebub, by whom do your followers drive them out? So then, they will be your judges. [20]But if I drive out demons by the finger of God, then the kingdom of God has come to you.

21"When a strong man, fully armed, guards his own house, his possessions are safe. 22But when someone stronger attacks and overpowers him, he takes away the armor in which the man trusted and divides up the spoils.

23"He who is not with me is against me, and he who does not gather with me, scatters.

24"When an evil*a* spirit comes out of a man, it goes through arid places seeking rest and does not find it. Then it says, 'I will return to the house I left.' 25When it arrives, it finds the house swept clean and put in order. 26Then it goes and takes seven other spirits more wicked than itself, and they go in and live there. And the final condition of that man is worse than the first."

27As Jesus was saying these things, a woman in the crowd called out, "Blessed is the mother who gave you birth and nursed you."

28He replied, "Blessed rather are those who hear the word of God and obey it."

The Sign of Jonah

29As the crowds increased, Jesus said, "This is a wicked generation. It asks for a miraculous sign, but none will be given it except the sign of Jonah. 30For as Jonah was a sign to the Ninevites, so also will the Son of Man be to this generation. 31The Queen of the South will rise at the judgment with the men of this generation and condemn them; for she came from the ends of the earth to listen to Solomon's wisdom, and now one*b* greater than Solomon is here. 32The men of Nineveh will stand up at the judgment with this generation and condemn it; for they repented at the preaching of Jonah, and now one greater than Jonah is here.

The Lamp of the Body

33"No one lights a lamp and puts it in a place where it will be hidden, or under a bowl. Instead he puts it on its stand, so that those who come in may see the light. 34Your eye is the lamp of your body. When your eyes are good, your whole body also is full of light. But when they are bad, your body also is full of darkness. 35See to it, then, that the light within you is not darkness. 36Therefore, if your whole body is full of light, and no part of it dark, it will be completely lighted, as when the light of a lamp shines on you."

Six Woes

37When Jesus had finished speaking, a Pharisee invited him to eat with him; so he went in and reclined at the table. 38But the Pharisee, noticing that Jesus did not first wash before the meal, was surprised.

39Then the Lord said to him, "Now then, you Pharisees clean the outside of the cup and dish, but inside you are full of greed and wickedness. 40You foolish people! Did not the one who made the outside make the inside also? 41But give what is inside ⌊the dish⌋*c* to the poor, and everything will be clean for you.

42"Woe to you Pharisees, because you give God a tenth of your mint, rue and all other kinds of garden herbs, but you neglect justice and the love of God. You should have practiced the latter without leaving the former undone.

Your Life Mission

LUKE 11:33–36

A "good eye" is a healthy, focused eye, which floods the body with light. In *Man's Search for Meaning*, Victor Frankl wrote that a person with a *why* to live can survive almost any *how*. What is your focused *why* for living? Try finishing this sentence: "My purpose for being on this earth is . . . ." Close your eyes and identify what gives you inner joy and fulfillment. What is your passion—your mission? Summarize this single vision in a sentence and write it on a small card, or express it artistically. Look at it from time to time and pray. How do you sense God's affirmation about being called in this direction?

See Meeting God in Community

---

a 24 Greek *unclean*   *b 31* Or *something*; also in verse 32   *c 41* Or *what you have*

Making Christ Known

LUKE 11:42–44; 12:1–3

Jesus Christ is reflected in us through the seamless integrity of our worship—expressed both in the words we whisper privately and in the love with which we carry out our deeds. The "yeast of the Pharisees"—hypocrisy of the heart—must be rooted out. Read this passage twice, slowly the second time. Sit quietly, allowing a word or phrase to stand out. Reflect on this word or phrase or action. Why is it meaningful to you? Use that word or phrase to pray back to God the truth God has given you. Be quiet before God and attentive to anything God may be showing you.

See Meeting God in Scripture

43"Woe to you Pharisees, because you love the most important seats in the synagogues and greetings in the marketplaces.

44"Woe to you, because you are like unmarked graves, which men walk over without knowing it."

45One of the experts in the law answered him, "Teacher, when you say these things, you insult us also."

46Jesus replied, "And you experts in the law, woe to you, because you load people down with burdens they can hardly carry, and you yourselves will not lift one finger to help them.

47"Woe to you, because you build tombs for the prophets, and it was your forefathers who killed them. 48So you testify that you approve of what your forefathers did; they killed the prophets, and you build their tombs. 49Because of this, God in his wisdom said, 'I will send them prophets and apostles, some of whom they will kill and others they will persecute.' 50Therefore this generation will be held responsible for the blood of all the prophets that has been shed since the beginning of the world, 51from the blood of Abel to the blood of Zechariah, who was killed between the altar and the sanctuary. Yes, I tell you, this generation will be held responsible for it all.

52"Woe to you experts in the law, because you have taken away the key to knowledge. You yourselves have not entered, and you have hindered those who were entering."

53When Jesus left there, the Pharisees and the teachers of the law began to oppose him fiercely and to besiege him with questions, 54waiting to catch him in something he might say.

Warnings and Encouragements

12 Meanwhile, when a crowd of many thousands had gathered, so that they were trampling on one another, Jesus began to speak first to his disciples, saying: "Be on your guard against the yeast of the Pharisees, which is hypocrisy. 2There is nothing concealed that will not be disclosed, or hidden that will not be made known. 3What you have said in the dark will be heard in the daylight, and what you have whispered in the ear in the inner rooms will be proclaimed from the roofs.

4"I tell you, my friends, do not be afraid of those who kill the body and after that can do no more. 5But I will show you whom you should fear: Fear him who, after the killing of the body, has power to throw you into hell. Yes, I tell you, fear him. 6Are not five sparrows sold for two pennies*a*? Yet not one of them is forgotten by God. 7Indeed, the very hairs of your head are all numbered. Don't be afraid; you are worth more than many sparrows.

8"I tell you, whoever acknowledges me before men, the Son of Man will also acknowledge him before the angels of God. 9But he who disowns me before men will be disowned before the angels of God. 10And everyone who speaks a word against the Son of Man will be forgiven, but anyone who blasphemes against the Holy Spirit will not be forgiven.

11"When you are brought before synagogues, rulers and authorities, do not worry about how you will defend yourselves or what you will say, 12for the Holy Spirit will teach you at that time what you should say."

a 6 Greek two assaria

The Parable of the Rich Fool

¹³Someone in the crowd said to him, "Teacher, tell my brother to divide the inheritance with me."

¹⁴Jesus replied, "Man, who appointed me a judge or an arbiter between you?" ¹⁵Then he said to them, "Watch out! Be on your guard against all kinds of greed; a man's life does not consist in the abundance of his possessions."

¹⁶And he told them this parable: "The ground of a certain rich man produced a good crop. ¹⁷He thought to himself, 'What shall I do? I have no place to store my crops.'

¹⁸"Then he said, 'This is what I'll do. I will tear down my barns and build bigger ones, and there I will store all my grain and my goods. ¹⁹And I'll say to myself, "You have plenty of good things laid up for many years. Take life easy; eat, drink and be merry." '

²⁰"But God said to him, 'You fool! This very night your life will be demanded from you. Then who will get what you have prepared for yourself?'

²¹"This is how it will be with anyone who stores up things for himself but is not rich toward God."

Do Not Worry

²²Then Jesus said to his disciples: "Therefore I tell you, do not worry about your life, what you will eat; or about your body, what you will wear. ²³Life is more than food, and the body more than clothes. ²⁴Consider the ravens: They do not sow or reap, they have no storeroom or barn; yet God feeds them. And how much more valuable you are than birds! ²⁵Who of you by worrying can add a single hour to his life*a*? ²⁶Since you cannot do this very little thing, why do you worry about the rest?

²⁷"Consider how the lilies grow. They do not labor or spin. Yet I tell you, not even Solomon in all his splendor was dressed like one of these. ²⁸If that is how God clothes the grass of the field, which is here today, and tomorrow is thrown into the fire, how much more will he clothe you, O you of little faith! ²⁹And do not set your heart on what you will eat or drink; do not worry about it. ³⁰For the pagan world runs after all such things, and your Father knows that you need them. ³¹But seek his kingdom, and these things will be given to you as well.

³²"Do not be afraid, little flock, for your Father has been pleased to give you the kingdom. ³³Sell your possessions and give to the poor. Provide purses for yourselves that will not wear out, a treasure in heaven that will not be exhausted, where no thief comes near and no moth destroys. ³⁴For where your treasure is, there your heart will be also.

Watchfulness

³⁵"Be dressed ready for service and keep your lamps burning, ³⁶like men waiting for their master to return from a wedding banquet, so that when he comes and knocks they can immediately open the door for him. ³⁷It will be good for those servants whose master finds them watching when he comes. I tell you the truth, he will dress himself to serve, will have them recline at the table and will come and wait on them. ³⁸It will be good for those servants whose master finds them ready, even if he comes in

---

Focused Solely on God

LUKE 12:22–34

"Indeed the very heart of this work is nothing else but a naked intent toward God for God's own sake. I call it a naked intent because it is utterly disinterested. In this work the perfect artisan does not seek personal gain or exemption from suffering. One desires only God and God alone. One is so fascinated by the God one loves and so concerned that God's will be done on earth that one neither notices nor cares about one's own ease or anxiety. In reality it amounts to a yearning for God, a longing to see and taste God as much as is possible in this life."

—ANONYMOUS,
The Cloud of Unknowing

---

a 25 Or *single cubit to his height*

Let Jesus Carry Your Stress

LUKE 12:49–53

Although we'd like to believe that the walk of faith is all light and warmth, we can't avoid the reality that it can also be fiery: "I have come to bring fire on the earth." Being a disciple of Jesus is costly. Loyalty to Jesus Christ may cause division rather than peace. Referring to the cross and his resurrection as a "baptism," Jesus says, "How distressed I am until it is completed!"

A life of faith isn't about being happy and popular, but about aligning ourselves with Jesus. Picture Jesus carrying each stress in your life to the cross, one by one, as each thought of a personal or family conflict comes to your mind. Finally, picture yourself being baptized—dying with Jesus, then rising to walk in newness of life.

the second or third watch of the night. ³⁹But understand this: If the owner of the house had known at what hour the thief was coming, he would not have let his house be broken into. ⁴⁰You also must be ready, because the Son of Man will come at an hour when you do not expect him."

⁴¹Peter asked, "Lord, are you telling this parable to us, or to everyone?"

⁴²The Lord answered, "Who then is the faithful and wise manager, whom the master puts in charge of his servants to give them their food allowance at the proper time? ⁴³It will be good for that servant whom the master finds doing so when he returns. ⁴⁴I tell you the truth, he will put him in charge of all his possessions. ⁴⁵But suppose the servant says to himself, 'My master is taking a long time in coming,' and he then begins to beat the menservants and maidservants and to eat and drink and get drunk. ⁴⁶The master of that servant will come on a day when he does not expect him and at an hour he is not aware of. He will cut him to pieces and assign him a place with the unbelievers.

⁴⁷"That servant who knows his master's will and does not get ready or does not do what his master wants will be beaten with many blows. ⁴⁸But the one who does not know and does things deserving punishment will be beaten with few blows. From everyone who has been given much, much will be demanded; and from the one who has been entrusted with much, much more will be asked.

Not Peace but Division

⁴⁹"I have come to bring fire on the earth, and how I wish it were already kindled! ⁵⁰But I have a baptism to undergo, and how distressed I am until it is completed! ⁵¹Do you think I came to bring peace on earth? No, I tell you, but division. ⁵²From now on there will be five in one family divided against each other, three against two and two against three. ⁵³They will be divided, father against son and son against father, mother against daughter and daughter against mother, mother-in-law against daughter-in-law and daughter-in-law against mother-in-law."

Interpreting the Times

⁵⁴He said to the crowd: "When you see a cloud rising in the west, immediately you say, 'It's going to rain,' and it does. ⁵⁵And when the south wind blows, you say, 'It's going to be hot,' and it is. ⁵⁶Hypocrites! You know how to interpret the appearance of the earth and the sky. How is it that you don't know how to interpret this present time?

⁵⁷"Why don't you judge for yourselves what is right? ⁵⁸As you are going with your adversary to the magistrate, try hard to be reconciled to him on the way, or he may drag you off to the judge, and the judge turn you over to the officer, and the officer throw you into prison. ⁵⁹I tell you, you will not get out until you have paid the last penny.ᵃ"

Repent or Perish

13 Now there were some present at that time who told Jesus about the Galileans whose blood Pilate had mixed with their sacrifices. ²Jesus answered, "Do you think that these Galileans were worse sinners than all the other Galileans because they suffered this way? ³I tell you,

ᵃ 59 Greek *lepton*

no! But unless you repent, you too will all perish. [4]Or those eighteen who died when the tower in Siloam fell on them—do you think they were more guilty than all the others living in Jerusalem? [5]I tell you, no! But unless you repent, you too will all perish."

[6]Then he told this parable: "A man had a fig tree, planted in his vineyard, and he went to look for fruit on it, but did not find any. [7]So he said to the man who took care of the vineyard, 'For three years now I've been coming to look for fruit on this fig tree and haven't found any. Cut it down! Why should it use up the soil?'

[8]"'Sir,' the man replied, 'leave it alone for one more year, and I'll dig around it and fertilize it. [9]If it bears fruit next year, fine! If not, then cut it down.'"

A Crippled Woman Healed on the Sabbath

[10]On a Sabbath Jesus was teaching in one of the synagogues, [11]and a woman was there who had been crippled by a spirit for eighteen years. She was bent over and could not straighten up at all. [12]When Jesus saw her, he called her forward and said to her, "Woman, you are set free from your infirmity." [13]Then he put his hands on her, and immediately she straightened up and praised God.

[14]Indignant because Jesus had healed on the Sabbath, the synagogue ruler said to the people, "There are six days for work. So come and be healed on those days, not on the Sabbath."

[15]The Lord answered him, "You hypocrites! Doesn't each of you on the Sabbath untie his ox or donkey from the stall and lead it out to give it water? [16]Then should not this woman, a daughter of Abraham, whom Satan has kept bound for eighteen long years, be set free on the Sabbath day from what bound her?"

[17]When he said this, all his opponents were humiliated, but the people were delighted with all the wonderful things he was doing.

The Parables of the Mustard Seed and the Yeast

[18]Then Jesus asked, "What is the kingdom of God like? What shall I compare it to? [19]It is like a mustard seed, which a man took and planted in his garden. It grew and became a tree, and the birds of the air perched in its branches."

[20]Again he asked, "What shall I compare the kingdom of God to? [21]It is like yeast that a woman took and mixed into a large amount[a] of flour until it worked all through the dough."

The Narrow Door

[22]Then Jesus went through the towns and villages, teaching as he made his way to Jerusalem. [23]Someone asked him, "Lord, are only a few people going to be saved?"

He said to them, [24]"Make every effort to enter through the narrow door, because many, I tell you, will try to enter and will not be able to. [25]Once the owner of the house gets up and closes the door, you will stand outside knocking and pleading, 'Sir, open the door for us.'

"But he will answer, 'I don't know you or where you come from.'

Set Free

LUKE 13:10–13

The wounds of people's infirmities rarely escape Jesus' notice and he is always ready to offer a healing touch. Walk around the room bent over, as the woman in this passage does, to see how the world looks from her vantage point. How does it feel to walk that way? What are the burdens that weigh you down and bend you over? Take a deep breath and stand up straight, offering your burdens to God. Raise your hands in praise to God, who declares you have been "set free!" Take note of any part of your body in which you feel tightness or pain—your neck, shoulders, lower back. Inhale and exhale deeply. From what does God want to set you free?

See Meeting God in the Created Order

---

*a 21 Greek three satas (probably about 1/2 bushel or 22 liters)

As a Hen Gathers Her Chicks

LUKE 13:31–35

As he contemplates Jerusalem, the Holy City of David, Jesus is filled with sorrow at the reluctance of God's chosen people to allow him to gather them in as a mother hen gathers, warms and protects her chicks.

Let this image of Jesus as nurturer guide you as you pray today. Read Psalm 91 to help you sharpen your awareness of God as your protector and nurturer. How can you nestle under the wings of God? In what ways do you need to be warmed in mind and spirit? What, if any, resistance are you experiencing as you contemplate this image?

See Meeting God in Scripture

²⁶"Then you will say, 'We ate and drank with you, and you taught in our streets.'
²⁷"But he will reply, 'I don't know you or where you come from. Away from me, all you evildoers!'
²⁸"There will be weeping there, and gnashing of teeth, when you see Abraham, Isaac and Jacob and all the prophets in the kingdom of God, but you yourselves thrown out. ²⁹People will come from east and west and north and south, and will take their places at the feast in the kingdom of God. ³⁰Indeed there are those who are last who will be first, and first who will be last."

Jesus' Sorrow for Jerusalem

³¹At that time some Pharisees came to Jesus and said to him, "Leave this place and go somewhere else. Herod wants to kill you."
³²He replied, "Go tell that fox, 'I will drive out demons and heal people today and tomorrow, and on the third day I will reach my goal.' ³³In any case, I must keep going today and tomorrow and the next day—for surely no prophet can die outside Jerusalem!
³⁴"O Jerusalem, Jerusalem, you who kill the prophets and stone those sent to you, how often I have longed to gather your children together, as a hen gathers her chicks under her wings, but you were not willing! ³⁵Look, your house is left to you desolate. I tell you, you will not see me again until you say, 'Blessed is he who comes in the name of the Lord.'ᵃ"

Jesus at a Pharisee's House

14 One Sabbath, when Jesus went to eat in the house of a prominent Pharisee, he was being carefully watched. ²There in front of him was a man suffering from dropsy. ³Jesus asked the Pharisees and experts in the law, "Is it lawful to heal on the Sabbath or not?" ⁴But they remained silent. So taking hold of the man, he healed him and sent him away.

⁵Then he asked them, "If one of you has a sonᵇ or an ox that falls into a well on the Sabbath day, will you not immediately pull him out?" ⁶And they had nothing to say.

⁷When he noticed how the guests picked the places of honor at the table, he told them this parable: ⁸"When someone invites you to a wedding feast, do not take the place of honor, for a person more distinguished than you may have been invited. ⁹If so, the host who invited both of you will come and say to you, 'Give this man your seat.' Then, humiliated, you will have to take the least important place. ¹⁰But when you are invited, take the lowest place, so that when your host comes, he will say to you, 'Friend, move up to a better place.' Then you will be honored in the presence of all your fellow guests. ¹¹For everyone who exalts himself will be humbled, and he who humbles himself will be exalted."

¹²Then Jesus said to his host, "When you give a luncheon or dinner, do not invite your friends, your brothers or relatives, or your rich neighbors; if you do, they may invite you back and so you will be repaid. ¹³But when you give a banquet, invite the poor, the crippled, the lame, the blind,

ᵃ 35 Psalm 118:26   ᵇ 5 Some manuscripts *donkey*

[14]and you will be blessed. Although they cannot repay you, you will be repaid at the resurrection of the righteous."

The Parable of the Great Banquet

[15]When one of those at the table with him heard this, he said to Jesus, "Blessed is the man who will eat at the feast in the kingdom of God."

[16]Jesus replied: "A certain man was preparing a great banquet and invited many guests. [17]At the time of the banquet he sent his servant to tell those who had been invited, 'Come, for everything is now ready.'

[18]"But they all alike began to make excuses. The first said, 'I have just bought a field, and I must go and see it. Please excuse me.'

[19]"Another said, 'I have just bought five yoke of oxen, and I'm on my way to try them out. Please excuse me.'

[20]"Still another said, 'I just got married, so I can't come.'

[21]"The servant came back and reported this to his master. Then the owner of the house became angry and ordered his servant, 'Go out quickly into the streets and alleys of the town and bring in the poor, the crippled, the blind and the lame.'

[22]" 'Sir,' the servant said, 'what you ordered has been done, but there is still room.'

[23]"Then the master told his servant, 'Go out to the roads and country lanes and make them come in, so that my house will be full. [24]I tell you, not one of those men who were invited will get a taste of my banquet.' "

The Cost of Being a Disciple

[25]Large crowds were traveling with Jesus, and turning to them he said: [26]"If anyone comes to me and does not hate his father and mother, his wife and children, his brothers and sisters—yes, even his own life—he cannot be my disciple. [27]And anyone who does not carry his cross and follow me cannot be my disciple.

[28]"Suppose one of you wants to build a tower. Will he not first sit down and estimate the cost to see if he has enough money to complete it? [29]For if he lays the foundation and is not able to finish it, everyone who sees it will ridicule him, [30]saying, 'This fellow began to build and was not able to finish.'

[31]"Or suppose a king is about to go to war against another king. Will he not first sit down and consider whether he is able with ten thousand men to oppose the one coming against him with twenty thousand? [32]If he is not able, he will send a delegation while the other is still a long way off and will ask for terms of peace. [33]In the same way, any of you who does not give up everything he has cannot be my disciple.

[34]"Salt is good, but if it loses its saltiness, how can it be made salty again? [35]It is fit neither for the soil nor for the manure pile; it is thrown out.

"He who has ears to hear, let him hear."

The Parable of the Lost Sheep

15 Now the tax collectors and "sinners" were all gathering around to hear him. [2]But the Pharisees and the teachers of the law muttered, "This man welcomes sinners and eats with them."

Hospitality Within the Heart of Christ

LUKE 14:12–14

"Let all guests who arrive be received like Christ, for he is going to say, 'I came as a guest, and you received me.' And to all let due honor be shown . . . In reception of the poor and of pilgrims the greatest care and solicitude should be shown, because it is especially in them that Christ is received."

—*The Rule of Saint Benedict*

Reassuring Words, Empowering Words

LUKE 15:11–32

Read this passage silently and create an "inner video" of it. Converse with each character: the younger prodigal son; the angry, perfectionist older son; the heartbroken father; and the unseen mother. With whom do you identify most? Why? Return to the older sibling, identifying your own dutiful, resentful feelings. Hear God's reassuring words: "You are always with me." God invites you to claim your inheritance: "Everything I have is yours." Repeat these empowering words. Let them become your prayer of thanksgiving as you offer yourself to God: "You are always with me, and everything I have is yours."

See *Meeting God in Scripture*

³Then Jesus told them this parable: ⁴"Suppose one of you has a hundred sheep and loses one of them. Does he not leave the ninety-nine in the open country and go after the lost sheep until he finds it? ⁵And when he finds it, he joyfully puts it on his shoulders ⁶and goes home. Then he calls his friends and neighbors together and says, 'Rejoice with me; I have found my lost sheep.' ⁷I tell you that in the same way there will be more rejoicing in heaven over one sinner who repents than over ninety-nine righteous persons who do not need to repent.

The Parable of the Lost Coin

⁸"Or suppose a woman has ten silver coins*ᵃ* and loses one. Does she not light a lamp, sweep the house and search carefully until she finds it? ⁹And when she finds it, she calls her friends and neighbors together and says, 'Rejoice with me; I have found my lost coin.' ¹⁰In the same way, I tell you, there is rejoicing in the presence of the angels of God over one sinner who repents."

The Parable of the Lost Son

¹¹Jesus continued: "There was a man who had two sons. ¹²The younger one said to his father, 'Father, give me my share of the estate.' So he divided his property between them.

¹³"Not long after that, the younger son got together all he had, set off for a distant country and there squandered his wealth in wild living. ¹⁴After he had spent everything, there was a severe famine in that whole country, and he began to be in need. ¹⁵So he went and hired himself out to a citizen of that country, who sent him to his fields to feed pigs. ¹⁶He longed to fill his stomach with the pods that the pigs were eating, but no one gave him anything.

¹⁷"When he came to his senses, he said, 'How many of my father's hired men have food to spare, and here I am starving to death! ¹⁸I will set out and go back to my father and say to him: Father, I have sinned against heaven and against you. ¹⁹I am no longer worthy to be called your son; make me like one of your hired men.' ²⁰So he got up and went to his father.

"But while he was still a long way off, his father saw him and was filled with compassion for him; he ran to his son, threw his arms around him and kissed him.

²¹"The son said to him, 'Father, I have sinned against heaven and against you. I am no longer worthy to be called your son.*ᵇ*'

²²"But the father said to his servants, 'Quick! Bring the best robe and put it on him. Put a ring on his finger and sandals on his feet. ²³Bring the fattened calf and kill it. Let's have a feast and celebrate. ²⁴For this son of mine was dead and is alive again; he was lost and is found.' So they began to celebrate.

²⁵"Meanwhile, the older son was in the field. When he came near the house, he heard music and dancing. ²⁶So he called one of the servants and asked him what was going on. ²⁷'Your brother has come,' he replied, 'and your father has killed the fattened calf because he has him back safe and sound.'

ᵃ8 Greek *ten drachmas,* each worth about a day's wages   *ᵇ21* Some early manuscripts *son. Make me like one of your hired men.*

28"The older brother became angry and refused to go in. So his father went out and pleaded with him. 29But he answered his father, 'Look! All these years I've been slaving for you and never disobeyed your orders. Yet you never gave me even a young goat so I could celebrate with my friends. 30But when this son of yours who has squandered your property with prostitutes comes home, you kill the fattened calf for him!'

31" 'My son,' the father said, 'you are always with me, and everything I have is yours. 32But we had to celebrate and be glad, because this brother of yours was dead and is alive again; he was lost and is found.' "

The Parable of the Shrewd Manager

16 Jesus told his disciples: "There was a rich man whose manager was accused of wasting his possessions. 2So he called him in and asked him, 'What is this I hear about you? Give an account of your management, because you cannot be manager any longer.'

3"The manager said to himself, 'What shall I do now? My master is taking away my job. I'm not strong enough to dig, and I'm ashamed to beg— 4I know what I'll do so that, when I lose my job here, people will welcome me into their houses.'

5"So he called in each one of his master's debtors. He asked the first, 'How much do you owe my master?'

6" 'Eight hundred gallons*a* of olive oil,' he replied.

"The manager told him, 'Take your bill, sit down quickly, and make it four hundred.'

7"Then he asked the second, 'And how much do you owe?'

" 'A thousand bushels*b* of wheat,' he replied.

"He told him, 'Take your bill and make it eight hundred.'

8"The master commended the dishonest manager because he had acted shrewdly. For the people of this world are more shrewd in dealing with their own kind than are the people of the light. 9I tell you, use worldly wealth to gain friends for yourselves, so that when it is gone, you will be welcomed into eternal dwellings.

10"Whoever can be trusted with very little can also be trusted with much, and whoever is dishonest with very little will also be dishonest with much. 11So if you have not been trustworthy in handling worldly wealth, who will trust you with true riches? 12And if you have not been trustworthy with someone else's property, who will give you property of your own?

13"No servant can serve two masters. Either he will hate the one and love the other, or he will be devoted to the one and despise the other. You cannot serve both God and Money."

14The Pharisees, who loved money, heard all this and were sneering at Jesus. 15He said to them, "You are the ones who justify yourselves in the eyes of men, but God knows your hearts. What is highly valued among men is detestable in God's sight.

Additional Teachings

16"The Law and the Prophets were proclaimed until

Choosing God's Riches

LUKE 16:10–13

We are being trained to be trustworthy with God's "true riches" when we are given little and prove trustworthy with it. Sometimes we struggle, however, to keep choosing "true riches" over worldly wealth. Read this passage twice. What word or phrase draws your attention? Reflect on this word or phrase. What comes to you as you reflect on it? Remain silent and open to insight from God. In what way does this passage touch your life today?

See Meeting God in Scripture

a 6 Greek *one hundred batous* (probably about 3 kiloliters)   *b* 7 Greek *one hundred korous* (probably about 35 kiloliters)

Letting Go of Possessions

LUKE 16:19–31

Jesus, in this story of the rich man and Lazarus, illustrates how difficult it is to love God and your neighbor when one's treasure is great wealth and possessions.

Imagine yourself in the scene of Lazarus and the rich man. With which character do you identify more? What would you like to ask each character? Try asking Jesus how you can let go of your attachment to money, intelligence and privilege. What would it mean to relinquish everything to God? (See also 18:18–30.)

John. Since that time, the good news of the kingdom of God is being preached, and everyone is forcing his way into it. ¹⁷It is easier for heaven and earth to disappear than for the least stroke of a pen to drop out of the Law.

¹⁸"Anyone who divorces his wife and marries another woman commits adultery, and the man who marries a divorced woman commits adultery.

The Rich Man and Lazarus

¹⁹"There was a rich man who was dressed in purple and fine linen and lived in luxury every day. ²⁰At his gate was laid a beggar named Lazarus, covered with sores ²¹and longing to eat what fell from the rich man's table. Even the dogs came and licked his sores.

²²"The time came when the beggar died and the angels carried him to Abraham's side. The rich man also died and was buried. ²³In hell,ᵃ where he was in torment, he looked up and saw Abraham far away, with Lazarus by his side. ²⁴So he called to him, 'Father Abraham, have pity on me and send Lazarus to dip the tip of his finger in water and cool my tongue, because I am in agony in this fire.'

²⁵"But Abraham replied, 'Son, remember that in your lifetime you received your good things, while Lazarus received bad things, but now he is comforted here and you are in agony. ²⁶And besides all this, between us and you a great chasm has been fixed, so that those who want to go from here to you cannot, nor can anyone cross over from there to us.'

²⁷"He answered, 'Then I beg you, father, send Lazarus to my father's house, ²⁸for I have five brothers. Let him warn them, so that they will not also come to this place of torment.'

²⁹"Abraham replied, 'They have Moses and the Prophets; let them listen to them.'

³⁰"'No, father Abraham,' he said, 'but if someone from the dead goes to them, they will repent.'

³¹"He said to him, 'If they do not listen to Moses and the Prophets, they will not be convinced even if someone rises from the dead.' "

Sin, Faith, Duty

17 Jesus said to his disciples: "Things that cause people to sin are bound to come, but woe to that person through whom they come. ²It would be better for him to be thrown into the sea with a millstone tied around his neck than for him to cause one of these little ones to sin. ³So watch yourselves.

"If your brother sins, rebuke him, and if he repents, forgive him. ⁴If he sins against you seven times in a day, and seven times comes back to you and says, 'I repent,' forgive him."

⁵The apostles said to the Lord, "Increase our faith!"

⁶He replied, "If you have faith as small as a mustard seed, you can say to this mulberry tree, 'Be uprooted and planted in the sea,' and it will obey you.

⁷"Suppose one of you had a servant plowing or looking after the sheep. Would he say to the servant when he comes in from the field, 'Come along now and sit down to eat'? ⁸Would he not rather say, 'Prepare my supper, get

ᵃ 23 Greek *Hades*

yourself ready and wait on me while I eat and drink; after that you may eat and drink'? ⁹Would he thank the servant because he did what he was told to do? ¹⁰So you also, when you have done everything you were told to do, should say, 'We are unworthy servants; we have only done our duty.' "

Ten Healed of Leprosy

¹¹Now on his way to Jerusalem, Jesus traveled along the border between Samaria and Galilee. ¹²As he was going into a village, ten men who had leprosy[a] met him. They stood at a distance ¹³and called out in a loud voice, "Jesus, Master, have pity on us!"

¹⁴When he saw them, he said, "Go, show yourselves to the priests." And as they went, they were cleansed.

¹⁵One of them, when he saw he was healed, came back, praising God in a loud voice. ¹⁶He threw himself at Jesus' feet and thanked him—and he was a Samaritan.

¹⁷Jesus asked, "Were not all ten cleansed? Where are the other nine? ¹⁸Was no one found to return and give praise to God except this foreigner?" ¹⁹Then he said to him, "Rise and go; your faith has made you well."

The Coming of the Kingdom of God

²⁰Once, having been asked by the Pharisees when the kingdom of God would come, Jesus replied, "The kingdom of God does not come with your careful observation, ²¹nor will people say, 'Here it is,' or 'There it is,' because the kingdom of God is within[b] you."

²²Then he said to his disciples, "The time is coming when you will long to see one of the days of the Son of Man, but you will not see it. ²³Men will tell you, 'There he is!' or 'Here he is!' Do not go running off after them. ²⁴For the Son of Man in his day[c] will be like the lightning, which flashes and lights up the sky from one end to the other. ²⁵But first he must suffer many things and be rejected by this generation.

²⁶"Just as it was in the days of Noah, so also will it be in the days of the Son of Man. ²⁷People were eating, drinking, marrying and being given in marriage up to the day Noah entered the ark. Then the flood came and destroyed them all.

²⁸"It was the same in the days of Lot. People were eating and drinking, buying and selling, planting and building. ²⁹But the day Lot left Sodom, fire and sulfur rained down from heaven and destroyed them all.

³⁰"It will be just like this on the day the Son of Man is revealed. ³¹On that day no one who is on the roof of his house, with his goods inside, should go down to get them. Likewise, no one in the field should go back for anything. ³²Remember Lot's wife! ³³Whoever tries to keep his life will lose it, and whoever loses his life will preserve it. ³⁴I tell you, on that night two people will be in one bed; one will be taken and the other left. ³⁵Two women will be grinding grain together; one will be taken and the other left.[d]

³⁷"Where, Lord?" they asked.

Praying With the Tenth Leper

LUKE 17:11–19

"If in your lifetime the only prayer you offer is Thanks, that would suffice," wrote Meister Eckhart. Sit comfortably, close your eyes and begin to repeat the word *gracias!* (Spanish for "thanks") or *grazia!* (Italian). Recall the events that have occurred in the last week (conversations with friends, small tasks accomplished, rest and relaxation, appointments kept) and, after each event comes to mind, offer thanks. Because *gracias!* (or *grazia!*) means "grace" as well as "thanks," you can continue praying this way when you think of difficulties. To the God who provides grace under pressure, you can say, "Thank you for being with me."

See Meeting God in Everyday Life

Receiving the Kingdom

LUKE 18:15–17

"Anyone who will not receive the kingdom of God like a little child will never enter it." What spiritual truth could you learn from children that would help you receive (take in or take possession of) the kingdom of God? Call to mind the faces of a child or two, or go to a place where you might spend time with children (a playground or church nursery). Recall the children you know—their questions, stories, attitudes about life. Ponder this question: What would it mean to "receive the kingdom of God" like a child? What would it mean for you to embrace the childlike faith within you?

See Meeting God in the Created Order

He replied, "Where there is a dead body, there the vultures will gather."

The Parable of the Persistent Widow

18 Then Jesus told his disciples a parable to show them that they should always pray and not give up. [2]He said: "In a certain town there was a judge who neither feared God nor cared about men. [3]And there was a widow in that town who kept coming to him with the plea, 'Grant me justice against my adversary.'

[4]"For some time he refused. But finally he said to himself, 'Even though I don't fear God or care about men, [5]yet because this widow keeps bothering me, I will see that she gets justice, so that she won't eventually wear me out with her coming!' "

[6]And the Lord said, "Listen to what the unjust judge says. [7]And will not God bring about justice for his chosen ones, who cry out to him day and night? Will he keep putting them off? [8]I tell you, he will see that they get justice, and quickly. However, when the Son of Man comes, will he find faith on the earth?"

The Parable of the Pharisee and the Tax Collector

[9]To some who were confident of their own righteousness and looked down on everybody else, Jesus told this parable: [10]"Two men went up to the temple to pray, one a Pharisee and the other a tax collector. [11]The Pharisee stood up and prayed about[a] himself: 'God, I thank you that I am not like other men—robbers, evildoers, adulterers—or even like this tax collector. [12]I fast twice a week and give a tenth of all I get.'

[13]"But the tax collector stood at a distance. He would not even look up to heaven, but beat his breast and said, 'God, have mercy on me, a sinner.'

[14]"I tell you that this man, rather than the other, went home justified before God. For everyone who exalts himself will be humbled, and he who humbles himself will be exalted."

The Little Children and Jesus

[15]People were also bringing babies to Jesus to have him touch them. When the disciples saw this, they rebuked them. [16]But Jesus called the children to him and said, "Let the little children come to me, and do not hinder them, for the kingdom of God belongs to such as these. [17]I tell you the truth, anyone who will not receive the kingdom of God like a little child will never enter it."

The Rich Ruler

[18]A certain ruler asked him, "Good teacher, what must I do to inherit eternal life?"

[19]"Why do you call me good?" Jesus answered. "No one is good—except God alone. [20]You know the commandments: 'Do not commit adultery, do not murder, do not steal, do not give false testimony, honor your father and mother.'[b]"

[21]"All these I have kept since I was a boy," he said.

[22]When Jesus heard this, he said to him, "You still lack one thing. Sell everything you have and give to the poor,

a 11 Or to   b 20 Exodus 20:12–16; Deut. 5:16–20

and you will have treasure in heaven. Then come, follow me."

²³When he heard this, he became very sad, because he was a man of great wealth. ²⁴Jesus looked at him and said, "How hard it is for the rich to enter the kingdom of God! ²⁵Indeed, it is easier for a camel to go through the eye of a needle than for a rich man to enter the kingdom of God."

²⁶Those who heard this asked, "Who then can be saved?"

²⁷Jesus replied, "What is impossible with men is possible with God."

²⁸Peter said to him, "We have left all we had to follow you!"

²⁹"I tell you the truth," Jesus said to them, "no one who has left home or wife or brothers or parents or children for the sake of the kingdom of God ³⁰will fail to receive many times as much in this age and, in the age to come, eternal life."

Jesus Again Predicts His Death

³¹Jesus took the Twelve aside and told them, "We are going up to Jerusalem, and everything that is written by the prophets about the Son of Man will be fulfilled. ³²He will be handed over to the Gentiles. They will mock him, insult him, spit on him, flog him and kill him. ³³On the third day he will rise again."

³⁴The disciples did not understand any of this. Its meaning was hidden from them, and they did not know what he was talking about.

A Blind Beggar Receives His Sight

³⁵As Jesus approached Jericho, a blind man was sitting by the roadside begging. ³⁶When he heard the crowd going by, he asked what was happening. ³⁷They told him, "Jesus of Nazareth is passing by."

³⁸He called out, "Jesus, Son of David, have mercy on me!"

³⁹Those who led the way rebuked him and told him to be quiet, but he shouted all the more, "Son of David, have mercy on me!"

⁴⁰Jesus stopped and ordered the man to be brought to him. When he came near, Jesus asked him, ⁴¹"What do you want me to do for you?"

"Lord, I want to see," he replied.

⁴²Jesus said to him, "Receive your sight; your faith has healed you." ⁴³Immediately he received his sight and followed Jesus, praising God. When all the people saw it, they also praised God.

Zacchaeus the Tax Collector

19 Jesus entered Jericho and was passing through. ²A man was there by the name of Zacchaeus; he was a chief tax collector and was wealthy. ³He wanted to see who Jesus was, but being a short man he could not, because of the crowd. ⁴So he ran ahead and climbed a sycamore-fig tree to see him, since Jesus was coming that way.

⁵When Jesus reached the spot, he looked up and said to him, "Zacchaeus, come down immediately. I must stay at your house today." ⁶So he came down at once and welcomed him gladly.

The Prayer of the Heart

LUKE 18:13,38

The ancient "Jesus prayer" is based on the words of the tax collector in the temple and of the blind beggar. Using this prayer can help you pray continually (see 1 Thessalonians 5:17). It can be done as naturally as breathing: "O Lord Jesus Christ, [Son of God] (*inhaling, receiving*), have mercy [on me, a sinner] (*exhaling, surrendering*)." Get up and do an everyday task (cook a meal, clean a bathroom, get dressed), reciting the "Jesus prayer" as you do so. Come back and rest in God's presence. Keep this prayer in your heart throughout the day; let the awareness of God's presence permeate all your activities.

See Meeting God in Worship

Jesus Notices "the Little People"

LUKE 19:1–10

Imagine that you are Zacchaeus, a hated tax collector. Consider how Zacchaeus may have felt when singled out in the crowd by Jesus, someone everyone wanted to meet. Jesus wants to talk to you—you are the focus of his attention. Picture the face of someone who is a reflection of Jesus' loving attention to you. Bask in the joy of being chosen and loved by God.

Now reflect on Zacchaeus's response to Jesus. Because Zacchaeus was "a short man," he was probably used to being overlooked. (The Hebrew word for "the poor" [v.8] also means "the little people" of the earth, those who may be discounted or overlooked.) Do you ever feel overlooked or passed over by people? What is your response to Jesus as he singles you out?

See Meeting God in Scripture

[7] All the people saw this and began to mutter, "He has gone to be the guest of a 'sinner.' "

[8] But Zacchaeus stood up and said to the Lord, "Look, Lord! Here and now I give half of my possessions to the poor, and if I have cheated anybody out of anything, I will pay back four times the amount."

[9] Jesus said to him, "Today salvation has come to this house, because this man, too, is a son of Abraham. [10] For the Son of Man came to seek and to save what was lost."

The Parable of the Ten Minas

[11] While they were listening to this, he went on to tell them a parable, because he was near Jerusalem and the people thought that the kingdom of God was going to appear at once. [12] He said: "A man of noble birth went to a distant country to have himself appointed king and then to return. [13] So he called ten of his servants and gave them ten minas.[a] 'Put this money to work,' he said, 'until I come back.'

[14] "But his subjects hated him and sent a delegation after him to say, 'We don't want this man to be our king.'

[15] "He was made king, however, and returned home. Then he sent for the servants to whom he had given the money, in order to find out what they had gained with it.

[16] "The first one came and said, 'Sir, your mina has earned ten more.'

[17] " 'Well done, my good servant!' his master replied. 'Because you have been trustworthy in a very small matter, take charge of ten cities.'

[18] "The second came and said, 'Sir, your mina has earned five more.'

[19] "His master answered, 'You take charge of five cities.'

[20] "Then another servant came and said, 'Sir, here is your mina; I have kept it laid away in a piece of cloth. [21] I was afraid of you, because you are a hard man. You take out what you did not put in and reap what you did not sow.'

[22] "His master replied, 'I will judge you by your own words, you wicked servant! You knew, did you, that I am a hard man, taking out what I did not put in, and reaping what I did not sow? [23] Why then didn't you put my money on deposit, so that when I came back, I could have collected it with interest?'

[24] "Then he said to those standing by, 'Take his mina away from him and give it to the one who has ten minas.'

[25] " 'Sir,' they said, 'he already has ten!'

[26] "He replied, 'I tell you that to everyone who has, more will be given, but as for the one who has nothing, even what he has will be taken away. [27] But those enemies of mine who did not want me to be king over them—bring them here and kill them in front of me.' "

The Triumphal Entry

[28] After Jesus had said this, he went on ahead, going up to Jerusalem. [29] As he approached Bethphage and Bethany at the hill called the Mount of Olives, he sent two of his disciples, saying to them, [30] "Go to the village ahead of you, and as you enter it, you will find a colt tied there, which no one has ever ridden. Untie it and bring it here. [31] If anyone

a 13 A mina was about three months' wages.

asks you, 'Why are you untying it?' tell him, 'The Lord needs it.' "

³²Those who were sent ahead went and found it just as he had told them. ³³As they were untying the colt, its owners asked them, "Why are you untying the colt?"

³⁴They replied, "The Lord needs it."

³⁵They brought it to Jesus, threw their cloaks on the colt and put Jesus on it. ³⁶As he went along, people spread their cloaks on the road.

³⁷When he came near the place where the road goes down the Mount of Olives, the whole crowd of disciples began joyfully to praise God in loud voices for all the miracles they had seen:

³⁸"Blessed is the king who comes in the name of the Lord!"[a]

"Peace in heaven and glory in the highest!"

³⁹Some of the Pharisees in the crowd said to Jesus, "Teacher, rebuke your disciples!"

⁴⁰"I tell you," he replied, "if they keep quiet, the stones will cry out."

⁴¹As he approached Jerusalem and saw the city, he wept over it ⁴²and said, "If you, even you, had only known on this day what would bring you peace—but now it is hidden from your eyes. ⁴³The days will come upon you when your enemies will build an embankment against you and encircle you and hem you in on every side. ⁴⁴They will dash you to the ground, you and the children within your walls. They will not leave one stone on another, because you did not recognize the time of God's coming to you."

Jesus at the Temple

⁴⁵Then he entered the temple area and began driving out those who were selling. ⁴⁶"It is written," he said to them, " 'My house will be a house of prayer'[b]; but you have made it 'a den of robbers.'[c]"

⁴⁷Every day he was teaching at the temple. But the chief priests, the teachers of the law and the leaders among the people were trying to kill him. ⁴⁸Yet they could not find any way to do it, because all the people hung on his words.

The Authority of Jesus Questioned

20 One day as he was teaching the people in the temple courts and preaching the gospel, the chief priests and the teachers of the law, together with the elders, came up to him. ²"Tell us by what authority you are doing these things," they said. "Who gave you this authority?"

³He replied, "I will also ask you a question. Tell me, ⁴John's baptism—was it from heaven, or from men?"

⁵They discussed it among themselves and said, "If we say, 'From heaven,' he will ask, 'Why didn't you believe him?' ⁶But if we say, 'From men,' all the people will stone us, because they are persuaded that John was a prophet."

⁷So they answered, "We don't know where it was from."

⁸Jesus said, "Neither will I tell you by what authority I am doing these things."

What Would the Stones Say?

LUKE 19:28–40

Picture yourself in the multitude during Jesus' triumphal entry and allow the scene to unfold. Imagine the sun beating down on your head, the shouts of the crowd, the odors of animals and people. Look how the people are spreading their cloaks in the road like a carpet. Join the chorus, "Blessed is the king who comes . . .! Peace in heaven and glory in the highest!" Notice the disapproval of the religious leaders: "Teacher, rebuke your disciples!" Jesus responds: "If they keep quiet, the stones will cry out." What would the stones say? Try expressing your unspoken cries of joy in your journal.

See Meeting God in Worship

Love the Questions!

LUKE 20:1–47

In Luke 20 the religious authorities ask Jesus three questions in order to trick him. Jesus responds by asking them twice as many questions and by telling them a parable. You might want to list the questions in this chapter of Luke and ponder why Jesus asks so many of them. Then ask yourself, "Do I respond to people's problems with *my* answers or do I listen to them and ask them helpful questions?" The poet Rainer Maria Rilke wrote, "Be patient toward all that is unsolved in your heart and try to love the questions themselves." Do you offer your own questions to God in your prayer life? Try writing a prayer consisting only of questions.

See Meeting God in Prayer

The Parable of the Tenants

⁹He went on to tell the people this parable: "A man planted a vineyard, rented it to some farmers and went away for a long time. ¹⁰At harvest time he sent a servant to the tenants so they would give him some of the fruit of the vineyard. But the tenants beat him and sent him away empty-handed. ¹¹He sent another servant, but that one also they beat and treated shamefully and sent away empty-handed. ¹²He sent still a third, and they wounded him and threw him out.

¹³"Then the owner of the vineyard said, 'What shall I do? I will send my son, whom I love; perhaps they will respect him.'

¹⁴"But when the tenants saw him, they talked the matter over. 'This is the heir,' they said. 'Let's kill him, and the inheritance will be ours.' ¹⁵So they threw him out of the vineyard and killed him.

"What then will the owner of the vineyard do to them? ¹⁶He will come and kill those tenants and give the vineyard to others."

When the people heard this, they said, "May this never be!"

¹⁷Jesus looked directly at them and asked, "Then what is the meaning of that which is written:

" 'The stone the builders rejected
  has become the capstone'ᵃ'ᵇ?

¹⁸Everyone who falls on that stone will be broken to pieces, but he on whom it falls will be crushed."

¹⁹The teachers of the law and the chief priests looked for a way to arrest him immediately, because they knew he had spoken this parable against them. But they were afraid of the people.

Paying Taxes to Caesar

²⁰Keeping a close watch on him, they sent spies, who pretended to be honest. They hoped to catch Jesus in something he said so that they might hand him over to the power and authority of the governor. ²¹So the spies questioned him: "Teacher, we know that you speak and teach what is right, and that you do not show partiality but teach the way of God in accordance with the truth. ²²Is it right for us to pay taxes to Caesar or not?"

²³He saw through their duplicity and said to them, ²⁴"Show me a denarius. Whose portrait and inscription are on it?"

²⁵"Caesar's," they replied.

He said to them, "Then give to Caesar what is Caesar's, and to God what is God's."

²⁶They were unable to trap him in what he had said there in public. And astonished by his answer, they became silent.

The Resurrection and Marriage

²⁷Some of the Sadducees, who say there is no resurrection, came to Jesus with a question. ²⁸"Teacher," they said, "Moses wrote for us that if a man's brother dies and leaves a wife but no children, the man must marry the widow

ᵃ 17 Or *cornerstone*   ᵇ 17 Psalm 118:22

and have children for his brother. ²⁹Now there were seven brothers. The first one married a woman and died childless. ³⁰The second ³¹and then the third married her, and in the same way the seven died, leaving no children. ³²Finally, the woman died too. ³³Now then, at the resurrection whose wife will she be, since the seven were married to her?"

³⁴Jesus replied, "The people of this age marry and are given in marriage. ³⁵But those who are considered worthy of taking part in that age and in the resurrection from the dead will neither marry nor be given in marriage, ³⁶and they can no longer die; for they are like the angels. They are God's children, since they are children of the resurrection. ³⁷But in the account of the bush, even Moses showed that the dead rise, for he calls the Lord 'the God of Abraham, and the God of Isaac, and the God of Jacob.'ᵃ ³⁸He is not the God of the dead, but of the living, for to him all are alive."

³⁹Some of the teachers of the law responded, "Well said, teacher!" ⁴⁰And no one dared to ask him any more questions.

Whose Son Is the Christ?

⁴¹Then Jesus said to them, "How is it that they say the Christᵇ is the Son of David? ⁴²David himself declares in the Book of Psalms:

> " 'The Lord said to my Lord:
> "Sit at my right hand
> ⁴³until I make your enemies
> a footstool for your feet." 'ᶜ

⁴⁴David calls him 'Lord.' How then can he be his son?"

⁴⁵While all the people were listening, Jesus said to his disciples, ⁴⁶"Beware of the teachers of the law. They like to walk around in flowing robes and love to be greeted in the marketplaces and have the most important seats in the synagogues and the places of honor at banquets. ⁴⁷They devour widows' houses and for a show make lengthy prayers. Such men will be punished most severely."

The Widow's Offering

21 As he looked up, Jesus saw the rich putting their gifts into the temple treasury. ²He also saw a poor widow put in two very small copper coins.ᵈ ³"I tell you the truth," he said, "this poor widow has put in more than all the others. ⁴All these people gave their gifts out of their wealth; but she out of her poverty put in all she had to live on."

Signs of the End of the Age

⁵Some of his disciples were remarking about how the temple was adorned with beautiful stones and with gifts dedicated to God. But Jesus said, ⁶"As for what you see here, the time will come when not one stone will be left on another; every one of them will be thrown down."

⁷"Teacher," they asked, "when will these things happen? And what will be the sign that they are about to take place?"

The Poor Widow, Our Teacher

LUKE 21:1–4

Luke shows Jesus pointing to forgotten people as agents of God's love to privileged people. Here a poor widow (typically a recipient of charity) becomes our teacher, prefiguring Jesus Christ's self-giving love. Can you recall an occasion when a person whom the world might ignore became a special symbol of God's love in your life or a window through which you could see God? Reflect on it with God. Whom might God be using to teach you now? Try exploring these questions in your journal and see if any connections come to you or reflect on this idea with a friend.

See Meeting God in Community

ᵃ 37 Exodus 3:6   ᵇ 41 Or *Messiah*   ᶜ 43 Psalm 110:1   ᵈ 2 Greek *two lepta*

Pay Attention to Today!

LUKE 21:7–38

Jesus warns about preoccupation with end-times predictions (21:8) and instead commands simple attentiveness to God's presence every moment of every day: "Be always on the watch" (21:36). How can you nurture what Jean-Pierre de Caussade called "the sacrament of the present moment"? He described it this way: "This discovery of divine action in everything that happens, each moment, is the most subtle wisdom possible regarding the ways of God in this life." What practices help you cultivate this simple attentiveness?

See Meeting God in Everyday Life

⁸He replied: "Watch out that you are not deceived. For many will come in my name, claiming, 'I am he,' and, 'The time is near.' Do not follow them. ⁹When you hear of wars and revolutions, do not be frightened. These things must happen first, but the end will not come right away."

¹⁰Then he said to them: "Nation will rise against nation, and kingdom against kingdom. ¹¹There will be great earthquakes, famines and pestilences in various places, and fearful events and great signs from heaven.

¹²"But before all this, they will lay hands on you and persecute you. They will deliver you to synagogues and prisons, and you will be brought before kings and governors, and all on account of my name. ¹³This will result in your being witnesses to them. ¹⁴But make up your mind not to worry beforehand how you will defend yourselves. ¹⁵For I will give you words and wisdom that none of your adversaries will be able to resist or contradict. ¹⁶You will be betrayed even by parents, brothers, relatives and friends, and they will put some of you to death. ¹⁷All men will hate you because of me. ¹⁸But not a hair of your head will perish. ¹⁹By standing firm you will gain life.

²⁰"When you see Jerusalem being surrounded by armies, you will know that its desolation is near. ²¹Then let those who are in Judea flee to the mountains, let those in the city get out, and let those in the country not enter the city. ²²For this is the time of punishment in fulfillment of all that has been written. ²³How dreadful it will be in those days for pregnant women and nursing mothers! There will be great distress in the land and wrath against this people. ²⁴They will fall by the sword and will be taken as prisoners to all the nations. Jerusalem will be trampled on by the Gentiles until the times of the Gentiles are fulfilled.

²⁵"There will be signs in the sun, moon and stars. On the earth, nations will be in anguish and perplexity at the roaring and tossing of the sea. ²⁶Men will faint from terror, apprehensive of what is coming on the world, for the heavenly bodies will be shaken. ²⁷At that time they will see the Son of Man coming in a cloud with power and great glory. ²⁸When these things begin to take place, stand up and lift up your heads, because your redemption is drawing near."

²⁹He told them this parable: "Look at the fig tree and all the trees. ³⁰When they sprout leaves, you can see for yourselves and know that summer is near. ³¹Even so, when you see these things happening, you know that the kingdom of God is near.

³²"I tell you the truth, this generation*a* will certainly not pass away until all these things have happened. ³³Heaven and earth will pass away, but my words will never pass away.

³⁴"Be careful, or your hearts will be weighed down with dissipation, drunkenness and the anxieties of life, and that day will close on you unexpectedly like a trap. ³⁵For it will come upon all those who live on the face of the whole earth. ³⁶Be always on the watch, and pray that you may be able to escape all that is about to happen, and that you may be able to stand before the Son of Man."

³⁷Each day Jesus was teaching at the temple, and each evening he went out to spend the night on the hill called

a 32 Or race

the Mount of Olives, ³⁸and all the people came early in the morning to hear him at the temple.

Judas Agrees to Betray Jesus

22 Now the Feast of Unleavened Bread, called the Passover, was approaching, ²and the chief priests and the teachers of the law were looking for some way to get rid of Jesus, for they were afraid of the people. ³Then Satan entered Judas, called Iscariot, one of the Twelve. ⁴And Judas went to the chief priests and the officers of the temple guard and discussed with them how he might betray Jesus. ⁵They were delighted and agreed to give him money. ⁶He consented, and watched for an opportunity to hand Jesus over to them when no crowd was present.

The Last Supper

⁷Then came the day of Unleavened Bread on which the Passover lamb had to be sacrificed. ⁸Jesus sent Peter and John, saying, "Go and make preparations for us to eat the Passover."

⁹"Where do you want us to prepare for it?" they asked.

¹⁰He replied, "As you enter the city, a man carrying a jar of water will meet you. Follow him to the house that he enters, ¹¹and say to the owner of the house, 'The Teacher asks: Where is the guest room, where I may eat the Passover with my disciples?' ¹²He will show you a large upper room, all furnished. Make preparations there."

¹³They left and found things just as Jesus had told them. So they prepared the Passover.

¹⁴When the hour came, Jesus and his apostles reclined at the table. ¹⁵And he said to them, "I have eagerly desired to eat this Passover with you before I suffer. ¹⁶For I tell you, I will not eat it again until it finds fulfillment in the kingdom of God."

¹⁷After taking the cup, he gave thanks and said, "Take this and divide it among you. ¹⁸For I tell you I will not drink again of the fruit of the vine until the kingdom of God comes."

¹⁹And he took bread, gave thanks and broke it, and gave it to them, saying, "This is my body given for you; do this in remembrance of me."

²⁰In the same way, after the supper he took the cup, saying, "This cup is the new covenant in my blood, which is poured out for you. ²¹But the hand of him who is going to betray me is with mine on the table. ²²The Son of Man will go as it has been decreed, but woe to that man who betrays him." ²³They began to question among themselves which of them it might be who would do this.

²⁴Also a dispute arose among them as to which of them was considered to be greatest. ²⁵Jesus said to them, "The kings of the Gentiles lord it over them; and those who exercise authority over them call themselves Benefactors. ²⁶But you are not to be like that. Instead, the greatest among you should be like the youngest, and the one who rules like the one who serves. ²⁷For who is greater, the one who is at the table or the one who serves? Is it not the one who is at the table? But I am among you as one who serves. ²⁸You are those who have stood by me in my trials. ²⁹And I confer on you a kingdom, just as my Father conferred one on me, ³⁰so that you may eat and drink at my

What It Means to Live in Christ

LUKE 22:24–27

"The church is the church only when it exists for others. To make a start, it should give away all its property to those in need. The church must share in the secular problems of ordinary human life, not dominating, but helping and serving. It must tell people of every calling what it means to live in Christ, to exist for others. It must not under-estimate the importance of human example (which has its origins in the humanity of Jesus and is so important in Paul's teaching); it is not abstract argument, but example, that gives its word emphasis and power."

—DIETRICH BONHOEFFER,
Letters and Papers from Prison

This Bitter Cup

LUKE 22:39–46

"Jesus, my gentle Jesus,
Walking in the dark of the
    garden—
The Garden of Gethsemane,
Saying to the three
    disciples:
Sorrow is in my soul—
Even unto death;
Tarry ye here a little while,
And watch with me.

"Jesus, my burdened Jesus,
Praying in the dark of the
    garden—
The Garden of Gethsemane.
Saying: Father,
Oh, Father,
This bitter cup,
This bitter cup,
Let it pass from me.

"Jesus, my sorrowing Jesus,
The sweat like drops of
    blood upon his brow,
Talking with his Father,
While the three disciples
    slept,
Saying: Father,
Oh, Father,
Not as I will,
Not as I will,
But let thy will be done."
                —JAMES WELDON JOHNSON,
                    "God's Trombones"

table in my kingdom and sit on thrones, judging the twelve tribes of Israel.

³¹"Simon, Simon, Satan has asked to sift you*a* as wheat. ³²But I have prayed for you, Simon, that your faith may not fail. And when you have turned back, strengthen your brothers."

³³But he replied, "Lord, I am ready to go with you to prison and to death."

³⁴Jesus answered, "I tell you, Peter, before the rooster crows today, you will deny three times that you know me."

³⁵Then Jesus asked them, "When I sent you without purse, bag or sandals, did you lack anything?"

"Nothing," they answered.

³⁶He said to them, "But now if you have a purse, take it, and also a bag; and if you don't have a sword, sell your cloak and buy one. ³⁷It is written: 'And he was numbered with the transgressors'*b*; and I tell you that this must be fulfilled in me. Yes, what is written about me is reaching its fulfillment."

³⁸The disciples said, "See, Lord, here are two swords."

"That is enough," he replied.

Jesus Prays on the Mount of Olives

³⁹Jesus went out as usual to the Mount of Olives, and his disciples followed him. ⁴⁰On reaching the place, he said to them, "Pray that you will not fall into temptation." ⁴¹He withdrew about a stone's throw beyond them, knelt down and prayed, ⁴²"Father, if you are willing, take this cup from me; yet not my will, but yours be done." ⁴³An angel from heaven appeared to him and strengthened him. ⁴⁴And being in anguish, he prayed more earnestly, and his sweat was like drops of blood falling to the ground.*c*

⁴⁵When he rose from prayer and went back to the disciples, he found them asleep, exhausted from sorrow. ⁴⁶"Why are you sleeping?" he asked them. "Get up and pray so that you will not fall into temptation."

Jesus Arrested

⁴⁷While he was still speaking a crowd came up, and the man who was called Judas, one of the Twelve, was leading them. He approached Jesus to kiss him, ⁴⁸but Jesus asked him, "Judas, are you betraying the Son of Man with a kiss?"

⁴⁹When Jesus' followers saw what was going to happen, they said, "Lord, should we strike with our swords?" ⁵⁰And one of them struck the servant of the high priest, cutting off his right ear.

⁵¹But Jesus answered, "No more of this!" And he touched the man's ear and healed him.

⁵²Then Jesus said to the chief priests, the officers of the temple guard, and the elders, who had come for him, "Am I leading a rebellion, that you have come with swords and clubs? ⁵³Every day I was with you in the temple courts, and you did not lay a hand on me. But this is your hour—when darkness reigns."

Peter Disowns Jesus

⁵⁴Then seizing him, they led him away and took him

a 31 The Greek is plural.   *b 37* Isaiah 53:12   *c 44* Some early manuscripts do not have verses 43 and 44.

into the house of the high priest. Peter followed at a distance. ⁵⁵But when they had kindled a fire in the middle of the courtyard and had sat down together, Peter sat down with them. ⁵⁶A servant girl saw him seated there in the firelight. She looked closely at him and said, "This man was with him."

⁵⁷But he denied it. "Woman, I don't know him," he said.

⁵⁸A little later someone else saw him and said, "You also are one of them."

"Man, I am not!" Peter replied.

⁵⁹About an hour later another asserted, "Certainly this fellow was with him, for he is a Galilean."

⁶⁰Peter replied, "Man, I don't know what you're talking about!" Just as he was speaking, the rooster crowed. ⁶¹The Lord turned and looked straight at Peter. Then Peter remembered the word the Lord had spoken to him: "Before the rooster crows today, you will disown me three times." ⁶²And he went outside and wept bitterly.

The Guards Mock Jesus

⁶³The men who were guarding Jesus began mocking and beating him. ⁶⁴They blindfolded him and demanded, "Prophesy! Who hit you?" ⁶⁵And they said many other insulting things to him.

Jesus Before Pilate and Herod

⁶⁶At daybreak the council of the elders of the people, both the chief priests and teachers of the law, met together, and Jesus was led before them. ⁶⁷"If you are the Christ,ᵃ" they said, "tell us."

Jesus answered, "If I tell you, you will not believe me, ⁶⁸and if I asked you, you would not answer. ⁶⁹But from now on, the Son of Man will be seated at the right hand of the mighty God."

⁷⁰They all asked, "Are you then the Son of God?"

He replied, "You are right in saying I am."

⁷¹Then they said, "Why do we need any more testimony? We have heard it from his own lips."

23 Then the whole assembly rose and led him off to Pilate. ²And they began to accuse him, saying, "We have found this man subverting our nation. He opposes payment of taxes to Caesar and claims to be Christ,ᵇ a king."

³So Pilate asked Jesus, "Are you the king of the Jews?"

"Yes, it is as you say," Jesus replied.

⁴Then Pilate announced to the chief priests and the crowd, "I find no basis for a charge against this man."

⁵But they insisted, "He stirs up the people all over Judeaᶜ by his teaching. He started in Galilee and has come all the way here."

⁶On hearing this, Pilate asked if the man was a Galilean. ⁷When he learned that Jesus was under Herod's jurisdiction, he sent him to Herod, who was also in Jerusalem at that time.

⁸When Herod saw Jesus, he was greatly pleased, because for a long time he had been wanting to see him. From what he had heard about him, he hoped to see him perform some miracle. ⁹He plied him with many ques-

The Lord Turns and Looks
LUKE 22:56-62

Jesus confronts his delinquent disciple, Peter, simply by looking at him. What sort of look might it have been? Hold in your hand an object that, for you, represents some kind of denial of Jesus' lordship in your life (money, a book, a certain piece of clothing). As you hold it, close your eyes. Imagine Jesus turning and gazing at you with eyes of rebuke—and love. Ask yourself, "Why have I held on to this? What makes me think I need it?" Let go of the object and look to Jesus again.

ᵃ 67 Or *Messiah*   ᵇ 2 Or *Messiah*; also in verses 35 and 39   ᶜ 5 Or *over the land of the Jews*

Meditating on Forgiveness at the Cross

LUKE 23:34

If you're experiencing pain in a relationship with a child, spouse, friend or coworker, picture Jesus on the cross, sharing the pain that you feel over the relationship. If there are persons you cannot forgive, open your arms wide, breathe deeply and let Jesus Christ pray within you: "Father, forgive them, for they do not know what they are doing." Feel free to admit that humanly you cannot forgive, but that with Jesus it is possible. Consider practicing this exercise several days a week, for a month. Don't be discouraged if a *feeling* of forgiveness doesn't come; for the time being, be content that God has forgiven those involved in the situation.

See Meeting God in Prayer

tions, but Jesus gave him no answer. [10]The chief priests and the teachers of the law were standing there, vehemently accusing him. [11]Then Herod and his soldiers ridiculed and mocked him. Dressing him in an elegant robe, they sent him back to Pilate. [12]That day Herod and Pilate became friends—before this they had been enemies.

[13]Pilate called together the chief priests, the rulers and the people, [14]and said to them, "You brought me this man as one who was inciting the people to rebellion. I have examined him in your presence and have found no basis for your charges against him. [15]Neither has Herod, for he sent him back to us; as you can see, he has done nothing to deserve death. [16]Therefore, I will punish him and then release him.[a]"

[18]With one voice they cried out, "Away with this man! Release Barabbas to us!" [19](Barabbas had been thrown into prison for an insurrection in the city, and for murder.)

[20]Wanting to release Jesus, Pilate appealed to them again. [21]But they kept shouting, "Crucify him! Crucify him!"

[22]For the third time he spoke to them: "Why? What crime has this man committed? I have found in him no grounds for the death penalty. Therefore I will have him punished and then release him."

[23]But with loud shouts they insistently demanded that he be crucified, and their shouts prevailed. [24]So Pilate decided to grant their demand. [25]He released the man who had been thrown into prison for insurrection and murder, the one they asked for, and surrendered Jesus to their will.

The Crucifixion

[26]As they led him away, they seized Simon from Cyrene, who was on his way in from the country, and put the cross on him and made him carry it behind Jesus. [27]A large number of people followed him, including women who mourned and wailed for him. [28]Jesus turned and said to them, "Daughters of Jerusalem, do not weep for me; weep for yourselves and for your children. [29]For the time will come when you will say, 'Blessed are the barren women, the wombs that never bore and the breasts that never nursed!' [30]Then

> " 'they will say to the mountains, "Fall on us!"
> and to the hills, "Cover us!" '[b]

[31]For if men do these things when the tree is green, what will happen when it is dry?"

[32]Two other men, both criminals, were also led out with him to be executed. [33]When they came to the place called the Skull, there they crucified him, along with the criminals—one on his right, the other on his left. [34]Jesus said, "Father, forgive them, for they do not know what they are doing."[c] And they divided up his clothes by casting lots.

[35]The people stood watching, and the rulers even sneered at him. They said, "He saved others; let him save himself if he is the Christ of God, the Chosen One."

[36]The soldiers also came up and mocked him. They of-

---

[a] 16 Some manuscripts him." [17]Now he was obliged to release one man to them at the Feast.   [b] 30 Hosea 10:8   [c] 34 Some early manuscripts do not have this sentence.

fered him wine vinegar ³⁷and said, "If you are the king of the Jews, save yourself."

³⁸There was a written notice above him, which read: THIS IS THE KING OF THE JEWS.

³⁹One of the criminals who hung there hurled insults at him: "Aren't you the Christ? Save yourself and us!"

⁴⁰But the other criminal rebuked him. "Don't you fear God," he said, "since you are under the same sentence? ⁴¹We are punished justly, for we are getting what our deeds deserve. But this man has done nothing wrong."

⁴²Then he said, "Jesus, remember me when you come into your kingdom.ᵃ"

⁴³Jesus answered him, "I tell you the truth, today you will be with me in paradise."

Jesus' Death

⁴⁴It was now about the sixth hour, and darkness came over the whole land until the ninth hour, ⁴⁵for the sun stopped shining. And the curtain of the temple was torn in two. ⁴⁶Jesus called out with a loud voice, "Father, into your hands I commit my spirit." When he had said this, he breathed his last.

⁴⁷The centurion, seeing what had happened, praised God and said, "Surely this was a righteous man." ⁴⁸When all the people who had gathered to witness this sight saw what took place, they beat their breasts and went away. ⁴⁹But all those who knew him, including the women who had followed him from Galilee, stood at a distance, watching these things.

Jesus' Burial

⁵⁰Now there was a man named Joseph, a member of the Council, a good and upright man, ⁵¹who had not consented to their decision and action. He came from the Judean town of Arimathea and he was waiting for the kingdom of God. ⁵²Going to Pilate, he asked for Jesus' body. ⁵³Then he took it down, wrapped it in linen cloth and placed it in a tomb cut in the rock, one in which no one had yet been laid. ⁵⁴It was Preparation Day, and the Sabbath was about to begin.

⁵⁵The women who had come with Jesus from Galilee followed Joseph and saw the tomb and how his body was laid in it. ⁵⁶Then they went home and prepared spices and perfumes. But they rested on the Sabbath in obedience to the commandment.

The Resurrection

24 On the first day of the week, very early in the morning, the women took the spices they had prepared and went to the tomb. ²They found the stone rolled away from the tomb, ³but when they entered, they did not find the body of the Lord Jesus. ⁴While they were wondering about this, suddenly two men in clothes that gleamed like lightning stood beside them. ⁵In their fright the women bowed down with their faces to the ground, but the men said to them, "Why do you look for the living among the dead? ⁶He is not here; he has risen! Remember how he told you, while he was still with you in Galilee: ⁷'The Son of Man must be delivered into the hands of sin-

---

Standing by Christ

LUKE 23:39–43

"What I call the haven is the Cross. If it cannot be given me to deserve one day to share the Cross of Christ, at least may I share that of the good thief. Of all the beings other than Christ of whom the Gospel tells us, the good thief is by far the one I most envy. To have been at the side of Christ and in the same state during the crucifixion seems to me a far more enviable privilege than to be at the right hand of his glory."

—SIMONE WEIL,
Waiting for God

Journeying to Emmaus

LUKE 24:13–36

Following the sequence of events in this passage, note the ways the hidden Christ is revealed. In your journal reflect how God speaks to you through the following elements:

- Body movement (walking, exercising)
- Conversation (discussing, talking)
- Listening (attentive to stories, feelings)
- Printed and spoken word (interpreting Scripture)
- Nature (sunset, beauty)
- Friendship (empathizing with sadness, joy)
- Hospitality (inviting, visiting)
- Prayer (blessing the bread)
- Communion (breaking the bread)
- Knowing without evidence (as he vanished they knew who he was)
- Surprise (the guest was really the host; the stranger was really a friend)
- Celebrating the memory (sharing how their hearts burned)

See *Meeting God in the Created Order*

ful men, be crucified and on the third day be raised again.' " [8]Then they remembered his words.

[9]When they came back from the tomb, they told all these things to the Eleven and to all the others. [10]It was Mary Magdalene, Joanna, Mary the mother of James, and the others with them who told this to the apostles. [11]But they did not believe the women, because their words seemed to them like nonsense. [12]Peter, however, got up and ran to the tomb. Bending over, he saw the strips of linen lying by themselves, and he went away, wondering to himself what had happened.

On the Road to Emmaus

[13]Now that same day two of them were going to a village called Emmaus, about seven miles[a] from Jerusalem. [14]They were talking with each other about everything that had happened. [15]As they talked and discussed these things with each other, Jesus himself came up and walked along with them; [16]but they were kept from recognizing him.

[17]He asked them, "What are you discussing together as you walk along?"

They stood still, their faces downcast. [18]One of them, named Cleopas, asked him, "Are you only a visitor to Jerusalem and do not know the things that have happened there in these days?"

[19]"What things?" he asked.

"About Jesus of Nazareth," they replied. "He was a prophet, powerful in word and deed before God and all the people. [20]The chief priests and our rulers handed him over to be sentenced to death, and they crucified him; [21]but we had hoped that he was the one who was going to redeem Israel. And what is more, it is the third day since all this took place. [22]In addition, some of our women amazed us. They went to the tomb early this morning [23]but didn't find his body. They came and told us that they had seen a vision of angels, who said he was alive. [24]Then some of our companions went to the tomb and found it just as the women had said, but him they did not see."

[25]He said to them, "How foolish you are, and how slow of heart to believe all that the prophets have spoken! [26]Did not the Christ[b] have to suffer these things and then enter his glory?" [27]And beginning with Moses and all the Prophets, he explained to them what was said in all the Scriptures concerning himself.

[28]As they approached the village to which they were going, Jesus acted as if he were going farther. [29]But they urged him strongly, "Stay with us, for it is nearly evening; the day is almost over." So he went in to stay with them.

[30]When he was at the table with them, he took bread, gave thanks, broke it and began to give it to them. [31]Then their eyes were opened and they recognized him, and he disappeared from their sight. [32]They asked each other, "Were not our hearts burning within us while he talked with us on the road and opened the Scriptures to us?"

[33]They got up and returned at once to Jerusalem. There they found the Eleven and those with them, assembled together [34]and saying, "It is true! The Lord has risen and has appeared to Simon." [35]Then the two told what had hap-

a 13 Greek *sixty stadia* (about 11 kilometers)   *b 26* Or *Messiah*; also in verse 46 pened on the way, and how Jesus was recognized by them when he broke the bread.

Jesus Appears to the Disciples

[36] While they were still talking about this, Jesus himself stood among them and said to them, "Peace be with you."

[37] They were startled and frightened, thinking they saw a ghost. [38] He said to them, "Why are you troubled, and why do doubts rise in your minds? [39] Look at my hands and my feet. It is I myself! Touch me and see; a ghost does not have flesh and bones, as you see I have."

[40] When he had said this, he showed them his hands and feet. [41] And while they still did not believe it because of joy and amazement, he asked them, "Do you have anything here to eat?" [42] They gave him a piece of broiled fish, [43] and he took it and ate it in their presence.

[44] He said to them, "This is what I told you while I was still with you: Everything must be fulfilled that is written about me in the Law of Moses, the Prophets and the Psalms."

[45] Then he opened their minds so they could understand the Scriptures. [46] He told them, "This is what is written: The Christ will suffer and rise from the dead on the third day, [47] and repentance and forgiveness of sins will be preached in his name to all nations, beginning at Jerusalem. [48] You are witnesses of these things. [49] I am going to send you what my Father has promised; but stay in the city until you have been clothed with power from on high."

The Ascension

[50] When he had led them out to the vicinity of Bethany, he lifted up his hands and blessed them. [51] While he was blessing them, he left them and was taken up into heaven. [52] Then they worshiped him and returned to Jerusalem with great joy. [53] And they stayed continually at the temple, praising God.

Pointing Toward Eternity

LUKE 24:39–53

"The day of resurrection!
Earth tell it out abroad;
the Passover of gladness,
the Passover of God.
From death to life eternal,
from earth unto the sky,
our Christ has brought us
over with hymns of victory."
—JOHN OF DAMASCUS

JOHN
Living in the Light

KEY VERSES:

The Word became flesh and made his dwelling among us. We have seen his glory . . . In him was life, and that life was the light of men.—John 1:14,4

"You called, you cried, you shattered my deafness. You sparkled, you blazed, you drove away my blindness. You shed your fragrance, and I drew in my breath, and I pant for you. I tasted and now I hunger and thirst. You touched me, and now I burn with longing for your peace."

—AUGUSTINE,
Confessions

The light is shining. It is a light that defies our ability to capture and define. The light has a voice that speaks life to us. The light has hands that hold and heal us. The light has a name—Jesus, the son of Mary, the Son of God.

The light became flesh. The light conquers darkness and turns death into life. Into situations as ordinary as a catering problem at a wedding or as deeply troubling as a death in the family, this light beams a transforming power. When the light is present, everything is changed. When the light is present in us, we are changed. We have eternal life. We are restored to the glory that our Creator God intended.

Many situations in the book of John may resemble your personal situations. As you read you might ask yourself, "What is God doing here, and how can I be open to allow God to work within me?" As you participate in a community of believers, you might ask, "What is God doing among us?"

John calls his community of Jews and non-Jews to follow the revolutionary—and sometimes unpopular—way of Jesus. He shows that the way of Jesus is full of challenge and adventure—full of the risk involved when we let go and trust. The way might be hard. But in Jesus we find grace and truth. In Jesus we will "have life, and have it to the full!" (John 10:10). John urges us to dwell in the light of Jesus, so that we might carry the death-defying love of God into the world.

The Word Became Flesh

1 In the beginning was the Word, and the Word was with God, and the Word was God. ²He was with God in the beginning.

³Through him all things were made; without him nothing was made that has been made. ⁴In him was life, and that life was the light of men. ⁵The light shines in the darkness, but the darkness has not understood*ᵃ* it.

⁶There came a man who was sent from God; his name was John. ⁷He came as a witness to testify concerning that light, so that through him all men might believe. ⁸He himself was not the light; he came only as a witness to the light. ⁹The true light that gives light to every man was coming into the world.*ᵇ*

¹⁰He was in the world, and though the world was made through him, the world did not recognize him. ¹¹He came to that which was his own, but his own did not receive him. ¹²Yet to all who received him, to those who believed in his name, he gave the right to become children of God— ¹³children born not of natural descent,*ᶜ* nor of human decision or a husband's will, but born of God.

¹⁴The Word became flesh and made his dwelling among us. We have seen his glory, the glory of the One and Only,*ᵈ* who came from the Father, full of grace and truth.

¹⁵John testifies concerning him. He cries out, saying, "This was he of whom I said, 'He who comes after me has surpassed me because he was before me.' " ¹⁶From the fullness of his grace we have all received one blessing after another. ¹⁷For the law was given through Moses; grace and truth came through Jesus Christ. ¹⁸No one has ever seen God, but God the One and Only,*ᵈ,ᵉ* who is at the Father's side, has made him known.

John the Baptist Denies Being the Christ

¹⁹Now this was John's testimony when the Jews of Jerusalem sent priests and Levites to ask him who he was. ²⁰He did not fail to confess, but confessed freely, "I am not the Christ.*ᶠ*"

²¹They asked him, "Then who are you? Are you Elijah?"

He said, "I am not."

"Are you the Prophet?"

He answered, "No."

²²Finally they said, "Who are you? Give us an answer to take back to those who sent us. What do you say about yourself?"

²³John replied in the words of Isaiah the prophet, "I am the voice of one calling in the desert, 'Make straight the way for the Lord.' "*ᵍ*

²⁴Now some Pharisees who had been sent ²⁵questioned him, "Why then do you baptize if you are not the Christ, nor Elijah, nor the Prophet?"

²⁶"I baptize with*ʰ* water," John replied, "but among you stands one you do not know. ²⁷He is the one who comes

---

ᵃ 5 Or darkness, and the darkness has not overcome ᵇ 9 Or This was the true light that gives light to every man who comes into the world ᶜ 13 Greek of bloods ᵈ 14,18 Or the Only Begotten ᵉ 18 Some manuscripts but the only (or only begotten) Son ᶠ 20 Or Messiah. "The Christ" (Greek) and "the Messiah" (Hebrew) both mean "the Anointed One"; also in verse 25. ᵍ 23 Isaiah 40:3 ʰ 26 Or in; also in verses 31 and 33

A Light Shines

JOHN 1:1–18

John's rich, resonating words sound out like a majestic overture. Imagine trumpets and drums as the great themes of this Gospel are declared: "In the beginning was the Word"; "in him was life"; "the light shines"; "darkness has not understood it." As you walk around the room, read this passage again aloud, as loudly as the text suggests to you. As you read, listen for a word or phrase that catches your attention. Repeat it and let it expand within your spirit. Sense its power. Give it the center stage of your consciousness and let it speak. When you are ready, let this experience serve as the foundation for a prayer of reflection.

See Meeting God in Scripture

Where Are You Staying?

JOHN 1:35–39

Two seekers ask Jesus where he is staying. Jesus says, "Come . . . and you will see." It is an invitation to his lodgings—and into discipleship with him.

Invite Jesus to come and see where you are staying. Invite him into your living space. Talk to him as you show him around. Show him those aspects of your home and your possessions that delight you. Then ask Jesus to sit with you. When Jesus asks where your spirit is residing, how might you respond? Write a dialogue with Jesus about where you are "staying." Be truthful. Trust him. Pray through the thoughts and emotions you experience during that dialogue. If appropriate, share your experience with someone you trust.

See Meeting God in Everyday Life

after me, the thongs of whose sandals I am not worthy to untie."

28This all happened at Bethany on the other side of the Jordan, where John was baptizing.

Jesus the Lamb of God

29The next day John saw Jesus coming toward him and said, "Look, the Lamb of God, who takes away the sin of the world! 30This is the one I meant when I said, 'A man who comes after me has surpassed me because he was before me.' 31I myself did not know him, but the reason I came baptizing with water was that he might be revealed to Israel."

32Then John gave this testimony: "I saw the Spirit come down from heaven as a dove and remain on him. 33I would not have known him, except that the one who sent me to baptize with water told me, 'The man on whom you see the Spirit come down and remain is he who will baptize with the Holy Spirit.' 34I have seen and I testify that this is the Son of God."

Jesus' First Disciples

35The next day John was there again with two of his disciples. 36When he saw Jesus passing by, he said, "Look, the Lamb of God!"

37When the two disciples heard him say this, they followed Jesus. 38Turning around, Jesus saw them following and asked, "What do you want?"

They said, "Rabbi" (which means Teacher), "where are you staying?"

39"Come," he replied, "and you will see."

So they went and saw where he was staying, and spent that day with him. It was about the tenth hour.

40Andrew, Simon Peter's brother, was one of the two who heard what John had said and who had followed Jesus. 41The first thing Andrew did was to find his brother Simon and tell him, "We have found the Messiah" (that is, the Christ). 42And he brought him to Jesus.

Jesus looked at him and said, "You are Simon son of John. You will be called Cephas" (which, when translated, is Peter[a]).

Jesus Calls Philip and Nathanael

43The next day Jesus decided to leave for Galilee. Finding Philip, he said to him, "Follow me."

44Philip, like Andrew and Peter, was from the town of Bethsaida. 45Philip found Nathanael and told him, "We have found the one Moses wrote about in the Law, and about whom the prophets also wrote—Jesus of Nazareth, the son of Joseph."

46"Nazareth! Can anything good come from there?" Nathanael asked.

"Come and see," said Philip.

47When Jesus saw Nathanael approaching, he said of him, "Here is a true Israelite, in whom there is nothing false."

48"How do you know me?" Nathanael asked.

Jesus answered, "I saw you while you were still under the fig tree before Philip called you."

49Then Nathanael declared, "Rabbi, you are the Son of God; you are the King of Israel."

a 42 Both *Cephas* (Aramaic) and *Peter* (Greek) mean *rock*.

[50]Jesus said, "You believe[a] because I told you I saw you under the fig tree. You shall see greater things than that." [51]He then added, "I tell you[b] the truth, you[b] shall see heaven open, and the angels of God ascending and descending on the Son of Man."

Jesus Changes Water to Wine

2 On the third day a wedding took place at Cana in Galilee. Jesus' mother was there, [2]and Jesus and his disciples had also been invited to the wedding. [3]When the wine was gone, Jesus' mother said to him, "They have no more wine."

[4]"Dear woman, why do you involve me?" Jesus replied. "My time has not yet come."

[5]His mother said to the servants, "Do whatever he tells you."

[6]Nearby stood six stone water jars, the kind used by the Jews for ceremonial washing, each holding from twenty to thirty gallons.[c]

[7]Jesus said to the servants, "Fill the jars with water"; so they filled them to the brim.

[8]Then he told them, "Now draw some out and take it to the master of the banquet."

They did so, [9]and the master of the banquet tasted the water that had been turned into wine. He did not realize where it had come from, though the servants who had drawn the water knew. Then he called the bridegroom aside [10]and said, "Everyone brings out the choice wine first and then the cheaper wine after the guests have had too much to drink; but you have saved the best till now."

[11]This, the first of his miraculous signs, Jesus performed at Cana in Galilee. He thus revealed his glory, and his disciples put their faith in him.

Jesus Clears the Temple

[12]After this he went down to Capernaum with his mother and brothers and his disciples. There they stayed for a few days.

[13]When it was almost time for the Jewish Passover, Jesus went up to Jerusalem. [14]In the temple courts he found men selling cattle, sheep and doves, and others sitting at tables exchanging money. [15]So he made a whip out of cords, and drove all from the temple area, both sheep and cattle; he scattered the coins of the money changers and overturned their tables. [16]To those who sold doves he said, "Get these out of here! How dare you turn my Father's house into a market!"

[17]His disciples remembered that it is written: "Zeal for your house will consume me."[d]

[18]Then the Jews demanded of him, "What miraculous sign can you show us to prove your authority to do all this?"

[19]Jesus answered them, "Destroy this temple, and I will raise it again in three days."

[20]The Jews replied, "It has taken forty-six years to build this temple, and you are going to raise it in three days?" [21]But the temple he had spoken of was his body. [22]After he was raised from the dead, his disciples recalled what he had said. Then they believed the Scripture and the words that Jesus had spoken.

[a] 50 Or Do you believe . . . ?   [b] 51 The Greek is plural.   [c] 6 Greek two to three metretes (probably about 75 to 115 liters)   [d] 17 Psalm 69:9

Doing What Jesus Says

JOHN 2:1–11

Sometimes the things God asks us to do just don't seem to make sense! Jesus says, "Fill the jars with water." But why fill up the jars with water when it is wine that has run out? Even though it seems to make no sense, the servants do as they are told. The water becomes premium wine. The hosts experience honor rather than shame.

You may ask, "What am I running out of? What shortages are my family, my faith community or my neighborhood likely to encounter?" Tell Jesus about them. What does Jesus ask you to do in response? What act of obedience does Jesus ask of you so that the situation might be transformed? What do you envision Jesus doing as you cooperate with him?

See *Meeting God in Community*

You Choose

JOHN 3:1–9

Nicodemus admires Jesus and has many questions to ask, but he has much to lose—security, position and power—if he is public about his admiration, so he seeks Jesus under the cover of darkness. Yet Jesus asks the Pharisee to do something much more profound and much more difficult than putting his lifestyle in jeopardy—he asks him to be born again.

Ask the Spirit to bless your imagination and your senses as you take your place in the story as Nicodemus. What is happening? What do you see? What do you hear—around you and from Jesus? Smell the evening air. Feel the breeze. Ask Jesus to speak to you about your fears and questions. Ask what being "born again" could mean for you right now. Let Jesus enlighten your lack of understanding, your stubborn resistance or your glad acceptance. Carry the experience in your heart during the coming week.

See Meeting God in Everyday Life

²³Now while he was in Jerusalem at the Passover Feast, many people saw the miraculous signs he was doing and believed in his name.[a] ²⁴But Jesus would not entrust himself to them, for he knew all men. ²⁵He did not need man's testimony about man, for he knew what was in a man.

Jesus Teaches Nicodemus

3 Now there was a man of the Pharisees named Nicodemus, a member of the Jewish ruling council. ²He came to Jesus at night and said, "Rabbi, we know you are a teacher who has come from God. For no one could perform the miraculous signs you are doing if God were not with him."

³In reply Jesus declared, "I tell you the truth, no one can see the kingdom of God unless he is born again.[b]"

⁴"How can a man be born when he is old?" Nicodemus asked. "Surely he cannot enter a second time into his mother's womb to be born!"

⁵Jesus answered, "I tell you the truth, no one can enter the kingdom of God unless he is born of water and the Spirit. ⁶Flesh gives birth to flesh, but the Spirit[c] gives birth to spirit. ⁷You should not be surprised at my saying, 'You[d] must be born again.' ⁸The wind blows wherever it pleases. You hear its sound, but you cannot tell where it comes from or where it is going. So it is with everyone born of the Spirit."

⁹"How can this be?" Nicodemus asked.

¹⁰"You are Israel's teacher," said Jesus, "and do you not understand these things? ¹¹I tell you the truth, we speak of what we know, and we testify to what we have seen, but still you people do not accept our testimony. ¹²I have spoken to you of earthly things and you do not believe; how then will you believe if I speak of heavenly things? ¹³No one has ever gone into heaven except the one who came from heaven—the Son of Man.[e] ¹⁴Just as Moses lifted up the snake in the desert, so the Son of Man must be lifted up, ¹⁵that everyone who believes in him may have eternal life.[f]

¹⁶"For God so loved the world that he gave his one and only Son,[g] that whoever believes in him shall not perish but have eternal life. ¹⁷For God did not send his Son into the world to condemn the world, but to save the world through him. ¹⁸Whoever believes in him is not condemned, but whoever does not believe stands condemned already because he has not believed in the name of God's one and only Son.[h] ¹⁹This is the verdict: Light has come into the world, but men loved darkness instead of light because their deeds were evil. ²⁰Everyone who does evil hates the light, and will not come into the light for fear that his deeds will be exposed. ²¹But whoever lives by the truth comes into the light, so that it may be seen plainly that what he has done has been done through God."[i]

John the Baptist's Testimony About Jesus

²²After this, Jesus and his disciples went out into the Judean countryside, where he spent some time with them,

---

a 23 Or *and believed in him* b 3 Or *born from above*; also in verse 7
c 6 Or *but spirit* d 7 The Greek is plural. e 13 Some manuscripts *Man, who is in heaven* f 15 Or *believes may have eternal life in him* g 16 Or *his only begotten Son* h 18 Or *God's only begotten Son* i 21 Some interpreters end the quotation after verse 15.

and baptized. [23]Now John also was baptizing at Aenon near Salim, because there was plenty of water, and people were constantly coming to be baptized. [24](This was before John was put in prison.) [25]An argument developed between some of John's disciples and a certain Jew[a] over the matter of ceremonial washing. [26]They came to John and said to him, "Rabbi, that man who was with you on the other side of the Jordan—the one you testified about—well, he is baptizing, and everyone is going to him."

[27]To this John replied, "A man can receive only what is given him from heaven. [28]You yourselves can testify that I said, 'I am not the Christ[b] but am sent ahead of him.' [29]The bride belongs to the bridegroom. The friend who attends the bridegroom waits and listens for him, and is full of joy when he hears the bridegroom's voice. That joy is mine, and it is now complete. [30]He must become greater; I must become less.

[31]"The one who comes from above is above all; the one who is from the earth belongs to the earth, and speaks as one from the earth. The one who comes from heaven is above all. [32]He testifies to what he has seen and heard, but no one accepts his testimony. [33]The man who has accepted it has certified that God is truthful. [34]For the one whom God has sent speaks the words of God, for God[c] gives the Spirit without limit. [35]The Father loves the Son and has placed everything in his hands. [36]Whoever believes in the Son has eternal life, but whoever rejects the Son will not see life, for God's wrath remains on him."[d]

Jesus Talks With a Samaritan Woman

4 The Pharisees heard that Jesus was gaining and baptizing more disciples than John, [2]although in fact it was not Jesus who baptized, but his disciples. [3]When the Lord learned of this, he left Judea and went back once more to Galilee.

[4]Now he had to go through Samaria. [5]So he came to a town in Samaria called Sychar, near the plot of ground Jacob had given to his son Joseph. [6]Jacob's well was there, and Jesus, tired as he was from the journey, sat down by the well. It was about the sixth hour.

[7]When a Samaritan woman came to draw water, Jesus said to her, "Will you give me a drink?" [8](His disciples had gone into the town to buy food.)

[9]The Samaritan woman said to him, "You are a Jew and I am a Samaritan woman. How can you ask me for a drink?" (For Jews do not associate with Samaritans.[e])

[10]Jesus answered her, "If you knew the gift of God and who it is that asks you for a drink, you would have asked him and he would have given you living water."

[11]"Sir," the woman said, "you have nothing to draw with and the well is deep. Where can you get this living water? [12]Are you greater than our father Jacob, who gave us the well and drank from it himself, as did also his sons and his flocks and herds?"

[13]Jesus answered, "Everyone who drinks this water will be thirsty again, [14]but whoever drinks the water I give him will never thirst. Indeed, the water I give him will become in him a spring of water welling up to eternal life."

Over the Line

JOHN 4:7–9

The Samaritans are considered "unclean." Jews don't associate with Samaritans, John reminds us. To do so is to cross over the line of propriety. And Jesus dares to talk to a Samaritan woman alone! The two discuss thirst (physical and spiritual), relationships and religion. As he speaks Jesus crosses the boundary of his culture's notion of what is acceptable and what is not. His disciples are surprised—even shocked (v.27).

Who is "over the line" in your way of thinking? How can you expand your ideas of what is acceptable so that you can meet the needs of "the unacceptable" as Jesus did? What is Jesus waiting to teach you and show you about yourself?

See Meeting God in Service

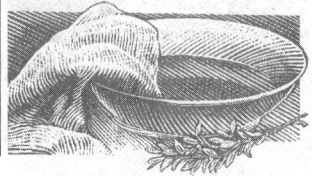

---

[a] 25 Some manuscripts *and certain Jews*   [b] 28 Or *Messiah*   [c] 34 Greek *he*
[d] 36 Some interpreters end the quotation after verse 30.   [e] 9 Or *do not use dishes Samaritans have used*

Living Water

JOHN 4:13–15

Walk around the room as you read verses 13 through 15 aloud three times. Put the Bible down and walk around the room again, reciting the text three more times. Now, seated comfortably, with this text and a glass of water in front of you, name your thirsts. Pray the same request that the Samaritan woman made of Jesus: "Sir, give me this water." Drink the water as you receive Jesus' gift, a spring of water that gushes up to eternal life. Rest in God's presence. As you go out into the world, let the water of eternal life flow through your heart and out to others through your words and actions.

See Meeting God in Scripture

¹⁵The woman said to him, "Sir, give me this water so that I won't get thirsty and have to keep coming here to draw water."

¹⁶He told her, "Go, call your husband and come back."

¹⁷"I have no husband," she replied.

Jesus said to her, "You are right when you say you have no husband. ¹⁸The fact is, you have had five husbands, and the man you now have is not your husband. What you have just said is quite true."

¹⁹"Sir," the woman said, "I can see that you are a prophet. ²⁰Our fathers worshiped on this mountain, but you Jews claim that the place where we must worship is in Jerusalem."

²¹Jesus declared, "Believe me, woman, a time is coming when you will worship the Father neither on this mountain nor in Jerusalem. ²²You Samaritans worship what you do not know; we worship what we do know, for salvation is from the Jews. ²³Yet a time is coming and has now come when the true worshipers will worship the Father in spirit and truth, for they are the kind of worshipers the Father seeks. ²⁴God is spirit, and his worshipers must worship in spirit and in truth."

²⁵The woman said, "I know that Messiah" (called Christ) "is coming. When he comes, he will explain everything to us."

²⁶Then Jesus declared, "I who speak to you am he."

The Disciples Rejoin Jesus

²⁷Just then his disciples returned and were surprised to find him talking with a woman. But no one asked, "What do you want?" or "Why are you talking with her?"

²⁸Then, leaving her water jar, the woman went back to the town and said to the people, ²⁹"Come, see a man who told me everything I ever did. Could this be the Christ[a]?" ³⁰They came out of the town and made their way toward him.

³¹Meanwhile his disciples urged him, "Rabbi, eat something."

³²But he said to them, "I have food to eat that you know nothing about."

³³Then his disciples said to each other, "Could someone have brought him food?"

³⁴"My food," said Jesus, "is to do the will of him who sent me and to finish his work. ³⁵Do you not say, 'Four months more and then the harvest'? I tell you, open your eyes and look at the fields! They are ripe for harvest. ³⁶Even now the reaper draws his wages, even now he harvests the crop for eternal life, so that the sower and the reaper may be glad together. ³⁷Thus the saying 'One sows and another reaps' is true. ³⁸I sent you to reap what you have not worked for. Others have done the hard work, and you have reaped the benefits of their labor."

Many Samaritans Believe

³⁹Many of the Samaritans from that town believed in him because of the woman's testimony, "He told me everything I ever did." ⁴⁰So when the Samaritans came to him, they urged him to stay with them, and he stayed two days. ⁴¹And because of his words many more became believers.

⁴²They said to the woman, "We no longer believe just because of what you said; now we have heard for ourselves, and we know that this man really is the Savior of the world."

a 29 Or Messiah

Jesus Heals the Official's Son

⁴³After the two days he left for Galilee. ⁴⁴(Now Jesus himself had pointed out that a prophet has no honor in his own country.) ⁴⁵When he arrived in Galilee, the Galileans welcomed him. They had seen all that he had done in Jerusalem at the Passover Feast, for they also had been there.

⁴⁶Once more he visited Cana in Galilee, where he had turned the water into wine. And there was a certain royal official whose son lay sick at Capernaum. ⁴⁷When this man heard that Jesus had arrived in Galilee from Judea, he went to him and begged him to come and heal his son, who was close to death.

⁴⁸"Unless you people see miraculous signs and wonders," Jesus told him, "you will never believe."

⁴⁹The royal official said, "Sir, come down before my child dies."

⁵⁰Jesus replied, "You may go. Your son will live."

The man took Jesus at his word and departed. ⁵¹While he was still on the way, his servants met him with the news that his boy was living. ⁵²When he inquired as to the time when his son got better, they said to him, "The fever left him yesterday at the seventh hour."

⁵³Then the father realized that this was the exact time at which Jesus had said to him, "Your son will live." So he and all his household believed.

⁵⁴This was the second miraculous sign that Jesus performed, having come from Judea to Galilee.

The Healing at the Pool

5 Some time later, Jesus went up to Jerusalem for a feast of the Jews. ²Now there is in Jerusalem near the Sheep Gate a pool, which in Aramaic is called Bethesda[a] and which is surrounded by five covered colonnades. ³Here a great number of disabled people used to lie—the blind, the lame, the paralyzed.[b] ⁵One who was there had been an invalid for thirty-eight years. ⁶When Jesus saw him lying there and learned that he had been in this condition for a long time, he asked him, "Do you want to get well?"

⁷"Sir," the invalid replied, "I have no one to help me into the pool when the water is stirred. While I am trying to get in, someone else goes down ahead of me."

⁸Then Jesus said to him, "Get up! Pick up your mat and walk." ⁹At once the man was cured; he picked up his mat and walked.

The day on which this took place was a Sabbath, ¹⁰and so the Jews said to the man who had been healed, "It is the Sabbath; the law forbids you to carry your mat."

¹¹But he replied, "The man who made me well said to me, 'Pick up your mat and walk.'"

¹²So they asked him, "Who is this fellow who told you to pick it up and walk?"

¹³The man who was healed had no idea who it was, for Jesus had slipped away into the crowd that was there.

¹⁴Later Jesus found him at the temple and said to him, "See, you are well again. Stop sinning or something worse

At a Distance

JOHN 4:46–54

"Anticipation. God is fixing it right now, even though I can't see how. Anticipation. While I am trying to figure it out, God has already worked it out. Learn how to wait with the expectancy that God is doing something about it. Anticipation. Faith is relational, not conceptual: 'What we will yet be, has not been revealed.'"

—JEREMIAH A. WRIGHT, JR.,
What Makes You So Strong

---

a 2 Some manuscripts Bethzatha; other manuscripts Bethsaida   b 3 Some less important manuscripts paralyzed—and they waited for the moving of the waters. ⁴From time to time an angel of the Lord would come down and stir up the waters. The first one into the pool after each such disturbance would be cured of whatever disease he had.

The Son Gives Life

JOHN 5:1–15

Jesus has challenged this man to change—a man who has good reasons for being the way he is. But still Jesus asks him, "Do you want to get well?" Jesus' question is purposely ambiguous.

Picture the scene with yourself in the role of the person with a disability. Jesus asks you, "Do you want to get well?" What do you think of the question? How does it make you feel? How do you answer Jesus? Ask the Spirit to enlighten your heart and mind. Write a letter to Jesus, asking him to help you discern any resistance to wellness that you hold within you.

See *Meeting God in Scripture*

may happen to you." [15]The man went away and told the Jews that it was Jesus who had made him well.

Life Through the Son

[16]So, because Jesus was doing these things on the Sabbath, the Jews persecuted him. [17]Jesus said to them, "My Father is always at his work to this very day, and I, too, am working." [18]For this reason the Jews tried all the harder to kill him; not only was he breaking the Sabbath, but he was even calling God his own Father, making himself equal with God.

[19]Jesus gave them this answer: "I tell you the truth, the Son can do nothing by himself; he can do only what he sees his Father doing, because whatever the Father does the Son also does. [20]For the Father loves the Son and shows him all he does. Yes, to your amazement he will show him even greater things than these. [21]For just as the Father raises the dead and gives them life, even so the Son gives life to whom he is pleased to give it. [22]Moreover, the Father judges no one, but has entrusted all judgment to the Son, [23]that all may honor the Son just as they honor the Father. He who does not honor the Son does not honor the Father, who sent him.

[24]"I tell you the truth, whoever hears my word and believes him who sent me has eternal life and will not be condemned; he has crossed over from death to life. [25]I tell you the truth, a time is coming and has now come when the dead will hear the voice of the Son of God and those who hear will live. [26]For as the Father has life in himself, so he has granted the Son to have life in himself. [27]And he has given him authority to judge because he is the Son of Man.

[28]"Do not be amazed at this, for a time is coming when all who are in their graves will hear his voice [29]and come out—those who have done good will rise to live, and those who have done evil will rise to be condemned. [30]By myself I can do nothing; I judge only as I hear, and my judgment is just, for I seek not to please myself but him who sent me.

Testimonies About Jesus

[31]"If I testify about myself, my testimony is not valid. [32]There is another who testifies in my favor, and I know that his testimony about me is valid.

[33]"You have sent to John and he has testified to the truth. [34]Not that I accept human testimony; but I mention it that you may be saved. [35]John was a lamp that burned and gave light, and you chose for a time to enjoy his light.

[36]"I have testimony weightier than that of John. For the very work that the Father has given me to finish, and which I am doing, testifies that the Father has sent me. [37]And the Father who sent me has himself testified concerning me. You have never heard his voice nor seen his form, [38]nor does his word dwell in you, for you do not believe the one he sent. [39]You diligently study[a] the Scriptures because you think that by them you possess eternal life. These are the Scriptures that testify about me, [40]yet you refuse to come to me to have life.

[41]"I do not accept praise from men, [42]but I know you. I know that you do not have the love of God in your hearts. [43]I have come in my Father's name, and you do not accept me; but if someone else comes in his own name, you will accept him. [44]How can you believe if you accept praise

[a] 39 Or *Study diligently* (the imperative)

from one another, yet make no effort to obtain the praise that comes from the only God[a]?

⁴⁵"But do not think I will accuse you before the Father. Your accuser is Moses, on whom your hopes are set. ⁴⁶If you believed Moses, you would believe me, for he wrote about me. ⁴⁷But since you do not believe what he wrote, how are you going to believe what I say?"

Jesus Feeds the Five Thousand

6 Some time after this, Jesus crossed to the far shore of the Sea of Galilee (that is, the Sea of Tiberias), ²and a great crowd of people followed him because they saw the miraculous signs he had performed on the sick. ³Then Jesus went up on a mountainside and sat down with his disciples. ⁴The Jewish Passover Feast was near.

⁵When Jesus looked up and saw a great crowd coming toward him, he said to Philip, "Where shall we buy bread for these people to eat?" ⁶He asked this only to test him, for he already had in mind what he was going to do.

⁷Philip answered him, "Eight months' wages[b] would not buy enough bread for each one to have a bite!"

⁸Another of his disciples, Andrew, Simon Peter's brother, spoke up, ⁹"Here is a boy with five small barley loaves and two small fish, but how far will they go among so many?"

¹⁰Jesus said, "Have the people sit down." There was plenty of grass in that place, and the men sat down, about five thousand of them. ¹¹Jesus then took the loaves, gave thanks, and distributed to those who were seated as much as they wanted. He did the same with the fish.

¹²When they had all had enough to eat, he said to his disciples, "Gather the pieces that are left over. Let nothing be wasted." ¹³So they gathered them and filled twelve baskets with the pieces of the five barley loaves left over by those who had eaten.

¹⁴After the people saw the miraculous sign that Jesus did, they began to say, "Surely this is the Prophet who is to come into the world." ¹⁵Jesus, knowing that they intended to come and make him king by force, withdrew again to a mountain by himself.

Jesus Walks on the Water

¹⁶When evening came, his disciples went down to the lake, ¹⁷where they got into a boat and set off across the lake for Capernaum. By now it was dark, and Jesus had not yet joined them. ¹⁸A strong wind was blowing and the waters grew rough. ¹⁹When they had rowed three or three and a half miles,[c] they saw Jesus approaching the boat, walking on the water; and they were terrified. ²⁰But he said to them, "It is I; don't be afraid." ²¹Then they were willing to take him into the boat, and immediately the boat reached the shore where they were heading.

²²The next day the crowd that had stayed on the opposite shore of the lake realized that only one boat had been there, and that Jesus had not entered it with his disciples, but that they had gone away alone. ²³Then some boats from Tiberias landed near the place where the people had eaten the bread after the Lord had given thanks. ²⁴Once the crowd realized that neither Jesus nor his disciples were

The Sovereign One

JOHN 6:13–15

The crowd that gathers around Jesus is impressed with him. They have seen him miraculously provide lunch for thousands. They want to make him king. But Jesus refuses to be co-opted.

Jesus will not be enlisted into our causes—no matter how laudable they may seem to us—if they do not conform to the will of God. Using the words of Psalm 139, invite God to examine your heart. Confess (perhaps in the presence of someone you trust) ways in which you have desired Jesus for what he could do for your cause, rather than desiring Jesus for himself. Spend some time with Jesus, enjoying him for his own sake. Repeat a simple phrase such as, "Jesus, you are all I want."

See Meeting God in Prayer

---

[a] 44 Some early manuscripts *the Only One*   [b] 7 Greek *two hundred denarii*
[c] 19 Greek *rowed twenty-five or thirty stadia* (about 5 or 6 kilometers)

Living Bread

JOHN 6:35

Think about how it feels to be hungry—hungry in your stomach and hungry in your soul. Then think of the best bread you have ever tasted. Smell its yeasty aroma. What does it look like? Feel its crust and its soft interior with your fingers. Taste it. Savor the experience. What kinds of things are like bread for you—savory, filling, satisfying? Write down some descriptive words that come to you. What does it mean for you to "eat" the bread Jesus offers? At your earliest opportunity (according to your custom), take your place at the communion table of the Lord and receive the bread of remembrance, the bread of life.

See Meeting God in Worship

there, they got into the boats and went to Capernaum in search of Jesus.

Jesus the Bread of Life

25 When they found him on the other side of the lake, they asked him, "Rabbi, when did you get here?"

26 Jesus answered, "I tell you the truth, you are looking for me, not because you saw miraculous signs but because you ate the loaves and had your fill. 27 Do not work for food that spoils, but for food that endures to eternal life, which the Son of Man will give you. On him God the Father has placed his seal of approval."

28 Then they asked him, "What must we do to do the works God requires?"

29 Jesus answered, "The work of God is this: to believe in the one he has sent."

30 So they asked him, "What miraculous sign then will you give that we may see it and believe you? What will you do? 31 Our forefathers ate the manna in the desert; as it is written: 'He gave them bread from heaven to eat.'*a*"

32 Jesus said to them, "I tell you the truth, it is not Moses who has given you the bread from heaven, but it is my Father who gives you the true bread from heaven. 33 For the bread of God is he who comes down from heaven and gives life to the world."

34 "Sir," they said, "from now on give us this bread."

35 Then Jesus declared, "I am the bread of life. He who comes to me will never go hungry, and he who believes in me will never be thirsty. 36 But as I told you, you have seen me and still you do not believe. 37 All that the Father gives me will come to me, and whoever comes to me I will never drive away. 38 For I have come down from heaven not to do my will but to do the will of him who sent me. 39 And this is the will of him who sent me, that I shall lose none of all that he has given me, but raise them up at the last day. 40 For my Father's will is that everyone who looks to the Son and believes in him shall have eternal life, and I will raise him up at the last day."

41 At this the Jews began to grumble about him because he said, "I am the bread that came down from heaven." 42 They said, "Is this not Jesus, the son of Joseph, whose father and mother we know? How can he now say, 'I came down from heaven'?"

43 "Stop grumbling among yourselves," Jesus answered. 44 "No one can come to me unless the Father who sent me draws him, and I will raise him up at the last day. 45 It is written in the Prophets: 'They will all be taught by God.'*b* Everyone who listens to the Father and learns from him comes to me. 46 No one has seen the Father except the one who is from God; only he has seen the Father. 47 I tell you the truth, he who believes has everlasting life. 48 I am the bread of life. 49 Your forefathers ate the manna in the desert, yet they died. 50 But here is the bread that comes down from heaven, which a man may eat and not die. 51 I am the living bread that came down from heaven. If anyone eats of this bread, he will live forever. This bread is my flesh, which I will give for the life of the world."

52 Then the Jews began to argue sharply among themselves, "How can this man give us his flesh to eat?"

a 31 Exodus 16:4; Neh. 9:15; Psalm 78:24,25   *b 45* Isaiah 54:13

⁵³Jesus said to them, "I tell you the truth, unless you eat the flesh of the Son of Man and drink his blood, you have no life in you. ⁵⁴Whoever eats my flesh and drinks my blood has eternal life, and I will raise him up at the last day. ⁵⁵For my flesh is real food and my blood is real drink. ⁵⁶Whoever eats my flesh and drinks my blood remains in me, and I in him. ⁵⁷Just as the living Father sent me and I live because of the Father, so the one who feeds on me will live because of me. ⁵⁸This is the bread that came down from heaven. Your forefathers ate manna and died, but he who feeds on this bread will live forever." ⁵⁹He said this while teaching in the synagogue in Capernaum.

Many Disciples Desert Jesus

⁶⁰On hearing it, many of his disciples said, "This is a hard teaching. Who can accept it?"

⁶¹Aware that his disciples were grumbling about this, Jesus said to them, "Does this offend you? ⁶²What if you see the Son of Man ascend to where he was before! ⁶³The Spirit gives life; the flesh counts for nothing. The words I have spoken to you are spirit[a] and they are life. ⁶⁴Yet there are some of you who do not believe." For Jesus had known from the beginning which of them did not believe and who would betray him. ⁶⁵He went on to say, "This is why I told you that no one can come to me unless the Father has enabled him."

⁶⁶From this time many of his disciples turned back and no longer followed him.

⁶⁷"You do not want to leave too, do you?" Jesus asked the Twelve.

⁶⁸Simon Peter answered him, "Lord, to whom shall we go? You have the words of eternal life. ⁶⁹We believe and know that you are the Holy One of God."

⁷⁰Then Jesus replied, "Have I not chosen you, the Twelve? Yet one of you is a devil!" ⁷¹(He meant Judas, the son of Simon Iscariot, who, though one of the Twelve, was later to betray him.)

Jesus Goes to the Feast of Tabernacles

7 After this, Jesus went around in Galilee, purposely staying away from Judea because the Jews there were waiting to take his life. ²But when the Jewish Feast of Tabernacles was near, ³Jesus' brothers said to him, "You ought to leave here and go to Judea, so that your disciples may see the miracles you do. ⁴No one who wants to become a public figure acts in secret. Since you are doing these things, show yourself to the world." ⁵For even his own brothers did not believe in him.

⁶Therefore Jesus told them, "The right time for me has not yet come; for you any time is right. ⁷The world cannot hate you, but it hates me because I testify that what it does is evil. ⁸You go to the Feast. I am not yet[b] going up to this Feast, because for me the right time has not yet come." ⁹Having said this, he stayed in Galilee.

¹⁰However, after his brothers had left for the Feast, he went also, not publicly, but in secret. ¹¹Now at the Feast the Jews were watching for him and asking, "Where is that man?"

¹²Among the crowds there was widespread whispering about him. Some said, "He is a good man."

"To Whom Shall We Go?"

JOHN 6:66-69

Sometimes the things Jesus says are just too hard. Many of Jesus' disciples just can't accept his teaching—that he is "the bread of life" (see 6:35-58). They decide to leave. What is Jesus asking you to face that seems too hard for you right now? To whom will you go? Your friend? Your counselor? Your therapist? Your spiritual adviser? They will surely help. But who has the words of eternal life? When life is too hard, do you *really* believe in the Holy One of God? It may help to write your response. Go to Jesus and tell him about those things that seem too hard for you.

---

a 63 Or Spirit   *b 8 Some early manuscripts do not have yet.*

Who Is This Man?

JOHN 7:25–29

"Whatever we now strive for, or are justly eager for, or blamelessly desire, when we come to the vision of God, we shall require no more . . . An impure heart cannot see that which is seen only by the pure in heart. You will be repelled, driven back from it, and will not see it."

—AUGUSTINE,
"Purity of Heart"

Others replied, "No, he deceives the people." ¹³But no one would say anything publicly about him for fear of the Jews.

Jesus Teaches at the Feast

¹⁴Not until halfway through the Feast did Jesus go up to the temple courts and begin to teach. ¹⁵The Jews were amazed and asked, "How did this man get such learning without having studied?"

¹⁶Jesus answered, "My teaching is not my own. It comes from him who sent me. ¹⁷If anyone chooses to do God's will, he will find out whether my teaching comes from God or whether I speak on my own. ¹⁸He who speaks on his own does so to gain honor for himself, but he who works for the honor of the one who sent him is a man of truth; there is nothing false about him. ¹⁹Has not Moses given you the law? Yet not one of you keeps the law. Why are you trying to kill me?"

²⁰"You are demon-possessed," the crowd answered. "Who is trying to kill you?"

²¹Jesus said to them, "I did one miracle, and you are all astonished. ²²Yet, because Moses gave you circumcision (though actually it did not come from Moses, but from the patriarchs), you circumcise a child on the Sabbath. ²³Now if a child can be circumcised on the Sabbath so that the law of Moses may not be broken, why are you angry with me for healing the whole man on the Sabbath? ²⁴Stop judging by mere appearances, and make a right judgment."

Is Jesus the Christ?

²⁵At that point some of the people of Jerusalem began to ask, "Isn't this the man they are trying to kill? ²⁶Here he is, speaking publicly, and they are not saying a word to him. Have the authorities really concluded that he is the Christ[a]? ²⁷But we know where this man is from; when the Christ comes, no one will know where he is from."

²⁸Then Jesus, still teaching in the temple courts, cried out, "Yes, you know me, and you know where I am from. I am not here on my own, but he who sent me is true. You do not know him, ²⁹but I know him because I am from him and he sent me."

³⁰At this they tried to seize him, but no one laid a hand on him, because his time had not yet come. ³¹Still, many in the crowd put their faith in him. They said, "When the Christ comes, will he do more miraculous signs than this man?"

³²The Pharisees heard the crowd whispering such things about him. Then the chief priests and the Pharisees sent temple guards to arrest him.

³³Jesus said, "I am with you for only a short time, and then I go to the one who sent me. ³⁴You will look for me, but you will not find me; and where I am, you cannot come."

³⁵The Jews said to one another, "Where does this man intend to go that we cannot find him? Will he go where our people live scattered among the Greeks, and teach the Greeks? ³⁶What did he mean when he said, 'You will look for me, but you will not find me,' and 'Where I am, you cannot come'?"

³⁷On the last and greatest day of the Feast, Jesus stood and said in a loud voice, "If anyone is thirsty, let him come

a 26 Or *Messiah*; also in verses 27, 31, 41 and 42

to me and drink. ³⁸Whoever believes in me, as*a* the Scripture has said, streams of living water will flow from within him." ³⁹By this he meant the Spirit, whom those who believed in him were later to receive. Up to that time the Spirit had not been given, since Jesus had not yet been glorified.

⁴⁰On hearing his words, some of the people said, "Surely this man is the Prophet."

⁴¹Others said, "He is the Christ."

Still others asked, "How can the Christ come from Galilee? ⁴²Does not the Scripture say that the Christ will come from David's family*b* and from Bethlehem, the town where David lived?" ⁴³Thus the people were divided because of Jesus. ⁴⁴Some wanted to seize him, but no one laid a hand on him.

Unbelief of the Jewish Leaders

⁴⁵Finally the temple guards went back to the chief priests and Pharisees, who asked them, "Why didn't you bring him in?"

⁴⁶"No one ever spoke the way this man does," the guards declared.

⁴⁷"You mean he has deceived you also?" the Pharisees retorted. ⁴⁸"Has any of the rulers or of the Pharisees believed in him? ⁴⁹No! But this mob that knows nothing of the law—there is a curse on them."

⁵⁰Nicodemus, who had gone to Jesus earlier and who was one of their own number, asked, ⁵¹"Does our law condemn anyone without first hearing him to find out what he is doing?"

⁵²They replied, "Are you from Galilee, too? Look into it, and you will find that a prophet*c* does not come out of Galilee."

[The earliest manuscripts and many other ancient witnesses do not have John 7:53–8:11.]

⁵³Then each went to his own home.

8 But Jesus went to the Mount of Olives. ²At dawn he appeared again in the temple courts, where all the people gathered around him, and he sat down to teach them. ³The teachers of the law and the Pharisees brought in a woman caught in adultery. They made her stand before the group ⁴and said to Jesus, "Teacher, this woman was caught in the act of adultery. ⁵In the Law Moses commanded us to stone such women. Now what do you say?" ⁶They were using this question as a trap, in order to have a basis for accusing him.

But Jesus bent down and started to write on the ground with his finger. ⁷When they kept on questioning him, he straightened up and said to them, "If any one of you is without sin, let him be the first to throw a stone at her." ⁸Again he stooped down and wrote on the ground.

⁹At this, those who heard began to go away one at a time, the older ones first, until only Jesus was left, with the woman still standing there. ¹⁰Jesus straightened up and asked her, "Woman, where are they? Has no one condemned you?"

¹¹"No one, sir," she said.

a 37,38 Or / *If anyone is thirsty, let him come to me. / And let him drink,* ³⁸*who believes in me. / As* *b 42* Greek *seed* *c 52* Two early manuscripts *the Prophet*

Let the Waters Flow

JOHN 7:37–39

Jesus is the source of living water. And this water is to have many conduits—the hearts of believers. From the believer's heart will flow streams of living water! Because it is sometimes hard to own the good that has happened through us, ask the Spirit to bring to mind people who have been refreshed by the living water of Jesus that has flowed from you. Give thanks for them. Pray that God will refresh them again today. Give thanks for the living water of Jesus.

See Meeting God in Prayer

Standing in the Light of Life

JOHN 8:1–11

In this passage Jesus declares to a shamed woman that she is not condemned, and then he invites her to leave her life of sin and walk in the light.

Sometimes we too readily believe another's words of condemnation rather than seek the word of Jesus. Jesus invites us to come out of the darkness and death of condemnation and into the light of life. Stand in sunlight or lamplight. Open yourself to Jesus as the light of the world. Welcome his light into your soul and ask Jesus to stand in that place with you. Let him transform the darkness in you into light.

See Meeting God in the Created Order

"Then neither do I condemn you," Jesus declared. "Go now and leave your life of sin."

The Validity of Jesus' Testimony

[12] When Jesus spoke again to the people, he said, "I am the light of the world. Whoever follows me will never walk in darkness, but will have the light of life." [13] The Pharisees challenged him, "Here you are, appearing as your own witness; your testimony is not valid."

[14] Jesus answered, "Even if I testify on my own behalf, my testimony is valid, for I know where I came from and where I am going. But you have no idea where I come from or where I am going. [15] You judge by human standards; I pass judgment on no one. [16] But if I do judge, my decisions are right, because I am not alone. I stand with the Father, who sent me. [17] In your own Law it is written that the testimony of two men is valid. [18] I am one who testifies for myself; my other witness is the Father, who sent me."

[19] Then they asked him, "Where is your father?"

"You do not know me or my Father," Jesus replied. "If you knew me, you would know my Father also." [20] He spoke these words while teaching in the temple area near the place where the offerings were put. Yet no one seized him, because his time had not yet come.

[21] Once more Jesus said to them, "I am going away, and you will look for me, and you will die in your sin. Where I go, you cannot come."

[22] This made the Jews ask, "Will he kill himself? Is that why he says, 'Where I go, you cannot come'?"

[23] But he continued, "You are from below; I am from above. You are of this world; I am not of this world. [24] I told you that you would die in your sins; if you do not believe that I am ˻the one I claim to be˼,[a] you will indeed die in your sins."

[25] "Who are you?" they asked.

"Just what I have been claiming all along," Jesus replied. [26] "I have much to say in judgment of you. But he who sent me is reliable, and what I have heard from him I tell the world."

[27] They did not understand that he was telling them about his Father. [28] So Jesus said, "When you have lifted up the Son of Man, then you will know that I am ˻the one I claim to be˼ and that I do nothing on my own but speak just what the Father has taught me. [29] The one who sent me is with me; he has not left me alone, for I always do what pleases him." [30] Even as he spoke, many put their faith in him.

The Children of Abraham

[31] To the Jews who had believed him, Jesus said, "If you hold to my teaching, you are really my disciples. [32] Then you will know the truth, and the truth will set you free."

[33] They answered him, "We are Abraham's descendants[b] and have never been slaves of anyone. How can you say that we shall be set free?"

[34] Jesus replied, "I tell you the truth, everyone who sins is a slave to sin. [35] Now a slave has no permanent place in the family, but a son belongs to it forever. [36] So if the Son sets

a 24 Or *I am he*; also in verse 28   *b 33* Greek *seed*; also in verse 37

you free, you will be free indeed. ³⁷I know you are Abraham's descendants. Yet you are ready to kill me, because you have no room for my word. ³⁸I am telling you what I have seen in the Father's presence, and you do what you have heard from your father.*ᵃ*"

³⁹"Abraham is our father," they answered.

"If you were Abraham's children," said Jesus, "then you would*ᵇ* do the things Abraham did. ⁴⁰As it is, you are determined to kill me, a man who has told you the truth that I heard from God. Abraham did not do such things. ⁴¹You are doing the things your own father does."

"We are not illegitimate children," they protested. "The only Father we have is God himself."

The Children of the Devil

⁴²Jesus said to them, "If God were your Father, you would love me, for I came from God and now am here. I have not come on my own; but he sent me. ⁴³Why is my language not clear to you? Because you are unable to hear what I say. ⁴⁴You belong to your father, the devil, and you want to carry out your father's desire. He was a murderer from the beginning, not holding to the truth, for there is no truth in him. When he lies, he speaks his native language, for he is a liar and the father of lies. ⁴⁵Yet because I tell the truth, you do not believe me! ⁴⁶Can any of you prove me guilty of sin? If I am telling the truth, why don't you believe me? ⁴⁷He who belongs to God hears what God says. The reason you do not hear is that you do not belong to God."

The Claims of Jesus About Himself

⁴⁸The Jews answered him, "Aren't we right in saying that you are a Samaritan and demon-possessed?"

⁴⁹"I am not possessed by a demon," said Jesus, "but I honor my Father and you dishonor me. ⁵⁰I am not seeking glory for myself; but there is one who seeks it, and he is the judge. ⁵¹I tell you the truth, if anyone keeps my word, he will never see death."

⁵²At this the Jews exclaimed, "Now we know that you are demon-possessed! Abraham died and so did the prophets, yet you say that if anyone keeps your word, he will never taste death. ⁵³Are you greater than our father Abraham? He died, and so did the prophets. Who do you think you are?"

⁵⁴Jesus replied, "If I glorify myself, my glory means nothing. My Father, whom you claim as your God, is the one who glorifies me. ⁵⁵Though you do not know him, I know him. If I said I did not, I would be a liar like you, but I do know him and keep his word. ⁵⁶Your father Abraham rejoiced at the thought of seeing my day; he saw it and was glad."

⁵⁷"You are not yet fifty years old," the Jews said to him, "and you have seen Abraham!"

⁵⁸"I tell you the truth," Jesus answered, "before Abraham was born, I am!" ⁵⁹At this, they picked up stones to stone him, but Jesus hid himself, slipping away from the temple grounds.

ᵃ 38 Or *presence. Therefore do what you have heard from the Father.*
ᵇ 39 Some early manuscripts *"If you are Abraham's children," said Jesus, "then*

What Makes You, You?

JOHN 8:31–33

Jesus is challenging a group of people whose identity is firmly entrenched in their religious culture. The Pharisees are proudly saying, "We are Abraham's descendants," as if that is all that is needed to be right with God.

Jesus calls us into the identity of being his disciples—into a truth that will set us free. What gives you your identity? A birth certificate or a passport? Your income or your education? A neighborhood or a relationship? Make a list of several aspects of your life that form the basis of your identity. Write the name of Jesus beside each one. Pray over each item on your list and ask that your allegiance to Jesus be the foundation of each aspect of your life.

Owning the Action of Jesus

JOHN 9:1–11,20–22

The Pharisees are hostile to Jesus and what he is doing. As a result, the parents of the blind man are fearful. We would expect them to be thankfully proclaiming that their son can see for the first time! They are afraid to speak up and testify to the power and goodness of the man who performed the miracle.

How free are you to speak of what Jesus has done for you? Whatever your situation, how can you let your gratitude to Jesus be as full as it needs to be? Name any hostile people or forces that you are encountering when you share your faith and bring them into the light of Jesus' redeeming power.

Jesus Heals a Man Born Blind

9 As he went along, he saw a man blind from birth. ²His disciples asked him, "Rabbi, who sinned, this man or his parents, that he was born blind?"

³"Neither this man nor his parents sinned," said Jesus, "but this happened so that the work of God might be displayed in his life. ⁴As long as it is day, we must do the work of him who sent me. Night is coming, when no one can work. ⁵While I am in the world, I am the light of the world."

⁶Having said this, he spit on the ground, made some mud with the saliva, and put it on the man's eyes. ⁷"Go," he told him, "wash in the Pool of Siloam" (this word means Sent). So the man went and washed, and came home seeing.

⁸His neighbors and those who had formerly seen him begging asked, "Isn't this the same man who used to sit and beg?" ⁹Some claimed that he was.

Others said, "No, he only looks like him."

But he himself insisted, "I am the man."

¹⁰"How then were your eyes opened?" they demanded.

¹¹He replied, "The man they call Jesus made some mud and put it on my eyes. He told me to go to Siloam and wash. So I went and washed, and then I could see."

¹²"Where is this man?" they asked him.

"I don't know," he said.

The Pharisees Investigate the Healing

¹³They brought to the Pharisees the man who had been blind. ¹⁴Now the day on which Jesus had made the mud and opened the man's eyes was a Sabbath. ¹⁵Therefore the Pharisees also asked him how he had received his sight. "He put mud on my eyes," the man replied, "and I washed, and now I see."

¹⁶Some of the Pharisees said, "This man is not from God, for he does not keep the Sabbath."

But others asked, "How can a sinner do such miraculous signs?" So they were divided.

¹⁷Finally they turned again to the blind man, "What have you to say about him? It was your eyes he opened."

The man replied, "He is a prophet."

¹⁸The Jews still did not believe that he had been blind and had received his sight until they sent for the man's parents. ¹⁹"Is this your son?" they asked. "Is this the one you say was born blind? How is it that now he can see?"

²⁰"We know he is our son," the parents answered, "and we know he was born blind. ²¹But how he can see now, or who opened his eyes, we don't know. Ask him. He is of age; he will speak for himself." ²²His parents said this because they were afraid of the Jews, for already the Jews had decided that anyone who acknowledged that Jesus was the Christ^a would be put out of the synagogue. ²³That was why his parents said, "He is of age; ask him."

²⁴A second time they summoned the man who had been blind. "Give glory to God,^b" they said. "We know this man is a sinner."

²⁵He replied, "Whether he is a sinner or not, I don't know. One thing I do know. I was blind but now I see!"

²⁶Then they asked him, "What did he do to you? How did he open your eyes?"

^a 22 Or *Messiah*   ^b 24 A solemn charge to tell the truth (see Joshua 7:19)

²⁷He answered, "I have told you already and you did not listen. Why do you want to hear it again? Do you want to become his disciples, too?"

²⁸Then they hurled insults at him and said, "You are this fellow's disciple! We are disciples of Moses! ²⁹We know that God spoke to Moses, but as for this fellow, we don't even know where he comes from."

³⁰The man answered, "Now that is remarkable! You don't know where he comes from, yet he opened my eyes. ³¹We know that God does not listen to sinners. He listens to the godly man who does his will. ³²Nobody has ever heard of opening the eyes of a man born blind. ³³If this man were not from God, he could do nothing."

³⁴To this they replied, "You were steeped in sin at birth; how dare you lecture us!" And they threw him out.

Spiritual Blindness

³⁵Jesus heard that they had thrown him out, and when he found him, he said, "Do you believe in the Son of Man?"

³⁶"Who is he, sir?" the man asked. "Tell me so that I may believe in him."

³⁷Jesus said, "You have now seen him; in fact, he is the one speaking with you."

³⁸Then the man said, "Lord, I believe," and he worshiped him.

³⁹Jesus said, "For judgment I have come into this world, so that the blind will see and those who see will become blind."

⁴⁰Some Pharisees who were with him heard him say this and asked, "What? Are we blind too?"

⁴¹Jesus said, "If you were blind, you would not be guilty of sin; but now that you claim you can see, your guilt remains.

The Shepherd and His Flock

10 "I tell you the truth, the man who does not enter the sheep pen by the gate, but climbs in by some other way, is a thief and a robber. ²The man who enters by the gate is the shepherd of his sheep. ³The watchman opens the gate for him, and the sheep listen to his voice. He calls his own sheep by name and leads them out. ⁴When he has brought out all his own, he goes on ahead of them, and his sheep follow him because they know his voice. ⁵But they will never follow a stranger; in fact, they will run away from him because they do not recognize a stranger's voice." ⁶Jesus used this figure of speech, but they did not understand what he was telling them.

⁷Therefore Jesus said again, "I tell you the truth, I am the gate for the sheep. ⁸All who ever came before me were thieves and robbers, but the sheep did not listen to them. ⁹I am the gate; whoever enters through me will be saved.ᵃ He will come in and go out, and find pasture. ¹⁰The thief comes only to steal and kill and destroy; I have come that they may have life, and have it to the full.

¹¹"I am the good shepherd. The good shepherd lays down his life for the sheep. ¹²The hired hand is not the shepherd who owns the sheep. So when he sees the wolf coming, he abandons the sheep and runs away. Then the wolf attacks the flock and scatters it. ¹³The man runs away because he is a hired hand and cares nothing for the sheep.

¹⁴"I am the good shepherd; I know my sheep and my

"I Was Blind but Now I See!"

JOHN 9:25

Fill a bowl with water. As you sit in a comfortable position, focus your attention on Jesus. Ask him to cover you and fill you with healing light. Ask him to show you some part of your life to which you are blind—perhaps a responsibility you don't see or an attitude that blinds you to the truth of a situation. Ask Jesus to enable you to see what he wants you to see. Wash your eyes with the water, praying that you may see with the eyes of Jesus. Ask Jesus to empower you to take whatever action your renewed spiritual sight requires.

See Meeting God in Prayer

The Good Shepherd

JOHN 10:11–18

Jesus is the Good Shepherd. The shepherd cares for you. He knows your name. He will protect you and guard you from those who want to destroy you. And he knows the path that lies ahead of you.

What is ahead of you right now? With crayon or paint, draw or paint a picture of it. Are you walking into green pastures or dark valleys? Draw Jesus in your picture. Think about the implications of Jesus' presence. Envisioning Jesus ahead of you as you walk, pray about what is happening to you.

See Meeting God in Everyday Life

sheep know me— ¹⁵just as the Father knows me and I know the Father—and I lay down my life for the sheep. ¹⁶I have other sheep that are not of this sheep pen. I must bring them also. They too will listen to my voice, and there shall be one flock and one shepherd. ¹⁷The reason my Father loves me is that I lay down my life—only to take it up again. ¹⁸No one takes it from me, but I lay it down of my own accord. I have authority to lay it down and authority to take it up again. This command I received from my Father."

¹⁹At these words the Jews were again divided. ²⁰Many of them said, "He is demon-possessed and raving mad. Why listen to him?"

²¹But others said, "These are not the sayings of a man possessed by a demon. Can a demon open the eyes of the blind?"

The Unbelief of the Jews

²²Then came the Feast of Dedication[a] at Jerusalem. It was winter, ²³and Jesus was in the temple area walking in Solomon's Colonnade. ²⁴The Jews gathered around him, saying, "How long will you keep us in suspense? If you are the Christ,[b] tell us plainly."

²⁵Jesus answered, "I did tell you, but you do not believe. The miracles I do in my Father's name speak for me, ²⁶but you do not believe because you are not my sheep. ²⁷My sheep listen to my voice; I know them, and they follow me. ²⁸I give them eternal life, and they shall never perish; no one can snatch them out of my hand. ²⁹My Father, who has given them to me, is greater than all[c]; no one can snatch them out of my Father's hand. ³⁰I and the Father are one."

³¹Again the Jews picked up stones to stone him, ³²but Jesus said to them, "I have shown you many great miracles from the Father. For which of these do you stone me?"

³³"We are not stoning you for any of these," replied the Jews, "but for blasphemy, because you, a mere man, claim to be God."

³⁴Jesus answered them, "Is it not written in your Law, 'I have said you are gods'[d]? ³⁵If he called them 'gods,' to whom the word of God came—and the Scripture cannot be broken— ³⁶what about the one whom the Father set apart as his very own and sent into the world? Why then do you accuse me of blasphemy because I said, 'I am God's Son'? ³⁷Do not believe me unless I do what my Father does. ³⁸But if I do it, even though you do not believe me, believe the miracles, that you may know and understand that the Father is in me, and I in the Father." ³⁹Again they tried to seize him, but he escaped their grasp.

⁴⁰Then Jesus went back across the Jordan to the place where John had been baptizing in the early days. Here he stayed ⁴¹and many people came to him. They said, "Though John never performed a miraculous sign, all that John said about this man was true." ⁴²And in that place many believed in Jesus.

The Death of Lazarus

11 Now a man named Lazarus was sick. He was from Bethany, the village of Mary and her sister Martha. ²This Mary, whose brother Lazarus now lay sick, was the

---

a 22 That is, Hanukkah   *b 24* Or *Messiah*   *c 29* Many early manuscripts *What my Father has given me is greater than all*   *d 34* Psalm 82:6

same one who poured perfume on the Lord and wiped his feet with her hair. ³So the sisters sent word to Jesus, "Lord, the one you love is sick."

⁴When he heard this, Jesus said, "This sickness will not end in death. No, it is for God's glory so that God's Son may be glorified through it." ⁵Jesus loved Martha and her sister and Lazarus. ⁶Yet when he heard that Lazarus was sick, he stayed where he was two more days.

⁷Then he said to his disciples, "Let us go back to Judea."

⁸"But Rabbi," they said, "a short while ago the Jews tried to stone you, and yet you are going back there?"

⁹Jesus answered, "Are there not twelve hours of daylight? A man who walks by day will not stumble, for he sees by this world's light. ¹⁰It is when he walks by night that he stumbles, for he has no light."

¹¹After he had said this, he went on to tell them, "Our friend Lazarus has fallen asleep; but I am going there to wake him up."

¹²His disciples replied, "Lord, if he sleeps, he will get better." ¹³Jesus had been speaking of his death, but his disciples thought he meant natural sleep.

¹⁴So then he told them plainly, "Lazarus is dead, ¹⁵and for your sake I am glad I was not there, so that you may believe. But let us go to him."

¹⁶Then Thomas (called Didymus) said to the rest of the disciples, "Let us also go, that we may die with him."

Jesus Comforts the Sisters

¹⁷On his arrival, Jesus found that Lazarus had already been in the tomb for four days. ¹⁸Bethany was less than two miles[a] from Jerusalem, ¹⁹and many Jews had come to Martha and Mary to comfort them in the loss of their brother. ²⁰When Martha heard that Jesus was coming, she went out to meet him, but Mary stayed at home.

²¹"Lord," Martha said to Jesus, "if you had been here, my brother would not have died. ²²But I know that even now God will give you whatever you ask."

²³Jesus said to her, "Your brother will rise again."

²⁴Martha answered, "I know he will rise again in the resurrection at the last day."

²⁵Jesus said to her, "I am the resurrection and the life. He who believes in me will live, even though he dies; ²⁶and whoever lives and believes in me will never die. Do you believe this?"

²⁷"Yes, Lord," she told him, "I believe that you are the Christ,[b] the Son of God, who was to come into the world."

²⁸And after she had said this, she went back and called her sister Mary aside. "The Teacher is here," she said, "and is asking for you." ²⁹When Mary heard this, she got up quickly and went to him. ³⁰Now Jesus had not yet entered the village, but was still at the place where Martha had met him. ³¹When the Jews who had been with Mary in the house, comforting her, noticed how quickly she got up and went out, they followed her, supposing she was going to the tomb to mourn there.

³²When Mary reached the place where Jesus was and saw him, she fell at his feet and said, "Lord, if you had been here, my brother would not have died."

³³When Jesus saw her weeping, and the Jews who had

Resurrection and Life

JOHN 11:21–26

Jesus is "the resurrection and the life." Is your perception of the future determined by the certainty of your death or by your faith in Jesus? Is your life determined by the ability to make life "happen" or by the power of Jesus' presence within you to give you life? Find a quiet place and a quiet moment. Quiet your body and slowly breathe the life of Jesus' presence in. Hold your breath and let your mind and heart say, "Jesus, my life!" Slowly breathe "death" out. Hold your breath and let your mind and heart say, "Jesus, my resurrection!" Repeat these phrases a few times. Let Jesus speak of resurrection and life to you.

See Meeting God in Scripture

Jesus Wept Too

JOHN 11:32–37

Jesus wept too. The Word made flesh knows the pain and the loss that death causes us. He does not minimize our feelings. He knows about our grief and is with us in the midst of it. Through today's newspaper, radio or television broadcast, or personal contact, learn about a situation that is likely to be causing grief to someone. Imagine yourself in that person's place. Grieve alongside him or her. Share that grief with Jesus. With the wings of imagination, go into that situation with Jesus, inviting him to "come and see" (v.34). Ask him to bring his resurrection life and light to the ones who are grieving. Just as Mary and Martha trusted him to know what to do, you trust him too.

See Meeting God in Everyday Life

come along with her also weeping, he was deeply moved in spirit and troubled. [34]"Where have you laid him?" he asked.

"Come and see, Lord," they replied.

[35]Jesus wept.

[36]Then the Jews said, "See how he loved him!"

[37]But some of them said, "Could not he who opened the eyes of the blind man have kept this man from dying?"

Jesus Raises Lazarus From the Dead

[38]Jesus, once more deeply moved, came to the tomb. It was a cave with a stone laid across the entrance. [39]"Take away the stone," he said.

"But, Lord," said Martha, the sister of the dead man, "by this time there is a bad odor, for he has been there four days."

[40]Then Jesus said, "Did I not tell you that if you believed, you would see the glory of God?"

[41]So they took away the stone. Then Jesus looked up and said, "Father, I thank you that you have heard me. [42]I knew that you always hear me, but I said this for the benefit of the people standing here, that they may believe that you sent me."

[43]When he had said this, Jesus called in a loud voice, "Lazarus, come out!" [44]The dead man came out, his hands and feet wrapped with strips of linen, and a cloth around his face.

Jesus said to them, "Take off the grave clothes and let him go."

The Plot to Kill Jesus

[45]Therefore many of the Jews who had come to visit Mary, and had seen what Jesus did, put their faith in him. [46]But some of them went to the Pharisees and told them what Jesus had done. [47]Then the chief priests and the Pharisees called a meeting of the Sanhedrin.

"What are we accomplishing?" they asked. "Here is this man performing many miraculous signs. [48]If we let him go on like this, everyone will believe in him, and then the Romans will come and take away both our place[a] and our nation."

[49]Then one of them, named Caiaphas, who was high priest that year, spoke up, "You know nothing at all! [50]You do not realize that it is better for you that one man die for the people than that the whole nation perish."

[51]He did not say this on his own, but as high priest that year he prophesied that Jesus would die for the Jewish nation, [52]and not only for that nation but also for the scattered children of God, to bring them together and make them one. [53]So from that day on they plotted to take his life.

[54]Therefore Jesus no longer moved about publicly among the Jews. Instead he withdrew to a region near the desert, to a village called Ephraim, where he stayed with his disciples.

[55]When it was almost time for the Jewish Passover, many went up from the country to Jerusalem for their ceremonial cleansing before the Passover. [56]They kept looking for Jesus, and as they stood in the temple area they asked one another, "What do you think? Isn't he coming to the Feast at all?" [57]But the chief priests and Pharisees had given orders that if anyone found out where Jesus was, he should report it so that they might arrest him.

a 48 Or temple

Jesus Anointed at Bethany

12 Six days before the Passover, Jesus arrived at Bethany, where Lazarus lived, whom Jesus had raised from the dead. ²Here a dinner was given in Jesus' honor. Martha served, while Lazarus was among those reclining at the table with him. ³Then Mary took about a pint*ᵃ* of pure nard, an expensive perfume; she poured it on Jesus' feet and wiped his feet with her hair. And the house was filled with the fragrance of the perfume.

⁴But one of his disciples, Judas Iscariot, who was later to betray him, objected, ⁵"Why wasn't this perfume sold and the money given to the poor? It was worth a year's wages.*ᵇ*" ⁶He did not say this because he cared about the poor but because he was a thief; as keeper of the money bag, he used to help himself to what was put into it.

⁷"Leave her alone," Jesus replied. "ₗIt was intendedₗ that she should save this perfume for the day of my burial. ⁸You will always have the poor among you, but you will not always have me."

⁹Meanwhile a large crowd of Jews found out that Jesus was there and came, not only because of him but also to see Lazarus, whom he had raised from the dead. ¹⁰So the chief priests made plans to kill Lazarus as well, ¹¹for on account of him many of the Jews were going over to Jesus and putting their faith in him.

The Triumphal Entry

¹²The next day the great crowd that had come for the Feast heard that Jesus was on his way to Jerusalem. ¹³They took palm branches and went out to meet him, shouting,

"Hosanna!*ᶜ*"

"Blessed is he who comes in the name of the
Lord!"*ᵈ*

"Blessed is the King of Israel!"

¹⁴Jesus found a young donkey and sat upon it, as it is written,

¹⁵"Do not be afraid, O Daughter of Zion;
see, your king is coming,
seated on a donkey's colt."*ᵉ*

¹⁶At first his disciples did not understand all this. Only after Jesus was glorified did they realize that these things had been written about him and that they had done these things to him.

¹⁷Now the crowd that was with him when he called Lazarus from the tomb and raised him from the dead continued to spread the word. ¹⁸Many people, because they had heard that he had given this miraculous sign, went out to meet him. ¹⁹So the Pharisees said to one another, "See, this is getting us nowhere. Look how the whole world has gone after him!"

Jesus Predicts His Death

²⁰Now there were some Greeks among those who went up to worship at the Feast. ²¹They came to Philip, who was from Bethsaida in Galilee, with a request. "Sir," they said,

---

Pouring Out Love

JOHN 12:1–8

Mary anoints Jesus in a grand and extravagant gesture of uninhibited love. Though others criticize her, Jesus accepts her gift and affirms her faith and love. She anoints him with nard, a fragrant ointment, in symbolic preparation for his death—his own gesture of love, a gesture so vast that it will have cosmic repercussions: The Son of God will pour out his life for the forgiveness of sins. What unexpected and extravagant act of love can you perform today? How can you be a gift to others? What can you do that will be a reflection of the love of Jesus?

See Meeting God in Service

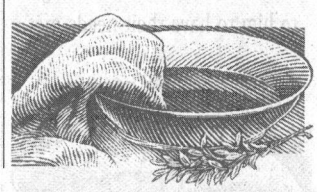

ᵃ 3 Greek *a litra* (probably about 0.5 liter)   *ᵇ 5* Greek *three hundred denarii*
ᶜ 13 A Hebrew expression meaning "Save!" which became an exclamation
of praise   *ᵈ 13* Psalm 118:25,26   *ᵉ 15* Zech. 9:9

That Jesus May Be Seen

JOHN 12:20–26

The Greeks come from a culture with a vast tradition of learning, philosophy and culture. Yet they come to see Jesus because they have needs.

In our own day we have an explosion of information available, but we are also more aware than ever that human need abounds. What human needs seem most urgent in our own day? Take a relaxed position. Breathe in and let your body and mind grow quiet. Imagine you are a sponge, soaking up the life of Jesus into every part of your being. Then pray that Jesus will be "lifted up"(v.32) and so visible in you that others will desire to know him for themselves and will go to him to have their needs met.

See *Meeting God in Service*

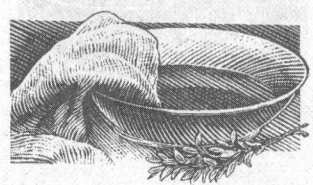

"we would like to see Jesus." 22Philip went to tell Andrew; Andrew and Philip in turn told Jesus.

23Jesus replied, "The hour has come for the Son of Man to be glorified. 24I tell you the truth, unless a kernel of wheat falls to the ground and dies, it remains only a single seed. But if it dies, it produces many seeds. 25The man who loves his life will lose it, while the man who hates his life in this world will keep it for eternal life. 26Whoever serves me must follow me; and where I am, my servant also will be. My Father will honor the one who serves me.

27"Now my heart is troubled, and what shall I say? 'Father, save me from this hour'? No, it was for this very reason I came to this hour. 28Father, glorify your name!"

Then a voice came from heaven, "I have glorified it, and will glorify it again." 29The crowd that was there and heard it said it had thundered; others said an angel had spoken to him.

30Jesus said, "This voice was for your benefit, not mine. 31Now is the time for judgment on this world; now the prince of this world will be driven out. 32But I, when I am lifted up from the earth, will draw all men to myself." 33He said this to show the kind of death he was going to die.

34The crowd spoke up, "We have heard from the Law that the Christ[a] will remain forever, so how can you say, 'The Son of Man must be lifted up'? Who is this 'Son of Man'?"

35Then Jesus told them, "You are going to have the light just a little while longer. Walk while you have the light, before darkness overtakes you. The man who walks in the dark does not know where he is going. 36Put your trust in the light while you have it, so that you may become sons of light." When he had finished speaking, Jesus left and hid himself from them.

The Jews Continue in Their Unbelief

37Even after Jesus had done all these miraculous signs in their presence, they still would not believe in him. 38This was to fulfill the word of Isaiah the prophet:

> "Lord, who has believed our message
> and to whom has the arm of the Lord been
> revealed?"[b]

39For this reason they could not believe, because, as Isaiah says elsewhere:

> 40"He has blinded their eyes
> and deadened their hearts,
> so they can neither see with their eyes,
> nor understand with their hearts,
> nor turn—and I would heal them."[c]

41Isaiah said this because he saw Jesus' glory and spoke about him.

42Yet at the same time many even among the leaders believed in him. But because of the Pharisees they would not confess their faith for fear they would be put out of the synagogue; 43for they loved praise from men more than praise from God.

44Then Jesus cried out, "When a man believes in me, he does not believe in me only, but in the one who sent me. 45When he looks at me, he sees the one who sent me. 46I

a 34 Or *Messiah*   b 38 Isaiah 53:1   c 40 Isaiah 6:10

have come into the world as a light, so that no one who believes in me should stay in darkness.

⁴⁷"As for the person who hears my words but does not keep them, I do not judge him. For I did not come to judge the world, but to save it. ⁴⁸There is a judge for the one who rejects me and does not accept my words; that very word which I spoke will condemn him at the last day. ⁴⁹For I did not speak of my own accord, but the Father who sent me commanded me what to say and how to say it. ⁵⁰I know that his command leads to eternal life. So whatever I say is just what the Father has told me to say."

Jesus Washes His Disciples' Feet

13 It was just before the Passover Feast. Jesus knew that the time had come for him to leave this world and go to the Father. Having loved his own who were in the world, he now showed them the full extent of his love.ᵃ

²The evening meal was being served, and the devil had already prompted Judas Iscariot, son of Simon, to betray Jesus. ³Jesus knew that the Father had put all things under his power, and that he had come from God and was returning to God; ⁴so he got up from the meal, took off his outer clothing, and wrapped a towel around his waist. ⁵After that, he poured water into a basin and began to wash his disciples' feet, drying them with the towel that was wrapped around him.

⁶He came to Simon Peter, who said to him, "Lord, are you going to wash my feet?"

⁷Jesus replied, "You do not realize now what I am doing, but later you will understand."

⁸"No," said Peter, "you shall never wash my feet."

Jesus answered, "Unless I wash you, you have no part with me."

⁹"Then, Lord," Simon Peter replied, "not just my feet but my hands and my head as well!"

¹⁰Jesus answered, "A person who has had a bath needs only to wash his feet; his whole body is clean. And you are clean, though not every one of you." ¹¹For he knew who was going to betray him, and that was why he said not every one was clean.

¹²When he had finished washing their feet, he put on his clothes and returned to his place. "Do you understand what I have done for you?" he asked them. ¹³"You call me 'Teacher' and 'Lord,' and rightly so, for that is what I am. ¹⁴Now that I, your Lord and Teacher, have washed your feet, you also should wash one another's feet. ¹⁵I have set you an example that you should do as I have done for you. ¹⁶I tell you the truth, no servant is greater than his master, nor is a messenger greater than the one who sent him. ¹⁷Now that you know these things, you will be blessed if you do them.

Jesus Predicts His Betrayal

¹⁸"I am not referring to all of you; I know those I have chosen. But this is to fulfill the scripture: 'He who shares my bread has lifted up his heel against me.'ᵇ

¹⁹"I am telling you now before it happens, so that when it does happen you will believe that I am He. ²⁰I tell you the truth, whoever accepts anyone I send accepts me; and whoever accepts me accepts the one who sent me."

Receiving and Giving

JOHN 13:1–20

Like Peter we may resist being served. When someone serves us we feel vulnerable and out of control. Despite our self-sufficiency and our need for control, Jesus wants to serve us—not just in order to benefit us, but also to show us how to serve others. Can you name something Jesus has done for you? Write about it or paint a representation of it. Discover the safety, love and grace within Jesus' service. Go and perform an act of loving service for another person. Celebrate the fact that when someone receives your service, Jesus is received also.

See Meeting God in the Created Order

ᵃ 1 Or *he loved them to the last*   ᵇ 18 Psalm 41:9

Love in Action

JOHN 13:34

"God also showed me that any 'love' for him meant *nothing* unless I was truly able to love from my heart my brother or sister in Christ. As the Lord put various names into my mind I began to write letters to about twelve people asking for forgiveness for hurting them, for still being inwardly angry against them—or whatever. It was the most painful pruning and purging I can remember in my entire Christian life. But fruitful! Already some replies to my letters have reduced me to tears!"

—DAVID WATSON,
Fear No Evil

21 After he had said this, Jesus was troubled in spirit and testified, "I tell you the truth, one of you is going to betray me."

22 His disciples stared at one another, at a loss to know which of them he meant. 23 One of them, the disciple whom Jesus loved, was reclining next to him. 24 Simon Peter motioned to this disciple and said, "Ask him which one he means."

25 Leaning back against Jesus, he asked him, "Lord, who is it?"

26 Jesus answered, "It is the one to whom I will give this piece of bread when I have dipped it in the dish." Then, dipping the piece of bread, he gave it to Judas Iscariot, son of Simon. 27 As soon as Judas took the bread, Satan entered into him.

"What you are about to do, do quickly," Jesus told him, 28 but no one at the meal understood why Jesus said this to him. 29 Since Judas had charge of the money, some thought Jesus was telling him to buy what was needed for the Feast, or to give something to the poor. 30 As soon as Judas had taken the bread, he went out. And it was night.

Jesus Predicts Peter's Denial

31 When he was gone, Jesus said, "Now is the Son of Man glorified and God is glorified in him. 32 If God is glorified in him,[a] God will glorify the Son in himself, and will glorify him at once.

33 "My children, I will be with you only a little longer. You will look for me, and just as I told the Jews, so I tell you now: Where I am going, you cannot come.

34 "A new command I give you: Love one another. As I have loved you, so you must love one another. 35 By this all men will know that you are my disciples, if you love one another."

36 Simon Peter asked him, "Lord, where are you going?"

Jesus replied, "Where I am going, you cannot follow now, but you will follow later."

37 Peter asked, "Lord, why can't I follow you now? I will lay down my life for you."

38 Then Jesus answered, "Will you really lay down your life for me? I tell you the truth, before the rooster crows, you will disown me three times!

Jesus Comforts His Disciples

14 "Do not let your hearts be troubled. Trust in God[b]; trust also in me. 2 In my Father's house are many rooms; if it were not so, I would have told you. I am going there to prepare a place for you. 3 And if I go and prepare a place for you, I will come back and take you to be with me that you also may be where I am. 4 You know the way to the place where I am going."

Jesus the Way to the Father

5 Thomas said to him, "Lord, we don't know where you are going, so how can we know the way?"

6 Jesus answered, "I am the way and the truth and the life. No one comes to the Father except through me. 7 If you really knew me, you would know[c] my Father as well. From now on, you do know him and have seen him."

---

a 32 Many early manuscripts do not have *If God is glorified in him.* *b 1* Or *You trust in God* *c 7* Some early manuscripts *If you really have known me, you will know*

⁸Philip said, "Lord, show us the Father and that will be enough for us."

⁹Jesus answered: "Don't you know me, Philip, even after I have been among you such a long time? Anyone who has seen me has seen the Father. How can you say, 'Show us the Father'? ¹⁰Don't you believe that I am in the Father, and that the Father is in me? The words I say to you are not just my own. Rather, it is the Father, living in me, who is doing his work. ¹¹Believe me when I say that I am in the Father and the Father is in me; or at least believe on the evidence of the miracles themselves. ¹²I tell you the truth, anyone who has faith in me will do what I have been doing. He will do even greater things than these, because I am going to the Father. ¹³And I will do whatever you ask in my name, so that the Son may bring glory to the Father. ¹⁴You may ask me for anything in my name, and I will do it.

Jesus Promises the Holy Spirit

¹⁵"If you love me, you will obey what I command. ¹⁶And I will ask the Father, and he will give you another Counselor to be with you forever— ¹⁷the Spirit of truth. The world cannot accept him, because it neither sees him nor knows him. But you know him, for he lives with you and will be*ᵃ* in you. ¹⁸I will not leave you as orphans; I will come to you. ¹⁹Before long, the world will not see me anymore, but you will see me. Because I live, you also will live. ²⁰On that day you will realize that I am in my Father, and you are in me, and I am in you. ²¹Whoever has my commands and obeys them, he is the one who loves me. He who loves me will be loved by my Father, and I too will love him and show myself to him."

²²Then Judas (not Judas Iscariot) said, "But, Lord, why do you intend to show yourself to us and not to the world?"

²³Jesus replied, "If anyone loves me, he will obey my teaching. My Father will love him, and we will come to him and make our home with him. ²⁴He who does not love me will not obey my teaching. These words you hear are not my own; they belong to the Father who sent me.

²⁵"All this I have spoken while still with you. ²⁶But the Counselor, the Holy Spirit, whom the Father will send in my name, will teach you all things and will remind you of everything I have said to you. ²⁷Peace I leave with you; my peace I give you. I do not give to you as the world gives. Do not let your hearts be troubled and do not be afraid.

²⁸"You heard me say, 'I am going away and I am coming back to you.' If you loved me, you would be glad that I am going to the Father, for the Father is greater than I. ²⁹I have told you now before it happens, so that when it does happen you will believe. ³⁰I will not speak with you much longer, for the prince of this world is coming. He has no hold on me, ³¹but the world must learn that I love the Father and that I do exactly what my Father has commanded me.

"Come now; let us leave.

The Vine and the Branches

15 "I am the true vine, and my Father is the gardener. ²He cuts off every branch in me that bears no fruit, while every branch that does bear fruit he prunes*ᵇ* so that

---

ᵃ 17 Some early manuscripts *and is*   ᵇ 2 The Greek for *prunes* also means *cleans.*

Troubles and Trust

JOHN 14:1

"Do not let your hearts be troubled." Jesus is saying we can trust him. He is telling us to "believe" in God—not a generic "god" but "the Father" to whom he leads us. We make a choice to trust him and the Father to bear our troubles for us.

So what is troubling you? Feel the intensity of that problem. Listen to its demands. Face its immensity and offer it in complete abandonment to God. Pray, "Lord, I choose you." Take the prayer with you and repeat it many times. Let God shoulder your trouble. Jesus is promising that you will not be orphaned and left to face your troubles alone.

See Meeting God in Prayer

Bearing Fruit

JOHN 15:1–5

Draw a vine. Watch each branch grow under your pencil. Note that no branch is more important than another. Each branch is dependent on the main stem. Let your vine do what vines are supposed to do, and draw some fruit growing from the branch that passes on all the necessary nutrients from the vine. Grounded in the self-giving love of Jesus, the true vine, talk with other people in your faith community about an action you can take together that will show love as visibly as fruit.

See Meeting God in Service

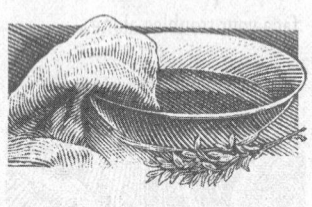

it will be even more fruitful. ³You are already clean because of the word I have spoken to you. ⁴Remain in me, and I will remain in you. No branch can bear fruit by itself; it must remain in the vine. Neither can you bear fruit unless you remain in me.

⁵"I am the vine; you are the branches. If a man remains in me and I in him, he will bear much fruit; apart from me you can do nothing. ⁶If anyone does not remain in me, he is like a branch that is thrown away and withers; such branches are picked up, thrown into the fire and burned. ⁷If you remain in me and my words remain in you, ask whatever you wish, and it will be given you. ⁸This is to my Father's glory, that you bear much fruit, showing yourselves to be my disciples.

⁹"As the Father has loved me, so have I loved you. Now remain in my love. ¹⁰If you obey my commands, you will remain in my love, just as I have obeyed my Father's commands and remain in his love. ¹¹I have told you this so that my joy may be in you and that your joy may be complete. ¹²My command is this: Love each other as I have loved you. ¹³Greater love has no one than this, that he lay down his life for his friends. ¹⁴You are my friends if you do what I command. ¹⁵I no longer call you servants, because a servant does not know his master's business. Instead, I have called you friends, for everything that I learned from my Father I have made known to you. ¹⁶You did not choose me, but I chose you and appointed you to go and bear fruit—fruit that will last. Then the Father will give you whatever you ask in my name. ¹⁷This is my command: Love each other.

The World Hates the Disciples

¹⁸"If the world hates you, keep in mind that it hated me first. ¹⁹If you belonged to the world, it would love you as its own. As it is, you do not belong to the world, but I have chosen you out of the world. That is why the world hates you. ²⁰Remember the words I spoke to you: 'No servant is greater than his master.'ᵃ If they persecuted me, they will persecute you also. If they obeyed my teaching, they will obey yours also. ²¹They will treat you this way because of my name, for they do not know the One who sent me. ²²If I had not come and spoken to them, they would not be guilty of sin. Now, however, they have no excuse for their sin. ²³He who hates me hates my Father as well. ²⁴If I had not done among them what no one else did, they would not be guilty of sin. But now they have seen these miracles, and yet they have hated both me and my Father. ²⁵But this is to fulfill what is written in their Law: 'They hated me without reason.'ᵇ

²⁶"When the Counselor comes, whom I will send to you from the Father, the Spirit of truth who goes out from the Father, he will testify about me. ²⁷And you also must testify, for you have been with me from the beginning.

16 "All this I have told you so that you will not go astray. ²They will put you out of the synagogue; in fact, a time is coming when anyone who kills you will think he is offering a service to God. ³They will do such things because they have not known the Father or me. ⁴I have told you this, so that when the time comes you will remember that I warned you. I did not tell you this at first because I was with you.

ᵃ *20* John 13:16 ᵇ *25* Psalms 35:19; 69:4

The Work of the Holy Spirit

5"Now I am going to him who sent me, yet none of you asks me, 'Where are you going?' 6Because I have said these things, you are filled with grief. 7But I tell you the truth: It is for your good that I am going away. Unless I go away, the Counselor will not come to you; but if I go, I will send him to you. 8When he comes, he will convict the world of guilt[a] in regard to sin and righteousness and judgment: 9in regard to sin, because men do not believe in me; 10in regard to righteousness, because I am going to the Father, where you can see me no longer; 11and in regard to judgment, because the prince of this world now stands condemned.

12"I have much more to say to you, more than you can now bear. 13But when he, the Spirit of truth, comes, he will guide you into all truth. He will not speak on his own; he will speak only what he hears, and he will tell you what is yet to come. 14He will bring glory to me by taking from what is mine and making it known to you. 15All that belongs to the Father is mine. That is why I said the Spirit will take from what is mine and make it known to you.

16"In a little while you will see me no more, and then after a little while you will see me."

The Disciples' Grief Will Turn to Joy

17Some of his disciples said to one another, "What does he mean by saying, 'In a little while you will see me no more, and then after a little while you will see me,' and 'Because I am going to the Father'?" 18They kept asking, "What does he mean by 'a little while'? We don't understand what he is saying."

19Jesus saw that they wanted to ask him about this, so he said to them, "Are you asking one another what I meant when I said, 'In a little while you will see me no more, and then after a little while you will see me'? 20I tell you the truth, you will weep and mourn while the world rejoices. You will grieve, but your grief will turn to joy. 21A woman giving birth to a child has pain because her time has come; but when her baby is born she forgets the anguish because of her joy that a child is born into the world. 22So with you: Now is your time of grief, but I will see you again and you will rejoice, and no one will take away your joy. 23In that day you will no longer ask me anything. I tell you the truth, my Father will give you whatever you ask in my name. 24Until now you have not asked for anything in my name. Ask and you will receive, and your joy will be complete.

25"Though I have been speaking figuratively, a time is coming when I will no longer use this kind of language but will tell you plainly about my Father. 26In that day you will ask in my name. I am not saying that I will ask the Father on your behalf. 27No, the Father himself loves you because you have loved me and have believed that I came from God. 28I came from the Father and entered the world; now I am leaving the world and going back to the Father."

29Then Jesus' disciples said, "Now you are speaking clearly and without figures of speech. 30Now we can see that you know all things and that you do not even need to have anyone ask you questions. This makes us believe that you came from God."

Dare to Be Different

JOHN 15:18–27

Jesus is referring to "the world" as a force opposed to him—a force that hates him and will hate his followers by association. Jesus and his followers are in many ways "countercultural." In what ways are you different from "the world"? How much do you participate in the world's games of "achieve, succeed and win"? Talk with others about how your church can be an "alternative community" controlled by God's love. Ask the Spirit to help you and your faith community pray for your church and for the world. Agree on a way in which you can focus your prayer for the next week.

See Meeting God in Community

---

a 8 Or *will expose the guilt of the world*

Pray Boldly

JOHN 16:23–33

We are called to pray boldly. With the kind of fervent prayer that brought down the Iron Curtain or the Berlin Wall, ask of the Father, in Jesus' name, that his power will overcome political corruption, economic bondage, pedophilia, terrorism or whatever problem God's love requires you to address. Pray against despair and discouragement in spite of the evidence of the power of evil, "for the Father himself loves you" (v.27). With holy imagination, see more "iron curtains" falling.

See Meeting God in Prayer

[31] "You believe at last!"[a] Jesus answered. [32] "But a time is coming, and has come, when you will be scattered, each to his own home. You will leave me all alone. Yet I am not alone, for my Father is with me.

[33] "I have told you these things, so that in me you may have peace. In this world you will have trouble. But take heart! I have overcome the world."

Jesus Prays for Himself

17 After Jesus said this, he looked toward heaven and prayed:

"Father, the time has come. Glorify your Son, that your Son may glorify you. [2] For you granted him authority over all people that he might give eternal life to all those you have given him. [3] Now this is eternal life: that they may know you, the only true God, and Jesus Christ, whom you have sent. [4] I have brought you glory on earth by completing the work you gave me to do. [5] And now, Father, glorify me in your presence with the glory I had with you before the world began.

Jesus Prays for His Disciples

[6] "I have revealed you[b] to those whom you gave me out of the world. They were yours; you gave them to me and they have obeyed your word. [7] Now they know that everything you have given me comes from you. [8] For I gave them the words you gave me and they accepted them. They knew with certainty that I came from you, and they believed that you sent me. [9] I pray for them. I am not praying for the world, but for those you have given me, for they are yours. [10] All I have is yours, and all you have is mine. And glory has come to me through them. [11] I will remain in the world no longer, but they are still in the world, and I am coming to you. Holy Father, protect them by the power of your name—the name you gave me—so that they may be one as we are one. [12] While I was with them, I protected them and kept them safe by that name you gave me. None has been lost except the one doomed to destruction so that Scripture would be fulfilled.

[13] "I am coming to you now, but I say these things while I am still in the world, so that they may have the full measure of my joy within them. [14] I have given them your word and the world has hated them, for they are not of the world any more than I am of the world. [15] My prayer is not that you take them out of the world but that you protect them from the evil one. [16] They are not of the world, even as I am not of it. [17] Sanctify[c] them by the truth; your word is truth. [18] As you sent me into the world, I have sent them into the world. [19] For them I sanctify myself, that they too may be truly sanctified.

Jesus Prays for All Believers

[20] "My prayer is not for them alone. I pray also for those who will believe in me through their message, [21] that all of them may be one, Father, just as you are in me and I am in you. May they also be in us so that the

---

[a] 31 Or *"Do you now believe?"*   [b] 6 Greek *your name*; also in verse 26
[c] 17 Greek *hagiazo* (set apart for sacred use or make holy); also in verse 19

world may believe that you have sent me. ²¹I have given them the glory that you gave me, that they may be one as we are one: ²³I in them and you in me. May they be brought to complete unity to let the world know that you sent me and have loved them even as you have loved me.

²⁴"Father, I want those you have given me to be with me where I am, and to see my glory, the glory you have given me because you loved me before the creation of the world.

²⁵"Righteous Father, though the world does not know you, I know you, and they know that you have sent me. ²⁶I have made you known to them, and will continue to make you known in order that the love you have for me may be in them and that I myself may be in them."

Jesus Arrested

18 When he had finished praying, Jesus left with his disciples and crossed the Kidron Valley. On the other side there was an olive grove, and he and his disciples went into it.

²Now Judas, who betrayed him, knew the place, because Jesus had often met there with his disciples. ³So Judas came to the grove, guiding a detachment of soldiers and some officials from the chief priests and Pharisees. They were carrying torches, lanterns and weapons.

⁴Jesus, knowing all that was going to happen to him, went out and asked them, "Who is it you want?"

⁵"Jesus of Nazareth," they replied.

"I am he," Jesus said. (And Judas the traitor was standing there with them.) ⁶When Jesus said, "I am he," they drew back and fell to the ground.

⁷Again he asked them, "Who is it you want?"

And they said, "Jesus of Nazareth."

⁸"I told you that I am he," Jesus answered. "If you are looking for me, then let these men go." ⁹This happened so that the words he had spoken would be fulfilled: "I have not lost one of those you gave me."ᵃ

¹⁰Then Simon Peter, who had a sword, drew it and struck the high priest's servant, cutting off his right ear. (The servant's name was Malchus.)

¹¹Jesus commanded Peter, "Put your sword away! Shall I not drink the cup the Father has given me?"

Jesus Taken to Annas

¹²Then the detachment of soldiers with its commander and the Jewish officials arrested Jesus. They bound him ¹³and brought him first to Annas, who was the father-in-law of Caiaphas, the high priest that year. ¹⁴Caiaphas was the one who had advised the Jews that it would be good if one man died for the people.

Peter's First Denial

¹⁵Simon Peter and another disciple were following Jesus. Because this disciple was known to the high priest, he went with Jesus into the high priest's courtyard, ¹⁶but Peter had to wait outside at the door. The other disciple, who was known to the high priest, came back, spoke to the girl on duty there and brought Peter in.

ᵃ 9 John 6:39

In Unity

JOHN 17:20–23

This is no typical deathbed prayer Jesus is praying. Jesus is praying for unity with God, asking the Father to make believers one as he and the Father are one. And Jesus is praying for his followers' oneness with him and with the Father.

Unity may be hard for us to achieve, but the glory of God is visible when we live in unity. When we do, the death-defying life of God is expressed. In what ways might you be experiencing disunity? Ask God to show you what actions you will need to take. Carry within your mind a picture of Jesus praying for unity.

See Meeting God in Community

Are You With Him?

JOHN 18:17

We are quick to point out and condemn the evil we see in Judas. But Peter? His betrayal is even more disturbing, perhaps because it is generated by Peter's need for self-preservation, a trait we recognize in ourselves. His loyalty to Jesus is requiring much more of him than he is prepared to give up—his safety and security.

Is there someone in your school, your workplace or your family who is asking something like, "You are not one of his disciples, are you?" What is your reply? Find an object that might symbolize your reply. What color is it? What properties does it have? When you are ready, speak to Jesus about your reflections.

See Meeting God in Scripture

17"You are not one of his disciples, are you?" the girl at the door asked Peter.

He replied, "I am not."

18It was cold, and the servants and officials stood around a fire they had made to keep warm. Peter also was standing with them, warming himself.

The High Priest Questions Jesus

19Meanwhile, the high priest questioned Jesus about his disciples and his teaching.

20"I have spoken openly to the world," Jesus replied. "I always taught in synagogues or at the temple, where all the Jews come together. I said nothing in secret. 21Why question me? Ask those who heard me. Surely they know what I said."

22When Jesus said this, one of the officials nearby struck him in the face. "Is this the way you answer the high priest?" he demanded.

23"If I said something wrong," Jesus replied, "testify as to what is wrong. But if I spoke the truth, why did you strike me?" 24Then Annas sent him, still bound, to Caiaphas the high priest.[a]

Peter's Second and Third Denials

25As Simon Peter stood warming himself, he was asked, "You are not one of his disciples, are you?"

He denied it, saying, "I am not."

26One of the high priest's servants, a relative of the man whose ear Peter had cut off, challenged him, "Didn't I see you with him in the olive grove?" 27Again Peter denied it, and at that moment a rooster began to crow.

Jesus Before Pilate

28Then the Jews led Jesus from Caiaphas to the palace of the Roman governor. By now it was early morning, and to avoid ceremonial uncleanness the Jews did not enter the palace; they wanted to be able to eat the Passover. 29So Pilate came out to them and asked, "What charges are you bringing against this man?"

30"If he were not a criminal," they replied, "we would not have handed him over to you."

31Pilate said, "Take him yourselves and judge him by your own law."

"But we have no right to execute anyone," the Jews objected. 32This happened so that the words Jesus had spoken indicating the kind of death he was going to die would be fulfilled.

33Pilate then went back inside the palace, summoned Jesus and asked him, "Are you the king of the Jews?"

34"Is that your own idea," Jesus asked, "or did others talk to you about me?"

35"Am I a Jew?" Pilate replied. "It was your people and your chief priests who handed you over to me. What is it you have done?"

36Jesus said, "My kingdom is not of this world. If it were, my servants would fight to prevent my arrest by the Jews. But now my kingdom is from another place."

37"You are a king, then!" said Pilate.

Jesus answered, "You are right in saying I am a king. In

a 24 Or (Now Annas had sent him, still bound, to Caiaphas the high priest.)

fact, for this reason I was born, and for this I came into the world, to testify to the truth. Everyone on the side of truth listens to me."

[38]"What is truth?" Pilate asked. With this he went out again to the Jews and said, "I find no basis for a charge against him. [39]But it is your custom for me to release to you one prisoner at the time of the Passover. Do you want me to release 'the king of the Jews'?"

[40]They shouted back, "No, not him! Give us Barabbas!" Now Barabbas had taken part in a rebellion.

Jesus Sentenced to Be Crucified

19 Then Pilate took Jesus and had him flogged. [2]The soldiers twisted together a crown of thorns and put it on his head. They clothed him in a purple robe [3]and went up to him again and again, saying, "Hail, king of the Jews!" And they struck him in the face.

[4]Once more Pilate came out and said to the Jews, "Look, I am bringing him out to you to let you know that I find no basis for a charge against him." [5]When Jesus came out wearing the crown of thorns and the purple robe, Pilate said to them, "Here is the man!"

[6]As soon as the chief priests and their officials saw him, they shouted, "Crucify! Crucify!"

But Pilate answered, "You take him and crucify him. As for me, I find no basis for a charge against him."

[7]The Jews insisted, "We have a law, and according to that law he must die, because he claimed to be the Son of God."

[8]When Pilate heard this, he was even more afraid, [9]and he went back inside the palace. "Where do you come from?" he asked Jesus, but Jesus gave him no answer. [10]"Do you refuse to speak to me?" Pilate said. "Don't you realize I have power either to free you or to crucify you?"

[11]Jesus answered, "You would have no power over me if it were not given to you from above. Therefore the one who handed me over to you is guilty of a greater sin."

[12]From then on, Pilate tried to set Jesus free, but the Jews kept shouting, "If you let this man go, you are no friend of Caesar. Anyone who claims to be a king opposes Caesar."

[13]When Pilate heard this, he brought Jesus out and sat down on the judge's seat at a place known as the Stone Pavement (which in Aramaic is Gabbatha). [14]It was the day of Preparation of Passover Week, about the sixth hour.

"Here is your king," Pilate said to the Jews.

[15]But they shouted, "Take him away! Take him away! Crucify him!"

"Shall I crucify your king?" Pilate asked.

"We have no king but Caesar," the chief priests answered.

[16]Finally Pilate handed him over to them to be crucified.

The Crucifixion

So the soldiers took charge of Jesus. [17]Carrying his own cross, he went out to the place of the Skull (which in Aramaic is called Golgotha). [18]Here they crucified him, and with him two others—one on each side and Jesus in the middle.

[19]Pilate had a notice prepared and fastened to the cross. It read: JESUS OF NAZARETH, THE KING OF THE JEWS. [20]Many of the Jews read this sign, for the place where Jesus was crucified was near the city, and the sign was written in Aramaic, Latin and Greek. [21]The chief priests of the Jews protested to

Here Is Your King

JOHN 19:1–15

Jesus is dressed in purple and wearing a crown that mocks him rather than honors him. Though Jesus looks nothing like royalty, Pilate says cynically, "Here is your king!" The tragedy of this moment is not only Jesus' impending death but that the people fail to recognize God in Jesus Christ.

Will you recognize your King today? Jesus may be in the child who needs you to listen to her troubles. Jesus may be in the neighbor who needs a ride to the doctor's office. Jesus may be in the person being shouted at and abused, for whom you might intervene. Ask Jesus to give you the vision to see him today. Ask for the grace to see Jesus in the people you meet so that you may serve your God and King (see Matthew 25:31–46).

See Meeting God in Worship

Jesus in the Hour of Death

JOHN 19:28–30

In great dignity, and in the serenity of complete trust, Jesus dies. The blood spilled, like the blood of the Passover lamb, is for our deliverance—the ultimate act of a heart generous with the fullness of God's love.

Pray for those who are dying. Pray for those who are dying for lack of love. Pray for yourself in the hour of your death. And in the presence of a love "so amazing, so divine," with confidence in your voice, sing:

> "When I tread the verge of
> Jordan,
> bid my anxious fears
> subside;
> death of death and hell's
> destruction,
> land me safe on Canaan's
> side.
> Songs of praises, songs of
> praises,
> I will ever sing to you; I will
> ever sing to you."
> —HARRY EMERSON FOSDICK,
> "Guide Me, O Thou Great Jehovah"

See *Meeting God in Worship*

Pilate, "Do not write 'The King of the Jews,' but that this man claimed to be king of the Jews."

²²Pilate answered, "What I have written, I have written."

²³When the soldiers crucified Jesus, they took his clothes, dividing them into four shares, one for each of them, with the undergarment remaining. This garment was seamless, woven in one piece from top to bottom.

²⁴"Let's not tear it," they said to one another. "Let's decide by lot who will get it."

This happened that the scripture might be fulfilled which said,

> "They divided my garments among them
> and cast lots for my clothing."*a*

So this is what the soldiers did.

²⁵Near the cross of Jesus stood his mother, his mother's sister, Mary the wife of Clopas, and Mary Magdalene. ²⁶When Jesus saw his mother there, and the disciple whom he loved standing nearby, he said to his mother, "Dear woman, here is your son," ²⁷and to the disciple, "Here is your mother." From that time on, this disciple took her into his home.

The Death of Jesus

²⁸Later, knowing that all was now completed, and so that the Scripture would be fulfilled, Jesus said, "I am thirsty." ²⁹A jar of wine vinegar was there, so they soaked a sponge in it, put the sponge on a stalk of the hyssop plant, and lifted it to Jesus' lips. ³⁰When he had received the drink, Jesus said, "It is finished." With that, he bowed his head and gave up his spirit.

³¹Now it was the day of Preparation, and the next day was to be a special Sabbath. Because the Jews did not want the bodies left on the crosses during the Sabbath, they asked Pilate to have the legs broken and the bodies taken down. ³²The soldiers therefore came and broke the legs of the first man who had been crucified with Jesus, and then those of the other. ³³But when they came to Jesus and found that he was already dead, they did not break his legs. ³⁴Instead, one of the soldiers pierced Jesus' side with a spear, bringing a sudden flow of blood and water. ³⁵The man who saw it has given testimony, and his testimony is true. He knows that he tells the truth, and he testifies so that you also may believe. ³⁶These things happened so that the scripture would be fulfilled: "Not one of his bones will be broken,"*b* ³⁷and, as another scripture says, "They will look on the one they have pierced."*c*

The Burial of Jesus

³⁸Later, Joseph of Arimathea asked Pilate for the body of Jesus. Now Joseph was a disciple of Jesus, but secretly because he feared the Jews. With Pilate's permission, he came and took the body away. ³⁹He was accompanied by Nicodemus, the man who earlier had visited Jesus at night. Nicodemus brought a mixture of myrrh and aloes, about seventy-five pounds.*d* ⁴⁰Taking Jesus' body, the two of them wrapped it, with the spices, in strips of linen. This was in accordance with Jewish burial customs. ⁴¹At the place

a 24 Psalm 22:18   *b 36* Exodus 12:46; Num. 9:12; Psalm 34:20   *c 37* Zech. 12:10   *d 39* Greek *a hundred litrai* (about 34 kilograms)

where Jesus was crucified, there was a garden, and in the garden a new tomb, in which no one had ever been laid. ⁴²Because it was the Jewish day of Preparation and since the tomb was nearby, they laid Jesus there.

The Empty Tomb

20 Early on the first day of the week, while it was still dark, Mary Magdalene went to the tomb and saw that the stone had been removed from the entrance. ²So she came running to Simon Peter and the other disciple, the one Jesus loved, and said, "They have taken the Lord out of the tomb, and we don't know where they have put him!"

³So Peter and the other disciple started for the tomb. ⁴Both were running, but the other disciple outran Peter and reached the tomb first. ⁵He bent over and looked in at the strips of linen lying there but did not go in. ⁶Then Simon Peter, who was behind him, arrived and went into the tomb. He saw the strips of linen lying there, ⁷as well as the burial cloth that had been around Jesus' head. The cloth was folded up by itself, separate from the linen. ⁸Finally the other disciple, who had reached the tomb first, also went inside. He saw and believed. ⁹(They still did not understand from Scripture that Jesus had to rise from the dead.)

Jesus Appears to Mary Magdalene

¹⁰Then the disciples went back to their homes, ¹¹but Mary stood outside the tomb crying. As she wept, she bent over to look into the tomb ¹²and saw two angels in white, seated where Jesus' body had been, one at the head and the other at the foot.

¹³They asked her, "Woman, why are you crying?"

"They have taken my Lord away," she said, "and I don't know where they have put him." ¹⁴At this, she turned around and saw Jesus standing there, but she did not realize that it was Jesus.

¹⁵"Woman," he said, "why are you crying? Who is it you are looking for?"

Thinking he was the gardener, she said, "Sir, if you have carried him away, tell me where you have put him, and I will get him."

¹⁶Jesus said to her, "Mary."

She turned toward him and cried out in Aramaic, "Rabboni!" (which means Teacher).

¹⁷Jesus said, "Do not hold on to me, for I have not yet returned to the Father. Go instead to my brothers and tell them, 'I am returning to my Father and your Father, to my God and your God.' "

¹⁸Mary Magdalene went to the disciples with the news: "I have seen the Lord!" And she told them that he had said these things to her.

Jesus Appears to His Disciples

¹⁹On the evening of that first day of the week, when the disciples were together, with the doors locked for fear of the Jews, Jesus came and stood among them and said, "Peace be with you!" ²⁰After he said this, he showed them his hands and side. The disciples were overjoyed when they saw the Lord.

²¹Again Jesus said, "Peace be with you! As the Father has sent me, I am sending you." ²²And with that he breathed

He Speaks Your Name

JOHN 20:1–18

Joseph of Arimathea offers a tomb for Jesus' body. Nicodemus says his good-bye to Jesus with a generous gift of burial spices (see 19:38–40). Peter and John (the "other disciple") see an empty tomb with the linen burial cloths "folded up". Mary weeps before the gardener—until he says her name!

Jesus, the risen One, knows your name too. Be very still and use every one of your senses. Listen as Jesus says your name. Listen. Sense, think and feel what it means for you to hear Jesus say your name.

See Meeting God in Scripture

1437

He Knows What We Need

JOHN 20:24-29

We are sometimes scornful of Thomas, giving him the nickname "doubting Thomas." But he is not unlike many of us. He needs the data. He needs the visuals. He needs to touch Jesus' wounds in order for his faith to take root and grow. Jesus accepts that. He knows what we need.

What do you need from Jesus in order for your faith to bloom? Write it down. Say it aloud. Tell another person perhaps. Tell Jesus. And wait, watch and wonder.

See Meeting God in Worship

on them and said, "Receive the Holy Spirit. ²³If you forgive anyone his sins, they are forgiven; if you do not forgive them, they are not forgiven."

Jesus Appears to Thomas

²⁴Now Thomas (called Didymus), one of the Twelve, was not with the disciples when Jesus came. ²⁵So the other disciples told him, "We have seen the Lord!"

But he said to them, "Unless I see the nail marks in his hands and put my finger where the nails were, and put my hand into his side, I will not believe it."

²⁶A week later his disciples were in the house again, and Thomas was with them. Though the doors were locked, Jesus came and stood among them and said, "Peace be with you!" ²⁷Then he said to Thomas, "Put your finger here; see my hands. Reach out your hand and put it into my side. Stop doubting and believe."

²⁸Thomas said to him, "My Lord and my God!"

²⁹Then Jesus told him, "Because you have seen me, you have believed; blessed are those who have not seen and yet have believed."

³⁰Jesus did many other miraculous signs in the presence of his disciples, which are not recorded in this book. ³¹But these are written that you may^a believe that Jesus is the Christ, the Son of God, and that by believing you may have life in his name.

Jesus and the Miraculous Catch of Fish

21 Afterward Jesus appeared again to his disciples, by the Sea of Tiberias.^{b} It happened this way: ²Simon Peter, Thomas (called Didymus), Nathanael from Cana in Galilee, the sons of Zebedee, and two other disciples were together. ³"I'm going out to fish," Simon Peter told them, and they said, "We'll go with you." So they went out and got into the boat, but that night they caught nothing.

⁴Early in the morning, Jesus stood on the shore, but the disciples did not realize that it was Jesus.

⁵He called out to them, "Friends, haven't you any fish?"

"No," they answered.

⁶He said, "Throw your net on the right side of the boat and you will find some." When they did, they were unable to haul the net in because of the large number of fish.

⁷Then the disciple whom Jesus loved said to Peter, "It is the Lord!" As soon as Simon Peter heard him say, "It is the Lord," he wrapped his outer garment around him (for he had taken it off) and jumped into the water. ⁸The other disciples followed in the boat, towing the net full of fish, for they were not far from shore, about a hundred yards.^{c} ⁹When they landed, they saw a fire of burning coals there with fish on it, and some bread.

¹⁰Jesus said to them, "Bring some of the fish you have just caught."

¹¹Simon Peter climbed aboard and dragged the net ashore. It was full of large fish, 153, but even with so many the net was not torn. ¹²Jesus said to them, "Come and have breakfast." None of the disciples dared ask him, "Who are you?" They knew it was the Lord. ¹³Jesus came, took the bread and gave it to them, and did the same with the fish.

^{a} 31 Some manuscripts *may continue to* ^{b} 1 That is, Sea of Galilee
^{c} 8 Greek *about two hundred cubits* (about 90 meters)

¹⁴This was now the third time Jesus appeared to his disciples after he was raised from the dead.

Jesus Reinstates Peter

¹⁵When they had finished eating, Jesus said to Simon Peter, "Simon son of John, do you truly love me more than these?"

"Yes, Lord," he said, "you know that I love you."

Jesus said, "Feed my lambs."

¹⁶Again Jesus said, "Simon son of John, do you truly love me?"

He answered, "Yes, Lord, you know that I love you."

Jesus said, "Take care of my sheep."

¹⁷The third time he said to him, "Simon son of John, do you love me?"

Peter was hurt because Jesus asked him the third time, "Do you love me?" He said, "Lord, you know all things; you know that I love you."

Jesus said, "Feed my sheep. ¹⁸I tell you the truth, when you were younger you dressed yourself and went where you wanted; but when you are old you will stretch out your hands, and someone else will dress you and lead you where you do not want to go." ¹⁹Jesus said this to indicate the kind of death by which Peter would glorify God. Then he said to him, "Follow me!"

²⁰Peter turned and saw that the disciple whom Jesus loved was following them. (This was the one who had leaned back against Jesus at the supper and had said, "Lord, who is going to betray you?") ²¹When Peter saw him, he asked, "Lord, what about him?"

²²Jesus answered, "If I want him to remain alive until I return, what is that to you? You must follow me." ²³Because of this, the rumor spread among the brothers that this disciple would not die. But Jesus did not say that he would not die; he only said, "If I want him to remain alive until I return, what is that to you?"

²⁴This is the disciple who testifies to these things and who wrote them down. We know that his testimony is true.

²⁵Jesus did many other things as well. If every one of them were written down, I suppose that even the whole world would not have room for the books that would be written.

The Food of Love

JOHN 21:1–19

Jesus turned water into wine at a wedding reception. He provided lunch for thousands. And in this passage, even after his glorious resurrection we see him caring for his own by providing fish and bread for breakfast.

In the same warm, companionable way, Jesus is with you now, asking, "Do you love me?" What is your reply? Jesus is asking you, "Do you truly love me?" How will you respond? Whether it is an honest "no," a "give me a bit more time," or an unequivocal "yes," Jesus wants to share his gifts of nourishment and life with you. He wants you to care for others with nothing less than his own love. As you conclude your reading of this Gospel, go out in the name of Jesus with a specific act or word of love.

See Meeting God in Service

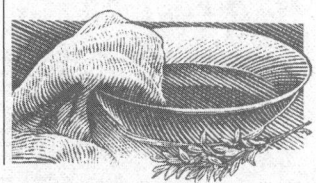

ACTS
The Good News Spreads Under the Spirit's Guidance

KEY VERSE:

*"But you will receive power when the Holy Spirit comes on you; and you will be my witnesses in
Jerusalem, and in all Judea and Samaria, and to the ends of the earth."—Acts 1:8*

"In this manner the church proceeds on its pilgrim way . . . with the persecutions of the world on one side, and on the other the consolations of God."
—AUGUSTINE,
The City of God

This book might well be called "The Acts of the Holy Spirit." From beginning to end the Spirit guides the spread of the gospel from Jerusalem to Rome itself. Poured out on the day of Pentecost with "a sound like the blowing of a violent wind" and "tongues of fire" (Acts 2:2–3), the Spirit changes lives, alters plans and transforms situations. The Spirit empowers the early Christians to stand up to authorities, to face down mobs, to speak to hostile audiences, and to hold fast through suffering even to death—all for the sake of the Good News of Jesus Christ. At the same time, the Spirit impels them far beyond their comfort zones into missions to the Samaritans and Gentiles and to people from all levels of society.

God's Spirit is active in our own lives—comforting, encouraging, strengthening, nudging. When have you felt led, like the early disciples, in a particular direction? When have you been the channel of God's love to someone else? When have you experienced a shower of grace when you needed it most? And when have you found resources of strength to do what seemed impossible? You have experienced the work of the Spirit, sent by Jesus Christ who, "exalted to the right hand of God . . . has received from the Father the promised Holy Spirit and has poured out what you now see and hear" (2:33).

Jesus Taken Up Into Heaven

1 In my former book, Theophilus, I wrote about all that Jesus began to do and to teach [2]until the day he was taken up to heaven, after giving instructions through the Holy Spirit to the apostles he had chosen. [3]After his suffering, he showed himself to these men and gave many convincing proofs that he was alive. He appeared to them over a period of forty days and spoke about the kingdom of God. [4]On one occasion, while he was eating with them, he gave them this command: "Do not leave Jerusalem, but wait for the gift my Father promised, which you have heard me speak about. [5]For John baptized with[a] water, but in a few days you will be baptized with the Holy Spirit."

[6]So when they met together, they asked him, "Lord, are you at this time going to restore the kingdom to Israel?"

[7]He said to them: "It is not for you to know the times or dates the Father has set by his own authority. [8]But you will receive power when the Holy Spirit comes on you; and you will be my witnesses in Jerusalem, and in all Judea and Samaria, and to the ends of the earth."

[9]After he said this, he was taken up before their very eyes, and a cloud hid him from their sight.

[10]They were looking intently up into the sky as he was going, when suddenly two men dressed in white stood beside them. [11]"Men of Galilee," they said, "why do you stand here looking into the sky? This same Jesus, who has been taken from you into heaven, will come back in the same way you have seen him go into heaven."

Matthias Chosen to Replace Judas

[12]Then they returned to Jerusalem from the hill called the Mount of Olives, a Sabbath day's walk[b] from the city. [13]When they arrived, they went upstairs to the room where they were staying. Those present were Peter, John, James and Andrew; Philip and Thomas, Bartholomew and Matthew; James son of Alphaeus and Simon the Zealot, and Judas son of James. [14]They all joined together constantly in prayer, along with the women and Mary the mother of Jesus, and with his brothers.

[15]In those days Peter stood up among the believers[c] (a group numbering about a hundred and twenty) [16]and said, "Brothers, the Scripture had to be fulfilled which the Holy Spirit spoke long ago through the mouth of David concerning Judas, who served as guide for those who arrested Jesus— [17]he was one of our number and shared in this ministry."

[18](With the reward he got for his wickedness, Judas bought a field; there he fell headlong, his body burst open and all his intestines spilled out. [19]Everyone in Jerusalem heard about this, so they called that field in their language Akeldama, that is, Field of Blood.)

[20]"For," said Peter, "it is written in the book of Psalms,

    " 'May his place be deserted;
      let there be no one to dwell in it,'[d]

and,

    " 'May another take his place of leadership.'[e]

A Question to Ponder

ACTS 1:11

Do you sometimes allow prayer, Bible study or other spiritual exercises to become substitutes for your mission as a Christian rather than allow them to become the power sources for that mission? Write a dialogue between yourself and God. Begin with God asking you what the angel asked the first Christians: "Why do you stand here looking into the sky?" How would you respond? What do you think God would say to your response? Writing it out will keep the dialogue focused.

Your Picture of the Spirit

ACTS 2:1–4

How do you picture the Holy Spirit? Here the Spirit is likened to a violent wind and tongues of fire. In Matthew 3:16 the Spirit is compared to a descending dove. Elsewhere the Spirit is experienced through various gifts (see 1 Corinthians 12:4–11) and fruit (see Galatians 5:22–23). Try praising God with your hands as you draw or paint your own image or images of the Spirit.

See *Meeting God in Worship*

²¹Therefore it is necessary to choose one of the men who have been with us the whole time the Lord Jesus went in and out among us, ²²beginning from John's baptism to the time when Jesus was taken up from us. For one of these must become a witness with us of his resurrection."

²³So they proposed two men: Joseph called Barsabbas (also known as Justus) and Matthias. ²⁴Then they prayed, "Lord, you know everyone's heart. Show us which of these two you have chosen ²⁵to take over this apostolic ministry, which Judas left to go where he belongs." ²⁶Then they cast lots, and the lot fell to Matthias; so he was added to the eleven apostles.

The Holy Spirit Comes at Pentecost

2 When the day of Pentecost came, they were all together in one place. ²Suddenly a sound like the blowing of a violent wind came from heaven and filled the whole house where they were sitting. ³They saw what seemed to be tongues of fire that separated and came to rest on each of them. ⁴All of them were filled with the Holy Spirit and began to speak in other tongues*ᵃ* as the Spirit enabled them.

⁵Now there were staying in Jerusalem God-fearing Jews from every nation under heaven. ⁶When they heard this sound, a crowd came together in bewilderment, because each one heard them speaking in his own language. ⁷Utterly amazed, they asked: "Are not all these men who are speaking Galileans? ⁸Then how is it that each of us hears them in his own native language? ⁹Parthians, Medes and Elamites; residents of Mesopotamia, Judea and Cappadocia, Pontus and Asia, ¹⁰Phrygia and Pamphylia, Egypt and the parts of Libya near Cyrene; visitors from Rome ¹¹(both Jews and converts to Judaism); Cretans and Arabs—we hear them declaring the wonders of God in our own tongues!" ¹²Amazed and perplexed, they asked one another, "What does this mean?"

¹³Some, however, made fun of them and said, "They have had too much wine.*ᵇ*"

Peter Addresses the Crowd

¹⁴Then Peter stood up with the Eleven, raised his voice and addressed the crowd: "Fellow Jews and all of you who live in Jerusalem, let me explain this to you; listen carefully to what I say. ¹⁵These men are not drunk, as you suppose. It's only nine in the morning! ¹⁶No, this is what was spoken by the prophet Joel:

¹⁷" 'In the last days, God says,
     I will pour out my Spirit on all people.
Your sons and daughters will prophesy,
     your young men will see visions,
     your old men will dream dreams.
¹⁸Even on my servants, both men and women,
     I will pour out my Spirit in those days,
     and they will prophesy.
¹⁹I will show wonders in the heaven above
     and signs on the earth below,
     blood and fire and billows of smoke.
²⁰The sun will be turned to darkness
     and the moon to blood

ᵃ 4 Or languages; also in verse 11   ᵇ 13 Or sweet wine

before the coming of the great and glorious day
of the Lord.
²¹And everyone who calls
on the name of the Lord will be saved.'ᵃ

²²"Men of Israel, listen to this: Jesus of Nazareth was a man accredited by God to you by miracles, wonders and signs, which God did among you through him, as you yourselves know. ²³This man was handed over to you by God's set purpose and foreknowledge; and you, with the help of wicked men,ᵇ put him to death by nailing him to the cross. ²⁴But God raised him from the dead, freeing him from the agony of death, because it was impossible for death to keep its hold on him. ²⁵David said about him:

" 'I saw the Lord always before me.
Because he is at my right hand,
I will not be shaken.
²⁶Therefore my heart is glad and my tongue rejoices;
my body also will live in hope,
²⁷because you will not abandon me to the grave,
nor will you let your Holy One see decay.
²⁸You have made known to me the paths of life;
you will fill me with joy in your presence.'ᶜ

²⁹"Brothers, I can tell you confidently that the patriarch David died and was buried, and his tomb is here to this day. ³⁰But he was a prophet and knew that God had promised him on oath that he would place one of his descendants on his throne. ³¹Seeing what was ahead, he spoke of the resurrection of the Christ,ᵈ that he was not abandoned to the grave, nor did his body see decay. ³²God has raised this Jesus to life, and we are all witnesses of the fact. ³³Exalted to the right hand of God, he has received from the Father the promised Holy Spirit and has poured out what you now see and hear. ³⁴For David did not ascend to heaven, and yet he said,

" 'The Lord said to my Lord:
"Sit at my right hand
³⁵until I make your enemies
a footstool for your feet." 'ᵉ

³⁶"Therefore let all Israel be assured of this: God has made this Jesus, whom you crucified, both Lord and Christ."

³⁷When the people heard this, they were cut to the heart and said to Peter and the other apostles, "Brothers, what shall we do?"

³⁸Peter replied, "Repent and be baptized, every one of you, in the name of Jesus Christ for the forgiveness of your sins. And you will receive the gift of the Holy Spirit. ³⁹The promise is for you and your children and for all who are far off—for all whom the Lord our God will call."

⁴⁰With many other words he warned them; and he pleaded with them, "Save yourselves from this corrupt generation." ⁴¹Those who accepted his message were baptized, and about three thousand were added to their number that day.

Rising to New Life

ACTS 2:24

"Christ has risen and death has been cast down. Christ has risen and the devils have fallen. Christ has risen and the angels rejoice. Christ has risen and there are no corpses left in the sepulcher. For Christ in rising from the dead is the firstfruits of those that sleep. To him be glory and power for ever and ever. Amen."

—JOHN CHRYSOSTOM,
"Those Invited"

ᵃ 21 Joel 2:28–32   ᵇ 23 Or of those not having the law (that is, Gentiles)
ᶜ 28 Psalm 16:8–11   ᵈ 31 Or Messiah. "The Christ" (Greek) and "the Messiah" (Hebrew) both mean "the Anointed One"; also in verse 36.
ᵉ 35 Psalm 110:1

The Gift You Really Need

ACTS 3:1–10

The beggar thinks he knows the extent of what he can ask for, but Peter gives him something much better. Do you limit God's giving by specifying what you want rather than receiving what God wants to give you? Imagine yourself as the beggar, crying out to Peter and John. What do you ask for? What do you really want? Healing of body or soul? Forgiveness? Hear Peter, as an instrument of Christ's Spirit, speak to you: "In the name of Jesus Christ of Nazareth . . ." What is the gift he offers?

See *Meeting God in Scripture*

The Fellowship of the Believers

⁴²They devoted themselves to the apostles' teaching and to the fellowship, to the breaking of bread and to prayer. ⁴³Everyone was filled with awe, and many wonders and miraculous signs were done by the apostles. ⁴⁴All the believers were together and had everything in common. ⁴⁵Selling their possessions and goods, they gave to anyone as he had need. ⁴⁶Every day they continued to meet together in the temple courts. They broke bread in their homes and ate together with glad and sincere hearts, ⁴⁷praising God and enjoying the favor of all the people. And the Lord added to their number daily those who were being saved.

Peter Heals the Crippled Beggar

3 One day Peter and John were going up to the temple at the time of prayer—at three in the afternoon. ²Now a man crippled from birth was being carried to the temple gate called Beautiful, where he was put every day to beg from those going into the temple courts. ³When he saw Peter and John about to enter, he asked them for money. ⁴Peter looked straight at him, as did John. Then Peter said, "Look at us!" ⁵So the man gave them his attention, expecting to get something from them.

⁶Then Peter said, "Silver or gold I do not have, but what I have I give you. In the name of Jesus Christ of Nazareth, walk." ⁷Taking him by the right hand, he helped him up, and instantly the man's feet and ankles became strong. ⁸He jumped to his feet and began to walk. Then he went with them into the temple courts, walking and jumping, and praising God. ⁹When all the people saw him walking and praising God, ¹⁰they recognized him as the same man who used to sit begging at the temple gate called Beautiful, and they were filled with wonder and amazement at what had happened to him.

Peter Speaks to the Onlookers

¹¹While the beggar held on to Peter and John, all the people were astonished and came running to them in the place called Solomon's Colonnade. ¹²When Peter saw this, he said to them: "Men of Israel, why does this surprise you? Why do you stare at us as if by our own power or godliness we had made this man walk? ¹³The God of Abraham, Isaac and Jacob, the God of our fathers, has glorified his servant Jesus. You handed him over to be killed, and you disowned him before Pilate, though he had decided to let him go. ¹⁴You disowned the Holy and Righteous One and asked that a murderer be released to you. ¹⁵You killed the author of life, but God raised him from the dead. We are witnesses of this. ¹⁶By faith in the name of Jesus, this man whom you see and know was made strong. It is Jesus' name and the faith that comes through him that has given this complete healing to him, as you can all see.

¹⁷"Now, brothers, I know that you acted in ignorance, as did your leaders. ¹⁸But this is how God fulfilled what he had foretold through all the prophets, saying that his Christ*a* would suffer. ¹⁹Repent, then, and turn to God, so that your sins may be wiped out, that times of refreshing may come from the Lord, ²⁰and that he may send the Christ, who has

a 18 Or Messiah; also in verse 20

been appointed for you—even Jesus. ²¹He must remain in heaven until the time comes for God to restore everything, as he promised long ago through his holy prophets. ²²For Moses said, 'The Lord your God will raise up for you a prophet like me from among your own people; you must listen to everything he tells you. ²³Anyone who does not listen to him will be completely cut off from among his people.'ᵃ

²⁴"Indeed, all the prophets from Samuel on, as many as have spoken, have foretold these days. ²⁵And you are heirs of the prophets and of the covenant God made with your fathers. He said to Abraham, 'Through your offspring all peoples on earth will be blessed.'ᵇ ²⁶When God raised up his servant, he sent him first to you to bless you by turning each of you from your wicked ways."

Peter and John Before the Sanhedrin

4 The priests and the captain of the temple guard and the Sadducees came up to Peter and John while they were speaking to the people. ²They were greatly disturbed because the apostles were teaching the people and proclaiming in Jesus the resurrection of the dead. ³They seized Peter and John, and because it was evening, they put them in jail until the next day. ⁴But many who heard the message believed, and the number of men grew to about five thousand.

⁵The next day the rulers, elders and teachers of the law met in Jerusalem. ⁶Annas the high priest was there, and so were Caiaphas, John, Alexander and the other men of the high priest's family. ⁷They had Peter and John brought before them and began to question them: "By what power or what name did you do this?"

⁸Then Peter, filled with the Holy Spirit, said to them: "Rulers and elders of the people! ⁹If we are being called to account today for an act of kindness shown to a cripple and are asked how he was healed, ¹⁰then know this, you and all the people of Israel: It is by the name of Jesus Christ of Nazareth, whom you crucified but whom God raised from the dead, that this man stands before you healed. ¹¹He is

"'the stone you builders rejected,
which has become the capstone.ᶜ'ᵈ

¹²Salvation is found in no one else, for there is no other name under heaven given to men by which we must be saved."

¹³When they saw the courage of Peter and John and realized that they were unschooled, ordinary men, they were astonished and they took note that these men had been with Jesus. ¹⁴But since they could see the man who had been healed standing there with them, there was nothing they could say. ¹⁵So they ordered them to withdraw from the Sanhedrin and then conferred together. ¹⁶"What are we going to do with these men?" they asked. "Everybody living in Jerusalem knows they have done an outstanding miracle, and we cannot deny it. ¹⁷But to stop this thing from spreading any further among the people, we must warn these men to speak no longer to anyone in this name."

¹⁸Then they called them in again and commanded them not to speak or teach at all in the name of Jesus. ¹⁹But Peter and John replied, "Judge for yourselves whether it is right in

Holy Boldness

ACTS 4:13–20

People are amazed at Peter and John's boldness as they preach the Good News in spite of warnings from the religious authorities. Are there areas of your own life in which you pay more attention to human rules than to God's call? Pray for opportunities to share the gospel and for the boldness to use those opportunities. You might also pray for pastors and missionaries, evangelists and others engaged in spreading the Word. Be specific as you pray.

See Meeting God in Prayer

ᵃ 23 Deut. 18:15,18,19   ᵇ 25 Gen. 22:18; 26:4   ᶜ 11 Or *cornerstone*
ᵈ 11 Psalm 118:22

The Blessed Community

ACTS 4:32–33

" 'See how these Christians love one another' might well have been a spontaneous exclamation in the days of the apostles. The Holy Fellowship, the Blessed Community has always astonished those who stood without it. The sharing of physical goods in the primitive church is only an outcropping of a profoundly deeper sharing of a Life, the base and center of which is obscured to those who are still oriented about self, rather than about God."

—THOMAS KELLY,
A Testament of Devotion

See Meeting God in Community.

God's sight to obey you rather than God. ²⁰For we cannot help speaking about what we have seen and heard."

²¹After further threats they let them go. They could not decide how to punish them, because all the people were praising God for what had happened. ²²For the man who was miraculously healed was over forty years old.

The Believers' Prayer

²³On their release, Peter and John went back to their own people and reported all that the chief priests and elders had said to them. ²⁴When they heard this, they raised their voices together in prayer to God. "Sovereign Lord," they said, "you made the heaven and the earth and the sea, and everything in them. ²⁵You spoke by the Holy Spirit through the mouth of your servant, our father David:

" 'Why do the nations rage
        and the peoples plot in vain?
²⁶ The kings of the earth take their stand
        and the rulers gather together
    against the Lord
        and against his Anointed One.[a][b]

²⁷Indeed Herod and Pontius Pilate met together with the Gentiles and the people[c] of Israel in this city to conspire against your holy servant Jesus, whom you anointed. ²⁸They did what your power and will had decided beforehand should happen. ²⁹Now, Lord, consider their threats and enable your servants to speak your word with great boldness. ³⁰Stretch out your hand to heal and perform miraculous signs and wonders through the name of your holy servant Jesus."

³¹After they prayed, the place where they were meeting was shaken. And they were all filled with the Holy Spirit and spoke the word of God boldly.

The Believers Share Their Possessions

³²All the believers were one in heart and mind. No one claimed that any of his possessions was his own, but they shared everything they had. ³³With great power the apostles continued to testify to the resurrection of the Lord Jesus, and much grace was upon them all. ³⁴There were no needy persons among them. For from time to time those who owned lands or houses sold them, brought the money from the sales ³⁵and put it at the apostles' feet, and it was distributed to anyone as he had need.

³⁶Joseph, a Levite from Cyprus, whom the apostles called Barnabas (which means Son of Encouragement), ³⁷sold a field he owned and brought the money and put it at the apostles' feet.

Ananias and Sapphira

5 Now a man named Ananias, together with his wife Sapphira, also sold a piece of property. ²With his wife's full knowledge he kept back part of the money for himself, but brought the rest and put it at the apostles' feet.

³Then Peter said, "Ananias, how is it that Satan has so filled your heart that you have lied to the Holy Spirit and have kept for yourself some of the money you received for the land? ⁴Didn't it belong to you before it was sold? And

a 26 That is, Christ or Messiah   *b 26* Psalm 2:1,2   *c 27* The Greek is plural.

after it was sold, wasn't the money at your disposal? What made you think of doing such a thing? You have not lied to men but to God."

[5]When Ananias heard this, he fell down and died. And great fear seized all who heard what had happened. [6]Then the young men came forward, wrapped up his body, and carried him out and buried him.

[7]About three hours later his wife came in, not knowing what had happened. [8]Peter asked her, "Tell me, is this the price you and Ananias got for the land?"

"Yes," she said, "that is the price."

[9]Peter said to her, "How could you agree to test the Spirit of the Lord? Look! The feet of the men who buried your husband are at the door, and they will carry you out also."

[10]At that moment she fell down at his feet and died. Then the young men came in and, finding her dead, carried her out and buried her beside her husband. [11]Great fear seized the whole church and all who heard about these events.

The Apostles Heal Many

[12]The apostles performed many miraculous signs and wonders among the people. And all the believers used to meet together in Solomon's Colonnade. [13]No one else dared join them, even though they were highly regarded by the people. [14]Nevertheless, more and more men and women believed in the Lord and were added to their number. [15]As a result, people brought the sick into the streets and laid them on beds and mats so that at least Peter's shadow might fall on some of them as he passed by. [16]Crowds gathered also from the towns around Jerusalem, bringing their sick and those tormented by evil[a] spirits, and all of them were healed.

The Apostles Persecuted

[17]Then the high priest and all his associates, who were members of the party of the Sadducees, were filled with jealousy. [18]They arrested the apostles and put them in the public jail. [19]But during the night an angel of the Lord opened the doors of the jail and brought them out. [20]"Go, stand in the temple courts," he said, "and tell the people the full message of this new life."

[21]At daybreak they entered the temple courts, as they had been told, and began to teach the people.

When the high priest and his associates arrived, they called together the Sanhedrin—the full assembly of the elders of Israel—and sent to the jail for the apostles. [22]But on arriving at the jail, the officers did not find them there. So they went back and reported, [23]"We found the jail securely locked, with the guards standing at the doors; but when we opened them, we found no one inside." [24]On hearing this report, the captain of the temple guard and the chief priests were puzzled, wondering what would come of this.

[25]Then someone came and said, "Look! The men you put in jail are standing in the temple courts teaching the people." [26]At that, the captain went with his officers and brought the apostles. They did not use force, because they feared that the people would stone them.

[27]Having brought the apostles, they made them appear before the Sanhedrin to be questioned by the high priest.

Rejoicing in Suffering

ACTS 5:41

Have you suffered "disgrace for the Name"? Has being faithful created uncomfortable situations for you? How did you respond? If you have never experienced firsthand the cost of discipleship, why do you think that is so? For the apostles, suffering was a badge of honor, a declaration of worthiness. Is your Christianity so low-key that it offends no one or even is unnoticed outside of the church setting? If no one knows for sure you are a Christian, what badge are you wearing?

See Meeting God in Everyday Life

---

[28]"We gave you strict orders not to teach in this name," he said. "Yet you have filled Jerusalem with your teaching and are determined to make us guilty of this man's blood."

[29]Peter and the other apostles replied: "We must obey God rather than men! [30]The God of our fathers raised Jesus from the dead—whom you had killed by hanging him on a tree. [31]God exalted him to his own right hand as Prince and Savior that he might give repentance and forgiveness of sins to Israel. [32]We are witnesses of these things, and so is the Holy Spirit, whom God has given to those who obey him."

[33]When they heard this, they were furious and wanted to put them to death. [34]But a Pharisee named Gamaliel, a teacher of the law, who was honored by all the people, stood up in the Sanhedrin and ordered that the men be put outside for a little while. [35]Then he addressed them: "Men of Israel, consider carefully what you intend to do to these men. [36]Some time ago Theudas appeared, claiming to be somebody, and about four hundred men rallied to him. He was killed, all his followers were dispersed, and it all came to nothing. [37]After him, Judas the Galilean appeared in the days of the census and led a band of people in revolt. He too was killed, and all his followers were scattered. [38]Therefore, in the present case I advise you: Leave these men alone! Let them go! For if their purpose or activity is of human origin, it will fail. [39]But if it is from God, you will not be able to stop these men; you will only find yourselves fighting against God."

[40]His speech persuaded them. They called the apostles in and had them flogged. Then they ordered them not to speak in the name of Jesus, and let them go.

[41]The apostles left the Sanhedrin, rejoicing because they had been counted worthy of suffering disgrace for the Name. [42]Day after day, in the temple courts and from house to house, they never stopped teaching and proclaiming the good news that Jesus is the Christ.[a]

The Choosing of the Seven

6 In those days when the number of disciples was increasing, the Grecian Jews among them complained against the Hebraic Jews because their widows were being overlooked in the daily distribution of food. [2]So the Twelve gathered all the disciples together and said, "It would not be right for us to neglect the ministry of the word of God in order to wait on tables. [3]Brothers, choose seven men from among you who are known to be full of the Spirit and wisdom. We will turn this responsibility over to them [4]and will give our attention to prayer and the ministry of the word."

[5]This proposal pleased the whole group. They chose Stephen, a man full of faith and of the Holy Spirit; also Philip, Procorus, Nicanor, Timon, Parmenas, and Nicolas from Antioch, a convert to Judaism. [6]They presented these men to the apostles, who prayed and laid their hands on them.

[7]So the word of God spread. The number of disciples in Jerusalem increased rapidly, and a large number of priests became obedient to the faith.

Stephen Seized

[8]Now Stephen, a man full of God's grace and power, did great wonders and miraculous signs among the people.

a 42 Or Messiah

⁹Opposition arose, however, from members of the Synagogue of the Freedmen (as it was called)—Jews of Cyrene and Alexandria as well as the provinces of Cilicia and Asia. These men began to argue with Stephen, ¹⁰but they could not stand up against his wisdom or the Spirit by whom he spoke.

¹¹Then they secretly persuaded some men to say, "We have heard Stephen speak words of blasphemy against Moses and against God."

¹²So they stirred up the people and the elders and the teachers of the law. They seized Stephen and brought him before the Sanhedrin. ¹³They produced false witnesses, who testified, "This fellow never stops speaking against this holy place and against the law. ¹⁴For we have heard him say that this Jesus of Nazareth will destroy this place and change the customs Moses handed down to us."

¹⁵All who were sitting in the Sanhedrin looked intently at Stephen, and they saw that his face was like the face of an angel.

Stephen's Speech to the Sanhedrin

7 Then the high priest asked him, "Are these charges true?"

²To this he replied: "Brothers and fathers, listen to me! The God of glory appeared to our father Abraham while he was still in Mesopotamia, before he lived in Haran. ³'Leave your country and your people,' God said, 'and go to the land I will show you.'ᵃ

⁴"So he left the land of the Chaldeans and settled in Haran. After the death of his father, God sent him to this land where you are now living. ⁵He gave him no inheritance here, not even a foot of ground. But God promised him that he and his descendants after him would possess the land, even though at that time Abraham had no child. ⁶God spoke to him in this way: 'Your descendants will be strangers in a country not their own, and they will be enslaved and mistreated four hundred years. ⁷But I will punish the nation they serve as slaves,' God said, 'and afterward they will come out of that country and worship me in this place.'ᵇ ⁸Then he gave Abraham the covenant of circumcision. And Abraham became the father of Isaac and circumcised him eight days after his birth. Later Isaac became the father of Jacob, and Jacob became the father of the twelve patriarchs.

⁹"Because the patriarchs were jealous of Joseph, they sold him as a slave into Egypt. But God was with him ¹⁰and rescued him from all his troubles. He gave Joseph wisdom and enabled him to gain the goodwill of Pharaoh king of Egypt; so he made him ruler over Egypt and all his palace.

¹¹"Then a famine struck all Egypt and Canaan, bringing great suffering, and our fathers could not find food. ¹²When Jacob heard that there was grain in Egypt, he sent our fathers on their first visit. ¹³On their second visit, Joseph told his brothers who he was, and Pharaoh learned about Joseph's family. ¹⁴After this, Joseph sent for his father Jacob and his whole family, seventy-five in all. ¹⁵Then Jacob went down to Egypt, where he and our fathers died. ¹⁶Their bodies were brought back to Shechem and placed in the tomb

Telling the Story of Salvation

ACTS 7:1–38

When Stephen talks about God's activity in human history, he starts with Abraham, Isaac, Jacob, Joseph and Moses.

Think of the ways you might recall the most important events and people in your life. For example, you might revisit your family home, reflect on a family tree, write in a journal or browse through a photo album. Can you, like Stephen, see God's hand in the big and small events of your life? Use paper and pen to briefly describe, or draw a picture of, an important event in your life. With the benefit of hindsight, where do you see God at work in what happened? How might this event fit into God's larger scheme for your life?

See Meeting God in Everyday Life

To Kill Virtue's Adversary

ACTS 7:24

"Moses teaches us to take our stand with virtue as with a kinsman and to kill virtue's adversary. The victory of true religion is the death of idolatry. So also injustice is killed by righteousness and arrogance is slain by humility."

—GREGORY OF NYSSA,
The Life of Moses Book II

that Abraham had bought from the sons of Hamor at Shechem for a certain sum of money.

[17]"As the time drew near for God to fulfill his promise to Abraham, the number of our people in Egypt greatly increased. [18]Then another king, who knew nothing about Joseph, became ruler of Egypt. [19]He dealt treacherously with our people and oppressed our forefathers by forcing them to throw out their newborn babies so that they would die.

[20]"At that time Moses was born, and he was no ordinary child.[a] For three months he was cared for in his father's house. [21]When he was placed outside, Pharaoh's daughter took him and brought him up as her own son. [22]Moses was educated in all the wisdom of the Egyptians and was powerful in speech and action.

[23]"When Moses was forty years old, he decided to visit his fellow Israelites. [24]He saw one of them being mistreated by an Egyptian, so he went to his defense and avenged him by killing the Egyptian. [25]Moses thought that his own people would realize that God was using him to rescue them, but they did not. [26]The next day Moses came upon two Israelites who were fighting. He tried to reconcile them by saying, 'Men, you are brothers; why do you want to hurt each other?'

[27]"But the man who was mistreating the other pushed Moses aside and said, 'Who made you ruler and judge over us? [28]Do you want to kill me as you killed the Egyptian yesterday?'[b] [29]When Moses heard this, he fled to Midian, where he settled as a foreigner and had two sons.

[30]"After forty years had passed, an angel appeared to Moses in the flames of a burning bush in the desert near Mount Sinai. [31]When he saw this, he was amazed at the sight. As he went over to look more closely, he heard the Lord's voice: [32]'I am the God of your fathers, the God of Abraham, Isaac and Jacob.'[c] Moses trembled with fear and did not dare to look.

[33]"Then the Lord said to him, 'Take off your sandals; the place where you are standing is holy ground. [34]I have indeed seen the oppression of my people in Egypt. I have heard their groaning and have come down to set them free. Now come, I will send you back to Egypt.'[d]

[35]"This is the same Moses whom they had rejected with the words, 'Who made you ruler and judge?' He was sent to be their ruler and deliverer by God himself, through the angel who appeared to him in the bush. [36]He led them out of Egypt and did wonders and miraculous signs in Egypt, at the Red Sea[e] and for forty years in the desert.

[37]"This is that Moses who told the Israelites, 'God will send you a prophet like me from your own people.'[f] [38]He was in the assembly in the desert, with the angel who spoke to him on Mount Sinai, and with our fathers; and he received living words to pass on to us.

[39]"But our fathers refused to obey him. Instead, they rejected him and in their hearts turned back to Egypt. [40]They told Aaron, 'Make us gods who will go before us. As for this fellow Moses who led us out of Egypt—we don't know what has happened to him!'[g] [41]That was the time they made an idol in the form of a calf. They brought sacrifices

[a]20 Or *was fair in the sight of God*   [b]28 Exodus 2:14   [c]32 Exodus 3:6
[d]34 Exodus 3:5,7,8,10   [e]36 That is, Sea of Reeds   [f]37 Deut. 18:15
[g]40 Exodus 32:1

to it and held a celebration in honor of what their hands had made. ⁴²But God turned away and gave them over to the worship of the heavenly bodies. This agrees with what is written in the book of the prophets:

> " 'Did you bring me sacrifices and offerings
> forty years in the desert, O house of Israel?
> ⁴³You have lifted up the shrine of Molech
> and the star of your god Rephan,
> the idols you made to worship.
> Therefore I will send you into exile'ᵃ beyond
> Babylon.

⁴⁴"Our forefathers had the tabernacle of the Testimony with them in the desert. It had been made as God directed Moses, according to the pattern he had seen. ⁴⁵Having received the tabernacle, our fathers under Joshua brought it with them when they took the land from the nations God drove out before them. It remained in the land until the time of David, ⁴⁶who enjoyed God's favor and asked that he might provide a dwelling place for the God of Jacob.ᵇ ⁴⁷But it was Solomon who built the house for him.

⁴⁸"However, the Most High does not live in houses made by men. As the prophet says:

> ⁴⁹" 'Heaven is my throne,
> and the earth is my footstool.
> What kind of house will you build for me?
> says the Lord.
> Or where will my resting place be?
> ⁵⁰Has not my hand made all these things?'ᶜ

⁵¹"You stiff-necked people, with uncircumcised hearts and ears! You are just like your fathers: You always resist the Holy Spirit! ⁵²Was there ever a prophet your fathers did not persecute? They even killed those who predicted the coming of the Righteous One. And now you have betrayed and murdered him— ⁵³you who have received the law that was put into effect through angels but have not obeyed it."

The Stoning of Stephen

⁵⁴When they heard this, they were furious and gnashed their teeth at him. ⁵⁵But Stephen, full of the Holy Spirit, looked up to heaven and saw the glory of God, and Jesus standing at the right hand of God. ⁵⁶"Look," he said, "I see heaven open and the Son of Man standing at the right hand of God."

⁵⁷At this they covered their ears and, yelling at the top of their voices, they all rushed at him, ⁵⁸dragged him out of the city and began to stone him. Meanwhile, the witnesses laid their clothes at the feet of a young man named Saul.

⁵⁹While they were stoning him, Stephen prayed, "Lord Jesus, receive my spirit." ⁶⁰Then he fell on his knees and cried out, "Lord, do not hold this sin against them." When he had said this, he fell asleep.

8 And Saul was there, giving approval to his death.

The Church Persecuted and Scattered

On that day a great persecution broke out against the

The Crowd at Stephen's Stoning

ACTS 7:54–60

This might be a good passage with which to try the Ignatian approach described in the article *Meeting God in Scripture*. Imagine yourself as part of the crowd at Stephen's stoning. Begin by rereading the story of Stephen's arrest and speech beginning at 6:8. Picture the crowded council room. Listen to the accusations against Stephen and to his defense against those allegations. How do those around you react to Stephen calling them "stiff-necked people . . . always resist[ing] the Holy Spirit"(v.51)? Try talking with them. How do you react? Follow the mob as they take Stephen out to stone him. How does his witness affect you? Do you get caught up in the mob's anger? You might "debrief" by writing a description of what you have seen, heard and felt.

ᵃ 43 Amos 5:25–27   ᵇ 46 Some early manuscripts *the house of Jacob*
ᶜ 50 Isaiah 66:1,2

Purchasing God

ACTS 8:18–21

Simon the sorcerer tried to buy the Spirit's power, and ever since that time the practice of purchasing church offices has been called "simony." There are less obvious ways we try to purchase God's favor. Sometimes we pray, "O God, if you'll do this [or give me that], then I'll be good [or go to church every Sunday or become a minister]." When have you tried to bargain with God? What is it that God really wants? (See Psalm 51:16–17 and Micah 6:8.) You might want to pray a brief prayer of surrender, freely offering God your heart, your will, your life—to use as he wills.

church at Jerusalem, and all except the apostles were scattered throughout Judea and Samaria. ²Godly men buried Stephen and mourned deeply for him. ³But Saul began to destroy the church. Going from house to house, he dragged off men and women and put them in prison.

Philip in Samaria

⁴Those who had been scattered preached the word wherever they went. ⁵Philip went down to a city in Samaria and proclaimed the Christ[a] there. ⁶When the crowds heard Philip and saw the miraculous signs he did, they all paid close attention to what he said. ⁷With shrieks, evil[b] spirits came out of many, and many paralytics and cripples were healed. ⁸So there was great joy in that city.

Simon the Sorcerer

⁹Now for some time a man named Simon had practiced sorcery in the city and amazed all the people of Samaria. He boasted that he was someone great, ¹⁰and all the people, both high and low, gave him their attention and exclaimed, "This man is the divine power known as the Great Power." ¹¹They followed him because he had amazed them for a long time with his magic. ¹²But when they believed Philip as he preached the good news of the kingdom of God and the name of Jesus Christ, they were baptized, both men and women. ¹³Simon himself believed and was baptized. And he followed Philip everywhere, astonished by the great signs and miracles he saw.

¹⁴When the apostles in Jerusalem heard that Samaria had accepted the word of God, they sent Peter and John to them. ¹⁵When they arrived, they prayed for them that they might receive the Holy Spirit, ¹⁶because the Holy Spirit had not yet come upon any of them; they had simply been baptized into[c] the name of the Lord Jesus. ¹⁷Then Peter and John placed their hands on them, and they received the Holy Spirit.

¹⁸When Simon saw that the Spirit was given at the laying on of the apostles' hands, he offered them money ¹⁹and said, "Give me also this ability so that everyone on whom I lay my hands may receive the Holy Spirit."

²⁰Peter answered: "May your money perish with you, because you thought you could buy the gift of God with money! ²¹You have no part or share in this ministry, because your heart is not right before God. ²²Repent of this wickedness and pray to the Lord. Perhaps he will forgive you for having such a thought in your heart. ²³For I see that you are full of bitterness and captive to sin."

²⁴Then Simon answered, "Pray to the Lord for me so that nothing you have said may happen to me."

²⁵When they had testified and proclaimed the word of the Lord, Peter and John returned to Jerusalem, preaching the gospel in many Samaritan villages.

Philip and the Ethiopian

²⁶Now an angel of the Lord said to Philip, "Go south to the road—the desert road—that goes down from Jerusalem to Gaza." ²⁷So he started out, and on his way he met an Ethiopian[d] eunuch, an important official in charge of all the trea-

---

[a] 5 Or Messiah   [b] 7 Greek unclean   [c] 16 Or in   [d] 27 That is, from the upper Nile region

sury of Candace, queen of the Ethiopians. This man had gone to Jerusalem to worship, ²⁸and on his way home was sitting in his chariot reading the book of Isaiah the prophet. ²⁹The Spirit told Philip, "Go to that chariot and stay near it."

³⁰Then Philip ran up to the chariot and heard the man reading Isaiah the prophet. "Do you understand what you are reading?" Philip asked.

³¹"How can I," he said, "unless someone explains it to me?" So he invited Philip to come up and sit with him.

³²The eunuch was reading this passage of Scripture:

"He was led like a sheep to the slaughter,
    and as a lamb before the shearer is silent,
    so he did not open his mouth.
³³In his humiliation he was deprived of justice.
    Who can speak of his descendants?
    For his life was taken from the earth."ᵃ

³⁴The eunuch asked Philip, "Tell me, please, who is the prophet talking about, himself or someone else?" ³⁵Then Philip began with that very passage of Scripture and told him the good news about Jesus.

³⁶As they traveled along the road, they came to some water and the eunuch said, "Look, here is water. Why shouldn't I be baptized?"ᵇ ³⁸And he gave orders to stop the chariot. Then both Philip and the eunuch went down into the water and Philip baptized him. ³⁹When they came up out of the water, the Spirit of the Lord suddenly took Philip away, and the eunuch did not see him again, but went on his way rejoicing. ⁴⁰Philip, however, appeared at Azotus and traveled about, preaching the gospel in all the towns until he reached Caesarea.

Saul's Conversion

9 Meanwhile, Saul was still breathing out murderous threats against the Lord's disciples. He went to the high priest ²and asked him for letters to the synagogues in Damascus, so that if he found any there who belonged to the Way, whether men or women, he might take them as prisoners to Jerusalem. ³As he neared Damascus on his journey, suddenly a light from heaven flashed around him. ⁴He fell to the ground and heard a voice say to him, "Saul, Saul, why do you persecute me?"

⁵"Who are you, Lord?" Saul asked.

"I am Jesus, whom you are persecuting," he replied. ⁶"Now get up and go into the city, and you will be told what you must do."

⁷The men traveling with Saul stood there speechless; they heard the sound but did not see anyone. ⁸Saul got up from the ground, but when he opened his eyes he could see nothing. So they led him by the hand into Damascus. ⁹For three days he was blind, and did not eat or drink anything.

¹⁰In Damascus there was a disciple named Ananias. The Lord called to him in a vision, "Ananias!"

"Yes, Lord," he answered.

¹¹The Lord told him, "Go to the house of Judas on Straight Street and ask for a man from Tarsus named Saul, for he is

---

Seeing Opportunities to Witness

ACTS 8:29–39

An angel of the Lord gives instructions to Philip and he is led to a chariot on a desert road. There he finds an unexpected occasion to tell the good news of Jesus. Such opportunities are all around us, though we often let them pass unnoticed. You might look back over the last day or so. Did you ignore someone's pain or offer polite sympathy instead of a word of hope or love? When might you have invited someone to come to a worship service or a Bible study? Were there occasions when you could have witnessed about your own faith? Ask God to give you the vision to see such opportunities in the coming days as well as the courage to act on them.

See *Meeting God in Service*

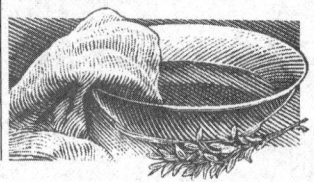

ᵃ 33 Isaiah 53:7,8   ᵇ 36 Some late manuscripts *baptized?"* ³⁷*Philip said, "If you believe with all your heart, you may." The eunuch answered, "I believe that Jesus Christ is the Son of God."*

Before and After

ACTS 9:13–16

Ananias is afraid to go to Saul (Paul) because he knows only who Saul *has been*, not who he *is becoming* since his encounter with Jesus Christ. You might try drawing simple cartoons to illustrate the "before" and "after" versions of Paul. What are the outward changes? How might you illustrate the inward ones? What if you were to try the same exercise with yourself? What changes has Jesus made in your life? What is still "in process"? You might go even further and illustrate the "ideal you" that you are becoming in Jesus.

praying. [12]In a vision he has seen a man named Ananias come and place his hands on him to restore his sight."

[13]"Lord," Ananias answered, "I have heard many reports about this man and all the harm he has done to your saints in Jerusalem. [14]And he has come here with authority from the chief priests to arrest all who call on your name."

[15]But the Lord said to Ananias, "Go! This man is my chosen instrument to carry my name before the Gentiles and their kings and before the people of Israel. [16]I will show him how much he must suffer for my name."

[17]Then Ananias went to the house and entered it. Placing his hands on Saul, he said, "Brother Saul, the Lord—Jesus, who appeared to you on the road as you were coming here—has sent me so that you may see again and be filled with the Holy Spirit." [18]Immediately, something like scales fell from Saul's eyes, and he could see again. He got up and was baptized, [19]and after taking some food, he regained his strength.

Saul in Damascus and Jerusalem

Saul spent several days with the disciples in Damascus. [20]At once he began to preach in the synagogues that Jesus is the Son of God. [21]All those who heard him were astonished and asked, "Isn't he the man who raised havoc in Jerusalem among those who call on this name? And hasn't he come here to take them as prisoners to the chief priests?" [22]Yet Saul grew more and more powerful and baffled the Jews living in Damascus by proving that Jesus is the Christ.[a]

[23]After many days had gone by, the Jews conspired to kill him, [24]but Saul learned of their plan. Day and night they kept close watch on the city gates in order to kill him. [25]But his followers took him by night and lowered him in a basket through an opening in the wall.

[26]When he came to Jerusalem, he tried to join the disciples, but they were all afraid of him, not believing that he really was a disciple. [27]But Barnabas took him and brought him to the apostles. He told them how Saul on his journey had seen the Lord and that the Lord had spoken to him, and how in Damascus he had preached fearlessly in the name of Jesus. [28]So Saul stayed with them and moved about freely in Jerusalem, speaking boldly in the name of the Lord. [29]He talked and debated with the Grecian Jews, but they tried to kill him. [30]When the brothers learned of this, they took him down to Caesarea and sent him off to Tarsus.

[31]Then the church throughout Judea, Galilee and Samaria enjoyed a time of peace. It was strengthened; and encouraged by the Holy Spirit, it grew in numbers, living in the fear of the Lord.

Aeneas and Dorcas

[32]As Peter traveled about the country, he went to visit the saints in Lydda. [33]There he found a man named Aeneas, a paralytic who had been bedridden for eight years. [34]"Aeneas," Peter said to him, "Jesus Christ heals you. Get up and take care of your mat." Immediately Aeneas got up. [35]All those who lived in Lydda and Sharon saw him and turned to the Lord.

[36]In Joppa there was a disciple named Tabitha (which,

a 22 Or Messiah

when translated, is Dorcas*a*), who was always doing good and helping the poor. ³⁷About that time she became sick and died, and her body was washed and placed in an upstairs room. ³⁸Lydda was near Joppa; so when the disciples heard that Peter was in Lydda, they sent two men to him and urged him, "Please come at once!"

³⁹Peter went with them, and when he arrived he was taken upstairs to the room. All the widows stood around him, crying and showing him the robes and other clothing that Dorcas had made while she was still with them.

⁴⁰Peter sent them all out of the room; then he got down on his knees and prayed. Turning toward the dead woman, he said, "Tabitha, get up." She opened her eyes, and seeing Peter she sat up. ⁴¹He took her by the hand and helped her to her feet. Then he called the believers and the widows and presented her to them alive. ⁴²This became known all over Joppa, and many people believed in the Lord. ⁴³Peter stayed in Joppa for some time with a tanner named Simon.

Cornelius Calls for Peter

10 At Caesarea there was a man named Cornelius, a centurion in what was known as the Italian Regiment. ²He and all his family were devout and God-fearing; he gave generously to those in need and prayed to God regularly. ³One day at about three in the afternoon he had a vision. He distinctly saw an angel of God, who came to him and said, "Cornelius!"

⁴Cornelius stared at him in fear. "What is it, Lord?" he asked.

The angel answered, "Your prayers and gifts to the poor have come up as a memorial offering before God. ⁵Now send men to Joppa to bring back a man named Simon who is called Peter. ⁶He is staying with Simon the tanner, whose house is by the sea."

⁷When the angel who spoke to him had gone, Cornelius called two of his servants and a devout soldier who was one of his attendants. ⁸He told them everything that had happened and sent them to Joppa.

Peter's Vision

⁹About noon the following day as they were on their journey and approaching the city, Peter went up on the roof to pray. ¹⁰He became hungry and wanted something to eat, and while the meal was being prepared, he fell into a trance. ¹¹He saw heaven opened and something like a large sheet being let down to earth by its four corners. ¹²It contained all kinds of four-footed animals, as well as reptiles of the earth and birds of the air. ¹³Then a voice told him, "Get up, Peter. Kill and eat."

¹⁴"Surely not, Lord!" Peter replied. "I have never eaten anything impure or unclean."

¹⁵The voice spoke to him a second time, "Do not call anything impure that God has made clean."

¹⁶This happened three times, and immediately the sheet was taken back to heaven.

¹⁷While Peter was wondering about the meaning of the vision, the men sent by Cornelius found out where Simon's house was and stopped at the gate. ¹⁸They called out, asking if Simon who was known as Peter was staying there.

What's Stopping You?

ACTS 10:9–16

Peter was unwilling to visit Gentiles because they ate unclean animals. Then God showed him a vision. You might put yourself in Peter's place. See a great sheet coming down and opening. What are the things inside that make you cry, "Surely not, Lord!"? What makes you hold back? A different race or ethnic group? A dirty house? A lifestyle you find strange or repugnant? As you look around you, hear God's word to you: "Do not call anything impure that God has made clean." What can you do to move from prayer to action?

See Meeting God in Service

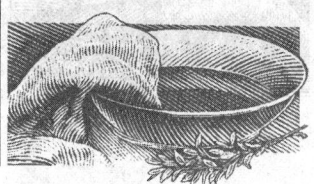

---

a 36 Both *Tabitha* (Aramaic) and *Dorcas* (Greek) mean *gazelle*.

Who Is Acceptable?

ACTS 10:34–35

"I now realize how true it is that God does not show favoritism but accepts men from every nation who fear him and do what is right." What an amazing statement! Turn this sentence over and over in your mind. Mull it over until you have extracted all its truth. Take it in little bites: no favoritism . . . every nation . . . accepts. What do you learn about God's love? What call do you hear to change your attitude toward others? What good news do you hear for yourself?

See Meeting God in Service

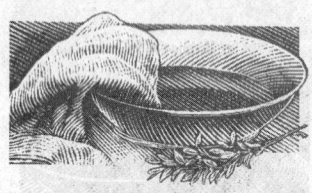

¹⁹While Peter was still thinking about the vision, the Spirit said to him, "Simon, three*a* men are looking for you. ²⁰So get up and go downstairs. Do not hesitate to go with them, for I have sent them."

²¹Peter went down and said to the men, "I'm the one you're looking for. Why have you come?"

²²The men replied, "We have come from Cornelius the centurion. He is a righteous and God-fearing man, who is respected by all the Jewish people. A holy angel told him to have you come to his house so that he could hear what you have to say." ²³Then Peter invited the men into the house to be his guests.

Peter at Cornelius' House

The next day Peter started out with them, and some of the brothers from Joppa went along. ²⁴The following day he arrived in Caesarea. Cornelius was expecting them and had called together his relatives and close friends. ²⁵As Peter entered the house, Cornelius met him and fell at his feet in reverence. ²⁶But Peter made him get up. "Stand up," he said, "I am only a man myself."

²⁷Talking with him, Peter went inside and found a large gathering of people. ²⁸He said to them: "You are well aware that it is against our law for a Jew to associate with a Gentile or visit him. But God has shown me that I should not call any man impure or unclean. ²⁹So when I was sent for, I came without raising any objection. May I ask why you sent for me?"

³⁰Cornelius answered: "Four days ago I was in my house praying at this hour, at three in the afternoon. Suddenly a man in shining clothes stood before me ³¹and said, 'Cornelius, God has heard your prayer and remembered your gifts to the poor. ³²Send to Joppa for Simon who is called Peter. He is a guest in the home of Simon the tanner, who lives by the sea.' ³³So I sent for you immediately, and it was good of you to come. Now we are all here in the presence of God to listen to everything the Lord has commanded you to tell us."

³⁴Then Peter began to speak: "I now realize how true it is that God does not show favoritism ³⁵but accepts men from every nation who fear him and do what is right. ³⁶You know the message God sent to the people of Israel, telling the good news of peace through Jesus Christ, who is Lord of all. ³⁷You know what has happened throughout Judea, beginning in Galilee after the baptism that John preached— ³⁸how God anointed Jesus of Nazareth with the Holy Spirit and power, and how he went around doing good and healing all who were under the power of the devil, because God was with him.

³⁹"We are witnesses of everything he did in the country of the Jews and in Jerusalem. They killed him by hanging him on a tree, ⁴⁰but God raised him from the dead on the third day and caused him to be seen. ⁴¹He was not seen by all the people, but by witnesses whom God had already chosen—by us who ate and drank with him after he rose from the dead. ⁴²He commanded us to preach to the people and to testify that he is the one whom God appointed as judge of the living and the dead. ⁴³All the prophets testify

a 19 One early manuscript *two*; other manuscripts do not have the number.

about him that everyone who believes in him receives forgiveness of sins through his name."

⁴⁴While Peter was still speaking these words, the Holy Spirit came on all who heard the message. ⁴⁵The circumcised believers who had come with Peter were astonished that the gift of the Holy Spirit had been poured out even on the Gentiles. ⁴⁶For they heard them speaking in tongues*a* and praising God.

Then Peter said, ⁴⁷"Can anyone keep these people from being baptized with water? They have received the Holy Spirit just as we have." ⁴⁸So he ordered that they be baptized in the name of Jesus Christ. Then they asked Peter to stay with them for a few days.

Peter Explains His Actions

11 The apostles and the brothers throughout Judea heard that the Gentiles also had received the word of God. ²So when Peter went up to Jerusalem, the circumcised believers criticized him ³and said, "You went into the house of uncircumcised men and ate with them."

⁴Peter began and explained everything to them precisely as it had happened: ⁵"I was in the city of Joppa praying, and in a trance I saw a vision. I saw something like a large sheet being let down from heaven by its four corners, and it came down to where I was. ⁶I looked into it and saw four-footed animals of the earth, wild beasts, reptiles, and birds of the air. ⁷Then I heard a voice telling me, 'Get up, Peter. Kill and eat.'

⁸"I replied, 'Surely not, Lord! Nothing impure or unclean has ever entered my mouth.'

⁹"The voice spoke from heaven a second time, 'Do not call anything impure that God has made clean.' ¹⁰This happened three times, and then it was all pulled up to heaven again.

¹¹"Right then three men who had been sent to me from Caesarea stopped at the house where I was staying. ¹²The Spirit told me to have no hesitation about going with them. These six brothers also went with me, and we entered the man's house. ¹³He told us how he had seen an angel appear in his house and say, 'Send to Joppa for Simon who is called Peter. ¹⁴He will bring you a message through which you and all your household will be saved.'

¹⁵"As I began to speak, the Holy Spirit came on them as he had come on us at the beginning. ¹⁶Then I remembered what the Lord had said: 'John baptized with*b* water, but you will be baptized with the Holy Spirit.' ¹⁷So if God gave them the same gift as he gave us, who believed in the Lord Jesus Christ, who was I to think that I could oppose God?"

¹⁸When they heard this, they had no further objections and praised God, saying, "So then, God has granted even the Gentiles repentance unto life."

The Church in Antioch

¹⁹Now those who had been scattered by the persecution in connection with Stephen traveled as far as Phoenicia, Cyprus and Antioch, telling the message only to Jews. ²⁰Some of them, however, men from Cyprus and Cyrene, went to Antioch and began to speak to Greeks also, telling them the good news about the Lord Jesus. ²¹The Lord's

---

Praising God for the Spirit's Work

ACTS 11:17-18

Peter was amazed when the Spirit was poured out on Cornelius and his household. The other disciples were also astonished to hear of it. But they praised God for giving grace "even [to] the Gentiles." As you think about the world around you, where does the Spirit's activity astound you? Name people whom you have written off as unreachable who are finding Jesus Christ. How are people experiencing the Spirit's power in ways that you find strange or that make you uncomfortable? What attitudes or traditions do you cherish that might be hindering God? What do you see that makes you praise God for this gift of "repentance unto life"?

---

a 46 Or *other languages*   *b 16* Or *in*

The Chains Fall Off

ACTS 12:1–18

Use your imagination to put yourself in Peter's place. Reread the passage. See the cell, the guards, the chains. What are the chains that bind you? What keeps you captive, unable to move freely? Even as you remain in bondage, know that others are praying for your release. You might join them, asking God for help. See an angel appear before you. Feel the angel's touch. Hear the words, "Quick, get up!" Picture yourself getting up as the chains fall off. You stand free, able to walk out of captivity. Hear the angel call you to follow him. Where can you go to tell what God has done for you? Whom do you need to tell?

See *Meeting God in Scripture*

hand was with them, and a great number of people believed and turned to the Lord.

²²News of this reached the ears of the church at Jerusalem, and they sent Barnabas to Antioch. ²³When he arrived and saw the evidence of the grace of God, he was glad and encouraged them all to remain true to the Lord with all their hearts. ²⁴He was a good man, full of the Holy Spirit and faith, and a great number of people were brought to the Lord.

²⁵Then Barnabas went to Tarsus to look for Saul, ²⁶and when he found him, he brought him to Antioch. So for a whole year Barnabas and Saul met with the church and taught great numbers of people. The disciples were called Christians first at Antioch.

²⁷During this time some prophets came down from Jerusalem to Antioch. ²⁸One of them, named Agabus, stood up and through the Spirit predicted that a severe famine would spread over the entire Roman world. (This happened during the reign of Claudius.) ²⁹The disciples, each according to his ability, decided to provide help for the brothers living in Judea. ³⁰This they did, sending their gift to the elders by Barnabas and Saul.

Peter's Miraculous Escape From Prison

12 It was about this time that King Herod arrested some who belonged to the church, intending to persecute them. ²He had James, the brother of John, put to death with the sword. ³When he saw that this pleased the Jews, he proceeded to seize Peter also. This happened during the Feast of Unleavened Bread. ⁴After arresting him, he put him in prison, handing him over to be guarded by four squads of four soldiers each. Herod intended to bring him out for public trial after the Passover.

⁵So Peter was kept in prison, but the church was earnestly praying to God for him.

⁶The night before Herod was to bring him to trial, Peter was sleeping between two soldiers, bound with two chains, and sentries stood guard at the entrance. ⁷Suddenly an angel of the Lord appeared and a light shone in the cell. He struck Peter on the side and woke him up. "Quick, get up!" he said, and the chains fell off Peter's wrists.

⁸Then the angel said to him, "Put on your clothes and sandals." And Peter did so. "Wrap your cloak around you and follow me," the angel told him. ⁹Peter followed him out of the prison, but he had no idea that what the angel was doing was really happening; he thought he was seeing a vision. ¹⁰They passed the first and second guards and came to the iron gate leading to the city. It opened for them by itself, and they went through it. When they had walked the length of one street, suddenly the angel left him.

¹¹Then Peter came to himself and said, "Now I know without a doubt that the Lord sent his angel and rescued me from Herod's clutches and from everything the Jewish people were anticipating."

¹²When this had dawned on him, he went to the house of Mary the mother of John, also called Mark, where many people had gathered and were praying. ¹³Peter knocked at the outer entrance, and a servant girl named Rhoda came to answer the door. ¹⁴When she recognized Peter's voice,

she was so overjoyed she ran back without opening it and exclaimed, "Peter is at the door!"

[15] "You're out of your mind," they told her. When she kept insisting that it was so, they said, "It must be his angel."

[16] But Peter kept on knocking, and when they opened the door and saw him, they were astonished. [17] Peter motioned with his hand for them to be quiet and described how the Lord had brought him out of prison. "Tell James and the brothers about this," he said, and then he left for another place.

[18] In the morning, there was no small commotion among the soldiers as to what had become of Peter. [19] After Herod had a thorough search made for him and did not find him, he cross-examined the guards and ordered that they be executed.

Herod's Death

Then Herod went from Judea to Caesarea and stayed there a while. [20] He had been quarreling with the people of Tyre and Sidon; they now joined together and sought an audience with him. Having secured the support of Blastus, a trusted personal servant of the king, they asked for peace, because they depended on the king's country for their food supply.

[21] On the appointed day Herod, wearing his royal robes, sat on his throne and delivered a public address to the people. [22] They shouted, "This is the voice of a god, not of a man." [23] Immediately, because Herod did not give praise to God, an angel of the Lord struck him down, and he was eaten by worms and died.

[24] But the word of God continued to increase and spread.

[25] When Barnabas and Saul had finished their mission, they returned from[a] Jerusalem, taking with them John, also called Mark.

Barnabas and Saul Sent Off

13 In the church at Antioch there were prophets and teachers: Barnabas, Simeon called Niger, Lucius of Cyrene, Manaen (who had been brought up with Herod the tetrarch) and Saul. [2] While they were worshiping the Lord and fasting, the Holy Spirit said, "Set apart for me Barnabas and Saul for the work to which I have called them." [3] So after they had fasted and prayed, they placed their hands on them and sent them off.

On Cyprus

[4] The two of them, sent on their way by the Holy Spirit, went down to Seleucia and sailed from there to Cyprus. [5] When they arrived at Salamis, they proclaimed the word of God in the Jewish synagogues. John was with them as their helper.

[6] They traveled through the whole island until they came to Paphos. There they met a Jewish sorcerer and false prophet named Bar-Jesus, [7] who was an attendant of the proconsul, Sergius Paulus. The proconsul, an intelligent man, sent for Barnabas and Saul because he wanted to hear the word of God. [8] But Elymas the sorcerer (for that is what his name means) opposed them and tried to turn the proconsul from the faith. [9] Then Saul, who was also called

Called Through Community

ACTS 13:1–3

How often do you pray for God to set apart and empower leaders for your church? How often is this need mentioned in prayer during worship or other group gatherings? You might want to suggest this concern during worship or at a meeting. You might even offer to lead such a time of prayer. Perhaps you could read this passage and then suggest a time of silent prayer, focusing on the need to hear God's call. Or you might pray for the spiritual empowerment of those who already have positions of leadership, mentioning them by name or even laying hands on them as you pray.

See *Meeting God in Community*

Perverting the Right Ways of the Lord

ACTS 13:8–12

When Paul speaks of perverting the right ways of the Lord, he is reacting to an opponent's attempt to distort the Christian message in order to attack it. Where in your own life have you found yourself falsely under attack? In what ways were you able to stand firm? How were you able to display the love of Jesus Christ? Recall ways in which God was gracious in supporting you. Ask God for forgiveness for those times in which you did not stand firm. Commit the incident into God's hands, knowing he can bring good out of it, as he did for Paul.

See Meeting God in Prayer

Paul, filled with the Holy Spirit, looked straight at Elymas and said, [10]"You are a child of the devil and an enemy of everything that is right! You are full of all kinds of deceit and trickery. Will you never stop perverting the right ways of the Lord? [11]Now the hand of the Lord is against you. You are going to be blind, and for a time you will be unable to see the light of the sun."

Immediately mist and darkness came over him, and he groped about, seeking someone to lead him by the hand. [12]When the proconsul saw what had happened, he believed, for he was amazed at the teaching about the Lord.

In Pisidian Antioch

[13]From Paphos, Paul and his companions sailed to Perga in Pamphylia, where John left them to return to Jerusalem. [14]From Perga they went on to Pisidian Antioch. On the Sabbath they entered the synagogue and sat down. [15]After the reading from the Law and the Prophets, the synagogue rulers sent word to them, saying, "Brothers, if you have a message of encouragement for the people, please speak."

[16]Standing up, Paul motioned with his hand and said: "Men of Israel and you Gentiles who worship God, listen to me! [17]The God of the people of Israel chose our fathers; he made the people prosper during their stay in Egypt, with mighty power he led them out of that country, [18]he endured their conduct[a] for about forty years in the desert, [19]he overthrew seven nations in Canaan and gave their land to his people as their inheritance. [20]All this took about 450 years.

"After this, God gave them judges until the time of Samuel the prophet. [21]Then the people asked for a king, and he gave them Saul son of Kish, of the tribe of Benjamin, who ruled forty years. [22]After removing Saul, he made David their king. He testified concerning him: 'I have found David son of Jesse a man after my own heart; he will do everything I want him to do.'

[23]"From this man's descendants God has brought to Israel the Savior Jesus, as he promised. [24]Before the coming of Jesus, John preached repentance and baptism to all the people of Israel. [25]As John was completing his work, he said: 'Who do you think I am? I am not that one. No, but he is coming after me, whose sandals I am not worthy to untie.'

[26]"Brothers, children of Abraham, and you God-fearing Gentiles, it is to us that this message of salvation has been sent. [27]The people of Jerusalem and their rulers did not recognize Jesus, yet in condemning him they fulfilled the words of the prophets that are read every Sabbath. [28]Though they found no proper ground for a death sentence, they asked Pilate to have him executed. [29]When they had carried out all that was written about him, they took him down from the tree and laid him in a tomb. [30]But God raised him from the dead, [31]and for many days he was seen by those who had traveled with him from Galilee to Jerusalem. They are now his witnesses to our people.

[32]"We tell you the good news: What God promised our fathers [33]he has fulfilled for us, their children, by raising up Jesus. As it is written in the second Psalm:

a 18 Some manuscripts *and cared for them*

" 'You are my Son;
today I have become your Father.'*a'b*

34The fact that God raised him from the dead, never to decay, is stated in these words:

" 'I will give you the holy and sure blessings
promised to David.'*c*

35So it is stated elsewhere:

" 'You will not let your Holy One see decay.'*d*

36"For when David had served God's purpose in his own generation, he fell asleep; he was buried with his fathers and his body decayed. **37**But the one whom God raised from the dead did not see decay.

38"Therefore, my brothers, I want you to know that through Jesus the forgiveness of sins is proclaimed to you. **39**Through him everyone who believes is justified from everything you could not be justified from by the law of Moses. **40**Take care that what the prophets have said does not happen to you:

41" 'Look, you scoffers,
wonder and perish,
for I am going to do something in your days
that you would never believe,
even if someone told you.'*e*"

42As Paul and Barnabas were leaving the synagogue, the people invited them to speak further about these things on the next Sabbath. **43**When the congregation was dismissed, many of the Jews and devout converts to Judaism followed Paul and Barnabas, who talked with them and urged them to continue in the grace of God.

44On the next Sabbath almost the whole city gathered to hear the word of the Lord. **45**When the Jews saw the crowds, they were filled with jealousy and talked abusively against what Paul was saying.

46Then Paul and Barnabas answered them boldly: "We had to speak the word of God to you first. Since you reject it and do not consider yourselves worthy of eternal life, we now turn to the Gentiles. **47**For this is what the Lord has commanded us:

" 'I have made you*f* a light for the Gentiles,
that you*f* may bring salvation to the ends of the
earth.'*g*"

48When the Gentiles heard this, they were glad and honored the word of the Lord; and all who were appointed for eternal life believed.

49The word of the Lord spread through the whole region. **50**But the Jews incited the God-fearing women of high standing and the leading men of the city. They stirred up persecution against Paul and Barnabas, and expelled them from their region. **51**So they shook the dust from their feet in protest against them and went to Iconium. **52**And the disciples were filled with joy and with the Holy Spirit.

His Poverty, Our Riches

ACTS 13:38–39

"Become like Christ, since Christ has become like us . . . He has become inferior to make us superior; he has become poor to enrich us by his poverty; he has taken the condition of a slave to procure freedom for us; he has come on earth to bring us to heaven; he has been tempted to see us triumph; he has been dishonored to cover us with glory; he has died to save us; he has ascended to heaven to draw us to himself, we who lie prostrate because of falling into sin."

—GREGORY OF NAZIANZUS,
"Sermon I: On Easter" in *The Paschal Mystery*

---

a 33 Or *have begotten you*   *b 33* Psalm 2:7   *c 34* Isaiah 55:3   *d 35* Psalm 16:10   *e 41* Hab. 1:5   *f 47* The Greek is singular.   *g 47* Isaiah 49:6

All Good Gifts

ACTS 14:17

A hymn reminds us, "All good gifts around us are sent from heaven above." Another urges us to count our blessings and to name them one by one. Now might be a good time to do that. Write them down to make the exercise more concrete. How long a list can you make of the blessings in your life—the people, things and events for which you are thankful? When you have run out of ideas, go back over the list again, thanking God for each of these good gifts. Keep the list handy so you can come back to it when you need to remind yourself of what you truly appreciate in your life.

See Meeting God in Worship

In Iconium

14 At Iconium Paul and Barnabas went as usual into the Jewish synagogue. There they spoke so effectively that a great number of Jews and Gentiles believed. ²But the Jews who refused to believe stirred up the Gentiles and poisoned their minds against the brothers. ³So Paul and Barnabas spent considerable time there, speaking boldly for the Lord, who confirmed the message of his grace by enabling them to do miraculous signs and wonders. ⁴The people of the city were divided; some sided with the Jews, others with the apostles. ⁵There was a plot afoot among the Gentiles and Jews, together with their leaders, to mistreat them and stone them. ⁶But they found out about it and fled to the Lycaonian cities of Lystra and Derbe and to the surrounding country, ⁷where they continued to preach the good news.

In Lystra and Derbe

⁸In Lystra there sat a man crippled in his feet, who was lame from birth and had never walked. ⁹He listened to Paul as he was speaking. Paul looked directly at him, saw that he had faith to be healed ¹⁰and called out, "Stand up on your feet!" At that, the man jumped up and began to walk.

¹¹When the crowd saw what Paul had done, they shouted in the Lycaonian language, "The gods have come down to us in human form!" ¹²Barnabas they called Zeus, and Paul they called Hermes because he was the chief speaker. ¹³The priest of Zeus, whose temple was just outside the city, brought bulls and wreaths to the city gates because he and the crowd wanted to offer sacrifices to them.

¹⁴But when the apostles Barnabas and Paul heard of this, they tore their clothes and rushed out into the crowd, shouting: ¹⁵"Men, why are you doing this? We too are only men, human like you. We are bringing you good news, telling you to turn from these worthless things to the living God, who made heaven and earth and sea and everything in them. ¹⁶In the past, he let all nations go their own way. ¹⁷Yet he has not left himself without testimony: He has shown kindness by giving you rain from heaven and crops in their seasons; he provides you with plenty of food and fills your hearts with joy." ¹⁸Even with these words, they had difficulty keeping the crowd from sacrificing to them.

¹⁹Then some Jews came from Antioch and Iconium and won the crowd over. They stoned Paul and dragged him outside the city, thinking he was dead. ²⁰But after the disciples had gathered around him, he got up and went back into the city. The next day he and Barnabas left for Derbe.

The Return to Antioch in Syria

²¹They preached the good news in that city and won a large number of disciples. Then they returned to Lystra, Iconium and Antioch, ²²strengthening the disciples and encouraging them to remain true to the faith. "We must go through many hardships to enter the kingdom of God," they said. ²³Paul and Barnabas appointed elders*ᵃ* for them in each church and, with prayer and fasting, committed them to the Lord, in whom they had put their trust. ²⁴After going through Pisidia, they came into Pamphylia, ²⁵and

ᵃ 23 Or Barnabas ordained elders; or Barnabas had elders elected

when they had preached the word in Perga, they went down to Attalia. [26]From Attalia they sailed back to Antioch, where they had been committed to the grace of God for the work they had now completed. [27]On arriving there, they gathered the church together and reported all that God had done through them and how he had opened the door of faith to the Gentiles. [28]And they stayed there a long time with the disciples.

The Council at Jerusalem

15 Some men came down from Judea to Antioch and were teaching the brothers: "Unless you are circumcised, according to the custom taught by Moses, you cannot be saved." [2]This brought Paul and Barnabas into sharp dispute and debate with them. So Paul and Barnabas were appointed, along with some other believers, to go up to Jerusalem to see the apostles and elders about this question. [3]The church sent them on their way, and as they traveled through Phoenicia and Samaria, they told how the Gentiles had been converted. This news made all the brothers very glad. [4]When they came to Jerusalem, they were welcomed by the church and the apostles and elders, to whom they reported everything God had done through them.

[5]Then some of the believers who belonged to the party of the Pharisees stood up and said, "The Gentiles must be circumcised and required to obey the law of Moses."

[6]The apostles and elders met to consider this question. [7]After much discussion, Peter got up and addressed them: "Brothers, you know that some time ago God made a choice among you that the Gentiles might hear from my lips the message of the gospel and believe. [8]God, who knows the heart, showed that he accepted them by giving the Holy Spirit to them, just as he did to us. [9]He made no distinction between us and them, for he purified their hearts by faith. [10]Now then, why do you try to test God by putting on the necks of the disciples a yoke that neither we nor our fathers have been able to bear? [11]No! We believe it is through the grace of our Lord Jesus that we are saved, just as they are."

[12]The whole assembly became silent as they listened to Barnabas and Paul telling about the miraculous signs and wonders God had done among the Gentiles through them. [13]When they finished, James spoke up: "Brothers, listen to me. [14]Simon[a] has described to us how God at first showed his concern by taking from the Gentiles a people for himself. [15]The words of the prophets are in agreement with this, as it is written:

[16] " 'After this I will return
    and rebuild David's fallen tent.
  Its ruins I will rebuild,
    and I will restore it,
[17]that the remnant of men may seek the Lord,
    and all the Gentiles who bear my name,
  says the Lord, who does these things'[b]
[18]   that have been known for ages.[c]

[19]"It is my judgment, therefore, that we should not make

Extra Burdens

ACTS 15:10

The earliest Christian leaders decided not to put on the necks of the disciples a yoke too heavy to bear. Though we could point to many instances where leaders do heap on extra burdens, perhaps the heaviest burdens are those we heap on ourselves. What expectations do you have for yourself that continue to be a source of guilt? What private vows do you find impossible to keep? You might imagine yourself yoked to all these burdens, bent down under their weight. Ask God to break the yoke, release you from the weight of guilt and help you to stand tall, supported with grace. Thank God for setting you free.

See Meeting God in Scripture

---

a 14 Greek *Simeon*, a variant of *Simon*; that is, Peter   *b 17* Amos 9:11,12
c 17,18 Some manuscripts *things'— / 18known to the Lord for ages is his work*

1463

Receiving Exhortations

ACTS 15:22–31

When the Jerusalem council met to deliberate and to discern God's will, they knew they needed the collective wisdom of the group. When the decision was delivered, "the people read it and were glad for its encouraging message." Imagine that a present-day equivalent of the council is addressing a pressing issue in your life. How difficult would it be for you to consider the prayerful insights of others? On the other hand, in what situations might God want you to rely on your own prayerful insight?

See Meeting God in Community

it difficult for the Gentiles who are turning to God. [20]Instead we should write to them, telling them to abstain from food polluted by idols, from sexual immorality, from the meat of strangled animals and from blood. [21]For Moses has been preached in every city from the earliest times and is read in the synagogues on every Sabbath."

The Council's Letter to Gentile Believers

[22]Then the apostles and elders, with the whole church, decided to choose some of their own men and send them to Antioch with Paul and Barnabas. They chose Judas (called Barsabbas) and Silas, two men who were leaders among the brothers. [23]With them they sent the following letter:

The apostles and elders, your brothers,

To the Gentile believers in Antioch, Syria and Cilicia:

Greetings.

[24]We have heard that some went out from us without our authorization and disturbed you, troubling your minds by what they said. [25]So we all agreed to choose some men and send them to you with our dear friends Barnabas and Paul— [26]men who have risked their lives for the name of our Lord Jesus Christ. [27]Therefore we are sending Judas and Silas to confirm by word of mouth what we are writing. [28]It seemed good to the Holy Spirit and to us not to burden you with anything beyond the following requirements: [29]You are to abstain from food sacrificed to idols, from blood, from the meat of strangled animals and from sexual immorality. You will do well to avoid these things.

Farewell.

[30]The men were sent off and went down to Antioch, where they gathered the church together and delivered the letter. [31]The people read it and were glad for its encouraging message. [32]Judas and Silas, who themselves were prophets, said much to encourage and strengthen the brothers. [33]After spending some time there, they were sent off by the brothers with the blessing of peace to return to those who had sent them.[a] [35]But Paul and Barnabas remained in Antioch, where they and many others taught and preached the word of the Lord.

Disagreement Between Paul and Barnabas

[36]Some time later Paul said to Barnabas, "Let us go back and visit the brothers in all the towns where we preached the word of the Lord and see how they are doing." [37]Barnabas wanted to take John, also called Mark, with them, [38]but Paul did not think it wise to take him, because he had deserted them in Pamphylia and had not continued with them in the work. [39]They had such a sharp disagreement that they parted company. Barnabas took Mark and sailed for Cyprus, [40]but Paul chose Silas and left, commended by the brothers to the grace of the Lord. [41]He went through Syria and Cilicia, strengthening the churches.

a 33 Some manuscripts them, 34but Silas decided to remain there

Timothy Joins Paul and Silas

16 He came to Derbe and then to Lystra, where a disciple named Timothy lived, whose mother was a Jewess and a believer, but whose father was a Greek. ²The brothers at Lystra and Iconium spoke well of him. ³Paul wanted to take him along on the journey, so he circumcised him because of the Jews who lived in that area, for they all knew that his father was a Greek. ⁴As they traveled from town to town, they delivered the decisions reached by the apostles and elders in Jerusalem for the people to obey. ⁵So the churches were strengthened in the faith and grew daily in numbers.

Paul's Vision of the Man of Macedonia

⁶Paul and his companions traveled throughout the region of Phrygia and Galatia, having been kept by the Holy Spirit from preaching the word in the province of Asia. ⁷When they came to the border of Mysia, they tried to enter Bithynia, but the Spirit of Jesus would not allow them to. ⁸So they passed by Mysia and went down to Troas. ⁹During the night Paul had a vision of a man of Macedonia standing and begging him, "Come over to Macedonia and help us." ¹⁰After Paul had seen the vision, we got ready at once to leave for Macedonia, concluding that God had called us to preach the gospel to them.

Lydia's Conversion in Philippi

¹¹From Troas we put out to sea and sailed straight for Samothrace, and the next day on to Neapolis. ¹²From there we traveled to Philippi, a Roman colony and the leading city of that district of Macedonia. And we stayed there several days.

¹³On the Sabbath we went outside the city gate to the river, where we expected to find a place of prayer. We sat down and began to speak to the women who had gathered there. ¹⁴One of those listening was a woman named Lydia, a dealer in purple cloth from the city of Thyatira, who was a worshiper of God. The Lord opened her heart to respond to Paul's message. ¹⁵When she and the members of her household were baptized, she invited us to her home. "If you consider me a believer in the Lord," she said, "come and stay at my house." And she persuaded us.

Paul and Silas in Prison

¹⁶Once when we were going to the place of prayer, we were met by a slave girl who had a spirit by which she predicted the future. She earned a great deal of money for her owners by fortune-telling. ¹⁷This girl followed Paul and the rest of us, shouting, "These men are servants of the Most High God, who are telling you the way to be saved." ¹⁸She kept this up for many days. Finally Paul became so troubled that he turned around and said to the spirit, "In the name of Jesus Christ I command you to come out of her!" At that moment the spirit left her.

¹⁹When the owners of the slave girl realized that their hope of making money was gone, they seized Paul and Silas and dragged them into the marketplace to face the authorities. ²⁰They brought them before the magistrates and said, "These men are Jews, and are throwing our city

Receiving God's Guidance

ACTS 16:6–10

How have you experienced God's call or God's guidance during your life? Through dreams like the one Paul had? Through "closed doors" you could come to accept as God's will? Have you heard God speak through the voices of friends, through unexpected opportunities, through gut feelings? As you listen prayerfully to the people, things and events in your life right now, where can you hear God? What responses could you make? What response will you make?

See Meeting God in Everyday Life

An Earthshaking Experience

ACTS 16:25–34

This is a powerful story to play out in the imagination. You might want to imagine yourself in the role of the jailer. As you drift off to sleep, you are puzzled to hear your prisoners singing God's praises while chained in their cells. Then you awake with a start as an earthquake shakes open the prison doors. Terrified, you hear Paul call out, "Don't harm yourself!" Imagine your unrestrained joy when you and all your family are baptized. What other emotions do you experience? What parallels do you see in your own Christian experience? You might conclude with rejoicing that you too have "come to believe in God."

See *Meeting God in Scripture*

into an uproar ²¹by advocating customs unlawful for us Romans to accept or practice."

²²The crowd joined in the attack against Paul and Silas, and the magistrates ordered them to be stripped and beaten. ²³After they had been severely flogged, they were thrown into prison, and the jailer was commanded to guard them carefully. ²⁴Upon receiving such orders, he put them in the inner cell and fastened their feet in the stocks.

²⁵About midnight Paul and Silas were praying and singing hymns to God, and the other prisoners were listening to them. ²⁶Suddenly there was such a violent earthquake that the foundations of the prison were shaken. At once all the prison doors flew open, and everybody's chains came loose. ²⁷The jailer woke up, and when he saw the prison doors open, he drew his sword and was about to kill himself because he thought the prisoners had escaped. ²⁸But Paul shouted, "Don't harm yourself! We are all here!"

²⁹The jailer called for lights, rushed in and fell trembling before Paul and Silas. ³⁰He then brought them out and asked, "Sirs, what must I do to be saved?"

³¹They replied, "Believe in the Lord Jesus, and you will be saved—you and your household." ³²Then they spoke the word of the Lord to him and to all the others in his house. ³³At that hour of the night the jailer took them and washed their wounds; then immediately he and all his family were baptized. ³⁴The jailer brought them into his house and set a meal before them; he was filled with joy because he had come to believe in God—he and his whole family.

³⁵When it was daylight, the magistrates sent their officers to the jailer with the order: "Release those men." ³⁶The jailer told Paul, "The magistrates have ordered that you and Silas be released. Now you can leave. Go in peace."

³⁷But Paul said to the officers: "They beat us publicly without a trial, even though we are Roman citizens, and threw us into prison. And now do they want to get rid of us quietly? No! Let them come themselves and escort us out."

³⁸The officers reported this to the magistrates, and when they heard that Paul and Silas were Roman citizens, they were alarmed. ³⁹They came to appease them and escorted them from the prison, requesting them to leave the city. ⁴⁰After Paul and Silas came out of the prison, they went to Lydia's house, where they met with the brothers and encouraged them. Then they left.

In Thessalonica

17 When they had passed through Amphipolis and Apollonia, they came to Thessalonica, where there was a Jewish synagogue. ²As his custom was, Paul went into the synagogue, and on three Sabbath days he reasoned with them from the Scriptures, ³explaining and proving that the Christ*ᵃ* had to suffer and rise from the dead. "This Jesus I am proclaiming to you is the Christ,*ᵃ*" he said. ⁴Some of the Jews were persuaded and joined Paul and Silas, as did a large number of God-fearing Greeks and not a few prominent women.

⁵But the Jews were jealous; so they rounded up some bad characters from the marketplace, formed a mob and started a riot in the city. They rushed to Jason's house in search of Paul and Silas in order to bring them out to the crowd.*ᵇ*

ᵃ3 Or Messiah   *ᵇ5 Or the assembly of the people*

6But when they did not find them, they dragged Jason and some other brothers before the city officials, shouting: "These men who have caused trouble all over the world have now come here, 7and Jason has welcomed them into his house. They are all defying Caesar's decrees, saying that there is another king, one called Jesus." 8When they heard this, the crowd and the city officials were thrown into turmoil. 9Then they made Jason and the others post bond and let them go.

In Berea

10As soon as it was night, the brothers sent Paul and Silas away to Berea. On arriving there, they went to the Jewish synagogue. 11Now the Bereans were of more noble character than the Thessalonians, for they received the message with great eagerness and examined the Scriptures every day to see if what Paul said was true. 12Many of the Jews believed, as did also a number of prominent Greek women and many Greek men.

13When the Jews in Thessalonica learned that Paul was preaching the word of God at Berea, they went there too, agitating the crowds and stirring them up. 14The brothers immediately sent Paul to the coast, but Silas and Timothy stayed at Berea. 15The men who escorted Paul brought him to Athens and then left with instructions for Silas and Timothy to join him as soon as possible.

In Athens

16While Paul was waiting for them in Athens, he was greatly distressed to see that the city was full of idols. 17So he reasoned in the synagogue with the Jews and the God-fearing Greeks, as well as in the marketplace day by day with those who happened to be there. 18A group of Epicurean and Stoic philosophers began to dispute with him. Some of them asked, "What is this babbler trying to say?" Others remarked, "He seems to be advocating foreign gods." They said this because Paul was preaching the good news about Jesus and the resurrection. 19Then they took him and brought him to a meeting of the Areopagus, where they said to him, "May we know what this new teaching is that you are presenting? 20You are bringing some strange ideas to our ears, and we want to know what they mean." 21(All the Athenians and the foreigners who lived there spent their time doing nothing but talking about and listening to the latest ideas.)

22Paul then stood up in the meeting of the Areopagus and said: "Men of Athens! I see that in every way you are very religious. 23For as I walked around and looked carefully at your objects of worship, I even found an altar with this inscription: TO AN UNKNOWN GOD. Now what you worship as something unknown I am going to proclaim to you.

24"The God who made the world and everything in it is the Lord of heaven and earth and does not live in temples built by hands. 25And he is not served by human hands, as if he needed anything, because he himself gives all men life and breath and everything else. 26From one man he made every nation of men, that they should inhabit the whole earth; and he determined the times set for them and the exact places where they should live. 27God did this so that men would seek him and perhaps reach out for him and

When in Athens

ACTS 17:16–32

When the apostle Paul speaks to the people of Athens, he addresses them in the context of their culture. He begins with a common area of interest and speaks to them with respect. He speaks of the "UNKNOWN GOD," with whom they are familiar. He uses vocabulary they understand. And yet he delivers the gospel in its entirety and without watering it down.

Do you know anyone who needs to hear the gospel? How can you present the gospel to that individual within the context of the culture he or she knows and understands? Think about the kind of vocabulary you might use. Pray for the wisdom and creativity to think of a way to approach that person.

See Meeting God in Community

Shaking off the Dust

ACTS 18:6

Sometimes we have to admit defeat in our efforts to spread the gospel. The hardest part of this process is learning to shake off the dust and get on with our lives. How do defeats, hurts or broken relationships still weigh you down? You might want to name the defeat, then shake out your clothes while saying, "I am leaving you behind. Through Jesus Christ you have no more power over me. I will go on as God leads me." What new beginning is God calling you to? (See also Acts 22:19–21 and Matthew 10:14.)

See Meeting God in Service

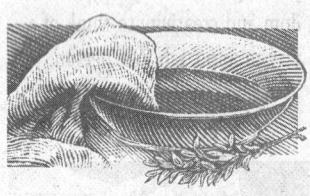

find him, though he is not far from each one of us. ²⁸'For in him we live and move and have our being.' As some of your own poets have said, 'We are his offspring.'

²⁹"Therefore since we are God's offspring, we should not think that the divine being is like gold or silver or stone—an image made by man's design and skill. ³⁰In the past God overlooked such ignorance, but now he commands all people everywhere to repent. ³¹For he has set a day when he will judge the world with justice by the man he has appointed. He has given proof of this to all men by raising him from the dead."

³²When they heard about the resurrection of the dead, some of them sneered, but others said, "We want to hear you again on this subject." ³³At that, Paul left the Council. ³⁴A few men became followers of Paul and believed. Among them was Dionysius, a member of the Areopagus, also a woman named Damaris, and a number of others.

In Corinth

18 After this, Paul left Athens and went to Corinth. ²There he met a Jew named Aquila, a native of Pontus, who had recently come from Italy with his wife Priscilla, because Claudius had ordered all the Jews to leave Rome. Paul went to see them, ³and because he was a tentmaker as they were, he stayed and worked with them. ⁴Every Sabbath he reasoned in the synagogue, trying to persuade Jews and Greeks.

⁵When Silas and Timothy came from Macedonia, Paul devoted himself exclusively to preaching, testifying to the Jews that Jesus was the Christ.ᵃ ⁶But when the Jews opposed Paul and became abusive, he shook out his clothes in protest and said to them, "Your blood be on your own heads! I am clear of my responsibility. From now on I will go to the Gentiles."

⁷Then Paul left the synagogue and went next door to the house of Titius Justus, a worshiper of God. ⁸Crispus, the synagogue ruler, and his entire household believed in the Lord; and many of the Corinthians who heard him believed and were baptized.

⁹One night the Lord spoke to Paul in a vision: "Do not be afraid; keep on speaking, do not be silent. ¹⁰For I am with you, and no one is going to attack and harm you, because I have many people in this city." ¹¹So Paul stayed for a year and a half, teaching them the word of God.

¹²While Gallio was proconsul of Achaia, the Jews made a united attack on Paul and brought him into court. ¹³"This man," they charged, "is persuading the people to worship God in ways contrary to the law."

¹⁴Just as Paul was about to speak, Gallio said to the Jews, "If you Jews were making a complaint about some misdemeanor or serious crime, it would be reasonable for me to listen to you. ¹⁵But since it involves questions about words and names and your own law—settle the matter yourselves. I will not be a judge of such things." ¹⁶So he had them ejected from the court. ¹⁷Then they all turned on Sosthenes the synagogue ruler and beat him in front of the court. But Gallio showed no concern whatever.

ᵃ 5 Or *Messiah;* also in verse 28

Priscilla, Aquila and Apollos

18Paul stayed on in Corinth for some time. Then he left the brothers and sailed for Syria, accompanied by Priscilla and Aquila. Before he sailed, he had his hair cut off at Cenchrea because of a vow he had taken. **19**They arrived at Ephesus, where Paul left Priscilla and Aquila. He himself went into the synagogue and reasoned with the Jews. **20**When they asked him to spend more time with them, he declined. **21**But as he left, he promised, "I will come back if it is God's will." Then he set sail from Ephesus. **22**When he landed at Caesarea, he went up and greeted the church and then went down to Antioch.

23After spending some time in Antioch, Paul set out from there and traveled from place to place throughout the region of Galatia and Phrygia, strengthening all the disciples.

24Meanwhile a Jew named Apollos, a native of Alexandria, came to Ephesus. He was a learned man, with a thorough knowledge of the Scriptures. **25**He had been instructed in the way of the Lord, and he spoke with great fervor*a* and taught about Jesus accurately, though he knew only the baptism of John. **26**He began to speak boldly in the synagogue. When Priscilla and Aquila heard him, they invited him to their home and explained to him the way of God more adequately.

27When Apollos wanted to go to Achaia, the brothers encouraged him and wrote to the disciples there to welcome him. On arriving, he was a great help to those who by grace had believed. **28**For he vigorously refuted the Jews in public debate, proving from the Scriptures that Jesus was the Christ.

Paul in Ephesus

19 While Apollos was at Corinth, Paul took the road through the interior and arrived at Ephesus. There he found some disciples **2**and asked them, "Did you receive the Holy Spirit when*b* you believed?"

They answered, "No, we have not even heard that there is a Holy Spirit."

3So Paul asked, "Then what baptism did you receive?"

"John's baptism," they replied.

4Paul said, "John's baptism was a baptism of repentance. He told the people to believe in the one coming after him, that is, in Jesus." **5**On hearing this, they were baptized into*c* the name of the Lord Jesus. **6**When Paul placed his hands on them, the Holy Spirit came on them, and they spoke in tongues*d* and prophesied. **7**There were about twelve men in all.

8Paul entered the synagogue and spoke boldly there for three months, arguing persuasively about the kingdom of God. **9**But some of them became obstinate; they refused to believe and publicly maligned the Way. So Paul left them. He took the disciples with him and had discussions daily in the lecture hall of Tyrannus. **10**This went on for two years, so that all the Jews and Greeks who lived in the province of Asia heard the word of the Lord.

11God did extraordinary miracles through Paul, **12**so that even handkerchiefs and aprons that had touched him were

---

Receive the Holy Spirit

ACTS 19:1–2

Paul asks, "Did you receive the Holy Spirit when you believed?" How have you experienced the Spirit in your life? In the extraordinary ways of speaking in tongues or performing miracles so often described in Acts? In the steady working of spiritual gifts? (See 1 Corinthians 12:4–11 and Ephesians 4:11–13.) In the quiet grace of the fruit of the Spirit? (See Galatians 5:22–23.) You might welcome the Spirit's presence with a hymn-prayer such as "Come, Holy Ghost, Our Souls Inspire," "Spirit of God, Descend Upon My Heart" or "Spirit of the Living God, Fall Afresh on Me."

See Meeting God in Worship

---

a 25 Or *with fervor in the Spirit*   *b 2* Or *after*   *c 5* Or *in*   *d 6* Or *other languages*

Who Must Lose?

ACTS 19:23–27

The silversmiths of Ephesus see the gospel as a threat to their livelihood. Certainly when lives are changed, those who profited from the old way must lose. What companies or businesses in your area would be threatened if more people took Christian discipleship seriously? Could they change? Or would they have to start over from scratch? What about your own livelihood? Are there changes you could implement in order to support a more Christian lifestyle?

See Meeting God in Community

taken to the sick, and their illnesses were cured and the evil spirits left them.

[13]Some Jews who went around driving out evil spirits tried to invoke the name of the Lord Jesus over those who were demon-possessed. They would say, "In the name of Jesus, whom Paul preaches, I command you to come out." [14]Seven sons of Sceva, a Jewish chief priest, were doing this. [15]One day, the evil spirit answered them, "Jesus I know, and I know about Paul, but who are you?" [16]Then the man who had the evil spirit jumped on them and overpowered them all. He gave them such a beating that they ran out of the house naked and bleeding.

[17]When this became known to the Jews and Greeks living in Ephesus, they were all seized with fear, and the name of the Lord Jesus was held in high honor. [18]Many of those who believed now came and openly confessed their evil deeds. [19]A number who had practiced sorcery brought their scrolls together and burned them publicly. When they calculated the value of the scrolls, the total came to fifty thousand drachmas.[a] [20]In this way the word of the Lord spread widely and grew in power.

[21]After all this had happened, Paul decided to go to Jerusalem, passing through Macedonia and Achaia. "After I have been there," he said, "I must visit Rome also." [22]He sent two of his helpers, Timothy and Erastus, to Macedonia, while he stayed in the province of Asia a little longer.

The Riot in Ephesus

[23]About that time there arose a great disturbance about the Way. [24]A silversmith named Demetrius, who made silver shrines of Artemis, brought in no little business for the craftsmen. [25]He called them together, along with the workmen in related trades, and said: "Men, you know we receive a good income from this business. [26]And you see and hear how this fellow Paul has convinced and led astray large numbers of people here in Ephesus and in practically the whole province of Asia. He says that man-made gods are no gods at all. [27]There is danger not only that our trade will lose its good name, but also that the temple of the great goddess Artemis will be discredited, and the goddess herself, who is worshiped throughout the province of Asia and the world, will be robbed of her divine majesty."

[28]When they heard this, they were furious and began shouting: "Great is Artemis of the Ephesians!" [29]Soon the whole city was in an uproar. The people seized Gaius and Aristarchus, Paul's traveling companions from Macedonia, and rushed as one man into the theater. [30]Paul wanted to appear before the crowd, but the disciples would not let him. [31]Even some of the officials of the province, friends of Paul, sent him a message begging him not to venture into the theater.

[32]The assembly was in confusion: Some were shouting one thing, some another. Most of the people did not even know why they were there. [33]The Jews pushed Alexander to the front, and some of the crowd shouted instructions to him. He motioned for silence in order to make a defense before the people. [34]But when they realized he was a Jew, they all shouted in unison for about two hours: "Great is Artemis of the Ephesians!"

[a] 19 A drachma was a silver coin worth about a day's wages.

[35]The city clerk quieted the crowd and said: "Men of Ephesus, doesn't all the world know that the city of Ephesus is the guardian of the temple of the great Artemis and of her image, which fell from heaven? [36]Therefore, since these facts are undeniable, you ought to be quiet and not do anything rash. [37]You have brought these men here, though they have neither robbed temples nor blasphemed our goddess. [38]If, then, Demetrius and his fellow craftsmen have a grievance against anybody, the courts are open and there are proconsuls. They can press charges. [39]If there is anything further you want to bring up, it must be settled in a legal assembly. [40]As it is, we are in danger of being charged with rioting because of today's events. In that case we would not be able to account for this commotion, since there is no reason for it." [41]After he had said this, he dismissed the assembly.

Through Macedonia and Greece

20 When the uproar had ended, Paul sent for the disciples and, after encouraging them, said good-by and set out for Macedonia. [2]He traveled through that area, speaking many words of encouragement to the people, and finally arrived in Greece, [3]where he stayed three months. Because the Jews made a plot against him just as he was about to sail for Syria, he decided to go back through Macedonia. [4]He was accompanied by Sopater son of Pyrrhus from Berea, Aristarchus and Secundus from Thessalonica, Gaius from Derbe, Timothy also, and Tychicus and Trophimus from the province of Asia. [5]These men went on ahead and waited for us at Troas. [6]But we sailed from Philippi after the Feast of Unleavened Bread, and five days later joined the others at Troas, where we stayed seven days.

Eutychus Raised From the Dead at Troas

[7]On the first day of the week we came together to break bread. Paul spoke to the people and, because he intended to leave the next day, kept on talking until midnight. [8]There were many lamps in the upstairs room where we were meeting. [9]Seated in a window was a young man named Eutychus, who was sinking into a deep sleep as Paul talked on and on. When he was sound asleep, he fell to the ground from the third story and was picked up dead. [10]Paul went down, threw himself on the young man and put his arms around him. "Don't be alarmed," he said. "He's alive!" [11]Then he went upstairs again and broke bread and ate. After talking until daylight, he left. [12]The people took the young man home alive and were greatly comforted.

Paul's Farewell to the Ephesian Elders

[13]We went on ahead to the ship and sailed for Assos, where we were going to take Paul aboard. He had made this arrangement because he was going there on foot. [14]When he met us at Assos, we took him aboard and went on to Mitylene. [15]The next day we set sail from there and arrived off Kios. The day after that we crossed over to Samos, and on the following day arrived at Miletus. [16]Paul had decided to sail past Ephesus to avoid spending time in the province of Asia, for he was in a hurry to reach Jerusalem, if possible, by the day of Pentecost.

Resurrection Power

ACTS 20:7–12

Even a wearying three-hour sermon can lead to an experience of God's resurrection power. When have you most vividly felt God's presence or power in worship? What made that experience come alive? As you reflect on the experience, what do you recognize about your own need for God? What can you learn about God's ways of reaching out to you? What difference did the presence of the worshiping community make?

See Meeting God in Worship

Genuine Community

ACTS 20:36–37

"I have community with others and I shall continue to have it only through Jesus Christ. The more genuine and the deeper our community becomes, the more surely will everything between us recede, the more clearly and purely will Jesus Christ and his work become the one and only thing that is vital between us."

—DIETRICH BONHOEFFER,
Life Together

17 From Miletus, Paul sent to Ephesus for the elders of the church. 18 When they arrived, he said to them: "You know how I lived the whole time I was with you, from the first day I came into the province of Asia. 19 I served the Lord with great humility and with tears, although I was severely tested by the plots of the Jews. 20 You know that I have not hesitated to preach anything that would be helpful to you but have taught you publicly and from house to house. 21 I have declared to both Jews and Greeks that they must turn to God in repentance and have faith in our Lord Jesus.

22 "And now, compelled by the Spirit, I am going to Jerusalem, not knowing what will happen to me there. 23 I only know that in every city the Holy Spirit warns me that prison and hardships are facing me. 24 However, I consider my life worth nothing to me, if only I may finish the race and complete the task the Lord Jesus has given me—the task of testifying to the gospel of God's grace.

25 "Now I know that none of you among whom I have gone about preaching the kingdom will ever see me again. 26 Therefore, I declare to you today that I am innocent of the blood of all men. 27 For I have not hesitated to proclaim to you the whole will of God. 28 Keep watch over yourselves and all the flock of which the Holy Spirit has made you overseers.*a* Be shepherds of the church of God,*b* which he bought with his own blood. 29 I know that after I leave, savage wolves will come in among you and will not spare the flock. 30 Even from your own number men will arise and distort the truth in order to draw away disciples after them. 31 So be on your guard! Remember that for three years I never stopped warning each of you night and day with tears.

32 "Now I commit you to God and to the word of his grace, which can build you up and give you an inheritance among all those who are sanctified. 33 I have not coveted anyone's silver or gold or clothing. 34 You yourselves know that these hands of mine have supplied my own needs and the needs of my companions. 35 In everything I did, I showed you that by this kind of hard work we must help the weak, remembering the words the Lord Jesus himself said: 'It is more blessed to give than to receive.' "

36 When he had said this, he knelt down with all of them and prayed. 37 They all wept as they embraced him and kissed him. 38 What grieved them most was his statement that they would never see his face again. Then they accompanied him to the ship.

On to Jerusalem

21 After we had torn ourselves away from them, we put out to sea and sailed straight to Cos. The next day we went to Rhodes and from there to Patara. 2 We found a ship crossing over to Phoenicia, went on board and set sail. 3 After sighting Cyprus and passing to the south of it, we sailed on to Syria. We landed at Tyre, where our ship was to unload its cargo. 4 Finding the disciples there, we stayed with them seven days. Through the Spirit they urged Paul not to go on to Jerusalem. 5 But when our time was up, we left and continued on our way. All the disciples and their wives and children accompanied us out of the city, and there on the

a 28 Traditionally *bishops*   *b 28* Many manuscripts *of the Lord* beach we knelt to pray. ⁶After saying good-by to each other, we went aboard the ship, and they returned home.

⁷We continued our voyage from Tyre and landed at Ptolemais, where we greeted the brothers and stayed with them for a day. ⁸Leaving the next day, we reached Caesarea and stayed at the house of Philip the evangelist, one of the Seven. ⁹He had four unmarried daughters who prophesied.

¹⁰After we had been there a number of days, a prophet named Agabus came down from Judea. ¹¹Coming over to us, he took Paul's belt, tied his own hands and feet with it and said, "The Holy Spirit says, 'In this way the Jews of Jerusalem will bind the owner of this belt and will hand him over to the Gentiles.' "

¹²When we heard this, we and the people there pleaded with Paul not to go up to Jerusalem. ¹³Then Paul answered, "Why are you weeping and breaking my heart? I am ready not only to be bound, but also to die in Jerusalem for the name of the Lord Jesus." ¹⁴When he would not be dissuaded, we gave up and said, "The Lord's will be done."

¹⁵After this, we got ready and went up to Jerusalem. ¹⁶Some of the disciples from Caesarea accompanied us and brought us to the home of Mnason, where we were to stay. He was a man from Cyprus and one of the early disciples.

Paul's Arrival at Jerusalem

¹⁷When we arrived at Jerusalem, the brothers received us warmly. ¹⁸The next day Paul and the rest of us went to see James, and all the elders were present. ¹⁹Paul greeted them and reported in detail what God had done among the Gentiles through his ministry.

²⁰When they heard this, they praised God. Then they said to Paul: "You see, brother, how many thousands of Jews have believed, and all of them are zealous for the law. ²¹They have been informed that you teach all the Jews who live among the Gentiles to turn away from Moses, telling them not to circumcise their children or live according to our customs. ²²What shall we do? They will certainly hear that you have come, ²³so do what we tell you. There are four men with us who have made a vow. ²⁴Take these men, join in their purification rites and pay their expenses, so that they can have their heads shaved. Then everybody will know there is no truth in these reports about you, but that you yourself are living in obedience to the law. ²⁵As for the Gentile believers, we have written to them our decision that they should abstain from food sacrificed to idols, from blood, from the meat of strangled animals and from sexual immorality."

²⁶The next day Paul took the men and purified himself along with them. Then he went to the temple to give notice of the date when the days of purification would end and the offering would be made for each of them.

Paul Arrested

²⁷When the seven days were nearly over, some Jews from the province of Asia saw Paul at the temple. They stirred up the whole crowd and seized him, ²⁸shouting, "Men of Israel, help us! This is the man who teaches all men everywhere against our people and our law and this place. And besides, he has brought Greeks into the temple area and defiled this holy place." ²⁹(They had previously seen Troph-

"Why Are You Weeping?"

ACTS 21:13–14

How can we best support loved ones who face trouble? Paul seems to find his companions' weeping less than helpful. Do you pray that your loved ones may find relief from their problems or that they may find the courage and strength to face them? Sometimes the best we can do is what Paul's friends did: Be silent except to say, "The Lord's will be done." For what friends or family members do you need to offer that prayer today? You might also want to pray for yourself, for the willingness to release them into God's care.

See Meeting God in Prayer

Paul's Conversion

ACTS 22:6–11

As Paul tells his story, you might try picturing the event as if you had been there with Paul as a traveling companion. See the road as you walk toward Damascus. Feel the heat of the sun, smell the animals, taste the blowing dust. Do you see the bright light or only Paul's reaction as he falls, blinded? Imagine yourself helping him up, asking what has happened. What does he say? What is your response? After imagining the story as a bystander, you might try putting yourself in the role of Paul. Is your experience of the event different?

See *Meeting God in Scripture*

imus the Ephesian in the city with Paul and assumed that Paul had brought him into the temple area.)

³⁰The whole city was aroused, and the people came running from all directions. Seizing Paul, they dragged him from the temple, and immediately the gates were shut. ³¹While they were trying to kill him, news reached the commander of the Roman troops that the whole city of Jerusalem was in an uproar. ³²He at once took some officers and soldiers and ran down to the crowd. When the rioters saw the commander and his soldiers, they stopped beating Paul.

³³The commander came up and arrested him and ordered him to be bound with two chains. Then he asked who he was and what he had done. ³⁴Some in the crowd shouted one thing and some another, and since the commander could not get at the truth because of the uproar, he ordered that Paul be taken into the barracks. ³⁵When Paul reached the steps, the violence of the mob was so great he had to be carried by the soldiers. ³⁶The crowd that followed kept shouting, "Away with him!"

Paul Speaks to the Crowd

³⁷As the soldiers were about to take Paul into the barracks, he asked the commander, "May I say something to you?"

"Do you speak Greek?" he replied. ³⁸"Aren't you the Egyptian who started a revolt and led four thousand terrorists out into the desert some time ago?"

³⁹Paul answered, "I am a Jew, from Tarsus in Cilicia, a citizen of no ordinary city. Please let me speak to the people."

⁴⁰Having received the commander's permission, Paul stood on the steps and motioned to the crowd. When they were all silent, he said to them in Aramaic[a]: **22** ¹"Brothers and fathers, listen now to my defense."

²When they heard him speak to them in Aramaic, they became very quiet.

Then Paul said: ³"I am a Jew, born in Tarsus of Cilicia, but brought up in this city. Under Gamaliel I was thoroughly trained in the law of our fathers and was just as zealous for God as any of you are today. ⁴I persecuted the followers of this Way to their death, arresting both men and women and throwing them into prison, ⁵as also the high priest and all the Council can testify. I even obtained letters from them to their brothers in Damascus, and went there to bring these people as prisoners to Jerusalem to be punished.

⁶"About noon as I came near Damascus, suddenly a bright light from heaven flashed around me. ⁷I fell to the ground and heard a voice say to me, 'Saul! Saul! Why do you persecute me?'

⁸" 'Who are you, Lord?' I asked.

" 'I am Jesus of Nazareth, whom you are persecuting,' he replied. ⁹My companions saw the light, but they did not understand the voice of him who was speaking to me.

¹⁰" 'What shall I do, Lord?' I asked.

" 'Get up,' the Lord said, 'and go into Damascus. There you will be told all that you have been assigned to do.' ¹¹My companions led me by the hand into Damascus, because the brilliance of the light had blinded me.

¹²"A man named Ananias came to see me. He was a de-

a 40 Or possibly *Hebrew*; also in 22:2

vout observer of the law and highly respected by all the Jews living there. ¹³He stood beside me and said, 'Brother Saul, receive your sight!' And at that very moment I was able to see him.

¹⁴"Then he said: 'The God of our fathers has chosen you to know his will and to see the Righteous One and to hear words from his mouth. ¹⁵You will be his witness to all men of what you have seen and heard. ¹⁶And now what are you waiting for? Get up, be baptized and wash your sins away, calling on his name.'

¹⁷"When I returned to Jerusalem and was praying at the temple, I fell into a trance ¹⁸and saw the Lord speaking. 'Quick!' he said to me. 'Leave Jerusalem immediately, because they will not accept your testimony about me.'

¹⁹" 'Lord,' I replied, 'these men know that I went from one synagogue to another to imprison and beat those who believe in you. ²⁰And when the blood of your martyr[a] Stephen was shed, I stood there giving my approval and guarding the clothes of those who were killing him.'

²¹"Then the Lord said to me, 'Go; I will send you far away to the Gentiles.' "

Paul the Roman Citizen

²²The crowd listened to Paul until he said this. Then they raised their voices and shouted, "Rid the earth of him! He's not fit to live!"

²³As they were shouting and throwing off their cloaks and flinging dust into the air, ²⁴the commander ordered Paul to be taken into the barracks. He directed that he be flogged and questioned in order to find out why the people were shouting at him like this. ²⁵As they stretched him out to flog him, Paul said to the centurion standing there, "Is it legal for you to flog a Roman citizen who hasn't even been found guilty?"

²⁶When the centurion heard this, he went to the commander and reported it. "What are you going to do?" he asked. "This man is a Roman citizen."

²⁷The commander went to Paul and asked, "Tell me, are you a Roman citizen?"

"Yes, I am," he answered.

²⁸Then the commander said, "I had to pay a big price for my citizenship."

"But I was born a citizen," Paul replied.

²⁹Those who were about to question him withdrew immediately. The commander himself was alarmed when he realized that he had put Paul, a Roman citizen, in chains.

Before the Sanhedrin

³⁰The next day, since the commander wanted to find out exactly why Paul was being accused by the Jews, he released him and ordered the chief priests and all the Sanhedrin to assemble. Then he brought Paul and had him stand before them.

23 Paul looked straight at the Sanhedrin and said, "My brothers, I have fulfilled my duty to God in all good conscience to this day." ²At this the high priest Ananias ordered those standing near Paul to strike him on the mouth. ³Then Paul said to him, "God will strike you, you whitewashed wall! You sit there to judge me according to the law,

Those We Cannot Reach

ACTS 22:19–21

Jesus told Paul to leave Jerusalem because Paul could not effectively preach the gospel to the people there. They knew too much of his past to accept his changed life. It can be both frustrating and humbling to admit that there are some people who will never listen to what we have to say. Whom have you tried to reach out to, only to be rebuffed? Relatives? Old friends? Inactive church members? Can you accept Jesus' permission to leave them and go on to others who may be more responsive? Express your love for them as you commit them to Jesus' care. Then listen for his call to pursue new opportunities.

Take Courage

ACTS 23:11

Who are your enemies? Are there people or groups who criticize you or belittle you personally? People who stand against what is important to you? What particular temptations must you struggle with? What spiritual powers seem to be opposing you? (See Ephesians 6:10–12.) You might try to picture your enemies surrounding you, trying to reach you. But Jesus stands next to you, and they cannot come into his light. Hear his word to you: "Take courage!" He tells you that your battle is not yet over, for he has more for you to do. As you stand with him in his light, hear again his words, "Take courage!"

yet you yourself violate the law by commanding that I be struck!"

[4]Those who were standing near Paul said, "You dare to insult God's high priest?"

[5]Paul replied, "Brothers, I did not realize that he was the high priest; for it is written: 'Do not speak evil about the ruler of your people.'[a]"

[6]Then Paul, knowing that some of them were Sadducees and the others Pharisees, called out in the Sanhedrin, "My brothers, I am a Pharisee, the son of a Pharisee. I stand on trial because of my hope in the resurrection of the dead." [7]When he said this, a dispute broke out between the Pharisees and the Sadducees, and the assembly was divided. [8](The Sadducees say that there is no resurrection, and that there are neither angels nor spirits, but the Pharisees acknowledge them all.)

[9]There was a great uproar, and some of the teachers of the law who were Pharisees stood up and argued vigorously. "We find nothing wrong with this man," they said. "What if a spirit or an angel has spoken to him?" [10]The dispute became so violent that the commander was afraid Paul would be torn to pieces by them. He ordered the troops to go down and take him away from them by force and bring him into the barracks.

[11]The following night the Lord stood near Paul and said, "Take courage! As you have testified about me in Jerusalem, so you must also testify in Rome."

The Plot to Kill Paul

[12]The next morning the Jews formed a conspiracy and bound themselves with an oath not to eat or drink until they had killed Paul. [13]More than forty men were involved in this plot. [14]They went to the chief priests and elders and said, "We have taken a solemn oath not to eat anything until we have killed Paul. [15]Now then, you and the Sanhedrin petition the commander to bring him before you on the pretext of wanting more accurate information about his case. We are ready to kill him before he gets here."

[16]But when the son of Paul's sister heard of this plot, he went into the barracks and told Paul.

[17]Then Paul called one of the centurions and said, "Take this young man to the commander; he has something to tell him." [18]So he took him to the commander.

The centurion said, "Paul, the prisoner, sent for me and asked me to bring this young man to you because he has something to tell you."

[19]The commander took the young man by the hand, drew him aside and asked, "What is it you want to tell me?"

[20]He said: "The Jews have agreed to ask you to bring Paul before the Sanhedrin tomorrow on the pretext of wanting more accurate information about him. [21]Don't give in to them, because more than forty of them are waiting in ambush for him. They have taken an oath not to eat or drink until they have killed him. They are ready now, waiting for your consent to their request."

[22]The commander dismissed the young man and cautioned him, "Don't tell anyone that you have reported this to me."

[a] 5 Exodus 22:28

Paul Transferred to Caesarea

²³Then he called two of his centurions and ordered them, "Get ready a detachment of two hundred soldiers, seventy horsemen and two hundred spearmen*a* to go to Caesarea at nine tonight. ²⁴Provide mounts for Paul so that he may be taken safely to Governor Felix."

²⁵He wrote a letter as follows:

²⁶Claudius Lysias,

To His Excellency, Governor Felix:

Greetings.

²⁷This man was seized by the Jews and they were about to kill him, but I came with my troops and rescued him, for I had learned that he is a Roman citizen. ²⁸I wanted to know why they were accusing him, so I brought him to their Sanhedrin. ²⁹I found that the accusation had to do with questions about their law, but there was no charge against him that deserved death or imprisonment. ³⁰When I was informed of a plot to be carried out against the man, I sent him to you at once. I also ordered his accusers to present to you their case against him.

³¹So the soldiers, carrying out their orders, took Paul with them during the night and brought him as far as Antipatris. ³²The next day they let the cavalry go on with him, while they returned to the barracks. ³³When the cavalry arrived in Caesarea, they delivered the letter to the governor and handed Paul over to him. ³⁴The governor read the letter and asked what province he was from. Learning that he was from Cilicia, ³⁵he said, "I will hear your case when your accusers get here." Then he ordered that Paul be kept under guard in Herod's palace.

The Trial Before Felix

24 Five days later the high priest Ananias went down to Caesarea with some of the elders and a lawyer named Tertullus, and they brought their charges against Paul before the governor. ²When Paul was called in, Tertullus presented his case before Felix: "We have enjoyed a long period of peace under you, and your foresight has brought about reforms in this nation. ³Everywhere and in every way, most excellent Felix, we acknowledge this with profound gratitude. ⁴But in order not to weary you further, I would request that you be kind enough to hear us briefly.

⁵"We have found this man to be a troublemaker, stirring up riots among the Jews all over the world. He is a ringleader of the Nazarene sect ⁶and even tried to desecrate the temple; so we seized him. ⁸By*b* examining him yourself you will be able to learn the truth about all these charges we are bringing against him."

⁹The Jews joined in the accusation, asserting that these things were true.

¹⁰When the governor motioned for him to speak, Paul

a 23 The meaning of the Greek for this word is uncertain.   *b 6–8* Some manuscripts *him and wanted to judge him according to our law.* *7But the commander, Lysias, came and with the use of much force snatched him from our hands* *8and ordered his accusers to come before you. By*

Doing Your Best

ACTS 24:16

"So I strive always to keep my conscience clear before God and man." What a statement Paul makes! Can you make such a claim? When are you inspired to do your best? When do you feel it is okay to slack off, to offer less than your best? What are some specific occasions recently when you have done less than you could have? Did you let others down? Did you let God down? What can you do now to clear your conscience? Is it enough to ask forgiveness, or are there other actions you need to take as well?

See Meeting God in Prayer

replied: "I know that for a number of years you have been a judge over this nation; so I gladly make my defense. ¹¹You can easily verify that no more than twelve days ago I went up to Jerusalem to worship. ¹²My accusers did not find me arguing with anyone at the temple, or stirring up a crowd in the synagogues or anywhere else in the city. ¹³And they cannot prove to you the charges they are now making against me. ¹⁴However, I admit that I worship the God of our fathers as a follower of the Way, which they call a sect. I believe everything that agrees with the Law and that is written in the Prophets, ¹⁵and I have the same hope in God as these men, that there will be a resurrection of both the righteous and the wicked. ¹⁶So I strive always to keep my conscience clear before God and man.

¹⁷"After an absence of several years, I came to Jerusalem to bring my people gifts for the poor and to present offerings. ¹⁸I was ceremonially clean when they found me in the temple courts doing this. There was no crowd with me, nor was I involved in any disturbance. ¹⁹But there are some Jews from the province of Asia, who ought to be here before you and bring charges if they have anything against me. ²⁰Or these who are here should state what crime they found in me when I stood before the Sanhedrin— ²¹unless it was this one thing I shouted as I stood in their presence: 'It is concerning the resurrection of the dead that I am on trial before you today.' "

²²Then Felix, who was well acquainted with the Way, adjourned the proceedings. "When Lysias the commander comes," he said, "I will decide your case." ²³He ordered the centurion to keep Paul under guard but to give him some freedom and permit his friends to take care of his needs.

²⁴Several days later Felix came with his wife Drusilla, who was a Jewess. He sent for Paul and listened to him as he spoke about faith in Christ Jesus. ²⁵As Paul discoursed on righteousness, self-control and the judgment to come, Felix was afraid and said, "That's enough for now! You may leave. When I find it convenient, I will send for you." ²⁶At the same time he was hoping that Paul would offer him a bribe, so he sent for him frequently and talked with him.

²⁷When two years had passed, Felix was succeeded by Porcius Festus, but because Felix wanted to grant a favor to the Jews, he left Paul in prison.

The Trial Before Festus

25 Three days after arriving in the province, Festus went up from Caesarea to Jerusalem, ²where the chief priests and Jewish leaders appeared before him and presented the charges against Paul. ³They urgently requested Festus, as a favor to them, to have Paul transferred to Jerusalem, for they were preparing an ambush to kill him along the way. ⁴Festus answered, "Paul is being held at Caesarea, and I myself am going there soon. ⁵Let some of your leaders come with me and press charges against the man there, if he has done anything wrong."

⁶After spending eight or ten days with them, he went down to Caesarea, and the next day he convened the court and ordered that Paul be brought before him. ⁷When Paul appeared, the Jews who had come down from Jerusalem stood around him, bringing many serious charges against him, which they could not prove.

⁸Then Paul made his defense: "I have done nothing wrong against the law of the Jews or against the temple or against Caesar."

⁹Festus, wishing to do the Jews a favor, said to Paul, "Are you willing to go up to Jerusalem and stand trial before me there on these charges?"

¹⁰Paul answered: "I am now standing before Caesar's court, where I ought to be tried. I have not done any wrong to the Jews, as you yourself know very well. ¹¹If, however, I am guilty of doing anything deserving death, I do not refuse to die. But if the charges brought against me by these Jews are not true, no one has the right to hand me over to them. I appeal to Caesar!"

¹²After Festus had conferred with his council, he declared: "You have appealed to Caesar. To Caesar you will go!"

Festus Consults King Agrippa

¹³A few days later King Agrippa and Bernice arrived at Caesarea to pay their respects to Festus. ¹⁴Since they were spending many days there, Festus discussed Paul's case with the king. He said: "There is a man here whom Felix left as a prisoner. ¹⁵When I went to Jerusalem, the chief priests and elders of the Jews brought charges against him and asked that he be condemned.

¹⁶"I told them that it is not the Roman custom to hand over any man before he has faced his accusers and has had an opportunity to defend himself against their charges. ¹⁷When they came here with me, I did not delay the case, but convened the court the next day and ordered the man to be brought in. ¹⁸When his accusers got up to speak, they did not charge him with any of the crimes I had expected. ¹⁹Instead, they had some points of dispute with him about their own religion and about a dead man named Jesus who Paul claimed was alive. ²⁰I was at a loss how to investigate such matters; so I asked if he would be willing to go to Jerusalem and stand trial there on these charges. ²¹When Paul made his appeal to be held over for the Emperor's decision, I ordered him held until I could send him to Caesar."

²²Then Agrippa said to Festus, "I would like to hear this man myself."

He replied, "Tomorrow you will hear him."

Paul Before Agrippa

²³The next day Agrippa and Bernice came with great pomp and entered the audience room with the high ranking officers and the leading men of the city. At the command of Festus, Paul was brought in. ²⁴Festus said: "King Agrippa, and all who are present with us, you see this man! The whole Jewish community has petitioned me about him in Jerusalem and here in Caesarea, shouting that he ought not to live any longer. ²⁵I found he had done nothing deserving of death, but because he made his appeal to the Emperor I decided to send him to Rome. ²⁶But I have nothing definite to write to His Majesty about him. Therefore I have brought him before all of you, and especially before you, King Agrippa, so that as a result of this investigation I may have something to write. ²⁷For I think it is unreasonable to send on a prisoner without specifying the charges against him."

Praying for Justice

ACTS 25:18–19

The quest for truth and justice is often a difficult one. How might you undergird it with prayer? One possibility might be to attend a trial in your area or follow a trial through newspaper accounts, not to come to some judgment but simply to pray for all of those involved: defendant and accuser, defense attorney and prosecutor, judge and jury. Pray for wisdom and courage and patience. Pray for the Spirit's guidance.

See Meeting God in Everyday Life

Kicking Against the Goads

ACTS 26:14–16

This third report of Paul's conversion is the first one to include these words of Jesus: "It is hard for you to kick against the goads." Where in your own life have you "kicked against" God's guidance? What have you lost by insisting on your own way rather than God's? How have you been hurt? What is God prodding you toward now? You might write out answers to three questions: What is God calling me to be? What is God calling me to do? What specific actions can I take to respond to these calls?

See Meeting God in Service

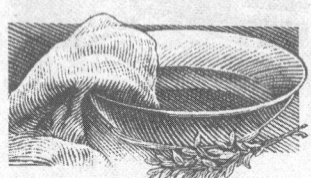

26 Then Agrippa said to Paul, "You have permission to speak for yourself."

So Paul motioned with his hand and began his defense: ²"King Agrippa, I consider myself fortunate to stand before you today as I make my defense against all the accusations of the Jews, ³and especially so because you are well acquainted with all the Jewish customs and controversies. Therefore, I beg you to listen to me patiently.

⁴"The Jews all know the way I have lived ever since I was a child, from the beginning of my life in my own country, and also in Jerusalem. ⁵They have known me for a long time and can testify, if they are willing, that according to the strictest sect of our religion, I lived as a Pharisee. ⁶And now it is because of my hope in what God has promised our fathers that I am on trial today. ⁷This is the promise our twelve tribes are hoping to see fulfilled as they earnestly serve God day and night. O king, it is because of this hope that the Jews are accusing me. ⁸Why should any of you consider it incredible that God raises the dead?

⁹"I too was convinced that I ought to do all that was possible to oppose the name of Jesus of Nazareth. ¹⁰And that is just what I did in Jerusalem. On the authority of the chief priests I put many of the saints in prison, and when they were put to death, I cast my vote against them. ¹¹Many a time I went from one synagogue to another to have them punished, and I tried to force them to blaspheme. In my obsession against them, I even went to foreign cities to persecute them.

¹²"On one of these journeys I was going to Damascus with the authority and commission of the chief priests. ¹³About noon, O king, as I was on the road, I saw a light from heaven, brighter than the sun, blazing around me and my companions. ¹⁴We all fell to the ground, and I heard a voice saying to me in Aramaic,ᵃ 'Saul, Saul, why do you persecute me? It is hard for you to kick against the goads.'

¹⁵"Then I asked, 'Who are you, Lord?'

"'I am Jesus, whom you are persecuting,' the Lord replied. ¹⁶'Now get up and stand on your feet. I have appeared to you to appoint you as a servant and as a witness of what you have seen of me and what I will show you. ¹⁷I will rescue you from your own people and from the Gentiles. I am sending you to them ¹⁸to open their eyes and turn them from darkness to light, and from the power of Satan to God, so that they may receive forgiveness of sins and a place among those who are sanctified by faith in me.'

¹⁹"So then, King Agrippa, I was not disobedient to the vision from heaven. ²⁰First to those in Damascus, then to those in Jerusalem and in all Judea, and to the Gentiles also, I preached that they should repent and turn to God and prove their repentance by their deeds. ²¹That is why the Jews seized me in the temple courts and tried to kill me. ²²But I have had God's help to this very day, and so I stand here and testify to small and great alike. I am saying nothing beyond what the prophets and Moses said would happen— ²³that the Christᵇ would suffer and, as the first to rise from the dead, would proclaim light to his own people and to the Gentiles."

²⁴At this point Festus interrupted Paul's defense. "You are

ᵃ *14 Or Hebrew*   ᵇ *23 Or Messiah*

out of your mind, Paul!" he shouted. "Your great learning is driving you insane."

²⁵"I am not insane, most excellent Festus," Paul replied. "What I am saying is true and reasonable. ²⁶The king is familiar with these things, and I can speak freely to him. I am convinced that none of this has escaped his notice, because it was not done in a corner. ²⁷King Agrippa, do you believe the prophets? I know you do."

²⁸Then Agrippa said to Paul, "Do you think that in such a short time you can persuade me to be a Christian?"

²⁹Paul replied, "Short time or long—I pray God that not only you but all who are listening to me today may become what I am, except for these chains."

³⁰The king rose, and with him the governor and Bernice and those sitting with them. ³¹They left the room, and while talking with one another, they said, "This man is not doing anything that deserves death or imprisonment."

³²Agrippa said to Festus, "This man could have been set free if he had not appealed to Caesar."

Paul Sails for Rome

27 When it was decided that we would sail for Italy, Paul and some other prisoners were handed over to a centurion named Julius, who belonged to the Imperial Regiment. ²We boarded a ship from Adramyttium about to sail for ports along the coast of the province of Asia, and we put out to sea. Aristarchus, a Macedonian from Thessalonica, was with us.

³The next day we landed at Sidon; and Julius, in kindness to Paul, allowed him to go to his friends so they might provide for his needs. ⁴From there we put out to sea again and passed to the lee of Cyprus because the winds were against us. ⁵When we had sailed across the open sea off the coast of Cilicia and Pamphylia, we landed at Myra in Lycia. ⁶There the centurion found an Alexandrian ship sailing for Italy and put us on board. ⁷We made slow headway for many days and had difficulty arriving off Cnidus. When the wind did not allow us to hold our course, we sailed to the lee of Crete, opposite Salmone. ⁸We moved along the coast with difficulty and came to a place called Fair Havens, near the town of Lasea.

⁹Much time had been lost, and sailing had already become dangerous because by now it was after the Fast.ᵃ So Paul warned them, ¹⁰"Men, I can see that our voyage is going to be disastrous and bring great loss to ship and cargo, and to our own lives also." ¹¹But the centurion, instead of listening to what Paul said, followed the advice of the pilot and of the owner of the ship. ¹²Since the harbor was unsuitable to winter in, the majority decided that we should sail on, hoping to reach Phoenix and winter there. This was a harbor in Crete, facing both southwest and northwest.

The Storm

¹³When a gentle south wind began to blow, they thought they had obtained what they wanted; so they weighed anchor and sailed along the shore of Crete. ¹⁴Before very long, a wind of hurricane force, called the "northeaster," swept down from the island. ¹⁵The ship was caught by the storm

---

Praying for Conversions

ACTS 26:28–29

Join your prayer to Paul's, praying that those who hear the gospel proclaimed may become Christians, whether in a "short time or long." It may help to make a list of friends, neighbors or family members who are not followers of Jesus. Through your praying bring each one into the presence of Jesus. Note that this kind of prayer is not the same as praying for these people to become members of your church or simply praying for your church to grow. All your concern should be focused on the goal that these individuals meet and follow Jesus, in Jesus' own way and time.

See Meeting God in Prayer

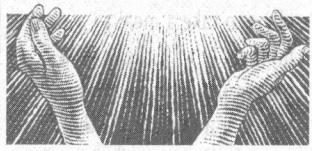

Encouraged by Rest, Food and Prayer

ACTS 27:33–36

After fourteen days of being pitched and tossed about on the Adriatic Sea, the crew is near exhaustion and ready to jump ship. Paul intervenes with much-needed food and encouragement.

In our days of fast food and hurried meals, we are tempted to overlook the ministry of a shared meal and the fellowship of breaking bread, as was common in the early church (see 2:46). A pot of bean soup or a loaf of freshly baked bread can communicate volumes of care and concern to one who is sad, lonely, discouraged or sick. Ask God to show you someone who needs encouragement. Make plans to take a meal to a shut-in. Include with the meal a written prayer or Scripture verse, or a book or CD that will nourish that person spiritually. Take a young person out to a good restaurant or invite a family to your home for a hearty meal soon.

See Meeting God in Community

and could not head into the wind; so we gave way to it and were driven along. ¹⁶As we passed to the lee of a small island called Cauda, we were hardly able to make the lifeboat secure. ¹⁷When the men had hoisted it aboard, they passed ropes under the ship itself to hold it together. Fearing that they would run aground on the sandbars of Syrtis, they lowered the sea anchor and let the ship be driven along. ¹⁸We took such a violent battering from the storm that the next day they began to throw the cargo overboard. ¹⁹On the third day, they threw the ship's tackle overboard with their own hands. ²⁰When neither sun nor stars appeared for many days and the storm continued raging, we finally gave up all hope of being saved.

²¹After the men had gone a long time without food, Paul stood up before them and said: "Men, you should have taken my advice not to sail from Crete; then you would have spared yourselves this damage and loss. ²²But now I urge you to keep up your courage, because not one of you will be lost; only the ship will be destroyed. ²³Last night an angel of the God whose I am and whom I serve stood beside me ²⁴and said, 'Do not be afraid, Paul. You must stand trial before Caesar; and God has graciously given you the lives of all who sail with you.' ²⁵So keep up your courage, men, for I have faith in God that it will happen just as he told me. ²⁶Nevertheless, we must run aground on some island."

The Shipwreck

²⁷On the fourteenth night we were still being driven across the Adriatic[a] Sea, when about midnight the sailors sensed they were approaching land. ²⁸They took soundings and found that the water was a hundred and twenty feet[b] deep. A short time later they took soundings again and found it was ninety feet[c] deep. ²⁹Fearing that we would be dashed against the rocks, they dropped four anchors from the stern and prayed for daylight. ³⁰In an attempt to escape from the ship, the sailors let the lifeboat down into the sea, pretending they were going to lower some anchors from the bow. ³¹Then Paul said to the centurion and the soldiers, "Unless these men stay with the ship, you cannot be saved." ³²So the soldiers cut the ropes that held the lifeboat and let it fall away.

³³Just before dawn Paul urged them all to eat. "For the last fourteen days," he said, "you have been in constant suspense and have gone without food—you haven't eaten anything. ³⁴Now I urge you to take some food. You need it to survive. Not one of you will lose a single hair from his head." ³⁵After he said this, he took some bread and gave thanks to God in front of them all. Then he broke it and began to eat. ³⁶They were all encouraged and ate some food themselves. ³⁷Altogether there were 276 of us on board. ³⁸When they had eaten as much as they wanted, they lightened the ship by throwing the grain into the sea.

³⁹When daylight came, they did not recognize the land, but they saw a bay with a sandy beach, where they decided to run the ship aground if they could. ⁴⁰Cutting loose the anchors, they left them in the sea and at the same time un-

---

[a] 27 In ancient times the name referred to an area extending well south of Italy.   [b] 28 Greek *twenty orguias* (about 37 meters)   [c] 28 Greek *fifteen orguias* (about 27 meters)

tied the ropes that held the rudders. Then they hoisted the foresail to the wind and made for the beach. **⁴¹**But the ship struck a sandbar and ran aground. The bow stuck fast and would not move, and the stern was broken to pieces by the pounding of the surf.

⁴²The soldiers planned to kill the prisoners to prevent any of them from swimming away and escaping. **⁴³**But the centurion wanted to spare Paul's life and kept them from carrying out their plan. He ordered those who could swim to jump overboard first and get to land. **⁴⁴**The rest were to get there on planks or on pieces of the ship. In this way everyone reached land in safety.

Ashore on Malta

28 Once safely on shore, we found out that the island was called Malta. **²**The islanders showed us unusual kindness. They built a fire and welcomed us all because it was raining and cold. **³**Paul gathered a pile of brushwood and, as he put it on the fire, a viper, driven out by the heat, fastened itself on his hand. **⁴**When the islanders saw the snake hanging from his hand, they said to each other, "This man must be a murderer; for though he escaped from the sea, Justice has not allowed him to live." **⁵**But Paul shook the snake off into the fire and suffered no ill effects. **⁶**The people expected him to swell up or suddenly fall dead, but after waiting a long time and seeing nothing unusual happen to him, they changed their minds and said he was a god.

⁷There was an estate nearby that belonged to Publius, the chief official of the island. He welcomed us to his home and for three days entertained us hospitably. **⁸**His father was sick in bed, suffering from fever and dysentery. Paul went in to see him and, after prayer, placed his hands on him and healed him. **⁹**When this had happened, the rest of the sick on the island came and were cured. **¹⁰**They honored us in many ways and when we were ready to sail, they furnished us with the supplies we needed.

Arrival at Rome

¹¹After three months we put out to sea in a ship that had wintered in the island. It was an Alexandrian ship with the figurehead of the twin gods Castor and Pollux. **¹²**We put in at Syracuse and stayed there three days. **¹³**From there we set sail and arrived at Rhegium. The next day the south wind came up, and on the following day we reached Puteoli. **¹⁴**There we found some brothers who invited us to spend a week with them. And so we came to Rome. **¹⁵**The brothers there had heard that we were coming, and they traveled as far as the Forum of Appius and the Three Taverns to meet us. At the sight of these men Paul thanked God and was encouraged. **¹⁶**When we got to Rome, Paul was allowed to live by himself, with a soldier to guard him.

Paul Preaches at Rome Under Guard

¹⁷Three days later he called together the leaders of the Jews. When they had assembled, Paul said to them: "My brothers, although I have done nothing against our people or against the customs of our ancestors, I was arrested in Jerusalem and handed over to the Romans. **¹⁸**They examined me and wanted to release me, because I was not guilty

Facing Fear

ACTS 28:1–10

After surviving a shipwreck, Paul gathers firewood and is bitten by a snake! Danger can strike in the midst of everyday activities. What "everyday" danger do you fear? How does that fear affect your life? What would happen if your worst fear came true? Can you offer your fear to God? You might want to draw your fear or sculpt it from wire or clay, so that you can face it as you pray for God's deliverance.

See Meeting God in Everyday Life

A Visit With Paul

ACTS 28:28–31

The book of Acts ends with Paul living serenely in Rome, where he "welcomed all who came to see him." You might imagine yourself as one of those visitors. What would you want to talk about with Paul? What would you ask him? How do you think he would answer? Your imagination will be more focused if you write out a "transcript" of your visit.

See Meeting God in Scripture

of any crime deserving death. ¹⁹But when the Jews objected, I was compelled to appeal to Caesar—not that I had any charge to bring against my own people. ²⁰For this reason I have asked to see you and talk with you. It is because of the hope of Israel that I am bound with this chain."

²¹They replied, "We have not received any letters from Judea concerning you, and none of the brothers who have come from there has reported or said anything bad about you. ²²But we want to hear what your views are, for we know that people everywhere are talking against this sect."

²³They arranged to meet Paul on a certain day, and came in even larger numbers to the place where he was staying. From morning till evening he explained and declared to them the kingdom of God and tried to convince them about Jesus from the Law of Moses and from the Prophets. ²⁴Some were convinced by what he said, but others would not believe. ²⁵They disagreed among themselves and began to leave after Paul had made this final statement: "The Holy Spirit spoke the truth to your forefathers when he said through Isaiah the prophet:

²⁶ " 'Go to this people and say,
   "You will be ever hearing but never
      understanding;
   you will be ever seeing but never perceiving."
²⁷ For this people's heart has become calloused;
      they hardly hear with their ears,
      and they have closed their eyes.
   Otherwise they might see with their eyes,
      hear with their ears,
      understand with their hearts
   and turn, and I would heal them.'ᵃ

²⁸"Therefore I want you to know that God's salvation has been sent to the Gentiles, and they will listen!"ᵇ

³⁰For two whole years Paul stayed there in his own rented house and welcomed all who came to see him. ³¹Boldly and without hindrance he preached the kingdom of God and taught about the Lord Jesus Christ.

ᵃ 27 Isaiah 6:9,10   ᵇ 28 Some manuscripts *listen!" ²⁹After he said this, the Jews left, arguing vigorously among themselves.*

ROMANS

The Old Self and the New Self

KEY VERSE:

God demonstrates his own love for us in this: While we were still sinners,
Christ died for us.—Romans 5:8

Like a parent giving a gift to a child out of pure love, God gives us the gift of salvation. We do not have to do anything to deserve it, and we never could be good enough to earn it. In the book of Romans, the apostle Paul writes a treatise on the love of God. God's love is redeeming love, for every one of us is "under sin" (3:9) and controlled by our human nature; we all "fall short of the glory of God" (3:23). God initiates our redemption even before we are aware of our need of it. In response to God's love, we are to turn our entire lives toward God so that, day by day, we are transformed—a process (5:1–4) that involves heart (2:29), mind (8:5–6), will (7:14–15) and actions (12:9–21)—as we become new persons who want what God wants (12:2).

Romans is a theological book, but it is also a realistic, practical discussion of how growing into fullness of life in Christ is a matter of mind, heart and spirit. Throughout our inner struggles and our struggles with others, we are drawn by God's incredible love in Christ Jesus, which seeks us out and bears us along in the spiritual life. Nothing that we have done, or ever could do, can separate us from the love that God offers us in Christ Jesus our Lord.

"Carefully note this point: When you find the phrase 'the righteousness of God' in Scripture, do not think that it means the essential, inner righteousness of God . . . . Otherwise you will be frightened by it. Know rather that . . . it means the grace and the mercy of God poured out into us through Christ, whereby we are considered pious and righteous before Him. And it is called the righteousness or the piety of God because not we but God works it in us by His grace."

—MARTIN LUTHER,
in What Luther Says, 3909

All Creation Is God's

ROMANS 1:19–21

God has made himself knowable and readily visible in the creation he has made. God's Spirit has been present in the world from its beginning. When we are observant, creation reveals the eternal power and wondrous beauty of the Creator.

Set aside a half hour to go for a stroll. As you walk, pray for awareness of anything that might speak to you of God. Breathe deeply. If something attracts you, stop and give it your full attention. Let God speak to you in whatever form that experience may take. Look for some small object to bring back with you as a reminder of your meeting with God, and place it where you can see it for the next few days.

See Meeting God in the Created Order

1 Paul, a servant of Christ Jesus, called to be an apostle and set apart for the gospel of God— [2]the gospel he promised beforehand through his prophets in the Holy Scriptures [3]regarding his Son, who as to his human nature was a descendant of David, [4]and who through the Spirit[a] of holiness was declared with power to be the Son of God[b] by his resurrection from the dead: Jesus Christ our Lord. [5]Through him and for his name's sake, we received grace and apostleship to call people from among all the Gentiles to the obedience that comes from faith. [6]And you also are among those who are called to belong to Jesus Christ.

[7]To all in Rome who are loved by God and called to be saints:

Grace and peace to you from God our Father and from the Lord Jesus Christ.

Paul's Longing to Visit Rome

[8]First, I thank my God through Jesus Christ for all of you, because your faith is being reported all over the world. [9]God, whom I serve with my whole heart in preaching the gospel of his Son, is my witness how constantly I remember you [10]in my prayers at all times; and I pray that now at last by God's will the way may be opened for me to come to you.

[11]I long to see you so that I may impart to you some spiritual gift to make you strong— [12]that is, that you and I may be mutually encouraged by each other's faith. [13]I do not want you to be unaware, brothers, that I planned many times to come to you (but have been prevented from doing so until now) in order that I might have a harvest among you, just as I have had among the other Gentiles.

[14]I am obligated both to Greeks and non-Greeks, both to the wise and the foolish. [15]That is why I am so eager to preach the gospel also to you who are at Rome.

[16]I am not ashamed of the gospel, because it is the power of God for the salvation of everyone who believes: first for the Jew, then for the Gentile. [17]For in the gospel a righteousness from God is revealed, a righteousness that is by faith from first to last,[c] just as it is written: "The righteous will live by faith."[d]

God's Wrath Against Mankind

[18]The wrath of God is being revealed from heaven against all the godlessness and wickedness of men who suppress the truth by their wickedness, [19]since what may be known about God is plain to them, because God has made it plain to them. [20]For since the creation of the world God's invisible qualities—his eternal power and divine nature—have been clearly seen, being understood from what has been made, so that men are without excuse.

[21]For although they knew God, they neither glorified him as God nor gave thanks to him, but their thinking became futile and their foolish hearts were darkened. [22]Although they claimed to be wise, they became fools [23]and exchanged the glory of the immortal God for images made

a 4 Or who as to his spirit   b 4 Or was appointed to be the Son of God with power   c 17 Or is from faith to faith   d 17 Hab. 2:4

to look like mortal man and birds and animals and reptiles.

²⁴Therefore God gave them over in the sinful desires of their hearts to sexual impurity for the degrading of their bodies with one another. ²⁵They exchanged the truth of God for a lie, and worshiped and served created things rather than the Creator—who is forever praised. Amen.

²⁶Because of this, God gave them over to shameful lusts. Even their women exchanged natural relations for unnatural ones. ²⁷In the same way the men also abandoned natural relations with women and were inflamed with lust for one another. Men committed indecent acts with other men, and received in themselves the due penalty for their perversion.

²⁸Furthermore, since they did not think it worthwhile to retain the knowledge of God, he gave them over to a depraved mind, to do what ought not to be done. ²⁹They have become filled with every kind of wickedness, evil, greed and depravity. They are full of envy, murder, strife, deceit and malice. They are gossips, ³⁰slanderers, God-haters, insolent, arrogant and boastful; they invent ways of doing evil; they disobey their parents; ³¹they are senseless, faithless, heartless, ruthless. ³²Although they know God's righteous decree that those who do such things deserve death, they not only continue to do these very things but also approve of those who practice them.

God's Righteous Judgment

2 You, therefore, have no excuse, you who pass judgment on someone else, for at whatever point you judge the other, you are condemning yourself, because you who pass judgment do the same things. ²Now we know that God's judgment against those who do such things is based on truth. ³So when you, a mere man, pass judgment on them and yet do the same things, do you think you will escape God's judgment? ⁴Or do you show contempt for the riches of his kindness, tolerance and patience, not realizing that God's kindness leads you toward repentance?

⁵But because of your stubbornness and your unrepentant heart, you are storing up wrath against yourself for the day of God's wrath, when his righteous judgment will be revealed. ⁶God "will give to each person according to what he has done."ᵃ ⁷To those who by persistence in doing good seek glory, honor and immortality, he will give eternal life. ⁸But for those who are self-seeking and who reject the truth and follow evil, there will be wrath and anger. ⁹There will be trouble and distress for every human being who does evil: first for the Jew, then for the Gentile; ¹⁰but glory, honor and peace for everyone who does good: first for the Jew, then for the Gentile. ¹¹For God does not show favoritism.

¹²All who sin apart from the law will also perish apart from the law, and all who sin under the law will be judged by the law. ¹³For it is not those who hear the law who are righteous in God's sight, but it is those who obey the law who will be declared righteous. ¹⁴(Indeed, when Gentiles, who do not have the law, do by nature things required by the law, they are a law for themselves, even though they

---

God's Kindness

ROMANS 2:4

"God's kindness leads [us] toward repentance"; all the means that God uses to bring us to faith are expressions of that kindness. Even before we are aware that we need or want to know God, he reaches out to draw us toward himself.

What is your first memory of awareness of God? What circumstances led you to repentance? Who was instrumental in bringing you to an awareness of God's love? Try to recall your first memory of praying or wanting to pray, the person who first mentioned God to you, the person who taught you your first "memory verse." In more recent times, who has helped you learn about God or inspired you to want to know God more deeply? Give thanks for the kindnesses that have nurtured your faith. Take the time to write a thank-you note to someone who has been an expression of God's kindness in your life.

See Meeting God in Everyday Life

A Matter of the Heart

ROMANS 2:28-29

Many common expressions acknowledge the importance of the heart in our daily language. When we speak openly and honestly, we "speak from the heart." To truly understand, we "get to the heart" of a matter. The heart is the place of deepest knowing. When the heart is cluttered, resistant or hardened, it can keep us closed to God and alienated from other people. An uncluttered heart is the work of a lifetime, a work we cannot achieve alone.

Set aside time to be quiet and ask Jesus to inspect your heart. Is it open and ready to welcome God? Or is it cluttered? What does the clutter look like? Write about, or draw a description of, the areas of your heart that are not prepared to welcome God. Tell Jesus why you have closed off those areas.

do not have the law, [15]since they show that the requirements of the law are written on their hearts, their consciences also bearing witness, and their thoughts now accusing, now even defending them.) [16]This will take place on the day when God will judge men's secrets through Jesus Christ, as my gospel declares.

The Jews and the Law

[17]Now you, if you call yourself a Jew; if you rely on the law and brag about your relationship to God; [18]if you know his will and approve of what is superior because you are instructed by the law; [19]if you are convinced that you are a guide for the blind, a light for those who are in the dark, [20]an instructor of the foolish, a teacher of infants, because you have in the law the embodiment of knowledge and truth— [21]you, then, who teach others, do you not teach yourself? You who preach against stealing, do you steal? [22]You who say that people should not commit adultery, do you commit adultery? You who abhor idols, do you rob temples? [23]You who brag about the law, do you dishonor God by breaking the law? [24]As it is written: "God's name is blasphemed among the Gentiles because of you."[a]

[25]Circumcision has value if you observe the law, but if you break the law, you have become as though you had not been circumcised. [26]If those who are not circumcised keep the law's requirements, will they not be regarded as though they were circumcised? [27]The one who is not circumcised physically and yet obeys the law will condemn you who, even though you have the[b] written code and circumcision, are a lawbreaker.

[28]A man is not a Jew if he is only one outwardly, nor is circumcision merely outward and physical. [29]No, a man is a Jew if he is one inwardly; and circumcision is circumcision of the heart, by the Spirit, not by the written code. Such a man's praise is not from men, but from God.

God's Faithfulness

3 What advantage, then, is there in being a Jew, or what value is there in circumcision? [2]Much in every way! First of all, they have been entrusted with the very words of God.

[3]What if some did not have faith? Will their lack of faith nullify God's faithfulness? [4]Not at all! Let God be true, and every man a liar. As it is written:

> "So that you may be proved right when you
>   speak
> and prevail when you judge."[c]

[5]But if our unrighteousness brings out God's righteousness more clearly, what shall we say? That God is unjust in bringing his wrath on us? (I am using a human argument.) [6]Certainly not! If that were so, how could God judge the world? [7]Someone might argue, "If my falsehood enhances God's truthfulness and so increases his glory, why am I still condemned as a sinner?" [8]Why not say—as we are being slanderously reported as saying and as some claim that we say—"Let us do evil that good may result"? Their condemnation is deserved.

[a] 24 Isaiah 52:5; Ezek. 36:22   [b] 27 Or who, by means of a   [c] 4 Psalm 51:4

No One Is Righteous

[9]What shall we conclude then? Are we any better[a]? Not at all! We have already made the charge that Jews and Gentiles alike are all under sin. [10]As it is written:

"There is no one righteous, not even one;
[11]   there is no one who understands,
     no one who seeks God.
[12]All have turned away,
     they have together become worthless;
there is no one who does good,
     not even one."[b]
[13]"Their throats are open graves;
     their tongues practice deceit."[c]
     "The poison of vipers is on their lips."[d]
[14]   "Their mouths are full of cursing and
         bitterness."[e]
[15]"Their feet are swift to shed blood;
[16]   ruin and misery mark their ways,
[17]and the way of peace they do not know."[f]
[18]   "There is no fear of God before their eyes."[g]

[19]Now we know that whatever the law says, it says to those who are under the law, so that every mouth may be silenced and the whole world held accountable to God. [20]Therefore no one will be declared righteous in his sight by observing the law; rather, through the law we become conscious of sin.

Righteousness Through Faith

[21]But now a righteousness from God, apart from law, has been made known, to which the Law and the Prophets testify. [22]This righteousness from God comes through faith in Jesus Christ to all who believe. There is no difference, [23]for all have sinned and fall short of the glory of God, [24]and are justified freely by his grace through the redemption that came by Christ Jesus. [25]God presented him as a sacrifice of atonement,[h] through faith in his blood. He did this to demonstrate his justice, because in his forbearance he had left the sins committed beforehand unpunished— [26]he did it to demonstrate his justice at the present time, so as to be just and the one who justifies those who have faith in Jesus.

[27]Where, then, is boasting? It is excluded. On what principle? On that of observing the law? No, but on that of faith. [28]For we maintain that a man is justified by faith apart from observing the law. [29]Is God the God of Jews only? Is he not the God of Gentiles too? Yes, of Gentiles too, [30]since there is only one God, who will justify the circumcised by faith and the uncircumcised through that same faith. [31]Do we, then, nullify the law by this faith? Not at all! Rather, we uphold the law.

Abraham Justified by Faith

4 What then shall we say that Abraham, our forefather, discovered in this matter? [2]If, in fact, Abraham was justified by works, he had something to boast about—but not

The Gift of Righteousness

ROMANS 3:21–24

Paul points out that, regardless of how "nice" or "good" we feel we are, to be human is to be deeply and terminally flawed. God in Christ Jesus covers us perfectly and fully with righteousness—flaws and all. Jesus loves us so much that he redeemed us at the price of his own life.

Imagine Jesus kneeling before you. He wants to pour out his love and grace to you; as a symbol of love and grace, he is pouring out water to wash your feet. As he gazes up at you with eyes of love and acceptance, what emotions do you experience? What will you say to him? What do you envision Jesus saying to you?

See Meeting God in Scripture

[a]9 Or *worse*   [b]12 Psalms 14:1–3; 53:1–3; Eccles. 7:20   [c]13 Psalm 5:9
[d]13 Psalm 140:3   [e]14 Psalm 10:7   [f]17 Isaiah 59:7,8   [g]18 Psalm 36:1
[h]25 Or *as the one who would turn aside his wrath, taking away sin*

Living in Faith

ROMANS 4:16–19

Abraham believed God even when things looked impossible; because of Abraham's faith, God considered him righteous. To have faith is to walk along a path without a map and to believe that Almighty God knows the way and walks with us. It is an act of will, not of emotion, when we hand over the control of our lives to the only One who will neither become lost nor lose us.

Think of some troubling situations that you would like to surrender to God's control. Is it difficult for you to think about letting go of them? Write a description of one of them on a piece of paper and place it in the palm of your hand. Then, raising your hands, transfer your concern to the nail-scarred palms of Jesus. What emotions do you experience? Talk to God about them, and listen carefully for God's response.

See Meeting God in Everyday Life

before God. ³What does the Scripture say? "Abraham believed God, and it was credited to him as righteousness."[a]

⁴Now when a man works, his wages are not credited to him as a gift, but as an obligation. ⁵However, to the man who does not work but trusts God who justifies the wicked, his faith is credited as righteousness. ⁶David says the same thing when he speaks of the blessedness of the man to whom God credits righteousness apart from works:

⁷"Blessed are they
    whose transgressions are forgiven,
    whose sins are covered.
⁸Blessed is the man
    whose sin the Lord will never count against
    him."[b]

⁹Is this blessedness only for the circumcised, or also for the uncircumcised? We have been saying that Abraham's faith was credited to him as righteousness. ¹⁰Under what circumstances was it credited? Was it after he was circumcised, or before? It was not after, but before! ¹¹And he received the sign of circumcision, a seal of the righteousness that he had by faith while he was still uncircumcised. So then, he is the father of all who believe but have not been circumcised, in order that righteousness might be credited to them. ¹²And he is also the father of the circumcised who not only are circumcised but who also walk in the footsteps of the faith that our father Abraham had before he was circumcised.

¹³It was not through law that Abraham and his offspring received the promise that he would be heir of the world, but through the righteousness that comes by faith. ¹⁴For if those who live by law are heirs, faith has no value and the promise is worthless, ¹⁵because law brings wrath. And where there is no law there is no transgression.

¹⁶Therefore, the promise comes by faith, so that it may be by grace and may be guaranteed to all Abraham's offspring—not only to those who are of the law but also to those who are of the faith of Abraham. He is the father of us all. ¹⁷As it is written: "I have made you a father of many nations."[c] He is our father in the sight of God, in whom he believed—the God who gives life to the dead and calls things that are not as though they were.

¹⁸Against all hope, Abraham in hope believed and so became the father of many nations, just as it had been said to him, "So shall your offspring be."[d] ¹⁹Without weakening in his faith, he faced the fact that his body was as good as dead—since he was about a hundred years old—and that Sarah's womb was also dead. ²⁰Yet he did not waver through unbelief regarding the promise of God, but was strengthened in his faith and gave glory to God, ²¹being fully persuaded that God had power to do what he had promised. ²²This is why "it was credited to him as righteousness." ²³The words "it was credited to him" were written not for him alone, ²⁴but also for us, to whom God will credit righteousness—for us who believe in him who raised Jesus our Lord from the dead. ²⁵He was delivered

[a] *3 Gen. 15:6; also in verse 22*   [b] *8 Psalm 32:1,2*   [c] *17 Gen. 17:5*
[d] *18 Gen. 15:5*

over to death for our sins and was raised to life for our justification.

Peace and Joy

5 Therefore, since we have been justified through faith, we[a] have peace with God through our Lord Jesus Christ, [2]through whom we have gained access by faith into this grace in which we now stand. And we[a] rejoice in the hope of the glory of God. [3]Not only so, but we[a] also rejoice in our sufferings, because we know that suffering produces perseverance; [4]perseverance, character; and character, hope. [5]And hope does not disappoint us, because God has poured out his love into our hearts by the Holy Spirit, whom he has given us.

[6]You see, at just the right time, when we were still powerless, Christ died for the ungodly. [7]Very rarely will anyone die for a righteous man, though for a good man someone might possibly dare to die. [8]But God demonstrates his own love for us in this: While we were still sinners, Christ died for us.

[9]Since we have now been justified by his blood, how much more shall we be saved from God's wrath through him! [10]For if, when we were God's enemies, we were reconciled to him through the death of his Son, how much more, having been reconciled, shall we be saved through his life! [11]Not only is this so, but we also rejoice in God through our Lord Jesus Christ, through whom we have now received reconciliation.

Death Through Adam, Life Through Christ

[12]Therefore, just as sin entered the world through one man, and death through sin, and in this way death came to all men, because all sinned— [13]for before the law was given, sin was in the world. But sin is not taken into account when there is no law. [14]Nevertheless, death reigned from the time of Adam to the time of Moses, even over those who did not sin by breaking a command, as did Adam, who was a pattern of the one to come.

[15]But the gift is not like the trespass. For if the many died by the trespass of the one man, how much more did God's grace and the gift that came by the grace of the one man, Jesus Christ, overflow to the many! [16]Again, the gift of God is not like the result of the one man's sin: The judgment followed one sin and brought condemnation, but the gift followed many trespasses and brought justification. [17]For if, by the trespass of the one man, death reigned through that one man, how much more will those who receive God's abundant provision of grace and of the gift of righteousness reign in life through the one man, Jesus Christ.

[18]Consequently, just as the result of one trespass was condemnation for all men, so also the result of one act of righteousness was justification that brings life for all men. [19]For just as through the disobedience of the one man the many were made sinners, so also through the obedience of the one man the many will be made righteous.

[20]The law was added so that the trespass might increase. But where sin increased, grace increased all the more, [21]so that, just as sin reigned in death, so also grace might reign

---

The Gift of Life

ROMANS 5:6–8

Our consumer-driven culture tempts us to speak glibly about sacrifice and self-denial: "I'd give my right arm for tickets to that game." "That ice cream is to die for." Do we take in the amazing reality of such wondrous love—that Jesus not only *offered* to die for us, but he actually did? If we fully absorbed this truth, would we not walk day by day in awe?

Repeat verse 8 slowly, personalizing it: "While I was still a sinner, Christ died for me." Can you understand why? Would you die for someone else? Would you willingly take the punishment someone else deserved? What kind of connection would you have to have with someone to put yourself in that person's place? Write a letter to the One who died for you, expressing what you think and feel about his wondrous sacrifice for you.

---

[a] 1,2,3 Or *let us*

Service That Frees

ROMANS 6:20–23

Every person serves something—giving his or her energies to some goal, desire, person or organization. And after we serve long enough, we identify with that master and take on its characteristics. What do you serve? Ask God to make you aware of your motives and loyalties. Set aside some time to think about how you are spending your time and energy. In what ways have you made choices to serve God? Are you growing more Christlike? Who, or what, claims your loyalty? Who are your other "gods"? What is the payoff for serving them?

See Meeting God in Service

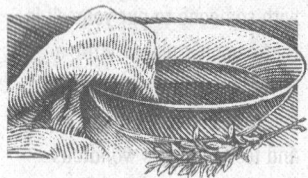

through righteousness to bring eternal life through Jesus Christ our Lord.

Dead to Sin, Alive in Christ

6 What shall we say, then? Shall we go on sinning so that grace may increase? [2]By no means! We died to sin; how can we live in it any longer? [3]Or don't you know that all of us who were baptized into Christ Jesus were baptized into his death? [4]We were therefore buried with him through baptism into death in order that, just as Christ was raised from the dead through the glory of the Father, we too may live a new life.

[5]If we have been united with him like this in his death, we will certainly also be united with him in his resurrection. [6]For we know that our old self was crucified with him so that the body of sin might be done away with,[a] that we should no longer be slaves to sin— [7]because anyone who has died has been freed from sin.

[8]Now if we died with Christ, we believe that we will also live with him. [9]For we know that since Christ was raised from the dead, he cannot die again; death no longer has mastery over him. [10]The death he died, he died to sin once for all; but the life he lives, he lives to God.

[11]In the same way, count yourselves dead to sin but alive to God in Christ Jesus. [12]Therefore do not let sin reign in your mortal body so that you obey its evil desires. [13]Do not offer the parts of your body to sin, as instruments of wickedness, but rather offer yourselves to God, as those who have been brought from death to life; and offer the parts of your body to him as instruments of righteousness. [14]For sin shall not be your master, because you are not under law, but under grace.

Slaves to Righteousness

[15]What then? Shall we sin because we are not under law but under grace? By no means! [16]Don't you know that when you offer yourselves to someone to obey him as slaves, you are slaves to the one whom you obey— whether you are slaves to sin, which leads to death, or to obedience, which leads to righteousness? [17]But thanks be to God that, though you used to be slaves to sin, you wholeheartedly obeyed the form of teaching to which you were entrusted. [18]You have been set free from sin and have become slaves to righteousness.

[19]I put this in human terms because you are weak in your natural selves. Just as you used to offer the parts of your body in slavery to impurity and to ever-increasing wickedness, so now offer them in slavery to righteousness leading to holiness. [20]When you were slaves to sin, you were free from the control of righteousness. [21]What benefit did you reap at that time from the things you are now ashamed of? Those things result in death! [22]But now that you have been set free from sin and have become slaves to God, the benefit you reap leads to holiness, and the result is eternal life. [23]For the wages of sin is death, but the gift of God is eternal life in[b] Christ Jesus our Lord.

a 6 Or *be rendered powerless*   *b 23* Or *through*

An Illustration From Marriage

7 Do you not know, brothers—for I am speaking to men who know the law—that the law has authority over a man only as long as he lives? ²For example, by law a married woman is bound to her husband as long as he is alive, but if her husband dies, she is released from the law of marriage. ³So then, if she marries another man while her husband is still alive, she is called an adulteress. But if her husband dies, she is released from that law and is not an adulteress, even though she marries another man.

⁴So, my brothers, you also died to the law through the body of Christ, that you might belong to another, to him who was raised from the dead, in order that we might bear fruit to God. ⁵For when we were controlled by the sinful nature,ᵃ the sinful passions aroused by the law were at work in our bodies, so that we bore fruit for death. ⁶But now, by dying to what once bound us, we have been released from the law so that we serve in the new way of the Spirit, and not in the old way of the written code.

Struggling With Sin

⁷What shall we say, then? Is the law sin? Certainly not! Indeed I would not have known what sin was except through the law. For I would not have known what coveting really was if the law had not said, "Do not covet."ᵇ ⁸But sin, seizing the opportunity afforded by the commandment, produced in me every kind of covetous desire. For apart from law, sin is dead. ⁹Once I was alive apart from law; but when the commandment came, sin sprang to life and I died. ¹⁰I found that the very commandment that was intended to bring life actually brought death. ¹¹For sin, seizing the opportunity afforded by the commandment, deceived me, and through the commandment put me to death. ¹²So then, the law is holy, and the commandment is holy, righteous and good.

¹³Did that which is good, then, become death to me? By no means! But in order that sin might be recognized as sin, it produced death in me through what was good, so that through the commandment sin might become utterly sinful.

¹⁴We know that the law is spiritual; but I am unspiritual, sold as a slave to sin. ¹⁵I do not understand what I do. For what I want to do I do not do, but what I hate I do. ¹⁶And if I do what I do not want to do, I agree that the law is good. ¹⁷As it is, it is no longer I myself who do it, but it is sin living in me. ¹⁸I know that nothing good lives in me, that is, in my sinful nature.ᶜ For I have the desire to do what is good, but I cannot carry it out. ¹⁹For what I do is not the good I want to do; no, the evil I do not want to do—this I keep on doing. ²⁰Now if I do what I do not want to do, it is no longer I who do it, but it is sin living in me that does it.

²¹So I find this law at work: When I want to do good, evil is right there with me. ²²For in my inner being I delight in God's law; ²³but I see another law at work in the members of my body, waging war against the law of my mind and making me a prisoner of the law of sin at work within my

---

The Reality of Struggle

ROMANS 7:15,21–25

Paul was no stranger to the struggle against the sinful nature. He knew what it was like to want to do one thing and yet do another. On a daily basis we fall short of being who God wants us to be and of doing what God wants us to do.

Is there one area of your life where you have experienced continual struggle, perhaps for years? Tell God about your struggles. End your prayer by reading Romans 8:1–2 as God's promise to you. Ask God's Spirit to live in you, and find some object to carry with you as a reminder of the Spirit within you—a cross, a small rock, a written verse from Scripture. Keep this symbol where you can touch it when you need to remember that you live by grace.

See Meeting God in Everyday Life

ᵃ5 Or the flesh; also in verse 25   ᵇ7 Exodus 20:17; Deut. 5:21   ᶜ18 Or my flesh

Enlightening Our Spirits

ROMANS 8:26–27

Watching 3-D movies requires special glasses. While wearing these glasses viewers see a dramatically different picture. The glasses make it possible to see to a depth or perspective that is otherwise impossible. Without the presence of the Holy Spirit in us, we cannot see with God's perspective. The Spirit enlightens "the eyes of [our] heart" (Ephesians 1:18) so we can understand the hope to which God calls us.

Pray for an awareness of God's Spirit within you. Then, allowing God's Spirit to give you perspective, take time to write about some issue—perhaps a difficult moment at work or at home, or something you've read about in the daily newspaper. Allow the Spirit to give you ongoing insight about what you have written.

See Meeting God in Everyday Life

members. [24]What a wretched man I am! Who will rescue me from this body of death? [25]Thanks be to God—through Jesus Christ our Lord!

So then, I myself in my mind am a slave to God's law, but in the sinful nature a slave to the law of sin.

Life Through the Spirit

8 Therefore, there is now no condemnation for those who are in Christ Jesus,[a] [2]because through Christ Jesus the law of the Spirit of life set me free from the law of sin and death. [3]For what the law was powerless to do in that it was weakened by the sinful nature,[b] God did by sending his own Son in the likeness of sinful man to be a sin offering.[c] And so he condemned sin in sinful man,[d] [4]in order that the righteous requirements of the law might be fully met in us, who do not live according to the sinful nature but according to the Spirit.

[5]Those who live according to the sinful nature have their minds set on what that nature desires; but those who live in accordance with the Spirit have their minds set on what the Spirit desires. [6]The mind of sinful man[e] is death, but the mind controlled by the Spirit is life and peace; [7]the sinful mind[f] is hostile to God. It does not submit to God's law, nor can it do so. [8]Those controlled by the sinful nature cannot please God.

[9]You, however, are controlled not by the sinful nature but by the Spirit, if the Spirit of God lives in you. And if anyone does not have the Spirit of Christ, he does not belong to Christ. [10]But if Christ is in you, your body is dead because of sin, yet your spirit is alive because of righteousness. [11]And if the Spirit of him who raised Jesus from the dead is living in you, he who raised Christ from the dead will also give life to your mortal bodies through his Spirit, who lives in you.

[12]Therefore, brothers, we have an obligation—but it is not to the sinful nature, to live according to it. [13]For if you live according to the sinful nature, you will die; but if by the Spirit you put to death the misdeeds of the body, you will live, [14]because those who are led by the Spirit of God are sons of God. [15]For you did not receive a spirit that makes you a slave again to fear, but you received the Spirit of sonship.[g] And by him we cry, *"Abba,[h] Father."* [16]The Spirit himself testifies with our spirit that we are God's children. [17]Now if we are children, then we are heirs—heirs of God and co-heirs with Christ, if indeed we share in his sufferings in order that we may also share in his glory.

Future Glory

[18]I consider that our present sufferings are not worth comparing with the glory that will be revealed in us. [19]The creation waits in eager expectation for the sons of God to be revealed. [20]For the creation was subjected to frustration, not by its own choice, but by the will of the one who subjected it, in hope [21]that[i] the creation itself will be lib-

---

[a] 1 Some later manuscripts *Jesus, who do not live according to the sinful nature but according to the Spirit,* [b] 3 Or *the flesh*; also in verses 4, 5, 8, 9, 12 and 13 [c] 3 Or *man, for sin* [d] 3 Or *in the flesh* [e] 6 Or *mind set on the flesh* [f] 7 Or *the mind set on the flesh* [g] 15 Or *adoption* [h] 15 Aramaic for *Father* [i] 20,21 Or *subjected it in hope.* [21]For

erated from its bondage to decay and brought into the glorious freedom of the children of God.

²²We know that the whole creation has been groaning as in the pains of childbirth right up to the present time. ²³Not only so, but we ourselves, who have the firstfruits of the Spirit, groan inwardly as we wait eagerly for our adoption as sons, the redemption of our bodies. ²⁴For in this hope we were saved. But hope that is seen is no hope at all. Who hopes for what he already has? ²⁵But if we hope for what we do not yet have, we wait for it patiently.

²⁶In the same way, the Spirit helps us in our weakness. We do not know what we ought to pray for, but the Spirit himself intercedes for us with groans that words cannot express. ²⁷And he who searches our hearts knows the mind of the Spirit, because the Spirit intercedes for the saints in accordance with God's will.

More Than Conquerors

²⁸And we know that in all things God works for the good of those who love him,[a] who[b] have been called according to his purpose. ²⁹For those God foreknew he also predestined to be conformed to the likeness of his Son, that he might be the firstborn among many brothers. ³⁰And those he predestined, he also called; those he called, he also justified; those he justified, he also glorified.

³¹What, then, shall we say in response to this? If God is for us, who can be against us? ³²He who did not spare his own Son, but gave him up for us all—how will he not also, along with him, graciously give us all things? ³³Who will bring any charge against those whom God has chosen? It is God who justifies. ³⁴Who is he that condemns? Christ Jesus, who died—more than that, who was raised to life—is at the right hand of God and is also interceding for us. ³⁵Who shall separate us from the love of Christ? Shall trouble or hardship or persecution or famine or nakedness or danger or sword? ³⁶As it is written:

> "For your sake we face death all day long;
> we are considered as sheep to be slaughtered."[c]

³⁷No, in all these things we are more than conquerors through him who loved us. ³⁸For I am convinced that neither death nor life, neither angels nor demons,[d] neither the present nor the future, nor any powers, ³⁹neither height nor depth, nor anything else in all creation, will be able to separate us from the love of God that is in Christ Jesus our Lord.

God's Sovereign Choice

9 I speak the truth in Christ—I am not lying, my conscience confirms it in the Holy Spirit— ²I have great sorrow and unceasing anguish in my heart. ³For I could wish that I myself were cursed and cut off from Christ for the sake of my brothers, those of my own race, ⁴the people of Israel. Theirs is the adoption as sons; theirs the divine glory, the covenants, the receiving of the law, the temple worship and the promises. ⁵Theirs are the patri-

---

Utterly Inseparable

ROMANS 8:35–39

"Can a mother forget the baby at her breast and have no compassion on the child she has borne? Though she may forget, I will not forget you! See, I have engraved you on the palms of my hands" (Isaiah 49:15–16).

Find an old tree whose roots are deeply entwined with the earth and with other roots, or find moss that has grown on a tree trunk. Or at the beach find a shell that has attached itself to a rock. Look for other examples of such deep inseparability. As you hold or look at these objects, speak the words of this passage, using them as a description for the One who holds you close.

See Meeting God in Scripture

---

a 28 Some manuscripts *And we know that all things work together for good to those who love God*   *b 28* Or *works together with those who love him to bring about what is good—with those who*   *c 36* Psalm 44:22   *d 38* Or *nor heavenly rulers*

A Greater Purpose

ROMANS 9:14–18,24

Paul reminds us that we are not aware of God's greater design. The reasons that he has mercy on some and not on others remain a mystery to our finite minds.

We do know, however, that God's infinite wisdom is motivated by his infinite love. He sometimes uses negative circumstances to achieve his divine purposes. What qualifies as a closed door or a momentous defeat today may look quite different a few months or years down the road. With God's involvement, what seems like defeat can become a door to life.

Look back on your life and identify events that seemed completely negative at the time. Can you see any good that God has brought from them? Can you see how they are like pieces of a puzzle that, when fit together, have made you the person you are today? Offer to God the memories and experiences that still make no sense to you and that continue to be a source of pain.

See Meeting God in Everyday Life

archs, and from them is traced the human ancestry of Christ, who is God over all, forever praised![a] Amen.

[6]It is not as though God's word had failed. For not all who are descended from Israel are Israel. [7]Nor because they are his descendants are they all Abraham's children. On the contrary, "It is through Isaac that your offspring will be reckoned."[b] [8]In other words, it is not the natural children who are God's children, but it is the children of the promise who are regarded as Abraham's offspring. [9]For this was how the promise was stated: "At the appointed time I will return, and Sarah will have a son."[c]

[10]Not only that, but Rebekah's children had one and the same father, our father Isaac. [11]Yet, before the twins were born or had done anything good or bad—in order that God's purpose in election might stand: [12]not by works but by him who calls—she was told, "The older will serve the younger."[d] [13]Just as it is written: "Jacob I loved, but Esau I hated."[e]

[14]What then shall we say? Is God unjust? Not at all! [15]For he says to Moses,

> "I will have mercy on whom I have mercy,
>   and I will have compassion on whom I have
>   compassion."[f]

[16]It does not, therefore, depend on man's desire or effort, but on God's mercy. [17]For the Scripture says to Pharaoh: "I raised you up for this very purpose, that I might display my power in you and that my name might be proclaimed in all the earth."[g] [18]Therefore God has mercy on whom he wants to have mercy, and he hardens whom he wants to harden.

[19]One of you will say to me: "Then why does God still blame us? For who resists his will?" [20]But who are you, O man, to talk back to God? "Shall what is formed say to him who formed it, 'Why did you make me like this?' "[h] [21]Does not the potter have the right to make out of the same lump of clay some pottery for noble purposes and some for common use?

[22]What if God, choosing to show his wrath and make his power known, bore with great patience the objects of his wrath—prepared for destruction? [23]What if he did this to make the riches of his glory known to the objects of his mercy, whom he prepared in advance for glory— [24]even us, whom he also called, not only from the Jews but also from the Gentiles? [25]As he says in Hosea:

> "I will call them 'my people' who are not my
>   people;
>   and I will call her 'my loved one' who is not my
>   loved one,"[i]

[26]and,

> "It will happen that in the very place where it was
>   said to them,
>   'You are not my people,'
>   they will be called 'sons of the living God.' "[j]

[a] 5 Or *Christ, who is over all. God be forever praised!* Or *Christ. God who is over all be forever praised!*   [b] 7 Gen. 21:12   [c] 9 Gen. 18:10,14
[d] 12 Gen. 25:23   [e] 13 Mal. 1:2,3   [f] 15 Exodus 33:19   [g] 17 Exodus 9:16
[h] 20 Isaiah 29:16; 45:9   [i] 25 Hosea 2:23   [j] 26 Hosea 1:10

[27]Isaiah cries out concerning Israel:

"Though the number of the Israelites be like the
sand by the sea,
only the remnant will be saved.
[28]For the Lord will carry out
his sentence on earth with speed and finality."[a]

[29]It is just as Isaiah said previously:

"Unless the Lord Almighty
had left us descendants,
we would have become like Sodom,
we would have been like Gomorrah."[b]

Israel's Unbelief

[30]What then shall we say? That the Gentiles, who did not pursue righteousness, have obtained it, a righteousness that is by faith; [31]but Israel, who pursued a law of righteousness, has not attained it. [32]Why not? Because they pursued it not by faith but as if it were by works. They stumbled over the "stumbling stone." [33]As it is written:

"See, I lay in Zion a stone that causes men to
stumble
and a rock that makes them fall,
and the one who trusts in him will never be put
to shame."[c]

10 Brothers, my heart's desire and prayer to God for the Israelites is that they may be saved. [2]For I can testify about them that they are zealous for God, but their zeal is not based on knowledge. [3]Since they did not know the righteousness that comes from God and sought to establish their own, they did not submit to God's righteousness. [4]Christ is the end of the law so that there may be righteousness for everyone who believes.

[5]Moses describes in this way the righteousness that is by the law: "The man who does these things will live by them."[d] [6]But the righteousness that is by faith says: "Do not say in your heart, 'Who will ascend into heaven?'[e]" (that is, to bring Christ down) [7]"or 'Who will descend into the deep?'[f]" (that is, to bring Christ up from the dead). [8]But what does it say? "The word is near you; it is in your mouth and in your heart,"[g] that is, the word of faith we are proclaiming: [9]That if you confess with your mouth, "Jesus is Lord," and believe in your heart that God raised him from the dead, you will be saved. [10]For it is with your heart that you believe and are justified, and it is with your mouth that you confess and are saved. [11]As the Scripture says, "Anyone who trusts in him will never be put to shame."[h] [12]For there is no difference between Jew and Gentile—the same Lord is Lord of all and richly blesses all who call on him, [13]for, "Everyone who calls on the name of the Lord will be saved."[i]

[14]How, then, can they call on the one they have not believed in? And how can they believe in the one of whom they have not heard? And how can they hear without someone preaching to them? [15]And how can they preach

Faith in Jesus

ROMANS 10:9–13

Paul's unequivocal affirmation—that faith in Jesus is the only possible way to become righteous before God—allows no theological room for legalism to creep into our thinking. Legalism kept the Pharisees from accepting God's grace, and it remains a snare today. Rule keeping allows one to be religious without relinquishing pride or power to Almighty God. It is a way of avoiding the necessity of saying "Jesus is Lord."

In what ways are you tempted to think legalistically? Are there any attitudes of self-righteousness, selfishness or pride that you hang on to? Do you rely on an illusion of your own goodness for spiritual security? Search the corners of your heart with the Spirit's help. Write a paragraph about that search, and then respond by relinquishing pride and control to Jesus. Conclude by writing "Jesus is Lord" across that paragraph.

[a]28 Isaiah 10:22,23   [b]29 Isaiah 1:9   [c]33 Isaiah 8:14; 28:16
[d]5 Lev. 18:5   [e]6 Deut. 30:12   [f]7 Deut. 30:13   [g]8 Deut. 30:14
[h]11 Isaiah 28:16   [i]13 Joel 2:32

God's Initiative, Our Response

ROMANS 10:21—11:1,5–6

Scripture tells many stories of men and women whose choice to believe that God is God has placed them among God's "remnant" people. It was not their deeds or their titles that qualified them, but their decision to remain in relationship to God and therefore open to his guidance, correction and saving faithfulness.

Read these verses from Romans aloud, slowly. Where do you find yourself in them? Holding out your hands to another? Turning away from a gift? Accepting it? Trying to work your way to God? Wherever you are led, use that as a topic for prayer. Tell God where you are being led, and give him your response. Remember that any experience of God is a gift of grace and not your own work.

See Meeting God in Scripture

unless they are sent? As it is written, "How beautiful are the feet of those who bring good news!"[a]

[16]But not all the Israelites accepted the good news. For Isaiah says, "Lord, who has believed our message?"[b] [17]Consequently, faith comes from hearing the message, and the message is heard through the word of Christ. [18]But I ask: Did they not hear? Of course they did:

> "Their voice has gone out into all the earth,
>   their words to the ends of the world."[c]

[19]Again I ask: Did Israel not understand? First, Moses says,

> "I will make you envious by those who are not a
>   nation;
> I will make you angry by a nation that has no
>   understanding."[d]

[20]And Isaiah boldly says,

> "I was found by those who did not seek me;
>   I revealed myself to those who did not ask for
>   me."[e]

[21]But concerning Israel he says,

> "All day long I have held out my hands
>   to a disobedient and obstinate people."[f]

The Remnant of Israel

11 I ask then: Did God reject his people? By no means! I am an Israelite myself, a descendant of Abraham, from the tribe of Benjamin. [2]God did not reject his people, whom he foreknew. Don't you know what the Scripture says in the passage about Elijah—how he appealed to God against Israel: [3]"Lord, they have killed your prophets and torn down your altars; I am the only one left, and they are trying to kill me"[g]? [4]And what was God's answer to him? "I have reserved for myself seven thousand who have not bowed the knee to Baal."[h] [5]So too, at the present time there is a remnant chosen by grace. [6]And if by grace, then it is no longer by works; if it were, grace would no longer be grace.[i]

[7]What then? What Israel sought so earnestly it did not obtain, but the elect did. The others were hardened, [8]as it is written:

> "God gave them a spirit of stupor,
>   eyes so that they could not see
>   and ears so that they could not hear,
> to this very day."[j]

[9]And David says:

> "May their table become a snare and a trap,
>   a stumbling block and a retribution for them.
> [10]May their eyes be darkened so they cannot see,
>   and their backs be bent forever."[k]

---

[a]15 Isaiah 52:7   [b]16 Isaiah 53:1   [c]18 Psalm 19:4   [d]19 Deut. 32:21
[e]20 Isaiah 65:1   [f]21 Isaiah 65:2   [g]3 1 Kings 19:10,14
[h]4 1 Kings 19:18   [i]6 Some manuscripts *by grace. But if by works,
then it is no longer grace; if it were, work would no longer be work.*
[j]8 Deut. 29:4; Isaiah 29:10   [k]10 Psalm 69:22,23

Ingrafted Branches

[11] Again I ask: Did they stumble so as to fall beyond recovery? Not at all! Rather, because of their transgression, salvation has come to the Gentiles to make Israel envious. [12] But if their transgression means riches for the world, and their loss means riches for the Gentiles, how much greater riches will their fullness bring!

[13] I am talking to you Gentiles. Inasmuch as I am the apostle to the Gentiles, I make much of my ministry [14] in the hope that I may somehow arouse my own people to envy and save some of them. [15] For if their rejection is the reconciliation of the world, what will their acceptance be but life from the dead? [16] If the part of the dough offered as firstfruits is holy, then the whole batch is holy; if the root is holy, so are the branches.

[17] If some of the branches have been broken off, and you, though a wild olive shoot, have been grafted in among the others and now share in the nourishing sap from the olive root, [18] do not boast over those branches. If you do, consider this: You do not support the root, but the root supports you. [19] You will say then, "Branches were broken off so that I could be grafted in." [20] Granted. But they were broken off because of unbelief, and you stand by faith. Do not be arrogant, but be afraid. [21] For if God did not spare the natural branches, he will not spare you either.

[22] Consider therefore the kindness and sternness of God: sternness to those who fell, but kindness to you, provided that you continue in his kindness. Otherwise, you also will be cut off. [23] And if they do not persist in unbelief, they will be grafted in, for God is able to graft them in again. [24] After all, if you were cut out of an olive tree that is wild by nature, and contrary to nature were grafted into a cultivated olive tree, how much more readily will these, the natural branches, be grafted into their own olive tree!

All Israel Will Be Saved

[25] I do not want you to be ignorant of this mystery, brothers, so that you may not be conceited: Israel has experienced a hardening in part until the full number of the Gentiles has come in. [26] And so all Israel will be saved, as it is written:

> "The deliverer will come from Zion;
> he will turn godlessness away from Jacob.
> [27] And this is[a] my covenant with them
> when I take away their sins."[b]

[28] As far as the gospel is concerned, they are enemies on your account; but as far as election is concerned, they are loved on account of the patriarchs, [29] for God's gifts and his call are irrevocable. [30] Just as you who were at one time disobedient to God have now received mercy as a result of their disobedience, [31] so they too have now become disobedient in order that they too may now[c] receive mercy as a result of God's mercy to you. [32] For God has bound all men over to disobedience so that he may have mercy on them all.

Connected

ROMANS 11:16

As branches grafted into a tree become part of the tree and dependent on the tree, taking on the character and nature of the tree, so we as believers are grafted into Jesus Christ.

With your eyes closed, picture a tree. Begin to imagine yourself as a part of the tree. You are connected to the sturdy central trunk and to all the other branches through that trunk. How did you become a part of this tree? What do you share? What is yours alone? Do you give anything to the tree? Stay with this picture, being open to whatever images and emotions come to you. Conclude by drawing or writing your experience, and use that as your prayer to God.

See Meeting God in Scripture

---

a 27 Or *will be*   *b 27* Isaiah 59:20,21; 27:9; Jer. 31:33,34   *c 31* Some manuscripts do not have *now.*

Creator, Creation and Call

ROMANS 12:3–6

Plants give off oxygen in photo-synthesis and thus provide oxygen for respiration for human beings and animals. Human beings and animals give off carbon dioxide for plants to use. This interdependence that God has built into all creation is the pattern for our life in Jesus Christ. We all worship the same God and face many of the same problems, yet each of us experiences life—and God—in unique ways. Our unique perspective may provide just the right pathway for others to gain insight to apply to their lives. Each of us belongs to others and each of us is to offer our unique gifts and talents to help the body grow.

What are your spiritual gifts? How do you use them as part of the body of Christ? Ask God to help you review your gifts and service. Are you mutually dependent on others in the body, or are you a "lone ranger"? In what ways can you offer yourself as a "living sacrifice" (v.1)?

See Meeting God in Community

Doxology

33 Oh, the depth of the riches of the wisdom and[a]
  knowledge of God!
  How unsearchable his judgments,
  and his paths beyond tracing out!
34 "Who has known the mind of the Lord?
  Or who has been his counselor?"[b]
35 "Who has ever given to God,
  that God should repay him?"[c]
36 For from him and through him and to him are all
  things.
  To him be the glory forever! Amen.

Living Sacrifices

12 Therefore, I urge you, brothers, in view of God's mercy, to offer your bodies as living sacrifices, holy and pleasing to God—this is your spiritual[d] act of worship. 2 Do not conform any longer to the pattern of this world, but be transformed by the renewing of your mind. Then you will be able to test and approve what God's will is—his good, pleasing and perfect will.

3 For by the grace given me I say to every one of you: Do not think of yourself more highly than you ought, but rather think of yourself with sober judgment, in accordance with the measure of faith God has given you. 4 Just as each of us has one body with many members, and these members do not all have the same function, 5 so in Christ we who are many form one body, and each member belongs to all the others. 6 We have different gifts, according to the grace given us. If a man's gift is prophesying, let him use it in proportion to his[e] faith. 7 If it is serving, let him serve; if it is teaching, let him teach; 8 if it is encouraging, let him encourage; if it is contributing to the needs of others, let him give generously; if it is leadership, let him govern diligently; if it is showing mercy, let him do it cheerfully.

Love

9 Love must be sincere. Hate what is evil; cling to what is good. 10 Be devoted to one another in brotherly love. Honor one another above yourselves. 11 Never be lacking in zeal, but keep your spiritual fervor, serving the Lord. 12 Be joyful in hope, patient in affliction, faithful in prayer. 13 Share with God's people who are in need. Practice hospitality.

14 Bless those who persecute you; bless and do not curse. 15 Rejoice with those who rejoice; mourn with those who mourn. 16 Live in harmony with one another. Do not be proud, but be willing to associate with people of low position.[f] Do not be conceited.

17 Do not repay anyone evil for evil. Be careful to do what is right in the eyes of everybody. 18 If it is possible, as far as it depends on you, live at peace with everyone. 19 Do not take revenge, my friends, but leave room for God's wrath, for it is written: "It is mine to avenge; I will repay,"[g] says the Lord. 20 On the contrary:

---

a 33 Or riches and the wisdom and the   b 34 Isaiah 40:13   c 35 Job 41:11
d 1 Or reasonable   e 6 Or in agreement with the   f 16 Or willing to do menial work   g 19 Deut. 32:35

"If your enemy is hungry, feed him;
        if he is thirsty, give him something to drink.
In doing this, you will heap burning coals on his
        head."[a]

[21] Do not be overcome by evil, but overcome evil with good.

Submission to the Authorities

13 Everyone must submit himself to the governing authorities, for there is no authority except that which God has established. The authorities that exist have been established by God. [2] Consequently, he who rebels against the authority is rebelling against what God has instituted, and those who do so will bring judgment on themselves. [3] For rulers hold no terror for those who do right, but for those who do wrong. Do you want to be free from fear of the one in authority? Then do what is right and he will commend you. [4] For he is God's servant to do you good. But if you do wrong, be afraid, for he does not bear the sword for nothing. He is God's servant, an agent of wrath to bring punishment on the wrongdoer. [5] Therefore, it is necessary to submit to the authorities, not only because of possible punishment but also because of conscience.

[6] This is also why you pay taxes, for the authorities are God's servants, who give their full time to governing. [7] Give everyone what you owe him: If you owe taxes, pay taxes; if revenue, then revenue; if respect, then respect; if honor, then honor.

Love, for the Day Is Near

[8] Let no debt remain outstanding, except the continuing debt to love one another, for he who loves his fellowman has fulfilled the law. [9] The commandments, "Do not commit adultery," "Do not murder," "Do not steal," "Do not covet,"[b] and whatever other commandment there may be, are summed up in this one rule: "Love your neighbor as yourself."[c] [10] Love does no harm to its neighbor. Therefore love is the fulfillment of the law.

[11] And do this, understanding the present time. The hour has come for you to wake up from your slumber, because our salvation is nearer now than when we first believed. [12] The night is nearly over; the day is almost here. So let us put aside the deeds of darkness and put on the armor of light. [13] Let us behave decently, as in the daytime, not in orgies and drunkenness, not in sexual immorality and debauchery, not in dissension and jealousy. [14] Rather, clothe yourselves with the Lord Jesus Christ, and do not think about how to gratify the desires of the sinful nature.[d]

The Weak and the Strong

14 Accept him whose faith is weak, without passing judgment on disputable matters. [2] One man's faith allows him to eat everything, but another man, whose faith is weak, eats only vegetables. [3] The man who eats everything must not look down on him who does not, and the man who does not eat everything must not condemn the man who does, for God has accepted him. [4] Who are

God Knows Our Needs

ROMANS 14:2–12

"Abbot Mark once said to Abbot Arsenius: It is good, is it not, to have nothing in your cell that just gives you pleasure? For example, once I knew a brother who had a little wildflower that came up in his cell, and he pulled it out by the roots. Well, said Abbot Arsenius, that is all right. But each man should act according to his own spiritual way. And if one were not able to get along without the flower, he should plant it again" (Thomas Merton, trans., *The Wisdom of the Desert*).

Take some time to think about the ways in which you worship best. Is it through prayer, solitude, serving others, working with your hands? Set aside a time to worship in that way. Or set aside time to worship in a setting that communicates joy and peace to you: in a garden, by a body of water, with another person, in silence, or using a piece of music or words of Scripture. Rest in that peace. All good things are gifts from God.

See Meeting God in Worship

The Gift of Harmony

ROMANS 15:5–6

The early Christians stood out in their culture because of the love and care they showed one another. The love they showed to each other is the same love they experienced from knowing Jesus Christ. "We love because [God] first loved us" (1 John 4:19). The heart of the gospel and the hope of our lives are connected: God's loving stead-fastness toward us gives us the resources to live with and to love each other.

Read these verses slowly aloud to yourself. As you read, what touches your heart? Stop reading and focus your attention on that point. What is the call, the hope, the concern or the need that these verses reveal to you, however faint it may be? Open your mind and heart to God's leading. Slowly read these verses again, taking the time to personalize them so that they become your own prayer of petition or prayer of response.

See Meeting God in Scripture

you to judge someone else's servant? To his own master he stands or falls. And he will stand, for the Lord is able to make him stand.

⁵One man considers one day more sacred than another; another man considers every day alike. Each one should be fully convinced in his own mind. ⁶He who regards one day as special, does so to the Lord. He who eats meat, eats to the Lord, for he gives thanks to God; and he who abstains, does so to the Lord and gives thanks to God. ⁷For none of us lives to himself alone and none of us dies to himself alone. ⁸If we live, we live to the Lord; and if we die, we die to the Lord. So, whether we live or die, we belong to the Lord.

⁹For this very reason, Christ died and returned to life so that he might be the Lord of both the dead and the living. ¹⁰You, then, why do you judge your brother? Or why do you look down on your brother? For we will all stand before God's judgment seat. ¹¹It is written:

> " 'As surely as I live,' says the Lord,
> 'every knee will bow before me;
>   every tongue will confess to God.' " [a]

¹²So then, each of us will give an account of himself to God.

¹³Therefore let us stop passing judgment on one another. Instead, make up your mind not to put any stumbling block or obstacle in your brother's way. ¹⁴As one who is in the Lord Jesus, I am fully convinced that no food[b] is unclean in itself. But if anyone regards something as unclean, then for him it is unclean. ¹⁵If your brother is distressed because of what you eat, you are no longer acting in love. Do not by your eating destroy your brother for whom Christ died. ¹⁶Do not allow what you consider good to be spoken of as evil. ¹⁷For the kingdom of God is not a matter of eating and drinking, but of righteousness, peace and joy in the Holy Spirit, ¹⁸because anyone who serves Christ in this way is pleasing to God and approved by men.

¹⁹Let us therefore make every effort to do what leads to peace and to mutual edification. ²⁰Do not destroy the work of God for the sake of food. All food is clean, but it is wrong for a man to eat anything that causes someone else to stumble. ²¹It is better not to eat meat or drink wine or to do anything else that will cause your brother to fall.

²²So whatever you believe about these things keep between yourself and God. Blessed is the man who does not condemn himself by what he approves. ²³But the man who has doubts is condemned if he eats, because his eating is not from faith; and everything that does not come from faith is sin.

15 We who are strong ought to bear with the failings of the weak and not to please ourselves. ²Each of us should please his neighbor for his good, to build him up. ³For even Christ did not please himself but, as it is written: "The insults of those who insult you have fallen on me."[c] ⁴For everything that was written in the past was written to teach us, so that through endurance and the encouragement of the Scriptures we might have hope.

⁵May the God who gives endurance and encouragement

a 11 Isaiah 45:23   *b 14* Or *that nothing*   *c 3* Psalm 69:9

give you a spirit of unity among yourselves as you follow Christ Jesus, ⁶so that with one heart and mouth you may glorify the God and Father of our Lord Jesus Christ.

⁷Accept one another, then, just as Christ accepted you, in order to bring praise to God. ⁸For I tell you that Christ has become a servant of the Jews*ᵃ* on behalf of God's truth, to confirm the promises made to the patriarchs ⁹so that the Gentiles may glorify God for his mercy, as it is written:

> "Therefore I will praise you among the Gentiles;
> I will sing hymns to your name."*ᵇ*

¹⁰Again, it says,

> "Rejoice, O Gentiles, with his people."*ᶜ*

¹¹And again,

> "Praise the Lord, all you Gentiles,
> and sing praises to him, all you peoples."*ᵈ*

¹²And again, Isaiah says,

> "The Root of Jesse will spring up,
> one who will arise to rule over the nations;
> the Gentiles will hope in him."*ᵉ*

¹³May the God of hope fill you with all joy and peace as you trust in him, so that you may overflow with hope by the power of the Holy Spirit.

Paul the Minister to the Gentiles

¹⁴I myself am convinced, my brothers, that you yourselves are full of goodness, complete in knowledge and competent to instruct one another. ¹⁵I have written you quite boldly on some points, as if to remind you of them again, because of the grace God gave me ¹⁶to be a minister of Christ Jesus to the Gentiles with the priestly duty of proclaiming the gospel of God, so that the Gentiles might become an offering acceptable to God, sanctified by the Holy Spirit.

¹⁷Therefore I glory in Christ Jesus in my service to God. ¹⁸I will not venture to speak of anything except what Christ has accomplished through me in leading the Gentiles to obey God by what I have said and done— ¹⁹by the power of signs and miracles, through the power of the Spirit. So from Jerusalem all the way around to Illyricum, I have fully proclaimed the gospel of Christ. ²⁰It has always been my ambition to preach the gospel where Christ was not known, so that I would not be building on someone else's foundation. ²¹Rather, as it is written:

> "Those who were not told about him will see,
> and those who have not heard will
> understand."*ᶠ*

²²This is why I have often been hindered from coming to you.

Paul's Plan to Visit Rome

²³But now that there is no more place for me to work in these regions, and since I have been longing for many

The Community of Prayer

ROMANS 15:23–32

We need each other. The faithfulness of the Christian community supports us when we stumble, and we support others in turn. Whether they like it or not, believers are woven together into a large, interdependent family. When we pray for another or are prayed for, we live out the reality of this connection.

Take a piece of woven fabric. Pull a thread or two out of the fabric and notice what happens to the remaining piece. Look at the threads you pulled out and notice their sudden isolation, smallness and weakness when compared to the larger fabric. Imagine God weaving the fabric, and imagine yourself as a thread in that fabric. How does that experience form and inform your prayer?

See Meeting God in Community

ᵃ8 Greek *circumcision*   *ᵇ9* 2 Samuel 22:50; Psalm 18:49
ᶜ10 Deut. 32:43   *ᵈ11* Psalm 117:1   *ᵉ12* Isaiah 11:10   *ᶠ21* Isaiah 52:15

Individual Greetings; Community Life

ROMANS 16:1–16

Even as much as Paul was teacher and theologian and apostle to the people of Rome, he was a good friend and "family" as well.

Who are the people who make up your spiritual network? Draw a "family tree" and name some of the members who share your branch. Include those you pray and worship with, your "soul friends" or authors who have taught and mentored you. Write notes of greeting and appreciation to some of them.

See Meeting God in Community

years to see you, ²⁴I plan to do so when I go to Spain. I hope to visit you while passing through and to have you assist me on my journey there, after I have enjoyed your company for a while. ²⁵Now, however, I am on my way to Jerusalem in the service of the saints there. ²⁶For Macedonia and Achaia were pleased to make a contribution for the poor among the saints in Jerusalem. ²⁷They were pleased to do it, and indeed they owe it to them. For if the Gentiles have shared in the Jews' spiritual blessings, they owe it to the Jews to share with them their material blessings. ²⁸So after I have completed this task and have made sure that they have received this fruit, I will go to Spain and visit you on the way. ²⁹I know that when I come to you, I will come in the full measure of the blessing of Christ.

³⁰I urge you, brothers, by our Lord Jesus Christ and by the love of the Spirit, to join me in my struggle by praying to God for me. ³¹Pray that I may be rescued from the unbelievers in Judea and that my service in Jerusalem may be acceptable to the saints there, ³²so that by God's will I may come to you with joy and together with you be refreshed. ³³The God of peace be with you all. Amen.

Personal Greetings

16 I commend to you our sister Phoebe, a servant^a of the church in Cenchrea. ²I ask you to receive her in the Lord in a way worthy of the saints and to give her any help she may need from you, for she has been a great help to many people, including me.

³Greet Priscilla^b and Aquila, my fellow workers in Christ Jesus. ⁴They risked their lives for me. Not only I but all the churches of the Gentiles are grateful to them.
⁵Greet also the church that meets at their house.
Greet my dear friend Epenetus, who was the first convert to Christ in the province of Asia.
⁶Greet Mary, who worked very hard for you.
⁷Greet Andronicus and Junias, my relatives who have been in prison with me. They are outstanding among the apostles, and they were in Christ before I was.
⁸Greet Ampliatus, whom I love in the Lord.
⁹Greet Urbanus, our fellow worker in Christ, and my dear friend Stachys.
¹⁰Greet Apelles, tested and approved in Christ.
Greet those who belong to the household of Aristobulus.
¹¹Greet Herodion, my relative.
Greet those in the household of Narcissus who are in the Lord.
¹²Greet Tryphena and Tryphosa, those women who work hard in the Lord.
Greet my dear friend Persis, another woman who has worked very hard in the Lord.
¹³Greet Rufus, chosen in the Lord, and his mother, who has been a mother to me, too.
¹⁴Greet Asyncritus, Phlegon, Hermes, Patrobas, Hermas and the brothers with them.
¹⁵Greet Philologus, Julia, Nereus and his sister, and Olympas and all the saints with them.

a 1 Or *deaconess*   *b 3* Greek *Prisca*, a variant of *Priscilla*

¹⁶Greet one another with a holy kiss.

All the churches of Christ send greetings.

¹⁷I urge you, brothers, to watch out for those who cause divisions and put obstacles in your way that are contrary to the teaching you have learned. Keep away from them. ¹⁸For such people are not serving our Lord Christ, but their own appetites. By smooth talk and flattery they deceive the minds of naive people. ¹⁹Everyone has heard about your obedience, so I am full of joy over you; but I want you to be wise about what is good, and innocent about what is evil.

²⁰The God of peace will soon crush Satan under your feet.

The grace of our Lord Jesus be with you.

²¹Timothy, my fellow worker, sends his greetings to you, as do Lucius, Jason and Sosipater, my relatives.

²²I, Tertius, who wrote down this letter, greet you in the Lord.

²³Gaius, whose hospitality I and the whole church here enjoy, sends you his greetings.

Erastus, who is the city's director of public works, and our brother Quartus send you their greetings.ᵃ

²⁵Now to him who is able to establish you by my gospel and the proclamation of Jesus Christ, according to the revelation of the mystery hidden for long ages past, ²⁶but now revealed and made known through the prophetic writings by the command of the eternal God, so that all nations might believe and obey him— ²⁷to the only wise God be glory forever through Jesus Christ! Amen.

To God Be the Glory

ROMANS 16:25–27

God has made known to us the mystery of faith: We can know God in an intimate way through the incarnation of Jesus Christ. God is accessible and available. God is "for us," and that is reason to shout and to sing: "To the only wise God be glory forever through Jesus Christ! Amen."

Let these last verses become a dialogue with God as you pray them. What particular word or phrase draws your attention? As you keep that word or phrase in your mind, let God lead you further: What do you need to disclose? How do you need to be strengthened? Comforted? What prompts you to cry, "Glory to God"? Return to these verses again, changing the wording so that it becomes your personal response to who God is and what God has done.

ᵃ 23 Some manuscripts *their greetings.* ²⁴*May the grace of our Lord Jesus Christ be with all of you. Amen.*

1505

Ways of MEETING GOD

Meeting God in Community

We were not created to live in isolation. No person "is an island, entire of itself," wrote the poet John Donne. While no one questions the need for periods of solitude and refreshment in our lives, faith tends to thrive most readily when shared and experienced with others. Without the connections community affords us, we experience what someone once called "spiritual loneliness." For we meet God not just as we sit alone in quiet corners but in and through the people with whom we live, work and interact as we go through our daily routine.

> **W**e meet God not just as we sit alone in quiet corners but in and through the people with whom we live, work and interact as we go through our daily routine.

Relationships present us with both a remarkable privilege and an awesome responsibility. Proverbs 27:17 tells us that "as iron sharpens iron, so one [person] sharpens [and shapes] another." As other people's lives touch ours, they help to form our faith and make us who we are. As we touch others, we reflect God's love to them.

Relationships with other believers have extraordinary power in our lives because Jesus is present in them. Jesus knew how important people are in conveying God's grace and presence. "Where two or three come together in my name," he said, "there am I with them" (Matthew 18:20). Within our churches, small groups, families and friendships, we learn from one another. We find encouragement. We challenge one another to follow God more faithfully. Other Christians enable us to walk as we should when we might otherwise have strayed or wandered. God uses relationships to form us, and relationships form us so that God can use us.

Power for Growth and Change. The Bible offers many examples of the formational power of relationships. The story of Ruth and Naomi demonstrates

1506

how the presence of other believers can enable us to do what we can't do alone. Ruth is a foreigner, a "Moabitess" who has married Naomi's son. When Naomi's husband and her sons (including Ruth's husband) die, she grieves, saying, "The LORD's hand has gone out against me!" (Ruth 1:13). Ruth, also widowed, chooses to stay with Naomi rather than return to her own kin. Ruth speaks the words that are well-known and much-loved: "Where you go I will go, and where you stay I will stay. Your people will be my people and your God my God" (Ruth 1:16). Just think of the magnitude of the change those words brought about! Something in this relationship makes Ruth willing to leave her family and country to adopt Naomi's faith. The younger woman seeks guidance from Naomi and in turn cares for her. Through their loving relationship Naomi is released from the bitterness of her losses, and Ruth is drawn into relationship with the God of Israel. Eventually Ruth even becomes the ancestor of Jesus the Messiah (see Matthew 1:5).

Elijah and Elisha offer an example of the way God uses the power of relationships to build strong leaders. God, employing Elijah as Elisha's mentor, makes a dramatic difference in the life of the younger man who is eager to serve God faithfully. Elijah, a famous prophet, is near the end of his ministry when God tells him to seek out and anoint Elisha as his successor. Elijah throws his cloak over Elisha's shoulders as the younger man walks behind his plow and his oxen, publicly calling Elisha to a new way of life. What a dramatic act! Elisha leaves his farm work to become Elijah's attendant (see 1 Kings 19:16–21), following the prophet and seeking to learn from him. He refuses to leave his mentor and asks for "a double portion" of the spirit that has made Elijah great (see 2 Kings 2:9). One man is clearly the teacher and the other the student, and, like Elijah, Elisha acknowledges that God is at the center of his life and ministry. Through his relationship with Elijah, he develops the courage, faith and skills to carry on the work of the prophet as God's spokesman.

In the New Testament Mary and Elizabeth offer us yet another example of how relationships help us mature in faith. Their relationship illustrates the value of sharing mutual insight and encouragement. According to the Gospel of Luke, young Mary is visited by the angel Gabriel, who tells her that she will bear a son who will be the Messiah. Mary, "greatly troubled at his words" (Luke 1:29), hurries to visit her older cousin Elizabeth, who is also pregnant. Though Mary has told the angel that she wants to be obedient to God's will, she is surely also confused and frightened. But after Elizabeth speaks to her, Mary breaks into a song of praise to God; her faith has been strengthened. Mary spends three months with Elizabeth, who supports her and in turn is supported in the joyful yet sacrificial work to which God has called both of them. Mary discovered, as many have, that when we are hesitant to face what lies ahead, spending time with someone who knows us and shares our faith can help us see more clearly and understand more deeply the issues we need to deal with. It fortifies us to move forward in faith.

Soul Friends. Throughout the history of the church, writers and leaders have echoed this message. In the twelfth century, Aelred of Rievaulx said that Christian friendship can be "a step to raise us to the love and knowledge of God." He also spoke of the joy of having a friend with "whom you need have no fear to confess your failings; one to whom you can unblushingly make known what progress you have made in the spiritual life; one to whom you can entrust all the secrets of your heart and before whom you can place all your plans." Teresa of Avila wrote in the sixteenth century of how "it is a great advantage for us to be able to consult someone who knows us, so that we may learn to know ourselves." John Wesley went so far as to declare that there is no such thing as a solitary Christian.

What these Christians from various times and places learned is that God uses close and continuing relationships to form us into the image of Jesus. As we share both our high moments and our low, pray for one another, help each other and work together toward common goals, we reflect Jesus and acknowledge Jesus' presence with us.

> At their best, relationships with other believers not only shield us in difficult times but also help us to confront our imperfections.

Nurturing Your Own Soul Friends. To begin to meet God in community you may want to reach out to other believers with whom you can discuss your spiritual journey. Such conversation helps you to sort out what you know about yourself and about God. It may be especially valuable if you make this a deliberate action. Ask one or two mature individuals—with whom you can exchange thoughts and prayers with confidence and assurance of confidentiality—to meet with you. This practice has traditionally been called "spiritual guidance," "spiritual direction" or "spiritual friendship." This kind of conversation may also occur in the context of worship services, church school classes and small groups. One-on-one relationships and small groups allow for a depth of interaction not possible in larger, more formal settings. They allow us to pray aloud for one another with potentially life-changing results. As Alan Jones, an essayist on Christian friendship, stated, "We cannot help but tremble on the brink of surrender, but it is our companions who give us the courage to jump."

Spend Time Observing the Lives of Faithful Christians. The New Testament tells us repeatedly that we become like Jesus by spending time with those who are his friends. We look at those who have led us, consider the outcome of their faith and then choose to imitate them (see Hebrews 13:7). Some find it a good discipline to think periodically about someone whose faith they admire. Consider approaching one or more such people to ask them how God has been at work in their lives. (For Biblical examples of this process, see 1 Corinthians 4:6; Philippians 3:17; 1 Thessalonians 1:6; and 2 Thessalonians 3:9.)

Stay Active in a Church Community. As happens within our immediate family circle, when we rub shoulders with others we are continually confronted with reminders of our weaknesses and brokenness. We wound others and are wounded by them. Romans 12:18 acknowledges that living with others can be difficult, urging, "If it is possible, as far as it depends on you, live at peace with everyone." While imperfections abound within what Paul calls "the body of Christ," God still uses the company of believers to grace our lives and transform the world (see Romans 12:4–5; 1 Corinthians 12:12; and Ephesians 5:30). We cannot do without our fellow believers. "Let us not give up meeting together," the writer of the letter to the Hebrews urges (Hebrews 10:25). At their best, relationships with other believers not only shield us in difficult times but also help us to confront our imperfections. We find a place to mutually speak "the truth in love" (Ephesians 4:15).

View Your Involvement With Other Believers as an Opportunity to Help. It is a privilege to nurture another person, to be trusted to hear another's dreams and concerns, to pray for someone. In so doing we may discover myriad ways to use the gifts that God has given us to benefit our family in Christ as well as for our own growth and enjoyment. As we help others, we too will be helped. As we comfort and teach and encourage, we will be comforted, taught and encouraged in turn. As we experience community, we find our own lives enriched, in turn providing us with more to give to others.

See Page 1586 for the next Ways of Meeting God *article.*

1 CORINTHIANS

The Way of Love

KEY VERSES:

Love is patient, love is kind. It does not envy, it does not boast, it is not proud. It is not rude, it is not self-seeking, it is not easily angered, it keeps no record of wrongs. Love does not delight in evil but rejoices with the truth. It always protects, always trusts, always hopes, always perseveres.

—1 Corinthians 13:4–7

"Love in its nature makes a human being like God, as far as is possible for a human being. The soul is intoxicated by the effects of it. Its characteristics are a fountain of faith, an abyss of patience, an ocean of humility."

—JOHN CLIMACUS,
in *Drinking from the Fountain:
A Patristic Breviary*

In the apostle Paul's first letter to the Corinthians we encounter a missionary whose spirit is being transformed by the Holy Spirit. Paul urges the people of the Corinthian church to be likewise transformed by the Spirit of God. Paul admits that he is not a clever, eloquent orator but a childlike man who is "foolish" enough to preach the cross (1:17—2:16). His servant posture cuts through the barriers of human factions to pull together a community of believers who will proclaim in one voice that Jesus is Lord.

As you read Paul's letter and meditate on it, imagine yourself in the presence of the apostle, a seasoned spiritual teacher who crowns his letter with the often–quoted essay on love. Envision yourself telling Paul how hard it is for you to uphold this standard of love when you've had a spat with your spouse or felt misunderstood by your friend. Then turn your thoughts toward God in prayer. Ask God to help you cross the bridge between love in the abstract ("Of course I love people, but I can't stand my next-door neighbor!") and love in the concrete ("I know if I can learn to love my neighbor, then it won't be so hard to love other people"). How might such prayerful interaction with what Paul writes help you to become more loving—and part of a more loving community in Jesus Christ?

1 Paul, called to be an apostle of Christ Jesus by the will of God, and our brother Sosthenes,

²To the church of God in Corinth, to those sanctified in Christ Jesus and called to be holy, together with all those everywhere who call on the name of our Lord Jesus Christ—their Lord and ours:

³Grace and peace to you from God our Father and the Lord Jesus Christ.

Thanksgiving

⁴I always thank God for you because of his grace given you in Christ Jesus. ⁵For in him you have been enriched in every way—in all your speaking and in all your knowledge— ⁶because our testimony about Christ was confirmed in you. ⁷Therefore you do not lack any spiritual gift as you eagerly wait for our Lord Jesus Christ to be revealed. ⁸He will keep you strong to the end, so that you will be blameless on the day of our Lord Jesus Christ. ⁹God, who has called you into fellowship with his Son Jesus Christ our Lord, is faithful.

Divisions in the Church

¹⁰I appeal to you, brothers, in the name of our Lord Jesus Christ, that all of you agree with one another so that there may be no divisions among you and that you may be perfectly united in mind and thought. ¹¹My brothers, some from Chloe's household have informed me that there are quarrels among you. ¹²What I mean is this: One of you says, "I follow Paul"; another, "I follow Apollos"; another, "I follow Cephas*ᵃ*"; still another, "I follow Christ."

¹³Is Christ divided? Was Paul crucified for you? Were you baptized into*ᵇ* the name of Paul? ¹⁴I am thankful that I did not baptize any of you except Crispus and Gaius, ¹⁵so no one can say that you were baptized into my name. ¹⁶(Yes, I also baptized the household of Stephanas; beyond that, I don't remember if I baptized anyone else.) ¹⁷For Christ did not send me to baptize, but to preach the gospel—not with words of human wisdom, lest the cross of Christ be emptied of its power.

Christ the Wisdom and Power of God

¹⁸For the message of the cross is foolishness to those who are perishing, but to us who are being saved it is the power of God. ¹⁹For it is written:

> "I will destroy the wisdom of the wise;
>   the intelligence of the intelligent I will
>   frustrate."*ᶜ*

²⁰Where is the wise man? Where is the scholar? Where is the philosopher of this age? Has not God made foolish the wisdom of the world? ²¹For since in the wisdom of God the world through its wisdom did not know him, God was pleased through the foolishness of what was preached to save those who believe. ²²Jews demand miraculous signs and Greeks look for wisdom, ²³but we preach Christ crucified: a stumbling block to Jews and foolishness to Gentiles, ²⁴but to those whom God has called, both Jews and

The Cross Is Good News

1 CORINTHIANS 1:17–18

Think of the cross on which the Savior of the world hung. The grisly story it tells seems to suggest anything but God's glory, yet by the sacrifice of Jesus Christ on the cross we are saved. Jesus, hanging in agony upon it, was powerless, yet in him resides the power to redeem humankind from sin and death. There is nothing eloquent about the cross, yet it preaches the world's best sermon.

Let the weight of this paradox sink into your heart. In what ways do you feel emotionally or spiritually weak? In what ways are you drained and exhausted? Are you living with self-condemnation or guilt? Write down your responses. Then rethink them in the light of the good news Paul conveys to the Corinthians in this powerful opening passage. Appropriate the power of God to renew your spirit with life and forgiveness.

See Meeting God in Worship

God's Secret Wisdom

1 CORINTHIANS 2:3–7

We live in a culture that values power and self-reliance. It seems that the Corinthians held the same assumptions about human righteousness that we do today: Moral standards are set by human wisdom, not by God's wisdom; privileges are acquired through noble birth, not by being born in a stable; truth is found in the testimony of clever minds, not in the fear and trembling uttered by humble prophets.

What, then, is the secret wisdom of which Paul speaks in this passage? What cherished illusions about the way to grow spiritually does it shatter? How does Paul's message prompt you to pray? For more perfect understanding? For a greater capacity for spiritual discernment? Or simply for putting on the mind of Christ Jesus?

See Meeting God in Prayer

Greeks, Christ the power of God and the wisdom of God. [25]For the foolishness of God is wiser than man's wisdom, and the weakness of God is stronger than man's strength.

[26]Brothers, think of what you were when you were called. Not many of you were wise by human standards; not many were influential; not many were of noble birth. [27]But God chose the foolish things of the world to shame the wise; God chose the weak things of the world to shame the strong. [28]He chose the lowly things of this world and the despised things—and the things that are not—to nullify the things that are, [29]so that no one may boast before him. [30]It is because of him that you are in Christ Jesus, who has become for us wisdom from God—that is, our righteousness, holiness and redemption. [31]Therefore, as it is written: "Let him who boasts boast in the Lord."[a]

2 When I came to you, brothers, I did not come with eloquence or superior wisdom as I proclaimed to you the testimony about God.[b] [2]For I resolved to know nothing while I was with you except Jesus Christ and him crucified. [3]I came to you in weakness and fear, and with much trembling. [4]My message and my preaching were not with wise and persuasive words, but with a demonstration of the Spirit's power, [5]so that your faith might not rest on men's wisdom, but on God's power.

Wisdom From the Spirit

[6]We do, however, speak a message of wisdom among the mature, but not the wisdom of this age or of the rulers of this age, who are coming to nothing. [7]No, we speak of God's secret wisdom, a wisdom that has been hidden and that God destined for our glory before time began. [8]None of the rulers of this age understood it, for if they had, they would not have crucified the Lord of glory. [9]However, as it is written:

> "No eye has seen,
>   no ear has heard,
>   no mind has conceived
>   what God has prepared for those who love
>   him"[c]—

[10]but God has revealed it to us by his Spirit.

The Spirit searches all things, even the deep things of God. [11]For who among men knows the thoughts of a man except the man's spirit within him? In the same way no one knows the thoughts of God except the Spirit of God. [12]We have not received the spirit of the world but the Spirit who is from God, that we may understand what God has freely given us. [13]This is what we speak, not in words taught us by human wisdom but in words taught by the Spirit, expressing spiritual truths in spiritual words.[d] [14]The man without the Spirit does not accept the things that come from the Spirit of God, for they are foolishness to him, and he cannot understand them, because they are spiritually discerned. [15]The spiritual man makes judgments about all things, but he himself is not subject to any man's judgment:

[a]31 Jer. 9:24   [b]1 Some manuscripts *as I proclaimed to you God's mystery*
[c]9 Isaiah 64:4   [d]13 Or *Spirit, interpreting spiritual truths to spiritual men*

[16] "For who has known the mind of the Lord
    that he may instruct him?"[a]

But we have the mind of Christ.

On Divisions in the Church

3 Brothers, I could not address you as spiritual but as worldly—mere infants in Christ. [2]I gave you milk, not solid food, for you were not yet ready for it. Indeed, you are still not ready. [3]You are still worldly. For since there is jealousy and quarreling among you, are you not worldly? Are you not acting like mere men? [4]For when one says, "I follow Paul," and another, "I follow Apollos," are you not mere men?

[5]What, after all, is Apollos? And what is Paul? Only servants, through whom you came to believe—as the Lord has assigned to each his task. [6]I planted the seed, Apollos watered it, but God made it grow. [7]So neither he who plants nor he who waters is anything, but only God, who makes things grow. [8]The man who plants and the man who waters have one purpose, and each will be rewarded according to his own labor. [9]For we are God's fellow workers; you are God's field, God's building.

[10]By the grace God has given me, I laid a foundation as an expert builder, and someone else is building on it. But each one should be careful how he builds. [11]For no one can lay any foundation other than the one already laid, which is Jesus Christ. [12]If any man builds on this foundation using gold, silver, costly stones, wood, hay or straw, [13]his work will be shown for what it is, because the Day will bring it to light. It will be revealed with fire, and the fire will test the quality of each man's work. [14]If what he has built survives, he will receive his reward. [15]If it is burned up, he will suffer loss; he himself will be saved, but only as one escaping through the flames.

[16]Don't you know that you yourselves are God's temple and that God's Spirit lives in you? [17]If anyone destroys God's temple, God will destroy him; for God's temple is sacred, and you are that temple.

[18]Do not deceive yourselves. If any one of you thinks he is wise by the standards of this age, he should become a "fool" so that he may become wise. [19]For the wisdom of this world is foolishness in God's sight. As it is written: "He catches the wise in their craftiness"[b]; [20]and again, "The Lord knows that the thoughts of the wise are futile."[c] [21]So then, no more boasting about men! All things are yours, [22]whether Paul or Apollos or Cephas[d] or the world or life or death or the present or the future—all are yours, [23]and you are of Christ, and Christ is of God.

Apostles of Christ

4 So then, men ought to regard us as servants of Christ and as those entrusted with the secret things of God. [2]Now it is required that those who have been given a trust must prove faithful. [3]I care very little if I am judged by you or by any human court; indeed, I do not even judge myself. [4]My conscience is clear, but that does not make me innocent. It is the Lord who judges me. [5]Therefore judge nothing before the appointed time; wait till the Lord

Building the House of God

1 CORINTHIANS 3:9–17

Have you ever had the experience of building your own home? If you have, you know about the importance of starting with a straight, solid foundation. Paul says any foundation other than Jesus Christ will never support the church. Anything built on any other foundation will one day topple over. What is the foundation of your spiritual life? What is the foundation of your worshiping community? Are there some things that must change in order for Jesus Christ to become the only foundation? Picture yourself building on this foundation, laying the first stone. Of what does it consist— "gold, silver, costly stones, wood, hay or straw" (3:12)? Is your house built in such a way that it is impervious to most natural disasters, or is it likely to fall down in a windstorm or collapse in a flood? How could you build it better?

See Meeting God in Scripture

Foolish for Christ

1 CORINTHIANS 4:9–13

Who would ever want to look like a fool? Yet that is what Paul asks followers of Christ to be. Who would ever want to come across as a spectacle? Yet Paul would show us off, in all our weakness, "to the whole universe, to angels as well as to men."

In what ways are you a fool for Christ? What behaviors and attitudes do others see as foolish in you: blessing those who curse you, enduring persecution and misunderstanding without comment, answering slander with kindness, letting others take precedence? Write such events in your spiritual journal or on a note card and review them with this passage in mind.

See *Meeting God in Everyday Life*

comes. He will bring to light what is hidden in darkness and will expose the motives of men's hearts. At that time each will receive his praise from God.

[6]Now, brothers, I have applied these things to myself and Apollos for your benefit, so that you may learn from us the meaning of the saying, "Do not go beyond what is written." Then you will not take pride in one man over against another. [7]For who makes you different from anyone else? What do you have that you did not receive? And if you did receive it, why do you boast as though you did not?

[8]Already you have all you want! Already you have become rich! You have become kings—and that without us! How I wish that you really had become kings so that we might be kings with you! [9]For it seems to me that God has put us apostles on display at the end of the procession, like men condemned to die in the arena. We have been made a spectacle to the whole universe, to angels as well as to men. [10]We are fools for Christ, but you are so wise in Christ! We are weak, but you are strong! You are honored, we are dishonored! [11]To this very hour we go hungry and thirsty, we are in rags, we are brutally treated, we are homeless. [12]We work hard with our own hands. When we are cursed, we bless; when we are persecuted, we endure it; [13]when we are slandered, we answer kindly. Up to this moment we have become the scum of the earth, the refuse of the world.

[14]I am not writing this to shame you, but to warn you, as my dear children. [15]Even though you have ten thousand guardians in Christ, you do not have many fathers, for in Christ Jesus I became your father through the gospel. [16]Therefore I urge you to imitate me. [17]For this reason I am sending to you Timothy, my son whom I love, who is faithful in the Lord. He will remind you of my way of life in Christ Jesus, which agrees with what I teach everywhere in every church.

[18]Some of you have become arrogant, as if I were not coming to you. [19]But I will come to you very soon, if the Lord is willing, and then I will find out not only how these arrogant people are talking, but what power they have. [20]For the kingdom of God is not a matter of talk but of power. [21]What do you prefer? Shall I come to you with a whip, or in love and with a gentle spirit?

Expel the Immoral Brother!

5 It is actually reported that there is sexual immorality among you, and of a kind that does not occur even among pagans: A man has his father's wife. [2]And you are proud! Shouldn't you rather have been filled with grief and have put out of your fellowship the man who did this? [3]Even though I am not physically present, I am with you in spirit. And I have already passed judgment on the one who did this, just as if I were present. [4]When you are assembled in the name of our Lord Jesus and I am with you in spirit, and the power of our Lord Jesus is present, [5]hand this man over to Satan, so that the sinful nature[a] may be destroyed and his spirit saved on the day of the Lord.

[6]Your boasting is not good. Don't you know that a little yeast works through the whole batch of dough? [7]Get rid of

[a] 5 Or *that his body*; or *that the flesh*

the old yeast that you may be a new batch without yeast—as you really are. For Christ, our Passover lamb, has been sacrificed. [8]Therefore let us keep the Festival, not with the old yeast, the yeast of malice and wickedness, but with bread without yeast, the bread of sincerity and truth.

[9]I have written you in my letter not to associate with sexually immoral people— [10]not at all meaning the people of this world who are immoral, or the greedy and swindlers, or idolaters. In that case you would have to leave this world. [11]But now I am writing you that you must not associate with anyone who calls himself a brother but is sexually immoral or greedy, an idolater or a slanderer, a drunkard or a swindler. With such a man do not even eat.

[12]What business is it of mine to judge those outside the church? Are you not to judge those inside? [13]God will judge those outside. "Expel the wicked man from among you."[a]

Lawsuits Among Believers

6 If any of you has a dispute with another, dare he take it before the ungodly for judgment instead of before the saints? [2]Do you not know that the saints will judge the world? And if you are to judge the world, are you not competent to judge trivial cases? [3]Do you not know that we will judge angels? How much more the things of this life! [4]Therefore, if you have disputes about such matters, appoint as judges even men of little account in the church![b] [5]I say this to shame you. Is it possible that there is nobody among you wise enough to judge a dispute between believers? [6]But instead, one brother goes to law against another—and this in front of unbelievers!

[7]The very fact that you have lawsuits among you means you have been completely defeated already. Why not rather be wronged? Why not rather be cheated? [8]Instead, you yourselves cheat and do wrong, and you do this to your brothers.

[9]Do you not know that the wicked will not inherit the kingdom of God? Do not be deceived: Neither the sexually immoral nor idolaters nor adulterers nor male prostitutes nor homosexual offenders [10]nor thieves nor the greedy nor drunkards nor slanderers nor swindlers will inherit the kingdom of God. [11]And that is what some of you were. But you were washed, you were sanctified, you were justified in the name of the Lord Jesus Christ and by the Spirit of our God.

Sexual Immorality

[12]"Everything is permissible for me"—but not everything is beneficial. "Everything is permissible for me"—but I will not be mastered by anything. [13]"Food for the stomach and the stomach for food"—but God will destroy them both. The body is not meant for sexual immorality, but for the Lord, and the Lord for the body. [14]By his power God raised the Lord from the dead, and he will raise us also. [15]Do you not know that your bodies are members of Christ himself? Shall I then take the members of Christ and unite them with a prostitute? Never! [16]Do you not

Honoring God With Your Body

1 CORINTHIANS 6:12–20

The bread of sincerity and truth that Paul advises us to eat nourishes the spirit much like a loaf of bread satisifies hunger. What happens, then, when sexual immorality replaces integrity? When overindulgence replaces self-control? The body is not separate from the soul; what nourishes one nourishes the other. What destroys or degrades one destroys or degrades the other.

If you were asked to speak to young people in your church about sexual morality and the sanctity of marriage, how might you paraphrase or expand the argument Paul gives here? How much of your own lecture do you need to hear?

See Meeting God in Everyday Life

---

[a] 13 Deut. 17:7; 19:19; 21:21; 22:21,24; 24:7   [b] 4 Or *matters, do you appoint as judges men of little account in the church?*

The Balm of Fidelity

1 CORINTHIANS 7:1–7,17–24

"Without a little wisp of fidelity simmering within, life can become distasteful enough to make a marriage come crashing down, to send men and women through foolish pursuits of power, gambling, promiscuity, and exotic interludes, to a feverish chase after fantasized heights through dangerous drugs. Nothing of this can heal the tediousness of a life lived outside simple loyalty to a daily task. No human banality can substitute for the balm of fidelity."

—ADRIAN VAN KAAM,
The Music of Eternity

know that he who unites himself with a prostitute is one with her in body? For it is said, "The two will become one flesh."[a] ¹⁷But he who unites himself with the Lord is one with him in spirit.

¹⁸Flee from sexual immorality. All other sins a man commits are outside his body, but he who sins sexually sins against his own body. ¹⁹Do you not know that your body is a temple of the Holy Spirit, who is in you, whom you have received from God? You are not your own; ²⁰you were bought at a price. Therefore honor God with your body.

Marriage

7 Now for the matters you wrote about: It is good for a man not to marry.[b] ²But since there is so much immorality, each man should have his own wife, and each woman her own husband. ³The husband should fulfill his marital duty to his wife, and likewise the wife to her husband. ⁴The wife's body does not belong to her alone but also to her husband. In the same way, the husband's body does not belong to him alone but also to his wife. ⁵Do not deprive each other except by mutual consent and for a time, so that you may devote yourselves to prayer. Then come together again so that Satan will not tempt you because of your lack of self-control. ⁶I say this as a concession, not as a command. ⁷I wish that all men were as I am. But each man has his own gift from God; one has this gift, another has that.

⁸Now to the unmarried and the widows I say: It is good for them to stay unmarried, as I am. ⁹But if they cannot control themselves, they should marry, for it is better to marry than to burn with passion.

¹⁰To the married I give this command (not I, but the Lord): A wife must not separate from her husband. ¹¹But if she does, she must remain unmarried or else be reconciled to her husband. And a husband must not divorce his wife.

¹²To the rest I say this (I, not the Lord): If any brother has a wife who is not a believer and she is willing to live with him, he must not divorce her. ¹³And if a woman has a husband who is not a believer and he is willing to live with her, she must not divorce him. ¹⁴For the unbelieving husband has been sanctified through his wife, and the unbelieving wife has been sanctified through her believing husband. Otherwise your children would be unclean, but as it is, they are holy.

¹⁵But if the unbeliever leaves, let him do so. A believing man or woman is not bound in such circumstances; God has called us to live in peace. ¹⁶How do you know, wife, whether you will save your husband? Or, how do you know, husband, whether you will save your wife?

¹⁷Nevertheless, each one should retain the place in life that the Lord assigned to him and to which God has called him. This is the rule I lay down in all the churches. ¹⁸Was a man already circumcised when he was called? He should not become uncircumcised. Was a man uncircumcised when he was called? He should not be circumcised. ¹⁹Circumcision is nothing and uncircumcision is nothing. Keep-

---

[a] 16 Gen. 2:24   [b] 1 Or "*It is good for a man not to have sexual relations with a woman.*"

ing God's commands is what counts. ²⁰Each one should remain in the situation which he was in when God called him. ²¹Were you a slave when you were called? Don't let it trouble you—although if you can gain your freedom, do so. ²²For he who was a slave when he was called by the Lord is the Lord's freedman; similarly, he who was a free man when he was called is Christ's slave. ²³You were bought at a price; do not become slaves of men. ²⁴Brothers, each man, as responsible to God, should remain in the situation God called him to.

²⁵Now about virgins: I have no command from the Lord, but I give a judgment as one who by the Lord's mercy is trustworthy. ²⁶Because of the present crisis, I think that it is good for you to remain as you are. ²⁷Are you married? Do not seek a divorce. Are you unmarried? Do not look for a wife. ²⁸But if you do marry, you have not sinned; and if a virgin marries, she has not sinned. But those who marry will face many troubles in this life, and I want to spare you this.

²⁹What I mean, brothers, is that the time is short. From now on those who have wives should live as if they had none; ³⁰those who mourn, as if they did not; those who are happy, as if they were not; those who buy something, as if it were not theirs to keep; ³¹those who use the things of the world, as if not engrossed in them. For this world in its present form is passing away.

³²I would like you to be free from concern. An unmarried man is concerned about the Lord's affairs—how he can please the Lord. ³³But a married man is concerned about the affairs of this world—how he can please his wife— ³⁴and his interests are divided. An unmarried woman or virgin is concerned about the Lord's affairs: Her aim is to be devoted to the Lord in both body and spirit. But a married woman is concerned about the affairs of this world—how she can please her husband. ³⁵I am saying this for your own good, not to restrict you, but that you may live in a right way in undivided devotion to the Lord.

³⁶If anyone thinks he is acting improperly toward the virgin he is engaged to, and if she is getting along in years and he feels he ought to marry, he should do as he wants. He is not sinning. They should get married. ³⁷But the man who has settled the matter in his own mind, who is under no compulsion but has control over his own will, and who has made up his mind not to marry the virgin—this man also does the right thing. ³⁸So then, he who marries the virgin does right, but he who does not marry her does even better.ᵃ

³⁹A woman is bound to her husband as long as he lives. But if her husband dies, she is free to marry anyone she wishes, but he must belong to the Lord. ⁴⁰In my judgment, she is happier if she stays as she is—and I think that I too have the Spirit of God.

ᵃ 36–38 Or ³⁶If anyone thinks he is not treating his daughter properly, and if she is getting along in years, and he feels she ought to marry, he should do as he wants. He is not sinning. He should let her get married. ³⁷But the man who has settled the matter in his own mind, who is under no compulsion but has control over his own will, and who has made up his mind to keep the virgin unmarried—this man also does the right thing. ³⁸So then, he who gives his virgin in marriage does right, but he who does not give her in marriage does even better.

Undivided Devotion

1 CORINTHIANS 7:35

"The greatest difficulty in conversion, is to win the heart to God; and the greatest difficulty after conversion, is to keep the heart with God."

—JOHN FLAVEL,
Keeping the Heart

Sowing the Seeds of Truth

1 CORINTHIANS 8:9–12

Many of the same issues that threatened to divide the Christian community in Corinth still plague us today. For example, the problem of an inflated ego (knowledge that puffs us up) is not easily overcome in a culture in which people make choices based on their own preferences and perceptions. The main challenge Paul proposes is that Christians are to be motivated first and foremost by love.

Search your conscience. How are your actions—no matter how justifiable or innocent they may seem in your eyes—likely to affect the faith of those who are not confident or strong in their faith? Is your exercise of Christian freedom likely to undermine someone's faith? Try to be specific. Ask God for forgiveness and guidance—and trust that you will reap the spiritual fruit of which Paul speaks.

See *Meeting God in Community*

Food Sacrificed to Idols

8 Now about food sacrificed to idols: We know that we all possess knowledge.[a] Knowledge puffs up, but love builds up. [2]The man who thinks he knows something does not yet know as he ought to know. [3]But the man who loves God is known by God.

[4]So then, about eating food sacrificed to idols: We know that an idol is nothing at all in the world and that there is no God but one. [5]For even if there are so-called gods, whether in heaven or on earth (as indeed there are many "gods" and many "lords"), [6]yet for us there is but one God, the Father, from whom all things came and for whom we live; and there is but one Lord, Jesus Christ, through whom all things came and through whom we live.

[7]But not everyone knows this. Some people are still so accustomed to idols that when they eat such food they think of it as having been sacrificed to an idol, and since their conscience is weak, it is defiled. [8]But food does not bring us near to God; we are no worse if we do not eat, and no better if we do.

[9]Be careful, however, that the exercise of your freedom does not become a stumbling block to the weak. [10]For if anyone with a weak conscience sees you who have this knowledge eating in an idol's temple, won't he be emboldened to eat what has been sacrificed to idols? [11]So this weak brother, for whom Christ died, is destroyed by your knowledge. [12]When you sin against your brothers in this way and wound their weak conscience, you sin against Christ. [13]Therefore, if what I eat causes my brother to fall into sin, I will never eat meat again, so that I will not cause him to fall.

The Rights of an Apostle

9 Am I not free? Am I not an apostle? Have I not seen Jesus our Lord? Are you not the result of my work in the Lord? [2]Even though I may not be an apostle to others, surely I am to you! For you are the seal of my apostleship in the Lord.

[3]This is my defense to those who sit in judgment on me. [4]Don't we have the right to food and drink? [5]Don't we have the right to take a believing wife along with us, as do the other apostles and the Lord's brothers and Cephas[b]? [6]Or is it only I and Barnabas who must work for a living?

[7]Who serves as a soldier at his own expense? Who plants a vineyard and does not eat of its grapes? Who tends a flock and does not drink of the milk? [8]Do I say this merely from a human point of view? Doesn't the Law say the same thing? [9]For it is written in the Law of Moses: "Do not muzzle an ox while it is treading out the grain."[c] Is it about oxen that God is concerned? [10]Surely he says this for us, doesn't he? Yes, this was written for us, because when the plowman plows and the thresher threshes, they ought to do so in the hope of sharing in the harvest. [11]If we have sown spiritual seed among you, is it too much if we reap a material harvest from you? [12]If others have this right of support from you, shouldn't we have it all the more?

But we did not use this right. On the contrary, we put up

---

[a] 1 Or "We all possess knowledge," as you say   [b] 5 That is, Peter   [c] 9 Deut. 25:4

with anything rather than hinder the gospel of Christ. [13]Don't you know that those who work in the temple get their food from the temple, and those who serve at the altar share in what is offered on the altar? [14]In the same way, the Lord has commanded that those who preach the gospel should receive their living from the gospel.

[15]But I have not used any of these rights. And I am not writing this in the hope that you will do such things for me. I would rather die than have anyone deprive me of this boast. [16]Yet when I preach the gospel, I cannot boast, for I am compelled to preach. Woe to me if I do not preach the gospel! [17]If I preach voluntarily, I have a reward; if not voluntarily, I am simply discharging the trust committed to me. [18]What then is my reward? Just this: that in preaching the gospel I may offer it free of charge, and so not make use of my rights in preaching it.

[19]Though I am free and belong to no man, I make myself a slave to everyone, to win as many as possible. [20]To the Jews I became like a Jew, to win the Jews. To those under the law I became like one under the law (though I myself am not under the law), so as to win those under the law. [21]To those not having the law I became like one not having the law (though I am not free from God's law but am under Christ's law), so as to win those not having the law. [22]To the weak I became weak, to win the weak. I have become all things to all men so that by all possible means I might save some. [23]I do all this for the sake of the gospel, that I may share in its blessings.

[24]Do you not know that in a race all the runners run, but only one gets the prize? Run in such a way as to get the prize. [25]Everyone who competes in the games goes into strict training. They do it to get a crown that will not last; but we do it to get a crown that will last forever. [26]Therefore I do not run like a man running aimlessly; I do not fight like a man beating the air. [27]No, I beat my body and make it my slave so that after I have preached to others, I myself will not be disqualified for the prize.

Warnings From Israel's History

10 For I do not want you to be ignorant of the fact, brothers, that our forefathers were all under the cloud and that they all passed through the sea. [2]They were all baptized into Moses in the cloud and in the sea. [3]They all ate the same spiritual food [4]and drank the same spiritual drink; for they drank from the spiritual rock that accompanied them, and that rock was Christ. [5]Nevertheless, God was not pleased with most of them; their bodies were scattered over the desert.

[6]Now these things occurred as examples[a] to keep us from setting our hearts on evil things as they did. [7]Do not be idolaters, as some of them were; as it is written: "The people sat down to eat and drink and got up to indulge in pagan revelry."[b] [8]We should not commit sexual immorality, as some of them did—and in one day twenty-three thousand of them died. [9]We should not test the Lord, as some of them did—and were killed by snakes. [10]And do not grumble, as some of them did—and were killed by the destroying angel.

[11]These things happened to them as examples and were

Building Up the Body of Christ

1 CORINTHIANS 10:23–24

" 'Everything is permissible'— but not everything is beneficial. 'Everything is permissible'—but not everything is constructive." Contrast Paul's sense of what it means to follow Jesus Christ in true liberation from the law with the "anything goes" freedom that allows the individual to do whatever feels right. How are Christians to balance freedom with concern for the good of others?

In what ways do gratification of desires, a need to acquire possessions, or a slavery to addictions replace Jesus Christ as your source of fulfillment? In what ways do you allow a judgmental attitude or a posture of superiority over weaker members to prevent you from accepting others in the body of Christ? How could you go about correcting these arrogant and judgmental traits in yourself as well as helping others to do so?

See Meeting God in Community

---

[a] 6 Or *types*; also in verse 11   [b] 7 Exodus 32:6

Overcoming Conflicts

1 CORINTHIANS 10:31–33

Disagreements, arguments, differences of opinion—such conflicts divide Christians from God and from one another. Handling the conflicts that threaten Christian unity is unthinkable without a spirit of charity. That spirit begins to grow when we put aside self-promotion and allow the love Jesus Christ plants in our hearts to permeate all of our attitudes and activities. Try to live the gospel today. As you eat your supper, drink a glass of water, drive your car, stop at the grocery store, speak to someone on the phone, dust the living room furniture, dress your child, write a letter or engage in any other ordinary activity, be conscious of doing it all thankfully, with a grateful disposition "for the glory of God."

See Meeting God in Everyday Life

written down as warnings for us, on whom the fulfillment of the ages has come. ¹²So, if you think you are standing firm, be careful that you don't fall! ¹³No temptation has seized you except what is common to man. And God is faithful; he will not let you be tempted beyond what you can bear. But when you are tempted, he will also provide a way out so that you can stand up under it.

Idol Feasts and the Lord's Supper

¹⁴Therefore, my dear friends, flee from idolatry. ¹⁵I speak to sensible people; judge for yourselves what I say. ¹⁶Is not the cup of thanksgiving for which we give thanks a participation in the blood of Christ? And is not the bread that we break a participation in the body of Christ? ¹⁷Because there is one loaf, we, who are many, are one body, for we all partake of the one loaf.

¹⁸Consider the people of Israel: Do not those who eat the sacrifices participate in the altar? ¹⁹Do I mean then that a sacrifice offered to an idol is anything, or that an idol is anything? ²⁰No, but the sacrifices of pagans are offered to demons, not to God, and I do not want you to be participants with demons. ²¹You cannot drink the cup of the Lord and the cup of demons too; you cannot have a part in both the Lord's table and the table of demons. ²²Are we trying to arouse the Lord's jealousy? Are we stronger than he?

The Believer's Freedom

²³"Everything is permissible"—but not everything is beneficial. "Everything is permissible"—but not everything is constructive. ²⁴Nobody should seek his own good, but the good of others.

²⁵Eat anything sold in the meat market without raising questions of conscience, ²⁶for, "The earth is the Lord's, and everything in it."ᵃ

²⁷If some unbeliever invites you to a meal and you want to go, eat whatever is put before you without raising questions of conscience. ²⁸But if anyone says to you, "This has been offered in sacrifice," then do not eat it, both for the sake of the man who told you and for conscience' sakeᵇ— ²⁹the other man's conscience, I mean, not yours. For why should my freedom be judged by another's conscience? ³⁰If I take part in the meal with thankfulness, why am I denounced because of something I thank God for?

³¹So whether you eat or drink or whatever you do, do it all for the glory of God. ³²Do not cause anyone to stumble, whether Jews, Greeks or the church of God— ³³even as I try to please everybody in every way. For I am not seeking my own good but the good of many, so that they may be saved. ¹Follow my example, as I follow the example of Christ.

Propriety in Worship

²I praise you for remembering me in everything and for holding to the teachings,ᶜ just as I passed them on to you.

³Now I want you to realize that the head of every man is Christ, and the head of the woman is man, and the head of Christ is God. ⁴Every man who prays or prophesies with

ᵃ 26 Psalm 24:1   ᵇ 28 Some manuscripts *conscience' sake, for "the earth is the Lord's and everything in it"*   ᶜ 2 Or *traditions* his head covered dishonors his head. ⁵And every woman who prays or prophesies with her head uncovered dishonors her head—it is just as though her head were shaved. ⁶If a woman does not cover her head, she should have her hair cut off; and if it is a disgrace for a woman to have her hair cut or shaved off, she should cover her head. ⁷A man ought not to cover his head,ᵃ since he is the image and glory of God; but the woman is the glory of man. ⁸For man did not come from woman, but woman from man; ⁹neither was man created for woman, but woman for man. ¹⁰For this reason, and because of the angels, the woman ought to have a sign of authority on her head. ¹¹In the Lord, however, woman is not independent of man, nor is man independent of woman. ¹²For as woman came from man, so also man is born of woman. But everything comes from God. ¹³Judge for yourselves: Is it proper for a woman to pray to God with her head uncovered? ¹⁴Does not the very nature of things teach you that if a man has long hair, it is a disgrace to him, ¹⁵but that if a woman has long hair, it is her glory? For long hair is given to her as a covering. ¹⁶If anyone wants to be contentious about this, we have no other practice—nor do the churches of God.

The Lord's Supper

¹⁷In the following directives I have no praise for you, for your meetings do more harm than good. ¹⁸In the first place, I hear that when you come together as a church, there are divisions among you, and to some extent I believe it. ¹⁹No doubt there have to be differences among you to show which of you have God's approval. ²⁰When you come together, it is not the Lord's Supper you eat, ²¹for as you eat, each of you goes ahead without waiting for anybody else. One remains hungry, another gets drunk. ²²Don't you have homes to eat and drink in? Or do you despise the church of God and humiliate those who have nothing? What shall I say to you? Shall I praise you for this? Certainly not!

²³For I received from the Lord what I also passed on to you: The Lord Jesus, on the night he was betrayed, took bread, ²⁴and when he had given thanks, he broke it and said, "This is my body, which is for you; do this in remembrance of me." ²⁵In the same way, after supper he took the cup, saying, "This cup is the new covenant in my blood; do this, whenever you drink it, in remembrance of me." ²⁶For whenever you eat this bread and drink this cup, you proclaim the Lord's death until he comes.

²⁷Therefore, whoever eats the bread or drinks the cup of the Lord in an unworthy manner will be guilty of sinning against the body and blood of the Lord. ²⁸A man ought to examine himself before he eats of the bread and drinks of the cup. ²⁹For anyone who eats and drinks without recognizing the body of the Lord eats and drinks judgment on himself. ³⁰That is why many among you are weak and sick, and a number of you have fallen asleep. ³¹But if we

---

The Bread of Life, the Cup of Salvation

1 CORINTHIANS 11:23–25

Because this passage brings us to the heart of our faith, it is important not to rush past it, but to consciously enter the presence of Almighty God. The Corinthians are taking the Eucharistic feast too lightly. Go with the apostle Paul to visit, in your imagination, into the upper room where Jesus ate the Last Supper with his disciples. Imagine yourself and Paul in that awesome setting with Jesus and the others. Picture all of the details of the setting. Hear Jesus' words concerning the bread and wine. Join in receiving the elements when they are passed. How do you feel about being present? Try to recall that feeling the next time you partake at the Lord's Table. How is Paul's perspective on that Last Supper evident in this passage?

See Meeting God in Worship

ᵃ 4–7 Or ⁴*Every man who prays or prophesies with long hair dishonors his head. ⁵And every woman who prays or prophesies with no covering ⌊of hair⌋ on her head dishonors her head—she is just like one of the "shorn women." ⁶If a woman has no covering, let her be for now with short hair, but since it is a disgrace for a woman to have her hair shorn or shaved, she should grow it again. ⁷A man ought not to have long hair*

Unity in Diversity

1 CORINTHIANS 12:4–6,13,26

Paul proposes that unity in diversity is central to life in the Christian community. He sees in the community different gifts but the same Spirit; different services and deeds but the same God working through them; an array of people called to be baptized—Jews and Greeks, slaves and free—who are part of the same body. How might the words of this passage influence the way you relate to people in the church? The way in which you pray? To bring the message of Paul closer to home, name someone you know who is suffering. Think of another person who has recently been honored or acknowledged in some way. Think of someone who exhibits each of the spiritual gifts listed in verses 28 through 30.

See Meeting God in Community

judged ourselves, we would not come under judgment. ³²When we are judged by the Lord, we are being disciplined so that we will not be condemned with the world.

³³So then, my brothers, when you come together to eat, wait for each other. ³⁴If anyone is hungry, he should eat at home, so that when you meet together it may not result in judgment.

And when I come I will give further directions.

Spiritual Gifts

12 Now about spiritual gifts, brothers, I do not want you to be ignorant. ²You know that when you were pagans, somehow or other you were influenced and led astray to mute idols. ³Therefore I tell you that no one who is speaking by the Spirit of God says, "Jesus be cursed," and no one can say, "Jesus is Lord," except by the Holy Spirit.

⁴There are different kinds of gifts, but the same Spirit. ⁵There are different kinds of service, but the same Lord. ⁶There are different kinds of working, but the same God works all of them in all men.

⁷Now to each one the manifestation of the Spirit is given for the common good. ⁸To one there is given through the Spirit the message of wisdom, to another the message of knowledge by means of the same Spirit, ⁹to another faith by the same Spirit, to another gifts of healing by that one Spirit, ¹⁰to another miraculous powers, to another prophecy, to another distinguishing between spirits, to another speaking in different kinds of tongues,ᵃ and to still another the interpretation of tongues.ᵃ ¹¹All these are the work of one and the same Spirit, and he gives them to each one, just as he determines.

One Body, Many Parts

¹²The body is a unit, though it is made up of many parts; and though all its parts are many, they form one body. So it is with Christ. ¹³For we were all baptized byᵇ one Spirit into one body—whether Jews or Greeks, slave or free— and we were all given the one Spirit to drink.

¹⁴Now the body is not made up of one part but of many. ¹⁵If the foot should say, "Because I am not a hand, I do not belong to the body," it would not for that reason cease to be part of the body. ¹⁶And if the ear should say, "Because I am not an eye, I do not belong to the body," it would not for that reason cease to be part of the body. ¹⁷If the whole body were an eye, where would the sense of hearing be? If the whole body were an ear, where would the sense of smell be? ¹⁸But in fact God has arranged the parts in the body, every one of them, just as he wanted them to be. ¹⁹If they were all one part, where would the body be? ²⁰As it is, there are many parts, but one body.

²¹The eye cannot say to the hand, "I don't need you!" And the head cannot say to the feet, "I don't need you!" ²²On the contrary, those parts of the body that seem to be weaker are indispensable, ²³and the parts that we think are less honorable we treat with special honor. And the parts that are unpresentable are treated with special modesty, ²⁴while our presentable parts need no special treatment. But God has combined the members of the body

ᵃ *10* Or *languages*; also in verse 28   ᵇ *13* Or *with; or in* and has given greater honor to the parts that lacked it, [25]so that there should be no division in the body, but that its parts should have equal concern for each other. [26]If one part suffers, every part suffers with it; if one part is honored, every part rejoices with it.

[27]Now you are the body of Christ, and each one of you is a part of it. [28]And in the church God has appointed first of all apostles, second prophets, third teachers, then workers of miracles, also those having gifts of healing, those able to help others, those with gifts of administration, and those speaking in different kinds of tongues. [29]Are all apostles? Are all prophets? Are all teachers? Do all work miracles? [30]Do all have gifts of healing? Do all speak in tongues[a]? Do all interpret? [31]But eagerly desire[b] the greater gifts.

Love

And now I will show you the most excellent way.

13 If I speak in the tongues[c] of men and of angels, but have not love, I am only a resounding gong or a clanging cymbal. [2]If I have the gift of prophecy and can fathom all mysteries and all knowledge, and if I have a faith that can move mountains, but have not love, I am nothing. [3]If I give all I possess to the poor and surrender my body to the flames,[d] but have not love, I gain nothing.

[4]Love is patient, love is kind. It does not envy, it does not boast, it is not proud. [5]It is not rude, it is not self-seeking, it is not easily angered, it keeps no record of wrongs. [6]Love does not delight in evil but rejoices with the truth. [7]It always protects, always trusts, always hopes, always perseveres.

[8]Love never fails. But where there are prophecies, they will cease; where there are tongues, they will be stilled; where there is knowledge, it will pass away. [9]For we know in part and we prophesy in part, [10]but when perfection comes, the imperfect disappears. [11]When I was a child, I talked like a child, I thought like a child, I reasoned like a child. When I became a man, I put childish ways behind me. [12]Now we see but a poor reflection as in a mirror; then we shall see face to face. Now I know in part; then I shall know fully, even as I am fully known.

[13]And now these three remain: faith, hope and love. But the greatest of these is love.

Gifts of Prophecy and Tongues

14 Follow the way of love and eagerly desire spiritual gifts, especially the gift of prophecy. [2]For anyone who speaks in a tongue[e] does not speak to men but to God. Indeed, no one understands him; he utters mysteries with his spirit.[f] [3]But everyone who prophesies speaks to men for their strengthening, encouragement and comfort. [4]He who speaks in a tongue edifies himself, but he who prophesies edifies the church. [5]I would like every one of you to speak in tongues,[g] but I would rather have you prophesy. He who prophesies is greater than one who speaks in tongues,[g] unless he interprets, so that the church may be edified.

Follow the Way of Love

1 CORINTHIANS 14:1

"The Holy Spirit has enabled people to speak with tongues, and to prophesy. But the light that most necessarily attends it is a light to discern the fallacies of flesh and blood, to reject the irreligious maxims of the world, and to practice those degrees of trust in God and love to people, whose foundation is not so much in the present appearances of things, as in some that are yet to come. The object which this light brings us most immediately to know is ourselves. And by virtue of this, one that is born of God and has a lively hope, may indeed see far into the ways of Providence and farther yet into the Holy Scriptures."

—JOHN WESLEY,
from his sermon "On the Holy Spirit"

Growing Spiritually Mature

1 CORINTHIANS 14:20–40

The Corinthian Christians continue to try Paul's patience. Instead of focusing on God in grateful unity, they persist in competing for the most impressive manifestation of spiritual gifts. Paul declares that they should "stop thinking like children" and conduct their worship in an orderly and fitting manner.

What are some childish behaviors you would like to correct in yourself as you grow spiritually mature? What about whining when things go wrong? Or calling attention to your accomplishments? Perhaps you choose the safer and more familiar course rather than take risks for the sake of spiritual maturity. Write a letter to yourself similar to one Paul might write to you.

See Meeting God in Everyday Life

[6]Now, brothers, if I come to you and speak in tongues, what good will I be to you, unless I bring you some revelation or knowledge or prophecy or word of instruction? [7]Even in the case of lifeless things that make sounds, such as the flute or harp, how will anyone know what tune is being played unless there is a distinction in the notes? [8]Again, if the trumpet does not sound a clear call, who will get ready for battle? [9]So it is with you. Unless you speak intelligible words with your tongue, how will anyone know what you are saying? You will just be speaking into the air. [10]Undoubtedly there are all sorts of languages in the world, yet none of them is without meaning. [11]If then I do not grasp the meaning of what someone is saying, I am a foreigner to the speaker, and he is a foreigner to me. [12]So it is with you. Since you are eager to have spiritual gifts, try to excel in gifts that build up the church.

[13]For this reason anyone who speaks in a tongue should pray that he may interpret what he says. [14]For if I pray in a tongue, my spirit prays, but my mind is unfruitful. [15]So what shall I do? I will pray with my spirit, but I will also pray with my mind; I will sing with my spirit, but I will also sing with my mind. [16]If you are praising God with your spirit, how can one who finds himself among those who do not understand[a] say "Amen" to your thanksgiving, since he does not know what you are saying? [17]You may be giving thanks well enough, but the other man is not edified.

[18]I thank God that I speak in tongues more than all of you. [19]But in the church I would rather speak five intelligible words to instruct others than ten thousand words in a tongue.

[20]Brothers, stop thinking like children. In regard to evil be infants, but in your thinking be adults. [21]In the Law it is written:

> "Through men of strange tongues
>   and through the lips of foreigners
>   I will speak to this people,
>   but even then they will not listen to me,"[b]
> says the Lord.

[22]Tongues, then, are a sign, not for believers but for unbelievers; prophecy, however, is for believers, not for unbelievers. [23]So if the whole church comes together and everyone speaks in tongues, and some who do not understand[c] or some unbelievers come in, will they not say that you are out of your mind? [24]But if an unbeliever or someone who does not understand[d] comes in while everybody is prophesying, he will be convinced by all that he is a sinner and will be judged by all, [25]and the secrets of his heart will be laid bare. So he will fall down and worship God, exclaiming, "God is really among you!"

Orderly Worship

[26]What then shall we say, brothers? When you come together, everyone has a hymn, or a word of instruction, a revelation, a tongue or an interpretation. All of these must be done for the strengthening of the church. [27]If anyone speaks in a tongue, two—or at the most three—should

---

[a] 16 Or *among the inquirers*   [b] 21 Isaiah 28:11,12   [c] 23 Or *some inquirers*
[d] 24 Or *or some inquirer*

speak, one at a time, and someone must interpret. ²⁸If there is no interpreter, the speaker should keep quiet in the church and speak to himself and God.

²⁹Two or three prophets should speak, and the others should weigh carefully what is said. ³⁰And if a revelation comes to someone who is sitting down, the first speaker should stop. ³¹For you can all prophesy in turn so that everyone may be instructed and encouraged. ³²The spirits of prophets are subject to the control of prophets. ³³For God is not a God of disorder but of peace.

As in all the congregations of the saints, ³⁴women should remain silent in the churches. They are not allowed to speak, but must be in submission, as the Law says. ³⁵If they want to inquire about something, they should ask their own husbands at home; for it is disgraceful for a woman to speak in the church.

³⁶Did the word of God originate with you? Or are you the only people it has reached? ³⁷If anybody thinks he is a prophet or spiritually gifted, let him acknowledge that what I am writing to you is the Lord's command. ³⁸If he ignores this, he himself will be ignored.ᵃ

³⁹Therefore, my brothers, be eager to prophesy, and do not forbid speaking in tongues. ⁴⁰But everything should be done in a fitting and orderly way.

The Resurrection of Christ

15 Now, brothers, I want to remind you of the gospel I preached to you, which you received and on which you have taken your stand. ²By this gospel you are saved, if you hold firmly to the word I preached to you. Otherwise, you have believed in vain.

³For what I received I passed on to you as of first importanceᵇ: that Christ died for our sins according to the Scriptures, ⁴that he was buried, that he was raised on the third day according to the Scriptures, ⁵and that he appeared to Peter,ᶜ and then to the Twelve. ⁶After that, he appeared to more than five hundred of the brothers at the same time, most of whom are still living, though some have fallen asleep. ⁷Then he appeared to James, then to all the apostles, ⁸and last of all he appeared to me also, as to one abnormally born.

⁹For I am the least of the apostles and do not even deserve to be called an apostle, because I persecuted the church of God. ¹⁰But by the grace of God I am what I am, and his grace to me was not without effect. No, I worked harder than all of them—yet not I, but the grace of God that was with me. ¹¹Whether, then, it was I or they, this is what we preach, and this is what you believed.

The Resurrection of the Dead

¹²But if it is preached that Christ has been raised from the dead, how can some of you say that there is no resurrection of the dead? ¹³If there is no resurrection of the dead, then not even Christ has been raised. ¹⁴And if Christ has not been raised, our preaching is useless and so is your faith. ¹⁵More than that, we are then found to be false witnesses about God, for we have testified about God that he raised Christ from the dead. But he did not raise him if

---

Saved by the Gospel

1 CORINTHIANS 15:1–2

Consider your journey of faith. Do you remember the moment when you accepted Jesus Christ as your Savior and Lord? When you decided that for the rest of your life you would "hold firmly to the word"? Let this passage ignite your commitment to let the Bible be your companion every day. Think of ways to pass on the saving word of the gospel to your spouse, children, friends, coworkers and even to the people you encounter in your daily routine. Conclude by meditating on Paul's bottom line: "By the grace of God I am what I am" (v.10).

See Meeting God in Scripture

ᵃ 38 Some manuscripts *If he is ignorant of this, let him be ignorant*   ᵇ 3 Or *you at the first*   ᶜ 5 Greek *Cephas*

Death Swallowed in Victory

1 CORINTHIANS 15:20-26

In radiant faith Paul proclaims the victory of the resurrection of the dead in the power of Christ Jesus. Read this passage slowly. Find some garden seeds. Hold one in the palm of your hand. Notice how small it is, perhaps no bigger than the head of a pin, how dry and dead it looks. Yet you know that if you bury it, it will produce a plant. Allow this simple illustration from nature to reawaken your awe in the resurrection. Let what happened on Easter morning fill your mind and imagination with wonder. Open your heart to contemplative prayer. Let the Orthodox greeting, "My Joy! Christ is risen!" be ever on your lips.

See Meeting God in Everyday Life

in fact the dead are not raised. ¹⁶For if the dead are not raised, then Christ has not been raised either. ¹⁷And if Christ has not been raised, your faith is futile; you are still in your sins. ¹⁸Then those also who have fallen asleep in Christ are lost. ¹⁹If only for this life we have hope in Christ, we are to be pitied more than all men.

²⁰But Christ has indeed been raised from the dead, the firstfruits of those who have fallen asleep. ²¹For since death came through a man, the resurrection of the dead comes also through a man. ²²For as in Adam all die, so in Christ all will be made alive. ²³But each in his own turn: Christ, the firstfruits; then, when he comes, those who belong to him. ²⁴Then the end will come, when he hands over the kingdom to God the Father after he has destroyed all dominion, authority and power. ²⁵For he must reign until he has put all his enemies under his feet. ²⁶The last enemy to be destroyed is death. ²⁷For he "has put everything under his feet."ᵃ Now when it says that "everything" has been put under him, it is clear that this does not include God himself, who put everything under Christ. ²⁸When he has done this, then the Son himself will be made subject to him who put everything under him, so that God may be all in all.

²⁹Now if there is no resurrection, what will those do who are baptized for the dead? If the dead are not raised at all, why are people baptized for them? ³⁰And as for us, why do we endanger ourselves every hour? ³¹I die every day—I mean that, brothers—just as surely as I glory over you in Christ Jesus our Lord. ³²If I fought wild beasts in Ephesus for merely human reasons, what have I gained? If the dead are not raised,

"Let us eat and drink,
for tomorrow we die."ᵇ

³³Do not be misled: "Bad company corrupts good character." ³⁴Come back to your senses as you ought, and stop sinning; for there are some who are ignorant of God—I say this to your shame.

The Resurrection Body

³⁵But someone may ask, "How are the dead raised? With what kind of body will they come?" ³⁶How foolish! What you sow does not come to life unless it dies. ³⁷When you sow, you do not plant the body that will be, but just a seed, perhaps of wheat or of something else. ³⁸But God gives it a body as he has determined, and to each kind of seed he gives its own body. ³⁹All flesh is not the same: Men have one kind of flesh, animals have another, birds another and fish another. ⁴⁰There are also heavenly bodies and there are earthly bodies; but the splendor of the heavenly bodies is one kind, and the splendor of the earthly bodies is another. ⁴¹The sun has one kind of splendor, the moon another and the stars another; and star differs from star in splendor.

⁴²So will it be with the resurrection of the dead. The body that is sown is perishable, it is raised imperishable; ⁴³it is sown in dishonor, it is raised in glory; it is sown in weakness, it is raised in power; ⁴⁴it is sown a natural body, it is raised a spiritual body.

a 27 Psalm 8:6   *b 32* Isaiah 22:13

If there is a natural body, there is also a spiritual body. [45]So it is written: "The first man Adam became a living being"[a]; the last Adam, a life-giving spirit. [46]The spiritual did not come first, but the natural, and after that the spiritual. [47]The first man was of the dust of the earth, the second man from heaven. [48]As was the earthly man, so are those who are of the earth; and as is the man from heaven, so also are those who are of heaven. [49]And just as we have borne the likeness of the earthly man, so shall we[b] bear the likeness of the man from heaven.

[50]I declare to you, brothers, that flesh and blood cannot inherit the kingdom of God, nor does the perishable inherit the imperishable. [51]Listen, I tell you a mystery: We will not all sleep, but we will all be changed— [52]in a flash, in the twinkling of an eye, at the last trumpet. For the trumpet will sound, the dead will be raised imperishable, and we will be changed. [53]For the perishable must clothe itself with the imperishable, and the mortal with immortality. [54]When the perishable has been clothed with the imperishable, and the mortal with immortality, then the saying that is written will come true: "Death has been swallowed up in victory."[c]

[55]"Where, O death, is your victory?
Where, O death, is your sting?"[d]

[56]The sting of death is sin, and the power of sin is the law. [57]But thanks be to God! He gives us the victory through our Lord Jesus Christ.

[58]Therefore, my dear brothers, stand firm. Let nothing move you. Always give yourselves fully to the work of the Lord, because you know that your labor in the Lord is not in vain.

The Collection for God's People

16 Now about the collection for God's people: Do what I told the Galatian churches to do. [2]On the first day of every week, each one of you should set aside a sum of money in keeping with his income, saving it up, so that when I come no collections will have to be made. [3]Then, when I arrive, I will give letters of introduction to the men you approve and send them with your gift to Jerusalem. [4]If it seems advisable for me to go also, they will accompany me.

Personal Requests

[5]After I go through Macedonia, I will come to you—for I will be going through Macedonia. [6]Perhaps I will stay with you awhile, or even spend the winter, so that you can help me on my journey, wherever I go. [7]I do not want to see you now and make only a passing visit; I hope to spend some time with you, if the Lord permits. [8]But I will stay on at Ephesus until Pentecost, [9]because a great door for effective work has opened to me, and there are many who oppose me.

[10]If Timothy comes, see to it that he has nothing to fear while he is with you, for he is carrying on the work of the Lord, just as I am. [11]No one, then, should refuse to accept

Death, Be Not Proud

1 CORINTHIANS 15:35–58

Death, be not proud,
    though some have called
    thee
Mighty and dreadful, for
    thou art not so;
For those whom thou
    think'st thou dost
    overthrow
Die not, poor Death, nor yet
    canst thou kill me.
From rest and sleep, which
    but thy pictures be,
Much pleasure; then from
    thee much more must
    flow
And soonest our best men
    with thee do go,
Rest of their bones, and
    soul's delivery.
Thou are slave to fate,
    chance, kings, and
    desperate men,
And dost with poison, war,
    and sickness dwell,
And poppy or charms can
    make us sleep as well
And better than thy stroke;
    why swell'st thou then?
One short sleep past, we
    wake eternally
And death shall be no more;
    Death, thou shalt die.

—JOHN DONNE,
"Holy Sonnets" 10

[a]45 Gen. 2:7   [b]49 Some early manuscripts *so let us*   [c]54 Isaiah 25:8
[d]55 Hosea 13:14

Sowing the Seeds

1 CORINTHIANS 16:1–2

Giving, says Paul, should be a way of life, not a spur-of-the-moment gesture. Set aside money regularly, planning prayerfully how much to give to your church and how much to contribute to other causes. Give joyfully and without condescension as you are blessed. Consider how by your giving you carry on the mission begun in Jesus Christ and continued by the apostle Paul—a mission of peace, courage and above all—love. End your reading of 1 Corinthians with a prayer for a heart of love. Starting today let your actions speak as loudly as your words.

See Meeting God in Service

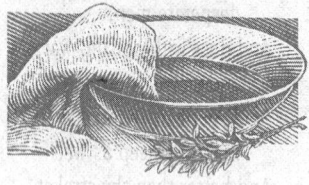

him. Send him on his way in peace so that he may return to me. I am expecting him along with the brothers.

¹²Now about our brother Apollos: I strongly urged him to go to you with the brothers. He was quite unwilling to go now, but he will go when he has the opportunity.

¹³Be on your guard; stand firm in the faith; be men of courage; be strong. ¹⁴Do everything in love.

¹⁵You know that the household of Stephanas were the first converts in Achaia, and they have devoted themselves to the service of the saints. I urge you, brothers, ¹⁶to submit to such as these and to everyone who joins in the work, and labors at it. ¹⁷I was glad when Stephanas, Fortunatus and Achaicus arrived, because they have supplied what was lacking from you. ¹⁸For they refreshed my spirit and yours also. Such men deserve recognition.

Final Greetings

¹⁹The churches in the province of Asia send you greetings. Aquila and Priscilla[a] greet you warmly in the Lord, and so does the church that meets at their house. ²⁰All the brothers here send you greetings. Greet one another with a holy kiss.

²¹I, Paul, write this greeting in my own hand.

²²If anyone does not love the Lord—a curse be on him. Come, O Lord[b]!

²³The grace of the Lord Jesus be with you.

²⁴My love to all of you in Christ Jesus. Amen.[c]

---

[a] 19 Greek *Prisca*, a variant of *Priscilla*   [b] 22 In Aramaic the expression *Come, O Lord* is *Marana tha*.   [c] 24 Some manuscripts do not have *Amen*.

2 CORINTHIANS

Our Hope for New Life

KEY VERSES:

Therefore, if anyone is in Christ, he is a new creation; the old has gone, the new has come! All this is from God, who reconciled us to himself through Christ and gave us the ministry of reconciliation: that God was reconciling the world to himself in Christ, not counting men's sins against them.

—2 Corinthians 5:17–19

One of the greatest obstacles facing us on the road to spiritual formation is our lack of appreciation for our infinite worth in the eyes of God. No matter what faults and failings may hamper us on our way home to our Father's house, God loves and forgives and welcomes us. One of the gifts the apostle Paul gives his readers in this ardent and honest letter is a renewed sense of worthiness to minister in the name of Jesus Christ. Paul applies correction but he also encourages his readers with an appraisal of their worth: They are "the aroma of Christ . . . the fragrance of life" (2:15–16); "Christ's ambassadors" (5:20); "God's fellow workers" (6:1); "the temple of the living God" (6:16). Paul's encouragement is not meant to produce pride in his readers but to remind them that "Christ Jesus is in [them]" (13:5). His Spirit forms, reforms and transforms us "into his likeness with ever-increasing glory" (3:18).

The spirit of servanthood dies, as Paul sees it, when we try to become "super-apostles" (12:11), incapable of admitting that we are vulnerable, suffering, wounded creatures. We can unlock the door to Christian service only with the key of our weaknesses. Paul boasts of his "weaknesses, so that Christ's power may rest on [him]" (12:9).

As you read this letter, reflect on your ministry, whatever it may be. What do you think makes you competent to serve? What are your strengths in Christ Jesus? How are his strengths apparent through your weaknesses?

> "The holy Church includes many people, men, women, and children without number. They are all quite different from one another in birth, in size, in nationality and language, in style of living and age, in trades and opinions, in clothes and customs, in knowledge and rank, in welfare and in appearance. They are nonetheless all of them in the self-same Church. Thanks to her, they are all reborn, newly created in the Spirit."
>
> —MAXIMUS THE CONFESSOR,
> in *Drinking from the Fountain: A Patristic Breviary*

Yes!

2 CORINTHIANS 1:3–11,18–22

Paul declares that "no matter how many promises God has made, they are 'Yes' in Christ." As you read these two passages, make a list of the verb phrases that describe God's promised actions toward us. Let them lead you to awareness of God's love and saving grace. Begin with the phrase "comforts us in all our troubles." After each phrase, think of an example of how God has kept that promise to you. Then write "Yes!" after each one, and keep the list in your Bible or journal.

See Meeting God in Prayer

1 Paul, an apostle of Christ Jesus by the will of God, and Timothy our brother,

To the church of God in Corinth, together with all the saints throughout Achaia:

²Grace and peace to you from God our Father and the Lord Jesus Christ.

The God of All Comfort

³Praise be to the God and Father of our Lord Jesus Christ, the Father of compassion and the God of all comfort, ⁴who comforts us in all our troubles, so that we can comfort those in any trouble with the comfort we ourselves have received from God. ⁵For just as the sufferings of Christ flow over into our lives, so also through Christ our comfort overflows. ⁶If we are distressed, it is for your comfort and salvation; if we are comforted, it is for your comfort, which produces in you patient endurance of the same sufferings we suffer. ⁷And our hope for you is firm, because we know that just as you share in our sufferings, so also you share in our comfort.

⁸We do not want you to be uninformed, brothers, about the hardships we suffered in the province of Asia. We were under great pressure, far beyond our ability to endure, so that we despaired even of life. ⁹Indeed, in our hearts we felt the sentence of death. But this happened that we might not rely on ourselves but on God, who raises the dead. ¹⁰He has delivered us from such a deadly peril, and he will deliver us. On him we have set our hope that he will continue to deliver us, ¹¹as you help us by your prayers. Then many will give thanks on our[a] behalf for the gracious favor granted us in answer to the prayers of many.

Paul's Change of Plans

¹²Now this is our boast: Our conscience testifies that we have conducted ourselves in the world, and especially in our relations with you, in the holiness and sincerity that are from God. We have done so not according to worldly wisdom but according to God's grace. ¹³For we do not write you anything you cannot read or understand. And I hope that, ¹⁴as you have understood us in part, you will come to understand fully that you can boast of us just as we will boast of you in the day of the Lord Jesus.

¹⁵Because I was confident of this, I planned to visit you first so that you might benefit twice. ¹⁶I planned to visit you on my way to Macedonia and to come back to you from Macedonia, and then to have you send me on my way to Judea. ¹⁷When I planned this, did I do it lightly? Or do I make my plans in a worldly manner so that in the same breath I say, "Yes, yes" and "No, no"?

¹⁸But as surely as God is faithful, our message to you is not "Yes" and "No." ¹⁹For the Son of God, Jesus Christ, who was preached among you by me and Silas[b] and Timothy, was not "Yes" and "No," but in him it has always been "Yes." ²⁰For no matter how many promises God has made, they are "Yes" in Christ. And so through him the "Amen" is spoken by us to the glory of God. ²¹Now it is God who makes both us and you stand firm in Christ. He anointed

a 11 Many manuscripts *your*   *b 19* Greek *Silvanus,* a variant of *Silas* us, ²²set his seal of ownership on us, and put his Spirit in our hearts as a deposit, guaranteeing what is to come.

²³I call God as my witness that it was in order to spare you that I did not return to Corinth. ²⁴Not that we lord it over your faith, but we work with you for your joy, because it is by faith you stand firm. ¹So I made up my mind that I would not make another painful visit to you. ²For if I grieve you, who is left to make me glad but you whom I have grieved? ³I wrote as I did so that when I came I should not be distressed by those who ought to make me rejoice. I had confidence in all of you, that you would all share my joy. ⁴For I wrote you out of great distress and anguish of heart and with many tears, not to grieve you but to let you know the depth of my love for you.

Forgiveness for the Sinner

⁵If anyone has caused grief, he has not so much grieved me as he has grieved all of you, to some extent—not to put it too severely. ⁶The punishment inflicted on him by the majority is sufficient for him. ⁷Now instead, you ought to forgive and comfort him, so that he will not be overwhelmed by excessive sorrow. ⁸I urge you, therefore, to reaffirm your love for him. ⁹The reason I wrote you was to see if you would stand the test and be obedient in everything. ¹⁰If you forgive anyone, I also forgive him. And what I have forgiven—if there was anything to forgive—I have forgiven in the sight of Christ for your sake, ¹¹in order that Satan might not outwit us. For we are not unaware of his schemes.

Ministers of the New Covenant

¹²Now when I went to Troas to preach the gospel of Christ and found that the Lord had opened a door for me, ¹³I still had no peace of mind, because I did not find my brother Titus there. So I said good-by to them and went on to Macedonia.

¹⁴But thanks be to God, who always leads us in triumphal procession in Christ and through us spreads everywhere the fragrance of the knowledge of him. ¹⁵For we are to God the aroma of Christ among those who are being saved and those who are perishing. ¹⁶To the one we are the smell of death; to the other, the fragrance of life. And who is equal to such a task? ¹⁷Unlike so many, we do not peddle the word of God for profit. On the contrary, in Christ we speak before God with sincerity, like men sent from God.

Are we beginning to commend ourselves again? Or do we need, like some people, letters of recommendation to you or from you? ²You yourselves are our letter, written on our hearts, known and read by everybody. ³You show that you are a letter from Christ, the result of our ministry, written not with ink but with the Spirit of the living God, not on tablets of stone but on tablets of human hearts.

⁴Such confidence as this is ours through Christ before God. ⁵Not that we are competent in ourselves to claim anything for ourselves, but our competence comes from God. ⁶He has made us competent as ministers of a new covenant—not of the letter but of the Spirit; for the letter kills, but the Spirit gives life.

The Fragrance of Christ

2 CORINTHIANS 2:14—3:6

Often what we remember about people is not so much what they said or did but who they were—their identity, their spirit. How do you want people to remember you? Pray that by your very presence you may spread the knowledge of Jesus Christ, the living God, as sweet fragrance fills a room. What kind of "letter of recommendation" for Christ does your life offer? What would you like to edit out or add? What do you want the Spirit of God to write on the hearts of people who serve you day by day as "ministers of a new covenant"?

See Meeting God in Everyday Life

A Treasure in Clay Jars

2 CORINTHIANS 4:5–7

Paul reflects on the mystery of God's transforming love. We are like humble, everyday clay pots and yet God has filled us with "the light of the knowledge of the glory of God in the face of Christ." God hides this treasure in ordinary vessels to show that the power is his, not ours. What do you see when you look at yourself—the simple clay pot or the divine glory it contains? What do others see in you—the glory of God in a clay pot, or a clay pot trying to look like a treasure chest? A clay pot with the lid tightly closed? A clay pot with a hole in the bottom? A pot with cracks through which God's glory shines? Pray for more awareness of God's presence in you and in everyone you meet.

See Meeting God in the Created Order

The Glory of the New Covenant

⁷Now if the ministry that brought death, which was engraved in letters on stone, came with glory, so that the Israelites could not look steadily at the face of Moses because of its glory, fading though it was, ⁸will not the ministry of the Spirit be even more glorious? ⁹If the ministry that condemns men is glorious, how much more glorious is the ministry that brings righteousness! ¹⁰For what was glorious has no glory now in comparison with the surpassing glory. ¹¹And if what was fading away came with glory, how much greater is the glory of that which lasts!

¹²Therefore, since we have such a hope, we are very bold. ¹³We are not like Moses, who would put a veil over his face to keep the Israelites from gazing at it while the radiance was fading away. ¹⁴But their minds were made dull, for to this day the same veil remains when the old covenant is read. It has not been removed, because only in Christ is it taken away. ¹⁵Even to this day when Moses is read, a veil covers their hearts. ¹⁶But whenever anyone turns to the Lord, the veil is taken away. ¹⁷Now the Lord is the Spirit, and where the Spirit of the Lord is, there is freedom. ¹⁸And we, who with unveiled faces all reflect[a] the Lord's glory, are being transformed into his likeness with ever-increasing glory, which comes from the Lord, who is the Spirit.

Treasures in Jars of Clay

4 Therefore, since through God's mercy we have this ministry, we do not lose heart. ²Rather, we have renounced secret and shameful ways; we do not use deception, nor do we distort the word of God. On the contrary, by setting forth the truth plainly we commend ourselves to every man's conscience in the sight of God. ³And even if our gospel is veiled, it is veiled to those who are perishing. ⁴The god of this age has blinded the minds of unbelievers, so that they cannot see the light of the gospel of the glory of Christ, who is the image of God. ⁵For we do not preach ourselves, but Jesus Christ as Lord, and ourselves as your servants for Jesus' sake. ⁶For God, who said, "Let light shine out of darkness,"[b] made his light shine in our hearts to give us the light of the knowledge of the glory of God in the face of Christ.

⁷But we have this treasure in jars of clay to show that this all-surpassing power is from God and not from us. ⁸We are hard pressed on every side, but not crushed; perplexed, but not in despair; ⁹persecuted, but not abandoned; struck down, but not destroyed. ¹⁰We always carry around in our body the death of Jesus, so that the life of Jesus may also be revealed in our body. ¹¹For we who are alive are always being given over to death for Jesus' sake, so that his life may be revealed in our mortal body. ¹²So then, death is at work in us, but life is at work in you.

¹³It is written: "I believed; therefore I have spoken."[c] With that same spirit of faith we also believe and therefore speak, ¹⁴because we know that the one who raised the Lord Jesus from the dead will also raise us with Jesus and present us with you in his presence. ¹⁵All this is for your benefit, so that the grace that is reaching more and more people may cause thanksgiving to overflow to the glory of God.

a 18 Or *contemplate*   *b 6* Gen. 1:3   *c 13* Psalm 116:10

¹⁶Therefore we do not lose heart. Though outwardly we are wasting away, yet inwardly we are being renewed day by day. ¹⁷For our light and momentary troubles are achieving for us an eternal glory that far outweighs them all. ¹⁸So we fix our eyes not on what is seen, but on what is unseen. For what is seen is temporary, but what is unseen is eternal.

Our Heavenly Dwelling

5 Now we know that if the earthly tent we live in is destroyed, we have a building from God, an eternal house in heaven, not built by human hands. ²Meanwhile we groan, longing to be clothed with our heavenly dwelling, ³because when we are clothed, we will not be found naked. ⁴For while we are in this tent, we groan and are burdened, because we do not wish to be unclothed but to be clothed with our heavenly dwelling, so that what is mortal may be swallowed up by life. ⁵Now it is God who has made us for this very purpose and has given us the Spirit as a deposit, guaranteeing what is to come.

⁶Therefore we are always confident and know that as long as we are at home in the body we are away from the Lord. ⁷We live by faith, not by sight. ⁸We are confident, I say, and would prefer to be away from the body and at home with the Lord. ⁹So we make it our goal to please him, whether we are at home in the body or away from it. ¹⁰For we must all appear before the judgment seat of Christ, that each one may receive what is due him for the things done while in the body, whether good or bad.

The Ministry of Reconciliation

¹¹Since, then, we know what it is to fear the Lord, we try to persuade men. What we are is plain to God, and I hope it is also plain to your conscience. ¹²We are not trying to commend ourselves to you again, but are giving you an opportunity to take pride in us, so that you can answer those who take pride in what is seen rather than in what is in the heart. ¹³If we are out of our mind, it is for the sake of God; if we are in our right mind, it is for you. ¹⁴For Christ's love compels us, because we are convinced that one died for all, and therefore all died. ¹⁵And he died for all, that those who live should no longer live for themselves but for him who died for them and was raised again.

¹⁶So from now on we regard no one from a worldly point of view. Though we once regarded Christ in this way, we do so no longer. ¹⁷Therefore, if anyone is in Christ, he is a new creation; the old has gone, the new has come! ¹⁸All this is from God, who reconciled us to himself through Christ and gave us the ministry of reconciliation: ¹⁹that God was reconciling the world to himself in Christ, not counting men's sins against them. And he has committed to us the message of reconciliation. ²⁰We are therefore Christ's ambassadors, as though God were making his appeal through us. We implore you on Christ's behalf: Be reconciled to God. ²¹God made him who had no sin to be sin[a] for us, so that in him we might become the righteousness of God.

6 As God's fellow workers we urge you not to receive God's grace in vain. ²For he says,

[a] 21 Or be a sin offering

An Appeal to Be Reconciled

2 CORINTHIANS 5:17–20

"What unparalleled condescension and divinely tender mercies are displayed in [these verses]! Did the judge ever beseech a condemned criminal to accept pardon? Does the creditor ever beseech a ruined debtor to receive an acquittal in full? Yet our almighty Lord, and our eternal Judge, not only vouchsafes to offer these blessings, but invites us, entreats us, and, with the most tender importunity, solicits us not to reject them."

—JOHN WESLEY,
Explanatory Notes Upon the New Testament

Temples of the Living God

2 CORINTHIANS 6:16–18

We are God's temple, for God dwells in us. It is through us that others see God's face. Through us others experience God's love, comfort, healing and forgiveness. Like all dwellings, sacred and secular, we are in need of maintenance.

What has to be swept out of your life today to make your whole being a more fitting dwelling for God? Whether you have to dust a little corner still permeated by the darkness of doubt or whether you have to run the vacuum throughout the house to sweep from your system the last traces of lingering sin is for you to decide. The important thing is to open wide the doors of your temple so that the Spirit of God can enter. Ask God to help you prepare a place for the One who wants to live in you and walk with you.

See Meeting God in Prayer

"In the time of my favor I heard you,
   and in the day of salvation I helped you."[a]

I tell you, now is the time of God's favor, now is the day of salvation.

Paul's Hardships

³We put no stumbling block in anyone's path, so that our ministry will not be discredited. ⁴Rather, as servants of God we commend ourselves in every way: in great endurance; in troubles, hardships and distresses; ⁵in beatings, imprisonments and riots; in hard work, sleepless nights and hunger; ⁶in purity, understanding, patience and kindness; in the Holy Spirit and in sincere love; ⁷in truthful speech and in the power of God; with weapons of righteousness in the right hand and in the left; ⁸through glory and dishonor, bad report and good report; genuine, yet regarded as impostors; ⁹known, yet regarded as unknown; dying, and yet we live on; beaten, and yet not killed; ¹⁰sorrowful, yet always rejoicing; poor, yet making many rich; having nothing, and yet possessing everything.

¹¹We have spoken freely to you, Corinthians, and opened wide our hearts to you. ¹²We are not withholding our affection from you, but you are withholding yours from us. ¹³As a fair exchange—I speak as to my children—open wide your hearts also.

Do Not Be Yoked With Unbelievers

¹⁴Do not be yoked together with unbelievers. For what do righteousness and wickedness have in common? Or what fellowship can light have with darkness? ¹⁵What harmony is there between Christ and Belial[b]? What does a believer have in common with an unbeliever? ¹⁶What agreement is there between the temple of God and idols? For we are the temple of the living God. As God has said: "I will live with them and walk among them, and I will be their God, and they will be my people."[c]

¹⁷"Therefore come out from them
   and be separate,
                                 says the Lord.
   Touch no unclean thing,
      and I will receive you."[d]
¹⁸"I will be a Father to you,
      and you will be my sons and daughters,
                                 says the Lord Almighty."[e]

7 Since we have these promises, dear friends, let us purify ourselves from everything that contaminates body and spirit, perfecting holiness out of reverence for God.

Paul's Joy

²Make room for us in your hearts. We have wronged no one, we have corrupted no one, we have exploited no one. ³I do not say this to condemn you; I have said before that you have such a place in our hearts that we would live or die with you. ⁴I have great confidence in you; I take great pride in you. I am greatly encouraged; in all our troubles my joy knows no bounds.

---

a 2 Isaiah 49:8   *b 15* Greek *Beliar*, a variant of *Belial*   *c 16* Lev. 26:12; Jer. 32:38; Ezek. 37:27   *d 17* Isaiah 52:11; Ezek. 20:34,41
e 18 2 Samuel 7:14; 7:8

⁵For when we came into Macedonia, this body of ours had no rest, but we were harassed at every turn—conflicts on the outside, fears within. ⁶But God, who comforts the downcast, comforted us by the coming of Titus, ⁷and not only by his coming but also by the comfort you had given him. He told us about your longing for me, your deep sorrow, your ardent concern for me, so that my joy was greater than ever.

⁸Even if I caused you sorrow by my letter, I do not regret it. Though I did regret it—I see that my letter hurt you, but only for a little while— ⁹yet now I am happy, not because you were made sorry, but because your sorrow led you to repentance. For you became sorrowful as God intended and so were not harmed in any way by us. ¹⁰Godly sorrow brings repentance that leads to salvation and leaves no regret, but worldly sorrow brings death. ¹¹See what this godly sorrow has produced in you: what earnestness, what eagerness to clear yourselves, what indignation, what alarm, what longing, what concern, what readiness to see justice done. At every point you have proved yourselves to be innocent in this matter. ¹²So even though I wrote to you, it was not on account of the one who did the wrong or of the injured party, but rather that before God you could see for yourselves how devoted to us you are. ¹³By all this we are encouraged.

In addition to our own encouragement, we were especially delighted to see how happy Titus was, because his spirit has been refreshed by all of you. ¹⁴I had boasted to him about you, and you have not embarrassed me. But just as everything we said to you was true, so our boasting about you to Titus has proved to be true as well. ¹⁵And his affection for you is all the greater when he remembers that you were all obedient, receiving him with fear and trembling. ¹⁶I am glad I can have complete confidence in you.

Generosity Encouraged

8 And now, brothers, we want you to know about the grace that God has given the Macedonian churches. ²Out of the most severe trial, their overflowing joy and their extreme poverty welled up in rich generosity. ³For I testify that they gave as much as they were able, and even beyond their ability. Entirely on their own, ⁴they urgently pleaded with us for the privilege of sharing in this service to the saints. ⁵And they did not do as we expected, but they gave themselves first to the Lord and then to us in keeping with God's will. ⁶So we urged Titus, since he had earlier made a beginning, to bring also to completion this act of grace on your part. ⁷But just as you excel in everything—in faith, in speech, in knowledge, in complete earnestness and in your love for us*ᵃ*—see that you also excel in this grace of giving.

⁸I am not commanding you, but I want to test the sincerity of your love by comparing it with the earnestness of others. ⁹For you know the grace of our Lord Jesus Christ, that though he was rich, yet for your sakes he became poor, so that you through his poverty might become rich.

¹⁰And here is my advice about what is best for you in this matter: Last year you were the first not only to give but also to have the desire to do so. ¹¹Now finish the work, so that your eager willingness to do it may be matched by your

---

Cultivating the Life of Holiness

2 CORINTHIANS 7:1

"The beginner must realize that in order to give delight to the Lord he is starting to cultivate a garden on very barren soil, full of abominable weeds. His Majesty pulls up the weeds and plants good seed .... And with the help of God we must strive like good gardeners to get these plants to grow and take pains to water them so that they don't wither but come to bud and flower and give forth a most pleasant fragrance to provide refreshment for this Lord of ours. Then He will often come to take delight in this garden and find His joy among these virtues."

—TERESA OF AVILA,
The Book of Her Life

From Contemplation to Action

2 CORINTHIANS 8:2–15

Teresa of Avila and John of the Cross remind us that the only true test of contemplation or oneness with God is the charity that flows from it. The apostle Paul declares, as he makes an appeal for financial support, that giving is an essential test of the sincerity of love. Even today it is not easy to ask people to reach into their pockets and contribute generously to a ministry. What do Paul's words of appeal and conviction communicate afresh to you? What examples of others' generosity inspire you to give more freely? What does it mean to give not only out of your abundance but also out of your poverty?

See Meeting God in Community

completion of it, according to your means. [12]For if the willingness is there, the gift is acceptable according to what one has, not according to what he does not have.

[13]Our desire is not that others might be relieved while you are hard pressed, but that there might be equality. [14]At the present time your plenty will supply what they need, so that in turn their plenty will supply what you need. Then there will be equality, [15]as it is written: "He who gathered much did not have too much, and he who gathered little did not have too little."[a]

Titus Sent to Corinth

[16]I thank God, who put into the heart of Titus the same concern I have for you. [17]For Titus not only welcomed our appeal, but he is coming to you with much enthusiasm and on his own initiative. [18]And we are sending along with him the brother who is praised by all the churches for his service to the gospel. [19]What is more, he was chosen by the churches to accompany us as we carry the offering, which we administer in order to honor the Lord himself and to show our eagerness to help. [20]We want to avoid any criticism of the way we administer this liberal gift. [21]For we are taking pains to do what is right, not only in the eyes of the Lord but also in the eyes of men.

[22]In addition, we are sending with them our brother who has often proved to us in many ways that he is zealous, and now even more so because of his great confidence in you. [23]As for Titus, he is my partner and fellow worker among you; as for our brothers, they are representatives of the churches and an honor to Christ. [24]Therefore show these men the proof of your love and the reason for our pride in you, so that the churches can see it.

9 There is no need for me to write to you about this service to the saints. [2]For I know your eagerness to help, and I have been boasting about it to the Macedonians, telling them that since last year you in Achaia were ready to give; and your enthusiasm has stirred most of them to action. [3]But I am sending the brothers in order that our boasting about you in this matter should not prove hollow, but that you may be ready, as I said you would be. [4]For if any Macedonians come with me and find you unprepared, we—not to say anything about you—would be ashamed of having been so confident. [5]So I thought it necessary to urge the brothers to visit you in advance and finish the arrangements for the generous gift you had promised. Then it will be ready as a generous gift, not as one grudgingly given.

Sowing Generously

[6]Remember this: Whoever sows sparingly will also reap sparingly, and whoever sows generously will also reap generously. [7]Each man should give what he has decided in his heart to give, not reluctantly or under compulsion, for God loves a cheerful giver. [8]And God is able to make all grace abound to you, so that in all things at all times, having all that you need, you will abound in every good work. [9]As it is written:

"He has scattered abroad his gifts to the poor;
    his righteousness endures forever."[b]

a 15 Exodus 16:18   *b 9* Psalm 112:9

[10]Now he who supplies seed to the sower and bread for food will also supply and increase your store of seed and will enlarge the harvest of your righteousness. [11]You will be made rich in every way so that you can be generous on every occasion, and through us your generosity will result in thanksgiving to God.

[12]This service that you perform is not only supplying the needs of God's people but is also overflowing in many expressions of thanks to God. [13]Because of the service by which you have proved yourselves, men will praise God for the obedience that accompanies your confession of the gospel of Christ, and for your generosity in sharing with them and with everyone else. [14]And in their prayers for you their hearts will go out to you, because of the surpassing grace God has given you. [15]Thanks be to God for his indescribable gift!

Paul's Defense of His Ministry

10 By the meekness and gentleness of Christ, I appeal to you—I, Paul, who am "timid" when face to face with you, but "bold" when away! [2]I beg you that when I come I may not have to be as bold as I expect to be toward some people who think that we live by the standards of this world. [3]For though we live in the world, we do not wage war as the world does. [4]The weapons we fight with are not the weapons of the world. On the contrary, they have divine power to demolish strongholds. [5]We demolish arguments and every pretension that sets itself up against the knowledge of God, and we take captive every thought to make it obedient to Christ. [6]And we will be ready to punish every act of disobedience, once your obedience is complete.

[7]You are looking only on the surface of things.[a] If anyone is confident that he belongs to Christ, he should consider again that we belong to Christ just as much as he. [8]For even if I boast somewhat freely about the authority the Lord gave us for building you up rather than pulling you down, I will not be ashamed of it. [9]I do not want to seem to be trying to frighten you with my letters. [10]For some say, "His letters are weighty and forceful, but in person he is unimpressive and his speaking amounts to nothing." [11]Such people should realize that what we are in our letters when we are absent, we will be in our actions when we are present.

[12]We do not dare to classify or compare ourselves with some who commend themselves. When they measure themselves by themselves and compare themselves with themselves, they are not wise. [13]We, however, will not boast beyond proper limits, but will confine our boasting to the field God has assigned to us, a field that reaches even to you. [14]We are not going too far in our boasting, as would be the case if we had not come to you, for we did get as far as you with the gospel of Christ. [15]Neither do we go beyond our limits by boasting of work done by others.[b] Our hope is that, as your faith continues to grow, our area of activity among you will greatly expand, [16]so that we can preach the

---

Sowing Generously

2 CORINTHIANS 9:5–12

"It is not enough to help the poor. We must help them with generosity and without grumbling. And it is not enough to help them without grumbling. We must help them gladly and happily. When the poor are helped there ought to be these two conditions: generosity and joy . . . . By showing great joyfulness you will succeed in enabling your brother or sister to overcome their sensitivity. They will understand that in your opinion receiving is just as beautiful as giving. By showing bad temper, on the other hand, far from cheering them up you will be depressing them even further. If you give gladly, even if you give only a little, it is a big gift. If you give unwillingly, even if you give a big gift, you turn it into a small one."

—JOHN CHRYSOSTOM,
On the Letter to the Romans

See Meeting God in Community

---

[a] 7 Or *Look at the obvious facts*   [b] 13–15 Or [13]*We, however, will not boast about things that cannot be measured, but we will boast according to the standard of measurement that the God of measure has assigned us—a measurement that relates even to you.* [14] . . . [15]*Neither do we boast about things that cannot be measured in regard to the work done by others.*

Boasting in the Cross

2 CORINTHIANS 11:21–30

The cross of Jesus Christ is the horizon against which Paul sees everything else. He sees in the cross the whole meaning of every imprisonment, every flogging, every exposure to death he endures. Picture yourself standing with Paul at the foot of the cross. Rub your fingers against the rough wood. Look up at the crossbars on which the Savior hung. Imagine the pain of this horrendous way of death. No wonder Paul boasts about his sufferings. What are they? All these sufferings have gained for him a wealth of meaning. What are you suffering for the cross of Christ? Are you growing in compassion through the pain? Growing in courage?

gospel in the regions beyond you. For we do not want to boast about work already done in another man's territory. [17]But, "Let him who boasts boast in the Lord."[a] [18]For it is not the one who commends himself who is approved, but the one whom the Lord commends.

Paul and the False Apostles

11 I hope you will put up with a little of my foolishness; but you are already doing that. [2]I am jealous for you with a godly jealousy. I promised you to one husband, to Christ, so that I might present you as a pure virgin to him. [3]But I am afraid that just as Eve was deceived by the serpent's cunning, your minds may somehow be led astray from your sincere and pure devotion to Christ. [4]For if someone comes to you and preaches a Jesus other than the Jesus we preached, or if you receive a different spirit from the one you received, or a different gospel from the one you accepted, you put up with it easily enough. [5]But I do not think I am in the least inferior to those "super-apostles." [6]I may not be a trained speaker, but I do have knowledge. We have made this perfectly clear to you in every way.

[7]Was it a sin for me to lower myself in order to elevate you by preaching the gospel of God to you free of charge? [8]I robbed other churches by receiving support from them so as to serve you. [9]And when I was with you and needed something, I was not a burden to anyone, for the brothers who came from Macedonia supplied what I needed. I have kept myself from being a burden to you in any way, and will continue to do so. [10]As surely as the truth of Christ is in me, nobody in the regions of Achaia will stop this boasting of mine. [11]Why? Because I do not love you? God knows I do! [12]And I will keep on doing what I am doing in order to cut the ground from under those who want an opportunity to be considered equal with us in the things they boast about.

[13]For such men are false apostles, deceitful workmen, masquerading as apostles of Christ. [14]And no wonder, for Satan himself masquerades as an angel of light. [15]It is not surprising, then, if his servants masquerade as servants of righteousness. Their end will be what their actions deserve.

Paul Boasts About His Sufferings

[16]I repeat: Let no one take me for a fool. But if you do, then receive me just as you would a fool, so that I may do a little boasting. [17]In this self-confident boasting I am not talking as the Lord would, but as a fool. [18]Since many are boasting in the way the world does, I too will boast. [19]You gladly put up with fools since you are so wise! [20]In fact, you even put up with anyone who enslaves you or exploits you or takes advantage of you or pushes himself forward or slaps you in the face. [21]To my shame I admit that we were too weak for that!

What anyone else dares to boast about—I am speaking as a fool—I also dare to boast about. [22]Are they Hebrews? So am I. Are they Israelites? So am I. Are they Abraham's descendants? So am I. [23]Are they servants of Christ? (I am out of my mind to talk like this.) I am more. I have worked much harder, been in prison more frequently, been flogged more severely, and been exposed to death again and again. [24]Five times I received from the Jews the forty lashes minus

[a] 17 Jer. 9:24

one. ²⁵Three times I was beaten with rods, once I was stoned, three times I was shipwrecked, I spent a night and a day in the open sea, ²⁶I have been constantly on the move. I have been in danger from rivers, in danger from bandits, in danger from my own countrymen, in danger from Gentiles; in danger in the city, in danger in the country, in danger at sea; and in danger from false brothers. ²⁷I have labored and toiled and have often gone without sleep; I have known hunger and thirst and have often gone without food; I have been cold and naked. ²⁸Besides everything else, I face daily the pressure of my concern for all the churches. ²⁹Who is weak, and I do not feel weak? Who is led into sin, and I do not inwardly burn?

³⁰If I must boast, I will boast of the things that show my weakness. ³¹The God and Father of the Lord Jesus, who is to be praised forever, knows that I am not lying. ³²In Damascus the governor under King Aretas had the city of the Damascenes guarded in order to arrest me. ³³But I was lowered in a basket from a window in the wall and slipped through his hands.

Paul's Vision and His Thorn

12 I must go on boasting. Although there is nothing to be gained, I will go on to visions and revelations from the Lord. ²I know a man in Christ who fourteen years ago was caught up to the third heaven. Whether it was in the body or out of the body I do not know—God knows. ³And I know that this man—whether in the body or apart from the body I do not know, but God knows— ⁴was caught up to paradise. He heard inexpressible things, things that man is not permitted to tell. ⁵I will boast about a man like that, but I will not boast about myself, except about my weaknesses. ⁶Even if I should choose to boast, I would not be a fool, because I would be speaking the truth. But I refrain, so no one will think more of me than is warranted by what I do or say.

⁷To keep me from becoming conceited because of these surpassingly great revelations, there was given me a thorn in my flesh, a messenger of Satan, to torment me. ⁸Three times I pleaded with the Lord to take it away from me. ⁹But he said to me, "My grace is sufficient for you, for my power is made perfect in weakness." Therefore I will boast all the more gladly about my weaknesses, so that Christ's power may rest on me. ¹⁰That is why, for Christ's sake, I delight in weaknesses, in insults, in hardships, in persecutions, in difficulties. For when I am weak, then I am strong.

Paul's Concern for the Corinthians

¹¹I have made a fool of myself, but you drove me to it. I ought to have been commended by you, for I am not in the least inferior to the "super-apostles," even though I am nothing. ¹²The things that mark an apostle—signs, wonders and miracles—were done among you with great perseverance. ¹³How were you inferior to the other churches, except that I was never a burden to you? Forgive me this wrong!

¹⁴Now I am ready to visit you for the third time, and I will not be a burden to you, because what I want is not your possessions but you. After all, children should not have to save up for their parents, but parents for their children. ¹⁵So

Walking in the Truth

2 CORINTHIANS 12:7–10

The classical definition of humility offered by Teresa of Avila is to walk in the truth of who we are. This means accepting our weaknesses and our limitations as gifts of God as well as our strengths and talents.

Given that definition, what does walking in the truth mean for you? How can you regard yourself as God regards you? How can you become more grateful for the way God has created you—in light of both your strengths and weaknesses? Meditate on these words and let them give you the courage to fulfill your calling as a minister of the new covenant. "My grace is sufficient for you, for my power is made perfect in weakness."

See Meeting God in Service

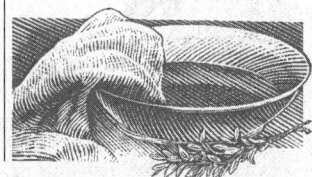

Spending All for God

2 CORINTHIANS 12:14–18

"As children of the darkness that rules through fear, self-interest, greed, and power, our great motivators are survival and self-preservation. But as children of the light who know that perfect love casts out all fear, it becomes possible to give away all that we have for others. As children of the light, we prepare ourselves to become true martyrs, people who witness with their whole lives to the unlimited love of God. Giving all thus becomes gaining all . . . . Every time I take a step in the direction of generosity, I know I am moving from fear to love."

—HENRI J. M. NOUWEN,
The Return of the Prodigal Son:
A Story of Homecoming

I will very gladly spend for you everything I have and expend myself as well. If I love you more, will you love me less? [16]Be that as it may, I have not been a burden to you. Yet, crafty fellow that I am, I caught you by trickery! [17]Did I exploit you through any of the men I sent you? [18]I urged Titus to go to you and I sent our brother with him. Titus did not exploit you, did he? Did we not act in the same spirit and follow the same course?

[19]Have you been thinking all along that we have been defending ourselves to you? We have been speaking in the sight of God as those in Christ; and everything we do, dear friends, is for your strengthening. [20]For I am afraid that when I come I may not find you as I want you to be, and you may not find me as you want me to be. I fear that there may be quarreling, jealousy, outbursts of anger, factions, slander, gossip, arrogance and disorder. [21]I am afraid that when I come again my God will humble me before you, and I will be grieved over many who have sinned earlier and have not repented of the impurity, sexual sin and debauchery in which they have indulged.

Final Warnings

13 This will be my third visit to you. "Every matter must be established by the testimony of two or three witnesses."[a] [2]I already gave you a warning when I was with you the second time. I now repeat it while absent: On my return I will not spare those who sinned earlier or any of the others, [3]since you are demanding proof that Christ is speaking through me. He is not weak in dealing with you, but is powerful among you. [4]For to be sure, he was crucified in weakness, yet he lives by God's power. Likewise, we are weak in him, yet by God's power we will live with him to serve you.

[5]Examine yourselves to see whether you are in the faith; test yourselves. Do you not realize that Christ Jesus is in you—unless, of course, you fail the test? [6]And I trust that you will discover that we have not failed the test. [7]Now we pray to God that you will not do anything wrong. Not that people will see that we have stood the test but that you will do what is right even though we may seem to have failed. [8]For we cannot do anything against the truth, but only for the truth. [9]We are glad whenever we are weak but you are strong; and our prayer is for your perfection. [10]This is why I write these things when I am absent, that when I come I may not have to be harsh in my use of authority—the authority the Lord gave me for building you up, not for tearing you down.

Final Greetings

[11]Finally, brothers, good-by. Aim for perfection, listen to my appeal, be of one mind, live in peace. And the God of love and peace will be with you.

[12]Greet one another with a holy kiss. [13]All the saints send their greetings.

[14]May the grace of the Lord Jesus Christ, and the love of God, and the fellowship of the Holy Spirit be with you all.

a 1 Deut. 19:15

GALATIANS

In Step With the Spirit

KEY VERSE:

Since we live by the Spirit, let us keep in step with the Spirit.—Galatians 5:25

Parades are fun to watch, but it takes great concentration to march in one, especially if one is playing an instrument or carrying a flag. Bands designate a leader to set the proper cadence; the challenge for each band member is to stay in step—and not only when the band is in front of the viewing stand!

Paul's letter to the Galatians explores some of the difficulties that can cause Christians to get out of step as they follow Jesus Christ. Paul warns his readers against misunderstanding the role of the law, pursuing the dead end of human effort, and concentrating on external religious practice while neglecting their inner life.

Paul's letter is a refreshing message for the Galatians—and for us today: We don't have to struggle to be in control of our spiritual life. God wants to guide us as we walk in step with the Holy Spirit so that we experience God's gracious freedom, guidance and renewing joy. As you read this letter, consider how your own lifestyle reflects the pace and power of the Holy Spirit. Be careful to notice those areas in which God is calling you to get in step with the Spirit.

"Is there not a soul among you who sometimes hears the Spirit of the Son crying in his inmost heart, 'Abba, Father'? (Galatians 4:6). Let him who feels himself loved by the Father realize that he is moved by the same Spirit as the Son. Trust without reserve. Be of good courage."

—BERNARD OF CLAIRVAUX,
Selected Works

Called by Grace

GALATIANS 1:13–17

As a zealous Pharisee, Paul had been out of step with God's Spirit. Steeped in a tradition of law, he had relied on his own strength and ability. But all that changed when he met Jesus on the road to Damascus. Getting in step with the Spirit meant discovering and following God's way, not his own.

Retrace your spiritual history. You may, like Paul, be able to pinpoint a specific occasion when you fell into step with Jesus Christ (Acts 9:1–19). Or your life might resemble the more gradual pattern of Timothy's experience (2 Timothy 3:14–15). How have you experienced God's grace? How has God revealed Jesus Christ to you? Where is God still calling you to change, to get in step with the Spirit? What is blocking you? You might ask for God's help in overcoming the obstacles or in listening for direction. Consider the possibility of recording your reflections in a journal as a way of deepening your experiences of God's grace.

See Meeting God in Everyday Life

1 Paul, an apostle—sent not from men nor by man, but by Jesus Christ and God the Father, who raised him from the dead— [2]and all the brothers with me,

To the churches in Galatia:

[3]Grace and peace to you from God our Father and the Lord Jesus Christ, [4]who gave himself for our sins to rescue us from the present evil age, according to the will of our God and Father, [5]to whom be glory for ever and ever. Amen.

No Other Gospel

[6]I am astonished that you are so quickly deserting the one who called you by the grace of Christ and are turning to a different gospel— [7]which is really no gospel at all. Evidently some people are throwing you into confusion and are trying to pervert the gospel of Christ. [8]But even if we or an angel from heaven should preach a gospel other than the one we preached to you, let him be eternally condemned! [9]As we have already said, so now I say again: If anybody is preaching to you a gospel other than what you accepted, let him be eternally condemned!

[10]Am I now trying to win the approval of men, or of God? Or am I trying to please men? If I were still trying to please men, I would not be a servant of Christ.

Paul Called by God

[11]I want you to know, brothers, that the gospel I preached is not something that man made up. [12]I did not receive it from any man, nor was I taught it; rather, I received it by revelation from Jesus Christ.

[13]For you have heard of my previous way of life in Judaism, how intensely I persecuted the church of God and tried to destroy it. [14]I was advancing in Judaism beyond many Jews of my own age and was extremely zealous for the traditions of my fathers. [15]But when God, who set me apart from birth[a] and called me by his grace, was pleased [16]to reveal his Son in me so that I might preach him among the Gentiles, I did not consult any man, [17]nor did I go up to Jerusalem to see those who were apostles before I was, but I went immediately into Arabia and later returned to Damascus.

[18]Then after three years, I went up to Jerusalem to get acquainted with Peter[b] and stayed with him fifteen days. [19]I saw none of the other apostles—only James, the Lord's brother. [20]I assure you before God that what I am writing you is no lie. [21]Later I went to Syria and Cilicia. [22]I was personally unknown to the churches of Judea that are in Christ. [23]They only heard the report: "The man who formerly persecuted us is now preaching the faith he once tried to destroy." [24]And they praised God because of me.

Paul Accepted by the Apostles

2 Fourteen years later I went up again to Jerusalem, this time with Barnabas. I took Titus along also. [2]I went in response to a revelation and set before them the gospel that I preach among the Gentiles. But I did this privately to those who seemed to be leaders, for fear that I was running

[a] 15 Or *from my mother's womb*   [b] 18 Greek *Cephas*

or had run my race in vain. ³Yet not even Titus, who was with me, was compelled to be circumcised, even though he was a Greek. ⁴This matter arose⌐ because some false brothers had infiltrated our ranks to spy on the freedom we have in Christ Jesus and to make us slaves. ⁵We did not give in to them for a moment, so that the truth of the gospel might remain with you.

⁶As for those who seemed to be important—whatever they were makes no difference to me; God does not judge by external appearance—those men added nothing to my message. ⁷On the contrary, they saw that I had been entrusted with the task of preaching the gospel to the Gentiles,ᵃ just as Peter had been to the Jews.ᵇ ⁸For God, who was at work in the ministry of Peter as an apostle to the Jews, was also at work in my ministry as an apostle to the Gentiles. ⁹James, Peterᶜ and John, those reputed to be pillars, gave me and Barnabas the right hand of fellowship when they recognized the grace given to me. They agreed that we should go to the Gentiles, and they to the Jews. ¹⁰All they asked was that we should continue to remember the poor, the very thing I was eager to do.

Paul Opposes Peter

¹¹When Peter came to Antioch, I opposed him to his face, because he was clearly in the wrong. ¹²Before certain men came from James, he used to eat with the Gentiles. But when they arrived, he began to draw back and separate himself from the Gentiles because he was afraid of those who belonged to the circumcision group. ¹³The other Jews joined him in his hypocrisy, so that by their hypocrisy even Barnabas was led astray.

¹⁴When I saw that they were not acting in line with the truth of the gospel, I said to Peter in front of them all, "You are a Jew, yet you live like a Gentile and not like a Jew. How is it, then, that you force Gentiles to follow Jewish customs?

¹⁵"We who are Jews by birth and not 'Gentile sinners' ¹⁶know that a man is not justified by observing the law, but by faith in Jesus Christ. So we, too, have put our faith in Christ Jesus that we may be justified by faith in Christ and not by observing the law, because by observing the law no one will be justified.

¹⁷"If, while we seek to be justified in Christ, it becomes evident that we ourselves are sinners, does that mean that Christ promotes sin? Absolutely not! ¹⁸If I rebuild what I destroyed, I prove that I am a lawbreaker. ¹⁹For through the law I died to the law so that I might live for God. ²⁰I have been crucified with Christ and I no longer live, but Christ lives in me. The life I live in the body, I live by faith in the Son of God, who loved me and gave himself for me. ²¹I do not set aside the grace of God, for if righteousness could be gained through the law, Christ died for nothing!"ᵈ

Faith or Observance of the Law

3 You foolish Galatians! Who has bewitched you? Before your very eyes Jesus Christ was clearly portrayed as crucified. ²I would like to learn just one thing from you: Did you receive the Spirit by observing the law, or by believing

---

New Life at the Center

GALATIANS 2:20

Imagine that someone has asked you to create a film of your life using this verse as the theme. What scenes would you include to represent your life before Jesus Christ came to live in you? After? What is different? Why? Whom would you cast for the major parts? What message do you hope your viewers will receive by watching your life? Pay attention to the details. Be open to ways in which you can thank God for the whole picture, even if some parts are painful to watch.

See Meeting God in Everyday Life

ᵃ 7 Greek *uncircumcised*   ᵇ 7 Greek *circumcised*; also in verses 8 and 9
ᶜ 9 Greek *Cephas*; also in verses 11 and 14   ᵈ 21 Some interpreters end the quotation after verse 14.

Consider Abraham

GALATIANS 3:6–9

Our society is hungry for heroes. So many of our "all-stars" in politics, entertainment, sports and even in the church have fallen and disappointed us. While Abraham was not perfect, he was different. He was a person of faith. The Bible speaks of faith as both belief (assenting to the content of Christianity) and trust (depending on God for all our needs). Living out that faith—living in step with the Spirit—is risky, especially in the uncertainties of life. God repeatedly asked Abraham to step out into the unknown.

Reflect on your own life. How have you been blessed in living by faith? In what way is God calling you to live by faith? Identify some contemporary heroes of faith who can encourage you to walk in step with God's Spirit.

See Meeting God in Everyday Life

what you heard? [3]Are you so foolish? After beginning with the Spirit, are you now trying to attain your goal by human effort? [4]Have you suffered so much for nothing—if it really was for nothing? [5]Does God give you his Spirit and work miracles among you because you observe the law, or because you believe what you heard?

[6]Consider Abraham: "He believed God, and it was credited to him as righteousness."[a] [7]Understand, then, that those who believe are children of Abraham. [8]The Scripture foresaw that God would justify the Gentiles by faith, and announced the gospel in advance to Abraham: "All nations will be blessed through you."[b] [9]So those who have faith are blessed along with Abraham, the man of faith.

[10]All who rely on observing the law are under a curse, for it is written: "Cursed is everyone who does not continue to do everything written in the Book of the Law."[c] [11]Clearly no one is justified before God by the law, because, "The righteous will live by faith."[d] [12]The law is not based on faith; on the contrary, "The man who does these things will live by them."[e] [13]Christ redeemed us from the curse of the law by becoming a curse for us, for it is written: "Cursed is everyone who is hung on a tree."[f] [14]He redeemed us in order that the blessing given to Abraham might come to the Gentiles through Christ Jesus, so that by faith we might receive the promise of the Spirit.

The Law and the Promise

[15]Brothers, let me take an example from everyday life. Just as no one can set aside or add to a human covenant that has been duly established, so it is in this case. [16]The promises were spoken to Abraham and to his seed. The Scripture does not say "and to seeds," meaning many people, but "and to your seed,"[g] meaning one person, who is Christ. [17]What I mean is this: The law, introduced 430 years later, does not set aside the covenant previously established by God and thus do away with the promise. [18]For if the inheritance depends on the law, then it no longer depends on a promise; but God in his grace gave it to Abraham through a promise.

[19]What, then, was the purpose of the law? It was added because of transgressions until the Seed to whom the promise referred had come. The law was put into effect through angels by a mediator. [20]A mediator, however, does not represent just one party; but God is one.

[21]Is the law, therefore, opposed to the promises of God? Absolutely not! For if a law had been given that could impart life, then righteousness would certainly have come by the law. [22]But the Scripture declares that the whole world is a prisoner of sin, so that what was promised, being given through faith in Jesus Christ, might be given to those who believe.

[23]Before this faith came, we were held prisoners by the law, locked up until faith should be revealed. [24]So the law was put in charge to lead us to Christ[h] that we might be justified by faith. [25]Now that faith has come, we are no longer under the supervision of the law.

[a]6 Gen. 15:6   [b]8 Gen. 12:3; 18:18; 22:18   [c]10 Deut. 27:26   [d]11 Hab. 2:4   [e]12 Lev. 18:5   [f]13 Deut. 21:23   [g]16 Gen. 12:7; 13:15; 24:7   [h]24 *Or charge until Christ came*

Sons of God

[26]You are all sons of God through faith in Christ Jesus, [27]for all of you who were baptized into Christ have clothed yourselves with Christ. [28]There is neither Jew nor Greek, slave nor free, male nor female, for you are all one in Christ Jesus. [29]If you belong to Christ, then you are Abraham's seed, and heirs according to the promise.

4 What I am saying is that as long as the heir is a child, he is no different from a slave, although he owns the whole estate. [2]He is subject to guardians and trustees until the time set by his father. [3]So also, when we were children, we were in slavery under the basic principles of the world. [4]But when the time had fully come, God sent his Son, born of a woman, born under law, [5]to redeem those under law, that we might receive the full rights of sons. [6]Because you are sons, God sent the Spirit of his Son into our hearts, the Spirit who calls out, *"Abba,[a] Father."* [7]So you are no longer a slave, but a son; and since you are a son, God has made you also an heir.

Paul's Concern for the Galatians

[8]Formerly, when you did not know God, you were slaves to those who by nature are not gods. [9]But now that you know God—or rather are known by God—how is it that you are turning back to those weak and miserable principles? Do you wish to be enslaved by them all over again? [10]You are observing special days and months and seasons and years! [11]I fear for you, that somehow I have wasted my efforts on you.

[12]I plead with you, brothers, become like me, for I became like you. You have done me no wrong. [13]As you know, it was because of an illness that I first preached the gospel to you. [14]Even though my illness was a trial to you, you did not treat me with contempt or scorn. Instead, you welcomed me as if I were an angel of God, as if I were Christ Jesus himself. [15]What has happened to all your joy? I can testify that, if you could have done so, you would have torn out your eyes and given them to me. [16]Have I now become your enemy by telling you the truth?

[17]Those people are zealous to win you over, but for no good. What they want is to alienate you ⌊from us⌋, so that you may be zealous for them. [18]It is fine to be zealous, provided the purpose is good, and to be so always and not just when I am with you. [19]My dear children, for whom I am again in the pains of childbirth until Christ is formed in you, [20]how I wish I could be with you now and change my tone, because I am perplexed about you!

Hagar and Sarah

[21]Tell me, you who want to be under the law, are you not aware of what the law says? [22]For it is written that Abraham had two sons, one by the slave woman and the other by the free woman. [23]His son by the slave woman was born in the ordinary way; but his son by the free woman was born as the result of a promise.

[24]These things may be taken figuratively, for the women represent two covenants. One covenant is from Mount Sinai and bears children who are to be slaves: This is Hagar.

God's Life in Us

GALATIANS 4:19

"True religion is a union of the soul with God, a real participation of the Divine nature, the very image of God drawn upon the soul, or, in the apostle's phrase, 'Christ is formed in you.'"

—HENRY SCOUGAL,
The Life of God in the Soul of Man

[a] 6 Aramaic for *Father*

Free to Love Responsibly

GALATIANS 5:13–15

While Christian freedom is a wonderful gift, it carries responsibility along with it. God expects those who follow the Spirit to walk in love rather than to serve the sinful nature. Furthermore, walking in step with the Spirit is communal as well as individual. Personal, spiritual formation is only half of the process. As representatives of Jesus Christ, we are called to live out our faith by loving our neighbor and treating others as if they were Jesus (see Matthew 25:35–36).

Use the newspaper or evening news broadcast to pray this Scripture. Consider which stories reflect love and which ones abuse freedom and reflect a lack of love. How do the news stories and this Scripture challenge you to some form of responsible action? If Jesus were watching the news with you, how might he respond and encourage you to respond?

See Meeting God in Community

²⁵Now Hagar stands for Mount Sinai in Arabia and corresponds to the present city of Jerusalem, because she is in slavery with her children. ²⁶But the Jerusalem that is above is free, and she is our mother. ²⁷For it is written:

> "Be glad, O barren woman,
>   who bears no children;
> break forth and cry aloud,
>   you who have no labor pains;
> because more are the children of the desolate
>   woman
>   than of her who has a husband."ᵃ

²⁸Now you, brothers, like Isaac, are children of promise. ²⁹At that time the son born in the ordinary way persecuted the son born by the power of the Spirit. It is the same now. ³⁰But what does the Scripture say? "Get rid of the slave woman and her son, for the slave woman's son will never share in the inheritance with the free woman's son."ᵇ ³¹Therefore, brothers, we are not children of the slave woman, but of the free woman.

Freedom in Christ

5 It is for freedom that Christ has set us free. Stand firm, then, and do not let yourselves be burdened again by a yoke of slavery.

²Mark my words! I, Paul, tell you that if you let yourselves be circumcised, Christ will be of no value to you at all. ³Again I declare to every man who lets himself be circumcised that he is obligated to obey the whole law. ⁴You who are trying to be justified by law have been alienated from Christ; you have fallen away from grace. ⁵But by faith we eagerly await through the Spirit the righteousness for which we hope. ⁶For in Christ Jesus neither circumcision nor uncircumcision has any value. The only thing that counts is faith expressing itself through love.

⁷You were running a good race. Who cut in on you and kept you from obeying the truth? ⁸That kind of persuasion does not come from the one who calls you. ⁹"A little yeast works through the whole batch of dough." ¹⁰I am confident in the Lord that you will take no other view. The one who is throwing you into confusion will pay the penalty, whoever he may be. ¹¹Brothers, if I am still preaching circumcision, why am I still being persecuted? In that case the offense of the cross has been abolished. ¹²As for those agitators, I wish they would go the whole way and emasculate themselves!

¹³You, my brothers, were called to be free. But do not use your freedom to indulge the sinful natureᶜ; rather, serve one another in love. ¹⁴The entire law is summed up in a single command: "Love your neighbor as yourself."ᵈ ¹⁵If you keep on biting and devouring each other, watch out or you will be destroyed by each other.

Life by the Spirit

¹⁶So I say, live by the Spirit, and you will not gratify the desires of the sinful nature. ¹⁷For the sinful nature desires what is contrary to the Spirit, and the Spirit what is contrary to the sinful nature. They are in conflict with each

---

ᵃ *27* Isaiah 54:1   ᵇ *30* Gen. 21:10   ᶜ *13* Or *the flesh*; also in verses 16, 17, 19 and 24   ᵈ *14* Lev. 19:18

other, so that you do not do what you want. ¹⁸But if you are led by the Spirit, you are not under law.

¹⁹The acts of the sinful nature are obvious: sexual immorality, impurity and debauchery; ²⁰idolatry and witchcraft; hatred, discord, jealousy, fits of rage, selfish ambition, dissensions, factions ²¹and envy; drunkenness, orgies, and the like. I warn you, as I did before, that those who live like this will not inherit the kingdom of God.

²²But the fruit of the Spirit is love, joy, peace, patience, kindness, goodness, faithfulness, ²³gentleness and self-control. Against such things there is no law. ²⁴Those who belong to Christ Jesus have crucified the sinful nature with its passions and desires. ²⁵Since we live by the Spirit, let us keep in step with the Spirit. ²⁶Let us not become conceited, provoking and envying each other.

Doing Good to All

6 Brothers, if someone is caught in a sin, you who are spiritual should restore him gently. But watch yourself, or you also may be tempted. ²Carry each other's burdens, and in this way you will fulfill the law of Christ. ³If anyone thinks he is something when he is nothing, he deceives himself. ⁴Each one should test his own actions. Then he can take pride in himself, without comparing himself to somebody else, ⁵for each one should carry his own load.

⁶Anyone who receives instruction in the word must share all good things with his instructor.

⁷Do not be deceived: God cannot be mocked. A man reaps what he sows. ⁸The one who sows to please his sinful nature, from that nature*a* will reap destruction; the one who sows to please the Spirit, from the Spirit will reap eternal life. ⁹Let us not become weary in doing good, for at the proper time we will reap a harvest if we do not give up. ¹⁰Therefore, as we have opportunity, let us do good to all people, especially to those who belong to the family of believers.

Not Circumcision but a New Creation

¹¹See what large letters I use as I write to you with my own hand!

¹²Those who want to make a good impression outwardly are trying to compel you to be circumcised. The only reason they do this is to avoid being persecuted for the cross of Christ. ¹³Not even those who are circumcised obey the law, yet they want you to be circumcised that they may boast about your flesh. ¹⁴May I never boast except in the cross of our Lord Jesus Christ, through which*b* the world has been crucified to me, and I to the world. ¹⁵Neither circumcision nor uncircumcision means anything; what counts is a new creation. ¹⁶Peace and mercy to all who follow this rule, even to the Israel of God.

¹⁷Finally, let no one cause me trouble, for I bear on my body the marks of Jesus.

¹⁸The grace of our Lord Jesus Christ be with your spirit, brothers. Amen.

Keeping in Step With the Spirit

GALATIANS 5:22–26

To be in step with the Spirit is to live in such a way that we reflect the fruit of the Spirit and the characteristics of Jesus Christ.

Slowly read this passage. What word or phrase attracts your attention? Reflect on this word or phrase. What new insights surface as you continue to meditate on it? How does it touch your emotions? How does it stir your heart to pray? Gently rest in silence, being open to any impressions from God. In a journal (or on any piece of paper) write down your impressions and experiences so you can return to them later in the day.

See *Meeting God in Scripture*

EPHESIANS

Rooted in Love

KEY VERSES:

And I pray that you, being rooted and established in love, may have power, together with all the saints, to grasp how wide and long and high and deep is the love of Christ.—Ephesians 3:17–18

> "Our real problem, in failing to center down, is not a lack of time; it is, I fear, in too many of us, lack of joyful, enthusiastic delight in [God], lack of deep, deep-drawing love directed toward him at every hour of the day and night."
>
> —THOMAS KELLY,
> *A Testament of Devotion*

Paul's letter to the Ephesians reminds us of the importance of roots. The health of a tree is dependent on the health of its root system. Roots reach deep into the soil to draw up the necessary nourishment to sustain the tree. Deep roots create stability and help the tree withstand the storms of life. Likewise, when we are rooted in the powerful and boundless love of Jesus, we are prepared to face the challenges of living in a stormy world.

This letter calls us to imitate God (5:1) as the means of developing healthy roots. That task is made possible by being in a community of love with other Christians (4:12–16). Furthermore, our life is energized by the unconditional grace of Jesus rather than by our own human efforts (2:4–10). Throughout this letter Paul offers prayers for his readers.

Pay attention to your own root system as you read and pray through Ephesians. Pray that Jesus Christ will dwell within your heart more and more so that you are equipped to face the realities of life. Consider the spiritual habits that have sustained you in the past. What new resources does this book offer to you? How can you encourage others in the healthy planting of their roots deep into Jesus?

1 Paul, an apostle of Christ Jesus by the will of God,

To the saints in Ephesus,[a] the faithful[b] in Christ Jesus:

²Grace and peace to you from God our Father and the Lord Jesus Christ.

Spiritual Blessings in Christ

³Praise be to the God and Father of our Lord Jesus Christ, who has blessed us in the heavenly realms with every spiritual blessing in Christ. ⁴For he chose us in him before the creation of the world to be holy and blameless in his sight. In love ⁵he[c] predestined us to be adopted as his sons through Jesus Christ, in accordance with his pleasure and will— ⁶to the praise of his glorious grace, which he has freely given us in the One he loves. ⁷In him we have redemption through his blood, the forgiveness of sins, in accordance with the riches of God's grace ⁸that he lavished on us with all wisdom and understanding. ⁹And he[d] made known to us the mystery of his will according to his good pleasure, which he purposed in Christ, ¹⁰to be put into effect when the times will have reached their fulfillment—to bring all things in heaven and on earth together under one head, even Christ.

¹¹In him we were also chosen,[e] having been predestined according to the plan of him who works out everything in conformity with the purpose of his will, ¹²in order that we, who were the first to hope in Christ, might be for the praise of his glory. ¹³And you also were included in Christ when you heard the word of truth, the gospel of your salvation. Having believed, you were marked in him with a seal, the promised Holy Spirit, ¹⁴who is a deposit guaranteeing our inheritance until the redemption of those who are God's possession—to the praise of his glory.

Thanksgiving and Prayer

¹⁵For this reason, ever since I heard about your faith in the Lord Jesus and your love for all the saints, ¹⁶I have not stopped giving thanks for you, remembering you in my prayers. ¹⁷I keep asking that the God of our Lord Jesus Christ, the glorious Father, may give you the Spirit[f] of wisdom and revelation, so that you may know him better. ¹⁸I pray also that the eyes of your heart may be enlightened in order that you may know the hope to which he has called you, the riches of his glorious inheritance in the saints, ¹⁹and his incomparably great power for us who believe. That power is like the working of his mighty strength, ²⁰which he exerted in Christ when he raised him from the dead and seated him at his right hand in the heavenly realms, ²¹far above all rule and authority, power and dominion, and every title that can be given, not only in the present age but also in the one to come. ²²And God placed all things under his feet and appointed him to be head over everything for the church, ²³which is his body, the fullness of him who fills everything in every way.

---

a 1 Some early manuscripts do not have *in Ephesus.*   *b 1* Or *believers who are*   *c 4,5* Or *sight in love.* *5He*   *d 8,9* Or *us. With all wisdom and understanding, 9he*   *e 11* Or *were made heirs*   *f 17* Or *a spirit*

Chosen by Love

EPHESIANS 1:3–8

When the Bible speaks of love it is more than a sentimental or romantic concept. Love reveals the compassionate heart of God for us and God's active presence with us. We recognize God's love by paying attention to what God does on our behalf. Notice the verbs Paul uses to describe God's actions:

- blessed
- chose
- predestined
- adopted
- given
- loves
- lavished

What does each verb express about God's nature? How does each verb invite you to experience your spiritual blessings in Christ? Write a brief paragraph or compose a poem about what you notice.

See Meeting God in Everyday Life

Built Into the Cornerstone

EPHESIANS 2:19–22

Imagine that you are watching God build a "household," a "holy temple" within the setting of your church community. What needs to be cleared away before the foundation can be laid? What is the foundation made of? Now God comes to add you to the building. Where does God place you? What is your function within the whole? How can you use your spiritual gifts to work alongside others in order to build up the church of Jesus Christ? What can you do to promote the building of this spiritual dwelling place for God?

See *Meeting God in Community*

Made Alive in Christ

2 As for you, you were dead in your transgressions and sins, ²in which you used to live when you followed the ways of this world and of the ruler of the kingdom of the air, the spirit who is now at work in those who are disobedient. ³All of us also lived among them at one time, gratifying the cravings of our sinful nature[a] and following its desires and thoughts. Like the rest, we were by nature objects of wrath. ⁴But because of his great love for us, God, who is rich in mercy, ⁵made us alive with Christ even when we were dead in transgressions—it is by grace you have been saved. ⁶And God raised us up with Christ and seated us with him in the heavenly realms in Christ Jesus, ⁷in order that in the coming ages he might show the incomparable riches of his grace, expressed in his kindness to us in Christ Jesus. ⁸For it is by grace you have been saved, through faith—and this not from yourselves, it is the gift of God— ⁹not by works, so that no one can boast. ¹⁰For we are God's workmanship, created in Christ Jesus to do good works, which God prepared in advance for us to do.

One in Christ

¹¹Therefore, remember that formerly you who are Gentiles by birth and called "uncircumcised" by those who call themselves "the circumcision" (that done in the body by the hands of men)— ¹²remember that at that time you were separate from Christ, excluded from citizenship in Israel and foreigners to the covenants of the promise, without hope and without God in the world. ¹³But now in Christ Jesus you who once were far away have been brought near through the blood of Christ.

¹⁴For he himself is our peace, who has made the two one and has destroyed the barrier, the dividing wall of hostility, ¹⁵by abolishing in his flesh the law with its commandments and regulations. His purpose was to create in himself one new man out of the two, thus making peace, ¹⁶and in this one body to reconcile both of them to God through the cross, by which he put to death their hostility. ¹⁷He came and preached peace to you who were far away and peace to those who were near. ¹⁸For through him we both have access to the Father by one Spirit.

¹⁹Consequently, you are no longer foreigners and aliens, but fellow citizens with God's people and members of God's household, ²⁰built on the foundation of the apostles and prophets, with Christ Jesus himself as the chief cornerstone. ²¹In him the whole building is joined together and rises to become a holy temple in the Lord. ²²And in him you too are being built together to become a dwelling in which God lives by his Spirit.

Paul the Preacher to the Gentiles

3 For this reason I, Paul, the prisoner of Christ Jesus for the sake of you Gentiles—

²Surely you have heard about the administration of God's grace that was given to me for you, ³that is, the mystery made known to me by revelation, as I have already written briefly. ⁴In reading this, then, you will be able to understand my insight into the mystery of Christ, ⁵which was not made

a 3 Or *our flesh*

known to men in other generations as it has now been revealed by the Spirit to God's holy apostles and prophets. [6]This mystery is that through the gospel the Gentiles are heirs together with Israel, members together of one body, and sharers together in the promise in Christ Jesus.

[7]I became a servant of this gospel by the gift of God's grace given me through the working of his power. [8]Although I am less than the least of all God's people, this grace was given me: to preach to the Gentiles the unsearchable riches of Christ, [9]and to make plain to everyone the administration of this mystery, which for ages past was kept hidden in God, who created all things. [10]His intent was that now, through the church, the manifold wisdom of God should be made known to the rulers and authorities in the heavenly realms, [11]according to his eternal purpose which he accomplished in Christ Jesus our Lord. [12]In him and through faith in him we may approach God with freedom and confidence. [13]I ask you, therefore, not to be discouraged because of my sufferings for you, which are your glory.

A Prayer for the Ephesians

[14]For this reason I kneel before the Father, [15]from whom his whole family[a] in heaven and on earth derives its name. [16]I pray that out of his glorious riches he may strengthen you with power through his Spirit in your inner being, [17]so that Christ may dwell in your hearts through faith. And I pray that you, being rooted and established in love, [18]may have power, together with all the saints, to grasp how wide and long and high and deep is the love of Christ, [19]and to know this love that surpasses knowledge—that you may be filled to the measure of all the fullness of God.

[20]Now to him who is able to do immeasurably more than all we ask or imagine, according to his power that is at work within us, [21]to him be glory in the church and in Christ Jesus throughout all generations, for ever and ever! Amen.

Unity in the Body of Christ

4 As a prisoner for the Lord, then, I urge you to live a life worthy of the calling you have received. [2]Be completely humble and gentle; be patient, bearing with one another in love. [3]Make every effort to keep the unity of the Spirit through the bond of peace. [4]There is one body and one Spirit— just as you were called to one hope when you were called— [5]one Lord, one faith, one baptism; [6]one God and Father of all, who is over all and through all and in all.

[7]But to each one of us grace has been given as Christ apportioned it. [8]This is why it[b] says:

> "When he ascended on high,
> he led captives in his train
> and gave gifts to men."[c]

[9](What does "he ascended" mean except that he also descended to the lower, earthly regions[d]? [10]He who descended is the very one who ascended higher than all the heavens, in order to fill the whole universe.) [11]It was he who gave some to be apostles, some to be prophets, some to be evangelists, and some to be pastors and teachers, [12]to pre-

A "Walking Prayer"

Perhaps because we use the word "love" so carelessly, people do not take it seriously. Listen to the conversations that fill your day. You will likely hear people say, "I love that car!" (or restaurant, dress, tie, CD).

Paul had a deeper and more formative principle in mind when he prayed that the Ephesians be "rooted and established in love." To be rooted in love is to experience the boundless love of Jesus Christ. Use this passage as a "walking prayer." As you go about your day, frequently and gently repeat the phrase "rooted in love." Pray this phrase as you meet people, participate in activities, make decisions, drive your vehicle, and so forth. What might happen to each person or activity if they were rooted in the love of Jesus Christ? What might happen to you?

See Meeting God in Everyday Life

---

[a] 15 Or *whom all fatherhood*   [b] 8 Or *God*   [c] 8 Psalm 68:18   [d] 9 Or *the depths of the earth*

The Language of Love

EPHESIANS 4:14–16

Love is never lived out in isolation; rather it is integrated into every relationship. As we become rooted in the love of Jesus, we grow in integrity and truth. Lying denies God's love (see v.25), while honesty inspires maturity and unity in any group of which we are members.

Prayerfully reflect on this Scripture, inviting Jesus to guide you as you review the ways in which you speak with others. How do you speak to God, to those closest to you and to others you meet throughout the day? How do you deal with difficult people? Try monitoring your speech for a few days, listening to how frequently you speak the language of love.

See Meeting God in Community

pare God's people for works of service, so that the body of Christ may be built up [13]until we all reach unity in the faith and in the knowledge of the Son of God and become mature, attaining to the whole measure of the fullness of Christ.

[14]Then we will no longer be infants, tossed back and forth by the waves, and blown here and there by every wind of teaching and by the cunning and craftiness of men in their deceitful scheming. [15]Instead, speaking the truth in love, we will in all things grow up into him who is the Head, that is, Christ. [16]From him the whole body, joined and held together by every supporting ligament, grows and builds itself up in love, as each part does its work.

Living as Children of Light

[17]So I tell you this, and insist on it in the Lord, that you must no longer live as the Gentiles do, in the futility of their thinking. [18]They are darkened in their understanding and separated from the life of God because of the ignorance that is in them due to the hardening of their hearts. [19]Having lost all sensitivity, they have given themselves over to sensuality so as to indulge in every kind of impurity, with a continual lust for more.

[20]You, however, did not come to know Christ that way. [21]Surely you heard of him and were taught in him in accordance with the truth that is in Jesus. [22]You were taught, with regard to your former way of life, to put off your old self, which is being corrupted by its deceitful desires; [23]to be made new in the attitude of your minds; [24]and to put on the new self, created to be like God in true righteousness and holiness.

[25]Therefore each of you must put off falsehood and speak truthfully to his neighbor, for we are all members of one body. [26]"In your anger do not sin"[a]: Do not let the sun go down while you are still angry, [27]and do not give the devil a foothold. [28]He who has been stealing must steal no longer, but must work, doing something useful with his own hands, that he may have something to share with those in need.

[29]Do not let any unwholesome talk come out of your mouths, but only what is helpful for building others up according to their needs, that it may benefit those who listen. [30]And do not grieve the Holy Spirit of God, with whom you were sealed for the day of redemption. [31]Get rid of all bitterness, rage and anger, brawling and slander, along with every form of malice. [32]Be kind and compassionate to one another, forgiving each other, just as in Christ God forgave you.

5 Be imitators of God, therefore, as dearly loved children [2]and live a life of love, just as Christ loved us and gave himself up for us as a fragrant offering and sacrifice to God.

[3]But among you there must not be even a hint of sexual immorality, or of any kind of impurity, or of greed, because these are improper for God's holy people. [4]Nor should there be obscenity, foolish talk or coarse joking, which are out of place, but rather thanksgiving. [5]For of this you can be sure: No immoral, impure or greedy person—such a man is an idolater—has any inheritance in the kingdom of Christ and of God.[b] [6]Let no one deceive you with empty words, for be-

[a] 26 Psalm 4:4   [b] 5 Or *kingdom of the Christ and God*

cause of such things God's wrath comes on those who are disobedient. [7]Therefore do not be partners with them.

[8]For you were once darkness, but now you are light in the Lord. Live as children of light [9](for the fruit of the light consists in all goodness, righteousness and truth) [10]and find out what pleases the Lord. [11]Have nothing to do with the fruitless deeds of darkness, but rather expose them. [12]For it is shameful even to mention what the disobedient do in secret. [13]But everything exposed by the light becomes visible, [14]for it is light that makes everything visible. This is why it is said:

> "Wake up, O sleeper,
> rise from the dead,
> and Christ will shine on you."

[15]Be very careful, then, how you live—not as unwise but as wise, [16]making the most of every opportunity, because the days are evil. [17]Therefore do not be foolish, but understand what the Lord's will is. [18]Do not get drunk on wine, which leads to debauchery. Instead, be filled with the Spirit. [19]Speak to one another with psalms, hymns and spiritual songs. Sing and make music in your heart to the Lord, [20]always giving thanks to God the Father for everything, in the name of our Lord Jesus Christ.

[21]Submit to one another out of reverence for Christ.

Wives and Husbands

[22]Wives, submit to your husbands as to the Lord. [23]For the husband is the head of the wife as Christ is the head of the church, his body, of which he is the Savior. [24]Now as the church submits to Christ, so also wives should submit to their husbands in everything.

[25]Husbands, love your wives, just as Christ loved the church and gave himself up for her [26]to make her holy, cleansing[a] her by the washing with water through the word, [27]and to present her to himself as a radiant church, without stain or wrinkle or any other blemish, but holy and blameless. [28]In this same way, husbands ought to love their wives as their own bodies. He who loves his wife loves himself. [29]After all, no one ever hated his own body, but he feeds and cares for it, just as Christ does the church— [30]for we are members of his body. [31]"For this reason a man will leave his father and mother and be united to his wife, and the two will become one flesh."[b] [32]This is a profound mystery—but I am talking about Christ and the church. [33]However, each one of you also must love his wife as he loves himself, and the wife must respect her husband.

Children and Parents

6 Children, obey your parents in the Lord, for this is right. [2]"Honor your father and mother"—which is the first commandment with a promise— [3]"that it may go well with you and that you may enjoy long life on the earth."[c]

[4]Fathers, do not exasperate your children; instead, bring them up in the training and instruction of the Lord.

Slaves and Masters

[5]Slaves, obey your earthly masters with respect and fear, and with sincerity of heart, just as you would obey Christ.

Good Roots Produce Healthy Fruit

EPHESIANS 5:8–11

God's love transforms us. As we begin to experience this incredible love we move from darkness to light. As a child of the light we bear the fruit of light and love. Imagine yourself as a fruit tree. Light a candle and, within its circle of illumination, draw your tree on paper with crayons or markers. What kind of fruit do you bear? Is your fruit the kind that "pleases the Lord"? Who is nourished by your fruit? How can you offer yourself and your fruit for God's glory?

See Meeting God in Worship

---

a 26 Or *having cleansed*   b 31 Gen. 2:24   c 3 Deut. 5:16

The Ministry of Intercession

EPHESIANS 6:18–20

Paul offers three helpful guidelines for rooting our lives in prayer: depending on the Spirit, praying wherever we are, and using different forms or methods. He reminds us that prayer confronts and weakens the powers of darkness (see v.12) that seek to destroy God's love. Being rooted in love calls us to pray for others.

As you pray, remember to intercede in love for those who are:

- struggling with depression or doubt
- facing persecution and turmoil
- seeking to communicate the gospel of Jesus Christ
- trying to find hope and direction
- wrestling with failing health

Establish the habit of intercessory prayer by writing the name of at least one person on each day of your planning calendar for the next month to remind you to pray daily for others.

See *Meeting God in Service*

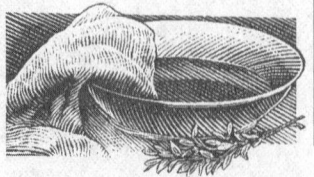

[6]Obey them not only to win their favor when their eye is on you, but like slaves of Christ, doing the will of God from your heart. [7]Serve wholeheartedly, as if you were serving the Lord, not men, [8]because you know that the Lord will reward everyone for whatever good he does, whether he is slave or free.

[9]And masters, treat your slaves in the same way. Do not threaten them, since you know that he who is both their Master and yours is in heaven, and there is no favoritism with him.

The Armor of God

[10]Finally, be strong in the Lord and in his mighty power. [11]Put on the full armor of God so that you can take your stand against the devil's schemes. [12]For our struggle is not against flesh and blood, but against the rulers, against the authorities, against the powers of this dark world and against the spiritual forces of evil in the heavenly realms. [13]Therefore put on the full armor of God, so that when the day of evil comes, you may be able to stand your ground, and after you have done everything, to stand. [14]Stand firm then, with the belt of truth buckled around your waist, with the breastplate of righteousness in place, [15]and with your feet fitted with the readiness that comes from the gospel of peace. [16]In addition to all this, take up the shield of faith, with which you can extinguish all the flaming arrows of the evil one. [17]Take the helmet of salvation and the sword of the Spirit, which is the word of God. [18]And pray in the Spirit on all occasions with all kinds of prayers and requests. With this in mind, be alert and always keep on praying for all the saints.

[19]Pray also for me, that whenever I open my mouth, words may be given me so that I will fearlessly make known the mystery of the gospel, [20]for which I am an ambassador in chains. Pray that I may declare it fearlessly, as I should.

Final Greetings

[21]Tychicus, the dear brother and faithful servant in the Lord, will tell you everything, so that you also may know how I am and what I am doing. [22]I am sending him to you for this very purpose, that you may know how we are, and that he may encourage you.

[23]Peace to the brothers, and love with faith from God the Father and the Lord Jesus Christ. [24]Grace to all who love our Lord Jesus Christ with an undying love.

PHILIPPIANS

A Work in Progress

KEY VERSE:

Being confident of this, that he who began a good work in you will carry it on to completion until the day of Christ Jesus.—Philippians 1:6

One of the characteristics of our contemporary culture is impatience. Advances in technology encourage us to demand ever more in less time. Unfortunately the continued pressure to rush everything has reduced our ability to wait for anything.

Some aspects of life, however, cannot be rushed. Spiritual growth is no different than physical growth—both require time and great patience. And when we experience growth, it is not always easy to detect. Progress sometimes seems meager. Perhaps that is why Christians have often been called a pilgrim people. Our lives reflect the process of God's work more than any polished final product.

In an age of instant gratification, the apostle Paul proclaims a countercultural message. He reminds us to be patient because God's work in us is not finished. Regardless of how long we have been concentrating on growing spiritually, we are still beginners—and always will be—until we reach heaven. Paul encourages us to press on and not give up. He emphasizes that Christian maturity is a process of cooperating with God's presence and power in our lives.

The message of Philippians is one of patience and hope. Perhaps this book will renew your stagnant life or give you permission to seek excellence rather than perfection in all you do. Regardless of where you find yourself, let these words inspire and invite you into deeper participation with the God who seeks to join you in spiritual partnership.

> "Those who think that they have arrived, have lost their way. Those who think they have reached their goal, have missed it. Those who think they are saints, are demons. An important part of the spiritual life is to keep longing, waiting, hoping, expecting."
>
> —HENRI J. M. NOUWEN,
> *The Genesee Diary*

God's Work Will Be Completed

PHILIPPIANS 1:3–6

In this letter Paul warmly and joyfully expresses the confidence that God will complete the work of faith and growth in those who are in Christ Jesus. Paul's prayer for his readers is that they may grow in love, in discernment and in the fruit of righteousness.

It's important to look at where we've been and where God is taking us in our spiritual lives (see Psalm 77:11; 105:5; 143:5). If you have been following Jesus for a number of years, recall what your life was like at the beginning of your journey. How have you grown? If you are a more recent Christian, reflect on the promises and faithfulness of God, who calls you to spiritual maturity. What specific aspect of hope or encouragement does this passage offer? Draw a picture that illustrates God's work in your life today. What colors will you select? Do the colors have any particular significance?

See Meeting God in Everyday Life

1 Paul and Timothy, servants of Christ Jesus,

To all the saints in Christ Jesus at Philippi, together with the overseers[a] and deacons:

[2]Grace and peace to you from God our Father and the Lord Jesus Christ.

Thanksgiving and Prayer

[3]I thank my God every time I remember you. [4]In all my prayers for all of you, I always pray with joy [5]because of your partnership in the gospel from the first day until now, [6]being confident of this, that he who began a good work in you will carry it on to completion until the day of Christ Jesus.

[7]It is right for me to feel this way about all of you, since I have you in my heart; for whether I am in chains or defending and confirming the gospel, all of you share in God's grace with me. [8]God can testify how I long for all of you with the affection of Christ Jesus.

[9]And this is my prayer: that your love may abound more and more in knowledge and depth of insight, [10]so that you may be able to discern what is best and may be pure and blameless until the day of Christ, [11]filled with the fruit of righteousness that comes through Jesus Christ—to the glory and praise of God.

Paul's Chains Advance the Gospel

[12]Now I want you to know, brothers, that what has happened to me has really served to advance the gospel. [13]As a result, it has become clear throughout the whole palace guard[b] and to everyone else that I am in chains for Christ. [14]Because of my chains, most of the brothers in the Lord have been encouraged to speak the word of God more courageously and fearlessly.

[15]It is true that some preach Christ out of envy and rivalry, but others out of goodwill. [16]The latter do so in love, knowing that I am put here for the defense of the gospel. [17]The former preach Christ out of selfish ambition, not sincerely, supposing that they can stir up trouble for me while I am in chains.[c] [18]But what does it matter? The important thing is that in every way, whether from false motives or true, Christ is preached. And because of this I rejoice.

Yes, and I will continue to rejoice, [19]for I know that through your prayers and the help given by the Spirit of Jesus Christ, what has happened to me will turn out for my deliverance.[d] [20]I eagerly expect and hope that I will in no way be ashamed, but will have sufficient courage so that now as always Christ will be exalted in my body, whether by life or by death. [21]For to me, to live is Christ and to die is gain. [22]If I am to go on living in the body, this will mean fruitful labor for me. Yet what shall I choose? I do not know! [23]I am torn between the two: I desire to depart and be with Christ, which is better by far; [24]but it is more necessary for you that I remain in the body. [25]Convinced of this, I know that I will remain, and I will continue with all of you for your progress and joy in the faith, [26]so that through my

a 1 Traditionally *bishops*   *b 13* Or *whole palace*   *c 16,17* Some late manuscripts have verses 16 and 17 in reverse order.   *d 19* Or *salvation*

being with you again your joy in Christ Jesus will overflow on account of me.

²⁷Whatever happens, conduct yourselves in a manner worthy of the gospel of Christ. Then, whether I come and see you or only hear about you in my absence, I will know that you stand firm in one spirit, contending as one man for the faith of the gospel ²⁸without being frightened in any way by those who oppose you. This is a sign to them that they will be destroyed, but that you will be saved—and that by God. ²⁹For it has been granted to you on behalf of Christ not only to believe on him, but also to suffer for him, ³⁰since you are going through the same struggle you saw I had, and now hear that I still have.

Imitating Christ's Humility

2 If you have any encouragement from being united with Christ, if any comfort from his love, if any fellowship with the Spirit, if any tenderness and compassion, ²then make my joy complete by being like-minded, having the same love, being one in spirit and purpose. ³Do nothing out of selfish ambition or vain conceit, but in humility consider others better than yourselves. ⁴Each of you should look not only to your own interests, but also to the interests of others.

⁵Your attitude should be the same as that of Christ Jesus:

⁶Who, being in very nature*ᵃ* God,
   did not consider equality with God something
      to be grasped,
⁷but made himself nothing,
   taking the very nature*ᵇ* of a servant,
   being made in human likeness.
⁸And being found in appearance as a man,
   he humbled himself
   and became obedient to death—
      even death on a cross!
⁹Therefore God exalted him to the highest place
   and gave him the name that is above every
      name,
¹⁰that at the name of Jesus every knee should bow,
   in heaven and on earth and under the earth,
¹¹and every tongue confess that Jesus Christ is
      Lord,
   to the glory of God the Father.

Shining as Stars

¹²Therefore, my dear friends, as you have always obeyed—not only in my presence, but now much more in my absence—continue to work out your salvation with fear and trembling, ¹³for it is God who works in you to will and to act according to his good purpose.

¹⁴Do everything without complaining or arguing, ¹⁵so that you may become blameless and pure, children of God without fault in a crooked and depraved generation, in which you shine like stars in the universe ¹⁶as you hold out*ᶜ* the word of life—in order that I may boast on the day of Christ that I did not run or labor for nothing. ¹⁷But even if I am being poured out like a drink offering on the sacrifice and service coming from your faith, I am glad and rejoice with all of you. ¹⁸So you too should be glad and rejoice with me.

Working In, Working Out

PHILIPPIANS 2:12–14

"You have to work out with concentration and care what God works in; not work your own salvation, but work it out, while you base resolutely in unshaken faith on the complete and perfect Redemption of the Lord . . . God is the source of your will, therefore you are able to work out [God's] will."

—OSWALD CHAMBERS,
My Utmost for His Highest

---

*ᵃ*6 Or *in the form of*   *ᵇ*7 Or *the form*   *ᶜ*16 Or *hold on to*

Claiming the Prize

PHILIPPIANS 3:12–14

In this passage the apostle Paul shares his vision of the eternal prize—a prize that Christ Jesus has already won, yet a prize that prompts the apostle to look heavenward.

What prize do you reach for? (See also 3:7–11.)

What vision do Paul's words prompt in you concerning your life in Christ? Be open to any insight or impressions from God. Based on this passage, write three goals for your own life in Christ.

See Meeting God in Scripture

Timothy and Epaphroditus

¹⁹I hope in the Lord Jesus to send Timothy to you soon, that I also may be cheered when I receive news about you. ²⁰I have no one else like him, who takes a genuine interest in your welfare. ²¹For everyone looks out for his own interests, not those of Jesus Christ. ²²But you know that Timothy has proved himself, because as a son with his father he has served with me in the work of the gospel. ²³I hope, therefore, to send him as soon as I see how things go with me. ²⁴And I am confident in the Lord that I myself will come soon.

²⁵But I think it is necessary to send back to you Epaphroditus, my brother, fellow worker and fellow soldier, who is also your messenger, whom you sent to take care of my needs. ²⁶For he longs for all of you and is distressed because you heard he was ill. ²⁷Indeed he was ill, and almost died. But God had mercy on him, and not on him only but also on me, to spare me sorrow upon sorrow. ²⁸Therefore I am all the more eager to send him, so that when you see him again you may be glad and I may have less anxiety. ²⁹Welcome him in the Lord with great joy, and honor men like him, ³⁰because he almost died for the work of Christ, risking his life to make up for the help you could not give me.

No Confidence in the Flesh

3 Finally, my brothers, rejoice in the Lord! It is no trouble for me to write the same things to you again, and it is a safeguard for you.

²Watch out for those dogs, those men who do evil, those mutilators of the flesh. ³For it is we who are the circumcision, we who worship by the Spirit of God, who glory in Christ Jesus, and who put no confidence in the flesh— ⁴though I myself have reasons for such confidence.

If anyone else thinks he has reasons to put confidence in the flesh, I have more: ⁵circumcised on the eighth day, of the people of Israel, of the tribe of Benjamin, a Hebrew of Hebrews; in regard to the law, a Pharisee; ⁶as for zeal, persecuting the church; as for legalistic righteousness, faultless.

⁷But whatever was to my profit I now consider loss for the sake of Christ. ⁸What is more, I consider everything a loss compared to the surpassing greatness of knowing Christ Jesus my Lord, for whose sake I have lost all things. I consider them rubbish, that I may gain Christ ⁹and be found in him, not having a righteousness of my own that comes from the law, but that which is through faith in Christ—the righteousness that comes from God and is by faith. ¹⁰I want to know Christ and the power of his resurrection and the fellowship of sharing in his sufferings, becoming like him in his death, ¹¹and so, somehow, to attain to the resurrection from the dead.

Pressing on Toward the Goal

¹²Not that I have already obtained all this, or have already been made perfect, but I press on to take hold of that for which Christ Jesus took hold of me. ¹³Brothers, I do not consider myself yet to have taken hold of it. But one thing I do: Forgetting what is behind and straining toward what is

ahead, [14]I press on toward the goal to win the prize for which God has called me heavenward in Christ Jesus.

[15]All of us who are mature should take such a view of things. And if on some point you think differently, that too God will make clear to you. [16]Only let us live up to what we have already attained.

[17]Join with others in following my example, brothers, and take note of those who live according to the pattern we gave you. [18]For, as I have often told you before and now say again even with tears, many live as enemies of the cross of Christ. [19]Their destiny is destruction, their god is their stomach, and their glory is in their shame. Their mind is on earthly things. [20]But our citizenship is in heaven. And we eagerly await a Savior from there, the Lord Jesus Christ, [21]who, by the power that enables him to bring everything under his control, will transform our lowly bodies so that they will be like his glorious body.

4 Therefore, my brothers, you whom I love and long for, my joy and crown, that is how you should stand firm in the Lord, dear friends!

Exhortations

[2]I plead with Euodia and I plead with Syntyche to agree with each other in the Lord. [3]Yes, and I ask you, loyal yoke-fellow,[a] help these women who have contended at my side in the cause of the gospel, along with Clement and the rest of my fellow workers, whose names are in the book of life.

[4]Rejoice in the Lord always. I will say it again: Rejoice! [5]Let your gentleness be evident to all. The Lord is near. [6]Do not be anxious about anything, but in everything, by prayer and petition, with thanksgiving, present your requests to God. [7]And the peace of God, which transcends all understanding, will guard your hearts and your minds in Christ Jesus.

[8]Finally, brothers, whatever is true, whatever is noble, whatever is right, whatever is pure, whatever is lovely, whatever is admirable—if anything is excellent or praiseworthy—think about such things. [9]Whatever you have learned or received or heard from me, or seen in me—put it into practice. And the God of peace will be with you.

Thanks for Their Gifts

[10]I rejoice greatly in the Lord that at last you have renewed your concern for me. Indeed, you have been concerned, but you had no opportunity to show it. [11]I am not saying this because I am in need, for I have learned to be content whatever the circumstances. [12]I know what it is to be in need, and I know what it is to have plenty. I have learned the secret of being content in any and every situation, whether well fed or hungry, whether living in plenty or in want. [13]I can do everything through him who gives me strength.

[14]Yet it was good of you to share in my troubles. [15]Moreover, as you Philippians know, in the early days of your acquaintance with the gospel, when I set out from Macedonia, not one church shared with me in the matter of giving and receiving, except you only; [16]for even when I was in Thessalonica, you sent me aid again and again when I was in need. [17]Not that I am looking for a gift, but I

Inventory of Peace

PHILIPPIANS 4:4–9

What images and impressions does the word "peace" create for you? The word peace has rich Biblical connotations of reconciliation, wholeness, health and unity. The apostle Paul often greets fellow Christians with the words *grace and peace* (see Romans 1:7; 1 Corinthians 1:3; Galatians 1:3).

Read and ponder these words of Scripture. Make two columns on a page of your journal. In one column list some of the things that rob you of peace. In the other column note some things that give you a sense of peace. Which column reflects the condition you find yourself in most often? How can this Scripture passage guide you into greater peace?

See *Meeting God in Scripture*

[a] 3 Or loyal Syzygus

Renewing Abundance

PHILIPPIANS 4:19

"Providence is the almighty and
ever present power of God by
which [God] upholds, as with
[God's] hand, heaven and earth
and all creatures, and so rules
them that leaf and blade, rain
and drought, fruitful and lean
years, food and drink, health
and sickness, prosperity and
poverty—all things, in fact,
come to us not by chance but
from [God's] fatherly hand."

—*Heidelberg Catechism,*
Lord's Day 10, Question and Answer 27

See *Meeting God in the Created Order*

am looking for what may be credited to your account. [18]I
have received full payment and even more; I am amply
supplied, now that I have received from Epaphroditus the
gifts you sent. They are a fragrant offering, an acceptable
sacrifice, pleasing to God. [19]And my God will meet all your
needs according to his glorious riches in Christ Jesus.

[20]To our God and Father be glory for ever and ever.
Amen.

Final Greetings

[21]Greet all the saints in Christ Jesus. The brothers who
are with me send greetings. [22]All the saints send you greetings, especially those who belong to Caesar's household.

[23]The grace of the Lord Jesus Christ be with your spirit.
Amen.[a]

[a] 23 Some manuscripts do not have *Amen.*

COLOSSIANS

A Heart Set on God

KEY VERSE:

Since, then, you have been raised with Christ, set your hearts on things above, where Christ is seated at the right hand of God.—Colossians 3:1

Sometimes we fool ourselves, believing it is more difficult to live today than two thousand years ago. However the Christians of the first century faced equal or greater challenges to their faith. The apostle Paul seeks to etch deeply into human hearts the truth that meaning and purpose do not come through any exclusive knowledge or superior spirituality. Rather they are firmly established in the life of Jesus Christ, in whom God was pleased to dwell with all the divine fullness. Paul understands the serious crisis before his readers and seeks to weave these words into a fabric of practical guidance that clothes them with hearts that seek to focus on God. In pondering these words of Scripture, remember that the Bible uses the word "heart" to speak of mind, soul and will. How can the book of Colossians help you devote your life to God in all of these areas?

"O to grace how great a
   debtor daily I'm
   constrained to be!
Let thy goodness, like a
   fetter, bind my wandering heart to thee.
Prone to wander, Lord, I feel
   it, prone to leave the
   God I love;
Here's my heart, O take and
   seal it; seal it for thy
   courts above."

—ROBERT ROBINSON,
"Come, Thou Fount of Every Blessing"

Motivated Living

COLOSSIANS 1:15–20

This beautiful hymn to Jesus Christ contains several wonderful images of his supremacy. List them using your own words. Then choose one of these images and meditate on it. Draw, paint or fashion some sort of creative expression that reflects your experience of pondering this Scripture. Keep it in your place of prayer to encourage you daily.

See Meeting God in the Created Order

1 Paul, an apostle of Christ Jesus by the will of God, and Timothy our brother,

²To the holy and faithful*ᵃ* brothers in Christ at Colosse:

Grace and peace to you from God our Father.*ᵇ*

Thanksgiving and Prayer

³We always thank God, the Father of our Lord Jesus Christ, when we pray for you, ⁴because we have heard of your faith in Christ Jesus and of the love you have for all the saints— ⁵the faith and love that spring from the hope that is stored up for you in heaven and that you have already heard about in the word of truth, the gospel ⁶that has come to you. All over the world this gospel is bearing fruit and growing, just as it has been doing among you since the day you heard it and understood God's grace in all its truth. ⁷You learned it from Epaphras, our dear fellow servant, who is a faithful minister of Christ on our*ᶜ* behalf, ⁸and who also told us of your love in the Spirit.

⁹For this reason, since the day we heard about you, we have not stopped praying for you and asking God to fill you with the knowledge of his will through all spiritual wisdom and understanding. ¹⁰And we pray this in order that you may live a life worthy of the Lord and may please him in every way: bearing fruit in every good work, growing in the knowledge of God, ¹¹being strengthened with all power according to his glorious might so that you may have great endurance and patience, and joyfully ¹²giving thanks to the Father, who has qualified you*ᵈ* to share in the inheritance of the saints in the kingdom of light. ¹³For he has rescued us from the dominion of darkness and brought us into the kingdom of the Son he loves, ¹⁴in whom we have redemption,*ᵉ* the forgiveness of sins.

The Supremacy of Christ

¹⁵He is the image of the invisible God, the firstborn over all creation. ¹⁶For by him all things were created: things in heaven and on earth, visible and invisible, whether thrones or powers or rulers or authorities; all things were created by him and for him. ¹⁷He is before all things, and in him all things hold together. ¹⁸And he is the head of the body, the church; he is the beginning and the firstborn from among the dead, so that in everything he might have the supremacy. ¹⁹For God was pleased to have all his fullness dwell in him, ²⁰and through him to reconcile to himself all things, whether things on earth or things in heaven, by making peace through his blood, shed on the cross.

²¹Once you were alienated from God and were enemies in your minds because of*ᶠ* your evil behavior. ²²But now he has reconciled you by Christ's physical body through death to present you holy in his sight, without blemish and free from accusation— ²³if you continue in your faith, established and firm, not moved from the hope held out in the gospel. This is the gospel that you heard and that has been proclaimed to every creature under heaven, and of which I, Paul, have become a servant.

ᵃ2 Or *believing*   *ᵇ2* Some manuscripts *Father and the Lord Jesus Christ*   *ᶜ7* Some manuscripts *your*   *ᵈ12* Some manuscripts *us*   *ᵉ14* A few late manuscripts *redemption through his blood*   *ᶠ21* Or *minds, as shown by*

Paul's Labor for the Church

²⁴Now I rejoice in what was suffered for you, and I fill up in my flesh what is still lacking in regard to Christ's afflictions, for the sake of his body, which is the church. ²⁵I have become its servant by the commission God gave me to present to you the word of God in its fullness— ²⁶the mystery that has been kept hidden for ages and generations, but is now disclosed to the saints. ²⁷To them God has chosen to make known among the Gentiles the glorious riches of this mystery, which is Christ in you, the hope of glory.

²⁸We proclaim him, admonishing and teaching everyone with all wisdom, so that we may present everyone perfect in Christ. ²⁹To this end I labor, struggling with all his energy, which so powerfully works in me.

2 I want you to know how much I am struggling for you and for those at Laodicea, and for all who have not met me personally. ²My purpose is that they may be encouraged in heart and united in love, so that they may have the full riches of complete understanding, in order that they may know the mystery of God, namely, Christ, ³in whom are hidden all the treasures of wisdom and knowledge. ⁴I tell you this so that no one may deceive you by fine-sounding arguments. ⁵For though I am absent from you in body, I am present with you in spirit and delight to see how orderly you are and how firm your faith in Christ is.

Freedom From Human Regulations Through Life With Christ

⁶So then, just as you received Christ Jesus as Lord, continue to live in him, ⁷rooted and built up in him, strengthened in the faith as you were taught, and overflowing with thankfulness.

⁸See to it that no one takes you captive through hollow and deceptive philosophy, which depends on human tradition and the basic principles of this world rather than on Christ.

⁹For in Christ all the fullness of the Deity lives in bodily form, ¹⁰and you have been given fullness in Christ, who is the head over every power and authority. ¹¹In him you were also circumcised, in the putting off of the sinful nature,ᵃ not with a circumcision done by the hands of men but with the circumcision done by Christ, ¹²having been buried with him in baptism and raised with him through your faith in the power of God, who raised him from the dead.

¹³When you were dead in your sins and in the uncircumcision of your sinful nature,ᵇ God made youᶜ alive with Christ. He forgave us all our sins, ¹⁴having canceled the written code, with its regulations, that was against us and that stood opposed to us; he took it away, nailing it to the cross. ¹⁵And having disarmed the powers and authorities, he made a public spectacle of them, triumphing over them by the cross.ᵈ

¹⁶Therefore do not let anyone judge you by what you eat or drink, or with regard to a religious festival, a New Moon celebration or a Sabbath day. ¹⁷These are a shadow of the things that were to come; the reality, however, is found in Christ. ¹⁸Do not let anyone who delights in false humility

---

Experiencing the Mystery

COLOSSIANS 1:27

Our western world has a strong desire to analyze and explain everything. While knowledge and understanding are essential for the Christian, there are some aspects of the faith that defy explanation. John Calvin, the sixteenth-century Swiss reformer, understood this. As he was struggling to understand Jesus' presence in the Lord's Supper, he reached a point where he confessed, "I would rather experience than understand it" (John Calvin, *Institutes of the Christian Religion*). What would it mean for you to experience this verse? Seek the Spirit's guidance as you pray and ponder the good news that Jesus Christ is in you. Use your imagination as you engage this Scripture and quietly rest in this mystery. Conclude your time with a prayer of gratitude and commitment. Create some symbol or picture to remind you of Christ's indwelling presence in your life.

See Meeting God in Scripture

ᵃ *11* Or *the flesh* ᵇ *13* Or *your flesh* ᶜ *13* Some manuscripts *us*
ᵈ *15* Or *them in him*

Guidelines for a Healthy Heart

COLOSSIANS 3:1–4

Your physical heart requires a balanced diet to remain healthy. Your spiritual heart is no different. It too requires a healthy diet to function and equip you to know the love, grace, forgiveness, wonder and joy of God.

Where do you normally set your heart? How does that help you experience God? How does that hinder you from experiencing God? What spiritual habits encourage you in cultivating a heart for God? What is the greatest competition for your heart? How does that affect your relationship with God? What one request would you like to ask of Jesus to help you set your heart on things above? Record it and pay attention to how God answers your prayer.

See Meeting God in Prayer

and the worship of angels disqualify you for the prize. Such a person goes into great detail about what he has seen, and his unspiritual mind puffs him up with idle notions. [19]He has lost connection with the Head, from whom the whole body, supported and held together by its ligaments and sinews, grows as God causes it to grow.

[20]Since you died with Christ to the basic principles of this world, why, as though you still belonged to it, do you submit to its rules: [21]"Do not handle! Do not taste! Do not touch!"? [22]These are all destined to perish with use, because they are based on human commands and teachings. [23]Such regulations indeed have an appearance of wisdom, with their self-imposed worship, their false humility and their harsh treatment of the body, but they lack any value in restraining sensual indulgence.

Rules for Holy Living

3 Since, then, you have been raised with Christ, set your hearts on things above, where Christ is seated at the right hand of God. [2]Set your minds on things above, not on earthly things. [3]For you died, and your life is now hidden with Christ in God. [4]When Christ, who is your[a] life, appears, then you also will appear with him in glory.

[5]Put to death, therefore, whatever belongs to your earthly nature: sexual immorality, impurity, lust, evil desires and greed, which is idolatry. [6]Because of these, the wrath of God is coming.[b] [7]You used to walk in these ways, in the life you once lived. [8]But now you must rid yourselves of all such things as these: anger, rage, malice, slander, and filthy language from your lips. [9]Do not lie to each other, since you have taken off your old self with its practices [10]and have put on the new self, which is being renewed in knowledge in the image of its Creator. [11]Here there is no Greek or Jew, circumcised or uncircumcised, barbarian, Scythian, slave or free, but Christ is all, and is in all.

[12]Therefore, as God's chosen people, holy and dearly loved, clothe yourselves with compassion, kindness, humility, gentleness and patience. [13]Bear with each other and forgive whatever grievances you may have against one another. Forgive as the Lord forgave you. [14]And over all these virtues put on love, which binds them all together in perfect unity.

[15]Let the peace of Christ rule in your hearts, since as members of one body you were called to peace. And be thankful. [16]Let the word of Christ dwell in you richly as you teach and admonish one another with all wisdom, and as you sing psalms, hymns and spiritual songs with gratitude in your hearts to God. [17]And whatever you do, whether in word or deed, do it all in the name of the Lord Jesus, giving thanks to God the Father through him.

Rules for Christian Households

[18]Wives, submit to your husbands, as is fitting in the Lord.

[19]Husbands, love your wives and do not be harsh with them.

[20]Children, obey your parents in everything, for this pleases the Lord.

[a] 4 Some manuscripts *our*   [b] 6 Some early manuscripts *coming on those who are disobedient*

²¹Fathers, do not embitter your children, or they will become discouraged.

²²Slaves, obey your earthly masters in everything; and do it, not only when their eye is on you and to win their favor, but with sincerity of heart and reverence for the Lord. ²³Whatever you do, work at it with all your heart, as working for the Lord, not for men, ²⁴since you know that you will receive an inheritance from the Lord as a reward. It is the Lord Christ you are serving. ²⁵Anyone who does wrong will be repaid for his wrong, and there is no favoritism.

4 Masters, provide your slaves with what is right and fair, because you know that you also have a Master in heaven.

Further Instructions

²Devote yourselves to prayer, being watchful and thankful. ³And pray for us, too, that God may open a door for our message, so that we may proclaim the mystery of Christ, for which I am in chains. ⁴Pray that I may proclaim it clearly, as I should. ⁵Be wise in the way you act toward outsiders; make the most of every opportunity. ⁶Let your conversation be always full of grace, seasoned with salt, so that you may know how to answer everyone.

Final Greetings

⁷Tychicus will tell you all the news about me. He is a dear brother, a faithful minister and fellow servant in the Lord. ⁸I am sending him to you for the express purpose that you may know about our*ᵃ* circumstances and that he may encourage your hearts. ⁹He is coming with Onesimus, our faithful and dear brother, who is one of you. They will tell you everything that is happening here.

¹⁰My fellow prisoner Aristarchus sends you his greetings, as does Mark, the cousin of Barnabas. (You have received instructions about him; if he comes to you, welcome him.) ¹¹Jesus, who is called Justus, also sends greetings. These are the only Jews among my fellow workers for the kingdom of God, and they have proved a comfort to me. ¹²Epaphras, who is one of you and a servant of Christ Jesus, sends greetings. He is always wrestling in prayer for you, that you may stand firm in all the will of God, mature and fully assured. ¹³I vouch for him that he is working hard for you and for those at Laodicea and Hierapolis. ¹⁴Our dear friend Luke, the doctor, and Demas send greetings. ¹⁵Give my greetings to the brothers at Laodicea, and to Nympha and the church in her house.

¹⁶After this letter has been read to you, see that it is also read in the church of the Laodiceans and that you in turn read the letter from Laodicea.

¹⁷Tell Archippus: "See to it that you complete the work you have received in the Lord."

¹⁸I, Paul, write this greeting in my own hand. Remember my chains. Grace be with you.

Supportive Care for Seeking Hearts

COLOSSIANS 4:7–9

Soul friends are a special gift from God. Tychicus served in that capacity for Paul by being a dear brother, a faithful minister and a fellow servant.

Do you have a Tychicus in your life? How has he or she supported you in your faith? When have you last told this person how glad you are to have him or her in your life? For whom are you a Tychicus? How do you seek to encourage his or her heart in Jesus Christ? Remember, in particular, the wonderful opportunity of supporting children and young people as they seek to know Jesus. This week select one person whose heart you can encourage for God.

See Meeting God in Service

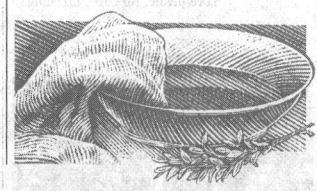

---

1 THESSALONIANS

Waiting in Holiness

KEY VERSE:

May [God] strengthen your hearts so that you will be blameless and holy in the presence of our God and Father when our Lord Jesus comes with all his holy ones.—1 Thessalonians 3:13

"Finish, then, thy new cre-
    ation; pure and spotless
    let us be;
Let us see thy great
    salvation perfectly
    restored in thee:
Changed from glory into
    glory, till in heaven we
    take our place,
Till we cast our crowns
    before thee, lost in
    wonder, love and
    praise."

—CHARLES WESLEY,
"Love Divine, All Loves Excelling"

How often don't we wish for a friend who could give us spiritual help—not just casual advice, but powerful counsel that would lead us to a closer relationship with God (2:12). The Christians of Thessalonica had such a friend in the apostle Paul. As he writes, Paul is open about his affection for them, his longing to be their guide and religious instructor, and his pride in their success in living lives worthy of God's calling. He is thrilled when Timothy reports that the faith and love Paul remembered as characteristic of them was still alive and flourishing among these faithful converts.

Paul's affection for the Thessalonians is so endearing that we might be reminded of a similar friend of our own. Imagine returning home one day and finding a letter waiting in the mail from just such an old friend. More than once you have wished you could sit and talk with this friend because he or she is a good listener and always knows just what to say to point you in the right direction.

Now imagine that this friend is someone like Paul, a person of considerable stature, who is keenly interested in the things you do, say and think. In your last letter to this friend, what did you write about? What was weighing heavily on your heart? What joys did you share? Now how does this person's letter of response to you begin? What concern seems most important? What does your friend wish for you most of all? Read the book of 1 Thessalonians as if it were such a letter, written just for you and your faith community.

We should search
the Scriptures carefully,
in humility and
with the counsel
of experienced people,
learning not merely theoretically
but by putting into practice
what we read.

PETER OF DAMASKOS (TWELFTH CENTURY?)
The Philokalia (Volume Three)

At any price,
give me the book of God!
Here is knowledge enough
for me. In God's presence
I open, I read this book,
for this end:
to find the way
to heaven.

JOHN WESLEY (1703-1791)

Sermons on Several Occasions

In our meditation we ponder the chosen text on the strength of the promise that it has something utterly personal to say to us for this day and for our Christian life.

DIETRICH BONHOEFFER (1906-1945)

Life Together

Just as you

do not analyze the words of someone you love, but accept them as they are said to you, accept the Word of Scripture and ponder it in your heart.

DIETRICH BONHOEFFER (1906-1945)

The Way to Freedom

1 Paul, Silas[a] and Timothy,

To the church of the Thessalonians in God the Father and the Lord Jesus Christ:

Grace and peace to you.[b]

Thanksgiving for the Thessalonians' Faith

[2]We always thank God for all of you, mentioning you in our prayers. [3]We continually remember before our God and Father your work produced by faith, your labor prompted by love, and your endurance inspired by hope in our Lord Jesus Christ.

[4]For we know, brothers loved by God, that he has chosen you, [5]because our gospel came to you not simply with words, but also with power, with the Holy Spirit and with deep conviction. You know how we lived among you for your sake. [6]You became imitators of us and of the Lord; in spite of severe suffering, you welcomed the message with the joy given by the Holy Spirit. [7]And so you became a model to all the believers in Macedonia and Achaia. [8]The Lord's message rang out from you not only in Macedonia and Achaia—your faith in God has become known everywhere. Therefore we do not need to say anything about it, [9]for they themselves report what kind of reception you gave us. They tell how you turned to God from idols to serve the living and true God, [10]and to wait for his Son from heaven, whom he raised from the dead—Jesus, who rescues us from the coming wrath.

Paul's Ministry in Thessalonica

2 You know, brothers, that our visit to you was not a failure. [2]We had previously suffered and been insulted in Philippi, as you know, but with the help of our God we dared to tell you his gospel in spite of strong opposition. [3]For the appeal we make does not spring from error or impure motives, nor are we trying to trick you. [4]On the contrary, we speak as men approved by God to be entrusted with the gospel. We are not trying to please men but God, who tests our hearts. [5]You know we never used flattery, nor did we put on a mask to cover up greed—God is our witness. [6]We were not looking for praise from men, not from you or anyone else.

As apostles of Christ we could have been a burden to you, [7]but we were gentle among you, like a mother caring for her little children. [8]We loved you so much that we were delighted to share with you not only the gospel of God but our lives as well, because you had become so dear to us. [9]Surely you remember, brothers, our toil and hardship; we worked night and day in order not to be a burden to anyone while we preached the gospel of God to you.

[10]You are witnesses, and so is God, of how holy, righteous and blameless we were among you who believed. [11]For you know that we dealt with each of you as a father deals with his own children, [12]encouraging, comforting and urging you to live lives worthy of God, who calls you into his kingdom and glory.

[13]And we also thank God continually because, when you

Thank You, My Friend in Christ

1 THESSALONIANS 1:1

The apostle Paul is very appreciative of his partners in ministry. In the opening verse of this letter, he mentions two of them, Silas and Timothy. Paul knows he needs others to share the mission of spreading the Good News as well as to bolster him when he is discouraged. Paul's gratitude prompts us to reflect on our own friendships rooted in a shared faith and a common mission.

Who are the people who have shared your journey and made a difference in your life with Jesus Christ? Sometimes a letter is the best way to tell them how grateful you are for their presence in your life. To which friend will you write today? How was that friend transparent enough to let the presence of Jesus shine through them on your behalf? How did that friend influence your prayer life? What plan do you have for writing your other friends?

See Meeting God in Community

---

[a] 1 Greek *Silvanus*, a variant of *Silas*   [b] 1 Some early manuscripts *you from God our Father and the Lord Jesus Christ*

A Pastor's Prayer

1 THESSALONIANS 3:9–13

What a wonderful prayer Paul offers for his friends in Thessalonica! Picture in your mind someone who has been important in helping you to grow in Jesus Christ: a former pastor, evangelist, teacher or other mentor. Picture this person praying for you with the same insight and concern Paul shows in these words. Read these words slowly and carefully so that they sink in. Rejoice in the knowledge that this person prays for you, if not with these exact words, then with other words of love flowing from their spirit.

Close your prayer time by thanking God for this person and the ways in which this person touches your life. Lift your thanks to God also for his continuing presence as he strengthens your heart in holiness.

See Meeting God in Community

received the word of God, which you heard from us, you accepted it not as the word of men, but as it actually is, the word of God, which is at work in you who believe. ¹⁴For you, brothers, became imitators of God's churches in Judea, which are in Christ Jesus: You suffered from your own countrymen the same things those churches suffered from the Jews, ¹⁵who killed the Lord Jesus and the prophets and also drove us out. They displease God and are hostile to all men ¹⁶in their effort to keep us from speaking to the Gentiles so that they may be saved. In this way they always heap up their sins to the limit. The wrath of God has come upon them at last.[a]

Paul's Longing to See the Thessalonians

¹⁷But, brothers, when we were torn away from you for a short time (in person, not in thought), out of our intense longing we made every effort to see you. ¹⁸For we wanted to come to you—certainly I, Paul, did, again and again—but Satan stopped us. ¹⁹For what is our hope, our joy, or the crown in which we will glory in the presence of our Lord Jesus when he comes? Is it not you? ²⁰Indeed, you are our glory and joy.

3 So when we could stand it no longer, we thought it best to be left by ourselves in Athens. ²We sent Timothy, who is our brother and God's fellow worker[b] in spreading the gospel of Christ, to strengthen and encourage you in your faith, ³so that no one would be unsettled by these trials. You know quite well that we were destined for them. ⁴In fact, when we were with you, we kept telling you that we would be persecuted. And it turned out that way, as you well know. ⁵For this reason, when I could stand it no longer, I sent to find out about your faith. I was afraid that in some way the tempter might have tempted you and our efforts might have been useless.

Timothy's Encouraging Report

⁶But Timothy has just now come to us from you and has brought good news about your faith and love. He has told us that you always have pleasant memories of us and that you long to see us, just as we also long to see you. ⁷Therefore, brothers, in all our distress and persecution we were encouraged about you because of your faith. ⁸For now we really live, since you are standing firm in the Lord. ⁹How can we thank God enough for you in return for all the joy we have in the presence of our God because of you? ¹⁰Night and day we pray most earnestly that we may see you again and supply what is lacking in your faith.

¹¹Now may our God and Father himself and our Lord Jesus clear the way for us to come to you. ¹²May the Lord make your love increase and overflow for each other and for everyone else, just as ours does for you. ¹³May he strengthen your hearts so that you will be blameless and holy in the presence of our God and Father when our Lord Jesus comes with all his holy ones.

Living to Please God

4 Finally, brothers, we instructed you how to live in order to please God, as in fact you are living. Now we ask you

---

[a] 16 Or *them fully* [b] 2 Some manuscripts *brother and fellow worker*; other manuscripts *brother and God's servant*

and urge you in the Lord Jesus to do this more and more. [2]For you know what instructions we gave you by the authority of the Lord Jesus.

[3]It is God's will that you should be sanctified: that you should avoid sexual immorality; [4]that each of you should learn to control his own body[a] in a way that is holy and honorable, [5]not in passionate lust like the heathen, who do not know God; [6]and that in this matter no one should wrong his brother or take advantage of him. The Lord will punish men for all such sins, as we have already told you and warned you. [7]For God did not call us to be impure, but to live a holy life. [8]Therefore, he who rejects this instruction does not reject man but God, who gives you his Holy Spirit.

[9]Now about brotherly love we do not need to write to you, for you yourselves have been taught by God to love each other. [10]And in fact, you do love all the brothers throughout Macedonia. Yet we urge you, brothers, to do so more and more.

[11]Make it your ambition to lead a quiet life, to mind your own business and to work with your hands, just as we told you, [12]so that your daily life may win the respect of outsiders and so that you will not be dependent on anybody.

The Coming of the Lord

[13]Brothers, we do not want you to be ignorant about those who fall asleep, or to grieve like the rest of men, who have no hope. [14]We believe that Jesus died and rose again and so we believe that God will bring with Jesus those who have fallen asleep in him. [15]According to the Lord's own word, we tell you that we who are still alive, who are left till the coming of the Lord, will certainly not precede those who have fallen asleep. [16]For the Lord himself will come down from heaven, with a loud command, with the voice of the archangel and with the trumpet call of God, and the dead in Christ will rise first. [17]After that, we who are still alive and are left will be caught up together with them in the clouds to meet the Lord in the air. And so we will be with the Lord forever. [18]Therefore encourage each other with these words.

5 Now, brothers, about times and dates we do not need to write to you, [2]for you know very well that the day of the Lord will come like a thief in the night. [3]While people are saying, "Peace and safety," destruction will come on them suddenly, as labor pains on a pregnant woman, and they will not escape.

[4]But you, brothers, are not in darkness so that this day should surprise you like a thief. [5]You are all sons of the light and sons of the day. We do not belong to the night or to the darkness. [6]So then, let us not be like others, who are asleep, but let us be alert and self-controlled. [7]For those who sleep, sleep at night, and those who get drunk, get drunk at night. [8]But since we belong to the day, let us be self-controlled, putting on faith and love as a breastplate, and the hope of salvation as a helmet. [9]For God did not appoint us to suffer wrath but to receive salvation through our Lord Jesus Christ. [10]He died for us so that, whether we are awake or asleep, we may live together with him. [11]Therefore encourage one another and build each other up, just as in fact you are doing.

Meeting the Lord

1 THESSALONIANS 4:16–18

When Paul talks about meeting the Lord in the air, the image is of a welcoming committee going out from a town to greet and escort a visiting dignitary.

Imagine that you are appointed to head such a welcoming committee to prepare for Jesus' coming to your church or your town. How would you greet him? What would you say? What parts of your community would you eagerly show him? What parts would you rather hide? How would your own life stand up to his gaze? What in your community or your life would you wish to change before he arrived? What might be preventing you from making the change? Why not begin right now?

See Meeting God in Scripture

---

[a] 4 Or *learn to live with his own wife; or learn to acquire a wife*

Demands and Priorities

Living a life of unity and peace with others can be difficult and demanding. Before you read (or reread) this section of Paul's letter, make your own list of the tough demands made on you by living with your family, spouse, children, parents, roommates and friends. Add the demands of your church life, your job or other role or responsibility. Then compare it with Paul's list. How are Paul's demands different from yours?

We set priorities by appraising the demands made by others in light of our own sense of our identity and our calling from God. As you look over your list, ask God to help you decide which demands need to be priorities and which demands need to be dismissed. Pray also for the strength and encouragement of the Holy Spirit as you seek to live out these decisions.

See Meeting God in Everyday Life

Final Instructions

¹²Now we ask you, brothers, to respect those who work hard among you, who are over you in the Lord and who admonish you. ¹³Hold them in the highest regard in love because of their work. Live in peace with each other. ¹⁴And we urge you, brothers, warn those who are idle, encourage the timid, help the weak, be patient with everyone. ¹⁵Make sure that nobody pays back wrong for wrong, but always try to be kind to each other and to everyone else.

¹⁶Be joyful always; ¹⁷pray continually; ¹⁸give thanks in all circumstances, for this is God's will for you in Christ Jesus.

¹⁹Do not put out the Spirit's fire; ²⁰do not treat prophecies with contempt. ²¹Test everything. Hold on to the good. ²²Avoid every kind of evil.

²³May God himself, the God of peace, sanctify you through and through. May your whole spirit, soul and body be kept blameless at the coming of our Lord Jesus Christ. ²⁴The one who calls you is faithful and he will do it.

²⁵Brothers, pray for us. ²⁶Greet all the brothers with a holy kiss. ²⁷I charge you before the Lord to have this letter read to all the brothers.

²⁸The grace of our Lord Jesus Christ be with you.

2 THESSALONIANS
A Life Worthy of God's Calling

KEY VERSE:

With this in mind, we constantly pray for you, that our God may count you worthy of his calling, and that by his power he may fulfill every good purpose of yours and every act prompted by your faith.—2 Thessalonians 1:11

The early church in Thessalonica is buzzing with predictions of Jesus' second coming. For some the fearful "end times" are troubling to contemplate. Others want only to wait passively for Jesus' return. The timing of this final event is uncertain, and many, in a state of paralysis, have given up their work and sit idly, awaiting the end of the world.

The author of this letter pointedly reminds his readers of who is in charge of all these things. The apostle Paul admonishes the Thessalonians not to be shaken but to have faith (2:2), remembering that God has chosen them.

Paul also confronts the destructiveness of fear and anxiety. They are to remain steadfast in their faith in the same way God is steadfast in his love for them (2:16). Idleness only adds to the problem of worry, he says; and he tells them to earn their own way (3:11–12) and live their lives as models of love and perseverance (3:5).

Take time to reflect on your fears as you read 2 Thessalonians. Which fears can you surrender to God? How could a fuller measure of faith in God dispel your feelings of being overwhelmed and hopeless in your daily life? What do you need to allow God to handle so that you can experience a turnabout in your ability to handle your fears? As you read this letter, let yourself experience the presence of the One who can calm all your fears.

"Some Christians seem to think that all the requirements of a holy life are met when there is very active and successful Christian work; and because they do so much for the Lord in public they feel a liberty to be cross and ugly and un-Christlike in private . . . If we are to walk as Christ walked, it must be in private as well as in public, at home as well as abroad; and it must be every hour all day long, and not at stated periods or on certain fixed occasions . . . It is in daily homely living, indeed, that practical piety can best show itself."

—HANNAH WHITALL SMITH,
The Christian's Secret of a Happy Life

A Portrait of a Church

2 THESSALONIANS 1:1–4

With just a few words, the author paints a picture of a thriving church that, despite problems, is filled with love, faith and steadfastness.

Try painting a portrait of your church. You might use words similar to those used in these verses. Or you might try representing your church pictorially, using crayons, markers or paints. What attributes would you honor? What problems would you need to illustrate?

As you work on this portrait, say a prayer for your church. Give thanks for what is good and confess problems that need God's correction. Ask God to bless all the individuals who are a part of your church, especially those in leadership positions.

1 Paul, Silas[a] and Timothy,

To the church of the Thessalonians in God our Father and the Lord Jesus Christ:

[2]Grace and peace to you from God the Father and the Lord Jesus Christ.

Thanksgiving and Prayer

[3]We ought always to thank God for you, brothers, and rightly so, because your faith is growing more and more, and the love every one of you has for each other is increasing. [4]Therefore, among God's churches we boast about your perseverance and faith in all the persecutions and trials you are enduring.

[5]All this is evidence that God's judgment is right, and as a result you will be counted worthy of the kingdom of God, for which you are suffering. [6]God is just: He will pay back trouble to those who trouble you [7]and give relief to you who are troubled, and to us as well. This will happen when the Lord Jesus is revealed from heaven in blazing fire with his powerful angels. [8]He will punish those who do not know God and do not obey the gospel of our Lord Jesus. [9]They will be punished with everlasting destruction and shut out from the presence of the Lord and from the majesty of his power [10]on the day he comes to be glorified in his holy people and to be marveled at among all those who have believed. This includes you, because you believed our testimony to you.

[11]With this in mind, we constantly pray for you, that our God may count you worthy of his calling, and that by his power he may fulfill every good purpose of yours and every act prompted by your faith. [12]We pray this so that the name of our Lord Jesus may be glorified in you, and you in him, according to the grace of our God and the Lord Jesus Christ.[b]

The Man of Lawlessness

2 Concerning the coming of our Lord Jesus Christ and our being gathered to him, we ask you, brothers, [2]not to become easily unsettled or alarmed by some prophecy, report or letter supposed to have come from us, saying that the day of the Lord has already come. [3]Don't let anyone deceive you in any way, for ˻that day will not come˼ until the rebellion occurs and the man of lawlessness[c] is revealed, the man doomed to destruction. [4]He will oppose and will exalt himself over everything that is called God or is worshiped, so that he sets himself up in God's temple, proclaiming himself to be God.

[5]Don't you remember that when I was with you I used to tell you these things? [6]And now you know what is holding him back, so that he may be revealed at the proper time. [7]For the secret power of lawlessness is already at work; but the one who now holds it back will continue to do so till he is taken out of the way. [8]And then the lawless one will be revealed, whom the Lord Jesus will overthrow with the breath of his mouth and destroy by the splendor of his coming. [9]The coming of the lawless one will be in

[a] 1 Greek *Silvanus*, a variant of *Silas*   [b] 12 Or *God and Lord, Jesus Christ*
[c] 3 Some manuscripts *sin*

accordance with the work of Satan displayed in all kinds of counterfeit miracles, signs and wonders, [10]and in every sort of evil that deceives those who are perishing. They perish because they refused to love the truth and so be saved. [11]For this reason God sends them a powerful delusion so that they will believe the lie [12]and so that all will be condemned who have not believed the truth but have delighted in wickedness.

Stand Firm

[13]But we ought always to thank God for you, brothers loved by the Lord, because from the beginning God chose you[a] to be saved through the sanctifying work of the Spirit and through belief in the truth. [14]He called you to this through our gospel, that you might share in the glory of our Lord Jesus Christ. [15]So then, brothers, stand firm and hold to the teachings[b] we passed on to you, whether by word of mouth or by letter.

[16]May our Lord Jesus Christ himself and God our Father, who loved us and by his grace gave us eternal encouragement and good hope, [17]encourage your hearts and strengthen you in every good deed and word.

Request for Prayer

3 Finally, brothers, pray for us that the message of the Lord may spread rapidly and be honored, just as it was with you. [2]And pray that we may be delivered from wicked and evil men, for not everyone has faith. [3]But the Lord is faithful, and he will strengthen and protect you from the evil one. [4]We have confidence in the Lord that you are doing and will continue to do the things we command. [5]May the Lord direct your hearts into God's love and Christ's perseverance.

Warning Against Idleness

[6]In the name of the Lord Jesus Christ, we command you, brothers, to keep away from every brother who is idle and does not live according to the teaching[c] you received from us. [7]For you yourselves know how you ought to follow our example. We were not idle when we were with you, [8]nor did we eat anyone's food without paying for it. On the contrary, we worked night and day, laboring and toiling so that we would not be a burden to any of you. [9]We did this, not because we do not have the right to such help, but in order to make ourselves a model for you to follow. [10]For even when we were with you, we gave you this rule: "If a man will not work, he shall not eat."

[11]We hear that some among you are idle. They are not busy; they are busybodies. [12]Such people we command and urge in the Lord Jesus Christ to settle down and earn the bread they eat. [13]And as for you, brothers, never tire of doing what is right.

[14]If anyone does not obey our instruction in this letter, take special note of him. Do not associate with him, in order that he may feel ashamed. [15]Yet do not regard him as an enemy, but warn him as a brother.

Prevenient Grace

2 THESSALONIANS 2:13–15

Sometimes we talk about making a decision for Jesus Christ as if our decision initiated God's presence in our lives. Here the author reminds the Thessalonians that God chose them for salvation and called them to the Lord Jesus Christ through Paul's preaching. Theologians speak of "prevenient" grace—God's gifts to us "coming before" we even thought or even knew to ask. God may have touched your life and drawn you through family devotions, a church school teacher or a Vacation Bible School program, a campfire sing-a-long, religious programming on television or Christian themes powerfully depicted in a movie, a Gideon Bible in a motel room, a friend whose example inspired you, or countless other ways.

Try making a list of different examples of prevenient grace in your life. Where can you see God going before you, drawing you nearer in ways that at the time you didn't recognize as God's grace at work in your life? Close by reading the list aloud and thanking God for each item.

Receiving God's Grace

2 THESSALONIANS 3:18

"We cannot escape the dangers, which abound in life, without the actual and continual help of God. Let us then pray to God for it continually. How can we pray to God without being with God? How can we be with God but in thinking of God often? And how can we often think of God, but by a holy habit, which we should form of it? . . . This is the best and easiest method I know; and as I use no other, I advise all the world to it."

—BROTHER LAWRENCE,
The Practice of the Presence of God

Final Greetings

¹⁶Now may the Lord of peace himself give you peace at all times and in every way. The Lord be with all of you.

¹⁷I, Paul, write this greeting in my own hand, which is the distinguishing mark in all my letters. This is how I write.

¹⁸The grace of our Lord Jesus Christ be with you all.

1 TIMOTHY

Guidelines for Godliness

KEY VERSE:

Watch your life and doctrine closely. Persevere in them, because if you do, you will save both yourself and your hearers.—1 Timothy 4:16

As the young pastor Timothy's mentor and friend, the apostle Paul writes to his "true son in the faith" with words of instruction and encouragement. Timothy is pastor of the Ephesian church, which is facing all the problems of a growing institution, not the least of which is keeping the church's love for Jesus Christ fresh and fervent (see Revelation 2:4). Timothy has to manage the church's internal affairs such as personnel, structure, worship and doctrinal struggles as well as to combat the continuing persecution and false teachings coming from outside and inside the church.

The book of 1 Timothy is primarily a call to godliness in the broadest sense. Paul summons the Ephesians to godliness characterized by right doctrine, orderly worship and holy relationships. He addresses the mission of the church, the qualifications of leaders and social concerns such as the care of widows.

To be godly is to imitate God in holiness; such a calling affects every part of our being, from our beliefs to our behavior, from our attitudes to our actions, and from our relationships to our worship. There isn't an element of human existence that isn't radically and profoundly altered by this call to Christian living that Paul refers to as godliness. Consider studying this book with a sheet of paper with the word "godliness" written at the top. Ask God to broaden your view of godliness and to remove the limits of how you might have previously defined godliness. Ask God to show you areas of your life that need to be anointed with new holiness.

> "As a good Christian should consider every place as holy because God is there, so he should look upon every part of his life as a matter of holiness because it is to be offered unto God."
>
> —WILLIAM LAW,
> *A Serious Call to a Devout and Holy Life*

Dynamic Hope

Paul calls Christ Jesus our "hope." The word "hope" (*elpis*) means something very different from "wishful thinking." This hope connotes absolute certainty. At the top of a sheet of paper write the words "Because of Jesus." Below it list all the "absolute certainties" you can count on because of Jesus Christ. What can you expect in this life? What certainties do you face in eternity? What is the difference between having this certain hope in a *person*—Jesus Christ—and having hope in a cause or a political agenda?

1 Paul, an apostle of Christ Jesus by the command of God our Savior and of Christ Jesus our hope,

²To Timothy my true son in the faith:

Grace, mercy and peace from God the Father and Christ Jesus our Lord.

Warning Against False Teachers of the Law

³As I urged you when I went into Macedonia, stay there in Ephesus so that you may command certain men not to teach false doctrines any longer ⁴nor to devote themselves to myths and endless genealogies. These promote controversies rather than God's work—which is by faith. ⁵The goal of this command is love, which comes from a pure heart and a good conscience and a sincere faith. ⁶Some have wandered away from these and turned to meaningless talk. ⁷They want to be teachers of the law, but they do not know what they are talking about or what they so confidently affirm.

⁸We know that the law is good if one uses it properly. ⁹We also know that law*ᵃ* is made not for the righteous but for lawbreakers and rebels, the ungodly and sinful, the unholy and irreligious; for those who kill their fathers or mothers, for murderers, ¹⁰for adulterers and perverts, for slave traders and liars and perjurers—and for whatever else is contrary to the sound doctrine ¹¹that conforms to the glorious gospel of the blessed God, which he entrusted to me.

The Lord's Grace to Paul

¹²I thank Christ Jesus our Lord, who has given me strength, that he considered me faithful, appointing me to his service. ¹³Even though I was once a blasphemer and a persecutor and a violent man, I was shown mercy because I acted in ignorance and unbelief. ¹⁴The grace of our Lord was poured out on me abundantly, along with the faith and love that are in Christ Jesus.

¹⁵Here is a trustworthy saying that deserves full acceptance: Christ Jesus came into the world to save sinners—of whom I am the worst. ¹⁶But for that very reason I was shown mercy so that in me, the worst of sinners, Christ Jesus might display his unlimited patience as an example for those who would believe on him and receive eternal life. ¹⁷Now to the King eternal, immortal, invisible, the only God, be honor and glory for ever and ever. Amen.

¹⁸Timothy, my son, I give you this instruction in keeping with the prophecies once made about you, so that by following them you may fight the good fight, ¹⁹holding on to faith and a good conscience. Some have rejected these and so have shipwrecked their faith. ²⁰Among them are Hymenaeus and Alexander, whom I have handed over to Satan to be taught not to blaspheme.

Instructions on Worship

2 I urge, then, first of all, that requests, prayers, intercession and thanksgiving be made for everyone— ²for kings and all those in authority, that we may live peaceful and quiet lives in all godliness and holiness. ³This is good, and pleases God our Savior, ⁴who wants all men to be

ᵃ 9 Or that the law

saved and to come to a knowledge of the truth. ⁵For there is one God and one mediator between God and men, the man Christ Jesus, ⁶who gave himself as a ransom for all men—the testimony given in its proper time. ⁷And for this purpose I was appointed a herald and an apostle—I am telling the truth, I am not lying—and a teacher of the true faith to the Gentiles.

⁸I want men everywhere to lift up holy hands in prayer, without anger or disputing.

⁹I also want women to dress modestly, with decency and propriety, not with braided hair or gold or pearls or expensive clothes, ¹⁰but with good deeds, appropriate for women who profess to worship God.

¹¹A woman should learn in quietness and full submission. ¹²I do not permit a woman to teach or to have authority over a man; she must be silent. ¹³For Adam was formed first, then Eve. ¹⁴And Adam was not the one deceived; it was the woman who was deceived and became a sinner. ¹⁵But women*a* will be saved*b* through childbearing—if they continue in faith, love and holiness with propriety.

Overseers and Deacons

3 Here is a trustworthy saying: If anyone sets his heart on being an overseer,*c* he desires a noble task. ²Now the overseer must be above reproach, the husband of but one wife, temperate, self-controlled, respectable, hospitable, able to teach, ³not given to drunkenness, not violent but gentle, not quarrelsome, not a lover of money. ⁴He must manage his own family well and see that his children obey him with proper respect. ⁵(If anyone does not know how to manage his own family, how can he take care of God's church?) ⁶He must not be a recent convert, or he may become conceited and fall under the same judgment as the devil. ⁷He must also have a good reputation with outsiders, so that he will not fall into disgrace and into the devil's trap.

⁸Deacons, likewise, are to be men worthy of respect, sincere, not indulging in much wine, and not pursuing dishonest gain. ⁹They must keep hold of the deep truths of the faith with a clear conscience. ¹⁰They must first be tested; and then if there is nothing against them, let them serve as deacons.

¹¹In the same way, their wives*d* are to be women worthy of respect, not malicious talkers but temperate and trustworthy in everything.

¹²A deacon must be the husband of but one wife and must manage his children and his household well. ¹³Those who have served well gain an excellent standing and great assurance in their faith in Christ Jesus.

¹⁴Although I hope to come to you soon, I am writing you these instructions so that, ¹⁵if I am delayed, you will know how people ought to conduct themselves in God's household, which is the church of the living God, the pillar and foundation of the truth. ¹⁶Beyond all question, the mystery of godliness is great:

> He*e* appeared in a body,*f*
> was vindicated by the Spirit,

Holy Hands

1 TIMOTHY 2:8

When Paul mentions "holy hands in prayer," many images might come to mind, but the two ideas Paul specifically mentions here are "without anger or disputing." Have you ever experienced extra difficulty in prayer while in the midst of a contentious relationship?

As you pray, look at your hands. Are they "holy hands"? Clench them into fists. What situations or people are making you angry? Ask God to take away your anger as you slowly relax and open your hands. What relationships need reconciliation or healing? Imagine the other person held in your hands as you lift him or her up to God. Ask for God's blessing on the relationship. Finally, spread your raised hands apart in praise and thanksgiving.

See Meeting God in Community

Taking Care of the Soul

1 TIMOTHY 4:11–16

Imagine that God gave you two plants to take care of, leaving you in charge of watering them, fertilizing them and making sure they get enough (but not too much) sun. In a way, Paul gives us this kind of challenge in verse 16. The two "plants" we are to watch over are our life and our doctrine. How can you create a favorable environment for both of these plants to grow? What essential elements do you provide for them? Write out a "gardening" plan for both your life and your doctrine.

was seen by angels,
was preached among the nations,
was believed on in the world,
was taken up in glory.

Instructions to Timothy

4 The Spirit clearly says that in later times some will abandon the faith and follow deceiving spirits and things taught by demons. ²Such teachings come through hypocritical liars, whose consciences have been seared as with a hot iron. ³They forbid people to marry and order them to abstain from certain foods, which God created to be received with thanksgiving by those who believe and who know the truth. ⁴For everything God created is good, and nothing is to be rejected if it is received with thanksgiving, ⁵because it is consecrated by the word of God and prayer.

⁶If you point these things out to the brothers, you will be a good minister of Christ Jesus, brought up in the truths of the faith and of the good teaching that you have followed. ⁷Have nothing to do with godless myths and old wives' tales; rather, train yourself to be godly. ⁸For physical training is of some value, but godliness has value for all things, holding promise for both the present life and the life to come.

⁹This is a trustworthy saying that deserves full acceptance ¹⁰(and for this we labor and strive), that we have put our hope in the living God, who is the Savior of all men, and especially of those who believe.

¹¹Command and teach these things. ¹²Don't let anyone look down on you because you are young, but set an example for the believers in speech, in life, in love, in faith and in purity. ¹³Until I come, devote yourself to the public reading of Scripture, to preaching and to teaching. ¹⁴Do not neglect your gift, which was given you through a prophetic message when the body of elders laid their hands on you.

¹⁵Be diligent in these matters; give yourself wholly to them, so that everyone may see your progress. ¹⁶Watch your life and doctrine closely. Persevere in them, because if you do, you will save both yourself and your hearers.

Advice About Widows, Elders and Slaves

5 Do not rebuke an older man harshly, but exhort him as if he were your father. Treat younger men as brothers, ²older women as mothers, and younger women as sisters, with absolute purity.

³Give proper recognition to those widows who are really in need. ⁴But if a widow has children or grandchildren, these should learn first of all to put their religion into practice by caring for their own family and so repaying their parents and grandparents, for this is pleasing to God. ⁵The widow who is really in need and left all alone puts her hope in God and continues night and day to pray and to ask God for help. ⁶But the widow who lives for pleasure is dead even while she lives. ⁷Give the people these instructions, too, so that no one may be open to blame. ⁸If anyone does not provide for his relatives, and especially for his immediate family, he has denied the faith and is worse than an unbeliever.

⁹No widow may be put on the list of widows unless she is over sixty, has been faithful to her husband,ᵃ ¹⁰and is well known for her good deeds, such as bringing up children, showing hospitality, washing the feet of the saints, helping those in trouble and devoting herself to all kinds of good deeds.

¹¹As for younger widows, do not put them on such a list. For when their sensual desires overcome their dedication to Christ, they want to marry. ¹²Thus they bring judgment on themselves, because they have broken their first pledge. ¹³Besides, they get into the habit of being idle and going about from house to house. And not only do they become idlers, but also gossips and busybodies, saying things they ought not to. ¹⁴So I counsel younger widows to marry, to have children, to manage their homes and to give the enemy no opportunity for slander. ¹⁵Some have in fact already turned away to follow Satan.

¹⁶If any woman who is a believer has widows in her family, she should help them and not let the church be burdened with them, so that the church can help those widows who are really in need.

¹⁷The elders who direct the affairs of the church well are worthy of double honor, especially those whose work is preaching and teaching. ¹⁸For the Scripture says, "Do not muzzle the ox while it is treading out the grain,"ᵇ and "The worker deserves his wages."ᶜ ¹⁹Do not entertain an accusation against an elder unless it is brought by two or three witnesses. ²⁰Those who sin are to be rebuked publicly, so that the others may take warning.

²¹I charge you, in the sight of God and Christ Jesus and the elect angels, to keep these instructions without partiality, and to do nothing out of favoritism.

²²Do not be hasty in the laying on of hands, and do not share in the sins of others. Keep yourself pure.

²³Stop drinking only water, and use a little wine because of your stomach and your frequent illnesses.

²⁴The sins of some men are obvious, reaching the place of judgment ahead of them; the sins of others trail behind them. ²⁵In the same way, good deeds are obvious, and even those that are not cannot be hidden.

6 All who are under the yoke of slavery should consider their masters worthy of full respect, so that God's name and our teaching may not be slandered. ²Those who have believing masters are not to show less respect for them because they are brothers. Instead, they are to serve them even better, because those who benefit from their service are believers, and dear to them. These are the things you are to teach and urge on them.

Love of Money

³If anyone teaches false doctrines and does not agree to the sound instruction of our Lord Jesus Christ and to godly teaching, ⁴he is conceited and understands nothing. He has an unhealthy interest in controversies and quarrels about words that result in envy, strife, malicious talk, evil suspicions ⁵and constant friction between men of corrupt mind, who have been robbed of the truth and who think that godliness is a means to financial gain.

⁶But godliness with contentment is great gain. ⁷For we

The Weight of Words

1 TIMOTHY 6:3-5

Throughout this letter, Paul addresses people who are fascinated with fanciful and false doctrines. Read through this list and try to discern any contemporary applications. What kinds of current discussions tend to do nothing but create controversy? What forms of debate lead to envy? Quarreling? Malicious talk? Evil suspicions? Constant friction? Now turn this around and imagine the kinds of conversation that build unity. Pray and think about ways in which your words can lead to encouragement instead of envy, reconciliation instead of quarreling, sincere appreciation instead of malicious talk, and expressions of confidence and support instead of evil suspicions. Ask God to allow you to turn at least one "controversial" conversation into a "unifying" one in the next twenty-four hours.

See Meeting God in Everyday Life

The Pursuit of Growth

1 TIMOTHY 6:11

Copy this verse down on a piece of paper (or commit it to memory), then go outside and start walking. Pick a point on the horizon and as you walk toward it, prayerfully consider what activities mentioned throughout this letter will help you to "pursue" righteousness and godliness. Start running (or at least pick up the pace) for just a short while. What is the significance of the sense of urgency Paul conveys (see also 1 Corinthians 9:24–25)? Once you reach your destination, turn around and walk back, prayerfully considering Paul's words about growing in endurance. Are your legs tired? What makes you spiritually tired? How can you get in better shape spiritually?

brought nothing into the world, and we can take nothing out of it. ⁸But if we have food and clothing, we will be content with that. ⁹People who want to get rich fall into temptation and a trap and into many foolish and harmful desires that plunge men into ruin and destruction. ¹⁰For the love of money is a root of all kinds of evil. Some people, eager for money, have wandered from the faith and pierced themselves with many griefs.

Paul's Charge to Timothy

¹¹But you, man of God, flee from all this, and pursue righteousness, godliness, faith, love, endurance and gentleness. ¹²Fight the good fight of the faith. Take hold of the eternal life to which you were called when you made your good confession in the presence of many witnesses. ¹³In the sight of God, who gives life to everything, and of Christ Jesus, who while testifying before Pontius Pilate made the good confession, I charge you ¹⁴to keep this command without spot or blame until the appearing of our Lord Jesus Christ, ¹⁵which God will bring about in his own time—God, the blessed and only Ruler, the King of kings and Lord of lords, ¹⁶who alone is immortal and who lives in unapproachable light, whom no one has seen or can see. To him be honor and might forever. Amen.

¹⁷Command those who are rich in this present world not to be arrogant nor to put their hope in wealth, which is so uncertain, but to put their hope in God, who richly provides us with everything for our enjoyment. ¹⁸Command them to do good, to be rich in good deeds, and to be generous and willing to share. ¹⁹In this way they will lay up treasure for themselves as a firm foundation for the coming age, so that they may take hold of the life that is truly life.

²⁰Timothy, guard what has been entrusted to your care. Turn away from godless chatter and the opposing ideas of what is falsely called knowledge, ²¹which some have professed and in so doing have wandered from the faith.

Grace be with you.

2 TIMOTHY
Faithfulness Under Pressure

KEY VERSE:

But you, keep your head in all situations, endure hardship, do the work of an evangelist, discharge all the duties of your ministry.—2 Timothy 4:5

Do you ever live through seasons in which the entire world seems bent on distracting you from God's calling? As you seek to serve God, are you hampered by pressures and opposition? If so, this letter will offer you profound encouragement. Whether your frustrations stem from the pressure of meeting many obligations, a feeling of weariness, or the experience of open opposition or ridicule, you will find empathy in Paul's and Timothy's experiences. Even as they face many of these same pressures, Paul urges Timothy to persevere and remain faithful in his ministry.

While most of the New Testament books are written to churches, this one is written to an individual. The situation in which Paul and Timothy find themselves is a veritable pressure cooker. Paul is in prison, the church is being persecuted, opposition is hot and fierce—even from those who call themselves Christians, and Timothy is trying to stay true to his work in the midst of doctrinal confusion and hardship. Paul's letter is a stirring call to Timothy to remain faithful under pressure, and its relevance has been proven in every generation.

Before you reflect on the specific teachings of this book, take a personal inventory of the challenges you have faced in serving God. What has made it most difficult for you to fulfill a calling that you believe God has given you? What is the biggest obstacle you currently face? Even as you confront your own struggles, prepare to be challenged and encouraged by Paul's words to his friend Timothy. Within these chapters you may find the keys to remaining faithful under pressure in your own life.

> "Trials are a further benefit to true religion because they not only manifest its truth but they also enhance its genuine beauty and attractiveness. True virtue is loveliest when it is oppressed. The divine excellency of real Christianity is best exhibited when it is under the greatest trials."
>
> —JONATHAN EDWARDS,
> *Treatise Concerning Religious Affections*

Guard the Truth

2 TIMOTHY 1:14

Picture yourself as a guard, like Timothy, given charge of protecting God's truth. Who, or what, are the enemies you need to watch out for? What might cause a guard to fail—weariness, lack of attention, carelessness, distractions? What arena would be the most probable scene of battle? Guards need proper equipment and good backup. What has God provided for you as you stand guard? What is the difference between guarding something against being corrupted or damaged and guarding something from being stolen? What is the particular challenge of guarding "truth" as opposed to guarding a person or physical object?

1 Paul, an apostle of Christ Jesus by the will of God, according to the promise of life that is in Christ Jesus,

²To Timothy, my dear son:

Grace, mercy and peace from God the Father and Christ Jesus our Lord.

Encouragement to Be Faithful

³I thank God, whom I serve, as my forefathers did, with a clear conscience, as night and day I constantly remember you in my prayers. ⁴Recalling your tears, I long to see you, so that I may be filled with joy. ⁵I have been reminded of your sincere faith, which first lived in your grandmother Lois and in your mother Eunice and, I am persuaded, now lives in you also. ⁶For this reason I remind you to fan into flame the gift of God, which is in you through the laying on of my hands. ⁷For God did not give us a spirit of timidity, but a spirit of power, of love and of self-discipline.

⁸So do not be ashamed to testify about our Lord, or ashamed of me his prisoner. But join with me in suffering for the gospel, by the power of God, ⁹who has saved us and called us to a holy life—not because of anything we have done but because of his own purpose and grace. This grace was given us in Christ Jesus before the beginning of time, ¹⁰but it has now been revealed through the appearing of our Savior, Christ Jesus, who has destroyed death and has brought life and immortality to light through the gospel. ¹¹And of this gospel I was appointed a herald and an apostle and a teacher. ¹²That is why I am suffering as I am. Yet I am not ashamed, because I know whom I have believed, and am convinced that he is able to guard what I have entrusted to him for that day.

¹³What you heard from me, keep as the pattern of sound teaching, with faith and love in Christ Jesus. ¹⁴Guard the good deposit that was entrusted to you—guard it with the help of the Holy Spirit who lives in us.

¹⁵You know that everyone in the province of Asia has deserted me, including Phygelus and Hermogenes.

¹⁶May the Lord show mercy to the household of Onesiphorus, because he often refreshed me and was not ashamed of my chains. ¹⁷On the contrary, when he was in Rome, he searched hard for me until he found me. ¹⁸May the Lord grant that he will find mercy from the Lord on that day! You know very well in how many ways he helped me in Ephesus.

2 You then, my son, be strong in the grace that is in Christ Jesus. ²And the things you have heard me say in the presence of many witnesses entrust to reliable men who will also be qualified to teach others. ³Endure hardship with us like a good soldier of Christ Jesus. ⁴No one serving as a soldier gets involved in civilian affairs—he wants to please his commanding officer. ⁵Similarly, if anyone competes as an athlete, he does not receive the victor's crown unless he competes according to the rules. ⁶The hardworking farmer should be the first to receive a share of the crops. ⁷Reflect on what I am saying, for the Lord will give you insight into all this.

⁸Remember Jesus Christ, raised from the dead, descended from David. This is my gospel, ⁹for which I am suffering even to the point of being chained like a criminal. But God's

word is not chained. [10]Therefore I endure everything for the sake of the elect, that they too may obtain the salvation that is in Christ Jesus, with eternal glory.

[11]Here is a trustworthy saying:

> If we died with him,
> we will also live with him;
> [12]if we endure,
> we will also reign with him.
> If we disown him,
> he will also disown us;
> [13]if we are faithless,
> he will remain faithful,
> for he cannot disown himself.

A Workman Approved by God

[14]Keep reminding them of these things. Warn them before God against quarreling about words; it is of no value, and only ruins those who listen. [15]Do your best to present yourself to God as one approved, a workman who does not need to be ashamed and who correctly handles the word of truth. [16]Avoid godless chatter, because those who indulge in it will become more and more ungodly. [17]Their teaching will spread like gangrene. Among them are Hymenaeus and Philetus, [18]who have wandered away from the truth. They say that the resurrection has already taken place, and they destroy the faith of some. [19]Nevertheless, God's solid foundation stands firm, sealed with this inscription: "The Lord knows those who are his,"[a] and, "Everyone who confesses the name of the Lord must turn away from wickedness."

[20]In a large house there are articles not only of gold and silver, but also of wood and clay; some are for noble purposes and some for ignoble. [21]If a man cleanses himself from the latter, he will be an instrument for noble purposes, made holy, useful to the Master and prepared to do any good work.

[22]Flee the evil desires of youth, and pursue righteousness, faith, love and peace, along with those who call on the Lord out of a pure heart. [23]Don't have anything to do with foolish and stupid arguments, because you know they produce quarrels. [24]And the Lord's servant must not quarrel; instead, he must be kind to everyone, able to teach, not resentful. [25]Those who oppose him he must gently instruct, in the hope that God will grant them repentance leading them to a knowledge of the truth, [26]and that they will come to their senses and escape from the trap of the devil, who has taken them captive to do his will.

Godlessness in the Last Days

3 But mark this: There will be terrible times in the last days. [2]People will be lovers of themselves, lovers of money, boastful, proud, abusive, disobedient to their parents, ungrateful, unholy, [3]without love, unforgiving, slanderous, without self-control, brutal, not lovers of the good, [4]treacherous, rash, conceited, lovers of pleasure rather than lovers of God— [5]having a form of godliness but denying its power. Have nothing to do with them.

[6]They are the kind who worm their way into homes and

Ripe or Rotting?

2 TIMOTHY 3:13–15

Paul contrasts two images in these verses. The first image is of evil men and impostors, who go from "bad to worse"; the second image is of Timothy, who continues to grow in keeping with the good start he received, becoming mature.

Imagine two pieces of fruit—one that has a rotten spot that is getting ever worse, and the other that is wholesome, firm and just beginning to ripen. What is there in your spiritual life that resembles the rotten fruit? What can be done to keep the rot from spreading? What is like the ripening fruit? What will keep it growing toward full maturity? Ask God for whatever help you need to prevent rot and encourage growth.

gain control over weak-willed women, who are loaded down with sins and are swayed by all kinds of evil desires, [7]always learning but never able to acknowledge the truth. [8]Just as Jannes and Jambres opposed Moses, so also these men oppose the truth—men of depraved minds, who, as far as the faith is concerned, are rejected. [9]But they will not get very far because, as in the case of those men, their folly will be clear to everyone.

Paul's Charge to Timothy

[10]You, however, know all about my teaching, my way of life, my purpose, faith, patience, love, endurance, [11]persecutions, sufferings—what kinds of things happened to me in Antioch, Iconium and Lystra, the persecutions I endured. Yet the Lord rescued me from all of them. [12]In fact, everyone who wants to live a godly life in Christ Jesus will be persecuted, [13]while evil men and impostors will go from bad to worse, deceiving and being deceived. [14]But as for you, continue in what you have learned and have become convinced of, because you know those from whom you learned it, [15]and how from infancy you have known the holy Scriptures, which are able to make you wise for salvation through faith in Christ Jesus. [16]All Scripture is God-breathed and is useful for teaching, rebuking, correcting and training in righteousness, [17]so that the man of God may be thoroughly equipped for every good work.

4 In the presence of God and of Christ Jesus, who will judge the living and the dead, and in view of his appearing and his kingdom, I give you this charge: [2]Preach the Word; be prepared in season and out of season; correct, rebuke and encourage—with great patience and careful instruction. [3]For the time will come when men will not put up with sound doctrine. Instead, to suit their own desires, they will gather around them a great number of teachers to say what their itching ears want to hear. [4]They will turn their ears away from the truth and turn aside to myths. [5]But you, keep your head in all situations, endure hardship, do the work of an evangelist, discharge all the duties of your ministry.

[6]For I am already being poured out like a drink offering, and the time has come for my departure. [7]I have fought the good fight, I have finished the race, I have kept the faith. [8]Now there is in store for me the crown of righteousness, which the Lord, the righteous Judge, will award to me on that day—and not only to me, but also to all who have longed for his appearing.

Personal Remarks

[9]Do your best to come to me quickly, [10]for Demas, because he loved this world, has deserted me and has gone to Thessalonica. Crescens has gone to Galatia, and Titus to Dalmatia. [11]Only Luke is with me. Get Mark and bring him with you, because he is helpful to me in my ministry. [12]I sent Tychicus to Ephesus. [13]When you come, bring the cloak that I left with Carpus at Troas, and my scrolls, especially the parchments.

[14]Alexander the metalworker did me a great deal of harm. The Lord will repay him for what he has done. [15]You too should be on your guard against him, because he strongly opposed our message.

[16]At my first defense, no one came to my support, but everyone deserted me. May it not be held against them. [17]But the Lord stood at my side and gave me strength, so that through me the message might be fully proclaimed and all the Gentiles might hear it. And I was delivered from the lion's mouth. [18]The Lord will rescue me from every evil attack and will bring me safely to his heavenly kingdom. To him be glory for ever and ever. Amen.

Final Greetings

[19]Greet Priscilla[a] and Aquila and the household of Onesiphorus. [20]Erastus stayed in Corinth, and I left Trophimus sick in Miletus. [21]Do your best to get here before winter. Eubulus greets you, and so do Pudens, Linus, Claudia and all the brothers.

[22]The Lord be with your spirit. Grace be with you.

Friends

2 TIMOTHY 4:19–21

In his pressure-packed pursuit to plant churches, live a holy life and serve God, Paul clearly remains a very relational person. At the end of this letter, Paul affectionately greets several friends, companions and fellow believers—a refreshing end to a somewhat somber letter. If you were writing a letter back to a member of your church, what friends might you inquire about? To whom would you want your greetings passed along? How do relationships encourage us in our pursuit of God? What role do relationships play in dealing with pressure? How might you begin to build additional "spiritual friendships"? (See Hebrews 10:24–25.)

See Meeting God in Community

WAYS of MEETING GOD

Meeting God in Everyday Life

"We live lives of little things," someone once said. We are occupied most often with the details of ordinary life. Driving to the office or factory, putting supper on the table, taking feverish kids to the doctor—these are the things that fill our hours. When we meet God, that encounter often takes place in and through everyday circumstances. Growing spiritually will mean "living to God on common occasions," as Horace Bushnell expressed it. Inevitably we cultivate our spiritual lives not just in quiet solitude but in the activity of everyday life. We realize that God speaks to us not just in sky-rending revelations but also in the intimacy of quiet conversation with our spouse, the freshness of a child's spontaneous observation, the warmth of a bubbling pot of chili, the comfort of a family-night ritual.

> The Bible leaves no doubt that God works through the inner and outer details of our everyday lives. And if God is present in such moments, we cannot let them slide into oblivion.

How do we meet God in the midst of our stressful, busy lives? How do we recognize the signs that, in Avery Brooke's wonderful phrase, lie "hidden in plain sight"?

Two intentions will help us:

Remember God's Deeds. The Bible leaves no doubt that God works through the inner and outer details of our everyday lives. And if God is present in such moments, we cannot let them slide into oblivion: "Watch yourselves closely so that you do not forget the things your eyes have seen or let them slip from your heart as long as you live" (Deuteronomy 4:9). The psalmist, recalling God's careful involvement in Israel's history, vowed, "I will remember the deeds of the LORD; yes, I will remember your miracles of long ago" (Psalm 77:11).

The act of remembering helped the people of Israel to keep events from the past vital in the present. Just as we pull out a photo album on a rainy day in order

to recall the significant moments of our lives—to review the snapshots of gradua-
tions and confirmations, visits and vacations—so God wanted the people of Israel
to keep their holy history vividly present in their minds. And they were to remember God's good deeds corporately, as a people. Recollection was a community
event. As they gathered in various ways, the people recalled aloud the moments
that had given them identity as people of God—when God led them to freedom
from Egyptian bondage, gave them commandments and instruction, gave them
life. "Remember the former things, those of long ago," Isaiah enjoined the people,
speaking on God's behalf (Isaiah 46:9). The Israelites' very identity depended on
the God who had acted in their history. To forget God's acts would have meant to
forget that God had called and chosen them.

God's call to remember carried over into New Testament times. Jesus urged his
followers to recall God's work of redemption in his own life, death and resurrection. "Do this in remembrance of me," Jesus said at the Last Supper (Luke 22:19).
Communion, in which we partake of the bread and the cup, is a supreme act of remembering. We also meet God through recalling what he has done for us personally. With David the psalmist we make certain that we "forget not all [God's]
benefits" in our daily lives (Psalm 103:2). To jog his readers' memories, David then
recited specific benefits. He was not indulging in nostalgia but was gleaning from
the past all that the Lord did and said. When we remember the Lord's deeds, we
likewise keep in the forefront of our minds what God has already shown us; we
live in continuity with the events that have shaped us. We recall the blessings of
last year and the hardships of last week, remembering how God walked beside us
and sometimes carried us in our moments of weakness and woundedness.

Conscious recollection requires discipline. In our live-for-the-moment culture, we
may find the act of remembering more difficult than ancient people did. We are
prone to become distracted by the details of the moment. We forget to "read life
backwards." But memory can be a powerful resource for keeping our spiritual perspective alive.

One practical aid to this holy remembering is keeping a journal. Many find it
helpful to jot down prayers, record insights from Bible readings or put on paper the
events that seem to be leading somewhere—events that have left an impression on
them. Keeping a journal can be done in a way that meets your own needs and
preferences. Journaling need not be an elaborate affair or something you slavishly
perform every day. It can be as simple as you wish and as occasional as meets
your need. If you have never used a journal, try taking a blank bound book, a spiral notebook or a binder full of paper—and then simply write. Make your writing
an act of sanctified listening. When you write down your thoughts and ideas and
emotions, they take definition and shape. You may find that as you write, you
begin to untangle your confusion about what you are hearing from God. You may

hear God speaking in ways in which you may not have been attentive otherwise.

Do not allow yourself to relegate to a fuzzy memory the significant things going on within and around you. "The simplest ink," says an old Chinese proverb, "is more reliable than the finest mind." Writing becomes a way to extract a deeper meaning from what has happened to you. It becomes an act of remembering.

Leaf back through your journal pages every few weeks. Notice how God's purposes seem to be emerging in what has happened—and in what hasn't happened. Thank God for prayers that have been answered. Continue to lift up to God themes that emerge from what you've written, themes that reveal your heart's desires. And watch for a greater sense of personal direction. Keeping a journal, wrote Ronald Klug, is "like walking into a messy room—toys and clothes and books piled around—and slowly picking things up and putting them in their right places again. The room 'feels good' and I can go on living there. In a similar way, my journal helps me sort out things in my life and restore some internal order."

We can practice the art of remembering when we meet with family and friends. Conversations at family reunions might move beyond talk of sports or vacations to reflections about how God has proven himself faithful in our family's past and present stories. And when we go to church, worship can be an exercise in remembering. Spiritual growth groups, church school classes—any gathering of believers—can be an occasion to track God's actions in our midst. We recall all the ways God has been faithful. We "testify." And as we do, we find ourselves reminded of who God is through what he has done.

O pen-eyed reflection allows us to see God's hand at work or grasp insights we might otherwise have been too busy to notice.

Reflect on God's Deeds. Reflection—alert awareness of what is happening now—returns us to the present moment. Open-eyed reflection allows us to see God's hand at work or grasp insights we might otherwise have been too busy to notice. The Bible sometimes uses the word "meditation" for this kind of thoughtful reflection. We are not talking about the meditation of Eastern religions, nor a privatized, overly individualistic quest for religious experience. Biblical meditation is always God-centered. It often focuses on God's Word revealed in Scripture. And it often has to do with God's activity. "I will meditate on your wonderful works," David exults in Psalm 145:5. Just three verses earlier he had vowed, "Every day I will praise you." An awareness of what God is doing and the impulse to praise God go hand-in-hand.

Events of daily life therefore belong in our daily prayers. In the Lord's Prayer

Jesus directed us to pray for God's will to be done on earth, not just in heaven—which means in our everyday lives as well. Knowing how much daily matters affect us, Jesus even encouraged his followers to pray for "daily bread"—the everyday sustenance that keeps our physical bodies going. The likelihood that Jesus worked as a carpenter during his early adult years implies that God, through Jesus Christ's incarnation, has for all time graced daily work. And God notices when "bad" things happen and operates through events so that, as the apostle Paul wrote, "we know that in all things God works for the good of those who love him" (Romans 8:28). All the realities of life, then, constitute the grist for our conversations with God.

As we pray about the things that happen to us from moment to moment, we will begin to cultivate a spiritual alertness. Jean-Pierre de Caussade wrote of "the sacrament of the present moment." He meant that the very place where we are, the very things that we do, can mediate God's presence. Writing of Mary and Joseph, Jesus' parents, de Caussade asks, "What do they discern beneath the seemingly everyday events which occupy them? What is seen is similar to what happens to the rest of [hu]mankind. But what is unseen, that which faith discovers and unravels, is nothing less than God fulfilling his mighty purpose . . . God reveals himself to the humble in small things."

This reflection can take place in the workplace, where many of us spend much of our time. Martin Luther, one of the prime figures of the Protestant Reformation, argued that not just priest or nun, but also milkmaid or blacksmith, could become deeply conscious of God's presence. This can happen in our family times and during our leisure times. Thomas Kelly writes, "a life of little whispered words of adoration, of praise, of prayer, of worship can be breathed all through the day."

Staying alert to God's presence may be as simple as pausing to acknowledge that God is near. It may mean taking a few moments to pray during a lunch hour or coffee break. It may mean occasionally looking out the window to drink in the beauty of God's creation or really paying attention to the people with whom we live. And it certainly means allowing everyday blessings—a sunset, a smile from a friend—to remind us of God and point us back to him in gratitude.

See Page 164 for the first Ways of Meeting God *article.*

TITUS
Keeping Your Focus

KEY VERSE:
The reason I left you in Crete was that you might straighten out what was left unfinished and appoint elders in every town, as I directed you.—Titus 1:5

"I earnestly beseech you all in the name of God, and for the sake of your people's souls, that you do not do your ministry carelessly and superficially. Do it vigorously and with all your might. Make it your great and serious business . . ."
—RICHARD BAXTER,
The Reformed Pastor

Have you ever heard of the phrase "medical triage"? It refers to the practice of responding to natural or human disasters. When the injured are so many and the physicians are so few, doctors and nurses must set priorities and work systematically; otherwise they'd be overwhelmed and the situation would take much longer to bring under control.

On a spiritual level, this was the challenge Titus faced. He is left on the Mediterranean island of Crete to supervise a church planted among a particularly unruly people. The people of Crete were renowned for their malicious savagery and unrestrained passions. The idiom "to play the Cretan" meant to be a liar. Even Epimenides, one of Crete's own philosophers, chastised his homeland's moral character. These are the issues Paul takes up with Titus. By giving concrete advice in a clear framework, Paul seems to be saying, "Don't be overwhelmed, stay focused, appoint qualified elders, challenge false teaching, pass on pure doctrine and don't forget the importance of good deeds."

In this letter Paul encapsulates the heart of true Christianity. Titus is overwhelmed, so Paul focuses only on what was most important. The challenge Titus faced long ago can result in something good for us today, for in this letter we are presented with the bedrock essence of our faith. If you were left alone on an island to nurture a Christian church that had been planted in this culture, what would you emphasize? How would you bring order? What would be your primary message?

1 Paul, a servant of God and an apostle of Jesus Christ for the faith of God's elect and the knowledge of the truth that leads to godliness— ²a faith and knowledge resting on the hope of eternal life, which God, who does not lie, promised before the beginning of time, ³and at his appointed season he brought his word to light through the preaching entrusted to me by the command of God our Savior,

⁴To Titus, my true son in our common faith:

Grace and peace from God the Father and Christ Jesus our Savior.

Titus's Task on Crete

⁵The reason I left you in Crete was that you might straighten out what was left unfinished and appoint*a* elders in every town, as I directed you. ⁶An elder must be blameless, the husband of but one wife, a man whose children believe and are not open to the charge of being wild and disobedient. ⁷Since an overseer*b* is entrusted with God's work, he must be blameless—not overbearing, not quick-tempered, not given to drunkenness, not violent, not pursuing dishonest gain. ⁸Rather he must be hospitable, one who loves what is good, who is self-controlled, upright, holy and disciplined. ⁹He must hold firmly to the trustworthy message as it has been taught, so that he can encourage others by sound doctrine and refute those who oppose it.

¹⁰For there are many rebellious people, mere talkers and deceivers, especially those of the circumcision group. ¹¹They must be silenced, because they are ruining whole households by teaching things they ought not to teach—and that for the sake of dishonest gain. ¹²Even one of their own prophets has said, "Cretans are always liars, evil brutes, lazy gluttons." ¹³This testimony is true. Therefore, rebuke them sharply, so that they will be sound in the faith ¹⁴and will pay no attention to Jewish myths or to the commands of those who reject the truth. ¹⁵To the pure, all things are pure, but to those who are corrupted and do not believe, nothing is pure. In fact, both their minds and consciences are corrupted. ¹⁶They claim to know God, but by their actions they deny him. They are detestable, disobedient and unfit for doing anything good.

What Must Be Taught to Various Groups

2 You must teach what is in accord with sound doctrine. ²Teach the older men to be temperate, worthy of respect, self-controlled, and sound in faith, in love and in endurance.

³Likewise, teach the older women to be reverent in the way they live, not to be slanderers or addicted to much wine, but to teach what is good. ⁴Then they can train the younger women to love their husbands and children, ⁵to be self-controlled and pure, to be busy at home, to be kind, and to be subject to their husbands, so that no one will malign the word of God.

⁶Similarly, encourage the young men to be self-controlled. ⁷In everything set them an example by doing what is good. In your teaching show integrity, seriousness ⁸and

---

The Power of a Pure Source

TITUS 1:15

Take out some food coloring and a clear drinking glass. Fill the glass with water; then add a few drops of food coloring. Notice how the small stain begins to spread. With a little stirring, it colors all the water. Imagine trying to separate the dye from the water. Sounds impossible, doesn't it?

Now hold the glass under a running faucet. Watch as eventually the clear, pure water completely replaces the dyed water in the glass. What might you infer about your spiritual life from this experiment? What are the stains that have colored your life? Anger, fear, despair, self-righteousness, addictions? Ask Jesus to give you the living water of the Spirit to blot out the stains and cleanse you completely.

---

a 5 Or ordain   b 7 Traditionally bishop

Changed Saints

"Even true Christians still have remnants of a contrary spirit and may even be guilty of behavior offensive to such a spirit. But this I affirm, there are no true Christians who live in the prevailing power of such a spirit so that it becomes truly their character. The Scripture speaks of no real Christians who have an ugly, selfish, angry, and contentious spirit. Nothing can be more contradictory than a morose, hard, closed, and spiteful Christian. [While] allowances must be made for our natural human temperament . . . we see that in the early church converts were remarkably changed."

—JONATHAN EDWARDS, *Treatise Concerning Religious Affections*

soundness of speech that cannot be condemned, so that those who oppose you may be ashamed because they have nothing bad to say about us.

⁹Teach slaves to be subject to their masters in everything, to try to please them, not to talk back to them, ¹⁰and not to steal from them, but to show that they can be fully trusted, so that in every way they will make the teaching about God our Savior attractive.

¹¹For the grace of God that brings salvation has appeared to all men. ¹²It teaches us to say "No" to ungodliness and worldly passions, and to live self-controlled, upright and godly lives in this present age, ¹³while we wait for the blessed hope—the glorious appearing of our great God and Savior, Jesus Christ, ¹⁴who gave himself for us to redeem us from all wickedness and to purify for himself a people that are his very own, eager to do what is good.

¹⁵These, then, are the things you should teach. Encourage and rebuke with all authority. Do not let anyone despise you.

Doing What Is Good

3 Remind the people to be subject to rulers and authorities, to be obedient, to be ready to do whatever is good, ²to slander no one, to be peaceable and considerate, and to show true humility toward all men.

³At one time we too were foolish, disobedient, deceived and enslaved by all kinds of passions and pleasures. We lived in malice and envy, being hated and hating one another. ⁴But when the kindness and love of God our Savior appeared, ⁵he saved us, not because of righteous things we had done, but because of his mercy. He saved us through the washing of rebirth and renewal by the Holy Spirit, ⁶whom he poured out on us generously through Jesus Christ our Savior, ⁷so that, having been justified by his grace, we might become heirs having the hope of eternal life. ⁸This is a trustworthy saying. And I want you to stress these things, so that those who have trusted in God may be careful to devote themselves to doing what is good. These things are excellent and profitable for everyone.

⁹But avoid foolish controversies and genealogies and arguments and quarrels about the law, because these are unprofitable and useless. ¹⁰Warn a divisive person once, and then warn him a second time. After that, have nothing to do with him. ¹¹You may be sure that such a man is warped and sinful; he is self-condemned.

Final Remarks

¹²As soon as I send Artemas or Tychicus to you, do your best to come to me at Nicopolis, because I have decided to winter there. ¹³Do everything you can to help Zenas the lawyer and Apollos on their way and see that they have everything they need. ¹⁴Our people must learn to devote themselves to doing what is good, in order that they may provide for daily necessities and not live unproductive lives.

¹⁵Everyone with me sends you greetings. Greet those who love us in the faith.

Grace be with you all.

PHILEMON
A Plea for Reconciliation

KEY VERSE:

So if you consider me a partner, welcome him as you would welcome me.—Philemon 17

This brief letter leads us into the middle of a difficult situation in the early church, one with parallels to our time. Philemon was a first-century Christian living in Asia Minor. His slave Onesimus escaped and met the imprisoned apostle Paul, who shared the gospel with him. Then Paul wrote this gracious and respectful letter encouraging Philemon to take back Onesimus—"no longer as a slave, but . . . as a dear brother" (v.16).

Consider Philemon's options. Should he free Onesimus and risk total chaos among the other slaves, who might fake conversions to win their freedom? Should he punish Onesimus for running away? Should he return Onesimus to Paul? Or should he do what Paul suggests—welcome him home as a brother in Christ Jesus?

Welcoming people into our church communities after they have a change of heart can be a problem for us. If they have hurt us in the past, we may want to offer only the cold heart and closed fist of judgment. We may feel little eagerness to remove the stigma associated with their former reputations. After all, what will everyone else think if it looks like we are too easy on them?

But Paul takes a different approach by regarding other Christians as family members. Philemon is twice addressed as "brother." Apphia is a "sister." Because Onesimus is now a Christian, he, too, must be called "brother." The apostle Paul encourages Philemon to do the hard thing—the right thing. His letter asks us to do the same in the difficult relationships we may face in our own churches.

> "We are to be gospel people. We are not to be our own law; we are not to be the centers of our own universe; we are not to be unaware, unconcerned, unlistening to all the others. We are to be the formers of the human community, and we are to be formed by it as well. That is the function of authority . . . Authority is more than the preservation of law or the maintenance of order. Authority is the call to growth."
>
> —JOAN CHITTISTER, O.S.B.,
> *Wisdom Distilled from the Daily:*
> *Living the Rule of St. Benedict Today*

Asking a Favor

PHILEMON 13–14

Paul writes to request a favor of a friend. He could use his authority to force Philemon to comply, but he wants Philemon to make the choice freely.

Paul's actions give us something to wonder about. How do we seek to get our way? Do we simply ask, or do we use authority, guilt or other forms of manipulation? You might ask those around you to help assess your approach.

It takes real faith—in others and in God—to state your case and then trust that whatever happens will be okay. Are you involved in urging an individual or group to make a particular decision? Ask God to give you the wisdom to present your opinion well and the courage to allow others the freedom to decide for themselves.

See Meeting God in Community

[1] Paul, a prisoner of Christ Jesus, and Timothy our brother,

To Philemon our dear friend and fellow worker, [2] to Apphia our sister, to Archippus our fellow soldier and to the church that meets in your home:

[3] Grace to you and peace from God our Father and the Lord Jesus Christ.

Thanksgiving and Prayer

[4] I always thank my God as I remember you in my prayers, [5] because I hear about your faith in the Lord Jesus and your love for all the saints. [6] I pray that you may be active in sharing your faith, so that you will have a full understanding of every good thing we have in Christ. [7] Your love has given me great joy and encouragement, because you, brother, have refreshed the hearts of the saints.

Paul's Plea for Onesimus

[8] Therefore, although in Christ I could be bold and order you to do what you ought to do, [9] yet I appeal to you on the basis of love. I then, as Paul—an old man and now also a prisoner of Christ Jesus— [10] I appeal to you for my son Onesimus,[a] who became my son while I was in chains. [11] Formerly he was useless to you, but now he has become useful both to you and to me.

[12] I am sending him—who is my very heart—back to you. [13] I would have liked to keep him with me so that he could take your place in helping me while I am in chains for the gospel. [14] But I did not want to do anything without your consent, so that any favor you do will be spontaneous and not forced. [15] Perhaps the reason he was separated from you for a little while was that you might have him back for good— [16] no longer as a slave, but better than a slave, as a dear brother. He is very dear to me but even dearer to you, both as a man and as a brother in the Lord.

[17] So if you consider me a partner, welcome him as you would welcome me. [18] If he has done you any wrong or owes you anything, charge it to me. [19] I, Paul, am writing this with my own hand. I will pay it back—not to mention that you owe me your very self. [20] I do wish, brother, that I may have some benefit from you in the Lord; refresh my heart in Christ. [21] Confident of your obedience, I write to you, knowing that you will do even more than I ask.

[22] And one thing more: Prepare a guest room for me, because I hope to be restored to you in answer to your prayers.

[23] Epaphras, my fellow prisoner in Christ Jesus, sends you greetings. [24] And so do Mark, Aristarchus, Demas and Luke, my fellow workers.

[25] The grace of the Lord Jesus Christ be with your spirit.

a 10 Onesimus means useful.

HEBREWS

A New and Better Way

KEY VERSE:

For this reason Christ is the mediator of a new covenant, that those who are called may receive the promised eternal inheritance—now that he has died as a ransom to set them free from the sins committed under the first covenant.—Hebrews 9:15

Some people think that, in religious matters, tradition is all-important. Some, on the other hand, will have nothing to do with tradition; they forever want to be on the "cutting edge." Ideally, though, the best of the new is that which grows from and builds on the depth and wisdom of the older traditions.

For the writer of Hebrews, the new covenant of Jesus Christ represented the fullness and completion of the revelation of God's love for humanity—the revelation God began with the old covenant. In fact the Old Testament itself pointed to the unfolding of the new covenant of love in Jesus Christ—a new and superior way that would supersede the old.

As you read and meditate on these pages of Scripture, notice how often they refer to Jesus' ministry as "superior to" or "better" than the ministry of the old covenant. This book is about faith—God's faithfulness to us in giving us his Son, "the radiance of God's glory and the exact representation of his being" (1:3), and our faithful response to "fix our eyes on Jesus" (12:2). Open up any areas in your life in which you need to renew your trust and dependence on the promises of God and the provisions of Jesus Christ through the Holy Spirit.

> "Our faith in Jesus is most real. We believe in those dear wounds of His as we believe in nothing else; there is no fact so sure to us as that He was slain, and He has redeemed us to God by His blood. We believe in the brightness of His glory; for nothing seems to us so necessarily true as that He who was obedient unto death should, as His due reward, be crowned with glory and honour."
>
> —CHARLES H. SPURGEON,
> *An All Around Ministry*

The Reflection of God's Glory

HEBREWS 1:1–4

Jesus Christ is the Son of God! Consider what that means to God. Then consider what that means to you. Notice what God has done through Jesus (spoken, created, sustained and saved). List some of the ways you have experienced this "superior" ministry of Jesus Christ in your life.

After reading and pondering this passage, close your eyes and imagine how you would depict Jesus through painting, sculpture, music or poetry based on this Scripture. What characteristics of Jesus would you try to emphasize? You might want to create the work of art you have imagined.

See Meeting God in Scripture

The Son Superior to Angels

1 In the past God spoke to our forefathers through the prophets at many times and in various ways, ²but in these last days he has spoken to us by his Son, whom he appointed heir of all things, and through whom he made the universe. ³The Son is the radiance of God's glory and the exact representation of his being, sustaining all things by his powerful word. After he had provided purification for sins, he sat down at the right hand of the Majesty in heaven. ⁴So he became as much superior to the angels as the name he has inherited is superior to theirs.

⁵For to which of the angels did God ever say,

> "You are my Son;
> today I have become your Father*ᵃ*"*ᵇ*?

Or again,

> "I will be his Father,
> and he will be my Son"*ᶜ*?

⁶And again, when God brings his firstborn into the world, he says,

> "Let all God's angels worship him."*ᵈ*

⁷In speaking of the angels he says,

> "He makes his angels winds,
> his servants flames of fire."*ᵉ*

⁸But about the Son he says,

> "Your throne, O God, will last for ever and ever,
> and righteousness will be the scepter of your kingdom.
> ⁹You have loved righteousness and hated wickedness;
> therefore God, your God, has set you above your companions
> by anointing you with the oil of joy."*ᶠ*

¹⁰He also says,

> "In the beginning, O Lord, you laid the foundations of the earth,
> and the heavens are the work of your hands.
> ¹¹They will perish, but you remain;
> they will all wear out like a garment.
> ¹²You will roll them up like a robe;
> like a garment they will be changed.
> But you remain the same,
> and your years will never end."*ᵍ*

¹³To which of the angels did God ever say,

> "Sit at my right hand
> until I make your enemies
> a footstool for your feet"*ʰ*?

¹⁴Are not all angels ministering spirits sent to serve those who will inherit salvation?

ᵃ5 Or *have begotten you*   ᵇ5 Psalm 2:7   ᶜ5 2 Samuel 7:14; 1 Chron. 17:13   ᵈ6 Deut. 32:43 (see Dead Sea Scrolls and Septuagint)   ᵉ7 Psalm 104:4   ᶠ9 Psalm 45:6,7   ᵍ12 Psalm 102:25–27   ʰ13 Psalm 110:1

Warning to Pay Attention

2 We must pay more careful attention, therefore, to what we have heard, so that we do not drift away. ²For if the message spoken by angels was binding, and every violation and disobedience received its just punishment, ³how shall we escape if we ignore such a great salvation? This salvation, which was first announced by the Lord, was confirmed to us by those who heard him. ⁴God also testified to it by signs, wonders and various miracles, and gifts of the Holy Spirit distributed according to his will.

Jesus Made Like His Brothers

⁵It is not to angels that he has subjected the world to come, about which we are speaking. ⁶But there is a place where someone has testified:

> "What is man that you are mindful of him,
>   the son of man that you care for him?
> ⁷You made him a little[a] lower than the angels;
>   you crowned him with glory and honor
> ⁸   and put everything under his feet."[b]

In putting everything under him, God left nothing that is not subject to him. Yet at present we do not see everything subject to him. ⁹But we see Jesus, who was made a little lower than the angels, now crowned with glory and honor because he suffered death, so that by the grace of God he might taste death for everyone.

¹⁰In bringing many sons to glory, it was fitting that God, for whom and through whom everything exists, should make the author of their salvation perfect through suffering. ¹¹Both the one who makes men holy and those who are made holy are of the same family. So Jesus is not ashamed to call them brothers. ¹²He says,

> "I will declare your name to my brothers;
>   in the presence of the congregation I will sing
>   your praises."[c]

¹³And again,

> "I will put my trust in him."[d]

And again he says,

> "Here am I, and the children God has given me."[e]

¹⁴Since the children have flesh and blood, he too shared in their humanity so that by his death he might destroy him who holds the power of death—that is, the devil—¹⁵and free those who all their lives were held in slavery by their fear of death. ¹⁶For surely it is not angels he helps, but Abraham's descendants. ¹⁷For this reason he had to be made like his brothers in every way, in order that he might become a merciful and faithful high priest in service to God, and that he might make atonement for[f] the sins of the people. ¹⁸Because he himself suffered when he was tempted, he is able to help those who are being tempted.

Freedom From Fear

HEBREWS 2:14–18

Life can be pretty scary! And the powers of darkness delight in shifting our focus from Jesus to our fears and problems. But listen to the good news: "Because he himself suffered when he was tempted, he is able to help those who are being tempted."

What are your greatest fears? In what ways do you feel enslaved by your fears? How do you feel about the process of aging and the reality that you (and all your loved ones) will someday die? Picture a situation in which you feel afraid. Invite Jesus to sit beside you. Slowly repeat verse 18. Memorize it and recall it whenever you feel that fear is taking control of your mind or emotions.

See *Meeting God in Scripture*

---

a 7 Or *him for a little while*; also in verse 9   *b 8* Psalm 8:4–6
c 12 Psalm 22:22   *d 13* Isaiah 8:17   *e 13* Isaiah 8:18   *f 17* Or *and that he might turn aside God's wrath, taking away*

Don't Be Disqualified!

HEBREWS 3:12–14

How sad to read the letters DNF ("did not finish") behind the name of an athlete for whatever the reason—a sprain, exhaustion, violation of a rule, or an equipment problem. It's sad, too, when we Christians don't finish "the race marked out for us" (see 12:1). One of our greatest spiritual challenges is to protect our hearts from becoming hardened and to stay receptive to God's action in our lives.

Take some time to gently examine your life. Are there any habits that draw you away from God? What helps you to draw nearer to Jesus Christ and deepen your relationship with him? Who has been your cheerleader—one who has encouraged you to be faithful? Conclude by renewing your commitment to God through a tangible act of dedication.

See Meeting God in Everyday Life

Jesus Greater Than Moses

3 Therefore, holy brothers, who share in the heavenly calling, fix your thoughts on Jesus, the apostle and high priest whom we confess. [2]He was faithful to the one who appointed him, just as Moses was faithful in all God's house. [3]Jesus has been found worthy of greater honor than Moses, just as the builder of a house has greater honor than the house itself. [4]For every house is built by someone, but God is the builder of everything. [5]Moses was faithful as a servant in all God's house, testifying to what would be said in the future. [6]But Christ is faithful as a son over God's house. And we are his house, if we hold on to our courage and the hope of which we boast.

Warning Against Unbelief

[7]So, as the Holy Spirit says:

> "Today, if you hear his voice,
> [8] do not harden your hearts
>   as you did in the rebellion,
>   during the time of testing in the desert,
> [9]where your fathers tested and tried me
>   and for forty years saw what I did.
> [10]That is why I was angry with that generation,
>   and I said, 'Their hearts are always going astray,
>   and they have not known my ways.'
> [11]So I declared on oath in my anger,
>   'They shall never enter my rest.' "[a]

[12]See to it, brothers, that none of you has a sinful, unbelieving heart that turns away from the living God. [13]But encourage one another daily, as long as it is called Today, so that none of you may be hardened by sin's deceitfulness. [14]We have come to share in Christ if we hold firmly till the end the confidence we had at first. [15]As has just been said:

> "Today, if you hear his voice,
>   do not harden your hearts
>   as you did in the rebellion."[b]

[16]Who were they who heard and rebelled? Were they not all those Moses led out of Egypt? [17]And with whom was he angry for forty years? Was it not with those who sinned, whose bodies fell in the desert? [18]And to whom did God swear that they would never enter his rest if not to those who disobeyed[c]? [19]So we see that they were not able to enter, because of their unbelief.

A Sabbath-Rest for the People of God

4 Therefore, since the promise of entering his rest still stands, let us be careful that none of you be found to have fallen short of it. [2]For we also have had the gospel preached to us, just as they did; but the message they heard was of no value to them, because those who heard did not combine it with faith.[d] [3]Now we who have believed enter that rest, just as God has said,

> "So I declared on oath in my anger,
>   'They shall never enter my rest.' "[e]

a 11 Psalm 95:7-11   b 15 Psalm 95:7,8   c 18 Or *disbelieved*   d 2 Many manuscripts *because they did not share in the faith of those who obeyed*   e 3 Psalm 95:11; also in verse 5

And yet his work has been finished since the creation of the world. [4]For somewhere he has spoken about the seventh day in these words: "And on the seventh day God rested from all his work."[a] [5]And again in the passage above he says, "They shall never enter my rest."

[6]It still remains that some will enter that rest, and those who formerly had the gospel preached to them did not go in, because of their disobedience. [7]Therefore God again set a certain day, calling it Today, when a long time later he spoke through David, as was said before:

"Today, if you hear his voice,
    do not harden your hearts."[b]

[8]For if Joshua had given them rest, God would not have spoken later about another day. [9]There remains, then, a Sabbath-rest for the people of God; [10]for anyone who enters God's rest also rests from his own work, just as God did from his. [11]Let us, therefore, make every effort to enter that rest, so that no one will fall by following their example of disobedience.

[12]For the word of God is living and active. Sharper than any double-edged sword, it penetrates even to dividing soul and spirit, joints and marrow; it judges the thoughts and attitudes of the heart. [13]Nothing in all creation is hidden from God's sight. Everything is uncovered and laid bare before the eyes of him to whom we must give account.

Jesus the Great High Priest

[14]Therefore, since we have a great high priest who has gone through the heavens,[c] Jesus the Son of God, let us hold firmly to the faith we profess. [15]For we do not have a high priest who is unable to sympathize with our weaknesses, but we have one who has been tempted in every way, just as we are—yet was without sin. [16]Let us then approach the throne of grace with confidence, so that we may receive mercy and find grace to help us in our time of need.

5 Every high priest is selected from among men and is appointed to represent them in matters related to God, to offer gifts and sacrifices for sins. [2]He is able to deal gently with those who are ignorant and are going astray, since he himself is subject to weakness. [3]This is why he has to offer sacrifices for his own sins, as well as for the sins of the people.

[4]No one takes this honor upon himself; he must be called by God, just as Aaron was. [5]So Christ also did not take upon himself the glory of becoming a high priest. But God said to him,

"You are my Son;
    today I have become your Father."[d][e]

[6]And he says in another place,

"You are a priest forever,
    in the order of Melchizedek."[f]

[7]During the days of Jesus' life on earth, he offered up prayers and petitions with loud cries and tears to the one who could save him from death, and he was heard because of his reverent submission. [8]Although he was a son, he

Help for the Asking

HEBREWS 4:14–16

What would it be like to "approach [God's] throne"? Does that phrase invoke a mental image of the angels and awesome glory of Isaiah 6? Read this passage again, lingering over the phrases "sympathize with our weaknesses . . . . tempted in every way, just as we are . . . . throne of grace." Imagine yourself approaching God's throne and finding Jesus there; he smiles and calls you "friend." What do you ask of him? What gift does he give you? You might conclude by singing a hymn such as "What a Friend We Have in Jesus" or "Jesus Is All the World to Me."

See Meeting God in Prayer

a 4 Gen. 2:2   *b 7* Psalm 95:7,8   *c 14* Or *gone into heaven*   *d 5* Or *have begotten you*   *e 5* Psalm 2:7   *f 6* Psalm 110:4

Confidence in God's Promises

HEBREWS 6:13–15

"One of the chief needs in our waiting upon God, one of the deepest secrets of its blessedness and blessing, is a quiet, confident persuasion that it is not in vain. Have courage and believe that God will hear and help. We are waiting on a God who could never disappoint His people."

—ANDREW MURRAY,
Waiting on God

learned obedience from what he suffered ⁹and, once made perfect, he became the source of eternal salvation for all who obey him ¹⁰and was designated by God to be high priest in the order of Melchizedek.

Warning Against Falling Away

¹¹We have much to say about this, but it is hard to explain because you are slow to learn. ¹²In fact, though by this time you ought to be teachers, you need someone to teach you the elementary truths of God's word all over again. You need milk, not solid food! ¹³Anyone who lives on milk, being still an infant, is not acquainted with the teaching about righteousness. ¹⁴But solid food is for the mature, who by constant use have trained themselves to distinguish good from evil.

6 Therefore let us leave the elementary teachings about Christ and go on to maturity, not laying again the foundation of repentance from acts that lead to death,ᵃ and of faith in God, ²instruction about baptisms, the laying on of hands, the resurrection of the dead, and eternal judgment. ³And God permitting, we will do so.

⁴It is impossible for those who have once been enlightened, who have tasted the heavenly gift, who have shared in the Holy Spirit, ⁵who have tasted the goodness of the word of God and the powers of the coming age, ⁶if they fall away, to be brought back to repentance, becauseᵇ to their loss they are crucifying the Son of God all over again and subjecting him to public disgrace.

⁷Land that drinks in the rain often falling on it and that produces a crop useful to those for whom it is farmed receives the blessing of God. ⁸But land that produces thorns and thistles is worthless and is in danger of being cursed. In the end it will be burned.

⁹Even though we speak like this, dear friends, we are confident of better things in your case—things that accompany salvation. ¹⁰God is not unjust; he will not forget your work and the love you have shown him as you have helped his people and continue to help them. ¹¹We want each of you to show this same diligence to the very end, in order to make your hope sure. ¹²We do not want you to become lazy, but to imitate those who through faith and patience inherit what has been promised.

The Certainty of God's Promise

¹³When God made his promise to Abraham, since there was no one greater for him to swear by, he swore by himself, ¹⁴saying, "I will surely bless you and give you many descendants."ᶜ ¹⁵And so after waiting patiently, Abraham received what was promised.

¹⁶Men swear by someone greater than themselves, and the oath confirms what is said and puts an end to all argument. ¹⁷Because God wanted to make the unchanging nature of his purpose very clear to the heirs of what was promised, he confirmed it with an oath. ¹⁸God did this so that, by two unchangeable things in which it is impossible for God to lie, we who have fled to take hold of the hope offered to us may be greatly encouraged. ¹⁹We have this hope as an anchor for the soul, firm and secure. It enters the inner sanctuary behind the curtain, ²⁰where Jesus, who

ᵃ 1 Or *from useless rituals*   ᵇ 6 Or *repentance while*   ᶜ 14 Gen. 22:17

went before us, has entered on our behalf. He has become a high priest forever, in the order of Melchizedek.

Melchizedek the Priest

7 This Melchizedek was king of Salem and priest of God Most High. He met Abraham returning from the defeat of the kings and blessed him, ²and Abraham gave him a tenth of everything. First, his name means "king of righteousness"; then also, "king of Salem" means "king of peace." ³Without father or mother, without genealogy, without beginning of days or end of life, like the Son of God he remains a priest forever.

⁴Just think how great he was: Even the patriarch Abraham gave him a tenth of the plunder! ⁵Now the law requires the descendants of Levi who become priests to collect a tenth from the people—that is, their brothers—even though their brothers are descended from Abraham. ⁶This man, however, did not trace his descent from Levi, yet he collected a tenth from Abraham and blessed him who had the promises. ⁷And without doubt the lesser person is blessed by the greater. ⁸In the one case, the tenth is collected by men who die; but in the other case, by him who is declared to be living. ⁹One might even say that Levi, who collects the tenth, paid the tenth through Abraham, ¹⁰because when Melchizedek met Abraham, Levi was still in the body of his ancestor.

Jesus Like Melchizedek

¹¹If perfection could have been attained through the Levitical priesthood (for on the basis of it the law was given to the people), why was there still need for another priest to come—one in the order of Melchizedek, not in the order of Aaron? ¹²For when there is a change of the priesthood, there must also be a change of the law. ¹³He of whom these things are said belonged to a different tribe, and no one from that tribe has ever served at the altar. ¹⁴For it is clear that our Lord descended from Judah, and in regard to that tribe Moses said nothing about priests. ¹⁵And what we have said is even more clear if another priest like Melchizedek appears, ¹⁶one who has become a priest not on the basis of a regulation as to his ancestry but on the basis of the power of an indestructible life. ¹⁷For it is declared:

> "You are a priest forever,
>   in the order of Melchizedek."ᵃ

¹⁸The former regulation is set aside because it was weak and useless ¹⁹(for the law made nothing perfect), and a better hope is introduced, by which we draw near to God.

²⁰And it was not without an oath! Others became priests without any oath, ²¹but he became a priest with an oath when God said to him:

> "The Lord has sworn
>   and will not change his mind:
> 'You are a priest forever.' "ᵃ

²²Because of this oath, Jesus has become the guarantee of a better covenant.

²³Now there have been many of those priests, since death prevented them from continuing in office; ²⁴but be-

An Anchor for the Soul

HEBREWS 6:17–20

Many people seem overwhelmed by a chronic, low-grade hopelessness. Adrift in a sea of busyness and pressure, they are looking for something to grab hold of—anything to keep them afloat.

What is your greatest source of hope? In what areas of your life are you most in need of hope? Hebrews speaks of hope as "an anchor for the soul." Reflect on that image. What other symbol or image would remind you of hope? Draw or find a picture of that item, and hang it in a prominent place where you can see it and let it strengthen you.

Jesus, Our Intercessor

HEBREWS 7:23–25

The good news is that Jesus never gives up! He continues until he completes each task that has been set before him. Jesus lives always to offer prayers for you. Sit quietly and imagine Jesus praying for you. What do you sense about his method of prayer? How does it feel to know that Jesus, the great high priest, is praying to the Father on your behalf? How might his prayers differ from your prayers for yourself? From the prayers of others on your behalf? How can Jesus help you as you intercede for other people?

See Meeting God in Prayer

cause Jesus lives forever, he has a permanent priesthood. [25]Therefore he is able to save completely[a] those who come to God through him, because he always lives to intercede for them.

[26]Such a high priest meets our need—one who is holy, blameless, pure, set apart from sinners, exalted above the heavens. [27]Unlike the other high priests, he does not need to offer sacrifices day after day, first for his own sins, and then for the sins of the people. He sacrificed for their sins once for all when he offered himself. [28]For the law appoints as high priests men who are weak; but the oath, which came after the law, appointed the Son, who has been made perfect forever.

The High Priest of a New Covenant

8 The point of what we are saying is this: We do have such a high priest, who sat down at the right hand of the throne of the Majesty in heaven, [2]and who serves in the sanctuary, the true tabernacle set up by the Lord, not by man.

[3]Every high priest is appointed to offer both gifts and sacrifices, and so it was necessary for this one also to have something to offer. [4]If he were on earth, he would not be a priest, for there are already men who offer the gifts prescribed by the law. [5]They serve at a sanctuary that is a copy and shadow of what is in heaven. This is why Moses was warned when he was about to build the tabernacle: "See to it that you make everything according to the pattern shown you on the mountain."[b] [6]But the ministry Jesus has received is as superior to theirs as the covenant of which he is mediator is superior to the old one, and it is founded on better promises.

[7]For if there had been nothing wrong with that first covenant, no place would have been sought for another. [8]But God found fault with the people and said[c]:

"The time is coming, declares the Lord,
    when I will make a new covenant
with the house of Israel
    and with the house of Judah.
[9]It will not be like the covenant
    I made with their forefathers
when I took them by the hand
    to lead them out of Egypt,
because they did not remain faithful to my
    covenant,
and I turned away from them,
                        declares the Lord.
[10]This is the covenant I will make with the house of
        Israel
    after that time, declares the Lord.
I will put my laws in their minds
    and write them on their hearts.
I will be their God,
    and they will be my people.
[11]No longer will a man teach his neighbor,
    or a man his brother, saying, 'Know the Lord,'
because they will all know me,

---

a 25 Or *forever*   *b 5* Exodus 25:40   *c 8* Some manuscripts may be translated *fault and said to the people.*

from the least of them to the greatest.
¹²For I will forgive their wickedness
   and will remember their sins no more."ᵃ

¹³By calling this covenant "new," he has made the first one obsolete; and what is obsolete and aging will soon disappear.

Worship in the Earthly Tabernacle

9 Now the first covenant had regulations for worship and also an earthly sanctuary. ²A tabernacle was set up. In its first room were the lampstand, the table and the consecrated bread; this was called the Holy Place. ³Behind the second curtain was a room called the Most Holy Place, ⁴which had the golden altar of incense and the gold-covered ark of the covenant. This ark contained the gold jar of manna, Aaron's staff that had budded, and the stone tablets of the covenant. ⁵Above the ark were the cherubim of the Glory, overshadowing the atonement cover.ᵇ But we cannot discuss these things in detail now.

⁶When everything had been arranged like this, the priests entered regularly into the outer room to carry on their ministry. ⁷But only the high priest entered the inner room, and that only once a year, and never without blood, which he offered for himself and for the sins the people had committed in ignorance. ⁸The Holy Spirit was showing by this that the way into the Most Holy Place had not yet been disclosed as long as the first tabernacle was still standing. ⁹This is an illustration for the present time, indicating that the gifts and sacrifices being offered were not able to clear the conscience of the worshiper. ¹⁰They are only a matter of food and drink and various ceremonial washings—external regulations applying until the time of the new order.

The Blood of Christ

¹¹When Christ came as high priest of the good things that are already here,ᶜ he went through the greater and more perfect tabernacle that is not man-made, that is to say, not a part of this creation. ¹²He did not enter by means of the blood of goats and calves; but he entered the Most Holy Place once for all by his own blood, having obtained eternal redemption. ¹³The blood of goats and bulls and the ashes of a heifer sprinkled on those who are ceremonially unclean sanctify them so that they are outwardly clean. ¹⁴How much more, then, will the blood of Christ, who through the eternal Spirit offered himself unblemished to God, cleanse our consciences from acts that lead to death,ᵈ so that we may serve the living God!

¹⁵For this reason Christ is the mediator of a new covenant, that those who are called may receive the promised eternal inheritance—now that he has died as a ransom to set them free from the sins committed under the first covenant.

¹⁶In the case of a will,ᵉ it is necessary to prove the death of the one who made it, ¹⁷because a will is in force only when somebody has died; it never takes effect while the one who made it is living. ¹⁸This is why even the first cov-

---

Inner Cleansing

HEBREWS 9:13–14

Making a good impression is important. Yet we may become so preoccupied with our outward appearance that we neglect our inner heart and conscience. Jesus comes to cleanse all aspects of our lives. His Spirit begins by renewing our hearts and his work radiates through our attitudes and actions. You may already be conscious of your faults. Are you as familiar with Jesus' cleansing? You might picture your faults as trash cluttering the floor of a room that represents your conscience. Let the Spirit pour through your inner room like a flood—cleansing, purifying and renewing. Envision the room transformed into a chapel where God is worshiped and glorified. You may want to conclude by slowly and reflectively repeating the Lord's Prayer.

ᵃ12 Jer. 31:31–34   ᵇ5 Traditionally the mercy seat   ᶜ11 Some early manuscripts are to come   ᵈ14 Or from useless rituals   ᵉ16 Same Greek word as covenant; also in verse 17

A New and Different High Priest

HEBREWS 9:25–28

The human priests of the Old Testament had to continually offer up sacrifices for themselves and the people they represented in order to be cleansed from their sin. Jesus is a different high priest. He offered his life as a sacrifice only once and for all time.

Allow yourself to reflect on the significance of Jesus' sacrifice. What does it mean to you? How does it affect the way in which you live? What words could you use to describe Jesus' extravagant gift to you? Record these words in your journal. How do you express your gratitude to God for Jesus, your high priest?

See Meeting God in Worship

enant was not put into effect without blood. ¹⁹When Moses had proclaimed every commandment of the law to all the people, he took the blood of calves, together with water, scarlet wool and branches of hyssop, and sprinkled the scroll and all the people. ²⁰He said, "This is the blood of the covenant, which God has commanded you to keep."[a] ²¹In the same way, he sprinkled with the blood both the tabernacle and everything used in its ceremonies. ²²In fact, the law requires that nearly everything be cleansed with blood, and without the shedding of blood there is no forgiveness.

²³It was necessary, then, for the copies of the heavenly things to be purified with these sacrifices, but the heavenly things themselves with better sacrifices than these. ²⁴For Christ did not enter a man-made sanctuary that was only a copy of the true one; he entered heaven itself, now to appear for us in God's presence. ²⁵Nor did he enter heaven to offer himself again and again, the way the high priest enters the Most Holy Place every year with blood that is not his own. ²⁶Then Christ would have had to suffer many times since the creation of the world. But now he has appeared once for all at the end of the ages to do away with sin by the sacrifice of himself. ²⁷Just as man is destined to die once, and after that to face judgment, ²⁸so Christ was sacrificed once to take away the sins of many people; and he will appear a second time, not to bear sin, but to bring salvation to those who are waiting for him.

Christ's Sacrifice Once for All

10 The law is only a shadow of the good things that are coming—not the realities themselves. For this reason it can never, by the same sacrifices repeated endlessly year after year, make perfect those who draw near to worship. ²If it could, would they not have stopped being offered? For the worshipers would have been cleansed once for all, and would no longer have felt guilty for their sins. ³But those sacrifices are an annual reminder of sins, ⁴because it is impossible for the blood of bulls and goats to take away sins.

⁵Therefore, when Christ came into the world, he said:

"Sacrifice and offering you did not desire,
　　but a body you prepared for me;
⁶with burnt offerings and sin offerings
　　you were not pleased.
⁷Then I said, 'Here I am—it is written about me in
　　the scroll—
I have come to do your will, O God.' "[b]

⁸First he said, "Sacrifices and offerings, burnt offerings and sin offerings you did not desire, nor were you pleased with them" (although the law required them to be made). ⁹Then he said, "Here I am, I have come to do your will." He sets aside the first to establish the second. ¹⁰And by that will, we have been made holy through the sacrifice of the body of Jesus Christ once for all.

¹¹Day after day every priest stands and performs his religious duties; again and again he offers the same sacrifices, which can never take away sins. ¹²But when this priest had offered for all time one sacrifice for sins, he sat down at the right hand of God. ¹³Since that time he waits for his ene-

a 20 Exodus 24:8　　*b 7* Psalm 40:6–8 (see Septuagint)

mies to be made his footstool, [14]because by one sacrifice he has made perfect forever those who are being made holy.

[15]The Holy Spirit also testifies to us about this. First he says:

[16]"This is the covenant I will make with them
 after that time, says the Lord.
 I will put my laws in their hearts,
 and I will write them on their minds."[a]

[17]Then he adds:

"Their sins and lawless acts
 I will remember no more."[b]

[18]And where these have been forgiven, there is no longer any sacrifice for sin.

A Call to Persevere

[19]Therefore, brothers, since we have confidence to enter the Most Holy Place by the blood of Jesus, [20]by a new and living way opened for us through the curtain, that is, his body, [21]and since we have a great priest over the house of God, [22]let us draw near to God with a sincere heart in full assurance of faith, having our hearts sprinkled to cleanse us from a guilty conscience and having our bodies washed with pure water. [23]Let us hold unswervingly to the hope we profess, for he who promised is faithful. [24]And let us consider how we may spur one another on toward love and good deeds. [25]Let us not give up meeting together, as some are in the habit of doing, but let us encourage one another—and all the more as you see the Day approaching.

[26]If we deliberately keep on sinning after we have received the knowledge of the truth, no sacrifice for sins is left, [27]but only a fearful expectation of judgment and of raging fire that will consume the enemies of God. [28]Anyone who rejected the law of Moses died without mercy on the testimony of two or three witnesses. [29]How much more severely do you think a man deserves to be punished who has trampled the Son of God under foot, who has treated as an unholy thing the blood of the covenant that sanctified him, and who has insulted the Spirit of grace? [30]For we know him who said, "It is mine to avenge; I will repay,"[c] and again, "The Lord will judge his people."[d] [31]It is a dreadful thing to fall into the hands of the living God.

[32]Remember those earlier days after you had received the light, when you stood your ground in a great contest in the face of suffering. [33]Sometimes you were publicly exposed to insult and persecution; at other times you stood side by side with those who were so treated. [34]You sympathized with those in prison and joyfully accepted the confiscation of your property, because you knew that you yourselves had better and lasting possessions.

[35]So do not throw away your confidence; it will be richly rewarded. [36]You need to persevere so that when you have done the will of God, you will receive what he has promised. [37]For in just a very little while,

"He who is coming will come and will not delay.

[a]16 Jer. 31:33   [b]17 Jer. 31:34   [c]30 Deut. 32:35   [d]30 Deut. 32:36; Psalm 135:14

The Overcoming Power of Faith

HEBREWS 10:19–25

Life is filled with pain and challenges that tax the human spirit. Some respond to life's pain by taking refuge in materialism and hedonism or by dulling the pain with addictions. Some people choose to become hard and bitter. But Jesus offers us a "new and living way," a way of hope and reconciliation.

Find a comfortable place where you can relax and read these verses with both your head and your heart. Read the passage twice, slowly. What phrase or word speaks to you? Examine that phrase or word more closely. What attracts you to it? What does it mean to you? Allow this phrase or word to touch your heart. What emotions does it stir within you? Turn it into a prayer for yourself or others. Continue to savor these verses. Open your heart and mind to any impressions God's Spirit may wish to communicate to you.

See Meeting God in Scripture

The Beauty of Faith

"Faith is a living, daring confidence in God's grace. It is so sure and certain that a [person] could stake his [or her] life on it a thousand times."

—MARTIN LUTHER

³⁸ But my righteous one^a will live by faith.
And if he shrinks back,
I will not be pleased with him."^b

³⁹But we are not of those who shrink back and are destroyed, but of those who believe and are saved.

By Faith

11 Now faith is being sure of what we hope for and certain of what we do not see. ²This is what the ancients were commended for.

³By faith we understand that the universe was formed at God's command, so that what is seen was not made out of what was visible.

⁴By faith Abel offered God a better sacrifice than Cain did. By faith he was commended as a righteous man, when God spoke well of his offerings. And by faith he still speaks, even though he is dead.

⁵By faith Enoch was taken from this life, so that he did not experience death; he could not be found, because God had taken him away. For before he was taken, he was commended as one who pleased God. ⁶And without faith it is impossible to please God, because anyone who comes to him must believe that he exists and that he rewards those who earnestly seek him.

⁷By faith Noah, when warned about things not yet seen, in holy fear built an ark to save his family. By his faith he condemned the world and became heir of the righteousness that comes by faith.

⁸By faith Abraham, when called to go to a place he would later receive as his inheritance, obeyed and went, even though he did not know where he was going. ⁹By faith he made his home in the promised land like a stranger in a foreign country; he lived in tents, as did Isaac and Jacob, who were heirs with him of the same promise. ¹⁰For he was looking forward to the city with foundations, whose architect and builder is God.

¹¹By faith Abraham, even though he was past age—and Sarah herself was barren—was enabled to become a father because he^c considered him faithful who had made the promise. ¹²And so from this one man, and he as good as dead, came descendants as numerous as the stars in the sky and as countless as the sand on the seashore.

¹³All these people were still living by faith when they died. They did not receive the things promised; they only saw them and welcomed them from a distance. And they admitted that they were aliens and strangers on earth. ¹⁴People who say such things show that they are looking for a country of their own. ¹⁵If they had been thinking of the country they had left, they would have had opportunity to return. ¹⁶Instead, they were longing for a better country—a heavenly one. Therefore God is not ashamed to be called their God, for he has prepared a city for them.

¹⁷By faith Abraham, when God tested him, offered Isaac as a sacrifice. He who had received the promises was about to sacrifice his one and only son, ¹⁸even though God had said to him, "It is through Isaac that your offspring^d will be reckoned."^e ¹⁹Abraham reasoned that God could raise the

^a 38 One early manuscript *But the righteous*   ^b 38 Hab. 2:3,4   ^c 11 Or *By faith even Sarah, who was past age, was enabled to bear children because she*   ^d 18 Greek *seed*   ^e 18 Gen. 21:12

dead, and figuratively speaking, he did receive Isaac back from death.

²⁰By faith Isaac blessed Jacob and Esau in regard to their future.

²¹By faith Jacob, when he was dying, blessed each of Joseph's sons, and worshiped as he leaned on the top of his staff.

²²By faith Joseph, when his end was near, spoke about the exodus of the Israelites from Egypt and gave instructions about his bones.

²³By faith Moses' parents hid him for three months after he was born, because they saw he was no ordinary child, and they were not afraid of the king's edict.

²⁴By faith Moses, when he had grown up, refused to be known as the son of Pharaoh's daughter. ²⁵He chose to be mistreated along with the people of God rather than to enjoy the pleasures of sin for a short time. ²⁶He regarded disgrace for the sake of Christ as of greater value than the treasures of Egypt, because he was looking ahead to his reward. ²⁷By faith he left Egypt, not fearing the king's anger; he persevered because he saw him who is invisible. ²⁸By faith he kept the Passover and the sprinkling of blood, so that the destroyer of the firstborn would not touch the firstborn of Israel.

²⁹By faith the people passed through the Red Sea*a* as on dry land; but when the Egyptians tried to do so, they were drowned.

³⁰By faith the walls of Jericho fell, after the people had marched around them for seven days.

³¹By faith the prostitute Rahab, because she welcomed the spies, was not killed with those who were disobedient.*b*

³²And what more shall I say? I do not have time to tell about Gideon, Barak, Samson, Jephthah, David, Samuel and the prophets, ³³who through faith conquered kingdoms, administered justice, and gained what was promised; who shut the mouths of lions, ³⁴quenched the fury of the flames, and escaped the edge of the sword; whose weakness was turned to strength; and who became powerful in battle and routed foreign armies. ³⁵Women received back their dead, raised to life again. Others were tortured and refused to be released, so that they might gain a better resurrection. ³⁶Some faced jeers and flogging, while still others were chained and put in prison. ³⁷They were stoned*c*; they were sawed in two; they were put to death by the sword. They went about in sheepskins and goatskins, destitute, persecuted and mistreated— ³⁸the world was not worthy of them. They wandered in deserts and mountains, and in caves and holes in the ground.

³⁹These were all commended for their faith, yet none of them received what had been promised. ⁴⁰God had planned something better for us so that only together with us would they be made perfect.

God Disciplines His Sons

12 Therefore, since we are surrounded by such a great cloud of witnesses, let us throw off everything that hinders and the sin that so easily entangles, and let us run with perseverance the race marked out for us. ²Let us fix

Heroes of Faith

HEBREWS 11:32–34

This eleventh chapter of Hebrews introduces us to some of the heroes of the faith who demonstrated both belief and action. Who are some of the men and women who have become your own heroes of the faith? How did the trials they faced strengthen them? In the past and the present, how have they assisted you in living your faith? Make a list of your heroes and place it at this passage as a bookmark.

See Meeting God in Everyday Life

Therefore, Consider Jesus!

HEBREWS 12:1–13

These verses are filled with action verbs. Notice the verb phrases used to describe Jesus' actions on our behalf. Reflect on what Jesus has done for the sake of "the joy set before him":

"endured the cross"

"scorning its shame"

"sat down"

Ponder the verb phrases that describe our response:

"throw off"

"run with perseverance"

"fix our eyes"

"consider him"

"not grow weary and lose heart"

How many of these action verbs capture the essence of your response to Jesus Christ? In what areas of your life would you like to deepen your faith? Spend some time in prayer with Jesus about that desire, repeating your need to him over the course of the next days and weeks.

See Meeting God in Everyday Life

our eyes on Jesus, the author and perfecter of our faith, who for the joy set before him endured the cross, scorning its shame, and sat down at the right hand of the throne of God. ³Consider him who endured such opposition from sinful men, so that you will not grow weary and lose heart.

⁴In your struggle against sin, you have not yet resisted to the point of shedding your blood. ⁵And you have forgotten that word of encouragement that addresses you as sons:

"My son, do not make light of the Lord's
discipline,
and do not lose heart when he rebukes you,
⁶because the Lord disciplines those he loves,
and he punishes everyone he accepts as a
son."[a]

⁷Endure hardship as discipline; God is treating you as sons. For what son is not disciplined by his father? ⁸If you are not disciplined (and everyone undergoes discipline), then you are illegitimate children and not true sons. ⁹Moreover, we have all had human fathers who disciplined us and we respected them for it. How much more should we submit to the Father of our spirits and live! ¹⁰Our fathers disciplined us for a little while as they thought best; but God disciplines us for our good, that we may share in his holiness. ¹¹No discipline seems pleasant at the time, but painful. Later on, however, it produces a harvest of righteousness and peace for those who have been trained by it.

¹²Therefore, strengthen your feeble arms and weak knees. ¹³"Make level paths for your feet,"[b] so that the lame may not be disabled, but rather healed.

Warning Against Refusing God

¹⁴Make every effort to live in peace with all men and to be holy; without holiness no one will see the Lord. ¹⁵See to it that no one misses the grace of God and that no bitter root grows up to cause trouble and defile many. ¹⁶See that no one is sexually immoral, or is godless like Esau, who for a single meal sold his inheritance rights as the oldest son. ¹⁷Afterward, as you know, when he wanted to inherit this blessing, he was rejected. He could bring about no change of mind, though he sought the blessing with tears.

¹⁸You have not come to a mountain that can be touched and that is burning with fire; to darkness, gloom and storm; ¹⁹to a trumpet blast or to such a voice speaking words that those who heard it begged that no further word be spoken to them, ²⁰because they could not bear what was commanded: "If even an animal touches the mountain, it must be stoned."[c] ²¹The sight was so terrifying that Moses said, "I am trembling with fear."[d]

²²But you have come to Mount Zion, to the heavenly Jerusalem, the city of the living God. You have come to thousands upon thousands of angels in joyful assembly, ²³to the church of the firstborn, whose names are written in heaven. You have come to God, the judge of all men, to the spirits of righteous men made perfect, ²⁴to Jesus the mediator of a new covenant, and to the sprinkled blood that speaks a better word than the blood of Abel.

²⁵See to it that you do not refuse him who speaks. If they

a 6 Prov. 3:11,12   *b 13* Prov. 4:26   *c 20* Exodus 19:12,13
d 21 Deut. 9:19

did not escape when they refused him who warned them on earth, how much less will we, if we turn away from him who warns us from heaven? ²⁶At that time his voice shook the earth, but now he has promised, "Once more I will shake not only the earth but also the heavens."ᵃ ²⁷The words "once more" indicate the removing of what can be shaken—that is, created things—so that what cannot be shaken may remain.

²⁸Therefore, since we are receiving a kingdom that cannot be shaken, let us be thankful, and so worship God acceptably with reverence and awe, ²⁹for our "God is a consuming fire."ᵇ

Concluding Exhortations

13 Keep on loving each other as brothers. ²Do not forget to entertain strangers, for by so doing some people have entertained angels without knowing it. ³Remember those in prison as if you were their fellow prisoners, and those who are mistreated as if you yourselves were suffering.

⁴Marriage should be honored by all, and the marriage bed kept pure, for God will judge the adulterer and all the sexually immoral. ⁵Keep your lives free from the love of money and be content with what you have, because God has said,

> "Never will I leave you;
>   never will I forsake you."ᶜ

⁶So we say with confidence,

> "The Lord is my helper; I will not be afraid.
>   What can man do to me?"ᵈ

⁷Remember your leaders, who spoke the word of God to you. Consider the outcome of their way of life and imitate their faith. ⁸Jesus Christ is the same yesterday and today and forever.

⁹Do not be carried away by all kinds of strange teachings. It is good for our hearts to be strengthened by grace, not by ceremonial foods, which are of no value to those who eat them. ¹⁰We have an altar from which those who minister at the tabernacle have no right to eat.

¹¹The high priest carries the blood of animals into the Most Holy Place as a sin offering, but the bodies are burned outside the camp. ¹²And so Jesus also suffered outside the city gate to make the people holy through his own blood. ¹³Let us, then, go to him outside the camp, bearing the disgrace he bore. ¹⁴For here we do not have an enduring city, but we are looking for the city that is to come.

¹⁵Through Jesus, therefore, let us continually offer to God a sacrifice of praise—the fruit of lips that confess his name. ¹⁶And do not forget to do good and to share with others, for with such sacrifices God is pleased.

¹⁷Obey your leaders and submit to their authority. They keep watch over you as men who must give an account. Obey them so that their work will be a joy, not a burden, for that would be of no advantage to you.

¹⁸Pray for us. We are sure that we have a clear conscience and desire to live honorably in every way. ¹⁹I particularly urge you to pray so that I may be restored to you soon.

Worship That Makes a Difference

HEBREWS 12:28–29

Worship is our grateful response to all that Jesus has accomplished and all he continues to do on our behalf. Unfortunately many people think of worship in terms of what they can receive from God rather than what they can offer to God.

What is your definition of worship? What happens when you gather with other Christians to worship? What principles does this passage provide to guide your worship? Read these verses before you worship next Sunday. As you worship seek to participate as fully and freely as possible. How conscious are you of God's awesome majesty? Of God's nearness and intimate love? Follow up by rereading this Scripture and reflecting on your experience in light of it.

See Meeting God in Worship

Receive the Benediction

The author of Hebrews offers you this blessing. What posture indicates openness or receptivity for you? You might adopt that posture as you receive this blessing. Reread it slowly. All of this is for you: Jesus Christ's death and resurrection; the new covenant; the perfect equipment for serving God; power to know and do God's will; participation in Christ's glory. Spend some time pondering each of these gifts, accepting each one and thanking God for it. Finish by singing the doxology "Praise God, From Whom All Blessings Flow."

See *Meeting God in Everyday Life*

[20]May the God of peace, who through the blood of the eternal covenant brought back from the dead our Lord Jesus, that great Shepherd of the sheep, [21]equip you with everything good for doing his will, and may he work in us what is pleasing to him, through Jesus Christ, to whom be glory for ever and ever. Amen.

[22]Brothers, I urge you to bear with my word of exhortation, for I have written you only a short letter.

[23]I want you to know that our brother Timothy has been released. If he arrives soon, I will come with him to see you.

[24]Greet all your leaders and all God's people. Those from Italy send you their greetings.

[25]Grace be with you all.

JAMES

Faith at Work

KEY VERSE:

Do not merely listen to the word, and so deceive yourselves. Do what it says.—James 1:22

James could be said to have one objective in writing this letter: to assist the churches to whom he writes to live well, that is, to work out their faith in good deeds and holy habits. The straightforward, commonsense approach of this letter is refreshing, although it might challenge and confront those who are comfortable in certain patterns of neglect or indifference toward others. "Do not . . . deceive yourselves" (1:22). "Take note of this" (1:19). "If you really keep the royal law . . . you are doing right" (2:8). These are the directives of a writer who is intent on reiterating or fleshing out the ancient words of the prophet Micah: "He has showed you, O man, what is good. And what does the LORD require of you? To act justly and to love mercy and to walk humbly with your God" (Micah 6:8).

As you contemplate these chapters, let them be like candles lighting your soul, life and habits. How do they describe you or your church? How do they challenge you toward greater faithfulness in loving others? In the down-to-brass-tacks spirit of this letter, consider this question throughout: What are specific and concrete ways in which I can respond to what I am reading? Ask God to lead you into authentic behaviors and attitudes that—in challenging ways and ways that may very well stretch you perhaps—will put your faith to work.

"For when we ask how good a person is, we do not ask what they believe or what they hope for but what they live."

—AUGUSTINE,
Enchiridion

Perseverance [Endurance]

JAMES 1:2–9

The word "endurance" appears often in James. The meaning of this word in Greek has to do with "rising above" a circumstance while at the same time "holding on" within that circumstance. The exercise of perseverance is central to James's lessons on faithfulness.

What are some circumstances in your life or in your church in which the practice of "rising above while holding on" is called for? What would it mean to regard these circumstances as "pure joy"? When in the past have you persevered in a difficult situation and found that it bore the fruit of joy?

1 James, a servant of God and of the Lord Jesus Christ,

To the twelve tribes scattered among the nations:

Greetings.

Trials and Temptations

²Consider it pure joy, my brothers, whenever you face trials of many kinds, ³because you know that the testing of your faith develops perseverance. ⁴Perseverance must finish its work so that you may be mature and complete, not lacking anything. ⁵If any of you lacks wisdom, he should ask God, who gives generously to all without finding fault, and it will be given to him. ⁶But when he asks, he must believe and not doubt, because he who doubts is like a wave of the sea, blown and tossed by the wind. ⁷That man should not think he will receive anything from the Lord; ⁸he is a double-minded man, unstable in all he does.

⁹The brother in humble circumstances ought to take pride in his high position. ¹⁰But the one who is rich should take pride in his low position, because he will pass away like a wild flower. ¹¹For the sun rises with scorching heat and withers the plant; its blossom falls and its beauty is destroyed. In the same way, the rich man will fade away even while he goes about his business.

¹²Blessed is the man who perseveres under trial, because when he has stood the test, he will receive the crown of life that God has promised to those who love him.

¹³When tempted, no one should say, "God is tempting me." For God cannot be tempted by evil, nor does he tempt anyone; ¹⁴but each one is tempted when, by his own evil desire, he is dragged away and enticed. ¹⁵Then, after desire has conceived, it gives birth to sin; and sin, when it is full-grown, gives birth to death.

¹⁶Don't be deceived, my dear brothers. ¹⁷Every good and perfect gift is from above, coming down from the Father of the heavenly lights, who does not change like shifting shadows. ¹⁸He chose to give us birth through the word of truth, that we might be a kind of firstfruits of all he created.

Listening and Doing

¹⁹My dear brothers, take note of this: Everyone should be quick to listen, slow to speak and slow to become angry, ²⁰for man's anger does not bring about the righteous life that God desires. ²¹Therefore, get rid of all moral filth and the evil that is so prevalent and humbly accept the word planted in you, which can save you.

²²Do not merely listen to the word, and so deceive yourselves. Do what it says. ²³Anyone who listens to the word but does not do what it says is like a man who looks at his face in a mirror ²⁴and, after looking at himself, goes away and immediately forgets what he looks like. ²⁵But the man who looks intently into the perfect law that gives freedom, and continues to do this, not forgetting what he has heard, but doing it—he will be blessed in what he does.

²⁶If anyone considers himself religious and yet does not keep a tight rein on his tongue, he deceives himself and his religion is worthless. ²⁷Religion that God our Father accepts as pure and faultless is this: to look after orphans and widows in their distress and to keep oneself from being polluted by the world.

Favoritism Forbidden

2 My brothers, as believers in our glorious Lord Jesus Christ, don't show favoritism. ²Suppose a man comes into your meeting wearing a gold ring and fine clothes, and a poor man in shabby clothes also comes in. ³If you show special attention to the man wearing fine clothes and say, "Here's a good seat for you," but say to the poor man, "You stand there" or "Sit on the floor by my feet," ⁴have you not discriminated among yourselves and become judges with evil thoughts?

⁵Listen, my dear brothers: Has not God chosen those who are poor in the eyes of the world to be rich in faith and to inherit the kingdom he promised those who love him? ⁶But you have insulted the poor. Is it not the rich who are exploiting you? Are they not the ones who are dragging you into court? ⁷Are they not the ones who are slandering the noble name of him to whom you belong?

⁸If you really keep the royal law found in Scripture, "Love your neighbor as yourself,"[a] you are doing right. ⁹But if you show favoritism, you sin and are convicted by the law as lawbreakers. ¹⁰For whoever keeps the whole law and yet stumbles at just one point is guilty of breaking all of it. ¹¹For he who said, "Do not commit adultery,"[b] also said, "Do not murder."[c] If you do not commit adultery but do commit murder, you have become a lawbreaker.

¹²Speak and act as those who are going to be judged by the law that gives freedom, ¹³because judgment without mercy will be shown to anyone who has not been merciful. Mercy triumphs over judgment!

Faith and Deeds

¹⁴What good is it, my brothers, if a man claims to have faith but has no deeds? Can such faith save him? ¹⁵Suppose a brother or sister is without clothes and daily food. ¹⁶If one of you says to him, "Go, I wish you well; keep warm and well fed," but does nothing about his physical needs, what good is it? ¹⁷In the same way, faith by itself, if it is not accompanied by action, is dead.

¹⁸But someone will say, "You have faith; I have deeds."

Show me your faith without deeds, and I will show you my faith by what I do. ¹⁹You believe that there is one God. Good! Even the demons believe that—and shudder.

²⁰You foolish man, do you want evidence that faith without deeds is useless[d]? ²¹Was not our ancestor Abraham considered righteous for what he did when he offered his son Isaac on the altar? ²²You see that his faith and his actions were working together, and his faith was made complete by what he did. ²³And the scripture was fulfilled that says, "Abraham believed God, and it was credited to him as righteousness,"[e] and he was called God's friend. ²⁴You see that a person is justified by what he does and not by faith alone.

²⁵In the same way, was not even Rahab the prostitute considered righteous for what she did when she gave lodging to the spies and sent them off in a different direction? ²⁶As the body without the spirit is dead, so faith without deeds is dead.

a 8 Lev. 19:18   *b 11* Exodus 20:14; Deut. 5:18   *c 11* Exodus 20:13; Deut. 5:17   *d 20* Some early manuscripts *dead*   *e 23* Gen. 15:6

Loving All the Same

JAMES 2:3–13

A rabbi asked the question of his disciples, "When do we know that light has appeared out of darkness?" One student answered, "When we can tell the difference between a dog and a lamb?" "No," said the rabbi. Another student answered, "When we can tell the difference between a palm tree and a fig tree?" "No," said the rabbi. "When, then, do we know?" the disciples asked their teacher. "We know that light has appeared out of darkness when someone can look in the face of any human being and see the face of a sister or brother."

See Meeting God in Service

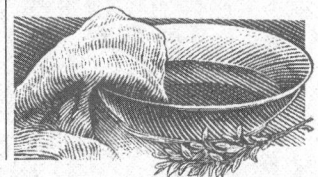

Guarding the Heart

JAMES 3:6–12

"A brother asked Abba Sisois, 'I long to guard my heart.' The old man said to him, 'And how can we guard the heart if our tongue leaves the door of the fortress open?' "

—from *Western Asceticism*

Taming the Tongue

3 Not many of you should presume to be teachers, my brothers, because you know that we who teach will be judged more strictly. ²We all stumble in many ways. If anyone is never at fault in what he says, he is a perfect man, able to keep his whole body in check.

³When we put bits into the mouths of horses to make them obey us, we can turn the whole animal. ⁴Or take ships as an example. Although they are so large and are driven by strong winds, they are steered by a very small rudder wherever the pilot wants to go. ⁵Likewise the tongue is a small part of the body, but it makes great boasts. Consider what a great forest is set on fire by a small spark. ⁶The tongue also is a fire, a world of evil among the parts of the body. It corrupts the whole person, sets the whole course of his life on fire, and is itself set on fire by hell.

⁷All kinds of animals, birds, reptiles and creatures of the sea are being tamed and have been tamed by man, ⁸but no man can tame the tongue. It is a restless evil, full of deadly poison.

⁹With the tongue we praise our Lord and Father, and with it we curse men, who have been made in God's likeness. ¹⁰Out of the same mouth come praise and cursing. My brothers, this should not be. ¹¹Can both fresh water and salt*ᵃ* water flow from the same spring? ¹²My brothers, can a fig tree bear olives, or a grapevine bear figs? Neither can a salt spring produce fresh water.

Two Kinds of Wisdom

¹³Who is wise and understanding among you? Let him show it by his good life, by deeds done in the humility that comes from wisdom. ¹⁴But if you harbor bitter envy and selfish ambition in your hearts, do not boast about it or deny the truth. ¹⁵Such "wisdom" does not come down from heaven but is earthly, unspiritual, of the devil. ¹⁶For where you have envy and selfish ambition, there you find disorder and every evil practice.

¹⁷But the wisdom that comes from heaven is first of all pure; then peace-loving, considerate, submissive, full of mercy and good fruit, impartial and sincere. ¹⁸Peacemakers who sow in peace raise a harvest of righteousness.

Submit Yourselves to God

4 What causes fights and quarrels among you? Don't they come from your desires that battle within you? ²You want something but don't get it. You kill and covet, but you cannot have what you want. You quarrel and fight. You do not have, because you do not ask God. ³When you ask, you do not receive, because you ask with wrong motives, that you may spend what you get on your pleasures.

⁴You adulterous people, don't you know that friendship with the world is hatred toward God? Anyone who chooses to be a friend of the world becomes an enemy of God. ⁵Or do you think Scripture says without reason that the spirit he caused to live in us envies intensely?*ᵇ* ⁶But he gives us more grace. That is why Scripture says:

ᵃ 11 Greek *bitter* (see also verse 14)   *ᵇ 5* Or *that God jealously longs for the spirit that he made to live in us;* or *that the Spirit he caused to live in us longs jealously*

"God opposes the proud
but gives grace to the humble."[a]

[7]Submit yourselves, then, to God. Resist the devil, and he will flee from you. [8]Come near to God and he will come near to you. Wash your hands, you sinners, and purify your hearts, you double-minded. [9]Grieve, mourn and wail. Change your laughter to mourning and your joy to gloom. [10]Humble yourselves before the Lord, and he will lift you up.

[11]Brothers, do not slander one another. Anyone who speaks against his brother or judges him speaks against the law and judges it. When you judge the law, you are not keeping it, but sitting in judgment on it. [12]There is only one Lawgiver and Judge, the one who is able to save and destroy. But you—who are you to judge your neighbor?

Boasting About Tomorrow

[13]Now listen, you who say, "Today or tomorrow we will go to this or that city, spend a year there, carry on business and make money." [14]Why, you do not even know what will happen tomorrow. What is your life? You are a mist that appears for a little while and then vanishes. [15]Instead, you ought to say, "If it is the Lord's will, we will live and do this or that." [16]As it is, you boast and brag. All such boasting is evil. [17]Anyone, then, who knows the good he ought to do and doesn't do it, sins.

Warning to Rich Oppressors

5 Now listen, you rich people, weep and wail because of the misery that is coming upon you. [2]Your wealth has rotted, and moths have eaten your clothes. [3]Your gold and silver are corroded. Their corrosion will testify against you and eat your flesh like fire. You have hoarded wealth in the last days. [4]Look! The wages you failed to pay the workmen who mowed your fields are crying out against you. The cries of the harvesters have reached the ears of the Lord Almighty. [5]You have lived on earth in luxury and self-indulgence. You have fattened yourselves in the day of slaughter.[b] [6]You have condemned and murdered innocent men, who were not opposing you.

Patience in Suffering

[7]Be patient, then, brothers, until the Lord's coming. See how the farmer waits for the land to yield its valuable crop and how patient he is for the autumn and spring rains. [8]You too, be patient and stand firm, because the Lord's coming is near. [9]Don't grumble against each other, brothers, or you will be judged. The Judge is standing at the door!

[10]Brothers, as an example of patience in the face of suffering, take the prophets who spoke in the name of the Lord. [11]As you know, we consider blessed those who have persevered. You have heard of Job's perseverance and have seen what the Lord finally brought about. The Lord is full of compassion and mercy.

[12]Above all, my brothers, do not swear—not by heaven or by earth or by anything else. Let your "Yes" be yes, and your "No," no, or you will be condemned.

Faith and Tomorrow's Work

JAMES 4:13–17

In the Mexican culture, *si Dios quiere* ("if God wishes") is a common expression that refers to the tenuous nature of daily living and future planning. James conveys the same idea. He prompts his readers to live by an awareness of the radical contingency of their lives: "Instead, you ought to say, 'If it is the Lord's will, we will live and do . . .' " Examine your life; in what ways do you act as though tomorrow and the future are within your own control? Consider ways in which you could be more intentional in surrendering your plans to God and more open to divine guidance.

See Meeting God in Everyday Life

The Community of Care

JAMES 5:13–20

Augustine once referred to the "walls of the church" as those braces and boundaries within which individuals who belong to the church are held. James closes his letter by describing those "walls" or means of grace—prayer, confession, healing, restoration—that benefit both the individual and the whole community. Recall an instance in which the church has provided for you in a time of specific need. Now think of less visible or dramatic ways in which your faith community has been a channel of God's grace in your life. In what ways can you become such a caring presence to a brother or sister, or to your congregation as a whole? Ask God to guide you in discerning and fulfilling that calling.

See Meeting God in Community

The Prayer of Faith

¹³Is any one of you in trouble? He should pray. Is anyone happy? Let him sing songs of praise. ¹⁴Is any one of you sick? He should call the elders of the church to pray over him and anoint him with oil in the name of the Lord. ¹⁵And the prayer offered in faith will make the sick person well; the Lord will raise him up. If he has sinned, he will be forgiven. ¹⁶Therefore confess your sins to each other and pray for each other so that you may be healed. The prayer of a righteous man is powerful and effective.

¹⁷Elijah was a man just like us. He prayed earnestly that it would not rain, and it did not rain on the land for three and a half years. ¹⁸Again he prayed, and the heavens gave rain, and the earth produced its crops.

¹⁹My brothers, if one of you should wander from the truth and someone should bring him back, ²⁰remember this: Whoever turns a sinner from the error of his way will save him from death and cover over a multitude of sins.

1 PETER

Christians Under Construction

KEY VERSE:

I have written to you briefly, encouraging you and testifying that this is the true grace of God. Stand fast in it. —1 Peter 5:12

Standing fast in the true grace of God transforms all of life. How simple it sounds. How seldom it is achieved! Peter knows this from personal experience. He knows how easy it is to wobble and fall. With a pastor's heart of compassion, he writes to Christians scattered in many places and facing a variety of tests and trials. His warm, encouraging letter reminds them first of the blessings and hope they already have in Jesus Christ. With that confident assurance they have every reason to be diligent in putting aside anything that could hold them back from full enjoyment of salvation.

The Christian life is no glowing dream world though. Peter is realistic. Believers are to hold on in the midst of political challenges, slavery, abuse, questions from unbelievers, and suffering and pain. Standing fast in these situations requires a clear sense of God's gracious presence. It also demands a disciplined commitment to living daily according to Jesus' example. Peter gives down-to-earth, specific guidance. This is Christianity in everyday clothes.

Even outright persecution is not to shake Jesus' followers from standing fast. As painful and puzzling as it is to suffer because of their faith, Peter's readers can be encouraged because of his gentle reminder that they share in Christ's sufferings.

Peter shows the care of a wise shepherd in the way he writes to his readers. His letter encourages us to care for others in the same way. Humbled, disciplined and strengthened by the power of Jesus Christ, we can stand firm in the amazing, true grace of God.

"The many uses of the word in English convince me that grace is indeed amazing—truly our last best word. It contains the essence of the gospel as a drop of water can contain the image of the sun. The world thirsts for grace in ways it does not even recognize; little wonder the hymn 'Amazing Grace' edged its way into the Top Ten charts two hundred years after composition. For a society that seems adrift, without moorings, I know of no better place to drop the anchor of faith."

—PHILIP YANCEY,
What's So Amazing About Grace?

Inheritance Guaranteed!

1 PETER 1:1–12

If you found out today that you had inherited a million dollars from a rich relative, what difference would it make to the way you live? Be specific: "I would . . ." Now come back from dreaming to reality! You actually do have an inheritance—and it is worth infinitely more than a million dollars. Read this entire passage and write down every word or phrase that speaks of the riches you have in Jesus Christ. Then repeat several times: "This is my inheritance. It can never perish, spoil or fade." What difference will this knowledge make in the way you live? Be specific. Write a thank-you letter to God, expressing what this inheritance means to you.

See Meeting God in Everyday Life

---

1 Peter, an apostle of Jesus Christ,

To God's elect, strangers in the world, scattered throughout Pontus, Galatia, Cappadocia, Asia and Bithynia, ²who have been chosen according to the foreknowledge of God the Father, through the sanctifying work of the Spirit, for obedience to Jesus Christ and sprinkling by his blood:

Grace and peace be yours in abundance.

Praise to God for a Living Hope

³Praise be to the God and Father of our Lord Jesus Christ! In his great mercy he has given us new birth into a living hope through the resurrection of Jesus Christ from the dead, ⁴and into an inheritance that can never perish, spoil or fade—kept in heaven for you, ⁵who through faith are shielded by God's power until the coming of the salvation that is ready to be revealed in the last time. ⁶In this you greatly rejoice, though now for a little while you may have had to suffer grief in all kinds of trials. ⁷These have come so that your faith—of greater worth than gold, which perishes even though refined by fire—may be proved genuine and may result in praise, glory and honor when Jesus Christ is revealed. ⁸Though you have not seen him, you love him; and even though you do not see him now, you believe in him and are filled with an inexpressible and glorious joy, ⁹for you are receiving the goal of your faith, the salvation of your souls.

¹⁰Concerning this salvation, the prophets, who spoke of the grace that was to come to you, searched intently and with the greatest care, ¹¹trying to find out the time and circumstances to which the Spirit of Christ in them was pointing when he predicted the sufferings of Christ and the glories that would follow. ¹²It was revealed to them that they were not serving themselves but you, when they spoke of the things that have now been told you by those who have preached the gospel to you by the Holy Spirit sent from heaven. Even angels long to look into these things.

Be Holy

¹³Therefore, prepare your minds for action; be self-controlled; set your hope fully on the grace to be given you when Jesus Christ is revealed. ¹⁴As obedient children, do not conform to the evil desires you had when you lived in ignorance. ¹⁵But just as he who called you is holy, so be holy in all you do; ¹⁶for it is written: "Be holy, because I am holy."[a]

¹⁷Since you call on a Father who judges each man's work impartially, live your lives as strangers here in reverent fear. ¹⁸For you know that it was not with perishable things such as silver or gold that you were redeemed from the empty way of life handed down to you from your forefathers, ¹⁹but with the precious blood of Christ, a lamb without blemish or defect. ²⁰He was chosen before the creation of the world, but was revealed in these last times for your sake. ²¹Through him you believe in God, who raised him from the dead and glorified him, and so your faith and hope are in God.

[a] 16 Lev. 11:44,45; 19:2; 20:7

²²Now that you have purified yourselves by obeying the truth so that you have sincere love for your brothers, love one another deeply, from the heart.ᵃ ²³For you have been born again, not of perishable seed, but of imperishable, through the living and enduring word of God. ²⁴For,

> "All men are like grass,
> and all their glory is like the flowers of the field;
> the grass withers and the flowers fall,
> ²⁵ but the word of the Lord stands forever."ᵇ

And this is the word that was preached to you.

2 Therefore, rid yourselves of all malice and all deceit, hypocrisy, envy, and slander of every kind. ²Like newborn babies, crave pure spiritual milk, so that by it you may grow up in your salvation, ³now that you have tasted that the Lord is good.

The Living Stone and a Chosen People

⁴As you come to him, the living Stone—rejected by men but chosen by God and precious to him— ⁵you also, like living stones, are being built into a spiritual house to be a holy priesthood, offering spiritual sacrifices acceptable to God through Jesus Christ. ⁶For in Scripture it says:

> "See, I lay a stone in Zion,
> a chosen and precious cornerstone,
> and the one who trusts in him
> will never be put to shame."ᶜ

⁷Now to you who believe, this stone is precious. But to those who do not believe,

> "The stone the builders rejected
> has become the capstone,ᵈ"ᵉ

⁸and,

> "A stone that causes men to stumble
> and a rock that makes them fall."ᶠ

They stumble because they disobey the message—which is also what they were destined for.

⁹But you are a chosen people, a royal priesthood, a holy nation, a people belonging to God, that you may declare the praises of him who called you out of darkness into his wonderful light. ¹⁰Once you were not a people, but now you are the people of God; once you had not received mercy, but now you have received mercy.

¹¹Dear friends, I urge you, as aliens and strangers in the world, to abstain from sinful desires, which war against your soul. ¹²Live such good lives among the pagans that, though they accuse you of doing wrong, they may see your good deeds and glorify God on the day he visits us.

Submission to Rulers and Masters

¹³Submit yourselves for the Lord's sake to every authority instituted among men: whether to the king, as the supreme authority, ¹⁴or to governors, who are sent by him to punish those who do wrong and to commend those who do right. ¹⁵For it is God's will that by doing good you should silence the ignorant talk of foolish men. ¹⁶Live as free men,

---

A Chosen People

1 PETER 2:9–10

How confident are you that you are personally chosen by God and that you really *belong*? The need for a strong sense of belonging touches deep and vulnerable places in the spirit. Gently envision God coming toward you right now. How close will you let God come? What posture does God take? What is your response? Do you move? Do you say anything? What emotions rise within you? Is there anything God wants to say to you? Describe the experience you envision by writing down or drawing what happens.

ᵃ22 Some early manuscripts *from a pure heart*   ᵇ25 Isaiah 40:6–8
ᶜ6 Isaiah 28:16   ᵈ7 Or *cornerstone*   ᵉ7 Psalm 118:22   ᶠ8 Isaiah 8:14

Free, Yet Costly Love

1 PETER 3:8–12

"Do not hesitate to love and to love deeply. You might be afraid of the pain that deep love can cause. When those you love deeply reject you, leave you, or die, your heart will be broken. But that should not hold you back from loving deeply. The pain that comes from deep love makes your love ever more fruitful. It is like a plow that breaks the ground to allow the seed to take root and grow into a strong plant."

—HENRI J. M. NOUWEN,
The Inner Voice of Love

but do not use your freedom as a cover-up for evil; live as servants of God. [17]Show proper respect to everyone: Love the brotherhood of believers, fear God, honor the king.

[18]Slaves, submit yourselves to your masters with all respect, not only to those who are good and considerate, but also to those who are harsh. [19]For it is commendable if a man bears up under the pain of unjust suffering because he is conscious of God. [20]But how is it to your credit if you receive a beating for doing wrong and endure it? But if you suffer for doing good and you endure it, this is commendable before God. [21]To this you were called, because Christ suffered for you, leaving you an example, that you should follow in his steps.

> [22]"He committed no sin,
> and no deceit was found in his mouth."[a]

[23]When they hurled their insults at him, he did not retaliate; when he suffered, he made no threats. Instead, he entrusted himself to him who judges justly. [24]He himself bore our sins in his body on the tree, so that we might die to sins and live for righteousness; by his wounds you have been healed. [25]For you were like sheep going astray, but now you have returned to the Shepherd and Overseer of your souls.

Wives and Husbands

3 Wives, in the same way be submissive to your husbands so that, if any of them do not believe the word, they may be won over without words by the behavior of their wives, [2]when they see the purity and reverence of your lives. [3]Your beauty should not come from outward adornment, such as braided hair and the wearing of gold jewelry and fine clothes. [4]Instead, it should be that of your inner self, the unfading beauty of a gentle and quiet spirit, which is of great worth in God's sight. [5]For this is the way the holy women of the past who put their hope in God used to make themselves beautiful. They were submissive to their own husbands, [6]like Sarah, who obeyed Abraham and called him her master. You are her daughters if you do what is right and do not give way to fear.

[7]Husbands, in the same way be considerate as you live with your wives, and treat them with respect as the weaker partner and as heirs with you of the gracious gift of life, so that nothing will hinder your prayers.

Suffering for Doing Good

[8]Finally, all of you, live in harmony with one another; be sympathetic, love as brothers, be compassionate and humble. [9]Do not repay evil with evil or insult with insult, but with blessing, because to this you were called so that you may inherit a blessing. [10]For,

> "Whoever would love life
> and see good days
> must keep his tongue from evil
> and his lips from deceitful speech.
> [11]He must turn from evil and do good;
> he must seek peace and pursue it.
> [12]For the eyes of the Lord are on the righteous

[a] 22 Isaiah 53:9

and his ears are attentive to their prayer,
but the face of the Lord is against those who do
evil."[a]

[13]Who is going to harm you if you are eager to do good? [14]But even if you should suffer for what is right, you are blessed. "Do not fear what they fear[b]; do not be frightened."[c] [15]But in your hearts set apart Christ as Lord. Always be prepared to give an answer to everyone who asks you to give the reason for the hope that you have. But do this with gentleness and respect, [16]keeping a clear conscience, so that those who speak maliciously against your good behavior in Christ may be ashamed of their slander. [17]It is better, if it is God's will, to suffer for doing good than for doing evil. [18]For Christ died for sins once for all, the righteous for the unrighteous, to bring you to God. He was put to death in the body but made alive by the Spirit, [19]through whom[d] also he went and preached to the spirits in prison [20]who disobeyed long ago when God waited patiently in the days of Noah while the ark was being built. In it only a few people, eight in all, were saved through water, [21]and this water symbolizes baptism that now saves you also—not the removal of dirt from the body but the pledge[e] of a good conscience toward God. It saves you by the resurrection of Jesus Christ, [22]who has gone into heaven and is at God's right hand—with angels, authorities and powers in submission to him.

Living for God

4 Therefore, since Christ suffered in his body, arm yourselves also with the same attitude, because he who has suffered in his body is done with sin. [2]As a result, he does not live the rest of his earthly life for evil human desires, but rather for the will of God. [3]For you have spent enough time in the past doing what pagans choose to do—living in debauchery, lust, drunkenness, orgies, carousing and detestable idolatry. [4]They think it strange that you do not plunge with them into the same flood of dissipation, and they heap abuse on you. [5]But they will have to give account to him who is ready to judge the living and the dead. [6]For this is the reason the gospel was preached even to those who are now dead, so that they might be judged according to men in regard to the body, but live according to God in regard to the spirit.

[7]The end of all things is near. Therefore be clear minded and self-controlled so that you can pray. [8]Above all, love each other deeply, because love covers over a multitude of sins. [9]Offer hospitality to one another without grumbling. [10]Each one should use whatever gift he has received to serve others, faithfully administering God's grace in its various forms. [11]If anyone speaks, he should do it as one speaking the very words of God. If anyone serves, he should do it with the strength God provides, so that in all things God may be praised through Jesus Christ. To him be the glory and the power for ever and ever. Amen.

Suffering for Being a Christian

[12]Dear friends, do not be surprised at the painful trial you

---

Gentle Answers

1 PETER 3:13–17

How attractive do Christians make Christianity? Gentle, respectful answers for the hope that is in us are made authentic when matched by the nonverbal messages of our attitudes and behavior. Think of three people with whom you have regular contact. Ask Jesus to help you as you formulate what you would say to each one if he or she asked about your faith in Jesus Christ. Speak your answers aloud as if the person were sitting opposite you. Now reflect on what each person sees and experiences in interaction with you in everyday life. Do your words and lifestyle match? Bring your answer to Jesus in prayer.

See Meeting God in Service

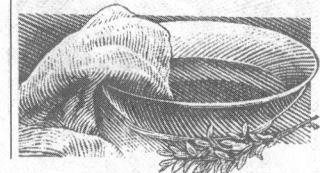

---

[a] 12 Psalm 34:12–16   [b] 14 Or *not fear their threats*   [c] 14 Isaiah 8:12
[d] 18,19 Or *alive in the spirit,* [19]*through which*   [e] 21 Or *response*

True Grace

1 PETER 4:12—5:14

Peter writes this letter to encourage his readers to stand fast in the true grace of God. Pause and expectantly open your heart for a gift of true grace personally underlined for you somewhere in this page of God's Word. Now read slowly right through the passage, noting any special phrases, words or verses that attract your attention. Choose the one that draws you most strongly and return to it. Read that phrase or verse aloud, emphasizing different key words on each reading. Then quiet your spirit and let the words nestle in a safe place within your heart. Let this gift of grace grow and bear fruit.

See *Meeting God in Scripture*

are suffering, as though something strange were happening to you. [13]But rejoice that you participate in the sufferings of Christ, so that you may be overjoyed when his glory is revealed. [14]If you are insulted because of the name of Christ, you are blessed, for the Spirit of glory and of God rests on you. [15]If you suffer, it should not be as a murderer or thief or any other kind of criminal, or even as a meddler. [16]However, if you suffer as a Christian, do not be ashamed, but praise God that you bear that name. [17]For it is time for judgment to begin with the family of God; and if it begins with us, what will the outcome be for those who do not obey the gospel of God? [18]And,

> "If it is hard for the righteous to be saved,
>   what will become of the ungodly and the
>   sinner?"[a]

[19]So then, those who suffer according to God's will should commit themselves to their faithful Creator and continue to do good.

To Elders and Young Men

5 To the elders among you, I appeal as a fellow elder, a witness of Christ's sufferings and one who also will share in the glory to be revealed: [2]Be shepherds of God's flock that is under your care, serving as overseers—not because you must, but because you are willing, as God wants you to be; not greedy for money, but eager to serve; [3]not lording it over those entrusted to you, but being examples to the flock. [4]And when the Chief Shepherd appears, you will receive the crown of glory that will never fade away.

[5]Young men, in the same way be submissive to those who are older. All of you, clothe yourselves with humility toward one another, because,

> "God opposes the proud
>   but gives grace to the humble."[b]

[6]Humble yourselves, therefore, under God's mighty hand, that he may lift you up in due time. [7]Cast all your anxiety on him because he cares for you.

[8]Be self-controlled and alert. Your enemy the devil prowls around like a roaring lion looking for someone to devour. [9]Resist him, standing firm in the faith, because you know that your brothers throughout the world are undergoing the same kind of sufferings.

[10]And the God of all grace, who called you to his eternal glory in Christ, after you have suffered a little while, will himself restore you and make you strong, firm and steadfast. [11]To him be the power for ever and ever. Amen.

Final Greetings

[12]With the help of Silas,[c] whom I regard as a faithful brother, I have written to you briefly, encouraging you and testifying that this is the true grace of God. Stand fast in it.

[13]She who is in Babylon, chosen together with you, sends you her greetings, and so does my son Mark. [14]Greet one another with a kiss of love.

Peace to all of you who are in Christ.

a 18 Prov. 11:31   *b 5* Prov. 3:34   *c 12* Greek *Silvanus,* a variant of *Silas*

2 PETER

Listening for Truth

KEY VERSE:

Grow in the grace and knowledge of our Lord and Savior Jesus Christ. —2 Peter 3:18

Would you prefer a godly life or a wallow in the mud (2:22)? Given the choice, most Christians would choose a godly life! Peter dramatically contrasts those two choices. He asserts that everything needed for living a godly life has already been given us in Christ Jesus; it is simply waiting to be appropriated. If this is the case, who would ever be diverted? "Well," says Peter, "plenty of people!" He pulls no punches. The examples he uses do not make for pleasant reading. Yet, shock tactics have their place in demanding our attention.

These particular shock tactics provide the basis for Peter's heartfelt exhortation that his readers be on the lookout for similar issues that might undermine their faith. God is patient and leaves time for each generation of believers to identify the options and choose salvation and life. But the day will come when time has run out. How much better to be actively involved in growing in grace than to be caught unprepared.

The message of this letter is very contemporary. Nothing has changed—God provides everything we need for a life of godliness. We face the same challenge the early Christians did—to grow in our knowledge and experience of holiness in Jesus Christ. Nothing has changed, either, in the human capacity to distort, scoff at or simply disbelieve the grace of God. We, like the recipients of Peter's letter, have been forewarned: Stay away from the mud and discover the green pastures of godliness!

> "Let all our employment be to *know* God: the more one *knows* him, the more one *desires* to know him. And as knowledge is commonly the measure of *love*, the deeper and more extensive our *knowledge* shall be, the greater will be our *love*: and if our *love* of God were great we would love him equally in pains and pleasures."
>
> —BROTHER LAWRENCE,
> *The Practice of the Presence of God*

You Have Everything You Need

2 PETER 1:1–4

"In technology you have this horizontal progress where you must start at one point and move to another and then another. But that is not the way to build a life of prayer. In prayer we discover what we already have. You start where you are and you deepen what you already have, and you realize that you are already there. We already have everything, but we don't know it and we don't experience it. Everything has been given to us in Christ. All we need is to experience what we already possess."

—THOMAS MERTON,
as quoted in *Thomas Merton/Monk: A Monastic Tribute*

1 Simon Peter, a servant and apostle of Jesus Christ,

To those who through the righteousness of our God and Savior Jesus Christ have received a faith as precious as ours:

²Grace and peace be yours in abundance through the knowledge of God and of Jesus our Lord.

Making One's Calling and Election Sure

³His divine power has given us everything we need for life and godliness through our knowledge of him who called us by his own glory and goodness. ⁴Through these he has given us his very great and precious promises, so that through them you may participate in the divine nature and escape the corruption in the world caused by evil desires. ⁵For this very reason, make every effort to add to your faith goodness; and to goodness, knowledge; ⁶and to knowledge, self-control; and to self-control, perseverance; and to perseverance, godliness; ⁷and to godliness, brotherly kindness; and to brotherly kindness, love. ⁸For if you possess these qualities in increasing measure, they will keep you from being ineffective and unproductive in your knowledge of our Lord Jesus Christ. ⁹But if anyone does not have them, he is nearsighted and blind, and has forgotten that he has been cleansed from his past sins.

¹⁰Therefore, my brothers, be all the more eager to make your calling and election sure. For if you do these things, you will never fall, ¹¹and you will receive a rich welcome into the eternal kingdom of our Lord and Savior Jesus Christ.

Prophecy of Scripture

¹²So I will always remind you of these things, even though you know them and are firmly established in the truth you now have. ¹³I think it is right to refresh your memory as long as I live in the tent of this body, ¹⁴because I know that I will soon put it aside, as our Lord Jesus Christ has made clear to me. ¹⁵And I will make every effort to see that after my departure you will always be able to remember these things.

¹⁶We did not follow cleverly invented stories when we told you about the power and coming of our Lord Jesus Christ, but we were eyewitnesses of his majesty. ¹⁷For he received honor and glory from God the Father when the voice came to him from the Majestic Glory, saying, "This is my Son, whom I love; with him I am well pleased."[a] ¹⁸We ourselves heard this voice that came from heaven when we were with him on the sacred mountain.

¹⁹And we have the word of the prophets made more certain, and you will do well to pay attention to it, as to a light shining in a dark place, until the day dawns and the morning star rises in your hearts. ²⁰Above all, you must understand that no prophecy of Scripture came about by the prophet's own interpretation. ²¹For prophecy never had its origin in the will of man, but men spoke from God as they were carried along by the Holy Spirit.

False Teachers and Their Destruction

2 But there were also false prophets among the people, just as there will be false teachers among you. They will

a 17 Matt. 17:5; Mark 9:7; Luke 9:35

secretly introduce destructive heresies, even denying the sovereign Lord who bought them—bringing swift destruction on themselves. ²Many will follow their shameful ways and will bring the way of truth into disrepute. ³In their greed these teachers will exploit you with stories they have made up. Their condemnation has long been hanging over them, and their destruction has not been sleeping.

⁴For if God did not spare angels when they sinned, but sent them to hell,ᵃ putting them into gloomy dungeonsᵇ to be held for judgment; ⁵if he did not spare the ancient world when he brought the flood on its ungodly people, but protected Noah, a preacher of righteousness, and seven others; ⁶if he condemned the cities of Sodom and Gomorrah by burning them to ashes, and made them an example of what is going to happen to the ungodly; ⁷and if he rescued Lot, a righteous man, who was distressed by the filthy lives of lawless men ⁸(for that righteous man, living among them day after day, was tormented in his righteous soul by the lawless deeds he saw and heard)— ⁹if this is so, then the Lord knows how to rescue godly men from trials and to hold the unrighteous for the day of judgment, while continuing their punishment.ᶜ ¹⁰This is especially true of those who follow the corrupt desire of the sinful natureᵈ and despise authority.

Bold and arrogant, these men are not afraid to slander celestial beings; ¹¹yet even angels, although they are stronger and more powerful, do not bring slanderous accusations against such beings in the presence of the Lord. ¹²But these men blaspheme in matters they do not understand. They are like brute beasts, creatures of instinct, born only to be caught and destroyed, and like beasts they too will perish.

¹³They will be paid back with harm for the harm they have done. Their idea of pleasure is to carouse in broad daylight. They are blots and blemishes, reveling in their pleasures while they feast with you.ᵉ ¹⁴With eyes full of adultery, they never stop sinning; they seduce the unstable; they are experts in greed—an accursed brood! ¹⁵They have left the straight way and wandered off to follow the way of Balaam son of Beor, who loved the wages of wickedness. ¹⁶But he was rebuked for his wrongdoing by a donkey—a beast without speech—who spoke with a man's voice and restrained the prophet's madness.

¹⁷These men are springs without water and mists driven by a storm. Blackest darkness is reserved for them. ¹⁸For they mouth empty, boastful words and, by appealing to the lustful desires of sinful human nature, they entice people who are just escaping from those who live in error. ¹⁹They promise them freedom, while they themselves are slaves of depravity—for a man is a slave to whatever has mastered him. ²⁰If they have escaped the corruption of the world by knowing our Lord and Savior Jesus Christ and are again entangled in it and overcome, they are worse off at the end than they were at the beginning. ²¹It would have been better for them not to have known the way of righteousness, than to have known it and then to turn their backs on the sacred command that was passed on to them. ²²Of them

Slave or Free?

2 PETER 2:17–20

Peter does not mince words: "A [person] is a slave to whatever has mastered [him or her]." Given all the examples he has just identified, we had better take his cautionary words seriously.

What controls you? What hinders your freedom and growth in Jesus Christ? Is it fear? The opinions of others? Laziness? An addiction? An unforgiving spirit? Greed? Or something else? Take time to let the Spirit reveal what enslaves you. Stand up and let your body feel as it would if bound with restricting ropes. Ask God to reveal the freedom Christ Jesus has won for you. As you see each rope being untied, move your body more and more freely and joyfully. End by assuming a posture that expresses your grateful commitment to true freedom.

ᵃ4 Greek *Tartarus*   ᵇ4 Some manuscripts *into chains of darkness*   ᶜ9 Or *unrighteous for punishment until the day of judgment*   ᵈ10 Or *the flesh*
ᵉ13 Some manuscripts *in their love feasts*

A Day to Look Forward To

2 PETER 3:1–18

As children, most of us felt as though Christmas day would never come. We looked forward to it eagerly for weeks—weeks that seemed like years! The anticipation filled us with excitement and imagination and prompted all kinds of preparation for the big day. Another big day is coming. But this time we don't know the date!

Suppose you knew that Jesus would return this year or next month or next week. What difference would that make in your plans and priorities? How would you feel? What preparation would you make? "Well, get on with it!" says Peter in effect. This could be the day. Let eager anticipation motivate your choices.

the proverbs are true: "A dog returns to its vomit,"[a] and, "A sow that is washed goes back to her wallowing in the mud."

The Day of the Lord

3 Dear friends, this is now my second letter to you. I have written both of them as reminders to stimulate you to wholesome thinking. [2]I want you to recall the words spoken in the past by the holy prophets and the command given by our Lord and Savior through your apostles.

[3]First of all, you must understand that in the last days scoffers will come, scoffing and following their own evil desires. [4]They will say, "Where is this 'coming' he promised? Ever since our fathers died, everything goes on as it has since the beginning of creation." [5]But they deliberately forget that long ago by God's word the heavens existed and the earth was formed out of water and by water. [6]By these waters also the world of that time was deluged and destroyed. [7]By the same word the present heavens and earth are reserved for fire, being kept for the day of judgment and destruction of ungodly men.

[8]But do not forget this one thing, dear friends: With the Lord a day is like a thousand years, and a thousand years are like a day. [9]The Lord is not slow in keeping his promise, as some understand slowness. He is patient with you, not wanting anyone to perish, but everyone to come to repentance.

[10]But the day of the Lord will come like a thief. The heavens will disappear with a roar; the elements will be destroyed by fire, and the earth and everything in it will be laid bare.[b]

[11]Since everything will be destroyed in this way, what kind of people ought you to be? You ought to live holy and godly lives [12]as you look forward to the day of God and speed its coming.[c] That day will bring about the destruction of the heavens by fire, and the elements will melt in the heat. [13]But in keeping with his promise we are looking forward to a new heaven and a new earth, the home of righteousness.

[14]So then, dear friends, since you are looking forward to this, make every effort to be found spotless, blameless and at peace with him. [15]Bear in mind that our Lord's patience means salvation, just as our dear brother Paul also wrote you with the wisdom that God gave him. [16]He writes the same way in all his letters, speaking in them of these matters. His letters contain some things that are hard to understand, which ignorant and unstable people distort, as they do the other Scriptures, to their own destruction.

[17]Therefore, dear friends, since you already know this, be on your guard so that you may not be carried away by the error of lawless men and fall from your secure position. [18]But grow in the grace and knowledge of our Lord and Savior Jesus Christ. To him be glory both now and forever! Amen.

a 22 Prov. 26:11   *b 10* Some manuscripts *be burned up*   *c 12* Or *as you wait eagerly for the day of God to come*

1 JOHN

Living in Love

KEY VERSE:

God is love. Whoever lives in love lives in God, and God in him. — *1 John 4:16*

John's letter paints a panoramic portrait of love the way God sees it. As we read and pray through these brief but powerful pages, two facets of Biblical love seem to stand out. First, before we are able to practice or walk in love, we must have some awareness of its nature. Love is grounded in God (4:8,16) and is most clearly depicted in Jesus Christ, who sacrificially offered his life for us (3:16; 4:10). John calls us to the same kind of sacrificial love in which our actions align with our words in truth (3:18).

Second, the apostle John connects love with obedience. Obedience is our joyful response to the love of Jesus Christ, which allows us to live in him and he in us (2:3–5; 2 John 5–6). We are commanded to walk in love not only when it is convenient for us but each day because we are children of God (5:2).

As you reflect on these words, review your experience of God's incredible love for you. Think about how you express that love to others. And as you join John in pondering this message, prayerfully ask God to help you to see him more clearly, love him more dearly and follow him more nearly as you mirror his love day by day.

"O most merciful Redeemer, friend and brother, may we know thee more clearly, love thee more dearly, and follow thee more nearly, for thine own sake."

—RICHARD OF CHICHESTER

Imitating Christ

1 JOHN 2:3–6

Jesus' message is clear and bracing: He commands us to follow him and walk in the same way in which he himself walked (see Matthew 8:22; John 21:19). It's not possible for us to do this through our own effort, but we can walk in him when he lives within us. Otherwise Jesus would not have given us this command!

As you reflect on these verses, describe in your own words how Jesus walked. How might you follow his example? How have you already experienced this? In what situations is it most difficult to practice? How will you ask for his help in fulfilling this command? Before turning away from this Scripture passage, think about a hymn or song that best captures this theme for you. Sing or hum it throughout the day as a way of internalizing this passage.

See *Meeting God in Everyday Life*

The Word of Life

1 That which was from the beginning, which we have heard, which we have seen with our eyes, which we have looked at and our hands have touched—this we proclaim concerning the Word of life. **2**The life appeared; we have seen it and testify to it, and we proclaim to you the eternal life, which was with the Father and has appeared to us. **3**We proclaim to you what we have seen and heard, so that you also may have fellowship with us. And our fellowship is with the Father and with his Son, Jesus Christ. **4**We write this to make our*a* joy complete.

Walking in the Light

5This is the message we have heard from him and declare to you: God is light; in him there is no darkness at all. **6**If we claim to have fellowship with him yet walk in the darkness, we lie and do not live by the truth. **7**But if we walk in the light, as he is in the light, we have fellowship with one another, and the blood of Jesus, his Son, purifies us from all*b* sin.

8If we claim to be without sin, we deceive ourselves and the truth is not in us. **9**If we confess our sins, he is faithful and just and will forgive us our sins and purify us from all unrighteousness. **10**If we claim we have not sinned, we make him out to be a liar and his word has no place in our lives.

2 My dear children, I write this to you so that you will not sin. But if anybody does sin, we have one who speaks to the Father in our defense—Jesus Christ, the Righteous One. **2**He is the atoning sacrifice for our sins, and not only for ours but also for*c* the sins of the whole world.

3We know that we have come to know him if we obey his commands. **4**The man who says, "I know him," but does not do what he commands is a liar, and the truth is not in him. **5**But if anyone obeys his word, God's love*d* is truly made complete in him. This is how we know we are in him: **6**Whoever claims to live in him must walk as Jesus did.

7Dear friends, I am not writing you a new command but an old one, which you have had since the beginning. This old command is the message you have heard. **8**Yet I am writing you a new command; its truth is seen in him and you, because the darkness is passing and the true light is already shining.

9Anyone who claims to be in the light but hates his brother is still in the darkness. **10**Whoever loves his brother lives in the light, and there is nothing in him*e* to make him stumble. **11**But whoever hates his brother is in the darkness and walks around in the darkness; he does not know where he is going, because the darkness has blinded him.

> **12**I write to you, dear children,
>   because your sins have been forgiven on
>   account of his name.
> **13**I write to you, fathers,
>   because you have known him who is from the
>   beginning.
>   I write to you, young men,
>   because you have overcome the evil one.

a 4 Some manuscripts *your*   *b 7* Or *every*   *c 2* Or *He is the one who turns aside God's wrath, taking away our sins, and not only ours but also*   *d 5* Or *word, love for God*   *e 10* Or *it*

I write to you, dear children,
  because you have known the Father.
¹⁴I write to you, fathers,
  because you have known him who is from the
    beginning.
I write to you, young men,
  because you are strong,
  and the word of God lives in you,
  and you have overcome the evil one.

Do Not Love the World

¹⁵Do not love the world or anything in the world. If anyone loves the world, the love of the Father is not in him. ¹⁶For everything in the world—the cravings of sinful man, the lust of his eyes and the boasting of what he has and does—comes not from the Father but from the world. ¹⁷The world and its desires pass away, but the man who does the will of God lives forever.

Warning Against Antichrists

¹⁸Dear children, this is the last hour; and as you have heard that the antichrist is coming, even now many antichrists have come. This is how we know it is the last hour. ¹⁹They went out from us, but they did not really belong to us. For if they had belonged to us, they would have remained with us; but their going showed that none of them belonged to us.

²⁰But you have an anointing from the Holy One, and all of you know the truth.ᵃ ²¹I do not write to you because you do not know the truth, but because you do know it and because no lie comes from the truth. ²²Who is the liar? It is the man who denies that Jesus is the Christ. Such a man is the antichrist—he denies the Father and the Son. ²³No one who denies the Son has the Father; whoever acknowledges the Son has the Father also.

²⁴See that what you have heard from the beginning remains in you. If it does, you also will remain in the Son and in the Father. ²⁵And this is what he promised us—even eternal life.

²⁶I am writing these things to you about those who are trying to lead you astray. ²⁷As for you, the anointing you received from him remains in you, and you do not need anyone to teach you. But as his anointing teaches you about all things and as that anointing is real, not counterfeit—just as it has taught you, remain in him.

Children of God

²⁸And now, dear children, continue in him, so that when he appears we may be confident and unashamed before him at his coming.

²⁹If you know that he is righteous, you know that everyone who does what is right has been born of him.

3 How great is the love the Father has lavished on us, that we should be called children of God! And that is what we are! The reason the world does not know us is that it did not know him. ²Dear friends, now we are children of God, and what we will be has not yet been made known. But we know that when he appears,ᵇ we shall be like him, for we

---

The Hollowness of Worldly Pursuits

1 JOHN 2:15–17

"This stage of love, then, is the time and place to cut out indulgent pleasures, to root out all vices, and to crush all false desires. He will be able to deal with other artificial desires, which need to be cut off as adulterous and as false branches that grow spontaneously. These are not so much desires as false appetites of the soul, the lust of the eye, and the ambitions of the world. He can then hope to make spiritual and true progress."

—BERNARD OF CLAIRVAUX,
The Love of God

ᵃ20 Some manuscripts *and you know all things*   ᵇ2 Or *when it is made known*

Love in Actions

1 JOHN 3:16–18

Many people think they *know* something when in reality they only know *about* it. They are limited by secondhand knowledge—a poor substitute for the real thing! We know the love of Jesus Christ because he laid down his life for us. And John reminds us that the best way to experience that love is to express it. How might you demonstrate that love to God? How might you demonstrate love to those who are closest to you, to your friends or associates at work, school, church, to those who are in need, or maybe even to a person you don't particularly like? Create a symbol or reminder to encourage you to make love visible to others. Carry it with you or place it on your mirror or in another prominent spot.

See Meeting God in Everyday Life

shall see him as he is. ³Everyone who has this hope in him purifies himself, just as he is pure.

⁴Everyone who sins breaks the law; in fact, sin is lawlessness. ⁵But you know that he appeared so that he might take away our sins. And in him is no sin. ⁶No one who lives in him keeps on sinning. No one who continues to sin has either seen him or known him.

⁷Dear children, do not let anyone lead you astray. He who does what is right is righteous, just as he is righteous. ⁸He who does what is sinful is of the devil, because the devil has been sinning from the beginning. The reason the Son of God appeared was to destroy the devil's work. ⁹No one who is born of God will continue to sin, because God's seed remains in him; he cannot go on sinning, because he has been born of God. ¹⁰This is how we know who the children of God are and who the children of the devil are: Anyone who does not do what is right is not a child of God; nor is anyone who does not love his brother.

Love One Another

¹¹This is the message you heard from the beginning: We should love one another. ¹²Do not be like Cain, who belonged to the evil one and murdered his brother. And why did he murder him? Because his own actions were evil and his brother's were righteous. ¹³Do not be surprised, my brothers, if the world hates you. ¹⁴We know that we have passed from death to life, because we love our brothers. Anyone who does not love remains in death. ¹⁵Anyone who hates his brother is a murderer, and you know that no murderer has eternal life in him.

¹⁶This is how we know what love is: Jesus Christ laid down his life for us. And we ought to lay down our lives for our brothers. ¹⁷If anyone has material possessions and sees his brother in need but has no pity on him, how can the love of God be in him? ¹⁸Dear children, let us not love with words or tongue but with actions and in truth. ¹⁹This then is how we know that we belong to the truth, and how we set our hearts at rest in his presence ²⁰whenever our hearts condemn us. For God is greater than our hearts, and he knows everything.

²¹Dear friends, if our hearts do not condemn us, we have confidence before God ²²and receive from him anything we ask, because we obey his commands and do what pleases him. ²³And this is his command: to believe in the name of his Son, Jesus Christ, and to love one another as he commanded us. ²⁴Those who obey his commands live in him, and he in them. And this is how we know that he lives in us: We know it by the Spirit he gave us.

Test the Spirits

4 Dear friends, do not believe every spirit, but test the spirits to see whether they are from God, because many false prophets have gone out into the world. ²This is how you can recognize the Spirit of God: Every spirit that acknowledges that Jesus Christ has come in the flesh is from God, ³but every spirit that does not acknowledge Jesus is not from God. This is the spirit of the antichrist, which you have heard is coming and even now is already in the world.

⁴You, dear children, are from God and have overcome them, because the one who is in you is greater than the one who is in the world. ⁵They are from the world and therefore speak from the viewpoint of the world, and the world listens to them. ⁶We are from God, and whoever knows God listens to us; but whoever is not from God does not listen to us. This is how we recognize the Spirit*a* of truth and the spirit of falsehood.

God's Love and Ours

⁷Dear friends, let us love one another, for love comes from God. Everyone who loves has been born of God and knows God. ⁸Whoever does not love does not know God, because God is love. ⁹This is how God showed his love among us: He sent his one and only Son*b* into the world that we might live through him. ¹⁰This is love: not that we loved God, but that he loved us and sent his Son as an atoning sacrifice for*c* our sins. ¹¹Dear friends, since God so loved us, we also ought to love one another. ¹²No one has ever seen God; but if we love one another, God lives in us and his love is made complete in us.

¹³We know that we live in him and he in us, because he has given us of his Spirit. ¹⁴And we have seen and testify that the Father has sent his Son to be the Savior of the world. ¹⁵If anyone acknowledges that Jesus is the Son of God, God lives in him and he in God. ¹⁶And so we know and rely on the love God has for us.

God is love. Whoever lives in love lives in God, and God in him. ¹⁷In this way, love is made complete among us so that we will have confidence on the day of judgment, because in this world we are like him. ¹⁸There is no fear in love. But perfect love drives out fear, because fear has to do with punishment. The one who fears is not made perfect in love.

¹⁹We love because he first loved us. ²⁰If anyone says, "I love God," yet hates his brother, he is a liar. For anyone who does not love his brother, whom he has seen, cannot love God, whom he has not seen. ²¹And he has given us this command: Whoever loves God must also love his brother.

Faith in the Son of God

5 Everyone who believes that Jesus is the Christ is born of God, and everyone who loves the father loves his child as well. ²This is how we know that we love the children of God: by loving God and carrying out his commands. ³This is love for God: to obey his commands. And his commands are not burdensome, ⁴for everyone born of God overcomes the world. This is the victory that has overcome the world, even our faith. ⁵Who is it that overcomes the world? Only he who believes that Jesus is the Son of God.

⁶This is the one who came by water and blood—Jesus Christ. He did not come by water only, but by water and blood. And it is the Spirit who testifies, because the Spirit is the truth. ⁷For there are three that testify: ⁸the*d* Spirit, the water and the blood; and the three are in agreement. ⁹We

---

God Is Love

1 JOHN 4:16–18

God is love. What a simple, yet powerful description of God's nature! Slowly and carefully read these verses again. What phrase captures your attention? Gently savor this Scripture. What attracts you to it? What does it mean to you? How have you experienced it in your life? As you continue to slowly ponder and pray this phrase, what emotions do you feel stirring within your heart? Allow God's Spirit the freedom to impress you with any insights, reminders or invitations. Conclude by thanking God for your time together.

See Meeting God in Scripture

---

a 6 Or *spirit*   *b* 9 Or *his only begotten Son*   *c* 10 Or *as the one who would turn aside his wrath, taking away*   *d* 7,8 Late manuscripts of the Vulgate *testify in heaven: the Father, the Word and the Holy Spirit, and these three are one.* ⁸*And there are three that testify on earth: the* (not found in any Greek manuscript before the sixteenth century)

Accept No Substitutes!

1 JOHN 5:21

God alone is worthy to receive our devotion and love. Sometimes, however, we allow people and things to take God's place at the center of our lives; they become idols.

Use your imagination and enter into a conversation with Jesus. Where are the two of you? What are you talking about? As your time unfolds, imagine Jesus gently but firmly asking, "My friend, who are the idols in your life? What competes with me for your love? I desire to fill you with my grace—with myself—and to be your first love." How is God's Holy Spirit calling you to respond? What do you notice about the look on Jesus' face? What emotions are you experiencing. Record your insights in your journal.

See *Meeting God in Everyday Life*

accept man's testimony, but God's testimony is greater because it is the testimony of God, which he has given about his Son. [10]Anyone who believes in the Son of God has this testimony in his heart. Anyone who does not believe God has made him out to be a liar, because he has not believed the testimony God has given about his Son. [11]And this is the testimony: God has given us eternal life, and this life is in his Son. [12]He who has the Son has life; he who does not have the Son of God does not have life.

Concluding Remarks

[13]I write these things to you who believe in the name of the Son of God so that you may know that you have eternal life. [14]This is the confidence we have in approaching God: that if we ask anything according to his will, he hears us. [15]And if we know that he hears us—whatever we ask—we know that we have what we asked of him.

[16]If anyone sees his brother commit a sin that does not lead to death, he should pray and God will give him life. I refer to those whose sin does not lead to death. There is a sin that leads to death. I am not saying that he should pray about that. [17]All wrongdoing is sin, and there is sin that does not lead to death.

[18]We know that anyone born of God does not continue to sin; the one who was born of God keeps him safe, and the evil one cannot harm him. [19]We know that we are children of God, and that the whole world is under the control of the evil one. [20]We know also that the Son of God has come and has given us understanding, so that we may know him who is true. And we are in him who is true—even in his Son Jesus Christ. He is the true God and eternal life.

[21]Dear children, keep yourselves from idols.

2 JOHN

Walking in Love

KEY VERSE:

As you have heard from the beginning, his command is that you walk in love.—2 John 6

The challenging words of Amy Carmichael mirror John's message: Biblical love is contagious! Love is a dynamic, blazing flame that awakens us by its power, passion and reality. However, our life experiences remind us that not everyone is inspired by the integrity of love. As strange as it may seem, some are equally motivated by error. This brief letter summarizes the battle being waged within the believer between walking in love and walking in error. True love—expressed in obedience—produces the richness of delight in God (v.6). But walking in error and heresy yields the emptiness of deception and danger (vv.7–11). John alerts us to the same potential pitfalls today. As you read this short book, don't underestimate the importance of its message. Whom or what do you welcome into your life? Do those people, activities and experiences encourage you to walk in love or in error?

"You will, I believe and trust, become more and more in love with a crucified Saviour. He wants lovers. Oh how tepid is the love of so many who call themselves by His name. How tepid our own—my own—in comparison with the lava fires of His eternal love. I pray that you may be an ardent lover, the kind of lover who sets others on fire."

—AMY CARMICHAEL,
Candles in the Dark,

Remember the Command: Walk in Love!

2 JOHN 4–6

Parents and teachers can readily grasp the message of these verses. John's heart is overflowing with joy that others within the church are living out the truth of walking in love. In our own day, when many relationships both within and outside the church are fractured by greed and the desire for ease and self-advancement, it is both wise and necessary to follow this Biblical counsel.

What does it mean for you to walk in love with those significant people in your life? What is the greatest hurdle you have to overcome to walk in love? How much joy does your church bring to Jesus Christ by the way its people interact inside the church? By the way those people interact with those outside the church? As you reflect on these questions write a "love letter" to Jesus about your intentions to walk in love.

See Meeting God in Community

¹The elder,

To the chosen lady and her children, whom I love in the truth—and not I only, but also all who know the truth—²because of the truth, which lives in us and will be with us forever:

³Grace, mercy and peace from God the Father and from Jesus Christ, the Father's Son, will be with us in truth and love.

⁴It has given me great joy to find some of your children walking in the truth, just as the Father commanded us. ⁵And now, dear lady, I am not writing you a new command but one we have had from the beginning. I ask that we love one another. ⁶And this is love: that we walk in obedience to his commands. As you have heard from the beginning, his command is that you walk in love.

⁷Many deceivers, who do not acknowledge Jesus Christ as coming in the flesh, have gone out into the world. Any such person is the deceiver and the antichrist. ⁸Watch out that you do not lose what you have worked for, but that you may be rewarded fully. ⁹Anyone who runs ahead and does not continue in the teaching of Christ does not have God; whoever continues in the teaching has both the Father and the Son. ¹⁰If anyone comes to you and does not bring this teaching, do not take him into your house or welcome him. ¹¹Anyone who welcomes him shares in his wicked work.

¹²I have much to write to you, but I do not want to use paper and ink. Instead, I hope to visit you and talk with you face to face, so that our joy may be complete.

¹³The children of your chosen sister send their greetings.

3 JOHN
Walking in Truth

KEY VERSE:

I have no greater joy than to hear that my children are walking in the truth.—3 John 4

What a startling comparison John paints on the canvas of this book of holy Scripture. Two specific individuals are mentioned by name to illustrate the importance of personal character. Diotrephes, who is characterized by self-love, exhibits an inhospitable attitude that ravages the Christian community (vv. 9–10). In stark contrast is Demetrius, whose reputation for truthful living is affirmed by everyone (v. 12). His life is marked by integrity, and John holds him up as a fitting model for his readers. It is evident from John's words that walking in truth is more than speaking the correct words. It requires the formation of character that is honest and is worthy of God. Indeed John's third letter could serve as a New Testament counterpoint to Micah's great ethical summary of the law: "He has showed you, O man, what is good. And what does the LORD require of you? To act justly and to love mercy and to walk humbly with your God" (Micah 6:8). What will you do today to rise to John Huss's challenges to pursue truth?

"Therefore, O faithful Christian, search for truth, hear truth, learn truth, love truth, speak the truth, hold the truth, defend the truth till death!"

—JOHN HUSS,
Exposition of Faith

The Source of True Health

3 JOHN 2–4

Our society is health conscious, a phenomenon that is clearly confirmed by the number of health publications, vitamins and supplements, kinds of exercise equipment and assorted experimental healing techniques that are available on the market. And modern medicine is finally discovering the reality, which Scripture has consistently communicated, that there is a connection between the health of our spirit and the health of our bodies. We rarely hear, however, that one of the basic principles of a healthful life is truth!

When our lives are characterized by honesty and integrity, we reduce the need to conceal or deceive. Our level of peace goes up and our stress level goes down. Jesus was telling the gospel truth when he reminded us that the truth sets us free (see John 8:32). Where do you most need this freedom in your life? How are you being challenged to walk in greater truth? Spend some moments quietly seeking and listening to God's Spirit. If possible, share your insights with a trusted friend who can pray with you and encourage you to walk in the truth.

[1]The elder,

To my dear friend Gaius, whom I love in the truth.

[2]Dear friend, I pray that you may enjoy good health and that all may go well with you, even as your soul is getting along well. [3]It gave me great joy to have some brothers come and tell about your faithfulness to the truth and how you continue to walk in the truth. [4]I have no greater joy than to hear that my children are walking in the truth.

[5]Dear friend, you are faithful in what you are doing for the brothers, even though they are strangers to you. [6]They have told the church about your love. You will do well to send them on their way in a manner worthy of God. [7]It was for the sake of the Name that they went out, receiving no help from the pagans. [8]We ought therefore to show hospitality to such men so that we may work together for the truth.

[9]I wrote to the church, but Diotrephes, who loves to be first, will have nothing to do with us. [10]So if I come, I will call attention to what he is doing, gossiping maliciously about us. Not satisfied with that, he refuses to welcome the brothers. He also stops those who want to do so and puts them out of the church.

[11]Dear friend, do not imitate what is evil but what is good. Anyone who does what is good is from God. Anyone who does what is evil has not seen God. [12]Demetrius is well spoken of by everyone—and even by the truth itself. We also speak well of him, and you know that our testimony is true.

[13]I have much to write you, but I do not want to do so with pen and ink. [14]I hope to see you soon, and we will talk face to face.

Peace to you. The friends here send their greetings. Greet the friends there by name.

JUDE

Standing Firm

KEY VERSE:

Keep yourselves in God's love as you wait for the mercy of our Lord Jesus Christ to bring you to eternal life.—Jude 21

This little book is short, sharp and salutary. Jude sets out to write an enthusiastic letter about the wonders of salvation but finds himself writing strong, stern words instead. He is motivated by love of God and love for his readers.

Jude (said by tradition to be the brother of Jesus as well as his servant) burns with passion for the purity of the faith; he can't bear to see it undermined. But that is exactly what is happening, and a warning must be issued. With anguish and energy Jude startles his readers into taking notice. At the beginning and end of the letter, Jude speaks of the mercy, peace, love, power and security that are available in Jesus Christ. In the middle of the letter, Jude gives graphic examples of the awful possibility of perverting what Jesus offers. Though the examples Jude gives certainly would have evoked powerful memories for his original readers, some of them may seem irrelevant to us in our culture and our time. We can't escape the significance of this letter however. God's Spirit, who inspired Jude's letter, asks us to consider what might pervert God's grace in our day. What behavior, lifestyle, attitudes or destructive talk do we need to address? Do we need to wake up? After all, we are nearer to the "last times" than Jude's readers were! May his passionate words kindle the fire of love in our hearts. Be warned. Take action. Keep yourself in the love of God.

"It is not easy under everyday conditions to learn and maintain the art of steadfast attention to God; yet no art could more certainly serve his purposes than this. 'One loving spirit sets another on fire.'"

—EVELYN UNDERHILL,
The Golden Sequence

Beware of Intruders!

Jude issues a wake-up call to those of his readers whose spiritual lives are being subtly undermined. There are intruders in the community of faith—distorters of the truth, who are turning abundant mercy, peace and love into waterless clouds and fruitless trees. Do you ever have the uncomfortable feeling that there is subtle conflict going on within you? Within your community of faith? Prayerfully reflect on your faith community. What symbols or descriptions might represent various influences, both negative and positive? Name what you can celebrate and that for which you can give thanks! Then ask for the Spirit's help to name and deal with the intruders that undermine your peace.

See Meeting God in Community

¹Jude, a servant of Jesus Christ and a brother of James,

To those who have been called, who are loved by God the Father and kept by*ᵃ* Jesus Christ:

²Mercy, peace and love be yours in abundance.

The Sin and Doom of Godless Men

³Dear friends, although I was very eager to write to you about the salvation we share, I felt I had to write and urge you to contend for the faith that was once for all entrusted to the saints. ⁴For certain men whose condemnation was written about*ᵇ* long ago have secretly slipped in among you. They are godless men, who change the grace of our God into a license for immorality and deny Jesus Christ our only Sovereign and Lord.

⁵Though you already know all this, I want to remind you that the Lord*ᶜ* delivered his people out of Egypt, but later destroyed those who did not believe. ⁶And the angels who did not keep their positions of authority but abandoned their own home—these he has kept in darkness, bound with everlasting chains for judgment on the great Day. ⁷In a similar way, Sodom and Gomorrah and the surrounding towns gave themselves up to sexual immorality and perversion. They serve as an example of those who suffer the punishment of eternal fire.

⁸In the very same way, these dreamers pollute their own bodies, reject authority and slander celestial beings. ⁹But even the archangel Michael, when he was disputing with the devil about the body of Moses, did not dare to bring a slanderous accusation against him, but said, "The Lord rebuke you!" ¹⁰Yet these men speak abusively against whatever they do not understand; and what things they do understand by instinct, like unreasoning animals—these are the very things that destroy them.

¹¹Woe to them! They have taken the way of Cain; they have rushed for profit into Balaam's error; they have been destroyed in Korah's rebellion.

¹²These men are blemishes at your love feasts, eating with you without the slightest qualm—shepherds who feed only themselves. They are clouds without rain, blown along by the wind; autumn trees, without fruit and uprooted—twice dead. ¹³They are wild waves of the sea, foaming up their shame; wandering stars, for whom blackest darkness has been reserved forever.

¹⁴Enoch, the seventh from Adam, prophesied about these men: "See, the Lord is coming with thousands upon thousands of his holy ones ¹⁵to judge everyone, and to convict all the ungodly of all the ungodly acts they have done in the ungodly way, and of all the harsh words ungodly sinners have spoken against him." ¹⁶These men are grumblers and faultfinders; they follow their own evil desires; they boast about themselves and flatter others for their own advantage.

A Call to Persevere

¹⁷But, dear friends, remember what the apostles of our Lord Jesus Christ foretold. ¹⁸They said to you, "In the last times there will be scoffers who will follow their own un-

---

ᵃ 1 Or *for;* or *in*   *ᵇ 4* Or *men who were marked out for condemnation*
ᶜ 5 Some early manuscripts *Jesus*

godly desires." ¹⁹These are the men who divide you, who follow mere natural instincts and do not have the Spirit.

²⁰But you, dear friends, build yourselves up in your most holy faith and pray in the Holy Spirit. ²¹Keep yourselves in God's love as you wait for the mercy of our Lord Jesus Christ to bring you to eternal life.

²²Be merciful to those who doubt; ²³snatch others from the fire and save them; to others show mercy, mixed with fear—hating even the clothing stained by corrupted flesh.

Doxology

²⁴To him who is able to keep you from falling and to present you before his glorious presence without fault and with great joy— ²⁵to the only God our Savior be glory, majesty, power and authority, through Jesus Christ our Lord, before all ages, now and forevermore! Amen.

Securely Loved

JUDE 20–25

Being made aware of the weak spots and the distortions in our life of faith can be a devastating as well as a defining experience. Where is the secure ground, we ask? How can we be sure we aren't following a wild wave or a wandering star to nowhere? Stay in the center of God's love, answers Jude. This is the axis around which faith, prayer, hope and mercy revolve. Close your eyes and picture the center "pole" of God's love. Where are you in relation to it? Let the prayer picture develop. Notice what the Spirit shows you. Afterward you may want to draw or write down your key insights. Read verses 24–25 as a final assurance of blessing and a powerful shout of praise to God.

REVELATION
A Kingdom of Priests

KEY VERSES:

To him who loves us and has freed us from our sins by his blood, and has made us to be a kingdom and priests to serve his God and Father—to him be glory and power for ever and ever! Amen.—Revelation 1:5–6

"Christ's Cross has become the key to a history whose purpose is to separate the City of God from the city of this world, which has Babylon for its symbolic name."

—THOMAS MERTON,
Bread in the Wilderness

The book of Revelation paints sweeping landscapes of two worlds: the sinful world that will pass away ("Fallen! Fallen is Babylon the Great!" [18:2]) and, in contrast, a new world established in Jesus Christ that is the true home of all believers ("I saw the Holy City, the new Jerusalem, coming down out of heaven from God" [21:2]).

There are many interpretations of this apocalyptic book. Some interpret it as exclusively futuristic and place the events of the book in the end times. This view, however, avoids the call to radical discipleship at the heart of John's vision. Revelation can be seen as a map of the Christian's spiritual journey from citizenship in Babylon to citizenship in the new Jerusalem. Babylon represents all the destructive, self-centered, dehumanizing effects of sin in this world, while Jerusalem represents the healing and liberation of new life in Christ. Redeemed in the blood of the Lamb of God, believers find a new identity in Jesus Christ and become "priests" of God who represent the presence of God in the fallen world.

As you meditate on John's vision, try to put aside all your preconceptions about Revelation and listen to the voice of the Spirit speaking to your heart about your true life as a "priest" in God's kingdom. Listen for God's call for you to become what you were created to be—a beloved child created in the image of God, a member of God's kingdom. Let the love of God become evident in you as you live in profound integrity and wholeness.

Prologue

1 The revelation of Jesus Christ, which God gave him to show his servants what must soon take place. He made it known by sending his angel to his servant John, ²who testifies to everything he saw—that is, the word of God and the testimony of Jesus Christ. ³Blessed is the one who reads the words of this prophecy, and blessed are those who hear it and take to heart what is written in it, because the time is near.

Greetings and Doxology

⁴John,

To the seven churches in the province of Asia:

Grace and peace to you from him who is, and who was, and who is to come, and from the seven spirits*ᵃ* before his throne, ⁵and from Jesus Christ, who is the faithful witness, the firstborn from the dead, and the ruler of the kings of the earth.

To him who loves us and has freed us from our sins by his blood, ⁶and has made us to be a kingdom and priests to serve his God and Father—to him be glory and power for ever and ever! Amen.

> ⁷Look, he is coming with the clouds,
>   and every eye will see him,
>   even those who pierced him;
> and all the peoples of the earth will mourn
>   because of him.
> So shall it be! Amen.

⁸"I am the Alpha and the Omega," says the Lord God, "who is, and who was, and who is to come, the Almighty."

One Like a Son of Man

⁹I, John, your brother and companion in the suffering and kingdom and patient endurance that are ours in Jesus, was on the island of Patmos because of the word of God and the testimony of Jesus. ¹⁰On the Lord's Day I was in the Spirit, and I heard behind me a loud voice like a trumpet, ¹¹which said: "Write on a scroll what you see and send it to the seven churches: to Ephesus, Smyrna, Pergamum, Thyatira, Sardis, Philadelphia and Laodicea."

¹²I turned around to see the voice that was speaking to me. And when I turned I saw seven golden lampstands, ¹³and among the lampstands was someone "like a son of man,"*ᵇ* dressed in a robe reaching down to his feet and with a golden sash around his chest. ¹⁴His head and hair were white like wool, as white as snow, and his eyes were like blazing fire. ¹⁵His feet were like bronze glowing in a furnace, and his voice was like the sound of rushing waters. ¹⁶In his right hand he held seven stars, and out of his mouth came a sharp double-edged sword. His face was like the sun shining in all its brilliance.

¹⁷When I saw him, I fell at his feet as though dead. Then he placed his right hand on me and said: "Do not be afraid. I am the First and the Last. ¹⁸I am the Living One; I was

Radical Reorientation

REVELATION 1:10–17

John is so disturbed when he encounters God that he falls "at his feet as though dead." God's presence has a way of disrupting our carefully structured world. We tend to expect God to fit neatly into our agendas, our perspectives and our lifestyle. Make a list of your attitudes that limit who God can be in your life. Alongside this list write down some characteristics of your lifestyle that could restrict God's presence in your activities. Also examine your expectations for the future. How could they hinder God's purposes for you? What would you need to do to let this awesome and merciful God disrupt the structures of your life?

See *Meeting God in Everyday Life*

Cold Orthodoxy

The Ephesian church appears to be strong; in reality it has a serious problem that threatens its very existence in the body of Christ. What is the nature of its "first love"? (See Acts 19:10,19–20.) What are the signs of its faithfulness? What are the signs of your faithfulness? Are there ways in which your discipleship has become a set of habits and not a living relationship with God? Write a letter to yourself or your church—one you could envision Jesus himself writing. In light of such a letter, what changes in your discipleship do you need to make?

dead, and behold I am alive for ever and ever! And I hold the keys of death and Hades.

¹⁹"Write, therefore, what you have seen, what is now and what will take place later. ²⁰The mystery of the seven stars that you saw in my right hand and of the seven golden lampstands is this: The seven stars are the angels[a] of the seven churches, and the seven lampstands are the seven churches.

To the Church in Ephesus

2 "To the angel[b] of the church in Ephesus write:

These are the words of him who holds the seven stars in his right hand and walks among the seven golden lampstands: ²I know your deeds, your hard work and your perseverance. I know that you cannot tolerate wicked men, that you have tested those who claim to be apostles but are not, and have found them false. ³You have persevered and have endured hardships for my name, and have not grown weary.

⁴Yet I hold this against you: You have forsaken your first love. ⁵Remember the height from which you have fallen! Repent and do the things you did at first. If you do not repent, I will come to you and remove your lampstand from its place. ⁶But you have this in your favor: You hate the practices of the Nicolaitans, which I also hate.

⁷He who has an ear, let him hear what the Spirit says to the churches. To him who overcomes, I will give the right to eat from the tree of life, which is in the paradise of God.

To the Church in Smyrna

⁸"To the angel of the church in Smyrna write:

These are the words of him who is the First and the Last, who died and came to life again. ⁹I know your afflictions and your poverty—yet you are rich! I know the slander of those who say they are Jews and are not, but are a synagogue of Satan. ¹⁰Do not be afraid of what you are about to suffer. I tell you, the devil will put some of you in prison to test you, and you will suffer persecution for ten days. Be faithful, even to the point of death, and I will give you the crown of life.

¹¹He who has an ear, let him hear what the Spirit says to the churches. He who overcomes will not be hurt at all by the second death.

To the Church in Pergamum

¹²"To the angel of the church in Pergamum write:

These are the words of him who has the sharp, double-edged sword. ¹³I know where you live—where Satan has his throne. Yet you remain true to my name. You did not renounce your faith in me, even in the days of Antipas, my faithful witness, who was put to death in your city—where Satan lives.

¹⁴Nevertheless, I have a few things against you: You have people there who hold to the teaching of Balaam, who taught Balak to entice the Israelites to sin by eat-

ing food sacrificed to idols and by committing sexual immorality. [15]Likewise you also have those who hold to the teaching of the Nicolaitans. [16]Repent therefore! Otherwise, I will soon come to you and will fight against them with the sword of my mouth.

[17]He who has an ear, let him hear what the Spirit says to the churches. To him who overcomes, I will give some of the hidden manna. I will also give him a white stone with a new name written on it, known only to him who receives it.

To the Church in Thyatira

[18]"To the angel of the church in Thyatira write:

These are the words of the Son of God, whose eyes are like blazing fire and whose feet are like burnished bronze. [19]I know your deeds, your love and faith, your service and perseverance, and that you are now doing more than you did at first.

[20]Nevertheless, I have this against you: You tolerate that woman Jezebel, who calls herself a prophetess. By her teaching she misleads my servants into sexual immorality and the eating of food sacrificed to idols. [21]I have given her time to repent of her immorality, but she is unwilling. [22]So I will cast her on a bed of suffering, and I will make those who commit adultery with her suffer intensely, unless they repent of her ways. [23]I will strike her children dead. Then all the churches will know that I am he who searches hearts and minds, and I will repay each of you according to your deeds. [24]Now I say to the rest of you in Thyatira, to you who do not hold to her teaching and have not learned Satan's so-called deep secrets (I will not impose any other burden on you): [25]Only hold on to what you have until I come.

[26]To him who overcomes and does my will to the end, I will give authority over the nations—

[27]'He will rule them with an iron scepter;
    he will dash them to pieces like pottery'[a]—

just as I have received authority from my Father. [28]I will also give him the morning star. [29]He who has an ear, let him hear what the Spirit says to the churches.

To the Church in Sardis

3 "To the angel[b] of the church in Sardis write:

These are the words of him who holds the seven spirits[c] of God and the seven stars. I know your deeds; you have a reputation of being alive, but you are dead. [2]Wake up! Strengthen what remains and is about to die, for I have not found your deeds complete in the sight of my God. [3]Remember, therefore, what you have received and heard; obey it, and repent. But if you do not wake up, I will come like a thief, and you will not know at what time I will come to you.

[4]Yet you have a few people in Sardis who have not soiled their clothes. They will walk with me, dressed in

---

Dead or Alive?

REVELATION 3:1–6

Imagine that you are a citizen of the impregnable city of Sardis, set atop a promontory. Only twice in many centuries has your city ever been captured by an enemy. On both occasions your ancestors were so confident in their security that they failed to set a watch during a siege. The enemy scaled the cliffs at night and captured the city. What is Jesus saying to you as a citizen of this city? How can you set a watch against the enemies of your soul? If Jesus were to come right now, would it be well with your soul? What changes do you need to make?

---

[a]27 Psalm 2:9   [b]1 Or *messenger*; also in verses 7 and 14   [c]1 Or *the sevenfold Spirit*

Opening the Door

REVELATION 3:14–22

Are there any closed doors in your heart? Are there doors that you have not dared open to allow Jesus in? What are the spiritual and emotional prisons that keep you from him? Try to still the inner "noise" of distracting thoughts and listen for Jesus' knock of love on the door. Picture yourself in a room with a closed door. What is the name on the door (indulgence, impatience, anger, lust, _____)? Go to that door. Open it to Jesus' presence. Give him permission to enter and nurture you to wholeness.

white, for they are worthy. ⁵He who overcomes will, like them, be dressed in white. I will never blot out his name from the book of life, but will acknowledge his name before my Father and his angels. ⁶He who has an ear, let him hear what the Spirit says to the churches.

To the Church in Philadelphia

⁷"To the angel of the church in Philadelphia write:

These are the words of him who is holy and true, who holds the key of David. What he opens no one can shut, and what he shuts no one can open. ⁸I know your deeds. See, I have placed before you an open door that no one can shut. I know that you have little strength, yet you have kept my word and have not denied my name. ⁹I will make those who are of the synagogue of Satan, who claim to be Jews though they are not, but are liars—I will make them come and fall down at your feet and acknowledge that I have loved you. ¹⁰Since you have kept my command to endure patiently, I will also keep you from the hour of trial that is going to come upon the whole world to test those who live on the earth.

¹¹I am coming soon. Hold on to what you have, so that no one will take your crown. ¹²Him who overcomes I will make a pillar in the temple of my God. Never again will he leave it. I will write on him the name of my God and the name of the city of my God, the new Jerusalem, which is coming down out of heaven from my God; and I will also write on him my new name. ¹³He who has an ear, let him hear what the Spirit says to the churches.

To the Church in Laodicea

¹⁴"To the angel of the church in Laodicea write:

These are the words of the Amen, the faithful and true witness, the ruler of God's creation. ¹⁵I know your deeds, that you are neither cold nor hot. I wish you were either one or the other! ¹⁶So, because you are lukewarm—neither hot nor cold—I am about to spit you out of my mouth. ¹⁷You say, 'I am rich; I have acquired wealth and do not need a thing.' But you do not realize that you are wretched, pitiful, poor, blind and naked. ¹⁸I counsel you to buy from me gold refined in the fire, so you can become rich; and white clothes to wear, so you can cover your shameful nakedness; and salve to put on your eyes, so you can see.

¹⁹Those whom I love I rebuke and discipline. So be earnest, and repent. ²⁰Here I am! I stand at the door and knock. If anyone hears my voice and opens the door, I will come in and eat with him, and he with me.

²¹To him who overcomes, I will give the right to sit with me on my throne, just as I overcame and sat down with my Father on his throne. ²²He who has an ear, let him hear what the Spirit says to the churches."

The Throne in Heaven

4 After this I looked, and there before me was a door standing open in heaven. And the voice I had first heard speaking to me like a trumpet said, "Come up here, and I will show you what must take place after this." ²At once I was in the Spirit, and there before me was a throne in heaven with someone sitting on it. ³And the one who sat there had the appearance of jasper and carnelian. A rainbow, resembling an emerald, encircled the throne. ⁴Surrounding the throne were twenty-four other thrones, and seated on them were twenty-four elders. They were dressed in white and had crowns of gold on their heads. ⁵From the throne came flashes of lightning, rumblings and peals of thunder. Before the throne, seven lamps were blazing. These are the seven spirits*a* of God. ⁶Also before the throne there was what looked like a sea of glass, clear as crystal.

In the center, around the throne, were four living creatures, and they were covered with eyes, in front and in back. ⁷The first living creature was like a lion, the second was like an ox, the third had a face like a man, the fourth was like a flying eagle. ⁸Each of the four living creatures had six wings and was covered with eyes all around, even under his wings. Day and night they never stop saying:

> "Holy, holy, holy
> is the Lord God Almighty,
> who was, and is, and is to come."

⁹Whenever the living creatures give glory, honor and thanks to him who sits on the throne and who lives for ever and ever, ¹⁰the twenty-four elders fall down before him who sits on the throne, and worship him who lives for ever and ever. They lay their crowns before the throne and say:

> ¹¹ "You are worthy, our Lord and God,
> to receive glory and honor and power,
> for you created all things,
> and by your will they were created
> and have their being."

The Scroll and the Lamb

5 Then I saw in the right hand of him who sat on the throne a scroll with writing on both sides and sealed with seven seals. ²And I saw a mighty angel proclaiming in a loud voice, "Who is worthy to break the seals and open the scroll?" ³But no one in heaven or on earth or under the earth could open the scroll or even look inside it. ⁴I wept and wept because no one was found who was worthy to open the scroll or look inside. ⁵Then one of the elders said to me, "Do not weep! See, the Lion of the tribe of Judah, the Root of David, has triumphed. He is able to open the scroll and its seven seals."

⁶Then I saw a Lamb, looking as if it had been slain, standing in the center of the throne, encircled by the four living creatures and the elders. He had seven horns and seven eyes, which are the seven spirits*a* of God sent out into all the earth. ⁷He came and took the scroll from the right hand of him who sat on the throne. ⁸And when he had taken it,

a 5 Or the sevenfold Spirit

Priestly Character

REVELATION 4:4–11

Read this vision of the throne of God several times and then reenact it as a prayerful recommitment to priestly discipleship. Make a paper crown for yourself and write on it "The Control of My Life." Falling down before God, acknowledge him with the prayer in verse 8. In a spirit of worship give him freedom to be God in your life. Finally, lay down your crown before him! Let him be in control of your life. Meditate on how you can carry into your daily life and relationships an inner attitude of falling down before God, worshiping him and placing your "crown" before him.

See Meeting God in Everyday Life

"Worthy Is the Lamb"

REVELATION 5:11–14

We may be among the many Christians who have a very well-developed intellectual understanding of Jesus, his life, his death, his resurrection and what it all means for us. But sometimes our spirit and emotions do not catch up with our intellect. Find a CD, cassette tape or record of Handel's *Messiah*. Play the selection "Worthy Is the Lamb" and let the music lead you into worship. Or for a more contemporary musical offering, play Michael Card's "You Are Worthy," from his CD *Unveiled Hope*. Let the music sink into your soul until it expresses your adoration of the Lamb. You might try something similar with the other songs on Card's CD, which sets many of the songs of praise and adoration in Revelation to music. Then try singing the Scripture in your heart and mind throughout the day.

See Meeting God in Worship

the four living creatures and the twenty-four elders fell down before the Lamb. Each one had a harp and they were holding golden bowls full of incense, which are the prayers of the saints. ⁹And they sang a new song:

> "You are worthy to take the scroll
>   and to open its seals,
> because you were slain,
>   and with your blood you purchased men for
>   God
>   from every tribe and language and people and
>   nation.
> ¹⁰You have made them to be a kingdom and priests
>   to serve our God,
>   and they will reign on the earth."

¹¹Then I looked and heard the voice of many angels, numbering thousands upon thousands, and ten thousand times ten thousand. They encircled the throne and the living creatures and the elders. ¹²In a loud voice they sang:

> "Worthy is the Lamb, who was slain,
>   to receive power and wealth and wisdom and
>   strength
>   and honor and glory and praise!"

¹³Then I heard every creature in heaven and on earth and under the earth and on the sea, and all that is in them, singing:

> "To him who sits on the throne and to the Lamb
>   be praise and honor and glory and power,
>   for ever and ever!"

¹⁴The four living creatures said, "Amen," and the elders fell down and worshiped.

The Seals

6 I watched as the Lamb opened the first of the seven seals. Then I heard one of the four living creatures say in a voice like thunder, "Come!" ²I looked, and there before me was a white horse! Its rider held a bow, and he was given a crown, and he rode out as a conqueror bent on conquest.

³When the Lamb opened the second seal, I heard the second living creature say, "Come!" ⁴Then another horse came out, a fiery red one. Its rider was given power to take peace from the earth and to make men slay each other. To him was given a large sword.

⁵When the Lamb opened the third seal, I heard the third living creature say, "Come!" I looked, and there before me was a black horse! Its rider was holding a pair of scales in his hand. ⁶Then I heard what sounded like a voice among the four living creatures, saying, "A quart*ᵃ* of wheat for a day's wages,*ᵇ* and three quarts of barley for a day's wages,*ᵇ* and do not damage the oil and the wine!"

⁷When the Lamb opened the fourth seal, I heard the voice of the fourth living creature say, "Come!" ⁸I looked, and there before me was a pale horse! Its rider was named Death, and Hades was following close behind him. They were given power over a fourth of the earth to kill by sword, famine and plague, and by the wild beasts of the earth.

ᵃ 6 Greek *a choinix* (probably about a liter)   *ᵇ 6* Greek *a denarius*

⁹When he opened the fifth seal, I saw under the altar the souls of those who had been slain because of the word of God and the testimony they had maintained. ¹⁰They called out in a loud voice, "How long, Sovereign Lord, holy and true, until you judge the inhabitants of the earth and avenge our blood?" ¹¹Then each of them was given a white robe, and they were told to wait a little longer, until the number of their fellow servants and brothers who were to be killed as they had been was completed.

¹²I watched as he opened the sixth seal. There was a great earthquake. The sun turned black like sackcloth made of goat hair, the whole moon turned blood red, ¹³and the stars in the sky fell to earth, as late figs drop from a fig tree when shaken by a strong wind. ¹⁴The sky receded like a scroll, rolling up, and every mountain and island was removed from its place.

¹⁵Then the kings of the earth, the princes, the generals, the rich, the mighty, and every slave and every free man hid in caves and among the rocks of the mountains. ¹⁶They called to the mountains and the rocks, "Fall on us and hide us from the face of him who sits on the throne and from the wrath of the Lamb! ¹⁷For the great day of their wrath has come, and who can stand?"

144,000 Sealed

7 After this I saw four angels standing at the four corners of the earth, holding back the four winds of the earth to prevent any wind from blowing on the land or on the sea or on any tree. ²Then I saw another angel coming up from the east, having the seal of the living God. He called out in a loud voice to the four angels who had been given power to harm the land and the sea: ³"Do not harm the land or the sea or the trees until we put a seal on the foreheads of the servants of our God." ⁴Then I heard the number of those who were sealed: 144,000 from all the tribes of Israel.

⁵From the tribe of Judah 12,000 were sealed,
from the tribe of Reuben 12,000,
from the tribe of Gad 12,000,
⁶from the tribe of Asher 12,000,
from the tribe of Naphtali 12,000,
from the tribe of Manasseh 12,000,
⁷from the tribe of Simeon 12,000,
from the tribe of Levi 12,000,
from the tribe of Issachar 12,000,
⁸from the tribe of Zebulun 12,000,
from the tribe of Joseph 12,000,
from the tribe of Benjamin 12,000.

The Great Multitude in White Robes

⁹After this I looked and there before me was a great multitude that no one could count, from every nation, tribe, people and language, standing before the throne and in front of the Lamb. They were wearing white robes and were holding palm branches in their hands. ¹⁰And they cried out in a loud voice:

"Salvation belongs to our God,
who sits on the throne,
and to the Lamb."

When the World Falls Apart

REVELATION 6:12–17

In this vision everything familiar to the people of the earth—the mighty and powerful people as well as the ordinary people—is shaken. The things that seem most permanent and dependable—the sun, moon, stars and sky—are passing away.

God has a way of disrupting our familiar landmarks—the settled ruts of our lives—leaving us disoriented among the broken pieces of our world, so that we learn to acknowledge his sovereign control in our lives. What are the familiar landmarks of your life? Values you've absorbed but never examined? Familiar but unbiblical ways of dealing with problems? Unhealthy patterns of relating to others? Into which of these do you sense God's presence as a disruption? How are you responding to that disruption?

See Meeting God in the Created Order

Prayer That Shakes the World

REVELATION 8:3–5

In John's vision the prayers of the saints are offered with fire as a sacrifice to God and God's power is released into the world, which is shaken to its foundations.

Choose the letter that best completes the sentence: Prayer (a) puts everything in God's hands; (b) changes me; (c) invites God's disruptive but transforming presence into my life; (d) is costly; or (e) all of the above. What do you need to sacrifice as an offering of prayer? Try this experiment: When praying about an urgent concern in your life, see if you can abandon (sacrifice) your desired "solution" and be genuinely receptive to God's resolution—no matter what it may be. Write down your prayer and preserve it at this point in your Bible. Keep track of how God answers.

See Meeting God in Prayer

¹¹All the angels were standing around the throne and around the elders and the four living creatures. They fell down on their faces before the throne and worshiped God, ¹²saying:

"Amen!
Praise and glory
and wisdom and thanks and honor
and power and strength
be to our God for ever and ever.
Amen!"

¹³Then one of the elders asked me, "These in white robes—who are they, and where did they come from?"

¹⁴I answered, "Sir, you know."

And he said, "These are they who have come out of the great tribulation; they have washed their robes and made them white in the blood of the Lamb. ¹⁵Therefore,

"they are before the throne of God
    and serve him day and night in his temple;
and he who sits on the throne will spread his tent
        over them.
¹⁶Never again will they hunger;
    never again will they thirst.
The sun will not beat upon them,
    nor any scorching heat.
¹⁷For the Lamb at the center of the throne will be
        their shepherd;
    he will lead them to springs of living water.
And God will wipe away every tear from their
        eyes."

The Seventh Seal and the Golden Censer

8 When he opened the seventh seal, there was silence in heaven for about half an hour.

²And I saw the seven angels who stand before God, and to them were given seven trumpets.

³Another angel, who had a golden censer, came and stood at the altar. He was given much incense to offer, with the prayers of all the saints, on the golden altar before the throne. ⁴The smoke of the incense, together with the prayers of the saints, went up before God from the angel's hand. ⁵Then the angel took the censer, filled it with fire from the altar, and hurled it on the earth; and there came peals of thunder, rumblings, flashes of lightning and an earthquake.

The Trumpets

⁶Then the seven angels who had the seven trumpets prepared to sound them.

⁷The first angel sounded his trumpet, and there came hail and fire mixed with blood, and it was hurled down upon the earth. A third of the earth was burned up, a third of the trees were burned up, and all the green grass was burned up.

⁸The second angel sounded his trumpet, and something like a huge mountain, all ablaze, was thrown into the sea. A third of the sea turned into blood, ⁹a third of the living creatures in the sea died, and a third of the ships were destroyed.

¹⁰The third angel sounded his trumpet, and a great star, blazing like a torch, fell from the sky on a third of the rivers

and on the springs of water— ¹¹the name of the star is Wormwood.ᵃ A third of the waters turned bitter, and many people died from the waters that had become bitter.

¹²The fourth angel sounded his trumpet, and a third of the sun was struck, a third of the moon, and a third of the stars, so that a third of them turned dark. A third of the day was without light, and also a third of the night.

¹³As I watched, I heard an eagle that was flying in midair call out in a loud voice: "Woe! Woe! Woe to the inhabitants of the earth, because of the trumpet blasts about to be sounded by the other three angels!"

9 The fifth angel sounded his trumpet, and I saw a star that had fallen from the sky to the earth. The star was given the key to the shaft of the Abyss. ²When he opened the Abyss, smoke rose from it like the smoke from a gigantic furnace. The sun and sky were darkened by the smoke from the Abyss. ³And out of the smoke locusts came down upon the earth and were given power like that of scorpions of the earth. ⁴They were told not to harm the grass of the earth or any plant or tree, but only those people who did not have the seal of God on their foreheads. ⁵They were not given power to kill them, but only to torture them for five months. And the agony they suffered was like that of the sting of a scorpion when it strikes a man. ⁶During those days men will seek death, but will not find it; they will long to die, but death will elude them.

⁷The locusts looked like horses prepared for battle. On their heads they wore something like crowns of gold, and their faces resembled human faces. ⁸Their hair was like women's hair, and their teeth were like lions' teeth. ⁹They had breastplates like breastplates of iron, and the sound of their wings was like the thundering of many horses and chariots rushing into battle. ¹⁰They had tails and stings like scorpions, and in their tails they had power to torment people for five months. ¹¹They had as king over them the angel of the Abyss, whose name in Hebrew is Abaddon, and in Greek, Apollyon.ᵇ

¹²The first woe is past; two other woes are yet to come.

¹³The sixth angel sounded his trumpet, and I heard a voice coming from the hornsᶜ of the golden altar that is before God. ¹⁴It said to the sixth angel who had the trumpet, "Release the four angels who are bound at the great river Euphrates." ¹⁵And the four angels who had been kept ready for this very hour and day and month and year were released to kill a third of mankind. ¹⁶The number of the mounted troops was two hundred million. I heard their number.

¹⁷The horses and riders I saw in my vision looked like this: Their breastplates were fiery red, dark blue, and yellow as sulfur. The heads of the horses resembled the heads of lions, and out of their mouths came fire, smoke and sulfur. ¹⁸A third of mankind was killed by the three plagues of fire, smoke and sulfur that came out of their mouths. ¹⁹The power of the horses was in their mouths and in their tails; for their tails were like snakes, having heads with which they inflict injury.

²⁰The rest of mankind that were not killed by these plagues still did not repent of the work of their hands; they

The Blindness of Sin

REVELATION 9:13–21

This portion of John's vision is a terrifying picture of the destructiveness of sin (vv.13–19). Even more frightening is the blindness of sin (vv.20–21). Name some people who are in a destructive bondage to sin and who persist in it, even though they know what the consequences will be. Are there Biblical restrictions or requirements that you'd rather not notice? What is the price you are paying to resist God's commands? What would obedience cost you? What behaviors would you have to change? What attitudes would you have to alter? What relationships would have to be different?

See *Meeting God in Everyday Life*

ᵃ *11* That is, Bitterness   ᵇ *11* *Abaddon* and *Apollyon* mean *Destroyer.*
ᶜ *13* That is, projections

Feeding on the Word

REVELATION 10:8–10

The promises of God's Word often seem "as sweet as honey" when we first receive them: "I have come that they may have life, and have it to the full" (John 10:10). When we begin to internalize the Word, however, we begin to realize that the promises may require a radical response from us: "If anyone would come after me, he must deny himself and take up his cross and follow me" (Matthew 16:24). There is a temptation to claim the promises without committing to the relationship with God in which the promises are grounded. Jot down a few of God's promises you claim for yourself. What are the commitments God is asking from you in response to each promise?

See Meeting God in Service

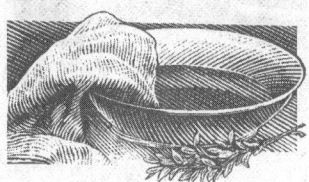

did not stop worshiping demons, and idols of gold, silver, bronze, stone and wood—idols that cannot see or hear or walk. ²¹Nor did they repent of their murders, their magic arts, their sexual immorality or their thefts.

The Angel and the Little Scroll

10 Then I saw another mighty angel coming down from heaven. He was robed in a cloud, with a rainbow above his head; his face was like the sun, and his legs were like fiery pillars. ²He was holding a little scroll, which lay open in his hand. He planted his right foot on the sea and his left foot on the land, ³and he gave a loud shout like the roar of a lion. When he shouted, the voices of the seven thunders spoke. ⁴And when the seven thunders spoke, I was about to write; but I heard a voice from heaven say, "Seal up what the seven thunders have said and do not write it down."

⁵Then the angel I had seen standing on the sea and on the land raised his right hand to heaven. ⁶And he swore by him who lives for ever and ever, who created the heavens and all that is in them, the earth and all that is in it, and the sea and all that is in it, and said, "There will be no more delay! ⁷But in the days when the seventh angel is about to sound his trumpet, the mystery of God will be accomplished, just as he announced to his servants the prophets."

⁸Then the voice that I had heard from heaven spoke to me once more: "Go, take the scroll that lies open in the hand of the angel who is standing on the sea and on the land."

⁹So I went to the angel and asked him to give me the little scroll. He said to me, "Take it and eat it. It will turn your stomach sour, but in your mouth it will be as sweet as honey." ¹⁰I took the little scroll from the angel's hand and ate it. It tasted as sweet as honey in my mouth, but when I had eaten it, my stomach turned sour. ¹¹Then I was told, "You must prophesy again about many peoples, nations, languages and kings."

The Two Witnesses

11 I was given a reed like a measuring rod and was told, "Go and measure the temple of God and the altar, and count the worshipers there. ²But exclude the outer court; do not measure it, because it has been given to the Gentiles. They will trample on the holy city for 42 months. ³And I will give power to my two witnesses, and they will prophesy for 1,260 days, clothed in sackcloth." ⁴These are the two olive trees and the two lampstands that stand before the Lord of the earth. ⁵If anyone tries to harm them, fire comes from their mouths and devours their enemies. This is how anyone who wants to harm them must die. ⁶These men have power to shut up the sky so that it will not rain during the time they are prophesying; and they have power to turn the waters into blood and to strike the earth with every kind of plague as often as they want.

⁷Now when they have finished their testimony, the beast that comes up from the Abyss will attack them, and overpower and kill them. ⁸Their bodies will lie in the street of the great city, which is figuratively called Sodom and Egypt, where also their Lord was crucified. ⁹For three and a half days men from every people, tribe, language

and nation will gaze on their bodies and refuse them burial. [10] The inhabitants of the earth will gloat over them and will celebrate by sending each other gifts, because these two prophets had tormented those who live on the earth.

[11] But after the three and a half days a breath of life from God entered them, and they stood on their feet, and terror struck those who saw them. [12] Then they heard a loud voice from heaven saying to them, "Come up here." And they went up to heaven in a cloud, while their enemies looked on.

[13] At that very hour there was a severe earthquake and a tenth of the city collapsed. Seven thousand people were killed in the earthquake, and the survivors were terrified and gave glory to the God of heaven.

[14] The second woe has passed; the third woe is coming soon.

The Seventh Trumpet

[15] The seventh angel sounded his trumpet, and there were loud voices in heaven, which said:

> "The kingdom of the world has become the
>   kingdom of our Lord and of his Christ,
>   and he will reign for ever and ever."

[16] And the twenty-four elders, who were seated on their thrones before God, fell on their faces and worshiped God, [17] saying:

> "We give thanks to you, Lord God Almighty,
>   the One who is and who was,
>   because you have taken your great power
>   and have begun to reign.
> [18] The nations were angry;
>   and your wrath has come.
>   The time has come for judging the dead,
>   and for rewarding your servants the prophets
>   and your saints and those who reverence your
>   name,
>   both small and great—
>   and for destroying those who destroy the
>   earth."

[19] Then God's temple in heaven was opened, and within his temple was seen the ark of his covenant. And there came flashes of lightning, rumblings, peals of thunder, an earthquake and a great hailstorm.

The Woman and the Dragon

12 A great and wondrous sign appeared in heaven: a woman clothed with the sun, with the moon under her feet and a crown of twelve stars on her head. [2] She was pregnant and cried out in pain as she was about to give birth. [3] Then another sign appeared in heaven: an enormous red dragon with seven heads and ten horns and seven crowns on his heads. [4] His tail swept a third of the stars out of the sky and flung them to the earth. The dragon stood in front of the woman who was about to give birth, so that he might devour her child the moment it was born. [5] She gave birth to a son, a male child, who will rule all the nations with an iron scepter. And her child was

The Depths of God's Love

REVELATION 12:1–6

How does this vision help you understand the phrase "the Lamb that was slain from the creation of the world," mentioned in Revelation 13:8? John here reveals to us the profound meaning of Jesus' redeeming death on the cross—not as a simple event, but as a revelation of the very nature of God. The cross is not simply something God *did*, but it is a revelation of who God *is*! God offers his very being to you for your healing. In what way are you wounded and in pain? Do you carry within you unhealed memories? Damaged emotions? Addiction? Picture God touching each place that hurts. See yourself receiving God's love, healing, protection and freedom as God transforms your broken spirit into a whole one.

See Meeting God in the Created Order

Seeing the Unseen

REVELATION 12:10–11

Paul says to the Corinthians, "Therefore we do not lose heart. Though outwardly we are wasting away, yet inwardly we are being renewed day by day. For our light and momentary troubles are achieving for us an eternal glory that far outweighs them all. So *we fix our eyes not on what is seen, but on what is unseen. For what is seen is temporary, but what is unseen is eternal*" (2 Corinthians 4:16–18, emphasis added). In light of this, and of this vision of God's victory in Jesus Christ, reflect on some event in your life from the past week. Did you perceive that event in terms of the impossible circumstances of the situation, or did you see it in the light of God's sure victory in Christ? How could you have lived it out differently? What lies ahead of you today? How do you think it looks through God's eyes?

See Meeting God in Everyday Life

snatched up to God and to his throne. ⁶The woman fled into the desert to a place prepared for her by God, where she might be taken care of for 1,260 days.

⁷And there was war in heaven. Michael and his angels fought against the dragon, and the dragon and his angels fought back. ⁸But he was not strong enough, and they lost their place in heaven. ⁹The great dragon was hurled down—that ancient serpent called the devil, or Satan, who leads the whole world astray. He was hurled to the earth, and his angels with him.

¹⁰Then I heard a loud voice in heaven say:

"Now have come the salvation and the power and
    the kingdom of our God,
and the authority of his Christ.
For the accuser of our brothers,
    who accuses them before our God day and
        night,
    has been hurled down.
¹¹They overcame him
    by the blood of the Lamb
    and by the word of their testimony;
they did not love their lives so much
    as to shrink from death.
¹²Therefore rejoice, you heavens
    and you who dwell in them!
But woe to the earth and the sea,
    because the devil has gone down to you!
He is filled with fury,
    because he knows that his time is short."

¹³When the dragon saw that he had been hurled to the earth, he pursued the woman who had given birth to the male child. ¹⁴The woman was given the two wings of a great eagle, so that she might fly to the place prepared for her in the desert, where she would be taken care of for a time, times and half a time, out of the serpent's reach. ¹⁵Then from his mouth the serpent spewed water like a river, to overtake the woman and sweep her away with the torrent. ¹⁶But the earth helped the woman by opening its mouth and swallowing the river that the dragon had spewed out of his mouth. ¹⁷Then the dragon was enraged at the woman and went off to make war against the rest of her offspring—those who obey God's commandments and hold to the testimony of Jesus. ¹And the dragon*ᵃ* stood on the shore of the sea.

The Beast out of the Sea

And I saw a beast coming out of the sea. He had ten horns and seven heads, with ten crowns on his horns, and on each head a blasphemous name. ²The beast I saw resembled a leopard, but had feet like those of a bear and a mouth like that of a lion. The dragon gave the beast his power and his throne and great authority. ³One of the heads of the beast seemed to have had a fatal wound, but the fatal wound had been healed. The whole world was astonished and followed the beast. ⁴Men worshiped the dragon because he had given authority to the beast, and they also worshiped the beast and asked, "Who is like the beast? Who can make war against him?"

ᵃ 1 Some late manuscripts And I

⁵The beast was given a mouth to utter proud words and blasphemies and to exercise his authority for forty-two months. ⁶He opened his mouth to blaspheme God, and to slander his name and his dwelling place and those who live in heaven. ⁷He was given power to make war against the saints and to conquer them. And he was given authority over every tribe, people, language and nation. ⁸All inhabitants of the earth will worship the beast—all whose names have not been written in the book of life belonging to the Lamb that was slain from the creation of the world.ᵃ

⁹He who has an ear, let him hear.

> ¹⁰If anyone is to go into captivity,
> into captivity he will go.
> If anyone is to be killedᵇ with the sword,
> with the sword he will be killed.

This calls for patient endurance and faithfulness on the part of the saints.

The Beast out of the Earth

¹¹Then I saw another beast, coming out of the earth. He had two horns like a lamb, but he spoke like a dragon. ¹²He exercised all the authority of the first beast on his behalf, and made the earth and its inhabitants worship the first beast, whose fatal wound had been healed. ¹³And he performed great and miraculous signs, even causing fire to come down from heaven to earth in full view of men. ¹⁴Because of the signs he was given power to do on behalf of the first beast, he deceived the inhabitants of the earth. He ordered them to set up an image in honor of the beast who was wounded by the sword and yet lived. ¹⁵He was given power to give breath to the image of the first beast, so that it could speak and cause all who refused to worship the image to be killed. ¹⁶He also forced everyone, small and great, rich and poor, free and slave, to receive a mark on his right hand or on his forehead, ¹⁷so that no one could buy or sell unless he had the mark, which is the name of the beast or the number of his name.

¹⁸This calls for wisdom. If anyone has insight, let him calculate the number of the beast, for it is man's number. His number is 666.

The Lamb and the 144,000

14 Then I looked, and there before me was the Lamb, standing on Mount Zion, and with him 144,000 who had his name and his Father's name written on their foreheads. ²And I heard a sound from heaven like the roar of rushing waters and like a loud peal of thunder. The sound I heard was like that of harpists playing their harps. ³And they sang a new song before the throne and before the four living creatures and the elders. No one could learn the song except the 144,000 who had been redeemed from the earth. ⁴These are those who did not defile themselves with women, for they kept themselves pure. They follow the Lamb wherever he goes. They were purchased from among men and offered as firstfruits to God and the Lamb. ⁵No lie was found in their mouths; they are blameless.

The Mark of the Beast

REVELATION 13:1–18

Read this chapter describing the beast out of the sea and beast out of earth. Write down a few words that describe each one. What emotions do these descriptions evoke in you? What happens within you as you reread verse 8? How do you picture the book of life that belongs to the Lamb? How does that verse encourage you? Reread also verses 10 and 18. How do these verses lead you to pray? In what ways might patient endurance and wisdom help you in the trials and tribulations you face today?

ᵃ 8 Or *written from the creation of the world in the book of life belonging to the Lamb that was slain* ᵇ 10 Some manuscripts *anyone kills*

Walking on Water

REVELATION 15:2–4

Those who have been victorious over the beast and his image stand beside the sea and sing the song of Moses and of the Lamb, a song of deliverance. Those who have conquered the world of fallen Babylon (the beast, its image and its number) "by the blood of the Lamb and by the word of their testimony" (12:11) can sing the song of God's deliverance today.

Throughout the morning today, reflect on God's great, amazing love that created you as God's beloved child (your identity and value) and calls you to wholeness (your purpose). During the afternoon, bow your heart in awe before the Holy One who is your true life. In the evening, look back on how the world's false values are crumbling beneath your feet.

See Meeting God in Worship

The Three Angels

⁶Then I saw another angel flying in midair, and he had the eternal gospel to proclaim to those who live on the earth—to every nation, tribe, language and people. ⁷He said in a loud voice, "Fear God and give him glory, because the hour of his judgment has come. Worship him who made the heavens, the earth, the sea and the springs of water."

⁸A second angel followed and said, "Fallen! Fallen is Babylon the Great, which made all the nations drink the maddening wine of her adulteries."

⁹A third angel followed them and said in a loud voice: "If anyone worships the beast and his image and receives his mark on the forehead or on the hand, ¹⁰he, too, will drink of the wine of God's fury, which has been poured full strength into the cup of his wrath. He will be tormented with burning sulfur in the presence of the holy angels and of the Lamb. ¹¹And the smoke of their torment rises for ever and ever. There is no rest day or night for those who worship the beast and his image, or for anyone who receives the mark of his name." ¹²This calls for patient endurance on the part of the saints who obey God's commandments and remain faithful to Jesus.

¹³Then I heard a voice from heaven say, "Write: Blessed are the dead who die in the Lord from now on."

"Yes," says the Spirit, "they will rest from their labor, for their deeds will follow them."

The Harvest of the Earth

¹⁴I looked, and there before me was a white cloud, and seated on the cloud was one "like a son of man"[a] with a crown of gold on his head and a sharp sickle in his hand. ¹⁵Then another angel came out of the temple and called in a loud voice to him who was sitting on the cloud, "Take your sickle and reap, because the time to reap has come, for the harvest of the earth is ripe." ¹⁶So he who was seated on the cloud swung his sickle over the earth, and the earth was harvested.

¹⁷Another angel came out of the temple in heaven, and he too had a sharp sickle. ¹⁸Still another angel, who had charge of the fire, came from the altar and called in a loud voice to him who had the sharp sickle, "Take your sharp sickle and gather the clusters of grapes from the earth's vine, because its grapes are ripe." ¹⁹The angel swung his sickle on the earth, gathered its grapes and threw them into the great winepress of God's wrath. ²⁰They were trampled in the winepress outside the city, and blood flowed out of the press, rising as high as the horses' bridles for a distance of 1,600 stadia.[b]

Seven Angels With Seven Plagues

15 I saw in heaven another great and marvelous sign: seven angels with the seven last plagues—last, because with them God's wrath is completed. ²And I saw what looked like a sea of glass mixed with fire and, standing beside the sea, those who had been victorious over the beast and his image and over the number of his name.

a 14 Daniel 7:13   *b 20* That is, about 180 miles (about 300 kilometers)

They held harps given them by God ³and sang the song of Moses the servant of God and the song of the Lamb:

"Great and marvelous are your deeds,
    Lord God Almighty.
Just and true are your ways,
    King of the ages.
⁴Who will not fear you, O Lord,
    and bring glory to your name?
For you alone are holy.
All nations will come
    and worship before you,
    for your righteous acts have been revealed."

⁵After this I looked and in heaven the temple, that is, the tabernacle of the Testimony, was opened. ⁶Out of the temple came the seven angels with the seven plagues. They were dressed in clean, shining linen and wore golden sashes around their chests. ⁷Then one of the four living creatures gave to the seven angels seven golden bowls filled with the wrath of God, who lives for ever and ever. ⁸And the temple was filled with smoke from the glory of God and from his power, and no one could enter the temple until the seven plagues of the seven angels were completed.

The Seven Bowls of God's Wrath

16 Then I heard a loud voice from the temple saying to the seven angels, "Go, pour out the seven bowls of God's wrath on the earth."

²The first angel went and poured out his bowl on the land, and ugly and painful sores broke out on the people who had the mark of the beast and worshiped his image.

³The second angel poured out his bowl on the sea, and it turned into blood like that of a dead man, and every living thing in the sea died.

⁴The third angel poured out his bowl on the rivers and springs of water, and they became blood. ⁵Then I heard the angel in charge of the waters say:

"You are just in these judgments,
    you who are and who were, the Holy One,
    because you have so judged;
⁶for they have shed the blood of your saints and
        prophets,
    and you have given them blood to drink as they
        deserve."

⁷And I heard the altar respond:

"Yes, Lord God Almighty,
    true and just are your judgments."

⁸The fourth angel poured out his bowl on the sun, and the sun was given power to scorch people with fire. ⁹They were seared by the intense heat and they cursed the name of God, who had control over these plagues, but they refused to repent and glorify him.

¹⁰The fifth angel poured out his bowl on the throne of the beast, and his kingdom was plunged into darkness. Men gnawed their tongues in agony ¹¹and cursed the God of heaven because of their pains and their sores, but they refused to repent of what they had done.

The Wrath of God

REVELATION 15:7–16:11

Imagine yourself sitting comfortably in an easy chair on the top of a hill. See yourself rejoicing that the trustworthiness of the law of gravity provides you with security and stability. Now picture yourself getting up and tripping, tumbling painfully down the hill. How has gravity changed? Has gravity suddenly become mean, punitive, judgmental, retributive, angry? Of course not! It's still gravity. Now apply that illustration to the sense of wholeness and well-being that accompanies your response to God's love and the sense of disruption and anxiety that comes when you reject God's love. Rejoice that, even in the midst of our self-imposed pain and anguish, God persistently seeks our redemption (note the reminder of the possibility of repentance in 16:9,11).

Fatal Attraction

REVELATION 17:4–6

John seems to be describing a horrendous monster who is, nonetheless, adorned with great beauty and power. Babylon the Great, the Mother of Prostitutes, is a vision of rich royal fabrics, jewels and gold. John is "greatly astonished."

What aspects of the world's allure attract you? Power? The promise of control? The security of abundance? The possibility of fame and popularity? Don't be too quick to deny any attraction to these. The time may be right for a spiritual inventory. Where does the needle of the compass of your soul point? Toward power or powerlessness? Toward control or consecration? Toward abundance or simplicity? Toward fame or humility? Toward popularity or servanthood?

See Meeting God in Prayer

[12]The sixth angel poured out his bowl on the great river Euphrates, and its water was dried up to prepare the way for the kings from the East. [13]Then I saw three evil[a] spirits that looked like frogs; they came out of the mouth of the dragon, out of the mouth of the beast and out of the mouth of the false prophet. [14]They are spirits of demons performing miraculous signs, and they go out to the kings of the whole world, to gather them for the battle on the great day of God Almighty.

[15]"Behold, I come like a thief! Blessed is he who stays awake and keeps his clothes with him, so that he may not go naked and be shamefully exposed."

[16]Then they gathered the kings together to the place that in Hebrew is called Armageddon.

[17]The seventh angel poured out his bowl into the air, and out of the temple came a loud voice from the throne, saying, "It is done!" [18]Then there came flashes of lightning, rumblings, peals of thunder and a severe earthquake. No earthquake like it has ever occurred since man has been on earth, so tremendous was the quake. [19]The great city split into three parts, and the cities of the nations collapsed. God remembered Babylon the Great and gave her the cup filled with the wine of the fury of his wrath. [20]Every island fled away and the mountains could not be found. [21]From the sky huge hailstones of about a hundred pounds each fell upon men. And they cursed God on account of the plague of hail, because the plague was so terrible.

The Woman on the Beast

17 One of the seven angels who had the seven bowls came and said to me, "Come, I will show you the punishment of the great prostitute, who sits on many waters. [2]With her the kings of the earth committed adultery and the inhabitants of the earth were intoxicated with the wine of her adulteries."

[3]Then the angel carried me away in the Spirit into a desert. There I saw a woman sitting on a scarlet beast that was covered with blasphemous names and had seven heads and ten horns. [4]The woman was dressed in purple and scarlet, and was glittering with gold, precious stones and pearls. She held a golden cup in her hand, filled with abominable things and the filth of her adulteries. [5]This title was written on her forehead:

MYSTERY
BABYLON THE GREAT
THE MOTHER OF PROSTITUTES
AND OF THE ABOMINATIONS OF THE EARTH.

[6]I saw that the woman was drunk with the blood of the saints, the blood of those who bore testimony to Jesus.

When I saw her, I was greatly astonished. [7]Then the angel said to me: "Why are you astonished? I will explain to you the mystery of the woman and of the beast she rides, which has the seven heads and ten horns. [8]The beast, which you saw, once was, now is not, and will come up out of the Abyss and go to his destruction. The inhabitants of the earth whose names have not been written in the book of life from the creation of the world will be astonished

a 13 Greek unclean

when they see the beast, because he once was, now is not, and yet will come.

9 "This calls for a mind with wisdom. The seven heads are seven hills on which the woman sits. 10 They are also seven kings. Five have fallen, one is, the other has not yet come; but when he does come, he must remain for a little while. 11 The beast who once was, and now is not, is an eighth king. He belongs to the seven and is going to his destruction.

12 "The ten horns you saw are ten kings who have not yet received a kingdom, but who for one hour will receive authority as kings along with the beast. 13 They have one purpose and will give their power and authority to the beast. 14 They will make war against the Lamb, but the Lamb will overcome them because he is Lord of lords and King of kings—and with him will be his called, chosen and faithful followers."

15 Then the angel said to me, "The waters you saw, where the prostitute sits, are peoples, multitudes, nations and languages. 16 The beast and the ten horns you saw will hate the prostitute. They will bring her to ruin and leave her naked; they will eat her flesh and burn her with fire. 17 For God has put it into their hearts to accomplish his purpose by agreeing to give the beast their power to rule, until God's words are fulfilled. 18 The woman you saw is the great city that rules over the kings of the earth."

The Fall of Babylon

18 After this I saw another angel coming down from heaven. He had great authority, and the earth was illuminated by his splendor. 2 With a mighty voice he shouted:

"Fallen! Fallen is Babylon the Great!
    She has become a home for demons
and a haunt for every evil[a] spirit,
    a haunt for every unclean and detestable bird.
3 For all the nations have drunk
    the maddening wine of her adulteries.
The kings of the earth committed adultery with
        her,
    and the merchants of the earth grew rich from
        her excessive luxuries."

4 Then I heard another voice from heaven say:

"Come out of her, my people,
    so that you will not share in her sins,
    so that you will not receive any of her plagues;
5 for her sins are piled up to heaven,
    and God has remembered her crimes.
6 Give back to her as she has given;
    pay her back double for what she has done.
    Mix her a double portion from her own cup.
7 Give her as much torture and grief
    as the glory and luxury she gave herself.
In her heart she boasts,
    'I sit as queen; I am not a widow,
    and I will never mourn.'

A Peculiar People

REVELATION 18:1–5

What does it mean to be a citizen of God's kingdom in a world shaped by the destructive and dehumanizing values of Babylon? List characteristics of your community that reflect the values and structures of fallen Babylon, especially those that impinge on your life. Reflect on what citizenship in the new Jerusalem looks like. What specific steps can you take to incarnate the liberating and healing presence of the new Jerusalem?

See *Meeting God in Community*

A Tenuous Livelihood

REVELATION 18:11–19

Isn't it interesting that economic issues are in the forefront of this passage about those who mourn the fall of Babylon? Economic issues were also central in the early days of the church (Acts 2:44–45)! The link between our attitudes toward money and our spiritual lives is reflected in Jesus' words: "For where your treasure is, there your heart will be also" (Matthew 6:21). What are the values that shape your economic philosophy? In a few paragraphs write a description of your economic worldview. Ask God to examine your values and priorities with you.

See Meeting God in Service

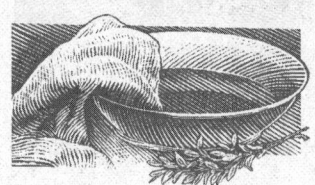

[8] Therefore in one day her plagues will overtake her:
  death, mourning and famine.
  She will be consumed by fire,
  for mighty is the Lord God who judges her.

[9] "When the kings of the earth who committed adultery with her and shared her luxury see the smoke of her burning, they will weep and mourn over her. [10] Terrified at her torment, they will stand far off and cry:

" 'Woe! Woe, O great city,
  O Babylon, city of power!
  In one hour your doom has come!'

[11] "The merchants of the earth will weep and mourn over her because no one buys their cargoes any more— [12] cargoes of gold, silver, precious stones and pearls; fine linen, purple, silk and scarlet cloth; every sort of citron wood, and articles of every kind made of ivory, costly wood, bronze, iron and marble; [13] cargoes of cinnamon and spice, of incense, myrrh and frankincense, of wine and olive oil, of fine flour and wheat; cattle and sheep; horses and carriages; and bodies and souls of men.

[14] "They will say, 'The fruit you longed for is gone from you. All your riches and splendor have vanished, never to be recovered.' [15] The merchants who sold these things and gained their wealth from her will stand far off, terrified at her torment. They will weep and mourn [16] and cry out:

" 'Woe! Woe, O great city,
  dressed in fine linen, purple and scarlet,
  and glittering with gold, precious stones and pearls!
[17] In one hour such great wealth has been brought to ruin!'

"Every sea captain, and all who travel by ship, the sailors, and all who earn their living from the sea, will stand far off. [18] When they see the smoke of her burning, they will exclaim, 'Was there ever a city like this great city?' [19] They will throw dust on their heads, and with weeping and mourning cry out:

" 'Woe! Woe, O great city,
  where all who had ships on the sea
  became rich through her wealth!
  In one hour she has been brought to ruin!
[20] Rejoice over her, O heaven!
  Rejoice, saints and apostles and prophets!
  God has judged her for the way she treated you.' "

[21] Then a mighty angel picked up a boulder the size of a large millstone and threw it into the sea, and said:

"With such violence
  the great city of Babylon will be thrown down,
  never to be found again.
[22] The music of harpists and musicians, flute players and trumpeters,
  will never be heard in you again.
No workman of any trade
  will ever be found in you again.
The sound of a millstone

will never be heard in you again.
²³ The light of a lamp
   will never shine in you again.
The voice of bridegroom and bride
   will never be heard in you again.
Your merchants were the world's great men.
   By your magic spell all the nations were led
      astray.
²⁴ In her was found the blood of prophets and of the
      saints,
   and of all who have been killed on the earth.'"

Hallelujah!

19

After this I heard what sounded like the roar of a great multitude in heaven shouting:

"Hallelujah!
Salvation and glory and power belong to our God,
²   for true and just are his judgments.
He has condemned the great prostitute
   who corrupted the earth by her adulteries.
He has avenged on her the blood of his servants."

³ And again they shouted:

"Hallelujah!
The smoke from her goes up for ever and ever."

⁴ The twenty-four elders and the four living creatures fell down and worshiped God, who was seated on the throne. And they cried:

"Amen, Hallelujah!"

⁵ Then a voice came from the throne, saying:

"Praise our God,
   all you his servants,
you who fear him,
   both small and great!"

⁶ Then I heard what sounded like a great multitude, like the roar of rushing waters and like loud peals of thunder, shouting:

"Hallelujah!
   For our Lord God Almighty reigns.
⁷ Let us rejoice and be glad
   and give him glory!
For the wedding of the Lamb has come,
   and his bride has made herself ready.
⁸ Fine linen, bright and clean,
   was given her to wear."
(Fine linen stands for the righteous acts of the saints.)

⁹ Then the angel said to me, "Write: 'Blessed are those who are invited to the wedding supper of the Lamb!'" And he added, "These are the true words of God."
¹⁰ At this I fell at his feet to worship him. But he said to me, "Do not do it! I am a fellow servant with you and with your brothers who hold to the testimony of Jesus. Worship God! For the testimony of Jesus is the spirit of prophecy."

The Bride and the Groom

REVELATION 19:5–8

"The bride sets all this perfection and preparedness before her beloved, the Son of God, with the desire that He transform her from the spiritual marriage, to which He desired to bring her in this Church Militant, to the glorious marriage of the Triumphant. May the most sweet Jesus, bridegroom of faithful souls, be pleased to bring all who invoke His name to this glorious marriage. To Him be honor and glory, together with the Father and the Holy Spirit, *in saecula saeculorum*. Amen."

—JOHN OF THE CROSS,
The Spiritual Canticle

Reigning With Christ

Compare Ephesians 2:1–6 with Revelation 20:4–6. Paul is describing in Ephesians what John is seeing in Revelation. Often we can grasp things with our minds (as Paul was so good at doing) more readily than with our hearts (as John was prone to do). These passages are excellent spiritual checklists: Are there vestiges of darkness in me? Have I claimed all my rights as a citizen of Christ's kingdom? Have I washed my soul in the blood of the Lamb of God? Is my life seated with him? Am I reigning with Christ? Am I living out my priestly life in Christ? If the images don't seem to have meaning for you, ask yourself why not. Choose the image that seems most difficult for you and ask God to make it a spiritual reality for you.

The Rider on the White Horse

[11]I saw heaven standing open and there before me was a white horse, whose rider is called Faithful and True. With justice he judges and makes war. [12]His eyes are like blazing fire, and on his head are many crowns. He has a name written on him that no one knows but he himself. [13]He is dressed in a robe dipped in blood, and his name is the Word of God. [14]The armies of heaven were following him, riding on white horses and dressed in fine linen, white and clean. [15]Out of his mouth comes a sharp sword with which to strike down the nations. "He will rule them with an iron scepter."[a] He treads the winepress of the fury of the wrath of God Almighty. [16]On his robe and on his thigh he has this name written:

KING OF KINGS AND LORD OF LORDS.

[17]And I saw an angel standing in the sun, who cried in a loud voice to all the birds flying in midair, "Come, gather together for the great supper of God, [18]so that you may eat the flesh of kings, generals, and mighty men, of horses and their riders, and the flesh of all people, free and slave, small and great."

[19]Then I saw the beast and the kings of the earth and their armies gathered together to make war against the rider on the horse and his army. [20]But the beast was captured, and with him the false prophet who had performed the miraculous signs on his behalf. With these signs he had deluded those who had received the mark of the beast and worshiped his image. The two of them were thrown alive into the fiery lake of burning sulfur. [21]The rest of them were killed with the sword that came out of the mouth of the rider on the horse, and all the birds gorged themselves on their flesh.

The Thousand Years

20 And I saw an angel coming down out of heaven, having the key to the Abyss and holding in his hand a great chain. [2]He seized the dragon, that ancient serpent, who is the devil, or Satan, and bound him for a thousand years. [3]He threw him into the Abyss, and locked and sealed it over him, to keep him from deceiving the nations anymore until the thousand years were ended. After that, he must be set free for a short time.

[4]I saw thrones on which were seated those who had been given authority to judge. And I saw the souls of those who had been beheaded because of their testimony for Jesus and because of the word of God. They had not worshiped the beast or his image and had not received his mark on their foreheads or their hands. They came to life and reigned with Christ a thousand years. [5](The rest of the dead did not come to life until the thousand years were ended.) This is the first resurrection. [6]Blessed and holy are those who have part in the first resurrection. The second death has no power over them, but they will be priests of God and of Christ and will reign with him for a thousand years.

[a] 15 Psalm 2:9

Satan's Doom

⁷When the thousand years are over, Satan will be released from his prison ⁸and will go out to deceive the nations in the four corners of the earth—Gog and Magog—to gather them for battle. In number they are like the sand on the seashore. ⁹They marched across the breadth of the earth and surrounded the camp of God's people, the city he loves. But fire came down from heaven and devoured them. ¹⁰And the devil, who deceived them, was thrown into the lake of burning sulfur, where the beast and the false prophet had been thrown. They will be tormented day and night for ever and ever.

The Dead Are Judged

¹¹Then I saw a great white throne and him who was seated on it. Earth and sky fled from his presence, and there was no place for them. ¹²And I saw the dead, great and small, standing before the throne, and books were opened. Another book was opened, which is the book of life. The dead were judged according to what they had done as recorded in the books. ¹³The sea gave up the dead that were in it, and death and Hades gave up the dead that were in them, and each person was judged according to what he had done. ¹⁴Then death and Hades were thrown into the lake of fire. The lake of fire is the second death. ¹⁵If anyone's name was not found written in the book of life, he was thrown into the lake of fire.

The New Jerusalem

21 Then I saw a new heaven and a new earth, for the first heaven and the first earth had passed away, and there was no longer any sea. ²I saw the Holy City, the new Jerusalem, coming down out of heaven from God, prepared as a bride beautifully dressed for her husband. ³And I heard a loud voice from the throne saying, "Now the dwelling of God is with men, and he will live with them. They will be his people, and God himself will be with them and be their God. ⁴He will wipe every tear from their eyes. There will be no more death or mourning or crying or pain, for the old order of things has passed away."

⁵He who was seated on the throne said, "I am making everything new!" Then he said, "Write this down, for these words are trustworthy and true."

⁶He said to me: "It is done. I am the Alpha and the Omega, the Beginning and the End. To him who is thirsty I will give to drink without cost from the spring of the water of life. ⁷He who overcomes will inherit all this, and I will be his God and he will be my son. ⁸But the cowardly, the unbelieving, the vile, the murderers, the sexually immoral, those who practice magic arts, the idolaters and all liars—their place will be in the fiery lake of burning sulfur. This is the second death."

⁹One of the seven angels who had the seven bowls full of the seven last plagues came and said to me, "Come, I will show you the bride, the wife of the Lamb." ¹⁰And he carried me away in the Spirit to a mountain great and high, and showed me the Holy City, Jerusalem, coming down out of heaven from God. ¹¹It shone with the glory of God, and its brilliance was like that of a very precious jewel, like a jasper, clear as crystal. ¹²It had a great, high wall with

All Things New

REVELATION 21:3-7

List the "old things" that hold you in bondage to your past—the hidden addiction that fills your hear with fear, the destructive habit that brings death to your hopes and dreams, the unhealed memories that cause you sorrow, the damaged emotions that inflict pain on your spirit. Then, at each point, read and affirm Revelation 21:3. When you sense in your spirit the reality of God's loving presence with you, hear God say, "I am making everything new!" This exercise may be helpful to you as a daily discipline until the awareness of God's deliverance and healing permeates your heart and calms your spirit.

See *Meeting God in the Created Order*

The Gates Are Open!

REVELATION 21:25—22:5

Access to God's realm, the new Jerusalem, is completely available to all who wash their robes in the blood of the Lamb. Its gates are never shut. Read this passage slowly and meditatively until a phrase or sentence stands out. Stay with that word or phrase until you hear God speaking to you. What response will you make? Rest in God's presence.

See Meeting God in Prayer

twelve gates, and with twelve angels at the gates. On the gates were written the names of the twelve tribes of Israel. [13]There were three gates on the east, three on the north, three on the south and three on the west. [14]The wall of the city had twelve foundations, and on them were the names of the twelve apostles of the Lamb.

[15]The angel who talked with me had a measuring rod of gold to measure the city, its gates and its walls. [16]The city was laid out like a square, as long as it was wide. He measured the city with the rod and found it to be 12,000 stadia[a] in length, and as wide and high as it is long. [17]He measured its wall and it was 144 cubits[b] thick,[c] by man's measurement, which the angel was using. [18]The wall was made of jasper, and the city of pure gold, as pure as glass. [19]The foundations of the city walls were decorated with every kind of precious stone. The first foundation was jasper, the second sapphire, the third chalcedony, the fourth emerald, [20]the fifth sardonyx, the sixth carnelian, the seventh chrysolite, the eighth beryl, the ninth topaz, the tenth chrysoprase, the eleventh jacinth, and the twelfth amethyst.[d] [21]The twelve gates were twelve pearls, each gate made of a single pearl. The great street of the city was of pure gold, like transparent glass.

[22]I did not see a temple in the city, because the Lord God Almighty and the Lamb are its temple. [23]The city does not need the sun or the moon to shine on it, for the glory of God gives it light, and the Lamb is its lamp. [24]The nations will walk by its light, and the kings of the earth will bring their splendor into it. [25]On no day will its gates ever be shut, for there will be no night there. [26]The glory and honor of the nations will be brought into it. [27]Nothing impure will ever enter it, nor will anyone who does what is shameful or deceitful, but only those whose names are written in the Lamb's book of life.

The River of Life

22 Then the angel showed me the river of the water of life, as clear as crystal, flowing from the throne of God and of the Lamb [2]down the middle of the great street of the city. On each side of the river stood the tree of life, bearing twelve crops of fruit, yielding its fruit every month. And the leaves of the tree are for the healing of the nations. [3]No longer will there be any curse. The throne of God and of the Lamb will be in the city, and his servants will serve him. [4]They will see his face, and his name will be on their foreheads. [5]There will be no more night. They will not need the light of a lamp or the light of the sun, for the Lord God will give them light. And they will reign for ever and ever.

[6]The angel said to me, "These words are trustworthy and true. The Lord, the God of the spirits of the prophets, sent his angel to show his servants the things that must soon take place."

Jesus Is Coming

[7]"Behold, I am coming soon! Blessed is he who keeps the words of the prophecy in this book."

[8]I, John, am the one who heard and saw these things.

---

[a] 16 That is, about 1,400 miles (about 2,200 kilometers)   [b] 17 That is, about 200 feet (about 65 meters)   [c] 17 Or *high*   [d] 20 The precise identification of some of these precious stones is uncertain.

And when I had heard and seen them, I fell down to worship at the feet of the angel who had been showing them to me. ⁹But he said to me, "Do not do it! I am a fellow servant with you and with your brothers the prophets and of all who keep the words of this book. Worship God!"

¹⁰Then he told me, "Do not seal up the words of the prophecy of this book, because the time is near. ¹¹Let him who does wrong continue to do wrong; let him who is vile continue to be vile; let him who does right continue to do right; and let him who is holy continue to be holy."

¹²"Behold, I am coming soon! My reward is with me, and I will give to everyone according to what he has done. ¹³I am the Alpha and the Omega, the First and the Last, the Beginning and the End.

¹⁴"Blessed are those who wash their robes, that they may have the right to the tree of life and may go through the gates into the city. ¹⁵Outside are the dogs, those who practice magic arts, the sexually immoral, the murderers, the idolaters and everyone who loves and practices falsehood.

¹⁶"I, Jesus, have sent my angel to give you[a] this testimony for the churches. I am the Root and the Offspring of David, and the bright Morning Star."

¹⁷The Spirit and the bride say, "Come!" And let him who hears say, "Come!" Whoever is thirsty, let him come; and whoever wishes, let him take the free gift of the water of life.

¹⁸I warn everyone who hears the words of the prophecy of this book: If anyone adds anything to them, God will add to him the plagues described in this book. ¹⁹And if anyone takes words away from this book of prophecy, God will take away from him his share in the tree of life and in the holy city, which are described in this book.

²⁰He who testifies to these things says, "Yes, I am coming soon."

Amen. Come, Lord Jesus.

²¹The grace of the Lord Jesus be with God's people. Amen.

The Spirit and the Bride

REVELATION 22:17

As the final notes of Revelation sound out, a clear bell of invitation chimes: "Come!"

Whoever is thirsty, whoever is in need, whoever will accept the free gift of the water of life is invited by the Spirit and the bride to simply "come." God awaits you with open hands—gentle, healing and life-giving hands. Read these final chapters of Revelation over until you hear the invitation of God resound in you. Then go out and, with joy, share the invitation with someone else who needs the gift of life.

WEIGHTS AND MEASURES

	BIBLICAL UNIT		APPROXIMATE AMERICAN EQUIVALENT	APPROXIMATE METRIC EQUIVALENT
WEIGHTS	talent	(60 minas)	75 pounds	34 kilograms
	mina	(50 shekels)	1 ¼ pounds	0.6 kilogram
	shekel	(2 bekas)	⅖ ounce	11.5 grams
	pim	(⅔ shekel)	⅓ ounce	7.6 grams
	beka	(10 gerahs)	⅕ ounce	5.5 grams
	gerah		1/50 ounce	0.6 gram
LENGTH	cubit		18 inches	0.5 meter
	span		9 inches	23 centimeters
	handbreadth		3 inches	8 centimeters
CAPACITY				
Dry Measure	cor [homer]	(10 ephahs)	6 bushels	220 liters
	lethek	(5 ephahs)	3 bushels	110 liters
	ephah	(10 omers)	⅗ bushel	22 liters
	seah	(⅓ ephah)	7 quarts	7.3 liters
	omer	(1/10 ephah)	2 quarts	2 liters
	cab	(1/18 ephah)	1 quart	1 liter
Liquid Measure	bath	(1 ephah)	6 gallons	22 liters
	hin	(⅙ bath)	4 quarts	4 liters
	log	(1/72 bath)	⅓ quart	0.3 liter

The figures of the table are calculated on the basis of a shekel equaling 11.5 grams, a cubit equaling 18 inches and an ephah equaling 22 liters. The quart referred to is either a dry quart (slightly larger than a liter) or a liquid quart (slightly smaller than a liter), whichever is applicable. The ton referred to in the footnotes is the American ton of 2,000 pounds.

This table is based upon the best available information, but it is not intended to be mathematically precise; like the measurement equivalents in the footnotes, it merely gives approximate amounts and distances. Weights and measures differed somewhat at various times and places in the ancient world. There is uncertainty particularly about the ephah and the bath; further discoveries may shed more light on these units of capacity.

Topical Index
to Entry Points
and Ways of Meeting God

Index of Quotations

TOPICAL INDEX
TO ENTRY POINTS AND WAYS OF MEETING GOD

INDEX OF QUOTATIONS
TO ENTRY POINTS AND WAYS OF MEETING GOD

Page 395 Francis de Sales (1567–1622) from *Introduction to the Devout Life*. Copyright ©1972. Published by Doubleday Image Books, New York.

Page 396 Mechtild of Magdeburg (c. 1212–c. 1280) from *Flowing Light of the Godhead*, Book I (*Classics of Western Spirituality Series*). Copyright ©1998. Published by Paulist Press, Mahwah, NJ.

Page 404 Francois Fenelon (1651–1715) from *Spiritual Letters* to Women (Letter 7). Copyright ©1984 by Zondervan Publishing House. Published by the Zondervan Corporation, Grand Rapids, MI.

Page 408 A quotation attributed to Pastor Martin Niemoeller (1892–1984).

Page 416 Augustine (354–430) from *Confessions*.

Page 426 From *Time for God* by Leslie D. Weatherhead. Copyright ©1967. Published by Abingdon Press, Nashville, TN.

Page 430 From *Taste and See: A Personal Guide to the Spiritual Life* by William O. Paulsell. Copyright ©1976. Published by Chalice Press, St. Louis, MO.

Page 433 Augustine (354–430) from *Enchiridion*.

Page 440 Augustine (354–430) from *On The Presence of God*, Letter 187, from *Augustine of Hippo: Selected Writings*, translation and introduction by Mary T. Clark. Copyright ©1984. Published by Paulist Press, Mahwah, NJ.

Page 447 From *The Talmud*, Numbers Rabba, Bemidhar, IV, 20, edited by Rabbi Steinsaltz. Copyright ©1998. Published by Random House, New York.

Page 452 From *The Talmud*, Deuteronomy Rabba, V, 1 and 3. Copyright ©1998. Published by Random House, New York.

Page 454 From *Taste and See: A Personal Guide to the Spiritual Life* by William O. Paulsell. Copyright ©1976. Published by Chalice Press, St. Louis, MO.

Page 456 From *People of the Lie* by M. Scott Peck. Copyright ©1983 by M. Scott Peck. Published by Simon & Schuster, New York.

Page 468 Evelyn Underhill (1875–1941) from *The Spiritual Life: Great Spiritual Truths for Everyday Life* (*Mystical Series of the World*). Copyright ©1955. Morehouse Publications, Harrisburg, PA.

Page 476 From *Workbook on the Seven Deadly Sins* by Maxie Dunham, Kimberly Dunham Reisman. Copyright ©1997 by Maxie Dunham, Kimberly Dunham Reisman. Published by Upper Room Books, Nashville, TN. Reprinted by permission of Upper Room Books. All rights reserved.

Page 488 From *Your God is Too Small* by J.B. Phillips. Copyright ©1976. Published by Simon & Schuster, New York.

Page 505 William Law (1686–1761) from *A Serious Call to a Devout and Holy Life*.

Page 509 From the *Lumen Gentium* Chapter 2, Vatican Council II, (1962–1965), *The Concilar and Post Concilar Documents*, edited by Austin Flannery, O.P. Copyright ©1975. Liturgical Press, Collegeville, MN.

Page 513 From *The Book of Discipline of the United Methodist Church*. Copyright ©1992. United Methodist Publishing House, Nashville.

Page 517 From *A Testament of Devotion* by Thomas R. Kelly. Copyright ©1941 by Harper & Row Publishers, Inc. Renewed ©1969 by Lois Lael Kelly Statler.

Page 520 From *Eighth Day of Creation* by Elizabeth O'Connor. Copyright ©1971. Word Books, Nashville, TN.

Page 522 Frederick Lucian Hosmer, "Forward through the Ages," # 555, United Methodist Hymnal (1908).

Page 525 Eberhard Arnold (1883–1935) from *God's Revolution*. Copyright ©1984. Plough Publishing of the Bruderhof Foundation, Farmington, PA.

Page 530 Cyprian of Carthage (d. 258). From *Letter 1*.

Page 534 Augustine (354–430) from *The City of God*, Book 17 Chapter 14.

Page 538 Charles Wesley (1707–1788) from a hymn.

Page 540　Macarius the Great (300–390). Quoted in *Sayings of the Desert Fathers*, edited by Sister Benedicta Ward. Copyright ©1975. Published by Cistercian Publications, Inc., Kalamazoo, MI.

Page 544　John Bunyan (1628–1688) from *Grace Abounding to the Chief of Sinners*.

Page 546　Cyprian of Carthage (d. 258). Treatise "On the Lord's Prayer."

Page 548　Thomas Merton (1915–1968) from *No Man Is an Island*. Copyright ©1955 by the Trustees of the Merton Legacy Fund. Published by Harcourt Brace, New York, NY.

Page 556　From Augustine (354–430) from *Confessions*, Book I.

Page 560　John Wesley (1703–1791) from *Journal*.

Page 565　From *The Cloud of Unknowing*, an anonymous, 14th century work. Copyright ©1981. Published by Paulist Press, Mahwah, NJ.

Page 572　Thomas à Kempis (1380–1471) from *The Imitation of Christ*.

Page 573　Anonymous Franciscan (late 19th century), often attributed to St. Francis. Hymn # 481, United Methodist Hymnal.

Page 576　Annie S. Hawks. "I Need Thee Every Hour," Hymn # 397, United Methodist Hymnal.

Page 583　Augustine (354–430) from *Confessions*.

Page 587　Ignatius of Loyola (1491–1556) from *The Spiritual Exercises*.

Page 592　George B. Robson. Hymn # 607, United Methodist Hymnal.

Page 594　Teresa of Avila (1515–1582) from *The Interior Castle*.

Page 597　From *Prayer and the Common Life* by Georgia Harkness. Copyright ©1948. Published by Abingdon/Cokesbury, Nashville, TN.

Page 599　Mius of Belos is quoted in *Sayings of the Desert Fathers*, edited by Sister Benedicta Ward. Copyright ©1975. Published by Cistercian Publications, Inc., Kalamazoo, MI.

Page 603　From *The Passover Haggadah* (traditional), edited by Nahum Glatzer. Copyright ©1953, 1969. Published by Schocken Books (Knopf), New York

Page 606　John Bunyan (1628–1688) from *Grace Abounding to the Chief of Sinners*.

Page 612　Francis de Sales (1567–1622) from *Introduction to the Devout Life*. Copyright ©1972. Published by Doubleday Image Books, New York.

Page 621　Dorothy Day (1897–1980) from *The Long Loneliness*. Copyright ©1952. Harper & Row, New York.

Page 624　From *Community and Growth* by Jean Vanier. Copyright ©1979. Published by Paulist Press Mahwah, NJ.

Page 627　Ephraim the Syrian, (c. 300), from *Repentance*. Copyright ©1984. Published by Paulist Press, Mahwah, NJ.

Page 635　Brother Lawrence (c.1605–1691) from *The Practice of the Presence of God*.

Page 637　Evelyn Underhill (1875–1941) from *The School of Charity*. Copyright ©1991. Published by Morehouse Publications, Harrisburg, PA.

Page 642　From *Reversed Thunder* by Eugene Peterson. Copyright ©1988 by Eugene Peterson. Published by HarperSan Francisco, San Francisco, CA.

Page 647　Dietrich Bonhoeffer (1906 1945) from *Ethics*, edited by Eberhard Bethge, translated by Neville Horton Smith. Copyright ©1995. Macmillan Publishing Co., New York.

Page 653　John of the Cross (1542–1591) from *The Dark Night of the Soul, from Selected Writings (Classics of Western Spirituality Series)*. Copyright ©1987. Published by Paulist Press, Mahwah, NJ.

Page 671　John of the Cross (1542–1591). *The Dark Night of the Soul* from *Selected Writings (Classics of Western Spirituality Series)*. Copyright ©1987. Published by Paulist Press, Mahwah, NJ.

Page 677　From *The Cloud of Unknowing*, an anonymous, 14th century work. Copyright ©1981. Published by Paulist Press, Mahwah, NJ.

Page 855   Hildegard of Bingen (1098–1179). *Scivias* from *Creation and Christ: The Wisdom of Hildegard of Bingen*, translated by Columba Hart and Jane Bishop; edited by Kathleen A. Walsh. Copyright ©1996. Published by Paulist Press, Mahwah, NJ.

Page 866   Phoebe Palmer (1807–1874) from *Entire Devotion to God.* Copyright ©1979. Published by Schmul Publishing, Salem, Ohio.

Page 870   Peter of Damaskos, (c 1100) from *Philokalia*, Vol. III compiled by St. Nikodimos of the Holy Mountain and St. Makarios of Corinth; translated from the Greek and edited by G.E.H. Palmer, Philip Sherrard, Kallistos Ware. Copyright ©1979, 1983. Published by Faber & Faber, London.

Page 873   Jean-Pierre de Caussade (1675–1751) from *The Sacrament of the Present Moment*, translated by Kitty Muggeridge. Copyright ©1989. Published by HarperSanFrancisco, San Francisco, CA.

Page 881   From *A Testament of Devotion* by Thomas R. Kelly. Copyright ©1941 by Harper & Row Publishers, Inc. Renewed ©1969 by Lois Lael Kelly Statler.

Page 887   Bernard of Clairvaux (1090–1153) from *Sermon XX on the Song of Songs.* Copyright ©1987. Published by Paulist Press, Mahwah, NJ.

Page 895   Blaise Arminjon from *The Cantata of Love: A Verse-by-Verse Reading of the Song of Songs,* translated by Nelly Marans. Copyright ©1988. Published by Ignatius Press, San Francisco, CA.

Page 897   Gerard Manley Hopkins (1844–1889). "God's Grandeur." From *Poems and Prose of Gerard Manley Hopkins.*

Page 904   Augustine (354–430) from *Sermon LIX:3.*

Page 908   C. S. Lewis (1898–1963) from *Mere Christianity.* Copyright ©1952. Published by Simon & Schuster, New York.

Page 910   Origen of Alexandria (c.185–c.254) from *Contra Celsus.*

Page 913   Bonaventure (1221–1274) from *The Life of St. Francis* translated by Ewart Cousins. Copyright ©1978. Published by Paulist Press, Mahwah, NJ.

Page 916   Julian of Norwich (c.1342–c.1413) from *Revelations of Divine Love.*

Page 921   Sister Wendy Beckett from *"Sister Wendy in Conversation with Bill Moyers.* Copyright ©1997. Broadcast by WGBH-TV Boston.

Page 924   Francis de Sales (1567–1622) from *Treatise of the Love of God.* Copyright ©1973. Published by Morehouse Publications, Harrisburg, PA.

Page 932   Evelyn Underhill (1875–1941) from *The Spiral Way.*

Page 935   George Herbert (1593–1633) from "Repentance" in *George Herbert: The Country Parson*, edited John Wal Jr. *(Classics of Western Spirituality Series).* Copyright ©1981. Published by Paulist Press, Mahwah, NJ.

Page 942   Julian of Norwich (c.1342–c.1413) from *Showings.*

Page 947   Hildegard of Bingen (1098–1179) from *"Symphony of the Blessed,* Vision 13, translated by Columba Hart and Jane Bishop. Copyright ©1990. Published by Paulist Press, Mahwah, NJ.

Page 954   Karl Barth (1886–1968) from *Church Dogmatics, Vol. 2,* edited by G.W. Bromiley, T.F. Torrance. Copyright ©1957. Published by Books International Inc., Herndon, VA.

Page 961   *Jewish Morning Prayer.* Copyright ©1956. Published by Prayer Book Press (subs. of Media Judaica, Inc.) Bridgeport, CT.

Page 968   Augustine (354–430) from *Confessions.*

Page 975   Friedrich von Hugel (1852–1925) from *Letters to a Niece (Letters from Baron Friedrich von Hugel to a Niece)*, edited by Gwendolyn Green. Copyright ©1928. Published by J.M. Dent & Sons, (subs of Orion House) London.

Page 978   From *A Testament of Devotion* by Thomas R. Kelly. Copyright ©1941 by Harper & Row Publishers, Inc. Renewed ©1969 by Lois Lael Kelly Statler.

Page 985   St. Ephraim of Syria, (c.300) from *Ephraim the Syrian,* edited by K. McVey *(Classics of Western Spirituality Series).* Copyright ©1989. Published by Paulist Press, Mahwah, NJ.

Page 1275 Teresa of Avila (1515–1582) from *The Interior Castle*.

Page 1279 John Calvin (1509–1564) from *Institutes of the Christian Religion*, edited by John T. McNeill. Copyright ©1960. Published by Westminster John Knox Press, Louisville, KY.

Page 1285 From *The Reality of the Spiritual World* by Thomas R. Kelly. Copyright ©1942. Published by PendleHill Publications, Wallingford, PA.

Page 1290 John Calvin (1509–1564) from *Institutes of the Christian Religion*, edited by John T. McNeill. Copyright ©1960. Published by Westminster John Knox Press, Louisville, KY.

Page 1293 Blaise Pascal (1623–1662) from *Pensees*.

Page 1301 Oswald Chambers (1874–1917) from *My Utmost for His Highest*. Copyright ©1935 by Dodd Mead & Co. Renewed ©1963 by The Oswald Chambers Publications Assn. Ltd., and is used by permission of Discovery House Publishers, Box 3566, Grand Rapids, MI. All rights reserved.

Page 1304 Oswald Chambers (1874–1917) from *My Utmost for His Highest*. Copyright ©1935 by Dodd Mead & Co. Renewed ©1963 by The Oswald Chambers Publications Assn. Ltd., and is used by permission of Discovery House Publishers, Box 3566, Grand Rapids, MI. All rights reserved.

Page 1313 Augustine (354–430) from *The City of God*.

Page 1317 Hannah Whithall Smith (1832–1911) from *The Christian's Secret of a Happy Life*.

Page 1321 John Calvin (1509–1564) from *Institutes of the Christian Religion*, edited by John T. McNeill. Copyright ©1960. Published by Westminster John Knox Press, Louisville, KY.

Page 1326 Dietrich Bonhoeffer (1906–1945) from *The Cost of Discipleship*. Copyright ©1995. Published by Simon & Schuster, New York.

Page 1329 Henri J.M. Nouwen from *The Way of the Heart: Desert Spirituality and Contemporary Ministry*. Copyright ©1981 by Henri J. M. Nouwen. Published by Seabury Press, New York.

Page 1331 Oswald Chambers (1874–1917) from *My Utmost for His Highest*. Copyright ©1935 by Dodd Mead & Co. Renewed ©1963 by The Oswald Chambers Publications Assn. Ltd., and is used by permission of Discovery House Publishers, Box 3566, Grand Rapids, MI. All rights reserved.

Page 1339 Oswald Chambers (1874–1917) from *My Utmost for His Highest*. Copyright ©1935 by Dodd Mead & Co. Renewed ©1963 by The Oswald Chambers Publications Assn. Ltd., and is used by permission of Discovery House Publishers, Box 3566, Grand Rapids, MI. All rights reserved.

Page 1346 From *How to Pray* by Jean Nicholas Grou. Copyright ©1982. Published by James Clark and Co., Cambridge, England.

Page 1352 Bernard of Clairvaux (1090–1153) from *Selections from the Writings of Bernard Clairvaux*, edited by Douglas V. Steere. Copyright ©1952. Published by A.R. Mowbray & Co., London.

Page 1355 Dietrich Bonhoeffer (1906–1945) from *Life Together*, translated by John W. Doberstein. Copyright ©1954. Published by Harper & Row, New York.

Page 1357 Aelred of Rievaulx (1109–1167) from "On Spiritual Friendship," translated by .Mary Eugenia Laker, SSND. Copyright ©1974. Published by Cistercian Publications Inc., Kalamazoo, MI.

Page 1365 Simone Weil (1909–1943) from *Waiting for God*. Copyright ©1973. Published by Putnam & Sons, New York, NY.

Page 1369 From *By the Rivers of Babylon* by Kaj Munk. Copyright ©1945. Published in Blair, Nebraska: Lutheran Publishing House, Copyright ©1945. Reprinted with permission from Augsburg Fortress Press, Minneapolis, MN.

Page 1378 Martin Luther (1483–1546). Quoted from "A Pamphlet on Prayer" in *Luther and the Mystics* edited by Bengt Hoffman. Copyright ©1976. Augsburg Fortress Press, Minneapolis, MN.

Page 1381 From *The Cloud of Unknowing*, an anonymous, 14th century work. Copyright ©1981. Published by Paulist Press, Mahwah, NJ.

Page 1385 From *The Rule of St. Benedict*. Copyright ©1975. Published by Liturgical Press, Collegeville, MN.

Page 1397 Dietrich Bonhoeffer (1906–1945) from *Letters and Papers from Prison*, edited by Eberhard Bethge. Copyright ©1971, 1972. Published by Simon & Schuster, New York.

Page 1398 James Weldon Johnson. "God's Trombones." Copyright ©1976. Published by Viking Penguin, New York.

Page 1401 Simone Weil (1909–1943) from *Waiting for God*. Copyright ©1973. Published by Putnam & Sons, New York, NY.

Page 1403 John of Damascus (c. 675–c. 749) from "The Day of Resurrection, #303, United Methodist Hymnal. Words translated by John Mason Neale.

Page 1404 Augustine (354–430) from *Confessions, X:27*.

Page 1411 From *What Makes You So Strong* by Jeremiah A. Wright, Jr. Copyright ©1993 by Jeremiah A. Wright, Jr. Published by Judson Press, Valley Forge, PA.

Page 1416 Augustine (354–430) from *Purity of Heart*.

Page 1428 From *Fear No Evil* by David Watson. Copyright ©1984. Published by Harold Shaw Publishing, Wheaton, IL.

Page 1436 Harry Emerson Fosdick. "God of Grace and God of Glory," Hymn #577, from the United Methodist Hymnal. Copyright by Elinor Fosdick Downs, Boston, MA.

Page 1440 Augustine (354–430) from *The City of God*, Book XVIII, r 51.

Page 1443 John Chrysostom (d.407) from "Those Invited," *A Paschal Sermon*. Copyright ©1969. Published by Alba House (Society of St. Paul), Staten Island, New York.

Page 1446 From *A Testament of Devotion* by Thomas R. Kelly. Copyright ©1941 by Harper & Row Publishers, Inc. Renewed ©1969 by Lois Lael Kelly Statler.

Page 1450 Gregory of Nyssa (330–395) from *The Life of Moses*, translated by Abraham Malherbe and Everett Ferguson. Copyright ©1978. Published by Paulist Press, Mahwah, NJ.

Page 1461 Gregory of Nazianzus (330–389) from "Sermon I: On Easter" in *The Paschal Mystery*.

Page 1472 Dietrich Bonhoeffer (1906–1945) from *Life Together*, translated by John W. Doberstein. Copyright ©1954. Published by Harper & Row, New York, NY.

Page 1477 Thomas à Kempis (1380–1471) from *The Imitation of Christ*.

Page 1485 Martin Luther (1483–1546). Quoted in *What Luther Says*, Section 3909.

Page 1501 Thomas Merton (1915–1968) from *The Wisdom in the Desert*. Copyright ©1990 by the Trustees of the Merton Legacy Fund. Published by New Directions, New York.

Page 1506 John Donne (1573–1631). *Holy Sonnets 10*.

Page 1508 Aelred of Rievaulx (1109–1167) from "On Spiritual Friendship," translated by Mary Eugenia Laker, SSND. Copyright ©1974. Published by Cistercian Publications Inc., Kalamazoo, MI.

Page 1508 From "Exploring Spiritual Direction: An Essay on Christian Friendship" by Alan Jones. Copyright ©1982. Published by Seabury Press, New York.

Page 1510 John Climacus (579–649) is quoted in *Drinking from the Hidden Fountain: a Patristic Breviary: Ancient Wisdom for Today's World* edited by Thomas Spidlik; translated by Paul Drake. Copyright ©1994. Published by Cistercian Publications Inc., Kalamazoo, MI.

Page 1516 *The Music of Eternity* by Adrian van Kaam. Copyright ©1990. Published by Ave Maria Press, Notre Dame, IL.

Page 1517 John Flavel (d.1691) from *Keeping the Heart*. Copyright ©1958. Published by Soli Deo Gloria, Morgan, PA.

Page 1523 John Wesley (1703–1791) from "On the Holy Spirit."

Page 1527 John Donne (1573–1631)."Death Be Not Proud" From *Holy Sonnets*.

Page 1529 Maximus the Confessor (c. 580–662) is quoted in *Drinking from the Hidden Fountain: A Patristic Breviary: Ancient Wisdom for Today's World,* edited by Thomas Spidlik; translated by Paul Drake. Copyright ©1994. Published by Cistercian Publications Inc., Kalamazoo, MI.

Page 1533 John Wesley (1703–1791) from *Explanatory Notes Upon the New Testament*.

Page 1535 Teresa of Avila (1515–1582) from *The Book of Her Life*.

Page 1537 John Chrysostom (d.407) from *On the Letter to the Romans.*

Page 1540 From *The Return of the Prodigal Son: A Story of Homecoming* by Henri J. M. Nouwen. Copyright ©1992 by Henri J.M. Nouwen. Published by Doubleday, Image Books, New York.

Page 1542 Bernard of Clairvaux (1090–1153) from *Selected Works,* translation and foreword by G.R. Evans. Copyright ©1987. Published by Paulist Press, Mahwah, NJ.

Page 1545 Henry Scougal (1650–1678) from *The Life of God in the Soul of Man.* Copyright ©1992. Published by GAM Publications, Sterling, VA.

Page 1548 From *A Testament of Devotion* by Thomas R. Kelly. Copyright ©1941 by Harper & Row Publishers, Inc. Renewed ©1969 by Lois Lael Kelly Statler.

Page 1555 From *The Genesee Diary* by Henri J. M. Nouwen. Copyright ©1981 by Henri J. M. Nouwen. Published by Image Books, Doubleday Publishing, New York.

Page 1557 Oswald Chambers (1874–1917) from *My Utmost for His Highest.* Copyright ©1935 by Dodd Mead & Co. Renewed ©1963 by The Oswald Chambers Publications Assn. Ltd., and is used by permission of Discovery House Publishers, Box 3566, Grand Rapids, MI. All rights reserved.

Page 1560 *Heidelberg Catechism.* Copyright ©1963. Published by Pilgrim Press, Cleveland, OH.

Page 1561 Robert Robinson. "Come Thou Fount of Every Blessing," #400, United Methodist Hymnal.

Page 1566 Charles Wesley (1707–1788). *"Love Divine, All Loves Excelling."*

Page 1571 Hannah Whithall Smith (1832–1911) from *The Christian's Secret of a Happy Life.*

Page 1574 Brother Lawrence (c.1605–1691) from *The Practice of the Presence of God.*

Page 1575 William Law (1686–1761) from *A Serious Call to a Devout and Holy Life.*

Page 1581 Jonathan Edwards (1703–1758) from *Treatise Concerning Religious Affections.*

Page 1583 From *Guard the Gospel: the Message of 2 Timothy* by John R.W. Stott. Copyright ©1973. Published in Downer's Grove, IL by Inter Varsity Press.

Page 1587 From *Sermons For New Life*, by Horace Bushnell; revised edition quoted in Weavings, May/June25, 1987. Copyright ©1901. Published in New York by Charles Scribner's Sons

Page 1588 Jean-Pierre de Caussade (1675–1751) from *The Sacrament of the Present Moment,* translated by Kitty Muggeridge. Copyright ©1989. Published in San Francisco by Harper & Row.

Page 1588 From *Keeping a Spiritual Journal* by Ronald Klug. Copyright ©1983. Published by Augsburg Press, Minneapolis, MN.

Page 1589 From *A Testament of Devotion* by Thomas R. Kelly. Copyright ©1941 by Harper & Row Publishers, Inc. Renewed ©1969 by Lois Lael Kelly Statler.

Page 1590 From *The Reformed Pastor* by Richard Baxter. Copyright ©1979. Published by Banner of Truth Publications, Carlisle, PA.

Page 1592 Jonathan Edwards (1703–1758) from a *Treatise Concerning Religious Affections.*

Page 1593 *Wisdom Distilled from the Daily: Living the Rule of St. Benedict Today* by Joan Chittister, OSB. Copyright ©1991. Published by HarperSanFrancisco.

Page 1595 Charles H. Spurgeon (1834–1892) from *An All Around Ministry.* Copyright ©1983. Published by Pilgrim Publications, Pasadena, TX.

Page 1600 Andrew Murray (1828–1917) from *Waiting on God.* Copyright ©1992. Published by the Christian Literature Crusade, Fort Washington, PA.

Page 1606 Martin Luther (1483–1546) from *Topical Encyclopedia of Living Quotations,* #1010, edited by Sherwood Wirt. Copyright ©1982. Published by Bethany House Publishers, Minneapolis, MN.

Page 1611 Augustine (354–430) from *Enchiridion.*

Page 1614 From *Western Asceticism*, edited by Owen Chadwick. Copyright ©1979. Published by Westminster John Knox Press, Louisville, KY.

Page 1617 From *What's So Amazing About Grace?* by Phillip Yancey. Copyright ©1997 by Phillip Yancey. Published by the Zondervan Corporation, Grand Rapids, MI. Used with permission.

SPIRITUAL FORMATION BIBLE:

GROWING IN INTIMACY WITH GOD THROUGH SCRIPTURE

General Editor, Timothy Jones

Project Management and Editorial, Ruth DeJager

Editorial Assistance, Natalie Block

Art Direction, Cindy Davis

Interior Design, Sharon Wright,
Belmont, MI

Interior Art, Clint Hanson

Calligraphic Design, Bruce Gore

Proofreading, Peachtree Editorial and Proofreading Service,
Peachtree City, GA

Interior Typesetting, Multnomah Graphics,
Troutdale, OR

Printing, R. R. Donnelley & Sons,
Crawfordsville, IN

GUARANTEE

CARE

*We suggest loosening the binding of your new Bible by gently
pressing on a small section of pages at a time from the center.
To ensure against breakage of the spine, it is best not to
bend the cover backward around the spine or to carry study
notes, church bulletins, pens, etc., inside the cover. Because a
felt-tipped marker will "bleed" through the pages, we recom-
mend use of a ball-point pen or pencil to underline favorite passages. Your Bible should not be exposed to excessive heat, cold,
or humidity. Protecting the gold or silver edges of the paper
from moisture will avoid spotting, streaking, or fading.*

DEFINITIONS

*Bonded leather: no less than 90% leather fibers with latex base.
Top-Grain leather: 100% pigskin
Cowhide: 100% cowhide*